Our Sunday Visitor's FAMILY GUIDE TO MOVIES AND VIDEOS

Edited by HENRY HERX

Our Sunday Visitor Publishing Division
Our Sunday Visitor, Inc.
Huntington, Indiana 46750

The reviews in this book are from the United States Catholic Conference
Department of Communications, Office for Film and Broadcasting.

International Standard Book Number: 0-87973-369-1
Library of Congress Catalog Card Number: 99-74729

Cover design by Tyler Ottinger

369

Introduction

Thanks to the electronic media of television, cable, and videocassette, many more people watch movies at home than in movie theaters. For those who find little of interest in contemporary theatrical fare, the home screen serves as an alternative by providing access to the vast library of films produced over the past century.

This has proved a marvelous opportunity for family viewers to select their own favorites — and find new ones — from among the classics of motion-picture art and entertainment. But in order to make the most of that opportunity, parents need to have sufficient information about the values and virtues of older movies, and that's not so easily come by.

For instance, newspaper TV-listings are simply inadequate for making an informed decision about whether or not a movie is worth several hours of anyone's time. Yet, most viewers have to make a choice based on the title, year of release, a hint of the plot situation, the names of a couple of actors, and perhaps a few words or a symbol indicating the fact that it is anything from a classic to a clunker.

While there are a number of film books offering plot summaries and critiques of vintage movies, most are written for movie fans and film students interested in Hollywood trivia and the medium's history.

Parents, of course, have other concerns in searching out movies with themes and values appropriate for their family. It is the intention of this guide to furnish them with information about the moral dimension of story and treatment, age suitability, and the artistic and entertainment quality of each of the movies listed in the following pages.

How to Use This Guide

Descriptions and evaluations are provided for virtually all motion pictures in national release to American theaters from 1966 through the first half of 1999. Many movies released prior to 1966 are also included, especially those that have particular relevance — good, bad, and indifferent — for family viewing. Most movie capsules consist of two sentences, the first summarizing the picture's plot or theme, and the second offering an evaluation of its relative merits as entertainment or enrichment, as well as suitability for various age groups.

Following each entry are the symbols used by two rating groups: the United States Catholic Conference's Office for Film and Broadcasting (USCC) followed within parentheses by that of the Motion Picture Association of America (MPAA). The USCC classifications indicate moral suitability as well as appropriateness for children, adolescents, and adults. The MPAA ratings are divided according to age suitability.

USCC CLASSIFICATIONS

A-I — general patronage

A-II — adults and adolescents

A-III — adults

A-IV — adults, with reservations (this refers to certain movies that require some analysis and explanation to avoid mistaken interpretations and false conclusions)

O — morally offensive

MPAA RATINGS

G — general audiences; all ages admitted

PG — parental guidance suggested; some material may not be suitable for children

PG-13 — parents are strongly cautioned to give special guidance for attendance of children under 13; some material may be inappropriate for young children

R — restricted; under 17 requires accompanying parent or adult guardian

X — no one under 17 admitted; age limit may vary in certain areas

NC-17 — no one 17 and under admitted; this rating replaced the X rating in 1990

In addition to the above, the MPAA in its first years used the symbols GP and later M for what today has become the PG category. However, the MPAA does not allow the automatic substitution of the present PG rating for these two former symbols unless it has officially changed these original designations. Consequently, though perhaps confusing, GP and M are used where appropriate.

Because MPAA ratings are changed occasionally, it was thought advisable to indicate such changes by a slash mark separating the original rating from the current one. For example, R/PG indicates that a movie originally rated as restricted has since been changed to the parental guidance category. Such changes may indicate that the distributor has cut the scenes responsible for the R rating, or that material previously deemed inappropriate for young viewers has subsequently been adjudged solely a matter of parental discretion. Though only one version of an MPAA-rated movie can be in distribution during its theatrical release, that same movie when released on video may have several different versions, each with its own separate MPAA rating or, for that matter, no rating at all.

Finally, the MPAA rating system has an appeal process by which a group of industry representatives can overrule the Rating Administration. Though this happens rarely, it was thought worth indicating those instances when the appeal process changed the rating. This is indicated by the word "appeal" following the new rating, as for example, (R/PG-13 appeal).

OTHER ABBREVIATIONS

nr — not rated (movies that have been released without applying for a rating from the MPAA or, in some cases, rejecting the one assigned to it)

br — before ratings (movies released before the MPAA classification system began in October 1968)

The Reason for Ratings

Finding a good movie can be difficult these days, especially for those concerned about the quality of screen fare for themselves and, even more, for those who depend upon their guidance. Youngsters are the most vulnerable to current screen excesses and need some assistance in selecting movies that help them grow without false values and wrong ideas. This was not always a problem for families.

The American movie industry began at the turn of the century as a mass medium of entertainment. During World War I, it grew to international stature, with Hollywood dominating the screens of the world until World War II. The genius of Hollywood was its ability to make movies that appealed to the entire family, relying primarily on simple stories told well. Going to the movies was relatively inexpensive and during the Great Depression became a regular habit for almost all American families.

After World War II, television brought popular entertainment, including movies, directly into the home. In the 1950s, Hollywood fought back by introducing 3-D devices and the wide screen, but neither effort brought back the family audience. In the 1960s, movie producers and exhibitors turned to more adult material than television would allow on the home screen. In doing so, however, the MPAA realized that it would have to advise viewers, especially parents, that certain movies were not for the young. The MPAA Rating Administration was created to replace the MPAA Production Code that had regulated the content of Hollywood movies since the 1930s. The MPAA ratings are determined by officials of the Rating Administration in Los Angeles and were initiated in October 1968.

USCC Movie Classification

The USCC Office for Film and Broadcasting classification system is an outgrowth of a program that began in 1934 with the founding of the National Legion of Decency and its initiation of moral ratings in 1936. Over the years, various modifications have been introduced in reflecting the development of movies from primarily escapist entertainment to a medium capable of serious artistic expression. It should be noted here that as older movies become available on video, the original Legion of Decency classifications have in some cases been updated in accordance with the current USCC rating system.

The classifications are the result of a consensus process involving OFB staff and, at times, outside consultants who contribute their perspective on the values, or lack thereof, in movies under consideration. This volunteer group is today an ecumenical one, representative of the general movie-going public, Catholic as well as non-Catholic.

The classifications serve busy parents as an instant means of identifying the age suitability and moral quality of a particular movie. But it is the capsule comments which provide parents with enough information to judge for themselves the level of maturity required by a given movie and whether it is worth their family's viewing.

In 1964, OFB's staff began writing reviews of the best of the new releases, and all movies since 1969 have been reviewed as well as classified. This volume represents the work of many individuals, both staff and consultants, who contributed their moral judgements, aesthetic sensibilities, and considerable writing talents to the task of movie evaluations. The present format makes their work accessible to anyone seeking guidance about movies.

Each week, OFB provides motion picture reviews, capsules, and ratings, as well as television and video reviews, to more than 150 Catholic newspapers via the Catholic News Service (CNS) in Washington, DC. For further information, contact your local diocesan newspaper or CNS at (202) 541-3250. CNS also reprints these reviews in its weekly "TV & Movie Guide" which is available for group or individual use. Those interested only in movies, however, may subscribe to the "Movie Guide Monthly" for $12.00 a year.

Through a grant from the Catholic Communication Campaign, OFB's capsule reviews and ratings of new releases are recorded each week and may be heard by dialing the toll-free number: 1-800-311-4222.

Capsule reviews of new releases are also posted each week on the United States Catholic Conference web site: www.nccbuscc.org.

Henry Herx, Director
Office for Film and Broadcasting
Department of Communications
United States Catholic Conference

Vatican Best Films List

On the occasion of the one-hundredth anniversary of cinema in 1995, the Vatican compiled this list of "great films." The 45 movies are divided into three categories: "Religion," "Values," and "Art." The USCC classification for each film follows its description.

Religion

Andrei Rublev (1969) Russian production about a fifteenth-century monk (Anatoli Solonitzine) who perseveres in painting icons and other religious art, despite the civil disruptions and cruel turmoil of his times. Director Andrei Tarkovsky visualizes brilliantly the story of a devout man seeking through his art to find the transcendent in the savagery of the Tartar invasions and the unfeeling brutality of Russian nobles. Subtitles. Stylized historical violence. The US Catholic Conference classification is A-II — adults and adolescents. Not rated by the Motion Picture Association of America. (Fox Lorber, $79.95)

Babette's Feast (1988) Screen version of a story by Isak Dinesen, set in a rugged fishing village in 1871 Denmark, shows the impact of a French housekeeper (Stephane Audran) on two pious sisters who carry on their late father's work as pastor of a dwindling religious flock. Danish director Gabriel Axel's understated but finely detailed work centers on the preparation and consumption of an exquisite Gallic meal, a sensuous labor of love which has a healing effect on the austere sect and the Frenchwoman who prepared it. Subtitles. Cerebral treatment. The US Catholic Conference classification is A-II — adults and adolescents. The Motion Picture Association of America rating is G — general audiences. (Orion, $19.98)

Ben-Hur (1959) Director William Wyler's classic Hollywood epic follows the Jewish prince of the title (Charlton Heston) after he's betrayed by his boyhood Roman friend (Stephen Boyd) and subjected to much misery, until finally achieving retribution for all his suffering. The narrative's conventional melodrama is transformed by the grand scale of its spectacle, especially the chariot race, and by the stirring performances of its principals, who manage to overcome the story's cliches and stereotypes. The US Catholic Conference classification is A-I — general patronage. The Motion Picture Association of America rating is G — general audiences. (MGM/UA, $29.98)

The Flowers of St. Francis (1950) Remarkable Italian production about the beginnings of the Franciscan Order as its founder sets the example of humility, simplicity, and obedience for his first followers at Portiuncula, a little chapel near Assisi, from which they depart into the world to preach peace. Directed by Roberto Rossellini from a script co-written with Federico Fellini, the movie's form is as simple and sincere as the subject of the narrative, which relates a series of little incidents realistically, yet with an infectious sense of joy marvelously conveyed by an anonymous cast of monks from a Roman monastery. Subtitles. The US Catholic Conference classification is A-I — general patronage. Not rated by the Motion Picture Association of America. (Facets Multimedia, $34.95)

Francesco (1989) Overwrought Italian production portrays St. Francis of Assisi (Mickey Rourke) as a spiritual agitator challenging the accepted values of his thirteenth-century contemporaries by embracing a life of utter poverty and simplicity. Director Liliana Cavani builds an elaborate picture of the period's social injustices, but fails to evoke any convincing sense of religious conviction from Rourke's embarrassingly vacuous performance. English-language version. Occasional scenes of violence, desperate poverty, and brief nudity. The US Catholic Conference classification is A-III — adults. The Motion Picture Association of America rating is PG-13 — parents are strongly cautioned that some material may be inappropriate for children under 13. (Hemdale, $89.95)

The Gospel According to St. Matthew (1966) Straightforward Italian dramatization of the evangelist's account of the life of Jesus and His message of salvation succeeds exceptionally well in placing the viewer within the Gospel events, avoiding the artificiality of most biblical movie epics. Director Pier Paolo Pasolini is completely faithful to the text while employing the visual imagination necessary for his realistic interpretation. Subtitles. The US Catholic Conference classification is A-I — general patronage. Not rated by the Motion Picture Association of America. (Water Bearer, $24.95)

La Passion de Notre Seigneur Jesus-Christ (1905) Though better known for one-reel crime melodramas, movie pioneer Ferdinand Zecca (1863-1947) also produced this two-reel (c. 30 minutes) dramatization of Christ's Passion. Distributed by Pathe, France's leading motion-picture company, it was reportedly quite popular in its time and was notable, according to film historian Georges Sadoul, for its "rudimentary" camera movements. (Not available on video)

A Man for All Seasons (1966) Engrossing drama of the last seven years in the life of Thomas More, Henry VIII's chancellor, who met a martyr's death rather than compromise his conscience during a period of religious turmoil. Robert Bolt's script is masterfully directed by Fred Zinnemann, with a standout performance by Paul Scofield in the title role, among other notable performances from a uniformly fine cast. The historical dramatization achieves an authentic human dimension that makes its sixteenth-century events more accessible and its issues more universal. Profoundly entertaining, but heavy-going for children. The US Catholic Conference classification is A-I — general patronage. The Motion Picture Association of America rating is G — general audiences. (Columbia TriStar, $19.95)

The Mission (1986) In the 1750s, the large and prosperous Jesuit Indian missions were divided between Spain and Portugal. In dramatizing these events, Robert Bolt's screenplay focuses not on the religious but on the sociopolitical dimension of the colonial era and its injustices. The epic production is visually splendid, but Roland Joffe's direction is erratic and bogs down in contrasting a nonviolent priest (Jeremy Irons) and one (Robert De Niro) who leads the Indians against a colonial army. Although dramatically flawed, the work recalls a past that provides a context for current Latin-American struggles. Some violence and ethnographic nudity. The US Catholic Conference classification is A-III — adults. The Motion Picture Association of America rating is PG — parental guidance suggested. (Warner, $19.98)

Monsieur Vincent (1947) Lucid, moving account of St. Vincent de Paul's work among the poor and the oppressed in seventeenth-century France, from his first labors in a plague-ravaged village and his appeals to the conscience of the aristocracy, to the founding of an order devoted to charitable works and his death in 1660. Director Maurice Cloche portrays the poverty of the times and the cruelty of the regime in starkly convincing fashion, providing a solid historical framework within which Pierre Fresnay's performance in the title role shines with a warm compassion and spiritual intensity which most viewers will find irresistibly compelling. Subtitles. High on the list of great religious movies. The US Catholic Conference classification is A-I — general patronage. Not rated by the Motion Picture Association of America. (Nostalgia, $29.95)

Nazarin (1958) Mexican story set in 1905 when a young priest comes into disfavor with his inflexible religious superiors, the civil authorities, and even the poor among whom he tries to live a life of simplicity, poverty, and charity. Though director Luis Bunuel's work is not very optimistic about the possibility of idealism winning over the world, it's not critical of religion, only pious hypocrisy. Subtitles. Perplexing themes. The US Catholic Conference classification is A-III — adults. Not rated by the Motion Picture Association of America. (Connoisseur, $69.95)

Ordet (1954) Challenging Danish production about different kinds of faith and various sorts of miracles, one of which restores a dead woman to life. Directed by Carl Dreyer, the austere narrative centers on a farming family troubled by the madness of a son (Preben Lerdorff Rye) who believes he is Jesus Christ until, regaining his balance, his faith in God achieves the miracle which brings the story to a positive though less than convincing conclusion some may find disappointingly ambiguous. Mature themes. The US Catholic Conference classification is A-III — adults. Not rated by the Motion Picture Association of America. (Nostalgia, $24.95)

The Passion of Joan of Arc (1928) Silent-screen masterpiece portraying the heresy trial, confession, recantation, and execution of the Maid of Orleans (Maria Falconetti), in a performance of such emotional power that it still stands as the most convincing portrayal of spirituality on celluloid. Directed by Carl Dreyer, the work is essentially the interior epic of a soul, consisting largely of close-ups of Joan's face and those of her interrogators accomplished in a fashion which is never static, as the camera explores the inner struggle between human frailties and spiritual strength. Some duplicitous churchmen, medicinal bloodletting, and a restrained torture scene. The US Catholic Conference classification is A-II — adults and adolescents. Not rated by the Motion Picture Association of America. (Nostalgia, $29.95)

The Sacrifice (1986) Swedish production in which a group of adults and a child pass through a night of confusion and fear, including portents of a nuclear-devastated landscape. Director Andrei Tarkovsky's murky religious allegory about an aging writer's bargaining with God to save others relies upon long silences, ritualized dialogue, and beautiful but static photography. Subtitles. A very personal film about love and compassion, the effect is strangely cold and distant. The US Catholic Conference classification is A-III — adults. The Motion Picture Association of America rating is PG — parental guidance suggested. (Pacific Arts, $29.95)

Therese (1986) French dramatization of the life of St. Therese de Lisieux from age 15, when she joined a cloistered convent of Carmelite nuns, to her death there nine years later of tuberculosis. Director Alain Cavalier's impressionistic account of the young woman (luminously portrayed by Catherine Mouchet) who found personal joy, spiritual liberation, and the sanctity of selfless simplicity within the restrictive traditions of an austere religious community will challenge contemporary viewers and confound some. The young may find its picture of nineteenth-century religious life more confusing than inspiring. Dubbed in English. The US Catholic Conference classification is A-III — adults. Not rated by the Motion Picture Association of America. (Palisades Home Video, 1-800-989-8576, $39.95)

Values

Au Revoir les Enfants (1988) When the Gestapo discover that a priest has hidden three Jewish youths in a Catholic boys' school, he and the boys are arrested and deported to concentration camps. French writer-producer-director Louis Malle re-creates a painful memory from his own youth in a restrained, humbling, well-acted dramatization of a boy's first-hand experience of the Holocaust. Subtitles. Some rough language. The US Catholic Conference classification is A-II — adults and adolescents. The Motion Picture Association of America rating is PG — parental guidance suggested. (Orion, $19.98)

The Bicycle Thief (1949) Simple yet compelling

study in desperation as a worker (Lamberto Maggiorani) must find his stolen bicycle or lose his new job. Ignored by the police and others, the man and his young son (Enzo Staiola) search the streets for it until, in despair, he himself tries to steal a bicycle. Scripted by Cesare Zavattini and directed by Vittorio De Sica, the result is an engrossing picture of the human realities of life on the edge of poverty, shot on the streets of Rome with a cast of nonprofessionals that brought a new realism to the postwar screen and a new emotional honesty to the stories it told. Subtitles. Some earthy references. The US Catholic Conference classification is A-II — adults and adolescents. Not rated by the Motion Picture Association of America. (Nostalgia Family, $69.95)

The Burmese Harp (1956) Badly wounded in Burma at the end of WW II, a Japanese soldier (Shoji Yasui) is nursed back to health by a Buddhist monk, then devotes himself to searching the jungle battlefields for the abandoned remains of dead soldiers to give them a decent burial. Directed by Kon Ichikawa, the Japanese production takes a strong anti-war stance through a series of flashbacks to the horrors of battle, but uses hauntingly poetic imagery to convey the main theme of life's value and the need to atone for its loss. Subtitles. Wartime violence. The US Catholic Conference classification is A-II — adults and adolescents. Not rated by the Motion Picture Association of America. (Connoisseur, $29.95)

Chariots of Fire (1981) Two young Englishmen (Ben Cross and Ian Charleson) overcome quite different obstacles to win gold medals at the Paris Olympics of 1924. One is a Jew determined to beat the anti-Semitic establishment at its own game, and the other is a devout Scot who runs for the glory of God. Directed by Hugh Hudson, it is a richly entertaining and highly inspiring movie for the whole family. Several coarse words. The US Catholic Conference classification is A-I — general patronage. The Motion Picture Association of America rating is PG — parental guidance suggested. (Warner, $19.98)

Decalogue (1988) Produced for Polish television, this series of ten hour-long programs explores the contemporary meaning of the Ten Commandments as seen in the lives of various residents of a drab Warsaw apartment complex. Directed by Krzysztof Kieslowski, none of the stories is religious, though all grapple with moral conflicts arising from ordinary situations and relationships which most viewers will not see as being at all foreign to them. Subtitles. Mature themes. The US Catholic Conference classification is A-III — adults. Not rated by the Motion Picture Association of America. (Not available on video)

Dersu Uzala (1978) Russian production about the friendship that grows between a turn-of-the-century explorer in Siberia and his guide, an aging Tungus hunter whose name gives the film its title. Japanese director Akira Kurosawa concentrates on evoking the vast remoteness of the Siberian wilderness, a world the Russian finds forbidding but one in which the hunter is perfectly at home. Subtitles. Finely acted, beautifully photographed, it is an admiring portrait of a man living in harmony with nature and with his fellow hunters. The US Catholic Conference classification is A-I — general patronage. The Motion Picture Association of America rating is G — general audiences. (Sultan, $29.98)

Gandhi (1982) Superb portrait of India's great political and spiritual leader comes to life in Ben Kingsley's authoritative yet sensitive performance. Director Richard Attenborough's epic-scale production re-creates Gandhi's life and times, especially his use of non-violence and hunger strikes to bring together the diverse peoples of India and unify them as a nation. Though its scenes of violence are not for children, the movie's vision of justice and peace is for everyone else, especially young people. The US Catholic Conference classification is A-II — adults and adolescents. The Motion Picture Association of America rating is PG — parental guidance suggested. (Columbia TriStar, $29.95)

Intolerance (1916) D.W. Griffith's epic masterpiece inter-cuts four stories of injustice — the fall of Babylon, the Crucifixion, the St. Bartholomew's Day massacre, and a contemporary American story of an innocent man sentenced to death. The movie develops parallel action in each of the stories, though centered principally on the tale of an impoverished couple whose wife tries to save her husband from being unjustly hanged , and the Assyrian conquest of Babylon which is presented on an epic scale. Though complex in narrative structure, each story is connected to the others by the simple image of a woman rocking a cradle, a device dropped as the tempo increases in the conclusion of the stories. The movie's brilliance in concept, execution, and editing is still impressive, dated only by its florid titles and melodramatic characterizations. Stylized violence, sexual references, and a few flashes of nudity. The US Catholic Conference classification is A-III — adults. Not rated by the Motion Picture Association of America. (Kino, $29.95)

It's a Wonderful Life (1946) Seasonal favorite about the joys and trials of a good man (James Stewart) who, facing financial ruin on the eve of Christmas, contemplates suicide, until his guardian angel (Henry Travers) shows him how meaningful his life has been to those around him. Director Frank Capra's unabashedly sentimental picture of mainstream American life is bolstered by a superb cast (including Lionel Barrymore as a conniving banker) and a wealth of good feelings about such commonplace virtues as hard work and helping one's neighbor. Young children may find the story's dark moments unsettling. The US Catholic Conference classification is A-II — adults and adolescents. Not rated by the Motion Picture Association of America. (Republic, 45th Anniversary Edition, $19.98)

On the Waterfront (1954) Classic labor film about

a punched-out boxer (Marlon Brando) who, despite the machinations of his shifty brother (Rod Steiger) and with some encouragement from the woman (Eva Marie Saint) he loves as well as a waterfront priest (Karl Malden), decides to stand up to the criminal boss (Lee J. Cobb) of a corrupt union of dock workers. Budd Schulberg's fact-based script is directed by Elia Kazan, with stand-out performances and a gritty realism grounded in a working-class milieu, abetted by Leonard Bernstein's rousing score and Boris Kauffman's atmospheric photography. Much menace and some violence. The US Catholic Conference classification is A-II — adults and adolescents. Not rated by the Motion Picture Association of America. (Columbia TriStar, $19.95)

Open City (1945) Composite picture of the resistance movement in German-occupied Rome focusing on an underground leader (Marcello Pagliero) hidden by a widow (Anna Magnani), until he's betrayed to the Gestapo, then tortured and executed along with a partisan priest (Aldo Fabrizi). Director Roberto Rossellini began filming while German troops were still in the city, and the result has a documentary quality giving a sense of immediacy to the period portrayal of events by a cast whose naturalistic acting captures the fervor and determination of diverse social types united in their opposition to Fascism. Subtitles. Wartime violence and some intense torture scenes. The US Catholic Conference classification is A-III — adults. Not rated by the Motion Picture Association of America. (Kino, $24.95)

Schindler's List (1993) Sobering account of an opportunistic German businessman (Liam Neeson) out to make his fortune by exploiting Jewish labor in occupied Poland, but the increasing barbarism of Nazi racial policies and the sadistic perversions of the local commandant (Ralph Fiennes) cause him to risk his life trying to save the Jews in his employ. Director Steven Spielberg re-stages this Holocaust story on an epic scale that gives horrifying dimension to one man's attempt to save some innocent lives, though providing little insight in the German's moral transformation or the individual lives of his Jewish workers. Realistically graphic treatment of an infamous historical period and its crimes against humanity, a few discreet sexual scenes, and occasional rough language. The US Catholic Conference classification is A-III — adults. The Motion Picture Association of America rating is R — restricted. (MCA/Universal, $29.98)

The Seventh Seal (1956) Intense medieval morality tale about a disillusioned knight (Max Von Sydow) returning from the Crusades to a plague-ravaged land, where he forestalls Death (Bengt Ekerot) by wagering his life on a game of chess, during the course of which he saves a traveling player named Joseph (Nils Poppe), his wife Mary (Bibi Andersson), and their infant son. Swedish director Ingmar Bergman convincingly re-creates the religious context of the Middle Ages, but the knight's quest to find meaning in a world of physical suffering and spiritual emptiness is more directly related to the contemporary search for life's meaning in our own age of doubt and uncertainty. Subtitles. Recurring images of death, some stylized violence, and instances of religious fanaticism. The US Catholic Conference classification is A-III — adults. Not rated by the Motion Picture Association of America. (Video Dimensions, $19.95)

The Tree of Wooden Clogs (1978) Quiet, richly textured Italian drama about the lives of four peasant families who work as tenant farmers on a Lombardy estate at the end of the last century. Beginning with the fall harvest and ending with the spring planting, the movie depicts the everyday life of rural people who endure with human dignity in spite of the oppressive system which exploits their labor. Written, photographed, and directed by Ermanno Olmi, this is a loving portrait of ordinary life in an age of social injustice. Some tense scenes. The US Catholic Conference classification is A-II — adults and adolescents. Not rated by the Motion Picture Association of America. (Fox/Lorber, $79.95)

Wild Strawberries (1958) During the day on which he is to be awarded an honorary degree from a nearby university, a 78-year-old retired scholar (Victor Sjostrom in a masterful performance) is visited with dreams and reveries about his past life, especially his failures and disappointments in personal relationships. Swedish director Ingmar Bergman brilliantly develops the man's interior journey from pangs of regret and anxiety to a refreshing sense of peace and reconciliation summed up in blissful images of his happy youth. One of the great films about aging that touches universal chords in mature viewers. English subtitles. The US Catholic Conference classification is A-III — adults. Not rated by the Motion Picture Association of America. (Connoisseur, $29.95)

Art

Citizen Kane (1941) When a Hearst-like newspaper tycoon (Orson Welles) dies, a reporter (William Alland) interviews the man's former associates (Joseph Cotton and Everett Sloane among them) and wives (Ruth Warrick and Dorothy Comingore) in an effort to pin down the essence of the contradictory, larger-than-life millionaire by discovering the meaning of his dying word, "Rosebud." Also co-written (with Herman J. Mankiewicz), produced, and directed by Welles, the movie is a landmark in American cinema, notable both for its superb use of film technique and its intriguing story of a man who came from nothing, acquired fame and fortune, but died without the love he sought. Marital infidelity. The US Catholic Conference classification is A-II — adults and adolescents. Not rated by the Motion Picture Association of America. (Turner, 50th Anniversary Edition includes a 30-minute documentary on the movie, $19.98)

8 1/2 (1963) With both career and marriage in chaos,

an Italian movie director (Marcello Mastroianni) protects his overgrown ego by retreating into surreal memories of the past and wild fantasies about the present. Director Federico Fellini has some self-indulgent fun with his profession, semi-biographical events from his youth, and themes from his movies, while taking viewers on a journey through the rich, at times bizarre, imagination of an artist whose attempts to cope with the demands of the real world are resolved in a final flood of optimism, as the director joins with all his characters in a human carousel of life. Subtitles. Ambiguous treatment of mature themes. The US Catholic Conference classification is A-IV — adults, with reservations. Not rated by the Motion Picture Association of America. (Vestron, $69.95)

Fantasia (1940) Walt Disney's only excursion into the world of the fine arts presents eight selections of classical music, including Dukas's "Sorcerer's Apprentice" with Mickey Mouse and a bucket brigade of brooms; Stravinsky's "Rite of Spring" with its massive, earthbound images; and the macabre vision of Musorgsky's "Night on Bald Mountain." Using different approaches and animation styles for each piece of music as performed by the Philadelphia Orchestra under conductor Leopold Stokowski, the imaginative work was not only Disney's most ambitious undertaking, but it remains an enjoyably creative introduction to fine music, especially for youngsters. The US Catholic Conference classification is A-I — general patronage. The Motion Picture Association of America rating is G — general audiences. (Disney, $24.99)

Grand Illusion (1937) Shot down during WW I, a French aristocrat (Pierre Fresnay) is treated as a brother officer by the German aristocrat (Erich von Stroheim) commanding the prisoner-of-war camp, then makes use of his special status to distract attention while two fellow prisoners (Jean Gabin and Dalio) make good their escape to Switzerland. Directed by Jean Renoir, the picture of life in the camp is rich in narrative incident and human detail, neatly supporting a theme dealing with the end of the aristocratic ideal of chivalry and its replacement by mass armies of commoners with no desire for war. Subtitles. Some ribald humor and tense situations. The US Catholic Conference classification is A-II — adults and adolescents. Not rated by the Motion Picture Association of America. (Home Vision, $29.95)

La Strada (1956) Two-bit circus strongman (Anthony Quinn) adds a simpleminded peasant (Giulietta Masina) to his act, treating her badly, until a tragic encounter with a bantering acrobat (Richard Basehart) who tries to help her. Italian director Federico Fellini's somber picture of lost souls on the back-roads of life has its emotional center in Masina's Chaplinesque performance as the poor waif struggling to keep her spirit from being crushed by the brute she serves. Subtitles. Some stylized violence and brutalizing conditions of life. The US Catholic Conference classification is A-III — adults. Not rated by the Motion Picture Association of America. (Sultan, $29.98)

The Lavender Hill Mob (1951) British comedy classic in which a timid bank employee (Alec Guinness) concocts a scheme to hijack a shipment of gold bullion with the aid of professional crooks (Sidney James and Alfie Bass), then melt it down in the foundry of an accommodating sculptor (Stanley Holloway), and recast it as Eiffel Tower souvenirs for export to Paris. Scripted by T.E.B. Clarke and directed by Charles Crichton, the tongue-in-cheek depiction of a perfect crime has one hilarious flaw after another, culminating in a wild police chase through London, and a neat twist ending in South America. Comic crime caper and mild menace. The US Catholic Conference classification is A-II — adults and adolescents. Not rated by the Motion Picture Association of America. (HBO, $19.98)

The Leopard (1963) Historical drama set against the background of Garibaldi's 1860 invasion of Sicily, where the prince (Burt Lancaster) of an old aristocratic family refuses to adapt to revolutionary times despite the marriage of his more egalitarian nephew (Alain Delon) to the daughter of a wealthy ex-peasant. Directed by Luchino Visconti from the novel by Giuseppe Di Lampedusa, the result captures a fascinating period of social, political, and economic change in a family saga filled with nostalgia for a past, more elegant age. Subtitles. Mature themes. The US Catholic Conference classification is A-III — adults. Not rated by the Motion Picture Association of America. (Not available on video)

Little Women (1933) Lovingly sentimental but firmly crafted adaptation of Louisa May Alcott's story of four New England girls cared for by their mother while their father is soldiering in the Civil War. Director George Cukor depicts the joys and woes of the loving March family household with warmth and sincerity, but most memorable is the ensemble performance of a remarkable cast headed by Katharine Hepburn as serious-minded Jo, Joan Bennett as vain Amy, Frances Dee as prosaic Meg, Jean Parker as waifish Beth, and Spring Byington as the girls' beloved Marmee. Prime family fare. The US Catholic Conference classification is A-I — general patronage. Not rated by the Motion Picture Association of America. (MGM/UA, $14.98)

Metropolis (1926) Silent classic of a future society ruled by an aristocracy living in luxury above ground, while the workers suffer miserably underground, comforted only by the religious faith of a young woman (Brigitte Helm), in whose likeness a sinister scientist (Rudolf Klein-Rogge) fashions a robot inciting the workers to rebel, but all ends in reconciliation. Directed by Fritz Lang, the story's melodramatic turns and woolly finale may be dated, but not its vivid pictorial sense, grandly expressionistic décor, and theme of social justice. Bleak picture of exploited workers, stylized violence, and some sexual innuendo. The US Catholic Conference classification is A-II — adults and adolescents. Not rated by the Motion Picture Association of America. (Nostalgia, $16.95)

Modern Times (1936) Charlie Chaplin's insightful fable of man versus machine centers in the artificiality of industrialized society and the anxieties caused by the Depression, as Charlie dances his way through the hazards of an assembly-line job. A model of silent comedic technique and refined slapstick humor, the movie marks the last appearance of the Little Tramp character, as Charlie takes his final walk down the long empty road, this time in the company of Paulette Goddard, who adds an element of freshness to the plot's old-fashioned romance. The US Catholic Conference classification is A-I — general patronage. The Motion Picture Association of America rating is G — general audiences. (CBS/Fox, $19.98)

Napoleon (1927) Epic silent chronicle of Napoleon Bonaparte (Albert Dieudonne) from his student days at a military academy, through his rise as an officer during the Revolution and Reign of Terror, until ending in 1796, when the Directory puts him in command of the army invading Italy. Directed by Abel Gance, the episodic narrative is heavily melodramatic, yet the sheer exuberance of the actors and the monumental staging of the action carry viewers along in richly visual experience made memorable by Gance's innovative use of portable cameras and triple screens. This reconstructed print runs 235 minutes, with music composed by Carmine Coppola. Stylized violence and brief sexual innuendo. The US Catholic Conference classification is A-II — adults and adolescents. Not rated by the Motion Picture Association of America. (MCA/Universal, $29.95)

Nosferatu (1922) Silent horror classic loosely based on Bram Stoker's novel *Dracula* centers on the vampire count (Max Schreck) who leaves his sinister castle in the Carpathian mountains to sail on a doomed ship bringing him to 1838 Bremen, where his dark deeds are undone by a brave young woman and the first light of dawn. Directed by F.W. Murnau, the German production is most notable for its eerie portrayal of the vampire in images which seem to personify evil and dread, in a movie even more remarkable for having been filmed mostly on location rather than in the controlled confines of a studio. Stylized violence and menace. The US Catholic Conference classification is A-II — adults and adolescents. Not rated by the Motion Picture Association of America. (Nostalgia, $19.95)

Stagecoach (1939) In this Western classic, a cowboy (John Wayne) wanted by the law on trumped-up charges joins an odd assortment of passengers (Claire Trevor, Thomas Mitchell, Donald Meek, John Carradine, and others) on the stage to Lordsburg in the midst of an Apache uprising. Directed by John Ford, the characters are a microcosm of frontier types, each of whom has a different reason for the journey whose dangers are played out against the majestic vistas of Monument Valley, with a brilliantly staged Indian attack and a final showdown on the streets of Lordsburg that brings the story to a rousing finish. Stylized violence. The US Catholic Conference classification is A-II — adults and adolescents. Not rated by the Motion Picture Association of America. (Warner, $19.98)

2001: A Space Odyssey (1968) Director Stanley Kubrick's epic work, co-written with Arthur C. Clarke, is both science fiction and metaphysical poetry using an unconventional mixture of visuals and music to bridge humanity's reconstructed past, identifiable present, and projected future, all tied together by the recurring image of a monolith as symbol of a superhuman existence. The central narrative follows the struggle of two astronauts (Keir Dullea and Gary Lockwood) to wrest control of their spacecraft from HAL, a talking computer (voice of Douglas Rain), on a half-billion-mile trip to Jupiter and the unknown. For young people and imaginative adults but too long, deep, and intense for children. The US Catholic Conference classification is A-II — adults and adolescents. The Motion Picture Association of America rating is G — general audiences. (MGM/UA, $19.98)

The Wizard of Oz (1939) Dorothy rides her cyclone to the magic land over the rainbow in director Victor Fleming's classic that skyrocketed Judy Garland's career and has given generations of families prime entertainment again and again. The fiftieth anniversary edition has 17 minutes of material not included in the original release. The US Catholic Conference classification is A-I — general patronage. The Motion Picture Association of America rating is G — general audiences. (MGM/UA, $24.98)

A la Mode (1994) Tepid French fantasy in which a hapless 17-year-old orphan (Ken Higelin) is apprenticed to a Jewish tailor (Jean Yanne) who adopts him, encourages his talents as a fashion designer, and helps him marry the girl of his dreams (Florence Darel). Director Remy Duchemin's bland success story avoids the troublesome pitfalls of youth to concentrate on the father-son relationship of tailor and apprentice, with feel-good results that may be too sweet for some tastes. Subtitles. Brief bedroom scene with nudity and implied premarital relationship. A-III (R)

A-Haunting We Will Go (1942) Tedious comedy directed by Alfred Werker in which aging comics Stan Laurel and Oliver Hardy get mixed up with stage magician Dante and gangsters searching for a missing corpse. Slapstick menace. A-I (br)

Aaron Loves Angela (1976) The story of a teenage romance between a black youth (Kevin Hooks) and a Puerto Rican girl (Irene Cara) is told in a lifeless movie that tries to get too much mileage out of the charm of its two young principals. Director Gordon Parks Jr.'s absurdly melodramatic conclusion involves violence between a brutal but soft-hearted heroin pusher (Robert Hooks) and some syndicate types. O (R)

Aaron Slick from Punkin Crick (1952) Lackluster musical comedy set in the 1890s with a country lass (Dinah Shore) off to Chicago after selling her farm to a slick operator (Robert Merrill), who expects to strike oil but doesn't, then schemes to get his money back until her rural beau (Alan Young) comes to town. Director Claude Binyon's broad, tongue-in-cheek tale of rural folk outsmarting city slickers lacks charm and has little appeal beyond cornball humor and forgettable songs. Romantic complications and confidence schemes. A-II (br)

Aaron's Magic Village (1997) Animated version of Isaac Bashevis Singer's stories about a Jewish village in Poland which becomes threatened by a wicked sorcerer's Golem until an orphaned lad helps save the hamlet and its foolish residents. Directed by Albert Hanan Kaminski and narrated by Fyvush Finkel, the humorous tale conveys the distinctive flavor of Jewish culture and tradition, though the story tends to drag in between lively musical numbers. A-I (G)

Abandon Ship! (1957) Taut moral exercise in life and death decisions face an officer (Tyrone Power) of a sunken ocean-liner who must choose which of 27 survivors should have a place in a lifeboat designed to hold 14 people. Writer-director Richard Sale realistically develops the hazards of the open sea while providing a human dimension for each survivor with harrowing consequences for all. Much menace and stylized violence. A-II (br)

Abbott and Costello in Hollywood (1945) Bud Abbott and Lou Costello play Los Angeles barbers who turn talent agents when they try to help a young singer (Robert Stanton) get a job. Director S. Sylvan Simon sets up a comic situation that goes nowhere as the boys clown their way through Metro-Goldwyn-Mayer's shooting stages and backlot with largely unamusing results. Slapstick humor. A-I (br)

Abbott and Costello in the Foreign Legion (1950) One of the pair's lesser efforts as directed by Charles Lamont follows the boys from Brooklyn to the Sahara Desert, where they get caught in the middle of shady dealings between a greedy legionnaire (Walter Slezak) and a bellicose sheik (Douglass Dumbrille). Comic violence. A-I (br)

Abbott and Costello Go to Mars (1953) Thin comedy directed by Charles Lamont in which two ignoramuses (Bud Abbott and Lou Costello) accidentally launch a space rocket, which lands in New Orleans during Marti Gras, then blasts off to Venus, whose queen (Mari Blanchard) sends them packing back to Earth. Comic menace and sexual innuendo. A-II (br)

Abbott and Costello Lost in Alaska (see: **Lost in Alaska**)

Abbott and Costello Meet Captain Kidd (1952) Tired costume comedy directed by Charles Lamont has the boys find a treasure map, then get shanghaied by the title pirate (Charles Laughton mugging outrageously) who's after the loot. Comic violence. A-I (br)

Abbott and Costello Meet Dr. Jekyll and Mr. Hyde (1953) Enterprising period comedy directed by Charles Lamont casts the two screen boobies as vintage London bobbies on the trail of Robert Louis Stevenson's Victorian monster (Boris Karloff). Comic menace. A-I (br)

Abbott and Costello Meet Frankenstein (1948) The comics deliver some crates to a spooky mansion, where they run into the title monster (Glenn Strange) along with Dracula (Bela Lugosi) and the Wolfman (Lon Chaney, Jr.). Directed by Charles Barton, the boys go through their usual routines spiced with some ghoulish nonsense about a brain exchange. Comic violence. A-II (br)

Abbott and Costello Meet the Ghosts (see: **Abbott and Costello Meet Frankenstein**)

Abbott and Costello Meet the Invisible Man (1951) This time around the boys play private detectives hired by a prizefighter (Arthur Franz), who's used an invisibility serum to escape the police after being framed for murder by a gangster (Sheldon Leonard). Directed by Charles Lamont, the formula comedy's highlight is a boxing match in which the inept Costello gets some help in the ring from his unseen client. Comic violence. A-II (br)

Abbott and Costello Meet the Killer (1949) Comic murder mystery with the boys finding, then trying to lose, a couple of corpses in a hotel whose guests include the usual likely suspects, including a sinister swami (Boris Karloff). Directed by Charles Barton, it's mildly amusing fare for the comedy team's fans. Comic violence. A-I (br)

Abbott and Costello Meet the Mummy (1955) Tired formula comedy directed by Charles Lamont has the boys helping an adventuress (Marie Windsor) search for a lost Egyptian tomb whose treasures are guarded by an unfriendly mummy. Comic menace. A-I (br)

Abby (1975) Low-budget, black version of **The Exorcist**, in which God and the Devil clash, this time in the form of a young woman (Carol Speed) possessed by a demon unleashed by her archaeologist father-in-law (William Marshall) who, fortunately, also happens to be a clergyman. Directed by William Girdler, it has all the defects and excesses of the original plus a few of its own. Exploitative sex and violence. O (R)

Abdication, The (1974) Having relinquished the Swedish throne for various religious reasons, Queen Christina (Liv Ullmann) arrives in Rome to prostrate herself before Pope Alexander VII. Suspecting a Protestant plot to discredit the Church, a cardinal (Peter Finch) is appointed to examine the ex-queen and his interrogation forms the bulk of the movie. It is a test the movie thoroughly fails, despite director Anthony Harvey's efforts to breathe fire into a tired historical drama with little historicity and less drama. A-III (PG)

Abductors, The (1972) Using local New Jersey talent and a story line that Mickey Spillane would have thrown in the wastebasket, writer-director Don Schain pits sexy, sadistic private eye Ginger (Cheri Caffaro) against a seedy gang who abduct young women, instruct them in the finer points of depravity, and then sell them to needy executives around the country. Trash with violence and nudity. O (R)

Abe Lincoln in Illinois (1940) Raymond Massey stars as the future president with Ruth Gordon playing Mary Todd in this well-acted drama based on Robert Sherwood's Pulitzer Prize-winning play. Directed by John Cromwell, the movie's emphasis is upon the development of Lincoln's character as a backwoodsman-turned-lawyer and his compassionate confrontation with adversity. A-I (br)

Abilene Town (1946) Sturdy Western with Randolph Scott as marshal of 1870 Abilene trying to stop a war between cattlemen and sodbusters, while the fearful townspeople stand on the sidelines. Director Edwin L. Marin paces the action with some comic relief (Edgar Buchanan's reluctant lawman), as well as Scott's romantic interest in a shopkeeper's daughter (Rhonda Fleming) and a dancehall beauty (Ann Dvorak). Frontier violence and menacing situations. A-II (br)

Abominable Dr. Phibes, The (1971) Horror movie featuring superb Art Deco sets and the campy good humor of Vincent Price as the nasty doctor (of both medicine and theology) who takes revenge on those he holds responsible for his wife's death by employing each of the ten plagues found in Exodus. Despite a certain wacky unreality running through the whole exercise, director Robert Fuest uses some gory visuals that may be a bit strong for any but devoted horror fans. A-III (PG)

Abominable Snowman, The (1957) Mild thriller follows British scientist Peter Cushing and crass American adventurer Forrest Tucker as they face the terrors of the unknown on the trail of the Yeti in the high Himalayas. Director Val Guest's low-budget effort is effective enough in building suspense from the off-screen presence of the legendary creatures, with a provocative glimpse of one just before the ending. Some menace and a minimum of stylized violence. A-I (br)

About Face (1952) Flat musical version of the military school comedy **Brother Rat** (1938) is unimaginatively directed by Roy Del Ruth, with Gordon MacRae as the leader of the pack and Eddie Bracken as the secretly married cadet who is about to become a father. Silly romantic situations. A-II (br)

About Last Night (1986) Romance set against the vulgar background of the singles scene, where the immaturity and insecurities of two young professionals (Demi Moore and Rob Lowe) doom to failure their struggle to form a lasting bond. Played for comedy by director Edward Zwick, the movie is socially, emotionally, and morally uninformed about the nature of a truly loving relationship. Rough language and nudity in a sexual context. O (R)

About Mrs. Leslie (1954) Sentimental tearjerker about a good-hearted nightclub singer (Shirley Booth) who takes an annual decompression holiday with an overly intense businessman (Robert Ryan), then cuts him dead when she discovers he's married. Directed by Daniel Mann, the bittersweet romance is told in maudlin flashbacks, though Booth's sunny performance is likeable, if not credible. Muddled romantic complications. A-III (br)

Above the Law (1988) Silly, convoluted detective yarn featuring a Chicago cop (Steven Seagal), whose martial-arts expertise and former involvement with the CIA make him a target for every macho crook and dirty dealing CIA agent in town. Directed by Andrew Davis, it's a disappointing, politically confused story focusing mainly on the martial arts for which Seagal is noted. Excessive violence, much grisly gore, and a liberal dose of profanity. O (R)

Absence of Malice (1981) Ambitious Miami reporter (Sally Field) is duped into reporting false information on the son of an organized-crime figure (Paul Newman). Though director Sydney Pollack slickly stacks the deck against the news media, the movie does succeed in raising serious issues about media responsibility and public opinion. Incidental details include suicide, abortion, and an illicit sexual relationship. A-II (PG)

Absent-Minded Professor, The (1961) Mildly amusing Disney comedy with Fred MacMurray as a daffy science professor who discovers a potion that lets people and objects defy the laws of gravity. The resulting silliness might best be appreciated by the very young. A-I (G)

Absolute Beginners (1986) Youth-oriented musical drama starring David Bowie as an ad man selling materialism to adolescents, represented by a teenage song-and-dance team (Eddie O'Connell and Patsy Kensit). British production directed by Julien Temple links the euphoria of young people in the late 1960s with the birth of a youth subculture and consumer market. Mainly, however, it celebrates lack of conscience and good judgment as the substance of adolescence. An intense scene of violence and a confused perspective on adolescent sexuality. A-III (PG-13)

Absolute Power (1997) Sleek but shallow suspense drama in which a jewel thief (Clint Eastwood) secretly witnesses a murder implicating the president (Gene Hackman), then decides to ruin the White House cover-up, at the risk of his own life and that of his daughter (Laura Linney). Also produced and directed by Eastwood, the fine performances can't quite cover the inconsistencies in the flawed narrative. Intermittent violence, including a stylized scene of sexual violence, recurring profanity, and occasional rough language. A-IV (R)

Absolution (1988) A priest (Richard Burton) at a British Catholic boys' school is driven to commit a grisly murder after his teenage protegé (Dominic Guard) torments the priest in confession with lies about sexual trysts and murder. Director Anthony Page invests the scenario with a promise of menace never fulfilled by screenwriter Anthony Shaffer. Remorseless, gruesome murders, and some profanity. O (R)

Abyss, The (1989) Derivative sea adventure tracking the attempt to rescue a US nuclear submarine which has sunk in waters inhabited by mysterious, benign alien creatures. Writer-director James Cameron drowns the fantasy in a sea of dopey interpersonal distractions and technological razzle-dazzle. Intense underwater action with drownings, resuscitations, and locker-room language. A-III (PG-13)

Accident (1967) Cryptic Harold Pinter script begins with an auto crash killing the young man engaged to an Oxford coed, after which the events and forces contributing to the "accident" are presented in flashback, including the rivalry of two dons for the woman student's affection. Director Joseph Losey and an excellent cast use the sparse dialogue and strained situations to give clues to the violence developing beneath the tranquil surface of academic life. Adult situation and treatment. A-III (br)

Accidental Tourist, The (1988) Poignant, whimsical adaptation of Anne Tyler's novel about an emotionally shut-down travel writer (William Hurt) struggling to cope with the death of his son and the disintegration of his marriage. Director Lawrence Kasdan depicts the gradual unfolding of this withered, weary man in relation to the two women in his life (Kathleen Turner and Geena Davis) in a sensitively told story of death and rebirth. A discreetly filmed bedroom scene and implied cohabitation without benefit of marriage. A-III (PG)

Accompanist, The (1993) After being hired as piano accompanist for an acclaimed classical singer (Elena Safonova) during the German occupation, a meek young Parisienne (Romane Bohringer) comes to resent her employer's rich life with an adoring husband (Richard Bohringer) and secret lover (Samuel Labarthe), while she remains in the background with no personal life of her own. Director Claude Miller's melancholy tale of love and loss skillfully uses the music track to reflect the characters' tortured emotions. Subtitles. An implied affair and an off-screen suicide. A-III (PG)

Accused, The (1948) Muddy melodrama in which a psychology professor (Loretta Young) kills a student (Douglas Dick) while fending off his advances, then lives in fear of being found out by the youth's smitten guardian (Robert Cummings) and the investigating policeman (Wendell Corey). Director William Dieterle sets up the premise in involving fashion, but the woman's plight grows overly contrived and ultimately tiresome. An act of violence and growing psychological tension. A-II (br)

Accused, The (1988) In a powerful story of violence and justice, a loose-living young woman (Jodie Foster) is brutally gang-raped in a bar and, after the rapists are sentenced to prison, the district attorney (Kelly McGillis) brings charges against the barflies who cheered them on. Though the rape is explicitly shown in flashback during the trial proceedings, director Jonathan Kaplan clearly portrays it as a crime of violence. Lengthy, graphic gang-rape sequence is excessively detailed and there is much profanity. O (R)

Accused of Murder (1956) Routine crime story directed by Joe Kane in which a police detective (David Brian) falls for a blonde singer (Vera Ralston), whom his partner (Lee Van Cleef) suspects murdered a shady lawyer (Sidney Blackmer). Stylized violence and romantic complications. A-II (br)

Ace Eli and Rodger of the Skies (1973) Cliff Robertson and Eric Shea play a father-son team of Kansas barnstormers in the early 1920s who are flying away from the tragic death of the woman in their life. For Eli, his wife's death triggers a streak of womanizing, while for his 11-year-old son, the loss of a mother brings out a raunchy maturity and wisdom far surpassing that of his father, but also the search for a new mother-figure. Director Bill Sampson's failed drama is a confusing and confused, largely unmotivated, concoction of scenes alternately nostalgic, crude, cruel, near-perverse, and sappy. A-III (PG)

Ace High (1969) Revenge with a humorous twist is the theme of this low-budget Italian Western starring Eli Wallach as a bug-ridden, babysitting Greek bandit. Director Giuseppe Colizzi's action is slapdash but unflagging enough to compensate for rough dubbing, poor color, and ragged editing. Stylized violence. A-II (M)

Ace in the Hole (1951) Cynical reporter (Kirk Douglas) parlays the local story of a man trapped in a New Mexico cave into a national news event by getting a corrupt sheriff to delay the weakening victim's rescue for a week. Director Billy Wilder's dark study of media manipulation and the public's appetite for sensationalism has few characters with any integrity, save the reporter's editor (Porter Hall), the tragic victim, and his devoted parents. Continuing menace and unsavory characters. A-II (br)

Ace Ventura: Pet Detective (1994) Deadening comedy in which a nerdy gumshoe (Jim Carrey) gets involved sexually with two women (Courtney Cox and Sean Young) while attempting to rescue kidnapped Miami Dolphins quarterback Dan Marino and the team mascot on the eve of the Super Bowl. Tom Shadyac directs what is little more than an obnoxious parade of scatological jokes, demeaning sexist remarks, and mindless violence. Realistic brutality played for laughs, some bedroom scenes, brief nudity, and occasional profanity. O (PG-13)

Ace Ventura: When Nature Calls (1995) The further adventures of the manic pet detective (Jim Carrey) land him in the African jungle, where he overcomes assorted dangers in rescuing a kidnapped white bat. Writer-director Steve Oedekerk gives rubber-faced Carrey free rein to mug his way through a series of inane physical skits whose humor ranges from the outrageous to the tasteless. Slapstick violence, occasional sexual innuendo, and fleeting nudity. A-III (PG-13)

Aces: Iron Eagle III (1992) Action-packed sequel follows former WW II fighter pilots (Louis Gossett, Jr., Horst Buchholz, Sonny Chiba, and Christopher Cazenove) to Peru, where they intend to blow up a cocaine factory with souped-up vintage aircraft. John Glen directs a predictable shoot-'em-up whose comic overtones make the violent outbursts and characters seem cartoonish. Recurring violence. A-III (R)

Aces High (1976) WW I tale of the Royal Flying Corps, as an idealistic English youth (Peter Firth) arrives in 1917 France at an airbase whose hardened commander (Malcolm McDowell) is sick of sending young pilots to their death. Directed by Jack Gold, the British production pays close attention to period details and stages numerous dogfights between vintage biplanes, but the picture's anti-war perspective and stereotyped characters are too familiar to make any fresh impression of their own. Wartime violence, sexual situations and innuendo, fleeting nude photos, and occasional profanity. A-III (PG)

Across 110th Street (1972) Anthony Quinn plays a tough old-time cop compelled for political reasons to work with a black new-breed policeman (Yaphet Kotto) in tracking down the three blacks who ripped off a syndicate-controlled, black-managed Harlem numbers bank. Unfortunately, director Barry Shear develops neither the broader implications of the story's social conflicts nor the potentially interesting personality clash of his principals, apparently too involved with the mechanics of all the violence that is so grossly in evidence. O (R)

Across the Great Divide (1977) Two orphans on the pioneer trail to Oregon in 1876 are guided through the perils of frontier America by a charming gambler (Robert Logan). Directed by Robert Raffill, it provides a familiar mixture of attractive characters, photogenic animals, and gorgeous scenery. The slick use of these wholesome elements at the expense of any realism may strike some viewers as rather calculated, but that does not lessen its value as fantasy entertainment for family audiences. A-I (G)

Across the Wide Missouri (1951) Colorful Western adventure about a mountain man (Clark Gable) taking a polyglot company of hunters into 1829 Montana country, where he weds a Blackfoot woman (Maria Elena Marques), then stays with her people to raise their son after she's killed by an Indian renegade (Ricardo Montalban). Director William A. Wellman does well with the rugged setting of the early West and its clash of cultures, but the narrative turns flat with subsequent domestic contrivances. Stylized violence and romantic situations. A-II (br)

Act of Aggression (1975) French vigilante movie about a man (Jean-Louis Trintignant) whose wife and daughter have been brutally raped and murdered, apparently by vicious bikers, and his lust both for revenge and for his wife's sister (Catherine Deneuve). Director Gerard Pires never grapples seriously with the vendetta theme but concentrates instead on the romance, employing some nudity and kinky sexuality. O (R)

Act of Murder, An (1948) After celebrating their 20th wedding anniversary, a judge (Fredric March) learns his wife (Florence Eldridge) has an incurable brain tumor and, as her condition grows increasingly painful, determines to end her suffering, but the wife has her own plans. Directed by Michael Gordon, the drama sets up the arguments for and against mercy killing with a copout ending that finds the judge legally innocent but morally guilty. Adult theme and treatment. A-III (br)

Act of the Heart, The (1970) Sensitive but flawed Canadian drama about a young woman (Genevieve Bujold) whose love for a priest (Donald Sutherland) results in his leaving the ministry, but his subsequent disillusionment with the world leads her to burn herself to death. Until this grisly conclusion, the movie had been a perceptive study of character and feeling in which director Paul Almond explored issues of loneliness, the search for self, and meaning in the contemporary world. Inadequately motivated, the violent act of self-immolation is a major miscalculation in what otherwise is a gentle story of idealism and love. A-IV (GP)

Act of Vengeance (1974) Exploitation melodrama about rape and the efforts of five victims, led by Joann Harris, to entrap their assailant, a sadist with a penchant for singing "Jingle Bells." Director Robert Kelljan seems less concerned about showing the degradation and humiliation of rape as an act of violence against women than as using an anti-rape theme as an excuse for displaying naked bodies as sex objects. O (R)

Action in the North Atlantic (1943) The captain (Raymond Massey), first mate (Humphrey Bogart), and crew (Alan Hale, Sam Levene, Dane Clark, etc.) of a torpedoed oil tanker sign on to another tanker in a convoy bound for Murmansk, heroically fighting off U-boats and air attacks along the way. Director Lloyd Bacon's lengthy tribute to the merchant marine may have stirred WW II audiences, but the action seems artificial now and the patriotic sentiments heavy-handed. Wartime violence. A-II (br)

Action Jackson (1988) The ultra-violent exploits of a Detroit police detective (Carl Weathers) are detailed in a contrived series of bloody killings, car chases, crashes, and explosions, perpetrated by an exotic collection of villains in the hire of a power-mad businessman (Craig T. Nelson). Director Craig R. Baxley laces the special-effects pyrotechnics with some sexual titillation and drug scenes. Excessive violence, some nudity, and much rough language. O (R)

Action of the Tiger (1958) Potboiler in which a Frenchwoman (Martine Carol) gets an American adventurer (Van Johnson) to help smuggle her blind brother out of Communist Albania, picking up a band of refugee children along the way. Directed by Terence Young, it has an exotic setting and some colorful action, but the story is plodding and predictable, including the silly twist ending. Stylized violence and sexual innuendo. A-III (br)

Activist, The (1969) Amateurish semi-documentary account of several months in the life of a Berkley student who is a dedicated militant in the protest movement. The best thing about this fictional reconstruction is some actual newsreel footage of campus demonstrations. Directed by Art and Jo Napoleon. Lengthy and explicit love-making scene lacks any dramatic purpose or justification. O (X)

Adalen '31 (1969) Swedish production re-creates a 1931 labor strike by focusing on the lives of individual workers involved in the struggle for subsistence. The political conflict and social commentary are crystal clear, but remarkably unobtrusive amid the vignettes of daily life in a small town during hard times. When scab workers arrive, a peaceful demonstration ends in violence and death. Using a mixture of romantic fiction and economic realities, director Bo Widerburg successfully combines social awareness with lyric beauty. Brief nudity and casual acceptance of abortion. A-IV (X)

Adam at 6 A.M. (1970) West Coast college professor (Michael Douglas), searching for the values of heartland America, spends a summer doing construction work in Missouri, decides to settle down and marry a local belle (Lee Purcell), but then realizes that life in the Midwest will be no less conformist than that of the world from which he has fled. Director Robert Scheerer employs a number of easy stereotypes to characterize America's geographic and cultural polarities, but beneath the movie's slick surface is a profoundly cynical commentary upon the country's heritage and the values of its people. A-IV (GP)

Adam Had Four Sons (1941) Artificial tearjerker, directed by Gregory Ratoff, about the travails of a French governess (Ingrid Bergman) in caring for the boys of a New York stockbroker (Warner Baxter) from 1907 until the youths enlist in WW I. The nub of the story turns on the devoted governess' determination to shield her preoccupied employer from learning that his son's wartime bride (Susan Hayward) is a greedy conniver. Sudsy picture of a virtuous woman contrasted with a selfish one. A-II (br)

Adam's Rib (1950) Sly romantic comedy about married attorneys (Spencer Tracy and Katharine Hepburn) battling over the issue of women's rights when she defends a wife (Judy Holliday) on trial for shooting her philandering husband (Tom Ewell), while he represents the wounded man. Director George Cukor injects the witty dialogue and visual comedy with screwball overtones and the Tracy-Hepburn exchanges are prime, though the feminist views seem tame today. Comic view of the battle of the sexes. A-II (br)

Adam's Rib (1992) Living in a cramped Soviet apartment, a twice-divorced working mother (Inna Churikova) tries to juggle taking care of her own aged mother; two troubled, unmarried daughters; and a new man in her life. Ukrainian director Vyacheslav Krishtofovich has nothing particularly new to say about mother-daughter relations or the travails of single women, though the cultural context may make them seem a little more interesting than our own domestic melodramas. Subtitles. Some discussion of sexual matters, a comically interrupted bedroom tryst, and minimal rough language. A-III (nr)

Addams Family, The (1991) Based on the tongue-in-cheek clan of grotesques created by cartoonist Charles Addams, the movie version revolves around a scheme to steal the family fortune from Gomez Addams (Raul Julia) and wife, Morticia (Anjelica Huston), by a man (Christopher Lloyd) claiming to be their long-lost relative, Fester. Directed by Barry Sonnenfeld, the anemic plot only gets in the way of the eccentric sets, outlandish make-up, sinister special effects, and intermittent bits of macabre humor. Much dark comedy, some bizarre comic violence, and mild sexual innuendo. A-II (PG-13)

Addams Family Values (1993) Macabre comedy sequel has the Addams children (Christina Ricci and Jimmy Workman) attempting to eliminate their mustachioed baby brother, while their lovestruck uncle (Christopher Lloyd) marries a murderous fortune hunter (Joan Cusack). Director Barry Sonnenfeld injects some outrageous black humor into a broad, predictable slapstick comedy that is more concerned about style than content. Frequent comic menace to a baby, violence played for laughs, and occasional sexual innuendo. A-II (PG-13)

Addicted to Love (1997) A heartbroken astronomer (Matthew Broderick) and a vengeful photographer (Meg Ryan) join forces to wreck a romance between their ex-flames (Kelly Preston and Tcheky Karyo). Director Griffin Dunne's overly contrived romantic comedy has a distinctly dark side, but relies heavily on the appeal of the rejected pair as they predictably turn to each other. Brief comic violence, fleeting shadowy nudity, and references to pre-marital affairs. A-III (R)

Addiction, The (1995) Slack horror tale set in New York City, where a philosophy student (Lili Taylor) is bitten by a vampire, becomes one herself, and infects others with the lust for blood. Director Abel Ferrara stages the action in a clumsy series of wooden scenes which unaccountably motivate characters to philosophical and religious digressions on the nature of evil. Stylized violence with unconvincing gore. A-III (nr)

Adding Machine, The (1969) An office worker (Milo O'Shea), saddled with a nagging wife (Phyllis Diller), has fantasies of an affair with his pretty assistant (Billie Whitelaw). When he kills his boss and a sentence of death is carried out, he ultimately winds up in a hell of adding machines. Adapted by producer-director Jerome Epstein from a '30's Elmer Rice play, the stagy result speaks less about the contemporary onslaught of automation and economic disparity than it does of a very dated kind of ideological indignation. A-III (PG)

Adelaide (1969) Director Jean-Daniel Simon was unable to elevate this pulp story of a widow whose new husband continues to carry on an affair with her teenage daughter. Static and introverted atmosphere, incomprehensible plot development, and determined underplaying by Ingrid Thulin and Jean Sorel supply no motivation for the senseless actions of the story's characters. O (R)

Adieu Philippine (1973) French production about a young man awaiting his army call-up who begins a flirtation with two girls who are intimate friends, a situation left unresolved by the boy's departure, but with the sense of embarking on a new, more mature phase of life. Directed by Jacques Rozier, this 1961 movie is a mosaic of scenes, beautifully photographed and evocative of the carefree romanticism of youth, carefully knit together by the jukebox music of the period. Without a traditional narrative, however, its appeal is mainly to those who enjoy watching a well-crafted film. A-III (nr)

Adios, Sabata (1971) Routine Italian Western with bounty hunter Yul Brynner polishing off great gobs of humanity in his relentless pursuit of a Mexican revolutionary and a share of Maximillian's gold. Taken seriously, all this violence would be alarming, but played tongue-in-cheek under Frank Kramer's direction, it's a comic fantasy for those who enjoy such action programs. A-II (GP)

Adjuster, The (1992) Bleak and boring look at the sexual perversions of an insurance adjuster (Elias Koteas); his wife (Arsinee Khanjian), who collects porno films; and a phony filmmaker (Maury Chaykin), who uses their home for his own murderous ends. Writer-director Atom Egoyan offers a sick view of characters who deliberately doom themselves and those around them. Frequent sexual references, a shadowy sexual encounter, some nudity, and intermittent rough language. O (R)

Adrift (1971) Czechoslovakian production about a fisherman who rescues a beautiful woman from drowning and his gradual disintegration (told in flashbacks mixing reality with fantasy) driven by desire for the girl (Paula Pritchett), who has become a member of his household. Although not entirely successful in its fancy time-sequences, director Jan Kadar's leisurely pace builds steadily towards his powerful conclusion concerning man's vulnerability to temptation. The erotic element of the film is a necessary one counterbalanced by the very human portrayals of the fisherman and his wife (Rade Markovic and Milena Dravic). A-IV (R)

Adventure (1946) Flat-footed seriocomic romance between a footloose sailor (Clark Gable) and an independent-minded librarian (Greer Garson) who clash, marry, and divorce, until reunited in a maudlin finish. Directed by Victor Fleming, the two leads are hopelessly miscast in a clunker that even wastes performances by Joan Blondell as the other woman and Thomas Mitchell as a sailor who's lost his soul. Stylized violence, sexual innuendo, and bogus virile posturing. A-III (br)

Adventure for Two (see: **The Demi-Paradise**)

Adventure in Baltimore (1949) Vacuous romantic comedy set in 1905 concerns an earnest young suffragette (Shirley Temple), whose unchaperoned meetings with a young man (John Agar) stir up considerable gossip just when her minister-father (Robert Young) is being considered for bishop. Director Richard Wallace treats the contrived proceedings in heavy-handed fashion, but especially tiresome is Temple's role as an idealistic meddler. A-I (br)

Adventure of Sherlock Holmes' Smarter Brother, The (1975) Gene Wilder directs, as well as stars in, a fairly conventional romantic comedy, except for his eclectic choice of comedy styles, including some heavy-handed vulgarities. Instead of satirizing mystery movies, the plot is a disconnected series of complications about a stolen document that is at last recovered by chance rather than by ratiocination. The movie's intermittent amusement is marred by some spectacularly tasteless visuals, double entendres, and a love scene that goes beyond comic intentions. O (PG)

Adventurers, The (1970) One man's experiences from childhood to early middle-age in a revolutionary South American country are the focus of this long, sprawling soap opera based on Harold Robbins's novel and directed by Lewis Gilbert. Motivation is frequently sacrificed for plot elements featuring brutality, pillage, rape, sadism, voyeurism, nudity, lesbianism, and adultery. O (R)

Adventures in Babysitting (1987) Teenage

babysitter (Elizabeth Shue) and her wards suffer through an evening of harrowing escapades while trying to rescue their runaway friend stranded in a downtown Chicago bus station. Flawed seriocomic tale deals with real urban dangers in a treatment made irresponsibly light and mundane by writer-director Chris Columbus. Some violence, sexual innuendo, and profanity mar this trite diversion aimed at youngsters. A-III (PG-13)

Adventures of Baron Munchausen, The (1989) The fantasy exploits of an 18th-century adventurer notorious for his exaggerated stories are re-created in a tongue-in-cheek tale about the wacky adventures of the Baron (John Neville) and his 10-year-old traveling companion (Sarah Polley) in a city besieged by Turks, during a trip to the moon, and in brushes with a volcano and a whale. Director Terry Gilliam's elaborate special effects will entrance all ages, but the plot is so bloated that few will find it interesting, and children may be more confused than entertained. Minimal sexual innuendo, a flash of nudity, and much comic-book violence. A-II (PG)

Adventures of Buckaroo Banzai, The (1984) Director W.D. Richter's sci-fi spoof is about a punk-rock, space-age neurosurgeon (Peter Weller) who stumbles into the eighth dimension, where he learns of an alien plot to destroy the world. How all this happens or, indeed, what happens, is not very clear. It's comic-book fantasy for people who are content to watch a lot of action and strange characters without asking too many questions. Very stylized violence. A-II (PG)

Adventures of Bullwhip Griffin, The (1967) Roddy McDowall deadpans for gold in the Wild West with Suzanne Pleshette along for romantic interest. The plot broadly spoofs Gold Rush days, with director James Neilson getting the most from its collection of jokes and sight gags. Karl Malden, Richard Haydn, and Mike Mazurki help make this pleasant comedy one of the better efforts by the Disney studios. A-I (br)

Adventures of Captain Sebastian (1951) Romantic potboiler set in pre-Civil War New Orleans, where an ambitious maid (Micheline Presle) on trial for murder is saved by a sea captain (Errol Flynn), whom she spurns so she can marry a devious merchant (Vincent Price), with dire consequences for all three. The result is a clumsy melodrama which sputters lifelessly along until its hokey climax. Directed by William Marshall. Stylized violence and sexual situations. A-III (br)

Adventures of Chico (1937) Simple tale produced by Stacy and Horace Woodard follows the ordinary activities of a Mexican goat-herder and his young son and their encounters with the rural area's wildlife, including a quail hunt and the father's tracking down a marauding cougar. Ineffective narration but fine nature photography. A-I (br)

Adventures of Ford Fairlane, The (1990) Blue stand-up comic Andrew Dice Clay plays the title's repulsive macho detective in search of a dimwitted blonde who holds the key to the murder of a heavy-metal rock star. Supposedly a comic thriller, director Renny Harlin's limp, mirthless vehicle serves only to showcase Clay's sewer mouth, sexist attitudes, and penchant for nasty, gratuitous violence. Constant rough language, excessive violence, and numerous demeaning sexual situations. O (R)

Adventures of Gallant Bess (1948) After training a wild mare to be a trick horse, a rodeo rider (Cameron Mitchell) is injured and his prize horse taken away by a crooked rodeo owner (James Millican). Directed by Lew Lander, the story of the bond between a cowboy and his horse is routine fare, though the location footage is colorful and questions are raised about training animals to perform in show business. Some tense situations. A-I (br)

Adventures of Huck Finn, The (1993) Spirited rendition of Mark Twain's tale of an irrepressibly mischievous lad (Elijah Wood) rafting down the Mississippi with a runaway slave (Courtney B. Vance), until a brush with disaster when they become involved with a pair of colorful con-men (Robbie Coltrane and Jason Robards). Adapted and directed by Stephen Sommers, the zestful performance of the young Wood brightens the fast-moving, handsomely mounted production that makes abundantly clear its anti-slavery stance. Some menace and stylized violence. A-II (PG)

Adventures of Huckleberry Finn, The (1960) Good production of the Mark Twain classic, though Eddie Hodges is a mite sweet as Huck and former boxing champ Archie Moore a bit stiff as the runaway slave, Jim. Director Michael Curtiz conveys much of the spirit of the original and gets amusing support from the colorful cast of characters, especially Tony Randall and Mickey Shaughnessy as the Mississippi con artists. Enjoyable family fare. A-I (br)

Adventures of Huckleberry Finn, The (for the 1931, 1939, and 1974 versions, see: **Huckleberry Finn**)

Adventures of Ichabod and Mr. Toad, The (1949) Disney animated double feature begins with Basil Rathbone narrating a lovely, fanciful adaptation of Kenneth Grahame's *Wind in the Willows*, followed by Bing Crosby singing, as well as telling, Washington Irving's "Legend of Sleepy Hollow," with its spooky Headless Horseman. Directed by Jack Kinney, Clyde Geronimi, and James Algar, the slight but enjoyable American tale pales alongside the bouncy, whimsical British children's classic. Quality family fare. A-I (br)

Adventures of Jack London, The (see: **Jack London**)

Adventures of Marco Polo, The (1938) Gary Cooper plays the curious 13th-century Venetian on his travels through China, where he discovers spaghetti, coal, and gunpowder while saving the throne of Kublai Khan (George Barbier) from a villainous court official (Basil Rathbone). Directed by Archie Mayo, the stylish spectacle is undercut by lackluster comedy and halting action. Stylized violence and romantic situations. A-II (br)

Adventures of Mark Twain, The (1944) Interesting piece of Americana follows Twain's life as Mississippi riverboat pilot, Western prospector, newspaper reporter, popular humorist, and acclaimed author. Irving Rapper directs Fredric March in a quite winning performance as the irascible humbug of the title, with Alexis Smith as his cherished wife, whose early death devastates the man and darkens his writing. Idealized view of Twain's life provides satisfying, meaningful entertainment. A-I (br)

Adventures of Mark Twain, The (1986) Combining elements of the author's life and times with excerpts from his writings, this animated fantasy will engage youngsters while providing older viewers with some insights into Twain's complex character. Will Vinton's use of clay animation, with fully modeled characters in imaginative sets, is a visual treat. Several scenes may be frightening for the very young but otherwise unusually fine family entertainment. A-I (G)

Adventures of Milo and Otis, The (1989) Fine Japanese live-action movie about a mischievous kitten named Milo and his puppy pal, Otis, who get lost in the autumn wilderness but eventually return home in the spring with their own mates and families. Zestfully narrated by actor Dudley Moore, director Masanori Hata's imaginative photography reveals the wonder of nature and the cycle of life, including brief shots of the birth of a kitten and puppy. Some mild tension in a few scenes involving wild animals, but otherwise it is a welcome, gentle experience for the young and adults who enjoy the beauty of nature. A-I (G)

Adventures of Pinocchio, The (1996) Charming tale about a kindly puppet carver (Martin Landau) whose enchanted wooden puppet (voice of Jonathan Taylor Thomas) yearns to become a real boy, but who must first learn not to lie and must pass through several dangers before he can make his wish come true. Director Steve Barron nicely blends the live cast with the impressively lifelike animatronic puppet for a luminous storybook look, although there are a few scary moments for preschoolers. A-I (G)

Adventures of Priscilla, Queen of the Desert, The (1994) A drag queen (Hugo Weaving) and his chums (Terence Stamp and Guy Pearce) travel by bus through the Australian outback, rehearsing their stage act for alternately friendly and hostile audiences before performing at a hotel where the drag queen's estranged wife and youngsters are waiting. Writer-director Stephan Elliott's lavish treatment of the flamboyant cross-dressers casts a comic eye on their extravagant excesses, but fails to address their inner conflicts with much insight. Sympathetic depiction of openly gay lifestyles, an implied homosexual affair, some crude sexual innuendo, and frequent rough language. A-IV (R)

Adventures of Robin Hood, The (1938) Rousing costume adventure tale pitting the good Robin (Errol Flynn), Lttle John (Alan Hale), Friar Tuck (Eugene Pallette), and the rest of the Merry Men of Sherwood Forest against the nasty Prince John (Claude Rains) and the Sheriff of Nottingham (Basil Rathbone), with the lovely Maid Marian (Olivia de Havilland) serving as pawn. Directed by Michael Curtiz and William Keighley, the story's fight against injustice is treated with sincerity but told playfully, the color photography adds zest to the action scenes, and the Warner Brothers' cast of supporting players seem to be having as good a time as the leads. Vintage but still sparkling. A-I (br)

Adventures of Sherlock Holmes, The (1939) Mysterious doings in fog-bound London keep Holmes (Basil Rathbone) and Watson (Nigel Bruce) busy safeguarding a client (Ida Lupino), while Professor Moriarty (George Zucco) prepares to snatch a priceless jewel from the Tower of London. Director Alfred Werker laces the suspense with sinister Victorian settings which help sustain the convoluted narrative to its satisfactory conclusion. Brief violence and some menace. A-I (br)

Adventures of Tartu, The (1943) British tale of derring-do in WW II, as a military explosives expert (Robert Donat) is sent to Czechoslovakia to steal the formula for a new poison gas, then destroy the factory about to manufacture it. Directed by Harold S. Bucquet, the patriotic adventure is awash in improbabilities and villainous Nazis, though helped by Donat's wry performance and some winsome members of the Czech underground (Valerie Hobson and Glynis Johns). Some intense menace. A-II (br)

Adventures of the Great Mouse Detective, The (see: **The Great Mouse Detective**)

Adventures of the Wilderness Family, The (1975) Los Angeles family, fed up with the problems of urban life, leave it all behind to set up housekeeping in a remote section of the Rocky Mountains. What follows is predictable, but director Stewart Raffill tells it with a disarming combination of artlessness and professional competence. Good wildlife adventure. A-I (G)

Adventures of Tom Sawyer, The (1938) Fine version of Mark Twain's classic yarn of boyhood in which a frisky Missouri lad (Tommy Kelly) witnesses a graveyard murder, saves the man accused (Walter Brennan) by identifying Injun Joe (Victor Jory) as the culprit, then rescues girlfriend Becky (Ann Gillis) when they get trapped in a mammoth cave. Directed by Norman Taurog, the dandy action sequences are nicely paced by sentimental domestic scenes laced with humor involving his Aunt Polly (May Robson), cousin Sidney, a schoolteacher, and a Sunday school official (Donald Meek). Some menacing moments. A-I (br)

Adventuress, The (1946) Wry British thriller set in WW II as an Irish colleen (Deborah Kerr) puts her hatred of England to work helping a German spy (Raymond Huntley), then has second thoughts and tries to flee pursuing German and British agents with the help of a smitten English officer (Trevor Howard). Directed by Frank Launder, the loosely plotted proceedings are not very convincing, but there are plenty of droll situations along the way and much good-natured kidding of British and Irish stereotypes. Stylized violence and comic national aspersions. A-II (br)

Adversary, The (1973) Indian production directed by Satyajit Ray tells the story of a former student who has high hopes of achieving more than a dead-end job but, when he falls in love, becomes a rural drug salesman, resigned to becoming part of the faceless Indian masses. Set in Calcutta, a city drowning in its mass of humanity, Ray's protagonist is society itself and the failure of the present system to humanize the process of industrialized urbanization. Ray's blending of human sensibility with a passion for social justice makes this an unusually important work. A-III (nr)

Advise and Consent (1962) Sprawling potboiler about Washington politics revolves around the nomination of a liberal academic (Henry Fonda) as secretary of state, with a vengeful Southern senator (Charles Laughton) getting a troubled clerk (Burgess Meredith) to charge the nominee with communism, while a wild-eyed junior senator (George Grizzard) tries to influence the hearings by blackmailing the committee chairman (Don Murray) over his homosexual past. Directed by Otto Preminger from Allen Drury's novel, the performances in this rogues' gallery of bickering politicians are enjoyably broad, though the melodramatic proceedings end abruptly with the death of the ailing president (Franchot Tone) and his ignored vice president (Lew Ayres) firmly taking charge. An off-screen suicide, sexual situations, and unethical political conduct. A-IV (br)

Advocate, The (1994) A 15th-century Paris lawyer (Colin Firth) has his illusions about the virtues of simple rural foHlk shattered after setting up practice in a small town ruled by fear, superstition, lust, and murder. Written and directed by Leslie Megahey, the glossy British production turns medieval life into a freak show of bizarre cases involving bestiality, witchcraft, and animals tried as criminals, but its titillating tabloid account lacks any dramatic — let alone historical — insights. Some graphic sex, exploitative nudity, and emphasis on religious hypocrisy. O (R)

Affair in Havana (1957) Turgid melodrama directed by Laslo Benedek and filmed in Cuba, where a visiting American pianist (John Cassavetes) falls for the greedy wife (Sara Shane) of a wheelchair-bound industrialist (Raymond Burr), who winds up murdered. Stylized violence and an adulterous relationship. A-III (br)

Affair to Remember, An (1957) Lush sentimental melodrama begins as light comedy with a shipboard romance between a wealthy bachelor (Cary Grant) and a former nightclub singer (Deborah Kerr), then plunges into heavyweight soap opera when their rendezvous in New York is prevented by an accident. Director Leo McCarey's remake of his 1939 **Love Affair** manages to keep the lumbering romance afloat with an old-fashioned mix of smiles and tears, a charming cast, and plush settings. Starry-eyed romance. A-II (br)

Affair with a Stranger (1953) Formula sudser starts with gossip about a Broadway playwright (Victor Mature) seeking to divorce his wife (Jean Simmons), then uses a series of flashbacks to trace the couple's courtship, marriage, growing fame, and adoption of a son before returning to the present and the predictable outcome. Directed by Roy Rowland, the sentimental story is well-intended, but has little charm and no surprises. Mild sexual innuendo. A-II (br)

Affairs of Annabel, The (1938) Comic misadventures of a movie star (Lucille Ball) cajoled by a dizzy press agent (Jack Oakie) into publicity stunts which invariably backfire, including one which results in her being kidnapped by bank robbers. Directed by Ben Stoloff, the no-frills production has a congenial cast and some wacky period humor aimed at the Hollywood studio system. Dated, but unpretentious and still largely fun. A-I (br)

Affliction (1998) Compelling drama charts the inevitable fall from grace of a small-town, part-time cop (Nick Nolte) after an acrimonious divorce, continued verbal abuse by his alcoholic father (James Coburn), and fears that his best friend may have murdered a union official. Director Paul Schrader's adaptation of Russell Bank's bleak novel uses spare dialogue and chilling imagery to show how a lifetime of emotional and physical violence has left a tortured soul unable to cope with his demons. Scattered violence, alcohol abuse, an implied affair, recurring rough language, and frequent profanity. A-III (R)

Afraid of the Dark (1992) Bizarre, disjointed thriller about a disturbed child (Ben Keyworth), his endangered baby sister, his mother (Fanny Ardant) who may or may not be blind, and a neighborhood slasher (Paul McGann). Director Mark Peploe's twisted tale of deadly menace and mayhem is badly structured and largely unintelligible. Exploitative violence, especially that involving two children, a lingering nude shot, and frequent nasty menace. O (R)

Africa Addio (1967) Cruelty, violence, blood, gore, and human indignity are highlighted in director Gualtiero Jacopetti's Italian documentary, which claims that its aim is to enlighten viewers concerning the "birth pangs" of emerging African nations. Exploitation of serious subject. O (R)

Africa Blood and Guts (see: **Africa Addio**)

Africa Screams (1949) The usual comedy of errors begins with Manhattan book clerks (Bud Abbott and Lou Costello) joining a crook (Hillary Brooke) on an African safari through cannibal-infested jungles in quest of diamonds. Director Charles Barton garners few laughs from the boys' tired routines while encountering domestic thugs, wild animals, puzzled natives, and real jungle veterans Clyde Beatty and Frank Buck. Slapstick violence and African stereotypes. A-I (br)

Africa — Texas Style (1967) Texas cowboys are hired to herd wild animals on the plains of Kenya because domestic cattle are turning the land into a dust bowl. The idea of switching from cattle-ranching to game-ranching is an intriguing one that director Andrew Marton keeps moving with old-fashioned Western action in exotic African settings. Good family entertainment. A-I (nr)

African Elephant, The (1971) Simon Trevor, a former African guide and game warden turned wildlife filmmaker, has made an in-depth birth-to-death documentary on the world's largest and strongest land mammal. Achieving its aims with beauty, sensitivity, and intelligence, the movie conveys an experience of the land, the surrounding wildlife, and the environment in which the elephant exists. Unlike many such movies, the violence which is so much a part of the wild is given a rationale and thoroughly integrated into the whole. Parents in search of suitable movies for children will find it a healthy, broadening experience for even their youngest. A-I (G)

African Fury (see: 1952's **Cry, the Beloved Country**)

African Queen, The (1951) Director John Huston's tale of high romantic adventure set in Africa during WW I features Katharine Hepburn as a prim missionary who enlists the aid of rough riverboat captain Humphrey Bogart in escaping capture by German forces. Sharing a harrowing voyage down a wild jungle river, they gradually develop a relationship that changes both their lives — for the better. Wartime violence. A-II (br)

African Safari (1969) Interesting and exciting documentary excursion into central and east Africa with beautiful photography of the area's wildlife and native customs. Directed and photographed by Ron E. Shanin, it is a rewarding experience both for young people and sophisticated moviegoers. A few graphically violent animal sequences. A-II (G)

After Dark, My Sweet (1990) Manipulative excop (Bruce Dern) involves a lonely widow (Rachel Ward) and an escaped mental patient (Jason Patric) in a deadly kidnapping plot. Intense performances prop up director James Foley's unsavory tale of three losers mired in mutual mistrust, until an unexpectedly moral ending provides a positive note. Brief violence and menace to a child, an extended sexual encounter, and minimal rough language. A-III (R)

After Hours (1985) A bored yuppie (Griffin Dunne) from Manhattan's fashionable East Side ventures into a dangerous part of town to meet an eccentric date (Rosanna Arquette), only to encounter a series of life-threatening misadventures before escaping back to the safety of his own turf in the dawn's early light. Director Martin Scorsese's black comedy lacks satiric bite, preferring instead to wring laughs out of mental instability and bizarre sexual practices. Sophomoric nihilism and some brief nudity. A-IV (R)

After Office Hours (1935) Dated but breezy newspaper yarn in which a crusading editor (Clark Gable) falls for a bright debutante (Constance Bennett) after using her to gain access to a philandering lawyer (Harvey Stephens) he suspects is a murderer. Scripted by Herman J. Mankiewicz and directed by Robert Z. Leonard, the far-fetched plot is of less interest than the witty dialogue and colorful characters. Stylized violence, sexual innuendo, and implied adultery. A-III (br)

After the Fox (1966) Scriptwriter Neil Simon and director Vittorio de Sica collaborated on this surprisingly flat and frequently overdone comedy revolving around a bungling ex-convict (Peter Sellers) who hatches a preposterous scheme to steal the fortune in gold that he has been hired to smuggle into Italy. There are some mildly vulgar jokes, but they offend only one's sense of humor. A-II (br)

After the Thin Man (1936) The first of five sequels to 1934's **The Thin Man** brings private eye Nick Charles (William Powell) and wife Nora (Myrna Loy) on a visit to her rich family in San Francisco, where Nick helps a local flatfoot (Sam Levene) solve a murder case. Though the mystery is not as perplexing as the original, director W.S. Van Dyke II makes it seem almost as much fun, thanks to the breezy byplay between the sleuthing couple and an odd gallery of suspects (notably James Stewart, Joseph Calleia, and George Zucco). Murder mystery menace. A-II (br)

After Tonight (1933) WW I romantic melodrama in which an Austrian officer (Gilbert Roland) falls in love with a nurse (Constance Bennett) while investigating reports of espionage at a military base, then discovers she's a Russian spy. Directed by George Archainbaud, the hokey mix of wartime romance and secret agents limps along without much conviction, until collapsing in a tacked-on happy ending. Menacing situations and romantic complications. A-II (br)

Afterglow (1997) The shaky marriages of two couples (Julie Christie and Nick Nolte; Lara Flynn Boyle and Jonny Lee Miller) are further complicated by an affair between the older husband (Nolte) and younger man's wife (Boyle), forcing each spouse to re-evaluate their relationships. Writer-director Alan Rudolph begins with a serious treatment of infidelity and its consequences, only to reduce the story to the level of bedroom farce leading to a bogus sunny conclusion. Sexual situations with nudity, brief violence, some rough language, and considerable profanity. A-III (R)

Against All Flags (1952) Colorful swashbuckler in which an English sea captain (Errol Flynn) joins a pirate crew in order to enter their impregnable island fortress, then destroy it. Directed by George Sherman, the formula plot focuses on the hero's problems with a suspicious buccaneer (Anthony Quinn), a lovely pirate captain (Maureen O'Hara), and the Grand

Mogul's captured daughter. Stylized violence and romantic situations. A-II (br)

Against All Odds (1984) Los Angeles bookie and entrepreneur (James Wood) sends his buddy, an aging pro-football star (Jeff Bridges), to find his runaway mistress (Rachel Ward). Director Taylor Hackford tries to build up a suspenseful and sinister mood but spends too much time developing the improbable romance that develops between fugitive and tracker. Hair-raising Sunset Boulevard chase scene, violence, graphic sex scenes, and rough language. O (R)

Against the Wind (1948) Absorbing WW II tale of a group of Allied agents (notably Simone Signoret, Jack Warner, Gordon Jackson, and Paul Dupuis) trained by British intelligence, then sent to Belgium on a mission led by a Catholic priest (Robert Beatty), in the course of which several die and one proves to be a traitor. Charles Crichton directs the episodic narrative with emphasis on the diverse motivations of the agents and how each responds to the dangers encountered. Wartime violence, much menace, and a captured agent who commits suicide. A-III (br)

Agatha (1979) Agatha Christie's never-explained 11-day disappearance in December 1926 provides the basis for director Michael Apted's romantic mystery, starring Vanessa Redgrave as the shy and retiring writer who strikes up a fragile and tender relationship with dapper journalist Dustin Hoffman. Rich in period atmosphere but muddled conclusion and mature theme and treatment. A-III (PG)

Agatha Christie's The Mirror Crack'd (see: **The Mirror Crack'd**)

Age of Consent (1970) Australian production about an artist (James Mason) who retreats to an island to be alone, but discovers it is already inhabited by a local child of nature (Helen Mirren) who has trouble keeping her shift on. When her gin-soaked grandmother obligingly falls off a cliff, the artist and his new model are free to romp artistically and amorously. Michael Powell directs a sorry little diversion that bogs down somewhere between Lolita and Paul Gaughin. O (R)

Age of Innocence, The (1993) Screen version of the Edith Wharton novel about a wealthy young lawyer (Daniel Day-Lewis) torn between his sweet, socially acceptable fiancé (Winona Ryder) and his love for her independent-minded cousin (Michelle Pfeiffer), who has left her faithless husband behind in Europe to face the chilly embrace of the disapproving New York elite in the 1870s. Director Martin Scorcese's visually opulent work skewers the shallow pretenses of high society while delicately exploring the emotions simmering behind the fragile facades of the three protagonists. Mild sexual references. A-II (PG)

Agent for H.A.R.M. (1966) Mediocre spy melodrama about an American secret agent (Mark Richman) assigned to keep a defecting foreign scientist from being grabbed by Iron Curtain operatives (led by heavy Martin Kosleck). Directed by Gerd Oswald, the formula is marred by heavy-handed violence and sexual suggestiveness. O (br)

Agent on Ice (1986) Dreary little melodrama about the separate efforts of the CIA and a crime syndicate to kill a double agent (Tom Ormeny) who knows too much. Director Clark Worswick's effort lacks suspense and drive but offers excessive amounts of bloodshed and stereotyping of Italian-Americans. O (R)

Agnes of God (1985) A psychiatrist (Jane Fonda) sent to a cloistered convent to evaluate the mental stability of a novice (Meg Tilly) accused of strangling her newborn baby provokes the determined opposition of the nun's superior (Anne Bancroft). With the psychiatrist looking for a rational explanation and the mother superior hoping for a supernatural one, director Norman Jewison's movie straddles the fence in a dramatically fraudulent conclusion. Although this pretentious and shallow movie is not meant to be anti-religious, some may be offended by its use of a religious setting. A-IV (PG-13)

Agony and the Ecstasy, The (1965) Adapted from Irving Stone's historical novel about Michaelangelo and the Renaissance papacy, the lavish production depicts the clash between two strong-willed individuals, as the artist (Charlton Heston) struggles to create the Sistine Chapel's frescoed ceilings while being badgered by Pope Julius II (Rex Harrison). Directed by Carol Reed, the movie is not as great as its subject, but it does provide considerable cultural background in an entertaining, though at times plodding, manner beyond the capacity of most youngsters. A-II (br)

Aguirre, the Wrath of God (1977) Ponderous and plodding story of gold-seeking, power-hungry conquistadors on an inglorious expedition into the jungle wilderness of 16th-century Peru. German director Werner Herzog's stark imagery reflects the madness of the venture, but Klaus Kinski in the title role looks so vicious as to become tiresome long before movie's end. Subtitles. Occasional violence, particularly a beheading. A-III (nr)

Aileen Wuornos: The Selling of a Serial Killer (1994) Provocative documentary follows the case of a Florida prostitute convicted in 1992 of multiple murders, with the focus on the pot-smoking lawyer who became her agent and a Christian fundamentalist who legally adopted her, both of whom appear primarily concerned with money from the media. Despite its sleazy tabloid aspects, British filmmaker Nick Broomfield concentrates on how the judgments of those representing the interests of an accused criminal can be warped by the potential for big bucks from book and movie rights. Graphic descriptions of sexual violence, recreational drug use, and some rough language. A-IV (nr)

Air America (1990) Jaded mercenary pilot (Mel Gibson) and an idealistic recruit (Robert Downey,

Jr.) fly missions over Laos in 1969 for a covert, CIA-backed airline being investigated by a US senator (Lane Smith). Director Roger Spottiswoode's blatantly cocky adventure yarn portrays the two mercenaries as incredibly cool daredevils whose grandstanding antics run rings around the grotesque cardboard characters of the senator and their military superiors. Idealized depiction of mercenaries, frequent foul language, and references to sex as a commodity. A-III (R)

Air Bud (1997) Thin but likeable story of a lonely boy (Kevin Zegers) who befriends a stray dog he names Buddy, then discovers the dog's talent for putting a basketball through the hoop, which is good enough for his team's coach (Bill Cobbs) to use Buddy as a substitute player in the big game. Directed by Charles Martin Smith, the proceedings are cheerfully manipulative in alternating heartwarming scenes with ones of slapstick silliness, though some threatening moments are provided by an abusive coach and the cruel master who wants his runaway dog back. Some scenes of menace and a few vulgarities. A-II (PG)

Air Bud: Golden Receiver (1998) Pedestrian sequel turns its talented canine basketball star into a gridiron sensation, catching passes for an inept junior-high school football team, while the dog's young master (Kevin Zegers) frets over the man (Gregory Harrison) dating his widowed mom (Cynthia Stephenson). Directed by Richard Martin, the predictable story includes a hammy pair of comic dognappers, who strike on the eve of the championship game, but all that really counts are the antics of its four-legged star, which will delight juveniles of all ages. A-I (G)

Air Cadet (1951) Routine service melodrama about a group of recruits training to become Air Force pilots, eventually centering on the conflict between a cadet (Richard Long) and a veteran instructor (Stephen McNally) whose estranged wife (Gail Russell) gets in the mix. Directed by Joseph Pevney, the movie is notable for having been filmed on Air Force bases using resident personnel, except for the leads. Romantic complications. A-II (br)

Air Force (1943) WW II tale of a B-17 Flying Fortress bomber crew (notably John Ridgely, Gig Young, Arthur Kennedy, Charles Drake, Harry Carey, and John Garfield) who arrive in Hawaii during the Japanese attack on Pearl Harbor, go on to Wake Island, then Manila, from which they escape to Australia while helping sink a Japanese task force enroute. Directed by Howard Hawks, the picture raised home-front morale by showing heroic Americans turning defeat into victory, but of more interest today is its well-crafted mix of studio battle scenes with actual combat footage. Wartime violence and anti-Japanese stereotyping. A-II (br)

Air Force One (1997) Violent political thriller in which terrorists (led by Gary Oldman) hijack the president's plane in order to force the Russians to release their imprisoned leader, unaware the president (Harrison Ford) is still aboard and determined to stop them. Directed by Wolfgang Petersen, the ensuing cat-and-mouse derring-do is very violent and jazzed up with all manner of complications, but none of it is very credible and the suspense grows tiresome. Vicious violence, brutal treatment of hostages, profanity, and rough language. A-IV (R)

Air Up There, The (1994) Arriving in Kenya to convince a tribal lad (Charles Gitonga Maina) to accept a basketball scholarship at his midwestern Catholic college, an ambitious assistant coach (Kevin Bacon) finds he must first win the chief (Winston Ntshona) over to the idea, as well as coach a crucial game the tribe has staked their land and cattle upon. Director Paul M. Glaser's light, slight movie is contrived and derivative, but its colorful tale of culture clashes is mildly diverting. Tribal bloodletting ceremony and a few instances of profanity. A-II (PG)

Airheads (1994) Armed with toy guns, three would-be rock stars (Brendan Fraser, Steve Buscemi, and Adam Sandler) seize control of a radio station and try to force the on-air disc jockey (Joe Mantegna) to play their demo tape while a throng of delirious supporters taunt the police outside. Director Michael Lehmann finds only shrill and mean-spirited humor in the mindless antics of rebellious young adults trying to get attention by toying with violence. Comic mayhem, brief violence, a bedroom scene, and crude gestures. A-III (PG-13)

Airplane (1980) This aviation-disaster spoof offers a sprinkling of bright and funny gags. If you don't like one, wait a minute and another will be along. Directed by Jim Abrahams, the comedy is moderately entertaining for those who don't mind an excess of silliness and a certain amount of crudity. A-III (PG)

Airplane II: The Sequel (1982) For those who liked the jokes in the original, here they are again, although many fewer and much farther between this time around under Ken Finkleman's direction. What was of questionable taste in the first movie, however, has now crossed the line into the downright offensive, including quite a bit of nudity. O (PG)

Airport (1970) Disaster movie based on Arthur Hailey's bestseller in which the fate of passengers and crew of an airborne 707 are in the hands of a mad bomber (Van Heflin). Director George Seaton's lumbering Hollywood blockbuster revels in its all-star cast of stereotyped characters and surface melodrama. Adult situations. A-III (G)

Airport 1975 (1974) This time disaster takes the form of a private plane piloted by Dana Andrews, who suffers a heart attack and crashes into a 747's cockpit, leaving chief stewardess Karen Black in command and responsible for landing the plane via radio instructions. On board is the usual all-star cast, and on the ground is a rescue team led by Charlton Heston and George Kennedy. Directed by Jack Smight, it has some entertaining thrills that will have viewers reaching to fasten their seatbelts. A-II (PG)

Airport '77 (1977) The third edition of the series has to do with a huge 747 crashing into the ocean, trapping a host of major stars in its watertight fuselage. It's all pretty silly but entertaining enough under Jerry Jameson's direction. Restrained violence and some mild profanity. A-II (PG)

Airport '79 (see: **The Concorde—Airport '79**)

A.K.A. Cassius Clay (1970) Documentary on the career of Muhammed Ali, also known as (A.K.A.) Cassius Clay, from his first interest in boxing at the age of 12 to involvement with the Black Muslims and the draft controversy. Fight fans may enjoy several of the clips from some now-classic bouts, but William Cayton's direction is amateurish and superficial, leaving many loose ends and unanswered questions. A-II (GP)

Akira Kurosawa's Dreams (1990) Beautiful Japanese production presents eight short fragments from the imagination of 80-year-old director Akira Kursosawa. These lyric, at times surreal, musings on childhood, tradition, toxic pollution, nuclear holocaust, art, and death are timeless, open-ended, and calculated to expand the mind of the viewer. Sparse subtitled dialogue. Some unsettling themes and a few frightening visuals. A-II (PG)

Al Capone (1959) Gritty gangster melodrama with Rod Steiger in the title role alternately scowling and smirking his way to the top in Chicago's gangland wars during Prohibition, then follows his downfall in the 1930s as the feds close in and send him to Alcatraz on a tax evasion conviction. Directed by Richard Wilson, this portrait of a ruthless criminal succeeds best in its re-creation of the era, but the slow-paced narrative holds only intermittent interest, despite a capable cast. Some hard-edged violence, much menace, and several sexual situations. A-III (br)

Al Jennings of Oklahoma (1951) Formula Western directed by Ray Nazarro about wronged brothers (Dan Duryea and Dick Foran) who turn outlaws, then try to go straight but are hounded by the law. Stylized violence and justice questions. A-II (br)

Aladdin (1992) Vibrant animated Arabian Nights tale of a genie (voice of Robin Williams), a commoner in love with a princess, and an evil vizier who connives to capture the genie and marry the princess. As produced and directed by John Musker and Ron Clements, the story is sweet, the animation delightful, and Williams's wisecracks wedded to lightning-fast sight-gags should hold adult interest. A-I (G)

Alamo, The (1960) John Wayne stars as Davy Crockett in a sprawling, over-sized blockbuster re-creating the heroic last stand in 1836 of a small band of Texans facing superior Mexican forces under Santa Ana. Also produced and directed by Wayne, the panorama of large-scale battle scenes is undercut by lumpy continuity, clunky dialogue, and stock frontier types. Patriotic entertainment but somewhat deficient in historical accuracy and ethnic stereotyping. A-I (br)

Alamo Bay (1985) On the Texas Gulf Coast in 1979, Vietnamese refugees working as shrimp fishermen arouse the animosity of local citizens, who feel their livelihood is being taken away from them. Director Louis Malle wastes some good material by bogging down in a melodramatic plot involving adultery and shallow characterizations. Violence and some nudity. A-III (R)

Alan Smithee Film: Burn Hollywood Burn, An (1998) Satirical movie-within-a-movie in which an enraged director (Eric Idle) steals the master negative of his movie after the producer (Ryan O'Neal) re-cuts his film. Directed by Alan Smithee from a script by Joe Eszterhas, the movie's inside jokes are self-serving in lionizing creative types who refuse to compromise their artistic vision. Brief stylized violence, sexual situations, constant rough language, and occasional profanity. A-III (R)

Alarmist, The (1998) Modest comedy-drama in which a naive alarm-systems salesman (David Arquette) becomes romantically involved with one of his clients (Kate Capshaw), then comes to suspect his boss (Stanley Tucci) when she's found murdered. Writer-director Evan Dunsky doesn't get too far with the story's comic elements, though the growing conflict between the two men leads to some genuine soul searching. Brief violence, a few sexual situations, intermittent rough language, and minimal profanity. A-III (R)

Alaska (1996) After their bush-pilot dad (Dirk Benedict) crashes in the Alaskan wilderness, two teens (Thora Birch and Vincent Kartheiser) set out on their own to find him, aided along the way by a plucky polar bear cub. Director Fraser C. Heston turns in a visually scenic but slow-paced rescue tale relying heavily on the cuteness factor of the frisky young bear. Some strong menace and a crude expression. A-II (PG)

Alberto Express (1992) Italian comedy about a panic-striken father-to-be (Sergio Castellitto) trying to raise money aboard a Rome-bound train in order to honor the family tradition of repaying his father (Nino Manfredi) every lira spent on his upbringing before his own first child is born. Director Arthur Joffe's amusing premise gets overworked by the lead character's hammy portrayal and an abundance of contrived situations. Subtitles. Comic treatment of stealing and some sexual innuendo. A-III (nr)

Albino Alligator (1997) When cops surround an after-hours bar, a trio of fugitives (Matt Dillon, Gary Sinise, and William Fichtner) take the other occupants (including Faye Dunaway) hostage, then bicker on how to escape alive. Director Kevin Spacey's shrill tale of miscreants and their innocent victims explores the dark side of humanity with chilling cynicism. Intermittent violence, frequent profanity, and incessant rough language. A-IV (R)

Alex and the Gypsy (1976) Seriocomic story of

an autumnal romance between a bail-bondsman (Jack Lemmon) and a gypsy (Genevieve Bujo l d) has problems of character motivation and a highly improbable ending. Although director John Korty has brought a strong sense of value and human dignity to what could have been a sordid situation, there is a rather extended sexual scene that is both graphic and boorish. O (R/PG)

Alex in Wonderland (1971) The only character of interest in this movie about the cinematic and familial hang-ups and private fantasies of a youngish, modish director (Donald Sutherland) is his rather ordinary, sweet, and appealing wife (Ellen Burstyn), who can't understand what her husband's problem is all about and won't pretend to be awed by its manufactured profundity. Director Paul Mazursky's self-indulgent effort, with themes and images borrowed from Fellini, wastes itself on condemning such easy targets as Hollywood and Los Angeles' pollution while praising sexual liberation and the peoples' revolution. O (R)

Alexander the Great (1956) Historical dramatization re-creates the life of the Macedonian prince (Richard Burton) who, after the Greek city-states fell to his father, Philip (Fredric March), went on to conquer the mighty Persian Empire in a 10-year campaign ending with his death in 323 B.C. at age 33. Written, produced, and directed by Robert Rossen, the result is both good history and fine drama with a solid cast, some well-staged action scenes, and a sense of spectacle, though the narrative is at times stilted and occasionally obscure. The stylized violence, sexual references, and political complications make it heavy-going for children. A-I (br)

Alf 'n' Family (1972) Screen version of the popular British television series, which was Americanized as "All in the Family," stars Warren Mitchell as Alf, the simple but ridiculously opinionated bigot. By movie's end, Alf is an isolated, pathetic man barely tolerated by his wife (Dandy Nichols) and married daughter. Though he justly deserves his fate, it is to the credit of Norman Cohen's direction of Johnny Speight's script that we feel pity for the old reprobate. Comedy of insult with a bit of rough language. A-III (PG)

Alfie (1966) A modern rake (Michael Caine) who regards women only as sexual objects is brought to the realization that his way of life is empty and sterile. Caine brilliantly interprets the title role with deadpan expression, flip Cockney dialogue, and occasionally addresses the audience directly in a film directed by Lewis Gilbert and adapted by Bill Naughton from his own play. Although the treatment includes a series of sexual escapades, this British production largely succeeds as a contemporary morality play. A-IV (PG)

Alfred the Great (1969) This elaborate British production re-creates ninth-century England when a youthful prince (later king) rallied the feuding, demoralized Saxon tribes against their common enemy, the Vikings. The barbarism of the period, only slighty leavened by an imperfectly realized brand of Christianity, is handled with some human credibility. Clive Donner's direction is marked by striking visual effects and well-controlled, through necessarily bloody, battle scenes. A-III (PG)

Alfredo, Alfredo (1973) Mildly entertaining, occasionally quite funny Italian sex farce directed by Pietro Germi, about a shy bank clerk (Dustin Hoffman) whose desperate attempts to avoid marriage to a predatory woman (Stefania Sandrelli) fail and his troubles begin. There are enough character bits pointing up the foibles, battles, and games that go on between the sexes to entertain those whose tastes do not run deep. A-III (R)

Algiers (1938) Exotic romance set in the Casbah, the native quarter in French Algiers, where a suave Paris crook (Charles Boyer) takes refuge, until a policeman (Joseph Calleia) uses a woman (Hedy Lamarr) to lure him out into the open. Directed by John Cromwell, this remake of **Pepe Le Moko** relies on moody visuals, tense emotions, and a fine cast to hold interest in the melodramatic story of a criminal undone by love. Stylized violence, unsavory characters, and romantic situations. A-II (br)

Ali Baba and the Forty Thieves (1944) When the Mongols capture Baghdad and kill its caliph (Maroni Olsen), his young son (Scotty Beckett) is given refuge by the legendary band of thieves, grows up to become their leader (Jon Hall), and wins back his throne by defeating the villainous Khan (Kurt Katch). Slack Arabian Nights adventure directed by Arthur Lubin with colorful sets, plodding action, and weak romance (Maria Montez). A-I (br)

Ali: Fear Eats the Soul (see: **Fear Eats the Soul: Ali**)

Alias Boston Blackie (1942) Enterprising series entry directed by Lew Landers in which the title crook-turned-crimefighter (Chester Morris) stages a Christmas Eve show in the big house, then has to find one of the convicts (Larry Parks), who escapes disguised as a clown after vowing to kill those who framed him. Stylized violence. A-I (br)

Alias Bulldog Drummond (see: **Bulldog Jack**)

Alias Nick Beal (1949) Interesting variation on the Faust theme has a sinister stranger (Ray Milland) with diabolic powers of persuasion trying to corrupt an honest district attorney (Thomas Mitchell) by promises of wealth and fame. Director John Farrow sets the tale in a gritty gangster context but with appropriately dark overtones that suggest more is at stake than simply criminal greed. Unsettling situation and menacing characters. A-II (br)

Alice (1990) After 16 years of marriage to a patronizing husband (William Hurt) and a brief guilt-ridden affair with a divorced musician (Joe Mantegna), a wealthy Manhattan housewife (Mia Farrow) seeks new directions in her life. As written and directed by Woody Allen, the film has substance as well as many humorous flights of fancy, though it tends to depict Catholics as more motivated by guilt than any true sense of morality. Adulterous relationships, benign treatment of recreational drug use, and minimal blasphemy. A-IV (PG-13)

Alice Doesn't Live Here Anymore (1975) A widow (Ellen Burstyn) takes her young son (Alfred Lutter) on a sojourn across the Southwest trying to pursue her dream of a singing career, but winds up as a waitress in a greasy spoon, where she is courted by a local rancher (Kris Kristofferson). Director Martin Scorsese's somewhat ambiguous and ambivalent picture of a singl e parent in a contemporary American landscape offers some interesting insights on women in a male chauvinistic society. Though some may be distressed by certain tawdry situations and rough language, the movie achieves its purpose of looking at its subject without too much sentimentality or idealization. A-IV (PG)

Alice in Wonderland (1951) Disney animated version of the Lewis Carroll classic about a schoolgirl who daydreams her way through a fantasy world of strange creatures and odd personages, such as the White Rabbit, the Mad Hatter, and the Cheshire Cat, is whimsical entertainment for the entire family, especially youngsters unfamiliar with the original. A-I (G)

Alice of Wonderland in Paris (1966) Animated movie by Gene Deitch on the further adventures of Alice, incorporating children's stories written by Ludwig Bemelmans, James Thurber, Eve Titus, and Crockett Johnson, and featuring the voices of Carl Reiner, Norma Macmillan, and Howard Morris. Youngsters will enjoy the stories, and the animation is passable. A-I (br)

Alice's Restaurant (1969) Based on the popular song by Arlo Guthrie, the movie loosely follows various events alluded to in its lyrics, a kind of personal odyssey in which Guthrie plays himself. Although not a very cohesive work, director Arthur Penn succeeds best in satiric bits done in the style and spirit of the song. Despite its stylistic lapses, the result is a balanced film, presenting the life of flower children neither as dismal nor utopian, but as human. Adult themes. A-III (PG)

Alien (1979) Science-fiction thriller about a deep-space freighter whose crew is ravaged by a hungry alien intruder which causes havoc on the long voyage home. Director Ridley Scott goes in for lots of noise and flashing lights rather than characterization, and the slick enterprise depends more on shock than on suspense. Considerable gore, graphic violence, and foul language make this unsuitable for youngsters. A-III (R)

Alien Nation (1988) Failed science-fiction thriller in which an alien (Mandy Patinkin) joins the Los Angeles police department and is teamed with a human cop (James Caan) out to find the alien who killed his former partner. Director Graham Baker has little talent for suspense, and the comical relationship between the mismatched partners falls flat. Excessive violence, much profanity, and vulgar sexual references. O (R)

Alien Resurrection (1997) Grim sci-fi sequel finds Ripley (Sigourney Weaver) revived on board a spaceship and teamed with a mysterious stranger (Winona Ryder) to rid the vehicle of rampaging aliens. Director Jean-Pierre Jeunet's mildly suspenseful thriller uses the stale aliens-on-the-loose premise mainly for grotesque combinations of incubating monsters grafted onto deformed human body-parts. Recurring gory violence, some profanity, and frequent rough language. A-III (R)

Alien 3 (1992) Crash landing on an unarmed penal colony whose criminal inmates have embraced Christian fundamentalism, a space officer (Sigourney Weaver) finds she has brought along a murderous alien monster whose female version is nesting inside her body. Though this sci-fi sequel covers familiar territory and the religious angle is undeveloped, director David Fincher ekes out sufficient suspense to sustain interest in the outcome. Sporadic shadowy violence and much rough language. A-III (R)

Aliens (1986) Sigourney Weaver returns in a sequel as the maternalistic super-heroine who single-handedly battles an egg-laden alien to prevent its infesting the galaxy with slimy creatures from hyperspace. Director James Cameron balances his affinity for moody sets and special effects with a satirical reversal of roles in which a woman dominates inept and witless macho males. Stylized violence and excessive sexually derived profanity. A-IV (R)

Alive (1993) Long, sometimes gruesome dramatization of the life-and-death struggle of survivors (including Ethan Hawke, Vincent Spano, and Josh Hamilton) of a plane crash high in the Andes where, stranded for 10 freezing weeks in 1972, some resort to eating the flesh of their dead companions in order to survive. Director Frank Marshall highlights the strength of the human spirit and the survivors' religious faith in both enduring their ordeal and justifying their actions. Violent air-crash with fatalities and restrained shots of cannibalism. A-II (R)

All About Eve (1950) Classic Broadway story in which a veteran star (Bette Davis) helps a seemingly innocent novice (Anne Baxter), then learns too late of the younger woman's duplicity in landing a role intended for the star by charming the play's author (Hugh Marlowe), its director (Gary Merrill), and the town's leading theater critic (George Sanders). Writer-director Joseph L. Mankiewicz keeps the proceedings churning with a steady stream of witty dialogue and pungent put-downs, but it is Davis's caustic performance as the flinty veteran actress that carries the picture to its wryly satisfying conclusion. Devious characters, sexual innuendo, and marital discord. A-III (br)

All-American, The (1953) Formula tale directed by Jesse Hibbs in which a college football star (Tony Curtis), sobered by his parents' death in a car accident, quits the gridiron and devotes himself to getting a degree in architecture, despite pressures from all sides to play again. College antics. A-I (br)

All American Boy, The (1973) Jon Voight stars as a boxer with great expectations in this precious, pretentious little exercise in destroying the myth of the small-town-boy-making-good. Directed by Charles Eastman, this reverse Horatio Alger story, with its poorly staged boxing scenes and amorous goings-on, is sprinkled with helpings of gratuitous nudity and truly foul language. O (R)

All Dogs Go to Heaven (1989) Dark, disappointing animated feature, set in 1930's Louisiana, charts the death and redemption of a rogue German shepherd (voice of Burt Reynolds) who, after being bumped off by a crooked business partner, cons his way from heaven back to earth, where he is reformed by his love for an adorable orphan (voice of Judith Barsi). The orphan proves the only shining light in director Don Bluth's predictable, derivative fantasy with forgettable music and unappealing lead characters. Some cartoon menace and intense moments of mortal danger. A-I (G)

All Dogs Go to Heaven 2 (1996) Animated musical sequel in which two canine angels (voices of Charlie Sheen and Dom DeLuise), in San Francisco to retrieve Gabriel's horn, help a runaway boy return home while outwitting a devilish duo. Directed by Paul Sabella and Larry Leker, the songs are sprightly, but the animation often looks washed-out in this cartoon-busy search-and-rescue tale. A-I (G)

All I Desire (1953) Turn-of-the-century sudser in which a woman (Barbara Stanwyck), whose life has gone downhill since running out on a small-town husband (Richard Carlson) and three young children, suddenly turns up years later to see her daughter's high-school play, then finds it difficult to leave. The reconciliation of a broken home makes a worthy theme, despite director Douglas Sirk's melodramatic excesses, including a malevolent villain (Lyle Bettger) who wants to resume the affair which caused the woman to leave in the first place. Domestic complications and implied infidelity. A-II (br)

All I Want for Christmas (1991) Harmless formula comedy about a young teen (Ethan Randall) and his little sister (Thora Birch) conspiring to reunite their divorced parents (Harley Jane Kozak and Jamey Sheridan) on Christmas Eve. Director Robert Lieberman's heavily contrived holiday offering is only lightly amusing, as the mischievous kids unfold their goofy plot with predictable syrupy results. A-I (G)

All Mine to Give (1958) Bright story of Scottish immigrants (Glynis Johns and Cameron Mitchell) pioneering in 1856 Wisconsin turns maudlin when both die, leaving their six youngsters faced with an orphanage unless the eldest can find a foster home for each by visiting their neighbors on Christmas Day. Director Allen Reisner details well the bond of love between parents and their growing brood amidst the harsh conditions of frontier life, but becomes increasingly morose as the orphans are parceled out in the downbeat, disheartening conclusion. A mixed bag of emotions for youngsters, whose parents can help by discussing the movie's portrayal of family life, death, and separation. A-I (br)

All My Sons (1948) Stodgy adaptation of Arthur Miller's play about a son (Burt Lancaster) learning that his father (Edward G. Robinson) framed his partner (Frank Conroy) to take the fall for shipping defective parts to the military during WW II. The subject of business ethics and personal morality is treated earnestly but gets lost in a welter of family melodramatics. Directed by Irving Reis. Suicide in plot resolution. A-III (br)

All Neat in Black Stockings (1969) Without too much imagination or subtlety, this British import centers on the amorous adventures of a young, irresponsible window cleaner (Victor Henry) and his buddy (Jack Shepherd), with whom he shares everything, including the woman he marries. While the visuals and dialogue rarely become offensive, the entire situation as developed in this film can hardly be considered wholesome adult entertainment. O (R)

All Night Long (1981) After being demoted from the executive ranks to manager of an all-night drugstore, a married man (Gene Hackman) finds himself being pursued by a seductive married housewife (Barbara Streisand). Streisand and Hackman are both good, and director Jean-Claude Tramont's movie has its moments, but it is basically shallow and mean-spirited rather than amusing. Casual acceptance of adultery. O (R)

All of Me (1984) Steve Martin plays a lawyer who becomes the host for the soul of a recently deceased client, a rich crank played by Lily Tomlin. Martin gives a bravura slapstick performance in trying to liberate himself of the possession, but director Carl Reiner's sense of humor is largely oriented to the sexual, with some needlessly crude dialogue. A-III (PG)

All Quiet on the Western Front (1930) Excellent adaptation of Erich Maria Remarque's novel about the lessons in life and death learned by a patriotic German youth (Lew Ayres) after enlisting in the Kaiser's army and serving at the front during the WWI. In showing the conflict's senseless waste of human life, director Lewis Milestone re-creates with vivid authenticity the horrors of trench warfare while underscoring the humanity of those on both sides of no-man's-land. Classic anti-war picture especially appropriate for older teenagers, despite some strong battlefield violence and a brief romantic interlude. A-II (br)

All Screwed Up (1976) Italian tragicomedy about the plight of a group of workers from the agrarian south who come to bustling, industrial Milan to seek a better life but wind up worse off than before. Director Lina Wertmuller's vision is pessimistic but pulsates with the vigor of life and a concern and affection for its characters. Earthy treatment of sex and ambiguous view of prostitution and abortion. A-IV (PG)

All That Heaven Allows (1956) Soggy suburban romance in which a rich widow (Jane Wyman) falls for the nurseryman (Rock Hudson), who tends her grounds, then has second thoughts when he's scorned by her wealthy neighbors and rejected by her two college-age children. Directed by Douglas Sirk, the sudsy plot is drearily predictable as the shy sophisticate is drawn to a simple, uncomplicated fellow who loves trees. Romantic complications and a drunk making sexual advances. A-II (br)

All That Jazz (1980) The story of an egotistical, womanizing Broadway director-choreographer who drives himself quite literally to death while rehearsing a new musical. Director Bob Fosse's semi-autobiographical movie stars Roy Scheider, who gives a fine performance demonstrating the pitfalls of living in the fast lane, obsessed with one's work while using drugs, sex, alcohol, and jazz to heal the pain. The nihilistic mood, and some lewd dance parodies, are wholly self-indulgent. O (R)

All That Money Can Buy (see: **The Devil and Daniel Webster**)

All the Brothers Were Valiant (1953) Middling 19th-century sea yarn about the captain of a New England whaler (Robert Taylor) who finds his missing brother (Stewart Granger) in the South Seas, then has to keep him from seizing the ship to search for a fortune in pearls. Directed by Richard Thorpe, the adventure combines the themes of greed and sibling rivalry with more talk than action. Stylized violence, some of it quite nasty. A-II (br)

All the King's Men (1949) Strong adaptation of Robert Penn Warren's novel about a poor country lawyer (Broderick Crawford) whose rise to political power during the Depression transforms him from a populist reformer into a ruthless demagogue with national ambitions. Directed by Robert Rossen, the picture is strikingly realistic in showing the corruption of democratic processes by a politician closely resembling Louisiana's Huey Long, though is less convincing in its portrayal of his personal failings and moral transgressions. Mature themes and treatment. A-III (br)

All the Loving Couples (1969) This extended stag film has its serious moments contemplating the morality and psychological ramifications of wife-swapping. Gross handling of the subject in graphic exploitation terms negates whatever serious intentions it may have had. O (X)

All the Marbles (1981) Peter Falk plays the manager of a tag-team of women wrestlers (Vicki Frederick and Laurene Landon), who battle in dinky arenas across the country on the way to the championship match in Reno. Directed by Robert Aldrich, the vulgar, slipshod story wavers between the farcical and the serious. Sadistic violence of the wrestling sequences, exploitative nudity, and general air of sleazy amorality. O (R)

All the Mornings in the World (see: **Tous les Matins du Monde**)

All the President's Men (1976) The investigation by two Washington Post reporters (Dustin Hoffman and Robert Redford) of the facts behind the 1974 Watergate break-in has been dramatized with restraint and objectivity. Director Alan Pakula's deliberately low-keyed, well-acted, and comprehensive account of a political scandal emphasizes the painstaking work involved in investigative journalism. Though it uses a few coarse words in a realistic context, the movie is one that most teenagers would benefit from seeing. A-III (R/PG)

All the Right Moves (1983) The hopes of a high-school senior (Tom Cruise) to escape the poverty of his blighted factory town by getting a college athletic scholarship seem doomed by a clash with his football coach (Craig T. Nelson). Although the situation is realistic enough, director Michael Chapman's shallow treatment lacks any moral perspective, especially in its depiction of the youth's relationship with his girlfriend. Graphic bedroom scene and a casual attitude toward abortion. O (R)

All the Right Noises (1971) Dull British production about a theatrical-lighting technician (Tom Bell) who succumbs to the charms of a lovely actress (Olivia Hussey) and seems quite content to divide his attentions between her and his pretty wife (Judy Carne) until the predictable complications ensue. Director Gerry O'Hara competently records this story of adultery without weighing any moral issues, so that the result is more a clinical report than a thoughtful, moving drama. A-III (GP)

All the Way, Boys (1974) Italian action comedy featuring the hi-jinks and misadventures of the "Trinity" boys (Terence Hill and Bud Spencer), this time as bush pilots in the Amazon, where they fly in supplies for emerald-mining outposts, and their gradual friendship with one particularly touched prospector (Cyril Cusack). Directed by Giuseppe Colizzi, the clumsy dubbing and sloppy editing seem only to enhance the modest fun offered by a chaotic plot, some whimsical mayhem, and the cheerful mugging of its principals. A-II (PG)

All the Young Men (1960) Routine Korean War story of a Marine patrol ordered to hold a critical mountain pass against an overwhelming enemy force. Written, produced, and directed by Hall Bartlett, the low-budget production is notable mostly for a subplot involving an inexperienced black sergeant (Sidney Poitier) and a veteran subordinate (Alan Ladd), whose conflict ends in a well-intended but mawkish demonstration of racial harmony. Wartime violence, including a battlefield amputation. A-II (br)

All Things Bright and Beautiful (1979) Genial family film about the work of a dedicated veterinarian (John Alderton) practicing in the Yorkshire countryside prior to the onset of WW II. Director Eric Till concentrates on the details of healing at the expense of characterization. Graphic depiction of the birth of a calf may be too intense for some youngsters. A-I (G)

All This and Glamour Too (see: **Vogues of 1938**)

All This and World War II (1977) Tasteless, misconceived documentary that reduces the newsreel footage of six years of agony that was the Second World War to a mindless light-show for rock enthusiasts grooving to Beatle's music. Director Susan Winslow spares viewers a magical mystery tour of Dachau, but not much else in a production so inane as to be beneath contempt. Wartime actualities. A-III (PG)

All Together Now (1970) Low-budget peep show narrated by a blonde corpse (Cileste Eslar) recounting how her experimentation with lesbianism and auto-eroticism drove her to suicide. Written and directed by William Louis Allan, the monochromic sex scenes photographed on closet-sized sets will stifle viewers more than shock them. O (nr)

Allan Quartermain and the Lost City of Gold (1987) Richard Chamberlain's overacting as the soldier of fortune and Gary Nelson's direction make the action-adventure yarn play with comic-book superficiality. Like **Indiana Jones**, this dramatically silly jungle adventure offers youngsters only laughable mock-heroics and exotic sets. Stylized violence. A-II (PG)

Alleghany Uprising (1939) When colonial backwoodsmen (led by John Wayne) use force to stop a trader (Brian Donlevy) from supplying Indians with guns and firewater, they are attacked as rebels by the local British military commander (George Sanders). Director William A. Seiter's wilderness adventure has some colorful action, more than a little patriotism, and a rambunctious frontierswoman (Claire Trevor) who can shoot as well as any of the men. Stylized violence. A-I (br)

Alligator (1981) Director Lewis Teague and writer John Sayles have taken the old chestnut about the baby alligator that grows to monstrous proportions after being flushed down into the sewer system and turned it into a moderately entertaining thriller with some tongue-in-cheek asides. Although the creature has a selective appetite, devouring villains for the most part, such violent actions are graphically depicted. A-III (R)

Alligator Eyes (1991) Three vacationing pals (Roger Kabler, Mary McLain, and Allen McCullough) pick up a blind hitchhiker (Annabelle Larsen) who tricks them into aiding her in committing a revenge murder. Writer-director John Feldman's low-budget psycho-thriller is low on thrills, medium on psychological character studies, but high on its own sense of luridly bizarre melodrama. Conscienceless murder, sexual exploitation with gratuitous full nudity, and intermittent rough language. O (R)

Alligator People, The (1959) Woefully inept monster movie in which wife Beverly Garland tries to keep hubby Richard Crane from being turned into a reptile by mad doctor George Macready's alligator serum. Directed by Roy Del Ruth, the backcountry setting is creepy, but the script is ludicrous, with acting to match. Stylized violence and menacing situations. A-II (br)

Allnighter, The (1987) Southern California college coed struggles to have a meaningful sexual encounter before graduation and finally succeeds after several failed attempts. Rock star Susanna Hoffs, directed by her mother, Tamar Simon Hoffs, fails to convey anything of significance in this surf-and-brew disaster, whose narrow view of life and permissive view of sex is annoyingly vapid. O (PG-13)

Almost an Angel (1990) An ex-convict (Paul Hogan), convinced he is being given a second chance to do good as an angel on probation, comes to the aid of a woman (Linda Kozlowski) and her wheelchair-bound brother (Elias Koteas), who run an impoverished kids' center. As written by Hogan and directed by John Cornell, the one-joke comedy runs out of steam long before the three leads affirm their belief in an afterlife. Very minor violence and minimal vulgar expressions. A-II (PG)

Almost Heroes (1998) Comedy clunker about inept explorers (Chris Farley and Matthew Perry) starting out from St. Louis in 1804 to beat the Lewis and Clark expedition to the Pacific Ocean. Directed by Christopher Guest, the witless wilderness proceedings are of the dumb-and-dumber variety and its crude sense of humor is tiresomely unamusing. Slapstick violence, sexual innuendo, outhouse humor, and profanity. A-III (PG-13)

Almost Perfect Affair, An (1979) American filmmaker (Keith Carradine) brings his movie to Cannes, is held up by customs officials, and has an affair with the helpful wife (Monica Vitti) of a movie producer (Raf Vallone). Toothless satire from director Michael Ritchie gets bogged down in private conceits, leaving only industry jokes and a carnival atmosphere in which adultery is condoned. O (PG)

Almost Summer (1978) Dull and sophomoric comedy about a class election at a southern California high school. Director Martin Davidson presents the school's suffocatingly materialistic and amoral environment in uncritical fashion. Gratuitous nudity and offensive jokes at the expense of the disabled. O (PG)

Almost You (1985) Manhattan couple (Brooke Adams and Griffin Dunne) have everything and are so miserable that the husband contemplates running off with his wife's physical therapist (Karen Young). Adam Brooks directs a trivial and boring effort. Rough language and adultery figure in the plot. A-III (R)

Aloha, Bobby and Rose (1975) Director Floyd Mutrux chronicles the tragic love affair between a tousled-haired auto mechanic (Paul Le Mat) and a starry-eyed, unwed mother (Diane Hull), apparently intending an object lesson in the dangers of too much law and order and too little justice. The message is not expressed at all convincingly in the contrived ending of this inept, low-budget melodrama, whose chief merit is the acting of the principals in creating characters for whom one feels real concern. A-III (PG)

Along the Great Divide (1951) Fairly tense Western in which a lawman (Kirk Douglas) saves an old man (Walter Brennan) from being lynched, then has to trek across the desert to get him safely to town for trial, despite the accused's ornery daughter (Virginia Mayo), pursuing ranchers, lack of water, and a sandstorm. Director Raoul Walsh handles the desert action convincingly enough, but the tension evaporates in a slick, hokey climax preventing a miscarriage of justice. Some stylized violence and menace make it unlikely fare for children. A-II (br)

Alpha Beta (1976) Screen version of E.A. Whitehead's two-character play about a couple (Albert Finney and Rachel Roberts) who feel trapped by marriage, a theme developed with wit and compassion. Although superbly acted and quite affecting, as a movie it suffers from being a straightforward recording of the play. Adult themes. A-III (nr)

Alphabet Murders, The (1966) Tony Randall badly mangles the role of Hercule Poirot, Agatha Christie's dapper Belgian detective, who is investigating a case in which a murderer is killing his victims, apparently in alphabetical order. British production directed by Frank Tashlin, the effort to add comedy to the mystery falls flat and badly hurts the rest of the movie. A-II (br)

Alphaville (1965) A secret agent (Eddie Constantine) in a future science-fiction world accomplishes his mission of destruction. Jean-Luc Godard directs his own script with imaginative visual gusto, ably abetted by Raoul Coutard's camerawork. The French production is enjoyable both as a spy spoof and as a satire on humanity threatened by the machine. Subtitles. Stylized violence and implied sexual affair. A-III (br)

Altered States (1981) The talents of director Ken Russell and writer Paddy Chayefsky have joined in this story about a scientist (William Hurt) who, in trying to find the essence of being, takes a hallucinogen and regresses into a primeval form. He is rescued from total chromosomal metamorphosis by his wife (Blair Brown), who proves that love conquers all. Rather than exploring the spiritual self-realization the character sought, the emphasis is on the physical and sexual, with instances of nudity. O (R)

Alvarez Kelly (1966) Standard Western in Civil War trappings as a cowboy (William Holden) who's making good money supplying beef for the Union Army has a cattle herd hijacked by a Confederate officer (Richard Widmark), who aims to drive them to his southern comrades. There is plenty of violent action in this colorful production, but director Edward Dmytryk has a hard time keeping all the motivations straight. Stylized violence and questions of loyalty. A-III (br)

Always (1989) Forced romantic fantasy about love, death, and the human spirit in which a daredevil firefighter pilot (Richard Dreyfuss) loses his life saving a fellow flier (John Goodman), but comes back to earth to help his girlfriend (Holly Hunter) and an inexperienced pilot (Brad Johnson). Directed by Steven Spielberg, the movie seems too studied and portentous to put across either the romance or its inspirational message that the spirit, however defined, outlives the body. Several intense scenes threatening human life and some vulgar language. A-II (PG)

Amadeus (1984) Director Milos Forman's gaudy evocation of the great age of the Baroque features Tom Hulce in the title role of the young, brash, often vulgar Wolfgang Amadeus Mozart. Though somewhat lacking in dramatic development, the result exquisitely details the pain and anguish of Mozart's spiritual and physical assassin, Salieri (F. Murray Abraham), who's driven by an overwhelming sense of divine injustice and abandonment. Too intense for youngsters. A-II (PG)

Amarcord (1974) Director Federico Fellini recalls his youth in the little seaside village of Rimini through a seemingly plotless series of recollections and fantasies, held together by a genially bombastic host-narrator-historian (Luigi Rossi) who provides social and historical commentary on events that typified life during the Fascist 1930s. Fellini is in full control of these various episodes, which have a powerful and warming effect as the artist looks back with mellow affection, compassion, and humor on experiences that shaped his creative life. In celebrating the dreams and schemes, petty and grandiose, of the ordinary folk of this little town, Fellini reminds us of our own past and our own humanity. Though there is some bawdy earthiness, it is a thoroughly humane work, seeing everything but judging no one. A-IV (R)

Amateur, The (1982) CIA technician John Savage forces the agency to train him as a field operative so that he can go behind the Iron Curtain to avenge his girlfriend's murder by terrorists. Director Charles Jarrott weaves a complex spy thriller which is not saved from mediocrity by the fine performances of Marthe Keller and Christopher Plummer in supporting roles. Stylized violence. A-III (R)

Amazing Grace (1974) Comedy with fine black performers, notably Moms Mabley as an earth-mother type who sets out, with the help of retired train conductor Slappy White, to bring Baltimore politician Moses Gunn back to the straight and narrow path. Though there are cameo appearances by such old-timers as Stepin' Fetchit and Butterfly McQueen, director Stan Lathan keeps his camera mainly on Moms' rolling of the eyes, toothless grins, and ceaseless line of hilarious homespun patter. Entertaining, frequently quite funny, and occasionally moving general-audience pleaser. A-I (G)

Amazing Grace and Chuck (1987) Little League baseball player (Joshua Zuehlke) and a pro-basketball star (Alex English) join in a protest against nuclear weapons. When the basketball star is suspiciously killed in a mid-air explosion, his death precipitates a US-Soviet accord on disarmament. Director Mike Newell provides a strained example of how the altruistic actions of the individual can make a difference. Given the complexity of the world affairs, the movie may be more confusing than inspiring for youngsters. A-II (PG)

Amazing Mr. X, The (see: **The Spiritualist**)

Amazing Panda Adventure, The (1995) Contrived escapade of an American youth visiting his estranged father on a panda preserve in the highlands of northern China, where the 10-year-old boy promptly gets lost in the wilds while trying to rescue a panda cub from a pair of gun-toting poachers. Despite the beautiful locales and cuddly cub, director Christopher Cain can't overcome the handicaps of an artificial story, undeveloped characters, and the spoiled lad's unconvincing juvenile exploits. Life-threatening menace and a needless scene with head shots of two youngsters in the buff. A-II (PG)

Amazon Women on the Moon (1987) Tasteless compilation of comic skits and parodies of TV fare from five directors and presented by John Landis. Irreverent satire, excessive gratuitous nudity, and rough language are low points of this sophomoric joke-fest, whose huge cameo cast is its only remarkable feature. O (R)

Ambition (1991) A failed writer (Lou Diamond Phillips) gains the trust of a released multiple murderer (Clancy Brown) in order to entice him into another killing. As written by Phillips and directed by Scott D. Goldstein, the skimpy production values, stiff acting, and clumsy staging further hamper this marginally suspenseful thriller. A gory murder, live-in relationship, flash of nudity, and minimal rough language. A-III (R)

Ambush (1949) Familiar Western tale of the growing antagonism between a seasoned scout (Robert Taylor) and a greenhorn cavalry officer (John Hodiak) on a mission to rescue a woman taken captive by the Apaches. Director Sam Wood puts the cast through the plot's well-worn hoops with enough energy to make it all seem to matter. Indian stereotypes and frontier violence. A-I (br)

Ambush at Cimarron Pass (1958) Routine Western directed by Jodie Copelan in which a handful of troopers (led by Sgt. Scott Brady) are joined by a few cowboys (including anti-Yankee Clint Eastwood) in crossing hostile Apache country but, after losing their horses in a raid, continue on foot, toting a load of repeating rifles that must be kept from Apache hands at all costs. Frontier violence. A-I (br)

Ambush Bay (1966) Slack WW II action movie with a group of Marines (Hugh O'Brien, Mickey Rooney, James Mitchum) battling on a Pacific island under Ron Winston's direction offers nothing new to the wartime violence formula. A-III (br)

Ambushers, The (1968) Dean Martin stars as Matt Helm in a mindless spy spoof that has an almost nonexistent plot and is full of devices from other and better movies. Directed by Henry Levin, the effort is little more than a device for spewing out a succession of smutty jokes and sexual encounters reducing women to objects. O (br)

America at the Movies (1976) The American Film Institute put together a bicentennial mosaic of 92 excerpts from 83 American movies, but the result fails to convey much of significance about our nation and way of life. Although the overall tone of the compilation is innocuous, it contains a few instances of strong language and a frank depiction of sex. A-III (PG)

American Anthem (1986) Shallow tale about a teenage athlete (Mitch Gaylord) who, demoralized after his arm is broken during a violent argument between his parents, finds romance and renews his competitive spirit. Olympic gold medallist Gaylord can't overcome the emotional limitations of a script that plays like a gymnastic music video. Acceptance of casual sex. A-III (PG-13)

American Buffalo (1996) After promising an eager youngster (Sean Nelson) the chance to pull off his first robbery, a junk-shop owner (Dennis Franz) instead gives the job to a small-time hustler (Dustin Hoffman). Directed by Michael Corrente from David Mamet's adaptation of his own 1975 three-person stage play, the result is a shrill, depressing character study of losers and their mutual betrayals. Fleeting violence, crude references, and incessant rough language, as well as some profanity. A-III (R)

American Cyborg: Steel Warrior (1994) Ultraviolent action movie set in a post-apocalyptic society in which a young woman (Nicole Hansen) carrying the world's last human fetus is aided by a mysterious stranger (Joe Lara) in trying to escape the unstoppable cyborg (John Ryan) programmed to kill them. The outlandish plot in director Boaz Davidson's tiresome chase movie is simply an excuse for endless scenes of body blows, bloodshed, and butchery as the body count mounts. Excessive violence, crude sexual references, and occasional rough language. O (R)

American Dream, An (1966) In this generally inept screen adaptation of the Norman Mailer novel, Stuart Whitman plays an ex-war hero who becomes a muckraking TV commentator. When his exposes are not making trouble for others, personal problems with his wife and mistress, and a supposedly "accidental" death come to the fore. Directed by Robert Gist, the treatment of some unappealing adult themes is offensive. O (br)

American Dream (1992) Gritty documentary chronicles the bitter and divisive 1985-86 strike by Austin, Minn., meatpackers against wage and benefit concessions demanded by Hormel management. Writer-director Barbara Kopple vigorously explores the human cost of corporate profits as union workers, their families, and the entire community experience the financial and emotional strains of the long labor dispute. Occasional rough language and shots of meat-house slaughtering. A-II (nr)

American Dreamer (1984) Director Rick Rosenthal's miserably failed comedy about an Ohio housewife (JoBeth Williams) who wins a trip to Paris and, after suffering a blow to the head, carries on like a female James Bond. Because of its ringing endorsement of adultery, the movie languishes in the realm of soap-opera fantasy derisively stereotyping women. O (PG)

American Empire (1942) Uneven Western about partners (Richard Dix and Preston Foster) who build a booming Texas ranch, then quarrel over its expansion, until joining forces to save their vast herds from a small army of rustlers (led by Leo Carrillo). Director William McGann achieves only mediocre results from a colorful plot featuring riverboat owners becoming cattle barons, Cajun rustlers from Louisiana, the advent of barbed wire on the open range, and a massive shootout for the climax. Stylized violence, including the death of a youngster caught in a stampede. A-I (br)

American Flyers (1985) Two brothers (Kevin Costner and David Grant), one with a fatal brain disorder, enter a high-speed bicycle race to face the grueling competition together one last time. A well-acted but mundane tearjerker directed by John Badham. Vulgar language and some casual sex. A-III (PG-13)

American Friend, The (1977) Murky psychological thriller in which a shadowy American (Dennis Hopper) is asked by a French gangster to murder an American criminal, but winds up getting a German to do the job instead. Although German director Wim Wenders is sensitive to the cultural milieu of his characters and there is some tension in certain scenes, the narrative fails to generate suspense and ultimately becomes trite and dull. Stylized violence. A-II (nr)

American Game, The (1979) Documentary contrasts the lifestyles, motivations, and family ties of two high-school basketball stars, a black from Brooklyn and a white from Hoosier country. Producer Anthony Jones follows the young men through a crucial decision-making period detailing the uncertainties and pressures of winning and losing in sports and in the game of life. Spotted with some rough locker-room language, but still worth the attention of teenagers facing similar problems. A-II (PG)

American Gigolo (1980) Richard Gere plays a man who lives off women, and Lauren Hutton is a politician's wife who falls for him, but his world collapses when he's accused of murder. Written and directed by Paul Schrader, this is a silly and pretentious movie with much nudity, graphic sexuality, and a quite muddled moral stance. O (R)

American Graffiti (1973) It's the last, long night of the summer of 1962, and for two recent California grads (Richard Dreyfuss and Ron Howard) jetting away to college in the morning, it's a last chance to taste the innocent fantasies of a teenage world about to be lost, perhaps forever. The hugely eventful evening is packed with high-school nostalgia but, despite the bemused smiles of its star-crossed lovers, the mood ultimately turns sober. Director George Lucas's delightful comedy not only captures the signs of former times but comments on them with eloquence and incisiveness. A-III (PG)

American Guerrilla in the Philippines (1950) Plodding, predictable war story in which a US naval officer (Tyrone Power), caught on Leyte after the Japanese occupation, joins the local resistance (Micheline Prelle among them) and establishes radio contact with American invasion forces. Director Fritz Lang mutes the situation's potential for action by concentrating on the mundane problems of life in the underground. Stylized violence and ethnic stereotypes. A-II (br)

American Heart (1993) Wrenching tale in which a paroled ex-con (Jeff Bridges) painfully learns to care about his long-estranged teenage son (Edward Furlong), while holding down a menial job and being pressured by his former partner-in-crime (Don Harvey) to pull a new heist. Director Martin Bell's gritty father-son drama captures the tough reality of rebuilding a shattered relationship, as well as the frustrations ex-cons face in trying to go straight in an uncaring society. Brief violence, several sexual situations, and some rough language. A-III (R)

American History X (1998) Violent melodrama in which the young leader of a California hate group (Edward Norton) is convicted of manslaughter for killing two African-Americans who had broken into his car, but is raped in prison by fellow skinheads, then is befriended by a black convict, before returning home a changed man. Directed by Tony Kaye, there is nothing subtle about the movie's anti-hate message and the reliance on hard-edged violence in the story's treatment, but the result is unconvincing as a human drama and provides no insights beyond the real danger to society of such groups. Intense violence (some of it gory), sexual situations, including a homosexual gang rape, brief nudity, racial epithets, recurring rough language, and some profanity. A-IV (R)

American Hot Wax (1978) Nostalgic rock 'n' roll musical focusing upon a few days in the life of 1950's disc jockey Alan Freed (Tim McIntire) before his last big show at the Brooklyn Paramount in 1959. The work, directed by Floyd Mutrux, will appeal to those who like the music and stars of the time. Occasional vulgarities. A-III (PG)

American in Paris, An (1951) Stylish musical romance set in elegant 1920's Paris, where an expatriate American painter (Gene Kelly) pursues a vision of beauty (Leslie Caron) while eluding the clutches of a wealthy patron (Nina Foch). Despite the flimsy plot, director Vicente Minnelli has no trouble delighting the ear with George Gershwin's music and brother Ira's lyrics, while charming the eye with stylized production numbers, evocative period sets, and a fine cast. Romantic complications. A-II (br)

American Justice (1986) Corrupt border police enslave illegal Mexican aliens in a movie that begins as an exploration of the problems of illegal aliens and ends in a blood-bath between good and bad lawmen. Excessive violence, some nudity, and rough language add to the unpleasantries in the desert. O (R)

American Me (1992) Graduating from juvenile delinquent to prison inmate, a Hispanic gangster (Edward James Olmos) uses his cell as the base of a crime network whose tentacles of violence reach deep into the LA barrio, only to engulf him after he is reformed by a good woman (Evelina Fernandez). Also directed by Olmos, the movie makes a powerful statement against the drug culture and its consequences for the young. Much graphic violence including executions and gang rapes, restrained bedroom scene, flash of nudity, and constant rough language. A-IV (R)

American Pop (1981) Animated feature by Ralph Bakshi presents a history of American popular music through the story of an immigrant family from the turn of the century to the present, with the great-grandson gaining fame as a rock star. Interesting concept, but the story lacks dramatic focus and many of the characters are unappealing, if not repulsive. Depiction of some sleazy environments and the use of drugs. A-III (R)

American President, The (1995) Fluffy romance with the nation's widowed chief executive (Michael Douglas) insisting on his right to carry on a love affair with a feisty lobbyist (Annette Bening), despite its potential to derail his chances for re-election. Thanks to the appealing treatment of the couple, producer-director Rob Reiner's feel-good romantic fantasy provides superficial entertainment while glossing over moral issues and political realities. References to an off-screen affair and a few instances of rough language. A-III (PG-13)

American Tail, An (1986) A family of Jewish mice emigrate from Russia to America in 1885 seeking a new life free from Cossack cats, but become separated during a storm at sea. While searching for his parents in New York City, a young mouse finds adventure and the meaning of the Statue of Liberty. Director Don Bluth uses Disney-style full animation in meticulous, loving detail on a story that may delight youngsters, but which some parents might find a bit too saccharine. A-I (G)

American Tail: Fievel Goes West, An (1991) Unexceptional sequel continues the animated adventures of feisty Fievel Mousekewitz and his family in the Wild West, where he must save them from crafty cats conniving to turn them into mouse-burgers. Directors Phil Nebbelink and Simon Wells deliver an uneven story whose pace and images range from gentle to chaotic. Some typical cartoon violence. A-I (G)

American Werewolf in London, An (1981) Trashy, sardonically muddled horror show by writer-director John Landis attempts to combine comedy and fright with a dash of steamy sex. The result is a squalid mess. Contains violence and explicit sex. O (R)

American Werewolf in Paris, An (1997) Inept horror movie in which an American tourist (Tom Everett Scott) saves a woman (Julie Delpy) as she jumps from the Eiffel Tower, but by the time he learns she is a bloodthirsty werewolf, he has become one himself. Directed by Anthony Waller, the slipshod story mixes gory special effects with airhead humor and sophomoric sex, though the combination proves grimly tiresome. Mindless fantasy violence, sexual situations with nudity, condom jokes, and gross language. O (R)

American Wilderness (1973) Little more than a collection of self-congratulatory home movies taken during the past decade or so by an Oregon sportsman named Art Dubs. Although it has a down-home folksiness, there are many other fine outdoor adventure documentaries that offer family viewers better camerawork and information on wildlife than this narrowly conceived, often poorly photographed movie. A-I (G)

Americanization of Emily, The (1964) Attached to an American military headquarters, a British volunteer (Julie Andrews) learns fast as a megalomaniacal admiral (Melvyn Douglas) tries to make a hero of himself, while his aide (James Garner) tries to take advantage of her and others. The conclusion to director Arthur Hiller's cynical look at life in WW II England is Emily's own compromise of her virtue and previously unimpeachable character. O (br)

Americano, The (1955) Muddled adventure in which a Texas rancher (Glenn Ford) escorts three prize Brahma bulls to Brazil's Matto Grosso, then finds the buyer murdered in a range war between a big rancher (Frank Lovejoy) and small ones (led by Ursula Thiess) backed by the local bandit chief (Cesar Romero). Directed by William Castle, the proceedings are colorful but slow-paced and confusingly disjointed. Stylized violence and sexual situations. A-III (br)

Americathon (1979) With America about to go bankrupt in this dismal comedy directed by Neil Israel, a massive telethon is held to rescue the national finances. Besides being unfunny, the movie employs objectionable language and graphic depictions of misconduct. O (PG)

Amin — The Rise and Fall (1981) Amateurish and exploitative account of the Uganda dictator's bloody career in a Kenyan production directed by Sahrad Patel. Posing as socio-political document, it offers little more than sensationalism through a disreputable mix of violence and sex. O (R)

Amistad ((1997) Uneven dramatization of the 1839 legal battle over the fate of 53 Africans who massacre the crew of a Spanish slave ship, then are captured by an American naval vessel and put on trial for murder and piracy in a case that ultimately reaches the Supreme Court, where former president John Quincy Adams (Anthony Hopkins) defends their right to freedom. Director Steven Spielberg's ambitious attempt to re-examine the contradictions of a society which proclaimed the equality of all and yet accepted slavery succeeds in dramatizing the obvious injustices done the enslaved Africans (led by Djimon Hounsou), but the legal and political issues argued in the lengthy case are treated in stiff historical tableaus. Some gory violence, brutalizing conditions of slavery, and brief frontal nudity. A-III (R)

Amityville Horror, The (1979) The anemic plot of this tepid horror movie about a suburban couple whose house is possessed by some demonic force doesn't allow for much in the way of a satisfactory resolution. Director Stuart Rosenberg's garish special effects are relatively restrained, but his superficial treatment of the story's religious dimension is ludicrous. A-III (R)

Amityville II: The Possession (1982) Set in a period previous to that of the original, director Damiano Damiani's sequel features Burt Young in a partly haunted-house story and a partly wretched remake of the **Exorcist**, highlighted by a ludicrously inept depiction of the religious rite of exorcism. Excessive violence and nudity. O (R)

Amityville 3-D (1983) The third in this dreary series features Tony Roberts as a writer who moves into the demonic house, confident he's gotten a real bargain. This silly mess is probably all the worse for viewers aggravated by the headache from the 3-D glasses. Absurd, spurious violence. A-III (PG)

Amongst Friends (1993) Three buddies (Joseph Lindsay, Steve Parlavecchio, Patrick McGaw) who grew up together in an affluent New York suburb take up a life of crime, leading them eventually to betrayal and deadly confrontations with each other. Writer-director Rob Weiss portrays the trio's smug lawbreaking and violent actions with raw energy but no insights into their wasted lives. Some nasty violence and cold-blooded murders, a bedroom scene, recreational drug use, brief nudity, and constant rough language. O (R)

Amorous Adventures of Moll Flanders, The (1965) Witless romantic folderol from Daniel Defoe's novel about a servant girl (miscast Kim Novak) in 18th-century England who, after being seduced and abandoned, sets out to find a rich husband but instead falls for a highwayman (Richard Johnson), with predictable results. Director Terence Young's attempt to turn the slow-paced proceedings into bawdy fun misfires badly in labored sequences more tiresome than amusing, though the fine supporting cast provides some droll moments. Heavy-handed sexual situations and innuendo. A-IV (br)

Amos & Andrew (1993) Clunky comedy about a prominent African-American (Samuel L. Jackson) mistaken for a thief, then taken hostage by a kooky crook (Nicolas Cage) in cahoots with a bone-headed police chief (Dabney Coleman) trying to turn the fiasco into a publicity stunt. Writer-director E. Max Frye gets off a few acidly funny lines in an otherwise overly broad, overwrought comedy heavily dependent on dopey stereotypes. Brief violence, shots of recreational drug use, and minimal rough language. A-III (PG-13)

Amsterdam Kill, The (1978) Robert Mitchum plays a disgraced but incorruptible ex-narcotics agent who finds himself caught in a bloody struggle among rival Chinese drug dealers in Hong Kong and Amsterdam. Director Robert Clouse's plot seems no more than a string of action sequences, none of which is very exciting, let alone entertaining. Stylized violence and high body count. A-III (R)

Amy (1981) This warm and amiable Disney movie, set in the early 1900s, tells the story of a determined young woman (Jenny Agutter) who leaves her wealthy but unloving husband (Chris Robinson) to teach at a school for the deaf. Director Vincent McEveety does well in developing the contrast between personal and social commitment in a film that is ideal for children, except for the marital estrangement in the plot. A-II (G)

Anaconda (1997) Overwrought thriller about an anthropological expedition taking a film crew (led by Jennifer Lopez and Ice Cube) far up the Amazon River in search of a primitive tribe, but they pick up a stranded snake-hunter (Jon Voight) who soon diverts them into tracking down a valuable but deadly 40-foot reptile. Director Luis Llosa's transparent plot is anchored by Voight's sinister performance, but the grotesque attacks by the undulating animatronic beast are so overdone they become almost comical. Intermittent violence, a few profanities, and an instance of rough language. A-III (PG-13)

Anais Observed (1974) Anais Nin was both participant in and observer of the avant-garde scene between the world wars. Robert Snyder's feature documentary reveals all the paradox implicit in her work of self-absorption bordering on the narcissistic, combined with a warm and encouraging interest in relating to others (as with some awed students who visit her). The viewer will have to judge, however, how valuable are her aesthetic judgments and personal philosophy. A-III (nr)

Analyze This (1999) Sporadically funny comedy in which a mob boss (Robert De Niro) suffering anxiety attacks enlists a nervous psychoanalyst (Billy Crystal) to treat and cure him before an imminent meeting of crime kingpins from around the country. Director Harold Ramis tempers the crude underworld setting with adult humor, some sentiment, and the gangster's reformation. Intermittent stylized violence, a brief sexual encounter, some sex references, occasional profanity, and much rough language. A-IV (R)

Anastasia (1956) Absorbing drama from Marcelle Maurette's play set in 1928 Paris, where a woman suffering from amnesia (Ingrid Bergman) is tutored by a White Russian general (Yul Brynner) to pass as the czar's youngest daughter, who somehow escaped the 1918 Bolshevik massacre of the royal family. Director Anatole Litvak portrays the émigré scene with enough conviction to sustain interest in the growing mystery of the woman's true identity, but most memorable are the scenes between the spunky yet vulnerable Bergman and Helen Hayes as the regal dowager empress whose compassion leads to an emotionally satisfying conclusion. A-I (br)

Anastasia (1997) Appealing animated musical

about the Czar's youngest daughter (voice of Meg Ryan), who survives the Bolshevik Revolution to grow up in an orphanage with only faint memories of her family, then meets a handsome con-man (voice of John Cusack), who takes her to Paris, where her one surviving relative lives. Directors Don Bluth and Gary Goldman turn history into a fairy tale with the enchantment of lush animation and spirited musical numbers. A-I (G)

Anatomy of a Murder (1959) Overlong courtroom drama in which a small-town lawyer (James Stewart) undertakes the defense of an Army officer (Ben Gazarra) charged with murdering the man who raped his wife (Lee Remick). Directed by Otto Preminger, the case is less interesting than Stewart's genial, intelligent performance, backed by a fine cast including Joseph N. Welch, the lawyer who gained fame in the 1954 Army-McCarthy hearings and is convincing here as the trial judge. Controversial at the time for its courtroom descriptions of the rape, it is relatively mild today. A-III (br)

Anchoress (1994) Lyric melodrama set in medieval England, where a dreamy adolescent (Natalie Morse) claims to have seen the Blessed Mother, is persuaded by the parish priest to be enclosed as a hermit within a cell adjacent to the local church, but eventually rebels and tunnels her way out to an uncertain freedom. Director Chris Newby's poetic black-and-white photography is imaginatively convincing in its depiction of the agrarian life and religious sensibility of the period, but the narrative is dramatically flawed with murky motivations and incoherent subplots that add up finally to little more than a feminist tract against the abuses of male authority. Ambiguous treatment of the conflict between individual conscience and Church authority, numerous sexual implications, and occasional crude language. A-IV (nr)

Anchors Aweigh (1945) Musical romance on the home front with a shy sailor (Frank Sinatra) and his slick buddy (Gene Kelly) on a four-day shore leave in Hollywood, where they meet an aspiring singer (Kathryn Grayson), promise her an audition with Jose Iturbi, then frantically try to meet the famed pianist. Directed by George Sidney, the thin plot offers plenty of period nostalgia, along with some well-staged musical numbers, notably Kelly's dance with animated mouse Jerry from the MGM "Tom and Jerry" cartoon series. A-I (br)

And Hope to Die (1972) In a considerably shortened version of a French production directed by Rene Clement (originally entitled **The Race of the Hare Across the Fields**), the plot itself seems to have gone the way of the Cheshire Cat. What remains is a series of interesting but capricious scenes involving a gang of colorful cut-throats (Robert Ryan, Jean-Louis Trintignant, Lea Massari, and Aldo Ray) that finally culminates in a "kidnapping" from police headquarters in the middle of Montreal. If Clement's intention was to liken this kind of adult entertainment to childhood games, something is missing in the translation. A-III (PG)

... And Justice for All (1979) Al Pacino stars as an honest but abrasive anti-establishment lawyer who is blackmailed into defending a "law and order" judge (John Forsythe) accused of rape. A heavy-handed and muddled potboiler directed by Norman Jewison. Foul language and sexual promiscuity. O (R)

And Now for Something Completely Different (1972) This random sampling of skits from "Monty Python's Flying Circus," the BBC zany comedy series, offers some distinctly British humor ranging from social satire and black comedy to broad slapstick and sexual jokes, most notably at the expense of homosexuals. Under director Ian MacNaughton, the young cast comes over as a quite likeable group of performers, which helps when jokes fall flat. Best of all, however, are Terry Gilliam's animated pieces linking the skits but also standing on their own as contemporary graphic humor. However, it is comedy not for all tastes. A-IV (PG)

And Now Miguel (1966) An engaging portrayal of a year in the life of a small boy (Pat Cardi) in New Mexico, whose only wish is to become a shepherd like his father (Michael Ansara). Produced by Robert B. Radnitz and based on Joseph Krumgold's prize-winning novel, the film emphasizes the strength of Hispanic family life rooted in mutual love and respect, with the natural beauty of the land and a credible cast contributing to its realistic picture of pastoral life. A-I (br)

And Now My Love (1975) French production using the history of Europe from WW I to the present as the backdrop to a love story tracing, in almost surrealistic fashion, the heritages and key events in the lives of a young Jewish heiress (Marthe Keller) and an ex-convict turned film director (Charles Denner). Beautifully produced and directed by Claude Lelouch, history is interestingly put at the service of love, and there is no denying that the optimism of his romantic fable makes one feel good, even though aware that its selective view of the past is being used only to make a romantic trifle seem more consequential than it really is. A-III (PG)

And Now the Screaming Starts (1973) British horror movie directed by Roy Ward Baker offers no more than an average example in this 18th-century tale of inherited guilt from a diabolically inspired family curse. Good production values and special effects. The cast includes horror veterans Peter Cushing, Patrick Magee, and Herbert Lom. A number of the plot elements involve rape and other forms of brutality, but their treatment is restrained. A-III (R)

And Now Tomorrow (1944) Creaky sudser directed by Irving Pichel in which a poor but earnest doctor (Alan Ladd) seeks to restore the hearing of a wealthy deaf woman (Loretta Young) while opening her eyes to the needs of the less fortunate and unlocking her heart to the throbs of true love. Romantic complications. A-II (br)

And Soon the Darkness (1971) Two pretty English lasses (Pamela Franklin and Michele Dotrice) on a bicycle tour of France have a row, and Dotrice disappears on the site of an unsolved grisly sex-murder, leaving Franklin to search for her friend while eluding the crazed killer. British thriller directed by Robert Fuest takes her up and down any number of verdant but blind alleys, establishing everyone she meets as a prime suspect, but even the pretty French countryside cannot compensate for the overall disappointment in the climax. A-III (GP)

And the Band Played On (1993) Ambitious but uneven docudrama from Randy Shilts's book about the first years of the AIDS epidemic begins in 1981 with the efforts of medical researchers (notably Matthew Modine) to identify a mystery disease seemingly limited to homosexuals, then details the indecisive action of government and medical officials in the battle against what was becoming a worldwide crisis. Directed by Roger Spottiswoode, the scenario's attempt to provide a comprehensive account of complex events results in an unwieldy narrative which gathers dramatic impact from its diverse picture of individuals confronting the reality of this deadly disease. Sympathetic treatment of homosexual relationships and a realistic depiction of the human tragedy of AIDS and the indifference of some to it. A-III (R)

And Then There Were None (1945) Mystery classic from the Agatha Christie novel in which 10 strangers invited for a weekend on a remote island are each charged by their unseen host with an unpunished capital crime, for which he begins to kill them one by one. Director Rene Clair and scriptwriter Dudley Nichols embroider the cunning plot with elaborate chills and deepening suspense, laced with gallows humor and carried off in style by an accomplished cast (led by Barry Fitzgerald, Walter Huston, Louis Hayward, and June Duprez). More menace than violence. A-II (br)

And There Came a Man (1968) Part documentary and part re-enactment, this screen biography of Pope John XXIII features Rod Steiger as narrator and stand-in for the person of the title. The Italian production is best in its unpretentious re-created scenes of Pope John's early boyhood, but director Ermanno Olmi is less successful in depicting his clerical career. A-I (br)

Anderson Platoon, The (1968) French documentary about the Vietnam War centers not on the issues of the war but on a few weeks in the lives of an airmobile unit under Lt. Joseph B. Anderson fighting in the central highlands. Directed by Pierre Schoendorffer, its focus on these men helps give a human perspective to the reality of combat, something the screen too often glamorizes. A-II (br)

Anderson Tapes, The (1971) Director Sidney Lumet almost succeeds in splicing together an exciting perfect heist narrative and an ironic statement about electronic eavesdropping, public and private. Sean Connery masterminds the robbery of an entire luxury apartment building, but all those he recruits for the job are already under surveillance by various law agencies, none of whom has a full picture of what is going on. Adult material with occasional violence that some may find excessive. A-IV (PG)

Andre (1994) Pleasant fact-based story of a family living on the Maine coast, where in the 1960s father (Keith Carradine) and daughter (Tina Majorino) rescue an orphaned seal pup, who becomes so attached to its adopted human family that for 24 years the seal makes its way back to them after every winter thaw. Director George Miller embroiders the playful antics of the personable seal with several subplots about prickly individuals and community misunderstandings in a sentimental story stressing positive parent-child relationships. A-I (PG)

Andrei Rublev (1969) Russian production about a 15th-century monk (Anatoli Solonitzine) who perseveres in painting icons and other religious art despite the civil disruptions and cruel turmoil of his times. Director Andrei Tarkovsky visualizes brilliantly the story of a devout man seeking through his art to find the transcendent in the savagery of the Tartar invasions and the unfeeling brutality of Russian nobles. Subtitles. Stylized historical violence. A-II (br)

Androcles and the Lion (1952) Satiric misfire from George Bernard Shaw's play about a group of Christians (headed by patrician Jean Simmons) who are saved from martyrdom in Rome's Colosseum by a lion from whose paw one of them (Alan Young) had once extracted a thorn. Directed by Chester Erskine, the sluggish narrative is buoyed by some droll exchanges on secular power vs. religious faith and many eccentric performances (aggressive pacifist Robert Newton, dim emperor Maurice Evans, shrewish wife Elsa Lanchester, etc.). Romantic situations and humorous probes into religious matters. A-III (br)

Andromeda Strain, The (1971) When a New Mexico hamlet is wiped out by extraterrestrial microbes, a team of top medical specialists try to find a way to destroy the deadly bacterium before it destroys the human race. Despite some overdone special effects and unnecessary plot complications, director Robert Wise's screen version of Michael Crichton's bestseller is gripping and its impact is sharp. A-II (G)

Andy (1965) The aging parents of a grown man (Norman Alden) with the mind of a small child are forced to make the decision to commit him to an institution. Writer-director Richard Sarafian captures the less than understanding attitudes of society toward the mentally handicapped but tinges the realism of the New York City locale with poetic images affirming the joys of simple existence. Challenging but worthwhile fare. A-III (br)

Andy Hardy Comes Home (1958) Clunker directed by Howard Koch tries to revive the Hardy series with the original cast (except family patriarch Lewis Stone). Best forgotten. A-I (br)

Andy Hardy Gets Spring Fever (1939) Judge

Hardy (Lewis Stone) falls for an aluminum scam while son Andy (Mickey Rooney) develops a crush on the new high-school drama teacher. Directed by W.S. Van Dyke II, it offers the usual family sitcom fare, though Andy's involvement with the school play has its moments. A-I (br)

Andy Hardy Meets a Debutante (1940) In order to rescue the town orphanage trust fund, Judge Hardy (Lewis Stone) journeys to New York City, taking the family along on a trip that threatens to disgrace Andy (Mickey Rooney) back home, until he's saved by a wealthy friend (Judy Garland). Directed by George B. Seitz, this edition of the Hardy series provides some period amusement as well as an incidental lesson in democracy. A-I (br)

Andy Hardy's Blonde Trouble (1944) As a college freshman, Andy (Mickey Rooney) gets off on the wrong foot with the dean (Herbert Marshall), a lovely co-ed (Bonita Granville), and a contrary blonde, who turns out to be identical twins (Lee and Lyn Wilde). Directed by George B. Seitz, it's one of the feebler efforts of the series, sorely lacking the interplay of the Hardy family circle. A-I (br)

Andy Hardy's Double Life (1942) While Judge Hardy (Lewis Stone) is preoccupied with an accident case, flirtatious Andy is perplexed by girlfriend Polly (Ann Rutherford) and her visiting pal (Esther Williams). Directed by George B. Seitz, the usual domestic misunderstandings culminate in a big finish at the train station seeing Andy off to college. A-I (br)

Andy Hardy's Private Secretary (1941) Disorganized Andy (Mickey Rooney) gets a secretary (Kathryn Grayson) to help him keep up with his busy activities as a Carvel High senior in a typical episode of the Hardy series under George B. Seitz's direction. A-I (br)

Andy Warhol's Dracula (1975) In this variation on the Dracula theme, the ever-thirsty Count must live on "wirgin's blood," as it is rendered in one of the dreadful accents abounding here. Besides the accents, there's no lack of other offensive elements in director Paul Morrissey's campy efforts in trying to make perversion seem hilarious. O (X/R)

Andy Warhol's Frankenstein (1974) Written and directed by Warhol's alter ego, Paul Morrissey, this version emphasizes the fatal and the perverse aspects of the Mary Shelley original, ever-escalating the campy hijinks for shock value. If one isn't offended by the gross nudity and kinky sex combinations, perhaps one will be by the gory charnel scraps flying all over the place. O (X/R)

Angel (1984) Advertised as "High-school honor student by day, Hollywood hooker by night" is all one needs to know about this dismal effort by director Robert Vincent O'Neil to tell the story of a young prostitute (Donna Wilkes), who helps a detective catch a psychopathic killer. Nudity, graphic sex, and violence. O (R)

Angel and the Badman (1947) Enjoyable low-key Western in which a wounded outlaw (John Wayne) is nursed back to health by a Quaker family, whose daughter (Gail Russell) tries to get him to hang up his guns rather than square accounts with a bushwhacker (Bruce Cabot). Directed by James Edward Grant, the unpretentious yet thoughtful story features a very likeable cast, including Harry Carey as the sage sheriff. Solid social values with some meaningful stylized violence. A-I (br)

Angel, Angel Down We Go (1969) An 18-year-old virgin (Holly Near), desperate to lose that state, is helped out by a rock singer (Jordon Christopher), who also gives sexual aid to her wealthy mother and father, and then destroys them all. Blaming a corrupt society for the depicted immoral activity, director Robert Thom's presentation tries to smooth over the guilt feelings of viewers slightly ashamed at their own voyeurism. Promiscuity and several insulting references to religion. O (R)

Angel Face (1953) Dark crime-melodrama in which an unhinged heiress (Jean Simmons) embroils an unwitting car mechanic (Robert Mitchum) in the murder of her wealthy stepmother (Barbara O'Neill), with dire consequences for both. Directed by Otto Preminger, the story is a mess of contrived situations and unconvincing characters. Stylized violence including suicide in the plot resolution. A-III (br)

Angel Heart (1987) Director Alan Parker's bloody, often disgusting depiction of one man's grappling with the devil and the consequences of his refusal to face the evil within him forms the core of this parable about a private eye (Mickey Rourke) hired to find a missing person, only to discover it is a missing soul. Graphic mix of sex and violence in a demonic setting, nudity, and vivid results of dismemberment. O (R)

Angel in My Pocket, An (1968) A newly ordained minister (Andy Griffith) comes to serve his first congregation in a small Kansas town, where he immediately becomes involved in the feud between two families that has wrecked the ministry of all his predecessors. Directed by Alan Rafkin, the comedy is broad and mindless, the characters stereotypes, and the sugary situations enough to give some viewers diabetes. A-I (G)

Angel Levine, The (1970) A devout old Jewish tailor (Zero Mostel) living in poverty in Harlem seems to have his prayers answered when a black man (Harry Belafonte) arrives claiming to be an angel who can help, but only if the tailor has faith in him. Though some viewers may find the tailor's wavering between belief and disbelief growing tiresomely repetitive, others will see it as the point of director Jan Kadar's brilliant allegory asserting people's need for belief and commitment for the sake of human survival. A-III (GP)

Angel on My Shoulder (1946) Seriocomic fantasy about a murdered gangster (Paul Muni) whom the Devil (Claude Rains) puts in the body of a look-alike judge to destroy the man's virtuous career, but things don't go according to plan. Though it doesn't make a whole lot of sense, director Archie Mayo has some fun creating the sulfuric pits of hell down below, as well as with the tough-talking mug's reformation by the judge's fiancé (Anne Baxter). Some stylized violence and devilish goings-on. A-II (br)

Angel Unchained (1970) Routine motorcycle melodrama about a biker (Don Stroud) who leaves his cycling buddies to join a commune, but when its peaceful members are harassed by the local cowboys he calls on his old friends to help even out the odds in the big showdown. Director Lee Madden's contrived plot provides the opportunity for some hard-hitting brawls, a touch of sex, an abundance of beer and pot, and, of course, plenty of daredevil bike riding. A-III (GP)

Angel with the Trumpet (1949) Sprawling saga of an Austrian family from 1888 through WW II, focusing on the Jewish wife (Eileen Herlie) of the family's head (Basil Sydney) as they struggle to survive the disasters of war, financial ruin, and the aged woman's suicide under Nazi rule. Directed by Anthony Bushell, the British production interweaves the drama of the family's changing fortunes with the history of the Austrian nation from monarchy to republic to occupation by the Germans, then the Allies. Wartime violence, suicide, and implied sexual affairs. A-III (br)

Angel Wore Red, The (1960) Muddled tale in which a priest (Dirk Bogarde) loses his faith during the Spanish Civil War, then falls in love with a kind-hearted prostitute (Ava Gardner), but winds up on his own safeguarding a holy relic sought by all sides. Written and directed by Nunnally Johnson, the unwieldy plot has interesting characters and compelling situations but grows increasingly unsure of where it is going with this mixture of love story, political fable, and saga of faith, until ending in a welter of sentimentality. Wartime violence, anti-clerical rhetoric, and illicit romance. A-III (br)

Angels & Insects (1996) Ponderous British drama of the 1860s centers on a penniless naturalist (Mark Rylance), whose happy marriage to the pretty daughter (Patsy Kensit) of a wealthy patron is shattered at discovering his wife's incestuous relationship with her worthless brother, causing him to turn to a woman (Kristin Scott Thomas) whose intelligence and interests match his own. Directed by Philip Haas, the multileveled Victorian narrative gains dramatic force through restrained performances and evocative visuals while probing the relationships between love and passion, beauty and intelligence, nature and environment, Darwinian materialism and the human spirit. Several gauzy but graphic bedroom scenes and restrained treatment of incest. A-IV (nr)

Angels Die Hard (1970) Unenlightened motorcycle movie about a gang of bikers who invade a small town, brutally torment the locals, then linger nearby to do it again. Underdeveloped conflicts center around the sheriff's blustering threats to shoot them down, especially since his teenage daughter is keen on joining them. Director Richard Compton leans to admiring shots of the gang riding the road, but the coarse customs and cruelty of these outlaw heroes far outweigh any suggestions of their benevolent humanity. O (R)

Angels in the Outfield (1994) Remake of the 1951 syrupy fantasy in which the surly baseball manager (Danny Glover) of the last-place California Angels starts relying on the advice of a young boy (Joseph Gordon-Levitt), who claims to see heavenly angels assisting various players during the games. William Dear directs a slow-paced, old-fashioned crowd-pleaser in which a foster child's prayer for a family is answered and cynical adults begin believing that, with a little faith, miracles can happen. Fleeting violence and a few instances of profanity. A-II (PG)

Angels with Dirty Faces (1938) Depression melodrama in which a gang of New York toughs (Billy Hallop, Leo Gorcey, and other Dead End Kids) regard a local gangster (James Cagney) as a hero until a priest (Pat O'Brien) who was his boyhood pal persuades him to help the boys by feigning cowardice on the way to the electric chair. Directed by Michael Curtiz, the simplistic plot is buttressed by convincing performances, especially the counterpoint between Cagney's cocky crook and O'Brien's sincere cleric. Stylized violence and justice questions. A-II (br)

Angels' Alley (1948) Formula slapstick comedy with the Bowery Boys (notably Leo Gorcey and Huntz Hall) battling a gang of car thieves whose sneering boss (Nestor Paiva) gets decked by a priest running the local youth center. A-I (br)

Angi Vera (1980) A marvelously subtle and complex Hungarian production set in 1948, the early days of the Communist regime, a tragic and confused era full of idealism and opportunism. Veronica Papp gives a flawless performance in the title role as a young woman with a talent for survival, who is sent by the Party to a political training-center, where she has an affair that could threaten her future. Director Pal Gabor shows that human nature has a way of infiltrating the most resistant of ideologies. Adult situations and politically complex themes. A-III (nr)

Angie (1994) Soggy tearjerker about a working-class Brooklyn girl (Geena Davis) who becomes pregnant by her plumber boyfriend (James Gandolfini), then dumps him for an eccentric high-class lawyer (Stephen Rea), who walks out after the baby is born, leaving her to face single parenthood with the support of loving family and friends. In trying to lighten the melodrama with humor, director Martha Coolidge never gets to the heart of her feminist heroine, whose struggle for independence is complicated by hostility for her stepmother and yearnings for the mother she never knew, though along the way there are some positive discoveries about the responsibilities of parenthood and the importance of family. Premarital relationships, a flash of nudity, some raunchy humor, and occasional rough language. A-IV (R)

Angry Harvest (1986) Set in a Polish village during WW II, a simple but devout farmer abuses the trust of a Jewish refugee he is sheltering by his lust for her. In the Polish production, director Agnieszka Holland offers a compelling portrait of a man whose loneliness undermines his basic moral character, resulting in betrayal and death. In this context, several brief scenes of partial nudity and simulated sex are anything but titillating. A-IV (nr)

Angry Hills, The (1959) As German troops occupy 1941 Athens, an American reporter (Robert Mitchum) is pursued by Gestapo agents (led by Stanley Baker) out to stop him from delivering a list of Nazi collaborators to the Allies, but he escapes with the help of Greek guerrillas fighting in the mountains. Directed by Robert Aldrich, the story is far-fetched, with little characterization and more muddy intrigue than action. Wartime violence and sexual situations. A-III (br)

Angry Red Planet, The (1959) Low-budget sci-fi adventure directed by Ib Melchior in which a US space mission lands on Mars, where its crew (Gerald Mohr, Nora Hayden, Les Tremayne, and Jack Kruschen) encounters a giant ameba and other bargain-basement monsters before returning to Earth with a Martian warning never to return. Stylized violence and menacing situations. A-II (br)

Angus (1995) Formula comedy in which a tubby teen (Charlie Talbert) must overcome low self-esteem and taunting classmates before finding courage to talk to the girl of his dreams (Ariana Richards). Cardboard characters and Patrick Read Johnson's dull direction result in a preachy, predictable tale about beauty being only skin-deep. Some sexual innuendo, comic roughhousing, crude slang, and a needless instance of rough language. A-III (PG-13)

Animal Behavior (1989) Muddled romance between a sincere music teacher (Armande Assante) and a spacey psychology professor (Karen Allen) who's too caught up in her communication research with a chimp to relate in a man-woman context. Directed by H. Anne Riley, the movie's dopey, implausible script and miscast, overwrought characters fail in a humorless attempt at screwball comedy. Minimal rough language and some sexual innuendo. A-III (PG)

Animal Crackers (1930) Marx Brothers comedy with Groucho as Captain Geoffrey T. Spaulding, the inveterate African explorer and improbable guest of honor at a party given by Margaret Dumont to unveil a valuable painting which is stolen, then replaced by two bogus ones. Chico and Harpo add a bit of music to the comic proceedings, Lillian Roth sings, and Zeppo, the fourth brother, plays Groucho's private secretary. Directed by Victor Heerman, the coarse slapstick of the early Marx Brothers comedies may not appeal to everyone's tastes, but their zany verbal and physical assaults on conventions of every kind continue to amuse comedy fans. A-II (G)

Animal House (see: **National Lampoon's Animal House**)

Animal Kingdom, The (1932) Stagy dramatization of Philip Barry's play about a playboy publisher (Leslie Howard), who weds a manipulative socialite (Myrna Loy) but is saved from being turned into a stuffed shirt by his former mistress (Ann Harding). Directed by Edward H. Griffith, the contrived situation is played for comedy, notably William Gargan's dippy role as a boxer-turned-butler, but the arch humor about the mating game has dated badly. Much sexual innuendo and comic treatment of marriage. A-III (br)

Animals Are Beautiful People (1975) Wildlife documentary filmed in a vast tract of desert, swamp, and mountains in southwest Africa, with an exotic variety of animal species. Director Jamie Uys provides some humorous as well as fascinating moments, marred slightly by a Disney-style anthropomorphic slant and what some might detect as a paternalistic attitude toward blacks. A-I (G)

Ann and Eve (1970) Swedish story of a jaded journalist (Gio Petre), who takes a young innocent (Marie Liljedahl) on a vacation to a Yugoslav resort, where she is initiated into a predictable series of sexual adventures around town. Arne Mattsson directs the lurid melodrama with clinical coldness toward the characters, who meander through arbitrary situations. Excessive nudity. O (nr)

Anna Karenina (1997) Opulent adaptation of Leo Tolstoy's 19th-century novel of Czarist Russia contrasts the hard-won love story of an eventually happy couple (Alfred Molina and Mia Kirshner) with the doomed romance of a married woman (Sophie Morceau), who forsakes husband and child to run off with a wealthy officer (Sean Bean). Screenwriter-director Bernard Rose's elaborate period piece is visually lush in portraying the hypocrisy of class distinctions and exploring characters who question the morality of their actions. Brief violence, fleeting bedroom scene, and a suicidal character's drug dependency. A-III (PG-13)

Anna Lucasta (1958) Lurid melodrama about a guilt-ridden old man (Rex Ingram) and his daughter (Eartha Kitt) who turned to prostitution after being driven from home as a teenager, but whom the family now insists return to wed a man whose money will benefit them. Directed by Arnold Laven from Philip Yordan's play, the contrived proceedings grow increasingly muddled, though convincing performances by an all-black cast hold interest, especially those of Kitt in the title role and Sammy Davis, Jr., as her ex-sailor lover. Sexual situations and innuendo. A-III (br)

Annabel Takes a Tour (1938) Thin Hollywood spoof in which a movie star (Lucille Ball) kicks off a studio publicity tour in Chicago, where her dizzy press agent (Jack Oakie) cooks up a romance with a viscount (Ralph Forbes), but she thinks it's on the level and quits show business. Directed by Lew Landers, the laughs come mainly from the wacky antics of Ball and Oakie, abetted by their dim studio

Hhead (Bradley Page) and his wise-cracking secretary (Ruth Donnelly). Romantic complications. A-I (br)

Annapolis Story, An (1955) Feeble service story of an elder brother (Kevin McCarthy) helping his younger sibling (John Derek) graduate from the Naval Academy, then both train as fighter pilots at Pensacola, fall for the same woman (Diana Lynn), and wind up in the Korean War, where the younger saves the life of the elder. Directed by Don Siegel, the weak story and unfocused characters don't make much of an impression, despite all the footage filmed at the Academy and other naval facilities. Some wartime violence and romantic complications. A-I (br)

Anne Frank Remembered (1996) Compelling documentary portrait of the Jewish teenager known to millions through the diary she kept while hiding with her family in Amsterdam until they were betrayed and sent to the Nazi death camps. Written, produced, and directed by British filmmaker Jon Blair, the film puts Anne's life in historical perspective by interviews with those who knew her as a child or met her in the camps, as well as the dramatic use of visuals provided by family photographs, period artifacts, and archival footage, including scenes of a 1941 wedding, at which Anne is briefly glimpsed. A work poignant with its sense of loss and painful visuals of the Holocaust. A-II (PG)

Anne of Green Gables (1934) Charming dramatization of the Lucy Maud Montgomery novel about a spunky teenaged orphan (Anne Shirley, who took her name from the heroine of these novels; she was previously known as Dawn O'Day), who overcomes assorted obstacles to win the hearts of a taciturn farmer (O.P. Heggie) and his domineering sister (Helen Westley) on Canada's Prince Edward Island at the turn of the century. Directed by George Nicholls, the story of a lonely waif finding the loving home of her dreams has special appeal for young viewers, while reminding older ones of youth's yearning for unconditional love. Fine family fare. A-I (nr)

Anne of the Thousand Days (1969) Screen version of Maxwell Anderson's play about the romance between Henry VIII (Richard Burton) and Anne Boleyn (Genevieve Bujold). Directed by Charles Jarrott, the story centers on all the dynastic complications that motivated Henry's break with Rome and his six-year pursuit of Anne. Though the action is limited, the acting is impressive, especially that of Anthony Quayle as Cardinal Wolsey. For those who are not history buffs, there is plenty of royal pageantry, colorful costumes, and well-preserved castles. In dealing with the period and its characters, there is some blood-letting and sexual candor. A-III (PG)

Anne of Windy Poplars (1940) Pedestrian sequel directed by Jack Hively follows the now-grown orphan (Anne Shirley) on her first teaching position in a small town whose nasty matriarch (Ethel Griffies) schemes to have her fired, until the woman's nephew (James Ellison) steps in to save the school's Christmas play, and Anne's fiancé (Patric Knowles) cures a local child's pneumonia. Though warmly played, the characters and situations are as predictable as the wholesome ending is saccharine. A-I (br)

Annie (1982) Although John Huston's direction of the screen version of the popular stage musical is somewhat cynical and definitely disappointing, it does preserve much of the exotic ambiance of the comic strip about the little orphan (Aileen Quinn) and Daddy Warbucks (Albert Finney). With awkward dance numbers, some coarse dialogue, and Carol Burnett's mean-spirited characterization, the movie's appeal is somewhat limited beyond uncritical viewers. A-I (PG)

Annie Get Your Gun (1950) Big and brassy version of the Irving Berlin musical in which rustic Annie Oakley (Betty Hutton) gets some polish while working with Frank Butler (Howard Keel) in a sharpshooting act, then finds fame and finally gets her man (Butler) after Buffalo Bill (Louis Calhoun) makes her a star in his Wild West Show. Directed by George Sidney, this show has lots of stunt riding, staged Indian attacks, and shoot-outs, which make a suitable backdrop for Hutton's overcharged performance, with the result memorable chiefly for its songs ranging from the romantic "The Girl That I Marry" to the comedic "Doing What Comes Naturally" and "Anything You Can Do" and the signature tune, "There's No Business Like Show Business." Romantic complications. A-II (br)

Annie Hall (1977) Director Woody Allen's romantic comedy about an on-again, off-again relationship between a Jewish comedian from New York (Allen) and a WASP from the Midwest (Diane Keaton). Although the movie is frequently very funny and has a touch of humanity lacking in Allen's earlier work, it falls far short of its more ambitious intention of making a serious statement about human relationships. Some rough language and much humor derived from sexual matters. A-III (PG)

Annie Oakley (1935) Robust story of an Ohio country girl (Barbara Stanwyck), whose prowess with a hunting rifle starts her on the way to fame as the star sharpshooter of Buffalo Bill's Wild West Show. Director George Stevens provides a lively picture of late 19th-century America, as well as a gentle story of Annie's love for a boastful trick-shooter (Preston Foster). Enjoyable both for its colorful Western action and appealing success story. A-I (br)

Anniversary, The (1968) Bette Davis overacts dreadfully as a dreadful mother who rules the lives of every member of the family. Director Roy Ward Baker's comedy of the outrageous fails in satirizing the evils of mom-ism because it lacks compassion, and its unhealthy humor is frequently tasteless. O (br)

Anonymous Venetian, The (1971) A young musician (Tony Musante) calls his estranged wife (Florinda Bolkan) to Venice and they spend their day revisiting scenes that had once brought them happiness, until the wife learns that, like the city, he and their marriage are dying. Italian production directed by Enrico Maria Salerno, it is a tragically lyric travelogue through the canals and streets of a great city, which by day's end slowly sinks into the sea, surrounded by the pollution and technology of modern times. With a little less sentimentality, its story of the fragility of human love and man-made beauty might have been more credible. A-III (GP)

Another Day in Paradise (1999) Abhorrent violence marks the tale of a callous thief (James Woods) and his junkie lover (Melanie Griffith), who take a similar younger couple (Vincent Kartheiser and Natasha Gregson Wagner) on the road for a big heist that goes murderously awry. Director Larry Clark's raw picture of not-so-innocent-youth-further-corrupted is less a cautionary tale than a glamorization of daily doses of drugs, alcohol, and deadly violence as an exciting lifestyle. Intermittent gory violence, sexual encounters with nudity, recurring substance abuse, as well as incessant profanity and rough language. O (R)

Another 48 HRS (1990) Eddie Murphy and Nick Nolte re-team as the convict and the cop in this savage sequel centering around their efforts to nail a drug kingpin before his gang ices them. Director Walter Hill revs up the violence to the max, with brutal shootups at close range taking precedence over story line, characterizations, and comic relief. Excessive violence, continuous raw language, and brief nudity. O (R)

Another Man, Another Chance (1977) French director Claude Lelouch's romantic sagebrush drama about a widowed veterinarian (James Caan) who falls in love with a charming widowed photographer (Genevieve Bujold). Despite the movie's striking photography and excellent acting, Lelouch's calculatedly relaxed style of characterization and glossy romanticism do not lend themselves well to the more austere mood of a Western. Brief violence in a scene of rape. A-III (PG)

Another Man's Poison (1951) Clumsily contrived doings on the English moors, where a wealthy mystery writer (Bette Davis) poisons her estranged husband, then tries to pass off a stranger (Gary Merrill) as the missing spouse — until a neighbor (Emlyn Williams) grows suspicious. Directed by Irving Rapper, the plot's melodramatic claptrap triggers a scenery-chewing performance by Davis as the deadly, willful schemer who cares more for her chestnut stallion than any human. Murder, menace, and some romantic trifling. A-II (br)

Another Part of the Forest (1948) Convoluted family saga set in an 1880 Southern town, whose wealthiest citizen (Fredric March) is despised by his neighbors as a Civil War profiteer, but his years of lording it over the townspeople and his own conniving offspring (Edmond O'Brien, Dan Duryea, and Ann Blyth) come to an end when his downtrodden wife (Florence Eldridge) reveals a dark secret from his past. Directed by Michael Douglas from Lillian Hellman's prequel to **The Little Foxes**, the melodramatic proceedings feature a fine cast, but the plotting is ragged and the ending is mawkishly contrived. Domestic tensions and justice questions. A-II (br)

Another Stakeout (1993) Uneven sequel to 1987's **Stakeout** re-teams Seattle detectives Richard Dreyfuss and Emilio Estevez with assistant DA Rosie O'Donnell posing as a make-believe family who rent a home next door to a couple (Dennis Farina and Marcia Strassman), who are the friends of a government witness (Cathy Moriarty) running for her life. Director John Badham opens and closes with murderous violence totally at odds with the hilarious meat of the movie, in which the innocent neighbors are constantly confused by mixed-up versions of the fake family's cover story. A live-in relationship, some intense violence, and a few off-color remarks. A-III (PG-13)

Another Thin Man (1939) Enjoyable sequel with Nick and Nora Charles (William Powell and Myrna Loy) in New York trying to solve the murder of a wealthy family friend (C. Aubrey Smith) while keeping his daughter (Virginia Grey); their one-year-old son, Nicky, Jr.; and canine cut-up, Asta, out of harm's way. Directed by W.S. Van Dyke II, the twisty plot has more red herrings than clues, with plenty of sinister suspects (Sheldon Leonard, Abner Biberman, and Don Costello) and comic relief from flustered cops (Otto Kruger and Nat Pendleton), as well as a children's party thrown by ex-cons. Stylized violence and muted sexual innuendo. A-II (br)

Another Time, Another Place (1958) Weepy sudser directed by Lewis Allen in which an American reporter (Lana Turner) in WW II London falls for a married BBC radio correspondent (Sean Connery), suffers a breakdown when he dies in an air crash, recovers after journeying to Cornwall to commiserate with his widow (Glynis Johns), then goes off with the man (Barry Sullivan) who has loved her all along. Unconvincing portrayals of cardboard characters and their hokey romantic affairs. A-III (br)

Another Woman (1988) On her 50th birthday, a philosophy professor (Gena Rowlands) is forced to face the fact that she is not as loved and respected as she previously assumed, nor is her life the success that it had seemed. In this serious examination of midlife regrets, writer-director Woody Allen continues to be sensitive to female protagonists. Brief, explicit talk of marital infidelity and a past abortion. A-III (PG)

Another You (1991) When a pathological liar (Gene Wilder) is released from a mental hospital, he is persuaded to pass himself off as a missing millionaire by a con-man (Richard Pryor). A needlessly convoluted script makes director Maurice Phillips's garbled comedy misfire badly with hardly a laugh to be had. Recurring rough language and mild sexual innuendo. A-III (R)

Antarctica (1984) When a 1957 Japanese expedition leaves its sled dogs behind at the South Pole, two of its members (Ken Takakura and Tsunehido Watase) return the next year to rescue any canine survivors. Director Koreyoshi Kurahara re-stages the fact-based story amidst spectacular polar landscapes, but the result succeeds better as a nature documentary than as a drama of polar scientists searching for their lost huskies. Dubbed. Life-threatening situations in a frozen wasteland make heavy sledding for children. A-II (G)

Antonia & Jane (1991) Bland comedy about two longtime acquaintances (Imelda Stauton and Saskia Reeves) individually recounting their sex lives, perceived failures, and resentments of each other to the same therapist (Brenda Bruce). Only rare moments of wit punctuate director Beeban Kidron's would-be comedy of two unhappy women. Benign attitude toward affairs, brief bedroom scenes with momentary nudity, and several sexual references. A-III (R)

Antonia's Line (1996) Multigenerational tale of a fiercely independent Dutch woman (Willeke van Ammelrooy) whose lesbian daughter and eventually her granddaughter and great-granddaughter live on the matriarch's farm, where all confront emotional crises over the decades, drawing strength from their female solidarity. Writer-director Marleen Gorris celebrates non-traditional families and the resilience of women in a whimsical story overpopulated with village eccentrics, misfit clerics, and disposable men. Subtitles. Several bedroom scenes with nudity, occasional violence including rape, an off-screen suicide, and an instance of rough language. A-IV (R)

Antonio Das Mortes (1970) Brazilian folk epic about a gunman hired by a feudal landlord to eliminate the leaders of a peasant rebellion in the hills, and how the hired assassin eventually joins the rebels himself. Using a gaudy color photography that suits his strange story and setting, director Glauber Rocha intermingles black and Indian rituals and ceremonies with Christian saints and symbols to create a world of bizarre superstitions and revolutionary fervor. It is an episodic movie of unusual power and beauty that some tastes may find too exotic. A-III (nr)

Antz (1998) Computer-animated tale of an ant colony in which a whiny worker ant (voice of Woody Allen) sets his sights on the ant queen's sassy daughter (voice of Sharon Stone), and defies his lowly status by becoming a warrior ant out to save the colony from the machinations of its dictatorial general (voice of Gene Hackman). Directors Eric Darnell and Tim Johnson provide the animation with a three-dimensional look, but the story about following one's dreams is on the bland side. Some crude expressions and fleeting cartoon violence. A-II (PG)

Any Number Can Play (1949) Dreary melodrama of a day in the life of a gambling-house owner (Clark Gable) with a bad heart, a loving wife (Alexis Smith), an estranged son (Darryl Hickman), a weak brother-in-law (Wendell Corey), and an exotic clientele, one of whom (Frank Morgan) is on a winning streak. Mervyn Le Roy directs a fine cast in a plodding scenario crowded with contrived incidents, including an attempted robbery and a hokey finish. Lots of anxiety and a bit of stylized violence. A-II (br)

Any Wednesday (1966) Jaded wealthy businessman (Jason Robards) is a good husband six days of the week, but Wednesday is reserved for a young lady (Jane Fonda) until his wife (Rosemary Murphy) forces a showdown, and his lady friend finds the man of her dreams (Dean Jones). Under Robert Ellis Miller's direction, it's a lively, sappy, broad comedy with some serious overtones about the pain of infidelity. A-III (br)

Any Which Way You Can (1980) An auto repairman and free-lance street-fighter (Clint Eastwood) finds happiness with a skittish prostitute (Sondra Locke). Director Buddy Van Horn's salute to machismo presents an abundance of violence and an atmosphere of sleazy immorality. O (R)

Anything Can Happen (1952) Sudsy romantic comedy in which an emigrant (Jose Ferrer) from Georgia, USSR, works hard at becoming a US citizen while falling along the way for one of the natives (Kim Hunter). Director George Seaton gives superficial treatment to the cultural differences facing a group of immigrants in New York City, preferring to portray them as quaint eccentrics with predictable problems in contrived circumstances. Well-intentioned but sugar-coated view of America's ethnic melting pot. A-I (br)

Anything Goes (1956) Halting musical in which a veteran performer (Bing Crosby) agrees to team with a rising newcomer (Donald O'Connor), then each signs a different leading lady (Mitzi Gaynor and Jeanmaire respectively) while vacationing in Europe, but they resolve the mix-up on the voyage home. Directed by Robert Lewis from Sidney Sheldon's leaden updating of the '36 film musical, the result lumbers along with stilted production numbers, surprisingly few laughs, and even the Cole Porter songs seem flat. Romantic complications and some sexual innuendo. A-II (br)

Anzio (1968) Huge, sprawling WW II epic about the Allied invasion at Anzio in southern Italy with Robert Mitchum, Peter Falk, and Robert Ryan in the thick of combat. Directed by Edward Dmytryk, the movie is graphic in its depiction of the grim images of battle, with appropriately harsh action and language. A-III (PG)

Apache (1954) When Geronimo and his band are sent to Florida in chains, one Apache warrior (Burt Lancaster) manages to escape and find his way back to New Mexico, where he makes his last stand with wife (Jean Peters) and infant son. Director Robert Aldrich treats the Indians with sympathy while showing the injustices against them, though the movie's clash-of-cultures theme is on the simplistic side, most notably in its corn-grows-in-the-badlands ending. Stylized violence. A-II (br)

Apache Drums (1951) Routine Western directed by Hugo Fregonese tells of an outcast gambler

(Stephen McNally) who risks his life trying to save the citizens of an 1880 border town from being massacred by Mescalero Apaches. Stylized violence. A-I (br)

Apache Territory (1958) Sluggish Western in which a seasoned cowboy (Rory Calhoun) tries to hold together a motley band of travelers (Barbara Bates and John Dehner, among them) caught in the desert by attacking Apaches. Director Ray Nazarro can't overcome a script that's more talk than action and a plot that's predictable from the start. Stylized violence. A-I (br)

Apache Uprising (1965) Formula Western in which a cowboy (Rory Calhoun) saves the stagecoach to Lordsburg from a badman (John Russell) who's being pursued by Indians for his crimes against them. Directed by R.G. Springsteen, it is noteworthy only for the remarkably bad acting of DeForest Kelley as a crazed gunman. Stylized violence. A-II (br)

Apartment, The (1960) Director Billy Wilder's comedy satire about the corporate rise and moral near-downfall of a garden-variety office-manager, whose sudden success in climbing the company ladder comes from loaning out his bachelor apartment to philandering executives. His falling in love with one of their girlfriends (Shirley MacLaine) leads to the usual moral comeuppances for all involved, but Wilder and his talented cast devise startling ways of arriving at the obvious, obligatory conclusion. A-III (br)

Apartment for Peggy (1948) Heavy-handed comedy about the post-war housing shortage causing a veteran on the GI Bill (William Holden) and his pregnant wife (Jeanne Crain) to move into the unused attic of an aging college professor (Edmund Gwenn) who's decided to commit suicide. Directed by George Seaton, the script turns maudlin when the wife's miscarriage makes the prof realize the value of his own life, but the movie's main value is as a treasure trove of the period's social attitudes and ideals. A-II (br)

Apartment Zero (1989) Unsettling hothouse thriller set in 1968 Buenos Aires delves into the uneasy relationship between a wealthy, repressed movie theater owner (Colin Firth) and his mysterious tenant (Hart Bochner), a professional assassin. Argentinian-born director Martin Donovan's tale of users and victims has an erotically charged atmosphere that culminates in grisly violence. Some profanity and suggestions of sexual promiscuity. O (R)

Ape Man, The (1943) Lethargic horror movie directed by William Beaudine with a newspaper reporter (Wallace Ford) on the trail of a mad scientist (Bela Lugosi), who's trained an ape to secure victims as needed for an experiment gone awry. Unimaginative fantasy provoking more yawns than scares. A-II (br)

Apocalypse Now (1979) Director Francis Ford Coppola's uneven attempt to transpose Joseph Conrad's *Heart of Darkness* to a Vietnam setting follows an intelligence officer (Martin Sheen) on a mission to kill a renegade Special Forces officer (Marlon Brando), who has set up a private domain deep in the Cambodian interior. Much ambiguous and unresolved soul-searching in between several brilliant battle sequences, but stealing the show is Robert Duvall's turn as a gung-ho helicopter commander. Much graphic violence and some rough language. A-IV (R)

Apollo 13 (1995) Fact-based story of the April 1970 moon launch aborted on its third day in space after an incapacitating problem diminished the oxygen, power, and computer systems, making the safe return of the three astronauts (Tom Hanks, Bill Paxton, Kevin Bacon) an almost insurmountable problem for Houston Mission Control. Director Ron Howard keeps emotional tensions taut and suspense levels high throughout this salute to the courage and perseverance of all involved in the dicey rescue mission. Fleeting sexual innuendo and minor profanity. A-II (PG)

Apostle, The (1997) When a Texas Pentecostal preacher (Robert Duvall) becomes distraught over losing his congregation and wife (Farrah Fawcett) to a younger minister, he bashes his rival's head with a baseball bat, then flees to a rural Louisiana community where he revitalizes an old church and starts a radio ministry, whose growing popularity leads to his arrest. Also written and directed by Duvall, this portrait of an evangelical preacher explores his religious zeal and personal failings as seen within the human context of a Southern community, all of which is played out with sincerity and conviction in an often compelling story. A strong scene of violence, menacing situations, and marital infidelity. A-III (PG-13)

Appaloosa, The (1966) Marlon Brando stars as a would-be rancher whose prize horse is stolen by Mexican bandits (led by John Saxon). British director Sidney J. Furie follows the action conventions of the Western but pays more attention to colorful camerawork than to developing character motivation. The result is a picture with lots of atmosphere but little human interest. Assorted stylized violence. A-II (br)

Apple, The (1999) Factual story about an elderly Iranian man and his blind wife who kept their 12-year-old twin daughters locked in their room since birth, followed by the efforts of a social worker to convince them to allow the children out to play and develop normally. Director Samira Makhmalbaf recreates the news story with the actual participants in a intriguing, sometimes baffling docudrama, whose depiction of innocents at the mercy of adults and bureaucracy raises social and political issues. Subtitles. A few vulgar expressions. A-II (nr)

Apple Dumpling Gang, The (1975) Western comedy about three little orphans left with a gold mine who con a suave gambler (Bill Bixby) into a marriage of convenience with a stagecoach driver (Susan Clark) to protect them from greedy townspeople and bungling robbers (Don Knotts and Tim Conway). Norman Tokar directs a standard Disney family entertainment. A-I (G)

Apple Dumpling Gang Rides Again, The (1979) Inept outlaws (Don Knotts and Tim Conway) try to go straight, with predictably disastrous results in this Disney sequel. Directed by Vincent McEveety, the comedy is not helped much by a bland romantic subplot (Tim Matheson and Elyssa Davalos), but the humor is carried by the manic efforts of a frenzied marshal (Kenneth Mars) to get the zany pair. A-I (G)

Applegates, The (see: **Meet the Applegates**)

Appointment, The (1968) Romantic melodrama about a successful lawyer (Omar Sharif) who comes to suspect that his wife (Anouk Aimee) was once a prostitute. When he tries to find out the truth, tragedy results. Directed by Sidney Lumet, the silly tale of a strange jealousy cannot sustain its length and comes to an unsatisfying conclusion. A-III (br)

Appointment in Honduras (1953) Murky melodrama directed by Jacques Tourneur follows an American adventurer (Glenn Ford) slogging through Honduran jungles with a hostage couple (Ann Sheridan and Zachary Scott) and some escaped convicts, who only get in the way of his mission to help the country's deposed leader stage a counter-revolution. Stylized violence, hokey menace, and romantic situations. A-III (br)

Appointment with Danger (1951) Contrived but fairly interesting crime story of a postal inspector (Alan Ladd) getting some help from a nun (Phyllis Calvert) in tracking the killer of a colleague, then foiling a million-dollar mail robbery. Director Lewis Allen handles the action with the hard-bitten crooks (Paul Stewart, Henry Morgan, and Jack Webb) better than the idealistic nun's reformation of a tough, cynical postal agent. Stylized violence. A-II (br)

Appointment with Death (1988) Lackluster adaptation of an Agatha Christie whodunit unfolds during a grand tour of Europe and the Middle East with an all-star cast, including Peter Ustinov as Belgian sleuth Hercule Poirot. Though Piper Laurie shines as a tyrannical stepmother, director Michael Winner pretty much wastes the rest of his cast in an effort that may bore diehard mystery fans but please those who enjoy travelogues. A few brief scenes of violence. A-II (PG)

Apprentice to Murder (1988) In rural 1927 Pennsylvania, an itinerant preacher-faith healer (Donald Sutherland) takes a 16-year-old youth (Chad Lowe) under his wing, but their friendship ends when an attempted exorcism causes the death of a local hermit (Knut Husebo), seemingly possessed by the devil. Moody, listless English-language Norwegian production directed by R.L. Thomas wastes Sutherland's considerable acting abilities. Brief graphic violence and several totally gratuitous sexual encounters. O (PG-13)

Apprenticeship of Duddy Kravitz, The (1974) Superior Canadian drama about an ambitious young man (Richard Dreyfuss), growing up in a Jewish ghetto in Montreal, who discovers that making money is not all there is to life. Directed by Ted Kotcheff, the moral problems and mistaken goals of youth are convincingly presented in terms of Duddy's relationships with family and those he meets along the way. More than the story of one man's greed, it is also the chronicle of a ghetto, finely evoking a detailed and realistic world whose humanity transcends any ethnic group, making all the more universal its picture of human self-centeredness. Some crude religious and sexual references used within a purposeful context. A-IV (R)

April Fool's Day (1986) Group of wealthy college students, acting like retarded adolescents, spend a weekend playing deadly tricks on each other at an island estate. Director Fred Walton treats the women involved solely as sexual objects, and the dialogue is preoccupied with profanity, sexual innuendoes, and off-color jokes. Accepts sexual promiscuity as a natural part of youthful behavior. O (R)

April Fools, The (1969) Director Stuart Rosenberg's comedy-drama involves a New York stockbroker (Jack Lemmon) and a jet-set beauty (Catherine Deneuve) who start a 24-hour romance by flying off to Paris and forsaking their own shallow previous marriages. The underlying seriousness of the film's healthy criticism of the "good" life creates definite moral problems and a credibility gap for its glib resolution, especially when set beside the film's slapstick routines and the unlikely liaison between the central characters. O (PG)

April in Paris (1952) Charmless musical fluff about a State Department underling (Ray Bolger) and the Broadway chorus girl (Doris Day) he mistakenly invites to represent the US at a world arts conference in Paris. Directed by David Butler, the thin story has the unlikely pair find romance with the help of a Gallic cupid (Claude Dauphin), though the witless proceedings are occasionally enlivened by Bolger's hoofing and Day's singing. Romantic complications and sexual innuendo keyed to a bogus wedding. A-III (br)

April Love (1957) Thin but pleasant musical romance in which a young man (Pat Boone) begins to enjoy his stay on his uncle's Kentucky horse farm after meeting the neighbor's daughter (Shirley Jones) and they start training an entry for a big trotting race. Directed by Henry Levin, the formula proceedings are held together by the easy-going songs, the personable performances of singers Boone and Jones, and, not least, the lovely bluegrass scenery. Wholesome family fare. A-I (br)

Apt Pupil (1998) Sinister tale in which a manipulative high-school senior (Brad Renfro), realizing an elderly neighbor (Ian McKellen) is an escaped Nazi war criminal, makes him recount in detail his deadly deeds or face exposure, but the old man devises his own means of controlling his tormentor. Director Bryan Singer's drama is a darkly cautionary tale with unexpected twists and a chilling view of calculated evildoing. Some harsh violence, fleeting nudity, brief sexual innuendo, and substance abuse, occasional profanity, and recurring rough language. A-III (R)

Arabella (1969) Italian comedy set in the 1920s tells the story of a young Roman aristocrat (Virna Lisi) who tries to help her grandmother (Margaret Rutherford) out of financial difficulties by fleecing various victims (all played by Terry Thomas). Whether director Mauro Bolognini means to satirize the Italian tax laws or indict Italian manners and morals, his farcical complications strain frantically and often repulsively for laughs that seldom materialize. A-III (PG)

Arabesque (1966) Muddled thriller in which an American exchange professor at Oxford (Gregory Peck) gets involved with several sets of Arab spies, one of whom (Sophia Loren) keeps shifting sides. Directed by Stanley Donen, villains and villainy abound, there's eye-catching violence and sexy romance, but it's all surface and no substance. A-III (br)

Arabian Adventure (1979) British fantasy is a thrilling flying-carpet adventure about a prince on a mission to foil the evil ambitions of sinister sorcerer Christopher Lee. Directed by Kevin Connor, the brisk costume-and-special-effects vehicle is devoid of violence or trite romanticism. Pleasant escapist fare for young and old. A-I (G)

Arabian Knight (1995) Thin animated tale of ancient Baghdad, where a young cobbler (voice of Matthew Broderick) wins the hand of his beloved princess (voice of Jennifer Beals) after saving the city from an evil sorcerer (voice of Vincent Price) in league with an army of one-eyed invaders. Directed by Richard Williams, the production is visually splendid, but the saccharine story line is padded out with the unamusing antics of a dim-witted thief (voice of Jonathan Winters), some charmless songs and much slapstick action of unlikely appeal to youngsters. A-I (G)

Arachnophobia (1990) A young doctor (Jeff Daniels) with an avid fear of spiders (arachnophobia) is put to the ultimate test when he relocates his family to a small town, unaware that a deadly new species is rapidly reproducing in his barn. Despite one glaring inconsistency in the plot, director Frank Marshall has crafted a deliciously menacing thriller whose moody cinematography and precise editing steadily build the suspense. Some graphic shots of dead bodies. A-II (PG-13)

Arch, The (1972) Hong Kong production presenting a doomed tale of unrequited passion in which a widow, true to the memory of her dead husband and her social position, refuses the love of a handsome captain, but then allows her daughter to marry him. The movie's deliberate, timeless creation of mood has been broken up with freeze-frames and some heavy-handed montages by its woman director, Shu Shuen. It is an oriental curio which may best be left to the romantically inclined. A-II (nr)

Arch of Triumph (1948) Muddled melodrama in which an Austrian doctor (Charles Boyer) hiding from the Nazis in 1938 Paris falls in love with a troubled woman (Ingrid Bergman), but loses her to a former lover while undertaking the murder of a visiting Gestapo officer (Charles Laughton), then is interned as an illegal alien at the start of WW II. Directed by Lewis Milestone from Erich Maria Remarque's novel, the tangled romance is too contrived to earn sympathy, though the movie's depiction of the uncertainties of refugee life still holds interest. Stylized violence, implied sexual relationships, and a veiled reference to a quack abortion. A-III (br)

Arise, My Love (1940) Uneven romantic comedy in which an eager reporter (Claudette Colbert) creates her own scoop by rescuing an American flier (Ray Milland) from a Spanish firing squad, then is fired for being with him instead of on the job when Hitler invades Poland, but she gets rehired when the liner taking both of them back to the States is torpedoed. Director Mitchell Leisen has lots of fun with the romantic fluff, but the laughs are chilled by the heavy period atmosphere and warnings about the Nazi menace. Veiled sexual situations and innuendo. A-III (br)

Aristocats, The (1970) Directed by Wolfgang Reitherman, the first animated feature from the Disney studio since Disney's death in 1966 tells the adventures of a family of felines who, after being made the heir of their millionaire mistress, are catnapped and ditched in the country, but then rescued by a pair of bumbling hounds, a couple of giggling geese, a rodent named Roquefort, and an alley cat named O'Malley. Enhanced by the voices of Eva Gabor, Phil Harris, Hermione Baddeley, and Sterling Holloway, with five songs thrown in for good measure, the result, while not purr-fect, is plentifully pleasing. A-I (G)

Arizona (1940) When a Tucson frontierswoman (Jean Arthur) faces loss of her booming freight business to a cheating competitor (Porter Hall) and his Confederate partner (Warren William), she gets some needed help from a smitten cowboy (William Holden). Directed by Wesley Ruggles, the plot is weak but sturdy enough to anchor the action, including Apache raids, North-South rivalries, well-staged shootouts, and a fitful courtship that ultimately proves quite charming. Stylized violence and assorted villainies. A-I (br)

Arizona Bushwhackers (1967) Routine Western directed by Lesley Selander in which a Confederate agent (Howard Keel) stops a renegade (Scott Brady) from selling a cache of rebel guns to the Indians, and the movie concludes happily with the end of the Civil War. A-I (br)

Arizona Raiders (1965) Formula Western in which one of Quantrill's Raiders (Audie Murphy) is let out of prison after the Civil War to help the Arizona Rangers stamp out the last of the now-outlawed band. Directed by William Witney, the flimsy plot is held together by the usual action scenes, but only the concluding segment involving a small Indian mission holds any interest. Stylized violence. A-II (br)

Arizona Whirlwind (1944) Grade-B Western starring Ken Maynard, Hoot Gibson, and Bob Steele as a team of lawmen who find a gang of jewel thieves (!) operating out of a frontier town. Director Robert Tansey's formula shoot-'em-up ends with a race against time to free a boy locked in a bank safe. Stylized violence. A-I (br)

Armageddon (1998) Bloated disaster flick in which the Earth will be destroyed by a humongous asteroid hurtling through space unless a crew of oil drillers (led by Bruce Willis and Ben Affleck) land on it and position a nuclear warhead deep in its center to blow it off its deadly trajectory. Director Michael Bay turns in an overlong, testosterone-fueled tale pumped up with special effects, then doused in weepy emotions. Explosive mayhem, an implied affair, occasional profanity, and an instance of rough language. A-III (PG-13)

Armed and Dangerous (1986) Posing as social spoof, this failed slapstick movie concerns security guards (John Candy and Eugene Levy) who fight organized crime by being more aggressive and antisocial than the criminals. Violent and destructive imagery sprinkled with profanity and sexual sight-gags that fail as burlesque. A-III (PG-13)

Army of Darkness (1993) Mindless sword-and-sorcery movie about a present-day macho guy (Bruce Campbell) zapped back to the Dark Ages, where he must rescue a damsel in distress (Embeth Davidtz) and do battle with legions of undead skeletons before he can return to his own time. Director Sam Raimi's inept attempt at comic horror fails miserable, save for a few briefly interesting special effects. Frequent comic violence and mild sexual innuendo. A-III (R)

Arnold (1973) At least half of this creaky horror-comedy takes place in a fog-bound graveyard, and all of it centers around a well-heeled, well-preserved cadaver (in the title role). The gimmick derives from a condition in the deceased's will that his wife (Stella Stevens), who married him hastily just after his demise, has to keep him near her for the rest of her life, a condition that leads to a number of murders and other preposterous goings-on. All director George Fenady can do with this bizarre material is to play it for laughs and these do come at reasonably close intervals. A-III (PG)

Around the World in 80 Days (1956) In Mike Todd's lavish production of the Jules Verne classic, an English armchair adventurer (David Niven) makes a bet that he can encircle the globe within 80 days and sets off with his valet (Cantinflas) to prove it. Michael Anderson's direction makes the most of the cultural splendor of the late Victorian period, visits just about every scenic locale worth a postcard, and offers an all-star marathon of cameo appearances. The result is a wonderful romp that is great fun for all. A-I (G)

Around the World Under the Sea (1966) Producer-director Andrew Marton's undersea adventure with scientists (Lloyd Bridges, David McCallum, Brian Kelly, Shirley Eaton) setting earthquake warning devices on the ocean floor and meeting monsters of the deep should appeal to most youngsters. A-I (br)

Arrangement, The (1969) Director Elia Kazan's screen version of his own novel suffers less from being ambitious than from being pretentious. Kirk Douglas plays a man who attempts suicide because his life has been a sham, a series of "arrangements" in business as well as with his mistress (Faye Dunaway) and his wife (Deborah Kerr). Among the many flaws in this failed work, the greatest is its reduction of personal crises to predominantly sexual conflicts and involvements. Rough language and some coy nudity. O (R)

Arrival, The (1996) After tracking extraterrestrial radio signals, a maverick astronomer (Charlie Sheen) risks his life in unraveling a massive conspiracy by aliens disguised as humans seeking to colonize the planet. Directed by David Twohy, the supremely silly plot and Sheen's wooden, wide-eyed intensity combine to limit the movie's appeal to undemanding sci-fi fans. Stylized violence, fleeting nudity, profanity, and an instance of rough language. A-III (PG-13)

Arrivederci, Baby! (1966) Dull, tasteless, and vulgar vehicle for Tony Curtis clownishly playing a con-man who marries and murders a series of wealthy women. Written, produced, and directed by Ken Hughes, the attempts at humor fall flat, making the proceedings all the more vulgar and pointless. O (br)

Arrow in the Dust (1954) Wooden Western directed by Lesley Selander in which an Army deserter (Sterling Hayden) masquerading as an officer winds up saving a wagon train from marauding Apaches. Frontier violence. A-I (br)

Arrowhead (1953) Dark Western in which an Indian-hating Army scout (Charlton Heston) helps the post's new commander (Brian Keith) put down an Apache uprising led by a messianic warrior (Jack Palance). Directed by Charles Marquis Warren, there's plenty of action, but most of it is as unconvincing as the vicious hostiles. Nasty Indian stereotypes and stylized violence. A-II (br)

Arruza (1972) Documentary by Budd Boetticher on the final years of the legendary Mexican bullfighter, Carlos Arruza. Narrated by Anthony Quinn, it fails to explore the make-up of the man, presenting instead a cold, distant portrait of the *torero* seen totally from the outside. What will impress most viewers, however, is only the foolish, cruel, and debasing side of this contest between man and beast. A-II (PG)

Arsenic and Old Lace (1944) Droll adaptation of Joseph Kesselring's madcap stage hit about an irascible theater critic (Cary Grant) whose dotty maiden aunts (Josephine Hull and Jean Adair) serve lonely old men elderberry wine laced with poison. Director Frank Capra's black comedy features a great cast, including Boris Karloff and Peter Lorre as criminal interlopers, but the wacky proceedings are not for all tastes. A-II (br)

Art of Love, The (1965) Clunky romantic comedy directed by Norman Jewison is set in Paris, where a poor artist (Dick Van Dyke) fakes suicide to raise the value of his canvases, then dons various disguises trying to get revenge on his larcenous roommate (James Garner), who's made off with his money and his girl (Elke Sommer). Slapstick conniving and romantic complications. A-II (br)

Artemisia (1998) Melodramatic French production based on the life of 17th-century Italian artist Artemisia Gentileschi (Valentina Cervi) who at age 17 falls in love with her drawing instructor (Miki Manojlovic), but after her father discovers them in bed, the lover is sentenced to prison for rape, and Artemisia goes off to start her own painting career. Writer-director Agnes Merlet changes the historical record of the 1612 rape trial into an upbeat feminist romance which turns Artemisia into a modern woman breaking with the artistic and moral conventions of her time. Subtitles. Several fairly graphic sex scenes, some nudity, and occasional rough language. A-IV (R)

Arthur (1981) A rich and spoiled young man named Arthur (Dudley Moore), who spends his days and nights drinking to excess and pursuing all sorts of women, falls in love with a waitress (Liza Minnelli). Director Steve Gordon tries to distill humor from the playboy's sexual weaknesses and from his indecision about meaningful commitment, but most of the humor comes from John Gielgud's performance as the snobbish, harsh-tongued valet. Adult situations. A-III (PG)

Arthur Rubenstein — Love of Life (1975) Extraordinary documentary about one of the world's greatest piano virtuosos is concerned not only with music but also with humanity. Directed by Francois Reichenbach, it captures the artist and the man at age 82 and is equally important as a commentary on classical music as it is a testament to a rare human being. Of far greater appeal than just to the specialized art audience. A-I (nr)

Arthur 2: On the Rocks (1988) Comedy sequel about the perpetually drunk millionaire wastrel (Dudley Moore) whose marriage to a perky waitress-shoplifter (Liza Minnelli) is threatened by a tycoon (Stephen Elliott) and his daughter (Cynthia Sikes). Though director Bud Yorkin adds some weight with a subplot about the couple's adoption of a baby, alcoholism is no laughing matter. Some vulgar language. A-III (PG)

Article 99 (1992) Fast-paced drama set in a veterans' hospital, where a dedicated doctor (Ray Liotta) and his new intern (Kiefer Sutherland) continually run afoul of the hospital's budget-conscious director (John Mahoney). Directed by Howard Deutch, the choppy mix of comedy and dramatic exaggeration focuses attention on the plight of sick and disabled veterans at the mercy of government bureaucracy. Brief violence, including several graphic shots of open-heart surgery, an instance of sexual innuendo, and recurring rough language. A-III (R)

Artists and Models (1955) Frenetic, fitfully amusing comedy about an artist (Dean Martin) who uses the vivid dreams of his nutty pal (Jerry Lewis) as the basis for a comic strip that attracts the attention of foreign agents. Director Frank Tashlin's outlandish brand of comedy is unusually flat-footed here, wasting Shirley MacLaine and Dorothy Malone as the romantic interests. Comic violence and sexual innuendo. A-III (br)

As Good As It Gets (1997) Acerbic comedy in which a misanthropic author (Jack Nicholson) tries to rejoin the human race after falling in love with a tolerant waitress (Helen Hunt) and befriending a broke homosexual artist (Greg Kinnear). Directed by James L. Brooks, the thin plot begins with the mean-spirited humor of Nicholson's nasty, self-centered sociopath, then turns mushy as he attempts to reform, but the proceedings are overlong and only sporadically amusing. Stylized violence, sexual situations, recurring rough language, and occasional profanity. A-IV (PG-13)

As the Earth Turns (1934) Rustic turn-of-the-century sudser directed by Alfred E. Green concerns the troubled romance between a woman (Jean Muir) who grew up on a farm and a city man (Donald Woods) who's determined to become a farmer. Sexual innuendo and romantic complications. A-II (br)

As You Like It (1936) British production of Shakespeare's comedy in which the banished princess Rosalind (Elisabeth Bergner) takes refuge in the forest of Arden, where she disguises herself as a man to test the love of the noble Orlando (Laurence Olivier). Directed by Paul Czinner, the gender mix-up is sweetly silly as is most else in these frivolous proceedings, though the talented cast is hampered by static staging, especially for such key speeches as "The Seven Ages of Man." A-I (br)

Ash Wednesday (1973) Dowdy middle-aged matron (Elizabeth Taylor), on the verge of losing her successful lawyer-husband (Henry Fonda) to a younger woman, undergoes body sculpture in a posh European clinic, but it will take Liz a good deal longer than the audience to figure out that no amount of face-lifting will change Henry's mind. Director Larry Peerce elicits solid performances from a good cast, and the plot moves along smoothly through a series of plush settings, but it is no more than a well-made but uninvolving melodrama without any perspective upon the actions and motivations of its characters and their lifestyle. A-III (R)

Aspen Extreme (1993) Two Detroit buddies (Paul Gross and Peter Berg) become Aspen ski instructors and end up paying a price for succumbing to the seductive dangers of life among the rich and glamorous. Writer-director Patrick Hasburgh fails to mount much of a story around his main focus — daredevil ski footage and impressive mountain scenery. Implied affair, brief nudity, a shot of drug abuse, and minimal rough language. A-III (PG-13)

Asphalt Jungle, The (1950) Classy crime caper in

which an aging criminal mastermind (Sam Jaffe) assembles a gang of specialized talents (notably Sterling Hayden, Louis Calhern, and James Whitmore) to pull off a million-dollar jewelry heist. Director and co-writer John Huston follows the crooks as they plan the robbery, carry it out, and suffer the consequences, but the focus is less on the crime than the characters, especially Calhern's corrupt lawyer with a weakness for blondes (notably Marilyn Monroe) and Hayden's bitter gunman with a yen to own a Kentucky horse farm. Stylized violence, menacing situations, and sexual innuendo. A-III (br)

Assassination (1987) Through his experience and cunning, a Secret Service agent (Charles Bronson) protects the wife (Jill Ireland) of the president of the United States from assassination. Directed by Peter Hunt, the movie is relatively restrained in its violence and sexual treatment. A-III (PG-13)

Assassination Bureau, The (1969) British tongue-in-cheek comedy set in the early 1900s about an international organization of killers-for-hire that is commissioned by a neophyte reporter (Diana Rigg) to kill their own leader (Oliver Reed). Good cast, marvelous settings, but Basil Dearden's direction is rather uncertain in its mixture of slapstick and satire. Comic violence. A-III (M)

Assassination File, The (1996) Thin thriller in which an ex-FBI agent (Sherilyn Fenn) uncovers a vast conspiracy behind the assassination of a presidential candidate (Paul Winfield), then can trust no one while dodging bombs, bullets, and car crashes to nail the baddies. Directed by John Harrison, the made-for-cable movie is mostly a woman-in-jeopardy exercise with the murky conspiracy plot generating little suspense. Stylized violence, sexual situations, brief nudity, and occasional profanity and rough language. A-III (R)

Assassination of Trotsky, The (1972) The death of the magnetic Russian revolutionary in his Mexican exile in 1924 is portrayed not from the political angle but the human, centering on the two protagonists — the sympathetic victim (Richard Burton) and the shadowy assassin (Alain Delon), who so clearly exhibits classic symptoms of psychological disturbance that his infiltration of the closely guarded Trotsky compound is simply not credible. Despite this central dramatic flaw, director Joseph Losey has fashioned a fascinating movie that succeeds in placing its figures into a historical time and place. A-III (R)

Assassins (1995) Ultra-violent tale of rival hit men (Sylvester Stallone and Antonio Banderas), each assigned to kill the same thief (Julianne Moore), who has possession of a computer disk containing compromising information. Director Richard Donner focuses on suspenseless bloodshed, since there is little story and no character development among this trio of hardened criminals. Numerous casual murders and much rough language. O (R)

Assault on a Queen (1966) Navy veterans (Frank Sinatra and Richard Conte) raise a sunken U-boat and use it to hijack and rob the Queen Mary in mid-ocean. Directed by Jack Donahue, it's routine escapist entertainment with the bad guys getting their just desserts and the good guys escaping, but without the loot. A-II (br)

Assignment, The (1997) Sordid thriller in which a callous CIA agent (Donald Sutherland) inveigles a Navy lieutenant (Aidan Quinn) into impersonating an international terrorist known as Carlos the Jackal in hopes this will lure the real Jackal (also Quinn) out of hiding. Directed by Christian Duguay, the loosely fact-based story emphasizes hard-edged violence in scenes of terrorism and murder committed by the lieutenant while masquerading as the merciless assassin. Much brutal violence, rationalization of adultery, some seamy sexual encounters, with full nudity, occasional profanity, and frequent rough language. O (R)

Assignment K (1968) Masquerading as a toy tycoon, a British agent (Stephen Boyd) matches wits with enemy spies and counterspies in rich and exotic European settings. Director Val Guest's weak spy melodrama is cluttered with plot complications whose only purpose is to afford changes of glamorous locales and chic costumes. Moderate violence. A-III (br)

Assignment to Kill (1968) Private detective (Patrick O'Neal) works his way up the ladder in an organization headed by a mobster, who sinks his own ships to collect the insurance. Threadbare plot directed by Sheldon Reynolds but with much action and many dead bodies. A-III (br)

Assisi Underground, The (1984) Fact-based story of a Franciscan friar (Ben Cross) who helps set up a network of hiding places for Jewish refugees in Assisi's monasteries, while the local bishop (James Mason) organizes their escape from German-occupied Italy. Directed by Alexander Ramati, the sincere portrayal of the religious setting adds a spiritual dimension to this example of the Christian resistance to Nazi inhumanity. Much menace and some stylized violence. A-II (PG)

Associate, The (1996) Meager one-joke comedy about a bright investment analyst (Whoopi Goldberg) who breaks into Wall Street's all-boys club by setting up a company with an imaginary white male partner. Directed by Donald Petrie, the inane script gets some laughs along the way in its jibes at sexism and racial prejudice, but the humor is mostly uninspired and the comic premise is too thin to credit. Sexual situations, brief nudity in a strip club, coarse language, and a profanity. A-III (PG-13)

Asylum (1971) British production of four psychological horror tales by Robert Bloch that are tied together by being set in an insane asylum run by Patrick Magee, and the gimmick of a puzzle to be unraveled by the end of the last episode. Director Roy Ward Baker provides a few mild chills, a handful of ironic chuckles, and a couple of nifty twists at the conclusion. A-II (PG)

At Any Price (1970) Poor Italian caper movie about a retiring curator of the Vatican museums (Walter Pidgeon) who, though blind, gathers a group of willing and unwilling professional accomplices to carry out the intricate heist of Vatican treasures. Directed by Emilio Miraglia, it is little more than a series of highly improbable, unmotivated, and badly dubbed escapades. A-II (PG)

At Close Range (1986) In director James Foley's harrowing, fact-based tale of youth corrupted by the seductive powers of evil, a son (Sean Penn) blindly follows his menacing, ruthless father (Christopher Walken) as he steals, murders, and betrays without remorse. Some brief nudity, profanity, and intense moments of violence. A-IV (R)

At First Sight (1999) Fact-based drama in which a well-adjusted blind man (Val Kilmer), at the urging of his architect girlfriend (Mira Sorvino), undergoes an operation which restores his sight but opens a Pandora's Box of other difficulties that come to jeopardize their relationship and his previously secure sense of self. While overly sentimental, director Irwin Winkler's romantic drama is emotionally involving in exploring the unexpected pitfalls of a sudden, drastic change in lifestyle. Discreet bedroom scenes, a flash of nudity, some profanity, and an instance of rough language. A-III (PG-13)

At Gunpoint (1955) Routine Western directed by Alfred Werker in which a storekeeper (Fred MacMurray) kills a bank robber, then finds he can't count on any help from the frightened town when the dead man's gang returns to kill him. Stylized violence. A-I (br)

At Long Last Love (1975) Tedious, boring musical about a New York millionaire (Burt Reynolds) who becomes romantically involved with a musical comedy star (Madeline Kahn) and, then, with a bankrupt socicty girl (Cybill Shepherd). Director Peter Bogdanovich has mastered the form of the 1930's Hollywood musicals but not their spirit, drive, or buoyant style. The miscast principals savage some lesser songs by Cole Porter. Permissive attitude toward casual sex. A-III (G)

At Play in the Fields of the Lord (1991) Ponderous adaptation of Peter Matthiessen's novel about the cultural chasm separating a group of US evangelical missionaries (John Lithgow, Daryl Hannah, Aidan Quinn, and Kathy Bates), the Amazonian tribe of aboriginals they hope to convert, and a part-Navaho bush pilot (Tom Berenger) who goes native. In laboring to re-create a remote jungle culture with some ethnographic integrity, director Hector Babenco fails to develop much interest in the colorless missionaries and their part in the human drama of a devastating encounter between civilization and a primitive society. Fairly graphic sexual encounter, much nudity, some violence, and occasional rough language. A-IV (R)

At Sword's Point (1952) Mediocre costumer in which the Four Musketeers' offspring (Cornel Wilde, Dan O'Herlihy, Alan Hale, Jr., and Maureen O'Hara) come to the aid of France's aging queen (Gladys Cooper). Directed by Lewis Allen, the foursome laugh a lot and wield their swords with gusto, but the plot is hardly worth the effort. Stylized violence. A-II (br)

At the Earth's Core (1976) Director Kevin Connor's low-budget science-fiction movie about finding a lost world of prehistoric creatures far beneath the earth's surface falls considerably short of its modest entertainment goals. Considerable special-effects violence and monsters. A-II (PG)

At the Max (1991) Concert film of the Rolling Stones rock band performing on tour in Turin, Berlin, and London during the summer of 1990 is presented in the IMAX format, which is 10 times larger than the conventional 35mm film frame and uses a six-channel four-way sound system. Location director Julien Temple uses the enormous size of the IMAX screen to record the spectacle of the stage sets and lighting, the mass energy of the fans and the full spectrum of amplified music as the band performs 15 of their hits from "Satisfaction" to "Rock and a Hard Place." Some vulgar words and gestures. A-II (nr)

At War with the Army (1950) Lame service comedy set mainly in the orderly room of a stateside tank company, where a zany PFC (Jerry Lewis) tries to help the top sergeant (Dean Martin) evade a persistent lady (Jean Ruth). Directed by Hal Walker, the disjointed script has some fun with the brass as well as the enlisted men, Lewis sneaks off base in drag, and a soda machine pays off in laughs. Comic treatment of a presumed unwed pregnancy. A-II (br)

Atlantic City (1944) Thin musical begins in 1915, when an ambitious showman (Brad Taylor) marries a singer (Constance Moore), then neglects her as his career grows with the New Jersey shore town, but it is she who bails him out when he goes bust in the 1920s. Directed by Ray McCarey, the formula plot is helped by period vaudeville acts, including that of Gallagher and Sheen, as well as musical numbers by Paul Whiteman and Louis Armstrong. Domestic tensions. A-II (br)

Atlantic City (1981) Aging, opportunistic con-man (Burt Lancaster) living in poverty in Atlantic City becomes involved with a young woman (Susan Sarandon). After her husband is killed in a heroin shipment, Lancaster is left with the proceeds from the sale. Director Louis Malle powerfully evokes the seedy side of casino life, as well as a portrait of a small-time loser who takes one last shot at the big time and thinks he can succeed. Some violence, scenes of drug dealing, and brief nudity. A-III (R)

Atlantis (1993) Nature documentary explores underwater sea life in such diverse locations as the Galapagos Islands, the Arctic Circle, Tahiti, and New Caledonia, focusing on endangered or unusual species such as the marine iguana, the striped-sweater sea snake, and the whale shark. Filmmaker Luc Besson's soothing, almost wordless record of life in a watery environment is certainly exotic, but it grows overlong with its repetitive parade of fish. A-I (nr)

Atlantis, the Lost Continent (1961) Lackluster adventures in the ancient world from producer-director George Pal has a Greek fisherman (Anthony Hall) return a shipwrecked princess (Joyce Taylor) to her title homeland, but there he's enslaved and almost turned into an animal by cruel scientists working on a death ray to conquer the world, until volcanic eruptions sink the continent into the Atlantic Ocean. Stylized violence, including some nasty brutality. A-II (br)

Atoll K (see: **Utopia**)

Atom Age Vampire (1961) Italian horror clunker directed by Anton Giulio Majano tells of a surgeon's attempt to restore a woman's disfigured face by experimenting with a radioactive substance that turns him by night into a mutant monster who kills only women. Dubbed. Stylized violence and some gruesome visuals. A-III (br)

Atragon (1964) Standard Japanese science-fiction fantasy about an evil undersea empire whose plans to rule the world are stopped by the underwater battleship of the title. Director Inoshiro Honda manages some nifty special effects in kiddie matinee story. A-I (br)

Attack! (1956) Gritty WW II story of a US infantry company thrown into the Battle of the Bulge, where its cowardly commander (Eddie Albert) is called to account by a platoon leader (Jack Palance) for wasting the lives of his men. Director Robert Aldrich sets up the situation in a convincingly realistic fashion, then goes overboard with the ending's desperate melodramatics. Wartime violence seen from the perspective of individual responsibilities. A-II (br)

Attack of the 50 Ft. Woman (1958) Supremely silly bargain-basement sci-fi directed by Nathan Hertz in which a wealthy, mixed-up heiress (Allison Hayes) grows to the size of a house after encountering an alien spacecraft, then sets off to seek revenge on her philandering husband (William Hudson). Cheesy menace and restrained portrayal of infidelity. A-III (br)

Attack on the Iron Coast (1968) Routine WW II action movie about the training of an elite British commando force (led by Lloyd Bridges) and their raid on German positions in France. Director Paul Wendkos adds nothing new to the old story of brave men who give their lives for their country. A-I (br)

Attica (1974) Documentary recounting the tragic events that took place in the 1971 New York prison revolt at Attica (43 dead, 200 wounded) from the point of view of the inmates, using footage shot inside the prison before and during the National Guard's attack, TV coverage of the state's official investigations, as well as its own interviews with participants. Directed by Cinda Firestone, it takes a clear advocacy position toward prison reform to insure no future Atticas. A-III (nr)

Au Hasard, Balthazar (1970) French production centering on a donkey as a device to tie together a series of vignettes of human injustice. In this unusual and challenging work, director Robert Bresson presents a view of selfishness and inhumanity that is unrelenting in its condemnation of evil. As austere and as uncompromising as any film he has made, it will be hard going for those unacquainted with his previous explorations of the human condition. A-III (nr)

Au Revoir les Enfants (1988) When the Gestapo discover that a priest has hidden three Jewish youths in a Catholic boys' school, he and the boys are arrested and deported to concentration camps. French writer-producer-director Louis Malle re-creates a painful memory from his own youth in a restrained, humbling, well-acted dramatization of a boy's first-hand experience of the Holocaust. Subtitles. Some rough language. A-II (PG)

Audrey Rose (1977) Slow-moving, low-voltage thriller about an 11-year-old girl who becomes an object of contention between a man (Anthony Hopkins) who claims that she is the reincarnation of his dead daughter and her shocked parents (Marsha Mason and John Beck). Although director Robert Wise's movie concerns the spiritual dimension of human existence, its poorly developed theme of reincarnation is confusing, and youngsters may be discomfited by some graphic scenes of the young girl's acute anguish. A-III (PG)

August (1996) The ordered routine of a Victorian estate in North Wales is shattered when an arrogant, elderly professor moves in with his brother-in-law (Anthony Hopkins), who falls hopelessly in love with the professor's bored young wife (Kate Burton). Hopkins directs a sometimes poignant adaptation of Chekhov's *Uncle Vanya* with its smatterings of farcical comedy amidst the ruins of dashed hopes and unfulfilled lives. Fleeting violence and romantic complications. A-II (PG)

Auntie Mame (1958) Uneven but never uninteresting comedy adapted from Dennis Patrick's play about an orphan's upbringing by an outrageously eccentric aunt (Rosalind Russell) who loses a fortune in the Depression, then gains another when she loses her husband (Forrest Tucker) in the Alps. Directed by Morton DaCosta, the result is stagy and overlong, but nothing distracts from Russell's delightfully exuberant performance as a self-centered extrovert whose loving concern for her nephew overcomes her wacky sense of propriety. Comic treatment of serious subjects, including an unwed pregnancy. A-III (PG)

Austin Powers: International Man of Mystery (1997) Lame James Bond spoof in which a British secret agent and his evil nemesis (Mike Myers in a dual role) are revived after both were cryogenically frozen during the swinging '60s and once again face off, with the agent trying to foil the villain's plot to destroy the planet. Also written by Myers with Jay Roach directing, it's merely a vanity vehicle for

Myers's tasteless asides and leadenly drawn-out skits. Fleeting sexual encounter, some comically intended violence, much crude humor, and an instance of profanity. A-III (PG-13)

Austin Powers: The Spy who Shagged Me (1999) Mindless sequel to the '97 spoof in which the swinging British secret agent (Mike Myers) time-travels back to the '60s to recover his libido and joins forces with a comely CIA agent (Heather Graham) to again save the world from the wacky machinations of Dr. Evil (Myers in a dual role). As directed by Jay Roach, the silly shenanigans alternate with gross toilet humor and puerile sexual innuendo for a mixed bag of goofy but tasteless entertainment. Comically intended violence, frequent sexual innuendo, crude references, rude gestures, and a few instances of profanity. A-III (PG-13)

Author, Author (1982) Armenian-American playwright (Al Pacino), left by his wife (Tuesday Weld) with five children on his hands, finds another woman (Dyan Cannon) to help him get through it all. While pleasant enough, director Arthur Hiller's romantic comedy is not especially funny and offers an intemperate moral outlook, viewing adultery and divorce as an inevitable part of self-development. A-III (PG)

Autumn Afternoon, An (1973) Japanese production about the transient joys of family life and the loneliness of parents after children leave home. Its story is of a widower (Chishu Ryu), who realizes that if his daughter devotes any more of her time to him, it will ruin her life. With his encouragement she eventually marries, and after the wedding the father returns home to the form of loneliness he has anticipated throughout the movie. Directed by Yasujiro Ozu, it is a movie rich in the rhythm of life, the warmth of humanity, and the web of relationships that sustain any individual. A-I (nr)

Autumn Leaves (1956) Slick tearjerker about a woman (Joan Crawford) who's spent her youth caring for an invalid father, then is swept into marriage by an insistent young suitor (Cliff Robertson), only to fear for her life from irrational outbursts triggered by his traumatic past. Though the wife suffers through heroically, director Robert Aldrich lards the threatening situation with contrived thrills and kinky romance between Robertson's ex-wife and his father (Vera Miles and Lorne Greene). Stylized violence, menace, and sexual situations. A-III (br)

Autumn Sonata (1978) Ingmar Bergman's bleak examination of a middle-aged woman (Liv Ullmann) and her relationship with her mother (Ingrid Bergman). What results is a film long on talk and short on characterization and dramatic action. Fine acting throughout, but the mother-daughter conflict may be too depressing for young people. A-III (PG)

Avalanche (1978) Scorning all ecological considerations, an entrepreneur (Rock Hudson) builds a luxurious ski resort on a Colorado mountainside, hoping to impress his estranged wife (Mia Farrow) enough to effect a reconciliation. With ludicrous dialogue and shallow characterizations, director Corey Allen's run-of-the-mill disaster movie deserves to be buried in the avalanche that follows. Nudity and suggestive sexual behavior. O (PG)

Avalanche Express (1979) Cold War thriller in which CIA agents (Lee Marvin and Linda Evans) try to spirit a defecting head of Soviet intelligence (Robert Shaw) out of Italy by train. Noisy ambushes, counter-spy intrigue, and conventional violence lets the steam out of the plot. Director Mark Robson's last film lacks humor and genuine excitement, with its climactic avalanche sequence midway derailing most of attempts at tension that follow. A-II (PG)

Avalon (1990) Multi-generational saga about a Russian Jewish immigrant (Armin Mueller-Stahl) who joins his four brothers in 1914 Baltimore, embraces life in his new land, and watches their extended family, especially his son (Aidan Quinn), pursue the American dream. Writer-director Barry Levinson's tribute to family values is well-acted, and its positive message is welcome, but the impact is blunted by the heavily nostalgic and sentimental treatment of the characters. A-I (PG)

Avanti! (1972) American businessman (Jack Lemmon), in attempting to bring his father's remains back to the US after the old man's death in an auto accident at an Italian resort, falls for the woman (Juliet Mills) his father has been meeting there for the last 10 years. Director Billy Wilder bludgeons the situation with some rather unfunny black humor, a good deal of vulgarity, much rough language, and a bit of gratuitous nudity. O (R)

Avengers, The (1998) Leaden updating of the 1960's TV series with unflappable British operatives Steed (Ralph Fiennes) and Mrs. Peel (Uma Thurman) battling a mad villain (Sean Connery), who's manipulating worldwide weather systems. Director Jeremiah Chechik misses the droll wit of the original, whose debonair agents are now smug and charmless while the villain is embarrassingly buffoonish. Stylized violence, mild sexual innuendo, and an instance of rough language. A-III (PG-13)

Avenging Waters (1936) Cowboy star Ken Maynard saves a rancher and his daughter (Beth Marion) from the evil designs of a neighboring cattleman (Ward Bond). Director Spencer Gordon Bennet stretches out the thin plot with some country music, stock footage of a stampede, and the devastation caused by a burst dam. The gunplay, fisticuffs, and natural disasters are anything but realistic. A-I (br)

Awakening, The (1980) The mummy of a dead Egyptian queen tries to fulfill an ancient prophecy with devastating consequences for the family of the archeologist (Charlton Heston) who opened her tomb. The best asset of director Mike Newell's plodding horror story is the location photography of the Valley of the Kings. Implications of incest and some gore. A-III (R)

Awakenings (1990) Refusing to give up on his chronically catatonic patients, a caring doctor (Robin Williams) experiments with a new drug which brings a man (Robert De Niro) out of a trance-like state after 30 years. Director Penny Marshall's sensitive, fact-based drama brings the viewer on a moving, emotional odyssey made all the more poignant by superior performances all around. Minimal rough language. A-II (PG-13)

Away All Boats (1956) Routine WW II action picture directed by Joseph Pevney chronicles the heroic exploits of a dedicated Navy captain (Jeff Chandler) and his brave crew (notably Lex Barker, Richard Boone, and David Janssen) in transporting troops for amphibious landings on enemy-held islands in the Pacific. Wartime violence and gobs of celluloid courage. A-I (br)

Awfully Big Adventure, An (1995) Dark, muddled tale of backstage romances set in 1947 Liverpool, where a dramatic troupe, headed by a cruelly arrogant director (Hugh Grant), is joined by a starry-eyed adolescent (Georgina Cates), who's seduced by the lead actor (Alan Rickman) with devastating consequences. Directed by Mike Newell, the unappealing story of manipulative adults and vulnerable adolescents offers a poorly focused mix of strained drama and mean-spirited comedy. Brief bedroom scenes with nudity, frequent sexual innuendo, fleeting violence, and an instance of rough language. A-IV (R)

Babar: The Movie (989) In a delightful, animated version of the children's books by Jean and Laurent de Brunhoff, King Babar recalls for his own kids how as a boy he saved Elephantland from the rhinos and became an unlikely hero. Director Alan Bunce's Canadian production underscores the value of commitment to friends and family, while Babar's fears in an alien jungle will be identifiable to young children just beginning to explore unfamiliar turf. The movie will enjoy a long life as a family video. A-I (G)

Babe (1995) Live-action barnyard charmer in which a kindly Australian farmer (James Cromwell) enters his unusual piglet (voice of Christine Cavanaugh) in a sheepdog competition, unaware that his farm animals can talk to one another as they pull together to make the little pig's dream of herding sheep come true. Director Chris Noonan's enchanting comic fable is filmed entirely from the animals' point-of-view, with delightful visuals and an endearing message of learning to live and work in harmony. A-I (G)

Babe, The (1992) Sprawling saga of baseball great George Herman "Babe" Ruth (John Goodman) from his youth in a home for "incorrigibles" through his exploits on and off the field to his final turn at bat in 1935. Directed by Arthur Miller, the emphasis is less on Ruth's record-setting career than on the simple-minded character whose antics and indiscretions made him one of the era's more colorful personalities. Discreet treatment of infidelity, a bedroom scene, and some coarse language. A-II (PG)

Babe: Pig in the City (1998) Darker sequel to the 1995 hit in which the farmer's wife (Magda Szubanski) takes the plucky porker (voice of E.G. Daily) of the title to the city, but when she's wrongly arrested, Babe and a gaggle of homeless animals he befriends have to fend for themselves against starvation and the machinations of nasty humans. Directed by George Miller, the less-endearing sequel retains the polite pig's innocence and generosity, but some of the perilous situations may be a bit intense for very young children. A-I (G)

Babe Ruth Story, The (1948) In his portrayal of baseball's fabled slugger, William Bendix can't do much with the hollow heroics and phony sentimentality of a bogus script. Director Roy Del Ruth makes mincemeat out of big-league baseball and applesauce out of the Bambino's exploits on and off the field. For undemanding fans of the national pastime. A-I (br)

Babes in Arms (1939) With the talkies having put their vaudeville parents out of work, their adolescent offspring (led by Mickey Rooney and Judy Garland) get together to earn some money by putting on a variety show. Director Busby Berkeley's period piece showcases Rooney's talents as a juvenile hoofer and madcap comic, but shortchanges the Rodgers and Hart musical upon which the zestful proceedings are based. Youthful optimism wins the day, despite the creaky plot cliches. A-I (br)

Babes in Toyland (1961) Disappointing Disney adaptation of the Victor Herbert operetta in which Mary Quite Contrary (Annette Funicello) is saved from the clutches of the villainous Barnaby (Ray Bolger) by a silly pair of apprentice toymakers (Gene Sheldon and Henry Calvin). Directed by Jack Donohue, the live-action musical works hard to create the fantasy of a fairytale world, but the result lacks the fun and charm of the 1934 Laurel and Hardy version (aka **March of the Wooden Soldiers**). The nursery rhyme characters and special effects will keep the children entertained but hold only sporadic interest for their elders. A-I (nr)

Babette's Feast (1988) Screen version of a story by Isak Dinesen, set in a rugged Danish fishing village in 1871, shows the impact of a French housekeeper (Stephane Audran) on two pious sisters, who carry on their late father's work as pastor of a dwindling religious flock. The conclusion follows the preparation and consumption of an exquisite French meal, with focus on its sensual and religious implications and its healing effect on the austere sect and the Frenchwoman who prepares it. Danish director Gabriel Axel's low-key and understated work is rich with detail and fine, controlled performances. Subtitles. Cerebral treatment. A-II (G)

Baby Blue Marine (1976) WWII boot camp washout (Jan-Michael Vincent) pretends to be a Marine Ranger and is received as a hero in a small Colorado town. When a waitress (Glynnis O'Connor) falls for him, he has to prove his courage. Although the story is abundantly sentimental, director John Hancock warmly evokes the people and the period, the acting is good, and the result is a fairly entertaining movie. A-II (PG)

Baby Boom (1987) High-powered businesswoman (Diane Keaton) chooses the transforming love of motherhood and the ego boost of self-employment when she inherits a baby whose parents have died tragically. Director Charles Shyer's wry and insightful situation comedy has the good sense to affirm that new life is more important than new clients. A-II (PG)

Baby Doll (1956) Meandering social satire set in rural Mississippi, where an Italian-American newcomer (Eli Wallach) takes revenge on the redneck (Karl Malden) who torched his cotton gin by seducing the man's bird-brained wife (Carroll Baker). Directed by Elia Kazan from Tennessee Williams's script, the halting narrative and eccentric characters never quite jell into a coherent story, though Boris Kaufman's photography provides haunting images of racial animosities, crumbling facades, and deep-seated rural poverty. Stylized violence, implied marital infidelity, and leering sexual situations. A-IV (br)

Baby Geniuses (1999) Comic misfire in which a megalomaniacal doctor (Kathleen Turner) intent on raising brilliant toddlers in a secret underground lab is outsmarted by two-year-old twins who wreck her elaborate plans. Director Bob Clark's insipid take on babies as miniature, wise-cracking adults is unappealing, dull, and overacted by both Turner and her clueless assistant, Christopher Lloyd. Some cartoon violence and mayhem and a few crude remarks. A-II (PG)

Baby, It's You (1983) Bright daughter of a Jewish doctor (Rosanna Arquette) and the son of working-class Catholic parents (Vincent Spano) fall in love when they're high-school seniors in Camden, N.J., in the late 1960s. Director John Sayles's perceptive, compassionate, if uneven, movie is made memorable by an absolutely pitch-perfect performance by Arquette and very good acting by Spano. Some needlessly graphic sex scenes and nudity. O (R)

Baby Love (1969) Psychotic teenager (Linda Hayden) is taken into a wealthy London home, where she proceeds to destroy each member of the family out of resentment against the father, who had had an affair with her own mother (Diana Dors). Alistair Reid directs the British production as if it were a manual on sexual pathology ranging from attempted rape to lesbianism, with plenty of nudity and little concern for characterization, consistent motivation, or common sense. O (R)

Baby Maker, The (1970) Barbara Hershey plays a freethinking hippie who agrees to bear a child for a couple who want a baby at least half theirs (the wife is infertile). Writer-director James Bridges provides an ending in which the wife is now insecure about her husband's affection, the husband has fallen for the girl, and she realizes she wants to keep the child after all. Because the basic immorality of the arrangement is never addressed, their various disappointments seem hollow and crass. O (R)

Baby: Secret of the Lost Legend (1985) American couple (William Katt and Sean Young) exploring in Africa discover a cute baby brontosaurus which they later reunite with its mama, from whom it had been separated by some villains. Directed by B.W.L. Norton, it's a pleasant enough adventure tale for most age groups. A violent battle scene and some mild vulgarity. A-II (PG)

Baby, Take a Bow (1934) Little Shirley Temple gets her first starring role as a preschooler who recovers the jewels her father (James Dunn) is accused of stealing, then helps nab the real thief. Directed by Harry Lachman, the formula melodrama has little interest other than its Depression-era family setting and, of course, the bubbly presence of its precocious star. Brief violence endangering a child. A-I (G)

Baby the Rain Must Fall (1964) Paroled convict (Steve McQueen) returns to his wife (Lee Remick), but her love and encouragement are not enough to reform his violent ways. Directed by Richard Mulligan, the narrative never quite jells into an understandable situation, though the backcountry locales and characters provide some interest. A-II (br)

Baby's Day Out (1994) Crawling away from three dopey kidnappers (Joe Mantegna, Joe Pantoliano, and Brian Haley), a nine-month-old infant blissfully enjoys visits to the zoo, a department store, and a construction site, all on his own, as the klutzy trio scrambles to recapture him. Director Patrick Read Johnson's mildly entertaining formula comedy gets its mileage out of the juxtaposition of the adorable baby (twins Adam and Jacob Worton) amidst incredible situations. Frequent slapstick violence and fantasy treatment of an infant in jeopardy. A-II (PG)

Baby-Sitters Club, The (1995) Seven enterprising pre-teen girls run a backyard day-camp for neighborhood children, while one of them (Schuyler Fisk) copes with the return of her father (Peter Horton) to the area, which he insists she keep secret from her mom and step-dad. Based on a popular series of children's books, director Melanie Mayron's lightweight summer-camp story is weakly developed, though it depicts resourceful, hard-working youngsters cheerfully providing emotional support for each other. Mild menace. A-I (PG)

Bachelor and the Bobby-Soxer, The (1947) Mild romantic comedy in which a level-headed judge (Myrna Loy) orders a rakish artist (Cary Grant) to date her 17-year-old sister (Shirley Temple), expecting this to cure the girl's infatuation for him, but results predictably go awry. Scripted by Sidney Sheldon and directed by Irving Reis, the veteran performers add some class and a great deal of charm to lightweight situations, the best of which are the competitive games at a town picnic and a chaotic nightclub scene. Dated family fare. A-I (br)

Bachelor Bait (see: **Adventure in Baltimore**)

Bachelor Flat (1962) Failed farce in which a hapless British archaeologist (Terry-Thomas) on the faculty of a California college has trouble fending off amorous American women, including the pretended advances of the adolescent daughter (Tuesday Weld) of his fiancé (Celeste Holm). Director Frank Tashlin gets few laughs from the tiresome misunderstandings and tasteless situations that pad out the proceedings. Much sexual innuendo. A-III (br)

Bachelor in Paradise (1961) Weak romantic comedy in which a playboy author (Bob Hope) moves into an exclusive California housing development to research the mating game among the affluent, then falls for its pert business manager (Lana Turner). Directed by Jack Arnold, the script's satiric pretensions fall flat, and the sexist humor wasn't funny even then. Much sexual innuendo and marital strife. A-III (br)

Bachelor Knight (see: **The Bachelor and the Bobby-Soxer**)

Bachelor Mother (1939) Flimsy romantic comedy revolves around a shop-girl (Ginger Rogers) who finds an abandoned infant, then tries to convince her boss (David Niven) that she's not the baby's mother.

Directed by Garson Kanin, the complications arising from this comic premise are broadly farcical yet always related to the inevitable sentimental ending. Veiled references to unwed motherhood. A-II (br)

Bachelor Party (1984) Prospective bridegroom Tom Hanks has a tasteless time with crude friends in director Neil Israel's sex farce full of gross, unfunny jokes, exploitative nudity, and demeaning raps about women. O (R)

Back at the Front (1952) Slack sequel to **Up Front** has veteran goldbricks Willie (Tom Ewell) and Joe (Harvey Lembeck) recalled to active duty in postwar Tokyo, where they are duped by smugglers (Mari Blanchard and Richard Long) and chased by MPs. Directed by George Sherman, the comic scrapes into which these retread GIs get themselves are overly familiar, the Japanese locations don't make them any fresher, and there's not a peep about the Korean War. A-I (br)

Back in the USSR (1991) Muddled thriller about a US tourist (Frank Whaley) in post-Soviet Russia, on the run from rival gangsters (Brian Blessed and Roman Polanski) after a priceless icon they think he's hidden. Directed by Deran Sarafian, the helter-skelter plot generates more confusion than suspense, though the Moscow locales add some interest. Stylized violence, a brief sexual encounter, and minimal rough language. A-III (R)

Back Roads (1981) A prostitute (Sally Field) and a cheerful down-and-outer (Tommy Lee Jones) hit the road for California, and in the course of their misadventure, fall in love. Under Martin Ritt's direction the performances are appealing, but the basic narrative has an air of sentimental romanticism. Its soapy mix of sexuality and occasional violence is disappointingly emphasized. A-III (R)

Back to Bataan (1945) WW II melodrama of an American officer (John Wayne) organizing an underground movement against the Japanese occupation of the Philippines, it pays tribute to the contribution of these guerrillas in the liberation of their homeland. Directed by Edward Dmytryk, the patriotic derring-do of the Filipino resistance fighters begins and ends with the freeing of Allied prisoner-of-war camps. Wartime violence and national stereotypes. A-II (br)

Back to God's Country (1953) Dim adventure directed by Joseph Pevney is set in the 1890s Yukon, where an American sea captain (Rock Hudson) struggles to protect his wife (Marcia Henderson) and cargo of furs from a vicious villain (Steve Cochran), whose nemesis is a murderous Great Dane. Stylized violence, including an attempted sexual assault. A-II (br)

Back to School (1986) Rodney Dangerfield provides his special brand of uncouth humor in this story about a self-made millionaire who returns to college to help his son, but finds that there are some things money can't buy. Alan Metter's direction keeps things moving in a somewhat tame sophomoric comedy about higher education. Brief instance of nudity and a bit of foul language. A-III (PG-13)

Back to the Beach (1987) Frankie Avalon and Annette Funicello return to the seashore and discover that the chaste relationships of the 1950s have evolved into the sexual alliances of the 1980s. Fanciful nostalgic trip from director Lyndall Hobbs is inconsistent in winking at the plot's implied premarital sex while offhandedly affirming the virtues of enduring marriage and fidelity. A-III (PG)

Back to the Future (1985) Above-average entertainment about a teenager (Michael J. Fox) who is transported back through time and obliged to serve as matchmaker for his parents or face retroactive nonexistence. A major problem is that his mother-to-be finds him far more attractive than she does his father-to-be. Directed by Robert Zemeckis, it is funny and clever with a bit of genuine sentiment that unfortunately is marred by casual profanity, the depiction of violence as manly, and, though there is no depiction of it, an implicit acceptance of sexual promiscuity as standard teenage behavior. A-III (PG)

Back to the Future Part II (1989) Mediocre sequel with the time-traveling doctor (Christopher Lloyd) taking Marty McFly (Michael J. Fox) and his girlfriend (Elizabeth Shue) to the year 2015 to save Marty's son (also Fox) from the ravages of destiny, and then back to 1955 to stop the growing power of arch-villain Biff (Thomas F. Wilson). Director Robert Zemeckis makes an empty show of technical wizardry out of a nonsensical script that features a succession of product endorsements, including a trailer for Part III. Minimal rough language laced with incidental sexual innuendoes. A-II (PG)

Back to the Future Part III (1990) Tame, tired second sequel finds Marty (Michael J. Fox) transported to the Old West of 1885, where his professor pal (Christopher Lloyd) has fallen in love but is about to take a bullet in the back. With little more to go on than cardboard characters, cartoon situations, and special effects that have by now grown stale, the team of writer Bob Gale and director Robert Zemeckis can't quite triplicate the sense of fun and ingenuity that made the original so appealing. Minimal street language and mild, cartoon-like violence. A-II (PG)

Backbeat (1994) Tragic, fact-based story of Stu Sutcliffe (Stephen Dorff), one of the original Beatles and close friend of John Lennon (Ian Hart), who left the band in order to remain in Hamburg with his fiancé (Sheryl Lee) and hopes of a career in painting, but dies months later of a brain hemorrhage. Director Iain Softley's downbeat movie is little more than a routine buddy story which fails to capture the quirky energy of the Beatles as they first burst onto the international scene. Restrained bedroom scenes, intermittent nudity, brief violence, drug use, and much rough language. A-III (R)

Backdraft (1991) Deep-rooted conflicts boil over when a rookie Chicago firefighter (William Baldwin) is placed under the command of his estranged brother

(Kurt Russell) during the investigation of a string of arson-related murders. With the terrifying nature of fire emerging as the real star of the movie, director Ron Howard ambitiously tackles a relationship story, a murder mystery, and a special-effects action movie with modest success. Some grisly shots of charred bodies, very brief nudity, fleeting sexual innuendo, occasional fisticuffs, and intermittent rough language. A-III (R)

Backfire (1950) Convoluted mystery in which an ex-GI (Gordon MacRae) tries to clear his missing buddy (Edmond O'Brien) of a murder rap with the help of a nurse (Virginia Mayo), another ex-GI (Dane Clark), and a mystery woman (Viveca Lindfors) with mob connections. Directed by Vincent Sherman, the muddled plot relies on murky flashbacks which never quite add up, even after the twist ending. Stylized violence, menacing situations, and romantic complications. A-II (br)

Backlash (1956) Murky Western in which a gunfighter (Richard Widmark) tracks down the lone survivor of an Apache massacre of Arizona gold miners to learn if his long-lost father (John McIntire) was among them. Directed by John Sturges, the quest is complicated by a woman traveler (Donna Reed), who keeps getting in the gunman's way, an Apache attack on a trading post, and an all-out range war pitting father against son. Assorted frontier violence and romantic complications. A-II (br)

Backtrack! (1969) Formula Western directed by Earl Bellamy in which a Wyoming cowboy (Doug McClure) sets off for Mexico to buy a prize bull, but gets entangled along the way with a trio of Texas Rangers (led by Neville Brand) on the trail of train robbers, with lame tongue-in-cheek results. Stylized violence and mild sexual innuendo. A-II (G)

Bad and the Beautiful, The (1952) Gritty Hollywood melodrama about the rise and fall of a ruthless producer (Kirk Douglas) as told in flashback by the director (Barry Sullivan) he exploited to get his start, an actress (Lana Turner) he pretended to love, and a screenwriter (Dick Powell) who blames him for the death of his wife (Gloria Grahame). Directed by Vincente Minnelli, the episodic story has a number of credible scenes about the business and craft of movie-making, but the troubled characters never emerge as anything more than familiar stereotypes. Sexual situtions and ambiguous treatment of Hollywood ethics. A-III (br)

Bad Behaviour (1993) Low-key comedy-drama set in London, where a long-married Irish couple (Stephen Rea and Sinead Cusack), tired with the daily grind of work and parenting, go through a restless phase in their marriage with good-humored impatience. Working without a script, director Les Blair gets convincing, down-to-earth performances from the actors meandering through droll slice-of-life situations that ring true to the discontents of mid-life malaise and the comforts of marital commitment. An implied sexual encounter, some heavy drinking, and occasional rough language. A-III (nr)

Bad Boys (1983) Sean Penn stars as a vicious young criminal sent to a reformatory in this brutal exploitation movie trying to pass itself off as socially significant. The uninspired direction of Richard Rosenthal of a cliche-littered script owes little to real life and everything to some five decades of Hollywood prison movies. Bereft of moral or social perspective, it places a heavy emphasis on violence and vengeance within the gruesome context of prison life. O (R)

Bad Boys (1995) Thin buddy movie of Miami detectives (Martin Lawrence and Will Smith) saddled with protecting a murder witness (Tea Leoni) while trying to recover a huge stash of heroin stolen from the police evidence room. Director Michael Bay's explosive action story is stuffed with wall-to-wall violence made to look like little more than manly fun and all part of a day's work for macho cops. Excessive violence, much sexual innuendo, fleeting nudity, and incessant rough language. O (R)

Bad Company (1969) French production composed of two dramatic variations on a single theme: loneliness is only masked by the companionship of equally lonely pals. Director Jean Eustache skillfully communicates the desperate bravado which hides the gnawing uncertainties of the immature youths in these two stories. Viewers may be put off by the movie's drab documentary style and some gross sexual language, but none will be unmoved by the pathetic nature of these young lives. A-IV (nr)

Bad Company (1972) Clean-cut Pennsylvanian youth (Barry Brown), fleeing conscription during the Civil War, joins up with a youthful band of Missouri toughs (led by Jeff Bridges), and as they make their way west, he becomes as adept as any of them at robbing banks and killing hombres. Directed by Robert Benton, its morality tale is not very profound, but the period piece is beautifully mounted and painstakingly detailed. One wonders, however, if all the cursing and updated sex talk is really credible for teenagers in 1862. A-IV (PG)

Bad Company (1995) Double-crosses abound in Ross Thomas's cynical story about a disgraced ex-CIA agent (Laurence Fishburne) who gets a job with a shady industrial-espionage firm, then plots with his partner (Ellen Barkin) to kill their boss (Frank Langella) and take over the company. Director Damian Harris supplies an edgy atmosphere and sleek visual style to an unsavory story about greedy cardboard characters. Several brief bedroom scenes, fleeting nudity, brief violence, and some rough language. A-III (R)

Bad Day at Black Rock (1955) Morality tale in the form of a tense thriller set in a small Western town whose residents are forced to face their guilty past when a one-armed stranger (Spencer Tracy) arrives in 1945 asking for the whereabouts of a Japanese-American farmer. Director John Sturges gets much suspense from the uneven odds against the lone, handicapped outsider confronted by increasingly hostile locals (Robert Ryan, Lee Marvin, and Ernest Borgnine). Growing menace and brief but painfully effective violence. A-II (br)

Bad Girls (1994) Superficial feminist Western in which disenchanted prostitutes (Madeleine Stowe, Mary Stuart Masterson, Andie MacDowell, and Drew Barrymore) flee a murder charge in Texas, only to run into a gang of sadistic outlaws (led by James Russo and Robert Loggia). Director Jonathan Kaplan's empty oater is coated with a slick Hollywood veneer, but its feeble story is nothing more than a string of tired Western cliches substituting female for male leads. Some gunfights, revenge murders, and frequent sexual references. A-III (R)

Bad Influence (1990) Stylish, menacing, and perverse thriller about a cunning drifter (Rob Lowe) who lures a wimpish yuppie (James Spader) into a decadent life of sex, lies, and murder. Director Curtis Hanson chillingly develops the cat-and-mouse relationship between his two doomed protagonists in a story updating the Faust legend to modern-day Los Angeles. Rough language, recreational drug use, some grisly violence, and several explicit sexual scenes with nudity. O (R)

Bad Lieutenant (1992) Rancid melodrama about the crackup of a New York City police detective (Harvey Keitel) who's over his head in gambling debts, drugs, and sex, all of which is compounded by self-pity and a warped sense of moral guilt. Director Abel Ferrara's disjointed exercise in the emotional turbulence of going over the edge lacks credibility and leads nowhere. Excessive violence, graphic sex, substance abuse, and rough language. O (NC-17)

Bad Man of Deadwood (1941) Roy Rogers and Gabby Hayes bring their medicine show to a crook-infested town and help its good citizens run the crooks out in a low-budget but good-natured Western directed by Joseph Kane. Simple, clean-cut action with some mild violence. A-I (br)

Bad Man's River (1973) Tame Italian Western with Gina Lollobrigida as a shady lady whose hobby is bilking amorous males (among them, Lee Van Cleef and James Mason) of whatever they're worth. Director Gene Martin stages a lot of forgettable action involving a sheriff's posse, a horde of revolutionary banditos, and the Mexican Army. Waste of time. A-III (PG)

Bad Medicine (1985) Misfit American students (led by Steve Guttenberg and Julie Hagerty) attend a bogus medical school in Central America. Director Harvey Miller's movie fails both as social satire and as broad comedy, offering little more than some insulting humor pointed at Hispanic stereotypes along with bad jokes about incest and drug abuse. O (PG)

Bad Men of Missouri (1941) Standard shoot-'em-up turns the Younger Brothers (Dennis Morgan, Wayne Morris, and Arthur Kennedy) into western Robin Hoods, robbing a villainous carpetbagger (Victor Jory) to save their neighbors' farms. Director Ray Enright provides some vigorous action, with occasional comic relief (Walter Catlett) and mild romance (Jane Wyman). Muddled justice theme and stylized violence. A-II (br)

Bad Moon (1996) Inept monster movie in which a man (Michael Pare) visiting his sister (Mariel Hemingway) and young nephew manages to keep them in the dark about spending his nights as a demon werewolf, but he can't fool the family's pet dog. Director Eric Red fails to build any interest in the characters as they plod through an inane story with some gruesome chills and cheesy special-effects gore. Mindless sex, violence, and rough language. O (R)

Bad News Bears, The (1976) Walter Matthau stars as a former minor leaguer who takes over a hopelessly misdirected and inept Little League baseball team and makes it a winner. Under Michael Ritchie's direction, the children are cute, but used to communicate a cynical, albeit humorous, critique of middle-class values. Profanity, especially from the mouths of children, not exemplary image-making. O (PG)

Bad News Bears Go to Japan, The (1978) The third and least accomplished in the series celebrating the exploits of the inept but lovable and cunning Little League team features Tony Curtis as a somewhat unsavory promoter who hopes to exploit the exhibition game he sets up for the Bears in Tokyo. Director John Berry keeps the language pretty much under control, but Curtis's visit to a geisha house is sexually suggestive. A-III (PG)

Bad News Bears in Breaking Training, The (1977) An estranged father (William Devane) of one of the team's players takes the Bears to the Astrodome for a taste of big league atmosphere, but the film's language is anything but tasteful. Director Michael Pressman's sequel, like the original, is too cynical in its view of human foibles to provide solid family entertainment. A-III (PG)

Bad Seed, The (1956) Muddled melodrama from Maxwell Anderson's play in which a mother (Nancy Kelly) comes to believe her bright, loving eight-year-old daughter (Patty McCormack) has inherited criminal tendencies after discovering she drowned a classmate. Directed by Mervyn LeRoy, the contrived proceedings gain a sinister atmosphere from McCormack's chilling performance, but the stagy treatment, hollow speeches about genetic influences, and hokey ending are uninviting. Menacing situations, domestic tensions, and an off-screen suicide. A-II (br)

Bad Timing: A Sensual Obsession (1980) Director Nicolas Roeg's coldly somber account of obsessive love in modern Vienna stars Art Garfunkel as a smug, domineering psychiatrist and Theresa Russell (whose performance gives the movie the only life it has) as an unstable American woman. Some very explicit sex scenes. O (X/R)

Badge 373 (1973) New York City detective (Robert Duvall), suspended from the force pending an investigation into the death of a Puerto Rican drug pusher, becomes a one-man crime-stopper. Director

Howard Koch places his violent action in the slums and dives of the big city, showing in gritty detail racism, graft, greed, and venality on every human level. Add constant coarse language and seamy situations, and the result is a cynical view of humanity. O (R)

Badlands (1974) Fact-based story of a drifter (Martin Sheen) who takes his teenage sweetheart (Sissy Spacek) on a bizarre shooting spree across South Dakota and Montana in the 1950s. Director Terrence Malik presents a panoramic view of American life and myths, looking at the reality and the fiction behind the American Dream from the perspective of two archetypal characters. It is a dark and troubling vision with senseless violence at its core. A-III (PG)

Badlanders, The (1958) Muddled Western teams ex-convicts (Alan Ladd and Ernest Borgnine) in a far-fetched scheme to steal gold ore from an abandoned shaft adjacent to a working mine. Director Delmer Daves has no trouble building suspense in the ramshackle mining sequences, but the rest of the proceedings are rather bogus, though of interest in depicting Mexican-Americans as an oppressed people who take a leading role in the story's conclusion. Stylized violence, sexual innuendo, and a restrained childbirth scene. A-III (br)

Badman's Territory (1946) Wild West yarn in which a Texas sheriff (Randolph Scott) on the run from trumped-up charges winds up in the Oklahoma panhandle, which serves as a sanctuary for outlaws such as the James Brothers and the Dalton gang. Directed by Tim Whelan, it's a good guy-bad guy muddlement with comic relief from Gabby Hayes. Stylized shoot-outs and fisticuffs. A-I (br)

Bagdad (1949) Clunky tale of desert intrigue directed by Charles Lamont pits an English-educated Bedouin princess (Maureen O'Hara) against the man (Paul Christian) accused of murdering her father, as well as the Turkish governor (Vincent Price) in cahoots with the real culprit (John Sutton), whose marauding Black Robes are terrorizing the desert tribes. Revenge tale with stylized violence and romantic bosh. A-II (br)

Bagdad Cafe (1988) Lovely little fable about the restorative powers of love and friendship set at the Bagdad Cafe, a rundown truckstop, luncheonette, and motel in the desert outside Las Vegas. German director Percy Adlon tracks the unlikely friendship between a German tourist (Marianne Sagebrecht) and the Bagdad's proprietor (CCH Pounder), a black single mother. Also in focus are the cafe's oddball regulars, including an old Hollywood set painter (Jack Palance), who falls for the tourist. Much profanity and some nudity in several brief scenes involving an artist's model. A-III (PG)

Ball of Fire (1942) Uneven romantic comedy about eight erudite professors (led by Gary Cooper) whose work writing an encyclopedia is disrupted by a burlesque queen (Barbara Stanwyck) hiding from the DA seeking an indictment of her gangster boyfriend (Dana Andrews). Directed by Howard Hawks, the fish-out-of-water plot generates some smiles but never quite measures up to the comic potential of the situation, which increasingly falters into sentimental melodrama. Romantic complications and comic menace. A-II (br)

Ballad of a Soldier (1960) A 19-year-old soldier, on a six-day furlough, makes his way home through the war-torn Russian countryside, encountering a variety of people, each with his or her own unique experience of WWII. Director Grigori Chukhrai avoids the blatant Soviet propaganda of previous Russian exports while fashioning a warm and humanistic tribute to the integrity and goodness of ordinary people. A-II (br)

Ballad of Cable Hogue, The (1970) Going to some absurd extremes is director Robert Altman's off-beat, turn-of-the-century Western about a man's last stand against the machine and the alienation that comes with it. Some violence, bawdiness, and profanity undercut Jason Robards's warmly credible performance. O (R)

Ballad of Gregorio Cortez, The (1983) Fact-based movie tells the story of Gregorio Cortez, a Hispanic-American (Edward James Olmos), who in 1901 Gonzales, Tex., shoots a sheriff when a mistake made by an interpreter turns a question into a threat. He flees for the Mexican border, pursued by a huge posse led by Texas Rangers, but surrenders when he learns that his wife and children are being held in prison. Director Robert M. Young's sensitive, restrained, beautifully photographed movie does justice to both sides in this clash of cultures. There is brief, if graphic, violence. A-II (PG)

Ballad of Josie, The (1967) Director Andrew McLaglen's plotless Western stars dungareed Doris Day and offers little else. The form of a ballad is simple and episodic whereas the movie, unfortunately, is merely simple-minded and fragmented. A-I (br)

Ballad of Little Jo, The (1993) Spurned by her proper Bostonian father after bearing an illegitimate child, a woman (Suzy Amis) ends up alone in a mining town in the Old West, where she forges a reclusive, hardworking life disguised as a man, eventually finding love with her Chinese cook (David Chung) when he discovers her secret and plays along. Writer-director Maggie Greenwald shatters the Hollywood image of the heroic male Westerner with a heavy-handed but provocative feminine perspective that is sympathetic in its treatment of women and immigrants. Some violence and bedroom scenes, fleeting nudity, and occasional opium use. A-III (R)

Ballad of Orin, The (1979) Japanese movie, set in the early part of this century, in which a blind girl raised by blind women becomes a social outcast after being raped, until she is befriended by an army deserter, the only person not to take advantage of her. Director Masahiro Shinoda uses the lyric tale as a vehicle of social criticism directed against Japanese militarism and the inferior status of women. Several restrained scenes of sexual activity. A-III (nr)

Ballad of the Sad Cafe, The (1991) Disappointing adaptation of Carson McCullers's twisted love story of a strong, independent woman (Vanessa Redgrave) in a Southern rural community during the Depression, whose downfall is engineered by a dwarfed hunchback (Cork Hubbert) she takes into her home and the husband (Keith Carradine) she threw out on their wedding night. Directed by Simon Callow, the narrative is slow and portentous, the characters unappealing, and the conclusion heavy-handed and unenlightening. Brutalizing fistfight between the protagonists and minimal rough language. A-III (PG-13)

Baltimore Bullet (1980) Moderately funny comedy about a master pool hustler (James Coburn) who takes on a young protégé (Bruce Boxleitner) in order to fulfill the veteran's dream of getting revenge on the greatest pool sharpster of them all (Omar Sharif). Sexual scenes played in a leering and demeaning manner make this Robert Ellis Miller-directed roadshow with Ronee Blakley unsuitably vulgar. O (PG)

Balto (1995) Uneven animated adventure about an outcast dog (voice of Kevin Bacon) who gets through an Alaskan blizzard in the winter of 1925 with the antitoxin needed to save snowbound Nome from a diphtheria epidemic. Directed by Simon Wells, the animation is more imaginative than the formula characters in a story which starts slowly, then becomes a series of thrills as Balto overcomes the perils of the frozen wilderness and a nasty canine rival. A-I (G)

Bambi (1942) Walt Disney's classic animated feature conveys the simplicity, charm, and excitement of Felix Salten's novel, especially in its appealing characterization of Thumper, Flower, and all the others who inhabit the young deer's forest world. The story has some intense moments, notably the forest-fire sequence and the death of Bambi's mother, though in a context not beyond the resources of most young viewers. A-I (G)

Bamboo Gods and Iron Men (1974) Honeymooning in the Orient, a black American couple (James Iglehart and Shirley Washington) get mixed up with a ruthless gang. The inept Philippine production, clumsily directed by Cesar Gallardo, spices up its dreary martial-arts violence with a massage parlor sequence. O (R)

Bamboo Saucer, The (1968) Thin sci-fi adventure directed by Frank Telford in which a U.S. team (led by Dan Duryea) parachutes into Red China to find a downed flying saucer, but they encounter a Soviet team (including Lois Nettleton) on the same mission and join forces to keep the alien spacecraft from falling into Chinese hands. Stylized violence and hokey menace. A-II (PG)

Bamse (1970) Swedish import about a young man who falls in love with his dead father's mistress, (Grynet Molvig) but she does not reciprocate his affections. The situation is far from being morally or psychologically healthy, but it is handled with restraint and artistic sensitivity. A-III (GP)

Banana Peel (1964) Enjoyable French crime spoof about a gang of con-artists (notably Jeanne Moreau and Jean-Paul Belmondo) trying their best to outswindle each other. Directed by Marcel Ophuls, the plot doesn't add up to much, but it's fast-paced and good-natured. Subtitles. Comic violence and sexual references. A-III (br)

Bananas (1971) Woody Allen's patchwork comedy is loosely tied to a Latin-American revolution, which serves as the excuse for the standard fare of tasteless insult and irreverence, chock-full of gratuitous nonsense dragged in seemingly because there was still a little film in the camera. As those familiar with Allen's approach might expect, religious orthodoxy comes in for its share of ecumenical jibes that many will find needlessly offensive. O (GP/PG-13)

Band of Angels (1957) Crowded Civil War sudser from the Robert Penn Warren novel in which the mulatto daughter (Yvonne De Carlo) of a bankrupt Kentucky aristocrat is sold at auction to a New Orleans cotton millionaire (Clark Gable) with a shady past, who treats her with respect and ultimately wins her love. Directed by Raoul Walsh, the script raises period issues of racial oppression and human rights, but they get lost in the stew of melodramatic action and tawdry characters. Stylized violence, sexual situations, injustices of slavery, and racial epithets. A-III (br)

Band Wagon, The (1953) Classy backstage musical in which a veteran Hollywood hoofer (Fred Astaire) tries to revive his flagging career by starring in a Broadway musical comedy authored by old pals (Nanette Fabray and Oscar Levant), but the production lays an egg after its pretentious director (Jack Buchanan) adds a serious Faustian theme and a temperamental ballet dancer (Cyd Charisse). Director Vincente Minnelli's loving spoof of show business serves up a delightful mix of Howard Dietz-Arthur Schwartz songs, including "That's Entertainment," "Dancing in the Dark," and "I Love Louisa," grand production ensembles ranging from ballet to tap and the show-stopping "Triplets" number with Astaire, Fabray, and Buchanan as manic toddlers. Mild romantic complications. A-II (br)

Bandit Queen (1995) Beaten and raped as a youngster, a low-caste Indian woman (Seema Biswas) joins a gang of thieves, eventually leading them on a murderous rampage against unarmed upper-caste men in 1981 following the murder of her lover. In a fact-based story with no tolerance for love or forgiveness, director Shekhar Kapur presents the title character as a furious feminist heroine, driven to revenge killings but lionized by the lower castes for her insistence on political and social equality. Subtitles. Excessive, bloody violence, including multiple rapes, a massacre, savage beatings, prolonged full nudity, and much rough language. O (nr)

Bandits (1988) Sentimental but stylish French

mystery-romance about an aging criminal (Jean Yanne), his daughter (Marie-Sophie L.), and a handsome, daring young crook (Patrick Bruel). Though Claude LeLouch's direction tends to be slick and glossy, there is some substance to the characters and their feelings. Several scenes of violence, brief nudity, and implied sexual situations. A-III (nr)

Bandolero (1968) Uneven Western starring Jimmy Stewart and Dean Martin as brothers who redeem their shady past in a battle against Mexican bandits. Directed by Andrew V. McLaglen, the characterizations are interesting, women are treated in a positive fashion, and the humor is sly and refreshing. Some vulgar language and violent climax. A-III (G)

Bandwagon (1997) Comic road movie in which four disparate youths (led by Lee Holmes) set out to make a name for their rock 'n roll band by playing gigs all over the South, until a record contract with strings attached threatens to break them up. Writer-director John Schultz uses some low-key, good-natured humor to make the proceedings mildly entertaining despite a thin story line and halting pace. Benign attitude towards theft, implied substance abuse, occasional profanity, and a few uses of rough language. A-III (nr)

Bang Bang Gang, The (1972) Relentlessly brutal, sex-obsessed exploitation movie directed by one Van Guylder, which details the rural escapades of two amateur gangster couples in the 1920s. O (X/R)

Bang, Bang, You're Dead (1966) Standard espionage story directed by Don Sharp in which an American (Tony Randall) gets swept away by romance and intrigue in Morocco. Stylized violence and a bedroom scene. A-III (br)

Bang the Drum Slowly (1973) Director John Hancock's humorous and touching portrait of a young baseball player who wants to play one last season before he dies made Robert De Niro a name to remember. Michael Moriarity co-starred as the best friend who shares his hopes and pains. Realistic but sensitive treatment of terminal illness. A-II (PG)

Bank Detective, The (see: **The Bank Dick**)

Bank Dick, The (1940) Classic W.C. Fields comedy in which he plays a small-town curmudgeon who accidentally foils a bank robbery, is rewarded with the job of bank guard, and winds up being hired to direct a movie. Director Edward Cline backs Fields's brand of eccentric humor with a suitably wacky supporting cast, including Franklin Pangborn as a near-sighted bank examiner, Grady Sutton as a prospective son-in-law, and Shemp Howard as an unflappable bartender. Comic treatment of insobriety. A-II (br)

Bank Robber (1993) Vapid surrealistic tale written and directed by Nick Mead features a moronic bank robber (Patrick Dempsey) hiding out in a seedy hotel room, where he is troubled by real and imaginary visitors. Explicit sex scenes, violence, drug abuse, and rough language. O (NC-17/R)

Bank Shot (1974) George C. Scott plays a safe-cracker sprung from jail in order to use his unique skills to direct a bank robbery. Director Gower Champion's fast-paced comedy is a satire on the criminal mind, but its theme may give youngsters the wrong impression that crime pays. A-III (PG)

Banning (1967) Director Don Winston's story of corruption among the operators and affluent members of a California golf club overdoes the plot elements of vice and greed. O (br)

B.A.P.S. (1997) Clumsy comedy set in Beverly Hills, where two dim young women (Halle Berry and Natalie Desselle) befriend a sickly millionaire (Martin Landau), then are nearly framed for a crime, but end up as wealthy heiresses. Director Robert Townsend's mushy comedy is straight out of the dumb-and-dumber school, though its central characters are likeable lug-heads. Fleeting comic violence, brief toilet humor, and some rough language. A-III (PG-13)

Barabbas (1962) Uneven costume epic follows the tormented path of the criminal (Anthony Quinn) who, after being freed instead of Christ by Pilate, is sentenced to the sulfur mines in Sicily, brought to Rome to be a gladiator (with Jack Palance as grimacing tutor-adversary), and finally crucified as a Christian under Nero. Directed by Richard Fleischer, the movie begins promisingly with a sequence counterpointing Christ and Barabbas, but the religious level gets lost in Quinn's one-note performance as the surly, ever-questioning survivor until reemerging in the ironic conclusion. Stylized violence. A-II (br)

Barb Wire (1996) Cheesy exploitation tale set in 2017, when the USA is wracked by a civil war, which is of no particular consequence to a busy nightclub owner (Pamela Anderson Lee) until the murder of her brother causes her to side with the rebels. Directed by David Hogan, the murky proceedings are transparently ridiculous, especially those in which the dour heroine teases men with her body before blowing them apart with assorted weaponry. Mindless violence, sexual situations, fleeting nudity, profanity, and coarse language. O (R)

Barbados Quest (see: **Murder on Approval**)

Barbarella (1968) French production about the misadventures of a vulnerable earth-woman (Jane Fonda) facing various perils in a science-fiction world, where evil has the upper hand. In a movie which is part comic strip and part Marquis de Sade, director Roger Vadim concentrates on the kinky and the unwholesome in this French production. Sexist theme and brief nudity. O (PG)

Barbarian and the Geisha, The (1958) Arriving in 1856 as the first American consul to Japan, Townsend Harris (a bemused John Wayne) is officially ignored until his efforts to stem a cholera epidemic bring an invitation to the Shogun's court, where he's marked for death by a patriotic nobleman. Directed by John Huston, the beautifully framed but largely static proceedings are a visual treat but lack character interest, especially the flimsy role of the geisha (Eiko Ando) as spy in the consul's household.

Pedestrian clash of cultures in a picturesque setting. A-I (br)

Barbarosa (1982) Country-western singer Willie Nelson plays the title role of a grizzled outlaw who is an unwilling participant in a 30-year old feud with the aristocratic Mexican family into which he married. Gilbert Roland is the patriarch who keeps sending out young men to kill him, and Gary Busey is the young farmer with whom he teams and who ultimately receives Barbarosa's mantle. Offbeat concept, mediocre script, but Nelson's performance is fine. Australian director Frank Schepsi's American debut contains restrained violence. A-II (PG)

Barcelona (1994) An American (Taylor Nichols) based in Barcelona reluctantly takes in an obnoxious cousin (Chris Eigeman) who suddenly turns up, but after becoming involved with two unpredictable local women (Mira Sorvino and Tushka Bergen), the cousins' old antagonisms resurface until resolved when one is nearly killed in a burst of anti-American violence. Writer-director Whit Stillman invests the somewhat bland story with an abundance of droll dialogue, gently mocking the political pretentions and sexual mores of 20-something Americans and Spaniards whose facade of sophistication masks their insecurities. Implied promiscuity, fleeting bedroom scenes, brief violence, and minimal profanity. A-III (PG-13)

Barefoot Executive, The (1971) The title character in this Disney spoof is a chimpanzee with an uncanny taste for quality TV programs. An ambitious office boy (Kurt Russell) uses the talents of his monkey friend to become the boy wonder of network programming. The movie is really stolen by dead-panning Wally Cox and a building-ledge sequence as well-timed and suspenseful as Harold Lloyd's silent comedies. A-I (G)

Barefoot in the Park (1967) Young married couple (Jane Fonda and Robert Redford) live in a five-flight walk-up which leads to a number of amorous mix-ups. Directed by Gene Saks, Neil Simon's adaptation of his own Broadway hit, offers surefire broad comedy with strong supporting cast (Mildred NatWick and Charles Boyer). A-III (br)

Barney's Great Adventure: The Movie (1998) Syrupy children's tale in which the purple dinosaur of the TV series befriends three youngsters as they follow a magical egg through a parade, into a circus, and alongside a gathering of hot-air balloons, with which the children take flight by using their imagination. Directed by Steve Gomer, the colorful musical numbers may amuse preschoolers, but the movie's hokey staging and frequent overacting will not be appreciated by their elders. A-I (G)

Baron Blood (1972) Italian horror movie about an evil medieval baron whose American descendent (Elke Sommer) rejuvenates him to continue his evildoings in the form of an invalid millionaire (Joseph Cotten). Director Mario Bava stresses a fine assortment of torture machines, but the story is a perfectly forgettable bit of nonsense. A-III (PG)

Baron's African War, The (1943) Feature version of a serial directed by Spencer Bennet in which an American secret agent (Rod Cameron) is sent to Casablanca to stop a Nazi spy ring from fomenting an Arab holy war against the Allies. Hokey violence and menace. A-I (br)

Barquero (1970) Uneven Western directed by Gordon Douglas about a ferryman (Lee Van Cleef) who takes on a horde of bandits who want to use and then destroy his barge to delay their pursuers. It proceeds as a battle of wits with some caustic dialogue, amusing characterizations, and occasional violence and sexual references. A-III (GP)

Barren Lives (1969) Brazilian production set in an arid area of the interior, where in 1940 a poor family looks for a place to settle and live like human beings instead of like migrant laborers the world over. Stark and unrelieved, filled with the accusing silence of the destitute, this work by director Nelson Pereira dos Santos visualizes a powerful sermon on social justice and the dignity of the human person. A-II (nr)

Barry Lyndon (1975) Delicate screen adaptation of William Makepeace Thackeray's novel about the manners and morals of 18th-century Europe is pictorially exquisite and has an appropriately elaborate musical score. Director Stanley Kubrick pays more attention to setting and mood than to the human dimensions that are part of its story of an ambitious young man (Ryan O'Neal) trying to rise to social prominence. Mature themes. A-III (PG)

Bartleby (1972) Adaptation of Herman Melville's short novel about a perplexed accountant (Paul Scofield) who can neither get his pallid clerk (John McEnery) to do the work desired, nor can he bring himself to fire him. Director Anthony Friedmann's austere movie is faithful to the spirit, if not the flavor, of the original and the acting is superb. However, the decision to update the period to the present can only be labeled an interesting failure. A-II (nr)

Barton Fink (1991) Lured to Hollywood by a fast-talking studio boss (Michael Lerner), a promising playwright (John Turturro) suffers writer's block until his beefy next-door neighbor (John Goodman) provides unexpected inspiration. The writing-directing team of Joel and Ethan Cohn have produced a dark satire and stylish evocation of Tinseltown in the 1940s that eventually falters with its morbid imagery. Some gory violence, discreet sexual innuendo, and minimal rough language. A-III (R)

Baseketball (1998) Comic misfire about a couple of lame-brained louts (Trey Parker and Matt Stone) who concoct a game combining baseball and basketball, which a mindless millionaire (Ernest Borgnine) turns into a national pastime, with the dim-witted pair as its beloved heroes. Directed by David Zucker, the movie starts as a satire of professional sports but quickly turns into little more than a tiresome exercise in bad taste. Crude sexual humor, brief rear nudity, much sophomoric vul-

nt rough language, and some profan-

(1992) Violent and sordid potboiler micide detective (Michael Douglas) d in an affair with a bisexual mur- on Stone), who throws suspicion ychiatrist girlfriend (Jeanne ected by Paul Verhoeven, this cat- s an empty exercise in audience ng graphic scenes of rough sex Exploitative mix of sex and vio- risly killings, and frequent rough

986) This totally offensive sex- ical satire has the look and sense , X-rated home videocassette. O

sketball Diaries, The (1995) Basketball star (Leonardo DiCaprio) in a Manhattan Catholic high school turns to crime with two buddies (Mark Wahlberg and James Madio) when he gets hooked on heroin, ending up in prison, where he mulls going straight. Directed by Scott Kalvert, the raw anti-drug tale graphically illustrates how drugs bankrupt body and soul, but the last-minute redemptive ending is weakly delivered, and the Catholic background is depicted mainly in negative stereotypes. Brief violence, graphic scenes of drug abuse and criminal activity, several sexual encounters, fleeting nudity, and continuous rough language. A-IV (R)

Basquiat (1996) Hollow dramatization of the short career of Jean-Michel Basquiat (Jeffrey Wright), a black graffiti artist in New York City who achieved international fame as a self-taught painter before dying from a drug overdose in 1988 at the age of 27. Written and directed by Julian Schnabel, the episodic script develops little emotional involvement in the character and lacks insight into his work or the bohemian art group which brought him fame. Frequent scenes of drug abuse, implied sexual encounters, profanity, and rough language. A-IV (R)

Bastard Out of Carolina (1996) Harrowing tale of domestic violence set in 1950's South Carolina, where a little girl is mercilessly beaten and eventually raped by her unstable stepfather (Ron Eldard), despite the efforts of her mom (Jennifer Jason Leigh) to protect her. Directed by actress Anjelica Huston, the disjointed narrative is relentlessly realistic in depicting the recurring violence to the child as well as the squalid working-class poverty of her relatives, but the result adds nothing new to the tragic topic of child abuse. Graphic violence, including a rape scene, and sexual references. A-IV (R)

Bat, The (1959) Modest thriller from the Mary Roberts Rinehart story of a mystery writer (Agnes Moorehead) vacationing in a spooky old mansion while the police hunt a missing fortune and a killer dressed as a bat. Directed by Crane Wilbur, the melodramatic proceedings creak along with the usual red herrings and obvious suspects (including Vincent Price), but it adds up to considerable fun for those in the mood. Mild menace and stylized violence. A-II (br)

Bat People (see: **It Lives by Night**)

Bat 21 (1988) Suspenseful, fact-based story of a high-level intelligence officer (Gene Hackman) who is shot down in the jungles of Vietnam and, lacking firsthand experience with combat survival skills, has to rely upon radio contact witn a spotter pilot (Danny Glover) who keeps him going until rescued. Compassionate interracial characterizations by Hackman and Glover, and crisp direction by Peter Markle make it one of the better films about Vietnam heroics. Intense but non-gratuitous fire-bombings and individual killings. Some locker-room language. A-III (R)

Bataan (1943) WWII melodrama about the battle for the Bataan peninsula, where a small group of American soldiers (including Robert Taylor, George Murphy, Thomas Mitchell, and Lloyd Nolan) die one by one holding a position against overwhelming enemy forces. Directed by Tay Garnett, the doomed squad is a composite of melting-pot America whose patriotic fervor turns defeat into a moral victory badly needed on the home-front then, and of some historical interest today. Much wartime violence and anti-Japanese stereotyping. A-II (br)

Bathing Beauty (1944) Slapdash musical comedy directed by George Sidney with Harry James, Xavier Cugat, and their orchestras trying to pick up the slack in the silly story of a songwriter (Red Skelton) enrolling in a woman's college in order to win back his estranged wife (Esther Williams), who's a teacher there. Romantic complications. A-II (br)

Batman (1966) Movie version of the TV series based on the comic-book characters of the Masked Marvel (Adam West) and the Boy Wonder (Burt Ward) has them battling a plot against the United Nations. Directed by Leslie H. Martinson. The very young will find the action exciting and those over 12 may be amused by the movie's consciously heavy-handed tongue-in-cheek treatment of events. A-I (br)

Batman (1989) Dark, haunting vision of the caped crusader (Michael Keaton) who must battle not only the evil Joker (Jack Nicholson) but the demons left over from his own tragic childhood. Director Tim Burton does not make the eternal fight between good and evil an easy one, but virtuoso performances by the leads and Anton Furst's production design of a Gotham City full of shadowy gothic and modernistic spires make the movie noteworthy. Some grisly comic-book violence and a suggested sexual encounter are too intense for preteens and impressionable younger adolescents. A-III (PG-13)

Batman & Robin (1997) Empty spectacle marks the fourth entry in the series, as Batman (George Clooney), Robin (Chris O'Donnell), and Batgirl (Alicia Sliverstone) tangle with deadly seductress Poison Ivy (Uma Thurman) while trying to save Gotham and its residents from being fast-frozen by demented scientist Mr. Freeze (Arnold Schwarzenegger). Directed by Joel Schumacher, it's an elaborate live-action cartoon, with villains who are somewhat more interesting than the bland superheroes, but the movie sags in between the visually frantic action sequences. Much cartoon-like violence and some sexual innuendo. A-II (PG-13)

Batman Forever (1995) Frenetic sequel with Batman (Val Kilmer) distracted by a sultry psychologist (Nicole Kidman) and a vengeance-crazed Robin (Chris O'Donnell) while battling two lunatics (Tommy Lee Jones and Jim Carrey) out to destroy the Caped Crusader. Director Joel Schumacher's dark comic fantasy has little narrative interest, relying instead on violent special effects, sleek visuals, and exaggerated performances by the two villains. Recurring stylized violence and brief sexual innuendo. A-III (PG-13)

Batman: Mask of the Phantasm (1993) Murky animated movie in which Batman tries to revive a failed romance while chasing after whoever is murdering Gotham gangsters dressed in a Batman-like outfit. Directors Eric Radomski and Bruce W. Timm exhibit a sleek visual style throughout, but the story line is too cluttered, confusing, and menacing for young children, while not sophisticated enough for parents. Frequent stylized violence. A-II PG

Batman Returns (1992) Bigger isn't better in this overproduced sequel in which Batman (Michael Keaton) must save crumbling Gotham City and himself from the fiendish Penguin (Danny DeVito), a schizophrenic Catwoman (Michelle Pfeiffer), and a power-crazed industrialist (Christopher Walken). Director Tim Burton leaves out the human element of the story in his zeal for mind-boggling mayhem that offers much sound and fury, but only signifies the shallowness of Hollywood's interpretation of pop culture. Much stylized violence, some of it quite nasty, and occasionally blatant sexual innuendoes. A-III (PG-13)

Batteries Not Included (1987) Failed fantasy about a group of tenement dwellers, headed by an old couple (Jessica Tandy and Hume Cronyn), who are being terrorized by thugs in the pay of a greedy real-estate developer until two miniature spaceships come to their rescue. Directed by Matthew Robbins, the alien reproducing metal-works are cute and there are some whimsical special effects, but the fantasy level of this urban melodrama never gets very far off the ground. Some scenes of intense menace and realistic violence. A-II (PG)

Battle Beneath the Earth (1968) Low-budget adventure fantasy directed by Montgomery Tully in which maverick Chinese Reds, undermining the United States with a network of tunnels containing atomic bombs, are stopped by a unit of Marines led by Kerwin Mathews. Stylized violence. A-II (br)

Battle Beyond the Stars (1980) Young volunteer Richard Thomas goes on a hunt to hire mercenaries to defend a planet threatened with conquest by an intergalactic tyrant. Scripted by John Sayles and directed by Jimmy T. Murakami with some style and humor, it is a moderately entertaining science-fiction action fantasy. Many sexually oriented jokes. A-III (PG)

Battle Command (1976) Old-fashioned war movie of uncertain origin — all the soldiers seem to be Italian no matter what their uniforms — done on a limited budget and with an appalling lack of skill. A-II (PG)

Battle Cry (1955) Hokey WWII sudser from the Leon Uris novel follows a Marine battalion from boot camp to combat, though most of the plot concerns a recruit (Tab Hunter) in a hopeless affair with an officer's wife (Dorothy Malone), and the reformation of his womanizing buddy (Aldo Ray) by a New Zealand war widow (Nancy Olson). Director Raoul Walsh sets the wartime scene convincingly enough, but its contrived romances and cardboard characters never rise beyond bad melodrama. Wartime violence, sexual situations, and an unwed pregnancy. A-III (br)

Battle for Anzio, The (see: **Anzio**)

Battle for the Planet of the Apes (1973) Final sequel to the series with Roddy McDowell heading up the ape cast and John Huston as a campy sort of simian Moses. Directed by J.Lee Thompson, the most entertaining sequences are excerpts from the previous movies used as the background of the story. A-II (G)

Battle Hymn (1957) Fact-based story of Col. Dean Hess, the "flying parson," who returns to service during the Korean War, takes command of a squadron of inexperienced fighter pilots, and starts an orphanage for the area's displaced children. Directed by Douglas Sirk, the dramatization will strike some as overly idealistic, though Rock Hudson gives a credible performance as the dedicated minister willing to fight for a just cause, yet troubled in conscience by the need for killing. Wartime violence. A-I (br)

Battle in Outer Space (1960) Aliens use the moon for an attack on Earth in this Japanese sci-fi clunker directed by Inoshiro Honda. The stoic heroics of the dubbed characters, cheesy model work, and cardboard special effects offer little excitement or interest. A-I (br)

Battle of Algiers, The (1967) The 1954-58 Algerian struggle for independence from French rule is re-created in this French production directed by Gillo Pontecorvo. Sympathetic to the rebels, yet compromising neither the facts nor the personalities involved, the film's documentary-like authenticity is achieved without resort to actual newsreel footage. It is a remarkable look at the process of revolutionary terror and counter-terror that victimizes ordinary citizens on both sides. Subtitles. Stylized violence. A-II (br)

Battle of Britain (1969) With the fall of France in 1940, Great Britain stood alone against the might of the German air force. The movie pays tribute to the smaller number of British fighter pilots who, in the months that followed, downed so many planes that the Luftwaffe was unable to mount its massive raids. Laurence Olivier, Michael Redgrave, and Trevor

Howard star in this huge and impressive British production directed by Guy Hamilton. Wartime violence. A-I (G)

Battle of Chile, The (1978) Documentary on the 1973 overthrow of the Allende government, it shows in painstaking detail the growing agony of a society on the verge of civil war and the inevitable brutal usurpation of power by the military. Assembled from footage smuggled out of Chile and edited in Cuba under the direction of Patricio Guzman, it is a partisan account, but one does not have to accept its Marxist politics in examining for oneself the visual record of events showing how the elected government of a constitutional democracy was subverted and overthrown. Some violent actualities. A-III (nr)

Battle of El Alamein, The (1971) Italian-French shoot-'em-up WWII movie seen from the Axis point-of-view, in which Rommel (Robert Hossein) loses to the superior British forces of Field Marshall Montgomery (Michael Rennie). Directed by Calvin Jackson, it's not strong on characterization, but it does have a sturdy string of exciting battle sequences. A-II (GP)

Battle of Neretva (1971) Yugoslavian production about the 1943 victory of Tito's Partisans over the German Army re-creates the horror of a ferocious battle, and is a tribute to their sacrifices enacted by a large international cast. Directed by Veljko Bulajic, the work is developed with little dramatic punctuation and evokes only mild sympathy and audience identification with the events it portrays. A-II (G)

Battle of Okinawa (1973) Japanese re-creation of the ferocious, last-ditch defense of the island of Okinawa by its undermanned garrison. Directed by Kihachi Okamoto, it has a semi-documentary objectivity that distances viewers from the considerable amount of special effects battle gore and mass suicide by part of the civilian population. A-II (nr)

Battle of Powder River (see: **Tomahawk**)

Battle of Rogue River (1954) Western clunker directed by William Castle is set in 1850's Oregon, where an Army officer (George Montgomery) averts an Indian war by nabbing the frontiersman (Richard Denning) who's been stirring up all the trouble. Stylized violence. A-I (br)

Battle of the Bulge (1965) Henry Fonda, Robert Shaw, and Robert Ryan star in a big-budget re-creation of the last, desperate German offensive against American forces in December 1944. In an ambitious, wide-ranging epic, director Ken Annakin tries to turn one of the most brutal battles of WWII into star-studded entertainment. Wartime violence. A-I (nr)

Battle of the Coral Sea (1959) Captured while gathering intelligence on the Japanese fleet, a US submarine captain (Cliff Robertson) escapes with his crew in time to help win the decisive 1942 naval battle of the title. Directed by Paul Wendkos, the main part of the narrative takes place in a P.O.W. camp, where the heroics are standard issue and the acting perfunctory. Some stylized violence and Japanese stereotyping. A-I (br)

Battle of the Worlds (1961) Dubbed Italian production directed by Anthony Dawson provides limp sci-fi thrills as Earth is threatened by an alien planet, which the military seek to vaporize before a cantankerous scientist (Claude Rains) can learn its secrets. Unconvincing models in space battles, mild tension, and weak romance. A-II (br)

Battleground (1949) Centering on the dogged resistance of an American infantry unit cut off in the Battle of the Bulge — Hitler's last desperate offensive in the West — the movie makes the most of its cross-section of GIs (Van Johnson, John Hodiak, Ricardo Montalban, James Whitmore, George Murphy, et. al.) as representative of the nation's ethnic, regional, and social diversity. Veteran director William Wellman keeps the action taut and credible, uses the battlefield's snow-filled terrain to add further misery to the unit's plight, and tries to keep his grab-bag collection of civilian-soldiers from turning into superheroes. Wartime violence and mild sexual references. A-I (br)

Battlestar Galactica (1979) A fleet of survivors of an alien attack travel through deep space in search of a refuge they call Earth. Lorne Greene is at the helm of the flagship avoiding the dreaded Cylons in this compilation of episodes from the television series. As directed by Richard A. Colla, the only peril is its worshipful portrayal of the military in contrast to a foolish civil government. A-I (PG)

Bawdy Adventures of Tom Jones, The (1976) Dull and unimaginative adaptation of a stage musical based on the Henry Fielding novel. More boring than bawdy, director Cliff Owens has made a sexual burlesque of the original, with much sexual innuendo and some partial nudity. O (R)

Baxter! (1973) British story of a London youngster with a speech defect (Scott Jacoby) who is crushed when his parents ignore his limited speech improvement, but his speech therapist (Patricia Neal) stands by him. Director Lionel Jefferies treats his sentimental melodrama with crisp dispatch, some gentle humor, and fine performances. It's a bit too serious for children, but others may find it quite rewarding entertainment. A-II (PG)

Be Yourself! (1930) Sappy musical romance in which a nightclub singer (Fanny Brice) turns a pug (Robert Armstrong) she's sweet on into a boxing champ, then helps the ex-champ defeat him when he takes up with a gold digger (Gertrude Astor). Directed by Thornton Freeland, it's a vehicle for Brice to show off her talents as singer, comedienne, and actress, though little else in this creaky melodrama is memorable. Some racy dialogue and sexual implications. A-III (br)

Beach Blanket Bingo (1965) Dated youth comedy in which California beach pals (Frankie Avalon and Annette Funicello) get involved with a smirky agent (Paul Lynde), whose publicity stunts for a new singer

(Linda Evans) end in her being kidnapped by a wacky biker (Harvey Lembeck). Directed by William Asher, the nonsensical story treads water with occasional songs, surfing, and skydiving sequences, a shy mermaid (Marta Kristen), and a hapless comic foil (Buster Keaton). Slick but empty merriment. A-II (br)

Beach Party (1963) Sun-baked youth comedy in which an ogling anthropologist (Bob Cummings) rents a California beach house to study the mating rituals of a pack of youthful surfers, then gets involved with one of them (Annette Funicello) to the dismay of her boyfriend (Frankie Avalon) and the researcher's faithful assistant (Dorothy Malone). Directed by William Asher, the banal proceedings are paced by surfing interludes, forgettable songs, bikini-clad dancers, and occasional brawls. Slapstick violence, sexual situations, and much sexual innuendo. A-III (br)

Beach Red (1967) Directed by and starring Cornel Wilde, the movie attempts to explore the inhumanity of war in the story of a WWII assault on a Pacific island, but it fails by its repetitious emphasis on the realistic details of carnage and its degrading treatment of women in flashbacks. O (br)

Beachcomber, The (1938) Droll romantic comedy from the Somerset Maugham tale of an English reprobate (Charles Laughton) carousing in the Dutch East Indies until reformed by the shrewish sister (Elsa Lanchester) of a missionary (Tyrone Guthrie), who herself is changed in the process. Producer-director Erich Pommer mixes narrative, character, and locale in wry fashion, abetted by the whimsical observations of the colonial governor (Robert Newton), but the real fun is the battle royal between the two principals. Comic treatment of human weaknesses and puritanical compunctions. A-II (br)

Beaches (1988) The ups and downs of the 30-year friendship between a California blueblood (Barbara Hershey) and a Jewish singer-dancer from the Bronx (Bette Midler) are tracked through rites of passage, life crises, petty jealousies, and ultimate tragedy. Director Garry Marshall's positive portrait of a committed friendship overcomes the story's weepy moments with many comedic and rousing musical sequences, but gets a tad too sudsy during the poignant climax. Some off-color language and vulgar humor, brief fisticuffs, and a risqué musical number. A-III (PG-13)

Beachhead (1954) Routine WWII adventure as Marines (Tony Curtis, Frank Lovejoy, and Skip Homeier) search a Pacific island for a French planter (Eduard Franz) and his daughter (Mary Murphy) to get information on Japanese forces in the area. Director Stuart Heisler stages the jungle action adequately, but the characters are cardboard and Curtis's heroics less than convincing. Stylized violence and mild sexual innunedo. A-II (br)

Bean (1997) Puerile comedy in which British comic Rowan Atkinson plays a bumbling British museum guard entrusted to deliver a priceless painting to a Los Angeles gallery — with predictable results. Directed by Mel Smith, the slapstick antics of Atkinson's nearly wordless character occasionally amuse, but usually fall flat. Brief drunkenness, nude pin-up photo, some toilet humor, and a streak of profanity. A-III (PG-13)

Bear, The (1989) Glorious nature drama set in turn-of-the-century British Columbia tracks the unlikely companionship of a wounded male Kodiak bear and an orphaned cub as they explore their natural habitat and fend off two relentless human predators. Director Jean-Jacques Annaud dramatizes the story from the bears' point of view, using impressive wildlife photography to connect these majestic animals to humans in astounding and unforgettable ways. Some bloodied dogs and horses, ongoing menace to the bears, and a realistically audible mating sequence may be too intense for very young children. A-I (PG)

Bear and the Doll, The (1971) Rather flat French farce about a radio cellist (Jean-Pierre Cassel) preoccupied with providing for a young son and four nieces and apparently the only man in France not willing to fall instantly at Brigitte Bardot's adorable feet. Directed by Michele Deville. There are some amusing moments in this adult comedy, but the two principals seem impossibly mismatched. A-III (GP)

Bear Tooth (1978) Settling into a backwoods cabin, a garrulous old codger (Dub Taylor) and a stray dog spend the winter in director Zack Belcher's low-budget production, which has little of interest except the Montana scenery. The result is often pretty to look at but lacks any human depth. A-I (G)

Bears and I, The (1974) A Vietnam veteran (Patrick Wayne) trying to find peace on a remote Indian reservation unknowingly breaks a tribal taboo when he starts raising three bear cubs whose mother has been killed by a poacher. Disney outdoor adventure directed by Vincent McEveety should please the younger set with its wilderness background and the cute antics of the baby cubs. A-I (G)

Beast, The (1988) Set in 1981 Afghanistan, the story begins with the brutal destruction of a village by a squadron of Soviet tanks, then follows its aftermath in which a lone, lost tank is stalked by Afghan rebels. Directed by Kevin Reynolds, the gruesome opening massacre is eventually counterpointed with philosophical and psychological conflicts, mainly between the heartless tank commander (George Dzundza) and a young tank driver (Jason Patric) who empathizes with the brutalized Afghans. Extremely graphic violence. A-IV (R)

Beast, The (1996) Formula marine thriller in which a hungry giant squid threatens an island resort's inhabitants and property values until a local fisherman (William Petersen) takes on the monster from the deep, while romancing a feminist Coast Guard officer (Karen Sillas). Directed by Jeff Bleckner from the Peter Benchley novel, the television production offers a cast of underdeveloped characters and an overdeveloped sea beast whose tentacles and beady eyes fail to arouse the same kind of fright as do the jaws of a shark. Stylized violence, menacing situations, and sexual innuendo. A-III (PG-13)

Beast in the Cellar, The (1971) Pair of dotty spinsters (Beryl Reid and Flora Robson) brick up their draft-age brother in the cellar rather than see him sent off to the Western Front. Director James Kelly's horror movie has its scary moments, but far too much is given over to the doting sisters trying to rationalize their past errors in rearing their now-mad sibling. Sordid seduction-murder scene. A-III (R)

Beast Must Die, The (1974) British thriller in which a millionaire (Calvin Lockhart) invites some guests (Peter Cushing, Tom Chadbon, Michael Bambon) to spend a weekend at his remote country estate, where everything is wired for sight and sound because the host knows that one of them will turn into a beast when the moon is full. Directed by Paul Annett, the updated werewolf tale offers some novelty and a fair amount of trumped-up horror and gore for fans of this kind thing. A-III (PG)

Beast of Blood (1970) Philippine horror movie in which a scientist (John Ashley), searching Blood Island for the crazed creature that shipwrecked him, discovers a mad surgeon (Eddie Garcia) experimenting on human head transplants. Directed by Eddie Romero, the spurting blood, slicing blades, and a rape scene will upset the squeamish. O (GP)

Beast of Hollow Mountain, The (1956) An American (Guy Madison) ranching in Mexico faces dastardly rustlers and a special-effects dinosaur. Directed by Edward Nassour and Ismael Rodriguez, the routine Western story is of little interest until the proceedings perk up with a prehistoric monster in a fantasy ending. Mild thrills for preschoolers. A-I (br)

Beast with Five Fingers, The (1946) Minor horror movie set in the Italian villa of a famous pianist (Victor Francen) whose sudden death brings terror after his sinister secretary (Peter Lorre) reports seeing the dead man's severed hand scuttling about, though the local police chief (J. Carrol Naish) is unconvinced. Directed by Robert Florey, the story's eerie atmosphere is sustained by Lorre's maniacal performance and fearsome visuals of the antic hand. Scenes of menace and suggestions of the occult, but rational explanations are never far away. A-II (br)

Beat, The (1988) Grim inner-city drama about some drugged-up aimless teens, who take a turn for the better when they befriend a weird new boy (David Jacobson) who slinks around reciting poetry. They all become poets and are drawn into the boy's mystical fantasy world. Director-writer Paul Mones provides no background on these derelict kids, and no explanation for the boy's spacey behavior. Wall-to-wall profanity, much violence, and a clear suggestion of teen sexual promiscuity. O (R)

Beat Street (1984) Skimpy plot involving the aspirations of young blacks and Hispanics in the Bronx loosely holds together a series of production numbers, many of which involve break dancing. Director Stan Lathan's lavish production fails because of its pretension and high gloss. Some rough language now and again, but the movie is innocuous for the most part. A-II (PG)

Beau Geste (1926) Silent adventure classic from Percival Christopher Wren's novel in which the title Englishman (Ronald Colman) enlists in the French Foreign Legion after a fabulous family gem disappears, then is joined by his brothers (Neil Hamilton and Ralph Forbes) in battling rebellious Arabs as well as a villainous sergeant (Noah Beery), until the two brothers return home for the truth about the missing gem. Directed by Herbert Brenon, the story revolves around deeds of loyalty, comradeship, and honor, with visually striking action scenes, the most memorable being the Viking's funeral in a Saharan fort manned by Legionnaire corpses. Stylized violence. A-I (br)

Beau Geste (1939) Dandy adventure classic from the P.C. Wren story about three brothers, two of whom (Ray Milland and Robert Preston) follow the eldest (Gary Cooper) into the French Foreign Legion, where they wind up in a Saharan outpost besieged by rebel Arabs and commanded by a sadistic sergeant (Brian Donlevy). Directed by William Wellman, this remake of the 1926 original retains the visual gusto of the silent's action scenes while getting strong performances from a fine cast, making the talkie version a success in its own right. Stylized violence. A-I (br)

Beau Geste (1966) The French Foreign Legion becomes the refuge for two English brothers (Dean Stockwell and Doug McClure) after the apparent theft of a family jewel worth a fortune. Well-done remake of classic adventure story, the movie is restrained in its treatment of military brutality and the violence inherent to a desert uprising. A-I (br)

Beau Ideal (1931) Weak sequel to **Beau Geste** shows how an American friend (Lester Vail) joins the French Foreign Legion to rescue the youngest Geste brother (Ralph Forbes) from a Legion penal battalion, then both get caught in the middle of an Arab uprising. Director Herbert Brenon's well-staged sequences of action in the desert can't rescue the dated adventure from the stilted acting style of the early talkies. Stylized violence and some silly romantic complications. A-II (br)

Beaumarchais, the Scoundrel (1997) Elaborate historical romp recounts the romantic and political exploits of the rakish 18th-century playwright (Fabrice Luchini) who, in addition to being jailed for ridiculing the French aristocracy, was an inventor, a magistrate, a spy, and a gun runner for American revolutionaries. Director Edouard Molinari's giddy approach to the title character's busy life unreels as a series of breathless misadventures without revealing much of Beaumarchais's character or motivations. Subtitles. Some sexual innuendo, fleeting nudity, and an instance of rough language. A-III (nr)

Beautician and the Beast, The (1997) Inane romantic comedy with TV sitcom star Fran Drescher as a brassy New York cosmetician mistakenly hired to tutor the children of an Eastern European leader (played by Timothy Dalton), with predictable results. Directed by Ken Kwapis, the lightweight proceedings are generally mirthless and depend entirely on one's tolerance for the star's nasal voice and abrasive manner. Some sexual innuendo. A-II (PG)

Beautiful Blonde from Bashful Bend, The (1949) Western farce in which a saloon singer (Betty Grable) skips town after shooting a judge (Porter Hall) instead of her two-timing lover (Cesar Romero), then is mistaken for the new schoolmarm in a mining town whose leading citizen (Rudy Vallee) woos her until learning of her past. Writer-director Preston Sturges turns the plot into a shambles of eccentric characters and slapstick action, some of it very funny, but most of the gags are overdone and rather witless. Comic violence, romantic complications, and sexual innuendo. A-III (br)

Beautiful Girls (1996) Returning to his Massachusetts hometown for a high-school reunion, a musician (Timothy Hutton) about to turn 30 compares notes with his buddies about girlfriends and the scary prospect of settling down. Director Ted Demme's relationship movie takes a sweetly comical look at young men trying to come to terms with adult responsibilities and the women who love them. Several sexual references about affairs, brief violence, and recurring rough language. A-III (R)

Beautiful Stranger (see: **Twist of Fate**)

Beauty and the Beast (1962) Tiresomely drawn-out fantasy set in medieval Italy, where a sorcerer's curse transforms a young duke (Mark Damon) into a beast by night, until the spell is broken by the true love of a count's daughter (Joyce Taylor). Director Edward L. Cahn's pedestrian treatment lacks imagination and the result has little to offer viewers of any age. A-I (br)

Beauty and the Beast (1991) Enchanting animated fairytale of a young maiden who rescues her father from a ferocious beast only to fall in love with the creature's gentler qualities. Computer graphics enhance classic Disney animation for eye-pleasing visuals enlivened by rousing musical numbers and delightful characterizations from directors Kirk Wise and Gary Trousdale. Brief scary scenes. A-I (G)

Beavis and Butt-head Do America (1996) Tiresomely crude comedy featuring two teenage cartoon cretins in a cross-country pursuit of illusory sex and toilet facilities. Directed by Mike Judge, the animation is appropriately as primitive as the humor. Adolescent obsession with sexual and scatological references, incessant coarse language, and occasional profanity. A-IV (PG-13)

Bebe's Kids (1992) Dull animated tale in which three bratty kids harass their babysitter (voice of Vanessa Bell Calloway), her little boy, and, most of all, her boyfriend (voice of Faizon Love), who is forced to take them all to an amusement park. Under Bruce Smith's direction, the African-American characters created by Robin Harris have plenty of sass and brass, but neither the story's treatment nor the animation shines. Comic violence and mild sexual innuendo. A-II (PG-13)

Because of You (1952) Sappy sudser directed by Joseph Pevney in which a woman (Loretta Young) loses both husband (Jeff Chandler) and young daughter when he discovers her secret criminal past, but she regains them after a stint as a magician's assistant. Hokey domestic misunderstandings. A-II (br)

Becoming Colette (1992) Dull, plodding picture of the French author Colette (Mathilda May) during her formative years in Paris at the turn of the century married to a hedonistic bounder (Klaus Maria Brandauer), who publishes her writings under his name until she leaves him to embark on her own career. Director Danny Huston turns an interesting subject into a lethargic object lesson in women's rights. Several depictions of sexual encounters with brief nudity. O (R)

Bed and Board (1971) Continuing French saga of Antoine Doinel (Jean-Pierre-Leaud) who, still somewhat delinquent and fumbling, marries his sweetheart (Claude Jade) and gets through the first year of marital adjustment: a change of jobs, the coming of their first child, and a test of conjugal fidelity. Director Francois Truffaut has etched a sensitive, compassionate, humorous, and exquisitely tasteful picture of the maturation of love and marriage. Whether one has seen the previous two films in the trilogy or not, this will delight, amuse, and captivate the imagination. A-III (GP)

Bed of Roses (1996) Frail drama in which an emotionally insecure investment banker (Mary Stuart Masterson) has difficulty accepting the unconditional love of a florist (Christian Slater) who wants to marry her. Writer-director Michael Goldenberg's sweet-natured but flimsy romance is so sketchy in its characterization of the young lovers they seem to just fade away in the story's limp conclusion. Implied live-in relationship. A-III (PG)

Bed-Sitting Room, The (1969) Three years after WWIII, which took place in less then two-and-a-half minutes, 20-odd survivors wander around the bizarre remains of London, including such grotesques as Sir Ralph Richardson turning, quite literally, into a bed-sitting room. Director Richard Lester's screen version of playwright Spike Milligan's surrealistic farce is meant to be a commentary on the horrors of war and middle-class morality, but the result is merely a disappointing jumble of British wit and rude humor. A-III (M)

Bedazzled (1968) A shy short-order cook (Dudley Moore) in love with a waitress (Eleanor Moore) sells his soul to a satanic figure (Peter Cook) for seven wishes, which turn out hilariously different from what was intended. Director Stanley Donen has reshaped the Faust legend to the cut of contemporary man, though the lust sequence gets a bit too sinful, and another satirizing the image of nuns may seem more distasteful than funny. A-IV (br)

Bedford Incident, The (1965) An American destroyer and a nuclear-armed Soviet submarine are on a collision course that, unless one of them yields, will cause an international incident. Director James Hill builds the psychological tension on board the destroyer as its cold-warrior captain (Richard Widmark) comes into conflict with an inquisitive journalist (Sidney Poitier) and others on deck (Martin Balsam, Eric Portman, and Wally Cox). Heavy seas for youngsters. A-II (br)

Bedknobs and Broomsticks (1971) In an English seaside village during WWII, a would-be witch (Angela Lansbury) invokes an army of spectral warriors to rout 20th-century German invaders and takes some trips with three children on her big brass bed. Director Robert Stevenson keeps this Disney musical moving merrily and emphasizes the smiling high spirits of the youngsters. A-I (G)

Bedlam (1946) Dark tale of London's infamous 18th-century insane asylum to which a sane woman (Anna Lee) is committed in order to silence her criticism of its head keeper (Boris Karloff). Produced by Val Lewton and directed by Mark Robson, the asylum's terrors are only suggested, but they work powerfully enough in the imagination to make credible the woman's plight and the viewer's fears. Menacing atmosphere and some brutality. A-II (br)

Bedroom Window, The (1987) Steve Guttenberg plays a young, carefree executive whose affair with his boss's wife (Isabelle Huppert) ends in her death when a killer-rapist they tried to bring to justice is freed. Directed by Curtis Hanson, the engaging, though convoluted, plot deals with themes of dishonesty and betrayal, and the treatment includes brief instances of violence, nudity, and profanity. A-III (R)

Bedtime for Bonzo (1951) Silly situation comedy in which a college psychology professor (Ronald Reagan) tries to prove the importance of environment over heredity by raising a chimp in his bachelor digs while employing a 22-year-old babysitter (Diana Lynn) as stand-in for the monkey's mama. Director Frederick de Cordova plays the premise straight, but employs the cast mainly as foils for cutesy monkey business, convoluted misunderstandings, and slapstick complications. A-I (br)

Bedtime Story (1964) Leaden sex comedy in which a womanizing Army corporal (Marlon Brando) meets a phony prince (David Niven) who preys on rich women, then the two compete in wooing an American (Shirley Jones), who they think is an heiress. Directed by Ralph Levy, the lackluster proceedings are brightened by the French Riviera setting, but the humor is less than sophisticated and Brando sadly lacks Niven's comic flair. Sexual situations and innuendo. A-III (br)

Been Down So Long It Looks Like Up to Me (1971) Episodic melodrama directed by Jeff Young about a college drop-out (Barry Primus) who, disenchanted by his odyssey in the real world, returns to college to mock everything it stands for, take drugs, and have sex. It's a bad trip. O (R)

Beethoven (1992) Slap-happy comedy about a fussy father (Charles Grodin) forced to accept a stray St. Bernard into the family, then has to rescue it from the snatches of dog-nappers and a mad doctor (Dean Jones). Director Brian Levant delivers a likeable, though strictly formula family entertainment. Some strong menace and comic violence. A-II (PG)

Beethoven's Nephew (1988) After winning custody of his teenage nephew (Dietmar Prinz), the composer Beethoven (Wolfgang Reichmann) monitors the boy's every move for 11 years. Director Paul Morrissey's fact-based story suggests more a jealous lover's obsession than extreme parental behavior on Beethoven's part, but these implications are never explored. Some nudity in several heterosexual situations, one of an explicit nature, and a graphic suicide attempt. O (R)

Beethoven's 2nd (1993) Highly contrived canine comedy in which the Newton family dog, Beethoven, and a neighboring St. Bernard have four puppies, which the Newton children try to hide from dear old dad (Charles Grodin) and a wicked dog-napper (Debi Mazur). Rod Daniel directs a cartoon-like sequel peopled with cardboard characters cavorting around the movie's chief attraction, a quartet of adorable puppies. Some menace, adolescent beer drinking, and violence played for laughs. A-II (PG)

Beetlejuice (1988) Good special effects overshadow a silly plot in which a couple of dim-witted ghosts (Alec Baldwin and Geena Davis) reluctantly use the services of a ghoulish demon (Michael Keaton) to scare off the eccentric family who have moved into the ghosts' picturesque New England home. Director Tim Burton's comic fantasy is loud and on the dippy side, with only Keaton's manic performance to maintain interest. Some vulgar language and bloody special effects. A-II (PG)

Before and After (1996) Fearing their missing teenage son (Edward Furlong) has killed his girlfriend, the boy's father (Liam Neeson) destroys all physical evidence of the crime, while his mother (Meryl Streep) struggles with her conscience over this obstruction of justice. After setting up initial uncertainty about the boy's guilt, director Barbet Schroeder concentrates on the emotional drama of a family nearly torn asunder by moral conflicts. Sexual references, fleeting violence, and some profanity. A-III (PG-13)

Before Sunrise (1995) The day before his flight back to the States, a young American tourist (Ethan Hawke) on board a Vienna-bound train meets a vivacious Sorbonne student (Julie Delpy) and persuades her to explore the city with him while seeking to discover if their mutual attraction could blossom into love. Director Richard Linklater fitfully captures typical 20-something yearnings through the extended conversations of two strangers searching for a meaningful relationship in an often uncaring world. An implied sexual encounter and occasional rough language. A-III (R)

Before the Rain (1995) Intertwining tales of doomed love begin in contemporary Macedonia, where a young monk (Gregoire Colin) is dismissed for hiding an Albanian refugee (Labina Mitevska), then turn to the monk's uncle (Rade Serbedzija), who leaves London career and married mistress (Katrin Cartlidge) to retire to his Macedonian village only to find the horrors of war at his doorstep. Writer-director Milcho Manchevski turns in a powerful, emotionally resonant anti-war movie despite the sometimes confusing narrative. Subtitles. Intense, sporadic violence, an attempted seduction, a partially nude shower scene, and occasional rough language. A-III (nr)

Before Winter Comes (1969) A Russian deserter (Topol) becomes the right-hand man of a British officer (David Niven) responsible for the care of refugees in an Austrian outpost after WWII. Director J. Lee Thompson focuses on the officer's dilemma of following orders to the letter or bending a little to help these displaced persons whose problems are convincingly detailed. A decent little film, but one of the problems is a woman (Anna Karina) who can't say no to anyone in uniform. A-III (PG)

Beginning of the End (1957) Hokey sci-fi tale of an agricultural specialist (Peter Graves) and a news reporter (Peggie Castle) trying to save Chicago from an invasion of giant locusts before the military nukes them and the city. Directed by Bert I. Gordon, the plot is flimsy, the acting phony, and the special-effects primitive, though the shot of superimposed grasshoppers on the Wrigley Building is a hoot. A-I (br)

Beguiled, The (1971) Civil War story in which a wounded Union soldier (Clint Eastwood) takes refuge in a Southern school for ladies, whom he must keep beguiled or risk being turned over to the Confederates. Directed by Don Siegel, this murky gothic horror story ends with the captive paying dearly for his ingratitude towards his captors' sick brand of Southern hospitality. In addition to the implied sexual situation, there is an explicit seduction followed by a gruesome amputation scene. A-IV (R)

Behind the Rising Sun (1943) Heavy-handed wartime booster in which the American-educated son (Tom Neal) of a Japanese government official (J. Carrol Naish) falls for the secretary (Margo) of an American engineer (Robert Ryan) in 1936 Tokyo, then is drafted to fight in China, where he participates in atrocities and, after Pearl Harbor, denounces his American friends as spies. Directed by Edward Dmytryk, the unconvincing melodrama finally ends with the father committing hari-kari over the crimes of his son and his nation's evil regime. Assorted wartime violence and savage anti-Japanese sterotyping. A-III (br)

Behold a Pale Horse (1964) Disappointing drama set 20 years after the Spanish Civil War, as an anti-Franco refugee (Gregory Peck) living in France crosses the border to kill an old foe (Anthony Quinn), who has become a brutal police chief. Directed by Fred Zinnemann, the slow-paced narrative bogs down in ideological explanations of the conflict, though the action scenes are gripping and the hard-working cast is first rate. Stylized violence and mild sexual innuendo. A-II (br)

Being Human (1994) In each of five vignettes ranging from the Bronze Age to today, Robin Williams portrays a man struggling to overcome a personal crisis that proves a turning point in his life. Writer-director Bill Forsyth's quintet of minor anecdotes on major themes of survival, freedom, and the importance of family demonstrate William's versatility as an actor but provide little insight on the human condition. Brief violence, a discreet sexual encounter, and minimal rough language. A-III (PG-13)

Being There (1980) Slender and austere comic tale directed by Hal Ashby from the screenplay by Jerzy Kosinski about a middle-aged, television-addicted gardener (Peter Sellers) who becomes a national celebrity when the rich and powerful mistake his slow-wittedness and ignorance for profound intelligence. This sardonic commentary about values in the television age has a seduction scene with Shirley MacLaine which places it in the adult category. A-III (PG)

Bela Lugosi Meets a Brooklyn Gorilla (see: **The Boys from Brooklyn**)

Belated Flowers (1972) Russian director Abram Room has taken a very early, uncharacteristically romantic story by Chekhov and made a simple but moving tale of doomed lovers. Room has fashioned a stylish set piece in which every artifice is used to establish and maintain a lyric mood of idealized romance. A-III (nr)

Believe in Me (1971) Michael Sarrazin plays a promising young intern who gets hooked on amphetamines, and Jacqueline Bisset is the girl he takes down the primrose path. Directed by Stuart Hagman, the story is one long TV hospital soap opera, but this one features a number of slow-motion love scenes. O (R)

Believers, The (1987) Desperate crime caper in which a New York City detective (Martin Sheen) tries to saves his son from a ritual death at the hands of a cultist group who derive power from human sacrifices. Director John Schlesinger's flawed, superficial treatment of a serious subject is marred by graphic shots of naked corpses, bloody animal entrails, gruesome murders, and a violent suicide. A-III (R)

Bell, Book and Candle (1958) Flat-footed romantic comedy from John Van Druten's play about a comely Manhattan witch (Kim Novak) who casts a spell on an engaged publisher (James Stewart), then falls in love with him. Director Richard Quine plays the romance for cloying sentimentality and fails to find much humor in the situation, despite witches Jack Lemmon, Elsa Lanchester, and Hermione Gingold, with Ernie Kovacs as a befuddled authority on the occult. Sexual inferences. A-III (br)

Bell for Adano, A (1945) Sturdy adaptation of John Hersey's WWII novel in which a US Army officer (John Hodiak) in charge of a liberated Italian town promises to find a replacement for a bell prized by the local community. Directed by Henry King, the story demonstrates the virtues of democracy as well as the common bond of humanity, put over by a good supporting cast, including Gene Tierney as an Italian girl pining for the safe return of her soldier boyfriend. Menacing situations and sexual innuendo. A-II (br)

Bell Jar, The (1979) Dreary, painful adaptation of the Sylvia Plath autobiography detailing a seemingly well-adjusted college girl's mental breakdown after the death of her father and her rude encounters with the realities of the New York publishing world. Director Larry Peerce resorts to extensive use of nudity groping for the muddled sexual basis for the tragic heroine's problems. O (R)

Belle de Jour (1968) The marital frigidity of a wealthy Parisian housewife (Catherine Deneuve) is traced to a religiously induced sense of guilt over a childhood incident which she seeks to expiate by working in a brothel. In this coldly elegant French production, director Luis Bunuel has some surrealistic fun with such themes as sexual perversity among the affluent, middle-class conservative values, and traditional concepts of religion. Degrading view of sexuality. O (br)

Belle of New York, The (1952) Thin musical romance features a turn-of-the-century playboy (Fred Astaire) transformed by his love for a crusading social reformer (Vera-Ellen). Director Charles Walters concentrates on the colorful decor and costumes of the period, as well as the staging of several flashy dance numbers, but the flat, predictable story line is uninvolving and the songs are pleasant but unmemorable. Mild romantic misunderstandings. A-I (br)

The Belles of St. Trinians (1955) Zany British comedy based on Ronald Searle's cartoons about a bizarre girl's school whose eccentric headmistress (Alastair Sim) vies with her shady brother (also Sim) over a racehorse stolen by students and hidden in the dorms. The result is a series of farcical vignettes involving the teachers, one of whom is an undercover police agent (Joyce Grenfell), and the students' extracurricular activities, including distilling gin in the chemistry lab and using a mallet to win a hockey tournament. Directed by Frank Launder. Comic violence and veiled sexual innuendo. A-II (br)

Bells of St. Mary's, The (1945) Director Leo McCarey's sequel to **Going My Way** (1944) pulls out all the emotional stops in a sugary confection that takes happy-go-lucky Father O'Malley (Bing Crosby) to a poor parish with a crumbling school run by overworked Sister Benedict (Ingrid Bergman). Though their conflicting views on education have less to do with the plot than the chasm between their personal relations, Bergman's shining performance as the idealistic nun is still worth watching. Sentimental yet warm picture of Catholic life in an age of innocence. A-I (br)

Belly (1998) Low-budget crime picture in which two African-American pals (DMX and Nas) rise high in the drug trade, then become fugitives from the police and rival drug traffickers until a bogus crime-doesn't-pay ending. Writer-director Hype Williams's disjointed gangster story gets lost in a welter of camera gimmicks pumping up the level of violence and the allure of crime's material rewards. Excessive violence, sexual encounters, nudity, drug abuse, and rough language. O (R)

Beloved (1998) Affecting tale of a Kentucky slave (Oprah Winfrey) whose horrific escape to freedom in Ohio one fateful night in 1855 comes back to haunt her 18 years later, when she is visited by an old friend (Danny Glover). Shortly afterward, a disturbed young woman (Thandie Newton) shows up on her doorstep, leading to further shocking revelations. Directed by Jonathan Demme from Toni Morrison's novel, the picture's unflinching look at slavery's legacy of shame and violence is powerfully acted, emotionally shattering, and suffused with a sense of mystery that helps to sustain the three-hour saga. Some intensely violent images, brief sexual encounters, full nudity, and intermittent profanity. A-IV (R)

Beloved Enemy (1936) Romantic melodrama set in 1921 Ireland, where a dashing rebel leader (Brian Aherne) falls for a British diplomat's daughter (Merle Oberon), with their unlikely romance complicating negotiations over the establishment of an independent Irish Republic. Director H.C. Potter makes the tensions of the period convincing in such scenes as a British military sweep in Dublin being harassed by children's pranks, but the love affair is heavy-handed and the ending hopelessly muddled. Some stylized violence, much menace, and soppy romantic situations. A-II (br)

Ben (1972) Ben (a rat) moves in with a musician-puppeteer (Lee Harcourt Montgomery) who, though he is recuperating from open heart surgery, exhausts himself trying to protect his new friend from unsympathetic adults. Director Phil Karlson passes the cheese to animal trainer Moe Di Sesso to generate some sympathy for the little fur balls, who kill just about everyone but their friendly host. Stylized violence. A-II (PG)

Ben-Gurion Remembers (1973) Israeli documentary on the twentyfifth anniversary of the embattled state of Israel pays tribute to the unique role played by David Ben-Gurion in its founding. Directed by Simon Hesers, it is a warm, personal portrait of a man not usually known for his congeniality, intermingling documentary footage and reminiscences with friends who today comprise the leadership of the country. A-I (nr)

Ben-Hur (1959) Director William Wyler's classic Hollywood epic follows the Jewish prince of the title (Charlton Heston) after he's betrayed by his boyhood Roman friend (Stephen Boyd) and subjected to much misery, until finally achieving retribution for all his suffering. The narrative's conventional melodrama is transformed by the grand scale of its spectacle, especially the chariot race, and by the stirring performances of its principals, who manage to overcome the story's cliches and stereotypes. A-I (G)

Bend of the River (1952) After escorting a wagon train of settlers to Oregon, two Kansas cowboys (James Stewart and Arthur Kennedy) find themselves on opposite sides in the battle between the new farmers and an influx of gold miners to the area. Directed by Anthony Mann, the pioneer setting is colorful and the action plentiful, but too many subplots weaken the dramatic focus. Stylized violence and romantic situations. A-I (br)

Beneath the Planet of the Apes (1970) Lame sequel has an astronaut (James Franciscus) reaching the bombed-out earth, where the ape people are warring with the subterranean remnants of the human race, a skinless colony of people who worship "the Holy Bomb," and these deformed humans destroy the planet in the final scene. Directed by Ted Post, it lacks the wit, excitement, and ingenuity of the original's warning to war-mongering, damage-prone humanity. A-III (G)

Beneath the 12-Mile Reef (1953) Colorful, unpretentious melodrama set in the Florida Keys, where the son (Robert Wagner) of a Greek-American sponge fisherman (Gilbert Roland) falls in love with the daughter (Terry Moore) of a redneck rival fisherman (Richard Boone). Director Robert D. Webb depicts the dangers awaiting sponge divers in the deep, then focuses on the problems of the young couple in winning over the girl's family. Brief violence and menacing situations. A-I (br)

Bengal Brigade (1954) Wooden drama set in imperial India, where a British officer (Rock Hudson) sacrifices his career to save his trapped native troops who, in turn, save him and other British captives (notably Arlene Dahl, Torin Thatcher, and Dan O'Herlihy) during the 1857 Sepoy Mutiny. Directed by Laslo Benedek, the unconvincing tale of loyalty overcoming colonial barriers offers more talk than action and stereotypes instead of characters. Stylized violence. A-I (br)

Bengal Rifles (see: **Bengal Brigade**)

Benji (1974) Tough little mongrel maintains his independence by begging food only from people who attach no strings, and ultimately becomes the hero of his small town by foiling some kidnappers. Directed by Joe Camp, it is light, wholesome entertainment with enough tension and false leads to keep children on the edge of the seats as the little dog toughs it out and wins on his own. A-I (G)

Benji the Hunted (1987) Stranded in a hostile wilderness after his master's boat capsizes, the courageous canine finds a new home for some orphaned mountain lion cubs. The Disney production directed by Joe Camp creates a sense of wildlife authenticity, and tells the story without any need for dialogue or voiceover narration. Charming simple tale for the very young. A-I (G)

Benny & Joon (1993) Offbeat love story with a mentally ill, homebound young woman (Mary Stuart Masterson) falling for a would-be mime (Johnny Depp), who encourages her independence despite the objections of her fiercely overprotective brother (Aidan Quinn). While director Jeremiah Chechik clearly romanticizes the two social outcasts, the movie's charm lies in its intermingling of sweet pathos, whimsical humor, and strong sense of family and caring. An implied sexual encounter and an instance of rough language. A-III (PG)

Benny Goodman Story, The (1955) Standard Hollywood biography of the popular bandleader (Steve Allen) from his youth in Chicago to his heyday in the 1940s, with Donna Reed as the romantic interest. Directed by Valentine Davies, the treatment is strictly superficial, but the nostalgic period music is good and plentiful. Not for fidgety youngsters. A-I (br)

Bernadette (1987) The story of Bernadette Soubirous and her visions of a beautiful lady in white at a grotto near Lourdes in 1858 is dramatically portrayed in this French production by veteran film director Jean Delannoy. Sidney Penny, a 17-year-old American actress, portrays the 15-year-old Bernadette with charming down-to-earth innocence, and the screen adaptation is simple, direct, and faithful to the religious drama of the events portrayed. The result is an uncompromising, spiritually moving picture of a young woman's faith, a story that still has meaning for contemporary viewers. Dubbed into English. A-I (PG)

Berserk (1967) Lurid story of a series of gruesome murders in a circus run by Joan Crawford is directed by Jim O'Connolly. Macabre atmosphere and violence. A-III (br)

Bert Rigby: You're a Fool! (1989) Clumsy show biz rags-to-riches fable stars British song-and-dance man Robert Lindsay, who succeeds best in mimicking such screen greats as Chaplin, Keaton, Kelly, and Astaire. However, the family-oriented musical numbers are poorly staged, and writer-director Carl Reiner injects too much sexual innuendo as well as vulgar references, name-dropping, and product endorsements in a misguided attempt to be trendy. Some rough language and brief nudity. A-III (R)

Besieged (1999) Offbeat drama in which an English pianist (David Thewlis) living in Rome falls for his African maid (Thandie Newton) who is studying for a medical degree while her husband remains a political prisoner in her homeland. Director Bernardo Bertolucci's intriguing attempts to convey romantic obsession ultimately disappoint as the characters barely communicate with one another, robbing the illogical outcome of emotional resonance. Fleeting violence, a sexual situation, some nudity, and brief alcohol abuse. A-III (R)

Best Defense (1984) Supremely unfunny vehicle

for the irreverent humor of comedian Eddie Murphy involves the development of a super-tank for the military. Director Willard Huyck tries desperately to revive the brain-dead comedy by resorting to graphic sex and tasteless jokes about sex and the Third World. O (R)

Best Foot Forward (1943) Flimsy Broadway musical comedy about a fading movie star (Lucille Ball) sneaking into a military prep school's graduation ball as a publicity stunt. Director Edward Buzzell stretches out the meager plot with some good period music by Harry James and orchestra, peppy comic bits from Nancy Walker, and a frivolous patriotic ending. Mild sexual innuendo. A-II (br) —

Best Friends (1975) Low-budget road picture about two discharged soldiers making their way home in a camper accompanied by their girlfriends. Whenever the action drags, a bit of violence or sexual exploitation is brought in. O (R)

Best Friends (1982) Burt Reynolds and Goldie Hawn play a happy Hollywood couple, a screenwriting team, who seem to have everything going for them until they put it all in jeopardy by deciding to get married. Director Norman Jewison offers a somewhat cynical comedy about the institution of marriage without insight into the values it represents. A-III (PG)

Best House in London, The (1969) A mansion in Victorian London, donated for the worthy purpose of serving as a residence for the rehabilitation of wayward girls, is soon turned into a high class bordello by a notorious profligate (David Hemmings). Directed by Philip Saville, this witless, tasteless satire on the hypocrisy of the Victorian Age is excessive in its use of nudity and sexual references. O (X)

Best Intentions, The (1992) Episodic Swedish family saga set in the early 1900s focuses on the troubled courtship and stormy marriage of a dour, strong-willed Lutheran minister (Samuel Froler) who had grown up in poverty and his bright, willful bride (Pernilla August) whose wealthy family had opposed their wedding. As directed by Bille August, Ingmar Bergman's autobiographical script offers a moody meditation on the emotional affinity of two completely opposite temperaments whose bond of love withstands the resulting clashes of personality and inevitable misunderstandings only because they are willing to forgive one another and go on together. Subtitles. Restrained scene of premarital relations with brief nudity, several scenes of domestic violence, a suicide, and a life-threatening scene involving a small child. A-III (nr)

Best Little Whorehouse in Texas, The (1982) Broadway musical about a Texas brothel threatened by a clean-up campaign has been made into a vehicle for Burt Reynolds and Dolly Parton. The characterizations and country music are so lackluster that the virtues of the original must remain a mystery to anyone who has not seen it. Director Colin Higgins resorts to quite a bit of nudity and several fairly graphic bedroom scenes. O (R)

Best Man, The (1964) To win presidential nomination at the national convention, an idealistic liberal candidate (Henry Fonda) seeks support from his party's leader (Lee Tracy), but is threatened by the unscrupulous tactics of a conservative rival (Cliff Robertson). Directed by Franklin Schaffner and adapted by Gore Vidal from his own stage play, the political back-room maneuverings seem depressingly familiar, though brightened by some sharply satiric humor. Ambiguous treatment of a candidate's religion. A-IV (br)

Best of Everything, The (1959) Glossy soap opera about the romantic travails of three secretaries in a Manhattan publishing firm, where Hope Lange settles for sad Stephen Boyd; Diane Baker is betrayed by wealthy Robert Evans; and Suzy Parker goes off the deep end because of arty Louis Jourdan. Directed by Jean Negulesco, the lugubrious proceedings alternate between heartthrobs and heartaches, furtive liaisons and gushy weddings, young employees and senior executives (bitter Joan Crawford and womanizing Brian Aherne). Sexual situations and veiled references to abortion. A-III (br)

Best of the Badmen (1951) Hokey tale of carpetbag justice after the Civil War, when a Union major (Robert Ryan) falsely accused of murder throws in with an outlaw band of former Confederate irregulars (Bruce Cabot, Walter Brennan, and Jack Buetel). Directed by William D. Russell, the story doesn't make a whole lot of sense, especially the wife (Claire Trevor) of the chief heavy (Robert Preston) throwing in with the outlaws. Stylized violence and a bad marriage. A-III (br)

Best of Times, The (1986) Slack comedy about middle-aged out-of-shape losers (Robin Williams and Kurt Russell) who get a second chance to replay the big football game they lost as high-school seniors. Starting with some wry, tongue-in-cheek humor, director Roger Spottiswoode lets the comic situation go downhill, and the quest of grown men for their lost youth grows ever more tiresome. Much rough language, some sexual innuendo, and a passing reference to locker-room drugs. O (PG-13)

Best Way, The (1978) From France comes a drab and pale little film devoted to the theme of sexual ambivalence. Director Charles Miller loosely sets the drama in a boys' camp in 1960, but provides undeveloped characters in a story about a sexual confrontation between two counselors (Patrick Dewaere and Patrick Bouchitey). Occasional nudity. O (nr)

Best Years of Our Lives, The (1946) Three WWII veterans (sergeant Fredric March, bombardier Dana Andrews, and sailor Harold Russell with hooks in place of hands) meet on their way home to resume civilian lives in the same small town, where they try to help each other readjust to peacetime. Director William Wyler gives sympathetic treatment to the post-war rehabilitation of returning GIs, portraying in fairly realistic detail their career difficulties as well as personal problems with wives and girlfriends (Myrna Loy, Teresa Wright, Virginia Mayo, and Cathy O'Donnell). Mature themes, including a broken marriage. A-III (br)

Betrayal (1983) Screen version of Harold Pinter's play about a love triangle is a pretentious and anemic exercise which hints at profundities that lie too deep for words, but never delivers the goods. The British production under the direction of David Jones squanders a talented cast (Patricia Hodge, Jeremy Irons, and Ben Kingsley). Single instance of obscene language. A-III (R)

Betrayed (see: **When Strangers Marry**)

Betrayed (1988) FBI undercover agent (Debra Winger) falls in love with a Nebraska farmer (Tom Berenger) suspected of involvement with a political terrorist group. Director Costa-Gavras achieves some credibility in his fictional portrayal of the shadowy world of American hate groups, and there are some tense moments, but the romance is silly and the movie's stance against racism requires a mature perspective. Some intense graphic violence, implied illicit sex, racial slurs, and other rough language. A-III (R)

Betsy, The (1978) Supremely trashy novel by Harold Robbins, adapted into a supremely trashy movie about the obsession for power, sex, and wealth among the upper echelon of the automobile industry (Laurence Olivier, Robert Duvall, and Katherine Ross). Director Daniel Petrie's potboiler contains nudity and is lacking completely in moral perspective. O (R)

Betsy's Wedding (1990) Mildly amusing look at a family's harried preparations for a lavish wedding that the father (Alan Alda) can't afford and the bride-to-be (Molly Ringwald) doesn't want. Also written and directed by Alda, the story lacks real dramatic tension, but the characters and situations are believable, even commonplace, resulting in a sweetly bland comedy, where everyone compromises so love can endure. Occasional rough language and a brief mob-related shootout. A III (R)

Better a Widow (1968) Weak Italian romantic comedy directed by Duccio Tessari about the daughter (Virna Lisi) of a Sicilian Mafia Don and an Englishman (Peter McEnery) who has come to build an oil refinery. Light treatment of murder and sex. A-III (PG)

Better Off Dead (1985) This crass comedy about teenage suicide has the gall to aim itself at teenage audiences and, indeed, proclaims all the verities of the genre, including the portrayal of parents as congenital idiots. Terribly inappropriate theme as well as jocular view of drug abuse. O (PG)

Betty (1993) When a concerned widow (Stephane Audran) takes in a drunken, depressed young wife (Marie Trintignant), the unhappy woman's marital crisis spills over into the older woman's life with disastrous results. Director Claude Chabrol's adaptation of a Georges Simenon novel painstakingly burrows into the psyche of two women who base their self-worth on their sexual relationships with men, an attitude which destroys them in different ways. Subtitles. Several discreet bedroom scenes, some brief nudity, an off-screen suicide, and an instance of rough language. A-III (nr)

Between Heaven and Hell (1956) Routine WWII melodrama directed by Richard Fleischer follows an affluent Southern landowner (Robert Wagner) who's turned into an egalitarian by his combat experiences on a Japanese-held island, especially through the friendship he forms under fire with a pre-war sharecropper (Buddy Ebsen). Fairly intense wartime violence and the psychological stress of combat. A-II (br)

Between Miracles (198O) Nino Manfredi directs and stars in this dull and insipid film about a not-too-bright young man who as a boy was saved from death by an apparent miracle, raised in a monastery, and then has difficulty coping with the problems he finds in the world outside. Some sexual situations. A-III (nr)

Between the Lines (1977) Rather aimless comedy-drama about the youthful staff of a once radical Boston newspaper attempting to come to terms with changing times. Though director Joan Micklin Silver gets some good acting from a young cast (John Heard, Stephen Collins, and Jill Eikenberry), the movie comes off as nothing more than a slick, run-of-the mill Hollywood production emphasizing nudity and sexual innuendo. O (R)

Beverly Hillbillies, The (1993) Clunky movie version of the 1962-71 TV series has billionaire Jed (Jim Varney) nearly robbed of his fortune by a scheming gold-digger (Lea Thompson) hired to teach refinement to his tomboy daughter (Erika Eleniak). Director Penelope Spheeris adds nothing to the cornpone formula of the original sitcom, nor to the cartoonish characters and situations that barely add up to a plot. Some blatant sexual innuendo, coarse gestures, and slapstick violence. A-III (PG)

Beverly Hills Cop (1984) For those who like the comedic crassness of Eddie Murphy, there's plenty of it in his role as a super-cool Detroit detective whose quest for justice in the shooting of a friend takes him to Los Angeles, where he bears the brunt of prejudice. Murphy's streetwise charm and cunning overcome a script infused with rough language and director Martin Brest's reliance upon violence, some brutality, and awkward stereotyping. A-III (R)

Beverly Hills Cop II (1987) Tiresome vanity production directed by Tony Scott features Eddie Murphy as the clever Detroit cop who helps his California friends break up a gang of thieves and gunrunners. Violence and brutality vie with extended demolition-derby chase sequence, unamusingly vulgar sight gags, rampant profanity, and topless dancers. O (R)

Beverly Hills Cop III (1994) Mindlessly violent sequel in which the resourceful Detroit cop (Eddie Murphy) tracks a killer to a Los Angeles theme park, where almost single-handedly he takes on its murderous security force and their counterfeiting operation. Murphy's slack performance fails to carry director John Landis's poorly plotted shoot-'em-up, which adds insult to injury in feeble attempts at hip humor. Excessive violence and much rough language. O (R)

Beverly Hills Ninja (1997) Dopey comedy in which a klutzy American (Chris Farley) raised in a Japanese martial-arts school trails a mysterious blonde (Nicollette Sheridan) to Los Angeles intent on rescuing her from a gangster boyfriend. Directed by Dennis Dugan, the Farley vehicle is more silly than funny, as his awkward physical comedy fails to compensate for the witless script. Much comic violence and some sexual innuendo. A-III (PG-13)

Beware My Brethren (1972) Beware indeed of this annoying British movie which tells of a fanatical evangelist (Patrick Magee) and his merciless influence upon a pathetically devout diabetic (Ann Todd) and her emotionally unstable son (Tony Beckley). Such things as rape, baptizing in blood, and crucifying are treated in detail by director Robert Hartford-Davis's disgusting little shocker that is an insult to moral sensibilities. O (R)

Beware, My Lovely (1952) Harrowing tale of a widow (Ida Lupino) held captive in her home by a mild-mannered handyman (Robert Ryan) who proves a terrifying mental case. Directed by Harry Horner, the threatening situation goes on far too long to sustain credibility, though Ryan's performance as the unbalanced menace is chillingly convincing. Not for the young and impressionable. A-II (br)

Beware of Blondie (1950) The twenty-eighth and final episode in this popular family-comedy series has the vacationing Mr. Dithers (Edward Earle) leave Dagwood (Arthur Lake) with a blank check for an upcoming deal, but he's swindled out of it by a beautiful imposter (Adele Jergens), then has terrifying nightmares of prison. Directed by Edward Bernds, the Bumstead family formula reaches its inglorious end with a plot hinged on a bogus sex-scam. Muted sexual innuendo. A-II (br)

Beware Spooks (1939) Silly slapstick comedy directed by Edward Sedgwick follows the follies of a bonehead policeman (Joe E. Brown) who becomes a hero while on his honeymoon by capturing an escaped killer (Marc Lawrence) after a wild chase through an amusement park's haunted house. Dated funny business with some comic menace and stylized violence. A-I (br)

Beware! The Blob (see: **Son of Blob**)

Beyond and Back (1978) The movie presents itself as a serious, scientific examination of certain alleged happenings that seem to indicate that there is life after death. The result, however, proves to be utterly uncritical in its treatment of data, and many of its conclusions are not merely absurd but at variance with some traditional religious beliefs. Its realistic depiction of death experiences may be too strong for the very young. A-III (G)

Beyond Bombasa (1957) Tepid African adventure follows a rugged American (Cornel Wilde) and his guides (Donna Reed, Leo Genn, and Christopher Lee) through the jungle to a mysterious mine discovered by his murdered brother. Filmed largely in Kenya by director George Marshall, the action is colorful, but the clumsy, far-fetched plot hinges on a religious murder cult and a mad humanitarian. African stereotypes and some stylized but nasty violence unsuitable for young imaginations. A-I (br)

Beyond Rangoon (1995) Stranded in 1988 Burma when her US passport is lost during student demonstrations against the military dictatorship, a newly widowed doctor (Patricia Arquette) and her elderly Burmese tour guide (U Aung Ko) struggle to evade murderous soldiers as they join the flood of desperate dissidents fleeing to the safety of the Thai border. Though director John Boorman's political thriller is overly contrived in developing the American woman's plight, it succeeds in calling attention to human rights violations in that beleaguered country. Intermittent scenes of military attacks on unarmed civilians. A-III (R)

Beyond Silence (1998) A young girl (Tatjana Trieb), whose parents (Howie Seago and Emmanuelle Laborit) are deaf, is encouraged by her aunt (Sibylle Canonica) to take up the clarinet, and proves to be musically gifted. After high school she (Sylvie Testud) leaves home to enroll in a conservatory, though her father is deeply hurt by what he considers his daughter's rejection of her family. Directed by Caroline Link, the German production puts across the warm, though sometimes painful, story of a hearing child being raised by deaf parents in an atmosphere of love, yet with occasional misunderstandings which have less to do with words than with emotions and relationships that are universal. Subtitles. Some intense domestic confrontations, several sexual situations, a toilet scene, and a crude expression. A-III (PG-13)

Beyond the Door (1975) Cheap horror movie directed by Oliver Hellman is an inept, tasteless attempt to combine **Rosemary's Baby** and **The Exorcist**. O (R)

Beyond the Fog (see: **Horror on Snape Island**)

Beyond the Law (1968) Novelist Norman Mailer's self-indulgent home movie about brutality in a New York City police station is offensive in its almost jocular use of violence and its coarse and obscene language. O (nr)

Beyond the Limit (1983) Director John Mackenzie's screen version of the Graham Greene novel *The Honorary Consul* is a plodding, uninspired effort given some merit only by Michael Caine's performance as the hapless diplomat in an Argentine backwater, whom an inept band of revolutionaries kidnap by mistake. Another mistake is Richard Gere as Greene's introspective protagonist. Extensive nudity in the context of an adulterous affair. O (R)

Beyond the Poseidon Adventure (1979) Tugboat

captain Michael Caine (aided and abetted by Karl Malden and Sally Field) try to salvage the Poseidon, moments after the climactic rescue of the previous disaster film. Producer-director Irwin Allen supplies only vacuous plot, dialogue, and resolution in a boring adventure yarn. A-II (PG)

Beyond the Reef (1981) This is a South Pacific idyll about a Polynesian lad and his pet shark, who helps him win the love of a rich man's daughter, despite interference from her greedy brother and unscrupulous land developers. Directed by Frank C. Clark, it's an amateurish little movie, save for some remarkable underwater photography and a school of apparently trained sharks. Some partial nudity and permissive attitude toward the lovers' affair. A-III (PG)

Beyond the Valley of the Dolls (1970) Director Russ Meyers's unfunny spoof of Hollywood lacks story, stars, and appeal. Boring as it may be, it abounds in unhealthy fantasies of sex, with some nudity, and violence. O (X)

Beyond Therapy (1987) Based on the Christopher Durang play, Robert Altman's emotionally anemic romance tries to find humor in the failures of modern psychoanalysis and in the flaws of a sexually confused cast (Jeff Goldblum, Julie Hagerty, Glenda Jackson, Tom Conti, and Christopher Guest). Shallow insights pervade the movie, which relies totally upon sexual innuendo, negative stereotypes, and some vulgar language for interest. O (R)

Beyond Tomorrow (1940) Dated Depression fantasy in which three aging business partners (Harry Carey, C. Aubrey Smith, and Charles Winninger) share the Christmas holidays with two needy New Yorkers (Richard Carlson and Jean Parker), but after the three die in a plane crash, the spirit of one of them lingers on earth to insure the young couple wed. Directed by A. Edward Sutherland, the sentimental melodrama has plenty of heartfelt warmth and a bit of soul-searching as the dead partners face eternity. Romantic complications involving a gold digger. A-II (br)

Bible, The (1966) Six episodes from Genesis (creation, Adam and Eve, Cain and Abel, Noah, the Tower of Babel, and Abraham) are pictured as literally as they were written, largely leaving their interpretation to the viewer. John Huston directs, narrates, and plays the part of Noah in this reverent but entertaining spectacular. George C. Scott as Abraham takes acting honors among a cast including Ava Gardner, Richard Harris, Ulla Bergryd, and Michael Parks. A-I (br)

Bicycle Thief, The (1949) Simple yet compelling study in desperation as a worker (Lamberto Maggiorani) must find his stolen bicycle or lose his new job. Ignored by the police and others, the man and his young son (Enzo Staiola) search the streets for it until, in despair, he himself tries to steal a bicycle. Scripted by Cesare Zavattini and directed by Vittorio De Sica, the result is an engrossing picture of the human realities of life on the edge of poverty, shot on the streets of Rome with a cast of non-professionals that brought a new realism to the postwar screen and a new emotional honesty to the stories it told. Subtitles. Some earthy references. A-II (br)

Bicycle Thieves (see: **The Bicycle Thief**)

Big (1988) When a lad of 12 (David Moscow) wakes up in a 30-year-old body (Tom Hanks), he rises to the top in a computer toy firm by beguiling his boss (Robert Loggia) and a female executive (Elizabeth Perkins) with his innocence and childlike exuberance. Under Penny Marshall's direction, the body-switching gimmick affords a sweet-natured look at the longings, dreams, and nightmares of children and adults. Some profanity and a brief, discreetly filmed sexual situation. A-II (PG)

Big Bang, The (1990) An astronomer, a gangster, a painter, a model, and a nun-philosopher are among the diverse mix of 19 individuals who tell what they think about love, life, death, the origins of the universe, and what lies beyond the grave. Director James Toback's documentary interweaves the interviews into a relatively painless talk show, offering an uneven grab-bag of ideas ranging from the provocative to the pretentious and, at times, preposterous. Some rough language and an explicit description of a sexual encounter. A-III (R)

Big Bird Cage, The (1972) Poorly-made Philippine movie directed by Jack Hill in which a woman (Pam Grier) smuggles her boyfriend into a women's prison camp in order to foment a rebellion. Much nudity, savagery, and raw language. O (R)

Big Blue, The (1988) Mysterious young Frenchman (Jean-Marc Barr), who was taught to dive long and deep by his fisherman father, sets the world diving record, but his affinity for dolphins ultimately ruins his chances for a normal life on land. Exquisite seascapes and beautiful underwater cinematography can't make up for a poorly realized script directed by Luc Besson. Two intense drowning sequences and fleeting nudity in a brief but explicit sexual encounter. A-III (PG)

Big Bounce, The (1969) Young drifter (Ryan O'Neal) becomes deeply involved with a supposedly lovable psychotic (Leigh Taylor-Young), whose desire for thrills eventually drives him away, but only after she has committed murder. Directed by Alex March, the heavy-handed melodrama is totally unconvincing. Several ludicrous nude scenes and much coarse language used so self-consciously as to emphasize its offensiveness. O (R/PG)

Big Bully (1996) Comedy clunker in which an author (Rick Moranis) returns to his hometown as a grade-school teacher, then learns the bully (Tom Arnold) who had made his life miserable as a child is on the faculty. Directed by Steve Miner, the unamusing situation has the two resume their childhood antagonism with grown-up intensity, while their boys do their own bully-victim routines. Much unfunny violence, some life-threatening situations, sexist humor, and occasional coarse language. A-III (PG)

Big Bus, The (1976) A parody of disaster movies, it follows the misadventures of a nuclear-powered bus on its maiden run non-stop from New York to Denver. The gags work about 30 percent of the time, not too bad an average for this type of film, and director James Frawley keeps a light touch on the often heavy-handed proceedings. Innocent, mostly sophomoric humor, except for several sexual references. A-III (PG)

Big Business (1988) Two sets of identical twin girls are mismatched at birth — one set ends up at the helm of a New York-based conglomerate, the other set is raised by a poor, rural couple in West Virginia. Director Jim Abrahams keeps the farce fast and funny in showing how the real twins (both sets are played by Bette Midler and Lily Tomlin) are reunited in New York City's Plaza Hotel, but not before confounding husbands, lovers, and all manner of co-workers and hotel employees. Much humor with sexual connotations and some rough language. A-III (PG)

Big Carnival, The (see: **Ace in the Hole**)

Big Cat, The (1949) Soured relations between rural neighbors in 1933 Utah worsen when the city nephew (Lon McCallister) of one (Forrest Tucker) arrives to take a job with the other (Preston Foster), but the feud is ended by a rampaging mountain lion. Director Phil Karlson delivers a credible period piece about simple country folk trying to survive hard times, but the melodramatic rivalry between the two men escalates from nastiness to brutality. Some fairly intense violence. A-II (br)

Big Chill, The (1983) Seven old friends (William Hurt, Kevin Kline, Glenn Close among them) from college days in the 1960s are reunited by the suicide of the most brilliant of their number. After the funeral they spend the weekend together soul-searching and, to some degree, mourning their lost innocence. Director Lawrence Kasdan indicates no political awareness on the part of his characters despite their supposed sophistication, and the result is an entertaining but shallow and contrived work. Brief nudity, rough language, and a benign attitude toward adultery. A-III (R)

Big Circus, The (1959) Big-top owner (Victor Mature) faces financial ruin, thanks to devious activities of a traitor working for a rival circus. Director Joseph M. Newman's hackneyed story line is buttressed by some good circus acts, a few thrills (notably aerialist Gilbert Roland walking a tightrope across Niagara Falls), and a cast including Vincent Price as the ringmaster and Peter Lorre as a clown. Some stylized violence and mild romance. A-I (br)

Big City, The (1967) From India comes this unassuming but dignified story of the problems that occur when a young mother must work in the city to help support her family. Director Satyajit Ray generates considerable human warmth out of a simple situation of ordinary Bengali family life that, despite the cultural differences, many will find universal. Subtitles. Domestic tensions. A-II (br)

Big Clock, The (1948) Intriguing suspense thriller embroils a crime magazine editor (Ray Milland) as the chief suspect in a murder committed by his megalomaniacal publisher (Charles Laughton). Directed by John Farrow, the tense narrative is nicely keyed to a collection of quirky characters (including Elsa Lanchester, George Macready, and Henry Morgan). Mounting menace and some stylized violence. A-II (br)

Big Combo, The (1955) Overheated crime story in which a weary but determined cop (Cornel Wilde) tries to bring down a ruthless syndicate boss (Richard Conte) by getting the criminal's unhappy mistress (Jean Wallace) to tell what she knows. Directed by Joseph Lewis, the plot plods along with the cop stymied at every turn, until a sudden break brings the downfall of the feared crime boss and his sadistic thugs. Brutal crime scenes and sexual innuendo. A-III (br)

Big Cube, The (1969) Lana Turner is sent over the psychic edge by George Chakiris, who has been spiking her medicine with LSD in order to control her fortune when she is declared incompetent. Director Tito Davison's low-budget melodrama shot in Mexico splices in some scenes of over-age hippies cutting up at drug parties. O (PG)

Big Easy, The (1987) Quirky romance about a Cajun detective (Dennis Quaid) and an assistant district attorney (Ellen Barkin) who weather a conflict of interests and the low moral atmosphere of New Orleans to solve a drug-related crime. Director Jim McBride's nervously stylistic movie stays light and often dopey, despite some gruesome flashes of murder victims, a shot of topless dancers, and an explicit, albeit fumbling, lovemaking scene. A-III (R)

Big Enough and Old Enough (1968) Family of Mexican migrant workers runs afoul of a motorcycle gang in this wretched movie directed by Joseph Prieto. Rape, mental and physical violence, sexually suggestive dialogue and visuals, and coarse language. O (br)

Big Fix, The (1978) A Los Angeles private eye (Richard Dreyfuss), a former 1960's campus radical, is now cynical, disenchanted, and divorced, scraping a living out of minor gumshoe jobs. When an old college friend (Susan Anspach) asks him to investigate a smear campaign against a political reformer, he is drawn back into the idealism of his youth. Director Jeremy Paul Kagan has made an entertaining though convoluted detective thriller that benefits greatly from the vitality of Dreyfuss's performance. Some of its humor and its less than adequate treatment of the political and moral issues it deals with make it mature fare. A-III (PG)

Big Green, The (1995) The economically depressed residents of a tiny Texas town get back their fighting spirit after a perky new teacher (Olivia d'Abo) from England, assisted by the local sheriff (Steve Guttenberg), shape the listless junior-high schoolers into a winning soccer team. Writer-director Holly

Goldberg Sloan's bland story of underdogs beating the odds is an innocuous, slightly amusing family film which never ventures beyond the thoroughly predictable. A-I (PG)

Big Gundown, The (1968) In this Italian-made Western, snickering ex-lawman (Lee Van Cleef) aids in tracking down a shifty Mexican (Tomas Millian) accused of rape and murder but, discovering his quarry's innocence, he then joins with him to punish the real culprits. Director Sergio Sollima's formula plot is simply an excuse to string together chases and places for the hero to exhibit his brutal brand of six-gun justice. Particularly objectionable in this film is sadistic violence and perversion perpetrated by and upon women. O (R)

Big Hand for the Little Lady, A (1966) Henry Fonda, Joanne Woodward, Jason Robards, Burgess Meredith, Paul Ford, and Kevin McCarthy are among the ensemble playing cards in the Old West's most comical and colorful poker game. Director Fielder Cook places emphasis on the personalities, and the plot's ingenious bluffing makes for fascinating entertainment, even without the clever surprise ending. A-II (nr)

Big Heat, The (1953) Gritty crime thriller in which a homicide detective (Glenn Ford), whose wife is murdered by a bomb intended for him, turns in his badge and goes it alone to bring down a powerful crime syndicate, its unsavory boss (Alexander Scourby), and his corrupt City Hall cronies. Directed by Fritz Lang, the melodrama's harsh action, sordid atmosphere, and seedy characters are relieved by the idealistic cop and a gangster's abused girlfriend (Gloria Grahame) who dies helping to crack the case. Much menace and stylized violence, some of it quite nasty. A-III (br)

Big Hit, The (1998) Repulsive action comedy in which a hitman (Lou Diamond Phillips) turns on his partner (Mark Wahlberg) when a kidnapping they engineered goes murderously awry. Director Che-Kirk Wong depicts vicious murders as dangerously glamorous deeds performed by macho heroes. Excessive, jokey violence, implied promiscuity and sexual references, brief nudity, and non-stop rough language. O (R)

Big House, U.S.A. (1955) Brutal crime picture in which the callous kidnapper (Ralph Meeker) of a schoolboy buries the ransom money in Colorado's Royal Gorge Park before being arrested and sent to prison, but his cellmates (led by Broderick Crawford) force him to join them in an escape to retrieve the loot. Directed by Howard W. Koch, the formula proceedings are paced by cruel action scenes including the death of the kidnapped boy and the use of a hammer and blow-torch to destroy a dead convict's identity. Considerable brutality. A-III (br)

Big Jake (1971) John Wayne Western in which he and his two grown sons (Patrick Wayne and Christopher Mitchum) trail the gang who kidnapped his grandson, with occasional pauses for bloodshed, to a Mexican village, where they take on villain Richard Boone and his band of eight cutthroats. Directed by George Sherman, it's a rather old-fashioned kind of shoot-'em-up, except some of the violence is overdone. A-III (GP)

Big Jim McLain (1952) Dated patriotic melodrama in which the title character (John Wayne) and his associate (James Arness) are investigators for the House Un-American Activities Committee. While ferreting out Red subversives in Hawaii, McLain finds romance with a loyal citizen (Nancy Olson). Directed by Edward Ludwig, the story plods along with more lectures than action, though the result may interest students of Cold War politics. Some stylized violence. A-I (br)

Big Jump, The (see: **Paratrooper**)

Big Knife, The (1955) Muddled Hollywood version of the conflict between art and commerce from the Clifford Odets play about a movie star (Jack Palance) blackmailed by an unscrupulous producer (Rod Steiger) into signing a contract for a movie he's dead-set against doing. Director Robert Aldrich's melodrama has little action, much high-minded dialogue, and good character bits by Ida Lupino, Jean Hagen, Shelley Winters, and Wendall Corey. Sexual references and suicide in plot resolution. A-III (br)

Big Land, The (1957) Routine oater in which a Texas cattleman (Alan Ladd) persuades Kansas farmers (led by John Qualen) to join him in getting a railroad spur to the area in order to end their mutual dependency on a crooked Missouri trader (Anthony Caruso). Director Gordon Douglas seems more comfortable with cattle drives and shootouts than frontier links to Eastern markets, and a sappy subplot involving a reformed alcoholic (Edmond O'Brien) and his marriageable sister (Virginia Mayo). Stylized violence. A-I (br)

Big Lebowski, The (1998) Leaden, foul-mouthed comedy in which a shiftless character (Jeff Bridges) and his volatile buddy (John Goodman) are duped into a kidnapping scam involving a variety of claimants to the ransom money. Co-written by director Joel Coen with his brother Ethan, the picture focuses on an unsavory collection of self-obsessed Los Angeles eccentrics whose mindless antics are more aggravating than amusing. Stylized violence, recreational substance abuse, an implied sexual encounter, brief nudity, some profanity, and constant rough language. O (R)

Big Lift, The (1950) During the Russian blockade of Berlin, an American (Montgomery Clift) in the massive airlift of supplies to the beleaguered city falls in love with a German resident, despite the advice of his anti-German buddy (Paul Douglas). Filmed on location in semi-documentary style by director George Seaton, this tribute to the airmen who braved the dangers of the Berlin route is convincingly authentic, though marred by the contrived love story and great gobs of patriotic rhetoric. An outburst of vengeful violence and a romance based on deceit. A-II (br)

Big Mo (see: **Maurie**)

Big Mouth, The (1967) Working from what seems an almost totally improvised script, director Jerry Lewis takes a bank clerk (Jerry Lewis) who happens to look exactly like a gangster (Jerry Lewis) through a tediously meandering story line. The look-alike gimmick sets up encounters with a hotel manager, a lunatic who thinks he's an FBI agent, a group of smugglers, amusement parlor police, cruel Orientals, and so on until its frantic conclusion. For Jerry Lewis fans. A-I (br)

Big Night (1996) Two Italian immigrants in the 1950s — a perfectionist chef (Tony Shalhoub) and his more pragmatic brother (Stanley Tucci) — risk bankruptcy by putting on a lavish banquet for celebrity Louis Prima in hopes the resulting publicity will attract business to their restaurant. As co-directed by Tucci and Campbell Scott, the bittersweet story is a warm-hearted celebration of family, community, and the fragile relationships that give life its flavor. Implied sexual affair, sporadic rough language, and minimal profanity. A-III (R)

Big One, The (1998) Thin video record of the mischievous adventures of corporate critic Michael Moore as he crosses the country promoting his book, *Downsize This!*, while giving talks to college students, visiting laid-off workers, and trying to see corporation heads, though he gets nowhere with the only one (Nike's Phil Knight) willing to meet with him. Also written, produced, and directed by Moore, it's the picture of a one-man band beating the drum for social justice, though his impish tactics of provocation grow tiresome along the way. Some mean-spirited humor about nuns and sporadic rough language. A-III (PG-13)

Big Parade, The (1925) Silent WWI epic centers on a small-town Army recruit (John Gilbert) who goes to France, falls in love with a village girl (Renee Adoree), joins in the Big Push at the front, and returns minus a leg. Director King Vidor mounts the large-scale sequences of troop movements and the chaos of battle with realistic vigor that, combined with small scenes of human tenderness and comic by-play, add up to a convincing picture of men in war and its inhuman cost. Wartime violence and romantic situations. A-II (br)

Big Picture, The (1989) Rambling satire of Hollywood focusing on an aspiring young filmmaker (Kevin Bacon) determined not to compromise his values on the way up the ladder of success — but, of course, he does. Director Christopher Guest beats his rags-to-riches-to-rags message into the ground with cornball fantasy sequences and show-biz in-jokes that make the result similar to the self-indulgent, high-gloss student films it seeks to lampoon. Sexual innuendoes and vulgar references. A-III (PG-13)

Big Red (1962) French-Canadian orphan (Gilles Payant) taken in by a wealthy dog breeder (Walter Pidgeon) devotes himself to raising a beautiful Irish setter who later saves his master's life. Director Norman Tokar's rather flat Disney production has plenty of picturesque scenery of the Quebec countryside, and youngsters will fancy the boy-dog story. A-I (br)

Big Red One, The (1980) Director Samuel Fuller's attempt to honor the bravery of the US Army in WWII has sadly resulted in an episodic and tedious work. Lee Marvin seems to be sleepwalking through his pivotal role as the sergeant in charge of a special infantry unit. Instead of conveying the sacrifice and futility of war, it doesn't get much beyond obnoxious characterizations of some of the GIs who fought it. Wartime violence and incidental vulgarities. A-III (PG)

Big Shots (1987) Two fatherless youngsters — a streetwise inner-city black and a naive suburban white — help each other through a series of dangerous mishaps while trying to locate one boy's father and the other's watch. Director Robert Mandel unnecessarily emphasizes the boys' recklessly anti-social antics, foul street talk, and some violence in what disappointingly amounts to no more than a conventional chase picture. A-III (PG-13)

Big Sky, The (1952) Kentucky frontiersmen Kirk Douglas and Dewey Martin join veteran mountain man Arthur Hunnicutt on a fur-trapping expedition up the Missouri River into hostile Indian territory. Long, sprawling Western adventure directed by Howard Hawks, the period details of the journey are more interesting than the slow pace of the narrative and its occasional bursts of action. Frontier violence and some veiled sexual references. A-II (br)

Big Sleep, The (1946) Classic hard-boiled crime caper with Raymond Chandler's private eye, Philip Marlowe (Humphrey Bogart), taking a routine blackmail case that turns into a convoluted murder mystery involving a millionaire's bewildering daughters (Lauren Bacall and Martha Vickers). Director Howard Hawks keeps the plot complications simmering with plenty of rugged action, colorful tough guys, much sardonic humor, snappy dialogue, and the promise of romance. Stylized violence and sexual innuendo. A-III (br)

Big Sleep, The (1978) In a remake of the 1946 Howard Hawks-Raymond Chandler private eye classic, writer-director Michael Winner makes a disastrous mistake by taking the hard-boiled yet soft-edged detective Philip Marlowe out of his era and environment and plunking him down in contemporary London. This cultural dislocation only adds further confusion to the story's flurry of killings, eccentric cast of characters, and incredibly complex plot. Under the circumstances, Robert Mitchum has no chance of competing with Humphrey Bogart's performance as Marlowe in the original. Violence, brutality, and some nudity. O (R)

Big Steal, The (1949) Nifty chase thriller on Mexican back-roads with a US Army officer (Robert Mitchum) fleeing arrest by a fellow officer (William Bendix) for the theft of an Army payroll, while

Mitchum pursues the real culprit (Patric Knowles) with the help of a Spanish-speaking American (Jane Greer). Director Don Siegel's cat-and-mouse tale has plenty of eccentric curves, some deftly paced comic relief, and appropriately tough characterizations. Stylized violence, mild romance, and mostly positive Mexican stereotypes. A-II (br)

Big Store, The (1941) Weak Marx Brothers vehicle in which the veteran comics play department store detectives who turn the place into a shambles before unmasking the gang of thieves (headed by Douglas Dumbrille) out to bankrupt the store. Directed by Charles Reisner, the story's a bust and the brothers' slapstick routines and zany wordplay are only intermittently amusing. Comic violence and double entendres. A-II (br)

Big T.N.T. Show, The (1966) Concert film directed by Larry Peerce featuring such performers as Roger Miller, Ray Charles, Joan Baez, Donavan, The Byrds, Petula Clark, Ike & Tina Turner, and Bo Diddley. Mixed bag of positive, wholesome songs and tribal chants whose lyrics are understandable only by rock cultists. A-II (br)

Big Time (1988) Theatrical concert film directed in contrived, artsy fashion by Chris Blum showcasing the eccentric talents of singer-songwriter-poet Tom Waits. Best for Waits's fans. Some vulgar comic banter. A-III (PG)

Big Top Pee-wee (1988) Zany child-man Pee-wee Herman (Paul Reubens) matures as a gentleman farmer with a talking pig, a hotdog tree, a school teacher fiancé (Penelope Ann Miller), and his first screen kiss with her rival, a trapeze artist (Valeria Golino). Directed by Randal Kleiser, its colorful circus activity and gorgeous production values are marred by hackneyed images implying Pee-wee's sexual blossoming and loss of virginity. A-II (PG)

Big Town, The (1987) Small-time hustler (Matt Dillon) tries his luck shooting dice for big-time operators (Lee Grant and Bruce Dern) while taking his time deciding between a nice girl (Suzy Amis) and a strip-teaser (Diane Lane). He learns some lame lessons in director Ben Bolt's dingy melodrama which offers sex, violence, and nudity instead of anything remotely uplifting. O (R)

Big Trail, The (1930) Colorful Western adventure in which a seasoned mountain man (John Wayne) tracks those who killed his friend to a wagon train, then serves as scout guiding the settlers across the wilderness while getting the goods on the killers. Directed by Raoul Walsh, the melodramatic plot fairly creaks today, though the picture still holds interest for its visual spectacle of a pioneer wagon train overcoming swollen rivers, rugged mountains, desert wastes, and wild Indians on the journey from Missouri to Oregon. Frontier violence. A-I (br)

Big Trees, The (1952) Wooden turn-of-the-century melodrama about a claim-jumping logger (Kirk Douglas) who tries to wheedle a California religious sect into letting him cut down the giant redwoods they revere as symbols of the eternal. Director Felix Feist's contrived plot lumbers along from one complication to another until the logger's unsurprising reformation. Beautiful forest scenery, stylized violence, and mild romantic allusions. A-II (br)

Big Trouble (1986) A zany pair of con-artists (Peter Falk and Beverly D'Angelo) force a broker (Alan Arkin) to become their unwilling accomplice in an insurance fraud until a detective (Charles Durning) nails the pair. Director John Cassavetes elicits amiable performances in this witty but slight farce. Some rough language and brief nudity. A-III (R)

Big Trouble in Little China (1986) Kurt Russell reveals a comic flair for mock heroics in an action-fantasy about a 2,000-year-old Chinese wizard who is determined to kidnap and marry the green-eyed girlfriend of one of Russell's pals. John Carpenter directs this martial-arts frolic in a movie teeming with special effects. Much profanity and sadistic violence. A-III (PG-13)

Big Wednesday (1978) Three young surfer fanatics spend their time boozing, fighting, and womanizing in director John Milius's vulgar glorification of the male bond, arrested in the adolescence of the beach-bum culture of the past, offering viewers little save scenes of nature's grandeur. O (PG)

Big Wheel, The (1949) Formula tale directed by Edward Ludwig in which the son (Mickey Rooney) of a famous race-car driver lands in a heap of trouble trying to emulate his dead dad, then straightens out in time to race in the Indianapolis 500. Racetrack accidents and sexual situations. A-III (br)

Bigamist, The (1953) Contrived melodrama in which a married sales executive (Edmond O'Brien) falls for a Los Angeles waitress (Ida Lupino), gets her pregnant, then weds her before seeking a divorce from his wife (Joan Fontaine) in San Francisco. Also directed by Lupino, the scenario treats the husband sympathetically as a gentleman motivated by a reluctance to hurt either woman, though viewers are likely to render a harsher judgment. Adult themes. A-III (br)

Bigger Than Life (1956) When a mild-mannered, underpaid, and overworked elementary school teacher (James Mason) falls ill, the drug used in his treatment has disastrous psychological aftereffects that make him a threat to his wife (Barbara Rush) and young son. Directed by Nicholas Ray, the well-meaning but slow-moving lesson in the pitfalls of becoming addicted to prescribed drugs is less than convincing. A-II (br)

Biggest Bundle of Them All, The (1967) Comic crime melodrama directed by Ken Annakin about the kidnapping of an American gangster relies excessively on sexual innuendo. O (br)

Bikini Beach (1964) Sun-baked youth comedy in which the owner (Keenan Wynn) of a seaside retirement home tries to rid the area of boisterous surfers whose leader (Frankie Avalon) is more concerned that his girlfriend (Annette Funicello) is falling for a British pop singer (also Avalon). Directed by William Asher, the banal plot adds drag-racing to the formula mix of song, dance, surfing, and brawling. Slapstick violence, sexual situations, and much sexual innuendo. A-III (br)

Bill & Ted's Bogus Journey (1991) In this moronic sequel to their 1989 clunker, the two young oafs (Keanu Reeves and Alex Winter) are murdered by robot lookalikes and, after sampling heaven and hell, force the Grim Reaper to return them to Earth to rescue their girlfriends. Peter Hewitt directs a lame fantasy whose lack of intelligence is no laughing matter. Some mock violence and minimal gutter talk. A-II (PG)

Bill & Ted's Excellent Adventure (1989) Two spacey teenagers (Keanu Reeves and Alex Winter) are saved from sure flunk-out with the help of a futuristic genie (George Carlin), whose magical phone booth enables them to nab some historic figures (Napoleon, Sigmund Freud, Billy the Kid, etc.) as show 'n' tell for a crucial oral history project. Director Stephen Herek's cheesy putdown of modern adolescent sensibilities includes moronic depictions of education and parenting. Some gratuitous vulgar references laced with sexual innuendo. A-III (PG)

Bill of Divorcement, A (1932) Stilted melodrama from Clemence Dane's play about a young woman (Katharine Hepburn) whose marriage prospects dim after her father (John Barrymore) returns from an asylum to find his wife (Billie Burke) has divorced him and is about to remarry. Directed by George Cukor, the maudlin proceedings gain interest mainly from Barrymore's cheerful delusions and Hepburn's acceptance of the situation. Questions of divorce and hereditary insanity. A-III (br)

Bill of Divorcement, A (1940) Remake of the 1932 original, with Maureen O'Hara as the young Englishwoman who learns insanity runs in her family when her father (Adolphe Menjou) returns from an asylum on Christmas Eve. Directed by John Farrow, the cast is fine, but the situations seem even more dated than in the original. Sympathetic treatment of divorce and dated view of hereditary insanity. A-III (br)

Billion Dollar Brain (1967) Filmed on location in Finland, the third in the British spy-with-horn-rimmed-glasses series starring Michael Caine as Harry Palmer goes gimmicky, humorless, and even offensive with some graphic lovemaking. Almost nothing of the original Palmer character is recognizable but the glasses, as Caine stumbles stolidly through acres of snow on a mission involving biowarfare and a Texas millionaire's giant computer. Director Ken Russell's elaborate satire on obsessive anti-Communist types is clear enough, but that's about all that is in this brainless film. Violence and sexual scenes. O (br)

Billy Bathgate (1991) Sluggish 1930s gangster movie about a Bronx youth (Loren Dean) learning the ropes under his idol, Dutch Schultz (Dustin Hoffman), while juggling a dangerous relationship with the mobster's seductive girlfriend (Nicole Kidman). Director Robert Benton's less-than-compelling guys-and-molls flick has more vapid valleys than high spots. Sporadic violence, a brief bedroom scene, momentary nudity, a homosexual reference, and some rough language. A-III (R)

Billy Budd (1962) Engrossing version of Herman Melville's story contrasting justice and the letter of the law when the seaman of the title (Terence Stamp) faces hanging aboard a British man-of-war in 1797 for striking an officer (Robert Ryan) who has falsely accused him of fomenting mutiny. Director Peter Ustinov (who also plays the vessel's vacillating captain) effectively evokes the twisted malevolence of the bullying master-at-arms, who cannot abide the simple innocence of the stammering seaman. Stylized violence and moral dilemmas. A-II (br)

Billy Jack (1971) Simple-minded story of the conflict between a redneck town and a school for runaway teenagers located on an Arizona Indian reservation, where the title hero (Tom Laughlin, who also directed) champions the area's oppressed Indians, Mexicans, blacks, and school's youngsters by fighting violence with violence. Besides the violent proceedings are a rape, brief nudity, and rough language. O (GP)

Billy Madison (1995) Dim-witted comedy in which a retiring billionaire (Darren McGavin) decides to leave control of his hotel empire to his loutish 27-year-old son (Adam Sandler), provided the wastrel manages to graduate grades 1-12 in six months, or else it all goes to the billionaire's scheming assistant (Bradley Whitford). Director Tamra Davis's dismal attempt to fashion a vehicle for Sandler's limited comic talents never rises above dumb toilet jokes and moronic situations, adding up to zero as entertainment. Occasional sexual innuendo and alcohol abuse, brief violence played for laughs, some crude bathroom humor, and an instance of rough language. A-III (PG-13)

Billy Rose's Diamond Horseshoe (1945) Lightweight musical romance directed by George Seaton and set in the New York nightclub of the title, where a medical student (Dick Haymes) woos a showgirl (Betty Grable) despite the objections of his showbiz father (William Gaxton). Artificial romantic complications. A-II (br)

Billy Rose's Jumbo (1962) Bright but overlong turn-of-the-century musical about a failing circus whose owner (Jimmy Durante) relies on his daughter (Doris Day) to keep things going, but she falls for a helpful stranger (Stephen Boyd) who's out to get their prize elephant for a rival circus. Directed by Charles Waters, the soggy Day-Boyd romance is a distinct handicap, but the comic by-play between Durante and Martha Raye as his longsuffering fiancé, the Rodgers and Hart musical numbers, and the colorful circus acts offer something for everybody. A-I (br)

Billy the Kid (1941) After switching sides in a range war between a conniving land-grabber (Gene

Lockhart) and a straight-arrow English rancher (Ian Hunter), the hard-bitten gunman of the title (Robert Taylor) becomes a peaceable cowboy, until the Englishman's murder causes him to seek vengeance on the killers, despite the warnings of his boyhood friend (Brian Donlevy), who is now the marshal. Directed by David Miller, the Western action is colorful but flawed by a romanticized plot and Taylor's wooden performance. Frontier violence with some sense of its tragedy and pain. A-I (br)

Billy the Kid vs. Dracula (1966) Director William Beaudine's low-budget attempt to graft the Western and horror movie strains results in a silly hybrid that youngsters might possibly sit through but anyone of the age of reason will find beyond endurance. A-I (br)

Billy Two Hats (1974) Two smalltime bank robbers (Gregory Peck and Desi Arnaz, Jr.) are on the run from a racist, Indian-hating marshal (Jack Warden) and his deputy (David Huddleston). Directed by Ted Kotcheff, the two friends in crime become symbolic reference points for the death of the Old West with the passing of the buffalo and the advent of the railroad. One very violent sequence. A-III (PG)

Billy's Hollywood Screen Kiss (1998) Failed homosexual romantic comedy in which a photographer (Sean P. Hayes) falls for a male model (Brad Rowe), pursues him with growing frustration, then finally realizes he's interested in another guy. Writer-director Tommy O'Haver tries to dress up the tired formula plot and its cardboard characters with colorful but hokey homosexual parties, but the inane results lack the intended human pathos that might have given the situation some interest. Uncritical treatment of homosexual relationships as well as occasional profanity and rough language. O (R)

Biloxi Blues (1988) Coming-of-age comedy adapted by Neil Simon from his autobiographical play about a New York would-be writer (Matthew Broderick) in a Mississippi boot camp at the close of WWII, who is constantly in hot water with his brain-damaged sergeant (Christopher Walken) and some of his company's more macho men. Tight direction by Mike Nichols enhances Simon's perceptive reflections on the milestones and meatheads one is forced to confront in such close quarters during wartime. Much rough language and a sexual situation involving a prostitute. A-III (PG-13)

Bingo (1991) Contrived fantasy has an amazingly clever little mutt saving a half-drowned boy (Robert J. Steinmiller, Jr.) and tailing him cross-country to become part of his family. Director Matthew Robbins's scrappy comedy is no more than a series of cutesy dog tricks in search of a movie. Some slapstick violence, menace to a child, and frequent toilet humor. A-II (PG)

Bingo Long Traveling All-Stars and Motor Kings, The (1976) Warmly nostalgic comedy about a black baseball team barnstorming through the Midwest during the Depression summer of 1939, an era when black players were barred from the major leagues. Starring Billy Dee Williams, James Earl Jones, and Richard Pryor as top players who start hamming it up in the style of the Harlem Globe Trotters to make their victories against white teams go down easier. Director John Badham's movie looks back at the way it was, good and bad, without finding villains or making excuses. Good entertainment, but coarse language and a brothel vignette unfortunately limit its appeal. A-III (PG)

Bio-Dome (1996) Mindless but obnoxious comedy directed by Jason Bloom in which the boorish antics of untalented comics Pauly Shore and Stephen Baldwin wreck an expensive environmental habitat, then put it back together for a bogus feel-good ending. Comic crudities, sexist humor, sophomoric sexual references, coarse expressions, and an instance of rough language. A-III (PG-13)

Birch Interval (1976) Charming and affecting movie produced by Robert B. Radnitz, about a preteen New York City girl (Susan McClung) who in 1947 confronts the emerging complexities of adult life when she is sent to stay with her grandfather (Eddie Albert) and uncle (Rip Torn) in a tranquil Amish community in Pennsylvania. Director Delbert Mann treats the marital problems of the uncle delicately, while depicting in close detail Amish country life. Episodic and a little slow-moving, the movie nonetheless is a refreshing view of family matters that parents and their teenagers might benefit from discussing. A-II (PG)

Bird (1988) Biography of troubled jazz saxophonist Charlie "Bird" Parker (Forest Whitaker), who died in 1955 at age 34 after ravaging his body with years of heroin and alcohol addiction, follows his last years on the road and with his common-law wife (Diane Venora). There's not a false note in this expressionistic, moody look at the jazz subculture of the 1950s. Directed by Clint Eastwood. Realistic view of the consequences of Parker's addiction, a graphic suicide attempt, sexual promiscuity, and an offhanded acceptance of out-of-wedlock pregnancy. A-IV (R)

Bird of Paradise (1932) Exotic romance on a remote South Sea island, where an American sailor (Joel McCrea) falls in love with the king's daughter (Delores Del Rio), who's destined to be sacrificed to save her people from the island's angry volcano. Directed by King Vidor, the couple's romantic idyll is picturesque but as emotionally hollow as the phony melodramatics of the contrived story. Sexual situations and fleeting semi-nudity. A-III (br)

Bird on a Wire (1990) Classy slam-bang chase thriller in which a former government witness (Mel Gibson) and his one-time sweetheart (Goldie Hawn) are on the run from vengeful drug dealers (David Carradine and Bill Duke) as well as assorted police agencies. Director John Badham maintains an air of romantic comedy throughout the desperate proceedings, mixing the screwball characterizations of the couple with some spectacular action stunts, notably in a jungle zoo. Much menace and demolition-derby violence, a bedroom scene, and some sexually suggestive dialogue. A-III (PG-13)

Bird with the Crystal Plumage, The (1970) Failed Italian thriller in which a passer-by (Tony Musante) saves a woman (Eva Renzi) from the black-cloaked knifer and then finds himself and his sleep-in girlfriend (Suzy Kendall) the target of the ripper. Directed by Dario Argento, the loose ends and false clues are so apparent that the state of terrifying suspense so necessary to such a film is never fully realized. A-III (GP)

Birdcage, The (1996) Comic complications ensue when the son of a gay Miami nightclub owner (Robin Williams) invites his fiancé and her ultra-conservative parents (Gene Hackman and Dianne Wiest) home for dinner and the gay man's lover (Nathan Lane) shows up in drag, pretending to be the son's mother. Producer-director Mike Nichols's remake of **La Cage aux Folles** (1979) pokes fun at flamboyant homosexuals and those who shun them while stressing the vulnerable humanity of both groups. Sympathetic depiction of the gay lifestyle, many sexual references, and intermittent rough language. A-IV (R)

Birdman of Alcatraz (1962) Fact-based prison saga of Robert Stroud (Burt Lancaster), whose death sentence for killing a guard in Leavenworth prison was commuted in 1916 to life in solitary confinement, which he spent becoming an eminent authority on birds before transfer in 1942 to Alcatraz, where he was deprived of anything to do with birds until transferred out in 1959. In showing Stroud's transformation from a vicious criminal to a dedicated ornithologist over 43 years in solitary, director John Frankenheimer probes the man's rehabilitation in relation to his mother (Thelma Ritter), wife (Betty Field), a sympathetic guard (Neville Brand), and a punitive prison warden (Karl Malden). Stylized violence and justice questions. A-II (br)

Birds, The (1963) Classy adaptation of Daphne du Maurier's story of nature in revolt begins leisurely as a romantic comedy that gradually shifts into high gear as a suspense thriller when seagulls, crows, and other usually harmless birds suddenly turn malignant and band together in murderous attacks on a seaside community. Director Alfred Hitchcock is up to his old tricks in transforming the ordinary into the menacing as he puts his vulnerable principals (Rod Taylor, Tippi Hedren, Jessica Tandy, and Suzanne Pleshette) through an emotional wringer trying to fend off nightmare attacks by the winged avengers. Mounting menace and special-effects violence, with a key sequence involving schoolchildren that youngsters may find especially frightening. A-II (PG-13)

Birds Do It (1966) Harmless comedy directed by Andrew Marton in which Tab Hunter plays a secret agent trying to get from Soupy Sales, whom he mistakes for a scientist, a secret ionizer that enables people to fly. Innocuous story which young children may find amusing. A-I (br)

Birds Do It, Bees Do It (1974) Documentary focuses on how living things make other living things from the world of microbes to that of human beings. Very graphic in depicting the mating of birds, bees, and just about everything else. For adults and older teens. A-III (R/PG)

Birds, the Bees and the Italians, The (1967) Director Pietro Germi's biting satire on Italian hypocrisy may prove offensive to some viewers because its story concerns adultery and because of coarse language. A-IV (br)

Birdy (1984) Vietnam vet (Matthew Modine) left virtually catatonic by a battlefield wound dreams about his past and his boyhood desire to be a bird, while a friend (Nicolas Cage) tries to bring him back to reality in the grim confines of an Army hospital. Director Alan Parker gets lost in sketchy characterizations and great globs of tedious monologues that seem pointless, especially recollections of youthful sexual encounters with graphic nudity. O (R)

Birth of a Nation, The (1915) D.W. Griffith's still controversial, still powerful picture of the Civil War and Reconstruction links the lives of two families, North and South, each sacrificing sons in the fratricidal conflict, then focuses on the Southern family's plight under greedy carpetbaggers and black opportunists until the Ku Klux Klan rides to the rescue in a swirl of racist propaganda. Griffith's mastery of the silent medium succeeds in combining the sweep of historical spectacle with the intimacy of individual lives in a fashion that still engages viewers' emotions. Though it has a place in film history as the first feature to demonstrate fully the dramatic potential of the medium, the work presents an uncritical view of 19th-century myths justifying white supremacy. Not for casual entertainment, but has a place in film study programs where its racist perspective can be properly addressed. A-IV (br)

Birthday Party, The (1968) Good adaptation of Harold Pinter's play about two overnight guests (Patrick Magee and Sydney Tafler) who entertain the permanent lodger (Robert Shaw) with disastrous consequences. Director William Friedkin succeeds in conveying the play's never-explained mood of fear that pervades the menacing rooms of the house and the acting is superb. Mature themes. A-III (G)

The Biscuit Eater (1940) Sentimental but unpretentious melodrama from James Street's story of a little white boy (Billy Lee) and his black chum who, despite numerous mishaps, train the seemingly worthless runt of the title into a champion bird dog, then face a tragic loss that will leave few viewers dry-eyed. Director Stuart Heisler makes effective use of the rural Georgia locales, including a fearsome swamp, but the heart of the movie is in the interaction between the boys and their beloved dog. Rewarding family fare. A-I (br)

Biscuit Eater, The (1972) A couple of kids (Johnny Whitaker and George Spell) train a rejected bird dog for the regional championships which, if it wins, will make Johnny's dad (Earl Holliman) look bad in the eyes of his boss (Lew Ayres). Director Vincent McEveety's version of the James Street classic will appeal mainly to the elementary school set since it follows the Disney formula of animals exceeding humans in intelligence. A-I (G)

Bishop's Wife, The (1947) A debonair, smartly tailored angel (Cary Grant) uses his heavenly powers to help the neglected wife (Loretta Young) of a busy Episcopalian bishop (David Niven) renew her husband's ministry to those in need rather than in raising the money for a new cathedral. Director Henry Koster's sentimental Christmas fable has the virtue of a good script, sincere performances, and some amusing moments with Grant's angelic powers and Monty Wooley as a softhearted old cynic. Most of the family will find it charming entertainment. A-II (nr)

Bite the Bullet (1975) Muddled Western directed by Richard Brooks dealing with a 700-mile horse race shortly after the turn of the century. Its hero (Gene Hackman) gives a coolly reasoned critique of the cruel stupidity of the race and its win-at-all-costs spirit, but not long afterwards he himself joins in and submits his horse to the brutal ordeal. Stylized violence. A-III (PG)

Bitter Moon (1994) Repellent shipboard melodrama in which a paralyzed American (Peter Coyote) and his sultry French wife (Emanuelle Seigner) lure a conventional British couple (Hugh Grant and Kristin Scott-Thomas) into joining them in deadly sadomasochistic sex games. Director Roman Polanski's darkly perverse look at extreme sexual obsession thoroughly dehumanizes its characters and despairs of any normal loving relationships. Brief graphic violence, numerous bedroom scenes with nudity, and much rough language. O (R)

Bitter Sugar (1996) The pro-Castro beliefs of a young Cuban student (Rene Lavan) are shaken to the core when he discovers his fiancé (Mayte Vilan) has taken to prostitution to survive, and his rebellious brother (Larry Villanueva) has deliberately injected himself with AIDS-tainted blood in protest against the repressive regime. Director Leon Ichaso's melodramatic political tract blends doomed romance and family crises into a scathing portrait of a beleaguered island whose economy caters to tourists at the expense of its own people. Subtitles. Brief spurts of violence, a discreet sexual encounter, and some rough language. A-III (nr)

Bitter Tea of General Yen, The (1933) Exotic tale set in war-torn China, where an American refugee (Barbara Stanwyck) is rescued from the fighting by a cruel but cultured warlord (Nils Asther) whom she finds strangely appealing, then unwittingly causes his downfall. Directed by Frank R. Capra, the romantic melodrama succeeds in creating the unsettled, menacing atmosphere of a war zone as the bandit patiently woos the rescued woman, then contemplates a double suicide upon learning she was responsible for his defeat. Stylized violence and sexual situations. A-III (br)

Bittersweet Love (1977) A couple (Meredith Baxter Birney and Scott Hylands) fall in love, but only after getting married and her pregnancy is well-advanced do they discover that they have the same father (Robert Lansing). Director David Miller takes a glossy soap opera approach to the theme of incest in a cloying and tedious film that raises issues about abortion and divorce without much insight. A- III (PG)

B.J. Lang Presents (1972) Only Mickey Rooney's hardiest fans may be able to endure a picture in which their idol rants and rages mercilessly as a movie director driven insane by fantasies of former glory. Director Yabo Yablonsky revels in flashy camera tricks, strobe lighting, and sound effects in a pointless exercise in horror. A-III (R)

Black and White in Color (1977) Extremely subtle and probing French comedy set in West Africa at the start of WW I, it tells the story of what happens when a small French settlement decides to attack a nearby German post. In looking at the human factors that lead to war, director Jean-Jacques Annaud avoids sentiment entirely, spares no one in this cast of characters and delivers an outrageous challenging and extremely funny anti-war film. Wartime violence and brief, incidental nudity. A-III (PG)

Black Angel (1946) Dark crime story from the Cornell Woolrich novel in which the wife (June Vincent) of a man convicted of murder joins forces with the victim's estranged husband (Dan Duryea) to find the real killer, whom they suspect is a shady nightclub owner (Peter Lorre). Director Roy William Neill goes for atmosphere rather than action, with plodding results and an unsurprising twist ending. More menace than violence and an alcoholic central character. A-II (br)

Black Bart (1948) Fanciful Western in which the title's smooth outlaw (Dan Duryea) throws in with a crooked banker (John McIntire) to rob Wells Fargo gold shipments, then is forced to take in a shifty ex-partner (Jeffrey Lynn) who gums up the works and both end in a hail of bullets. Directed by George Sherman, the tale is embroidered with a visit by Lola Montez (Yvonne De Carlo), who falls for the dashing outlaw in a brief interlude adding a wistful note to the otherwise tough-minded proceedings. Stylized violence and mild romance. A-II (br)

Black Beauty (1971) British version of the classic tale of a boy (Mark Lester) and his horse comes to the screen under the direction of James Hill. It is lovely to look at but, unfortunately, it is flawed by stilted scripting and wooden performances which, one hopes, will not spoil it for younger audiences. A-I (G)

Black Beauty (1994) Richly pictorial version of Anna Sewell's 1877 children's classic in which the spirited horse of the title recounts (as voiced by Alan Cumming) his life under good masters (Sean Bean, Jim Carter, and David Thewlis) and bad (Eleanor Bron, Peter Cook, and Alun Armstrong) until, old and broken, he's given a home by the former stable boy who had grown to love him. Scripted by director Caroline Thompson, the movie captures the beauty of the animal world and the picturesque nature of the Victorian era, though the woes seem to outweigh the joys in this episodic chronicle teaching youngsters the responsibility of caring for animals. Scenes of the horse's mistreatment and endangerment by sickness, fire, and flood may distress the very young. A-I (G)

Black Belt Jones (1974) Black kung-fu movie with Jim Kelly and Gloria Hendry fighting to keep their school of self-defense in the Watts area of L.A. from falling into the hands of the Mafia. Director Robert Clouse goes in for a lot of clowning and sight gags, leading to a sudsy climax in a car-wash gone berserk, an approach which makes the movie fairly tolerable despite its deep-down mindlessness and brutality. A-III (R)

Black Bird, The (1976) Unfunny spoof of **The Maltese Falcon** private-eye classic with George Segal playing Sam Spade, Jr., and Stephane Audran as the femme fatale who has not quite mastered the American idiom. Director David Giler strains hard for laughs, even trying for some religious parody, but nothing works. The language is frequently blasphemous. O (PG)

Black Caesar (1973) Black crime movie in which Fred Williamson takes over a Harlem-South Bronx crime syndicate by acquiring pay-off ledgers incriminating New York politicians. Written, produced, and directed by Larry Cohen, it trades exclusively in ruthless violence, sex, and street language.O (R)

Black Cauldron, The (1985) Disney's animated adventure about the brave attempts of a peasant boy to prevent the evil Horned King from gaining possession of a black cauldron capable of producing an army of supernatural warriors. The result is a delightful fantasy saga during which the boy learns about love, loyalty, courage, and the importance of friendship over power. Some creepy moments. A-I (PG)

Black Christmas (1975) Nasty Canadian horror movie directed by Bob Clark follows the exploits of a maniac who terrorizes a sorority house over the Christmas holidays. The incoherent script attempts to bridge the gap between the gruesome murder of coeds and the obscene telephone calls that are disgusting. O (R)

Black Dog (1998) Contrived action thriller in which an ex-con truck driver (Patrick Swayze) is coerced into transporting assault weapons across state lines while pursued by murderous hijackers and federal agents. Directed by Kevin Hooks, the result is standard TV-movie fare. Intermittent violence, occasional profanity, and an instance of rough language. A-III (PG-13)

Black Dragons (1942) Wartime clunker directed by William Nigh concerns an Axis spy ring using a Nazi plastic surgeon (Bela Lugosi) to transform Japanese espionage agents into bogus American businessmen. Period anti-Japanese stereotypes. A-II (br)

Black Eye (1974) Black private eye Fred Williamson is searching Los Angeles for an antique cane stuffed with heroin and for a missing girl who is reportedly being held in a commune of Jesus freaks. Jack Arnold's direction is fast-paced, but muddying the waters is a sub-plot involving a bisexual relationship between our hero, his girlfriend (Teresa Graves), and her girlfriend (Rosemary Forsyth). Routine violence. A-IV (PG)

Black Girl (1972) Uneven drama of a black American family portrays the tensions and conflicts, the misplaced love and bitterness, that stem from a kind of collective familial sense of inferiority. Directed by Ossie Davis, the movie seems largely aimed against its own members, particularly those who attempt to break the mold and escape the family's self-imposed cultural limitations. A-III (PG)

Black Godfather, The (1974) Low-budget black exploitation movie with heavy doses of unrelieved brutality and shrill racism. Written, produced, and directed by John Evans, it offers a low view of humanity in general and of black life in particular. O (R)

Black Gold (1947) An Indian rancher (Anthony Quinn) and his wife (Katherine DeMille) adopt an orphaned Chinese boy, become millionaires when oil is discovered on their land, and enter a horse they've raised from a colt in the Kentucky Derby. Despite a rambling narrative with predictable plot complications, director Phil Karlson holds it together by focusing on the rancher's mare and her colt, abetted by warm performances from the human principals. An animal story with heart and some social consciousness. A-I (br)

Black Gunn (1973) Black crime movie features Jim Brown as a posh nightclub owner drawn into a confrontation with the mob when they kill his younger brother for knocking off a numbers parlor. Directed by Robert Hartford-Davis, the story provides ample opportunities for violence of every description, some casual sex, and coarse language. O (R)

Black Hand (1950) After his father is murdered by the criminal society of the title, a young Italian American (Gene Kelly) determines to drive the gang from his turn-of-the-century New York neighborhood, getting help along the way from a dedicated city detective (J. Carrol Naish). Directed by Richard Thorpe, the formula story is told with vigor, plenty of period atmosphere, and strong performances from the two leads. Stylized violence and much menace. A-II (br)

Black Hole, The (1980) Disney science-fiction movie with some fine special effects and a mediocre plot about a maverick scientist (Maximilian Schell) and his mysterious space laboratory. Unfortunately, director Gary Nelson has made the experience no more intriguing than a ride at Disneyland. Incidental violence. A-II (PG)

Black Jesus (1971) Awkward Italian production about a black African revolutionary (Woody Strode) who tries to maintain a peaceful course in the midst of leading an energetic revolution. Director Valerio Zurlini's narrative suffers from interminable, badly-dubbed dialogue, an agonizingly slow pace, and a mechanical plot device drawing rather simplistic and superficial parallels to the passion of Jesus. Some brutal violence. A-III (GP)

Black Knight, The (1954) A blacksmith (Alan Ladd) wins knighthood and his lady fair (Patricia Medina) by saving King Arthur (Anthony Bushell), Camelot, and Christianity from the treachery of Cornwall's pagan king (Andre Morell) and his Saracen allies (led by Peter Cushing). Directed by Tay Garnett, the ludicrous plot turns the Arthurian legend into a pulp fantasy whose erratic action, including Arthur's sacking of Stonehenge, may bemuse adult viewers while seeming exciting for those too young to know better. Much stylized violence and a ridiculous Druid orgy. A-I (br)

Black Mama (1976) A black woman raising her child in a Los Angeles ghetto is gradually radicalized by her experiences in just trying to survive. Although director Haile Gerima uses an impressionistic style, alternating between objective reality and subjective fantasy, its message is clear that the dehumanizing conditions of poverty and racism are intolerable. A-III (nr)

Black Mama, White Mama (1973) Philippine story of two women (Pam Grier and Margaret Markhov) who escape from a prison camp handcuffed together. Director Eddie Romero, no stranger to this kind of thing, features lots of whipping, stripping, and degradation. O (R)

Black Marble, The (1980) Joseph Wambaugh adapted his own novel for this movie about the romance that develops between two police officers (Paula Prentiss and Robert Foxworth). Director Harold Becker succeeds with some fine characterizations and valid emotions but fails to integrate a major subplot involving a hapless, bungling dognapper (Harry Dean Stanton). The film's decent edge is blunted by some violence and an acceptance of a premarital relationship. A-III (PG)

Black Mask (1999) Routine Hong Kong martial-arts flick in which a genetically enhanced human (Jet Li) joins forces with a cop (Lau Ching Wan) to battle an elite group of super-soldiers intent on world domination. Directed by Daniel Lee, the threadbare story is merely an excuse to demonstrate myriad ways to maim and slaughter opponents. Excessive violence with gore, a rough-sex encounter, much rough language, and an instance of profanity. O (R)

Black Moon (1975) French surrealistic fantasy in which a young girl (Cathryn Harrison), fleeing a bloody civil war between men and women combatants, finds refuge in an isolated country house in which live a bedridden old woman (Therese Gieshe), a brother, and sister (Joe Dallesandro and Alexandra Stewart) and a band of children. While battles rage round the estate, the girl is preoccupied with her bizarre surroundings which include a talking unicorn, crying flowers, and an enormous rat named Humphrey. Director Louis Malle is less concerned with the theme of innocence than with the modern preoccupation with death and sex. Mature themes. A-IV (R)

Black Moon Rising (1987) Seething raw sexuality and toughness, Tommy Lee Jones slithers through this implausible drama from director Harley Cokliss as a thief hired to obtain some tax-court evidence. He hides his findings in a prototype racing car which is then stolen. The casual sex, brutal beatings, and hair-raising stunts he puts up with to retrieve the data are not worth the viewing time. O (R)

Black Orchid, The (1959) Slow but feeling drama of the pitfalls facing a happy-go-lucky widower (Anthony Quinn) in courting a proud widow (Sophia Loren), whom his grown daughter (Ina Balin) regards with contempt. Director Martin Ritt gets good performances in a nicely textured story of Italian-American life in New York City, but the plot complications with offspring, relatives, and friends keep getting in the way until an entirely predictable conclusion. Troubled characters and perplexing situations make it unlikely fare for young children. A-I (br)

Black Orpheus (1959) Vibrant intercultural feast updating the Greek myth to Rio de Janeiro, where trolley driver Orpheus (Breno Mello) accidentally kills his beloved Eurydice (Marpessa Dawn) while trying to protect her from a stalker costumed as Death and, after a religious cult fails to revive her, he sets out with her body for burial until another fatal accident intervenes. Directed by Marcel Camus, the appealing leads are supported by a spirited cast, who play out the mythic tragedy amidst the gaiety of Rio's Carnival with its colorful parades of dancing bands, backed by a haunting music score and spectacular views of Rio's picturesque locales. Subtitles. Stylized violence, sexual situations, and innuendo. A-III (br)

Black Patch (1951) Western misfire about a one-eyed marshal (George Montgomery) and a mixed-up widow (Diane Brewster) in a one-street town, whose nasty boss (Sebastian Cabot) sends an alienated youngster (Tom Pittman) to kill the lawman. Writer-director Allen H. Miner never gets beyond the bogus motivations of one-dimensional characters in a convoluted but pointless plot. Heavy-handed stylized violence, sordid atmosphere, and sexual inferences. A-III (br)

Black Pearl, The (1977) A young lad (Mario Custodio) in a small Mexican village, whose livelihood depends upon pearl-diving, is taught to respect the power of the sea by an old Indian (Gilbert Roland). Produced in Mexico and directed by Saul Swimmer, the movie's greatest strength lies in its beautiful natural setting and in its depiction of a youngster coming to terms with his religious beliefs and his doubts about himself. The very young may find the scenes with a sea monster quite scary. A-II (PG)

Black Peter (1971) Czechoslovakian movie of a 17-year-old boy (Ladislav Jakim) growing up with all the anguished diffidence of adolescence in his dealings with parents and friends, his first job, and his shy curiosity about girls. The first feature of director Milos Forman, made in 1964, it is a string of small gems crystallizing the final, wonderfully hazy days of uncommitted youth the world over. A-III (nr)

Black Rain (1989) Glossy crime thriller celebrates the hard-edged cynicism of an American cop (Michael Douglas), who bludgeons his way through Japan in pursuit of an escaped criminal but ultimately is taught a lesson in honor by a self-effacing Japanese detective (Ken Takakura). Director Ridley Scott devotes his energies to endless chase scenes in an exotic foreign culture, but is unable to work up any sympathy for the foul-mouthed, small-minded, anti-hero portrayed by Douglas. Much excessive violence and incessant rough language. O (R)

Black Raven, The (1943) Hokey mystery thriller directed by Sam Newfield takes place in a country inn, whose sinister owner (George Zucco), addled assistant (Glenn Strange), and assorted lodgers spend a stormy night searching for a murderer. Pedestrian proceedings with bogus menace. A-I (br)

Black Robe (1991) After arriving in 17th-century New France, a Jesuit missionary (Lothaire Bluteau), guided by Algonquins, endures both a dangerous journey through the Canadian wilderness and an Iroquois attack to reach a distant Huron mission. Only towards the end does director Bruce Beresford manage to put the cultural clash between the humorless priest and the unbelieving Native-Americans in a moving spiritual context. Some brief but graphic violence and several shadowy sexual encounters with momentary nudity. A-III (R)

Black Rodeo (1972) Documentary about a contingent of black cowboys who bring a Wild West show to New York, which serves to make people aware of the black contribution to the heritage of the American West. Directed by Jeff Kanew and narrated by Woody Strode, the result has some expert slow-motion photography and a soundtrack full of pop songs commenting ironically on the action in the arena. A-I (G)

Black Rose, The (1950) Colorful 13th-century adventure in which a troubled Saxon noble (Tyrone Power) and a simple bowman (Jack Hawkins) flee Norman England for the Orient, where they enter the service of a Mongol general (Orson Welles), aid a Crusader's daughter (Cecile Aubry), and wind up prisoners in a besieged Chinese town. Director Henry Hathaway keeps the pot boiling as the embittered Saxon tests his courage, samples the wisdom of the East, and finally returns to England a better man. Stylized violence and mild sexual innuendo. A-II (br)

Black Samson (1974) Familiar story of black versus white in the struggle over inner-city turf, though the hero this time is a rather whimsical ghetto bar owner (Rockne Tarkington) who wants to keep his Los Angeles neighborhood drug- and crime-free. Directed by Charles Bail, it wastes its potential by taking the predictable, brutal path leading to the inevitable bloodbath climax. Violence, rough language, and numerous glimpses of the casual nudity in a topless bar. O (R)

Black Scorpion, The (1957) Hokey monster tale directed by Edward Ludwig in which an American geologist (Richard Denning) investigating a volcanic eruption in Mexico discovers a fissure leading to a cavern filled with gigantic prehistoric scorpions, one of which escapes to attack Mexico City. Stylized violence and menace. A-I (br)

Black Sheep (1996) Inept comedy in which a well-meaning oaf (Chris Farley) nearly ruins his brother's chances to be elected governor, despite the efforts of a campaign staffer (David Spade) to keep the bumbler out of the public eye. A limp script and tepid physical comedy make director Penelope Spheeris's movie look more like an extended TV sitcom. Some slapstick violence, brief substance abuse, minor sexual innuendo, intermittent profanity, and an instance of rough language. A-III (PG-13)

Black Shield of Falworth, The (1954) Uneven medieval romance set in England during the reign of Henry IV (Ian Keith), as a youthful rustic (Tony Curtis) is befriended by a nobleman (Herbert Marshall) and his daughter (Janet Leigh), then is made a knight and saves the king and his son Hal (Dan O'Herlihy) from a traitor (David Farrar). Directed by Rudolph Maté from Howard Pyle's novel, the period action is colorful, especially a section showing the stages in the training of a knight, but the story's development is sluggish and the characters one-dimensional. Period violence. A-I (br)

Black Sheep, The (1956) Week horror hokum directed by Reginald Le Borg in which a Victorian surgeon (Basil Rathbone), abetted by his butler (Bela Lugosi) and a gypsy henchman (Akim Tamiroff), uses an ancient drug to induce a death-like trance on subjects needed for brain experiments, with deformed survivors (notably John Carradine, Lon Chaney, Jr., and Tor Johnson) kept chained in the cellar. Grisly concept but boring treatment with few scares and little tension. A-II (br)

Black Six, The (1974) Black motorcycle movie with Gene Washington as the leader of a bike pack of Vietnam War veterans, who seem to find nothing but trouble wherever they go. Excessive violence and rough language. O (R)

Black Stallion, The (1979) Strikingly visualized tale about the magical relationship between a youngster (Kelly Reno) and the horse he finds shipwrecked on a deserted island becomes a beautiful metaphor for the force of youthful ambition taming the raw power of nature. Directed by Carroll Ballard from the Walter Farley story, the drama is the perfect children's movie — unsentimental, gripping, and good stimulation for the young imagination. A-I (G)

Black Stallion Returns, The (1983) Uninspired sequel directed by Robert Dalva in which the stallion's original owners spirit it back to Morocco, while its present master (teenaged Kelly Reno) pursues them, making his way across the desert to reclaim his beloved horse. The climax, of course, is a horse race, but perhaps the dullest ever committed to film. Corny, muddled, and a bore. A-I (PG)

Black Starlet (1976) A serious topic, the exploitation of women, is handled ineptly and is not above incorporating a bit of what it pretends to decry. O (R)

Black Sunday (1977) Palestinian extremist group plots to commit a terrorist atrocity at the Super Bowl while Israeli agent (Robert Shaw) tries frantically to avert it. Director John Frankenheimer's thriller is exciting enough but it unfortunately exploits some larger issues for the sake of entertainment. Some intense violence. A-III (R)

Black Swan, The (1942) When England agrees to end piracy on the Spanish Main, a reformed pirate (Tyrone Power) sets out to stop the last of the buccaneers (George Sanders), and, for his troubles, wins the heart of the English envoy's daughter (Maureen O'Hara). Though handicapped by a lame plot, director Henry King manages to keep the adventure afloat with swashbuckling action and manly humor, some of which is quite sexist. Stylized violence and romantic complications. A-II (br)

Black Thursday (1974) On July 16, 1942, Paris police rounded up 13,000 Jews for deportation to Nazi concentration camps, from which all but 30 failed to return after the war. Director Michael Mitrani has reconstructed in semi-documentary style that terrible Black Thursday, using as his script the account of a young student who attempted to save those he could. A-III (nr)

Black Whip, The (1956) Clunky Western directed by Charles Marquis Warren in which a former Rebel officer (Hugh Marlowe) saves four prostitutes held hostage by the last of Quantrill's Raiders (led by whip-wielding Paul Richards). Stylized violence and sexual situations. A-III (br)

Black Widow (1987) Debra Winger and Theresa Russell square off in a confrontation of cunning and guile when a Justice Department data analyst (Winger) tries to put an end to the series of seductions and murders of wealthy men by a mysterious and deadly woman (Russell). The double-bluff conclusion is as flawed as the sensually toned melodrama, which has a brief instance of nudity and a decidedly adult treatment by director Bob Rafelson. A-III (R)

Black Windmill, The (1974) Above average British thriller about an espionage agent (Michael Caine), whose son has been kidnapped by enemy agents, and, in trying to get him back, he is suspected of being a double agent by his superior (Donald Pleasence). Directed by Don Siegel, the highly charged movie's rapid pace and sharp action gloss over the obvious holes and inconsistencies in the plot, but the real interest is in Caine's characterization and a conclusion that for once is not cynical but rather optimistic. A-III (PG)

Blackbeard the Pirate (1952) With grimaces, guffaws, and rolling eyes, Robert Newton hams his way through the title role as the 17th-century scourge of the Spanish Main in a muddled story involving buried treasure, a dead pirate's daughter (Linda Darnell), a captive surgeon (Keith Andes), and Blackbeard's arch-enemy, Sir Henry Morgan (Torin Thatcher). Director Raoul Walsh plays the disjointed script mainly for laughs, relying on the occasional swashbuckling action to hold interest. It doesn't. Much stylized violence, considerable brutality, and some sexual innuendo. A-III (br)

Blackbeard's Ghost (1968) Disney comedy in which some elderly New England ladies are saved from eviction through the invisible machinations of pirate Blackbeard (Peter Ustinov), who helps the inept local school track-team win a meet and lots of money. Director Robert Stevenson's simple-minded slapstick and special effects provide laughs, but the team's coach (Dean Jones), after being thoroughly ridiculed for objecting to Blackbeard's tactics, gets into the act himself. Children may get the impression that cheating is O.K. if you can't win honestly. A-II (G)

Blackboard Jungle, The (1955) Screen version of Evan Hunter's novel about an idealistic English teacher (Glenn Ford) confronting juvenile delinquents in an inner city high school to win over a potential drop-out (Sidney Poitier) and the rest of his class. Directed by Richard Brooks, the movie called attention to the growing problems of public education after WW II and, though dated by its melodramatic treatment, its tribute to the teaching profession is as valid today as then. Some nasty violence and much menace, especially that directed at the teacher's pregnant wife. A-III (br)

Blackjack Ketchum, Desperado (1956) Formula Western directed by Earl Bellamy in which a retired gunman (Howard Duff) pins on a badge to rid his valley of a local badman (Victor Jory) and his gang. Frontier violence. A-I (br)

Blackmail (1929) Intriguing crime thriller in which the girlfriend (Anny Ondra) of a jaunty Scotland Yard detective (John Longden) kills an overly amorous artist (Cyril Ritchard), then is blackmailed by a petty crook (Donald Calthrop), whom the police mistakenly link to the crime and chase into the British Museum for a smashing climax. Directed by Alfred Hitchcock, the first British talkie may seem fairly creaky today, though the unsentimental treatment of the characters and the visual flair of the action scenes still hold interest. Stylized violence, a sexual situation, and much tension. A-III (br)

Blacula (1972) African prince (William Marshall), seeking Dracula's signature on a petition abolishing slavery, is instead bitten by the Transylvanian count, entombed in the cellar, and liberated two centuries later by a pair of swishy interior decorators, whereupon he begins teething on the town. Director Bill Crain provides a few genuine thrills on the horror side but, for the most part, the movie tries to have some simple fun with its horror premise. A-II (PG)

Blade (1998) Ultra-violent horror fantasy adapted from a comic strip about the battle between a city full of vampires (led by Stephen Dorff) and three armed-to-the-teeth humans (Wesley Snipes, Kris Kristofferson, N'Bushe Wright) bent on exterminating them. Director Stephen Norrington's gory, stomach-turning tale of hatred and murder wallows in constant scenes of brutality, butchery, and bloodshed. Excessive violence, much profanity, and constant rough language. O (R)

Blade Runner (1982) Science-fiction thriller about a private eye (Harrison Ford) whose job is to hunt down and dispose of out-of-control humanoids. His work gets complicated when he falls in love with an advanced prototype who doesn't know she's not human (Sean Young). Director Ridley Scott's moody atmosphere and futuristic sets evoke an ecologically fouled and spiritually demoralized metropolis, but the disappointing script meanders listlessly. Excessive violence and partial nudity. O (R)

Blame It on Rio (1984) Businessman (Michael Caine) yields to the seduction of the daughter of his best friend (Joseph Bologna), who is depending upon him to help trap the daughter's lover. Director Stanley Donen's misguided celebration of male sexual fantasies tries to milk humor from a promiscuous situation and its use of partial nudity. O (R)

Blame It on the Bellboy (1992) Screwball complications abound when a bellboy (Bronson Pinchot) in a Venice hotel mixes up delivery of messages intended for a meek English worker (Dudley Moore), a philandering mayor (Richard Griffiths), and a hitman (Bryan Brown). Writer-director Mark Herman concocts a lively, fast-paced comedy, whose silly antics make for innocuous escapist entertainment. Some stylized violence and ethnic stereotyping played for laughs, a fleeting bedroom scene, and many double entendres. A-III (PG-13)

Blank Check (1994) After taking a blank check from a gangster (Miguel Ferrer) in return for his damaged bike, a resourceful 11-year-old (Brian Bonsall) fills it out to the tune of one million dollars, successfully cashes it, and goes on a spending spree, with three buffoonish crooks and an undercover FBI agent (Karen Duffy) in hot pursuit. Director Rupert Wainwright's silly comedy looks like a commercial for oversize toys and computer gadgets, with plotting and characterizations tossed in as an afterthought. Some violence played for laughs and a child's greedy excesses. A-II (PG)

Blankman (1994) Dopey comedy in which a wacky inventor (Damon Wayans) turns into a masked crime-fighter whose ineptitudes require frequent rescues by an exasperated older brother (David Alan Grier). Director Mike Binder's dumb, cartoon-like comedy downplays plot and characterization in favor of goofy gadgets and gizmos that enable the would-be super-hero to defeat villains and get the girl (Robin Givens). Comic violence, vulgar humor, and occasional profanities. A-III (PG-13)

Blast From the Past (1999) Amusing comedy in which a 35-year-old (Brendan Fraser), born and raised in a fallout shelter by parents (Christopher Walken and Sissy Spacek) fearful of a nuclear attack, finally emerges and asks a skeptical local girl (Alicia Silverstone) to help him find a wife. Director Hugh Wilson orchestrates some goofy fun as the innocent breezes through the complexities of mean-spirited modern life, never forgetting his manners and winning friends with his unshakable wholesomeness. Mild sexual references, occasional profanity, and an instance of rough language. A-III (PG-13)

Blast Off (see: **Those Fantastic Flying Fools**)

Blaze (1989) Failed dramatization of the love affair between a striptease performer (Lolita Davidovitch) and Louisiana Governor Earl Long (Paul Newman). Written and directed by Ron Shelton, the movie offers little insight into the characters or the era of the 1950s. Sympathetic treatment of adultery and several extended sex scenes. O (R)

Blaze of Noon (1947) The dangers of early aviation plague barnstorming brothers (William Holden, Sonny Tuffs, Sterling Hayden, and Johnny Sands) when they turn airmail pilots in the 1920s, with tragic results. Director John Farrow gets suitable tension from the flight sequences but can't hold interest in the earthbound romance between Holden and nurse Anne Baxter. Restrained treatment of air calamities. A-I (br)

Blazing Saddles (1974) Vulgar and broad satire on Westerns has not so much a plot as a series of wacky situations and comic stereotypes, including black sheriff Cleavon Little, rail baron Harvey Korman, and barroom singer Madeline Kahn. Directed by Mel Brooks, it offers some funny moments, but the overall tone of its humor runs solidly toward the coarse, the smutty, and the scatological. O (R)

Bless the Beasts and Children (1971) Failed melodrama about a handful of adolescent misfits wanting to set free a herd of captive buffalo. Directed by Stanley Kramer, the obvious aim was to deal with man's inhumanity to wildlife and youth, but the result is a heavy-handed succession of mini-soap operas that wrench the emotions without any semblance of insight. Some rough language. A-III (GP)

Blind Date (1987) Bruce Willis goes on a blind date with Kim Basinger but forgets to keep her away from alcohol. The consequences are traditional slapstick sequences of reckless abandon and funny sight gags in this romance from director Blake Edwards. Jealous ex-boyfriend John Larroquette supplies most of the genuine humor, but Basinger shows some flare for the zany. Brief nudity, casual treatment of alcoholism, and some rough language are adult fare. A-III (PG-13)

Blind Dead, The (1973) Spanish-Portuguese horror movie in which three young people, camping amidst the ruins of a medieval monastery, fall prey to the vampire specters of 12th-century Crusaders. Directed by Amando De Ossorio, the story is silly and the horror is minimal. Some sexual innuendo and spilling of blood. A-III (PG)

Blind Fury (1989) Blind Vietnam vet (Rutger Hauer) uses a samurai sword to skewer a far-flung network of gun-happy criminals. Director Philip Noyce's inept rip-off of the Japanese **Zatoichi** series, about a blind swordsman in medieval Japan, proves a bloody exercise in the ludicrous with blade pitted against bullets in a modern American setting. Excessive violence and occasional rough language. O (R)

Blindfold (1966) Complicated espionage story directed by Philip Dunne starts in Central Park, where a psychiatrist (Rock Hudson) is approached by a G-man and asked to treat a top government scientist, but when he does, enemy agents and the patient's sister (Claudia Cardinale) get on his trail. Moderately entertaining with some mildly romantic interludes. A-II (br)

Blindman (1972) Italian Western in which the hobo hero of the title (Tony Anthony) is robbed of the 50 women he is delivering to a Texas mining camp by two hairy bandits (Ringo Starr and Lloyd Batista), who have other plans for them. Time and again senseless slaughter follows sadistic torture as blind man and bad men match wits under Ferdinando Baldi's routine direction. Most objectionable is its presentation of women as objects to be abused. O (R)

Blink (1994) When a blind musician (Madeleine Stowe), whose sight is gradually returning after an operation, glimpses a serial killer, she becomes involved in a steamy affair with the detective (Aidan Quinn) assigned to find the killer before she becomes his next victim. Director Michael Apted's formula cop-and-endangered-female thriller moves slickly along to an unconvincing climax amid a persistent atmosphere of casual promiscuity. Some violence, several bedroom scenes, recurring nudity, and much rough language. O (R)

Bliss (1986) An advertising executive (Barry Otto) dreams that he has died and gone to hell but, when shocked out of this nightmare, tries to change his already hellish and misdirected life. Directed by Ray Lawrence, this Australian import has difficulty finding a balance between social commentary and sex farce. Nudity and some profanity. O (R)

Bliss (1997) Ludicrous exploitation piece in which a husband (Craig Sheffer) goes to a quirky sex therapist (Terence Stamp) to learn how to satisfy his frigid wife (Sheryl Lee), whose problems stem from having been sexually abused as a child. Writer-director Lance Young's dramatically unconvincing story is a dreary mix of Western psychobabble, Eastern sexual lore, and simulated sex scenes which, of course, are the whole point of this bogus enterprise. Exploitative sex scenes and sexually graphic dialogue. O (R)

Bliss of Mrs. Blossom, The (1968) Shirley MacLaine plays a housewife with a devoted and hard-working husband (Richard Attenborough) while keeping a male admirer (James Booth) hidden in the attic. Whether or not this is the romantic daydream of all housewives, it does have a comic potential that this *menage-a-trois* fantasy plays with until the situation wears thin and then falls flat because of an over-inflated script. Though director Joe McGrath's broadly exaggerated treatment keeps the questionable shenanigans within the bounds of good taste, the basic material will not appeal to everyone. A-III (PG)

Blithe Spirit (1945) Noel Coward's witty comedy about spectral complications after the late wife (Constance Cummings) of a happily remarried writer (Rex Harrison) returns from "the other side" during a seance conducted by an enthusiastic but inept medium (Margaret Rutherford). Director David Lean has fun with the unexpected twists in the silly proceedings and their wry jabs at middle-class pretensions, but does best with Rutherford's zesty performance as a good-natured eccentric. Marital misunderstandings, satiric treatment of infidelity, and supernatural hokum. A-III (br)

Blob, The (1958) Tongue-in-cheek sci-fi adventure follows a resourceful youth (Steve McQueen) trying to save his small town from annihilation when it's invaded by a lethal gooey substance from outer space. Directed by Irvin S. Yeaworth, Jr., the premise is a hoot with zero credibility, yet it has a goofy charm, thanks to a lot of hard-working extras and low-budget but imaginative special effects. Some menace and stylized violence. A-II (br)

Blob, The (1988) Technical wizardry highlights this remake of a 1958 horror movie which centers on the efforts of a preppy cheerleader (Shawnee Smith) and a juvenile delinquent (Kevin Dillon) to save their town from being sucked up by an insatiable blob of plasma. Directed by Chuck Russell, there are several grisly, bloody blob encounters, a sense of menace, some profanity, and a dumb segment involving a condom. A-III (R)

Blonde Crazy (1931) Snappy period piece about a calculating hotel bellhop (James Cagney) and the blonde chambermaid (Joan Blondell) he ditches along the way for supposedly easy money with a veteran swindler (Louis Calhern), then wins back years later after her embezzling husband (Ray Milland) double-crosses him. Director Roy Del Ruth presents the rise and downfall of a wise guy in zestful, if dated, fashion, but it's Cagney's performance as a likeable heel that's worth watching. Benign view of crime and sexual innuendo. A-III (br)

Blonde Dynamite (1950) Formula slapstick comedy directed by William Beaudine in which the Bowery Boys (Leo Gorcey, Huntz Hall, and the rest) open a male escort service, then help a pal (Gabriel Dell) out of a jam involving a gang of bank robbers. Comic violence and sexual innuendo. A-II (br)

Blondie Brings Up Baby (1939) Formula family comedy directed by Frank Strayer in which Baby Dumpling (Larry Simms) starts school, then becomes the object of a frantic search when he wanders off looking for his pooch, Daisy, but both are found with a rich man's daughter, who has discarded her wheelchair to play with them. A-I (br)

Blondie for Victory (1942) Formula family comedy directed by Frank R. Strayer in which Dagwood (Arthur Lake) pretends to join the Army in an attempt to make Blondie (Penny Singleton) realize that looking after the Bumstead household is more important to the war effort than working as a volunteer in the home-front activities of the Housewives of America (a fictional patriotic organization). A-I (br)

Blondie Goes Latin (1941) Formula family comedy directed by Frank R. Strayer exports the Bumstead's domestic complications south of the border on a cruise ship, where Dagwood (Arthur Lake) tries his best as the drummer in a conga band and Blondie (Penny Singleton) gets to warble a few songs. A-I (br)

Blondie Goes to College (1942) Formula family comedy directed by Frank R. Strayer in which the Bumsteads put Baby Dumpling in a military school while they go back to college enrolled as singles, with Blondie (Penny Singleton) being courted by the campus hero (Larry Parks) and Dagwood (Arthur Lake) befriended by a rich co-ed (Janet Blair) until he loses the big crew boat race. A-I (br)

Blondie Has Servant Trouble (1940) Formula family comedy directed Frank R. Strayer has some fun with the Bumsteads (Arthur Lake, Penny Singleton, and Larry Sims) moving into a reputed haunted house with strange servants (Arthur Hohl and Ester Dale) and even stranger goings-on, none which have anything to do with spooks. Mild racial stereotyping. A-I (br)

Blondie Hits the Jackpot (1949) Formula family comedy directed by Edward Bernds has Dagwood (Arthur Lake) send son Alexander (Larry Simms) to a birthday party for a client's spoiled daughter, who manages to get Dagwood fired, but he becomes a hero when he spots structural flaws on a construction job just before Blondie (Penny Singleton) wins a radio contest. A-I (br)

Blondie in Society (1941) Formula family comedy directed by Frank R. Strayer has Dagwood (Arthur Lake) getting into trouble with his boss (Jonathan Hale), a dog owner (William Frawley), and a kennel manager (Arthur Kennedy) over a pedigreed Great Dane which Blondie (Penny Singleton) turns into a prizewinner at a dog show. A-I (br)

Blondie in the Dough (1947) Formula family comedy directed by Abby Berlin starts with Dagwood (Arthur Lake) getting fired and Blondie (Penny Singleton) turning breadwinner by selling homemade cookies which are tasty enough for a baking manufacturer (Hugh Herbert) to buy the recipe. A-I (br)

Blondie Knows Best (1946) Formula family comedy directed by Abby Berlin with predictable complications as Mr. Dithers (Jonathan Hale) tries to get a construction contract from a man (Jerome Cowan) he's insulted by switching places with Dagwood (Arthur Lake), who's on the run from a near-sighted process server (Shemp Howard). A-I (br)

Blondie Meets the Boss (1939) Formula family comedy directed by Frank R. Strayer in which Blondie (Penny Singleton) goes to work for Mr. Dithers (Jonathan Hale) while Dagwood (Arthur Lake) does the household chores until Blondie mistakenly suspects he's involved with another woman. A-I (br)

Blondie on a Budget (1940) Formula family comedy directed by Frank Strayer in which Dagwood (Arthur Lake) is visited by an old sweetheart (Rita Hayworth), whom Blondie (Penny Singleton) suspects is up to no good. A-I (br)

Blondie Plays Cupid (1940) Formula family comedy directed by Frank R. Strayer has Blondie (Penny Singleton) take the family on a visit to her aunt in the country, where they meet a nice young couple (Glenn Ford and Luana Walters), then help them elope. A-I (br)

Blondie Takes a Vacation (1939) Formula family comedy directed by Frank R. Strayer follows the Bumsteads to a resort, where, after a run-in with the manager (Donald MacBride), they check into a small nearby hotel which they help turn into a booming business when the resort is overrun by skunks (released by Donald Meek). A-I (br)

Blondie's Anniversary (1947) Formula family comedy directed by Abby Berlin in which Dagwood (Arthur Lake) celebrates his fifteenth wedding anniversary by getting fired after Blondie (Penny Singleton) thinks he's given her a $300 watch belonging to his boss (Jerome Cowen), then compounds the mix-up by buying a cheap replacement with money borrowed from a loan shark (William Frawley). A-I (br)

Blondie's Big Deal (1949) Formula family comedy directed by Edward Bernds in which Dagwood (Arthur Lake) invents a fire-repellent paint, then burns down the summer home of his boss (Jerome Cowen) after rivals for a construction contract switch the paint, leaving it up to Blondie (Penny Singleton) to save the day by getting proof of the theft. A-I (br)

Blondie's Big Moment (1947) Formula family comedy directed by Abby Berlin in which Dagwood is fired by his new boss (Jerome Cowan) after letting his son's classmates visit his office, but he gets his job back when one of the youngsters proves to be the key to buying a tract of land needed by the firm. A-I (br)

Blondie's Blessed Event (1942) Formula family comedy directed by Frank R. Strayer has Dagwood (Arthur Lake) off at a convention in Chicago when Blondie (Penny Singleton) gives birth to their second child, Cookie, then he returns home with a penniless playwright (Hans Conried), who settles in with them until Blondie lays down the law. Comic treatment of pregnancy and birth. A-II (br)

Blondie's Hero (1950) Formula family comedy directed by Edward Bernds has Dagwood (Arthur Lake) join the Army reserve and on his first weekend of training is visited by Blondie (Penny Singleton), who spends the day chasing Daisy around the firing range and taking a hair-raising spin in a tank before the Bumsteads return home to find it has been sold by a swindler (William Frawley). A-I (br)

Blondie's Holiday (1947) Formula family comedy directed by Abby Berlin in which Dagwood (Arthur Lake) plays the big shot by insisting on paying the tab for Blondie's high-school reunion dinner, then gets fired because of a stodgy banker (Grant Mitchell) and winds up in jail after trying to raise the money at a betting parlor. A-I (br)

Blondie's Lucky Day (1946) Formula family comedy directed by Abby Berlin in which Dagwood (Arthur Lake) is fired for hiring a demobilized WAC sergeant (Marjorie Kent), then tries to set up his own construction firm, going so far as to pose as a masseur to land a big client, before Mr. Dithers (Jonathan Hale) takes him back. A-I (br)

Blondie's Reward (1948) Formula family comedy directed by Abby Berlin has Dagwood (Arthur Lake) demoted to office boy after buying the wrong lot for his boss (Jerome Cowen), but all turns out for the best when the lot proves precisely the property needed to swing a big construction deal. A-I (br)

Blondie's Secret (1948) Formula family comedy directed by Edward Bernds in which Dagwood (Arthur Lake) is kept from going on vacation by his boss (Jerome Cowan), who needs him to correct some construction plans, with comic complications arising over the Bumstead's stolen luggage, a gang of counterfeiters, and Daisy in the dog pound suspected of having rabies. A-I (br)

Blood Alley (1955) After Chinese villagers spring an American sea captain (John Wayne) from a Red prison, he agrees to transport their entire village in a stolen ferry through the heavily guarded Formosa Straits to freedom in Hong Kong. Director William A. Wellman's formula adventure thriller has a couple of tense action scenes, a bit of romance (Lauren Bacall as an American who grew up in China), some virile humor, and lots of anti-Communist asides. Stylized violence and sexual innuendo. A-II (br)

Blood and Lace (1971) Orphanage operator (Gloria Grahame) has runaways killed by a cleaver-wielding lunatic (Len Lesser) and stashed in the freezer, lest she lose the monthly state subsidy for each orphan. That's only the plot premise of director Philip Gilbert's movie which goes on to add some sexual titillation to its low-budget bloody horror formula. O (GP)

Blood and Sand (1941) Slow-paced romantic melodrama from the Vincente Blasco Ibanez novel about a rising bullfighter (Tyrone Power) who marries his childhood sweetheart (Linda Darnell), becomes Spain's leading matador, then falls for a wealthy playgirl (Rita Hayworth), with tragic results. Director Rouben Mamoulian endeavors to bolster the story's credibility by establishing a strong sense of the Spanish cultural context with numerous songs, flamenco dancing, discussions of bullfighting lore, and Catholic religious expressions. Off-screen violence, life-threatening situations, and marital infidelity. A-III (br)

Blood and Wine (1997) A stolen diamond necklace and an alluring Cuban nanny (Jennifer Lopez) drive an unreachable wedge between a sullen young man (Stephen Dorff) and his thieving stepdad (Jack Nicholson) as each aims to get the girl and prevent the other from keeping the ice. Director Bob Rafelson finds most of his characters struggling with their consciences, but it's often a losing proposition in this serpentine crime thriller. Some violence, intermittent rough language, and recurring profanity. A-III (R)

Blood Beach (1981) A nasty-looking creature devours bathers before they can even get their feet wet, sucking them down into the sand, in this mindless, wholly inept little horror movie directed and written by Jeffrey Bloom. Excessive violence. O (R)

Blood Feud (1980) Fascist Italy is the setting for director Lina Wertmuller's seriocomic melodrama about a vengeance-crazed widow (Sophie Loren), who enlists the aid of her two lovers (Marcello Mastroianni and Giancarlo Giannini) to avenge the murder of her husband. Considering the talents involved, the result is a disappointing but ambitious failure. Violence, a frank approach to sex, and the complex social, religious, and political background serve as sources for the movie's satiric drive. A-IV (R)

Blood from the Mummy's Tomb (1972) Mild British horror tale taken from a Bram Stoker novel about a professor (Andrew Keir) who gives his daughter (Valerie Leon) a ruby ring pilfered from the hand of an ancient Egyptian princess, who returns to take her revenge. Directed by Seth Holt, it plays the game rather well and is worth exploring for a few chuckles, if not chills. A-II (PG)

Blood Guts Bullets and Octane (1999) Empty thriller about foul-mouthed used-car salesmen (Joe Carnahan and Dan Leis) whose quest of easy money results in their becoming the target of drug traffickers, hit-men, and federal agents. Also written and directed by Carnahan, the phony action consists mostly of frenetic dialogue scenes, some unconvincing mayhem, and a twist ending as meaningless as the title. Gory violence, menacing situations, constant rough language, and much profanity. A-IV (R)

Blood Mania (1971) Wealthy surgeon's daughter (Maria De Aragon) administers a heart stimulant to speed up her father's death which opens the door to other crimes of passion and greed. Between acts of violence, there are some bouts of nude lovemaking that place this pathetically sensational melodrama directed by Robert O'Neil in the sticky mire of the sex-violence formula. O (R)

Blood Money (see: **Requiem for a Heavyweight**)

Blood of Dracula's Castle (1969) Vampire couple (Paula Raymond and Alex D'Arcy) keep a collection of young women guests manacled in the cellar of a deserted desert castle, where they have taken residence, until a new owner (Robert Dix) arrives and tries to evict them. Directed by Al Adamson, the only horrifying aspect of this synthetic foolishness is seeing a fine character actor, John Carradine, playing a moon-baying butler. A-II (M)

Blood of Heroes, The (1990) Excruciatingly violent post-apocalyptic sports adventure that tracks a band of nomadic players, who challenge similar teams to brutal competitions resembling football and rugby. Director David Webb Peoples fails to make sense of his desolate landscape, his dazed characters, and the degrading sport in which players fend off opponents with chains, poles, and bared teeth. Gratuitous, graphic, grisly violence, and some implied promiscuous sexual situations. O (R)

Blood of the Condor (1973) Bolivian documentary investigating charges that a Peace Corps medical clinic had been sterilizing Indian women who came for treatment without telling them what they were doing. Director Jorge Sanjines places the report in the context of Indian culture and politics and has made a quite sophisticated film out of a direct and simple story. A-III (nr)

Blood of the Vampire (1958) British horror clunker set in 1874 Transylvania, where a physician (Vincent Ball) wrongly convicted of murder winds up in a prison for the criminally insane, run by a mad doctor (Donald Wolfit) with a blood deficiency and a deformed assistant (Victor Maddern). Directed by Henry Cass, the wooden production's witless proceedings are fueled by references to the doctor's experiments on helpless prisoners with boring rather than scary results. Stylized violence with gory effects and much hokey menace. A-III (br)

Blood on My Hands (see: **Kiss the Blood Off My Hands**)

Blood on Satan's Claw, The (1971) Failed British chiller set in bucolic 16th-century England, where an unsuspecting plowman unearths the remains of a devil who comes to life, and, with the aid of a seductive local recruit (Linda Hayden), manages to terrify the local yokels. Directed by Piers Haggard, the movie has its gory moments, but it is severely undercut by a clumsy emphasis on the sexual side of witchcraft. O (R)

Blood on the Moon (1948) Convoluted Western in which a cowboy (Robert Mitchum) switches sides in the fight against a rancher (Tom Tully) waged by homesteaders whose wily leader (Robert Preston) is interested only in making himself a quick fortune. Directed by Robert Wise, the action propels the story through a tangle of intrigues involving, among others, the rancher's two daughters (prim Phyllis Thaxter and tomboy Barbara Bel Geddes). Frontier violence and romantic complications. A-II (br)

Blood on the Sun (1945) American reporter (James Cagney) in 1930s Tokyo tries to get a document containing Japan's plans for world conquest out of the country with the help of an Oriental double agent (Sylvia Sidney). Director Frank Lloyd's espionage thriller has some dandy action scenes and not a little suspense but too often bogs down in anti-Japanese rhetoric. Racial stereotypes and stylized violence. A-II (br)

Blood Queen (see: **Little Mother**)

Blood Simple (1985) A young wife (Frances McDormand) runs away from her Texas saloon-owner husband (Dan Hedaya), who hires a seedy private detective (M. Emmet Walsh) to kill both her and her lover. Joel and Ethan Coen's cleverly plotted, well-acted tale of love, hate, and vengeance, in which nothing works out as the hapless characters intended, proves to be a work of somber, quirky brilliance, with glints of black humor. Some bloody violence subordinated to plot and characterizations. A-IV (R)

Blood Thirst (1972) Low-budget Philippine horror import about an American detective (Robert Winston) called to Manila to investigate a series of murdered women found drained of blood. Producer-director Newt Arnold handles the standard nonsense with the fast economy of a black-and-white movie and nary a gown is shed nor a vein slit before the camera pulls away. A-III (GP)

Bloodbrothers (1978) The tension between father (Tony Lo Bianco) and son (Richard Gere) is at the core of this movie about a tightly knit Italian-American working-class family living in the Bronx, which is under siege from other ethnic groups. The father and his brother (Paul Sorvino) bestow all their hopes for the future on the young lad, but he is not sure that he wants to follow in their footsteps. Director Robert Mulligan's work has a certain amount of raw power, but it is far too melodramatic and lacking in ethnic authenticity to be able to deal convincingly with the important moral and social issues it raises. Excessive profanity and an uncritical attitude toward sexual promiscuity. O (R)

Bloodhounds of Broadway (1989) Interweaving four Damon Runyon stories about Broadway denizens on New Year's Eve, 1928, this rambling tale of broken hearts and big bucks gambled, won, and lost is narrated by a newspaper scribe (Josef Sommer). Stand-outs are Randy Quaid and Matt Dillon as comical losers whose luck turns bright. Director Howard Brookner's labor of love will be most effective for those familiar with Runyon's work, distinctive language, and characters. Some cartoon violence, sexual innuendoes, and intimations of promiscuous liaisons. A-III (PG)

Bloodline (1979) Audrey Hepburn, surrounded by a host of veteran actors, inherits control of a vast pharmaceutical empire and becomes the target of a killer. Director Terence Young's treatment of the story adapted from Sidney Sheldon's bestseller reeks of sexual exploitation, sadistic violence, and a sleep-inducing plotline. O (R)

Bloodsuckers (1972) British horror movie about a vampire cult in the ruins of ancient Greece and an Oxford professor (Patrick Mower) who believes that vampirism is a remedy for impotency. Directed by Robert Hartford-Davis, the film has some stunning photography of Greece, but the disjointed plot doesn't hold together. Some graphic shots of body mutilations and nudity. O (R)

Bloodthirsty Butchers (1970) Poor British horror movie about a Fleet Street barber who shaves patrons too closely, his sadistic assistant who separates their components with his cleaver, and a baker's wife who sells assorted anatomic pies. The real victims are the viewers partaking of this low-budget exercise in sex and cruelty. O (R)

Bloody Mama (1970) Sordid crime melodrama about the 1930's Ma Barker gang with Shelley Winters in the title role. Directed by Roger Corman, the character is presented as a psychopath and the treatment includes excessive violence and the vagaries of sexual appetites. O (R)

Blow Out (1981) A movie soundman (John Travolta) records an auto accident, rescues a young woman (Nancy Allen), and then attempts to bring to light an assassination plot. Director Brian De Palma's thriller is short on suspense and long on sadism, employs ludicrously self-conscious techniques, and offers a shamelessly confused moral outlook. Mixture of violence and nudity in a sexual context. O (R)

Blow-Up (1967) In this British production, director Michaelangelo Antonioni takes on the themes of alienation in modern society and the uncertain relationship between illusion and reality in a story about an egocentric man (David Hemmings) who becomes indirectly involved in a murder. His cold and impersonal film, however, is unconvincing in its pessimistic vision of modern life. Nudity in a sexual context. O (br)

Blown Away (1994) Boston bomb squad cop (Jeff Bridges) with a secret past tries frantically to flush out a vengeful Irish bomber (Tommy Lee Jones) who is hellbent on killing the cop's family and friends. Director Stephen Hopkins's murky melodrama of underwritten characters and overblown special effects fails to involve the audience in the human dimension of the story, focusing instead on a series of gigantic explosions for bogus thrills. Intermittent deadly bombings and some rough language. A-III (R)

Blue (1968) A failed Western in which Terence Stamp stars as the adopted blue-eyed gringo son of a Mexican bandit chief (Ricardo Montalban). The son sides with the American settlers against his former comrades but is torn between the two cultures for the duration of this muddled movie. Beautiful landscapes, but English director Sylvio Narizzano offers only a superficial development of a complex theme. Winked-at bedroom encounter. A-III (br)

Blue (1993) After a car crash kills her composer husband and little girl, a Parisian widow (Juliette Binoche) attempts to withdraw from all human contact until her late husband's assistant (Benoit Regent) begins work on the composer's unfinished symphony, prompting her creative collaboration and tentative emotional recovery. Director Krzysztof Kieslowski's mournful story of a woman entrenched in grief blends evocative images and thunderous bursts of music within a slim narrative that remains distant and largely abstract, despite its hopeful ending. Subtitles. Fleeting nudity and implied sexual encounters. A-III (R)

Blue Bird, The (1940) Heavy-handed fantasy from the Maurice Maeterlinck story of two children (Shirley Temple and Johnny Russell) searching for the blue bird of happiness in the land of the past, the domain of luxury, and the world of the future, until finding it at home. Directed by Walter Lang, the allegorical settings are colorful, but the fanciful narrative has little charm or imagination, save the visit to the future's beclouded nursery filled with children waiting to be born. Best for the younger members of the family. A-I (G)

Blue Bird, The (1976) Filmed in Leningrad, this American-Soviet co-production presents Maurice Maeterlinck's children's classic about two peasant youngsters searching for the blue bird that will bring health and happiness to the sick daughter of a neighboring family. George Cukor directs this intermittently beautiful but ultimately earthbound musical fantasy, whose songs thankfully pass almost unnoticed. The child actors, (Todd Lookinland and Patsy Kensit) are fine, which cannot be said of the adult cast (Elizabeth Taylor, Jane Fonda, Ava Gardner, Cicely Tyson). Ponderous but innocuous entertainment. A-I (G)

Blue Chips (1994) Desperate to add three talented players (Shaquille O'Neal, Anfernee "Penny" Hardaway, and Matt Nover) to his losing college basketball team, a normally straight-arrow coach (Nick Nolte) okays a wealthy alum's recruitment bribes, but the sweet taste of victory cannot salve the coach's conscience. Director William Friedkin's examination of corruption in college sports is undercut by a contrived, melodramatic script and Nolte's scenery-chewing performance. Ambiguous treatment of ethical issues, some sexual references, and minimal rough language. A-III (PG-13)

Blue City (1986) A sour and violent story depicting vigilante ambitions on the part of a wayward adolescent (Judd Nelson) who returns home to discover his dad has been murdered. Under Michelle Manning's direction, Nelson and co-star Ally Sheedy give wretched performances as they mix violence, casual sex, and sexually derived profanity in this blue movie. O (R)

Blue Collar (1978) Screenwriter Paul Schrader's directing debut looks at the frustrations of three Detroit auto workers (Harvey Keitel, Richard Pryor, and Yaphet Kotto), trapped in a grueling environment while being taken advantage of by their union and management. A dim, failed work, it exploits such serious issues as factory conditions, union corruption, management oppression, economic distress, and marital tensions, rather than explore them in some coherant and intelligent fashion. Crass cynicism and harsh language. O (R)

Blue Country (1978) The setting for this French

comedy is a gorgeous bucolic valley into which comes a little stream of expatriates from the city in search of a more humane existence. What they find is that the natives are themselves longing for the easy life of the city. Unfortunately, writer-director Jean-Charles Tacchella has burdened his delightful cast and comic anecdotal style with the weight of a seriously flawed broadside against the institution of marriage. O (PG)

Blue Dahlia, The (1946) Dark crime tale in which a returned war veteran (Alan Ladd) eludes the police while seeking the murderer of his two-timing wife (Doris Dowling), with a little help from the estranged wife (Veronica Lake) of a nightclub owner (Howard da Silva). Directed by George Marshall from Raymond Chandler's screenplay, the murky plot offers some hard-boiled action and tough characters, notably William Bendix as the vet's shell-shocked pal and Will Wright as a sleazy house dick. Stylized violence and references to marital infidelity. A-II (br)

Blue Hawaii (1961) Routine musical in which a young man (Elvis Presley) returns from military service to declare his independence from wealthy parents (Angela Landsbury and Roland Winters), takes a job with an addled tourist agent (Howard McNear), and romances a lovely Hawaiian (Joan Blackman). Directed by Norman Taurog, the thin sitcom plot benefits greatly from the picturesque Hawaiian locales and some agreeable songs. Romantic complications, mild sexual innuendo, and a dance-hall brawl. A-II (PG)

Blue in the Face (1995) A Brooklyn tobacco shop managed by Harvey Keitel serves as a meeting place for an assortment of neighborhood characters to talk about the community as well as their quirky personal relationships. Co-directed by Wayne Wang and Paul Auster, this improvised sequel to **Smoke** takes on a mellow but uneven comedic tone in dealing with the vibrant ethnic diversity and spirit of its urban neighborhood. A few sexually suggestive scenes, fleeting nudity, and intermittent rough language. A-III (R)

Blue Lagoon, The (1980) Two marooned children (Brooke Shields and Christopher Atkins) grow through puberty to the discovery of sex and parenthood on a deserted island paradise. Director Randal Kleiser exploits teen sexuality with cute, peek-a-boo nudity, and the only innocence on the screen is its unawareness of the realities of life in the tropics. O (R)

Blue Lamp, The (1950) Unarmed London policemen hunt for a robber (Dirk Bogarde) who made his getaway by shooting down an officer (Jack Warner), eventually cornering him among the crowd at a greyhound race track. Director Basil Dearden details the normal routine of police work, humanizing the constables as decent, ordinary individuals who can count on the public and even professional criminals to apprehend a thug with a gun. Some menace and the death of a sympathetic major character. A-II (br)

Blue Max, The (1966) Saga of a German flying ace (George Peppard) toward the end of World War I details his exploits in sky, as well as on the ground with the wife (Ursula Andress) of a general (James Mason) who has turned him into a hero. Directed by John Guillermin, the movie soars with the scenes of biplanes in action but falters on the earthbound melodramatic problems of its characters. Two excessively explicit scenes of lovemaking. O (br)

Blue Skies (1946) Episodic musical spanning the Roaring Twenties to WW II recounts the rivalry between a nightclub owner (Bing Crosby) and a Broadway musical star (Fred Astaire), once vaudeville pals but now contenders for the affections of the same woman (Joan Caulfield). Director Stuart Heisler employs the arch, unconvincing narrative mainly as filler between musical set pieces featuring Irving Berlin songs and colorful production numbers. Romantic complications, including divorce. A-III (br)

Blue Sky (1994) In 1962 Alabama, an unfaithful, manic-depressive Army wife (Jessica Lange) pulls herself together to rescue her devoted husband (Tommy Lee Jones) from a mental hospital, where he's being kept to silence him over an Army cover-up of a nuclear testing accident. Despite an increasingly implausible script, director Tony Richardson gets choice performances from the two stars in a domestic melodrama about a couple's struggle to maintain their marriage at all costs. Fleeting nudity, brief bedroom scenes, and minor violence. A-III (PG-13)

Blue Steel (1990) Visually stunning, graphically violent thriller in which a rookie female cop (Jamie Lee Curtis) is stalked by a commodities broker (Ron Silver) who is also a closet psychopath. Director Kathryn Bigelow's artful depiction of a young woman's struggle to be a New York cop deteriorates into a gruesome night-stalker thriller which sees a female victim turn on her male victimizer with horrifying fury. Excessive grisly violence, some profanity, and a sexual incident with brief nudity. O (R)

Blue Thunder (1983) Tough, dedicated police helicopter pilot (Roy Scheider) and his callow but brainy sidekick (Daniel Stern) thwart the efforts of some sinister government types to use real people in testing a super-helicopter designed to put down urban riots. The unbelievable plot, however, serves only as a pretext for some slam-bang aerial action in a callous and cyncial movie directed by John Badham. Much violence and an utterly gratuitous nude sequence. O (R)

Blue Velvet (1986) Adolescent (Kyle MacLachlan) confronts the mostly darker sides of sexual desire in a small town when he comes across a severed human ear in a field and is drawn into a web of sadistic sex and eroticism. Director David Lynch's sinister fable of sex and violence in small-town America leaves only a vivid after-image of decadence and brutality. O (R)

Blue Water, White Death (1971) Wildlife filmmaker Peter Gimbel sets out to find and photograph the magnificent Great White shark in its natural surroundings of the open sea. Apart from the menacing sharks themselves, Gimbel's documentary dwells on a number of other forms of sea life and offers some ecological observations on the approaching extinction of the whale. Some terrifying moments with attacking sharks. A-II (G)

Bluebeard (1944) Moody chiller set in 19th-century Paris, where a melancholy puppeteer (John Carradine) attracts the interest of a pert fashion designer (Jean Parker) as the police hunt a serial killer who strangles young women, then paints their portrait before dumping their bodies in the Seine. Directed by Edgar G. Ulmer, the overly contrived plot provides a few fearsome moments, though the main interest is Carradine's tortured Jekyll-and-Hyde performance in the title role. Stylized violence, brutal off-screen murders, and sexual innuendo. A-III (br)

Bluebeard (1972) Richard Burton stars as the infamous lady-killer in a dull version of the story set in pre-Nazi Germany. Some of his victims (Raquel Welch, Virna Lisi, Nathalie Delon) play it for snickers, while others play it very straight. Directed by Edward Dmytryk, the movie doesn't succeed either as spoof or as melodrama. Restrained violence and much coy nudity. O (R)

Blues Brothers, The (1980) Two blues singers (John Belushi and Dan Aykroyd) try to raise money for an orphanage by putting a band together and playing some concert dates. The plot is interspersed with scenes of wholesale destruction and frenzied chases which are spectacularly unfunny and uninvolving. Some good musical portions from Cab Calloway and Ray Charles, but not enough depth from director John Landis to save this zany comedy from milking cheap laughs from rough language and crude situations. A-III (R)

Blues Brothers 2000 (1998) Feel-good musical in which Blues Brother Dan Aykroyd reunites his band after 18 years and takes it on the road, pursued by cops who think he kidnapped an orphan. Director John Landis's sequel is crippled by its feeble story line, but enlivened by top musicians and the comical moves of the black-suited Blues Brothers, including new member John Goodman. Suggestive dancing with brief rear nudity, some comic violence, occasional crude expressions, and an instance of profanity. A-III (PG-13)

Blues Busters (1950) Formula slapstick comedy directed by William Beaudine in which Sach (Huntz Hall) begins crooning like Bing Crosby after his tonsils are removed, then becomes a hit singer when the Bowery Boys (Leo Gorcey and company) open their own nightclub. Comic violence and some sexual innuendo. A-II (br)

Blues for Lovers (1966) Well-intentioned but weak melodrama directed by Paul Henreid about how a little blind boy with an over-protective widow-mother gets comfort and help from blind musician Ray Charles (playing himself). The mother's illicit relationship with a boyfriend makes it mature fare. A-III (br)

Blume in Love (1973) Beverly Hills divorce lawyer (George Segal), who loses his wife (Susan Anspach) when she catches him committing adultery, tries desperately to win her back in this uneven, sometimes amusing, romantic comedy directed by Paul Mazursky. Some casual nudity and harsh language. A-III (R)

Blush (1996) The fate of two prostitutes and a wealthy client become tragically entwined after the Red Chinese victory in 1949 when their brothel is closed, his property is nationalized, and he marries one of them when the other turns him down. Director Li Shaobong explores the effects of sudden grinding poverty on previously pampered individuals, bringing out their humanity even as one strengthens, another despairs, and one resolutely resists coming to terms with changed circumstances. Subtitles. Some sexual innuendo. A-III (nr)

Boardwalk (1979) Aging Brighton Beach Jewish couple (Lee Strasberg and Ruth Gordon) suffer through the deterioration of their health and of their neighborhood in this inept and heavy-handed moral tale from director Stephen Verona. Although some serious issues are presented, the conclusion is crude and melodramatic, over-baked with violence and a frank treatment of sex. A-III (nr)

Boat, The (see: **Das Boot**)

Boat Is Full, The (1981) A desperate party of Jewish refugees arrives in Switzerland vainly seeking asylum from Nazi persecution. An outstanding Swiss production written and directed by Markus Imhoof, it is a convincing and quite moving depiction of the plight of these refugees and the various attitudes of the Swiss toward them. A richly human treatment of a grim but important subject. A-II (PG)

Boatniks, The (1970) Typical Disney romp follows the slapstick misadventures of a bumbling Coast Guard officer (Robert Morse) and a master jewel thief (Phil Silvers) trying to leave the country with the loot. There's a seasoning of innocuous adult humor to interest the parents watching with their youngsters. A-I (G)

Bob & Carol & Ted & Alice (1969) When Bob & Carol (Robert Culp and Natalie Wood) introduce their friends Ted & Alice (Elliott Gould and Dyan Cannon) to the new freedom of being honest about their feelings, it is only a question of time before the two couples go to bed together. Director Paul Mazursky's modern morality tale about the new morality spoofs much that deserves spoofing but ultimately fails because it exploits the many opportunities for comic titillation worked into the obvious script. Excessive nudity and sexual references. O (R)

Bob Roberts (1992) Bemused parody of contemporary media politics follows a fictional campaign for the US Senate made by a folksy millionaire Pennsylvania candidate (Tim Robbins) as seen from the perspective of a BBC documentary filmmaker (Brian

Murray). Also directed by Robbins, the picture of the smarmy, cynical candidate, his proto-Fascist advisors, and their manipulation of a complacent news media is provocative but not especially amusing as the campaign drags on to its bogus conclusion. Satiric exaggerations of serious realities, a political assassination attempt, and some rough language. A-III (R)

Bobbie Jo and the Outlaw (1976) Inane and brutal western from director Mark Lester about a band of robbers whose antics seem designed as an obvious attempt to grind out a cheap Bonnie and Clyde copy, replete with excessive violence and some nudity. O (R)

Bobby Deerfield (1977) Plodding romantic melodrama directed by Sydney Pollack about a famous racing car driver (Al Pacino) and his relationship with an Italian aristocrat (Marthe Keller) who is dying of an incurable disease. Scenic, sentimental, and predictable, the film's theme and brief nudity make it mature fare. A-III (PG)

Bobo, The (1967) Penniless clown with two guitars but no voice (Peter Sellers) aims at becoming Spain's first singing matador, but he must first seduce a girl-about-town (Brett Ekland) in three days if he is to get a contract. Director Robert Parrish's dreary comedy is neither moving nor hilarious and it was aiming at both. Sexual innuendo. A-III (br)

Bodies, Rest & Motion (1993) Static story of four aimless young adults (Bridget Fonda, Phoebe Cates, Tim Roth, and Eric Stoltz) who exchange sexual partners as listlessly as they plan their futures. Michael Steinberg directs a pointless story about the young and the restless who are going nowhere and are unconcerned about anything beyond enjoying the moment. Acceptance of casual sex, recreational drug use, white collar crime, and much rough language. O (R)

Body, The (1971) With an impressive list of technical advisers, doctors, scientists, and educators, producer Tony Garnett and director Roy Battersby have set about a visual exploration of the fabric and functions, inside and out, of the human body. While their intentions may be pure, the explicit nature of the sexual material has no place in a movie theater and its use either in classroom or home is highly questionable. O (X)

Body and Soul (1947) During the Depression, a jobless youth (John Garfield) uses his fists to make money in the ring but, on his way to becoming champ, alienates his mom (Anne Revere), loses his girlfriend (Lili Palmer), and winds up in hock to a crooked promoter who eventually wants him to take a dive. It's an old story, but director Robert Rossen gives it a convincingly gritty look and Garfield's compelling performance is supported by a fine cast (Canada Lee, William Conrad, Joseph Pevney, Hazel Brooks, and others). Intense boxing scenes, alcohol abuse, and romantic complications. A-II (br)

Body Beneath, The (1971) Venerable British family of vampires, threatened by an infusion of bad blood and local harassment, decides to emigrate to America. The movie suffers from an infusion of bad acting, ludicrous scripting, and an over-generous display of sex, gore, and psychedelic nonsense. O (nr)

Body Chemistry (1990) A kinky affair between the project director (Marc Singer) of a sex research lab and one of the lab's clients (Lisa Pescia) gets out of control with disastrous results. Directed by Kristine Peterson, the slack tale of a woman's sexual obsession is as predictable as it is pointless. Several scenes of simulated sex with nudity, gory violence, and occasional rough language. O (R)

Body Double (1984) Director Brian De Palma's attempt at concocting an imitation Hitchcock thriller once again combines voyeurism and violence directed at women. Hitchcock might have been cruel but he was clever, while De Palma is only cruel and banal. A self-indulgent travesty with an unnecessary detailed depiction of the vicious murder of a woman and excessive use of nudity. O (R)

Body Heat (1981) Passing through a small Florida town, a smalltime lawyer (William Hurt) tarries to pursues a married woman (Kathleen Turner), who persuades him to rid her of an unwanted and very wealthy husband. Written and directed by Lawrence Kasdan, it's a labored imitation of a dark romantic melodrama of the 1940s, with the only modern touch being its extensive and explicit depiction of sex. O (R)

Body of Evidence (1993) Trashy thriller in which a conniving sadomasochist (Madonna), accused of murdering her wealthy lover, seduces her married defense attorney (Willem Dafoe) and manipulates other lovers (Frank Langella and Jurgen Prochnow) in an attempt to win acquittal. Director Uli Edel's tawdry melodrama glamorizes sexual perversity while ignoring human values. Sexually explicit scenes, several drug abuse reference, climactic gory violence, and frequent rough language. O (R)

Body Parts (1991) Schlocky horror movie in which the limbs of a man executed for mass murder replace those of accident victims (Jeff Fahey, Brad Dourif, and Peter Murnik), who then experience personality changes with deadly consequences. Director Eric Red sinks a potentially interesting psychological thriller in a bucket of blood, blotting out Fahey's credible performance and a tense car chase. Excessive violence and much rough language. O (R)

Body Rock (1984) Middling youth movie directed by Marcelo Epstein about a youngster (Lorenzo Lamas) who turns his back on friendships to pursue a career as a dance club disc jockey. Focus is on the hormonal rather than the moral. A-III (PG-13)

Body Snatcher, The (1945) Gruesome chills from a Robert Louis Stevenson story in which a doctor (Henry Daniell) in 1831 Edinburgh buys cadavers for his medical school from a grave-robber (Boris Karloff), who turns to murder when cemetery guards cut off his supply. Produced by Val Lewton and directed by Robert Wise, the setting and characters hold interest while the dark, sinister atmosphere provides goosebumps as do some ghoulish plot twists. Minimal violence but much menace and suspense. A-III (br)

Body Snatchers (1994) Innocently arriving at a military base where individuals are being systematically replaced by alien clones as they sleep, a scientist (Terry Kinney), his wife (Meg Tilly), and their youngsters (Gabrielle Anwar and Reilly Murphy) begin to distrust each other as they try to escape their fearful fate. Director Abel Ferrara's tired remake of **Invasion of the Body Snatchers** (1956) relies more on horror than the sci-fi thrills of the original and does little with the theme of the loss of individuality in a conformist society. Some violence, including an off-screen suicide, much menace, brief nudity, and occasional rough language. A-III (R)

Bodyguard, The (1992) Sluggish would-be romantic thriller about an Oscar-nominated singer-actress (Whitney Houston) and a former Secret Service agent (Kevin Costner) hired to protect her from a very determined and resourceful killer. Directed by Mick Jackson, the slow-moving action and stilted romance are matched by some unintentionally funny dialogue. Brief violence, an implied sexual encounter, and frequent rough language. A-III (R)

Bofors Gun, The (1968) British adaptation of John McGrath's play about a long night of guard's duty in a munitions depot, during which a fanatic Irish rebel-poet (Nicol Williamson) turns his rage on an ineffectual upper-class superior (David Warner) in an increasingly nightmarish situation. Director Jack Gold builds the growing antagonism between the two characters to the busting point. Harrowing tension and barracks' language. A-IV (nr)

Bogus (1996) Fantasy misfire in which a seven-year-old orphan (Haley Joel Osment), reluctantly cared for by his foster-aunt (Whoopi Goldberg), finds comfort in talking with an invisible grown-up pal (Gerard Depardieu). Director Norman Jewison's soggy salute to the power of a child's imagination is an awkward, unconvincing blend of comedy, drama, and fantasy. A fatal car crash and fleeting violence. A-II (PG)

Bohemian Girl, The (1936) Musical comedy in which gypsies (Stan Laurel and Oliver Hardy) raise a lost child, unaware she is a nobleman's daughter. She grows up to be reunited with her family. Directed by James Horne and Charles Rogers from William Balfe's operetta, the lackluster story and indifferent songs are made palatable by some very funny routines from Stan and Ollie. Some comic menace. A-I (br)

Boiling Point (1993) Violent crime story in which a Treasury agent (Westley Snipes) tracks down the two badmen (Dennis Hopper and Viggo Mortensen) who murdered his partner. Director James B. Harris's formula action movie is little more than a series of nasty shootouts, in between which women are showcased as sexual playthings ripe for abuse. Several violent shootouts, implied sexual encounters, and much rough language. O (R)

Bolshoi Ballet 67 (1966) Using the framework of a tour through the school of this famous troupe, the documentary affords a privileged view of the discipline and training that develop its leading dancers after years of effort. Much of the movie consists of performances including the spectacular "Pagnanini" and the colorful "Bolero." A-I (br)

Bombardier (1943) The tribulations and hijinks of Army Air Force trainees (Randolph Scott, Robert Ryan, Eddie Albert, etc.) under a demanding officer (Pat O'Brien) who readies them for the demands of airborne combat. Director Richard Wallace's dated WW II relic is little more than a wooden exercise in patriotic flag-waving. Wartime violence and stereotyped enemies. A-I (br)

Bombay Talkie (1970) Western pulp author (Jennifer Kendal) visits India, falls in love first with a screenwriter and then with a young film star but, constantly trailing misery in her wake, she completely ruins both their lives. Directed by James Ivory, the plot is low-key and conventional, with interest lying in the psychological development of the relationships and the unique setting. A-III (GP)

Bombers B-52 (1957) Formula service romance in which a veteran Air Force sergeant (Karl Malden) objects to his hot-shot squadron commander (Efram Zimbalist, Jr.) dating his daughter (Natalie Wood), then decides he's misjudged the officer. Directed by Gordon Douglas, the real romance is that of a man and his profession as the sergeant drops plans for retirement to provide the maintenance required to keep the new super-bombers of the title in combat readiness. A sequence of wartime violence and some menacing situations. A-I (br)

Bon Voyage, Charlie Brown (And Don't Come Back!) (1980) This fourth animated feature starring Charlie Brown and his friends brings them to France as exchange students, where they find themselves quartered in a spooky chateau. Written by Charles Schulz, the comic strip's creator, and directed by Bill Melendez, the movie is pretty thin fare, talky and episodic, but youngster and Peanuts fans will love it. A-I (G)

Bonaventure (see: **Thunder on the Hill**)

Bone (1974) Beverly Hills household of a used car tycoon (Andrew Duggan) and his repressed wife (Joyce Van Patten) is invaded by a black rapist (Yaphet Kotto) in a movie that apparently intended to show the hypocrisies of the affluent and contemporary American racial attitudes. Incoherently written and badly directed by Larry Cohen, all it shows is human ugliness. O (R)

Bonfire of the Vanities, The (1990) When a wealthy Wall Street broker (Tom Hanks) and his mistress (Melanie Griffith) accidentally run over a black youth in the Bronx, a desperate newspaper reporter (Bruce Willis) helps turn the ensuing court case into a political hot potato and media circus. Producer-director Brian De Palma has turned Tom Wolfe's satirical bestseller into a nasty, overblown, and very vulgar comedy having little human dimension. Many sexual references, racial epithets, and rough language. O (R)

Bonjour Amour (1978) Shy, studious high-school lad falls in love with a 17-year-old shopgirl, and despite objections from his parents, he tries to run away with her. French director Roger Andrieux is handicapped by a script that oversimplifies and romanticizes the serious problem of irresponsible teenage sexuality. O (nr)

Bonjour Tristesse (1958) Glossy sudser from Francoise Sagan's vapid novel about a world-weary 18-year-old Parisienne (Jean Seberg) recalling the tragic consequences of her callow efforts the previous summer to break up the impending marriage of her rich playboy father (David Niven) to a lovely, intelligent woman (Deborah Kerr). Producer-director Otto Preminger films the teenager's present melancholy in black-and-white scenes while the summer's events are in color, but this adds nothing to the thinly contrived proceedings and the slack performances of good actors in cardboard roles. Implied promiscuity, sexual situations, and innuendo. A-III (br)

Bonnie and Clyde (1967) Warren Beatty's production stars himself and Faye Dunaway, with supporting cast of Gene Hackman, Estelle Parsons, and Michael J. Pollard, in a vivid and strikingly real recreation of the treadmill existence of the Barrow Gang, ill-fated bank robbers of the Depression. Director Arthur Penn brings a human perspective to the gang's wildly distorted legend and their senselessly violent deaths which leaves viewers to ponder the brutal frontier ethic of American justice. Scenes of strong violence. A-IV (M)

Bonnie's Kids (1972) Lurid crime melodrama about deceitful, promiscuous sisters (Tiffany Bolling and Robin Mattson) who flee their shanty town after killing their lecherous stepfather, become models, and end as pawns in a big robbery. Writer-director Arthur Marks bases much of the plot on sexual jealousies from which stem this story of murder and suicide. O (R)

The Boogie Man Will Get You (1942) Slack comedy directed by Lew Landers involves daffy experiments in the cellar of a decrepit colonial tavern, where a screwball professor (Boris Karloff) and the local coroner (Peter Lorre) try to turn traveling salesmen (notably, Maxie Rosenbloom) into supermen to defeat the Axis. Comic menace in a setting with secret passages, murderous loonies, lively corpses, and a Fascist saboteur. A-I (br)

Boogie Nights (1997) Gritty melodrama about the sleazy world of porn movie-makers begins in 1977 with the rise of a new star (Mark Wahlberg), who after a few years of big money and drugs hits the skids, until being rehired by the director (Burt Reynolds) who gave him his start. Writer-director Paul Thomas Anderson doesn't glamorize the dysfunctional characters and their self-destructive way of life, but this attempt to humanize the porn trade lacks any larger moral or social perspective. Gory scenes of violence, explicit sex acts, full nudity, recurring rough language, and occasional profanity. O (R)

Book of Love (1991) Middle-aged man recalls his fumbling adventures as a teen (Chris Young) when he tried, with the aid of a nerdy buddy (Keith Coogan), to juggle the girl he wanted (Josie Bissett) with the girl who wanted him (Tricia Leigh Fisher). Director Robert Shaye's sophomoric comedy pays more attention to the 1950's soundtrack and pop artifacts than any semblance of a real story. Benign depiction of teenage drinking, mild sexual innuendo, brief partial nudity, and an instance of harsh language. A-III (PG-13)

Book of Numbers (1973) Pair of fast-talking slickers (Raymond St. Jacques and Philip Michael Thomas) set up a wildly successful numbers game in a small but monumentally venal Tennessee town, much to the chagrin of some local criminals. Also directed by St. Jacques, some bitter lessons in free enterprise and the futility of bucking the system are put over with lots of broad slapstick and sight gags. Some violence, a suggestive sex scene, and rough language. A-III (R)

Boom (1968) Screen version of Tennessee Williams's play in which a wealthy woman (Elizabeth Taylor) who is terminally ill is visited by the Angel of Death (Richard Burton) in her posh Mediterranean villa. Director Joseph Losey fails to give life to what is essentially a play of not very profound ideas. Mature themes with excessively crude sexual references. O (br)

Boomerang! (1947) Semi-documentary account of the arrest and trial of a vagrant (Arthur Kennedy) for the murder of a clergyman in a Connecticut town whose local prosecutor (Dana Andrews) is unsatisfied with the circumstantial evidence presented by the police chief (Lee J. Cobb). Director Elia Kazan's low-key treatment of the fact-based events involves viewers in the police investigation and political pressures to solve the case. Tense scenes and legal ambiguities. A-II (br)

Boomerang (1992) Belabored romantic comedy has the tables turned on a cocky playboy (Eddie Murphy) in the glamorous cosmetics industry when his sexy new boss (Robin Givens) rebuffs his advances. Director Reginald Hudlin gets limited comic mileage out of a trite story whose mostly shallow characters grow quickly tiresome. A few bedroom scenes, sexually suggestive references, and much rough language. A-III (R)

Boost, The (1988) Insecure, young Los Angeles tax shelter salesman (James Woods) and his devoted wife (Sean Young) are caught in the downward spiral brought about by financial speculation and drug addiction. Director Harold Becker takes a harrowing, painfully depressing look at a couple who throw away a promising life due to drugs. Graphic cocaine use, some violence, rough language, and brief nudity. A-III (R)

Boot Hill (1973) Flat Italian Western about a pair of adventurers (Terence Hill and Bud Spencer) who help some Colorado miners fight a corrupt boss (Victor Buono). Unfortunately, rather than try to make any sense out of the story, director Giuseppe Colizzi relies mostly on his cast's acrobatic antics and close-ups of their snickering faces. Some violence. A-II (GP)

Booty Call (1997) Dully repetitive sex farce in which two men (Jamie Foxx and Tommy Davidson) overcome complications before bedding their respective dates (Vivica A. Fox and Tamala Jones). Directed by Jeff Pollack, the result is a non-stop exercise in witless sexual situations with blue humor that leaves nothing to the imagination. Exploitative sexual situations and constant rough language. O (R)

Bopha! (1993) Fact-based story of a black South African policeman (Danny Glover) torn between the system he has always upheld, and his responsibility to wife (Alfre Woodard) and son (Maynard Eziashi) when he learns the youth is being sought for leading a student protest against apartheid in 1980. In dramatizing one family's story, director Morgan Freeman gives a human perspective to the tragedy of institutionalized racism in South Africa. Intermittent violence, fleeting nudity, and some rough language. A-II (PG-13)

Bora Bora (1970) Sex-exploitation movie in which a husband pursues his wife to the South Seas, where they engage in various affairs before reuniting for a happy ending that has no redeeming value. Except for the Polynesian setting, the movie is truly boring, boring. O (R)

Bordello of Blood (see: **Tales of the Crypt Presents Bordello of Blood**)

Border, The (1982) A member of the Border Patrol (Jack Nicholson) is appalled by the corruption of his fellow officers, but then begins himself to take small bribes from poor Mexicans because of his spendthrift wife (Valerie Perrine). Thoroughly muddled in both intentions and structure, director Tony Richardson keeps the narrative limping along until the sustained burst of improbable violence that concludes it. Also profanity and some brief nudity. A-III (R)

Borderline (1950) Seriocomic crime story of a Treasury agent (Claire Trevor) and a Los Angeles police detective (Fred MacMurray) who manage to infiltrate a Mexican narcotics ring (led by Raymond Burr), each unaware the other is a law officer. Directed by William A. Seiter, the tricky situation plays itself out in mostly amusing fashion, though the drug traffickers add some suitable menace to the proceedings. Stylized violence and romantic situations. A-II (br)

Born Again (1978) Based on Chuck Colson's book about his years in the Nixon White House, his trial, his prison term, and conversion to fundamentalist Christianity, director Irving Rapper's well-intentioned but inadequate movie fails to move, much less convince, because it equates religious conviction with sentimentality. The result is both an insult to those who take religion seriously and an occasion for contempt to those who look down on any form of belief as intellectually indefensible. A-III (PG)

Born American (1986) Absurdly implausible action-adventure yarn about three college lads who, while vacationing in the Arctic, cross into the Soviet Union for a lark. Imprisoned and brutalized by Soviet guards, one of these All-American boys turns into a mini-Rambo, visiting death and destruction on their tormentors. Profanity, graphic torture sequences, excessive violence, and an imbecilic perspective on international relations. O (R)

Born Black (to White Parents) (1972) German-Italian attempt at soft-core titillation whose title refers to a black child born of Caucasian parents, the result of a sperm transfer, not by promiscuity. O (R)

Born Free (1966) Endearing wildlife story of an African game warden (Bill Travers), his wife (Virginia McKenna), and Elsa (their pet lion), who when grown must be taught how to survive in the jungle rather than being confined in a zoo. Director James Hill relishes the natural beauty of the Kenyan game preserve and gets warm performances from the leads, but nothing can stop Elsa from stealing the picture. Splendid family fare. A-I (PG)

Born in East L.A. (1987) Cheech Marin writes, directs, and stars in this mild social satire about a Mexican-American's accidental deportation and his struggle to get back into the country. The film gives some sense of the immigration problems of illegal aliens but opts for slapstick humor, sexual innuendo, and excessive profanity instead of emotional depth. A-III (R)

Born on the Fourth of July (1989) Emotionally wrenching story of an idealistic youth (Tom Cruise) who returns from Vietnam a crippled war hero, grows increasingly disillusioned and alienated from family and friends, turns to alcohol and sex, but then rediscovers a purpose in life as part of the anti-war movement. Adapted from Ron Kovic's book by Kovic and director Oliver Stone, the movie captures the period in which the nation became polarized by the war, and provides some insight into the problems of Vietnam veterans, but Stone's overly graphic depiction of violence and a sequence in a bordello are not for the faint-hearted. Disturbing depiction of violence, a scene with nudity in a sexual context, and much rough language A-IV (R)

Born to Be Wild (1995) Formula adventure tale about a rebellious 14-year-old (Wil Horneff) who frees an abused, sign-language-trained gorilla from its cage and attempts to make it across the Canadian border before police and reward seekers can capture them. Director John Gray's sappy, youth-targeted movie puts boy and beast through predictable antics and dangers in contrived attempts to mix laughter with tears. Minor slapstick violence. A-II (PG)

Born to Kill (1947) Murky crime tale of a psychotic killer (Lawrence Tierney) and the mixed-up woman

(Claire Trevor) who is drawn to him, with dire results for both. Directed by Robert Wise, the plot is hackneyed but the hard-edged action is quite nasty with mostly amoral characters, including a Bible-quoting private eye (Walter Slezak). Stylized violence and a marriage for money. A-III (br)

Born to Win (1971) Czech director Ivan Passer's first American movie concerns a Times Square junkie (George Segal) who becomes involved with a woman (Karen Black) after stealing her car but, despite her help and his dreams of breaking his habit, he is a born loser. Though occasionally funny, too many scenes are played simply for their sexual content and the sensationalism of the drug counter-culture. O (R)

Born Wild (1968) Sordid melodrama directed by Maury Dexter about the conflict engendered by the bigoted treatment of Mexican-American students in a Southern California high school is excessive in its sensationalized treatment of sex and violence. O (PG)

Born Wild (see: **The Young Animals**)

Born Yesterday (1950) Witty social comedy from Garson Kanin's play about the moral transformation of a not-so-dumb blonde (Judy Holliday), who's the mistress of a corrupt government contractor (Broderick Crawford), after he pays a hard-up journalist (William Holden) to improve her mind. Director George Cukor gets much wry humor from the trio's shifting relationships as the reporter's introduction to political democracy, human rights, and true romance finally pays off in the self-discovery of a liberated woman. Implied sexual relationship. A-III (br)

Born Yesterday (1993) Weak updating of the 1950 Judy Holliday comedy in which a shady land developer (John Goodman), wheeling and dealing in Washington, D.C., gets more than his money's worth when he hires a savvy reporter (Don Johnson) to smarten up his embarrassingly dumb girlfriend (Melanie Griffith). Director Luis Mandoki's flat comedy develops the romantic triangle with no subtlety or interesting characterizations to lift it above the level of mindless adult humor. A live-in relationship and momentary violence. A-III (PG)

Borrower, The (1991) Gory sci-fi horror flick about two detectives (Rae Dawn Chong and Don Gordon) chasing an alien monster who borrows human heads to disguise himself. Director John McNaughton uses gross imagery and ugly humor in a violent, repelling horror fantasy. Excessive violence, fleeting nudity, and much rough language. O (R)

Borrowers, The (1998) Whimsical fantasy in which a villainous banker (John Goodman) sets out to drive a family of three from their home, only to discover he is up against a resourceful family of miniature people also living on the premises. Based on Mary Norton's children's stories and directed by Peter Hewitt, the movie doesn't lack for charm or gentle humor as the two families join forces to outwit big bully Goodman. Some menace and comic violence. A-II (PG)

Borsalino (1970) French gangster story set in 1930 Marseilles (the Chicago of its day) follows the rise of two petty crooks (Jean-Paul Belmondo and Alain Delon) until they control the city's rackets and are targets for other ambitious criminals. The point is not so much the story as it is the relationship between the two men and the evocation of the mood and feeling of life in the 1930s. Directed by Jacques Deray. A-III (GP)

Boss Nigger (1975) Fred Williamson, co-producer and star of this most recent rip-off of Kurosawa's samurai epic **Yojimbo**, surrounds himself here with a set of supposed actors even more inept then he, with a fine disregard for race, creed, color, or natural ability. Gratuitous violence and sex limit this to uncritical adults. A-III (PG)

Boston Blackie and the Law (1946) Formula crime series caper directed by D. Ross Lederman in which the title crime-buster (Chester Morris) puts on a Thanksgiving magic show at the local prison, then is accused of helping a woman inmate escape during his act, and has to find her to clear his name. Stylized violence. A-I (br)

Boston Strangler, The (1968) Fact-based movie about a sex murderer who terrorizes a city and the investigation which resulted in his capture. Director Richard Fleischer treats the case in plodding semi-documentary style, devoting the first half to the women victims and the last to the compulsive killer (Tony Curtis). Though well-intentioned, its graphic detailing of these brutal sex crimes is needless and offensive. O (R)

Bostonians, The (1984) Interesting adaptation of the Henry James novel about a strong woman (Vanessa Redgrave), a domineering male (Christopher Reeve), and an innocent young woman (Madeleine Potter), whom both are trying to influence. Director James Ivory gets some notable performances, though Potter lacks the magnetism to be the focal point for the ensuing struggle between feminist and chauvinist, but it does succeed in conveying 19th-century American attitudes about sexual roles. A-II (nr)

Botany Bay (1953) Transporting convicts to Australia in 1787, a cruel British sea captain (James Mason) makes life miserable for all aboard, notably an unjustly imprisoned American medical student (Alan Ladd) and a comely thief (Patricia Medina). Directed by John Farrow, the ocean voyage is eventful enough but the action flags after reaching the colony and a contrived ending. Stylized violence and romantic complications. A-II (br)

Bottle Rocket (1996) Failed comedy in which a bungling thief (Owen C. Wilson) persuades his equally dense buddies (Luke Wilson and Stephen Dignan) to attempt an ill-fated armed robbery. Writer-director Wes Anderson's unremittingly stupid characters are as tiresome as their penny-ante antics. Benign view of theft, some minor violence, implied sexual encounter, recurring profanity, and some rough language. A-III (R)

Bottom of the Bottle, The (1956) Dull tale of shifting psychological conflicts between a prosperous lawyer (Joseph Cotten) and his alcoholic brother (Van Johnson), an escaped convict trying to slip across the Mexican border. Director Henry Hathaway can't work up much interest in a contrived plot about cardboard characters. Stylized violence and excessive drinking. A-II (br)

Boulevard Nights (1979) Inner-city Hispanic brothers strive for contrasting ideals. One wants a better life, the other wants gang supremacy. Director Michael Pressman's superficial examination of the macho rituals of gang violence and drug dependence in the Mexican-American community generates bogus excitement, relying too heavily upon their graphic depiction. O (R)

Bound (1996) Nasty thriller in which the wily mistress (Jennifer Tilly) of a gangster (Joe Pantoliano) teams with her lesbian lover (Gina Gershon) to cheat the mob out of $2 million by framing the gangster. Co-written and directed by Larry and Andy Wachowski, the movie's soulless characters and non-stop brutality on-screen overwhelm the stylishly shot visuals. Excessive violence, graphic bedroom scene with nudity, and constant rough language and profanity. O (R)

Bound for Glory (1977) Screen adaptation of the 1943 autobiography of folk singer Woody Guthrie (David Carradine) follows his odyssey among America's dispossessed, from the Oklahoma Dust Bowl to migrant labor camps in California, where his songs about these experiences led to a national radio career. The outstanding achievement of director Hal Ashby's dramatization is its faithful re-creation of the Depression era and Guthrie's passion for social justice. Restrained depiction of promiscuity. A-III (PG)

Bounty, The (1984) Revisionist account of the mutiny aboard the "HMS Bounty" portrays Lt. William Bligh (Anthony Hopkins) as a flawed hero and Fletcher Christian (Mel Gibson) as an unstable young man bewitched by a Tahitian beauty. Roger Donaldson directs with intelligence and visual flare, but despite fine acting no real sparks ignite the drama because of a weak script. Extensive Polynesian nudity. A-IV (PG)

Bounty Killer, The (1965) After barely surviving an ambush that killed his partner, a bounty hunter (Dan Duryea) becomes a crazed avenger, using a sawed-off shotgun to get those responsible. Directed by Spencer G. Bennet, the hokey plot has equally unconvincing action despite a parade of veteran Western actors (Richard Arlen, Johnny Mack Brown, Bob Steele, and Buster Crabbe). Stylized violence and a hero who goes over the edge. A-II (br)

Bowery Bombshell (1946) Formula series entry directed by Phil Karlson in which the Bowery Boys (led by Leo Gorcey) capture some bank robbers (led by Sheldon Leonard) by pretending to be out-of-town mobsters. Slapstick violence and mild sexual innuendo. A-II (br)

Bowery Buckaroos (1947) Formula slapstick comedy directed by William Beaudine takes the Bowery Boys (Leo Gorcey, Huntz Hall, and company) out West, where they battle Indians and badmen while looking for a lost gold mine, a killer, and an orphaned girl. Mild comic menace. A-I (br)

Box of Moonlight (1997) While spending a long weekend with a rebellious young woodsman (Sam Rockwell), an uptight family man (John Turturro) learns to abandon his rigid perspective on life by indulging in some giddy lawlessness and cheating on his wife. Writer-director Tom DiCillo elicits some engaging performances, but his scenario is premised on the feeble notion that breaking society's laws and one's own moral code is a liberating experience which somehow turns a dull fellow into a better person. Positive treatment of criminal acts and marital infidelity, brief violence, intermittent male nudity, much profanity, and intermittent rough language. O (R)

Boxcar Bertha (1972) Trashy melodrama about a former labor unionizer turned bank robber (David Carradine), his woman companion of the title (Barbara Hershey), and some drifters (Barry Primus and Bernie Casey) picked up along the way. Directed by Martin Scorsese, the movie rumbles along through a tacky morass of redneck police and hired railroad thugs, pausing only for a shotgun blast in the chest here or a frolic in the buff there. There is a climactic massacre that leaves Carradine nailed cruciform to the side of a boxcar. O (R)

Boxer, The (1997) Against the backdrop of a shaky IRA cease-fire, the efforts of a Belfast IRA ex-con (Daniel Day-Lewis) to resume a boxing career and romance his old flame (Emily Watson) are complicated by the fact that she is now the wife of an IRA political prisoner. Director Jim Sheridan explores IRA infighting in a grim yet hopeful drama that stresses surviving in a culture of violence. Some violence, much rough language, and intermittent profanity. A-III (R)

Boxing Helena (1993) Tawdry horror tale in which an unbalanced surgeon (Julian Sands) amputates the limbs of the woman (Sherilyn Fenn) he loves, but who does not love him. Director Jennifer Chambers Lynch makes this nightmare of sexual obsession even more repulsive by treating it in the slick manner of a sentimental romance. Excessively graphic sex scenes, perverse violence, and occasional language. O (R)

Boy, a Girl and a Dog, A (1946) Sentimental WW II tale in which a city lad (Jerry Hunter) finds a mutt, to the delight of a young neighbor (Sharyn Moffett). When neither is allowed to keep the dog, they enlist him to the Army canine corps, and his trainer (Lionel Stander) takes him to the Pacific, where the dog becomes a war hero. Battlefield violence. A-I (br)

Boy and His Dog, A (1976) A not very bright boy (Don Johnson) and his extremely intelligent dog try to survive in a nuclear-ravaged world. The two, moreover, can communicate telepathically with one another, until the inevitable love triangle is introduced

(Susan Benton). The acting, including that of the dog, is very good, but the violence and sex are questionable elements in this black comedy from director L.Q. Jones based upon the Harlan Ellison novella. A-IV (R)

Boy Called Hate, A (1996) An alienated youth (Scott Caan) rescues a cynical teenager (Missy Crider) from being raped by shooting the attacker, then both become fugitives from the law after killing a highway patrolman they mistakenly assumed was going to arrest them. Writer-director Mitch Marcus's shrill road movie is of minimal interest save for a redemptive ending which underscores the grave consequences of violent behavior. Sporadic violence, a discreet sexual encounter, and much rough language. A-IV (R)

Boy, Did I Get a Wrong Number (1966) Hopeless comedy directed by George Marshall in which a real-estate operator (Bob Hope) lets a movie actress (Elke Sommer) hide out from the studio in an unsold estate, causing all kinds of implausible complications with his wife (Marjorie Lord) and maid (Phyllis Diller). Sexual innuendo. A-III (br)

Boy Friend, The (1972) British spoof of 1930s Hollywood backstage musicals with Twiggy as the understudy who becomes the star. Writer-producer-director Ken Russell turns Sandy Wilson's romantic musical set in the 1920s into an extravaganza of Busby Berkeley-like production numbers done on a lavish scale. Old-fashioned escapist fare, though a bit over-long for the small fry. A-I (G)

Boy from Oklahoma, The (1953) Amiable but pale Western in which a laconic cowpoke (Will Rogers, Jr.) takes the job of sheriff in a corrupt cow-town, where he uses his head and a lariat rather than six-shooters to solve the murder of his predecessor, whose feisty daughter (Nancy Olson) has caught his eye. Director Michael Curtiz spends more time on the muddled plot's exposition than on its potential for humor and action. Stylized violence and mild romance. A-I (br)

Boy in Blue, The (1986) Based on the life of a legendary Canadian scull-racing champion, the movie not only lacks a romantic vision but features a wholly anachronistic portrayal by Nicolas Cage in what becomes a teenage macho study of false pride and determination in 1870's America. Moronic teen romance and brief nudity. A-III (R)

Boy Named Charlie Brown, A (1969) First animated movie version of the Peanuts comic strip characters created by George Schulz centers on Charlie Brown's obsession with failure as he enters a national spelling bee contest. The animation team under director Bill Melendez has been completely faithful to the stylized world of the comic strip in giving movement and voice to the small-fry characters. Refreshing but meaningful amusement for both youngsters and grownups. A-I (G)

Boy of Two Worlds (1970) After the death of his parents, a West Indian boy is sent to live with his maiden aunt in a small Danish village. When she dies, he runs away and lives in the forest rather than stay in an orphanage. All ends happily in a very engaging children's movie directed by Astrid and Bjare Henning-Jensen that will also interest adults. A-I (G)

Boy on a Dolphin (1957) Murky adventure in Aegean waters as a dedicated archaeologist (Alan Ladd) vies with a conniving collector of antiquities (Clifton Webb) over the title art-treasure found on an ancient sunken ship by a local diver (Sophia Loren). Directed by Jean Negulesco, the convoluted tale of dark intrigue and pale romance has less appeal than the picturesque Greek backgrounds and some examples of ancient artworks. Sexual situations. A-III (br)

Boy Ten Feet Tall, A (1965) Orphaned boy journeys alone across the length of Africa to find an aunt and matures considerably during the course of his adventures. Directed by Alexander Mackendrick, the story is slight but very appealing, especially for youngsters. A-I (G)

Boy Who Could Fly, The (1986) A teenage girl befriends an autistic boy and tries to help him overcome his muteness in a tender and sensitive fable about the importance of friendship for those growing up in a socially inflexible environment. Nick Castle directs this unpretentious, life-affirming movie that uses brief but effective special-effects fantasy to provide some good-natured fun for youngsters. A-I (PG)

Boy Who Cried Werewolf, The (1973) Inept semi-horror movie about a youngster (Scott Sealey) whose father (Kerwin Matthews) is bitten by a werewolf near the family's secluded summer cabin, but no one will listen as the locals are decimated in traditional fashion. Lethargically directed by Nathan Juran, it may frighten youngsters insecure in their parental relationships, but lycanthropy lovers can only lament this travesty of a cherished movie myth. A-II (PG)

Boy with Green Hair, The (1948) Runaway war orphan (Dean Stockwell) tells social worker (Robert Ryan) how he was scorned and rejected after his hair suddenly turned green. Producer Dore Schary's earnest but preachy parable about prejudice gets heavy-handed direction from Joseph Losey, though Pat O'Brien's breezy performance as the lad's whimsical guardian adds some life to an otherwise dour story. A-I (br)

Boyfriends and Girlfriends (1988) French director-writer Eric Rohmer tracks the shifting romantic alliances between four young men and women living and working in a Paris suburb. Its sparkling depiction of the warm friendship between the two women (Emmanuelle Chaulet and Sophie Renoir) is marred by the story's implied cohabitation of unmarried couples. Subtitles. A-III (PG)

Boys (1996) Dull adolescent fantasy in which a troubled prep-school lad (Lukas Haas) falls for a young woman (Winona Ryder) in trouble over a stolen car and a missing baseball player. Written and directed by Stacy Cochran, the dragged-out proceedings invite little interest and less sympathy for the would-be rebel teen or his aimless rich girlfriend. Sexual situations and references, crude expressions, profanity, and an instance of rough language. A-III (PG-13)

Boys from Brazil, The (1978) Fanatical Nazi war criminal (Gregory Peck) oversees the care and feeding of some Hitler clones born in Brazil and distributed throughout the world. Laurence Olivier plays his opponent, an aging Jewish Nazi hunter. Some good acting but, for the most part, director Franklin Schaffner achieves only an overwrought melodrama with a large dose of graphic, sadistic violence. A-III (R)

Boys from Brooklyn, The (1952) Comic clunker directed by William Beaudine with Duke Mitchell and Sammy Petrillo (inept Dean Martin-Jerry Lewis imitators) lost on a South Seas island, where Bela Lugosi is experimenting on the evolutionary link between men and monkeys. Unamusing antics, including sexual innuendo. A-III (br)

Boys in Company C, The (1978) Directed by Sidney J. Furie with a cast of unknown actors, this muddled movie about a company of young Marines in boot camp and subsequent combat in Vietnam focuses on drugs, atrocities, greed, and cynicism. Veering from slapstick to supposedly real emotion, the movie uses foul language, bereft of any significant context, while failing to give any moral or political dimension to the drama. O (R)

Boys in the Band, The (1970) Screen version of a stage play about a birthday party attended by eight homosexual and one heterosexual college friends. Directed by William Friedkin, it is a gripping, frighteningly honest view of human relationships and the introverted homosexual psyche with all its anxiety, bitterness, depression, and solitude. A-IV (R)

Boys Next Door, The (1986) Two socially disadvantaged youths, about to graduate from high school and take on dull factory jobs, vent their frustrations and anxieties in a series of brutal encounters with innocent strangers who have the misfortune to cross their path. Director Penelope Spheeri's exploration of the dark side of maladjusted youth exploits only the violent consequences of alienation without a compassionate insight into adolescent behavior. Excessive use of brutality and foul language. O (R)

Boys on the Side (1995) After accidentally killing her abusive partner, a pregnant woman (Drew Barrymore) flees with a lesbian musician (Whoopi Goldberg) and a woman with AIDS (Mary-Louise Parker) to Tucson, where they supply moral support for each other in facing a series of emotional crises. Director Herbert Ross's big-hearted and sentimental tragicomedy concentrates on themes of love, forgiveness, and commitment, though the result is handicapped by its contrived treatment of numerous romantic complications ranging from the bizarre to the maudlin. Brief but intense violence, multiple implied affairs, fleeting nudity, sympathetic depiction of a frustrated homosexual, some crude sexual references, and intermittent rough language. A-IV (R)

Boys of Paul Street, The (1969) Hungarian movie in which two bands of schoolboys vie for possession of a vacant lot in 1902 Budapest, but the outcome of their skirmishes proves as disillusioning to them as the battles they will fight a few years later in World War I. Director Zoltan Fabri's nostalgic production recreates the historical period as well as the innocent earnestness with which the boys regard their secret societies and strange rituals. Good family fare. A-I (G)

Boys of St. Vincent, The (1994) Fictional dramatization of fact-based events in Canada centers in a Catholic orphanage run by religious brothers who sexually molest the youngsters in their care but, because of a cover-up, are not brought to trial until 15 years later. Shown originally as a four-hour TV program, the 1992 Canadian production directed by John N. Smith is a powerful indictment of those who abuse positions of trust as well as a sensitive, non-exploitational portrayal of the damage done their victims and the community, with convincing performances by a fine cast headed by Henry Czerny as the tormented chief offender. Strong fare but responsibly treated, relying on suggestion rather than graphic depiction of the sexual abuse of minors, with much pent-up emotional churnings, some outbursts of violence, and occasional profanity. A-III (nr)

Boys Town (1938) Sentimental but emotionally honest story of how Father Flanagan (Spencer Tracy) built his school for homeless and delinquent youths during the Depression. Directed by Norman Taurog, the Hollywood version centers in the conflict between the priest's charismatic powers of persuasion and a street-tough (Mickey Rooney) who only thinks he's hard-boiled. Tracy's Oscar-winning performance as a role model for those in need of one was a credible blend of the idealistic and the pragmatic. A-I (br)

Boyz N the Hood (1991) Drugs, gang warfare, and broken homes take their toll on a determined black youth (Cuba Gooding, Jr.) and two brothers (Ice Cube and Morris Chestnut) who are his closest friends in a violent South Central Los Angeles neighborhood. Writer-director John Singleton's first feature is a harrowing and powerful pro-family, anti-drug statement, though frequently undermined by the preachy tone of its heavy-handed dialogue. Excessive rough language and gutter talk, repeated mindless violence, drug and alcohol abuse, and brief bedroom shots with flashes of nudity. A-IV (R)

Braddock: Missing in Action III (1988) Brutal sequel in which superhero Col. Jim Braddock (Chuck Norris) returns to Vietnam, this time to rescue his Vietnamese wife, presumed killed in the fall of Saigon; the son he didn't know he had; and a terrorized group of Amerasian youngsters. Ploddingly directed by Aaron Norris, the movie's threadbare plot serves only as a pretext for extravagant mayhem, laced with comic-book heroics and exaggerated Oriental villains. Excessive violence. O (R)

Brady Bunch Movie, The (1995) Fluffy comedy updating the 1970's TV sitcom family of three boys and three girls (headed by parents Shelley Long and Gary Cole) into the troubled 1990s, where the Bradys remain do-goody innocents despite scornful schoolmates and the sleazy attempts of a greedy real estate agent (Michael McKean) to yank their home out from under them. As blandly directed by Betty Thomas, the threadbare plot and broad characterizations seem likely to appeal only to the sitcom's fans, leaving others to wonder why it merited the theatrical treatment. Intermittent sexual innuendo, including the jokey depiction of a frustrated lesbian character, mild slapstick violence, and a few crude expressions. A-III (PG-13)

Brain, The (1969) French comedy in which a master criminal (David Niven), whose brain is so large he has trouble keeping his head erect, comes up with a million dollar scheme that becomes an international cops and robbers chase. Director Gerard Oury has made an old-fashioned romp with a couple of good laughs, but many scenes are over-extended and full of cliches. Comic violence. A-II (G)

Brain Donors (1992) A trio of loonies (John Turturro, Bob Nelson, and Mel Smith) persuades a rich widow (Nancy Marchand) to sponsor them in the formation of a ballet company. Director Dennis Dugan's wacky farce repeats all manner of comic cliches from Marx Brothers comedies before it lurches out of control and runs out of genuine laughs. Mild sexual innuendo. A-II (PG)

Brain That Wouldn't Die, The (1963) Horror clunker directed by Joseph Green in which a mad doctor (Herb Evers) rescues his girlfriend's head after it's severed in a car accident, then keeps it alive while searching for a suitable body upon which to attach it, but an earlier botched experiment gets in the way. Stylized violence, hokey menace, and sexual innuendo. A-III (br)

Brainstorm (1983) Some dedicated scientists invent a device to enable one person to experience another's thoughts and sensations, but some nasty military types try to take it over for their own purposes. Directed by Douglas Trumbull, starring Natalie Wood and Christopher Walken, the movie is more interested in its special effects than in developing the human dimensions of its characters. Brief but graphic sex scene. A-III (PG)

Bram Stoker's Dracula (1992) Tawdry retelling of the vampire classic as a doomed love story begins in Transylvania, where Count Dracula (Gary Oldman) has his handmaidens seduce a young English realtor (Keanu Reeves), then moves to London in order to ravage the realtor's bride (Winona Ryder) before a cunning professor (Anthony Hopkins) orchestrates the vampire's demise. Director Francis Ford Coppola's erotic version of the Gothic tale gets lost in garishly titillating images that fail to evoke the basic simplicity of the struggle between good and evil and undercut the stark horror of the story. Perverse, sexually suggestive scenes with recurring nudity and intermittent gory violence, including several decapitations. O (R)

Brand X (1970) Taylor Mead stars in an underground movie satirizing TV programming with a self-conscious grab bag of humorous improvisations. Some of the skits are indeed witty, but the majority are crude, tasteless, vulgar, and indeed indecent. O (nr)

Branded (1950) Uneven Western in which a tough badman (Alan Ladd) poses as the long-lost son of a rich rancher (Charles Bickford), but a change of heart leads him to seek out the real son. Directed by Rudolph Maté, the story picks up interest when the missing youth is located south of the border, where he has been raised as the son of a Mexican bandit (Joseph Calleia). Frontier violence and divided family loyalties. A-I (br)

Brannigan (1975) John Wayne, violating civil rights at home and abroad, plays a police officer sent to England to extradite a hood with whom he has a personal score to settle. British production directed by Douglas Hickox focuses on Wayne's character as contemptuous of all legal restraint, an attitude in which he is joined ultimately by his London counterpart (Richard Attenborough). He-man violence. A-III (PG)

Brass Legend, The (1956) Pedestrian Western directed by Gerd Oswald pits steely-eyed sheriff Hugh O'Brien against wanted outlaw Raymond Burr with predictable results. Stylized violence. A-II (br)

Brass Target (1979) Yarn blurring the border between history and fiction about a failed attempt to assassinate General Patton (George Kennedy) who wants to retrieve the German gold high-ranking American staff officers have hijacked. John Hough's direction smothers suspense but inflates the violence, making the movie unsuitable for youngsters. A-III (PG)

Brassed Off (1997) British story set in a depressed 1992 Yorkshire mining town, where the mine's band leader (Pete Postlethwaite) insists the group carry on with their music sessions in hopes of winning a national band contest. Writer-director Mark Herman's spirited drama goes overboard in its indictment of Tory social policies, but is otherwise a winning, warmly human story of a working-class community coping with economic ruin. Brief sexual innuendo, fleeting locker-room nudity, minor violence, and intermittent rough language. A-III (R)

Bravados, The (1958) Grim, troubling Western follows a revengeful rancher (Gregory Peck) as he seeks the gang (notably Stephen Boyd, Henry Silva, and Lee Van Cleef) who killed his wife and child. Directed by Henry King, the trail is long and bloody, but by its end the rancher realizes that justice is not achieved at the end of a gun. Strong stylized violence and vigilante theme. A-II (br)

Brave Little Toaster, The (1987) Animated feature in which five old appliances — Toaster, Radio, Lampy, electric blanket Blanky, and vacuum cleaner Kirby — left in a summer cottage and yearning for the boy who used to use them, set off on an arduous, at times dangerous, journey to the big city to find their young master. Though the story doesn't bear much adult scrutiny and the Taiwan-Japanese animation is not up to Disney standards, most preteen viewers will find the adventures of the unlikely but lively five-some imaginative fun and be impressed by the loyalty and perseverance exhibited by the appliances. For all, though several menacing scenes may frighten the very young. A-I (nr)

Brave One, The (1956) Sentimental yet engaging tale of a young Mexican lad (Michel Ray) who raises a champion bull from a calf, then tries to save his pet when it is mistakenly shipped to the bull ring in Mexico City. Directed by Irving Rapper from an Oscar-winning script by Robert Rich (aka blacklisted Dalton Trumbo), the bond between the little boy and his noble beast is dramatized with enough conviction to tug at the hearts of all but confirmed cynics, with the added bonus of picturesque Mexican settings and a positive depiction of the story's cultural context, including the art of bullfighting. Some menacing situations and the bull ring's violence make it unlikely fare for preschoolers. A-I (br)

Brave Warrior (1952) With the aid of Chief Tecumseh (Jay Silverheels), Americans (led by Jon Hall) put down a British-instigated Shawnee uprising at Tippecanoe, Ind., in 1811. Directed by Spencer G. Bennet, it's a minor Western with grade-school heroics and some stylized violence. A-I (br)

Braveheart (1995) Bloody historical epic in which 13th-century Scotsman William Wallace (Mel Gibson), spurred on by the murder of his wife, attempts to unite the bickering Scottish noblemen under Robert the Bruce (Angus McFadyen) in a fight for independence against the ruthless English King Edward I (Patrick McGoohan). Also directed by Gibson, the lavish production focuses on savage battles, betrayals, and murders of revenge, softened by a smattering of royal romance, but its many scenes of nasty brutality tend to overwhelm this romanticized biography of Scotland's national hero. Much gory violence on and off the battlefield, a few fleeting bedroom scenes, brief nudity, and minimal rough language. A-IV (R)

Brazil (1986) This production combines the failed utopian vision of **Blade Runner** with the whimsical outlook of the Monty Python comedy troupe in a playful, expressionistic fantasy of a madcap totalitarian England, where nothing works. Director Terry Gilliam's mix of mirth and menace proclaims the futility of the hero's slapstick struggle to combat conformity and complacency with romantic love. A-III (R)

Bread and Chocolate (1978) In this tragicomedy from director Franco Brusati, Nino Manfredi plays an Italian immigrant worker desperately trying to make a go of it in Switzerland so that he can bring home some money to his family. Light social satire contrasting the unfeeling bourgeoisie with the passionate working-class loser, it resorts to some indecent exposure and a gratuitous incident in which a priest is involved in a bizarre murder. O (nr)

Break, The (1998) Absorbing story of an IRA gunman (Stephen Rea) who escapes from an Ulster prison, takes refuge in New York City, then uses his terrorist expertise to help Guatemalan refugees (Alfred Molina and Rosana Pastor) assassinate one of their country's oppressors. Directed by Robert Dornhelm, the British production is less a political drama than a character study in which Rea gives a convincing performance as a man who has lived by the gun and cannot change his destiny to die by the gun. Hard-edged violence, sexual situations, brief nudity, and occasional rough language. A-III (R)

Breakdown (1997) When his wife (Kathleen Quinlan) is kidnapped on a remote desert road after their jeep stalls, the distraught husband (Kurt Russell) must track down four murderous thugs (led by J.T. Walsh) to save her. Director Jonathan Mostow's twisty action thriller offers solid suspense, despite occasionally nasty violence. Some vicious violence, frequent profanity, and recurring rough language. A-III (R)

Breaker, Breaker (1977) An amateurish little movie directed by Don Hulette about a martial-arts master and trucker (Chuck Norris) who cleans out a nest of thugs and criminals with the help of a fleet of trucks called in by CB radio. Considerable violence and some rough language. A-III (PG)

Breaker Morant (1980) During the Boer War, three officers of an Australian unit (led by title character Edward Woodward) are court-martialed for shooting prisoners. Despite uniformly fine performances and well-staged action scenes, Australian director Bruce Beresford's fact-based courtroom drama never quite comes to grips with the issues raised about the irregular nature of combat against guerrilla forces as well as the defense of following orders. Mature themes and battlefield violence. A-III (PG)

Breakfast at Tiffany's (1961) Bright romantic comedy from Truman Capote's tale of Holly Golightly (Audrey Hepburn), a bubble-headed beauty whose kooky behavior wows Manhattan's social set and bowls over an earnest young writer (George Peppard) despite complications (Patricia Neal). Director Blake Edwards lances the bogus glitter of the big city and paces the action with humor (notably Mickey Rooney's broad performance as an irascible Japanese neighbor) but the movie's main attraction is Hepburn's ability to portray the innate innocence of the free-spirited Holly. Mature themes. A-III (br)

Breakfast Club, The (1985) Five teenagers spend a Saturday detention in their school library. After much abrasive interchange and a little marijuana, they become downright chummy when they realize they share common attitudes about adult authority figures, drugs, and sex. Under John Hughes's direction the movie lacks any critical perspective, seeming to justify antisocial behavior, casual sex, and the concept of drugs as a harmless escape, if not a liberating experience. O (R)

Breakfast for Two (1937) Flimsy romantic comedy in which a Texas oil heiress (Barbara Stanwyck) reforms a penniless playboy (Herbert Marshall). Directed by Alfred Santell, the labored plot features a bright cast and some droll funny business, including a wedding disrupted by wacky window-washers. Some heavy drinking and romantic complications. A-I (br)

Breakheart Pass (1976) This Charles Bronson vehicle is an interesting Western that is part mystery and part suspense. Although the action takes place mostly on a train, outside is the world of the US cavalry vs. the Indians. The movie's production values and Tom Gries's direction are tops, but there is some brutal violence. A-III (PG)

Breakin' (1984) Director Joel Silberg's quickie movie cashing in on the break-dancing craze is innocuous, light entertainment. A classical dancer, going nowhere as a waitress (Lucinda Dickey), joins up with break dancers Adolfo "Shabba-Doo" Quinones and Michael "Bongaloo Shrimp" Chambers, and the three conquer the prejudice of the dance establishment and make it to Broadway. There is some charm in its unpretentiousness but little, if any, style. A-II (PG)

Breakin' 2: Electric Boogaloo (1985) Break-dancing sequel is this time a case of "putting on a show of our own" in the old Judy Garland-Mickey Rooney tradition. The necessary ingredient is the dancing, with the plot being only the occasion for it. The performers are pleasantly exuberant and the whole exercise is innocuous. A-II (PG)

Breaking Away (1979) Light comedy chronicling a summer in the lives of four teenagers in mid-America who are determined to stay together, despite community and hometown college pressures to the contrary. In centering on one youth (Dennis Christopher) and his bemused parents (Barbara Barrie and Paul Dooley), director Peter Yates reveals a depth and feeling for character that gives weight to the movie's exploration of youthful determination culminating in a vivid bicycle race. A-II (PG)

Breaking Glass (1981) Brian Gibson directs an offbeat movie that takes a hard look at British society and the empire of pop music. It gets a bit too slick and sentimental at the end, but despite its defects it's fairly entertaining and provocative, thanks in large part to the talent of actress-singer-composer Hazel O'Connor. Restrained portrayal of the seamy side of life. A-III (PG)

Breaking In (1989) Refreshing, low-key buddy caper with Burt Reynolds as a graying, gimpy professional safecracker who teaches a young, goofy protégé (Casey Siemaszko) the tricks of his dying trade. Scottish director Bill Forsyth peoples his Portland landscape with nutty characters and doesn't glamorize his two harmless protagonists and their whimsical, non-menacing heists. No violence, though some profanity and suggested sexual encounters with prostitutes. A-III (R)

Breaking Point, The (1950) Gritty melodrama about the captain of a California charter boat (John Garfield) whose need for money gets him involved with a crooked lawyer (Wallace Ford) and some illegal cargos that cost the life of his shipmate (Juano Hernandez) and very nearly his own. Directed by Michael Curtiz from the Ernest Hemingway novel, *To Have and Have Not*, the action is lean and convincing, with well-defined characters that add some emotional depth to the story's desperate developments. Some nasty stylized violence, menacing situations, and sexual innuendo. A-III (br)

Breaking Point, The (1976) Bo Svenson plays the abused, honest citizen tracked by the hoods against whom he testified in this typically brutal and mindless variation on the revenge theme. Canadian director Bob Clark's viewers are subjected to an assault of violence, maiming, and a brutal rape. O (R)

Breaking the Waves (1996) Provocative but uneven drama set in Scotland, where a mentally confused woman (Emily Watson) comes to believe God will cure her paralyzed husband (Stellan Skarsgard) if she has sex with other men, a morally bizarre concept leading to dangerous situations and a seemingly miraculous outcome. Danish writer-director Lars Von Trier's contrived yet absorbing narrative centers in the emotional saga of a simple-minded, deeply religious heroine who goes over the edge trying to save her husband by sacrificing herself, with ambiguous results. Restrained sex scenes and sexual references, brief nudity, and occasional rough language and profanity. A-IV (R)

Breaking the Rules (1992) Maudlin male-bonding saga of estranged friends (Jonathan Silverman and C. Thomas Howell) accompanying a leukemia-stricken buddy (Jason Bateman) on the drive from Cleveland to Los Angeles so the dying man can appear on a cherished TV quiz show, but pick up a woman (Annie Potts) along the way instead. The trio's journey flounders in over-cute dialogue, sophomoric pranks, artificial tears, and pretentious musings on what it all means. Directed by Neil Israel. Recurring sexual references, a seduction scene, satiric treatment of religion, and occasional profanity. O (PG-13)

Breakout (1975) Down-on-his-luck pilot (Charles Bronson) contracts to fly a wrongly accused American out of a Mexican prison and finds himself involved with a rogue CIA operation. Directed by Tom Gries, it's an old-fashioned adventure yarn, with the emphasis on action rather than violence, except for a grisly depiction of a villain being killed by an airplane propeller. A-III (PG)

Breakthrough (1950) WW II story of a US Army platoon led by a green lieutenant (John Agar) and a veteran sergeant (Frank Lovejoy) from its training in

England to the D-Day invasion and through the hedgerows of Normandy, until linking with Patton's Third Army to break through the German lines at St. Lo. Director Lewis Seiler underplays the individual heroics and effectively inter-cuts actual combat footage with the staged battle scenes. Wartime violence. A-I (br)

Breathless (1983) Remake of Jean-Luc Godard's 1963 movie about a petty criminal betrayed by love is a self-indulgent exercise in graphic sex and sentimentality. Neither of the two lovers (Richard Gere and Valerie Kaprisky) shows sufficient humanity to stake a claim on our interest but, to be fair, both are constantly upstaged by a blaring rock score and the slick, flashy, altogether shallow technique of director Jim McBride. O (R)

Breezy (1973) May-December romance blooms when divorced L.A. realtor (William Holden) finds a 17-year-old flower child (Kay Lenz) on his doorstep, and soon they are off romping together until, of course, he meets her friends and she, his. Directed by Clint Eastwood, the romantic twaddle makes frequent use of nudity and pointless profanity. O (R)

Brenda Starr (1992) Flat adventure fantasy with the comic-strip ace reporter of the title (Brooke Shields) chasing a scoop to Brazil, where a mysterious stranger (Timothy Dalton) and the strip's cartoonist (Tony Peck) help out in her encounters with foreign agents and a rival reporter (Diana Scarwid). Director Robert Ellis Miller's clumsy treatment of the tedious proceedings is unamusing, going from comic strip to live action in an erratic mix of time periods as senseless as the rest of this misfire. Comic violence and romantic situations. A-II (br)

Brewster McCloud (1971) Failed allegory about a fallen angel (Sally Kellerman) who inspires a boy (Bud Cort) to fly under the power of his own homemade wings. Director Robert Altman manages to wring spirited performances from a fine supporting cast but not from his principals, and the result is a confused narrative with only flashes of humor and satire, much of it bawdy but toothless. A-III (R)

Brewster's Millions (1985) Richard Pryor stars in another remake of the venerable chestnut about a man who inherits a vast fortune on the condition that he squander a modest one. Under Walter Hill's direction, it's funny enough and fairly good entertainment, though the present version introduces too many needless complications. Some vulgar language. A-II (PG)

Brian Wilson: I Just Wasn't Made for These Times (1995) Sympathetic though ultimately sad portrait of the innovative musician who led the Beach Boys to the top of the music charts in the 1960s, then suffered a breakdown in the mid-1970s and became a recluse, until recently reemerging on the music scene. Interweaving a 1994 recording session with vintage filmclips and a wide variety of interviews, Don Was's documentary does a better job exploring Wilson's considerable musical accomplishments than in grappling with the personal problems which interrupted his brilliant career. Numerous references to substance abuse and a few coarse expressions. A-III (nr)

Bride, The (1985) In this freely adapted remake of **Bride of Frankenstein**, the mad doctor (rock star Sting) decides to keep for himself the mate (Jennifer Beals) he has fashioned for his creature (Clancy Brown). Unfortunately, director Franc Roddam is unable to bring this fine-looking but inert movie to life. Innocuous save for a brief sequence involving nudity. A-III (PG-13)

Bride Came C.O.D., The (1941) Screwball romantic comedy in which an aviator (James Cagney) is hired to bring an eloping heiress (Bette Davis) back to her millionaire father (Eugene Pallette), but their plane crash lands in a desert ghost town. Directed by William Keighley, the fun comes mostly from the battling Cagney-Davis combination, but the good supporting cast and some twists on an old formula plot are added dividends. Some comic violence and romantic complications. A-II (br)

Bride of Chucky (1998) Mindless horror sequel in which the title killer doll (voice of Brad Dourif) and his nasty doll girlfriend (voice of Jennifer Tilly) seek to take human form in the bodies of two teenagers. The result is a tiresome hodgepodge of gruesome killings depicted in grisly tongue-in-cheek fashion intended to evoke laughter from immature viewers. Directed by Ronnie Yu. Excessive gory violence, sexual situations, a flash of rear nudity, rough language, and profanity. O (R)

Bride of Frankenstein (1935) In a horror sequel better than the 1931 original, the macabre Dr. Praetorious (Ernest Thesiger) forces the reluctant Frankenstein (Colin Clive) to create a mate (Elsa Lanchester) for the unhappy monster (Boris Karloff). Director James Whale treats the dire proceedings with dry wit (a prologue featuring Lanchester as author Mary Wollstonecraft Shelley) and dark humor (timorous Una O'Connor), though the picture is best remembered for the poignant sequence in which the hunted monster is befriended by a blind hermit (O.P. Heggie). Stylized violence and considerable menace. A-II (br)

Bride of the Monster (1955) Horror clunker with Bela Lugosi as a mad doctor trying to create a master race with the help of a Tibetan mute (Tor Johnson) in a swampland laboratory protected by an octopus! Directed by Edward D. Wood, Jr., the low-budget proceedings are more silly than scary. Hokey menace. A-II (br)

Bride Wore Black, The (1968) Superior murder-thriller starring Jeanne Moreau as a revenge-obsessed bride who sets out to kill the five men responsible for her bridegroom's death. Directed by Francois Truffaut, the French production is an exercise in suspense of the Hitchcock variety. Subtitles. Restrained violence. A-III (br)

Brides of Dracula, The (1960) The cult of the undead lives on in Transylvania at the end of the 19th century as Dr. Van Helsing (Peter Cushing) tracks down a vampire baron (David Peel) who preys on young women. British director Terence Fisher makes effective use of eerie rural settings, fearful villagers, garlic garlands, and other vampire lore in an inventive script zestfully put over by a talented cast (notably Martita Hunt and Miles Malleson). Stylized violence and threatening situations. A-II (br)

Brides of Fu Manchu, The (1966) This time the Oriental master criminal (Christopher Lee) plans to conquer the world by forcing kidnapped scientists to develop a weapon utilizing intensified sound waves to destroy selected targets. Directed by Don Sharp, the action features mild violence and sexual innuendo. A-II (br)

Bridge at Remagen, The (1969) While the Germans try to destroy the last bridge across the Rhine in WW II, an American unit (led by George Segal) races to capture it. Director John Guillerman does well in building the tension and suspense inherent in the situation, but the human level of the relationships between the soldiers comes across as affected and shallow. Much wartime violence and strong language. A-III (PG)

Bridge on the River Kwai, The (1957) Epic WW II adventure based on Pierre Boulle's novel about British POWs in Burma, who build a military supply bridge for their Japanese captors while British commandos make their way through the jungle to blow it up. Though the anti-war ending is more hollow than ironic, director David Lean excels in depicting the rigors of prison camp life, the military discipline that sustains the prisoners, and, at the story's center, the battle of wills between the British commander (Alec Guinness) and his Japanese counterpart (Sessue Hayakawa) over who will command the work details. Some wartime violence and harrowing camp punishments. A-I (br)

Bridge Too Far, A (1977) Director Richard Attenborough's epic re-creation of the tragic Allied offensive code-named Market Garden details the fate of the massive paratroop force dropped behind German lines in Holland during WW II. The excellent all-star cast includes Dirk Bogarde, Anthony Hopkins, Laurence Olivier, Robert Redford, Ryan O'Neal, Gene Hackman, and Elliot Gould. Although the violence is unusually graphic, the movie has value as an historical dramatization that has tried to be faithful to the facts. A-III (PG)

Bridges at Toko-Ri, The (1954) Korean War melodrama from James A. Michener's novel about a lawyer (William Holden) recalled to active service as a jet pilot on an aircraft carrier (commanded by Fredric March) sent to destroy the heavily defended target of the title. Director Mark Robson does equally well with the shipboard camaraderie (notably Mickey Rooney, Earl Holliman, and Charles McGraw) as with the short visit of the pilot's wife (Grace Kelly), all of which strengthens the emotional impact of the pilot's final mission. Tense wartime action and a scene in a unisex Japanese bathhouse. A-II (br)

Bridges of Madison County, The (1995) Glossy woman's romance from Robert James Waller's novel set in 1965 Iowa, where a middleaged farm wife (Meryl Streep) spends several days in an intense relationship with a traveling photographer (Clint Eastwood) while her husband and teenage children are at a state fair, but chooses to stay in her marriage and not disrupt the lives of her loved ones. Also directed by Eastwood, the tastefully told love story walks a fine line between romanticizing adultery and affirming a positive moral choice. Restrained treatment of infidelity, fleeting shadowy nudity, minimal profanity, and an instance of rough language. A-IV (PG-13)

Brief Encounter (1945) Bittersweet British romance about a suburban housewife (Celia Johnson) and a married doctor (Trevor Howard) whose chance meeting in a train station becomes a weekly event that deepens into an emotional involvement neither had anticipated. Director David Lean shows this mutual attraction to be more spiritual than physical, as conveyed in exquisitely understated performances and evocative Rachmaninov piano concerto on the music track. The question of marital infidelity is treated within a moral framework. A-II (br)

Brief History of Time, A (1992) Documentary on British physicist Stephen Hawking, whose speculations on the origins of the universe and related matters have been achieved despite his progressive disablement since 1963 from the muscular disease ALS. Directed by Errol Morris, the result is a challenging introduction to Hawking's cosmological theories and ambivalence over the question of its Creator, but what's most impressive here is the human portrait of a determined individual overcoming the confinements of a wheelchair and inability to speak except through a voice synthesizer. Big concepts may confuse small children. A-II (G)

Brief Season (1971) Pia Degermark and Christopher Jones play a pair of Roman dropouts desperately having a go at life by bedding down, joy-riding in the woods and buying expensive gifts before taking their own lives. Director Renato Castellani's attempt to make alienation seem glamorous reduces everything to the most boring and inane level. A-III (R/GP)

Brief Vacation, A (1975) Italian portrait of a woman (Florinda Bolkan), her health broken from overworking to support three children and several relatives, who is sent to a sanitarium to regain her strength. There she has a brief affair with a younger man, but he comes from another class and her life remains unchanged. Director Vittorio de Sica contents himself with a realistic portrayal of a complex human being, letting viewers draw their own conclusions about the larger social implications in his story of the plight of the poor. Mature themes. A-III (PG)

Brigadoon (1954) Fanciful but thin Lerner and Loewe musical with vacationing Americans (Gene Kelly and Van Johnson) lost in the Scottish countryside, where they stumble upon an 18th-century village that appears for just one day every 100 years. Kelly's love for village lass Cyd Charisse isn't strong enough to keep director Vincente Minnelli's colorful fantasy from falling disappointingly flat, though the songs are lovely and Kelly's choreography worth watching. For the romantics in the family. A-I (G)

Brigand of Kandahar, The (1965) Turgid British melodrama about troubles on Victorian India's Northwest Frontier when a fanatic rebel leader (Oliver Reed) teams with a half-caste English officer (Ronald Lewis) seeking revenge on his bigoted commander (Duncan Lamont). Writer-director John Gilling's studio-bound production plods through an unconvincing story of adventure, romance and muddled loyalties. Stylized violence, romantic complications, and racial stereotypes. A-II (br)

Bright Angel (1991) An innocent 18-year-old Montana youth (Dermot Mulroney) and a world-weary runaway (Lili Taylor) who hopes to secure her brother's release from prison encounter a series of unsavory, at times deadly, characters. Cynicism and hopelessness pervade director Michael Fields's pathetic tale of easily exploited youngsters and jaded adults who have given up on life or chosen brutality to get what they want. A nihilistic view of life, occasional violence, sexual references, brief nudity, and much rough language. O (R)

Bright Eyes (1934) Sentimental but sturdy tale of a five-year-old orphan (Shirley Temple) whose loving godfather (James Dunn) risks his life piloting a plane through a ferocious storm to save the child from adoption by a grasping family. Directed by David Butler, the thin plot has plenty of heart with little Shirley at the center of things, whether stowing aboard a dangerous plane flight or singing "On the Good Ship Lollipop." A-I (PG)

Bright Leaf (1950) Tangled revenge tale of a man with a grudge (Gary Cooper) who in 1894 partners with a cigarette machine inventor (Jeff Corey), a con-man (Jack Carson), and a woman (Lauren Bacall) whose savings enable them to build a cigarette monopoly, which the man uses to ruin a snooty tobacco magnate (Donald Crisp) and marry his cunning daughter (Patricia Neal). Directed by Michael Curtiz, the beginnings of the cigarette industry are more interesting than the soppy story of a man who knows more about hate than love. Stylized violence, including a suicide, sexual innuendo, and marital strife. A-III (br)

Bright Lights, Big City (1988) Lurid adaptation of Jay McInerney's bestseller tracing the downward spiral of a young, aspiring novelist (Michael J. Fox) into sordid New York club life, drugs, and alcohol. Director James Bridges fails to fully develop the one-dimensional, dissipated lead character, doing a disservice to Fox's fans, who may be led to believe that drug and alcohol abuse are not addictive or lethal. Excessive scenes of substance abuse, some profanity, and hedonistic sexual activity within the NYC club scene. O (R)

Bright Shining Lie, A (1998) Fact-based account of the unfulfilled life of career Army officer John Paul Vann (Bill Paxton) who clashes with his superiors in 1964 Vietnam, then returns as civilian obsessed with showing the military how to win the war, until his death in a 1972 helicopter crash. Directed by Terry George from Neil Sheehan's 1988 Pulitzer Prize-winner, the dramatization portrays Vann as a flawed, contradictory figure whose actions in Vietnam raise questions about the war that divided Americans then and are still troubling today. Wartime violence, sexual situations, rough language, and profanity. A-III (R)

Bright Victory (1951) Blinded by a sniper's bullet in 1943 North Africa, an Army sergeant (Arthur Kennedy) learns to cope with sightlessness in a rehabilitation center, then finds his rich fiancé (Julia Adams) unable to accept his disability, but another can (Peggy Dow). Sensitively directed by Mark Robson, the movie succeeds best in showing the blinded soldier's rehabilitation but the love story and a racial theme are woodenly contrived. A-I (br)

Brighton Beach Memoirs (1986) Screen adaptation of Neil Simon's lighthearted play about a Jewish adolescent (Jonathan Silverman) coming of age in 1937 Brooklyn. Director Gene Saks re-creates the look and atmosphere of pre-WW II America and its traditional family values while finding humor in the young lad's struggle with the onset of puberty. Some discussion of masturbation, adolescent sexuality, and a sight gag featuring a nude postcard. A-III (PG-13)

Brighton Strangler, The (1945) Hokey thriller directed by Max Nosseck in which an actor (John Loder), starring as a maniacal murderer in a London play, is knocked senseless during the Blitz and awakens remembering only his stage character's compulsion to kill. Tepid menace and several scenes of stylized violence. A-II (br)

Brighty of the Grand Canyon (1967) Brighty, a brave burro with a natural instinct for distinguishing between good people and bad, helps track down the killer of an old prospector. Written and directed by Norman Foster, based on a book by Marguerite Henry, the outdoors adventure offers some dandy suspense as well as glorious photography of Arizona's Grand Canyon country. No violent visuals. A-I (br)

Brimstone (1949) Standard Western directed by Joseph Kane pits an undercover lawman (Rod Cameron) against the mean title outlaw (Walter Brennan) and his ornery sons, with the local sheriff (Forrest Tucker) causing complications for both sides. Shootouts and fistfights. A-I (br)

Bring Me the Head of Alfredo Garcia (1974) Down-at-the-heels American (Warren Oates) takes the grisly job of tracking down a man in Mexico and delivering his head to a millionaire, but in the process has to kill more and more people until he becomes mad with bloodlust. Director Sam Peckinpah turns the story into sordid essay on the pornography of violence. O (R)

Bringing Up Baby (1938) Classic screwball comedy in which a serious-minded paleontologist (Cary Grant) gets mixed up with a zany socialite heiress (Katherine Hepburn) whose pet leopard, Baby, is mistaken for an escaped killer leopard, as confusions multiply until girl gets boy. Howard Hawks directs the hilarious proceedings with flair and style, abetted by a playful plot, madcap performances by Hepburn and Grant, and a great supporting cast (including Charlie Ruggles, May Robson, Barry Fitzgerald, and Walter Catlett). Absurdly silly and utterly delightful. A-I (br)

Brink's Job, The (1978) Director William Friedkin focuses on the crooks (Peter Falk, Peter Boyle, and Allen Goorwitz) involved in a spectacular 1950 robbery in Boston, providing a fascinating picture of the underside of society in a particular time and place. Laced with wry humor, the movie has almost no violence, the language is relatively restrained, but there is moral ambiguity in its somewhat romanticized view of criminal life. A-III (PG)

Britannia Hospital (1983) Crude, muddled British satire about a hospital celebrating its 500th anniversary, and whose preparations for a visit from the Queen become reduced to chaos as various factions within and without clash. Director Lindsay Anderson obviously intends the clash of special interest groups as a metaphor of the condition of Britain herself and the world in general. Violence, nudity, and a general air of cynical amorality. O (R)

Broadcast News (1987) News producer (Holly Hunter) in the Washington bureau of a TV network finds herself drawn away from a hardworking reporter whom she admires (Albert Brooks) by an off-again, on-again attraction to a handsome but unprofessional reporter (William Hurt) being groomed as network news anchor. Written, produced, and directed by James L. Brooks, the romantic comedy is often quite funny and also worthwhile in its satiric portrait of television news being more concerned with image and packaging than with the news story itself. Permissive attitude toward casual sex, several explicit sexual references, and some rough language. A-IV (R)

Broadway Bill (1934) Slight but bright comedy in which a race horse owner (Warner Baxter) marries the daughter (Helen Vinson) of a sour millionaire (Walter Connolly), but can't stand her stuffy family and leaves determined to win the Derby with the champion horse of the title. Directed by Frank Capra, the comic complications are rich in devious racetrack characters (Raymond Walburn, Lynne Overman, Douglass Dumbrille, and others) but the owner perseveres with the help of the horse's trainer (Clarence Muse), a rooster mascot, and his wife's sister (Myrna Loy) who's in love with him. An attempt to fix a race and a broken marriage. A-III (br)

Broadway Danny Rose (1984) Director Woody Allen's nostalgic essay on showbiz self-deception is a droll and almost provincial tribute to the smalltime theatrical agents who, like Danny Rose (Allen), labor with scant hope of monetary reward for some fourth-rate talent. The plot, revolving around reviving the career of a has-been singer (Nick Apollo Forte) only to be betrayed at the point of success, is thin and only mildly amusing. Some Italian stereotyping. A-III (PG)

Broken Arrow (1950) Thoughtful Western set in 1870 Arizona, where an ex-Army officer (James Stewart) persuades the warring Apache leader, Cochise (Jeff Chandler), to make peace, then takes an Apache bride (Debra Paget) who's soon killed by vengeful whites out to break the treaty. Directed by Delmer Daves, the fact-based story has plenty of colorful period action, some Indian lore, and a bit of romance, but was more notable at the time for its sympathetic treatment of Native Americans as fellow humans rather than howling savages. Frontier violence in a meaningful context. A-I (br)

Broken Arrow (1996) Violent tale set in a remote area of the Southwest, where an Air Force bomber pilot (John Travolta) has hidden two nuclear warheads to extort a fortune from the Pentagon, unaware his copilot (Christian Slater) is out to foil his plan with the help of a spunky park ranger (Samantha Mathis). Director John Woo's handsomely mounted, explosive action thriller is fast-paced escapist fare until the mindless, ever-escalating violence goes ballistic in the last half-hour. Excessive violence, intermittent profanity, and frequent rough language. O (R)

Broken Blossoms (1919) Simple but heart-felt romantic tragedy from Thomas Burke's *Limehouse Nights* in which an impoverished, disillusioned Chinese immigrant (Richard Barthelmess) befriends a London street waif (Lillian Gish) terrified of her drunken, sadistic father (Donald Crisp). Director D. W. Griffith demonstrates his abilities to work in a small, intimate drama that conjures with the fragile innocence of an adolescent caught in the ugly reality of an intolerant and unjust adult world. Moral complexities. A-III (br)

Broken Dreams (1932) Mawkish melodrama about a man (Randolph Scott) whose grief over his wife's death during childbirth compels him to leave the infant with his parents while he goes off to Vienna to become a pediatrician, then returns, remarries, and, after many complications, reclaims his son. Domestic discord and a drunk making sexual advances. A-II (br)

Broken English (1997) New Zealand production about the daughter (Aleksandra Vujcic) of a Croatian family living in Auckland who brings her stern, nationalistic father (Rade Serbedzija) to violence when she persists in her decision to marry a Maori (Julian Arahanga). Directed by Gregor Nicholas, the story is ambitious in showing the harm of racial and cultural prejudices, but it becomes overly contrived and is flawed by melodramatic scenes of violence and sex. Some nasty violence, a graphic sex scene, sexual situations, denigrating racial expressions, and much rough language. O (NC-17)

Broken Harvest (1995) A farm boy (Darren McHugh) in 1950's Ireland gradually becomes aware that bitter enmities dating from the 1920's civil war still divide his rural community and indirectly cause the death of his father (Colin Lane). Co-written and directed by Maurice O'Callaghan, the Irish production is a slight but evocative anecdote about a boy's introduction into the adult world of politics and its consequences, though the context of Irish republicanism may be lost on American viewers. Stylized violence, some sexual innuendo. and an occasional profanity. A-II (nr)

Broken Lance (1954) Western family saga in which a ruthless, aging cattle baron (Spencer Tracy) tries to keep the inroads of civilization and the law from limiting his rule of the range, while his sons (Richard Widmark, Hugh O'Brian, and Earl Holliman) feud with their stepbrother (Robert Wagner) over the future of the family empire. Directed by Edward Dmytryk, some rugged outdoor action helps pace the story of a domineering father whose spiteful sons conspire to take over his vast ranchlands, with tragic results. Stylized violence and family conflicts. A-II (br)

Broken Mirrors (1987) Dutch import directed by feminist Marleen Gorris examines the ruthless and abusive relationships between men and women as viewed by two women who try to free themselves from the spiritual suffocation of working in an Amsterdam brothel. As a lesson for women to escape victimization, the amateurish production resorts too often to extreme and explicit examples of injustice, sadistic brutality, and abuse. Foul language and brief nudity are intermittent. O (nr)

Bronco Billy (1980) Offbeat story of a modern-day shoe salesman from New Jersey (Clint Eastwood) who puts together a modest but competent Wild West Show with other dreamers and misfits like himself. Also directed by Eastwood, the comedy is surprisingly amiable and relaxed, though marred by the inclusion of a brutal fight sequence. A-III (PG)

Bronco Bullfrog (1972) British story of a young worker who falls in love with an underage girl, but its principal intent is to describe a deadening environment which has already condemned him to a life without hope. Directed by Barney Platt-Mills, the 1969 semi-documentary is an honest portrayal of young people's alienation from the modern world. There are subtitles for those who can't catch the Cockney dialogue. A-III (nr)

Bronx Tale, A (1993) Growing up in the 1960s, an Italian-American youth (Lillo Brancato) is torn between the decent values his bus-driver father (Robert De Niro) and the easy-money life of the neighborhood crime boss (Chazz Palminteri), who treats him like his own son. Also directed by De Niro, the well-realized drama makes a convincing moral statement in its picture of a youth who comes to recognize the emptiness of dirty money and the deadly violence it spawns. Some violence, racial slurs, sexual references, and much rough language. A-III (R)

Brood, The (1979) Canadian movie in which a mentally disturbed woman (Samantha Eggar) generates such intense hatred that she gives birth to children of rage who go out and murder the objects of her enmity. Directed by David Cronenberg, some good acting is overwhelmed by blood and gore, building to an even more bloody conclusion. O (R)

Broth of a Boy (1959) Whimsical tale set in Ireland, where a London TV producer (Tony Wright) chances upon the world's oldest man (Barry Fitzgerald) and his "wee" middle-aged son (Harry Brogan), then makes plans to broadcast his 110th birthday celebration, but the old reprobate refuses to cooperate. Directed by George Pollack, the Irish production overdoes the quaint village types, though the Abbey Theater cast plays them with comic gusto and Fitzgerald has a lot of fun with the cantankerous oldster's shenanigans. A-I (br)

Brother, Can You Spare a Dime (1975) Slap-dash documentary supposedly dealing with the hard times of the Depression is not so much edited as spliced together. The vulgarity captured belongs not to the 1930s, but to the people who produced it. A-II (PG)

Brother Carl (1972) Study of four tortured individuals (Gunnel Lindbloom, Genevieve Page, Laurent Terzieff, and Keve Hjelm) who for no apparent reason torment themselves and one another. Director Susan Sontag's effort falls flat because, lacking an understandable human context, it is too abstract to evoke an emotional response from viewers. A-IV (nr)

Brother from Another Planet, The (1984) Black extraterrestrial crashes to Earth and finds sanctuary in Harlem from two bounty hunters determined to find and return him to his home planet. Moderately entertaining social satire from writer-director John Sayles has some profanity and a relatively restrained sexual scene. A-III (nr)

Brother John (1971) Returning to Alabama for his sister's funeral, a world traveler and keen observer of humanity (Sidney Poitier) arouses the suspicions of some townspeople when he involves himself in the life of the community. Though there is a certain amount of enjoyment to be had in the movie's vague suggestions about the mysterious title character's otherworldly origins, James Goldstone's heavy-handed direction only emphasizes the emptiness of a story concept that has nowhere to go other than its banal conclusion. Some mature themes. A-III (PG-13)

Brother of Sleep (1996) Confusing tale of a tormented musical prodigy (Andre Eisermann) in a 19th-century Alpine village, where his love for a passionate woman (Dana Vavrova), compulsion for music, and the unwanted amorous attentions of his best friend (Ben Becker) eventually lead to insanity. Directed by Joseph Vilsmaier, the German production lurches from grandiose emotions to grim reflections on opposing views of spirituality. Subtitles. Briefly intense violence including murder and suicide, scene with a nude boy, and a restrained sexual encounter. A-III (R)

Brother of the Wind (1975) Kindly old mountain dweller raises four cuddly, frisky wolf cubs amid the scenic splendor of the Canadian Rockies. Short on plot but long on shots of nature, the movie introduces the quartet to a variety of wildlife and, alas, a snowmobile-riding, shotgun-wielding hunter. Though younger children might be frightened by a few scenes depicting hunting and killing in the wild, the beauty of the scenery and the intimate glimpses of wildlife make it a pleasant experience for all. A-I (G)

Brother Orchid (1940) Seriocomic tale of a gang boss (Edward G. Robinson) returning from a vacation in Europe to find his mob has a new leader (Humphrey Bogart), but he escapes being rubbed-out by hiding in a monastery, where he works as a gardener while plotting his comeback — until he has a change of heart. Director Lloyd Bacon mixes some droll comedy and a bit of spiritual upliftment into a standard crime melodrama, with surprisingly agreeable results. Stylized violence and criminal menace. A-II (br)

Brother Sun, Sister Moon (1973) Director Franco Zeffirelli's version of the oft-told story of Francis of Assisi (Graham Faulkner) treats him as secular saint and social heretic, emphasizing parallels between his age and our own. The strength of the movie lies in its rich visualization of the natural beauties of the Umbrian hills and the Romanesque architecture of medieval Assisi. While the lush and lavish production has nothing to do with the Franciscan spirit of poverty and simplicity, it is a pictorially beautiful movie which succeeds quite well in celebrating nature and the quest for finding more to life than accumulating material goods. A-II (PG)

Brother's Keeper (1992) Compelling documentary about the Ward brothers, four illiterate and elderly dairy farmers in upstate New York, one of whom is put on trial for the 1990 mercy killing of an older brother. Produced and directed by Joe Berlinger and Bruce Sinofsky, the film provides an eloquent portrait of the rural community, which regarded the brothers as eccentric but harmless recluses and came to the defense of the accused brother, whom they believed incapable of murder. Some complex justice questions and a graphic scene of a pig being slaughtered. A-III (nr)

Brotherhood, The (1969) When a Mafia member (Kirk Douglas) kills one of the crime bosses (Luther Adler), he flees to Sicily and the mob sends his younger brother (Alex Cord) to kill him. The core of the movie is the contrast between the older brother's reverence for tradition and the younger one's ambitious pragmatism. Directed by Martin Ritt. Some graphic violence. A-III (M)

Brotherhood of Satan (1971) Coven of devil worshippers (led by Strother Martin) in their quest for eternal youth abduct 13 children while killing their parents in bizarre, bloody fashion that confounds a dim-witted sheriff (L.Q. Jones) as their bodies accumulate in the local ice-house. Director Bernard McEveety ladles out his witchcraft murders with remarkable ineptitude. Visual gore and a conclusion in which evil triumphs over good. A-III (GP)

Brotherly Love (1970) Peter O'Toole gives an outstanding performance as a Scottish lord caught up in a longstanding and unhealthy relationship with his sister (Susannah York), but the story fails to come alive. Directed by J. Lee Thompson, the movie's unexplained motivations, the slow pacing, and unpleasant characterizations contribute to a sense of disinterest in what is happening. A-IV (R)

Brothers (1977) Fictionalized and highly romanticized account of the friendship between imprisoned radical George Jackson (Bernie Casey) and Communist intellectual and philosophy professor Angela Davis (Vonetta McGee). Although the movie directed by Arthur Barron is obviously sympathetic towards its central characters, it offers intelligent and compassionate insights into the agony of prison life. Rough language, violence, and borders on justifying political terrorism. A-III (R)

Brothers McMullen, The (1995) Sturdy but flawed comic drama set in New York City, where three brothers (Jack Mulcahy, Mike McGlone, and Edward Burns) share their muddlements over love, sex, relationships, and commitment from the perspective of their Irish-Catholic upbringing. Also written and directed by Burns, the low-budget picture succeeds best in portraying the close family bond helping the brothers face individual moral quagmires as best they can without benefit of ties to parish or sacraments. Sexual situations occasioning much discussion of morality with sporadic profanity and rough language. A-IV (R)

Brothers Rico, The (1957) Formula crime melodrama about a mob member (Richard Conte) who tries to save his two brothers from being killed by the gang, then turns to the law to bring down his former associates. Directed by Phil Karlson, the story is not very credible but Conte's intense performance holds viewer interest. Much menace and some stylized violence. A-II (br)

Browning Version, The (1951) Affecting drama in which a disillusioned classics teacher (Michael Redgrave), nicknamed "the Himmler of the lower fifth," resigns after 18 years because of ill health and a wife (Jean Kent) who's having an affair with a science teacher (Nigel Patrick), then suddenly gets a new lease on life because of a student's gift of Browning's translation of *Agamemnon*. Directed by Anthony Asquith from Terence Rattigan's play, the story may be sentimentally contrived, but the school setting is keenly realistic and the performances are heart-felt, especially Redgrave's burnt-out academic whose spirit is revived by a student's act of kindness. Implied adultery. A-II (br)

Browning Version, The (1994) British production

of Terence Rattigan's play about a sour, dispirited classics teacher (Albert Finney) who, on the eve of his forced retirement from a posh boys school, finds the gumption to stand up to his unfaithful wife (Greta Sacchi) and a manipulative headmaster (Michael Gambon) because of a thoughtful, end-of-term gift from a student (Ben Silverstone). Directed by Mike Figgis, the failed attempt to update the original's setting from the 1950s to present undercuts the story's credibility, save for Finney's compelling performance as the dried-up pedant who comes to realize too late his failures as educator and husband. Implied adulterous liaisons and some rough language. A-III (R)

Brubaker (1980) Henry Brubaker (Robert Redford) is a prison warden and reformer who goes inside a prison disguised as a convict to find out what is wrong with the system. Director Stuart Rosenberg's fact-based movie is uncompromising and harrowingly realistic with graphic and implied violence, a brief scene of nudity, and much profanity. A-III (R)

Brute and the Beast, The (1969) Formula Italian Western directed by Lucio Fulciin in which a cowboy (Franco Nero) returns to his home town, finds it dominated by a petty land-baron's band of gunfighters, and proceeds to right the wrongs done his family and friends. Some four dozen men, women, and children are killed as the unimaginative story unfolds. Much stylized violence and brutality. A-III (M)

Brute Force (1947) Hard-bitten prison story in which convicts (led by Burt Lancaster and Charles Bickford) battle brutal guards led by a sadistic captain (Hume Cronyn) in a desperate attempt to escape. Director Jules Dassin keys the action to the convicts' pent-up anger over what is convincingly depicted as the inhuman conditions of an overcrowded, poorly run penitentiary, relieved only by occasional flashbacks to the women in the inmates' lives. Considerable hard-edged violence and brutality. A-III (br)

B.S., I Love You (1971) Young advertising hustler (Peter Kastner) stumbles into high position by making it with both mother and daughter. Director Steven Hillard concentrates upon the sexual aspects of the narrative portrayed in a series of supposedly humorous, but terribly tasteless, scenes. O (R)

Buccaneer, The (1938) Lively historical dramatization in which pirate Jean Lafitte (Fredric March) joins forces with Gen. Andrew Jackson in 1815 to save New Orleans from invading British forces, thereby winning a pardon for his brave followers and a hour's head-start for himself. Directed by Cecil B. DeMille, the colorful Louisiana settings and an interesting gallery of period characters easily hold attention between rousing action scenes and romantic complications. Stylized violence. A-I (br)

Buccaneer, The (1958) The pirate band of Jean Lafitte (Yul Brynner) help the American forces led by Andrew Jackson (Charlton Heston) defeat the British at the Battle of New Orleans in 1815. Produced by Cecil B. DeMille and directed by Anthony Quinn, the production is good-looking with colorful characters and action but little sense of credibility. Stylized violence. A-I (br)

Buccaneer's Girl (1950) Tongue-in-cheek romantic adventure directed by Frederick de Cordova in which a New Orleans singer (Yvonne De Carlo) turns against a pirate (Philip Friend) after discovering his secret identity as a respected sea captain engaged to the governor's daughter (Andrea King), then helps rescue him from prison to nab the real culprits. Stylized violence and romantic complications. A-II (br)

Buchanan Rides Alone (1958) Formula Western directed by Budd Boetticher in which a fast-shooting cowboy (Randolph Scott) intervenes to save a Mexican from being hanged in a corrupt border town ruled by a wildly dysfunctional family. Frontier violence. A-I (br)

Buck and the Preacher (1972) Sidney Poitier plays guide and wagon-master for a group of freed slaves moving West after the Civil War, but they face wild Indians and a gang of outlaws. Also directed by Poitier, it is little more than a standard shoot-'em-up, though Harry Belafonte's cunningly exaggerated performance as an opportunist-preacher with a six-shooter in his Bible adds some much-needed humor. A-III (GP)

Buck Benny Rides Again (1940) Dated comedy in which radio comedian Jack Benny tries to impress a singer (Ellen Drew) by pretending to own a Nevada ranch, but his bogus cowboy antics take a serious turn when real badmen (Ward Bond and Morris Ankrum) show up. Directed by Mark Sandrich, the weak proceedings are padded out with musical production numbers and comic routines by Benny's radio cast, including Phil Harris, Dennis Day, and Eddie Robinson as Benny's butler, Rochester, who here sings and dances as well as makes wry comments about his stingy boss. A-I (br)

Buck Privates (1941) The first of many vehicles starring the comedy team of Bud Abbott and Lou Costello has the boys mistakenly enlisting in the Army, where they make a shambles of basic training but wind up leading their unit to victory during field maneuvers. Director Arthur Lubin strings together a series of gags involving several of the team's familiar flimflam routines, little guy Lou's talent for slapstick, and a tame romantic subplot with the Andrew Sisters belting out "The Boogie Woogie Bugle Boy of Company B." It's a dated period piece, but that's part of its pleasure and the gags still draw smiles, especially from youngsters. A-I (br)

Buck Privates Come Home (1947) Uneven comedy directed by Charles Barton has Bud Abbott and Lou Costello smuggling a war orphan back from Europe, then as civilians trying to find jobs and a suitable home for their young charge. Sentimental but unpretentious fun, especially for youngsters. A-I (br)

Buck Rogers in the 25th Century (1979) An American astronaut (Gil Gerard) gets caught in a time warp and flashes forward 500 years, just in time to save Earth from evil invaders sent by a sensuous but immature princess (Pamela Hensley). Director Daniel Haller's gadget-ridden, lighthearted space adventure has a few mild double entendres, but is reasonably diverting pulp for sci-fi fans. A-II (PG)

Buckskin (1968) Formula Western directed by A.C. Lyles about a marshal (Barry Sullivan) who thwarts the plans of a crook (Wendell Corey) to force out the homesteaders and sell their land to the railroad. Restrained gunplay. A-I (br)

Bucktown (1975) Vicious, mindless black exploitation movie, the first half of which offers racism and violence (Fred Williamson and friends wiping out the corrupt white police force of a southern sin city) and the second half dealing solely with violence (black against black). Director Arthur Marks ends it in a bloody, drawn-out fist fight, witnessed by a little boy, who chortles the movie's last line about how happy he is to be a man. Ugh. O (R)

Buddy (1997) Often charming, fact-based story of a wealthy, animal-loving eccentric (Rene Russo), whose 1920's New York menagerie includes a sickly infant male gorilla she tenderly raises as a human child until his massive size and natural jungle instincts become a danger to the household. Director Caroline Thompson captures the almost-human qualities of chimps and gorillas in an unexciting but sweetly old-fashioned story of love and loss. A few scenes of violence by the mature gorilla. A-II (PG)

Buddy Buddy (1981) Ill-conceived attempt by director Billy Wilder and writer I.A.L. Diamond to turn a mediocre French farce about the chance meeting of a ruthless hit-man and a suicidal cuckold into a vehicle for Walter Matthau and Jack Lemmon. The result is achingly unfunny, vulgarly sentimental, and generally tasteless. Profanity and incidental nudity. O (R)

Buddy Holly Story, The (1978) Straight-forward screen biography of one of the pioneers of rock 'n' roll music, from his initial success in 1956 to his death in a plane crash three years later at the age of 22. The script by Robert Gittler is extremely competent, as is Steve Rash's direction. The movie's best feature, however, is the genial singing and acting of Gary Busey in the title role. A-III (PG)

Buddy System, The (1984) Unwed mother (Susan Sarandon) is brought together with a would-be novelist working as a security guard (Richard Dreyfuss) by her nine-year-old son (Wil Wheaton). Although director Glenn Jordan takes a long time to set up a rather obvious situation, the rest is a gentle romantic comedy, with some sensitive and perceptive moments. Vulgar language and a benign view of a premarital relationship. A-III (PG)

Buffalo Bill (1944) Fanciful story of the frontiersman (Joel McCrea) whose exploits were celebrated in dime novels and led to his success touring the world with his own Wild West Show. Directed by William Wellman, the Western action is colorful but hokey, with Maureen O'Hara and Linda Darnell as romantic interests. Frontier violence and Indian stereotypes. A-I (br)

Buffalo Bill and the Indians Or Sitting Bull's History Lesson (1976) Starting with the fact that Chief Sitting Bull once toured with Buffalo Bill's Wild West Show, director Robert Altman proceeds to show Buffalo Bill (Paul Newman) as a mere braggart with no real accomplishments, in contrast to the unfailingly noble and heroic Indian chief. The movie is entertaining enough, with some flashes of brilliance and humor, but strikes few genuine sparks in its repetitious debunking of the Western myth. Coarse language. A-III (PG)

Buffy the Vampire Slayer (1992) Insipid horror comedy about a high-schooler (Kristy Swanson) who's given the mission of ridding Southern California of marauding vampires. Director Fran Rubel Kuzui starts with some amusing satire of the valley girl mentality, but soon relies on cartoonish mayhem to sustain a brainless story line. Frequent stylized violence and a few off-color references. A-III (PG-13)

Buena Vista Social Club (1999) Documentary about a group of aging Cuban musicians who were brought together by American guitarist Ry Cooder for a 1996 pop-music album that became an international hit, with much filming of them in and around Havana, as well as of their concerts in Amsterdam and New York's Carnegie Hall. Directed by Wim Wenders, the result showcases the group's vibrant brand of swing music with a Latin beat while profiling each of the performers, whose ages range from the 70s to the 90s, but whose zestful spirits are as youthful and full of energy as their music. Subtitles. Occasional sexual innuendo and a few coarse words. A-II (G)

Bug (1975) Bradford Dillman, playing a variant of that hoary staple of horror movies, the mad scientist, brings to the role hyperbolic histrionics. Director Jeannot Szwarc's unsubtle special effects are much more likely to provoke nausea than terror, and the degree to which the film steps over the line in its depiction of brutal, degrading incidents should cause parents serious concern. O (PG)

Bug's Life, A (1998) Vividly animated tale of a spunky ant (voice of Dave Foley) who rounds up several performing circus bugs, mistaking them for warriors needed to defend his endangered ant colony against marauding grasshoppers. Directed by John Lasseter and Andrew Stanton, the animation and pacing are outstanding, but young children may find the intensity of the menace quite upsetting. Some scenes of physical abuse and verbal intimidation. A-II (G)

Bugs Bunny's 3rd Movie: 1001 Rabbit Tales (1982) A compilation of vintage theatrical "Merry Melodies" and "Looney Tunes" cartoons bridged by some new material which isn't nearly as good. Stringing together a 90-minute feature of such cartoon shorts may be too much of a good thing for some, especially youngsters. Cartoon violence. A-I (G)

Bugs Bunny/Road Runner (1979) Feature-length compilation of vintage Warner Brothers cartoons created by Chuck Jones has some new material featuring a retired Bugs and the typical Road Runner brand of cartoon violence that some parents may find unsuitable for their very young children. A-I (G)

Bugsy (1991) Bloated soap opera details the volatile relationship between gangster Bugsy Siegel (Warren Beatty) and his Hollywood mistress (Annette Bening) as he recklessly squanders mob money in building a posh casino hotel in Las Vegas during the 1940s. Despite a cast including Ben Kingsley and Joe Mantegna, director Barry Levinson's melodramatic narrative fails to sustain interest in its callous and conscienceless characters. Intermittent violence, an adulterous relationship, and frequent rough language. A-III (R)

Bugsy Malone (1976) Director Alan Parker's unique musical is a crime melodrama spoof done with a cast whose average age is twelve. Unique, however, does not mean good. Jodie Foster gives the only redeeming performance, the music is at best inoffensive, the humor consistently misfires, and some may note a touch of sexual ambivalence in moppets posturing as adults. A-I (G)

Bull Durham (1988) Romantic comedy about a minor-league baseball team features action on and off the field by such quirky folks as a has-been catcher (Kevin Costner), a rookie pitcher (Tim Robbins), and an overage groupie (Susan Sarandon) who tutors rookies in the fine art of baseball and lovemaking. Writer-director Ron Shelton gets the baseball scene right but turns the Sarandon character into a male fantasy figure. Thematic acceptance of promiscuity, several sexually explicit encounters, and much rough language. O (R)

Bulldog Jack (1934) Comic British caper in which a resourceful playboy (Jack Hulbert) assumes the identity of injured detective Bulldog Drummond (Athole Fleming) in order to rescue a kidnapped woman (Fay Wray) from a gang led by a master jewel thief (Ralph Richardson), who tries to escape on a stolen subway train in the wild climax. Directed by Walter Forde, the understated humor grows fairly antic as the unarmed hero uses wooden boomerangs to rout gun-toting robbers in the British Museum, then leads the pursuit through the London Underground after discovering the gang's hideout in an abandoned subway station. Stylized violence and criminal menace. A-II (br)

Bullet for Pretty Boy, A (1970) Bloody account of the life of 1930's gangster Pretty Boy Floyd (Fabian Forte), who commits some daring crimes and is eventually gunned down in a violent shoot-out. Directed by Larry Buchanan, it is of minimal interest. A-III (PG)

Bulletproof (1988) Comic-book thriller in which the hero, cop-secret agent Gary Busey, manages to wipe out an entire band of communist-trained terrorists stationed in Mexico and recapture a high-powered US Army tank without tarnishing his "bulletproof" reputation. Busey makes a likeable macho hero, but director Steve Carver can't do anything with the ridiculous script. Intense, gruesome violence from start to finish and a scene with nudity. O (R)

Bulletproof (1996) Trashy buddy movie about an undercover cop (Damon Wayans) who befriends a drug underling (Adam Sandler), then sets him free after they are pursued by a drug kingpin (James Caan) intent on murdering both of them. Director Ernest Dickerson's brainless action comedy does little but glamorize crime, drugs, and greed. Recurring deadly violence, fleeting nudity, brief video-porn scene, recreational drug abuse, and much profanity, as well as rough language. O (R)

Bullets Over Broadway (1994) Prohibition-era comedy in which a high-minded playwright (John Cusack) accepts backing for his latest work from a gangster (Joe Viterelli) who wants his showgirl mistress (Jennifer Tilly) in the cast, then during rehearsals falls for the play's fading star (Dianne Wiest) and rewrites his script in collaboration with the mistress' hard-boiled bodyguard (Chazz Palminteri). Directed by Woody Allen, the lightweight period proceedings are intermittently amusing, and the exaggerated performances are fun for a while, but the theme's skewering of pretentiousness is heavy-handed and the philosophical asides lack wit and originality. Occasional stylized violence, some sexual situations and references, as well as a few instances of profanity. A-III (R)

Bullies (1986) A city family moves to a rural town in British Columbia, only to be terrorized by a clan of demented toughs. A nasty little Canadian production, directed by suspense-terror specialist Paul Lynch, the movie ends in a crescendo of vengeance and retribution as the family's teenage son kills all the bullies. Profanity, promiscuity, rape, brutality, murder, and other assorted acts of violence. O (R)

Bullitt (1968) When an underworld informer is killed while in the protective custody of a San Francisco police detective (Steve McQueen), he sets up a ruse in order to smoke out those responsible. Under the direction of Peter Yates, the action thriller displays a convincing degree of realism, thanks to close attention to police work details, harrowing car chases through city streets, and McQueen's tight-lipped performance. Some graphic violence and sexual references. A-III (PG)

Bulworth (1998) Dark satire in which a US Senator (Warren Beatty), having taken out a contract on his own life, feels free to talk about how politics is used to keep the rich in power at the expense of all others. Also directed by Beatty, the black comedy aims at being provocative, but is marred by simplistic political ideas and a murky romantic subplot (with Halle Berry). Some crude sexual references, fleeting violence, substance abuse, constant rough language, and occasional profanity. A-IV (R) — (Fox, rental)

Bunny Lake Is Missing (1965) Suspenseful thriller about a child who appears to have been abducted, but who, in fact, may never have existed. Otto Preminger directs Keir Dullea and Carol Lynley as a properly mysterious couple, with Laurence Olivier as a quietly effective London policeman. Mature themes. A-III (br)

Bunny O'Hare (1971) Disguised as hippies, a pair of mature citizens (Bette Davis and Ernest Borgnine) pull off a series of bank robberies under Gerd Oswald's unimaginative direction. Their antics supply the framework for some heavy-handed, pseudo-satiric statements on everything from a migrant worker's savings and police intelligence to psychiatry and youthful protestors. A-III (GP)

Buona Sera, Mrs. Campbell (1969) American Air Force unit has a reunion in the Italian village, where it had been stationed in WW II, and three of the group learn that each has been supporting a local "widow" (Gina Lollobridgida), who has told each one he is the father of her daughter (Janet Margolin). The complications that make up this situation comedy are fairly predictable, but writer-director Melvin Frank comes up with a lively mixture of satire and sight gags making the most of the comic possibilities in an inherently serious plot. Adult humor. A-III (PG)

'burbs, The (1989) Burdened with too much free time and vivid imaginations that seem to have frozen in adolescence, three neighbor pals (Tom Hanks, Bruce Dern, and Rick Ducommun) create havoc when they investigate their mysterious new neighbors. Director Joe Dante's innocuous boys-will-be-boys comedy will make its biggest success on the home video circuit as a Halloween rental. Incidental vulgar references. A-II (PG)

Burglar (1987) Whoopi Goldberg is a cat burglar implicated in a murder which she has to solve in order to stay out of jail. The unflattering vanity production directed by Hugh Wilson offers little chance for Goldberg's talent to sparkle. Instead it is buried under false and demeaning stereotyping of women, brief nudity, and mild profanity. A-III (R)

Burglars, The (1972) French crime caper with Jean-Paul Belmondo stealing a cool million in emeralds and then playing cat-and-mouse games with Omar Sharif as a sadistic cop who uses Dyan Cannon and her striptease club as one way of persuading Belmondo to share the gems with him. Director Henri Verneuil opts for speed over suspense, and the beautiful scenery on the Greek island of Corfu helps him get away with a preposterous script. A-III (PG)

Burmese Harp, The (1956) Badly wounded in Burma at the end of WW II, a Japanese soldier (Shoji Yasui) is nursed back to health by a Buddhist monk, then devotes himself to searching the jungle battlefields for the abandoned remains of dead soldiers to give them a decent burial. Directed by Kon Ichikawa, the Japanese production takes a strong anti-war stance through a series of flashbacks to the horrors of battle, but uses hauntingly poetic imagery to convey the main theme of life's value and the need to atone for its loss. Subtitles. Wartime violence. A-II (br)

Burn! (1970) Complex Italian dramatization of a 19th-century revolution that takes place on a Caribbean island, where the conflict centers on a British agent (Marlon Brando) and the black leader (Evaristo Marquez) he creates and then has to destroy. Directed by Gillo Pontecorvo, there are some uncomfortable modern parallels in the movie's vivid statement that violence only begets more violence. A-III (GP)

Burn Hollywood Burn (see: **An Alan Smithee Film: Burn Hollywood Burn**)

Burning Hills, The (1956) Halting Western in which a young cowboy (Tab Hunter) on the run from a gang of rustlers (led by Skip Homeier) gets some help from a downtrodden senorita (Natalie Wood), a half-breed tracker (Eduard Franz), and a passing band of Comanches. Directed by Stuart Heisler, the story starts well but falters along the way as romance blossoms during lulls in the chase. Frontier violence and sexual innuendo. A-II (br)

Burnt by the Sun (1995) In 1936, a retired Red Army hero (Nikita Mikhalkov) enjoys a summer's day in the country with his young wife and six-year-old daughter, until the unexpected appearance of the wife's former lover (Oleg Menchikov), who eventually reveals the sinister political mission which has brought him there. Also directed by Mikhalkov, the visually exquisite movie portrays a loving familial relationship ripped asunder by Stalin's paranoid purges of potential enemies. Subtitles. Brief but intense violence, a suicide, and a discreet bedroom scene. A-III (R)

Burnt Offerings (1976) Inept horror movie about a family living in a haunted house in which the odds are hopelessly stacked against the best efforts of Oliver Reed, Bette Davis, and Karen Black to survive the proceedings. In trying to inject some interest in this rather nasty business, director Dan Curtis relies heavily on visual shock. A-III (PG)

Bus Is Coming, The (1971) Black Vietnam veteran (Mike Simms) returns home to discover that his brother has been murdered by a racist policeman, gets caught between a black militant group and redneck cops, and eventually becomes the moderate spokesman for his people. Directed by Wendell James Franklin, the movie manages to avoid a simplistic approach to its subject matter. A-II (GP)

Bushbabies, The (see: **The Bushbaby**)

Bushbaby, The (1970) Young girl (Margaret Brooks) leaves the ship taking her back to England in order to return her pet monkey to an East African jungle and winds up trekking through the hinterland with a faithful black (Lou Gosset) to escape the police, who suspect that he has kidnapped her. Though not explicit, the movie's attitude towards the black natives is condescending, making it less suitable as family entertainment. A-I (G)

Bushwhacked (1995) On the run after being framed for murder, a dopey delivery man (Daniel Stern) pretends to be the savvy guide assigned to take six children on an overnight camping trip into the wilds, with an FBI agent (Jon Polito) and the real guide (Brad Sullivan) in hot pursuit. Director Greg Beeman's forgettable comedy is an conventional mishmash of slapstick sketches and hammy acting with resourceful youngsters predictably helping the clumsy tenderfoot prove his innocence. Brief cartoon violence and bathroom humor, scenes of children in jeopardy, a mild sexual reference, and an instance of profanity. A-II (PG-13)

Buster (1988) Disjointed look at a small-time thief (Phil Collins) who hit the big time as a conspirator in England's 1963 Great Train Robbery. Director David Green focuses more on his relationship with his saintly wife (Julie Walters) while on the lam than on the infamous caper itself. Some violence, fleeting beach nudity, some sexually suggestive behavior, and rough language. A-III (R)

Buster and Billie (1974) The story of a high-school romance in a sleepy Georgia town in 1948 in which the boy (Jan-Michael Vincent) gives up his sweetheart (Pamela Sue Martin) when he falls in love with a girl from the wrong side of the tracks (Joan Goodfellow). Director Daniel Petrie's sappy and predictable movie has a feel for the era, the locale, and the people but indulges in an excess of violence and nudity. O (R)

Buster Keaton Story, The (1957) Disappointing dramatization with Donald O'Connor in the title role as the great comedian of the silent screen, who takes to drink when his career is eclipsed by the arrival of talkies. Directed and co-written by Sidney Sheldon, its picture of the early days of Hollywood and the biographical details of Keaton's life have little to do with historical reality, though O'Connor is worth watching as he reprises some classic bits from the films of this master of physical comedy. Restrained treatment of alcoholic excess. A-I (br)

Bustin' Loose (1981) Richard Pryor and Cicely Tyson star in this frumpy comedy about an ex-con forced into taking a group of developmentally disabled youths and their teacher across the country in a decrepit bus. Scripted by Pryor and directed by Oz Scott, the result is outrageously sentimental with a few laughs and some rough language. A-II (R)

Busting (1974) Two honest L.A. vice squad cops (Elliott Gould and Robert Blake) attempt to nail a crime boss (Allen Garfield) but eventually accept the inevitability of defeat under a corrupt system of justice. Director Peter Hyams throws in some comedy but too much violence, nudity, and profanity. O (R)

But Not for Me (1959) Leaden romantic comedy in which an aging Broadway producer (Clark Gable) turns a turkey into a hit with the help of his 22-year-old secretary (Carroll Baker), who thinks she loves him but marries another while he returns to his ex-wife (Lilli Palmer). Directed by Walter Lang, the comic potential of the May-December romance withers from heavy-handed treatment and pedestrian pace, though Gable gives an amusing performance as a man too vain to admit his age. Romantic complications. A-II (br)

Butch and Sundance: The Early Days (1979) Buddy movie directed by Richard Lester features William Katt and Tom Berenger as the not-very-dynamic duo stuck in a lifeless series of comedically failed situations involving their bumbling quest for notoriety. Sparse vulgar language and violence is less objectionable than the film's romantization of the lawless, irresponsible lifestyle. A-III (PG)

Butch Cassidy and the Sundance Kid (1969) Stylish seriocomic Western set at the end of the 19th century when a pair of outlaws, Butch (Paul Newman) and the Kid (Robert Redford), realize that civilization has overtaken their profession and head for the Bolivian frontier. Director George Roy Hill brings off the action scenes with gusto and the proper amount of humor, though beneath the surface of the laughter and the silly mishaps there are enough realistic scenes to show that their criminal exploits have serious consequences. Much stylized violence and a sexually suggestive situation. A-III (PG)

Butcher, The (see: **Le Boucher**)

Butcher Boy, The (1998) Darkly disturbing tale of a 1960's Irish lad (Eamonn Owens) veering into murderous madness following his mother's suicide, the death of his alcoholic father (Stephen Rea), and what he perceives as his only friend's betrayal. Director Neil Jordan captures the youth's psychic pain as well as the inability of family, clergy, or professionals to redirect his volatile rage before tragedy results. Some gory violence, sexual situations, intermittent profanity, and recurring rough language. A-IV (R)

Butcher's Wife, The (1991) Glossy romantic comedy about the clairvoyant bride (Demi Moore) of a Greenwich Village butcher (George Dzunzda) whose advice complicates the romantic relationships in the neighborhood, especially those of the local shrink (Jeff Daniels) and a prim choir teacher (Mary Steenburgen). Directed by Terry Hughes, it's mostly fluffy fantasy that stumbles in a brief subplot that hints a scorned woman might be happier with another woman. Implied lesbian relationship, mild sexual innuendo, and an instance of rough language. A-IV (PG-13)

Buttercup Chain, The (1971) Four crazy, mixed-up kids (Hywel Bennett, Jane Asher, Sven-Bertil Taube, and Leigh Taylor-Young), resort to a thoroughgoing and deliberate demonstration of the various illicit pairings that lead to regret, tragedy, and moral awakening. Director Robert Ellis Miller's clumsy treatment lets the movie run amok in pseudo-serious tangles that only emphasize the sexual misadventures. O (R)

Butterflies Are Free (1972) Good screen version of Leonard Gershe's play about a blind youth (Edward Albert), the cheerfully amoral kook in the apartment next door (Goldie Hawn) who becomes emotionally attached to him, and his over-protective but ultimately very wise and sensible mother (Eileen Heckart). Director Milton Katselas keeps the romantic melodrama moving along quite nicely, the acting is quite good, and the clash between the new morality and the old is treated very gently. A-III (PG)

Butterfly (1982) This is the story of a scheming and manipulative girl who uses seduction as a weapon, in this frivolous and inept screen version of the grim James M. Cain novel about incest ... or supposed incest. With Pia Zadora in the lead role, Stacey Keach and Orson Wells fail to rise above director Matt Cimber's offhanded material. Some nudity and a general air of sleazy amorality. O (R)

Bwana Devil (1952) Adventure clunker set in 1898 Kenya, where a railroad engineer (Robert Stack) must destroy the pair of man-eating lions preying on his construction workers or else abandon the project. Writer-director Arch Oboler turns in a slackly plotted tale, notable only for being the first feature filmed in a 3-D process. Stylized violence and much menace. A-II (br)

By the Blood of Others (1978) A French production about an escaped maniac who holds a woman and her younger daughter hostage while demanding that he be sent the prettiest girl in town. The melodramatic situation turns into a static problem play, as the mayor (Bernard Blier) and other townspeople debate what to do, until action is taken by the mayor's daughter (Mariangela Melato). Some fine acting and interesting observations about people under crisis, but not enough to compensate for the flat and predictable script and a brutal rape scene. A-III (nr)

By the Light of the Silvery Moon (1953) The small-town Indiana family of **On Moonlight Bay** returns in a sequel centering on the misunderstandings between the strong-willed daughter (Doris Day) and her World War I sweetheart (Gordon MacRae), with a comic subplot involving the upright father (Leon Ames) and a French actress. Directed by David Butler, the proceedings are lighthearted, wholesome family fun, with charming musical numbers and warm period nostalgia. A-I (br)

By the Sword (1993) Returning as an instructor in a New York City fencing academy whose owner he had killed 20 years earlier, a regret-filled ex-con (F. Murray Abraham) tries to undo the harm caused by the man's son (Eric Roberts) in teaching the students to use ruthless methods to win at all costs. Though director Jeremy Kagan develops the characters' emotional and competitive antagonisms in strictly routine fashion, the tale ends on a redemptive note in a climactic showdown between the dead man's son and the new instructor. Fleeting bedroom scenes, a violent duel, and occasional rough language. A-III (R)

Bye Bye Birdie (1963) Clumsy, unlikable musical comedy about a vapid teenager (Ann-Margaret) who goes gaga when her Elvis Presley-like idol (Jesse Pearson) comes to town for a last concert before being drafted. Directed by George Sidney, the adults in the cast (Janet Leigh, Dick Van Dyke, Paul Lynde, and Maureen Stapleton) are even birdier than the teen fans, the extravagant production numbers are flat-footed, and the songs unmemorable, save for "Put on a Funny Face." Blatant sexual innuendo. A-III (G)

Bye Bye Blues (1990) With her husband (Michael Ontkean) missing in action during WW II, a young Canadian mother (Rebecca Jenkins) gradually builds a singing career, falls in love with her marriage-minded bandleader (Luke Reilly), and ultimately faces a painful choice when her husband returns. Sensitively written and directed by Anne Wheeler, the movie's simple but evocative images, spare dialogue, and fine acting build understanding for the sacrifices and uncertainties of those who remained on the home-front. A subplot concerning marital infidelity and the question of abortion is treated in a responsible manner. A-II (PG)

Bye Bye Braverman (1968) In a seriocomic drama, four Jewish friends (George Segal, Joseph Wiseman, Jack Warden, and Sorrell Booke) spend an afternoon trying to find the funeral of Braverman, their mutual friend. In concentrating on the mourner's attitudes, hopes, and fears, director Sidney Lumet misses more than he scores in a flawed film that culminates in a graveyard soliloquy seeking to find some kind of meaning in an alien universe. A-III (br)

Bye Bye, Love (1995) Sputtering comic misfire as three divorced dads (Matthew Modine, Randy Quaid, and Paul Reiser) spend a weekend with variously aged offspring, spar with ex-wives, and make fools of themselves with other women. Directed by Sam Weisman, the episodic script jumbles together a series of skits, of which only Quaid's blind date with a looney Janeane Garofalo has some amusing moments, mainly sugarcoating the pain of divorce with artificial sentimentality revolving around their children. Sexual situations, a youngster driving while drinking, occasional profanity, and an instance of rough language. A-III (PG-13)

CB4 (1993) Satiric misfire in which a fictional black rap group (Chris Rock, Allen Payne, and Deezer D) zoom to the top of the charts by patterning their anti-social lyrics and behavior on a local hood who escapes prison promising revenge on his phony imitators. Directed by Tamra Davis, the result never gets much beyond glossy exaggerations of rappers who revel in the obscene, the absurd, and the vile. Some unfunny violence and simulated sex scenes, as well as much rough language. O (R)

C.C. and Company (1970) Ann-Margret acts bored and Joe Namath doesn't act at all in this aimless, trashy motorcycle melodrama directed by Seymour Robbie. Exploitative sex scenes. O (R/PG)

C'est la Vie (1990) Two young French sisters (Julie Bataille and Candice Lefranc) begin a carefree summer at the shore with their cousins, but the vacation is marred as their parents (Nathalie Baye and Richard Berry) inch closer to divorce. Director Diane Kury's ensemble cast and her well-written screenplay sensitively capture the innocent joys of childhood and the confusion and pain that offspring feel when parents separate. In French with English subtitles. References to an adulterous liaison, restrained domestic violence, and a flash of nudity. A-III (nr)

C'mom, Let's Live a Little (1966) Silly college campus musical about a country yokel (Bobby Vee) and the dean's lovely daughter (Jackie De Shannon). Directed by David Butler, nothing much happens, but there is enough innocent romance to appeal to some teenagers. A-II (br)

Cabaret (1972) Bouncy Liza Minnelli stars as an exploited and exploiting American showgirl performing in a decadent Berlin cabaret circa 1930. Showing a nation headed toward moral and political bankruptcy in a spirited musical format results in an entertainment with several levels of meaning given sharp ironic bite by director Bob Fosse. Themes of Nazi brutality, twisted sexual relationships, and a bizarre nightclub setting provide some challenging fare for grown-ups. A-III (PG)

Cable Guy, The (1996) One-note comedy stemming from the unstable character of a manic cable installer (Jim Carrey) who becomes a dangerous pest when he tries to make a friend out of a customer (Matthew Broderick). Directed by Ben Stiller, the thin concept is dragged out in weak skits yielding few laughs until finally ending with the title character going completely over the edge. Unfunny life-threatening predicaments, sexual situations and language, coarse expressions, and occasional profanity. A-III (PG-13)

Cabin Boy (1994) Sophomoric fantasy in which a spoiled rich youth (Chris Elliott) accidentally boards a grungy fishing boat and is forced to serve as cabin boy to four old salts as they navigate past a six-armed seductress, a vengeful giant, and a man-shark. The half-witted humor in director Adam Resnick's comedy clunker is stuck at half-mast in an insipid vehicle for cult comedian Elliott. Implied sexual encounters, some mock comic violence, and occasional profanity and gutter-talk. A-III (PG-13)

Cabin in the Cotton (1932) Dated but still interesting melodrama of Southern sharecroppers battling exploitative landowners until a local youth (Richard Barthelmess), who's in love with a farmer's daughter (Dorothy Jordan) but infatuated with a rich girl (Bette Davis), brings the two sides together. Directed by Michael Curtiz, the story of the young man's emotional turmoil pales beside the realistic depiction of oppressed farm-workers and their unequal struggle for a better life. Scenes of social and economic injustice, some stylized violence, including a lynching, and a restrained sexual situation. A-II (br)

Cabinet of Caligari, The (1962) Belabored psychological claptrap in which a woman (Glynis Johns) suffering from a mental breakdown is treated in an asylum by a doctor (Dan O'Herlihy) she imagines is keeping her captive. Scripted by Robert Bloch and directed by Roger Kay, the embarrassingly inept movie borrows the premise from its illustrious 1919 German predecessor but, despite a game cast, does nothing with it. Much sexual innuendo, most of it silly. A-III (br)

Cactus Flower, The (1969) Screen adaptation of the Broadway version of a French comedy about a prosperous Manhattan dentist (Walter Matthau) caught between a dizzy young girlfriend (Goldie Hawn) and his devoted but staid receptionist (Ingrid Bergman), who ultimately blooms like the prickly cactus on her desk. Director Gene Saks adds proper comic timing to the absurd complications of the light-weight romance, but it is the comic vitality of a talented cast that makes it enjoyable. A-III (PG)

Cactus in the Snow (1972) Movie entirely devoted to the attempts of an Army private (Richard Thomas) to have his first sexual experience with a teenager (Mary Layne) he has met on a weekend pass. Directed by Martin Zweiback, the movie is quite explicit about contraceptive devices and even resorts to having the soldier tutored by a prostitute. With crude sexual references throughout, it is reprehensible to aim this at young audiences. O (R/GP appeal)

Caddie (1981) Australian domestic drama about a young wife (Helen Morse) who walks out on her brutal and adulterous husband and makes a living for herself and her two young children by working as a barmaid in Sydney during the Great Depression. Morse gives a winning performance, and director Donald Crombie's period re-creation is finely detailed, but the story is listless and lacks dramatic force. A-III (nr)

Caddy, The (1953) Thin comedy directed by Norman Taurog in which a golf pro's nervous son

(Jerry Lewis) helps a fisherman's ambitious son (Dean Martin) win a place in a national golf tournament, but when their high-jinks on the course get them thrown out, they land a contract in show business and go on to be headliners. A-I (br)

Caddyshack (1980) Bill Murray and Chevy Chase cavort in this buffoonish slapstick comedy about a caddy's summer adventures at a loony country club. Director Harold Ramis counts on an assortment of obnoxious characters, lewd jokes, and brief nudity to energize a sophomoric plot. O (R)

Caddyshack II (1988) Dim-witted sequel with Jackie Mason causing havoc as a garish construction tycoon who crashes and finally trashes the snooty Bushwood Country Club. Cameos by Chevy Chase, Dan Aykrod, and a pesky golf club gopher highlight this humorless effort directed by Alan Arkush. Some profanity and vulgar humor. A-III (PG)

Cadence (1991) An Army private (Charlie Sheen) confined in the post stockade infuriates his racist jailer (Martin Sheen) by bonding with the black prisoners and rejecting favored treatment. Director Martin Sheen turns out a subtle, understated film about bigotry, mixing humor with drama and fleshing out the characters without resorting to empty stereotypes. Brief violence, some racial epithets, and a fleeting sexual reference. A-II (PG-13)

Cadillac Man (1990) Forced, unpleasant comedy in which a fast-talking car salesman (Robin Williams) tries to pacify a crazed gunman (Tim Robbins) who takes everyone hostage after bursting into the car agency in search of his wife's lover. Director Roger Donaldson gets few smiles out of the salesman's two mistresses, ex-wife, and runaway daughter, and, despite Williams's comic talents, the hostage situation is no laughing matter. A tacked-on happy ending does not compensate for the movie's emphasis on sexual promiscuity, nor its depiction of terrorized hostages and use of rough language. O (R)

Cafe au Lait (1994) Zany French farce set in Paris, where a young West Indian (Julie Mauduech) informs her two lovers — one African (Hubert Kounde), the other Jewish (Mathieu Kassovitz) — she is pregnant, whereupon the two men cease their rivalry to look after the woman they love until the baby is born. Also directed by Kassovitz, the situation is a comic fantasy emphasizing the male responsibilities that come with pregnancy and the common bond of humanity which transcends race. Subtitles. Unwed pregnancy, occasional comic violence, and a character given to rough language. A-III (nr)

Cafe Express (1981) Nino Manfredi plays a Sicilian selling coffee on a train, contrary to the rules of the railroad, with the action taking place in the course of one night's run. Italian comedy directed by Nanni Loy has its moments but is no more than a vignette, and the balance between the comic and the tragic falters. Earthy dialogue and a comic sexual incident. A-III (nr)

Cafe Society (1997) Plodding fact-based story from 1952 New York City, where an undercover cop (Peter Gallagher) goes after a high-class vice ring by befriending a nasty playboy (Frank Whaley) who's heir to a fortune, then nailing him for turning his girlfriend (Lara Flynn Boyle) into a prostitute. Writer-director Raymond De Felitta fails to work up much interest in the period characters and their sleazy activities, then bogs down in the cop's troubles with a headline-seeking DA. Sexual situations, brief nudity, and intermittent profanity, as well as rough language. A-IV (R)

Caged (1950) Harrowing tale of an innocent young woman (Eleanor Parker) wrongly sent to prison, where she suffers many woes, especially at the hands of a corrupt matron (Hope Emerson), then becomes embittered and emerges a hardened criminal a few years later. Directed by John Cromwell, the brutalizing conditions of prison life are convincingly enacted by a good cast, and the result supplies an emotional perspective to the issue of prison reform. Stylized violence and justice questions. A-II (br)

Caged Men Plus One Woman (1972) The various manifestations of homosexuality in prison provide sensational subject matter for Edward J. Forsyth's movie about an incredibly ignorant victim (Ross Stephanson) who just as incredibly wreaks bloody revenge on his tormentors inside, as well as on the girlfriend outside who had betrayed him. O (R)

Cahill, U.S. Marshal (1973) John Wayne stars in a contemporary Western about an overworked peace officer whose two neglected sons are involved in a robbery he is investigating. When Wayne decides to make his pursuit of the criminals into an object lesson for his sons, director Andrew V. McLaglen's movie seems to condone the use of guns in the hands of the young. Worse than the violence is what youngsters may make of the story's muddled morality. A-III (PG)

Cain and Mabel (1936) Flimsy romantic comedy in which a prizefighter (Clark Gable) and a showgirl (Marion Davies) decide to quit their careers and get married, despite efforts by their agents to break up the planned nuptials. Director Lloyd Bacon short-changes the comedy for elaborate production numbers that pad out the contrived plot. Romantic complications and stylized fight scenes. A-I (br)

Caine Mutiny, The (1954) Involving drama from the Herman Wouk novel in which young Navy officers (Fred MacMurray and Robert Francis) take control of their ship from a veteran captain (Humphrey Bogart) seemingly in funk during a typhoon, then are defended in a court martial by an officer (Jose Ferrer) who doesn't relish proving the captain's instability. Director Edward Dmytryk gets a powerful performance from Bogart as the shell-shocked Captain Queeg but does less well with the theme of military discipline and questionable commands. Psychological problems. A-I (br)

Cal (1984) Set against the background of the present conflict in Northern Ireland is the story of a doomed love affair between the widow (Helen Mirren) of a slain policeman and a shy, sensitive young man (John Lynch) who was inadvertently involved in her husband's death. Director Pat O'Connor has fashioned a nuanced morality tale of human beings caught in a divided world but there is some use of nudity and a fairly graphic love scene. A-IV (R)

Calamity Jane (1953) Agreeable Western musical in which the title character (Doris Day) forsakes her rough cowboy ways to learn feminine demeanor from a novice showgirl (Allyn McLerie), then sets her bonnet on an Army officer (Phil Carey) but winds up instead in the arms of her friendly rival, Wild Bill Hickok (Howard Keel). Director David Butler paces the romance with plenty of comic action and a bushel of tunes, notably "Deadwood Stage," "A Woman's Touch," and "Secret Love." A-I (br)

Calamity Jane and Sam Bass (1949) Routine Western in which Hoosier tenderfoot Bass (Howard Duff) comes to Texas, meets a good woman (Dorothy Hart), and plans to buy a ranch, then gets swindled in a horse race and becomes an outlaw with the help of Calamity (Yvonne De Carlo). Directed by George Sherman, the story of a good man who goes bad starts well, then bogs down in formula proceedings. Stylized violence and muddled justice questions. A-II (br)

Calendar Girl (1947) Formula musical directed by Allan Dwan mixes romance with comedy, as the daughter (Jane Frazee) of a New York fireman (Victor McLaglen) is torn between a poor songwriter (William Marshall) and the playboy artist who makes her the Calendar Girl of 1901. Unpretentious fun for those in the mood. A-I (br)

Calendar Girl (1993) Witless comedy about three 18-year-olds (Jason Priestley, Gabriel Olds, Jerry O'Connell) driving to Hollywood in the summer of 1962 hoping to have a date with movie goddess Marilyn Monroe. Director John Whitesell panders to adolescent male fantasies in a boringly inept, woefully unfunny movie. A sexist view of women, some nudity, fleeting bedroom scene, brief violence, and minimal rough language. O (PG-13)

California (1946) Disappointing Western in which an Army deserter (Ray Milland), a willful adventuress (Barbara Stanwyck), and a feisty farmer (Barry Fitzgerald) arrive in Monterey during the 1849 gold rush, then get involved in a scheme to seize the territory led by a lunatic sea captain (George Coulouris). Director John Farrow makes the most of the colorful situations, but the disjointed story flounders in a tangle of personal ambitions that end badly. Stylized violence and muddled motivations. A-II (br)

California Passage (1950) Formula Western directed by Joseph Kane in which an honest gambler (Forrest Tucker) has a showdown with his dishonest partner (Jim Davis), whom he suspects is behind a series of gold robberies and, even worse, has evil designs on a good woman (Adele Mora). Frontier violence. A-I (br)

California Split (1974) Magazine writer (George Segal) befriends a small-time hustler (Elliott Gould) whose wild antics intrigue, but this leads him deeper and deeper into the gambling underworld of dumb call girls, tough losers, impatient bookies, sleazy bars, and hole-in-the-wall games. Director Robert Altman's off-beat comedy ends with Segal's realization that he, unlike Gould, doesn't really care about winning, suggesting that with this knowledge, his obsession to gamble has been exorcised. Questionable attitude toward casual sex. A-IV (R)

California Suite (1978) Screen version of Neil Simon's play integrates the original's four one-acters into a single narrative with a good cast, including Jane Fonda, Alan Alda, Maggie Smith, and Michael Caine. Although not a completely successful adaptation from the stage, director Herbert Ross's movie is good fun for the most part and sometimes unexpectedly moving. Mature themes. A-III (PG)

Caligula (1981) The R-rated version of the X-rated original is no less a dreary exploitation movie awash with sex and violence. Directed by Tinto Brass, it brings not a trace of insight to the historical figures of the Roman Empire or to this period of history. O (R)

Call Me (1988) Basically soft porn all fancied up with an inane plot about hoods on the trail of a woman (Patricia Charbonneau) who inadvertently witnesses a murder and who enjoys trading phone turn-ons with an obscene caller. Director Sollace Mitchell offers an abundance of gory violence, much profanity, and rough language of an explicit sexual nature and a total insensitivity to the offensiveness of real obscene phone calls. O (R)

Call Me Bwana (1963) Generally funny but mindless Bob Hope comedy about a space scientist (Hope) who is easily distracted by the feminine wiles of a foreign agent (Anita Ekberg) from his mission of retrieving a space capsule that has landed in the African jungle. Directed by Gordon Douglas, it consists of typical Hope one-liners and double entendres. A-II (br)

Call Me Mister (1951) Musical romance set in post-war Japan, where an infantry sergeant (Dan Dailey) tries to win back his estranged wife (Betty Grable) by going AWOL to take part in a musical revue she's staging for the troops. Directed by Lloyd Bacon, the thin plot is stitched together with period songs, weak dance numbers, and dated comic skits of service life. Romantic complications and sexual innuendo. A-III (br)

Call Northside 777 (1948) Fact-based story in which a Chicago newspaper reporter (James Stewart) digs into the case of a convicted cop-killer (Richard Conte) and finds evidence of his innocence. Filming on Chicago locations, director Henry Hathaway gets the flavor of the city's ethnic neighborhoods and sustains the credibility of the reporter's dogged leg work in following leads until the convict's ultimate release in a downbeat ending emphasizing his lost years in prison and ruined marriage. Sobering justice theme. A-II (br)

Call of the Forest (1949) Routine outdoor adventure directed by John F. Link in which a young boy (Charlie Hughes) gentles a wild black stallion, then is saved by the horse from the villain (Robert Lowery) who killed his father (Ken Curtis). Enjoyable wildlife scenes, especially those with a bear cub and a family of skunks. A-I (br)

Call of the Wild, The (1935) Romantic melodrama from Jack London's outdoor adventure in the frozen 1900 Yukon, where the search for gold leads a woman (Loretta Young) whose husband has been lost in the snowy wastes to throw in with a rugged adventurer (Clark Gable), whose only assets are a courageous sled dog and a bumbling partner (Jack Oakie), with a formidable foe (Reginald Owen) on their trail. Directed by William Wellman, the result is well-crafted but predictable entertainment, leaving viewers with little that sticks in the mind or touches the heart. Some rough frontier humor, occasional menace, and a few tender moments. A-II (br)

Call of the Yukon (1938) Adventure programmer in which a hunter (Richard Arlen) rescues a writer (Beverly Roberts) from a deserted Eskimo village besieged by ravenous wolves and wild dogs. Directed by B. Reaves Eason, the rugged location photography gives credibility to the couple's dangerous trek through the icy wastes before turning to romance in the melodramatic ending. Romantic complications and menacing situations. A-II (br)

Camelot (1967) Director Josh Logan's screen version of the Broadway musical on the King Arthur legend offers the charming Lerner and Loewe score and lyrics, luxurious fantasy settings, and a grand cast (Richard Harris, Vanessa Redgrave, Franco Nero, and David Hemmings). Emphasizing the human implications of the legend rather than its romanticism, the musical shows that power is not strength and that compassion is not weakness. Never has adultery carried so high a price — the downfall of Camelot. A-II (br)

Cameraman, The (1928) Buster Keaton plays a newsreel cameraman sent to Chinatown, where he finds himself in the middle of a chaotic Tong War. Still hilarious today, the mark of his genius in physical comedy is present in almost every frame of the picture. It was his last silent feature and the last movie in which he was in complete control. A-I (br)

Camila (1985) The daughter of a wealthy family in 19th-century Argentina falls in love with a Jesuit priest in this tragic love story with modern political implications. In this Argentinean production, director Maria Luisa Bemberg deals with difficult historical matters as well as the sacrilegious character of the love affair. Powerful but problematic, with one brief but excessively graphic love scene. A-IV (nr)

Camille Claudel (1989) Bittersweet story of French sculptress (Isabelle Adjani) whose troubled life (1864-1943) as a trailblazer in a male-dominated field ended in a mental asylum after an emotionally devastating May-December affair with her mentor, sculptor Auguste Rodin (Gerard Depardieu). Directed by Bruno Nuytten, it's powerfully acted but confusing as to chronology and characters. Unmarried sexual liaisons and nude models in studio scenes. A-III (R)

Camille 2000 (1969) In updating Dumas' tubercular heroine, director Radley Metzger has changed the flighty and unstable Camille into an amoral jet-setter who fills her days with hip slang, liquor, drugs, and sex. The plot is no more than a flimsy structure for scenes replete with nudity, joyless orgies, and 20th-century guilt-ridden anxieties. O (R)

Camouflage (1981) Meditative essay on the corruptive nature of any bureaucratic system and the destructive games people play in seeming to conform to what is expected of them. The Polish production's success lies in an intelligent script and perceptive direction by Krzysztof Zanussi. Several sexual situations. A-III (nr)

Camp Nowhere (1994) Nitwit comedy in which a bunch of adolescents (led by Jonathan Jackson and Andrew Keegan) hire an unemployed drama teacher (Christopher Lloyd) to impersonate a responsible camp owner in order to dupe their parents into sending them to an abandoned campsite for a summer of unsupervised fun. There's nothing funny about director Jonathan Prince's lame attempt at innocent hijinks, with the youngsters eventually confessing all to parents who appear to be less bright than their inventive offspring. Mild sexual innuendo and a few profanities. A-III (PG)

Can Hieronymus Merkin Ever Forget Mercy Humppe and Find True Happiness? (1969) Writer-director Anthony Newley plays a star entertainer making a movie about his career and using fragmented and surrealistic techniques both for the film and the film-within-the-film. Apparently an attempt to make a statement about the artist's quest for identity, the result is an incoherent failure, floundering in excesses of explicit sexual adventures and moral relativism that leave viewers with little to share other than the character's lack of self-knowledge and the director's lack of ability to control his material. O (X/R)

Can't Buy Me Love (1987) Suburban nerd (Patrick Dempsey) pays a popular cheerleader (Amanda Peterson) to date him for a month in director Steve Rash's comic exploration of teen mores which condemns in-crowd conformism and self-deception but passively conveys a permissive attitude toward adolescent sex. A-III (PG-13)

Can't Hardly Wait (1998) Failed coming-of-age comedy in which various couples at an unsupervised high-school graduation party break up, make up, or attempt to act wild and crazy. Co-directed by Harry Elfont and Deborah Kaplan, the tiresome proceedings feature stereotyped characters lurching uneasily between looniness and loneliness. An implied sexual encounter, some underage drinking, and verbal crudity with minimal profanity and rough language. A-III (PG-13)

Can't Help Singing (1944) Flat musical romance in which a US senator's daughter (Deanna Durbin) runs off to join an Army officer posted to California during the Gold Rush of 1849, then falls in love with a gambler (Robert Paige) she meets along the way. Directed by Frank Ryan with music by Jerome Kern and lyrics by E.Y Harburg, the weak script makes disappointing use of the colorful era, the comic relief (Akim Tamiroff and Leonid Kinsky) fizzles, and the songs are mostly forgettable. Frontier violence and romantic complications. A-II (br)

Can't Stop the Music (1980) This vehicle for The Village People, a disco singing group, is a high-energy, low-IQ, 100-percent synthetic product. Directed by Nancy Walker, the silly comedy about the music publishing and recording business is marked by sexual situations and jokes, as well as a homosexual sheen coloring most of the production numbers. A-III (PG)

Canadian Bacon (1995) Limp political satire in which a US president (Alan Alda) determines to boost his popularity by uniting the country against a foreign enemy, but all his aides (Rip Torn and Kevin Pollak) can come up with is a media campaign charging a Canadian plot to take over North America. Writer-director Michael Moore's comic premise is too thin to support a feature, though his scattershot spoof of political, military, and business leaders yield some smiles and a few laughs. Some profanity and crude language. A-II (PG)

Cancel My Reservations (1972) Bob Hope plays the henpecked half of a husband-wife TV talk-show team who falls victim to a gang of murderous Arizona land-grabbers. Wife Eva Marie Saint races to Hope's rescue and ultimately learns that a woman's place is in the home. Director Paul Bogart strikes out with tired gags and dated topical humor. A-II (G)

Candidate, The (1972) Robert Redford stars in the title role as a California lawyer who finds himself in the middle of a hot race for US senator. Director Michael Ritchie, working with an excellent cast and a literate script, has constructed a fast-paced, cool, and very slick movie about the process of electing a candidate for major office. How power politics and the hard-sell work, as seen from the inside, is all laid bare in this realistic and frequently quite funny political satire. A-III (PG)

Candidate for a Killing (1972) Itinerant sportsman (John Richardson) is used by a businessman (Fernando Rey) in a scheme to extort gold from the Congo and becomes a target for assassins as he races around Europe accompanied by a questionable ally (Anita Ekberg). Director Sidney Pink pads his picture with silly conversations and irrelevant interludes, many of them of a teasing sexual nature. O (R)

Candleshoe (1978) Jodie Foster plays a Los Angeles juvenile delinquent whom confidence man Leo McKern uses to hoodwink wealthy Helen Hayes into thinking is her long-lost granddaughter. Standard Disney fare from director Norman Tokar that tends towards slapstick rather than anything more gentle and satisfying. A-I (G)

Candy (1969) Screen version of the Southern-Hoffenberg novel about the travail of a threatened virgin (Ewa Aulin) is no more than a gross sex farce that reinforces all the behavioral patterns it supposedly satirizes. Christian Marquand directs a big-name cast with a sensitivity only for the vulgar remark, the suggestive sequence, and the explicitly titillating. O (R)

Candy Tangerine Man, The (1975) Black exploitation movie makes a hero out of a vicious black procurer and serves up the sex and violence that is the standard of the genre. O (R)

Candyman (1992) Idiotic horror story relates the problems of a skeptical graduate student (Virginia Madsen) after she conjures up a 19th-century hook-handed ghoul (Tony Todd) who goes on a murderous rampage. Writer-director Bernard Rose's badly scripted tale of brutal mayhem in a gang-ravaged Chicago ghetto slowly drowns in its own gore. Excessive violence, continuing deadly menace to an infant, and occasional nudity. O (R)

Candyman: Farewell to the Flesh (1995) Repellent slasher sequel in which a horribly mutilated black man (Tony Todd), killed for impregnating his white lover in the 1890s, returns to life in present-day New Orleans, wreaking murderous revenge on the family whose ancestors betrayed him and anyone else who gets in his way. Employing strictly one-dimensional characters, director Bill Condon exploits violence and hateful racial animosities in a dreary series of grisly killings. Excessive violence and gore, fleeting shots of simulated sex, and occasional profanities and rough language . O (R)

Cannibal Girls (1973) The title refers to three beauties in a remote Canadian town, whose diner serves beefy portions of male travelers whom they have seduced and slaughtered. Director Ivan Reitman's low-budget movie romps in sex and gore to no entertaining end. O (R)

Cannon for Cordoba (1970) George Peppard, leader of a undisciplined platoon in Pershing's Mexican expedition, is responsible for the loss of cannon and supplies, and subsequently must recapture or destroy them. Directed by Paul Wendkos, the far-fetched adventure is seasoned with torture and violence, in ludicrous fashion. A-III (R/GP)

Cannonball Run, The (1981) Banal and tedious cross-country car race movie with Burt Reynolds and Farrah Fawcett, directed by ex-stunt coordinator Hal Needham. Some vulgarity and sexual innuendo. A-III (PG)

Cannonball Run II (1984) Sequel with Burt Reynolds and friends is a sort of cinematic "People Magazine"-on-wheels. Stuntman Hal Needham's direction of this demolition-derby comedy is geared toward dangerous auto stunts and off-color jokes. A-III (PG)

Canterville Ghost, The (1944) Oscar Wilde fantasy updated to WW II finds American GIs quartered in an English castle inhabited by its seven-year-old heiress (Margaret O'Brien) and a 17th-century ghost (Charles Laughton) doomed by his cowardice to remain there until a kinsman (Robert Young) performs a brave deed on his behalf. The wartime American presence adds little to the sentimental amusement provided by the serious-minded little girl and the rougish antics of her cowardly ancestor. Directed by Jules Dassin. Mild comic menace and spooky fun. A-I (br)

Canyon Passage (1946) Tangled Western in which a rugged individualist (Dana Andrews) pioneers a delivery service in 1856 Oregon, though distracted by a woman (Susan Hayward) engaged to a crooked banker (Brian Donlevy) and an Indian uprising incited by the banker's lustful henchman (Ward Bond). Directed by Jacques Tourneur, the contrived plot gains interest from the wilderness setting and colorful characters, including Hoagy Carmichael as a frontier minstrel. Stylized violence, including an off-screen rape. A-II (br)

Canyon River (1956) On a cattle drive from Oregon to Wyoming, a rancher (George Montgomery) hires ex-outlaws (led by Alan Hale, Jr.) to get the herd past rustlers in cahoots with his best friend (Peter Graves). Standard outdoor shoot-'em-up directed by Harmon Jones. Stylized violence. A-I (br)

Cape Fear (1962) Stomach-churning suspense thriller in which a vengeful ex-convict (Robert Mitchum) sets out to brutalize the wife (Polly Bergen) of the lawyer (Gregory Peck) he blames for his imprisonment. Director J. Lee Thompson's picture of an ordinary decent citizen pitted against a cunning sadistic criminal builds the tension to the breaking point on a boat in a lonely North Carolina bayou. Well-crafted exercise in terror, not for the nervous or faint-of-heart. A-III (br)

Cape Fear (1991) Violent remake of the 1962 thriller has a Bible-spouting psychopath (Robert De Niro), imprisoned for viciously violating a woman, returning to terrorize his former lawyer (Nick Nolte) and to rape the man's wife and teenage daughter (Jessica Lange and Juliette Lewis). Director Martin Scorsese loses the atmospheric terror of the original in favor of graphic brutality and a relentlessly ugly vision of the law as powerless to protect the innocent. Excessive violence, perverse sexual innuendo, adult endorsement of teen drug abuse, and minimal rough language. O (R)

Caper of the Golden Bulls, The (1967) Stephen Boyd and Yvette Mimieux star in a hokey caper movie about a jewel robbery. Directed by Russell Rouse and set in Pamplona, Spain, the only point of interest is the bullring and its environs. Some violence. A-III (br)

Capone (1975) The rise of Al Capone (Ben Gazzara) from Brooklyn street mug to Chicago's top mobster is depicted with excessive resort to violence and sexual displays. Directed by Steve Carver, the movie is a sleazy, slapdash effort. O (R)

Caprice (1967) Spy spoof misfires badly as an undercover agent (Doris Day) for a cosmetics firm tries to steal a water-repellant hairspray from a rival company, then falls for a quirky double agent (Richard Harris) and winds up solving the murder of her Interpol father years before. Directed by Frank Tashlin, the slapdash proceedings don't make much sense and the treatment swings erratically from slapstick to suspense, with tiresome results. Stylized violence, menacing situations, and sexual innuendo. A-III (br)

Capricious Summer (1968) In this Czechoslovakian production set in a small country village between the world wars, three aging friends make fools of themselves over a young woman in a traveling circus and, by summer's end, they realize that their courting days are over. Director Jiri Menzel captures the elegiac mood of period and character with a tolerance of human foibles. Adult situations. A-III (br)

Capricorn One (1978) Three astronauts are persuaded by a NASA official (Hal Holbrook) to fake a landing on Mars to save the threatened space program, but a hot-shot reporter (Elliott Gould) eventually saves the day. Director Peter Hyams has come up with a solid if unspectacular entertainment with some clever twists. A-II (PG)

Captain Apache (1971) Poor Western about an Indian scout for the US Cavalry who becomes the unwilling victim of a plot to fake an uprising that will see the Indians cruelly exiled to uninhabitable territory. Director Alexander Singer's message of brotherhood is as subtle as his battle sequences. Stylized violence and sexual innuendo. A-III (GP)

Captain Blood (1935) Swashbuckling adventure begins in 1685 England as an Irish doctor (Errol Flynn) is unjustly arrested with a band of rebels against King James II, then condemned to slavery in Jamaica under a brutal commander (Lionel Atwill), until the plucky doctor organizes their escape by sea to become pirates. Directed by Michael Curtiz, the lively proceedings include well-staged sea battles, the doctor's romance with the commander's niece (Olivia de Havilland) after rescuing her from a French buccaneer (Basil Rathbone), and justice for the rebels from the new English monarch, William of Orange. Assorted period violence. A-I (br)

Captain Blood, Fugitive (see: **Captain Pirate**)

Captain Carey, U.S.A. (1950) Former OSS officer (Alan Ladd) returns to northern Italy after WW II to search out the traitor who betrayed his underground unit to the Gestapo. Director Mitchell Leisen makes the foreign locales more interesting than the captain's murky, slow-paced quest to avenge his dead comrades. Stylized violence. A-II (br)

Captain Horatio Hornblower (1951) Fanciful sea yarn with C.S. Forester's title character (Gregory Peck) commanding a British man-of-war battling the Spanish allies of Napoleon off the Central American coast, then the French fleet in their home waters, escaping capture to return home a hero, with the Duke of Wellington's sister (Virginia Mayo) as his prize. Director Raoul Walsh packs in a fair amount of colorful action and some humor, but the far-fetched plot is meandering at best. Stylized sea battles and romantic complications. A-I (br)

Captain January (1936) Formula sudser with loveable orphan Shirley Temple cared for by lighthouse keeper Guy Kibbee until the loss of his job forces him to seek out the child's rich relatives. Director David Butler covers the bases with occasional song-and-dance numbers, some playful humor, and a capable supporting cast (Slim Summerville, Buddy Ebsen, and Jane Darwell). Easy-going, unpretentious family fare. A-I (G)

Captain John Smith and Pocahontas (1953) Dull low-budget programmer directed by Lew Landers plods through the story of how Smith (Anthony Dexter) and Jamestown are saved by the daughter (Jody Lawrance) of Algonquian Chief Powhatan (Douglass Dumbrille). Stylized violence and romantic complications. A-II (br)

Captain Kidd (1945) Tepid swashbuckler directed by Rowland V. Lee is set in 1699, when the title pirate (a subdued Charles Laughton except for his unkempt hair) bamboozles William III into sending him to escort a British treasure ship from India, making easy plunder for his henchman (John Carradine, Gilbert Roland and Sheldon Leonard), until confronted by the son (Randolph Scott) of one of their previous victims. Stylized violence. A-I (br)

Captain Kronos: Vampire Hunter (1974) Classy British horror import in which the itinerant Kronos (Horst Janson) is called to rid a village of a vampire who has been putting the bite on local maidens, which he accomplishes with his able hunchback assistant (John Cater). Director Brian Clemens maintains the proper chilling atmosphere for hair-raising encounters with the hooded fiend, who comes to a grisly end. Stylized violence and sexual implications. A-III (R)

Captain Lightfoot (1955) Colorful but artificial blather about the rebel hero of the title (miscast Rock Hudson) whose adventures in 1815 Ireland consist mainly of falling in and out of the hands of British dragoons and local traitors. Directed by Douglas Sirk, the color comes mainly from the costumes and the Irish locations, but the contrived story is hammy and the acting is worse. Stylized violence and menace. A-II (br)

Captain Nemo and the Underwater City (1970) Jules Verne's Nemo (Robert Ryan) rescues a group of landlubbers (Nanette Newman, Bill Fraser, Kenneth Connor, and Chuck Connors) on condition that they not attempt an escape from his self-sufficient city 20,000 leagues under the sea. Directed by James Hill, the special effects, the underwater city, and the dramatic complications are intriguing enough to engross a child's imagination in this generally pleasing, utopian anti-war fantasy. A-I (G)

Captain Newman, M.D. (1963) WW II comedy-drama set in an Army Air Force psychiatric ward, where the title's dedicated officer (Gregory Peck) labors to help deeply troubled patients, notably a suicidal colonel (Eddie Albert), a guilt-ridden survivor (Bobby Darin), and an autistic pilot (Robert Duvall). Directed by David Miller from Leo Rosten's novel, the result is an uneasy blend of serious psychological problems, the doctor's sarcastic wit, and the zany antics of ward attendants Tony Curtis and Larry Storch. Stylized violence, menacing situations, and sexual references. A-II (br)

Captain Pirate (1952) Mediocre swashbuckler about a reformed pirate (Louis Hayward) who once again hoists the Jolly Roger in order to stop a Caribbean buccaneer using his name. Directed by Ralph Murphy, this sequel to **Captain Blood** (1935) meanders aimlessly in search of compelling adventure but only comes up with some colorful action scenes. Stylized violence. A-II (br)

Captain Ron (1992) Inept comedy about a Chicago family (headed by Martin Short and Mary Kay Place) who take a Caribbean dream cruise on an inherited sailboat, whose disreputable captain (Kurt Russell) involves them with guerrillas and pirates. Director Thom Eberhardt's waterlogged plot soon sinks under the weight of its contrived situations and leaden script. Brief shadowy nudity, some sexual innuendo, stylized violence, and an instance of rough language. A-III (PG-13)

Captain Scarlett (1953) Humdrum swashbuckler directed by Thomas H. Carr in which the French hero of the title (Richard Greene) rights the wrongs done by villainous royalists back in power after Napoleon's defeat. Routine swordplay and romantic complications. A-II (br)

Captain Sinbad (1963) Silly Arabian Nights fantasy pits the title hero (Guy Williams) against a dastardly magician-ruler (Pedro Armendariz) who's abducted a lovely princess (Heidi Bruhl). Directed by Byron Haskin, the European co-production limps along with a weak story line but some passable special effects. A few hideous creatures and grizzly fight scenes may scare the very young. A-I (br)

Captains Courageous (1937) Spencer Tracy won an Oscar for his performance as Manuel, the simple Portuguese fisherman in Rudyard Kipling's story of a spoiled rich boy (Freddie Bartholomew) rescued at sea and turned into a good shipmate by the kind-hearted veteran sailor. Director Victor Fleming provides a gruff but appealing picture of life aboard the fishing boat, backed by some memorable sea scenes and the unsentimental transformation of the youth's character under Manuel's manly yet compassionate influence. Youngsters may get teary-eyed at Manuel's death, but all is emotionally resolved in the lad's homecoming. A-I (br)

Captains of the Clouds (1942) Happy-go-lucky but bored Yank aviator (James Cagney) joins the Royal Canadian Air Force before US entry in WW II, rebels against military discipline, then comes through in heroic action against the Luftwaffe. Director Michael Curtiz's patriotic melodrama has plenty of human interest with a good cast (Alan Hale, Dennis Morgan, George Tobias, as well as RCAF veterans). Stylized violence and a marriage in name only. A-II (br)

Captive Girl (1950) Adventure programmer directed by William Berke in which Jungle Jim (Johnny Weissmuller) saves a wild jungle woman (Anita Lhoest) from capture by the witch doctor (John Dehner) who had murdered her anthropologist parents years before and now seeks to dispose of Jim with help from a greedy treasure hunter (Buster Crabbe), until a thundering swarm of gibbons comes to the rescue. Stylized violence. A-I (br)

Captive Heart, The (1946) WW II drama about life in a German POW camp for a group of British officers, one of whom proves to be a Czech (Michael Redgrave) who escaped from a concentration camp and took the papers of a dead British officer just before the fall of France in 1940. Directed by Basil Dearden, the British production is warmly human in its depiction of the camp inmates coping with four years of imprisonment and the plight of the dead officer's family when the Czech imposter turns up in place of their expected son. A-I (br)

Captives (1996) Angry and confused over her divorce from an unfaithful husband, a woman (Julia Ormond) begins working as a dentist in a London prison, then falls into a passionate affair with a lonely inmate (Tim Roth) who can't protect her when she's blackmailed by a fellow prisoner. Director Angela Pope sets up the situation credibly enough, but has trouble sustaining the risky romance which follows, then turns the ending into a conventional thriller. Some nasty violence, a fairly graphic sex scene, and occasional rough language. A-IV (R)

Capture, The (1950) Muddled melodrama directed by John Sturges in which an American (Lew Ayres) working for a Mexican oil company kills a suspect in a payroll robbery, then marries his widow (Teresa Wright), becomes convinced he shot an innocent man, and sets out to find the real culprit. Stylized violence and sexual situations. A-III (br)

Car, The (1977) In a new and not-at-all entertaining twist to the possession theme, an evil spirit takes over a huge car and terrorizes a Southwestern town. Directed by Elliot Silverstein, everything about the movie is embarrassingly bad, save for the special effects of Albert Whitlock. Some violence and a lot of stupidity. A-III (PG)

Car 54, Where Are You? (1994) Trigger-happy movie version of the 1960s TV series teams a rookie Brooklyn patrolman (John McGinley) with a bumbling veteran (David Johansen) on the tail of a mob don (Daniel Baldwin) who is trying to rub out a government witness (Jeremy Piven). Director Bill Fishman has trouble stringing together assorted witless sketches which fail to capture the amiable kookiness of the original sitcom. Recurring violence played for laughs, some sexual innuendo, and occasional toilet humor. A-III (PG-13)

Car Wash (1976) Director Michael Schultz's touching, sometimes extremely funny movie follows the course of a day at an inner city car wash, where the employees keep a jive rhythm to their work and to their joking. Richard Pryor, Ivan Dixon, the Pointer Sisters, and George Carlin supply the wit and energy in this comic tale of streetwise survival. Some rough language, sexual innuendo, and casual acceptance of drug use. A-III (PG)

Caravans (1978) A young State Department official (Michael Sarrazin) in 1948 Iran is ordered to locate a missing American (Jennifer O'Neill) reportedly in the mountainous domain of a nomad chief (Anthony Quinn). Directed by James Faro, the effort is a silly misfire, with a rambling and unfocused plot line, atrocious dialogue, and lead-footed pacing. A bloody execution as well as a sequence involving a homosexual dancer make it mature fare. A-III (PG)

Carbine Williams (1952) Gritty fact-based story of a North Carolina moonshiner (James Stewart) who gets 30 years for his part in the death of a revenue agent, then is pardoned after the prison warden (Wendall Corey) allows him to perfect a lightweight rifle, which the Army adopts for use in WW II as the M1 carbine. Directed by Richard Thorpe, the story is awkwardly told in flashbacks, much of them devoted to his mistreatment on a chain gang and at the prison farm, with the rest providing a sentimental before-and-after picture of his relations with his large farm family, as well as supportive wife (Jean Hagen) and puzzled son. Stylized violence, justice questions, and contemplation of divorce. A-II (br)

Carbon Copy (1981) Successful businessman (George Segal) marries the boss's shrewish daughter (Susan St. James) but finds his snug, affluent nest disrupted when a black youth (Denzel Washington) shows up one day claiming to be his illegitimate son. Director Michael Schultz's crude and heavy-handed comedy attempts to get laughs by some cheap shots at religion, not excluding a dose of male chauvinism. Strong language and two rather distasteful bedroom scenes. A-III (PG)

Cardinal, The (1963) Sprawling melodrama from Henry Morton Robinson's novel about the ecclesiastical rise of an Irish-American priest (Tom Tryon) from 1917 Boston to a 1924 post in the Vatican, then he becomes a bishop after tangling with the KKK in 1934 Georgia and is made a cardinal after tangling with the Nazis in 1938 Austria. Directed by Otto Preminger, the movie makes good use of the religious backgrounds and clerical roles (dying pastor Burgess Meredith, Boston Cardinal John Huston, and Vatican prelate Raf Vallone), but the central figure is pure cardboard and his moral crises unconvincing. Stylized violence, racial epithets, and such moral issues as saving the life of the infant rather than the mother in a troubled childbirth and the temptation to leave the priesthood for the love of a woman. A-III (br)

Care Bears Adventures in Wonderland, The (1987) Vastly superior sequel to the 1985 original, the Canadian animated feature is a lively, colorful, complexly designed and orchestrated travelogue through Wonderland with the Bears and a little girl named Alice who must save the kingdom from a power-hungry wizard. Director Raymond Jafelice holds even adult interest with his fast cuts and engaging fantasy characters. A-I (G)

Care Bears Movie, The (1985) The Care Bears are sweet little pastel-colored creatures who inhabit a saccharine world called Care-a-Lot. Unless they teach the earth to care, Care-a-Lot will fall into ruin. Only very young children will care very much about this sentimental, mediocre effort. A-I (G)

Career Girls (1997) British drama of a woman (Lynda Steadman) renewing her friendship with a former college roommate (Katrin Cartlidge) on a weekend visit which recalls their frenetic, uncertain lives as undergraduates and how much each has changed in the six years since then. Written and directed by Mike Leigh, the impressionistic narrative is loosely assembled from scenes of past and present, relying mainly on improvisational performances, but the result is too disjointed to add up to more than a tentative understanding of how much progress the two have made in their lives since college. Sexual encounter with brief nudity, sexual situations, recurring rough language, and occasional profanity. A-IV (R)

Career Opportunities (1991) A novice janitor (Frank Whaley) and a lonely shoplifter (Jennifer Connelly), locked overnight in a department store, become friends while warding off a pair of dim-witted thieves. Writer John Hughes and director Bryan Gordon bomb out with a terminally dumb comedy of humorless stick figures and glaringly bad plotting. Mock comic violence and very suggestive double entendres. A-III (PG-13)

Carefree (1938) Wacky musical comedy about a psychiatrist (Fred Astaire) whose best friend (Ralph Bellamy) asks him to treat his marriage-shy girlfriend (Ginger Rogers), but matters get complicated when the patient falls for the doctor. Directed by Mark Sandrich, the thin plot takes some very giddy turns, with the added bonus of appealing Irving Berlin tunes, including "I Used to Be Color Blind" danced in slow motion by Rogers and Astaire, as well as Astaire's stand-out syncopated solo on the golf links. Silly romantic complications. A-I (nr)

Careful He Might Hear You (1984) Sensitive, extremely well-acted Australian movie about a 1930's custody fight between two sisters over the six-year-old son of a third sister who died in childbirth. Director Carl Schultz has done well with showing the effect of all this upon the boy, partly in a less-than-wholesome attraction of a woman for a young child. A-III (PG)

Carey Treatment, The (1972) Hip California doctor (James Coburn) comes to a conservative Boston hospital, where he uncovers the murder of the chief of staff's daughter and the disappearance of large amounts of hospital drugs. Director Blake Edward employs a good deal of rather self-conscious vulgarity and profanity but worse is its casual attitude toward abortion and marital commitments. O (PG)

Caribbean (1952) Convoluted swashbuckler in which an 18th-century English pirate (Cedric Hardwicke) sends an agent (John Payne) to lead a slave uprising on the island plantation of his foe (Francis L. Sullivan), whose daughter (Arlene Dahl) is the cause of their enmity. Directed by Edward Ludwig, the implausible narrative has a hardworking cast and exotic settings, but the muddled plot falters with cardboard characters, aimless action, and throwaway ending. Stylized violence. A-II (br)

Cariboo Trail, The (1950) Routine Western directed by Edwin L. Marin with Montana cowboys (Randolph Scott and Bill Williams) taking a herd of cattle into the gold fields of British Columbia, where they tangle with the crooked local boss (Victor Jory), make a gold strike with the aid of an old prospector (George "Gabby" Hayes), and stake out some rich grazing land belonging to hostile Indians. Frontier violence. A-I (br)

Carlito's Way (1993) Planning to leave crime and New York City gangsters behind for a new life in the Bahamas with his girlfriend (Penelope Ann Miller), a newly released convict (Al Pacino) pays a high price for his friendship with the corrupt lawyer (Sean Penn) who got him out of jail on a technicality. Director Brian De Palma overstuffs his bleak crime drama with a profusion of morally bankrupt characters who glibly rationalize their murderous acts. Much violence, incessant rough language, some drug abuse, ethnic slurs, topless dancers, and brief sexual encounters. O (R)

Carmen (1983) During the rehearsals for a dance version of Bizet's opera about the gypsy temptress whose infidelities end in murder, the choreographer (Antonio Gades) falls in love with the young woman (Laura del Sol) in the title role, and their affair offstage follows the same scenario as that enacted onstage. Carlos Saura directs the Spanish production, which is filled with stunning flamenco dance numbers. Its story of life imitating art is intriguing at first but gradually bogs down in operatic melodrama. Subtitles. Mature theme and treatment. A-III (nr)

Carmen Jones (1954) Bizet's tragic opera is updated to WW II, when a soldier (Harry Belafonte) falls for a pretty worker (Dorothy Dandridge) in a southern parachute factory, then goes AWOL to follow her to Chicago, where he strangles her after she dumps him for a prizefighter. Directed by Otto Preminger, the strong period Americana and fine African-American cast can't overcome the disappointment of the movie's flatly dubbed singing and stiffly staged musical numbers. Sexual situations and innuendo. A-III (br)

Carmen Miranda: Bananas Is My Business (1995) Brought to Hollywood in 1940, the popular Brazilian samba singer was quickly typecast as a comic figure who wore bizarre hats and spoke mangled English in a career increasingly ridiculed by her countrymen and American moviegoers. Directed and narrated by Helena Solberg, the documentary presents a sobering account of the unhappy personal life and tragically early death of a performer whose vivacious talents were misused by Hollywood, resulting in a career sadly lost between two cultures. Discreet treatment of sexual affairs. A-III (nr)

Carnal Knowledge (1971) Producer-director Mike Nichols and screenwriter Jules Feiffer collaborate on a movie with three episodes spanning two decades (late 1940s to late 1960s) in the lives of two men (Jack Nicholson and Art Garfunkel), tracing their non-maturation from sex-starved college students to sex-saturated, middle-aged men in professional life. It is a feeble morality play which preaches once again, with pathetic exploitation, that the wages of sin is impotence. Brief nudity and rough language. A-IV (R)

Carnival of Souls (1962) Low budget but effective horror tale directed by Herk Harvey follows the eerie experiences of a church organist (Candace Hilligoss) after she emerges from a car crash in a Kansas river, until her reunion weeks later with others who died in the same accident. Sinister, unsettling atmosphere and sexual situations. A-III (br)

Carnival Story (1954) Shabby melodrama directed by Kurt Neumann in which an impoverished German woman (Anne Baxter) finds work with a touring American carnival, then is torn between an amorous but brutal barker (Steve Cochran) and the caring high diver (Lyle Bettger) whom she marries with disastrous results. An off-screen murder and tawdry sexual situations. A-III (br)

Carny (1980) Set against the background of a traveling carnival is a triangle theme involving a teenage runaway (Jody Foster), a clown (Gary Busey), and his best friend (Robbie Robertson). The theme, however, is undeveloped, because director Robert Kaylor is more interested in documenting carnival life, especially its seamy side, with generous amounts of violence, sex, and rough language. O (R)

Caroline and the Rebels (1955) Vapid French melodrama directed by Jean Devaivre follows the romantic misadventures of a Spanish noble (Jean-Claude Pascal) who goes off to fight the French during the Napoleonic Wars, then finds proof he was an adopted child and is free to marry his loving sister (Brigitte Bardot). Dubbed. Stylized violence and sexual situations. A-III (br)

Carousel (1956) Rodgers and Hammerstein musical from Ferenc Molnar's tragic romance in which a macho carnival worker (Gordon MacRae) dies in a robbery trying to provide for his pregnant wife (Shirley Jones), then gets a chance to come back in spirit to set things right for his still-grieving widow and teen daughter. Directed by Henry King, the dramatic portions seem stilted and out of place in the lovely 19th-century New England setting, though the production numbers are eye-filling and the songs memorable, notably "If I Loved You" and "You'll Never Walk Alone." Romantic complications. A-II (br)

Carpetbaggers, The (1964) Trashy melodrama from Harold Robbins's novel in which a troubled youth (George Peppard) after WW I parlays his inherited wealth into a mighty business empire, pioneers an airline corporation, and dabbles in the movie industry. Directed by Edward Dmytryk, the glossy production is a saga in nastiness as the egotistical tycoon enjoys mistreating his stepmother (Carroll Baker), his wife (Elizabeth Ashley), and his mentor (Alan Ladd), among others, though redemption awaits in the final reel. Psychological as well as physical violence, sexual situations, and alcoholic excess. A-III (br)

Carpool (1996) Taking hostage a workaholic dad (David Paymer) and five school-kids in a minivan, a bumbling but goodhearted robber (Tom Arnold) gradually turns them into accomplices as they elude pursuing police cars. Director Arthur Hiller's witless chase movie frequently stalls out, thanks to its tired, lowest-common-denominator brand of humor. Indulgent treatment of kidnapping and theft, comically intended violence, and brief toilet humor. A-III (PG)

Carrie (1952) Elaborate sudser from the Theodore Dreiser novel about a country girl (Jennifer Jones) who gets a job in turn-of-the-century Chicago, is seduced by a salesman (Eddie Albert), then runs off with a married man (Laurence Olivier) to New York, where she leaves him flat while finding fame on the stage. Director William Wyler's studied period piece arouses little interest in the characters and their woes, though Olivier's descent into penury gains some sympathy. Mature theme and treatment. A-III (br)

Carrie (1976) A repressed high-school student (Sissy Spacek) discovers that she has telekinetic powers, which she uses at the senior prom to wreak a bloody revenge on taunting classmates and her religious fanatic mother. Director Brian De Palma's horror movie is too ludicrous and overdrawn to scare, but succeeds in the shock value of its callous, unhealthy mix of nudity and violence. O (R)

Carried Away (1996) Pretentious tale of a middle-aged country schoolteacher (Dennis Hopper) who throws himself into a passionate affair with a 17-year-old student (Amy Locane) to the consternation of his friends and the widow (Amy Irving) who wants to marry him. Director Bruno Barreto captures the gritty reality of the rural Texas setting and characters but turns the story into romanticized claptrap, portraying the teacher's affair with a dangerously mixed-up teenager as a minor indiscretion which supposedly reawakens his passion for the widow. Graphic sex scenes, frontal nudity, and occasional profanity and rough language. O (R)

Carrington (1995) Fact-based story of the live-in relationship between homosexual author Lytton Strachey (Jonathan Pryce) and painter Dora Carrington (Emma Thompson), who remain devoted to one another while carrying on a series of affairs with other men. Writer-director Christopher Hampton establishes the pair's deep mutual affection while indulging their sexual appetites with others, but leaves their part in the British cultural scene between the world wars a disappointing blank. Uncritical treatment of sexual promiscuity, brief bedroom scenes with fleeting nudity, an off-screen suicide, and a few instances of rough language. A-IV (R)

Carry It On (1970) Documentary on an anti-Vietnam draft resister, David Harris, sentenced to a three-year term in federal prison, focuses on his last meeting with his wife, folk singer Joan Baez, and then on her activities with the anti-war movement. Robert Jones, Christopher Knight, and James Coyne have assembled a very moving and effective statement against war. A-III (GP)

Carry On Camping (1972) Rude British send-up of summer campers employs such familiar funsters as Sidney James, Kenneth Williams, and Joan Sims. Director Gerald Thomas has assembled a grab-bag of comic skits but too often strains for double entendres and vulgar sexual shenanigans to carry the day. O (R)

Carry On Cleo (1965) Thin British farce directed by Gerald Thomas follows enslaved English rustics in ancient Rome, where their bumbling antics help save Caesar (Kenneth Connor) from a plot concocted by Marc Antony (Sidney James) and Cleopatra (Amanda Barrie). Slapstick violence and bawdy humor. A-III (br)

Carry On Cruising (1962) Slack British farce from director Gerald Thomas follows a two-week Mediterranean cruise aboard a ship whose dour captain (Sidney James) bullies inept crew replacements (notably Kenneth Williams and Kenneth Connor) on the prowl for romantic passengers (Liz Fraser and Dilys Laye). Broad sexual innuendo and slapstick vulgarity. A-III (br)

Carry On Doctor (1972) Director Gerald Thomas commits his comic cronies (Sidney James, Frankie Howerd, Kenneth Williams, Hattie Jacques, Barbara Windsor, and Jim Dale) to a hospital, but the operation results in the same old monkey business. There is a generous share of double entendres, but the ribaldry is fairly tame. A-III (PG)

Carry On Henry VIII (1972) The latest offering in this series from director Gerald Thomas concerns two previously undiscovered wives of King Henry and their topsy-turvy effect on the beleaguered monarch and his court. Coarse language and blatant double entendres. O (GP)

Carry On Jack (1964) Thin British farce directed by Gerald Thomas in which a barmaid (Juliet Mills) gets aboard a Navy frigate in the uniform of a midshipman (Bernard Cribbins), then the two become heroes in the Napoleonic Wars by saving the ship from mutiny, pirates, and Spanish galleons. Slapstick swashbuckler with broad sexual innuendo. A-III (br)

Carry On Nurse (1959) Feeble British farce in which director Gerald Thomas finds few laughs, as hospital patients (Kenneth Connor, Charles Hawtrey, Wilfrid Hyde-White and others) suffer various indignities while engaging in hijinks at the expense of haughty administrators (led by Hattie Jacques), befuddled attendants (notably Shirley Eaton), and each other. Sexual innuendo and vulgar situations. A-III (br)

Carson City (1952) Routine Western directed by Andre de Toth in which a determined engineer (Randolph Scott) builds a railroad line by tunneling through the mountainous terrain between Carson City and Virginia City, despite a gang of outlaws (led by Raymond Massey) out to stop it. Frontier violence. A-I (br)

Carson City Kid (1940) Routine Roy Rogers Western in which he gets help from sheriff Gabby Hayes and gold miner Noah Berry, Jr., in tracking down the gambler who killed his brother. Mild chases, brawls and gunplay. A-I (br)

Cartouche (1957) Stilted adventure in 18th-century France, as a hunted nobleman (Richard Basehart) tries to find the culprit who committed the murder for which he has been blamed, getting help along the way from an actress (Patricia Roc) with a traveling troupe of players. Directed by Steve Sekely, the period story is flat, and the action has less flair than the picture's colorful costumes and ornate settings. Stylized violence and muted sexual innuendo. A-II (br)

Casa Assassinada, A (1974) Brazilian story of an eccentric family of shabby aristocrats living on a crumbling, neglected plantation, into which comes a woman who throws the entire household into turmoil and finally violence. Director Paulo Cesar Saraceni's study of creeping moral and mental deterioration is heavily melodramatic but visually powerful in its images of the simultaneous fecundity and decay of the jungle surroundings. Explicit sex scene in a story which otherwise unfolds through indirection. A-IV (nr)

Casablanca (1942) Classic romantic melodrama set in the refugee crossroads of French North Africa, where an American expatriate (Humphrey Bogart) helps the woman who broke his heart (Ingrid Bergman) and her husband (Paul Henreid), an underground leader, escape the Nazi dragnet. Directed by Michael Curtiz, the story is replete with WW II intrigue, sardonic humor, punchy dialogue ("Here's looking at you, kid!"), and a great cast, including Claude Rains as a suave Vichy police officer and Dooley Wilson's rendition of "As Time Goes By." Time stands still for this one, though the wartime atmosphere may be too menacing for the children. A-II (br)

Casanova Brown (1944) Disappointing romantic comedy about a college professor (Gary Cooper) whose marriage is over almost before it starts, then learns months later that his ex-wife (Teresa Wright) has become a mother. Except for a hilarious house-burning sequence, director Sam Wood treats the situation with such deadly coyness that all involved appear to be congenital idiots. Sophomoric treatment of marriage and parenthood. A-II (br)

Casanova's Big Night (1954) Mistaken for the notorious lover Casanova (Vincent Price), a tailor's apprentice (Bob Hope) escapes imprisonment by the doge of Venice (Arnold Moss) to save a woman (Audrey Dalton) from dishonor and win the heart of his true love (Joan Fontaine). Director Norman Z. McLeod's listless comedy wastes a good cast in a leaden 18th-century period piece from which Hope wrings only a few smiles. Mild sexist humor. A-II (br)

Case of the Naves Brothers, The (1972) Brazilian director Luiz Sergio Person tells the fact-based story of two peasant brothers sentenced in 1938 for an apparent murder, but even when the supposed victim resurfaced several years later, it was not until 1963 that the brothers were released on parole. The story of a miscarriage of justice contains all too graphic depictions of torture. A-III (nr)

Casey's Shadow (1978) An irascible but basically good-hearted Cajun horse trainer (Walter Matthau) has to make an agonizing decision whether or not to run a horse with an injured leg in a race that could mean fame and fortune for him and his three sons. Director Martin Ritt captures the colorful world of quarter-horse racing in the Southwest, but the movie's benign attitude toward the trainer's moral failings and the frequent use of profanity make it mature fare. A-III (PG)

Cash McCall (1959) Low-powered romantic drama in which a shrewd corporate raider (James Garner) buys a stagnant company in order to woo the daughter (Natalie Wood) of its owner (Dean Jagger), but things get complicated when the deal produces millions in unexpected profits. In tracking the devious turns of the business world, director Joseph Pevney generates little interest in the characters and even less in their personal problems. Romantic situations and sexual innuendo. A-III (br)

Casino (1995) Increasingly violent story of the rise and fall of a mob-backed Las Vegas casino manager (Robert De Niro), married to a money-obsessed drug addict (Sharon Stone) who seduces her husband's best friend (Joe Pesci), a murderous gangster she hopes will kill the husband she despises. Director Martin Scorsese spins a well-acted, compelling yarn ultimately ruined by an excess of sadistic violence. Much graphic violence, adulterous affairs, fleeting nudity, substance abuse, and incessant rough language. O (R)

Casper (1995) A lonely 13-year-old (Christina Ricci) is befriended by the cuddly ghost of the title when her widowed therapist dad (Bill Pullman) is hired to coax some menacing spirits out of a mansion rumored to be hiding buried treasure. Director Brad Silberling pumps up the cuteness factor, but there is not much of a story or little else to engage audiences beyond a few novel special effects. Some comic violence, a couple of profanities, and a crude expression. A-II (PG)

Casper, A Sprited Beginning (1997) Made-for-video sequel to the 1995 feature shows how Casper became a friendly ghost after missing out on ghost training and winding up in a small town, where he's befriended by a lonely 10-year-old (Brendon Ryan Barrett) who introduces him to a trio of ghosts haunting a mansion scheduled for demolition by the boy's father (Steve Guttenberg). Directed by Sean McNamara, the formula story develops at a pedestrian pace with the live-action proceedings of less interest than the animated ghosts and their special-effects antics. Slapstick violence, some bathroom humor, and occasional coarse language. A-II (PG)

Cassandra Crossing, The (1977) George Pan Cosmatos directs a disaster epic about a train-load of international stars (including Sophia Loren, Burt Lancaster, Richard Harris, and Ava Gardner), a crowd of extras, and a lovable Basset hound, who are exposed to a lethal germ, must cross a decaying bridge, and are victims of a witless, only fitfully exciting story line. Extremely violent conclusion and some rough language. A-III (R)

Cast a Giant Shadow (1966) Standard Hollywood biography with Kirk Douglas playing David (Mickey) Marcus, New York lawyer and WW II hero, who helped whip the young Israeli army into shape. Written and directed by Melville Shavelson, the dramatization is at times painfully stilted but for the most part human and likeable. Extramarital attachment and wartime violence. A-III (br)

Castaway Cowboy, The (1974) James Garner plays a shanghaied Texas cowboy who jumps ship in Hawaii and is persuaded by potato-farm widow Vera Miles to stay around long enough to teach her lazy, fun-loving islanders how to round up the wild cattle which are trampling and eating her farm out of business. Disney director Vincent McEveety makes the most of the sunny story, the location scenery, and a good cast, but adults may find it less than riveting. A-I (G)

Castilian, The (1963) Poorly dubbed Spanish production re-creates the rivalry between the royal houses of Castile and Navarre until they join to stop the Moors from conquering all of Spain. Director Javier Seto does best in staging the clash of medieval armies on the Spanish plains but gets nowhere with the personal problems of the characters (notably Cesar Romero, Broderick Crawford, Fernando Rey, and Alida Valli), despite occasional commentary by an earnest troubadour (Frankie Avalon). Much stylized violence and several sexual references. A-II (br)

Castle, The (1969) German adaptation of Franz Kafka's unfinished novel about a land surveyor (Maximilian Schell) trying to report for a job assignment but frustrated by an absurdist bureaucracy and a dehumanized populace. Director Rudolf Noelte's production is strangely flat, despite its effective use of photography, settings, and peasant faces to convey a mood of grim eerieness. Perhaps in our era, faceless bureaucracy has become too facile and cliched a target. A-III (nr)

Castle, The (1999) Sophomoric satire in which a goodhearted Australian family of nitwits refuses to let a planned airport expansion rob of them of their home, and the case goes to Australia's highest court. Director Robert Sitch's goofy underdog tale is undercut by heavy-handed treatment of the comical situations. Minor menace and vandalism, occasional profanity, and recurring rough language. A-III (R)

Castle in the Desert (1942) Playful murder mystery with Charlie Chan (Sidney Toler) on the job in a spooky 16th-century castle built in the Mojave Desert by a reclusive millionaire (Douglass Dumbrille), whose wife is suspected of poisoning a visitor. There's a fortune at stake in a twisty story involving real and bogus murders, almost as many red herrings as suspects (notably Richard Derr, Henry Daniell, Steve Geray, and Ethel Griffies), and some comic relief from Chan's Number Two Son (Victor Sen Yung). Directed by Harry Lachman. Menacing situations. A-I (br)

Castle Keep (1969) Screen version of novelist William Eastlake's surrealistic satire on the absurdity of war is set in a Gothic chateau with its priceless art treasures, where an American major (Burt Lancaster) and a company of infantrymen prepare to make a stand against the German army's offensive at Bastogne. Regrettably, director Sydney Pollack fails to incorporate a convincing human and moral dimension to counter-balance the senseless heroics and casual sexual relationships that result. O (R)

Castle of Fu Manchu, The (1973) With weapons developed by kidnapped scientists, Fu (Christopher Lee) broadcasts his intention to rule the world, but Scotland Yard sleuth Nayland Smith (Richard Greene) manages to come to the rescue. This is not accomplished until the screen has been deluged with flimsy skirmishes, unsynchronized voices, and stock footage of a sinking ship, a bursting dam, and an exploding house. Fu-ey. Directed by Jess Franco. A-II (PG)

Casual Sex (1988) Unfunny comedy about two young single women (Lea Thompson and Victoria Jackson) who, in search of a healthy way to meet Mr. Right, sign on for a vacation at a singles health spa. Director Genevieve Robert uses humor to portray contemporary issues of sexuality and the AIDS epidemic in a frank if non-cerebral manner. Much blunt sex talk and a non-sexual nude-beach sequence. O (R)

Casualties of War (1989) Fact-based story of an atrocity committed by an American patrol during the Vietnam War centers on the moral dilemma of a soldier (Michael J. Fox) who tries to prevent his unit (led by Sean Penn) from gang raping and murdering a Vietnamese woman. Director Brian DePalma's treatment of the atrocity and the war's violence is extremely graphic. Intense violence and much foul language. A-IV (R)

Cat, The (1966) Poorly done outdoor adventure story in which a boy (Dwayne Redlin) gets lost on a camping trip, then is saved by a mountain lion who befriends him. Directed by Ellis Kadison, it would only be of interest to the very young and the gullible. A-I (br)

Cat and Mouse (1970) German adaptation of the Gunter Grass novel about a young man's groping for maturity under the Nazi regime, and his subjective way of facing reality and his own handicaps. Directed with precision and style by Hansjurgen Pohland, it is of interest for what it shows of the period but also has some insights for those working with adolescents. A-III (nr)

Cat and Mouse (1978) Unorthodox police inspector (Serge Reggiani) is baffled by what appears to be a millionaire's murder and theft of his art collection, but as the case progresses nothing is quite what it seems, and the viewer is never exactly sure where the abundance of clues will lead. Written and directed by Claude Lelouch, the mystery comedy is both intelligent and playful, especially with its offbeat cast of characters acted with style by the likes of Michele Morgan and Philippe Leotard. A-III (nr)

Cat and the Canary, The (1927) Classic silent thriller in which a dead man's relatives gather in a spooky manor for the reading of his will at the stroke of midnight, then learn his entire fortune goes to a young woman (Laura La Plante) who comes to fear for her life before the stormy night's end. Directed by Paul Leni, the picture is awash in eccentric characters and bizarre plot twists as a menacing figure flits about the eerie candle-lit house, whose dark shadows, sliding panels, and secret passages provide some scary moments. Stylized violence, menacing situations, and mild sexual innuendo. A-II (br)

Cat Ballou (1965) Wild romp out West as the daughter (Jane Fonda) of a murdered rancher (John Marley) seeks justice by enlisting the aid of an over-the-hill gunfighter (Lee Marvin), an Indian ranch hand (Tom Nardini), and a pair of con-men (Michael Callan and Dwayne Hickman). Director Elliot Silverstein's frontier spoof has comic flair, droll performances (Marvin also doubles as the chief villain), and musical commentary by balladeers Nat King Cole and Stubby Kaye. Comic violence and mild sexual innuendo. A-II (br)

Cat from Outer Space, The (1978) A stricken spaceship piloted by a very sophisticated cat lands on earth for repairs and is aided by an odd assortment of friendly scientists (Ken Berry, Sandy Duncan, and McLean Stevenson) to get airborne again despite interference from the military (Henry Morgan) and the charms of an earth cat named Lulubelle. Surviving Norman Tokar's unsubtle direction, it proves better than average Disney fare. A-I (G)

Cat O'Nine Tails, The (1971) Italian director Dario Argento's B-grade murder mystery centers on a series of killings in a medical research center which are eventually unraveled by newspaper reporters (James Francisus and Karl Malden). The assorted graphic murders and death agonies are utterly pointless, as are the sex interludes with Catherine Spaak and a ludicrous encounter in a gay nightclub. O (GP)

Cat People (1942) Effectively understated horror movie in which a husband (Kent Smith) tries to help his bride (Simone Simon) conquer her fear of an old Serbian legend about humans cursed with the power to turn into deadly panthers. In their first effort to wring suspense from low-budget melodramas, producer Val Lewton and director Jacques Tourneur create a sinister atmosphere and some scary scenes — notably in a hotel swimming pool — but are less successful with the weak plot. Much menace and a broken marriage. A-II (br)

Cat People (1982) Very loosely based on Val Lewton's 1942 horror classic, this one is tediously explicit in showing the tribulations of a brother and sister (Malcolm McDowell and Nastassia Kinski) who turn into black panthers at odd moments and must kill to regain their human form. Paul Schrader's direction offers clumsy, heavy-handed doses of blood and gore, graphic sex, and nudity. O (R)

Cat's Eye (1985) Three episodes that are an unstable blend of suspense, violence, and black humor linked together tenuously by the presence of the same cat in each. Directed by Lewis Teague from a screenplay by horror writer Stephen King, these are moderately entertaining with relatively restrained violence. A-II (PG-13)

Catch My Soul (1974) Uneven rock opera version of Shakespeare's *Othello* turns the wicked Iago (Lance Le Gault) into the devil incarnate dressed as a hippie, and the noble Moor (Richie Havens) is now a pacifist preacher who heads a hippie commune. The score by Havens and Tony Joe White is quite good, but Jack Good's script ranges from the sublime to the ridiculous in its mixture of Shakespearean imagery, Biblical diction, and contemporary argot. As directed by Patrick McGoohan and photographed by Conrad Hall, the New Mexico locations are an impressive backdrop for the opera, but the contemporary rarely meshes smoothly with the classic. A-III (PG)

Catch 22 (1970) Screen version of Joseph Heller's black comedy about a bomber squadron in Italy during WW II and its troubled airman, Yossarian (Alan Arkin). Although skillfully done under Mike Nichols' direction, it is more pretentious than profound in its statement that war is madness. Brief nudity and some graphic depiction of wartime casualties. A-IV (R)

Catherine & Co. (1976) French production about an English prostitute, played with nauseating coyness by Jane Birkin, who decides to incorporate herself as a business enterprise. Thoroughly unfunny and offensive sex comedy directed by Michael Boisrond. O (R)

Catherine the Great (1934) Historical drama centers on the troubled marriage of German princess Catherine (Elisabeth Bergner) to Russia's Grand Duke Peter (Douglas Fairbanks, Jr.), who becomes Czar after the death of the empress (Flora Robson), but his unstable personality and despotic rule lead to his murder and Catherine's being acclaimed empress. Directed by Paul Czinner, the British production has elaborate sets, endless court intrigues, Peter's mad antics, and Catherine's triumphant smile. Implied sexual affairs. A-III (nr)

Catlow (1971) Flip outlaw (Yul Brynner) shoots his way across the Southwest and part of Mexico with a quixotic marshal (Richard Crenna) in hot pursuit. Directed by Sam Wanamaker, action rather than plot is all this meandering, seriocomic Western shoot-'em-up has to offer. Stylized violence. A-III (GP)

Catman of Paris, The (1946) Low-budget horror movie set in 1896 Paris, where a famous author (Carl Esmond) suffers blackouts whenever a serial murderer strikes, leaving victims clawed to ribbons. Directed by Lesley Selander, the author is hounded by a police inspector (Gerald Mohr), defended by his literary agent (Douglass Dumbrille), and troubled by an ancient legend of a cat monster, before the story reaches its predictable conclusion. Stylized violence and scary menace. A-II (br)

Cats Don't Dance (1997) Animated feature in which a young hep-cat (voiced by Scott Bakula) from Kokomo, Indiana, comes to 1930's Hollywood to sing and dance his way to movie stardom but can only get a job as an animal extra, until proving he and his friends are top talents. Directed by Mark Dindal, the colorful animation is lost in the threadbare animal story of an unknown's break into showbiz, with most of the humor directed at the era's movie stars and studio moguls, but the result offers little to charm the imagination of young viewers. A-I (G)

Cattle Annie and Little Britches (1981) Two teenage girls (Amanda Plummer and Diane Lane) join a once famous outlaw gang (led by Burt Lancaster) and inspire its aging members to live up to their reputation. Director Lamont Johnson's contrived Western does not measure up to its whimsical intentions and takes a benign view of immorality of various sorts, including sexual. A-III (PG)

Cattle Drive (1951) Western adventure in which the spoiled teenage son (Dean Stockwell) of a railroad owner (Leon Ames) gets lost in the wilds and is rescued by a cowboy (Joel McCrea), who teaches him the value of work and self-discipline while driving a herd of cattle to Santa Fe. Directed by Kurt Neumann, it's *Captains Courageous* on horseback with an agreeable cast and colorful outdoor vistas. A-I (br)

Cattle King (1963) Tired formula Western about an 1880's Wyoming range war between a big rancher (Robert Taylor) and the hired guns of a city boss (Robert Middleton). Directed by Tay Garnett, there's nothing new here, though it does touch on the question of government land policy. Stylized shoot-outs and fisticuffs. A-I (br)

Cattle Queen of Montana (1954) Routine Western directed by Allan Dwan has an undercover government agent (Ronald Reagan) give some needed assistance to the title character (Barbara Stanwyck) in the fight to save her ranch from an ambitious land-grabber (Gene Evans) and his Indian allies. Stylized violence. A-I (br)

Caught (1996) Slow-paced drama of the close friendship that develops between a Jersey City fishmonger (Edward James Olmos) and the young drifter (Arie Verveen) he takes into his home, but things turn nasty when the fishmonger's wife (Maria Conchita Alonso) takes a fancy to the boarder and they begin an affair. Directed by Robert M. Young, the picture develops its working-class environment and characters in credible fashion, then gets swept away in the torrid depiction of an increasingly passionate affair whose tragic ending falls flat. Simulated sex scenes with nudity and occasional profanity and rough language. O (R)

Caught in the Draft (1941) Trying to impress a colonel's daughter (Dorothy Lamour) by pretending to enlist in the Army, a spineless movie actor (Bob Hope) finds himself in uniform and blunders his way through boot camp, until eventually becoming a hero during a war game. Director David Butler relies on Hope's droll delivery of one-liners and hapless double-takes to provide most of the humor in this standard peacetime service comedy. Mild sexual innuendo. A-II (br)

Caught Up (1998) Formula thriller set in L.A.'s South Central 'hood, where an ex-con (Bokeem Woodbine) falls for a woman (Cynda Williams) who gets him involved with the loot from a big jewel heist, then finds he's been set up to take the fall for the crime. Writer-director Darin Scott offers a slick but uneven reworking of the old story of an innocent man caught up in a web of desperate doings which he must unravel at the risk of his life. Gory violence, a sexual encounter with brief nudity, numerous sexual references, and much rough language. A-IV (R)

Cauldron of Blood (1971) Far-fetched, not-scary would-be chiller about a mad housewife (Viveca Lindfors) who won't tell her blind sculptor-hubby (Boris Karloff) the source of the skeletons she supplies for him to use as models for his lifelike statues. A bubbly vat of acid has the title role. Directed by Edward Mann, it is pure hokum, but innocuous enough for hardy, undemanding adults. A-III (GP)

Cause for Alarm (1951) Gimmicky suspense thriller directed by Tay Garnett follows a panicky housewife (Loretta Young) as she tries to retrieve a letter written by her demented husband (Barry Sullivan) just before his death, charging that she and his doctor (Bruce Cowling) are lovers plotting his murder. Threatening situations and irrational behavior. A-II (br)

Cavalcade (1933) Dated family saga from the Noel Coward play contrasts the changing fortunes of an upper-class London couple (Clive Brook and Diana Wynyard) with those of their servants (Herbert Mundin and Una O'Connor) from the turn of the century to the Great Depression. Director Frank Lloyd's stagy portrayal of parents and offspring suffering through wars, personal tragedies, and socio-economic upheavals is so understated that its picture of the times has little historical interest today and even less emotional impact. Some wartime violence and veiled sexual references. A-II (br)

Cavalry Command (1963) American troopers (John Agar and Richard Arlen) in 1902 Luzon battle nationalist guerrillas and local rebels while trying to help the residents of the village in which they have been stationed. Writer-director Eddie Romero simplifies the historical realities underlying this tangled tale of the US occupation of the Philippines after the Spanish-American War. Stylized violence. A-I (br)

Cave of Outlaws (1951) Routine Western directed by William Castle in which an ex-con (Macdonald Carey) is tailed by a Wells Fargo agent (Edgar Buchanan) while searching for stolen gold hidden in an Arizona cave, then tangles with a ruthless copper baron (Victor Jory) who wants to marry the local newspaper owner (Alexis Smith). Frontier violence and romantic complications. A-II (br)

Caveman (1981) Prehistoric slapstick comedy with Ringo Starr, John Matuszak, and Barbara Bach has at least the virtue of being unpretentious, yet garners few laughs along the way. Director Carl Gottlieb's sense of humor is only for those whose weakness for buffoonery and vulgarity borders on total insensibility. A-III (PG)

Cease Fire (1985) A Vietnam veteran has difficulty adjusting to civilian life because of the traumatic effect of his war experiences. Good acting by Don Johnson and Lisa Blount, but the film itself is superficial and not very moving. Some rough language and use of narcotics. A-III (R)

Ceiling Zero (1935) Stilted action melodrama from Frank Wead's Broadway play glorifies the male bond between pioneer aviators (Pat O'Brien, James Cagney, and Stu Erwin) flying the mail in canvas crates and stormy weather, as the women who love them fret on the ground. Director Howard Hawks focuses on the pilot's bantering camaraderie in dealing with the hazards of flight and their relations with women. Airborne dangers and sexual innuendo. A-III (br)

Celebration, The (1998) At a family dinner celebrating the 60th birthday of the family patriarch (Henning Moritzen), his eldest son (Ulrich Thomsen) rises to accuse his father of having sexually abused him and his dead twin sister when they were children, and after a night of consternation, the family buries the revelation as a dark secret and ostracizes the offender from their circle. Directed by Thomas Vinterberg, the Danish production works up a great deal of emotional energy on a tragic subject, then lets it dissipate in a flat conclusion that avoids dealing with its consequences. Subtitles. A theme involving incest, stylized violence, sexual situations and innuendo, fleeting nudity, heavy drinking, and occasional rough language. A-IV (R)

Celebration at Big Sur (1971) Lackluster documentary about a rock/folk music festival at California's Big Sur with performances by Joan Baez, Joni Mitchell, Crosby Stills Nash & Young, John B. Sebastian, and, best of all, Dorothy Morrison and the Combs Sisters. The inevitable shots of casual nudity and drug-taking are brief, but they are there almost as tokens of the music scene which, in itself, is very sad indeed. A-III (GP)

Celebrity (1998) Flat series of seriocomic sketches about a small-time New York writer (Kenneth Branagh) whose work brings him into the circle of the rich and famous but, instead of these contacts furthering his career, he gets lost in a series of sexual affairs while his ex-wife (Judy Davis) remarries and finds happiness as a TV celebrity. Writer-director Woody Allen's spoofing of the empty glitter surrounding real and fictional celebrities is only occasionally amusing, and his comic treatment of the neurotic writer's inability to resist his sexual urges comes across as hollow and rather sad, with the end result labored and hardly worth the effort. Numerous sexual situations, some gross sexual humor, a scene of domestic violence, frequent rough language, and occasional profanity. A-IV (R)

Celestial Clockwork (1996) Giddy French comedy in which a would-be opera singer (Ariadna Gil) leaves Venezuela for Paris, where her attempts to audition for the lead in the Rossini opera *Cinderella* is thwarted by a series of comic complications, eccentric characters, and whimsical situations. Though writer- director Fina Torres tries to set the absurd proceedings in the grander context of the foolish nature of mortals, the lightweight result proves little more than a hit-or-miss mixture of good-natured frivolity and general silliness. Subtitles. Some sexual inferences, a few coarse words, and an instance of profanity. A-III (nr)

Celluloid Closet, The (1996) Documentary from Vito Russo's book on the portrayal of homosexuality in mainstream American movies from the comic sissy of the silents, through the Production Code's ban on homosexual references, to the present mix of movies that range from gay bashing to positive depictions. Produced and directed by Rob Epstein and Jeffrey Friedman, the work uses clips from over 100 Hollywood movies and interviews with filmmakers in presenting a sympathetic account of how homosexuals have emerged from a shadowy, furtive existence on the screen to a new visibility still to be defined in terms of mainstream attitudes. Excerpted scenes of violence, sexual encounters with nudity, and rough language. A-IV (R)

Celtic Pride (1996) Weak sports comedy in which two fanatical Boston Celtics basketball fans (Daniel Stern and Dan Aykroyd) kidnap the rival team's star player (Damon Wayans) to better the odds of the Celts in the NBA finals. Director Tom DeCerchio elicits only bland humor out of a one-joke situation as the threesome awkwardly move from insulting one another to camaraderie. Fleeting violence, some vulgar expressions, minimal profanity, and an instance of rough language. A-III (PG-13)

Cement Garden, The (1994) After their mother (Sinead Cusack) dies, four orphaned youngsters bury her body in the cellar and live on their own, as an incestuous relationship develops between teenage brother (Andrew Robertson) and sister (Charlotte Gainsbourg), and their seven-year old brother (Ned Birkin) takes to dressing as a girl and reverting to using baby bottles. British director Andrew Birkin seems interested only in the shock value of a repellant story about self-possessed teenaged siblings who are knowing and willful in their sexual appetites and indifferent to their little brother's pathetic deterioration. Graphic depiction of sibling incest, recurring nudity, frequently implied masturbation, and much rough language. O (nr)

Cemetery Club, The (1993) Strained comedy about three close-knit Jewish widows (Ellen Burstyn, Olympia Dukakis, and Diane Ladd) whose halting readjustment to single life is complicated by a romantically inclined widower (Danny Aiello). Despite crackerjack performances and often witty dialogue, director Bill Duke ultimately lets the story wallow in maudlin sentimentality. An implied sexual encounter and minimal rough language. A-III (PG-13)

Central Station (1998) Stark Brazilian drama in which a cynical spinster (Fernanda Montenegro) reluctantly agrees to escort a nine-year-old boy (Vincius De Oliveira), whose mother was killed at the Rio bus station, to the disreputable father he's never met in the remote reaches of the country. Director Walter Salles's poignant road movie becomes a humanist voyage of discovery as the woman's tender emotions are rekindled by sacrificing for the child. Subtitles. Fleeting violence, petty thievery, minor profanity, crude expressions, and a few instances of rough language. A-III (R)

Ceremony, The (1974) With this chronicle of an influential family that spans from 1946 to the present, director Nagisa Oshima has taken the measure of the Japanese upper-class and found it wanting. His picture of the convoluted relationships within this archetypal family stresses the unthinking ritualistic approach to life which was harmful in the past and even more dangerous today. Violence. A-III (nr)

Cesar and Rosalie (1972) French romance about a liberated woman (Romy Schneider) who divides her time between her young daughter, her current lover (Yves Montand), and her first love (Sami Frey) just returned from America but in the end she leaves them both. Directed by Claude Sautet, the movie is a fine character study of middle-aged people and their feelings about life, though some may find the implied sexual relationships offensive. A-IV (R)

Chain Gang Women (1972) Two convicts (Michael Stearns and Robert Lott) escape from a Georgia prison farm, and two women provide them with places of refuge and plenty of sexual satisfaction. As directed by Lee Frost and Wes Bishop, the women's complicity hardly justifies the title but, in any event, its sex and violence are excessive. O (R)

Chain of Desire (1993) Dreadfully dull tale of the jaded sex lives of assorted Manhattanites (including Malcolm McDowell, Linda Fiorentino, and Grace Zabriskie) who patronize a sleazy transvestite nightclub. Writer-director Temistocles Lopez attempts a feeble cautionary tale in the age of AIDS but fails to develop the situations or characters beyond meager sketches without wit or insight. Various sexual perversions and encounters, brief nudity and drug abuse, minimal violence, and intermittent rough language. O (nr)

Chain Reaction (1996) Slack action thriller in which a fugitive (Keanu Reeves), hunted by the FBI for blowing up a hydrogen energy project, uncovers a rogue government operation and blows it sky-high. Directed by Andrew Davis, the weakly contrived proceedings are filled with high-tech machinery and special-effects violence, but the formula plot and stock characters generate little genuine suspense and even less interest. Assorted violence, much menace, and intermittent profanity. A-III (PG-13)

Chained Heat 2 (1993) Soft-core rot directed by Lloyd Simandl in which an American tourist (Kimberley Kates) winds up in a Prague women's prison whose warden (Brigitte Nielsen) farms out the inmates as prostitutes and porn-movie fodder just before the fall of Czechoslovakia's Communist regime. Numerous sexual situations with nudity, stylized violence, and occasional rough language. O (R)

Chairman, The (1969) A scientist (Gregory Peck) goes to Red China to steal a secret formula at the urging of Western military intelligence who implant a pill-sized transmitter in his skull. J. Lee Thompson directs an entertaining secret-agent melodrama that is mildly suspenseful yet also raises hypothetical questions about US cold-war policies and procedures. Adult situations. A-III (PG)

Chalk Garden, The (1964) Subdued adaptation of Enid Bagnold's play set in a British seaside manor whose eccentric owner (Edith Evans) entrusts her troubled 16-year-old granddaughter (Hayley Mills) to a governess with a mysterious past (Deborah Kerr). Directed by Ronald Neame, the fine cast manages to overcome a glossy, melodramatic production and give some point to a quirky tale of wounded psyches and love denied. Psychological problems. A-II (br)

Challenge to Be Free (1976) Mike Mazurki plays a trapper who accidentally shoots a policeman and leads a posse on a two-month chase through the depths of an Alaskan winter. A family film directed by Tay Garnett, the flimsy plot is no more than a pretext for showing the austere, rugged beauty of Alaska and a number of photogenic animals that children will love. A-I (G)

Challenge to Lassie (1949) After an aged sheepherder (Donald Crisp) is killed by robbers in 1860 Edinburgh, the dog he had trained from a pup overcomes all manner of obstacles to keep vigil beside her master's grave each night. Directed by Richard Thorpe, the fact-based story of a dog's steadfast loyalty is prime fare for youngsters, though older viewers may be more interested in the legal conflict between Lassie's defender (Edmund Gwenn) and the town magistrate (Alan Napier). Engaging family fare. A-I (br)

Challenges, The (1973) Three-part Spanish movie knit together by using American actor Dean Selmier in three separate roles, each as an outsider doomed to disaster in a foreign land, simply doesn't go very far with its basic theme of alienation. The interplay between cultures and people is a fascinating subject, but each segment is treated with disappointing shallowness by its director (Claudio Guerin, Jose Luis Egea, and Victor Erice). Violence. A-III (GP)

Chamber, The (1996) Somber drama from John Grisham's novel about the dark secrets uncovered by a novice lawyer (Chris O'Donnell) in his stubborn attempt to win a stay of execution in Mississippi for his racist grandfather (Gene Hackman), convicted of murdering twin boys decades earlier. Directed by James Foley, the result is not particularly suspenseful, but offers an absorbing character study of the convicted man coming to terms with the life he has led. Sporadic violence, racial epithets, and an instance of profanity. A-III (R)

Chamber of Horrors (1966) Hy Averback directs a weak murder mystery with wax museum setting and a cast including Cornel Wilde, Wildred Hyde-White, and Patrice Wymore. Stylized violence and a sequence set in a brothel. A-III (br)

Chameleon Street (1991) Bored by his blue-collar job and pressured to make big bucks by his wife (Angela Leslie), a handsome charmer (Wendell B. Harris, Jr.) passes himself off as a Harvard-trained surgeon, a Time magazine journalist, a Yale student, and a human rights attorney. Harris wrote, starred in, and directed this fact-based movie, infusing it with lively originality and sardonic humor that generally makes up for the disjointed narrative. Sporadic rough language and some sexual innuendo. A-III (R)

Champ, The (1979) Over-the-hill boxing champ (Jon Voight) tries a comeback for the sake of his adoring son (Ricky Schroder) in director Franco Zeffirelli's romanticized remake of the 1931 classic. Racetrack atmosphere and Voight's performance are more interesting than the melodramatic plot, but the boxing sequences may be too brutally intense for younger teens. A-II (PG)

Champagne for Caesar (1950) Dated but still enjoyable comedy about a congenial genius (Ronald Colman) who goes on a double-or-nothing TV quiz program intending to win enough money to bankrupt the show's nasty sponsor (Vincent Price), despite the charms of a classy siren (Celeste Holm) hired to distract him. Directed by Richard Whorf, the spoof of quiz shows and greedy advertisers is no novelty today, but the humor remains good-natured and the broad characterizations are still fun. Mild sexual innuendo. A-II (br)

Champagne Murders, The (1967) Uneven French murder mystery about a jaded playboy (Maurice Ronet) who is being made to believe that he has murdered several women in drunken blackouts. Director Claude Chabrol is more interested in showing upper-class corruption than working out the details of a rather complicated plot. Scenes of immorality and decadence tend to be excessive for their purpose. O (br)

Champagne Safari, The (1996) Documentary about ambitious American businessman Charles Bedeaux, who made a fortune in the 1920s marketing his efficiency system to increase worker productivity, lavishly refurbished a French chatteau in which to entertain Europe's rich and powerful during the 1930s, then collaborated with the Nazis after the fall of France and, facing US treason charges, committed suicide in 1944. Director George Ungar's picture of a self-promoter's growing delusions of grandeur is interspersed with footage taken by Hollywood cameraman Floyd Crosby of Bedeaux's bizarre 1934 expedition through the Canadian Rockies loaded down with luxury goods. Justice questions and marital infidelity. A-II (nr)

Champion (1949) Gritty version of Ring Lardner's story about the rise and fall of a Chicago tough (Kirk Douglas) who becomes a ruthless prizefighter, dumps his manager (Paul Kelly) to get a shot at the middleweight title, and, after winning it, proves an even worse heel than before. Produced by Stanley Kramer and directed by Mark Robson, the result is as much about corruption in the fight game as the harm done by the conscienceless boxer. Gory boxing scenes and implied sexual relationships. A-III (br)

Chances Are (1989) Delightful fantasy fluff about a beautiful 40-year-old widow (Cybill Shepherd) who is reunited with her beloved husband when he returns to life 20 years later in the body of a young aspiring journalist (Robert Downey, Jr.). Director Emile Ardolino has fashioned a classy comedy romance that makes the most of a good cast and offers a feeble message about the healthy necessity of moving on after the death of a loved one. Some sexual innuendoes. A-III (PG)

Chandler (1971) Private eye (Warren Oates) falls in love with the French woman (Leslie Caron) he's been hired to follow in a ruse concocted by government agents to flush an underworld biggie out of the shadows. Director Paul Magwood's confused, convoluted plot is a poor imitation of a Raymond Chandler mystery. Stylized violence. A-III (GP)

Change of Habit (1969) Three coy nuns don civilian clothes to work in a Spanish-Harlem ghetto clinic run by doctor Elvis Presley who, unaware of the convent's experimental program, naturally falls in love with one of them (Mary Tyler Moore). William Graham directs with plenty of sentimentality, cliches, and stereotypes of the 1940s variety that some modern nuns may not appreciate. A-II (G)

Change of Mind (1969) A white district-attorney in a Southern town who is dying of cancer survives by means of a medical operation that transplants his brain into the healthy body of a black accident-victim (Raymond St. Jacques). Though burdened with stereotypes, cliches, and a far-fetched premise, director Robert Stevens achieves an allegory with some insights into how race affects people's perceptions and actions. Some adult situations and dialogue limit it to mature audiences. A-III (R)

Change of Seasons, A (1980) Shirley MacLaine plays a loving wife who, shocked to learn that her husband (Anthony Hopkins) is having an affair with a woman young enough to be their daughter (Bo Derek), jumps into an affair with a younger man (Michael Brandon). This pretentious, meandering, excruciatingly cute effort, directed by Richard Lang and written by Erich Segal, features extravagant nudity and lack of any positive moral perspective. O (R)

Changeling, The (1980) An unusually subtle and intelligent haunted-house melodrama starring George C. Scott as the man who rents a huge, isolated old mansion, where soon the fun begins with strange noises, eerie manifestations, and a seance that reveals the secret of the house. Directed by Peter Medak, its mood of horror and flashes of violence are remarkably restrained, though there is a scene depicting the cruel murder of a child. A-III (R)

Changes (1969) A college student (Kent Lane) leaves home looking for a more authentic meaning to his life than he has experienced from his parents and passes through a series of relationships in his quest for self-identity. Writer-director Hall Bartlett's restatement of the problems and inner conflicts confronting youth in an affluent American society is well-intentioned but abounds in cliches, both in its romantic visuals and probes of adult hypocrisies. A-III (PG)

Chant of Jimmie Blacksmith, The (1980) Powerful and disturbing Australian movie set at the turn of the century tells the story of a half-white, mission-educated aborigine (Tommy Lewis) who breaks under the strain of constant exploitation and goes on a mad rampage of revenge. Adapted by director Fred Schepisi from a novel by Thomas Keneally, the picture is a searing indictment of injustice and a grim warning of the consequences it can provoke. Though the theme has much contemporary relevance, its depiction of graphic violence and sordid environment may be too strong for some adults. A-IV (nr)

Chaplin (1992) Respectful, plodding biography of screen great Charles Chaplin (1889-1977), from his impoverished youth in London to his meteoric rise in WW I Hollywood, decades of popular success and critical acclaim, exile as a political undesirable after WW II, and triumphal return to Hollywood for a special Academy Award a few years before his death. Directed by Richard Attenborough, the episodic chronicle captures the changing historical context but not, for all Robert Downey Jr.'s evocative performance in the title role, the essence of the man or his genius for visual comedy. Muted sexual references, incidental nudity, and occasional rough language. A-III (PG-13)

Chaplin Revue, The (1972) Three silent featurettes written, directed, and starring Charles Chaplin for First National were originally released as **A Dog's Life** (April 1918), **Shoulder Arms** (October 1918), and **The Pilgrim** (1923). This sampler of films from what may have been Chaplin's most inventive period helps to explain better than anything else why he will endure in the memory of the movie public. A-I (G)

Chappaqua (1967) In an autobiographical semi-documentary featuring himself, Conrad Rooks chronicles his treatment for drug dependence in a private hospital abroad. Disjointed montage of images convey the nightmarish existence of an addict in the physical agony of withdrawal. A-III (br)

Chapter Two (1979) A successful writer (James Caan) marries an actress (Marsha Mason), but the memory of his dead wife threatens their happiness in this adaptation of a Neil Simon play. Under Robert Moore's direction, the one-liners are still funny, but the attempt to deal with more serious material is beset with problems, chief of which is the lack of dramatic action. Attempted adultery figures in a subplot, though it is far from being condoned. A-III (PG)

Character (1998) Absorbing Dutch production set in 1930s Rotterdam, where the man (Fedja van Huet) arrested for murdering the city's powerful, much-hated bailiff (Jan Decleir) turns out to be the dead man's illegitimate son, who explains to the police how the father he never knew came to dominate his life. Writer-director Mike van Diem turns a fairly conventional murder mystery into a compelling character study of a bright youth who tries to overcome the stigma of his birth and impoverished upbringing, then comes to fear his vengeful father is out to ruin his chances of success. Subtitles. Some gory violence, sexual references, brief nudity, and an instance of profanity. A-III (R)

Charade (1963) Black romantic comedy about a rich widow (Audrey Hepburn) who is hounded by criminals (James Coburn and Walter Matthau) and seeks help from a mysterious, debonair stranger (Cary Grant) whom she must learn to trust. Director Stanley Donen makes exquisite use of the Parisian locales and Henry Mancini's memorable score. Stylized violence, menacing situations, and romantic complications. A-II (br)

Charge at Feather River, The (1953) Standard Western starts with a squad of misfit troopers (led by Guy Madison) rescuing two reluctant women (Vera Miles and Helen Westcott) from their Cheyenne captors, then being pursued and forced to make a stand against waves of attackers. Director Gordon Douglas alternates pitched battles against the Indians with dissension within the rescue party but achieves only slack results. Much stylized violence and veiled sexual references. A-II (br)

Charge of the Lancers (1954) Slack war story of a French captain (Pierre Aumont) attached to British forces in the Crimea War, who gets help from a gypsy (Paulette Goddard) in rescuing an English officer held by the Russians in Sevastapol. Directed by William Castle, the action is tediously unconvincing, though the preposterous situation has unintended amusing moments. Stylized violence and minor romantic complications. A-II (br)

Charge of the Light Brigade, The (1936) Loosely drawn from Tennyson's poem on an incident in the Crimean War, the Hollywood version saves it for the finale in the story of brothers (Errol Flynn, Patric Knowles) who have a falling-out over a woman (Olivia de Havilland) while soldiering in Imperial India, then meet again in 1856 when the nobler of the two leads 600 lancers against an artillery emplacement at Balaclava. Director Michael Curtiz downplays the sudsy romance in favor of military action, with the Indian massacre of a British outpost as motivation for the famous charge, vividly re-created here in a sweeping set-piece of men and horses dashing across a landscape riddled with shot and shell. The result is stirring entertainment with some noble sentiments but little regard for history. A-I (br)

Charge of the Light Brigade, The (1968) Heavy-handed account of the 1853-56 British campaign against the Russian forces in the Crimea, set in the context of the power politics and social inequalities of the Victorian age. Director Tony Richardson fails to keep the scale of the spectacle from reducing the stature of its characters, thereby wasting a large and talented cast. Anti-war violence. A-III (br)

Chariots of Fire (1981) Two young Englishmen (Ben Cross, Ian Charleson) overcome quite different obstacles to win gold medals at the Paris Olympics of 1924. One is a Jew determined to beat the anti-Semitic establishment at its own game, and the other is a devout Scot who runs for the glory of God. Directed by Hugh Hudson, it is a richly entertaining and highly inspiring movie for the whole family. Several coarse words. A-I (PG)

Chariots of the Gods? (1974) Eric von Daniken's account of the mammoth constructions of prehistory, from the pyramids to Easter Island, relates their creation to spacemen from more highly developed planets than Earth. The mysteries of man's past are many and awesome, but this pseudo-documentary sheds little light on them. A-I (G)

Charles — Dead or Alive (1972) Swiss movie in which a successful businessman (Francois Simon) decides one day that he hates his daily routine and goes off to think about his future. His son, frantic about the welfare of the business and afraid of publicity, hires a detective to locate his father, then commits him to an insane asylum. Director Alain Tanner's story about a mid-life crisis is also a criticism of Swiss conformity but done in such a light-hearted and gently human way that it is first-rate entertainment and not just a social lesson. Mature themes. A-III (nr)

Charles and Lucie (1980) Uneven French sentimental comedy about a middle-aged Parisian couple whom swindlers leave penniless and on the run from the police in the picturesque south of France. What follows is a series of comic misadventures and absurd encounters that director Nelly Kaplan handles somewhat haphazardly in a mixture of farce, satire, and whimsy. Holding the film together are the marvelous performances of Ginette Garcin and Daniel Ceccaldi as the struggling couple who steadfastly face adversity with a comic dignity that is in the best tradition of screen comedy. A-III (nr)

Charley and the Angel (1973) After Fred MacMurray is informed by angel Harry Morgan that he has only a short time on earth, he changes his ways and becomes a dedicated family man. Director Vince McEveety handles the Disney Depression-era story with a suitably light touch that allows Harry Morgan a maximum amount of fun while emphasizing the positive messages of the story. A-I (G)

Charley One-Eye (1973) Fugitive black soldier (Richard Roundtree) makes his way across the Mexican desert in 1866 in the company of a lame, half-breed Indian (Roy Thinnes), occasionally bothered by Mexican bandits and a bounty hunter (Nigel Davenport). Directed by Don Chaffey, the movie is shallow, ponderous, and considerably violent. A-III (R)

Charley Varrick (1973) Unusual, action-packed, and curiously disturbing film about a seemingly ordinary individual (Walter Matthau) who supplements his income as a crop-duster pilot by robbing small-town banks on his mornings off. When he happens to rob a bank used by gangsters, he winds up being chased by the mob as well as the police. Director Don Siegel's movie is tense and occasionally quite brutal, with an undercurrent of amorality in the dog-eat-dog atmosphere of the underworld. A-III (PG)

Charley's Aunt (1930) Creaky British farce in which two Oxford students persuade an older chap (Charles Ruggles) to dress up as a wealthy aunt from Brazil — "where the nuts come from" — because they need a chaperon to entertain their girlfriends in the dorm, but the counterfeit lady spends the day being chased by aged suitors. Directed by Al Christie, the stagy result is mainly an exercise in period silliness, though Ruggles has a lot of fun in the flamboyant role of female impersonator. Sexual innuendo. A-II (br)

Charlie Bubbles (1968) Seriocomic think-piece about a sensitive, generous, popular writer of romantic novels who discovers that success is more trouble than it's worth but can't go back again. Though some may not care for the movie's non-narrative style and may even find Charlie's boredom contagious, others will find it thoughtful and provocative. Directed by Albert Finney, who also plays the lead, it has a fine supporting cast (Billie Whitelaw, Colin Blakely, and Liza Minnelli). Adult situations. A-III (br)

Charlie Chan and the Curse of the Dragon Queen (1981) Called out of retirement to help the San Francisco police solve a series of bizarre murders, Charlie Chan (Peter Ustinov) trades leaden aphorisms with a dotty in-law, her daffy servants, and a cloddish Number One Grandson. Ineptly directed by Clive Donner, this witless farce relies on vulgarity and profanity for laughs. A-III (PG)

Charlie Chan and the Golden Eye (see: **The Golden Eye**)

Charlie Chan at Monte Carlo (1938) Convoluted mystery in which Chan (Warner Oland) aids Monaco's police chief (Harold Huber) in solving several murders tied to missing bonds, with suspects including their owner (Sidney Blackmer), his secretary (Robert Kent), a rival financier (Edward Raquello), a former model (Virginia Field), and an American bartender (George Lynn). Directed by Eugene Forde, the murky proceedings are lightened by the bumbling efforts of Chan's Number One Son (Keye Luke) and marks Oland's final appearance in the role. Stylized violence and romantic complications. A-II (br)

Charlie Chan at the Circus (1936) Enjoyable mystery in which the title Honolulu detective (Warner Oland) takes his wife and dozen offspring to the circus, then solves the murder of its grasping co-owner (Paul Stanton). Directed by Harry Lachman, Charlie gets some bumbling help from Number One Son (Keye Luke) in tracking suspects, including the dead man's partner (Francis Ford), an animal trainer (J. Carrol Naish), and a host of circus performers. Menacing situations. A-I (br)

Charlie Chan at the Olympics (1937) Mystery and intrigue abound as Chan (Warner Oland) follows the trail of a stolen military device to the 1936 Olympic Games in Berlin, where he gets help from the German police in cracking the case while freeing Number One Son (Keye Luke) from kidnappers. Directed by H. Bruce Humberstone, the suspects include the device's inventor (Morgan Wallace), its manufacturer (Jonathan Hale), and an arms dealer (C. Henry Gordon), though the Nazi swastika is conspicuously absent from the newsreel footage of the Berlin Games. Stylized violence and menace. A-I (br)

Charlie Chan at the Opera (1936) Elaborate mystery with Chinese-American detective Chan (Warner Oland) aiding the Los Angeles police after an opera diva (Margaret Irving) is murdered during the opening night's performance, with the lead suspect being an escaped mental case (Boris Karloff). Directed by H. Bruce Humberstone, the twisty plot is paced by scenes from the opera (composed by Oscar Levant) and the backstage activities of the performers, with comic relief from Chan's Number One Son (Keye Luke) and a dim flat-foot (William Demarest). Menacing situations. A-I (br)

Charlie Chan at the Race Track (1936) Standard mystery directed by H. Bruce Humberstone with Honolulu detective Chan (Warner Oland) getting some unwanted help from Number One Son (Keye Luke) in solving the murder of a racehorse owner aboard an ocean-liner, with suspects including gamblers, crooked jockeys, and racetrack rivals. Offscreen murder and comic racial stereotyping. A-I (br)

Charlie Chan at the Wax Museum (1940) Eerie mystery directed by Lynn Shores in which the title Honolulu detective (Sidney Toler) and his Number Two Son (Sen Yung) spend an evening in a New York crime museum owned by a plastic surgeon (C. Henry Gordon), whose criminal clientele includes an escaped murderer (Marc Lawrence) and his former partner (Ted Osborn). Menacing situations and shadowy frights. A-II (br)

Charlie Chan at Treasure Island (1939) Engrossing mystery in which Chan (Sidney Toler) seeks to link the murder of a friend (Louis Jean Heydt) to a blackmailing psychic, with some help from a magician (Cesar Romero) performing at the San Francisco World's Fair. Directed by Norman Foster, the proceedings have some eerie moments involving illusions created by the phony psychic, as well as the unsettling powers of the magician's mental telepathist, but the focus is on the twisty case and its surprise solution. Menacing situations. A-I (br)

Charlie Chan in City in Darkness (see: **City in Darkness**)

Charlie Chan in Egypt (1935) Eerie mystery as Chan (Warner Oland) arrives in Luxor to investigate the theft of ancient artifacts from a newly excavated tomb, then discovers the body of the archeologist in charge hidden in mummy wrappings inside a sarcophagus. The murderer's motive involves a secret treasure hidden in the tomb, with the suspects including the dead man's brother (Frank Conroy), other members of the expedition, and several Egyptians (notably Rita Cansino, aka Hayworth), with comic relief from expedition menial Stepin Fetchit. Directed by Louis King. Some scary moments, menacing situations, and period racial stereotyping. A-II (br)

Charlie Chan in Honolulu (1938) Despite the comic-relief antics of Number Two Son (Sen Yung), Chan (Sidney Toler) manages to solve two murders and the theft of $300,000 aboard a freighter carrying a menagerie of wild animals, as well as the usual suspects (Phyllis Brooks, George Zucco, Eddie Collins, Marc Lawrence, and Robert Barrat). Directed by H. Bruce Humberstone, this was Toler's first appearance as Chan, who nabs the killer just before the birth of his first grandchild. Menacing situations. A-I (br)

Charlie Chan in London (1934) Intricate mystery set in England, where Chan (Warner Oland) has only three days in which to save an innocent man (Douglas Walton) from the gallows by finding the real killer among his circle of country gentry friends (Alan Mowbray, Ray Milland, and others). Directed by Eugene Forde, Chan perseveres despite snooty servants, uncooperative witnesses, another murder, an attempt on his own life, and a puzzling military connection, before laying an ingenious trap for the killer. Stylized violence and some intense menace. A-II (br)

Charlie Chan in Panama (1940) Formula mystery with Chan (Sidney Toler) trying to save the US Fleet from being blown up while moving through the Canal, but the saboteur's trail leads to a Czech refugee (Jean Rogers), a Chicago schoolteacher (Mary Nash), an Egyptian tobacconist (Frank Puglia), a nightclub owner (Jack La Rue), and an Austrian scientist (Lionel Royce). Directed by Norman Foster, much of the plot is lifted from the 1934 espionage thriller **Marie Galante** and the bumbling antics of Number Two Son (Sen Yung) are mostly tiresome. Menacing situations. A-I (br)

Charlie Chan in Paris (1935) Intriguing mystery as Chan (Warner Oland) gets some unneeded help from Number One Son (Keye Luke), as well as the head of the Paris police (Minor Watson), while solving the murder of an apache dancer (Dorothy Appleby) who had information about counterfeit bank bonds. Directed by Lewis Seiler, the case turns on a recurring mysterious figure, a double disguise, and a secret room in the Paris sewers. Stylized violence and menacing situations. A-II (br)

Charlie Chan in Reno (1939) Convoluted mystery with Chan (Sidney Toler) coming to Nevada's divorce mill to save a friend's wife (Pauline Moore) accused of murdering the woman (Louise Henry) who stole her husband's affections. Directed by Norman Foster, the plot is loaded with suspects (notably Ricardo Cortez, Phyllis Brooks, and Kay Linaker) and much comic relief from Number Two Son (Sen Yung), the local sheriff (Slim Summerville), and a daffy cab driver (Eddie Collins). Stylized violence and messy divorce proceedings. A-II (br)

Charlie Chan in Rio (1941) Formula mystery with Chan (Sidney Toler) helping Rio de Janeiro's police chief (Harold Huber) solve the murders of a nightclub singer (Jacqueline Dalya) and her butler (Leslie Denison), with suspects including the dead woman's secretary (Kay Linaker), fiancé (Ted North), ex-husband (Truman Bradley), jealous girlfriend (Mary Beth Hughes), and a Hindu mystic (Victor Jory). Directed by Harry Lachman, the heavy-handed plot hinges on the woman's unsavory past, with rather dour results, despite the comic diversions of Number Two Son (Sen Yung) and Toler's silly mugging while smoking a supposedly drugged cigarette. Stylized violence and romantic complications. A-II (br)

Charlie Chan in Shanghai (1935) Formula mystery in which Chan (Warner Oland) visits Shanghai on a holiday with Number One Son (Keye Luke) but his real objective is nabbing a ring of opium smugglers. Directed by James Tinling, Chan and the city's police commissioner (Halliwell Hobbes) have matters well in hand until an American G-man (Russell Hicks) gets in their way. Stylized violence and menacing situations. A-I (br)

Charlie Chan on Broadway (1937) Twisty mystery in which Chan (Warner Oland) helps a New York homicide detective (Harold Huber) solve the murder of a blackmailer (Louise Henry) whose diary was sought by gangster Leon Ames, nightclub owner Douglas Fowley, newspaper editor J. Edward Bromberg, and ace reporter Donald Woods. Directed by Eugene Forde, the story is tightly plotted, paced with comic relief from Chan's Number One Son (Keye Luke), and matters are wrapped up in satisfactory fashion. Menacing situations. A-I (br)

Charlie Chan's Murder Cruise (1940) Formula mystery with Chan (Sidney Toler) joining an ocean cruise because among the ship's passengers (notably Lionel Atwill, Leo G. Carroll, Don Beddoe, Charles Middleton, and Cora Witherspoon) is a killer whose strangled victims include a Scotland Yard colleague (Montague Shaw). Directed by Eugene Forde, the plot involves a recurring mysterious figure, a double disguise, and a bitter divorce, with the usual comic relief from Number Two Son (Sen Yung). Some gruesome murders and much menace. A-II (br)

Charlie Chan's Secret (1936) Convoluted mystery in which Chan (Warner Oland) comes to San Francisco in search of a missing heir, who turns up dead in a spooky house during a seance held by his aunt (Henrietta Grossman). Directed by Gordon Wiles, Chan easily unmasks the trickery of the seance's phony psychics (Gloria Roy, Arthur Edmund Carew), but finding the killer proves less simple and a lot more dangerous. Sinister situations. A-I (br)

Charlie, the Lonesome Cougar (1967) Disney wildlife documentary featuring an agile cougar named Charlie, who has outgrown the north-woods lumber camp where he was raised and finds happiness with a female cougar in a nearby game preserve. Charlie is a very photogenic animal but his "adventures" are on the cute side and begin to wear thin. A-I (br)

Charlotte's Web (1973) Charming animated musical version of E.B. White's classic fable about a piglet named Wilbur, who develops from runt of the litter into the county-fair champ with the help of his friends, most notably the spider of the title. Directed by Charles A. Nichols, the Hanna-Barbera production is a gentle introduction to the natural cycle of life that will entertain youngsters and most others in the family. A-I (G)

Charly (1968) Mentally retarded adult (Cliff Robertson) becomes a genius during a medical experiment that has only one drawback, and it's a heartbreaker. A somewhat sentimental adaptation of Daniel Keyes's short story "Flowers for Algernon," the intriguing plot is delicately handled by director Ralph Nelson and given dramatic impact by the range of Robertson's performance in the title role. Mature treatment of romantic subplot. A-III (br)

Charro! (1969) Elvis Presley sings only one song, and that off-camera, in a silly Western vehicle about a gang of outlaws and a golden cannon in Old Mexico. Directed by Charles Marquis Warren, it contains stylized violence, a bit of sadism, and some double entendres. A-III (G)

Charulata (1974) Director Satyajit Ray's story is of a wife neglected by her husband's total commitment to his work. As the film ends with a freeze-frame of the couple reaching for each other, the picture reaches far beyond the boundaries of Ray's native Bengal. A-II (nr)

Chase, The (1966) When an escaped convict (Robert Redford) makes his way home, the entire community dissolves in outbreaks of hate and violence, putting a local sheriff (Marlon Brando) on the spot in trying to uphold the law. An outstanding cast flounders in a murky political allegory directed by Arthur Penn from Lillian Hellman's adaptation of Horton Foote's play. Confused treatment of significant themes, including racism, greed, lust, alcoholism, and religious fanaticism. A-III (br)

Chase, The (1994) Failed black comedy in which a convicted bank-robber (Charlie Sheen) escapes from the law by taking a young woman (Kristy Swanson) hostage, then heads for Mexico in her car with hordes of police in high-speed pursuit. Written and directed by Adam Rifkin, the juvenile fantasy miscalculates the viewer's tolerance for endless scenes of reckless driving, car crashes, exploding vehicles, media goons, police cretins, repeated protestations of innocence by a gun-wielding loser, and a feather-headed woman who falls in love with her abductor. Comic treatment of violence and life-threatening situations, a restrained sexual fantasy, occasional profanity, and much crude language. A-III (PG-13)

Chase a Crooked Shadow (1958) Limp British thriller directed by Michael Anderson is set in Barcelona, where a South African diamond heiress (Anne Baxter) comes to fear for her life after a stranger (Richard Todd) shows up claiming to be her brother, with a preposterous twist ending. Some fairly intense menace makes it unlikely fare for children. A-I (br)

Chase for the Golden Needles, The (see: **Golden Needles**)

Chasing Amy (1997) When a lesbian (Joey Lauren Adams) falls for a love-struck male (Ben Affleck), their affair is shattered by his friend (Jason Lee) revealing details of her kinky bisexual past. Writer-director Kevin Smith mines the topic of sexual identity for some weak laughs in a raunchy, long-winded tale that views promiscuity as harmless fun. Sexual situations, blue humor, drug abuse, and constant rough language with occasional profanity. O (R)

Chastity (1969) Produced by Sonny and starring Cher, the movie intends to be a personal statement about dropping out and searching for identity and true relationships, here depicted in time-honored trial-and-error fashion. Directed by Alessio De Paola, it unfortunately suffers from a lack of sophistication and insight, as well as the severe technical limitations that are common in small-budget films. A-IV (R)

Chato's Land (1972) Failed Western about a half-breed Indian (Charles Bronson) who is goaded into killing a brutish sheriff and becomes the object of an intense manhunt led by an ex-Confederate officer (Jack Palance), which ends in the parched Indian country of the title. Directed by Michael Winner, the problem is that once the movie gets into the groove of steady killing, it becomes both tedious and glaring in its cumulative brutality. A-III (PG)

Chattahoochee (1990) Dark, tedious account of an emotionally disturbed Korean War hero (Gary Oldman), who in the mid-1950s is sent to a degrading mental institution from which he, with the aid of his sister, alerts officials to the brutal mistreatment of the inmates, resulting in legislation that improved treatment of the mentally ill across the country. Mick Jackson's unimaginative direction dilutes the power of the young man's gradual transformation into a mature person committed to social justice. Graphic scenes of brutality, shower room nudity, implicit masturbation, and locker-room language. A-IV (R)

Che! (1969) Dramatization of different points of view on the life and career of Ernesto (Che) Guevara (Qmar Sharif), the Argentinean who was the theoretician and moving spirit behind Cuban revolutionary Fidel Castro (Jack Palance). Directed by Richard Fleischer, it's a boring and lifeless illustrated lecture, devoid of the passion, politics, urgency, and conflict that might have involved viewers in potentially interesting and significant political realities. A-II (PG)

Cheap Detective, The (l978) Overdone parody of the private-eye melodramas of the 1940s with Peter Falk as a Humphrey Bogart-like detective searching for the murderer of his partner, smashing a smuggling ring led by John Houseman doing a Sidney Greenstreet interpretation, and helping a Free French agent gain passage to Oakland. Robert Moore directs a Neil Simon script lacking in wit and invention, sporting tired jokes and some sexually derived humor. A-III (PG)

Cheaper by the Dozen (1950) Warm family comedy about the unusual domestic arrangements in the New Jersey household of a no-nonsense efficiency expert (Clifton Webb), his equally proficient wife (Myrna Loy), and their 12 children (Jeanne Crain is the eldest). Set in the early part of the century, director Walter Lang's episodic, fact-based story has a strong nostalgic appeal along with a genial sense of humor about family life, some of which proves more than funny (e.g., Mildred Natwick as a bemused planned-parenthood representative). Still pleases. A-I (br)

Cheaper to Keep Her (1981) A divorce lawyer (Tovah Feldshuh), concerned about late alimony payments, hires a private investigator (Mac Davis) who is newly divorced himself in a dreadfully acted, determinedly vulgar attempt by director Ken Annakin at romantic comedy. The humor, when not lewd, comes at the expense of homosexuals and Hispanics. O (R)

Checkered Flag or Crash (1977) Joe Don Baker plays a driver in a 1,000-mile road race in the Philippines, with Susan Sarandon as an intrepid photographer-journalist. Directed by Alan Gibson, it is mindless even by the modest standards of racing movies and exhibits a disregard for human life. A-III (PG)

Checking Out (1989) Failed, badly written comedy about one man's fear of mortality when an airline executive (Jeff Daniels) flips out after the sudden death of his best friend (Allen Havey). Director David Leland offers little beyond tasteless ethnic jokes, tired coronary gags, numbingly selfish characters, and a particularly gross sex scene. O (R)

Cheech and Chong's Next Movie (1980) Second movie with the comedy team of Cheech and Chong (Cheech Marin and Thomas Chong) assaults thc audience with drugs, foul language, crude sexual references, and a plot that goes nowhere. Directed by Chong. O (R)

Cheech and Chong's Nice Dreams (1981) The dopey duo this time out are entrepreneurs dealing marijuana from an ice cream truck, which leads to the usual rambling misadventures with drugs and sex. O (R)

Cheech and Chong's "The Corsican Brothers" (1984) Cheech and Chong take the plot of the venerable old swashbuckler and bedeck it with their usual slapstick gags, though this time they avoid drugs and nudity. Directed by Thomas Chong, however, it's all very unfunny, especially its gross sexual humor. O (R)

Cheers for Miss Bishop (1941) Sentimental drama of an unmarried teacher (Martha Scott) at a Midwestern college, from her student days in the 1870s to her retirement in the 1930s. Directed by Tay Garnett, the result has plenty of heart in its depiction of the teacher's failed romances (William Gargan and Sidney Blackmer) and her dedication to niece, grandniece, and students, as well as a patriotic theme equating knowledge with democracy. Romantic complications. A-II (br)

Cheetah (1989) Disney live-action adventure of two teenagers who adopt an orphaned cheetah cub while spending the summer with their parents in Kenya. Directed by Jeff Blyth, the movie may bore parents familiar with the similar, better movie **Born Free**, but children will be content with the movie's nature photography and the warm friendship that develops between the American youngsters and a local Masai lad who shows them the wonders of his world. A-I (G)

Chef in Love, A (1997) Engaging romantic fantasy set on the eve of the Russian Revolution, as a French chef (Pierre Richard) opens a restaurant in Tbilisi, where he lives happily with a Georgian princess (Nino Kirtadze) until their loving relationship is tragically shattered by the arrival of the Bolsheviks. Directed by Nana Djordjadze, the French-Georgian co-production uses an impressionistic stream of anecdotes filled with strange, almost surreal images of Georgian life to tell the story of an irrepressible adventurer whose zest for life is certainly refreshing, sometimes amusing, and occasionally exhilarating. Subtitles. Implied sexual relationship, a restrained bedroom scene, and flashes of nudity. A-III (PG-13)

Cher Victor (1976) French black comedy to which director Robin Davis brings a hard-edged sensibility in a story of two old men for whom petty quarrels turn into a vendetta that ends in tragedy. Bernard Blier and Jacques Dufilho, two great character actors, give performances worth seeing as the geriatric odd couple who are locked in a symbiotic relationship neither can break. The movie is amusing, yet underneath lurks the truth that the frailties of old age await each viewer. A-III (nr)

Cherry, Harry and Raquel (1970) Marijuana operation in the Arizona desert is interfered with by a pesky Indian. Sex-exploitation job directed by Russ Meyer with extensive nudity and perverse acts. O (X/R)

Chess Players, The (1978) Indian director Satyajit Ray tells a 19th-century story of British encroachments on a small Moslem kingdom in the north of India, using as his focus two idle aristocrats who pass their days in playing chess, oblivious of the danger that threatens their land and its poet-king. Based on an actual incident and told with some humor and much irony, the film suffers from being overly talky and stagy. Its greatest asset for American viewers is its careful re-creation of a vanished era. A-II (nr)

Cheyenne (1947) Thin Western directed by Raoul Walsh is set in the Wyoming Territory of 1867, where a gambler (Dennis Morgan) working for Wells Fargo nabs a stagecoach robber known as the Poet (Bruce Bennett), chiefly by playing footsy with the outlaw's wronged wife (Jane Wyman). Stylized violence and implied marital infidelity. A-III (br)

Cheyenne Autumn (1964) Western epic of Indian courage in the face of the white man's neglect and broken promises in the story of a Cheyenne tribe who leave a squalid reservation for their homeland, and an officer (Richard Widmark) who sympathizes with their plight but whose orders are to bring them back. Director John Ford's rugged locales match the grandeur of the trek even though the melodramatic narrative falters at times. A-I (nr)

Cheyenne Social Club, The (1970) Jimmy Stewart, a cowboy with moral inhibitions, inherits a brothel, but his ownership of the building depends on the ladies remaining there. Sidekick Henry Fonda jumps in and out of ladies' beds, while Stewart stammers his way through an excruciatingly silly seduction scene (complete with maid in transparent blouse). An exercise in off-color humor directed by Gene Kelly, the result lacks wit, taste, and interest. O (GP)

Chicago Cab (1998) Sour slice-of-life treatment of a day the life of a harried taxi driver (Paul Dillon), as seen in his interaction with a strange assortment of fares ranging from the rich and boorish to drunks, junkies, and weirdos. The colorful Chicago backgrounds provide more visual interest than the cab's depressing interior, though the largely failed attempt to deal with the potential human drama in all this is not without interest. Directed by Mary Cybulski and John Tintori. Some nasty menace, sexual situations and references, much rough language, and occasional profanity. A-IV (R)

Chicago Joe and the Showgirl (1990) Stationed in WW II London, a GI (Kiefer Sutherland) and an exotic dancer (Emily Lloyd) take their Hollywood-inspired crime fantasies to deadly lengths within days of meeting each other. Directed by Bernard Rose, the fact-based movie re-stages the pair's murderous rampage without offering any insight into such cold-blooded behavior. Brutal depictions of violent crimes, brief shots of sexual activity, and partial nudity. A-III (R)

Chicago 70 (1970) Witty anti-establishment satire intertwines the Chicago conspiracy trial of Bobby Seale and Abbie Hoffman with Lewis Carroll's *Alice in Wonderland*. Director Kerry Feltham photographed the stage play as performed by the Toronto Workshop, with its bizarre, colorful costumes and a minimum of props in a black limbo setting. Mature themes. A-III (nr)

Chicken Chronicles, The (1977) Obnoxious youth-oriented comedy set in the late 1960s about a self-indulgent Beverly Hills high-school senior determined to get his girlfriend into bed. Though avoiding nudity, director Francis Simon's treatment of sex, drugs, and alcohol is exploitative. O (PG)

Chief Crazy Horse (1955) Impelled by a boyhood vision, the Lakota Sioux warrior of the title (Victor Mature) unites rival tribes against the invading whites, but after Custer's defeat his allies disperse, and he finally surrenders, only to be murdered by a Lakota outcast (Ray Danton). Director George Sherman gives sympathetic treatment to the Indian struggle for their homelands, though handicapped by the weak device of the chief's story being told by an unlikely white friend (John Lund). Frontier violence. A-I (br)

Child's Play (1972) Failed screen version of Robert Marasco's play about the tragedy of evil that grows from the school rivalry between a paranoiac Latin teacher (James Mason) and a jovial paternalistic English teacher (Robert Preston) who has come to hate him. The only mystery is why director Sidney Lumet weakened what was originally a straight chiller by throwing in all kinds of sidelong glances, creaky doors, murky corridors, and unsubtle theatrical effects. A-III (PG)

Child's Play (1988) A widow (Catherine Hicks) buys a talking doll for her son's sixth birthday, but the doll is possessed by the soul of a psychopath (Brad Dourif). Although the boy (Alex Vincent) knows the doll is deadly, no one believes him, including the

Chicago cop (Chris Sarandon) investigating the doll's murder victims. Director Tom Holland overdoes the doll's brutal rampages in a tasteless horror movie exploiting a child as ghoul bait. O (R)

Child's Play 2 (1990) Chucky, the doll possessed by the spirit of a psychopath, is reassembled and goes on another murderous rampage, as he tries to get his hands on the little boy (Alex Vincent) he's determined to inhabit. Director John Lafia's schlocky sequel is as predictable as it is trite and repulsive. Intermittent gory violence and recurring rough language and gestures. O (R)

Child's Play 3 (1991) Formula horror sequel has killer doll Chucky (voice of Brad Dourif) at a military academy intent on transferring his soul into an eight-year-old (Jeremy Silvers) unless a previously intended victim (Justin Whalin) can prevent it. Director Jack Bender sets the foulmouthed doll on another killing rampage in a contrived plot centering on murder and mayhem. Excessive violence, continual menace to a child, and much rough language. O (R)

Childhood II (1973) Group encounter sessions held in the nude because, we are told, without clothes people can be more honest and open with one another. Martin J. Spinelli's documentary indicates that this technique is as inadequate as most other shortcuts to mental health. O (nr)

Children, The (1980) An orange radioactive cloud turns a group of children into nasty creatures bent upon murder in director Max Kalmanowicz's cheap, amateurish horror movie that overdoes the blood and gore. O (R)

Children of a Lesser God (1986) A deaf girl (Marlee Matlin) who has resigned herself to a life of solitude and mediocrity painfully comes to accept the love and admiration of a professor (William Hurt) at the school for the deaf where she works as a janitor. A well-acted sentimental love story, its potential insights into the problems of interpersonal communication are undercut by director Randa Haines's concentration on the sexual aspects of the lovers' relationship. Nudity and harsh language. A-III (R)

Children of Fate (1993) Compelling documentary focuses on an abused wife and mother in a Sicilian slum plagued by childhood mortality and pervasive unemployment, where boys aspire to join the Mafia. As directed and edited by Andrew Young and Susan Todd, the documentary combines 30-year-old footage of the mother's sorry situation then with her family's current conditions, resulting in a moving family portrait of poverty's lasting effects upon generations of the disadvantaged. Subtitles. Several references to wife-beating, drugs, sexual situations, and criminal lifestyles. A-III (nr)

Children of Heaven (1999) Charming story set in Tehran, where a nine-year-old Iranian boy loses his little sister's only shoes, forcing the two to share wearing his sneakers to school, until he hears of a footrace in which the third prize is a pair of new shoes. Director Majid Majidi spins a slender but sweetly evocative tale of genuine childhood stress made bearable by bonds of love and their generosity to an even less fortunate child. Subtitles. Depictions of poverty and brief menace. A-II (PG)

Children of Rage (1975) Set in 1968, after the disastrous Arab losses in the Six Day War, this movie tries to explain why the Palestinians adopted the desperate policy of terrorism in their fight against the state of Israel. An embarrassingly amateurish production directed by Arthur Allan Seidelman, its failure to explain in any coherent fashion can only serve to exacerbate the feelings of both sides. Violence. A-III (PG)

Children of the Corn (1984) Some nasty kids, in the sway of a demonic power, slaughter all the adults in a Midwestern town where a doctor and his wife (Peter Horton and Linda Hamilton) chance to stop on an auto trip. Fritz Kiersch directs this dull, predictable horror movie adapted from a story by Stephen King. Violence. A-III (R)

Children of the Revolution (1997) Australian cold-war spoof starts with a dedicated party member (Judy Davis) being wooed by Stalin (F. Murray Abraham) at a 1952 Moscow congress, returning home pregnant and raising her son, Joe (Richard Roxburgh), to be like her, but he grows up more like the father he never knew. Writer-director Peter Duncan's lighthearted political comedy grows increasingly heavy-handed as communism self-destructs and Joe seeks political power in 1990 at the head of a police union. A restrained sex scene, sexual situations, brief nudity, some rough language, and occasional profanity. A-IV (R)

Children of Theatre Street, The (1978) American documentary on the famous ballet school in Leningrad that produced Nijinsky and whose more recent graduates include Nureyev, Makarova, and Baryshnikov. Directed by Robert Dornhelm and narrated by Princess Grace of Monaco, it offers some lovely, if fragmented, ballet sequences and some fine views of Peter the Great's city, but the narrative tends to be bland and repetitive, pursuing its subject in rather aimless fashion. A-I (nr)

Children's Hour, The (1962) After opening a girl's school in a small town, two women (Audrey Hepburn and Shirley MacLaine) become the victims of a malicious student's comments about their close friendship, which leads the children's parents to conclude the two are lovers, with tragic results for all. Directed by William Wyler from Lillian Hellman's adaptation of her own play, the slow-moving picture grows heavy-handed as the town reacts irrationally to the gossip and the conclusion taxes credibility. Discreet implications of a lesbian relationship and a suicide. A-III (br)

Chilly Scenes of Winter (see: **Head Over Heels**)

China (1943) WW II morale-booster in which an American neutral (Alan Ladd) selling fuel to the Japanese invaders reluctantly gives a lift to a stranded

American teacher (Loretta Young) and her Chinese women students, but when his truck is strafed and a baby killed by Japanese planes, he joins the Chinese guerrillas just before Pearl Harbor. Directed by John Farrow, the story is simplistic and emotionally manipulative but is still watchable today as one of the better examples of the patriotic melodramas that flourished in the war years. Stylized violence, much menace, and some sexual innuendo. A-II (br)

China Gate (1957) Creaky melodrama set in 1954 Indochina, where an American explosives expert (Gene Barry) joins a French commando team to blow up the key munitions dump supplying the Vietnamese Reds, then learns their guide through enemy lines is his Eurasian wife (Angie Dickinson) whom he deserted five years before. Writer-director Samuel Fuller handles the raid with much unconvincing derring-do, and the characters are as shallow as the themes, though it has interest as Hollywood's first look at the Vietnam conflict. Wartime violence, marital rancor, and racial prejudice. A-II (br)

China Girl (1987) Interracial teen romance blooms amid a climate of gang warfare in New York's Chinatown and Little Italy. Director Abel Ferrara emphasizes action and setting over characterization and an understanding of ethnic loyalties and traditions of prejudice that rule the lives of two generations of Chinese and Italians. Bloody violence, a lovemaking scene, and profanity abounds. O (R)

China Is Near (1968) Italian satire on the country's politics and morals centers on a man's campaign for office in a small town where everything revolves around sex, politics, and religion. Marco Bellocchio's confusing direction lacks a clear enough viewpoint to support its heavy-handed and at times offensive treatment. A-IV (br)

China Moon (1994) Grim crime thriller in which a Florida homicide detective (Ed Harris) falls for a troubled woman (Madeleine Stowe), and after she kills her abusive, wealthy husband (Charles Dance) helps her cover up the crime, only to wind up accused of having committed it. Director John Bailey's elaborately twisted tale of sexual obsession, murder, and betrayed loyalties has a game cast of hardworking actors and plenty of arty photography, but the pulp story, bogus plot contrivances, and empty ending aren't worth the bother. Some graphic violence and sex scenes, extramarital relationships, nudity, and occasional rough language. O (R)

China Sky (1945) WW II melodrama from the Pearl S. Buck story of American doctors (Randolph Scott and Ruth Warrick) providing care for Chinese guerrillas (led by Anthony Quinn) in a mountain base betrayed to Japanese paratroopers by a treacherous prisoner (Richard Loo). Directed by Ray Enright, the routine action story falters in a clunky romantic subplot involving Scott's cowardly wife (Ellen Drew). Wartime violence and romantic complications. A-II (br)

China Syndrome, The (1979) Director James Bridges's prophetic drama suspensefully deals with nuclear safety issues in a movie featuring Jack Lemmon as an executive and Jane Fonda as a news reporter whose consciences won't let them conceal the imminent danger of a nuclear meltdown at a power plant. Thoughtful entertainment. A-II (PG)

Chinatown (1974) Jack Nicholson plays a private eye trying to unravel a murder bound up with a civic scandal in the Los Angeles of the 1930s. Faye Dunaway is the mysterious, frightened woman at the center of the plot, along with wealthy tycoon John Huston. Director Roman Polanski plays a sinister heavy. A superior entertainment altogether adult in its theme of social and personal corruption, especially its implication of incest. A-IV (R)

Chinatown at Midnight (1949) Low-budget crime thriller directed by Seymour Friedman is set in San Francisco, where a cunning crook (Hurd Hatfield) commits a murder, then tries to throw the police off his trail by planting evidence pointing to a Chinese perpetrator. Stylized violence. A-II (br)

Chinese Box (1998) Disjointed pastiche of scenes from the unhappy life of a dying British reporter (Jeremy Irons) in Hong Kong on the eve of the Crown Colony's return to Chinese sovereignty. Directed by Wayne Wang, the use of the dying reporter as a metaphor for the end of British rule only gets in the way of what is essentially an impressionistic picture of Hong Kong as a cultural crossroads of East and West, which its new rulers will likely find as puzzling as American viewers. Sexual situations and some rough language. A-III (R)

Chinese Connection, The (1973) Martial-arts movie with Bruce Lee revenging the murder of his beloved teacher. In the end, the hero goes to jail for his murderous deeds, affording him one last snickering kick at the audience as he's led away. Director Lo Wei employs excessive violence and a totally irrelevant striptease by a geisha girl. O (R)

Chinese Ring, The (1947) Formula Charlie Chan mystery directed by William Beaudine follows the Chinese-American detective (Roland Winters) on the case of a murdered Chinese princess involved in a scheme to smuggle US fighter planes to her compatriots, with token comic relief from Chan's chauffeur (Mantan Moreland) and Number Two Son (Victor Sen Yung). Some menace and period racial stereotyping. A-I (br)

Chipmunk Adventure, The (1987) Animated feature plays like a musical revue of pop tunes, as Alvin and his Chipmunk friends sing and race around the world with their female cousins, the Chipettes, in hot-air balloons inadvertently delivering stolen diamonds for their wicked human guardians. Director Janice Karman's charming, lighthearted diversion for the younger set includes a sweet song about motherhood and the critters' comical conversation. A-I (G)

Chisum (1970) Boisterous, good old-fashioned Western stars John Wayne as cattle baron John Chisum, who figured prominently in the bloody Lincoln County cattle wars involving the likes of Pat Garrett and Billy the Kid. Directed by Andrew V. McLaglen with the usual oversimplification of moral issues in the taming of the West, the movie will appeal to those who like action at the expense of historical accuracy. A-I (G)

Chitty Chitty Bang Bang (1968) Widowed inventor (Dick Van Dyke) takes his two children and girlfriend (Sally Ann Howes) on a magical mystery tour of the imagination involving an evil baron (Gert Frobe), a cavernous castle in the air, the rescue of imprisoned children, and the strange flying car of the title. Though adults may be disappointed by the indifferent lyrics and lackluster special effects of this musical fantasy directed by Ken Hughes, there is still more than enough good fun for the young and uncritical. A-I (G)

Chloe in the Afternoon (1972) French drama about a married man (Bernard Verley) with a wonderful wife (Francoise Verley), lovely daughter, secure job, and serene life, who is drawn into intimacy with a sensuous woman (Zouzou) that takes him to the brink of actual infidelity. The final episode in director Eric Rohmer's series of **Six Moral Tales** is an elegant, sophisticated story of a smug, self-absorbed man, who viewers will have to decide was strong enough to resist temptation or simply not nervy enough to indulge it. Restrained nudity. A-III (R)

Chocolat (1989) Set in the French Cameroons on the eve of independence in the late 1950s, this picture of life in colonial Africa is seen through the eyes of the young daughter (Cecile Ducasse) of a colonial official (Francois Cluzet). Director Claire Denis takes an unsettling look at the inhumanity of master-servant relationships, especially the anger and sexual frustration arising between the lady of the house (Giulia Boschi) and the devoted family manservant (Isaach de Bankole). Subtitles. Fleeting nudity. A-III (PG-13)

Chocolate War, The (1989) When a sadistic Brother (John Glover) in a parochial school for boys unreasonably pushes his students to sell huge quotas of candy to boost his administrative aspirations, one student (Ilan Mitchell-Smith) refuses and is subjected to abusive reprisals from the teacher and the school's secret fraternity of sociopathic thugs. Writer-director Keith Gordon makes parallels between teen peer-pressure and Fascist repression, but his ponderous, metaphoric script and artsy camerawork do little to raise the heavy-handed effort beyond mindless mediocrity. A warped, unbalanced view of parochial school education, vulgar language laced with sexual innuendoes, and some intense violence. O (R)

Choirboys, The (1977) The screen adaptation of Joseph Wambaugh's novel seems to imply that Los Angeles would be a relatively peaceful city if it could only get rid of its corrupt, drunken, violent, perverted, and vicious police force. Scriptwriter Christopher Knopf has thrown together a pointless series of clumsy, presumably black-comedy sketches of police antics which director Robert Aldrich treats in cynical, leering fashion. Excessive profanity. O (R)

Choke Canyon (1986) Cowboy-scientist (Stephen Collins) fights for his rights against big business, foils the flying hit-man (Bo Swenson) sent to silence him, exposes the effort to turn his canyon lab into a toxic waste site, saves his horse, gets the girl, and manages to complete his experiment turning sound waves into energy. Supposedly about integrity and personal initiative, the story gets derailed by juvenile action scenes, pyrotechnics, romance, and a small bit of rough language. A-II (PG)

C.H.O.M.P.S. (1979) Young engineer (Wesley Eure) invents the perfect home-protection device — a robot watchdog — and wins the hand of the boss's cute daughter, despite the machinations of some inept industrial spies. This weak little comedy from Hanna-Barbera might be of passing interest to very young children if its producers had not seen fit to add a sizable amount of vulgar language. A-II (PG/G)

Choose Me (1984) Smug, irritating little comedy-drama about a man (Keith Carradine) who gets involved with three very talkative women who are supported by their lovers in Los Angeles. He suffers, but viewers suffer more. Directed by Alan Rudolph, it has a benign view of sexual amorality. O (R)

Chopper Chicks in Zombietown (1991) The inhabitants of a sleepy desert town are threatened by the arrival of eight tough motorcycle babes and a host of flesh-eating zombies. Writer-director Dan Hoskins's cheap horror spoof lumbers along, mired in hackneyed characterizations and dripping with gory dismemberments and witless, vulgar humor. Excessive violence played for laughs, intermittent rough language, some sexual innuendo, and a flash of nudity. O (R)

Chorus Line, A (1985) Screen version of the hit stage musical provides a close-up view of backstage fears and emotions at a Broadway audition. Directed by Richard Attenborough, the film tries too hard to translate the theatrical experience to the big screen. Discussion of adult sexual themes. A-IV (PG-13)

Chorus of Disapproval, A (1989) Uninspired movie adaptation of British playwright Alan Ayckbourn's comedy about a handsome widower (Jeremy Irons) who joins a light-opera company for companionship but instead becomes the obsession of two married women (Jenny Seagrove and Prunella Scales). Local gossip provides some comic tension, but director Michael Winner imparts little energy to a well-acted but otherwise lackluster play within a play. Satiric adulterous liaisons and some rough language. A-III (PG)

Chosen, The (1978) Italian production about an industrial magnate (Kirk Douglas), building a super nuclear-power plant in a Third World country, who learns that one of the major backers of the project is the devil and that the Antichrist waiting to take over is none other than his own son (Simon Ward). Director Alberto De Martino's supernatural slash-'em, crunch-'em movie is abysmal drivel exploiting nudity and gory violence. O (R)

Chosen, The (1982) Set in Brooklyn during and immediately after WW II, different views of life and religious faith confront two Jewish teenagers (Robby Benson and Barry Miller), one the son of a revered Hassidic rabbi (Rod Steiger), the other the son of a secular scholar (Maximilian Schell). Directed by Jeremy Paul Kagan, the only shortcoming in the screen adaptation of the Chaim Potok novel is a certain lack of dramatic tension. A-II (PG)

Chosen Survivors (1974) A group of people (Bradford Dillman, Jackie Cooper, Diana Muldaur, Barbara Babcock, Alex Cord, and a handful of others) are thrown together in a self-contained underground environment and told that they are the only survivors of a nuclear holocaust. Their problems begin, however, when vampire bats start invading the ventilating system. Directed by Sutton Rolley, it is a scary movie psychologically, especially if bats are not quite your dish. A-III (PG)

Christa (1971) Swedish story about a woman (Birte Tove) looking for someone with whom she'd be sexually compatible and who would make a nice father for her illegitimate son. Producer-director Jack O'Connell seems interested only in putting as much of his actress on display as the law allows. O (R)

Christian Licorice Store, The (1971) Beau Bridges plays a California tennis pro whose descent into the nether world of casual sex with proper Hollywood strangers and into TV product endorsements affords neither food for thought nor dramatic morsels to chew. When he winds up killing himself, it is simply stupid, not tragic. Director James Frawley's slick, shallow work is all style and no substance. O (GP)

Christian the Lion (1977) George Adamson, whose story was dramatized in **Born Free,** again becomes involved with the task of rehabilitating a tame lion cub to survive in the perils of its natural African habitat. Assisting in this real-life adventure are the stars of **Born Free**, Virginia McKenna and Bill Travers, who co-directed the film with James Hill. Beautifully photographed in Kenyan game preserve, it is an engrossing picture of wildlife and worthwhile family fare. A-I (G)

Christine (1983) Adaptation of Stephen King's novel about a 1959 car that kills people either for the sheer fun of it or because they're rude to its teenage owner (Keith Gordon), who rescued it from a junkyard and restored it to pristine splendor. Director John Carpenter's plodding, mediocre movie has foul language, sex, violence, and an unwholesome view of family life. O (R)

Christine Jorgensen Story, The (1970) The story of a sex-change operation certainly has a place in medical annals, but whether it's a proper subject for a movie, except perhaps in a documentary, is another matter. Directed by Irving Rapper, the result is neither entertaining nor illuminating. A-IV (R)

Christmas Carol, A (1938) Sturdy version of the Dickens classic in which miserly Ebenezer Scrooge (Reginald Owen) fires clerk Bob Cratchitt (Gene Lockhart) on Christmas Eve, then undergoes a change of heart after being visited later that night by his dead partner, Marley (Leo G. Carroll), and three ghosts. Directed by Edwin L. Marin, the adaptation is faithful to the spirit of the original, though it lightens the tone with some comic relief and makes the 1843 London setting more quaint than grim. A-I (br)

Christmas Carol, A (1951) This British version of the Dickens's classic has worn well over the years, principally because of Alistair Sim's zestful performance as Scrooge, the old humbug whose transformation into a loving human being is a pleasure to behold. Director Brian Desmond Hurst's period piece does well with its 19th-century London setting, and the ghostly visitations are done simply but with considerable flair. The result is dandy family viewing. A-I (br)

Christmas Eve (1947) Sentimental melodrama directed by Edwin L. Marin in which a greedy nephew (Reginald Denny) tries to have his wealthy aunt (Ann Harding) declared incompetent, but the old lady's three adopted sons (playboy George Brent, gangster George Raft, and rodeo cowboy Randolph Scott) show up on Christmas Eve to save her. Mixed in with the sticky proceedings is a violent confrontation with a Nazi war criminal, a baby adoption racket, and assorted romantic complications. A-II (br)

Christmas in Connecticut (1945) Breezy romantic comedy in which the unmarried writer (Barbara Stanwyck) of a popular homemaker column has to invent a husband, baby, and country home after her unsuspecting publisher (Sydney Greenstreet) invites a war hero (Dennis Morgan) to celebrate Christmas with her "family." Directed by Peter Godfrey, the slickly contrived proceedings benefit from a capable cast, but the slapdash humor is uneven and the romance less than convincing. Romantic situations, sexual innuendo, and much comic duplicity. A-III (br)

Christmas Story, A (1983) Adapted from Jean Shepherd's nostalgic piece of whimsy *In God We Trust, All Others Pay Cash*, the movie re-creates what it was like to be a boy (Peter Billingsley) yearning for a genuine Red Ryder air rifle for Christmas in the Midwest of the 1940s. Director Bob Clark gets some good performances from Darren McGavin and Melinda Dillon as the understanding parents, and the period atmosphere is nicely conveyed in what is essentially a warm celebration of a more innocent, less sophisticated America. A few vulgar syllables. A-II (PG)

Christmas Tree, The (1969) Wealthy widower (William Holden), told that his only child is dying of leukemia, lavishes all his attention on the boy during his final months. Director Terence Young treats the subject of death with a good deal of sense and sensibility, and by focusing on the son's acceptance of his terminal condition infuses the film with vitality (and even some humor), instead of the static and fruitless sentimentality that is common in such films. A-II (G)

Christopher Columbus — The Discovery (1992) Disappointing theatrical version of the first voyage of the Genoese navigator (George Corraface) who sets off from Spain in 1492 to reach Cathay by sailing west, but finds the New World instead. Though director John Glen tries to inject some sense of adventure into the proceedings, the script by Mario Puzo and others settles for comic-book history, bogus thrills, and politically correct ambiguities, none of which illuminates either the character of Columbus or the nature of the times. Muddled historical context, assorted violence, and partial nudity. A-III (PG-13)

Chrome and Hot Leather (1971) When the girlfriend of a Green Beret (Tony Young) is accidentally killed by a motorcycle gang, he and three of his Green Beret comrades set out to avenge her death. Directed by Lee Frost, the routine biker movie contains occasional and relatively restrained sex and violence. A-III (GP)

Chronicle of Anna Magdalena Bach, The (1969) Unusual concert performance film with brief dramatic scenes from the life of the 18th-century composer connecting the musical presentations. Directed by Jean-Marie Straub, the German production is static, with almost no camera movement, but the ornate settings and elaborate costuming contribute to a rare musical experience in this performance of works by Johann Sebastian Bach. A-I (nr)

Chu Chu and the Philly Flash (1981) Alan Arkin and Carol Burnett struggle desperately for laughs in director David Lowell Rich's contrived mishmash of a comedy about a panhandler and failed showgirl who find secret government documents. Some profanity. A-III (PG)

Chubasco (1968) Story of the regeneration of a rebellious young man (Christopher Jones) through hard work with a tuna fisherman (Joe De Santis) and the love of a young woman (Susan Strasberg), who marries him despite her father's (Richard Egan) objections. Writer-director Allen H. Miner has given fresh life to an old plot by selecting San Diego's tuna fleet as its setting and utilizing to the full the excitement and dangers of deep-sea tuna fishing. A-II (br)

C.H.U.D. (1984) Run-of-the-mill horror movie about monsters created by toxic waste. Ineptly directed by Douglas Cheek, it contains violence and gore. A-III (R)

Chuka (1967) Slack Western directed by Gordon Douglas about a lone gunfighter (Rod Taylor) who arrives at an Army fort filled with misfit soldiers just before it is attacked by starving Indians. Much violence and some sexual innuendo. A-III (br)

Chump at Oxford, A (1940) As a reward for upsetting a bank robbery, Stan Laurel and Oliver Hardy are sent to England for a college education at Oxford, where they get into all kinds of comic trouble. Directed by Alfred Goulding, the hodgepodge script has some very funny routines as the boys get lost in a shrub maze; unwittingly insult the dean; and Stan, after getting conked on the head, turns into a mental giant, lording it over the flustered Ollie. Uneven slapstick comedy with some hilarious bits. A-I (br)

Chungking Express (1996) After being dumped by their girlfriends, two single cops (Tony Leung and Takeshi Kaneshiro) in bustling Hong Kong cling to the hope of reconciliation, even as mysterious new women (Faye Wang and Brigitte Lin) complicate their lives. Writer-director Wong Kar-Wai's gently comic look at the lovelorn is impressive for visual technique but barely maintains its wispy narrative thrust. Subtitles. Some sexual innuendo and brief stylized violence. A-III (PG-13)

Ciao! Manhattan (1973) John Palmer and David Weisman have fashioned a semi-documentary about the sorry life of Edie Sedgwick, a New York society girl who in 1965, at age 28, overdosed on pills. The result proves sophomoric and smart-alecky, with not a little exploitation of the girl's debilitated state of mind and scarred, siliconed body. O (R)

Ciao, Professore! (1994) When a highly cultured teacher (Paolo Villaggio) is accidentally transferred from northern Italy to an impoverished Neapolitan village, he learns much about life by teaching streetwise third-graders, many of whom are already working to support their families. Director Lina Wertmuller puts a gently comic spin on the poverty and crime rampant in the area, but the uneven narrative frequently stoops to soggy sentimentality. Subtitles. Fleeting violence, much graphic slang, and frequent rough language. A-III (R)

Cimarron (1960) Big, sprawling, and generally lethargic Western from the Edna Ferber novel, stretching from the 1889 Oklahoma land-rush to WW I, tells the story of a would-be rancher (Glenn Ford) who becomes a crusading newspaper editor but alienates his wife (Maria Schell) by fighting crime and bigotry instead of getting rich. Director Anthony Mann scores on the big action scenes but bores with the domestic soap operatics. Stylized frontier violence and marital rifts. A-I (br)

Cimarron Kid, The (1951) Routine Western in which corrupt lawmen turn a genial Oklahoma cowboy (Audie Murphy) into a genial outlaw on a crime spree, until turned in by his fiancé (Beverly Tyler) so they can settle down after he serves his time. Director Budd Boetticher's sympathetic portrait of a good badman is strictly cardboard melodrama, with clumsily staged shootouts and a laughably desperate desperado (Hugh O'Brien). Much stylized violence and criminal activity. A-II (br)

Cincinnati Kid, The (1965) The title character is an enterprising young card-shark (Steve McQueen) in 1930's New Orleans who takes on the gambling world's top poker-player (Edward G. Robinson) in a high-stakes game of stud. Directed by Norman Jewison, the narrative takes too long in setting up the characters and their motivations, especially the Kid's problems with women (Tuesday Weld and Ann-

Margret), but when the big game finally gets underway, it's a real gripper. Some violence, including a cockfight, and sexual situations. A-III (br)

Cinderella (1950) Disney animated feature tells the traditional tale of the downtrodden stepdaughter who leaves her chores to attend the prince's ball in a pumpkin coach and shod in glass slippers. Directors Wilfred Jackson, Hamilton Luske, and Clyde Geronimi pace the proceedings with comedy supplied by playful mice Jaq and Gus-Gus, a mean old cat aptly named Lucifer, and an amusingly daffy fairy godmother. Enjoyable entertainment for all the family. A-I (G)

Cinderella Liberty (1973) A sailor (James Caan) becomes involved with a bar-girl (Marsha Mason) and her young son, who understandably acts surly towards his mother's night-time visitor. Caan and Mason establish a stable arrangement of sorts, but this unusual family unit is brought to the brink of ruin by various sappy plot devices. Director Mark Rydell coats the transparent soap opera with heartbreak, misery, pathos, and, of course, a happy ending. Much foul language and some nudity. O (R)

Cindy and Donna (1971) The title duo are a pair of teenybopper sisters who use their Southern California environment to pollute the screen with any number of crude displays. With adulterous sots as parents, it's a picture of family to be avoided at all costs. O (X/R)

Cinema Paradiso (1990) In this Italian production, a film director (Jacques Perrin) returns to his hometown for the funeral of the movie projectionist (Philippe Noiret) who befriended him as a youthful patron of the local movie house, a social mecca where viewers caroused and the parish priest censored every celluloid kiss and embrace. In comic, nostalgic flashbacks, writer-director Giuseppe Tornatore shows how the movies over the years have enriched people's everyday lives. Dubbed or subtitled. Some fleeting sexually suggestive scenes and vulgar antics. A-III (PG)

Circle of Deceit (1982) German production directed by Volker Schlondorff follows the random wanderings of a journalist through the horrors of strife-torn Beirut, Lebanon. Although some of the terrible madness of urban civil warfare is apparent, there is little clear thinking or real drama in a movie marred by an extremely explicit bedroom scene. O (R)

Circle of Friends (1995) Irish coming-of-age tale set in 1957 Dublin, where a young Catholic couple (Minnie Driver and Chris O'Donnell) struggle to abstain from premarital sex, while the girl's scheming friend (Saffron Burrows) carries on an affair with a wealthy Protestant (Colin Firth) which leads only to deceit and betrayal. Based on Maeve Binchy's novel and directed by Pat O'Connor, the visually pretty movie focuses on the sudsy upheavals of first love complicated by matters of conscience which are only superficially resolved. Brief bedroom scene and a few profanities. A-III (PG-13)

Circle of Iron (1979) Ambitious but botched recounting of the adventures of a mythic hero (David Carradine) on a Far Eastern journey toward enlightenment. In homage to martial-arts king Bruce Lee, director Richard Moore's action adventure relies too heavily on stylized violence and a ridiculously inappropriate sex scene which reflects the movie's overall inversion of the values its hero seeks. O (R)

Circus, The (1928) Charles Chaplin wrote, directed, produced, and starred in this silent feature, for which he has written a musical score as well as a song for the sound version. Charlie, on the run from the police, hides in the circus and becomes a prop man but inadvertently proves funnier than the clowns. He falls in love with the bareback rider (Merna Kennedy), but she loves the high-wire artist and the circus goes on, leaving Charlie walking off alone. Admittedly not his best, it is nevertheless a real gem of comic invention and sympathetic understanding of human nature and the human condition. A-I (G)

Cisco Pike (1971) Kris Kristofferson plays a faded flower-child forced by narcotics detective Gene Hackman to re-enter the drug-dealing world he hoped was all in the past. As directed by Bill Norton, there are some kinky sex scenes and meanderings through the California drug scene. O (R)

Citadel of Crime (see: **A Man Betrayed**)

Citizen Kane (1941) When a Hearst-like newspaper tycoon (Orson Welles) dies, a reporter (William Alland) interviews the man's former associates (Joseph Cotten and Everett Sloane, among them) and wives (Ruth Warrick and Dorothy Comingore) in an effort to pin down the essence of the contradictory, larger-than-life millionaire by discovering the meaning of his dying word, "Rosebud." Also co-written (with Herman J. Mankiewicz), produced and directed by Welles, the 1941 movie is a landmark in American cinema, both for its superb use of film technique and its intriguing story of a man who came from nothing, acquired fame and fortune, but died without the love he sought. Marital infidelity. A-II (nr)

Citizen Ruth (1996) Ridiculing both sides of the abortion issue is this failed satire in which the pregnant title character (Laura Dean) cares more about getting money for her next glue-sniffing high than whether she has her baby or not. Director Alexander Payne treats both supporters and opponents of abortion as wild-eyed, power-hungry fanatics, while wrong-headedly trying to build sympathy for the benumbed addict whose glue-sniffing is a danger to herself and her unborn child. Trivialization of a serious subject, a sexual encounter, substance abuse, and frequent rough language. O (R)

Citizens Band (see: **Handle with Care**)

City Across the River (1949) Plodding melodrama about a Brooklyn youth gang (Peter Fernandez, Richard Jaekel, Tony Curtis, and others), two of whom murder their high-school shop teacher, then are hunted down by the police (led by Jeff Corey). Director Maxwell Shane gets some gritty realism from filming on Brooklyn locations, but the sprawling story is unfocused and dramatically less than satisfying. Stylized violence and sexual innuendo. A-II (br)

City for Conquest (1940) Sentimental but sturdy tale set in New York City, where a trucker (James Cagney) turns prizefighter to put his kid brother (Arthur Kennedy) through music school, but loses his girl (Ann Sheridan) and his eyesight in the process. Directed by Anatole Litvak, the formula plot is saved from phoniness by the gritty urban setting and effective performances from a fine cast, including Elia Kazan as a gangster from the old neigborhood. Stylized violence and romantic complications. A-II (br)

City Hall (1996) Gritty political drama set in New York City, where the deputy mayor (John Cusack) is determined to protect the mayor (Al Pacino), an effective politician he much admires, from being ensnared in a burgeoning judicial scandal. Director Harold Becker skillfully turns the screws in an absorbing plot that explores backroom political compromises, where ethics get lost in power struggles and wheeling-dealing. Brief violence and much rough language. A-III (R)

City Heat (1984) A police detective (Clint Eastwood) and a private eye (Burt Reynolds) talk rudely to each other whenever their paths cross during the course of a mob war in Depression-era Kansas City. Director Richard Benjamin apparently means these exchanges to be terribly funny, but they're not. Amidst all the shooting, carnage, and violence, the in-joke nature of the two macho stars becomes quite wearying. A-III (PG)

City in Darkness (1939) Period mystery with Charlie Chan (Sidney Toler) helping the bumbling assistant (Harold Huber) of the Paris Prefect of Police (C. Henry Gordon) solve the murder of a shady financier (Douglass Dumbrille) during the city's blackout on Sept. 12, 1938, as war looms over the Czech crisis. Directed by Herbert I. Leeds, the mystery revolves around such suspects as the dead man's butler (Pedro de Cordoba), partner (Noel Madison), ex-secretary (Richard Clark), and a foreign agent (Dorothy Tree), with the war jitters of the period providing an unusually interesting backdrop for the action. Stylized violence, menacing situations, and mild sexual innuendo. A-II (br)

City Jungle, The (see: **The Young Philadephians**)

City Lights (1931) Classic feature comedy with Charlie Chaplin as the Little Tramp who falls in love with a blind flower-seller (Virginia Cherrill), gets the money needed for her eye operation, then, in the poignant fade out, awaits her reaction when she sees him for the first time. Also produced, written, and directed by Chaplin, the movie's cheerful bouts with urban adversity make good use of sound effects, though there is no spoken dialogue. A-I (G)

City of Angels (1998) Wispy tale of an angel (Nicolas Cage) who longs to become human after falling in love with a Los Angeles heart surgeon (Meg Ryan). Director Brad Silberling explores the limitations of science and the mystery of faith within the framework of a visually striking but ultimately sappy love story. Minor violence, discreet sexual situations, and fleeting nudity. A-III (PG-13)

City of Hope (1991) Powerful drama shows how corruption in a fictional New Jersey city affects a wide spectrum of individuals, including an easily compromised contractor (Tony Lo Bianco), his estranged son (Vincent Spano), a victimized teacher (Bill Raymond), and an earnest councilman (Joe Morton). Writer-director John Sayles's cynical, realistic movie ties up many divergent, finely-acted stories in a shattering conclusion that resonates with irony. Brief violence, frequent rough language, and a marital bedroom scene with a flash of nudity. A-III (R)

City of Industry (1997) Gritty crime story in which four armed men pull off a big jewel heist, then a murderous double-cross by one of them (Stephen Dorff) causes another (Harvey Keitel) to go gunning for him. Director John Irvin's violent tale of betrayal and revenge is a dark study of hardened criminals, most of whom pay for their greed with their lives. A morally ambiguous ending, intermittent nasty violence, fleeting nudity, and much rough language. A-IV (R)

City of Joy (1992) The poorest section of Calcutta provides the vivid backdrop for a humanistic drama revolving around the family of an impoverished rickshaw-puller (Om Puri) and an alienated American doctor (Patrick Swayze) who serves the residents of the area in an endangered clinic. Director Roland Joffe dramatically captures the spiritual and material desperation of his characters in a story that accentuates the resiliency of the human spirit despite its simplistic ending. Brief violence and mild sexual innuendo. A-II (PG-13)

City of Women (1981) Italian director Federico Fellini offers a heavy-handed analysis of the male ego threatened by feminist demands for sexual equality in a story about an aging Lothario (Marcello Mastroianni) and his erotic daydreams. There are touches of the old Fellini magic, but his penchant for the grotesque has grown wearisome, his imagery repetitious, and his studio artifice annoyingly obvious. O (R)

City on Fire (1979) One of the most disastrous disaster movies ever made, the title tells the entire plot. The Canadian production directed by Alvin Rakoff is unbelievably dull and pedestrian. Violence involving fire victims. A-III (R)

City of Lost Children, The (1995) Grotesque fantasy set in a grungy futuristic world, where a brawny simpleton (Ron Perlman) gets help from a street-smart preteen orphan (Judith Vittet) in rescuing kidnapped children from the clutches of a mad scientist and his diabolical minions. Sluggishly directed by Jean-Pierre Jeunet and Marc Caro, the movie's elaborate art design is more interesting than the bizarre characters and their convoluted actions. Subtitles. Some stylized violence and much menace. A-III (R)

City Slickers (1991) Three New York City pals (Billy Crystal, Bruno Kirby, and Daniel Stern) tackle their individual midlife crises while trying to survive a working vacation on a cattle drive in the Southwest. Director Ron Underwood's insightful buddy comedy takes on issues of commitment, family, and fidelity in a generally entertaining story. Occasional sexual references and vulgar expressions. A-II (PG-13)

City Slickers II: The Legend of Curly's Gold (1994) Disappointing sequel in which an Old West map indicating the location of a cache of stolen gold prompts three New Yorkers (Billy Crystal, Daniel Stern, and Jon Lovitz) to head back west, where the deceased map owner's twin brother (Jack Palance) joins their greedy treasure hunt. Director Paul Weiland's mildly funny rehash of the three urban cowboys' misadventure is diluted by plot holes and its copycat approach to the characterizations and settings. A money-hungry theme incorporating several off-color remarks, toilet humor, incidental violence, and an instance of profanity. A-III (PG-13)

City That Never Sleeps (1953) Murky crime picture in which a Chicago cop (Gig Young) on the verge of leaving his wife for a honky-tonk dancer (Mala Powers) gets mixed up with a crooked lawyer (Edward Arnold), whose wife (Marie Windsor) is about to run off with a thug (William Talman). Directed by John H. Auer, the convoluted story is of less interest than the location photography of the action during the cop's nighttime tour of duty, which ends with a deadly chase along the tracks of the Chicago El. Heavy stylized violence and sexual innuendo. A-III (br)

Civil Action, A (1998) Fact-based courtroom drama in which an ambitious Boston ambulance chaser (John Travolta) is pitted against a cunning corporate attorney (Robert Duvall) while representing families whose children's deaths appear linked to industrial pollution. Directed by Steve Zaillian, the movie focuses on moral and ethical issues, but its tragic story is sluggishly dramatized. Minimal rough language and fleeting profanity. A-II (PG-13)

Clair de Femme (1980) A recent widower (Yves Montand) and a woman (Romy Schneider) who has just lost her daughter in an auto accident and her husband to insanity meet, and a love affair ensues, apparently meant to be the salvation of both. The melancholy romance is directed by Costa-Gavras in pretentious and tedious fashion, wasting the talents of those involved in this French production. Treatment of sex makes this adult fare. A-III (PG)

Claire's Knee (1971) Amusing but cerebral French drama in which a middle-aged diplomat (Jean-Claude Brialy) is introduced to a young woman (Laurence de Monaghan) and becomes disconcertingly obsessed with her knee. Director Eric Rohmer's fifth in his series of **Six Moral Tales** is a droll study of a rather pompous man's self-deception in trying to rationalize his fixation in a movie of literate conversations about everything from love to philosophy. A-III (GP)

Clambake (1967) In order to know whether he is liked more for his money than himself, a tycoon's son (Elvis Presley) switches identities with a penniless water-ski instructor (Will Hutchins). Directed by Arthur Nadel, the results are entirely predictable, with Elvis singing a few subdued ballads and driving in a speed-boat race that is the movie's highlight. A-I (br)

Clan of the Cave Bear, The (1986) Based on Jean Auel's popular novel about prehistoric times, this movie plods along with its band of dull-witted Neanderthals who raise an orphaned Cro-Magnon child, Ayla. Except for the scenery, not much happens until Ayla grows intelligent enough to leave the clan to its caves. Several scenes of simulated sex and some violence. O (R)

Clara's Heart (1988) Wise Jamaican housekeeper (Whoopi Goldberg) takes her employer's adolescent son (Neil Patrick Harris) under her wing when she sees that he's being ignored by his estranged, shallow parents. Director Robert Mulligan's cliched story of interracial friendship lacks emotional insight into its characters. Extramarital affairs, some rough language, and verbal recollections of a mother's rape by her son. A-III (PG-13)

Clarence the Cross-eyed Lion (1965) The comic adventures of conservationists (Marshall Thompson and Betsy Drake) in an African wildlife preserve, where they fight off a gang of poachers with the help of their friend of the title. Directed by Andrew Marton, the animals are cute, the action mild, and the result painless for the younger members of the family. A-I (G)

Clash by Night (1952) Dark dramatization of the Clifford Odets play about a sullen, unhappy woman (Barbara Stanwyck) who marries a good-hearted fishing-boat captain (Paul Douglas), then falls for his cynical movie projectionist pal (Robert Ryan). Director Fritz Lang portrays the human tragedy caused by disordered passions in convincing fashion, with contrasting figures of hope and despair among the citizens of a California fishing town and adjacent cannery. Theme of infidelity and its moral consequences. A-II (br)

Clash of the Titans (1981) Greek mythology plays second fiddle to a whole medley of not especially enthralling special effects in director Desmond Davis's languid and hopelessly episodic reworking of the Perseus-Andromeda legend. The immense talents of Laurence Olivier, Burgess Meredith, Claire Bloom, Sian Phillips, and Flora Robson are helpless in this mess of a movie. Incidental nudity. A-III (PG)

Class (1983) Jacqueline Bisset plays a woman who has an affair with a teenage boy (Andrew McCarthy), later discovering that he is her son's (Rob Lowe) best friend. Director Lewis John Carlino can't decide whether to play the contrived, ill-considered effort as romantic comedy, slapstick farce, or serious drama.

The result settles for adolescent vulgarity and the sensationalism of graphic sex. O (R)

Class Act (1992) Two teens, one a parolee (Christopher Martin), the other a brilliant scholar (Christopher Reid), whose academic records were accidentally switched in their new high school, decide to continue the charade. Director Randall Miller's aimed-at-teens rap-music comedy has the nerd vs. hip types down pat, but sends out all the wrong messages about casual sex. A teenage sexual encounter with parental approval, much double entendre, and frequent violence played for laughs. O (PG-13)

Class Action (1991) A lawsuit charging a giant automobile manufacturer with negligence causing deaths and injuries brings an estranged father (Gene Hackman) and daughter (Mary Elizabeth Mastrantonio) together — as opposing counsels. Director Michael Apted's first-rate courtroom drama is craftily portrayed by the leads, and trenchant dialogue raises important moral questions about corporate responsibility and personal ethics. Restrained sexual innuendo and minimal rough language. A-III (R)

Class of '44 (1973) Director Paul Bogart's quarter-baked sequel to the half-baked **Summer of '42** takes two of the adolescent boys of the earlier movie into college and one into the Marines. When it is not being either sentimental or tasteless (sex on campus), it is something like an old Henry Aldrich comedy. A-III (PG)

Class of Miss MacMichael, The (1979) Dedicated, embattled teacher (Glenda Jackson) struggles with a classroom of maladjusted youngsters and an incompetent headmaster (Oliver Reed). Director Silvio Narizzano can't decide on either a serious or farcical mood for this British story whose flow of obscenities and depiction of sexual misbehavior are objectionable. O (R)

Class of 1999 (1990) Experimental androids posing as teachers go berserk in this ultra-violent film in which a student just released from prison discovers the teachers are systematically killing troublesome kids. Producer-director Mark L. Lester's darkly atmospheric tale quickly descends into a nonstop bloodbath, overpowering the suspense with gory special effects and a grisly pileup of corpses. Extremely graphic violence, drug use, and rough language throughout. O (R)

Class of Nuke 'em High Part 2: Sub-humanoid Meltdown (1991) Sex-crazed high-school students go on a rampage with mutant sub-humanoids inside a defective nuclear power-plant. Director Eric Louzil's sick flick is endlessly amateurish and badly acted, with depraved and dehumanizing humor. Gross sexual exploitation, much nudity, mindless cartoonish violence, and sporadic rough language. O (R)

Class of '74 (1973) Three aggressive college coeds teach a fourth how to dispel memories of harsh parents and develop into a sexually liberated woman. Directed by Arthur Marks and Mack Bing, the low-budget package grossly exploits its intended young audience. O (R)

Claudine (1974) Diahann Carroll stars as a welfare mother of six, with James Earl Jones as a sanitation man who likes being her lover but who cannot cope with the idea of becoming her husband. Directed by John Berry, it is an interesting and at times dramatically compelling attempt to create a compassionate, realistic picture of black city-life tempered with both humor and bitterness. Some raunchy humor with street vocabulary to match. A-III (PG)

Clay Pigeon (1971) Returned Vietnam war hero (Tom Stern) resents a ruthless narcotics agent (Telly Savalas) setting him up in order to nab LA's top dope-dealer, especially when it causes the death of some of the vet's playmates. Also produced and directed by Stern, the result is full of pretense and good intentions, but empty of real achievement. Though against hard drugs, it is in favor of soft ones. Some nudity and rough language. O (R)

Clay Pigeons (1998) Smug black comedy in which a Montana gas station attendant (Joaquin Phoenix) finds himself framed for murders by his friend, his slutty lover, and a serial killer (Vince Vaughn) who wanders into town. Director David Dobkin's slick story can't disguise its implausibilities by piling up the corpses, then delivering a pat solution. Jokey depiction of sexual violence, a suicide, several murders, sexual encounters with nudity and profanity, and constant profanity and rough language. O (R)

Clean and Sober (1988) Gutsy drama directed by Glenn Gordon Caron chronicles the toll of alcohol and cocaine addiction on a successful sales executive (Michael Keaton) and his subsequent slow, painful road to recovery. Realistic characterization by Keaton takes him from criminal behavior and denial to fighting his dependency with the help of some recovering addicts (M. Emmet Walsh and Kathy Baker) and a hard-nosed detox counselor (Morgan Freeman). Much locker-room language, some explicit scenes of drug and alcohol abuse, and brief nudity. A-III (R)

Clean Slate (1994) Affable vehicle for comic Dana Carvey, who plays an amnesia-prone private eye bluffing his way through a danger-laden case involving a duplicitous beauty (Valeria Golina), a murderous mobster (Michael Gambon), and a stolen coin worth millions. Director Mick Jackson maintains a breezy tempo in a goofy plot that hits as often as it misses its comic targets. Fleeting violence, implied affairs, and an instance of rough language. A-III (PG-13)

Clear and Present Danger (1994) Classy political thriller in which a top CIA official (Harrison Ford) discovers that he is being set up to take the blame when the president (Donald Moffat) approves an illegal covert military operation (under Willem Dafoe) against a Colombian drug cartel. Director Phillip Noyce balances a dense plot with rich characterizations, lean performances, taut editing, and intriguing moral ambiguities for a crackling good tale of suspense. Intermittent intense violence and an instance of rough language. A-III (PG-13)

Cleopatra (1963) Lumbering Hollywood epic of suds along the Nile, as Egypt's queen (Elizabeth Taylor) makes a conquest of Julius Caesar (Rex Harrison), then after his assassination ensnares his avenger, Mark Antony (Richard Burton), but both commit suicide when cornered by the legions of Octavius (Roddy McDowall). Director Joseph L. Mankiewicz manages to hold interest for the first hour, chiefly in Harrison's portrayal of a man consumed by his ambitions, but the next three seem interminable as the gassy love story bogs down in tedium and the visual spectacle wears thin, save for the sea battle at Actium. Stylized violence, sexual situations, and much sexual innuendo. A-III (br)

Cleopatra (1972) Japanese cartoon for adults retells the story of the Egyptian queen, but its main interest is in the mangled pronunciations of historical names and observing the color scheme used for the animation. Directed by Osamu Tezula and Eilichi Yamamoto, the movie's sexual appeal centers mostly in topless cartoon characters and a few mildly erotic abstractions. O (nr)

Cleopatra Jones (1973) Black adventuress (towering Tamara Dobson) is used by the US government to shake up the illegal drug traffic worldwide, but most of the action unfolds in the LA Watts neighborhood as Cleo carries out a personal vendetta. Directed by Jack Starrett, the movie goes down pretty easily as light, action-packed adult entertainment. A-III (PG)

Cleopatra Jones and the Casino of Gold (1975) Tamara Dobson, tall, black, and beautiful, is the main ingredient of a plot whose chief villain is the Dragon Lady (Stella Stevens). Directed by Chuck Bail, it features extravagant violence with a bit of sexual exploitation thrown in for bad measure. O (R)

Clerks (1994) Raunchy gutter-talk comedy about a day in a New Jersey convenience store whose bored cashier (Brian O'Halloran) passes the time in graphic sexual conversations with a cretinous buddy (Jeff Anderson), as well as past and present lovers (Lisa Spoonhauer and Marilyn Ghigliotti). Writer-director Kevin Smith presents a limited assortment of young adults, including drug users and sellers, all of whom regard promiscuity as casual fun to be enjoyed without thought of commitment or consequences. Extensive graphic descriptions of oral sex, positive view of teenage sexual relationships, off-screen necrophilia, brief drug abuse, and constant rough language. O (R)

Client, The (1994) Indifferent thriller from the John Grisham bestseller in which an 11-year-old (Brad Renfro) with information about a mob murder turns to a novice lawyer (Susan Sarandon) for protection from hit-men out to silence him, as well as from an aggressive US attorney (Tommy Lee Jones) determined to pry the truth from the fearful boy. Directed by Joel Schumacher, the story is moderately interesting and well-acted, yet doesn't adequately build enough suspense to qualify as riveting viewing. Some violence and recurring menace and profanity. A-III (PG-13)

Cliffhanger (1993) A former member of the Rocky Mountain Rescue team (Sylvester Stallone) and his estranged girlfriend (Janine Turner) attempt to save a colleague (Michael Rooker) who's been captured by a murderous bandit gang (led by John Lithgow) stranded on a mountain peak. Director Renny Harlin's relentlessly contrived action fantasy ultimately overdoes the violence with brutal savagery and gruesome humor. Excessive violence and much rough language. O (R)

Clifford (1994) Dismally dumb comedy about a devilish 10-year-old (Martin Short in kiddy clothes) making life miserable over the course of a week for his babysitting uncle (Charles Grodin), who wants to impress his fiancé (Mary Steenburgen) with how much he loves children. Director Paul Flaherty fails to produce any laughs from the script's witless, unamusing situations. Mild comic violence, fleeting ethnographic nudity, and a few instances of profanity. A-II (PG)

Climax, The (1967) Italian satire about a polygamist (Ugo Tognazzi), happily married to three women and raising three sets of families. Equally devoted to each, he dies of sheer exhaustion. Deftly directed by Pietro Germi, the black comedy pushes a rather silly male sex fantasy to its absurd conclusion. A-III (nr)

Clive of India (1935) Sanitized life of Robert Clive (1725-74), who made his fortune with the East India Company by driving the French from southern India and establishing British rule, but leaving him with a reputation besmirched by charges of corruption. The sweep of Empire is mostly off-camera, as is his devoted wife (Loretta Young), giving Ronald Colman little to do in the role of Clive except brood, posture, and declaim. Directed by Richard Boleslawski. Some stylized violence. A-II (br)

Cloak and Dagger (1946) Midwestern professor (Gary Cooper) is sent to Switzerland during WW II to spy on German attempts to develop an atomic bomb. With Lilli Palmer as the love interest, director Fritz Lang almost succeeds in making something more than another espionage thriller, though Ring Lardner, Jr.'s, screenplay offers little more than wartime intrigue. A-II (br)

Cloak and Dagger (1984) Lonely young boy (Henry Thomas) escapes from reality by playing super-spy, but when reality obtrudes and he witnesses a murder, nobody will believe him — except the killers. Directed by Richard Franklin, it's well-acted, fast-paced escapist fare, but its violent situation makes it questionable entertainment for pre-teens. A-II (PG)

Clock, The (1945) Arriving in New York City on a two-day pass, an Army corporal (Robert Walker) bumps into a nice young woman (Judy Garland) who spends her Sunday showing him some of the sights and, after a late night dinner, they help a milkman (James Gleason) finish his route, get separated in the subway, reunite in Penn Station, and decide to get married. Director Vincent Minnelli's wartime romance is too sweet to be charming, but the couple's small-town innocence shines in the big city setting and one wishes them well, even after the predictably soggy ending. Romantic complications ending in a impulsive wedding. A-II (br)

Clockers (1995) Determined to get at the truth of what is behind the murder of a Brooklyn drug dealer, a dogged homicide detective (Harvey Keitel) disregards the confession of a hard-working family man (Isaiah Washington) and puts the screws on his younger dope-pushing brother (Mekhi Phifer). Directed by Spike Lee from Richard Price's gritty ghetto novel, the harrowing morality tale indicts black-on-black violence and graphically dramatizes the ripple effects of drug dealing on an entire neighborhood. Numerous shots of bloodied corpses, several murders, brutal beatings, and constant rough language. A-IV (R)

Clockmaker, The (1976) A good-hearted, middle-aged clockmaker (Philippe Noiret) is visited one morning by a police inspector (Jean Rochefort) and told that his son is wanted for murder. Though the father has never understood his son, he stands by him at the trial and afterwards. Bertrand Tavernier directs what is essentially a character study of the father without any sentimentality, yet with sufficient quiet charm and convincing performances to earn one's interest. A-II (nr)

Clockwatchers (1998) Office drama in which four temporary secretaries bond, then are gradually torn apart when they come under suspicion after other employees' personal items begin disappearing. Director Jill Sprecher's character study proceeds sluggishly but succeeds in exploring the frustrations of being treated as a disposable corporate cog. Sexual references, petty thievery, a few profanities, and an instance of rough language. A-III (PG-13)

Clockwise (1986) British import about a headmaster (John Cleese) whose neurotic obsession with punctuality makes him suffer inordinately through a series of complications impeding his attempt to arrive at a headmasters' convention in time to deliver his presidential address. Dry wit, gentle humor, and general silliness pervade a farce illustrating the futility of a rigid approach to life. A-II (PG)

Clockwork Orange (1972) Produced, directed, and written by Stanley Kubrick, the urban scene of the 1962 Anthony Burgess novel is ruled by day by the forces of law and order, and by punk teenagers like Alex (Malcolm McDowell), the central character, and his pals by night. The Kubrick-Burgess message about the human right to a free will is not very new or startling, and only Burgess's marvelous language and Kubrick's grandiose style have made it seem at all fresh and significant. Excessive violence and nudity in a sexual context. O (X/R)

Cloportes (1966) Uneven French gangster movie in which a Paris underworld character (Lino Ventura) takes his revenge on those who left him in the lurch during a robbery. Directed by Pierre Granier-Deferre, The film's the acting is superior, but its treatment of the criminal world and its liberal use of nudity are excessive. O (br)

Close Encounters of the Third Kind (1977) Richard Dreyfuss stars in director Steven Spielberg's epic about UFOs and the humanistic, hopeful, and, for some, religious theme of mankind's close encounter with an extra-galactic life-form. The scenes involving simple person-to-person relationships may be somewhat flat, but the movie boasts some dazzling special effects and is tinged with a feeling of awe rare in science-fiction works. Some effects might frighten the very young. A-II (PG)

Close to Eden (1992) Dwelling in a one-room hut on the steppes of China's Inner Mongolia, an isolated herding family (Badema and Bayaertu) find that life is not as simple as it was for their ancestors when the outside world intrudes in the form of a stranded Russian truck driver (Vladimir Gostukhin) and the government's population policy. Directed by Nikita Mikhalkov, the French-Russian co-production contrasts the natural rhythm of life on the vast treeless steppes with the inevitable changes brought by the country's growing industrialization, whose impact on one Mongol family is shown with charm, good humor, and respect for the human spirit and nature's beauty. Subtitles. Some discussion of contraception, graphic shots of a lamb being slaughtered, and occasional rough language. A-III (nr)

Closely Watched Trains (1968) Czechoslovakian director Jiri Menzel's story about a young man's blundering search for maturity seems to imply that the transition to manhood cannot be made without the experience of sex. A-IV (br)

Closer, The (1991) Forced into early retirement, a tenacious salesman's (Danny Aiello) strained relationships with his family (Diane Baker, Justine Bateman, and Tim Quill) come to a head over Thanksgiving dinner as he interviews two potential successors (Michael Pare and Joe Cortese). Sharp dialogue but unfinished characterizations mark director Dimitri Logothetis's well-acted drama of what price ambition. Some rough language. A-II (PG-13)

Closet Land (1991) A government interrogator (Alan Rickman) uses psychological terror and physical torture on an author of children's books (Madeleine Stowe) in hopes of obtaining a false confession of subversive activities. Writer-director Radha Bharadwaj dramatizes the violent methods of a repressive regime in an intimate one-room setting that, despite fine acting, seems better suited to the confines of a two-character stage play. Constant menace, a few depictions of torture, and some sexual innuendo. A-III (R)

Clouded Yellow, The (1951) British mystery thriller in which a former secret-service agent (Trevor Howard) helps a woman wanted for murder (Jean Simmons) escape the police, until the real culprit tries to kill her. Directed by Ralph Thomas, the plot gets off to a slow start, but the tension builds in the taut chase sequences through northern England's Lake District, until the killer is unmasked in a twist ending. More menace than violence. A-II (br)

Clouds over Europe (1939) Amusing British spy caper joins eccentric counter-spy Ralph Richardson, newspaper reporter Valerie Hobson, and test pilot Laurence Olivier in solving the mystery of military planes disappearing on test flights. Director Tim Whelan's comic-book adventure of villainous agents with a secret ray gun are no match for the sterling trio and their tongue-in-cheek endeavors. Stylized violence. A-I (br)

Clowns, The (1971) Federico Fellini directs a highly imaginative documentary about the disappearance of laughter and fantasy in modern life, concentrating on the tradition of the circus and various kinds of clowns, citing them as sources of his own cinematic inspiration. Most viewers will find more than enough to satisfy their curiosity about the subject and will be abundantly entertained as well. A-I (G)

Club Paradise (1986) Robin Williams and numerous other comics try to create some fun and frolic in the Jamaican sun. The mild satire of the Club Med scene features Jimny Cliff, his music, and predictable drug and sex references which do very little for the funny bone. A-III (PG-13)

Clue (1985) Parker Brothers's board game comes to life in a mildly entertaining screen version that is being circulated with three different endings. Although for some it will be nostalgic fun, slapstick comedy prevails. A-II (PG)

Clueless (1995) Teen-targeted comedy about a rich, popular Beverly Hills high-school student (Alicia Silverstone) who blissfully plays Cupid for friends and teachers alike before deciding to sleep with her college-student stepbrother (Paul Rudd). Writer-director Amy Heckerling's satire about self-obsessed teenagers brightly captures their inexperienced perspective but leaves the impression that there is nothing wrong with teenagers experimenting with sex, drugs, and alcohol. Ridicule of virginity, implied affairs, and casual substance abuse by adolescents. O (PG-13)

Cluny Brown (1946) Slight but trim romantic comedy set in 1938 England, where a plumber's niece (Jennifer Jones) is put in service to "learn her place" as parlor maid for a posh family, whose houseguest is an unconventional Czech refugee (Charles Boyer). Director Ernst Lubitsch has some gentle fun with British class distinctions and stuffy manners, buttressed by plenty of plot misunderstandings and witty dialogue, but the chief attraction is the affinity between bemused older man (Boyer) and the naive young woman of the title. Romantic situations. A-II (br)

Coal Miner's Daughter (1980) Sissy Spacek, who does all her own singing, gives a warm and utterly winning performance as Loretta Lynn. In this semi-biographical story, director Michael Apted depicts her life from poverty and obscurity in the Kentucky hills to undreamed-of riches and success. Tommy Lee Jones plays Loretta's husband who escorts her along the rocky road to stardom. Frank language about sex and a wedding-night sequence would rule out younger children. A-II (PG)

Coast to Coast (1980) Mediocre chase comedy with Dyan Cannon and Robert Blake as an odd couple — she's a runaway from a mental institution and he's a hard-luck trucker — who make their way across the country pursued by various characters with hostile intentions. Directed by Joseph Sargent, the slapstick grows tedious and often abrasive. Some rough language. A-III (PG)

Cobb (1994) After a sportswriter (Robert Wuhl) accepts an offer to write a book about pioneering baseball star Ty Cobb (Tommy Lee Jones), he spends months in the cantankerous company of the dying 72-year-old man, both fascinated with his greatness as an athlete and repelled by his aberrant, mean-spirited behavior, until he must finally decide whether to print the unvarnished truth about the man or preserve the legend of a sports hero. Writer-director Ron Shelton focuses on the growing friendship between these two completely opposite characters, though some viewers may not care to subject themselves to such detailed treatment of a sociopath's private life. Frequent outbursts of angry violence, sexual situations, bigoted references, much rough language, and occasional profanity. A-IV (R)

Cobra (1986) Sylvester Stallone as the ace crime-stopper of the Los Angeles Police Department single-handedly blows away an army of cultist serial murderers in director George Cosmatos's excessively violent treatment to the vigilante spirit. O (R)

Cobra, The (1968) Failed adventure melodrama directed by Mario Sequi about an American agent (Dana Andrews) fighting an Oriental drug-smuggling ring. Fairly heavy violence and sexual innuendo. A-III (br)

Cobra Woman (1944) Adventure fantasy directed by Robert Siodmak in which a South Seas islander (Jon Hall) tracks his kidnapped fiancé (Maria Montez) to Cobra Island, where her wicked twin sister (Montez again) rules as high priestess over an oppressed people, whom he tries to liberate with some help from his friends (Sabu and Lon Chaney, Jr.). Dated escapist fare with the usual stylized violence and romantic complications. A-II (br)

Coca-Cola Kid, The (1985) American whiz-kid troubleshooter (Eric Roberts) for Coca-Cola arrives in Australia determined to boost sales but is stymied by one small town that is content with its own local soft drink. In visiting its manufacturer, the American discovers a competitor who is every bit as fanatical as himself. Directed by Dusan Makavejev, the movie begins with some satiric promise but becomes unglued midway and spins off in several different directions. Despite some good acting and clever touches, it's a disappointing failure. Some nudity and a needlessly graphic bedroom scene. O (nr)

Cockeyed Cowboys of Calico County, The (1970) Lumbering blacksmith (Dan Blocker) in a small Western town is bilked when he sends for a mail-order bride, and sympathetic townsfolk (Mickey Rooney, Jim Backus, Wally Cox, Stubby Kaye) enlist the aid of a local dance-hall girl (Nanette Fabray) to take her place. Director Tony Leader's silly charade ends in true love. Youngsters may enjoy the Western setting and broad acting. A-I (G)

Cockleshell Heroes, The (1956) After rigorous training under an unorthodox commander (Jose Ferrer) and his by-the-book subordinate (Trevor Howard), 10 Royal Marines use canoes to slip past the German defenses guarding Bordeaux's harbor and mine the naval vessels moored there. Also directed by Ferrer, the fact-based WW II story moves haltingly until the unit reaches its objective and a fiery climax. Wartime violence. A-II (br)

Cocktail (1988) Young New York bartender (Tom Cruise) learns the ropes about life and love from a heavy drinking, womanizing mentor (Bryan Brown) but manages to jump off the fast track before it's too late for honest success and a good woman (Elizabeth Shue). Australian director Roger Donaldson's colossal bore lacks interesting characterizations and dramatic credibility. Sexual promiscuity, unwed pregnancy, excessive alcohol consumption, off-camera suicide, and some profanity. A-III (R)

Cocoon (1985) Three old Rover Boys, young at heart, become young in body as well when they take a dip in a swimming pool being used as a rejuvenating force by some genial extraterrestrials. Good acting from some veterans, especially Don Ameche, but the plot premise is weakly contrived and the view of rejuvenation banally condescending. Directed by Ron Howard, the movie reinforces the stereotypes of old age as sexless and of women as passive. Some locker-room humor and an emphasis upon the sexual aspect of rejuvenation. A-II (PG-13)

Cocoon: The Return (1988) Disappointing sequel sees the temporary return to Earth of the original's aliens and senior citizens (Don Ameche, Wilford Brimley, Hume Cronyn, Gwen Verdon, Maureen Stapleton, and Jessica Tandy) who delightfully debunk aging stereotypes. Director Daniel Petrie has trouble pulling various plot threads together, and the rescue of an alien cocoon is suspenseless. Some locker-room language and mild sexual innuendoes. A-II (PG)

Code of Silence (1985) Chuck Norris stars as a Chicago detective who uses his martial-arts skills to combat evil. Directed by Andy Davis, it's fairly standard action fare, though a cut above Norris's earlier efforts. Violence and profanity. A-III (R)

Code of the Fearless (1939) Formula Western directed by Raymond K. Johnson in which a singing Texas Ranger (Fred Scott) pretends to break the law in order to join an outlaw band and arrest its leader (John Merton). Vigorous fistfights and unconvincing gunplay. A-I (br)

Code of the Secret Service (1939) B-budget action programmer follows federal agent Brass Bancroft (Ronald Reagan) and his sidekick Gabby (Eddie Foy, Jr.) south of the border as they smash a counterfeiting ring holed up in an abandoned monastery. Directed by Noel Smith, it's a pallid mix of juvenile theatrics and dated ethnic stereotypes. Stylized violence. A-I (br)

Coffy (1973) Black exploitation picture of a woman (Pam Grier) who seeks revenge on the drug pushers who turned her little sister into a catatonic hospital patient. Her weapons range from sawed-off shotguns to her full-blown figure, which lets the sex and violence crowds have it both ways. Directed by Jack Hill, it is a low-grade exploitation piece. O (R)

Cold Comfort Farm (1996) Suddenly destitute in the 1930s Depression, a crisply optimistic London socialite (Kate Beckinsale) moves in with a near-dozen gloomy, eccentric relatives on a dilapidated farm, turning all their lives upside down and right side up in short order. Director John Schlesinger's sprightly comedy of manners deftly pokes fun at rich and poor alike in a delightfully wacky send-up of life on the farm. Brief sexual innuendo and an instance of profanity. A-III (PG)

Cold Feet (1989) Quirky black comedy about a cache of stolen emeralds and a trio of eccentric con-artists, one of whom (Keith Carradine) runs out and hides on his honest brother's Montana horse ranch until tracked down by his two cohorts (Sally Kirkland and Tom Waits). Throughout the course of the movie's wacky encounters, director Robert Dornhelm shows empathy for his offbeat characters and a feel for the heartland. In the end, family values remain intact, but there is much profanity laced with sexual vulgarities and some grisly violence. A-III (R)

Cold Sweat (1974) Formula crime story about a Korean War veteran (Charles Bronson) living in the south of France, where some old Army buddies (led by James Mason) try to force him into a drug smuggling caper by holding his wife (Liv Ullman) and teen stepdaughter hostage. Directed by Terence Young, the French-Italian co-production is weakly plotted, lethargically acted, and poorly dubbed. Stylized violence, menacing situations, some coarse language, and momentary nudity. A-III (PG)

Cold Turkey (1971) Led by the local minister (Dick Van Dyke), a small town in Iowa accepts an offer of $25 million from a cigarette adman (Bob Newhart) provided the townspeople stop smoking for 30 days. Director Norman Lear sets out to satirize rural America, Madison Avenue, and all points in between, but the movie's slight sense of humor is overworked to the point of tedium. Some vulgar language, tasteless sexual references, and snide portrayal of a venal, self-serving clergyman. A-III (GP)

Colditz Story, The (1957) Fact-based WW II drama set in a German castle serving as a prison for Polish,

Dutch, French, and British POWs who have tried to escape other camps. Directed by Guy Hamilton, the 1954 British production balances the boredom of prison life with ingenious plans of escape, particularly that of British officer John Mills. A-I (br)

Cole Younger, Gunfighter (1958) Formula Western directed by R.G. Springsteen with outlaw Younger (Frank Lovejoy) saving an innocent man (James Best) charged with murdering carpetbaggers in 1873 Texas. Frontier violence. A-I (br)

Collector, The (1965) Glossy adaptation of the John Fowles thriller about a warped butterfly collector (Terence Stamp) who tries to make a young woman (Samantha Egger) fall in love with him while he holds her captive. Directed by William Wyler, the plight of a woman imprisoned by a psychopath capable of destroying what he cannot have is properly unsettling. Though treated with restraint, its study of a disturbed individual is not casual entertainment. A-IV (br)

Color Me Dead (1969) Australian production about a man (Tom Tryon) who becomes unwittingly involved in an uranium swindle and is then given a dose of slow-working poison, a plot device allowing him to spend the rest of the movie looking for his own murderer. Director Eddie Davis's remake of **D.O.A.** (1949) is slow-moving and not very inventive, but at least the unfamiliar Australian locales give it some interest. Permissive attitude toward sex and a nightclub striptease make it mature fare. A-III (R)

Color of Money, The (1986) An aging poolroom pro (Paul Newman) is obsessed with turning a young pool player (Tom Cruise) into a champion. Directed by Martin Scorsese, this disappointing sequel to **The Hustler** lets its conflict of personal integrity vs. the lure of money get lost in the clash of male egos. Brief nudity and extensive profanity. A-III (R)

Color of Night (1994) Trashy potboiler in which a psychologist (Bruce Willis) has a steamy affair with an aspiring actress (Jane March) while trying to save himself from being killed by one of his five group-therapy patients. With its emphasis on sadistic violence and promiscuity, director Richard Rush's ludicrous melodrama displays a slick, sick sense of humor and reduces troubled characters to empty caricatures. Some gruesome violence, sexual encounters with nudity, and much rough language. O (R)

Color Purple, The (1985) Steven Spielberg's glossy screen version of Alice Walker's Pulitzer Prize-winning novel about a young black woman (Whoopi Goldberg) growing up in rural Georgia between the two world wars. The screen adaptation lacks cohesion and unwittingly reinforces damaging racial and sexual stereotypes. O (PG-13)

Colorado Territory (1949) Gritty Western about an escaped badman (Joel McCrea) agreeing to pull one last job — a train robbery that goes awry, leaving him rejected by the woman he loves (Dorothy Malone) and helped by a woman (Virginia Mayo) for whom he feels nothing. Director Raoul Walsh's remake of **High Sierra** uses the Western setting well, but the characters and relationships lack the dramatic weight of the original. Stylized violence and sexual innuendo. A-III (br)

Colors (1988) Violent crime movie explores the conflict between a volatile rookie cop (Sean Penn) and his laid-back veteran partner (Robert Duvall) as they battle youth gangs in East Los Angeles. Realistically directed by Dennis Hopper, with gritty cinematography by Haskell Wexler, the emphasis is often less on the cops than on the chaotic and complex subculture of the street gangs. Many scenes of extremely intense violence, heavy drug use, a few graphic sexual encounters, and brief nudity. O (R)

Colossus: The Forbin Project (see: **The Forbin Project**)

Colossus of New York, The (1958) When a brilliant scientist (Ross Martin) dies in a tragic accident, his surgeon-father (Otto Kruger) keeps the son's brain alive, then places it in control of an oversized robot fashioned by his other son (Robert Hutton), but the robot runs amok until, like the Golem, it is stopped by a child. Directed by Eugene Lourie, the pulp proceedings are memorable only for the robot's eerie appearance and laser-beam eyes. Stylized violence and a rather ghoulish premise. A-II (br)

Colt .45 (1950) Formula Western directed by Edwin L. Marin is set in the 1850s when an outlaw (Zachary Scott) steals two of the first Colt repeating pistols from a salesman (Randolph Scott), who tracks him down with the help of some Indians (led by Chief Thundercloud) and the wife (Ruth Roman) of one of the outlaw's gang (Lloyd Bridges). Frontier violence. A-I (br)

Column South (1953) Routine Western directed by Frederick de Cordova in which a cavalry officer (Audie Murphy) tries to prevent his commanding officer (Ray Collins) from stirring up an Indian uprising on the eve of the Civil War. Frontier violence. A-I (br)

Coma (1978) Screen version of Robin Cook's novel about a spunky Boston doctor (Genevieve Bujold) who uncovers a murderous scheme involving trafficking in human organs. Michael Crichton directs a suspenseful, well-acted drama with a relatively sophisticated plot and some rather graphic operating room scenes, incidental nudity, and the casual treatment of an affair. A-III (PG)

Comanche (1956) Standard Western directed by George Sherman in which a US Cavalry scout (Dana Andrews) tries to arrange peace talks with the chief (Kent Smith) of a warring Comanche tribe while battling white troublemakers, renegade Indians, and a testy woman (Linda Cristal) he rescues along the way. Frontier violence and contrasting stereotypes of noble and savage Indians. A-I (br)

Comanche Station (1960) Lone cowboy (Randolph Scott) rescues a woman (Nancy Gates) taken captive by Comanches and gets her safely back to her husband, despite running into a badman (Claude Akins) along the way. Directed by Budd Boetticher, the story starts and ends well, but the journey between bogs down in the two men's past rivalry. Frontier violence and muted sexual implications. A-I (br)

Comanche Territory (1950) Formula Western directed by George Sherman in which frontiersman Jim Bowie (MacDonald Carey) and a temperamental friend (Maureen O'Hara) try to keep the peace by stopping greedy whites from mining silver on Comanche land. Mild frontier violence and romantic complications. A-II (br)

Comancheros, The (1961) Outlandish but colorful Western in which a Texas Ranger (John Wayne) and a fugitive gambler from New Orleans (Stuart Whitman) join forces in the 1840s to take on a highly organized band of white renegades in league with Comanche raiders. Director Micahel Curtiz adds some romance (Ina Balin) and a lot of rough humor to the action formula with only middling results, though Lee Marvin has a memorable bit as a half-scalped gunrunner. Assorted stylized violence and much horseplay. A-I (br)

Come Back Charleston Blue (1972) Raymond St. Jacques and Godfrey Cambridge repeat their **Cotton Comes to Harlem** roles as two detectives in a caper movie about a black gang's attempt to wrest control of the Harlem drug traffic from white mobsters. Under Mark Warrren's direction, there is a good deal of violence and killing but enough authentic references to ghetto life to cloak the escapist action fantasy with a pathos that was probably not intended. A-III (PG)

Come Back, Little Sheba (1952) Strong story from William Inge's play about a middle-aged housewife (Shirley Booth) and her chiropractor husband (Burt Lancaster), a recovering alcoholic who goes off the wagon when a pert college student (Terry Moore) becomes their boarder. Director Daniel Mann keeps emotions churning as the couple's sad past and the harrowing consequences of alcoholism slowly emerge, but what remains most memorable is Booth's Oscar-winning performance as the pathetic wife. Implied premarital relations, sexual situations, and alcoholic violence. A-III (br)

Come Back to Me (see: **Doll Face**)

Come Blow Your Horn (1963) Feeble romantic comedy in which a Manhattan playboy (Frank Sinatra) initiates his kid brother (Tony Bill) in the life of a swinging bachelor but is so appalled at the result that he quits philandering to marry his true love (Barbara Rush). Directed by Bud Yorkin from the Neil Simon play, the brothers' bickering parents (Lee J. Cobb and Molly Picon) add some shrill ethnic humor to the otherwise stale proceedings. Sexual situations and innuendo. A-III (br)

Come Fill the Cup (1951) Tough-minded story of an alcoholic newsman (James Cagney) who sobers up with some help from an ex-drunk (James Gleason), gets his old job back, and winds up helping the publisher's nephew (Gig Young) beat the bottle and a murderous mobster (Sheldon Leonard). Directed by Gordon Douglas, Cagney gives a standout performance in a busy melodrama which stretches credibility but never loses interest. Scenes of alcoholic excess, stylized violence, and romantic complications. A-III (br)

Come Fly with Me (1963) Slick romantic fluff directed by Henry Levin in which airline stewardesses (Pamela Tiffin, Delores Hart, and Lois Nettleton) on a flight from New York to Paris get involved with prospective husbands (Hugh O'Brian, Karl Boehm, and Karl Malden respectively). Romantic complications. A-II (br)

Come Have Coffee with Us (1973) Italian black comedy about a middle-aged man (Ugo Tognazzi) who decides to settle down and marries an aging, grotesque heiress. His virile prowess eventually extends to her two equally unattractive sisters, but when the maid catches his eye, nature strikes him down in an ending that is both fitting and hilarious. Directed by Alberto Lattuada, the rise and fall of this figure of smug satisfaction will not please those who object to earthy humor. A-IV (nr)

Come Play with Me (see: **Grazie Zia**)

Come See the Paradise (1990) A Japanese-American (Tamlyn Tomita) defies her family by marrying a Caucasian (Dennis Quaid) who is drafted at the start of WW II, while she and their daughter are forced to live in an internment camp with thousands of other Japanese-Americans. Director Alan Parker sheds some light on this shameful episode in American history but gets bogged down in the interracial love story which is not the movie's real focus. A very restrained sexual encounter, references to suicide, occasional rough language, and a flash of nudity. A-III (R)

Come September (1961) Flagging romantic comedy about a rich but dull American (Rock Hudson) and his girlfriend (Gina Lollobrigida) who turn up unannounced at his Italian villa only to discover it's being run as a hotel by his caretaker (Walter Slezak). Directed by Robert Mulligan, the clumsy comic premise leads to all manner of contrived misunderstandings, none of them very amusing, until an unconvincing moral ending. Thinly veiled sexual innuendo. A-II (br)

Come Spy with Me (1967) Failed spy spoof directed by Marshall Stone about an agent (Troy Donahue) in the Caribbean who joins a scuba diving contest as a blind while he investigates several murders. Stylized violence and mild sexual innuendo. A-II (br)

Come to the Stable (1949) Sentimental but amusing picture from Clare Booth Luce's story of two French nuns (Loretta Young and Celeste Holm) trying to establish a hospital in New England with some help from an eccentric artist (Elsa Lanchester) and a cynical songwriter (Hugh Marlowe). Director Henry Koster gets some smiles from the nuns' adapting to American ways and the bemused reactions of the locals to the newcomers' otherworldly simplicity, with mostly heartwarming results. Unpretentious, generally high-minded fun. A-I (br)

Comedians, The (1967) Multi-leveled tragicomedy about a man (Richard Burton) who finds himself involved in a plot to overthrow a ruthless dictatorship in Haiti. Strong cast (Alec Guinness, Peter Ustinov, Elizabeth Taylor, Lillian Gish, Cicely Tyson, and James Earl Jones), thoughtful script by Graham Greene from his own novel, and assured direction by Peter Glenville result in a powerful movie about personal commitment in the context of political injustice. Some brutal violence and much tension. A-III (br)

Comes a Horseman (1978) Somber, slow-moving Western set in 1945, when a small rancher (Jane Fonda) stands up to the encroachments of a cattle baron (Jason Robards) by enlisting the help of a discharged serviceman (James Caan). The best parts of director Alan J. Pakula's movie are its Colorado setting and the depiction of the warming relationship between Fonda and Caan, but the film's violence and the nature of their relationship rule out younger viewers. A-III (PG)

Cometogether (1971) Made in Italy by Saul Swimmer, the story of an offbeat *menage-a-trois* is a compendium of bad production techniques that serve only to emphasize the sordid characters and relationships without satisfying those voyeurs who expect the visuals to exploit the potential of the subject matter. O (R)

Comfort and Joy (1984) The melancholy-comic chronicle of the worst Christmas week ever spent by an aging Scottish disc jockey (Bill Peterson) who, deserted by his mistress, throws himself into his work and becomes involved as mediator in a local ice-cream war. Directed by Bill Forsyth, there's not much of interest here except for the Glasgow locale. A-II (PG)

Comfort of Strangers, The (1991) While on holiday in Venice, a young English couple (Natasha Richardson and Rupert Everett) are entertained by a mysterious older couple (Christopher Walken and Helen Mirren) who have very sinister designs on the young man. Directed by Paul Schrader from Harold Pinter's screenplay, the belabored pace and morbidly aberrant characterizations in this exasperating, erotic drama greatly detract from its theme of innocence corrupted. Fairly restrained sexual encounters with some nudity, heavy sadomasochistic references, occasional rough language, and minimal violence. A-IV (R)

Comic, The (1969) Although this Dick Van Dyke movie is about a silent-screen comedian, it is not a comedy. Van Dyke's performance as Billy Bright incorporates some unamusing parodies of physical comedy from the slapstick era, but Carl Reiner's direction lacks any sense of nostalgia or even sentimentality in what is essentially a maudlin presentation of Bright's various problems with alcohol and women. A-III (PG)

Coming Apart (1969) Rip Torn plays a psychiatrist who uses a hidden camera to record his own disintegration through a series of sexual encounters with neurotic women. The characters, however grotesque, are recognizably human rather than sex-fantasy objects, but director Milton Moses Ginsberg hopelessly dilutes any potential insights into psychological anguish and need by indulging in sheer sensationalism. O (nr)

Coming Home (1978) When a Marine captain (Bruce Dern) is assigned to Vietnam in 1968, his wife (Jane Fonda) volunteers to work in a veterans' hospital, where she falls in love with a paraplegic Vietnam casualty (Jon Voight). Good performances by Fonda and Voight and fine camerawork by Haskell Wexler, but director Hal Ashby's movie lacks the political sophistication to examine the war issue and concentrates instead only on the theme of romantic love. Brief nudity in a sexual context and acceptance of adultery. O (R)

Coming to America (1988) The pampered heir to an African throne (Eddie Murphy) travels to New York to find a bride he can both love and respect — a fast-food restaurant owner's daughter (Shari Headley) — but his parents (James Earl Jones and Madge Sinclair) have an arranged marriage all set up for him. Director John Landis spices up this Cinderella story with lush African sets and production numbers. Some nudity and much profanity (but not from Murphy). A-III (R)

Command, The (1954) Pale Western in which a doctor (Guy Madison) is the only officer left to command the cavalry squadron escorting a wagon train through hostile Indian country. Directed by David Butler, the hokey proceedings include an outbreak of chicken pox and the doctor's unorthodox military tactics, which include dressing some troopers in women's outfits. Frontier violence. A-I (br)

Command Decision (1948) The sacrifice of American bombing crews in daylight raids over Germany weighs heavily on the general (Clark Gable) responsible for selecting the targets. The setting is an airbase in England, where the necessity of launching a series of risky attacks is questioned by the general's fellow officers (Walter Pidgeon, Brian Donlevy, Ray Collins, and John McIntire), a congressman (Edward Arnold), and a war correspondent (Charles Bickford). Directed by Sam Wood. Conflicting views of patriotism and its cost. A-I (br)

Commandments (1997) Blaming God for his pregnant wife's drowning and other personal tragedies, a distraught widower (Aidan Quinn) vows to break all 10 commandments, in the process falling for his late wife's sister (Courteney Cox) whose marriage to a womanizer (Anthony La Paglia) is on the rocks. Writer-director Daniel Taplitz treats the protagonist's heartfelt loss of faith in jarringly comic terms that become sappy and ultimately ludicrous. Fleeting sexual encounters, brief violence, intermittent rough language, and some profanity. A-III (R)

Commando (1985) When the daughter of a retired Army martial-arts expert (Arnold Schwarzenegger) is kidnapped by a Latin-American strongman to force him to assassinate a political rival, he turns, instead, to assassinating the kidnapper's entire army. Mark Lester's direction has a certain leavening of comic-book humor, but it won't seem especially funny unless you happen to think there is something intrinsically amusing about sudden death. Unrelenting celebration of violence. O (R)

Commandos Strike at Dawn, The (1942) After the German Army occupies Norway in 1940, a fisherman (Paul Muni) assassinates the German commandant of his village, then spots a camouflaged enemy airbase, escapes to Britain, and returns with a commando unit to destroy it. Director John Farrow's wartime morale booster is quite effective in its depiction of innocent villagers (Lillian Gish, Ray Collins, and others) brutalized by a cruel enemy and the bravery of Norwegian patriots in league with their British allies. Wartime violence and much menace. A-I (br)

Commissar (1988) In a small Ukrainian village after the Bolshevik Revolution, a pregnant commissar (Nonna Mordukova) is given shelter by a poor Jewish family. Russian director Aleksandr Askoldov's 1967 movie shows compassion for the family whose lives are threatened by local anti-Semites and by political enemies of the commissar. Subtitles. Some rough language, an intense childbirth scene, and a harrowing anti-Semitic children's game. A-III (nr)

Commitments, The (1991) Soul music, 1960s-style, resurfaces in, of all places, Dublin, when an unemployed Irish youth (Robert Arkins) fashions a band out of an experienced trumpeter (Johnny Murphy) and nine cheeky working-class youngsters. Director Alan Parker's vibrant, gritty movie ultimately goes over the top but not before it has energetically celebrated hope amidst poverty, the vitality of youth, and the power of music. Much rough language, intermittent sexual innuendo, and minimal violence. A-III (R)

Committee, The (1969) Stage revue featuring the antics of eight young West Coast comics was videotaped during a performance and the results were then transferred to color film. Produced and directed by Del Jack, the program consists of 18 sometimes lively skits, often spiked with adult language, that concentrate on exposing the foibles of everyday life, especially of young couples, married and unmarried. Though there are some good laughs, it's for those who appreciate satire even when it misses. A-III (GP)

Companeros! (1972) Italian-Spanish-German production shot mostly in English and set in turn-of-the-century Mexico finds Franco Nero running guns during the revolution. Director Sergio Corbucci clutters the story with plenty of loudly-staged massacres, a fair share of unusual tortures, and a bit of sexual innuendo. A-III (R)

Company of Killers (1970) Van Johnson heads a special police squad trained for unusual assignments, while Ray Milland sets the wheels in motion for a murder to help his financial designs. Routine crime melodrama directed by Jerry Thorpe contains mild doses of violence, sex, and some ambiguous religious themes. A-II (G)

Competition, The (1980) Rival concert pianists (Richard Dreyfuss and Amy Irving) fall in love but have problems because of his sense of insecurity in a romantic melodrama written and directed by Joel Oliansky. Despite good performances, it is but mediocre entertainment marred by crude sexual references and a graphic bedroom scene. O (PG)

Compromising Positions (1985) A former journalist (Susan Sarandon), caught up in an investigation into the murder of a womanizing dentist (Joe Mantegna), does some snooping on her own and comes into conflict with the detective in charge (Raul Julia). Director Frank Perry's shallow, contrived, and unpleasant comedy-mystery leans heavily on crude, sexually oriented humor. A-III (R)

Computer Wore Tennis Shoes, The (1970) Typical Disney comedy in which none-too-bright college student (Kurt Russell) accidentally has his brain computerized and becomes an intellectual phenomenon, who by chance threatens the operations of a racketeer (Cesar Romero). Director Robert Butler's movie is a zany, very superficial comedy intended to amuse youngsters. A-I (G)

Comrade X (1940) Wacky romantic comedy set in Moscow, where an American reporter (Clark Gable) woos a patriotic streetcar conductor (Hedy Lamarr) while trying to keep track of Kremlin intrigues. Director King Vidor's dated spoof of life in the Soviet Union has some very funny moments but not enough to sustain interest in the slapstick plot and belabored East-West romance. Comic political menace and romantic complications. A-II (br)

Con Air (1997) Overly violent action thriller in which a gang of hardened prisoners (led by John Malkovich) seize control of their federal transport plane, unaware that a parolee (Nicolas Cage) on board is undermining their efforts to escape the country. Director Simon West's shrilly overwrought action movie offers only the empty excitement of pumped-up brutality, murder, and deadly chaos. Excessive violence, glamorized mayhem, frequent rough language, and an instance of profanity. O (R)

Conan the Barbarian (1982) Based on a pulp hero's violent exploits in savage prehistoric times, the movie's preliterate narrative ponderously details how the slow-witted Conan (Arnold Schwarzenegger) revenges the slaughter of his parents. John Milius directs with heavy emphasis on brutality, violence, and some graphic sex. O (R)

Conan the Destroyer (1984) Director Richard Fleischer's sequel may be more polished and less gory than the original, but with Arnold Schwarzenegger again in the title role, the result is still nothing more than a lead-footed, muscle-bound costume epic with an extremely high violence quotient. O (PG)

Concert for Bangladesh (1972) Saul Swimmer's documentary record of a landmark benefit concert in New York's Madison Square Garden features the performances of Bob Dylan, Billy Preston, Eric Clapton, Leon Russell, Ravi Shankar, and Ringo Starr, to name a few of those who appeared. A-I (G)

Concorde — Airport '79, The (1979) Another in the series of airport movies with the usual multitude of disasters and film stars (Alain Delon, Susan Blakely, Robert Wagner, et. al.) who can do nothing with the script's ineptness. Directed by David Lowell Rich, it contains harsh language and casual love affairs. O (PG)

Concrete Jungle, The (1982) Low-budget women-in-prison melodrama is directed by Tom De Simone as another exploitative sex-and-violence movie. Much nudity. O (R)

Condemned Women (1938) Formula prison tale directed by Lew Landers focuses on an embittered inmate (Sally Eilers) who falls for the idealistic prison doctor (Louis Hayward), then, thinking her love will bring him disgrace, joins a hardened con (Lee Patrick) in making a jail break. Stylized violence and penal injustices. A-II (br)

Conduct Unbecoming (1975) Set on India's Northwest Frontier in 1878, the honor of the regiment is at stake when a flirtatious widow (Suzannah York) accuses a young subaltern (James Faulkner) of assaulting her. With an idealist (Michael York) appointed to defend him, the movie turns from larger issues of conflicting claims of duty and loyalty and becomes no more than a whodunit of only moderate ingenuity. Directed by Michael Anderson, the movie offers a very talented cast, magnificent locales, and exotic costumes but only mediocre drama. A-III (PG)

Coneheads (1993) Having crash-landed on planet Earth, Mr. and Mrs. Conehead (Dan Aykroyd and Jane Curtin) pursue the American dream in their own weird ways while raising a precocious teenager (Michelle Burke) and avoiding immigration agents anxious to deport them back to the planet Remulak. Director Steve Barron stitches together a pleasantly daffy assemblage of episodic skits inspired by Akyroyd and Curtin's original 1970's Conehead sketches on TV's "Saturday Night Live." Some mild sexual innuendo, fleeting rear nudity, and occasional tasteless humor. A-II (PG)

Coney Island (1943) Standard musical romance directed by Walter Lang with a colorful 1890's honky-tonk background for a story of longtime competitors (George Montgomery and Cesar Romero) out-tricking each other over a popular singer (Betty Grable) who has a mind of her own. Duplicitous romantic complications and ethnic stereotypes. A-III (br)

Confession, The (1970) Dramatic re-creation of the 1951 Czechoslovakian Purge Trials in which 14 dedicated Party members were convicted of high treason, to which all confessed, though none were involved in any kind of political plot. Director Costa-Gavras focuses on one of them (Yves Montand), showing the process by which the man's idealistic faith in the Party was used against him in obtaining his confession. A-III (GP)

Confessions of Tom Harris (1972) The story of a tough mob enforcer (Don Murray) whose chance encounter with a woman (Linda Evans) led to his religious conversion at her father's commune for the spiritual and physical rehabilitation of alcoholics. Murray also wrote and produced, but neither he nor co-directors John Derek and David Nelson seem capable of capturing the spiritual malaise or, for that matter, the religious convictions of the characters in their drama. The result is a series of incidents, ranging all the way from a rape to a symbolic re-creation of the Last Supper, which convey little of human or religious significance. A-III (PG)

Confessions of a Police Captain (1972) Italian story of corruption in high places features a police official (Martin Balsam) who will use any method, including assassination, to get rid of crooks, and a young prosecutor (Franco Nero) who is an honest but ineffectual bureaucrat. Directed by Damiano Damiani, the result is little more than a potboiler with considerable violence. A-III (PG)

Confessions of a Window Cleaner (1974) Infantile sex comedy with a pimply young apprentice window-washer (Robin Askwith) as he makes his predictable rounds of surburban London. Witless sniggering and leering sex. O (R)

Confidential Report (see: **Mr. Arkadin**)

Confirm or Deny (1941) Hokey wartime romance between an American newspaperman (Don Ameche) and a British teletypist (Joan Bennett) bogs down in his attempt to get a scoop involving military secrets. Director Archie Mayo invests the trite tale with the tense atmosphere of London during the Blitz and good chunks of both comedy and pathos from the supporting cast (Roddy McDowall, Arthur Shields, and Raymond Walburn). Wartime violence and romantic situations. A-II (br)

Conformist, The (1971) Italian movie about a man (Jean-Louis Trintingnant) who joins the Fascist party and is eventually entrusted with a mission to kill one of his former university professors who is now causing trouble for the regime. Director Bernardo Bertolucci's portrait of a man who goes along with those in authority is frighteningly real and much more dangerous than any political fanatic. The central theme of the movie is a cautionary one for any politically threatened society, though it has powerful scenes of violence and sexual inferences including that of homosexuality. A-IV (R)

Confrontation (1976) In 1936 a Jewish medical student assassinated the leader of the Nazi Party in Switzerland, an event and an era that this Swiss production has succeeded in re-creating with vivid force. Directed by Rolf Lyssy, the movie does not defend political murder but poses the kind of moral problems individuals must face in a time when injustice is an accepted national policy. A-III (nr)

Congo (1995) Love, greed, and scientific pursuits bring together a zoologist (Dylan Walsh), a tough corporate executive (Laura Linney), and a bogus philanthropist (Tim Curry), who hire a savvy guide (Ernie Hudson) to get them into and out of a abandoned camp in war-torn Zaire, where a fabled diamond mine and a previously unknown species of killer apes await them. Director Frank Marshall's visually impressive but contrived thriller pits high-tech humans against the forces of nature, but the campy performances and plastic dialogue have a lame comic-book effect. Brief bloody violence, much menace, and a few profanities. A-II (PG-13)

Congo Crossing (1956) Wooden adventure tale directed by Joseph Pevney in which a surveyor (George Nader) finds a tract of unclaimed land and helps a group of fugitives (Virginia Mayo, Peter Lorre, Rex Ingram, and others) settle there. Stylized violence and sexual innunedo. A-II (br)

Congo Maisie (1940) Wisecracking, man-savvy Maisie (Ann Sothern) turns up in darkest Africa to chastise a wolf (John Carroll), save a marriage (Rita Johnson and Shepperd Strudwick), and quell a native uprising. Directed by H.C. Potter, it's an early offering of the breezy comedy series featuring the likeable Maisie in formula plots with thin-bare budgets. Some racial stereotyping and mild sexual innuendo. A-II (br)

Conjugal Bed, The (1994) Despairing melodrama set in contemporary Romania, where a brutally abusive husband (Gheorghe Dinica), lusting after his mistress-turned-prostitute, determines to kill his pregnant wife, then hangs himself when she survives his hammering a nail into her brain. Director Mircea Daneliuc ineptly attempts to satirize a post-Communist society by picturing its unstable economy as the principal reason virtually all of the characters act irrationally. Graphic spousal abuse, gory violence, mindless promiscuity, much nudity, and frequent rough language. O (nr)

Connecticut Yankee in King Arthur's Court, A (1949) Uneven musical fantasy derived from Mark Twain's tale of a blacksmith (Bing Crosby) hit on the head in turn-of-the-century New England, then awakened in sixth-century Camelot by a knight (William Bendix) of the Round Table. Directed by Tay Garnett, Crosby's bemused Sir Boss is entirely agreeable and Sir Cedric Hardwicke's Arthur is drolly dense, but the action rarely measures up to its comic potential and the forgettable songs add little to the entertainment. Brief stylized violence. A-I (br)

Conqueror, The (1956) Epic clunker about the early years of 12th-century Mongol leader Genghis Khan (John Wayne,) who kills a powerful ally (Thomas Gomez) after his brothers (Pedro Armendariz and William Conrad) prove his treachery, then goes on to defeat the Tartar chief (Ted de Corsia) and wed his daughter (Susan Hayward). Directed by Dick Powell, there is plenty of bloody action in large-scale battles as well as individual combat, but the characters are cardboard primitives who happen to speak broken English. Much stylized gore and some sexual situations. A-III (br)

Conqueror Worm, The (1968) Inept British horror movie about a 17th-century witch-hunter (Vincent Price) who combines his delight in human suffering with the profits he makes out of his trade. Directed by Michael Reeves, it offers little more than a series of sadistic episodes. O (br)

Conquest of Cochise (1953) The 1853 Gasden Purchase brings a US cavalry unit (led by Robert Stack) to the former Mexican town of Tuscon, where the title's Apache chief (John Hodiak) agrees to keep the peace despite American troublemakers. Directed by William Castle, the period is colorful with a rich mixture of Indians, Mexicans, and gringos, but the action is not in the least credible. Frontier violence. A-I (br)

Conquest of Space (1955) Ordered to pilot a rocketship to Mars from the space station he's just constructed, a colonel (Walter Brooke) en-route develops religious scruples over tampering with the universe and tries to destroy craft and crew (Eric Fleming, Mickey Shaughnessy, Phil Foster, and others). Produced by George Pal and directed by Byron Haskin, the heavy-handed plot and wooden acting are overshadowed by the special effects and novel notions of space flight. Menacing situations and occasional sexual innuendo. A-III (br)

Conquest of the Planet of the Apes (1972) This fourth attempt at reworking the same material marks the fatal deterioration of a series that had some good moments. This time around all the apes on earth are abject slaves, until a new Moses (Roddy McDowell) leads them in revolt against their cruel masters. Under J. Lee Thompson's direction there is too much violence for youngsters who might otherwise buy this stale stuff, but it won't satisfy anyone else. A-III (PG)

Conrack (1974) Jon Voight gives a convincingly exuberant performance as the idealistic white teacher who comes to a remote sea island off the coast of South Carolina to teach the island's black children. The problems he encounters in adjusting to the island's timeless way of life, in reaching his students with useful knowledge, and in dealing with suspicious adults and cranky school officials form the core of an unusual and often moving work. Director Martin Ritt does well with a movie that is enjoyable, funny, sad, poignant, full of hope, and real feeling for people. A-II (PG)

Consenting Adults (1992) Sleazy thriller in which a musician (Kevin Kline) is framed for murdering the wife (Rebecca Miller) of his diabolical next-door neighbor (Kevin Spacey), who then takes up with the musician's wife (Mary Elizabeth Mastrantonio). Director Alan J. Pakula glosses over gaping plot implausibilities with a manipulative scenario glamorizing marital infidelity and making insurance fraud seem an easy solution to financial problems. Brief graphic violence, a titillating wife-swapping scene, many sexual references, occasional nudity, and minimal rough language. O (R)

Consolation Marriage (1931) Creaky romantic

melodrama in which a wisecracking reporter (Pat O'Brien) marries a shopkeeper (Irene Dunne) for a lark after both are jilted by their true loves (Myrna Loy and Leslie Vail), then face divorce when their former beaus resurface several years — and a child — later. Director Paul Sloane's sentimental sudser is helped considerably by a likeable cast, though its sappy treatment of the mating game turns heart-throbs into empty contrivances. Shallow view of marriage. A-III (br)

Conspiracy Theory (1997) Convoluted melodrama in which a paranoid New York cabbie (Mel Gibson) tries to convince a skeptical attorney (Julia Roberts) that they're in mortal danger from government agents after them for unknown reasons. Although overlong and far-fetched, director Richard Donner's elaborate thriller is engrossing escapist entertainment, with Gibson's quirky performance a standout. Some violence and a few instances of profanity. A-III (R)

Contact (1997) Visually impressive sci-fi movie based on Carl Sagan's 1985 novel about a radio astronomer (Jodie Foster) who receives an extraterrestrial communication with instructions for building a spacecraft capable of transporting one human to the aliens' distant habitat. Director Robert Zemeckis focuses on the obsessed astronomer's determination to be the one selected for the flight while also touching on the scientific and spiritual implications of intergalactic life. Some sexual innuendo and fleeting violence. A-III (PG)

Contest Girl, The (1966) Superficial British movie debunking beauty contests tells the story of a newspaper editor (Ian Hendry) teaching a nobody (Janette Scott) the tricks of the beauty game. Produced and directed by Val Guest, the movie and its moral are skin deep. Suggestive costuming and some sexual innuendo. A-III (br)

Continental Divide (1981) A hotshot Chicago newspaperman (John Belushi) and an ornithologist who studies eagles in the Rockies (Blair Brown) fall in love, though both are lost outside of their chosen habitat. The attempt to resurrect a 1940's type of romantic comedy comes to grief because of Lawrence Kasdan's lackluster script and Michael Apted's uncertain direction. Winks at premarital sex and some brief nudity. A-III (PG)

Conversation, The (1974) Intricate story about the world of electronic eavesdropping in which a colorless professional bugger (Gene Hackman) is hired to spy on a young couple but then finds himself being spied upon. Directed by Francis Ford Coppola, it is beautifully acted, meticulously paced, and of interest because it looks at some of the ambiguities and shades of responsibility in the subterranean area of electronic snooping as practiced by anonymous professionals for hire. Some violence. A-III (PG)

Convicted Woman (1940) Dated women-behind-bars story directed by Nick Grinde tells of an innocent inmate (Rochelle Hudson) who, aided by a sympathetic reporter (Glenn Ford), blows the whistle on prison abuses and helps turn the place into a model rehabilitation facility. Stylized violence, including an inmate's suicide. A-II (br)

Convoy (1978) Kris Kristofferson plays a free-spirited trucker who finds himself turned into a folk hero when he leads a group of fellow truckers across state lines in protest against police harassment. Ali MacGraw goes along for the ride. Director Sam Peckinpah lends some visual energy to an otherwise muddled, pretentious, and often quite ludicrous movie displaying casual sex and a sophomoric disregard for the law. O (PG)

Coogan's Bluff (1968) Arizona deputy (Clint Eastwood) runs amok in Manhattan while tracking down an escaped prisoner. Action director Don Siegel emphasizes sex and sadism in a plot based on the premise that law enforcement should not be bound by constitutuional restraints. Excessive violence and sex. O (br)

Cook, the Thief, His Wife and Her Lover, The (1990) Boring when not repellent British production about a feral mobster (Michael Gambon) and his wife (Helen Mirren) who spend their evenings in a restaurant owned by the husband — he gorging himself on delicacies prepared by a French chef (Richard Bohringer) while she makes love to a bookseller between courses in an affair that has dire, gruesome results. Written and directed by Peter Greenaway, it's a pointless exercise in moral decadence treated in tedious, pretentious fashion. Excessive violence, unremitting brutality, exploitative sex scenes, and rough language. O (NC-17)

Cookie (1989) Director Susan Seidelman tracks the comic transformation of an 18-year-old alienated adolescent (Emily Lloyd) into a street-smart Mafia princess who saves the life of her mobster father (Peter Falk) and unifies an offbeat family, including the mobster's wife (Brenda Vaccaro) and mistress (Dianne Wiest). Colorful performances, however, cannot make up for a far-fetched ending, a weak attempt at mob satire, and an uninsightful look at an offbeat father-daughter relationship. Much profanity and a cavalier attitude toward murder and adultery. A-III (R)

Cookie's Fortune (1999) Droll Southern comedy of manners in which an imperious spinster (Glenn Close) and her dim-witted sister (Julianne Moore) attempt to cover up the suicide of their aunt (Patricia Neal), which results in the arrest of the aunt's devoted caretaker (Charles S. Dutton). Director Robert Altman stresses the human dimension of the movie's quirky characters as their gently comic interactions provide subtle charms. A suicide, an implied affair, and some profanity. A-III (PG-13)

Cool Breeze (1972) Black exploitation movie traces the generally downhill course of a gang of thieves (Thalmus Rasulala, Raymond St. Jacques, Jim Watkins, and Lincoln Kilpatrick). Written and directed by Barry Pollack, it has atrocious dialogue covering every racial stereotype and gripe in the book, flashy violence, gratuitous nudity, and a particularly offensive attitude toward black women. O (R)

Cool Hand Luke (1967) Nonconformist loner (Paul Newman), sentenced to a brutal Southern prison farm, gains the respect of his fellow inmates for standing up to the guards' degrading treatment and cruel punishments. Director Stuart Rosenberg relieves the grim situation with some well-paced humor, and Newman's memorable performance in the title role transforms Luke from a pathetic victim of an unjust system into a symbol of the rebellious spirit that refuses to accept the legitimacy of power. A few scenes of brutality that some might consider excessive. A-IV (GP)

Cool Ones, The (1967) Once-popular singing idol (Gil Peterson) tries to stage a comeback, but his struggles are complicated by a budding romance that his manager (Roddy McDowall) threatens to ruin. Director Gene Nelson contributes much ado about nothing. A-I (br)

Cool Runnings (1993) Coached by a disgraced former Olympian (John Candy), four feisty Jamaicans (Leon, Doug E. Doug, Malik Yoba, and Rawle D. Lewis) who had never even seen snow arrive in Calgary, Canada, in hopes of representing their country in the 1988 Winter Olympics by qualifying as a bobsled team. Jon Turteltaub directs a high-spirited, loosely fact-based underdog story that never loses its sense of good, clean fun as the foursome practice on junkyard parts under a tropical sun, ignoring ridicule and impossible odds. Fleeting violence. A-II (PG)

Cool World (1992) Catapulted into his own two-dimensional comic-strip world, a cartoonist (Gabriel Byrne) is seduced into helping one of his vampy creations (Kim Basinger) cross over to the real world, where they are pursued by a hard-boiled detective (Brad Pitt) who knows their secret. Director Ralph Bakshi's manic mix of busy animation and live action produces an outlandishly uneven movie, more adult in its sexual content than the juvenile story would suggest. Cartoon violence and suggestive sexual situations. A-III (PG-13)

Cooley High (1975) Director Michael Schultz' story of young blacks, graduating seniors, in Chicago in the mid-1960s, has some good acting (Glynn Turman and Lawrence-Hilton Jacobs) and flashes of honesty and insight about ghetto life, but its narrative is by turns clumsy and pretentious. More seriously, sexual promiscuity is either played largely for laughs, despite the hurt looks on the faces of the girls cast aside, or, in the case of its hero, given lyrical treatment hard to condone in a work aimed at a young audience. O (PG)

Coonskin (1975) Ralph Bakshi's animated feature with some live action tells the story of three southern blacks (a rabbit, bear and fox) who go to Harlem, take over the rackets and vanquish a corrupt white policeman and a gross Mafia don's brood of murderous homosexual sons. Though it has some effective scenes of indignation at the squalor and hopelessness of ghetto life, the satire places heavy emphasis upon violent action, brutal caricature, and a heavy-handed use of sex. O (R)

Cop (1988) Exploitative crime thriller with James Woods as an obsessed Los Angeles detective who concocts a profile of a serial killer responsible for 15 years of unsolved murders of a young women. Written and directed by James B. Harris, the unpalatable, implausible cop melodrama features a detective whose blatant sexism and vigilante mentality are totally repugnant. Extreme violence, gratuitous sex, graphic shots of murder victims, and profanity. O (R)

Cop, The (1971) In order to avenge the death of a fellow policeman, an honest cop (Michel Bouquet) takes the law into his own hands, becoming as ruthless as the gangsters he hunts. Director Yves Boisset has made a fast-moving action film, hard-edged in violence, but with all elements completely integrated in expressing his theme of moral and social corruption. A-IV (GP)

Cop-Out (1968) Failed British murder mystery directed by Pierre Rouve has a generation-gap story of alcoholic lawyer (James Mason) whose neglect of his daughter (Geraldine Chaplin) leads to her joining the wrong crowd. Muddled story line fails to integrate several sexually suggestive sequences and a near rape. O (br)

Cop and a Half (1993) Cantankerous police detective (Burt Reynolds) humors an eight-year-old (Norman D. Golden II) by making him a member of the Tampa police force in order to get details of a murder the child witnessed, all the while having to protect the boy from the killers. Director Henry Winkler's one-joke comedy wears thin fast and may give children the wrong impression about the very real dangers inherent in police work. Menace to a child, frequent violence depicted comically, and occasional toilet humor. A-II (PG)

Cop Land (1997) Gritty thriller in which the two-bit sheriff (Sylvester Stallone) of a sleepy New Jersey town discovers the group of New York City cops (notably Harvey Keitel) living there are ruthlessly corrupt and about to murder one of their own (Michael Rapaport). Writer-director James Mangold's attempt at a character study of people who compromise their principles is woefully simplistic in a plot resolved by a climactic shootout. Some intense violence, sexual references, occasional profanity, and much rough language. A-III (R)

Cops and Robbers (1973) Nifty comedy about two New York policemen (Joe Bologna and Cliff Gorman) who hatch the perfect crime in a scheme to steal and sell $10 million in bearer bonds to the Mafia. Director Aram Avakian breaks up the humor by building in some taut sequences showing the risks and demands of day-to-day police work in a big city environment, keeping the viewer from asking the sort of logical questions that might puncture the plot. Stylized violence. A-III (PG)

Cops and Robbersons (1994) Tepid comedy in which a crusty police detective (Jack Palance) sets up a stakeout in the home of a bumbling dad (Chevy Chase) who jeopardizes the operation by his unwanted, over-eager participation. Director Michael Ritchie allows Chase his familiar klutzy persona and Palance his wry snarls, but never does much with either in this unengaging one-joke comedy. Some violence, mostly of a comic nature, brief nudity with mild sexual innuendo, and a sprinkling of profanity. A-III (PG)

Copacabana (1947) Lame musical comedy in which a jobless comic (Groucho Marx) persuades his former partner (Carmen Miranda) to audition for the title nightclub, first as a Brazilian singer, then a French one, and the club's unwitting owner (Steve Cochran) hires both. Directed by Alfred E. Green, the comic premise of one singer masquerading as two is frantic but tiresome, with Groucho limited to occasional one-liners, leaving the entertainment mostly in musical numbers featuring Miranda, Andy Russell, and the club's showgirls. Romantic complications and mild sexual innuendo. A-II (br)

Copper Canyon (1950) Slack Western in which an ex-Confederate colonel (Ray Milland) saves some fellow Southerners from losing their Arizona copper mine to a villainous Northern lawman (Macdonald Carey). Directed by John Farrow, there's nothing new here, though Hedy Lamarr is pleasantly restrained as the romantic interest. Stylized violence. A-II (br)

Copper Sky (1957) Small Western in which a hard-drinking drifter (Jeff Morrow) and a prim schoolmarm fresh from Boston (Coleen Gray) escape an Apache massacre and head for safety in a wagon, then on foot. Directed by Charles Marquis Warren, this variation on **The African Queen** makes some intelligent use of the Old West setting, but the mismatched couple never becomes anything more interesting than stereotypes. Stylized violence and mild sexual innuendo. A-II (br)

Copycat (1995) Twisted thriller in which a San Francisco homicide detective (Holly Hunter) tries to nab a cunning serial killer with the reluctant aid of an expert criminal psychologist (Sigourney Weaver), who's still traumatized by a murderous encounter with a patient. Directed by Jon Amiel, the plot has interest until disintegrating into a repellent horror show featuring the gruesome killer and his tortured victims. Excessive violence and gore, brief nudity, and much rough language. O (R)

Corky (1973) Amateur hotshot speedster (Robert Blake) wants to make the big-time as a professional driver, but from the very first scene when he beats out another car at a stoplight, endangering wife, children, and best friend, it is obvious this is the story of a loser. Directed by Leonard Horn, the track footage has class, the Southern locales and people are evoked quite well, and Blake's performance as a man whose delusions lead to inevitable self-destruction is first-rate. A-III (PG)

Corn Is Green, The (1945) Fine adaptation of the Emlyn Williams play set in 1895, when a dedicated teacher (Bette Davis) wins over a Welsh mining town and the local lord (Nigel Bruce) through her perseverance in starting a school and preparing her prize student (John Dall) to take the entrance exam for Oxford. Directed by Irving Rapper, the performances and period setting convincingly demonstrate the value of universal education, though an unwed pregnancy seriously complicates matters. A-III (br)

Cornbread, Earl and Me (1975) When a black youth (Keith Wilkes) is shot accidentally by two policemen, one black and one white, the city administration engages in a cover-up, but a lawyer (Moses Gunn), hired by the parents, clears their son's name. Directed by Joe Manduke, the movie deals well with the complexity of black-white relations and has a fine, convincing cast. Mature treatment. A-III (PG)

Cornered (1945) Tough thriller in which a Canadian airman (Dick Powell) tracks the Nazi agent responsible for his wife's death to Buenos Aires, where he stumbles into a nest of escaped war criminals and their Argentinean collaborators (notably Walter Slezak). Director Edward Dmytryk keeps the tension high as the vengeful veteran blunders through the devious intrigues of Fascist agents and counter-agents in quest of personal justice. Stylized violence, some of it quite nasty. A-II (br)

Coroner Creek (1948) Taut, no-frills Western about a cowboy (Randolph Scott) seeking to find the man (George Macready) who robbed a stagecoach and killed all its passengers. Directed by Ray Enright, the plot is anything but subtle yet holds sufficient interest until the final shootout. Stylized violence. A-II (br)

Corpse Grinders, The (1972) Felines feeding on a new brand of cat food made from grain, exhumed corpses, and freshly dispatched winos acquire a desire to attack their slovenly mistresses. Producer-director-editor Ted V. Mikels has made his dumb little movie in dim, closet-size settings which render transparent any horror that the disgusting plot and mangy characters might suggest. A-III (R)

Corpse Vanishes, The (1942) Creaky chiller directed by Wallace Fox with Bela Lugosi as a mad botanist who has bred an orchid that emits a scent inducing a death-like paralysis in young women, from whom he extracts a vital fluid needed for rejuvenating his aged wife (Elizabeth Russell). Horror hokum, flavored with sinister atmosphere and dark sexual undertones. A-III (br)

Corrina, Corrina (1994) Sentimental exercise in which a seven-year-old girl (Tina Majorino) is helped over the trauma of her mother's death by the take-charge housekeeper (Whoopi Goldberg) hired by her songwriter father (Ray Liotta), who slowly comes to appreciate how much the newcomer means to his daughter and, finally, to himself. Despite idealized characters and artificial situations, writer-director Jessie Nelson effectively manipulates viewers' deep-felt emotions about family, friends, romance, and race in a story that has its heart in the right place. Some romantic complications and occasional racial epithets. A-II (PG)

Corruption (1968) Routine British thriller directed by Robert Hartford-Davis about a mad doctor (Peter Cushing) who murders women for their pituitary gland in a vain effort to restore the burned flesh of his beloved (Sue Lloyd). Graphic violence. A-III (br)

Corruptor, The (1999) Violent action film set in New York City's Chinatown, where a white police detective (Mark Wahlberg) is partnered with a respected but corrupt Chinese superior (Chow Yun-Fat) as they attempt to nail a murderous gang intent on usurping power from rival gangsters. Director James Foley's formulaic story of friendship and betrayal is densely plotted with shootouts, car crashes, and lame moral rationalizing. Excessive violence, sexual situations with nudity, and much rough language. O (R)

Corvette K-225 (1943) Patriotic WW II melodrama directed by Richard Rosson follows the captain (Randolph Scott) and crew (Barry Fitzgerald, Andy Devine, and others) of the title Canadian warship in engagements with German submarines preying on a convoy they are escorting across the Atlantic. Wartime violence. A-I (br)

Corvette Summer (1978) Innocent California high-school senior (Mark Hamill) goes to Las Vegas to track down a car stolen from his shop class, but things get very complicated once there. Boy meets aspiring hooker (Annie Potts), boy loses girl, and regains his former ideals. Director Matthew Robbins's movie shows a much too benign acceptance of the affair between the two youngsters. O (PG)

Cosi (1997) Airy Australian comedy in which an easygoing college dropout (Ben Mendelsohn) is hired to stage an Italian opera in a mental institution using the unruly patients as the cast. Director Mark Joffe's well-acted ensemble piece is a warm-hearted look at the humanity of those with mental problems, demonstrating that creativity is not limited to the brilliant. Fleeting violence, a live-in relationship, and rough language. A-III (R)

Cotton Club, The (1985) Big splashy celebration of the famous white-owned, black-talent nightclub that flourished in Harlem in the 1920s and 1930s has some entertaining moments, but it lacks emotional power and fails to mesh its two diverse elements: gangsters and show business. Directed by Francis Coppola with Richard Gere and Gregory Hines heading a good cast, the movie contains some very graphic violence and two restrained bedroom scenes. A-III (R)

Cotton Comes to Harlem (1970) In a high-powered action story focusing on a big-time con game up in Harlem, two bumbling-but-uncanny detectives (Godfrey Cambridge and Raymond St. Jacques) unmask the fraud being worked by a back-to-Africa preacher (Calvin Lockhart). Directed by Ossie Davis, the dialogue and visuals are harsh and raunchy, with a lot of black racial humor and much gore to round things out. A-IV (R)

Cougar Country (1972) Semi-documentary on the life and hard times of a young cougar in the Great American Northwest makes a fine wildlife story, especially the earlier sequences showing the young animal learning to cope with life within its natural habitat. The going gets a little tougher when the grown cougar has to outwit human invaders of its domain. For the young and curious and all who enjoy the world of nature. A-I (G)

Count Five and Die (1958) Fact-based story of a WW II espionage unit (headed by Jeffrey Hunter and Nigel Patrick) whose mission is to convince German intelligence that the Allies plan to invade Holland rather than Normandy. Directed by Victor Vicas, the dramatic tension centers on neutralizing a double agent (Ann-Marie Duringer) within the London unit rather than on the morality of deliberately sacrificing members of the Dutch underground as part of the deception. Challenging fare. A-II (br)

Count Three and Pray (1955) Muddled tale of a Civil War veteran (Van Heflin) whose experiences at Vicksburg transform him from hardened roughneck to self-styled preacher, but his backwoods community has trouble accepting his new role as pastor, especially when he takes in an orphaned adolescent (Joanne Woodward). Director George Sherman spends more energy in detailing the melodramatic conflicts between the characters than in probing the theme of a simple man's struggle to follow his conscience. Interesting but largely failed attempt to portray the power of faith. A-II (br)

Count Yorba, Vampire (1970) Fairly old-fashioned kind of horror movie with an involving, almost believable plot, underplayed stereotypes of good-and-innocent vs. evil-and-ghoulish, plus a very effective ending. Director Bob Kelljan suggests more than he shows of the story's sex, blood, and violence. A-III (G)

Countdown (1968) Exciting visual exploration of the frantic behind-the-scenes activity surrounding a space launch. James Caan stars as the NASA astronaut whose life as a scientist spaceman is complicated by domestic troubles. Directed by Robert Altman, the location photography in the Houston ground-control center and at Cape Kennedy overshadows the otherwise routine drama. A-I (br)

Countdown at Kusini (1976) Directed by Ossie Davis and filmed in Nigeria, the movie's theme of struggle against neocolonialism in Africa is never treated seriously and leads to no new insights into the old story of exploitation. Its muddled structure and melodramatic plot, however, wreak havoc with its credibility and do little to further the black image on the screen. A-III (PG)

Counter-Attack (1945) Soviet partisans (Paul Muni and Marguerite Chapman) hit a German command post to get vital information for an upcoming offensive, then spend most of the movie trapped in an underground bunker with their prisoners. Directed by Zoltan Korda, the patriotic paean to our WW II allies is short on both military and dramatic credibility. Stylized violence. A-II (br)

Counterfeit Constable, The (1966) Droll British comedy directed by Robert Dhery about a Frenchman (Dhery) in England on the run from a publicity-seeking actress (Diana Dors), the police and his fiancé. Mild sexual innuendo. A-II (br)

Counterfeit Killer (1968) Routine story of counterfeiters and treasury agents directed by Josef Leytes with Jack Lord as the undercover man who infiltrates the gang and Shirley Knight as the waitress who falls in love with him. Fairly graphic violence. A-III (br)

Counterpoint (1968) The fate of an entire symphony orchestra lies in the balance when a German general (Maximilian Shell) insists that they perform a concert and their conductor (Charlton Heston) refuses. Directed by Ralph Nelson, the WW II meldodrama's only merit is its classical music soundtrack. Wartime violence. A-II (br)

Countess Dracula (1972) Aging countess (Ingrid Pitt) discovers quite by accident that her youth is revived by quick dips in virgin's blood. Directed by Peter Sasdy, the horror aspect is lost in a story line in which almost every relationship turns about the anticipation of a nude sexual encounter. O (R/PG)

Countess from Hong Kong, A (1967) The last movie directed by Charlie Chaplin is unfortunately an over-produced, heavy-handed romantic comedy about an impoverished countess (Sophia Loren) who tries to get into the US by stowing away in the stateroom of an American diplomat (miscast Marlon Brando). The laughs are provided mainly by fellow passengers Margaret Rutherford and Patrick Cargill. Sexual situations and inferences. A-III (br)

Country (1984) An Iowa family (Jessica Lange and Sam Shepard) trying to hold on to their farm while burdened with the interest due on massive government loans extended in more prosperous times. Nicely directed by Richard Pearce, it may be a little too predictable and its heroine a bit too courageous and noble, but it's an admirable achievement nevertheless. The only reservation for preteens is some humorous by-play occasioned by a contraceptive. A-II (PG)

Country Boy (1966) Randy Boone of TV's "The Virginian" stars in a story of grassroots patriotism. Scenario and catchy country-western songs by Paul Crabtree. A-I (br)

Country Gentlemen (1936) Lame comedy directed by Ralph Staub in which a bumbling pair of swindlers (Ole Olsen and Chic Johnson) on the run from charges of selling phony gold-mining stock arrive in a rural area, where they start selling oil stock but, unsurprisingly, oil's well at movie's end. Comic dishonesty and muted sexual innuendo. A-II (br)

Country Life (1995) After many years away, a pompous London-based theatre critic (Michael Blakemore) returns to 1919 Australia to visit an outback ranch, whose owner (John Hargreaves) and the local doctor (Sam Neill) fall hopelessly in love with his young, bored wife (Greta Scacchi). Adapted from Chekov's *Uncle Vanya* by writer-director Blakemore, the slowly paced drama of unrequited romances has sprightly comic moments and stresses the humanity of its characters as they learn to accept life's disappointments with good grace. Momentary violence, fleeting nudity, and romantic complications. A-II (PG-13)

Country Music (1972) Marty Robbins's company put together what is essentially a feature-length commercial for his kind of music. Directed by Robert Hinkle, the best that can be said for it as a movie is that there is a certain fascination in its naive artlessness as well as its unconscious humor. A-I (G)

Country Music Daughter (see: **New Girl in Town**)

County Fair (1937) Low-budget adventure directed by Howard Bretherton in which a suspended jockey (John Arledge) battles racetrack crooks while helping a brother and sister enter their horse in a race at the local fair, despite the opposition of their puritanical father (J. Farrell McDonald). Criminal activities and romantic complications. A-II (br)

Coup de Grace (1978) Sober but rather dull German movie about the entangled passions of three German aristocrats set against the chaotic background of post-WW I Latvia. Starring Margarethe von Trotta and Matthias Habich, director Volker Schlondorff's tale of unrequited love and its wasteful consequences is for the patient and mature. A-III (nr)

Coup de Tete (1980) French comedy about a maverick soccer player (Patrick Dewaere) who wins the big match and becomes the hero of his hometown, which once scorned him as a feckless ne'er-do-well but which now is ready to believe that his conviction for rape was a miscarriage of justice. Though the acting is good and director Jean-Jacques Annaud's flair for satire occasionally hits home, the rape's central place in the plot makes for heavy going in a comedy. A-IV (nr)

Coupe de Ville (1990) On orders from their father (Alan Arkin), three battling brothers drive a 1954 Cadillac Coupe de Ville from Detroit to Florida as a birthday gift for their mother but wreck the car along the way. This mildly entertaining coming-of-age comedy is directed in predictable fashion by Joe Roth, with appealing performances by Patrick Dempsey, Daniel Stern, and Arye Gross as the brothers. Some locker-room language laced with sexual vulgarities and an incident of premarital sex. A-III (PG-13)

Courage Mountain (1990) Uninspired but wholesome story of 14-year-old Heidi (Juliette Caton), who is forced from an Italian boarding school into a rat-infested orphanage by the disruptions of WW I. Director Christopher Leitch strains credibility with some far-fetched action as Heidi and her friends escape across the Alps to Switzerland in the dead of winter. Children will enjoy hissing the despicable orphanage owners, and young adolescents may be charmed by the hints of a blossoming romance between Heidi and her dashing soldier friend (Charlie Sheen). Some comic-book menace and minimal battlefield carnage. A-I (PG)

Courage of Lassie (1946) A lost, wounded pup is nursed back to health and raised as a sheepdog by a young girl (Elizabeth Taylor), then winds up as a heroic Army canine, shell-shocked and ultimately vicious, until fate brings him back to his loving mistress and rehabilitation as a sweet-tempered companion. Directed by Fred Wilcox, Lassie goes through her appealing paces as Bill, the dog whose incredible adventures most youngsters will find irresistible, though their elders may be more interested in the story's post-war rehabilitation theme and the gorgeous Sierra locales. Brief wartime violence and some fairly intense scenes of menace. A-I (G)

Courage of the North (1934) Formula outdoor adventure directed by Robert Emmet in which Sgt. Morton (John Preston) of the Canadian Mounted Police gets some help from his wonder horse Dynamite and his dog Captain in capturing a gang stealing pelts from the trap lines of fur traders. Stylized violence and menacing situations. A-II (br)

Courage Under Fire (1996) Returning from the Gulf War, an Army commander (Denzel Washington) feeling guilty over his part in a friendly fire incident doggedly pursues discrepancies in the recommendation of a posthumous medal of honor for a Medevac pilot (Meg Ryan). Director Edward Zwick blends the differing versions of the pilot's actions under fire with compelling character studies as a series of flashbacks gradually reveals how all concerned behaved under the stress of mortal combat. Intense battlefield violence, a suicide, substance abuse, and frequent rough language, as well as profanity. A-III (R)

Courageous Mr. Penn (1941) Earnest but plodding account of the religious persecution facing aristocrat William Penn (Clifford Evans) after joining the Quakers in 1667 London, his marriage to a good woman (Deborah Kerr), her death, and his founding of Pennsylvania as a Quaker refuge in the American wilderness. Directed by Lance Comfort, the episodic script is dramatically weak and rather superficial in its treatment of the historical period and Penn's religious convictions. Heavy-going for children. A-II (br)

Courier, The (1989) Irish import with narrow appeal zeroing in on the victims of a notorious Dublin drug dealer (Gabriel Byrne) who'll stop at nothing to protect his criminal operation. Directed by Frank Deasy and Joe Lee, the movie's contrived romance and revenge plot are poorly focused and surprisingly uninvolving given its gritty subject and working-class setting. Some profanity, clumsy violence, and implied heterosexual and homosexual promiscuity. A-III (R)

Court Jester, The (1955) Delightful costume comedy with Danny Kaye in top form masquerading alternately as a clown and an assassin in order to help a band of rebels overthrow a corrupt king (Cecil Parker) and his treacherous ally (Basil Rathbone) while saving a damsel in distress (Glynis Johns). Written and directed by Norman Panama and Melvin Frank, the silly court intrigues and mistaken identities are clever nonsense, there are some pleasant songs, and Kaye delivers the laughs stylishly, especially in his patter routine with Mildred Natwick about "the brew that is true." Enjoyable romp for the family. A-I (br)

Courtney Affair, The (see: **The Courtneys**)

Courtneys, The (1947) Plodding British saga of an aristocratic family from 1900, when the Courtney heir (Michael Wilding) weds his mother's Irish maid (Anna Nagle), through their ups and downs over the years, until ending in 1945 with the engagement of their grandson to a working-class girl. Producer-director Herbert Wilcox details the changes in British society from the Boer War to WW II in grand soap-opera fashion which still holds appeal for undemanding romantics. A-I (br)

Courtneys of Curzon Street, The (see: **The Courtneys**)

Courtship of Andy Hardy, The (1942) Judge Hardy (Lewis Stone) asks son Andy (Mickey Rooney) to squire the neglected daughter (Donna Reed) of a custody case, but he does such a good job she wants to marry him. George B. Seitz directs an episode whose subplots include mechanic Andy's troubles with the FBI and sister Marian (Cecilia Parker) taking up with a playboy. A-I (br)

Courtship of Eddie's Father, The (1963) Treacly romantic comedy about a widower (Glenn Ford) with a precocious six-year-old (Ronny Howard) who nixes his father's wooing of a bubble-headed drummer (Stella Stevens) and a ritzy fashion consultant (Dina Merrill) in favor of a wholesome divorcee (Shirley Jones). Director Vincente Minnelli can do little with the contrived plot's artificial situations, and the result is an embarrassment for all concerned. Sticky romantic complications. A-II (br)

Cousin Angelica (1977) A middle-aged man (Jose Luis Lopez Vazquez) returns to the village where he had been a boy during the Spanish Civil War, and his recollections help explain his alienation as an adult. Carlos Saura directs the Spanish production with controlled intensity, making the individual's story credible but also using it to show the Spanish character and culture at war with itself. A-III (nr)

Cousin Bette (1998) Strained black comedy set in 1840's Paris, where a wily spinster (Jessica Lange) exacts revenge on her selfish relatives and a young sculptor (Aden Young) she had saved from starvation. Based on the Honore de Balzac novel, director Des McAnuff's period piece is only fitfully amusing in conveying the simmering fury of a woman long taken for granted. Fleeting sexual encounter, intermittent nudity, brief violence, and a comic theme of vengeance. A-IV (R)

Cousin Bobby (1992) Affirmative documentary profile of Episcopal Father Robert Castle, the white rector of a mostly black parish in Harlem, chronicling his decades of social activism in championing minority rights despite countless arrests since the 1960s. Director Jonathan Demme's portrait of his activist cousin is in part an easygoing home movie, but the pastor's undiminished idealism and involvement with his parishioners shines through his own laid-back commentary. Minimal street language. A-II (nr)

Cousin, Cousine (1976) A married man and a married woman (Victor Lanoux and Marie-Christine Barrault) meet at their relatives' wedding that makes them cousins and are immediately drawn to each other. The story of marital infidelity that results is an amusing, malicious trifle which has more to do with wish fulfillment than reality. Under the good-humored surface of this French production directed by Jean-Charles Tachella is a pervading acceptance of adultery. Some nudity. O (R)

Cousins (1989) Remake of the 1976 French satire, **Cousin, Cousine**, centers in the adulterous liaisons between the partners of two unhappily married couples related by marriage (Isabella Rossellini, William Petersen, Ted Danson, and Sean Young). Director Joel Schumacher features some delightful ethnic family weddings, but the film's romanticization of adultery and premarital sex are morally objectionable. Discreet nudity and rough language laced with sexual vulgarities. O (PG-13)

Covenant with Death, A (1966) Suspenseful drama about an innocent man (Earl Holliman), wrongfully convicted of a crime and sentenced to death, whose fight for his life results in the death of another and a dilemma for a small-town judge (George Maharis). Director Lamont Johnson's lackluster production lets an intriguing moral-ethical-legal premise get lost in side issues. Casual love affair condoning seduction. O (br)

Cover Girl (1944) Mediocre musical with Rita Hayworth as a nightclub dancer catapulted into stardom after being put on the cover of a magazine whose publisher (Otto Kruger) had wooed her grandmother, but she's torn between wedding a Broadway impresario (Lee Bowman) and returning to the nightclub owner (Gene Kelly) who loves her. Directed by Charles Vidor, Hayworth looks good in the part but is outshone by Kelly's performance as a song-and-dance man in a flimsy plot bolstered by comic relief from Eve Arden and Phil Silvers. Romantic complications and sexual innuendo. A-II (br)

Cover Me Babe (1970) Bad movie about a student filmmaker (Robert Forster) whose wrongheaded ideas about moviemaking alienate his coworkers, girlfriend (Sondra Locke), and department instructor (Robert Fields). Directed by Noel Black, the movie suffers many of the faults it seems to be criticizing, including an exploitative emphasis on sex. O (R/PG)

Cowards (1970) Draft-age youth (John Ross), pondering the alternatives to imminent induction, moves in with his girlfriend (Susan Sparling) and takes part in a raid to destroy draft files. Writer-producer-director Simon Nuchtern makes light of the moral issues, preferring instead to anchor his hero in absolute confrontations with an overloaded anti-war tract disseminated by supporting characters. A-IV (nr)

Cowboy (1958) Rawhide coming-of-age story from the Frank Harris novel in which a callow Chicago hotel clerk (Jack Lemmon) learns from a hardened cattle-herder (Glenn Ford) that cow-punching is hard work but, as the youth's character toughens on the trail, that of his mentor mellows. Director Delmer Daves get some modest enjoyment out of the tenderfoot's education, but it is Ford's performance as the veteran cowman that dominates the picture. Dangers of the trail from snakebite to a brush with Comanches, some mild romance, rough humor, and an off-screen suicide. A-I (br)

Cowboy and the Girl, The (see: **A Lady Takes a Chance**)

Cowboy and the Lady, The (1938) Romantic comedy in which a presidential candidate's daughter (Merle Oberon) falls for a rodeo rider (Gary Cooper) who mistakes her for a maid, then after they marry, the bride has to square matters with him and her wealthy family. Directed by H.C. Potter, the contrived plot premise provides some dizzy amusement with a fine supporting cast (notably Walter Brennan, Patsy Kell,y and Harry Davenport) until the artificial egalitarian ending. A-I (br)

Cowboys, The (1972) When the local cowpokes join the Gold Rush to California, a tough old rancher (John Wayne) resorts to hiring some schoolboys (ages nine to 15) to drive his cattle to the railhead, teaching them the dangerous craft of cow-punching along the trail. In a traditionally violent finale, the young adolescents slaughter a gang of cattle rustlers who have brutally murdered the rancher (one of the rare roles in which Wayne is not invincible). Well directed by Mark Rydell, but definitely not for the youngsters or the squeamish. A-III (GP)

Cowboy Way, The (1994) Witless comic adventure of two rodeo stars (Woody Harrelson and Kiefer Sutherland) in New York City on the trail of the vicious killer (Dylan McDermott) who has murdered their buddy and kidnapped his daughter. Director Gregg Champion's slack handling of the chases and shootouts in the derivative plot is made worse by Harrelson's clumsy overacting. Intermittent violence, brief bedroom scene with rear nudity, and an instance of rough language. A-III (PG-13)

Crack in the World (1965) Doomsday scenario unleashes widening series of earthquakes caused when a scientist (Dana Andrews) explodes a nuclear bomb to tap the energy at the earth's core. Director Andrew Marton gets some frightening moments in an otherwise sluggish script ending with the earth's getting a second moon. Stylized violence and a menacing premise. A-II (br)

Crack-Up (1946) Intriguing mystery thriller opens with an art specialist (Pat O'Brien) found raving about a train wreck that police establish never occurred but which eventually leads to evidence of forged masterpieces. Director Irving Reis invests the puzzling proceedings with suitably sinister atmosphere, taut suspense, and a solid cast of suspicious characters (Claire Trevor, Herbert Marshall, Ray Collins, and Wallace Ford). Stylized violence. A-II (br)

Crackers (1984) Donald Sutherland plays the ringleader of an inept band of San Francisco characters who devise an elaborate plot to break into their local pawnshop and repay its cranky owner (Jack Warden) by cracking open his safe. Director Louis Malle spends more time trying to find some new angles on the old caper formula than on character development, a miscalculation that results in a flat, lackluster comedy with some sexual situations and a benign view of petty crime. A-III (PG)

Craft, The (1996) Cliche-ridden horror clunker in which four Catholic high-school girls-turned-witches (led by Fairuza Balk) cast evil spells on classmates until one of the quartet (Robin Tunney) tries to stop them from doing further harm. Directed by Andrew Fleming, the occult nonsense employs thousands of snakes and maggots, though some of the spells have deadly results. Stylized violence, brief sexual innuendo, several crude expressions, and an instance of rough language as well as a profanity. A-III (R)

Crash (1997) Repellent picture of kinky sex and deadly violence as a spacey Canadian couple (James Spader and Deborah Kara Unger) switch from casual adultery to group sex in a cult using car crashes as a turn-on. Writer-director David Cronenberg compounds the absurdity of all this by an absence of plot and character development, focusing instead on highways being turned into demolition derbies and frenzied simulations of sexual activities. Graphic sex scenes, substance abuse, and occasional rough language. O (NC-17)

Crash Dive (1943) WW II tale in which a PT-boat commander (Tyrone Power) is ordered to duty on a submarine, then clashes with its captain (Dana Andrews) over a nurse (Anne Baxter) just before putting out to sea, where they resolve their differences after torpedoing a German Q-raider and destroying its base. Directed by Archie Mayo, the naval derring-do is depicted in rousing patriotic fashion, but the love triangle is the story's central focus. Wartime violence and romantic complications. A-II (br)

Crashing through Danger (1938) Romantic melodrama directed by Sam Newfield in which a foreman in the city's power utility department is killed on the job and members of his crew (James Newill and Ray Walker) join in looking after his daughter (Sally Blane) until she falls in love with one of them. Dangers facing power-line workers and romantic complications. A-II (br)

Crawling Hand, The (1963) Cheesy sci-fi horror from director Herbert L. Strock in which the forearm of an astronaut who died in a moon-shot turns up on a California beach, then scuttles about at night trying to strangle people. Some stylized violence and hokey menace. A-II (br)

Crazies, The (1973) Backwoods Pennsylvanians go wild when their water supply is contaminated by Army chemicals, and they react viciously when troops are sent in to pacify them. Directed by George A. Romero, the title belongs to the moviegoers who would sit through this frantic, inconclusive, blood-spurting exercise in silly mayhem. A-III (R)

Crazy House (1943) Chaotic comedy directed by Edward F. Cline with zanies Ole Olson and Chic Johnson trying to produce a movie with financing from phony millionaire Percy Kilbride. Filmed at Universal, many of their contract players (Basil Rathbone, Billy Gilbert, Andy Devine, et al.) drift in and out of the proceedings, which include musical numbers by Count Basie, Allan Jones, and Cass Daley. Dated silliness. A-I (br)

Crazy Joe (1974) Peter Boyle plays the late Joe Gallo, a maverick Brooklyn mobster who paid for his crimes with his life, thanks to the mob's rough system of instant justice. Director Carlo Lizzani's movie is grade-A trash in its pretensions on the "noble savage" theme, and the dialogue is ridiculous. Worthless, especially in view of its misguided sense of morality. O (R)

Crazy People (1990) Madison Avenue ad executive (Dudley Moore), fed up with the lies and deception of his profession, writes some bluntly honest ad copy and is quickly shunted off to a sanitarium, where he befriends some wacky mental patients. Director Tony Bill blends a predictable satire on the ad game with a heartwarming comic fairytale about good guys winning out over bad. Includes much overt product advertising and takes a flip, patronizing attitude towards mental illness. Some profanity laced with vulgarities and numerous sexual references. A-III (R)

Crazy Quilt (1966) Burgess Meredith narrates this offbeat attempt at spanning the whole life of a married couple who have completely different outlooks on life. Producer-director John Korty's use of realistic images in unpretentious, semi-documentary style greatly enhances the movie's keen perceptions of human relationships. Mature themes. A-III (br)

Crazy World of Julius Vrooder, The (1974) Vietnam veteran (Timothy Bottoms) is a genially demented soul in a California psychiatric hospital who continues to live out war-game fantasies until a comely nurse (Barbara Seagull Hershey) solves his problems by applying large doses of affection. Directed by Arthur Hiller, it's all attractively packaged nonsense but glazed with a gooey sweetness that may thrust some viewers into diabetic comas. Some rough language. A-III (PG)

Crazy World of Laurel and Hardy, The (1969) Compilation of highlights from the comedy team's many shorts and features from 1927 through the 1940s. The boys are still irresistible, as their simple-minded logic reduces a seemingly rational universe to complete absurdity. Short on narration, the excerpts emphasize their two-reelers, most notably **The Music Box**, their only Academy Award-winner. Though their work still plays on television, they are seen to best advantage on the big screen. A-I (nr)

Creator (1985) Harry (Peter O'Toole), the hero of this sentimental comedy-drama directed by Ivan Passer, is a Nobel laureate widely believed by his jealous rivals to be a bit over the hill. Constantly talking about God and the Big Picture, Harry is obsessed with, among other things, finding a way to clone his dead wife. Though it deals with ideals, the movie undercuts them by its lack of discipline and its tendency to veer off into excess, especially scenes involving nudity and graphic sexuality. O (R)

Creature from the Black Lagoon, The (1954) A scientific expedition (Richard Carlson, Julie Adams, and Richard Denning among them) exploring a tributary of the Amazon River find in its murky depths a bizarre humanoid creature with gills (Ricou Browning) that doesn't take kindly to the idea of being captured. Directed by Jack Arnold, the low-budget monster movie is not very scary but has a few tense moments, plenty of atmosphere reflecting humans faced with the unknown and a funny-looking but ultimately sympathetic creature. A-I (br)

Creature with the Atom Brain (1955) Penny-ante sci-fi scenario directed by Edward L. Cahn pits a police medical examiner (Richard Denning) against a revenge-warped gangster using radioactivity to revive dead men, then programming them to kill his enemies. Stylized violence and hokey tension. A-II (br)

Creature with the Blue Hand (1972) Murky German mystery based on an Edgar Wallace novel in which a man (Klaus Kinski) is unjustly committed to an insane asylum, then allowed to escape so that he might be blamed for a series of murders. Director Alfred Vohrer employs rats and serpents, secret passageways and poisoned potions, stodgy police inspectors and shadowy villains in a fast-paced tale that cares little for clarifying motives amidst all the dark doings. A-III (GP)

Creatures the World Forgot (1971) British story of the struggle between twin brothers for leadership of a prehistoric band of nomads and the love of primitive pin-up girl Julie Ege. It's entirely forgettable entertainment from director Don Chaffey, but there is enough violence and buttock-and-bosom shots for parents to strongly discourage their youngsters from seeing. A-III (GP)

Creepers (1985) Maniac terrorizes a Swiss girls' school in this inept Italian horror movie written and directed by Dario Argento. Profusion of blood and gore. O (R)

Creeping Flesh, The (1973) Fair British horror movie about Victorian brothers (Peter Cushing and Christopher Lee) who find the bones of a giant human skeleton that grows flesh when wet; they try to cash in on their discovery results in a predictable ending. Horror buffs will find this adequate fare for a rainy day. Directed by Freddie Francis. A-III (PG)

Creepshow (1982) Screenwriter Stephen King and director George Romero join forces in this omnibus of five horror stories, each featuring an abundance of disgusting gore. Although an undercurrent of humor runs though each story, there is a nasty edge to the movie, especially in its depiction of graphic violence. O (R)

Creepshow 2 (1987) Producer-writer George Romero resurrects the pulp horror form in this group of three tales based on Stephen King ghost stories. Light on fright and nudity but heavy on sadistic violence, the moral lessons of the gory fables are bogus and not worth the viewing effort. O (R)

Crescendo (1972) British melodrama in which a writer (Stefanie Powers) researching the life of a famous composer is invited by his widow (Margaretta Scott) to visit her estate and soon discovers herself in the middle of some very kinky goings-on involving sex and drugs. Unfortunately, director Alan Gibson never manages to work up much interest in the proceedings, let alone the intensity of the title in the disappointing climax. A-III (R/PG)

Cria! (1977) Fragile nine-year-old (Ana Torrent) lives with her ultraconservative family in a big house in Madrid, where she mourns the death of her mother and ponders the actions of the adults around her. In attempting to present a child's view of the world, Spanish director Carlos Saura shows that while childhood is not all oblivious innocence, children do have a resilience enabling them to bounce back from all but the most traumatic experience. Brief non-erotic nudity. A-III (nr)

Cries and Whispers (1973) Director Ingmar Bergman presents an anguished study of four women, each representing a different aspect of woman as victim. Harriet Anderson plays a spinster deprived of love from the time she was a child; Ingrid Thulin has been destroyed by marriage and five children who mean nothing to her; Liv Ullmann is the empty-headed coquette who must attract everyone but who can be faithful to none; and Kari Sylwan is the simple, uneducated maid who is the only one capable of an active, outgoing love. It is filled with emotional insights, but it takes a dark view of human nature in an alienated world. A-IV (R)

Crime and Passion (1976) A dark and murky murder comedy filmed in Austria about an unscrupulous financier (Omar Sharif) who encourages his assistant (Karen Black) to marry one of the world's richest men so she can bail him out when his speculations go bust. Director Ivan Passer loses control of his plot quite early on and never recovers. Attempted cuteness about sex throughout and some nudity. O (R)

Crime Doctor (1943) Hokey tale of an amnesia victim (Warner Baxter) who becomes an eminent psychiatrist under the name Dr. Ordway, then recovers the memory of his past life as head of a robbery ring and turns himself in, with predictable results.

Directed by Michael Gordon and based on a popular radio series created by Max Marcin, the movie proved successful enough to sustain nine sequels over the next six years. Some menacing situations. A-I (br)

Crime Doctor's Courage, The (1945) Standard mystery-series entry directed by George Sherman in which the title sleuthing psychiatrist (Warner Baxter) solves a locked-room murder case with numerous suspects, including the bride (Hillary Brooke) of the victim, whose first two wives had died in suspicious accidents, and a pair of Spanish dancers reputed to be vampires. Stylized violence, menacing situations, and mild sexual innuendo. A-II (br)

Crime Doctor's Diary, The (1949) Final series entry directed by Seymour Friedman involves the title psychiatrist (Warner Baxter) in a murder case whose victim was accused of arson by the man (Stephen Dunne) sent to prison for committing it but who was paroled just before the murder. Stylized violence and mild menace. A-I (br)

Crime Doctor's Warning, The (1945) Disjointed series entry directed by William Castle in which the title psychiatrist (Warner Baxter) gets mixed up in a case involving two murdered models with numerous suspects from the art world (including John Abbott, Eduardo Ciannelli, Miles Mander, and J.M. Kerrigan). Stylized violence and menacing situations. A-II (br)

Crimebusters (1979) Terence Hill and Bud Spencer play rough-and-tumble vigilantes who enjoy beating up crooks, so they join the police force and continue on their merry way. Director Enzo Barboni's Italian spoof of American crime melodrama is tediously violent and vulgar in service of heavy-handed social satire. A-III (PG)

Crimes and Misdemeanors (1989) Writer-director Woody Allen once again examines the limits of our moral universe by focusing on an influential ophthalmologist (Martin Landau) who has his mistress (Angelica Huston) murdered when she threatens to spill the beans to his wife (Claire Bloom) and reveal his embezzlement of philanthropic funds. Allen uses humor, pathos, and melodrama to depict the man's struggles with feelings of guilt and accountability ingrained in him by his devout Jewish father, while interweaving a tapestry of other Manhattanites who have moral choices to make as well. Some rough language, explicit sexual innuendoes, and a ruthless, off-camera murder. A-III (PG-13)

Crimes of Passion (1984) Director Ken Russell's sordid and squalid melodrama about a prostitute (Kathleen Turner), a sexually frustrated married man (John Lauglin), and a crazed minister (Anthony Perkins) leads to little but graphic sex and violence. O (R)

Crimes of the Heart (1986) Mutual love and acceptance keep three sisters (Sissy Spacek, Diane Keaton, and Jessica Lange) together and help them survive their personal problems in this adaptation of Beth Henley's play. Bruce Beresford's direction elicits performances of insight, tenderness, and forgiveness. Casual attitude toward infidelity and some crude language. A-III (PG-13)

Criminal Law (1989) Cocky defense lawyer (Gary Oldman) wins the acquittal of a wealthy murderer-rapist (Kevin Bacon), then is conscience-stricken when he realizes the psycho is back on the street brutalizing women. A cat-and-mouse game ensues between the murderer, who regards himself as an anti-abortion avenger since he was almost aborted, and the lawyer, who thinks he can achieve justice outside the judicial system. Director Martin Campbell's muddled crime thriller is not credible on any level — legal, moral, or technical. Grisly shots of corpses, some violence, much menace, and a rough sex scene. A-III (R)

Crimson Blade, The (1963) Dark doings in 1648 England when a troop of Cromwell's Roundheads under a turncoat officer (Lionel Jeffries) occupy the royalist stronghold of a rebel leader (Jack Hedley), whom the turncoat's daughter (June Thorburn) and a double-agent (Oliver Reed) try to protect. Directed by John Gilling, the British production labors through the muddled narrative with meager results. Much menace and stylized violence. A-I (br)

Crimson Cult (1970) Noteworthy only as Boris Karloff's last major screen appearance, the weak British horror movie concerns a local expert in witchcraft (Karloff) who investigates the mysterious disappearance of a young man. Directed by Vernon Sewell, the plot elements involve ancient cults, witch-burning ceremonies, strange dreams, and a brief love affair. A-III (PG)

Crimson Kimono, The (1959) While protecting a witness (Victoria Shaw) in a murder case, two LA police detectives fall in love with her, then have a falling out when she chooses the Japanese-American (James Shigeta) over his best friend (Glenn Corbett). Writer-director Samuel Fuller makes good use of the colorful Little Tokyo setting and Nisei characters in a story that starts as a murder mystery, then focuses on the interracial romance and resulting misunderstandings. Stylized violence, racial tensions, and romantic complications. A-III (br)

Crimson Pirate, The (1952) Colorful 18th-century swashbuckler in which the title's pirate captain (Burt Lancaster) puts justice ahead of profits by siding with revolutionaries on a Caribbean island and leading them to victory with the powerful weapons furnished by an inventor (James Hayter), then rallies his mutinous crew (led by Torin Thatcher) to capture the escaping galleon of the villain (Lesley Bradley). Directed by Robert Siodmak, the plot is riddled with intrigues, acrobatic action, and desperate characters, much of which is given tongue-in-cheek treatment, especially Lancaster's brief masquerade as a woman. Stylized period violence. A-I (br)

Crimson Tide (1995) Slack thriller about a breakdown in the chain of command aboard a US submarine when its captain (Gene Hackman) and executive officer (Denzel Washington) battle over launching a pre-emptive nuclear strike on a Russian missile base seized by rebel forces. Director Tony Scott sets up the political situation realistically enough, then fritters away the suspense in military and technological jargon, underdeveloped characters, and portentous verbal sparring between the two principals. Stylized violence, a bit of profanity, and intermittent rough language. A-III (R)

Cripple Creek (1952) Standard Western fare from director Ray Nazarro is set in 1893 Colorado, where undercover federal agents (George Montgomery and Richard Egan) masquerade as outlaws in order to stop a murderous band of gold robbers. Stylized violence. A-I (br)

Crisis (1950) Honeymooning in Latin America, a US doctor (Cary Grant) and his wife (Paula Raymond) are forced to remain as the "guests" of a dictator (Jose Ferrer) in need of an operation for a brain tumor, while outside the palace an opposition leader (Gilbert Roland) readies a revolution. Writer-director Richard Brooks's political melodrama works hard at setting up the contrived situation, but is undone by a flabby plot and ideological posturing. Some stylized violence and menace. A-II (br)

Criss Cross (1949) Dark crime caper in which an armored-car driver (Burt Lancaster) joins a mobster (Dan Duryea) in a payroll robbery by which the poor sap hopes to win back the mobster's doublecrossing girlfriend (Yvonne De Carlo). Director Robert Siodmak deftly meshes a twisty crime plot with a brooding love triangle detailing the destruction of a man blinded by his obsession for a manipulative woman. Some stylized violence and heavy sexual innuendo. A-III (br)

CrissCross (1992) Distraught over the divorce of his parents, a 12-year-old boy (David Arnott) attempts to sell cocaine so his impoverished mom (Goldie Hawn) can afford to quit a humiliating job as a stripper. Director Chris Menges presents a sad perspective on the tragedy of broken homes, but its deadpan tone undercuts the story's dramatic power. Some suggestive dancing with partial nudity, implied sexual encounter, occasional scenes of drug abuse, rough language, and minimal violence. A-III (R)

Critic's Choice (1963) Flat comedy directed by Don Weis has a New York drama critic (Bob Hope) mumbling distempered one-liners when his would-be playwright wife (Lucille Ball) teams with a Broadway producer (Rip Torn) on a domestic comedy that she demands he not review. Marital misunderstandings and sexual innuendo. A-III (br)

Critical Care (1997) Uneven medical satire concerns the efforts of a caring resident doctor (James Spader) to do what's best for a terminal patient despite the patient's venal daughter (Kyra Sedgwick) trying to blackmail him into pulling the plug immediately so she can collect a huge inheritance. Director Sidney Lumet raises provocative issues about a flawed health-care system in seriocomic style, although a contrived ending mutes the points made about greed and dehumanization. Serious treatment of euthanasia, a brief sexual encounter, and occasional profanity and rough language. A-IV (R)

Critical Condition (1987) Richard Pryor is the failed con-man who tries to plead insanity to avoid going to prison, where he's sure to be killed by the mobsters with whom he inadvertently got busted when undercover cops caught them making a deal. Director Michael Apted's keen social satire contrasts the insane patients and the insane administrators of the institution. Although the language is vulgar and incessantly harsh, its message about personal and professional integrity is significant. A-III (R)

Critters (1986) Small, fuzzy space aliens invade a small farm community and terrorize a captive family of four who fight off the hungry little beasts with the help of two bounty hunters from outer space. The critters might give young children the jitters as they ferociously bite everything in sight. A subtitled profanity in an otherwise mildly amusing sci-fi movie. A-II (PG-13)

Crocodile Dundee (1986) Central premise of this Australian comedy is the clash of cultures when a wild and woolly crocodile hunter from Down Under (Paul Hogan) visits New York City accompanied by an attractive journalist (Linda Kozlowski) assigned to do a human interest story on the Crocodile Man. Director Peter Faiman is more concerned about fashioning a vehicle showcasing Hogan's charming mannerisms than about achieving the lighthearted romance the movie pretends to be. Mild satire of some of the seamier sides of urban life. A-II (PG-13)

Crocodile Dundee II (1988) Now a savvy New Yorker, the Australian adventurer (Paul Hogan) saves his journalist girlfriend (Linda Kozlowski) from some Colombian drug dealers (Hechter Ubary and Juan Fernandez) and spirits her away to Australia, one step ahead of the heavies. Directed by John Cornell, much of the movie's laid-back humor comes as Dundee confounds the crooks on his own turf. Some rough language and comic-book violence. A-II (PG)

Cromwell (1970) Alec Guinness and Richard Harris star as king and commoner in the British Civil War of 1640-49. Director Ken Hughes succeeds in telescoping the wide reaches of the action into a manageable sequence of events centering on the two principals. The lavish historical spectacle, the issues it raises, and the competence of its performances make interesting viewing, especially for those studying its history in school. A-I (G)

Cronos (1994) Gruesome vampire tale in which a dying industrialist (Claudio Brook) and his sadistic nephew (Ron Perlman) try to rob an antiques dealer (Federico Luppi) of an ancient gold scarab which has restored the dealer's youth at the price of turning him into a vampire. Mexican writer-director Guillermo del Toro's arty black comedy of horrors eventually disintegrates into a dehumanizing mess of gory blood-fests witnessed by an innocent child. Some subtitles.

Excessive, sadistic violence, and recurring rough language. O (R)

Crook, The (see: **Simon the Swiss**)

Crooked Circle, The (1957) Routine prizefight tale directed by Joe Kane in which a novice boxer (John Smith) drops his honest manager (Robert Armstrong) to make more money with a new manager who is tied up with gamblers, whom he finally helps a sportswriter (Steve Brodie) expose. Stylized violence. A-I (br)

Crooked Hearts (1991) Three grown sons (Vincent D'Onofrio, Noah Wyle, and Peter Berg) in a close-knit family are badly affected by a fleeting affair their father (Peter Coyote) had when they were children. Writer-director Michael Boatman's poorly scripted story offers such hollow dialogue and illogical developments as to invite laughter during what is intended to be a tragedy. Several sexual references, some rough language, brief fisticuffs, and a flash of nudity. A-III (R)

Crooklyn (1994) Uneven, seriocomic picture of an African-American family living in Brooklyn during a summer in the 1970s, seen mostly through the experiences of a 10-year-old girl (Zelda Harris) with loving but troubled parents (Alfre Woodward and Delroy Lindo) and four rambunctious brothers. Director Spike Lee brings sensitivity to this portrait of a youngster whose childhood ends with a death in the family, but the result is squandered in aimless by-play with her raucous brothers, overbearing aunt, and neighborhood eccentrics. Domestic turmoil, a sexual situation, a bathroom scene, petty thefts, glue-sniffing, and coarse language. A-III (PG-13)

Cross and the Switchblade, The (1970) Fact-based dramatization about David Wilkerson, a Protestant minister from rural Pennsylvania, who converted two rival Harlem gangs by the power of his personal dedication and forceful preaching. Directed by Don Murray and starring Pat Boone, it is honest and sincere in its message that the cure for drugs, slums, and youthful rebellion is to be found in the simple acceptance of religious faith. A-II (GP)

Cross Creek (1983) Screen biography of author Marjorie Kinnan Rawlings (*The Yearling*) begins in 1928, when Rawlings (Mary Steenburgen) walks out on an unhappy marriage and drives to the tiny settlement of Cross Creek, Florida, where she finds herself as a writer. Directed by Martin Ritt, the movie vividly evokes the period and place, has solid acting, and is centered in a compassionate regard for human values. A-II (PG)

Cross My Heart (1987) Blatant sex comedy about two young singles (Annette O'Toole and Martin Short) who wind up in bed on their third date. There are some comic moments, but the seduction and sex scenes are heavy-handed and sour. Directed by Armyan Bernstein. Nudity, simulated sex, and rough language. O (R)

Cross My Heart (1991) When the mother of a fatherless boy (Sylvain Copans) dies, his schoolmates conspire to keep it a secret so he will not be sent away to an orphanage. Writer-director Jacques Fansten captures the innocence and resourcefulness of youngsters in this touchingly funny, bittersweet story of childhood friendship. Subtitles. Some mild sexual references. A-II (nr)

Cross of Iron (1977) WW II movie about a hardened-yet-humane German Army sergeant (James Coburn) who finds himself fighting not only the Russians but his glory-hungry company commander (Maximilian Schell) as well. Though Sam Peckinpah directs the action with convincing authenticity, the movie proves little more than a sophomoric celebration of nihilism and the bond that shared hardship forges between males. Much violence, some nudity, and brutality in a sexual context. O (R)

Crossed Swords (1978) Director Richard Fleischer's version of Mark Twain's *The Prince and the Pauper* wisely exploits its potential for romance and spectacle. Starring Mark Lester in the dual role of the street urchin who trades places with the Prince of Wales, the story provides sound lessons in trust and loyalty. Well-mounted historical production and good performances from a fine cast (George G. Scott, Rex Harrison, Charlton Heston, and Oliver Reed) but there is some graphic violence. A-II (PG)

Crossfire (1947) Tightly wound thriller in which a police detective (Robert Young) investigating a murder case links the fact that the victim (Sam Levene) was a Jew to a rabid bigot among a group of soldiers (Robert Ryan, Robert Mitchum, and others). Director Edward Dmytryk handles the theme of anti-Semitism directly yet with some sensitivity as the convincing story of a hate crime is unraveled by a persistent cop. Stylized violence, considerable psychological tension, and some racist epithets. A-II (br)

Crossing Delancey (1988) A 33-year-old New York career woman (Amy Irving) is aghast when her meddling grandmother (Reizl Bozyk) and a matchmaker friend (Sylvia Miles) pair her up with a Lower East Side pickle-seller (Peter Riegert), but soon finds herself falling for the guy. Director Joan Micklin Silver's wonderful, sweet-natured story of the collision between old-world and modern-day customs features some fine performances and a knowing portrayal of New York life. Some rough language and sexual situations outside marriage. A-III (PG)

Crossing Guard, The (1995) Affecting story involving a grief-stricken dad (Jack Nicholson) determined to murder the drunken driver (David Morse) who killed his little girl when the remorseful young man is released from prison. Writer-director Sean Penn plumbs dark emotional territory in a sensitive character study exploring self-loathing, bitterness, and the ultimate futility of violence. Minimal violence, implied one-night stands, recurring strip-joint nudity, and much rough language. A-III (R)

Crossing the Bridge (1992) Slow-starting coming-of-age movie in which three aimless youths (Josh Charles, Jason Gedrick, and Stephen Baldwin) stumble into a major drug deal, then have to decide what to do. Writer-director Mike Binder's low-key story improves gradually as the trio finally comes to grips with their floundering lives. Brief violence and drug abuse, frequent drinking, much rough language, and an implied sexual encounter. A-III (R)

Crossplot (1970) Harried ad agency executive (Roger Moore) is romantically involved with a model (Claudie Lang) who knows too much about a forthcoming assassination planned by her aunt (Martha Hyer). Shallow but diverting intrigue with a lot of fast action, a dash of violence and nudity, some beautiful photography of the English countryside, and a few good laughs. A-III (PG)

Crossroads (1986) This musically inclined teen romance relates the story of an aspiring adolescent music student who frees an old blues musician from confinement in a nursing home and helps him win back his soul from the Devil. Walter Hill's musical allegory about determination and growing up is weakened by rough language and a permissive attitude toward casual adolescent sex. A-III (R)

Crow, The (1994) Ultra-violent revenge fantasy in which a murdered man (Brandon Lee) returns to life with the express intention of killing the gang of thugs who raped and murdered his fiancé and flung him to his death on the night before their wedding. Director Alex Proyas wastes sleek, dark visuals on a dreary depiction of the varied sadistic and brutal ways in which this undead creature exterminates his prey. Excessive violence, rationalization of murder, brief nudity, drug use, and much rough language. O (R)

Crow: City of Angels, The (1996) Clunky pulp sequel in which a dead man (Vincent Perez) returns from a watery grave to wreak vengeance on his evil killers with the help of a magical crow and a tender-hearted tattoo artist (Mia Kirshner). Directed by Tim Pope, the thin mythic premise provides the basis for an episodic gore-fest as exploitative as the bogus atmosphere supplied by occult trappings and pseudo-religious references. Excessive violence, sexual situations, fleeting nudity, some profanity, and much rough language. O (R)

Crowd, The (1928) Extraordinary picture of ordinary American life follows a young man (James Murray) as he comes to New York, gets work as a clerk in a big company, marries (Eleanor Boardman), tries to make good, but loses his job and goes on the skids, until the tragic death of his little boy shocks him out of self-pity and into trying again. Director King Vidor's silent masterpiece achieves its impact not through plot or story devices but by capturing the human details of everyday life, from its simple joys to it humdrum routines that viewers recognize as not far different from their own. Domestic problems and the intensely felt loss of a child. A-II (br)

Crowded Sky, The (1960) Dull disaster vehicle stars Dana Andrews as a troubled commercial airline pilot, with the usual assortment of passengers and problems aboard a flight that ends on a collision course with a Navy jet piloted by Efrem Zimbalist, Jr. Director Joseph Pevney alternates the airborne ennui with soapy flashbacks detailing the troubled lives of its cardboard characters. Marital problems and sexual situations. A-III (br)

Crucible, The (1996) A group of girls stir hysteria in 1692 Salem, Massachusetts, when they confess seeing some of their neighbors consorting with the Devil, but matters get out of hand after a Boston magistrate (Paul Scofield) arrives and the number of accused grows to include the wife (Joan Allen) of a farmer (Daniel Day-Lewis) denounced by a teenage girl (Winona Ryder), who wants to marry him. Directed by Nicholas Hytner from Arthur Miller's adaptation of his 1953 play, the drama vividly re-creates the period's fear of witchcraft and the children's exploitation of it, though the personal level of the tragedy lacks the same emotional conviction. Period violence including torture and hangings, brief nudity, and a few coarse words. A-III (PG-13)

Crucible of Horror (1971) Eerie British horror item about a sadistic father (Michael Gough), whose pretty daughter (Sharon Gurney) and long-suffering wife (Yvonne Mitchell) hatch a scheme to be rid of the old man. Director Viktors Ritelis keeps the proceedings taut until the last 20 minutes, when it becomes just another routine chiller. A-III (GP)

Cruel Intentions (1999) Pandering tale of lustful teenagers, one of whom (Ryan Phillippe) bets his hypocritical stepsister (Sarah Michelle Gellar) he can seduce the wholesome daughter (Reese Witherspoon) of the school's new headmaster. Writer-director Roger Kumble updates an 18th-century French novel about decadent aristocrats to the adolescent offspring of wealthy Manhattanites, but the result is little more than teen hothouse fantasy. Numerous sexual situations and explicit references, drug abuse, and frequent rough language as well as profanity. O (R)

Cruel Sea, The (1953) Convincing dramatization of Nicholas Monsarrat's WW II novel about the captain (Jack Hawkins) of a British convoy escort battling U-boats in the Atlantic, until the ship is torpedoed and he finishes the war in command of a corvette guarding convoys bound for the Russian port of Murmansk. Director Charles Frend gets a sense of realism by filming the action in semi-documentary style, but what makes the picture memorable is its understated story of a conscientious captain, a sensible crew made up mostly of civilian conscripts, and their courage in facing the enemy, as well as the perils of the sea. Wartime violence. A-I (br)

Cruel Tower, The (1956) Low-budget tale of a troubled drifter (John Ericson) who's befriended by some steeplejacks (Charles McGraw, Steve Brodie, and Peter Whitney) and their business manager (Mari Blanchard), then things go haywire when McGraw discovers his wife is having an affair with Brodie. Directed by Lew Landers, the portrayal of camaraderie between steeplejacks who risk their lives working at great heights is more convincing than the melodramatic plot about blue-collar carousing and its harmful consequences. Stylized violence and sexual situations. A-III (br)

Cruise, The (1998) Quirky black-and-white documentary in which eccentric New York City double-decker bus-tour guide Timothy "Speed" Levitch is seen on the job describing the Big Apple in florid terms, and after hours roaming the streets while ranting about his personal gripes and insecurities. Director Bennett Miller maintains a lively pace following the loquacious oddball around, but the film's sole focus on Levitch's self-absorbed verbiage ultimately grows tiresome. Frequent sexual references and an instance of profanity and rough language. A-III (PG-13)

Cruising (1980) Al Pacino plays an undercover cop assigned to find a killer who preys upon homosexuals in New York City's sadomasochistic underground. Murky, muddled movie from director William Friedkin depicts a series of gory murders, male nudity, and bizarre sexual practices without a single redeeming bit of humanity anywhere to be found. O (R)

Crumb (1995) Disturbing documentary explores the life and work of cult comic-strip illustrator R. Crumb, creator of Fritz the Cat and the Keep on Truckin' logo, while probing the effects of the abusive upbringing endured by the misogynistic Crumb and his two emotionally troubled brothers. Director Terry Zwigoff's portrait of the controversial artist deals with his blatant racism and sexism, yet is not without sympathy for the flawed humanity of the Crumb brothers. Many illustrations with graphic sexual content and discussions with explicit sexual references, painful recollections of child abuse, and recurring rough language. A-IV (R)

Crusades, The (1935) Epic costume melodrama in which England's Richard the Lionhearted (Herbert Wilcoxson) escapes from marrying the sister (Katherine DeMille) of the French king (C. Henry Gordon) by joining the crusade to free the Holy Land from the Saracens, but along the way he agrees to wed the King of Navarre's daughter (Loretta Young) to get provisions for his men, then falls in love with her. Once again, director Cecil B. DeMille turns history into pageantry, but the dramatic spectacle of the crusaders' victory at Acre turns to bathos as Richard seeks to free his captured wife from the crafty Saladin (Ian Keith). Stylized violence and religious conflict. A-II (br)

Crush, The (1993) Dumb, witless thriller about a precocious teenager (Alicia Silverstone) whose obsession with a handsome journalist (Cary Elwes) living in her parents' guest-house results in her attempting to kill the man's girlfriend (Jennifer Rubin). The vampy teenage character leers and mugs her way through the entirely predictable proceedings. Written and directed by Alan Shapiro. Brief stylized violence, fleeting nudity, an implied sexual encounter, and occasional rough language. A-III (R)

Cry-Baby (1990) Musical comedy about the star-crossed romance between a handsome teen gang-leader from the wrong side of the tracks (Johnny Depp) and a wealthy good girl (Amy Locane) in 1954 Baltimore. With some rousing production numbers, eccentric casting, and much period humor, writer-director John Waters satirizes the innocence of mid-1950's teenage rebellion and the problems of conformity. Best for baby-boomers who survived the period. Some Keystone Cops violence, sexually suggestive action, and rude language with vulgar sexual innuendoes. A-III (PG-13)

Cry Blood, Apache (1971) Irate Indian stalks the gold-seeking murderers of his family who also abducted his sister and only Jody McCrea, who protects the girl from the lecherous prospectors, will survive his revenge. Directed by Jack Starrett, it's a terribly tedious little Western with failed pretensions of being something more. Some nasty violence. A-III (R)

Cry Freedom (1987) The story of Steve Biko (Denzel Washington), a black South African leader who died in 1977 from police mistreatment, is told by Donald Woods (Kevin Kline), a white editor who had to escape from his native land to reveal the truth of what had occurred. Director Richard Attenborough's large-scale dramatization re-creates an authentic picture of the enormity of South Africa's racist policy of apartheid and effectively conveys the need for racial harmony in effecting social and political changes in that tragic land. A-II (PG)

Cry in the Dark, A (1988) Grim fact-based story of an Australian couple (Meryl Streep and Sam Neill) who were unjustly convicted of killing their nine-week-old daughter in 1980 because of media-induced hysteria in reports of religious sacrifice (the husband was a Seventh Day Adventist pastor) and personal gossip. Australian director Fred Schepisi indicts the media's frightening influence on public opinion and provides a stirring reminder of religious intolerance. Graphic scene of a wild dog attacking an infant. A-III (PG-13)

Cry in the Wild, A (1990) A teenage boy (Jared Rushton) survives a plane crash but finds the fight for his life has only begun when he realizes he's now alone in the uninhabited Canadian wilderness. The pristine scenery is the most interesting aspect of an adventure movie which ambles along without any sense of urgency to its expected conclusion. Minor menace and flash of rear nudity. A-II (PG)

Cry of the Banshee (1970) Mild-mannered medieval witch hunter (Vincent Price) is cursed by an old hag for having killed some of her young followers, and his own children begin to die as the curse runs its course. Directed by Gordon Hessler, the movie relies on graphic shock effects, with blood and gore, torture, promiscuity, nudity, and a casual disrespect for life. O (GP)

Cry of the City (1948) Moody crime melodrama set in New York City, where a relentless cop (Victor Mature) pursues a wounded but ruthless crook (Richard Conte) with whom he had grown up in an Italian-American neighborhood but who is now being hunted as a cop-killer and jewel thief. Directed by Robert Siodmak, the narrative is well-paced with unexpected plot twists and colorful characters, but the focus is on the personal battle between one-time pals who have chosen opposite sides of the law. Stylized violence and menacing situations. A-II (br)

Cry of the Owl, The (1991) A melancholy stranger (Christophe Malavoy) disrupts the relationship of an engaged couple (Mathilda May and Jacques Penot) as puzzling deaths seem to follow him everywhere. French director Claude Chabrol's routine suspense drama lags throughout as the irrational behavior of the characters throttles the movie's credibility. Subtitles. Occasional violence, a suicide, implied live-in relationship, and minimal sexual references. A-III (nr)

Cry of the Wild (1974) Fascinating documentary study of the elusive Arctic wolf, as well as an interesting chronicle of Bill Mason's adventures in photographing these wild creatures. Spending months alone in the Arctic, his perseverance and ingenuity has resulted in some stunning wildlife footage. Its raw picture of hunting and carnage in the wild, and also its matter-of-fact presentation of courting and birth in a wolf pack, suggest it is not for young children unless they see it with their parents. A-II (PG)

Cry, the Beloved Country (1952) Compelling British production of Alan Paton's story about bridging South Africa's racial divide, as a black Anglican minister (Canada Lee) leaves his rural parish to seek his missing son in Johannesburg, finds him condemned to death for murdering the son of a white farmer, and the tragedy brings the two aged fathers together in mutual understanding and respect. Directed by Zoltan Korda, the location photography documents the oppressive conditions in the black slums bordering the city, but the story's rich assortment of characters, including Sidney Poitier's pragmatic city curate, puts matters in a human context transcending racial differences. Stylized violence, sexual references, and justice questions. A-II (br)

Cry, the Beloved Country (1995) Fine adaptation of Alan Paton's novel set in 1946 South Africa, where a black minister (James Earl Jones), whose son has killed a white man, reconciles with the victim's father (Richard Harris) in a story exploring the artificial barriers of racial differences. Director Darrell James Roodt emphasizes the human dignity of the characters, the equality of all in the sight of God, and the injustice of a society based on racism. Restrained violence and sexual references in a justice context. A-II (PG-13)

Cry Uncle! (1971) Paunchy New York private detective (Allen Garfield) fornicates his way through half the ranks of the city's netherworld of streetwalkers and porno actresses whilst tracking down a murderous, blackmailing filmmaker. Director John Avildsen apparently intended this to be funny, though it is anything but amusing. O (R)

Crying Game, The (1992) Quirky tale of an IRA gunman (Stephen Rea) who, after the bungled slaying of a British soldier (Forest Whitaker), escapes Belfast for London, where his attempt to make amends to the dead soldier's lover (Jaye Davidson) turns his life upside down. Writer-director Neil Jordan starts with the unnatural violence of republican terrorists and ends with the unnatural relationship of two of society's outcasts in a picture filled with ironic contrivances, bizarre situations, and human frailties. The plot hinges on transvestitism, as well as contains some scenes of hard-edged violence, a flash of frontal nudity and recurring rough language. A-IV (R)

Cuba (1980) Sean Connery plays a soldier of fortune who arrives in 1959 to help the Baptista regime in its struggle against Castro's rebels. Connery meets a former love (Brooke Adams), now happily married, and their rekindled relationship provides some unresolved conflict working against director Richard Lester's remarkable evocation of period and setting. Adventure romance contains violence and a desultory striptease in a half-empty night club. A-III (R)

Cube (1998) Bizarre futuristic thriller in which six strangers wake up imprisoned inside interlocking steel cubes and must combine their varied skills to find a way out of the mysterious, booby-trapped maze. Director Vincenzo Natali leaves much of the mystery unresolved but develops gradual psychological suspense as the claustrophobic situation brings out the characters' best and worst survival instincts. Some brief but intense violence, intermittent rough language, and an instance of profanity. A-III (R)

Cujo (1983) Stephen King's script of his own horror story about a vicious dog that goes on a rampage and eventually threatens a mother (Dee Wallace) and her young son trapped in their car. Lewis Teague directs the mediocre horror movie, which has some considerable blood and gore. A-III (R)

Cul-De-Sac (1966) British thugs threaten a man (Donald Pleasance) and his wife (Francoise Dorleac) in a pointless exercise in terror directed by Roman Polanski. Perverse violence and sex. O (br)

Culpepper Cattle Co., The (1972) Gary Grimes signs on as the cook's helper for a particularly gritty cattle drive way out in the Old West. Directed by Dick Richards, the movie reaches a climax of sorts when Grimes and a couple of trigger-happy cowhands decide to make their stand protecting some Quaker squatters, but this degenerates into a pointless bloodbath, making Grimes's final renunciation of the gun a hollow act. A-III (PG)

Curdled (1996) Ghoulish comedy in which a woman (Angela Jones) with a morbid fascination about murder is hired by a company cleaning up murder sites, where she encounters a psycho killer (William Baldwin) returned to the scene of his crime. Directed by Reb Braddock, this tongue-in-cheek horror fantasy uses a lot of fake gore in stretching out its thin sick-joke premise, but the result is as tedious as it is tasteless. Several off-screen decapitations, some cruel but stylized violence, bloody murder sites, and occasional profanity and rough language. A-IV (R)

Cure, The (1995) Poignant tearjerker in which an AIDS-infected 11-year-old Minnesota boy (Joseph Mazzello) is scorned by all but his loving mom (Annabella Sciorra) and the surly kid next door (Brad Renfro), with whom he runs off to Louisiana in search of a reputed cure for the fatal illness. Despite an increasingly implausible narrative, director Peter Horton's downbeat yet ultimately uplifting drama explores the transforming power of friendship with genuine sensitivity. Mild sexual innuendo, brief menace, and an instance of profanity. A-II (PG-13)

Curious Female, The (1970) Sex-exploitation movie using a frame device of 25th-century voyeurs watching a 20th-century sex-exploitation movie. That's as imaginative as it gets. O (R)

Curly Sue (1991) Formula comedy has a hobo (James Belushi) and his nine-year-old orphan pal (Alisan Porter) winning the affections of a yuppie Chicago lawyer (Kelly Lynch) who has no time for tender emotion in her life. Writer-producer-director John Hughes's trite story is loaded with heartstring music that doesn't quite drown out the cloying and insipid dialogue. Several instances of slapstick violence. A-II (PG)

Curly Top (1935) Lesser Shirley Temple vehicle directed by Irving Cummings in which the little charmer leaves the orphanage behind after captivating a millionaire (John Boles), then helps him realize he's in love with her older sister (Rochelle Hudson). Contrived but still fun thanks to Shirley's zestful screen presence and playful way with such numbers as "Animal Crackers in My Soup." A-I (G)

Curse of Dracula, The (see: **The Return of Dracula**)

Curse of Frankenstein, The (1957) Rather lurid retelling of Mary W. Shelley's story of Baron Victor Frankenstein (Peter Cushing), who seeks to create a perfect man out of stolen body parts, then kills to get the brain of a brilliant professor, but it's damaged by a horrified colleague (Robert Urquhart) and the resulting creature (Christopher Lee) proves malevolent. Directed by Terence Fisher, the picture plays up the story's ghoulish angles while turning the mad baron into a womanizer who makes love to the maid (Valerie Gaunt), then lets the creature kill her after becoming engaged to his cousin (Hazel Court) and winds up sentenced to the guillotine for the maid's murder. Stylized violence, gruesome menace, and sexual situations. A-III (br)

Curse of the Cat People, The (1944) Sequel to **Cat People** in which a lonely child is befriended by the spirit of her father's first wife (Simone Simon), who met a dire end in the original as a woman unhappily cursed with the power to turn into a panther. Directed by Gunther v. Fritsch and Robert Wise, the fantasy is not one of horror but of fear for the child's safety. Some eerie scenes evoking dread of the unknown. A-II (br)

Curse of the Demon (1958) Uneven thriller in which an American psychologist (Dana Andrews) comes to England to debunk the leader (Niall MacGinness) of a satanic cult, then finds himself pursued by diabolical forces. Directed by Jacques Tourneur, the eerie proceedings rely more on suggestion than visuals, though there are several effective scenes with a demonic figure. Stylized violence and menacing situations. A-II (br)

Curse of the Fly (1965) Addled sequel to **The Fly** in which a third generation of Montreal scientists assist their father (Brian Donlevy) in trying to perfect a machine transmitting matter through space, despite the human toll in failed experiments. Directed by Don Sharp, the British production limps along with stereotyped characters in a muddled plot, none of which makes much sense. Stylized violence and menace. A-II (br)

Curse of the Mummy's Tomb, The (1964) When an American showman (Fred Clark) transports the mummy of an ancient Egyptian prince to London for a 1900 exhibition, the mummy comes to life seeking revenge on those who unearthed it. In a British thriller directed by Michael Carreras, the archaeological trappings provide some chills in a fizzled plot done in by the mummy's cursed-with-eternal-life brother. Occasional stylized violence and menace. A-II (br)

Curse of the Undead (1959) Western curio about a preacher (Eric Fleming) pitted against a gunfighter (Michael Pate) who turns out to be a Mexican vampire draining locals of their blood. Writer-director Edward Dein's tale of a vampire on the loose in the Old West fails to mesh the horror elements with the Western action, though there are some effective moments. Stylized violence and hokey menace. A-II (br)

Curse of the Vampires (1970) Family honor, religious piety, and a romantic love story provide the diverting background of this low-budget Philippine horror movie. Unfortunately, its plot about the father of a noble family who cannot preserve the secret that his mother is a vampire is alternately confusing and unintentionally amusing. A-II (GP)

Curse of the Werewolf, The (1961) Pedestrian monster movie set in 18th-century Spain, where an illegitimate child is given a good home but grows up to be a wolfman (Oliver Reed), with predictable results. Directed by Terence Fisher, the story makes little sense, and Reed's troubled character as the werewolf fails to elicit the intended sympathy. Gory violence, hokey menace, and some sexual situations. A-III (br)

Custer of the West (1968) Epic-sized Western reduces both the legend of the general (Robert Shaw) and the history of the times to postage-stamp dimensions. Filmed in Spain and directed by Robert Siodmak, the re-creation rings as hollow as the motivations of the various characters. Stylized violence. A-II (G)

Cutter and Bone (1981) Bitter, crippled Vietnam

veteran (John Heard), despite objections from his neglected wife (Lisa Eichorn), teams up with his best friend (Jeff Bridges), an aging and feckless beach boy, in a quixotic, obsessive attempt to smoke out a fat-cat oil magnate whom they believe to be responsible for the brutal murder of a teenage girl. Director Ivan Passer's uneven thriller contains strong language, violence, and a frank depiction of sex. A-III (R)

Cutter's Way (see: **Cutter and Bone**)

Cutthroat Island (1995) Rousing 17th-century adventure in which a fearless female pirate (Geena Davis) teams with a dashing thief (Matthew Modine) to beat her murderous uncle (Frank Langella) in finding a huge cache of pirate treasure. Producer-director Renny Harlin's lavish swashbuckler is fast-paced escapist fun as assorted blackguards engage in fiery, death-defying stunts on ship and shore. Frequent stylized violence and some sexual innuendo. A-III (PG-13)

Cutting Edge, The (1992) Routine love story about a pampered figure skater (Moira Kelly) who must accept a gruff ice-hockey player (D.B. Sweeney) as her new skating partner if she wants a shot at winning Olympic gold. The predictable story with its expected spills and comebacks is as thin as ice in director Paul M. Glaser's blandly cheerful romance. Several implied promiscuous encounters and an instance of alcohol abuse. A-III (PG)

Cyborg (1989) Venomous post-apocalypse pirates, led by a blue-eyed sadist (Vincent Klyn), kidnap a cyborg (a robot that's partly human, played by Dayle Haddon) who holds the cure for a killer plague, but they're pursued by a martial-arts expert (Jean-Claude Van Damme) who's out to avenge the slaughter of his loved ones. Director Albert Pyun drowns the somber, badly acted, inept sci-fi scenario in too much grisly violence, compounded by dabs of profanity and nudity. O (R)

Cyclops, The (1957) Low budget sci-fi thriller directed by Bert I. Gordon is set in a remote area of Mexico, where a woman (Gloria Talbot) seeks her missing fiancé but finds a one-eyed giant and other monsters caused by radiation poisoning. Cheesy special effects and hokey threats. A-II (br)

Cynara (1932) Dated period melodrama directed by King Vidor features a staid English barrister (Ronald Colman) who seeks forgiveness from his wife (Kay Francis) after his brief affair with a shopgirl (Phyllis Barry) ends in her suicide. Restrained treatment of infidelity and its painful consequences. A-III (br)

Cyrano de Bergerac (1950) Uneven version of Edmond Rostand's verse play set in 17th-century France, where the title's long-nosed soldier-wit-poet (Jose Ferrer) secretly loves his cousin, Roxanne (Mala Powers), but she fancies a handsome, inarticulate cadet (William Prince), for whom Cyrano writes impassioned love letters that win her heart. Directed by Michael Gordon, the adaptation is stagy and the young lovers' romance is never more than tepid, but Ferrer's robust performance as the best swordsman in Paris, as well as the most idealistic, compensates for the flaws. Period violence and romantic complications. A-II (br)

Cyrano de Bergerac (1990) Swashbuckling 17th-century poet (Gerard Depardieu), despairing of romance because of his enormous nose, helps a young soldier (Vincent Perez) win the heart of the poet's cousin and true love, Roxanne (Anne Brochet), by composing love letters for him. Director Jean-Paul Rappeneau imbues Edmond Rostand's 19th-century French play with fresh energy and cinematic beauty but the centerpiece is Depardieu's towering performance as the tragic, unrequited lover. Subtitles. Battlefield violence. A-II (PG)

D-Day the Sixth of June (1956) Glossy WW II sudser in which a married American officer (Robert Taylor) stationed in London has an affair with an English Red Cross worker (Dana Wynter) while her British commando beau (Richard Todd) is off fighting the war. Directed by Henry Koster, the messy triangle gets resolved on the bloody beaches of Normandy, but the trite ending is embarrassingly banal. Sexual situations. A-III (br)

D.O.A. (1950) Involving thriller in which a vacationing accountant (Edmond O'Brien) discovers he has been given a lethal dose of a toxic poison, then backtracks trying to find his killer before he dies. Directed by Rudolph Maté, the premise is simple but effective, with O'Brien's frantic performance as the doomed man adding a sense of urgency to the proceedings. Stylized violence and emotionally intense situations. A-II (br)

D.O.A. (1988) During an all-night drinking binge, a burned-out college professor (Dennis Quaid) somehow chugs a cocktail spiked with slow-acting poison and, with only 24 hours to live and the aid of a naive student (Meg Ryan), he maniacally tracks down his killer. Directed by British husband-wife team Rocky Morton and Annabel Jankel, the remake of the 1949 Hollywood thriller is entertaining but intense and not for the squeamish. Much violence and incidental profanity. A-IV (R)

D3: The Mighty Ducks (1996) Thin sequel about the problems of the now-teen hockey team at a posh prep school, where they encounter hostile students. Their old coach (Emilio Estevez) is replaced by a grim new one (Jeffrey Nordling). The formula story is a contrived mixture of youthful pranks and emotional struggles leading up to the big game and its bone-crunching physical contact. Some dangerous stunts, vulgar humor, and a few coarse expressions. A-II (PG)

D2: The Mighty Ducks (1994) Thoroughly predictable sequel takes the peewee hockey team to the Junior Goodwill Games, where the coach (Emilio Estevez) becomes temporarily distracted by lucrative sports endorsements while his young players prepare to take on the mean, lean team from Iceland. Director Sam Weisman piles on the hockey footage as the cliche-ridden narrative steadily sinks under various characters' dull sermonizing about the commercialization of athletes and the nobility of team sports. Some rough play on the ice and a sprinkling of profanity. A-II (PG)

Da (1988) Literate, poignant adaptation by Hugh Leonard of his own play and novel about a middle-aged playwright (Martin Sheen) who returns to Ireland to bury his dad (Barnard Hughes) and make peace with his ghost. Director Matt Clark gets outstanding performances from the two leads, which helps overcome some confusing flashbacks and jolting sequence featuring the attempted drowning of a pet dog. Some profanity. A-II (PG)

Dad (1989) When a heart attack fells the domineering wife (Olympia Dukakis) of a 78-year-old man (Jack Lemmon), he relearns independence from his adult son (Ted Danson), but then suffers a series of illnesses that require new priorities for the family. Though writer-director Gary David Goldberg's sudsy seriocomic effort has various plot lapses and excessive climaxes, it offers some worthwhile insights on the subject of parenting one's parents and coping with their illnesses and death. Mild sexual innuendo and minimal rough language. A-II (PG)

Daddy Nostalgia (1991) Following her father's near-fatal heart attack, a middle-aged daughter (Jane Birkin) tries to form closer ties with her frightened mother (Odette Laure) and vulnerable father (Dirk Bogarde). French director Bertrand Tavernier elicits luminous performances that enable the theme of reconciliation to emerge with emotional honesty from the film's deliberately slow pace and lack of high drama. Subtitles. Serious treatment of mortality. A-II (PG)

Daddy's Gone A-Hunting (1969) Urban thriller in which a wife (Carol White) and her husband (Paul Burke) are terrorized by her manic ex-boyfriend (Scott Hylands), who seeks revenge for the child that years before she had aborted without his consent. Director Mark Robson manages to work up a little tension in a rather thin story of people living in fear which, together with some silly but non-prurient bits of nudity, make it mature fare. A-III (PG)

Daisy Kenyon (1947) Classy sudser in which a fashion illustrator (Joan Crawford) finally realizes the futility of her affair with a wealthy, married lawyer (Dana Andrews) and weds a likeable, bemused architect (Henry Fonda), only to find herself still pursued by the heel who's now getting a divorce. Director Otto Preminger dresses up the brittle heroine's saga of romantic woes with some good performances and ironic humor but the tears are all artificial. Stylized treatment of infidelity and a broken marriage. A-III (br)

Daisy Miller (1974) Good adaptation of the Henry James story about a rich American (Cloris Leachman) touring Europe with her spoiled son (James McMurty) and impetuous daughter (Cybill Shepard). Directed by Peter Bogdanovich, the slight story is a gentle probe of the American character, but what makes the movie so charming and absorbing is the director's care in visualizing the mannered style of a past age. A-II (G)

Dakota (1945) Routine Western in which a cowboy (John Wayne) and a railroad baron's daughter (Vera Hruba Ralston) wed, then head for Fargo, N. D., where they get in the way of a devious land speculator (Ward Bond). Directed by Joseph Kane, the battle to save the farmers from being cheated ends in a furious night shootout as burning wheat fields light the prairie. Frontier violence and comic racial stereotyping. A-II (br)

Dakota (1988) Alienated California teenager (Lou Diamond Phillips), accidentally responsible for his younger brother's death, motorcycles away from his father's wrath, gets a job on a Texas thoroughbred ranch, befriends the owner's disabled 12-year-old son (Jordan Burton), and becomes a love interest for the boy's older sister (DeeDee Norton). Director Fred Holmes makes the story more interesting than its contrivances and ultimately encourages young viewers to face life's difficulties instead of running away from them and to commit to positive values. Chaste kisses, brief fisticuffs, and climactic heroics in a raging fire. A-II (PG)

Dakota Incident (1956) Formula Western in which the stagecoach to Laramie breaks down and its occupants (notably Linda Darnell, Dale Robertson, John Lund, and Ward Bond) take refuge in a gully, where they are besieged by a band of Cheyenne raiders. Directed by Lewis R. Foster, the unlikely proceedings are not without interest, though the peaceable resolution is a considerable stretch. Much frontier violence and muted sexual innuendo. A-II (br)

Dallas (1950) Laconic Western in which a former Confederate officer (Gary Cooper) comes to Texas seeking the outlaw raiders (Raymond Massey and Steve Cochran) who torched his home and killed his family in wartime Georgia. Directed by Stuart Heisler, the formula plot has some interesting wrinkles as Cooper pretends to be a US marshal, saves a Mexican ranch from land-grabbers, and finds true romance (Ruth Roman) along the way. Frontier violence and romantic complications. A-II (br)

Dam Busters, The (1954) Engrossing story of how the German steel mills in the Ruhr valley were flooded by British bombers (led by Richard Todd) using an ingenious bouncing bomb designed by a scientist (Michael Redgrave) to penetrate the area's fortified dams. Directed by Michael Anderson from R.C. Sheriff's script, the well-paced narrative details the bomb's invention, the training of the bomber crews and the dangers of the mission. A-I (br)

Damage (1992) Dreary look at the downfall of a British government minister (Jeremy Irons) whose out-of-control passion for the fiancé (Juliette Binoche) of his son (Rupert Graves) destroys several lives. Producer-director Louis Malle's dull, one-dimensional drama offers little more than the raw physical aspects of a sexually obsessive affair whose tragic consequences are emotionally barren. Explicit scenes of adulterous encounters, some nudity, and occasional rough language. O (R)

Damien — Omen II (1978) Sequel follows Damien the Antichrist (Jonathan Scott-Taylor), now 13 and living with wealthy Chicago aunt and uncle (Lee Grant and William Holden), as the special-effects department disposes of everyone who can reveal his secret. Directed with some intelligence by Don Taylor, the horror movie contains some gory violence and a dubious use of scripture. O (R)

Damn the Defiant! (1962) Handsomely mounted sea yarn of a British man-of-war whose seasoned captain (Alec Guiness) has his hands full dealing with a sadistic chief officer (Dirk Bogarde), a mutinous crew (led by Anthony Quayle), and Napoleon's fleet. Directed by Lewis Gilbert, the shifting conflict between the honorable captain and his villainous officer gets lost in a busy plot that ultimately proves less interesting than its lavishly detailed picture of life at sea, with some dandy naval battles along the way. Stylized violence, some of it quite brutal, especially that directed at a young lad aboard. A-I (br)

Damn Yankees (1958) Uneven screen version of the Broadway musical about a middle-aged real estate agent who sells his soul to the devil (Ray Walston) to become a baseball star (Tab Hunter) with the Washington Senators as they battle the New York Yankees for the pennant. Directed by George Abbott and Stanley Donen, the plot limps fitfully along in between some zesty musical numbers, the most memorable of which feature Gwen Verdon as Lola, the devil's seductive assistant. Comic sexual innuendo and situations. A-III (br)

Damnation Alley (1977) The survivors of a nuclear holocaust trek across a devastated America in search of a haven in this muddled and unexciting disaster film directed by Jack Smight and starring Jan-Michael Vincent, Dominique Sanda, and George Peppard. Some violence. A-III (PG)

Damned, The (1969) Using the story of a corrupt aristocratic family (Dirk Bogarde, Ingrid Thulin, and Helmut Berger) whose immense wealth derives from steel and armaments, director Luchino Visconti has fashioned a disquieting picture of the moral decadence within German society that made possible the rise of Hitler. The result has the primitive force of a Wagnerian opera in its mixture of fury and spectacle portraying the obscene lusts not only of the flesh, but of power and greed. Scenes of sexual perversity (incest, child molestation, homosexuality) are repulsive and anti-erotic, all part of a fabric that includes the obscenities of mass murder and unlimited violence on the part of those who ruled totalitarian Germany. A-IV (X/R)

Damned Don't Cry, The (1950) Slick but unconvincing melodrama of a woman (Joan Crawford) leaving a small-town, blue-collar husband to seek her fortune in the big city, where she uses an infatuated accountant (Kent Smith) to meet the big syndicate boss (David Brian), then becomes his mistress until learning crime doesn't pay. Directed by Vincent Sherman, the Crawford vehicle showcases her emotional range from earnest housewife to cynical playgirl, though in the midst of all this corruption, Smith's portrayal of a decent fellow steals the show. Stylized violence and sexual situations. A-III (br)

Damned in the U.S.A. (1992) British television

documentary on the 1990 controversy over the National Endowment for the Arts funding of sexually explicit and anti-religious works, as well as the obscenity trial of the 2 Live Crew rap group. Director Paul Yule presents both points of view through TV news coverage of events, interviews with those against pornography (notably Rev. Donald Wildmon of the American Family Association) and those for free expression (notably Cincinnati museum director Dennis Barrie), and a running commentary on the issues by Boston topical humorist Jimmy Tingle. Some brief shots of the works in question and occasional rough language. A-IV (nr)

Damsel in Distress, A (1937) Fluffy musical romance set in England, where an American hoofer (Fred Astaire) overcomes numerous comic complications to win the love of an earl's daughter (Joan Fontaine), then faces losing her because of a boastful press agent (George Burns) and his dizzy secretary (Gracie Allen). Directed by George Stevens, the result is a pleasant mix of romantic charm, zany humor, and mellow Gershwin tunes, with a zestful production number in an amusement park as the highlight. A-I (br)

Dance, Girl, Dance (1940) Creaky melodrama about an aspiring dancer (Maureen O'Hara) who takes a job in a burlesque show as the comic stooge of its spiteful star (Lucille Ball), then a wealthy playboy (Louis Hayward) breaks her heart before her talent is discovered by an uptown impresario (Ralph Bellamy). Directed by Dorothy Arzner, the formula story has dated badly, but the women characters are interesting period types and O'Hara has a classic scene in which she stops her burlesque routine to blast the male spectators for degrading women. Stylized violence, sexual innuendo, alcoholic excess, and light treatment of marriage. A-III (br)

Dance of Death (1979) Claustrophobic rendering of Strindberg's play about an embittered army captain (Laurence Olivier), commander of a remote and unimportant fortress off the coast of Sweden, and his love/hate relationship with his wife (Geraldine McEwan). Director David Giles preserves the relentless pessimism of the play, which expresses the dreary results of the couple's inability to find the grace of reconciliation. A-III (G/PG)

Dance with Me (1998) Overblown musical romance with a Latin beat as a Cuban youth (Chayanne) finds work in a Texas dance studio owned by the man (Kris Kristofferson) he is certain is his father, then falls for one of the studio's dance instructors (Vanessa L. Williams). Directed by Randa Haines, the thinly developed story relies on increasingly elaborate dance routines to provide the interest missing from stereotyped situations and characters, until all is resolved happily in a wildly upbeat dance-competition ending. Romantic complications and a benign view of unmarried sexual relationships. A-III (PG)

Dances with Wolves (1990) Set in the Dakota Territory of the 1860s, the story centers on a soldier (Kevin Costner) at a deserted frontier fort who embarks on a voyage of self-discovery when he is befriended by a Sioux tribe and falls in love with a white woman (Mary McDonnell) adopted by them. Also directed by Costner, the film's sensitive treatment of Native-Americans, exceptional cinematography, and fine performances compensate for its excessive three-hour-plus length. Much gory battlefield violence; minimal, restrained lovemaking; and a flash of rear nudity. A-III (PG-13)

Dancer, Texas: Pop. 81 (1998) Four high-school buddies vow to leave their tiny town and move to Los Angeles as soon as they graduate, then begin reconsidering their plan over the course of the graduation weekend. Writer-director Tim McCanlies's family-centered tale is sweet-natured and punctuated with wry humor, but its narrative is predictable and sluggishly paced. A scene with a drunken adult and implied promiscuity. A-III (PG)

Dancing at Lughnasa (1998) Wistful tale set in 1936 rural Ireland where five impoverished, unmarried sisters (led by schoolmarm Meryl Streep) are visited by their sickly priest brother (Michael Gambon) back from 25 years in Africa, and the youngest sister's wandering lover, whose 8-year-old son the sisters are jointly raising. Director Pat O'Connor beautifully bittersweet movie captures the sisters' indelible bond of love despite crushing emotional and financial hardships. An unmarried relationship and a rude expression. A-III (PG)

Dandy in Aspic (1968) A British secret agent (Laurence Harvey) also happens to be a Soviet double agent but has become expendable to both sides. Directed by Anthony Mann, the film is marked by interesting Berlin locales wasted on a confused plot that gets lost in its own web of intrigue. Stylized violence. A-III (br)

Danger Lights (1930) Pat romantic triangle as a gruff railroad boss (Louis Wohlheim) loses his fiancé (Jean Arthur) to the down-on-his-luck locomotive engineer (Robert Armstrong) he had befriended. Directed by George B. Seitz, the melodramatic plot is less memorable than its naturalistic picture of railroad life in the age of steam, with a dandy train race-against-time to Chicago for the finale. Romantic complications and a crippling train accident. A-II (br)

Dangerous Beauty (1998) Vapid period piece based on the diary of a 16th-century Venetian courtesan (Catherine McCormack) who uses her beauty and sexual allure to seduce the French king and to rally her lovers to protect her from the Inquisition. Director Marshall Herskovitz's mushy yarn romanticizes its heroine as a role model for repressed women of her day in what amounts to a lame historical bodice-ripper. A glamorized depiction of prostitution, brief sexual encounters with nudity, some violence, and occasional rough language. O (R)

Dangerous Game (1993) Dulling movie-within-a-movie features a sex-obsessed director (Harvey Keitel) filming the story of a homicidal yuppie (James

Russo) enraged that his wife (Madonna) is no longer willing to take part in drug-filled orgies. Abel Ferrara directs little more than one long, shrill stream of curses, drugs, drinks, empty sex, and repugnant characters. Recurring sexual violence against women including rape, some brief nudity, much substance abuse, and incessant rough language. O (R)

Dangerous Ground (1997) Violent melodrama in which an African-American (Ice Cube) returns on a visit to his native South Africa and finds his brother is a drug addict dangerously in debt to a merciless drug lord (Ving Rhames). Directed by Darrell Roodt, this portrait of the burgeoning drug trade in the new South Africa relies on a formula tale of explosive bloodshed and smug revenge. Acceptance of vigilante justice, much violence, recreational drug use, brief nudity, much rough language, and intermittent profanity. O (R)

Dangerous Liaisons (1988) In Paris before the French Revolution, a rogue aristocrat (John Malkovich) and his female counterpart (Glenn Close) weave a web of sexual intrigue and treachery to attain the lovers they covet and to destroy those who interfere. British director Stephen Frears portrays the psycho-sexual tug of war between the two selfish protagonists as devoid of moral or social considerations. Explicit sexual encounters with some nudity, acceptance of adultery as the norm within its historic context, and much sexual innuendo. O (R)

Dangerous Minds (1995) When an ex-Marine (Michelle Pfeiffer) turns to teaching high-school English to a chaotic class of tough minority students, she becomes involved in their personal problems while showing them that poetry offers practical insights in facing life's struggles. Director John N. Smith's fact-based story stresses uplifting themes about staying in school and rejecting despair, but the slick script rarely rises beyond shallow characterizations and pat solutions. Brief violence, some sexual references, and much crude slang and rough language. A-III (R)

Dangerous Mission (1954) Lackluster thriller directed by Louis King in which a New York cop (Victor Mature) tracks a terrified witness (Piper Laurie) in a gang slaying to a resort in National Glacier Park, then has to save her from a professional hit-man (Vincent Price) sent to silence her. Much unconvincing menace and some stylized violence. A-I (br)

Dangerous Money (1946) Weak shipboard murder mystery directed by Terry Morse with Charlie Chan (Sidney Toler) getting help from No. 2 Son (Victor Sen Yung) and chauffeur (Willie Best) in tracking the killer of a treasury agent to Samoa, where they find a cache of hot money. Comic racial stereotypes. A-I (br)

Dangerous Moonlight (1941) Dated WW II tearjerker in which a Polish pianist (Anton Walbrook) fights the invading Germans as a fighter pilot, then escapes to America, performs concerts for the Polish Relief Fund, and weds a wealthy supporter (Sally Gray) before enlisting in the RAF during the Battle of Britain. Directed by Brian Desmond Hurst, the movie opens with the pianist hospitalized with amnesia after his plane rams a German bomber, with the rest of the picture told in flashbacks triggered by the arrival of his wife. Wartime violence. A-I (br)

Dangerous Woman, A (1993) A simple-minded woman (Debra Winger), raised by an overprotective aunt (Barbara Hershey), falls in love with an alcoholic drifter (Gabriel Byrne) who finally admits to fathering her child after she's institutionalized for killing a former co-worker (David Strathairn). Director Stephen Gyllenhall's unconvincing melodrama presents several well-meaning characters who make major mistakes in their lives, then concludes the story with a terribly unrealistic happy ending. A few bedroom scenes with fleeting nudity, brief gory violence, some heavy drinking, and recurring rough language. A-III (R)

Dangerously Close (1986) Director Albert Pyun's hard-edged depiction of a high-school breeding ground for Rambo-styled vigilantes is a disturbing look at what some fear may be a contemporary trend. Starring and co-written by John Stockwell, the drama has no message, but its observation of the dread and menace caused by adolescent "law and order" Fascists is a cautionary tale. Some violence, brutality, and profanity. A-III (R)

Daniel (1983) Fictional treatment of the execution of Julius and Ethel Rosenberg for treason in the 1950s and its effect on their son (Timothy Hutton) as he grows into adulthood in the 1960s, determined to learn the truth about his parents' trial and their guilt or innocence. Sidney Lumet directs a well-intentioned but murky treatment of political events and personal relationships treated in a rather simplistic and romantic manner. It succeeds best, however, in showing the continuity of social justice issues and movements over the last half-century. Graphic electrocution scene. A-III (R)

Daniel Boone (1936) Frontier adventure with the title woodsman (George O'Brien) leading a pioneer wagon train through the wilderness to settle in 1775 Kentucky, despite Indian raids led by white renegade Simon Girty (John Carradine) and greedy colonial officials (notably Ralph Forbes). Directed by David Howard, the melodrama is fairly routine, though the frontier re-creations have a rugged credibility and the pioneer characters are quite colorful. Stylized violence. A-I (br)

Daniel Boone, Trail Blazer (1956) Simple outdoors adventure directed by Albert C. Gannaway and Israel Rodriquez in which the title frontiersman (Bruce Bennett) helps a band of settlers fight off attacks by Shawnee Indians and their British allies until Boone manages to make peace with his blood brother, the Shawnee chief (Lon Chaney, Jr.). Frontier violence and children in peril. A-I (br)

Danny (1979) A little girl (Rebecca Page) acquires a horse, nurses it back to health, and then rides it to victory over the nasty and spoiled little rich girl who formerly abused it. Director Gene Feldman's simple tale about the positive effects of caring should appeal to a family audience wishing to sensitize youngsters to the virtues of gentility and compassion. A-I (G)

Danny Boy (1945) Sentimental melodrama directed by Terry Morse in which a war dog is returned to its young master (Robert "Buzzy" Henry) after serving with the Marines in the South Pacific, then irritates a nasty neighbor who tries to have it destroyed as a menace, until the dog saves a toddler from an oncoming train. A-I (br)

Dante's Inferno (1935) Well-crafted melodrama in which a penniless go-getter (Spencer Tracy) turns an amusement-park show about the Italian poet Dante into a gold mine after marrying the niece (Claire Trevor) of its studious owner (Henry B. Walthall), then gets into trouble with the law and sinks all his money in a gambling boat destroyed by fire on its first outing. Directed by Harry Lachman, the acting, photography, and set design put over a formula story whose moral is underlined by a grandiose sequence patterned on the Dore illustrations of Dante's description of hell. Stylized violence, criminal acts, and fleeting nudity. A-III (br)

Dante's Peak (1997) Seeing signs that a long-dormant volcano is becoming dangerously active, a geologist (Pierce Brosnan) urges a nearby town to evacuate, then tries to save the town's mayor (Linda Hamilton) and her two young children when the eruption begins. Director Roger Donaldson's formula disaster picture has spectacular special effects of mass destruction amid an idyllic setting, but is otherwise a tame, even lackluster tale. Disaster injuries and fatalities, fleeting sexual innuendo, and a few instances of profanity. A-II (PG-13)

Danton (1984) Polish director Andrzej Wajda has made a stark and powerful film about the conflict between two leading figures of the French Revolution, the cold ideologue Robespierre (Wojciech Pszoniak) and the warm, passionate humanist Danton (Gerard Depardieu). The dubbed French production is essentially an intimate drama, revolving around the personality of its two protagonists. Although no prior knowledge of the intricacies of this revolutionary period is required, those who want to appreciate all the nuances of the situation may be motivated to do some reading in the history of the time. Some graphic violence. A-II (PG)

Danzon (1992) When her weekly dance partner disappears, a forty-ish telephone operator (Maria Rojo) journeys from Mexico City to Veracruz in hopes of finding him but discovers instead a fresh perspective on her regimented life. Director Maria Novaro presents a sensitive but haltingly told story of assorted transients reaching out to help one another over the potholes on life's highway. Subtitles. An implied sexual encounter. A-III (PG-13)

Darby O'Gill and the Little People (1959) Though none believe his blarney about capturing the king of the leprechauns, wily old Darby (Albert Sharpe) has indeed bagged the magical trickster and won't let him go until granting a wish for his daughter (Janet Munro) and her young man (Sean Connery). Directed by Robert Stevenson, the Disney production spins a pleasing yarn of Irish fantasy that is both warm-hearted and fun, though it has a few scary scenes to keep youngsters on the edge of their seats. A-I (G)

Daredevil, The (1972) George Montgomery plays an aging, amoral dirt-track race driver forced by the mob to run heroin shipments across Florida, and Terry Moore is the local schoolteacher who tries to reclaim him. Directed by Robert W. Stringer, the story and action are so inept that some will find it unintentionally entertaining. Some rough language. A-III (PG)

Daring Game (1967) Bubbly underwater action-adventure movie starring Lloyd Bridges, Nico Minardos, and Joan Blackman, who don rubber suits and flippers in an attempt to rescue a man held prisoner on a desert isle by a Banana Republic dictator. Director Laslo Benedek pumps up the action in attempting to supply some mediocre fun for all. A-I (br)

Dark Alibi (1946) Formula Charlie Chan mystery directed by Phil Karlson in which the Chinese-American detective (Sidney Toler) cracks a murder case involving planted fingerprints stolen from prison records, with some lame comedy from Chan's son Tommy (Benson Fong) and chauffeur (Mantan Moreland). Mild racial stereotyping. A-I (br)

Dark Angel, The (1935) Creaky sudser set in England, where a woman (Merle Oberon) chooses between two childhood friends when they go off to World War I, but the one (Herbert Marshall) who returns is not the man she loves (Fredric March), who's alive but unwilling to inflict his blindness on her. Directed by Sidney A. Franklin from Guy Bolton's play, the production is elegant and the characters have style, but the sentimental melodrama is dizzily contrived with complications only a romantic could find plausible. Implied premarital relations. A-III (br)

Dark at the Top of the Stairs, The (1960) Muddled melodrama from William Inge's play about the mid-life crisis of a man (Robert Preston) in 1920's Oklahoma when he loses his job, alienates his wife (Dorothy McGuire), and turns to a friendly widow (Angela Lansbury) before making a new start with his family. Director Delbert Mann portrays the period's changing economy, sexual mores, racial prejudice, and religious bigotry in more compelling fashion than the man's problems with himself and his family. Domestic tensions and sexual situations. A-III (br)

Dark Avenger, The (see: **The Warriors**)

Dark City (1950) Gritty crime thriller in which Chicago gamblers (Charlton Heston, Jack Webb, and Ed Begley) fleece a visiting businessman (Dan DeFore) whose suicide brings his psycho older brother (Mike Mazurki) to hunt them down one by one. Directed by William Dieterle, the stark proceedings focus on Heston's cynical character as he gradually softens under the influence of a torch singer (Lizabeth Scott) and the dead man's widow (Viveca Lindfors). Stylized violence, menacing atmosphere, and sexual innuendo. A-III (br)

Dark City (1998) Mysterious sci-fi thriller in which a man (Rufus Sewell) discovers aliens have manufactured his memories and physical surroundings in order to steal his soul. Directed by Alex Proyas, the nightmarish premise relies on sleek visuals to compensate for the narrative's murky logic. Occasional violence and brief nudity. A-III (R)

Dark Command (1940) After losing both the job of sheriff and his girl (Claire Trevor) to a Texas hayseed (John Wayne), an embittered Kansas schoolteacher (Walter Pidgeon) heads a band of pro-slavery raiders as the Civil War nears. Director Raoul Walsh stages some sweeping action scenes, and the supporting players (Roy Rogers, Gabby Hayes, Marjorie Main, and Porter Hall) add flavor to a contrived but fanciful script. Stylized violence. A-I (br)

Dark Corner, The (1946) Routine crime caper in which a private eye (Mark Stevens) is framed on a murder rap by an art dealer (Clifton Webb), but the gumshoe's devoted secretary (Lucille Ball) helps save the day. Directed by Henry Hathaway, the plot doesn't measure up to its hardboiled intentions, though William Bendix excels as a callous killer. Some hard-edged violence. A-II (br)

Dark Crystal, The (1983) Muppet masters Jim Henson and Frank Oz join in directing a Tolkein-like fairytale about the restoration of a shattered crystal to wholeness, which will bring about a never-ending reign of justice and peace. Although its story of good versus evil is a bit thin, the inventiveness of the puppetry and special effects is magical. Some scary moments for the very young. A-I (PG)

Dark Eyes (1987) Aging philanderer (Marcello Mastroianni) shares reminiscences of his love-life unknowingly with the husband of the mysterious lover who abandoned him. Sumptuous Italian period romance from Russian director Nikita Mikhalkov is both an affectionate celebration and comic denunciation of the self-centered blindness of male chauvinism. A-III (nr)

Dark Half, The (1993) Half-baked psychological thriller in which an established author decides to stop writing sleazy but lucrative crime novels under a pseudonym, then finds himself implicated in a series of brutal murders that seem incredibly the work of his literary alias. Director George Romero works hard at creating a suitably eerie atmosphere and keeps the violent shocks largely off-screen but fails to make much sense out of Stephen King's novel involving a malignant twin brother with supernatural powers. Some graphic violence, much menace, and occasional rough language and references. A-III (R)

Dark Journey (1937) Muddled spy melodrama of World War I follows two master agents (Vivien Leigh and Conrad Veidt) to neutral Stockholm, where they fall in love, though on opposite sides. Director Victor Saville's shadowy tale of spy and counterspy is filled with period detail and a properly tense atmosphere, but the bittersweet romance of the two secret agents seems as counterfeit as their assumed identities. Wartime menace and romantic complications. A-II (br)

Dark Mirror, The (1946) Psychological thriller in which a homicide detective (Thomas Mitchell) gets a psychologist (Lew Ayres) to examine identical twin sisters (Olivia de Havilland in a dual role) hoping to learn which of them committed a murder. Directed by Robert Siodmak, the plot turns on the doctor falling for one of the sisters, which pushes the other over the edge in a twisty ending that compensates for the movie's slow pacing. Menacing situations. A-II (br)

Dark Obsession (1991) Caring nothing that he has killed a woman in a hit-and-run accident and that one of the passengers (Douglas Hodge) may go to the police, a wealthy English aristocrat (Gabriel Byrne) is consumed by the fear that his wife (Amanda Donohoe) is unfaithful. Director Nick Broomfield's murky tale of violent sexual obsession offers a world of callous immorality, where the sole well-intentioned character pays dearly for his pangs of conscience. A number of explicit sexual encounters, other scenes with nudity, implied incest, calculated indifference to human life, and minimal rough language. O (NC-17)

Dark of the Night (1986) Lightweight Gothic tale about a woman (Heather Bolton) whose life is saved by the ghost of the former owner of her recently purchased vintage Jaguar. Directed by Gaylene Preston, the New Zealand import plays like a children's mystery devoid of any visual shocks and only mild suspense. A-I (nr)

Dark of the Sun (1967) Sleazy but gripping action-adventure melodrama about the efforts of mercenary soldiers Rod Taylor and Jim Brown to retrieve a fortune in uncut diamonds from their Congo employer's jungle outpost that has fallen into the hands of bloodthirsty rebels. British production directed by Jack Cardiff emphasizes gory slayings, tortures, and some sexual situations. O (PG)

Dark Passage (1947) Offbeat crime melodrama about a man (Humphrey Bogart) who escapes prison, is sheltered by a woman (Lauren Bacall) who believes him innocent, and has a plastic surgeon change his face in order to find the culprit who framed him. Directed by Delmer Daves, there are some interesting plot twists, fine use of San Francisco locations, and a good gallery of intriguing characters. A-II (br)

Dark Past, The (1948) Dated melodrama in which a psychiatrist (Lee J. Cobb) held prisoner by an escaped killer (William Holden) in an isolated country cottage passes the time by seeking the cause of the man's homicidal urges. Directed by Rudolph Maté, the threatening situation is made convincing enough, but the killer's psychiatric "cure" through dream analysis seems incredibly naive today. On-going menace and occasional physical violence. A-II (br)

Dark Places (1974) British horror movie about a man (Robert Hardy) who inherits the creepy estate of a wealthy maniac and then must defend it against outsiders (Joan Collins, Christopher Lee, and Herbert Lom) looking for the fortune stashed somewhere in the house. Directed by Don Sharp, the dark places are spooky enough for the undemanding horror buff. A dollop of blood and gore and some subtle sex. A-III (PG)

Dark Victory (1939) Classic tearjerker in which an energetic socialite (Bette Davis) is felled by a brain tumor, then falls in love with the surgeon (George Brent) who saved her life but knows she has only a few months to live. Directed by Edmund Goulding, the emotional manipulation of the plot is shamelessly transparent, but what still holds interest today is Davis's spunky, smiling-through-the-tears performance. Romantic complications and tense discussions of death. A-II (br)

Darker Than Amber (1970) Adaptation of a John MacDonald mystery with Rod Taylor as Travis McGee up to his neck in a tangle of brutal murders that begin when he falls in love with a woman (Suzy Kendall) he tries to protect from killers. Directed by Robert Clouse, the violence and brutality go beyond bounds of taste and restraint, as do some sex scenes. O (R/GP)

Darkman (1990) Extremely violent action thriller in which a scientist (Liam Neeson) seeks revenge on those who hideously disfigured him with acid by using his invention of synthetic skin to assume various identities in stalking his victims. Written and directed by Sam Raimi, the movie's production values add little to its dismal parade of grisly killings and human torture. Excessive violence and some rough language. O (R)

Darling (1965) Realistic British examination of the emptiness that characterizes the purposeless lives of the jet set. Directed by John Schlesinger with unrelenting honesty, the episodic movie follows the rise of a young woman (Julie Christie) through a series of affairs until she marries a wealthy prince whose palace becomes a sterile prison. A-IV (br)

Darling Lili (1970) Uneven musical comedy set in World War I about a London music hall entertainer (Julie Andrews) who feigns romance with an Allied pilot (Rock Hudson) in order to ferret military secrets for the Germans. Produced and directed by Blake Edwards, Andrews's charming performance and the lavish re-creation of the period's rickety automobiles and biplane aircraft are generally pleasing, but some lovemaking scenes and a couple of strip-tease numbers place it in the adult category. A-III (G)

Darwin Adventure, The (1972) Jack Couffer directs a historical dramatization of the events that led to Charles Darwin (Nicholas Clay) writing *Origin of Species* with loving attention to the world of nature but little feel for the human conflicts and emotional crises aroused by the scientist's theories. A-II (G)

D.A.R.Y.L. (1985) Sci-fi version of Pinocchio in which government scientists experimenting with artificial intelligence develop a robot that is like a boy in almost every respect. Some nasty higher-ups decide to put an end to the project when the robot transforms into a living boy with loving foster parents. Predictable story line, but director Simon Wincer maintains interest, and save for a few ill-considered vulgar expletives, it would have been quite suitable for young children. A-II (PG)

Das Boot (1982) Authentic WW II picture of a German submarine's final cruise in the North Atlantic, where U-boats were the terror of Allied convoys. Director Wolfgang Petersen emphasizes the claustrophobic conditions and dangers of sub duty with creative camerawork and first-rate performances, especially that of Jurgen Prochnow, whose haggard face as the captain is likely to haunt the viewer for some time. For all its virtues as a war movie, the moral dilemma of serving one of the worst causes in history is treated only indirectly. Subtitles or dubbed. Sexual references and crude language abound in this all-male environment. A-III (R)

Date with an Angel (1987) Plodding romantic comedy about a young man with a brain tumor (Michael E. Knight) who alienates his fiancé (Phoebe Cates) when he rescues an angel with a broken wing (Emmanuelle Beart). Writer-director Tom McLoughlin turns what might have been a lightweight, bouncy comedy into a leaden, earthbound fantasy. Some sexual innuendo, brief nudity, and verbal vulgarities. A-III (PG)

Date with Judy, A (1948) Thin teenage romance with 16-year-old Santa Barbara high-schoolers (Jane Powell in the title role with Elizabeth Taylor as her stuck-up rival) falling for a WW II veteran (Robert Stack) working his way through college as a soda jerk. Director Richard Thorpe's sentimental picture of small-town family life is invincibly innocent in its treatment of such contrivances as Judy's father (Wallace Beery) secretly taking lessons from a rhumba dancer (Carmen Miranda) in order to surprise his wife (Selena Royle) but causing Judy to fear he's having an affair. Adolescent mix-ups. A-I (br)

Date with the Falcon, A (1941) Routine mystery directed by Irving Reis has the sardonic series crime-fighter (George Sanders) chasing a gang after a synthetic diamond formula while being pursued by his neglected fiancé (Wendy Barrie) and bewildered police (led by James Gleason). Stylized violence and weak romance. A-II (br)

Daughter of Rosie O'Grady, The (1950) Pleasant 1890's musical in which a young woman (June Haver) disgruntles her father (James Barton) by trying to emulate her deceased mom's vaudeville success with the help of a top singer (Gordon MacRae) and a star hoofer (Gene Nelson). Directed by David Butler, the sentimental proceedings offer an agreeable mix of romance, comedy, and musical numbers, with Barton especially good as the obstinate father and veteran song-and-dance performer. Romantic complications and mild sexual innuendo. A-II (br)

Daughters of Darkness (1971) Delphine Seyrig plays a glamorous 300-year-old vampire in a very bizarre but very stylish horror fantasy directed by Harry Kumel. The Belgian production is a nightmarish study in mood and atmosphere with contemporary settings used to brilliant effect, but its explicit treatment of the sexual perversity usually only implicit in such horror movies is offensive. O (R)

Daughters of Satan (1972) Philippine devil-cult huff and puff their way through a ritual murder of the reincarnated Inquisitor responsible for the burning of three witches in 1592. Innocent of any coherence of plot, acting (Tom Selleck, Barra Grant, Tani Phelps Guthrie) or direction (Hollingsworth Morse), the movie carries the burden of several gratuitous scenes featuring sadism and nudity. O (R)

Daughters of the Dust (1991) Lyrical, feminist period piece set on an island off the South Carolina, coast where a family clan descended from West African slaves gather on a summer's day in 1902 to discuss their plans for moving to the mainland. Writer-director Julie Dash's highly imaginative and very stylized work contrasts those who want to pursue the American dream with the majority who are adamant about preserving the African traditions and mystical tales that have sustained them through countless generations. Some familial bickering and mild sexual references. A-II (nr)

Dave (1993) Conniving White House Chief of Staff (Frank Langella) dupes a patriotic businessman (Kevin Kline) into impersonating the comatose President while the estranged First Lady (Sigourney Weaver) grows increasingly suspicious as the lookalike begins to reform the government. In typical Hollywood fashion, director Ivan Reitman's lightweight comedy affably presents populist themes and simplistic solutions grounded in feel-good fantasy. Brief bedroom scene, fleeting shadowed nudity, and an instance of profanity. A-III (PG-13)

David and Bathsheba (1951) In Philip Dunne's somber biblical adaptation, King David (Gregory Peck) secretly orders one of his commanders (Kieron Moore) killed in battle so he can marry the man's widow (Susan Hayward), then faces God's wrath on him and his people. By avoiding the ostentatious spectacle usually associated with biblical epics, director Henry King weakens the impact of David's youthful triumphs shown in flashbacks, but strengthens the narrative's main focus on the king's moral weaknesses and the complexity of their consequences — human and divine. Mature theme and treatment. A-III (br)

David and Goliath (1961) Minor Italian production retelling the biblical story of David from boyish shepherd to manly Israelite champion (Ivo Payer) in the court of King Saul (Orson Welles). Directed by Richard Pottier and Ferdinando Baldi, the earnest but clumsy script is lost in hokey spectacle and bad acting. Stylized violence. A-I (br)

David and Lisa (1962) Two disturbed teenagers (Keir Dullea and Janet Margolin) in a mental institution form a loving relationship that helps each gain some emotional stability with the encouragement of a caring psychologist (Howard da Silva). Director Frank Perry with wife Eleanor's fact-based script turns the tale of damaged youths into an uplifting experience of love conquering despair, though some may find it all a bit too pat and unconvincing. Psychological problems of troubled adolescents. A-II (br)

David Copperfield (1935) Classic adaptation of the Charles Dickens story about an orphan (Freddie Bartholomew) saved from the wicked designs of a cruel stepfather (Basil Rathbone) with the help of his aunt (Edna May Oliver) and a host of friends (Maureen O'Sullivan, Jessie Ralph, Lionel Barrymore, Herbert Mundin, etc.). Director George Cukor captures the flavor of Dickens's mix of whimsy and melodrama with the proper Victorian atmosphere and an outstanding cast portraying its rich ensemble of characters, not least of whom is W.C. Fields's Micawber besting Roland Young's Uriah Heep. Outstanding family fare. A-I (br)

Davy Crockett and the River Pirates (1956) Disney sequel directed by Norman Foster has Davy (Fess Parker) and his genial sidekick (Buddy Ebsen) in a Mississippi boat race against riverman Mike Fink (Jeff York), then the slapstick violence turns a little more serious when they tangle with some hostile Indians. Mostly unpretentious juvenile fun. A-I (br)

Davy Crockett, King of the Wild Frontier (1955) Disney Western with coonskin-hatted Fess Parker as the Tennessee frontiersman of the title and Buddy Ebsen as his faithful partner in a series of adventures that end at the Alamo. Directed by Norman Foster, the setting is phony and the humor cornball, but the camaraderie is appealing and the action exciting enough to hold interest. Stylized violence. A-I (br)

Dawn at Socorro (1954) Formula Western directed by George Sherman in which an aristocratic Southern gunfighter (Rory Calhoun) comes out of retirement to help a troubled woman (Piper Laurie) by shooting it out with an old rival (Alex Nichol) and a crooked gambler (David Brian). Numerous gun battles and some sexual innuendo. A-II (br)

Dawn of the Dead (1979) Survivors of a previous night of the living dead are now besieged in a shopping mall. George Romero's campy pulp yarn has metaphorical pretensions as social satire, but essentially what's on the screen, peppered with rough language, is a relentless exploitation of gore and violence and the repulsive effects of violence. O (R)

Dawn Patrol, The (1930) World War I as fought in the air by a squadron of British fighter pilots whose commander (Neil Hamilton) buckles under the strain of sending men to their death and is replaced by one of the squadron's pilots (Douglas Fairbanks, Jr.). Directed by Howard Hawks from John Monk Saunders's script, the early talkie seems creaky today in romanticizing the desperate bravado of those who survive the deadly toll of daily air missions, but the aerial combat sequences are gripping enough to carry the picture. Wartime violence. A-I (br)

Dawn Patrol, The (1938) Remake of the 1930 movie about World War I fighter pilots in a British squadron whose stressed commander (Basil Rathbone) is replaced by one of the pilots (Errol Flynn). Directed by Edmund Goulding, the heroics here lack the raw edge of the original, though the acting is much more polished and the action better paced with sardonic humor. Wartime violence. A-I (br)

Dawning, The (1988) Sensitive coming-of-age drama set in the political troubles of 1920 Ireland, where an Anglo-Irish girl (Rebecca Pidgeon), being raised by an affluent aunt (Jean Simmons), turns 18 and drops her crush on a local stockbroker (Hugh Grant) after meeting a mysterious stranger (Anthony Hopkins) hiding in an abandoned beach house. Viewers know long before the girl does that the stranger is an IRA gunman planning a ruthless terrorist action which will unleash an equally ruthless response, with traumatic results for the innocent teenager. Directed by Robert Knights. Brief gory violence and menacing situations. A-III (PG)

Day for Night (1973) Director Francois Truffaut presents an amusing day-to-day diary of how a melodrama gets filmed in a studio on the French Riviera and himself plays the role of the director battling production difficulties while trying to deal with various complications in the (mostly love) lives of his cast (Jacqueline Bisset, Jean-Pierre Leaud, Valentina Cortese, and Jean-Pierre Aumont). It not only has some charming comedy, but it provides viewers with a real insight into how movies are made. A-III (PG)

Day in October, A (1992) A single Jewish family (Tovah Feldshuh, Daniel Benzali, and Kelly Wolf) serves as the dramatic focus in this tribute to the people of Denmark who helped the vast majority of their Jewish fellow citizens escape to neutral Sweden in October 1943, a day before the Germans ordered the arrest of every Jew in Denmark. Director Kenneth Madsen's well-intentioned dramatization bogs down in a lethargic, cliché-ridden script about a wounded Danish resistance fighter (D.B. Sweeney) who is helped by the Jewish family and who in turn helps them. Extraordinary heroism in the context of wartime violence and a muted romantic scene. A-II (PG-13)

Day in the Death of Joe Egg, A (1972) Intense drama about the parents (Alan Bates and Janet Suzman) of a hopelessly retarded, spastic 12-year-old raises issues of abortion and euthanasia but is hardly a propaganda piece for either faction. Directed by Peter Medak, the ambiguities of its characters and situation are left unresolved and casual moviegoers are likely to find it a difficult, draining, and confusing experience. A-IV (R)

Day James Dean Died, The (see: **24 Hours of the Rebel**)

Day of Anger (1969) Routine Italian Western about a gunman (Lee Van Cleef) and his hero-worshipping young assistant (Giuliano Gemna) who take over a small town by blackmailing its leading citizens. Directed by Tonino Valeri, bullets fly quite readily but the violence is controlled. A-III (PG)

Day of Fury, A (1956) Far-fetched Western directed by Harmon Jones in which a gambler (Dale Robertson) conspires to take over a town whose local marshal (Jock Mahoney) refuses to intervene until the local citizens turn to vigilante action. Stylized violence and sexual innuendo. A-II (br)

Day of the Animals (1977) A depletion in the atmosphere's ozone layer provokes Rocky Mountain wildlife into a wholesale attack upon humans. There is some elemental terror and suspense in this silly plot premise, but director William Girdler quickly depletes the suspension of disbelief by ineptly staging the resulting violence, including an attempted rape. A-III (PG)

Day of the Bad Man, The (1958) Hokey Western directed by Harry Keller in which a judge (Fred MacMurray) sentences a murderer to death, but the fearful townspeople leave him on his own to face the man's avenging brothers (notably John Middleton, Skip Homeier, and Lee Van Cleef), though an old friend (Edgar Buchanan) lends a helping hand. Frontier violence, considerable menace, and romantic complications. A-II (br)

Day of the Dead (1985) Director-writer George Romero's third low-budget zombie chiller provides a loathsome and unimaginative mix of violence, blood, gore, and some sexual references demeaning to women. O (nr)

Day of the Dolphin, The (1973) Dedicated scientist George C. Scott, privately funded and working in secret, has begun teaching a dolphin to talk. What he doesn't know is that he and the dolphin are being used by a mysterious clique of powerful officials in an assassination attempt. Director Mike Nichols's melodramatic plot about the corruption of the innocent is only intermittently interesting, but at least the movie serves as a reminder of the accelerated dangers of modern science. A-II (PG)

Day of the Evil Gun (1968) Routine but interesting Western stars Glenn Ford as a long-lost rancher who returns home to find not only that his wife and child have been carried off by Apaches, but that she was about to marry a neighbor anyway. Search for them he must, though, and director Jerry Thorpe packs the ensuing adventures with action, suspense, and some stylized violence. A-II (G)

Day of the Jackal, The (1973) Screen version of Frederick Forsyth's novel stars Edward Fox as a professional assassin hired by a rightist group of military officers to murder the president of France. Directed by Fred Zinnemann, this superbly crafted thriller succeeds not only as a gripping action movie but also as a serious probe into a theme of political expediency and amorality. A-III (PG)

Day of the Locust, The (1975) Aspiring artist (William Atherton) plumbs the emotional depths of the glittering 1930's Hollywood in director John Schlesinger's adaptation of the Nathaniel West novel about the superficial values and exploitative relationships that bind the Tinseltown community together. Karen Black is one of the victims who works as an extra and is obsessed by the dream of future stardom. Provoking at times, but ultimately a disappointing melodrama, with unnecessarily graphic violence. A-IV (R)

Day of the Outlaw (1959) Grim Western directed by Andre de Toth is set in a snowbound Wyoming town terrorized by a fleeing band of gold robbers (led by Burl Ives) who hole up there until persuaded by a local rancher (Robert Ryan) that he can lead them across the mountains to safety. Stylized violence, some of it quite nasty, and romantic situations. A-III (br)

Day of the Triffids, The (1963) Effective sci-fi thriller from John Wyndham's story in which a shower of meteorites engenders hordes of walking, carnivorous vines, as well as causes humans around the world to go blind, except for a sea captain (Howard Keel), a young woman (Nicole Maurey), and a couple of scientists (Kieron Moore and Janette Scott) seeking to destroy the killer vegetation. Director Steve Sekely makes the premise convincing enough to sustain interest through a meandering, uneven plot. Much menace and occasional stylized violence. A-II (br)

Day That Shook the World, The (1977) Yugoslavian re-creation of the 1914 assassination of the Archduke Ferdinand and his wife (Christopher Plummer and Florinda Bolkan) at Sarajevo, the tragic incident that triggered World War I. Director Veliko Bulajic captures the period atmosphere and historical background but fails to bring its characters to life, the result being merely a colorful but unmoving pageant. Excessively graphic torture sequence. A-IV (R)

Day the Earth Stood Still, The (1951) Science fiction classic about a humane alien (Michael Rennie) landing a flying saucer in Washington, D.C., on a mission to warn the world of self-annihilation if wars continue, makes the point by demonstrating his superior powers and then, with some help from a widow (Patricia Neal) and her boy, departs in peace. Director Robert Wise treats the fantasy premise in sober, underplayed fashion, giving the anti-war theme unusual credibility by relying more on the viewer's imagination and intelligence than on the hokum of the special effects department. Unsettling atmosphere of menace and some stylized violence. A-II (br)

Day the Fish Came Out, The (1967) When dying fish surface around a small Aegean island teeming with tourists, it's the result of an accidentally jettisoned nuclear weapon contaminating its waters, and world doom is forecast. Michael Cacoyannis wrote, produced, and directed this satiric morality play starring Candace Bergen and Tom Courteney that tries to do too many things and none of them well. Some sexual references concerning homosexuality. A-III (br)

Day the World Ended (1956) Low-budget production in which seven survivors of a global nuclear apocalypse try to cope with radioactive mists while fending off a mutated desert monster. Director Roger Corman's pulp tale focuses more on the dangers from within than from outside as a petty crook (Touch "Mike" Connors) tries to wrest control of the group from an upright geologist (Richard Denning), with predictable results. Menacing situations with occasional violence and an attempted rape. A-II (br)

Day They Gave Babies Away, The (see: **All Mine to Give**)

Daydreamer, The (1966) A little boy runs away from home and has a series of adventures, most of them taking place in his imagination. Jules Bass directs a part-animation, part live-action children's entertainment combining the biblical concept of Paradise with the fancy of Hans Christian Anderson and the result adds up to a diverting fantasy. A-I (br)

Daydreamer, The (1976) French comedy starring Pierre Richard (who also wrote and directed) as an eager but completely absent-minded art director for an advertising agency, where his wacky ideas prove so sensationally successful that they finally arouse the public to violence. In satirizing the vagaries of a consumer society, Richard's talent for remaining oblivious to all the chaos caused by his innocent eccentricities is in the best tradition of visual comedy. Minor romantic complications. A-III (PG)

Daylight (1996) A former medical emergency worker (Sylvester Stallone) single-handedly attempts to rescue a dozen trapped survivors when a tunnel connecting Manhattan to New Jersey collapses at both ends following a fiery explosion. Director Rob Cohen's formula disaster movie works up considerable concern over the fate of the frightened victims as their peril mounts from fires, flooding and collapsing supports. Some charred corpses, accident-related fatalities, and occasional profanity. A-III (PG-13)

Days and Nights in the Forest (1973) Indian movie about four men on holiday in a large forest preserve, where they meet a number of interesting individuals, not least, two women of wit and intelligence. Director Satyajit Ray's character study offers very little of dramatic action, but it is fascinating to observe the interplay of characters who are as authentic as our own circle of friends. A-II (nr)

Days of Glory (1944) WW II melodrama directed by Jacques Tourneur pays tribute to our then-Soviet allies in the story of a brave partisan leader (Gregory Peck) operating behind enemy lines, only to find his true love (Tamara Toumanova) just before joining in the Red Army's counterattack against the German invaders. Wartime violence, including atrocities against civilians, and romantic complications. A-II (br)

Days of Heaven (1978) In a drama set in 1916, a

Chicago mill-worker (Richard Gere), his common-law wife (Brooke Adams), and his kid sister (Linda Manz) work their way West as migrant farm laborers until they are hired by a wealthy Texas wheat-grower (Sam Shepherd). There is unfortunately not much in the characterizations or the plot's passionless romantic triangle to match the grandeur of Nelson Alemendros's camerawork and its visual homage to the land and those who work it. Directed by Terrence Malick. A-III (PG)

Days of Jesse James (1939) Standard Western directed by Joseph Kane in which singing lawman Roy Rogers nabs crooked banker Harry Woods for robbing his own bank, then blaming the theft on the James gang. Stylized violence and good badmen. A-I (br)

Days of Thunder (1990) Trained by a crusty racecar builder (Robert Duvall), a determined young driver (Tom Cruise) is pushed by his physician girlfriend (Nicole Kidman) to confront his fears head-on at the Daytona 500. Director Tony Scott surrounds Cruise's winning performance with wall-to-wall racing action in a formula underdog plot that builds to a rousing feel-good ending. Several sexual situations, a restrained bedroom scene, intense car crashes, and a few instances of rough language. A-III (PG-13)

Days of Wine and Roses (1962) Sobering tale of alcoholism as public-relations flack Jack Lemmon pulls wife Lee Remick into the bottle with him, then can't persuade her to quit when he joins Alcoholics Anonymous. Directed by Blake Edwards, the tragic narrative is rendered with harrowing realism but with enough compassion to earn sympathy for all involved. Many scenes of alcohol abuse and its consequences. A-II (br)

Daytrippers, The (1997) When a happily married teacher (Hope Davis) finds a love letter to her husband (Stanley Tucci), she spends the day with her concerned family (including mom Anne Meara, dad Pat McNamara, and sister Parker Posey) driving around Manhattan searching for an explanation from her elusive husband. Adroitly mixing comedy and drama, writer-director Greg Mottola explores intimate and family relationships with realism and sympathy for the very human characters who flesh out the story. Some sexual innuendo, some profanity, and occasional rough language. A-III (R)

Dazed and Confused (1993) A group of high-school seniors (including Jason London, Michelle Burke, and Ben Affleck) honor the custom of taunting and beating incoming freshmen (including Wiley Wiggins and Christin Hinojosa) after school and then at an all-night pot-smoking, drunken beer-bash. Writer-director Richard Linklater's plotless nostalgia about the excesses of free-spirited '70s adolescents is boringly inept but harmful in suggesting that doing drugs is simply a fun part of growing up. Constant teen drug and alcohol abuse, sexist attitudes, brief violence, and much rough language. O (R)

D.C. Cab (1983) Fifth-rate taxi company on the verge of extinction suddenly shapes up and plays a heroic role in foiling a kidnapping. Cast includes Gary Busey, Adam Baldwin, and Mr. T. Badly written and directed by Joel Schumacher, this vulgar comedy is dreary and unfunny, with foul language and some nudity. O (R)

De Sade (1969) The aging Marquis de Sade (Keir Dullea), in between bouts of prison and the insane asylum, returns to the decaying family mansion, where he recalls significant events in his life. Instead of providing any insight into the relationships and misfortunes that formed his character, director Cy Enfield's kindergarten Freud lacks even a thread of intelligibility or coherence. Numerous orgy sequences and a leering depiction of sadism. O (R)

Dead, The (1987) James Joyce's story of a family gathering on the Feast of the Epiphany in 1904 Dublin makes a small but beautifully crafted mood piece that ends somberly in the reverie of a wife (Anjelica Huston) on the long-ago death of a boy who was in love with her, and the reflections of her husband (Donal McCann) on the transitory nature of love, life, and the world. Director John Huston's warm evocation of the period and its characters is enlivened by the excellent performances of a largely Irish cast. A few indelicate words and mature references. A-II (PG)

Dead Again (1991) A reincarnation theme fuels this slick romantic thriller in which a private eye (Kenneth Branagh) and a fearful amnesiac (Emma Thompson) use a hypnotist (Derek Jacobi) to uncover their past lives — which had intersected violently. Also directed by Branagh, it's an eerie, crackling-good suspense movie, only partially marred by a strident music score and gory climax. Some brief, intense violence, intermittent rough language, and mild sexual innuendo. A-III (R)

Dead Are Alive, The (1972) Muddled European thriller about a series of murders occurring around the Etruscan excavations of an archaeologist (Alex Cord) who has some enemies (Samantha Eggar and John Marley). Director Armando Crispino's treatment of the story's abundant sex and violence can only be described as neo-Paleolithic. O (R)

Dead Calm (1989) Australian director Philip Noyce turns in a taut psychological thriller about a couple (Sam Neill and Nicole Kidman) terrorized at sea by a psychopath (Billy Zane) who overtakes their sailing yacht. A real nail-biter with powerful technical effects and a refreshingly resourceful female heroine, it's hampered by images of horrific violence and a brief but graphic sexual encounter. A-IV (R)

Dead End (1937) Gritty screen version of Sidney Kingsley's play about the cycle of poverty focuses on a fugitive gangster (Humphrey Bogart), an aspiring architect (Joel McCrea), and a union worker (Sylvia Sidney) worried over an adolescent brother (Billy Halop) who's hanging out with a gang of street toughs (Leo Gorcey, Huntz Hall, Gabriel Dell, and others) in a New York City block of tenements next to a luxury apartment building. Directed by William

Wyler, the story portrays a classic example of the slums as breeding ground for crime but ends with some hope of change. Stylized violence. A-II (br)

Dead Heat on a Merry-Go-Round (1966) Crass ex-con (James Coburn) engineers a bank robbery at the Los Angeles airport timed to coincide with the arrival of the Soviet premier. Directed by Bernard Girard, the emphasis is less on the crime aspects than on depicting its amoral hero who not only gets the loot but ditches his girlfriend. Some violence. A-III (br)

Dead Image (see: **Dead Ringer**)

Dead Man on Campus (1998) Contrived black comedy in which two failing college freshmen (Tom Everett Scott, Mark-Paul Gosselaar) try to provoke a succession of depressed roommates into committing suicide, in which case their bad grades would be excused. As directed by Alan Cohn, the bizarre premise is unconvincing, and lighthearted scenes of recreational drugs, underage drinking, casual sex, and troubled students are highly unamusing. Jokey treatment of substance abuse and promiscuity, fleeting nudity, and much rough language and profanity. O (R)

Dead Man Walking (1995) Powerful fact-based dramatization about a Louisiana nun (Susan Saradon) offering spiritual comfort to a hard-bitten prisoner (Sean Penn) condemned to death for the rape and murder of two teenagers, while at the same time attempting to share in the painful loss of the victims' grieving parents. Directed by Tim Robbins, the picture is balanced between the nun's respect for the dignity of every individual, even the despicable killer, and the parents' quest for justice in the state's execution of their children's murderer, leaving viewers at the end to ponder what moral or social purpose is served by capital punishment. Flashbacks to savage crimes, the depiction of an execution, racial slurs, and several instances of rough language. A-III (R)

Dead Men Don't Wear Plaid (1982) Steve Martin playing a 1940's private eye cavorts with famous stars of the period, thanks to some clever editing of footage from old Hollywood detective movies. Affectionate and moderately entertaining spoof directed by Carl Reiner, it's a one-joke movie, but the joke holds up fairly well. Some sexually oriented humor. A-III (PG)

Dead of Night (1945) Classic British horror movie recounts five chilling tales, the best of which concerns the troubles of a ventriloquist (Michael Redgrave) with his dummy, unfolding within the frame story of an architect (Mervyn Johns) whose recurrent nightmare finally becomes a reality. Produced by Michael Balcon with various directors for the individual stories, the result is an eerie spellbinder, relying on the intelligence as well as the imagination of the viewer. Low-key menace and several instances of stylized violence. A-II (br)

Dead of Summer (1971) Wealthy neurotic American (Jean Seberg), in a desolate Moroccan city beset by sweltering heat and a howling sandstorm, spends the day in her elegant apartment (with broken air conditioner) making various attempts to communicate with others. Director Nelo Risi's boring existential study has several needlessly extended erotic sequences. O (R)

Dead of Winter (1987) Aspiring actress becomes the pawn in a blackmail attempt which proves fatal to her captors and to the rich woman who's the target of their extortion. Director Arthur Penn's unconvincing thriller features Mary Steenburgen in a triple role. Unnecessarily explicit violence at the conclusion make the film unsuitable for youngsters. A-III (R)

Dead Poets Society (1989) A teacher (Robin Williams) returns in 1959 to the tony New England prep school for boys from which he had graduated, determined to turn his students on to poetry and into free-thinkers, but his unorthodox methods inspire the impressionable youths to take personal risks not always in their best interests. Director Peter Weir's thought-provoking period drama raises more questions than it answers in exploring such issues as peer pressure, child rights, values clarification, teen suicide. and the price of nonconformity. Mild locker-room language and an unsettling, unresolved teen suicide. A-III (PG)

Dead Pool, The (1988) With some assistance from his Chinese-American partner (Evan Kim), San Francisco homicide detective "Dirty Harry" Callahan (Clint Eastwood) makes Swiss cheese out of both the mob and a psycho killer but is no match for a bomb-laden miniature sports car. Veteran stunt coordinator Buddy Van Horn directs the bloody action and graphic mayhem with a questionable sense of humor. Excessive violence and much profanity. O (R)

Dead Presidents (1995) Crime melodrama in which a black youth (Larenz Tate) returns to the mean streets of the Bronx after serving four years in Vietnam, then turns to crime to support his family. Directed by Albert and Allen Hughes, the story of a disillusioned veteran becoming an armed robber is not new, but the African-American context gives it a fresh vitality. Some intense violence, sexual situations, and rough language. A-IV (R)

Dead Ringer (1964) Baldly contrived suspense thriller with Bette Davis in dual roles as an embittered sister who kills her treacherous twin, then assumes the sister's life as a wealthy widow. Directed by Paul Henreid, the paper-thin plot is given some class by Davis's highly charged performance until a good cop (Karl Maudlin) and a worthless womanizer (Peter Lawford) get in the way. Some stylized violence and implied marital infidelity. A-III (br)

Dead Ringers (1988) Twin gynecologists (Jeremy Irons plays both roles), unable to establish their own individual identities, ultimately find their lives and successful practice in ruins due to the love relationship between one of the brothers and a strong-willed actress (Genevieve Bujold). Director David Cronenberg and actor Irons happily do not exploit the obvious horror show potential of this chilling psychological thriller, but the explicit gynecological discussions of female anatomy and some graphic, kinky sexual encounters are excessive enough. Also much profanity and a gruesome, bloody finale. O (R)

Dead Run (1969) Petty German pickpocket steals some secret government papers and becomes the target for undercover agents all over Europe. Humdrum foreign intrigue melodrama starring Peter Lawford and directed by Christian-Jacque, its only saving feature is that it does not take itself seriously. Scenes of violence and torture and one featuring a strip tease. O (R)

Dead Tired (see: **Grosse Fatigue**)

Dead Zone (1983) Good screen version of the Stephen King novel about a man (Christopher Walken) who awakens after being in a coma for five years to discover that he has the gift of second sight, enabling him to tell things of the future and past of anyone with whom he comes into physical contact. Such a gift has its drawbacks, of course, and director David Cronenberg does well in exploring them. More a psychological suspense thriller than a horror film, its strong supporting cast includes Brooke Adams, Tom Skerrit, and Herbert Lom. Passably entertaining for a mature audience. A-III (R)

Dead-Bang (1989) Unsatisfying Los Angeles cop drama featuring a troubled homicide detective (Don Johnson) on the trail of a vicious cop-killer who's tied to a grassroots white-supremacist movement. Director John Frankenheimer fails to pull together the cop's messed up personal life and the growing threat of white racists in the Southwest. Much grisly violence, a gratuitous sex scene, and profanity. O (R)

Deadfall (1968) Convoluted tale about a cat burglar (Michael Caine) who, linking up with a married couple of jewel thieves (Eric Portman and Giovanna Ralli), falls in love with the wife, which is all right with the husband because he's a homosexual; but, than again, maybe he's really her father. Obscure British production directed by Bryan Forbes fails both as action thriller and psychological drama with its implications of incest and homosexual relationships. O (br)

Deadlier Than the Male (1967) Bulldog Drummond detective adventure starring Richard Johnson on the trail of a pretty pair of female assassins (Elke Sommer and Sylvia Koscina) whose specialty is murdering key executives involved in business mergers. Dim-witted British production directed by Ralph Thomas, it offers a frothy mixture of sex and violence adding up to some very distasteful entertainment. O (br)

Deadline (1987) Reporter assigned to Beirut (Christopher Walken) not only loses his big story but gets caught between warring factions and has to flee for his life. Directed by Nathaniel Gutman, the personal story gets lost in the chaos and confusion of the war-torn city, whose violence is depicted in realistic, stomach-churning fashion. Much bloody violence with vivid and gruesome scenes of the dead and dying. A-IV (R)

Deadline at Dawn (1946) Uneven murder mystery from the Cornell Woolrich story in which a drunken sailor (Bill Williams) comes to in a room with a dead woman, then gets help from a novice actress (Susan Hayward) and a cab driver (Paul Lukas) in searching through the night for clues to the real killer's identity. Directed by Harold Clurman from Clifford Odets's script, the tense proceedings get increasingly complicated until the twist ending, though relieved along the way by a romantic subplot and the cabby's philosophic musings. Much menace and occasional stylized violence. A-II (br)

Deadline U.S.A. (1952) High-minded editor (Humphrey Bogart) tries to save his newspaper from being sold to a competitor by assigning his ace reporters (notably Ed Begley, Paul Stewart, and Jim Backus) to get the goods on the city's crime boss, despite threats, murdered witnesses, and the editor's own problems trying to win back his ex-wife (Kim Hunter). Writer-director Richard Brooks keeps the pot boiling with a plot full of newspaper cliches, occasional sermons on the value of a free press, and a protracted downbeat ending. Stylized violence, gritty underworld characters, and some sexual innuendo. A-III (br)

Deadly Affair, The (1967) Screen version of a John Le Carre novel about an aging government agent (James Mason) who, just before retirement, discovers he must carry out one last investigation that probably will shatter whatever small security he has left in life. Director Sidney Lumet gets fine performances from a cast which includes Simone Signoret, Harriet Andersson, and Harry Andrews in this taut British spy thriller for grown-ups. A-III (br)

Deadly Bees, The (1967) Halting British thriller in which a pop singer (Suzanna Leigh) arrives for a needed vacation on a sleepy island, where a horde of bees begins killing people. Directed by Freddie Francis, the slow-moving plot makes it fairly obvious which of the island's two beekeepers (Frank Finlay or Guy Doleman) is responsible, though the swarm of killer bees provides some uncomfortable moments. Stylized violence and menace. A-II (br)

Deadly Fathoms (1973) Documentary explores the graveyard of sunken ships that were involved in the 23 atomic bomb tests in South Pacific waters near the atoll of Bikini. Despite a no-nonsense narration by Rod Serling, these grotesque monuments to the nuclear age often only serve the purposes of an undersea adventure directed by Michael Harris. A-I (G)

Deadly Friend (1986) A strange but mild-mannered horror movie about a teenager who brings his girlfriend back to life by implanting a computer chip in her brain. She thereupon kills her abusive father and the nasty old lady next door. Director Wes Craven makes little of this, or anything else, in a dull and pedestrian tale. Restrained violence. A-II (R)

Deadly Hero (1976) After killing an unarmed man

(James Earl Jones) who has been terrorizing a cultured musician (Diahn Williams), a violence-prone New York policeman (Don Murray) becomes enraged when his career is put in jeopardy by her telling the truth. Director Ivan Nagy gets convincing performances and evokes the gritty atmosphere of the big city, but his creative energies flag midway, and it becomes little more than another woman-stalked-by-terror movie relying on violence and the sexual menace it generates. O (R)

Deadly Trackers, The (1973) Excessively violent story of Western revenge in which a sheriff (Richard Harris) sees his family murdered by a band of outlaws, follows them to Mexico, and kills them one by one, until a Mexican sheriff, upholding law and order, kills the American sheriff. Directed by Barry Shear, much of the movie is devoted to bloody fights and shootouts as well as expounding a simplistic notion of law and justice. O (PG)

Deadly Trap, The (1972) Frank Langella and Faye Dunaway play an uneasily married couple living in Paris troubled by a series of peculiar occurrences that culminate in the disappearance of their two children. Badly failed French suspense thriller directed by Rene Clement, the plight of the two young children might be distressing for some preteens. A-II (PG)

Deaf Smith and Johnny Ears (1973) Italian Western filmed in sunny Spain and set in frontier Texas, where Anthony Quinn and Franco Nero spend most of their time preventing a particularly nefarious Mexican general from taking over the Southwest. Director Paolo Cavara provides numerous fistfights, shootouts, rattling Gattling guns, and lots of explosions, with an occasional visit to the local bordello. A-III (PG)

Deal of the Century (1983) Chevy Chase and Gregory Hines play traveling salesmen selling bargain-basement weaponry to Third World governments and those who are trying to overthrow them. It might have worked as a satire on the illicit arms trade, but as a straight slapstick comedy, it is merely disappointing and only sporadically funny. Directed by William Friedkin, it is marred by some outrageous stereotyping of Hispanics, both in Latin America and in this country. A-III (PG)

Dealers (1989) British import takes a satirical look at the bankrupt ethic pushing high-powered financial traders to substance abuse and suicide in a story about the love-hate relationship between a flamboyant young trader (Paul McGann) and his new supervisor, a sexy American (Rebecca DeMornay) who's sleeping with their married boss. Directed by Colin Bucksey, the financial mumbo jumbo and male-female cat-and-mouse games divert attention from the pressures that drive such individuals to succeed at any cost. Brief sexual encounters and some scenes of drug abuse. A-III (R)

Dealing: Or The Berkeley-To-Boston Forty-Brick Lost-Bag Blues (1972) Harvard law student (Robert F. Lyons) flies out to Berkeley to pick up a marijuana shipment for the campus pusher (John Lithgow) and meets a liberated woman (Barbara Hershey), but they run into a corrupt cop (Charles Durning). Directed by Paul Williams, the supposed comedy views pot as amusing and contains nudity and rough language. O (R)

Dear America: Letters Home from Vietnam (1988) Based on the book of the same name, this feature-length documentary uses compelling newsreel footage to visualize the feelings and impressions recorded in the letters sent home by American soldiers who saw the war firsthand. Directed by Bill Couterie, the off-camera readers include a fine array of actors from Tom Berenger to Robin Williams, and excellent use is made of the many songs engendered by the bitter conflict on the home-front. Realistic footage, some of it very intense, depicting the obscenity of war. A-II (PG-13)

Dear Brigitte (1965) Failed comedy about an underpaid humanities professor (James Stewart), his down-to-earth wife (Glynis Johns), and their eight-year-old mathematical prodigy (Billy Mumy) whose facility with numbers is put to use picking racetrack winners, though the boy prefers writing love letters to French actress Brigitte Bardot. Directed by Henry Koster, the picture aims at heartwarming whimsy (Ed Wynn is the hapless narrator) but settles for artificial sentimentality and noxious treacle. Pretentious time-waster. A-I (br)

Dear Detective (1978) Two former college classmates, now in their mid-40s, bump into each other (quite literally) and discover that he's still a bachelor (Philippe Noiret) and she's divorced (Annie Girardot). The main source of humor in this French comedy directed by Philippe de Broca is how their romance is complicated by each other's professions — he's a college professor and she's a police inspector. Cheerful little comedy with two charming, talented performers. Some Gallic wit about the war between the sexes and brief partial nudity. A-III (PG)

Dear God (1996) Feeble comedy in which a con-artist working as a postal employee (Greg Kinnear) and his wacky co-workers get in hot water after he opens letters addressed to God and they begin helping the needy letter-writers. Despite a talented comedic supporting cast, director Garry Marshall's sentimental tale is clumsily contrived, generating few laughs and mostly bogus emotions. Fleeting violence and mild sexual innuendo. A-II (PG)

Dear Heart (1964) Synthetic romance unfolds during a postmaster's convention in New York City, where a wistful Ohio delegate (Geraldine Page) beguiles a sales executive (Glenn Ford) about to wed a level-headed widow (Angela Lansbury). Directed by Delbert Mann, the plot contrivances are too calculated to imbue the characters with the script's intended charm. Sexual situations and innuendoes. A-III (br)

Dear John (1966) Swedish movie written and directed by Lars Magnus Lindgren is intended to explore the beginnings of a meaningful love relationship through a couple's physical experience of sex. It deals only superficiality with the human dimension of its characters and never gets much beyond the physical. Graphic portrayal of sexual activity. O (br)

Dear Ruth (1947) Wacky romantic comedy in which a high-school girl (Mona Freeman) secretly writes love letters to a WW II bombardier (William Holden) using her older sister's name and photo (Joan Caulfield) in a deception which comes to involve the entire household when the soldier shows up for a visit on a two-day furlough. Directed by William D. Russell from Norman Krasna's play, the situation grows ever more confusing, nicely paced with comic bits by a solid supporting cast (notably Edward Arnold, Mary Philips, and Billy De Wolfe) until the agreeably sentimental ending. Romantic complications and much duplicity. A-II (br)

Dear Wife (1949) Less amusing sequel to **Dear Ruth** employs the same cast, but director Richard Haydn can't do much with them in a story centered on the growing tensions between Ruth (Joan Caulfield) and her ex-soldier husband (William Holden) when he runs against her father (Edward Arnold) for the state senate. Domestic disputes. A-I (br)

Death and the Maiden (1994) Somber adaptation of Ariel Dorfman's play set in a South American country recently liberated from a brutal dictatorship, one of whose victims (Sigourney Weaver) happens upon a man (Ben Kingsley) she is certain tortured her and, with the unwilling help of her husband (Stuart Wilson), binds and brutally tries to force him to confess his guilt. Director Roman Polanski fails to turn the one-set stage piece into more than a static movie with overly theatrical performances, yet the human rights theme is rightly troubling in this raw, ugly treatment of violence's cyclical nature. Intense scenes of physical brutality and life-threatening menace, detailed verbal descriptions of torture, brief nudity, and occasional profanity. A-IV (R)

Death Becomes Her (1992) Satire and fantasy clash in this black comedy about two aging celebrities (Goldie Hawn and Meryl Streep) ready to kill each other over an alcoholic plastic surgeon (Bruce Willis). The humor is decidedly plastic in director Robert Zemeckis's frenzied movie, with Streep's finely nuanced performance the sole merit. Comic violence, some sexual references, and a flash of nudity. A-III (PG-13)

Death Before Dishonor (1987) Trite, almost propagandistic account of hostilities between Arab terrorists and US Marines assigned to protect a US Embassy in a small Middle Eastern country. Fred Dryer plays a clone of Clint Eastwood's **Heartbreak Ridge** gunnery sergeant in director Terry Leonard's failed drama. Much violence, graphic brutality, and recurring rough language. O (R)

Death by Hanging (1974) Japanese movie made in 1968 presents a scathing attack on capital punishment with the sub-theme of Japanese racist attitudes towards Koreans. Directed by Nagisa Oshima, its originality in structure and technique takes chances in combining documentary and dramatic styles but is unusually successful in making an exciting movie on a most provocative subject. A-III (nr)

Death Collector (1976) Crime syndicate melodrama about a rash but engaging young hoodlum (Joseph Cortese) who refuses to stay in line and suffers the ultimate penalty. Aided by some talented actors, director Ralph De Vito's effort, for all its low-budget defects, has a tough sense of reality and some intelligence but resorts to excessive violence and some nudity. O (R)

Death Hunt (1981) Lee Marvin plays a grizzled Mountie tracking Charles Bronson, a wrongly accused fugitive, in the 1930s Canadian backwoods, both men aware that they are the last of the old breed upon whom civilization is fast closing in. Routine outdoor melodrama directed by Peter R. Hunt with some rough language and violence. A-III (R)

Death in Venice (1971) Fine adaptation of the Thomas Mann novel in which an artist (Dirk Bogarde), in the twilight of his career and unwilling to chance personal encounters with others, is taken with the beauty of a golden-haired youth, setting off within him an unresolved conflict between mind and body. Directed by Luchino Visconti, it is a movie of character and mood rather than of plot, with the interior drama being much more significant than any external actions. A-III (GP)

Death of a Bureaucrat (1979) Cuban director Tomas Gutierrez Alea fashions a satire on the hypocrisy of government bureaucracy. A widow must retrieve the work card buried with her husband in order to receive her pension. Black comedy with wry moments but a bit too sardonic and cynical for some tastes. A-III (nr)

Death of a Gunfighter (1969) Western town trying to attract Eastern industry wants to get rid of its tough, old-fashioned sheriff (Richard Widmark), but he won't resign. So, in the interest of civic progress, the town fathers decide to have him gunned down. Though given little to do, Lena Horne as a madam who marries the sheriff adds some interest to a disappointingly thin story whose fitful proceedings were directed by the pseudonymous Allen Smithee. Stylized violence and sexual situations. A-III (PG)

Death of a Hooker (see: **Who Killed Mary What's'ername**)

Death of a Jew (1973) Captured Israeli agent (Assaf Dayan) is befriended by an old Arab policeman (Akim Tamiroff), a promising situation which goes nowhere except to a very predictable conclusion. The 1970 Israeli production is a well-intentioned parable on the brotherhood of man, but it is without a shred of insight into people or politics and the direction of Denys de la Patalliere is hopelessly lackluster. A-III (PG)

Death of a Salesman (1951) Interesting adaptation of the Arthur Miller play charting the downward spiral of a middle-aged man (Fredric March) who cannot cope with the reality that his company and customers consider him redundant. Though the movie has limitations as popular drama, director Laslo Benedek generates empathy for the liked-but-not-well-liked salesman who relies on empty optimism to mask his growing doubts and then despair. The cautionary tale about defining one's life in terms of what one does for a living is too intense for children. A-II (nr)

Death of an Angel (1986) This unconvincing drama attempts to contrast a rationalistic vs. charismatic approach to matters of faith. An Episcopal priest (Bonnie Bedelia) confronts her doubts about her own religious belief and the integrity of a seemingly dishonest faith healer (Nick Mancuso) patronized by poor, destitute, and crippled Mexican peasants. In addition to several instances of harsh language, writer-director Petro Popescu offers several scenes of needless sadistic brutality and ambiguous sexual references. O (PG)

Death of Tarzan, The (1968) This Czechoslovakian version of the Tarzan legend has the ape-man return to Europe in order to make its point that human society can be more predatory than that of the jungle. A dark comedy directed by Jaroslav Balik, it nevertheless demonstrates that love is a more basic part of human nature than greed or violence. A-II (br)

Death on the Nile (1978) An heiress (Lois Chilez) is murdered on a honeymoon cruise up the Nile and Hercule Poirot (Peter Ustinov), Agatha Christie's Belgian sleuth, is on hand to interrogate such suspects as Bette Davis, Angela Lansbury, Maggie Smith, Mia Farrow, and George Kennedy. Directed by John Guillermin, it is an intricately plotted whodunit that plays the game fairly in laying out clues to challenge the mystery fan. A lavishly produced 1930's period piece with exotic Egyptian locales, it's solid escapist entertainment for those who don't mind rather graphic depictions of murder. A-III (PG)

Death Race 2000 (1975) Satire about the American passion for violence and speed set against the background of a transcontinental auto race in the year 2000, when America is ruled by a dictatorship whose main method of control is the bread-and-circus device. Director Paul Bartel exploits what supposedly he is satirizing, including a unneeded sampling of sex and nudity. O (R)

Death Rides a Horse (1969) After a gruesome opening in which a small boy watches his whole family brutalized and killed by outlaws, director Giulio Petroni's Italian Western moderates the violence as it follows the pursuit of the killers by the boy (John Phillip Law) 15 years later. While it's somewhat lower on the violence scale than many others of the genre, it also registers fairly low on the scale of originality. A-III (M)

Death Ship (1980) George Kennedy and other unfortunates perform in a witless story about a Nazi ghost ship that roams the Atlantic ramming passenger ships and seeking the blood of the survivors to keep its ghoulish act going. Besides considerable gore and violence, director Alvin Rakoff's horror movie trades upon memories of the Holocaust to give substance to its cheap and grisly thrills. O (R)

Death Valley (1982) Homicidal maniac (Steve McHattie) menaces a young boy (Peter Billingsley) in a terribly inept thriller that starts out like **Kramer vs. Kramer** and ends up like **The Texas Chainsaw Massacre**. Directed by Dick Richards, it traffics in explicit violence, bloodshed, and nudity. O (R)

Death Warrant (1990) A spate of unexplained killings inside a Los Angeles prison prompts a former Canadian Mountie (Jean-Claude Van Damme) to pose as a newly arrived con and likely target for the next hit. Directed by Deran Sarafian, the routine kickboxing action movie features mediocre performances in a predictable plot with the expected pay-off of increasingly brutal, bloodthirsty fights. Excessive violence and some rough language. O (R)

Death Wish (1974) New York executive (Charles Bronson) sets about avenging the vicious assaults upon his wife and daughter by systematically doing away with the criminal population of the city. Director Michael Winner treats his judge-and-jury actions as if they were an admirable example of civic consciousness. Objectionable are not only the movie's incessantly bloody visuals but even more so its dangerous vigilante message. O (R)

Death Wish II (1982) Charles Bronson reprises his role of the decent citizen turned murderous vigilante in a sequel utterly condoning unlawful actions. Directed by Michael Winner with graphic violence, including sexual violence. O (R)

Death Wish III (1985) Urban vigilante Charles Bronson again mows down felons in this third outing directed by Michael Winner with a variation on the theme increasing the body count to the point of utter absurdity. Unremitting and exploitative violence, including sexual violence. O (R)

Death Wish V: The Face of Death (1994) Following the mutilation and murder of his fiancé (Lesley-Anne Down), the series's aging vigilante (Charles Bronson) methodically tracks down and executes the gangster (Michael Parks) and goons responsible. Writer-director Allan A. Goldstein's paean to vigilante justice is hackneyed and predictable in its mindless brutality. Graphic violence, some nudity, and occasional rough language. O (R)

Deathmaster (1972) Stale story of a vampire (Robert Quarry) who employs brainless hippies to bring victims (Bill Ewing and Brenda Dickson) to his isolated beach mansion. Lifelessly directed by Ray Danton, the movie indulges in some raw dialogue and a bit of coy nudity. A-III (PG)

Deathtrap (1982) A washed-up playwright (Michael Caine) contemplates murdering an up-and-coming one (Christopher Reeve) and stealing his play in this competent if uninspired movie version of Ira Levin's Broadway comedy-thriller. Though it drags and the ending is weak, director Sidney Lumet gets first-rate performances from a cast including Dyan Cannon and Irene Worth. Brutal murders and some rough language. A-III (PG)

Debut, The (1971) Quiet little Russian comedy about a young woman worker who is selected to play Joan of Arc in a movie production and her affair with a married man. Director Gleb Pantilov gently contrasts proletarian life and attitudes with those of the official class of state artists and functionaries. A-III (nr)

Decalogue (1988) Produced for Polish television, this series of ten hour-long programs explores the contemporary meaning of the Ten Commandments as seen in the lives of various residents of a drab Warsaw apartment complex. Directed by Krzysztof Kieslowski, none of the stories is directly religious though all grapple with moral conflicts arising from ordinary situations and relationships, which most viewers will not see as being at all foreign to them. Subtitles. Mature themes. A-III (nr)

Decameron, The (1971) Italian director Pier Paolo Pasolini's adaptation of some tales from Boccaccio's 14th-century volume of 100 stories is faithful to the original in burlesquing religious beliefs and practices in favor of the joys of the natural life, especially those relating to sex and greed. Though splendid in its robust evocation of Renaissance Italy, its explicit visualizations of sexual encounters is seriously offensive. O (X)

Decameron Nights (1953) Escaping from war-torn 14th-century Florence, the writer Boccaccio (Louis Jourdan) is given refuge by a widow (Joan Fontaine) and her women friends, then proceeds to entertain them with three stories in which a wife's fidelity is tested. Directed by Hugo Fregonese, the period setting is picturesque, but the performances are as flat as the dramatized stories which clumsily contrive to tone down the ribald nature of the original. Stylized violence, romantic complications, and sexual innuendo. A-III (br)

Deceived (1991) A young widow (Goldie Hawn) discovers that her museum curator husband (John Heard) was leading a double life, putting her and her little girl (Ashley Peldon) in mortal danger. Director Damian Harris's nifty thriller is packed with implausibilities but scores on atmosphere and emotionally involving suspense. Momentary violence and mild sexual innuendo. A-II (PG-13)

Deceiver (1998) Talky psychological thriller in which a rich murder suspect (Tim Roth) undergoes a series of lie detector tests administered by two detectives (Chris Penn, Michael Rooker), with occasional flashbacks to the crime, as well as pivotal events in the lives of the three men. Written and directed by Josh and Jonas Pate, the movie sets up an intriguing situation but soon gets lost in increasingly bizarre plot twists which make the story unlikely and the characters unlikable. Criminal violence, intense menace, sexual situations, recurring rough language, and occasional profanity. A-IV (R)

Deceivers, The (1988) Lackluster historical crime movie about a British officer (Pierce Brosnan) in 19th-century India who infiltrates and exposes a murderous cult that preys on unsuspecting travelers. Director Nicholas Meyer makes every effort to re-create the period and place but forgets to inject any energy into the scenario or examine the circumstances that fostered the cult. Much violence, brief flashes of nudity, and a hallucinatory sexual encounter with a prostitute. A-III (PG-13)

December (1991) Listless story tells of the effect the Japanese attack on Pearl Harbor has on five teens at a New England boys academy who stay up all night arguing about whether to enlist the next morning. Writer-director Gabe Torres's adolescent gab-fest merely voices the boys' fears and naive patriotism without emotional involvement or any insights. Momentary violence. A-II (PG)

Decision at Sundown (1957) Revenge Western directed by Budd Boetticher presents the unconvincing story of a town's reformation after its corrupt boss (John Carroll) is forced into a showdown with a straight-shooting Texan (Randolph Scott) who's come to avenge his wife's death. Frontier violence and murky plot of personal vengeance. A-III (br)

Decline and Fall of a Birdwatcher (1969) Delightful screen version of Evelyn Waugh's 1928 novel about a naive school teacher (Robin Phillips) who becomes involved with the elegant Lady Margot Beste-Chetwynde (Genevieve Page) and her vice ring and winds up taking the rap for her and going to prison. Director John Krish has caught the satirically solemn flavor of the original, and his fine British cast never cracks a smile in carrying on with Waugh's outrageous lampooning of English high and low life. Stylish comedy even for those who don't usually like British humor. A-III (PG)

Decline of Western Civilization Part II: The Metal Years, The (1988) Penelope Spheeris's documentary focuses mostly on the posturing, wanton performers and fans in the L.A. heavy-metal scene, whose hedonistic and clearly self-destructive lifestyles have nothing to commend them. Much profanity, bragging about sexual promiscuity, drug and alcohol abuse, some nudity, and several sexually provocative scenes. O (R)

Deconstructing Harry (1997) Impressionistic account of how a writer (Woody Allen, who also directed) views his life and work, with the imagined characters of his stories often getting mixed up with people and events from real life. There are some witty situations and funny one-liners, but the result is an often painful picture of a glib egoist who is only interested in self-gratification and turning his experiences of it into fiction. Compulsive infidelity, sexual situations, repeated references to oral sex, brief nudity, recurring rough language, and some profanity. A-IV (R)

Dee Snider's Strangeland (1998) Senselessly violent clunker in which writer-producer Dee Snider stars as a mad murderer who uses the Internet to lure his victims to gruesome deaths by torture. Directed by John Pieplow, the dreary formula plot mixes inept action scenes of the police hunt for the killer with perverse images of his sadistic activities. Excessive violence, graphic torture scenes, sexual references, brief nudity, incessant rough language, and some profanity. O (R)

Deep, The (1977) Screen version of Peter Benchley's novel about an unmarried couple (Jacqueline Bisset and Nick Nolte) whose scuba diving on a Bermuda vacation leads to sunken treasure and the help of a salvage expert (Robert Shaw) in outwitting a crew of black villains (led by Louis Gosset). Simple-minded but clunky melodrama directed by Peter Yates, it has at least the Bermuda scenery and underwater photography to recommend it. Otherwise it makes much of a blissful premarital relationship, stereotypes blacks as threats, offers a particularly brutal fight scene, and mixes an abundance of highly calculated titillation with sexual menace. O (PG)

Deep Cover (1992) Violent, drug-themed movie has a corrupt attorney (Jeff Goldblum) outsmarted by an undercover narcotics cop (Larry Fishburne) who then succumbs to drugs and their profits when he becomes disillusioned. Director Bill Duke's thoroughly cynical movie sends the wrong message about the war against drugs and overdoses on gory killings. Excessive violence, morally ambiguous theme, sexually suggestive scenes, and frequent rough language. O (R)

Deep End (1971) London adolescent (John Moulder-Brown) gets a job in a public bathhouse, becomes involved with one of the girl attendants (Jane Asher), and ruins his life and hers. Directed by Jerzy Skolimowski, the seedy environment is of more interest than the human characters within it. Some bizarre, graphic sex scenes. O (R)

Deep End of the Ocean, The (1999) Emotional drama in which a mother (Michelle Pfeiffer) copes with heartbreak when her three-year-old son disappears, then has to realize she is only a stranger to the boy when he is found nine years later. Directed by Ulu Grosbard, the story deals with substantive issues of family life, but the treatment is disappointingly superficial and the result serves principally as an overwrought vehicle for its star. A traumatic family crisis, domestic tensions, and occasional profanity and rough language. A-III (PG-13)

Deep Impact (1998) Low-voltage disaster movie focuses on a TV network anchor (Tea Leoni) and a teen astronomy buff (Elijah Wood) after the president (Morgan Freeman) announces that a manned spacecraft (headed by Robert Duvall) has failed to deflect a huge comet from its deadly collision course with Earth. Directed by Mimi Leder, the spectacular special effects are brief and fleeting, while the personal stories are contrived and schmaltzy. A massive natural catastrophe, suicidal and sexual references, occasional profanity, and an instance of rough language. A-III (PG-13)

Deep in the Heart (1984) A rape victim (Karen Young) gains vengeance upon the rapist (Clayton Day), an amoral but respectable attorney who is a gun enthusiast, by learning how to use a pistol and then turning this symbol of male dominance against him. Directed by Tony Garnett, this British production relies on exploitative violence and nudity. O (R)

Deep Red (1976) David Hemmings stars in a badly acted, worse-dubbed Italian horror movie in which director Dario Argento devotes most of his attention to depicting a series of gory, sadistic murders. O (R)

Deep Rising (1998) Scary monster movie in which nearly all the passengers aboard a luxury cruise ship are drained of their blood by a serpentine sea monsters, leaving a motley band of thieves and innocents (led by Treat Williams) trying to evade the relentless creatures. Writer-director Stephen Sommers doesn't bother with character development, relying instead on fearsome special effects as the horrific monsters chase their prey. Frequent fantasy violence, some rough language, and a few instances of profanity. A-III (R)

Deep Six, The (1958) Because of his pacifist Quaker upbringing, a WW II naval officer (Alan Ladd) isn't sure he can fire at the enemy until going on a mission to rescue US airmen downed on a Japanese-held island. Directed by R. Maté, the theme of conscience gets lost amidst the cliches of wartime action and the interplay between the destroyer's crew (including James Whitmore, Keenan Wynn, William Bendix, and Joey Bishop). Interesting premise superficially developed with routine heroics and mild sexist humor. A-I (br)

Deep Throat (1972) This is the first thoroughly hardcore porno feature to receive a sophisticated national promotion campaign, enabling it to reach beyond the porno theater circuit. It is not about cough remedies. O (X)

Deep Thrust — The Hand of Death (1973) Mindless Hong-Kong Kung-Fu story about a woman's revenge on the man who seduced her sister. Directed by Heang Feng, it is explicit in its physical violence almost to the point of nausea. O (R)

Deepstar Six (1989) Submerged for six months in the Pacific, some underwater experts unsettle a mysterious monster when they dynamite its sea cave for a US missile site. Despite a likeable cast (Taurean Blacque, Nancy Everhard, and Greg Evigan, among others) and the prerequisite monster of no known species, its mindless plot and unimaginative direction by Sean S. Cunningham generate about as much menace as a clogged drain. Some sexual suggestiveness, rough language, and several incidents of gruesome gore. O (R)

Deer Hunter, The (1979) Three small-town steelworkers (Robert De Niro, Christopher Walken, and John Savage) have their mettle tested by the horrors of Vietnam in director Michael Cimino's harsh evocation of the effects of war on friendship and spirit. Somewhat racist and chauvinistic treatment and the film's brutal and intense moments of violence play on gut emotions overriding any serious intent to explore the painful tragedy of Vietnam. O (R)

Deerslayer, The (1957) Slack version of James Fennimore Cooper's tale in which the title character (Lex Barker) and his Mohican ally, Chingachgook (Carlos Rivas), try to save a revenge-obsessed hunter (Jay C. Flippen), his daughters (Rita Moreno and Cathy O'Donnell), and a greedy woodsman (Forrest Tucker) from a Huron war party. Directed by Kurt Neumann, the slow-paced narrative mixes cardboard characters with far-fetched action. Frontier violence. A-I (br)

Def by Temptation (1990) While visiting a friend (Kadeem Hardison) in the Big Apple, a southern divinity student (James Bond III) finds himself drawn to a beautiful sorceress (Cynthia Bond) who lures men into her bed before killing them. Bond III also wrote, produced, and directed this comedy of horrors which exploits sex and violence for shock value and cheap thrills. Excessive violence, fairly explicit sexual activity with frontal nudity, and some rough language. O (R)

Def Jam's How to Be a Player (1997) Raunchy sex comedy about a smug womanizer (Bill Bellamy) trying to keep each of his bevy of girlfriends from learning about the others. Directed by Lionel C. Martin, this African-American version of the playboy philosophy of lust as a male game was done on the cheap, and its sexist humor is even more impoverished. Simulated sex scenes, nudity, and much rough language. O (R)

Defector, The (1966) Muddled espionage story about an American scientist (Montgomery Clift) recruited as a CIA spy and an East German scientist (Hardy Kruger) recruited by the Reds to get him to defect. The plot has some gaping holes, and the Cold War politics are heavy-handed. Directed by Raoul Levy. Mild violence and romance. A-II (br)

Defending Your Life (1991) After dying in separate accidents, a mild-mannered ad exec (Albert Brooks) and his new love interest (Meryl Streep) face individual trials in the hereafter which will determine whether they progress to a higher plane or return to Earth to try again. Also written and directed by Brooks, this vaguely defined comic fantasy is a smoothly soothing salute to the redemptive powers of love, given some needed sparks from Lee Grant and Rip Torn as prosecutor and defending counsel in the afterlife trial proceedings. References to reincarnation and extremely mild sexual innuendo. A-II (PG)

Defenseless (1991) Lurid murder mystery has an LA police detective (Sam Shepard) tightening the screws on the attorney (Barbara Hershey) who is defending the wife (Mary Beth Hurt) of her murdered client-lover. Director Martin Campbell maintains suspense with a capable cast but favors the sensational in this dense and derivative plot. Intermittent gory violence, recurring sexual innuendo, fleeting partial nudity, and some rough language. A-IV (R)

Defiance (1980) Young merchant seaman (Jan-Michael Vincent) leads the terrorized residents of a New York ghetto neighborhood in a vigilante assault on their tormentors. The oft-told tale, directed by John Flynn, is run-of-the-mill entertainment with some graphic violence. A-III (PG)

Defiant Ones, The (1958) Interracial chase thriller in which a black convict (Sidney Poitier) and a Southern redneck (Tony Curtis) flee a chain gang shackled together and needing each other if they are to make good their escape. Director Stanley Kramer's message movie about the chains of prejudice may be a little too pat and melodramatic in developing the stark situation, but the incidents along the way more than sustain interest until the finale. Some nasty stylized violence and racial epithets. A-III (nr)

Degree of Murder (1969) German crime melodrama about a waitress who casually recruits two young men to help her dispose of the body of an ex-lover she has just as casually, though accidentally, killed. Director Volker Schlondorff's study of unfeeling, amoral youth emphasizes the matter-of-fact hedonism of the three as they enjoy themselves while going about their grisly errand. The treatment of these incidents is excessively graphic and undermines whatever serious intentions the movie may have had. O (R)

Delicate Delinquent, The (1957) Jerry Lewis in his first solo comedy plays a klutzy janitor pushed around by young toughs until a friendly cop (Darren McGavin) gets him into the police academy and he earns his badge. Writer-director Don McGuire showcases the star's zany clowning, especially his stunts in the academy, but the sentimental story built around the character takes itself so seriously the picture becomes leaden. Some stylized violence and a bit of sexist humor. A-I (br)

Delinquents, The (1957) Unconvincing story of a teenager (Tom Laughlin) getting into serious trouble after falling in with a gang of young punks. Written, produced, and directed by Robert Altman, the low-budget production was filmed in Kansas City, Mo., and has some interest in terms of the period rather than the phony plot. Stylized violence, sexual innuendo, heavy drinking, and anti-social attitudes. A-III (br)

Delirious (1991) Weak comic fantasy in which an injured soap-opera writer (John Candy) wakes up inside his own TV story and proceeds to write himself a role as a dashing hero to the two leading ladies (Emma Samms, Mariel Hemingway). Director Tom Mankiewicz spoofs nighttime soaps with a good cast but not enough wit to excuse its saccharine predictability. Infrequent slapstick violence, discreet sexual references, and minimal profanity. A-II (PG)

Deliverance (1972) Challenging screen version of the James Dickey novel about four Atlanta businessmen (Burt Reynolds, Jon Voight, Ned Beatty, and

Ronny Cox) who decide to spend a weekend canoeing down a hazardous mountain river on a wilderness journey that turns into a nightmare. Director John Boorman's powerful and absorbing adventure piece tries fitfully to provide some insights on masculinity, civilization, and nature. Those deciding to take the trip should be prepared for some harrowing violence and a brutal homosexual assault. A-IV (R)

Delta Force (1986) Lee Marvin and Chuck Norris replay the 1985 Lebanese hijacking of an American airliner in a fictional account portraying a US Army Special Forces team successfully routing Arab terrorists while rescuing every American hostage. Excessive violence, unacceptably justified by patriotic fervor, runs consistently throughout the film. O (R)

Delta Force 2 (1990) An elite US Army unit sends its most lethal muscleman (Chuck Norris) to capture a Latin-American drug lord (Billy Drago) who is holding three Americans hostage. Director Aaron Norris's action movie is a strictly formula affair with hackneyed dialogue, no originality, and an unending stream of machine-gun fire and bloodied bodies. Excessive violence and occasional raw language. O (R)

Delusions of Grandeur (1975) Set in 17th-century Spain, this costume drama from director Gerard Oury stars Louis De Funes whose frenetic zest carries the comedy about avarice and pride. As the dismissed minister of finance for the Spanish king, he concocts an absurd plot whereby his valet (Yves Montand) is to make compromising advances to the beautiful queen. Innocent, light farce in French with English subtitles. A-II (PG)

Dementia 13 (1963) Failed horror movie filmed in Ireland by writer-director Francis Coppola tells a preposterous tale of a wealthy family (mother Eithne Dunn, daughter-in-law Luana Anders, and sons William Campbell and Bart Patton) terrorized by a demented axe murderer until a sinister doctor (Patrick Magee) intervenes. Several gory murders, some gruesome graphics, and menacing situations. A-III (br)

Demetrius and the Gladiators (1954) In this meandering sequel to **The Robe**, the Greek Christian of the title (Victor Mature) is made a Roman tribune after renouncing his faith, then falls under the spell of Messalina (Susan Hayward) until her husband, Claudius (Barry Jones), replaces the mad Caligula (Jay Robinson) as emperor, and Demetrius regains his faith. Directed by Delmer Daves, the gaudy proceedings have less to do with early Christianity than with the brutal world of the gladiators (Ernest Borgnine, William Marshall, Richard Egan), the luxury of Caligula's court and his increasingly bizarre behavior. Stylized violence and sexual innuendo. A-II (br)

Demi-Paradise, The (1943) Soviet engineer (Laurence Olivier) gets a taste of British life when sent to the UK in 1939 to oversee the casting of an innovative propeller for an icebreaker, then returns with an improved design in 1941 just as the USSR is invaded by Nazi Germany. Director Anthony Asquith pokes some gentle fun at British eccentricities while affirming its national virtue of "making the best of things" in this curious relic of mutual admiration by wartime allies. Good-spirited but dated comedy of manners. A-I (br)

Demolition Man (1993) An explosive LA cop (Sylvester Stallone) is pitted against a madman (Wesley Snipes) bent on mass destruction in the rigidly conformist society of 2032, where they are revived after being cryogenically frozen 36 years earlier. Director Marco Brambilla's boring action flick is an overproduced assault on the senses which glorifies mindless mayhem and a sick, dehumanizing sense of humor. Excessive violence, some nudity, and much rough language. O (R)

Demon (1977) Inept thriller about a New York detective (Tony Lo Bianco) trying to solve the mystery behind an outbreak of random murders in which the killers say that God told them to do it. Directed by Larry Cohen, the movie is marked by violence, nudity, and a tawdry use of religious references. O (R)

Demon Seed (1977) Proteus IV, a thinking computer, focuses on the problem of giving its mind a body and propagating itself with the unwilling assistance of the wife (Julie Christie) of its creator (Fritz Weaver). The special effects are exceptional but director Donald Cammell's treatment dwells on the vulnerability of a helpless woman, in the degrading context of its depiction of procreation via computer. Brief nudity and some profanity. O (R)

Demons (1974) Masterless samurai, duped by a woman out of the money he needs to redeem his honor, sets out on a rampage of violence to revenge himself on everyone associated with his betrayer. Directed by Toshio Matsumoto, its theme is the senseless wastefulness of any code of "honor" based on revenge. Stylized violence. A-III (R)

Dennis the Menace (1993) Hank Ketcham's comic-strip characters come to life with the cherubic-looking five-year-old (Mason Gamble) continually discombobulating his curmudgeonly neighbor (Walter Matthau) while unwittingly outwitting a dimwitted thief (Christopher Lloyd). Matthau's crotchety performance is the best thing in the comedy's aimless assortment of pranks, mischief, and pratfalls blandly directed by Nick Castle and scripted by John Hughes, who tacks on the same little-boy-vs.-nasty-thief situation from his earlier **Home Alone** movies. Momentary violence and many slapstick incidents. A-II (PG)

Denver and Rio Grande, The (1952) Standard Western with a troubleshooter (Edmond O'Brien) for the title railroad battling an unscrupulous rival (Sterling Hayden) over the only route through the mountains. Director Byron Haskin mixes the skullduggery with some comedy and a lot of action, including two empty trains racing into a head-on smash-up. Stylized violence. A-I (br)

Deranged (1974) Roberts Blossom plays an aging Mama's boy in a sick study of incestuous necrophilia, with Cosette Lee as the late object of his present affection, and a host of unknowns filling in as his erstwhile victims. Directed by Jeff Gillen, the grisly movie lives up to its title. O (R)

Derby (1971) Documentary by Robert Kaylor on the Roller Derby in Dayton, Ohio, focuses on the players, the hopefuls, and the fans. Though it contains some unexpected humor and pathos, the violence and crude appeal of the sport is what it's all about. A-III (R/GP)

Dersu Uzala (1978) Russian production about the friendship that grows between a turn-of-the-century explorer in Siberia and his guide, an aging Tungus hunter whose name gives the film its title. Japanese director Akira Kurosawa concentrates on evoking the vast remoteness of the Siberian wilderness, a world the Russian finds forbidding but one in which the hunter is perfectly at home. Finely acted, beautifully photographed, it is an admiring portrait of a man living in harmony with nature and with his fellow hunters. A-I (G)

Desert Bloom (1986) An idealistic young girl (Annabeth Gish) runs away from her family she has tried to keep together when she sees her father (Jon Voight) making a drunken pass at her visiting aunt (Ellen Barkin). Set in Las Vegas during the 1950s era of atomic testing, the movie by first-time director Eugene Coor expresses the adaptability and resilience of a compassionate teenager's growing maturity as she returns to try to bring her troubled parents back together. Brief scene of domestic violence. A-II (PG)

Desert Fox, The (1951) Intelligent dramatization of Desmond Young's biography of German Field Marshal Erwin Rommel (James Mason) from his defeat in 1943 North Africa to his part in the failed 1944 plot to assassinate Hitler, ending in his suicide to save his family from Nazi retribution. Directed by Henry Hathaway, this homage to a valiant foe makes credible use of the wartime settings, but Mason's performance as a brilliant general who's also a decent human being makes it absorbing fare. Wartime violence and an off-screen suicide. A-II (br)

Desert Hawk, The (1950) Routine adventure in ancient Persia, where the rebel hero of the title (Richard Greene) battles a despotic ruler (George Macready) while winning the love of Bagdad's princess Scheherazade (Yvonne De Carlo). Directed by Frederick de Cordova, the cliched story derives some mild amusement from the comic antics of Aladdin (Jackie Gleason) and Sinbad (Joe Besser). Stylized violence and sexual innuendo. A-II (br)

Desert Hearts (1986) Awaiting the finalizing of her divorce at a ranch near Reno, Nev., a 1950's professional woman creates a new self-image during a sexual relationship with a younger woman. Director Donna Deitch's very personal romantic vision treats homosexuality as basically a matter of sexual preference and sex as the fundamental basis for a meaningful commitment between the film's main characters. Lengthy nude scene. O (R)

Desert Legion (1953) Second-rate Shangri-La tale directed by Joseph Pevney is set in 19th-century Algeria, where a captain (Alan Ladd) in the French Foreign Legion discovers deep in the mountains a prosperous utopian city whose ruler (Oscar Beregi) and daughter (Arlene Dahl) are threatened by a rebel chieftain (Richard Conte). Several battles, including a spear duel, and mild romance. A-I (br)

Desert Rats, The (1953) Standard war picture honors the exploits of an Australian battalion under an English officer (Richard Burton) during the 1941 siege of Tobruk by Desert Fox Rommel (James Mason). Directed by Robert Wise, the battle scenes are exciting but less than credible, further burdened by Burton who agonizes unconvincingly over his abilities as a commander. Wartime violence. A-I (br)

Desert Song, The (1953) Plodding musical from the 1926 Sigmund Romberg operetta about the romance between a French general's daughter (Kathryn Grayson) and a hunted Riff leader (Gordon MacRae) fighting a villainous Moroccan sheik (Raymond Massey). Directed by Bruce Humberstone, the plot is as dated as the acting is wooden, but the songs still soar and the desert landscapes are picturesque. Stylized violence and romantic misunderstandings. A-I (br)

Deserter, The (1971) Cynical Western about the US Cavalry's recruiting an Indian-hating deserter (Bekim Fehmiu) to lead a raid against an Apache stronghold. Mediocre Italian production directed by Burt Kennedy, the movie exploits its subject for the sake of brutish violence. O (GP)

Deserter U.S.A. (1969) Swedish production about US servicemen who defected during the Vietnam War to take refuge in Sweden is atrociously acted by the deserters themselves staging "typical" situations. Written and directed by Lars Lambert and Olle Sjogren, the pseudo-documentary's anti-American, anti-establishment bias is excessively heavy-handed and its production values are barely adequate. O (nr)

Designated Mourner, The (1997) Three actors seated in a studio give a reading of a text in which one (Mike Nichols) ruminates about his strained marriage to the daughter (Miranda Richardson) of a famous poet (David de Keyser), both of whom add their own version of events until perishing in a revolution, which leaves him mourning the end of the culture they represented. Written by Wallace Shawn and directed by David Hare, the readings are as mannered as the artificial script, whose observations about life, art and the human condition range mostly from the banal to the pretentious. Sexual references, rough language, and several instances of profanity. A-III (R)

Desire in the Dust (1960) Hothouse trash directed by William F. Claxton revolves around the thwarted love affair between a cloddish Louisiana sharecropper (Ken Scott) and the amoral daughter of a politically ambitious aristocrat (Raymond Burr) whose guilty bag of secrets includes a dotty wife (poor Joan Bennett). Sordid sexual situations, including suggestions of incest, and some stylized violence. A-III (br)

Desire under the Elms (1958) Stagy adaptation of the Eugene O'Neill drama of greed and lust set in 19th-century New England, where the angry son (Anthony Perkins) of a grasping, dour farmer (Burl Ives) falls in love with his father's new wife (Sophia Loren). Directed by Delbert Mann, the dramatic conflict between father, son, and stepmother are treated in heavy-handed theatrical fashion that grows wearisome long before the conclusion's moral retribution. Mature themes, including infanticide. A-III (br)

Desiree (1954) Stilted historical drama begins in 1794 Marseilles, where a silk merchant's daughter, Desiree (Jean Simmons), falls for penniless general Napoleon Bonaparte (Marlon Brando), but he discards her after being recalled to Paris and turns to the politically astute Josephine (Merle Oberon), leaving Desiree to wed the brilliant general Bernadotte (Michael Rennie) who becomes Sweden's king and Bonaparte's foe. Directed by Henry Koster, there is plenty of costume pageantry, but Desiree is less a character than a commentator on Napoleon's off-stage rise and fall, giving Brando little to do but strut, glower, and disclaim. Romantic complications and veiled sexual innuendo. A-II (br)

Desk Set (1957) It's mind over machine in this breezy romantic comedy about an eccentric automation expert (Spencer Tracy) who more than meets his match in the mental prowess of the woman (Katharine Hepburn) heading the TV network research department he's been hired to modernize. As directed by Walter Lang from William Marchant's play, the comic battle of wits between the two leads is charming, genial fun, abetted by the kooky hijinks of staff researchers Joan Blondell and Dina Merrill as well as some satirical jabs at corporate manners and mix-ups. A-II (br)

Despair (1979) Expatriate White Russian (Dirk Bogarde) living in Berlin prior to Hitler's takeover, grows in madness and desperation, eventually killing a stranger and trying to change his identity. Portrait of a fragmented psyche from director Rainer Werner Fassbinder based on the Vladimir Nabokov novel also delves deeply and graphically into the antihero's sexual perversities. O (nr)

Desperado (1995) Violent bandito Western in which a mariachi musician (Antonio Banderas) turns killer as he shoots his way through Mexican border towns searching for the drug lord (Joaquim de Almeida) responsible for his girlfriend's murder. Despite its darkly satirical elements, writer-director Robert Rodriguez's revenge yarn is ultimately reduced to a series of mindless, jokey bloodbaths. Excessive violence, sexual encounters with nudity, and much rough language. O (R)

Desperadoes, The (1943) Standard Western tale of a wronged outlaw (Glenn Ford) teaming with a straight-shooting sheriff (Randolph Scott) to get the goods on a crooked banker and his gang. Directed by Charles Vidor, the routine plot gains interest from some lively action sequences and a solid cast (including Claire Trevor, Edgar Buchanan, and Guinn "Big Boy" Williams). Stylized violence. A-I (br)

Desperados, The (1969) Substandard Western about an outlaw family fathered by a mad, Bible-quoting parson (Jack Palance) who vows vengeance against his son (Vince Edwards) when he decides to go straight. Under Henry Levin's direction, everyone concerned looks embarrassingly ridiculous in a movie that emphasizes violence and toys with nudity, suggestive costuming, prostitutes, and a little aberrant sex thrown in for good measure. O (M)

Desperate Characters (1971) Middle-class, childless couple (Shirley MacLaine and Kenneth Mars) live comfortably in New York City until urban realities of crime and vandalism begin to unravel their sense of security. Written and directed by Frank D. Gilroy, there is a hollow staginess about this affluent but loveless couple that makes it difficult to share their plight. Graphic, violent, and, yes, desperate bedroom scene. A-IV (R)

Desperate Hours (1990) The home of an estranged couple (Mimi Rogers and Anthony Hopkins) is invaded by an escaped psychopathic killer (Mickey Rourke) who terrorizes them as he awaits the arrival of his lawyer/lover (Kelly Lynch). Director Michael Cimino's psychological thriller relies more on Rourke's chillingly nasty performance than on a coherent plot to carry the tale to its melodramatic finish. Some violence, much menace, occasional rough language, and flashes of nudity. A-III (R)

Desperate Journey (1942) Shot down over WW II Germany, a RAF bomber crew (notably Errol Flynn, Ronald Reagan, and Arthur Kennedy) escape their Nazi captor (Raymond Massey) to commit various acts of sabotage while making their way back to England. Directed by Raoul Walsh, the brave derring-do has all the credibility of a romp with the Rover Boys and provides only dated wartime hokum today. Stylized violence with flag-waving rhetoric. A-I (br)

Desperate Measures (1998) Violent thriller in which a brainy homicidal convict (Michael Keaton) tries to escape from the San Francisco hospital, where he has volunteered to undergo a bone marrow transplant to save the dying son of a cop (Andy Garcia), who now must recapture the escaped man alive or lose his boy. Directed by Barbet Schroeder, the wild chase through the hospital is too improbably contrived to be emotionally satisfying, and the result answers none of the moral questions raised about the cop's responsibility to both son and public. Much hard-edged violence, life-threatening situations, and occasional rough language as well as profanity. A-IV (R)

Desperate Ones, The (1968) Uneven melodrama about two Polish brothers (Maximilian Schell and Raf Vallone) who escape from a Siberian labor camp during WW II and, as they make for the Afghanistan border, elude the NKVD, survive the elements, and have improbable love affairs. Directed by Alexander Ramati, it has some good moments, but its sentiments are too often cloying. A-III (br)

Desperately Seeking Susan (1985) A New Jersey housewife (Rosanna Arquette) exchanges identities with a Manhattan playgirl (Madonna) in this screwball comedy directed by Susan Seidelman. Bright at moments but for the most part limp. Benign view of adultery and some exploitation of nudity. O (PG-13)

Destination Moon (1950) Pedestrian story of American know-how in getting a manned rocket to the moon, but once there the crew (John Archer, Warner Anderson, Tom Powers, and Dick Wesson) have some difficulties getting back. Produced by George Pal and directed by Irving Pichel, the narrative is rather tedious and the characters one-dimensional, though what is interesting now is how closely this picture of an imaginary moon shot resembles the one which actually took place 19 years later. A-I (br)

Destination Tokyo (1943) Wartime morale booster about an American submarine (captained by Cary Grant) sneaking into Tokyo Bay to guide bombers from nearby aircraft carriers in the first air attack on Japan's capital. Though dated by its patriotic rhetoric, this tribute to the "silent service" is directed by Delmer Daves, with credible attention to the tensions of duty aboard a sub, abetted by a good cast (Alan Hale, John Garfield, and Dane Clark among them), suspenseful battle sequences, and a textbook emergency appendectomy. Wartime violence and menace. A-I (br)

Destroy All Monsters (1969) It is 1999 and such monsters as Godzilla and Rodan have been exiled to Monsterland in remote Oceania from which they are unleashed by space aliens who want to make Earth their new home. Director Ishiro Honda's model work and special effects are unconvincing but fun for those who liked earlier editions of these Japanese monster movies. A-I (G)

Destroyer (1943) Patriotic WW II programmer from director William Seiter follows the course of a retired Navy seaman (Edward G. Robinson) who wangles sea duty on a troubled destroyer, bullies its crew (including Glenn Ford), but proves a hero under enemy fire. Wartime violence. A-I (br)

Destructors, The (1974) Drug-syndicate thriller about a Paris-based U.S. narcotics agent (Anthony Quinn) who goes outside the law to nab the heads of rival syndicates (Michael Caine and James Mason). Directed by Robert Parrish, it is for those who like escaspist action entertainment. Some violence in an amoral atmosphere. A-III (PG)

Destry (1954) Mediocre sequel in which the son (Audie Murphy) of the mild-mannered sheriff in **Destry Rides Again** uses his wits instead of guns to tame a lawless Western town run by a crooked gambler (Lyle Bettger) whose casino features a gold-digging showgirl (Mari Blanchard). Director George Marshall recycles many of the characters and situations from its 1939 predecessor, but the result lacks the zest and charm which gave the original its appeal. Frontier violence and sexual innuendo. A-III (br)

Destry Rides Again (1939) Western sheriff (James Stewart) uses his wits rather than his dead aim with a six-shooter to rid a lawless town of its ruthless boss (Brian Donlevy). Director George Marshall mixes humor and action in equal measure abetted by a solid all-around cast, including Marlene Dietrich as a barroom singer ("See What the Boys in the Back Room Will Have") who shows her mettle in a knockdown brawl with Una Merkel. Stylized gunplay and fisticuffs. A-II (br)

Detective, The (1954) British adaptation of the adventures of G.K. Chesteron's amateur sleuth, Father Brown. Directed by Robert Hamer and with Alec Guinness in the title role, the movie offers a dandy mystery and some intelligent entertainment. A-I (br)

Detective, The (1968) Tough but honest New York cop (Frank Sinatra) has a number of problems, including railroading an innocent psychotic into the electric chair and a bad marriage to a nymphomaniac (Lee Remick). Gordon Douglas's flat-footed direction bludgeons home its condemnation of big city crime and corruption, mostly through rather lurid depictions of homosexual practices and much crude language. O (br)

Detective Belli (1971) Failed Italian crime melodrama in which crooked Rome cop (Franco Nero) supplements his paycheck by keeping the precocious son of a rich lawyer (Aldolfo Celli) out of harm's way. The plot is jumbled enough without director Romolo Guerreri adding to the confusion with jump cuts, flashy zooms, and ragged editing. Stylized violence and brief nudity. A-III (R)

Detective Story (1951) Powerful adaptation of Sidney Kingsley's play about a day in a New York City police station, beginning with the arrest of a shoplifter (Lee Grant) and ending with a dying cop's Act of Contrition. At the center of events is an idealistic but overbearing detective (Kirk Douglas) who brings in a petty thief (Craig Hill), slaps around an abortionist (George Macready), breaks up with his wife (Eleanor Parker), and stops an escaping crook (Joseph Wiseman). Director William Wyler keeps the set piece humming with finely honed character types including the weary precinct captain (Horace MacMahon) and a sympathetic cop (William Bendix). Veiled references to abortion and stylized violence. A-II (br)

Detour (1945) Dire bad-luck story in which a jobless club pianist (Tom Neal) hitchhiking from New York to Los Angeles is picked up by a driver who dies accidentally, and the pianist, fearing he'll be blamed, takes off with the man's car and wallet, only to be blackmailed by a nasty woman hitchhiker (Ann Savage). Directed by Edgar G. Ulmer, the tension mounts as the hapless fellow's predicament worsens, but the effort is too contrived with improbabilities to hold interest until the inconclusive ending. Menacing situations. A-II (br)

Detour (1969) Touching Bulgarian story of a chance meeting of two former lovers who had had a brief affair 17 years before when they were idealistic college students. Their nostalgic remembrances are told succinctly and with restraint, while their renewed affections and awkward present situations are handled sympathetically and with grace. A-III (PG)

Detroit 9000 (1973) The title is the signal used by the Detroit police force to indicate an officer in need of assistance, and the predictable story is of a cop (Alex Rocco) who doesn't want any assistance, let alone that of the black partner (Hari Rhodes) assigned him. Director Arthur Marks handles the action and super-tough dialogue quite well, although the constant grittiness of both is eventually enervating. Excessive violence and brief nudity. O (R)

Devil and Daniel Webster (1941) Crackerjack adaptation of Stephen Vincent Benet's story about a New England farmer (James Craig) who sells his soul to the devil (John Huston), then hires lawyer Webster (Edward Arnold) to argue his case before a jury from hell. Directed by William Dieterle, it's a classic piece of regional Americana whose fantasy elements range from the sunny and playful to the dark and sinister, owing much of its success to Joseph August's evocative photography. Highly entertaining tussle between good and evil, though some fairly intense scenes for young children. A-II (br)

Devil and Max Devlin, The (1980) Fiendishly unfunny fantasy in which a miserly landlord (Elliott Gould) plummets into hell after being struck by a bus, then makes a deal with Satan's left-hand man (Bill Cosby) to escape damnation if he delivers the souls of three young people. Directed by Steven Hill Stern, the inane Disney production gives Cosby next to nothing to do and Gould, especially charmless here, has far too much. Some mild vulgarity. A-II (PG)

Devil at 4 O'Clock, The (1961) Turgid melodrama set on a small island near Tahiti, where a convict (Frank Sinatra) helps a dyspeptic, worn-out priest (Spencer Tracy) save his flagging faith as well as the children in an isolated leper hospital after volcanic eruptions begin convulsing the island. Director Mervyn LeRoy sentimentalizes the flawed character of both priest and convict, then turns them into doomed heroes long after viewers have lost interest. Much menace and some sexual innuendo. A-II (br)

Devil Bat, The (1941) Horror clunker in which a revenge-obsessed doctor (Bela Lugosi) breeds giant bats trained to kill those wearing the lotion he provides his victims, until a Chicago reporter (Dave O'Brien) gets wise. Directed by Jean Yarborough, the pulp story has cheesy special effects, though Lugosi's quietly menacing performance almost makes it worth seeing. A-II (br)

Devil by the Tail (1969) Breezy, exuberant French comedy about a once-noble family who maintain their ancient chateau by running it as a hotel, helped by the local garage mechanic's disabling of passing automobiles, one of which belongs to a bank robber (Yves Montand) whose loot could permanently solve the family's financial woes. Directed by Philippe de Broca, the plot weaves in and out of comic situations with amazing speed and vivacity. Its amoral and unscrupulous stereotyped characters are in the great tradition of frothy farce. Adult situations. A-III (PG)

Devil Commands, The (1941) Low-budget horror movie directed by Edward Dmytryk with mad scientist Boris Karloff trying to establish contact with his dead wife through the brain waves of spiritualist Anne Revere and a coven of cadavers. Gruesome concept and treatment. A-III (br)

Devil-Doll, The (1936) When a dying inventor (Henry B. Walthall) demonstrates his discovery for shrinking people to one-sixth their size, an escaped convict (Lionel Barrymore) determines to use it as an instrument of vengeance on the Paris bank officials who had framed him for their own crimes. Directed by Tod Browning, the bizarre story centers in Barrymore's masquerade as an old lady running a doll shop, assisted by the inventor's wild-eyed sister (Rafaela Ottiano), with imaginative special effects making the human dolls a credible horror premise. Menacing situations and morally ambiguous ending. A-II (br)

Devil Doll (1964) Limp British thriller directed by Lindsay Shonteff in which a stage hypnotist (Bryant Halliday) doubles as a ventriloquist whose wooden dummy moves and talks on its own, which causes a curious reporter (William Sylvester) to search for the performer's missing assistant. Stylized violence, menacing situations, and sexual innuendo. A-III (br)

Devil in a Blue Dress (1995) Hired to find a mysterious woman sought by rival mayoral candidates in 1948 Los Angeles, a down-on-his-luck veteran (Denzel Washington) becomes trapped in a case of double murder the cops are willing to pin on him if he doesn't quickly find the actual killer. Writer-director Carl Franklin spins an atmospheric, engrossing tale of deceit and racial tension, marred only by one character's casual reliance on violence to solve problems. A discreet bedroom scene, some intense violence, and an instance of rough language. A-III (R)

Devil in Love, The (1968) An Italian comedy in which a devil (Vittorio Gassman), sent by Satan to provoke war between Renaissance Florence and the Papal States, falls in love with a princess and loses his diabolical powers. Directed by Ettore Scola, the movie has a sniggering script with a lascivious, overacted central character and nasty jabs at religious figures. Sexually suggestive situations and dialogue. O (br)

Devil Is a Woman, The (1975) Italian potboiler with Glenda Jackson as the mother superior of what seems to be a cross between a medieval monastery and an early 1960's Italian Holiday Inn. Director Damiano

Damiani postulates institutional religion as a repressive force that stifles any sense of self-determination. Not only is the movie hopelessly adrift in depicting religious belief and practice, but its sexual implications are offensive. O (R)

Devil Rider (1971) Low-budget motorcycle movie about a biker gang hanging around Miami Beach and terrorizing two sisters and those who try to help them. Director Brad F. Grinter exploits an amateur cast with an emphasis on brutality and leering sex. O (R)

Devil Within Her, The (1976) After many mysterious complications, a pregnant woman (Joan Collins) gives birth to a murderous baby in a clumsy, repulsive British horror movie directed by Peter Sasdy. Gore and nudity. O (R)

Devil's Advocate, The (1997) Overwrought fantasy in which an ambitious criminal attorney (Keanu Reeves) nearly sacrifices his morals and loses his wife (Charlize Theron) when lured into a powerful New York law firm by the devil in disguise (Al Pacino). Drama and comedy clash badly in director Taylor Hackford' shrill potboiler which relies on a lame cliche to reach its drawn-out conclusion. Gory violence, explicit sexual encounters, recurring full nudity, and much rough language with profanity. O (R)

Devil's Bride, The (1968) Adequate British horror movie in which Christopher Lee is the hero in fighting a sect of devil worshippers. Directed by Terence Fisher, there is a lot of hokum about black magic, but the forces of good are more than equal to those of darkness. Mild violence. A-II (br)

Devil's Brigade, The (1968) WW II movie based on the training and battle experiences in Italy of the Special Service Force, the forerunner of the Green Berets. William Holden stars in the rather routine men-in-battle epic directed by Andrew V. McLaglen showing the hard work that prepares soldiers for the stress and grimness of combat. Wartime violence. A-III (br)

Devil's Canyon (1953) Bottom-drawer Western in which a former lawman (Dale Robertson) is jailed in the same prison as a vicious cutthroat (Stephen McNally) who's vowed to kill him. Directed by Alfred Werker, the clumsy plot has the badman's girl (Virginia Mayo) turn up as a convict to lead a prison break. Forget it. Stylized violence. A-II (br)

Devil's Disciple, The (1959) Bumpy adaptation of Bernard Shaw's play about British incompetence in the American Revolution as seen in the person of dapper General Burgoyne (Laurence Olivier) who carelessly mistakes a Presbyterian minister (Burt Lancaster) for a rebellious unbeliever (Kirk Douglas), thereby goading the peaceful parson into joining the colonial militia. Directed by Guy Hamilton, the result is more an action piece than a witty send-up of British imperialism and attitudes, but the flavor of Shaw's satiric intentions remain in Olivier's wry asides about the inefficiencies of Empire and a narration setting the scenes with animated graphics. Wartime violence and some comic banter about Christian as well as other kinds of hypocrites. A-II (br)

Devil's Doorway (1950) Decorated for bravery as a Union soldier in the Civil War, a Shoshone Indian (Robert Taylor) returns to his Wyoming ranch, but a fanatic Indian-hater (Louis Calhern) tries to drive him and his people off their fertile lands by stirring up a range war. Director Anthony Mann handles the vanishing-American theme with much sympathy and plenty of action culminating in a truly tragic last stand. Stylized violence. A-I (br)

Devil's Eight, The (1969) A federal agent (Christopher George) springs a group of convicts (led by Ross Hagan) from a Southern prison and cowers them into helping him crack a whiskey-running operation. Producer-director Burt Topper manages to mix questions of law enforcement, racial justice and the hippie philosophy together with scenes of violent action, fast cars, and suggestions of promiscuity without any sense of priorities, taste, or judgment. O (M)

Devil's Island (1939) Boris Karloff stars as a brain surgeon wrongly sentenced to the tropical French penal colony, where he is mistreated by its corrupt military commandant (James Stephenson), then helped to escape by the officer's wife (Nedda Harrigan) after saving her injured daughter. Though the script is filled with melodramatic cliches, director William Clemens depicts the prison island's dehumanizing conditions strongly enough to make the surgeon's ordeal convincing. Stylized violence in a theme of injustice. A-II (br)

Devil's Mask, The (1946) Hokey crime caper from the "I Love a Mystery" radio series in which San Francisco detectives Jack Packard (Jim Bannon) and Doc Long (Barton Yarborough) solve a case involving a missing Amazon explorer, his frightened daughter (Anita Louise), and a shrunken head found aboard a crashed airliner. Directed by Henry Levin, the picture has plenty of colorful characters and ominous situations, but they never jell into a coherent plot and the solution is too contrived to be satisfying. Stylized violence and menace. A-II (br)

Devil's Own, The (1997) Solid thriller in which an upright New York policeman (Harrison Ford) welcomes an Irish immigrant (Brad Pitt) into his home, unaware the young man is an IRA agent whose attempt to buy stinger missiles inadvertently enmeshes the cop, his family, and his police partner (Ruben Blades) in a web of violence. Director Alan J. Pakula focuses on the complex moral dilemmas facing the cop and the IRA man while skillfully building the suspense in the gripping narrative. Intermittent violence, recurring rough language, and some profanity. A-III (R)

Devil's Rain (1975) Routine horror movie stars Ernest Borgnine who gives an embarrassingly broad performance in his central role as a satanic recruiter. Director Robert Fuest's gimmick of having most of the cast melt away at the end is in keeping with his lack of interest in the logical and religious nuances of the subject in favor of simple gory visuals. A-III (PG)

Devil's Widow, The (see: **Tam Lin**)

Devils, The (1971) Failed British adaptation of the Aldous Huxley novel about the demonic possession of a 17th-century French convent (led by Vanessa Redgrave) and the burning of a local priest (Oliver Reed) for his alleged commerce with the devil. Director Ken Russell's attempts to shock with scenes such as nuns cavorting at the altar in the nude are pathetic both in their imagination and in their execution. O (X/R)

Diabolique (1954) Gripping French thriller in which the brutal headmaster (Paul Meurisse) of a shabby boy's school grows so abusive to wife (Vera Clouzot) and mistress (Simone Signoret) that they join in a pact to kill him, then become frantic when his corpse disappears and they fear he may still be alive. Director Henri-Georges Clouzot slowly unfolds the desperate murder plot, then builds the uncertainty and suspense over the missing body until a twist ending provides the dreadful pay-off. Subtitles. Themes of violence and betrayal, much unsettling suspense and several grisly graphics. A-III (br)

Diabolique (1996) Drawn-out remake of the 1955 French film in which the wife (Isabelle Adjani) and mistress (Sharon Stone) of a Catholic boarding school headmaster (Chazz Palminteri) conspire to murder him, only to have the body disappear and a nosy private detective (Kathy Bates) inch closer to the truth. Director Jeremiah Chechik's heavy-handed treatment of the nasty thriller robs it of suspense and crudely overplays the irony of a religious setting in which evil thrives. Brief adulterous sex scene, implied lesbian relationship, fleeting full nudity, murderous violence, and recurring rough language and profanity. O (R)

Dial M for Murder (1954) Talky suspense thriller from Frederick Knott's play about a London cad (Ray Milland) whose plan to murder his wealthy wife (Grace Kelly) boomerangs, thanks partly to a shrewd police inspector (John Williams) and the wife's ardent friend (Robert Cummings). Director Alfred Hitchcock handles the intricately plotted narrative deftly but without his usual flair for edge-of-the-seat tension. Intermittent menace and stylized treatment of a grisly murder. A-II (br)

Diamond Head (1962) Hothouse Hawaiian hooey directed by Guy Green involves a rich hypocrite (Charlton Heston) who breaks up the romance between his sister (Yvette Mimieux) and a native islander, despite the fact that his own mistress is a beautiful Hawaiian. Trashy sudser with colorful scenery and cardboard characters whose sexual philandering and racial bigotry are supposedly redeemed by tragedy. A-III (br)

Diamond Horseshoe (see: **Billy Rose's Diamond Horseshoe**)

Diamond Hunters, The (1956) Intriguing melodrama set in Latin America, where a small band of refugees from a miner's revolt against a dictatorial regime head for the Brazilian border on a river boat, then on foot through the jungle. Directed by Luis Bunuel, the dubbed Mexican production sets up a desperate situation testing the moral fiber of the fleeing characters, including a prostitute (Simone Signoret), a con-man (Georges Marchal), an elderly miner (Charles Vanel), and a priest (Michel Piccoli). Stylized violence, sexual situations, and muddled justice themes. A-III (br)

Diamond Queen, The (1953) Lame adventure in which a jewel merchant (Fernando Lamas) and a military officer (Gilbert Roland) sail from 1659 France to India to trade the invention of the grenade for a flawless blue diamond to top the crown of Louis XIV. Directed by John Brahm, the pair's halting encounters with an Indian princess (Arlene Dahl) and a Mogul emperor (Sheldon Leonard) are more hokey than colorful. Stylized violence and mild sexual innuendo. A-II (br)

Diamonds (1975) Dull jewel-heist caper with an ex-con (Richard Roundtree) and girlfriend (Barbara Seagull Hershey) being recruited by a wealthy London jeweler (Robert Shaw) to break into a mammoth jewelry exchange in Jerusalem. Director Menahem Golan succeeds much better as an Israeli travelogue than as crime melodrama with fleeting nudity and crude language. A-III (PG)

Diamonds Are Forever (1971) This time James Bond's antagonist is intent on cornering the world diamond market in order to finance still worse villainy. British production directed by Guy Hamilton lacks the wit and wizardry with which the 007 series began, and everything about this entry seems tired including Sean Connery's performance. Usual stylized violence and sexual by-play. A-III (GP)

Diary of a Chambermaid (1964) Remake of the 1946 movie has a Parisian maid (Jeanne Moreau) coping with the bizarre family of a wealthy provincial household until a little girl's brutally violated body is found in the woods nearby, and she determines to prove the family's Fascist groundskeeper was responsible. Director Luis Bunuel has a field day playing around with sexual fantasies and middle-class parasites but succeeds best in depicting the nationalistic excesses of the political right in 1930's France. Stylized violence, sexual situations and innuendo, anti-clerical views, and anti-Semitic invective. A-IV (br)

Diary of a Country Priest (1951) Director Robert Bresson's classic adaptation of the Georges Bernanos novel is a study in anguish, doubt, and frustrated zeal set in the bleak Normandy countryside, where a dedicated priest tries to revitalize a run-down parish but is regarded with suspicion by the locals. The diary format serves to evoke the interior life of a lonely soul who accepts his trials and ultimately finds peace within himself. The subtitled French production presents aspects of religious faith and human responses that make it ideal for study and discussion. A-II (br)

Diary of a Mad Housewife (1970) Attractive Manhattan housewife (Carrie Snodgrass in a fine performance) rebels against her frustrating domestic life with an egotistical, social-climbing lawyer husband (Richard Benjamin) by acquiring a lover (Frank Langella) who proves an equally unenlightened male chauvinist. Director Frank Perry's exercise in women's liberation issues is ultimately unsatisfying in its melodramatic conclusion with the mental breakdown of its affluent but unfulfilled housewife-victim. Some harsh language and brief nudity. A-IV (R)

Diary of a Madman (1963) Pedestrian psychological thriller set in 19th-century France, where a respected magistrate (Vincent Price) is driven to commit murder after he comes to believe he is possessed by a demon. Director Reginald Le Borg fails to create any sense of the supernatural and gets only limp suspense out of this talky exercise in horror. Overwrought menace and a few scenes of stylized violence. A-II (br)

Diary of a Schizophrenic Girl (1970) Disappointing dramatization of the recovery of a mentally disturbed patient (Ghislaine D'Orsay) through the ministrations of a woman therapist (Margarita Lozano). Director Nelo Risi's plodding study spends too much time documenting the background and course of illness rather than on the cure. A-III (GP)

Diary of a Shinjuku Burglar (1973) Pretentious Japanese movie uses a young couple's confusion about their sexual identity to supposedly mirror the conflicting realities of the Tokyo student district of Shinjuku. Director Nagisa Oshima uses a number of confusing techniques that don't reflect much of anything for American viewers. Several very graphic sex sequences. O (nr)

Diary of Anne Frank, The (1959) Somber dramatization of the long ordeal facing an adolescent girl (Millie Perkins), her parents (Joseph Schildkraut and Gusti Huber), and another Jewish family (including Shelley Winters, Lou Jacobi, and Ed Wynn) hiding from the Nazis in a secret room above a warehouse in WW II Amsterdam. Directed by George Stevens, the fact-based account painstakingly conveys the group's determination to survive their desperate plight, but the effort is flawed by a strangely limp performance in the title role. Much tension and menacing atmosphere. A-I (br)

Diary of Forbidden Dreams (see: **What?**)

Dick Tracy (1945) Chester Gould's comic-strip police detective (Morgan Conway) rescues girlfriend Tess Trueheart (Anne Jeffreys) from knife-wielding serial killer Splitface (Mike Mazurki) in a low-budget production slackly directed by William Berke. Stylized violence. A-II (br)

Dick Tracy (1990) Chester Gould's comic-strip detective (Warren Beatty, who also produced and directed) tries to get the goods on a mob syndicate headed by Big Boy Caprice (Al Pacino) with some help along the way from a seductive singer (Madonna), a streetwise orphan (Charlie Korsmo), and the hero's steadfast girlfriend, Tess Trueheart (Glenne Headley). Beatty deadpans his way through a plodding, threadbare cops-and-robbers script, Pacino chews up all the scenery in sight, and a notable supporting cast languishes under mounds of make-up, leaving viewers disappointed with everything but Richard Sylbert's evocative 1930's set designs. Several relatively mild double entendres and much comic-book violence ranging from menace to elaborate shoot-outs. A-II (PG)

Dick Tracy, Detective (see: 1945's **Dick Tracy**)

Dick Tracy Meets Gruesome (1947) Low-budget crime caper directed by John Rawlins with Ralph Byrd as Chester Gould's comic-strip crime-stopper and Boris Karloff as the sinister ex-con of the title who robs a bank using an experimental gas that freezes people in mid-motion. Unreal situations with some menacing characters. A-II (br)

Dick Tracy vs. Crime, Inc. (1951) Feature version of a serial co-directed by William Witney and John English pits federal agent Tracy (Ralph Byrd) against the Ghost, a mad criminal who uses laser rays to become invisible while committing such dastardly deeds as setting off an earthquake to unleash a tidal wave destroying New York City in some good model shots. Comic-strip heroics and fantasy violence. A-II (br)

Dick Tracy vs. Cueball (1946) Formula crime caper directed by Gordon M. Douglas has Tracy (Morgan Conway) on the trail of a bald ex-con responsible for a series of murders stemming from a diamond robbery. Stylized violence and comic-strip heroics. A-II (br)

Dick Tracy's Dilemma (1947) Chester Gould's comic-strip cop (Ralph Byrd) cracks a fur robbery case and nabs a murderer known as the Claw in a routine effort directed by John Rawlins. Occasional stylized violence and menace. A-II (br)

Dick Tracy's G-Men (1939) Feature version of 15-episode serial co-directed by William Witney and John English has the comic-strip crime-stopper (Ralph Byrd) joining the FBI to stop a gang of spies led by an evil mastermind (Irving Pichel). Some stylized violence and a lot of far-fetched menace. A-II (br)

Did You Hear the One about the Traveling Saleslady? (1968) A corny, cliche-ridden vehicle for comedienne Phyllis Diller who plays a player-piano peddler in a Missouri town circa 1910. Tedious. A-I (br)

Die! Die! My Darling! (1965) Overwrought British chiller about a loony religious fanatic (Tallulah Bankhead) who holds her dead son's former fiancé (Stephanie Powers) prisoner while trying to purify her soul, even if it kills her. Directed by Silvio Narizzano, the picture's wild-eyed melodramatics are ludicrously contrived, with Bankhead's game but wrong-headed performance in her final screen role providing the only interest. Stylized violence, menacing situations, and sexual innuendo. A-III (br)

Die Hard (1988) When a band of savvy terrorists

take over a LA high-rise on Christmas Eve, they're no match for a New York cop (Bruce Willis) who happens to be there visiting his estranged wife (Bonnie Bedelia). Director John McTiernan mixes thrills and chills with humorous banter and in-jokes, but its picture of conscienceless terrorist brutalities contains excessive graphic violence and rough language. O (R)

Die Hard 2 (1990) This time detective John McClane (Bruce Willis) takes on an elite band of terrorists who have taken control of Washington DC's Dulles airport while the plane his wife (Bonnie Bedelia) is in is rapidly running out of fuel in the raging blizzard overhead. As directed by Renny Harlin, this sequel matches the intense excitement, explosive special effects, and welcome comic relief of the original film while surpassing its level of violence with constant, calculated, and cold-blooded slaughters. Excessively graphic brutality and violence, much rough language, and brief male nudity. O (R)

Die Hard with a Vengeance (1995) Third special-effects marathon featuring the hardened, unlikable New York super-cop (Bruce Willis) who here gets some help from a nervy Harlem shopkeeper (Samuel L. Jackson) in going after the international terrorist (Jeremy Irons) behind a series of bombings designed to keep the police occupied while his Fascist band of bad guys loot Manhattan's Federal Reserve gold vaults. Director John McTiernan's leaden action fantasy turns New York City into a terrorist's delight, with its vulnerable populace threatened by a ludicrously contrived plot which spends most of its energy on setting up bloody encounters between formula characters. Excessive violence, mindless menace, racial epithets, occasional profanity, and recurring rough language. O (R)

Die Laughing (1980) Young cabdriver (Robby Benson, who also worked on the screenplay), accused of murdering a famous nuclear scientist, tries to clear himself with the aid of his girlfriend (Linda Grovenor) and a monkey. Directed by Jeff Werner, the lame comedy-mystery is mediocre entertainment in every respect. Violence. A-III (PG)

Die, Monster, Die (1966) Weak British horror movie directed by Daniel Haller with Boris Karloff playing a sort of contemporary wizard. Mild violence. A-II (br)

Different for Girls (1997) British drama in which a bike messenger (Ruppert Graves) is attracted to a woman (Steven Mackintosh) whom he finally recognizes is an old school buddy after a sex-change operation and proceeds unwittingly to wreck his old friend's new life, then tries to make amends. Directed by Richard Spence, the story's bizarre situation is given some plausibility by the credible performances of the two leads and the serious treatment given to the human dignity of a person who's attempted to switch genders. Troubling theme of transsexuality, several sexual encounters with brief nudity, and some rough language. A-IV (R)

Different Story, A (1978) Failed romantic comedy in which boy meets girl (Perry King and Meg Foster) and, though both are homosexual, they settle down to a happily married life, complete with baby. Directed by Paul Aaron, there are few amusing lines and a good performance from Foster, but its rough language and a nude sequence are excessive. O (R/PG)

Digby, the Biggest Dog in the World (1974) British children's fantasy in which a lonely boy (Richard Beaumont) loses his dog when it consumes a secret growth chemical, expands to the size of three elephants and terrorizes the countryside. Director Joseph McGrath makes the most of a good cast of zanies (Jim Dale, Spike Milligan, Milo O'Shea, and Victor Spinetti) who come to the lad's rescue in a shaggy-dog story that relies on funny dialogue and comic gesture rather than transparent special effects. For the kids, but most parents will get some enjoyment too. A-I (G)

Diggstown (1992) An ex-con (James Woods) outcons a con-man (Bruce Dern) by betting millions on an aging ex-boxer (Louis Gossett, Jr.) being able to beat 10 men in the ring in a single night. Director Michael Ritchie serves up lowest-common-denominator humor in brutally physical conflicts whose dramatic elements are sacrificed for cheap laughs. Extended bloody bouts, some sexual innuendo, and recurring rough language. A-III (R)

Dillinger (1973) The crime odyssey of John Dillinger (Warren Oates) through the 1930's Midwest is paralleled with the obsession of FBI agent Melvin Purvis (Ben Johnson) to capture the fear of criminals and the respect of the public. Written and directed by John Milius, the acting and period settings are very good and the special effects are appropriately brutal and eye-catching. Although extremely violent, one should emerge from the experience a little more reflective about our national fascination with guns. A-IV (R)

Dimples (1936) Shirley Temple vehicle set in pre-Civil War New York, where the little star plays a street urchin cared for by a rascally dishonest grandfather (Frank Morgan) until he's reformed by a wealthy matron (Helen Westley) interested in the girl's welfare. Director William A. Seiter peps up the sentimental plot with appealing musical numbers and colorful period settings, including scenes from "Uncle Tom's Cabin" with Shirley in the tragic role of Little Eva. Black stereotyping typical of the era. A-I (PG)

Diner (1982) Low-keyed, humane, and often very funny movie about several young men whose favorite hangout is a diner in 1959 Baltimore. Now in their early twenties, they still want to cling to the carefree life of high-school days. Writer-director Barry Levinson has come up with an offbeat and entertaining piece which in its modest way is also a worthwhile one. A major portion of the dialogue is concerned with sex and there is a sequence involving a lewd practical joke. A-III (R)

Dinner at the Ritz (1937) Dated but still enjoyable murder mystery in which the daughter (Annabella) of a French financier (Stewart Rome) sets out to find her father's killer despite the protests of her fiancé (Paul Lukas) and the interference of a British detective (David Niven) posing as a dippy playboy. Directed by Harold D. Schuster, the mystery plot isn't much, but the high-fashion settings, polished cast, and comic misunderstandings between amateur and professional sleuths still have appeal. A-I (br)

Dinner Game, The (1999) Wry French comedy in which a snooty married publisher (Thierry Lhermitte) intending to humiliate his dimwitted dinner guest (Jacques Villeret) has the tables turned on him when the guileless guest accidentally reveals the husband's infidelity to his wife and unintentionally sets him up for a scathing tax audit. Writer-director Francis Verber hilariously contrasts the smug yuppie with the earnest dullard to steady comic effect enhanced by excellent acting. Subtitles. Adulterous references and a few instances of rough language. A-III (nr)

Dinosaurus! (1960) Woefully inept fantasy directed by Irvin S. Yeaworth, Jr., takes place on a remote island whose inhabitants panic when a caveman and a couple of dinosaurs are dynamited out of their suspended animation and into the 20th-century. Much silliness and some stylized violence. A-I (br)

Dionysus in '69 (1970) Filmed performance of an experimental play loosely based on Euripides depends mainly on its own uninhibited eroticism and the unrestrained participation of the audience. Director Brian De Palma records the proceedings in wave after wave of split-screen nakedness and orgiastic behavior that has little to do with art but seems more related to cheap exploitation. O (nr)

Dirigible (1931) Rugged adventure tale in which a daredevil Navy pilot (Ralph Graves) crashes while flying an explorer over the South Pole, then is rescued from the Antarctic's frozen wastes by a Navy dirigible piloted by an officer (Jack Holt) he considers a rival. Directed by Frank R. Capra, the perilous action sequences are still gripping, despite a hokey subplot about the daredevil's wife (Fay Wray) being fed up with his risky hijinks. Life-threatening situations and contemplation of divorce. A-II (br)

Dirt Gang, The (1972) Rampaging biker gang invades a Western movie set and proceeds to terrorize and otherwise debauch the movie-makers until a movie stuntman (Michael Forest) pummels the gang's leader to death in a bike duel. Directed by Jerry Jameson, its combination of sex and violence is grossly offensive. O (R)

Dirty Dancing (1987) Coming-of-age story set in the 1960s about a middle-class girl (Jennifer Grey) and a local dancer (Patrick Swayze) who teaches her a few bold new steps. Director Emile Ardolino's lightweight effort at evoking the teen scene of a generation ago uses an ill-conceived plot contrivance about an abortion, brief nudity, and an acceptance of casual sex. A-III (PG-13)

Dirty Dingus Magee (1970) Western spoof with Frank Sinatra in the title role as an outlaw involved with a town where the mayor (Anne Jackson) is also a madam whose brothel business thrives on a cavalry clientele, and to keep them around she orders the sheriff (George Kennedy) to incite an Indian uprising. Director Burt Kennedy has a field day altering allegiances in a mad cacophony of discordant sequences that are juvenile in their attempts to ridicule the Old West and tiresome in their constant leering. Boisterous, bawdy, and dumb. A-III (GP/PG-13)

Dirty Dozen, The (1967) WW II story about a freewheeling officer (Lee Marvin) and the dozen army convicts he trains to destroy the headquarters of the German General Staff. Directed by Robert Aldrich, the movie is savage in its violence, yet raises questions about authorized brutality. A-IV (br)

Dirty Game, The (1966) Jumbled European-produced espionage movie with Henry Fonda, Vittorio Gassman, Robert Ryan, and three directors (Terence Young, Christian-Jaque, and Carlo Lizzani). Some violence and sexual innuendo. A-III (br)

Dirty Hands (1976) Silly, convoluted plot about a wife (Romy Schneider) who plots with lover to murder drunken, maudlin husband (Rod Steiger in a self-indulgent performance). French production written and directed by Claude Chabrol is a sordid little story of marital infidelity and contains some nudity. O (R)

Dirty Harry (1971) Clint Eastwood stars as a hardboiled detective of the San Francisco homicide squad who takes the law into his own hands when a psychotic killer is released on a technicality. Director Don Siegel keeps the action tightly-wound and fast-paced, but his cynical superhero is basically irresponsible in endangering the lives of innocent people in his personal crusade against criminals. Harry is clearly dangerous and so is a movie which evades the complex legal problems and moral issues of vigilante justice. Sadistic brutality and graphic violence. O (R)

Dirty Little Billy (1973) The story of how and why Billy the Kid (Michael J. Pollard) began his life of crime is told by director Stan Dragoti by making him the victim of the times and circumstances, an idea neither very new nor very stimulating and, at any rate, goes nowhere. Contains a barrage of gritty, peripheral sex, and violence. A-IV (R)

Dirty Mary, Crazy Larry (1974) Peter Fonda and Adam Roarke extort big money from supermarket executive Roddy McDowall, pick up Susan George, and destroy every car in sight while trying to escape with the cash. Directed by John Hough, it is thin action entertainment with an abundance of rough language. A-III (PG)

Dirty O'Neil (1974) Small-town policeman (Morgan Paull) finds his job less challenging than trying to bed the area's entire female population until three thugs come to town and sodomize his steady girl friend. Directors Howard Freen and Lewis Teague start with a sex farce that ends in sordid, sickening violence. O (R)

Dirty Outlaws, The (1972) Pallid Italian Western directed by Franco Rossetti tells the story of a desperado (Chip Corman) who seeks gold and discovers that his heart is made of it. Some fairly benign violence. A-III (R)

Dirty Rotten Scoundrels (1988) Two rogues (dapper Michael Caine and slovenly Steve Martin) who specialize in conning women out of their money in a lucrative Riviera resort vie in a comic battle to bilk an American (Glenne Headly) out of $50,000. Director Frank Oz makes the most of his gorgeous Riviera setting, but the film lacks major laughs and a heart in its cynical attitude toward women as easily conned targets. Mild sexual innuendo and bathroom humor. A-III (PG)

Dirty Tricks (1981) Harvard history professor (Elliott Gould) and a television newswoman (Kate Jackson) are the unwitting targets of gangsters and government men in this inane comedy-thriller directed by Alvin Rakoff. Some leering humor. A-III (PG)

Dirty Work (1998) Leaden comedy in which two losers (Norm Macdonald and Artie Lange) start a revenge-for-hire business, then are tricked into doing an undeserved nasty deed for a smarmy tycoon (Christopher McDonald), upon whom they turn the tables. Director Bob Saget tries unsuccessfully to cobble together a series of pranks, pratfalls, and silly stunts performed by the dumb-and-dumber duo in this creaky clunker. Some slapstick violence, sexual innuendo, brief nudity, and frequent crude humor. A-III (PG-13)

Dirtymouth (1971) At the time of his death, controversial comedian Lenny Bruce was the center of a legal storm that has far-reaching implications about the freedom of expression in modern society. Viewers of Herbert Altman's documentary will get little insight into the man and, more importantly, will come away without any perspective on his times. The failure exploits an already tragic career. O (nr)

Disclosure (1994) With his computer firm is on the verge of a crucial merger, a troubled family man (Michael Douglas) jeopardizes the deal and his job by bringing charges of sexual harassment against his new boss (Demi Moore), a manipulative former lover out to destroy his career while enhancing her own. Director Barry Levinson makes slick entertainment out of corporate back-stabbing while reducing the painful subject of sexual harassment to the level of glossy escapist fare. Restrained depiction of a near-seduction scene, verbally graphic descriptions of it, and intermittent rough language. A-III (R)

Discreet Charm of the Bourgeoisie, The (1972) Director Luis Bunuel's surrealistic satire on the lives of the very rich presents an incredibly complicated series of events, such as dreamers dreaming of other dreamers, that grows more satisfying as the narrative becomes more outrageously illogical. The central recurring situation is that of six wealthy friends (Fernando Rey, Delphine Seyrig, Stephane Audran, Bulle Ogier, Jean-Pierre Cassel, and Michel Piccoli) about to sit down to dinner but always being interrupted by something which prevents them from being able to proceed with the meal. The movie is meant to be enjoyed as something as playful as the title itself. A-III (PG)

Disembodied, The (1957) Hokey jungle horror from director Walter Grauman in which an adventurer (Paul Burke) beating his way through a bushy studio backlot gets mixed up with a medical researcher whose unfaithful wife (Allison Hayes) is secretly the leader of a local voodoo cult. Minor-league supernatural hooey, sexual situations, and native stereotyping. A-III (br)

Disorderlies (1987) The Fat Boys, a rap music group, star as health-care interns who unwittingly foil the plot of an inept nephew (Anthony Geary) to do in his wealthy uncle (Ralph Bellamy). Director Michael Schultz's not-exactly-uplifting comedy relies on purely physical slapstick brought off amiably by the funky boys and is marred only by some mildly crude language and a brief nude swimming scene. A-II (PG)

Disorderly Orderly, The (1964) Leaden comedy set in a sanatorium, where an accident-prone aide (Jerry Lewis) creates havoc by trying to help patients, especially the woman (Susan Oliver) he had secretly admired in high school. Director Frank Tashlin embroiders the one-note plot with a grab-bag of sight gags and slapstick zaniness, but the result is drowned in hokey sentimentality. Romantic complications. A-I (br)

Disorganized Crime (1989) Four seasoned cons (Ruben Blades, Fred Gwynne, Lou Diamond Phillips, and William Russ) plan the heist of a small-town Montana bank without their ringleader (Corbin Bernsen) who is dodging the clutches of two dimwitted detectives (Ed O'Neill and Daniel Roebuck). Though all the disorganized running around makes for slapstick moments, director Jim Kouf doesn't take full advantage of his actors' potential. Rough language, cartoon violence, and phony glamorization of career criminals. A-III (R)

Distance (1976) Black sergeant (Paul Benjamin) on a Georgia army post in 1956 becomes estranged from his German wife (Eija Pokkinen), a woman desperately trying to save her marriage and her own sense of worth. With good acting, strong characterizations, and period authenticity, Anthony Lover directs a meaningful story of alienation, but the fragile web of relationships that had been developing so well is finally overwhelmed by a needlessly melodramatic climax. Adult situations. A-III (R)

Distant Drums (1951) Disappointing historical yarn set in 1840 Florida, where an Army expedition (led by Gary Cooper) boats across a lake to destroy a former Spanish fort used by smugglers supplying guns to the Seminoles, then has to fight its way back on foot to the American lines. Directed by Raoul Walsh, the stock characters work up little interest in a formula plot that offers surprisingly little action and scant information about the Seminole Wars. Frontier violence and Indian stereotyping. A-II (br)

Distant Thunder (1975) Indian production about a young Brahman couple whose quiet, secure lives in a small Bengali village are disrupted and their modest expectations destroyed in the terrible famine of 1943, when more than five million people starved to death. Showing the gradual breakdown of village society as rice shortages and hunger grow, director Satyajit Ray makes the viewer share his compassion and anger for the fate of those anonymous victims of a catastrophe caused by WW II. Moving but unsentimental, it is also a cogent parable for our own times. A-II (nr)

Distant Voices, Still Lives (1989) Visually beautiful but tedious autobiographical movie dramatizing filmmaker Terence Davies's working-class family roots in Liverpool, England, during the 1940s and 1950s. Impressionistic shots of various family rites of passage wear thin and ultimately tend to confound viewers about the family's troubled dynamics in which Catholic ritual and period music seem the only positive unifying forces. Several rough scenes of family violence and verbal abuse. A-III (PG-13)

Distinguished Gentleman, The (1992) Artificial comedy about a sleazy Florida con-artist (Eddie Murphy) who gets elected to Congress, goes far on the government gravy train, then has an improbable change of heart by going public with evidence of graft on the part of his political mentor (Lane Smith). Director Jonathan Lynn plays **Mr. Smith Goes to Washington** for laughs but doesn't get many out of a clumsy comic vehicle for a performer who's made a career out of insincere grins and foul language. Comic depiction of a sexual encounter, much sexual innuendo, and recurring rough language. A-III (R)

Disturbing Behavior (1998) Slack teen thriller in which a transfer student from Chicago (Steve Marsden) arrives in an idyllic island community to find the local high school has a growing number of too-perfect students whose minds, he discovers at his peril, are being controlled by a mad psychiatrist. Directed by David Nutter, there are occasional scenes of bizarre violence and nightmare suspense, but the plot makes little sense and, worse, sometimes evokes unintended laughs. Stylized violence, sexual situations and innuendo, a flash of nudity, occasional rough language, and some profanity. A-III (R)

Diva (1982) Bright French production recounting the adventures of a romantic 18-year-old postman (Frederic Andrei), obsessed with an opera diva (Wilhelmenia Wiggins Fernandez), but when he records her performance at a concert, his tape gets mixed up with one incriminating some gangsters and the chase is on through the streets and subways of Paris. Jean-Jacques Beineix directs a diverting tongue-in-cheek thriller that's an all-style, no-substance entertainment. Violence and brief nudity. A-III (R)

Divine Mr. J., The (1974) Thoroughly mindless, abysmally inept, yawningly unfunny attempt to satirize the New Testament. Cast as a Flatbush-accented Virgin Mary, Bette Midler appears to be totally without any redeeming talent, a condition afflicting the rest of the cast in this low satire. O (R)

Divine Nymph, The (1979) Italian study of upper-class decadence after WW I from director Giuseppe Patroni Griffi tells the story of an insensitive woman (Laura Antonelli) who drives one lover (Terence Stamp) to suicide and another (Marcello Mastroianni) to join the Fascists. The theme of the destructive force of thwarted passion is given surface treatment as is the unclothed figure of its heroine. O (nr)

Divorce American Style (1967) Dick Van Dyke and Debbie Reynolds have to decide whether to call it a day after 17 years of marriage and one of separation in their divorce-riddled California community. Producer-writer Norman Lear and director Bud Yorkin have come up with an entertaining satire that touches all the bases: the senseless rift, the well-meant advice, the legal razzle-dazzle, the shuffled offspring, the social plight of disconnected spouse, the financial bite. Well-paced and occasionally very funny, it's a good try that largely succeeds. A-III (br)

Do the Right Thing (1989) After 25 years of selling pizza in the same Bedford-Stuyvesant neighborhood, now black and Hispanic, Italian-American Sal (Danny Aiello) attempts to squash racial tensions before they destroy his family business. Writer-director-actor Spike Lee concocts a powerful look at racism with passionate characters, sharp satire, savvy musical counterpoints, theatricality, and much humor. Its incendiary point of view — that violence may be a potentially justified means to an end — will unsettle many and force viewers to confront stereotypes. Heavy profanity, racial and ethnic slurs, intense climactic racial violence, and a brief sexual scene with fleeting nudity. A-IV (R)

Do You Love Me? (1946) Lightweight musical romance in which the staid dean (Maureen O'Hara) of a rustic music college tries out some attractive outfits on a trip to New York, then finds herself pursued by both a bandleader (Harry James) and a radio crooner (Dick Haymes). Directed by Gregory Ratoff, the thin plot is chiefly of interest as a vehicle for the music and songs of the big-band era. Mild romantic complications. A-I (br)

Doberman Gang, The (1972) Enterprising gang (Byron Mabe, Julie Parrish, and Hal Reed) use a pack of Doberman pinscher attack dogs in an intricate, highly-orchestrated bank robbery. Director Byron Chudnow's inventive low-budget heist movie depends on an element of terror that attack dogs provide and has some mild lovemaking scenes. A-III (PG/G)

Doc (1971) Stacy Keach stars as legendary gunfighter and gambler Doc Holliday. Director Frank Perry's re-creation of an oft-told tale attempts to turn the events leading up to the gunfight at the OK Corral into some sort of allegory about American involvement in Vietnam, and the movie collapses under the weight of its pretensions. Considerable violence. A-III (PG)

Doc Hollywood (1991) En route to a lucrative plastic surgery practice in Beverly Hills, a young doctor (Michael J. Fox) is stranded by a car mishap in a folksy Southern town eager to keep him as their general practitioner. The corn is higher than an elephant's eye in director Michael Caton-Jones's syrupy, contrived, and predictable tribute to small-town life. Scene with full frontal nudity and minimal vulgar language. A-III (PG-13)

Doc Savage: The Man of Bronze (1975) Pulp adventure hero of the 1930s becomes a dud on the big screen as Savage (Ron Ely) takes his WW I buddies, dubbed the Fabulous Five, to South America, where they encounter an Indian snake-cult guarding a pool of gold deep in the jungle. Directed by Michael Anderson, the adventures are as foolish as the acting is flat, though the John Philip Souza score adds some welcome energy to the proceedings. Stylized violence, comic-strip menace, and mild sexual innuendo. A-II (G)

Docks of New Orleans (1948) Formula Charlie Chan mystery directed by Derwin Abrahams involves the Chinese-American detective (Roland Winters) in the case of a chemical manufacturer murdered by poison gas from a shattered radio tube. Comic racial stereotyping of Chan's chauffeur (Mantan Moreland) and No. 2 Son (Victor Sen Yung). A-I (br)

Doctor, The (1991) Stricken with throat cancer, an arrogant physician (William Hurt) bristles at his treatment as a lowly patient but, inspired by a fellow sufferer (Elizabeth Perkins) and supported by his neglected wife (Christine Lahti), the experience unexpectedly enriches his life. Director Randa Haines gets some fine performances while fully developing the human element that often gets lost in modern, impersonal hospital settings. A suggestive song lyric, minimal rough language, and graphic shots of open-heart surgery. A-II (PG-13)

Doctor and the Devils, The (1985) An often-too-gleefully gruesome dramatization of a famous 19th-century case involving a prominent surgeon (Timothy Dalton) who refuses to inquire into the source of the cadavers furnished him for his lectures in anatomy. It's well-directed by Freddie Francis from an exceptionally literate script by Ronald Harwood based on a Dylan Thomas scenario plumbing its theme of ends and means. Stylized violence, sordid environment, and brief nudity. A-III (R)

Doctor Blood's Coffin (1961) Pedestrian horror story in which a mad scientist (Kieron Moore) returns to his country village to use its abandoned tin mines as the site for ghoulish experiments in human transplants. Director Sidney Furie's low-budget British production is a poor Frankenstein variation that creates little sense of terror, though it does have a horrific finish. Stylized violence. A-II (br)

Doctor Death: Seeker Of Souls (1973) John Considine plays the dastardly doctor who specializes in giving a new lease on life to the ailing by finding a body into which his client's soul can be liberated. Directed by Eddie Saeta, it is so witless in plot and execution that its bloody excesses become equally meaningless and boring. A-III (R)

Doctor Detroit (1983) A mild-mannered but oddball English professor (Dan Aykroyd) assumes the role of Doctor Detroit, a real bad gangster, in order to protect four prostitutes who have been abandoned by their pimp (Howard Hesseman). The shuttle back and forth between the two identities is the basis for most of the comedy, but under Michael Pressman's direction the laughs are infrequent and mild at best. Sexually oriented humor, brief shots from a pornographic movie, and a benign view of drug use. O (R)

Doctor Dolittle (1967) Gentle, turn-of-the-century musical fantasy about an eccentric animal doctor's adventures searching for the Great Pink Sea Snail. Rex Harrison stars as the doctor who can talk to animals in an attractive but slow-moving production directed by Richard Fleischer. Movie musical purists may be disappointed in Leslie Bricusse's uninspired screenplay, music, and lyrics but others, especially children, may be charmed. A-I (G)

Doctor Faustus (1968) British adaptation of Christopher Marlowe's Elizabethan drama about the German university professor (Richard Burton) who sells his soul to the devil for knowledge, power, and a woman (Elizabeth Taylor). Directed by Burton and Nevill Coghill, the result is something of a witch's brew of scenes depicting the emptiness of the world, the flesh, and the devil. Brief nudity. A-III (br)

Doctor, You've Got to Be Kidding (1966) Glamorized treatment of teenage pregnancy in director Peter Tewksbury's vacuous movie starring Sandra Dee and George Hamilton is offensive, especially considering the juvenile audience to which it is directed. O (br)

Doctor Zhivago (1965) Boris Pasternak's novel has been turned into a romantic epic of the Russian Revolution and its effects upon various individuals (Julie Christie, Omar Sharif, and Alec Guinness) struggling to survive in difficult times. The Revolution serves as a rich backdrop for a bittersweet love story reflecting the disruption of lives and values caused by the turmoil of the time. Adapted by Robert Bolt and directed by David Lean. Restrained treatment of violence. A-II (PG/PG-13)

Doctors' Wives (1971) Dyan Cannon and Richard Crenna star in an adult soap opera about doctors in a posh California medical clinic who dally with the nurses while their wives find diversion elsewhere. A colleague's fatal heart attack provides the necessary scandal and shame to motivate everyone back into their proper and respective beds. Ploddingly directed by George Schaefer, the shenanigans are mostly off-camera and recounted in euphemistic dialogue. Gruesome open-heart surgical sequence, but the movie itself has no heart or any real emotion for that matter. O (R)

Dodge City (1939) Ex-Confederate officer (Errol Flynn) heads a cattle drive to the railhead in Dodge, becomes sheriff of the lawless town, and takes on the entire gang of its worst badman (Bruce Cabot). Director Michael Curtiz's action-packed Western includes a cattle stampede, an epic barroom brawl, and shoot-outs galore, given some pace by romantic misunderstandings (Olivia de Havilland) and rough frontier humor (Alan Hale, Frank McHugh, and Guinn Williams). Stylized violence. A-I (br)

Dog Day Afternoon (1975) Al Pacino stars as a hapless Brooklyn bankrobber whose plans go awry when the police arrive before he and an accomplice can flee. In a taut, well-acted drama with comic overtones, director Sidney Lumet is consistently entertaining in his treatment of this fact-based incident, but the bisexual character of the hero (who needed money for his partner's sex-change operation), the rough language, and the disquieting look at the seamy side of life limit its appeal. A-IV (R)

Dog of Flanders, A (1959) In a turn-of-the-century Antwerp suburb, an old man (Donald Crisp) and his small grandson (David Ladd) rescue a dog left to die at the roadside. Produced by Robert B. Radnitz and directed by James B. Clark, the movie shows how unselfish love and understanding bring happiness even under conditions of dire poverty. Fine family fare. A-I (br)

Dogfight (1991) Coming-of-age story about a teenage Marine (River Phoenix) who, on his last night stateside in 1963, finds friendship and romance with the shy waitress (Lili Taylor) he originally picked up as part of a game to find the ugliest date. Director Nancy Savoca examines male peer pressure and lances sexist attitudes with some sensitivity but gets only lukewarm results. Implied premarital encounter, some sexual innuendo, and frequent rough language. A-III (R)

Dogpound Shuffle (1975) Tap-dancing vagrant (Ron Moody) teams up with an itinerant harmonica player (David Soul) in order to make enough money to retrieve his impounded dog. Director Jeffrey Bloom's frequently moving study of the interaction between the two has an affirmative, spunky quality marred by an unnecessarily bloody fight scene and a few expletives. A-II (PG)

Dogs of War, The (1981) Screen version of Frederick Forsyth's novel about mercenaries (headed by Christopher Walken) hired to oust a bloody West African tyrant in order to replace him with a man just as bad but who will be more amenable to foreign business-interests. Though the movie lacks sympathetic and well-defined central characters, the narrative's action is handled quite well by director John Irvin. The result is an interesting melodrama with serious but ambiguous implications and some graphic violence. A-III (R)

Doll Face (1945) Brassy but sentimental low-budget clunker directed by Lewis Seiler transforms a burlesque queen (Vivian Blaine) into a Broadway musical star, despite misunderstandings with her manager boyfriend (Dennis O'Keefe). Romantic complications and sexual innuendo. A-III (br)

Doll's House, A (1973) Director Patrick Garland interprets Ibsen's play as anything but a repudiation of the married state. Fine cast (Claire Bloom, Anthony Hopkins, Ralph Richardson) conveys those qualities of maturity, compassion, and respect for the integrity of the individual without which human growth and fulfillment in marriage is impossible. It is a film for women who yearn to be emancipated, for women who have been, and for men who have wondered why Women's Lib was even necessary. A-II (G)

$ (Dollars) (1971) Richard Brooks wrote and directed this only occasionally amusing Hamburg bank-heist action-drama that features Warren Beatty as the brains of the bank's security system and Goldie Hawn as his brainless, high-priced hooker accomplice. Unfortunately, Brooks's fascination with electronic gadgetry impedes the pace of the action which creaks along too implausibly to maintain much interest. Short on comedy and high on ugly twists and brutal turns, the movie has large doses of nudity, sexual innuendo, and crude language. O (R)

Dolores Claiborne (1995) Absorbing psychological melodrama from the Stephen King novel about a brittle New York journalist (Jennifer Jason Leigh) returning to a remote Maine village to help her estranged mother (Kathy Bates), who years earlier was suspected of murdering her husband (David Strathairn) and now stands accused of killing her elderly employer (Judy Parfitt). Director Taylor Hackford builds suspense through a series of flashbacks gingerly unwrapping secrets of the damaged mother-daughter relationship. Fleeting violence, references to sexual abuse, and intermittent rough language. A-III (R)

Dominick and Eugene (1988) Lovely story of an unlikely pair of 25-year-old fraternal twins - a mentally damaged garbage man (Tom Hulce) and a moody medical student (Ray Liotta) - following the traumas and conflicts that threaten to disrupt their close sibling bond and the positive changes that result. Director Robert M. Young sensitively underplays a child-abuse subplot and does not exploit the violent potential of several incidents. A few sexually suggestive scenes and some profanity. A-III (PG-13)

Domino Kid (1957) Dour revenge Western directed by Ray Nazarro in which an ex-Rebel (Rory Calhoun) returns home to Texas, learns his rancher father was murdered by cattle rustlers, then sets out to find and kill them without waiting for the law to do the job. Vigilante justice. A-III (br)

Domino Principle, The (1977) Gene Hackman plays a convict recruited by a powerful and mysterious group to carry out an assassination whose intended victim apparently is the President of the United States. Director Stanley Kramer disappointingly fails to deal with the political paranoia of our times in any significant fashion, settling instead for another pointless and simple-minded melodrama with violence. A-III (R)

Don Giovanni (1979) Great voices and sumptuously romantic Italian landscapes predominate in director Joseph Losey's screen version of the Mozart opera about a jilted woman (Kiri Te Kanawa) obsessed with her husband's damnation. Realistic treatment of the Don's compulsive sexuality takes on Marxist significance as a reflection of the conflict of the old regime with the working class. A cultural artifact whose romantic vision of adultery requires a mature perspective. A-IV (nr)

Don Is Dead, The (1973) Crime godfather (Anthony Quinn) suffers a heart attack, triggering a power struggle to fill the vacuum. Directed by Richard Fleischer, it is a dull, mindless variation on a theme. Excessive violence. O (R)

Don Juan DeMarco (1995) Featherweight romantic comedy in which a delusional patient (Johnny Depp) claims to be legendary lover Don Juan, whose embroidered tales of loves won and lost inspire his weary psychiatrist (Marlon Brando) to rediscover romance with his delighted wife (Faye Dunaway). Writer-director Jeremy Leven's fanciful movie offers a wafer-thin narrative of limited appeal beyond a charming veneer which coyly blurs the line between fantasy and reality. Frequent sexual references, fleeting nudity, brief stylized violence, and an instance of rough language. A-III (PG-13)

Don Juan, My Love (1991) Riotous Spanish comedy in which the legendary 16th-century lover Don Juan escapes Purgatory to do good on earth and earn a heavenly reward, only to be mistaken for a lookalike, drug-smuggling actor (Juan Luis Galiardo in a dual role) who is playing the part of Don Juan in a Seville production rife with backstage amorous intrigues. Director Antonio Mercero handles this screwball bedroom farce in good taste, and Galiardo fully captures both the gentler nature of the well-intentioned Don Juan and the arrogance of his latter-day counterpart. Some bawdy humor, frequent sexual innuendo, and brief rear nudity. A-III (nr)

Don Quixote (1973) A performance by the Australian Ballet Company of the Cervantes classic, co-directed by Rudolph Nureyev and Robert Helpmann, with Helpmann in the title role and Nureyev dancing that of the young Basilio. A-I (G)

Donnie Brasco (1997) Fact-based story of an undercover FBI agent (Johnny Depp) who infiltrates a New York mob family in the late 1970s by befriending an aging, low-level hood (Al Pacino), despite the agent's moral dilemmas over neglecting his own family while betraying a man who has treated him like a son. Director Mike Newell delivers an absorbing character study of a good guy nearly destroyed by his dedication to the job, while never glamorizing the vicious brutality of the gangsters. Brief graphic violence, flash of nudity, intermittent profanity, and much rough language. A-III (R)

Donovan's Brain (1953) Strange horror tale of a doctor (Lew Ayres) who keeps the brain of a ruthless financier alive, then finds himself compelled by the brain to carry on the dead man's business affairs. Directed by Felix Feist, the low-budget production succeeds in building up the story's suspense mainly through Ayres's solid performance as a likeable fellow who falls victim to his own scientific curiosity. Bizarre fantasy premise. A-II (br)

Donovan's Reef (1963) Throwaway situation comedy with WW II vets (John Wayne, Lee Marvin, and Jack Warden) beach-combing on a South Pacific isle, when the daughter (Elizabeth Allen) of one of them makes a surprise visit. Director John Ford plays around with his familiar themes of male camaraderie and manly rivalry, as well as the freedom of nature versus the restraints of civilization, but the result is less than original and only fitfully engaging. Slapstick violence and comic bathos. A-II (br)

Don't Be a Menace to South Central While Drinking Your Juice in the Hood (1996) Lame spoof of black ghetto movies gets few laughs from a disjointed series of tired skits featuring a gun-toting homeboy (Marlon Wayans) and a naive newcomer (Shawn Wayans). Directed by Paris Barclay, it's an exercise in the obvious pushed to the extremes of bad taste, mean-spirited parody, and sophomoric crudities. Simulated sex scenes, comic violence, and constant rough language. O (R)

Don't Bother to Knock (1952) Churning thriller in which a hotel house-detective (Richard Widmark) tries to cope with a deranged babysitter (Marilyn Monroe) threatening to kill herself and the little girl in her charge. Directed by Roy Ward Baker, the situation develops slowly, then matters turn decidedly nasty with mounting tension until an unconvincing ending, though Monroe's tenuous performance as a mental case is worth seeing. Intense menace to a child and sexual innuendo. A-III (br)

Don't Cry, It's Only Thunder (1982) Uneven dramatization of the fact-based story of an Army private (Dennis Christopher) in 1967 Saigon who becomes obsessed with finding food and supplies for a Vietnamese orphanage run by two nuns. Directed by Peter Werner, the transformation of the soldier from a scheming wheeler-dealer into a dedicated do-gooder is handled less credibly than the scenes with the various orphans, especially the 12-year-old girl he wants to adopt. Sexual references and occasional profanity. A-III (PG)

Don't Cry with Your Mouth Full (1975) Pastoral symphony about a not-very-eventful summer spent by a family in the south of France is lovely to look at, but drama consists of more than holding a mirror up to reality. The only element of tension is the older teenage daughter's impending loss of virginity, but even this is not exploited and nothing is allowed to get beneath the shimmering surface of things. Beautiful, human, naturalistic, but disappointing. A-IV (nr)

Don't Drink the Water (1969) Hapless Newark

caterer (Jackie Gleason) tours Europe with wife (Estelle Parsons) and daughter (Joan Delaney), but in the process their plane is hijacked to Vulgaria, an Iron Curtain country, where the family is mistaken for American spies. Written by Woody Allen and directed by Howard Morris, the comedy's brightest moments come during the credits, when the family is preparing for the trip which itself proves less than memorable. Obligatory, but tastelessly handled, romance between the daughter and the American ambassador's son (Ted Bessell) brings the whole affair to its inevitable happy conclusion. A-III (G)

Don't Give Up the Ship (1959) Feeble comedy about a pea-brained naval officer (Jerry Lewis) accused of losing a destroyer escort. Directed by Norman Taurog, the episodic nonsense taxes the patience more than it tickles the funny-bone. Sexual innuendo, especially wedding-night references. A-III (br)

Don't Go in the House (1980) When a little boy whose mother burns him as punishment for being naughty grows up, he doesn't want to set the world on fire, only mama and every other woman who reminds him of her. Starring Dan Grimaldi and directed by Joseph Ellison, it's a grisly piece of trash exploiting violence and nudity. O (R)

Don't Go Near the Water (1957) Lumbering WW II comedy about a naval press-relations unit (commanded by Frank Clark) on a Pacific island, where one of the officers (Glenn Ford) falls for a local resident (Gia Scala) while carrying out various hare-brained assignments. Directed by Charles Walters, the episodic story line has a few funny moments, notably Mickey O'Shaughnessy's foul-mouthed sailor, but not nearly enough to save the rest of the picture. Sexual situations and innuendo. A-III (br)

Don't Just Stand There (1968) Brainless comedy in which two Americans (Mary Tyler Moore and Robert Wagner) in Paris deal with the problems caused by an author who has gone on a pleasure cruise, leaving the last chapter of her new sex novel unwritten. Directed by Ron Winston, the plot complications don't make much sense and, even if they did, they aren't very amusing. Excessive sexual innuendo. O (br)

Don't Look Back (1967) Feature documentary on folk singer Bob Dylan produced by D.A. Pennebaker during Dylan's 1965 concert tour of England. Filming the singer in performance and off stage, the documentary records his expression of the doubts, depressions and joys of his generation without comment or explanation. Some crude language. A-II (br)

Don't Look Now (1969) Zany slapstick WW II comedy done with style by Terry-Thomas, Bourvil, and Louis de Funes about the confused attempts of the crew of a downed British bomber to escape from occupied France. Written and directed by Gerard Oury, the comedy routines and sight gags may not be entirely new, but they are done imaginatively and with verve by three great film clowns. The period supplies suspense and is never used to make wartime look like a lark. The Disney release provides superior entertainment for audiences of all ages. A-I (G)

Don't Look Now (1973) English couple (Donald Sutherland and Julie Christie), distraught about the drowning of their only child, attempt to regain their emotional balance as he helps restore a crumbling church in Venice. Sutherland's gift of second sight is pivotal to both their dead child and their deteriorating marriage in this psychic potboiler directed by Nicholas Roeg with moody, atmospheric photography. Extended scene of explicit lovemaking. O (R)

Don't Make Waves (1967) California beach-blanket movie geared towards the easy-living teenage set revolving around the attempts of undernourished Tony Curtis to woo shapely Sharon Tate away from her muscle-bound surfer boyfriends. Directed by Alexander Mackendrick, the movie's lightheaded attitudes towards teenage sexuality make it somewhat tainted fare, especially for impressionable viewers. O (br)

Don't Raise the Bridge, Lower the River (1968) Jerry Lewis stars in and directs a British-made comedy about a semi-shady promoter who likes to do things the hard way. Most of the humor is typical Lewis farce, with some really funny sight (and sound) gags, as well as some slack stretches. Gap-toothed Terry-Thomas, Bernard Cribbins, and some other British comedy pros lend some extra spark. A-II (G)

Don't Tell Her It's Me (1990) A meddling sister (Shelley Long) tries to make a writer (Jami Gertz) fall in love with her insecure brother (Steve Guttenberg) by coaching him in assuming a swaggering macho personality complete with motorcycle and foreign accent. The laughs are meager in director Malcolm Mowbray's dimwitted comedy whose sappy situations and dialogue are well below the talents of Long and Guttenberg. Sexual references and a discreet scene of unmarried intimacy. A-III (PG-13)

Don't Tell Mom the Babysitter's Dead (1991) With mom in Australia for the summer, five kids enjoy life without supervision when their elderly babysitter dies suddenly, leaving a 17-year-old (Christina Applegate) to juggle a fashion job and pay the bills. Director Steven R. Herek's contrived comedy is really a female adolescent success fantasy that sags for long stretches after its one-joke premise wears thin. Uncritical depiction of teens smoking pot as well as occasional sexual references and vulgarities. A-III (PG-13)

Doolins of Oklahoma, The (1949) Routine Western about an outlaw gang in the 1890s whose leader (Randolph Scott) decides to marry a good woman (Louise Allbriton) and settle down to farming, but the gang blows his cover and he returns to a life on the run from lawmen (notably, implacable George Macready). Directed by Gordon Douglas, the action is formula fare, but the result is fairly thoughtful in depicting the unglamorous life of an outlaw. Much stylized violence. A-II (br)

Doors, The (1991) Fact-based musical biography of the pivotal 1960s rock band of the title whose hedonistic leader Jim Morrison (Val Kilmer) died at age 27, following years of constant drug and alcohol abuse. Director Oliver Stone presents an overblown, self-important "rockumentary" detailing Morrison's endless sexual escapades, non-stop boozing, and drug highs, while treating him as the tragic rock-poet and cultural demigod of the age. Much promiscuity with full nudity, pervasive substance abuse, and continual rough language. O (R)

Doppelgaenger (see: **Journey to the Far Side of the Sun**)

Dorian Gray (1971) Italian adaptation of the Oscar Wilde story about a young man (Helmut Berger) who watches a painting of himself take on the spiritual decay of his soul while his physical exterior remains unblemished. Director Massimo Dallamano treats the story's perversions, ranging from sodomy to murder, in such coy fashion that its hero's many vices are as lackluster as they are corrupting. O (R)

Dossier 51 (1979) Tediously subjective melodrama about a minor French diplomat harassed by all the technique and technology an intelligence agency can bring to bear against him. Director Michel Deville's deliberate but failed attempts at humor and extensive use of nudity make the unexciting plot even more mindless. O (nr)

Double Con, The (see: **Trick Baby**)

Double Dragon (1994) Popcorn action fantasy set in the post-earthquake ruins of 2007 Los Angeles, where two brothers (Mark Dacascos, Scott Wolf) use their martial-arts skills against an arch-criminal (Robert Patrick) after an ancient Chinese medallion with superhuman powers. Directed with tongue-in-cheek gusto by James Yukich, the young heroes have a jolly time cracking skulls in the gang-ridden streets of the devastated movie capital, but the simpleminded action grows tiresome long before their inevitable victory, as might be expected from a movie based on a video game. Considerable martial-arts violence and much menace. A-III (PG-13)

Double Dynamite (1951) Tepid comedy directed by Irving Cummings flounders in misunderstandings when mousy bank teller Frank Sinatra is suspected of embezzlement after gangster Nestor Paiva tips him to winning a fortune on the horses, then lavishes expensive gifts on coworker Jane Russell with encouragement from friendly waiter Groucho Marx. Minor stylized violence and sexual innuendo. A-II (br)

Double Edge (1992) Provocative drama views the Palestinian-Israeli conflict through the helter-skelter experiences of a newspaper reporter (Faye Dunaway) on a three-week assignment in Jerusalem, where she is romanced by an Israeli writer (Amos Kollek). Also written and directed by Kollek, the result tries to be evenhanded in its treatment of both sides, including statements from actual leaders in the region, while showing how the news media are manipulated by all factions in the conflict. Realistic depiction of political tensions that occasionally erupt in violence, an implied sexual relationship, and some rough language. A-III (PG-13)

Double Happiness (1995) Rigidly traditional Chinese parents insist their 22-year-old Canadian daughter (Sandra Oh), an aspiring actress, live at home while arranging dates for her with their idea of suitable marital partners, unaware she is involved with a Caucasian graduate student. Director Mina Shum casts a wryly bittersweet look at cultural stereotyping on the job and culture clashes at home as the young woman seeks her own identity. Some subtitling. A discreet bedroom scene and brief homosexual innuendo. A-III (PG-13)

Double Impact (1991) Bloody martial-arts movie about identical twins (Jean-Claude Van Damme), separated as infants but reunited 25 years later in Hong Kong, where they hunt down their parents' drug-dealing murderers. Director Sheldon Lettich grinds out another slick action-movie that exists solely to showcase escalating, mindless violence in an heroic setting that justifies murder as righteous vengeance. Excessive violence, a scene with nudity, and intermittent rough language. O (R)

Double Indemnity (1944) Dark crime classic adapted from James M. Cain's novel about a treacherous woman (Barbara Stanwyck) who conspires with an insurance agent (Fred MacMurray) to make her husband's murder look like an accident, but before they can collect on his policy, a company investigator (Edward G. Robinson) begins to get wise. Directed by Billy Wilder, who also gets credit for co-writing the script with Raymond Chandler, the intricate plot centers on the furtive, greedy pair whose mistrust of each other finally ends in mutual betrayal. Riveting tale of crime and punishment, with hard-bitten performances, brightly cynical dialogue, and darkly atmospheric imagery. A-II (br)

Double Life, A (1947) Overdone melodrama about a veteran actor (Ronald Colman) who plays the part of Othello so well that the role begins to affect his offstage life, until he finally loses control and in a fit of jealous rage kills an overly friendly waitress (Shelley Winters). Directed by George Cukor, the story creaks with obvious plot contrivances, but its backstage picture of theatrical life is often witty, and Colman's Oscar-winning performance is worth seeing. Stylized violence and muted sexual innuendo. A-II (br)

Double Life of Veronique, The (1991) Two young women, one Polish and one French, are strangely linked by identical looks, musical talents, and frail hearts. Director Krzystof Kieslowski's lyrical tale of unexplained spiritual bonding is given considerable emotional force by Irene Jacob's ethereal and haunting performance as the two Veroniques. Subtitles. A few restrained scenes of sexual encounters with some nudity. A-III (nr)

Double Man, The (1968) Far-fetched spy caper (a British production directed by Franklin J. Schaffner) in which Soviet operatives lure a top US agent (Yul Brynner) to a Swiss ski resort, where, thanks to plastic surgery, his double has been prepped to take his place, though an old pal (Clive Revill) and a new friend (Britt Ekland) complicate matters. The dour dueling between the two Brynners adds a bit of novelty to otherwise standard espionage fare amidst picturesque mountain locales. Stylized violence. A-I (br)

Double Ransom (see: **The Terrorists**)

Double Team (1997) Violent action tale in which a former CIA operative (Jean-Claude Van Damme) teams with an oddball arms dealer (Dennis Rodman) to save his wife and newborn from death at the hands of a revenge-bent assassin (Mickey Rourke). While technically glossy, director Tsui Hark's muddled plot features endlessly brutal fights, deadly shootouts, and massive explosions. Excessive violence, some gore, and repulsive menace to an infant. O (R)

Double Trouble (1967) Elvis Presley vehicle casts the singer as a nightclub entertainer playing London and pleasantly plagued by pretty, love-struck fan Annette Day. Directed by Norman Taurog, the plot includes a parental attempt to break up the romance, a spate of spies, and nine well-swiveled song numbers. A-II (br)

Doug's 1st Movie (1999) Uninspired feature-length cartoon based on a children's TV series in which two 12-year-old boys hide an E.T.-like creature that fled a polluted lake until it can be safely relocated to a new home. Director Maurice Joyce's flat and nearly static animation makes the skimpy tale seem even more drawn-out that it already is. A-I (G)

Dove, The (1974) Fact-based odyssey of a 16-year-old (Joseph Bottoms) who sets out to sail around the world in a 23-foot sloop of the title until he meets an Australian girl (Deborah Raffin) and decides to marry, but she convinces him to complete his journey first. Directed by Charles Jarrott and beautifully photographed by Sven Nyquist, the entertaining adventure would appeal to youngsters, but the moral ambiguities of the early stages of the Bottoms-Raffin relationship warrant labeling it as adult fare. A-III (PG)

Down and Out in Beverly Hills (1986) Nick Nolte portrays a super-tramp who relieves everyone's misery in a jaded and spoiled Beverly Hills household. Director Paul Mazursky's movie is an overly simplified tale of manners and morals poking fun at the tribulations of a suddenly rich family headed by Richard Dreyfuss and Bette Midler. Its farcical treatment of sex as a remedy for all ills marks it as a misguided burlesque, carefully avoiding any sense of conviction or consequence. O (R)

Down Argentine Way (1940) Elaborate but silly musical romance directed by Irving Cummings goes south of the border to involve an American heiress (Betty Grable) with the love-struck son (Don Ameche) of a rich Argentinean horse-breeder (Henry Stephenson) who happens to loathe the American's father. Romantic complications and family tensions. A-II (br)

Down by Law (1986) This lighthearted comedy begins with a breezy introduction to three likeable but corrupt residents of Louisiana's bayou country. The friendship and humorous camaraderie which develops after they are wrongfully sent to jail propels them to escape detention and try to start new and more rewarding lives for themselves. Some profanity and nudity. A-III (R)

Down in the Delta (1998) Uplifting tale in which a drug-addicted single mom (Alfre Woodard) and her two young children leave the inner city to make a fresh start in rural Mississippi with her righteous uncle (Al Freeman Jr.) and Alzheimer's-afflicted aunt (Esther Rolle). Directed by Maya Angelou, this hopeful story of the healing power of family is flawed only by the apparent ease with which the troubled woman is transformed once she escapes urban temptations. A scene of substance abuse and a fleeting reference to prostitution. A-II (PG-13)

Down Missouri Way (1946) Corny musical comedy directed by Josef Berne follows the misadventures of a movie company filming a hillbilly picture on location in the Ozarks, where the locals cause the director (John Carradine) much grief over a mule required by the script. A-I (br)

Down Periscope (1996) Thin comedy about a Navy officer (Kelsey Grammer) whose career is over unless he can turn an old diesel submarine and its motley crew into a winning team during war games against a superior force. Directed by David S. Ward, the predictable plot about misfits and underdogs has a few good laughs but far more yawns. Sexual innuendo, bathroom humor, and instances of profanity and rough language. A-III (PG-13)

Down Went McGinty (see: **The Great McGinty**)

Downhill Racer (1969) Robert Redford plays a surly American skier with enough recklessness and skill to challenge the best Europeans but who is unwilling to listen to his team's tough, long-suffering coach (admirably played by Gene Hackman) in preparing for the big skiing competition. Though the personal drama follows the formula of such sports movies, director Michael Ritchie concentrates on providing a vivid overview of a dangerous and photogenic sport and the fallible people who compete in it for the psychological rewards that some find worth all its rigors and traumatic nervous strain. A-III (PG)

Downtown (1990) Hot-headed black cop (Forest Whitaker) and rookie white cop (Anthony Edwards) make a mismatched but likeable team in inner-city Philadelphia, as they investigate a psycho cop-killer and a drug-smuggling operation that smells like an inside job. Director Richard Benjamin injects some humanizing family touches and nutty humor, but the contrived drug-bust scenario ambles along to a predictable grisly close that sees the good guys win validation for their unorthodox police work amidst much bloodshed. Much profanity laced with sexual vulgarities; grisly, gratuitous violence, and a flash of nudity. O (R)

Dr. Bethune (1993) Fact-based story of the fiery Canadian surgeon (Donald Sutherland) who was considered a radical for promoting socialized medicine in the 1920s, served as a doctor with the anti-Franco forces in the Spanish Civil War, and died in 1939 China while serving as chief medical officer in the Communist army. Despite the narrative's confusing chronology, director Phillip Borsos's international production offers a complex portrait of a selfless medical humanitarian who was also a hard-drinking womanizer, as well as a lifelong political idealist. Some battlefield violence, alcohol abuse, and sexual innuendo. A-III (nr)

Dr. Cyclops (1940) Fanciful low-budget thriller set in the Amazon jungle, where a mad scientist (Albert Dekker) tries to hide his uranium experiments from unwanted visitors (Charles Halton, Janice Logan, Thomas Coley, and Victor Kilian) by shrinking them to the size of dolls. Directed by Ernest B. Schoedsack, the uneven battle between the near-sighted doctor and his undersized victims is worked out rather neatly with simple but imaginative special effects. Occasional stylized violence and much menace. A-II (nr)

Dr. Dolittle (1998) Comedy clunker about a San Francisco physician (Eddie Murphy) whose life becomes complicated when he starts talking to animals but no one else can hear what they say to him. Director Betty Thomas treats the thin proceedings with bogus sentimentality while pursuing laughs from sophomoric vulgarities and crude invective. Much bathroom humor, coarse language, and several instances of profanity. A-III (PG-13)

Dr. Frankenstein on Campus (1971) Contemporary namesake of the legendary scientist is a college student who doesn't fit in very well with the rest of the campus scene. Director Gilbert W. Taylor's attempt to update a classic story flounders in scenes more suited to sex-exploitation movies than to the horror genre. O (R)

Dr. Giggles (1992) Grisly horror movie about an escaped lunatic (Larry Drake) who returns to his hometown to avenge the death of his physician father by murdering everyone in sight with specially designed medical instruments. Lame, sick humor predominates director Manny Coto's boring exercise in medical mass murder, unrelieved by any sense of drama or suspense. Excessive gory violence, heavy sexual innuendo, brief nudity, and some rough language. O (R)

Dr. Goldfoot and the Bikini Machine (1965) Witless farce directed by Norman Taurog is set in San Francisco, where a novice secret agent (Frankie Avalon) tangles with the title mad scientist (Vincent Price) who's using bikini-clad female robots to lure rich men into marriage in order to get their wealth. Slapstick violence, comic menace, and sexual innuendo. A-II (br)

Dr. Goldfoot and the Girl Bombs (1966) Inept farce directed by Mario Bava in which the title mad scientist (Vincent Price) uses bikini-clad female robots to blow up NATO generals as part of his plan to rule the world. Slapstick violence, comic menace, and sexual innuendo. A-II (br)

Dr. Jekyll and Mr. Hyde (1920) Silent version of the Robert Louis Stevenson novel about London physician Jekyll (John Barrymore) whose experiments in separating the good from the bad in the human soul result in his evil alter ego taking control of his person as Hyde, with tragic results. Directed by John S. Robertson, the adaptation is visualized in somber fashion, with a compelling performance from Barrymore, who's able to change on camera from Jekyll to Hyde by facial contortions rather than special effects. Stylized violence and sexual innuendo. A-II (br)

Dr. Jekyll and Mr. Hyde (1932) Classic adaptation of Robert Louis Stevenson's story about idealistic London doctor Jekyll (Fredric March) seeking a drug to separate the soul's good and bad elements, but the result frees his evil side to emerge as the bestial Hyde, who kills a prostitute (Miriam Hopkins), among other acts of wanton violence. Directed by Rouben Mamoulian, the story is creatively visualized, well-paced, and convincingly acted, with March's Oscar-winning performance greatly aided by the make-up department. Nasty violence and sexual situations. A-III (br)

Dr. Jekyll and Mr. Hyde (1941) Elaborate studio production of the Robert Louis Stevenson tale starring Spencer Tracy as Jekyll, the 19th-century London physician whose experiments keep him from his fiancé (Lana Turner) while transforming him into the evil Hyde, who brutally mistreats a prostitute (Ingrid Bergman) and ultimately becomes a murderer. Directed by Victor Fleming, the acting is first-rate and there are many effective scenes, including some terrifying dream sequences, but the halting narrative never quite gels as a satisfying whole. Stylized violence and sexual innuendo. A-II (br)

Dr. Jekyll and Ms. Hyde (1995) Dreary sex farce turns the Robert Louis Stevenson story into that of a chemist (Tim Daly) working in a perfume laboratory, where he concocts a formula transforming him into a predatory female (Sean Young). Directed by David Price, the plot's adolescent preoccupation with sexual titillation is an embarrassment for all concerned. Exploitative sex and intermittent profanity. O (PG-13)

Dr. Jekyll and Sister Hyde (1972) British horror movie directed by Roy Ward Baker features Ralph Bates as Jekyll and Martine Beswick as his alter egoess. It is at its best when it slyly rings the changes on the 19th-century story, but it offers a lot of just-beneath-the-surface sexual ambience. A-III (PG)

Dr. Phibes Rises Again (1972) Vincent Price as Phibes is still trying to bring his beautiful wife back to life while he fends off Robert Quarry's devious attempts to locate the elixir of life beneath an Egyptian mountain. Directed by Robert Fuest, much of the fun comes from Phibes's ingenious manner of dispatching his enemies against Brian Eatwell's amusing art deco sets. Restrained violence. A-II (PG)

Dr. Strangelove or: How I Learned to Stop Worrying and Love the Bomb (1964) Peter Sellers is president of the United States, as well as the mad doctor of the title, when a fanatical general (Sterling Hayden) launches a nuclear bomber strike on the USSR. Director Stanley Kubrick's black comedy shows the absurdity of a world quaking under the threat of annihilation by its own artifacts. It may not be everyone's cup of tea, but sifting the leaves remains a provocative challenge even today. A-IV (GP)

Dr. Terror's House of Horrors (1965) Uneven British horror movie about a railroad journey during which an ominous stranger (Peter Cushing) uses tarot cards to reveal the terrible fate awaiting each of five passengers. Directed by Freddie Francis, the lesser tales involve an ancestral curse, a killer plant with a brain, and a voodoo taboo, but more ambitious are those dealing with an artist (Michael Gough) whose severed hand pursues an art critic (Christopher Lee) and a doctor (Donald Sutherland) who marries a vampire (Jennifer Jayne). More menace than violence. A-II (br)

Dr. Who and the Daleks (1966) Derived from the British TV science fiction series, the movie shows how the good doctor (Peter Cushing) stops the Daleks, a tribe of mutants, from using their robot army to destroy their neighbors, the peaceful Thais people. Directed by Gordon Flemyng, the fantasy with all its colorful gadgetry will please the children and Dr. Who fans. A-I (br)

Dracula (1931) Antiquated but venerable horror classic from the Bram Stoker novel about the dread vampire Count Dracula (Bela Lugosi) who leaves his Transylvanian castle to take up residence in England, where a trail of bloodless corpses lead to his undoing by the determined Professor Van Helsing (Edward Van Sloan). Director Tod Browning establishes the vampire premise with macabre gusto, then bogs down in stilted English settings, but for all its dated qualities, this early talkie still evokes goosebumps in the struggle to overcome evil. Restrained menace with off-screen violence. A-II (br)

Dracula (1979) Clever British version of the horror story features Frank Langella re-creating his Broadway role as the ruthless vampire romantically obsessed with the daughter of a madhouse caretaker (Kate Nelligan). Director John Badham's ill-considered use of violence directed against seemingly willing female victims and the gory and bloody killings of the Count's henchmen make the movie an exercise in excess. O (R)

Dracula (see: 1958's **Horror of Dracula** and 1992's **Bram Stoker's Dracula**)

Dracula A.D. 1972 (1972) Fairly mild British horror movie in which the vampire count (Christopher Lee) returns to settle a score with the descendant (Peter Cushing) of the man who last put Dracula to sleep back in the 1870s. Director Alan Gibson holds attention with some gaudy twists and turns in the modern setting and with the usual amount of gory effects. A-III (PG)

Dracula: Dead and Loving It (1995) Slack spoof of Bela Lugosi's 1931 Dracula, with Leslie Nielsen hamming it up as the title Transylvanian vampire whose bloody nighttime antics in 1893 England are stymied by a quirky metaphysician (Mel Brooks). Also directed by Brooks, the familiar vampire tale is laced with slapstick comedy and verbal gags, but the uneven humor seldom relieves the tedium of the tongue-in-cheek melodramatics. Comic gory effects and sexual innuendo. A-III (PG-13)

Dracula Has Risen from the Grave (1969) When Dracula (Christopher Lee) is accidentally un-entombed from a frozen mountain stream, he proceeds to take his revenge on the cleric (Rupert Davies) who exorcised his castle and barred its doors with a large cross. British production directed by Freddie Francis, this version of the old horror tale takes a much more sensual approach to the vampire's bloodlust, and its young hero (Barry Andrews) is an outspoken atheist. Graphic blood and gore. A-III (G)

Dracula, Prince of Darkness (1966) Routine British vampire movie directed by Terence Fisher with Christopher Lee as the revived Count preying on unwary visitors to his castle. Mild violence. A-II (br)

Dracula's Daughter (1936) Creaky horror tale in which the 500-year-old count's 100-year-old daughter (Gloria Holden) seeks release from the living dead by turning to a London psychiatrist (Otto Kruger) but, despairing of a cure, determines to share her eternal life with the doctor, until her disgruntled servant (Irving Pichel) intervenes. Directed by Lambert Hillyer, the thin plot is bolstered by strong performances and eerie settings with uneven results. More fantasy menace than violence. A-II (br)

Dragnet (1987) Police sergeant Joe Friday (Dan Aykroyd) and his partner (Tom Hanks) foil a group of PAGANs (People Against Goodness and Normalcy) headed by a minister (Christopher Plummer) wishing to take over Los Angeles. Director Tom Mankiewicz's updated spoof of the popular 1960's television show provides little genuine humor in sarcastic putdowns of virginity, anti-pornography groups, personal integrity, and public morality. Vulgar sexual gestures, brief nudity, and rough language. O (PG-13)

Dragon Seed (1944) Laborious Hollywood tribute to the Chinese people's struggle in WW II from Pearl Buck's novel about the daughter-in-law (Katharine Hepburn) of a rural clan leader (Walter Huston) who finally convinces him to resist the Japanese invaders by torching the village and retreating into the hills. Directed by Jack Conway and Harold S. Bucquet, the flag-waving result is tedious as wartime propaganda and unconvincing as melodrama. Stylized violence and racial stereotyping. A-II (br)

Dragon: The Bruce Lee Story (1993) Fact-based biography of the late martial-arts screen-actor (played by Jason Scott Lee) tells of his relocation from Hong Kong to the US, interracial marriage, founding of his own martial-arts academy, and his imminent crossover to movie stardom at the time of his death under mysterious circumstances in 1973. Despite being based on the rose-tinted memoirs of Lee's widow, the Rob Cohen-directed movie captures Lee's personal life and struggle against discrimination while blending in numerous intense but well-choreographed fight sequences. A discreet bedroom scene and several violent martial-arts confrontations. A-III (PG-13)

Dragon Chow (1988) Two illegal Pakistani aliens (Bhasker and Buddy Uzzaman) attempt to settle into permanent homes and jobs in Hamburg, Germany. German director Jan Schutte offers a heartbreaking view of immigrants caught in a bureaucratic web of exploitation. Subtitles. Its theme and incidental rough language make it inappropriate for younger adolescents. A-II (nr)

Dragon Flies, The (1975) Martial-arts story of a police inspector (Jimmy Wang Yu) in pursuit of the chief drug dealer in the Far East. It's all an excuse, of course, for running the gamut of Kung Fu brutality with some incidental interracial romance thrown in for good measure. Once again, however, the cardboard violence is vicious and the police are as reprehensible as the criminals. O (R)

Dragonfly (1976) Released from a mental institution where he was committed at age 13, a young man (Beau Bridges) is helped by a sympathetic woman (Susan Sarandon) to find out the truth about his past and the mother (Mildred Dunnock) he fears he has killed. Well-acted and sensitively directed by Gilbert Cates, the movie has much to recommend it, in spite of an uneven script and an overwrought conclusion that leaves some significant loose ends. Heavy-handed seduction scene. A-III (PG)

Dragonheart (1996) Medieval fantasy in which an honorable knight (Dennis Quaid), disillusioned after the prince he trained becomes a tyrannical king, joins forces with a mammoth talking-dragon (voice of Sean Connery) to lead a peasant revolt. Director Rob Cohen's noble-minded story is remarkable for its magnificent, computer-generated beast, but is otherwise a flat-footed spectacle hampered by terribly corny dialogue. Stylized battlefield violence. A-II (PG-13)

Dragonslayer (1981) Sorcerer's apprentice (Peter MacNicol) has to battle the fierce dragon terrorizing a distant kingdom in order to fulfill a promise made by his dead master (Ralph Richarson). Directed by Matthew Robbins, this above-average Disney co-production unravels in the latter third of the story, with showy special effects diminishing the simple human elements of romance and gallantry. Extremely unsettling sequence of a gory death, several other scenes of violence, and very brief nudity. A-III (PG)

Draughtsman's Contract, The (1983) Mannered and pretentious period piece set in late 17th-century England, depicts an artist (Anthony Higgins) and the lady of a manor (Janet Suzman) caught up in a web of evil and hostility. Written and directed by Peter Greenway, the period re-creation is stylish, but its too-clever plot eventually becomes boring, undone by its carelessness and its airs. Considerable male nudity and a general air of amorality. O (R)

Dream a Little Dream (1989) Incomprehensible teen comedy/romance about a loving middle-aged couple (Jason Robards, Piper Laurie) who, through dream telepathy, swap psyches with a deadbeat teenage couple (Corey Feldman, Meredith Salenger) who redirect their adolescent anger into sweet romance and deflate their peers' anti-social behavior. Director Marc Rocco can't make sense out of the mess resulting from this misfire of the old-young body-switch gimmick. Much rough language laced with sexual vulgarities. A-III (PG-13)

Dream City (1977) A troubled artist and his wife are invited to join a utopian community hidden in a remote area of Africa but, upon arrival, find that they are prisoners in an asylum run by the mad inmates. German production directed by Johannes Schaaf, this allegory on society and human nature is stunning to the eye but leaves the heart and imagination untouched. Several scenes are given a voyeuristic emphasis. O (R)

Dream Lover (1986) Psychological thriller starring Christy McNichol as a young girl tormented by a recurring nightmare in which she repeatedly stabs an intruder and potential rapist. Under a dream state induced to cure her, she envisions her own rape, the stabbing of her father, and an unsuccessful leap off a 40-story building. Needless repetition of excessively violent acts. O (R)

Dream Lover (1994) Glossy melodrama in which the contented life of a prosperous young architect (James Spader) is shattered when he discovers his alluring wife (Madchen Amick) is not what she seems. Writer-director Nicholas Kazan creates an aura of suspense with intriguing characters, but the static narrative barely moves beyond the central premise of a naive husband and his malevolent wife. A few bedroom scenes with nudity, adulterous references, brief violence, and intermittent rough language. A-III (R)

Dream of Kings, A (1969) Uneven screen version of the Harry Mark Petrakis novel about a Greek-American (Anthony Quinn in a larger-than-life performance) who, desperate for the money to take his terminally ill son to Greece to be cured by breathing the air of their noble ancestors, is caught cheating at dice and is brutally beaten. But his pride and dreams are saved by his long-suffering wife (Irene Papas). Daniel Mann's direction puts more emphasis on character study than on Chicago's Greek community, but the result has vitality and compassion for human struggle and endurance. A-III (R)

Dream of Passion (1978) Aging international star (Melina Mercouri), back in her native Greece to play

Medea, finds herself drawn to an American (Ellen Burstyn) imprisoned for killing her three children in revenge for her husband's infidelity. Director Jules Dassin's muddled attempt to give a modern slant to the Medea theme suffers from some dreadful acting (save for Burstyn), fatuous dialogue, and a general mood of self-indulgence. Some rough language and violent emotions. A-III (R)

Dream Team, The (1989) Contrived comedy about four mental patients (Michael Keaton, Christopher Lloyd, Peter Boyle, and Stephen Furst) on the loose in New York City as they outwit murderous cops to save their comatose therapist (Dennis Boutsikaris). Valiant performances can't pump life into this uncomfortable mix of comedy and pathos about mental illness, leadenly directed by Howard Zieff. Brief violence, a flash of nudity, and some rough language. A-III (PG-13)

Dream with the Fishes (1997) Dreary tale of a suicidal peeping Tom (David Arquette) and a dying, drug-addicted thief (Brad Hunt) who become buddies after stealing a car and setting out in search of quirky adventures on the road. Writer-director Finn Taylor's drawn-out story of male bonding attempts to gain misplaced sympathy for the rebellious pair by depicting their criminal behavior as just a lark. Positive view of euthanasia and drug abuse, a live-in relationship, intermittent nudity, minor violence, and rough language. O (R)

Dreamchild (1985) A lovely movie full of genuine sentiment based upon the 1932 trip of 80-year-old Alice Hargreaves (Coral Browne) — the same Alice who inspired Lewis Carroll (Ian Holm) 70 years before — to New York City to celebrate the centenary of the author's birth. The trip unlocks a flood of memories in the old woman's mind as she recalls the past with a wisdom that comes only with age. Directed by Gavin Millar, the movie makes evident that the writer's love for the little girl, though kept within proper bounds, was more intense than it should have been. A-II (PG)

Dreamer (1979) Unranked amateur (Tim Matheson) becomes national bowling champ in director Noel Nosseck's insignificant little film about athletic determination. Implication of premarital sex further mars a bland plot and second-rate performances. A-III (PG)

Dreamer, The (1970) Israeli story of a vague young handyman working in an old age home who, after a love affair with a woman visitor, decides he is happier with the old folks. It is a beautifully photographed, quiet paced study in loneliness, with gentle human and some winning emotions, but it lacks any sort of dramatic depth or narrative interest. A-III (R)

Dreamlife of Angels, The (1999) Somber French drama in which the friendship of two impoverished young females is jeopardized when one (Elodie Bouchez) tries to force the other (Natacha Regnier) to recognize she is only being used and demeaned by a callous rich lover (Gregoire Colin). Director Erick Zonca's astute character study contrasts one woman's tentative maturing with her friend's destructive lack of self-esteem. Subtitles. A suicide, a harsh sexual encounter, brief substance abuse, intermittent nudity, and an instance of profanity. A-III (R)

Dreams of Glass (1969) Trite and banal romance between a rather irresponsible California youth (John Denos) and a charming Japanese girl (Caroline Barrett) whose trysting place in an abandoned warehouse is wrecked one day by a group of young thugs. Lacking a story with substance, director Robert Clouse relies on stylish camerawork and luscious photography. Visually beautiful but emotionally vapid. A-III (PG)

Dreamscape (1984) Absurd melodrama with a hero (Dennis Quaid) who enters the nightmares of disturbed people and performs instant repairs on their wounded psyches. Pulp fantasy movie directed by Joseph Ruben. A torrid but relatively restrained love scene. A-III (PG-13)

Dressed to Kill (1946) Modestly intriguing mystery as Sherlock Holmes (Basil Rathbone) and Dr. Watson (Nigel Bruce) seek to connect three music boxes made by a convict in Dartmoor prison with stolen Bank of England plates for printing five-pound notes. Directed by Roy William O'Neill, it was the 12th and final episode in the low-budget series of Holmes's modern adventures begun in 1942. Some menace and stylized violence. A-I (br)

Dressed to Kill (1980) Young prostitute (Nancy Allen) witnesses the brutal murder of a woman (Angie Dickinson) and, with the help of the woman's son (Keith Gordon), searches for the killer, a transvestite in a blond wig. An urbane psychiatrist (Michael Caine) is also part of the mix. Director Brian De Palma's suspense thriller, with its slipshod story line, flat dialogue, and paper-thin characters, is an empty, sterile exercise in fantasy sex and violence directed against women. O (R)

Dresser, The (1983) Albert Finney and Tom Courtenay score twin triumphs in a splendid adaptation of the play by Ronald Harwood on the symbiotic relationship between a vain, doddering Shakespearean actor (Finney) and his dresser (Courtenay). The main portion of the action takes place during a performance of King Lear given in the midst of an air raid in the darkest days of WW II. Peter Yates's direction helps greatly to make this an inspired adaptation of a stage play, though for some tastes it may be too theatrical. A-II (PG)

Dressmaker, The (1989) Somber British movie about three troubled women living too close for comfort in a WW II Liverpool flat — two aging sisters (Joan Plowright and Billie Whitelaw) and their young niece (Jane Harrocks) whose failed romance with an American soldier has tragic consequences. Director Jim O'Brien's emphasis on mundane details of the women's everyday life detracts from illuminating the contradiction between one's outward appearance and actual character and the ultimate cost of repressed feelings and misdirected rage. A graphic scene of violence, sexual overtones, and brief nudity. A-III (nr)

Driftwood (1947) Contrived but enjoyable tale of a small-town doctor (Dean Jagger) whose life becomes complicated when he adopts a little girl (Natalie Wood) after the death of her great-grandfather (H.B. Warner), a retired preacher who had been raising her in a Nevada ghost town. Director Allan Dwan derives plenty of whimsy from the small-town characters, with Wood especially good as the child who unwittingly embarrasses people by telling the truth. A-I (br)

Drive, He Said (1971) Self-indulgent story of a college basketball star (William Tepper) who divides his time between working out in the gym and the front seat of his car with the wife (Karen Black) of the drama prof (Robert Towne). Directed by Jack Nicholson, it is a mindless exercise in sexual explicitness and rough language. O (X/R)

Drive-In (1976) Star-crossed teenagers, youth-gangs, inept armed robbers, nasty children, and a variety of other characters converge upon a Texas drive-in to see a movie called Disaster '76. Under Rod Amateau's direction, the results are sometimes amusing, but more often unfunny with some backseat romancing and use of marijuana. A-III (PG)

Driver, The (1978) In this somber crime movie, Ryan O'Neal plays a criminal who specializes in driving getaway cars, and Bruce Dern is an obsessed detective out to get him even if he has to break the law to do it. Written and directed by Walter Hill, the confrontations between policeman and criminal lack any deeper resonance than that of other routine melodramas. Violence. A-III (R)

Driver's Seat, The (1975) Uneven adaptation of Muriel Spark's story is a mood piece about a psychotic spinster (Elizabeth Taylor) who travels to the South of Italy to seek her lover-murderer . Director Giuseppe Patroni Griffi complicates the narrative by inter-cutting past and future scenes with the present, and the result offers little insight into the characters' motives and actions. Its themes of alienation, the elusiveness of reality, and the relationship between sexuality and violence will appeal only to a limited audience. A-IV (R)

Driving Miss Daisy (1989) Exquisite adaptation of Alfred Uhry's Pulitzer Prize-winning play about the growing friendship between a wealthy Jewish widow (Jessica Tandy) and her black driver (Morgan Freeman) that begins in 1948 and spans 25 years of turbulent change in the South. Without stooping to sentiment or racial and ethnic stereotypes, director Bruce Beresford sensitively tackles the issues raised by this whimsical friendship, including bigotry, the difficulties of change, the death of the old, and birth of the new. The prejudices characterizing the period may be misunderstood by young children. A-II (PG)

Drop Dead Fred (1991) A jilted wife (Phoebe Cates) moves back home to her tyrannical mother (Marsha Mason) and finds her horrid imaginary childhood pal (Rik Mayall) has reappeared to complicate her interpersonal relationships. Director Ate De Jong's failed fantasy is one long and boring parade of mindless mayhem not suitable for kids and too witless for grownups. Sporadic comic book violence and sexual references, a flash of nudity, and occasional profanity. A-III (PG-13)

Drop Squad (1994) Failed satire in which an underground African-American group (led by Vondie Curtis-Hall and Ving Rhames) kidnaps an arrogant black yuppie (Eriq LaSalle) and subjects him to physical humiliation in order to rid him of attitudes undermining their common racial heritage. Director David Johnson's shrill attempts at provocative racial humor become increasingly tiresome and mean-spirited as the kidnappers squabble over the politics of black separatism. Some moderate brutality and much rough language. A-III (R)

Drop Zone (1994) Revenge-themed action flick in which a suspended US marshal (Wesley Snipes) goes undercover to get evidence against his brother's killers, who turn out to be a group of highly skilled skydivers (led by Gary Busey) planning to break into DEA headquarters to steal information on undercover drug agents. Director John Badham focuses so intently on skydiving action and escalating violence that the characters become a blur and the narrative a bore. Excessive violence and recurring rough language. O (R)

Drowning by Numbers (1991) As the movie's characters play endless games involving numbers, three related women (Joan Plowright, Juliet Stevenson, and Joely Richardson) drown their husbands and get the coroner (Bernard Hill) to falsify the death certificates by implying possible sexual favors in return. British writer-director Peter Greenaway has nothing worthwhile to say in this pretentiously arty film that fails as black comedy and substitutes warped values for wit. Casual acceptance of murder, adultery, and juvenile suicide, nude sexual encounters, and minimal rough language. O (R)

Drowning Pool, The (1975) Uninspired adaptation of a Ross MacDonald mystery with Paul Newman as the low-key private eye hired by frightened, rich Joanne Woodward. Director Stuart Rosenberg does better conveying the local flavor of New Orleans than he does stirring the plot's distasteful gumbo of corrupt police, sadistic oil men, blackmail, and genteel depravity. The treatment of sexual elements in the story is marred by some ill-considered attempts at comic relief and by the use of a very young actress in an especially distasteful role. O (PG)

Drugstore Cowboy (1989) Set in 1971 Portland, Oregon, this movie neither romanticizes nor condemns its protagonist — a drug-loving junkie who knocks off pharmacies to feed his habit and those of his pals. Director Gus Van Sant, Jr., uses stark realism, jazzy music, and hallucinatory flourishes to tell a tale of 1960's hippie holdouts whose renegade leader finally cleans up his act. Much profanity, some violence, incidental sexual innuendoes, and graphic scenes of drug abuse. A-IV (R)

Drum, The (see: **Drums**)

Drum Beat (1954) Slow-moving story of an Indian fighter (Alan Ladd) sent by President Grant to make peace with the leader (Charles Bronson) of a renegade band of Oregon's Modoc Indians. Written and directed by Delmer Daves, it's an earnest effort to show that not all Indians were bad nor all whites good, but the Western action is unconvincing. Frontier violence. A-I (br)

Drums (1938) Colorful adventure in India's Northwest Frontier, where a young prince (Sabu) saves the British resident (Roger Livesey), his wife (Valerie Hobson), and a British garrison from being massacred by the lad's treacherous uncle (Raymond Massey). Director Zoltan Korda gets off to a slow start in setting the scene and relationships, but the preliminaries pay off handsomely in the action-filled conclusion. Stylized violence. A-I (br)

Drums Across the River (1954) Convoluted Western directed by Nathan Juran in which a crook (Lyle Bettger) after gold on Ute land tries to start an Indian war, but standing in his way is a youth (Audie Murphy) whose father (Walter Brennan) is a friend of the Ute chief. Frontier violence, a hostage situation, and sexual innuendo. A-II (br)

Drums Along the Mohawk (1939) Sparkling outdoor adventure saga of a colonial couple (Claudette Colbert and Henry Fonda) who settle in New York's Mohawk Valley, where they are beset by Indian attacks led by English officers during the Revolutionary War. Directed by John Ford, the picture alternates lovely sequences of bucolic farming life with stirring action scenes and plenty of rough frontier humor. Some stylized violence but in a meaningful context holding appeal for all members of the family except preschoolers. A-I (br)

Drums in the Deep South (1951) Cheesy Civil War adventure directed by William Cameron Menzies in which a Georgia belle (Barbara Payton) aids a Confederate officer (James Craig) in a battle with Union forces led by an old friend from West Point (Guy Madison). Stylized violence and sexual innuendo. A-II (br)

Drums of Africa (1963) Charting the course for a railroad through East Africa, a turn-of-the-century explorer and his ward (Frankie Avalon) wind up trying to free a woman (Mariette Hartley) captured by slavers. Director James B. Clark makes extensive use of stock footage trying to give some sense of adventure to an otherwise lackluster effort. Stylized violence and mild sexual innuendo. A-I (br)

Drums of Tahiti (1954) Routine programmer about an American expatriate (Dennis O'Keefe) smuggling arms for an 1877 Polynesian uprising against the French that is ended before it starts by a typhoon and a volcanic eruption. Directed by William Castle, the movie's only bright spots are Patricia Medina as O'Keefe's battling bride and Francis L. Sullivan as the shrewd French police commissioner. Some stylized violence and romantic complications. A-II (br)

Dry White Season, A (1989) Wrenching adaptation of Andre Brink's novel about the 1976 Soweto uprisings and a conscience-stricken white Afrikaner (Donald Sutherland) who becomes an anti-apartheid activist after his black gardener and the gardener's young son die from police brutality. Black woman-director Euzhan Palcy depicts the moral bankruptcy of those supporting racist policies which leads to the slaughter of defenseless blacks. Brief but graphic scenes of violence. A-III (R)

Du Barry Was a Lady (1943) Cheerful screen version of the Cole Porter musical opens in a nightclub whose hatcheck attendant (Red Skelton) moons over a singer (Lucille Ball), then dreams he's Louis XV and she's Madame DuBarry in 1743 France. Directed by Roy Del Ruth, the opening features some period club acts, including the singer's tap-dancing suitor (Gene Kelly) and comic relief from Rags Ragland and Virginia O'Brien, with many of them playing dual roles in the dream sequences, but the stagy treatment often gets in the way of the fun. Romantic complications and sexual innuendo. A-III (br)

Duck, You Sucker! (1972) Director Sergio Leone spins out another of his endless, blood-drenched Western epics, this one telling how Rod Steiger and James Coburn win the Mexican Revolution. The story is far too long to hold up either its story line or the viewer's sagging attention. Much preposterous violence. A-III (PG)

DuckTales: The Movie — Treasure of the Lost Lamp (1990) Meandering animated adventure involving a lost magic lamp whose genie takes refuge with Scrooge McDuck's clan to avoid capture by the evil sorcerer Merlock. Despite sprightly characters and busy story line, the result is a rather lame feature cartoon stemming from the Disney television series. Produced and directed by Bob Hathcock, some of the highlights are Richard Libertini's sly voice as Merlock's light-fingered lackey and a few moments of striking animation. Minimum of scary menace. A-I (G)

Dude Goes West, The (1948) Mild comedy in which a bookish gunsmith (Eddie Albert) leaves 1876 Brooklyn for lawless Arsenic City, Nev., then proves a straight-shooter in encounters with various outlaws (Barton MacLane, Gilbert Roland, and Binnie Barnes), becomes the blood brother of an Paiute chief, and helps a woman (Gale Storm) claim a lost gold mine. Directed by Kurt Neumann, the proceedings provide some agreeable fun, as Albert's idealistic tenderfoot relies more on his intelligence than his shooting ability. Frontier violence. A-I (br)

Duel at Diablo (1966) Sidney Poitier, James Garner, and Bibi Andersson star in a Western rife with brutal killings and wife-kidnapping by Apache Indians, with Dennis Weaver as a vengeful husband who cannot forgive his wife for surviving her ordeal. Director Ralph Nelson disguises his movie's shortcomings with a complicated plot and larger-than-life characters, but can't hide its violent excesses. O (br)

Duel at Silver Creek, The (1952) Routine Western directed by Don Siegel in which a marshal (Stephen McNally) hunting gold robbers gets wounded and has to rely upon his young deputy (Audie Murphy) to help nab the gang, despite complications caused by a woman (Faith Domergue) in cahoots with the bad guys. Frontier violence. A-I (br)

Duel in the Sun (1946) Overripe Western melodrama in which the wife (Lillian Gish) of a Texas cattle baron (Lionel Barrymore) gives a home to a cousin's orphaned half-breed daughter (Jennifer Jones), who falls in love with their upright elder son (Joseph Cotten), but is seduced by his devil-may-care brother (Gregory Peck), with tragic results. Directed by King Vidor, the picture has plenty of visual spectacle and occasional high drama, notably the rancher's stand against the railroad, but the effort is undone by its hokey story of an unfortunate woman's struggle to be more than an object of lust. Frontier violence, sexual situations, and much sexual innuendo. A-III (br)

Duel of the Titans (1961) Dubbed Italian production directed by Sergio Corbucci retells the eighth-century B.C. legend of Romulus (Steve Reeves) and Remus (Gordon Scott) from their rescue as babies by a she-wolf to their flight from the Sabines and the founding of Rome. Considerable stylized bloodshed. A-II (br)

Duellists, The (1978) Screen version of a Joseph Conrad story about two hussar officers in Napoleon's army (Keith Carradine and Harvey Keitel) who fight a series of duels over two decades. Director Ridley Scott excels in his re-creation of the settings, costumes, and general flavor of the era and does well with a delightful supporting cast (notably Albert Finney and Diana Quick). These virtues cannot compensate, however, for a large hole at the center of the story due to inept performances by the two principals. Violence. A-III (PG)

Duet for Cannibals (1969) Young man and his girlfriend become involved with a fantasy-ridden political activist and his unstable wife in a relationship that becomes sexually bizarre and potentially murderous. Writer Susan Sontag's debut as a director is an interesting failure in its black-and-white variations on a theme of the corruption of innocence. A-IV (nr)

Duet for One (1987) Brilliant, world-renowned concert violinist (Julie Andrews) struggles to overcome the anger and depression she feels when her talents are diminished by multiple sclerosis. Frightened by the realization of her mortality, she finds consolation in her psychiatrist (Max von Sydow) only after two adulterous affairs and a failed suicide attempt. Director Andrei Konchalovsky stresses righteous indignation as a life-sustaining virtue over spiritual renewal. Alan Bates costars in this morbid and morally muddled melodrama. Brief nudity. O (R)

Duffy (1968) James Coburn plays a pop-erotic artist living in Tangiers who becomes involved in a complicated piracy plot with relatives of wealthy James Mason, who has a few surprises in store for those trying to rob him. Instead of a sophisticated comedy, director Robert Parrish has come up with a shallow, low-grade bore whose sexual references are occasionally offensive. O (PG)

Dulcima (1972) Rustic British movie traces the relationship between a cunning country lass (Carol White) who moves in as a "housekeeper" for a wealthy, much older farmer (John Mills), but the arrival of a handsome newcomer results in a shocking finale. Director Frank Nesbitt keeps things admirably subdued, although he is uncompromising in terms of the earthy language and lusty pursuits of his isolated characters. A-III (PG)

Dumb and Dumber (1994) Aptly named comedy follows two dimwits (Jim Carrey and Jeff Daniels) from Providence to Aspen as they blunder along trying to return an attaché case stuffed with ransom money left by a beautiful woman (Lauren Holly) for kidnappers who, in turn, pursue the dopey duo. When not concentrating on scatological humor, director Peter Farrelly gets occasional laughs from this example of lowest-common-denominator comedy. Much vulgar toilet humor, exaggerated violence played for laughs, and fleeting sexual innuendo. A-III (PG-13)

Dumbo (1941) In this classic Disney animated feature, a baby elephant with oversized ears, the laughing stock of the entire circus troupe to which he belongs, is befriended by a sympathetic mouse. What happens to the diminutive pachyderm shows children how self-respect and self-confidence can be gained by making the most of one's imagination and inventive initiative. A-I (G)

Dune (1984) Dark, quirky adaptation of Frank Herbert's science fiction trilogy about four factions struggling for control of a desert planet and its wondrous spices. Directed by David Lynch, much of the story is incomprehensible to anyone who has not read the original, and the staging of the action sequences is absurd rather than imaginative. Some graphic violence and vulgarity. A-III (PG-13)

Dungeonmaster (1985) Dreadful hodgepodge of a movie, with no less than seven directors, about a computer wizard who must overcome a series of challenges of the sort found in the game that gives this clunker its title. Sadistic violence. O (PG-13)

Dunston Checks In (1996) Goofy comedy in which chaos threatens to overtake a swanky Manhattan hotel when an orangutan trained to steal escapes his odious owner and is hidden by the mischievous son of the frazzled hotel manager (Jason Alexander). Director Ken Kwapis makes screwball show business out of manic monkey business in a generally genial movie of simian silliness. Slapstick violence, mild sexual innuendo, and a vulgar expression. A-II (PG)

Dunwich Horror, The (1970) Young warlock (Dean

Stockwell), despite the warnings of his grandfather (Sam Jaffe), strives to conjure up some devil-monsters from the underworld but is foiled by a professor of witchcraft (Ed Begley). Director Daniel Haller's weak horror movie has some sexually suggestive scenes. O (M)

Dusty and Sweets McGee (1971) Semi-documentary by Floyd Mutrux on the tragic lives of drug addicts and pushers parades the dehumanizing effect, the withdrawals, and death which drugs produce. The result is a talk piece which poses tough questions about real people but gets nowhere in what ultimately proves to be a surface examination of substantive matters. A-IV (R)

Dutch (1991) Often tacky road movie in which the blue-collar boyfriend (Ed O'Neill) of a timid divorcée (JoBeth Williams) snatches her snobby adolescent son (Ethan Randall) from his Atlanta private academy to drive him home to Chicago for Thanksgiving dinner. Director Peter Faiman gets only cheap laughs from writer-producer John Hughes's simplistic and obvious comedy where rich is bad, poor is good, and brawn wins over brains. Blatant sexual innuendo, intermittent sophomoric violence, and an instance of rough language. A-III (PG-13)

Dutchess and the Dirt-Water Fox, The (1976) Western comedy about a bumbling gambler (George Segal) and a dance-hall girl (Goldie Hawn) whose avarice brings them together in a series of cliched chases and misadventures. Director Melvin Frank's mostly unfunny effort collapses under the weight of incessant visual and verbal vulgarities, double entendres, and some crude satire at the expense of Mormons and Jews. O (PG)

Dying Young (1991) A young man (Campbell Scott) stricken with leukemia hires a beautiful woman (Julia Roberts) to help him through chemotherapy treatment and encourages her love while misleading her about his condition. The emotional honesty of the characters in this compassionate movie from director Joel Schumacher eventually overcomes the romanticized Hollywood formula of poor girl meeting rich boy. Discreet unmarried sexual encounters, intermittent rough language, and a flash of rear nudity. A-III (R)

Dynamite Chicken (1972) Director Ernie Pintoff's low-budget collection of skits on pot smoking, campus rebellion, Madison Avenue hucksterism, nudity, LBJ, Lenny Bruce, and other dated topical items, is merely trite and self-consciously offensive. O (R)

E

Each Dawn I Die (1939) Crime melodrama about a crusading reporter (James Cagney) framed for manslaughter and sent to prison, where he helps a gang leader (George Raft) who later helps the reporter clear his name. Directed by William Keighley, the conditions of prison life are harshly detailed, but the plot is hackneyed and taxes credibility. Some hard-edged violence and ambiguous treatment of criminals. A-III (br)

Eagle and the Hawk, The (1950) Slack Western in which a Texas Ranger (John Payne) takes a federal agent (Dennis O'Keefe) into 1863 Mexico to stop a traitor (Fred Clark) smuggling US arms to rebels fighting the French forces of Emperor Maximillian. Directed by Lewis R. Foster, the proceedings are colorful but mired in muddled intrigues and patriotic blather. Stylized violence and implied suicide of a central character. A-III (br)

Eagle Has Landed, The (1977) Director John Sturges's lethargic adventure yarn based on the fictional premise involving a German plot to kidnap Winston Churchill during WW II is a conventional spy melodrama. Michael Caine, Robert Duvall, and Donald Sutherland star in the suspenser, which is marred by some graphic violence, sexual by-play, and profanity. A-III (PG)

Eagle in a Cage (1971) Exiled after Waterloo on the barren isle of St. Helena in the middle of the South Atlantic, Napoleon wages an unequal contest of will with the English garrison and its overbearing commander. Director Fielder Cook's direction simply reflects the strength and weakness of an uneven script, though it does capitalize on the grandeur of the Yugoslavian location where it was filmed. A-III (GP)

Early Spring (1974) Japanese study of a man's alienation from job and home until a series of events jolts him out of his benumbed apathy, and he decides to make the best of things. Directed in 1956 by Yasujiro Ozu, the movie conveys the density of feeling and the richness of relationships that make up ordinary life. A-II (nr)

Earth Girls Are Easy (1989) When three fuzzy aliens crash-land into a ditzy manicurist's pool, she (Geena Davis) is torn between her love for her philandering fiancé (Charles Rocket) and her attraction to one of the aliens (Jeff Goldblum). Director Julien Temple's satire of California glitz, consumerism, and grade-B alien movies sinks in a sea of poorly integrated musical numbers, sexual innuendoes, and an offensive, denigrating view of women. Endorses sexual promiscuity. O (PG)

Earth Is Our Sinful Song, The (1975) Director Rauni Mollberg's extraordinary picture of life in a Finnish Lapland village tells the story of a father's ill-considered act of vengeance provoked by the pregnancy of his unmarried daughter. The story taking place beneath the awesome, brooding northern sky has the authenticity of a documentary but also the power of drama about lust and love, passion, and remorse. Some sexual scenes that are graphic but not titillating and some violence that is brutal but not gratuitous. Some may find this picture of another, more elemental culture disturbing. A-IV (R)

Earth vs. the Flying Saucers (1956) Effective sci-fi thriller in which refugees from a decaying solar system demand the nations of Earth surrender or be destroyed, but a US scientist (Hugh Marlowe) comes to the rescue with an ultrasonic weapon to stop the alien invaders. Directed by Fred F. Sears, the low-budget production establishes its fantasy premise with Ray Harryhausen's credible special effects, including the destruction of famous Washington, DC, landmarks in the climactic battle. Fantasy violence. A-I (br)

Earth vs. the Spider (1958) Hokey horror directed by Bert I. Gordon in which a pair of teenagers discover a giant spider living in a cave from which it emerges to panic a nearby town, then retreats back into its cave, where it is electrocuted by the high-school science teacher (Ed Kemmer). Stylized violence and menacing situations. A-II (br)

Earthling, The (1981) Dying man (William Holden) teaches a lost orphan (Ricky Schroder) how to survive in the wilds of the Australian bush in this import from director Peter Collinson. The photography of Don McAlpine is outstanding with its lavish scenic splendor, but the story's stilted dialogue and sketchy characterizations make for a long sit. Mild profanity and threatening wild animals. A-II (PG)

Earthquake (1974) Moderately entertaining disaster spectacle of Los Angeles before, during, and after a cataclysmic earthquake. Directed by Mark Robson, Charlton Heston stars but is outclassed by the special effects. Unfortunately, in an attempt to include something for everyone, there is a seduction here, an attempted rape there, and a certain amount of strong language. A-III (PG)

Earth's Final Fury (see: **When Time Ran Out**)

East of Java (see: **South Sea Sinner**)

East of Shanghai (see: **Rich and Strange**)

East of Sumatra (1953) Adventure clunker in which an engineer (Jeff Chandler) excavating a tin mine on an East Indies island gets into trouble with the local ruler (Anthony Quinn) over a woman (Suzan Ball), though he really has his eye on the fiancé (Marilyn Maxwell) of his boss (John Sutton). Directed by Budd Boetticher, the contrived proceedings feature some artificial action scenes but not enough to distract from the artificial romancing. Stylized violence, romantic complications, and sexual innuendo. A-III (br)

East Side Kids Meet Bela Lugosi, The (see: **Ghosts on the Loose**)

Easter Parade (1948) Irving Berlin musical about

a vaudeville dancer (Fred Astaire) who loses one dancing partner (Ann Miller) but gains stardom with another (Judy Garland). Directed by Charles Walters, the story's little more than adequate, but the principals make it all seem to matter and the songs and dance numbers are bright and cheery. A-I (br)

Easy Come, Easy Go (1967) Formula musical with Elvis Presley diving for sunken treasure aided by a bandleader (Pat Harrington), a beatnik artist (Dodie Marshall), and a seasick salvager (Frank McHugh). Directed by John Rich, the treasure hunt is strung out by inane complications, weak comic relief, and a handful of Presley songs. Stylized violence and sexual innuendo. A-II (PG)

Easy Living (1937) Pleasing screwball comedy about a secretary (Jean Arthur) whose chance meeting with a financier (Edward Arnold) over an errant fur coat leads to a wild variety of misunderstandings about their relationship, one of which happens to cause a stock market panic. Written by Preston Sturges and directed by Mitchell Leisen, the laughs are guaranteed by a solid cast including Luis Alberni as a desperate hotel owner and Ray Milland as an addled automat attendant who turns out to be the financier's son. Mild romantic situations. A-II (br)

Easy Living (1949) Slack sports picture in which a top pro-quarterback (Victor Mature) faces the end of his football career because of a heart condition, but his biggest problem is his overly ambitious wife (Lizabeth Scott). Directed by Jacques Tourneur, the movie's focus is on the player's strained marriage, which is complicated futher by his friendship with a sympathetic secretary (Lucille Ball) in the front office. Marital tensions. A-II (br)

Easy Money (1983) Happily married lout (Rodney Dangerfield), given to drinking, gambling, philandering, and narcotics, is forced to clean up his act when his wealthy mother-in-law (Geraldine Fitzgerald) leaves him a fortune on condition that he reforms completely. This dreary, witless failed comedy, directed by James Signorelli and written by Dangerfield and half a dozen others, passes off some nudity, obscenity, and a benign attitude towards drugs as supposedly harmless gags. O (R)

Easy Rider (1969) Two drifters (Peter Fonda and Dennis Hopper), with a wad of cash from a drug transaction, motorcycle through the Southwest encountering a disparate variety of Americans (standout is Jack Nicholson as a small-town lawyer) on their way to a tragic end in New Orleans. Also directed by Hopper, the journey may lead nowhere, but the beauty of the natural landscape provides a lyrical context for this excursion through the troubled byways of contemporary American life. Thoughtful and provocative, it is marred by some graphic violence, a foggy mixture of sex and religion, and a benign view of drugs. A-IV (R)

Eat a Bowl of Tea (1989) Wry comedy about family life in New York's Chinatown circa 1949, depicting the pressures on one newly married Chinese-American couple (Russell Wong and Cora Miao) to have children. Because of immigration restrictions, Chinese-American communities of the period had many old men but few women, making the couple's marriage, child-bearing abilities, and his impotence fraught with intergenerational and cultural pressures humorously and touchingly evoked by director Wayne Wang. Brief graphic violence, an adulterous liaison, and some rough language laced with sexual innuendoes. A-III (PG-13)

Eat Drink Man Woman (1994) Three grown daughters weather unexpected romances while living under the roof of their stoic, long-widowed Taiwanese father (Sihung Lung), who expresses his love for them by cooking extraordinarily elaborate gourmet meals. Director Ang Lee offers a sumptuous plate of satisfying interlocking stories with full-bodied characters in a narrative richly seasoned with subtle humor and a benevolent view of the human condition. Subtitles. Fleeting bedroom scene. A-III (nr)

Eat My Dust (1976) Ron Howard stars in a brainless romp, a kind of live-action Roadrunner cartoon, about some youngsters obsessed with fast cars. Directed by Charles Griffith, it is an inane vision of youth culture and glorifies a dangerous pastime. A-III (PG)

Eating (1991) A group of women gather for a birthday party for three women (Lisa Richards, Mary Crosby, and Marlena Giovi) which becomes a true-confessions session exploring the partygoers' relationships to each other, to men, and especially to food. Writer-director Henry Jaglom's lively, mildly insightful look at Americans' shallow obsession with being thin as a measure of self-worth makes its points well before the party's over. Several casual references to adultery and abortion, occasional rough language, and momentary nudity. A-III (R)

Eboli (1980) The political exile of Italian anti-Fascist writer and artist Carlo Levi is the subject of director Francesco Rosi's warmly human dramatization. Though it does convey some of the complexities of Levi's social, political, and artistic concerns, it is more interested in the man and his place in the context of the times. Serious subject matter and complex background might be confusing for young viewers. A-III (PG)

Echo Park (1986) In a rare unglamorous view of Los Angeles, an aspiring actress (Susan Dey) who is a single parent finds security and devotion with a down-to-earth younger man (Tom Hulce). The gritty drama contrasts blind ambition and false illusions with the rewards of patience and kindness. Director Robert Dornhelm's harshly realistic but truthful treatment counterbalances a sexually explicit nude scene, some foul 1anguage, and violence. A-IV (R)

Echoes of a Summer (1976) Young girl (Jodie Foster) dying of a heart defect conveys stoic acceptance of her condition and provides the inspiration for her family to deal gracefully with impending tragedy. Good cast, with Lois Nettleton as the mother,

Geraldine Fitzgerald as the tutor, and Richard Harris, who also co-produced, as the father. Director Don Taylor is a bit heavy-handed, but the sentiment is genuine. A-II (PG)

Ed (1996) Flat baseball-themed comedy about the friendship between a minor-league rookie (Matt LeBlanc) who chokes at the bat and a chimp who is promoted from team mascot to third-base player and inspires the rookie to loosen up. Director Bill Couturie barely patches together predictable monkey antics to form a tired underdog-triumphant plot. Fleeting violence, frequent scatological humor, and an instance of profanity. A-II (PG)

Ed Wood (1994) Romanticized story of the untalented but enterprising Wood (Johnny Depp), considered Hollywood's all-time worst director, in which he befriends aging has-been actor Bela Lugosi (Martin Landau) to star in his pathetic, shoestring-budget sci-fi fantasies. Director Tim Burton casts a comic and madly affectionate eye on transvestite Wood, but it is Landau's canny portrayal as the 1930's horror great reduced to an impoverished morphine addict which gives the movie some heart in an otherwise campy black-and-white re-staging of Wood's schlock 1950s moviemaking. An implied live-in relationship, some crude remarks, and occasional rough language. A-III (R)

Eddie (1996) When a New York Knicks fan (Whoopi Goldberg) is named coach by the basketball club's devious new owner (Frank Langella), it's no joke as she proceeds to transform a losing team into a winner. Directed by Steve Rash, the thin formula comedy gets few laughs with worn-out cliches from similar underdog stories, and its premise of a woman NBA coach yields more smirks than smiles. Sexual situations and references, many coarse expressions, and an instance of rough language. A-III (PG-13)

Eddie and the Cruisers (1983) A reporter (Ellen Barkin) investigates the fate of a 1960's rock group whose sudden disappearance raises questions about the apparent suicide of its lead singer (Michael Paré). Director Martin Davidson, hampered by a mediocre script, fails to create any visual or narrative interest. Mildly vulgar dialogue. A-II (PG)

Eddie Cantor Story, The (1953) Clunky screen biography directed by Alfred E. Green with Keefe Brazelle doing a ludicrous imitation of the eccentric title comic as he goes from headliner in the Ziegfeld Follies to losing his money in the stock market crash of 1929, then suffers a heart attack, from which he recovers with the help of his loving wife (Marilyn Erskine) and resumes his career on stage, screen, and radio. A-I (br)

Eddy Duchin Story, The (1956) Sentimental journey through the life and career of pianist Duchin (miscast Tyrone Power), who becomes a band leader in the 1930s, loses his wife (Kim Novak) in the 1940s, and is crippled with leukemia in the 1950s. Director George Sidney overplays the innocence of the youthful Duchin, then his morose brooding over personal woes, relieved only by some bright musical numbers and occasional glimpses of the country's changing social context. Heavy going for children. A-I (br)

Eden (1998) Poignant drama in which a young mother (Joanna Going) afflicted with multiple sclerosis slips into a lingering coma while her patronizing husband (Dylan Walsh) and one of his students (Sean Patrick Flanery), who cares deeply about her, clash over her treatment. Although muddled by a subplot involving the woman's belief in astral projection, writer-director Howard Goldberg's sensitive story emphasizes the personal growth of the three characters as they come to terms with life-and-death choices. Fleeting substance abuse, occasional profanity, and some rough language. A-III (R)

Edge, The (1997) Stranded in the Alaskan wilderness and trailed by a hungry Kodiak bear, a billionaire (Anthony Hopkins) and a fashion photographer (Alec Baldwin) struggle to survive the elements and their mutual mistrust over the rich man's much younger wife (Elle Macpherson). Directed by Lee Tamahori, the harrowing adventure is well acted, tautly edited, and psychologically suspenseful, despite a few lapses in logic. Some intense violence, threatening situations, intermittent profanity, and recurring rough language. A-III (R)

Edge of Eternity (1959) Arizona deputy (Cornel Wilde) takes his time searching for a killer whose three victims all worked at a local gold mine until it was shut down 20 years before. Set in and around the Grand Canyon, director Don Siegel has a spectacular backdrop for a meandering mystery with a thrilling finish high atop a cable car used to transport bat guano from a mountain cave. Minimal stylized violence. A-I (br)

Edison, the Man (1940) Spencer Tracy plays the American go-getter who sells his first invention to Western Electric in order to set up his own laboratory, saves it by chancing upon the phonograph, then in 1886 achieves his dream of the electric light. Director Clarence Brown uses occasional comic touches to keep the idealized biography from getting too sentimental, but Tracy's likeable performance is what makes it worth watching. Its picture of science in the service of humanity as well as the virtues of dedication and hard work will not be lost on the young. A-I (br)

EDtv (1999) Stale comedy in which a video-store clerk (Matthew McConaughey) is paid to have his daily life televised, but the sudden fame alienates his new girlfriend (Jenna Elfman) and leads to embarrassing revelations about his folks and siblings. Director Ron Howard goes for cheap laughs while poking fun at the cult of celebrity, but the predictable plot and skimpy characterizations are of the dumb-and-dumber variety. Implied affairs, fleeting nudity, numerous sexual references, and intermittent profanity. A-III (PG-13)

Educating Rita (1983) This British production

adapted from Willy Russell's play and directed by Lewis Gilbert stars Michael Caine as a disillusioned, drunken professor of English in Dublin who becomes involved with a spunky housewife (Julie Walters) determined to get an education. The Pygmalion relationship has some charm, but Walter's characterization is somewhat crude and ethnically stereotyped. A-III (PG)

Education of Little Tree, The (1997) Uneven adaptation of Forrest Carter's novel about an eight-year-old part-Cherokee orphan (Joseph Ashton) being raised by his grandparents (James Cromwell and Tantoo Cardinal) in the Great Smokies of 1935 Tennessee, where he learns the mountaineer craft of making moonshine, the values of his Cherokee heritage, and the injustices of the white world. Directed by Richard Friedenberg, the movie benefits from convincing performances amidst the natural beauty of the mountain setting, but the story romanticizes the rustic virtues of backwoods folk while depicting urban society as hopelessly corrupt. Brief but brutal beatings, the death of close family members, instances of religious hypocrisy, occasional profanity, and vulgar language. A-II (PG)

Education of Sonny Carson, The 1974) Screen biography of a black militant (Rony Clanton), graduating from the Brooklyn ghetto to reform school and prison, embittered by the brutal cops and uncaring parole officials. Directed by Michael Campus, this attempt to show a world of racial injustice suffers from an onslaught of foul language, disjointed episodes, jarring switches in movie styles, and an excessively prolonged scene of a merciless beating by a racist cop. O (R)

Edvard Munch (1976) Written and directed by Peter Watkins, this is the story of the Norwegian artist Edvard Munch (1863-1944), who, as one of the founders of Expressionism, has had a great influence upon the direction of contemporary art. Watkins interweaves three main strands of narrative: the historical, the intellectual, and the personal. Beautifully photographed, with the feel of a semi-documentary, the movie's treatment of the tormented life of this artist is at times intense, but diffused by the cultural context. A-II (nr)

Edward Scissorhands (1990) A gentle humanoid (Johnny Depp) with grotesque blades for hands is adopted by a family (Dianne Wiest, Alan Arkin, and Winona Ryder) and prized by the community for his haircutting and lawn sculpting talents, until exploited by the daughter's boyfriend. Director Tim Burton's offbeat fantasy is an oddly appealing mix of mild comedy and mock tragedy despite its phony pastel suburban setting and stereotyped residents. Brief stylized violence and sexual innuendo. A-II (PG-13)

Edward II (1992) Bizarre adaptation of Christopher Marlowe's 16th-century play about King Edward II (Steven Waddington), his male lover (Andrew Tiernan), and his wife, Queen Isabella (Tilda Swinton), who concocts a murderous revenge. British director Derek Jarman wallows in sexually violent images in a medieval story jarringly joined to scenes of modern-day gay-bashing. Much sexual activity with nudity and bloody violence including scenes of torture and cannibalism. O (R)

Effect of Gamma Rays on Man-in-the-Moon Marigolds, The (1972) Joanne Woodward stars in the screen version of Paul Zindel's play about a desperate middle-aged mother living in an urban hovel, abandoned by her husband, and struggling to raise two teenaged daughters (Nell Potts and Roberta Wallach). Producer-director Paul Newman's ambitious but flawed exploration into the labyrinthine workings of the human heart is largely redeemed by Woodward's superb performance. A-III (PG)

Effi Briest (1977) Tragedy based on Theodor Fontane's nineteenth-century romantic novel about a 17-year-old girl, married to a middle-aged Prussian official, who makes the mistake of having an affair, ultimately leading to her destruction. Directed by Rainer Werner Fassbinder, the German production is a haunting black-and-white evocation of a bygone age with some insight into the morals of the times. A-III (nr)

Efficiency Expert, The (1992) Gentle Australian comedy about the irresistible effect of the human factor on a rigidly methodical management consultant (Anthony Hopkins) who has been hired to modernize a hopelessly out-of-date family-run shoe factory. Director Mark Joffe's sentimental fantasy centers in its good-natured depiction of the foibles and eccentricities of the factory workers and the idea that there is more to a business than making money. Some violence to property and minor romantic complications. A-II (PG)

Egg and I, The (1947) Postwar comedy in which a city couple (Claudette Colbert and Fred MacMurray) buy a broken-down chicken farm, then learn about country life the hard way from rustic neighbors Ma and Pa Kettle (Marjorie Main and Percy Kilbride). Directed by Chester Erskine, the fish-out-of-water proceedings provide mild fun, with Colbert especially good as the bemused, spunky wife, until taking a turn into romantic melodrama for a sentimental finish. Domestic misunderstandings. A-II (br)

Egyptian, The (1954) Muddled epic from Mika Waltari's novel about a physician (Edmund Purdom) in ancient Thebes who loses his idealism, then regains it during the 13th-century B.C. reign of Akhnaton (Michael Wilding), the pharaoh who tried to replace all the old gods with the one all-powerful Sun-God, Aton. Directed by Michael Curtiz, the overlong, thinly contrived melodrama overplays the hero's downfall with a Babylonian courtesan (Bella Darvi), while giving scant attention to his true love (Jean Simmons), best friend (Victor Mature), and wily servant (Peter Ustinov), then gets lost in the court intrigues against the pharaoh and his introduction of monotheism. Stylized violence and sexual situations. A-III (br)

Eiger Sanction, The (1975) An art professor (Clint Eastwood, who also directed) moonlights as an assassin for an intelligence outfit run by a former Nazi. The movie is exploitative in its treatment of sexual promiscuity and brutality. O (R)

8 1/2 (1963) With both career and marriage in chaos, an Italian movie director (Marcello Mastroianni) protects his overgrown ego by retreating into surreal memories of the past and wild fantasies about the present. Director Federico Fellini has some self-indulgent fun with his profession, semi-biographical events from his youth, and themes from his movies, while taking viewers on a journey through the rich, at times bizarre, imagination of an artist whose attempts to cope with the demands of the real world are resolved in a final flood of optimism, as the director joins with all his characters in a human carousel of life. Subtitles. Ambiguous treatment of mature themes. A-IV (br)

8 Heads in a Duffel Bag (1997) Sophomoric black comedy about a gangster (Joe Pesci) pursuing a vacationing medical student (Andy Comeau) who accidentally took a duffel bag containing the heads of eight rivals the gangster was to deliver to a mob boss. Writer-director Tom Schulman's tasteless chase comedy finds redundant humor in the horrified reactions of a half-dozen people who chance upon the decapitated heads but never bother to notify the police. Brief violence with frequent mistreatment of body parts for comic effect, much profanity, and some rough language. A-IV (R)

Eight Iron Men (1952) Low-budget WW II story of a US infantry squad pinned down by a German machine-gunner while awaiting replacements in a bombed-out town. Directed by Edward Dmytryk, the gritty but stagy situation consists mostly of the by-play between the stereotyped cross-section of soldiers and the sergeant (Lee Marvin) who wants to leave with the same number of men he came with. Wartime violence. A-II (br)

Eight Men Out (1988) Based on the 1919 scandal of bribe-taking Chicago White Sox players in the World Series won by the Cincinnati Reds, this morality tale is about compromising a lifetime of professional credibility for big bucks and revenge on a stingy ball-club owner (Clifton James). Writer-director John Sayles does well contrasting honest and dishonest players, but the movie bogs down in too much detail and too many indistinguishable characters. Some locker-room language and a theme involving bribery and threats of violent retribution. A-III (PG)

Eight Millimeter (1999) Nihilistic tale of a righteous investigator (Nicolas Cage) who is corrupted and becomes a murderous avenger once he determines a teenage girl was butchered as the final scene of a porno film production. Offering no insights, director Joel Schumacher's very violent thriller is content to wallow in the beastly world of pornographers, blood-lusting killers, and insatiable millionaires. Excessive brutality and deadly sexual violence, rationalization of vigilante justice, some nudity, and much rough language. O (R)

8 Million Ways to Die (1986) In this heartless murder mystery, Jeff Bridges plays a reformed alcoholic ex-cop who breaks up a drug ring as he finds a prostitute's killer. Violence, ethnic stereotyping, extreme amounts of profanity, and some nudity. O (R)

8 Seconds (1994) Dramatization of the brief but eventful life of world champion bull-rider Lane Frost (Luke Perry), who gained rodeo fame alongside best friend and competitor Tuff Hedeman (Stephen Baldwin), while weathering stormy relationships with his wife (Cynthia Geary) and demanding father (James Rebhorn). Director John G. Avildsen turns out a flavorsome rodeo movie with inspirational themes of friendship and forgiveness, which are unfortunately expressed through corny dialogue and an overly sentimental treatment. Very discreet references to adultery and some rodeo injuries. A-II (PG-13)

18 Again (1988) When a grandfather and grandson switch spirits after an almost-fatal car-crash, the 81-year-old grandpa (George Burns) manages to enjoy some college antics as an 18-year-old, while his grandson (Charlie Schlatter) learns a thing or two about social savvy from his grandfather's example. Directed by Paul Flaherty, the potentially sweet-natured comedy is marred by some off-color, sexist jokes with sexual inferences, sophomoric humor, and brief nudity. A-III (PG)

Eighth Day, The (1997) Separated from his wife and family, a depressed salesman (Daniel Auteuil) is transformed by a young man (Pascal Duquenne) afflicted with Down's Syndrome, whom he finds on the road and has difficulty returning to a mental institution. Writer-director Jaco Van Dormael's French movie about a man finding his inner child by opening his heart to a needy innocent is a bold blend of affecting drama, colorful fantasy sequences, and unabashed sentimentality. Subtitles. Ambiguous treatment of a suicide, brief violence, a restrained bedroom scene, and a few crude gestures. A-IV (nr)

84 Charing Cross Road (1987) Screen version of New Yorker Helene Hanff's autobiography telling of her 20-year transatlantic correspondence with a London bookseller, starting with an inquiry about some rare books in 1949 and ending with his death in 1969. Though they never meet, the book seller (Anthony Hopkins) and the book lover (Anne Bancroft) come sharply into focus through letters sharing their mutual love of literature and other cultural matters. Director David Jones does extremely well in conveying the spiritual meeting of minds underlying their long-distance friendship. This uplifting celebration of kind and gentle souls may be above the heads of the very young, but they would benefit from seeing it with their parents. A-I (PG)

80 Steps to Jonah (1969) Young drifter (Wayne Newton), innocently implicated in a car theft, takes refuge in a camp for blind children, where he finds commitment and a new purpose in life. Romance and exoneration follow in director Gerd Oswald's simple, somewhat sentimental tale of spiritual renewal that has special appeal for youngsters. A-I (G)

El Condor (1970) Big, bold Jim Brown joins up with skinny, mean Lee Van Cleef in this gory Western about getting Maximilian's vast gold horde out of El Condor, which is guarded by cruel Patrick O'Neal. Director John Guillermin rightfully pays little attention to the shoddy script but, unfortunately, devotes his energies to heavy-handed violence and sex scenes. O (R)

El Dorado (1967) When a band of cut-throats terrorize the town, an aging sheriff (Robert Mitchum), who drinks too much, fights them off with the help of his old partner (John Wayne), who suffers occasional spinal spasms. Producer-director Howard Hawks mixes the action formula with farcical situations and unconventional characters in this tribute to the old cowboy heroes of screen legend. Stylized violence. A-III (br)

El Greco (1966) Mel Ferrer and Rosanna Schiaffino star in a very melodramatic romance based loosely on the life of the 16th-century Spanish painter. European production directed by Luciano Salce features beautiful location photography, but art is secondary to a presentation of the artist's tempestuous romance with a high-born lady. A-III (br)

El Mariachi (1993) Increasingly violent comedy in which a mariachi guitarist (Carlos Gallardo) finds himself caught up in a killing spree when a series of menacing strangers mistake him for a vicious hit-man (Reinol Martinez) out to murder a traitorous drug dealer (Peter Marquardt). Though its dark humor is occasionally funny, writer-director Robert Rodriguez's low-budget movie trivializes murder and the worth of human life. Subtitles. Much gratuitous violence and a conclusion justifying deadly violence to exact personal revenge. O (R)

El Norte (1984) Fleeing from terrorists who kill their father and kidnap their mother, two Guatemalan teenagers head towards "El Norte," meaning the US, where they hope to begin a new life free from fear and exploitation. After a journey with further terrors, they reach Los Angeles, get jobs, and have a taste of the good life they have dreamed about, before one becomes seriously ill and the other is deported as an illegal alien. Director Gregory Nava has made a splendid film about human dignity and the exploitation of undocumented workers, with some good-natured humor keeping matters from getting too solemn. Subtitles aplenty with much of the dialogue in Spanish and Mayan. Several scenes of intense violence. A-III (R)

El Paso (1949) Muddled Western in which a lawyer (John Payne) turns outlaw in order to bring justice to a crooked town. Directed by Lewis R. Foster, the melodrama's heavies (Sterling Hayden and Dick Foran), comic relief (Gabby Hayes), and romantic interest (Gail Russell) get lost in a welter of vigilante justice, sharply contrasted with a law-abiding Mexican community across the Rio Grande. Much stylized violence, including lynchings. A-III (br)

El Super (1979) Unpretentious and affecting movie about a former Havana bus conductor (Raymundo Hidalgo-Gato) struggling to get through his 10th New York winter as a building superintendent, supported by his loving wife (Zully Montero) but troubled by their promiscuous, drug-taking daughter (Elizabeth Pena). Directed by Leon Ichaso and Orlando Jimenez-Leal, the slice-of-life portrait is brightened by wit and humor, bridging the gap between North American and Latin cultures with low-budget ingenuity and cultural integrity. A-II (nr)

El Topo (1971) Argentinean director Alexandro Jodorowsky presents the story of a man's spiritual journey through life and the contradictions that arise between physical and moral power. The form is the time-honored Western with its gunfighters, open landscapes, and frontier towns. But in addition to using the Western conventions, the film also employs religious imagery, and sections of the Bible serve as its ideological frame of reference. Some will find its images of violence, sexuality, and venality to be unsettling, if not offensive. A-IV (nr)

Eldridge Cleaver (1970) William Klein's documentary on political refugee Cleaver, an American whose radical ideas are uncongenial to the majority of his fellow citizens, uses the rhetoric of violence in presenting his views on revolution. Viewers will make their own judgment about the validity of his statements according to their knowledge and experience. A-IV (nr)

Election (1999) Biting satire in which an idealistic but flawed teacher (Matthew Broderick) goes overboard in trying to prevent a scheming senior (Reese Witherspoon) from being elected president of the student council. Director Alexander Payne's sharply observed comedy examines with ironic, sometimes nasty, wit such human foibles as sexual obsession, hypocrisy, and rationalizing such behavior. Several sexual situations, fleeting nudity, crude sex references, recurring rough language, and an instance of profanity. A-IV (R)

Electra Glide in Blue (1973) Ironic slice-of-life movie about a motorcycle cop (Robert Blake) in a small Southwestern town who revels in his splendid uniform and rugged equipment but yearns for the status he might have as a detective. A short stint with the local marshal (Mitch Ryan) cures him of that, and a botched twist ending leaves a bad aftertaste. Embarrassingly pretentious but empty movie, painfully directed by James Guercio, it contains violence, rough language, and sexual references. A-III (PG)

Electric Dreams (1984) Bland, innocuous British romantic comedy from director Steve Barron about a computer which falls in love with a woman. Youth-oriented movie features Lenny von Dohlen, Virginia Madsen, and Bud Cort, who manage to cavort in bed together, but this is implied rather than depicted. A-III (PG)

Electric Horseman, The (1979) Television reporter (Jane Fonda) teams up with over-the-hill rodeo star (Robert Redford) to save a gallant racehorse from commercial exploitation. Low voltage but cheerful and unassuming movie directed by Sydney Pollack. Treatment of the romantic involvement between the two principals makes it mature viewing fare. A-III (PG)

Eleni (1985) A New York newspaper reporter (John Malkovich), born in Greece, returns to his native land to find the man responsible for the execution of his mother (Kate Nelligan) in the Greek Civil War 30 years earlier. Despite the emotional power intrinsic to its fact-based subject, director Peter Yates has made a flat and unmoving movie, due largely to a pedestrian script and miscasting. Some scenes of wartime violence. A-II (PG)

Elephant Boy (1937) Sturdy little adventure in the jungles of colonial India, where a local youth (Sabu) helps a British hunting party on the trail of a great elephant herd. Co-directed by Robert Flaherty and Zoltan Korda, the simple story focuses on young Sabu's winning performance, though the film's semi-documentary style mixes the authentic with the phony, including making elephants appear to dance. For all its dated qualities, the movie still delights youngsters. A-I (br)

Elephant Called Slowly, An (1971) Director James Hill offers a rambling account of a return visit by Bill Travers and Virginia McKenna, the stars of **Born Free**, to a Kenyan game preserve, where they are befriended by a baby elephant. Nothing much happens, but this album of wildlife is so low-keyed and innocent that parents, especially accompanied by their youngsters, will find it a pleasant, relaxing experience. A-I (G)

Elephant Man, The (1980) Touching fact-based portrait of an impoverished man deformed by a rare disease who is rescued from a London freak show by a dedicated doctor, only to become the curiosity of fashionable Victorian society. Directed by David Lynch with evocative black-and-white photography, it features a fine performance by Anthony Hopkins as the concerned physician who rehabilitates the outcast (John Hurt under great wads of make-up). Some intense scenes of brutality. A-III (PG)

Elephant Walk (1954) Heavy goings-on in Ceylon when a tea plantation owner (Peter Finch) brings home an English bride (Elizabeth Taylor) who can't understand his obsession with the colonial past and turns for sympathy to the plantation's manager (Dana Andrews). Directed by William Dieterle, the glossy romantic melodrama goes in circles until nature takes its revenge through drought, plague, and an elephant rampage razing the planter's mansion and bringing him to his senses. Mild romantic triangle and stylized violence. A-II (br)

11 Harrowhouse (1974) Routine caper movie in which jewel thieves (Charles Grodin and Candice Bergen) get some inside help from a dissident employee (James Mason). Director Aram Avakian does make the most of his London setting and especially the metallic glint of the sophisticated detection devices in the basement of the diamond exchange. A-II (PG)

Elizabeth (1998) Historical dramatization of the political intrigues and religious conflicts besetting England as the Protestant Elizabeth succeeds her half-sister, the Catholic Mary, to the throne, then comes to rely on the sinister Walsingham to break the power of the Catholic nobles and other potential enemies to her reign, after which Elizabeth rules in her own right as the Virgin Queen. Directed by Shekhar Kapur, the picture turns a complex and confusing period of history into a series of highly dramatic tableaus focusing on Elizabeth's development as a royal feminist, though the result never probes beneath the surface of events or motivations. Intense period violence including religious persecutions, torture and executions, sexual situations, and brief nudity. A-IV (R)

Elizabeth of Ladymead (1948) British melodrama in four acts, each a variation on the bewilderment of an Army officer upon returning home to find his wife (Anna Neagle in each case) has changed while he was off soldiering in, alternately, the Crimean War, the Boer War, and World Wars I and II. Director Herbert Wilcox shows how far the cause of women's equality has come since 1854, but ends in 1946 with scant comprehension of the changes ahead. Mild sexual innuendo. A-II (br)

Ellen (see: **The Second Woman**)

Elmer Gantry (1960) Vivid dramatization of the Sinclair Lewis novel about a cunning sharpster (Burt Lancaster) who attaches himself to the entourage of a barnstorming evangelist (Jean Simmons) in the 1920s, then falls in love with her. In exploring the commercialization of religion and some of the techniques used by religious charlatans, writer-director Richard Brooks makes good use of the period's hypocrisy and people's credulity. Critical view of religion's exploitation, some sexual references, and occasional stylized violence. A-III (br)

Elusive Pimpernel, The (1950) Disappointing remake of **The Scarlet Pimpernel** features David Niven as the daredevil Englishman who risks his life rescuing French aristocrats from the bloodthirsty Reign of Terror. Written and directed by Michael Powell and Emeric Pressburger, the disjointed narrative fails to sustain interest despite a variety of swashbuckling action, a failure compounded by bland characters who tend to get lost in the colorful settings. Stylized violence and murky intrigue. A-I (br)

Elvira Madigan (1967) Romantic 19th-century tale of a cavalry officer (Thommy Berggren) and a young circus performer (Pia Degermark) who run away to the Danish countryside for a summer's idyll, but, as the chill of fall sets in, realize their future is doomed. Director Bo Widerberg's sensitive, straight-forward version of a popular Swedish legend is lushly beautiful with a darkly somber ending. Subtitles. Mature theme. A-III (PG)

Elvira, Mistress of the Dark (1988) A buxom TV horror show hostess (Cassandra Peterson) gets into trouble trying to bankroll a Las Vegas song-and-dance act with her aunt's paranormal inheritance. Directed by James Signorelli, its wall-to-wall sex jokes, a tasteless orgiastic picnic, and a tassel-twirling finale manage to reduce it to the level of soft-porn comedy. O (PG-13)

Elvis on Tour (1972) Pierre Adidge's documentary of a 15-day concert tour by Elvis Presley reveals nothing new about the man behind the legend, but devotees of the legend will find it entertaining enough. A-I (G)

Elvis: That's the Way It Is (1970) Documentary profile of rock 'n' roll superstar Elvis Presley beginning with the rehearsals and exhausting preparations for a gala opening night performance at the International Hotel in Las Vegas. The performance itself is a winner, giving fans of old swivel-hips 30 songs to savor. Director Denis Sanders captures the quality of the man as performer and conveys that special Elvis magic that is part put-on and part solid singing conviction. A-II (G)

Embalmer, The (1972) Ensconced in a sunken monastery beneath a fancy hotel in Venice, a psychotic frogman enshrines the beautiful women he has abducted and drowned in the canal, until he tries to nab a lovely tourist who has caught the eye of a handsome reporter staying at the hotel. Dino Travella directs this failed 1966 Italian thriller with absolutely no imagination, but a few red herrings mildly seasoned with sexual innuendo. A-III (PG)

Embryo (1976) Scientist (Rock Hudson) injects a human embryo with a drug that speeds growth to save the baby of a woman who has committed suicide. The result is a young girl (Barbara Carrera) with a photographic memory that creates terrifying results. Director Ralph Nelson's sci-fi horror story contains graphic, but brief, nudity and a shockingly violent conclusion. O (PG)

Emerald Forest, The (1985) An American father (Powers Booth) searches the Amazonian jungle for 10 years until he finds the son who was kidnapped by Indians. The boy, however, now a teenager, has no desire to return to civilization. Under John Boorman's direction, the exotic setting provides some interest to this simplistic and melodramatic story of noble and ignoble savages and the ravages wrought on nature by commercial exploitation. Passable entertainment, but strictly for mature audiences because of a great deal of nudity and some rather graphic violence. A-IV (R)

Emigrants, The (1972) Superb Swedish production starring Liv Ullmann and Max von Sydow about a young couple who leave their native land in the early 19th century to find a new home in Minnesota. Directed by Jan Troell, the re-creation of the era is finely detailed and the acting is first rate. A-II (PG)

Emil and the Detectives (1964) A group of boys play detective and thwart the plans of a trio of comically sinister bank robbers in West Berlin. Disney production directed by Peter Tewksbury may please the young and uncritical. A-I (br)

Emily Bronte's Wuthering Heights (1992) This adaptation of the 19th-century romantic tale of doomed lovers turns Heathcliff (Ralph Fiennes) into a despicable woman-basher and all-around heel after Cathy (Juliet Binoche) marries and dies, then takes his revenge on Cathy's grown daughter 20 years later. Directed by Peter Kosminsky, the result is an episodic thicket of sour people and bitter events that has more to do with madness and folly than with unrequited love. Stylized violence and sexual situations. A-III (PG)

Eminent Domain (1991) Bland Cold War drama in which a Polish Politburo member (Donald Sutherland) strikes back after he is summarily stripped of his position and power with disastrous results for his wife (Anne Archer) and child (Johdi May). A threadbare story line and a lumbering pace make director John Irvin's movie a slack and tepid affair of minimal suspense. Momentary violence and an instance of rough language. A-II (PG-13)

Emitai (1972) Fact-based Senegalese movie about a small village whose men are conscripted by France during WW II, but, when they refuse a year later to give up all their rice, the remaining villagers are massacred. Directed by Ousmane Sembene, much of the story is told solely through its expressive images, and these visuals are the great strength of the movie. The title is the name of one of the tribe's gods who represents the passage from one stage of life to a new and better one. Stylized violence. A-II (nr)

Emma (1996) Bright adaptation of Jane Austen's 1816 novel about a supremely self-confidant young woman (Gwyneth Paltrow) who busily, though ineptly, sets about matchmaking for those around her, but, in the process, nearly overlooks the perfect match for herself. Writer-director Dough McGrath's British production of the romantic classic captures the subtle snobbery of the English class system without losing sight of the charming frailties of the story's many characters. Romantic complications. A-II (PG)

Emperor Jones, The (1933) Stage-bound adaptation of Eugene O'Neill's play about a poor but ambitious black youth (Paul Robeson) who becomes a Pullman porter, gets in trouble with the law, escapes from a chain gang, and winds up the oppressive ruler of a small Caribbean island. Director Dudley Murphy's low-budget production relies on dark, expressionistic sets in staging a story of the corrupting nature of power, but the result is most notable for what it shows of Robeson's talent as a dramatic actor. Stylized violence and menace. A-III (br)

Emperor of the North (1973) Brutal, altogether unsubtle drama about a clash between a hobo (Lee Marvin) and a sadistic train guard (Ernest Borgnine) set in the era of the Great Depression. It captures some of the mood of the 1930s, with out-of-work men living in hobo camps and riding the rails, but this is only used as the context for director Robert Aldrich's myopic vision of the male mystique and the cult of violence. A-IV (PG)

Emperor's Shadow, The (1998) Violent historical drama set in 210 B.C., as a ruthless warlord (Jiang Wen) conquers surrounding kingdoms to unite China under his tyrannical reign, but cannot control the rebellious spirit of his court musician (Ge You) who has dared to take the dictator's daughter (Xu Qing) as his lover. Director Zhou Xiaowen provides intriguing character studies of the two men, and the picture's visual spectacle is impressive, but the constant period barbarity overwhelms the narrative. Subtitles. Much stylized violence, discreet sexual encounters, and fleeting nudity. A-III (nr)

Empire of the Sun (1987) Adventure saga of a British lad (Christian Bale) who has to learn to survive on his own after being separated from his parents when the Japanese capture Shanghai and intern him for the duration of WW II. Director Steven Spielberg uses a large-scale action canvas to tell with some feeling and conviction the story of a youth growing up in the midst of wartime inhumanity. Some realistic violence and a scene indicating the boy's curiosity about sex. A-II (PG)

Empire Strikes Back, The (1980) Gallant intergalactic rebels led by Luke Skywalker (Mark Hamill), Han Solo (Harrison Ford), Princess Leia (Carrie Fisher), and lovable android companions continue the fight against the evil Empire aided by Yoda, a remarkable creature who safeguards the Force and teaches moderation in all things. Some intense fight sequences punctuate director Irvin Kershner's sci-fi fantasy action. A-II (PG)

Enchanted April (1992) Charming period piece about the transformation four world-weary London women (Joan Plowright, Miranda Richardson, Josie Lawrence, and Polly Walker) experience when they impulsively rent a medieval castle for a month in sunny Italy. Director Mike Newell's offers up a sweetly fanciful film, based on Elizabeth von Armin's 1922 novel, about characters removed from their drab routines who learn the value of tolerance and renewed commitment to relationships. Very mild sexual innuendo. A-II (PG)

Enchanted Cottage, The (1945) Fragile romantic fantasy about a disfigured WW II veteran (Robert Young) and a plain-looking maid (Dorothy McGuire), each of whom sees the beauty of the other through the eyes of love. Directed by John Cromwell, the sentimentality is old-fashioned, but the theme of true love is universal. A-I (br)

Enchantment (1948) Romantic melodrama centers on an aged British general (David Niven) who recalls the lost love (Teresa Wright) of his youth when visited during WW II by her son (Farley Granger) who falls for the daughter (Evelyn Keyes) of the general's mean-spirited sister (Jayne Meadows). Directed by Irving Reis, the parallel romances of past and present are neatly contrived and unabashedly sentimental. Tough sledding for children and non-romantics. A-I (br)

Encino Man (1992) Sophomoric comedy has two California teens (Sean Astin and Pauly Shore) unearthing a frozen caveman (Brendan Fraser) whom they defrost and pass off as a really cool high-school exchange student. Director Les Mayfield's innocuous romp is just a drawn-out unreeling of gooney antics with no attempt at plot or characterization. Minor brawling and very mild sexual innuendo. A-II (PG)

End, The (1978) Except for the buffoonery of Dom Deluise, this is a painfully unfunny Burt Reynolds comedy about how not to commit suicide. Also directed by Reynolds, it contains an explicit love scene, some highly insulting ethnic jokes, and disrespectful treatment of a religious rite. O (R)

End of a Priest (1970) Seriocomic Czechoslovakian tale about villagers rehearsing for a play during which the sexton becomes saintly playing the role of a priest, and the teacher becomes an unimaginative buffoon in the role of mayor. The movie's theme is not the conflict between church and state but the difference between doing good and talking about it. Though it has a moral, director Evald Schorm is mainly concerned with its characters and the high comedy of the absurd. A-III (nr)

End of Innocence, The (1991) Rejected by her younger lover (Steve Meadows) and hooked on pills, a middle-aged woman (Dyan Cannon) begins to find herself after checking into a rehab center. Also written and directed by Cannon, the movie lacks any subtlety in its shrill look at one woman's long-overdue conclusion that she must accept herself. Discreet sexual encounters, recreational drug use, minor violence, and rough language. A-III (R)

End of the Game, The (1976) Screen version of a Friedrich Duerrenmatt novel about a Swiss detective (Martin Ritt) who is obsessed with bringing to belated justice a former friend (Robert Shaw), now possessed of immense wealth and power, who 30 years earlier had killed a young woman. Director Maximilian Schell elicits strong performances from the cast, which also includes Jacqueline Bisset and Jon Voight, in this convincing crime melodrama about retribution and redemption. A-III PG)

End of the Line (1988) In order to protest the closing of their town's rail yard, veteran Arkansas railroad workers (Wilford Brimley and Levon Helm) go to Chicago to confront the railroad's chairman of the board, who helps them teach his weaselly son-in-law, the company president, a lesson in humanity. Director and co-writer Jay Russell and executive producer and co-star Mary Steenburgen have collaborated on an authentic and uncloying evocation of rural American life. Fine ensemble acting, but some rough language. A-II (PG)

End of the Road (1970) Screen version of John

Barth's novel about a catatonic (Stacy Keach) who falls into the hands of a mad doctor (James Earl Jones) practicing multimedia shock treatment on his insane patients. Directed by Aram Avakian, vignettes of perversion, sadism, masochism, and fetishism are woven into a story of adultery and exploitation, ending in a gross abortion sequence. O (X)

End of Violence, The (1997) Murky drama in which a movie mogul (Bill Pullman) suspected of killing two hitmen goes on the lam, then finds himself being spied upon by a top-secret government agency. Director Wim Wenders endeavors to show how one act of violence comes to affect many people but gets lost in dense story strands that are finally tied together laboriously and with little impact. Brief violence, fleeting nudity, some profanity, and recurring rough language. A-III (R)

Endangered Species (1982) Ex-cop from New York City (Robert Urich) settles in Colorado to find peace and quiet but instead becomes involved in a bizarre case of cattle mutilations. Director Alan Rudolph manages to obscure a theme about chemical warfare by focusing upon the romance between the local sheriff (Jobeth Williams) and the boorish, foul-mouthed ex-cop. Some violence, nudity, and rough language. A-III (R)

Endless Love (1981) Glossy fantasy about teenage love takes an inexplicable turn when the boy (Martin Hewitt) sets fire to the house in which the girl (Brooke Shields) and her family are sleeping. Directed by Franco Zeffirelli, the lovemaking scenes and needless nudity dissolve all pretense of sensitivity. O (R)

Endless Summer, The (1966) Two young experts (Robert August and Mike Hinson) travel to Africa, New Zealand, Tahiti, and Hawaii in search for the perfect wave. Producer-director Bruce Brown pictures the pleasures of surfing with enthusiasm and humor. A-I (br)

Endless Summer II, The (1994) Joyous sequel to the classic 1966 surfer documentary about the search for the perfect wave shows off the new wave of world-class surfers (notably Pat O'Connell and Robert "Wingnut" Weaver) as they hang ten in the surf off the varied coastlines of Alaska, Costa Rica, Biarritz, South Africa, Brisbane, and Bali. Director Bruce Brown's sometimes corny narration can't dampen his love of the sport in this lengthy but always upbeat, often humorous, and handsomely shot tribute to the art of surfing. Fleeting shots of topless bathers. A-II (PG)

Endurance (1999) Semi-documentary account of Ethiopian distance runner Haile Gebrselassie's life from rural childhood in a large farm family to years of training with a track club in Addis Ababa and his record-setting 10,000-meter run in the 1996 Atlanta Olympics. Except for the Olympic footage, everything else has been re-created by writer-director Leslie Woodhead in scenes showing Gebrselassie's affinity for running, his father's attempts to make him give it up, and the hard work that pays off in his Atlanta triumph, but the slow-paced result is more a snapshot of the runner than a portrait of the man. A-I (G)

Enemies, A Love Story (1989) Brilliant adaptation of Isaac Bashevis Singer's novel about a troubled Holocaust survivor (Ron Silver) who shuttles between three wives (Margaret Sophie Stein, Lena Olin, and Anjelica Huston) as he struggles with his disillusionment with God and the chaos that his lies have caused. In capturing the feel of Jewish émigré life in 1949 New York City, director Paul Mazursky helps viewers empathize with the tragic flaws of the character and the courage of the women he loves. Sexually promiscuous protagonist, several sexual encounters with nudity, some violence, and a climactic suicide. A-IV (R)

Enemy Below, The (1957) Tense WW II tale in which the skipper (Robert Mitchum) of an American destroyer relentlessly pursues a German submarine, despite all the wily stratagems of its veteran captain (Curt Jurgens). Directed by Dick Powell, it's a battle of wit as well as weapons, with realistic situations and credible performances, though the chivalrous ending is a bit much. Wartime violence. A-I (br)

Enemy General, The (1960) Limp WW II adventure directed by George Sherman has a US officer (Van Johnson) working with the French underground to rescue a turncoat German general from the Gestapo despite his part in executing French civilians, including the officer's girlfriend. Transparent hooey with unconvincing violence and menace. A-II (br)

Enemy Mine (1985) In a science-fiction parable about the solidarity of intelligent life forms, a human (Dennis Quaid) and a reptilian alien (Louis Gossett, Jr.), enemies from warring star systems, find themselves marooned on an uninhabited planet, where they must work together or perish. Plodding script by Edward Khmara and leaden direction by Wolfgang Petersen make the premise more silly than it might have been. Violence and a confusing sequence involving the reptilian reproductive process. A-III (PG-13)

Enemy of the State (1998) Glossy political thriller in which a Georgetown lawyer (Will Smith) is being framed for murder by a corrupt government surveillance agent (Jon Voight) unless a mysterious former agent (Gene Hackman) can outsmart the operative at his own game. Tony Scott directs a relentlessly high-tech chase film that, by stressing elaborate surveillance gizmos and tracking satellites, fails to become emotionally involving. Sporadic violence, sexual references, some profanity, and intermittent rough language. A-III (R)

Enforcer, The (1977) Clint Eastwood again plays Dirty Harry, the sadistic San Francisco policeman who, with a female partner (Tyne Daly) in tow, is on the job tracking down an underground terrorist group. Director James Fargo's crime melodrama has scant concern for plot consistency but just enough realism for its excessive violence to be offensive. O (R)

England Made Me (1973) British screen version

of the Graham Greene novel about a crooked Swedish tycoon (Peter Finch) and an ineffectual loser (Michael York) who gets in his way. By changing the locale from Depression Sweden to Hitler's Germany, director Peter Duffell focuses more on Nazi villainy than on the individual problems of the characters. The drama rejects the confused morality of its characters but lacks the sense of guilt that characterized Green's moral universe. A-IV (PG)

English Patient, The (1996) Romantic mystery unfolds as a burn victim (Ralph Fiennes) with a British convoy of wounded in WW II Italy slowly recalls bits and pieces of his ill-fated affair with a married woman (Kristin Scott Thomas) on a prewar mapping survey of the Egyptian desert. Director Anthony Minghella immerses their romance in shimmering desert imagery which churns up some emotional heat, though the burn patient's story and that of his nurse (Juliette Binoche) add up to little more than soapy melodrama. Some stylized violence, several sexual encounters with brief nudity, and occasional rough language. A-IV (R)

Englishman Who Went Up a Hill but Came Down a Mountain, The (1995) Quaint but long-winded tale set in 1917 Wales, where a sharp innkeeper (Colm Meaney) goads his fellow villagers into hauling mounds of dirt to add some 16 feet to their local mountain in order to keep English surveyors (Hugh Grant and Ian McNeice) from downgrading it officially to a hill. Writer-director Christopher Monger gives epic treatment to a fact-based bit of whimsy, piling on scenes of picturesque Welsh landscapes, eccentric characters, hectic community action, and a bit of romance, with uneven results. An implied sexual relationship, some sexual innuendo, and a couple of rude expressions. A-III (PG)

Enigma (1983) French-British production has an agent (Martin Sheen) sent on a perilous mission behind the Iron Curtain in this stodgy thriller directed by Jeannot Szwarc. Supporting cast, headed by Brigitte Fossey and Sam Neil, can do nothing to lift it above the conventional and mediocre. Some violence, brief nudity, and a general air of moral ambiguity. A-III (PG)

Enough Rope (1966) French adaptation of a Patrica Highsmith mystery about a wife-killer (Gert Frobe), a man who would like to kill his wife (Maurice Ronet), and a police inspector (Robert Hossein) who gives them enough rope to wrap up his case. Directed by Claude Autant-Lara, the plot is intriguing in bringing together two strangers-in-crime, but the inspector's extra-legal methods are questionable. Mature themes. A-III (br)

Ensign Pulver (1964) Lackluster sequel to **Mister Roberts** resumes the running battle between crew (led by Robert Walker, Jr., in the title role, with Walter Matthau as Doc) and the egocentric captain (Burl Ives) of a WW II cargo ship in the South Pacific. Director Joshua Logan misses the original's zesty humor and sense of wartime purpose, with few compensations from a game cast and largely witless script. Mild sexual innuendo. A-I (br)

Enter Laughing (1967) Autobiography based on comedian Carl Reiner's first break into show biz. Reni Santoni is somewhat bland as the young comic, but Elaine May creates an outlandishly laughable neurotic and Michael J. Pollard adds a fine folksy touch to the laughter. Also directed by Reiner. Viewers will exit, if not laughing, at least smiling. A-I (br)

Enter the Dragon (1973) Domestic martial-arts exercise with Bruce Lee, Jim Kelly, and John Saxton as secret agents out to get the goods on a dope-and-prostitution ring by taking part in a Kung Fu competition staged by the gang. Directed by Robert Clouse, the complications are simply an endless repetition or brutal beatings, undifferentiated by the participant's race, creed, or sex. O (R)

Entertainer, The (1960) Downbeat British drama of a seedy music-hall comic (Laurence Olivier) whose dishonest scheme to put on a big London show is scotched by his famed vaudevillian father (Roger Livesey), with tragic results. Directed by Tony Richardson from John Osborne's play, the result is a harsh character study of a third-rate showman whose human failings have made life miserable for his downtrodden wife (Brenda de Banzie) and struggling offspring (Joan Plowright, Alan Bates, and Albert Finney). Off-screen infidelity, sexual innuendo, and alcoholic excess. A-III (br)

Entertaining Angels: The Dorothy Day Story (1996) Compelling dramatization of the early life of Catholic Worker founder Dorothy Day (Moira Kelly) as a young journalist whose agonizing over failed love affairs leads her to reflect on her life and, in doing so, discovers God, then meets Peter Maurin (Martin Sheen) and puts his ideas of social justice into practice during the Depression. Directed by Michael Ray Rhodes, the biographical movie depicts a woman's spiritual journey in convincing dramatic fashion, though it is largely interior, deeply religious, and specifically Catholic in its sensibilities. Realistic treatment of love affairs, an abortion, and a suicide, as well as some coarse language. A-II (PG-13)

Entertaining Mr. Sloane (1970) British screen version of Joe Orton's black comedy about an unscrupulous young man (Peter McEnery) being wooed and won simultaneously by a pathetic aging doxy (Beryl Reid) and her fastidious brother (Harry Andrews). Director Douglas Hickox gets too close to the corruption of human nature without the distancing of laughter that was intended, leaving most viewers incredulous about the film's surface reality and unconcerned about any inner meaning that might be there. A-IV (nr)

Entrapment (1999) Mindless escapist caper in which a wily insurance investigator (Catherine Zeta-Jones) joins forces with the world's craftiest art thief (Sean Connery) to nail him red-handed. Jon Amiel's sluggish direction and the bogus emotions on display limit suspense in this glossy fantasy of doublecrossing daredevils defying the odds and each other. A romanticized view of crime, fleeting violence and a few instances of rough language and profanity. A-IV (PG-13)

Equinox (1971) The forces of good and evil emerge to do battle, this time in an inept and highly ludicrous story of devils and monsters and invisible castles. Directed by Jack Woods, this cornball exercise in fright and horror has phony special effects that could only scare the very young. A-II (PG)

Equinox Flower (1977) Gentle Japanese domestic comedy about a father's foolish concerns over his daughter's marriage. Directed in 1958 by Yusujiro Ozu, the story is infused with his loving brand of insight into character and situation that transcends national boundaries. A-II (nr)

Equus (1977) Director Sidney Lumet has brought Peter Shaffer's play to the screen with Richard Burton as the psychiatrist who treats a 17-year-old boy (Peter Firth) accused of blinding six horses. The tedium is made bearable only by Burton's presence and the work of a fine supporting cast. The fearful punishment that heterosexuality takes, the violence of the blinding, and the nude scene are unwarranted and insensitive. O (R)

Eraser (1996) A federal agent (Arnold Schwarzenegger) fends off a murderous colleague (James Caan) while protecting the innocent executive (Vanessa Williams) who reported a plot to channel advanced weapons to the Russian Mafia. Charles Russell directs a sleek, fast-paced thriller glamorizing explosive mayhem, huge guns, and vigilante justice. Excessive violence, intermittent profanity, and recurring rough language. O (R)

Ernest Goes to Camp (1987) TV commercial legend Jim Varney plays the slap-happy goon of the title who bears the brunt of juvenile pranks and the callous villainy of some land developers in director John R. Cherry III's lame and often violent slapstick comedy set in a children's summer camp. Ex-football star Lyle Alzado's convincingly brutal beating of the Chaplin-like clown and Ernest's numerous pratfalls are too realistic to be funny. A-III (PG)

Ernest Goes to Jail (1990) When loveable, bumbling bank janitor Ernest (Jim Varney) switches places with a hardened death-row inmate (also Varney), he must escape before he's electrocuted and his lookalike robs the bank. Director John Cherry keeps the slapstick gags flowing nonstop, including one with Ernest as a riotous human magnet and the silly antics of his yokel bank-guard buddies (Gailard Sartain and Bill Byrge). Some prison menace and comic-book violence with extended scenes showing Ernest being zapped with electric shocks. A-II (PG)

Ernest Saves Christmas (1988) A Florida cabby (rubber-mouthed comic Jim Varney) picks up Santa (Douglas Seale) at the Orlando Airport and takes him into town in quest of a younger man to replace him at the North Pole, but they meet up with some disbelief. Directed by John Cherry, it's a holiday hoot with some good virtues for the youngsters. Some hectic traffic pile-ups and tense aerial moments. A-II (PG)

Ernest Scared Stupid (1991) Child-kidnapping troll upsets the Halloween festivities of a small town until a slow-witted resident (Jim Varney) teams with an eccentric recluse (Eartha Kitt) to stop the supernatural monster. Director John Cherry's lame slapstick comedy gets precious few laughs from Varney's labored mugging and goofy anti-troll devices. Recurring threats to children, some frightening special effects, and a few vulgar expressions. A-II (PG)

Erotic Three, The (see: **Scratch Harry**)

Escape Artist, The (1982) Teenager (Griffin O'Neal), trying to measure up to his dead father's reputation as a magician, puts his lock-picking and wallet-lifting skills to good use in exposing a ring of corrupt politicians. Director Caleb Deschanel's offbeat adventure story has a rather underdeveloped plot, but what makes it worth seeing is O'Neal's precocious performance as the plucky youngster who beats an adult world at its own shady game. A-II (PG)

Escape from Alcatraz (1979) Clint Eastwood stars as a convict who attempts the impossible in a taut prison drama about one man's struggle to free himself from the conflicts and brutalities of the one-time island fortress known as the Siberia of prisons. Don Siegel's direction is grim but compelling. Some graphic violence. A-III (PG)

Escape from Fort Bravo (1953) A captured Confederate officer (John Forsythe) is helped by a friend (Eleanor Parker) to escape from a Union outpost in the Arizona badlands, but they're recaptured by a Yankee captain (William Holden), then ambushed by Mescalero Indians. Directed by John Sturges, the cliched story only comes to life in the climactic Indian battle amidst the rugged splendor of Death Valley locales. Stylized violence. A-I (br)

Escape from L.A. (1996) After being separated from the mainland by an earthquake, Los Angeles in 2013 serves as a prison island for undesirables into which a war hero-turned-criminal (Kurt Russell) is sent by the president (Cliff Robertson) to retrieve a doomsday device from a power-mad anarchist (George Corraface). Director John Carpenter's derivative sequel to **Escape from New York** (1981) is chock full of gunfights, chases, and sleek special effects that add up to mindless escapism. Recurring stylized violence, some rough language, and an instance of profanity. A-III (R)

Escape from New York (1981) Futuristic fantasy written and directed by John Carpenter imagines the island of Manhattan as a prison for incorrigible criminals who have taken captive the US president (Donald Pleasence) and a seedy, cynical war hero (Kurt Russell) is sent in to bring him out. It's a clunker with excessive violence, brutality, and sexual innuendo. A-III (R)

Escape from the Planet of the Apes (1971) Third in the series features Roddy McDowall and Kim Hunter as the upright apes from the future who whisk through the time barrier to land in the USA of today. The chaos resulting from mankind's inhumanity to apes provides a so-so adventure that ends in tragedy but hope for the future in the birth a baby ape. The appeal of director Don Taylor's movie is less in its ragged story than in its creation of an imaginative situation and the zesty performances of its two leads. A-I (G)

Escape to Athena (1979) Mediocre WW II movie has to do with a raid on a Nazi communications station in the Mediterranean led by some old familiar faces (Roger Moore, Telly Savalas, Elliott Gould, and David Niven). British production directed by George Pan Cosmatos, it has considerable violence and a few brothel scenes. A-III (PG)

Escape to Burma (1955) Director Allan Dwan wastes a good cast in a dully contrived potboiler set in the Burmese jungles, where an accused murderer (Robert Ryan) gets a job on a teak plantation and wins the heart of its owner (Barbara Stanwyck) until a police officer (David Farrar) arrives looking for him. Some stylized violence and period colonial stereotypes. A-II (br)

Escape to Happiness (see: **Intermezzo**)

Escape to Nowhere (1974) French spy thriller about a physicist (Lino Ventura) who is fleeing for his life from Soviet agents and whose only chance of survival is to trade a Soviet spy for his life. Director Claude Pinoteau has given new life to the old conventions of suspense, with menace and threat everywhere and the most ordinary places concealing potential dangers. A-II (PG)

Escape to the Sun (1972) Heavy, melodramatic escape adventure about a pair of Soviet Jews who hijack an Aeroflot jetliner to land at an abandoned airstrip and pick up a group of Jews hiding nearby. Director Menahem Golan's story is grim in outlook and execution, especially a long torture sequence, and its political implications require mature perspective and sensitivity. A-III (PG)

Escape to Witch Mountain (1975) Above-average Disney adventure about two orphans with supernatural powers who become runaways sought by a greedy millionaire, muddled police, gangsters who think they are witches, and even their own mysterious relatives from another solar system. Younger children will love the fantasy of kids having powers adults don't, but parents may wish that director John Hough had put a little more zest in the action. A-I (G)

E.T., The Extra-Terrestrial (1982) Ugly-duckling fable in which a boy (Henry Thomas) befriends a stranded alien creature from outer space and helps him return to his home. Director Steven Spielberg fashions an inspiring image of youthful innocence and courage in a story that some may find overly sentimental. Nevertheless, the childlike fantasy conveys some genuine emotion and a message of trust and peace that the family might enjoy sharing. A-I (PG)

Eternally Yours (1939) Sour romantic comedy in which a daredevil magician (David Niven) tries to win back his ex-wife (Loretta Young) while she is honeymooning with her new husband (Broderick Crawford). Director Tay Garnett plays up the stylish magic tricks and handcuffed parachute jumps but can't disguise the sentimental applesauce required in healing the broken marriage. Romantic complications and mild sexual innuendo. A-II (br)

Eternity and a Day (1999) Lyric Greek production in which an aging author (Bruno Ganz) prepares to be hospitalized for what he's certain is a terminal illness, then turns his attention to helping a 10-year-old Albanian refugee keep out of harm's way as an undocumented alien, though his thoughts often wander into reveries about past events, real and imaginary. Directed by Theo Angelopoulos, the portrait of a man at the end of his life combines the writer's interior concerns over matters still unresolved in his life with his present efforts on behalf of the young boy in a narrative that uses evocative visuals and compelling performances to intertwine the spiritual and material aspects of human experience. Subtitles. Menacing situations involving children. A-II (nr)

Ethan Frome (1993) Turn-of-the-century love triangle revolves around an impoverished New England farmer (Liam Neeson), his gloomy invalid wife (Joan Allen), and the tragedy that unfolds when her vibrant young cousin (Patricia Arquette) comes to care for her. Based on Edith Wharton's 1911 novel and directed by John Madden, the movie's skillful performances, exquisite cinematography, and evocative music beautifully capture the moral dilemma of the farmer and his wife's cousin. Implied extramarital relationship. A-II (PG-13)

Europa, Europa (1991) Stirring, fact-based story of a Jewish adolescent (Marco Hofschneider) who survives the Holocaust through an incredible series of events, including posing as an Aryan and being sent to an elite Hitler Youth school. Writer-director Agnieszka Holland's superb script is laced with ironic humor and a rich portrait of a youngster grappling with conflicting identities. Subtitles. Some wartime violence, fleeting sexual situations, and occasional male nudity. A-III (R)

Europeans, The (1979) Screen version of the Henry James novel is a quiet comedy of manners about the unsettling effect of their European cousins (Lee Remick and Robin Ellis) upon the Wentworths, a proper Bostonian family. Though pleasant enough to watch, director James Ivory's moderately entertaining period piece lacks a sense of vitality and the feel for life that is to be found in the original. A-II (nr)

Eve of Destruction (1991) Anti-terrorist expert (Gregory Hines) sets out to destroy a rogue robot that looks exactly like its creator (Renee Soutendijk) but is equipped with a nuclear capability that could destroy Manhattan. Duncan Gibbins directs an appallingly slick sci-fi thriller with little on its mind but assaulting viewers. Excessive violence, constant rough language, nasty sexual innuendo, brief nudity, and menace to a child. O (R)

Eve's Bayou (1997) Poignant drama set in 1962 Louisiana, where a precocious 10-year-old (Jurnee Smollett) observes how her family is affected by the womanizing of their prosperous doctor father (Samuel L. Jackson), which culminates in a violent tragedy. Writer-director Kasi Lemmons's beautifully lyric tale probes human failings, though the result is marred by the action's melodramatic treatment. Mature theme of adultery, fleeting sexual encounters, brief violence, intermittent rough language, and profanity. A-III (R)

Evel Knievel (1971) Dramatization, with George Hamilton playing a real-life character whose story this slapdash movie purports to be, from growing up in Butte, Montana, and getting started on the motorcycle circuit, to preparing for his impossible jump over 19 cars. Director Marvin Chomsky's portrayal of a man driven by the desire to forever outdo himself in order to fend off personal insecurities has a passing interest, but Evel's amiable antics do not completely redeem the immaturity of his feelings about death or the cynical attitude of those fans who watch hoping for the worst. A-III (GP)

Even Cowgirls Get the Blues (1994) Failed adaptation of Tom Robbins's 1976 seriocomic novel about an aimless hitchhiker (Uma Thurman) who falls into a lesbian affair with the leader (Rain Phoenix) of a ranch taken over by radical feminist cowgirls. Writer-director Gus Van Sant's disjointed narrative features wooden dialogue delivered by vacuous performers in this thoroughly forgettable look at the counterculture of the '70s. Restrained treatment of a lesbian relationship, fleeting nudity, brief violence, recreational drug use, and minimal rough language. A-III (R)

Even Dwarfs Started Small (1972) Pretentious German movie in which the head of some kind of correctional institution is forced to barricade himself inside his office while crude male and female midget inmates wreak havoc upon the facilities and one another. Director Werner Herzog has come up with a visually striking, emotionally disturbing, curiosity piece which will tax the patience of most viewers. A-IV (nr)

Evening Star, The (1996) Spirited sequel to 1983's **Terms of Endearment** continues the story of the strong-willed grandmother (Shirley MacLaine) and her problems with the three grandchildren she raised as she pursues romance with a decades-younger therapist (Bill Paxton), despite the opposition of her long-time maid (Marion Ross), and adoring neighbor (Donald Moffat). Writer-director Robert Harling paces the drama with plenty of heart and comic sassiness as the imperious matriarch comes to terms with her progeny's independence and her own mortality. Restrained bedroom scenes, minimal rough language, and an instance of profanity. A-III (PG-13)

Evening with the Royal Ballet, An (1965) Filmed on stage at the Royal Opera House in London, the work features Margot Fonteyn and Rudolph Nureyev in the performance of four ballets and two encores. Directed by Anthony Asquith and Anthony Havelock-Allan, it is a record of a prime ballet event marred only by static camerawork. A-I (br)

Event, An (1970) Yugoslavian adaptation of a short story by Chekhov relates a simple, tragic tale of a little boy and his grandfather who take a horse to the market and are waylaid on their return. Directed by Vatroslav Mimica, the hauntingly beautiful photography and credible acting of the small cast help make this small but terrible event an emotional experience of universal dimension. A-III (nr)

Event Horizon (1997) Gory sci-fi clunker in which the captain (Laurence Fishburne) of a rescue mission to a derelict spaceship finds it controlled by an evil force that decimates his crew. Directed by Paul Anderson, the films' futuristic spaceship sets are more imaginative than the muddled plot, which winds down in pools of blood and other grisly special effects. Excessive violence, flashes of nudity, and much rough language. O (R)

Ever After (1998) Medieval romance from the Cinderella story of a young Frenchwoman (Drew Barrymore) whose wicked stepmother (Anjelica Huston) has raised her as little more than a servant until her wit, beauty, and intelligence win the heart of the bemused crown prince (Dougray Scott), though many complications intervene before the traditional happy ending. Directed by Andy Tennant, the 16th-century setting and costumes provide a fairytale atmosphere for proceedings built around a spunky, self-sufficient heroine who takes the lead in the action, with often amusing and, at times, heartwarming results. Some stylized violence, menace, and crude language. A-II (PG-13/PG)

Everlasting Secret Family, The (1989) Unconvincing Australian drama about a government official (Arthur Dignam) who operates a secret society that procures young prep students for affluent homosexuals. Directed by Michael Thornhill, the movie largely romanticizes its story of sexual and political corruption. Some nudity in explicit, titillating homosexual encounters. O (nr)

Every Bastard a King (1970) Israeli movie set during the Six Day War is a contrived potboiler about an American journalist (William Berger) trying to understand the new society of Israel. Director Uri Zohar's title refers to the Israeli's spirit of democracy, but the movie itself manages to turn an interesting subject into a mediocre and incredibly muddled melodrama. A-III (GP)

Every Girl Should Be Married (1948) Heavy-handed romantic comedy directed by Don Hartman in which a strong-willed young woman (Betsy Drake) sets out to marry a happy bachelor pediatrician (Cary Grant) but, along the way, has to fend off the unwanted attentions of a wealthy would-be suitor (Franchot Tone). Romantic complications. A-II (br)

Every Little Crook and Nanny (1972) The nanny of the title (Lynn Redgrave) revenges the loss of her dancing school by kidnapping the young son of the crime boss responsible (Victor Mature). Director Cy Howard plays the situation comedy for dumb, at times coarse, laughs. A-III (PG)

Every Other Weekend (1991) Quiet, poignant French production in which a divorced actress (Nathalie Baye) impulsively takes her two young children out of Paris in violation of her custody agreement and heads for Spain with them, with her anxious ex-husband (Miki Manojlovic) in pursuit. Director Nicole Garcia's melancholy first feature takes a vague and inconclusive look at a woman's self-absorption and the price she and her family pay for it. Subtitles. Family arguments with minor violence. A-II (nr)

Every Time We Say Goodbye (1986) Iowa minister's son (Tom Hanks) joins the British Royal Air Force during WW II, meets a Jewish-Hispanic girl living in Palestine, and convinces her to wait for him to return after the war. The overdone, glossy romance has some positive value in exploring the meaning of full commitment required for marriage. Bedroom scene and some violence. A-III (PG-13)

Every Which Way But Loose (1979) Clint Eastwood stars as a footloose trucker and barroom brawler who falls in love with a fickle country-western singer (Sondra Locke). Supporting characters includes an orangutan and Ruth Gordon as a foul-mouthed old lady whose antics and vocabulary are supposed to be funny. Director James Fargo's slipshod movie features unremitting violence and sick humor. O (PG)

Everybody Does It (1949) Domestic comedy about a would-be singer (Celeste Holm) whose disapproving husband (Paul Douglas) is encouraged by an opera star (Linda Darnell) to become a professional singer. Directed by Edmund Goulding, this remake of **Wife, Husband and Friend** has a great cast, plenty of laughs, but never quite pulls it all together. Romantic situations. A-II (br)

Everybody Sing (1937) Fanciful Depression-era comedy about a wacky theatrical family (Billie Burke and Reginald Owen) saved from the poor house when their adolescent daughter (Judy Garland) teams up with the family's cook (Allan Jones) and maid (Fanny Brice) to stage a smash Broadway revue. Directed by Edwin L. Marin, the performances are spirited, but the material is badly dated (including Garland's black-face number) and the songs unmemorable. More a curiosity piece than entertaining fare for youngsters today. A-I (br)

Everybody Wins (1990) Sexually promiscuous, emotionally unstable New England woman (Debra Winger) baffles a private detective (Nick Nolte) with her puzzling offer to help him prove his client did not murder her physician. Scriptwriter Arthur Miller, director Karel Reisz, and a gifted cast sustain the thriller's mood of intrigue, but can't salvage the muddled exposition nor fill the holes in a plot involving judicial corruption. Some menace and promiscuity with veiled nudity, a graphic scene of violence, and incidental rough language. A-III (R)

Everybody's All-American (1988) The 25-year-saga of the rise and fall of a Louisiana football hero (Dennis Quaid) and his Southern-belle wife (Jessica Lange). Director Taylor Hackford's entertaining romance raises questions about hero worship and also touches on integration and other cultural changes affecting the South from 1956 to 1981. Brief sexual scenes, a flash of nudity, some bloody violence, and vulgar language. A-III (R)

Everybody's Cheering (see: **Take Me Out to the Ball Game**)

Everybody's Fine (1991) Poignant family drama follows an elderly Sicilian patriarch (Marcello Mastroianni) as he travels across Italy to visit his five grown children on a journey that proves full of bittersweet surprises and revelations. Director Giuseppe Tornatore blends Mastroianni's superlative performance into a wryly observed depiction of modern Italian life and personal predicaments. Subtitles. References to premarital pregnancy, promiscuity, suicide, and a flash of nudity. A-III (PG-13)

Everyone Says I Love You (1996) Frivolous musical comedy centering on the flighty love lives of an extended family of wealthy New Yorkers, including Drew Barrymore, Alan Alda, and Goldie Hawn, whose neurotic ex-husband, Woody Allen, lives in Paris. Also written and directed by Allen, the low-key story uses a cast of non-singers to gently spoof movie musical conventions, but the results are decidedly mixed. An extramarital affair, occasional profanity, and an instance of rough language. A-III (R)

Everything but the Truth (1956) Saccharine formula comedy directed by Jerry Hopper centers on the escalating problems caused when a young boy (Tim Hovey) accuses a local politician of graft, refuses to recant, then becomes a national celebrity after his teacher (Maureen O'Hara) gets a syndicated columnist (John Forsythe) to come to the boy's defense. Romantic complications and a child subjected to various adult pressures. A-I (br)

Everything You Always Wanted to Know About Sex But Were Afraid to Ask (1972) Writer-director Woody Allen's take-off on Dr. David Reuben's book and the curiosity that made it a bestseller does better debunking sex obsessions than sex itself. The result is an uneven jumble of sketches, most of which go on too long, and range from the witty to the perverse, from hilarious sight gags to crudely offensive material. O (R)

Everything's Ducky (1961) Mindless comedy drags out the slapstick efforts of numbskull sailors Mickey Rooney and Buddy Hackett to save a talking duck from being used in a Navy missile experiment. Directed by Don Taylor, the situation is tiresome, though the duck proves easier to take than his booby pals. Unimaginative fare without charm or appeal for young minds. A-I (br)

Evil Mind, The (1934) Creaky but intriguing British melodrama directed by Maurice Elvey in which a music-hall mind-reader (Claude Rains) gets into serious trouble after making accurate predictions of the future when his psychic powers are triggered by a woman admirer (Jane Baxter) until his wife (Fay Wray) intervenes. Some stylized violence and romantic complications. A-II (br)

Evil of Frankenstein, The (1964) Returning to his crumbling chateau in the mountains of Karlstaad, Dr. Frankenstein (Peter Cushing) discovers his monster (Kiwi Kingston) frozen in a glacier, but after being revived the creature goes on a crime spree under the control of a greedy hypnotist (Peter Woodthrope). Directed by Freddie Francis, the British production is let down by an unimpressive monster and a hokey script which offers little in the way of suspense. Stylized violence and a brief sexual situation. A-II (br)

Evil That Men Do, The (1984) Soldier-of-fortune (Charles Bronson) is hired to kill a political despot. Director Lee J. Thompson's violent action vehicle is set against the background of an oppressive regime in Central America, but sidesteps any serious political commentary in favor of the usual excessively brutal melodrama. O (R)

Evil Under the Sun (1982) Hercule Poirot (Peter Ustinov) is the thoughtful sleuth on a mission in the Adriatic in this fairly amusing adaptation of the Agatha Christie story. Director Guy Hamilton's British production turns the mystery into a travelogue which, lacking suspense, allows a talented cast free reign. The dialogue contains a few double entendres meant as witty insults. A-II (PG)

Evita (1996) Lavish adaptation of the Andrew Lloyd Webber musical about Eva Peron (Madonna), who rose from illegitimacy and poverty to marry Argentinean dictator Juan Peron (Jonathan Pryce) and attract the adulation of the masses before dying of cancer in 1952 at age 33. Writer-director Alan Parker's polished but hardly riveting musical drama explores the conflicting images of Evita as both saint and sinner. Premarital promiscuity and violent riot scenes. A-III (PG)

Excalibur (1981) Long and lavish retelling of the legendary story of King Arthur (Nigel Terry) and his tutor Merlin (Nicol Williamson) is distinguished by an earnest sincerity and by its impressive settings, visual effects, and cinematography. The treatment emphasizes the folk magic elements of the legend rather than its early Christian origin. In striving for effect, however, director John Boorman overdoes the sex and violence. O (R)

Excess Baggage (1997) Mirthless comedy in which a neglected teen (Alicia Silverstone) tires to stage her own kidnapping by getting in the trunk of a car, which is then stolen by a thief (Benicio Del Toro) unaware of her presence. Directed by Marco Brambilla, the witless narrative rambles aimlessly on as a host of unsympathetic characters vie to cash in on the ransom. Brief violence, underage drinking, sexual innuendo, and intermittent profanity. A-III (PG-13)

Execution Protocol, The (1993) Challenging documentary takes a clear-eyed view of what capital punishment means to those sentenced to die as well as to those responsible for executing them. Filmed by Steven Trombley at Missouri's Potosi Correction Center, where the death sentence is carried out by a lethal injection machine, officials explain its humane application while death-row inmates describe it as "premeditated murder," leaving viewers confronting capital punishment not as a legal abstraction but as a troubling human reality. Grim subject and unsettling treatment. A-III (nr)

Executioner, The (1970) British spy thriller about an agent (George Peppard) who suspects a top-level government security leak and takes it upon himself to execute the person he believes responsible. Director Sam Wanamaker emphasizes gray areas of conscience and morality in a setting of violence and intrigue, but the plot is unnecessarily complicated and lacking in subtlety, sympathy, and credibility. A-III (GP)

Executive Action (1973) Failed political thriller about a conspiracy of right-wing millionaires who are behind the assassination of President John F. Kennedy neglects to offer any coherent, convincing demonstration of its fictional premise. Director David Miller wastes a good cast (Robert Ryan, Burt Lancaster, and Will Geer) in a static movie that is disturbing only in its inability to stir even pathos for the fallen president. A-III (PG)

Executive Decision (1996) Unbeknownst to the fanatical terrorist (David Suchet) holding 400 passengers hostage on a jumbo jet headed to Washington, DC, a hostage rescue team (led by Kurt Russell) is in the freight deck desperately trying to defuse a bomb attached to enough nerve gas to decimate the East Coast upon landing. Director Stuart Baird's action thriller offers several unexpected plot twists, but is overlong and overly complicated, weakening it in the suspense department. Some violence, recurring profanity, and an instance of rough language. A-III (R)

eXistenZ (1999) Muddled sci-fi tale in which an electronic-game designer (Jennifer Jason Leigh) and her inexperienced bodyguard (Jude Law) get lost in the labyrinths of her latest virtual-reality creation, then return to the real world with a blurred sense of what is actual and what imaginary. Directed by David Cronenberg, the story is a "Twilight Zone" type of fantasy, but the meandering plot grows increasingly arbitrary and ultimately tiresome long before the bogus twist ending. Stylized fantasy violence, ghoulish body plugs and game pods, sexual innuendo, and occasional rough language. A-III (R)

Ex-Mrs. Bradford, The (1936) Suave amateur detective (William Powell) teams with dizzy ex-wife (Jean Arthur) to solve a series of racetrack murders along the way to inevitable remarriage. Director Stephen Roberts gets surprisingly little comic mileage out of the Powell-Arthur pairing in a routine mystery which resembles but lacks the class of the **Thin Man** series. Mild menace. A-I (br)

Exodus (1960) Long and lavish adaptation of the Leon Uris novel about the birth of Israel follows the exploits of a Jewish underground leader (Paul Newman) in rescuing refugees interned by the British on Cyprus, freeing partisans from a British prison in Acre, and saving a Jewish village from Arab attack after the 1948 UN partition of Palestine. Directed by Otto Preminger, the idealistic narrative is partly seen through the perspective of an American widow (Eva Marie Saint) whose visit to the Near East brings romance and an understanding of the need for a Jewish state. Some graphic violence including terrorist acts and sexual references. A-III (br)

Exorcist, The (1974) Strong screen version of the William Blatty novel about the demonic possession of a young girl (Linda Blair) and the attempts of two priests (Jason Miller and Max von Sydow) to exorcise the devil from her. Directed by William Friedkin, the movie is on shaky ground theologically, and its special effects are horrific, but the result is an exciting horror fantasy for those with strong stomachs. Its graphic violence, obscene references, and foul language make it strictly adult fare. A-IV (R)

Exorcist II: The Heretic (1977) It is four years later and Reagan (Linda Blair), still bothered by a demon, is in the care of a psychiatrist (Louise Fletcher) who gets some help from a priest (Richard Burton) assigned to investigate the case. Director John Boorman's crass sequel, through simple ineptitude or outright ignorance, manages to denigrate a whole range of religious values. Some violence and profanity. O (R)

Exorcist III, The (1990) Heavy-handed sequel pits an intelligent Georgetown detective (George C. Scott) against the diabolical deeds committed by an executed serial killer (Brad Dourif) whose soul has taken possession of the body of the priest (Jason Miller) who was killed at the conclusion of the original. Writer-director William Peter Blatty turns in a flawed horror movie with a slack plot but plenty of colorful characters and eerie photography. Several grisly scenes of demonic violence, many detailed verbal descriptions of bizarre murders, and some instances of defiled religious symbols. A-IV (R)

Exotica (1995) Dark, quirky puzzler about lost lives slowly unwinds in a sleazy strip club whose young star (Mia Kirschner) becomes an obsession for a regular customer (Bruce Greenwood), until one night he's brutally ejected from the club by its nasty disk jockey (Elias Koteas), then returns to get revenge with the aid of a homosexual smuggler (Don McKellar). Canadian director Atom Egoyen's lurid club setting dominates the narrative's sluggish story line, which has little meaning until the final reel and then seems hardly worth the effort. Voyeuristic nudity, implied sexual encounters, and occasional rough language. O (R)

Experiment Perilous (1944) Clumsy turn-of-the-century melodrama in which a doctor (George Brent) tries to save a woman (Hedy Lamarr) from the cruel manipulations of her psychotic husband (Paul Lukas). Directed by Jacques Tourneur, the story unfolds in lumpy flashbacks that belabor the obvious. Psychological blather and stylized violence. A-II (br)

Explorers, The (1985) Three 12-year-old boys, inspired by dreams, rig up their own spaceship and have some unusual close encounters. Moderately entertaining, but too much time is spent on the preliminaries with the outer-space payoff not packing the punch that it was meant to, namely some kind of profound lesson that lies beyond the cinematic vocabulary of director Joe Dante. Some profanity in the mouths of the young space cadets. A-II (PG)

Explosion (1970) Canadian movie about a disturbed youth (Gordon Thomson) whose anti-Vietnam views supposedly cause him to rape a woman, flee to Canada, and join a local hippie (Don Stroud) on an orgy of sex and violence in British Columbia. Director Jules Bricken's one-dimensional melodrama is hopelessly confused with flashbacks and fantasy sequences that rely for interest on bloodshed and nudity. O (R/GP)

Exposed (1983) Wisconsin farm girl (Nastassia Kinski) becomes a hot New York model and falls for a concert violinist (Rudolf Nureyev) who turns out to be a notorious terrorist tracking down his mother's murderer (Harvey Keitel). Director James Toback's shallow and silly vehicle exploits serious issues in an attempt to appear chic and witty. Excessive graphic sexuality. O (R)

Exterminating Angel, The (1967) A number of wealthy party guests find that after a long night in the home of their host, they are unable to leave, held by some mysterious force. In the days that follow, their veneer of politeness disintegrates until raw ego shows through. When finally released from each other's presence, they gather in a church to celebrate their deliverance, only to discover themselves once again unable to leave. Director Luis Bunuel's 1962 surrealistic satire amusingly suggests that hell is other people. A-III (br)

Exterminator, The (see: **The Inheritor**)

Extraordinary Seaman, The (1969) WW II action fantasy in which a captain in the Royal Navy (David Niven) who died in 1914 is granted a celestial reprieve to vindicate an inglorious death by taking on the Japanese Navy with his dilapidated island steamer. Director John Frankenheimer fails in an embarrassingly bad effort to keep this seagoing bomb afloat. A-II (G)

Extreme Close-Up (1973) Researching a story on electronic surveillance techniques, a reporter (James McMullan) becomes obsessed with the easily obtainable gadgets of the trade and their potential for invading the private lives of innocent people. Director Jeannot Szwarc uses Michael Crichton's screenplay simply as a vehicle for spying upon the sexual escapades of a rather dull group of characters. O (R)

Extreme Measures (1996) Routine thriller in which a doctor (Hugh Grant) stumbles onto a diabolical conspiracy led by a famed neurosurgeon (Gene Hackman) who's using homeless men as disposable human guinea pigs in medical experiments. Directed by Michael Apted, the story builds initial suspense, then succumbs to the cliches of a mad-scientist plot with a far-fetched, overwrought finale. Sporadic violence, much profanity, and rough language. A-III (R)

Extreme Prejudice (1987) Nick Nolte plays a bulletproof Texas Ranger poised to stamp out a drug-traffic kingpin (Powers Boothe) with the aid of a ruthless commando group made up of legally dead Vietnam vets headed by a double-crossing major (Michael Ironside). Director Walter Hill's lengthy sequences of excessively brutal gunplay and some nudity mark this as a conventional blood-and-guts time-waster. O (R)

Extremities (1986) A woman (Farrah Fawcett) is the target of a sadistic rapist (James Russo) whom she manages to restrain and molest in turn. Film plays upon the vulnerability of women in a man's world and suggests that fighting back is an essential survival tactic. It concludes somewhat weakly that justice must be tempered with mercy in spite of possible further endangerment. Instead of being thought-provoking, the film brutalizes the viewer with explicit scenes of sadism, violence, and foul language. O (R)

Eye for an Eye (1996) When the cold-blooded murderer (Kiefer Sutherland) of her teenage daughter is freed on a legal technicality, then threatens her five-year-old, a terrified mother (Sally Field) plots to kill him and get away with it. Director John Schlesinger's emotionally manipulative melodrama blurs the distinction between premeditated murder and justified self-defense. Brief but intense violence including rape, ambiguous treatment of murder, and intermittent rough language. A-IV (R)

Eye for an Eye, An (1966) Routine Western directed by Michael Moore in which a former bounty hunter (Robert Lansing) teams with a young bounty hunter (Pat Wayne) to take revenge on the villains who brutally murdered his wife and son. Stylized violence, and the revenge is accomplished through self-defense. A-II (br)

Eye of God (1997) Brooding drama set in rural Oklahoma, where a distraught, orphaned teen (Nick Stahl) is befriended by a troubled young woman (Martha Plimpton) who has married a born-again ex-con (Kevin Anderson) despite his refusal to reveal the crime for which he was imprisoned. Writer-director Tim Blake Nelson builds the mystery-laden narrative to a shattering climax in a tale of psychotic madness hiding behind fundamentalist ravings. Brief violence with grisly shots of corpses, an explicit abortion scene, fleeting nudity, and some rough language, as well as profanity. A-IV (R)

Eye of the Cat (1969) San Francisco mansion full of cats is the setting for the story of two nephews (Michael Sarrazin and Tim Henry) scheming to eliminate a rich, but ailing, aunt (Eleanor Parker) and each other in order to inherit her fortune. Director David Lowell Rich manipulates the cats for shock and suspense effect but not enough to cover the gaping holes in the plot. Some violence and sexual implications. A-III (PG)

Eye of the Devil (1967) The head of an aristocratic French family (David Niven) journeys to his ancestral chateau to offer himself as a victim in a religious rite practiced by his forbears. Under the direction of J. Lee Thompson, the performances of Niven and Deborah Kerr compensate for a plot that often strains credibility. A-III (br)

Eye of the Needle (1981) Mediocre British screen version of Ken Follett's WW II thriller in which a coldly proficient German spy (Donald Sutherland) becomes distracted from his mission when he encounters a love-starved woman (Kate Nelligan) on a bleak island off the coast of Scotland. Directed by Richard Marquand, the unabsorbing melodrama combines a conventional espionage plot with a needlessly explicit depiction of a love affair. O (R)

Eyes of a Stranger (1981) Sadistic rapist-murderer (John DiSanti) stalks the blind adolescent sister (Jennifer Jason Leigh) of a television reporter (Lauren Tewes) in this sleazy, amateurish horror movie. Director Ken Wiederhorn's suspense thriller forfeits finesse in favor of stomach-churning violence and nudity. O (R)

Eyes of Hell (see: 1961's **The Mask**)

Eyes of Laura Mars, The (1978) Failed thriller about a series of brutal murders that happen exactly as seen in the premonitions of a top New York fashion photographer (Faye Dunaway). The shallow, slick, kinky movie directed by Irvin Kershner leeringly exploits sex and violence. O (R)

Eyes Wide Shut (1999) A failed cautionary tale about a mixed-up Manhattan physician (Tom Cruise) who sneaks into a satanic cult's sex orgy, from which he barely escapes with his life to return home a more sober husband to his wife (Nicole Kidman). Director Stanley Kubrick's final picture is a major disappointment in its cold-hearted, heavy-handed treatment of shallow characters in thinly contrived situations that fail to elicit any empathy. Graphic sex scenes, full nudity, drug use, and rough language. O (R)

Eyewitness (1981) A young janitor (William Hurt) falls in love with a television reporter (Sigourney Weaver) whom he has never met, and, when she asks him questions about a murder committed in his building, he pretends to know more about the crime than he actually does. Director Peter Yates's romantic mystery succeeds better in terms of characterization of the young couple than its muddled attempts at suspense. Some violence and a rather graphic bedroom scene. A-III (R)

F for Fake (1973) Rambling documentary narrated by Orson Welles, who uses the examples of an admitted art forger named Elmyr de Hory and Clifford Irving, author of a bogus biography of Howard Hughes, to expound on the relationship between illusion, reality, and truth. Also directed by Welles, the result is a slipshod essay in flimflam which tries too hard to be amusing. Ambiguous treatment of forgery and brief nudity. A-III

FM (1978) Lightweight, derivative comedy about a popular radio station which is taken over by its disc jockeys because they refuse to contaminate their music with unsuitable commercials. Under John A. Alonzo's direction, the characters are uninteresting and the jokes feeble. Some highly suggestive dialogue. A-III (PG)

F.T.A. (1972) Filmed record of performers Jane Fonda, Donald Sutherland, and troupe staging a series of anti-war shows outside military bases in the US and in the Pacific. The group as a whole looks rather sappy, but the show's politics, which is what it is all about, is as worthy of a platform as those of Bob Hope's Christmas troupe. A-III (nr)

F/X (1986) Tough suspense thriller concerning a movie special-effects expert (Bryan Brown) asked by a government agency to stage a fake killing, but who then finds himself hunted by the police for murder and shot at by unknown assassins. The plot is full of holes, but director Robert Mandel rivets attention on the action's twists and turns. There is some intense violence, but because the movie is about the trickery of special effects, the fake blood and gore is unlikely to offend most adult moviegoers. A-IV (R)

F/X 2 — The Deadly Art of Illusion (1991) A special-effects expert (Bryan Brown) and a retired detective (Brian Dennehy) re-team to uncover why a cop (Tom Mason) was set up by his boss (Philip Bosco) to be rubbed out. Brown and Dennehy's appealing chemistry partially makes up for the contrived and convoluted plot in director Richard Franklin's rough, action-packed movie. Intermittent gory violence and brief shower nudity. A-III (PG-13)

Fabulous Baker Boys, The (1989) Demoralized piano-playing brother team (Jeff and Beau Bridges) on the Seattle cocktail-lounge circuit briefly revitalize their stale act with a sultry female singer (Michelle Pfeiffer), who catalyzes the men to face some hard, personal realities. The acting of the principals is fine and writer-director Steve Kloves has a feel for these fringe performers and the poignant unraveling of family ties. Some profanity laced with sexual vulgarities and brief sexual situations with a flash of nudity. A-III (R)

Fabulous Dorseys, The (1947) The Dorsey brothers play themselves in this screen biography, as trombonist Tommy and saxophonist Jimmy leave Pennsylvania to take their jazz band on the road in the 1920s, then quarrel and go their separate ways to fame and fortune with their own dance bands. Directed by Alfred E. Green, the routine dramatization overplays the bickering brothers' rivalry, though the main attraction here is the movie's showcase of pop standards performed by the Dorseys, Paul Whiteman and other period bands. A-I (br)

Face in the Crowd, A (1957) Cautionary tale about an Arkansas drifter (Andy Griffith) whose homespun appeal is discovered by a local radio producer (Patricia Neal). He then goes on to become a national television star, but his ambitious ego and nasty disposition ultimately make him a dangerous political force. Directed by Elia Kazan from Budd Schulberg's savvy script, the result takes a close look at the media's power to influence and manipulate, a theme given credibility by Griffith's chilling two-faced performance, but the story itself grows increasingly contrived and predictable. Sexual situations and innuendo. A-III (br)

Face of a Fugitive (1959) Clumsy Western in which a man (Fred MacMurray) on the run from a false charge of murder arrives in a town where he's unknown, then risks discovery by staying on to help its citizens, including the sheriff. Director Paul Wendkos can do little with a contrived plot, talky script, and wooden acting. Stylized violence. A-II (br)

Face to Face (1976) Stockholm psychiatrist (Liv Ullmann) discovers that she must heal herself when she suffers from a nervous breakdown in director Ingmar Bergman's clinical investigation into the realm of the feminine psyche. Ullmann's magnificent performance conveys the failure of psychiatry as a remedy to the disappointments and contradictions of her guilt-ridden life. The movie includes some harrowing scenes, including an attempted rape, but the emphasis is on the interior journey to peace of soul. A-III (R)

Face/Off (1997) Ultra-violent action movie in which the faces of a crusading federal agent (John Travolta) and a sociopathic terrorist (Nicolas Cage) are surgically switched, enabling the criminal to pose as the law officer in deadly pursuit of his nemesis. Directed by John Woo, the slickly contrived premise is used mainly to provide many protracted and gratuitous scenes of murderous bloodshed and mayhem. Excessive violence, sexual innuendo, and much profanity and rough language. O (R)

Faces (1968) Director John Cassavetes' intense study of the marital crisis of a middle-aged, middle-class couple (Gena Rowlands and John Marley) who discover that divorce isn't the answer to their personal emptiness and despairing search for meaning in life. Troubling, sardonic, somewhat depressing treatment of a mature theme that is part of so many contemporary relationships. Some rough language, sexual innuendo, and a suicide attempt. A-IV (R)

Faces of Love (1978) A movie director (Jean-Louis Trintignant) tries to win back his ex-wife (Delphine Seyrig) by starring her in an adaptation of Chekhov's *The Three Sisters* (with Lea Massari and Valerie Mairesse as the other leads). Swiss director Michael Soutter wastes a talented cast on what is in effect a shallow exercise in psychodrama. A-III (nr)

Faculty, The (1998) Inept sci-fi horror tale in which a malevolent alien force from outer space begins taking over the teachers, then the students, of a decrepit high school, until a diverse group of students (led by Elijah Wood as the school nerd) go into action. Directed by Robert Rodriguez, the derivative plot has some scary effects but little suspense, with the slack taken up by the teenagers' preoccupation with sex and drugs. Gory violence, sexual references and innuendo, the use of narcotics as a plot device, recurring rough language, and occasional profanity. O (R)

Fade to Black (1980) Muddled, unsavory tale directed by Vernon Zimmerman centers on a frustrated young man (Dennis Christopher) who escapes the rigors of reality by living in a dream world nourished by murderous fantasies derived from movies. Excessive violence and sordid atmosphere. O (R)

Fahrenheit 451 (1966) A fireman (Oskar Werner) reforms his book-burning ways in this adaptation of Ray Bradbury's science-fiction novel about a society that forbids the printed word. First rate performances by Julie Christie in a dual role as two women in the fireman's life and Cyril Cusack as a smiling fanatic help sustain the dream-like reality of director Francois Truffaut's allegorical fantasy. Menacing atmosphere. A-II (br)

Fail Safe (1964) A mechanical failure makes impossible the recall of nuclear bombers headed for Russia in a movie questioning the ability of humans to control their inventions. Sidney Lumet directs Henry Fonda, Dan O'Herlihy, and various machines with mounting suspense. A-II (br)

Fair Game (1995) Senseless thriller about a Miami cop (William Baldwin) protecting a confused lawyer (Cindy Crawford) from a hit squad of ex-Soviet agents on a computer fraud caper. Directed by Andrew Sipes, the hammy performances match the cheesy marathon of violent special effects and bloody shootouts which pass for the plot. Excessive violence, a shadowy sexual encounter, flashes of nudity, and much rough language. O (R)

Fair Wind to Java (1953) Fair adventure tale of a Yankee sea captain (Fred MacMurray) fighting pirates in the Dutch East Indies while getting some help from a native dancer (Vera Ralston) in locating a treasure in diamonds hidden on the volcanic island of Krakatoa just before it explodes in 1883. Directed by Joseph Kane, the action is slowed by various conspiracies aboard ship and ashore, but the ending is suitably suspenseful and the volcano's eruption is quite spectacular even by today's standards. Stylized violence including a torture scene and a woman assaulted by a drunken sailor. A-II (br)

Fairy Tale: A True Story (1997) Romanticized account of the controversy stirred in 1917 England by two little girls whose photographs of what they said were tiny fairies frolicking in their garden aroused the skepticism of Harry Houdini (Harvey Keitel), though were proclaimed genuine by Sir Arthur Conan Dthey oyle (Peter O'Toole). Director Charles Sturridge spins an enchanting tale of childhood innocence in a sweet family film marred by a few rude words. Serious argumentation over the existence of fairies and fleeting mild language. A-II (PG)

Faithful (1996) Nasty black comedy in which a depressed wife (Cher) turns the tables on her philandering husband (Ryan O'Neal) and the hitman (Chazz Palminteri) he has hired to kill her on their 20th wedding anniversary. The laughs are hollow in director Paul Mazursky's talky and mean-spirited look at marital infidelity. Off-screen murders, many adulterous references, minimal profanity, and constant rough language. O (R)

Falcon and the Co-eds, The (1943) Creaky murder mystery directed by William Clemens in which the suave private eye (Tom Conway) of this detective series investigates several deaths connected with a girl's school. Stylized violence and mild sexual innuendo. A-II (br)

Falcon and the Snowman, The (1985) Some boyhood friends, now young men (Timothy Hutton and Sean Penn), sell secret data to the Soviets. How all this happened and why is an engrossing and very well-acted story, but director John Schlesinger has left too many loose ends and tends to sentimentalize these treasonous actions as mistaken idealism. Brief nudity, some drug use, and ambivalent treatment of a complex subject. A-III (R)

Falcon in Danger, The (1943) Intriguing mystery directed by William Clemens with series hero (Tom Conway) cracking a case involving a pilotless plane, a kidnapped industrialist, blackmailers, and murder. Some stylized violence and threatening situations. A-I (br)

Falcon in San Francisco, The (1945) Thin series entry directed by Joseph H. Lewis in which the title sleuth (Tom Conway) and his assistant (Edward Brophy) interrupt their 'Frisco vacation to help a distressed child (Sharyn Moffett) overcome problems caused by a bickering gang of murderous smugglers. Stylized violence and veiled sexual innuendo. A-II (br)

Falcon Out West, The (1944) Change of pace for this mystery series, as director William Clemens takes the dapper crime-buster (Tom Conway) from his usual Manhattan haunts to find a murderer on a Texas ranch complete with cowboys and Indians. Stylized violence and romantic complications. A-II (br)

Falcon Strikes Back, The (1943) Formula mystery directed by Edward Dmytryk with the series sleuth (Tom Conway) and his wise-cracking aide (Cliff Edwards) suspected of stealing war bonds in a caper whose suspects include a resort manager (Harriet Hilliard) and a veteran puppeteer (Edgar Kennedy). Minimal violence and romantic by-play. A-II (br)

Falcon's Adventure, The (1945) Tired formula mystery directed by William Berke with series hero (Tom Conway) and comic sidekick (Edward Brophy) in Miami thwarting a gang after a formula for making synthetic diamonds. Minimal stylized violence. A-I (br)

Falcon's Alibi, The (1946) Routine mystery directed by Ray McCarey in which the suave private eye (Tom Conway) nabs a murderer after locating some missing pearls in a case involving, among other, a radio disk-jockey (Elisha Cook, Jr.) and his two-timing wife (Jane Greer). Some stylized violence and romantic complications. A-II (br)

Falcon's Brother, The (1942) Routine murder case directed by Stanley Logan leads to the smashing of an Axis spy ring, but the plot is most notable for killing off the series' dapper sleuth, Gaylord Lawrence (George Sanders), and replacing him with his brother Tom (Tom Conway, Sanders real-life brother). Stylized violence. A-I (br)

Fall of the House of Usher, The (see: **House of Usher**)

Fall of the Roman Empire, The (1964) In this lavish historical re-creation, Rome's wise old emperor Marcus Aurelius (Alec Guinness) is poisoned by his corrupt son (Christopher Plummer), whose savage policies against the barbarians brings the teetering empire to its ruin. Directed by Anthony Mann, the three-hour dramatization has an autumnal splendor that one can admire, yet find the spectacle unmoving on a human level. Stylized battle scenes and other assorted violence may frighten young children. A-I (br)

Fallen (1998) Silly supernatural chiller in which a homicide detective (Denzel Washington) realizes he is being framed for murders committed by the demonic spirit of an executed serial killer. Directed by Gregory Hoblit, the ridiculous premise is more ludicrous than suspenseful in depicting the dead man's spirit making use of host bodies to commit evil deeds. Brief violence, menacing situations, much rough language, and intermittent profanity. A-III (R)

Fallen Angel (1945) Convoluted tale in which a con-man (Dana Andrews) weds a small-town church organist (Alice Faye) planning to clean out her safety deposit box and skip town with a sultry waitress (Linda Darnell), who turns up murdered before he can get the money. Directed by Otto Preminger, the darkly contrived proceedings aren't very plausible, though the small-town setting has an interesting mix of eccentrics (Anne Revere, Percy Kilbride, and John Carradine), as well as a sinister detective (Charles Bickford). Stylized violence, a feigned marriage, and heavy sexual innuendo. A-III (br)

Fallen Sparrow, The (1943) When a Spanish Civil War veteran (John Garfield) uncovers a nest of Nazi agents in 1940 New York, he goes after their leader (Walter Slezak), convinced he's found the limping man who tortured him in a Spanish prison. Directed by Richard Wallace, the result has plenty of period atmosphere and dark doings, but the meandering plot and surfeit of sinister characters fail to add up to more than a halting thriller. Stylized violence and menacing situations. A-II (br)

Falling Down (1993) Pointless, ugly saga of a bitterly divorced, unemployed defense worker (Michael Douglas), who freaks out one day and goes on a one-man killing spree in LA, while a persistent cop (Robert Duvall) doggedly tracks him down. Director Joel Schumacher presents a repulsive view of contemporary America, where murderous behavior is seen as an inevitable response to mundane frustrations of modern urban life. Trivialization of deadly violence and much rough language, including racial and ethnic epithets. O (R)

Falling from Grace (1992) Melancholy tale of a popular country singer (John Mellencamp) come home to rural Indiana, where he cheats on his wife (Mariel Hemingway) with an old girlfriend (Kay Lenz) while considering how to proceed with the rest of his life. Also directed by Mellencamp, the ponderous story crawls along under the burden of static characters shuffling through midlife crises with little hint of resolution or personal growth. Discreet bedroom scene, references to adulterous affairs, fleeting violence, and an instance of rough language. A-III (PG-13)

Falling in Love (1984) Two train commuters (Robert De Niro and Meryl Streep) fall in love, have a secret affair, and part, never resolving their true feelings and their commitments to others. Although the story is essentially about adultery, the whole enterprise is so lacking in substance that moral principles hardly seem relevant. Director Ulu Grosbard fails to convey adequately the moral dilemma which was meant to be the core of the film's romantic theme. A-II (PG-13)

Falling in Love Again (1980) Elliott Gould plays the middle-aged owner of a Beverly Hills garment store who spends his time in nostalgic daydreams about his Bronx origins, much to the chagrin of his wife (Susannah York) in this contrived and determinedly simple-minded little movie written and directed by Steven Paul. A bedroom sequence and a certain moral ambiguity makes this mature fare. A-III (PG)

Fame (1980) Irene Cara and several other talented youngsters from various ethnic and racial backgrounds learn the showbiz ropes studying in New York City's High School for the Performing Arts. Following them from audition to graduation, director Alan Parker's movie is a vibrant showcase for physical prowess, not the least of which is demonstrated in some scenes involving nudity in a sexual context. Permissive sexual attitudes and irreverent treatment of religion overshadow the film's portrait of youngsters expressing their creativity and striving for professionalism. O (R)

Family, The (1987) Interesting Italian production recounting the lives of several generations of a family inhabiting an elegant apartment in Rome from the turn of the century to the present. Directed by Ettore Scola, the family portrait recalled by an aging man (Vittorio Gassman) is limited to the domestic life within the rooms of the apartment over the years. Many will find its fragmentary vignettes of personal drama surprisingly remote and lacking in emotional involvement. Some mature themes. A-III (PG)

Family Affair, A (1937) Fine old-fashioned and full-blooded family melodrama in which Judge Hardy (Lionel Barrymore) rescues the town from an aqueduct scam while saving the marriage of his eldest daughter (Cecilia Parker). Directed by George B. Seitz, the picture's strong success spawned 15 sequels in a series that came to focus more on the judge's teenage son (Mickey Rooney) than the role of sage family patriarch created by Barrymore, but thereafter played by Lewis Stone. In 1942 the series received a special Oscar for "representing the American way of life." The original is dated entertainment but still of interest for its idealistic view of family life. A-I (br)

Family Business (1989) Muddled comedy-drama about a crooked grandfather (Sean Connery), his reformed son (Dustin Hoffman), and his bright grandson (Matthew Broderick), who join forces to commit the perfect theft in an improbable caper that proves self-destructive for the entire family. Directed by Sidney Lumet, there is much father-son business to resolve, but the poor script and oddball casting only get in the way. Much profanity, some sexual innuendo, and an unresolved moral perspective on crime as a career. A-III (R)

Family Game, The (1984) Japanese director Yoshimitsu Morita fashions a gentle and noble comedy of family life and incisively chronicles their problems and how they resolve them. For those willing to read subtitles, the film will be an enjoyable as well as rewarding experience of the universality of family themes. A-II (nr)

Family Honor (1973) New York cop (Anthony Page) seeks revenge on the policemen who set up his father, also a member of the force, for opposing their taking payoffs from mobsters. Director Clark Worswick's crime movie is remarkable only in its consistent mediocrity, which follows a predictable course of killings, drug traffic, warehouse confrontations, and corruption in high places. Some Italian-Americans may be offended by ethnic stereotyping. A-III (R)

Family Jewels, The (1965) Sentimental slapstick comedy in which a nine-year-old orphan (Donna Butterworth) inherits her parents' millions, then ponders which of seven unlikely uncles (all Jerry Lewis) to choose as her guardian. Also produced and directed by Lewis, the self-indulgent proceedings offer little amusement for any but dedicated Lewis fans. A-I (br)

Family Plot (1976) Director Alfred Hitchcock turns in a below-par thriller about the efforts of a not-quite-bogus medium (Barbara Harris) and her not-too-bright boyfriend (Bruce Dern) to match wits with a pair of diabolically clever kidnappers (William Devane and Karen Black). The movie is peppered with profanity and unwitty double entendres, perhaps meant to inject some life into a slack picture. A-III (PG)

Family Prayers (1993) Melancholy tale set in 1969 as a sensitive Jewish boy (Tzvi Ratner-Stauber) prepares for his bar mitzvah while the marriage of his parents (Joe Mantegna and Anne Archer) unravels under the strain of his father's compulsive gambling. Despite its heartfelt intentions, director Scott Rosenfelt's earnest drama is a familiar story marred by flat direction and weak scripting. Minor violence and an ongoing sense of menace from loan sharks. A-II (PG)

Family Thing, A (1996) Suddenly learning he is half-black, an older Southerner (Robert Duvall) travels to Chicago to meet his half-brother, an African-American cop (James Earl Jones) who shuns him, but whose blind aunt insists he stay a few days and get to know the family. Directed by Richard Pearce, the plot may be contrived, but Jones and Duvall give interesting performances in what proves a touching story of coping with life's surprises. Fleeting violence, mild sexual references, and occasional epithets, profanity, and rough language. A-III (PG-13)

Family Way, The (1967) The lives of a young married couple (Hywell Bennett and Hayley Mills) are fraught with problems, including the groom's temporary inability to consummate their union. The groom's well-meaning but domineering father (John Mills) stands in his son's way, but it is the strengths of family life that save the day. Directed by Roy Boulting with musical score by Paul McCartney. A-IV (br)

Famine Within, The (1992) Thought-provoking documentary about female obsession with body shape examines how, increasingly, young girls and women are suffering serious eating disorders as they define their worth by their weight. Writer-producer-director Katherine Gilday perceptively questions society's adulation of ultra-thin models and actresses in disturbing interviews with young female bulimics and anorectics. Brief shower-room nudity. A-II (nr)

Fan, The (1981) Young psychopath (Michael Biehn) stalks a glamorous star (Lauren Bacall) with whom he has become obsessed, striking with a razor at those whom he believes are preventing her from seeing him. Bacall is very good, but here she lends her presence and talent to a cheap, exploitative movie by director Ed Bianchi, who seems obsessed with delivering brutal visual shocks. Extremely graphic violence. O (R)

Fan, The (1996) Nasty thriller in which a psychotic baseball fan (Robert De Niro) kills a San Francisco Giants ballplayer and terrorizes another (Wesley Snipes). Directed by Tony Scott, the disturbing story concerns a troubled man's disintegration into insanity with murderous results. Some violence with gore, sporadic profanity, and much rough language. A-IV (R)

Fanatic (see: **Die! Die! My Darling!**)

Fancy Pants (1950) Mistaken for an English butler, a jobless American actor (Bob Hope) is hired to bring some class to the household of a newly rich cattle baron whose sparky daughter (Lucille Ball) grows fond of the inept tenderfoot. Director George Marshall's enjoyable Western comedy — a variation of **Ruggles of Red Gap** — offers a winning pair of screen clowns at the top of their form and a script that has room for wit as well as pratfalls. A-I (br)

Fandango (1985) It's May 1971, and five newly minted Texas college graduates go off on a car trip to the Mexican border in search of their lost youth — fleeing Vietnam, marriage, regular jobs, and other fearful specters. Written and directed by Kevin Reynolds, the movie is sporadically amusing but more often sentimental, self-important, and tedious. Some brief nudity meant to be comic. A-II (PG)

Fanny and Alexander (1983) Directed by Ingmar Bergman, this autobiographical mood piece set at Christmas in 1907 examines family ties through the eyes of a 10-year-old boy. Replete with the themes of earlier films, the period drama has none of the depth and perception of Bergman at his best but does offer the spectacle of a lavish re-creation. Scatological and sexually derived humor and some brief nudity set the naturalistic tone of this decidedly mature tale of Swedish provincial life. A-IV (R)

Fantasia (1940) Walt Disney's only excursion into the world of the fine arts presents eight selections of classical music, including Dukas' *Sorcerers Apprentice* with Mickey Mouse and a bucket brigade of brooms, Stravinsky's *Rite of Spring* with its massive, earth-bound images, and the macabre vision of Musorgsky's *Night on Bald Mountain.* Leopold Stokowski conducts the Philadelphia Orchestra as each piece of music is visualized in different animation styles, and the imaginative result was not only Disney's most ambitious undertaking, but it remains an enjoyably creative introduction to fine music, especially for youngsters. A-I (G)

Fantastic Animation Festival (1977) Compilation consisting of 16 award-winning animated films. The majority are solidly entertaining, especially two featuring the clay figures of Will Vinton. For youngsters, it's a chance to view other approaches to the art of frame-by-frame moviemaking in contrast to Saturday-morning cartoon fare. A-II (PG)

Fantastic Disappearing Man, The (see: **The Return of Dracula**)

Fantastic Planet (1973) Lovely, haunting animated feature set in the far distant future, where humans have become miniscule vermin in a world of purple reptilian giants who periodically exterminate the humans, just as people today routinely exterminate rodents and roaches. For adults, this unusual picture, the creation of Rene Laloux and a Franco-Czech production team, can be a fascinating experience, heightened by its surrealistic imagery and eerie electronic soundtrack. Youngsters, however, might be disturbed by the occasional brutalities and the type of nudity associated with tribes living in a savage state. A-III (R/PG)

Fantastic Voyage (1966) The miniaturization of a medical team to the size of a molecule and their injection into a stroke patient's bloodstream is the only possible way to save the life of an important scientist. Director Richard Fleischer's incredible plot premise yields rich dividends in the form of exacting special effects re-creating the surreal world within the human body. Much suspense and some tense moments. A-I (PG)

Fantomas (1966) Gimmicky French-Italian superhero story about a master of disguise who battles all manner of Parisian criminals is directed by Andre Hanebelle in the melodramatic style of the old Saturday matinee adventure serials. Innocuous escapist fare. A-I (br)

Far and Away (1992) Sprawling, brawling romantic adventure about the rebellious daughter (Nicole Kidman) of an Irish landowner and a scrappy tenant farmer (Tom Cruise) who wind up in Boston, where they share quarters in order to save enough to get to the 1893 Oklahoma land rush. Director Ron Howard orchestrates rousing, feel-good entertainment whose romanticized predicaments detract little from the spirited performances of the two principals. Some sexual innuendo and bloody fisticuffs. A-III (PG-13)

Far Country, The (1955) After taking a herd of cattle from Oregon to the gold camps of Alaska, a rancher (James Stewart) and aging sidekick (Walter Brennan) get in the way of a crooked judge (John McIntire) and his claim-jumping cohorts. Directed by Anthony Mann, the rugged setting appropriately frames the tough characters in an action picture that winds up with the usual shoot-out heroics. Some stylized violence and mild romance. A-I (br)

Far from Home: The Adventures of Yellow Dog (1995) Bland family picture concerns a 14-year-old (Jesse Bradford) and his Labrador shipwrecked and stranded for weeks in the Pacific Northwest on a thickly forested, uninhabited island, as his worried parents (Bruce Davison and Mimi Rogers) continue to hope they will be rescued. Writer-director Phillip Borsos presents a formula survival story, surprising only in its consistent predictability. A-I (PG)

Far from the Madding Crowd (1967) Excellent British screen version of Thomas Hardy's romantic melodrama of early Victorian country life, with Julie Christie being pursued by Peter Finch, Terence Stamp, and Alan Bates. Director John Schlesinger avoids the pitfalls of the formula blockbuster and comes up with a superbly realistic, atmospheric production filmed entirely on location in Hardy's Dorset. A-II (br)

Far Horizons, The (1955) Colorful but wooden recreation of the Lewis (Fred MacMurray) and Clark (Charlton Heston) expedition (1803-06) exploring the upper reaches of the Missouri River and across the Rockies to the Pacific Ocean. Directed by Rudolph Maté, the scenery is certainly picturesque, but the adventure is too fanciful to be convincing, especially the hokey romance between Clark and the expedition's Indian guide, Sacajawea (a badly miscast Donna Reed). Some stylized violence and Native-American stereotypes. A-I (br)

Far Off Place, A (1993) Contemporary African adventure with a 14-year-old American girl (Reese Witherspoon) and young friend (Ethan Randall) fleeing murderous ivory poachers by trekking 1,000 miles across the Kalahari desert with only an African Bushman (Sarel Bok) as guide. Director Mikael Salomon combines a lively story, delightful cast, and exquisite cinematography for an old-fashioned outdoor adventure with modern environmental sensibilities. Brief violence, occasional profanity, and continuing menace. A-II (PG)

Far Out Man (1990) Terminally revolting movie about the aimless wanderings of an aging, leftover hippie (Tommy Chong) who takes to the road to forget his long-lost wife and son but accidentally chances upon them. Chong wrote, directed, and stars (along with assorted relatives) in this warped tribute to the drug culture and sexual promiscuity. Much rough language, sexually suggestive scenes with nudity, promotion of drug abuse, and a variety of gross, violent, and vulgar acts. O (R)

Faraway, So Close (1993) Poetic fantasy of invisible guardian angels watching over the untidy affairs of people living in contemporary Berlin, until one of them (Otto Sander) becomes a mortal man in order to save a child's life, then suffers a series of misadventures as a human. German director Wim Wenders's playfully creative but overlong journey is one of discovery in seeing modern life as experienced by a pure-hearted angel trying to cope with such things as alcohol, pornography, and arms trafficking. Subtitles. Some stylized violence and sexual references. A-III (PG-13)

Farewell My Concubine (1993) Long but colorful multi-leveled epic spanning the various political changes in China from 1925 to 1977, as seen in the lifelong friendship of two Peking Opera stars, one (Zhang Fengyi) famous for virile roles and the other (Leslie Cheung) for his performance of female leads, though the bond between them is strained after the former marries a prostitute (Gong Li). In intermixing the political with the personal, director Chen Kaige is particularly harsh on the excesses of the Cultural Revolution (1966-77), but his primary focus is on the world of the stage and those who make it their life. Subtitles. Some scenes of violence, sexual situations, including implications of homosexuality, and occasional rough language. A-III (R)

Farewell, My Lovely (1975) Hulking ex-convict (Jack O'Halloran) hires private investigator Philip Marlowe (Robert Mitchum) to find his girlfriend, though she hasn't bothered to write while he served a seven-year sentence for bank robbery. Director Dick Richards's version of the Raymond Chandler mystery is skillfully crafted, and Mitchum gives an outstanding performance. Some violence and incidental nudity. A-III (R)

Farewell to Arms, A (1957) Disappointing version of the Hemingway novel about an American ambulance driver (miscast Rock Hudson) serving with the Italian Army during WW I and his ill-fated romance with a British nurse (Jennifer Jones). Director Charles Vidor portrays the swirl and confusion of events in a war zone with greater conviction than his wooden treatment of an intimate relationship which ends in a tragic pregnancy. Wartime violence and sexual situations. A-III (br)

Farewell to the King (1989) Epic set in the jungles of Borneo during the final months of WW II, where an American survivor of Corregidor (Nick Nolte) winds up as the adopted "king" of a tribe of headhunters, whom he tries to protect from annihilation when they are forced to fight against the Japanese by a British Special Forces unit. Director John Milius leaves little doubt about who the true savages are in this uncomplicated, old-fashioned adventure movie. Intense battle carnage and minimal rough language. A-III (PG-13)

Farewell Uncle Tom (1972) Gualtiero Jacopetti and Franco Prosperi have been responsible for a long and dismayingly popular series of pseudo-documentaries, but this time their subject is a historical one, slavery in the United States. Their voyeuristic treatment of the subject is simply vicarious flesh-peddling and the concluding section, specially prepared for the American version of this Italian film, can only deepen racial misunderstanding. O (X)

Fargo (1996) A debt-ridden Minnesota car dealer (William H. Macy) hires two thugs to kidnap his wife and split the hefty ransom her wealthy father would pay, but all goes horribly awry, resulting in several murders doggedly investigated by a small-town chief of police (Frances McDormand). Finding black comedy in this loosely fact-based tragedy, filmmakers Joel and Ethan Coen chillingly depict earnest small-towners caught up in shocking violence, although justice eventually prevails in the unlikely form of a folksy, very pregnant police officer. Recurring gory violence and much rough language. A-IV (R)

Farinelli (1995) Elaborate costume drama about the personal and artistic relationship between an acclaimed 18th-century *castrato* singer (Stefano Dionisi) and his ambitious composer-brother (Enrico Lo Verso), who had had him castrated as a youth. It focuses on their pact of sharing women, until the singer's sexual frustrations jeopardize their relationship. Director Gerard Corbiau's visually lush production works primarily on the level of a passionately acted musical soap-opera whose two main characters view sexual conquests as their artistic due, although the narrative also explores the psychological harm on those castrated in the name of art. Subtitles.

A suicide, several bedroom scenes with nudity, and a cavalier attitude toward sexual matters. A-IV (R)

Farmer, The (1977) Revenge story of a WW II veteran (Gary Conway) has arty pretensions but not a spark of intelligence. Mechanically directed by David Berlatsky, it is excessively brutal and sexually degrading. O (R)

Farmer & Chase (1997) Nasty crime drama in which a career criminal (Ben Gazzara) accepts his admiring son (Todd Field) as his new partner as well as the young man's gun-toting girlfriend (Lara Flynn Boyle), but their botched bank robbery ends in multiple deaths. Writer-director Michael Seitzman's drawn-out tale of mindless lowlifes who rob out of boredom or greed is emotionally uninvolving and dramatically uninsightful. A romanticized view of crime, several murders and beatings, fleeting drug use, brief sexual encounter, some profanity, and constant rough language. O (R)

Farmer's Daughter, The (1947) Enjoyable comedy about a Swedish-American country lass (Loretta Young) who wins the love of a bachelor congressman (Joseph Cotten) and the affection of his party-boss mom (Ethel Barrymore) when she comes to work for them as a maid, but her wholesome virtues and honest candor lead to her nomination as the congressional candidate of the rival party. Directed by H.C. Potter, some fun is had with crooked politicians and a smear campaign that backfires, but the main attraction is Young's Oscar-winning performance as the country girl whose commonsense wisdom wins over the city slickers. A-I (br)

Fast Break (1979) Very funny movie about a new basketball coach (Gabe Kaplan) who recruits a motley collection of youths to give an obscure college a winning season. Directed by Jack Smight, it contains some rough language and several mildly suggestive sexual scenes. A-III (PG)

Fast Charlie ... The Moonbeam Rider (1979) Failed period road-comedy about a WW I vet (David Carradine) who enlists the aid of some of his old buddies to help him enter a transcontinental motorcycle race. Director Steve Carver's thin story is amiable but not very funny. Permissive attitude toward casual sex. A-III (PG)

Fast Forward (1985) Some bright and talented teenagers from Sandusky, Ohio, go to New York to win a dance contest without bothering to inform their parents. The poor kids have to hang on for a month or so before they make it to the top. Mediocre entertainment, disappointingly directed by Sidney Poitier. Some vulgar language, nose-thumbing at parental authority, and teenage drinking presented as humorous. A-III (PG)

Fast Talking (1986) A modern artful dodger lies, cheats, and steals his way out of high school and into the brave new world of self-sufficiency in reaction to flawed family, alienated friends, and a social order which offers little positive encouragement. But it's hard to accept the amiable, resourceful teenager as someone incapable of finding positive options. The film points to the moral and political inadequacies of adult society but in less than constructive fashion. A-III (nr)

Fast Times at Ridgemont High (1982) Director Amy Heckerling's examination of teen mores in the suburban jungle of shopping malls, discos, and the playing fields of southern California has some insights. However, for the most part it is a crass, insensitive, and superficial movie with an unsettling nastiness lurking just beneath its pleasant surface. Some extremely graphic nudity and a scene of adolescents discussing oral sex. O (X/R)

Fastest Gun Alive, The (1956) Contrived Western about a peaceful but fast-drawing storekeeper (Glenn Ford) who, after much soul-searching, saves his town from a crazed gunslinger (Broderick Crawford). Director Russell Rouse badly overplays the far-fetched situation, then muddles the hero's motivations in a coy conclusion that leaves viewers flat. Stylized violence. A-I (br)

Fat City (1972) Complex character study of two boxers, one a has-been (Stacy Keach) and the other a youth of 19 (Jeff Bridges) whose prospects on the B-grade California boxing circuit are at best uncertain. Director John Huston's theme of wasted lives and loves and the hopes of youth for affluence and success (the ironic meaning of the title) are evocative but unsatisfying in terms of the dramatic whole. Well-staged, realistic fight sequences. A-III (PG)

Fat Man, The (1951) Weak murder mystery directed by William Castle has the rotund detective (J. Scott Smart) created for radio by Dashiell Hammett employing a dull assistant (Clinton Sundberg) in following the trail of a dentist's killer, which leads along the way to an ex-con (Rock Hudson) and a circus clown (Emmett Kelly). The usual stylized violence and menace. A-II (br)

Fat Man and Little Boy (1989) Fine production values and serviceable acting highlight this dramatization of the creation of the atomic bomb beginning in 1942 and focusing on the professional and personal agendas motivating the two key players, Gen. Leslie R. Groves (Paul Newman) and physicist J. Robert Oppenheimer (Dwight Schultz). Director Roland Joffe creates an air of scientific and historical accuracy together with a sense of visual tension, and the result helps clarify the moral issues debated by those who made the bomb. An adulterous encounter with nudity, a grisly death from radiation, and minimal rough language. A-III (PG-13)

Fata Morgana (1974) German director Werner Herzog's interior journey to Africa is a stunning portrait of the North African landscape, where people are transformed into fragments of an alien, dreamlike world. For those adventurous enough to take a trip without the security of guideposts, it will most likely prove a consciousness-expanding experience. A-III (nr)

Fatal Attraction (1987) Ambitious, hard-driving

but happily married lawyer (Michael Douglas) has a fling with a compulsive admirer (Glenn Close), and both suffer the dangerous consequences. Director Adrian Lyne's fatalistic romance begins as a moral tale and ends in a melodramatic bloodbath. Several graphic lovemaking scenes but violence and rough language dominate. O (R)

Fatal Instinct (1993) Strained send-up of movie thrillers in which Armand Assante is the thoroughly dense object of affection and/or extinction by his wandering wife (Kate Nelligan), simpering secretary (Sherilyn Fenn), and kooky client (Sean Young). The slapstick and sight gags in director Carl Reiner's weak, goofy parody are only fitfully funny and often crude. Some vulgar sexual innuendo, brief nudity, and sporadic violence played for comic effect. A-III (PG-13)

Fate Is the Hunter (1964) Middling melodrama starts with a jetliner crash killing 53 people, including the pilot (Rod Taylor), whom an airline executive (Glenn Ford) spends the rest of the movie trying to clear of blame by interviewing those who knew him (notably Dorothy Malone, Nancy Kwan, Wally Cox, and Mark Stevens). Director Ralph Nelson plods through numerous flashbacks of the pilot's freewheeling life before a stewardess (Suzanne Pleshette) who survived the crash supplies the clue to its cause. Superficial treatment turns a serious subject into undemanding fare. A-I (br)

Father Goose (1964) An unusually disheveled Cary Grant plays a beachcomber reformed by a prim but high-spirited French schoolmarm (Leslie Caron) and her seven girl pupils when they are stranded together on a Pacific island during WW II. Director Ralph Nelson handles the romantic comedy deftly enough, though the plot is entirely predictable as wartime dangers are overcome with affable, good-natured humor. A-I (br)

Father of the Bride (1950) Delightful comedy from Edward Streeter's novel about a self-assured suburbanite (Spencer Tracy) suddenly thrust into the unfamiliar world of wedding preparations and financial obligations when his only daughter (Elizabeth Taylor) announces her engagement. Brightly directed by Vincente Minnelli, Tracy is superb as the caring but confused head of the household, helped by patient wife Joan Bennett to come to terms with their daughter's vision of the perfect wedding. Amusing yet perceptive view of middle-class life and family values. A-I (br)

Father of the Bride (1991) Trite remake of the 1950 Spencer Tracy-Elizabeth Taylor charmer, this time has father Steve Martin battling the emotional loss of daughter Kimberly Williams, while wife Diane Keaton tries to cushion the financial drain of a big wedding. A hilarious scene early on is outweighed by mawkish sentimentality in director Charles Shyer's drawn-out comedy. Fleeting sexual innuendo. A-II (PG)

Father of the Bride, Part II (1995) Warm-hearted sequel (and remake of the 1951 **Father's Little Dividend**) in which good-natured dad (Steve Martin) copes with the pregnancies of both his daughter (Kimberly Williams) and wife (Diane Keaton) while feeling too young to be called "Gramps," but too old to be pushing a baby buggy. Director Charles Shyer's sentimental domestic comedy is frequently funny in its wholesome depiction of family life. Mild sexual innuendo. A-II (PG)

Father's Little Dividend (1951) **Father of the Bride** cast returns in a heavy-handed sequel turning good old dad (Spencer Tracy) into an unsympathetic grouch dismayed by the demands of impending grandfather-hood. Nor does director Vincente Minnelli find much humor in the predictable problems of expectant parents Elizabeth Taylor and Don Taylor in naming the baby, false labors, and in-law competition over the heir apparent. Confusing situations for youngsters. A-II (br)

Fathers and Sons (1992) Shallow drama of a widower (Jeff Goldblum) trying to help his teenage son (Rory Cochrane) confront the perils of contemporary urban life — gangs, drugs, alcohol, sex, cults, and street crazies. Written and directed by Paul Mones, the well-intended effort realistically portrays the youth's problems while mawkishly handling the father's inept attempts to communicate with his son until a contrived ending. Restrained depiction of moral problems requiring a mature perspective. A-III (R)

Fathers' Day (1997) Needing help in searching for her 16-year-old runaway son (Charlie Hofheimer), a desperate mom (Nastassja Kinski) separately tells two former lovers (Robin Williams and Billy Crystal) that the boy is their biological son, and the two join forces to find him. Director Ivan Reitman lets Williams and Crystal improvise in the style of Hope and Crosby in an amusing, though overly sentimental, tale of unexpected bonding between strangers. Intermittent comic violence, several sexual references, and humorous treatment of past sexual escapades. A-III (PG-13)

Fathom (1967) Mindless spy intrigue with Raquel Welch being pursued by plane, by boat, by harpoonist, and by bull (both figuratively and literally). Directed by Leslie Martinson, the star vehicle becomes tiresome long before the ending. A-II (br)

Fatso (1980) Actress Anne Bancroft fails to convey much sincerity or intelligence in her directorial debut. Her comedy stars Dom DeLuise as a compulsive eater who is so shocked by the early death of an obese cousin that he determines to lose weight. The humor is weighted down, however, by foul language and silly sight gags in a social satire which provides little insight into a serious malady. A-III (PG)

Faust (1994) Playfully absurd fantasy in which a man (Petr Cepek) finds himself in a Prague theater playing the role of Faust, sometimes on the stage or in a medieval setting, but most often in a marionette version, all of which inevitably ends with Mephistopheles (again Cepek) claiming the man's soul. Writer-director Jan Svankmajer's Czech production is a surrealistic blend of live action, puppetry, and clay animation, but the traditional story gets lost in a welter of shifting scenes and bizarre images with Faust as a contemporary Everyman bumbling his way through a mythic world of good and evil. Sparse dubbed dialogue. A demonic incantation, some bawdy humor, and sexual innuendo. A-III (nr)

Favor, the Watch and the Very Big Fish, The (1992) Strained comedy has an earnest photographer (Bob Hoskins) of religious tableaux and the model he uses for Jesus (Jeff Goldblum) falling for the same woman (Natasha Richardson). Writer-director Ben Lewin's mildly naughty black comedy is too self-conscious and contrived to inspire more than forced laughter from the wacky situations. Much sexual innuendo, brief nudity, comic violence, and minimal rough language. A-III (R)

Fear (1996) Manipulative thriller in which a psycho youth (Mark Wahlberg) seduces a 16-year-old girl (Reese Witherspoon), then goes on a murderous rampage when her father (William Peterson) interferes. Directed by James Foley, the premise is ridiculously contrived in escalating threatening situations into the frightful scares of its absurd climax. Excessive violence, intense menace, graphic sexual situations, occasional profanity, and recurring rough language. O (R)

Fear and Loathing in Las Vegas (1998) Repulsive tale in which a continually stoned journalist (Johnny Depp) and his menacing sidekick (Benicio Del Toro) lurch through a boozy, destructive Las Vegas weekend, sampling every drug they can lay their hands on. Based on gonzo journalist Hunter S. Thompson's 1971 novel, director Terry Gilliam's salute to the acid-tripping subculture wallows in gleeful excess and gaudy nihilism. Constant substance abuse, brief nudity, and non-stop profanity and rough language. O (R)

Fear City (1984) Psychotic killer of New York City strippers is hunted by an ex-boxer (Tom Berenger) and his exhibitionist girlfriend (Melanie Griffith) in a sleazy exploitation feature directed by Abel Ferrara. Excessive violence, much nudity, and recurring rough language. O (R)

Fear Eats the Soul — Ali (1974) German movie in which a 60-year-old cleaning woman meets a young Moroccan mechanic, and out of mutual loneliness and a desperate need for some special other person, they marry and encounter the same rejection and discrimination suffered by minorities everywhere. Directed by Rainer Werner Fassbinder, the story is simply told, yet is profoundly human and affecting in its picture of two ordinary people persecuted by a hypocritical society. A-IV (nr)

Fear in the Night (1947) Muddled but involving mystery in which a bank clerk (DeForest Kelley) awakens from a nightmare convinced he's murdered a man, gets his cop brother-in-law (Paul Kelly) to investigate, and the clues eventually lead to a hypnotist. Directed by Maxwell Shane from a story by William Irish, the intriguing plot has some surreal visuals, including the multi-images reflected in an octagonal mirrored room, but the pacing is pedestrian and the solution is anticlimactic. Stylized violence, including an attempted suicide, menacing situations, and infidelity as a plot element. A-III (br)

Fear Is the Key (1973) Adaptation of Alistair MacLean thriller about an ex-salvage operator (Barry Newman) who, by reason of a wild and complex chain of events, finds himself in the palatial home of an oil heiress (Suzy Kendall), and given the task of dredging up a sunken treasure. Director Michael Tuchner's wildly improbable melodrama in which nothing is what it seems is moderately entertaining, mercifully short on sex and violence, but awfully hard to swallow. A-II (PG)

Fear No Evil (1981) Bright but popular high-school student is possessed by the devil in this inept horror film written and directed by Frank Laloggia. Excessive violence, nudity, and exploitation of religious themes. O (R)

Fear Strikes Out (1957) Fact-based story of Boston Red Sox baseball player Jimmy Piersall (Anthony Perkins) whose father (Karl Malden) raises him to be a star outfielder, but the pressure of making good brings on a nervous breakdown requiring psychiatric treatment before he's able to return to the club. Directed by Robert Mulligan, the movie presents a realistic picture of a youth trying to measure up to the high expectations of a well-meaning but ambitious father, with convincing performances from both Malden and Perkins. Brief but intense scenes of emotional instability. A-I (br)

Fearless (1993) In the months following a plane crash with many fatalities, a euphoric survivor (Jeff Bridges) feels disconnected from wife (Isabella Rossellini) and child, a situation aggravated by his determination to help a severely depressed survivor (Rosie Perez) adjust to the loss of her baby in the crash. Director Peter Weir realistically captures the spiritual anguish and psychological trauma of survivors trying to pull their lives together after a profound disaster completely changes their outlook on life. Violent aftermath of a crash with fleeting shots of the human carnage, minor sexual innuendo, and occasional rough language. A-II (R)

Fearless Frank (1969) The Second City gang have put together a super-spoof of crime movies with some digs at sex and religion. Jon Voight plays Frank, a Superman character flying through the air and fighting evil wherever it rears its ugly head. Director Philip Kaufman's campy, superficial adult comedy is of limited quality and appeal. A-III (G)

Fearless Vampire Killers, The (1967) Offbeat horror spoof in which an old scholar of the occult (Jack McGowran) and his young assistant (Polanski) seek out a vampire's castle in the hills of Transylvania, using the tools of garlic, the cross, and a wooden stake in their research, but the vampires are released to spread throughout the world. Also directed by Polanski, it is imitation camp at best, all very short on humor, and long on blood-drinking and sexual innuendo. A-III (br)

Feast of July (1995) Bittersweet romantic tragedy set in Victorian England, where a woman (Embeth Davidtz) deserted by her lover is taken in by a kindly working-class family whose three grown sons compete for her affection. Directed by Chris Menaul, the handsome production presents the story in stately, understated fashion with a growing sense of doom for its ill-fated characters. Brief but intense violence and discreet bedroom encounters with fleeting nudity. A-III (R)

Feathered Serpent, The (1948) Formula Charlie Chan mystery directed by William Beaudine with the Chinese-American detective (Roland Winters) interrupting a Mexican vacation to join in the search for a missing archeologist and a lost Aztec temple, with comic relief from Chan's No. 1 son (Keye Luke), No. 2 son (Victor Sen Yung), and chauffeur (Mantan Moreland). A-I (br)

Fedora (1979) Down-on-his-luck Hollywood producer (William Holden) journeys to the Greek island of Corfu to persuade a legendary actress (Marthe Keller) to come out of retirement and play the lead in his movie. German production directed by Billy Wilder is a failed curiosity piece about the old and the new wave of moviemakers. Some adult situations. A-III (PG)

Feds (1988) The saga of two women (Rebecca De Mornay, Mary Gross) determined to graduate from the male-dominated FBI Academy takes some unexpected turns that upgrade it from mere fluff to a fairly respectable view of women in a traditionally male occupation. Directed by Dan Goldberg, it reverses the convention, in contrived humorous fashion, of weak-kneed women and super men. Some locker room and sexually vulgar language. A-III (PG-13)

Feeling Minnesota (1996) Bleak screwball comedy about the sibling rivalry between two shiftless brothers which erupts into violence and mayhem when one (Vincent D'Onofrio) marries a conniving prostitute (Cameron Diaz) and the other (Keanu Reeves) runs off with her. Writer-director Steven Baigelman makes a mirthless mess out of a contrived, manipulative story about repugnant characters and their grotesque escapades. Simulated sex scenes, brief nudity, extensive violence, some profanity, and much rough language. O (R)

Fellini Satyricon (1970) Federico Fellini's self-indulgent vision of ancient Rome presents, not a story, but a series of sequences juxtaposed with little or no cause-and-effect relationship. Buried beneath its array of imagery ranging from the sensuous and opulent to the grotesque and orgiastic are such unconnected themes as youth's search for fulfillment, the destruction of the artist by his patrons, and the collapse of a society burdened by the luxury of wealth. Though an extraordinary visual experience, it is disappointing in its lack of structure, logic, and viewer engagement. Many scenes of sex and violence. A-IV (R)

Fellini's Casanova (1977) Director Federico Fellini's first English-language production concentrates on the sordid details of the sexual legend surrounding Giacomo Casanova without concern for any human dimensions of the worldly lover. Technically brilliant but lacking emotion, it is an empty work. Some nudity and consistently gross and perverse imagery becomes tedious and excessive. O (R)

Fellini's Roma (1972) Director Federico Fellini's imaginary tour of Rome is founded on an indulgent nostalgia for the 1930s and 1940s as against the city's present-day traffic jams, tourist traps, and imported lifestyles. His dramatic re-creations of the past are at times heavy-handed (the pathetic contrast between cheap and high-class bordellos) or coy (an ecclesiastical fashion show) but, for the most part, they are fond and playful evocations of a Rome that no longer exists except in memory. Some grotesque images may be troubling. A-IV (R)

Female Animal, The (1958) Soapy romance directed by Harry Keller in which a Hollywood extra (George Nader) is pursued by a glamorous movie star (Hedy Lamarr), her rebellious daughter (Jane Powell), and a faded screen actress (Jan Sterling). Hokey romantic complications and much sexual innuendo. A-III (br)

Female Animal, The (1970) Biographical account of a young woman (Arlene Tiger) who became a prostitute because of family and social pressures. Its gross treatment of basically immoral situations nullifies whatever social value it may have intended. O (nr)

Female Bunch, The (1972) Drugs, sex, and sadism are the routine for a group of women at a remote ranch, where some lustful admirers (Russ Tamblyn and Lon Chaney, Jr.) become tortured victims of the gang. Sex-exploitation Western directed by Al Adamson and John Cardos. O (R)

Female on the Beach (1955) Tawdry romantic thriller in which a rich but hard-as-nails widow (Jane Crawford) moves into a luxury beach community, falls for a smooth hustler (Jeff Chandler), then fears he intends to kill her for her money. Directed by Joseph Pevney, the result is a muddle of badly contrived situations and unconvincing performances punctuated by nasty dialogue. Heavy sexual innuendo. A-III (br)

Female Response, The (1972) Sex exploitation story of a newspaper lovelorn columnist (Raina Barrett) exploring the sex lives of five women. Voyeuristic trash directed by Tim Kincaid. O (R)

Femme de Personne (1986) In a French production directed by Christopher Frank, four women try to work out their individual problems in relationships with stereotyped males in an over-long drama whose message is that men are a lost cause and that women must sustain and support themselves. Promiscuity and infidelity are treated as positive strategies for women's survival in an alienating world of insensitive men. Some nudity. O (nr)

FernGully ... The Last Rain Forest (1992) Animated children's fantasy tells how the tiny fairy Crysta (voice of Samantha Mathis) employs her magical powers to save a pristine forest and its lively creatures, including a wacky bat (voice of Robin Williams), from being destroyed by the pollution monster, Hexxon (voice of Tim Curry). Directed by Bill Kroyer, the animation of the natural world is lovely to see and the action is sufficiently fanciful, but the well-intentioned story is thin and its ecological message saccharine. Some tense scenes. A-I (G)

Ferris Bueller's Day Off (1986) Director John Hughes turns in a lighthearted spoof about a teenager (Matthew Broderick) who has made a science out of truancy because he likes to take a break now and then to observe the world around him. The cheerfully implausible plot serves as the catalyst in changing the attitudes of his sister and best friend. Some vulgar language. A-II (PG-13)

Fever Heat (1968) Low-budget melodrama about a former stock-car racer (Nick Adams) who becomes romantically involved with the widow (Jeannine Riley) of a racer, and she overcomes her fear of the dirt track. Director Russell S. Doughten Jr. does better with the world of racing than with the development of the personal relations of his characters. A-II (br)

Fever Pitch (1985) Sportswriter (Ryan O'Neal) addicted to gambling is sent to Las Vegas to do a story about compulsive gamb lers. A well-intentioned drama about the evils of gambling that, unfortunately, becomes dull and repetitive, with a neat upbeat ending that undercuts the seriousness of the problem. Brief nudity and vulgar language. A-III (R)

Few Days with Me, A (1989) French director Claude Sautet tracks the travails of a depressed department store heir (Daniel Auteuil) who falls for a free-spirited young woman (Sandrine Bonnaire) but is unable to win her love. Despite hints of promiscuous relationships, this lightly comic tale is not about sex but about one frustrated man's inability to communicate love and affection for people in ways other than buying, selling, and psychological manipulation. Minimal violence. A-III (PG-13)

Few Good Men, A (1992) Insecure but glib Navy lawyer (Tom Cruise), goaded by a strong-willed Internal Affairs attorney (Demi Moore), takes on the politically sensitive murder trial of two Marines (James Marshall and Wolfgang Bodison) who are being used as scapegoats by their commanding officer (Jack Nicholson). Director Rob Reiner's tautly constructed courtroom drama bristles with intense performances while tackling prickly issues of honor, responsibility, and personal integrity. An off-screen suicide, a blatantly sexist remark, and intermittent rough language. A-III (R)

ffolkes (1980) Eccentric soldier of fortune (Roger Moore) and his crack team of underwater commandos are recruited by Her Majesty's Government to battle a sinister duo (Anthony Perkins and Michael Parks) and their dastardly gang of hijackers. Moore is in top form in director Andrew V. McLaglan's thriller which, unfortunately, has somewhat more graphic violence than necessary. A-III (PG)

Fiddler on the Roof (1971) Fine screen adaptation of Joseph Stein's Broadway musical about Tevye (Topol), a milk-seller in a Czarist Russian village whose life of Jewish Orthodoxy is filled with joy and sadness but always buoyed by the human spirit and eternal hope. Struggling in a time of cultural and political flux to find suitable husbands for his three dowry-less daughters, Tevye's faith and hope and sheer love of life and humankind keep him and the family going. Norman Jewison's direction does full justice to a rich and appealing musical that the whole family can enjoy. A-I (G)

Field, The (1990) Obsessed with acquiring the field he has slavishly cultivated for his only surviving son (Sean Bean), an impoverished Irishman (Richard Harris) comes into mortal conflict with an American (Tom Berenger) who outbids him for the land. With Harris's commanding performance at the center, writer-director Jim Sheridan's extravagantly crafted morality tale fully exploits the austere beauty of the Irish landscapes to reflect the primal emotions that the story evokes. Intermittent violence and a very restrained sexual encounter. A-III (PG-13)

Field of Dreams (1989) When an Iowa farmer (Kevin Costner) begins hearing voices, he and his supportive wife (Amy Madigan) use the family savings to turn a cornfield into a baseball field, whereupon the spirit of Shoeless Joe Jackson (Ray Liotta) and others appear to play ball, with their visions and voices enabling a reconciliation between the farmer and his deceased father. Adapted by director Phil Alden Robinson from W. P. Kinsella's novel, it's filled with happy, confounding surprises that some may dismiss as heavy-handed fantasy, though others will be refreshed by its positive point of view, wonderful mystical characters, love of baseball lore, and respect for those who follow their dreams. Minor rough language. A-II (PG)

Fiend Who Walked the West (1958) Cornball Western in which a reformed badman (Hugh O'Brian) helps a lawman (Stephen McNally) nab a psychotic killer (Robert Evans), then fears for his family's welfare when the killer escapes. Directed by Gordon Douglas and loosely based on the gangster movie **Kiss of Death** (1947), the dismal results are compounded by Evans's off-the-wall imitation of Richard Widmark's vicious hit-man. Sadistic violence. A-III (br)

Fiendish Plot of Dr. Fu Manchu, The (1980) Peter Sellers, in his last movie, plays both the diabolical 168-year-old Fu Manchu and his now-retired nemesis, Nayland Smith of Scotland Yard. Seller's forte as a character actor is not supported by any comic imagination behind either the clumsy script or the flat direction of Piers Haggard. Some vulgar expletives and a mildly suggestive striptease. A-II (PG)

Fierce Creatures (1997) Zany comedy in which the staff (headed by John Cleese) of an English zoo resists the efforts of their venal new owner and his son (Kevin Kline in a dual role), as well as their corporate representative (Jamie Lee Curtis), to commercialize their beloved animals. Co-directed by Robert Young and Fred Schepisi, the zippy comedy broadly satirizes rampant commercialization in the unlikely setting of a bucolic zoo, but the proceedings never quite achieve the intended level of madcap lunacy. Much sexual innuendo, brief comic violence, and an instance of rough language. A-III (PG-13)

Fifth Avenue Girl (1939) Routine Depression-era comedy in which a jobless woman (Ginger Rogers) helps a millionaire (Walter Connolly) win back his wife and straighten out his grown children. Directed by Gregory LaCava, the predictable plot is heavy-handed and its proletarian humor without much bite. Mild romantic mix-ups. A-II (br)

Fifth Element, The (1997) Uneven sci-fi action fantasy set 300 years in the future, when a space-taxi driver (Bruce Willis) saves a mysterious superhuman woman (Milla Jovovich) who has the power to destroy an evil planet hurtling towards Earth. Director Luc Besson uses the silly mythological premise for some tongue-in-cheek humor, as well as a sappy love story between human hero and otherworldly heroine which only gets in the way of the action plot. Fantasy violence, sexual innuendo, brief nudity, coarse language, and profanity. A-IV (PG-13)

Fifth Floor, The (1980) A young woman (Diane Hull) is wrongly committed to an institution for the insane in this exploitation movie directed by Howard Avedis. Contains much nudity and violence. O (R)

5th Musketeer, The (1979) Uninspired Austrian remake of the 1939 American movie **The Man in the Iron Mask** stars a miscast Beau Bridges in the dual role of Louis XIV and his twin brother, with aged musketeers Jose Ferrer, Cornel Wilde, Alan Hale, Jr., and Lloyd Bridges assuring that the good twin ascends the throne. Director Ken Annakin's lackluster adventure includes some adult situations. A-III (PG)

54 (1998) Empty retelling of the rise and demise of Studio 54, New York City's wildest disco in the late 1970s, as seen through the eyes of a pleasure-seeking bartender (Ryan Phillippe). Written and directed by Mark Christopher, the movie proves a lifeless assemblage of decadent disco scenes in search of a story, and the result offers no lessons to be learned from life in the fast lane. Uncritical portrayal of substance abuse, promiscuity, and theft, as well as brief nudity and much rough language. O (R)

55 Days at Peking (1963) With the encouragement of the Manchu dowager empress (Flora Robson), the forces of the 1900 Boxer Rebellion lay siege to the walled compound in the Chinese capital, where the foreign community tries to hold out until an international relief force arrives. Director Nicholas Ray's wide-screen spectacular has impressive sets and energetic action scenes, but the cast (US Marine officer Charlton Heston, British diplomat David Niven, Russian baroness Ava Gardner, and the rest) are cardboard characters adding little human dimension to a script of limited historical proportion. Stylized violence and romantic interludes. A-I (br)

52 Minutes to Midnight (See: **Hot Rods to Hell**)

52 Pick-up (1986) A wealthy industrialist and unfaithful husband (Roy Scheider), who dabbles in the sleazy underworld of drugs and sex, is taped in a liaison with a young girl that implicates him in her subsequent murder. The demand for b1ackmail motivates him to use his money to set the killers against themselves. The nasty peep-show ambiance of the proceedings, directed by John Frankenheimer, wallows in brutish violence, nudity, drugs, and profanity. O (R)

Fighter Attack (1953) Routine war picture directed by Lesley Selander follows a downed American pilot (Sterling Hayden) as he helps an Italian partisan band (led by J. Carrol Naish) destroy a mountain tunnel held by the Nazis. Wartime violence and mild romance. A-I (br)

Fighter Squadron (1948) Standard exploits of an Air Force unit (headed by Edmond O'Brien) in winning the war against the Luftwaffe despite the loss of brave pilots (notably Robert Stack). Director Raoul Walsh makes good use of actual combat footage, but the movie flags on the ground with the usual arguments over tactics, conflicts with the brass, and sporadic comic relief. Wartime violence. A-I (br)

Fighting Back (1982) Inner-city Italian-American (Tom Skerrit) organizes his neighbors to fight crime. Despite a muddled homage to the complexity of big city problems and an attempt to give some sort of moral perspective, the end result is the usual formula of simplistic violence as the way to solve all problems. Director Lewis Teague's movie is too morally confused to avoid giving the impression of extolling the virtues of vigilantism. Abundant violence. O (R)

Fighting Father Dunne (1948) Inspirational tale of a Catholic priest (Patrick O'Brien) in 1905 St. Louis who starts a residence for homeless boys, then struggles to find adequate funding as his efforts expand in rehabilitating a growing number of youths, one of whom (Darryl Hickman) proves incorrigible. Directed by Ted Tetzlaff, the subject is certainly worthy and the treatment sincere but the result suffers from a bland sentimentality which wears thin today. A-I (br)

Fighting Fools (1949) Formula slapstick comedy in which the Bowery Boys (Leo Gorcey, Huntz Hall, and company) help a prizefighter (Frankie Darro) win the title by getting the goods on the champ's crooked manager. Stylized violence. A-I (br)

Fighting Kentuckian, The (1949) Novel adventure in which a Kentucky rifleman (John Wayne) marching home with his militia regiment after the Battle of

New Orleans stops off in 1819 Alabama to woo a French belle (Vera Ralston) while saving a group of Napoleonic exiles from a land swindle. Directed by George Waggner, the improbable plot provides more intrigue than action, with some notable comic relief from Oliver Hardy as Wayne's sidekick. Frontier violence and romantic complications. A-II (br)

Fighting Mustang (1938) Formula Western directed by Oliver Drake with Sunset Carson as a Texas Ranger safeguarding a local referendum to extend the county's jurisdiction over badlands used by rustlers as their hideout. Mild frontier action. A-I (br)

Fighting O'Flynn, The (1949) Leaden blarney about an aging Irish adventurer (Douglas Fairbanks, Jr.) who wins his lady fair (Helena Carter) after saving the British garrison in Dublin from capture by a traitor (Richard Greene) working for Napoleon. Directed by Arthur Pierson, the tongue-in-cheek adventure flounders in heavy-handed comedy, lackluster swashbuckling, and Fairbank's energetic but charmless performance. Mild violence and romantic complications. A-II (br)

Fighting Pimpernel, The (see: **The Elusive Pimpernel**)

Fighting Prince of Donegal, The (1966) Young Irish prince tries to unite his country against the occupation by soldiers of Queen Elizabeth. Directed by Michael O'Herlihy, this Walt Disney production is an unpretentious action piece with adequate acting by young leads Peter McEnery and Susan Hampshire, with Gordon Jackson excelling in the villainy department. A-I (br)

Fighting Seabees, The (1944) Patriotic WW II programmer in which a civilian contractor (John Wayne) joins forces with a Navy officer (Dennis O'Keefe) in training a naval construction battalion, called the Seabees, which proves itself by building a fuel depot on an island under Japanese attack. Directed by Edward Ludwig, the formula plot includes a war correspondent (Susan Hayward) who's torn between the two until Wayne becomes a posthumous hero. Wartime violence. A-I (br)

Fighting 69th, The (1940) Cheerfully sentimental flag-waver celebrates the WW I exploits of New York's Irish infantry regiment, centering on its compassionate chaplain, Father Duffy (Pat O'Brien), and a feisty recruit (James Cagney) who proves a coward, then redeems himself by jumping on a German grenade to save a comrade (Alan Hale). Director William Keighley mixes broad ethnic humor, roughneck pranks, battlefield heroics and reverential moments into a colorful melodrama that can still be watched with interest. Wartime violence in an idealistic context that contemporary viewers may find unconvincing. A-I (br)

Fighting Sullivans, The (see: **The Sullivans**)

Figures in a Landscape (1971) Enigmatic chase movie begins with two escaped prisoners (Robert Shaw and Malcolm McDowell), hands bound, fleeing across a desolate Spanish countryside, pursued by a helicopter that occasionally shoots at them. Director Joseph Losey never explains who the fugitives are, nor from whom they are fleeing, in a movie that has only a middle, an unexplained antagonism between the principals, and a landscape in which both figures and viewers become lost. A-III (GP)

File of the Golden Goose (1969) Yul Brynner portrays a tough, determined American CIA agent trying to infiltrate a British counterfeiting gang. Director Sam Wanamaker's rather pedestrian British spy thriller contains some rather gruesome killings, coarse language, and homosexual references of questionable taste. A-III (PG)

Files on Thelma Jordan, The (1949) Darkly contrived melodrama directed by Robert Siodmak in which a district attorney (Wendell Corey) gives up home, honor, and career in order to protect a murderess (Barbara Stanwyck) who he believes loves him, only to learn she's played him for a sucker. Stylized violence, romantic situations, and hollow retribution. A-III (br)

Fillmore (1972) Documentary record of the final days and closing night at Fillmore West, the pioneering San Francisco rock-house, showing rock producer Bill Graham in action, for instance, haggling with the managers of groups he wants to perform in the farewell concert. Those who do include Jefferson Airplane, Santana, Quicksilver, New Riders of the Purple Sage, and Hot Tuna. Director Richard T. Heffron has not only captured some of the bittersweet moments of a memorable event, but has made an enlightening work about the rock world. Scatter-shot profanity in an otherwise wholesome and entertaining movie. A-III (R)

Film Actress (1988) Japanese director Kon Ichikawa has fashioned an enlightening look at the life and times of film actress Kinuyo Tanaka (1909-1977), showing the rise and role of this strong-minded and talented female artist (played by Sayuri Yoshinaga) in the history of Japanese cinema through the early 1950s. Rather flat dramatized biographical segments are inter-cut with narrated documentary sequences that include excerpts from her movie performances. Subtitles. Premarital cohabitation. A-III (nr)

Film Portrait (1974) The year before his death in 1972, Jerome Hill put together this picture which consists of his reflections on the magic of cinema and on how his own life got so intimately bound up with it. Definitely for film students, but the casual moviegoer may also enjoy it because it's an interesting look at an individual taking stock of his life's work and finding it, on the whole, something still filled with wonder. A-I (nr)

Final Analysis (1992) Overripe Gothic thriller stars Richard Gere as a San Francisco psychiatrist duped into being a defense witness for a patient's sister (Kim Basinger) accused of murdering her abusive husband (Eric Roberts). Director Phil Joanou blends nifty plot twists with nicely shaded performances to heighten suspense, then drops the ball with a wildly melodramatic ending. Brief violence, short scene of adultery with nudity, and intermittent rough language. A-III (R)

Final Chapter — Walking Tall (1977) Like the previous two movies about Tennessee Sheriff Buford Pusser and his fight against crime in McNairy County, Tennessee, director Jack Starrett's version is crude and simplistic in its good guys vs. bad guys approach. Bo Svenson in the Pusser role is a sensitive and appealing performer with a fine presence which, unfortunately, is wasted in the rigors of excessive violence and bloodshed. O (R)

Final Comedown, The (1972) Black exploitation movie with Billy Dee Williams as a young man on his way to death and destruction is a quite simple story cluttered unnecessarily by a raft of flashbacks. Written, produced, and directed by Oscar Williams, the movie pits the violence of ghetto blacks against the fears of middle-class whites and relies on prejudice and stereotype for effect. Relentless stream of vile epithets and a generous helping of gratuitous nudity. O (R)

Final Conflict, The (1981) Lackluster concluding episode in **The Omen** trilogy with the now-adult Damien (Sam Neill) growing desperate as his days as the Antichrist are drawing to an end. Graham Baker's plodding direction of Andrew Birkin's witless script strings together a boring series of scenes with gory violence. a touch of sadomasochistic sex, and absurd theological allusions. O (R)

Final Countdown, The (1980) The premise of this film is clever even if a bit too reminiscent of "Twilight Zone"-type television drama. Kirk Douglas, Martin Sheen, and James Farentino are aboard the *USS Nimitz* when it slips through a time warp in the year 1980 and reappears at Pearl Harbor in December 1941. It is a clever premise, but the most interesting aspect of director Don Taylor's drama is the aircraft carrier herself, which, photographed in detail, constitutes an overwhelming presence. Some brief, but intense violence. A-II (PG)

Final Crash, The (see: **Steelyard Blues**)

Final Option (1983) Elite anti-terrorist unit battles fanatical peace activists who take over an embassy in an extremely violent and simplistic melodrama directed by Ian Sharp from a screenplay by Reginald Rose. Mediocre entertainment with cardboard characters tries to justify excessive gunplay and brutal retribution for political crimes. A-III (R)

Find a Place to Die (1973) Routine Italian Western about a disgraced Texas Ranger (Jeffery Hunter) who tries to regain his honor by helping a widow (Pascale Petit) recover the gold stolen by the outlaws who murdered her husband. Director Hugo Fregonese's movie is notable only as the last performance of Hunter before his untimely death at age 40. Some brutal violence. A-III (R)

Finders Keepers (1984) Director Richard Lester's attempt at screwball comedy concerns a variety of characters (of which only David Wayne has a sense of comedy) trying to get their hands on a stolen $5 million in the course of a transcontinental train ride. The failed comedy revels in tastelessness, foul language, and an offensively unfunny sexual sequence. O (R)

Fine and Dandy (see: **The West Point Story**)

Fine Madness, A (1966) Sean Connery stars in a quaintly stereotyped role as an eccentric, romantically inclined Irish poet who is totally out of place in normal society. Unfortunately, director Irvin Kershner's movie places its emphasis on his promiscuity, which undercuts what might in other circumstances have been a very funny adult satire. O (br)

Fine Mess, A (1986) When two friends (Ted Danson and Howie Mandel) win big money on a crooked horse race, they find themselves being chased by loony Mafia thugs (Stuart Margolin and Richard Mulligan) as well as the promiscuous wife (Maria Conchita Alonzo) of the Mafia boss (Paul Sorvino). Writer-director Blake Edwards turns the slapstick comedy into a burlesque of the sexual-tease variety. The result provides an unwholesome acceptance of social and sexual irresponsibility, largely in scenes of an adulterous affair. O (PG)

Fine Pair, A (1969) Square New York police detective (Rock Hudson) gets involved with a fey crook (Claudia Cardinale), and after innumerable plot complications they wind up as a couple of lighthearted jewel thieves. Director Francesco Maselli's romance gets overly serious in its treatment of the supposedly idyllic love affair of the unprincipled principals, completely out of keeping with the movie's humorous intentions. O (PG)

Fine Romance, A (1992) Middle-aged engineer (Marcello Mastroianni) and a doctor's wife (Julie Andrews) living in Paris meet to discuss the fact that their mates are having an affair and end up becoming romantically involved with each other. Director Gene Saks's slight comedy depends upon a frail sense of humor about marital infidelity and human weakness. Uncritical attitude toward extramarital affairs. A-III (PG-13)

Finest Hours, The (1964) British documentary on the life and times of Winston Churchill presents an overview of his accomplishments and defeats as statesman, orator, author, soldier, and painter. Narrated by Orson Welles and good selection of photographs and newsreel footage. A-I (br)

Fingers (1978) Crude, pretentious crime melodrama with Harvey Keitel as a would-be concert pianist who supports himself by collecting bad debts for his loan-shark father (Michael V. Gazzo), and hotly pursues a blank-eyed young woman (Tisa Farrow). Directed by James Toback, the resulting confrontations, including random sex and violence, make no sense at all. O (R)

Finian's Rainbow (1968) Screen version of a 1940's Broadway musical offers a variation on the girl-meets-boy plot, with a cantankerous father (Fred

Astaire) and a lonely leprechaun (Tommy Steele) and some broad racial humor thrown in for good measure. Director Francis Ford Coppola brings off an enjoyable entertainment, not quite the lighthearted romantic fantasy that it might have been, but something that is pleasant to watch and, more especially, to listen to. A-I (G)

Finishing School (1934) Dated romance has a student (Ginger Rogers) at an exclusive women's academy falling in love with a poor medical intern (Bruce Cabot) then, helped by a pal (Frances Dee) and the blessings of her father, she escapes the repressive hold of empty-headed mother and conniving principal for marriage. Directed by Wanda Tuchock and George Nicholls, Jr., the contrived story has meager interest save for the period background and populist view of class distinctions. Sexual situations and alcohol abuse. A-III (br)

Fire (1997) Sudsy tale from India in which two sisters-in-law are thrown together and begin a lesbian affair after one husband insists on celibacy while the other prefers sleeping with his mistress. Writer-director Deepa Mehta stacks the deck by stereotyping men as selfish and cruel while presenting the women as virtually forced to turn to each other for love and sexual fulfillment. Defensive treatment of lesbian behavior, bedroom scenes including masturbation, brief nudity, fleeting violence, and some rough language. O (nr)

Fire and Ice (1983) Animated feature created by Ralph Bakshi about a war between good and evil wizards — the good one's weapon is fire, the bad one's is ice — displays in abundant detail Bakshi's obsession with grotesque sex and extravagant violence. All the more disheartening is to see such material appearing in a format traditionally reserved for family entertainment. O (PG)

Fire and Ice (1987) Series of spectacular stunts on skis, bobsleds, wind sleds, and skateboards are strung together by the flimsy device of a Canadian skier (John Eaves) searching for the girl of his dreams (Olympic skier Suzy Chaffee). German production photographed and directed by Willy Bogner offers plenty of winter feats with a pounding rock score and the limited dramatic talent of his principals. Some brief nudity in a bedroom scene. A-III (PG)

Fire Birds (1990) Brash Army helicopter pilot (Nicolas Cage) must convince his envious training instructor (Tommy Lee Jones) to select him for a dangerous air strike on a South American drug cartel, while coping with a feminist girlfriend (Sean Young) who despises his macho attitudes. Director David Green's rousing but simplistic tale of winning the drug war with a single military mission makes the characters secondary to the swooping aerial action and explosive special effects. Violent scenes of air combat, crude double entendres, and a fairly restrained bedroom scene. A-III (PG-13)

Fire Down Below (1997) Formula action movie in which an indestructible EPA agent (Steven Seagal) single-handedly saves an Appalachian community's water supply from a greedy mogul (Kris Kristofferson) while also rescuing a beautiful woman (Marg Helgenberger) from her abusive brother (Stephen Lang). Directed by Felix Enriquez Alcala, the plot is predictable, the characters are one-dimensional, and Seagal's macho heroics tiresome. Much stylized violence, sexual references, occasional profanity, and several instances of rough language. A-III (R)

Fire in the Sky (1993) Five Arizona loggers (led by Robert Patrick), suspected of murdering a vanished co-worker (D.B. Sweeney), are cleared when he returns to their midst five days later, dazed by terrifying memories of his abduction by a UFO. Director Robert Lieberman's dramatization of a supposedly fact-based 1975 incident uses imaginative special effects to suggest the alien encounter but avoids questions of extraterrestrial life by concentrating on the mundane plight of the loggers. A scene of menacing aliens physically abusing the main character. A-II (PG-13)

Fire on the Mountain (1996) Documentary about the formation and military achievements during WW II of the US Army's 10th Mountain Division, the only American infantry corps specifically trained for mountain warfare. Co-directors Beth and George Gage engagingly document the division's three years of training in the Rockies, its assault on German positions in the Italian Apennines, and the how surviving members of the 10th helped to popularize skiing in postwar America. Some combat footage. A-II (nr)

Fire with Fire (1986) Awkward teen romance with a bright and pretty convent schoolgirl (Virginia Madsen) being consumed by love for a boy (Craig Sheffer) from a nearby juvenile offenders' work camp. Directed by Duncan Gibbons, the plot of teenagers against a passionless adult world is dramatically unjustified. Instances of profanity and violence as well as scene of sexual gropings in a graveyard. A-III (PG-13)

Fire Within, The (1969) Taut, well-constructed, and thoroughly engrossing French movie records two days in the life of an alcoholic ex-playboy (Maurice Ronet) desperately searching for security, understanding, and meaning in his life. Director Louis Malle's 1963 drama presents a stinging indictment of upper middle-class life in a work whose theme is one of soul-searching despair. A-III (nr)

Fireball 500 (1966) Frankie Avalon plays a tough stockcar racer with Fabian Forte as his chief rival for the racing high-stakes and for the dimpled hand of sweet Annette Funicello as well. William Asher directs this dumb, garden-variety teenage vehicle, which has everything that used to happen in those beach-blanket-bingo movies of the early 1960s, except that instead of bikinis the bouncing babes are wearing abbreviated racing duds. The giggles and inane songs are the same, though. A-III (br)

Firecreek (1968) Henry Fonda terrorizes the town

where Jimmy Stewart is sheriff in a Western reminiscent of the showdown situation immortalized in **High Noon,** but it lacks that movie's punch. Director Vincent McEveety can't make up his mind whether the climactic shootout is a good thing or not, so why bother? Stylized violence. A-II (br)

Firefox (1982) Clint Eastwood stars as an American pilot traumatized by his Vietnam experiences who sneaks into the Soviet Union and steals a secret super-plane. Also directed by Eastwood, the action movie is plodding and unexciting, but does feature some graphic violence. A-III (PG)

Firelight (1998) Gauzy British period romance begins in 1838, when an impoverished Swiss governess (Sophie Marceau) is paid by an anonymous gentleman (Stephen Dillane) to bear his child, then give up the infant for him to raise, but seven years later she finds the two when hired as governess to the little girl. Writer-director William Nicholson fashions intriguing characters for the trio, but lets the narrative gradually descend into romanticized melodrama. Ambiguous treatment of euthanasia, discreet sexual encounters with nudity, and an instance of rough language. A-IV (R)

Fireman's Ball, The (1968) Unpretentious Czechoslovakian comedy deals with the foibles of average people in the story of a small-town fire brigade's annual ball. Disorganized and inept, the brigade bungles through in the face of stolen raffle prizes, an embarrassing beauty contest, and finally a real fire, while the ball continues as if nothing had happened. Directed by Milos Forman, the film is done with such good humor and loving care that the viewer cannot help but enjoy its affirmation that people are good, no matter how silly or stupid they may act. Some mature material. A-III (br)

Firepower (1979) Retired hit-man (James Coburn) is recruited by the Justice Department to kidnap a crooked financier from his Caribbean sanctuary and bring him back to stand trial in the States. The lavishly mounted British production has lots of lovely scenery, but director Michael Winner's trite melodrama overdoses on heavy-handed action and violence, made even more repugnant by its sleazy moral outlook. O (R)

Firestorm (1998) Hokey thriller in which forest firefighters (led by superhero Howie Long) rescue a woman (Suzy Amis) taken hostage by convicts (led by villainous William Forsythe) who have torched the woods to cover their escape. Directed by Dean Semler, the picture's cardboard characters and contrived situations add up to little more than a smoke-filled time-waster. Much violence and menace, some sexual innuendo, and occasional rough language and profanity. A-III (R)

Firestarter (1984) Screen version of Stephen King horror story about a little girl (Drew Barrymore) who is kidnapped by a secret government agency who want to use her psychokinetic power to make things burst into flames. Martin Sheen and George C. Scott make an interesting contrast in villains, but director Mark Lester's treatment of the premise is more absurd than frightening. Youngsters, however, may be negatively influenced by and even delight in the film's theme of a child's revenge against a cruel adult world. A-III (R)

Firewalker (1986) Simple but plodding action-adventure yarn about a woman (Melody Anderson) who hires two soldiers-of-fortune (Chuck Norris and Louis Gossett Jr.) to hunt for ancient Mayan treasure in Central America. J. Lee Thompson's direction is amiable but slack in its treatment of the usual assortment of villains and plot complications. Stylized, almost slapstick, violence. A-II (PG)

Firm, The (1993) After accepting a lucrative job offer from a small Memphis law firm, a novice lawyer (Tom Cruise) discovers his bosses are laundering mob money and must decide whether to risk his life copying their files for the FBI or be indicted if he doesn't cooperate. Director Sydney Pollack translates John Grisham's bestseller into a tense thriller whose cat-and-mouse maneuverings are sometimes confusing, but whose wily performances by Cruise, Gene Hackman, Holly Hunter, and Gary Busey are consistently absorbing. Brief violence, some sexual innuendo, and intermittent rough language. A-III (R)

First Blood (1982) Sylvester Stallone plays John Rambo, a disillusioned Vietnam veteran who reacts to police brutality in a small northwestern town by waging a one-man war against the local police force and the National Guard. Though Ted Kotcheff's direction is effective in fashioning a quite brutal action melodrama, it offers nothing of substance about the plight of the Vietnam veteran. Violence and rough language. A-III (R)

First Charge of the Machete (1974) In 1868, Cuban nationalists declared their independence from the Spanish colonial regime and defeated the army sent against it by using machetes in hand-to-hand combat. Manuel Octovio Gomez re-creates this patriotic episode as if it were a documentary filmed as the events occurred, interviewing participants of both sides and using high-contrast photography to effect a period feeling. A-II (nr)

First Circle, The (1973) Screen adaptation of Russian author Aleksandr Solzhenitsyn's account of the spiritual and physical torments of a political prisoner under Stalinist oppression is a deeply felt one, but its meaning never gets beyond the literal level of story and dialogue. Director Alexander Ford's graphic depictions of sadistic brutalization and sexual degradation needlessly depart from the rest of the movie's stylized visualization of prison-camp oppression. A-IV (R)

First Deadly Sin, The (1980) Frank Sinatra stars as an aging New York detective in pursuit of a deranged killer while worrying about his bedridden wife (Faye Dunaway). Brian G. Hutton directs a deeply flawed but entertaining enough crime melodrama with some gratuitous violence. A-III (R)

... First Do No Harm (1997) Fact-based drama in which a mother (Meryl Streep) refuses a risky brain operation for her epileptic four-year-old son and turns instead to a dieting treatment which has been successful for others. Directed by Jim Abrahams, the provocative story takes a harshly critical view of the medical establishment, while not sparing viewers the sight of a helpless child's agonizing convulsions or of the strain the boy's deteriorating condition places on his distressed family. Harrowing depiction of a suffering child and resulting domestic tensions. A-II (PG-13)

First Family (1981) Awkward, unfunny comedy starring Bob Newhart, Madeline Kahn, and Gilda Radner as the US presidential family. Buck Henry directs with total reliance upon humor derived from vulgar language and crude sight gags, combined with a few implicitly racist scenes. O (R)

First Kid (1996) Lightweight comedy in which a genial Secret Service agent (Sinbad) assigned to guard the president's 13-year-old son (Brock Pierce) spends his time building the neglected youngster's self-esteem by teaching him to box, dance, and be a regular kid. Directed by David Mickey Evans, the appealing story turns needlessly nasty at the end when a deranged individual sets out to shoot the boy. Some violence, deadly menace to a child, and fleeting nudity. A-II (PG)

First Knight (1995) After Lancelot (Richard Gere) rescues the soon-to-be Queen Guinevere (Julia Ormond) from the clutches of a power-mad rival (Ben Cross), King Arthur (Sean Connery) makes him a knight of the Round Table, then is devastated to discover his bride and trusted knight have fallen in love. Lovely to behold, rousingly paced with an emphasis on the virtues of honor and selflessness, director Jerry Zucker retells the legend of Camelot in a splendid swirl of romance and adventure whose contrived happy ending is the only false note. Stylized battlefield violence and romantic complications. A-II (PG-13)

First Love (1970) Romanticized German tale of fantasy and imagination in which a young lad falls in love with a slightly older flirt who has moved in next door, only to find out that his father (Maximilian Schell) is sleeping with the girl. Also directed by Schell, the movie concentrates on atmosphere and mood with bucolic settings and lush photography, but its lack of plot and shallow substance will leave most viewers yawning. A-III (R)

First Love (1977) College student (William Katt) looking for a lasting relationship catches a rich coed (Susan Dey), loses her to a married man, gets her back, but then doesn't want her any more because the "magic" is gone. Director Joan Darling's overripe soap opera of instant gratification takes itself so seriously that it would be laughable if its nudity, simulated intercourse, and coarse language were not so offensive. O (R)

First Men in the Moon (1964) H.G. Wells's tale of an eccentric English inventor (Lionel Jeffries) who uses his discovery of anti-gravity to take a couple (Edward Judd and Martha Hyer) on a trip to the moon in 1899. Directed by Nathan Juran, the preliminaries are mildly amusing, but matters turn serious after the trio find an advanced civilization of human-sized insects living in tunnels beneath the lunar surface. Some scary special effects by Ray Harryhausen. A-I (br)

First Monday in October (1981) Walter Matthau and Jill Clayburgh star in this drama about the first woman appointed to the US Supreme Court. On the surface, director Ronald Neame's movie deals with liberal-conservative conflicts but essentially demonstrates that women have the same problems as men in dealing with the complex and often unfair American justice system. A pornography case involves a needless nude insert and mature line of dialogue. A-III (R)

First Nudie Musical, The (1977) Shoddy production about a producer who is inspired to put on a pornographic musical to save his seedy company from ruin. Directors Mark Haggard and Bruce Kimmel emphasize sophomoric vulgarities and exploit nudity. O (R)

First of the Few, The (see: 1942's **Spitfire**)

First Position (1973) Inside look at the training of ballet students in which the real test is whether they have sufficient talent and determination to devote their lives to the pursuit of artistic perfection. Produced and directed by William Richert, the documentary succeeds admirably in conveying the hard work that goes into the learning of any art and the self-doubts of students as they look to the future. A-II (nr)

First Power, The (1990) A Los Angeles homicide detective (Lou Diamond Phillips) and a psychic (Tracy Griffith) play cat-and-mouse games with the satanic spirit of an executed serial killer (Jeff Kober) who possesses the bodies of weak humans and keeps on killing. Writer-director Robert Resnikoff's inventive stunt work does not save this cop thriller from deteriorating into a predictable, overlong horror show. Much menace, grisly violence, and bloody gore. O (R)

First Texan, The (1956) Agreeable Hollywood history of former Tennessee governor Sam Huston (Joel McCrea) coming to San Antonio in 1832 to set up a law practice, then agreeing to lead the fight against the Mexican forces of Santa Anna (David Silva) after the fall of the Alamo. Though director Byron Haskin doesn't make the events very exciting, the story of Huston's part in Texan independence holds interest, helped considerably by McCrea's credible performance as the heroic leader. Stylized violence. A-I (br)

First Time, The (1969) Empty-headed movie based on the supposition that the average American boy yearns to visit a house of prostitution and that listening to teenagers talk naively about sex is amusing.

Directed by James Neilson, the treatment of characters and situation lacks any sensitivity or insight, and the movie is slapped together so badly as to give the impression of being an amateur production. O (M)

First Time, The (1978) Easygoing, highly indulgent memoir about a 16-year-old boy's first sexual encounter gives some warm and positive details of French family life, but the view of sex presented here is morally wanting. Directed by Claude Berri, the movie is further marred by offensive dialogue and graphic depictions of sexual behavior. O (X)

First Time Felon (1997) Gritty fact-based tale of a Chicago youth (Omar Epps) sentenced to five years in prison for selling drugs but, because it's his first offense, he gets the chance instead to undergo four months of military-style discipline in a prison boot-camp program from which he returns home a better person, then finds no one will hire a convicted drug dealer. Directed by actor Charles S. Dutton, this television movie about a dead-end kid in an urban African-American community manages to overcome its cliched plot and characters to evoke the sense of alienation that breeds inner-city crime as well as the plight of those who try to escape it. Some degrading violence and much foul language. A-III (R)

First to Fight (1967) Standard WW II tale in which a Marine (Chad Everett) wins a Congressional Medal of Honor on 1942 Guadalcanal, then gets married on a war-bond tour, tires of training recruits, and is sent back into action, until he freezes with fright when his platoon hits the beach at Saipan. Directed by Christian Nyby, there's nothing new in this reworking of the old theme portraying true heroism as doing your duty despite being afraid. Wartime violence and romantic complications. A-II (br)

First Turn-On, The (1984) Exploitation film about a female guide and four teenage male campers who become trapped in a cave and pass the time describing their first sexual experiences. Nudity in a sexual context. O (R)

First Wives Club, The (1996) Deserted by wealthy husbands who have callously lined up younger replacements, three irate wives (Bette Midler, Goldie Hawn, and Diane Keaton) scheme to humiliate and financially drain their estranged spouses. Directed by Hugh Wilson, the revenge-themed comedy is weighed down by unconvincing plot contrivances, despite spirited performances and caustically funny dialogue. Some sexual innuendo, an off-screen suicide, fleeting comic violence, and an instance of profanity. A-III (PG)

Firstborn (1984) Divorced mother (Terri Garr) falls for a brutish loser (Peter Weller) who moves in and precipitates domestic violence with resentful teenage sons. Trite melodrama directed by Michael Apted tries to be a cautionary tale about distraught women making desperate commitments to men before knowing anything about them. Brutality rules out youngsters. A-III (PG-13)

Fish Called Wanda, A (1988) Black comedy by veteran British director Charles Crichton involves an uptight barrister (John Cleese) with a bizarre gang of jewel thieves (Jamie Lee Curtis, Kevin Kline, Michael Palin) whose methods stop at nothing, including sex and violence. The comic performances are weakened by running gags offending animal lovers, stutterers, and probably everyone else. Sexual promiscuity for laughs, much profanity and vulgar humor. O (R)

Fish Hawk (1980) The story of the friendship between a farmer's young son (Charlie Fields) and the lone Indian (Will Sampson) living in a white community in the Ozarks at the turn of the century is an unremarkable but pleasant and unpretentious entertainment directed by Donald Shebib. The acting is excellent, and the outdoor adventures of the two principals will appeal to younger children. A-I (G)

Fish That Saved Pittsburgh, The (1979) Dreadfully inept comedy about the rejuvenation of a basketball franchise through applied astrology, with Stockard Channing as the team astrologer, has been thrown together in slapdash fashion by director Gilbert Moses. Several instances of vulgar language. A-II (PG)

Fisher King, The (1991) Extravagant fantasy about a guilt-ridden former talk-show host (Jeff Bridges) and his feisty live-in love (Mercedes Ruehl) who try to help a tragically widowed homeless man (Robin Williams) win over a new love (Amanda Plummer). Director Terry Gilliam's exuberant dramatic comedy is a boldly imagined and beautifully cast fable of redemption that lurches out of control as it nears its sentimental wrap-up. Momentary gory violence, a live-in relationship, frequent rough language, and fleeting, shadowy nudity. A-III (R)

F.I.S.T. (1978) Sylvester Stallone stars in a deeply flawed, highly romanticized saga of the labor movement, which draws heavily upon the history of the Teamsters Union and the rise and fall of James Hoffa. Director Norman Jewison works on a large canvas telling a story that begins with hope and ends in corruption. The violence along the way is set in the context of a well-intentioned theme of social justice. A-III (PG)

Fistful of Dollars, A (1967) The spaghetti Western that launched Clint Eastwood's meteoric career as the squinting, black-hatted, cheroot-chomping gunslinger known as "The Man with No Name" who hires himself out to one side or the other, and occasionally both at once, in the settling of a border dispute. Directed with style by Sergio Leone, the action is swift, the violence plentiful, and the vengeance all Clint's. O (br)

Fistful of Dynamite (see: **Duck, You Sucker**!)

Fists of Fury (1973) Kung fu artist Bruce Lee takes on a gang of Bangkok dope smugglers, dispatching them with axes and clubs, and in countless stabbings and slashings with knives and swords. Viewers will gasp at the gore more than at the hero's prowess in this inept action movie written and directed by Lo

Wei. Excessive violence and nudity in a brothel scene. O (R)

Fists of the Double K (1973) Karate and kung fu are among the lethal means of killing people in this worthless action movie whose violence is bloody and interminable, interrupted only by some sex scenes by way of an attempted rape of a blind girl and a homosexual bad-guy. O (R)

Fitzwilly (1967) Breezy variation of the Robin Hood theme with a canny butler (Dick Van Dyke) running a thievery racket with other domestics in order to keep up the household of his once-rich New York employer (Dame Edith Evans). Directed by Delbert Mann, it has its amusing moments but, in spite of a comment on the dishonesty of bilking insurance companies, it still implies that what people don't know won't hurt them. A-III (br)

5 Against the House (1955) Bored with college studies, three Korean War veterans (Brian Keith, Alvy Moore, and Kerwin Matthews) concoct a "foolproof" plan to rob a Reno gambling casino but need another vet (Guy Madison) and his girlfriend (Kim Novak) to pull it off. Director Phil Karlson's routine crime caper takes a long time getting away from the phony campus setting and some soggy romance before heading for Reno and a heist complicated by one of the vets being an ex-psychiatric case. Criminal situations and mild sexual innuendo. A-III (br)

Five Bloody Graves (1971) Violent Western in which foolhardy Robert Dix, trailing the Yaqui warrior who slaughtered his wife, encounters sneaky Indians, stubborn homesteaders, stranded stagecoach passengers, wily gunrunners, and a half-breed renegade — all of whom dispatch one another before several suns have set. Women are not exempt from bullets or arrows, and producer-director Al Adamson treats one rape-murder in an especially cruel manner. O (R/GP)

Five Card Stud (1968) Mediocre Western mystery pits Dean Martin as a fast-talking, fast-loving gambler against Robert Mitchum as a hellfire preacher who also carries a gun. Director Henry Hathaway spins a simple story of retribution motivated by the lynching of a card cheat but the identity of the revengeful killer is fairly obvious. Gory violence, sexual innuendo, and a questionable use of religion. A-III (PG)

Five Days One Summer (1982) Produced and directed by Fred Zinnemann, this is the story of a 1930's romance set against the stunning background of the Swiss Alps, where a man and his niece (Sean Connery and Betsy Brantley) try to pass themselves off as husband and wife during a skiing vacation. The well-crafted movie has very good acting and acknowledges in no-nonsense fashion the existence of good and evil. Several love scenes handled with much restraint. A-II (PG)

Five Easy Pieces (1970) Jack Nicholson gives an outstanding performance as a young man who has lost his sense of identity and is wasting his life searching and unsatisfied. Directed with precision by Bob Rafelson, the movie's best scene is when Nicholson breaks down and confesses his loneliness to his stroke-victim father. The movie's moral ambiguity makes it more suitable for serious viewing rather than casual entertainment. A-IV (R)

5 Fingers (1952) Fact-based dramatization of WW II espionage in neutral Turkey, where the British ambassador's valet (James Mason) finances early retirement by selling top-secret embassy documents to the Germans, only to be doublecrossed by a Polish countess (Danielle Darrieux) and his Nazi paymasters. Director Jospeh L. Mankiewicz does best with Mason's coolly intelligent portrayal as the enterprising spy code-named Cicero, but dampens the effect with sporadic wry humor, while comic Nazi stereotypes undercut the irony of German agents discarding the plans for the Normandy invasion because they feared Cicero was a double agent. Wartime dangers and mild romance. A-I (br)

5 Fingers of Death (1973) Hong Kong martial-arts movie directed by Cheng Chang Ho shows the training of a young disciple of a kung fu master and their problems with thugs from a rival school. The atrocious dubbing of this thin effort makes the action seem at first to be played for laughs but it proves, unfortunately, to be deadly serious. Acrobatic violence. A-III (R)

Five Golden Dragons (1967) Lame crime thriller directed by Jeremy Summers is set in Hong Kong, where a genial American visitor (Bob Cummings) gets mixed up in a gold-smuggling ring (led by Brian Donlevy, Dan Duryea, George Raft, and Christopher Lee in cameos), with predictable results. Stylized violence and mild sexual innuendo. A-II (br)

Five Graves to Cairo (1943) Intriguing WW II thriller in which a British officer (Franchot Tone) masquerades as a porter in a Sahara Desert hotel occupied by Rommel (Erich von Stroheim) in order to learn where the Germans have hidden advance-supply depots for invading Egypt. Director Otto Preminger relieves the tension with occasional humor in the relations between the bogus porter and the hotel staff (Akim Tamiroff and Anne Baxter), though the situation itself is less than credible. Wartime violence and menace. A-II (br)

Five Heartbeats, The (1991) The career and personal lives of a fictional black singing-group in the '60s is charted in this musical drama starring Robert Townsend, Michael Wright, and Leon. Also directed by Townsend, the warm-hearted but vapid nostalgia trip has lots of corn but little bite. Considerable sexual innuendo, occasional violence, and some rough language. A-III (R)

Five Man Army, The (1970) Peter Graves plays the leader of an odd collection of renegades whom he has brought together to rob a shipment of gold from the Mexican government at the turn of the century. Substandard Western directed by Don Taylor has a lumpy doublecross plot that fails to bridge the credibility gap. Some of the violence gets a bit gruesome in spots. A-III (PG)

Five Million Years to Earth (1968) Above-average British science-fiction movie in which workers digging a London subway extension find skeletons and an indestructible spacecraft with a prehistoric secret that threatens the entire human race until a brave scientist (James Donald) discovers the origins and meaning of the craft. With good acting, dialogue, and special effects, director Roy Ward Baker's unpretentious effort sustains interest and an air of plausibility. Mild violence. A-II (br)

Five on the Black Hand Side (1973) Good screen version of a play by Charlie L. Russell tells a simple but humorous story of the varying effect black awareness has on a middle-class family living in Los Angeles. Under the direction of Oscar Williams, the performances are warm and engaging, with Clarice Taylor and Leonard Jackson as the parents and Glynn Turman, Bonnie Banfield, and D'Urville Martin as their grown children. The ultimate message is one of positive respect for oneself and others, which in turn leads to a sense of solidarity and community. A-III (G/PG)

Five Pennies, The (1959) Dour screen bio of coronet-player Red Nichols (Danny Kaye), whose Dixieland quintet became famous in the 1920s, but he quit the music business when his daughter contracted polio in the 1930s, then made a comeback after she recovered in the 1940s. Directed by Melville Shavelson, Kaye's acerbic performance as Nichols is mellowed somewhat by the interaction of wife Barbara Bel Geddes, pal Harry Guardino, and jazz king Louis Armstrong himself, but the characters prove less interesting than the era's music. A-I (br)

Fixed Bayonets! (1951) Korean War tale in which a platoon left behind to cover the withdrawal of a US infantry division sets up a position in a narrow ravine, then holds on despite attacks by enemy troops, mortar barrages, and, finally, tanks. Writer-director Samuel Fuller focuses on individual members of the platoon, notably a veteran sergeant (Gene Evans) and a troubled corporal (Richard Basehart) who freezes in combat. Battlefield violence. A-I (br)

Fixer, The (1968) Set during a time of pogroms in Czarist Russia, the movie tells the story of a simple carpenter (Alan Bates) who is falsely accused of the ritual murder of a young boy. The man's stubborn refusal to confess to the crime makes his case internationally famous and the country which holds him prisoner must force his confession in order to save its good name. Director John Frankenheimer's intense but thought-provoking adaptation of the Bernard Malamud novel confronts viewers with a universal theme of intolerance and abuse of power. Solid fare for adults and older adolescents. A-III (PG)

Flame and the Arrow, The (1950) Energetic adventure set in medieval Italy, where a grinning outlaw (Burt Lancaster) leads the citizens of Lombardy in a revolt against a cruel Hessian despot (Frank Allenby) whose niece (Virginia Mayo) sides with the rebels. Directed with gusto by Jacques Tourneur, the script gives full bent to Lancaster's acrobatic skills and those of his partner, Nick Cravat, in this overbusy Robin Hood variation. Stylized violence and considerable menace. A-II (br)

Flame and the Fire (1966) French documentary about the Stone Age lives of primitive tribes in remote areas of South America, Africa and the Pacific. Directed by Pierre Dominique Gaisseau, it is not sensationalistic but some of its elements may prove distasteful or shocking to sensitive viewers. A-IV (br)

Flame in My Heart, A (1990) Sexually explicit black-and-white meditation on the drawbacks of obsessive love as observed in the life of a Parisian actress (Myriam Mezieres) who is stalked by one lover while she herself becomes obsessed with a casual stranger. While perhaps titillating to its Swiss director, Alain Tanner, this borderline porn movie is a hardcore bore and should be avoided at all costs. Subtitles. Numerous scenes of graphic sex including full frontal nudity. O (nr)

Flame of Araby (1951) Halting romantic adventure directed by Charles Lamont in which an Arabian princess (Maureen O'Hara) avoids being married to a boorish Corsair pirate by proposing to wed the winner of a horse race, then cajoles a likeable Bedouin (Jeff Chandler) to enter the race riding an unbeatable black stallion. Stylized violence, romantic complications, and some sexual innuendo. A-II (br)

Flame of New Orleans, The (1941) Romantic comedy about antebellum foreign belle (Marlene Dietrich) who hooks a rich suitor (Roland Young) but can't land him because of the unwanted attentions of a dashing sea captain (Bruce Cabot). French director Rene Clair fails to get much mirth out of the silly situations, though Dietrich is fun to watch and the period costumes are eye-fetching. Romantic complications and borderline black stereotyping. A-II (br)

Flame of the Barbary Coast (1945) Routine melodrama directed by Joseph Kane in which a Montana cowboy (John Wayne) competes with a ritzy casino owner (Joseph Schildkraut) for the affections of San Francisco's prettiest showgirl (Ann Dvorak), but it takes the 1906 earthquake to resolve the situation. Romantic complications. A-II (br)

Flame of the Islands (1958) Dreary hokum directed by Edward Ludwig in which a woman (Yvonne De Carlo) becomes partners with a crook (Kurt Kasznar) in a Nassau casino, where she takes revenge on the wealthy man (Howard Duff) who had gotten her pregnant as a teenager. Stylized violence and sexual situations. A-III (br)

Flame Over India (1959) Rattling good adventure thriller follows a British officer (Kenneth Moore) escorting a six-year-old Hindu prince and his governess (Lauren Bacall) on a dangerous train journey to safety during a 1905 Moslem uprising on the Northwest Frontier. Directed by J. Lee Thompson, the well-paced narrative includes a traitor among the passengers (Herbert Lom, Wilfred Hyde-White, Ursula Jeans, et al.) in the prince's coach, which is drawn by an antiquated steam engine with a personality all its own. Some reassuring humor and compensating values amidst the tale's suspense and stylized violence. A-I (br)

Flaming Feather (1951) Routine Western directed by Ray Enright follows the 1877 exploits of a hardened Arizona rancher (Sterling Hayden) and a veteran cavalry officer (Forrest Tucker) in tracking down a white renegade called the Sidewinder (Victor Jory) whose band of Ute warriors are the terror of the territory. Frontier violence. A-I (br)

Flaming Frontier, The (1968) Ludicrous German Western directed by Alfred Vohrer based on the Old Shatterhand character created by Karl May appears here as Old Surehand (Stewart Granger), who tries to keep peace between the Indians and frontier settlers. Mild violence. A-I (G)

Flaming Star (1960) Standard Western in which the son (Elvis Presley) of a pioneer Texas rancher (John McIntire) and his Kiowa wife (Delores Del Rio) is torn between fighting for or against his mother's people when they make war on his father's people. Directed by Don Siegel, the story of how the family tries to stay out of the fighting falls apart when the whites prove as bloodthirsty as the Indians, and tragedy looms for all. Frontier violence and menacing situations make it unlikely fare for young children. A-I (br)

Flamingo Kid, The (1985) Brooklyn youth of 18 (Matt Dillon) gains some maturity in the summer of 1963 while working at an affluent Long Island beach club, an experience that confirms his blue-collar father's traditional values over those of the would-be rich and famous. Director Garry Marshall's work is slickly fashioned but contrived and superficial. Sympathetic depiction of sexual promiscuity. O (PG-13)

Flamingo Road (1949) Gritty romantic melodrama in which a stranded carnival dancer (Joan Crawford) gets romantically involved with a man (Zachary Scott) being groomed for political office by the local sheriff (Sidney Greenstreet), who keeps trying to run her out of town. Directed by Michael Curtiz, the story's sudsy romance is fairly tepid, but the escalating battle between former dancer and corrupt sheriff is what still holds interest. Stylized violence and sexual situations. A-III (br)

Flanagan (1985) Middle-aged out-of-work actor (Philip Bosco), burdened with family and personal problems, is forced to drive a taxi while he struggles along trying to be ready to seize the big chance when it comes his way. Directed and co-scripted by Scott Goldstein, it's an interesting, often moving little film, though the script is too episodic and the happy ending is several shades too improbable. Mature treatment of the hero's marital problems and some rough language. A-III (R)

Flap (1970) Anthony Quinn plays Flapping Eagle in a seriocomic attempt to decry the mistreatment and indifference endured by today's Native-Americans. Flap fights police prejudice and highway construction in trying to preserve his people's cultural heritage but, regrettably, the movie fails to confront far deeper issues of discrimination and, indeed, stereotypes Indians as deceitful, debauched (by Madam Shelley Winters and her girls), and destructive daredevils. British director Carol Reed's movie is an embarrassment that will seem funny only to the most ill-informed viewer. A-III (GP)

Flareup (1969) Shallow chase film with little suspense and much trite characterization stars James Stacey as a mentally unbalanced, jealous husband who thinks go-go dancer Raquel Welch has broken up his marriage. Directed by James Neilson, the movie's bumbling treatment of violence, nudity, drugs, and homosexuality only further encumbers an already weak film. O (PG/PG-13)

Flash Gordon (1980) Neither Sam J. Jones as the comic-strip hero nor Melody Anderson as Dale Arden are especially memorable in this lush and campy Dino De Laurentis production, whose witless script is directed by Mike Hodges. What moderate entertainment value the movie has to offer comes from the non-stop action, the inspired tackiness of the costumes and sets, and the performances of Max von Sydow as Ming the Merciless and Brian Blessed as a jovially barbaric hawk-man. Much stylized violence and sexual innuendo. A-III (PG)

Flash of Green, A (1985) Reporter in a small Florida town lets himself be drawn into the orbit of a corrupt politician intent on enriching himself in fronting for an ecologically destructive resort development. An interesting, very well-acted but flawed movie based on a John D. MacDonald novel and directed by Victor Nunez. Violence and a fairly graphic bedroom scene. A-III (nr)

Flashback (1990) Mismatched-buddy picture that pits a wily old 1960s radical (Dennis Hopper) against a young play-by-the-rules FBI rookie (Kiefer Sutherland) assigned to escort the aging prankster to court. Director Franco Amurri badly juggles at least five themes here, including a buddy action-adventure, a generation-gap comedy, a drama about self-acceptance, and an Abbott and Costello farce. Brief gratuitous violence, some sexual innuendo, and profanity. A-III (R)

Flashdance (1983) Director Adrian Lyne romanticizes the rags-to-riches story of a working-class female (Jennifer Beals) who overcomes hardships to fulfill her dreams of becoming a professional dancer. Blatantly exploiting female anatomy, the musical tries to overcome the commercial sexism with a love story about self-reliance. Some nudity. O (R)

Flashpoint (1984) Two Border Patrol officers (Kris Kristofferson and Treat Williams) in a remote part of Texas find themselves the targets of ruthless covert agents after they discover a jeep long buried in the desert. Director Bill Tannen's moderately entertaining action adventure has restrained violence, but because of its somber mood and extremely rough language, it is not for younger viewers. A-III (R)

Flat Top (1952) Formula WW II picture directed by Lesley Selander in which a veteran fighter pilot (Sterling Hayden) on an aircraft carrier pushes a squadron of recruits so hard they resent him until actual combat makes them realize the value of what he has taught them. Wartime violence. A-I (br)

Flatliners (1990) Bizarre aftereffects plague ambitious medical students (Kiefer Sutherland, Julia Roberts, Kevin Bacon, and others) when they engage in dangerous experiments aimed at taking them momentarily to whatever lies beyond death's threshold. Directed by Joel Schumacher, the pretentious fantasy thriller falls flat with illogical plot developments, frantic sound effects, and generally unsympathetic characters. Rationalization of suicidal behavior, depictions of promiscuity, sporadic violence, and some rough language. O (R)

Flavor of Green Tea over Rice (1973) Japanese drama shows the changes in the traditional view of marriage during the post-war era in the story of a woman's passage from indifference to rebellion and finally to a new appreciation of herself and her husband. Director Yasujiro Ozu's movie, made in 1952, is another of his quiet studies of family life, very intimate and warm with the special quality of humanity that Ozu manages to evoke from his characters. A-I (nr)

Flea in Her Ear, A (1968) Dull French bed-sitting room farce in which Rex Harrison and Rosemary Harris lead a parade of comically malcontent marrieds who get themselves into an essentially innocent tangle of mistaken identities and intentions that result in much door-slamming, sneaking around corners, and hallway chases at a disreputable Paris hotel. Directed by Jacques Charon, the proceedings are energetic, but lack the sense of timing and pace required for farce. A-III (PG)

Fled (1996) Violent action flick in which two escaped convicts (Laurence Fishburne and Stephen Baldwin) dodge Atlanta cops, feds, and murderous Cuban mobsters while trying to locate a stolen computer disc and a stash of five million dollars. Director Kevin Hooks keeps the guns blasting in this trashy tale of deceit, corruption, and crime paying off handsomely. Excessive violence, brief nudity, some profanity, and much rough language. O (R)

Flesh and Bone (1993) Emotionally scarred in childhood by a violent father (James Caan), a Texas loner (Dennis Quaid) becomes romantically involved with an abused wife (Meg Ryan), unaware they had met years earlier under deadly circumstances, which return to haunt him when his father reappears on the scene. Skillfully building on an atmosphere of menacing doom, writer/director Steve Kloves's contemporary film noir focuses on a well-meaning man who becomes unwittingly trapped in a moral dilemma. A few bedroom scenes with brief nudity, some violence, and intermittent rough language. A-III (R)

Flesh and Fantasy (1943) Three moody stories of the supernatural tell of a Mardi Gras mask transforming a plain woman (Betty Field) into a beauty; a palm-reader (Thomas Mitchell) foretelling the terrible fate of a smug lawyer (Edward G. Robinson); and a tightrope walker (Charles Boyer) meeting the woman (Barbara Stanwyck) he dreamed caused his death. Director Julien Duvivier works up a lot of sinister atmosphere and tense suspense, but the stories are only intermittently interesting and the limp comic wraparounds by Robert Benchley can't tie them together as a package. A-II (br)

Flesh and Fury (1952) Lightweight drama about a deaf-and-dumb boxer (Tony Curtis) torn between two women (Jan Sterling and Mona Freeman), while his trainer (Wallace Ford) gets him ready for a shot at the welterweight title. Directed by Joseph Pevney, the story turns hokey after an operation restores the boxer's hearing but ruins his concentration in the ring. Pugilistic violence and romantic complications. A-II (br)

Flesh Gordon (1974) Witless spoof on both the old Flash Gordon and Buck Rogers serials and the new porno movies. Sophomorically smutty humor, nudity, rough language, and cheap thrills. O (X/R)

Fletch (1985) This is a vehicle for comedian Chevy Chase to showcase several disguises and display his somewhat limited talent for accents. He plays a reporter trying to break a drug case with everybody against him, even his editors. Chase fans should enjoy this, but others are less like1y to. The humor runs heavily to the vulgar side, with the emphasis on the scatological and the anatomical. A-II (PG)

Fletch Lives (1989) Cheesy comedy sequel with Chevy Chase reprising his role as a wise-guy investigative reporter who this time is up against a sinister plot to rid him of his inherited Louisiana plantation. Chase fans may chuckle over his nutty disguises, corny names, and sappy one-liners, but director Michael Ritchie finds little humor, save in a satiric subplot about a sleazy TV faith-healer (R. Lee Ermey). Rough language laced with vulgar references, sexual innuendoes, and a casual attitude toward sex. A-III (PG)

Flight (1929) Creaky service melodrama in which a bonehead college recruit (Ralph Graves) flunks out as pilot in the Marine Corps flying school but is kept on as a mechanic by his flight instructor (Jack Holt), whom he flies to safety when the squadron is sent to aid Marines besieged by rebels in Nicaragua. Directed by Frank R. Capra, the crux of the story is the bond between the two men which surmounts their rivalry over a Marine nurse (Lila Lee), though of more interest today is the aerial photography of period biplanes in action. Stylized violence and romantic complications. A-II (br)

Flight Commander (see: **The Dawn Patrol** of 1930)

Flight for Freedom (1943) Soggy melodrama in which a woman aviator (Rosalind Russell) chooses her country over her first love (Fred MacMurray) and financial backer (Herbert Marshall) by sacrificing her life aiding US naval intelligence gain data on secret Japanese bases in the Pacific. Directed by Lothar Mendes, the movie succeeds best in portraying the dramatic rise of an aviatrix much like Amelia Earhart, though it rings hollow in celebrating a suicidal mission as an act of patriotism. Muddled treatment of suicide and romantic complications. A-III (br)

Flight from Ayisha (1964) Melodramatic story of three pilots (Richard Widmark, Yul Brynner, and George Chakiris) in the Air Rescue Service who use a helicopter to pick up the survivors of a Japanese freighter sunk in a typhoon. Directed by Michael Anderson, the script keeps interrupting the sea rescue with flashbacks revealing past woes in the lives of the rescuers. Strong menace and sexual situations. A-III (br)

Flight Lieutenant (1942) Contrived melodrama directed by Sidney Salkow in which a disgraced pilot (Pat O'Brien) keeps making problems for his aviator son (Glenn Ford), then tries to make amends by taking his place on a dangerous military test flight. Some hard-drinking and fatal airplane crashes. A-II (br)

Flight of the Doves (1971) Young brother and sister (Jack Wild and Helen Raye) escape the crushing rule of their stepfather (William Rushton) in gray Britain for their dear granny (Dorothy McGuire) in green Ireland. Learning that the children are heirs to a large fortune, they are pursued by a menacing uncle (Ron Moody) who intends to dispose of them and claim the money for himself. Director Ralph Nelson, steering clear of the scary potential of the situation, produces a fancy, frothy entertainment package, stuffed with colorful set pieces, songs, and sentimentality. The confection may be too sweet for adults, but young children will especially enjoy Moody's magic tricks and bag of disguises. A-I (G)

Flight of the Eagle, The (1983) Swedish director Jan Troell's fact-based drama illustrates an ill-fated attempt to reach the North Pole by a group of explorers (Max von Sydow, Goran Stangertz, and Sverre Anker Ousdal) making use of a hydrogen balloon. Though beautifully photographed and well-told, the somber nature of the story and the intensity of its treatment make it inappropriate for younger viewers. A-II (G)

Flight of the Innocent (1993) Engrossing fact-based story of feuding clans in southern Italy, where a young boy flees for his life after his entire family is slaughtered, then finds he is being pursued for the ransom money paid to the kidnappers of a rich man's son. Director Carlo Carlei turns the sympathetic youth's desperate attempts to escape his deadly trackers into a suspenseful chase movie that effectively condemns the culture of violence in which these events take place. Subtitles. Graphic violence, a youth in continuing jeopardy, and occasional rough language. A-III (R)

Flight of the Intruder (1991) Demoralized by futile bombing missions over North Vietnam in 1972, a Navy pilot (Brad Johnson) and his bombardier (Willem Dafoe) defy their commander (Danny Glover) to bomb an off-limits weapons site in downtown Hanoi. Directed by John Milius, the predictable plot uses dazzling, high-flying visuals and rah-rah music to portray war as the ultimate macho adventure while skirting the story's moral conflicts. Intermittent aerial and battlefield violence, a restrained extramarital encounter, and some crude bathroom humor. A-III (PG-13)

Flight of the Lost Balloon (1961) Clunky low-budget adventure in which a top-hatted Englishman (Marshall Thompson) transverses equatorial Africa by balloon in 1878 to reach an explorer (Douglas Kennedy) held captive by a crafty Hindu (James Lanphier) on an island in Lake Victoria. Written and directed by Nathan Juran, the plot takes an unwholesome turn when the explorer proves willing to see his fiancé (Mala Powers) tortured to death rather than reveal the location of Cleopatra's lost treasure. Stylized violence and some grotesque native stereotyping. A-II (br)

Flight of the Navigator (1986) A youngster (Joey Kramer) gets trapped in a time warp when he's transported to and from a distant world in the blink of an eye. Although he has not aged, he has been away from his family eight years and must decide if this is really home. The alien spacecraft which transported him figures prominently and humorously in this good-natured and unpretentious family movie directed by Randal Kleiser. A-I (PG)

Flight of the Phoenix (1966) Uneven disaster movie in which an airplane with the usual motley collection of male passengers crashes in the Arabian desert somewhere off-course and without a working radio. Their only chance of survival is to build a new plane from the wreckage of the old, which leads to friction between the pilot (James Stewart) and the German aircraft-designer who proposes to do it. Directed by Robert Aldrich, the situation is overly extended but provides enough suspense and excitement to please most old and young adventure fans. A-I (br)

Flight That Disappeared, The (1961) Low-budget fantasy directed by Reginald LeBorg in which an airliner loses contact with earth after being drawn into the future, where three passengers (Craig Hill, Paula Raymond, and Dayton Lummis) are questioned about their work on a new super-bomb, then are sent back in the airliner, which causes consternation by landing 24 hours behind schedule. A-I (br)

Flight to Tangier (1953) Cold War clunker about Americans (Joan Fontaine and Jack Palance) trying to outfox Communist agents in Algeria. Directed by Charles Marquis Warren, the clumsy scenario is made worse by stilted action scenes, silly romantic situations, and woolly patriotic asides.

Stylized violence and romantic complications. A-III (br)

Flim-Flam Man, The (1967) Aging confidence man (George C. Scott) tutors a young Army deserter (Michael Sarrazin) in the subtle art of capitalizing on the greed of his fellow man as the unlikely pair go on some genuinely hilarious adventures across the Kentucky countryside. Scott plays the role with carefree flamboyance and glimpses of the pathos that is part of a drifter's loneliness, and Sarrazin is appealing as the AWOL farm boy who is finally brought to his senses by pretty Sue Lyon. Directed by Irvin Kershner, it has beautiful location photography, first-rate dialogue, and a uniformly capable supporting cast that help make the movie enjoyable for all but the very young. A-II (br)

Flintstones, The (1994) Jaunty live-action version of the caveman cartoon series in which guileless Fred Flintstone (John Goodman) is the patsy in an embezzlement scheme at the quarry, which nearly wrecks his marriage to Wilma (Elizabeth Perkins) and threatens his friendship with neighbors Barney and Betty (Rick Moranis and Rosie O'Donnell). Director Brian Levant's colorful, big-budget comedy offers moderately enjoyable nostalgia for grown-up fans of the TV series and, despite some mild sexual innuendo, whimsical fun for children. A-I (PG)

Flipper (1963) After a young boy (Luke Halpin) rescues an injured dolphin, his fisherman father (Chuck Connors) releases it back into the sea, but later, when his son's life is in danger, the grateful dolphin returns to save the lad. Directed by James B. Clark, the story is simple but well-told, the scene-stealing title character is as personable as any in the cast, and the Florida nature footage, including a hurricane, is very watchable. Solid family fare, but especially appealing for youngsters. A-I (G)

Flipper (1996) Forced to spend the summer in the Florida Keys with his beach-bum uncle (Paul Hogan), a lonely 14-year-old (Elijah Wood) befriends an orphaned dolphin whose life is threatened by a villain (Jonathan Banks) dumping toxic waste in the local waters. Writer-director Alan Shapiro's environmentally themed update of the 1963 movie treads water with a listless story line despite likable performances and colorful underwater sequences. Brief menace and a fleeting profanity. A-I (PG)

Flipper's New Adventure (1964) Lame sequel with the agile dolphin and his friend (Luke Halpin) saving a family whose yacht has been hijacked by escaped convicts. Directed by Leon Benson, the aquatic scenes are still lovely to watch, but the story evokes little interest and less credibility. Some menace and fisticuffs. A-I (G)

Flirting (1992) Endearing Australian coming-of-age story set in the mid-1960s follows a stuttering Aussie lad (Noah Taylor) and an intellectual Ugandan girl (Thandie Newton) from neighboring private academies through the stages of interracial friendship and romance that gradually win the respect of their adolescent peers. Writer-director John Duigan treats the young characters with respect and affection in a story that gathers substance as the students mature beyond juvenile sexist and racist attitudes. An implied sexual encounter, flash of nudity, and brief brawling. A-III (R)

Flirting with Disaster (1996) Mindless comedy about a young couple (Ben Stiller and Patricia Arquette) on a cross-country search for the husband's biological parents with the help of an adoption agency worker (Tea Leoni) and a homosexual couple they meet along the way. Written and directed by David O. Russell, the journey's disasters are too predictable to be amusing and the sexual by-play between the quirky travelers is too heavy-handed to be comic, though occasional giggles are supplied by veteran performers in supporting roles. Sexual situations and innuendo, tasteless humor, drug jokes, and some rough language. A-IV (R)

Float Like a Butterfly, Sting Like a Bee (1970) Though boxing fans may be disappointed at the sparsity of ring action in this documentary on Muhammad Ali (aka Cassius Clay), it succeeds in being objective and entertaining while exploring the racial ramifications of Ali's success and notoriety, as well as providing insight into his life and character. A-III (nr)

Flood Tide (1958) Hokey melodrama directed by Abner Biberman in which an engineer (George Nader) tries to save an innocent man (Russ Conway) who's been convicted of murder on the false testimony of a crippled 10-year-old boy (Michel Ray), who fears losing his widowed mom (Cornell Borchers) to another male. Psychological problems and menacing situations. A-II (br)

Flower Drum Song (1961) Uneven Rodgers and Hammerstein musical about a picture-bride (Miyoshi Umeki) from Hong Kong who arrives illegally in San Francisco, but instead of marrying a night-club owner (James Soo) as arranged, she falls for a college grad (James Shigeta) who's hooked on a singer (Nancy Kwan). Directed by Henry Koster, the formula plot and mediocre songs are less interesting than the Chinatown settings and a strong Asian-American cast. Romantic complications. A-II (br)

Flower of My Secret, The (1996) Bittersweet romance from Spain in which a middle-aged woman (Marisa Paredes) attempts suicide after learning her husband has left her, then recovers with her mother's help and begins life anew with the aid of a would-be beau (Juan Echove). Directed by Pedro Almodovar, the story is basically a 1940s tearjerker, though enlivened by zestful characters and surreal comic moments. Subtitles. Sexual situations and occasional rough language. A-III (R)

Flowers in the Attic (1987) Failed suspense thriller about four youngsters locked in the upper story of a remote mansion, where their lives are endangered by unknown hands. Writer-director Jeffrey Bloom's heavy-handed treatment of the situation becomes boringly repetitive long before the movie's grisly resolution. Mature themes and some violence. A-III (PG-13)

Flowers of St. Francis, The (1950) Remarkable Italian production about the beginnings of the Franciscan Order as its founder sets the example of humility, simplicity, and obedience for his first followers at Portiuncula, a little chapel near Assisi, from which they depart into the world to preach peace. Directed by Roberto Rossellini from a script co-written with Federico Fellini, the movie's form is as simple and sincere as the subject of the narrative which relates a series of little incidents realistically, yet marvellously conveyed with an infectious sencse of joy by an anonymous cast of monks from a Roman monastery. Subtitles. A-I (br)

Flubber (1997) Weak remake of 1961's **The Absent-Minded Professor** has a distracted professor (Robin Williams) leaving his college-president bride (Marcia Gay Harden) at the altar while inventing flying rubber to save their debt-ridden college. Director Les Mayfield flubs it with an excess of jokey special effects at the expense of story and characterization. Frequent slapstick violence and fleeting sexual innuendo. A-II (PG)

Fluffy (1965) Comic misfire from director Earl Bellamy is a feeble slapstick affair featuring a research scientist (Tony Randall) and his tame lion on the run from California police, who regard both of them as highly dangerous. Few smiles from an unappealing premise based on the stupidity of all concerned. A-I (br)

Fluke (1995) Lame mystery-fantasy in which a family man killed in a car crash is reborn as a dog who sets out to determine if his business partner (Eric Stoltz) did him in and is after his wife (Nancy Travis) and son (Max Pomeranc). Working with a feeble narrative, director Carlo Carlei tries to impose comic touches on this canine caper by featuring frisky dogs who communicate by mental telepathy, but this too falls flat, resulting in a lumpy hodgepodge of mystery and comedy. Fleeting sexual innuendo and repeated scenes of a fatal car crash. A-II (PG)

Fly, The (1958) Classic horror-fantasy in which a French-Canadian scientist (David Hedison) invents a machine capable of reducing an object to a stream of molecules for transmission and reassembly elsewhere, but in trying the process on himself, his molecules get mixed up with those of a housefly. Directed by Kurt Neumann, the story unfolds in flashbacks during the investigation of the scientist's disappearance, with the memorable payoff as the man's brother (Vincent Price) and a Montreal policeman (Herbert Marshall) discover a fly with a human head caught in a spider's web. Some menace, a few frights and the killing of two half-human creatures. A-II (br)

Fly, The (1986) Tender romance fades quickly when a biological experiment intermixing human and insect genes fails. The result is a mutant in the form of a sexually powerful human fly (Jeff Goldblum) who gets some compassion from his lover (Geena Davis), but his condition, like director David Cronenberg's beauty-and-the-beast allegory, degenerates into an unhealthy mix of sex, brutality, and disgustingly grotesque imagery. Explicit sexual scenes, nudity, and some profanity. O (R)

Fly II, The (1989) When the son (Eric Stoltz) of the original mutant fly-man grows up to realize that his body and brains are being exploited by a dastardly industrialist (Lee Richardson), the boy tries to free himself from his damaged chromosomes before it's too late. Remarkable creature effects and an involving struggle between good and evil don't make up for director Chris Walas's exploitation of gore and a frightening subplot about zapping test animals in microwave devices. Keep impressionable kids away from this or they may try something similar with family pets. Gratuitous sex, gore, and some rough language. O (R)

Fly Away Home (1996) Sweetly charming story of a 13-year-old Ontario girl (Anna Paquin) who rescues a nest of orphaned wild goslings, then gets some help from her estranged dad (Jeff Daniels) in trying to teach them to fly so they can migrate South to survive the winter. Director Carroll Ballard combines captivating nature scenes with a warmly human tale of family bonding and tenacious inventiveness. Implied live-in relationship and mild menace. A-II (PG)

Flying Leathernecks (1951) WW II Marine pilots fight the war in the Pacific while their commander (John Wayne) quarrels with his executive (Robert Ryan) about the best way to do it. Directed by Nicholas Ray, the extensive use of actual combat footage makes the script's heroics seem all the more hollow and phony. Documentary war footage and assorted stylized violence. A-I (br)

Flying Matchmaker, The (1970) Israeli musical comedy set in a 19th-century East European Jewish community with a busy matchmaker promoting happy weddings, but silly confusion runs rampant when an impersonator of a prospective groom shows up. Directed by Mordechai Navon, the colorful production stars Mike Burstein, Lillian Lux, and Pesach Burstein, but the poorly dubbed comedy grows a bit tedious for those unaccustomed to its conventions. A-II (G)

Flying Missile, The (1950) Routine military story of a submarine commander (Glenn Ford) who perseveres in his attempts after WW II to prove to the Navy that missiles can be launched from under the sea. Directed by Henry Levin, a romantic subplot involving a coworker (Viveca Lindfors) takes a backseat to improving the nation's defenses. A-I (br)

Flying Tigers (1942) WW II tribute to the title's volunteer group of US airmen flying P-40 fighters against Japanese Zeros in China before Pearl Harbor, in a story centering on the antagonism between the squadron's determined leader (John Wayne) and the fun-loving recruit (John Carroll) he blames for the death of a veteran pilot (Paul Kelly). Directed by David Miller, the melodrama's patriotic rhetoric is dated, but what counts most is its rousing depiction of the small band's heroics, despite the air action's obvious reliance on model airplanes. Wartime violence. A-I (br)

Fog, The (1980) Victims of a century-old shipwreck caused by a false beacon stalk the descendants of their murderers under the cover of a lethal fog. Director John Carpenter's listless and heavy-handed thriller has little intelligence and much violence. A-III (R)

Fog Island (1945) Low-budget thriller set on a desolate island to which a ruined businessman (George Zucco) invites those (notably Lionel Atwill, Jerome Cowen, Veda Ann Borg, and Ian Keith) he suspects framed him, from which none are to return save his stepdaughter (Sharon Douglas) and an innocent young man (John Whitney). Directed by Terry Morse, the creaky proceedings feature an old house with sliding panels, hidden passages, and a room rigged as a death trap. More menace than violence. A-II (br)

Folks! (1992) Aging parents (Don Ameche and Anne Jackson) persuade their cash-strapped son (Tom Selleck) that they must be killed so he can collect their insurance. Insensitivity toward the elderly abounds in director Ted Kotcheff's witless black comedy. Suicidal behavior and violence treated comically, mild sexual innuendo, and minimal profanity. A-III (PG-13)

Follow Me (1969) Three American youths travel the globe in search of the perfect surfing wave in a movie that lacks any wit or style. Director Gene McCabe's material is so repetitious that one has time to question the young surfers' value system and sense of social consciousness. A-II (G)

Follow Me, Boys! (1966) Disney family movie with Fred MacMurray as a small-town Scoutmaster who devotes his life to helping the boys in his troop. Director Norman Tokar emphasizes the ideals of scouting, has the period atmosphere of a generation ago and benefits from the capable acting of Lillian Gish and Charles Ruggles. Though a sentimental formula picture, it has more than enough spirited action to keep most viewer's interest. A-I (G)

Follow That Bird (1985) In the first Sesame Street movie, a do-gooder type persuades Big Bird that he should be living with his own feathered kind and places him with the Dodo family in the distant Midwest. Pining for home, Big Bird heads East and immediately becomes the innocent object of a bird-hunt. In Sesame Street style, the movie maintains a gentle, whimsical spirit rather than going for the big laughs. As such it will succeed best with younger children and least well with teenagers. A-I (G)

Follow That Dream (1962) Mild comedy about modern homesteaders (Arthur O'Connell, Elvis Presley, Anne Helm, and three little orphans) settling on state land along the Florida coast, where they thrive until a gambler (Simon Oakland) sets up shop next to them. Directed by Gordon Douglas, the humor revolves around the family's unsophisticated innocence in disarming all attempts to dislodge them. Brief comic violence. A-I (br)

Follow the Boys (1944) Patriotic WW II time capsule in which a top screen-hoofer (George Raft) organizes the show-biz community to go on tours entertaining the troops, while his wife (Vera Zorina) smolders at his lengthy absences. As directed by A. Edward Sutherland, Universal Studio's tribute to Hollywood's part in the war effort features a lot of emotional applesauce along with such star-turns as magician Orson Welles sawing Marlene Dietrich in half, W.C. Fields displaying his prowess at a pool table, and tunes by the Andrew Sisters. Uneven assortment of period entertainment acts, double entendres, and domestic misunderstandings. A-II (br)

Follow the Fleet (1936) Sturdy musical about an easy-going sailor (Fred Astaire) trying to win back his former hoofing partner (Ginger Rogers) while her schoolteacher sister (Harriet Hilliard) pines for his shipboard buddy (Randolph Scott). Directed by Mark Sandrich, the appealing characters make the thin plot worth following, helped by some wry humor, delightful Astaire-Rogers dance routines, and lively Irving Berlin songs. Romantic complications. A-I (br)

Food of the Gods, The (1976) Directed by Bert I. Gordon and loosely based on a H.G. Wells story, the gross science-fiction movie delights in gore and vicious attacks by giant rats and insects on hapless explorers (Marjoe Gortner and Pamela Franklin). Excessive violence. O (R)

Fool for Love (1986) Under Robert Altman's direction, Sam Shepard's adaptation of his own play about a brutalizing love-hate relationship between kissing cousins (Shepard and Kim Basinger) is unremittingly violent, both physically and psychologically. Sexual coarseness in dialogue and unresolved ambiguity of a theme of incest. O (R)

Fool Killer, The (1969) Young runaway (Edward Albert) escaping from severe foster parents meets a brooding war veteran (Tony Perkins) bitter about his own excessively strict religious upbringing, but the youth comes to find a home, while the man is doomed to wandering. Although the comparatively lighthearted atmosphere of the first part of movie does not prepare the viewer for the darker tone of the later sequences, director Servando Gonzalez keeps the story consistently interesting. A-II (nr)

Fool There Was, A (1915) Silent melodrama in which an upright millionaire forgets wife, child, and all sense of honor after falling under the spell of a heartless vamp (Theda Bara) who seduces men, breaks their spirit, and leaves them penniless outcasts. Based on Rudyard Kipling's poem, "The Vampire," and directed by Frank Powell, the production is fairly primitive and the florid melodramatics border on the silly, yet the simple cautionary tale reflects the moral attitudes of its time in still interesting fashion. Unenticing sexual situations. A-II (br)

Foolin' Around (1980) Failed update of 1930's screwball comedy has a callow college freshman (Gary Busey) falling for an heiress (Annette O'Toole) and ruining her engagement to a boorish sophisticate. Directed by Richard Heffron, the slapstick overwhelms the few funny moments, while an implication of pre-marital sex and some rough language rule out younger viewers. A-III (PG)

Fools (1970) Aging actor tired of being typed in low-budget horror movies (Jason Robards) and a rich girl drifting away from her status-seeking spouse (Katharine Ross) traipse around San Francisco feebly attempting to forget life's frustrations by hopping into bed half-a-dozen times. Directed by Tom Gries, the movie is singularly devoid of any feelings for humanity that might justify one's interest in the intimate affairs of the neurotic pair. O (GP)

Fools of Fortune (1990) After avenging the murder of his father and sisters, which caused the tragic suicide of his mother (Julie Christie), a young Irishman (Iain Glen) flees the law, leaving behind his pregnant lover (Mary Elizabeth Mastrantonio). Director Pat O'Connor's post-WW I historical drama is marred by jarring flash-forwards, a profusion of characters, and tedious pacing which detracts from the film's primitive visual beauty and shimmering performances. Some violence with gore and a very restrained sexual encounter. A-III (PG-13)

Fools' Parade (1971) With money earned in prison, lovable ex-cons James Stewart, Strother Martin, and Kurt Russell want to set up a general store, but mean prison-captain George Kennedy wants their dollars and their lives. Perhaps director Andrew McLaglen intended a cornball-campy spoof, but the result is a disappointing chase melodrama that is sometimes silly but only occasionally funny. Some violence and sexual references. A-III (GP)

Fools Rush In (1997) Marriage proves a daunting clash-of-cultures for a workaholic WASP (Matthew Perry) and his fiery Mexican wife (Salma Hayek), who wed in haste because she became pregnant on the night they met. While director Andy Tennant's sweet romantic comedy is too sentimental, it errs on the side of an earnest couple striving to build a lasting love relationship and honor their commitments, not to mention the film's vibrant portrait of a large and nurturing Mexican-Catholic family. Sexual innuendo, occasional profanity, and an instance of rough language. A-III (PG-13)

Footlight Glamour (1943) Formula comedy in the **Blondie** series has Dagwood (Arthur Lake) in trouble when his boss insists he bring a client's daughter (Ann Savage) home as a boarder, and she talks Blondie (Penny Singleton) into going on the stage. Directed by Frank Strayer, the resulting theatrical follies are entirely predictable, though Blondie's explanation of WW II ration cards has period interest. Mild sexual innuendo. A-II (br)

Footloose (1984) A city boy (Kevin Bacon), brought to live in a small Bible Belt town which has an ordinance against dancing in public places, promptly gets in trouble with the local preacher (John Lithgow) over dating his daughter (Lori Singer), but eventually wins over the town. Director Herbert Ross tries to give the story line as much weight as the dazzling scenes of acrobatic dancing, but the simplistic script's treatment of issues is woefully inadequate. A-III (PG)

For a Few Dollars More (1967) Spaghetti Western directed by Sergio Leone with Clint Eastwood playing the cheroot-smoking Man with No Name and Lee Van Cleef, garbed all in black, as his not-to-be-trusted partner. Clint squints, Lee snarls, and dozens of Mexican banditos bite the dust in a routine shoot-'em-up involving Clint's vengeance for a doublecross. A-III (br)

For All Mankind (1990) Original footage and audio from NASA's nine manned lunar flights (1968-72) are edited together to create a composite lunar mission from lift-off to landing. Filmmaker Al Reinert provides glorious visuals and new astronaut interviews, but viewers will be confounded by his unidentified mix and melding of Apollo astronauts and launches into one mission. With clarifying introductory remarks, it may benefit young students of space exploration as well as interest veteran space buffs. A-I (nr)

For Better, For Worse (see: **Zandy's Bride**)

For Keeps (1988) Romantic melodrama about two high-school seniors (Molly Ringwald and Randall Batinkoff) whose plans for college and careers have to be deferred when they decide to face an unintended pregnancy by getting married and raising their child. Though the result is less than realistic in its treatment of the consequences of teen sex, director John G. Avildsen's movie is emotionally on the side of the miracle of human life and the value of the family bond. Some direct sexual references and a harrowing childbirth scene are not for the young and impressionable. A-III (PG-13)

For Love of Ivy (1968) Sidney Poitier plays a slick gambler who falls in love with a beautiful but ambitious maid (Abbey Lincoln), but what might have been an interesting romantic comedy is confounded by the overabundance of phony plot complications. As directed by Daniel Mann, whatever message the movie might have intended is lost in its glossy upper-class setting, pop songs, and a pair of "hip" youngsters. Mature themes. A-III (G)

For Love or Money (1993) To gain financial backing for his dream hotel in New York City, an ambitious concierge (Michael J. Fox) agrees to look after the young mistress (Gabrielle Anwar) of a busy, older tycoon (Anthony Higgins) — with predictable results. Director Barry Sonnenfeld turns in a tired formula romantic comedy in which integrity belatedly conquers materialism and wedding bells peal. A-III (PG)

For Me and My Gal (1942) Soppy romantic musical in which an ambitious song-and-dance team (Judy Garland and Gene Kelly) plan to wed once they've played the Palace, New York's vaudeville showcase, but WW I intervenes. Directed by Busby Berkeley, the sentimental story turns into patriotic mush as Kelly is transformed from heel to hero, though some first-rate musical numbers brighten the way. Romantic complications and a subplot about draft-dodging. A-II (br)

For Pete's Sake (1974) Barbra Streisand vehicle about a Brooklyn housewife who borrows money to speculate on the commodities market in order to finance her husband's college diploma, and then gets into trouble with a succession of unsavory characters who pressure her to pay back the loan. Director Peter Yates lets the promising comedy turn sour, and not even a final hilarious chase sequence can save it. Some grim twists and bizarre plot turns, including the housewife taking a job as a part-time prostitute. A-III (PG)

For Queen & Country (1989) Grim drama about a black British soldier (Denzel Washington) returning to civilian life in his crime-ravaged London neighborhood, where he resists illegal pursuits until he finds that, due to some legal loophole, he is no longer a British citizen. Director Martin Stellman stacks the cards against his ill-fated war hero and provides little insight into the grim community depicted. Profanity, sexual promiscuity, and grisly scenes of street violence. A-IV (R)

For Richer or Poorer (1997) Thin comedy in which wealthy yuppies (Tim Allen and Kirstie Alley) hide from the IRS by posing as newcomers in an Amish community, whose simple hardworking lifestyle inspires them to change their ways and renew their marital commitment. Directed by Bryan Spicer, the fish-out-of-water premise is wholly predictable, but the actors manage to wring some measure of humor from their unlikely predicament. Mild sexual innuendo, recurring coarse expressions, and an instance of rough language. A-III (PG-13)

For Roseanna (1997) Big-hearted comedy set in rural Italy, where a devoted husband (Jean Reno) promises his sickly wife (Mercedes Ruehl) the last plot in the local cemetery alongside their little daughter, then goes to extremes trying to ensure that no one else dies first. Director Paul Weiland goes from pathos to screwball comedy in this implausible, but poignantly funny, tale of love, buried treasure, and well-meaning deceit. Brief violence, fleeting bedroom scene, sexual references, and an instance of profanity. A-III (PG-13)

For Sasha (1992) Tangled love story set on a kibbutz during Israel's 1967 Six Day War involves a young woman (Sophie Marceau), the teacher (Richard Berry) she has followed there from Paris, and three lifelong friends (Fabien Orcier, Niels Dubost, and Frederic Quiring) who come to visit her. Alexandre Arcady directs a sentimental story of imperiled love that is more notable for its stirring portrayal of commitment to the Israeli cause. Subtitles. Fleeting sexual encounter and nudity, a live-in relationship, battlefield violence, and suicidal references. A-III (nr)

For Singles Only (1968) Living in a swinging Southern California hotel for unmarrieds, a serious but poor graduate student (John Saxon) bets that he can seduce a high-principled coed (Mary Anne Mobley). She goes along because winning the bet will pay off his overdue tuition bills, and then really cooperates because they are in love and are going to get married anyway. Directed by Arthur Dreifuss, the witless movie lacks any human texture or intelligence. Justifies premarital sex. O (br)

For the Boys (1991) Episodic melodrama about an earthy singer (Bette Midler) and a facile song-and-dance man (James Caan) who become a team entertaining the troops in WW II, then spend the next 50 years bickering on and off about their careers, families, and personal relationship. Director Mark Rydell gets a standout performance from Midler as the gutsy entertainer at the center of events, but the trivial show-business story fails to gain any human or social significance by pegging it to milestones of the period. Several graphic sequences of battlefield violence, an adulterous liaison, some sexual innuendo, and occasional rough language. A-III (R)

For the Love of Benji (1977) Extremely entertaining sequel with the lovable canine hero, this time on vacation in Greece, becoming the unwitting central figure in an international oil conspiracy, and the chase is on through the streets and byways of picturesque Athens. Director Joe Camp's lively adventure is surefire entertainment for younger children, and it goes down easily for parents as well. A-I (G)

For the Love of Mike (1960) Sentimental tale in which an Indian boy (Danny Bravo) races the thoroughbred horse he's raised from a colt in order to win the money needed by his ailing parish priest (Arthur Shields) to build a new church, then runs away when a man (Rex Allen) claims the horse belongs to him. Director George Sherman dresses up the formula story with a subplot about the poor Indian parish's kindly new curate (Richard Basehart), but the contrived results are less compelling than the rugged beauty of the Southwestern locales and the youth's tense encounter with a mountain lion. Thin but well-intended inspirational fare. A-I (br)

For the Moment (1996) Doomed romances bloom at a pilot-training school for Allied flyers in 1942 Manitoba when the American flight instructor and an Aussie recruit (Russell Crowe) fall in love with two married women whose husbands are fighting abroad. Writer-director Aaron Kim Johnston gingerly explores bittersweet relationships and wartime anxieties in an otherwise formula story. Recurring sexual innuendo with fleeting nudity, brief violence, and minimal profanity. A-III (PG-13)

For Whom the Bell Tolls (1943) Uneven adaptation of the Ernest Hemingway novel set in 1937 Spain, where an American (Gary Cooper) serving in the republican cause is sent to blow a bridge behind the insurgent lines with help from local partisans, one of whom (Ingrid Bergman) comes to love him. Directed by Sam Wood, the human cost in destroying the bridge proves all for naught in a movie which has less to do with the politics of the Spanish Civil War than the doomed romance between an idealistic veteran and a sympathetic novice. Stylized violence, romantic complications, and sexual innuendo. A-III (br)

For Your Eyes Only (1981) Uninspired, derivative spy caper with British agent James Bond (Roger Moore) out to retrieve a top-secret device from a sunken British ship. Directed by John Glen, the flimsy plot strings together a number of spectacular stunts amidst the tongue-in-cheek violence and disposable women which are fixtures in the 007 fantasy world. Nudity in an underwater sequence. O (PG)

Forbidden (1932) Creaky sudser about a librarian (Barbara Stanwyck) who falls for a married lawyer (Adolphe Menjou), lets him raise their baby daughter while he pursues a political career, then kills a newspaperman (Ralph Bellamy) to keep him from revealing the truth. Writer-director Frank R. Capra gives the formula story a classy treatmen, but the premise of the long-suffering mistress is unlikely to ring true with modern viewers. Adulterous affair and its ramifications. A-III (br)

Forbidden (1953) Convoluted underworld tale directed by Rudolph Maté is set in the Portuguese colony of Macao, where a woman (Joanne Dru) fleeing Philadelphia mobsters is given refuge by a local gambling boss (Lyle Bettger), but their wedding plans are spoiled when her ex-boyfriend (Tony Curtis) turns up with orders from the mob to kill her. Stylized violence, twisted loyalties, and romantic complications. A-III (br)

Forbidden Island (1959) Tawdry vanity piece written, produced, and directed by Charles B. Griffith, with Jon Hall diving for a priceless emerald in a sunken ship off a Pacific atoll while falling for the wife of his psychopathic employer. Some nasty violence and sexual innuendo. A-III (br)

Forbidden Planet (1956) Engaging sci-fi outing with a space expedition (led by Leslie Nielsen) fighting unseen monsters of the Id on a planet, where the powers of a superior, long-extinct civilization are being harnessed by a maverick scientist (Walter Pidgeon) with the help of his daughter (Anne Francis) and a very personable robot named Robby. Directed by Fred M. Wilcox, the premise echoes Shakespeare's *The Tempest*, but the movie has its own suspenseful plot developments, intriguing gadgetry, and colorful sets, flawed only by some clunky dialogue and desultory action. Occasional stylized violence and much menace. A-II (br)

Forbidden Quest, The (1994) Drama in which a documentary filmmaker interviews an aged Irish sailor (Joseph O'Conor) who reveals what became of his ill-fated crewmates, all thought to be lost on the Hollandia's 1905-06 voyage from Norway to the South Pole. Dutch writer-director Peter Delpeut creates an atmosphere of mystery and suspense in telling the fictional story of a doomed ship by marrying actual Antarctic exploration footage from the early 20th century to the old salt's crusty tale of a perilous and deadly voyage. Much menace and the shooting of a bear. A-II (nr)

Forbin Project, The (1970) An enormous self-sustaining and unhackable computer complex coordinating all US military defenses locates a Soviet counterpart, and together they plan a benevolent dictatorship guaranteeing peace and a better way of life for the peoples of the world at the expense of their freedom. A kind of horror film with contemporary allusions, director Joseph Sargent's movie has moments of genuine interest in its depiction of a modern electronic Frankenstein controlling humanity's fate but incapable of any human emotion or spiritual growth. Mild bedroom sequence. A-III (GP)

Force of Arms (1951) Earnest picture of a sergeant in the Fifth Army (William Holden) who gets a battlefield commission in 1943 Italy, then falls in love with a WAC lieutenant (Nancy Olson) while on leave in Naples but after they marry, he goes back in the line and is among the missing in a German counterattack. Directed by Michael Curtiz, the convincing battle scenes give considerable poignancy to the wartime romance, which ends in suitably uplifting fashion. Wartime violence. A-II (br)

Force of Evil (1948) Gritty crime picture in which a dishonest lawyer (John Garfield) helps a gangster (Roy Roberts) take control of the New York numbers racket, then gets his reluctant older brother (Thomas Gomez) involved, which leads to his death when a rival mob muscles in and the police get evidence of the lawyer's leading part in the racket. Directed by Abraham Polonsky, the story focuses on the gradual awakening of the greedy lawyer's conscience to the evil consequences of what he has done, though it is Garfield's edgy performance and George Barnes's evocative location photography which most hold interest today. Stylized violence and criminal activities. A-II (br)

Force of One, A (1980) Run-of-the-mill melodrama about how karate champ Chuck Norris breaks up a narcotics ring. Justice triumphs by means of the martial arts instead of superior firepower, with the violence being skillfully choreographed and kept in check by director Paul Aaron. A-II (PG)

Force 10 from Navarone (1979) Penny-ante sequel to **The Guns of Navarone** follows the mission of two American Rangers (Robert Shaw and Edward Fox) in Yugoslavia to blow up a bridge before the Germans can use it to attack the Partisans. Director Guy Hamilton's limp war movie is filled with cliches and occasional graphic violence. A-III (PG)

Forces of Nature (1999) Lackluster romantic comedy in which a wedding-bound bridegroom (Ben Affleck) finds himself drawn to a free-spirited traveling companion (Sandra Bullock) after a plane mishap forces them to continue on by train, bus, and car. As directed by Bronwen Hughes, an appealing cast gives the loopy proceedings some bounce, but it fails to achieve its intended screwball-comedy status. Fleeting violence, sexual situations and references, occasional profanity, and an instance of rough language. A-III (PG-13)

Foreign Affair, A (1948) Romantic intrigue in postwar Berlin with a visiting Iowan Congresswoman (Jean Arthur) falling for a US officer (John Lund) who's involved with the wife (Marlene Dietrich) of a hunted Nazi criminal. Directed by Billy Wilder, the comedy is sharply barbed and often cynical, scoring best in the rivalry between homespun Arthur and sultry Dietrich. Much sexual innuendo. A-III (br)

Foreign Correspondent (1940) With war threatening in Europe, a bumptious American newspaper reporter (Joel McCrea) stumbles upon a Nazi spy ring in Holland, escapes to London, where he falls for the daughter (Laraine Day) of a peace leader (Herbert Marshall) and, after various attempts on his life, finally manages to get his story of a Nazi plot to the American public. Director Alfred Hitchcock turns in a masterful suspense thriller with some chuckles and a lot of clever business along the way, from an official's assassination amidst a rain-swept maelstrom of umbrellas to a plane crash at sea, but the characters are cardboard and the script's anti-Fascist rhetoric is dated. Much menace. A-II (nr)

Foreign Student (1994) On a semester's scholarship to a Virginia college in 1956, a Parisian student (Marco Hofschneider) learns about campus life from a redneck Southerner (Rick Johnson) while falling in love with a black maid (Robin Givens) who can't believe they could marry and live without discrimination in Paris. Director Eva Sereny soft-peddles the pronounced prejudices of the era to deliver an almost nostalgic look at a bittersweet interracial romance and the clash of cultures surrounding it. Brief bedroom scene with shadowy nudity and some rough language. A-III (R)

Forest Rangers, The (1942) Romantic adventure in a national forest whose head ranger (Fred MacMurray) arouses the jealousy of a local tomboy (Susan Hayward) by wedding a wealthy tourist (Paulette Goddard), but the sticky situation burns itself out in a forest fire. Directed by George Marshall, the humor and horseplay in the rugged outdoors setting proves more interesting than the thin plot and its cardboard characters. Romantic complications and fiery menace. A-II (br)

Forever Amber (1947) Romantic potboiler set in 17th-century England, where an enterprising country lass (Linda Darnell) follows a dashing cavalier (Cornel Wilde) to London, then is left with his baby and a fierce determination to become his wife by gaining title and fortune through loveless bedroom intrigues in the corrupt court of Charles II (George Sanders). Directed by Otto Preminger, the pulp romance lumbers fitfully along to its unhappy conclusion, succeeding better with the period costumes and settings than the story's superficial characters and shallow emotions. Sexual situations. A-III (br)

Forever Darling (1956) Sentimental comic fantasy about the midlife blues of a couple whose marriage is saved when the daffy wife (Lucille Ball) is persuaded by her guardian angel (James Mason) to join research-chemist husband (Desi Arnaz) on a field trip testing a new insecticide. Directed by Alexander Hall, there are some playful moments in an otherwise routine domestic comedy whose fantasy device falls flat. A-I (br)

Forever Female (1953) Stodgy romantic comedy in which a novice writer (William Holden) changes his play to suit a Broadway producer (Paul Douglas) who wants it tailored for his ex-wife (Ginger Rogers) until realizing the role requires a younger actress (Pat Crowley). Directed by Irving Rapper, the show business setting is more interesting than the predictable and largely unamusing romantic complications. Sexual innuendo. A-III (br)

Forever in Love (see: **Pride of the Marines**)

Forever Mary (1991) A caring teacher (Michele Placido) tries to make a difference at a boys' reformatory in Sicily, where the staff and guards treat their adolescent charges like hardened criminals. Italian director Marco Risi's fact-based drama is a grimly moving expose of a harsh penal system that apparently writes off youthful first-time offenders, thus encouraging their continued antisocial behavior. Subtitles. Scenes of brief but intense violence, occasional sexual harassment, and innuendo and frequent vulgar language. A-III (nr)

Forever Young (1992) A secret experiment to briefly freeze a 1939 test pilot (Mel Gibson) goes awry and, instead, he wakes up 53 years later when a single mom (Jamie Lee Curtis) and her little boy (Elijah Wood) help him find someone from his past. Director Steve Miner's sweet old-fashioned romantic fantasy is resolved far too suddenly, blunting the story's emotional impact. Brief violence. A-II (PG)

Forever Young, Forever Free (see: **Lollipop**)

Forget Paris (1995) The on-again, off-again courtship and marriage of a pro-basketball referee (Billy Crystal) and an airline executive (Debra Winger), who originally met and fell in love in Paris, is recounted in a restaurant by friends who are awaiting the couple's arrival to learn if they have reconciled. As blandly directed by Crystal, the uneven romantic comedy is better at one-liners than at sustaining interest in the relationship between quirky lovers. An implied premarital affair. A-III (PG-13)

Formula, The (1980) Failed crime story of a police detective (George C. Scott) determined to see justice done when his investigation of a murder is blocked by a powerful oil tycoon (Marlon Brando). The messy script is directed by John Avildsen, who loses hold of its plot strings halfway through with the result proving utterly unintelligible. Some violence, rough language, and a suggestive night club sequence. A-III (R)

Forrest Gump (1994) Inspired by the faith his mother (Sally Field) has in him, a slow-witted Southerner (Tom Hanks) becomes a football All-American, Vietnam hero, and millionaire entrepreneur, despite intermittent rejection by his troubled, lifelong friend and sweetheart (Robin Wright). Director Robert Zemeckis's big-hearted love story cleverly incorporates gimmicks into the narrative without ever losing focus on the emotional and spiritual development of the title character. A few discreet bedroom scenes, some intense battlefield violence, fleeting drug use, and an instance of rough language. A-III (PG-13)

Fort Apache (1948) Elegiac Western in which a glory-seeking colonel (Henry Fonda) arrives from the East to command a cavalry post, arrogantly refuses the counsel of a seasoned subordinate (John Wayne), and leads his troop into a massacre by superior Indian forces. In contrasting the colonel's ignorance and scorn of the foe with the captain's experience and respect for the Indian, director John Ford acknowledges the reality of how the West was won, while recognizing the need to turn it into a myth. Stylized violence. A-I (br)

Fort Apache, the Bronx (1981) Paul Newman stars as a tough but compassionate police officer striving to do his job in a precinct that has the highest crime rate in New York City. Director Dan Petrie's standard urban melodrama is marked by excellent acting and fine cinematography, but, though it has occasional insights, it tends to exploit a serious and tragic subject. Some tough scenes involving sex and violence. A-IV (R)

Fort Dobbs (1957) Routine Western directed by Gordon Douglas in which a cowboy (Clint Walker) on the run from a posse pauses to rescue a widow (Virginia Mayo) and her boy from raiding Comanches, then brings them to safety and gets his chance to prove his innocence. Frontier violence and veiled sexual innuendo. A-II (br)

Fort Massacre (1958) Murky Western set in 1879 New Mexico, where a cavalry column is ambushed by hostile Apaches and the survivors, led by an Indian-hating sergeant (Joel McCrea), hide out in some adobe ruins to await reinforcements. Directed by Joseph M. Newman, the routine action vehicle contrives a tragic climax to the sergeant's private war against the Apache nation. Frontier violence and an ending which may confuse some youngsters. A-I (br)

Fort Osage (1952) Formula Western directed by Lesley Selander in which a frontiersman (Rod Cameron) saves a wagon train of settlers from being swindled by corrupt agents and scalped by outraged Indians. Stylized violence. A-I (br)

Fort Ti (1953) Adventure programmer set in colonial New York, where a captain (George Montgomery) in Rogers Rangers helps the British capture Fort Ticonderoga during the French and Indian Wars. Hokey violence and romantic complications. A-II (br)

Fort Utah (1968) Formula Western directed by Lesley Selander with a retired gunslinger (John Ireland) helping an Indian agent (Robert Strauss) find the Army deserter (Scott Brady) whose gang provoked an Indian uprising after murdering the soldiers in the area's only fort. Frontier violence and muted allusions to prostitution. A-II (br)

Fort Vengeance (1953) Formula Western set in Canada, where a good Montana cowboy (James Craig) and his devious brother (Keith Larsen) enlist in the North West Mounted Police, then have a falling-out as the Mounties (led by Reginald Denny) try to stop Sitting Bull from stirring an Indian uprising after the Custer Massacre. Directed by Lesley Selander, the predictable story has some good action scenes but is most notable for contrasting the Canadian policy of protecting its Indian peoples with the US policy of suppressing them. Frontier violence. A-I (br)

Fort Worth (1951) Tangled Western directed by Edwin L. Marin in which a reformed gunman (Randolph Scott) joins the staff of Fort Worth's crusading newspaper, then turns from editorials to bullets as the only way to stop a shrewd land-grabber (David Brian) from taking control of the city. Frontier violence and menace. A-II (br)

Fortune, The (1975) Jack Nicholson and Warren Beatty play a bumbling pair of 1920s con-men and would-be murderers who try to do in heiress Stockard Channing. Director Mike Nichols's comedy is contrived, clumsy, and only intermittently funny. Some sexual innuendo. A-III (PG)

Fortune and Men's Eyes (1971) Jailed on a minor narcotics rap, a young man (Wendell Burton) in fear of homosexual assault by the other prisoners lets a prison tough (Zooey Hall) protect him in return for exclusive rights to his body, and eventually he himself becomes one of the brutalizers that he had once so feared. Directed by Harvey Hart, the movie examines homosexuality in prison not only as a sexual release but as a means of wielding power. The treatment, however, is heavy-handed to the point of exploiting an important subject. O (R)

Fortune Cookie, The (1966) Shyster lawyer (Walter Matthau) gets brother-in-law (Jack Lemmon) to feign injuries in hopes of a million-dollar settlement. Directed by Billy Wilder, the situation is at first amusing but grows increasingly cynical and mean-spirited. Vulgar language and low morals. A-III (br)

Fortunes of Captain Blood (1950) The further adventures of the Irish doctor-turned-pirate (Louis Hayward) take him ashore in the Caribbean to rescue his men from a Spanish dungeon, then sail away in a captured galleon. Gordon Douglas directs the tame swashbuckler with little conviction and less interest. Stylized violence. A-I (br)

Forty Carats (1973) Very slight romantic comedy about a 40-year-old divorcée (Liv Ullmann) who falls in love with a man (Edward Albert) half her age during a holiday in Greece. Directed by Milton Katselas, it's lighthearted and entertaining enough, thanks primarily to gorgeous Hellenic scenery and Ullmann's bright performance. A-III (PG)

40 Guns to Apache Pass (1967) Routine Western about a US Cavalry captain (Audie Murphy) saving an Arizona outpost from marauding Apaches and a treacherous white man (Kenneth Tobey) by getting through with a shipment of repeating rifles. Directed by William Whitney, the formula action scenes are held together by a cliched narration. Stylized violence. A-I (br)

Forty Naughty Girls (1937) Weak murder mystery directed by Edward Cline in a series featuring spinster sleuth Hildegarde Withers (here played by Zazu Pitts) and New York City homicide inspector Oscar Piper (James Gleason), teamed this time in finding a backstage killer at a Broadway musical. Mild stylized violence and romantic complications. A-II (br)

40 Pounds of Trouble (1963) Predictable comedy in which a Nevada casino manager (Tony Curtis) finds a five-year-old girl left on the premises, then dodges a detective over alimony owed his ex-wife by taking the child and a casino singer (Suzanne Pleshette) to Disneyland. Directed by Norman Jewison, the sentimental proceedings rework the plot of **Little Miss Marker**, with the updated casino setting and sprawling theme-park adding some visual zest. Romantic complications. A-II (br)

48 Hours (see: **Went the Day Well?**)

48 Hrs. (1982) San Francisco police detective (Nick Nolte) springs a convict (Eddie Murphy) on a 48-hour pass in order to get his help tracking down some vicious killers. Directed by Walter Hill's slam-bang action thriller is filled with entirely disagreeable characters who indulge in extreme violence, crude sights gags, and rough language. O (R)

49th Man, The (1953) Cold War potboiler directed by Fred F. Sears in which a federal agent (John Ireland) tries to save San Francisco from annihilation by a Soviet spy ring which has smuggled a portable nuclear bomb into the country. Pulp menace. A-I (br)

Forty-Second Street (1933) Prototypical backstage musical in which a member of the chorus (Ruby Keeler) wins stardom when the frantic director (Warner Baxter) has her take over for the disabled leading lady (Bebe Daniels) on opening night. Directed by Lloyd Bacon, the Depression-era setting, slangy dialogue, and zesty cast (Ginger Rogers, Una Merkel, and Dick Powell, among them) are still fun, abetted by Al Dubin and Harry Warren's brassy music and topped off by Busby Berkeley's inventive production numbers for the title song, "I'm Young and Healthy" and "Shuffle Off to Buffalo." Some romantic complications and mild sexual innuendo. A-II (nr)

Foul Play (1978) Goldie Hawn and Chevy Chase are teamed in this comic melodrama about a feisty librarian and a police detective who foil a plot to assassinate the pope during a visit to San Francisco. Colin Higgins directs an above-average comedy that is frequently very funny but yet maintains enough tension to be enjoyable as a thriller too. Some crude language and a casual attitude toward premarital sex. A-III (PG)

Fountain of Love, The (1970) German sex farce about a little town which has a spring that bolsters the virility of all who bathe in it. The mayor's attempt to keep people from using it succeeds as badly as a meandering plot sprinkled with voyeurism and nudity. O (R)

Fountainhead, The (1949) Pretentious melodrama from the Ayn Rand novel about a brilliant architect (Gary Cooper) whose uncompromising standards win the friendship of a self-made millionaire (Raymond Massey) and the love of his wife (Patricia Neal) before the architect dynamites a housing complex whose construction has deviated from his designs. The muddled plot is treated with such pompous gravity by director King Vidor that it becomes a monumental bore with unconvincing characters spouting self-important twaddle. Sexual situations and suicide in plot resolution. A-III (br)

Four Adventures of Reinette and Mirabelle (1989) Wispy French comedy tracking the friendship between a country girl (Joelle Miquel) and a Parisian college student (Jessica Forde) as they explore Mother Nature and the nature of rude city waiters, homeless panhandlers, shoplifters, and a woman hustler in a train station. Director Eric Rohmer explores the contrasting thoughts and actions of the two young women — one innocent and rigidly didactic, the other more worldly and open-minded. A-II (nr)

4 Clowns (1970) Robert Youngson's compilation deals with the art of visual comedy as shown in the work of four of its leading buffoons: Charley Chase, Buster Keaton, Stan Laurel, and Oliver Hardy. The selection of excerpts is fine, the narration is helpful and the silent comedy is timeless. A-I (G)

4D Man (1959) Halting sci-fi tale in which a dose of radiation from a lab project enables a scientist (Robert Lansing) to dissolve his body's molecular structure and pass through solid matter such as walls, but the process ages him rapidly and can be reversed only by draining the life out of others. Directed by Irvin S. Yeaworth, Jr., the special effects showing Lansing melting through material objects are simple but effective, though the formula story bogs down in a subplot of the scientist's fiancé (Lee Meriwether) falling for his younger brother (James Congdon). Stylized violence and romantic complications. A-II (br)

Four Days in November (1964) Straightforward documentary account of the assassination of President John Fitzgerald Kennedy in Dallas on Friday, Nov. 22, 1963, his funeral services in the nation's capital, and burial in Arlington Cemetery on Monday, Nov. 25. Produced and directed by Mel Stuart, with a terse yet moving narration by Theodore Strauss eloquently read by Richard Baseheart, this memorial to the slain president provides a record of the nation's trauma over the tragic event as well as the sorrow and sense of loss reflected in the solemn pageantry of his funeral. A-I (br)

Four Days in September (1998) Gripping yet thoughtful fact-based thriller about the 1969 kidnapping of the US Ambassador to Brazil (Alan Arkin) by an underground group seeking to force the country's military dictatorship to release some of their imprisoned comrades. Directed by Bruno Barreto, the step-by-step account of the kidnapping and police search is quite suspenseful, but the treatment clearly shows the kidnapping as a brutal act of terrorism no less morally repugnant than the regime against which it is directed. Subtitles. Scenes of violence including torture, menacing situations, and occasional rough language. A-III (R)

Four Deuces, The (1975) Apparently intended as a spoof, this clunker about gangland warfare during Prohibition gets its laughs all in the wrong places. Director William H. Busnell Jr. directs the lavish period sets better than he does his floundering cast, and there is nothing funny about the movie's violent brutality and view of women as sex objects. A misdeal from the title on. O (R)

Four Faces West (1948) Small but flavorful Western in which an earnest cowboy (Joel McCrea) robs a bank to save his father's ranch, then helps some people (notably Frances Dee and Joseph Calleia) along the way while fleeing from a tough but fair-minded sheriff (Charles Bickford). Directed by Alfred E. Green, the stereotyped characters are warmly portrayed, with emphasis on the cowboy's basic honesty and determination to repay the stolen money. Frontier violence. A-I (br)

Four Feathers, The (1939) When his regiment is ordered to join Kitchener's 1895 campaign to recapture Khartoum, an officer (John Clements) resigns his commission, thereby earning white feathers of cowardice from three comrades (Ralph Richardson among them) and fiancé (June Duprez). How he redeems them by aiding his friends in the Sudan disguised as a native makes an exciting but far-fetched adventure directed by Zoltan Korda with much spectacle, some good humor (notably C. Aubrey Smith's account of "the thin red line" at Balaclava), and no little flag-waving. Assorted stylized violence, but for a higher purpose than imperialism. A-I (br)

Four Flies on Grey Velvet (1972) Italian director Dario Argento pursues his usual theme of homicidal paranoia in a story about a rock drummer (Michael Brandon) who, fearing his life is in danger, sends his raspy wife (Mimsy Farmer) out of town, seeks help from a bohemian friend (Bud Spencer), hires an effeminate private eye (Jean-Pierre Marielle), and hops into the bathtub with his visiting cousin (Francine Racette). If anyone cares, there is unsettling violence, coarse language, illicit sex, and a cast of unwholesome characters. O (PG)

4 for Texas (1963) Bloated comic Western in which rival sharpsters (Frank Sinatra and Dean Martin) fight for control of a Galveston gambling boat, then unite against a crooked banker (Victor Buono), with help from a couple of shady ladies (Anita Ekberg and Ursula Andress). Producer-director Robert Aldrich gets little comic mileage out of his two leads who are more at home with double entendres than six-shooters. Stylized violence and sexual innuendo. A-III (br)

Four Friends (1981) Young immigrant from Yugoslavia (Craig Wasson) comes of age in 1960's Indiana in Steve Tesich's uneven semi-autobiographical screenplay directed by Arthur Penn. Few effective moments are evident in this often outrageously sentimental melodrama, which tries to evoke something of significance about the era and the Midwest. Permissive attitude toward adolescent sex and some brief nudity. A-III (R)

Four Girls in Town (1956) Glossy picture of life in Hollywood as a movie studio mounts a talent search for an actress to play the title role in the biblical story of Esther with Julie Adams, Marianne Cook, Elsa Marinelli, and Gia Scala selected for screen tests under novice director George Nader. Writer-director Jack Sher spends more time on the women's romances than their work at the studio, with meager results on both scores. Sexual situations and innuendoes. A-III (br)

Four Guns to the Border (1954) Halting Western in which four gunmen head for Mexico after robbing a bank, but three (John McIntire, Jay Silverheels, and George Nader) are killed saving an old man (Walter Brennan) and his daughter (Colleen Miller) from Apache raiders, then the fourth (Rory Calhoun) faces a showdown with the sheriff (Charles Drake). Directed by Richard Carlson, the action scenes are wasted in a muddled subplot of settling old scores and the daughter's love for the surviving gunman. Stylized violence, romantic complications, and sexual situations. A-III (br)

4 Little Girls (1997) Moving documentary revisits Birmingham, Alabama, where on a Sunday morning in 1963, four young girls were murdered in the racially motivated bombing of a Southern Baptist Church. Director Spike Lee interviews relatives of the victims to put human faces on the tragedy, as well as examines how these cruel killings served to focus public condemnation of white extremists and increased support for the civil rights movement. Some grisly photos of corpses and news footage of police brutality. A-II (nr)

Four Men and a Prayer (1938) When their father (C. Aubrey Smith) is murdered, four English brothers (George Sanders, Richard Greene, David Niven, and William Henry) set off to solve the crime, with some help from an American debutante (Loretta Young). Directed by John Ford, the uneven melodrama mixes in a arms trafficking ring, a Latin American revolution, and some silly romance, but it all works reasonably well thanks to a fine supporting cast (Barry Fitzgerald, Alan Hale, John Carradine). Sterling virtues triumph over stylized violence. A-I (br)

Four Musketeers, The (1975) Oliver Reed, Raquel Welsh, Richard Chamberlain, and Faye Dunaway star in director Richard Lester's sequel to his previous movie based on the Dumas novel. The style is halfway between spoof and in earnest with both pratfalls and bloodshed. The uneasy mix makes for rather uncertain entertainment, and the violence makes it questionable fare for younger viewers. A-III (PG)

Four Nights of a Dreamer (1972) French adaptation of a Dostoevsky story about a lonely artist in need of someone to personify his ideals of beauty who saves a young woman from suicide, and they meet for the next three nights to talk, but on the last night, the lover she thought untrue returns to claim her. The artist is again a solitary dreamer, but now he has an ideal based upon reality. Directed by Robert Bresson, adults will find this a tender and loving film, and a warm, if predictable, exercise in romantic fantasy. A-III (nr)

Four Rooms (1995) Inept quartet of skits about a hotel bellhop (Tim Roth) spending New Year's Eve with a coven of witches, a homicidal husband, two children left on their own, and a movie producer's drunken party. Directors Allison Anders, Alexandre Rockwell, Robert Rodriguezand, Quentin Tarantino play around with bizarre situations and hammy performances in a campy misfire lacking coherence, wit, style, or interest. Assorted violence, sexual references, partial nudity, profanity, and rough language. O (R)

Four Seasons, The (1981) Three couples (Alan Alda and Carol Burnett; Len Cariou and Sandy Dennis; Jack Weston and Rita Moreno) maintain a friendship despite various ups and downs, most having to do with marital problems. Written and directed by Alda, the entertaining but superficial comedy tries to elicit some sense of the complacency of middle-aged, middle-class suburban lifestyles. Mature subject matter, some crude gags, and profanity. A-III (PG)

Four Skulls of Jonathan Drake, The (1959) Minor horror film directed by Edward L. Cahn in which a professor of the occult (Henry Daniell) becomes the instrument of a deadly curse imposed by Amazonian headhunters on an English trader and his descendants (notably Eduard Franz). Hokey headless horrors. A-III (br)

Four Weddings and a Funeral (1994) Offbeat British comedy in which a genial but dim London bachelor (Hugh Grant) falls in love with a self-assured American visitor (Andie MacDowell) who proceeds to marry another, then turns up months later at his wedding with the news that she's left her husband. Under Mike Newell's bright direction, Richard Curtis's clever script delivers much verbal wit and visual gags, especially at the expense of British manners and eccentricities, but its scatterbrained treatment of love and marriage fails to gain any depth by tacking on the somber funeral of a monogamous homosexual. Several stylized bedroom scenes, discussion of sexual affairs, and comically intended rough language. A-IV (R)

1492: Conquest of Paradise (1992) Plodding chronicle follows Christopher Columbus (Gerard Depardieu) from his first voyage to the New World through his eventual fall from favor with the Spanish crown. Director Ridley Scott's hollow re-creation of history offers some breathtaking visuals but never probes very deeply into the character of the explorer or his times. Some savage violence, a common-law marriage, and tribal nudity. A-III (PG-13)

Fourth Protocol, The (1987) Searing spy suspenser about an attempt to detonate a small nuclear device at a US military base in England in order to destroy the NATO alliance pits KGB agent Pierce Brosnan against British spy-chaser Michael Caine. Director John MacKenzie's realistic drama has enough nudity and brutal killings to make it off-limits for youngsters. A-III (R)

Fourth War, The (1990) Lackluster Cold War thriller about maverick American and Soviet colonels (Roy Scheider and Jurgen Prochnow) who personally battle it out on the 1988 West German-Czech border. Director John Frankenheimer fails to invest his infantile characters or their senseless actions with any interest or suspense. Some profanity and pointless violence. A-III (R)

Fox (1976) German melodrama directed by Rainer Werner Fassbinder tells of the rise and fall of a naive worker (played by Fassbinder himself) who is exploited by the bourgeoisie and then discarded when no longer useful. It's the old Hollywood story of the corruption of an innocent by the power placed within the context of the homosexual world. Devoid of any kind of sexual sensationalism, the movie is more about the evils of capitalism than about homosexuality. A-IV (nr)

Fox and the Hound, The (1981) A fox and hound raised as friends have to confront the consequences of the roles assigned them by humans and nature in this Disney animated feature directed by Art Stevens, Ted Berman, and Richard Rich. Based on the book by Daniel P. Mannix, it should make pleasant entertainment for the young, though its sentimentality and cloying cuteness will put off older and more demanding viewers. A-I (G)

Foxes (1980) Director Adrian Lyne's grim, depressing tale of four teenage girls (Jodie Foster, Marilyn Kagan, Cherie Currie, and Kandice Stroh) left to their own devices amid the urban and moral squalor of Los Angeles. Fairly interesting, but the viewer stops caring about a third of the way through. Rough language and a superficial depiction of adult and youthful decadence. A-III (R)

Foxfire (1955) Soapy melodrama set in Arizona, where a rich vacationer (Jane Russell) and a half-Apache mining engineer (Jeff Chandler) impulsively wed, then spend the rest of the picture trying to bridge their cultural differences. Directed by Joseph Pevney, the Native-American aspects are treated superficially with cardboard characters and a contrived plot that bogs down in the search for a lost gold mine. Domestic tensions and sexual innuendo. A-III (br)

Foxy Brown (1974) Pam Grier busts up a ring of ghetto drug dealers out of revenge in a movie directed by Jack Hill with more foul language, more horrible violence (rape and castration), and an even wider variety of sexual kinkiness than is usual for this kind of black exploitation movie. O (R)

Fragment of Fear (1971) When his aunt (Flora Robson) turns up strangled in the ancient ruins of Pompeii, a reformed drug addict (David Hemmings) resolves to track down her killer. Director Richard C. Sarafian initiates a crackling good study of the effect of the past on the present of a recovering addict but those interested in it as a mystery thriller will be infuriated at its abrupt surprise ending. A-II (GP)

Fragrance of Wild Flowers, The (1979) Yugoslavian movie in which a successful actor gets fed up with life, takes up residence on a friend's river barge, and winds up being celebrated by the media as a fashionable rebel, more in demand than ever. The alienation theme is a familiar one, but director Srdjan Karnovic handles it with incisive human detail and, amidst all the ironies, some warmly gentle humor. A-III (nr)

Framed (1975) Wronged man (Joe Don Baker) comes out of prison to wreck a quite literal bloody vengeance upon his oppressors. Directed by Phil Karlson, it is a vicious movie that goes all out in its depiction of brutal violence, especially against women. O (R)

Frances (1984) Impassioned film biography of Frances Farmer, the 1930's Hollywood starlet who bucked the system, got involved with alcohol, drugs, and strange men, and whose mother had her placed in a mental institution where she was abused, raped, and received a lobotomy. Jessica Lange's fine performance makes this sincere, non-exploitative but rather plodding and episodic movie worth seeing. Director Graeme Clifford's depiction of Frances's suffering and fate is so unremittingly cruel, that the movie will be too harsh for many viewers. A-IV (R)

Francesco (1989) Overwrought Italian production portrays St. Francis of Assisi (Mickey Rourke) as a spiritual agitator challenging the accepted values of his 13th-century contemporaries by embracing a life of utter poverty and simplicity. Director Liliana Cavani builds an elaborate picture of the period's social injustices but fails to evoke any convincing sense of religious conviction from Rourke's embarrassingly vacuous performance. English-language version. Occasional scenes of violence, desperate poverty, and brief nudity. A-III (PG-13)

Francis (1949) One-joke comedy directed by Arthur Lubin in which the talking mule of the title (voice of Chill Wills) helps a bumbling second lieutenant (Donald O'Connor) become a hero in WW II Burma. The picture succeeded well enough to spawn a series of six sequels. Comic violence. A-I (br)

Francis Goes to the Races (1951) Formula series entry directed by Arthur Lubin in which the talking mule of the title (voice of Chill Wills) helps a bumbling young man (Donald O'Connor) save a woolly Kentucky horse-breeder (Cecil Kellaway) and his pretty granddaughter (Piper Laurie) from losing a fixed race. Crooked gamblers. A-I (br)

Francis Goes to West Point (1952) Formula comedy series entry directed by Arthur Lubin in which the talking mule of the title (voice of Chill Wills) keeps a bumbling cadet (Donald O'Connor) from being kicked out of the Academy by helping him win the big football match against Navy. A-I (br)

Francis Joins the WACS (1954) Formula service comedy directed by Arthur Lubin in which an Army lieutenant (Donald O'Connor) gets into predictable mix-ups after he is mistakenly posted to a WAC base, with the talking mule of the title adding to the comic confusion. Tame gender jokes. A-I (br)

Francis of Assisi (1961) Uneven dramatization of the life of the 13th-century saint (Bradford Dillman), who founds a religious community based on absolute poverty, seeks its approval by the pope (Finlay Currie), encourages longtime friend Clare (Dolores Hart) to head a similar women's order, then journeys to the Holy Land, preaches to the sultan (Pedro Armendariz), and returns to find his order spreading but changing. Directed by Michael Curtiz, the production is well-mounted and well-intended, but the script is a muddle of historical fact and dramatic fiction, with results that barely scratch the surface of Franciscan spirituality. A-I (br)

Frankenhooker (1990) Clunky horror farce about a New Jersey "bio-electro technician" (James Lorinz) who saves his girlfriend's head after she is chewed up by a power mower and attaches it to various body parts selected from a bevy of Manhattan prostitutes. Directed by Frank Honenlotter, it's soft-core trash whose few droll moments are buried in low-budget gore. Repellent violence, sex scenes with nudity, and drug abuse. O (nr)

Frankenstein (1931) Stylish horror classic from Mary Shelley's novel about the obsessed Dr. Frankenstein (Colin Clive) who robs graves to complete his composite creation (Boris Karloff), which is brought to life during an electrical storm, then breaks free to the consternation of the local village. The tampering-with-nature fable succeeds largely because of Karloff's sympathetic portrayal of the monster as tormented victim, and director James Whale's treatment of the ghoulish proceedings as something more than mere horror fare. Stylized violence and recurring menace. A-II (br)

Frankenstein and the Monster from Hell (1974) Peter Cushing again assumes the role of the mad doctor who, with his assistant (Shane Briant), assembles a creature from assorted parts they collect at the insane asylum in which they are residents. Directed by Terence Fisher, the gore is both sickening and sick. O (R)

Frankenstein Conquers the World (1967) Dubbed Japanese import directed by Inoshiro Honda begins with a Nazi submarine delivering the monster's still-living heart to Hiroshima, from whose A-bombed ashes emerges a giant-sized Frankenstein, but his awful make-up fails to frighten an earnest American scientist (Nick Adams) who sticks around for the finale involving another bargain-basement monster.

Flimsy menace and scale-model violence. A-I (br)

Frankenstein Created Woman (1967) Monster mishmash in which the mad doctor (Peter Cushing) restores life to a drowned woman (Susan Denberg) by transferring the soul of his guillotined assistant (Robert Morris) into her body, with gory results. Directed by Terence Fisher, the British production has a good cast, but the tangled plot mixes a nonsensical premise with bad melodrama. Stylized violence and sexual situations. A-III (br)

Frankenstein Meets the Wolf Man (1943) Uneven series entry in which the late Lawrence Talbot (Lon Chaney, Jr.) is revived when grave robbers open his tomb during the full moon, then journeys to the ruins of Frankenstein's castle seeking release from his life as a werewolf, but finds instead the baron's frozen monster (Bela Lugosi) and a watery grave. Directed by Roy William Neill, the result has some spooky scenes, much eerie atmosphere, and a good cast (Maria Ouspenskaya, Ilona Massey, Patric Knowles, and others), though Lugosi's role is miniscule and the last part of the picture is tiresomely predictable. Stylized violence and menacing situations. A-II (br)

Frankenstein Must Be Destroyed (1970) Mediocre British installment in the Frankenstein saga with the mad doctor (Peter Cushing) fanatically intent on perfecting his experiments in brain transplants. Directed by Terence Fisher, the macabre setting and atmosphere are good, but the gore, with heads being lopped off and blood splattering freely, is less effective than the earlier convention of suggesting such shock effects. A-III (PG)

Frankenstein Unbound (see: **Roger Corman's Frankenstein Unbound**)

Frankenstein's Daughter (1959) Bargain-basement horror from director Richard Cunha offers a pedestrian tale of Frankenstein's grandson (John Ashley) working in southern California, where he creates a female monster with a teenager's brain. Sexual situations and hokey menace. A-III (br)

Frankie and Johnny (1966) Elvis Presley vehicle with plenty of rock-'n'-roll music, fist-swinging action, and cutsie-poo romance. Allegedly based on the famous folk-ballad, Presley plays a two-timing but ultimately redemptive riverboat gambler, with Donna Douglas as his tried but true love, Frankie. Directed by Frederick de Cordova, it's lightweight fun. A-II (br)

Frankie and Johnny (1991) Moderately engaging love story about a fed-up-with-men waitress (Michelle Pfeiffer) in a Manhattan diner who doesn't want a relationship with the new cook (Al Pacino), an ex-con who wants to offer her love, marriage, and a family. With Pacino in fine form here, producer-director Garry Marshall tackles themes of hope, renewal, and family ties, despite the confines of an overly talky romance. Brief shots of lovemaking, numerous sexual references, and some rough language. A-III (R)

Frankie Starlight (1995) Quirky drama set in Ireland, where a lonely adult dwarf (Corban Walker) recalls the story of how his French WW II refugee mother (Anne Parillaud) raised him with the help of an Irish family, whose oldest daughter finds unexpected romance with him years later. Director Michael Lindsay-Hogg's bittersweet tale of offbeat romances over two generations is full of charm and pathos, yet comes up short in defining the central character of the mother. Brief violence including suicides, a bedroom scene, and occasional rough language. A-III (R)

Frantic (1988) Well-crafted suspense thriller about an American couple (Harrison Ford and Betty Buckley) who, on a visit to Paris, get caught up in a dangerous game of international intrigue. Director Roman Polanski provides the chills and thrills with appropriately sinister camerawork and a strong performance by Ford, but several bizarre scenes involving drugs and a grotesque corpse are not for the squeamish. Restrained violence, drug use, brief nudity, and some street language. A-III (R)

Fraternity Row (1977) Shallow and sentimental look at fraternity life in the mid-1950s in a story about an idealistic young man who becomes a pledge at a prestigious college fraternity and runs afoul of a sadistic bully. Director Thomas J. Tobin takes an uncritical view of the frat system on American campuses. Some sexual references. A-III (PG)

Fraternity Vacation (1985) Frat nerds place a wager on who will seduce Britt Ekland first. Directed by James Frawley, this **Animal House** clone offers nothing but the usual nudity and gross, vulgar humor. O (R)

Fraulein Doktor (1969) WW I German spy (Suzy Kendall) engineers the sinking of Lord Kitchener's ship, steals a poison gas formula from a French scientist (Capucine), and supervises the theft of the master battle-plan from Allied headquarters in Belgium. Alberto Lattuada directs the movie in an almost documentary style that encourages a suspension of disbelief. Though uneven and deliberately devoid of emotional involvement, its events are often grimly absorbing and hard to dismiss. A-III (M)

Freaks (1932) Tod Browning, a director specializing in the field of horror and the grotesque, centered this story around a group of circus freaks who take in a normal woman in need of refuge, but she betrays them. Browning endows the movie with an unusual sympathetic quality in not exploiting the deformities and monstrous appearance of his characters. The result is a unique film of the horror genre, a real classic of its kind, that is not easily forgotten by even the most sophisticated cinema-addict. A-II (nr)

Freaky Friday (1977) Mother and teenage daughter (Barbara Harris and Jodie Foster) vehemently wish to trade places for a single day, only to have the wish granted, to their mutual discomfiture. Gary Nelson directs a typical Disney slapstick comedy bolstered by good performances in the leads. A-I (G)

Freckles (1960) Earnest but tedious tale directed by Andrew V. McLaglen follows the adventures of a one-armed Chicago youth (Martin West) as he gets a job with a small Western logging company, then saves it from an enterprising gang of timber thieves. Well-intentioned but painfully slow and uninvolving. A-I (br)

Freckles Comes Home (1942) Formula homespun adventure in which the title character (Johnny Downs) returns from college, then saves his small Indiana town from a swindler (Bradley Page), getting help along the way from his high-school girlfriend (Gale Storm) and a bumbling sheriff (Irving Bacon). Some stylized violence. A-I (br)

Freddy's Dead: The Final Nightmare (1991) Hideous Freddy Krueger (Robert Englund) continues to lure teenagers into suicidal nightmares until he is vanquished by his revenge-inspired daughter (Lisa Zane). Director Rachel Talalay spends more time on dream imagery and special effects than actual murders, but the movie is still designed to invite laughter at adolescents being tortured and viciously slaughtered. Deadly violence depicted as entertaining and recurring rough language. O (R)

Free Willy (1993) After befriending a killer whale trapped in a cramped marine park, a rebellious 12-year-old (Jason James Richter) persuades his foster parents (Michael Madsen and Jayne Atkinson) and two park workers (Lori Petty and August Schellenberg) to help free the giant animal before it is killed for the insurance money. Director Simon Wincer's beguiling relationship story affirms family values, though it must be noted the adults cavalierly break the law in saving the whale. Fleeting violence. A-II (PG)

Free Willy 2: The Adventure Home (1995) In this spirited sequel, the now 14-year-old youth (Jason James Richter) joins forces with his eight-year-old half-brother (Francis Capra) to rescue the trapped killer whale he had befriended two years earlier and, in turn, the whale saves him from a perilous situation. Director Dwight Little combines exceptional nature photography with an incident-filled narrative and uplifting values for a pleasing family film. Young children may be frightened by scenes of other youngsters in jeopardy. A-I (PG)

Free Willy 3: The Rescue (1997) Tired sequel in which the lad (Jason James Richter) who befriended the title whale attempts to protect him and his pregnant mate from being harpooned by a deadly whaler pursuing them on the high seas. Although the wildlife photography is still stunning, director Sam Pillsbury generates little suspense in the narrative, and the boy-with-whale footage has become overly familiar. Brief barroom brawl and some rationalization of misdeeds. A-II (PG)

Free Woman, A (1974) German drama of a woman (Margarethe von Trotta) struggling for self-identity and fulfillment following her divorce and bitter court battle for custody of her little boy. Directed by Volker Schlondorff, it seethes with a restrained anger that leads to occasionally brutal characterizations of male stereotypes but avoids the pitfalls of exploiting women in the process. A-III (nr)

Freejack (1992) Ultra-violent, futuristic tale of a race-car driver (Emilio Estevez) pursued by a ruthless killer (Mick Jagger) intent on selling the racer's body to a dying magnate (Anthony Hopkins). Director Geoff Murphy just marks time with his cast between the bloody shootouts that are the movie's only apparent reason for having been made. Excessive violence, implied live-in relationship, and occasional rough language. O (R)

Freebie and the Bean (1974) Two freewheeling San Francisco cops careen dangerously around the city to protect a mobster they plan to arrest when the time is ripe for a promotion. In director Richard Rush's failed comedy, Bean (Alan Arkin) and Freebie (James Caan) are gun-crazy psychopaths who enjoy indulging their penchant for foul language, ethnic slurs, kinky sex, and beating up hapless individuals whenever they get a chance. O (R)

Freedom on My Mind (1994) Compelling documentary recalls the civil rights struggle in the early 1960s to register black voters in the segregated State of Mississippi. Produced and directed by Connie Field and Marilyn Mulford, the tautly edited archival footage, inter-cut with frank commentary by those who were actively involved in the movement, provides a chilling portrait of institutionalized racism as well as heartening testimony to the power of committed individuals to effect change. Scenes of racial violence. A-II (nr)

Freedom to Love (1970) Presented in the form of a serious examination of sexual freedom, interspersed with some shallow commentary, the movie is merely a poor excuse to present scenes of graphic sex and nudity. O (nr)

Freeze-Die-Come to Life (1990) The foolhardy pranks of a young Russian boy (Pavel Nazarov) living near Stalin's WW II labor camps put him and his friend (Dinara Drukarova) in peril from both state authorities and a gang of cutthroat thieves. Director Vitaly Kanevski's grimly autobiographical account depicts life reduced to the level of self-preservation, where children find little warmth and are quickly hardened. Subtitles. Several instances of violence, nudity, and minimal rough language. A-III (nr)

French Connection, The (1971) Tough, unorthodox New York detective Popeye Doyle (Gene Hackman) and his partner (Roy Scheider) track down a massive heroin cache in this tense, exciting, very violent look at the darker side of law enforcement. Director William Friedkin makes excellent use of New York City locations in giving his fast-paced story the grimy look of reality and the acting of the leads is first-rate. The violent action and language are in the context of a sobering, perhaps shocking, portrayal of the kill-or-be-killed undercover world of cops and dope dealers. A-IV (R)

French Connection II (1975) Gene Hackman repeats his role as fanatical detective Popeye Doyle in a sequel set in France and directed by John Frankenheimer. Not nearly as successful as its predecessor, the movie is marred by its ambivalent attitude towards Doyle's ruthless methods, some strong violence, and rough language. A-IV (R)

French Conspiracy, The (1973) Dramatic re-creation of the events in a political scandal that rocked the French government in the late 1960s when Ben Barka, a Moroccan revolutionary exile, was kidnapped in France, with the apparent complicity and cooperation of some French officials. Directed by Yves Boisset, the result is not an espionage thriller, but rather a careful exposition of the intelligence community that operates beneath the surface of modern governments. Stars Gian-Maria Volonte, Michael Piccoli, and Jean-Louis Trintignant. A-II (PG)

French Cousins, The (see: **From Ear to Ear**)

French Detective, The (1979) Gaelic version of an American police thriller features a tough cop (Lino Ventura) and his young assistant (Patrick Dewaere) who encounter a dishonest political machine while investigating a murder. Director Pierre Granier-Deferre spends too much time on philosophical exchanges between his policemen by Hollywood standards, but its abuse of citizen's rights are familiar enough to American moviegoers. There is enough violence and moral ambiguity to make it adult fare. A-III (nr)

French Kiss (1995) Dizzy romantic comedy in which an uptight housewife-to-be (Meg Ryan) jets to Paris to save her callow fiancé (Timothy Hutton) from a French siren, getting help along the way from a scheming French thief (Kevin Kline) whose crass outlook on life naturally masks a sensitive soul. Director Lawrence Kasdan's attempts to be bright and witty come over as merely slick and superficial, further handicapped by an unamusing series of altercations between scorned woman and Gaelic opportunist. Some sexual situations and innuendo, occasional coarse expressions, and several instances of rough language. A-III (PG-13)

French Lessons (1986) Producer David Puttnam's somewhat anachronistic romance details the first sexual experience of a British exchange student in Paris. Jane Snowden gives a sensitive portrayal of the youth experimenting in adult responsibilities but the dialogue is so awful and the script so woefully inadequate that the movie never achieves any credibility. O (PG)

French Lieutenant's Woman, The (1981) Scriptwriter Harold Pinter's adaptation of John Fowles's novel uses a movie-within-a-movie gimmick so that the story of a wealthy gentleman's pursuit of a mysterious governess in the Victorian Age also becomes a tale of two performers carrying on an adulterous affair in the present. Meryl Streep and Jeremy Irons play the dual roles of the lovers. Director Karel Reisz's result is interesting, but too pretentious and humorless for its own good. Rather graphic bedroom scene. A-III (R)

French Line, The (1954) Leaden musical romance in which a Texas oil millionaire (Jane Russell) ducks fortune hunters on an ocean-liner to Europe by hiring a woman to pose as her, then falls for a Frenchman (Gilbert Roland) who turns out to be more interested in her stand-in until voyage's end. Directed by Lloyd Bacon, the slow-paced proceedings grow tiresome with predictable comic complications and clunky musical numbers. Sexual situations and innuendo. A-III (br)

French Postcards (1979) Lighthearted but aimless movie about a trio of American students in Paris (Miles Chapin, Blanche Baker, and David Marshall Grant) and their various amorous misadventures. Director Willard Huyck's episodic, listless, and anti-intellectual effort seeks unearned viewer sympathy for feckless youths whose acting ability seems more suited to amateur night at the fraternity house. The movie's implicit endorsement of sexual promiscuity makes it unacceptable entertainment. O (PG)

French Provincial (1976) Interesting French melodrama about a seamstress (Jeanne Moreau) who marries into a bourgeois family in the south of France and becomes the one who holds it together from the early 1930s to the 1970s. Director Andre Techine integrates the episodic family chronicle within the larger frame of the changes taking place within France during that period. A-III (nr)

French Way, The (see: **Love at the Top**)

Frenchman's Creek (1944) Romantic potboiler from Daphne du Maurier's novel in which a nobleman's wife (Joan Fontaine) flees 1668 London to escape her husband's lecherous friend (Basil Rathbone), arrives at the family's long-vacant manor on the coast of Cornwall, and falls for the French pirate (Arturo de Cordova) using it as his base. Director Mitchell Leisen gets some gusto in the period action scenes, but the romantic proceedings are woodenly acted and emotionally contrived. Stylized violence, implied marital infidelity, and a tacked-on moral ending. A-III (br)

Frenzy (1972) Alfred Hitchcock's masterful suspense thriller focuses on a deranged strangler preying on women in contemporary London. The central character is an innocent man (Jon Finch) whose careless way of living implicates him as the serial murderer who dispatches his victims by means of a characteristic necktie, with accompanying perverse violence. The suspense is built on whether the wrong man will be punished for the crimes, something which is not resolved until the very last moment. Though of the same caliber as Hitchcock's best works, it lamentably resorts to some very explicit violence and brief nudity. A-IV (R)

Fresh (1994) Disturbing story of a 12-year-old drug courier (Sean Nelson) who aims to take his addicted sister (N'Bushe Wright) out of their Brooklyn 'hood by pitting rival drug lords against each other, then offering to testify against them in exchange for admission to the Witness Protection program. Writer-director Boaz Yakin spares viewers no end of vicious, foul-mouthed characters in a harrowing narrative about the limited options an African-American youth has for survival in a poisonous environment of deadly violence. Some stylized violence, brief nudity, and incessant rough language with frequent racial and sexual slurs. A-IV (R)

Fresh Horses (1988) A college senior (Andrew McCarthy) drops his wealthy fiancé for a rural girl (Molly Ringwald) too young, uneducated, and married to give him anything but grief. In this mood-piece about obsession, director David Anspaugh provides little understanding of the characters and ignores intriguing plot-lines. Off-camera illicit sex, brief violence, and minimal rough language. A-III (PG-13)

Freshman, The (1990) Shortly after arriving in New York City, a college freshman (Matthew Broderick) is bewildered to find himself involved with a Godfather-like businessman (Marlon Brando), his marriage-minded daughter, a giant lizard, federal agents, and the threat of jail. Writer-director Andrew Bergman serves up an amiable comedy more distinguished by an amusing cast than the story's less-than-riveting dialogue and perfunctory pacing. Minimal rough language. A-II (PG)

Freud (1962) Earnest, plodding drama recounts the turning point for Dr. Sigmund Freud (Montgomery Clift) as a neurologist in 1885 Vienna, where his treatment of a troubled patient (Susannah York) leads to his theory of childhood sexual repression, a concept rejected by his closest colleague (Larry Parks) and scorned by his peers. Director John Huston's dramatization of psychiatry's beginnings may be simplistic, especially the dream sequences, but demonstrates the limitations of the physical sciences in treating emotional disorders. Though handled with sensitivity, the subject matter may be distasteful for some viewers. A-IV (br)

Friday (1995) An unemployed black youth (Ice Cube) and his pot-head pal (Chris Tucker) spend the day in their South Central neighborhood of Los Angeles swapping wisecracks while observing the antics of their neighbors, ogling females, eluding a drug dealer, and tangling with the local bully. Directed by Gary Gray, the low-budget production strings together a series of crude comedy-sketches about ghetto life, most of which viewers will find appalling rather than amusing, though at least it doesn't glamorize guns and drugs. Sexual innuendo, bathroom humor, stylized violence, pot smoking, and incessant rough language. A-IV (R)

Friday Foster (1976) Director Arthur Marks wastes some talented performers (Yaphet Kotto, Godfrey Cambridge, Eartha Kitt, and Pam Grier) in a black exploitation number adapted from a comic strip but without whatever depth and subtlety the original may have had. Excessive sex and violence. O (R)

Friday the 13th (1980) Homicidal maniac menaces teenagers at a summer camp. Crude, mindless exploitation cheapie directed by Sean S. Cunningham with much blood and violence and graphic sex scenes. O (R)

Friday the 13th, Part II (1981) Disgusting horror sequel with the homicidal maniac once more stalking slow-witted camp counselors who have sex on their minds rather than self-preservation. Wholly uninspired direction and script are by Steve Miner and Ron Kurz, with the usual unhealthy mix of nudity and graphic violence. O (R)

Friday the 13th, Part III (1982) The 3-D version directed by Steve Miner is no better than its predecessors in the blood and gore department. O (R)

Friday the 13th — The Final Chapter (1984) Jason the ghoulish maniac is on the loose again as director Joseph Zito fills the screen with the usual gore and violence mixed with crude language and much nudity. O (R)

Friday the 13th, Part V — A New Beginning (1985) Directed by Danny Steinmann, this time out Jason the maniac stalks a home for disturbed children. Violent, gory horror flick whose only goal is to shock. O (R)

Friday the 13th, Part VI: Jason Lives (1986) The demonic killer is brought back from the dead via a lightning bolt to torment, terrorize, and molest the descendants of his killers. This excessively violent sequel, written and directed by Tom McLoughlin, consists of little more than a succession of bloody slaughter scenes with a little explicit sex between minors thrown in for good measure. O (R)

Friday the 13th Part VIII — Jason Takes Manhattan (1989) Sick horror show in which bionic corpse Jason (Kane Hodder) dismembers recent grads of Crystal Lake High on a tour ship bound for Manhattan and pursues the survivors into the subways and alleys of the Big Apple. Writer-director Rob Hedden zeroes in on every gory detail in a movie that also offers profanity, recreational teen cocaine use, and fleeting nudity in a brief teen sexual encounter. O (R)

Fried Green Tomatoes (1991) The youthful reminiscences of a nursing-home resident (Jessica Tandy) about an unsolved, half-century-old murder mystery involving two spunky Alabama women (Mary Stuart Masterson and Mary-Louise Parker) inspire her newfound friend, a frustrated Southern housewife (Kathy Bates), to put her own house in order. An initially sluggish script hampers director Jon Avnet's beautifully acted movie but can't submerge its warm-hearted tribute to friendship, female solidarity, and respect for people of color. Very brief violence and a few sexual references. A-II (PG-13)

Frieda (1947) Just before WW II's end, a British airman (David Farrar) arrives home with a German bride (Mai Zetterling) whom he wed after she helped him escape a POW camp, but anti-German feelings of the locals drive her to attempt suicide. Directed by

Basil Dearden, the well-crafted but slow-paced melodrama examines the theme of collective guilt from a variety of angles, some uncomfortably close to Nazi racial doctrine. Stylized violence and anti-German sentiments. A-III (br)

Friend of the Family (1965) Weak French comedy directed by Robert Thomas about a toy inventor (Pierre Dux) and his wife (Danielle Darrieux) whose serenity is upset by a rival manufacturer (Jean Gabin) and his interest in their teenage daughter (Sylvie Vartan). A-III (br)

Friend of the Deceased, A (1998) Glumly comic tale set in Kiev, Ukraine, where an unemployed translator (Alexandre Lazarev) hires a hit-man to kill him, then changes his mind but has no way to cancel the contract except by hiring another hit-man to kill the first one. Director Vyacheslav Krishtofovich creates grim social satire out of the economic instability in post-communist Ukraine, which is seen as having left ordinary people adrift without a moral compass. Subtitles. Brief violence, fleeting nudity and sexual situations. A-III (R)

Friendly Persuasion (1956) Winning adaptation of Jessamyn West's novel about a Quaker household (Gary Cooper, Dorothy McGuire, and Tony Perkins) at the time of the Civil War. Director William Wyler's lyric treatment of family life and human relationships heightens the conflict between the hard realities of the war and the pacifist convictions of the Quaker faith. Still a warm and cheering experience for family viewers. A-I (nr)

Friends (1971) Soapy, sappy sudser about two unhappy teens (Sean Bury and Anicee Alvina) running away from cruel homes who meet in the Paris Zoo and flee to a seaside refuge, where instead of being friends they become lovers and parents in the pseudo-lyrical style of director Lewis Gilbert. The explicitness of their barely post-pubescent sexual awakening is not only offensive but a saddening exploitation of minors in the name of box-office romance. O (R)

Friends & Lovers (1999) Inept sex farce in which a group of old pals away for a ski weekend all find new sexual partners except for the preening stud (Stephen Baldwin) in their midst. Writer-director George Haas's lame ensemble comedy is utterly contrived, badly staged, and filled with bogus sentiments. A few fairly graphic sexual encounters, full frontal nudity, positive treatment of the gay lifestyle, and recurring profanity and rough language. O (nr)

Friends of Eddie Coyle, The (1973) Solid adaptation of a George V. Higgins's novel about a tired, smalltime Boston crook (Robert Mitchum), who wants to retire on one last job but gets caught in the middle of con-men, cops, and criminals, and tries desperately to find an out. Directed by Peter Yates, the story is given a fine, naturalistic treatment, tough and complex, but tight. The powerful effect of the conclusion is achieved through the movie's careful accumulation of detail, though some may be unwilling to wait for the final turn of events because of the harsh and uncompromising depiction of criminal life. A-III (R)

Fright Night (1985) This horror movie attempts to evoke chills in a quite ordinary setting, when a high-school youth (William Ragsdale) becomes convinced that his new neighbor (Chris Sarandon) is a vampire. A major problem with writer-director Tom Holland's approach is its uncertain tone in veering between straight horror and a spoof of horror movies. The conclusion is dominated by gory pull-out-all-the-stops special effects. Benign view of extramarital sex. O (R)

Frighteners, The (1996) Tawdry horror comedy in which a minor scam-artist (Michael J. Fox) is suspected of being behind a rash of mysterious heart attacks killing townspeople, though he is actually trying to stop the malevolent ghost causing the killing spree. Director Peter Jackson's overwrought special-effects fantasy lurches badly from a comic depiction of goofy characters into the darker territory of a mass murderer returned from the grave to claim more victims. Stylized violence with some gore, fleeting sexual innuendo, and recurring profanity. A-III (R)

Fringe Dwellers, The (1987) Insightful portrait of a young Australian aborigine girl's coming of age while struggling to break the cycle of poverty and oppression that crushes youthful ambition and enthusiasm. The contrived plot supplies an abrupt solution to a complex series of social and moral problems, but the overall perspective of director Bruce Beresford's movie provides an uplifting vision of community values and strong family ties. A-III (PG)

Frisco Kid, The (1979) A rabbi (Gene Wilder), sent cross-country on horseback during the Gold Rush to head a congregation in San Francisco, endures many misadventures that are potentially hilarious but prove only mildly funny under Robert Aldrich's direction. Harrison Ford as the badman who brings him cross-country unscathed, makes the long journey as enjoyable as the material allows. Contains some hard-edged violence and profanity. A-III (PG)

Fritz the Cat (1972) Foul-mouthed comic-book feline has been brought to the screen in an animated feature that lacks not only a clever script but a sense of humor. Under director Ralph Bakshi's slapdash direction, all attempts at satire regularly succumb to sexual sordidness, putting Fritz and his friends in the same category as the humans who toil in porno pictures. O (X)

Frogmen, The (1951) Standard WW II tale directed by Lloyd Bacon in which the new commander (Richard Widmark) of an underwater demolition team (Dana Andrews, Jeffrey Hunter, Robert Wagner, and others) alienates his men during the invasion of a South Pacific island, then wins them over in a raid on a Japanese submarine pen. Wartime violence. A-I (br)

Frogs (1972) Harmless-looking frogs and toads send an army of snakes, leeches, snapping turtles, and alligators to invade the home of Ray Milland on his swampy tropical island. Instead of playing the silly horror fantasy for laughs, director George McGowen tries for gasps in scene upon grisly scene with a transparent ecology message about nature taking its revenge. A-III (PG)

From Beyond the Grave (1976) British horror movie composed of four tales linked together by the device of a sinister antique shop and its affable proprietor (Peter Cushing). Director Kevin Connor can't improve upon the weak script, but he gets some fine performances (Ian Bannen, Donald Pleasance, and Margaret Leighton as an eccentric medium right out of Noel Coward). The blood flows a little too freely in one of the stories but, other than that, it's a relatively mild little chiller. A-III (PG)

From Dusk to Dawn (1996) Repellent tale of fleeing gangster brothers (George Clooney and Quentin Tarantino) holding a minister's family hostage across the Mexican border in a sleazy strip joint, where the performers turn out to be blood-thirsty vampires. Director Robert Rodriquez assaults viewers' sensibilities with a stream of gross visuals, mixing hardcore action and gory horror intended as sick, hip humor. Graphic violence, lurid sexual references, considerable nudity, and incessant rough language. O (R)

From Hell It Came (1957) Ludicrous horror fantasy directed by Dan Milner is set on a Pacific island whose superstitious natives are saved by US doctors (Tod Andrews and Tina Carver) from a murderous tree monster that walks on two legs. A yawner with some stylized violence and supernatural hokum. A-II (br)

From Here to Eternity (1953) Somber picture of life on an Army base in 1941 Hawaii centers on a company whose bugler (Montgomery Clift) is punished for refusing as a matter of conscience to join the unit's boxing team, with only a hapless private (Frank Sinatra) supporting his obstinacy. Directed by Fred Zinnemann from the James Jones novel, the story also involves an affair between the company's top sergeant (Burt Lancaster) and his commander's unhappy wife (Deborah Kerr), as well as the bugler's romance with a club hostess (Donna Reed), all of which gains tragic dimension from the Japanese sneak attack on Pearl Harbor at movie's end. Sexual situations and stylized violence, including a fatal beating and a knife fight. A-III (br)

From Noon Till Three (1976) Seriocomic Western about an outlaw (Charles Bronson) whose sexual dalliance with a zany widow (Jill Ireland) blossoms into true love. The cast's wooden performance, the script's utter banalities, and Frank Gilroy's inept direction obscure the theme of mistaken identities and half-truths becoming the basis for a legend. Excessive sex scenes. O (PG)

From Russia with Love (1964) Stealing a top-secret decoder from the Soviet Embassy in Istanbul, British super-spy James Bond (Sean Connery) takes the Venice-bound Orient Express, fighting off a wicked assortment of assassins (notably Robert Shaw and Lotte Lenya) along the way. Directed by Terence Young, the slick, tongue-in-cheek espionage thriller is marred by some scenes of sadistic violence, casual sexual encounters, and suggestive dialogue. O (PG)

From the Earth to the Moon (1958) Hokey sci-fi fantasy from a Jules Verne tale set in 1868 when a US armaments maker (Joseph Cotten) discovers a source of infinite energy, then uses it to propel a projectile to the moon with himself and an arch-rival (George Sanders) aboard. Director Byron Haskin trades on the story's parallels with modern nuclear power, but the effort is handicapped by an inept script and ham acting. Life-threatening situations. A-I (br)

From the Hip (1987) Law clerk (Judd Nelson) uses deceit and bravado to advance his career, but when he is given an unwinnable murder case, his defense of a psychotic literature professor (John Hurt) brings about a change of heart and conscience. Bob Clark directs this optimistic yuppie portrait with care and wit. Some vulgar language and a brief outburst of courtroom violence. A-II (PG)

From the Journals of Jean Seberg (1996) Fictional autobiography of the screen actress whose 1957 debut in Preminger's **Saint Joan** was mercilessly panned, then found brief fame in France in Godard's 1960 **Breathless,** after which she combined an indifferent screen career with several unhappy marriages, growing difficulties related to her support of the Black Panthers, and ultimately her suicide in 1979 at age 40. Written and directed by Mark Rappaport, the film uses Mary Beth Hurt to present Seberg's imagined recollections as the victim of her profession and times, with provocative asides about the movies as business and art, the relationship between talent and celebrit,y as well as the politics of pop culture. Ambiguous treatment of fact and fiction. A-III (nr)

From the Life of the Marionettes (1980) Disappointing exploration of the homicidal psyche details the killing and sexual violation of a prostitute by a sullen businessman. Director Ingmar Bergman's narrative is devoted to flashbacks and flash-forwards that supposedly shed some light on the what caused this irrational act. Darkly clinical and emotionally sterile, the movie is obscure and troubling. Extensive nudity. O (R)

From the Mixed-Up Files of Mrs. Basil E. Frankweiler (1973) Two preteen runaways (Sally Prager and Johnny Doran) find a haven in New York City's Metropolitan Museum of Art until discovered by a rich, eccentric recluse (Ingrid Bergman), from whom they learn a lesson in human integrity. In director Fielder Cook's well-intentioned but disappointing family movie, few things work the way they are supposed to, though young children may enjoy some of the midnight wanderings through the museum. A-I (G)

From the Terrace (1960) Slick melodrama from John O'Hara's novel about a WW II vet (Paul Newman) rejecting his wealthy parents (Myrna Loy and Leon Ames) to make good on his own with a wife (Joanne Woodward) whose father's Wall Street firm leads to the top, but along the way he decides to share his success with another woman (Ina Balin). Director Mark Robson turns in a glossy picture of life in the fast lane with cardboard characters, contrived plot, and superficial treatment of serious themes. A-IV (br)

From This Day Forward (1946) Still interesting picture in which a WW II veteran (Mark Stevens) recalls courting his girl (Joan Fontaine) and getting married during the lean years of the Depression, as he fills out forms trying to get a job and provide for his wife and family after the war. Directed by John Berry, the prewar flashbacks present a realistic context for a veteran's postwar problems and his hopes for the future. Some sexual innuendo. A-II (br)

Front, The (1976) Tragicomedy set during the early 1950s about a born loser (Woody Allen) who fronts for blacklisted writers by submitting their work under his name until he himself is turned in by a blacklisted actor (Zero Mostel) whose subsequent suicide is the story's turning point. Many of those associated with the movie, including director Martin Ritt and writer Walter Bernstein, were themselves blacklisted during that period. It is an interesting look at a tragic era, but the drama and humor do not mix easily. Some rough language and comic sexual references. A-III (PG)

Front Page, The (1974) New edition of the Charles MacArthur-Ben Hecht play about tough Chicago newspapermen in the 1920s pits Jack Lemmon as the ace reporter against Walter Matthau as his wily editor. Directed by Billy Wilder, there is plenty of sharp, fast comedy straight out of the original, but nicely put over by a fine cast and a few neat touches of the director. Some, however, will be put off by the constant stream of pressroom profanity. A-III (R/PG appeal)

Frontier Hellcat (1966) Dubbed German production directed by Alfred Vohrer offers juvenile Western adventure with novelist Karl May's cardboard heroes, Old Surehand (Stewart Granger) and Winnetou, his faithful Apache friend, saving pioneers (such as Elke Sommer) from Indians and badmen. Cliches galore, with the only twist as the good Indians, rather than the cavalry, arrive in the nick of time to save the encircled wagon train. Frontier violence. A-I (br)

Frozen Dead (1967) Failed horror movie about a good-bad scientist (Dana Andrews) who thaws out former Nazi military leaders after their 25 years of deep-freeze existence. Ineptly directed by Herbert J. Leder, its story of suspended animation and revivification is stupid but innocuous. A-I (br)

Fugitive, The (1947) Underrated screen version of Graham Greene's novel *The Power and the Glory*, about an all-too-human priest (Henry Fonda) who is hunted down by a puritanical officer (Pedro Armendariz) after the Mexican Revolution proscribes the free practice of religion. Director John Ford's flawed masterpiece uses deeply felt religious symbolism in telling the story of a weak man who, despite his fear of death, continues ministering to the spiritual needs of a poor community. Menacing atmosphere may be inappropriate for young children. A-I (nr)

Fugitive, The (1993) Having escaped while being transported to the state pen, a Chicago surgeon (Harrison Ford) convicted of murdering his wife must evade the ever-tightening net of a relentless US Marshall (Tommy Lee Jones) while desperately tracking down the one-armed man (Andreas Katsulas) who actually killed her. Director Andrew Davis knits together a strong narrative, crackerjack performances, and taut editing for a fine thriller not dependent on constant, glorified violence for mounting suspense. Brief, sporadic violence. A-II (PG-13)

Full House (see: **O. Henry's Full House**)

Full Life, A (1972) Japanese movie whose title indicates the goal that a young woman (Ineko Arima) sets for herself after leaving her worthless husband. Nothing very dramatic happens in director Susumu Hani's 1962 work, but the accumulation of small details of life in a large urban complex makes the woman's realization that she needs friends and social commitment seem quite real. A-III (nr)

Full Metal Jacket (1987) Director Stanley Kubrick's moody essay on the dehumanizing effects of basic training and combat during the Vietnam era traces the transformation of a typical Marine Corps recruit from observer to participant. Sexual come-ons by hookers, graphic bloodshed, and excessive profanity provide the realistic texture for the expression of diminishing spiritual sensitivity and moral ambiguity. A-IV (R)

Full Monty, The (1997) Desperate to earn some needed cash, an unemployed British steelworker (Robert Carlyle) convinces five jobless buddies there's easy money to be made performing in a one-night male strip show. Director Peter Cattaneo, the Brisish comedy downplays the sleazy aspects of the narrative, focusing instead on the characters' financial needs and inept dancing abilities. Benign view of petty theft, brief rear nudity, fleeting homosexual innuendo, occasional profanity, and recurring rough language. A-IV (R)

Full Moon in Blue Water (1988) The Mr. Nice Guy owner (Gene Hackman) of a rundown bar and grill on the Texas Gulf coast spends too much time mourning the loss of his wife and not enough time salvaging his business or courting the feisty woman who loves him (Teri Garr). Directed by Peter Masterson, the compact character study follows the nutty turn of events that motivate the laid-back hero to put the past to rest and get on with life. Constant stream of vulgar language spouted by the protagonist's senile father-in-law (Burgess Meredith) and implied sexual promiscuity. A-IV (R)

Fun and Fancy Free (1947) Disney omnibus of cartoon stories, with Dinah Shore narrating the misadventures of slow-learning circus-bear Bongo, but the main attraction features Mickey, Donald, and Goofy in "Jack and the Beanstalk" as told by Edgar Bergen with occasional interruptions from Charlie McCarthy. Good family fun, but only the Jack tale is memorable entertainment. A-I (G)

Fun in Acapulco (1963) Lightweight escapist fare as an American stranded in Mexico (Elvis Presley) divides his time between two lovely locals (Ursula Andress and Elsa Cardenas) while singing in a posh resort and using the pool's high-dive to recover his lost nerve as a circus aerialist. Director Richard Thorpe buries the lame plot in colorful Mexican settings, lots of Presley songs in a Latino tempo, and a cute urchin who becomes the singer's partner. Sexual situations. A-III (PG)

Fun with Dick and Jane (1977) Leaden comedy about an upwardly mobile suburban couple (Jane Fonda and George Segal) who suddenly find their direction reversed when the husband loses his job as an aerospace executive. After trying welfare and food stamps, they take to armed robbery and succeed beyond all measure. Apparently director Ted Kotcheff was aiming at satire, a task too formidable for the modest talents involved. Besides the movie's general insensitivity to genuine social ills, it employs coarse language and a tasteless bathroom scene. O (PG)

Funeral, The (1996) Depression-era tale of how two Italian-American gangster brothers (Christopher Walken and Chris Penn) avenge the murder of their younger brother (Vincent Gallo). Director Abel Ferrara sluggishly probes the dark psyches of brothers trained as killers by their father but constantly rebuked for their crimes by their devout Catholic wives (Isabella Rosellini and Annabella Sciorra). Some gory violence, a sexual encounter with nudity, and much rough language. A-IV (R)

Funeral in Berlin (1967) In a sequel to **The Ipcress File**, Michael Caine returns as the disreputable British intelligence agent, Harry Palmer. The plot's intermingling of German, Russian, British, and Israeli spies defies synopsis, but the action is plentiful and exciting. The British production directed by Guy Hamilton succeeds in brilliantly contrasting the ways of life in East and West Berlin. A winner for those who enjoy undercover work. Restrained violence. A-III (br)

Funeral Parade of Roses (1973) Failed Japanese experimental work by Toshio Matsumoto is a mishmash of scenes filmed at a gay bar in Tokyo. Never have fragmented images of eroticism and bloodshed looked more boring than those concocted here in a venture that adds nothing to our understanding of human nature. O (nr)

Funhouse (1981) A monster stalks four extremely dim young people trapped in a carnival funhouse in a loathsome horror movie written and directed by Tobe Hooper. More likely to sicken than frighten, the film exploits sex and violence in grotesque and ugly ways. O (R)

Funniest Man in the World, The (1970) Douglas Fairbanks Jr. narrates a documentary on Charlie Chaplin's early career as shown through excerpts from his work at the Keystone, Essanay, and Mutual studios and makes a good introduction to the comic art of silent comedy. Chaplin's admirers, however, may wince at the way some of his movies have been chopped up and comic routines presented out of context in a compilation assembled by Vernon P. Becker. A-I (nr)

Funny About Love (1990) Touching comedy about a cartoonist (Gene Wilder) whose belated but overwhelming desire for fatherhood drives his wife (Christine Lahti) to leave him and results in a precarious relationship with a much younger woman (Mary Stuart Masterson). Though director Leonard Nimoy's comedy is fairly predictable, its humor, good-hearted characters, and occasional sparkling dialogue make it light-hearted but strictly adult fare. Unmarried sexual relationships, several double entendres, a flash of nudity, and minimal rough language. A-III (PG-13)

Funny Bones (1995) Disjointed tale in which a failed Las Vegas comic (Oliver Platt) hopes to get some inspiration from visiting the seaside English town where his successful comedian father (Jerry Lewis) got his start, but learns instead that dad stole his comic routines from others and left behind a troubled illegitimate son (Lee Evans). Director Peter Chisholm finds occasional flashes of whimsical comedy in a busy but ultimately pointless narrative mixing intense family conflicts with awkward stabs at eccentric humor. Brief violence, sexual references, and several instances of rough language. A-III (R)

Funny Face (1957) Elegant musical romance in which an American gamin (Audrey Hepburn) is turned into a top Paris model by a love-smitten photographer (Fred Astaire) in cahoots with his fashion-magazine editor (Kay Thompson). Director Stanley Donen fleshes out the thin narrative with lovely musical numbers by George and Ira Gershwin as well as lots of gorgeous Paris scenery and a rainbow palette of color photography. Pleasant escapist fare for all but unromantic youngsters. A-I (br)

Funny Farm (1988) When a couple (Chevy Chase and Madolyn Smith) leave New York City behind for the joys of life in a Vermont farmhouse, their speedy disenchantment comes through many comic situations, some of them hackneyed. Though they're nicely acted, director George Roy Hill tends to let scenes drag on pointlessly. Some profanity and a skewed picture of rural folk as greedy nasties. A-III (PG)

Funny Girl (1968) Big, glossy musical gives the sentimental treatment to the rise of comic singer Fanny Brice (Barbra Streisand) to fame as the Ziegfeld Follies queen whose marriage to a gambler

(Omar Sharif) fails in spite of their love. Director William Wyler turns Streisand's movie debut into a personal triumph for the popular singer. The subject's troubled personal life is not children's fare. A-II (G)

Funny Lady (1975) Barbara Streisand musical comedy in which she brings some depth to her portrayal of the maturing Fanny Brice trapped by her love for a professional gambler (Omar Sharif) and her attraction to a Broadway producer (James Caan), without losing any of her zest in interpreting the Billy Rose songs and elaborate dance routines. Directed by Herbert Ross, the serious moments tend to drag, but the comic ones are hilarious, and the verve and nostalgia of the revue help to conceal a flawed plot. Basic plot situations and some of the dialog are adult fare. A-III (PG)

Funny Thing Happened on the Way to the Forum, A (1966) Wacky and ribald Broadway hit about a cunning slave (Zero Mostel) in ancient Rome who has great fun in exploiting a series of mistaken identities and in misinterpreting various orders in an effort to gain his freedom. Director Richard Lester keeps the humor swift and visual, backed by such fine screen-clowns as Buster Keaton, Phil Silvers, Jack Gilford, and Michael Hordern in a crisp and stylish musical burlesque of ageless low-comedy routines. A-III (br)

Funnyman (1971) Photographer-director John Korty applies his sensitivity and compassion to create a sort of fictional documentary about a young coffeehouse comic (perfectly played by Peter Bonerz) who aspires to more intellectual work as a writer-actor and is forever feeling disappointed with himself. Matter-of-fact acceptance of casual sex and some lingering shots of an artist's nude model are questionable elements in an otherwise perceptive study of a talented young man's aspirations. A-IV (nr)

Furies, The (1950) Overblown Western directed by Anthony Mann is mired in a convoluted narrative about a greedy cattle baron (Walter Huston) who doublecrosses his iron-willed cowgirl daughter (Barbara Stanwyck), causing her to throw in with a bitter family enemy (Wendell Corey) to bring her father's ruin. Stylized violence, including hanging and disfigurement, assorted obsessive behavior, and romantic complications. A-III (br)

Further Adventures of Ma and Pa Kettle, The (see: **Ma and Pa Kettle**)

Further Adventures of the Wilderness Family, The (1979) A sequel to the 1976 film about a family who leaves Los Angeles to live in the Rocky Mountains. This time Dad (Robert Logan) is caught in an avalanche and jumped by a cougar; however, the main crisis involves Mom, who is coming down with double-pneumonia and visited by a nasty pack of wolves. None of these perils are treated realistically by director Frank Zuniga, however, and even the younger children should be able to bear up and even enjoy them. A-I (G)

Fury (1936) Mistaken for a murderer, an innocent man (Spencer Tracy) escapes a small-town lynch mob and, despite his loving wife (Sylvia Sidney), becomes an embittered criminal obsessed with revenge. German director Fritz Lang's first Hollywood effort is a powerful picture of ordinary Americans struggling to survive hard times and hardened hearts during the Depression, though it falters in a melodramatic conclusion. The lynching sequence is a harrowing but classic portrayal of irrational mob violence. A-II (br)

Fury, The (1978) Kirk Douglas plays a man who tries to rescue his son from a sinister government agency that wants to use the boy's psychic powers for its own ends. Director Brian De Palma's crude, heavy-handed melodrama wallows in violence and gore. O (R)

Fury of the Congo (1951) Formula adventure directed by William Berke in which Jungle Jim (Johnny Weissmuller) helps a native tribe defeat a band of white men who have invaded their lands in quest of an animal whose glands yield a valuable narcotic. Stylized violence. A-I (br)

Futureworld (1976) Sequel to **Westworld** takes viewers back among those rambunctious robots. The plot gimmick this time is a scheme to replace world leaders with robots, but enterprising journalists Peter Fonda and Blythe Danner foil the bad guys. Under Richard T. Heffron's direction, it's all pretty silly but mildly diverting entertainment, thanks mostly to Danner's decidedly non-robotized performance. Some scenes involving sexually programmed robots. A-III (PG)

Futz (1969) Filmed performance by New York's La Mama Repertory Troupe of a play by Rochelle Owens about a farmer who is murdered by the community because, failing to find human love, he loves his pig. Supposedly an allegory about freedom and personal responsibility, its deliberately shocking and disgusting elements are less intolerable than its pretentious air of self-righteousness. O (nr)

Fuzz (1972) Police satire about the bumbling crime-fighting antics of writer Ed McBain's mythical 87th Precinct in Boston, where detective Burt Reynolds and subordinates Jack Weston, Tom Skerritt, and Raquel Welch as a policewoman decoy fail to take seriously Yul Brynner's extortion demands. Their inept performances are about as laughable as director Richard Colla's inept comedy ever gets. Viewers who find murder, attempted rape, and the burning of helpless hobos less than hilarious may wish to take a pass on this one. A-III (PG)

G.I. Blues (1960) Formula romance in which an American soldier (Elvis Presley) stationed in West Germany bets he can get a local nightclub dancer (Juliet Prowse) to let him stay the night in her apartment, then falls in love with her and tries to call the bet off. Directed by Norman Taurog, the result is a thin mix of sexist leers, occasional Presley songs, and some picturesque scenery of the Frankfurt area. Sexual situations and innuendo, including an unwed mother. A-III (br)

G.I. Jane (1997) Hokey melodrama in which a woman naval-officer (Demi Moore) undergoes the rigorous training program for the Navy's elite SEALS combat force, graduates despite various sexist obstacles, and soon becomes a battlefield hero. Directed by Ridley Scott, the picture offers no real insights about women in the military, concentrating instead on the character's endurance of physical pain and emotional suffering to prove she's as tough as any man, but the result is hardly worth the effort. Much brutality, some violence, several sexual situations, a flash of nudity, occasional profanity, and recurring rough language. A-IV (R)

Gabbeh (1997) Lyrical Iranian tale about a lovelorn maiden whose father keeps their nomadic tribe just out of reach of her beloved, a mysterious horseman who shyly follows their caravan. Writer-director Moshen Makhmalbaf interweaves fantasy with reality in this visually stunning story of a sheep-herding tribe whose handcrafted wool carpets illustrate the events in their lives. Subtitles. An off-screen juvenile death and an ambiguous reference to culturally condoned violence. A-II (nr)

Gable and Lombard (1976) Nostalgic love story about two famous Hollywood stars (James Brolin and Jill Clayburgh) is a slick but embarrassingly bad job of storytelling by British director Sidney J. Furie. Sympathetic and romanticized presentation of infidelity. O (R)

Gabriel over the White House (1933) Curious relic from Depression-era Hollywood in which a machine politician (Walter Huston) is elected president, then emerges from a brush with death to shed his party ties, suspend Congress, and declare martial law, using his executive powers to put the unemployed to work on federal projects, repeal Prohibition, and crush the crime syndicates with Army tanks. Directed by Gregory La Cava, the political fantasy of a homegrown American dictator solving the desperate problems of the day takes plenty of strange turns, not least of which is draping its Fascist hero in the mantle of Lincoln and linking his actions to the heavenly messenger of the title. Stylized violence, discreet sexual innuendo, and rationalization of the end justifying the means. A-III (br)

Gaby — A True Story (1987) Uneven dramatization of the story of Gabriella Brimmer (Rachel Levin), a successful Mexican writer who was born severely handicapped with cerebral palsy, and the peasant house-worker (Norma Aleandro) who became her nanny and eventually her guardian. The inspirational drama, as directed by Luis Mandoki, is somewhat frustrating in its failure to explore the motivations of a number of central characters, especially the mother (Liv Ullmann). Awkward and unnecessarily extended scenes of Gaby's attempts to express her sexuality. A-III (R)

Gaily, Gaily (1969) Ben Hecht, swaddled in adolescent innocence, makes his way to Chicago in 1910, and director Norman Jewison milks his autobiographical recollections into a nostalgic portrait capturing both the naivety of the young man and the corruption of the times. Illuminating satire stars Brian Keith, Beau Bridges, and Hume Cronyn. A-III (M)

Galaxina (1981) Low-budget, tediously sophomoric spoof of science-fiction films stars Dorothy R. Stratten in the title role. Directed by William Sachs, Stratten is made the target for a unrelenting series of sexually suggestive remarks. A-III (R)

Galileo (1975) Producer Ely Landau's screen version of the Bertolt Brecht play about the 16th-century scientist (Topol) and his confrontation with the Church and with his own conscience comes across brilliantly. Directed by Joseph Losey, the work presents Galileo, not as a hero, but as a loving portrait of a great man who becomes the victim of ordinary creature comforts. A-III (PG)

Gallant Hours, The (1960) Reverential portrait of Adm. William F. Halsey (James Cagney), under whose command the battle for Guadalcanal ended in November 1942, with the first American victory against Japanese forces since Pearl Harbor. Produced and directed by Robert Montgomery, the movie relies on Cagney's performance rather than battle scenes to convey the tense five weeks it took Halsey to turn a desperate situation around, though those unfamiliar with the campaign may find the details sketchy and the music by the Robert Wagner Chorale overbearing. A-I (br)

Gallipoli (1981) Enthusiastic young Australians (Mel Gibson and Mark Lee) enlist for service in WW I and soon have their romantic notions of the war as a glorious and noble adventure dissolved. Director Peter Weir contrasts naive patriotism with youthful idealism in this superbly rendered period drama. Intense battle scenes and a depiction of a brothel. A-III (PG)

Gambit (1966) Shirley MacLaine and Michael Caine set out to steal a priceless sculpture from wily Herbert Lom in the familiar plot about a perfect crime gone wrong. Director Ronald Neame comes up with a couple of new twists and some fine acting to distinguish it from a host of other romantic thrillers. A-I (br)

Gambler, The (1974) Static story of a compulsive gambler (James Caan) who betrays his bookies (Paul Sorvino and Carmine Caridi), his too-forgiving mother (Jacqueline Brookes), his doting grandfather (Morris Carnovsky), and his lovely girlfriend (Lauren Hutton) as he degrades himself on the path to self-destruction. Directed by Karel Reisz, the story is obvious from the beginning and there is no attempt to make the viewer care a whit about the characters and their problems. A-III (R)

Gambler's Choice (1944) Formula tale directed by Frank McDonald in which a trio of urchins meet again as adults in 1911 New York City, where one (Chester Morris) runs a gambling casino, another (Russell Hayden) is a police captain, and the third (Nancy Kelly) is a singer loved by both in this unimaginative reworking of **Manhattan Melodrama**. Stylized violence and corrupt characters. A-II (br)

Gambling House (1950) Muddled, mostly hokey tale directed by Ted Tetzlaff in which a cynical crook (Victor Mature) runs afoul of a double-crossing gangster (William Bendix), then faces deportation as an illegal alien until a social worker (Terry Moore) helps him appreciate the red, white, and blue. Stylized gang violence, some of it quite nasty. A-III (br)

Game, The (1997) Twisty drama about an arrogant San Francisco investment banker (Michael Douglas) whose birthday gift from his estranged brother (Sean Penn) is a bizarre game which puts the banker's life and fortune in constant danger from unknown assailants. Directed by David Fincher, the wildly imaginative proceedings are absorbing, suspenseful, and patently illogical. Stylized violence, occasional profanity, and frequent rough language. A-III (R)

Game Is Over, The (1967) French adaptation of an Emile Zola novel about a woman (Jane Fonda), married to a ruthless businessman (Michel Piccoli), falls fatefully in love with her husband's son (Peter McEnery). Directed by Roger Vadim, the movie's emphasis on nudity and eroticism is excessive. O (br)

Game of Death, A (1946) Adventure thriller in which a big-game hunter (John Loder) is shipwrecked on an island inhabited by a madman (Edgar Barrier) who finds hunting humans with a bow and arrow more challenging than shooting wild beasts. Directed by Robert Wise, this remake of **The Most Dangerous Game** works well enough but lacks the moody suspense and colorful characterizations that made the original a classic. Stylized violence and considerable menace. A-II (br)

Games (1967) Mediocre thriller about a bored couple (James Caan and Katharine Ross) and a mysterious stranger (Simone Signoret) who introduces them to some macabre games that end in murder. Some viewers will feel cheated by the twist ending which explains the illogical situations which precede it. Directed by Curtis Harrington. Mature themes and stylized violence. A-III (br)

Games, The (1970) Ponderous Olympic-marathon movie tracing the personal stories of various competitors, including an obnoxious American long-distance runner (Ryan O'Neal), his British counterpart (Michael Crawford), an exploited Australian aborigine (Athol Compton), and a patriotic Czech runner (Charles Aznavor). Forgettable British production directed by Michael Winner, it goes on and on to no point. Some sexual references. A-III (G)

Gandhi (1982) Superb portrait of India's great political and spiritual leader comes to life in Ben Kingsley's authoritative yet sensitive performance. Director Richard Attenborough's epic-scale production re-creates Gandhi's life and times, especially his use of nonviolence and hunger strikes to bring together the diverse peoples of India and unify them as a nation. Though its scenes of violence are not for children, the movie's vision of justice and peace is for everyone else, especially young people. A-II (PG)

Gang Related (1997) Shoddy crime story in which two corrupt cops (Tupac Shakur and James Belushi) unwittingly murder an undercover DEA agent, then try to frame a homeless drunk (Dennis Quaid) for what they did. Writer-director Jim Kouf's shrill tale is lamely scripted, poorly acted, and bereft of suspense. Intermittent violence, rationalization of murder, brief nudity, much profanity, and nonstop rough language. O (R)

Gang That Couldn't Shoot Straight, The (1972) Failed screen version of Jimmy Breslin's novel about a bunch of inept South Brooklyn hoods bent on "takin' ovah da territory" features ethnic humor that tends to give credence to the efforts of the Italian-American Anti-Defamation League. So inept are director James Goldstone's satirical irreverences that an adult perspective seems to be a basic requirement for viewing. A-III (PG/PG-13)

Gang's All Here, The (1943) Wartime musical extravaganza in which a nightclub singer (Alice Faye) falls in love with a soldier (James Ellison) who happens to be engaged to someone else. Directed by Busby Berkeley, things work out happily between the big musical numbers, including Carmen Miranda's "The Lady in the Tutti Frutti Hat." Innocent but dated fun. A-I (br)

Ganja & Hess (1973) Mindless horror movie about an anthropologist who is addicted to human blood and a beautiful young woman who is both smitten and bitten by the evil doctor. The story never gets much beyond this, though director Bill Gunn adds a number of silly sex interludes suggesting even more unhealthy goings-on than plasma addiction. O (R)

Garbo Talks (1984) Sentimental comedy about a loving son (Ron Silver) who spares no effort to fulfill the wish of his dying mother (Anne Bancroft) to meet Greta Garbo. Directed by Sidney Lumet, it is modestly entertaining, but a little hard to take unless you share the Garbo mystique and don't mind watching a callous depiction of the collapse of a marriage. A-III (PG-13)

Garden of Allah, The (1936) Dated romantic melodrama in which a troubled woman (Marlene Dietrich) seeks peace of soul in the Algerian desert, where she falls in love with a goodhearted but mysterious fellow (Charles Boyer) whom she weds, then learns he is a Trappist monk who fled his order to satisfy his curiosity about the material pleasures of the world. Director Richard Boleslawski relies on exotic Arab locales and characters to sustain interest in a soggy scenario about human and divine love, spiritual joy and personal happiness, desire and disillusionment. Despite its redemptive but hokey ending, the story's strange combination of elements is unlikely children's fare. A-I (br)

Garden of Delights, The (1971) Spanish director Carlos Saura has fashioned a quietly haunting, surreal black comedy about an aristocratic Madrid family perverted by greed. The story focuses on the aged family patriarch (Jose Luis Lopez Vasquez), struggling to regain his facilities after an auto accident, and is insightful study of a man coming to terms with the deceit and selfishness of loved ones. A-III (GP)

Garden of Evil (1954) Far-fetched, slow-paced adventure in 1850 Mexico, where an American (Susan Hayward) hires a former lawman (Gary Cooper), a gambler (Hugh Marlowe), and two tinhorns (Richard Widmark and Cameron Mitchell) to rescue her injured husband from his gold mine in hostile Indian country. Directed by Henry Hathaway, the plodding scenario sputters along in depicting the characters' mistrust of one another until the tense, action-packed finale. Stylized violence and some sexual innuendo. A-II (br)

Garden of the Finzi-Continis (1971) Director Vittorio De Sica's drama about the effects of Fascist anti-Semitism on the Jewish community in a small Italian town tells the story of a poor Jewish college student (Lino Capolicchio) who loves the beautiful daughter (Dominique Sanda) of a wealthy Jewish family. Structured as a somber nostalgic romance in which old class divisions prove stronger than racial bonds, the movie develops into a disturbing elegy for the loss of human dignity. A-III (R)

Gardens of Stone (1987) Director Francis Coppola's mildly nostalgic and insightful vision of the military as family contrasts the beliefs and aspirations of a decorated combat-vet (James Caan) with those of a raw recruit (D.B. Sweeney) assigned to his Old Guard Arlington National Cemetery unit during the difficult Vietnam War years. Tragic story of the meaning of military service has some rough language and sexual situations which mark it for mature audiences. A-III (R)

Gas Food Lodging (1992) Bittersweet tale of a starry-eyed teenage girl (Fairuza Balk) coming to accept the reality of life with her exhausted waitress-mom (Brooke Adams) after her roaming dad (James Brolin) leaves and her rebellious sister (Ione Skye) runs away. Allison Anders directs a realistic drama of a broken home that is not without modest insights into female solidarity. A few discreet sexual encounters, brief nudity, and minimal rough language. A-III (R)

Gaslight (1944) Sleek thriller set in Victorian London, where a rich young bride (Ingrid Bergman) is slowly being driven loony by her slick, greedy husband (Charles Boyer), until an old friend (Joseph Cotten) of her late aunt intervenes. Director George Cukor overplays the wife's passive acceptance of her mate's overbearing manipulations as she declines into a state of helplessness, but the contrived situation pays dividends after slowly building to its highly charged conclusion. Much menace. A-II (br)

Gas-s-s-s (1970) When the country's over-30 generation is wiped out by an accident with experimental nerve gas, a group of the under-30 crowd go for a cross-country romp, encountering demented cowboys, motorcycle freaks, a paramilitary football squad, a teenage brain surgeon, and so on and on. Director Roger Corman's silly, disjointed fantasy ends in a harmonious youth celebration, long before which most viewers will have sought some fresh air. Some adult material. A-III (PG)

Gate, The (1987) Modern fairytale for the younger set about the dangers of toying with the darker side. Preteens accidentally unleash suburban demons while parents are away and need a heavy-metal album, courage, and pure hearts to chase them back through the "gate" from which they escaped. Director Tibor Takacs provides some mild scares in a simple good-vs.-evil tale. A-II (PG-13)

Gateway (1938) Routine melodrama about a group of immigrants on a voyage ending at Ellis Island, with the focus on an Irish singer (Arleen Whelan) who gets help from a smitten newsman (Don Ameche) in her troubles with a slick gangster (Gilbert Roland). Directed by Alfred L. Werker, the contrived story is of less interest than the reenactment of the period's immigration procedures and patriotic view of America as melting pot. Some stylized violence and mild romance. A-I (br)

Gathering of Eagles, A (1963) Routine service drama directed by Delbert Mann in which an Air Force colonel (Rock Hudson) makes many enemies as the new commander of an under-performing wing of the Strategic Air Command. A-I (br)

Gator (1976) Burt Reynolds stars in and directs this story of an undercover agent's attempt to send the Mr. Big of a corrupt Southern county to prison. Mediocre entertainment at best, the movie veers in mood from slapstick to melodrama to soap opera and back again. Violence. A-III (PG)

Gattaca (1997) Weak sci-fi yarn of a future in which genetic engineering has created a master race that treats those conceived naturally as inferiors, one of whom (Ethan Hawke) carries off an elaborate masquerade to become a trusted member of the genetic elite until a murder investigation threatens to reveal his true identity. Writer-director Andrew Niccol sets up the premise of a regimented world ruled by dispassionate logic but succeeds too well in showing how dull such a place would be, even with all the scientific subterfuge used to fool computerized identity checks and the disruptions caused by swarms of investigators on the trail of an impostor. Stylized violence, sexual situations, and occasional rough language and profanity. A-III (PG-13)

Gauntlet, The (1977) Not-too-bright Phoenix police officer (Clint Eastwood) goes to Las Vegas to extradite a convicted prostitute (Sandra Locke), only to discover that both of them have been marked for death. Eastwood also directed the shoddy, violent movie which is little more than a pretext for an extravagant display of gunplay, a steady stream of verbal obscenities, and a bit of sex and nudity. O (R)

Gay Deceivers (1969) Young men pose as homosexuals to avoid military induction, but the charade backfires when they have to convince parents, girlfriends, and teachers that they are straight. Stereotyped characters may offend members of the gay community, while the instances of nudity and lovemaking add little to director Bruce Kessler's muddled social satire. A-IV (R)

Gay Divorce, The (see: **The Gay Divorcee**)

Gay Divorcee, The (1934) Comic misunderstandings abound in this dated musical fluff about an American (Ginger Rogers) whose lawyer (Edward Everett Horton) hires a professional co-respondent in order to obtain a divorce in England, then mistakes an unwanted admirer (Fred Astaire) for the unseen hireling. Director Mark Sandrich turns the farcical situation into a lighthearted musical comedy with no real substance beyond its charming songs and dances, notably "The Continental," and comic routines so ancient, they seem almost classic. Comic treatment of the war between the sexes with divorce as a plot device. A-III (br)

Gay Purr-ee (1962) Animated musical recounting the adventures of a country cat (voice of Judy Garland) who goes to Paris, where she falls into the clutches of con-artists (voices of Hermione Gingold and Paul Frees) until rescued by the cat (voice of Robert Goulet) she left behind. Director Abe Levitow's UPA cartoon feature has some pleasant but forgettable songs for older viewers and some broad comedy for the youngsters, but the story lacks strong appeal for either age group. A-I (G)

Geisha Boy, The (1958) Jerry Lewis plays a fumbling out-of-work magician who gets into a wearisome series of jams as a member of a USO troupe entertaining troops stationed in Japan. Director Frank Tashlin mixes the usual Lewis pratfalls with cloying sentimentality over the rabbit used in his magic act and a sad Japanese boy who finds the gawky American hilarious. Mild sexual innuendo. A-II (br)

General, The (1927) Epic silent comedy set in the Civil War has Buster Keaton as a Southern railroad engineer pursuing the Northern spies who have stolen his locomotive, outwitting them, and driving it back in time to stop an attack by the Union Army. Keaton's mastery of physical comedy is seen at its best here as he stoically overcomes all manner of obstacles in the path of his speeding but recalcitrant locomotive. A beautifully crafted work, with an appropriate musical score, it's a treat for all ages. A-I (br)

General, The (1998) Fact-based account of the criminal career of Martin Cahill (Brendan Gleeson), Dublin's best-known gangster, who graduated from petty thefts in the slums to running his own mob from an expensive home in a posh neighborhood, where he lived with his wife and children, as well as from another home, where he lived with his wife's sister, always one step ahead of the police until his assassination by an Irish Republican Army gunman in 1994. Directed by John Boorman, the picture views Cahill with some sympathy as a rebel against conventional society, the police, the Church, and the IRA, which demanded a share of his loot, but balances its colorful depiction of his criminal exploits with some of their painful consequences, including his brutal death. Some hard-edged violence, detailed criminal activities, sexual situations, brief nudity, frequent rough language, and occasional profanity. A-IV (R)

General's Daughter, The (1999) Lurid military thriller in which an Army criminal investigator (John Travolta), assigned to solve the brutal strangulation of a promiscuous female captain (Leslie Stefanson), is pressured to participate in a cover-up after he unravels a widespread criminal conspiracy of many years' standing. Despite sleek visuals and some strong performances, director Simon West delivers a deeply cynical and at times grotesque potboiler. Sporadic intense violence including rape with full nudity, videotape of a sadistic sexual encounter and much sexual innuendo, frequent rough language, and intermittent profanity. O (R)

General Idi Amin Dada (see **Idi Amin Dada**)

Generation (1969) Hippie (Pete Duel) and little rich girl (Kim Darby) move in together in Greenwich Village and decide to have a baby by natural childbirth. Anti-establishment comedy based on William Goodhart's play doesn't have the sharp edges of the original but preserves its wit and charm, thanks to director George Schaefer's toned-down treatment. A-III (PG)

Genghis Khan (1965) Lumbering historical epic follows the Mongol warrior (Omar Sharif) who rises to head the Gobi Desert tribes by defeating his rival (Stephen Boyd) and marrying his wife (Francoise Dorleac). Director Henry Levin stages a lot of colorful action scenes, but the script is cliched, the dialogue unintentionally funny, and the acting overdone ham. Much stylized violence and some sexual situations. A-III (br)

Gentle Giant (1967) Engaging but less-than-credible adventure yarn about a young boy (Clint Howard) who rescues a bear cub in the Florida Everglades and raises him into a 650-pound house-pet. Dennis Weaver is the boy's put-upon but understanding dad, with Ralph Meeker as an antagonist of sorts. Directed by James Neilson, the problems of the situation are all very predictable, but they are still fun, especially for the youngsters. A-I (br)

Gentle Sergeant, The (see: **Three Stripes in the Sun**)

Gentlemen Don't Eat Poets (1997) Gloomy drama with comic undertones is set in a decaying 1940s English manor whose owner (Alan Bates) falls prey to the manipulations of a cunning butler (Sting) after a guest at the estate is murdered. Director John-Paul Davidson's tale of seduction and betrayal is lethargically paced, and its dreary one-dimensional characters are of little interest. Several sexual encounters with nudity, some violence, minimal profanity, and recurring rough language. A-IV (R)

Gentleman Jim (1942) Period success-story unfolds as James Corbett (Errol Flynn) rises from lowly San Francisco bank clerk to cocky prizefighter, ultimately winning the heavyweight championship in 1892 by knocking out John L. Sullivan (Ward Bond). Director Raoul Walsh alternates scenes of Jim's prowess in the ring with his relations, often comic, with his working-class Irish-American family and his on-again, off-again romance with a society debutante (Alexis Smith). Stylized boxing sequences and brawls. A-I (nr)

Gentlemen's Agreement (1947) Earnest story of a journalist (Gregory Peck) who writes a series of articles about his encounters with anti-Semitic bigots and woolly hypocrites while posing as a Jew, despite the problems this causes his son (Dean Stockwell) and fiancé (Dorothy McGuire). Directed by Elia Kazan from Laura Z. Hobson's novel, the result may seem obvious today, but the picture has interest in showing how far we've come since then, especially in regard to the tacit form of prejudice referred to in the title. Mild violence, romantic complications, and some racial epithets. A-II (br)

George! (1973) The title character is a Saint Bernard whose clumsy exuberance embarrasses one and all, until he and his guardian (Marshall Thompson) rescue each other from an avalanche in the Swiss Alps. Director Wallace C. Bennett concentrates on the gorgeous Alpine locales, providing some distraction for audiences who may tire of watching actors engage in pratfalls for the benefit of a dopey, if loveable, dog. A-I (G)

George Balanchine's The Nutcracker (1993) Shimmering movie version of Tschaikovsky's Christmas-themed ballet (performed by the New York City Ballet) in which a little girl (Jessica Lynn Cohen) dreams her nutcracker toy-soldier comes to life (as Macaulay Culkin) to rescue her from the giant Mouse King and then transport her to the enchanted Land of Sweets, where magical fairies enchant them with dances. With Kevin Kline's brief narration setting the scenes, director Emile Ardolino presents a straightforward filming of the Balanchine choreography in a production captivating for its glorious music and splendid dancers, though without any dialogue small children and some adults may get restless. A-I (G)

George of the Jungle (1997) Engagingly silly live-action comedy based on a 1960's animated TV series about a jungle-raised primitive (Brendan Fraser) smitten with a beauty (Leslie Mann) on safari to escape her overbearing fiancé. Director Sam Weisman's good-natured spoof of Tarzan movies is amusingly self-mocking and drags only when the action moves from the jungle to the big city. Some mild sexual references, toilet humor, and occasional slapstick violence. A-II (PG)

George Raft Story, The (1961) Lackluster star-biography directed by Joseph M. Newman begins in 1920's New York, where Raft (Ray Danton) is a dancer who becomes involved with the mob, goes West to protect his health, and becomes a Hollywood movie star, then fades into cameo roles. Stylized violence, sexual innuendo, and a benign view of organized crime. A-III (br)

Georgia (1995) Brittle drama in which an impassioned but untalented younger sister (Jennifer Jason Leigh) vainly tries to copy the personal and professional success of her singer-composer sister (Mare Winningham). Powerful performances distinguish director Ulu Grosbard's multi-layered, often unpleasant, study of sibling rivalry for which there is no easy resolution. A bedroom scene with nudity, adulterous references, recurring substance abuse, and frequent rough language. A-III (R)

Georgia, Georgia (1972) Written by Maya Angelou and directed by Stig Bjorkman, this story of a beautiful black singer on tour in Sweden quickly lapses into a romantic interracial interlude between the singer (Diana Sands) and a photographer (Dirk Benedict). Clumsy insertion of coy material focusing on the homosexual appetites of the singer's manager and a jarring climax that shocks but without providing an adequate resolution. A-IV (R)

Georgy Girl (1966) Tragicomedy of a goodhearted, awkward young woman (Lynn Redgrave) who tries to make a life of her own after her friends (Alan Bates and Charlotte Rampling) break up and leave her to care for their neglected child. Under Silvio Narizzano's direction, Redgrave brings warmth and credibility to the title role, with James Mason adding a wry, slightly self-mocking performance as the aging millionaire who has long pursued her. Frank treatment of sexual matters. A-IV (nr)

Germinal (1994) Evocative French adaptation of Emile Zola's novel about the inhuman working conditions of 19th-century coal miners who decide on a strike (led by Gerard Depardieu) when their meager wages are cut, but with hunger, soldiers, and scab labor undercutting their resolve, some return to work, only to be trapped when the mine is flooded by an anarchist (Laurent Terzieff). Director Claude Berri's sprawling, large-scale production dramatically re-creates the historical period, portraying its oppressive social injustices from the perspective of an impoverished worker's family and their struggle for elemental human rights and some modest measure of human dignity. Subtitles. Restrained depiction of labor violence, including soldiers firing on workers and their families, and the castration of a dead body, casual sexual relationships, and brief nudity. A-III (R)

Geronimo: An American Legend (1993) Leaden Western about the efforts of General Crook (Gene Hackman) and two of his officers (Jason Patric and Matt Damon) to recapture Geronimo (Wes Studi) and his small band of renegade Apaches hiding out on Arizona-Mexico border in 1885-86. In pretentious, stilted fashion, director Walter Hill alternates scenes of brutal shootouts by both sides with the depiction of the government's unjust treatment of Native Americans. Frequent bloody violence. A-III (PG-13)

Get Carter (1971) Violent British crime melodrama in which Michael Caine plays a gangland killer-enforcer whose investigation into his brother's death finds him in and out of danger, bed, and dens of rival gangsters. Directed by Mike Hodges, the movie's principle is kill or be killed in coldly brutal, cruel style, varied only by scenes of graphic sex and nudity. O (R)

Get Charlie Tully (1977) Tedious British comedy directed by Cliff Owen about two con-men who, after bilking a foreign industrialist, find themselves on the run from the mob. A plot gimmick about the numbers of a secret Swiss account tattooed where anyone familiar with this kind of British humor can probably guess is the occasion for a good deal of female nudity. O (PG)

Get on the Bus (1996) Documentary-like road movie explores the attitudes and emotions of 15 African-American residents of Los Angeles as they bus across the country to attend the 1995 Million Man March in Washington, DC. Directed by Spike Lee, the fictional characters engage in lively discussions of racial and family issues that often turn serious and thoughtful but seldom preachy. Fleeting violence, some racial epithets, sporadic rough language, and occasional profanity. A-III (R)

Get Out Your Handkerchiefs (1979) Very uneven French comedy in which a not-too-bright, but good-natured, husband (Gerard Depardieu) is willing to go to any lengths to cure his wife (Carole Laure) of a galloping case of boredom, even to propositioning a stranger (Patrick Dewaere) on her behalf. While entertaining a few clever moments, director Bertrand Blier's attempts to sustain the one-joke affair are more frantic than successful, and its nudity and sexual immorality are seriously offensive. O (R)

Get Shorty (1995) Black comedy finds parallels between moviemaking and racketeering when a gangster (John Travolta) tries to collect a debt owed by an inept movie producer (Gene Hackman), then decides to produce movies with him instead. Directed by Barry Sonnenfeld from Elmore Leonard's novel, the fast-paced, wickedly funny satire lampoons the Hollywood world of unabashedly greedy would-be movers and shakers. Brief violence, restrained bedroom scenes, and recurring rough language. A-III (R)

Get to Know Your Rabbit (1972) Inane sex-farce features Tom Smothers as a high-powered corporate dropout who turns road magician and lover to a veritable parade of naked females. Director Brian De Palma's self-indulgent comedy is an utterly sophomoric burlesque posing as a spoof of conventional society. O (R)

Getaway, The (1972) Released from prison through the connivance of a crooked politician, Steve McQueen has to return the favor by robbing a bank and sharing the proceeds. When the heist goes bad, McQueen and Ali McGraw skip town with the law in hot pursuit. The movie, however, goes nowhere under Sam Peckinpah's heavy-handed direction, which resorts to some fairly ugly violence and a little sex. A-IV (PG)

Getaway, The (1994) Sprung from jail after agreeing to pull off a million-dollar heist, a cool-headed killer (Alec Baldwin) and his steely wife (Kim Basinger) keep the stolen cash and shoot their way out of myriad doublecrosses along the way to freedom in Mexico. Director Roger Donaldson's steamy remake of the '72 chase movie pours on the brutal violence and makes sympathetic heroes out of the murderously greedy couple, right up to the crime-certainly-does-pay ending. Excessive violence, several bedroom scenes with nudity, a suicide, and much rough language. O (R)

Getting Away with Murder (1996) Seriocomic misfire set in Boston, where a college ethics professor (Dan Aykroyd) murders his next-door neighbor (Jack Lemmon) because he was a Nazi war criminal, then learns the man was innocent and tries to atone by marrying his grieving daughter (Lily Tomlin). Writer-director Harvey Miller's convoluted plot struggles vainly to get laughs from serious justice issues, but the flat characters and their heavy-handed motivations are neither funny nor thought-provoking. Muddled justice questions, several restrained sex scenes, some crude humor, occasional profanity, and an instance of rough language. A-III (R)

Getting Even with Dad (1994) An ex-con (Ted Danson) is thoroughly discombobulated when his long-estranged 11-year-old son (Macaulay Culkin) unexpectedly appears on his doorstep, hides the proceeds of his latest robbery, and forces his dad to spend time with him and reconsider the theft. Director Howard Deutch's tepid comedy has heartwarming elements as the child seemingly reforms the adult, but the humor is limited to predictable complications and poorly staged pratfalls by the father's klutzy cronies. A parent's skeptical moral reformation, some minor violence, and a few instances of profanity. A-III (PG)

Getting It Right (1989) Coming-of-age British comedy directed by American Randal Kleiser about the social and sexual blossoming of a shy hairdresser (Jesse Birdsall) who loses his virginity to a lonely older woman (Lynn Redgrave), befriends a wacky heiress (Helena Bonham Carter), and finally takes a proper bride (Jane Horrocks). It's well-acted, often engaging material, with astute nuances about the wounded humanity of its characters. Suggestive sexual banter and an adulterous encounter with brief nudity. A-IV (R)

Getting of Wisdom, The (1980) Spirited Australian girl (Susannah Fowle) at a stuffy academy for young women in turn-of-the-century Sydney gives teachers, classmates, long-suffering mother, and various other people a run for the money before she settles down and graduates with honors. Unfortunately, director Bruce Beresford's heroine remains unlikable and self-absorbed from first to last, making the result less than engaging entertainment. A-II (nr)

Getting Straight (1970) Superficial survey of some elements of campus unrest in the story of a graduate student (Elliott Gould) and his encounters with sloganeering students, black militants, self-satisfied professors, insensitive administrators, bloodthirsty riot police, promiscuity, narcotics use, draft-dodging, profanity. Directed by Richard Rush, the movie exploits serious social issues, without any attempt to put them in context or provide a perspective for trying to understand them. O (R)

Gettysburg (1993) Long but compelling historical re-creation of the Civil War battle focuses on the decisive action of Union general Buford (Sam Elliott) in seizing the high ground at the start, the role of Union colonel Chamberlain (Jeff Daniels) in holding the Little Round Top, and the disastrous charge led by Confederate general Pickett (Stephen Lang) which ended the battle. Adapted by director Ronald F. Maxwell from Michael Shaara's novel, "The Killer Angels," the military actions are depicted on an epic scale that succeeds as spectacle but only occasionally as human drama. Much battlefield carnage. A-II (PG)

Ghidrah, the Three-Headed Monster (1965) Japanese rubber-suited monsters threaten miniatures of Tokyo in a standard fantasy thriller directed by Inoshiro Honda. Stylized violence. A-II (br)

Ghost (1990) The ghost of a murdered young banker (Patrick Swayze) uses a phony spiritualist (Whoopi Goldberg) to warn his lover (Demi Moore) that she too is in deadly peril until he can discover why he was killed and stop those responsible. Director Jerry Zucker's offbeat but uneven blend of fantasy, horror, and comedy is an engagingly sentimental thriller plump with quirky characters and edgy performances. Some grisly violence, acceptance of premarital sex, and occasional profanity. A-III (PG-13)

Ghost and Mr. Chicken, The (1966) Don Knotts comedy vehicle in which he spends a night in a haunted house is ineptly directed by Alan Rafkin. A-I (br)

Ghost and Mrs. Muir, The (1947) Amusing sentimental fantasy set in the early 1900s, when a sensible English widow (Gene Tierney) moves into an inexpensive seaside cottage, finds it haunted by the dead sea captain (Rex Harrison) who once lived there, and, as the years pass, falls in love with his cantankerous ghost. Directed by Joseph L. Mankiewicz, the proceedings are mostly sweet and often droll, though matters take a nasty turn when the widow is pursued by a man (George Sanders) she doesn't know is already married. Muted sexual innuendo. A-II (br)

Ghost and the Darkness, The (1996) After scores of construction workers fall victim to a relentless pair of marauding lions in 1898 East Africa, an Irish engineer (Val Kilmer) and an American big-game hunter (Michael Douglas) join forces to track down the beasts and shoot them. Directed by Stephen Hopkins, the fact-based action adventure is a dark and grisly story of two men in a land being unwillingly tamed by outside forces. Many scenes of maulings, gory shots of corpses, and minimal profanity. A-III (R)

Ghost Breakers, The (1940) Comic chiller in which a witless radio crime-reporter (Bob Hope) flees an irate gangster for Cuba, where he helps an heiress (Paulette Goddard) move into a creaky old castle complete with a resident zombie, assorted spooks, secret passageways, and a hidden treasure. Director George Marshall plays the eerie situation mainly for laughs, though with mild frights and a few scares along the way. Still a lot of fun for those in the mood, but small children may need the reassuring presence of an older viewer. A-I (br)

Ghost Dad (1990) Drawn-out, one-joke comedy about a widower (Bill Cosby) who is the victim of a fatal car accident, but whose spirit returns determined to insure the financial security of his three orphaned children. Director Sidney Poitier relies on broad, often vulgar, visual gags and inconsistent use of the ghost gimmick, but the silly plot is occasionally brightened by Cosby's likeable performance as a caring father and some special-effects wizardry that might frighten young children. A number of vulgarities, some sexual references, and several instances of profanity. A-II (PG)

Ghost in the Invisible Bikini, The (1966) Failed horror spoof in which the heirs (Tommy Kirk, Deborah Walley, Basil Rathbone, and Patsy Kelly) of a famous magician (Boris Karloff) gather for the reading of his will in a spooky mansion soon overrun by partying college students, a motorcycle gang, hired assassins, and the title ghost (Susan Hart). Directed by Don Weis, the seventh and final entry in the **Beach Party** series is a jumble of weak gags, silly frights, and tedious plot devices. Comic menace and sexual innuendo. A-II (br)

Ghost in the Machine (1993) Absurd sci-fi horror tale in which the brain of a serial killer lives on in a computer mainframe tracking the movements of his next victim (Karen Allen) and her teenage son (Wil Horneff), while a computer expert (Chris Mulkey) works feverishly to prevent the killings. Director Rachel Talalay tosses together routine suspense elements with lots of razzle-dazzle computer graphics and high-tech lingo in a story so silly it would be funny were it not so pathetic. Intermittent stylized violence, fleeting sexual innuendo, and an instance of rough language. A-III (R)

Ghost Story (1981) Fred Astaire, Melvyn Douglas, Douglas Fairbanks Jr., John Houseman, and Patricia Neal appear in director John Irvin's lavishly produced but intellectually impoverished film version of Peter Straub's novel about a vengeful spirit (an extremely fleshy spirit) stalking four old codgers who sent her to the bottom of a Vermont pond 50 years before. Ectoplasmic nudity and graphic spooky sexuality. O (R)

Ghostbusters (1984) Three parapsychologists (Bill Murray, Dan Aykroyd, and Harold Ramis), bounced from Columbia University because of the dubious nature of their research, go into private practice as ghost exterminators and find that all hell is about to break loose, quite literally. There are some very funny moments, largely due to Murray, but director Ivan Reitman lets the spectacular special effects begin to dominate midway and the humor fades. Some adult ribald jokes. A-III (PG)

Ghostbusters II (1989) Has-been Manhattan spook-chasers (Dan Aykroyd, Bill Murray, Harold Ramis, and Ernie Hudson) reunite to save the same lady in distress (Sigourney Weaver) from losing her baby to a 16th-century evil spirit (Wilhelm Von Homburg). The ghostly special effects are comical and mostly non-menacing, the guys are funny, and director Ivan Reitman satirizes the Big Bad Apple and yuppie trends without a heavy hand. Some sexual innuendo and mildly vulgar language. A-II (PG)

Ghosts Italian Style (1969) Italian romantic comedy about newlyweds trying to save their sputtering marriage by living rent-free in a decaying baroque mansion haunted by a womanizing count. Sophia Loren and Vittorio Gassman turn social satire into farce as director Renato Castellani tries to make something out of a story about false impressions and mistaken identities. A-III (G)

Ghosts of Mississippi (1996) Fact-based drama chronicles the struggle of a dedicated Mississippi prosecutor (Alec Baldwin), prompted by Medgar Evers's widow (Whoopi Goldberg), to retry and convict the white supremacist (James Woods) guilty of the 1963 slaying of the civil-rights leader nearly 30 years after two mistrials had left him a free man. Producer-director Rob Reiner's provides a straightforward, though emotionally involving, account of an infamous instance of institutionalized racism finally rectified. Scenes depicting the victim's bloody murder and a few instances of profanity. A-II (PG-13)

Ghosts on the Loose (1943) Formula comedy directed by William Beaudine with the East Side Kids (Leo Gorcey, Huntz Hall, Bobby Jordan, etc.) helping newlyweds (Ava Gardner and Rick Vallin) move into a supposedly haunted house, which proves to be the hide-out of a Nazi spy ring (led by Bela Lugosi). Dated fun. A-I (br)

Ghoulies (1985) Shameless, thoroughly inept rip-off of **Gremlins**, it is directed by Luca Bercovici, and has some brief partial nudity and gore but not too much in the way of real violence. A-III (PG-13)

Giant (1956) Sentimental but stylish adaptation of Edna Ferber's sprawling family saga of life and love in Texas oil country from the turn of the century to the early 1950s, with Dennis Hopper as the clean-cut, intense son of Texas patriarchs Elizabeth Taylor and Rock Hudson, while James Dean gives his most moving performance as the inarticulate cowhand who strikes it rich. Directed by George Stevens, the plot is less important than its themes of changing times, the generation gap, racial prejudice, the waste of war, and marital incompatibility. Over three hours long, so children may find it a taxing experience. A-I (G)

Giant Behemoth, The (1959) Low-budget British monster movie directed by Eugene Lourie pits a marine biologist (Gene Evans) against a prehistoric sea creature that's been roused from the deep by A-bomb tests, then proceeds to ravage the coast of Cornwall in radioactive fury, before heading up the Thames River to London. Scenes of destruction and radiation victims. A-II (br)

Giant Claw, The (1957) Sci-fi time-waster directed by Fred F. Sears concerns a colossal bird from outer space attacking Earth with dime-store special effects until stopped by a cornball electronics engineer (Jeff Morrow). The crunching of unconvincing models is more silly than scary. A-I (br)

Giant of Thunder Mountain, The (1992) When a little girl (winningly played by Noley Thornton) befriends a lonely, oversized woodsman (Richard Kiel) living on a nearby mountain, the villagers determine to drive him away, but have a change of heart after he saves them from a gang of cutthroats. Written by Kiel and directed by James Roberson, the story of a child's ability to see the goodness in a man foolishly misjudged by her elders is ultimately heartwarming and certainly eye-filling in its turn-of-the-century Western setting but suffers from a lumpy plot with too much violent action. Initial scenes of parents being killed by a grizzly bear, life-threatening situations involving children as well as adults, and frightening scenes of vigilante justice. A-II (PG)

Giant Spider Invasion, The (1975) Sci-fi clunker directed by Bill Rebane involves a meteoric shower of space geodes on a farm near Gleason, Wis., which is soon overrun by a spider as big as a house, until it's stopped by a pair of scientists (Steve Brodie and Barbara Hale) and the local sheriff (Alan Hale). Hokey violence and some sexual innuendo. A-II (PG)

Gidget (1959) Dated coming-of-age story set in sunny California, where a 16-year-old (Sandra Dee), whose nickname is a contraction of "girl midget," pals around with some would-be beach bums (led by beatnik Cliff Robertson) and learns about love from one of them (James Darren). Directed by Paul Wendkos, the slickly superficial proceedings feature the usual addled parents, empty-headed teenyboppers, partying young males, and a free-spirited, clay-footed social dropout. Romantic complications, sexual innuendo, and a sexual situation involving an adolescent. A-III (br)

Gidget Goes Hawaiian (1961) Flimsy sequel with teenage Gidget (Deborah Walley) joining her parents on a Waikiki vacation after breaking up with her boyfriend (James Darren), though he shows up in time to help when she fears that her missing parents are off philandering. Director Paul Wendkos downplays the adolescent hormones in a contrived plot providing a simplistic lesson in trust and faith in others, no matter how guilty their actions may seem. Mild sexual innuendo and some excessive social drinking. A-II (br)

Gidget Goes to Rome (1963) Tired sequel about the goofy misadventures and romantic mix-ups of 18-year-old Gidget (Cindy Carol) while touring the Eternal City with her boyfriend (James Darren), four of their chums, and a dotty aunt (Jessie Royce Landis) of one of them going along as chaperon. Directed by Paul Wendkos, the lame plot is occasionally relieved by visits to Rome's ancient monuments, historic buildings, and ritzy restaurants. Long sit for youngsters, though it may have nostalgic value for some of their elders. A-I (br)

Gigi (1958) Soured Lerner and Loewe musical from the Colette story about a 1890's Parisian adolescent (Leslie Caron) who balks at her family's efforts to train her as a courtesan until she meets a charming young man (Louis Jourdan). Directed by Vincente Minnelli, the plush production makes good use of French locales and has a splendid cast, but its theme, as enunciated in Maurice Chevalier's smirking rendition of "Thank Heaven for Little Girls," has lost the sense of sophisticated charm that was once considered amusing. Considerable sexual innuendo. A-III (br)

Gigot (1962) Seriocomic tale of a simple-minded French mute (Jackie Gleason) whose problems become increasingly serious after he gives shelter to a homeless woman and her child. Directed by Gene Kelly, the contrived plot provides an unlikely vehicle for a star whose sense of physical comedy and pathos of character in the role will not suit all tastes. Sentimental results that rarely touch the heart. A-I (br)

Gilbert and Sullivan (see: **The Story of Gilbert and Sullivan**)

Gilda Live (1980) Concert film by director Mike Nichols of comedienne Gilda Radner's Broadway stage show should appeal to fans of "Saturday Night Live," but leave others flat. Most of the amusing moments come from Don Novello as Father Guido Sarducci. Some rough language and Novello's occasional (and highly original) ventures into theology make this mature fare. A-III (R)

Gildersleeve on Broadway (1943) Feeble comedy directed by Gordon Douglas transports the small-town title bachelor (Harold Peary) to New York, where he gets involved through a series of comic misunderstandings with a dizzy heiress (Billie Burke) as well as a brassy gold digger. The laborious romantic complications include female impersonation. A-II (br)

Gimme Shelter (1970) Straightforward documentary gives an honest picture of what it was like to tour America with the Rolling Stones rock group and their notorious Altamont Speedway free concert, where a fan was beaten to death by a member of the Hell's Angels. Directed by David Maysles, Albert Maysles and Charlotte Zwerin, it is a disturbing picture of the dark side of the American Dream. A-IV (R)

Ginger and Fred (1986) Ginger (Giulietta Masina) and Fred (Marcello Mastroianni), a former vaudeville team who imitated Hollywood's Rogers and Astaire, are invited to perform in a Christmas television special. In this Italian production about the disappointments of old age and the commercialization of contemporary life, director Federico Fellini pays homage to performers important in his career, while at the same time indulging his penchant for visual cascades of freakish humanity. Some earthy proverbs about sex and several ambiguous references to religion. A-III (PG-13)

Gingerbread Man, The (1998) Murky thriller from John Grisham's novel about a Savannah lawyer (Kenneth Branagh) whose attraction to a vulnerable client (Embeth Davidtz) who's being stalked by her unstable father ensnares him in a murderous plot that threatens the safety of his two young children. Directed by Robert Altman, the sinister proceedings are wrapped in a thick Southern Gothic atmosphere that fails to compensate for a less-than-credible script. Brief violence, an implied affair, fleeting nudity, occasional rough language, and some profanity. A-III (R)

Girl and the General, The (1967) Muddled Italian movie set in WW I in which an Austrian general (Rod Steiger) is captured by an Italian private (Umberto Orsini) and a peasant waif (Virna Lisi). Directed by Pasquale Festa Campanile, it has wartime violence and brief nudity. A-III (br)

Girl Crazy (1943) Giddy musical in which a New York publisher sends his playboy son (Mickey Rooney) to a rugged, all-male college in the backlands of the Southwest, where he falls for the dean's granddaughter (Judy Garland) and saves the school from financial ruin by making it coeducational. Directed by Norman Taurog, the thin story line features buoyant lead performances, comic routines by Rags Ragland and Nancy Walker, and, best of all, upbeat songs by George and Ira Gershwin, ending with Busby Berkeley's staging of the big production number, "I Got Rhythm." A-I (br)

Girl for Joe, A (see: **Force of Arms**)

Girl from Petrovka, The (1974) Romance between a Russian woman (Goldie Hawn) and an American journalist (Hal Holbrook) based in Moscow blossoms into true love, but she is picked up by the police while on an errand of mercy and sentenced to prison. Directed by Robert Ellis Miller, the story is thin and watery and treated in ponderously sentimental style. Some ludicrously inappropriate nudity. A-III (PG)

Girl Getters, The (1966) British look at contemporary society through the eyes of young rebels without goals. Michael Winner's direction of Peter Draper's episodic script captures something of the cynical innocence of its subject. A-III (br)

Girl Happy (1965) Dim musical in which a band leader (Elvis Presley) secretly chaperones a gangster's daughter (Shelley Fabares) during the college spring-break at Fort Lauderdale. Director Boris Sagal focuses on nubile coeds and their sophomoric hijinks with largely mirthless results. Sexual situations. A-III (br)

Girl Hunters, The (1963) Low-budget crime picture directed by Roy Rowland in which author Mickey Spillane plays his own fictional private eye, Mike Hammer, who sobers up long enough to help a federal agent (Lloyd Nolan) capture a team of Soviet assassins. Brutal violence, including a suspect held for the police by nailing his hand to the floor, and sexual innuendo. A-III (br)

Girl in Blue, The (1974) David Selby crisscrosses picturesque Ontario looking for the blue-clad girl (Maud Adams) he encountered long ago. He also lives with his girlfriend (Gay Rowan) just in case the girl in blue never materializes. Directed by George Kaczender, the hackneyed exercise in romantic sentimentality is so slight and silly that even the occasional expletive and glimpse of nudity seem innocuous. A-III (nr)

Girl in the Picture, The (1986) Slight romantic comedy about a young Glasgow commercial photographer (John Gordon-Sinclair) who ends his live-in relationship with an art student (Irina Brook), only to realize he loves her after she moves out. Writer-director Cary Parker develops the characters in warmly human fashion and makes good use of the photographer's trade, but the overly familiar plot has no surprises. Sexual situations and occasional coarse language. A-III (PG-13)

Girl Most Likely, The (1957) Musical remake of the 1941 comedy **Tom, Dick and Harry**, with Jane Powell in the Ginger Rogers role as a woman torn between three suitors (rich Keith Andes, salesman Tommy Noonan, and carefree Cliff Robertson). Director Mitchell Leisen gets some smiles from the daffy romantic complications, but the song and dance numbers in the dream sequences add little zest to the lightweight proceedings. A-I (br)

Girl Named Tamiko, A (1962) Unsavory sudser about an embittered Eurasian (Laurence Harvey) working as a photographer in Tokyo but trying to use a rich American (Martha Hyer) as his passport to the US until falling for the lady of the title (France Nuyen). Directed by John Sturges, the only thing authentic about this ludicrous, anti-romantic account of a mean-spirited opportunist is the beautiful Japanese location photography. Implied sexual encounters. A-III (br)

Girl of the Golden West, The (1938) Wildly fanciful Nelson Eddy-Jeanette MacDonald musical set in California pioneer days, when a notorious bandit leader (Eddy) is reformed by the love of a good woman (MacDonald) who runs the saloon in a rough mining town whose sheriff (Walter Pigeon) wants to hang the bandit and marry her. Directed by Norman Z. Leonard, the creaky, melodramatic plot is helped by a bizarre assortment of characters, though the Sigmund Rohmberg-Gus Kahn songs are entirely forgettable. Old-fashioned escapist fare with some well-intentioned ethnic stereotypes. A-I (br)

Girl of the Year (see: **The Petty Girl**)

Girl on a Motorcycle, The (1968) The woman of the title (Marianne Faithfull) relives her past as she speeds down the highway early one morning to meet her lover and her fate. Failing to come to grips with the motivation of the character's past actions, director Jack Cardiff understandably concentrates on the travelogue aspects of a ride through the beautiful French and German countryside. Frequent and explicit depictions of scenes of physical intimacy are dramatically as well as morally unjustified. O (X/R)

Girl Was Young, The (see: **Young and Innocent**)

Girl Who Couldn't Say No, The (1969) Bland Italian comedy of a young surgeon (George Segal) who frequently falls in and out of love with an energetic Virna Lisi, who's a soft touch for distressed persons. Directed by Franco Brusati, its permissive attitude toward sex is treated farcically, but with excessive detail. O (PG)

Girl Who Dared, The (1944) Mystery programmer directed by Howard Bretherton is set on a stormy night in an isolated house where several people are murdered, with no way to contact the police until an insurance investigator (Peter Cookson) turns up to find the killer. Stylized violence, menace, and family conflicts. A-II (br)

Girl Who Knew Too Much, The (1969) Mystery story about a hired gun (Adam West) caught between the love for a slain crime-boss's girl (Nancy Kwan) and his job of uncovering a Communist plot to take over the syndicate. Director Francis D. Lyon features a full-length strip-tease to enliven the dull, but brutally violent, proceedings. O (R)

Girl with Green Eyes (1964) British coming-of-age drama about a naive young country girl (Rita Tushingham) who, on her first experience of living on her own away from home, becomes infatuated with a middle-aged writer (Peter Finch). Directed by Desmond Davis, the tale is slight, but the acting is fine and the girl's problems quite convincing. Sexual situations. A-IV (br)

Girlfriends (1978) Director Claudia Weill's contrasting portrait of two New York women (Melanie Mayron, Anita Skinner) and the measures they take to find romance and commitment. Realistic treatment of sex and use of profanity override what little sensitivity and insight the film conveys. O (PG)

Girls Just Want to Have Fun (1985) Standard teen movie in which two plucky, clean-cut kids (Sarah Jessica Parker and Lee Montgomery) win a dance contest. Competent but mediocre light entertainment. A-II (PG)

Girls on the Beach, The (1965) Witless youth comedy in which some college coeds try to pay off the mortgage on their sorority house by putting on a concert with the Beatles, then discover they've been hoaxed and have to substitute for them. Directed by William N. Witney, there's little going on here other than bikini-clad coeds frolicking in the sand and cavorting to the music of the Beach Boys and other period performers. Considerable sexual innuendo. A-III (br)

Girly (see: **Mumsy, Nanny, Sonny and Girly**)

Give 'Em Hell, Harry (1976) James Whitmore gives his interpretation of Harry Truman in a film recording of his one-man performance in the Samuel Gallu play. Directed by Steve Binder, Whitmore brings a passion, a conviction, and a dauntless energy that engenders some understanding for the man and his controversial political career. The language is sometimes rough, but it is in the service of honest emotions. A-II (PG)

Give Her the Moon (1970) Unpretentious French comedy in which an American industrialist is so determined to get a French maid (Marthe Keller) that he transports her entire village to New York, where culture shock becomes amusingly apparent. Though there is some romance, director Philippe de Broca concentrates on the contrasting lifestyles with some gentle satire of both. Its an old-fashioned escapist movie that may be lost on the young. A-II (G)

Give My Regards to Broadway (1948) When vaudeville flops in the 1920s, a juggler (Charles Winninger) awaits its return by taking a factory job while developing a family act with his son (Dan Dailey) and two daughters, who grow up to pursue more fruitful careers. Directed by Lloyd Bacon, the movie offers some entertaining stage routines, nostalgic songs, and a sentimental but generally pleasing story of family solidarity despite changing times. A-I (br)

Gizmo (1980) Howard Smith's delightfully zany little film uses newsreels from the 1920s and 1930s to chronicle the dogged if flawed ingenuity of a host of inventors whose creations did not become household words. Very entertaining. A-I (G)

Glacier Fox, The (1979) Outstanding Japanese wildlife documentary, narrated by Arthur Hill, presents the story of a glacier fox, his mate, and their five pups who live on the Okhotsk Sea coast of Hokkaido, a region blasted in winter by frigid winds that blow down from Siberia. Directed by Koreyoski Kurahara, the photography is stunning as it captures the intrinsic drama and humor in the life cycle of this fox family. Though it does not shy from some of the grimmer aspects of life in the wild, there are no visuals that might prove too strong for younger children, making it perfectly suited for the whole family. A-I (G)

Gladiator (1992) Routine prizefight picture in which a venal promoter (Brian Dennehy) pits a Chicago high-schooler (James Marshall) against his best friend (Cuba Gooding, Jr.) in illegal boxing matches so the youth can pay off his father's gambling debts. Capitalizing on the popularity of the two young actors, director Rowdy Herrington goes down for the count with this strictly formula story. Brief teen bedroom scene, much graphic violence in the ring, and intermittent rough language. A-III (R)

Glass Bottom Boat, The (1966) A secretary (Doris Day) and a scientific genius (Rod Taylor) get involved with each other and assorted spies, gadgets, and contrivances. The comedy has a number of good sight gags, some clever situations, and a fine supporting cast. As put together by director Frank Tashlin, it adds up to a lot of fun. A-II (br)

Glass Houses (1972) Broken family seeks self-revelation through group-encounter therapy at a California spa. Director Alexander Singer's ill-conceived satire features Jennifer O'Neil as a mistress and Deirdre Lenihan as the daughter of a business-type who contend for his sexual attention. Most viewers will experience a gagging sensation rather than a catharsis. O (R)

Glass Key, The (1942) Hardboiled crime picture from the Dashiell Hammett novel about a machine politician (Brian Donlevy) saved from a murder rap by his right-hand man (Alan Ladd), despite various complications created by the victim's sister (Veronica Lake). Directed by Stuart Heisler, the murder mystery is less perplexing than the relationships between the principals and the efforts of the hoods (Joseph Calleia and William Bendix) to benefit from the situation. Stylized violence, some of it quite nasty, and romantic complications. A-II (br)

Glass Menagerie, The (1950) Uneven adaptation of the Tennessee Williams play set in St. Louis, where an aging Southern belle (Gertrude Lawrence) tries to get her shy, lame daughter (Jane Wyman) interested in more than her collection of glass animals by having her son (Arthur Kennedy) invite his friend (Kirk Douglas) for a visit. Directed by Irving Rapper, the stagy proceedings are saved by Wyman's sensitive, convincing performance as the physically handicapped young woman who is more realistic about her situation than the others. Mild sexual innuendo. A-II (br)

Glass Shield, The (1995) Idealistic African-American rookie (Michael Boatman) in a corrupt, all-white Los Angeles sheriff's unit joins another outcast, a Jewish female deputy (Lori Petty), in attempting to find evidence of police cover-ups of past and present crimes. Writer-director Charles Burnett centers on the rookie's moral conflicts in working with rogue cops in a drawn-out narrative downplaying violence in favor of exploring racial and justice issues. Some brief violence, a racial slur, and an implied live-in relationship. A-III (PG-13)

Glass Slipper, The (1955) Pretty-looking but stilted rendering of the Cinderella story, this time with a waif (Leslie Caron) suffering under an ill-tempered stepmother (Elsa Lanchester) until the magic powers of a local eccentric (Estelle Winwood) help her win the love of a handsome prince (Michael Wilding). Director Charles Walters's slow-moving narrative is brightened by some elaborate fantasy numbers, but there is little magic or humor in this version of the classic romance, and the songs are strictly forgettable. For romantics of any age, though a long sit for children. A-I (br)

Glass Sphinx (1968) Inept European production directed by Luigi Scattini about an archaeological expedition led by Robert Taylor in searching the Egyptian desert for a lost tomb containing the art treasure of the title. Some violence and sexual innuendo. A-III (br)

Glass Web, The (1953) Muddled thriller directed by Jack Arnold in which a TV crime show's writer (John Forsythe) and his story consultant (Edward G. Robinson) become romantically involved with a blackmailing actress (Kathleen Hughes), whose unsolved murder becomes the subject of one of their shows and leads to the killer's apprehension. Minimal violence, some menace, and an implied extramarital affair. A-II (br)

Gleaming the Cube (1989) When an alienated teen (Christian Slater) decides to investigate the death of his adopted Vietnamese brother (Art Chudabala), he employs daredevil skateboard wizardry against the many meanies who get in his way. Set in a southern California Vietnamese community, director Graeme Clifford's contrived murder mystery uses a lot of fancy footwork to divert attention from its flimsy plot. Mild rough language, some violence, and comic-book menace. A-II (PG-13)

Glen and Randa (1971) After a thermonuclear apocalypse has destroyed contemporary civilization, two lost innocents (Steven Curry and Shelly Plimpton) live like primitive natives among the debris of Howard Johnson restaurants and deserted superhighways. Director Jim McBride's failed allegory about the primacy of animal passions becomes pretentious in execution and offensive in treatment, employing crude sex scenes, and frontal nudity. O (X/R)

Glengarry Glen Ross (1992) Screen version of David Mamet's play about four real-estate salesmen (Jack Lemmon, Al Pacino, Ed Harris, and Alan Arkin) who, under threat of being fired unless they close some deals within the week, commit desperate acts which ultimately backfire. James Foley's tautly directed movie delivers intense performances with blistering dialogue while depicting the characters' moral disintegration in a dehumanizing pressure-cooker where money is everything. Much rough language and some sexual references. A-III (R)

Glenn Miller Story, The (1954) James Stewart gives an ingratiating performance as the trombone player who starts his own band, discovers the "sound" that makes it a national favorite, then dies in a WW II flight over the English Channel. Directed by Anthony Mann, the story's interesting and the acting good (June Allyson as his supportive wife) with plenty of examples of Miller's music and appearances by many of the era's musicians. A-I (br)

Glimmer Man, The (1996) Mindless action thriller in which two Los Angeles homicide detectives (Steven Seagal and Keenan Ivory Wayans) break up a gang of international terrorists while after a serial killer who crucifies his victims. Directed by John Gray, the muddled plot alternates the search for a religious fanatic with hunting down the terrorist masterminds in numbingly dumb fashion. Numerous gruesome deaths, nudity, some rough language, and occasional profanity. O (R)

Gloria (1980) Independent filmmaker John Cassavetes tries to transport a 1930's crime melodrama to the 1980 streets of New York in the story of a middle-aged gun moll (Gena Rowlands), who retires from the mob, then suddenly finds herself responsible for a young boy marked for death by her old gang. The movie's strength lies in the extraordinary performance of Rowland, which more than makes up for some of the narrative's incoherence. A-III (PG)

Gloria (1999) Hollow crime tale in which a tough jailbird (Sharon Stone) tangles with her old gang when they try to rub out a seven-year-old boy who knows too much. Directed by Sidney Lumet, there are plenty of desperate chase scenes through gritty Manhattan locales, but the result lacks the emotional credibility of Gena Rowlands's title performance in the 1980 original. Some hard-edged violence, sexual references and innuendo, brief rear nudity, recurring rough language, and some profanity. A-IV (R)

Glorifying the American Girl (1929) Interesting relic from the early talkies in which an ambitious shop-girl (Mary Eaton) joins a vaudeville song-and-dance act, then gains fame in a Ziegfeld musical revue while losing the beau she left behind (Edward Crandall) to a devoted co-worker (Olive Shea). Directed by Willard Webb, the story line creaks and the sound quality is primitive, but the result has historical interest as a record of Ziegfeld's florid production style, stage routines by Eddie Cantor, Helen Morgan, and Rudy Vallee, glimpses of period personalities, and lots of New York locations. Some sexual situations and double entendres. A-III (br)

Glory (1956) Sentimental bluegrass tale directed by David Butler revolves around a penniless young Kentucky lass (Margaret O'Brien) who finds romance and the means to keep a cherished thoroughbred racehorse with the help of her aunt (Charlotte Greenwood) and a longtime friend (Walter Brennan). Good-natured formula hokum. A-I (br)

Glory (1989) The story of the 54th Regiment of Massachusetts Volunteer Infantry, the first black fighting unit raised during the Civil War, focuses on its enlightened white commander (Matthew Broderick), who molded field hands and runaway slaves into proud, heroic Union soldiers. Director

Edward Zwick raises consciousness about the little-known regiment and re-creates some harrowing battle scenes but, unfortunately, gives shallow attention to the themes of racism and the obscenity of war. Stereotyping of key black characters, much grisly wartime violence, and some profanity. A-III (R)

Glory Boy (1971) WW II vet (Michael Moriarty) returns to the family farm with two of his buddies (William Devane and Mitchell Ryan) with the intention of proving to his patriotic father (Arthur Kennedy) that there is no glory on the battlefield, but things get out of hand. Director Edwin Sherin's movie about the dehumanizing effects of war goes to excess in depicting rape and murder and its use of nudity and foul language. O (R)

Glory Guys, The (1965) Formula Western in which a cavalry captain (Tom Tryon) and an Army scout (Harve Presnell) vie for the love of a widow (Senta Berger) before both go off to fight the Sioux in a campaign led by a glory-seeking general (Andrew Duggan). Directed by Arnold Laven, this variation on Custer's Last Stand grows tiresome with barrack hijinks and barroom brawls long before the main event finally gets underway, then abruptly finishes. Frontier violence and romantic complications. A-II (br)

Gnome-Mobile, The (1967) A lumber baron takes his two grandchildren to one of his forests, discovers some lonely gnomes, and helps them find another gnome-infested forest. Walter Brennan is excellent in a dual role as the kindly grandfather and a waspish, irascible little old man. Robert Stevenson directs the colorful Walt Disney fantasy whose good humor and many finely executed special effects will divert just as many adults as children. A-I (G)

Go (1999) Smirky comedy divides its time between a smalltime drug-deal gone awry with near deadly consequences and a gambling jaunt to Las Vegas by four pals also culminating in violence. Director Doug Liman's mindless comedy takes a benign view of drug abuse and treats dealing as a lucrative lark as long as no one actually dies. Recreational drug use, a *ménage à trois*, some nudity, brief instances of violence, grand larceny, occasional profanity, and much rough language. O (R)

Go-Between, The (1971) British period romance features Michael Redgrave reminiscing about his childhood role as the innocent messenger between lovers (Julie Christie and Alan Bates) who are separated by the gulf of social class. Director Joseph Losey handles with sensitivity the boy's growing awareness of the nature of the couple's relationship and how, on his 13th birthday, he is directly confronted with the physical realities of adult life. A-III (GP)

Go for Broke! (1951) Worthy, entertaining account of a WW II Japanese-American infantry unit and its exploits on the battlefields of Italy and France. Writer-director Robert Pirosh provides a convincing picture of the unit's perseverance, not only against the German foe, but also in the face of prejudice from fellow Americans, including one of their own officers (Van Johnson). Wartime violence. A-I (br)

Go, Johnny, Go! (1958) Formula success story of a frustrated singer (Jimmy Clanton) who leaves an orphanage for New York, where he's turned into overnight rock 'n' roll star by disk jockey Alan Freed. Directed by Paul Landres, the simplistic tale is sandwiched between performances by such period music notables as Chuck Berry, Eddie Cochran, Ritchie Valens, and Jackie Wilson. Attempted robbery. A-II (br)

Go Naked in the World (1961) Trashy romantic clunker directed by Ranald MacDougall revolves around a young man (Tony Franciosa) being turned to mush after discovering that the woman he loves (Gina Lollabrigida) is a high-priced prostitute. Preposterous twaddle equating promiscuity with boredom and includes an off-screen suicide among its unconvincing contrivances. A-III (br)

Go Now (1998) A young soccer-playing Scotsman (Robert Carlyle) working as a plasterer in Bristol, England, begins a serious love affair (with Juliet Aubrey), only to find himself facing life in a wheelchair when he is diagnosed with multiple sclerosis. Director Michael Winterbottom chronicles the effects of the insidious ailment on the athlete and his lover with unsentimental gravity that gives way to an uplifting climax. Sexual encounters, brief nudity, occasional profanities, and frequent rough language. A-III (R)

Go Tell the Spartans (1978) Burt Lancaster plays an overage major who commands a small American cadre working with a motley collection of regular Vietnamese troops, mercenaries, and militia in the hostile countryside during the early days of the Vietnam involvement. Director Ted Post handles the action sequences extremely well and, as a whole, the movie is intelligent, well-acted, and moving. Violence and rough language, but conveys the contradictions and pathos of the Vietnam struggle. A-IV (R)

Goal! (1967) Good sports documentary highlights the skill and endurance of the champion soccer teams which vied for the 1966 World Cup in England. Octavio Senoret's production does well in showing the differences in the style of play of the 16 countries represented, and Nigel Patrick's narration helps explain the worldwide popularity of a sport in which no substitutions are allowed during the game. A-I (br)

Goat, The (see: **La Chevre**)

Goat Horn, The (1974) Bulgarian folk-tale set during the time of Turkish rule, when a goatherd raises his daughter as if she were a boy so that she will never be the victim, as was her mother, of the lust of their despotic master. Though it all ends badly, director Metodi Andonov conveys the sense of powerlessness of a subject people, not through dialogue, but through small details showing the daily life of the period. A-IV (nr)

Gobots, Battle of the Rock Lords (1986) This animated action-adventure movie features constant combat between humanoids, robots, and other silicon-based life-forms, perpetuating the exploitation of the preteen market. Parents should consider the merits of further exposure of the very young to increased levels of hostility depicted in this movie. A-II (G)

God Forgives, I Don't (1969) Professional gambler (Terence Hill) tracks down a notorious outlaw for personal reasons rather then to bring him to justice. Directed by Giuseppe Colizzi, the tale of a personal vendetta has little action or sense, but maintains an atmosphere throughout of brutality and needless violence. O (M)

God Gave Him a Dog (see: 1940's **The Biscuit Eater)**

God Said, 'Ha!' (1999) Filmed performance of comedian Julia Sweeney's one-woman show in which she gives a humorous account of putting her life on hold in her mid-30s to care for a brother dying of cancer, then facing further complications after her parents move in to help, and she herself is shortly later diagnosed as having cervical cancer. Also directed by Sweeney, the monologue is mildly amusing in its self-deprecating anecdotes about the comedian's Irish-Catholic upbringing, her torturous but loving family relationship, as well as her "amicable" divorce and expectations of single life, but the performance withers on the big screen and the thin material fails to sustain feature-length interest. Comic but never mean-spirited treatment of serious matters involving family, religion, sex, and medical procedures, as well as a reference to flatulence. A-III (PG-13)

Goddess, The (1958) Episodic story follows the unhappy formative years of a young woman (Kim Stanley) who goes on to movie stardom, growing more self-destructive with each success. Scripted by Paddy Chayevsky and directed by John Cromwell, the period details of the 1930s-50s provide a credible context for this psychological probe of a troubled woman driven by the need to be loved, yet unable to believe that she deserves anyone's love. Mature themes and treatment. A-III (br)

Godfather, The (1972) Blockbuster screen version of the Mario Puzo novel about a Mafia family's rise, decline, and resurgence in the murderous world of New York racketeering. Marlon Brando plays the aging but indomitable Don, with James Caan and Al Pacino as leading family members. Francis Ford Coppola's direction is a study in control and pacing with all the right touches in establishing the proper 1940's ambience. The murders are plentiful and gruesome, with little spared in detailing the intricacies of mob life. A-III (R)

Godfather, Part II, The (1974) Lacking the original's grace, majesty, and energy, the sequel follows the rise to power of a crime boss (Robert De Niro) and the subsequent use of that power by his son (Al Pacino). Produced and directed by Francis Ford Coppola, the unmanageably complex scenario shifts interminably from Lake Tahoe to the Kefauver hearings, from the lower East Side to Florida base of a crime kingpin (Lee Strasberg). The effect is unsettling and there is much graphic violence. A-III (R)

Godfather Part III, The (1990) Having shed all ties with the underworld, Michael Corleone (Al Pacino) seeks respectability and profits by investing in a Vatican holding company run by corrupt financiers whose business tactics include murder. Directed by Francis Ford Coppola, the narrative strives for tragedy, but settles for melodrama after losing its way in the vague, shadowy world of international finance and the intrigues of certain church officials. Some scenes of intense violence, the twisted morality of criminal retribution, rough language, and an unedifying fictional depiction of some religious figures. A-IV (R)

Gods and Monsters (1998) Offbeat, fictionalized buddy movie set in 1957 Hollywood, where terminally ill, openly gay horror-film director James Whale (Ian McKellan) befriends his young, macho gardener (Brendan Fraser) who overcomes his revulsion of homosexuals to offer compassionate, platonic friendship to the frail old man. Writer-director Bill Condon finds the humanity below the surface of the two very different men, as well as Whale's Catholic maid (Lynn Redgrave), in a subtle tale of manipulation and devotion. Fleeting violence, much homosexual innuendo, brief full frontal nudity, a shadowy sexual encounter, sporadic rough language, and an instance of profanity. A-IV (R)

Gods and the Dead, The (1972) Brazilian turn-of-the-century drama about cocoa plantation owners who try to destroy each other, with the ultimate survivor being a peasant who discovers that, just as he has been victimized by the owners, so too they were victimized by international business interests. Director Ruy Guerra's movie about the unequal distribution of wealth is filled with poetic imagery of the struggle for social justice. A-III (nr)

Gods Must Be Crazy, The (1983) An African bushman discovers a discarded Coke bottle and, after it causes dissension among his people, undertakes a trek to throw it off the edge of the world, but in the course of the journey he runs into some very peculiar civilized people. Director Jamie Uys's simple comedy-adventure explores amiably the cultural differences between industrial society and ritualized tribal folkways. Some violence. A-II (PG)

Gods Must Be Crazy II, The (1990) Mildly amusing but overly contrived sequel set in Africa's Kalahari Desert, where three different sets of strangers (a pair of poachers, two soldiers from opposing sides, and a couple whose plane has crashed) get lost but are helped periodically by a bemused bushman (N!xau) looking for his two missing children. Written and directed by Jamie Uys, the South African production has much broad visual comedy and some charming moments with the lost youngsters, but the endless predicaments of the strangers strain patience and credibility. Bare-bottomed Bushmen and several gags involving a woman's undergarments. A-II (PG)

Gods of the Plague (1977) German crime-melodrama made in 1969 about a young gangster who teams up with a killer for another robbery but is betrayed by one his girlfriends. Director Rainer Werner Fassbinder overdoes the murky underworld atmosphere, in which violence needs no motivation or justification, and the film has little point other than as an exercise in criminal brutality. O (nr)

Godsend, The (1980) Foundling with a nasty disposition knocks off, one by one, the natural children of her foster parents, who seem to be inordinately slow to get the drift. Director Gabrielle Beaumont's tepid British thriller has little to recommend it and, though all of its violence is off-camera, it creates a foreboding atmosphere and features a rather graphic birth scene. A-III (R)

Godson, The (1972) Chilling psychological study of a lonely criminal (Alain Delon) whose life is held in a delicate balance between the gang and the law. French director Jean-Pierre Melville unfolds this lone wolf's struggle to survive police pursuits, the distrust of his gangland associates, and the false sympathy of a woman in a restrained and highly visual manner without the violent excesses associated with gangster films. A-II (PG)

Godspell (1973) Sparkling screen version of musical based loosely on the Gospel according to Matthew, featuring an off-Broadway cast with Victor Garber as the Christ figure and David Haskell as both John the Baptist and Judas. What makes the movie so high-spirited is director David Greene's turning the entire city of New York into a giant stage-set, with its buildings, streets, and parks all strikingly used for great effect. The parables are presented in imaginative skits, many of which serve as springboards for the irresistible tunes, such as "Day by Day" and "God Save the People!," that made the play so popular. A-I (G)

Godzilla (1998) Undistinguished monster movie in which New York City's landmarks and citizens are stomped upon by the giant beast, whose hatching eggs prove an even greater threat, especially to a quartet (led by Matthew Broderick) in imminent danger. Director Roland Emmerich's special-effects thriller lacks the consistent excitement or goofy humor that would make it an escapist lark. Recurring fantasy violence with much mayhem and intermittent profanity. A-III (PG-13)

Godzilla, King of the Monsters (1956) Japanese monster movie in which an American newsman (Raymond Burr) reports on a 30-story-high prehistoric reptile named Godzilla, who rises from the Pacific after being revived by H-bomb tests, razes central Tokyo, then disappears back into the sea, apparently stopped by a scientist's "oxygen destroyer." In the dubbed American version, director Inoshiro Honda's thin story line, barebones model work, and rubber-suited monster provide little indication that this would spawn numerous sequels. Unconvincing special-effects violence and menace. A-II (br)

Godzilla 1985 (1985) You can't keep a good monster down and Japan's favorite has risen again, along with his old pal Raymond Burr, in a fairly competent new version. Godzilla fans everywhere should have reason to be happy with the results, though all the crashing and banging might frighten young children. A-II (PG)

Godzilla on Monster Island (1972) Dubbed Japanese monster movie directed by Jun Fukuda has alien cockroaches from a dying planet assume human form, then try to rule the world through space monsters Ghidrah and Gigan but, as they start destroying Tokyo, Godzilla and his pal Angillus come to the rescue. Much stylized violence and a few crude remarks. A-II (G)

Godzilla vs. Gigan (see: **Godzilla on Monster Island**)

Godzilla vs. Mechagodzilla (see: **Godzilla vs. the Cosmic Monster**)

Godzilla vs. Monster Zero (see: **Monster Zero**)

Godzilla vs. Mothra (see: **Godzilla vs. the Thing**)

Godzilla vs. the Cosmic Monster (1974) Dubbed Japanese monster movie directed by Jun Fukuda is centered in Okinawa, where alien primates in human guise construct Mechagodzilla, a metal super-monster modeled on Godzilla, but their plans for world conquest hit a snag when the real thing turns up. Stylized violence, some gore, and a few crude remarks. A-II (G)

Godzilla vs. the Sea Monster (1966) Dubbed Japanese production has the sleeping Godzilla awaken halfway through the movie to do battle with a denizen of the deep and squash a secret island base producing nuclear weapons, with winged Mothra coming to the rescue of the islanders. Formula action plot with assorted stylized violence. A-II (br)

Godzilla vs. the Smog Monster (1972) Godzilla tangles with a smog monster that bloats itself on factory and automobile wastes, and succeeds in frustrating its ambition to feed on the sacred fumes of Mt. Fuji. Wry social satire on pollution from director Yoshimitu Banno, whose use of blurry, grainy, anemic color photography here is for once thematically motivated. A-I (GP/G)

Godzilla vs. the Thing (1964) Mild Japanese monster movie directed by Inoshiro Honda pits Godzilla, angered by an industrial development, against the dying Mothra, a colossal moth trying to protect its giant egg which, when hatched, proves Godzilla's undoing. Stylized fantasy menace. A-I (br)

Godzilla's Revenge (1971) Young boy's conversation with Godzilla (who is in retirement on Monster Island) and also with his son teach him a few tricks which help thwart a pair of bankrobbers who are hiding near his home. Director Ishiro Honda resurrects his collection of monsters for another round of campy adventures. A-I (G)

Goin' Down the Road (1970) Canadian movie in

which two Nova Scotians come to Toronto in search of a better life but soon find themselves back on the highway, a little less likely of ever finding their place in the world. Directed by Donald Shebib, it is best in its celebration of the city and its environs, but its young people (Doug McGrath, Paul Bradley, and Jane Eastwood) are so sincere and earnest in their idealism that they almost overcome the handicap of stereotyped roles. A-III (R/GP)

Goin' South (1978) Jack Nicholson directs his own performance as a raffish outlaw who is saved from hanging when a young woman (Mary Steenburgen) agrees to marry him. Her sole interest is a hired hand to help her work a supposedly exhausted gold mine, but, naturally, romance blooms in the desert air. Moderately entertaining comedy Western with some sexually oriented humor. A-III (PG)

Going All the Way (1997) Satiric misfire about two Korean War vets returning to their Indianapolis homes to spend a summer pursuing women, the dim one (Ben Affleck) having effortless success, while the other (Jeremy Davies) is an introverted clod who suffers from his moralistic upbringing. Directed by Mark Pellingtoin from Dan Wakefield's 1970 novel, the movie's leering focus on sex makes it seem like a one-dimensional cartoon, made all the more off-putting by Davies's unlikable portrayal of a borderline sociopath. Sexual encounters with nudity, sexual situations including masturbation, rough language, and profanity. O (R)

Going Ape! (1981) Three orangutans provide the madcap antics in director Jeremy Joe Kronsberg's inept and witless situation comedy about a young man (Tony Danza) who inherits a fortune with the requirement that he care for the apes. Danny De Vito helps him protect the beasts from a greedy zoological society that also tries to get the dough. Much vulgarity and frequent profanity. A-III (PG)

Going Berserk (1983) Collection of skits loosely joined together by the gimmick of having television comic John Candy handcuffed to an escaped convict. Written and directed by David Steinberg, the farce offer little other than much foul language and some gross sexually oriented humor. O (R)

Going Hollywood (1933) Slight but bubbly musical romance in which a teacher (Marion Davies) falls for a radio crooner (Bing Crosby), follows him to Hollywood, then tangles with his temperamental French co-star (Fifi D'Orsay). Directed by Raoul Walsh, there's still some fun in its spoofing period radio shows and movie-making, with a good supporting cast (Ned Sparks, Stuart Erwin, and Patsy Kelly) and bouncy production numbers, but the plot's hokey Cinderella romance has aged rather badly. Some sexual innuendo, an implied liaison, and a comic black-face routine. A-III (br)

Going Home (1971) Jan-Michael Vincent plays a man who as a young child saw his father (Robert Mitchum) kill his mother in a drunken rage and now seeks to avenge her by raping the paroled father's new bride-to-be (Brenda Vaccaro). Producer-director Herbert Leonard's failed drama deals in the cliches of abnormal psychology without any serious analysis of characters and their actions, nor is there any meaningful resolution of its muddled plot. Some violence. A-III (GP)

Going in Style (1980) Three oldsters on pension (George Burns, Art Carney, and Lee Strasberg), fed up with feeding pigeons in a Queens park, decide to rob a Manhattan bank. Only George Burns's fine performance makes director Martin Brest's flat and uninspired geriatric farce at all worth watching. Some rough language and its benign view of the crime. A-III (PG)

Going My Way (1944) Bing Crosby ambles amiably through the role of Father O'Malley, the crooning curate sent to assist the aging, crotchety pastor (Barry Fitzgerald) of a poor parish in need of change. Director Leo McCarey's sentimental story is well-paced, with humor and songs such as "Swinging on a Star," but at its sugary center is the theme of new ways replacing the old as conveyed amusingly but with feeling by the two principals. The definitive Hollywood version of Catholic life in an age of innocence, the picture retains appeal today mainly as a well-crafted vehicle of popular entertainment. A-I (nr)

Going Places (1974) Pair of petty thieves (Gerard Depardieu and Patrick Dewaere) graduate to auto theft, kidnapping, and assault as they wander aimlessly through the French countryside, with a sex encounter of some sort at every stop. Directed by Bertrand Blier, the movie's amoral view of life is conveyed in gross language and even grosser, occasionally degrading, images. O (R)

Gold (1974) Though its plot is a rather tiresome affair about the manipulations of an international gold syndicate, this large-scale disaster movie offers an exotic catastrophe (the flooding of an entire gold mining area), fresh South African locations, and some gripping action sequences and spectacular special effects. Director Peter Hunt, however, fights a losing battle against an inept script. Some double entendres and an illicit romance make it inappropriate for youngsters. A-III (PG)

Gold Diggers: The Secret of Bear Mountain (1995) Formula adventure in which a vacationing city girl (Christina Ricci) pals around with a local tomboy (Anna Chlumsky) in the wilds of the Pacific Northwest, where they foolishly risk their lives searching for a lost gold mine. Directed by Kevin James Dobson, the story is less about the gold escapade than the relationship between the two young teens and their widowed moms, one of whom has an abusive boyfriend. Life-threatening perils from nature and an evil human. A-II (PG)

Gold Rush, The (1925) Classic silent comedy with Charlie Chaplin as the Little Tramp searching for gold in the Klondike, where he gets snowed in with a starving prospector (Mack Swain) and has a bittersweet romance with a dance-hall girl (Georgia Hale). It's

Chaplin at his best, with memorable comic highlights including a tilting cabin perched on the edge of a precipice, a Thanksgiving dinner made out of a boiled shoe, and a charming dance performed by bread rolls. Delightful family fare. A-I (br)

Goldbergs, The (see: **Molly**)

Golden Blade, The (1953) Halting but colorful adventure set in ancient Bagdad, where a desert nobleman (Rock Hudson) finds a magic sword enabling him to save the king's daughter (Piper Laurie) from marriage to the cruel son (Gene Evans) of her father's wicked vizier (George Macready). Directed by Nathan Juran, the formula story of right overcoming might has some good action sequences, but the plot plods and the acting ranges from wooden to hammy. Stylized violence. A-I (br)

Golden Boy (1939) Clifford Odets's romantic melodrama about a Depression youth (William Holden) who turns in his violin for boxing gloves, then falls for the girlfriend (Barbara Stanwyck) of his manager (Adolphe Menjou). Directed by Rouben Mamoulian, the ham-fisted story of material wealth versus human values is earnest but obvious, though its critical attitude towards prizefighting is quite effective. Stylized treatment of violence in the ring and romantic entanglements. A-II (br)

Golden Calf, The (1974) The stratagems of a confidence man (Sergei Yursky) in the Soviet Union of the late 1920s backfire with slapstick regularity, and when one of his schemes finally brings in a million rubles, he learns that money does not buy happiness and returns to his con-games. Directed by Mikhail Shveitser, it is an amusing change of pace from the usual socialist realism of Soviet cinema. A-I (nr)

Golden Child, The (1986) A private detective (Eddie Murphy) is charged with rescuing from evil kidnappers a Tibetan toddler, revered by a cult as their sacred leader. A tiresome Murphy vehicle, more irreverent than funny, replete with some unwholesome seduction humor, many indecent expressions, and other harsh language, as well as much violent action and gruesome images. O (PG-13)

Golden Eye, The (1948) Fairly enjoyable Charlie Chan mystery from director William Beaudine follows the Chinese-American detective (Roland Winters) from San Francisco to an Arizona gold mine to solve the murder of its owner, with some help from Number Two Son (Victor Sen Yung) and his chauffeur (Mantan Moreland). Some eerie menace and a gun-toting bogus nun. A-I (br)

Golden Hawk, The (1952) Slapdash 17th-century swashbuckler directed by Sidney Salkow features a womanizing French privateer (miscast Sterling Hayden) who's rebuffed by an attractive English pirate (Rhonda Fleming), then wins her love and aid in sacking the Spanish stronghold at Cartagana. Stylized violence, sexual situations, and marital infidelity. A-III (br)

Golden Horde, The (1951) Far-fetched adventure from Harold Lamb's story about a band of English Crusaders (led by David Farrar) trying to save Samarkand and its princess (Ann Blyth) from Genghis Khan's Tatars in A.D. 1220. Directed by George Sherman, the swordplay is secondary to the bickering between knight and princess over whether to save the city by force of arms or feminine wiles. Stylized violence and feigned seduction. A-II (br)

Golden Hour, The (see: **Pot o' Gold**)

Golden Needles (1974) Fair adventure movie in which Elizabeth Ashley, acting for aging millionaire Burgess Meredith, hires Joe Don Baker to obtain an Oriental statuette whose seven gold needles are said to be able to restore youth and virility to its possessor. Directed by Robert Clouse, there are some generous helpings of kung fu and karate fights and enough love scenes to put it in the adult class, but otherwise it is an escapist movie that doesn't take itself seriously. A-III (PG)

Golden Raiders, The (see: **Escape to Athena**)

Golden Seal, The (1983) Isolated by a storm, a lonely boy (Torquil Campbell) living on an island in the Aleutians befriends a mother seal and protects it from family and poachers. There is a lot of profanity, including some dark pearls from the mouth of our young hero, and a bit of violence. A-II (PG)

Golden Voyage of Sinbad, The (1974) John Phillip Law as Sinbad sails off to find the Fountain of Destiny, harassed by a variety of demons and other nasty types conjured up by Ray Harryhausen's imaginative special effects, which upstage the human cast. Director Gordon Hessler's lighthearted and entertaining adventure movie brings a treat for youngsters and those adults who wish to recapture some of the magic of childhood. A-I (G)

GoldenEye (1995) Action-packed escapist fare in which British agent 007 (Pierce Brosnan), abetted by a savvy computer programmer (Izabella Scorupco), is out to prevent Soviet-based villains (Sean Bean and Famke Janssen) from activating satellite weaponry set to destroy London. Martin Campbell directs a showy, explosive tale of death-defying stunts whose plot-line almost vanishes among all of Bond's frenzied escapes and rescues. Much stylized mayhem, brief bedroom scenes, and some sexual innuendo. A-IV (PG-13)

Goldengirl (1979) Muddled potboiler about the merchandizing of an Olympic sprinter (Susan Anton) by a promoter (James Coburn), who discovers that her scientist father (Curt Jurgens) has been giving her periodic injections of a dangerous growth hormone. Directed by Joseph Sargent, the movie is against the commercialization of sports and the manipulation of human beings, but compromises itself by attempting to merchandize an attractive model as an actress. A number of rather crude sexual references. O (PG)

Goldfinger (1964) British super-agent James Bond (Sean Connery) is on the trail of international smuggler Goldfinger (Gert Frobe) and his chief henchman, Oddjob (Harold Sakata), and with a little help from the ladies (Shirley Easton and Honor Blackman), he thwarts their plan to rob Fort Knox. Directed by Guy Hamilton, the fast-paced plot contains the usual assortment of gimmicky action and tongue-in-cheek sexual references, but adults who enjoy escapist entertainment will find it harmless, campy fun. A-III (GP)

Goldwyn Follies, The (1938) Overblown, undernourished musical in which a failing Hollywood producer (Adolphe Menjou) hires an ordinary moviegoer (Andrea Leeds) to advise him on how to make his next picture a box-office hit. Directed by George Marshall, the script mixes high art (ballet's Vera Zorina) with low comedy (the Ritz Brothers) in an aimless grab-bag of indifferent skits featuring a Gershwin score, singer Kenny Baker, and occasional mischief contributed by Charlie McCarthy and Edgar Bergen. Something for everybody adds up here to pleasing almost no one. A-I (br)

Golem, The (1920) Classic silent fantasy set in 16th-century Prague, where Rabbi Loew saves his people from expulsion by calling to life the clay monster (Paul Wegener) of the title, whose Samson-like strength convinces the emperor to rescind his decree; but the monster, unwilling to return to clay, rampages through the ghetto until being disarmed by a little child. Also directed by Wegener, the mythic narrative is powerfully visualized with expressionistic sets, an ominous atmosphere, and a memorable monster. Stylized violence and romantic complications. A-II (br)

Gone Are the Days (1963) Good-natured satire about the withering of the Old South, as Purlie Victorious (Ossie Davis) returns after 20 years to his family of Georgia sharecroppers, determined to end their exploitation by the local plantation owner (Sorrell Brooke). Directed by Nicholas Webster from a play by Davis, the story's farcical situations and comic misunderstandings ridicule a wide variety of racial stereotypes, and despite the movie's stagy production, the humor comes through in amusingly broad performances by a fine cast, including Ruby Dee, Beah Richards, Godfrey Cambridge, and Alan Alda. Satiric treatment of racism. A-II (br)

Gone Fishin' (1997) Inept comedy about two disaster-prone pals (Joe Pesci and Danny Glover) on a Florida fishing trip which turns into a tedious hunt for a nasty killer. Directed by Christopher Cain, the slow-paced, dim-witted proceedings are an unamusing mixture of large-scale comic destruction and pathetically dumb humor. Much slapstick violence, a menacing killer, and coarse language. A-II (PG)

Gone to Earth (see: **The Wild Heart**)

Gone with the Wind (1939) Epic romance spanning 20 years in the troubled lives of its ambitious southern heroine (Vivian Leigh), the man she loves (Leslie Howard), and the man she finally marries (Clark Gable). Produced by David O. Selznick and directed by Victor Fleming, the movie re-creates, not the history, but the myth of the Old South and its destruction in the Civil War and Reconstruction. Though blacks are treated in the stereotyped fashion of its time, the picture is sympathetic towards its main black characters, particularly Hattie McDaniel, who received an Academy Award for her performance. Wartime violence, romantic complications, and black stereotyping. A-II (G)

Gong Show Movie, The (1980) Chuck Barris's television game-show featuring out-takes too deplorable to show on television form the basis for this monument to bad taste and witless vulgarity. O (R)

Good Burger (1997) Weak comedy about the extremes to which two aged fast-food workers (Kel Mitchell and Kenan Thompson) go to keep a rival burger joint from stealing their secret sauce recipe, which is saving their store from bankruptcy. Director Brian Robbins keeps up a peppy pace as the bumbling buddies are put in and out of an insane asylum in their quest to save their jobs. Some slapstick violence, mild sexual innuendo, and a few crude expressions. A-II (PG)

Good Day for a Hanging (1958) Lethargic Western in which a lawman (Fred MacMurray) captures a killer (Robert Vaughn), gets him convicted, and prepares to carry out the sentence of hanging, then faces a town who thinks he's too vindictive. Directed by Nathan Juran, the result fails to overcome its muddled plot and wooden acting. Frontier violence. A-I (br)

Good Fairy, The (1935) Charming romantic comedy from the Molnar play is set in Hungary, where a naive young graduate (Margaret Sullavan) from an orphanage finds work as a movie usher, is befriended by a fatherly waiter (Reginald Owen), and sidetracks an amorous businessman (Frank Morgan) by getting him to help a struggling lawyer (Herbert Marshall) whom she claims is her husband. Directed by William Wyler, the slight plot is carried by Sullavan's shining performance as the innocent whose good intentions and fertile imagination cause hilarious complications. Sexual situations. A-III (br)

Good Father, The (1987) Middle-aged executive (Anthony Hopkins), troubled and resentful because of his broken marriage, uses his anger and a male-dominated legal system to pressure an unhappy friend into divorce and a child-custody battle in a somber British drama directed by Mike Newell. Hopkins's statement about lost idealism is conveyed with quiet rage as he rejects the feminism he once championed and seeks vengeance vicariously through the court battle of another, gaining only a greater sense of remorse. A-II (R)

Good Guys and the Bad Guys, The (1969) Aging marshal Robert Mitchum joins forces with aging outlaw George Kennedy to thwart a train robbery in this tongue-in-cheek tribute to the senior side of the generation gap. Director Burt Kennedy's entertaining, energetic Western spoofs the New West of inept bad men, greedy politicians, and complacent townspeople. Its aging stars' heroics are more slapstick than swashbuckling. A-III (PG)

Good Guys Wear Black (1979) Mediocre action adventure directed by Ted Post concerns the vengeful exploits of the leader (Chuck Norris) of an elite unit that was betrayed and almost wiped out in the last days of the Vietnam War. Standard violence and sexual hijinks in the service of eye-for-an-eye justice. A-III (PG)

Good Luck (1997) Well-intended but unconvincing tale of a blind ex-athlete (Vincent D'Onofrio) and a paraplegic dental technician (Gregory Hines) working together to compete in a whitewater rafting race. Directed by Richard LaBrie, the movie succeeds in a positive portrayal of the disabled, though the story's development is predictable and the situations are laced with off-putting dark humor and language. Sexual situations, toilet humor, profanity, and rough language. A-III (R)

Good Man in Africa, A (1994) Tasteless culture-clash comedy in which a skirt-chasing British junior diplomat (Colin Friels) and his fatuous boss (John Lithgow) assigned to a West African outpost attempt to influence a local election in hopes of getting a promotion out of the country. Director Bruce Beresford also manages to waste the talents of Sean Connery and Diana Rigg in a series of failed farcical situations that never approach real humor or incisive wit. Brief bedroom scenes with nudity, many crude sexual references, and occasional rough language. A-III (R)

Good Morning, Babylon (1987) Directors Paolo and Vittoria Taviani take an operatic tour of the early days of Hollywood as two brothers, emigrants from Italy, learn that creativity and passion don't last as long as movies and cathedrals. The Italian production is visually and emotionally engaging in paying homage to the silent movie era while celebrating life, love, brotherhood, and paternal obligations. Some subtitles. Brief nudity. A-III (PG-13)

Good Morning, Vietnam (1987) Robin Williams stars as a wacky US Armed Forces radio disc jockey brought to boost troop morale in 1965 Vietnam, but his unmilitary sense of humor brings him into conflict with those in charge of the station. Directed by Barry Levinson, the seriocomic movie has some hilarious routines but also considerable raunchy sexual humor, rough language, and irreverence, only somewhat redeemed by being placed within the context of the obscenity of war. A-IV (R)

Good Neighbor Sam (1964) Uneven romantic comedy with a married advertising executive (Jack Lemmon) working on a wholesome ad campaign for a fussy new client (Edward G. Robinson) while pretending to be the husband of a divorced neighbor (Romy Schneider), who will lose an inheritance if she's unmarried. Directed by David Swift, the frantic proceedings are played for slapstick effect, leaving little room for wit or clever plot developments. Romantic complications and sexual innuendo. A-II (br)

Good News (1947) Nostalgic musical set in 1927 with a giddy plot about the college football star (Peter Lawford) chasing a snooty new girl on campus (Patricia Marshall) while getting some needed tutoring from a bookish student (June Allyson), who by the finale has won his heart. Directed by Charles Walters, the cheerful proceedings feature the usual romantic complications, but the real fun is in the period dance numbers and such songs as "The Varsity Drag" and "Pass the Peace Pipe." Innocent fun from another age. A-I (br)

Good Sam (1948) Failed social comedy about a bumbling Good Samaritan (Gary Cooper) who's finally repaid a substantial loan and uses the money as down payment on the house wanted by his long-suffering wife (Anne Sheridan), but all seems lost when he's robbed on Christmas Eve. Director Leo McCarey's manipulative treatment of the sentimental plot is too obvious for any genuine emotions, though the fine cast at least makes the treacly proceedings watchable. Domestic tensions and veiled references to adultery and abortion. A-II (br)

Good Son, The (1993) Staying with relatives after his mother's death, a distraught youth (Elijah Wood) becomes convinced that his young cousin (Macaulay Culkin) is evil and bent on murder, but no one will believe him. Director Joseph Ruben's atmospheric thriller is handsomely shot and nicely acted, though the contrast between the angelic and diabolic boys is overly simplistic and the denouement unnerving. Brief violence, menace to children, and an instance of rough language. A-III (R)

Good, the Bad, and the Ugly, The (1968) Typically cynical, brutal spaghetti Western with Clint Eastwood, Lee Van Cleef, and Eli Wallach looking for some stolen gold at the time of the Civil War. Directed with some class by Sergio Leone, the movie's good is overwhelmed by the bad and the ugly. O (br)

Good Times (1967) Sonny and Cher star as themselves in a spoofy, puffy vehicle allowing them to try out various types of Hollywood roles and generally have a lot of fun fooling around in fancy costumes on colorful sets. Directed by William Friedkin, it's a cheerful, unassuming little movie. A-I (br)

Good Wife, The (1987) Seemingly faithful and modest wife (Rachel Ward) tries to overcome a sexual crisis in her marriage by having an affair with her brother-in-law and succumbing to the temptations of an aggressive stranger (Sam Neill). Bryan Brown is the unexciting lumberjack who suffers through his wife's sexual odyssey with the hope of putting their marriage back together. Director Ken Cameron makes it trashy with too many simulated sex scenes and confused moral perspective. O (R)

Good Will Hunting (1997) Feel-good drama about a tough South Boston youth (Matt Damon) with a brilliant mind and deep-seated emotional problems whom an MIT professor (Stellan Skarsgard) wants to rush into a top professional job while a psychologist (Robin Williams) pushes him to deal first with his problems, then decide on his future. Directed by

Gus Van Sant, the theme of a wounded psyche being made whole is helped greatly by credible performances from a talented cast, but the story is highly manipulative and the treatment needlessly vulgarized. Stylized violence, an implied sexual relationship, a restrained bedroom scene, sexual jokes, recurring rough language, and occasional profanity. A-IV (R)

Goodbye Again (1961) Bittersweet tearjerker from Francoise Sagan's novel set in Paris, where a 40-year-old interior decorator (Ingrid Bergman), fearing growing old alone and unloved, has an affair with a callow, rich American (Anthony Perkins), then settles for marriage with a longtime but unfaithful beau (Yves Montand). Directed by Anatole Litvak, the situation is lushly romantic, but the characters engage in endless self-justification of their muddled sexual relationships. Empty moralizing about love and relationships. A-III (br)

Goodbye, Columbus (1969) Uncompromising screen version of Philip Roth's novel about the generation gap in early 1960s America in a story about an affluent Jewish family whose daughter (Ali MacGraw) is pursued by an ambitious young man (Richard Benjamin). The conflicting social and generational attitudes result in general disillusionment for almost everyone involved. Directed by Larry Peerce, the young couple's sexual relationship is treated quite frankly. A-IV (R/PG)

Goodbye Gemini (1970) Surrounded with an aura of evil and perversion, maladjusted twins (Judy Geeson and Martin Potter) take up residence in a London fantasy world of their own making and become involved in a series of senseless and promiscuous escapades ending in murder. Director Alan Gibson's foul black comedy is replete with rape and other violence, nudity, and implied incest. O (R)

Goodbye Girl, The (1977) Aspiring actor from Chicago (Richard Dreyfuss) sublets a New York apartment from a friend and finds it already furnished with a 33-year-old divorcée (Marsha Mason) and her 10-year-old daughter (Quinn Cummings). Neil Simon's romantic comedy, directed by Herbert Ross, is pleasant and entertaining. though unfortunately flawed by occasional vulgarities and the acceptance of premarital sex. O (PG)

Goodbye Lover (1999) Tawdry comic thriller in which a faithless husband and wife (Dermot Mulroney and Patricia Arquette) conspire to murder his brother (Don Johnson), then turn on each other as a cynical police detective (Ellen DeGeneres) watches the body count mount. Director Roland Joffe attempts to blend comedy with film *noir*, but the humor is forced, and the smug ending predictable. Jokey treatment of murder and promiscuity, kinky sexual situations with nudity, some violence, recurring profanity, and constant rough language. O (R)

Goodbye, Mr. Chips (1939) Warmly affectionate, occasionally humorous story spans 50 years in the life of a dedicated but stodgy classics teacher (Robert Donat) whose love of learning eventually wins the respect and devotion of students, faculty, and the woman who becomes his supportive wife (Greer Garson). Directed by Sam Woods, this tribute to the teaching profession still touches the emotions, largely because of Donat's charmingly low-keyed, Oscar-winning performance. A-I (nr)

Goodbye, Mr. Chips (1969) Musical version of the James Hilton novel with Peter O'Toole as the distracted, unbending schoolmaster who is set upon, conquered, and finally humanized by a hoydenish music-hall performer (Petula Clark). Director Herbert Ross shifts the focus from the academic to the happy marriage of such unlikely opposites, with pleasantly unobtrusive songs by Leslie Bricusse pacing an old-fashioned romance some will find quite charming, though youngsters are less apt to be enchanted by the sentimental proceedings. A-I (G)

Goodbye, My Fancy (1951) Turgid romantic melodrama about a high-powered Congresswoman (Joan Crawford) accepting an honorary degree from a college whose dean (Robert Young) she had loved as a student, while a photographer (Frank Lovejoy) covering the event is another of her old flames. Directed by Vincent Sherman, the characters are as contrived as the plot's hokey triangle, though the college setting provides some period nostalgia and reminders of women's struggle for equality. Romantic complications. A-II (br)

Goodbye, Norma Jean (1976) Director Larry Buchanan's obsessive exploitation of the speculative and sordid details of Marilyn Monroe's rise to stardom is a dreadful little film trading on tabloid sensationalism, sexual intimacies, and demeaning images of women. O (R)

GoodFellas (1990) The heady rise — and eventual downfall — of three Brooklyn hoods (Ray Liotta, Robert De Niro, and Joe Pesci) are shown from one gangster's warped point of view in this fact-based story spanning 30 years. Director Martin Scorsese synthesizes flowing cinematography, an eye for details, and commanding performances into a chilling re-creation of the empty glamour, endless greed, and sick violence that characterizes mob life. Much graphic violence and rough language. A-IV (R)

Goofy Movie, A (1995) One of the stalwarts of the early Mickey Mouse cartoons was the sweetly dizzy pooch Goofy, who deserves better than this flat, hokey animated feature which transforms him into a dopey single dad (voice of Bill Farmer) trying to win over his surly adolescent son, Max (voice of Jason Marsden). Directed by Kevin Lima, the tiresome story revolves around a camping trip upon which the dull father drags the unwilling son who's nursing a bad case of puppy love, which sets up some saccharine songs, a couple of slapstick near-disasters on the road, and an occasional weak smile. A few scary moments for preschoolers and much tedium for the rest of the family. A-I (G)

Goonies, The (1985) A gang of kids search for pirate treasure to save their homes from foreclosure. A scaled-down version of **Indiana Jones** aimed squarely at children, but many parents will have reservations about exposing their preteens to the vulgar expletives that pepper the dialogue, supposedly as all part of the fun. A-II (PG)

Gordon's War (1973) Former Green Beret captain (Paul Winfield) declares war on Harlem drug-pushers with the help of three other Vietnam vets (Carl Lee, Tony King, and David Dowling). It is unfortunate that the movie dishes up so much unrelenting street violence, frank nudity, and unconscious acceptance of the hero as righteous avenger, because director Ossie Davis obviously has a moral point to make about the social evil of substance addiction. O (R)

Gordy (1995) Formula family movie in which the title's talking piglet sets off to rescue his family from the slaughterhouse, is helped along the way by the daughter (Kristy Young) of a country musician (Doug Stone), and eventually becomes a national celebrity before resuming his original quest. Directed by Mark Lewis, the busy cornpone narrative depends entirely upon the willingness to accept the fantasy of a cute talking-animal, something youngsters may find more congenial than their elders. Some comic menace and threatening images of a sausage factory. A-I (G)

Gorgo (1961) A sea captain (Bill Travers) captures a gigantic prehistoric monster off the coast of Ireland and sells it to a London circus, but not even Britain's military might can save the city from destruction when the monster's mother comes looking for its missing youngster. Directed by Eugene Lourie, the British production's low-budget special effects suit the unpretentious nature of the fantasy and, indeed, add a measure of sympathy, if not charm, to the put-upon monsters. Tense crowd scenes and much damage to models of London landmarks. A-I (br)

Gorgon, The (1964) Sluggish British horror movie in which the ancient Greek monster of the title takes over the body of a young woman (Barbara Shelley) in a turn-of-the-century German town and begins turning its residents to stone. Director Terence Fisher concentrates on the clash between the town doctor (Peter Cushing) who wants to hush matters up and a university professor (Christopher Lee) who wants to stop them. Unconvincing menace and occasional stylized violence. A-II (br)

Gorilla, The (1939) Creaky comic thriller directed by Allan Dwan has a trio of knuckle-headed detectives (the Ritz Brothers) guarding a financier (Lionel Atwill) from death threats in a spooky mansion containing the man's niece (Anita Louise), sinister butler (Bela Lugosi), nervous maid (Patsy Kelly), and a mysterious intruder (Joseph Calleia). Menacing atmosphere with few thrills and even fewer laughs. A-II (br)

Gorilla at Large (1954) Mystery clunker about brutal murders in an amusement park whose owner (Anne Bancroft) does a trapeze act with a gorilla blamed for the crimes, though there are plenty of human suspects (Cameron Mitchell, Raymond Burr, and others). Directed by Harmon Jones, the hokey plot is full of holes, and the solution isn't worth the bother. Stylized violence, mild menace, and unsavory sexual innuendo. A-III (br)

Gorillas in the Mist: The Adventure of Dian Fossey (1988) Sigourney Weaver stars as Dian Fossey, whose dedication over 18 years to saving the endangered mountain gorillas of central Africa alienated many and ended tragically with her murder in 1985. Sensitive direction by Michael Apted and Weaver's fine performance make this an inspiring but heartrending account of human courage and an unwavering commitment to wildlife preservation. An adulterous love affair, much rough language, and explicit attacks against gorillas. A-III (PG-13)

Gorky Park (1983) Disappointing adaptation of the Martin Cruz novel about murder in Moscow, with William Hurt playing the honest, apolitical detective in charge of the investigation, but his listless, mannered portrayal proves deadening. Director Michael Apted reduces Cruz's ingenious story to a run-of-the-mill mystery with a brief but graphic love scene, some violence, and several gruesome sequences involving corpses. A-IV (R)

Gospa (1995) When reported visions of Mary draw throngs of pilgrims to Medjugorje in 1981, Yugoslavia's communist authorities ban them as illegal public assemblies, then put the local pastor (Martin Sheen) on trial for breaking the law. The Croatian production directed by Jakov Sedlar uses the visions as the context for a melodramatic story, more political than spiritual, in which the priest stands up for his faith and his fellow Croatians by defying an unjust Serbian-led regime. Stylized violence and murky political machinations. A-II (PG)

Gospel According to St. Matthew, The (1966) Straightforward Italian dramatization of the evangelist's account of the life of Jesus and His message of salvation. It succeeds exceptionally well in placing the viewer within the Gospel events, avoiding the artificiality of most biblical movie epics. Director Pier Paolo Pasolini is completely faithful to the text while employing the visual imagination necessary for his realistic interpretation. Subtitles. A-I (nr)

Gospel According to Vic, The (1987) Tom Conti is a schoolmaster teaching learning-impaired children in a school in Scotland. Pride and public opinion lead him to believe that he's a miracle worker, but he slowly discovers that his special gifts of love, courage, and generosity are so rare that they are often mistaken for divine providence. Some profanity and implied sex impose upon an otherwise thoroughly gentle and uplifting story. A-III (PG-13)

Gospel Road (1973) Produced by Johnny Cash and filmed in locales around Jerusalem, the movie is a very personal and sincere interpretation of the public ministry of Jesus Christ. Directed by Robert Elfstrom (who is often seen as the Christ figure), it avoids for the most part a literal portrayal of the events of the New Testament and wisely opts for a symbolic visualization. Cash appears as on-screen narrator as well as vocalist backed by a country-folk musical score and the result reflects, better than most, the spirit of the Gospels. A-I (G)

Gotcha! (1985) A college boy (Anthony Edwards), eager to rid himself of his virginity, vacations in Europe, meets an agreeable older woman, but becomes the target of real bullets instead of the liquid air-gun pellets used in a campus game called "Gotcha." Director Jeff Kanew's sophomoric fantasy is neither funny nor exciting. Benign view of sexual promiscuity. O (PG-13)

Gothic (1987) Director Ken Russell's muddled exploration of the nightmarish roots of creativity is set during a Victorian-era weekend visit by poet Percy Shelley and fiancé Mary to the weird villa of Lord Byron. This grotesque vision of the darker side of the imagination features an unpleasant mix of nudity in a sexual context, images of death, deprivation, and degeneracy. O (R)

Government Girl (1943) Creaky wartime morale booster is set in overcrowded Washington, D.C., where a Detroit executive (Sunny Tufts) boosts bomber production by cutting through government red tape, which almost gets him fired until his secretary (Olivia de Havilland) defends him. Written, produced, and directed by Dudley Nichols, the result is an embarrassing mix of patriotic sloganeering, witless satire, and inept slapstick comedy. Mild sexual innuendo. A-II (br)

Grace of My Heart (1996) Hard-knocks music tale spans the years 1958-70, during which a songwriter (Illeana Douglas) with singing ambitions gains professional success while undergoing personal setbacks on the road to finding inner strength and her own true voice. Writer-director Allison Anders's familiar story is quite well-acted but suffers from predictability and sluggish pacing. Mature themes, including marital infidelity, abortion, and suicide, as well as intermittent rough language and profanity. A-IV (R)

Grace Quigley (1985) Aged widow (Katharine Hepburn) hires a professional hit-man (Nick Nolte) to do her in and then becomes his agent. A satiric comedy that went dreadfully wrong, despite the efforts of director Anthony Harvey and talented cast. Because of the movie's ineptness and its lack of satiric point, the view of suicide is more benign than not. O (PG)

Graduate, The (1968) Fresh out of college, an aimless middle-class youth (Dustin Hoffman) is seduced by a suburban housewife (Anne Bancroft) but redeemed by his love for her daughter (Katharine Ross). Directed by Mike Nichols, this satiric tale of an innocent in a corrupt world harpoons the emptiness of materialistic values but offers little in its place. Questionable treatment of adultery and some strong language. A-IV (PG)

Graffiti Bridge (1990) A brooding musician (Prince) and a rival rock-artist (Morris Day) compete over ownership of a dance club and the attentions of an elusive girl (Ingrid Chavez). Also written and directed by Prince, this vanity production is simply a feature-length music video with sleekly expressionistic visuals, catchy choreography, and awful acting. Females depicted primarily as sex objects and suggestive dancing. A-III (PG-13)

Grand Canyon (1991) Contemporary drama featuring an ensemble cast (Danny Glover, Kevin Kline, Steve Martin, Mary McDonnell, and Alfre Woodard) grappling with increasing lawlessness in a big city as they weather personal mid-life crises. Though the pace is sluggish, director Lawrence Kasdan credibly blends some dozen characters and situations for a sobering but ultimately hopeful look at the fragility of modern life. Brief violence, adulterous references, momentary nudity, and recurring rough language. A-III (R)

Grand Illusion (1937) Shot down during WW I, a French aristocrat (Pierre Fresnay) is treated as a brother officer by the German aristocrat (Erich von Stroheim) commanding the prisoner-of-war camp, then makes use of his special status to distract attention while two fellow prisoners (Jean Gabin and Dalio) make good their escape to Switzerland. Directed by Jean Renoir, the picture of life in the camp is rich in narrative incident and human detail, neatly supporting a theme dealing with the end of the aristocratic ideal of chivalry and its replacement by mass armies of commoners with no desire for war. Subtitles. Some ribald humor and tense situations. A-II (br)

Grand Prix (1967) Large-scale production takes viewers around the 10 courses of Europe's Grand Prix auto-racing circuit that conveys in almost documentary fashion the experience of racing. Director John Frankenheimer interweaves the story of four drivers (Yves Montand, James Garner, Brian Bedford, and Antonio Sabata) but is less successful with their off-track romances. A-III (br)

Grand Slam (1968) European production in which a retired teacher (Edward G. Robinson) plans the complex robbery of a Brazilian diamond firm during the time of the Rio Carnival and with some inside assistance (Janet Leigh). Tautly directed by Giuliano Montaldo, crime does not pay, but a seduction scene is not for youngsters. A-III (br)

Grapes of Wrath, The (1940) Outstanding adaptation of John Steinbeck's novel about an Okie family who lose their farm and join other Dust Bowl refugees on the road to exploitation as migrant workers. Told with gritty realism but with a compassion that still engages viewers a half-century later, director John Ford's definitive portrait of uprooted and dispossessed Americans during the Depression features compelling performances by a superior cast, including Henry Fonda as young Tom Joad, perplexed and angry that people are starving in a land of plenty, and Jane Darwell as the formidable Ma Joad, whose perseverance and optimism keep the family together. Brutalizing conditions of poverty and some violence. A-II (nr)

Grass Harp, The (1996) Screen version of Truman Capote's 1951 novel about an orphaned boy (Edward Furlong) growing up in a small Southern town during the Depression, looked after by two spinster sisters (Piper Laurie and Sissy Spacek) whose tranquil home is suddenly shattered by a terrible dispute between them, forcing him and the rest of the town to take sides. Directed by Charles Matthau, the result is a lovely little movie re-creating the charms of a past era without sentimentalizing its account of the boy's encounters with the adult world and odd behavior of his quirky elders (including retired judge Walter Matthau, swindler Jack Lemmon, servant Nell Carter, and barber Roddy McDowall). Some violence and strong domestic tension. A-II (PG)

Grass Is Greener, The (1960) Lackluster romantic comedy in which a British aristocrat (Cary Grant) is pursued by a friendly local lass (Jean Simmons) while his wife (Deborah Kerr) is being charmed by a visiting American (Robert Mitchum), with predictable results. Directed by Stanley Donen, there is little humor and less wit in the shallow characters and their unconvincing amorous temptations. Comic treatment of marital fidelity. A-III (br)

Grasshopper, The (1970) Small-town Canadian girl Jacqueline Bisset comes to Los Angeles for romance, but ends up as a showgirl who becomes an executive's mistress and then a prostitute. Director Jerry Paris's sordid and pessimistic melodrama resorts to frequent use of nudity. O (R)

Grave Indiscretion (see: **Gentlemen Don't Eat Poets**)

Grave Robbers from Outer Space (see: **Plan 9 from Outer Space**)

Grave Secrets (1990) Muddled thriller directed by Donald P. Borchers goes nowhere with the dull tale of a psychic researcher (Paul LeMat) aiding a woman (Renee Soutendijk) haunted by a headless ghost. Off-screen murder and infanticide, with a few spooky special effects. A-III (R)

Graveyard Shift (see **Stephen King's Graveyard Shift**)

Gravy Train, The (1974) Pair of brothers from the hills of West Virginia (Stacy Keach and Frederic Forrest) join in a complex armored-car robbery only to be ripped off by the caper's mastermind (Barry Primus). What follows is a downhill race against time to intercept the loot before it is sold to a fence. Director Jack Starrett has an eye for pell-mell action and an ear for racy backwoods expletives and witticisms. But the killings and cursing, plus a gratuitous massage parlor visit, tends to put a sour edge on the action. A-IV (R)

Gray Lady Down (1978) Reconditioned nuclear submarine on a shakedown cruise is struck by a freighter and sinks into a deep sea-canyon, from which the Navy tries to rescue the survivors. Charlton Heston, as the sub commander, and Stacy Keach, as the officer in charge of the rescue operation, are properly taut-jawed and grimly heroic, while for variety's sake, David Carradine is relaxed and cheerfully heroic as the pilot of a small experimental submarine. Director David Greene plumbs the depths and comes up with some fairly good entertainment. A-II (PG)

Gray's Anatomy (1997) Screen version of Spaulding Gray's one-man stage-play chronicling how he sought to avoid a delicate eye-operation by trying a series of alternative therapies, including a Native American sweating ceremony and the dubious intervention of a Filipino psychic surgeon. Director Steven Soderburgh relies on an array of changing backgrounds for visual interest as Gray deftly blends neurotic narcissism with self-deprecating humor in telling a story that is wry, dry, and usually engaging. Some sexual references and an anecdote about substance abuse. A-III (nr)

Grayeagle (1978) A dying Indian chief commissions a warrior to kidnap a supposed white woman who is, in fact, his daughter so that he might see her before he dies. Not even the presence of Ben Johnson helps this embarrassingly bad Western written, produced, and directed by Charles B. Pierce (who also does some dreadful acting in it). Violence and some partial nudity make it a tall tale for adults. A-III (PG)

Grazie Zia (1969) Ironic Italian fable about a rich young psychopath (Lou Castel) who torments his attractive aunt (Lisa Gastoni), a doctor trying to cure his affliction. Director Salvatore Samperi reduces the theme of good and evil to a unrelenting series of sexual games and perverse role-reversals ending in self-destruction. O (PG)

Grease (1978) Nostalgic 1950s musical romance in which John Travolta plays the leader of a slick-haired, leather-jacketed gang, and Olivia Newton-John is a sweet high-school transfer student from Australia whose attraction for him transforms her into a tough, sensual leather groupie. Though director Randal Kleiser plays it for simple-minded fun, the teen fantasy glamorizes negative role models and is preoccupied with sex in its dialogue and lyrics. O (PG)

Grease 2 (1982) Taking up where the original musical left off, an English youth (Maxwell Caulfield) enrolls at Rydel High School and learns to ride a motorcycle to impress his girlfriend (Michelle Pfeiffer). Set in the 1960s, director Patricia Birch's movie is bland and synthetic, but its gaping moral vacuum, emphasis on conformity at all costs, and sexual innuendo in the lyrics make it unsuitable for younger viewers. A-III (PG)

Greased Lightning (1977) The usually comic Richard Pryor gives an extremely restrained and effective performance as a stock-car racer in the deep South who has to overcome racial prejudice to succeed. Despite director Michael Schultz's blunting of the story's conflict and tension by inappropriate humor, Pryor's charm and skill along with an excellent supporting cast provide some buoyant and entertaining moments. A-II (PG)

Greaser's Palace (1972) Director Robert Downey's wacky fable juxtaposes the old movie West with the Second Coming of Christ (by parachute), a comic concept that deteriorates into a meandering string of sight gags. Those who find nothing funny in religious irreverence should be warned that this is definitely not their movie. Some explicit sexual and scatological references are excessive. O (nr)

Great Balls of Fire! (1989) Director Jim McBride's biography of rock legend Jerry Lee Lewis (Dennis Quaid) sacrifices a serious look at the troubled musician for glossy, romanticized pop entertainment. Little is made of the fact that radio stations in the late 1950s banned his records for being sexually suggestive. Also glossed over is his controversial marriage to his 13-year-old second cousin (Winona Ryder), which led to his career doldrums. Sexual innuendo, brief violence, and a sexually suggestive encounter. A-III (PG-13)

Great Bank Hoax, The (1979) Fine but ill-used cast headed by Ned Beatty, Burgess Meredith, and Michael Murphy is unable to get anything but a mild chuckle or two from this leaden-paced, awkward comedy about an attempt to cover up an embezzlement by staging a mock robbery. Director Joseph Jacoby adds an adult flavor to the jokes and slapstick situations. A-III (PG)

Great Bank Robbery, The (1969) Sophomoric Western spoof stars Zero Mostel and Kim Novak as the Rev. Pious Blue and Sister Lyda who try to save a small Western town from themselves as well as from some bandits. Directed by Hy Averback, a seduction sequence, a tasteless comic nude scene, and double-entendre sermonizing are not for youngsters, and probably most adults. A-III (PG)

Great Battle, The (1974) Inept Soviet dramatization depicting the bitter and dramatic siege of the Russian city of Kursk by German forces in 1943. The badly dubbed movie has little interest either historically or dramatically, and its scenes of carnage are not for young children. A-II (PG)

Great Catherine (1969) Chaotic flight-of-fancy based on George Bernard Shaw's bedroom farce opposes Peter O'Toole as a British dragoon and Jeanne Moreau as the 18th-century Russian empress. Director Gordon Flemyng manages to erode Shaw's fragile, pungent satire of pompous British aristocracy and unbridled Russian passion with slapstick humor, frantic chases, and crude caricatures. A-III (G)

Great Chase, The (1963) Choice chase scenes from the silent screen's weekly adventure serials, Mack Sennett comedies, and such features as D.W. Griffith's **Way Down East**, Douglas Fairbanks's **The Mark of Zorro**, W.S. Hart's **Tumbleweeds**, and Buster Keaton's **The General**. Written and edited by Harvey Cort, the compilation offers some fine action-highlights from movies relying more on creative imagination than special-effects technology. Menacing situations may frighten young children. A-I (br)

Great Dan Patch, The (1949) Routine tale about the title racehorse as it's raised by an Indiana farmer (Henry Hull) and turned into a champion by the man's son (Dennis O'Keefe), whose financial problems later force him to sell the horse which is celebrated as the greatest pacer of all time when it's retired in 1906. Directed by Joe Newman, the racing lore is well-handled, but the story's focus is on the son's unhappy marriage to a snob (Ruth Warrick) and his growing love for a horse-trainer's daughter (Gail Russell). Divorce in the plot resolution. A-III (br)

Great Dictator, The (1940) In this satirical indictment of Nazi totalitarianism, writer-producer-director Charles Chaplin plays dual roles as Hynkel, a European dictator modeled on Hitler, and as the lookalike Jewish barber who takes his place. As the barber's lady-love, Paulette Goddard shines luminously, even when banging storm-troopers over the head with a frying pan, and Jack Oakie steals some scenes with a goofy Mussolini take-off. Its treatment of serious themes makes it unlikely fare for the very young. A-II (G)

Great Escape, The (1963) Thrilling rendition of a fact-based story about an elaborate escape of Allied prisoners from a German POW camp during WW II. Steve McQueen is the most ambitious of a crew that includes James Garner, Charles Bronson, James Coburn, and Richard Attenborough as they plot a mass escape which becomes an intriguing, highly entertaining suspense gripper. With John Sturges directing, it all builds to a stunning, sobering climax that both tugs at the heart and keeps it racing. A-I (br)

Great Expectations (1998) In this reworked and updated version of the Charles Dickens classic, a poor Florida youth (Ethan Hawke) is given the chance to make good in the New York art world, thanks to an anonymous patron (Robert De Niro), but his expectations center on winning the love of the cruel girl (Gwyneth Paltrow) he has idealized from his youth. Directed by Alfonso Cuaron, the movie keeps the core of Dickens's story while making considerable changes in adapting it to a contemporary American setting, but the coming-of-age tale that results is dramatically uneven and the characters uncompelling. Stylized violence, sexual situations, brief nudity, occasional profanity, and some rough language. A-III (R)

Great Flamarion, The (1945) Moody melodrama in which a carnival sharpshooter (Erich von Stroheim) is seduced by his lovely assistant (Mary Beth Hughes) who persuades him to kill her husband (Dan Duryea), then takes a powder, leaving him broke and obsessed with revenge. Directed by Anthony Mann, Stroheim's strong performance as the man undone by a bad woman almost makes it worth seeing. Stylized violence and sexual innuendo. A-III (br)

Great Gatsby, The (1974) Lavish but disappointing screen version of F. Scott Fitzgerald's novel about the fatally ill-matched love of a millionaire (Robert Redford) for another man's wife (Mia Farrow). Director Jack Clayton's lush production gives more attention to the movie's set design and costuming than to Francis Ford Coppola's very literate but frequently literal adaptation. The result is beautiful to watch but proves an empty experience. Mature themes. A-III (PG)

Great Gildersleeve, The (1943) Lackluster movie version of a radio comedy-series about the pompous but goodhearted title character (Harold Peary) who faces losing custody of his orphaned niece and nephew unless he marries the judge's daughter (Mary Field). Director Gordon Douglas manages only a few genuine chuckles from a comic vehicle that has dated badly. Unexceptional family fare. A-I (br)

Great Guy (1936) Routine melodrama directed by John G. Blystone with James Cagney as the feisty head of the city bureau of weights and measures who takes on a corrupt gang of chiselers (headed by Henry Kolker) with some help from his girlfriend (Mae Clarke) and an old pal (Edward Brophy). Stylized violence. A-I (br)

Great Imposter, The (1960) Intriguing fact-based story of Ferdinand W. Demara, Jr. (Tony Curtis), who carried off his curious compulsion to assume false identities with convincing assurance as military officer, Trappist novice, prison warden, doctor on a Canadian warship, and schoolteacher. Director Robert Mulligan uses a fine supporting cast to give weight to the circumstances of each impersonation, with Curtis easy to take in the role of a likeable fraud who uses bogus credentials in ways that help others. Some menace and mild romantic complications. A-II (br)

Great Lover, The (1949) Mild comic thriller with Bob Hope as the dimwitted leader of a boy's scouting troop aboard an ocean-liner, where he gets involved with a cunning high-stakes murderer (Roland Young) while trying to romance an amiable duchess (Rhonda Fleming). Director Alexander Hall centers on Hope's blundering ineptitudes, which comically confound the proceedings until inevitably saving the day. Stylized violence and mild romantic complications. A-II (br)

Great Man, The (1957) Talky melodrama about a radio journalist (Jose Ferrer) hired to do a memorial program about a popular network broadcaster after his sudden death, who then has qualms of conscience when interviews with those who knew him reveal that the man was a heel and his career a fraud. Also directed by Ferrer, it's a smug variation on **Citizen Kane** without the flashbacks and moral ambiguity, despite a standout bit from Ed Wynn as a decent human being in the broadcast business. Private vices of a public figure. A-II (br)

Great Man Votes, The (1939) Dated but enjoyable fable on the virtues of democracy and the strength of family ties is set in 1923, when a city election swings on the vote of an alcoholic ex-Harvard professor (John Barrymore) whose bright but practical children (Virginia Wedler and Peter Holden) help him rise to the occasion. Director Garson Kanin gets a roguishly winning performance from Barrymore, abetted by blustery Donald MacBride as the local ward-heeler and a lightweight but heartwarming script. Cheerful family fun, despite the comic treatment of Prohibition-era intemperance. A-I (br)

Great Man's Lady, The (1942) Western sudser in which a 100-year-old recluse (Barbara Stanwyck) tells an aspiring biographer (Katharine Stevens) the secret of her marriage to a famous pioneer (Joel McCrea) who, after making a rich silver strike, had been mistakenly told of her death, remarried, and embarked on a political career which she protected over the years by her silence. Director William A. Wellman can't hold the contrived, episodic plot together, especially the title character's ambiguous friendship with a gambler (Brian Donlevy), though individual scenes and period characters have interest. Domestic difficulties. A-II (br)

Great McGinty, The (1940) Wacky political spoof in which an enterprising soup-line refugee (Brian Donlevy) is hired as a muscleman by a big-city machine boss (Akim Tamiroff), then takes over the organization, gets elected governor, and is undone only when he decides to run an honest administration. Written and directed by Preston Sturges, the daffy turns of fortune are as incongruous and untidy as the political corruption they satirize, all of which is treated with bemused wonderment rather than cynical disdain. Tongue-in-cheek electoral hijinks and minor stylized violence. A-II (br)

Great McGonagall, The (1975) Spike Milligan directs and stars in an offbeat movie about a poor 19th-century Scottish weaver who late in life gives up everything to write truly atrocious poetry and dies unknown and impoverished. Milligan's comedy lacks the anarchistic zest of his glory days on BBC radio and only occasionally reflects the madcap fancy of simpler times. A brief nude dance only compounds the movie's many problems. O (nr)

Great Mouse Detective, The (1986) Disney animated feature relates the adventures of Basil of Baker Street (voice of Barrie Ingham), the Sherlock Holmes of mouse-land, while rescuing a little-girl mouse's kidnapped father from the nefarious Professor Ratigan (voice of Vincent Price). While not one of Disney's finest, producer/co-director Burny Mattinson's sprightly take-off on the Holmes stories still manages charming characterizations throughout. A-I (G)

Great Muppet Caper, The (1981) Jim Henson directs his incomparable cast of Muppets as wisecracking Kermit and song-and-dance lady Miss Piggy lead the troupe off to England to thwart Charles Grodin's plan to rob fashion queen Diana Rigg of her jewels. Great silly fun for adults and children. A-I (G)

Great Northfield, Minnesota Raid, The (1972) Western melodrama about one of the last of the great outlaw bands contrasts the nonviolent, philosophical

Cole Younger (Cliff Robertson) and the murderous, Bible-spouting Jesse James (Robert Duvall). Director Philip Kaufman's mix of character study and a demythologizing of the frontier experience has many good moments but is flawed and derivative. Graphic violence and some incidental nudity. A-III (PG)

Great Outdoors, The (1988) Director Howard Deutch chronicles the botched summer vacation spent by two mismatched brothers-in-law (John Candy and Dan Aykroyd) and their families in the Canadian North Woods. Scripted by John Hughes, the humor comes from its two stars whose characters seem to be hilarious retreads from "Saturday Night Live." Some vulgar language. A-II (PG)

Great Race, The (1965) Slapstick potpourri of sight gags and broad characterizations abound in a turn-of-the-century automobile race from New York to Paris via Alaska, Russia, and western Europe. While Tony Curtis and Jack Lemmon ham it up outrageously as the chief racing rivals, Blake Edwards directs the low comedy-farce in high-comedy style. A-I (nr)

Great Santini, The (1980) Solid portrait of a gung-ho but aging Marine fighter-pilot (Robert Duvall) who, having no war to fight in 1962, brings his own war home to cause conflict with his wife (Blythe Danner), and especially his teenage son (Michael O'Keefe). Though flawed with some heavy melodrama and a contrived resolution, director John Lewis Carlino's story of family life has much heart, strong values, warm humor, and three marvelous performances to more than compensate. Some rough language and the intensity of emotional family conflict. A-II (PG)

Great Scout and Cathouse Thursday, The (1976) Lee Marvin plays a veteran scout out to avenge a swindle worked on him by former partner Robert Culp, but in the process he falls in love with a young prostitute. Director Don Taylor's Western spoof is tedious, unfunny, occasionally brutal, and unremittingly vulgar in its attempts at bawdy hijinks. O (PG)

Great Sioux Massacre, The (1965) After the death of Col. Custer (Philip Carey) and 251 of his men at the Little Big Horn, an Army court of inquiry learns how it happened from two officers (Joseph Cotten and Darren McGavin) who survived the attack. Directed by Sidney Salkow, the dramatization depicts Custer as a glory-seeker whose political ambitions led to the massacre, but the action scenes are largely unconvincing. Frontier violence, including Army and civilian atrocities against Indians. A-II (br)

Great Sioux Uprising, The (1953) When a greedy rancher (Lyle Bettger) steals a herd of Sioux ponies to sell to the Union cavalry during the Civil War, the local veterinarian (Jeff Chandler) teams with a horse dealer (Faith Domergue) to keep the peace. Directed by Lloyd Bacon, the pedestrian narrative offers little but stock characters and an unimaginative plot. Frontier violence. A-I (br)

Great Schnozzle, The (see: **Palooka**)

Great Spy Chase, The (1966) Flat French spy-spoof directed by Georges Lautner in which the world's leading secret agents pursue the blonde widow (Mireille Darc) of a manufacturer who left her his papers on a devastating new weapon. Much sexual innuendo. A-III (br)

Great Texas Dynamite Chase, The (1977) Two young women carry out a bank-robbing spree and live happily ever after. Despite oafish attempts at tongue-in-cheek satire, director Michael Pressman's farce sinks into gratuitous sex and violence with degrading female stereotypes. O (R)

Great Train Robbery, The (1979) Sean Connery stars as a debonair Victorian con-man who carries off the first high-speed train robbery in history, with the aid of accomplished locksmith Donald Sutherland and girlfriend Lesley Anne Down. British production boasts hair-raising hijinks and an impressive re-creation of the period by director-writer Michael Crichton. There is a fair amount of lighthearted double entendres and an acceptance of less-than-virtuous behavior. A-III (PG)

Great Waldo Pepper, The (1975) Robert Redford stars as a 1920s stunt pilot who realizes his fantasy of meeting a great German ace in air combat. Director George Roy Hill's movie is rather flat, but its aerial photography of the great old biplanes is entertainment enough. Some strong language. A-III (PG)

Great Wall, A (1986) Gentle but keenly observed comedy of cultural collision when a Chinese-American family visits relatives in Peking in the first American feature produced its mainland China. Directed by Peter Wang, the movie provides an entertaining and informative dissection of the humorous pitfalls of stereotyping. A-I (PG)

Great Waltz, The (1938) In 1845 Vienna, composer Johann Strauss II (Fernand Gravet) finds a publisher (Hugh Herbert) for his waltz music, marries his sweetheart (Luise Rainer), then is saved from arrest as a revolutionary by an opera singer (Miliza Korjus) with whom he falls in love, until his adoring wife finally intervenes. Directed by Julien Duvivier, the period drama is visually rich and well-acted, the romantic triangle is delicately handled, and the action is paced by the lovely music of Strauss's Viennese waltzes. Romantic complications. A-II (br)

Great Waltz, The (1972) Failed musical extravaganza tracing the life and times of 19th-century German composer Johann Strauss II, from when he first eclipsed his father as the most popular songwriter of Old Vienna, through the middle period when Strauss chased skirts and the muse with equal fervor, to his moment of triumph when he presented "On the Beautiful Blue Danube" at the 1872 Boston World Peace Jubilee. Horst Bucholz as Strauss looks like he is ready to gag on a steady diet of producer-writer-director Andrew L. Stone's preposterous dialogue. And the audience might gag on the saccharine treatment of this controversial composer's life. A-II (G)

Great White Hope, The (1970) Fictionalized but hardly sanitized story based on the life of prizefighter and onetime heavyweight champion of the world Jack Johnson, here named Jack Jefferson. Set in the early decades of the century, the narrative traces the swift rise and sudden, prolonged fall of the giant black boxer, played with burning intensity by James Earl Jones. Directed by Martin Ritt, the movie is a stinging indictment of the racial attitudes of the time. A strong film both visually and verbally, it should be approached with clear eyes and an open mind. A-III (GP/PG-13)

Great White Hype, The (1996) Scatterbrained spoof of prizefighting as a tacky slice of show business has a greedy promoter (Samuel L. Jackson) go for the big bucks by ballyhooing a match between the black heavyweight champ (Damon Wayans) and an unlikely white contender (Peter Berg) who once boxed as an amateur. Directed by Reginald Hudlin, the comic send-up of the fight game ranges from low farce to high comedy in a loose grab-bag of uneven sketches on a subject which itself borders on self-parody. Pugilistic violence, sexual situations, ethnic and racial jibes, profanity, and much rough language. A-IV (R)

Great Ziegfeld, The (1936) The life of Broadway producer Florenz Ziegfeld (William Powell) is told in terms of the various performers he turned into headliners, including wives Anna Held (Luise Rainer) and Billie Burke (Myrna Loy). Directed by Robert Z. Leonard, the result is an eye-filling cornucopia of musical extravaganzas, stylish showgirls, and vintage acts, including Fanny Brice and Ray Bolger as themselves. Mild sexual innuendo and romantic complications. A-II (br)

Greatest, The (1977) Entertaining but rather flat and patched-together film version of Muhammad Ali's autobiography, with Ali playing himself. Director Tom Gries's dramatization seems to have simplified a great deal, and the effect is to show the heavyweight boxing champion with no warts at all. Ring violence and religious stereotyping. A-III (PG)

Greatest Story Ever Told, The (1965) While not the greatest movie ever made, director George Stevens's vision of the Gospel story presents a consistent, traditional view of Christ as the God Incarnate. The movie, despite its epic Hollywood scale, is well-acted, tastefully and realistically written, beautifully photographed, and Max von Sydow's believable portrayal of the Christ is the most essential element in its success. A-I (G)

Greed (1924) Director Erich von Stroheim's silent masterpiece is based on the Frank Norris novel *McTeague*, about a self-taught San Francisco dentist who loses his license because of a jealous friend, is driven by poverty to kill his miserly wife and escape with her money into the scorching desert wastes of Death Valley in one of the screen's most memorable endings. Though cut by the studio from ten hours to two, the realism of the result has an almost documentary quality in what it shows of America at the turn of the century, especially its materialistic values and their corrupting influence on the human person. Powerful parable on the wages of greed, with a few scenes of intense but non-graphic violence. A-II (br)

Greedy (1994) Failed comedy about a cagey multimillionaire (Kirk Douglas) whose grasping relatives lure his favorite nephew (Michael J. Fox) home to distract the old codger from a sexy young companion (Olivia d'Abo) who poses a threat to their inheritance. Director Jonathan Lynn gets slack results from a dreary combination of predictable proceedings, plodding pace, and perfunctory performances. A premarital relationship, frequent sexual innuendo, flash of nudity, brief comic violence, and an instance of rough language. A-III (PG-13)

Greek Tycoon (1978) Tabloid melodrama in which a Greek shipping-magnate (Anthony Quinn) woos and wins the chic widow (Jacqueline Bisset) of an assassinated president of the United States. Directed by J. Lee Thompson, the movie is trashy to the core in its shameless trafficking in actual events viewed through the distorting glass of malicious gossip and innuendo, compounded by rough language and a graphic nude scene. O (R)

Green Berets, The (1968) John Wayne stars in and co-directs (with Ray Kellogg) this ghastly commercial for US involvement in Vietnam. Based on the popular Robin Moore novel, the movie follows Wayne and his green-bereted force as they slaughter wave upon wave of slant-eyed commies. Racial stereotyping and wartime violence depicted in much the same manner as the old Hollywood WW II movies set in the Pacific. A-III (G)

Green Card (1990) Unexpected romance develops after two strangers marry in name only so he (Gerard Depardieu) can remain in the US and she (Andie MacDowell) can move into a marrieds-only apartment. Written, produced, and directed by Peter Weir, the outcome is never in doubt, but the rocky road to love makes a sweet journey in this light-as-air romantic comedy. Mild sexual innuendo and minimal rough language. A-III (PG-13)

Green Fire (1954) Soggy adventure in Columbia's backcountry, where a pair of engineers (Stewart Granger and Paul Douglas) tunnel into a mountain searching for a lost emerald mine despite bandits, cave-ins, and the owner (Grace Kelly) of a coffee plantation in the valley below. Though director Andrew Marton makes the action in the wilderness setting seem credible, there is little he can do with an unconvincing plot and its cardboard characters. Some stylized violence, menacing situations, and mild romantic complications. A-II (br)

Green for Danger (1946) British murder mystery with a devious Scotland Yard inspector (Alastair Sim) ferreting out a killer among a small-town hospital staff (notably Leo Genn, Trevor Howard, and Sally Gray), with Hitler's buzz bombs adding to the tension. Director Sidney Gilliat neatly paces the suspense with some well-timed humor, though the staff's romantic involvements are the stuff of soap opera.

Minimal violence, some scary moments, and romantic situations. A-II (br)

Green Glove, The (1952) Uneven thriller set in southern France, where a former US paratrooper (Glenn Ford) gets in the way of a murderous art dealer (George Macready) who's after a jeweled gauntlet stolen from a local shrine during WW II. Directed by Rudolph Maté, the interesting French locales, taut chase scenes, and charming romantic interest (Geraldine Brooks) help compensate for the story's erratic development. Stylized violence and romantic complications. A-II (br)

Green Hell (1940) Seasoned explorer (Douglas Fairbanks) leads an expedition (Alan Hale, George Bancroft, George Sanders, Noah Berry, Jr., etc.) into the Peruvian jungle in search of pre-Incan treasures, but the local natives turn against them. The standard adventure plot is distinguished by director James Whale's effective use of exotic settings, threatening atmosphere, and a solid cast, including Joan Bennett as a romantic complication. Stylized violence and considerable menace. A-II (br)

Green Mansions (1959) Overcooked version of W.H. Hudson's turn-of-the-century romance about a political refugee (Anthony Perkins) who escapes into the Amazonian jungle, where he falls in love with a young woman (Audrey Hepburn) feared as an evil spirit by the local natives. Directed by Mel Ferrer, the romantic pretensions of the narrative are undone by the overacting of the principals, including Sessue Hayakawa and Henry Silva as tribal notables. Stylized violence and ethnic stereotyping. A-I (br)

Green Pastures, The (1936) Warmly sympathetic, gently humorous fantasy from Marc Connelly's Pulitzer Prize-winning play portraying stories from the Old Testament as imagined in the cultural idiom of black youngsters in a rural Sunday school of a long-ago segregated South. Directed by Connelly and William Keighley, the all-black cast carries off the narrative's mixture of whimsy and reverence in high style, with a commanding performance by Rex Ingram as De Lawd and appropriate gospel music by the Hall Johnson choir. Considered a positive portrayal of black folk-culture and religious feeling by audiences of the time, the work still has considerable charm and emotional appeal today, especially for those interested in the history of the African-American community. Parents, however, should be sensitive that its picture of blacks may be misunderstood as patronizing or demeaning unless seen in historical context. A-I (br)

Green Promise, The (1949) Uneven family picture in which a proud but foolish widower (Walter Brennan) moves to a farm with his four children, then makes a mess of things by refusing to take the advice of the local agricultural agent (Robert Paige). Director William D. Russell succeeds best in showing how the downtrodden youngest child (Natalie Wood) is transformed by joining in the rural community's 4-H activities, but the father's reformation after his farm is ruined by a terrible rainstorm brings the picture to an unconvincing close. A-I (br)

Green Room, The (1979) French director Francois Truffaut's adaptation of two short stories by Henry James is a philosophical meditation on the subject of death and the transcendence of the human spirit. Truffaut himself plays the WW I soldier who returns safely from the trenches to find that his wife has died. A masterful exercise in the cinema of atmosphere and characterization, but some may find the hero's obsession with death morbid. A-III (PG)

Green Slime, The (1969) A big mushroom from outer space plays the title role, with support from earthlings Robert Horton and Richard Jaeckel. Forgettable Japanese sci-fi production directed by Kinji Fukasaku. A-I (G)

Green Wall, The (1972) Young couple have carved out a homestead in the jungle of Peru's interior, fighting the lush vegetation for each acre of arable land. When their young son is bitten by a poisonous snake, the movie becomes a race to get the vaccine that will save the child, underlining the isolation of every frontier community. Writer-director Armando Robles Godoy has constructed his script around that one fateful day, with flashbacks filling out the story. Discreet lovemaking scene. A-III (R)

Green-Eyed Woman (See: **Take a Letter, Darling**)

Greenwich Village (1944) While visiting 1922 New York, a music teacher from Witchita (Don Ameche) falls for a nightclub singer (Vivian Blaine) whose boss (William Bendix) wants to use his concerto in a Broadway revue. Directed by Walter Lang, the colorful musical is thin on plot but has plenty of zestful numbers from a talented cast headed by vivacious Carmen Miranda. Romantic complications. A-II (br)

Greetings (1968) Brian De Palma directs a way-out satire on draft-dodgers, computer dating, and other aspects of 1960's society. The effort is sometimes humorous, but when wit fails, it turns to sex, nudity, and tasteless situations. O (X)

Gregory's Girl (1982) A charming movie about the travails of adolescence in urban Scotland. Written and directed by Bill Forsyth, it retains to the end its capacity to surprise with its daffy, yet at times touching, incongruity. A-II (PG)

Gremlins (1984) Bouncy, but often repulsively dark, comedy about nasty little creatures spawned by a cute, furry little Christmas gift an inventor (Hoyt Axton) buys for his son (Zach Galligan). A strained moral tale about the consequences of not following directions, the fantasy directed by Joe Dante is steeped in fierce, violent, savage sight gags which lead to mindless mischief, mayhem, and murder. A-III (PG)

Gremlins 2: The New Batch (1990) This time the fearsome creatures run amuck in a Manhattan skyscraper, where the adolescents (Zach Galligan and Phoebe Cates) from the original must save the day or the vicious gremlins will overrun the Big Apple during the night. Despite an elaborate visual design and wacky sight gags, director Joe Dante's sequel is a rather drawn-out testament to murderous mayhem, with plodding predictability, insipid characters, and an overkill quotient of violence disguised as nasty fun. Many scenes of intense menace and violence. A-III (PG-13)

Grey Fox, The (1983) Stagecoach robber (Richard Farnsworth), released after 30 years in prison into a world without stagecoaches, heads for Canada and starts robbing trains. Leisurely directed by Philip Borsos, the beautiful locales and some fine acting obscures the Canadian production's basically antisocial theme. A-III (PG)

Grey Gardens (1976) Documentary about two women, an aging mother and a middle-aged daughter, once wealthy but who now live as recluses in a crumbling mansion in an exclusive community which wants them out. Directed by Albert and David Maysles, the often moving, often troubling portrait of rugged individualism invades their privacy but presents them as noble and heroic women who refuse to compromise their ideals to the standards of society. A-III (PG)

Greyfriars Bobby (1961) Disney movie about a 19th-century dog in Scotland whose faithfulness in staying by his master's grave in an Edinburgh cemetery makes him a town legend. Director Don Chaffey's fine cast (Donald Crisp, Alex MacKenzie, Laurence Naismith, Gordon Jackson) and solid staging make it superior family entertainment that young children especially will enjoy. A-I (br)

Greystoke: The Legend of Tarzan, Lord of the Apes (1984) Director Hugh Hudson's visually stunning, extremely intelligent, well-acted retelling of the Edgar Rice Burroughs popular classic about a boy raised by apes and returned to civilization only to recoil from its moral savagery. The violence in the jungle sequences is very strong stuff, and there is also a brief bedroom sequence and some male nudity. A-III (PG)

Gridlock'd (1997) Failed comedy about two dope-addicted musicians (Tupac Shakur and Tim Roth) who halfheartedly attempt to enter a rehab program while hunted by cops for murdering their dealer and by the actual killer for stealing his heroin. In treating his lowlife addicts with boundless sympathy, writer-director Vondie Curtis Hall implies that trying to kick the habit is more trouble than it's worth. Benign view of drug abuse, some gory violence, brief nudity, a few racial epithets, and incessant rough language. O (R)

Grifters, The (1990) A mother (Anjelica Huston), her son (John Cusack), and his lover (Annette Bening) are con-artists in a bizarre triangle which gets deadly when the two women turn on each other. Director Stephen Frears's tale of twisted relationships presents a totally bleak view of humanity where decency, conscience, or even hope have no place. Intermittent intense violence, casual promiscuity with nudity, and minimal rough language. O (R)

Grimm's Fairy Tales for Adults (1971) Pretentious sex-fantasy with two impotent bumpkins seeking their fortune in the deep woods, where they have encounters with Snow White, Sleeping Beauty, and Cinderella. Director Rolf Thiele allays his own subconscious anxieties by lacing the uncouth un-doings with gory details in a German-produced strudel full of raw and rotten apples. O (nr)

Grissom Gang, The (1971) Perverse tale of a poor little rich girl (Kim Darby) who finds true love with one of her kidnappers (Scott Wilson) in director Robert Aldrich's excessively violent movie set in Prohibition-era Kansas City. O (R)

Grizzly (1976) Inept action-thriller about a 15-foot grizzly bear attacking unwary campers in a national park. Starring Christopher George and directed by William Girdler, it is no more than a tedious exercise in special-effects mayhem, totally inappropriate for youngsters. A-III (PG)

Grizzly Adams (see: **The Life and Times of Grizzly Adams**)

Grizzly Mountain (1997) Dull wilderness tale in which two youngsters (Dylan Haggerty and Nicole Lund) exploring an Oregon cave travel back in time to 1870, where they help an idealistic mountain man (Dan Haggerty) save the area from greedy developers. Directed by Jeremy Haft, the vanity production offers spectacular scenery but is marred by an inept script and wooden acting. A-I (G)

Groove Tube, The (1974) Satirical skits spoofing the state of television programming by imagining what it would be like if there were no sacred cows and the predominant color were blue. Directed by Ken Shapiro, the result is wild satire, mad slapstick and, as might be expected, adolescent smut, gross scatological humor, and a garden variety of tastelessness. O (X/R)

Gross Anatomy (1989) Seriocomic look at the trials and tribulations of first-year medical students, with focus on an obnoxious class clown (Matthew Modine) and the dissection professor (Christine Lahti) who inspires his overnight, unlikely transformation into a responsible student. Directed by Thom Eberhardt, it features a tensionless plot and unappealing, one-dimensional characters. Some rough language and an off-camera sexual liaison. A-III (PG-13)

Grosse Fatigue (1995) A burned-out French celebrity (Michel Blanc as himself) allows his double to impersonate him while he goes off to write in seclusion, but upon his return finds even his best friend (actress Carole Bouquet) rejects him as a pathetic impostor. Also written and directed by Blanc, the droll comedy hits as many high as flat notes but is generally amusing in its observations on the fleeting and sometimes unpleasant nature of fame. Subtitles. Some nudity, sexual innuendo, comic violence, and intermittent rough language. A-III (R)

Grosse Pointe Blank (1997) A cold-blooded hit-man (John Cusack) dodges rival assassins (including Dan Aykroyd) out to kill him while trying to win back an old flame (Minnie Driver) at his hometown high-school reunion. Director George Armitage's empty black comedy romanticizes a killer as a lovable fellow whose success at murdering for profit is seen merely as a minor character flaw. Morally bankrupt characters, some nasty violence, brief sexual situations, and recurring rough language. O (R)

Ground Zero (1988) Poorly realized political thriller about the British testing of atomic bombs during the 1950s and 1960s in the Australian desert and the military cover-ups that hid the tests' toll on soldiers and aborigines. Political fact and fiction is made so indistinguishable here by Australian directors Michael Pattinson and Bruce Myles that this, unfortunately, can too easily be dismissed as escapist fare. An overall sense of menace culminating in climactic violence and death, with a brief unsettling shot of stockpiled corpses. A-III (PG-13)

Groundhog Day (1993) Lightweight romantic fantasy in which a sarcastic weatherman (Bill Murray) slowly goes bonkers when inexplicably caught in a time warp in Punxsutawney, Pa. where, in daily reliving the same Groundhog Day, he gradually falls in love with his sweet-natured producer (Andie MacDowell). Despite appealing performances and numerous chuckles, director Harold Ramis's comic invention falls victim to the movie's own theme of repetitiveness. Occasional sexual innuendo and comic treatment of theft and suicide. A-II (PG)

Groundstar Conspiracy, The (1972) Mediocre espionage thriller about a plot to sabotage an important government nuclear-research center focuses mainly on George Peppard's ruthless, amoral methods of flushing out the traitor at the top. Directed by Lamont Johnson, the movie's hazy philosophical-political attitudes, as well as a romantic subplot, are not for the immature. A-III (PG)

Group, The (1966) Screen version of Mary McCarthy's novel about the private lives of eight Vassar girls capitalizes on the comeliness of its principals, particularly Candice Bergen, Elizabeth Hartman, and Johanna Pettet, to the detriment of real dramatic interest and human values. Lumpily directed by Sidney Lumet, the screen adaptation emphasizes the young ladies' sexual proclivities as they pursue husbands and careers in the 1930s. O (br)

Grumpy Old Men (1993) A half-century rivalry between two old pranksters (Walter Matthau and Jack Lemmon) escalates when an attractive widow (Ann-Margret) moves in across the street from them. Director Donald Petrie's contrived romantic comedy benefits greatly from the veteran actors' crusty portrayals despite the formula script and a feel-good finish. An implied sexual encounter, some crude sexual references, mild menace, and a few instances of profanity. A-III (PG-13)

Grumpier Old Men (1995) Genial sequel in which the bickering of fishing buddies (Jack Lemmon and Walter Matthau) is escalated by a voluptuous newcomer (Sophia Loren) who dares to turn their favorite bait shop into an Italian restaurant. While slim on story line, director Howard Deutch's romantic comedy depicts a half-dozen seniors as spirited citizens still open to loving relationships. Sexual innuendo, vulgar expressions, and an instance of profanity. A-III (PG-13)

Guadalcanal Diary (1943) WW II picture celebrating the first US victory against the Japanese in the hard-fought battle for Guadalcanal in the Solomon Islands after the Marine landing on August 7, 1942. Director Lewis Seiler's dated morale booster intersperses heroic action-scenes with patriotic musings from the ranks (notably Lloyd Nolan, William Bendix, Anthony Quinn, and Richard Jaekel) and the moral example of a Catholic chaplain (Preston Foster). Wartime violence. A-I (br)

Guardian, The (1990) Failed horror movie about a supernatural being (Jenny Seagrove) who masquerades as a nanny in order to steal infants and sacrifice them to some woodland deity. Director William Friedkin works hard at building an eerie, foreboding atmosphere, but the story is a clunker that doesn't make much sense and the special effects of a tree whose limbs kill people isn't worth the effort. Excessive gory violence, extended nudity, and an explicit sex scene. O (R)

Guarding Tess (1994) Reassigned to a second, unwanted three-year stint protecting an imperious former First Lady (Shirley MacLaine), a Secret Service agent (Nicolas Cage) is devastated when she's kidnapped while he's on duty. Though marketed as a comedy, director Hugh Wilson's uneven work succeeds better as a dramatic portrait of a lonely woman who's treated as a discarded figurehead by all but the ambitious agent who ultimately comes to care about her wellbeing. Fleeting violence and an instance of rough language. A-II (PG-13)

Guelwaar (1993) When the body of a murdered political activist in Senegal disappears just before his Catholic burial, his upset family and friends go to the Muslim cemetery where they believe he was mistakenly interred, but meet armed Muslims who will not allow the grave in question to be disturbed. Writer-director Ousmane Sembene touches upon religious animosities, widespread political corruption, and the need for African self-sufficiency in a straightforward narrative that is rich in complex characters and cultural observations. Subtitles. Some sexual innuendo, brief nudity, and momentary violence. A-III (nr)

Guernica (1976) Fernando Arrabal's movie presents a surrealistic history of the Spanish Civil War, making grotesques out of the Nationalists and idealizing the Republicans. It is basically a series of theatrical set pieces whose best images are filled with pain, sadness, and longing, but the imagery frequently operates on the level of shocking violence and anti-religious references. O (nr)

Guess What We Learned in School Today? (1971) Pretending to parody puritanical attitudes toward the sex education of the young in affluent suburbia, director John G. Avildsen's satire teaches its paltry lessons mainly with redundant nudity and protracted promiscuity. The movie's various sex-obsessed caricatures are embodied by passable unknown performers. O (R)

Guess Who's Coming to Dinner (1967) Pat comedy starring Spencer Tracy and Katharine Hepburn as parents whose daughter (Katharine Houghton) suddenly announces her plans to marry a distinguished black physician (Sidney Poitier). Directed by Stanley Kramer, the movie has some good comic moments, and by showing the efforts of both families to cope with the racial issues and the generation gap, it achieves a dimension of truth. A-II (nr)

Guilt of Janet Ames, The (1947) Hokey psychological sudser in which a troubled newsman (Melvyn Douglas) soothes his conscience by helping the widow (Rosalind Russell) of a WW II hero come to terms with her loss. Director Henry Levin does better with the expressionistic decor of the dream sequences than with the banal insights about the causes of the characters' bruised psyches. Murky delving into emotional self-delusions. A-II (br)

Guilty as Sin (1993) A defense attorney (Rebecca De Mornay) discovers her wily client (Don Johnson) is in fact a lady-killer who can frame her as an accomplice if she doesn't get him off the hook. Despite an implausible plot, director Sidney Lumet still manages to inject some suspense into the cat-and-mouse proceedings of this sinister courtroom melodrama. Briefly intense violence, an implied sexual encounter, and intermittent rough language. A-III (R)

Guilty by Suspicion (1991) The House Un-American Activities Committee in the early 1950s pressures a director (Robert De Niro) to name Communist sympathizers in the movie industry or face the complete destruction of his career. Director Irwin Winkler takes a compelling yet sobering look at the profound effect the loss of jobs and friends had on members of the Hollywood community who were blacklisted during the McCarthy era. Scene of suicide and occasional rough language. A-II (PG-13)

Guilty of Treason (1950) Uneven dramatization of the 1949 Communist show trial of Hungary's Cardinal Mindszenty (Charles Bickford) on bogus charges of treason, the injustice of which is reported by an American journalist (Paul Kelly) stationed in Budapest. Directed by Felix Feist, the melodrama turns historical events into a superficial dramatization, though the result has interest as an example of the period's anti-Red crusading. Stylized violence and psychological duress. A-I (br)

Gulliver's Travels (1939) Max Fleischer's animated version of Jonathan Swift's tale of the shipwrecked Englishman who is washed ashore in Lilliput, a diminutive land by whose scale Gulliver is a full-blown giant. The adaptation still goes over well with youngsters bemused by the images of tiny people coping with an oversized man, the movie's comic invention more than compensates for the silly subplot of neighboring kingdoms warring over a royal wedding and the songs are pleasant, if not memorable. A-I (br)

Gulliver's Travels Beyond the Moon (1966) Young children will like this Japanese-produced but Western-geared animated feature about a little boy, a pup dog, and a tin soldier, who join forces with old Lemuel Gulliver on an adventuresome trip by spaceship to the distant star of Hope. Charming and worthwhile. A-I (br)

Gumball Rally, The (1976) Mindless cross-country car race featuring a cast of characters led by Michael Sarrazin. Stunt coordinator-turned-director Chuck Bail tries some leering sex at the pit-stops. O (PG)

Gumby (1996) Animated feature directed by Art Clokey from the 1950's children's TV show about the green-clay title figure (voice of Charles Farrington) and his friends, who here battle a pair of Block Heads making robotic replicas of them in a scheme to steal a dog who cries pearls. The simple clay figures and their fantasy exploits have some appeal for youngsters, though their elders are unlikely to share it. A-I (G)

Gummo (1997) Incoherent picture of emotionally disturbed adolescents in small-town Ohio, who kill stray cats, sniff glue, have sex with a retarded girl, pull the plug on an old woman's respirator, and the like. Writer-director Harmony Korine has assembled a random collection of repugnant scenes which do no more than exploit the subject of youngsters growing up without parental guidance or social intervention. Perverse view of teen violence, sex, substance abuse, and foul language. O (R)

Gumshoe (1972) British movie in which Albert Finney plays a man who imagines himself as a hard-boiled private eye of the Raymond Chandler and Dashiell Hammett school, and these fantasies get him involved in a nasty but highly implausible case of gun-running and murder. Directed by Stephen Frears, the movie is fun at first, but it lacks a solid plot and therefore bogs down very quickly in its nonstop allusions to old detective movies. Violence and sexual innuendo. A-III (GP)

Gun Battle at Monterey (1957) Hokey Western in which a gunslinger (Sterling Hayden), left for dead after being shot in the back by an outlaw (Ted de Corsia), changes his name, hunts the outlaw down, then turns him over to the law to be charged with his own murder. Directed by Carl K. Hittleman and Sidney Franklin, Jr., the result is a dour revenge tale, with a tacked-on "moral" ending that makes matters even worse. Stylized violence, some of it quite nasty, and sexual situations. A-III (br)

Gun Brothers (1956) Routine Western directed by Sidney Salkow about a square-shooter (Buster Crabbe) who tries to reform his outlaw younger brother (Neville Brand), then tangles with the worst of his brother's confederates (Michael Ansara) over a good woman (Ann Robinson). Stylized violence and some sexual innuendo. A-II (br)

Gun for a Coward (1957) Standard Western about a rancher (Fred MacMurray) who's raised two younger brothers, one becoming a hothead (Dean Stockwell) while the other (Jeffrey Hunter) avoids confrontations until he's forced to prove his mettle. Directed by Abner Biberman, the predictable proceedings equate manhood with the ability to use one's fists as well as shoot straight. Stylized violence and romantic complications. A-I (br)

Gun Fury (1953) Standard Western about a woman (Donna Reed) abducted by an outlaw (Phil Carey) who's then tracked down by her fiancé (Rock Hudson). Directed by Raoul Walsh, the plot is tedious and the outcome entirely predictable. Stylized violence and sexual references. A-II (br)

Gun Glory (1957) Stewart Granger plays a gunfighter who wants to hang up his six-shooter but can't until he stops the cattleman (James Gregory) terrorizing the local sod-busters. Director Roy Rowland can't work up much interest in tired situations and formula plot, though Chill Wills does a nice turn as a down-to-earth preacher. The violence makes it unlikely children's fare. A-I (br)

Gun Hawk, The (1963) Western clunker in which a lawman (Rory Calhoun) pursues a mortally wounded gunslinger (Rod Cameron) who uses his approaching demise to deter a youth (Rod Lauren) from following in his footsteps. Directed by Edward Ludwig, the thinly plotted narrative revolves around pretentious characters and unconvincing motivations. Stylized violence, including a suicidal situation, and sexual references. A-III (br)

Gun Moll (see: **Jigsaw**)

Gun That Won the West, The (1955) Two veteran plainsmen (Dennis Morgan and Richard Denning) leave a Wild West show to serve as Indian scouts for a troop being equipped with a new-model Springfield rifle. Directed by William Castle, the story is pure Hollywood hokum which recycles action footage from earlier, better Westerns. Indian stereotyping and stylized violence. A-I (br)

Gunfight, A (1971) Retired gunfighters Kirk Douglas and Johnny Cash have little more to look forward to than an inevitable showdown with each other or with a younger, faster gun, so they stage their own final shootout. Director Lamont Johnson, aiming at audience participation in the ambiguous outcome, settles for heavy symbolism spotted with some rough language and a brief nude scene. A-III (PG)

Gunfight at Dodge City, The (1959) Routine Western directed by Joseph H. Newman follows the exploits of gambler-gunman Bat Masterson (Joel McCrea) in cleaning up Dodge after its marshal — his brother — is shot in the back. Frontier violence and romantic complications. A-II (br)

Gunfight at the O.K. Corral (1957) Overblown version of the shootout pitting sheriff Wyatt Earp (Burt Lancaster) and his cynical gun-slinging pal, Doc Holliday (Kirk Douglas), against the Clanton gang of rustlers. Directed by John Sturges, the ambitious production strives to stretch the thin proceedings into a meaningful story, but the result is too often pretentious and the overacting of its two stars undercuts the action's credibility. Some nasty violence and blatant sexual situations. A-III (br)

Gunfighter, The (1950) Pensive tale of an aging 1880's gunslinger (Gregory Peck) looking to outrun his reputation and settle down, but his past fame makes him a target for every aspiring gunman in the Southwest. Director Henry King delivers an intelligent Western drama with plenty of atmospheric Americana and fine performances from Peck, Millard Mitchell as the local sheriff, and Richard Jaeckel and Skip Homeier as would-be gunfighters. Some tense menace and stylized violence. A-I (br)

Gunfighters (1947) Formula Western directed by George Waggner in which a reformed gunman (Randolph Scott) finds himself in the middle of a range war, then is accused of murder and, despite the pleas of two contrary sisters (Barbara Britton and Dorothy Hart), straps on his guns to get the rustlers (Bruce Cabot and Forrest Tucker) responsible. Stylized violence and romantic complications. A-II (br)

Gunfighters of Casa Grande (1964) Routine European-made Western in which a gringo gunman (Alex Nichol) offers his gang to help protect Mexican ranchers from a bandit horde while planning to steal their cattle herds himself. The usual stylized violence and an off-screen rape. A-II (br)

Gung Ho! (1943) Standard WW II morale-booster directed by Ray Enright focuses on the training of a Marine Raider battalion (led by Randolph Scott) and their exploits after landing by submarine on a Japanese-held Pacific island. Battlefield violence with much period patriotism and some sexist comments. A-II (br)

Gung Ho (1986) Michael Keaton stars in this comedy about the reluctance of US workers to accept the standards of performance imposed upon them when a Japanese management team takes over a defunct auto-manufacturing plant in a small Pennsylvania town. Offering a multitude of stale one-liners and sight gags, the script seems somewhat insensitive in the stereotyping of Japanese businessmen as obsessively concerned with efficiency and saving face. Failed comedy with low humor, harsh language, and ethnic stereotyping. A-III (PG-13)

Gunga Din (1939) Classic adventure yarn loosely based on the Rudyard Kipling poem about a water carrier (Sam Jaffe) in Victoria's India who here dies as a hero with a bugle, warning British forces of an ambush. Director George Stevens focuses the action on three seasoned sergeants (Victor McLaglen, Cary Grant, and Douglas Fairbanks, Jr.) whose bickering comradeship provides some hardy fun while fighting Thugs, a long-suppressed murder cult led by a formidable foe (Eduardo Ciannelli). Old-fashioned "manly" celebration of such virtues as loyalty, courage, and steadfastness, though with plenty of stylized violence. A-I (br)

Gunman's Walk (1958) Tough-minded Western in which a pioneer rancher (Van Heflin) comes to regret being too indulgent in raising his motherless boys after the elder son (Tab Hunter) becomes a remorseless killer and the younger (James Darren) sides with the sister (Kathryn Grant) of an Indian his brother murdered. Director Phil Karlson relies on the clash of sharply contrasting characters to sustain the contrived proceedings till the final showdown between father and trigger-happy son. Tragic family theme with some harrowing stylized violence. A-III (br)

Gunn (1967) Seamy, occasionally brutal feature based on the once-popular "Peter Gunn" TV detective series features Craig Stevens as impeccable as ever in the title role. It's a minor effort from director Blake Edwards, offering little more than routine private-eye segments, a passel of cameo appearances by screen stars, and an unoriginal twist ending. Excessive violence and sexual situations. O (br)

Gunpoint (1965) Substandard Western directed by Earl Bellamy in which Audie Murphy plays a lawman chasing an outlaw band. Stylized violence. A-I (br)

Guns at Batasi (1964) A sudden political coup in a newly independent African country creates turmoil in its British-led army and leads a by-the-book but racist sergeant-major (Richard Attenborough) to challenge the takeover. Directed by John Guillerman, the situation starts credibly enough, but the tension evaporates in reams of rhetoric about the issues of the conflict until a final burst of action provides an inconclusive finale. Much menace with some stylized violence and sexual situations. A-III (br)

Guns for San Sebastian (1968) Mexican rebel (Anthony Quinn), mistaken for the priest expected by the inhabitants of a village ravaged by Indians and bandits, teaches them how to fight back and drive off the marauders. Directed by Henri Verneuil, the 18th-century setting is beautifully evoked, but the story is somewhat far-fetched and on the sentimental side. Stylized violence. A-II (br)

Guns of a Stranger (1973) Boring Western in which Marty Robbins plays a straight-shooter who comes to the rescue of a damsel-in-distress (Dovie Beams) whose boozy grandfather (Chill Wills) is about to lose his ranch to a cattle baron (William Foster). Robert Hinkle directs Robbins who is a singer but no cowboy, and certainly no actor. A-I (G)

Guns of August, The (1965) Based on Barbara Tuchman's book about the immediate causes of WW I, the documentary popularizes its scholarly account of the national aspirations of Balkan minorities, the political miscalculations of the Great Powers, and their diplomatic blunders. Director Nathan Kroll and his film researchers have accumulated a mass of familiar and unfamiliar footage on the outbreak of the war, presented in a straight-forward, factual manner. Heavy sledding for children. A-I (br)

Guns of Fort Petticoat, The (1957) With their men away fighting for the Confederacy, a bevy of Texas women (Kathryn Grant, Hope Emerson, and others) are helped by a Union officer (Audie Murphy) to defend themselves against an Indian uprising. Director George Marshall has trouble sustaining interest in the women's plight, though he stretches it out with broad humor, a band of outlaws, and an action-packed ending. Stylized violence and Indian stereotypes. A-I (br)

Guns of Hate (1948) Formula Western directed by Lesley Selander in which an Arizona cowboy (Tim Holt) goes after the man (Steve Brodie) who killed an old prospector and made off with his map to the Lost Dutchman Mine. Stylized violence. A-I (br)

Guns of Navarone, The (1961) Over-sized WW II action yarn from Alistair MacLean's novel about Allied commandos (Gregory Peck, David Niven, Anthony Quinn, Stanley Baker, and Anthony Quayle) sent to destroy a German artillery emplacement atop a Greek island. Director J. Lee Thompson notches the suspense tightly along the way to a bang-up finish, but the spectacle's impact is lessened by scant attention to the tale's human dimension. Wartime violence. A-I (br)

Guns of the Magnificent Seven (1969) Mercenaries try to outwit superior forces in this sequel set in revolutionary Mexico. Plot operates on the level of gunfights rather than coherent story, with George Kennedy trying hard, but simply not the taciturn strong-man type. Best is the historical background which director Paul Wendkos occasionally brings in. A-II (G)

Guns of the Timberland (1960) Routine Western pitting loggers (Alan Ladd and Gilbert Roland) against ranchers (Jeanne Crain among them) who fear their lands will be flooded after the trees are cut down. Directed by Roland D. Webb, the threadbare plot undercuts the colorful outdoor action. The usual fisticuffs and gunplay. A-I (br)

Gunslinger (1956) Muddled Western in which a lady marshal (Beverly Garland) and the gunman (John Ireland) hired to kill her happen to fall in love instead, though they can't avoid a final showdown. Directed by Roger Corman, the two-bit premise proves more ludicrous than quirky in a tiresomely inconsistent plot. Numerous cold-blooded murders and sexual situations. A-III (br)

Gunsmoke (1953) Convoluted Western directed by Nathan Juran in which a gunslinger (Audie Murphy) is hired to force a rancher (Paul Kelly) off his land, but when he wins the ranch at cards instead, he protects it from another imported gunslinger (Charles Drake) sent by the man (Donald Randolph) who hired him. Frontier violence and sexual innuendo. A-II (br)

Gunsmoke in Tucson (1958) Formula Western directed by Thomas Carr in which an Arizona marshal (Forrest Tucker) hunts down his bitter outlaw brother (Mark Stevens) while trying to stop a range war. Frontier violence, including a lynching. A-II (br)

Guru, The (1969) English pop singer (Michael York) journeys to Bombay to learn to play the sitar, where his teacher (Uptal Dutt) tries but fails to convert him to the spiritual values of the East. Rita Tushingham plays a wandering hippie fleeing Western materialism. Director James Ivory's uneven story is essentially a study in contradictions, with humorous overtones between two cultures and their outlook on life. A-II (G)

Guru, the Mad Monk (1971) The title character is a maniacal chaplain of a prison island where Central Europe sends its prisoners to be tortured and executed. The film's blood and sex diversions are complicated with a silly vampire and a hodgepodge of religious symbolism offensive to all faiths. O (nr)

Gus (1976) Above-average Disney comedy about a mule who kicks field goals. Vincent McEveety directs the lively, fast-moving entertainment, especially suitable for children. A-I (G)

Guyana: Cult of the Damned (1980) Dull fact-based dramatization of the 1978 Jonestown tragedy in which 900 followers of the Reverend James Jones went to their death with their deranged leader. Stuart Whitman stars as the false prophet in director Rene Cardona, Jr.'s, Mexican production, which is not as sensational as it might have been but neither does it have the least merit. A scene featuring nudity and another involving physical punishment are gratuitous and offensive. O (R)

Guys and Dolls (1955) Overstuffed screen version of Jo Swerling and Abe Burrows's stage musical based on Damon Runyon's colorful 1920's Broadway types in the story of a bet by a two-bit gambler (Frank Sinatra) that leads ultimately to the reformation of a big-time gangster (Marlon Brando) by a Salvation Army lass (Jeanne Simmons). Directed by Joseph L. Mankiewicz, the result is an uneven mix of Hollywood and Broadway styles, with some bright production numbers and Frank Loesser tunes, notably Stubby Kaye's "Sit Down, You're Rocking the Boat," but the parts never quite jell into a satisfying whole. Considerable sexual innuendo. A-III (br)

Gypsy Blood (see: **The Wild Heart**)

Gypsy Girl (1966) Slight British story of a retarded girl (Hayley Mills), fatherless and neglected by her alcoholic mother, whose tragic young life is changed when a handsome gypsy pays attention to her, and she learns what it means to be loved. Directed by John Mills, it is a well-done study of the simplicity of childlike people. The girl's prolonged sadness and her fights with her mother make it inappropriate for young children. A-II (br)

Gypsy Moths, The (1969) Burt Lancaster, Gene Hackman, and Deborah Kerr star in an unusual action movie about a rough-and-tough team who make a living as skydivers performing at state fairs across the Midwest. Director John Frankenheimer's aerial photography, especially the actual dive sequences, is absolutely breathtaking, but the dramatic portions unfolding on terra firma, having to do with the personal lives and problems of the divers, lack credibility. A-III (R)

Gypsy Wildcat (1944) Lackluster costume adventure directed by Roy William Neill in which an infant raised by gypsies turns out to be a countess (Maria Montez) whose lands have been seized by an evil baron (Douglass Dumbrille) but are regained when he's defeated by the king's envoy (Jon Hall). Stylized violence. A-I (br)

HMS Defiant (see: **Damn the Defiant!**)

Hackers (1995) Jumbled crime story in which a computer expert (Fisher Stevens) electronically steals millions from a corporation, then attempts to frame a group of teenage computer-freaks for the crime. Director Iain Softley relies more on zippy pacing than narrative logic in an over-busy script which ignores the teens' penchant for illegally breaching computer-security systems. Ambiguous treatment of white-collar crime, fleeting nudity, and an instance of rough language. A-III (PG-13)

Hagbard and Signe (1968) Scandinavian medieval romance based on the Romeo and Juliet theme is set against the stunning landscape of Iceland. Though there is much that is compelling and authentic in director Gabriel Axel's beautifully crafted movie, its treatment is regrettably marred by excessive nudity and graphic depictions of brutality. O (br)

Hail, Hero (1969) Generation-gap movie about a college dropout (Michael Douglas) who returns to the ranch to announce to his indifferent parents that he's joining the Army. Character portrait from director David Miller conveys an overly optimistic embodiment of joyous vitality and spiritual awareness. Disjointed comments about family ties, first love, prejudice, and war. A-III (M)

Hail! Mafia (1966) Forgettable crime melodrama directed by Raoul Levy about a paid killer involved in a gang war. Violence. A-III (br)

Hail Mary (1985) The Gospel account of the Incarnation and Virgin Birth is updated to present-day Switzerland in this French production. Though seriously intended, director Jean-Luc Godard's movie is not only tedious and disjointed, but its extensive use of nudity and extremely rough language in a context so sacred to Christians will be offensive to many. O (nr)

Hail the Conquering Hero (1944) Wacky home-front comedy about a WW II recruit (Eddie Bracken) who is rejected by the Marines because of chronic hay-fever but, thanks to some veterans of the fighting in the Pacific (led by William Demarest), returns home a reluctant war hero and is elected mayor in spite of himself. Written and directed by Preston Sturges, the tongue-in-cheek premise relies on the comic interplay between Bracken's mousy, non-heroic civilian, Demarest's tough, brassy veteran, and the patriotic fervor of a small American town whose sensible values emerge happily in the end. Memorable for its witty dialogue and slapstick situations. A-II (nr)

Hail to the Chief (1973) Occasionally hilarious, more often sophomoric, spoof of presidential politics stars Dan Resin as the nation's chief executive who is more than slightly demented about stamping out dissent in the land. Directed by Fred Levinson, there are some sterling gags of sight and sound but also a malicious sense of humor in regard to American politics. A-III (PG)

Hair (1979) Key Broadway musical of the 1960s was as much a slick exploitation of the flower children phenomenon as it was a celebration of it. Director Milos Forman's 1970s screen version keeps intact its virtues, including its measure of sincerity, and its defects, including its large dose of showbiz phoniness. For the most part, Forman does not romanticize his characters (John Savage, Treat Williams, Beverly D'Angelo, Charlotte Rae), though there are huge, lavish dance numbers and a restrained depiction of scenes with drugs, promiscuity, nudity, and some rough language. A-IV (PG)

Hairspray (1988) Underground writer-director John Waters makes a successful transition into the mainstream with this campy musical comedy tracing the rise of a chubby teenager (Ricki Lake) as the unexpected star of a 1962 Baltimore TV dance show. The story line includes teen rivalry, outrageous stage parents, and a nice subplot about integration, all of which is enlivened by toe-tapping period music and rousing dance numbers. Some off-color remarks. A-II (PG)

Hairy Ape, The (1944) Interesting misfire from the Eugene O'Neill play about a cocky steamship stoker (William Bendix) who goes haywire after a rich passenger (Susan Hayward) calls him an animal, then seeks her out ashore to put her straight. Director Alfred Santell treats the inverted beauty-and-the-beast theme in melodramatic fashion, pitting dim but good-natured working stiff against lovely but selfish socialite, with an obvious but unconvincing moral. Stylized violence and menace. A-II (br)

Half a Sixpence (1968) Director George Sidney's expanded version of the stage musical stars Tommy Steele as an exuberant dancing, singing draper's clerk who pledges his love to a working-class lass (Julia Foster), then inherits a fortune and nearly marries a society girl before returning to his true love, a bit sadder and wiser. Though overlong and somewhat lacking in variety, its handsome sets and soft-lens photography give the movie an Edwardian storybook quality that many viewers will find delightful. A-I (br)

Half-Baked (1998) Dreary collection of drug jokes revolving around a spaced-out addict (Dave Chappelle) getting money to bail a half-wit pal (Harland Williams) out of jail by becoming a dealer in marijuana. Directed by Tamra Davis, the low-budget proceedings are of the dumb-and-dumber variety with witless fantasies that smoking weed is no crime but only harmless fun. Unamusing trivialization of the drug culture, sexual encounters, brief nudity, and frequent rough language. O (R)

Half Moon Street (1986) Intelligent and attractive woman (Sigourney Weaver) supplements her meager salary as a London researcher by working as a part-time prostitute for upper-class clients. When one of them (Michael Caine) falls in love with her, she finds herself in the middle of a Middle Eastern power struggle that nearly costs her her life. Director Bob Swaim's routine tale of scandal among the British power-elite apparently intends to show how badly women are exploited, but it only does more of the same. Violence, nudity, and simulated sex. O (R)

Half Shot at Sunrise (1930) Creaky comedy directed by Paul Sloane has vaudevillians Bert Wheeler and Robert Woolsey clowning around as AWOL doughboys in 1918 Paris, where they give the MPs the runaround while romancing the colonel's daughter (Dorothy Lee) until their antics mistakenly take them to the front. Sexual situations, double entendres, and antisocial attitudes. A-III (br)

Hallelujah, I'm a Bum (1933) Fine musical comedy about the Depression in which Al Jolson stars as the mayor of Central Park, a bum respected by every tramp in New York City, until he falls in love and gets a regular job. Directed by Lewis Milestone, the movie is one of a kind in providing a socially conscious, rather than escapist, Hollywood musical. A-III (nr)

Halloween (1978) Criminally insane patient escapes to his hometown on Halloween, the 15th anniversary of the brutal murder for which he was locked up, and becomes a deadly menace to unsuspecting babysitters in director John Carpenter's low-budget horror show. Mixture of some nudity with much violence. O (R)

Halloween: H2O (1998) Twenty years after failing to kill his sister (Jamie Lee Curtis), a presumed-dead homicidal maniac tracks her down to a private academy, intent on finishing the job. Director Steve Miner pays some attention to characterization, making the slasher sequel seem less excessive and mildly suspenseful. Recurring shadowy violence, mild sexual innuendo, intermittent rough language, and an instance of profanity. A-III (R)

Halloween: The Curse of Michael Myers (1995) More mindless gore from the title's unstoppable homicidal maniac (George Wilbur), who this time is bent on killing his niece (Mariann Hagen) and snatching an infant boy, despite his old psychiatric nemesis (Donald Pleasence). Director Joe Chappelle stages some gross murders but wrings little menace or suspense out of a fright formula long since grown stale. Graphic violence, sexual innuendo, and rough language. O (R)

Halloween II (1981) The further adventures of the homicidal maniac and his relentless pursuit of babysitter Jamie Lee Curtis. Directed by Rick Rosenthal, it is just as bad as the original with its nauseating violence, sadism, tastelessness, and general senselessness. O (R)

Halloween III: Season of the Witch (1982) Director Tommy Lee Wallace's sequel uses a plot about a fiendish toy manufacturer (Dan O'Herlihy), intent upon giving the tots of America a Halloween to remember, as an excuse for trotting out the usual sickening special-effects violence and gore, as well as some nudity. O (R)

Halloween 4: The Return of Michael Myers (1988) Michael (George P. Wilbur) is back in Haddonfield, Ill., and this time he's escaped the mental ward to kill his little niece (Danielle Harris) on Halloween, despite his psychiatrist (Donald Pleasence). Director Dwight H. Little is unsuccessful in trying to turn the formula plot into a psychological thriller. Excessive violence, intense menace, a brief sex scene, and fleeting nudity. O (R)

Halloween 5: The Revenge of Michael Myers (1989) Director Dominique Othenin-Girard senselessly exploits Michael's psychic power over his young niece (Danielle Harris), who survived last year's installment and is once again her uncle's major target when he returns to terrorize young, Halloween revelers in Haddonfield, Ill. Mindless menace, remorseless violence, and a sexually suggestive encounter. O (R)

Halls of Anger (1970) Sixty white students are bused to a large, all-black high school, where the lid is kept on by a disciplinarian who happens to be a former athlete (Calvin Lockhart). Director Paul Bogart handles the desegregation issue with some authenticity but resorts to typical cliches and easy solutions. Much violence and brief nudity. A-III (PG)

Halls of Montezuma (1950) Gritty WW II picture of a Marine assault on a Japanese-held island during which a lieutenant (Richard Widmark) is ordered to take a platoon on a mission to locate and destroy an enemy missile-battery. Director Lewis Milestone tribute to the Marine Corps does well in placing the platoon's action within the larger context of the battle for the island, but the result suffers from the usual stereotyped characters and situations. Wartime violence, including a berserk Marine shooting prisoners. A-II (br)

Hamburger Hill (1987) A group of American grunts rest, recuperate, talk about their differences, while making failed attempts to capture a Vietnamese-held hilltop before a final bloody assault. Directed by John Irvin, it is more a testament to blind obedience and the absurdities of war than to the virtues of teamwork and determination. Excessive violence and profanity, some nudity, and false stereotyping. O (R)

Hamburger ... The Motion Picture (1986) Former football star Dick Butkus is the harsh and talkative coach teaching management techniques to trainees at a special college dedicated to Lyman Funk's All Bull Buster Burgers. What begins as social satire upon callous commercialism quickly collapses into an unfunny sex farce with profanity, nudity, and violence. O (R)

Hamlet (1969) Director Tony Richardson's intimate rendering of the Shakespearean tragedy emphasizes personal confrontations, heroic solitude, and, in the title role, Nicol Williamson's penchant for caustic repartee. Some omissions detract from the spirit of the original text, but this occasionally boisterous version still provides a poignant portrait of a man's obsessive search for truth. Stylized violence. A-II (G)

Hamlet (1990) Crazed by grief, the despairing Prince of Denmark (Mel Gibson) seeks the truth surrounding the death of his father (Paul Scofield) and the precipitous marriage of his mother (Glenn Close) to his murderous uncle (Alan Bates). Franco Zeffirelli's fluid direction of Shakespeare's classic is emotionally charged, cinematically beautiful, and boasts uniformly superior acting. Stylized violence. A-II (PG)

Hamlet (1996) Splendid screen version of Shakespeare's tragedy played out in 19th-century Denmark, where the troubled prince Hamlet (Kenneth Branagh) plots revenge after learning his uncle (Derek Jacobi) had murdered his father in order to wed Hamlet's mother (Julie Christie). Also directed by Branagh, the four-hour production is superbly acted and brought to the screen with a keen sense of drama and remarkable visual flair. Stylized violence and fleeting flashbacks of bedroom scenes. A-II (PG-13)

Hammer (1972) Black exploitation movie about an ex-dockworker (Fred Williamson) who becomes a boxer ,but when the mob wants him to take a dive, he takes them on and lays them out. Directed by Bruce Clark, the production values are good and the violence is toned down but it suffers from weak characterization and too-familiar story line. Some raw sex scenes and rough language. O (R)

Hammer of God, The (1973) Mindless martial-arts movie about Japanese karate fighters who slaughter students of a Chinese kung fu school, but a survivor bolsters himself with iron fist techniques and takes revenge on the baddies. Usual amount of violence, except for a savage rape of a woman who has nothing to do with the story. O (R)

Hammerhead (1968) An American soldier of fortune (Vince Edwards) and his companion (Judy Geeson) spend most of their time tracking down an international spy posing as an art collector (Robert Vaughn). Sluggish espionage melodrama directed by David Miller. Nasty violence and sexually suggestive treatment. O (R)

Hammersmith Is Out (1972) Sluggish variation on the Faust legend in which a psycho-ward attendant (Beau Bridges) is promised strength, wealth, and a hash-house waitress (Elizabeth Taylor) if he will let an inmate (Richard Burton) escape. From there it is a murderous journey to the upper reaches of corruption in a movie directed by Peter Ustinov with a total lack of wit and vigor. Some graphic sex and violence and much crude language. O (R)

Hammett (1983) Mediocre melodrama about Dashiell Hammett (Frederic Forrest), the creator of Sam Spade, getting started as a writer in 1928 San Francisco, but becoming sidetracked by a murder case in which he absorbs the same kind of punishment that would later appear in his hardboiled detective stories. Directed by Wim Wenders, the result proves to be a pretentious, sentimental, and uninspired tribute to old Hollywood murder mysteries, and at times borders on self-parody. Some vulgar expletives and some violence. A-II (PG)

Hamsun (1997) Fine historical dramatization explores the last years of famed Norwegian author Knut Hamsun (1859-1952) who as an old man destroyed his reputation by writing in support of the hated Quisling regime during the Nazi occupation and his punishment after Norway's liberation. Directed by Jan Troell, the absorbing period account helps explain, but doesn't excuse, Hamsun's wartime collaboration, though the human drama is made compelling by Max von Sydow's brilliant performance as the proud old writer who foolishly believes he can influence events he doesn't understand, then is left in disgrace to make peace with himself and his estranged wife (Ghita Norby). Subtitles. Wartime violence, ambiguous political attitudes, and intense marital conflicts. A-III (nr)

Hand, The (1981) Successful cartoonist (Michael Caine) loses his drawing hand in a freak accident and then imagines that the severed hand, never recovered, is pursuing him and threatening those who arouse his anger, especially his restless wife (Andrea Marcovicci). Director Oliver Stone achieves some scary effects, but it's otherwise a gloomy, depressing story with cardboard characters. Some graphic sex and violence. O (R)

Hand in Hand (1960) A British movie about the childhood friendship between a Catholic boy and a Jewish girl who discover that God is everywhere, watching over everyone. Directed by Philip Leacock, it is a fine little film, especially for family audiences. A-I (br)

Hand That Rocks the Cradle, The (1992) Callous suspense movie has an infant and a little girl (Madeline Zima) entrusted to a psychotic nanny (Rebecca De Mornay) out to kill the brood's young mother (Annabella Sciorra). Curtis Hanson directs a manipulative, highly contrived, and predictable thriller emphasizing violence and menace to helpless children. Exploitation of violence to women and children, occasional nudity, sexual references, and some rough language. O (R)

Handful of Dust, A (1988) Based on Evelyn Waugh's 1934 novel satirizing the British upper classes in the guise of a beautiful young couple (James Wilby and Kristin Scott Thomas) whose contented country life is destroyed by the wife's infidelity. Directed by Charles Sturridge, it plays more like romantic tragedy than social satire, with the wife as an especially remorseless, conscienceless character. A-III (PG)

Handle with Care (1958) When a third-year law class holds a mock grand-jury investigation of the town's elected officials, a cocky student (Dean Jones) accuses one of them (Thomas Mitchell) of having embezzled tax monies during the Depression. Directed by David Friedkin, the contrived proceedings are chiefly of interest for posing a case in which justice and the law are in conflict. Unlikely fare for children. A-I (br)

Handle with Care (1977) Good-natured, warm-hearted little comedy set in a small California town, where a citizens' band radio enthusiast (Paul Le Mat) dashes about rescuing people and doing other good deeds, though not always with the approval of his pensive girlfriend (Candy Clark). Director Jonathan Demme contrives an ending that tries to pull all his diverse story elements together, but it's forced and out of keeping with the relaxed mood of the rest of the movie. A sub-plot about a bigamous trucker and his two wives is adult fare. A-III (PG)

Handmaid's Tale, The (1990) Muddled fable about a Fascist state of the near future, where pollution and radioactivity have made most women barren and the fertile few are enslaved as "handmaids" to breed children for the state's rulers. Though director Volker Schloendorff's visuals summon up the image of Nazi Germany, the story of one particular handmaid (Natasha Richardson) gets lost in a dreary depiction of a dehumanized, male-dominated world. Several excessively graphic simulations of sexual intercourse, brief nudity, some rough language, and an ambiguous treatment of religion as contributing to a repressive society. O (R)

Hands across the Table (1935) Light romantic comedy about a manicurist (Carole Lombard) out to marry for money instead of love, but the rich man's son (Fred MacMurray) she's after proves penniless and himself is seeking a wealthy spouse, while the crippled millionaire (Ralph Bellamy) who truly loves her waits patiently in the wings. Director Mitchell Leisen keeps the frothy plot bubbling with comic wit and slapstick pranks as the cheerfully hardboiled gold-diggers charm each other and the viewer until an agreeably sentimental ending. Romantic complications and situations. A-III (br)

Hands of Orlac, The (see: **Mad Love**)

Hands of the Ripper (1972) A pioneer psychoanalyst (Eric Porter) tries to cure the daughter of Jack the Ripper (Angharad Rees) who has inherited her father's tendency to slash things in moments of stress. Fairly well-done British horror movie, but too violent for younger viewers. A-III (R)

Hang 'em High (1968) Vigorous Western starring Clint Eastwood as a former lawman who journeys into the Nebraska Territory where he is promptly hanged — but not high enough to keep him from coming back to enforce a rough version of justice on the range. Directed by Ted Post, the result is clever without being campy and, unusual for an action-packed Eastwood vehicle, without too much violence. A-III (PG-13)

Hangar 18 (1981) Within the title edifice are the remains of a wrecked flying saucer kept undercover as part of a government cover-up in this anemic little movie directed by James Conway and starring Darren McGavin and Robert Vaughn. Some incidental violence. A-II (PG)

Hangfire (1990) Feeble super-cop thriller directed by Peter Maris in which escaping convicts take a New Mexico town hostage until a local lawman (Brad Davis) rounds them up, despite interference from a trigger-happy National Guard commander (Jan-Michael Vincent). Lots of violence with graphic gore, nasty menace, and occasional coarse language. O (R)

Hanging Garden, The (1998) Pretentious Canadian clunker about a homosexual (Chris Leavins) who returns home after a 10-year absence to attend his sister's wedding, then wallows in painful recollections of his abusive childhood and unhappy adolescence. Writer-director Thom Fitzgerald paints an ugly picture of a wildly dysfunctional Irish-Catholic family in picturesque Nova Scotia, but the inter-cutting of past and present, the real and the imaginary, proves hopelessly artificial, and emotionally unconvincing. Some depiction of sex acts, religious caricature, bathroom humor, incessant rough language, and frequent profanity. O (R)

Hanging Tree, The (1959) Western melodrama set in an 1873 Montana mining camp, where a troubled doctor (Gary Cooper) restores the eyesight of a Swiss immigrant (Maria Schell), then saves her from a lustful prospector (Karl Malden) only to face being lynched for his troubles. Delmer Daves directs the turgid plot with more attention to the colorful details of mining life than the quirky relationships between the main characters. Stylized violence, sexual innuendo, and an attempted rape. A-II (br)

Hangman's Knot (1952) After robbing a Union gold shipment, a Confederate major (Randolph Scott) and his small band (including Lee Marvin and Claude Jarman, Jr.) learn the war is over and they are being hunted as outlaws. Directed by Roy Huggins, the action centers in a stagecoach relay station, where the group is besieged by local gunmen after the gold. Stylized violence and several muted sexual references. A-II (br)

Hanky Panky (1982) Limp and tedious comedy-adventure in which a mild-mannered architect from Chicago (Gene Wilder) finds himself suspected of murder and pursued by all sorts of hostile people, among them a mystery woman (Gilda Radner). Directed by Sidney Poitier, the poor effort contains a scene involving the beating and murder of a woman and some strong language. A-III (PG)

Hanna's War (1988) Based on the short, courageous life of WW II martyr Hanna Senesh (Maruschka Detmers), a Hungarian Jew who relocated to Palestine after high school graduation in 1938, but returned to Hungary on a secret RAF mission to help save her fellow Jews. Director Menahem Golan's glossy, superficial epic leaves more questions than it answers about Hanna's courageous life in Palestine and Hungary during the war. Intense prison scenes and brutal off-camera torture. A-III (PG-13)

Hannah and Her Sisters (1986) Writer-director

Woody Allen's disappointing treatment of infidelity and adultery in the lives of three sisters (Mia Farrow, Dianne Wiest, and Barbara Hershey). Although it shows the struggle and disappointments of people searching for a better life, it romanticizes amoral behavior and dishonesty as a natural consequence of contemporary urban lifestyles. A-IV (PG-13)

Hannibal Brooks (1969) British WW II POW (Oliver Reed) escapes in the company of an elephant to Switzerland. Director Michael Winner's pacifist fable resorts to some large-scale but graphically restrained guerrilla warfare to conclude the escape but preserves the lighthearted adventure motif of this generally amiable satire. A-II (M)

Hannie Caulder (1972) A rancher's wife (Raquel Welch) learns to take justice and a six-shooter into her own hands after being raped and widowed by three bumbling bandits (Strother Martin, Ernest Borgnine, and Jack Elam). Director Burt Kennedy's erratic Western focuses on a simpleminded and unquestioned theme of vengeance. Exploitative rape sequence, bloody violence, and coarse language. O (R)

Hanoi Hilton, The (1987) Michael Moriarty is the Christ-like crucified leader of a group of US POWs tortured by callous North Vietnamese until their release at the end of the war. Canadian director Lionel Chetwynd intends this as a tribute to their uncommon bravery but manages to convey an insidious jingoistic notion that duty to country is equal to Christian virtue. Profanity, male nudity, and scenes of brutality and torture are more prominent than religious references. O (R)

Hanover Street (1979) Dashing American bomber pilot (Harrison Ford) falls in love with a married woman (Lesley-Anne Down) during a 1943 London air raid, they have an affair, and then he winds up on a secret mission in France with her nice-guy husband (Christopher Plummer). Written and directed by Peter Hyams, it is an inept attempt to make an old-fashioned wartime romance without the skill or intelligence to evoke any genuine emotions or feelings. Though it does not condone adultery, its glossy and graphic treatment of it is offensive. O (PG)

Hans Christian Andersen (1952) Pleasant family musical based on the life of the Danish author (1805-75) whose fairytales are among the favorites of children's literature. Directed by Charles Vidor, the biography is pure Hollywood hokum, but Danny Kaye is particularly good as the gentle storyteller, and Frank Loesser's delightful musical numbers, including "Thumbelina," "The Ugly Duckling," and "The King Is in the Alltogether," are simple, singable, and just plain fun. Best for young children, though their elders will find sufficient charm in the proceedings to offset the sentimentality. A-I (nr)

Hans Christian Andersen's Thumbelina (1994) Animated musical version of the Danish fairytale about a tiny girl (voice of Jodi Benson) beset by misadventures and unwanted suitors before being reunited with her beloved fairy prince (voice of Gary Imhoff). Produced and directed by Don Bluth and Gary Goldman, the pastel-pretty, extremely sugary story features some lilting tunes by Barry Manilow, but the bland characters and lazy pace may challenge the attention span of both children and adults. A-I (G)

Happiest Days of Your Life, The (1950) Whimsical British comedy stemming from the education ministry's witless relocation of a girls' school to a boys' academy, with farcical results involving eccentric teachers (notably Joyce Grenfell) and rambunctious teen students. Directed by Frank Launder from John Dighton's play, the initial clash between stuffy headmaster (Alastair Sim) and steely headmistress (Margaret Rutherford) turns into a frantic partnership of necessity as they try to keep visiting parents from learning the truth. Romantic complications and mild sexual innuendo. A-II (br)

Happiest Millionaire, The (1967) Musical biography of Anthony J. Drexel Biddle (Fred McMurray), an eccentric turn-of-the-century millionaire who kept alligators as pets, collected prizefighters, and alternated a family program of physical fitness with hymn-singing. Directed by Norman Tokar, it has all the usual Disney staples: some innocent romance, a sentimental view of family life, and amusing animals. It is, however, overlong, and the music by Richard and Robert Sherman is undistinguished. A-I (G)

Happily Ever After (1990) Snow White and her prince are about to be married, but the dead queen's evil brother intervenes, casting a spell on the prince and dooming Snow White unless the Seven Dwarfs' cousins, the Dwarfelles, can rescue them. Filmation Studio's animated sequel to the Grimm Brothers fairytale fails to capture the magic of the 1937 Disney classic, but zippy pacing, the musical numbers, and positive messages for children make it lighthearted family fare. A-I (G)

Happiness (1934) Soviet silent slapstick comedy about a peasant misfit who is put in the Czarist army but after the Revolution returns home to what is now part of a collective farm, where he is as much of a misfit as ever. Directed by Alexandre Medvedkine, the action has the zany absurdity that is universal to visual comedy, though the ending is predictably didactic as the peasant learns that happiness is working for the common good. Some earthy humor. A-III (nr)

Happiness (1998) Unsettling psychodrama probing the dysfunctional emotional lives of three sisters (Lara Flynn Boyle, Cynthia Stevenson, and Jane Adams), their aged parents (Ben Gazarra and Louise Lasser), a pedophile husband (Dylan Baker), and an obscene phone-caller (Philip Seymour Hoffman), with depressing results. Written and directed by Todd Solondz, this is not an entertainment but a painful, often disturbing experience of the inner torments of sexually troubled individuals whose portrayal achieves enough human dimension to invite some compassion, though most adults will have no interest in sharing their misery. Non-graphic sexual content including fornication, masturbation and pedophilia, brief nudity, much rough language, and some profanity. A-IV (nr)

Happiness Cage, The (1972) Army private (Christopher Walken) receives some experimental brainwave treatment to control his schizophrenic behavior, administered by a neurosurgeon (Joss Ackland) who is trying to learn how to rehabilitate undesirables. Directing an adaptation of Dennis Reardon's play, Bernard Girard fails to provide enough information or human feeling about the scientific conditioning process to make the movie anything more than an old-fashioned horror movie. Patients rant and curse periodically. A-III (PG)

Happy Birthday, Gemini (1980) Screen version of Albert Innaurato's play about a poor Italian-American youth (Alan Rosenberg) who receives a surprise visit on his 21st birthday from two wealthy classmates, a brother and sister, but he thinks he loves the brother more than he does the sister. Directed by Richard Benner, the youth's sexual ambivalence is used as the hook upon which to hang all sorts of vignettes of working-class life but the movie is loud, messy, and overacted. Lacks any moral perspective on the sexual identity question, and features crude ethnic stereotypes, vulgarity, and profanity. O (R)

Happy Birthday to Me (1981) Simpleminded Canadian horror movie about a disturbed student (Melissa Sue Anderson) at an exclusive school whose friends start disappearing. The climax is her birthday party, at which they all show up rather the worse for wear. Directed by J. Lee Thompson, it is senselessly nauseating in its gore and violence. O (R)

Happy Birthday, Wanda June (1971) Screen version of the Kurt Vonnegut, Jr., play in which an explorer (Rod Steiger), presumed dead after disappearing in the Amazon jungles eight years before, returns home to discover that his wife (Susannah York) is about to marry a doctor (George Grizzard). Director Mark Robson's stage-bound adaptation is a muddled black comedy about the destructive he-man image of masculinity, the nature of aggression, and the status of women. Though there are some amusing bits, they do not add up to a coherent whole and the number of verbal obscenities becomes needlessly excessive. O (R)

Happy Ending, The (1969) Uneven drama begins with a disillusioned couple (John Forsythe and Jean Simmons) questioning each other's love on their 16th wedding anniversary and, after various complications, concludes with the wife asking her husband whether, if he had to do it over again, he would marry her. Directed by Richard Brooks, this examination of a rocky marriage is as unenlightening as it sounds and more than a little cliched. A-III (PG)

Happy Gilmore (1996) Desperately unfunny comedy about an inept hockey player (Adam Sandler) who earns big bucks by turning his slap-shot into power drives on the pro-golf tour. Directed by Dennis Dugan, the feeble proceedings are as unamusing as the violent antics of the ill-tempered boor of the title. Slapstick violence, sexual innuendo, and coarse language. A-III (PG-13)

Happy Go Lovely (1951) British musical comedy in which a penniless American producer (Cesar Romero) mounts a show in Edinburgh by starring a showgirl (Vera-Ellen), whom he mistakenly thinks is the girlfriend of a local millionaire (David Niven). Directed by H. Bruce Humberstone, the comic misunderstandings provide some giddy moments thanks mainly to Niven, but the musical numbers are flat and unmemorable. Romantic complications. A-II (br)

Happy Go Lucky (1943) Labored romantic comedy directed by Curtis Bernhart has Caribbean beachcombers Dick Powell and Eddie Bracken come to the aid of gold-diggers Mary Martin and Betty Hutton in pursuing millionaire Rudy Vallee by supplying them with a voodoo love potion which predictably backfires. Sexual situations and innuendo. A-III (br)

Happy Hooker, The (1975) Lynn Redgrave struggles gamely to give some life and glamour to the essentially sordid trade of prostitution. Though there are some humorous touches and a minimum of offensive graphics and vulgar speech, director Nicholas Sgarro's movie fails to justify its existence as either art or entertainment. O (R)

Happy Mother's Day ... Love, George (1973) A young lad (Ron Howard), searching for his unknown father, comes to a New England fishing village inhabited by a bizarre set of characters (Cloris Leachman, Patricia Neal, and Tessa Dahl). Ineptly directed by Darren McGavin, the film's gory violence, supposedly motivated by sexual repression, is an unsavory fantasy. O (PG)

Happy New Year (1973) French comedy about a pair of jewel thieves (Lino Ventura and Charles Gerard) who meticulously plan a heist on New Year's Eve, set it in action, and have it fail because one of them falls completely for the charming owner (Francoise Fabian) of an antique shop next door. Director Claude Lelouch succeeds in presenting a crime caper in a human context that has some moral weight to it. A-III (PG)

Happy Years, The (1950) A mischievous youth (Dean Stockwell) is sent by his exasperated father (Leon Ames) to a boys' boarding school, where he is straightened out by classmates (Darryl Hickman, Scotty Beckett, and numerous other juveniles) and a caustic but fatherly Latin teacher (Leo G. Carroll). Director William A. Wellman stresses the healthy nature of the boys' hijinks while poking some gentle fun at the manner and mores of 1896 New Jersey society. Pleasant exercise in nostalgia with special appeal for young viewers. A-I (br)

Hard Contract (1969) Hired-gun James Coburn gets amorously sidetracked by Lee Remick on his way to murder three people in Europe. He has a change of heart but struggles with his own lack of sensitivity. Talkathon by director-writer S.Lee

Pogostin questions how much authority figures are responsible for society's dehumanization. A-IV (R)

Hard Eight (1997) Dark melodrama in which a seasoned gambler (Philip Baker Hall) teaches a young loser (John C. Reilly) the tricks of the casino trade, then helps him and his bride (Gwyneth Paltrow) escape a bungled extortion, after which he kills a man threatening to reveal why he has become a second father to the young man. Writer-director Paul Thomas Anderson tautly focuses on the relationship between the veteran and the novice, but the movie takes a wrong turn into hard-edged, melodramatic action and an unsatisfying climax. Brief but graphic violence, sexual situations, much rough language, and some profanity. A-IV (R)

Hard Promises (1992) Lifeless romantic comedy concerns a young mother (Sissy Spacek) torn between marrying her solid, dependable fiancé (Brian Kerwin) or taking back her dashing ex-husband (William Petersen) who shows up on the eve of the wedding. Aside from its trite characters and sheer predictability, director Martin Davidson makes positive values look positively dull. Some sexual references, momentary fisticuffs, and occasional profanity. A-II (PG)

Hard Rain (1998) Waterlogged thriller about an armored-car robbery during a flashflood, from which a guard (Christian Slater) escapes with the moneybags, pursued by the robbers (headed by Morgan Freeman) and the local police (led by Randy Quaid) until the dam breaks to sweep the cat-and-mouse proceedings to a long-delayed finish. Directed by Mikael Salomon, the plot is set in a flood-evacuated town with powerboats chasing through partially submerged buildings, but the contrived situations and improbable action grow increasingly tiresome. Stylized violence, much menace including a sexual situation, recurring profanity, and a sexual expletive. A-III (R)

Hard Ride, The (1971) Vietnam vet (Robert Fuller) escorts home the body of his black buddy who had wanted his motorcycle pals to be present at his funeral, but, in trying to fulfill this request, he is killed in a bikers' brawl and is buried with his friend. Directed by Burt Topper, the movie mutes the usual sex and violence to make the point that being a road bum is a senseless way of life. A-III (GP)

Hard Target (1993) Hard-core violence is a constant in this repulsive tale of an unemployed New Orleans merchant sailor (Jean-Claude Van Damme) determined to single-handedly stop a pack of sadistic killers who hunt down and slaughter homeless veterans for sport. Director John Woo assaults viewers with deafening sounds of human torture and death as violence and vengeance are glorified to a sickening degree. Nonstop hardcore violence and much rough language. O (R)

Hard Times (1975) Tough loner (Charles Bronson), down on his luck during the Depression, picks up money by street fighting, an elemental no-holds-barred kind of contest whose payoff comes from the bets wagered. Director Walter Hill gets the period right and does well with the New Orleans locales, but the movie has no pretensions to being anything but good pulp-fiction and it succeeds on this level. Some brutal fighting scenes. A-III (R/PG)

Hard to Hold (1984) A rock star (Rick Springfield) falls madly in love with a sophisticated lady (Janet Eilber) whom he meets in a traffic accident. Director Larry Peerce's listless, awkward movie features bad acting by all concerned. A benign view of sex outside of marriage and some rough language are adult fare. A-III (PG)

Hard to Kill (1990) Los Angeles detective (Steven Seagal) awakens from a coma to avenge the bloodthirsty slaughter of his family seven years before by agents of a corrupt congressman. Though martial-arts master Seagal is depicted as a loving family man, director Bruce Malmuth emphasizes his grisly means of retribution. Excessive graphic violence and acts of vigilantism. O (R)

Hard Traveling (1986) Dan Bessie directs a grim, fact-based story of the Depression years about a down-and-out farmer convicted of murder. Although this movie offers a depressing vision of social injustices and their causes, its sensitive portrayals and strong period details lessen its pessimistic outlook. A-III (PG)

Hard Way, The (1991) Workaholic macho cop (James Woods) on the track of a serial killer (Stephen Lang) is stymied by his happy-go-lucky temporary partner (Michael J. Fox), a movie star along for the ride as he prepares for a new role. Director John Badham's formula comedy of stick figures and car chases is helped by its fast pace and lively climax of cliffhangers. Recurring stylized violence and rough language with vulgar expressions. A-III (R)

Hardbodies (1984) California smut-in-the-sun movie about three middle-aged lechers who engage a teenage lothario (Grant Cramer) to instruct them in the art of seduction. Badly directed by Mark Griffiths, it features abundant nudity, graphic sex, and utter disregard of every moral consideration. O (R)

Hardcore (1979) Deeply committed Christian from the Midwest (George C. Scott) hires a Los Angeles detective (Peter Boyle) to find his 15-year-old daughter who has disappeared while attending a religious youth-convention in California. When she turns up in a porno film, Scott is plunged into the pornographic underworld trying to find her. Writer-director Paul Schrader's movie deals with a serious subject, but on the whole is crude and simplistic, its characters shallow, and its melodramatic resolution unbelievable. Nudity and frequent rough language. O (R)

Harder They Come, The (1973) The movie, in English but frequently subtitled because of the thickly accented Jamaican speech, stars Jimmy Cliff as a country boy come to Kingston town seeking fame and fortune and winding up with the wrong sort of the one and none of the other. Directed by Perry Henzell, the result is a fast-paced picture full of color and action, sometimes violent and harsh, occasionally confusing, but constantly bursting with energy and interest. A-III (R)

Harder They Fall, The (1956) Crooked fight-promoter Rod Steiger hires veteran sportswriter Humphrey Bogart to build interest in a muscle-bound Argentinean boxer who's being set up to lose big. Director Mark Robson gets convincing performances from a strong cast in an adaptation of Budd Schulberg's novel about the callous types behind the brutal fight-racket. Some menace and stylized ring violence. A-II (br)

Hardly Working (1981) Jerry Lewis directs as well as stars in the role of an out-of-work circus clown who tries to hold down a string of varied jobs, ranging from chef to postman, with predictably disastrous results. As usual in his comedies, there are some genuinely funny moments, but otherwise this is for die-hard Lewis fans only. Some mild and incidental profanity. A-II PG)

Hardware (1990) Horrific sci-fi tale in which a scrap-metal sculptress (Stacey Travis) is given discarded robot parts by her lover (Dylan McDermott), unaware that the parts will reassemble into a rampaging, merciless killer-cyborg. Writer-director Richard Stanley captures the stark ugliness of a ravaged, futuristic society, but his nihilistic story concentrates on constant, unrelenting gore. Excessive violence, an extended sex scene with nudity, recreational drug use, and rough language. O (R)

Hardys Ride High, The (1939) When Judge Hardy (Lewis Stone) learns he may be the heir to a $2 million estate, he takes the family to Detroit to verify his claim. Directed by George B. Seitz, the episode is unusually playful in testing the family's small-town values when faced with sudden wealth, as well as providing some romance for Andy's maiden aunt Millie (Sara Hayden). A-I (br)

Harem Holiday (see: **Harum Scarum**)

Harlan County, U.S.A. (1977) Filmed during a bitter 13-month coal strike in eastern Kentucky, the documentary examines the strike's origins, the working and living conditions of the miners. and the violence that breaks out between the pickets and the strikebreakers. Though flawed by a clumsy narrative structure that is sometimes confusing, filmmaker Barbara Kopple's stirring picture of the still-unfinished struggle for labor justice has the raw power of reality and the passion of the worker's cause. A-II (PG)

Harlem Globetrotters, The (1951) Small but effective tale of a college All-American (Bill Walker) trying to make good with the title basketball team, whose African-American players are renowned for mixing clowning with sharpshooting. Directed by Phil Brown, the players give convincing performances as themselves on and off the court, but it's left to the Trotters's white manager (Vincent Gomez) to spell out the team's motivation to excel as representatives of their race. A-I (nr)

Harlem Nights (1989) Action comedy set in 1938 Harlem pits black nightclub-owners (Richard Pryor and Eddie Murphy) against a bloodthirsty white gangster (Michael Lerner) and his cop henchman (Danny Aiello). Written, produced, and directed by Murphy, the uninspired, derivative movie is saved from tedium by nutty running gags from a notable supporting cast (Redd Foxx, Della Reese, Stan Shaw, and Arsenio Hall). Excessive profanity, racial epithets, comic violence, and suggestive sexual encounters. O (R)

Harley Davidson and the Marlboro Man (1991) Ultra-violent action movie about a biker (Mickey Rourke) and a cowboy (Don Johnson) whose bungled armed robbery sets a corrupt banker and a quintet of killers on their trail. Pedestrian direction by Simon Wincer glamorizes trashy macho heroics while rationalizing murderous behavior. Excessive violence, positive depiction of crime as well as vigilante justice, brief nudity, and frequent rough language. O (R)

Harlow (1965) Glossy fictional picture about 1930s movie star Jean Harlow (game but miscast Carroll Baker) and her relationships with her mother (Angela Lansbury), stepfather (Raf Vallone), agent (Red Buttons), leading men (Leslie Nielsen and Michael Connors), and the impotent studio executive (Peter Lawford) she marries, with tragic results. Directed by Gordon Douglas, the picture mangles both the Hollywood period and the details of Harlow's life in its simplistic portrayal of the actress as a victim of the studio era. Stylized violence, sexual situations, and alcoholic excesses. A-III (br)

Harmonists, The (1999) Beguiling fact-based story set in early 1930s Germany recounts the rise of a beloved six-man singing group, the Comedian Harmonists, who were forced to break up at the height of their popularity because three members were Jewish. Director Joseph Vilsmaier's handsome period drama resonates with the understated horror of the growing Nazi threat that was soon to engulf the world in war. Subtitles. Fleeting violence, sexual situations, and brief nudity. A-III (R)

Harold and Maude (1971) Bud Cort plays an immature youth who finds a sympathetic older woman to help him grow up in the person of an eccentric woman bordering on 80 (Ruth Gordon). Cort is a neurotic smothered by the love of his mother (Vivian Pickles), upon whom he takes his revenge by acting out all kinds of elaborate fake suicides. Hal Ashby directs with a good photographer's eye, but his emphasis on the cute is out of place. A-III (PG)

Harper (1966) Paul Newman stars as a hardboiled private eye hired to track down a missing millionaire, and his various leads include Lauren Bacall, Shelley Winters, Robert Wagner, and Julie Harris. Director Jack Smight's mystery thriller has an intricate plot that sustains interest, solid performances by a good cast, and a satisfying pay-off. Restrained violence. A-III (br)

Harper Valley P.T.A. (1979) When the hypocritical board of a small-town PTA sends a nasty letter to a fun-loving widow (Barbara Eden), scolding her for her behavior and threatening to expel her daughter from junior-high school, they get much more than they bargained for. Based upon a hit song of the late 1960s, this unsophisticated comedy is standard drive-in fare, though the actors add an enjoyable zest to the proceedings. Some vulgar and risqué humor. A-III (PG)

Harrad Experiment, The (1973) James Whitmore plays the dean of an experimental coed college at which controlled group experience in premarital sex is the major item of the curriculum. Directed by Ted Post, the movie has much unintentional comedy, but it's message of sexual indulgence as primal cure for all attitudinal problems comes off as such sentimental hogwash that only the most naive college freshman will be deceived. Some nudity. O (R)

Harriet the Spy (1996) Dark, overlong tale of an 11-year-old (Michelle Trachtenberg) whose nanny (Rosie O'Donnell) inspires her to write down everything she sees, but this causes much heartache when her sixth-grade classmates read what she has written in her notebook about each of them. Directed by Bronwen Hughes from Louise Fitzhugh's novel, the movie turns into a nasty revenge story which is then slickly resolved in an unconvincing conclusion. The cruelty of youngsters and some crude language. A-II (PG)

Harry and Son (1984) Meant to be a warmhearted comedy that tugs at the heartstrings, this woeful misfire about a laid-off construction worker (Paul Newman, who also produced, directed, and did the screenplay) and his sensitive son (Robby Benson) is painful to sit through. Not the least oppressive element is Benson's insufferably cloying acting style. Aside from some rough language, the movie would be entirely innocuous if the filmmakers had not tried to get some comic mileage out of a sexually liberated secretary bestowing her favors on the heroes. O (PG)

Harry and the Hendersons (1987) Northwest fantasy tale directed by William Dear in which John Lithgow and family try to protect a big-foot primal creature they name Harry from the media, the police, and a French-Canadian hunter while learning, along the way, a bit about the human links to the animal kingdom. Violent auto chases in an otherwise mild-mannered picture of family values and the virtues of teamwork. A-II (PG)

Harry and Tonto (1974) Art Carney stars as Harry, the 72-year-old retired teacher who, after being evicted from his New York apartment, takes to the road with his cat Tonto, sees different aspects of contemporary American life, and reaches California to continue his struggle alone. Written, produced, and directed by Paul Mazursky, the subtle, sensitive, bittersweet comedy about old age and loneliness is marred only by the needless inclusion of many vulgarisms that may not be suitable for the young. A-III (R)

Harry and Walter Go to New York (1976) James Caan is crafty Harry and Elliott Gould is guileless Walter, two safecrackers so inept that, according to gentleman safecracker Michael Caine, "they would require practice to become oafs." But that doesn't stop them from trying to beat Caine to the biggest safe of them all, with the competent assistance of Diane Keaton. Director Mark Rydell's slack, tepid gaslight-era comedy has overcooked a satirical breast fetish scene and some crude verbal gags. A-III (PG)

Harry in Your Pocket (1973) James Coburn fills the title role as a pickpocket working some of the Northwest's most photogenic watering places in collusion with Walter Pidgeon and Trish Van Devere. Directed by Bruce Geller, it misses as an offbeat crime movie but does offer lovely travelogue footage of the posh resorts visited by the gang, and some silly romantic sex and hip humor. A-III (PG)

Harum Scarum (1965) One of Elvis Presley's sillier musicals is set in the Middle East, where a Hollywood action hero (Presley) is kidnapped by Arab rebels, who want him to assassinate the ruler of a remote mountain kingdom. Directed by Gene Nelson, the numerous songs and comic relief (Jay Novello as a greedy thief) are lost in the exotic hokum of Arabian intrigues. Stylized violence and mild sexual innuendo. A-II (br)

Harvey (1950) Amusing adaptation of the Mary Chase play about affable imbiber Elwood P. Dowd (James Stewart) whose drinking companion is an invisible six-foot rabbit, which leads to some zany mix-ups when Elwood's slightly dotty sister (Josephine Hull) tries to have her brother committed. Directed by Henry Koster, the stagy but amiable comedy centers in Stewart's winning performance as the good-natured eccentric, with much goofy by-play from a fine supporting cast, especially the incomparable Hull, Cecil Kellaway as the bemused asylum director, and Jesse White as a bemused attendant. Comic inebriation. A-II (br)

Harvey Girls, The (1946) Lightweight musical set in the Old West, where a railroad town is tamed by the opening of a Harvey restaurant, one of whose waitresses (Judy Garland) separates an honest casino owner (John Hodiak) from his greedy dance-hall girlfriend (Angela Lansbury). Directed by George Sidney, the songs are agreeable, with comic diversions supplied by Ray Bolger, Virginia O'Brien, Marjorie Main, and Chill Wills, but the cast is a lot better than the thin story deserves. Frontier violence, including a roomful of brawling women, and romantic complications. A-II (br)

Has Anybody Seen My Gal? (1952) Sentimental comedy in which a hard-pressed small-town family during the 1920s takes in an aging boarder (Charles Coburn) who transforms their lives before revealing he's a millionaire. Directed by Douglas Sirk, the contrived story is of less interest than Coburn's standout performance and the nostalgic period detail. A-I (br)

Hasty Heart, The (1949) Affecting adaptation of

John Patrick's play in which a proud Scot (Richard Todd) recovering from a battle wound in an Allied hospital in Burma at the end of WW II refuses the friendship offered by his Canadian nurse (Patricia Neal) and fellow soldiers (notably Ronald Reagan), who know he has a terminal condition. Directed by Vincent Sherman, the contrived situation is laced with humor, including a running gag about what a Scotchman wears under his kilt, but the performances of those in the hospital ward evoke enough genuine emotion to support the pathos Todd achieves as the lonely, vulnerable soldier. A-I (br)

Hatchet for the Honeymoon (1973) Spanish-Italian movie about a bridal-wear designer (Stephen Forsyth) who cannot bear to see his young models leave to get married because at age 12, the poor paranoiac hacked up his mother when she remarried, and ever since, well, never mind. Badly directed by Mario Bava, the bloodier frames have been chopped from the picture, leaving only a stuffy sexual aura to put adults to sleep. A-III (GP)

Hate (1996) Gritty French movie about 24 hours in the lives of three unemployed youths from a public housing-project in a Paris suburb, where they take drugs, argue, and elude aggressive cops, until inevitably a violent confrontation occurs. Writer-director Mathieu Kassovitz's stark, documentary-like portrait of dead-end youth pitted against brutal police takes a hard look at ghetto violence and despair. Subtitles. Intermittent violence, drug abuse, crude sexual references, and incessant rough language. A-IV (nr)

Haunted Honeymoon (1986) Light and uneventful horror-spoof written and directed by Gene Wilder with silly performances by Wilder, Gilda Radner, and Dom DeLuise as radio actors. When Wilder develops a strange malady, some of his friends try to frighten him out of it during his honeymoon at his aunt's weird mansion. Slapstick violence and a bit of rough language. A-II (PG)

Haunted Palace, The (1963) Pedestrian horror movie directed by Roger Corman in which a man (Vincent Price) brings his bride (Debra Paget) to an 1875 New England town to take possession of his evil ancestor's estate, then struggles to keep his devil-worshipping relative's spirit from possessing him. Stylized violence, menacing situations, and sexual innuendo. A-II (br)

Haunting, The (1963) Eerie version of Shirley Jackson's novel about Hill House, an isolated 19th-century New England mansion, where reports of psychic phenomena are investigated by a parapsychologist (Richard Johnson), a skeptic (Russ Tamblyn), and two potential psychic mediums (Julie Harris and Claire Bloom). Director Robert Wise generates mounting tension from the spooky atmosphere of the long-empty house and the terror of unseen forces lurking within it. Scary proceedings, mostly in the imagination, but no less effective for that. A-II (br)

Haunting of Julia, The (1981) Mia Farrow, playing a grief-stricken mother who has just lost her young daughter in a tragic accident, moves into an old house which comes completely furnished, including just the kind of unholy secret one would expect to find in this kind of place and this kind of movie. Director Richard Loncraine's muddled and tedious movie utterly lacks the inner logic that a good ghost story must have. Some violence. A-III (R)

Hav Plenty (1998) Talky comedy taking place over a New Year's weekend during which a trio of African-American women individually attempt to seduce a penniless writer (Christopher Scott Cherot), who turns his memory of the experience into his first screenplay. Also written, directed, and edited by Cherot, the fitfully funny story explores a theme of what-do-women-want in somewhat witty but largely superficial fashion. Mild sexual innuendo, an instance of profanity, and much rough language. A-III (R)

Havana (1990) On the eve of the Cuban Revolution, an American gambler (Robert Redford) gets caught up in rescuing the beautiful wife (Lina Olin) of a wealthy revolutionary (Raul Julia). Director Sydney Pollack has fashioned an intriguing though overlong love story, bolstered by strong performances and scenes of a decadent Havana overrun by American gangsters. Restrained sexual references, minor violence, and occasional rough language. A-III (R)

Having Wonderful Crime (1945) Wacky comic thriller with a Chicago lawyer (Pat O'Brien) staying with newlywed friends (Carole Landis and George Murphy) at a resort hotel, where they try to solve the murder of a vanishing magician (George Zucco). Directed by Eddie Sutherland, the trio's comic by-play is intermittently amusing, but the plot's murky menace adds little to the entertainment. Stylized violence, threatening situations, and mild sexual innuendo. A-II (br)

Hawaii (1966) Big, boring movie based on the sweeping epic by James A. Michener concentrates on the struggle between missionary Max von Sydow and the islands' pagan way of life. Von Sydow does as well as possible in his one-dimensional role of religious fanatic, while Julie Andrews is patient and long-suffering and Jocelyne Le Garde is delightful as the Hawaiian ruler. Though the spectacular re-creates its locale convincingly, it romanticizes the natives and vilifies the missionaries. Some nudity and harrowing childbirth scene. A-III (br)

Hawaiians, The (1970) Readers of James A. Michener's sweeping novel **Hawaii** will be disappointed that almost none of its spirit and style has survived in this sequel. Its witless, wordy screenplay avoids every opportunity for action in telling the potentially lively story of the lusty sea captain (Charlton Heston) who brought the pineapple to Hawaii. Though at times showing a nice sense of place, the lethargic direction of Tom Gries fails to do much with his cast. Silly nude bathing scene. O (GP)

Hawk, The (1993) Overwrought British thriller in which a woman (Helen Mirren) comes to suspect her travelling-salesman husband (George Costigan) is the serial killer, but, given her history of mental illness, the police discredit her story with tragic results. Director David Hayman's attempts to reveal the woman's increasingly shaky state of mind never get far beyond booming music and exaggerated sound effects. Brief violence, some sexual references, and intermittent rough language. A-III (R)

Hawks (1989) Manic British lawyer (Timothy Dalton) and depressed American football hero (Anthony Edwards), both terminally ill, team up for one last adventure in an Amsterdam bordello, but are instead sidetracked into a journey of self-discovery by two offbeat, refreshing women (Janet McTeer and Camille Coduri). Director Robert Ellis Miller's black comedy about death and dying is quirky, bittersweet, and poignant. Much vulgar humor, profanity, sexual innuendo, and incidental nudity. A-IV (R)

Hawks and the Sparrows, The (1967) Italian movie about the human journey on the road of life is a simple but strikingly photographed allegory in two acts which reject both Christian and Communist ideologies in favor of a very earthbound vision of humanity. Director Pier Paolo Pasolini offers a sketchy probe rather than a finished statement, and it is an interesting challenge for seasoned moviegoers. A-IV (br)

Hawmps (1976) The Army's attempt to replace horses with camels in the rugged terrain of the Southwest was ended by the Civil War and the railroad. Director Joe Camp's comic version of that attempt does have its occasional moments, but the humor never gets beyond the level of silliness. The camels steal every scene they're in, and only character actor Jack Elam comes close to out-mugging them. Children will find it fun, but parents may wish for a little less slapstick. A-I (G)

Hazel's People (1978) When a New York hippie goes to rural Pennsylvania for the burial of a student-activist friend, he finds himself at home with the simple, anti-materialistic people of the local Mennonite community, but finally leaves to find his own way. What the film lacks in moviemaking polish, it makes up for in sincerity, photogenic locale, and superb performances by Pat Hingle and Geraldine Page. A-II (PG)

He Got Game (1998) Muddled drama in which the country's top high-school basketball player (Ray Allen) is pressured about his choice of college or turning pro by manipulative friends and relatives, especially his estranged father (Denzel Washington), whose jail sentence will be shortened only if he can convince his son to attend the governor's alma mater. Writer-director Spike Lee convincingly explores the exploitation of student athletes, but is less successful in developing the father-son relationship which is at the story's core. Some violence, a brief but graphic sexual encounter with nudity, racial slurs, sexual references, and recurring rough language. A-IV (R)

He Knows You're Alone (1980) Psychotic killer of young brides-to-be is the focus of director Armand Mastroianni's low-budget exploitation thriller. Physical and psychological violence, sexual titillation, and occasional profanity. O (R)

He Married His Wife (1940) Thin screwball comedy in which a racehorse owner (Joel McCrea), tired of paying alimony, tries to get his ex-wife (Nancy Kelly) to wed another, but a series of misunderstandings while they're weekend guests of a daffy divorcée (Mary Boland) lead them to remarry. Directed by Roy Del Ruth, there are plenty of humorous turns from a good cast, but the plodding plot is too predictable to be more than mildly amusing. Comic treatment of marriage and some double entendres. A-III (br)

He Rides Tall (1964) Dreary Western directed by R.G. Springsteen in which a sheriff (Tony Young) has to kill his foster-father's nasty son, then many complications later, kills the dastardly villain (Dan Duryea) responsible for all his troubles. Much brutal violence and some sexual situations. A-III (br)

He Said, She Said (1991) Two rival journalists (Kevin Bacon and Elizabeth Perkins), who are live-in lovers, analyze their rocky relationship from their separate points of view. As co-directed from the male perspective by Ken Kwapis and from a female vantage by Marisa Silver, the movie's self-absorbed yuppie couple presents a talky, sometimes tacky, and insipid look at the war of the sexes. Acceptance of promiscuity and cohabitation and a flash of nudity. A-III (PG-13)

He Walked by Night (1948) Case history of a cunning cop-killer (Richard Basehart), who evades the Los Angeles police department for months until routine leg work by a persistent detective (Scott Brady) leads to his apprehension. Though dated by a heavy-handed narration, director Alfred Werker's dramatization effectively stages the action scenes in semi-documentary style with notable success, especially the climactic chase through the city's storm drains. Stylized violence. A-II (br)

He Who Must Die (1957) French drama adapted from the Nikos Kazantzakis novel about the inevitable fate of some Greek refugees in a Turkish occupied village. Whether seen as religious allegory or political tract, director Jules Dassin has made an emotionally arresting motion picture. A-III (br)

Head (1968) Flashy vehicle for the Monkees musical group (Peter Tork, Davy Jones, Mickey Dolenz, and Michael Nesmith) juxtaposes a nonsensical melange of scenes against a background chromatically and acoustically gone berserk. Directed by Robert Rafelson, the Monkees themselves are simply four very ordinary young men trying to imitate the Beatles but without the British group's spontaneity and sense of fun. Some tasteless spoofs. A-II (G)

Head Above Water (1997) Laborious comic misfire in which a staid judge (Harvey Keitel) grows manic trying to dispose of the corpse of his wife's former lover (Billy Zane) while she (Cameron Diaz) comes to fear her husband murdered him, then suspects it was the caretaker (Craig Scheffer). Directed by Jim Wilson, the lame series of misunderstandings that escalate into homicidal violence are too witless to be amusing, and the plot is too capricious to hold interest. Comic violence, grisly situations, sexual innuendo, and coarse language. A-III (PG-13)

Head Over Heels (1979) Minor bureaucrat (John Heard) has had a brief affair with a married woman (Mary Beth Hurt), but when she returns to her husband, he is obsessed to win her back. Directed by Joan Micklin Silver, the story is told in a series of flashbacks interspersed with scenes of the poor fellow's cheerless present life. All in all, it is a deadly dull affair. A-III (PG)

Headline Story (see: **The Hometown Story**)

Health (1979) Labored spoof of health addicts, the electoral process, and people in general, as a health organization gathers to elect a new president from its slate of candidates (Lauren Bacall, Glenda Jackson, and Paul Dooley), while a White House aide (Carol Burnett), a TV talk-show host (Dick Cavett), and a horde of zanies get in the way. Director Robert Altman gets few smiles and less coherence from this disjointed collection of dim characters and their witless antics. Numerous sexual references, several sexual situations, some vulgar language, and occasional profanity. A-III (PG)

Hear My Song (1992) Jaunty comedy follows a conniving London concert promoter (Adrian Dunbar) back to Ireland to lure a famous tenor (Ned Beatty) out of retirement for a reunion with his old flame (Shirley-Anne Field). Director Peter Chelsom's scenic joyride across Ireland is littered with plucky characters, romantic sentiment, and broad humor that's as silly as it is charming. Fleeting bedroom scene with nudity, momentary violence, and occasional rough language. A-III (R)

Hear No Evil (1993) Unaware that a priceless stolen coin has been hidden in her pager, a deaf woman (Marlee Matlin) and her boyfriend (D.B. Sweeney) face mortal danger from the corrupt cop (Martin Sheen) who orchestrated the theft and wants the coin back. Director Robert Greenwald delivers only mild suspense in a thriller which gets sidetracked by a dull romance. Intermittent violence, a discreet bedroom scene, fleeting nudity, and minimal rough language. A-III (R)

Hearse, The (1980) Supernatural thriller starring Trish Van Devere, who is recovering from a nervous breakdown and haunted by visions of a hearse. Directed by George Bowers, the film contains some graphic violence, and devil worship figures in the plot. A-III (PG)

Heart and Souls (1993) Schmaltzy comedy-fantasy in which a yuppie banker (Robert Downey, Jr.) becomes the reluctant medium for four strangers (Charles Grodin, Alfre Woodward, Kyra Sedgwick, and Tom Sizemore), killed in a bus crash as he was being born, to each have one more chance at doing something they need to complete before moving on to the afterlife. Director Ron Underwood's tiresome fantasy is as inept as it is doggedly warmhearted, straining to wring rich emotions out of contrived situations. Some sexual innuendo, fleeting violence, and an instance of profanity. A-III (PG-13)

Heart Beat (1980) Anemic screen biography of 1950s writer Jack Kerouac (John Heard) focuses on his friendship with fellow Beat Generation figures, Neal and Carolyn Cassady (Sissy Spacek and Nick Nolte). John Byrum's simplistic script and direction waste good performances and suggest nothing of the force and passion that must have driven Kerouac. Some use of nudity and a muddled moral outlook. O (R)

Heart Condition (1990) Bigoted slob of a Los Angeles vice-cop (Bob Hoskins) is hounded by the ghost of his heart-transplant donor (Denzel Washington), a slick black attorney out to protect his heart and solve his murder. Writer-director James D. Parriott skirts over the crime-thriller aspects of the story to focus on the comic antagonisms between the two offbeat characters and, along the way, make some valid points about healthy hearts and racial stereotypes. Some sexually suggestive scenes involving prostitutes, climactic violence, and rough language, including racial slurs. A-III (R)

Heart Is a Lonely Hunter, The (1968) Sensitive adaptation of a Carson McCullers story about the frustrated attempts of a deaf-mute man (Alan Arkin) to help others, yet his friendship with a teenager (Sondra Locke) proves not enough to compensate for his isolation in a world of utter silence. Director Robert Ellis Miller successfully treads the line between sentiment and sentimentality. A-II (G)

Heart Like a Wheel (1983) Fact-based story of Shirley Muldowny, who overcame prejudice in a man's profession to achieve success as a racing car driver, but her career triumphs cost heartbreak and bitterness in her personal life. With Bonnie Bedelia giving a wonderful performance in the role, director Jonathan Kaplan catches the human level of the story in moving and poignant fashion. Because adultery figures in the plot, it is not for younger viewers. A-III (PG)

Heart of Dixie (1989) Deep South saga in which a 1950s college coed (Ally Sheedy) blossoms from shallow sorority-sister into a vocal integrationist under the tutelage of a worldly photojournalist (Treat Williams), who has returned to his home turf to document civil-rights activity. Directed by Martin Davidson, the characters in this soapy stew are so thin and stereotyped, and the pivotal issues of sexism and racism are so poorly developed, that this scattershot tale is best forgotten. Much sexual innuendo, some vulgar references, and brief violence. A-III (PG)

Heart of Glass (1978) German movie about a town of glass blowers in the 18th century who find their livelihood threatened when the secret of a unique scarlet glass dies with a master craftsman. Werner Herzog directs a muddled parable so ponderous and dense, so inane in story line and dialogue that the whole enterprise lies beyond parody. A-III (nr)

Heart of Midnight (1989) Inheriting a former sex-club from her sleazy uncle (Sam Schacht), a disturbed young woman (Jennifer Jason Leigh) hopes to turn it into a classy nightclub but is tormented by unseen demons that seem to haunt the place or her mind. An empty-headed psychological thriller with muddled artsy direction by Matthew Chapman. Includes a brief but brutal rape, sexually suggestive scenes, nudity, profanity, intense menace, and gratuitous grisly violence. O (R)

Heartbeat (1946) Uneven romantic comedy set in Paris, where a reform-school escapee (Ginger Rogers) joins a school for pickpockets (run by Basil Rathbone), gets caught by a diplomat (Adolphe Menjou), and winds up in love with an embassy official (Jean-Pierre Aumont). Directed by Sam Woods, the romance is somewhat bubbly, but the humorous situations tend to go flat. Romantic complications. A-II (br)

Heartbeeps (1981) Dreadful futuristic comedy about two robots who fall in love and run off together is an endless one-joke situation with no place to go. Andy Kaufman and Bernadette Peters have an impossible task as the romantic robots, and the banality of John Hill's script is underscored by the ineptness of Allan Arkush's direction. To be avoided at all costs. A-I (PG)

Heartbreak Hotel (1988) Hoping to cheer up his ditzy mother (Tuesday Weld), a teenager (Charlie Schlatter) kidnaps Elvis Presley (David Keith) after a 1972 concert, and the singer rejuvenates the boy's troubled family by injecting some clean-living values, self-respect, and hope where none existed before. Though well-intended by writer-director Chris Columbus, the first half of this fable has a decidedly nasty tone. Some rough language and implications of illicit sexual liaisons. A-III (PG-13)

Heartbreak Kid, The (1973) Adult comedy about an immature Jewish bridegroom (Charles Grodin) who is stung by a WASP (Cybill Shepherd) on his Miami Beach honeymoon with his ill-fated bride (Jeannie Berlin) is a marvelous but uneven combination of strengths, especially those of Elaine May's deft direction. The movie bristles with telling barbs about contemporary life, some of which are merely entertaining, but many of which are truly enlightening and occasionally frightening. A-III (PG)

Heartbreak Ridge (1986) Flag-waving portrait of a Marine sergeant (Clint Eastwood, who also directed), a hardened veteran whose last assignment before retirement is to train a reconnaissance troop for combat. His brutal methods and end-justifies-the-means philosophy supposedly prepare his troop for victory in Grenada. Violent combat footage, scenes of dramatic brutality, and excessive profanity and vulgar language. O (R)

Heartbreakers (1985) Two friends (Peter Coyote and Nick Mancuso) in the throes of midlife crisis share everything, even their girlfriends. Shallow, unsympathetic characterizations under the direction of Bobby Roth. Nudity and a graphic sex scene. O (R)

Heartburn (1986) Meryl Streep and Jack Nicholson are professionals whose marriage dissolves over his infidelity. Director Mike Nichols's essentially pessimistic view of the contemporary state of romance in the 1980s implies more than it expresses, but focuses amiably on the plight of women who must find options to the American male's fear of commitment and responsibility. Adult theme, harsh language, and sexual innuendo. A-III (R)

Heartland (1981) Poor widow (Conchata Ferrell) takes her seven-year-old daughter to Wyoming in the first decade of the century, where she has signed on as housekeeper of a dour and laconic Scotsman (Rip Torn) on a remote ranch. During the long months of a hard and terrible winter, they realize that life would be better together, and the rancher proposes marriage. Director Richard Pearce's optimistic conclusion doesn't seem justified by the couple's poor circumstances, but this low-budget effort is unusually effective, both in its emotional force and fine performances by Ferrell and Torn. Extremely realistic birth sequence and some scenes of slaughtering farm animals are inappropriate for younger viewers. A-II (PG)

Hearts and Minds (1975) Hard-hitting documentary on the Vietnam War avoids the political realities that shaped the conflict and polarized the nation, presenting instead a painful picture of American soldiers lost in a moral quagmire. Director Peter Davis has compiled a selective history of the war as a visceral experience, which may touch some hearts and open some minds about the moral paradox that Vietnam represented for the American people. Graphic scenes of battlefield carnage with military and civilian casualties, as well as some explicit scenes of prostitution. A-IV (R)

Hearts of Darkness: A Filmmaker's Apocalypse (1991) Documentary on the making of **Apocalypse Now!** — the 1979 Vietnam War movie loosely based on Joseph Conrad's novel, *Heart of Darkness* — shows how the production ballooned from modest-budget project into high-cost epic as director Francis Ford Coppola struggled with his ambitions, complicated logistics on Philippine locations, and an incredible run of bad luck. In their fascinating behind-the-scenes account, Fax Bahr and George Hickenlooper make extensive use of footage shot during the course of production by Coppola's wife, Eleanor, and recent interviews with many of those involved in what proves a fascinating account of a creative moviemaker on the edge of self-destruction. Sporadic violence, recreational drug use, rough language, and a flash of rear nudity. A-III (R)

Hearts of the West (1975) Would-be writer of Westerns (Jeff Bridges) gets a job in 1930s Hollywood as a cowboy extra, but on his rise to stardom he has to dodge some crooks who are out to recover the loot he took by mistake. Director Howard Zieff's old-fashioned narrative makes an enjoyable comedy of character and situation, though for a film based on the innocence of its young hero, the needless scene of a stag party with a stripper interrupts the fun and makes it adult fare. A-III (PG)

Heat (1972) Sylvia Miles, Joe Dallesandro, and Andrea Feldman play characters living on the fringes of Hollywood and using sex to help their careers or assuage their loneliness. Director Paul Morrissey has made the **Sunset Boulevard** of independent cinema, but his characters here drown in a heavily-convoluted and sexually explicit narrative. O (R)

Heat (1987) Extremely dull exercise in pointless mayhem directed by D.M. Richards pits a compulsive gambler (Burt Reynolds) against a Las Vegas crime mob in a dreary series of revenge murders. Excessive violence. O (R)

Heat (1995) Violent tale of vicious criminals (notably Robert De Niro and Val Kilmer) determined to pull off a $12-million bank robbery, despite the dogged efforts of a police detective (Al Pacino) to nab them. Writer-director Michael Mann's drawn-out attempt at a grim study of criminal characters and their pursuers is overwhelmed by extended scenes of graphic bloodshed and nasty brutality. Excessive violence, restrained bedroom scenes, and much rough language. O (R)

Heat and Sunlight (1989) Self-indulgent movie directed by and starring Rob Nilsson as a troubled photojournalist who agonizes through the last 16 hours of his affair with a dancer (Consuelo Faust). It's not clear why their relationship is on the skids or why he is still depressed by a Biafran photo assignment 20 years before. Graphic sexual encounter with much frontal nudity and some profanity laced with sexual vulgarities. O (nr)

Heathers (1989) Disturbing satire of remorseless, self-serving, compassionless adolescents who seek revenge on equally nasty peers by murdering them and passing off the deaths as suicide. Winona Ryder is excellent as the movie's muddled voice of reason, but her character never quite makes sense, nor does the ease with which she conspires with the school psychopath (Christian Slater). Director Michael Lehmann has a feel for teenage narcissism, but this grisly account of it seems pointless. Much intense profanity, teen promiscuity, and mocking the value of human life. O (R)

Heaven and Earth (1991) Historical epic set in feudal Japan traces the rivalry of two fierce samurai (Takaaki Enoki and Masahiko Tsugawa) to become the most powerful warlord of the day. Director Haruki Kadokawa paints a vast canvas of colorful pageantry and immense battle scenes of greatest interest to armchair warriors and students of Japanese history. Subtitles. Intermittent battlefield violence. A-II (PG-13)

Heaven and Earth (1993) Growing up during the Vietnam War, a peasant girl (Hiep Thi Le) sees her family torn apart, is brutalized by both sides, then faces continuing problems after settling in San Diego as the wife of a Marine sergeant (Tommy Lee Jones) suffering from post-war stress. Writer-director Oliver Stone's fact-based dramatization paints a vivid portrait of a woman — and symbolically of her country — victimized and devastated by the ravages of war, but the movie's anti-war theme is overwhelmed by its narrow focus on the lurid and melodramatic aspects of her story. Much wartime violence including rape and torture, brief bedroom scenes and nudity, off-screen suicides, and recurring rough language. A-III (R)

Heaven Can Wait (1943) After a lifetime which he sums up as "one continuous misdemeanor," a deceased but still dapper playboy (Don Ameche) seeks accommodations from the Devil (Laird Cregar) rather than applying "upstairs." Director Ernst Lubitsch's zesty comedy of family life in late 19th-century New York makes good use of a splendid cast (Gene Tierney, Charles Coburn, Eugene Pallette, and Marjorie Main) and a witty script with a droll afterlife fantasy opening and close. Mild sexual innuendo. A-II (br)

Heaven Can Wait (1978) Charming remake of the 1941 comedy **Here Comes Mr. Jordan** has a past-his-prime quarterback (Warren Beatty) die prematurely, but the bungling angel responsible (James Mason) places him in the body of an eccentric millionaire just as he is done in by his wife (Dyan Cannon) and her lover (Charles Grodin). Enlisting the aid of his former coach (Jack Warden) to get his new body into playing form, the now-rich quarterback returns to the gridiron and wins the love of a good woman (Julie Christie). Co-directed by Beatty and Buck Henry, the entertainment succeeds in being very innocent and yet wise and funny. A-II (PG)

Heaven Help Us (1985) The adventures of four desperate misfits in a Catholic boys' school in Brooklyn in 1965. Though Catholic education of the era does take its lumps, the underlying feeling is one of affection. Written by Charles Purpura and directed by Michael Dinner, the movie is flawed, especially with regard to its fragmented story line, but the overall result is moderately entertaining. Some rough language and sexually oriented humor. A-III (R)

Heaven Knows, Mr. Allison (1957) Lightweight but good-natured WW II yarn in which a shipwrecked Marine (Robert Mitchum) washes up on a Pacific island, meets an Irish nun (Deborah Kerr) who had stayed behind to care for a dying priest, and, when Japanese troops set up a base there, the two take refuge in a cave to await the arrival of the Navy. Directed by John Huston, the story centers on the friendship forged in harrowing circumstances between two people whose very different outlooks on life are the subject of much earnest discussion and some humor, though on one occasion the Marine gets drunk and does not act like a gentleman. Some wartime violence. A-I (br)

Heaven with a Gun (1969) Glenn Ford plays a gunslinging preacher who mediates between feuding ranchers and sheepherders, punctuating his sermons with gunplay. Director Lee Katzin trades on the family-type Western to introduce a sexually oriented saloon encounter, a graphic rape scene, and a brief but totally gratuitous nude scene. A-III (M)

Heaven's Gate (1980) Bloated Western written and directed by Michael Cimino takes up the familiar theme of ranchers-vs.-settlers and is set in late 19th-century Wyoming, with lavish and exhausting attention to period authenticity. However, the characters are shallow, the story lacks dramatic force, and the whole thing becomes a pretentious bore. Extravagant nudity in one bedroom scene and it lacks any moral frame of reference. O (R)

Heaven's Prisoners (1996) Slack thriller in which a former New Orleans cop (Alec Baldwin) seeks vengeance after his wife (Kelly Lynch) is brutally murdered by a sadistic trio answering to an unknown boss. Directed by Phil Joanou, some atmospheric visuals provide the only interest in a tawdry tale of predictable betrayals and deadly revenge. Recurring murderous violence, fleeting drug use, brief full nudity, some profanity, and much rough language. O (R)

Heavenly Bodies (1985) Canadian movie directed by Lawrence Dane in which rival aerobic academies face off in a winner-take-all marathon workout. This **Flashdance** sequel makes the original look like a somber work of art. Excessive sex and nudity and some foul language. O (R)

Heavenly Creatures (1994) Fact-based dramatization about an obsessive friendship between two fantasy-prone adolescent girls (Melanie Lynsky and Kate Winslet) in 1950s New Zealand, which leads them to murder one of the girl's mothers when she (Sarah Peirse) refuses to let her 15-year-old daughter move to South Africa with the other. By employing the romanticized diary entries of one of the girls to furnish the movie's perspective, writer-director Peter Jackson's cautionary story of a terrible family tragedy tends to get sidetracked by its giddy depiction of the girls' developing lesbian attraction. A gory bludgeoning, brief heterosexual encounter, and increasing homosexual overtones. A-IV (R)

Heavenly Days (1944) Radio characters Fibber McGee and Molly (Jim and Marion Jordan) leave Wistful Vista for wartime Washington, where Fibber tries to make a speech from the Senate gallery and winds up being named the Average Man by the Gallup Poll. Director Howard Estabrook spends more time waving the flag than tickling the funny-bone in this dated patriotic comedy. A-I (br)

Heavenly Kid, The (1985) Feeble effort telling of a teenager who had been killed in the early 1950s and sent back to Earth in the 1980s to earn his wings by helping a gawky teen to become a success with the girls. Written and directed by Gary Medoway, the movie is contrived, clumsy, not very funny, and manipulatively sentimental. A-III (PG-13)

Heavy (1996) Slow-paced character study set in a rural New York tavern whose aging owner (Shelly Winters) hires a young part-time waitress (Liv Tyler), who soon fascinates the owner's overweight, slow-witted son (Pruitt Taylor Vince) but only irritates the tavern's regular waitress (Deborah Harry). Writer-director James Mangold develops the slight situation in a fashion some will find ponderous, though others may appreciate for focusing on the tenuous nature of human relationships. Sexual situations, excessive drinking, and occasional rough language. A-III (R)

Heavy Metal (1981) Feature-length cartoon made in a variety of styles and backed by the music of various rock groups offers six science-fiction tales loosely tied together by the appearance of a malevolent green sphere of death and destruction. The animation is far more imaginative than the narratives themselves, which never rise above the elemental level of pulp comic books. Abundance of cartoon sex and violence. O (R)

Heavy Petting (1989) Nostalgic, relatively non-judgmental compilation movie that looks back at the forces shaping and controlling teen sexuality and dating mores during the 1950s. Directors Obie Benz and Josh Waletzky use clips from old sex-ed and Hollywood teen films, topical period news, and TV footage to catalog the type of propaganda used to contain teen libidos of the period. Incidental explicit sexual terminology and some reminiscences about sexual promiscuity. A-III (R)

Heavy Traffic (1973) Director Ralph Bakshi and producer Steve Krantz animated feature about black and white love in the gritty streets of New York is infantile in technique and scabrous in theme and image. The film seems to have set out to offend just about everybody, and has generally succeeded with a constant flow of racial, ethnic, sexual, and religious slurs. O (X/R)

Heavyweights (1995) Comedy clunker about a summer camp catering to overweight boys (including Aaron Schwartz, Shaun Weiss, and Kenan Thompson) taken over by a fitness freak (Ben Stiller) who instigates draconian measures to slim down the youngsters in order to produce an infomercial hawking his weight-loss program. Writer-director Steven Brill attempts to spoof America's fitness craze, but his script is a weak collection of sitcom situations, lame fat jokes, and interchangeable youngsters, who predictably rebel and triumph in their search for just desserts. Minor violence and occasional toilet humor. A-II (PG)

Heidi (1937) One of Shirley Temple's better vehicles comes from the Johanna Spyri children's classic about a little Swiss orphan who brings cheer into the morose life of her grandfather (Jean Hersholt), then is taken from him to be the companion of a crippled rich girl in Frankfurt, where, after helping the child to walk again, she is spirited away by a hateful housekeeper (Mary Nash). As directed by Allan Dwan, curly-haired Shirley smiles her way through considerable woes until rescued from near tragedy on Christmas Eve. Best for young children with the reassuring presence of a parent. A-I (G)

Heidi (1953) Swiss version (directed by Luigi Comencini) of the Spyri story about an eight-year-old girl (Elsbeth Sigmund) brought from the Alps to 1900 Frankfurt to cheer a sick child, then returns home to her overjoyed grandfather (Heinrich Gretler). The Alpine scenery and period settings add interest to the simple tale, though the English dubbing sometimes gets in the way. A-I (br)

Heidi (1968) Updated version takes the little Alpine charmer (Eva Maria Singhammer) to present-day Frankfurt, whose bustling traffic makes her ache all the more for her peaceful mountains, despite the comforts of the wealthy city household where she reanimates the spirits of a wheelchair-bound youngster. Directed by Werner Jacobs, the 1965 Austrian production is true to its source, beautifully photographed, and well dubbed into English. A-I (br)

Heidi (1993) Fine adaptation of the 1881 children's classic from Germany about a sweet little orphan (Noley Thornton) living in the mountains with her cranky but loveable grandfather (Jason Robards) until taken from him to serve as companion to a crippled city girl (Lexi Randall) in the care of a nasty governess (Jane Seymour). Directed by Michael Rhodes with handsome location photography of Salzburg and the Austrian Alps, the appealing family film stresses many positive themes for children about love, death, forgiveness, and the joys of reading. A-I (G)

Heidi's Song (1982) Hanna-Barbera's animated, musical version of the popular story about an orphan girl who brings cheer into the life of her grandfather, a crippled child, and all sorts of other people is an entertaining film for younger children. A nightmare sequence in which Heidi is menaced by rats might be rather scary for the very young. A-I (G)

Heiress, The (1949) Stark adaptation of "Washington Square," Henry James's story of 1890s New York, where a plain-looking, sweet-natured innocent (Olivia de Havilland) succumbs, despite the warnings of her wealthy father (Ralph Richardson), to the blandishments of a handsome suitor (Montgomery Clift) interested only in her inheritance. Director William Wyler's bleak tale of dashed expectations and dour retribution relies on strong performances to give some psychological depth to the melodramatic situation. False love and its heartbreaking consequences. A-II (br)

Helen of Troy (1955) Crowded chronicle of the Trojan War begins as Paris (Jacques Sernas) escapes Sparta with Helen (Rosanna Podesta), the wife of King Meneleus (Niall MacGinnis), who pursues them to Troy, where his Greek allies sack the city after a 10-year siege by hiding soldiers in a wooden horse. Directed by Robert Wise, the heroic characters in this ancient myth spend more time talking than acting, but the historical spectacle is visually satisfying, especially the concluding sequence of Troy's fall. Period violence and sexual situations. A-II (br)

Helga (1968) German sex-education motion picture is too superficial for adults, too detailed for adolescents, and has no place in movie theaters. It might have use in a classroom or the home where, parents could put the material in a moral context. A-IV (br)

Helicopter Spies, The (1968) Episodic spy-caper directed by Boris Sagal follows the TV formula of "The Man from U.N.C.L.E." series with super-agents Robert Vaughn and David McCallum stealing a secret weapon from an Iranian scientist (John Dehner), then losing it to a diabolical criminal (Bradford Dillman). The usual artificial thrills, stylized violence, and sexual innuendo. A-III (br)

Hell Bent for Leather (1960) Muddled Western about an innocent man (Audie Murphy) being hunted down as a murderer by a sadistic marshal (Stephen McNally), whose motivation for chasing a man he knows is innocent proves disappointingly unconvincing when revealed in the final reel. Directed by George Sherman, the premise works up some initial interest, but the senseless chase grows tiresome until the flat conclusion. Stylized violence and romantic complications. A-II (br)

Hell Boats (1970) Routine WW II story about an American (James Franciscus) in the British navy whose difficult mission is to destroy a German base on Sicily which has proven impenetrable from the sea and the air. The focus in on the American's relationship to the men under his command and a romantic involvement with his superior's wife, but, though the acting leaves a bit to be desired, action buffs should be pleased with the special effects. A-III (PG)

Hell in the Pacific (1968) Two enemy soldiers (Lee Marvin and Toshiro Mifune), marooned on a tiny Pacific island during WW II, struggle first against each other, then against their adverse environment as they join forces in trying to build a raft. Directed by John Boorman, the cast of two makes a striking contrast not only in culture but also in acting styles, which helps make very watchable what is essentially an allegory on the nature of aggression and the will to survive. A-II (G)

Hell Is for Heroes (1962) Gritty WW II tale about a US infantry squad reaching the fortified Siegfried Line on the German border, where they're ordered to hold out until reinforcements arrive. As the tension mounts, director Don Siegel concentrates on defining the characters (grim loner Steve McQueen, seasoned veterans Fess Parker, and Harry Guardino, with Bobby Darin and Bob Newhart as comic relief) which pays off when the battlefield erupts in attacks and counterattacks. Wartime violence and questions about its morality. A-II (br)

Hell on Frisco Bay (1955) Hard-bitten crime story of an ex-cop (Alan Ladd) who serves five years in San Quentin for manslaughter, then comes after the waterfront boss (Edward G. Robinson) who framed him. Director Frank Tuttle can't do much with the hackneyed script and cliched characters, though the Italian-American setting and its Catholic flavor add some interest. Stylized violence, muted sexual references, and a troubled marriage. A-II (br)

Hell to Eternity (1960) Uneven dramatization follows WW II hero Guy Gabaldon (Jeffrey Hunter) as he's raised by a Japanese-American family during the Depression, then joins the Marines after Pearl Harbor, and during the battle for Saipan uses his knowledge of Japanese to persuade the defeated general (Sessue Hayakawa) to surrender. Directed by Phil Karlson, the irony of Gabaldon's foster-family being interned is sensitively handled, though an extended sequence of carousing on leave is embarrassingly phony. Much battlefield violence and sexual innuendo. A-III (br)

Hell Up in Harlem (1974) Fred Williamson fights his way to the top as a black mobster before turning onto the straight-and-narrow and becoming a family man of sorts. Larry Cohen's writing and direction are third-rate and the acting of Williamson and cast is even worse. Excessive violence. O (R)

Hell with Heroes, The (1968) Cynical WW II veteran (Rod Taylor) needing cash to bail out the air-freight business he started in Algeria gets involved with a black marketeer (Harry Guardino) and then falls for the criminal's mistress (Claudia Cardinale). Directed by Joseph Sargent, the entirely predictable melodrama has some excessive brutality and sexually suggestive scenes. O (br)

Hell's Angels on Wheels (1967) Overly violent motorcycle-gang movie directed by Richard Rush exploits sex and brutality for their own sake. O (br)

Hell's Angels 69 (1969) Two wealthy playboys (Tom Stern and Jermey Slate) infiltrate the Hell's Angels gang in order to use them as a diversionary front to pull off a casino heist. Biker girl (Conny Van Dyke) upsets the plan, and the rather dull climax of director Lee Madden's cycle flick is a bumpy cross-country chase ending in death. Notable only in that the real Hell's Angels tried a stint at acting. A-III (M)

Hell's Belles (1969) A young, roughhewn, stoic rancher (Jeremy Slate) sets out alone to retrieve his valuable bike, and the girl (Jocelyn Lane) swapped for it, from the lawless gang that stole it. Director Maury Dexter's motorcycle epic features violent action and a moral theme, but the film is too steeped in adolescent rat-pack thinking. A-III (M)

Hell's Bloody Devils (1971) The title characters are beefy motorcyclists in the pay of a German counterfeiter who has a deal with Las Vegas mobsters to help finance a worldwide resurgence of Nazism. Director Al Adamson tosses into this noxious mix some FBI agents, wily blondes, and a Jewish woman searching for the war criminal who executed her parents. Much violence and gratuitous sex. O (GP)

Hell's Half Acre (1954) Muddled melodrama in which a war widow (Evelyn Keyes) comes to Hawaii after her husband (Wendall Corey) turns up suspected of murdering his mistress (Nancy Gates). Directed by John H. Auer, the picture centers on the husband who became a racketeer after escaping death at Pearl Harbor and his attempt to trap the real killer (Philip Ahn) in the Honolulu red-light district of the title. Stylized violence and sexual situations. A-III (br)

Hell's House (1932) Dated Prohibition-era story in which a naive youth (Junior Durkin) takes the rap for a friendly bootlegger (Pat O'Brien) and winds up in a brutal reform school, then is saved when the adult culprit comes clean. Directed by Howard Higgin, it's strictly formula fare, save for O'Brien's breezy portrayal of the likeable heel and Bette Davis's minor role as his girlfriend. Some stylized violence, including a boy's death from mistreatment at the reformatory. A-II (br)

Hellbound: Hellraiser II (1988) Blood oozes from every frame of director Tony Randel's horror movie sequel in which a teenager (Ashley Laurence) is tagged for evisceration by the skinless souls of the nether-world who have been released from hell by an ancient puzzle box. Excessive, senseless, and repulsive gore, some simulated sex, brief nudity, and periodic profanity. O (R)

Hellcats of the Navy (1957) Routine WW II picture directed by Nathan Juran follows the cardboard exploits of submarine commander Ronald Reagan charting a passage through mined waters leading a battle fleet into the Sea of Japan, with Navy nurse Nancy Davis awaiting his safe return. The usual wartime heroics, tempered with questions of risking the crew's safety to rescue one of its members. A-I (br)

Heller in Pink Tights (1960) Silly but stylish and very self-indulgent Western directed by George Cukor follows an itinerant theatrical troupe (headed by Anthony Quinn) whose star performer (Sophia Loren) has a weakness for separating men from their money, a failing which keeps the company on the run from one town to the next. Some stylized violence and considerable sexual innuendo. A-III (br)

Hellfighters (1968) John Wayne heads an oil well fire-fighting team whose highly dangerous profession take them worldwide at a moment's notice, but his worries are about his daughter (Katherine Ross) whose marriage is in danger of winding up like that of his estranged wife (Vera Miles). Directed by Andrew McLaglen, the marital comparisons are strained and of less interest than the grand pyrotechnics of flaming oil wells and vintage Wayne action, including the expected but totally irrelevant barroom brawl. A-II (G)

Hellions, The (1962) Nasty clunker about a demented outlaw (Lionel Jeffries) and his four brutish sons terrorizing a frontier town and its one police officer (Richard Todd) in 1860s South Africa. Directed by Ken Annakin, the plot is as ludicrous as the acting is hammy. Much senseless violence and some sexual references before the inevitable retribution. A-II (br)

Hello Again (1987) Failed romantic comedy about a housewife (Shelley Long) brought back from the dead by an occult incantation of her sister (Judith Ivey) to find that her husband is now married to her best friend. Frank Perry's pedestrian direction of a rather dull and unimaginative script provides few laughs and almost no romance. Some sexual innuendo, vulgar situations, and coarse language. A-III (PG)

Hello, Dolly! (1969) Zesty New York Jewish widow and matchmaker (Barabra Streisand) gets emotionally involved with a rich client (Walter Matthau). Lavish musical extravaganza is a vehicle for Streisand's melodious talents staged and directed by Gene Kelly with exhilarating, albeit synthetic, Hollywood effervescence. Thornton Wilder's play is memorably infused with Jerry Herman's music. A-I (G)

Hello Down There (1969) An Ivan Tors production with plenty of marine life to entertain the kiddies, the adventure yarn situates a family with three teenagers complete with guitars in an experimental undersea house to sample living on the ocean floor and save their father's job. Plot centers around how the youngsters will get their music published while down under. A-I (G)

Hello-Goodbye (1970) Languid European triangle features Curt Jurgens as a baron with a love for antique autos, Genevieve Gilles as a baroness with a roving eye, and Michael Crawford as a lover of ladies and fine cars. Millions were spent on the cars, sets, and costumes, but not a penny's worth of action, dialogue, or characterization to break up the sheer boredom. Director Jean Negulesco's agonizing pace makes both the inept acting and slack moral values all the more apparent. O (PG)

Hellraiser: Bloodline (1996) Sadistic horror fantasy in which the descendents of a toy-maker (Bruce Ramsay) continue a centuries-long battle against a pinheaded demon (Doug Bradley) loosed from hell by their ancestor. Directed by Alan Smithee (a pseudonym), the fourth in the series lumbers clumsily along from one bloody death to another in a meaningless jumble of noxious pulp waste. Excessive violence, sexual situations, and rough language. O (R)

Hellraiser III: Hell on Earth (1992) Revolting horror tale continues the gruesome killing spree of satanic monster Pinhead (Doug Bradley) as he vies with a TV newswoman (Terry Farrell) over a magical box that can return him to Hell. Director Anthony Hickox fills the screen with an incessant parade of young people being tortured, murdered, and mutilated. Excessive dehumanizing violence, crude mockery of religion, a sex encounter with nudity, and intermittent rough language. O (R)

Hellstrom Chronicle, The (1971) Odd mixture of fascinating yet unsettling documentary footage of insect life in all its forms, from kindly moths and ladybugs to deadly fire ants and black-widow spiders. Unfortunately, director Walon Green's movie uses scare tactics in arguing that the world is on the brink of an ecological disaster from which insects will emerge as the dominant form of life. Though the information is neither startling nor precise, the insect footage is stunning. A-II (G)

Help! (1965) Madcap musical comedy with the Beatles on the run from Oriental religious fanatics (Leo McKern and Eleanor Bron) seeking a ring which Ringo can't get off his finger. Director Richard Lester uses a lot of clever editing, but the chase's frantic pace eventually grows tiresome, not that Beatles's fans will mind a whit. Comic menace and slapstick violence. A-I (br)

Hennessy (1975) Routine thriller about an Irishman (Rod Steiger) who decides to blow up Parliament after seeing his family killed by the British, but trying to stop him are a brutal British police officer (Richard Johnson) and an Irish widow tired of all the bloodshed (Lee Remick). Director Don Sharp works every conceivable variation on the chase, but the thrills aren't there and the result is quite ordinary melodrama. A-III (PG)

Henry: Portrait of a Serial Killer (1990) Former cellmates (Michael Rooker and Tom Towles) team in videotaping the tortured death throes of their random victims until one murderer kills the other. Director John McNaughton's pointless exercise in sadistic mayhem is little more than a voyeur's guide to psychopathic behavior. Excessively graphic scenes of brutal slayings, including torture, dismemberment, rape, and necrophilia. O (nr)

Henry & June (1990) Boring dramatization of the adulterous affair between writers Anais Nin (Maria de Medeiros) and Henry Miller (Fred Ward) in 1931 Paris. Director Philip Kaufman's dull and pretentious account alternates Nin's breathless musings about "sexual liberation" with scenes of simulated sex acts, lesbian as well as heterosexual. In attempting to justify a promiscuous lifestyle, the treatment resorts to explicit depictions of sex and much rough language. O (NC-17)

Henry V (1945) Brilliant adaptation of Shakespeare's play opens on the stage of the Globe Theater in 16th-century London, then transports the viewer to 1415 France, where the English king (Laurence Olivier) leads his forces to victory over the French at Agincourt. Also directed by Olivier, the result blends theater into film very nicely, with rousing action scenes capped by the English bowmen's decimation of the heavily armored French knights. Period violence and some ribald humor. A-II (br)

Henry V (1989) This version of the Shakespeare play features a powerful performance by Kenneth Branagh in the title role and makes good use of close-ups to bring intimacy and immediacy to Henry's mission to reclaim the French throne. Also directed and adapted by Branagh, the St. Crispin's Day speech of unity and the bloody battle at Agincourt are especially memorable, driving home the fact that war is hell and that faith is a strong instrument in survival. Graphic hanging scene and an intense, bloody climactic battle. A-II (PG)

Henry Fool (1998) Urged by a pompous would-be author (Thomas Jay Ryan) to write down his dark thoughts, a garbage man (James Urbaniak) gains literary fame and respect while his mentor marries the trash-man's sister (Parker Posey) and inherits his menial job. Writer-director Hal Hartley's wry fable touches on art, politics, family relations, and personal redemption in a tale marked by black humor and bizarre twists. Brief violence including suicide, a sexual encounter, fleeting nudity, some scatological humor, intermittent rough language, and an instance of profanity. A-IV (R)

Henry VIII and His Six Wives (1974) Keith Michell gives a memorable performance in a role that spans Henry's entire reign from the boyish energy of the young king to the quiet suffering of an amorous man betrayed by age and disease. Director Waris Hussein turns the historical events into personal drama, with each of the wives getting their fair share of attention, and the result proves as satisfying for the average viewer as for the specialist in Tudor history. A-II (PG)

Her Alibi (1989) A novelist (Tom Selleck) suffering from writer's block acts as an alibi for a beautiful Romanian murder suspect (Pauline Porizkova) intending to use her as a subject for his next book, and they end up falling in love despite their mutual distrust and lack of chemistry. Ineptly directed by Bruce Beresford, it's a poor excuse for a romantic thriller. Mild sexual innuendo, incidental vulgar references, and some minor comic-book violence. A-III (PG)

Her Twelve Men (1954) Sentimental bromide directed by Robert Z. Leonard in which a widow (Greer Garson) turns to teaching in a posh boarding school for boys, struggles to win over her class of 10-year-olds, and winds up with marriage proposals from the school's head teacher (Robert Ryan) and a student's father who happens to be a rich widower (Barry Sullivan). Treacle then and even more artificial now. A-I (br)

Herbie Goes Bananas (1980) The little car with a personality takes a Caribbean cruise to Panama this time, where it and its young owners become involved with villains looting ancient ruins. Director Vincent McEveety's effort is dismal, the Disney production is substandard, and it is hard to see how children would like it any more than their parents. Sprinkling of double entendres, presumably for adults accompanying their tots. A-I (G)

Herbie Goes to Monte Carlo (1977) Disney's "Love Bug" Volkswagen with a personality makes a comeback to win the Trans-France car race, a feat complicated by a diamond theft and his falling in love with a sleek sports car. Director Vincent McEveety makes the mildly amusing fantasy with the two cars much easier to take than the human actors (Dean Jones, Don Knotts, and Julie Sommars). Strictly for the kids. A-I (G)

Herbie Rides Again (1974) Sequel to **The Love Bug** with Herbie the lovable Volkswagen back, not as a race car, but as the well-kept companion of eccentric dowager Helen Hayes, who is trying to keep her home from being bulldozed by snarling land developer Keenan Wynn. Directed by Robert Stevenson, it's all lots of witless fun in the standard Disney vein. A-I (G)

Hercules (1959) Dubbed Italian production directed by Pietro Francisci offers a thin tale of adventure as the ancient Greek demigod of the title (Steve Reeves) helps Jason recover the Golden Fleece and reclaim the throne taken by his uncle. Comic-book violence. A-I (br)

Hercules (1983) Lou Ferrigno, better known as the Incredible Hulk, brings his massive pectorals to the role of the classic strongman, but not even Ferrigno's muscles can hoist John Thompson's languid direction and Lewis Coates's silly script out of the slough of mediocrity. Some mild violence. A-II (PG)

Hercules (1997) Buoyantly animated tale about the ancient Greek hero of the title (voice of Tate Donovan) who is kidnapped from Mt. Olympus as a baby and raised as a mere mortal, until, with a little help from a wisecracking teacher (voice of Danny De Vito), he proves himself a true hero by rescuing a damsel (voice of Susan Egan) from the fiery god of the underworld (voice of James Woods). Co-directed by John Musker and Ron Clements, the colorful adventure is a music-filled celebration of today's pop culture, using toga-clad figures from a mythological past, but tainting the fun midway is a shamelessly blatant plug for Disney products. A few scenes of menace may frighten toddlers. A-I (G)

Hercules Against the Moloch (1963) Dubbed Italian production directed by Giorgio Ferroni with a Greek prince (Gordon Scott) pretending to be Hercules in order to rally support against a despotic god-king. Formula hokum with stylized violence and sexual situations. A-III (br)

Here Come the Girls (1953) Lame Bob Hope vehicle places him on turn-of-the-century Broadway as a ham actor whose attempts to woo an actress (Arlene Dahl) rile her murderous boyfriend (Robert Strauss). Director Claude Binyon's comedy has a flat script and unappealing characters, despite some good musical numbers with Rosemary Clooney. Unamusing sexual innuendo and comic violence. A-III (br)

Here Come the Waves (1944) Stale musical comedy directed by Mark Sandrich has Navy recruits (Bing Crosby and Sonny Tufts) at cross purposes romancing twin-sister Wave recruits (Betty Hutton in a dual role). Bing sings, Tufts connives, and Hutton gets to play a prim brunette as well as her usual daffy blonde in this wartime morale booster. The usual romantic mix-ups. A-II (br)

Here Comes Every Body (1973) British filmmaker John Whitmore photographed a week's worth of encounter therapy at California's Esalen Institute, where participants are encouraged to remove their clothing as part of the treatment. The mostly young group grope frantically and vituperate fiercely, but seem to be acting more for the camera than to learn anything about themselves. Exploitative nudity. O (nr)

Here Comes Mr. Jordan (1941) Whimsical fantasy in which a saxophone-playing prizefighter (Robert Montgomery) is saved just before dying in an plane crash by an over-eager novice angel (Edward Everett Horton) and then has to find a new body in which to live his allotted span. Directed by Alexander Hall, the quest for a suitable replacement may not be very logical but is lots of fun, thanks chiefly to its comic twists, otherworldly special effects, and a fine cast, including James Gleason as an incredulous boxing manager and Claude Rains in the title role as the head angel. Not for literal-minded youngsters. A-II (nr)

Here Comes the Groom (1951) Affable journalist (Bing Crosby) comes home with two war-orphans after three years in France to find his long-suffering fiancé (Jane Wyman) about to marry a genial millionaire (Franchot Tone). Director Frank Capra's musical comedy suffers from a surfeit of cuteness, a tired plot, and an aging Crosby, though Wyman is surprisingly good in a lightweight role and Alexis Smith scores as a stuffy heiress who learns to unbend. Romantic complications. A-II (br)

Here We Go Round the Mulberry Bush (1968) British sex comedy in which a 17-year-old lad (Barry Evans) wants to be initiated into the mysteries of sex, gets involved with a string of girls who are easily available, but when he gets the one pure girl who is not, she turns out to be no better than the rest. Directed by Clive Donner, the predictable course of the story tries to hide behind overdone optical effects, and its humor tends toward the sordid. Unnecessary prolonged nude sequence. O (br)

Here's Your Life (1969) Exceptional seriocomic coming-of-age Swedish movie about an idealistic youth's (Eddie Axberg) experiences, beautifully evoked with period and location details, shortly before WW I. Director Jan Troell's gentle, warm, and sincere drama reveals the youthful search for the spiritual significance of life, sex, and brotherhood. Brief nudity in a sexual situation. A-III (PG)

Heritage of the Desert (see: **When the West Was Young**)

Hero (1992) After rescuing 54 passengers from a crashed, burning jetliner, a small-time crook (Dustin Hoffman) is cheated out of a million-dollar reward when a homeless man (Andy Garcia) takes credit and is lionized by a TV reporter (Geena Davis). Director Stephen Frears's stylish comedy about heroism and media manipulation blends its flawed characters into an intricate plot that is both thoughtful and entertaining. Some morally ambiguous situations and minimal rough language. A-III (PG-13)

Hero, The (1972) Richard Harris stars as an aging football player with feet of clay who is befriended by a 10-year-old runaway (Kim Burfield). Produced in Israel, the banality of the script by Wolf Mankowitz is exceeded only by the ineptness of its direction by Harris. A-II (PG)

Hero Ain't Nothin' But a Sandwich, A (1978) Benjie (Larry B. Scott) is a black 13-year-old living with his mother (Cicely Tyson) and grandmother (Helen Martin) in a Los Angeles ghetto, and his inability to accept his mother's lover (Paul Winfield) leads to school problems, the wrong companions, and drug addiction. Produced by Robert Radnitz and directed by Ralph Nelson, the movie deals realistically with the ghetto environment whose problems go far beyond those of drugs, but it does so from a perspective of hope and human potential. Some coarse street language and the depiction of Benjie shooting heroin and the agony of withdrawal. Good for parents to see with their older children and discuss afterwards. A-III (R/PG appeal)

Hero and the Terror (1988) Los Angeles detective (Chuck Norris) comes up against a psychotic murderer (Jack O'Halloran) of almost superhuman strength. Director William Tannen attempts to turn karate-champ Norris into a sensitive, reluctant hero whose lady love (Brynn Thayer) and their new baby are as important as his job, but it just doesn't wash. Numerous graphic neck-breaking scenes, gruesome half-naked corpses, the hero's unwed union, and some locker-room language. O (R)

Hero at Large (1980) Disarming romantic comedy about a struggling young actor (John Ritter) who, returning from a job still dressed in a superhero costume, routs a pair of thugs robbing a grocery, becomes a media celebrity, and is then exploited by a smooth public-relations man (Bert Convy). Director Martin Davidson's contrived story runs out of invention about two-thirds of the way through, but it has the prime asset of Ritter's warm appeal in the role, and Anne Archer is extremely likable as the disdainful neighbor eventually won over by his charm and decency. Despite its melodramatic ending, the comedy has a generous amount of good humor and the romance is unabashedly sentimental. Occasional burst of rough language. A-II (PG)

Hero's Island (1962) When an 18th-century colonial family comes to settle on an island off the North Carolina coast, a hostile band of local fishermen (Rip Torn, Dean Stanton, and others) tries to drive them off until a mysterious castaway (James Mason) takes a hand in the proceedings. Written and directed by Leslie Stevens, the uneven tale of frontier justice focuses on the nonviolent principles of the widow (Kate Manx) heading the family and the stranger's curious reluctance to intervene, though his skill with a cutlass is more than a match for the local bullies. Some violence, much menace, and children in peril. A-I (br)

Heroes (1977) Henry Winkler plays a mentally disturbed Vietnam War veteran who treks cross-country with Sally Field to meet old buddies and set up a worm farm. Director Jeremy Paul Kagan tries for seriocomic social relevance but manages only some underdeveloped ideas about the psychic toll wrought by war. Violent fight scene makes this less suitable for youngsters. A-III (PG)

Heroes of Telemark, The (1966) Norwegian resistance fighters (Kirk Douglas, Richard Harris, and Ulla Jacobson) try to stop the Nazis from developing the atom bomb. Director Anthony Mann accomplishes a lot with the action scenes but the story line keeps getting in the way. Stylized violence. A-II (br)

Hester Street (1975) Lively tale of Jewish immigrant life in New York's Lower East Side just before the turn of the century tells of the conflict between a husband (Steven Keats), who wants to forget all traces of his origins, and his wife (Carol Kane), who refuses to abandon the Russian Jewish traditions in which she was raised. Directed by Joan Micklin Silver, it is a film to be seen as a piece of Americana but also to be savored for the many brilliant little scenes that comprise a pulsating mosaic of the immigrant experience shared by so many Americans of diverse national origins. A-III (PG)

Hex (1973) Motorcycle gang led by Keith Carradine fall upon a little Nevada town on their way to California but are decimated by two comely farm girls (Hilarie Thompson and Tina Herazo). The year is 1919, and the girls are daughters of an Indian medicine-man whose legacy to them is the power of witchcraft. Directed by Leo Garen, the unintentionally comic proceedings are distinguished only by their attempt at an erotic atmosphere which is as silly as it is unnecessary. O (PG)

Hexed (1993) Crude spoof of violent thrillers in which a bored hotel-clerk (Arye Gross) assumes a fake identity and gets romantically involved with a homicidal model (Claudia Christian). Writer-director Alan Spencer's emphasis on shrill, vulgar, and nasty humor is a cheap substitute for comic wit. Extended sex scene, much nudity and rough language, and frequent comic violence. O (R)

Hey Good Looking (1982) Animated feature by Ralph Bakshi about juvenile-gang warfare in Brooklyn in the 1950s is extremely ugly and distasteful. It has an unremitting emphasis upon sex and violence. O (R)

Hi Diddle Diddle (1943) Dopey hit-or-miss comedy directed by Andrew L. Stone in which the wedding plans of a doltish sailor (Dennis O'Keefe) and his fiancé (Martha Scott) are complicated by his con-man father (Adolphe Menjou), the wealthy concert singer (Pola Negri) to whom he's married, the bride's mother (Billie Burke), and a genial nightclub singer (June Havoc). Much sexual innuendo. A-III (br)

Hi, Mom! (1970) After failing as a porno-film maker, a serious young lad (Robert De Niro) finds success as an urban guerrilla. Director Brian De Palma's movie is a put-on put-down of present American customs and culture. However, its clumsy satirizing of contemporary fads and fashions will also outrage the moral sense of some of its viewers. O (R)

Hi-Lo Country, The (1998) Western-themed melodrama set in 1946 New Mexico, where two cowboy buddies (Woody Harrelson and Billy Crudup) court tragedy after falling in love with the same married woman (Patricia Arquette). Directed by Stephen Frears, the backdrop of the dying cowboy culture proves of more interest than the twisted loyalties of the tangled threesome. Sporadic violence, frequent heavy drinking, discreet sexual encounters, some profanity, and an instance of rough language. A-III (R)

Hickey and Boggs (1972) When Los Angeles private eyes Bill Cosby and Robert Culp take a simple case of finding a missing person, they are soon embroiled in a sticky mess involving murder, a fortune in stolen currency, Chicago bank robbers, the Mafia, brutal cops, and black militants. Also directed by Culp, the movie starts promisingly enough but soon bogs down in plot complications and ends on a bitter, hopeless note. Hard-edged look at the tribulations of crime-fighting, it is extremely violent. A-IV (PG)

Hidden, The (1987) An alien from another galaxy inhabits the bodies of a series of individuals, turning them into homicidal maniacs, until finally stopped by a good alien (Kyle MacLachian) and a Los Angeles detective (Michael Nouri). Jack Sholder directs all the mayhem with mindless gusto. Excessive violence, brief nudity, and rough language. O (R)

Hidden Agenda (1990) Fictionalized though fact-based political thriller about a British policeman (Brian Cox) sent to Belfast to investigate the slaying of an American civil-rights lawyer (Brad Dourif) by Ulster security forces, who he discovers are systematically terrorizing the populace with the secret complicity of the British government. Director Ken Loach's chilling indictment of British policy in Northern Ireland is fueled by republican sympathies, but there is little reference to the IRA's men of violence to balance its picture of Orange fanaticism and a heavy-handed ending about a Fascist conspiracy among Britain's top leaders. Some graphic violence and brutalizing tension, a few instances of rough language, and references to an illicit sexual relationship. A-III (R)

Hidden Homicide (1959) Plodding British mystery directed by Tony Young in which a man (Griffith Jones) framed for the murder of his wealthy cousin gets some help from his girlfriend (Patricia Laffan) and a newspaper reporter (Bruce Seton) in unmasking the three disguises used by the real killer (James Kenney). Stylized violence and sexual innuendo. A-III (br)

Hidden Room, The (1949) Intriguing British thriller in which a London psychiatrist (Robert Newton) with an unfaithful wife (Sally Gray) abducts her flippant American boyfriend (Phil Brown), keeps him chained in a cellar until the police abandon the search, then sets out to kill him and dissolve the corpse in an acid bath. Directed by Edward Dmytryk, the grisly plot gains plausibility from Newton's mild-mannered performance as the wronged husband whose ingenious plan to commit a perfect crime doesn't include a small dog and a Scotland Yard veteran (Naunton Wayne). Mounting suspense over an impending murder. A-II (br)

Hide in Plain Sight (1980) Taut, fact-based story about a divorced factory worker (James Caan) whose two small children disappear when the government gives a new identity to his ex-wife's new husband, who has turned state's witness against the mob. Also directed by Caan, the emphasis is upon characterization rather than action and the acting is uniformly convincing. The measure of its success is its ability to convey an authentic sense of reality with but the most sparing use of violence and rough language. A-II (PG)

Hideaways, The (see: **From the Mixed-Up File of Mrs. Basil E. Frankweiler**)

Hideaway (1995) Clunky horror fantasy in which a resuscitated car-accident victim (Jeff Goldblum) discovers that his hallucinations stem from the mind of a psychotic teen (Jeremy Sisto) out to add the man's wife (Christine Lahti) and daughter (Alicia Silverstone) to his collection of mutilated, deceased females. Director Brett Leonard's overuse of jarring special effects and cinematic cliches drains most of the suspense from the Dean R. Koontz novel on which this predictable thriller is based. Intermittent snippets of nasty violence and some rough language. A-III (R)

Hiding Place, The (1975) Interesting story of two Dutch Christians, Corrie and Betsie ten Boom, who gave shelter to Jews during the Nazi occupation, but when discovered one of them (Julie Harris) was sent to her death in Ravensbruck, while her sister (Jeannette Clift) was released by mistake. Produced by Billy Graham's World Wide Pictures and directed by James F. Collier, the movie is quite well-done, though the script belabors the theological questions raised by the evil of Fascism to the point of becoming preachy. Harsh violence. A-III (PG)

High Anxiety (1978) Mel Brooks spoof of suspense thrillers has Brooks as the new director of the Institute for the Very, Very Nervous, the unwitting target of a staff (Harvey Korman and Cloris Leachman) who want him out of the way so they can continue to rip off wealthy patients. Though dedicated to Hitchcock, the entirely predictable plot consists of one-liners, outrageous slapstick, and a mixture of sexual and tasteless humor that some may find offensive. A-IV (PG)

High Art (1998) Morose tale in which a female magazine-editor (Radha Mitchell) becomes sexually involved with a lesbian photographer (Ally Sheedy) who has been sharing a decadent heroin habit with her jealous longtime lover (Patricia Clarkson). Writer-director Lisa Cholodenko attempts to explore sexually charged intimate relationships, but the fuzzy characterizations get blurred in repetitive, woozy scenes of recreational boozing and drug use. An uncritical acceptance of homosexual lifestyles, sexual situations with nudity, recurring substance abuse, and much rough language. O (R)

High Command, The (1937) Creaky British melodrama directed by Thorold Dickinson in which the general (Lionel Atwill) commanding a 1930s West African garrison is implicated in the murder of an unscrupulous medical officer (Leslie Perrins) when police find evidence in the victim's room tying the commander to the death of a romantic rival in 1921 Ireland. Complicating matters is the attraction between the dead officer's cousin (James Mason) and the estranged wife (Lucie Mannheim) of a local businessman (Steve Geray). Stylized violence and romantic implications. A-II (br)

High Commissioner, The (1968) Entertaining crime melodrama in which Rod Taylor plays an Australian policeman sent to London to arrest his country's leading diplomat (Christopher Plummer) for murder but thwarts a plot to assassinate him instead. Directed by Ralph Thomas, the action holds one's attention, the acting is more than adequate, and it accomplishes its purpose of painless diversion. Stylized violence. A-III (br)

High Fidelity — The Adventures of the Guarneri String Quartet (1989) The musicians who comprise the oldest and most successful string quartet performing today are the subject of a spirited documentary in which the four men recall how they met and how they've managed to co-exist and flourish as a team for 25 years. Directed by Allan Miller, it is an enervating blend of biography, backstage banter, bickering, and virtuoso performances filmed stateside and on tour in Europe. Mild profanity. A-II (nr)

High Gear (1933) Creaky melodrama directed by Leigh Jason in which a hotshot race-car driver (James Murray) loses his nerve after a smash-up kills his mechanic, but returns to his winning ways on the track after saving the life of the mechanic's son (Jackie Searl). Stylized violence, menace, and romantic complications. A-II (br)

High Heels (1991) Unappealing Spanish melodrama about an estranged mother and daughter (Marisa Paredes and Victoria Abril), both of whom are suspected of murdering the daughter's husband (Feodor Atkine) who was also the mother's lover. None of the sappy, manufactured emotions rings true in writer-director Pedro Almodovar's kinky soap opera whose comic overtones fall distinctly flat. Subtitles. Brief sex scene with fleeting nudity plus lesbian and sexual references. A-III (R)

High Hopes (1989) Low-key British satire focuses on one working-class couple (Ruth Sheen and Philip Davis) and their interaction with family members and wealthy neighbors who don't share their concern about economic reform. Writer-director Mike Leigh offers an especially savage portrait of *nouveau riche* relatives, snooty yuppies, and a painfully real family dynamic in which communication and love play minimal roles. Some rough language laced with sexual vulgarities, brief abuse within an adulterous liaison, and a common-law cohabitation. A-IV (nr)

High Noon (1952) Message Western in which a

veteran sheriff (Gary Cooper) is left on his own to face four vengeful gunmen when the citizens of the town he had freed of outlaws refuse to get involved. Tautly directed by Fred Zinnemann, the isolated frontier setting is used to probe the psychology of fear which immobilizes a law-abiding community before the inevitable showdown whose outcome will affect them all. Stylized violence. A-II (br)

High Plains Drifter (1973) Clint Eastwood directs and stars in a pretentious, if not perverse, tale of a stranger with no name who destroys a town for its cowardly collaboration in the murder of a marshal opposing the local mining-company's appropriation of federal land. Eastwood's celebration of sadistic vengeance applied by an individual outside the law features repeated graphic brutalities and a sexist attitude toward women, in particular the male fantasy that women cannot fail to respond to rape. In short, an utterly despicable movie. O (R)

High Risk (1981) American adventurers (James Brolin, Bruce Davison, and Cleavon Little) meddle in the affairs of a Latin American drug-ring in a trite melodrama directed by Stewart Raffill. Excessive violence. O (R)

High Road to China (1983) Spoiled rich girl Bess Armstrong, 1920s vintage, hires hard-drinking, disillusioned WW I ace Tom Selleck to fly her from Turkey to China to find her father (Wilford Brimley) who has disappeared in the midst of a civil war. Jack Weston is good as Selleck's mechanic-sidekick and Brian Blessed scores as a vividly nasty war-lord. Director Brian G. Hutton's consistently entertaining adventure movie does not rely upon sex and extravagant violence to keep the viewer's interest. A-II (PG)

High School High (1996) Dopey comedy in which an affable high-school history teacher (Jon Lovitz) tries to motivate his rowdy inner-city class and winds up infiltrating a neighborhood crime ring preying on the students. Director Hart Bochner gleans limited humor from a feeble script and cartoon-like characters. Comic violence, sexual innuendo, fleeting rear nudity, intermittent crude expressions, and minimal profanity. A-III (PG-13)

High Society (1956) Flat musical version of **The Philadelphia Story** with Grace Kelly about to marry doltish John Lund when ex-husband Bing Crosby and reporters Frank Sinatra and Celeste Holm show up to complicate matters. Directed by Charles Walters, the Cole Porter score has some good numbers, especially Crosby's duet with Louis Armstrong on "Now You Has Jazz," but they can't save the updated proceedings from terminal dullness. Romantic complications. A-II (br)

High Spirits (1988) When an impoverished Irish nobleman (Peter O'Toole) attempts to save his rotting, debt-ridden ancestral castle by luring American tourists with a promise of ghostly sightings, he doesn't bargain for the arrival of the real ghosts of his ancestors (Daryl Hannah and Liam Neeson) who meet and co-mingle with his guests. Writer-director Neil Jordan's noisy, haphazard farce has few likeable characters and the sexual co-mingling of humans and ghosts is a tad dopey. Much foul language laced with sexual vulgarities, explicit sexual seduction, and the implied deflowering of a would-be priest. O (PG-13)

High Street (1977) Belgian movie of the Holocaust which has the haunting central figure of a woman (Annie Cordy) whose Jewish husband was taken one night to the camps and their child killed in the confusion. Twenty years later, living in a Brussels slum and regarded as a harmless eccentric, she awaits her husband's return, irrationally screaming profanities at passersby, until an expatriate American artist (Mort Shuman) befriends her and shares her plight with the world. Told simply but with emotional directness, director Andre Ernotte's powerful indictment of people's unconcern for the suffering of others is an eloquent reminder of the indifference that made the Nazi camps a tragic part of human history. A-III (nr)

High Time (1960) Tired vehicle for Bing Crosby in the role of the wealthy founder of a burger-restaurant chain who goes back to school as a 51-year-old college freshman and proves he's not too old to make the grade scholastically or romantically with French prof Nicole Maurey. Director Blake Edwards injects some energy through zippy montages of college life, concluding with Crosby's sappy but soaring graduation valedictory. Youthful hijinks and frolicking co-eds. A-I (br)

High, Wild and Free (1968) Fairly interesting documentary about fishing and hunting in British Columbia and Alaska with sportsman Gordon Eastman as the guide. Also directed and narrated by Eastman, the emphasis is on the beauty of nature, conservation, and ecology. A-I (br)

High Wind in Jamaica, A (1965) Some children fall into the hands of pirates (Anthony Quinn and James Coburn) who see to it that they are unharmed in the hazardous events that follow. Director Alexander Mackendrick's exciting adventure is an excursion into the uncertain world of childish logic, but the action is too intense for younger children. A-II (br)

Higher and Higher (1943) Low-budget musical comedy directed by Tim Whelan revolves around bankrupt millionaire Leon Errol who contrives with servants Jack Haley, Mary Wickes, and others to revive the household fortunes by marrying off scullery maid Michele Morgan to phony English nobleman Victor Borge, with neighbor Frank Sinatra helping out occasionally with a song. Dizzy romantic complications and mild sexual innuendo. A-II (br)

Higher Learning (1995) Provocative melodrama set in a racially tense university, where the African-American student (Omar Epps) comes to terms with prejudice, the woman student (Kristy Swanson) questions her gender preference after a date-rape, and a disturbed misfit (Michael Rapaport) turns into a skinhead. Writer-director John Singleton juggles so many characters and contemporary social issues that the narrative's potential for deadly violence comes to overshadow its uplifting themes of accepting personal responsibility and perseverance in educational studies. Brief but intense violence including suicide, a few restrained bedroom scenes, fleeting substance abuse, some racial slurs, and much rough language. A-III (R)

Highlander (1986) Action-adventure fable of good conquering evil offers a positive hero (Christopher Lambert) as one of group of immortals who must battle to the death throughout history until only one survives. Director Russell Mulcahy's mix of action and diverse period settings lifts the movie somewhat above the average for this kind of escapist fantasy. Some foul langauge, brief nudity, and several less-than-realistic decapitations. A-III (R)

Highlander: The Final Dimension (1995) Dark action-fantasy pitting good against evil through a pair of centuries-old opponents (noble Christopher Lambert and murderous Mario Van Peebles), each skipping around the globe seeking to behead the other, with the fate of mankind hanging somehow in the balance. Director Andy Morahan's murky, special-effects-laden sequel barely makes sense as it tries to stitch together a hodgepodge of pretentious visuals. Stylized violence with off-screen decapitations, a fleeting bedroom scene, and an instance of profanity. A-III (PG-13)

Highlander 2: The Quickening (1991) Attempting to release the Earth from the force-shield destroying its atmosphere, two extraterrestrials (Christopher Lambert and Sean Connery) are confronted by an archenemy (Michael Ironside) from their home planet. The dark, flashy visuals and overused special effects in director Russell Mulcahy's lame sequel only magnify the wooden acting and plot incoherence. Intermittent violence and minimal rough language. A-III (R)

Highway Dragnet (1954) Routine crime tale directed by Nathan Juran in which a Marine (Richard Conte) escapes a Las Vegas murder charge by hitching a ride with a photographer (Joan Bennett) and a model (Wanda Hendrix), then takes them into the desert to get proof of his innocence, but is unprepared for what he finds there. Stylized violence, menace, and sexual innuendo. A-II (br)

Highway 61 (1992) Drug-smuggling roadie (Valerie Buhagiar) cons a naive musician (Don McKellar) into driving a corpse from Ontario to New Orleans, then meets en-route a devil-obsessed crackpot (Earl Pastko) who steals the body. Director Bruce McDonald's surreal vision of America is an exasperating assortment of lost souls on the road to nowhere. Brief sexual encounter, momentary nudity, minimal violence, and occasional rough language. A-III (R)

Highwayman, The (1951) With help from an innkeeper's daughter (Wanda Hendrix), an impoverished nobleman (Philip Friend) in George II's England becomes a masked bandit stealing from the rich to give to the poor while battling the corrupt aristocrats (Charles Coburn and Victor Jory) who ruined his father. Directed by Lesley Selander, the movie opens and closes with stanzas from the title poem by Alfred Noyes, but the formula proceedings in between are rarely more than pedestrian. Period violence, including a torture scene, and romantic complications. A-II (br)

Hilary and Jackie (1998) Evocative portrayal of the close but tormented relationship between two musically gifted sisters, famed cellist Jaqueline du Pre (Emily Watson) and flutist Hilary (Rachel Griffiths), as their lives go in different directions, then are complicated by Jackie's struggle with multiple sclerosis, from which she dies in 1987 at age 42. Directed by Anand Tucker, the British production succeeds in showing how growing up in a competitive household affected the sisters' development, then focuses on Jackie's increasingly erratic behavior, especially her insistence on sleeping with Hilary's husband, as her condition worsens. Sexual situations and references, brief nudity, some rough language, and occasional profanity. A-IV (R)

Hill, The (1965) WW II British military prison is the setting for a story of human injustice with Sean Connery as a prisoner who bucks the system and Harry Andrews as the chief warder. Sidney Lumet directs a tightly wound script that is a brutal, agonizing experience, yet a meaningful one. A-IV (br)

Hills Have Eyes, The (1977) Amateurish little horror about a family on a trip who are attacked by some very nasty people but whom they eventually beat at their own game. Director Wes Craven overdoes the blood and gore. O (R)

Hills Run Red, The (1967) Bottom-drawer Italian Western directed by Lee W. Beavers (aka Carlo Lizzani) tells of an ex-Confederate soldier (Thomas Hunter) seeking vengeance on a double-crossing compatriot. The usual assortment of meaningless violence. A-III (br)

Hindenburg, The (1975) Based upon the ill-fated last voyage of the famous German zeppelin in May 1937, the movie half-heartedly proposes that the disaster was caused by anti-Nazi sabotage. Director Robert Wise's thin plot and its Grand Hotel collection of passengers is of less interest than the majestic airship in flight (the special effects are quite effective). The final tragedy is too intense for youngsters. A-II (PG)

Hired Gun, The (1957) Routine Western directed by Ray Nazarro in which a veteran gunslinger (Rory Calhoun) is deputized to bring back an escaped murderess (Anne Francis), but along the way he becomes convinced of her innocence and saves her from hanging by finding the real killer. Stylized violence. A-I (br)

Hired Hand, The (1971) Offbeat, sensitive, and quiet little Western directed by and starring Peter Fonda. The tale of a young man turning away from his life as a drifter in order to return to the wife, child, and farm he deserted years before is probably too slow for most Western fans. But those who stick with it will find the movie rewarding in the way it attempts to sort out human values and relationships. Warren Oates as Fonda's sidekick gives a subtle performance and figures in a gentle resolution that follows a climactic outburst of frontier violence. A-III (GP)

Hireling, The (1973) Superb British screen version of the L.P. Hartley novel about a high-born lady (Sarah Miles) recovering from a breakdown who hires a brooding WW I veteran (Robert Shaw) to drive her to her mother's house in Bath. Thus begins a slow and somber character study, which under the painstaking direction of Alan Bridges results in a painful awareness of the tragic limitations of a class-conscious society. Mature themes. A-III (PG)

Hiroshima, Mon Amour (1960) Evocative adaptation of the Marguerite Duras story in which a French actress (Emmanuele Riva) falls for a Japanese architect (Eiji Okada), but their affair sets off tragic memories of her love for a German soldier during the occupation, while he recalls the wartime loss of his loved ones. Director Alain Resnais interweaves present and past flawlessly, providing psychological insights into the character of the two principals while turning their relationship into a metaphor for international peace and the abolition of nuclear arms. Subtitles. Wartime violence and sexual situations. A-III (br)

His Double Life (1933) Famous English painter (Roland Young) lets the public believe him dead in order to settle down to a life of domestic bliss with a devoted wife (Lillian Gish) — until his new paintings give him away. Directed by Arthur Hopkins, the dated satire has some good moments, such as attending his own funeral at Westminster Abbey and his trial as forger and bigamist, but it's mostly a pedestrian affair. A-III (br)

His Kind of Woman (1951) Twisty crime thriller, directed by John Farrow, in which a small-time gambler (Robert Mitchum) is sent to an out-of-the-way Mexican resort, where a deported crime boss (Raymond Burr) is waiting to kill him and assume his identity back in the States. The resort is filled with tourists, one of whom is a ham movie-actor (Vincent Price) whose ability with a rifle plays a key part in the showdown, while his girlfriend (Jane Russell) has little to do but sing and pout. Stylized violence, sexual innuendo, and romantic complications. A-III (br)

His Majesty O'Keefe (1954) Escaping a mutiny on his ship in the South Seas, an American captain (Burt Lancaster) lands on the island of Yap in 1870, organizes the natives to gather copra (coconut meat), then defeats pirates raiding the island for slaves, and is proclaimed king until the German Navy arrives with other plans. As directed by Byron Haskin, adventure fans may be put off by the details of Yap life and customs, though others may find this more interesting than the action sequences. Stylized violence and romantic complications. A-II (br)

His Other Woman (see: **The Desk Set**)

History of the Blue Movie, A (1970) Blurry 16mm stag-films are not only hard on the eyes but quite deadening to the spirit, especially when accompanied by dreary, pseudo-sociological commentary. Alex de Renzy's compilation is really nothing more than a long advertisement for the more technically proficient pornography that he is in the business of putting out. O (nr)

History Of The World, Part I (see: **Mel Brooks' History of the World, Part I**)

Hit! (1973) Billy Dee Williams plays a hard-nosed federal agent whose daughter's death from an overdose determines him to mastermind a plot to exterminate the entire drug syndicate of Marseilles. Director Sidney J. Furie's movie uses all the essential story devices of the traditional detective movie but needlessly laced with casual sex, nudity, and rough language. O (R)

Hit Man (1973) Bernie Casey plays a hood stalking the killer of his brother through some of the seamier sites of East Los Angeles, where his quest takes him into the arms of some of the ghetto's most unliberated but libidinous ladies. George Armitage's sharp direction is well above black exploitation standards, but it is squandered in a plot featuring graphic sex and super-graphic violence. O (R)

Hit Me (1998) Grim tale in which a dumb bellhop (Elias Koteas) becomes involved with a seductive guest (Laure Marsac) who ensnares him in a major hotel heist that goes murderously awry. Director Steven Shainberg laboriously unreels the undoing of an ordinary guy who allows lust and greed to transform him into a callous killer. Some gory violence, discreet sexual encounter, fleeting drug use, brief profanity, and much rough language. A-IV (R)

Hit the Saddle (1937) Low-budget Western directed by Mack V. Wright features the Three Mesquiteers (Robert Livingston, Ray Corrigan, and Max Terhune), who save a wild herd of Pinto horses from being destroyed by a greedy rancher. A-I (br)

Hitcher, The (1986) Homicidal maniac (Rutger Hauer) terrorizes a teenage driver (C. Thomas Howell) who has unwisely given him a lift one rainy night on a lonely southwestern highway. Director Robert Harmon makes excessive use of violence and scenes of bloodshed to propel the narrative to its gory conclusion. O (R)

Hitchhikers, The (1973) Pregnant runaway (Misty Rowe) finds happiness with a group of hippies who subsist by seducing and robbing lonely motorcyclists. Its a bum trip of sex and violence from low-budget filmmakers Ferd and Beverly Sebastian. O (R)

Hitler (1962) Historically weak dramatization of the personal life of the Nazi dictator (Richard Basehart) centers on his mother complex and apparent sexual impotence, as seen in his relationships with his niece (Cordula Trantow) and Eva Braun (Maria Umo). Director Stuart Heisler inter-cuts period German footage with the backroom dramatizations, but the result is notable only for Basehart's portrayal of an increasingly psychotic megalomaniac. Wartime violence and sexual situations. A-III (br)

Hitler—Dead or Alive (1942) Home-front morale booster with German-speaking gangsters from Milwaukee (Ward Bond, Warren Hymer, and Paul Fix) parachuting into Nazi Germany in order to collect the million-dollar reward offered by a scientist (Russell Hicks) for getting rid of Hitler. Directed by Nick Grinde, the ludicrous proceedings include the captured hoods' escape from the Dachau concentration camp with some help from an anti-Nazi countess (Dorothy Tree), but the movie's pulp melodramatics provide only some dated fun and hokey wartime situations. Stylized violence, including the execution of children, and patriotic rhetoric. A-II (br)

Hitler: The Last Ten Days (1973) The paradox of this movie directed by Ennio de Concini is that, while it is very well-made and has an excellent performance by Alec Guinness as Hitler, it misses the boat historically by getting all the details right but without giving them the meaning of their context. The result is a faithful but impossibly constricted dramatization which reduces a genuine monster to a figure of morbid curiosity and becomes little more than a footnote to a much more complex and significant chapter of human history. A-II (PG)

Hitler's Children (1943) Simple but effective anti-Nazi picture in which a Hitler Youth member (Tim Holt) falls for a naturalized American student (Bonita Granville) in 1933 Berlin, then they meet again in 1939 when he is a Gestapo officer and she is sent to a labor camp because of her German birth. Directed by Edward Dmytryk, the story emphasizes the evils of the Nazi regime and the dangers facing Germans who oppose them, including a Catholic bishop (H.B. Warner) and the Gestapo officer-turned-patriot. Off-screen violence, Nazi racial rhetoric and a strong condemnation of the Nazis' use of sterilization. A-II (br)

Hoa-Binh (1971) Low-key French drama about life in a Vietnamese village as seen through the eyes of an 11-year-old boy. The child, who has never known a day of peace, loses his sick mother to death, and all that keeps the boy going is his hope that some day he and his sister will be reunited with their father, who is presumed to have joined the Viet Cong. Directed by Raoul Coutard, it is a film of compassion and not polemics. A-II (GP)

Hobson's Choice (1954) Amusing British tale set in 1890s Manchester, where a smug shoe-store owner (Charles Laughton) gets his comeuppance when his eldest daughter (Brenda de Banzie) marries an uneducated but skilled shoemaker (John Mills) and they open a rival shoe-shop. Directed by David Lean, the story of a wise daughter outsmarting her foolish dad has plenty of ironic humor, a zestful music score, and a grandly comic performance from Laughton. Period sexism and romantic complications. A-II (br)

Hocus Pocus (1993) Three witches (Bette Midler, Sarah Jessica Parker, and Kathy Najimy), brought back to life in a Halloween prank by teenagers, scour a New England village for children whose life-force they need to survive beyond the break of day. Directed by Kenny Ortega, the spooky comedy misfires by lavishing its attention on ghoulish special effects, rather than the contrived predicaments of silly youngsters and dopey adults. Multiple vivid frights and some sexual innuendo. A-II (PG)

Hoffa (1992) Key moments in the career of Teamster Union boss Jimmy Hoffa (Jack Nicholson) are recalled by a long-time aide (Danny DeVito) as they wait for a meeting with a powerful crime-lord (Armand Assante) on the last day of their lives. Also directed by DeVito, the energetic but erratic production has its center in Nicholson's convincing performance as a man of action, equally willing to use his fists or cut a deal to achieve his ends, but precisely what they were and what Hoffa wanted out of life remains an enigma. Some graphic violence, several sexual situations, brief nudity, and recurring rough language. A-III (R)

Hold Back the Dawn (1941) Stylish sentimental romance set in a Mexican border-town, where a shrewd European refugee (Charles Boyer) is barred from entering the US, until he woos an American schoolteacher (Olivia de Havilland), intending to become a citizen by marriage, then leaves her for another (Paulette Goddard). Directed by Mitchell Leisen from a script by Charles Brackett and Billy Wilder, the would-be immigrant's cynical deception of the naive teacher becomes heartbreaking, with enough genuine emotion to compensate for all the contrivances. False courtship and veiled sexual references. A-II (br)

Hold 'Em Jail (1932) Dated madcap comedy in which novelty salesmen (Bert Wheeler and Robert Woolsey) are framed for a hold-up and sent to prison, where they irritate the warden (Edgar Kennedy) while charming his sister (Edna May Oliver) and daughter (Betty Grable), then star on the prison's football team. Directed by Norman Taurog, the result is a loose collection of slapstick gags and one-liners put over by a cast whose shenanigans still draw some chuckles. Mild sexual innuendo. A-II (br)

Hold Me, Thrill Me, Kiss Me (1993) After accidentally killing his girlfriend (Sean Young), a thief (Max Parrish) hides out in a trailer park, where he gets involved with a crude stripper (Andrea Naschak), her younger sister (Adrienne Shelly), and other nasty types. Writer-director Joel Hershman's vicious comedy is a degrading parade of mean-spirited characters in ugly relationships that are pointedly unfunny. Much promiscuity and rough language, comic depiction of murders, and frequent nudity. O (R)

Hold On (1966) Mindless youth film directed by Arthur Lubin about a rock-music group is utterly innocuous and eminently forgettable. A-I (br)

Hold That Baby! (1949) Formula slapstick comedy directed by Reginald LeBorg in which Louie (Bernard Gorcey) lets the Bowery Boys (Leo Gorcey, Huntz Hall, and company) use the back of his sweet shop for a laundromat, where a troubled mom leaves her baby who turns out to be the heir to a fortune. Comic violence. A-I (br)

Hold That Co-Ed (1938) Wacky comedy in which a governor (John Barrymore) running for the Senate bets the election on the outcome of a college football game in which a woman student (Joan Davis) makes the key play. Directed by George Marshall, there's a little bit of romance (George Murphy-Marjorie Weaver and Jack Haley-Davis), some musical numbers, and a lot of funny business with Barrymore as a flamboyant politician. A-I (br)

Hold That Ghost (1941) In one of their better efforts, Bud Abbott and Lou Costello join a group of strangers (including Richard Carlson, Joan Davis, and Marc Lawrence) stranded in a spooky, abandoned hotel, where a fortune in criminal loot is hidden. Directed by Arthur Lubin, the comedy gets double mileage out of a setting honeycombed with sliding panels and secret passages abetting both the eerie goings-on, including a peripatetic corpse, and the wacky hijinks of Costello and Davis at her best. Comic menace and slapstick violence. A-I (br)

Hole in the Head, A (1959) Sentimental tale of a widower (Frank Sinatra) and his loving young son (Eddie Hodges) who knows his dad's an impractical dreamer about to lose his Miami hotel unless he gets a loan from his unsympathetic brother (Edward G. Robinson), whose wife (Thelma Ritter) wants to raise the boy in New York. Director Frank Capra takes some sharp swings at measuring success in dollar signs, but overplays the emotional tangle of family relationships in a story ending with unconvincingly high hopes that the boy's irresponsible father will change his ways. Comic insults and sexual innuendo. A-II (br)

Holiday (1938) Sophisticated romantic comedy in which an honest go-getter (Cary Grant) becomes engaged to a millionaire's glamorous-but-materialistic daughter (Doris Nolan), only to discover he's really in love with her more intelligent and winningly down-to-earth sister (Katharine Hepburn). George Cukor directs the Philip Barry play in high style, and the fine cast (including Lew Ayres, Edward Everett Horton, and Ruth Donnelly) easily ridicule the emptiness of upper-class pomposity in favor of the more substantive values of ordinary people. Entertaining, meaningful fare for all but the very young. A-I (nr)

Holiday Affair (1949) Undemanding sentimental romance in which a war widow (Janet Leigh) with a young son is torn between a steady but dull lawyer (Wendell Corey) and a hard-working but dreamy salesman (Robert Mitchum). Directed by Don Hartman, the warmth of the Christmas season setting and likeable performances by the principals make the sentimental proceedings hard to resist. A-I (br)

Holiday Inn (1942) Easy-going musical romance in which two veteran song-and-dance men (Bing Crosby and Fred Astaire) fall for the same woman (Marjorie Reynolds) while performing together in a rural inn open only on holidays. Directed by Mark Sandrich, the slim plot mainly provide an amiable context for Astaire's eye-fetching dance numbers and Crosby's crooning some pleasant Irving Berlin songs, including "White Christmas" for the first time. Romantic complications. A-I (br)

Hollow Reed (1997) Searing drama in which a divorced homosexual (Martin Donovan) sues for full custody of his nine-year-old son on the grounds the child is being physically abused by the live-in boyfriend (Jason Flemyng) of his ex-wife (Joely Richardson). Director Angela Pope movingly explores the characters' human passions and frailties in an insightful tale of prejudice, betrayal, and self-deception. Brief homosexual activity with some nudity, some violence including child beating, intermittent profanity, and instances of rough language. A-IV (nr)

Hollywood Babylon (1972) Director Van Guylder's movie uses a few photos and brief footage of famous silent movie personalities, then dresses-up actors of no ability to resemble them and stages reenactments of their reputed escapades. Wallowing in explicit sex sequences, it is solely of prurient interest. O (nr)

Hollywood Horror House (1975) Miriam Hopkins plays an aging former movie-star whose reveries are interrupted by a psychopathic visitor (John David Garfield) to her remote Beverly Hills estate. Thoroughly B-grade film with sex and violence directed against women. O (R)

Hollywood Knights (1980) Writer-director Floyd Mutrux's vulgar attempt at slapstick comedy recounts the misadventures of a cretinous Beverly Hills car club on Halloween night. Its crudity and graphic sexuality are seriously offensive. O (R)

Hollywood or Bust (1956) Anemic comedy about the misfortunes of an unlucky gambler (Dean Martin) while driving from New York to LA with an idiotic movie fan (Jerry Lewis), his Great Dane, and a shapely singer (Pat Crowley). Director Frank Tashlin fails to get many smiles from the witless clowning of Lewis, while Martin's supposed romantic charm has even less appeal than the unmemorable songs. Tiresome sexual innuendo. A-III (br)

Hollywood Shuffle (1987) Writer-producer-director Robert Townsend provides satirical comment on black stereotyping in the movie business in a story contrasting the career aspirations of the central character (also Townsend) with his sense of dignity. The low-budget feature is fairly successful as a social satire of unconscious racial discrimination. Profanity in the context of a streetwise environment. A-II (R)

Holocaust 2000 (see: **The Chosen**)

Holy Man (1998) Tepid tale of a failing home-shopping network that is turned around when two employees (Jeff Goldblum and Kelly Preston) invite a wandering holy-man (Eddie Murphy) onto the shows, and his non-materialistic message sells products anyway. Directed by Stephen Herek, the feel-good comedy-drama promotes love, harmony, and self-esteem in simplistic terms that lack the spark of conflict.

Some sexual references and minimal profanity. A-II (PG)

Holy Outlaw, The (1971) Documentary about Daniel Berrigan, Jesuit priest, poet, and pacifist, examines the man's personal witness against human indifference and the horror of war. Filmmakers Don Lenzer and Lee Lockwood rely mainly on interviews with Father Berrigan, members of his family, close friends, and his religious superior, during a four-month period when the FBI was seeking to arrest him. A-II (nr)

Homage (1996) Plodding account of the murder of a TV actress (Sheryl Lee) by a troubled young man (Frank Whaley), as recounted by the victim's mother (Blythe Danner), his lawyer (Bruce Davison), and a prison guard (Danny Nucci). Directed by Ross Kagan Marks from Mark Medoff's play, the disjointed narrative unfolds in flashbacks providing little insight on media fame, unbalanced fans, tabloid reporting, or mother-daughter relationships. Stylized violence, sexual situations including masturbation, profanity, and crude language. A-IV (R)

Homage to Chagall: The Colours of Love (1977) Documentary on the occasion of Marc Chagall's 90th birthday pays tribute both to the beauty of his art and the humanity of the artist. With a script based upon Chagall's own writing and featuring hundreds of his paintings, murals, and stained-glass windows, director Harry Rasky searches for the vision that inspired their creation, a quest helped immensely by a remarkable interview with Chagall himself. A-I (nr)

Hombre (1967) White man living as an Apache (Paul Newman) is on an ambushed stagecoach with people he neither likes nor trusts and who neither like nor trust him, but, in the course of a struggle for survival, he wins their admiration. Directed by Martin Ritt, the picture's story of injustice is brutal in spots, but it serves a purpose in this above-average Western. A-II (br)

Home Alone (1990) A large family takes off for Christmas in Paris, accidentally leaving behind their timid eight-year-old (Macaulay Culkin) who becomes very resourceful in defending the house against a persistent pair of bungling burglars (Joe Pesci and Daniel Stern). The laughter ebbs and wanes in director Chris Columbus's contrived comedy, but the pace is peppy and the family message heartwarming. Minor violence and robbery played for laughs. A-II (PG)

Home Alone 2: Lost in New York (1992) Formula sequel places the resourceful 10-year-old (Macaulay Culkin) on his own in the big city, this time determined to prevent the same bone-brained bandits (Joe Pesci and Daniel Stern) from ripping off a toy store on Christmas Eve. Writer-producer John Hughes and director Chris Columbus repeat their popular comic paces in a similar lively adventure similarly hampered by exaggerated comic violence and cloying sentiment. Much slapstick violence and some menace to a child. A-II (PG)

Home Alone 3 (1997) Unimaginative comedy sequel in which an eight-year-old boy (Alex D. Linz), quarantined with chicken pox, booby-traps his home against four crooks determined to retrieve a stolen computer-chip from inside his toy truck. Writer-producer John Hughes and director Raja Gosnell repeat the basic premise of the original with few variations, resulting in little more than redundant comic mayhem. Much slapstick violence. A-II (PG)

Home and the World, The (1985) Indian director Satyajit Ray's screen version of Nobel laureate Rabindranath Tagore's novel set in 1907 Bengal centers on a triangle involving a wealthy and idealistic landowner, his willful and naive wife, and his best friend who is a charismatic revolutionary who has feet of clay. Though static and talky, it provides a fascinating glimpse into a bygone era and aspects of human nature that are universal. A-II (nr)

Home for the Holidays (1995) Uneven comedy about a stressed-out single mom (Holly Hunter) who flies home to spend Thanksgiving with her dysfunctional family, including meddling mother (Anne Bancroft), dotty aunt (Geraldine Chaplin), and gay brother (Robert Downey, Jr.). Directed by Jodie Foster, the formula sitcom of a family reunion beset by emotional clashes displays a mean-spirited tone in its treatment of family relationships as something to be endured rather than enjoyed. Assorted sexual references, fleeting violence, and frequent profanity. A-III (PG-13)

Home Fries (1998) Comic misfire about two dim-witted brothers who accidentally kill their philandering stepfather, whose pregnant girlfriend (Drew Barrymore) falls for one brother (Luke Wilson), while the other (Jake Busey) tries to kill her to please their crazy mom. Director Dean Parisot's drawn-out tale of dysfunctional characters is a mindless, mirthless, but not painless experience. Brief menace and violence, some sexual innuendo, and occasional profanity. A-III (PG-13)

Home in Oklahoma (1947) Small-town newspaper editor Roy Rogers and St. Louis reporter Dale Evans team up to solve a murder and save a young boy from being done out of his inheritance by greedy relations in a modern-day Western directed by William Witney. Simple formula fare with a minimum of stylized violence. A-I (br)

Home Movies (1980) Failed attempt at a screwball comedy about a high-school student (Keith Gordon) who tries to become something more than "an extra in my own life" by turning it into a film about himself with the help of an instructor (Kirk Douglas). Director Brian De Palma's embarrassingly bad movie achieves the level of an almost unwatchable student-film exercise. Sexual nature of some of the gags is adult fare. A-III (PG)

Home of Our Own, A (1993) Leaving Los Angeles for rural Idaho in 1962, a penniless mother (Kathy Bates) of six tries to make a home for her family out of a crumbling shack, with the reluctant help of her 15-year-old (Edward Furlong) and the generosity of the landowner (Soon-Tek Oh). Tony Bill directs a gritty, often downbeat story of a loving but dictatorial matriarch who scorns charity as well as religion, but vividly instills the work ethic in her children so the family can stay together under their own roof. Fleeting violence and sexual innuendo, occasional profanity, and the mother's antagonistic attitude toward organized religion. A-III (PG)

Home of the Brave (1949) WW II story of a black soldier (James Edwards) being treated by an Army psychiatrist (Jeff Corey) for paralysis resulting from his experiences on a five-man reconnaissance mission to a Japanese-held island, where he's taunted by a racist corporal (Steve Brodie) and sees the death of a boyhood friend (Lloyd Bridges). Directed by Mark Robson from Arthur Laurents's play, its realistic treatment of racial prejudice holds up better than the psychiatrist's finding the soldier disabled by his guilt over feeling glad it was his friend who died and not him. Wartime violence and racial epithets. A-I (br)

Home of the Brave (1986) In a concert performance, composer-director Laurie Anderson offers a musical diversion for the cultivated few who appreciate Far Eastern-inspired pointillist melody, Dadaist minimalism, and the poetry of alienation. Musically and visually dull, the concert does not demonstrate the potential of its all-digital sound track. A-II (nr)

Homebodies (1974) Handful of oldsters living in a creaking Cincinnati tenement doomed to be torn down rebel against the wrecker's ball, first by sabotaging the encroaching construction sites, then by taking more direct guerrilla actions that culminate in murder. Thanks to a sprightly set of aging character actors (Paula Trueman, Frances Fuller, Peter Brocco), it is a gripping and macabre little slice of black comedy. Director Larry Yust's ending is as grisly as it is illogical, yet its theme that the lives of old people, like those quaint Victorian houses, are all too often wasted in the face of "progress" remains to haunt the viewer. A-III (PG)

Homegrown (1998) Dreary tale of three dope-heads (Hank Azaria, Billy Bob Thornton, and Ryan Phillippe) who unwittingly promise to sell their murdered boss's marijuana crop to both a dealer and to the mob. Director Stephen Gyllenhaal's lurching mix of supposed comedy, drama, and suspense is an abysmal failure which treats drug sales as a highly profitable lark. Stylized violence, sexual encounters, brief nudity, benign attitude toward substance abuse, and other criminal activity, as well as much rough language and profanity. O (R)

Homer (1970) Midwest farm-boy (Don Scardino) likes to swill cheap wine, spark his girl (Tisa Farrow), smoke a little pot, and bug his dad by refusing to get a haircut and staging a one-man anti-war demonstration outside the local VFW Hall. Before mercifully ending the picture by running away, Scardino manages to sing or listen to enough songs to fill a soundtrack album, which seems about all that director John Trent has on his mind. A-III (PG)

Homer and Eddie (1990) Loveable brain-damaged man (James Belushi) and homicidal maniac with a brain tumor (Whoopi Goldberg) team up in a search for long-lost parents and $87 in stolen cash. Director Andrei Konchalovsky builds no empathy for Goldberg's repulsive role, and, despite Belushi's endearing performance, the result is little more than a parade of brain-damaged freaks. Much profanity and some grisly, pointless violence. A-III (R)

Hometown Story, The (1951) Capitalist tract from writer-director Arthur Pierson in which a defeated state legislator (Jeffrey Lynn) returns as editor of the town paper (staffed notably by Alan Hale, Jr., and Marilyn Monroe), then goes after the local manufacturer (Donald Crisp) he blames for his defeat, until the industrialist uses his plane to save the life of a third-grader. Stylized violence and mild sexual innuendo. A-II (br)

Homeward Bound: The Incredible Journey (1993) Left temporarily with a friend, an aging golden retriever (voice of Don Ameche), a sassy cat (voice of Sally Field), and a frisky bulldog puppy (voice of Michael J. Fox) embark on a perilous journey across the wilds of the Sierra Mountains to get home to the family they so desperately miss. In this remake of a 1963 Disney feature, director Duwayne Dunham's lethargic pacing weakens the appeal of a mostly charming live-action animal adventure that stresses perseverance and the importance of family and friendship. A-I (G)

Homeward Bound II: Lost in San Francisco (1996) Frisky sequel to the popular 1993 family film has a scrappy bulldog (voice of Michael J. Fox), sassy Himalayan cat (voice of Sally Field), and trusty golden retriever (voice of Ralph Waite) separated from their human family at the San Francisco airport and forced to deal with an urban gang of stray dogs and other misadventures as they wend their way home. Director David R. Ellis's shaggy-dog story incorporates a mushy puppy-love subplot to bolster the already familiar plot of talking pets persevering to reunite with their worried owners. A-I (G)

Homicidal (1961) Hokey thriller about a very strange lady (Jean Arless) who kills a justice of the peace, then returns to her duties caring for an aged invalid (Eugenie Leontovitch) in the home of a man about to inherit a fortune. Directed by William Castle, the menace is laboriously contrived to sustain a story which makes little sense until a twist ending involving a dual performance. Stylized violence and menacing situations. A-II (br)

Homicide (1991) Powerful drama centering on an inner-city cop (Joe Mantegna) who belatedly identifies with his Jewish heritage when investigating a murder with possible anti-Semitic overtones. Writer-director David Mamet's riveting action-thriller resonates with added layers of depth as the cop faces a moral dilemma that threatens to destroy all that he has steadfastly believed in. Intermittent brutal violence and much rough language. A-III (R)

Hondo (1954) Lean Western about a hard-riding, straight-shooting cowboy (John Wayne) who gives up his independent ways to stand by a woman (Geraldine Page) whose husband has abandoned her and their young son during an Apache uprising. Directed by John Farrow, the obligatory action scenes of fistfights, cavalry patrols, and Indian battles are less interesting than Wayne's strong title performance as the mythic Western hero who respects women, children, and the Indian way of life. Frontier violence. A-I (br)

Honey, I Blew Up the Kid (1992) When a two-year-old toddler is accidentally enlarged to a 112-foot giant by his inventor dad (Rick Moranis), he tucks his teenage brother and babysitter (Robert Oliveri and Keri Russell) into his pocket and heads for the bright lights of the big city. Director Randal Kleiser's sequel makes the most of a one-joke premise with amiable characters and amusing special effects. Comic treatment of the destruction and menace caused by the giant child. A-II (PG)

Honey, I Shrunk the Kids (1989) A nutty professor (Rick Moranis) mistakenly throws out his own and his neighbors' youngsters out with the garbage after one of his inventions accidentally shrinks them to a quarter-inch in height. Director Joe Johnston does a great job concocting a backyard full of hurdles, including giant insects, for these miniature kids to conquer on their way back to the house. Very young children may be frightened, but older ones will enjoy the dizzy array of special effects and appealing young actors. Witless parents, some menace, and minimal sexual innuendo. A-II (PG)

Honey Pot, The (1967) Pretending to be dying, a bachelor (Rex Harrison) summons three women (Susan Hayward, Edie Adams, and Capucine) from his past and says that one of them will become his sole heir. Intricate plot twists and a murder in his Venetian palace reveal his real motives. Typically witty, urbane performance by Harrison, who also manages to make the cynical and crafty bachelor a touching figure as well. Written and directed by Joseph L. Mankiewicz, the movie's mixture of satire and suspense doesn't quite jell but will please sophisticated tastes. A-III (br)

Honeycomb (1972) Spanish psychological study of a young wife (Geraldine Chaplin), who is emotionally still a child, and of her middle-aged husband (Per Oscarsson), whose chief interest is business. Directed by Carlos Saura, the story takes place over the course of a weekend, during which their suppressed marital discontents emerge through dreams, fantasies, and murderous games in a destructive pattern worthy of an abnormal psychology textbook. Intense psychological and some physical violence. A-IV (PG)

Honeymoon (1947) Tiresome romantic comedy set in Mexico City, where a US consulate official (Franchot Tone) tries to help a 17-year-old Minnesota girl (Shirley Temple) and an American corporal (Guy Madison) get married, despite endless complications, which arouse the suspicions of his own fiancé (Lina Romay). Directed by William Keighley, Temple's petulant, empty-headed character elicits little sympathy, and the repetitive situations draw few smiles, though the colorful Mexican settings and characters add some badly needed interest. Romantic complications. A-II (br)

Honeymoon Academy (1990) Failed attempt at slapstick comedy has a honeymooning ex-State Department courier (Kim Cattrall) and her naive husband (Robert Hays) pursued around Madrid by brainless foreign agents and sinister figures, all searching for counterfeit-currency plates that could ruin the US economy. Writer-director Gene Quintano lacks any subtlety in treating cartoonish characters with utterly predictable reactions, strained chase scenes, and routine shootouts. Several abrupt deaths and an instance of rough language. A-II (PG-13)

Honeymoon in Vegas (1992) Hours before the wedding, the prospective groom (Nicolas Cage) squares his losses in a Vegas card game by loaning his fiancé (Sarah Jessica Parker) for a platonic weekend with a wealthy, older man (James Caan) who really wants to marry her himself. Writer-director Andrew Bergman's slight comedy uses a convention of international Elvis impersonators as a diverting gimmick, but the story sometimes lags behind the laughs. An unmarried sexual relationship, flash of nudity, and an instance of rough language. A-III-(PG-13)

Honeymoon Killers, The (1970) Fact-based story of a professional gigolo and the 200-pound nurse he loves as they bilk and kill off a number of female victims responding to lonely hearts club letters. Without any real distinction on the part of the actors (Tony LoBianco and Shirley Stoler) or director (Leonard Kastle), the movie quickly descends into a quagmire of sick, morbidly sexual and violent situations, offensive both in theme and treatment. O (R)

Honeymoon Machine, The (1961) Naval officer (Steve McQueen) and computer expert (Jim Hutton) join in a scheme to beat the roulette wheel at a Venice casino, but their girlfriends (Paula Prentiss and Brigid Bazlen) and an admiral (Dean Jagger) complicate matters. Director Richard Thorpe's lightweight romantic comedy has a few good moments but should have had more. Harmless escapist fare. A-I (br)

Honeysuckle Rose (1980) Boring romantic triangle involves a singing star (Willie Nelson), his wife (Dyan Cannon), and a young musician (Amy Irving). The three principals give good performances but are up against a trite script, uninspired direction (Jerry Schatzberg), and poor editing. Course language, the use of marijuana, and an adult theme. A-III (PG)

Hong Kong (1951) Formula melodrama directed by Lewis R. Foster in which a down-on-his-luck American (Ronald Regan) tries to steal a valuable statuette from a little orphaned Chinese refugee, but the heel is transformed by the love of a Red Cross worker (Rhonda Fleming). Stylized violence and various threats to a child. A-I (br)

Hong Kong Cat, The (see: **Karado, the Hong Kong Cat**

Honkers, The (1972) James Coburn, free spirit and sometime rodeo-performer, returns to sometime-wife Lois Nettleton and son Ted Eccles in between one-night stands. Directed by Steve Ihnat, the movie gives no reason why viewers should be expected to sympathize with an aging adolescent loser who is incapable of making responsible decisions or understanding their consequences. A-III (GP)

Honky (1972) Black teenager (Brenda Sykes) and a white classmate (John Neilson) fall in love, cut class to hustle some pot, crack up daddy's flashy car, and split for the Coast, where the girl is raped and the boy beaten to a pulp. Director William A. Graham's story of adolescent folly is a shallow dramatic effort with a matching moral sensibility in its treatment of drugs and sex, teen irresponsibility, and parental unresponsiveness. O (R)

Honky Tonk Freeway (1981) Converging on a small Florida town, which is trying to effect its own exit ramp from a new superhighway, are a dozen or so uninteresting motorists, including some New York bank-robbers, a would-be writer, a cocaine-sniffing hitchhiker, a Kentucky waitress, and other vacationers. Director John Schlesinger's failed satire of American road-culture is an incoherent hodgepodge of silly sight gags and insulting stereotypes. A number of scenes involve casual sex. O (PG)

Honkytonk Man (1982) Hard-living, hard-drinking honky-tonk singer-composer (Clint Eastwood), accompanied by his 14-year-old nephew (played by Kyle Eastwood, Eastwood's own son), goes to an audition in Nashville for the Grand Old Opry. A brink-of-death recording session insures supposedly a measure of posthumous glory. Also directed by Eastwood, there are some good moments, but most of it suffers from self-indulgence. Not only does the hero goes to bed with a 16-year-old girl, but he pays a prostitute to introduce his nephew to sex. O (R)

Hoodlum (1997) Stylish but violent tale of the deadly struggle between upstart gangster Bumpy Johnson (Laurence Fishburne) and mobster Dutch Schultz (Tim Roth) for control of the numbers racket in 1934 Harlem. Director Bill Duke's ambitious, loosely fact-based drama tends to glamorize the criminals' lifestyle until they finally pay with their own lives or those close to them. Ambiguous depiction of crime, recurring gory violence, brief sexual encounters, continual rough language, and much profanity. A-IV (R)

Hook (1991) Enormously elaborate modern fairytale in which a grown-up, workaholic Peter Pan (Robin Williams) is spirited back to Neverland by tiny Tinkerbell (Julia Roberts) to rescue his kids (Charlie Korsmo and Amber Scott) from the dastardly Captain Hook (Dustin Hoffman). Director Steven Spielberg goes overboard on story embellishments, extravagant set designs, and dizzying production numbers, almost burying the positive family message in the visual spectacle of his high-flying adventure. Some swashbuckling violence, a juvenile death, and brief toilet humor. A-II (PG)

Hook, The (1963) Tense Korean War moral poser in which a veteran sergeant (Kirk Douglas) and two enlisted men (Robert Walker, Jr., and Nick Adams) take a captured North Korean pilot aboard a freighter evacuating their gasoline supply depot, then receive a radio message from headquarters directing them to execute their prisoner. Director George Seaton sustains interest in a situation revolving around an unjust order, military discipline, and human nature until the melodramatic, cop-out ending. Much menace and wartime violence. A-II (br)

Hook, Line & Sinker (1969) Informed by his doctor that he has only a few months to live, Jerry Lewis embarks on a trip around the world in order to indulge his favorite sport — fishing. Director George Marshall's alleged comedy also involves his wife (Anne Francis) and doctor (Peter Lawford) attempting to cash in on the peripatetic fisherman's large insurance policy by pulling a switcheroo in the local morgue. Unfunny stuff. A-II (G)

Hooker's Revenge (see: **They Call Her One Eye**)

Hoop Dreams (1994) Engrossing documentary follows two black youths from Chicago's inner city whose hopes of playing professional basketball sustain them through four years of high school, one in a local public school and the other in a suburban Catholic school, with the self-confidence of each buffeted by difficulties and disappointments, until graduation brings them athletic scholarships to different colleges but the same uncertain future. Filmmakers Steve James, Frederick Marx, and Peter Gilbert capture the excitement of high-school basketball competition while showing some of its pressures on young players aspiring to become professional athletes, though what enriches the film's nearly three-hour length is its intimate portrait of the disadvantaged youths, their families, and friends, struggling with the blighted realities of a ghetto environment and their limited opportunities to escape it. Unwed teen parenthood, drug references, and instances of profanity and rough language. A-II (PG-13)

Hooper (1978) Aging Hollywood stuntman (Burt Reynolds) faces competition from a young newcomer (Jan-Michael Vincent) who is seeking to displace him, just as he had done to a top stuntman (Brian Keith) 20 years earlier. Directed by former stuntman Hal Needham, the movie is little more than a succession of stunts (barroom fights, car crashes, helicopter jumps, chariot races, and so on) set within a film-within-a-film being directed by Robert Klein. Bawdy humor, rough language, and seems to justify the reckless endangerment of life for profit. O (PG)

Hoosier Schoolboy (1937) Simple period tale directed by William Nigh in which a small-town youth (Mickey Rooney) gets help from a new teacher (Anne Nagel) in coping with problems caused by his shell-shocked, war-hero father who, in the end, risks death to resolve the community's bitter milk-strike. A-I (br)

Hoosiers (1987) Dedicated but dictatorial coach (Gene Hackman) leads a small-town high-school basketball team to the 1952 Indiana state championship while effecting some attitude adjustments in the community and rebuilding his self-esteem along the way. Director David Anspaugh's film recalls and celebrates a vanishing American rural ethic, where integrity is everything and winning is the spice of life. Brief instances of mildly vulgar language and a courtside scuffle. A-I (PG)

Hope and Glory (1987) Fine British dramatization about a young boy growing up amid the terror and excitement of the London blitz during WW II. Director John Boorman's fact-based re-creation eloquently expresses a child's sense of wonder and hopefulness in contrast to the anxiety-ridden, pessimistic, and socially conscious lives of the adults around him. Seriocomic treatment of several restrained sexual scenes and some rough language. A-III (PG-13)

Hopscotch (1980) When a veteran CIA agent (Walter Matthau) is demoted by his incompetent superior (Ned Beatty), he goes underground to write an expose of international covert operations, trying to stay one step ahead of liquidation by the world's spy organizations. Matthau is in top form as the maverick agent and Glenda Jackson is fine as his helpful friend in a highly entertaining chase thriller directed by Ronald Neame. It has intelligence and wit, but also some rough language. A-III (R)

Horizons West (1952) Standard Western in which two brothers return to their Texas home after the Civil War, with one (Robert Ryan) using a gang of outlaws to gain wealth and power, while the other (Rock Hudson) works the family ranch, then is made sheriff and sets out to bring his corrupt brother to justice. Directed by Budd Boetticher, the formula plot is largely devoted to showing how a good man goes bad, then loses all in a swift crime-does-not-pay ending. Some nasty stylized violence and a bad marriage. A-II (br)

Horizontal Lieutenant, The (1962) Lame service-comedy from director Richard Thorpe follows the misadventures of an incompetent intelligence officer (Jim Hutton) assigned to stop the pilferage of military supplies on a Pacific island during WW II, with weak romantic interest provided by a spunky nurse (Paula Prentiss). Occasional sexual innuendo. A-II (br)

Horn Blows at Midnight, The (1945) Trumpet-playing angel (Jack Benny) is sent to Earth to destroy the troublesome planet by tooting a few notes from the top of a New York skyscraper, but his good intentions — and two fallen angels — get in the way. Director Raoul Walsh's whimsical fantasy features Benny in a role well-tailored to his deadpan style of comedy, but the humor of the situation fades well before the sentimental ending. Apocalyptic premise may be confusing for youngsters. A-II (br)

Hornet's Nest (1970) Trapped behind enemy lines in Italy during WW II, rugged Marine Rock Hudson assembles a ragtag army of kids too young to join the Resistance but old enough to smell blood, Hollywood-style. Phil Karlson directs an improbable and confused war adventure-movie that resorts to several rape scenes and excessive gore, made all the more gruesome by using youngsters in violent, foul-mouthed roles. O (M)

Horoscope (1970) Slow-paced Yugoslavian movie about some aimless young men in a sweltering small town on the Adriatic who, for want of anything better, try to seduce a pretty new shopkeeper, with tragic results. Without becoming overly moralistic, director Boro Draskovic provides an engrossing vignette of youth trapped in a wasteland of inactivity. A-IV (nr)

Horror House (1970) When Frankie Avalon leads a group of youths in exploring an old house, one of them is killed and the audience is led to believe that the psychopath responsible is the lover of one of the girls, but Frankie finally unmasks the mental case. Directed by Michael Armstrong, there's lots of tension, plenty of false alarms, and a couple of bloody murders. A-III (PG)

Horror of Blackwood Castle, The (1973) German murder-mystery spoof about a retired ship's captain (Otto Stern) whose apparent demise brings daughter and former crew members to search for pirated jewels. Directed by Alfred Vohrer, it's good fun with an intricate, fast-moving plot, a bushel of snakes and scary props, at least three surprise endings, and a batch of frisky characters. A-II (PG)

Horror of Dracula (1958) British version of the Bram Stoker horror classic with Professor Van Helsing (Peter Cushing) battling the vampire count (Christopher Lee) in 1885 Germany. Director Terence Fisher establishes a properly eerie atmosphere and keeps the action brisk, with the two leads convincingly matched, as Lee's sneering count unleashes his diabolical powers against Cushing's intense professor, whose weapons are the traditional ones of cross, garlic, wooden stake, and sunlight. Restrained scenes of blood-sucking vampires, much menace, and some sexual innuendo. A-III (br)

Horror of Frankenstein (1971) When the monster finally appears in this fresh reworking of the Mary Shelley classic, he is considerably less frightening than his creator (Ralph Bates), whose total lack of human feeling is chilling. Directed by Jimmy Sangster with understated black humor, whose tone is established by Dennis Price as a discreet grave robber, this proves to be witty, literate, and a cut above the usual horror fare. A-III (R)

Horror of the Blood Monsters (1971) After arriving by plastic rocket-ship on a planet remarkably like Earth, astronaut John Carradine tussles with the Tubertons, fang-toothed archetypal vampires. Meanwhile, mission controllers Robert Dix and Vicki Volante take time out to engage in electronically controlled lovemaking. Producer-director Al Adamson has slapped together a flimsy science-fiction adventure that is not worth anybody's traveling time. A-III (GP)

Horror on Snape Island (1972) Archaeological expedition searches a long-abandoned island off the English coast for a Phoenician burial site after some youths are found there slaughtered by ancient weapons. Unfortunately, British writer-director Jim O'Connolly, unable to sustain much suspense with his story, settles for a tacky mixture of nudity and mayhem. O (R)

Horse in the Gray Flannel Suit, The (1968) Weak Disney comedy about the problems of a widowed advertising man (Dean Jones) in finding ideas for his client, a horse for his daughter, and a romance for himself. Directed by Norman Tokar, there is some colorful photography and trained horses, but parents will likely find it a long sit. A-I (G)

Horse Soldiers, The (1959) Sprawling Civil War tale of a Union colonel (John Wayne) leading an 1863 cavalry raid to cut Vicksburg's railroad lines but runs into plenty of trouble from Southern civilians, Confederate regulars, and a boy's military academy. Director John Ford stages the action scenes with his usual gusto but places them in an unusually somber context through the comments of the troop's doctor (William Holden), who opposes the colonel's scorched-earth tactics and their heavy casualties. Wartime violence. A-I (br)

Horse Whisperer, The (1998) When a 14-year-old girl (Scarlett Johansson) is seriously injured in a gruesome accident which traumatizes her beloved horse, her career-driven mother (Kristin Scott Thomas) enlists the help of a Montana horse-healer (Robert Redford) with whom the mother falls in love during the long healing process. Also directed by Redford, the sensitively observed drama makes a moral point while exploring painful adult and parent-child relationships in a rural setting, which has a calming effect on the troubled characters. A gory vehicular accident, mild sexual innuendo, and a few instances of profanity. A-II (PG-13)

Horse's Mouth, The (1958) Wacky satire from the Joyce Cary novel in which a cantankerous artist (Alec Guinness) moves into the empty residence of an art collector (Robert Coote) and gradually turns it to rubble as he pursues his obsession of painting a giant mural, despite the best efforts of his caring friends (notably Renee Houston). Scripted by Guinness and directed by Ronald Neame, the story is subsidiary to the portrait of the artist as slightly mad, entirely egocentric, and yet, for all his nastiness, an endearing old reprobate touched with genius — a challenging role not for all tastes. Some sexual innuendo and disdain for property rights and people in general. A-III (br)

Horsemen, The (1971) Failed adventure movie filmed in the mountains of Afghanistan about a man who is driven to prove his bravery, but in the process loses his leg and ultimately his pride. Directed by John Frankenheimer, the narrative is incongruous and its movie stars (Omar Sharif, Leigh Taylor-Young, Jack Palance) are ridiculously out of place among the rugged mountain tribesmen. What it offers is plenty of violent action and feats of horsemanship. A-III (GP)

Horseman on the Roof, The (1996) Fleeing Austrian bounty hunters in 1832, an Italian nationalist (Olivier Martinez) makes his way through cholera-ravaged southern France alongside a beautiful, mysterious noblewoman (Juliette Binoche) he is determined to deliver to the safety of her family. Directed by Jean-Paul Rappeneau from the Jean Giono novel, the result is a visually splendid romantic adventure awash in danger, mystery, and the selfless hero's incredible gallantry. Subtitles. Sporadic brief violence and fleeting nudity. A-III (R)

Hospital, The (1971) Uneven black comedy about a series of deaths in a big-city hospital whose chief of surgery (George C. Scott) begins to suspect that what is going on is not simply gross medical incompetence but the work of a madman on the loose. Brilliantly written by Paddy Chayefsky and well directed by Arthur Hiller, some of the situations are hilarious, but the feeling is one of giddiness, followed by the bite of terror. Language and uncompromising situations make it for adult patients only. A-III (GP/PG-13)

Hostile Guns (1967) Routine Western directed by R.G. Springsteen in which a marshal (George Montgomery) and his deputy (Tab Hunter) fight off murderous bushwhackers while on the trail to a Texas jail with four prisoners, one of whom (Yvonne de Carlo) causes dissension between the two lawmen. Stylized violence and mild sexual innuendo. A-II (br)

Hot Blood (1955) Ludicrous romantic melodrama in which the leader of a Gypsy clan (Luther Adler) arranges a marriage between his young brother (Cornel Wilde), who doesn't want a wife, and a woman (Jane Russell) from another clan, who only wants the dowry. Making matters worse, director Nicholas Ray plays the material as grand grotesque evoking much unintended laughter. Some silly sexual innuendo and unflattering Gypsy stereotypes. A-III (br)

Hot Box, The (1972) Philippine production in which four foul-mouthed nurses become tortured objects of lust, first at the hands of jungle revolutionaries who kidnap them, then at the hands of government troops who rescue them. Director Joe Viola simply alternates scenes of nudity with displays of bloodshed. O (R)

Hot Dog ...The Movie (1984) Featuring Patrick Houser and Tracy Smith, this Animal House-on-skis is about a rivalry between clean-cut but lecherous American skiers and some sneaky and unsportsmanlike Europeans. Director Peter Markle's mindless diversion features action on the slopes by day and in hot tubs by night. Graphic sex and nudity. O (R)

Hot Lead and Cold Feet (1978) Poor Disney Western satire in which twin brothers of markedly different character (both played by Jim Dale) inherit a vast fortune with the stipulation that they engage in a winner-take-all competition. The talented Dale does as well as he can with the script's slapstick cliches and the support offered by Karen Valentine, Don Knotts, and Jack Elam. But not even children are likely to enjoy director Robert Butler's effort very much; the very young won't understand the jokes and the older children won't find them very funny. A-I (G)

Hot Millions (1968) Deft British comedy in which an embezzler (Peter Ustinov) takes revenge on the computer system which caused his previous imprisonment by setting up phony companies, for which he has programmed the computer to make regular payments. Aiding and abetting the comedy are Maggie Smith, Karl Malden, and Bob Newhart, with director Eric Till contributing some fine comic visuals and gags. Mild romantic complications. A-II (G)

Hot Pants Holiday (1971) Harried New York housewife (Tudi Wiggins) on holiday in the Caribbean shares lust with native sex-symbol (Christopher St. John), but after a voodoo ceremony as inept as it is lewd, housewife discovers that her native is two-timing her. Directed by Edward Mann, there are no surprises here. O (X/R)

Hot Pursuit (1987) Weak attempt to build romance around the madcap efforts of a college student (John Cusack) to catch up to his girlfriend's vacationing family stretches credibility. Director Steve Lisberger's contemporary comedy-adventure set in the West Indies has some ambiguities about drugs, premarital sex, and heroism, which are further obscured by improbable plot devices and concluding gunplay. A-III (PG-13)

Hot Rock, The (1972) Lighthearted caper movie in which four bumbling crooks (Robert Redford, George Segal, Ron Leibman, and Paul Sand) are hired by an African diplomat (Moses Gunn) to steal a huge uncut diamond that was taken from his country and now resides inside a heavily guarded display case in the Brooklyn Museum. Directed by Peter Yates, the fast-paced entertainment has a number of intriguing twists, but Gunn and Zero Mostel steal the picture in their supporting roles. A-II (GP)

Hot Rod Action (1969) Feature documentary celebrating America's penchant for speed and danger uses footage from Indianapolis, Daytona, and other speedways without commentary or narrative structure. For racing car buffs and anthropologists. A-I (G)

Hot Rods to Hell (1967) Trite cautionary tale directed by John Brahm has a family driving for its life on California back-roads terrorized by hot-rodding young punks, until the husband (Dana Andrews) hides wife (Jeanne Crain) and offspring in a gully, then confronts their pursuers. Some stylized violence, much menace, and sexual situations. A-III (br)

Hot Shots! (1991) Mildly entertaining spoof has daredevil Navy pilot (Charlie Sheen) rescuing a jinxed mission under the bumbling command of a scatter-brained admiral (Lloyd Bridges). Director Jim Abraham's lightweight comedy doesn't stay aloft long, with leaden Sheen in the cockpit and the helter-skelter inclusion of unrelated scenes spoofing other movies. Intermittent sexual innuendo, minor slapstick violence, and an instance of rough language. A-III (PG-13)

Hot Shots! Part Deux (1993) Goofy spoof in which a love-scarred Marine (Charlie Sheen) heading a hostage-rescue mission in the Middle East stumbles upon an old flame (Valeria Golino) in the thick of the fray, which turns into an assassination plot led by the numbskull US president (Lloyd Bridges). Director Jim Abrahams's silly but scrappy sequel is a pot-luck grab-bag of rapid-fire sight gags, spills, shootouts, and visual jokes spoofing earlier movies. Much comic violence, a racy bedroom scene, some toilet humor, and an instance of rough language. A-III (PG-13)

Hot Spot (see: **I Wake Up Screaming**)

Hot Spot, The (1990) A bankrobber (Don Johnson) falls for a teenage blackmail victim (Jenifer Connelly) while trying to conceal his crime from his boss's sex-crazed wife (Virginia Madsen). Limply directed by Dennis Hopper, the slow-moving narrative lacks the subtlety and character interest needed to overcome holes in the plot. Adulterous relationship, recurring partial nudity, brief violence, and occasional rough language. O (R)

Hot Stuff (1979) Routine comedy directed by Dom DeLuise, who also has the leading role, about a police burglary taskforce who set up a phony fencing ring to ensnare thieves and run afoul of the Mafia. Some adult humor and an abundance of profanity. A-III (PG)

Hot to Trot (1988) Loony young man (Bob Goldthwait) inherits a talking horse named Don (voiced by John Candy), and, amidst some hair-raising moments, the horse comes up with stock tips and a winning racing form to help out its dim-witted owner. A knuckle-headed insult to Mr. Ed fans, director Michael Dinner's unfunny comedy features some embarrassing performances by Dabney Coleman, Virginia Madsen, and Cindy Pickett. Much rough language laced with sexual vulgarities. A-III (PG)

Hotel (1967) Screen version of Arthur Hailey's novel about a New Orleans hotel famous for its old-fashioned hospitality, but losing money and facing a takeover. Richard Quine directs an old-fashioned melodrama using the hotel as the site for dramatic events in the lives of those staying there. Standing out among the large cast of stars are Melvyn Douglas as the aristocratic hotel owner and Karl Malden as a sneak thief. Escapist entertainment with some adult situations. A-III (br)

Hotel New Hampshire (1984) Eccentric New England family (Natassja Kinski, Jodie Foster, Beau Bridges, and Rob Lowe) jokes and cavorts in the face of human mortality in this glib and shallow adaptation of the John Irving novel adapted and directed by Tony Richardson. A kind of absurdist **You Can't Take It with You**, it affects a benign view of all sorts of sexual activity, including incest. O (R)

Hotel Paradiso (1966) British bedroom farce set in Paris at the turn of the century has a fine cast (Alec Guinness, Gina Lollobrigida, Robert Morley, and Akim Tamiroff) and a plot filled with mistaken identities and broad characterizations. Unfortunately, Peter Glenville's direction lacks the fast pace and timing required by this sort of comedy. A-III (br)

Hotel Sorrento (1995) Leisurely paced dramatization of Hannie Rayson's play about the strained reunion of three sisters when the eldest (Caroline Gillmer), a widow who stayed at home in Australia to care for a young son and aged father, is visited by the youngest (Tara Morice) from New York, and the middle sister (Caroline Goodall) from London, where she wrote an acclaimed autobiographical novel which now becomes a matter of contention between them. Director Richard Franklin can't quite pull together the past and present strands of a diffuse narrative dealing as much with Australian nationalism, cultural imperialism, and a writer's imagination as with sibling rivalries, though the abundant dialogue is always literate and often witty. Implied extramarital affair, some profanity, and occasional rough language. A-III (R)

Hotel Terminus: The Life and Times of Klaus Barbie (1988) Four-and-a-half-hour documentary by Marcel Ophuls about the infamous war criminal termed the "Butcher of Lyons" for his brutal crimes against humanity in 1944-45 France, as well as on his work after the war under the protection of a US agency. Relying mainly on interviews with Barbie's victims and coworkers, there are some redundancies and much sarcasm. Explicit recounting of Nazi torture. A-III (nr)

Houdini (1953) Tony Curtis plays Harry Houdini (1874-1926), the escape artist whose loyal wife (Janet Leigh) assists his rise to international fame but cannot deter his growing interest in the supernatural and death-defying escapes, one of which kills him. Directed by George Marshall, the Hollywood version greatly fictionalizes Houdini's life and manner of death, turning it into a colorful period melodrama of an engaging couple whose domestic bliss is paced by ever more dangerous escape acts. A-I (br)

Hound of the Baskervilles, The (1939) The first and one of the best in a series based on Sir Arthur Conan Doyle's stories of Sherlock Holmes, featuring Basil Rathbone as the Victorian detective, with Nigel Bruce as Dr. Watson. Director Sidney Lanfield paces the action with mysterious murders on the moors, a baying hound, old cemetery ruins, ancestral curses, eccentric neighbors, a young couple in love, and an escaped convict on the prowl. Entertaining thriller but a little scary for children. A-II (br)

Hound of the Baskervilles, The (1959) Uneven British version of the Conan Doyle story in which Holmes (Peter Cushing) and Watson (Andre Morell) try to save the last of the Baskervilles (Christopher Lee) from a cunning murderer. Directed by Terence Fisher, the slow-paced tale opens with the nasty origin of the family curse, then follows the present dark doings on the Dartmoor moors until the final showdown in the ruins of an abbey. Stylized violence and sexual innuendo. A-II (br)

Hound of the Baskervilles, The (1977) Failed British spoof directed by Paul Morrissey stitches together a series of wildly eccentric skits with Peter Cook as Holmes, Dudley Moore as Watson, and a badly used supporting cast (Terry Thomas, Hugh Griffith, and Joan Greenwood among them), leaving the hound literally to steal the picture. Much sexual innuendo, comic vulgarities, and unamusing sallies in bad taste. A-III (nr)

Hour of the Gun (1967) Standard Western about Marshal Wyatt Earp (James Garner) defending Tombstone against the Clantons (led by Robert Ryan) in the famed gunfight at the OK Corral. After the bloody shoot-out, Earp begins taking the law into his own hands until Doc Holliday (Jason Robards) straightens him out. John Sturges directs with a steady hand for convincing action sequences. A-II (br)

House (1986) Director Sean Cunningham's parody of **Poltergeist** has some fun and fright in the story of a divorced novelist (William Katt) rescuing his captive son from angry spirits which infest his grandmother's house. Unfortunately, there is excessive gore and harsh language in Vietnam War flashbacks that flow, intermittently, from the hero's memory. O (R)

House II: The Second Story (1987) Inventive fantasy with touches of horror in which Arye Gross digs up his ancestor Royal Dano, kept alive for a century by a magical skull. Director Ethan Wiley takes the funhouse approach, which wreaks more terror upon the cast than on the young audience which the movie's weirdness is certain to engage. Brief violence, ghoulish faces, and silly female stereotypes. A-II (PG-13)

House Arrest (1996) Contrived comedy about a number of parents (Jamie Lee Curtis, Kevin Poolak, Jennifer Tilly, and others) being kept locked in a basement by their children, who won't release them until they solve their interpersonal problems. Directed by Harry Winter, the premise of dysfunctional adults grounded by their own youngsters is largely ridiculous, though it has some touching moments before reaching its sappy happy ending. Comic marital discord, fleeting fisticuffs, and brief tippling by minors. A-III (PG)

House Calls (1978) Walter Matthau plays a doctor who enthusiastically pursues women after the death of his wife, only to get his comeuppance from an independent-minded divorcée (Glenda Jackson). Director Howard Zieff's tepid little comedy looks like a slipshod reworking of **Cactus Flower** and is thoroughly adult in theme and dialogue. A-III (PG)

House of Cards (1968) Handsome, footloose American tutor (George Peppard) is up against fanatical Algerian ex-patriots. Good wins over evil despite conventional mystery-melodrama trimmings from director John Guillermin, who uses the commonplace as a source of horror. Attractively lush Parisian milieu, some spurts of violence, and gratuitous (though silly) attempts at sexual titillation. A-III (G)

House of Cards (1993) Traumatized by her father's sudden death, a six-year-old (Asha Menina) withdraws into a silent dream-world, from which her mother (Kathleen Turner) tries to extricate her using her own intuitive approach which clashed with the more traditional methods of a skeptical child psychiatrist (Tommy Lee Jones). Writer-director Michael Lessac mixes elements of mystery and near-mysticism in a visually lovely movie that compares medical science unfavorably with a loving mother's desperate attempts to save her child from becoming autistic. A child's emotional trauma and a few scenes of a youngster in mortal danger. A-II (PG-13)

House of Dark Shadows (1970) Movie version of a daytime television series about a family of vampires features Jonathan Frid re-creating his role of Barnabas, the 175-year-old owner of the spooky Collinwood estate, with Joan Bennett and Grayson Hall as residents. Directed by Dan Curtis, the melodrama often slips into a mire of gushing blood and gore amidst all the vampire lore required by diehard horror fans. Others are likely to be repulsed. A-III (PG)

House of Dracula (1945) Murky monster tale of an idealistic doctor (Onslow Stevens) who cures the Wolfman (Lon Chaney, Jr.) after killing the prowling Dracula (John Carradine), then discovers he's been contaminated by the vampire's blood and becomes one himself until reviving the Frankenstein monster (Glenn Strange) for a fiery finale. Directed by Erle C. Kenton, the feverish plot is as unconvincing as the monsters, though the spooky visuals and eerie atmosphere offer some scary moments. Stylized violence, menacing situations, and hokey moralizing. A-II (br)

House of Exorcism (1976) Playing the role of a suave butler in a sinister mansion is Telly Savalas, who seems to be making it up as he goes along, in a standard Italian-Gothic horror movie, filled with gore and nudity, and innocent of the least trace of taste or wit. O (R)

House of Fear, The (1945) Intriguing entry in the mystery series brings Sherlock Holmes (Basil Rathbone) and Dr. Watson (Nigel Bruce) to an isolated residence on the Scottish coast, where the members of a club of wealthy retirees are being murdered and their bodies mutilated. Directed by Roy William Neill, the murder plot keeps one guessing as suspects are killed off one by one in a house the locals believe haunted. Much menace. A-II (br)

House of Frankenstein (1944) Sprawling horror fantasy in which a mad doctor (Boris Karloff) and his hunchbacked assistant (J. Carrol Naish) escape prison, have a brief encounter with Dracula (John Carradine) on the way to Frankenstein's ruined estate, then free his monster (Glenn Strange) and the Wolfman (Lon Chaney, Jr.) from an ice-bound cave, until their antics are ended by the local villagers. Directed by Erle C. Kenton, this disjointed parade of familiar screen monsters tries to find some fresh angles on old formulas, but the result offers little in the way of originality. Stylized violence and menacing situations. A-II (br)

House of Games (1987) Eminent psychiatrist (Lindsay Crouse) becomes involved with a con-artist (Joe Mantegna) and some of his shady games of deception, with disastrous results for both. Writer-director David Mamet succeeds fairly well in conning the viewer with a plot in which nothing is quite what it seems. Some brutal violence, rough language, and a restrained bedroom scene. A-III (R)

House of Strangers (1949) Brooding tale of a domineering Italian-American banker (Edward G. Robinson) whose harsh treatment of his four sons has earned their enmity, but when three of them conspire against him, he seeks revenge through the fourth (Richard Conte). Directed by Joseph L. Mankiewicz, the twisty plot holds dramatic interest, while its vivid portrayal of Italian-American family life contrasts the values of an older generation with those of a younger one. Stylized violence and intense family conflicts. A-II (br)

House of the Seven Gables, The (1940) Stale version of Nathaniel Hawthorne's novel set in 1840s Massachusetts, where a greedy lawyer (George Sanders) causes the imprisonment of his innocent brother (Vincent Price) in order to find a legendary fortune hidden in the ill-gotten family home of the title. Director Joe May gets some moody atmosphere from the curse haunting the family since the 17th-century witchcraft trials, but succeeds best with the perseverance of the love between imprisoned brother and aging fiancé (Margaret Lindsay). Tough sledding for children. A-I (br)

House of the Spirits, The (1994) Impressive adaptation of Chilean author Isabel Allende's multigenerational novel about a wealthy South American family whose cruel, reactionary patriarch (Jeremy Irons) tries to control the lives of his spinster sister (Glenn Close), clairvoyant wife (Meryl Streep), and fiery, defiant daughter (Winona Ryder), who's involved with a peasant rebel leader (Antonio Banderas). Director Bille August's portrait of an impassioned family caught up in a half-century of political upheaval starting in the 1920s is flawed by the narrative's somnambulistic pacing and Iron's stilted performance, but does succeed in showing the power of love and forgiveness in coping with adversity. Intermittent political violence and some sexual encounters with brief nudity. A-III (R)

House of Usher (1960) Melancholic dramatization of the Edgar Allan Poe story in which a man (Mark Damon) arrives at the Usher estate to find his cataleptic fiancé (Myrna Fahey) buried alive by her troubled brother (Vincent Price). Director Roger Corman gets properly edgy performances in the story of a waning family living in a crumbling mansion, which is destroyed in a great fire. Some stylized violence and much moody menace. A-II (br)

House of Wax (1953) After being horribly deformed when arson destroys his wax museum, a crazed sculptor (Vincent Price) takes to killing people, coating the bodies in wax, and placing them on exhibit in his new waxworks, until an intended victim (Phyllis Kirk) spots her missing friend (Carolyn Jones) displayed as Joan of Arc. Though the visuals are relatively tame and Price plays the monstrous villain for sympathy, director Andre de Toth provides a few scary moments and much sinister atmosphere in the waxworks, relieved by some diverting, if extraneous, 3-D effects, notably a barker with paddleballs. More menace than violence. A-II (br)

House of Women (1962) Uneven melodrama directed by Walter Doniger is set in a women's prison, where inmates are allowed to live with their children until the age of three, but the attempt of a new warden (Andrew Duggan) to change the policy sets off a prison-wide riot when he separates an inmate (Shirley Knight) from her child. Stylized violence, menacing situations, and an implied sexual affair. A-III (br)

House of Yes, The (1997) Darkly comic tale in which an unstable young woman (Parker Posey) becomes unhinged when her brother (Josh Hamilton), who was once her lover, returns from college with a fiancé (Tori Spelling). Director Mark Waters's talky story shows its stage-play origins while depicting a thoroughly dysfunctional family, but instead of being madly amusing, its humor is often tasteless. Fleeting violence, implied sexual encounters, flippant treatment of incest, occasional profanity, and rough language. A-IV (R)

House on Carroll Street, The (1988) Romantic thriller set in 1951 New York features a gutsy, blacklisted photo editor (Kelly McGillis), who uncovers a politically sanctioned conspiracy aimed at hiding Nazi war criminals in the US. The Hitchcockian influence is poorly realized by director Peter Yates in a stylish-looking but far-fetched movie about political hypocrisy, scripted by once-blacklisted screenwriter Walter Bernstein. Brief nudity and some graphic violence. A-II (PG)

House on Chelouche Street, The (1974) Israeli movie about a widow (Gila Almagor) in 1946 Tel Aviv who decides to remarry to give her family some security, but her adolescent son (Ophir Shalitan) resents her choice, has a brief affair with an older woman (Michal Bat-Adam), and learns something about adult responsibilities. Written and directed by Moshe Mizrahi, it proves an engaging and interesting portrayal of human problems and makeshift solutions in a time of great turmoil. A-III (PG)

House on Haunted Hill (1958) At the suggestion of his wife (Carol Ohmart), a sardonic millionaire (Vincent Price) holds a party in an isolated mansion with a history of grisly murders, promising to reward any of his guests (including Richard Long, Alan Marshall, and Elisha Cook, Jr.) who spend the night. Director William Castle has some fun in the low-budget fright department, ranging from spooky effects to bizarre deaths, but the tangled plot is full of holes. Menacing atmosphere and a few scares. A-II (br)

House on Skull Mountain, The (1974) Weak horror vehicle directed by Ron Honthaner begins with the death of a wealthy black woman whose heirs, one of whom is white (Victor French), gather in her remote mansion for the reading of the will, only to be beset by deadly voodoo spells. Muddled hokum with some eerie atmosphere, a few chills, and occasional sexual inferences. A-III (PG)

House Party (1990) Grounded by his well-meaning dad (Robin Harris), a black, middle-class teenager (Christopher Reid) is determined to attend a pal's house party. Black director Reginald Hudlin plays up the comic obstacles that get in the way, including a gang of toughs and some buffoonish white cops. Though this growing-pains comedy has a clear anti-drug and alcohol message, it also implies that the kids are sexually active. Nonstop rough language with much sexually explicit dialogue and black rap, some bathroom humor, and incidental cartoon violence. A-IV (R)

House Party 2 (1991) Vulgar sequel follows a black youth (Christopher Reid) to college, where he discovers his tuition check has been stolen, prompting his playboy buddy (Christopher Martin) to throw a steamy pajama party on campus to raise the needed cash. Producers-directors Doug McHenry and George Jackson inject lots of bouncy energy into the rapping and dancing, but the racial and sexual stereotyping defeat the movie's attempt at comedy. Much rough language and sexual innuendo, racial stereotyping, implied sexual encounters, a flash of nudity, and brief violence. A-IV (R)

House Party 3 (1994) Vulgar sequel in which a black youth (Christopher Martin) sets up a raunchy bachelor party for a friend (Christopher Reid) after they take money from a music promoter for a singing act they can't deliver. Director Eric Mesa throws together a rap-music situation comedy whose marginal humor is sexist, mean-spirited, and features a trio of very young boys who are casual lawbreakers. Implied promiscuity, partial nudity, many racial slurs, sexist insults, comic violence, and much rough language. O (R)

House That Dripped Blood, The (1971) Four tired tales of the preternatural are linked by the weak device of a haunted house that supposedly influences the behavior of its inhabitants. British director Peter Duffell fails to develop the least sense of dread, and the only surprise is that the screenplay is by veteran horror writer Robert Bloch. A-II (GP)

House That Screamed, The (1971) Lilli Palmer plays the turn-of-the-century proprietress of a French finishing-school for wealthy girls, and, while her 15-

year-old son (John Moulder-Brown) pursues the girls, they pursue the local deliveryman. The promiscuous pursuits at the school are finally relieved by several bloody murders, but by then, director Narciso Ibanez Serrador's attempts at horror are lost in a sophomoric sex-teaser. O (GP)

Houseboat (1958) Anemic romantic comedy in which a Washington, D.C., widower (Cary Grant) hires an Italian tourist (Sophia Loren) as housekeeper for his three youngsters, then falls in love with her. Director Melville Shavelson spends more time trying to wring laughs from silly plot complications, such as the antique houseboat they try to turn into a home, than in infusing charm for artificial characters as their mutual antipathy turns to love. Romantic complications. A-II (br)

Houseguest (1995) Flimsy feel-good comedy in which an overgrown underachiever (Sinbad) flees murderous loan-sharks by passing himself off as the expected Memorial weekend guest of an affluent suburban family, whose domestic problems he straightens out before squaring his debt and writing a bestseller. Director Randall Miller strings together a slapdash series of silly situations that are too predictable to be amusing, though Sinbad's cheerful exuberance helps relieve some of the tedium. Slapstick violence, some sexual inferences, a drunken party, and occasional vulgar language. A-III (PG)

Household Saints (1993) Multigenerational story set in New York City's Little Italy, where a superstitious mother-in-law (Judith Malina) frightens her daughter-in-law (Tracey Ullman), who subsequently bears a daughter (Lili Taylor) so obsessed with serving God that she eventually loses touch with reality, as well as morality. Director Nancy Savoca's confusing treatment of the role of Catholicism in the life of an Italian-American family robs the drama both of human credibility and a positive spiritual dimension. A few bedroom scenes, fleeting nudity, a suicide, gory shot of a stillborn baby, and superstitions depicted as part of Catholicism. O (R)

Housekeeping (1987) Interesting seriocomic probe into small-town family life in the 1950s tells the story of two girls who, after their mother's suicide, are raised by their aunt (Christine Lahti), a woman of somewhat strange and erratic behavior. Scottish director Bill Forsyth's look at growing up in an unconventional American household that's frowned upon by conformist neighbors, is quite often amusing and frequently very touching. Unresolved tensions between individual and social values. A-II (PG)

Housesitter (1992) Kooky pathological liar (Goldie Hawn) pretends she's married to an architect (Steve Martin), who hopes to make his ex-girlfriend (Dana Delany) jealous. Director Frank Oz's misguided comedy features perky performances, but falls flat with phony motivations and contrived sitcom humor. An implied bedroom encounter and much sexual innuendo. A-III (PG)

Housewife (see: **Bone**)

How Do I Love Thee? (1970) Longsuffering, Bible-thumping wife (Maureen O'Hara) desires only to instill a fear of God in her college-professor son (Rick Lenz) and to pray for the conversion of her atheist husband (Jackie Gleason), who is fooling around with a client (Shelley Winters). Director Michael Gordon, failing to elicit any depth or purposeful narrative, settles for prolonged and vacuous discussions of religion, remarkably tasteless sexual innuendo, and a generally witless sense of the comic. O (PG)

How Funny Can Sex Be? (1976) Tedious Italian sex-farce starring Giancarlo Giannini in a series of six ribald stories that, under Dino Risi's direction, vie with one another in lack of wit and general tastelessness and feature considerable nudity. O (R)

How Green Was My Valley (1941) Nostalgic chronicle of family ties based on the Richard Llewellyn novel about a Welsh coal-mining village at the turn of the century trying to maintain its traditional way of life, despite changing industrial times and the power of the mine owners. Director John Ford's episodic picture of a community in transition is depicted largely through an emotionally rich, often sunny, but sometimes tragic portrait of the close-knit Morgan family and its proud father (Donald Crisp), who rejects his five sons when they join the union, the mediating mother (Sara Allgood) who reconciles them, the daughter (Maureen O'Hara) who marries unhappily when rebuffed by the village's new minister (Walter Pidgeon), and the youngest of the Morgans (Roddy McDowall) recalling the family's past as a grown man leaving his beloved but now-depressed valley. Muted treatment of romantic complications and some stylized violence, including the sadistic caning of a youth and a harrowing mine disaster. A-II (nr)

How I Got into College (1989) Mediocre high-school senior (Corey Parker) aims to be accepted by the same top college that his secret heartthrob (Lara Flynn Boyle), the smartest and most popular girl in his class, hopes to attend. Directed by Savage Steve Holland, it's an innocuous, pleasant teen comedy about the very real anxieties suffered by college hopefuls and their parents. Mild rough language and sexual innuendoes. A-II (PG-13)

How I Won the War (1967) Unusual British anti-war movie ridicules the military concept of war as a noble game and debunks the cliches and slogans of belligerents. Michael Crawford stars as an inexperienced lieutenant assigned to build an advanced cricket-field in WW II North Africa, with John Lennon as the compliant everyman of the unit which deserts at the Rhine. Directed with comic ingenuity by Richard Lester, its pacifist view of war may be controversial, but it is neither anti-religious nor anti-patriotic, and it merits attention and reflection. Stylized violence. A-II (br)

How Stella Got Her Groove Back (1998) Glossy romance from Terry McMillan's novel about a 40-year-old, career-driven single mom (Angela Bassett) who ultimately finds happiness with a man (Taye Diggs) half her age while vacationing in Jamaica. Director Kevin Rodney Sullivan delivers an idealized, comic romantic fantasy in which a one-night stand matures into a committed relationship. Benign treatment of premarital sex, fleeting nudity, and some rough language. A-IV (R)

How Sweet It Is! (1968) James Garner and Debbie Reynolds star in a comedy-melodrama about a crazy, mixed-up American family sightseeing in Europe. Basically a happy couple, in the midst of complications caused by their son and his girlfriend, they find themselves on the brink of extracurricular flirtations. Forgettable froth directed by Jerry Paris. A-III (br)

How Tasty Was My Little Frenchman (1973) Brazilian movie set in the early colonial times, when a Frenchman is taken captive by a cannibal tribe and is held for execution at an upcoming festival. The final horror (and key to the title) in this black comedy is the cheerful smile of the young girl who has been his native wife as she prepares to eat her allotted portion of his dead body. Director Nelson Pereira Dos Santos does not romanticize or sentimentalize the savages or the Europeans, but neither does his movie miss the joy of life that exists in every culture. Scenes of nudity in this semi-ethnographic movie are without any sense of sexual exploitation. A-IV (nr)

How the West Was Won (1962) Sprawling Cinerama epic tracing the way West from the mountain men (James Stewart and Henry Fonda) to the settlers coming by riverboat (Karl Malden and Agnes Moorehead), wagon train (Debbie Reynolds and Gregory Peck), and railroad (Richard Widmark and George Peppard), with a Civil War stopover at Shiloh (John Wayne and Henry Morgan). Mostly directed by Henry Hathaway, with John Ford directing the Civil War sequences and George Marshall the railroad segment, the result is picturesque entertainment, stereotyped history, and bloated melodrama, chiefly of interest as a compendium of Western screen conventions. Some tense but stylized violence. A-I (br)

How to Beat the High Cost of Living (1980) Three housewives (Susan Saint James, Jane Curtin, and Jessica Lange) conspire to replenish their depleted finances by stealing the money displayed in a huge plastic ball in a shopping-center promotion. Director Robert Scheerer's comedy has some tart humor, but is pretty mediocre going and sometimes mean-spirited to boot. Adult humor and situations. A-III (PG)

How to Commit Marriage (1969) When the daughter of real-estate agent (Bob Hope) and his wife of 19 years (Jane Wyman) learns that her parents are about to be divorced, she goes off to live out of wedlock with the son of a cynical agent for rock groups (Jackie Gleason). How everyone, including Gleason and his girlfriend Tina Louise, is eventually legally united or reunited might have been the basis for some good satire, but director Norman Panama treats both his characters and the institution of marriage in a consistently grotesque and sleazy fashion. Though there are a few scattered laughs, this is not a funny picture. O (PG)

How to Frame a Figg (1971) Dim-witted city-hall clerk (Don Knotts) accidentally uncovers some shady dealings by the boys in the backroom, who promote him to a high-paying, no-sweat job, but eventually he figures out why and then blows the whistle on the corrupt officials. The comedy's humor revolves around the inane personality of Knotts, as well as around the far-fetched situations he bumbles into and out of. Alan Rafkin directs the appropriately juvenile script as if it were an extended TV sitcom. A-I (G)

How to Get Ahead in Advertising (1989) Biting British satire of the advertising business centers on an ad-man burnout (Richard E. Grant), who grows a boil that talks on his neck, with which he carries on a running debate over the evils of the ad game. Although writer-director Bruce Robinson's work is thought-provoking and technically sound, the satire deteriorates into a manic, mad show starring a ghoulish boil. Much profanity, sexually vulgar language, and an intense, though humorous, depiction of madness. A-IV (R)

How to Make a Monster (1957) Pedestrian thriller directed by Herbert L. Strock in which a veteran movie make-up artist (Robert H. Harris) takes revenge on the studio executives who fired him by using hypnotized actors dressed in monster make-up to kill them. Stylized violence and hokey menace. A-II (br)

How to Make an American Quilt (1995) Unsure over her recent engagement, a graduate student (Winona Ryder) spends the summer with her grandmother (Ellen Burstyn) and six quilting-bee cronies, who influence the young woman's decision with tales of their own troubled romantic relationships over the years. Director Jocelyn Moorhouse salutes sisterly solidarity in a sentimental but pokey tale of age bringing emotional maturity. Fleeting bedroom scenes, sexual references, and an instance of recreational drug use. A-III (PG-13)

How to Make Love to a Negro Without Getting Tired (1990) Offensively titled French-Canadian production takes a lightweight look at racial and sexual stereotypes in Montreal, where a black Haitian immigrant (Isaach de Bankole) engages in writing a novel while enjoying the sexual favors of several white women. Directed by Jacques Benoit, the result is blatantly exploitative in its positive portrayal of casual sex and promiscuity. Several simulated sex scenes, petty thievery shown as fun, and some rough language. O (nr)

How to Marry a Millionaire (1953) Lightweight comedy in which three Manhattan models (Lauren Bacall, Marilyn Monroe, and Betty Grable) hope to snare rich husbands by renting a luxury apartment, but love proves stronger than greed when each marries a guy with little income (Rory Calhoun, David Wayne, and Cameron Mitchell, who's actually a multimillionaire). Directed by Jean Negulesco, the one-note comic premise provides some good-natured humor, but the real fun comes from the cast's droll ensemble playing. Romantic complications and mild sexual innuendo. A-II (br)

How to Murder Your Wife (1965) Feeble comedy in which a happily unwed cartoonist (Jack Lemmon) wakes from a drunken spree married to an Italian beauty-contestant (Virna Lisi), but, many contrivances later, his initial antipathy turns into love until faced with murder charges when she disappears. Director Richard Quine tries to keep the dim-witted situation light and breezy, but its tongue-in-cheek praise of bachelor-hood grows increasingly tiresome, culminating in a leadenly satiric courtroom sequence denouncing marriage. Sexual innuendo and comic treatment of sexist views. A-III (br)

How to Save a Marriage ... and Ruin Your Life (1968) Eli Wallach and Anne Jackson play an adulterous couple under investigation by bachelor Dean Martin who mistakenly identifies Stella Stevens as Wallach's compliant girlfriend in a divorce action. Fielder Cook directs a not-so-funny marriage-go-round comedy that goes cheerfully around in circles leading nowhere. A-III (br)

How to Seduce a Woman (1974) Witless one-joke sex comedy with Angus Duncan is ineptly directed by Charles Martin. O (R)

How to Steal a Million (1966) Wacky romantic comedy set in Paris, where the daughter (Audrey Hepburn) of an art forger (Hugh Griffith) enlists a willing accomplice (Peter O'Toole) in a complicated scheme to steal her dad's bogus masterpiece from a museum exhibit before it can be revealed as a fraud. Director William Wyler handles the droll proceedings with sophisticated elegance, but the comic results may be too slow-paced for some tastes. A-I (br)

How to Stuff a Wild Bikini (1965) Sun-baked youth comedy in which a naval reservist (Frankie Avalon) on duty in the Pacific gets a local witch-doctor (Buster Keaton) to keep tabs on his California girlfriend (Annette Funicello) through a pelican and a bikini-clad lovely (Beverly Adams), which results in fending off a suitor (Dwayne Hickman). Directed by William Asher, the zany plot-strands and throwaway humor are more tiresome than amusing, especially the overdone motorcycle race at the conclusion. Slapstick violence, sexual situations, and much sexual innuendo. A-III (br)

How to Succeed in Business Without Really Trying (1967) Robert Morse and Rudy Vallee whoop it up at the World Wide Wicket Company in a zestful adaptation of the Broadway musical about an ex-window-washer's schemes to reach the top of a big corporation in the shortest possible time. Director David Swift's sharp, witty spoof retains most of the original's running gags and Frank Loesser's music. A-II (nr)

Howard the Duck (1986) This caustic, cynical, and malevolent fantasy-adventure features a fully costumed duck from outer space trying to find his way home after having been accidentally transported to a hostile Earth. Director Willard Huyck fills the screen with too much vulgarity, violent destruction, and sadistic humor to make the movie of interest to any sensitive earthling. O (PG)

Howards End (1992) Exquisitely done drama based on E.M. Forster's novel about an aristocratic widower (Anthony Hopkins) in turn-of-the-century England who cheats a young woman (Emma Thompson) out of property left her by his wife (Vanessa Redgrave) but then falls in love with her, much to the dismay of her egalitarian younger sister (Helena Bonham Carter). Enhanced by the ensemble cast's splendid performances, the sensitive collaboration of director James Ivory, producer Ismail Merchant, and screenwriter Ruth Prawer Jhabvala does justice to Forster's ironic and witty story of class distinctions and their sometimes tragic outcomes. Discreet sexual innuendo and fleeting violence. A-II (PG)

Howards of Virginia, The (1940) Longwinded saga of a colonial rustic (Cary Grant) helped by neighbor Tom Jefferson (Richard Carlson) to wed the sister (Martha Scott) of an aristocratic planter (Cedric Hardwicke) and then build his own plantation in the Shenandoah wilderness before joining Washington's ragged army at Valley Forge. Directed by Frank Lloyd, the historical dramatization is painfully artificial, with the script's patriotic intentions too obvious to be effective. Domestic misunderstandings and wartime hardships. A-I (br)

Howling, The (1981) Trashy but flashy horror movie written by John Sayles and directed by Joe Dante in which a television newswoman (Dee Wallace) finds herself in dire straits when her companions at a psychiatric retreat turn out to be a pack of werewolves. The special effects by Rob Bottin are remarkable, but not enough to justify what is essentially a sex-and-violence exploitation movie. O (R)

Huckleberry Finn (1931) Creaky version of Mark Twain's adventure story directed by Norman Taurog follows Huck (Jackie Coogan) on his Mississippi River adventures with escaped slave Jim, including their encounter with the Lost Dauphin (Eugene Pallette). Dated as a movie production but still some fun. A-I (br)

Huckleberry Finn (1939) Still one of the best screen adaptations of the Twain classic, with Mickey Rooney properly scrappy in the title role and Rex Ingram strong and dignified as his companion, the freedom-seeking Jim, with Walter Connolly and William Frawley as the confidence men they meet along the river. Director Richard Thorpe captures much of the youthful wonderment and the spirit of adventure that makes the original such enjoyable reading. Fine family fare. A-I (br)

Huckleberry Finn (1974) Sugary musical version of the Twain classic, with script and lyrics written by the Sherman Brothers, features Jeff East in the title role and Paul Winfield as Jim. Directed by J. Lee Thompson, it contains a clutter of supremely forgettable musical numbers, entirely misses the book's point, and adds up only to a minor children's matinee entry. A-I (G)

Hud (1963) Powerful drama pits a hard-working Texas rancher (Melvyn Douglas) against his cynical no-good son (Paul Newman) who, while scheming to take the ranch from his aging father, amuses himself by making a play for the old man's housekeeper (Patricia Neal) and trying to corrupt his young nephew (Brandon de Wilde). Directed by Martin Ritt, the picture's sympathies are with the old man and his high moral standards, but Newman's swaggering, devil-may-care performance turns the title character into an attractive anti-hero, which goes against the story's grain and adds ambiguity to the result. Stylized violence, including attempted rape, and a noxious central character. A-III (br)

Hudson Hawk (1991) A reformed cat-burglar (Bruce Willis) and his pal (Danny Aiello) are coerced into stealing art objects from the Vatican for a power-crazed couple (Sandra Bernhard and Richard E. Grant), while an undercover nun (Andie MacDowell) tries to foil the plan. Director Michael Lehmann's turkey crash-lands with a maddeningly overwritten script cluttered with underdeveloped characters and moronic musical duets. Much cartoon violence and rough language. A-III (R)

Hudsucker Proxy, The (1994) By appointing a naive mail-clerk (Tim Robbins) as company president, the chairman of the board (Paul Newman) aims to manipulate stock prices, but the plan goes awry when the young man invents a successful product, and his secretary (Jennifer Jason Leigh), an undercover investigative reporter, digs into what's behind the wheeling-dealing. Produced and directed by brothers Ethan and Joel Coen, the attempt to re-create a Capraesque populist fantasy proves grandly enjoyable, despite some clumsy imitations of 1930s movie conventions and acting styles. Comic treatment of suicide and fleeting violence. A-II (PG)

Hue and Cry (1947) Amusing British comedy in which some London youngsters take it upon themselves to stop a gang of thieves after the police ignore their discovery of a link between a series of recent robberies and information provided in stories written by a decidedly odd author (Alastair Sim) for a weekly comic magazine. Scripted by T.E.B. Clarke and directed by Charles Crichton, the result has some menacing scenes but is mostly good-natured fun, with a rollicking climax as thousands of boys descend on a bombed-out area of the city to nab the crooks. Youngsters in perilous situations. A-II (br)

Hugh Hefner: Once Upon a Time (1992) Uncritical documentary chronicles the millionaire publisher's Methodist upbringing, marital dissatisfactions, the growth, and eventual decline of his "Playboy" business up to his present May-December marriage and second shot at fatherhood. Robert Heath's unctuous direction and a fawning narration voiced by actor James Coburn attempt to lionize Hefner for supposedly liberating a generation of sexually repressed males but, in the process, unintentionally reveal the man's enormous ego and spiritual emptiness. Acceptance of promiscuity, sexist attitudes, frequent nudity, and minimal rough language. O (R)

Hugo Pool (1997) Failed seriocomic tale of a Los Angeles pool-cleaner (Alyssa Milano) who gets some help from her drug-addict dad (Malcolm McDowell) and obsessive gambler mom (Cathy Moriarity) in dealing with such customers as a threatening gangster (Richard Lewis), a loony film director (Robert Downey, Jr.), and a helpless man in a wheelchair (Patrick Dempsey), whom she comes to love. Directed by Robert Downey, the disjointed story line is pumped up with quirky characters and bizarre humor, but little of it works and the culminating romance lacks the charm intended. Sexual situations, drug references, and occasional rough language and profanity. A-III (R)

Hugs and Kisses (1968) Swedish movie about a triangular relationship that develops between a woman, her husband, and his bumbling friend. Written and directed by Jonas Cornell, the fragmentary story and its seriocomic incidents are at best ambiguous in developing a theme about human relationships. Unnecessarily graphic nude sequence. O (br)

Human Factor, The (1975) When the family of a computer expert (George Kennedy) at a NATO base in Naples is murdered by international terrorists, he tracks down the villains and slaughters them in an orgy of violence. Despite the title and Kennedy's efforts to give his role some human dimension, Edward Dmytryk directs his story of vigilante vengeance with little feeling for any of its characters. O (R)

Human Factor, The (1980) Nicol Williamson plays a quiet family man, working for British Intelligence but also leaking information to the Russians, who has a crisis of conscience that causes him to risk everything. Also with Richard Attenborough and Derek Jacobi, the performances are excellent, and Tom Stoppard's too-literal adaptation of the Graham Greene novel and Otto Preminger's plodding direction results in a movie that entertains, but does not excite or have the moral complexity of the original. Suggestive nightclub dance scene. A-III (R)

Human Revolution, The (1974) Japanese dramatization of the 1930s beginnings and beliefs of the Nichiren Shoshu Academy (a Buddhist sect numbering some 20 million adherents). Directed by Toshiro Masuda, it is a handsome and intelligent production whose philosophical, rather than religious, message is that the world can only become better through the inner change of each individual. A-II (G)

Humanoids from the Deep (1980) Meddling scientists tampering with genetic laws turn some prehistoric creatures, who are minding their own business at the bottom of the sea, into sex maniacs. Directed by Barbara Peeters, the penny-ante dreadful contains excessive violence and nudity. O (R)

Hunchback of Notre Dame, The (1939) Sprawling medieval melodrama from Victor Hugo's story of Quasimodo (Charles Laughton), the misshapen cathedral bell-ringer who rescues a kind Gypsy dancer (Maureen O'Hara) from the gallows, then saves her from the clutches of the evil judge (Cedric Hardwicke) who had been his benefactor. Directed by William Dieterle, the 15th-century Paris setting is vibrantly rendered, the crowded plot moves briskly, and, at the center of the piece, Laughton's feeling performance transcends the character's grotesque features to win audience sympathy. Stylized violence and romantic complications. A-II (br)

Hunchback of Notre Dame, The (1996) Touching animated tale set in 15th-century Paris, where the cathedral's deformed bell-ringer, Quasimodo (voice of Tom Hulce), rescues a kindhearted Gypsy (voice of Demi Moore) from the clutches of his cruel guardian (voice of Tony Jay), who raised Quasimodo as a monster unfit for human contact. Directors Gary Trousdale and Kirk Wise stay true to the comic characters, with sprightly songs and a happily-ever-after ending to the colorful proceedings. A-I (G)

Hunger, The (1983) Catherine Deneuve and David Bowie play vampires whose love has stood the test of time until he, after dining on punk rockers, begins to die, and she falls in love with the doctor (Susan Sarandon) called in to try to save him. Director Tony Scott's relentlessly slick and shallow movie consists of elegant surroundings and extravagant doses of blood and gore, nudity, graphic sexuality, and not one bit of plausibility. O (R)

Hunger for Love (1973) Brazilian drama presents a socio-psychological survey of contemporary values in the story of a young man who decides to run away with the wife of his best-friend. Directed in 1969 by Nelson Pereira Dos Santos, the beautifully crafted movie will appeal most to those interested in themes of social justice. A-III (nr)

Hunt, The (1967) Spanish movie in which three old friends spend a day hunting rabbits while the pressure of resentments caused by changed fortunes grows in each, until the occasion culminates in senseless tragedy. Director Carlos Saura's veiled political allegory about the Spanish Civil War makes a subtle anti-Fascist statement. A-III (br)

Hunt for Red October, The (1990) Cold War thriller based on Tom Clancy's novel tracks the near clash of US and USSR submarines in the Atlantic when a maverick Soviet sub captain (Sean Connery) plots to defect. Director John McTiernan captivates viewers with the suspenseful story, fine ensemble cast, and masterful production design without resorting to gratuitous violence for thrills and chills. Some intense menace and climactic violence. A-II (PG)

Hunted, The (1995) Graphically violent tale of an American businessman (Christopher Lambert) in Japan who is pursued by a deadly band of ninja warriors (led by John Lone) after witnessing their ritualistic murder of a prostitute (Joan Chen). Writer-director J.L. Lawton unleashes a continual torrent of bloodshed and murder in an absurd, inept movie glorifying mindless, murderous mayhem. Mostly subtitled. Excessive violence, including decapitations, and implied sexual encounters with brief, full nudity. O (R)

Hunter, The (1980) Steve McQueen plays a modern-day bounty hunter hired by bail bondsmen to bring back clients who have jumped bail. Though McQueen is very good, director Buzz Kulik's action movie is put together in slipshod fashion with an excess of plot threads that never come together. Good deal of violence. A-III (PG)

Hunting Party, The (1971) Repulsive Western about a wife (Candice Bergen) kidnapped by a sex-crazed outlaw (Oliver Reed) and pursued by a blood-lusting husband (Gene Hackman). Directed by Don Medford, its depiction of sex and nudity is mild in comparison to its graphic presentation of senseless violence and sadistic brutalities. O (R)

Hunting Scenes (1970) German movie about a young man who becomes the object of ridicule in his small village when a rumor starts that he is a homosexual, and he kills someone in a vain attempt to escape his persecutors. Writer-director Peter Fleischmann's story is not about homosexuality but about a tightly-knit community whose fear of those who are different unites them, and may be seen as referring to Hitler's popular support. A-III (nr)

Hurlyburly (1998) Pointless couple of hours spent in the company of a manic, doped-up Hollywood agent (Senn Penn), his mixed-up pals (Kevin Spacey, Chazz Palminteri, and Garry Shandling), and a few women they mistreat along the way. Directed by Anthony Drazan from David Rabe's 1984 play, the one-dimensional characters are chiefly defined by their drug, alcohol, and sexual preferences in stagy proceedings dominated by Penn's delusional ranting and raving, but none of it has any dramatic interest or human insight. Nasty violence, sexual situations and references, frequent substance abuse, constant rough language, and occasional profanity. O (R)

Hurricane (1979) Listless, mediocre remake of the 1937 John Ford movie about ill-fated South Sea lovers (Mia Farrow and Dayton Ka'Ne) was filmed in Bora Bora, but the spectacle of the climatic hurricane does not measure up to the Hollywood original. Director Jan Troell's melodramatic script and its shallow characterizations waste a good cast, including Jason Robards, Max Von Sydow, and Trevor Howard. Erotic dance sequences and distasteful pre-marriage ritual. O (PG)

Hurricane Streets (1998) Urban-youth drama in which a depressed Manhattan teen (Brendan Sexton III), whose thieving pals are verging on more serious crime, gets involved in an accidental killing just as he's about to move to New Mexico with a troubled girlfriend (Isidra Vega). Writer-director Morgan J. Freeman's gritty tale presents adolescent frustrations with some sensitivity, but the narrative is drawn out to a contrived, unconvincing finish. Brief violence, numerous thefts, some recreational drug use, and much rough language. A-III (R)

Hurry Sundown (1967) Michael Caine plays a Cockney-accented cracker and Jane Fonda is his somewhat bruised Georgia peach. Director Otto Preminger's superficial depiction of social, marital, and racial unrest in a small Southern town during the 1940s is patronizing in its treatment of racial attitudes and also demeaning in its approach to sex. O (br)

Hurry Up, or I'll Be 30 (1973) Young man in Brooklyn (John Lefkowitz), crushed by thoughts that he is almost 30, tries vainly to break out of his sterile lifestyle. Director Joseph Jacoby's generally sappy narrative involves George's frustrating job in his father's small print-shop and his brief affair with an aspiring Broadway actress (Linda DeCoff). Entirely predictable movie about boring people; the occasional nudity is totally gratuitous. O (R/GP)

Husbands (1970) Long Island commuters (John Cassavetes, Ben Gazzara, and Peter Falk) attend the burial of a mutual friend suddenly carried off by a coronary, and their own sense of mortality becomes both the catalyst and context for the drunken antics, middle-aged frustrations, and inarticulate revelations that follow. For all of its excesses, from a lavatory vomiting scene to a crude sex-romp in a London hotel, director John Cassavetes injects a compassion for his male misfits that redeems many of the glaring faults in his treatment of the proceedings. A-III (GP/PG-13)

Husbands and Wives (1992) An insecure and childless couple (Mia Farrow and Woody Allen) starts questioning their own marriage when their close friends (Sydney Pollack and Judy Davis) separate after 20 years and rush into hasty affairs. Also written and directed by Allen, the movie presents a cynical view of the permanence of love while deftly skewering older men's flirtations with much younger women. Theme of marital disharmony and infidelities, with some rough language. A-III (R)

Hush (1998) Inept thriller in which a possessive mom (Jessica Lange) tries to get her son (Jonathan Schaech) back by murdering his pregnant wife (Gwyneth Paltrow). Directed by Jonathan Darby, the trashy plot is too predictable to hold interest, and the schemes of the evil mother are too obvious to sustain credibility, with ludicrous results. Menacing situations, an attempted rape, a difficult childbirth sequence, fleeting nudity, and profanity. A-III (PG-13)

Hush ... Hush, Sweet Charlotte (1965) Creaky suspense thriller about a neurotic recluse (Bette Davis) haunted by 30-year-old memories of the hatchet murder of her fiancé and smothered by the attentions of her cousin (Olivia Havilland) and an old friend (Joseph Cotten). Directed by Robert Aldrich, the cast is better than the bogus plot and its belabored sinister atmosphere. Much psychological menace. A-III (br)

Hustle (1975) Los Angeles detective (Burt Reynolds), whose mistress is an expensive call-girl (Catherine Deneuve), finds nothing but corruption in places high and low during his investigation of a young girl's death. Director Robert Aldrich's muddled movie is not above purveying a bit of the corruption it seems to be decrying. Excessive sex and violence. O (R)

Hustler, The (1961) Fine character study of a small-time pool shark (Paul Newman) who muffs his chance to make it to the big-time by crumbling under the pressure of playing against a top veteran (Jackie Gleason), then gets a second chance when he falls for a troubled woman (Piper Laurie) and gets the backing of a manipulative gambler (George C. Scott). Director Robert Rossen captures the smoky netherworld of seedy pool-rooms and the tension of the gambling action, but it is the ensemble performances which sustain interest in this downbeat portrait of a loser and his struggle to be something more. Several scenes of stylized violence, including an off-screen suicide, shady activities, and a live-in relationship. A-III (br)

I

I.F. Stone's Weekly (1973) Fine documentary by Jerry Bruck, Jr., is primarily a study of Stone as a reporter's reporter, whose labors have made him an ebullient force in contemporary journalism. Not least of the film's virtues is its rare picture of a man who thoroughly enjoys what he does for a living and even feels a little guilty that he gets paid for it. A-II (nr)

I Am a Dancer (1973) Pierre Jourdan's documentary records Rudolf Nureyev as he rehearses, in performance, and working with promising novices. John Percival has written a reverent, rather adulatory, narration for the movie, which is pleasantly read by Bryan Forbes. A-I (nr)

I Am Curious (Blue) (1970) The Blue version is just as boring as its Yellow predecessor. Though it contains fewer erotic sequences, its social and political subject-matter is as intemperate, irrelevant, and uninteresting to an American audience as previously. O (nr)

I Am the Cheese (1983) Story of an adolescent's identity crisis, adapted from the novel by Robert Cormier, presents a rather bleak and depressing portrait of the hurt child under psychiatric care. Director Robert Jiras has some insight into ways children might deal with the loss of parents but it is not a movie youngsters will find engaging. A-II (PG)

I Can't Sleep (1995) Composite picture of urban alienation as seen through a series of sketches about immigrants, homosexuals, and other social outsiders living in a Paris neighborhood, where a serial killer is on the loose. French director Claire Denis develops some interesting characters, chiefly a young Lithuanian woman (Katerina Golubeva) hoping to find work as an actress, but the result is uneven and too disjointed to jell into a satisfying whole. Subtitles. Some grisly visuals of elderly corpses, implied homosexual relationships, brief frontal nudity, and some domestic tensions. A-III (nr)

I Come in Peace (1990) A Houston cop (Dolph Lundgren) teams with an obnoxious FBI agent (Brian Benben) to track down a serial killer who is actually an intergalactic drug-dealer (Matthias Hues). Director Craig R. Baxley's routine action-flick limps from one violent scene to the next, and the wooden acting doesn't help an already ludicrous plot. Excessive violence, much rough language, and partial nudity. O (R)

I Confess (1953) Murky thriller set in Quebec City, where a murderer (O.E. Hasse) confesses his crime to a priest (Montgomery Clift) who, bound by the seal of the confessional, refuses to answer certain questions of a police inspector (Karl Malden) and winds up on trial for the murder. Directed by Alfred Hitchcock from a play by Paul Anthelme, the situation is further muddled by a troubled woman (Anne Baxter) from the priest's youth, but the stark location photography picks up some of the narrative slack and the suspenseful conclusion is handled with the director's usual flair. Stylized violence, menacing situations, and romantic complications. A-II (br)

I Could Never Have Sex with Any Man Who Has So Little Regard for My Husband (1973) Dreary, psuedo-sophisticated sex comedy written by Dan Greenburg and directed by Robert McCarty is set in a rainy Martha's Vinyard, where Carmine Caridi, Cynthia Harris, Andrew Duncan, and Lynne Lipton play strip hide-and-seek while they wait for the weather to clear. Monogamy wins in the end, but till then, it's a low comedy exercise in sexual brinkmanship. A-III (R)

I Don't Give a Damn (1988) Disappointing Israeli melodrama about the emotional and physical problems of a wounded soldier (Ika Sohar) who despairs of adjusting to life as a paraplegic. Director Samuel Imberman centers on the soldier's fears of sexual inadequacy with little subtlety or insight. Several fairly explicit bedroom scenes, brief nudity, and much rough language. A-IV (R)

I Don't Want to Talk About It (1994) Fable set in 1930s South America, where a widowed mother (Luisina Brando) worries over her adolescent dwarf daughter (Alejandra Podesta) when a much older man (Marcello Mastroianni) falls deeply in love with the girl and asks to marry her. Argentinean director Maria Luisa Bemberg manages to treat each character with respect for their frailties in a lyrical and very human story about the mystery and unpredictability of love. Subtitles. Some sexual innuendo and fleeting violence. A-III (PG-13)

I Dream of Jeanie (1952) Sentimental tale of Cincinnati accountant Stephen Foster (Bill Shirley) whose 1849 song, "Oh! Susannah" becomes a hit but brings him not a penny until he takes a job as songwriter for the popular minstrel shows of E.P. Christy (Ray Middleton). Directed by Allan Dwan, the lackluster production and thin story line offer little beyond some spirited renditions of Foster's ballads of the Old South. A-I (br)

I Drink Your Blood (1971) Low-budget horror movie exploiting the hippie and drug scene begins with some phony occult rites and ends in a ridiculous rabies epidemic. Directed by David Durston, it is devoid of style and notable only for the way in which it proceeds to turn trash into garbage. O (X/R)

I Eat Your Skin (1971) Routine horror movie is set on a mysterious island with voodoo ceremonies, secret medical experiments, and roaming zombies. It has all been done before and with much more dash than writer-producer-director Del Tenney has been able to come up with, though the zombie makeup does add a little craft to tiresome proceedings. A-III (GP)

I Escaped from Devil's Island (1973) Held prisoner in the forbidding French penal colony circa 1918,

Jim Brown and Christopher George are brutalized by sadistic guards until they flee through shark-infested waters and the teeming jungle. Director William Witney's tough and sweaty movie has excessive violence and a lengthy nude scene. O (R)

I Know What You Did Last Summer (1997) Formula thriller in which four teens accidentally kill a pedestrian and hide his body, then a year later begin receiving threatening notes from an unknown sender, whom they try to identify in hopes of saving their lives. Directed by Jim Gillespie, the manipulative proceedings elicit the expected jolts in a slickly photographed but rather gory suspense picture. Intermittent violence, fleeting sexual innuendo, some rough language, and occasional profanity. A-III (R)

I Like It Like That (1994) After her husband (Jon Seda) is jailed for stealing a stereo, a Bronx housewife (Lauren Velez) provides for their three children by taking a job with a Manhattan music producer (Griffin Dunne), which leads to a marital split when the husband accuses her of infidelity and acknowledges his own affair with a neighbor. Written and directed by Darnell Martin, the inner-city drama is most effective in depicting the tensions of ghetto life and the struggle to transcend its deprivations, though the wife's growth in personal self-confidence is portrayed largely in terms of sexual liberation. Frequent sexual situations and references, a fairly graphic bedroom scene, a strong anti-drug scene involving a minor, some profanity, and recurring rough language. A-IV (R)

I Love My Wife (1971) Selfish, overgrown adolescent surgeon (Elliott Gould) spends increasing amounts of time with his mistresses while ignoring his wife (Brenda Vaccaro), who had put him through medical school and whom he loves deep-down inside. Director Mel Stuart indulges Gould's shaggy-panda style, which generates the barest number of painful laughs and a great deal of embarrassment at his frantic sex-life. O (R)

I Love Trouble (1994) Tiresome, often tasteless, romantic comedy in which rival Chicago newspaper reporters (Julia Roberts and Nick Nolte) join forces in more ways than one to uncover a billion-dollar corporate scam. Directed by Charles Shyer, the result is a romantic misfire set in a weak comedy whose only compensations are some minor-league thrills. Some stylized violence and scenes of menace, much sexual innuendo, and a few instances of profanity. A-III (PG)

I Love You, Alice B. Toklas (1968) Peter Sellers plays a Beverly Hills attorney drawn by love into the hippie lifestyle in what begins as an amusing satirical farce harpooning both the establishment as well as the counter-culture. Directed by Hy Averback, it eventually turns into a sex comedy with graphic sexual scenes, hash parties, and coarse language. O (R)

I Love You ... Don't Touch Me! (1998) Slender tale of a 25-year-old Jewish virgin (Maria Schaffel) who finally succumbs to a slick womanizer (Michael Harris), while her platonic best friend (Mitchell Whitfield) impatiently waits in the wings. Writer-director Julie Davis plumbs single female angst with some earnestness, but the narrative's narrow focus on its characters' sex lives is ultimately tiresome. Sexual situations with brief nudity, some profanity, and recurring rough language. A-III (R)

I Love You, I Kill You (1972) German movie set in the future, where there is a village existing only to maintain a game preserve for the ruling class and whose inhabitants are kept happy by popping pills. Written and directed by Uwe Brandner, the movie operates on many levels of love-hate relationships, but it is primarily a political parable about Fascism and freedom. For those who have the inclination to interpret its languid, dreamlike visuals, it is a demanding exercise but worth the experience. A-IV (nr)

I Love You, I Love You Not (1997) Wispy portrait of a bookish high-school student (Claire Danes) whose emotional insecurities get in the way when she begins dating the school's heartthrob (Jude Law), despite the unconditional moral support of her loving grandmother (Jeanne Moreau), a Holocaust survivor. Director Billy Hopkins tends to sentimentalize the problems of adolescence as well as the student's grappling with her Jewish identity, and the result is disappointingly superficial in its reliance on glossy visuals and slick melodramatics. Stark Holocaust images, sexual innuendo, occasional rough language, and an instance of profanity. A-III (nr)

I Love You, Rosa (1973) Israeli movie about an 11-year-old boy who wants to marry his brother's widow (Michal Bat-Adam), and as he grows older and more insistent, she finally has to take him seriously. Writer-director Moshe Mizrahi's story is set in late 19th-century Jerusalem and is told with a charmingly poetic, humorously sentimental glow that romantics will find hard to resist, though it does indulge in some nudity, crude dialogue, and a casual attitude about premarital sex. A-IV (nr)

I Love You to Death (1990) One-joke film about a loving wife (Tracey Ullman) who tries and fails to murder her philandering Italian husband (Kevin Kline). As directed by Lawrence Kasdan, this fact-based scenario is cartoonish at best, with oddball casting that showcases Joan Plowright as the Lothario's murderous Yugoslavian mother-in-law and buries William Hurt and Keanu Reeves as two nit-wit, drug-addicted assassins. Jokey attitude towards adultery and a cavalier acceptance of murder as a viable solution, some rough language, and fleeting nudity in a sexual context. O (R)

I Married a Monster from Outer Space (1958) Low-budget clunker directed by Gene Fowler, Jr., in which a woman (Gloria Talbott) marries the man of her dreams (Tom Tryon) only to discover that he and the rest of the town's male population are being replaced by alien creatures seeking to continue their species. Silly **Body Snatcher** rip-off with few chills and no thrills. A-II (br)

I Married a Witch (1942) Amusing romantic fantasy in which a witch (Veronica Lake) returns to torment a descendant (Fredric March) of the Puritan elder responsible for her execution 270 years before, but, despite her devilish father (Cecil Kellaway), she falls in love with him instead. Director Rene Clair puts the wacky premise to good comic effect with multiple misunderstandings and simple but witty special effects in a tale of love conquering wickedness. Comic sexual situations and innuendo. A-III (br)

I Married an Angel (1942) Thin musical comedy about a Hungarian count (Nelson Eddy) who dreams he has married an angel (Jeanette MacDonald), then awakens to make it come true. Directed by Maj. W.S. Van Dyke II, the limp plot hinges on the count's position as the head of a Budapest bank which faces ruin unless he reforms his playboy ways, but the Rodgers and Hart songs and bizarre settings are the main attractions. Romantic situations. A-II (br)

I Married You for Fun (1969) Monica Vitti displays comic flair as the "kooky" swinging wife of a young man from an absurdly stuffy background in this Italian sex-farce posing as a satire on marriage. Director Luciano Salce opens with a suicide attempt and goes on to employ a decadent orgy scene and nudity in a sexual context. O (X)

I Met My Love Again (1938) Creaky sudser begins in 1925 Vermont, where the fiancé (Joan Bennett) of a college student (Henry Fonda) runs off to Paris with a hotshot writer (Alan Marshall), then after his death 10 years later returns with her daughter to find her former beau is a college professor being romanced by a rich student (Louise Platt). Directed by Arthur Ripley and Joshua Logan, the formula script gains interest from engaging performances by a fine cast. Romantic complications. A-II (br)

I Never Promised You a Rose Garden (1977) The parents of a teenage schizophrenic (Kathleen Quinlan) reluctantly place her in a mental institution. Quinlan and Bibi Andersson as the psychiatrist give superb performances in this drama of mental illness directed by Anthony Page. The realistic depiction of the teenager's fantasy world and some brief nudity are inappropriate for youngsters. A-III (R)

I Never Sang for My Father (1970) Gilbert Cates directs a solid adaptation of the Robert Anderson play about a grown son (Gene Hackman) forced to come to some decision about how to care for his aging father (Melvyn Douglas). Both give remarkable performances, filled with compassion and understanding, and their scenes together are charged with the love and hate that simultaneously bind them together and make them strangers. It would be fine for adolescents, save for a rather frank bedroom scene. A-III (PG)

I Ought to Be in Pictures (1982) Superficial seriocomic Neil Simon story about a teen (Dinah Manoff) who reunites with the father (Walter Matthau) who had deserted her in order to become a Hollywood writer. Directed by Herbert Ross, the movie tries to make light of an adulterous, misguided character, and offers little insight into parent-child relations. Brief nudity and the father's dealings with a mistress (Ann-Margaret). A-III (PG)

I Remember Mama (1948) Engaging, warm-hearted version of the John Van Druten play in which a daughter (Barbara Bel Geddes) recalls the nurturing influence of her mother (Irene Dunne) on her Norwegian-American brood in San Francisco circa 1910. Produced and directed by George Stevens, the interplay of family life is richly depicted through good times and bad, convincingly portrayed by a cast including Oscar Homolka as the family patriarch, Ellen Corby as the spinster aunt, and Edgar Bergan as her mousy beau). Sincere, affecting, and universal in theme and appeal. A-I (br)

I Saw What You Did (1965) Modest thriller in which two teen girls amuse themselves by making random phone calls using the title sentence to get a rise out of those who answer, until dialing a man (John Ireland) who just killed his wife and now seeks to silence the caller. Directed by William Castle, the proceedings begin as a sophomoric prank which turns dangerously serious, with increasingly tense scenes and a violent climax. Stylized violence and menacing situations involving young people. A-III (br)

I See a Dark Stranger (see: **The Adventuress**)

I Shot Andy Warhol (1996) Dramatizing a minor but highly publicized part of the turbulent 1960s is this picture of Valerie Solanas (Lili Taylor), a radical feminist who lived on the fringes of New York's trendy counterculture but whose paranoid perceptions of its rejection boiled over in 1968, when she seriously wounded pop artist Warhol (Jared Harris). Directed by Mary Harron, the result is a vivid re-creation of one of the more bizarre fragments of the period's cultural ferment, but the treatment lacks a larger frame of reference and is uncritical of the antisocial ideas and behavior so amply portrayed. Stylized violence, sexual situations, brief nudity, casual drug usage, and frequent rough language. O (nr)

I Still Know What You Did Last Summer (1998) Pointless horror sequel in which a quartet of college students vacationing at a remote Caribbean island hotel find the staff murdered and face a similar fate from a relentless, hook-handed killer. Any thrills are bogus and the plot predictable in director Danny Cannon's mindless parade of gory slaughters and mutilated corpses. Excessive violence, sexual innuendo, recurring profanity, and much rough language. O (R)

I, the Jury (1982) Gross remake of the 1953 Mickey Spillane private-eye melodrama features Armand Assante as the sullen Mike Hammer out to avenge a dead friend by smashing a rogue CIA operation which uses a sex clinic as a front. Director Richard T. Heffron relies on a repulsive mix of sex and violence. O (R)

I Wake Up Screaming (1941) Twisty, atmospheric

thriller directed by H. Bruce Humberstone in which the sister (Betty Grable) of a murdered model (Carole Landis) falls for the leading suspect (Victor Mature), then helps him elude being framed by a vindictive cop (Laird Cregar) while searching for the real killer. Restrained violence, moody menace, and some sexual innuendo. A-II (br)

I Walk Alone (1948) Halting crime yarn in which a Prohibition bootlegger (Burt Lancaster) exits prison after 14 years to find his slick ex-partner (Kirk Douglas) has cheated him out of his share in a swanky nightclub, then winds up being framed for the murder of his best friend (Wendall Corey). Directed by Byron Haskin, the confrontations between the former partners become increasingly explosive, but the meandering narrative loses focus in a romantic subplot involving the club's pianist (Lizabeth Scott). Stylized violence including a brutal beating, romantic complications, and some sexual innuendo. A-II (br)

I Walk the Line (1970) Taking its title from a bittersweet Johnny Cash country-western song, the movie concerns a redneck Tennessee sheriff (miscast Gregory Peck) and his romance with a moon-shiner's daughter (Tuesday Weld). Director John Frankenheimer reduces the story to a series of heavy, melodramatic surface strokes without any social or moral complexity, resulting in a movie without any substance. A-III (GP)

I Walked with a Zombie (1943) Effective horror tale set on a Haitian plantation whose American owner (Tom Conway) employs a nurse (Frances Dee) to care for his strangely afflicted wife (Edith Barrett), who has had some dealings with a local voodoo cult. Produced by Val Lewton and directed by Curt Siodmak, the plot offers little more than the eerie situation's ominous atmosphere and scary visuals suggesting more than they show. Threatening situations and romantic complications. A-II (br)

I Wanna Hold Your Hand (1978) Three New Jersey high-school girls enact an elaborate scheme to get to see their heroes, the Beatles, on the day the singing group is to appear on the Ed Sullivan Show in 1964. Director Robert Zemeckis's farcical style, rough language, and a tasteless scene with a prostitute make it a decidedly adult comedy. A-III (PG)

I Want to Live! (1958) Compelling fact-based drama about a small-time crook and occasional prostitute (Susan Hayward) who in 1955 is convicted of a vicious murder on questionable evidence and, after many lengthy appeals, is executed in a California gas chamber. Directed by Robert Wise, the movie does not minimize the woman's criminal past, but, by suggesting she was railroaded on the murder charge, its harrowing portrayal of her execution becomes a powerful indictment of capital punishment as well as earning Hayward's Oscar for her tough yet sympathetic performance as a victim of injustice. Adult themes and detailed depiction of an execution. A-III (br)

I Want What I Want (1972) Anne Heywood playing both the before and after role in the story of a transsexual struggles sincerely, if not quite convincingly. Directed by John Dexter, the result is wanting in such basics as dramatic interest and clarity, as well as depth in treating the psychological, medical, and moral dimensions. A-III (R)

I Want You (1952) Contrived melodrama of the turmoil within a small-town family (headed by Dana Andrews and Dorothy McGuire) when one of its eligible males (Farley Granger) is drafted during the Korean War. Directed by Mark Robson, the soggy proceedings may be of some sociological interest, but the characters are cardboard patriots more concerned about safeguarding democracy here and abroad than about the drama of their personal lives. Dated political rhetoric and civic moralizing. A-II (br)

I Was a Communist for the F.B.I. (1951) Patriotic melodrama based on the experiences of Matt Cvetic (Frank Lovejoy), a Pittsburg steel worker who joined the Communist Party in order to inform the Feds of its activities. Directed by Gordon Douglas, the picture emphasizes the dangers Cvetic faced working as an undercover agent for nine years, with a subplot involving a Party member (Dorothy Hart) who risks her life to break with her Communist associates. Stylized violence. A-I (br)

I Was a Male War Bride (1949) Uneven romantic comedy in which a suave French officer (Cary Grant) and his sharp WAC aide (Ann Sheridan) bicker on and off the job in occupied Germany, then decide to wed, but getting "an alien spouse of female military personnel" into the US turns into a comic nightmare. Directed by Howard Hawks, the romantic mix-ups in Germany have some bright moments, but the frustrated Frenchman's problems with US military and immigration officials is tiresomely contrived, despite Grant's comic attempts at female impersonation. Romantic complications and sexual situations. A-III (br)

I Was a Teenage Frankenstein (1957) Ludicrous horror tale directed by Herbert L. Strock in which a mad doctor (Whit Bissell) constructs a creature (Gary Conway) out of teen body-parts, then faces the wrath of his creation. Jokey violence, some of it quite nasty, and sexual innuendo. A-III (br)

I Was a Teenage Werewolf (1957) Horror clunker from director Gene Fowler, Jr., in which the experimental treatment used by a doctor (Whit Bissell) on an emotionally disturbed high-school senior (Michael Landon) turns the troubled youth into a werewolf, with disastrous results for both. Stylized mayhem, hokey menace, and some sexual innuendo. A-III (br)

I Went Down (1997) Irish crime story in which a goodhearted parolee (Peter McDonald) is forced by a mob boss (Tony Doyle) to team with a blundering ex-con (Brendan Gleeson) in hunting down the gangster's doublecrossing partner (Peter Caffrey). Director Paddy Breathnach contrives to inject ditzy humor into an increasingly dark tale of revenge with unsatisfying results. Some nasty violence, a sexual encounter with nudity, occasional profanity, and much rough language. A-IV (R)

I Will, I Will ... For Now (1976) Limp sex-farce about sexually based marital problems stars Elliott Gould and Diane Keaton. Directed by Norman Panama, the movie's tasteless humor is structured as a parody of a sex manual with vulgar jokes and negative female stereotypes. O (R)

I'd Rather Be Rich (1964) Plodding remake of **It Started with Eve** in which a dying millionaire (Maurice Chevalier) is rejuvenated when his granddaughter (Sandra Dee) introduces a stranger (Robert Goulet) as her fiancé. Directed by Jack Smight, the merriment of the original is missing and Chevalier comes nowhere near matching Laughton's mischievous humbug. Romantic complications. A-II (br)

I'll Be Home for Christmas (1998) Witless road movie in which a manipulative college student (Jonathan Taylor Thomas) must get cross-country by Christmas Eve to claim a luxury car while worrying a romantic rival will steal his girlfriend. As blandly directed by Arlene Sanford, the comic situations are highly contrived and the student's transformation from smug to sweet is unconvincing. An indulgent attitude toward lying, cheating, and stealing, as well as fleeting sexual innuendo. A-III (PG)

I'll Be Seeing You (1944) Wartime romance blossoms between a lonely soldier (Joseph Cotten) and the woman (Ginger Rogers) who invites him to spend the Christmas holidays with her relatives, though she gradually realizes he's suffering from battle fatigue, and he finally learns she's a convict on a 10-day furlough. Directed by William Dieterle, the contrived situation is less than credible, though its celebration of ordinary people and small-town virtues touches the heart. Some menacing situations and an attempted sexual assault. A-II (br)

I'll Cry Tomorrow (1955) Strong fact-based story of singer Lillian Roth (Susan Hayward), a child vaudeville star pushed by her mother (Jo Van Fleet) to Hollywood and Broadway fame in the 1930s but, after romantic disappointments and a disastrous marriage (to Richard Conte), winds up an alcoholic on Skid Row, from which she emerges with the help of an Alcoholic Anonymous worker (Eddie Albert). Director Daniel Mann depicts with harrowing realism the effects of compulsive drinking as well as the courage needed for rehabilitation, but much of the credit for the movie's emotional impact belongs to the performances. Effective cautionary tale with discreet treatment of sordid details, including suicidal despair. A-II (br)

I'll Do Anything (1994) Given custody of his six-year-old spitfire of a daughter (Whittni Wright), a divorced actor (Nick Nolte) struggles with parenting while juggling romance with a junior movie-executive (Joely Richardson) in hopes that her self-obsessed boss (Albert Brooks) will give him an acting job. Pithy dialogue and sly humor surface intermittently in writer-director James L. Brooks' rambling yet engaging satire about fostering relationships amid Hollywood's phony values. An implied affair, a bedroom scene, a flash of nudity, and an instance of rough language. A-III (PG-13)

I'll Never Forget What's'isname (1968) Failed British melodrama about an advertising whiz (Oliver Reed) who, disillusioned with success, an unsatisfying marriage, and two mistresses, decides to throw it all away and return to making an honest living but learns one can't recapture a lost innocence. Directed by Michael Winner, there is some satirical goring of TV commercials and the emptiness of affluence, but the plot goes nowhere and ends in cynicism. Excessive gory violence and graphic sex-scenes. O (br)

I'll See You in My Dreams (1951) Sentimental biography of songwriter Gus Kahn (Danny Thomas) tracks his start during WW I, marriage (to Doris Day), and Tin Pan Alley triumphs, then Depression doldrums, until renewed success in Hollywood. Directed by Michael Curtiz, the engaging performance by Thomas almost overcomes the script's showbiz cliches and formula obstacles, but Day's credible as the supportive wife and, along the way, is an enjoyable review of Kahn lyrics, including the title song. Restrained treatment of marital misunderstandings and domestic difficulties. A-II (br)

I'm Dancing as Fast as I Can (1982) Disappointing dramatization of television producer Barbara Gordon's account of her struggle to overcome an addiction to tranquilizers, partly because Jill Clayburgh's characterization casts little light upon why she is so driven to drugs. The result is an unnerving melodrama rather than anything deeper ,as director Jack Hofsiss details the horrors of quitting "cold turkey," with violence and rough language used to realistic effect. A-III (R)

I'm Gonna Git You Sucka (1989) Writer-director Keenen Ivory Wayans also stars in this comic parody of 1970s black-exploitation films, which sees a former wimp (Wayans) avenge the death of his brother with the help of some over-the-hill black heroes (Bernie Casey, Issac Hayes, and Jim Brown, among others). Tacky, too self-mocking, and unfocused, it will hardly inspire audiences to question the media's role in perpetuating offensive black stereotypes. Much profanity laced with sexual vulgarities and intense comic-book violence. O (R)

I'm Not Rappaport (1996) Offbeat comedy in which a crusty retiree (Walter Matthau), instead of moving in with his daughter (Amy Irving), involves another old-timer (Ossie Davis) in assorted neighborhood causes to fend off resigning themselves to rocking chairs. Adapted form his own stage-play by writer-director Herb Gardner, the leisurely paced movie is a talky but acidly funny rejection of stereotypes about the elderly, with the result depending largely on Matthau's feisty performance and that of Davis as his gullible foil. Fleeting violence, brief recreational drug use, and intermittent profanity. A-III (PG-13)

I've Lived Before (1956) Pulp tale directed by Richard Bartlett in which an airline pilot (Jock

Mahoney) has vivid recollections of a previous life as a US Army aviator who died when shot down in a dogfight over 1918 France. Murky treatment of reincarnation theme. A-II (br)

Ice (1970) Writer-director Robert Kramer has made a fictional movie with a documentary look about shadowy revolutionary groups joining together to plan, then carry out, a regional show of force in preparation for a nationwide uprising. Though its surface realities seem to have little connection with any actual violence of radical groups, it does offer a chilling picture of the fantasies engendered in those frustrated by their hopes for social change. A-IV (nr)

Ice Castles (1979) When a talented young skater (Lynn-Holly Johnson) training for the Olympics is blinded in an accident, her father (Tom Skerritt) and boyfriend (Robby Benson) persuade her to resume her career. Director Donald Wrye gets good performances in this mildly inspirational tale, but the movie is undone by frequent rough language and its sympathetic attitude towards premarital sex on the part of its teenage heroine. O (PG)

Ice Follies of 1939 (1939) After out-of-work ice-skaters marry, the wife (Joan Crawford) becomes a movie star, while the husband (James Stewart) creates a smash ice-revue eventually reuniting them when it's made into a movie (the final reel is in Technicolor). Directed by Reinhold Schunzel, the story is only an excuse for stringing together ice-skating acts in a dated programmer of limited interest except for its stars. A-I (br)

Ice Pirates, The (1984) Lackluster science-fiction story about the hijacking of spaceships that supply ice to waterless planets tries but fails to get by as a spoof. Directed by Stewart Raffill and starring Robert Urich and Mary Crosby, it indulges in some sexually oriented humor, a relatively mild bedroom sequence, and an air of pervasive vulgarity. A-III (PG)

Ice Station Zebra (1968) Uneven screen version of Alistair MacLean's thriller in which a nuclear submarine captain (Rock Hudson) is ordered to bring a British spy (Patrick McGoohan), a friendly Russian (Ernest Borgnine), and a detachment of Marines to an Arctic weather station, where they come into conflict with the Soviets over a downed surveillance satellite. Directed by John Sturges, the ponderous plot relies on double agents and a Cold War showdown to keep up adult interest and plenty of icebound adventure for younger viewers. Some stylized violence and menace. A-I (G)

Ice Storm, The (1997) Somber drama set during Thanksgiving week in 1973, when a suburban housewife (Joan Allen) learns her husband (Kevin Kline) is having an affair with a neighbor (Sigourney Weaver), while the neglected adolescent offspring of both families furtively explore their sexuality until a sudden ice storm causes a sobering tragedy. Directed by Ang Lee, the movie does a marvelous job in recreating the era and its discontents while following the disordered emotional lives of its characters and the consequences of their parental neglect of family responsibilities. Numerous sexual situations, occasional profanity, and some rough language. A-IV (R)

Iceman (1984) Talented Australian director Fred Schepisi has too little to work with in a script by Chip Proser and John Drimmer about an Arctic expedition revivifying a frozen Neanderthal man (John Lone). There is a running argument between a scientist-humanist (Timothy Hutton) and a more clinical type (Lindsay Crosue) as to what to do with him, but it fails to generate enough heat to thaw out anything. Some mild vulgarities. A-II (PG)

Ichabod and Mr. Toad (see: **The Adventures of Ichabod and Mr. Toad**)

Icy Breasts (1975) French suspense movie set on the Riviera in winter, when a hack writer (Claude Brasseur) sees a striking blonde (Mireille Darc) with a hurt, gamin-like quality, and sets out in pursuit but is stopped by her lawyer (Alain Delon), who tells him she is unstable and a murderess. Director Georges Lautner has made a taut, spare thriller with talented performers and luxurious settings. Some brief nudity which the context makes far from erotic. A-IV (R)

Ideal Husband, An (1999) Oscar Wilde's 1895 drawing-room comedy of manners finds a rising London politician (Jeremy Northam) in danger of losing his career and adored wife (Cate Blanchett) unless a spoiled bachelor ally (Rupert Everett) distracted by a new love interest (Minnie Driver) can outwit a blackmailing *femme fatale* (Julianne Moore). Writer-director Oliver Parker's pokily paced adaptation is visually and verbally elegant, with an able ensemble cast skewering the era's social pretensions. Fleeting nudity and sexual innuendo, references to fraud, and deceitful behavior. A-III (PG-13)

Identification Marks: None (1969) Impressionistic Polish drama about a youth waiting to enter military service. Directed by Jerzy Skolimowski, the movie poetically evokes the confusions and personal conflicts of young people in a bleak, repressive society. A-III (nr)

Idi Amin Dada (1976) Self-portrait of the Ugandan leader shows Amin as a dangerous dictator perhaps more effectively than if director Barbet Schroeder had been permitted to make his own objective documentary. Its display of the ruler's gross self-indulgence in the midst of such an impoverished nation is a valuable part of the historical record as well as a warning of the excesses of unchecked political power. A-II (nr)

Idle Hands (1999) Gross horror-comedy in which a pot-smoking teen (Devon Sawa) cannot control his murderous hand, and even after he chops it off, the disembodied hand continues on its bloody killing spree at the Halloween school dance. As directed by Rodman Flender, the sick humor isn't amusing, and a tasteless parade of death scenes just adds insult to injury. Nasty violence with much gore, pervasive teen drug abuse, crude sexual references, brief nudity, occasional profanity, and recurring rough language. O (R)

Idol, The (1966) Self-centered American art student in England (Michael Parks), pursued by his friend's girlfriend, is more interested in seducing his pal's mother (Jennifer Jones). Director Daniel Petrie fails to make clear why anyone would find his confused, boorish hero of the slightest interest, let alone appeal. Adult themes and treatment. A-III (br)

Idolmaker, The (1980) Ray Sharkey turns in a fine performance as a Svengali-like manager who turns two marginally talented youngsters (Peter Gallagher and Paul Land) into rock stars in the early 1960s. Although the picture runs out of energy and interest about two-thirds of the way through, director Taylor Hackford's portrait of the power-hungry is superior entertainment up till then. Some sexual references. A-III (PG)

If (1969) British schoolboys (among them, Malcolm McDowell) rebel against the abuses of a social and educational system out of step with their yearnings and fantasies for a life of freedom from unenlightened authority. Director Lindsay Anderson's complex fable halfheartedly accepts violence as a means to social change and uses nudity as a symbol of liberation. A-IV (X/R)

If a Man Answers (1962) Dull romantic comedy in which a wealthy debutante (Sandra Dee) marries a struggling fashion photographer (Bobby Darin), then tries to keep him from straying by inventing an imaginary lover. Directed by Henry Levin, the glossy proceedings have little humor and no wit. Sexual situations and comic treatment of infidelity. A-III (br)

If Ever I See You Again (1978) Self-indulgent story about a hugely successful commercial songwriter (Joe Brooks) who after 12 years rediscovers, loses, and, at movie's end, wins his college sweetheart (Shelley Hack) while echoes of "Venite Adoremus" are heard on the sound track. Also directed by Brooks, it is so gloppy it makes **Love Story** look like a Tolstoy novel. Some scenes, by suggestion at least, are adult. A-III (PG)

If He Hollers, Let Him Go (1968) Black automechanic (Raymond St. Jacques), wrongly convicted of a capital crime, escapes prison and saves the life of a wealthy woman (Dana Wynter), who offers all the financial aid necessary to prove his innocence. Written, produced, and directed by Charles Martin, its story of racism and injustice is little more than a cheap exploitation of explicit sex and brutality. O (R)

If I Had a Gun (1973) The setting is a small rural village in Slovakia, the state created after the Nazi occupation of Czechoslovakia, during the last years of WW II. The central figure is a young boy living through the normal problems of early adolescence, which are compounded by the extraordinary conditions of wartime. Director Stephen Uher does not sentimentalize his subject but suggests that the effect of violence upon the young is the most terrible heritage that the adult world has to bestow. A-III (nr)

If I Were King (1938) Stylish tale of 14th-century vagabond poet Francois Villon (Ronald Colman), who saves Louis XI (Basil Rathbone) and Paris from Burgundian invaders by leading an army of the city's poor against the enemy. Directed by Frank Lloyd from a script by Preston Sturges, the result has some witty fun with the shifting relationship between crafty king and bright commoner, but the historical pageantry is pure Hollywood hokum. Stylized violence and mild romantic complications. A-II (br)

If It's Tuesday, This Must Be Belgium (1969) Drip-dry comedy about American tourist stereotypes, camera- and luggage-ladened, on an economy tour of Europe. Both the people and the places make easy targets for director Mel Stuart to poke fun at. Less funny is a romantic complication involving tourist Suzanne Pleshette, who tries a fling with grabby guide Ian McShane. A-III (G)

If Looks Could Kill (1991) Mistaken for an American secret-agent, a high-school senior (Richard Grieco), in Europe with his French class, is called upon to save the continent from the murderous machinations of a madman (Roger Rees). Director William Dear's spectacularly awful spy-movie spoof is a grab bag of screen cliches, all the more pronounced by the script's being underdeveloped and overacted. Much comic book violence and some sexual innuendo. A-III (PG-13)

If Lucy Fell (1996) Vapid romantic comedy about two socially inept roommates (Sarah Jessica Parker and Eric Schaeffer) who have made a pact to kill themselves if they haven't found true love by age 30. Also written and directed by Schaeffer, the premise is embarrassingly dumb, but the charmless characters are dumber still, with some crude humor making matters even worse. Sexual innuendo, vulgarity, profanity, and rough language. A-III (R)

If You Could See What I Hear (1982) Based upon the college experiences of blind singer-entertainer Tom Sullivan (Marc Singer), this muddled movie offers both crude slapstick and pathos with very little in between. Sullivan's pursuit of women and an off-again, on-again religious dimension is conveyed in a crude, insensitive manner by director Eric Till. A-III (PG)

Ikiru (1960) Universal tale from Japan in which a petty municipal bureaucrat (Takashi Shimura) learns he has stomach cancer but can find no solace either from family or empty diversions, until he determines to give some meaning to his life by cutting through the red tape of city agencies to build a children's playground in a poor neighborhood, as told in flashbacks at the man's wake. Directed by Akira Kurosawa, the 1952 production turns the story of a dying man into a convincing affirmation of life as he recovers the lost sense of his own human worth by helping others, in a movie filled with compelling performances and honest emotions, including its touching theme song, "Life Is So Short." Subtitles. Focus on terminal illness and some sexual references. A-III (br)

Il Bidone (1965) Italian drama about a confidence man (Broderick Crawford) who begins to realize that he is too old for the small-time rackets in which he is engaged. Directed by Federico Fellini, the 1955 production is episodic and the characters (including Giulietta Masina, Richard Basehart, and Franco Fabrizi) somewhat sentimentalized. Subtitles. Mature themes. A-III (br)

Il Ladro di Bambini (1993) Assigned to escort two youngsters to a distant children's home after their mother is arrested on a morals charge, a young policeman is at first exasperated, then appalled at their sullen, withdrawn behavior and endangers his career by responding to their desperate need for someone to trust and make them feel safe. Director Gianni Amelio's engrossing Italian production offers a small but emotionally rich story of an ordinary man whose sense of decency compels him to try to help undo the damage done to abused youngsters robbed of childhood's innocence. Subtitles. Veiled references to the sexual exploitation of a minor. A-II (nr)

Il Postino (**The Postman**) (1995) Touching, fact-based story set in 1952 Italy, where a simple country postman (Massimo Troisi) befriends Chilean political exile Pablo Neruda (Philippe Noiret), a renowned poet whose sensuous words inspire the girl-shy mailman to win the hand of the local beauty (Maria Grazia Cucinotta) he has admired from afar. Director Michael Radford's humanistic picture of love, friendship, and the transforming power of art is elevated by Troisi and Noiret's affecting performances and the sumptuous visual beauty of the rural setting. Subtitles. Mild sexual references. A-II (PG)

Illustrated Man, The (1969) Failed attempt to tie in three unrelated tales with the story of a man (Rod Steiger) whose body is covered from head to foot with tattoos in which others see their future. Directed by Jack Smight, the movie wavers between horror, thriller, and science fiction with unsatisfying results. Some violence and brief nudity. A-III (PG)

Images (1972) Psychological thriller in which events are seen through the eyes and mind of a troubled woman (Susannah York) and leaving, until the final shot, the audience to determine which of her perceptions are real and which imaginary. Director Robert Altman demonstrates a technical mastery of his medium, a willingness to take chances in achieving an effect, and a talent for eliciting strong performances from his actors. Mature themes. A-III (R)

Imaginary Crimes (1994) Picture of dysfunctional family life in which the doomed moneymaking schemes of a widowed, loving father (Harvey Keitel) in 1960s Oregon continually disappoint his young daughters (Fairuza Balk and Elisabeth Moss), forcing him to confront his basic dishonesty and poor parenting when arrested for fraud. Director Anthony Drazan builds a small but poignant drama out of the older daughter's attempt to raise her younger sister while struggling to forgive her flawed con-man dad. Fleeting sexual innuendo and several profanities. A-II (PG)

Imaginary Sweetheart (see: **Professional Sweetheart**)

Imagine: John Lennon (1988) Director Andrew Solt's documentary intersperses interviews with film footage to provide a portrait of the prolific singer, songwriter, and ex-Beatle. There's a lot of great music, but as much about the fans and the period in which the music was written as about Lennon, who comes across as a mature, positive image late in life. Some rough language and fleeting nudity. A-III (R)

Immediate Family (1989) In an open-adoption arrangement, a childless middle-class couple (Glenn Close and James Woods) take in a pregnant working-class teenager (Mary Stuart Masterson) and, while nervously awaiting the arrival of the child, they interact tentatively and with conflicting emotions. Director Jonathan Kaplan's predictable, bittersweet story shows adoption as neither an easy solution for the childless couple nor an easy way out for the pregnant teen. Minor rough language laced with sexual innuendoes. A-III (PG-13)

Imitation of Life (1959) Tawdry romantic claptrap about a struggling actress (Lana Turner), the self-effacing black woman (Juanita Moore) who becomes her best friend, and their daughters, one of whom (Sandra Dee) falls for her mother's beau (John Gavin) while the other (Susan Kohner) tries desperately to pass for white. Director Douglas Sirk's silly tearjerker changes the credible premise of the 1934 original for an empty scenario full of bad acting and bogus sentimentality. Some sexual innuendo, stylized violence, and unenlightened racial attitudes. A-III (br)

Immortal Bachelor, The (1980) Claudia Cardinale serves on the jury trying the case of a charwoman (Monica Vitti) on trial for murdering her philandering husband. Vitti's defense is that she could not possibly murder a man who was unequaled among lovers. Director Marcello Fondato's mood of artificiality undercuts the social satire while his emphasis upon marital infidelity makes this adult fare. A-III (PG)

Immortal Battalion, The (see: **The Way Ahead**)

Immortal Beloved (1994) Sprawling biographical portrait of Ludwig van Beethoven (Gary Oldman) is told in flashback after his death in 1827, leaving all to an unnamed mystery woman, the search for whom leads a devoted aide (Jeroen Krabbe) to a variety of women (Johanna Ter Steege, Valeria Golina, and Isabella Rossellini) and gradual insights into the composer's turbulent personal life. Writer-director Bernard Rose fashions a handsome, if highly romanticized, story of the composer in which his music is a backdrop to the mysterious romance that supposedly fueled his passionate music. Brief nudity, numerous sexual references, and an attempted suicide. A-III (R)

Immortal Story (1969) Orson Welles directs as well as stars in this solemn tale about a merchant baron's grotesque obsession with transforming pretense into reality. Jeanne Moreau appears in a cameo in this haunting, elusively obscure fable about the futility of wealth and power to provide fulfillment. A-III (nr)

Impact (1949) Convoluted murder yarn in which a wealthy businessman (Brian Donlevy) escapes being killed by his wife's lover, who dies instead, with the businessman charged with his murder. Directed by Arthur Lubin, the contrived plot turns on the search for a missing witness (Anna May Wong) by a veteran cop (Charles Coburn) and a woman (Ella Raines) who believes in his innocence. Stylized violence and marital infidelity. A-III (br)

Impasse (1969) Salvage-company owner (Burt Reynolds) reassembles four members of an Army detail which had buried a fortune in gold bullion in the tunnels of Corregidor just before its surrender to the Japanese. What could have been an interesting action melodrama in Philippine locales is ruined by a confused screenplay, formula characters, and the unsavory cynicism with which director Richard Benedict treats a love affair that eventually causes failure for the entire operation. Some violence, coarse language, and a rather graphic lovemaking scene. O (M)

Imported Bridegroom, The (1990) Thinking it will earn him a place in paradise, a pompous Jewish businessman (Eugene Troobnick) brings a bashful Talmudic scholar (Avi Hoffman) from Poland to marry his social-climbing Bostonian daughter (Greta Cowan). Produced and directed by Pamela Berger, the film is an affectionate look at a turn-of-the-century Jewish household with humorously ethnic dialogue, but the film is diluted by the actors' studied and self-conscious performances. A-I (nr)

Impossible on Saturday (1966) Mediocre French import. A-II (br)

Impossible Years, The (1969) Sappy situation comedy about a university professor (David Niven), a supposed authority on teenage behavior, who is unaware that his own teenage daughter (Christina Ferrare) is secretly married (to Chad Everett). The girl's permissive standards of conduct become the source of irreverent generation-gap humor, which director Michael Gordon plays badly as adult farce. A-III (G)

Impostors, The (1998) Screwball comedy set in the 1930s follows two hapless actors (Stanley Tucci and Oliver Platt) who become stowaways on-board a liner whose passengers include a mad terrorist (Tony Shalhoub) out to blow up the ship. Also written and directed by Tucci, the pacing is uneven, but the overall effect enjoyable thanks to a large ensemble cast portraying all manner of shipboard eccentrics. Comically intended sexual encounters, double entendres, occasional profanity, and some rough language. A-III (R)

Impromptu (1991) Enchanted by Chopin's music, female novelist George Sand (Judy Davis) sets her sights on having an affair with the sickly musician (Hugh Grant), unaware that the jealous mistress (Bernadette Peters) of Franz Liszt (Julian Sand) has thrown a wrench in the works. Despite an appealing cast, director James Lapine's comedy fails to rise beyond the level of silly period piece. Minor violence, casual acceptance of affairs, and minimal rough language. A-III (PG-13)

Improper Channels (1981) Alan Arkin stars as a screwball architect who is unjustly accused of child abuse when his five-year-old daughter hits her head, and a social worker misjudges the situation. Canadian production directed by Eric Till elicits a few comic moments but refuses to deal with the real questions of domestic violence and children's rights. A-II (PG)

Impulse (1984) Young couple (Meg Tilly and Tim Matheson) return to her hometown to find that everyone has gone berserk, indulging in bloody violence and promiscuous sex. Director Graham Baker's horror movie is as ridiculous as it is vicious. O (R)

Impulse (1990) Murky crime drama about a Los Angeles undercover female vice-cop (Theresa Russell) whose distorted priorities, problems with men, and near burnout become life-threatening when she's almost killed during a drug sting. Despite its intriguing female protagonist and impressive direction by Sondra Locke, the script is clumsily plotted and strangely lacking in female perspective. Some profanity, grisly violence, and a sexual encounter with shadowed nudity. A-III (R)

Impure Thoughts (1987) Four recently deceased friends are reunited in purgatory and reminisce about their 1960s Catholic upbringing. Some mildly irreverent humor is offset by director Michael Simpson's exploration of religious values and family life. Some crude language and sexual references. A-III (PG)

In a Lonely Place (1950) Uneven suspense tale in which a moody screenwriter (Humphrey Bogart) is cleared as a murder suspect by the testimony of a neighbor (Gloria Grahame) with whom he then becomes romantically involved until his violent outbursts of anger make her fear for her life. Directed by Nicholas Ray, the result is of interest more for its unglamorous picture of Hollywood life than its melodramatic story of a bright but dangerously volatile individual in need of professional help rather than sympathy. Stylized violence and threatening situations. A-II (br)

In & Out (1997) Sex farce about the comic confusions of a 40-year-old small-town teacher (Kevin Kline) whose life goes topsy-turvy days before his wedding when an Oscar-winning former student announces to the world that the teacher is gay. Director Frank Oz mixes warmhearted humor with broadly funny performances as the farcical proceeding poke fun at gay and straight stereotypes. Flippant treatment of homosexuality, brief male kissing scene, occasional profanity, and an instance of rough language. A-IV (PG-13)

In Celebration (1975) British adaptation of the David Storey play about three sons (Alan Bates, James Bolam, and Brian Cox) who return home to a coal-mining town to celebrate their parents' 40th wedding anniversary. Director Lindsay Anderson's incisive portrait of family relations and each individual's struggle to cope with the bonds of the past is emotionally powerful and will deeply involve most viewers. Mature themes. A-III (PG)

In Cold Blood (1967) Meaningful screen version of Truman Capote's nonfiction novel about the senseless 1959 slaying of a Kansas family and the apprehension and hanging of their killers (Robert Blake and Scott Wilson). Director Robert Brooks takes a semi-documentary approach in re-creating these events with shattering realism but with compassion and a notable lack of sensationalism. It also explores the backgrounds and the motivations of the two criminals as well as scrutinizes the practice of capital punishment. Strong stuff but the experience is thought-provoking. A-III (R)

In Country (1989) Old wounds are opened when a recent high-school grad (Emily Lloyd) begins to question her grandmother (Peggy Rea) and uncle (Bruce Willis) about her father, who died in Vietnam before her birth. Director Norman Jewison's poignant drama about how one rural Kentucky family deals with the unfinished business and personal tragedy caused by the unpopular conflict also includes the crucial element of healing that must occur within all individuals touched by war. Sexual involvement by the young, female protagonist, some rough language laced with sexual innuendo, and brief wartime violence. A-III (R)

In Custody (1994) In rural India, a college professor (Om Puri) encounters myriad frustrations in attempting to get the country's leading Urdu-language poet (Shashi Kapoor) to audiotape his verse for posterity. Director Ismail Merchant takes poignant note of the virtual disappearance of the ancient Urdu language in a wafer-thin narrative that inches along, gradually building minor interest through its gently comic sensibility. Subtitles. Mild sexual innuendo. A-II (PG)

In Dreams (1999) Murky thriller in which a mother (Annette Bening) is so terrified by vivid visions of a child-killer (Robert Downey, Jr.) she is institutionalized as mentally ill, but the killer really exists and goes on to murder her daughter and husband (Aidan Quinn). Director Neil Jordan's muddled jumble of murder, clairvoyance, and insanity fails to mesh into a coherent narrative, and the result barely rises above the level of a schlocky horror movie. Recurring gory violence, deadly menace to children, some profanity, and much rough language. A-IV (R)

In Enemy Country (1968) Limp WW II spy thriller about the exploits of a French intelligence agent (Tony Franciosa) behind German lines. The mediocre effort is directed by Harry Keller with no moral considerations beyond that of all is fair in love and war. Some violence and sexual situations. A-III (br)

In God We Trust (1980) Marty Feldman's inept and hugely unfunny comedy, intended as a satire on the exploitation of people in the name of religion, displays a tasteless, irreverent, crude mocking of religious beliefs. O (PG)

In Harm's Way (1965) Bloated WW II saga of US naval operations in the Pacific after Pearl Harbor centers less in military action than in the personal lives of its characters, particularly an extramarital affair between a tough commander (John Wayne) and a sympathetic nurse (Patricia Neal). Producer-director Otto Preminger churns the emotions in grand soap-opera fashion but to little purpose and only empty effects. Stylized violence and sympathetic treatment of sexual liaisons. A-III (br)

In Like Flint (1967) Dreary sequel to **Our Man Flint** in which the title super-agent (James Coburn) battles an international women's conspiracy to take over the world by substituting an actor for the US president (Andrew Duggan), then seizing control of a nuclear-armed space station. Directed by Gordon Douglas, the intended spoof is too overdone to be amusing and the slow-paced proceedings are embarrassingly witless. Slapstick violence and sexist humor. A-II (br)

In Love and War (1958) Soapy WW II sudser directed by Philip Dunne focuses on the love-life of three Marines — gung-ho sergeant Jeffrey Hunter and pregnant Hope Lange; cowardly recruit Robert Wagner and pragmatic Sheree North; and wealthy idealist Bradford Dillman engaged to flip socialite Dana Wynter, but in love with Hawaiian nurse France Nuyen. Dated romantic twaddle laced with sexual situations and occasional wartime violence. A-III (br)

In Love and War (1997) Fact-based account of the bittersweet wartime romance in 1918 Italy between two American Red Cross volunteers, the idealistic 19-year-old Ernest Hemingway (Chris O'Donnell) and a 26-year-old nurse (Sandra Bullock) torn between marrying the love-struck youth or a wealthy, older Italian doctor. Director Richard Attenborough displays keen visual skills in re-creating the WW I era, but fails to get beneath the surface of the characters and the result is little more than a superficial love story. Brief battlefield violence, a bedroom scene with shadowy nudity, and minimal profanity. A-III (PG-13)

In Old California (1942) Routine Western directed by William McGann in which a Boston druggist (John Wayne) sets up shop in Sacramento just before the gold strike at Sutter's Mill, then tangles with the town's corrupt boss (Albert Dekker) over a dance-hall singer (Binnie Barnes), but comes through in the end to save the gold fields from a typhoid epidemic. Frontier violence. A-I (br)

In Old Oklahoma (see: **War of the Wildcats**)

In Person (1935) Hokey romantic comedy directed by William Seiter in which an exhausted movie star (Ginger Rogers) hides from press and fans in a country cabin, where she falls for the man (George Brent) hired to guard her privacy. Some sexual situations and innuendo. A-III (br)

In Praise of Older Women (1979) Hopelessly episodic, shallow, and sexually exploitative Canadian movie about a young Hungarian émigré (Tom Berenger) and his amorous adventures with the likes of Karen Black and Susan Strasberg. Directed by George Kaczender, events never stray far from the bedroom. O (R)

In Search of Gregory (1970) British female Don Quixote fantasy set in the 20th century centers on a young woman (Julie Christie) who is told by her wealthy father (Adolfo Celi) and neurotic brother (Peter Hurt) about a young man (Michael Sarrazin) who will bring romance and fulfillment into her life. Directed by Peter Wood, the story is so murky and its execution so undisciplined that its moral about not taking fantasy for reality becomes bogged down in its own tedium, making the occasional nudity and brother-sister incest theme even more offensive than they might have been. O (PG)

In Search of Historic Jesus (1980) Pseudo-documentary by Henning G. Schellerup moves from a summary of the life of Jesus to a detailed examination of the significance of the Shroud of Turin, believed by many to be Jesus' burial cloth. Ludicrous dramatizations and dubious embellishments of the Gospel story suggest parental discretion in exposing youngsters to such a grab-bag selection of material, no matter how orthodox it is in regard to Christian doctrine. A-I (G)

In Search of Noah's Ark (1977) Semi-documentary sets out to prove the literal truth of the biblical account of the Flood, basing its case largely on conjecture and hypothesis. Directed by James Conway, its inept dramatization of the building and stocking of the Ark makes it appear ridiculous and undercuts the religious significance of the biblical story. A-I (G)

In Search of the Castaways (1962) Disney adventure fantasy from Jules Verne's story of a girl (Hayley Mills) and two siblings searching for their missing explorer-father with the help of an eccentric professor (Maurice Chevalier). As the 19th-century expedition makes its way from South America to Australia, director Robert Stevenson pays less attention to the characters than to the excitement along the way with natural disasters, strange creatures, and exotic natives. Youngsters in peril. A-I (br)

In the Army Now (1994) Tiresome time-waster with dopey comic Pauly Shore joining the Army Reserves for the money, then getting called up for active duty in the African desert, where he happens to knock out an enemy missile-site. Director Daniel Petrie, Jr., strings together a series of service comedy cliches that are as stale as Shore's dumb brand of humor is inept. Heavy sexual innuendo, stylized violence, and coarse language. A-III (PG)

In the Company of Men (1997) Disturbing picture of two callous corporate colleagues (Aaron Eckhart and Matt Malloy) who decide to pay back female rebuffs by deliberately romancing, then abruptly dumping, a vulnerable deaf secretary (Stacy Edwards), though things don't quite work out as planned. Writer-director Neil LaBute chillingly explores the vicious nature of office and sexual politics without settling for a simple good-triumphs-over evil outcome. Harrowing depiction of deceitful activities, an implied affair, and much rough language, as well as profanity. A-IV (R)

In the Good Old Summertime (1949) Pleasant musical version of **The Shop Around the Corner** is set in an 1890s Chicago music store whose head salesman (Van Johnson) and a new saleslady (Judy Garland) nurse their mutual dislike until each discovers the other is the lonely heart's pen-pal they have grown to love. Directed by Robert Z. Leonard, the romance is abetted by the charming period setting, some agreeable songs, and the cheerful antics of the shop's owner (S.Z. Sakall) and his befuddled nephew (Buster Keaton). A-I (br)

In the Heat of the Night (1967) When an industrialist is murdered in Sparta, Mississippi, the local police chief (Rod Steiger) has to rely on the scientific experience of a black homicide expert (Sidney Poitier) who is passing through town. The superior acting of the two principals and the sure hand of director Norman Jewison turn a rather muddled mystery plot into a balanced expression of the complex racial, legal, and intellectual prejudice permeating many areas of American life. Some stylized violence and sexual situations. A-III (br)

In the Land of the Deaf (1994) French documentary chronicles the daily life of deaf people of various age groups, ultimately concentrating on a small class of grade school students struggling to learn to speak under the watchful guidance of devoted teachers. Using sparse dialogue, director Nicolas Philibert's unsentimental, non-manipulative work allows its subjects to vividly communicate through sign language their feelings about the richness of life despite hearing problems. Subtitles. Several references to prejudices and stereotypes about the deaf. A-II (nr)

In the Line of Fire (1993) While bragging about his imminent plans to assassinate the incumbent president, a methodical killer (John Malkovich) taunts an aging Secret Service agent (Clint Eastwood) on the phone about his failure to save JFK in Dallas and promises history will repeat itself. Director Wolfgang Petersen's cat-and-mouse thriller is far better on characterization than on action as Eastwood and Malkovich's exchanges are shrewdly revealing, but the climax is unconvincingly staged. Intermittent violence and some rough language. A-III (R)

In the Meantime, Darling (1944) Flimsy WW II comedy about the scarcity of off-base housing for married officers (principally Frank Latimore and Jeanne Craine) during their months of training before being sent overseas. Directed by Otto Preminger, it wasn't very funny then and is just another dated period-piece now. Romantic complications. A-II (br)

In the Mood (1987) Teenage Lothario (Patrick

Dempsey) hits the headlines during the mid-1940s war years by running away with an older married woman — twice. Fact-based farce from director Phil Aiden Robinson romanticizes adultery and derides the idea of matrimony. Some implied sex scenes involving a minor. O (PG-13)

In the Mouth of Madness (1995) Dreary horror fantasy about an insurance investigator (Sam Neill) on the trail of a missing author (Jurgen Prochnow), whose horror bestsellers are set in a fictional New England village that suddenly materializes to engulf the investigator and an editor (Julie Carmen) in terrifying encounters with menacing children, slimy monsters, and the demonic author himself. In telegraphing every plot development, director John Carpenter crushes any element of suspense in what is, in any event, a trite and largely incoherent story. Numerous but very brief flashes of violence, an off-screen suicide, much menace, and occasional rough language. A-III (R)

In the Name of the Father (1974) Italian drama about a boys' school run by a corrupt religious order, into which comes a new teacher (Yves Beneyton), a man of efficiency, pragmatism, and scientific bent, who dedicates himself to reforming the old ways and introducing a new regime. Director Marco Bellocchio's talent is everywhere in evidence, though his political allegory about Fascism will probably seem to viewers with little knowledge of Italian culture as a rather strange and tedious fable. A-III (nr)

In the Name of the Father (1993) Based on the 1975 case of the "Guildford Four," the narrative centers on an aimless Belfast lad (Daniel Day-Lewis) grabbed by the British police and tortured into confessing complicity in an IRA bombing for which he is sentenced to life — with long prison terms for other falsely accused co-defendants, including his father (Pete Postlethwaite) — until 15 years later his lawyer (Emma Thompson) uncovers proof of his innocence hidden from the court by the police. Director Jim Sheridan focuses on the human dimensions of this political miscarriage of justice but spends more time exploring the generational conflicts between the imprisoned father and son than on the larger issues of the Ulster conflict and the battle to win public opinion. Recurring menace and violence, unresolved justice questions, and occasional rough language. A-III (R)

In the Realm of the Senses (1977) Japanese director Nagisa Oshima's study of perverse sex and its consequences is a tale of a former prostitute working as a maid whose affair with the owner of an inn culminates in her killing him and mutilating his body in horrible fashion. Pretentious mix of violence and eroticism. O (nr)

In the Shadow of Kilimanjaro (1986) Gritty wildlife adventure, based on an actual event at a game preserve in Kenya during a severe drought, turns into a gruesome carnage as thousands of starving baboons attack humans. Timothy Bottoms and John Rhys-Davies are featured in the bloody rampage, which relies too heavily on visual shock, including gory scenes of dismemberment. A-III (R)

In the Spirit (1990) Spacey New Age widow (Marlo Thomas) patches up her differences with a spoiled matron (Elaine May) in order to join forces in trapping a murderous stalker. Director Sandra Seacat misses a grand opportunity to explore intriguing questions about women and middle age, friendship and self-reliance, in this otherwise disjointed female buddy-caper comedy. Some rough language laced with explicit sexual references. A-III (R)

In the Year of the Pig (1969) Emile de Antonio's documentary recounts the political history of Vietnam from French colonial days to the American military involvement. Less an anti-war tract than a lucid examination of the complex political realities that have made Vietnam an American tragedy, it's a valuable document worthy of retrospective scrutiny. A-II (nr)

In Which We Serve (1942) WW II British classic in which the survivors (notably Noel Coward, John Mills, and Bernard Miles) of a destroyer sunk in the 1940 battle of Crete recall their lives ashore and at sea, especially in helping rescue British soldiers trapped on the beaches of Dunkirk. Also scripted by Coward, who co-directed with David Lean, the result is an absorbing mix of wartime naval action and the ardors of the home-front, with well-defined characters whose human appeal and patriotic fervor have not dimmed over the years. Wartime violence and sexual innuendo. A-II (br)

In-Laws, The (1979) Prominent New York dentist (Alan Arkin) and a seedy CIA agent (Peter Falk) are brought together when their children are engaged, and the hapless dentist finds himself unexpectedly plunged into a wild adventure in a corrupt Central American dictatorship. Directed by Arthur Hiller, the pairing of Arkin and Falk is bright and the comedy frequently hilarious. Some comic violence and a few mild vulgarities. A-II (PG)

Inadmissible Evidence (1968) Midlife crisis of a successful London lawyer (Nicol Williamson) triggers fears of an unsure future and concerns about failures of the past, especially his relations with women. Director Anthony Page's adaptation of the John Osborne play is claustrophobic and introspective but it is Willamson's tortured performance that makes it worth seeing. A-IV (br)

Inchon (1982) Expensively staged but wretched retelling of General Douglas MacArthur's amphibious victory in the early stages of the Korean War. Though Laurence Olivier plays MacArthur, supported by an international star cast, director Terence Young can't overcome the poor script, leaving only wartime melodrama and pyrotechnics for interest. A-III (PG)

Incident, The (1967) Dynamic social drama about a group of passengers riding the New York subway late at night and being terrorized by two hoodlums

(Tony Musante and Martin Sheen). Tautly directed by Larry Peerce, it is not a pleasant story, but gripping and thought-provoking. A-IV (br)

Incident at Oglala (1992) Documentary recounts events culminating in the 1975 killing of two FBI agents on South Dakota's Pine Ridge Sioux reservation and argues that the subsequent conviction of Leonard Peltier for the crime is a miscarriage of justice. Directed by Michael Apted and narrated by Robert Redford, the film's use of newsreel footage and interviews with many of the principals succeeds in explaining the context of violence on the reservation and the disputed evidence used to convict Peltier. Raises contemporary justice issues in realistic fashion. A-II (PG)

Incorrigible (1980) French director Philippe De Broca's wan comedy in which a hyperactive flimflam artist (Jean-Paul Belmondo) meets his match in a lovely and quick-witted social worker (Genevieve Bujold). The dash and charm of these two actors are the saving grace of the movie. Some sexual references. A-III (nr)

Incredible Mr. Limpet, The (1964) Part animation, part live-action, but mostly silly fantasy directed by Arthur Lubin follows the WW II underwater adventures of a meek clerk (Don Knotts) who, after falling into the ocean and turning into a cartoon fish, helps the Navy clear the Atlantic of Nazi subs. Mildly diverting for children but limp comic fare for their elders. A-I (br)

Incredible Journey, The (1963) Fact-based Walt Disney story of a 250-mile trek through the Canadian wilds undertaken by an English bulldog, a Labrador retriever, and a Siamese cat to rejoin their owner who had left them with friends while on vacation. Director Fletcher Markle allots most of the time to his four-footed actors who prove more engaging than the human characters and an over-cute narration. A-I (G)

Incredible Sarah, The (1976) Pop bio of French actress Sarah Bernhardt (Glenda Jackson) lacks the warmth or stateliness that might have conveyed the magnetism of the reputedly great performer. Incredibly misdirected by Richard Fleischer and filmed in England with little sense of the misfortune in her life and career. A-II (PG)

Incredible Shrinking Man, The (1957) Imaginative sci-fi tale from Richard Mathesen's novel about an ordinary fellow (Grant Williams) whose boating encounter with a radioactive mist starts him shrinking away to nothing, his diminishing size making him the target of the family cat and eventually a basement spider. Director Jack Arnold keeps viewer interest in the poor man's predicament by a judicious use of perspective, over-sized props, and special effects. Some tense scenes. A-I (br)

Incredible Shrinking Woman, The (1981) Lily Tomlin plays a harried suburban housewife and mother who suddenly finds that she is shrinking due to an allergy from all the chemical additives in her household products. Strained allegorical slapstick comedy directed by Joel Schumacher falls far short of satire despite its jibes at consumerism and its consequences. Mild sexual innuendo. A-III (PG)

Incredible Two-Headed Transplant, The (1971) Disappointed medical student (Bruce Dern) grafts the head of a homicidal maniac onto the shoulders of a retarded brute, and the maniac takes over, escapes, and is not caught until he has committed half-a-dozen murders. Director Anthony Lanza's low-budget horror movie supplies only a few grisly laughs here and there. A-III (GP)

Incredibly Strange Creatures Who Stopped Living and Became Mixed-up Zombies, The (1963) Inept exercise in nonsensical horror from director Ray Dennis Steckler centers on a carnival fortuneteller (Brett O'Hara) who has the power to turn bad actors into horribly made-up creatures for no discernible purpose. Hokey violence and sexual situations. A-III (br)

Incredibly True Adventure of Two Girls in Love, The (1995) Having broken up with her boyfriend, a bright high-school senior (Nicole Parker) initiates an affair with her pot-smoking lesbian classmate (Laurel Holloman), sending friends and families of both girls into furious hysterics. Writer-director Maria Maggenti casts a comic eye on the sexual experimentation of the teenagers, portraying it, as well as drug abuse, to be harmless fun and just part of growing up. Positive depiction of an adolescent lesbian affair and recreational substance abuse, a sexual encounter with nudity, fleeting violence, and much rough language. O (R)

Indecent Proposal (1993) Trite romantic triangle involves a wealthy stranger (Robert Redford) who pays a cash-strapped married couple (Demi Moore and Woody Harrelson) a million dollars to sleep with the wife for one night, then continues his romantic pursuit of the woman as her marriage crumbles. Director Adrian Lyne's thoroughly transparent and suspenseless movie revolves around cardboard characters who rationalize their every act without ever considering the moral dimensions of their behavior. Materialistic view of life, brief bedroom scene, fleeting nudity, and occasional rough language. O (R)

Independence Day (1983) Small-town girl (Kathleen Quinlan) yearns for success as a photographer in Los Angeles and must choose between love and ambition. Director Robert Mandel's predictable story has a subplot of wife abuse, but only Quinlan's vibrant performance is of interest. There is a love affair and a relatively sympathetic depiction of suicide. A-III (R)

Independence Day (1996) Compelling sci-fi thriller in which huge alien spaceships level three American cities before the President (Bill Pullman), a computer whiz (Jeff Goldblum), and a Marine pilot (Will Smith) mount a last-ditch effort to disable the spacecraft's impenetrable shields. Director Roland Emmerich's patriotic-themed disaster flick is powered by an action-packed story line, spectacular special effects, and sympathetic characters who provide some human dimension to the proceedings. Intense depiction of massive destruction but little gore, brief sexual innuendo, and minimal profanity. A-III (PG-13)

Indian in the Cupboard, The (1995) Unremarkable fantasy in which three-inch-high plastic toys belonging to a nine-year-old boy (Hal Scardino) magically come to life as a miniature Onondaga Indian (Litefoot) and an Old West cowboy (David Keith). Based on a bestselling children's book, director Frank Oz's special-effects movie is pleasant if undramatic fare, mostly retaining the quality of a bedtime story except for minor violence and fleeting sexual innuendo. A-I (PG)

Indian Paint (1965) Naive, sometime dramatically inept, account of the testing of an adolescent Indian brave (Johnny Crawford). Directed by Norman Foster, the movie's chief interest is in its authentic native lore and insights into the honorable values of another culture. A-I (br)

Indian Runner, The (1991) Violence-prone Vietnam veteran (Viggo Mortensen) returns to Nebraska in the late '60s, marries his pregnant girlfriend (Patricia Arquette), and settles down, yet remains a walking time-bomb despite the best efforts of his patrolman brother (David Morse). Writer-director Sean Penn paints a moving portrait of a tortured soul and the effect he has on those around him, but the plot is too drawn-out to sustain its paltry insights. Some brutal violence including suicide, brief male nudity, a graphic birth scene, much rough language, and a glimpse of recreational drug use. A-III (R)

Indian Summer (1993) Seriocomic ensemble piece concerns an aging summer-camp owner (Alan Arkin) who holds a week's reunion for his seven favorite campers of the past (notably Elizabeth Perkins, Vincent Spano, Kevin Pollak, and Diane Lane) during which they act like kids while evaluating their adult lives. Writer-director Mike Binder's nostalgia-drenched story offers situations of limited interest and characters whose puerile pranks soon grow tiresome. Brief recreational drug use, an implied sexual encounter, and an instance of rough language. A-III (PG-13)

Indiana Jones and the Last Crusade (1989) The adventure trilogy ends by pairing Indy (Harrison Ford) with his father (Sean Connery), a medieval scholar trying to save the Holy Grail from 1930s Nazis. Director Steven Spielberg's eye-popping stunts and intense comic-book violence are balanced by the humorous interaction between father and son, whose survival depends on their resolving longstanding conflicts. Exhilarating, old-fashioned action movie, much too intense for youngsters but less threatening to older adolescents. Minor sexual innuendo and rough language. A-III (PG-13)

Indiana Jones and the Temple of Doom (1984) Director Steven Spielberg's sequel to **The Raiders of the Lost Ark** has Indiana (Harrison Ford), with the help of a chorus girl (Kate Capshaw) and a Chinese war orphan (Ke Huy Quan), rescue a stone from a nasty Indian sect and return it to its rightful owners. Nonstop stunts take precedence above all else, making it entertaining for action fans, but the comic-book violence is a little intense, especially a sequence involving the removal of a human heart. A-III (PG)

Indiscreet (1931) Creaky romantic sudser directed by Leo McCarey in which a woman (Gloria Swanson) tries to save her sister from marrying a wealthy cad with whom she had had an unhappy romance, without revealing her past to the sister or her own upright fiancé (Ben Lyon). Despite getting to sing a couple of soppy songs, one while taking a bath, Swanson's self-styled role as "a modern girl with an old-fashioned conscience," is flat and unappealing, with McCarey providing scant comic relief. Sexual situations and innuendo. A-III (br)

Indiscreet (1958) Slick romantic comedy grows increasingly slack as a London stage-star (Ingrid Bergman) falls for a married NATO official (Gary Grant), then seeks revenge after learning he's single. Director Stanley Donen treats the contrived situation more for glamour and sentiment than humor, with the result depending upon one's empathy for the two veteran leads. Comic treatment of an implied sexual affair. A-III (br)

Indiscretion of an American Wife (1954) When the married woman of the title (Jennifer Jones) says farewell to the man (Montgomery Clift) she met on a holiday in Rome, he persuades her to catch the next train while he tries to convince her to stay with him rather than return to her husband and child in the States. Director Vittorio De Sica tries for realism, but the longwinded evening of dialogue proves more soapy than bittersweet on the way to a predictable conclusion. Discreet treatment of a theme of marital infidelity. A-II (br)

Indochine (1992) Romantic family saga set in 1930s French Indochina, where a rubber plantation owner's daughter (Catherine Deneuve) has a brief affair with a French naval officer (Vincent Perez), but her adopted Vietnamese daughter (Linh Dan Pham) falls in love with him, and the two wind up fleeing the French authorities by hiding out with Communist revolutionaries. Director Regis Wargnier maintains interest in the romantic story line by developing it in tandem with the changing political balance between French colonists and Vietnamese nationalists. Subtitles. Mature themes and treatment. A-III (PG-13)

Infinite Tenderness, An (1973) French documentary on the world of a brain-damaged, physically handicapped child confined to a wheel chair, unable to speak, but trying desperately to communicate with his nurse and the other children in the hospital. It chronicles his friendship with another youngster even more crippled than himself, their joy in being together, their little spats, and, finally, the termination of their friendship by death. Directed by Pierre Jallaud, it is a remarkable achievement, treating its subject creatively yet with complete integrity. There is no commentary, no dialogue, only the natural sounds of the children and their environment. A-II (nr)

Infinity (1996) Drama covers 1934-45 in the life of Nobel Prize-winning physicist Richard Feynman (Matthew Broderick), who married his high-school sweetheart (Patricia Arquette) despite the fact she had highly contagious tuberculosis and saw her through the terminal disease while working for the government on the secret Los Alamos project to split the atom. As sluggishly directed by Broderick, a sweetly melancholy love story emerges, leaving Feynman's feelings about his involvement in the creation of the atomic bomb unexplored. Discreetly implied premarital affair and an instance of profanity. A-II (PG)

Informer, The (1935) Powerful adaptation of Liam O'Flaherty's novel about oafish Gypo Nolan (Victor McLaglen) who betrays a comrade (Wallace Ford) to the Black and Tans for the reward, then squanders the blood money on drink trying to drown his guilty conscience and fear of being found out by the rebel Organization. Director John Ford's poetic evocation of 1922 strife-torn Dublin builds pity for the slow-witted Gypo, but only revulsion for his deeds in a tightly wound story of betrayal, retribution, and forgiveness. Stylized violence and veiled references to prostitution. A-II (br)

Inherit the Wind (1960) Loosely based on the 1925 Scopes "monkey trial" in which a small-town Tennessee teacher (Dick York) charged with breaking the law against teaching evolution is prosecuted by an aging populist politician (Fredric March) and defended by a prominent Northern attorney (Spencer Tracy), as a cynical Baltimore reporter (Gene Kelly) stirs up headlines. Directed by Stanley Kramer, the courtroom clash between religious convictions and scientific principles is portrayed mostly as yokels pitted against sophisticates, but worth seeing are the dramatic fireworks between March's smug, self-righteous prosecutor and Tracy's tenacious legal crusader, who regrets that the only way he can win the case is by discrediting a man whom he respects. Intense disagreements over biblical interpretations may confuse youngsters. A-III (br)

Inheritor, The (1973) Slick French mystery adventure in which a ne'er-do-well playboy (Jean-Paul Belmondo) investigates the circumstances of his industrialist father's death, and his search leads to some dark secrets in his own family as well as to the top leadership of Europe's industrial giants. Director Philippe Labro takes some elegant jabs at high society and the swaggering Belmondo has some discreet fun with the ladies. A-III (PG)

Inheritors, The (1998) Violent class conflicts embroil a 1930s Austrian village after a hateful farmer upsets the neighboring landowners by leaving all his property to his peasant workers, hoping his actions will lead to bloodshed on both sides. Writer-director Stefan Ruzowitzky creates vivid characterizations and incorporates wry humor into a dark tale of the peasants' dashed egalitarian dreams. Subtitles. Intermittent violence including rape, brief sexual encounter, fleeting nudity, and a few instances of profanity and rough language. A-III (R)

Inn of the Sixth Happiness, The (1958) Ingrid Bergman gives a warmly sympathetic performance as a Christian missionary in 1930s China, where her patience and sincerity gradually win over the district's crafty mandarin (Robert Donat), his people, and a cynical Eurasian army officer (Curt Jurgens), until the Japanese invasion forces her to lead a column of orphans across the mountains to safety. Director Mark Robson finds some delicious humor in the worldly mandarin's increasing bafflement at the woman's selfless kindness, then grows quite serious as her spiritual convictions are tested amidst the ravages of war. Despite tense moments and wartime violence, it's richly rewarding family fare. A-I (br)

Inner Circle, The (1991) Life in the Soviet Union from 1939 to 1953 as seen by Stalin's personal movie projectionist (Tom Hulce), whose faith in the dictator is unshaken despite party purges, the persecution of his neighbors, the suicide of his wife (Lolita Davidovich), and the blighted life of an orphan (Bess Meyer) befriended by his wife. Directed by Andrei Konchalovsky, the Italian production was filmed inside the Kremlin and around Moscow with a largely Russian cast that gives its picture of a totalitarian state more interest than the dramatic contrivances of the narrative. Some brief but strongly felt violence, a restrained bedroom scene, and some rough language. A-III (PG-13)

Innerspace (1987) Martin Short is the victim of industrial espionage as he tries to safely return the miniaturized capsule floating through his body and piloted by Dennis Quaid to the lab which created it. Madcap comedy from director Joe Dante falls short of large laughs, but has some genuinely charming, albeit dumb, moments of clean fun. A-II (PG)

Innocence Unprotected (1971) Yugoslavian director Dusan Makavejev's 1968 work is a documentary about the making of the first Serbian talking feature (done in 1942 under the nose of the Nazis). The central figure is acrobatic strongman Dragoljub Aleksic, a national hero whose feats of strength have to be seen to be believed. Makavejev captures the warmth and vitality of the 1942 filmmakers so that his movie becomes a commentary on society's changing values with a nostalgia for the innocence that is missing from our own "enlightened" times. A-II (nr)

Innocent, The (1979) Italian director Luchino Visconti's last movie tells of a turn-of-the-century Roman aristocrat (Giancarlo Giannini) who makes no secret of his infidelities to his wife (Laura Antonelli) until she pursues an affair of her own which has tragic consequences. Although the feel for the period and place is assured, the suicide of a major character is completely unmotivated. Extravagant, at times ludicrously so, use of nudity. O (R)

Innocent, The (1995) Sluggish thriller set in 1950s Berlin, where a gruff American spy (Anthony Hopkins) gets help tapping Russian phone-lines from a naive Englishman (Campbell Scott) who falls for a volatile German (Isabella Rossellini), who herself may be a spy. Directed by John Schlesinger from Ian McEwan's novel, the plot twists hold interest until the final portion gets lost in heavy melodramatics. Brief gory violence, a few discreet sexual encounters, shadowy partial nudity, and occasional profanity. A-III (R)

Innocent Blood (1992) Violent, trashy vampire parody features an undercover cop (Anthony LaPaglia) who risks having sex with a vampire (Anne Parillaud) while pursuing a mobster-turned-vampire (Robert Loggia) who is preying on other gangsters. Director John Landis is at his heavy-handed worst treating a gross parade of vicious killings as a comic lark. Extended kinky sex scene, much gory violence, rough language, and recurring nudity. O (R)

Innocent Bystanders (1973) Substandard British spy movie in which an aging agent (Stanley Baker), in order to save his job, has to find a scientist escaped from a Siberia camp before other agents bring him in. Peter Collinson's awkward direction highlights the story's violence, sadism, and cynical view of humanity. Particularly distasteful is a just off-screen torture sequence involving Geraldine Chaplin. O (PG)

Innocent Man, An (1989) Wrongfully accused and convicted citizen (Tom Selleck) ends up in maximum-security prison, where he is beaten and forced to kill another inmate (Bruce A. Young) to survive. Directed by Peter Yates, Selleck's transition from nice guy to tough dude is laughable, and the plot's far-fetched premise strains credibility in its cartoonish depiction of our judicial and penal systems. Racist undertones, vigilante ending, grisly violence, and profanity. O (R).

Innocent Sleep, The (1997) Murky thriller in which a homeless London drunk (Rupert Graves) witnesses a murder, then enlists the help of an investigative reporter (Annabella Sciorra) after realizing he's now being tailed by a corrupt police detective (Michael Gambon). Director Scott Mitchell's fuzzy melodrama vaguely hints at an international conspiracy, but fails to establish any rationale behind the murder. Intermittent violence, brief sexual innuendo, some rough language, and occasional profanity. A-III (R)

Innocents, The (1961) Powerful adaptation of Henry James's *The Turn of the Screw* centers on the new governess (Deborah Kerr) hired to care for two young children on an isolated English estate, where she comes to fear her charges are in grave danger from the dead spirits of their former governess and her evil lover. Directed by Jack Clayton, the moody visuals and eerie soundtrack evoke a marvelous sense of the supernatural, though events can also be construed as the dark product of a Victorian woman's troubled imagination. Menacing situations and youngsters in physical as well as moral peril. A-III (br)

Inserts (1976) There are fitful glints of serious intent amid the dreary chaos of this vulgar, pretentious movie about a once-brilliant Hollywood director (Richard Dreyfuss) reduced to making stag movies. Though Dreyfuss gives a convincing portrayal of a man bored with himself, director John Byrum has made nothing of consequence out of the movie's vulgarities and considerable nudity. O (X)

Inside (1997) Drawn-out South African prison drama in which a post-apartheid investigator (Louis Gossett Jr.) painstakingly uncovers how a racist prison warden (Nigel Hawthorne) drove an idealistic white professor (Eric Stoltz) being held without charges to the point of suicide. Static direction by Arthur Penn brings little that is insightful or emotionally involving to this harrowing but familiar tale of extreme police brutality tolerated under the former racist government. Recurring bloody beatings, a few instances of profanity, and frequent rough language. A-III (nr)

Inside Daisy Clover (1965) Caustic tale of 1930s Hollywood from Gavin Lambert's novel in which a feisty 15-year-old gamin (Natalie Woods) is put on the fast road to movie stardom by a cynical studio mogul (Christopher Plummer), breaks her heart over a philandering actor (Robert Redford), then has an emotional breakdown when her beloved, eccentric mother (Ruth Gordon) dies. Director Robert Mulligan's acerbic but unconvincing picture of the studio era flounders in a melodramatic plot and stilted acting. Some violence, including a comic suicide attempt, sexual situations, and coarse language. A-III (br)

Inside Moves (1980) Director Richard Donner's melodrama is set in a neighborhood bar patronized by men who have physical disabilities but who team up to help each other. Crippled John Savage regains his love of life and goes on to play pro basketball. Some rough language and crude sexual references mar an otherwise articulate story about regaining one's self-esteem. A-III (R/PG)

Inspector Clouseau (1968) Miscast Alan Arkin gamely plays the role Peter Sellers made his own but is let down by an unfunny script and lethargic direction by Bud Yorkin. Those with a taste for simple pratfalls may find some amusement in this crime comedy. A-III (G)

Inspector General, The (1949) Uneven Danny Kaye costume vehicle places him at the center of all manner of comic misunderstandings when the corrupt officials (Gene Lockhart, Alan Hale, etc.) of a central European town mistake a meek vagabond (Kaye) for the Emperor's feared inspector. Directed by Henry Koster, the 19th-century Gogol story is turned into a musical farce, broadly played by Kaye and company often to the point of tedium. Mild romantic subplot. A-I (br)

Instinct (1999) Failed drama in which a psychiatrist (Cuba Gooding, Jr.) probes why imprisoned

American anthropologist Anthony Hopkins chose to abandon civilization for life among Rwandan gorillas, culminating in his killing two park rangers. As directed by Jon Turteltaub, the steely performances of the two actors compensate somewhat for a simplistic script and formula scenes of prison brutality. Intermittent violence and a few instances of rough language and profanity. A-III (R)

Interiors (1978) Written and directed by Woody Allen, the plot involves three sisters (Diane Keaton, Marybeth Hurt, and Kristin Griffith), their mother (Geraldine Page), their father (E.G. Marshall), and his new wife (Maureen Stapleton). Save for the last named, all the rest of the characters are locked in their narcissistic prisons, the exquisite interiors Allen strives mightily to explore, but the dense theme often leaves the viewer staring into space rather than focusing on the profound. The claustrophobic and pessimistic movie communicates a sense of nihilistic ennui. A-IV (PG)

Interlude (1957) Glossy tearjerker in which an American (June Allyson) working in Munich falls for a famous orchestra conductor (Rossano Brazzi), then leaves him when she learns he's married to a tragically disturbed woman (Marianne Cook), and departs for home with a romantic American doctor (Keith Andes). Directed by Douglas Sirk, the soppy romance is slickly contrived, but the picture's only emotional appeal comes from the lovely Austrian backgrounds. Romantic situations. A-II (br)

Interlude (1968) Married orchestra conductor (Oskar Werner) conducts both the Royal Philarmonic and an affair with a London reporter half his age (Barbara Ferris). Director Kevin Billington's romantic tearjerker treats adultery as a bittersweet affair. A-III (br)

Intermezzo (1939) Sentimental tale of a doomed romance as a world-renowned violinist (Leslie Howard) abandons wife (Edna Best) and family to go off with a student pianist (Ingrid Bergman) until she realizes their affair has no future. Director Gregory Ratoff's remake of the 1936 Swedish movie treats the illicit interlude delicately, building compassion for all involved, though the errant husband invites little sympathy in the concluding scenes of family tragedy and reconciliation. Well-handled theme of marital infidelity. A-II (br)

Internal Affairs (1990) When a Los Angeles detective (Andy Garcia) in the department's Internal Affairs Division begins to investigate a routine misconduct case, he uncovers a web of police corruption masterminded by a well-respected veteran cop (Richard Gere). British director Michael Figgis creates a dark but shallow thriller depicting women as sexual playthings and exploiting the corrupt cop's pathological acts of blackmail, seduction, and murder. Much sexual promiscuity including a flash of nudity, graphic violence, and sexually vulgar language. O (R)

International House (1933) Zany comedy in which business rivals (Stuart Erwin, Bela Lugosi, and Lumsden Hare) reach Wu Hu, China, to bid on a television invention, but their hotel (staffed by Franklin Pangborn, George Burns, and Gracie Allen) becomes bedlam after an erratic professor (W.C. Fields) arrives by helicopter. Directed by Edward Sutherland, the nonsensical plot affords plenty of throwaway gags by vintage screen comics, while the gleeful inventor (Edmund Breese) of the "radioscope" pulls in stage routines by Col. Stoopnagle and Budd, Rudy Vallee, Cab Calloway, and other period performers. Daffy sexual innuendo and comic dipsomania. A-II (br)

International Velvet (1978) Lavishly produced and entertaining sequel to **National Velvet** (1944) now has the adult Velvet (Nanette Newman) living with a writer (Christopher Plummer) and her newly orphaned niece from America (Tatum O'Neal), who goes on to win the gold medal in the Olympic equestrian competition. Directed by Bryan Forbes, there is a little violence and the unmarried state of the two adults raises questions of propriety for younger viewers. A-II (PG)

Intersection (1994) A successful Vancouver architect (Richard Gere) vacillates about whether to build a new home with his lover (Lolita Davidovich) or to return to the life he has built with his estranged wife (Sharon Stone) and 13-year-old daughter (Jenny Morrison), until a car crash affects the situation. The shallow central characters make director Mark Rydell's exploration of a tortured romantic triangle slow going, though the final ironies are a nice touch. A theme of marital infidelities, flashes of nudity, and minimal rough language. A-III (R)

Interval (1973) Sentimental romance with Merle Oberon as an unattached woman traveling through an amber-colored Yucatan while fending off any number of mature males who become enchanted with her ageless beauty, one of whom (Robert Wolders) finally catches up with her. Aside from some quite pleasant travelogue footage of Mayan ruins, director Daniel Mann's movie is so trite as to be an embarrassment, and all the gauze over the close-up camera lens and the fireworks at climactic moments of passion only serve to emphasize its dated soap-opera origins. A-III (PG)

Interview with the Vampire (1994) Gore-filled fantasy from the Anne Rice novel in which a listless vampire (Brad Pitt) recounts his past 200 years beginning in 1791 New Orleans, where he was changed into one of the undead by a merciless master vampire (Tom Cruise), then helps turn a little girl (Kirsten Dunst) into a blood-lusting killer before journeying to Europe in search of his own kind. Director Neil Jordan's gruesome horror movie exploits the vampire myth in its empty depictions of the nightmare creatures' ceaseless cycle of draining and discarding their human prey. Excessive gore, graphic violence, stylized depictions of sexual perversions, an extended scene with full nudity, and a child depicted as an eager instrument of death. O (R)

Intervista (1992) In this 1987 Italian production, director Federico Fellini takes viewers on an imaginative tour of moviemaking at the famed Cinecitta Studios in the suburbs of Rome. Fellini's leisurely-paced valentine to the joys and confusion of the film-making process radiates a fondness for all around him but is best energized in scenes of a nostalgic reunion with his **La Dolce Vita** (1961) stars, Marcello Mastroianni and Anita Ekberg. Subtitles. A flash of shadowy nudity, some vulgar references, and minimal rough language. A-III (nr)

Intimate Lighting (1969) A Prague cellist, together with his girlfriend, returns to his hometown for a few days and stays with a childhood chum and his family. Director Ivan Passer's loving portrait of Czech life, culture, and people is done with affection and earthy humor. A-III (nr)

Intimate Relations (1997) Dreary fact-based tale is set in 1954 England, where a young lodger (Rupert Graves) with a troubled past is seduced by a dotty middle-aged landlady (Julie Walters) whose romantic illusions ultimately lead to a gory domestic tragedy. Writer-director Philip Goodhew takes a sardonic view of the characters and their relationships but the humorous treatment sours as their abnormal behavior grows increasingly bizarre long before the disturbingly violent conclusion. Gory violence, sexual situations and occasional rough language and profanity. A-IV (R)

Into the Night (1985) A man (Jeff Goldblum), bored with such problems as insomnia and an unfaithful wife, finds life noticeably more exciting when a beautiful woman (Michelle Pfeiffer) dives into his car with a quartet of assassins in hot pursuit. Crude, unimaginative effort from director John Landis,, with excessive violence and nudity. O (R)

Into the West (1993) When a magnificent white horse wanders into their Dublin slum, two motherless waifs (Ruaidhri Conroy and Ciaran Fitzgerald) ride off into the countryside, pretending to be Wild West cowboys, with their sobered father (Gabriel Byrne) and the police in hot pursuit. Director Mike Newell presents a sensitive yet rousing tale of emotionally neglected children whose fertile imaginations help them transcend an impoverished home. Fleeting violence, children in jeopardy, and a few profanities. A-II (PG)

Into Thin Air: Death on Everest (1997) Fact-based TV dramatization of an ill-fated 1996 expedition to scale Mount Everest which costs eight climbers their lives when they are enveloped by a fast-moving blizzard. Directed by Robert Markowitz from the book by Jon Krakauer, who was one of the survivors, the production has some awesome footage of the Austrian Alps as well as of the doomed climbers' desperate struggle to survive the savage storm, but the individuality of the characters gets lost behind hoods and snow masks. Life-threatening situations and the lethal power of nature. A-II (nr)

Intolerance (1916) D.W. Griffith's silent epic inter-cuts four stories of injustice — the fall of Babylon, the Crucifixion, the St. Bartholomew's Day massacre and a contemporary American story in which a wife (Mae Marsh) tries to save her innocent husband (Robert Harron) from execution. The narrative is developed through parallel action of the stories, each of which is connected to the others by the simple image of a woman rocking a cradle, a device dropped as the tempo increases in the conclusion of the stories. The movie's brilliance in concept, execution, and editing is still impressive, dated only by its florid titles and melodramatic characterizations. Stylized violence, sexual references, and a few flashes of nudity. A-III (br)

Intruder in the Dust (1949) Engrossing social drama from William Faulkner's novel about an aloof black farmer (Juano Hernandez) arrested for killing a white man, then saved from lynching by a Southern mob after an earnest youth (Claude Jarman, Jr.) and an elderly lady (Elizabeth Patterson) prove his innocence. Director Clarence Brown uses the puzzling murder-mystery to hold interest while exploring the motivations of the characters and the ethos of a small town (filmed in Oxford, Miss.) where racial prejudice is an accepted way of life. Excellent study of racial attitudes and human rights, though some scenes may be too intense for young children. A-I (br)

Invaders from Mars (1953) Sci-fi saga of a young boy who sees a spacecraft land behind his house but has a hard time convincing the authorities that aliens are taking the place of the townspeople. Director William Cameron Menzies uses the special effects sparingly, relying on the power of suggestion to give dramatic credibility to the lad's fears, thereby making the plot premise all the more unsettling. Well-sustained suspense may be too intense for some youngsters. A-I (br)

Invaders from Mars (1986) Inferior remake of the 1953 original about a little boy (Hunter Carson) who tries to warn his parents that their neighbors are being taken over by Martians. Director Tobe Hooper concentrates on the period settings to the detriment of some talented performers (Laraine Newman and Timothy Bottoms). Although the movie resorts to bullets as the answer to a communication problem, the movie is light enough for family entertainment. A-I (PG)

Invasion of the Blood Farmers (1973) Moronic movie about descendants of an ancient Druid cult who depopulate a rural area of upstate New York searching for the perfect specimen whose transfused blood would revive their catatonic queen. Director Ed Adlum's low-budget horror involves a cast of amateurs in excessively gory murders and tortures, with some teasing sexual allusions. O (GP)

Invasion of the Body Snatchers (1956) Classic sci-fi thriller in which a small-town doctor (Kevin McCarthy) and his girlfriend (Dana Wynter) discover that their fellow citizens are being replaced by pod people from outer space. Tautly directed by Don Siegel, the nightmarish concept becomes frighteningly credible as the townspeople gradually turn into their emotionless alien counterparts bent on keeping the terrified pair from escaping to warn the outside world. Mounting suspense, menacing atmosphere and an incidental marital complication. A-II (br)

Invasion of the Body Snatchers (1979) Mediocre remake of the 1956 thriller in which aliens from outer space take over the identity of earthlings through a pod producing a double of the sleeping victim. Its basic failing is director Philip Kaufman's inability to turn the banal pod-people into villains worth rooting against. Donald Sutherland and Brooke Adams try to stem the tide, but Kevin McCarthy and Dana Wynter did it better in the low-budget, yet more imaginative, original. Some excessive scenes of blood and gore and gratuitous nudity. O (PG)

Invasion of the Saucer Men (1957) Sci-fi dud directed by Edward L. Cahn in which teenagers evaporate some little green aliens with big heads and deadly long fingernails, but nobody believes them because the aliens' flying saucer has been obliterated by a secret Army unit whose mission is to erase all evidence of extraterrestrial contacts. Stylized violence, hokey menace, and a benign view of teen sex. A-III (br)

Invasion U.S.A. (1985) Group of Soviet terrorists sneaks ashore at Miami Beach and proceeds to wreak havoc until stopped by karate champion Chuck Norris and director Joseph Vito's simple-minded script. Unremitting violence. O (R)

Inventing the Abbotts (1997) Contrived romantic melodrama set in a 1950s Midwest town, where two poor teenage brothers (Billy Crudup and Joaquin Phoenix) uncover long-buried family secrets when they start dating three sisters (Liv Tyler, Jennifer Connelly, and Joana Going) from the community's wealthiest family. Directed by Pat O'Connor, the story's melodramatics detract from the bittersweet portrayal of frail, youthful characters coping with a troubled past. A few discreet bedroom scenes with fleeting nudity, momentary violence, recurring profanity, and intermittent rough language. A-III (R)

Investigation of a Citizen Above Suspicion (1970) Italian drama of a police chief (Gian Maria Volonte) who murders his girlfriend (Florinda Bolkan), then leaves a trail of evidence that inescapably reveals his identity. Director Elio Petri's narrative interweaves the investigation of the crime with flashbacks establishing its motivation. The engrossing thriller has many implications about the role of authority in maintaining an ordered society, but some may find its realistic scenes of sex and violence rather unsettling. A-IV (R)

Invisible Invaders (1959) Pulp sci-fi thriller directed by Edward L. Cahn in which invisible aliens from the moon invade Earth by taking over the bodies of dead humans until a scientist (Philip Tonge) gets help from an Army colonel (John Agar) in using sound waves to destroy "the walking dead." Hokey violence and menacing situations. A-I (br)

Invisible Kid, The (1988) Failed teen-comedy about a youth (Jay Underwood) who discovers his deceased father's secret formula for invisibility and uses it for a series of adolescent hijinks, including a foray into a girls' locker-room and the bedroom of a pretty cheerleader neighbor. Written and directed by Avery Crounse, the potential for humor in the dull-witted situation is stretched painfully thin. A-III (PG)

Invisible Man, The (1933) Gripping adaptation of the H.G. Wells story about a scientist (Claude Rains) who succeeds in perfecting a serum making him invisible but loses his sanity in the process and winds up terrorizing the countryside as an unseen menace. Directed by James Whale, Rains is impressive though his performance consists mostly of a maniacal disembodied voice, neatly abetted by convincing special effects and suitably terrified extras. Excellent fantasy fare with minimal stylized violence. A-I (br)

Invisible Man Returns, The (1940) In an uneven sequel to the 1933 original, a man (Vincent Price) convicted of murdering his brother uses the invisibility serum to bring the real killer to justice. Directed by Joe May, the plot nicely balances the invisible gimmickry with the wry ingenuity of the police inspector (Cecil Kellaway) in charge of the case. Some stylized violence. A-I (br)

Invisible Man's Revenge, The (1944) Muddled thriller set in England, where an obsessed killer (Jon Hall) is made invisible by an eccentric doctor (John Carradine), then tries to regain the riches he claims are rightfully his. Producer-director Ford Beebe manages to dress up the thin plot with some suspense and sinister atmosphere, but the pallid result is hardly worth the effort. More menace than violence. A-II (br)

Invisible Ray, The (1936) Slow-moving sci-fi tale in which a scientist (Boris Karloff) discovers an element more powerful than radium but, poisoned by its deadly rays, he goes mad and turns it on those he believes betrayed him, including a colleague (Bela Lugosi) and his own wife (Frances Drake). Directed by Lambert Hillyer, the formula story has a few interesting twists and some good visual effects, including the contaminated scientist glowing in the dark. Stylized violence and marital tensions. A-II (br)

Invisible Woman, The (1941) Low-budget comedy in which a crackpot professor (John Barrymore) invents a machine making objects invisible, then tests it on a $16.50-a-week model (Virginia Bruce), but the havoc caused by her invisible antics enables gangsters (led by Oscar Homolka) to steal the machine. Director A. Edward Sutherland gets some laughs out of the farcical situations, helped greatly by a comical supporting cast and Barrymore's hammy clowning. Mild sexual innuendo. A-II (br)

Invitation, The (1975) Pleasant little Swiss movie about a shy, awkward bachelor (Michel Robin) who invites his fellow office workers to a Sunday afternoon gathering at his rather plush home. Though everyone gets a little drunk, nothing much really happens in director Claude Goretta's adroitly precise celebration of ordinary people and their mundane foibles. A-III (nr)

Ipcress File, The (1965) Len Deighton's story of spy and counter-spy amuses as it confuses, de-glamorizing the business of secret agents to some extent with humor, while the story moves by tricky plot twists, some of which do not bear later examination. Michael Caine is excellent as the uncertain hero and director Sidney Furie holds everything together with a lightly satiric touch. A-II (br)

Iphigenia (1977) Greek adaptation of Euripides' play faithfully retells the story of King Agamemnon (Costa Kazakos), who is told to sacrifice his daughter, Iphigenia (Tatiana Papamoskou), in order to assure safe passage for his fleet to Troy. Considering the difficulties inherent in bringing Greek tragedy to the screen — not just translating one art form to another, but overcoming the cultural diversities of two millennia — producer-director Michael Cacoyannis's work represents a considerable accomplishment. Mature theme and some incidental nudity. A-III (nr)

I.Q. (1994) Pleasant romantic comedy in which an aging Albert Einstein (Walter Matthau) and his Princeton colleagues conspire to encourage romance between his scholarly niece (Meg Ryan) and an amiable auto-mechanic (Tim Robbins) by passing him off as a brilliant, self-taught physicist. Director Fred Schepisi's sweet but featherweight concoction floats along on the cuteness factor of cuddly old men hovering over an appealing young couple, until the young woman realizes that academic degrees aren't a prerequisite to true love. Occasional double entendres. A-II (PG)

Irene (1940) Dated romantic comedy in which an attractive Irish-American seamstress (Anna Neagle) is catapulted into New York's high society by a wealthy fashion designer (Ray Milland) and a Long Island playboy (Alan Marshal), both of whom are in love with her. Directed by Herbert Wilcox, the sentimental proceedings are helped by a strong supporting cast, but the plot contrivances are artificial at best and the egalitarian humor falls flat. Mild sexual innuendo. A-II (br)

Iron & Silk (1991) A 22-year-old American (Mark Salzman) arrives in China in 1982 to teach English and absorb the culture, but spends much of his time training under the skeptical eye of a famed kung-fu master (Pan Qingfu). Producer-director Shirley Sun's fact-based account of the youth's two years in China alternates martial-arts sequences with an earnest, low-keyed glimpse of Chinese society which hints at the government crackdown to come at decade's end. Restrained kung-fu segments. A-II (nr)

Iron Eagle (1986) Taking seriously his high-school commencement speech about accepting adult responsibilities, Air Force brat (Jason Gedrick) steals a Phantom jet fighter and, with a little help (Lou Gossett Jr.), blasts his way through an unfriendly Arab country to free his captive father. Self-righteous adolescent fantasy directed by Sidney J. Furie justifies excessive violence in the service of youthful idealism. Negative role model and extremely foul language. O (R)

Iron Eagle II (1988) The sequel tracks the US and Soviet brass as they unite misfit American and Soviet pilots in a joint mission to knock out a hot nuclear warhead in the Middle East. With Lou Gossett, Jr., in a respectable reprise of his original role, director Sidney J. Furie's sincere but cliched effort offers an innocuous vision of international cooperation and world peace. Cartoon violence and some locker-room language. A-II (PG)

Iron Eagle III (see: **Aces: Iron Eagle III**)

Iron Man (1951) Uneven boxing melodrama directed by Joseph Pevney in which a coal miner (Jeff Chandler) is turned into a prizefighter by his gambler brother (Stephen McNally), then develops a taste for the ring despite its physical toll, the boos of the crowd, and the threat of losing his wife (Evelyn Keyes). Brutal boxing scenes and domestic misunderstandings. A-II (br)

Iron Mask, The (1929) Silent version of the Dumas tale in which the aging D'Artagnon (Douglas Fairbanks) and the Three Musketeers set out to rescue young Louis XIV (William Bakewell) after he's kidnapped by a powerful noble (Ulrich Haupt), then locked in an iron mask while his evil twin (also Bakewell) takes his place on the throne. Directed by Allan Dwan, the 17th-century costume spectacle is lavishly mounted, but the story's melodramatic action fairly creaks, even in the 1940 sound version narrated by Douglas Fairbanks, Jr. Stylized violence and muted sexual innuendo. A-II (br)

Iron Maze (1991) Unsavory tale of the attempted murder of a Japanese businessman (Hiroaki Murakami) as recounted to the Pennsylvania police in contradictory versions by the victim, his US bride (Bridget Fonda), and her volatile lover (Jeff Fahey). Director Hiroaki Yoshida's clumsy melodrama sheds little light on the nature of truth or the clash of cultures and is further marred by choppy exposition and underdeveloped characters. Repeated staging of a violent confrontation, restrained lovemaking, and recurring rough language. A-III (R)

Iron Mistress, The (1952) Muddled tale of frontiersman Jim Bowie (Alan Ladd) who leaves the Louisiana bayous for New Orleans in 1825, makes a fortune in land speculation, but, played false by a local belle (Virginia Mayo), pulls up stakes for Texas where he marries a señorita (Phyllis Kirk). Directed by Gordon Douglas, the unconvincing period romance is paced by occasional duels and fights with Bowie's specially designed knife, which he ditches in the Mississippi at movie's end. Stylized violence and romantic complications. A-III (br)

Iron Petticoat, The (1957) Failed Cold War comedy directed by Ralph Thomas in which a strait-laced

Soviet aviator (Katherine Hepburn) on official business in London falls for the wacky charms of a US Air Force officer (Bob Hope) who convinces her of the superiority of the capitalist system in this pale take-off on **Ninotcha**. Much unamusing sexual innuendo. A-III (br)

Iron Sheriff, The (1957) Muddled Western in which a dour sheriff (Sterling Hayden) gives evidence convicting his son (Darryl Hickman) of murdering a stage driver in a robbery, then sets out to prove the lad's innocence. Directed by Sidney Salkow, the contrived proceedings and cliched characters have only intermittent interest. Stylized violence and sexual innuendo. A-II (br)

Iron Will (1994) Old-fashioned underdog tale in which a South Dakota youth (Mackenzie Astin) in 1917 attempts to save the family farm and earn college tuition by competing for the $10,000 prize in a grueling, 522-mile dogsled race from Winnipeg to St. Paul, Minnesota, in the dead of winter. Director Charles Haid's outdoors adventure is rousingly rendered despite downright corny dialogue and several cardboard villains. Some menace and brief violence. A-II (PG)

Ironweed (1987) Story set in 1936 Albany, N.Y., about a hobo (Jack Nicholson) who visits the wife (Carroll Baker) and family he had deserted 22 years before after having drunkenly caused the death of his infant son. Scripted by William Kennedy from his own novel and directed by Hector Babenco, the result is less the story of a few days in the life of a Depression-era bum than it is a challenging meditation on the quality of lost souls. Some adults will be repelled by its depiction of the brutalizing conditions in which derelicts live, as well as several needlessly explicit sex scenes. A-IV (R)

Irreconcilable Differences (1984) Preteen girl (Drew Barrymore) sues to be free of her parents (Ryan O'Neal and Shelley Long) who have been driven to distraction by life in the Hollywood fast lane. Some parents may be chagrined over the legal and emotional precedent of the child-rights issue, but director Charles Shyer can't choose whether this is light comedy or fairly serious drama. Very brief nudity in a comic context. A-III (PG)

Is Paris Burning? (1966) Jean-Paul Belmondo, Charles Boyer, and Leslie Caron head an international cast in this epic tribute to the French people who fought so valiantly to save Paris from the senseless destruction ordered by Hitler. In concentrating on the sweep of events rather than the character of the individuals involved, director Rene Clement has made a work that is convincing as history but fails on the level of human drama. Wartime violence. A-I (br)

Is There Sex After Death? (1971) Writer-director Alan Abel plays a sexologist who, when not attending local patients, roams the country asking pointed questions of people on the street. A few familiar personalities contribute risqué routines or scatological interviews, but for the most part the porno parade is strictly amateur night. O (X/R)

Isabel (1968) French-Canadian story of a young woman (Genevieve Bujold) who returns to a stifling back-country environment upon the death of her mother and finds herself unable to escape from her strange family, whose history is tied to the land. Written, produced, and directed by Paul Amond, it has plenty of lushly beautiful country scenes, but its moody, sinister interiors with their turgid, murky implications of incest do not add up to a satisfying experience. A-III (br)

Isadora (see: **The Loves of Isadora**)

Ishtar (1987) Warren Beatty and Dustin Hoffman play failed songwriters who find themselves pawns in a dangerously ironic game of international intrigue in director Elaine May's failed buddy comedy set in the Moroccan desert. Essentially a story about the saving grace of comradeship, the exotic romantic adventure has some rough language, brief slapstick violence, and a momentary flash of nudity. A-II (PG-13)

Island, The (1980) Clumsy, brutish thriller about a writer (Michael Caine) and his young son who inadvertently come across the descendents of 16th-century pirates still plying their bloodthirsty trade in the shelter of the Bermuda Triangle. Director Michael Ritchie's fantasy veers wildly between the cruel, ridiculous, and downright nasty. Excessive violence, some nudity, and profantiy. O (R)

Island at the Top of the World, The (1974) Disney version of a Ian Cameron novel about an American archaeologist (David Hartman) and a British adventurer (Donald Sinden) who journey to the Arctic, where they discover a tropical island atop a polar ice cap inhabited by the descendents of the Vikings. Directed by Robert Stevenson, it is burdened by a ragged screenplay, some lackluster special effects, and many atrocious performances. Harmless family fun, but it could have been so much better. A-I (G)

Island Escape (see: **No Man Is an Island**)

Island of Dr. Moreau, The (1977) Second screen version of H.G. Wells's novel about a scientist's obsession to turn animals into human beings starts out promisingly enough with a shipwrecked engineer (Michael York) finding himself on a remote Pacific island presided over by a kind but somewhat sinister doctor (Burt Lancaster). Once Moreau's secret is out, however, director Don Taylor's movie degenerates into rather clumsy and ineffective melodrama with considerable violence and bloodshed. The 1932 version with Charles Laughton is the one to see. A-III (PG)

Island of Dr. Moreau, The (1996) Murky updating of H.G. Wells's 1896 horror tale of an airplane-crash survivor (David Thewlis) held prisoner on a remote island, where the experiments of a mad scientist (Marlon Brando) in turning animals into humans have resulted in grotesque mutants who come to rebel against their demented creator. Directed by John Frankenheimer, the menacing visuals aren't enough to involve the viewer in the fate of the picture's ill-defined characters. Intermittent violence and mindless mayhem. A-III (PG-13)

Island of Lost Souls (1932) Horror classic from H.G. Wells's story of a shipwrecked sailor (Richard Arlen) turning up on an uncharted South Sea island, where a mad doctor (Charles Laughton) is hard at work trying to turn wild beasts into humans. Director Erle C. Kenton makes the grisly situation effectively menacing, though the misshapen refugees from the House of Pain are treated with some sympathy. Very stylized violence, but the thematic implications of animal vivisection are not for children. A-II (br)

Island of Lost Women (1958) Clunky adventure directed by Frank W. Tuttle with a radio newscaster (Jeff Richards) landing his disabled aircraft on an uncharted Pacific island inhabited by a scientist (Alan Napier) raising three daughters there because he's certain the civilized world will destroy itself in nuclear warfare. Of interest only as an example of the period's fears of nuclear annihilation. A-I (br)

Island of Terror (1966) Halting horror tale directed by Terence Fisher in which London pathologists (Peter Cushing and Edward Judd) are summoned to an island off the east coast of Ireland to deal with a rapidly multiplying organism that turns people and animals into jelly by devouring their bones. Stylized violence with some gruesome visuals and hokey menace. A-III (br)

Island of the Blue Dolphins (1964) Engrossing adaptation of Scott O'Dell's children's story about the 19th-century adventures of a young Indian girl (Celia Kaye) who learns to fend for herself when stranded on a remote island off the coast of California. Produced by Robert B. Radnitz and directed by James B. Clark, the movie captures the wondrous beauty of nature and its sense of ecology provides a delightful lesson for youngsters. A-I (br)

Island of the Burning Damned (1971) Standard British science-fiction programmer with Christopher Lee and Peter Cushing combating extraterrestrial beings who invade a country inn. Director Terence Fisher engenders as much suspense as possible with invaders who resemble nothing so much as bubbling, crawling neon pancakes. A-III (GP)

Island of the Burning Doomed (see: **Island of the Burning Damned**)

Islands in the Stream (1977) George C. Scott stars as an expatriate American living in the Bahamas who is jolted out of his self-pitying sense of failure as a man and as an artist by the demands of WW II. Franklin Schaffner has directed this adaptation of the posthumous Ernest Hemingway novel with considerable success in focusing upon the interior world of the central character, the prototypical Hemingway hero acting with style under pressure. A-II (PG)

Isle of the Dead (1945) Science faces the supernatural during the 1912 Balkan War when a stern Greek general (Boris Karloff) quarantines an island beset by plague and gripped by fears of a vampire. Producer Val Lewton and director Mark Robson team to fashion a quite effective tale of psychological dread filled with dark, moody photography and talk of the living dead. Mostly spooky effects but some stylized violence. A-II (br)

Istanbul (1957) Director Joseph Pevney's lackluster remake of **Singapore** (1947) follows the return of an American pilot (Errol Flynn) to Turkey after WW II to retrieve some hidden diamonds, then discovers that the woman (Cornell Borchers) he had once loved but thought dead is an amnesiac married to another. Some stylized violence and hokey romantic complications. A-II (br)

It! (1967) Hokey horror with Rabbi Loew's medieval Golem turning up in a British museum, where loony assistant curator Roddy McDowall brings it to life but can't control it. Writer-producer-director Herbert J. Leder updates the Golem legend with snatches of other horror movies, including **Psycho**, but with little sense of suspense and less credibility. Stylized violence and sexual situations. A-III (br)

It Came from Beneath the Sea (1955) Fair sci-fi thriller in which a nuclear-sub commander (Kenneth Tobey) has a mid-Pacific run-in with a gigantic radioactive octopus, then teams with a marine biologist (Faith Domergue) to keep the monster from destroying San Francisco. Director Robert Gordon handles the formula story rather blandly, except for some feminist asides and Ray Harryhusen's effective special effects as the animated monster savages the Golden Gate Bridge and menaces the 'Frisco waterfront. Some stylized violence, menace, and mild romance. A-I (br)

It Came from Outer Space (1953) Chilling science fiction from Ray Bradbury's story about an amateur astronomer (Richard Carlson) who sights a UFO landing in the Arizona desert, then discovers that the area's inhabitants, including his girlfriend (Barbara Rush), are being taken over by aliens. Director Jack Arnold uses the isolated desert setting to heighten the sense of menace in the strange proceedings, though the aliens' intentions ultimately prove more benign than threatening. Imaginative family fare with an upbeat ending. A-I (br)

It Conquered the World (1956) Hokey sci-fi tale directed by Roger Corman in which an alien creature from Venus takes control of an isolated rural community with the help of a disgruntled scientist (Lee Van Cleef), until his wife (Beverly Garland) and a fellow scientist (Peter Graves) intervene. Fantasy violence and menace. A-I (br)

It Could Happen to You (1994) After promising, in place of a tip, to split any lottery winnings with a waitress (Bridget Fonda), a New York City cop (Nicolas Cage) wins $4 million and gives her half, infuriating his money-hungry wife (Rosie Perez). Director Andrew Bergman's Capraesque romantic comedy makes good use of the Big Apple setting in this crowd-pleasing tale of blue-collar decency triumphing over deceit and greed. Fleeting violence and an implied affair. A-III (PG)

It Grows on Trees (1952) Comic fantasy of a small-town housewife (Irene Dunne) whose worries about family finances are solved after planting two odd trees in the backyard, one of which proceeds to grow five-dollar bills while the other sprouts tens. Directed by Arthur Lubin, the "dream-come-true" premise develops some playful complications, but the proceedings turn more serious than the lightweight situation can bear. A-I (br)

It Happened Here (1966) Imagining what life might have been like if Hitler had succeeded in invading Great Britain is shown in the story of a nurse who is drawn into collaboration with the puppet regime under the German Occupation. Directed by Kevin Brownlow and Andrew Mollo, it is an interesting inquiry into the nature of Nazi totalitarianism, with some scenes of brutality that, though not vivid, are extremely realistic and not for children. A-II (br)

It Happened One Night (1934) Delightful romantic comedy in which a just-fired reporter (Clark Gable) sees a scoop in helping a runaway heiress (Claudette Colbert) escape her father (Walter Connolly), detectives, and the press by roughing it from Miami to New York via buses, roadside tourist cabins, and even on foot. Director Frank Capra's screwball Depression road-show has the charm of matching opposites in Gable's hardboiled working man and Colbert's spoiled rich girl whose unsentimental journey ends with the falling "Walls of Jericho," a running gag which finally brings them together. Memorable romantic classic with plenty of fun as well as social and personal values. A-II (br)

It Happened to Jane (1959) Enjoyable comedy in which a widow (Doris Day) with two children and a lobster business gets her lawyer friend (Jack Lemmon) to sue the railroad for ruining one of her shipments, but the company's mean-spirited representative (Ernie Kovacs) escalates the case into a national media circus. Directed by Richard Quine, it's a predictable underdog story of small-town widow and lawyer persevering until they win the case and each other, with plenty of comic confusions along the way. A-I (br)

It Happens Every Spring (1949) Lightweight but very enjoyable comedy about a chemistry professor (Ray Milland) who concocts a wood-repellent formula that makes baseballs immune to contact with bats. Directed by Lloyd Bacon, the comic premise turns the prof into an instant big-league star whose pitches defy top-hitting batters and confound his veteran catcher (Paul Douglas). Family fun, even for those who don't like baseball. A-I (br)

It Happens Every Thursday (1953) Dated but pleasantly sentimental comedy in which a city couple (Loretta Young and John Forsythe) buy a failing small-town newspaper, then try various schemes to make it a success. Director Joseph Pevney uses the veteran supporting cast (Frank McHugh, Edgar Buchanan, Jane Darwell, and others) to keep the couple's problems from getting too serious in a picture affirming the homespun virtues of honesty, loyalty, and hard work. Mild sexual innuendo. A-II (br)

It Lives Again (1978) Cheap and shoddy horror movie about an epidemic of monstrous infants who kill with superhuman force. Director Larry Cohen's blood-and-gore thriller is excessive not only in its concept but also its graphic visuals. O (R)

It Lives by Night (1974) When a honeymooning couple (Steward Moss and Marianne McAndrew) run into a bat while frolicking in a Western cave and the husband is bitten, he goes around by night killing people, including the local tourist trade. Directed by Jerry Jameson, it is an innocuous bottom-drawer horror movie, but a love scene and some grisly gore make it inappropriate fare for the youngsters. A-III (PG)

It Only Happens to Others (1971) Written and directed by Nadine Trintignant, this is a very personal movie about the loss of a child (the Trintignants lost their child when Jean-Louis was filming **Z**). With Marcello Mastroianni and Catherine Deneuve playing the grieving parents, the result is a movie that seems to mourn over the loss of a sweet, precious toy rather than for a human life. The director seems to have kept her own feelings private while distracting viewers with both the luminous personalities of her players and the glossy plastic backgrounds against which they emote. A-III (GP)

It Started with Eve (1941) When a dying millionaire (Charles Laughton) insists on meeting his son's fiancé, the dizzy lad (Robert Cummings) brings home a hatcheck girl (Deanna Durbin), and the confusion contributes to the old man's recovery. Directed by Henry Koster, Laughton steals the picture in a sly performance that goes from death bed to dance floor, imparting much needed charm to an otherwise artificial romantic comedy. A-I (br)

It Takes Two (1995) Innocuous comedy in which two lookalike nine-year-olds (Mary-Kate and Ashley Olsen) contrive to match up one's billionaire widowed father (Steve Guttenberg) with the other's would-be adoptive mother (Kirstie Alley). Director Andy Tennant's insipid remake of 1961's **The Parent Trap** is dully drawn-out and drably predictable. Mild cursing. A-II (PG)

It! The Terror from Beyond Space (1958) When the sole survivor (Marshall Thompson) of a 1973 space shot to Mars is rescued by a back-up ship, no one believes his story of a Martian monster killing the others until it's corroborated on the return voyage by a murderous stowaway (Ray Corrigan). Director Edward L. Cahn's low-budget sci-fi thriller has a tin-can spacecraft and novice acting, but the concept of an alien killer hunting human prey on a four-month journey through space holds enough interest without the gruesome graphics featured in its 1979 re-make, **Alien**. Stylized violence and much menace. A-I (br)

It's a Great Life (1943) Formula family comedy

in the **Blondie** series starts with Dagwood (Arthur Lake) sent by Mr. Dithers (Jonathan Hale) to buy a house but he winds up with a horse instead, then is invited to ride in a fox hunt held by a wealthy eccentric (Hugh Herbert) Dithers needs for a business deal. Directed by Frank Strayer, it's a typical example of the series, except that Daisy, the Bumstead's dog, gets to say a few words at movie's end. A-I (br)

It's a Mad Mad Mad Mad World (1963) Overlong, overdone comedy spectacular about a random assortment of ordinary citizens who become greedy competitors in a madcap race to recover a fortune hidden by a bankrobber (Jimmy Durante). Producer-director Stanley Kramer misuses practically every Hollywood comedian of the period (from Buster Keaton and Jack Benny to Jonathan Winters and Carl Reiner, not to mention actors such as Spencer Tracy and Peter Falk) in a ponderous attempt to wring laughs from car crashes and other forms of slapstick carnage. The main value of this misguided effort is its all-star gallery of comics who manage to keep the heavy-handed vehicle at least fitfully funny. A-I (br)

It's a Wonderful Life (1946) Seasonal favorite about the joys and trials of a good man (James Stewart) who, facing financial ruin on the eve of Christmas, contemplates suicide, until his guardian angel (Henry Travers) shows him how meaningful his life has been to those around him. Director Frank Capra's unabashedly sentimental picture of mainstream American life is bolstered by a superb cast (including Lionel Barrymore as a conniving banker) and a wealth of good feelings about such commonplace virtues as hard work and helping one's neighbor. Young children may find the story's dark moments unsettling. A-II (br)

It's Alive (1977) Thoroughly nauseating movie in which a newborn baby turns out to be a bloodthirsty monster who kills some 20 people before the police stop it. Director Larry Cohen is most interested in using gore and graphic brutality for shock value alone. O (PG)

It's in the Bag (1945) Radio comedian Fred Allen stars as a flea-circus owner who inherits a fortune from a distant relative, then learns the proceeds were hidden in one of five chairs sold at auction and sets out to find the buyers, one of whom is radio rival Jack Benny. Directed by Richard Wallace, the halting plot serves mainly as a peg for an uneven assortment of comic skits, notably a wartime excursion to an over-crowded movie theater. Stylized violence and mild sexual innuendo. A-II (br)

It's Love Again (1936) British musical comedy in which an aspiring performer (Jessie Matthews) decides to break into show business by pretending to be the mystery lady all London is talking about but no one has seen, because she exists only in the columns of the society writer (Robert Young) who dreamed her up. Director Victor Saville treats the resulting mix-ups and misunderstandings with amusing tongue-in-cheek earnestness while singer-dancer-comedienne Matthews pours on the charm. Romantic complications and sexual inferences. A-III (br)

It's My Party (1996) Facing imminent blindness and possible dementia from AIDS, a prosperous architect (Eric Roberts) throws a two-day farewell party for family and friends, reconciling with his estranged lover (Gregory Harrison) just before taking a lethal dose of sleeping pills. Written and directed by Randal Kleiser, the script's attempts at gallows humor only intensify the maudlin tone of a movie affirming a man's decision to end his own life. Rationalization of suicide, homosexual references, fleeting full nudity, and occasional profanity, as well as rough language. O (R)

It's My Turn (1980) Jill Clayburgh plays an intelligent independent woman who meets an out-going man (Michael Douglas) and knows enough to dump the man she has been living with (Charles Grodin). Director Claudia Weill's attempt at a Tracy-Hepburn romantic comedy lacks the essential chemistry between the principals and its delineation of sexual as well as feminist themes requires a mature perspective. Some rough language. A-III (R)

It's Only Money (1962) Labored slapstick comedy with Jerry Lewis as a klutzy TV repairman unwittingly escaping murder attempts by a crooked lawyer (Zachary Scott) and his henchman (Jack Weston) after the fortune he doesn't know he's inherited. Directed by Frank Tashlin, the thin plot relies mainly on one's tolerance for Lewis's clowning and wacky sight gags. Comic menace and fleeting sexual innuendo. A-I (br)

It's Only Money (see: **Double Dynamite**)

It's Showtime (1976) Compilation of excerpts from Hollywood movies whose stars were four-footed, furry, winged, or other varieties of the animal kingdom. The clips have charming appeal in their lively and nostalgic remembrance of a time when movies were perhaps less sophisticated, but definitely more fun. Good family viewing. A-I (G)

It's Your Thing (1970) Produced by brothers Ronald, Rudolph, and O'Kelly Isley, who also top-line the marquee and perform the title number, the movie records a June evening in 1969 when New York's Yankee Stadium shook with the Gospel singers and pop groups who strut and stomp inexhaustibly. Jackie "Moms" Mabley steals the show with a heartfelt interpretation of "Abraham, Martin, and John." Some revealing costumes as well as suggestive lyrics and movements. A-III (G)

Italian Connection, The (1973) German-Italian B-grade gangster movie about a Milan pimp (Mario Adorf) who has been set up by the mob as scapegoat for a missing shipment of heroin sought by two American hit men (Henry Silva and Woody Strode), and the result is endless mayhem and violence. Director Fernando Di Leo punctuates the physical action with lots of sex and nudity. O (R)

Italian Job, The (1969) Tongue-in-cheek spoof of heist thrillers follows the hijacking of $4 million in gold as it is being transferred from the Turin airport to the bank by staging the world's most spectacular traffic jam. Michael Caine organizes the job for mastermind Noel Coward, who operates from an English prison. Before director Peter Collinson brings it all to a close with a maniacal, hair-raising auto chase, there's some good visual satire, and a lot of busy acting to make up for the loose ends in the plot. A-II (G)

Italiano Brave Gente (1965) The plight of Italian soldiers fighting on the Russian front during WW II is portrayed in the fate of four individuals, with Peter Falk and Arthur Kennedy as part of an impressive international cast. Director Giuseppe De Santis's large-scale epic manages to retain some feeling for the human pain of war. Fairly intense battle scenes. A-III (br)

Ivanhoe (1952) The age of chivalry comes to life in this version of Sir Walter Scott's novel about 12th-century England, where Saxon knight Ivanhoe (Robert Taylor) battles a host of Norman nobles, wins the hand of his lady fair (Joan Fontaine), and rescues a Jewish merchant (Felix Aymler) and his comely daughter (Elizabeth Taylor). Director Richard Thorpe's good cast does well in a story chock-full of romance, ideals, villainy, and medieval derring-do, including tournaments, the storming of a castle, and the ransom of good King Richard. Stylized violence. A-I (br)

Ivanhoe Donaldson (1965) Feature documentary about the work of Donaldson, field secretary of a civil-rights organization, as he helps conduct voter registration drives, freedom marches, and rallies in the South during 1963. Its footage showing the sincere commitment of those involved and their reliance on nonviolence in the face of provocation makes it a valuable part of the record of the times. A-II (br)

Ivory Hunter (1952) With the moral support of wife (Dinah Sheridan) and young son, a British game warden (Anthony Steel) perseveres in establishing East Africa's first wildlife preserve, despite pestilence, bureaucrats, native resistance, and greedy poachers. Writer-director Harry Watt's earnest drama features colorful action in the bush as well as an inspiring story with humane values. Entertaining family fare. A-I (br)

Ivy (1947) Uneven thriller set in early 1900s England, where a coldly ambitious woman (Joan Fontaine) poisons her penniless husband (Richard Ney) and pins the deed on her doctor-lover (Patric Knowles) in order to be free to marry a millionaire (Herbert Marshall). Directed by Sam Wood, the story turns on the persistence of a police inspector (Cedric Hardwicke) out to see justice done, but interest wanes long before that is achieved by an empty elevator shaft. Conscienceless criminal acts. A-II (br)

J

JFK (1991) Choppy dramatization chronicles the efforts of New Orleans District Attorney Jim Garrison (Kevin Costner) to refute the Warren Commission's conclusion that Lee Harvey Oswald (Gary Oldman) was the sole assassin of President Kennedy and instead charges conspiracy at the highest levels of government by bringing to trial a local gay businessman (Tommy Lee Jones) with alleged CIA connections. Director Oliver Stone freely mixes fact with speculation to validate Garrison's views in a long, unwieldy movie that is dramatically persuasive in reconstructing its version of events. Brief but recurring shots of violence, including staged and documentary footage of the assassination and subsequent autopsy, fleeting scene of a homosexual party, and intermittent rough language. A-III (R)

J.W. Coop (1972) Cliff Robertson plays a rugged rodeo champ fresh out of prison after serving 10 years for forging a check and raring to get back on the circuit to catch up with his life and the times. Also written, produced, and directed by Robertson, the success story may be a bit long in the telling, but its picture of a man who grits his teeth and gets on with the job of regaining a hold on life provides reasonably intelligent entertainment. Questionable romantic entanglement. A-III (GP/PG-13)

Jabberwocky (1977) British farce inspired by some lines of Lewis Carroll and shaped by the comic spirit of the Monty Python gang tells of a medieval country bumpkin (Michael Palin), who suffers all manner of indignities until he finally becomes a hero by slaying a monster. Directed by Terry Gilliam, much of the humor is of the British bathroom variety, with some comic gore and brief nudity adding up to a movie less offbeat than it is offensive. O (PG)

Jack (1996) Bittersweet comedy in which a 10-year-old boy (Robin Williams) who's aging at four times the normal rate persuades his overly protective parents to let him attend school and make friends his own age, despite looking like a 40-year old man. Directed by Francis Ford Coppola, the interaction between Williams and the children is intermittently amusing, though the life-affirming theme is heavy-handed, achieving more sentimentality than the intended poignancy. Some blatant sexual innuendo, several crude expressions, and occasional toilet humor. A-III (PG-13)

Jack and the Beanstalk (1952) Pedestrian comic fantasy in which Lou Costello falls asleep on a babysitting job and, together with sidekick Bud Abbott, enters the fairytale as the lad who bests the giant and escapes with his riches. Directed by Jean Yarbrough, the fantasy portion is filmed in color, but that doesn't make the forgettable songs and slapstick routines any brighter. Innocuous entertainment for young children. A-I (nr)

Jack and the Beanstalk (1976) Japanese animated musical version of the childhood classic has insipid songs and rather primitive animation. Still, it moves along at a lively enough pace and may amuse younger children. A-I (G)

Jack & Sarah (1996) When his wife dies in childbirth, a devastated London solicitor (Richard E. Grant) hires a friendly American waitress (Samantha Mathis) to be the infant's nanny, and their working relationship blossoms into romance. Writer-director Tim Sullivan furnishes a warmhearted story with appealing characters in what amounts to a sentimental feel-good movie. Some sexual references, as well as occasional profanity and rough language. A-III (R/PG)

Jack Frost (1966) Russian version of the Cinderella story with wicked stepmother, beautiful maid, and handsome prince set in a wintry countryside and told with charm. Adults will enjoy the gorgeous scenery, colorful costuming, and doll-like performances, even if they don't appreciate the old fairy tale as much as the youngsters do. A-I (br)

Jack Frost (1998) Flaky tale in which a deceased dad (Michael Keaton) briefly returns to life as a snowman in order to help his glum 12-year-old son (Joseph Cross). Bogus emotions and contrived situations only underline the gimmicky nature of director Troy Miller's fantasy meltdown. Some menace and a fleeting profanity. A-II (PG)

Jack London (1943) Lightweight biography of author London (1876-1916) starts with his experiences at sea and in the Yukon gold fields, then touches on his growing fame as a writer, before concluding with his warnings about Japan's plans for world conquest after covering the 1905 Russo-Japanese War as a newspaper correspondent. Director Alfred Santell gets a sincere but stolid performance from Michael O'Shea in the title role, but the episodic script never gets beyond cliches until the flag-waving conclusion for WW II viewers. Some nasty violence and period stereotyping. A-II (br)

Jack of Diamonds (1967) Mild suspense thriller about a suave international jewel thief (George Hamilton) who plans a big haul at a posh Bavarian ski resort lodging Zsa Zsa Gabor, Carroll Baker, Lilli Palmer, and their jewelry boxes, but meets a rival in pretty Marie Laforet who's equally adept at light-fingering the ice. Directed by Don Taylor, it's diverting if familiar entertainment. A-II (br)

Jack Slade (1953) Routine Western directed by Harold Schuster in which the title character (Mark Stevens) is hired to clean out the rustlers and outlaws plaguing a Colorado stagecoach line, but in the process he becomes a hardened gunman himself, with tragic results. Numerous shootouts among whose victims are several children. A-II (br)

Jack the Bear (1993) A boozy, grieving widower (Danny De Vito) moves his two young sons (Robert

J. Steinmiller, Jr., and Miko Hughes) to northern California, where a sinister neighbor (Gary Sinese) decides to kill the boys after an imagined hurt. Director Marshall Herskovitz treats deadly danger to children with the same weight as the father's comic antics as a TV monster-show host and one son's case of puppy-love, making for a jumbled, disturbing movie. Continuing menace, brief but nasty violence directed at a child, and an instance of rough language. A-III (PG-13)

Jack the Giant Killer (1961) When an English princess (Judi Meredith) is stolen away by an evil sorcerer (Torin Thatcher), a country youth (Kerwin Matthews) battles his way through an assortment of magic spells, witches, and giant creatures to rescue her — with the help of a wee leprechaun. Directed by Nathan Juran, the Edward Small production features some dandy special effects and fanciful settings, though the story and acting are pedestrian. Stylized violence and some scary moments. A-I (br)

Jackal, The (1997) Updated but uninspired remake of 1973's **The Day of the Jackal** this time around teams an FBI agent (Sidney Poitier) with a temporarily paroled IRA gunman (Richard Gere) to prevent a major assassination by a notorious terrorist (Bruce Willis). Directed by Michael Caton-Jones, the action formula moves efficiently forward but never achieves the level of gripping suspense of its predecessor. Some gory violence, intermittent rough language, and occasional profanity. A-IV (R)

Jackie Brown (1997) Drawn-out tale of a cunning flight attendant (Pam Grier) caught between a federal agent (Michael Keaton) and her murderous gun-dealer boss (Samuel L. Jackson) who manages to outfox both and grab a half-million bucks to boot. Writer-director Quentin Tarantino's crime story is talky, lethargically dramatized, and rationalizes felonies as a clever survival strategy. Several casual murders, a fleeting sexual encounter, recreational drug abuse, constant rough language, and recurring profanity. O (R).

Jackie Chan's First Strike (1997) Comic action thriller taking the likeable Hong Kong super-cop (Jackie Chan) to Eastern Europe and Australia on a wild espionage caper involving a nuclear warhead stolen by the Russian Mafia. Directed by Stanley Tong, the plot is loaded with double agents and energetic stunt work, but the fun is more violent than some might want. Martial-arts violence, a flash of rear nudity, and occasional coarse language. A-III (PG-13)

Jackie Robinson Story, The (1950) Robinson stars as himself in a dramatized account of his life, from college athlete and WW II service to being hired in 1946 by Brooklyn Dodgers president Branch Rickey (Minor Watson) as the first black player in major league baseball. Directed by Alfred E. Green, the low-budget production emphasizes Robinson's prowess on the field and his resolve to be a credit to his race, despite insults and threats by white bigots. Halting but sincere treatment of its era's struggle for racial equality. A-I (br)

Jacknife (1989) While an old Vietnam War buddy (Robert De Niro) tries to jolt a depressed friend (Ed Harris) out of drowning his memories of the war in drink and drugs, a tender middle-aged love story unfolds between the visitor and the troubled vet's shy sister (Kathy Baker). Director David Jones does a subtle job of weaving this low-key story to its conclusion in a well-acted slice of war-at-home life that sensitively explores the ghosts haunting Vietnam vets. Some profanity, brief violence, and a discreetly filmed bedroom scene. A-III (R)

Jackson County Jail (1976) While driving cross-country to a new job, a young woman (Yvette Mimieux) is raped by a small-town sheriff whom she kills in self-defense and then flees with an accused murderer (Tommy Lee Jones). Director Michael Miller conveys with some care and sensitivity a fugitive's view of ruthless authority, and the rape scene, though intense, is treated as a repugnant act of violence. A-IV (R)

Jacob the Liar (1977) East German movie about some Polish Jews forced to serve the Nazis as laborers, whose spirits are kept up by reports on advancing Allied troops by one of their number who pretends to have a secret radio. Under Frank Beyer's direction, the acting of Vlastimil Brodsky in the title role helps redeem a somewhat thin story line, though its theme of hope born of invention has universal appeal. Stylized violence. A-II (nr)

Jacob's Ladder (1990) A Vietnam veteran (Tim Robbins) suspects the Army is behind the terrifying hallucinations that are plaguing him and others in his unit. It's a case of style over substance in director Adrian Lyne's atmospheric thriller that jumpstarts from one menacing scene to the next, showcasing eerie cinematography but coming up short on satisfactory story line. Intermittent gory violence and rough language, recurring partial nudity, and a live-in relationship. A-III (R)

Jacqueline Susann's Once Is Not Enough (1975) Kirk Douglas stars as a washed-up movie producer who marries rich Alexis Smith so he can continue providing motherless daughter Deborah Raffin with a luxurious lifestyle, even though he realizes that his new wife is having a lesbian affair with Melina Mercouri, who is also sleeping with George Hamilton. Directed by Guy Green, the movie is simpleminded trash whose formula is to reduce every human relationship to its genital components. O (R)

Jacques Brel Is Alive and Well and Living in Paris (1975) Lively, freewheeling collage of bittersweet romantic songs written and composed by Brel makes a charming piece of cabaret entertainment. Directed by Denis Heroux, it has a good cast, including Elly Stone, Mort Schuman, Joe Masiell, and, of course, Jacques Brel. A-III (PG)

Jacquot (1993) Warmly nostalgic re-creation of the

formative years of filmmaker Jacques Demy (1931-90) follows his childhood in Nantes during WW II, enthrallment with marionettes, operettas, and then movies, teen attempts at filming with an amateur camera, and, finally, making his father realize he does not want to become a mechanic but go to film school in Paris. Directed by Agnes Varda, the 1991 French production is not only a loving tribute to her husband, playfully exploring the sources of his creative imagination by inter-cutting excerpts from his movies with episodes of his youth, but it also beautifully evokes the universal passage from childhood to the brink of adulthood. Subtitles. Wartime destruction and tensions, minor domestic disputes, and several scenes of youthful curiosity about sex. A-III (PG)

Jade (1995) Sordid potboiler in which an aggressive San Francisco prosecutor (David Caruso) finds his chief suspect in a murder case involving prostitution and political blackmail is his ex-lover (Linda Fiorentino), now the wife of a powerfully connected attorney (Chazz Palminteri). Director William Friedkin alternates wild car-chases with seamy bedroom scenes in an cynical tale of sex, power, and greed. Violence, grisly corpses, full nudity, numerous sexual encounters, and much rough language. O (R)

Jagged Edge (1985) Woman attorney (Glenn Close), defending a client (Jeff Bridges) accused of murdering his wife, begins to fall in love with him while becoming increasingly convinced of his guilt. Director Richard Marquand tries for Hitchcock-style suspense, but the plot line is implausible and the ending disappointing. Graphic violence, foul language, and nudity. O (R)

Jail, The (1974) Documentary, originally aired on public television, takes viewers within the walls of San Francisco County Jail to experience the daily life of the inmates and guards. Filmmakers Michael Anderson, Paul Jacobs, Saul Landau, and Bill Yahraus have collaborated in an effort to show that even in a relatively humane prison, keeping people locked away behind bars is an inhuman condition. A-III (nr)

Jail Bait (1977) German movie about a 14-year-old girl who has an affair with a 19-year-old boy, gets pregnant, and persuades the boy to kill her father for trying to keep them apart. Director Rainer Werner Fassbinder's unsavory tale about adolescent relationships and middle-class hypocrisy is seriously marred by excessive nudity. O (nr)

Jailhouse Rock (1957) Formula melodrama directed by Richard Thorpe in which a country boy (Elvis Presley) imprisoned for manslaughter learns about pop singing from a cellmate (Mickey Shaughnessy) and, after release, is helped by a music promoter (Judy Tyler) to become a top recording star, then gets lost in success until straightened out by his friends. Romantic complications and a surly attitude towards authority. A-III (br)

Jake Speed (1986) Self-indulgent action-adventure yarn in which a deadpan, not-too-perfect hero (Wayne Crawford) saves a college coed (Karen Kopins) from white slavers. Filmed in Zimbabwe, director Andrew Lane's pulp drama lacks comedic flair which might have saved its stodgy characterizations. Comic book violence. A-II (PG)

James and the Giant Peach (1996) A nine-year-old orphan living in England escapes two vicious aunts by magically entering a huge peach filled with six scrappy insects, who become his adopted family as the peach soars aloft to transport them to a new home in New York City. Director Henry Selick creatively combines live action with stop-motion animation in a visually remarkable adaptation of Roald Dahl's 1961 children's story that may be too sinister and scary for the under-10 set. Frequent menace. A-II (PG)

Jamilya (1972) Lyric Russian movie evoking the life of a peasant village during WW II in which a 12-year-old parts with his childhood as he witnesses his sister-in-law's clandestine affair with a convalescent soldier and their subsequent flight from her ruthless husband. Director Irina Poplavskaya paints her celluloid picture in predominantly sepia tones reflecting the primitive locale and a people whose personal emotions are habitually overshadowed by communal devotion to duty. A-III (nr)

Jane Eyre (1944) Moody dramatization of Charlotte Brontë's dark romance about a lonely orphan (Peggy Ann Garner) in 19th-century England who grows to womanhood (Joan Fontaine) in a cruel school for unfortunates, then is hired as governess for the lonely ward (Margaret O'Brien) of a wealthy eccentric (Orson Welles) tormented by a tragic secret. Director Robert Stevenson makes good use of the bleak school and remote Yorkshire settings to deepen sympathy for the unhappy heroine's loveless childhood and later emotional yearnings for a brooding employer who has hidden away his demented wife. Romantic complications. A-II (br)

Jane Eyre (1996) Fine adaptation of Charlotte Brontë's 1847 literary classic in which an English orphan becomes governess (Charlotte Gainsbourg) in a strange household, where she struggles to hide growing romantic feelings for her mercurial employer (William Hurt). Director Franco Zeffirelli gradually reveals a tale rich in intrigue as the virtuous governess brings love back into a home withering from emotional sterility and a dark secret. Fleeting violence and romantic complications. A-II (PG)

Janis (1975) Documentary on blues singer Janis Joplin is less a coherent chronicle of a life or a pop-music era than an assemblage of available footage, some of it quite elegant, but much rough-edged film clips people were willing to let directors Howard Alk and Seaton Findlay use in their musical portrait. The segments don't add up to a whole person (none of the personal problems that contributed to her death of a drug overdose in 1970 are broached), but it does have some of her finest numbers as seen in performance. Some rough language. A-III (R)

January Man, The (1989) Implausible New York cop thriller about a serial strangler wastes its time on the eccentric antics of a super-sleuth investigator (Kevin Kline), his possibly crooked brother (Harvey Keitel), the frustrated women in their lives (Susan Sarandon and Mary Elizabeth Mastrantonio), and the loud-mouthed Mayor (Rod Steiger) orchestrating the investigation. Irish director Pat O'Connor fails to mesh an erratic portrait of irreverent Irish-American New Yorkers with a crime story of serious intent. Excessive profanity laced with sexual vulgarities, sexual promiscuity, and some nudity. O (R)

Jason and the Argonauts (1963) Plodding fantasy from classical mythology follows Jason (Todd Armstrong) and his heroic crew as they sail the Argo from Thessaly to the ends of the earth in quest of the Golden Fleece. Director Don Chaffey does little more than string together Jason's adventures in confronting the Olympian gods (Niall MacGinnis as Zeus and Honor Blackman as Hera), a bronze giant, winged harpies, mountain slides, a seven-headed hydra, skeleton warriors, and other special effects created by Ray Harryhausen. Exciting but rather empty spectacle. A-I (br)

Jason Goes to Hell: The Final Friday (1993) Mindless horror sequel in the **Friday the 13th** series with its unkillable killer (Kane Hodder) on another murderous rampage until stopped by a female relative (Erin Gray) plunging a magic dagger through the monster's heart. Directed by Adam Marcus, the repetitious action of the formula script is as tiresome as its gory variations of special-effects mayhem are repulsive. Excessive violence, sexual situations, gross humor, and rough language. O (R)

Jason's Lyric (1994) Muddled melodrama of two brothers in a black neighborhood on the outskirts of Houston centers in the hardworking Jason (Allen Payne) whose growing ambition to leave the ghetto for a better life elsewhere is inspired by his love for girlfriend Lyric (Jada Pinkett), but his criminal brother (Bokeem Woodbine) gets entangled in a bungled robbery, which eventually engulfs all of them in tragedy. Director Doug McHenry overburdens the thin, predictable story line with the brothers' bond of guilt as youngsters who killed their abusive father, then wildly romanticizes Jason's love affair and ends in a bloodbath of gang violence. Graphic brutality and gore, several simulated sex acts, and occasional rough language. O (R)

Jawbreaker (1999) Feeble black comedy in which three arrogant high-school beauties accidentally kill a classmate, then proceed to transform the class geek into a vixen to guarantee her silence about the crime. Writer-director Darren Stein's catty dialogue lamely satirizes snooty cliques, but the stale results are unamusing and derivative. Brief violence, fleeting sexual encounter, frequent innuendo, intermittent rough language, and an instance of profanity. A-III (R)

Jaws (1975) Solid thriller about a killer shark first establishes the monster's reality by the effect of its attacks on the tourist trade of a seaside community, and then becomes the all-out battle of three men (Roy Scheider, Robert Shaw, and Richard Dreyfuss) against a malignant force of nature. Aided by good acting and superior special effects, Steven Spielberg directs the hunt and killing of the monster with sustained and riveting dramatic intensity. Graphic scenes of the shark attacks may be far too strong for younger viewers. A-III (PG)

Jaws 2 (1978) Roy Scheider re-creates his role of an embattled sheriff pitted against a great white shark in this dull sequel directed by Jeannot Szwarc. Violence, teenage promiscuity, and vulgar language. A-III (PG)

Jaws 3-D (1983) This second sequel to the big blockbuster only demonstrates there is a world of difference between technology and creativity. The 3-D effects are really rather effective in a grisly sort of way, but the movie itself is slow-moving, talky, and generally dull. The big fish inspires little fear, the plot inspires little excitement, and director Joe Alves tries to rescue his mediocre effort by emphasizing the violence. A-III (PG)

Jaws: The Revenge (1987) The great white shark tries to eat up the remainder of the Brody family but can't get past Mom (Lorraine Gary). Failed attempt by director Joseph Sargent to milk the suspense and shock of Steven Spielberg's original offers only mild scares for the small fry and dull, repetitive bloody visual effects. A-II (PG-13)

Jayhawkers, The (1959) Twisted tale of friendship focuses on the ruthless gunman (Jeff Chandler) whose band is terrorizing 1850s Kansas and an outlaw (Fess Parker) who agrees to betray him in return for a pardon. Director Melvin Frank fails to give much credibility to a convoluted plot which gallops off in too many directions, though individual action scenes are memorable. Stylized violence, some of it nasty, and sexual references. A-III (br)

Jazz Singer, The (1927) Sentimental tale of an aspiring singer (Al Jolson) who left his Jewish immigrant family as a boy rather than become a cantor like his father (Warner Oland), then years later his lucky break in a Broadway revue is jeopardized when his beloved mother (Eugenie Besserer) implores him to reconcile with his dying father. Directed by Alan Crosland from a play by Samson Raphaelson, the result has historic importance as the first talkie (songs and a few snatches of dialogue), but the picture is still worth seeing on its own merits. Strong domestic conflicts and Jolson's blackface routines. A-II (br)

Jazz Singer, The (1953) Korean War vet (Danny Thomas) wants to break into show business with the help of a singer (Peggy Lee) he met in service rather than succeed his father (Eduard Franz) as cantor of a Philadelphia synagogue. Directed by Michael Curtiz, the updated remake of the 1927 original is awash in sentimentality, though the actors lend it some dignity and the music is enjoyable. A-I (br)

Jazz Singer, The (1980) Neil Diamond stars as the cantor's son who pursues a career in show business, with Laurence Olivier as his grieving father and Lucie Arnez as the woman who promotes the son's career. Director Richard Fleischer's dim, sentimental tearjerker has more cliches than either the 1927 or 1953 versions. A-III (PG)

J.C. (1971) Strange biker movie about an itinerant preacher (William F. McGaha) whose motorcycling congregation share his rootless, searching way of life and return with him to his Alabama hometown. Its redneck sheriff (Slim Pickens) torments them and the story quickly resolves itself by violent confrontations ending in death. Also produced and directed by McGaha, the movie may strike some as an interesting parable about an outcast heralding peace, while others will dismiss it as glamorizing an irresponsible vision of life. A-IV (R)

J.D.'s Revenge (1976) The vengeful spirit of a slain hoodlum takes control of a clean-cut black law student who becomes a vicious sadist. Director Arthur Marks's tale of demon possession is a tiresome and disagreeable affair revolving around sex and violence. O (R)

Je T'Aime, Je T'Aime (1972) French movie about a failed suicide (Claude Rich) who agrees to participate in a scientific experiment aimed at sending him one year into the past, where he becomes lost in the labyrinth of bits and pieces of his life, centering mostly around the tragic love affair which led to his attempted suicide. Director Alain Resnais dazzles viewers with mental gymnastics and some uncharacteristic humor, but this excursion into the memories of a man who has no future is only a minor exercise by a major director marking time. A-II (nr)

Jean de Florette (1987) The first in a two-part adaptation of Marcel Pagnol's novel about a crafty farmer (Yves Montand) who in the early 1900s cheats a man from the city (Gerald Depardieu) out of the farm he has inherited by blocking the spring that is its only source of water, a wrong righted in the second part, **Manon of the Spring**. Directed by Claude Berri, the French production is beautifully crafted, and its sympathetic characterizations make the suffering and final tragic ruin of the city man, his wife, and their small daughter all the more affecting. Realistic depiction of the unfortunate family's hardships and a passing sexual reference. A-II (PG)

Jefferson in Paris (1995) Leaden dramatization of the five years (1784-89) spent by Thomas Jefferson (Nick Nolte) as ambassador to France are lamely focused on his Paris romances with an artist's flitty wife (Greta Scacchi) and the 15-year-old slave girl (Thandie Newton) with whom he supposedly fathered four children. Director James Ivory turns in a stiff costume drama which only superficially addresses the theme of a man who opposed slavery philosophically while personally benefiting from it. Much sexual innuendo. A-III (PG-13)

Jeffrey (1995) Unamusing series of skits centering on a homosexual (Steven Weber) whose fear of contracting AIDS turns him into a celibate, until he finally succumbs to peer pressures by taking a chance on sex with an HIV-positive lover (Michael T. Weiss). Directed by Christopher Ashley from Paul Rudnik's play, the results are generally flat and painfully heavy-handed, with some mean-spirited jabs at a gay Catholic priest (Nathan Lane). Sympathetic treatment of immoral acts. O (R)

Jennifer (1953) Thin melodrama directed by Joel Newton goes nowhere with an unimaginative story about the new caretaker (Ida Lupino) of a lonely country mansion who comes to suspect her predecessor was murdered by one of the locals (Howard Duff). Ominous atmosphere and a few scary moments. A-II (br)

Jennifer (1978) Mediocre thriller about a poor girl (Lisa Pelikan) in a posh private school on a scholarship who gets her revenge on the vicious and snobbish girls persecuting her by using her family training in snake-handling. John Gavin and Nina Foch in supporting roles lend whatever dignity there is to director Brice Mack's low-budget effort whose violence makes it adult fare. A-III (PG)

Jennifer 8 (1992) Obsessed with trying to protect his blind girlfriend (Uma Thurman) from a serial killer of blind women, a northern California cop (Andy Garcia) finds himself framed for the murder of his partner (Lance Henriksen). Writer-director Bruce Robinson's limp thriller finally falls apart in a ludicrous ending. Brief violence, some menace, a flash of nudity, and much rough language. A-III (R)

Jennifer on My Mind (1971) Pretentious story starts with the death of a young woman (Tippy Walker) and then proceeds through flashbacks and tape-recordings to chronicle the life of cute pot-smokers and heroin-shooters. Director Noel Black has rendered something that would have been merely boring as straightforward narrative into something insipid and absurd. Its most serious flaw is a total absence of any perspective, moral or otherwise. A-III (R)

Jenny (1969) Marlo Thomas stars in the title role as a patient, intelligent, resolute girl who intends to keep her baby even though born out of wedlock. She meets and marries Alan Alda, a self-centered filmmaker trying to avoid the draft. Director George Bloomfield's superficial melodrama reverses itself and manages to demonstrate how familiarity slowly leads to mutual respect and responsibility, and ultimately a deep regard and tender affection. A-III (PG)

Jeremiah Johnson (1972) Robert Redford stars in the story of a 19th-century mountain man from his arrival in the Rockies through his years as a self-sufficient trapper, then as family man, and, finally, a Crow Indian fighter of legendary proportions. Director Sydney Pollack's story offers the awesome natural spectacle of the mountain locales, the swift frontier action, intense cultural conflict, and colorful characters rendered without the burdens of sentimentality and contrivance. Stylized violence. A-II (GP)

Jeremy (1973) Robby Benson stars in the title role as a shy New York high-school sophomore who finds true love with a pretty senior transfer-student (Glynnis O'Conner), but they are parted when her father gets his old job back in Detroit. Directed by Arthur Barron, the slickly sentimental tearjerker is so phony in its contrivances that it should make any self-respecting teenager retch. A-III (PG)

Jerk, The (1980) Steve Martin plays a poor sharecropper who goes from rags to riches in a dreary, relentlessly vulgar, and foul-mouthed comedy directed by Carl Reiner. Sexual innuendo and racial stereotyping. O (R)

Jerky Boys, The (1995) Urban lowlifes (Johnny Brennan and Kamal Ahmed) act nasty on the phone and in person, amusing themselves but riling a humorless mob boss (Alan Arkin) in a dreary vanity production posing as a comedy and ineptly directed by James Melkonian. Incessant vulgar humor ranging from moronic insults to scatological tirades, some sexual references, and rough language. A-III (R)

Jerry Maguire (1996) Uneven comedy-drama in which a razzle-dazzle sports agent (Tom Cruise) winds up with a single client (Cuba Gooding, Jr.) while becoming romantically involved with a single mother (Renee Zellweger). Director Cameron Crowe satirizes the crass commercialization of athletes with some wit, but tackles male fear of commitment in a contrived, soggy fashion that rings false. Shadowy sexual encounters, locker-room nudity, brief violence, and recurring rough language with occasional profanity. A-III (R)

Jerusalem File, The (1972) Idealistic American student (Bruce Davison), against the advice of his college professor (Nicol Williamson) and an Israeli intelligence officer (Donald Pleasence), sets up a tragic meeting between some moderate Arab nationalists and a group of Israeli students. Director John Flynn handles the mechanics of the espionage caper adequately enough but cannot disguise what ultimately is a naive, unnecessarily muddled narrative. A-III (PG)

Jesse James (1939) Sympathetic portrait of the Missouri outlaw (Tyrone Power) who forms a gang with his brother Frank (Henry Fonda) to rob the trains of a railroad whose agents killed his mother (Jane Darwell), then is shot in the back in 1882 when he tries to go straight at the age of 34. With Jesse presented as a family man and local hero for exacting retribution from a railroad robber-baron (Donald Meek), director Henry King paces the story with six-shooter action, hard-riding chases, and narrow escapes, some comic relief, and the love a good woman (Nancy Kelly) who tries to reform the outlaw before it's too late. Stylized violence and muddled motivations. A-II (br)

Jesse James Meets Frankenstein's Daughter (1966) Inept clunker directed by William Beaudine is set on the Mexican border, where the famed outlaw (John Lupton) holes up in the abandoned mission being used by the mad doctor's granddaughter (Narna Onyx) for her own monstrous medical experiments. Tame Western shootouts, bargain-basement brain transplants, and lame romance. A-II (br)

Jesus (1979) Originally intended for educational purposes, this screen version of the Gospel of St. Luke is more a picture album illustrating the Good News Bible translation than a creative attempt to use the power of the film medium. Directed by Peter Sykes, the presentation is more likely to provoke boredom than stir admiration among young viewers. A-I (G)

Jesus Christ Superstar (1973) Screen version of the Andrew Lloyd Webber and Tim Rice musical adds a completely new dimension and drive to the music by virtue of a cinematography that enhances the original songs but also threatens to overwhelm them. Director Norman Jewison presents a visual recording, with optical embellishment, of a performance of the rock opera based on the last days of Christ's life on earth, ending in his crucifixion. Entertaining as musical theater, it can also be seen as a sincere if naive effort to tell the story of Jesus in contemporary musical and ethical terms. Some scenes require a mature perspective. A-III (G)

Jesus of Montreal (1990) Challenging French-Canadian drama about a young actor (Lothaire Bluteau) who takes seriously an invitation to modernize a traditional Passion Play staged annually at a local shrine. Though his new version is a dramatic success, its unorthodoxy causes the shrine's religious authorities to withdraw permission for future performances, resulting in a crisis for all concerned. Written and directed by Denys Arcand, this provocative movie places the Gospel story in the midst of the contemporary world, suggesting parallels to events in the life of Christ with what happens to the dedicated young actor. While some viewers may be dismayed by the work's critical attitude toward the institutional Church and its intermingling of the historical Jesus with unseemly aspects of modern life, others may gain some refreshing insights and perspectives on Christianity's continuing relevance in our own times. A-IV (R)

Jet over the Atlantic (1959) Disaster clunker directed by Byron Haskin in which the crew of a propeller-driven airliner die from a lethal-gas device planted aboard by a crazed Englishman (George Macready), leaving the fate of the plane and its 80 passengers in the hands of a former bomber pilot (Guy Madison), who happens to be an escaped killer in the custody of a federal agent (George Raft). Low-budget menace and cheap thrills. A-II (br)

Jet Pilot (1957) Addled Cold War drama in which a US Air Force officer (John Wayne) is vamped by a Soviet spy (Janet Leigh) masquerading as a defecting Russian aviator. Directed by Josef von Sternberg, the slack proceedings grow increasingly dim with silly on-again, off-again romancing and dull ideological clashes that wind up in a preposterous All-American finish. Sexual situations and innuendo. A-III (br)

Jetsons: The Movie (1990) Feature-length cartoon based on the popular television series about a space-age family follows George Jetson into outer space, where Mr. Spacely's sprocket factory is under siege by little creatures bent on sabotage. The producer-director team of William Hanna and Joseph Barbera sustain the upbeat personalities of the gadget-crazy Jetsons, but fail to mesh two opposing animation styles — the characteristically flat Jetsons look alongside the more dimensional, computerized animation. Musical interludes sung by teen pop-stars Tiffany and Shane serve only as forgettable fillers. A-I (G)

Jewel of the Nile, The (1985) Jack and Joan (Michael Douglas and Kathleen Turner) take off in their yacht for the Middle East to rescue a special kind of "jewel" in this disappointing sequel to **Romancing the Stone**. The zest of adventure has faded and even the comic touches seem forced in a ponderous plot with endless chase sequences and little suspense. Some mature subject matter and mild vulgarity. A-III (PG)

Jewish Gauchos, The (1976) Entertaining Argentinean movie about a group of Jewish refugees from pogroms in Czarist Russia who settle in the ranchlands of Argentina. A nostalgic version of immigrant history not too far different from our own, it tells the story of how these Jewish gringos become gauchos with robust action, comedy, and romance, helped by some lovely songs sung by Ginamaria Hildalgo. Restrained but intense scene of violence. A-II (PG)

Jigsaw (1949) Lame crime caper directed by Fletcher Markle in which a DA (Franchot Tone) takes on a shadowy hate group run by racketeers (notably Marc Lawrence) after finding evidence linking them to the murder of a newsman friend (Myron McCormick). Some brutal violence and sexual situations. A-III (br)

Jigsaw Man, The (1984) Laurence Olivier, Michael Caine, and Susan George are wasted in a dismal spy movie pitting a Soviet double agent against British Intelligence. Director Terence Young fails to make all the intrigue and plot contrivances of the slightest interest. A-II (PG)

Jim, the World's Greatest (see: **Story of a Teenager**)

Jim Thorpe — All-American (1951) Interesting dramatization of the Native American athlete (Burt Lancaster) who turns to professional football when the medals he won in the 1912 Olympics are taken from him on a technicality, then hits the skids when his son dies of polio. Director Michael Curtiz handles the sport sequences convincingly, but the objective portrayal of Thorpe's ordeals weakens their emotional impact. Consequences of prejudice including domestic difficulties. A-II (br)

Jimi Hendrix (1974) Documentary on pop singer Hendrix who died tragically in 1971, ending at age 27 his meteoric rise in the glittering constellation of rock music. An unusual and occasionally profound work assembled by Joe Boyd from mostly familiar footage of Hendrix performances interspersed with interviews and reminiscences of people who were close to him. Some rough language and crude gestures. A-III (R)

Jimmy Hollywood (1994) Angered by the constant crime committed on the once glamorous, now seedy streets of Hollywood, a cocky would-be actor (Joe Pesci), aided by a dense sidekick (Christian Slater), finds fame as a masked vigilante, a role he is unwilling to give up even if it means losing his girlfriend (Victoria Abril) or his life. Director Barry Levinson's fuzzy, seriocomic look at two losers who round up criminals with incredible ease is simplistic at best and increasingly unamusing as the narrative bogs down in the title character's dangerous obsession with playacting. Ambiguous treatment of vigilante methods, brief violence, a live-in relationship, and recurring rough language. A-III (R)

Jingle All the Way (1996) Macho-themed comedy set on Christmas Eve as a harried dad (Arnold Schwarzenegger) and a frantic postman (Sinbad) chase around the city, desperate to get the last Turbo Man doll each has promised his son. Director Brian Levant's extended sitcom substitutes rudely aggressive behavior for genuine humor in a contrived series of tiresome skirmishes. Frequent slapstick violence and fleeting sexual innuendo. A-II (PG)

Jinxed (1982) Unhappy wife (Bette Midler) of a seedy gambler (Rip Torn) teams up with a blackjack dealer (Ken Wahl) to get rid of her unwanted husband whom the dealer believes is a jinx. Director Don Siegel's attempt at black comedy is an embarrassing, unqualified disaster resorting to vulgarity and profanity as sources of humor. A-III (R)

Jitterbugs (1943) Halting comedy directed by Mal St. Clair in which zoot-suit musicians (Stan Laurel and Oliver Hardy) team with a con man (Robert Bailey) to help a woman (Vivian Blaine) recover money stolen by a pair of scam artists. Notable bits include the boys dancing a jitterbug number, Stan dressing in drag and Oliver pretending to woo a lady crook. Various scams and mild sexual innuendo. A-II (br)

Jivaro (1954) Bedraggled adventure directed by Edward Ludwig in which a witless American (Rhonda Fleming) travels up the Amazon River to find her fiancé, learns he is after gold in the land of the title headhunters and persuades a local trader (Fernando Lamas) to take her to him, with predictable results. Stylized violence and sexual innuendo. A-II (br)

Jo Jo Dancer, Your Life Is Calling (1986) Richard Pryor directs as well as stars in a tragicomic story of a comedian on his deathbed, reliving his past, assessing what went wrong and finally affirming the value of his life. Pryor takes some chances, with what many will see as autobiographical material, as he exposes the hurt and anger that was the source of the comedian's personalized brand of humor. Excessive harsh language and some nudity, but utilized as an authentic reflection of the environment in which the action takes place. A-IV (R)

Joan of Arc (1948) Sincere but static adaptation of the Maxwell Anderson play about the peasant girl (Ingrid Bergman) who follows her voices to lead the Dauphin's forces to victory over the English, but after his coronation as Charles VII, she was captured by the English, condemned as a heretic by a Church court, and burned at the stake in 1431. Directed by Victor Fleming, Bergman's performance is bright but artificial in a studio-bound production, occasionally relieved by hokey battle scenes, but even worse than these dramatic limitations is its failure to find a spiritual dimension in the proceedings. Period violence. A-I (br)

Joan of Paris (1942) Routine WW II morale booster in which a RAF bomber crew downed in France flee Nazi pursuers (Laird Cregar and Alexander Granach) while helped by a priest (Thomas Mitchell), an underground agent (May Robson), and a waitress (Michele Morgan) who falls for the crew's Free French captain (Paul Henreid). Directed by Robert Stevenson, the grim situation yields some suspenseful moments, but the doomed romance and pious references to Joan of Arc only underline the anti-Nazi theme. Wartime violence and justice questions. A-II (br)

Joanna (1968) Pretentious British movie about a 19-year-old innocent (Genevieve Waite) who comes to London to live with her grandmother and study art, but the wrong friends and the urban lifestyle lead her astray. Directed by Michael Sarne, the movie is supposedly about the need for an authentic value system but its graphic sex scenes are excessive. O (R)

Jock Petersen (1975) Australian sex-exploitation movie directed by Tim Burstall is distinguished only by some pretty travelogue footage of Qantas-land. O (R)

Joe (1970) Low-budget look at a blue-collar worker (Peter Boyle) whose hatred of hippies leads him to join in the search of an executive (Dennis Patrick) for his lost daughter and in their forays into the youth subculture, they participate in orgies of promiscuity and pot-smoking with tragic results. Written by Norman Wexler and directed by John G. Avildsen, the movie deals with the conflict between rebellious youth and conventional society in terms of stereotypes, yet Boyle's performance as a bigoted hard-hat has a three-dimensional quality. A-IV (R)

Joe and Maxi (1980) Documentary made by Maxi Cohen about her father, Joe, who learned he was dying of cancer during the filming. The result is utterly lacking in style and point of view, raising only questions of the propriety in continuing a project which the dying man insists be stopped. Perhaps it has some educational use in classroom discussions of death and family relationships. A-II (nr)

Joe Butterfly (1957) Faltering comedy in which Army journalists (Audie Murphy, George Nader, and others) stationed in post-war Tokyo are helped out of a scrape with a civilian reporter (Keenan Wynn) by a wily Japanese con-man (Burgess Meredith) in league with an Army hustler (Eddie Firestone). Directed by Jesse Hibbs, the plot complications are more hectic than amusing, and its depiction of Japanese culture is colorful but patronizing. Mild sexual innuendo. A-II (br)

Joe Dakota (1957) Drab Western in which a town gets testy when a stranger (Jock Mahoney) arrives seeking an Indian friend whose land he finds occupied by a man (Charles McGraw) drilling for oil. Directed by Richard Bartlett, the result is a pale imitation of 1955's **Bad Day at Black Rock**. Stylized violence, including a veiled reference to a rape. A-I (br)

Joe Hill (1971) Turn-of-the-century labor saga of an itinerant union organizer for the International Workers of the World (IWW or more commonly, the Wobblies), about whom little is known except that he wrote a number of songs popular in the labor movement. Swedish director Bo Widerberg has taken this almost mythical character and fleshed out a personality that is more poetic than real, yet Tommy Berggren's appealing performance as Joe makes credible his dedication to society's unfortunate and downtrodden. A-II (GP)

Joe Kidd (1972) Predictable Western in which an Eastern land-grabber (Robert Duvall), needing to get rid of the Mexican American (John Saxon) standing in the way of his scheme, hires a shiftless gunman (Clint Eastwood) who eventually gets around to seeing that justice is done his way. Directed by John Sturges, the justice-of-the-gun theme is distanced by the Western myth and can be dismissed as simple fantasy. A-III (PG)

Joe Louis Story, The (1953) Movie biography in which a sportswriter (Paul Stewart) recalls how Louis (Coley Wallace) was guided in his early boxing career by a talented trainer (James Edwards), then became the world heavyweight champion (1937-49) and retired undefeated, until making a sadly futile attempt to regain the title. Directed by Robert Gordon, the dramatization simplifies much, touching on racism chiefly in Louis's two bouts with Germany's Max Schemeling, but by inter-cutting newsreel footage of Louis in the ring, the result is a convincing tribute to a great prizefighter and a leading African-American of the era. A-I (br)

Joe Palooka (see: **Palooka**)

Joe Panther (1976) Unpretentious story of a Seminole youth (Ray Tracey) who gets a job on a Miami charter fishing boat by capturing a 13-foot alligator for its captain (Brian Keith), then discovers one of the crew is taking the boat at night to smuggle aliens, and in going after them his best friend (A Martinez) is killed. Directed by Paul Krasny, the plot becomes overly contrived towards the end, but this doesn't get in the way of the story's theme of cultural conflict, which is refreshingly presented through the experiences of the young Seminole and his people. Stylized violence and menacing situations. A-II (G)

Joe Versus the Volcano (1990) When a burned-out romantic (Tom Hanks) learns that he has only six months to live, he quits his grim job and jumps at an offer to spend 20 carefree days on a remote South Seas island, after which he will serve as a human sacrifice to the island's volcano. As written and directed by John Patrick Shanley, this delightful comic fantasy about realizing one's dreams before it's too late recalls earlier Hollywood fantasies with its magical set design, nutty romantic touches, and endearing performances. Some minor sexual innuendoes. A-II (PG)

Joe's Apartment (1996) Witless comedy in which a lad from Iowa (Jerry O'Connell) finds his dingy apartment in New York City infested with talking cockroaches who demonstrate more intelligence than any of the movie's human characters. Writer-director John Payson strings together a series of vulgar skits marked with toilet humor and coarse expressions, but the only thing animated about this clunker are the relentlessly crude roaches. Tasteless humor, slapstick violence, sexual innuendo, coarse language, and mild profanity. A-III (PG-13)

John and Mary (1969) Dud melodrama focusing on the relationship between two young singles (Mia Farrow and Dustin Hoffman) after they spend the night together. Director Peter Yates's essay on sexual morality in a liberated age raises questions about love and commitment but capitalizes on nudity and bogs down in endless discussions about sex. O (R/PG)

John Carpenter's Vampires (1998) Trashy horror flick about contemporary mercenaries (James Woods and Daniel Baldwin) hired to slay vampires led by a centuries-old vampire priest under the protection of a corrupt cardinal (Maximilian Schell). Carpenter's nonsensical gore-fest wallows in brutal violence, misogyny, and cynical disdain of religion. Frequent gory dismemberment, some nudity, occasional profanity, and non-stop rough language. O (R)

John Grisham's The Rainmaker (1997) Bland drama in which a novice attorney (Matt Damon) falls for a battered wife (Claire Danes) while in litigation with a smug corporate lawyer (Jon Voight) for a soulless insurance company which allowed a young man to die rather than pay for treatment. Francis Ford Coppola's pedestrian direction results in a predictable tale of a greedy corporation brought down to size by an idealistic underdog. Brief but intense violence. A-III (PG-13)

John Paul Jones (1959) Stilted biography of the Scottish sea captain (1747-92), who became an American naval hero during the Revolutionary War, and his subsequent service in the Russian navy. Except for the desperate sea battle with Britain's "Serapis," writer-director John Farrow offers a stiff, wordy portrait of Jones (Robert Stack) as high-minded but misunderstood patriot seeking support from such famous contemporaries as Ben Franklin (Charles Coburn) and Catherine the Great (Bette Davis). Stodgy patriotic exercise with colorful historical backgrounds. A-I (br)

Johnny Angel (1945) The mystery of a deserted freighter adrift on the high seas is solved by the thin-lipped merchant-ship captain of the title (George Raft) in this tale of smuggled gold, double-crossers, a two-timing wife (Claire Trevor), and a fearful witness (Signe Hasso). Director Edwin L. Marin keeps the mystery afloat with shady characters and taut action until the final showdown. Stylized violence. A-II (br)

Johnny Apollo (1940) In trying to get money to spring his embezzler father (Edward Arnold) from prison, a devoted son (Tyrone Power) turns to an influential gangster (Lloyd Nolan), becomes his front man, and winds up in prison along with dad. Director Henry Hathaway's tough crime melodrama takes some nasty turns, including an ice-pick murder, before the son is reformed by prison and a goodhearted woman (Dorothy Lamour). Stylized violence and sympathetic treatment of criminals. A-III (br)

Johnny Be Good (1988) When a top high-school quarterback (Anthony Michael hall) is courted by sleazy college-football recruiters promising fame and fortune, he exposes their slimy tactics by choosing to play for a school where he'll get a good education. Badly directed by Bud Smith, the movie has much jock humor and rough language, several situations that vulgarize women, and brief nudity. A-III (PG-13)

Johnny Belinda (1948) Sensitive turn-of-the-century drama about the transformation of a deaf-mute woman (Oscar-winning performance by Jane Wyman) when taught to read and sign by the new doctor (Lew Ayres) in a poor Nova Scotia community, but then is raped by a drunken fisherman (Stephen McNally) and threatened with the loss of the child she bears as a result. Director Jean Negulesco makes good use of the isolated rural setting in telling the story of a young woman who overcomes the inner isolation of her physical disability as well as the unenlightened prejudices of her neighbors. Several scenes of stylized violence, including the off-screen sexual assault. A-II (br)

Johnny Cash: The Man, His World, His Music (1970) Documentary follows Cash on his tours, at home, and behind the scenes in warm, intimate sessions with friends and admirers. There is plenty of music for the fans, and its above-average production values contribute to an enjoyable and entertaining movie. Some passages of dialogue are not for youngsters. A-II (GP)

Johnny Concho (1956) Bogus Western about a puny parasite (Frank Sinatra) who bullies a town cowed by his gunfighter brother until a mean hombre (William Conrad) shows up with the news that he's just killed the feared gunman. Under Don McGuire's uncertain direction, the script's contrived transformation of a nasty little coward into a righteous citizen is unearned, unconvincing, and, even worse, uninteresting. Stylized violence. A-II (br)

Johnny Dangerously (1984) Michael Keaton stars as a man who turns to crime in order to pay for his mother's multiple medical crises. Director Amy Heckerling's spoof of 1930s gangster movies, with Keaton doing a take-off on James Cagney, is defeated by an unfunny script emphasizing vulgar language and sexual situations. A-III (PG-13)

Johnny Dark (1954) Thin tale directed by George Sherman centers on an automobile company worker (Tony Curtis) who designs a super sports car, then drives it in a three-day race to prove its superiority and win the girl of his dreams (Piper Laurie). A-I (br)

Johnny Doesn't Live Here Anymore (1944) Dated farce in which a WW II gremlin causes a defense worker (Simone Simon) seven weeks of bad luck, starting with her getting an apartment to which the former tenant had given keys to all his friends. Directed by Joe May, the situation brings a stream of wacky visitors, including two suitors, but she can't decide whether to marry the Marine (William Terry) or the sailor (James Ellison) until a fantasy 1949 epilogue showing her with three kids and four husbands. Ribald romantic complications and sexual innuendo. A-III (br)

Johnny Got His Gun (1971) Dalton Trumbo directs his own adaptation of his 1938 novel about the hideous ironies of war, specifically the limbless, faceless, senseless, but conscious trunk which is all that remains of a WW I soldier (Timothy Bottoms). The story of an innocent sent out by his elders to make the world safe for democracy is told in straightforward, homey flashback scenes with a warmth and poignancy that makes ordinary American life wondrously appealing. It is remarkable for its achievement as a disturbing moral statement about the immorality of war, though many will turn away from its uncompromising treatment. A-IV (R/GP)

Johnny Handsome (1989) Downbeat drama about a disfigured felon (Mickey Rourke) who is given a second chance at life by a plastic surgeon, but even a new face, an honest job, and the love of a good woman (Elizabeth McGovern) do little to turn this low-life around. Director Walter Hill's grisly, pointless effort also features a sadistic pair of nasties (Ellen Barkin and Lance Henriksen). Assorted violence, much profanity, and brief nudity. O (R)

Johnny Minotaur (1971) Sojourning on Crete with the intention of making a movie about the myth of the Minotaur, surrealist poet and painter Charles Henri Ford evidently became preoccupied with the shiftless lifestyle of some young Greeks he retained to help with his project. The result is an amateur movie documenting homosexual diversions in graphic detail. O (nr)

Johnny Mnemonic (1995) Nasty action film from William Gibson's story in which a greedy courier (Keanu Reeves) bearing crucial data on a computer chip implanted in his brain and programmed to explode if not downloaded within 24 hours is pursued by assorted villains intent on decapitating him before he can deliver the goods. Director Robert Longo's sci-fi thriller is one long murderous chase after another inter-cut with slick computer graphics but lacking any appealing characters or human dimension. Excessive violence, some sexual innuendo, and much rough language. O (R)

Johnny Nobody (1965) Unusual British mystery about a priest (Nigel Patrick) who becomes an amateur sleuth when a writer is murdered in front of him and his entire congregation. Also directed by Patrick, the plot has some suspenseful twists, and the star is quite credible as a clergyman. A-II (br)

Johnny Rocco (1958) Interesting melodrama directed by Paul Landres in which a boy (Richard Eyer) is badly shaken after seeing his gangster father (Stephen McNally) involved in a murder, and the gang, fearing the lad might tip the police, decides to silence him and his dad. The troubled youth gets some help from a dedicated teacher (Coleen Gray), a concerned parish priest, and a homicide detective before his father's showdown with the gang. Stylized violence and menacing situations. A-I (br)

Johnny Stecchino (1992) Italian comedy of mistaken identity concerns a mild-mannered bus-driver who looks like a gangster-turned-informer (Roberto Benigni in a dual role), whose wife (Nicoletta Braschi) sets up the busman to be killed by the mob instead. As also written and directed by Benigni, the madcap movie's manic energy tends to compensate for the thin premise. Subtitles. Comic depiction of gunplay, drug abuse, and insurance fraud, mild sexual innuendo, and minimal rough language. A-III (R)

Johnny Suede (1992) Vacuous story of a vain would-be country singer (Brad Pitt) who drifts through intimate relationships, gaining no insight into himself or his pathetic schemes. Writer-director Tom DiCillo's ironic humor doesn't overcome a pointless script that treats the lead character's continual promiscuity with great bemusement. Several promiscuous relationships, sexist attitudes, minor violence, and frequent rough language. O (R)

Johnny Tiger (1965) Set in Florida Everglade country is the story of a half-breed Seminole Indian (Chad Everett) and a teacher (Robert Taylor) who tries to help him in a mediocre melodrama directed by Paul Wendkos. Some violence and mature themes. A-III (br)

johns (1997) Overlong account of 24 hours in the life of two male prostitutes (David Arquette and Lucas Haas) in Hollywood out to earn some quick cash on Christmas Eve so the younger can celebrate his 21st birthday in style. Writer-director Scott Silver's shrill tale of hustlers and their violent customers offers few insights into its one-dimensional characters. Restrained treatment of homosexual behavior, some recreational drug abuse, sporadic violence, occasional profanity, and constant rough language. O (R)

Joke, The (1970) Czechoslovakian story of a man (Josef Somr), sent to prison and his career ruined for holding political ideas that 20 years later have become fashionable, who determines to take revenge on those mouthing the new line as glibly as they had the old. Director Jiromil Jires infused his 1966 movie with a sense of quiet outrage, a sour and acerbic protest against the intolerance of the past and a warning for the present. A-III (nr)

Joke of Destiny, A (1984) Director Lina Wertmuller's satire on modern life and Italian politics is a disappointing misfire. Plodding and heavy-handed, the movie's comic invention fails badly after a brilliant opening. Adult situations. A-III (PG)

Joker Is Wild, The (1957) Overlong, painful biography of singer Joe E. Lewis (Frank Sinatra), whose vocal chords were slashed by Chicago mobsters in the late 1920s, but who reemerges in 1937 as an acerbic nightclub comic with the aid of a socialite (Jeanne Crain), whom he shabbily discards to wed a showgirl (Mitzi Gaynor), whom he treats even more shabbily. Director Charles Vidor does best with the period recreations but the portrayal of Lewis as his own worst enemy is repetitious enough to tax one's patience. Stylized violence, alcoholism, and unstable relationships. A-III (br)

Jokers, The (1967) British comedy about two brothers (Michael Crawford and Oliver Reed) who concoct a scheme to steal the crown jewels from the Tower of London, but the zany lark gets out control when one brother double-crosses the other. Director Michael Winner keeps the plot boiling all the time, not in the least concerned that there are a number of gaping holes in it. Viewers who like fast-paced humor won't mind either, especially with the picturesque London setting. A-II (br)

Jonah Who Will Be 25 in the Year 2000 (1976) Whimsical, very talky and coolly detached movie from Swiss director Alain Tanner about the effects of today's sexual and political upheavals on the lifestyles of several young adults. Its focus is on the future, and, as its title implies, it is fundamentally optimistic about people and their ability to survive. Some frank talk about sexual relationships and brief nudity. A-IV (nr)

Jonathan (1973) German horror movie about an isolated area, where Dracula maintains a reign of terror until a student leads the villagers in a raid driving the vampire hordes to their destruction in the sea. Writer-director Hans W. Geissendorfer's plot is secondary to its theme that total helplessness leads ultimately to revolt. Highly stylized but graphic images of the bizarre and the demonic. A-IV (nr)

Jonathan Livingston Seagull (1973) Richard Bach's pretentious little fable about a seagull who makes a number of discoveries, personal and cosmic, has been turned into a big pretentious movie. Director Hall Bartlett's reverential treatment of Bach's jumbled bits and scraps of mystical adages only highlights the weaknesses of the source, an effect helped not at all by the drone of Neil Diamond's uninspired ballads. A-I (G)

Joni (1982) Fact-based story of Joni Eareckson, a talented athlete who breaks her neck a month after graduation from high school and is sent to a wheelchair for the rest of her life. Director James F. Collier details her fight to rebuild her life and the central part played by her religious conversion. Inspiring and often deeply moving, it is made quite special by Eareckson's performance as herself. Restrained but realistic hospital scenes. A-I (G)

Jory (1972) Dim Western with Robby Benson in the title role as a 15-year-old who witnesses his father's murder, avenges it, repeats the pattern for a friend, and gets involved in a range war before riding off into the sunset. Directed by Jorge Fons, the tale of a youth coming to renounce violence by first bathing in blood is familiar to the point of being trite as well as poorly done. Stylized violence. A-II (PG)

Joseph Andrews (1977) Failed British adaptation of Henry Fielding's 18th-century farce about a virtuous servant lad (Peter Firth) beset by lustful females (Ann-Margret among them). Director Tony Richardson offers little more than a tedious and distasteful exercise in period lechery with gratuitous nudity and rough language. O (R)

Josh and S.A.M. (1993) Shuttled between divorced, self-absorbed parents (Stephen Tobolowsky and Joan Allen), two unhappy youngsters take off cross-country for Canada because the 12-year-old (Jacob Tierney) has convinced his seven-year-old brother (Noah Fleiss) that he is a US government humanoid rigged with a secret weapon that will detonate unless he escapes the country. Director Billy Weber's concern about neglected children of divorce being used as pawns by parents gets lost in an increasingly bizarre narrative that utterly defies credibility. Brief violence, frequent juvenile theft and lying, some menace to children, and sexual references. A-II (PG-13)

Joshua Then and Now (1985) Jewish writer (James Woods) from Montreal finds true love in London with a woman (Gabrielle Lazure) who comes from one of Montreal's first families, but, upon returning to Canada, their happy marriage threatens to come apart under pressure of their quite different social and religious backgrounds. Directed by Ted Kotcheff, it is an entertaining if uneven and often awkward movie that occasionally presents some serious ideas in provocative fashion. Extremely crude and vulgar language and situations, including brief nudity. A-IV (R)

Josette (1938) Lightweight romantic comedy in which two rich brothers (Don Ameche and Robert Young) fall for a singer (Simone Simon) after mistaking her for a gold-digger out to fleece their daffy father (William Collier, Sr.). Directed by Allan Dwan, the comic complications are easy to take, Bert Lahr and Joan Davis contribute some humor, and Simon is appealing, though her singing is less than noteworthy. Romantic fluff. A-II (br)

Journey into Fear (1942) Strange suspense thriller in which an American munitions expert (Joseph Cotten) becomes a bewildered pawn in a deadly game of international espionage aboard a Black Sea freighter carrying an odd assortment of passengers (including Delores Del Rio, Agnes Moorehead ,and Jack Moss), one of whom is a Nazi agent. Adapted from Eric Ambler's exotic tale of foreign intrigue, it was largely directed by Orson Welles (who also plays a cunning Turkish intelligence officer), though finished by the studio and credited to Norman Foster. Sinister atmosphere and stylized violence. A-II (br)

Journey into the Beyond (1977) Shoddy documentary which purports to be a serious inquiry into life after death is little more than tabloid exploitation of footage that is by turns tedious and revolting. O (R)

Journey of August King, The (1995) Engrossing drama set in 1815 North Carolina, where a farmer (Jason Patric) returning from market encounters a runaway slave (Thandie Newton), and, despite the consequences if caught, hides her in his cart while passing slave hunters and other travelers, then sets her on the trail North to freedom. Directed by John Duigan, the story is told uncommonly well, the two principals are characters viewers come to care deeply about, and the moral theme of common humanity makes it worth seeing. Menacing situations with some harsh violence and sexual innuendo. A-II (PG-13)

Journey of Hope (1991) The dream of a better life in Switzerland for a Turkish couple (Necmettin Cobanoglu and Nur Surer) and their little boy (Emin Sivas) is shattered when smugglers leave the three in the frozen Alps to find their own way across the border. Swiss director Xavier Koller's Oscar-winning fact-based drama is a powerful, straightforward appeal to the emotions regarding the plight of desperate, easily exploited immigrants from third world countries. Subtitles. A violent beating and scenes of intense menace. A-II (nr)

Journey of Natty Gann, The (1985) Courageous young girl (Meredith Salenger) searches for her father on a dangerous but wondrous trek cross-country, accompanied by a protective drifter (John Cusack) amidst the political unrest, social upheaval, and economic hardship of the 1930s Depression. Though unabashedly sentimental, this Disney movie under the direction of Jeremy Kagan is enjoyable family entertainment, filled with life-affirming people and situations. A-I (PG)

Journey through Rosebud (1972) Well-intentioned but inept movie about an Indian tribe's refusal to accept US government restrictions on their hunting rights involves a draft dodger (Kristoffer Tabori) who unwittingly causes the suicide of the tribe's demoralized leader (Robert Forster). Written by Albert Ruben and directed by Tom Greis, the movie's attempt to explore the causes of the Indians' bitter behavior gets lost in a welter of history, psychology, and contemporary sociology that most will find difficult to unravel. A-III (GP)

Journey through the Past (1974) Basically a home movie for the fans of rock superstar Neil Young, vaguely structured and larded with interview clips and lots of musical numbers recalling Young's early work with other groups. Its scenes showing his relationship with a screen actress are of dubious taste if not morality. A-IV (R)

Journey to Shiloh (1967) Seven young Texans join the Confederate Army to take part in what they believe will be a grand and glorious adventure, but soon become disillusioned with the war, and all but one (James Caan) are killed at the bloody Battle of Shiloh. Directed by William Hale, the melodramatic story is carelessly patched together and ineptly told, especially the badly handled battle action. Violence and a bedroom scene. A-III (br)

Journey to the Center of Time (1967) Low-budget sci-fi story directed by David L. Hewitt in which three scientists (Abraham Sofaer, Gigi Perreau, and Anthony Eisley) take their disgruntled financial backer (Scott Brady) on an excursion into the future world of 6968 A.D., then back to prehistoric times but, on the return home, they find themselves lost in time. Menacing situations. A-II (br)

Journey to the Center of the Earth (1959) Enjoyable adventure from the Jules Verne fantasy set in 1880 Iceland, where a Scottish scientist (James Mason), his student assistant (Pat Boone), a Swedish widow (Arlene Dahl), and a local guide (Peter Ronson) descend through a network of caves leading to a vast ocean at the earth's core, from which they return to the surface through an Italian volcano. Director Henry Levin paces the subterranean excitements — cave-ins, giant reptiles, the lost city of Atlantis, and a sinister interloper (Thayer David) — with some wry humor, imaginative sets, and plenty of convincing special effects. Lively family entertainment. A-I (br)

Journey to the Far Side of the Sun (1969) Sci-fi melodrama with astronauts Roy Thinnes and Ian Hendry setting out on a deep-space voyage to explore a newly discovered planet. Directed by Robert Parrish, the British production features an intriguing story of duplicate universes, with unexpected results. Menacing situations. A-II (G)

Jovita (1970) Polish story of illusion and ennui about a young long-distance runner who meets a girl at a masquerade party, and, in his attempts to find her again, makes a few self-discoveries along the way. Directed Janusz Morgenstern, the simple romance has a bit of athletics and classical music, but is chiefly of interest as one of the last performances of its star, Zbigniew Cybulski. A-III (nr)

Joy Luck Club, The (1993) A San Francisco bon voyage party becomes the occasion for four immigrant Chinese mothers (France Nuyen, Lisa Lu, Kieu Chinh, Tsai Chin) to reflect on their past lives and present prickly relationships with their Americanized daughters (Rosalind Chao, Lauren Tom, Tamlyn Tomita, Ming-Na Wen). Wayne Wang directs the adaptation of Amy Tang's novel with considerable sensitivity, insightfully exploring the love and pain that go into nurturing mother-daughter bonds complicated by parent and child having grown up in vastly different cultures. Brief violence including a suicide, a discreet sexual encounter, much sexual innuendo, and minimal rough language. A-III (R)

Joy of Living (1938) Wacky romantic comedy about a down-to-earth Broadway musical star (Irene Dunne) and a rich nonconformist (Douglas Fairbanks, Jr.) who insists she drop her career and bevy of idle relatives to sail away for a carefree life as his wife on their own island in the South Seas. Director Tay Garnett keeps the odd-couple situation amusing as practical star resists free-spirited suitor until the inevitable happy ending. Romantic complications. A-II (br)

Ju Dou (1991) The setting is a Chinese village in the 1920s, where a young bride (Gong Li), abused by her aged, impotent husband (Li Wei), finds refuge in the arms of his adopted nephew (Li Baotian), but the son they conceive brings disaster to all of them. As directed by Zhang Yimou, the melodrama is a beautifully shot, bittersweet love story condemning the feudal system that so regimented people's lives. Subtitles. Very discreet sexual encounters and some restrained violence. A-III (PG-13)

Jubal (1956) Dour Western directed by Delmer Daves is set on a Wyoming ranch whose straight-arrow foreman (Glenn Ford) gets into a heap of trouble because of an envious cowhand (Rod Steiger) and the unfaithful wife (Valerie French) of their boss (Ernest Borgnine). Stylized violence and sexual inferences. A-II (br)

Jubilee Trail (1954) Sprawling Western romance in which a trader (John Russell) and his bride (Joan Leslie) befriend a singer (Vera Ralston) in 1845 New Orleans, then hit the trail for California, where the husband is killed, leaving his widow and infant boy in the care of the singer and a frontier guide (Forrest Tucker). Directed by Joseph Inman Kane, the result is soap opera in Western dress, with much bathos and unconvincing melodramatics. Frontier violence, romantic complications, and references to a premarital affair. A-II (br)

Jude (1996) Grim adaptation of Thomas Hardy's bleak 1896 novel **Jude the Obscure**, in which a would-be scholar (Christopher Eccleston) runs off with his high-spirited cousin (Kate Winslet) to start a family despite each being married to another. Director Michael Winterbottom employs overly explicit visuals in depicting a harrowing story of star-crossed lovers suffering from their defiance of social mores. Graphic scenes of birth, death, and sexual encounters with full nudity. A-IV (R)

Judex (1966) French-Italian action melodrama about a daredevil champion of justice (Channing Pollack) who fights crime in the era just before WW I. Directed by Georges Franju, it will appeal to those who enjoy the innocent adventures of the superheroes of yesteryear. Stylized violence. A-II (br)

Judge Dredd (1995) In a chaotic future society where magistrates have the power to execute felons on the spot, an uncompromising judge (Sylvester Stallone) is framed for murder by a homicidal maniac (Armand Assante) long thought dead. Director Danny Cannon's violent sci-fi action movie shows its comic-book roots in ludicrous plotting, one-dimensional characters, exaggerated campy performances, and slick, cynical humor. Much mindless murder and mayhem, a twisted sense of law enforcement, and a few instances of profanity. O (R)

Judge Hardy and Son (1939) While the judge (Lewis Stone) saves an old woman (Maria Ouspenskaya) from losing her home, Mom Hardy (Fay Holden) battles pneumonia, and Andy (Mickey Rooney) has his usual trouble with the girls. Directed by George B. Seitz, the point of the episode is that parents must be honored and listened to, as Andy does in one of the longest man-to-man talks in the series. A-I (br)

Judge Hardy's Children (1938) Judge Hardy (Lewis Stone) takes son Andy (Mickey Rooney) and family to Washington, D.C., for a patriotic excursion in the Hardy series under the direction of George B. Seitz. A-I (br)

Judge Priest (1934) Warmly sentimental tale derived from Irvin S. Cobb's stories about a wise small-town judge (Will Rogers) in 1890 Kentucky who saves an innocent man (David Landau) from prison by having the local parson (Henry B. Walthall) testify to the accused's bravery in fighting for the Confederacy. Directed by John Ford, the picture stereotypes the jury's nostalgia for the Southern cause with as much good-natured humor as its depiction of the town's black characters (notably Stepin Fetchit and Hattie McDaniel). Stylized violence, veiled references to illegitimacy, and comic period stereotypes. A-II (br)

Judgment at Nuremberg (1961) Heavy dramatization in which four German justices (notably Burt Lancaster and Werner Klemperer) stand accused of war crimes in an American tribunal headed by a fair-minded judge (Spencer Tracy), prosecuted by a vengeful US Army officer (Richard Widmark), and defended by a shrewd German lawyer (Maximilian Schell). Scripted by Abby Mann and directed by Stanley Kramer, the lengthy courtroom drama examines Nazi crimes against humanity, with emotion-laded testimony from victims (Judy Garland and Montgomery Clift), as well as sad remonstrances from a German officer's widow (Marlene Dietrich), but on trial are less the four judges than the German people and, indeed, the Western world. Important subject but turgid treatment. Some newsreel footage of Nazi atrocities. A-II (br)

Judgment Night (1993) While taking a shortcut through a dark, deserted Chicago slum, four pals (Emilio Estevez, Cuba Gooding, Jr., Jeremy Piven,

Stephen Dorff) happen to witness a murder and are pursued by the killer (Denis Leary) and his goons. Director Stephen Hopkins's edgy thriller tempers scenes of violence with fitful attempts to portray the positive nature of masculinity and the bonds of friendship. Much violence and rough language. A-III (R)

Judith (1966) Sophia Loren plays a concentration camp refugee in Palestine after the war who joins an anti-Arab group in order get revenge on her ex-husband (Hans Verner), a former Nazi now working for the Arabs. Directed by Daniel Mann, it's melodramatic hokum, though some may enjoy its picturesque locales and a supporting cast including Peter Finch and Jack Hawkins. Restrained violence. A-II (br)

Judo Saga (1972) Japanese movie about the moral discipline necessary for a student of judo to best the rival followers of jujitsu is set in 1882, when Japan was emerging from feudalism under the Meiji restoration and contrasts the changes of the period with the constant values of a moral code. Directed by Akira Kurosawa in 1943, his first movie already reveals the characteristic narrative style that so distinguishes his later, internationally popular works. A-I (nr)

Juggernaut (1974) Demolition expert Richard Harris tries to disarm seven bombs placed by a madman aboard Omar Sharif's luxury liner carrying some 1,200 passengers. Director Richard Lester deftly turns a routine thriller into a grand, fast, and suspenseful entertainment. A-II (PG)

Juggler, The (1953) Arriving in a refugee camp in 1949 Haifa, a troubled Holocaust survivor (Kirk Douglas) runs away, injures a policeman, and eventually takes refuge in a kibbutz. Directed by Edward Dmytryk, the uneven script doesn't do justice to the subject, though the movie's location photography in Israel and Douglas's game attempt to portray a professional juggler who appeals especially to children are worth seeing. Stylized violence, threatening situations, and romantic complications. A-II (br)

Juice (1992) Unrelentingly ugly story of four young Harlem thieves, one of whom (Tupac Shakur) relishes killing and turns with deadly force on his three friends (Omar Epps, Jermaine Hopkins, and Khalil Kain). Director Ernest R. Dickerson presents a shrill movie where hatred, violence, and drug use is the norm and has no moral implications. Mindless violence, momentary bedroom scene, some casual drug use, and sexual references and constant rough language. O (R)

Julia (1977) Recollections by writer Lillian Hellman (Jane Fonda) of her friendship with Julia (Vanessa Redgrave), an extraordinary Englishwoman whose struggle to help Jews and anti-Nazis flee Hitler's Germany ends in tragedy. Directed by Fred Zinnemann, it is rather slow-moving, but its good acting and stress on human dignity in the face of inhumanity compensate for its dramatic flaws. A-II (PG)

Julia and Julia (1988) Failed thriller about a young widow (Kathleen Turner) inexplicably reunited with her husband six years after his death and pulled unnervingly between two worlds, until finally pushed to murder and mental collapse. Despite its eerie Italian setting and Turner's valiant effort to reflect the terror felt by her character, director Peter Del Monte is unable to combine the psychological and supernatural in a plausible narrative. Considerable nudity, graphic sex ,and some violence. O (R)

Julia Has Two Lovers (1991) A young man (David Duchovny) who gets his kicks sweet-talking strangers on the phone, then seducing them in their homes, falls for his latest victim (Daphna Kastner) just as she is about to marry her callous lover (David Charles). Director Bashar Shbib's low-budget movie traps the viewer into hearing details of the pathetic characters' perverse sexual encounters. Much sexual exploitation and recurring nudity. O (R)

Julia Misbehaves (1948) Sentimental comedy set in 1936 as a struggling music-hall performer (miscast Greer Garson) returns to the home of her wealthy husband (Walter Pidgeon) after a 20-years separation to attend the wedding of their daughter (Elizabeth Taylor). Directed by Jack Conway, the hokey story features a solid supporting cast (including Cesar Romero as an acrobat), but there's not much to smile about amidst all the cliches and Garson's vain attempts to put over her songs and comic routines. Romantic complications and much sexual innuendo. A-III (br)

Julie (1956) Soapy thriller begins with Doris Day as a hysteric married to a psychopath (Louis Jourdan) whom she suspects murdered her first husband and fears will kill her. Writer-director Andrew L. Stone offers one implausible twist after another until a ludicrous climax with airline hostess Day at the controls of a pilot-less passenger plane. Irrational violence and menacing situations are shaky fare for children. A-I (br)

Juliet of the Spirits (1965) Federico Fellini's first movie in color centers on a middle-aged woman (Giulietta Masina) trying to take stock of her life by sorting through her problems, memories, and illusions. Fellini's imaginative imagery and Masina's aging gamin make the reveries and evocations a delight to the eye and the spirit. Ambiguous treatment of mature themes. A-IV (br)

Julius Caesar (1953) Lavish Hollywood version of Shakespeare's play in which the noble Brutus (James Mason) joins the conspiracy to assassinate Caesar (Louis Calhern) in order to preserve the Republic, but two years later his forces are crushed by Mark Antony (Marlon Brando) at Philippi in 42 B.C. Writer-director Joseph L. Mankiewicz has boiled down the play to its essentials and the fine cast does well with the Elizabethian language, but the drama is too static to be entirely satisfying. Period violence, including suicide. A-I (br)

Julius Caesar (1970) Failed version of Shakespeare's tragedy directed by Stuart Burge with awkward staging, uniformly poor performances (Charlton Heston as Antony and Jason

Robards as Brutus), and gauche Roman costuming right out of an Italian muscle-movie. Even a desperate teacher, willing to try anything to motivate English students, had best beware this slack effort. A-II (PG)

Jumanji (1995) Eye-popping fantasy adventure about a jungle-wildlife board-game which springs to life, threatening to destroy a whole town unless its players (notably Robin Williams) successfully complete the game. Director Joe Johnston provides some frightening thrills as spectacular special effects put humans at the mercy of rampaging animals and a deadly hunter. Frequent life-threatening menace and intermittent gunfire. A-II (PG)

Jumbo (see **Billy Rose's Jumbo**)

Jumpin' Jack Flash (1986) Whoopi Goldberg plays a compassionate but fiercely independent computer operator who saves the life of a British intelligence agent trapped in an Iron Curtain country when she communicates with him via computer terminal. Director Penny Marshall's raucous but lighthearted spoof of the spy genre is chilled by an extraordinary amount of sexually derived expletives. A-III (R)

Jumping Jacks (1952) Predictable but congenial service comedy directed by Norman Taurog as nightclub entertainers (Dean Martin and Jerry Lewis) manage to wind up together in the paratroopers clowning their way through boot camp under a blustery sergeant (Robert Strauss), with antic highlights by Lewis on field maneuvers and jumping without a parachute. A-I (br)

Jun (1980) Japanese movie about a maladjusted Tokyo worker who gives vent to his frustrations by molesting women on crowded commuter trains. Written and directed by Hiroto Yokoyama, its pretentious vision of urban alienation becomes a heavy-handed display of graphic sexual excesses. O (nr)

June Bride (1948) Uneven romantic comedy in which the editor (Bette Davis) of a woman's magazine assigns an old beau (Robert Montgomery) to cover an Indiana wedding, whose unexpected problems bring the two back together. Directed by Bretaigne Windust, the witty sparring between these veteran professionals is more amusing than the romantic guff of a story predicated on the male calling the shots. Sexual situations. A-III (br)

Jungle Book, The (1942) Uneven adaptation of the Rudyard Kipling story in which an infant boy (Sabu) is raised by wolves in the wilds of India, then protects an ancient treasure from a trio of greedy villagers (led by Joseph Calleia). Directed by Zoltan Korda, the jungle with its exotic animals has greater appeal than the village and its human tribe. Some graphic violence. A-II (br)

Jungle Book, The (1967) Rudyard Kipling's adventure-filled story of Mowgli, a boy-child reared by obliging wolves in the jungles of India, has been freely but nicely adapted in this Disney animated feature directed by Wolfgang Reitherman. Using genial humor and the voices of Phil Harris as Baloo the lovable bear, George Sanders as Shere Khan the suave, menacing tiger, and Sterling Holloway as an opportunistic python, the movie will amuse everyone in the household. A-I (G)

Jungle Fever (1991) A married African-American architect (Wesley Snipes) becomes an outcast to his Harlem family, as does his Italian-Catholic girlfriend from Brooklyn (Annabella Sciorra) when their interracial affair is exposed. Written, produced, and directed by co-star Spike Lee, the ugliness of racism is provocatively exposed, and the human toll of drug addiction is harrowingly portrayed while religion comes off as something ineffectual or negative. An adulterous relationship, short outbursts of violence, brief partial nudity, and much rough language. A-IV (R)

Jungle Jim (1948) Standard adventure directed by William Berke in which the title character (Johnny Weissmuller) guides a scientist (Virginia Grey) to a lost temple in quest of a cure for polio, but a gold-hunting photographer (George Reeves) and hostile natives get in their way. Stylized violence and threatening situations. A-I (br)

Jungle Jim in the Forbidden Land (1952) Adventure programmer directed by Lew Landers in which Jim (Johnny Weissmuller) fights a panther, a hippopotamus, ivory poachers, and a fearsome tribe of giant people who stand in the way of rescuing an elephant herd trapped by a flood. Stylized violence. A-I (br)

Jungle Man-Eaters (1954) Adventure programmer directed by Lee Sholem pits Jungle Jim (Johnny Weissmuller) against a renegade band of native warriors led by a French crook looking for a secret diamond mine. Stylized violence. A-I (br)

Jungle Manhunt (1951) Formula adventure directed by Lew Landers in which Jungle Jim (Johnny Weissmuller) helps a reporter (Sheila Ryan) locate a missing millionaire war-hero (football star Bob Waterfield), then frees natives forced to mine radioactive ore which a greedy scientist (Lyle Talbot) converts into synthetic diamonds. Stylized violence. A-I (br)

Jungle 2 Jungle (1997) Workaholic Wall Street trader (Tim Allen) learns to bond with his visiting, newly discovered 13-year-old son (Sam Huntington) who was raised by his estranged wife in a Venezuelan rainforest. Director John Pasquin's clash-of-cultures comedy limps fitfully along, depending heavily on Allen's appeal as a TV sitcom star. Implied premarital relationship, comic violence, and some coarse humor. A-III (PG)

Jungle Woman (1944) Horror clunker directed by Reginald LeBorg in which a doctor (J. Carrol Naish) comes to fear that one of his patients (Aquanetta) is really an ape that a mad scientist (John Carradine) has transformed into a woman. Stylized violence and hokey menace. A-II (br)

Junior (1994) Low-brow comic fantasy in which a fertility specialist (Danny DeVito) tests an anti-miscarriage drug by injecting a fertilized egg into a willing male colleague (Arnold Schwarzenegger), who then refuses to end the experiment after the first trimester and goes to term with the pregnancy while romancing the woman (Emma Thompson) whose frozen egg was used without her knowledge. Director Ivan Reitman's one-joke premise of a pregnant man relies on common stereotypes of expectant women for its laughs while presenting fetal experimentation as all part of a nutty plot-line that gets increasingly bizarre. Comic treatment of reproductive technology, references to casual sexual relations, and an instance of profanity. A-III (PG-13)

Junior Bonner (1972) Aging cowboy Steve McQueen has one big challenge left to meet in the form of a brahma bull that nearly killed him last time around. The film is stolen, however, by Robert Preston as Junior's wild Pa and Ida Lupino as his heartbroken, long-suffering but tough Ma in their superb and emotionally wrenching scenes together. Unlike some of his violent Westerns, director Sam Peckinpah has here devoted his talents to constructing a well-balanced, well-paced, and well-acted rodeo movie. A-II (PG)

Junk Mail (1998) Offbeat black comedy in which a grungy Oslo mailman (Robert Skjaerstad) becomes unwittingly involved with a suicidal woman (Andrine Saether) who is reluctantly holding stolen money for a criminal acquaintance. Director Pal Sletaune finds quirky romance in this wry Norwegian tale of alienated urban workers whose glum lives offer little hope of human fulfillment. Subtitles. Brief violence, full nudity, occasional profanity, and an instance of rough language. A-III (nr)

Jupiter Menace, The (1983) Narrated by George Kennedy with a straight face, this is one of those psuedo-scientific, quasi-religious documentaries which forecasts the end of the world. It may scare the wits out of those not inclined to take it all with several grains of salt, but then, fear is sometimes good for the soul. A-II (PG)

Jurassic Park (1993) A bizarre theme-park featuring genetically re-created dinosaurs becomes a potential deathtrap when the carnivorous monsters break loose, endangering some visiting scientists (Sam Neill, Laura Dern, and Jeff Goldblum) and two very frightened young children (Joseph Mazzelo and Ariana Richards). Director Steven Spielberg's monster fantasy downplays plot and characterization in favor of spectacle and horrific special effects in which the realistic-looking creatures hunt down their human prey. Much intense menace to children and several stylized scenes of violent death. A-II (PG-13)

Juror, The (1996) Preposterous, dragged-out thriller involving the murder trial of a gang boss who unleashes a psychotic hit-man to threaten a jury member and her child with death unless she convinces her fellow jurors to acquit the accused. Directed by Brian Gibson, the cat-and-mouse struggle of the woman to placate her twisted tormentor, then attempt to kill him, has some nasty thrills but is too slow-moving and painfully contrived to hold attention. Sadistic threats, various murders, a sexual encounter with brief nudity, occasional profanity, and some rough language. A-IV (R)

Jury Duty (1995) Unamusing comedy in which a homeless juror (Pauly Shore) prolongs deliberations over the guilt of an alleged serial killer in order to enjoy free bed and board on a sequestered jury. Directed by John Fortenberry, Shore's dumb antics go from the inane to the obnoxious in a laughless time-waster. Some sleazy sexual innuendo, slapstick violence, and several instances of profanity. A-III (PG-13)

Just Another Girl on the I.R.T. (1993) Gritty cautionary tale of a bright but flip African-American teen (Ariyan Johnson) who aims to go to college and become a doctor but falls for a jock with a jeep (Kevin Thigpen), gets pregnant, and winds up a single mother enrolled in a community college. Writer-director Leslie Harris's low-budget account of coming of age in Brooklyn's public housing projects makes good use of the harsh urban landscape and blighted social conditions, but fails to create much sympathy for the girl's character and provides little insight in her predicament. Some restrained bedroom scenes, explicit discussions of contraception and abortion, an intense birth scene, attempted infanticide, and much rough language. A-IV (R)

Just Around the Corner (1938) After her architect father (Charles Farrell) loses his job in the Depression, his little girl (Shirley Temple) helps him get it back by appealing to a millionaire (Claude Gillingwater) whom she mistakes for Uncle Sam. Director Irving Cummings pads out the formula plot with a little comic relief (Bert Lahr and Joan Davis) and some musical numbers with Shirley and Bill Robinson. Thin sentimental fare for the undemanding. A-I (G)

Just Before Nightfall (1975) French psychological melodrama in which an ordinary man (Michel Bouquet) murders his mistress and then, overcome by guilt, decides to confess, but his wife (Stephane Audran) takes steps to prevent him from disgracing the family name. Director Claude Chabrol tells his story of conscience and middle-class morality with one ironic twist after another, confronting viewers with an ambiguous conclusion that implicitly indicts the emptiness of materialistic values. Brief nudity. A-IV (PG)

Just Between Friends (1986) Marital infidelity is the starting point for a seriocomic treatment of the relationship between a naive housewife and an independent career woman. When the man in their lives is killed in an accident, the wife (Mary Tyler Moore) discovers his affair with her friend (Christine Lahti) who is now pregnant with his child. The women ultimately find grounds for reconciliation and mutual support after the baby's birth. Directed by Allan Burns, the sitcom format and soap-opera characterizations offer little inspiration and less justification for a frivolous handling of a serious theme. A-III (PG-13)

Just Cause (1995) Tawdry melodrama in which a Harvard law professor (Sean Connery) is persuaded by his lawyer wife (Kate Capeshaw) to make a last-ditch effort at overturning the murder conviction of a Florida death-row inmate (Blair Underwood) whose confession had been coerced by a brutal police detective (Laurence Fishburne). Director Arne Glimcher maintains moderate suspense through a darkly twisted plot abetted by some fine performances, until the narrative goes haywire with a lurid, ludicrous ending. Some intense violence including grisly shots of corpses, fleeting shadowy nudity, and recurring rough language. (A-III) (R)

Just for You (1952) Routine musical in which a widowed Broadway producer (Bing Crosby) tries to woo a stage star (Jane Wyman) while coping with an adolescent son (Bob Arthur) who has a crush on her, and a daughter (Natalie Wood) who wants to enroll in a posh academy whose headmistress (Ethel Barrymore) proves uncommonly wise. Directed by Elliott Nugent, the narrative lumbers fitfully along, though matters brighten considerably whenever Barrymore is on screen in her small but pivotal role. Romantic complications. A-II (br)

Just Like a Woman (1994) Tossed out by his wife, a transvestite (Adrian Pasdar) falls in love with his new landlady (Julie Walters) who accepts his romancing and cross-dressing while trying to help him regain his lost job. Director Christopher Monger's belabored comedy strains to sustain a semblance of slightly naughty humor in a one-joke situation stretched out to accommodate a formula plot. A few discreet bedroom scenes, fleeting nudity, and an indulgent depiction of cross-dressing. A-III (nr)

Just Like at Home (1979) Hungarian director Marta Meszaros explores the relationship between a precocious 11-year-old girl (Zsuzsa Czinkoczy) and a rash and bedeviled man in his 30s. A flawed but nonetheless absorbing movie, it conveys the somber texture of life in contemporary Hungary. Mature themes. A-III (nr)

Just One of the Guys (1985) An ambitious high-school girl (Joyce Hyser) who wants to be a journalist decides that no one takes her work seriously because she's too pretty, so she disguises herself as a boy. Director Lisa Gottlieb's plodding, mediocre comedy has a heavy emphasis on vulgarity and sexually oriented humor. Worse, outright promiscuity is portrayed as perfectly normal. O (PG-13)

Just Tell Me What You Want (1980) Long-time mistress (Ali McGraw) of a greedy tycoon (Alan King) tries to break away by marrying a New York playwright (Peter Weller), and the tycoon's devious efforts to get her back provide the thrust for most of the plot in a sour and vulgar comedy directed by Sidney Lumet. Though it has a lot of action, it has little purpose and no heart. Condones immoral actions and features foul language. O (R)

Just the Ticket (1999) Dreary romantic melodrama in which a New York ticket scalper (Andy Garcia) intends to win back his lost love (Andee MacDowall) by making a fortune selling outrageously priced tickets to see the visiting pope at Yankee Stadium, but things don't work out the way he planned. Writer-director Richard Wenk fails to work up much human interest in these thin proceedings about street hustlers and scam artists, but the biggest disappointment is Garcia's shrilly, unlikable performance which sours the romantic angle and curdles the picture of commercial greed surrounding the papal visit. Stylized violence, a sexual encounter, tasteless treatment of Catholic matters, frequent rough language, and occasional profanity. A-IV (R)

Just the Way You Are (1984) Crippled musician (Kristy McNichol) goes to bed with a succession of men at home and during a vacation at a Swiss ski resort, where she hides her affliction with a plaster cast. Directed by Edouard Molinaro, the dull and listless attempt at light romance takes an entirely benign view of the heroine's promiscuous behavior. O (PG)

Just You and Me, Kid (1979) Retired comedian (George Burns) finds a teenage girl (Brooke Shields) in the trunk of his vintage Pierce-Arrow clad in nothing but an old inner tube. Neither the plot explanation nor the attempts at humor are convincing in director Leonard Stern's generation-gap bore which has some brief laughs from John Schuck and Andrea Howard as nosy neighbors. Some violence and strong language. A-II (PG)

Justine (1969) The last days of the British involvement in Egypt frame this complicated story featuring Anouk Aimee as the somber, crafty medium of the title, Michael York as a spineless schoolmaster, and Anna Karina as the tubercular dancer he comes to love. Director George Cukor uses the city of Alexandria to convey the social and moral decadence of the late 1930s. Graphic rendering of homosexuality and excessive use of nudity. O (R)

K2 (1992) The lifelong friendship of two amateur mountain-climbers (Michael Biehn and Matt Craven) is put to the ultimate test in the Himalayas, where they become stranded atop the world's most dangerous mountain peak. While the physical dangers in this adventure movie are predictable, director Franc Roddam enhances the spectacular action sequences with gripping character studies of the two men as they face impending death. Some sexual innuendo, rough language, and a flash of nudity. A-III (R)

K-9 (1989) Lame story of a hotheaded San Diego narcotics cop (James Belushi) and his police-dog partner. Director Rod Daniel tracks this unlikely cop team as they corner a slick drug czar (Kevin Tighe), but much of this comedy caper focuses on implausible macho heroics with intense comic-book violence, rough language, and vulgar sexual innuendoes. A-III (PG-13)

Kafka (1991) Interesting excursion into the dark imagination of absurdist author Franz Kafka (Jeremy Irons), whose dull duties as an insurance clerk in 1919 Prague spark nightmare images of an oppressive regime secretly operating from the medieval castle overlooking the city. Directed by Steven Soderbergh, the narrative is by turns moody, bizarre, and ironic but never quite achieves the dreamlike logic that would make it work as something more than an elaborate exercise of the emotions. Morosely unsettling atmosphere, some nasty stylized violence, and a glimpse of a nude photo. A-III (PG-13)

Kagemusha (1980) Grand period spectacle set in 16th-century Japan, when a thief (Tatsuya Nakadai) is trained to impersonate a dead warlord whose clan is fighting for its survival against a powerful rival. Director Akira Kurosawa's austere but powerful treatment of the historical material is filled with fierce martial pageantry, stirring action, and poignant ironies as the story of a clan's downfall unfolds. Subtitles. Tragic theme and violent battle sequences. A-II (PG)

Kaleidoscope (1966) Sophisticated comedy thriller involving the con-games of a suave American gambler (miscast Warren Beatty) on the loose in London and on the Continent. Though the plot is overly complicated, the largely British cast (notably Susannah York, Clive Revill, and Eric Porter) is excellent, and director Jack Smight keeps matters diverting enough for those who like this kind of derring-do. Stylized violence and romantic complications. A-III (br)

California (1993) Violent road movie in which a cash-strapped couple (David Duchovny and Michelle Forbes) unwittingly share cross-country car-ride expenses with another couple, a dimwitted innocent (Juliette Lewis) and her boyfriend (Brad Pitt), a cold-blooded murderer. Director Dominic Sena allows the drama to wallow in the vicious brutality of a callous killer and the conversion of a normal guy into a vengeful executioner, depicting it all with flippant black humor. Excessive violence, positive portrayal of a revenge murder, rough sexual encounters, nude photos, and occasional rough language. O (R)

Kama Sutra: A Tale of Love (1997) Convoluted romantic melodrama set in 16th-century India, where a king (Naveen Andrews) marries a princess (Sarita Choudhury) but is seduced by her envious servant (Indira Varma), who goes on to become a courtesan, falls in love with a sculptor (Ramon Tikaram), and ultimately incurs the king's wrath. Directed by Mira Nair, the exotic period setting is stylishly visualized, but the story proves little more than a soap-opera saga of English-speaking cardboard characters and their shallow emotional lives. Several restrained sex scenes with nudity, some sexual references, and brief violence. A-IV (R)

Kamouraska (1975) French-Canadian movie set in the early 19th-century, in which a passionate and headstrong young woman (Genevieve Bujold) marries the boorish master of a remote estate (Philippe Leotard), leaves him to return to civilization, and has a romance with a doctor (Richard Jordan) that ends in murder. Directed by Claude Jutra, the movie captures a vanished era, has excellent acting, and the beauty of its settings, but its story of hot passion in a cold climate is heavily melodramatic. Some incidental nudity and scenes of questionable taste. A-IV (R)

Kansas City (1996) Dour crime-story set in 1934 centers on the kidnapping of a politician's wife (Miranda Richardson) by a woman (Jennifer Jason Leigh) trying to free her husband (Dermot Mulroney) from a black gang-leader (Harry Belafonte). Directed by Robert Altman, the tension of the kidnapping plot is dissipated by leisurely digressions into corrupt Missouri politics, lengthy monologues by the gang leader, asides on Hollywood movies, and lively sessions in a jazz club. Considerable menace, hard-edged violence, sexual innuendo, drug abuse, racial epithets, profanity, and rough language. A-IV (R)

Kansas City Bomber (1972) Raquel Welsh plays a top skater on the Roller Derby scene with Kevin McCarthy as the team owner trying to promote a bigger and better franchise. Burdened with some unconvincing, if decorative, performances, director Jerrold Freedman's inept and shallow melodrama manages to make the Roller Derby look boring. Some rough language. A-III (PG)

Kansas City Confidential (1952) Tough-minded tale of an ex-con (John Payne) who's wrongly implicated in an armored-car robbery, then trails those who did it to Mexico for the final showdown. Directed by Phil Karlson, the gritty but contrived proceedings feature a gang (Jack Elam, Neville Brand, and Lee Van Cleef) whose leader (Preston Foster) insists they all wear masks so none will know the identity of the others. Some deadly violence and intermittent brutality. A-III (br)

Kansas Pacific (1953) Standard Western directed by Ray Nazarro tells how a Union officer (Sterling Hayden) built the title railroad while fighting off Quantrill's Raiders during the Civil War. Stylized violence. A-I (br)

Kansas Raiders (1950) Muddled Western in which Jesse James (Audie Murphy), his brother Frank (Richard Long), Cole Younger (James Best), and Kit Dalton (Tony Curtis) join Confederate Col. William Clarke Quantrill (Brian Donlevy) to fight Yankees but wind up terrorizing Kansas citizens instead. Directed by Ray Enright, the contradictory plot tries to have it both ways as young Jesse protests atrocities while continuing to participate in them. Terrorist violence against civilians, much brutality, and an implied sexual relationship. A-III (br)

Kaos (1986) Comprised of four fables of Italian peasant life drawn from Luigi Pirandello's short stories, this Italian production by the Taviani brothers offers a range of sensitive characterizations expressing simple but profound truths. Each segment is a self-contained tale on a social, political, or moral theme. Visually rich and dramatically provocative, the film's life-affirming narrative is well worth its running time of over three hours. A brief shot of partial nudity and a gruesome shot of a decapitated head punctuate an otherwise pastoral vision. A-III (R)

Karado, the Hong Kong Cat (1973) Martial-arts champion returns to the island of his birth and finds himself between two opposing factions. Non-stop violent encounters in which everything from chain whips to revolvers come into play, as well as some sex scenes. O (R)

Karate Kid, The (1984) High school student (Ralph Macchio) learns about life, friendship, and the martial arts from a kindly Japanese-American gardener (Pat Morita) who shows him how to deal with the bullies tormenting him. Directed by John G. Avildsen, the movie is made extremely appealing by the performances of the two principals despite its message that violence solves all ills. Parents should be sure that their youngsters realize karate is considerably more lethal than depicted here. A-II (PG)

Karate Kid Part II, The (1986) Repeating his role in the sequel, Pat Morita gives a winning performance as the martial-arts teacher who brings his young student (Ralph Macchio) to Okinawa in a gentle story re-affirming the importance of devotion, loyalty, and the sweet-and-sour of life as seen from the perspective of old age. Unabashedly moralistic without being didactic, it is high-spirited, engaging entertainment. A-I (PG)

Karate Kid Part III, The (1989) Against the wishes of his karate mentor (Noriyuki "Pat" Morita), young Daniel (Ralph Macchio) is coerced by sleazy martial-artists into defending his championship title. Director John G. Avildsen puts more emphasis on the smirking heavies and grisly brutality than on the anti-violence values of the earlier series. The exploitative nature of the violence is unsuitable for preteens or impressionable younger adolescents. A-III (PG)

Katerina Izmailova (1969) Russian production of Shostakovich's opera features the performance of Galina Vishnevskaya, first soprana of the Bolshoi. Director Mikhail Shapiro provides a fluid rendering of tragic lovers who resort to murder to preserve their relationship, but, while imprisoned in Siberia, their love gradually turns, through mutual recriminations and the man's infidelity, into hatred. Dreary moral tale in Russian with English subtitles. A-III (nr)

Kathy's Love Affair (see: **The Courtneys**)

Kaya, I'll Kill You (1969) Yugoslavian import conveys the simplicity of life in a pre-war Croatian village, and the terror which is unleashed by the emergence of its own hometown Fascists inebriated by power. Symbolic narrative set in exotic locales and directed by Vatroslav Mimica makes obscure points about the nature of violence and militarism. A-III (nr)

Kazaam (1996) Trashy comic fantasy in which a 12-year-old brat (Francis Capra) and a 5,000-year-old genie (Shaquille O'Neal) tangle with some nasty thugs in a rap-music racket, after which the boy reconciles with a father he hasn't seen in 10 years, as well as the man his divorced mom plans to marry. Directed by Paul Michael Glazer, the witless proceedings are noisy, the characters are generally unlikable, and there's nothing magical about the clumsy special effects. Stylized violence, menacing situations, domestic tensions, coarse language, and a profanity. A-II (PG)

Kazablan (1974) Israeli musical pits the Sephardim against Ashkenazim in the Jaffa slums of Tel Aviv, telling the story of two lovers from different sides of the ethnic gap. Director Menahen Golan's economy-sized extravaganza of dancing and singing has some natural charm, and its salty taunting and gesture are submerged in its theme of finding one's heart by relaxing one's prejudices. A-III (PG)

Keep, The (1983) Nazi unit guarding an ancient fortress in Romania runs into some odd events in this arty, pretentious, and thoroughly muddled drama of the supernatural written and directed by Michael Mann, and starring Scott Glenn and Ian McKellan. Vicious rape scene and some graphic sex. O (R)

Keep On Rockin' (1974) Documentary of the 1969 Toronto Rock and Roll Revival features performances by Chuck Berry, Little Richard, Jerry Lee Lewis, and Bo Didley. Made by D.A. Pennebaker, the film captures the infectious energy of the performers, and the drive of their music. A-II (PG)

Keeper, The (1997) Gritty drama in which an idealistic Brooklyn prison-guard (Giancarlo Esposito) tries to help a Haitian immigrant (Isaach de Bankole) he believes is wrongly accused of rape by paying his bail and taking him home, then turns on him when he imagines the man is after his wife (Regina Taylor). Writer-director Joe Brewster probes the psychological effects of the prison environment on its workers with some insight before opting for an overly melodramatic ending. Brief violence, several racial slurs, and constant rough language. A-III (nr)

Keeper of the Flame (1942) Contrived melodrama in which a journalist (Spencer Tracy) sets out to gather material for a tribute to a late public-leader, falls for his widow (Katharine Hepburn), then discovers the truth about the man's death and secret subversive plans. Director George Cukor's woolly tale of home-grown Fascism starts slowly and grows increasingly portentous until ending in typical period flag-waving. Muddled attempt to justify murder. A-III (br)

Keetje Tippel (1976) Dutch drama about a 19th-century woman, forced by her mother into prostitution to support the family, who learns from a middle-class lover how to act and dress like a lady, and eventually marries a wealthy social reformer. Director Paul Verhoeven's masterful depiction of the terrible poverty of the working class and their first stirrings of revolt is overshadowed by obsessive detailing and graphic treatment of sexual encounters. O (nr)

Kelly and Me (1957) Flat melodrama directed by Robert Z. Leonard tells of an ambitious vaudeville hoofer (Van Johnson) who breaks into the movies in 1930, thanks to his befriending a dog whose screen talents prove more valuable to the studio than those of his master. Formula fare of little appeal, save for those who appreciate canine antics. A-I (br)

Kelly's Heroes (1970) Clint Eastwood and Telly Salvalas lead a group of US soldiers (including Don Rickles and Donald Sutherland) 30 miles behind German lines to pull off a gold heist. Directed by Brian Hutton, the movie's premise is that all Germans are stupid, that American pragmatism is invincible, and that the realities and deadly rituals of warfare make engrossing entertainment. A-III (PG)

Kennel Murder Case, The (1933) Twisty murder mystery in which S.S. Van Dine's gentleman sleuth, Philo Vance (William Powell), proves that a dead man in a room locked from the inside is no suicide, then uses a dog to trick the killer into making a confession. Directed by Michael Curtiz, the mystery is intelligently plotted and unfolds in witty fashion, with Eugene Pallette's bungling cop especially amusing. Stylized violence and menacing situations. A-II (br)

Kentuckian, The (1955) Rough-hewn but unconvincing frontier tale of an 1820s backwoodsman (Burt Lancaster) torn between starting a new life in Texas with a servant girl he's rescued (Dianne Foster) or settling down in a small Kentucky town with a schoolteacher (Diana Lynn). Also directed by Lancaster, the plot is a haphazard series of complications delaying the predictable choice between frontier and civilization until the final scene. Assorted violence, some of it quite nasty, and romantic complications. A-III (br)

Kentucky Fried Movie, The (1977) Unfunny collection of sketches spoofing television and movies, especially movie trailers. Director John Landis finds vulgarity a proper source of humor, but even on a simple slapstick level his satire is often tasteless and sexually exploitative. O (R)

Kentucky Rifle (1955) Formula Western directed by Carl K. Hittleman has Kentucky frontiersmen (Lance Fuller and Chill Wills) save a wagon loaded with settlers and long rifles from being captured by Comanche raiders. Frontier violence. A-I (br)

Kes (1970) British movie set in a small, drab Yorkshire coal mining town tells the story of a lonely, sullen boy (David Bradley) whose life is momentarily given meaning by his experience in raising and training a baby kestrel, a European falcon. Directed by Ken Loach, the movie is a compassionate study of the blighted conditions and brutalizing life of this youth, which in its final scenes indicates the possibility of his rising above his environment. Fine experience for adults and older adolescents. A-III (GP)

Key, The (1958) Curious WW II tale in which an American skipper (William Holden) joins a squadron of British tugboats used to rescue torpedoed ships, is befriended by a veteran captain (Trevor Howard), and given a duplicate key to the apartment of a woman (Sophia Loren), who has given lodging to a succession of tugboat captains after her fiancé died on a rescue mission. When his friend is killed, the American must decide whether to move in, throw away the key, or pass it on to another. Director Carol Reed crafts the wartime action scenes with satisfying conviction but never quite gets a handle on the character of the sad, lonely woman who comes with the key. Wartime violence and implied cohabitation. A-III (br)

Key Exchange (1985) Young novelist (Ben Masters), unsure of his feelings about a young woman (Brooke Adams), joins a friend (Dan Jenny), whose wife deserted him, in prowling the singles-bar jungle before the inevitable happy ending. A very slight sex farce with little wit or charm, directed by Barnet Kellman. Nudity, graphic depiction of sex, benign view of adultery, and fornication. O (R)

Keys of the Kingdom, The (1944) Underrated adaptation of A.J. Cronin's novel about a Scottish priest (Gregory Peck) sent to China at the end of the 19th century, where he rebuilds a ruined mission, endures misunderstanding, war, and disease, but perseveres through humility and cheerful service to win many converts and friends, until retirement in Scotland fishing for supper rather than souls. Directed by John Stahl, the narrative is interestingly contrived, and Peck's characterization is entirely likeable and sincere, though, like so many vintage Hollywood pictures about religion, lacking much spiritual depth. A-I (br)

Khartoum (1966) Exciting action adventure with modern overtones about the British involvement in the Sudan during the 19th century pits the Empire's most famous general (Charlton Heston) against the ferocious leader of the desert tribes (Laurence Olivier). Directed by Basil Dearden, the movie has the sweep of history and some good characterizations. Stylized violence. A-I (br)

Kickboxer (1989) Belgian martial-arts whiz Jean-Claude Van Damme is pitted against a deadly Thai kick-boxing champ (Tong Po), who crippled his brother in the ring. Featuring some amateurish acting, melodramatic scripting, and heavy-handed direction by David Worth and Mark DiSalle, the movie is entertaining when it focuses on Van Damme's strict training sessions with a mysterious Thai mentor (Dennis Chan), but the kick-boxing fight scenes are brutal. Intense ring violence and profanity. O (R)

Kicking and Screaming (1995) Self-indulgent picture of four college men who hang around campus months after graduation to mull their future while chasing co-eds, with intermittent flash-backs as one (Josh Hamilton) moons over a lost love (Olivia d'Abo). Writer-director Noah Baumbach's comic treatment of the narcissism of aimless youths shirking adult responsibilities is too superficial to be truly amusing or insightful. Sexual situations and innuendo with much mindless rough language. A-IV (R)

Kid Blue (1973) Petty outlaw (Dennis Hopper) gives up on crime to make his way honestly in the little Texas town of Dime Box, whose single industry is a ceramic novelty factory, finds honest hard work, and decides to rob the factory payroll. James Frawley's direction makes the most of the comic potential of an uneven script, which stretches to make contemporary references to everything from the drug culture to the plight of the American Indian. Brief but explicit seduction scene. A-III (PG)

Kid Dynamite (1943) East Side Kids caper directed by Wallace Fox has bullying Muggs (Leo Gorcey) trying to outdo mild Danny (Bobby Jordan) in the boxing ring, then in a jitterbug contest, but the hapless Danny gets tired of being pushed around and joins the Army in a patriotic finish. Slapstick violence. A-I (br)

Kid for Two Farthings, A (1955) Uneven British fable set among the residents of London's Petticoat Lane market, where a boy (Jonathan Ashmore) buys a small goat with one horn, convinced it's a unicorn whose magical powers will help his friends and bring his father back from South Africa. Directed by Carol Reed from Wolf Mankowitz's novel, the narrative tries to parallel the boy's power of imagination with the changing fortunes of others (notably seamstress Diana Dors who wants her beau, bodybuilder Joe Robinson, to earn some money wrestling veteran Primo Carnera), but what works best is the tender relationship between the lad and a wise tailor (David Kosoff). Stylized violence and menacing situations. A-II (br)

Kid from Brooklyn, The (1946) Uneven musical comedy in which a meek milkman (Danny Kaye) is made to believe he's a prizefighter by a manager (Walter Abel), who pays his opponents to take a dive until left on his own in a title fight with the middleweight champ (Steve Cochran). Directed by Norman Z. McLeod, this remake of Harold Lloyd's **The Milky Way** adds some big production numbers featuring the milkman's girlfriend (Virginia Mayo) and his sister (Vera-Ellen), but the result is less funny than the original, and Kaye's performance proves more irritating than amusing. Stylized violence and romantic complications. A-II (br)

Kid from Left Field, The (1953) Corny sports fun directed by Harmon Jones in which the nine-year-old son (Billy Chapin) of a former baseball player (Dan Dailey) goes from batboy to manager of a faltering major-league club, bringing it out of the cellar and into pennant contention. Just the right speed for little leaguers, with enough heart for older members of the family willing to suspend their disbelief. A-I (br)

Kid from Spain, The (1932) After being expelled from college for a prank in the women's dorm, an over-aged zany (Eddie Cantor) winds up in Mexico helping a friend (Robert Young) by masquerading as the son of a famous bullfighter. Director Leo McCarey wrings some laughs from predictable situations, aided by a good cast and inventive Busby Berkeley production numbers. Some sexual innuendo and comic menace. A-III (br)

Kid from Texas, The (1950) Routine account of Billy the Kid (Audie Murphy) begins in 1879 Lincoln, New Mexico, where he's hired as a ranch hand by an Englishman (Sheppherd Strudwick) who's murdered in a range war, leaving Billy a hunted man until killed at age 21 by Sheriff Pat Garrett (Frank Wilcox). Director Kurt Neumann's shoot-'em-up fails to work up much sympathy for this vengeful, hot-tempered youth, who died with 21 notches in his gun. Numerous shootouts and muted sexual innuendo. A-II (br)

Kid Galahad (1962) In this remake of the 1936 original, a young auto-mechanic (Elvis Presley) is turned into a prizefighter by a needy promoter (Gig Young), then falls for the man's sister (Joan Blackman). Directed by Phil Karlson, Presley is unconvincing as a boxer, but is otherwise likeable as an earnest fellow who wants to make enough money to wed and open his own auto shop. Mild fight scenes and romantic complications. A-II (br)

Kid in King Arthur's Court, A (1995) Magically transported from his Southern California baseball field to 12th-century Camelot, a timid teenager (Thomas Ian Nicholas) finds the inner resources to rescue King Arthur's daughters (Paloma Baeza and Kate Winslet) from a villainous usurper (Art Malik). Director Michael Gottlieb's unimaginative fantasy-adventure strings together a sluggish series of routine obstacles for the lad to overcome, often with 20th-century gizmos from his backpack. Minor violence. A-II (PG)

Kid Millions (1934) Vintage Eddie Cantor musical follows him to Egypt to claim a fortune left by his archeologist father, but along the way he has to fend off an assortment of other claimants (Ethel Merman, Warren Hymer, Ann Sothern, and George Murphy). Directed by Roy Del Ruth, the plot is sappy and the songs forgettable, but it's a lot of silly fun, including the final reel with Eddie's ice-cream factory in Technicolor. Some stylized violence and mild sexual innuendo. A-II (br)

Kid Rodelo (1966) Passable melodrama about a drifter (Don Murray) who is forced to protect a young woman (Janet Leigh) from a rough band of former convicts who are looking for gold. Director Richard Carlson moderates the violence in favor of the action adventure. A-II (br)

Kidnapped (1938) Melodramatic adaptation of Robert Louis Stevenson's tale of an 18th-century orphaned youth (Freddie Bartholomew) befriended by a Scottish rebel (Warner Baxter) who tries to help the lad gain his stolen inheritance while fighting the English. Director Alfred L. Werker's good vintage cast (John Carradine, C. Aubrey Smith, Nigel Bruce, and Reginald Owen) keep the adventure exciting, if not quite what Stevenson had mind. Stylized violence. A-I (br)

Kidnapped (1948) Low-budget version of Robert Louis Stevenson's classic adventure in 18th-century Scotland, with William Beaudine directing Roddy McDowall as the wronged youth and Dan O'Herlihy as the anti-English rebel in a generally lackluster production. Stylized violence. A-I (br)

Kidnapped (1960) Disney version of the Robert Louis Stevenson adventure classic about a 18th-century Scottish youth (James MacArthur) done out of his inheritance and sold into servitude as a cabin boy by his treacherous uncle, then rescued by a dashing Jacobite rebel (Peter Finch) during the course of his battles with the English. Director Robert Stevenson is faithful to the spirit of the original, though some of the action may be a bit too intense for the preteen crowd. Stylized violence. A-I (br)

Kipnapped (1972) British adaptation of the Robert Louis Stevenson story of the young David Balfour (Lawrence Douglas), who is rescued from the villainy of his uncle (Donald Pleasence) by Alan Breck (Michael Caine), the heroic Stuart who opposes English rule over Scotland. Directed by Delbert Mann, it is still a classic children's adventure story, though there is some violence that might disturb young children. A-II (G)

Kidnapping of the President, The (1980) South American terrorist (Miguel Fernandes), laden with dynamite, handcuffs himself to the president of the United States (Hal Holbrook), but the villains are no match for the head of the Secret Service (William Shatner). Canadian director George Mendeluk's routine suspense thriller features unnecessarily graphic violence in the opening sequence. A-III (PG)

Kids (1995) A day in the so-called life of a group of feral inner-city youths shows them to be aimless dropouts from home, school, and the human race as they pass the time in pursuit of sex, drugs, cheap booze, petty larceny, and outbursts of violence. Director Larry Clark uses a lot of handheld camera shots in filming a cast of adolescent nonactors in New York locations, but manages to bring no sense of reality, let alone insight or perspective, to tawdry situations which never develop beyond surface sensationalism. Exploitative treatment of sex, violence, substance abuse, and rough language. O (nr)

Kids Are Alright, The (1979) Performance and interview film featuring the antics and music of the British rock group The Who. Director Jeff Stein's poorly organized documentary is marked by very little revelation, some vulgar language, and sexual references. A-III (PG)

Kids in the Hall Brain Candy (1996) Canadian comedy troupe brings its TV antics to the big screen in a half-baked spoof of a pharmaceutical firm rushing an anti-depression pill to market before testing its side effects. Directed by Kelly Makin, the result is a hodgepodge of weak skits relying on males in drag, ludicrous situations, and frequent bad taste. Sexual innuendo, rear nudity, occasional profanity, and recurring rough language. A-IV (R)

Kika (1994) Strained sex-farce about a ditzy hairdresser (Veronica Forque), her lovers, a rapist, a talk-show host (Victoria Abril), and a serial killer. Director Pedro Almodovar never strays far from the sexual eccentricities of his surreal characters in this tiresome, unamusing send-up of rape and mass murder. Subtitles. Some graphic sexual encounters, flippant treatment of rape, much nudity, several gory murders, and rough language. O (nr)

Kill a Dragon (1967) Run-of-the-mill action-adventure movie set in the Orient with contrived plot and unbelievable scenes of bravado. Directed by Michael Moore, it follows a predictable course of sex and violence. A-III (br):

Kill and Kill Again (1981) Martial-arts master (James Ryan) is hired to rescue a scientist from the clutches of a villain who wants to control the world in this slapdash, simpleminded melodrama produced in South Africa. Directed by Ivan Hall, the movie's violence is far less fierce than the accompanying grunts and groans. A-III (PG)

Kill-Off, The (1990) A bedridden crone (Loretta Gross) indulges in malicious phone gossip, and before long the objects of her invective, including her younger, unfaithful husband (Steve Monroe), are thinking deadly thoughts about silencing her. Jim Thompson's hardboiled novel is lifelessly directed by Maggie Greenwald with plodding pace, hesitant acting, and heavy-handed music. Intermittent partial nudity, fairly restrained violence, and minimal rough language. A-III (R)

Kill or Be Killed (1950) Hokey melodrama directed by Max Nosseck in which an American engineer (Lawrence Tierney), working in Brazil flees a false murder charge, hides as a laborer on a jungle plantation, then falls for the wife (Marissa O'Brien) of its malevolent owner (Rudolph Anders), whose partner (George Coulouris) wants to kill the American. Stylized violence, menacing situations, and sexual innuendo. A-III (br)

Kill the Umpire (1950) Lame-brained comedy about a fanatic baseball fan (William Bendix) who hates umpires but becomes one when he needs a job. Directed by Lloyd Bacon, the good supporting cast (notably Una Merkel, Ray Collins, and William Frawley) is wasted by the weak, slapstick script. For undemanding fans. A-I (br)

Kill Them All and Come Back Alone (1970) Italian Western in which Chuck Conners heads a band of Confederate renegades out to steal gold from a Yankee mining camp. Director Enzo G. Castellari lets the killings run their course until only anti-hero Conners remains. Extreme violence. O (R)

Killer Ape (1953) Formula jungle-adventure directed by Spencer G. Bennet in which Jungle Jim (Johnny Weissmuller) gets some help from a wild ape-man (Ray Corrigan) in stopping foreign agents (led by Nestor Paiva) from using animals to experiment on a drug that destroys "the will to resist." Stylized violence. A-I (br)

Killer Bats (see: **The Devil Bat**)

Killer Elite, The (1975) James Caan and Robert Duvall give fine performances as professional assassins working for a secret government agency in a suspense drama directed by Sam Peckinpah. Though flawed and lapsing into melodrama at times, the film raises questions of undercover agencies. Some brutal violence. A-III (PG)

Killer Force (1976) Peter Fonda plays the leader of a raid on the vaults of a diamond mine in South Africa, and after much muddlement escapes with the loot. Directed by Val Guest, the plot twists in this movie are so arbitrary that they are not worth following. Excessive gory violence. O (R)

Killer Grizzly (see: **Grizzly**)

Killer Klowns from Outer Space (1988) The aliens of the title turn the residents of a small town, most notably a disagreeable police officer (John Vernon), into pods of fodder. Directed by Stephen Chiodo, the inane thriller is silly and nasty by turns. Much noisy violence, some of it quite bloody, and some vulgar language. A-III (PG-13)

Killers, The (1946) Convoluted thriller from the Ernest Hemingway story starts with a former prizefighter (Burt Lancaster) being killed by two hit-men, leaving a puzzled insurance investigator (Edmond O'Brien) to search for the woman (Ava Gardner) involved. Directed by Robert Siodmak, one clue leads to another as the ex-boxer's part in a payroll heist and its aftermath is reconstructed in flashbacks that ultimately end in some measure of justice. Stylized violence and some menace. A-II (br)

Killing Fields, The (1984) Powerful and visually overwhelming movie about the friendship of an American correspondent (Sam Waterston) and his Cambodian assistant (Haing S. Ngor) set against the background of the fall of Cambodia and the slaughter of millions by the Khmer Rouge. Director Roland Joffe's fact-based drama makes an extraordinary human document in the tragic history of an entire nation. Graphically realistic but not overdone scenes of carnage. A-II (R)

Killing Floor, The (1984) Arresting, meaningful drama of a black sharecropper (Damien Leake) who comes to Chicago during WW I, gets a job in the stockyards, joins the union, and becomes an organizer, until the union is crushed in the race riots of 1919. Directed by William Duke, the personal drama has considerable force in the context of the union's struggle to achieve ethnic and racial solidarity in its battle against the meatpackers. Period racism and some nasty stylized violence. A-II (PG)

Killing Game, The (1968) Pretentious French murder mystery directed by Alain Jessua has excessive nudity. O (br)

Killing of a Chinese Bookie, The (1976) Owner of a cheap nightclub (Ben Gazzara) undertakes a murder to pay off the gambling debt he owes gangsters. Director John Cassavetes's quest for authenticity and spontaneity takes an indecorous turn down a blind alley, at the end of which one becomes sandbagged by sex and violence in a tedious drama that doesn't ring true. O (R)

Killing of Sister George, The (1969) British story about a fading soap-opera actress (Beryl Reid) whose lover (Susannah York) has been seduced by another woman (Coral Browne). Director Robert Aldrich fails to treat lesbianism with any depth, opting instead for heavy-handed melodrama and a rather clinical demonstration of lovemaking with ample peek-a-boo nudity. O (X/R)

Killing Zoe (1994) Brought to Paris for a bank robbery, an American safecracker (Eric Stoltz) spends part of the night with a prostitute (Julie Delpy), then parties with the gang of drugged-out thieves (led by Jean-Hughes Anglade), who next day storm into the bank, shooting patrons and employees on their way to the vault, where they're cornered in a final bloodbath. Writer-director Roger Avary's pointless exercise in movie mayhem has nothing else in mind than showing off its technical artifice in depicting vicious thugs killing and being killed. Excessive violence, a graphic sexual encounter, and some rough language. O (R)

Kim (1950) The orphaned son (Dean Stockwell) of an English soldier in Kipling's India is befriended by a Tibetan lama (Paul Lucas), sent briefly to military school, and then introduced to the "great game" of British intelligence by a dashing native agent (Errol Flynn). Directed by Victor Saville, the young lad's adventures in the colonial land of the British Raj are colorful enough, but the movie suffers from a plodding script and lackluster action. Some stylized violence. A-I (br)

Kind Hearts and Coronets (1949) Stylish black comedy set in Edwardian England, where eight members of an aristocratic family (all played by Alec Guinness) die in fatal accidents arranged by a distant relative (Dennis Price) in order to attain the dukedom he believes is rightfully his. Robert Hamer directs the proceedings with wit, elegance, and much irony, as related in flashbacks by the smoothly caustic perpetrator on the eve of his execution, though Guinness steals the show with his satirical parade of stuffy, doomed aristocrats. Cynical attitude towards murder. A-III (br)

Kindergarten Cop (1990) Posing as a kindergarten teacher, an undercover cop (Arnold Schwarzenegger) tries to protect a mother (Penelope Ann Miller) and her little boy from her ex-husband, a deadly drug dealer (Richard Tyson). Misleadingly marketed as a kid-appeal comedy, director Ivan Reitman has produced an unsettling mix of menace, mirth, and contrived romance that repels as often as it entertains. Recurring violence with menace to children and brief sexual innuendo. A-III (PG-13)

King and Country (1966) The court martial and execution of a British deserter during WW I is the grim story told by this impressive indictment of war and its injustices. Tom Courtenay is the passive and withdrawn victim of the military system, and Dirk Bogarde plays his sincere but ineffectual defense counsel. Director Joseph Losey's anti-war statement at times stretches for symbols but its sense of moral outrage is perfectly clear. A-III (br)

King and I, The (1956) Imaginative screen adaptation of the Rodgers and Hammerstein musical tells the story of a 19th-century British governess (Deborah Kerr) who comes to Thailand as tutor to the large brood of children in the royal court but finds her biggest job is enlightening its obstreperous king (Yul Brynner). Director Walter Lang creates a lovely fantasy version of an Asian kingdom, Kerr nicely abets Brynner's Oscar-winning performance, and the songs, especially the sweeping "Shall We Dance," are delightful. Fine family fare with some solid moral values. A-I (nr)

King and I, The (1999) Tuneful animated version of the Rodgers and Hammerstein musical in which the imperious king of 19th-century Siam (voice of Martin Vidnovic) hires a prim English schoolmarm (voice of Miranda Richardson) to teach his many children Western ways but discovers he has much to learn himself. Director Richard Rich's pretty animation is overshadowed by the splendid music and well-known lyrics that should entertain viewers of every age. A-I (G)

King Creole (1958) Crime story set to music as a high school dropout (Elvis Presley) defies his weak father (Dean Jagger) to take a job singing in a nightclub, then gets mixed up with a crooked club owner (Walter Matthau) and his boozy moll (Carolyn Jones). Director Michael Curtiz makes good use of the New Orleans setting but fails to mesh the show-biz fantasy with the underworld melodrama, and Presley's surly performance doesn't help much. Some stylized violence and sexual situations. A-III (PG)

King David (1985) For half its length, this is a superb biblical film in which the sex, violence, and pageantry usually emphasized in this genre do not obscure the central theme of God's intervention in humanity's messy affairs. However, the last half of director Bruce Beresford's work seems badly truncated, which, together with a miscast Richard Gere in the title role, make it a severely flawed film, but nonetheless one worth seeing. There is some nudity and considerable violence, but they are subordinated to the theme and not exploitative. A-III (PG-13)

King in New York, A (1957) Produced, written, and directed by Charles Chaplin, the movie is a rather mild satire of the 1950s witch hunts and black listings, as well as some of the foibles in American life. It is a less-than-profound work but a reminder of a past political hysteria that barred a great comedian from working in America. A-I (G)

King Kong (1933) The screen's best-remembered monster takes on New York City in a desperate attempt to regain the blonde beauty (Fay Wray) lost by the beast when captured on an uncharted island by an intrepid showman (Robert Armstrong). Produced and directed by Merian C. Cooper and Ernest B. Schoedsack, this classic adventure fantasy succeeds largely because of the giant ape's sympathetic treatment and Willis H. O'Brien's imaginative special effects in animating Kong and the prehistoric world of Skull Island. Scary situations and stylized violence, some of it quite brutal. A-II (br)

King Kong (1977) The Empire State Building and Fay Wray are in no danger of being outdone by the World Trade Towers and Jessica Lange in a moderately entertaining but uninspired remake of the 1933 classic. Director John Guillerman's lack of creative energy contrasts unfavorably with the naive vigor of the original. Some semi-nudity and graphic violence. A-III (PG)

King Kong Escapes (1968) Japanese monster movie directed by Inoshiro Honda has a modern setting but unwisely goes out of its way to try to duplicate a number of sequences from the 1933 original and comes up looking somewhat ludicrous. For the undemanding only. A-I (G)

King Kong Lives (1986) After an open-heart operation revives his comatose state, Kong returns to find a mate, father a child, and be killed in a better-safe-than-sorry military action. Needlessly detailed and extended scenes of bloodshed, both of the heart operation and fight sequences, and a very suggestive sexual encounter. A-III (PG-13)

King Kong vs. Godzilla (1963) Dubbed Japanese monster movie directed by Inoshiro Honda in which giant gorilla Kong is taken from his Pacific island home but escapes his captors just in time to save Tokyo from being destroyed by revived prehistoric dinosaur Godzilla. Rubber-suited monsters and the destruction of model sets. A-I (br)

King Lear (1971) Director Peter Brook's adaptation of Shakespeare's tragedy is a brilliant, stunning production, almost overwhelmingly powerful, owing to the combined strengths of the bold direction and the brilliance of a cast boasting Paul Scofield as Lear,

Irene Worth as Goneril, and Alan Webb as Gloucester. It stands as one of the screen's most striking homages to the Bard of Avon. A-II (GP)

King Murray (1969) Semi-documentary centers on Murray King, an overbearing, loud-mouthed Long Island insurance agent who caters exclusively to a wealthy clientele. Director Jonathan Gordon's fictionalized reenactment follows King through business deals, lunch breaks, and finally a Las Vegas excursion replete with obscene stories and the typical vulgarities of character the film suggests go hand-in-hand with a dehumanizing profession. O (nr)

King of Comedy, The (1983) Robert De Niro plays an aspiring standup comedian who kidnaps a famous talk-show host (Jerry Lewis) in order to obtain an appearance on his show. Director Martin Scorsese transforms an act of desperation into a black comedy in an offbeat and menacing study of a social misfit. Attempted seduction scene is done with restraint. A-III (PG)

King of Hearts (1966) Seriocomic commentary on the insanity of war makes its point in a WW I story of a sane British soldier (Alan Bates) who happens upon a town taken over by the inmates of a lunatic asylum after the villagers have fled. Directed by Philippe De Broca, the dubbed French production's awkward interplay of realism and fantasy just barely manages to avoid both sheer comedy and fresh insight. A-III (br)

King of Kings (1961) Stolid screen spectacular presents the life of Christ within the historical context of Jewish resistance to Roman rule. Uncomfortably cast in the title role is Jeffrey Hunter, though more effective are Siobhan McKenna as his mother, Robert Ryan as John the Baptist, Hurd Hatfield as Pilate, Rip Torn as Judas, and Harry Guardino as Barabbas. Directed by Nicholas Ray, the script is preoccupied with the period's political unrest but treats the Gospel account reverentially, if with more dramatic license than some might find acceptable. A-IV (br)

King of Marvin Gardens, The (1972) Jack Nicholson and Bruce Dern play two brothers who get together for a reunion in wintry Atlantic City to muse about their problems and wander around the near-deserted resort with girlfriends (Ellen Burstyn and Julia Anne Robinson) in tow. Directed by Bob Rafelson, nothing much happens, but the setting and situation seem to suggest that life is a game, and a fixed one at that. Several sexual scenes. A-IV (R)

King of Masks, The (1999) Operatic melodrama set in 1930s China, where an elderly artist discovers the scruffy street child he bought to continue his art is actually female, after which she is reduced to his devoted servant, but her actions accidentally put his life in mortal danger. Director Wu Tianming tugs on the heartstrings as the rejected child and the frustrated old man come to value love and sacrifice over gender and materialism in a well-acted, beautifully crafted tale. Subtitles. Fleeting juvenile nudity and an instance of rough language. A-II (nr)

King of New York (1990) Vigilante cops target a well-connected psychopath (Christopher Walken) who is killing off New York City's drug lords in order to take over the trade and use its profits to fund a children's hospital. Director Abel Ferrara's stylishly photographed night-time cityscapes mask a bleakly nihilistic vision of a doomed city where life is cheap, lawlessness is everywhere, and police readily resort to murder. Excessive violence, glamorized drug use, some nudity, and intermittent rough language. O (R)

King of the Grizzlies (1970) Disney adventure about a 1,300-hundred pound mountain bear who roams the Canadian Rockies, and his friend, a young Cree Indian of the bear clan, who must choose between his sympathy for the animal and his position as foreman of a cattle ranch. Ron Kelly directs with fine wildlife footage with a mildly dramatic story suitable for youngsters. A-I (G)

King of the Gypsies (1978) Young New York Gypsy (Eric Roberts) is appointed king of the clan by his grandfather (Sterling Hayden), passing over his father (Judd Hirsch), who hires two men to kill him. Sven Nykvist's beautifully photographed vision of a little-known world directed by Frank Pierson conveys a wholly negative portrait of Gypsy life characterized by rough language and brutal violence. O (R)

King of the Hill (1993) Depression-era drama in which an impoverished 12-year-old schoolboy (Jesse Bradford) lives by his wits out of a shabby St. Louis hotel room after his mom (Lisa Eichhorn) is put in a sanatorium, his kid brother (Cameron Boyd) is sent to live with an uncle, and his father (Jeroen Krabbe) goes on the road selling door-to-door. Writer-director Steven Soderburgh's adaptation of A.E. Hotchner's childhood memoir captures the pervasive hard times and growing desperation of its characters, while revealing the resourcefulness of a child coping courageously with basic survival and hopes of reuniting his family. A suicide, brief violence, and discreet sexual innuendo. A-II (PG-13)

King of the Khyber Rifles (1953) Disappointing tale of a British garrison on India's North-West Frontier, where an 1857 uprising by local mountain tribes is crushed by the half-caste British officer of the title (Tyrone Power) who leads his Moslem troopers into battle using knives rather than bite the pig-greased cartridges needed for their new Enfield rifles. Directed by Henry King, the slow-paced story centers on the inequities of British class consciousness and the evils of racial prejudice, but the treatment lacks subtlety and the characters are little more than tired stereotypes. Battlefield violence. A-I (br)

King of the Mountain (1981) Banal and pretentious movie whose anemic plot concerns the empty-headed romance between a woman singer and a young mechanic who loves to race his Porsche down a treacherous California road. Director Noel Nosseck celebrates the teen obsession with death-defying speed and takes a permissive attitude toward casual sex. A-III (PG)

King of the Wild Stallions (1958) Standard Western directed by R.G. Springsteen in which a cowboy (George Montgomery) and his old pard (Edgar Buchanan) save a widow (Diane Brewster) from losing her land to a crooked rancher. Youngsters may be more interested in scenes of the wild herd and the role of the widow's young son in capturing the horse of the title. Minimal stylized violence. A-I (br)

King, Queen, Knave (1975) Gawky, naive nephew (John Moulder-Brown) is initiated into the ways of love by his earthy aunt (Gina Lollobrigida), while his urbane uncle (David Niven) tends to his own affairs. Director Jerzy Skolimowski turns Vladimir Nabokov's novel into a sex farce lacking in humanity and humor. O (R)

King Ralph (1991) The throne of England is inherited by a goodhearted American slob (John Goodman) who chases a common shop-girl (Camille Coduri), much to the dismay of his most proper royal secretary (Peter O'Toole). Writer-director David S. Ward's clash-of-cultures comedy is a lightweight effort, equal parts affable and forgettable. Occasional vulgar expressions, double entendres, and flash of rear nudity. A-II (PG)

King Rat (1965) Japanese prisoner-of-war camp, with George Segal as the American opportunist of the title and James Fox as the British officer who tries to befriend him. Director Bryan Forbes's story of the human spirit under duress does not gloss over the rigors of captivity and its depiction of degradation is strong fare. A-III (br)

King Solomon's Mines (1937) Dated African adventure in which a veteran safari-guide (Cedric Hardwicke), his clients (John Loder and Roland Young), and a mysterious native (Paul Robeson) aid a young Irishwoman (Anna Lee) in searching for her father, who disappeared into the interior seeking the fabulous diamond mines of the title. Directed by Robert Stevenson from the H. Rider Haggard novel, the narrative builds to a rousing dramatic climax, as Robeson's claim to be his tribe's rightful king unleashes a civil war, and the diamond mines are buried in a volcanic eruption. Stylized violence and fleeting nudity. A-I (br)

King Solomon's Mines (1950) Rousing good version of the H. Rider Haggard adventure yarn about an Englishwoman (Deborah Kerr) who hires a guide (Stewart Granger) to search for her lost brother (Richard Carlson) in the African jungle, where they also find fabulous diamond mines. Directed by Compton Bennett and Andrew Marton, the movie's picturesque sights and colorful action make this a first-rate family safari. A-I (br)

King Solomon's Mines (1985) Richard Chamberlain stars in an extremely silly action-adventure spoof of the search for King Solomon's fabled diamond mines. Directed by J. Lee Thompson, the movie is not only exceedingly violent but also has unacceptable racial attitudes. O (PG-13)

King's Row (1942) Soapy melodrama from Henry Bellamann's novel about a young man (Robert Cummings) who grows up in the small town of the title, becomes a psychiatrist in pre-WW I Vienna, then returns to help his best friend (Ronald Reagan) cope with the loss of both legs in a rail-yard accident. Directed by Sam Wood, the story revolves around a number of troubled characters, not least a sadistic surgeon (Charles Coburn), a sour physician (Claude Rains), and his spooky daughter (Betty Field), as well as some noble women (Maria Ouspenskaya and Ann Sheridan), but the contrived proceedings are of less interest than the period's class distinctions and gender inequalities. Stylized violence and muted sexual innuendo. A-II (br)

Kingdom in the Clouds (1971) Rumanian fairytale about a young man who goes in search of a fabulous kingdom where no one ever grows old, survives various tests on the way, and at last wins the hand of the princess of the deathless kingdom. Adequately directed by Elisabeta Bostan, it has colorful characters in picturesque locales that will satisfy younger members of the audience. A-I (G)

Kingdom of the Spiders (1978) Complacent community in Arizona finds itself suddenly besieged by a horde of hungry mutant tarantulas. Director John Cardos's camp chiller features William Shatner and Tiffany Bolling trying to stop the revolt-of-nature nightmare in a fairly routine but mindless entertainment for the undemanding. A-II (PG)

Kingpin (1996) Dopey comedy in which a boozy, has-been bowling champ (Woody Harrelson) persuades a naive Amish bowling-prodigy (Randy Quaid) to compete in a million-dollar tournament, whose frontrunner (Bill Murray) had ruined the drunk's promising career years earlier. Directed by Peter and Bobby Farrelly, there is something to turn off nearly everyone in this occasionally funny hodgepodge of politically incorrect and scatological humor. Much tasteless humor, some stylized violence, brief sexual innuendo, and minimal profanity. A-III (PG-13/R)

Kings Go Forth (1958) Soggy romance set in 1944 on the French Riviera, where two GIs (Frank Sinatra and Tony Curtis) vie for the affection of a young mademoiselle (Natalie Wood) whose deceased father was an African-American jazz player. Director Delmer Daves alternates the romantic rivalry of the soldiers with their battlefield heroics, but the result is largely unconvincing. Wartime violence and romantic complications. A-II (br)

Kings of the Road (1976) German story about a movie-projector repairman and a hitchhiker who share their dissatisfaction with contemporary life and search for some way to change things. Director Wim Wenders's exploration of alienation reaches towards positive affirmation about the future. Some matter-of-fact nudity and a scene depicting a bodily function that would affront some viewers. A-IV (nr)

Kinjite: Forbidden Subjects (1989) When a Los Angeles detective (Charles Bronson) is ordered to find a missing Japanese girl, he must stifle his bigotry to help the girl's family get her back before a pimp (Juan Fernandez) turns her into a big-buck call girl. Director J. Lee Thompson plays up suggestions of exotic sex to titillate viewers and exploits the violence used to crush the baddies. Much gratuitous violence, rough language, and sexually suggestive scenes with some nudity. O (R)

Kipps (see **The Remarkable Mr. Kipps**)

Kismet (1955) Ponderous musical spectacle from the Broadway show about a cunning thief (Howard Keel) who outwits Bagdad's wicked vizier (Sebastian Cabot), thereby winning the affection of one of the vizier's bored wives (Delores Gray), while the love-smitten caliph (Vic Damone) determines to wed the thief's daughter (Ann Blyth). Directed by Vincente Minnelli, the muddled plot has some amusing buffoonery but is otherwise largely inert, leaving viewers to be entertained by the movie's elaborate Arabian Nights settings and use of Borodin's haunting themes for songs such as "Stranger in Paradise." Some sexual innuendo and occasional menace. A-II (br)

Kiss, The (1988) Cliched vampire movie about a curse passed down from aunts to nieces that makes a New York teenager (Meredith Salenger) the target of her afflicted aunt from the Belgian Congo (Joanna Pacula). Directed by Pen Densham, there is much grisly violence, nudity within several graphic sex scenes, and some rough language. O (R)

Kiss Before Dying, A (1956) Slick thriller in which a greedy college youth (Robert Wagner) kills his pregnant girlfriend (Joanne Woodward) after learning she'll be disinherited by her wealthy father (George Macready), then turns to romancing her sister (Virginia Leith), until a criminologist (Jeffrey Hunter) gets wise. Directed by Gerd Oswald, the suspense involved in the first murder is quite effective, though the tension slackens considerably as the proceedings grow increasingly contrived till the villain is paid in kind. Stylized violence, some intense menace, and sexual situations. A-III (br)

Kiss Before Dying, A (1991) Refusing to believe that her twin sister committed suicide, a young bride (Sean Young) uncovers a trail of murders that lead back to her own husband (Matt Dillon). Writer-director James Dearden delivers an engrossing thriller, carefully scripted, sleekly shot, and nicely acted, but the death scenes are unnecessarily gruesome. Some gory violence, several bedroom scenes with brief nudity, and minimal rough language. A-III (R)

Kiss in the Dark, A (1949) Mild romantic comedy directed by Delmer Daves in which a self-absorbed concert pianist (David Niven) gets a new outlook on life after investing in a New York apartment building with an eccentric landlord (Victor Moore) and an odd mix of tenants, including a photographer's model (Jane Wyman) with a jealous boyfriend (Wayne Morris). Intermittently amusing fish-out-of-water premise with the usual romantic complications. A-II (br)

Kiss Me Goodbye (1982) Dull, plodding remake of a popular Brazilian sex farce in which an about-to-be-married widow (Sally Field) is haunted by the ghost of her dead husband (James Caan) who tries to scare off the fiancé (Jeff Bridges). Directed by Robert Mulligan, the situation is so poorly contrived as to be embarrassing. Restrained sex scene. A-III (PG)

Kiss Me Kate (1953) Halting version of Cole Porter's musical comedy about the backstage bickering between husband and wife (Kathryn Grayson and Howard Keel) starring in a Broadway production of Shakespeare's *The Taming of the Shrew*. Director George Sidney gets lost in low-comedy routines with an aspiring starlet (Ann Miller) and a gangster duo (Keenan Wynn and James Whitmore), while Porter's musical numbers are squandered in raucous style. Sexual innuendo and domestic turmoil. A-III (br)

Kiss of Death (1947) Tough crime story about a crook (Victor Mature) who informs on his gang after they harm his family, but he needs more than police protection when a crazy killer (Richard Widmark) comes gunning for him. Though it's a fairly standard melodrama of the bad-man-goes-straight variety, director Henry Hathaway achieves a suitably gritty atmosphere by filming on the mean streets of New York City, and Widmark's performance as the gunman with a maniacal laugh is still chilling. Some nasty stylized violence. A-II (br)

Kiss of Death (1995) Dark, hardboiled melodrama in which an ex-con (David Caruso) fights for his life after being pressured by a ruthless prosecutor (Stanley Tucci) into providing evidence against a psychotic gangster (Nicolas Cage), whose cunning lawyer promptly gets the charges dropped. Director Barbet Schroeder's gritty crime thriller forgoes the understated aura of danger in the 1947 movie of the same title in favor of a sleazy atmosphere charged with violence as the ex-con struggles to outwit crass lowlifes on both sides of the law. Some nasty violence, recurring topless barroom nudity, and much rough language. A-IV (R)

Kiss of Evil (see: **Kiss of the Vampire**)

Kiss of Fire (1955) Soppy historical romance directed by Joseph M. Newman is set in 1700 New Mexico, where a notorious brigand (Jack Palance) agrees to guide a Spanish princess (Barbara Rush) and her small entourage through hostile Comanche territory, but the journey's dangers are compounded by traitorous Spanish soldiers and the growing attraction between the leads. Stylized violence and romantic complications. A-II (br)

Kiss of the Spider Woman (1985) Brazilian political prisoner (Raul Julia) shares a cell with a relatively flamboyant homosexual (William Hurt), who helps both of them pass the time by giving detailed descriptions of old Hollywood movies. Much musing about politics and sex, about verities of love and of betrayal, but there is not enough intelligence and wit in the script to carry off the high purpose that Argentinean director Hector Babenco obviously had in mind. Mature subject matter. A-IV (R)

Kiss of the Vampire (1962) British horror movie set in a remote province of pre-WW I Austria, where English newlyweds stumble into a nest of aristocratic vampires from which they are extracted by a professor (Noel Willman) versed in the black arts. Directed by Don Sharp, the eerie proceedings promise more than they deliver, though the climax has some chilling moments. Stylized violence and sexual innuendo. A-II (br)

Kiss or Kill (1997) Australian chase thriller in which a youthful pair of thieves (Frances O'Connor and Matt Day) skip town after one of their victims dies, then, while fleeing pursuing police through the vast vistas of the outback, several other murders occur, causing each to fear the other is a compulsive killer. Writer-director Bill Bennett fashions a dark but stylish crime movie out of a quirky plot and even quirkier characters, but its attempt to earn some sympathy for the young fugitives falls flat. Stylized violence and menace, sexual situations, a flash of nudity, recurring rough language, and occasional profanity. A-IV (R)

Kiss the Blood Off My Hands (1948) Tediously dark thriller about an American seaman (Burt Lancaster) hunted by the police after accidentally killing a man in post-war London, then befriended by an idealistic woman (Joan Fontaine) who helps him refashion his life, until a nasty blackmailer (Robert Newton) turns up. Director Norman Foster treats the narrative in such portentous fashion that the overacting becomes more tiresome than the improbable plot twists. Stylized violence and menace. A-II (br)

Kiss the Girls (1997) Lurid thriller in which a police psychologist (Morgan Freeman) hunts down a serial killer holding his niece and other young women, one of whom (Ashley Judd) escapes to join in the cop's desperate race to find the psycho and his prey. Director Gary Fleder's formula police drama is moderately suspenseful but rather brutal in its depiction of life-and-death confrontations. Some vicious violence, frequent rough language, and a few instances of profanity. A-IV (R)

Kiss the Girls and Make Them Die (1966) Failed Italian spy spoof about a CIA agent (Michael Connors) on the trail of a power-mad industrialist (Raf Vallone) who has developed a satellite which can render the entire world sterile. Directed by Henry Levin, the result is largely unamusing and mildly sexually suggestive. A-III (br)

Kiss Them for Me (1957) Flat, unamusing comedy directed by Stanley Donen in which WW II Navy pilots (Cary Grant, Ray Walston, and Larry Blyden) find romance (Suzy Parker and Jayne Mansfield) while getting into assorted troubles on leave in San Francisco. Sexual innuendo, marital complications, and alcoholic excess. A-III (br)

Kissin' Cousins (1964) Silly Elvis Presley vehicle about rebellious Tennessee mountaineers blocking the Army's plan to build an ICBM missile site in the Great Smoky Mountains. Directed by Gene Nelson, the dumb yokel humor is tiresome, the songs forgettable, and Elvis is doubly bad in dual roles. Sexual innuendo. A-III (br)

Kissing a Fool (1998) Slack romantic comedy in which an engaged playboy (David Schwimmer) decides to see if his fiancé (Mili Avital) will be faithful to him by asking his best friend (Jason Lee) to try to seduce her. Director Doug Ellin's crass romantic triangle is utterly predictable with few comic sparks along its tired route. A live-in relationship, drug references, occasional profanity, and much rough language. A-III (R)

Kissing Bandit, The (1948) Witless musical comedy set in Spanish-ruled California, where the bookish son (Frank Sinatra) of a famous bandit reluctantly agrees to lead his father's old gang, then falls in love with the governor's daughter (Kathryn Grayson), and winds up masquerading as the king's envoy. Directed by Laslo Benedek, the silly proceedings never jell into anything more than a weak vehicle for its bemused star. Romantic complications. A-II (br)

Kitchen Toto, The (1988) A 12-year-old Kikuyu boy (Edwin Mahinda) is tragically caught between his devotion to a kind British police chief (Bob Peck) and the 1950 terrorist Mau Maus fighting to liberate Kenya from British rule. Director Harry Hook shows how children are victimized by political strife. Some grisly violence and an adulterous affair. A-III (PG-13)

Kitten with a Whip (1964) Tawdry cautionary tale directed by Douglas Heyes in which a crafty 17-year-old delinquent (Ann-Margret) threatens to accuse a hapless San Diego businessman (John Forsythe) of molesting her unless he drives her and two threatening young men across the Mexican border, with dire results. Stylized violence, unconvincing menace, and sexual situations. A-III (br)

Kitty (1945) Droll tale of a 1783 London guttersnipe (Paulette Goddard) befriended by a cynical schemer (Ray Milland) and his eccentric aunt (Constance Collier), who turn her into such a proper lady with so many suitors that she ultimately becomes a duchess. Directed by Mitchell Leisen, the Pygmalion story offers some wry twists as the woman's romantic adventures overcome the oppressive gulf separating aristocrats and commoners. Sexual situations and romantic complications. A-III (br)

Kitty Foyle (1940) Subtitled "The Natural History of a Woman," the dated tearjerker spins the tale of a "white-collar girl" (Ginger Rogers) torn between the rich, handsome man of her dreams (Dennis Morgan) and the steady, down-to-earth beau (James Craig) who wants to marry her. Directed by Sam Woods, Rogers won an Oscar in the role of a woman who refuses to compromise her working-class principles to the upper-class snobbery of Philadelphia mainliners. Sexual situations and innuendo. A-III (br)

Klansman, The (1974) Adaptation of William Bradford Huie's novel about white-garbed fanatics set upon preserving racial purity by stopping a voter registration rally. Director Terence Young and his cast (Richard Burton, Lee Marvin, and O.J. Simpson) can do nothing with a dated scenario placed in a contemporary setting. It is an irresponsible premise for a repellent motion picture that makes rape, castration, murder, and racist terror into spectator sports. O (R)

Klondike Fury (1942) Hokey low-budget melodrama directed by William K. Howard in which a pilot (Edmund Lowe) crashes in the Canadian wilderness and spends the winter in a remote trading post, where, in order to save the life a brain tumor victim, he reveals his past as a brain surgeon who quit because of a malpractice suit. Romantic complications. A-II (br)

Klute (1971) Taut thriller about a savvy-yet-pathetic call-girl (Jane Fonda) and an unruffled, methodical private eye (Donald Sutherland), whose lives intersect when he comes to New York to search for a missing friend and uncovers a sadistic murderer (Charles Cioffi). Director Alan J. Pakula takes a serious, unflinching view of his characters, their actions, and the dark world they inhabit. Challenging subject matter but not treated exploitatively. A-IV (R)

Knickerbocker Holiday (1944) Lightweight version of the Kurt Weill-Maxwell Anderson musical comedy about Peter Stuyvesant (Charles Coburn), the peg-legged governor of 1647 New Amsterdam, whose political conniving is thwarted by an uprising led by a gadfly printer (Nelson Eddy). Directed by Harry Joe Brown, the stagy production hampers the story's pace, but the result is worth seeing for its droll humor and enjoyable musical numbers, especially Coburn's "September Song." Comic violence and romantic complications. A-II (br)

Knife in the Head (1980) Swiss drama in which a totally apolitical scientist (Bruno Gans) becomes the political pawn of leftists and police while recovering from a police gunshot wound which has left him an amnesiac. Director Reinhard Hauff focuses on the man's lonely struggle to regain his identity and personality in an alienated world. Violence and frank treatment of sex. A-IV (nr)

Knightriders (1981) Writer-director George A. Romero's lengthy and over-ambitious attempt to recreate the Arthurian legend in the saga of a troupe of daredevils who joust on motorcycles instead of horses. The idea is promising and the acting is appealing enough, but the plot is simple-minded at best, with too little action and too much gratuitous sex. O (R)

Knights of the Round Table (1953) Stiff costume drama about the rise of Camelot and its fall after Lancelot (Robert Taylor) is banished by Arthur (Mel Ferrer) because of his love for Guinevere (Ava Gardner). Director Richard Thorpe's picture of King Arthur's court is pretty but lifeless, save for the villainy of Modred (Stanley Baker) and some battle scenes. The ideals of chivalry are wrapped up in empty spectacle and stylized violence. A-I (br)

Knock Off (1998) In this high-tech, low-concept action-thriller, a crook-turned-businessman (Jean-Claude Van Damme) battles renegade American and Russian agents using Hong Kong as their base for terrorizing the world with miniature super-bombs. Directed by Tsui Hark, the result is a shoddy piece of merchandise which doesn't bother trying to make any sense of its contrived plot, stock characters, and cliched situations, all of which serve only to set up the mindless violence of unimaginative and tiresomely predictable action scenes. Excessive and occasionally graphic violence, some sexual innuendo, foul language, and occasional profanity. O (R)

Knock on Wood (1954) Standard Danny Kaye comedy in which he plays a troubled ventriloquist on a European tour, where he falls in love with a psychiatrist (Mai Zetterling), gets involved unknowingly with rival spies, and winds up wanted for murder by the London police. Written, produced, and directed by Norman Panama and Melvin Frank, the thin plot serves as a vehicle for typical Kaye routines in an Irish pub, an automobile showroom, and, the comedy highlight, an on-stage ballet performance. Some stylized violence and romantic complications. A-I (br)

Knockout, The (1941) Routine melodrama about the rise and fall of a prizefighter (Arthur Kennedy), his faithful wife (Olympe Bradna), faithless friend (Virginia Field), and crooked manager (Anthony Quinn). Directed by William Clemens, it's well-played but telegraphs all its punches. Stylized violence and mild romantic complications. A-II (br)

Knocks at My Door (1996) Political thriller set in a repressive Latin-American country, where two nuns risk their lives by sheltering a hunted rebel, then are betrayed and have to decide whether to renounce him and go free or defy the evil regime and be executed. Directed by Alejandro Saderman, the 1993 Venezuelan production creates a realistic picture of two women religious whose piety deepens their commitment to helping the poor and the oppressed. Subtitles. Stylized violence and menace in a justice context. A-II (nr)

Knute Rockne, All American (1940) Pat O'Brien gives a sturdy, likeable performance as Rockne (1888-1931), the dedicated football coach whose winning teams made the Fighting Irish of Notre Dame a national favorite after WW I. Director Lloyd Bacon pays equal attention to Rockne's qualities on and off the field, both as devoted family man and charismatic molder of youths into men, the most memorable example of which has to do with halfback George Gipp (Ronald Reagan). Inspiring period portrait of a legendary coach who believed in the character-building values of collegiate competition. A-I (br)

Kolya (1997) Heartwarming Czech drama set in 1989 Prague, where a womanizing, middle-aged cellist (Zdenek Sverak) marries a Russian woman who only wants a visa and promptly moves to West Germany, leaving him with her five-year-old son (Andrej Chalimon). Also scripted by Sverak and directed by his son, Jan Sverak, the picture convincingly captures the gradual transformation of a self-centered ladies' man into a caring stepfather willing to make great personal sacrifices for the child's welfare. Subtitles. Restrained bedroom scenes. A-III (PG-13)

Kona Coast (1968) Lurid melodrama with Richard Boone playing a brutally vengeful father out to crush the dope peddlers responsible for his daughter's death. The lush Hawaiian setting is the movie's only asset as director Lamont Johnson's treatment of drug trafficking lacks substance and credibility. Tends to condone taking the law violently into one's own hands. O (br)

Kon Tiki (1951) Documentary of the 5,000-mile sea voyage made by archeologist Thor Heyerdahl and five colleagues, which ends in Polynesia 101 days after leaving Peru on a balsa-wood raft. Though there's plenty of excitement along the way with weather, whales, and sharks, the journey is more than an adventure, as it was undertaken to prove that Incan balsa rafts were able to cross the ocean 1,500 years ago, making the Incas a possible source of the culture found in the islands of the Pacific. A-I (br)

Konga (1961) Cheesy British monster movie directed by John Lamont in which a mad botanist (Michael Gough) uses a plant extract to accelerate the growth of a chimpanzee until it reaches the size of a house, then becomes testy and stalks off for a stroll through London until the British Army arrives. Fantasy violence, hokey menace, and sexual innuendo. A-II (br)

Korczak (1991) A humanitarian doctor (Wojtek Pszoniak) heroically struggles to save the lives of 200 doomed orphans in Warsaw's Jewish ghetto during the Nazi occupation. A moving testament to one person's indomitable spirit, Polish director Andrzej Wajda's starkly powerful chronicle of this horrific fact-based story is at odds with its surreal fantasy ending. Subtitles. Brief wartime violence and shots of discarded nude corpses. A-II (nr)

Kotch (1971) Walter Matthau captures to perfection the eccentric but loveable grandfather who adores children and befriends an unwed teenage mother (Deborah Winters) when his son (Charles Aldman) places him in an old-age home. Directed by Jack Lemmon, it's an old-fashioned sentimental melodrama, full of warmth and fun, but avoids some of the serious implications of the situation. A-III (GP)

Krakatoa, East of Java (1969) Lavish disaster movie built around the 1883 eruption of a small volcanic island in the Dutch East Indies features the skipper (Maximilian Schell) of a vessel searching for sunken treasure but also transporting a gang of convicts to an island prison. Directed by Bernard L. Kowalski, the grand scale of the eruption is awesome on the big screen, but the cliche-studded story that precedes it is a yawner. Its terribly melodramatic dialogue and some romantic liaisons make it less appropriate for youngsters. A-II (G)

Kramer vs. Kramer (1979) Superficial treatment of child custody battle between angry wife (Meryl Streep) and resentful husband (Dustin Hoffman). Director Robert Benton conveys the tragedy of divorce by putting the emphasis on the father's attempts at parenting but neglects the child's perspective. Some harsh language and a sex scene witnessed by the young child. A-IV (PG)

Krays, The (1990) Harrowing fact-based drama about twin brothers (Gary and Martin Kemp) who ruthlessly murder their way to the top of the London crime scene in the 1960s while maintaining a slavish devotion to their overprotective mother (Billie Whitelaw). With excellent performances by the Kemp brothers, director Peter Medak's coldly fascinating portrait captures the twins' rise from lower-class origins and domineering females without glamorizing the lurid crimes that eventually caught up with them. Occasional graphic violence, homosexual innuendo, intermittent rough language, and a flash of nudity. A-III (R)

Kremlin Letter, The (1970) Screen version of Noel Behn's spy novel about a scramble among the world's intelligence agencies to obtain a letter outlining US policy in case of war between Russia and Red China. Director John Huston has fashioned a complex, action-packed and occasionally very cruel and violent Cold War thriller whose twists and turns leave nearly all its characters, which include Patrick O'Neal, Richard Boone, Nigel Green, Dean Jagger, and George Sanders, either murdered or revealed as double or even triple agents. A-III (PG)

Krippendorf's Tribe (1998) Dreadful comic misfire in which an anthropologist (Richard Dreyfuss) squanders his six-figure research grant, then pretends to have discovered an unknown primitive tribe by filming his children in bogus puberty rituals. Directed by Todd Holland, the crass comedy has the whole family happily profiting from their dishonesty and feeling smug about it. Positive view of major theft, fraud, constant lying, and a one-night stand, as well as crude sexual references and an instance of profanity. O (PG-13)

Kronos (1957) Routine sci-fi thriller in which a scientist (Jeff Morrow) attempts to destroy the monstrous title device sent from another planet to drain earth of all its energy, despite interference from the scientist's boss (John Emery), who's under the aliens' control. Directed by Kurt Neumann, the special effects are low-budget but effective, especially the multi-storied, mechanical Kronos and its four-pillar locomotion. More menace than violence. A-I (br)

Krull (1983) Director Peter Yates cannot quite bring into focus his tale of a mythical land, an enchanted weapon, and an evil monster. There are too many characters (a cyclops, a wizard, a spiderwoman, a magician, a seer, etc.), too many illogical jumps in the plot, and the familiar quest to save a damsel in distress has been done better before by others. A-II (PG)

Krush Groove (1985) Backstage saga of the rap-music scene, featuring some dynamic young performers under the direction of Michael Schultz. Disarming and energetic, the movie nevertheless suffers from a weak story-line and the very specialized nature of music that is for rap fans on1y. Some vulgar language. A-II (R)

Kuffs (1992) Addle-brained comedy about an irresponsible young man (Christian Slater) who becomes a cop to avenge the murder of an older brother (Bruce Boxleitner) killed in the line of duty. Director Bruce A. Evans uses a clumsy Slater-talking-to-the-camera technique as moronic humor trivializes the graphic shootouts. Excessive violence, positive portrayal of vigilante justice, premarital and adulterous affairs, and minimal rough language. O (PG-13)

Kull the Conqueror (1997) Brawny action-fantasy in which a soldier-turned-king (Kevin Sorbo) is cheated out of his kingdom by a sorceress (Tia Carrere), then regains the throne with the help of a beautiful slave (Karina Lombard). Director John Nicolella's sword-and-sorcery tale has some visual appeal, but its overacting and stilted dialogue are less than fantastic. Recurring stylized violence, brief bedroom scenes, some sexual innuendo, and several crude expressions. A-III (PG-13)

Kundun (1997) Dramatization of the early life of Tibet's 14th Dalai Lama (Tenzin Thuthob Tsarong), whose faith in nonviolence is put to the test when Red China occupies his country in 1950, his appeals to the West go unanswered, and the growing repression of his people forces him into exile in 1959 at age 24. Director Martin Scorsese provides an evocative picture of an ancient people whose mountainous isolation protects them from the changing world outside until suddenly invaded by a 20th-century army, but the result succeeds more as spectacle than as human drama, political history, or spiritual experience. Scenes of violence in a meaningful context. A-II (PG-13)

Kung Fu Master! (1989) French import about an implausible infatuation between a 40-year-old divorced mother (Jane Birkin) and the 15-year-old friend (Mathieu Demy) of her adolescent daughter. Director Agnes Varda provides no clue to this woman's amoral obsession for a youth who's obsessed with the "Kung Fu Master!" video game. Numerous AIDS warnings are inexplicable public service messages. No on-screen sex, but the cuddling and chaste kisses are unsettling. O (R)

Kurt and Courtney (1998) One-sided documentary views the 1994 suicide of grunge-rock star Kurt Cobain through interviews questioning the role his performer wife, Courtney Love, may have played in his death. Director Nick Broomfield trots out a bizarre assortment of mostly lowlifes to speculate on the couple's drug-addled relationship in what comes across as an scathing portrait of Love, who infuriated the filmmaker by attempting to have the documentary's funding halted. Many substance abuse and sexual references, threats of violence, much rough language, and occasional profanity. A-IV (nr)

Kwaidan (1966) Visually rich Japanese fantasy retelling three ghost stories from the days of the samurai will engross, if not enthrall, viewers. Directed by Masaki Kobayashi, the narratives are so simple, direct, and carefully paced that one is lulled into acceptance of their eerie logic. Based on stories by Lafcadio Hearn, an American writer who lived in Japan at the turn of the century, the movie helps one see why he found their culture so fascinating. Subtitles. Stylized violence and ghostly visitations. A-II (br)

L

L.A. Confidential (1997) Stylish cop drama set in 1950s Los Angeles, where three police detectives (Kevin Spacey, Russell Crowe, and Guy Pearce) working on apparently unrelated homicides begin to see all may be related to a ring of corrupt officials. Directed by Curtis Hanson, the darkly cynical story is densely plotted with murders most foul as the detectives work their way through a miasma of chicanery and deceit. Recurring violence, fleeting nudity, recurring sexual innuendo, some profanity, and intermittent rough language. A-IV (R)

L.A. Story (1991) A TV weatherman (Steve Martin) is chased by a bouncy blonde (Sarah Jessica Parker) while he, with a little help from a magical freeway sign, pursues a reserved English journalist (Victoria Tennant). Directed by Mick Jackson from Martin's script, the result takes a wry view of the trendy populace of Los Angeles, which proves more diverting than the fairly bland fantasy-romance story line. Casual attitude toward premarital sex and minimal rough language. A-III (PG-13)

L-Shaped Room, The (1963) British drama about an unwed French mother-to-be (Leslie Caron) who moves into a shabby London rooming house, gets involved with its odd lot of tenants, especially a would-be writer (Tom Bell), and broods about having her baby. Director Bryan Forbes handles the young woman's rejection of abortion and hopeful acceptance of the future with sensitivity while also probing the unconventional lives of her fellow lodgers, including a jazz musician (Brock Peters), a couple of prostitutes, and a lesbian actress. A mixed bag of moral muddlement and insight. A-IV (br)

La Bamba (1987) Pop biographical homage to teenage rock-singer Ritchie Valens (Lou Diamond Phillips). Director Luis Valdez sets Valens's meteoric success and tragic death against the poverty and oppression of the barrios of Southern California and ethnic bias of middle-class suburbia. Effective study of Valens's struggle against cultural stereotyping and his relationship with his wayward brother (Esai Morales). Scenes of domestic violence, a brief instance of nudity, and some profanity are overcome by the film's overall inspirational tone and depiction of positive youthful aspirations. A-II (PG-13)

La Boca del Lobo (1989) Gripping Peruvian production about a civilian atrocity committed by government forces in their struggle to crush the rebel movement known as the Shining Path. Director Francisco J. Lombardi centers the narrative on a young city-bred recruit (Antonio Vega) whose growing sympathy for the Indians being victimized by both army and terrorists causes him to refuse to obey the order to fire on a group of peaceful villagers. Some graphic depictions of violence. A-III (nr)

La Bohème (1965) Puccini's opera as performed on stage by the La Scala Opera company with musical direction by Herbert Von Karajan and stage direction by Franco Zeffirelli. The singing apparently was recorded separately, with the result that the excitement associated with a live performance is missing. A-II (br)

La Bohème (1989) Lackluster, updated adaptation of the Puccini opera about the frail, impoverished Mimi (Barbara Hendricks), whose love affair with the penniless poet Rodolfo (Luca Canonici) is doomed by her health, but not before we hear them sing of love, jealousy, and heartbreak, and watch as their playful bohemian friends fall in and out of love. Unimaginatively directed by Luigi Comencini, the classic work is plagued with bad lighting, stiff performances, and choppy editing. Implied sexual liaisons. A-III (nr)

La Cage aux Folles (1979) Transvestite nightclub owner (Ugo Tognazzi) lives with the club's revue star (Michel Serrault), a situation he wishes to conceal from his son, who returns to announce his marriage to the daughter of a sanctimonious town official. Directed by Edouard Molinaro, this French farce revels in comic deceptions and misconceptions using homosexuality as the context for poking fun at moralistic hypocrites, flamboyant transvestites, and society in general. Subtitles. Comic sexual situations not for all tastes. A-IV (R)

La Cage aux Folles II (1981) Sequel to the popular French comedy about a homosexual couple isn't up to the original. But thanks to Ugo Tognazzi and Michel Serrault, re-creating their original roles, director Edouard Molinaro's movie has some diverting moments before getting bogged down in an improbable plot that has the heroes becoming involved in a counterespionage operation. Subtitles. Comic sexual situations not for all tastes. A-IV (R)

La Cérémonie (1996) Hired to keep house for a wealthy family of four (headed by Jacqueline Bisset and Jean-Pierre Cassel), a secretive young woman (Sandrine Bonnaire) is befriended by a sulky postal clerk (Isabelle Huppert), who turns the domestic against her employers with startling results. Veteran French director Claude Chabrol constructs a Hitchcock-like thriller with a sense of anticipated dread that builds to an unanticipated conclusion. Subtitles. Some gory violence. A-III (nr)

La Chamade (1969) Bland, ménage-à-trois melodrama with Catherine Deneuve as mistress to both wealthy graying Michel Piccoli and young, handsome, and not-so-wealthy Roger Van Hool. Adapted from a Francoise Sagan novel and directed by Alain Cavalier, there is little to recommend in its frothy cliches, stock characters, and passionless bedroom scenes, but its moral meaning is clear in showing how such vapid relationships are unfulfilling and provide no real meaning or stability to one's life. A-IV (R)

La Chévre (1982) When a French industrialist's accident-prone daughter disappears in Mexico, he tries to find her by teaming a veteran detective (Gerard Depardieu) with an accountant (Pierre Richard) as unlucky as the missing young woman. Directed by Francois Veber, the wacky comedy has some very funny moments as the tough detective comes to learn that bad luck can be turned to good. Subtitles. Stylized violence, sexual innuendo, and occasional crude language. A-III (nr)

La Chienne (1976) A drab accountant and henpecked husband (Michel Simon) falls hopelessly in love with a crass prostitute who is only interested in getting every cent he has. A familiar story of passion and ruin, the 1931 French production is of interest chiefly for Simon's rich performance and as an example of the early sound work of director Jean Renoir. A-III (nr)

La Collectionneuse (1971) French story of a stuffy young wastrel (Patrick Bauchau) who meets an attractive woman (Haydee Politoff) staying at his friend's country estate, becomes totally infatuated, but, in the end, through a quirk of fate and not entirely of his own volition, he rejects her. Director Eric Rohmer's third in his series of *Six Moral Tales* presents a picture of a not very sympathetic male chauvinist who has to rationalize the woman's lack of interest in him. A-III (nr)

La Discréte (1992) A wily publisher (Maurice Garrel) convinces a self-important writer (Fabrice Luchini) to select a woman at random, make her (Judith Henry) fall in love with him, at which point he will seduce and abandon her, turning over the intimate details for publication. French director Christian Vincent's mildly comic movie is a sluggish, talky affair peppered with small charms along the way, primarily in Ms. Henry's gently dignified performance. Subtitles. An unmarried sexual relationship and several promiscuous references. A-III (nr)

La Dolce Vita (1960) Lengthy episodic Italian drama about a troubled journalist (Marcello Mastroianni) who mingles in the circles of Rome's high society (including Anita Ekberg, Anouk Aimee, and Alain Cuny), alternately fascinated, bemused, and repelled by what he observes. Director Federico Fellini's crowded picture of the moral ills as well as the human foibles and positive values of various segments of Italian society mixes realism with satire and a tragic sense of wasted lives. Subtitles. Critical treatment of immoral situations. A-IV (br)

La Femme Infidele (1969) French director Claude Chabrol manages to generate suspense with many layers of tension, ambiguity, and passion seething under a placid surface. Here he examines the apparently happy suburban marriage of insurance man Michel Bouquet and wife Stephane Audran, but the husband's growing suspicions of his wife's infidelity are confirmed, and he confronts and kills the other man (Maurice Ronet). Though Chabrol's style is coolly detached, viewers will be caught up in an inquiry into the human potential for evil. A-III (R)

La Femme Nikita (1991) A convicted killer (Anne Parillaud) working as an assassin for the French government wants out when she falls for an innocent store-clerk (Jean-Hughes Anglade). Writer-director Luc Besson's sleek action-thriller goes somewhat overboard on violence during the protagonist's journey to redemption via the healing power of love. Subtitles. Some grisly violence, a live-in relationship, flash of nudity, and occasional rough language. A-IV (R)

La Fuga (1966) Italian dramatization of the psychiatric treatment of a disturbed 27-year-old wife whose marital problems are related to latent lesbian tendencies. Directed by Paolo Spinola, the effort is well-intentioned, but the graphic treatment of several sexual scenes is excessively explicit. O (br)

La Grande Illusion (see: **Grand Illusion**)

La Grande Vadrouille (see: 1969's **Don't Look Now**)

La Lectrice (1989) French literary comedy in which a woman (Miou-Miou) fantasizes that she is the heroine of a novel about a woman who makes a living as a professional reader. Directed by Michel Deville, the dual role leads to some delightful vignettes about the woman's interaction with her eccentric clients and the literary works she deems suitable for each. The charm wears off, however, when she becomes both reader and sex surrogate to a frustrated client. Several gratuitous sexual encounters. O (R)

La Passion de Notre Seigneur Jésus-Christ (1905) Though better known for one-reel crime melodramas, movie pioneer Ferdinand Zecca (1863-1947) also produced this two-reel (about 30 minutes) dramatization of Christ's Passion. Distributed by Pathé, France's leading motion-picture company, it was reportedly quite popular in its time and was notable, according to film historian Georges Sadoul, for its "rudimentary" camera movements. (No ratings)

La Peau Douce (see: **The Soft Skin**)

La Prisonnière (1969) French import about a woman who finds herself first intrigued by, and then hopelessly attracted to, an art dealer (Laurent Terzieff), who proves to be a sadistic voyeur incapable of love. Director Henri-Georges Clouzot affects a detached, noncommittal attitude toward his subject, forcing viewers to share the voyeurism which his characters are experiencing. O (nr)

La Promesse (1997) Belgian drama in which a venal contractor (Olivier Gourmet) lets one of his illegal alien employees die rather than hospitalize him, resulting in his teenage son (Jeremie Renier) attempting to help the dead man's wife and infant without turning in his dad to the authorities. Directed by Jean-Pierre and Luc Dardenne, the movie probes the good and dark sides of its characters while creating a powerful portrait of desperate immigrants and those who callously exploit them. Subtitles. Brief violence and a few instances of rough language. A-II (nr)

La Rupture (1975) Contrived French mystery about a woman (Stephane Audran) seeking a divorce from her deranged husband in order to protect herself and her child, without realizing that her rich father-in-law (Michel Bouquet) will stop at nothing to get custody of his grandson. Director Claude Chabrol has used the theme of social decadence and moral corruption to better effect in other movies, but this one is little more than an interesting exercise in the modern gothic imagination. A-III (nr)

La Salamandre (1972) Engrossing Swiss drama about the collaboration between a journalist and a fiction writer on a television play based on a recent case of a young woman's shooting of a relative, but when they finally meet her (Bulle Ogier) she is too chameleon-like for them to continue the project. Director Alain Tanner's story seems on the surface an amusing anecdote about whether imagination or fact reveals the truth better, but underneath is the question of survival in a destructive post-industrial society where by movie's end it is clear that the woman has made the most progress toward self-liberation. Mature themes and treatment. A-III (nr)

La Scorta (1994) Compelling Italian drama focusing on four government bodyguards (led by Enrico Lo Verso) assigned to protect a crusading judge (Carlo Cecchi) from the bullets of Mafia hit-men while he investigates a case that implicates corrupt officials in his own department who will stop at nothing to have him silenced. Director Ricky Tognazzi puts in human terms the price being paid by brave individuals in the arduous effort to crush generations of mob-related activities in Sicily. Subtitles. Brief violence, much menace, and intermittent rough language. A-III (nr)

La Strada (1956) Two-bit strongman (Anthony Quinn) adds a simple-minded peasant (Giulietta Masina) to his circus act, treating her badly until a tragic encounter with a bantering acrobat (Richard Basehart) who tries to help her. Italian director Federico Fellini's somber picture of lost souls on the back-roads of life has its emotional center in Masina's Chaplinesque performance as the poor waif struggling to keep her spirit from being crushed by the brute she serves. Subtitles. Some stylized violence and brutalizing conditions of life. A-III (br)

La Tia Tula (1965) Delicate Spanish tale of a beautiful woman (Aurora Bautista) who rejects the love of her late sister's husband, then comes to regret her proud aloofness too late. Director Miguel Picazo treats the woman's fears of marriage in the context of her cultural and religious upbringing, investing the character with a tragic human dimension that earns respect and leaves a sense of loss. Subtitles. Sexual situations, including an attempted rape. A-III (br)

La Vie de Chateau (1967) Set in Normandy just before D-Day, the story is about a wealthy orchard farmer (Philippe Noiret), his lively wife (Catherine Deneuve), a lovelorn leader of the Resistance (Henri Garein), and a detachment of German soldiers quartered there. Some haphazard heroics take place on the beautiful old estate before it finally becomes the landing point for Allied paratroopers. A-II (br)

La Visita (1966) Middle-aged spinster (Sandro Milo) uses the personal columns to arrange a meeting with a seemingly eligible suitor (Francois Perier). The day they spend together is both amusing and touching as they come to discover the truth about their personalities. Director Antonio Pietrangeli's seriocomic tale is minor but deftly played. A-III (br)

Labyrinth (1986) Menagerie of Muppet goblins and related little folk tries to defer a young girl from solving the puzzle of the labyrinth and saving her infant brother from the snare of the Goblin King (David Bowie). Directed by Muppet-master Jim Henson, the movie is a colorful but overlong intricate visual romp for the young. Some bathroom humor. A-I (PG)

Labyrinth of Passion (1990) Spanish farce portraying the interaction of various sexually promiscuous and perverse characters in the streets, clubs, and boudoirs of Madrid. Director Pedro Almodovar pokes fun at incest, rape, nymphomania, bisexuality, transvestitism, homosexuality, frigidity, infertility, psychotherapy, and plastic surgery, most of which are acted out on camera. Despite the frothy satiric point of view, its graphic depiction of sexual acts, as well as a particularly gross bathroom joke, are excessive. O (nr)

Lacemaker, The (1977) The heroine of Swiss director Claude Goretta's film is an 18-year-old Parisian (Isabelle Huppert) who falls in love with wealthy, educated gentleman (Ives Beneyton), and their relationship results in her mental breakdown. It's a carefully etched melodrama about class consciousness, false impressions, and male irresponsibility. A-IV (nr)

Lacombe, Lucien (1974) Excellent French WW II drama about a 17-year-old farm boy (Pierre Blaise) who wants to join the Resistance but, when he is turned down as too young and irresponsible, joins the French collaborators of the local German police. Directed by Louis Malle, the movie succeeds admirably as a chilling story of an immature youth, but it also adds considerable insight to our knowledge of the history of this period. A-II (nr)

Lad: A Dog (1962) With the blessings of his owners (Peter Breck and Peggy McCay), the champion collie of the title and his two pups help a crippled little rich girl (Angela Cartwright) walk again, despite the canine phobia of her stuffy father (Carroll O'Connor). Directed by Aram Avakian and Leslie H. Martinson, the sentimental tale is plain and simple but too threadbare for older viewers, even with some menace supplied by a disgruntled poacher, who sets fire to the barn housing the pups. For wee ones and Lassie fans. A-I (br)

Ladies and Gentlemen, the Rolling Stones (1975) Pop concert documentary with Mick Jagger and crew at their slightly satanic but self-parodying best. Directed by former ad-man Rollin Binzer, it is bright, swift, and irresistible for adult rock-fans. A-III (PG)

Ladies of Leisure (1930) Pedestrian tearjerker in

which a gold digger (Barbara Stanwyck) is reformed by a love-struck artist (Ralph Graves) whose rich family persuades her to give him up, then fate takes a hand. Directed by Frank R. Capra, the creaky plot is strictly formula fare, but the breezy characters add some period vitality, and Stanwyck manages to make the most of her role as a hustler redeemed by love. Sexual situations, drunken parties, and a suicide attempt. A-III (br)

Ladies' Day (1943) Lightweight comedy about a baseball pitcher (Eddie Albert) who's no good on the mound after marrying an impulsive movie star (Lupe Velez) in the middle of a pennant race, forcing teammates and their wives (notably Patsy Kelly and Iris Adrian) to take bizarre measures in keeping the newlyweds apart until after the World Series. Director Leslie Goodwins tries for the daffy tone of a Ring Lardner story, but the mildly comic proceedings are strictly slapstick. Brief violence and romantic situations. A-II (br)

Ladies' Man, The (1961) Uneven farce with Jerry Lewis playing a klutzy handyman in a mansion whose its owner (opera singer Helen Traubel) has turned into a women's school for aspiring performers. Also directed and co-written by Lewis, the self-indulgent exercise juggles an erratic mix of sight gags, pratfalls, spoofs, and double-takes, but Lewis's tiresome mugging gets fewer laughs than Kathleen Freeman's cheerful performance as the mansion's dizzy maid. For Lewis fans. A-I (br)

Lady and the Tramp (1955) Walt Disney's animated feature about a cute little cocker spaniel in a Victorian family who loses her place in the couple's affections with the birth of their first child, but who is reinstated through the efforts of a freedom-loving mongrel. The cast of lovable dog characters and some delightful songs by Peggy Lee still appeal to youngsters. A-I (G)

Lady at Midnight (1948) Lackluster mystery directed by Sherman Scott in which a couple (Richard Denning and Frances Rafferty) discovers someone wants to get custody of their adopted daughter and is willing to kill anyone who interferes. Stylized violence and sexual implications. A-II (br)

Lady Beware (1987) A window dresser (Diane Lane), with a penchant for the erotic, decides to turn the tables on a psychotic admirer who terrifies her. Director Karen Arthur's clumsy chiller relies heavily on male and female nudity rather than developing any feminist insights. O (R)

Lady Caroline Lamb (1973) Robert Bolt wrote and directed this vehicle for Sarah Miles about a high-born but promiscuous lady who consorts with poets and other male playthings during the early 19th century. Miles's non-acting is complemented by Richard Chamberlain's non-limping parody of Byron, and the sincere efforts of Jon Finch as her stoical husband, Willie, cannot offset the movie's overall absurdity. Brief nudity. A-III (PG)

Lady Chatterley's Lover (1982) French director Just Jaeckin's skin-deep adaptation of the D.H. Lawrence novel, with Sylvia Kristel and Nicholas Clay, is a dulling exercise in commercial eroticism. Graphic sex. O (R)

Lady Eve, The (1941) Playful romantic comedy in which a con-artist (Barbara Stanwyck) falls for a millionaire's guileless son (Henry Fonda), but when he breaks with her, she seeks revenge by visiting his father's Long Island estate masquerading as a British aristocrat's daughter. Writer-director Preston Sturges centers the comedy on the attraction of opposites as the socially inept Fonda is hopelessly confused by the sophisticated Stanwyck in a series of ridiculous situations held together by a splendid supporting cast (Charles Coburn, Eugene Pallette, William Demerest, and Eric Blore). Romantic complications with some sexual situations. A-III (br)

Lady for a Day (1933) Cheerfully sentimental comedy from the Damon Runyon story about an aging Broadway apple-seller (May Robson) who gets help from a dapper crook (Warren William) and a phony judge (Guy Kibbee) in masquerading as a wealthy socialite when her convent-educated daughter (Jean Parker) arrives from Spain with her fiancé. Director Frank Capra mixes the pathos of the Depression-era situation with plenty of comic zest provided by an odd assortment of New York types ranging from underworld thugs to high society swells, as the improbable proceedings turn big-city cynics into fancy do-gooders. An elaborate deception and mild sexual innuendo. A-II (br)

Lady Frankenstein (1972) When her fanatic father (Joseph Cotten) dies at the hands of the demented creature he created, his daughter (Sara Bey) vows to create a perfect superman to destroy her father's murderer. Unfortunately in this Italian penny-dreadful directed by Mel Welles, she has to seduce her subjects for surgery, and graphic sex sequences only detract from the blood-drenched horror fantasy. O (R)

Lady from Cheyenne, The (1941) Uneven romantic comedy set in Wyoming after the Civil War, when a schoolteacher (Loretta Young), infuriated by her town's corrupt boss (Edward Arnold), tricks the new legislature into giving women the right to vote. Directed by Frank Lloyd, the unlikely tale involves the schoolmarm's love-hate relationship with the smooth lawyer (Robert Preston) fronting for the villain, though the movie undercuts the theme of women's rights by ending with the heroine vowing to become a meek housewife. Frontier violence and mild sexual innuendo. A-II (br)

Lady from Louisiana, The (1941) Routine melodrama directed by Bernard Vorhaus in which a crusading lawyer (John Wayne) is brought to pre-Civil War New Orleans to battle the wealthy group controlling the city's popular lottery, then falls for the daughter (Ona Munson) of one of them. Stylized violence and romantic complications. A-II (br)

Lady Gambles, The (1949) Hokey cautionary tale

directed by Michael Gordon recounts the downward spiral of the troubled wife (Barbara Stanwyck) of a Chicago newspaperman (Preston Foster) after a visit to Las Vegas turns her into a compulsive gambler who gets mixed up with a big-time operator (Stephen McNally), then hits the skids. Psychological tension and domestic misunderstandings. A-II (br)

Lady Godiva (1955) Historical charade set in 11th-century England, where a Saxon earl (George Nader) is imprisoned for battling Norman intriguers in the court of Edward the Confessor (Eduard Franz), but is freed when wife Godiva (Maureen O'Hara) proves Saxon fidelity by taking her famed bare-but-for-her-hair ride through the streets of Coventry. Director Arthur Lubin's shallow costume melodrama is a frivolous exercise in popular history. Period violence and mild sexual innuendo. A-II (br)

Lady Godiva of Coventry (see: **Lady Godiva**)

Lady Hamilton (see: **That Hamilton Woman**)

Lady Ice (1973) Middling diamond-heist caper in which an insurance investigator (Donald Sutherland) gets involved with a diamond fence (Jennifer O'Neill) and a hard-bitten US Justice Department agent (Robert Duvall), who adds a bit of class, but his scenes get lost in the shuffle. Directed by Tom Gries, the complex, and at times confusing, plot doesn't add up to much. A-II (PG)

Lady in a Cage (1964) Sadistic exercise in urban violence opens with an ailing widow (Olivia de Havilland) spending the July 4th weekend alone, until an electrical outage traps her in the house elevator while her wealthy home is robbed by street people (Jeff Corey and Ann Sothern), and her life threatened by a trio of punks (led by James Caan). Directed by Walter Grauman, the menace escalates in nastiness, until the woman's struggle for survival becomes as barbaric as the acts of her attackers. Cynical treatment undermines its pretensions as social commentary. O (br)

Lady in Cement (1968) Hardboiled private detective (Frank Sinatra) gets involved in the murder of a woman in the title, but director Gordon Douglas provides neither credibility nor atmosphere in the rambling, loosely plotted proceedings that create an ersatz excitement only by resorting to brutal violence and some sleazy sexual distractions. O (R/PG)

Lady in Question, The (1940) Muddled tale set in France, where a shopkeeper (Brian Aherne) called to serve on a murder case convinces his fellow jurors that the accused (Rita Hayworth) is innocent, then gives her a job in his shop, but comes to believe the worst when his son (Glenn Ford) falls for her. Directed by Charles Vidor, the sketchy characters and ambiguous situations fail to achieve the comic pathos intended, and the sunny ending is particularly flat. Sexual innuendo. A-II (br)

Lady in the Car with Glasses and a Gun, The (1970) Failed mystery thriller in which Samantha Eggar takes a holiday drive in the sSouth of France, and, after a number of puzzling incidents happen to her, she discovers a body in the trunk of the car she got from her boss (sinister Oliver Reed). Director Anatole Litvak goes overboard trying to create some suspense, but the result of all his efforts is no more than pure cleverness and empty contrivance. Some adult mayhem. A-III (R)

Lady in the Dark (1944) Lame screen version of the Moss Hart musical about a fashion magazine editor (Ginger Rogers) who gets help from a psychoanalyst (Barry Sullivan) in resolving her troubled relations with a married man (Warner Baxter), a movie star (Jon Hall), and an irritating associate (Ray Milland). Directed by Mitchell Leisen, the halting proceedings are short on wit and imagination, with charmless production numbers and a couple of Kurt Weill-Ira Gerschwin songs which don't help matters much. Sexual situations and innuendo. A-III (br)

Lady in the Lake (1946) Hardboiled private eye Philip Marlowe (Robert Montgomery) is hired to find the missing wife of a publisher (Leon Ames) in a twisty case involving the man's business associate (Audrey Totter), a devious cop (Lloyd Nolan), and a mystery woman (Jayne Meadows). Also directed by Montgomery from the Raymond Chandler novel, the picture is memorable for the camera taking Marlowe's place, filming events as if seen through his eyes, with the actor seen only in mirror shots, but the result isn't helped by a confusing plot, the Christmas setting, and phony cynical tone. Stylized violence, menacing situations, and veiled sexual innuendo. A-II (br)

Lady in White (1988) Supernatural thriller about a small-town boy (Lukas Haas) who comes face to face with the ghost of a girl murdered 10 years before, as well as with her murderer. With breathtaking special effects and cinematography, director Frank LaLoggia's unique fantasy attains wonderful interplay between the boy, his family, and the ghosts, in a lovely re-creation of life in 1962. Graphic violence directed toward children and some particularly chilling supernatural occurrences. A-III (PG-13).

Lady Jane (1986) The innocence and altruism of youth are contrasted with the deceit and treachery of the adult world in this period drama about the religious power-struggle following the reign of King Henry VIII. Its romantic treatment of adult themes contains a brief scene of nudity and a brutal scene of flogging. A-III (PG-13)

Lady Liberty (1972) When Sophia Loren flies into JFK Airport to rejoin her fiancé, she has a 20-pound mortadella sausage under her arm, and the crisis this causes at Customs promises one of those coarse peasant comedies the Italians do so well. Unfortunately, director Mario Monticelli presents a freak show of grisly New York stereotypes in a cynical blend of contempt, distrust, and generally low opinion of humanity. A-IV (PG)

Lady of Burlesque (1943) Tepid Hollywood cheesecake is mixed with corny jokes as a not-very-exotic dancer (Barbara Stanwyck) teams with a not-very-funny comic (Michael O'Shea) to solve two backstage murders in a ramshackle burlesque theater. Directed by William A. Wellman from Gypsy Rose Lee's novel *The G-String Murders*, the search for the killer plays second fiddle to the picture's sentimental hokum about goodhearted strippers. Some stylized violence and much sexual innuendo. A-III (br)

Lady on the Tracks, The (1968) Czechoslovakian musical fantasy about a lady streetcar driver in Prague (Jirina Bohdalova) who mounts a campaign for women's rights when she discovers her husband's love affair. Directed by Ladislav Rychman, its musical numbers are done in 1930s Hollywood style, and the result is a warm and humorous tale of one woman's dreams of glory. A-II (br)

Lady Says No, The (1951) Comedy clunker in which a feminist author (Joan Caulfield) repudiates her anti-male bestseller after she falls for a suave photographer (David Niven) who ridicules her lack of romantic experience. Directed by Frank Ross, the clumsy script gets few laughs from heavy-handed plot twists transforming the prim author into a calculating vamp. Sexist humor. A-III (br)

Lady Scarface (1941) Routine crime melodrama directed by Frank Woodruff in which a Chicago cop (Dennis O'Keefe) trails a gang of robbers (notably Arthur Shields and Marc Lawrence) to New York City, then nabs its notorious boss (Judith Anderson) with the aid of a photographer (Frances Neal). Stylized violence and sexual innuendo. A-II (br)

Lady Sings the Blues (1972) Diana Ross stars as Billie Holiday in a screen biography that reduces the famous singer's life to a series of cliches and soap opera theatrics. A very good performance by Ross can't save director Sidney J. Furie's failed movie. Rough language and sordid situations. A-IV (R)

Lady Takes a Chance, A (1943) Breezy romantic comedy in which a New York tourist (Jean Arthur) falls for a genial rodeo-cowboy (John Wayne), then pursues him despite his avowed intention to remain a bachelor, with amusingly predictable results. Director William A. Seiter gets good-natured performances from the two leads as they mix romantic situations with rough-and-tumble comedy, helped along the way by a good supporting cast (especially Charles Winninger and Phil Silvers). Comic violence and romantic complications. A-II (br)

Lady Takes a Flyer, The (1958) Predictably bumpy romance directed by Jack Arnold in which a lady aviator (Lana Turner) marries a hotshot pilot (Jeff Chandler) who gets so wrapped up in trying to build his own airline that he neglects wife and child, with predictable results. Domestic tensions and sexual situations. A-III (br)

Lady Vanishes, The (1938) Mystery classic in which a kind old lady (Dame May Whitty) abruptly disappears from a train traveling through central Europe without anyone noticing, until a frantic search by fellow passengers (Margaret Lockwood and Michael Redgrave) uncovers a ring of secret agents (led by Paul Lukas). Director Alfred Hitchcock leavens the mystery's suspense with some keen humor (notably Basil Radford and Naunton Wayne as woolly English travelers) and rich characterizations by a fine British cast (not least of which is Catherine Lacey as a counterfeit nun). Stylized violence and menacing situations. A-II (br)

Lady Yakuza (1974) Japanese gangster movie in which a young woman (Junko Fuji) takes over the leadership of a gang after her father's murder and ultimately is able to avenge his death. As directed by Kosaku Yamashita, there is plenty of violence, but used within a context of group loyalty and personal friendship. A-III (nr)

Ladybird Ladybird (1994) Blistering portrait of a loving but violent-tempered unwed mother of four (Crissy Rock) whose children are taken from her when British authorities deem her an unfit parent, only to do the same when she has two children by a caring foreigner (Vladimir Vega) who has taken her in. Director Ken Loach's superbly acted, fact-based examination of a flawed bureaucratic system compounded by a woman who is her own worst enemy is emotionally heart-rending and intellectually challenging, though the narrative lacks any insight into why she fails to learn from past mistakes. Troubling theme of unwed motherhood, brief but intense violence, and constant rough language. A-IV (nr)

Ladybugs (1992) A salesman (Rodney Dangerfield) whose promotion depends on successfully coaching his company-sponsored all-girls soccer team gets his fiancé's son (Jonathan Brandis) to play disguised as a girl in order to ensure a winning season. Sidney J. Furie directs a genial sports comedy peppered with Dangerfield's snappy one-liners. Mild sexual innuendo and double entendres. A-II (PG-13)

Ladyhawke (1985) Medieval sword-and-sorcery epic looks beautiful but tells a silly story of a curse which changes two true-lovers into a hawk (Michelle Pfeiffer) and a wolf (Rutger Hauer). Directed by Richard Donner, it is rife with bad dialogue, bad acting, and anachronisms. Aside from some violent swordplay, it is innocuous. A-II (PG-13)

Ladykillers, The (1955) Droll British comedy in which a daffy gang of crooks (Alec Guinness, Cecil Parker, Herbert Lom, Peter Sellers, and Danny Green) take a London flat as their hideout while planning a big heist, until their sweet old landlady (Katie Johnson) innocently gums up the works. Director Alexander Mackendrick rings in the comic changes adroitly, going from whimsical to black comedy as the bumbling thieves try to murder the old woman but wind up killing each other instead, then topping it off with a wryly innocent conclusion. Comic treatment of violence and criminal activities. A-I (br)

Lair of the White Worm, The (1988) Director Ken Russell's update of a 1911 Bram Stoker novel has a vampire (Amanda Donohoe) lure humans into the lair of an ancient serpent still living in an English town, with two sisters (Catherine Oxenberg and Sammi Davis) as key targets. The satiric elements are diluted by Russell's fascination with sexual debauch, involving dream sequences of the blood-splattered rape of nuns by pagan soldiers in front of a serpent-draped cross. Explicit sexual seduction, fleeting nudity, and intense vampire attacks. O (R)

Lamb (1995) Distraught over his father's death and the punitive atmosphere at the Irish school for troubled boys where he teaches, a Christian brother (Liam Neeson) flees to England with a 10-year-old student (Hugh O' Conor) he wants to help, but is unprepared to deal with the boy's debilitating epileptic seizures. Director Colin Gregg's frail story summons up much sympathy for the vulnerable boy and the plight of the well-intended brother, whose initial mistake of kidnapping the child ultimately has tragic consequences. Brief violence borne of despair and some rough language. A-III (nr)

Lambada (1990) High-school math-teacher (J. Eddie Peck) moonlights in an East Los Angeles barrio disco, where he dances and educates young Latinos so they can pass their high-school equivalency exams. Director Joel Silberg plays up the gyrations of the scantily clad female dancers, as well as a student's lust for her teacher in this cut-and-paste exploitation of adolescent male sexual fantasies. Much sexual innuendo and vulgar language. A-III (PG)

Lamerica (1995) Eager to make a fortune in post-communist Albania, an Italian con-man (Enrico Lo Verso) sets up a phony scheme involving a confused old man (Carmelo Di Mazzarelli) who spent 50 years as a political prisoner, then becomes ashamed of exploiting the elderly man's simple love and trust. Director Gianni Amelio's moving human drama strikes a universal chord, both in its small-scale story of the two men and in the larger picture of impoverished Albanians desperate for a better life abroad. Subtitles. Occasional rough language. A-II (nr)

L'Amour (1973) Andy Warhol's counterculture denizens flutter around Paris in this generally vapid put-on, which Warhol co-directed with Paul Morrissey. In tune with Warhol's philosophy, the camerawork is grainy, the color is anemic, and the parade of verbal and visual vulgarities is constant. O (R)

Lancelot of the Lake (1975) French director Robert Bresson takes the Arthurian legend and interprets it in austere realistic fashion, focusing on the decline of the Knights of the Round Table after their failure in the quest of the Grail. His treatment purges the legend of its magic and romance, searching for some historical substance, which for some will have more interest than the story. Subtitles. Some realistic violence. A-III (nr)

Lancer Spy (1937) WW I tale of a British agent (George Sanders) arriving in Berlin in the place of a lookalike captured German spy and using a beautiful woman (Delores Del Rio) as an unwitting accomplice in ferreting out war secrets. Director Gregory Ratoff builds the cat-and-mouse suspense as the agent arouses the growing suspicions of the German military (Peter Lorre, Joseph Schildkraut, and others). Implausible but diverting enough espionage thriller. A-I (br)

Land and Freedom (1996) Joining the Communist-backed Republican forces in their fight against Franco's Fascist-backed army in the 1936 Spanish Civil War, an idealistic young Brit (Ian Hart) becomes disillusioned by the violent in-fighting among the Stalinists and their peasant allies. Director Ken Loach re-creates the struggle with documentary-like intensity, dramatizing the view that political treachery by the communists undermined the republican cause. Battlefield violence, sexual references, and much rough language. A-IV (nr)

Land Before Time, The (1988) Delightful animated feature about the exploits of five young dinosaurs of differing species who band together for survival. Plagued by hunger and threats from meat-eating dinos, the leaf-eating tykes make their way to the Great Valley for food. Director Don Bluth offers some cute little characters, quality animation, and a lovely message of solidarity and courage. A brief, nicely handled sequence of a mother dino's death. A-I (G)

Land of the Pharaohs (1955) Uneven tale in which a ruler of ancient Egypt (Jack Hawkins) forces a captive architect (James Robertson Justice) to build a great pyramid housing a tomb that proves spacious enough not only for the pharaoh but also for his greedy, treacherous second wife (Joan Collins). Director Howard Hawks turns in a historical spectacle on a scale far grander than required for the soap opera antics of a conniving royal gold digger. Stylized violence and sexual situations. A-III (br)

Land Raiders (1970) Telly Savalas plays a loud, overbearing rancher who stirs up trouble with a local Indian tribe, is discovered to have killed his brother's girl, and gets his just desserts when the Indians go on the warpath. Directed by Nathan Juran, it's a poorly done Western with some gory violence and sexual references. A-III (PG)

Land That Time Forgot, The (1975) Doug McClure, John McEnery, and Susan Penhaligon are among the survivors of a WW I U-boat attack who find themselves in a strange land filled with prehistoric beasts. Routine British fantasy adventure directed by Kevin Connor. Restrained violence. A-II (PG)

Land Unknown, The (1957) When a Navy helicopter crash-lands in a fog-enshrouded valley in Antarctica, its commander (Jock Mahoney), two crew members, and a woman reporter (Shawn Smith) find themselves in a volcanic hothouse threatened by giant prehistoric animals and the mad survivor (Henry Brandon) of a previous expedition. Director Virgil Vogel's tame adventure-fantasy features bargain-basement sets and monsters, though the formula plot takes some intriguing twists along the way. Stylized violence, contrived thrills, and mild sexual innuendo. A-II (br)

Landlord, The (1970) Rich young man (Beau Bridges) becomes a ghetto landlord in some vague hope that by renovating a decaying Brooklyn brownstone, tenanted by justly suspicious blacks, he can rebuild his empty life. Directed by Hal Ashby, the seriocomic drama has some good performances (Diana Sands and Lou Gossett) and lyric photography, but lacks depth and coherence. Interesting failure with some mature themes. A-IV (R/PG)

Landscape After Battle (1978) Polish drama directed by Andrzej Wajda is a compilation of short stories by Tadeusz Borowski, survivor of Auschwitz and suicide victim. Some brief nudity, but the somberness of the theme makes this a movie for mature viewers. A-III (nr)

Landscape in the Mist (1990) Two runaways, a girl (Tania Palaiologou) and her little brother (Michalis Zeke), hitchhike and sneak onboard trains all across Greece in a pitiful attempt to reach Germany, where they seek the father they have never seen. Director Theo Angelopoulos's film is rich in striking imagery and symbolism, but its ponderous pace and theme of innocents set adrift in a world of mostly hostile adults is a decidedly downbeat experience. Greek production with English subtitles. Off-screen rape of the girl. A-III (nr)

Larger Than Life (1996) Feeble comedy in which a hapless chap (Bill Murray) inherits his father's performing elephant, then struggles to personally escort the unruly pachyderm across the country to an impatient buyer. Directed by Howard Franklin, the comic proceedings are pleasant enough, though they never venture far beyond its limited odd-couple premise. Fleeting profanity and brief menace. A-II (PG)

Las Vegas Hillbillys (1966) Ferlin Husky comes out of the hills and gains success in Las Vegas in a mindless story directed by Arthur C. Pierce. A-I (br)

Las Vegas Story, The (1952) Flimsy melodrama set in the title's gambling capital to which a fraudulent financier (Vincent Price) brings his wife (Jane Russell), whose ex-flame (Victor Mature), now a police detective, rescues her from a killer. Directed by Robert Stevenson, the romantic triangle flounders in mutual animosities, until murder leads to kidnapping and a helicopter chase for a big but empty finish. Some nasty violence, romantic complications, and a sexual situation. A-III (br)

Lassie (1994) A stray collie befriends a lonely boy (Thomas Guiry) adjusting to life in Virginia's Shenandoah Valley, where his Baltimore parents (Helen Shaver and Jon Tenney) are attempting to make a go of a sheep ranch despite stiff competition from an unprincipled neighbor (Frederic Forrest). Director Daniel Petrie delivers a postcard-pretty, very sentimental boy-and-his-dog story in which the brave collie predictably helps save the ranch and brings the family closer together. Fleeting violence and brief menace to children. A-II (PG)

Lassie Come Home (1943) Before television, the faithful collie got her start in this story of a poor English family who have to sell their dog, Lassie, but the canny canine crosses the Scottish highlands, despite the elements and all manner of hazards, to return to the little boy (Roddy McDowall) who loves her. Directed by Fred M. Wilcox, the movie's charm holds up quite well as family entertainment, especially for youngsters enthralled by Lassie's intelligence and perseverance. A-I (nr)

Lassiter (1984) Tom Selleck stars as a womanizing detective forced to become a spy in this espionage thriller directed by Roger Young and set in London just before WW II. Lauren Hutton is the German Mata Hari with a kinky appetite for blood, sex, and brutality. Violence and nudity. O (R)

Last Action Hero (1993) Overproduced parody of action movies follows an 11-year-old boy (Austin O'Brien) as he magically enters the movie he's watching to join his hero, a trigger-happy cop (Arnold Schwarzenegger), in countless chases and shootouts. Director John McTiernan does little but stitch together the mindless mayhem wrought by assorted weapons and the pyrotechnics engineered by the special-effects unit for a clunky and uninvolving pastiche that glamorizes violence and equates heroism with macho posturing and big guns. Much mean-spirited comic violence, positive treatment of phony male heroics, sexist images of women, and an instance of rough language. O (PG-13)

Last Adventure, The (1968) Episodic French movie about the comradeship between two men (Alain Delon and Lino Ventura) and a young woman (Joanna Shimkus), with the trio winding up on a dangerous search for sunken treasure. Directed by Robert Enrico, the emphasis is less on their adventures than on the qualities of loyalty and respect that keep the three together. A-II (br)

Last American Hero, The (1973) Story of champion stock-car driver Junior Johnson (Jeff Bridges) who evolved from running corn whiskey over the back-roads of North Carolina to earning $100,000 a year racing cars. Directed by Lamont Johnson, the movie's gritty atmosphere is evoked beautifully, supported by a fine cast (Art Lund, Geraldine Fitzgerald, Gary Busey, and Ned Beatty). A-III (PG)

Last Big Thing, The (1998) Ineffective satire in which a man (Dan Zukovic), obsessed with the lack of creativity in modern popular culture, seeks out pop performers to ridicule and insult, while a troubled follower (Susan Heimbinder) chronicles his bizarre exploits. Also written and directed by Zukovic, the comic concept is too thin to be sustained as a feature, though its wacky jabs at pop-culture icons provide some amusement along the way. Sexual situations and references, dark pranks, outrageous deceptions, and occasional rough language. A-IV (R)

Last Blitzkrieg, The (1958) Uneven WW II tale in which an English-speaking German officer (Van Johnson) heads a group of saboteurs dressed in

American uniforms during the Battle of the Bulge. Directed by Arthur Dreifuss, the story's conflict of loyalties to nation and to common humanity is well-intended but muddled. Wartime violence and an attempted sexual assault. A-II (br)

Last Boy Scout, The (1991) A former Secret Service agent (Bruce Willis) and a drug-addicted ex-football player (Damon Wayans) constantly court death while attempting to stop the assassination of a corrupt senator. Director Tony Scott's sleazy bloodbath is an affront to human sensibilities disguised as slick action entertainment. Excessive violence, incessant rough language, and brief nudity. O (R)

Last Command, The (1955) Historical dramatization centers on the exploits of Jim Bowie (Sterling Hayden) with the Texans, led by William Travis (Richard Carlson), and some Tennessee volunteers under Davy Crockett (Arthur Hunnicutt) at the 1836 Battle of the Alamo against the Mexican forces of Santa Anna (J. Carrol Naish). Directed by Frank Lloyd, the movie sets the scene with some sequences helping define the characters, as well as the political issues leading to the battle which is reenacted with convincing gusto. Battlefield violence. A-I (br)

Last Dance (1996) Flawed drama in which a novice lawyer (Rob Morrow) is stymied by the legal system and backroom politics in struggling to gain clemency for a young woman (Sharon Stone) sentenced to death for a brutal double-slaying. Director Bruce Beresford focuses on the humanity of a death-row inmate in a simplistic story questioning the state's right to take human life. Brief gory shots of murder victims, fleeting sexual innuendo, and recurring profanity as well as rough language. A-III (R)

Last Days of Disco, The (1998) Wryly observed tale, set in early 1980s New York City, follows the fluctuating social lives and fledgling careers of a half-dozen recent college grads who frequent a trendy disco over the course of a year. Writer-director Whit Stillman's talky comedy serves as a cautionary tale in exploring opinionated characters who discover there are consequences to sexual permissiveness. Momentary violence, a fleeting sexual encounter and nudity, implied affairs, a character's substance abuse, and a few instances of profanity. A-III (R)

Last Days of Dolwyn, The (1949) Stodgy British production about a village in 19th-century Wales which must be abandoned before its valley is turned into a reservoir, until a widow (Edith Evans) rejects any compensation from the project's agent (Emlyn Williams) and refuses to leave. Also written and directed by Williams, the Welsh setting is quite appealing, but the story grows increasingly melodramatic until a heavy-handed ironic ending. Stylized violence, including an accidental death by fire. A-II (br)

Last Days of Man on Earth, The (1977) Failed British satire set against the background of a post-nuclear disaster in which a group of scientists led by a ruthless woman (Jenny Runacre) force a brilliant young man to help them in an attempt to create a new breed of super-humans. Directed by Robert Fuest, the exotic settings are far more interesting than the action occurring in them. Excessive nudity. O (R)

Last Days of Pompeii, The (1935) Creaky but colorful tale in which a happy Pompeii blacksmith (Preston Foster) turns dour seeking wealth as a gladiator, then finds it as a trader in Judea, where his boy is cured by the miracle worker later crucified by Pontius Pilate (Basil Rathbone). But back home, the unworldliness of his now-Christian son puzzles the rich old man, then inspires him to save others in the volcanic eruption of Vesuvius. Directed by Ernest B. Schoedsack, the episodic story of a good man changing into a greedy one, then shedding selfishness in the face of disaster plods fitfully along until the spectacular effects depicting the city's destruction. Stylized violence. A-I (br)

Last Detail, The (1974) Career sailors (Jack Nicholson and Otis Young), assigned to escort a young seaman (Randy Quaid) to the Marine brig, stop off along the way to give him a last fling, which proves to be his first. Directed by Hal Ashby, it is fairly consistent but very coarse adult entertainment. Brothel scene with brief nudity and unrelenting flow of rough language are part of the movie's apparent definition of manliness. A-IV (R)

Last Dragon, The (1985) A kind of black Kung Fu movie that doesn't take itself too seriously. Although it has a banal story line about a good martial-arts expert vanquishing a nasty one, director Michael Schultz is helped out by lively high-spirited performers. Some restrained violence and vulgar language. A-II (PG-13)

Last Embrace (1979) Florid melodrama directed by Jonathan Demme about a government agent (Roy Scheider) who has a mental breakdown after his wife is killed in a shootout in which he inadvertently involved her. A mysterious graduate student (Janet Margolin) is somehow involved in a flimsy plot loaded with red herrings. Generous doses of brutality and sexual scenes. O (R)

Last Emperor, The (1988) Sweeping historical saga of Pu Yi (1906-67) who, after being crowned emperor at age three of the fading Manchurian dynasty, becomes a passive pawn amidst political power plays, until ending his life as a humble gardener under Chinese Communist rule. Italian director Bernardo Bertolucci's movie boasts exquisite historical detail, beautiful costumes, extraordinary location sets in the Forbidden City, and breathtaking pageantry, but oddly lacks dramatic punch. Some scenes of violence, sex, and opium smoking, though brief and integral to the cultural context. A-III (PG-13)

Last Escape, The (1970) Stuart Whitman leads an Allied operation in the final months of WW II to smuggle a leading rocket scientist out of war-scarred Germany while the Russians are attempting to do the same. Director Walter Grauman compensates for an obvious script and wooden acting by a lot of wartime action scenes with remarkably little bloodshed. A-II (G)

Last Exit to Brooklyn (1990) Repugnant view of working-class life during a 1952 shipping strike in a waterfront neighborhood, where thugs amuse themselves terrorizing passersby, the local union strike leader (Stephen Lang) destroys himself in a homosexual affair, and an aspiring hooker (Jennifer Jason Leigh) winds up the victim of a stand-in-line gang rape. Director Uli Edel's dark picture of human degradation makes several feeble gestures affirming the values of family and union solidarity, but they ring hollow and fail to add any significance to the dehumanized proceedings. Excessive violence and sexual exploitation. O (R)

Last Flight of Noah's Ark (1980) Elliott Gould agrees to fly missionary Genevieve Bujold and a menagerie of domestic animals to a South Pacific island, but, when the plane crash lands, they discover two child stowaways (Ricky Schroder and Tammy Lauren). Directed by Charles Jarrott, the Disney production is disarming and has a lighthearted grace that is irresistible. Appealing fare for young and old. A-I (G)

Last Frontier, The (1955) Standard Western in which a fur trapper (Victor Mature) becomes an Army scout during a Sioux uprising, then saves the fort after its deranged commander (Robert Preston) is killed in a futile attack, with his widow (Anne Bancroft) showing interest in the scout. Directed by Anthony Mann, the formula plot has a boisterous performance by Mature as the hard-drinking, free-spirited trapper whose antics are colorful but not very credible. Frontier violence and romantic complications. A-II (br)

Last Grenade, The (1970) British agent Stanley Baker tramps up and down the hills bordering Hong Kong in pursuit of Alex Cord, a grinning sadist working for the other side. Director Gordon Flemyng's chase story, in which an adulterous affair plays a part, doesn't make much sense, and the movie is a dud. A-III (M)

Last Hard Men, The (1976) Ugly, distasteful Western about an escaped convict (James Coburn) who is determined to get revenge upon the retired sheriff (Charlton Heston) who put him in jail. Coburn manages to be interesting and Michael Parks contributes a few bright moments, but all director Andrew V. McLaglen's movie really has on its mind is the usual rape and other brutalities that go with simple-minded debasements of the Western myth. O (R)

Last House on the Left, The (1972) Two teenagers (Lucy Grantham and Sandra Cassel) are kidnapped, tormented, raped, and slaughtered while a foolish sheriff bungles his investigation, and the parents of one girl take their own brutal revenge. Written and directed by Wes Craven, this lurid movie indulges in gore, sex, and profanity. O (R)

Last Hunt, The (1956) In the 1880s, with the last of the great buffalo herds nearing extinction, a cynical gunman (Robert Taylor) persuades a veteran hunter (Stewart Granger) to join him in going after buffalo hides, with predictably disastrous results. Director Richard Brooks reduces the plot to a simplistic contrast between the noble hunter and the cold-blooded gunman who not only kills people as wantonly as buffalo but also brutalizes an Indian woman (Debra Paget) he has taken captive. Much stylized violence and sexual situations. A-III (br)

Last Hurrah, The (1958) Uneven screen version of Edwin O'Connor's novel about the end of a colorful era in urban-machine politics as seen in the final campaign of fictional Boston Mayor Frank Skeffington (Spencer Tracy). Directed by John Ford, the story's contrast between the old and the new TV breed of politicians is less interesting than its nostalgia for a more human, if much flawed, American past, as evoked by a cast of veteran character actors (Pat O'Brien, Frank McHugh, James Gleason), as well as some of Ford's own stock company (Donald Crisp, Jane Darwell, John Carradine), who balance the thick sentimentality with broad humor. Lingering demise of the main character. A-II (br)

Last Man on Earth, The (1964) Halting horror tale in which the sole survivor (Vincent Price) of a worldwide plague, whose victims become vampires, manages to fend off their attacks for three years, then is suddenly confronted by a group of mutants who fear him more than they do the vampires. Directed by Sidney Salkow from a story by Richard Matheson, the picture is thinly plotted and unevenly acted, though Price's performance more than holds interest until the muddled ending in a church sanctuary. Stylized violence and considerable menace. A-II (br)

Last Man Standing (1996) Arriving in a Texas border town overrun by rival Prohibition-era bootleggers, a trigger-happy tough guy (Bruce Willis) hires himself out to both sides, then systematically kills them all. Willis smirks his way through one boring shootout after another in an empty story of violence from writer-director Walter Hill. Heroic treatment of a brutal murderer, excessive violence, a sexual encounter, and much profanity. O (R)

Last Married Couple in America, The (1980) George Segal and Natalie Wood begin to doubt the validity of their own relationship when the marriages of all their friends shatter around them. Directed by Gilbert Cates, it is a clumsy, shapeless affair, poorly scripted and badly acted. Some nudity and a great deal of foul language. O (R)

Last Metro, The (1981) Uninvolving wartime melodrama directed by Francois Truffaut about a harried actress-theater manager (Catherine Deneuve) who tries to keep her theater open and her Jewish husband (Heinz Bennent) hidden during the German Occupation of Paris. It is a romantic and sophisticated production lacking depth and passion. Adultery figures in the plot. A-III (PG)

Last Mile, The (1932) Awaiting execution, a vicious murderer (Preston Foster) takes control of death row in an attempt to exchange a hostage for freedom. Directed by Sam Bischoff from John Wexley's play, the action is stagy but viscerally effective, as the tension mounts within the cell block and among the prison guards surrounding it. Stylized violence in a desperate situation. A-III (br)

Last Mile, The (1959) Remake of the 1932 original, with Mickey Rooney giving a hard-edged performance as a condemned killer leading seven prisoners in an ill-fated takeover of death row. Director Howard W. Koch sets a somber scene with a Catholic chaplain preparing an inmate to face execution, but the brutal action in taking over the ward is nasty and conscienceless. Realistic violence. A-III (br)

Last Movie, The (1971) Failed story about the bizarre and tragic effects a movie company has on a community of primitive Peruvian Indians whose village they use as a location. Directed by Dennis Hopper, who also stars, the movie's concept is an intriguing one that, unfortunately, is not realized in a work totally out of control, with incredible lapses of logic and jumbled time sequences. Graphic scenes of sexual encounters and a demeaning attitude toward Indian culture and religious beliefs. O (R)

Last of His Tribe, The (1992) Stolid human drama based on the book by anthropologist Alfred Kroeber (Jon Voight) about his 1911 discovery of Ishi (Graham Greene), the last survivor of the Yahi, an Indian tribe long thought extinct, and his work in trying to preserve its language and culture. Director Harry Hook gives a rather flat account of an aboriginal man's learning to live in the 20th century and Kroeber's attempts to reconstruct the lost Yahi way of life. Some heart-rending scenes of violence and a restrained sexual episode. A-III (PG-13)

Last of Sheila, The (1973) Film producer (James Coburn) invites some friends (Richard Benjamin, Joan Hackett, Dyan Cannon, James Mason, Raquel Welch, and Ian McShane) for a week's cruise in the Mediterranean celebrating the first anniversary of the hit-and-run killing of his wife, whose name graces both the yacht and the movie's title. Director Herbert Ross is so busy being slick and clever in his parody of Hollywood types that he creates an elaborate hoax rather than a plausible whodunit. A-III (PG)

Last of the Comanches (1952) After Comanches massacre a troop of US Cavalry, six survivors (led by Broderick Crawford) along with several civilians (including Barbara Hale) take refuge in an abandoned mission and hold off waves of attackers until reinforcements arrive. Directed by Andre de Toth, the result is little more than standard action fare ending in a tribute to the bravery of the fallen. Frontier violence. A-I (br)

Last of the Dogmen (1995) Tall tale comes up short in telling how a bounty hunter (Tom Berenger) and an anthropologist (Barbara Hershey) discover a tribe of Cheyenne Indians who have managed to stay undetected for 128 years in a Montana valley hidden behind a waterfall. Writer-director Tab Murphy has the makings of a robust Western yarn but wastes the opportunity on a pedestrian treatment of cliched characters and sentimental situations. Some brutal violence and needless profanity. A-III (PG)

Last of the Fast Guns, The (1958) Convoluted Western in which a gunfighter (Jock Mahoney) hired to find an American missing in Mexico teams with a local adventurer (Gilbert Roland) who has his own reasons for joining in the search. Directed by George Sherman, the contrived plot has some colorful characters, notably a backcountry padre (Eduard Franz), but the quest becomes tiresome long before its improbable ending. Stylized violence. A-I (br)

Last of the Finest, The (1990) Suspended veteran Los Angeles cop (Brian Dennehy) and his three young cronies bust a big-time drug and money-laundering racket tied to Central American gunrunners. Directed in plodding, unimaginative fashion by John MacKenzie, this implausible cop adventure justifies vigilantism as patriotism. Some profanity, sexual expletives, bathroom humor, and explosive comic-book violence. A-III (R)

Last of the Mobile Hot-Shots (1970) Failed screen version of a play by Tennessee Williams presents a muddled and superficially symbolic story of Southern racial attitudes involving James Coburn, Robert Hooks, and Lynn Redgrave. Directed by Sidney Lumet, this talky affair has an excess of crude dialogue and several unnecessarily explicit sex scenes in the flashbacks. O (X/R)

Last of the Mohicans, The (1992) When the French and Indian War erupts on New York's colonial frontier, heroic woodsman Hawkeye (Daniel Day-Lewis) cannot save a British force from being massacred in the wilderness, but at least he's able to rescue its commander's daughter (Madeleine Stowe) from a wicked Huron warrior (Wes Studi). In adapting the James Fenimore Cooper classic to the screen, director Michael Mann updates its romanticized version of pioneer life amidst noble woodland savages by dwelling in realistic detail on the inhuman cruelties of hand-to-hand combat. Many graphic depictions of deadly violence and bloodshed. A-III (R)

Last of the Red Hot Lovers (1972) Failed screen version of the Neil Simon comedy about a man (Alan Arkin) who uses his unsuspecting mother's apartment for sex in the afternoon. Directed by Gene Saks, it tries desperately to be amusing, but, except for the occasional one-liner, it is boring when it's not irritating in its search for euphemisms for sin. A-III (PG)

Last of the Renegades (1966) Routine European-made Western directed by Harald Rinl is an old-fashioned cowboy and Indian movie with Lex Barker and Anthony Steel trying to avert an Indian war while both pursue the same Indian maiden (Karin Dor). Stylized violence. A-I (br)

Last of the Secret Agents?, The (1966) Stupid undercover spoof directed by Norman Abbott features the tiresome slapstick antics of comics Marty Allen and Steve Rossi. Overemphasis on the sexually suggestive. O (br)

Last Outlaw, The (1936) Unpretentious Western

in which an aged bank robber (Harry Carey) is released after 25 years in prison, then takes on some Detroit gangsters with the help of an old-time lawman (Henry B. Walthall) and a young rancher (Hoot Gibson). Directed by Christy Cabanne from a story by John Ford, Carey is in fine form portraying the old badman's bemusement at the changes in the modern West as well as his disdain at seeing a movie with singing cowboys. Shootout to free a woman held hostage by the gangsters. A-I (br)

Last Outpost, The (1951) Raiding Union supply lines along the Santa Fe Trail, a Confederate officer (Ronald Reagan) comes across his brother (Bruce Bennett), who happens to be a Yankee officer, and the two join forces to stop an Apache uprising. Director Lewis R. Foster treats the far-fetched yarn as if it were a Rover Boys adventure in blue and gray. Stylized violence. A-I (br)

Last Picture Show, The (1971) Bleak picture of life in a dust-stricken and culturally depressed little town in 1951 Texas. Director Peter Bogdanovich captures brilliantly the banal details of time and place, but portrays the town's inhabitants (Timothy Bottoms, Jeff Bridges, Cybill Shepherd, Ellen Burstyn, Cloris Leachman, and Ben Johonson) as a hopeless lot whose only interests are sexual experimentation and watching TV soap operas and quiz shows. There's more to life than that, even in a small town. Brief nudity. O (PG)

Last Rebel, The (1971) Joe Namath smirks his way through a puerile Western as an ex-Confederate adventurer who shoots up a few rivals, hustles some local pool sharks, and makes merry with ladies high and low. Director Denys McCoy's movie has crude language, stylized violence, and brief nudity, but its major offense is being so witless and dull that an adult will find it hard to sit through. A-III (GP)

Last Remake of Beau Geste, The (1977) Witless and boring spoof of a classic adventure movie stars Ann-Margret and Michael York, who are less embarrassing to watch than the struggle of a cast of comedians in the clutches of a dreary script. Director Marty Feldman relies almost solely on vulgar sight gags and crude humor to keep the French Foreign Legion afloat. A-III (PG)

Last Resort (1986) Charles Grodin takes his movie family on an island resort vacation in this failed satire about the crude excesses of the travel business. The sex maniacs who run the resort manage to corrupt the middle-class values of mom, dad, and the kids in this unfunny farce obsessed with crude sexual innuendo and sight gags, the drug-and-booze culture, and profanity. O (R)

Last Rites (1988) Donald P. Bellisario directs a trashy, twisted tale of a New York priest (Tom Berenger) who falls in love with a woman (Daphne Zuniga) seeking to protect him from a Mafia gang headed by the priest's father (Dane Clark). Several simulated sex scenes, some bloody violence, and occasional rough language. O (R)

Last Romantic Lover, The (1979) French sex farce begins with a male beauty contest sponsored by a women's magazine and ends with the runner-up romancing the supposedly liberated woman editor with such old-fashioned techniques as tenderness. The movie is directed by Just Jaeklin with all the gloss and glamour that he learned as a fashion photographer. Except for some partial nudity, it is a throwback to an earlier age of sexual comedy that feminists may find more objectionable than moralists. O (R)

Last Run, The (1971) George C. Scott plays an old-time professional getaway driver hired to breakout a young convict (Tony Musante), and he handles all the ensuing ambushes, chases, and double-crosses with credible assurance. Directed by Richard Fleischer, the flawed narrative is of less interest than Scott's bravura performance. Some violence and sexual references. A-III (GP)

Last Safari, The (1967) Mediocre British adventure directed by Henry Hathaway with Stewart Granger as a safari guide. The original version featured extensive nudity, which was edited out of the American release. A-I (br)

Last Seduction, The (1994) After stealing the proceeds of a drug deal from her hapless husband (Bill Pullman), a manipulative woman (Linda Fiorentino) hides out in a small town until she ensnares a lovestruck chump (Peter Berg), hoping to get him in the clear by having him kill her spouse. Director John Dahl's cynical crime-thriller twists its way through a hard-edged narrative of greed and lust perpetrated by colorful, if despicable, characters. Brief sexual encounters with partial nudity, crude sexual references, fleeting violence, and much rough language. A-III (R)

Last Shot You Hear, The (1969) Unintriguing thriller dealing with a renowned marriage counselor (Hugh Marlowe) who, after refusing to give his wife a divorce, is murdered by her lover. Director Gordon Hessler's movie concludes fatuously attempting to elicit sympathy for the murderers. O (PG)

Last Starfighter, The (1984) High-school senior (Lance Guest), a whiz at electronic games, finds himself defending the frontiers of the universe against ruthless space invaders in a touching, romantic, humorous fantasy from director Nick Castle. Some of the violence might be too much for younger viewers. A-II (PG)

Last Summer (1969) Suntanned teenagers (Richard Thomas, Bruce Davison, and Barbara Hershey) exploring adolescent limits of mutual trust and confidence and the tragic destruction of a self-possessed young girl (Kathy Burns) form the background and structure of the movie. Director Frank Perry's vision of upper-class youths contending with their curiosity about each other's physique and psyche features a terrifying rape sequence in which the antics and silliness in the first part of the film turn to dread. Though its use of nudity is questionable, this journey of sorts into self-discovery is a provocative examination of physical and spiritual maturation. A-IV (X/R/GP/R)

Last Summer in the Hamptons (1995) Talky comedy in which a theatrical family's matriarch (Viveca Lindfors), who has put on Chekovian dramas at her summer estate for years, gathers the clan and a young Hollywood star (Victoria Foyt) to stage their swan-song production before the property is sold. Director Henry Jaglom's rambling look at several generations beset by romantic and professional longings has occasional scenes of wry dialogue sprinkled throughout its rather drawn-out gabfest. Numerous sexual references, an attempted suicide, and intermittent rough language. A-III (R)

Last Sunset, The (1961) Western clunker in which a US lawman (Rock Hudson) trails a killer (Kirk Douglas) to Mexico, then both help a rancher (Joseph Cotten) on a cattle drive to Texas, where they finally shoot it out. Directed by Robert Aldrich, the inert script focuses on the outlaw's relationship with the rancher's wife (Dorothy Malone) and teen daughter (Carol Lynley), with incest as a plot gimmick. Superficial treatment of mature themes. A-III (br)

Last Supper, The (1996) Empty satire in which idle graduate students indulge their sense of superiority by inviting those they regard as less enlightened right-wingers, e.g., pro-lifers, anti-Semites, and homophobes, to dinner each week, then poisoning their wine, until the tables are turned by a pragmatic TV commentator (Ron Perlman). Directed by Stacy Title, the ludicrous premise merely gives license to outrageous political and social stereotypes in a static story which is pointless, unamusing, and devoid of any moral perspective, let alone wit or ideas. Callous murders, racist rhetoric, sexual innuendo, occasional profanity, and much rough language. O (R)

Last Tango in Paris (1973) Middle-aged man (Marlon Brando), numb with despair at the suicide of his wife, happens upon a woman (Maria Schneider) inspecting a vacant apartment, and they immediately engage in sex. She returns again and again to the apartment for further encounters, but when he eventually proposes marriage, she runs away, and in pursuing her he is killed. Directed by Bernardo Bertolucci, the romantic twaddle about tortured, alienated people adds up to very little, and the sex scenes, while not pornographic, are needlessly extended and explicit. O (X/R/NC-17)

Last Temptation of Christ, The (1988) Deeply flawed screen adaptation of the Nikos Kazantzakis novel probing the mystery of the human nature of Jesus Christ, the Son of God, fails because of artistic inadequacy, rather than anti-religious bias. Director Martin Scorsese's wrong-headed insistence on gore and brutality, as well as a preoccupation with sexual rather than spiritual love, is compounded by screenwriter Paul Schrader's muddled script, shallow characterizations, and flat dialogue delivered woodenly by William Dafoe in the title role. Excessively graphic violence, several sexually explicit scenes, and some incidental nudity. O (R)

Last Time I Committed Suicide, The (1997) Weak dramatization of the Denver youth of Neal Cassady (Thomas Jane), one of the 1950s Beat literary group, follows his affairs with a suicidal secretary (Claire Forlani) and a wild teenager (Gretchen Mol), as well as drinking bouts with a pool-hall buddy (Keanu Reeves). Writer-director Stephen Kay's hectic narrative is a chaotic series of vignettes picturing a shiftless young man more interested in fun than art. Sexual situations, some rough language, and occasional profanity. A-III (R)

Last Time I Saw Paris, The (1954) Sentimental tearjerker in which an American in Paris at the end of WW II marries a lovely woman (Elizabeth Taylor), becomes a reporter, inherits some money, turns into an alcoholic, then sobers up to return to wife and child. Directed by Richard Brooks from F. Scott Fitzgerald's updated story, the result is a glossy but unconvincing sudser. Romantic complications and alcohol abuse. A-II (br)

Last Train from Gun Hill (1959) Uneven Western in which a marshal (Kirk Douglas) tracks down a killer (Earl Holliman) whose victim was the lawman's Indian wife, then has to get him out of a town loyal to the culprit's father (Anthony Quinn). Despite an overly contrived plot and muddled relationships, director John Sturges effectively depicts the consequences of racial prejudice while wringing considerable suspense out of the lawman's predicament. Stylized violence and justice questions. A-II (br)

Last Tycoon, The (1976) Uninspired film version of the unfinished F. Scott Fitzgerald novel about an Irving Thalberg-like producer (Robert De Niro) who slowly works himself to death. Despite the handsomely mounted production, director Elia Kazan runs out of creative ideas of what to do with a cast (Robert Mitchum, Jeanne Moreau, and Tony Curtis) seemingly adrift in the setting. Occasional rough language and an overextended nude sequence. A-IV (PG)

Last Unicorn, The (1982) Animated feature about a lonely unicorn (voice of Mia Farrow) who goes off in a quest to learn what happened to the others of her kind. Though the animation is not very imaginative, the Rankin and Bass production has some superb voice-over talent (Alan Arkin, Angela Lansbury, Keenan Wynn, Christopher Lee, and Tammy Grimes), and the story itself is likeable enough. The result provides some pleasant fantasy for younger children. A-I (G)

Last Valley, The (1971) Omar Sharif plays a man of letters fleeing the 17th-century wars of religion and nationalism in the Germanies who takes refuge in an out-of-the-way, untouched village, but soon it is also found by a band of freebooters (led by Michael Caine). Written, produced, and directed by James Clavell, it is of more historical than dramatic interest, and its scenes of mass slaughter and individual cruelty coupled with the moral ambiguities of life under duress make it decidedly mature fare. A-III (GP)

Last Voyage, The (1960) When the boiler in an aging ocean-liner blows, the captain (George Sanders) delays evacuating the sinking vessel while his chief engineer (Edmond O'Brien) tries to contain the damage. Writer-director Andrew L. Stone's so-so disaster movie centers on the plight of a trapped woman (Dorothy Malone) whose husband (Robert Stack) gets heroic help from one of the crew (Woody Strode). Much menace, including a terrified child. A-I (br)

Last Wagon, The (1956) Muddled clash-of-cultures Western set in 1873 Arizona, where a man (Richard Widmark) raised by Comanches and wanted for murder risks his life to save the few survivors of a wagon train massacred by Apaches. Directed by Delmer Daves, the well-intentioned story flounders in bad dialogue about big issues — revenge, lynching, racial prejudice — and less-than-credible action scenes. Frontier violence and themes of unlikely interest to children. A-I (br)

Last Waltz, The (1978) This is a cinematic record of the last concert given by a rock group called The Band. Supplemented by interview footage and some numbers shot in a studio, director Martin Scorsese has put it all together extremely well, but its primary appeal is to rock fans. Some coarse language and an amoral attitude on the part of some of the performers. A-III (PG)

Last Wave, The (1979) Staid Australian lawyer (Richard Chamberlain) defends four aborigines accused of murder, but a mysterious tribal seer divines that the lawyer is the precursor of some cycle-ending event of cataclysmic proportions. Director Peter Weir evokes a strangely eerie sense of the aborigine's transcendental link with nature, in stark contrast to the sterile mechanistic environment of the city in which the trial takes place. Increasingly heavy atmosphere of the occult and foreboding of human disaster. A-III (PG)

L'Atalante (1934) Lyrically romantic French classic tells of a barge captain (Jean Daste) who brings his country bride (Dita Parlo) to live aboard his boat, but when they reach Paris, she goes off to see the sights and gets left behind until the crusty old mate (Michel Simon) reunites the unhappy couple. Director Jean Vigo's simple tale of love and its complications is marked by strange, yet lovely, surreal passages, Simon's masterfully eccentric performance and Boris Kaufman's poetic photography of life along the river. Several references to prostitution and a scene of erotic yearning. A-III (nr)

Latcho Drom (1994) Dramatically unstructured presentation of gypsies performing their music, song, and dance as filmed in such diverse locales as Romania, Spain, and India. In stringing together this sampling of musical performances, director Tony Gatlif provides a broad sense of Gypsy musical traditions from joyous celebrations of life to lamentations of their persecution through the ages, but gives little insight into their history and culture. Subtitles. Fleeting nudity. A-II (nr)

Late Autumn (1973) Fine Japanese drama made in 1961 about a young woman who rejects marriage because she does not wish to leave her widowed mother alone, but the mother tricks her into getting engaged. Director Yasujiro Ozu lightens the mood with some gentle humor, especially pointed at insufferable male smugness in a society in which women are dependent upon men. A-I (nr)

Late for Dinner (1991) Silly fantasy about a young family man (Brian Wimmer), frozen with his mildly retarded brother-in-law (Peter Berg) in 1962, and thawing 29 years later to return to his now middle-aged wife (Marcia Gay Harden) and grown daughter (Colleen Flynn). Producer-director W.D. Richter's inept attempt at heartfelt drama, comedy, and fantasy overplays the story's sappy sentiment. Momentary violence. A-II (PG)

Late Great Planet Earth, The (1979) Screen version of a book proving the imminent destruction of earth using prophecies from the Old and New Testament is a mishmash of interviews with experts of greater and lesser authority, portentous narration, and stock newsreel footage, with a touch of pseudo-biblical drama thrown in. Its distorted idea of the nature and purpose of biblical prophecy makes it unsuited to young and impressionable viewers. A-III (PG)

Late Liz, The (1973) Anne Baxter plays a hard-drinking woman who sifts through multiple marriages and attempted suicide before salvation hits her through the guidance of a local clergyman. Directed by Dick Ross, its rather bogus sentimentality and adult situations make it adult fare. A-III (GP)

Late Show, The (1977) Art Carney as the aging private eye (who spends most of his time watching old movies on television) feels compelled to solve the murder of his old partner (Howard Duff), who shows up on his doorstep with a fatal bullet wound. Lily Tomlin teams up in the sleuthing and the result is an above-average crime entertainment directed by Robert Benton. Occasional violence and crude language. A-III (PG)

Late Spring (1972) Japanese story of a dutiful daughter who refuses to leave her widowed father until he finally is forced to trick her into marriage. Director Yasujiro Ozu's 1949 movie is a lyric study of the abiding strength of family life and relationships, warmly told and universal in its values. A-I (nr)

Latitude Zero (1970) Japanese science-fiction movie with Joseph Cotton and Cesar Romero pitted against each other as the classic counterparts of good and evil. Directed by Inoshiro Honda, an underwater city in the Jules Verne vein, grotesque monsters, and some excellent miniature work make it a must for sci-fi fans. A couple of grisly scenes are inappropriate for small children. A-II (PG)

Laughing Policeman, The (1973) Detective thriller

about a brutal mass-murder on a San Francisco bus that veteran detective Walter Matthau pursues because his partner is one of those killed, and the clues point to a previous unsolved murder case. There's the basis for a good yarn here, but director Stuart Rosenberg puts too much emphasis on violence, crude language, and an exploration of the city's tawdry side. O (R)

Laughter in Paradise (1951) Clever British comedy in which the relatives of late prankster Hugh Griffith inherit his estate under certain conditions, namely that pulp-fiction writer Alastair Sim spend a month in jail, meek bank clerk George Cole rob his own bank, self-centered spinster Fay Compton spend a month as a domestic servant, and shiftless playboy Guy Middleton marry. Director Mario Zampi gets chortles from the predicaments of all four, especially Sim and Cole, but bogs down in showing how each is changed for the better in trying to fulfill the will's stipulations. Mild sexual innuendo. A-II (br)

Laughter in the Dark (1969) British drama about a man of some intelligence and breeding being destroyed by his infatuation for an unscrupulous schemer. The performance of Nicol Williamson, as the titled art dealer victimized by a dreadful cinema usherette (Anna Karina), is skillful, and Tony Richardson's direction evidences serious intentions, but the cumulative effect is merely ludicrous with more than a little nudity and explicit depiction of sex. O (X)

Laura (1944) Sparse mystery embroidered with moody romance from Vera Caspary's novel about a police detective (Dana Andrews) investigating the reported murder of the beautiful title character (Gene Tierney) whose rise in the New York social set was aided by an influential radio commentator (Clifton Webb at his waspish best). Things, of course, are not what they seem, as director Otto Preminger probes the dark side of high-society life while focusing on the dour detective's growing fascination with the glamorous Laura and the vitriolic journalist's feelings for his former protégé. More for romantics than mystery fans, there are some scenes of menace, stylized violence, and implied sexual encounters. A-II (nr)

Laurel and Hardy's Laughing Twenties (1966) Affectionate look back at the great comedy team of Stan Laurel and Oliver Hardy in a collection of excerpts from their silent two-reelers. The narrative is helpful and the sight gags irresistible. A-I (br)

Lavender Hill Mob, The (1951) British comedy classic in which a timid bank employee (Alec Guinness) concocts a scheme to hijack a shipment of gold bullion with the aid of professional crooks (Sidney James and Alfie Bass), then melt it down in the foundry of an accommodating sculptor (Stanley Holloway) and recast it as Eiffel Tower souvenirs for export to Paris. Scripted by T.E.B. Clarke and directed by Charles Crichton, the tongue-in-cheek depiction of a perfect crime has one hilarious flaw after another, culminating in a wild police chase through London and a neat twist ending in South America. Comic crime caper and mild menace. A-II (br)

Law and Disorder (1974) A taxi driver (Carrol O'Connor) and a hairdresser (Ernest Borgnine) form a number of their New York neighbors into an auxiliary police force to put a stop to an invasion of muggers, thieves, and exhibitionists. Directed by Ivan Passer, there is some sharp satire on contemporary urban crime and middle-class frustrations. Some intense violence, very rough language, and a number of embarrassing sexual references. A-IV (R)

Law and Jake Wade, The (1958) Contrived Western in which an outlaw (Richard Widmark) seeks revenge on a one-time partner (Robert Taylor) who ran out on him with the loot from a bank robbery, then settled down as sheriff of a small town. Directed by John Sturges, the clumsy narrative has the lawman and his fiancé (Paricia Owens) taken captive and forced to lead the outlaw's gang to the missing loot on a journey ending in a ghost town during a Comanche uprising. Stylized violence and much menace. A-II (nr)

Law and Order (1953) Routine Western directed by Nathan Juran in which a retired sheriff (Ronald Reagan) refuses to help a town rid itself of a brutal gang (headed by Preston Foster), but changes his mind after they kill his brother (Alex Nicol). Frontier violence, some of it quite nasty. A-II (br)

Law of the Lawless, The (1963) When a former gunman-turned-judge (Dale Robertson) arrives in town to try the son (John Agar) of an old friend (Barton MacLane) for murder, he faces a gunman (Bruce Cabot) hired to kill him. Director William F. Claxton can't do much with the contrived script, but a game cast of veterans (Yvonne De Carlo, William Bendix, Richard Arlen, Kent Taylor, and Lon Chaney, Jr.) do their best to make it seem interesting. While the movie's anti-gun message is laudable, its use of violence makes it unlikely fare for children. A-I (br)

Lawless Breed, The (1952) Routine Western directed by Raoul Walsh presents a sympathetic account of the life of famed Texas badman John Wesley Hardin (Rock Hudson), a preacher's son who claimed he killed only in self-defense but was sentenced to a long prison term for his crimes, after which he became a peaceable family man. Shootouts and justice questions. A-II (br)

Lawless Street, A (1955) Cliched Western in which a veteran marshal (Randolph Scott) outguns all his foes and wins back the wife (Angela Lansbury) who had left him years before because she disdained bloodshed. Director Joseph H. Lewis is more interested in shootouts and barroom brawls than in trying to make some sense out of a silly plot-line. Much violence and implied adultery. A-III (br)

Lawman (1971) Straight-shooting marshal Burt Lancaster attempts to round up seven murder suspects in a town where long-time sheriff Robert Ryan has learned to compromise with local cattle-baron Lee J. Cobb. The situation results in bloodshed with justice depending upon the fastest, surest gun. Director Michael Winner seems to have pretensions about examining what or who is the law, but the conclusion solves nothing. Stylized violence and bloodshed. A-III (GP)

Lawn Dogs (1998) Disturbing tale in which a 10-year-old girl (Mischa Barton) stubbornly seeks out the friendship of a dirt-poor 21-year-old laborer (Sam Rockwell), but their innocent relationship is misunderstood by vicious adults, with tragic results. Director John Duigan's delivers a darkly manipulative drama of class prejudices, which stacks the deck by pitting an entire community against a brash but well-meaning youth. Sexual situations, some full nudity, scattered violence, and intermittent profanity, as well as rough language. A-IV (R)

Lawnmower Man, The (1992) Failed sci-fi movie about a driven doctor (Pierce Brosnan) whose experiments turn a retarded man (Jeff Fahey) into a killer with psychic powers. Directed by Brett Leonard, it's little more than a computer-graphics variation on the mad-scientist theme, with thoroughly unappealing characters and images. Recurring violence, including a sadistic cleric, brief sexual encounters with momentary nudity, and some rough language. A-III (R)

Lawrence of Arabia (1963) Set within the frame of a grand adventure is this interesting study of British hero-author T.E. Lawrence (Peter O'Toole), whose WW I exploits in leading the Arabs against the Turks made his literary works popular in the 1920s. Director David Lean focuses on the diverse aspects of the man with an ambiguity suitable to the mystery still surrounding this mythic figure. Bloody wartime battles and implications of a homosexual incident. A-II (PG)

Laws of Gravity (1992) Shrill drama about two hot-tempered Brooklyn thugs (Peter Greene and Adam Trese) trying to hold on to their women (Edie Falco and Arabella Field) while secretly conniving to rip off a cache of stolen guns. Writer-director Nick Gomez blunders through a meaninglessly violent story of brutish, boastful thieves, told in ear-splitting obscenities. Some graphic violence, including abuse of women, much heavy drinking, and nonstop rough language. O (R)

Lawyer, The (1970) Routine crime melodrama in which a hotshot lawyer (Barry Newman) races around California in his beat-up camper trying to get his client, philandering Dr. Jack Harrison (Robert Colbert), off the hook for murdering his wife. Directed by Sidney J. Furie, it contains frequent nudity and crude dialogue. O (R)

Lay of the Land, The (1997) Pathetic seriocomic tale of husband-and-wife college professors (Sally Kellerman and Ed Begley, Jr.) trying to ease mid-life crises by having madcap affairs, which only magnify their marital problems. Writer-director Larry Arrick's juvenile attempt at poignant comedy is pretentiously misconceived, atrociously acted, and badly edited. Comic treatment of adultery, brief violence, some nudity, occasional profanity, and intermittent rough language. A-III (R)

Le Beau Mariage (1982) French comedy of manners and morals from director Eric Rohmer proves to be an amusing yet perceptive exploration of courtship rituals and mating practices not far different from our own. Its young heroine (Beatrice Romano), fed up with the complications of her affair with a married man, decides to get married and sets out to find her own husband. The result is a comedy of situations seen from a feminine perspective. A-III (PG)

Le Boucher (1972) Excellent psychological thriller about a schoolteacher (Stephane Audran) and the butcher of the title (Jean Yanne), who live in a small French village, where a series of insane murders have taken place. Written and directed by Claude Chabrol, the script is marvelously tight and disciplined, and the characterizations have an unusually solid psychological foundation. There are some shocks, but they are done with all the authority of the old master, Hitchcock himself. A-III (GP)

Le Chat (1975) French study of a couple (Simone Signoret and Jean Gabin) who have been married for 25 years but whose ardor has cooled and turned to rancor. Directed by Pierre Granier-Deferre, the script is one of unrelieved bleakness, yet the two principals invest their roles with a rich human dimension as two imperfect individuals who stubbornly go on, fueled by hate, but they sometimes remember love. A-III (nr)

Le Départ (1968) Belgian story of an assistant hairdresser (Jean-Pierre Leaud) who is so obsessed with the idea of entering an upcoming motor rally that he neglects his girlfriend in trying to find a suitable car. Director Jerzy Skolimowski treats his self-indulgent youth with stinging humor but also with some sympathy. A-III (br)

Le Magnifique (1976) Jean-Paul Belmondo stars in a failed satire of super-spy adventures of the James Bond variety. Forgettable French production directed by Phillipe de Broca. A-III (nr)

Le Mans (1971) Steve McQueen combines his acting and racing skills in a convincing portrait of a driver in the famed Le Mans competition in France. Directed by Lee H. Katzin, the drama is on the track and racing fans will find much satisfaction in the authenticity of the driving and in the beauty of the machines A-I (G)

Le Petit Théâtre de Jean Renoir (1969) Three short nostalgic sketches present a Christmas fantasy, a wildly funny opéra bouffe, and a tribute to the French game of boules. A charming interlude, sung by Jeanne Moreau, complements this homage to life by director Jean Renoir, who introduces each of his tales with an unpretentious explanation of his reasons for bringing it to life on film. Lovely, quaint, and sentimental by turn, but with some mature themes. A-III (nr)

Le Retour d'Afrique (1973) Swiss drama about a

young couple who decide to join a friend in Africa to help fashion a better world. After a final farewell party, a telegram arrives from their friend telling them not to come, and that the explanation is in the mail. Awaiting the letter in their empty flat, they begin to confront themselves and their relationship to society. Director Alain Tanner's theme of real change coming only from within is a bit pretentious and stilted, yet it does raise questions about coping in a post-industrial society. A-III (nr)

Le Sex Shop (1973) Unfunny French sex-farce about the owner of a failing bookstore (Claude Berri) who opens a shop selling erotic books and related mechanical contraptions, and then becomes obsessed with his merchandise and starts experimenting. Also written and directed by Berri, what might have been a satire on contemporary sexual mores itself becomes obsessed with the subject, and the explicit nature of its treatment is at best tasteless and at worst grossly offensive. O (X/R)

Le Trio Infernal (1974) Failed French black-comedy depicting the moral bankruptcy of society following WW I, the plot details the murder-for-profit of two German sisters (Romy Schneider and Mascha Gomska) by a French war hero (Michel Piccoli). Directed by Francis Girod, what begins as a Gallic sex farce soon becomes mired in details of ghoulish dismemberments and bizarre sex. O (nr)

Leadbelly (1976) Screen biography tracing the troubled life of neglected Huddie Ledbetter, legendary black folksinger and master of the twelve-string guitar, whose work became part of the post-WW II folk renaissance. Director Gordon Parks downplays the racial themes in favor of a musical tribute, while eliciting a colorfully authentic performance from Roger E. Mosley as Huddie. A-III (PG)

League of Their Own, A (1992) In a spirited, often amusing drama about the formation of a women's professional baseball league during WW II, the narrative follows the course of a season with a team whose odd assortment of players includes sibling rivals (Geena Davis and Lori Petty), a backwoods slugger (Megan Cavanagh), streetwise fielders (Madonna and Rosie O'Donnell), and a washed-up rummy as manager (Tom Hanks). Directed by Penny Marshall, the story uses the baseball diamond as an arena of team solidarity and personal self-discovery rather than as an ideological soapbox, though its feminist perspective is abundantly evident. A few mild sexual references, some vulgar language, and occasional tasteless humor, including a toilet joke. A-II (PG)

Lean on Me (1989) Formula feel-good bio of controversial Paterson, N.J., high-school principal Joe Clark (Morgan Freeman) focuses on his mission to clean up the crime and graffiti-infested school, restore student self-pride, and raise their abysmal reading scores. Fearless, funny, and nasty, Freeman is a standout as he rejuvenates the school. Director John G. Avildsen's cartoon movie-heroics may be simplistic, and the screenplay may play fast and loose with the facts, but the film should speak to older urban adolescents faced with similar school blight. Much rough language, some violence, and menace and a flash of nudity. A-III (PG-13)

Leap of Faith (1992) During a three-day revival in a backwater Kansas town, a bogus faith-healer (Steve Martin) and his mercenary manager (Debra Winger) each experience minor transformations when he witnesses a possible real miracle, and she is moved by the decency of the local sheriff (Liam Neeson). Director Richard Pearce's serio-comedy of religious hucksterism has few laughs and little meaning, made all the more unsatisfactory by a vague, feel-good ending. Comic depiction of religious sentiment exploited for profit and an implied sexual encounter. A-III (PG-13)

Learning Tree, The (1969) Director Gordon Park's lifeless cinematic version of his autobiographical novel is a highly romantic, colorful recreation of a black adolescent's coming-of-age in a mixed atmosphere of gentleness and violence, honesty, hypocrisy, and bigotry. The result has more a sense of a photographic essay than of a realistic portrait of the rural black experience. A-III (PG)

Leather Boys, The (1966) British story of a failed marriage, with Rita Tushingham as a teenager who weds to escape her appalling home, Colin Campbell as the immature husband, and Dudley Suttton as his calculating friend. Though the episodic story is loosely motivated, the acting is first-rate, and Sidney Furie's direction has the ring of authenticity. A-III (br)

Leathernecks Have Landed, The (1936) Dated pulp-adventure in movie-land China, where an ex-Marine (Lew Ayres) turns gunrunner, then winds up back in the Corps by saving his former buddies from a rebel attack. Director Howard Bretherton does little with the standard melodramatics, though a likeable cast (James Ellison, Isabel Jewell, and Ward Bond) makes it relatively painless. Stylized violence. A-I (br)

Leave Her to Heaven (1945) Contrived potboiler in which a beautiful fruitcake (Gene Tierney) proves a moral monster after jilting her powerful fiancé (Vincent Price) for a sensitive author (Cornel Wilde), then lets his handicapped brother drown, kills her unborn child in a fall, and commits suicide in a manner that makes her adopted sister (Jeanne Crain) seem the killer. Directed by John M. Stahl, the lush settings have more interest than the thin characterizations and hokey plot. Stylized violence and domestic tensions. A-II (br)

Leave It to Beaver (1997) Formula adaptation of the popular 1957-63 TV family series follows the trouble Beaver Cleaver (Cameron Finley) gets into after his bike is stolen and he continually skips football practice. Directed by Andy Cadiff, the thin proceedings rely on a child star whose appeal isn't strong enough to carry the weak, derivative comedy. Mild sexual innuendo, brief deception by a child, and minor comic violence. A-II (PG)

Leave It to Blondie (1945) Formula family comedy directed by Abby Berlin follows the misadventures of the Bumsteads after Blondie (Penny Singleton) gets Dagwood (Arthur Lake) to enter a songwriting contest. A-I (br)

Leaving Las Vegas (1995) Sterile story of a washed-up, alcoholic Hollywood writer (Nicolas Cage) who goes to Las Vegas to drink himself to death and the hardened prostitute (Elisabeth Shue) who helps him along the way because she finds some comfort in his company. Director Mike Figgis's self-indulgent elegy for self-destructive losers evokes as much emotional depth as watching TV test patterns. Graphic sex, occasional violence including a gang rape, and much rough language. O (R)

Leaving Normal (1992) A runaway battered wife (Meg Tilly) and a hard-bitten cocktail waitress (Christine Lahti) hitchhike to Alaska in hopes of finally putting down roots. Director Edward Zwick's combination female buddy and road movie is too contrived to be convincing. Recurring rough language and some sexual innuendo. A-III (R)

Leech Woman, The (1960) Clunky horror tale directed by Edward Dein in which a doctor (Philip Terry) finds an African potion capable of making the old young again, but a human sacrifice is needed to activate it. This is no problem for the doctor's aging wife (Coleen Gray), who maintains her youth by a series of killings, beginning with her cruel husband. Nasty stylized violence, sexual situations, and marital antagonisms. A-III (br)

Left Hand of God, The (1955) Fanciful melodrama set in 1947 China, where an American pilot (Humphrey Bogart) downed in WW II and forced to fight for the local warlord (Lee J. Cobb) finally escapes by assuming the identity of a dead Catholic missionary, then tries to save the priest's mission from the warlord's vengeance. Directed by Edward Dmytryk, the conflict between pilot and bandit has some interest, but the priestly masquerade and the romantic feelings it arouses in a mission aide (Gene Tierney) are pure Hollywood hokum. Bogus clergyman and romantic complications. A-II (br)

Left-Handed Gun, The (1958) Western misfire in which Billy the Kid (Paul Newman) determines to kill the four men who ambushed his English employer, but after finishing the job, his one-time friend and now sheriff Pat Garrett (John Dehner) tracks him down. Directed by Arthur Penn from Gore Vidal's TV drama, the choppy narrative keeps going off on tangents, and the acting is rooted more in the New York stage than in the sagebrush, with disappointing results. Hard-edged violence and sexual innuendo. A-III (br)

Legacy (1976) Middle-aged woman (Joan Hotchkis) is too busy to notice that she is on the verge of a breakdown in director Karen Arthur's attempt to turn a myriad of feminist themes into a movie. Her treatment of a woman's repressed sexuality and guilt feelings about her life might have some use for women's discussion groups but not as a popular entertainment. O (R)

Legacy, The (1979) Inferior horror movie of the satanic, let's-make-a-deal sub-genre depicts the misadventures of a bright, unmarried young couple (Katharine Ross and Sam Elliot) in a Gothic English manor. Directed by Richard Marquand, the story is extremely silly and excessively gory. O (R)

Legal Eagles (1986) Robert Redford tries his best to be funny, charming, and resourceful as the lawyer whose political ambitions get sidetracked when two women, a lawyer (Debra Winger) and her client (Daryl Hannah), implicate him in an art fraud that turns into a murder case. Director Ivan Reitman's shallow comedy is marred by female stereotyping and casual sex. A-III (PG)

Legend (1986) Director Ridley Scott's sumptuous fairytale contrasts exceptionally cruel evil with extraordinarily sweet innocence in a quest to redeem a frozen world from the control of the Lord of Darkness. Tom Cruise is the hero who vanquishes the devil (Tim Curry) in an astonishing visual delight, but some instances of grotesque imagery, especially the Lord of Darkness, may frighten very young children. A-II (PG)

Legend of Billy Jean, The (1985) Four teenagers unwittingly become outlawed folk heroes. The value system represented is so confused that the movie is inappropriate for its intended adolescent audience. Some vulgar language. A-III (PG-13)

Legend of Boggy Creek, The (1973) Little town in Arkansas is bothered by a hairy monster, with a dubious footprint or two as evidence of its existence. In the fictionalized speculations about the monster's attacks, an actor made up with a lot of hair is photographed from the rear and sides in shadowy condition; he is as skillful at evading pursuing dogs and townsmen as he is the camera. A-I (G)

Legend of Hell House, The (1973) Good British horror movie in which a skeptical physicist (Clive Revill), his wife (Gayle Hunnicutt), and two mediums (Pamela Franklin and Roddy McDowell) attempt to unravel the source of the ghastly murders that occurred when a previous group of scientists attempted to penetrate the mysteries of a deserted gothic mansion on the outskirts of London. Directed by John Hough, it has plenty of atmosphere, not a little suspense, but also some intense violence and a suggestion of perverse sexuality. A-III (PG)

Legend of Lylah Clare, The (1968) Sudsy, sentimental soap opera in which a young starlet (Kim Novak) is coached by a has-been movie director (Peter Finch) who exhibits untoward interest in her that leads to tragedy. Directed by Robert Aldrich, it's a clunker with sexually suggestive scenes. O (R)

Legend of Nigger Charley, The (1972) Runaway slaves (Fred Williamson, D'Urville Martin, and Don Pedro Colley) are pursued by a bloodthirsty slave-tracker (Keith Prentice). Directed by Martin Goldman, the mindless action movie indulges in some foul language and incidental nudity. A-IV (PG)

Legend of the Lone Ranger, The (1981) Klinton Spilsbury plays the masked champion of justice who, with the aid of Tonto (Michael Horse), rescues President Grant (Jason Robards) from the clutches of a badman (Christoper Lloyd). While moderately entertaining, director William A. Fraker's Western has considerable violence and occasional rough language. A-III (PG)

Legend of the Lost (1957) Uneven adventure tale starts in Timbuktu with an Italian doctor (Rossano Brazzi) hiring a veteran guide (John Wayne) to search for a lost city in the Sahara Desert, but the quest is complicated by taking along a local cafe entertainer (Sophia Loren) seeking to reform her life. Directed by Henry Hathaway, the travails of the journey and the secret of the abandoned city are lost in the men's sputtering rivalry over their female companion, with mostly slack results. Life-threatening situations and romantic complications. A-II (br)

Legend of Tom Dooley, The (1959) Unaware of Lee's surrender, Confederate raiders (including Michael Landon) attack a Union coach, kill some passengers, and become fugitives from Northern justice. Directed by Ted Post, the narrative is clumsily pegged to a song about doomed lovers, but the action is largely unconvincing. Stylized violence and romantic complications. A-II (br)

Legends of the Fall (1994) Set on the sprawling Montana spread of their rancher-father (Anthony Hopkins), the fate of three close brothers (Brad Pitt, Aidan Quinn, and Henry Thomas) is powerfully affected by the arrival of the youngest brother's captivating fiancé (Julia Ormond), whom all three want to marry. Directed by Edward Zwick, the melodramatic tale of family tragedy and doomed romance gains some historical sweep by tying the narrative to the young mens' service abroad in WW I, the mistreatment of Native Americans, and the ongoing backdrop of radically changing times for ranchers in the vanishing Old West. Some intense battlefield violence and revenge-motivated murders, brief bedroom scene with fleeting nudity, and minimal rough language. A-III (R)

Legions of the Nile (1960) Soapy Italian-Spanish co-production directed by Vittorio Cottafavi in which Cleopatra (Linda Cristal) is caught between court intriguers and invading Roman armies. The English-language version alternates muscle-bound heroics with ludicrous sexual situations and innuendo. A-III (br)

L'Elégant Criminel (1992) Before he is guillotined in 1836, a notorious French murderer (Daniel Auteuil) writes his memoirs rationalizing his life of crime. Director Francis Girod's overlong, fact-based period film leaves several key characters unexplained and fails to come to grips with what motivated the killer's callous behavior. Subtitles. Occasional violence and fleeting bedroom shots. A-III (nr)

Lemon Drop Kid, The (1951) Frantic adaptation of a Damon Runyon story in which a small-time bookie (Bob Hope) schemes to raise the money owed a gangster by setting up bogus sidewalk Santa Clauses supposedly collecting money for an old people's home. Directed by Sidney Lanfield, the script is tailored to suit Hope's talents for sight gags and one-liners, but the humor is too fitful to sustain the cumbersome plot and phony Christmastime sentimentality. Mild sexual innuendo. A-II (br)

Lemon Sisters, The (1990) Three lifelong girlfriends (Diane Keaton, Carol Kane, and Kathryn Grody), self-dubbed Atlantic City's singing "Lemon Sisters," support each other through personal and career crises. Director Joyce Chopra's comedy features endearing performances and some heartwarming moments, but is so lightweight it never gets beyond being a sentimental tribute to friendship. Brief instances of rough language. A-II (PG-13)

Lenny (1974) Screen version of Julian Barry's play about comic Lenny Bruce's problems with drugs and obscenity prosecution of his routines takes a semi-documentary stance by way of interviews with Bruce's widow, mother, agent, and others. Bob Fosse has directed an intelligent, complex, and often disturbing film, with Dustin Hoffman extraordinarily fine in the title role. No viewer should be surprised to hear a good deal of crude language. A-IV (R)

Leo and Lorrie (1980) A young actor and actress (Danny Most and Linda Purl), struggling for fame in television, fall in love, and encourage and console each other in this featherweight romantic comedy directed by Jerry Paris. The unabashed approval of unmarried cohabitation has enough substance to be morally offensive. O (PG)

Leo the Last (1970) The title character (Marcello Mastroianni), the last of an exiled European royal line, lives in the elegant family mansion in the heart of London's West Indian ghetto. When Leo realizes that the family fortune depends entirely on the rental income from these ghetto flats, he leads a peasant's revolt to blow up his mansion. The final frames show those who took part milling aimlessly around the rubble, wondering along with the audience what purpose director John Boorman's symbolic gesture served. Several relatively graphic sex scenes. A-IV (R)

Leolo (1993) A dreamy young boy (Maxime Collin) growing up in a strict Montreal family plagued by mental illness escapes his troubled surroundings by acting out murderous and sexual fantasies before going completely over the edge. Writer-director Jean-Claude Lauzon's self-indulgent and ugly view of life makes almost no human connections and gains added repulsion when seen through a child's eyes. Subtitles. Fierce murderous attacks, sexual perversions, some nudity, crude toilet humor, and rough language. O (nr)

Leon the Pig Farmer (1993) After learning that he is the product of artificial insemination in which the test tubes were accidentally switched, a Jewish Londoner (Mark Frankel) moves in with his natural father (Brian Glover), an earthy pig farmer in Yorkshire. Produced and directed by Gary Sinyor and Vadim Jean, the social comedy relies heavily on the contrasts between Jewish and gentile stereotypes for its satirical edge, but its exaggerated humor manages to be fitfully funny without being mean-spirited. Discreet bedroom scene with fleeting nudity and an irreverent depiction of religious traditions. A-III (nr)

Leonard Part 6 (1987) Comic misfire directed by Paul Weiland with writer-producer Bill Cosby starring as a CIA super-agent trying to win back his estranged wife while foiling a plot to control the world by turning ordinary animals into killer beasts. Unamusing claptrap with special-effects violence and conspicuous sexual innuendo. A-III (PG)

Leopard, The (1963) Historical drama set against the background of Garibaldi's 1860 invasion of Sicily, where the prince (Burt Lancaster) of an old aristocratic family refuses to adapt to revolutionary times despite the marriage of his more egalitarian nephew (Alain Delon) to the daughter of a wealthy ex-peasant. Directed by Luchino Visconti from the novel by Giuseppe Di Lampedusa, the result captures a fascinating period of social, political, and economic change in a family saga filled with nostalgia for a past, more elegant age. Subtitles. Mature themes. A-III (br)

Leopard Man, The (1943) Producer Val Lewton's dark, eerie thriller is set in a New Mexico town, where a singer's agent (Dennis O'Keefe) rents a leopard as a publicity stunt, but the animal's escape is followed by a series of deaths which the agent begins to suspect are the work of a madman. Director Jacques Tourneur overcomes a weak plot by using the power of suggestion to fill the situation with dread and suspense, while making good use of the Hispanic locale and character, including a religious procession in the climax. Menacing atmosphere. A-II (br)

Leopard Son, The (1996) Nature documentary follows two years in the growth of a male leopard from cub to adulthood on Africa's Serengeti Plains. Narrated by John Gielgud and directed by Hugo van Lawick, the dramatically photographed chronicle of life in the wild provides an uncompromising portrait of the survival of the fittest, with some fairly graphic scenes of animal kills. A-I (G)

Lepke (1975) Crime melodrama about a top Jewish member (Tony Curtis) of Murder Incorporated who has the unenviable distinction of being the only upper-echelon gang leader to suffer capital punishment. Directed by Menahem Golan, the problem of working up sympathy for a ruthless criminal, though a dedicated family man, is not surmounted by the talents involved. The treatment is restrained except for one excessive scene combining both sexuality and violence. O (R)

Leprechaun (1993) Feeble horror movie written and directed by Mark Jones strings out a series of disjointed encounters with the title's nasty little creature (Warwick Davis) who's in the US to recover a cache of gold coins. Intermittent violence with some graphic gore and occasional coarse language. A-III (R)

Leprechaun 2 (1994) Predictable horror sequel in which the title's murderous little monster (Warwick Davis) plans to marry a kidnapped teenager (Shevonne Durkin) but becomes distracted when her boyfriend (Charlie Heath) steals one of his precious gold coins. An inane script and Rodman Flender's lackluster direction result in a failed attempt at thrills and chills. Some brief gore with occasional sexual innuendo and fleeting nudity. A-III (R)

Les Biches (1968) Corruption is the theme of this subtle French production about the complicated relationship between a man and two women. Director Claude Chabrol is above all a moralist in telling the story of an innocent artist destroyed by the lavish excesses of wealthy society. Its context is psychologically ambiguous and seemingly amoral, and it ends in an outburst of madness. Chabrol's work raises questions about life rather than resolves them, and for this reason will not be very satisfying for the casual filmgoer. Others, however, will find it a thoughtful experience. A-IV (br)

Les Demoiselles de Rochefort (see: **The Young Girls of Rochefort**)

Les Diaboliques (see: **Diabolique**)

Les Enfants Terribles (1975) Jean Cocteau's story about the perennial revolt of youth against all that established society represents was brought to the screen in 1950 by director Jean-Pierre Melville. A remarkable achievement in many ways, some of its themes of alienation and self-destruction are troubling and even anarchistic but serve as a reminder that life is not as tidy and rational as one might wish. A-IV (nr)

Les Gauloises Bleues (1968) While his wife is giving birth in the hospital, the husband (Jean-Pierre Kalfon) waits, his thoughts of his own unhappy childhood and troubles as a young man. Written and directed by Michel Cournot, the surrealistic flow of these memories reflect the man's insecurity about himself and his relations with others, but many viewers will be put off by the obscurity of much of it. A-III (G)

Les Girls (1957) Uneven musical comedy about a 1930s European tour of a cabaret dance troupe (Mitzi Gaynor, Kay Kendall, and Taina Elg) headed by an American hoofer (Gene Kelly), as told in flashbacks during an English libel trial over the publication of Kendall's memoirs. Director George Cukor gets some bright moments from the Cole Porter songs and talented cast, but not enough to sustain an overlong narrative and some lame comedy routines. Romantic complications and considerable sexual innuendo. A-III (br)

Les Miserables (1935) Classic screen version of Victor Hugo's novel set in early 19th-century France, where a former convict (Fredric March) is inspired by the kindness of a bishop (Cedric Hardwicke) to turn his life around and become a highly respected citizen, though relentlessly pursued by a legalistic policeman (Charles Laughton). Directed by Richard Boleslawski, the narrative is well-paced and convincingly acted, with the theme of justice based on human dignity triumphing over that of the letter of the law. Stylized violence and an unwed mother. A-II (br)

Les Miserables (1995) Updated version of Victor Hugo's epic novel follows the attempts of a French laborer (Jean-Paul Belmondo) to spirit a Jewish family out of Nazi-occupied France, punctuated by periodic readings from the novel paralleling Jean Valjean's struggles with those of the laborer. Director Claude Lelouch's grandly ambitious adaptation retains the sweeping humanist themes of the original work but proves unwieldy in straining to mirror the novel's characters with those in WW II. Subtitles. Recurring intense violence including suicides and a brief sexual encounter. A-III (R)

Les Miserables (1998) Splendid adaptation of Victor Hugo's classic focuses on reformed convict Jean Valjean (Liam Neeson) and his efforts to elude the implacable Inspector Javert (Geoffrey Rush) while tenderly raising the daughter (Claire Danes) of a deceased prostitute (Uma Thurman). Director Bille August exquisitely brings out the novel's universal themes, integrating strong performances into vigorous narrative enhanced by striking visuals evoking the tumult of early 19th-century France. Some violence including a suicide and veiled sexual innuendo. A-II (PG-13)

Les Parapluies de Cherbourg (see: **The Umbrellas of Cherbourg**)

Les Violons du Bal (1974) French director Michel Drach has constructed a film-within-a-film dealing with the various problems he encountered in making a feature based upon his WW II memories of a Jewish childhood. The essential merit of this work lies in its strong evocation of the love uniting a family caught up in the terrors of the Nazi era. It succeeds admirably as a fragmentary remembrance of a child's struggling to cope with events beyond his comprehension. A-III (nr)

Les Voleurs (1996) Downbeat drama in which a coldhearted cop (Daniel Auteil), while investigating the murder of his gangster brother, becomes romantically involved with a very troubled female suspect (Laurence Cote) who's having an affair with her college instructor (Catherine Deneuve). Director Andre Techine explores the tense emptiness between characters whose inability to experience a loving relationship makes their lives joyless. Subtitles. A lesbian affair, a bedroom scene with full nudity, fleeting violence, and recurring rough language. A-IV (R)

Less Than Zero (1987) Failed cautionary tale about the terrible consequences of the drug scene for three bright high-school students in an affluent California community. Director Marek Kanievska spends most of his energies depicting the high-gloss drug scene so that none of the main three earn viewer sympathy or interest. Several excessive scenes of simulated sex and a pervasive atmosphere of the sordid depths of the drug culture. O (R)

Let Him Have It (1991) Plodding, fact-based drama about the 1952 London murder of a policeman by a teenager (Paul Reynolds) too young to be executed, although his 19-year-old accomplice (Chris Eccleston), who did not participate in the shooting, was hanged. A snail-like pace and unanswered questions mar director Peter Medak's miscarriage-of-justice movie that makes a strong case against capital punishment. Brief violence and recurring rough language. A-III (R)

Let It Be (1970) Filmed practice session of The Beatles as they rehearse various songs and clown around a bit. Directed by Michael Lindsay-Hogg in semi-documentary fashion with no real focal point or direction, but does give an interesting and informal low-key look behind the scenes. A-I (G)

Let Joy Reign Supreme (1976) French director Betrand Tavernier details the abuses of the aristocratic regime that led to the French Revolution. Philippe Noiret, Jean Rochefort, and Jean Pierre Marielle tend to get lost in a narrative preoccupied with noblemen's debauchery and clergymen's corruption in a manner closer to the excesses of sex farce than historical drama. O (nr)

Let the Good Times Roll (1973) Director Sid Levin's documentary shows the story of the Golden Age of Rock, and does it with a dazzling array of stars and an extraordinary balance of intelligence, artistry, and warm good humor. Stars Chuck Berry, Little Richard, Fats Domino, Chubby Checker, Bill Haley and the Comets, and Bo Diddley. A-II (PG)

Let's Dance (1950) Musical tearjerker in which a USO singer (Betty Hutton) in 1944 England turns down a fellow trouper (Fred Astaire) to wed a rich Army pilot who dies in the war, leaving her with a son whom she must support by re-teaming with her ex-beau or lose the child to her late spouse's domineering grandmother (Lucile Watson). Directed by Norman Z. McLeod, the sentimental proceedings are helped by some Frank Loesser tunes, Astaire's genial nonchalance, and occasional comic relief. Domestic problems and mild sexual innuendo. A-II (br)

Let's Do It Again (1975) Sidney Poitier (who also directed) and Bill Cosby play two lodge brothers from Atlanta who, in order to get money for a new meeting hall, get involved in a prize fight and the gangsters who go with it. Once the situation is set up, the comedy begins to flag and the gags become repetitious. It would be fine for children except for two sequences involving illicit lovemaking and an off-color verbal exchange. A-III (PG)

Let's Get Lost (1989) Disturbing documentary portrait of jazz trumpet great Chet Baker in youth and tragic middle age. Director Bruce Weber includes much performance footage and interviews with drug-dazed Chet at the end of his life, as well as with his wives, lovers, colleagues, and family. Though Baker's self-destructive lifestyle is not romanticized, there are explicit references to sexual promiscuity, drug and spouse abuse, and other anti-social behavior. A-IV (nr)

Let's Kill Uncle (1966) Offbeat British thriller about a young boy (Pat Cardi) who finds out his uncle (Nigel Green) is plotting to murder him and so contrives with his girlfriend (Mary Badham) to kill uncle. Produced and directed by William Castle, Green is excellent in the preposterous situation, but children may find the suspense a bit too intense. A-II (br)

Let's Make Love (1960) Clumsy romantic comedy about a billionaire playboy (Yves Montand) who falls for an actress (Marilyn Monroe) in a comedy revue, gets a role in the show, and then hires Bing Crosby, Gene Kelly, and Milton Berle to teach him to sing, dance, and tell jokes. They can't, and that's about as amusing as it gets in director George Cukor's laborious quest to wring some smiles out this lackluster star vehicle. Some sexually suggestive musical numbers. A-III (br)

Let's Scare Jessica to Death (1971) Zohra Lampert plays a young woman who goes to a remote farmhouse to recover from a nervous breakdown, only to find herself beset with eerie voices from beyond the grave. Unpretentious little horror movie directed with some intelligence by John Hancock. Some instances of sudden, graphic violence. A-III (GP)

Let's Talk About Men (1976) Italian director Lina Wertmuller's 1965 movie with four vignettes depicting the foibles of the male gender is a moderately entertaining parable with Nino Manfredi playing five roles that humorously contrast definitions of manhood. A-III (PG)

Let's Talk About Sex (1998) Clunky sexploitation fare intersperses pseudo-documentary footage of women being interviewed about their sex lives and desires with the sappy story of the interviewer (Troy Beyer, who also wrote and directed this amateur exercise in sleaze), her two roommates, and their troubled sex lives. The bogus proceedings exploit sexuality, though the result proves more boring than provocative or titillating. Sexually explicit situations and dialogue, nudity, and recurring rough language. O (R)

Lethal Weapon (1987) Mel Gibson is a deadly effective Los Angeles cop almost psychotically ruthless in getting his job done. He's teamed with a veteran policeman (Danny Glover) whose family is threatened by drug dealers headed by a former Vietnam Special Forces and CIA operative. Gibson's square-jawed version of a legalized Rambo and Richard Donner's powerfully frenetic direction festers with excessive violence, brutality, and profanity. O (R)

Lethal Weapon 2 (1989) Mindless, excessively violent sequel has the black-white cop team (Danny Glover and Mel Gibson) turn vigilante to squash a ruthless South African diplomat (Joss Ackland) behind a Los Angeles drug operation. Director Richard Donner forgoes human interest and suspense by stringing together an endless stream of intense chases, death-defying stunts, and numbing, bloody carnage. Some profanity and a sexual encounter with shadowed nudity. O (R)

Lethal Weapon 3 (1992) Tired sequel has two LA detectives (Mel Gibson and Danny Glover) out to get stolen, high-powered weapons off the streets — with a little help from an Internal Affairs officer (Rene Russo) and an overeager real-estate agent (Joe Pesci). Director Richard Donner's dull formula story and lame macho humor descends into a series of meaningless, glorified shootouts. Excessive violence, an implied sexual encounter, and much rough language. O (R)

Lethal Weapon 4 (1998) Mel Gibson and Danny Glover re-team as LA detectives pursuing a ring of Chinese counterfeiters while each copes with the imminent prospect of becoming a father and a grandfather respectively. Despite the cops' appealing camaraderie, director Richard Donner relies on the tired action formula of constant jokey violence and deadly mayhem masquerading as exciting fun. Excessive violence and brutality, occasional profanity, and much rough language. O (R)

Letter, The (1940) In a Singapore courtroom, the wife (Bette Davis) of a rubber-plantation owner (Herbert Marshall) stands trial for killing a man she claims tried to assault her, but his Eurasian widow (Gale Sondergaard) turns up with a letter proving it was an act of murder. Under William Wyler's moody direction, Davis gives a chilling performance in the coldly unsympathetic role as the faithless wife who ruins her life and the happiness of those around her. Restrained treatment of infidelity and its consequences. A-III (br)

Letter of Introduction, A (1938) When an aging movie star (Adolphe Menjou) learns that an aspiring actress (Andrea Leeds) is his daughter, he tries to launch her Broadway career, to the distress of her boyfriend (George Murphy). Director John M. Stahl's sentimental melodrama gets some welcome comic relief from Edgar Bergen's Charlie McCarthy. Mild romantic complications. A-I (br)

Letter to Brezhnev (1986) Two tough working-class girls in Liverpool search for romance and a way out of the narrow confines of their dull lives. This uncompromisingly realistic but lighthearted slice-of-life comedy, directed by Chris Bernard, features Peter Firth as a Russian sailor who provides a possible new direction for one of the girls (Alexandra Pigg). Harsh language and sexual innuendo. A-III (R)

Letter to Three Wives, A (1949) Classic sudser in which three suburban women (Jeanne Crain, Linda Darnell, and Ann Sothern) receive a note from a friend saying she has left town with one of their husbands (businessman Jeffrey Lynn, schoolteacher Kirk Douglas, and chain-store owner Paul Douglas, respectively). Writer-director Joseph L. Mankiewicz centers on each woman as she recalls her marriage in flashbacks laced with witty dialogue and contemporary social jabs which have dated badly, though the sentimental twist ending will never go out of style. Romantic complications. A-II (br)

Leviathan (1989) Tedious deep-sea monster movie in which an aborted Russian genetic experiment dooms a US mining team, turning most of its divers into amphibious beasts. Director George P. Cosmatos renders his cast (Richard Crenna, Amanda Pays, Peter Weller, and Daniel Stern) comatose long before the big pay-off, where the moral issue of using human guinea pigs loses out to showcasing the monsters. Moderate grisly gore and profanity. A-III (R)

Lianna (1983) Young wife (Linda Griffiths) falls in love with another woman (Jane Hallaren) and impulsively abandons her philandering husband and two children, only to find that she has traded one set of problems for another. Written, produced, and directed by John Sayles, it is a sensitive account of a lesbian relationship but lacks any but the most rudimentary of moral perspectives. Graphic and unnecessarily extended lovemaking sequence. O (R)

Liar Liar (1997) Unremarkable comedy in which a divorced dad (Jim Carrey) who is an habitual liar, especially when defending clients in court, is thrown for a loss when his little boy's birthday wish that Dad stop lying comes true. Directed by Tom Shadyac, Carrey's eccentric brand of physical humor is the only reason to see this sappy but occasionally risqué tale of a father learning about honesty and caring from his child. Brief comic violence, some sexual references, and an instance of profanity. A-III (PG-13)

Liberation of L.B. Jones, The (1970) Melodrama about the determined efforts of an upright black undertaker (Roscoe Lee Browne) to get a divorce from his unfaithful wife whose lover happens to be the white deputy of the little Tennessee town in which they live. Though perhaps overlong and cluttered with subplots, director William Wyler tells his story of racial justice in straightforward and dignified fashion. A-III (R)

License to Drive (1988) After failing his driver's exam, a 16-year-old (Corey Haim) borrows his grandfather's car to take out the girl of his dreams (Heather Graham). In the ensuing havoc, director Greg Beeman highlights the follies of peer pressure, puberty, and driving without a license. Fleeting rough language and a tasteless sex reference. A-II (PG-13)

Licence to Kill (1989) British agent James Bond (Timothy Dalton) has a personal vendetta as he tracks down a sadistic Latin-American drug lord (Robert Davi). As directed by John Glen, the usual nutty stunts, mechanical gizmos, and various Bond in-jokes fail to perk up this clone of every other Ramboesque action-adventure movie currently on the market. Grisly deaths by torture, intense chases, explosive violence, and implied sexual promiscuity. O (PG-13)

Lickerish Quartet, The (1970) Producer-director Radley Metzger's dreary sex melodrama is set in a decaying Italian castle occupied by a decadent husband, wife, and son, who spend their time watching porno movies and having sex with a houseguest (Silvana Venturelli). O (R)

Liebestraum (1991) Morbid melodrama about a love triangle (Kevin Anderson, Pamela Gidley, and Bill Pullman) that develops much like a decades-old murder mystery recalled by a dying woman (Kim Novak). Written and directed by Mike Figgis, this dark and plodding tale shows more style than substance as it winds down to an unsatisfying conclusion. Brief adulterous encounters, a flash of nudity, minimal stylized violence, and recurring rough language. A-III (R)

Lies My Father Told Me (1975) Warm, lyric picture of a boy's growing up in Montreal's Jewish ghetto, with a careful exploration of the customs and values of a ritualistic culture. Directed by Jan Kadar, it is a delicate poem about being Jewish and, at the same time, about being human. Some sexual elements make it mature fare. A-III (PG)

Life (1999) Bittersweet comedy in which Eddie Murphy and Martin Lawrence spend six cantankerous decades stuck together on a Mississippi prison farm after being wrongly convicted of murder. Director Ted Demme attempts to blend profane comedy with more serious concerns about injustice and institutionalized racism, but it's an overlong, rocky road. Some violence, mild sexual innuendo, intermittent profanity, and recurring rough language. A-III (R)

Life and Nothing But (1990) A war-weary major (Philippe Noiret) in post WW I France finds unexpected romance when a wealthy woman (Sabine Azema) enlists his help in locating her husband, who was reported missing in action and presumed dead. Director Bertrand Tavernier's uneven film makes pointed anti-war statements in an ironic context, but the movie is drearily drawn-out and mostly of interest for the principals' assured and impassioned performances. A minimum of vulgar expressions. A-II (PG)

Life and Times of Grizzly Adams, The (1976) Dan Haggerty stars as a late 19th-century trapper who lived with and befriended the animals of the Rocky Mountains. Directed by Richard Friedenberg, the movie is less a story than an occasion to show sun-drenched photography of picturesque landscapes and frolicsome animals that will appeal to very small children and undemanding adults. A-I (G)

Life and Times of Judge Roy Bean, The (1972) Director John Huston has a great deal of fun with this seriocomic tale of frontier justice as administered by the legendary "hanging judge" of Vinegaroon, Texas (Paul Newman). Some viewers, however, may not be as readily amused by its loud, coarse, and bawdy humor or repetitive use of fantasy violence. A-III (PG)

Life at the Top (1966) Laurence Harvey continues his callow progress in a sequel to **Room at the Top**.

Directed by Ted Kotcheff, the movie's realistic treatment of his groping for some kind of personal integrity in a rootless and corrupting society will seem excessive to some. A-IV (br)

Life Begins at 8:30 (1942) Maudlin melodrama about an aged, alcoholic actor (Monty Woolley) who relies on his dutiful daughter (Ida Lupino) to care for him, until a young man (Cornel Wilde) persists in courting her. Directed by Irving Pichel, the theme of filial devotion vs. personal happiness is painfully contrived, and Woolley's acerbic character wears thin long before film's end. A-II (br)

Life Begins for Andy Hardy (1941) The Hardy boy (Mickey Rooney) leaves Carvel to prove he's a man by getting a job in New York City, spurns help from a wealthy friend (Judy Garland), and learns the hard way that he's not ready for independence. Directed by George B. Seitz, this edition of the Hardy series is a bit more realistic than the others but equally sentimental about small-town virtues. A-I (br)

Life Is a Long Quiet River (1990) Two families react quite differently when told that each has a child that belongs to the other family. Director Etienne Chatiliez uses the plot primarily to pinpoint unflattering contrasts in the lifestyles of a smugly wealthy bourgeois family and a lower-class family of thieves whose greed is boundless. Some unwholesome sexual references and occasional vulgar expressions. A-III (nr)

Life Is Beautiful (1998) Bittersweet comic fable in which an Italian-Jewish bookseller (Roberto Benigni) uses his imagination to convince his little son that their grim existence in a Nazi concentration camp is just an elaborate contest, and that they are sure to win the grand prize. Also co-written and directed by Benigni, the story starts off as a slapstick comedy, with the young man courting his future wife, then midway becomes a touchingly human story of a parent's irrepressible determination to protect his child from terror and misery. Subtitles. Theme of genocide. A-II (PG-13)

Life Is Cheap But Toilet Paper Is Expensive (1990) Disjointed story of a Chinese-American (Spencer Nakasako) wandering through the strange byways of contemporary Hong Kong's commercialized culture. Directed by Wayne Wang, the fictional situation is undeveloped, and the movie's critical perspective of this culture is superficial. Some very graphic violence and brief clinical nudity. O (nr)

Life Is Sweet (1991) Richly observed story of good-natured English parents (Alison Steadman and Jim Broadbent) and their totally dissimilar twin daughters — one a placid plumber (Claire Skinner), the other (Jane Horrocks) a secretive anorexic hostile to one and all. Director Mike Leigh sensitively blends his characters' comic eccentricities with the heartfelt misery of a young woman's frightened search for herself made bearable by her supportive family. Brief bedroom scene with nudity and occasional rough language. A-III (nr)

Life Less Ordinary, A (1997) Romantic-fantasy clunker in which two angels (Holly Hunter and Delroy Lindo) are assigned to make a spoiled heiress (Cameron Diaz) and her dimwitted kidnapper (Ewan McGregor) fall in love and marry. Director Danny Boyle attempts to mix unexpected violence with screwball comedy, but the results are strained and unconvincing. Some violence, sexual innuendo, and intermittent profanity and rough language. A-III (R)

Life, Love, Death (1969) French director Claude Lelouch examines the apprehension, trial, and execution of a murderer (Amidou). The drama indicts capital punishment, suggesting that it dehumanizes those who demand it, and especially, those who carry it out. Coldly intellectual, his treatment responsibly distances the viewer from a subject easily sensationalized. A-III (R)

Life, Loves, and Operas of Giusepppi Verdi, The (1974) Mediocre European dramatization of Verdi's career, with Tito Gobbi and Mario Del Monaco appearing in excerpts from his major works. The production is lavish, the personal dimension is not interesting, but the music is for all who love opera. A-I (nr)

Life of Brian (1979) Monty Python movie about a hapless fellow named Brian, a contemporary of Jesus, who is mistaken for the Messiah and eventually crucified by the Romans. The nihilistic, anything-for-laughs thrust of director Terry Jones's comedy deliberately exploits much that is sacred to Christian and Jewish religious tradition. Especially offensive is the mocking parody of the crucifixion scene. O (R)

Life of Emile Zola, The (1937) Uplifting dramatization follows the French author and crusading journalist (Paul Muni) from obscurity in 1862 Paris to his first popular novel, *Nana*, then growing prosperity from a prolific writing career, until his final triumph in achieving the vindication of Captain Alfred Dreyfus (Joseph Schildkraut) after his unjust 1894 conviction for treason. Directed by William Dieterle, the production's convincing re-creation of the historical setting adds credibility to Muni's sympathetic performance as an idealist upholding the cause of the powerless against the injustices of those in power. Discreet reference to prostitution. A-I (br)

Life of Jack London, The (see: **Jack London**)

Life of Riley, The (1948) Screen version of a popular radio-comedy series about a working-class family headed by a goodhearted but dimwitted factory worker (William Bendix), whose constant mix-ups are smoothed over by his sage wife (Meg Randall). Written, produced, and directed by Irving Brecher, the plot revolves around Riley's money problems and the romantic concerns of his college-age daughter (Rosemary DeCamp). Still some fun, despite dated family stereotypes. A-I (br)

Life of the Party, The (1930) Ragged sex comedy directed by Roy del Ruth in which two gold-diggers from Brooklyn (Winnie Lightner and Irene Delroy) con an expensive wardrobe out of a fashion designer, then go to a Havana resort, where they snare a soft-drink millionaire (Jack Whiting) and a Kentucky horse-breeder (Charles Butterworth). Some sexual situations and considerable innuendo. A-III (br)

Life on the Edge (1992) Witless satire about the southern Californian lifestyle is set at a trendy LA party, where the shallow guests (including Jeff Perry, Jennifer Holmes, and Andrew Prine) must cope with the aftermath of an earthquake. Director Andrew Yates turns out an amateurish comedy whose characters' predictable sexual escapades are of little interest and no value. Adulterous theme, lesbian encounter with nudity, some violence, and occasional rough language. O (nr)

Life Stinks (1991) Betting he can live for 30 days on LA's skid row without any money, a cocky billionaire (Mel Brooks) finds love with a bag lady (Lesley Ann Warren) and becomes a crusader for the homeless. When not chewing up the scenery, producer-director Brooks's absurd populist fantasy offers occasional moments of madcap lunacy that sparkle in an otherwise forgettable comedy. Implied sexual encounter, comic-book violence, and an instance of rough language. A-III (PG-13)

Life Study (1973) Low-budget feature directed by Michael Nebbia tells the story of a girl chasing a reluctant boy encompasses 30 years of screen cliches done with such awkward sincerity as to evoke laughter in all the wrong spots. A-IV (nr)

Life with Blondie (1946) Formula family comedy directed by Abby Berlin begins with the Bumstead dog, Daisy, gaining fame as a Navy pin-up, then being turned into a high-priced advertising model until kidnapped by a gangster (Marc Lawrence). A-I (br)

Life with Mikey (1993) An irresponsible former child-star (Michael J. Fox) becomes a substitute father figure when he turns a sassy, 10-year-old pickpocket (Christina Vidal) into a cookie commercial star in hopes of salvaging his nearly bankrupt juvenile talent agency. Director James Lapin gets limited comic mileage out of the odd coupling though the twosome's positive changes become mildly heartwarming. Dysfunctional family circumstances. A-II (PG)

Lifeforce (1985) Vampires from outer space wreak havoc in director Tobe Hooper's disjointed sci-fi end-of-the-world movie which tries to sell itself by exploiting sex, nudity, and gore. O (R)

Lifeguard (1976) This is a paean to arrested adolescence, an uninspired soap opera on the beach. Director Daniel Petrie's bland, morally insensitive account of the growing pains of a 32-year-old lifeguard (Sam Elliott) is sheer male romanticism with a dash of nudity. A-III (PG)

Light at the Edge of the World, The (1971) Brutal adaptation of a Jules Verne story about a lighthouse keeper (Kirk Douglas) whose rock-ribbed Cape Horn isle is invaded by bloodthirsty pirates (under Yul Brynner) who, after impaling Douglas's co-workers, hack apart the hapless passengers aboard the first ship they manage to drive upon the rocks. Samantha Eggar is preserved, however, for a series of fates worse than death. Produced by Douglas and directed by Kevin Billington, it's literal visualizations of violence are excessive. O (GP)

Light of Day (1987) A brother-sister music team (Michael J. Fox and Joan Jett) have their self-centered attitudes toward life changed when faced with the death of their mother (Gena Rowlands). Awkward but naturalistic portraits of misdirected young adults in this film spotted with rough language are somewhat elevated by Rowlands's exquisite cameo performance. A-III (PG-13)

Light Sleeper (1992) Veteran drug-dealer (Willem Dafoe) takes desperate action when his shrewd boss (Susan Sarandon) decides to start a legitimate business without him and his ex-girlfriend (Dana Delany) meets a sudden, drug-related death. Writer-director Paul Schrader trivializes the harmful consequences of the drug culture with characters whose supposed transformation rings hollow. Narcotic trafficking shown as easy and highly profitable, brief violence, a sexual encounter with nudity, and much rough language. O (R)

Light That Failed, The (1939) Romanticized version of Rudyard Kipling's story about a newspaper illustrator (Ronald Colman) who receives a saber cut above the eye during a battle in the Sudan, then achieves fame as a London artist until going blind and returning to the Sudan to die with the troops. Producer-director William A. Wellman centers the movie's emotional weight on the artist's compulsion to finish his masterpiece before his eyesight fails and his despair on learning the painting has been destroyed by the street waif (Ida Lupino) who posed for it. Some wartime violence, sexual inferences, and suicidal bravado. A-III (br)

Lighthorsemen, The (1987) Unable to dislodge the Turks from Gaza during WW I, the British mount a surprise attack on Beersheba in a daring frontal assault by an Australian troop of Light Horse Infantry. Director Simon Wincer's Australian production is a visually compelling picture of war in the desert, with mass formations of soldiers riding to battle or marking time in camp, though its focus on several troopers (Jon Blake and Peter Phelps) and their problems is less than interesting. Stylized violence and several flashes of rear nudity. A-II (PG)

Lightning Jack (1994) Failed Western comedy teams a vain bank-robber (Paul Hogan) with an inept, mute assistant (Cuba Gooding, Jr.) as they attempt to score one successful hold-up. With Hogan's cliche-ridden script, director Simon Wincer turns in a dull, sometimes crude, oater in which the tumbleweeds have more substance than the characters. Implied affairs, sympathetic portrayal of outlaws, and a few shootouts. A-III (PG-13)

Lightning Strikes Twice (1951) Muddled mystery in which an actress (Ruth Roman) arrives at a dude ranch for a needed rest, then falls for a man (Glenn Ford) suspected of murdering his wife, and sets out to find the real killer. Directed by King Vidor, the story fairly creaks with melodramatic turns and formula characters, though the Southwestern locales supply some visual interest along the way. Stylized violence and romantic complications. A-II (br)

Lights of Variety (see: **Variety Lights**)

Lights Out (see: **Bright Victory**)

Lightship, The (1986) Obscure drama centered in a contest of wills between a Coast Guard skipper (Klaus Maria Brandauer) and a Southern con-man (Robert Duvall) who needs the skipper's boat to make a getaway. Aiming at a parable about freedom and determination, the movie has a dark and foreboding air, some explicitly violent murders, and some harsh language as it builds up to an abrupt and muddled conclusion. A-III (PG-13)

Like Father Like Son (1987) Fantasy about father-son role reversals brought about accidentally when the father (Dudley Moore) ingests a brain-transference potion. Director Rod Daniel's sitcom conveys the necessity for understanding and love between parents and children but has some rough language, a failed seduction scene, and some brief violence. A-II (PG-13)

Like Water for Chocolate (1993) Culinary magic is the main ingredient in this romantic melodrama set in 1910 revolutionary Mexico, where a family's youngest daughter (Lumi Cavazos) cooks up all manner of mischievous dishes for her family when her beloved (Marco Leonardi) asks her hand but is made to marry her older sister (Yareli Arizmendi) instead. Mexican director Alfonso Arau cleverly blends comedy and tragedy into this beguiling period movie about repressed love sublimated into a passion for cooking. Subtitles. A few bedroom scenes, some nudity, and minor violence. A-III (R)

Li'l Abner (1959) Flatfooted musical based on Al Capp's comic-strip yokels who save their Southern town of Dogpatch from becoming an A-bomb test site. Written by Norman Panama and Melvin Frank with Panama producing and Frank directing, the stage-bound proceedings are generally witless, with clunky choreography and wooden acting (especially by Peter Palmer as Abner and Leslie Parrish as Daisy May), though Stubby Kaye puts over a couple of catchy Johnny Mercer songs. Much sexual innuendo and barnyard humor. A-III (br)

Lilies of the Field (1963) When an itinerant jack-of-all-trades (Sidney Poitier) stops to help a group of German nuns newly arrived in New Mexico, his cheerful generosity is disdained by the stern, demanding Mother Superior (Lilia Skala) until he builds them a chapel with the aid of the local Mexican-American community. Directed by Ralph Nelson, the movie's simple little story of the triumph of faith coupled with good will has enormous charm in the winning performances of the two principals, some good-natured comedy, and an infectious theme song that will leave viewers humming "Amen." A-I (nr)

Lily in Love (1985) Stage actor (Christopher Plummer) disguises himself to get the romantic movie role for which his screenwriter wife (Maggie Smith) thinks he's entirely unsuited, and she begins falling in love with her husband's new persona. Witty, sophisticated comedy from Hungarian director Karoly Makk, it's a game of who's playing a trick on whom. A-II (PG-13)

Limbo (1972) Sincere tearjerker based on the stateside emotional and financial hardships of a group of Vietnam POW-MIA wives (Kathleen Nolan, Katherine Justice, and Kate Jackson). Despite its obvious melodrama, director Mark Robson makes the situation ring true much of the time by showing the human side of women trying to keep their family and emotional lives intact without any certainty about their husbands or the future. Nolan's performance, strong yet vulnerable, is worth seeing. Mature themes. A-III (PG)

Limbo (1999) Escaping a boat where a murder has taken place, a fisherman (David Strathairn), his new girlfriend (Mary Elizabeth Mastrantonio), and her estranged teen daughter (Vanessa Martinez) find themselves stranded on an Alaskan island, unsure if the killers will find them, the elements will kill them, or a search plane will rescue them. Writer-director John Sayles meticulously explores the roiling emotions of troubled characters as they struggle to survive, or at least make peace with one another in a drama some may find flawed by its ending. An off-screen sexual encounter, fleeting off-screen violence, recurring rough language, and occasional profanity. A-III (R)

Limelight (1952) Written, produced, and directed by Charles Chaplin, the story is about a WW I music-hall comic (Chaplin) who helps a ballerina (Claire Bloom), but the movie's importance comes from the light it casts on Chaplin as an artist and a man. Deeply steeped in Victorian sentimentality and simplistic affirmations of nature's goodness, the narrative may seem hopelessly dated and artificial, but its sensibilities are sincere, deeply felt, and enduring. Challenging but well worth seeing. A-II (G)

Limit, The (1972) Yaphet Kotto gets in over his head as writer, director, and star in a film about a Los Angeles cop having trouble justifying his job and the special demands it makes on him because he is black. As a director, Kotto is unable to overcome the insurmountable problems of an underdeveloped script and an obviously bargain-basement budget. Some mature themes. A-III (PG)

L'Immortelle (1969) Director Alain Robbe-Grillet's existential love story set in Istanbul about a man who dies trying to unravel the mystery behind the woman he loved and lost in a car accident. Narrative unfolds jumping back and forth in time and space in an attempt to make a cinematic (and philosophical) comment upon the nature of illusion and reality. An exercise for film buffs and poets. A-III (nr)

Lincoln Conspiracy, The (1977) Revisionist account of Lincoln's assassination alleges that Secretary of War Stanton and other high officials were involved in the plot directed at the President. As history, the movie relies upon still questionable documentation. As entertainment, director James L. Conway's stiff, instructive treatment would be more suited to a slide lecture. A-II (G)

Lion Has Seven Heads, The (1974) Brazilian production about African neo-colonialism and revolution told not in narrative form but through a series of highly stylized scenes conveying various forms of social, economic, and ideological exploitation. As directed by Glauber Rocha, one may object to some of the excesses in imagery, but there is no question it does contribute a sense of the revolutionary ferment in underdeveloped parts of the world. A-IV (nr)

Lion in Winter, The (1968) Toward the end of her life, Eleanor of Aquitane (Katharine Hepburn) engages in a running duel with her husband, Henry II of England (Peter O'Toole), over which of their sons should ascend the throne. Director Anthony Harvey does not allow history to get in the way of the principals, whose full-blown performances make absorbing entertainment. Adult themes. A-III (PG)

Lion King, The (1994) Animated tale of an African lion cub (voice of Jonathan Taylor Thomas) who, led to believe he caused the death of his father the king (voice of James Earl Jones), runs away in shame, enabling his evil uncle (voice of Jeremy Irons) to assume the throne, until he returns a full-grown lion (voice of Matthew Broderick) to discover the truth and reclaim the kingdom. Directors Roger Allers and Rob Minkoff combine stunning animation with deft comic touches and stirring musical numbers for an evocative allegorical story of a young lion coming of age and learning to assume responsibility as an adult leader. Some intense moments. A-I (G)

Lion of the Desert (1981) Director Moustapha Akkad's homage to Libyan hero, Omar Mukhtar (Anthony Quinn), who defied Mussolini's forces for 20 years until his capture and execution in 1931. Some of the desert battle scenes and those involving Italian reprisals are both extremely violent and poorly staged. A-III (PG)

Lion of Thebes, The (1963) Fleeing the fall of Troy, Helen (Yvonne Fumeaux) and her Spartan protector (Mark Forest) land in Egypt, where they become pawns in the political intrigue of the pharaoh's court. Directed by Giorgio Ferroni, the Italian production features colorful sets and a large cast of unknowns in a story that has more plot than sense. Dubbed American version. Stylized violence. A-II (br)

Lion's Love (1969) French director Agnes Varda's homage to and criticism of the Hollywood ethos is little more than a series of cameos with show-business types and pop-art personalities who seem terribly phony trying to act genuine. The amoral lifestyle espoused by its principals severely limits the movie's appeal and acceptability. O (nr)

Lionheart (1991) A French Foreign Legionnaire (Jean-Claude Van Damme) goes AWOL to Los Angeles to provide for his murdered brother's wife (Lisa Pelikan) and child (Ashley Johnson) by winning a series of high-stakes, no-holds-barred fights. Director Sheldon Lettich pulls out all the stops — destitute widow with cute tot, bloodthirsty crowds, and animal-like brutality — in an utterly transparent and trashy exercise. Excessive violence, much rough language, and rear nudity. O (R)

Lipstick (1976) Lamont Johnson directs this tawdry melodrama in which a woman (Margaux Hemingway), after being raped by a man who is freed and later attacks her younger sister (Mariel Hemingway), takes justice into her own hands. Exploitation of serious social problems offers only violence and brutality instead of insight. O (R)

Liquidator, The (1966) British spy thriller directed by Jack Cardiff about a tough intelligence agent (Rod Taylor) assigned to liquidate a number of folks the agency considers to be security risks. One of them is Jill St. John, and this complicates things, much to boss Trevor Howard's dismay. Routine action movie with stylized violence. A-III (br)

Lisa (1990) Nasty thriller in which a serial killer (D.W. Moffett) stalks the mother (Cheryl Ladd) of a precocious 14-year-old (Staci Keanan) who's been annoying him with prank telephone calls. Directed by Gary Sherman, the manipulative cat-and-mouse scenario is stretched out in mostly lethargic fashion until the bloody climax. Women-in-peril situations and sexual references. A-III (R/PG-13 appeal)

Lisbon (1956) Muddled intrigue with a classy crook (Claude Rains) hiring a suave smuggler (Ray Milland) to pick up an American industrialist from an Iron Curtain prison, but complications arise when the industrialist's wife (Maureen O'Hara) falls for the smuggler. Also directed by Milland, the contrived proceedings are woefully unconvincing despite lovely Portuguese locales. Stylized violence, romantic complications, and a wife ordering her husband's murder. A-III (br)

List of Adrian Messenger, The (1963) Gimmicky murder-mystery in which a retired British spy (George C. Scott) seeks a killer whose victims were all survivors of a Japanese POW camp in Burma, where one of them turned traitor. Directed by John Huston, the movie has a good cast (including Kirk Douglas, Clive Brook, and Dana Wynter) with the killer masked in various disguises which are as easy to see through as those sported by Robert Mitchum, Burt Lancaster, Frank Sinatra, and Tony Curtis in campy cameo roles. Though stylized, the violence makes it unlikely children's fare. A-I (br)

Listen, Let's Make Love (1969) Inept Italian soap opera directed by Ferdinando Scarfiotti purports to describe the pitfalls and insecurity of a young gigolo enmeshed in the opulent decadence of Milanese society. Excessive sexual depictions. O (R)

Listen to Me (1989) Campus hi-jinks at a posh California college focus on the school debating team, which at the end of the year vies for a national championship led by two freshman (Kirk Cameron and Jami Gertz) arguing in the affirmative that abortion is wrong. Written and directed by Douglas Day Stewart, the movie laboriously delays the inevitable romance between its two principals and plays both sides of the street on the abortion issue, though it ends affirming the pro-life view. Several suggestive sex scenes, sophomoric sex jokes, and a bit of rough language, but seen from a perspective critical of contemporary moral permissiveness. A-III (PG-13)

Listen Up: The Lives of Quincy Jones (1990) Portrait of the composer-producer's musical development and career achievements plus details of his personal life, including a harsh ghetto background and failed marriages. The colorful, kaleidoscopic "rockumentary" from director Ellen Weissbrod is done via interviews with Jones, his daughter, and famed musical collaborators in a somewhat lengthy and reverential study of what makes Quincy Jones tick, tempered by his refreshingly honest self-appraisal. Minimal rough language and racial epithets. A-II (PG-13)

Little Ark, The (1972) Director James B. Clark tells the story of two children (Philip Frame and Genevieve Ambas) who are separated from their parents during the 1953 floods in northern Holland. It has an intelligent message about human community, but the children face some intense dangers best left unexperienced by small children. A-II (G)

Little Big League (1994) Lightweight comedy in which an 11-year-old (Luke Edwards) inherits ownership of the Minnesota Twins baseball team from his grandfather (Jason Robards) and appoints himself manager, determined to inspire the players (including Timothy Busfield and Jonathan Silverman) out of a losing slump. Though director Andrew Scheinman doesn't deliver a home-run baseball comedy, he does fashion the breezy story-line and likable characters into a generally appealing, minor-league movie. Fleeting sexual innuendo and an instance of profanity. A-II (PG)

Little Big Man (1970) Dustin Hoffman as the sole survivor of Custer's Last Stand relives the story of his life and times on the frontier. Although not tightly conceived or executed, director Arthur Penn's large canvas provides a major overview of the Old West and its conflicts between Indians and pioneers. A-III (PG)

Little Boy Lost (1953) Contrived sudser directed by George Seaton features Bing Crosby as a US newsman in post-war France seeking his young son who disappeared after his mother was killed by the Gestapo. Good use of French locales and a fine performance by Gabrielle Dorziat as the sage nun running an orphanage, but the muddled plot about a father's anguish grows tiresome long before its flat, sentimental ending. A-I (br)

Little Buddha (1994) Traveling to the mountain kingdom of Bhutan with his dad (Chris Isaak), a nine-year-old Seattle boy (Alex Wiesendanger) learns about the life of Buddha (Keanu Reeves) from a monk (Ying Ruocheng) who thinks the child may be the reincarnation of a revered lama. Director Bernardo Bertolucci's visually stunning work crosscuts skillfully from the contemporary reincarnation story to the ancient tale of a troubled prince who became the Buddha after he learned compassion for all living things. Positive treatment of universal spiritual values as well as Buddhist beliefs, including reincarnation. A-II (PG)

Little Cigars (1973) Sadistically abused woman (Angel Tompkins) takes refuge with a group of midgets in a traveling sideshow, where she runs an aphrodisiac candy bar while having an affair with the head midget (Billy Curtis). Directed by Chris Christenberry, it is an utterly cruel and tasteless movie, with the worst big-woman, little-man joke ever devised. O (PG)

Little Colonel, The (1935) Rejecting his daughter (Evelyn Venable) for marrying a Yankee (John Lodge) after the Civil War, an irascible Kentucky colonel (Lionel Barrymore) is finally won over by their spunky little girl (Shirley Temple). Director David Butler's old-fashioned melodrama of family reconciliation centers in the interplay between youngster and grandfather as well as the child's friendship with black servants, notably in scenes with Hattie McDaniel at a river baptism and some stylish tap-dancing with Bill Robinson upstairs and down. Still a lot of fun, though flawed by regional and racial stereotypes. A-I (PG)

Little Darlings (1980) Silly but nasty little movie wasting the talents of young Kristy McNichol and Tatum O'Neal in a story that has to do with a group of girls at a summer camp making a bet that places loss of virginity into the category of a competitive sport. Besides some distasteful visuals and offensive language, director Ronald F. Maxwell's movie condones immoral behavior, despite some moralistic hedging at the end. O (R)

Little Drummer Girl, The (1984) Lackluster screen adaptation of the John Le Carre novel about an actress (Diane Keaton) recruited by Israeli agents to trap a terrorist. Director George Roy Hill appears unconcerned for politics, characterization, or moral details. Considerable violence, some nudity, and rough language. A-III (R)

Little Fauss and Big Halsy (1970) Routine motorcycle-racing movie that dotes upon the idiosyncrasies of one of its stars (Michael J. Pollard) and the good looks and sexual prowess of the other (Robert Redford). Sidney J. Furie directs an undistinguished clunker which has a permissive attitude toward casual sex. A-IV (R)

Little Foxes, The (1941) Engrossing adaptation of Lillian Hellman's play about a woman (Bette Davis) and her two brothers (Charles Dingle and Carl Benton Reid) who conspire to get the money needed for a business deal from her estranged but wealthy, seriously ill husband (Herbert Marshall). Directed by William Wyler and strikingly photographed by Gregg

Toland, the post-Civil War drama centers on the Southern family's conniving among themselves and ultimately against each other, with Davis memorable as the shrewd, conscienceless wife. Fascinating portrait of self-defeating greed. A-II (br)

Little Giants (1994) Strained comedy in which a single dad (Rick Moranis) is persuaded by his tomboy daughter (Shawna Waldron) to coach a preteen football squad composed of rejects from the town's official peewee team coached by his arrogant brother (Ed O'Neill), a former gridiron star. Director Duwayne Dunham's sentimental exercise in youthful hi-jinks is flat and often in bad taste, resulting in a picture whose contrived underdog situations are as largely unamusing as the inept title team's unlikely triumph on the field is entirely predictable. Vulgar language, crotch jokes, a running gag about breaking wind, and a ludicrous instance of "comic" profanity. A-II (PG)

Little Girl Who Lives Down the Lane, The (1977) Jodie Foster plays a mysterious, self-sufficient 13-year-old in a Maine village who is befriended by a teenage boy (Scott Jacoby) and threatened by an unstable adult (Martin Sheen) because she has something to hide. Pat, unbelievable Canadian melodrama directed by Nicholas Gessner, the movie condones teenage promiscuity and makes an adolescent the object of sexual titillation. O (PG)

Little Indian, Big City (1996) Raised by his French mom (Miou Miou) in the Amazon rain forest, a mischievous 13-year-old boy (Ludwig Briand) goes to Paris for the remarriage of his workaholic dad (Thierry Lhermitte), where his jungle-bred behavior turns his dad's life around. Director Herve Palud's dubbed 1994 fish-out-of-water comedy stresses the evolving father-son bonding as the father begins to reassess his priorities in positive ways. A premarital live-in relationship, fleeting violence, and an instance of profanity. A-III (PG)

Little Lord Fauntleroy (1936) Old-fashioned but not creaky adaptation of the Frances Hodgson Burnett tale in which a nine-year-old lad (Freddie Bartholomew) leaves 1880s Brooklyn to take his place as the heir of his titled English grandfather (C. Aubrey Smith), whom he transforms for the better, including his reconciliation with the boy's widowed mother (Delores Costello Barrymore). Directed by John Cromwell, the gradual softening of the old curmudgeon by his goodhearted grandson is delightfully sentimental, with some patriotic humor involving his American pals (Guy Kibbee and Mickey Rooney). A-I (br)

Little Man Tate (1991) Poignant drama concerns a lonely, genius-level seven-year-old (Adam Hann-Byrd) torn between his love for his unmarried, barmaid mom (Jodie Foster) and the intellectual stimulation offered by the book-bound psychologist (Dianne Wiest) who takes him away from home. Also directed by Foster, the movie presents an affecting story about the emotional vs. intellectual needs of one gifted child, but cops out with a typical Hollywood happy ending. Brief bedroom scene. A-II (PG)

Little Man, What Now? (1934) With his wife (Margaret Sullavan) pregnant, an insecure clerk (Douglass Montgomery) desperately seeks work in the depths of Weimar Germany's economic depression. Director Frank Borzage depicts the couple's problems realistically within the context of Germany's social and political turmoil, but the sentimental treatment weakens the story's impact today. Marital problems, some sexual innuendo, and unsavory characters. A-III (br)

Little Men (1940) Lackluster adaptation of Louisa May Alcott's novel about the reformation of a young scoundrel (Jimmy Lydon) left by a pair of con-men (George Bancroft and Jack Oakie) in a boarding school (run by Kay Francis). Directed by Norman Z. McLeod, the result is old-fashioned entertainment with some amusing moments, though the effort is dated by its sentimental treatment. A-I (br)

Little Men (1998) Uneven tale of an 1871 Boston street urchin (Michael Caloz) who makes great progress in a rural boarding school, until his scrappy city pal (Ben Cook) turns up and causes severe problems for the dedicated couple (Mariel Hemingway and Chris Sarandon) who run the school. Directed by Rodney Gibbons from Louisa May Alcott's novel, the dramatization does well in re-creating the look and feel of the period, but fails to bring any fresh insights to the sentimental story and its sentimentalized characters. A bloody fistfight, a dangerous game with a knife, and a few curse words. A-II (PG)

Little Mermaid, The (1989) Enchanting Disney animated feature adds a hopeful, happy ending to the Hans Christian Andersen fairytale about a feisty mermaid (voice of Jodi Benson) who falls in love with a human prince. Written and directed by John Musker and Ron Clements, the characters are delightful, the music is exhilarating, and the underwater animation is magical. Youngsters will love how its enterprising heroine faces up to typical parental pressures and learns to take responsibility for her own choices. A-I (G)

Little Minister, The (1934) Artificial but fanciful romance from the James M. Barrie play in which a young minister (John Beal) in 1840 Scotland revitalizes a village of dour weavers, then falls for a mysterious gypsy (Katharine Hepburn) who joins the weavers in their strike against an unjust local lord (Frank Conroy) before revealing her true identity. Directed by Richard Wallace, the whimsical plot contrivances seem downright silly today, though the spirited performances of the fine cast are still fun to watch. Murky intrigues and romantic complications. A-II (br)

Little Miss Marker (1980) Adaptation of the Damon Runyon story about a six-year-old (Sara Stimpson) who is left as security (a marker) for a bet with a bookie (Walter Matthau). Although director Walter Bernstein's reliance upon one-liners keeps the movie lively, and his treatment of the romance between Matthau and Julie Andrews is light, the original 1934 version remains unequalled by this remake. Occasional rough language. A-II (PG)

Little Monsters (1989) Sophomoric comedy about a sixth-grader (Fred Savage) who befriends a 200-year-old monster (Howie Mandel) from the demon world beneath his bed, where the boy almost becomes a monster himself. Directed by Richard Alan Greenberg, the plot is witless and the fantasy effects are nothing special. Bad taste abounds in its crude, at times gross, humor, comic violence, and coarse language. A-III (PG)

Little Mother (1973) Exploitative fictional life of Eva Peron hypothesizes a woman's rise to power in Argentinean politics through the use of her body and various forms of murder, torture, and brutality. Director Radley Metzger's ridiculous sexual obsessions will satisfy neither voyeurs nor students of Latin-American politics. O (R)

Little Murders (1971) Screen version of Jules Feiffer's black comedy about an apathetic man (Elliott Gould) who is awakened to a need for personal relationships by an aggressive young woman (Marcia Rodd), but when she is senselessly murdered by a sniper, he joins in the insanity that surrounds him. Directed by Alan Arkin, the film's object apparently is to sensitize its audience to the alienation of urban life by shocking it with sudden violence and a barrage of profanity. Viewers willing to undergo such an experience will find enough insights to justify the approach. A-IV (R/PG)

Little Nemo: Adventures in Slumberland (1992) Animated tale about the dreams of a boy at the turn of the century, who in his sleep enters Slumberland, where he must rescue kindly King Morpheus from the evil clutches of the Nightmare King. Based on Winsor McCay's classic comic strip, directors Masami Hata and William Hurtz's delicate backdrops are visually pretty, but the many characters and busy story may not hold small children's attention. A-I (G)

Little Night Music, A (1978) Screen version of the Broadway musical about ill-matched spouses and lovers who sort out their differences and find happiness in the coarse of a turn-of-the-century summer night. Harold Prince's uninspired direction and some unfortunate casting (Elizabeth Taylor is sadly unsuited to the central role of the charming and magnetic Desiree) cause what should have been a light and airy sophistication to become rather earthbound. The situations and dialogue make it mature viewing fare. A-III (PG)

Little Nuns, The (1965) Sentimental Italian comedy about two persistent nuns (Didi Perego and Catherine Spaak) who get an airline to change the route of its planes from passing over their orphanage. Director Luciano Salce treats the naivety of provincial sisters in sophisticated Rome with broad visual comedy, yet with enough charm to make the situation pleasantly diverting. Dubbed. Unpretentious entertainment. A-I (br)

Little Odessa (1995) Returning to his Russian-Jewish neighborhood in Brooklyn to carry out a contract killing, a hardened hit-man (Tim Roth) re-enters the lives of his dying mother (Vanessa Redgrave), embittered father (Maximillian Schell), and worshipful younger brother (Edward Furlong), with tragic consequences for them all. Writer-director James Gray's bleak study of murder and betrayal in a tightly knit ethnic community dramatizes the senseless nature of violence, but offers few insights into its remorseless central character. Several point-blank shootings, a bedroom scene with partial nudity, and much rough language. A-IV (R)

Little Prince, The (1974) Musical version of Antoine de Saint Exupery's classic fable about a planet-hopping child prince (Steven Warner) who relates his adventures to a pilot (Richard Kiley) who's crash-landed in the Sahara. Directed by Stanley Donen, the result is warm and upbeat, with engaging acting, pleasant Lerner and Loewe songs, and some clever dancing, but the story ends with a gentle letdown that may bring a wee tear to the eyes of the very young. A-I (G)

Little Princess, The (1939) Delightfully sentimental children's story of a poor little rich girl (Shirley Temple) put to work as a servant in a ritzy boarding school when her father (Ian Hunter) is reported dead during the Boer War, but she persists in searching for him among the convoys of wounded. Directed by Walter Lang, the story is not only a good heart-tugger, but gives Shirley a chance to sing, dance, and dream of being a queen. Charming family movie. A-I (G)

Little Princess, A (1995) Delightful family movie from the Frances Hodgson Burnett novel in which a British widower sent to the front in WW I places his young daughter (Liesel Matthews) in a private school in New York City, where she befriends a servant girl (Vanessa Lee Chester), then becomes one herself when her father is reported dead, leaving her penniless and at the mercy of the heartless headmistress (Eleanor Bron). Directed by Alfonso Cuaron, this visually splendid adaptation highlights the story's adventurous qualities and comical aspects as it affirms interracial friendships and the power of a child's imagination to encourage and inspire others. A-I (G)

Little Rascals, The (1994) Weak, overly cute comedy tries to update the **Our Gang** shorts of the 1930s to the present, as Spanky (Travis Tedford) and the other little imps are horrified when trusty Alfalfa (Bug Hall) falls for a girl (Brittany Ashton Holmes) who is being courted by a spoiled rich kid (Blake Ewing). Director Penelope Spheeris strings together a succession of mildly comic scenes in which the youngsters look adorable but unconvincing in the role of rib-tickling mischief-makers. Comic violence, mild double entendres, and boyish disdain of girls. A-II (PG)

Little Romance, A (1979) Romantic comedy about two teenagers in Paris, an American girl (Diane Lane) and a French boy, who run away to Venice to kiss under the Bridge of Sighs in fulfillment of a legend told to them by a romantic pickpocket (Laurence Olivier). Director George Roy Hill's treatment of adolescent love is affectionately tender, with only two risqué asides about human anatomy conveyed in the context of honest curiosity. A-II (PG)

Little Sex, A (1982) Romantic comedy about a newly married young man (Tim Matheson) who has trouble remaining faithful to his wife (Kate Capshaw). Director Bruce Paltrow's nearsighted sexual soap opera offers a sniggery bit of irreverent cynicism. O (R)

Little Shop of Horrors (1986) The wit and charm of the stage musical's b1ack comedy about a carnivorous plant has been mistaken for the theater of cruelty. Director Frank Oz concentrates on literal depictions of the plant's feeding sessions and use of foul language, the sadism and masochism of various characters, including Steve Martin in a madcap cameo, and constant references, both visual and verbal, to killing and brutality. O (PG-13)

Little Shop of Horrors, The (1960) Low-budget comic chiller in which a dim florist's clerk (Jonathan Haze) nurtures a small carnivorous plant, then winds up killing people to feed its insatiable appetite as it grows to monstrous size. Directed by Roger Corman, the tongue-in-cheek proceedings range from the weird to the gruesome, including a masochist (Jack Nicholson) who enjoys visiting dentists and a plant that calls out "Feed me," when it's hungry. Comic violence, menacing situations, and sexual innuendo. A-III (br)

Little Thief, The (1989) Opening in a rural village in 1950, this curious bittersweet French movie about a 16-year-old (Charlotte Gainsbourg) follows her life of lies and petty theft after being abandoned by her parents to the care of grim relatives. Directed by Claude Miller, it's a sensitive character study of a postwar survivor, adrift without love or guidance, although her miraculous change-of-heart at final fade-out is mere fairytale thinking. Teenage promiscuity, adultery, brief nudity, some violence, and rough language. A-IV (R)

Little Tough Guy (1938) Formula melodrama directed by Harold Young in which a youth (Billy Halop) joins the Dead End Kids (Huntz Hall, Gabriel Dell, and others) in a crime spree after his father is executed for killing a cop during a strike, but he gives himself up and is rehabilitated in reform school. Stylized violence. A-I (br)

Little Treasure (1985) An erotic dancer (Margot Kidder) and a down-on-his-luck ex-seminarian (Ted Danson) team up in Mexico to find the loot from a Depression-era bank robbery her father had buried there. Alan Sharp wrote and directed a morality tale with serious overtones but not enough substance, despite some good acting and dialogue. Dance sequence involving nudity and some rough language. A-IV (R)

Little Vera (1989) Non-political Russian movie about an aimless high-school graduate (Natalya Negoda) who feigns pregnancy to get her working-class parents to consent to her marrying a playboy student (Andrei Sokolov), and, when he moves in with them, her father's alcoholism and mother's nagging end the relationship. Director Vasily Pichul's frank look at an imperfect Russian family and teen sexuality is convincing, though melodramatic. An explicit sex scene with nudity, occasional locker-room language, and some violence. A-IV (nr)

Little Voice (1998) Engaging British comedy-drama in which a third-rate talent agent (Michael Caine) tries to make a singing star out of the reluctant but talented daughter (Jane Horrocks) of a desperately man-hungry widow (Brenda Blethyn). Writer-director Mark Herman's slim story features astute character studies brought to life by a fine cast. Fleeting violence, an implied affair, brief nudity, some profanity, and recurring rough language. A-III (R)

Little Women (1933) Lovingly sentimental but firmly crafted adaptation of Louisa May Alcott's story of four New England girls cared for by their mother while their father is soldiering in the Civil War. Director George Cukor depicts the joys and woes of the loving March family household with warmth and sincerity, but most memorable is the ensemble performance of a remarkable cast headed by Katharine Hepburn as serious-minded Jo, Joan Bennett as vain Amy, Frances Dee as prosaic Meg, Jean Parker as waifish Beth, and Spring Byington as the girls' beloved Marmee. Prime family fare. A-I (br)

Little Women (1949) Charming remake of the Alcott classic of adolescents — studious Jo (June Allyson), practical Meg (Janet Leigh), flighty Amy (Elizabeth Taylor), and sickly little Beth (Margaret O'Brien) — being raised by their mother (Mary Astor) during the Civil War. Director Mervyn LeRoy's version is nicely cast, makes good use of color in filming the lush period costumes and settings, and tempers the sentimental nature of the narrative with some lively action. Fine family entertainment. A-I (br)

Little Women (1994) Pretty, sentimental version of Louisa May Alcott's classic 1868 novel about four daughters growing up in New England during the Civil War under the watchful eye of an idealistic mother (Susan Sarandon) centers on independent-minded Jo (Winona Ryder), who spurns a wealthy suitor (Christian Bale) to pursue her dreams of becoming a writer. Director Gillian Armstrong's warm characterizations stress unfailing generosity, love, forgiveness, and feminine strength in a sweetly charming but dramatically bland production. A-I (PG)

Littlest Hobo, The (1958) Overlong children's picture featuring a bright German Shepherd who drops off a freight train, saves an orphaned lad's pet lamb from a slaughterhouse, eludes the town's police hunt for a mad dog while bringing the lamb back to the boy, then hops the next freight out of town. Directed by Charles Rondeau, the canine hero holds attention, but some of his adventures get heavy-handed, especially in a slum mission and among a gang of hungry hobos, resulting in an uneven mixture of fantasy and realism. Mild violence and much menace. A-I (br)

Littlest Horse Thieves, The (1977) Directed by Charles Jarrott, this Disney production is set in England around 1909 in a coal mining town in Yorkshire. Three children (Andrew Harrison, Chloe Franks, and Benjie Bolgar) try to save the ponies who haul the coal from the mines and who are about to be taken to the slaughterhouse and replaced by machinery. There is an ingenious twist, however, which provides a happy ending, though with a bittersweet touch. A-I (G)

Littlest Rebel, The (1935) The Civil War serves as a vehicle for a Shirley Temple heart-tugger in which she plays the daughter of a Confederate officer (John Boles) condemned to death as a spy until she wheedles a reprieve from Abraham Lincoln. Director David Butler's sentimental melodrama creaks with slave stereotypes (notably Stepin Fetchit), but is saved by Bill Robinson's dignified portrayal of a trusted servant whose song-and-dance routines with Shirley are not to be missed. Clear anti-war theme, but youngsters may need help with the movie's racial overtones. A-I (PG)

Live a Little, Love a Little (1968) Elvis Presley puts some new twists into his twenty-eighth screen effort, directed by Norman Taurog, his ninth collaboration with Presley. The gyrations are vintage swivel hips, but there's an attempt to update the stock dialogue and situations with the introduction of double entendre and sexual titillation. A-III (PG)

Live a Little, Steal a Lot (1975) Failed crime melodrama about the petty thief, Murph the Surf (Don Stroud), who stole the Star of India from New York's Museum of Natural History, is a yawner. Directed by Marvin Chomsky, it tries to glamorize its immature hero and the peek-a-boo sex is dreary going. O (PG)

Live and Let Die (1973) James Bond (Roger Moore) takes on hokey mixture of Harlem hoods (led by Yaphet Kotto) and Caribbean voodoo worshippers, all eager to chop him up before he blows the whistle on their plan to saturate the US with heroin. Directed by Guy Hamilton, the plot is preposterous, the humor more tasteless than spicy, and the special-effects department works overtime to hold the spectator's flagging attention. A-III (PG)

Live Fast, Die Young (1958) Low-budget tale of a California teen runaway (Norma Eberhardt) who graduates from petty crime to a big-time diamond robbery (led by Michael Connors), just before her older sister (Mary Murphy) catches up with her in time for a cautionary ending. Directed by Paul Henreid, the gritty proceedings feature familiar criminal types, though of more interest are the decent citizens met along the way, including a group of likeable hoboes. Criminal rackets, sexual situations, and innuendo. A-III (br)

Live Flesh (1998) Overwrought Spanish melodrama in which an unjustly convicted ex-con (Liberto Ribal) becomes involved with the wives of the two police detectives who arrested him seven years earlier. Writer-director Pedro Almodovar transforms Ruth Rendell's 1986 novel into a soapy tale of betrayals, guilt, and belated forgiveness. Subtitles. Several sexual encounters, brief nudity, fleeting violence, recreational drug abuse, recurring rough language, and occasional profanity. A-IV (R)

Live for Life (1967) Long rambling story about the late maturing of a French photographer (Yves Montand) and his wife (Annie Giradot) after his affair with a model (Candice Bergen). Director Claude Lelouch sustains interest in a superficial, sentimental story with beautiful photography, locales, music, and talented actors. A-III (br)

Live Today for Tomorrow (see: **An Act of Murder**)

Live Wires (1946) Formula roughhouse comedy directed by Phil Karlson in which the Bowery Boys (led by Leo Gorcey) take on a mobster (Mike Mazurki) and break up his gang. Stylized violence. A-II (br)

Lives of a Bengal Lancer, The (1934) Gary Cooper and Franchot Tone play British officers who save the colonel's son (Richard Cromwell) and the honor of the regiment by quelling a rebellion on India's Northwest Frontier. Directed by Henry Hathaway, the rousing military adventure features a tall but lively tale of comradeship and bravery with some good action sequences and not a little humor. Stylized violence includes an off-screen torture scene. A-I (br)

Livin' Large (1991) Strained comedy about a young black man (T.C. Carson) whose overnight success as a TV reporter goes to his head and results in an identity crisis. Michael Schultz directs a situation comedy whose early promise disintegrates into an extended, one-joke routine, punctuated by some wry observations about today's ratings-mad television news coverage. Fleeting sexual encounter, a very crude double entendre, and some rough language. A-III (R)

Living Daylights, The (1987) Timothy Dalton plays the new, more altruistic James Bond, who foils an arms and drug-dealing scheme by KGB bigwig Jeroen Krabbe and ruthless dealer Joe Don Baker. Mellow treatment of spy thriller by director John Glen includes a conventional romance with agent Maryam d'Abo and violence toned down to a level more acceptable for adults and mature teens. A-II (PG)

Living Free (1972) Sequel to Joy Adamson's **Born Free** tells of her attempts to rescue a trio of Elsa's orphaned lion cubs. Many adults will find their patience in short supply as Adamson (Susan Hampshire) and her gamekeeper-husband (Nigel Davenport) pursue their silly and sentimental ends in the name of humanitarianism while the cubs damage property and endanger themselves. Children, however, will only see cute wildlife antics. A-I (G)

Living It Up (1954) Lackluster musical remake of the screwball comedy, **Nothing Sacred**, with Jerry Lewis as the supposed victim of radium poisoning, Dean Martin as his doctor, and Janet Leigh as a reporter taking them to New York to exploit their media potential. Director Norman Taurog fails to find any charm, let alone human interest, in the glossy proceedings whose humor will escape all but the team's fans. Undemanding escapist fare. A-I (br)

Living in Oblivion (1995) Tedious farce about a low-budget movie production whose cast (Catherine Keener and James Le Gros) and crew (Steve Buscemi, Dermot Mulroney, Danielle Von Zerneck, etc.) are beset with problems on and off the set, most of which stem from their own personal shortcomings and professional pretensions. Writer-director Tom DiCillo spoofs the struggling filmmakers with obvious fondness, though the contrived situations and broad performances are more tiresome than amusing, even for film enthusiasts. Implied sexual liaisons, brief nudity, intermittent profanity, and rough language. A-III (R)

Living Out Loud (1998) Sweet-natured story of a lonely, newly divorced Manhattan nurse (Holly Hunter) and her depressed doorman (Danny DeVito), who befriend each other for different reasons, then help each other get on with their lives. Writer-director Richard La Gravenese's small story has big-hearted characters whose mid-life crises ring true, thanks to nicely nuanced performances. Some sexual innuendo, minor substance abuse, and intermittent profanity and rough language. A-III (R)

Liztomania (1975) Ken Russell directs an extravagant tribute to composer Franz Liszt, whom he presents as a 19th-century pop-star (Roger Daltrey) whose concerts are mobbed by shrieking teenage girls who tetter on the verge of hysteria whenever his fingers touch the piano keys. Though there is much here that is good, funny, and on-target, the movie flounders in excesses of every variety, most frequently sexual. O (R)

Local Hero (1983) Hotshot young executive (Peter Riegert), comes to buy up a remote Scottish village to turn into an oil refinery but goes native, while the natives themselves pant after the millions he came to give them. Director Bill Forsyth's delightful comedy keeps taking strange but enjoyable turns, and the prevailing mood is low-keyed zany. Some mild adult humor. A-II (PG)

Lock, Stock and Two Smoking Barrels (1999) Smug, convoluted caper in which four young Brits in heavy debt to a loan shark snatch a fortune in drug money from murderous thugs, who have just ripped off a dealer intent on killing everyone involved in the theft. Writer-director Guy Ritchie treats the constant bloody violence as a lark all in a day's work of making a fast buck. Jokey treatment of multiple murders, benign view of crime, brief nudity, intermittent profanity, and much shrill rough language. O (R)

Lock Up (1989) Sylvester Stallone plays another violent cartoon-hero in a behind-bars drama pitting good prisoners against bad prison-officials (notably warden Donald Sutherland). Directed by John Flynn, Stallone's Mr. Nice Guy is appealing, but the grisly violence that befalls him and his inmate cohorts make this especially off-limits for youthful Rocky fans. Intense, sadistic violence, and some profanity. O (R)

Lock Up Your Daughters (1969) Musical farce about three sex-starved sailors is a blend of two British Restoration comedies with their stock characters and scenes cluttering its ribald scenario of permissive "wenching." Christopher Plummer stars and Peter Coe directs the slapstick action and humor at the level of TV sitcom, spiced with nudity and sexual jokes. O (R)

Locket, The (1946) Muddled psychological tale of a very troubled woman (Lorraine Day) as told to her fiancé (Gene Raymond) by her former beaus (Brian Aherne and Robert Mitchum) in flashbacks-within-flashbacks reaching to her childhood. Directed by John Brahm, the contrived melodrama becomes tiresome long before its predictable ending. Romantic complications. A-II (br)

Locusts, The (1997) Tawdry tale of domestic dysfunction on a 1960s Kansas ranch whose promiscuous owner (Kate Capshaw) treats her disturbed son (Jeremy Davies) like a slave, until a defiant new employee (Vince Vaughn) decides to help the lad stand up to her. Writer-director John Patrick Kelly's intended tragedy is overwrought with so many lurid revelations it fails to register as a credible story with any emotional resonance. Brief but ugly violence including off-screen suicides, many perverse sexual references, implied sexual encounters, some profanity, and minimal rough language. A-IV (R)

Lodger, The (1944) Suspenseful tale in 1880s London, where a couple (Cedric Hardwicke and Sara Allgood) rent a room to a mysterious stranger (Laird Cregar), then come to suspect he's Jack the Ripper, and turn to a Scotland Yard inspector (George Sanders) to protect their niece (Merle Oberon). Directed by John Brahm, the sinister proceedings are heightened by Cregar's creepy performance and Lucien Ballard's moody photography. Off-screen murders, menacing situations, and a psychopathic character. A-II (br)

Logan's Run (1976) Futuristic social order is a hedonistic paradise except that its citizens are automatically exterminated at age 30. Instead of submitting, Michael York and Jenny Agutter make a run for it, pursued by zealous policeman Richard Jordan. Director Michael Anderson's rather simple-minded sci-fi chase movie is made moderately entertaining by its sets, special effects, and the talents of its three principals. Some incidental nudity and disappointing downbeat conclusion. A-III (PG)

Lola (1971) Charles Bronson, terribly miscast as an aging American writer living in Britain, is smitten with a 16-year-old girl (Susan George) and marries her, with predictable results. Directed by Richard Donner, the story has some interest but ultimately fails on the dramatic levels of coherence and acting. A-III (GP)

Lola Montes (1969) Heavily romantic treatment of the life of the 19th-century's most famous courtesan (Martine Carol) and her romance with King Ludwig of Bavaria (Anton Walbrook). Produced in 1955, director Max Ophul's visually masterful and lavish evocation of the age of Romanticism plays down the heroine's amorality, and paints, instead, a compassionate portrait of a pathetic and tragic figure who ends as a circus attraction for the curious. A-IV (nr)

Lolita (1962) Mangled, meandering adaptation of Vladimir Nabakov's controversial novel about a mild university professor (James Mason) and his passion for a 14-year-old girl (Sue Lyon). Director Stanley Kubrick uses a comic menace (Peter Sellers) to surface the professor's guilt and shame at his vague, undefined obsession, but the result leads nowhere. Mature themes related to abnormal psychology. A-IV (br)

Lolita (1998) Glossy but empty version of Vladimir Nabokov's novel about a middle-aged man (Jeffrey Irons) whose sexual obsession with a 12-year-old girl (Dominique Swain) ends tragically. Director Adrian Lyne's titillating treatment of the pair's cross-country sexual odyssey lacks any sense of a larger human context other than that of a troubled pedophile. Gory violence, frontal nudity, explicit sexual situations, brief drug abuse, occasional profanity, and an instance of rough language. O (R)

Lollipop (1976) Ailing white orphan (Norman Knox) from a Catholic mission in South Africa flees from his Afrikaner grandmother to the hills, where he nearly freezes to death. Director Ashley Lazarus tells a poignant tale about racial prejudices and interracial brotherhood, somewhat sentimentalizing his stereotyped characters, yet for many reasons, it is rewarding fare for young viewers. A-I (G)

Lollipop Cover (1966) Retired prizefighter (Don Gordon) and a nine-year-old girl (Carol Selfinger) help each other come to terms with their problems. The low-budget production is directed by Everett Chambers, and the fine acting of the principals helps keep the slight but uplifting story convincing. A-II (br)

Lolly-Madonna XXX (1973) Two neighboring Tennessee mountain families (headed by Rod Steiger and Robert Ryan) engage in a modern-day Hatfield-McCoy feud over a piece of pasture land, and an innocent passer-by (Season Hubley) is held captive by one clan who thinks she belongs to the other. Directed by Richard C. Sarafian, the self-indulgent movie seems only interested in graphic displays of violence, including rape and the threat of rape. O (R/PG)

Lone Gun, The (1954) Routine Western directed by Ray Nazzaro in which a Texas sheriff (George Montgomery) takes on a gang of rustlers (led by Neville Brand) while saving a genial gambler (Frank Faylen) from being framed for the murder of a rancher (Skip Homeier), who has a lovely sister (Dorothy Malone). Frontier violence. A-I (br)

Lone Hand, The (1953) Routine Western in which a young boy (Jimmy Hunt) doesn't know what to do when his widowed dad (Joel McCrea) takes up with outlaws, then marries a local girl (Barbara Hale). Directed by George Sherman, the dad's criminal activities are not what they seem, and all ends well after a furious shootout. Frontier violence. A-I (br)

Lone Prairie, The (1942) B-Western star Russell Hayden and singing sidekick Bob Wills save a rancher from losing his land to a villainous railroad speculator. Director William Berke paces the formula action with comic relief from Dub Taylor. Stylized violence. A-I (br)

Lone Ranger, The (1956) Disappointing movie version of the radio and TV series pits the Masked Man (Clayton Moore) and his faithful Indian companion, Tonto (Jay Silverheels), against a crooked rancher (Lyle Bettger) who's trying to provoke an Indian war so he can mine the mountain of silver he's discovered on their reservation. Directed by Stuart Heisler, the formula script with its pedestrian plot and stock villains offers little of interest. Frontier violence. A-I (br)

Lone Ranger, The (see: **The Legend of the Lone Ranger**)

Lone Star (1952) In 1845, Andrew Jackson (Lionel Barrymore) sends a pioneer cattleman (Clark Gable) to convince Sam Houston (Maroni Olsen) that Texas must join the Union, but along the way he gets entangled with an ambitious empire-builder (Broderick Crawford) and a lovely local editor (Ava Gardner). Director Vincent Sherman and a fine cast make the far-fetched Western adventure at least credible entertainment, if dubious history. Though the action is simple and robust, murky political intrigues keep complicating matters. A-I (br)

Lone Star (1996) Tangled tale of justice unfolds in the story of a Texas sheriff (Chris Cooper) investigating a 40-year-old murder implicating his former-sheriff father and his dad's corrupt, trigger-happy predecessor (Kris Kristofferson). Writer-director John Sayles slowly juggles the narrative strands and character relationships, eventually pulling them all together in a thoughtful story about prejudice, integrity, and healing. Fleeting bedroom encounter, brief violence, and occasional rough language. A-III (R)

Lone Wolf and His Lady, The (1949) Slack mystery directed by John Hoffman in which the title reformed jewel thief (Ron Randell) helps a newspaper reporter (June Vincent) cover the exhibition of the world's third largest diamond, then is suspected of stealing it in a formula entry notable only as the last in the series. Stylized violence and sexual innuendo. A-II (br)

Lone Wolf Keeps a Date, The (1941) Routine series entry directed by Sidney Salkow in which the title's reformed crook (Warren William) goes after a gang of kidnappers when they try to grab his client (Frances Robinson) but make off instead with his collection of rare stamps. Stylized violence. A-I (br)

Lone Wolf McQuade (1983) Martial-arts star Chuck Norris plays a modern Texas Ranger out to get a nasty arms smuggler (David Carradine), with Barbara Carrera on hand to look sultry and utter her share of the sappy dialogue. There is considerable violence, though treated by director Steve Carver in rather stylized and unrealistic fashion. A-III (PG)

Lone Wolf Strikes, The (1940) Twisty series entry directed by Sidney Salkow in which the title reformed jewel-thief (Warren William) retrieves a pearl necklace from a robber (Alan Baxter) by impersonating a crooked Dutch dealer (Montagu Love), then rescues the necklace's kidnapped owner (Joan Perry). Stylized violence and sexual innuendo. A-II (br)

Lone Wolf Takes a Chance, The (1941) Routine series entry directed by Sidney Salkow in which the title crime-buster (Warren William) saves a kidnapped inventor (Lloyd Bridges) from a gang of counterfeiters (led by Walter Kingsford). Stylized violence. A-I (br)

Loneliness of the Long Distance Runner, The (1962) British reform-school inmate (Tom Courtenay) mulls over his troubled past while making practice runs in training for the big cross-country race that the institution's head (Michael Redgrave) wants him to win. Alan Sillitoe's story of a working-class youth's rebellion against authority is directed by Tony Richardson with a gritty social realism that convincingly reflects, if not explains, the boy's alienation from a hypocritical adult world. Bleak study of the making of a juvenile delinquent. A-III (br)

Lonely Are the Brave (1962) Thoughtful, contemporary Western in which a free-spirited cowboy (Kirk Douglas) tries to break a pal out of jail, then gallops off for the protective wilderness of the mountains as a police manhunt (led by Walter Matthau) closes in. Director David Miller's engrossing narrative provides a penetrating character study of a nonconformist who has to pay the penalty for his refusal to adapt to changing times. Stylized violence. A-II (br)

Lonely Guy, The (1984) Steve Martin plays a writer of greeting-card verses, thrown out by his lover and wandering in Central Park, where he meets Charles Grodin who initiates him into the Lonely Guy fraternity. Director Arthur Hiller's comedy has sparse humor, stemming mainly from the encounters between Martin and Grodin. Some mild sexual humor. A-III (PG)

Lonely Lady (1983) Screen version of Harold Robbins's novel stars Pia Zadora as a young writer who cannot find happiness as she wins fame and fortune in Hollywood. Crass, sleazy vanity production directed by Peter Sasdy has graphic sex scenes and much nudity. O (R)

Lonely Man, The (1957) Mawkish Western about an aging gunfighter (Jack Palance) who tries to make amends with the grown son (Anthony Perkins) he had abandoned as a child. Directed by Henry Levin, there's a lot of clumsy talk and gunplay before the long-delayed but expected father-son reconciliation. Stylized violence. A-I (br)

Lonely Passion of Judith Hearne, The (1987) Disappointing movie version of the 1955 Brian Moore novel about a middle-aged Dublin spinster (Maggie Smith) who mistakes a gentleman's attentions as romantically intended and suffers a nervous breakdown when she discovers the truth. Elegantly directed by Jack Clayton, the novel's religious dimension is underdeveloped, and the spinster becomes a pathetic figure of sheer desperation. Some sexual scenes involving a teenaged maid. A-III (R)

Lonely Trail, The (1936) Routine Western directed by Joseph Kane in which a Texas rancher (John Wayne) who fought for the Union returns after the war to an unfriendly welcome from neighbors, then steps in to protect them from a corrupt carpetbagger (Cy Kendall). Stylized violence and minor racial stereotyping. A-II (br)

Lonely Woman Seeks Life Companion (1990) Somber Soviet comedy about a 43-year-old woman (Irina Kupchenko) who posts signs around her Moscow neighborhood for a mate and then is harassed by a drunken respondent. Directed by Viacheslav Krishtofovich, this is grim stuff with a stereotypic portrait of a single woman as desperate, cranky, and past consideration as a potential mate. Minimal rough language and some sexual innuendoes. A-III (nr)

Lonesome Cowboys (1969) Minimal Western spoof from pop artist Andy Warhol treats its homosexual characters with repellent cruelty and is little more than an adolescent peep-show exhibition of sexual acts. O (nr)

Long Ago, Tomorrow (1971) British love story of a man (Malcolm McDowell), paralyzed from a soccer injury, and a quiet, attractive polio victim (Nanette Newman) who reside in a nursing home for the disabled. Director Bryan Forbes's story of their determination to marry in spite of their limitations is cut short by her death, but the movie handles a delicate subject with great sensitivity. A-III (GP)

Long Dark Hall, The (1951) Dim British melodrama in which the murder of a showgirl is pinned on an innocent man (Rex Harrison) whose blindly loyal wife (Lilli Palmer) is stalked by the real killer (Anthony Dawson). Directed by Anthony Bushell and Reginald Beck, the turgid proceedings belabor the obvious until justice triumphs in the last five minutes. Implied extramarital affair. A-II (br)

Long Day Closes, The (1993) Uneventful, impressionistic look at life in mid-1950s Liverpool through the eyes of an 11-year-old lad as he takes part in the daily routines of his working-class family and neighbors. Writer-director Terence Davies's autobiographical movie is warmly nostalgic in treating his Catholic childhood, loving mother, and older siblings, but the period music and visually arresting images do not sustain what amounts to a slow-moving, highly personal reminiscence. Several racist references. A-II (PG)

Long Day's Dying, The (1968) British WW II drama about three soldiers (David Hemmings, Tom Bell, and Tony Beckley) trying to get back to their lines with a German prisoner. Directed by Peter Collinson, the realistic brutality used in this anti-war movie to convey the horror of war will strike some as excessive. A-IV (br)

Long Duel, The (1967) British India is the setting for this stiff-upper-lip story starring Trevor Howard as a nonconformist official who wants to treat even an outlaw native chief (Yul Brynner) with man-to-man justice. British production directed by Ken Annakin is routine escapist affair. A-II (br)

Long Good Friday, The (1982) Tough British gangster movie in which Bob Hoskins gives a remarkable performance as a London gang-lord done in by his own pride. Director John Mackenzie invests his brutal underworld story with grim but intelligent realism that some will find unnerving. Some intense scenes of violence. A-IV (R)

Long Goodbye, The (1973) Raymond Chandler's private eye, Philip Marlowe (Elliott Gould), by helping a friend out of a jam, finds himself picked up by the police and booked as an accessory to murder and left to sort through a tangle of murder, deception, robbery, suicide, and double-crossing. Directed by Robert Altman, the action is handled quite well as is the tacky atmosphere, but Marlowe and his moralities are hopelessly confused. Some rough language and brief nudity. A-IV (R)

Long Gray Line, The (1955) Sentimental, overlong, but ultimately rewarding picture of Sgt. Marty Maher (Tyrone Power), an Irish immigrant who became a physical-training instructor at West Point in a 50-year career which spanned two world wars and made him a beloved father-figure for generations of cadets. Director John Ford pays affectionate tribute to both Maher and the Academy in a story focused on the values of home (Maureen O'Hara plays Maher's wife) and the military, with many patriotic asides and rowdy good humor. Idealized yet interesting piece of Americana. A-I (br)

Long Hot Summer, The (1958) Uneven adaptation of the William Faulkner story about a wealthy Southern family whose uncouth patriarch (Orson Wells) hires a reputed barn-burner (Paul Newman), comes to appreciate the man's grit and ambition, then tries to get him to marry his independent-minded daughter (Joanne Woodward). Director Martin Ritt does well enough with the rural southern setting and gets good performances from the leads, but the script is flabby and the subsidiary roles seem more plot devices than characters. Minimal violence and some sexual innuendo. A-III (br)

Long John Silver (1953) Uninspired sequel in which the roguish pirate of the title (Robert Newton) returns to Treasure Island with young Jim Hawkins among his shipmates, but they have to fight off a variety of rivals before getting the treasure back to England, where Silver faces marriage to an doughty innkeeper (Connie Gilchrist). Directed by Byron Haskin, the Australian production is watchable entertainment, but the narrative's adventure is less than original and overindulges Newton's penchant for outrageous mugging. Swashbuckling violence and mild sexual innuendo. A-II (br)

Long Kiss Goodnight, The (1996) Overly violent tale of an amnesia victim (Geena Davis) who teams with a hired investigator (Samuel L. Jackson) to discover she was an assassin employed by a secret government agency, which now has her on its hit list. Director Renny Harlin's overwrought thriller is stuffed with brutality and murderous clashes but lacks character development and coherent plotting. Excessive violence, deadly menace to a child, some sexual innuendo, occasional profanity, and much rough language. O (R)

Long, Long Trailer, The (1954) Thin but mostly agreeable situation comedy in which newlyweds (Lucille Ball and Desi Arnaz) buy a trailer for their honeymoon in the mountains of Colorado, then face one calamity after another. Directed by Vincente Minnelli, the slapstick proceedings are mostly those of man-against-machine, in a story sprinkled with domestic arguments and sweet reconciliations. A-I (br)

Long Ride Home, The (1967) Vicious psychological triangle set at the end of the Civil War pitting Union officer Glenn Ford against Confederate counterpart George Hamilton with Inger Stevens in the middle. Dwarfed by the magnificence of its Grand Canyon locations, the characters lack human interest, and director Phil Karlson's movie ends up somewhere between muddled comment on the brutality of war at best and distorted, misguided melodrama at worst. A-III (br)

Long Riders, The (1980) Slow-paced, somber Western starring the Carradine, Keach, and Quaid brothers re-enacting the James and Younger gangs' disastrous raid on the bank in Northfield, Minn. Though it has its moments, director Walter Hill's effort is a little too pretentious to be really entertaining or enlightening. Some graphic violence and a realistic bordello scene. A-IV (R)

Long Voyage Home, The (1940) Compelling dramatization of four one-act plays by Eugene O'Neill about merchant seamen (Thomas Mitchell, Barry Fitzgerald, Ward Bond, and John Wayne, among them) sailing on a British tramp-freighter from a Caribbean port of call to the US, where they take on a cargo of munitions and head through the war zone for London. Director John Ford fashions an emotionally involving picture of life at sea, focusing on the camaraderie of the crew as they face the voyage's dangers from nature and human folly, as well as the temptations ashore at journey's end. Some menace and sexual references. A-II (nr)

Long Walk Home, The (1990) The 1955 bus boycott by blacks in Montgomery, Alabama, forces a wealthy white socialite (Sissy Spacek) to see her long-suffering black maid (Whoopi Goldberg) as a person and not just a personal convenience. Directed by Richard Pearce, the leads give shining performances, but its attempt to contrast black and white families is flawed by one-dimensional characterizations. Numerous racial epithets and brief violence. A-II (PG)

Longest Day, The (1962) The Allied invasion of Normandy on June 6, 1944, is re-created on an epic scale in this three-hour dramatization of the operational preparations, behind-the-line activities, but mostly the ferocious battle itself, with particular attention to the American landings at Omaha Beach. Directed by Ken Annakin, Andrew Marton, and Bernard Wicki, the result is an absorbing account of D-Day from both sides of the battlefield, with convincing portrayals of men in combat from an international cast headed by John Wayne, Robert Mitchum, and Henry Fonda. Wartime violence seen in the context of a righteous cause. A-I (br)

Longest Yard, The (1974) Burt Reynolds stars as an imprisoned ex-pro quarterback who leads a team of fellow convicts against a team made up of guards. Directed by Robert Aldrich, the movie has a careless, slapped-together look and relies heavily on violence and foul language. A-III (R)

Longhorn, The (1951) Standard Western directed by Lewis Collins with a rancher from Wyoming (Wild Bill Elliot) buying a herd of cattle in Oregon, then meeting trouble with the cowpunchers he's hired for the drive back, among whom are reformed gunmen and a traitor in cahoots with a gang of rustlers. The usual frontier violence. A-I (br)

Longtime Companion (1990) Moving but somewhat idealized portrait of how the AIDS epidemic affected the lives of three homosexual couples in New York City from 1981 to 1989. Directed by Norman Rene, the movie captures the human dimension of the illness without sensationalism or sentimentality, using understated performances to reveal the everyday heroism of "longtime companions" caring for their terminally ill loved ones. Frank depiction of homosexual life, including male kissing and embraces, casual drug use, and sporadic rough language. A-IV (R)

Look Out, Mr. Moto (see: **Mr. Moto Takes a Chance**)

Look Who's Laughing (1941) Radio comedian Edgar Bergen and puppet Charlie McCarthy team with radio's most popular comic couple, Fibber McGee and Molly (Jim and Marion Jordan), in director Allan Dwan's feeble effort to wring smiles from a convoluted plot about building an airplane factory in Wistful Vista rather than in a rival town. Limited fun, especially for youngsters. A-I (br)

Look Who's Talking (1989) Lame comedy about an unmarried career woman (Kirstie Alley) whose married lover (George Segal) leaves her pregnant and searching for the perfect father (John Travolta) for her baby son, who "talks" (voice of Bruce Willis) to the audience as he evolves from energized sperm and embryo through birth and toddler stages. Writer-director Amy Heckerling manages through the baby's sarcastic comments to vulgarize the process of conception, trivialize childbirth, and make a three-ring fantasy out of single parenthood. Much vulgar sexual humor, some rough language, and a cavalier attitude toward adultery. O (PG-13)

Look Who's Talking Now (1993) Witless sequel in which two family dogs (voices of Danny DeVito and Diane Keaton) trade insults while the husband (John Travolta) fends off a lecherous boss (Lysette Anthony) determined to keep him away from worried wife (Kirstie Alley) and children over Christmas. Director Tom Ropelewski's comedy clunker tacks a talking-dogs gimmick onto a contrived marital crisis of insipid sitcom proportions. Some sexual innuendo, crude remarks, and an intense dogfight. A-II (PG-13)

Look Who's Talking Too (1990) Silly sequel in which busy toddler Mikey (voice of Bruce Willis) confronts toilet training, a new baby sister (voice of Roseanne Barr), and his mom (Kirstie Alley) being on the outs with his new dad (John Travolta). Since virtually nothing happens in the movie, director Amy Heckerling is reduced to stringing together a lot of adorable baby shots until the grown-ups get their act together. Minor fantasy violence, sexual references, and much bathroom humor. A-III (PG-13)

Looker (1981) Beverly Hills plastic surgeon (Albert Finney) uncovers a plot by a conglomerate (headed by James Coburn) to hypnotize television viewers into buying products advertised in commercials. The scheme involves the murder of several actresses who are turned into computerized images. Writer-director Michael Crichton's confused story substitutes superficiality for social satire and flashiness for mystery. Some violence and brief nudity. A-III (PG)

Lookin' to Get Out (1982) Two luckless gamblers (Jon Voight and Burt Young) in debt to gangsters flee New York for Las Vegas, where they stake a down-on-his-luck gambling whiz (Burt Remsen) to one last try at the jackpot. Director Hal Ashby's movie written by Voight is a total disaster, utterly lacking in charm, with unremitting vulgar language, some brief nudity, and a benign view of the easy sex to be had in a resort. A-III (R)

Looking for Mr. Goodbar (1977) Director Richard Brooks's harrowing account of some of the consequences of the sexual revolution stars Diane Keaton as a wildly self-destructive young single on the prowl for love and commitment. Drama tries to evoke the moral confusion that pervades the lives of young people caught up in the liberated lifestyles of the 1970s, but says little about the options open to them. Details of the singles drug and sex scene, including a graphic rape and murder, hammer home the obvious. O (R)

Looking for Richard (1996) Playful documentary

exploring the historical background, Elizabethan language, and dramatic stagecraft of Shakespeare's *Richard III* as undertaken by actor Al Pacino and his cohorts in preparing for an American version of the play. Also directed by Pacino, the result is an amusing hodgepodge of fact and whimsy, sometimes serious, but often frivolous and at times self-indulgent, especially Pacino's hammy run-throughs in the title role. Dramatized violence, sexual references, and occasional rough language. A-III (PG-13)

Looking Glass War, The (1970) Failed screen version of John Le Carre's story of a Polish national (Christopher Jones) who jumps ship in Britain and is promised asylum by a group of British intelligence agents (led by Ralph Richardson) who cynically plan to use him for their own espionage ploys. Directed by Frank R. Pierson, the adaptation misses the interest and suspense of the original by bogging down in unmotivated and barely credible incidents, including his affair with a German woman (Pia Degermark). A-III (PG)

Looking Up (1977) Documentary directed by Linda Yellen offers a fragmented chronicle of the lives of three generations of a Jewish family seeking upward mobility and success in America. Although it's used to establish character, there are instances of vulgar language that may offend some viewers. A-III (PG)

Looney Looney Looney Bugs Bunny Movie, The (1981) Compilation of vintage Warner Brothers cartoon shorts with some new material. The artwork and the style of the animation are light-years removed from the crude fare offered a new generation watching Saturday morning television. A-I (G)

Loose Cannons (1990) Witless action comedy about two screwball cops (Gene Hackman and Dan Aykroyd) whose investigation of a bizarre murder-case leads to a sleazy porno-king (Dom DeLuise) linked to foreign agents seeking a lost reel of Nazi pornography. Director Bob Clark's sophomoric exercise in minimalist comedy strings together a series of dumb gags, weak spoofs, sex jokes, and special-effects mayhem. Much demeaning sexual humor, senseless violence, and some very offensive language. O (R)

Loot (1972) British black comedy by Joe Orton in which a mortician-bank robber (Hywel Bennett), his adoring pal (Roy Holder), the pal's freshly widowed father (Milo O'Shea), the dead wife's piously amoral nurse (Lee Remick), and a batty Scotland Yard inspector (Richard Attenborough) get mixed together in a tacky Brighton hotel with a fresh but rapidly stiffening corpse. Directed by Silvio Narizzano, the result is flat, chewy, but indigestible. O (R/PG)

Lord Jim (1965) Disappointing screen version of Joseph Conrad's novel about courage and cowardice as seen in the Far Eastern adventures of a British sailor (Peter O'Toole), a flawed hero driven to redeem himself in his own eyes. Directed by Richard Brooks, the theme is lost in a superficial and disjointed pageant, though handsomely photographed and containing many effective individual scenes. Some scenes of violence. A-II (nr)

Lord Love a Duck (1966) Uneven black comedy starring Roddy McDowall and Tuesday Weld in a story of high-school youths in southern California which offers some biting commentary on the meaningless lives of an affluent segment of American society. While there are some good laughs at the expense of ready targets, George Axelrod's direction relies on adult treatment and dialogue, including a plot complication involving hypnosis to regulate the love lives of students. A-IV (br)

Lord of Illusions (1995) Thin but gruesome horror movie in which a private detective (Scott Bakula) tracks some bizarre murders to a fanatic cult whose diabolical leader (Daniel Von Bargen) returns from the grave on a mission to destroy the world. Writer-director Clive Barker punches up the slow-moving fantasy with periodic bloodbaths and rabid occult ravings, but the picture flounders in a slack plot, one-dimensional characters, and unimaginative special effects. Excessive graphic violence, implied sexual encounters, partial nudity, and intermittent profanity and rough language. O (R)

Lord of the Flies (1990) Pointless remake of William Golding's 1954 novel about a contingent of schoolboys who deteriorate quickly into savages while marooned on an uninhabited tropical island. With too much emphasis on the island's lush wildlife and not enough on the characters, director Harry Hook's use of novice performers, Americanisms, and popular-culture asides detracts from the story's parable of good vs. evil. Much profanity and some grisly, conscienceless violence between the adolescents. A-III (R)

Lord of the Rings, The (1978) Ralph Bakshi's animated film version of the J.R.R. Tolkien epic of Middle Earth deals with the darker side of the trilogy. Since the monsters, and not the Hobbits, make a stronger impression, parents may want to think twice about their smaller children seeing this often frightening film. A-II (PG)

Lords of Discipline, The (1983) David Keith stars as a decent young cadet at a Southern military academy who tries to stop the hazing of a black freshman by a brutal clique trying to force him to quit the academy. Director Franc Roddam uses some fairly graphic violence and very rough language in depicting the ravages of prejudice and abuse of power. A-III (R)

Lords of Flatbush, The (1974) Small saga of leather-jacketed kids coming of age in Brooklyn in the late 1950s. Co-directed by Stephen F. Verona and Martin Davidson, it is not very probing, but it does have some good performances by Perry Kind, Sylvester Stallone, and Henry Winkler, as well as offering considerably more humanity and substance than most such nostalgia films. Some graphic depiction of sexual encounters and crude language. A-III (PG)

Lords of the Deep (1989) Set in the underwater

world of 2020, when Earth has become virtually uninhabitable due to environmental disasters, a motley crew of scientists meet a colony of friendly aliens who settled at the bottom of the sea when their planet was similarly destroyed. Low-budget ecological warning produced by Roger Corman suffers from cheesy sets and costumes, derivative script, and amateurish direction by Mary Ann Fisher. Mild rough language, sexual innuendo, and comic-book menace. A-II (PG-13)

Lorenzo's Oil (1992) Confronted with the devastating news that their five-year-old son (Zack O'Malley Greenburg) is dying of a rare terminal disease, his desperate parents (Nick Nolte and Susan Sarandon) defy medical science by setting out on their own to find some way to prolong their boy's life. Without shielding viewers from the relentless progress of the child's degenerative illness, director George Miller presents a grueling but incredible fact-based story of a couple who, with no medical training and while agonizing over their son's constant suffering, beat tremendous odds in discovering a treatment that has since saved hundreds of afflicted boys. Harrowing scenes of a child's physical deterioration and some intense arguments. A-II (PG-13)

Lorna Doone (1951) Lumpy costume melodrama from the Richard D. Blackmore novel in which a 17th-century English farmer (Richard Greene) leads the local peasantry to revolt against the greedy relatives of a traitorous lord, though in love with his oppressor's daughter (Barbara Hale) who ultimately proves the noblest of all. Director Phil Karlson manages a few good action scenes, especially on the brink of a waterfall, but the characters are as cardboard as the romance is pasty. Swashbuckling violence and assorted villainy. A-II (br)

Losers, The (1970) Motorcycle gang goes to Vietnam, and they blast their way into a Viet Cong stronghold to rescue a CIA official. Director Jack Starrett's action movie is appalling in its excessive bloodshed, glamorized violence, cheap moralizing, and phony patriotism. O (R)

Losing Chase (1996) Recovering at home from a nervous breakdown, a hostile mother (Helen Mirren) of two little boys initially resents, then comes to love, the patient young woman (Kyra Sedgwick) hired to care for them, though their closeness creates problems for the wife's hapless husband (Beau Bridges). Kevin Bacon directs a sensitive and very human story of juvenile and adult characters trying to cope with the ravages of chronic depression. Some sexual innuendo, occasional profanity, and an instance of rough language. A-III (R)

Losing Isaiah (1995) Having discovered that the infant she abandoned before overcoming her crack addiction has been adopted by a white couple (Jessica Lange and David Strathairn), an African-American single mother (Halle Berry) goes to court to regain custody of the now three-year-old toddler. Director Stephen Gyllenhaal probes touchy social concerns over parental rights and racial identity with some sensitivity, although the contrived ending compromises the hard issues raised by the story. Brief drug and alcohol abuse, sexual references, and a few instances of rough language. A-III (R)

Lost and Found (1979) George Segal, a widowed professor of English at a second-rate university, meets sharp-tongued divorcée Glenda Jackson while on a sabbatical in Europe. They marry, return to the States, only to have everything fall apart. Melvin Frank's uninspired direction doesn't help the offhanded message that commitment dulls romance. A few vulgar turns of dialogue and some cynical humor concerning marriage. A-III (PG)

Lost & Found (1999) Wan comedy in which complications arise after a restaurant owner (David Spade) infatuated with a French cellist (Sophie Marceau) steals her dog in order to be the hero when he returns it. As directed by Jeff Pollack, the thin premise makes the comic antics seem little more than a stretched-out sitcom. A few crude sexual references, fleeting nudity, much toilet humor, and an instance of profanity. A-III (PG-13)

Lost Angels (1989) Aimless but gifted Los Angeles youth (Adam Horovitz) pals around with his delinquent older brother (Don Bloomfield) and ends up being sent to a private mental hospital for adolescents, where an overburdened therapist (Donald Sutherland) tries to help him. British director Hugh Hudson paints a grim, at times heavy-handed, picture of upper-class parents whose broken marriage and self-involvement have disastrous consequences for their kids. Much profanity, some intense violence, and a brief, graphic sex scene. A-IV (R)

Lost Boys, The (1987) Strained parable of the evils of drugs and sex couched in a story about a gang of teenage vampires headed by Kiefer Sutherland trying to get the new kid in town (Jason Patric) to join them. Director Joel Schumacher leaves it up to preteens to foil the pack via the gruesomely violent, albeit traditionally effective, stake-in-the-heart bit. A-III (R)

Lost Command, The (1966) French paratroopers retaliate by atrocity and torture against the terrorists whom they are fighting in Algeria. Directed by Mark Robson, the politics may be muddled, but the acting is good (Anthony Quinn and Alain Delon) and the action well-staged, with realistic violence. A-III (br)

Lost Continent, The (1968) British horror movie in which a ship, beleaguered in the Sargasso Sea, finds a centuries-old Spanish galleon whose strange occupants (Hildegard Knef, Daryl Read, and Eddie Powell) are the descendents of the original crew and passengers. Director Michael Carreras offers a senseless mix of threatening violence and sexual innuendo. A-III (br)

Lost Flight, The (1971) Innocuous little melodrama about a planeful of people marooned on a remote South Sea island as a result of engine failure. Gallant pilot Lloyd Bridges tries to maintain peace among his passengers while awaiting rescue from various plot contrivances under the uninspired direction of Leonard J. Horn. A-II (G)

Lost Highway (1997) Surreal melodrama in which a husband (Bill Pullman) convicted of murdering his wife (Patricia Arquette) is inexplicably transformed into a different younger man (Balthazar Getty), who becomes murderously involved with a seductress identical to the murdered woman. Director David Lynch's darkly bizarre film is glamorously photographed, but its concentration on loveless sex and heinous crime becomes tiresomely repulsive. Excessive, gory violence, extended sex scenes with much nudity, recurring rough language, and some profanity. O (R)

Lost Honor of Katharina Blum, The (1976) Written and directed by Volker Schlondorff and Margarethe von Trotta, this is a plodding adaptation of Heinrich Boll's 1974 novel about an ordinary citizen (Angela Winkler) who is victimized by the police and the press because they mistakenly believe she is part of a terrorist group. The movie makes it too easy to condemn police excesses, while not clearly defining its complex political theme. A-III (PG)

Lost Horizon (1937) Producer-director Frank Capra's classic yarn about the kidnapping of a British consul (Ronald Colman) who is brought to Shangri-La, a thriving utopian community in the High Himalayas, as the chosen successor to its dying leader (Sam Jaffe). Restored in 1986 as closely as possible to the original release print, its picture of an ideal society whose people live in peace and harmony has as much meaning for our own troubled times as it did for audiences on the eve of WW II. A-I (nr)

Lost Horizon (1973) Producer Ross Hunter's mammoth, lavish musical version of the 1937 Frank Capra classic is an enormous dud. Director Charles Jarrott wastes a fine cast and good story in a welter of forgettable Burt Bacharch-Hal David tunes. Charles Boyer as the ancient High Lama wisely succumbs midway. A-I (G)

Lost in Alaska (1952) Routine Bud Abbott and Lou Costello comedy directed by Jean Yarbrough with the boys in 1890s San Francisco, where they save a despondent prospector, then help him search for his lost gold-mine in the frozen North. Comic menace and mild sexual innuendo. A-II (br)

Lost in America (1985) Slight comedy about a yuppie couple (Albert Brooks and Julie Hagerty) who buy a Winnebago and go off in search of America when he's fired instead of promoted at the ad agency. Also written and directed by Brooks, their misadventures lead to no greater insight than his going back to the ad game, though viewers will see the emptiness of their materialistic values. Some rough language in a humorous context. A-II (R)

Lost in Space (1998) While rocketing to a distant planet, an intergalactic family (headed by William Hurt and Mimi Rogers) is confronted by an evil stowaway (Gary Oldman), who causes their spaceship to careen off-course into various dangers. Directed by Stephen Hopkins, the result is a noisy, big-budget version of the 1960s TV series, but here the special effects win out over a jumbled, overly busy storyline. Frequent fantasy violence, mild sexual references, and occasional coarse expressions. A-II (PG-13)

Lost in Yonkers (1993) When their father must take a job on the road for almost a year, two teenagers (Brad Stoll and Mike Damus) move in with a fearsomely cruel grandmother (Irene Worth), a ditzy romantic aunt (Mercedes Ruehl), and a shady uncle (Richard Dreyfuss) hiding out from gangsters. Adapted from Neil Simon's WW II-era play, director Martha Coolidge's drama of comic one-liners is unabashedly sentimental in its humanist treatment of a flawed family struggling to accept each other despite varied emotional problems. Fleeting violence, mild sexual references, and minimal profanity. A-II (PG)

Lost Man, The (1969) A decent man (Sidney Poitier) engages in robbery to get money needed for the families of jailed black militants. Director Robert Alan Aurthur's movie refuses to grapple with the real issues posed by the black movement, yielding only a mixed-up story of revolution born of despair and an ethic based on the end justifying the means. A-III (PG)

Lost Patrol, The (1934) Classic desert adventure set in WW I Mesopotamia, where a British cavalry patrol shelters for the night in an abandoned oasis, then tries to survive attacks by an unseen Arab enemy. Director John Ford turns the desperate situation into a character study of men with little in common except their uniforms under a seasoned sergeant (Victor McLaglen) holding out with a few regulars and a squad of recruits, including a disgraced aristocrat (Reginald Denny), a steady conscript (Wallace Ford), a comical Cockney (Billy Bevan), and a religious fanatic (Boris Karloff). Wartime violence in a context weighing personal values and group loyalties. A-II (br)

Lost Tribe, The (1949) Formula adventure series entry directed by William Berke in which some friendly gorillas help comic-book hero Jungle Jim (Johnny Weissmuller) save a city hidden in Africa's interior from a cutthroat gang of diamond thieves. Stylized violence. A-I (br)

Lost World: Jurassic Park, The (1997) Uninspired sequel to the 1993 blockbuster again puts a scientific team (notably Jeff Goldblum and Julianne Moore), as well as a rival group of armed mercenaries, against a rampaging colony of genetically re-created dinosaurs who are now thriving on another remote tropical isle. Director Steven Spielberg delivers the expected jolts of terror with special-effects wizardry, but the cardboard characters and formula narrative make the movie less than involving. Several violent deaths and much intense menace. A-II (PG-13)

Lottery Bride, The (1930) Bleak musical romance

set in Norway, where a misunderstanding between college sweethearts drives the boy (John Garrick) off to work in an Arctic mining-camp to which, by chance, a matrimonial agency sends the girl (Jeanette MacDonald) to be raffled off as a "picture bride" in a miner's lottery. Directed by Paul L. Stein, the songs are as turgid as the heavy-handed plot, though matters turn downright giddy after an Italian dirigible sets down on its way to the North Pole and an ending amidst the Northern Lights. Sexual innuendo and hokey menace. A-III (br)

Louisa (1950) Dated sitcom in which romantic oldsters (Edmund Gwenn and Charles Coburn) vie to marry an eligible widow (Spring Byington) who thinks she's become a burden for her son (Ronald Reagan) and his family. Director Alexander Hall puts the aging trio through some undignified antics which prove more silly than amusing, though Byington emerges with some dignity and not a little charm. A-I (br)

Louisiana Purchase (1941) Stagy musical-comedy directed by Irving Cummings in which a venal state official (Bob Hope) uses a poor Austrian refugee (Vera Zorina) to compromise a Yankee Senator (Victor Moore) investigating political corruption in New Orleans. Dated topical humor with sexual situations and innuendo. A-III (br)

Louisiana Story (1948) Robert Flaherty's evocative documentary about life deep in the Louisiana bayous revolves around a Cajun youth whose first contact with the outside world comes when an oil company begins drilling in the area. With music by Virgil Thompson and photography by Philip Leacock, the story contrasts the boy's easy relationship with nature and his innocent wonderment at the modern utilities and new ways brought by the oil-drillers. Lyrical blending of the primitive and the modern with an optimistic sense that progress is more beneficial than destructive. A-I (br)

Love (1973) Hungarian drama about the wife (Mari Torocsik) of a man imprisoned by the Stalinist regime who tries to keep her aged mother-in-law (Lili Darvas) from learning the truth about her son's absence. Director Karoly Makk's work is simple, unpretentious, and quite honest in its celebration of such sentiments as love, fidelity, and sacrifice. Subtitles. A-I (nr)

Love Affair (1939) Buoyant romance between a suave French playboy (Charles Boyer) and a sprightly American (Irene Dunne) blossoms aboard an ocean-liner, but matters take a tragic turn when their plans to meet at the Empire State building are disrupted by a serious accident. Director Leo McCarey lightens the sentimental story with humorous situations, brisk pacing, and lively dialogue, but what makes the movie memorable are the truly affecting performances of the leads. Romantic complications. A-II (br)

Love Affair (1994) Sentimental remake of the 1939 the orgininal in which a couple (Warren Beatty and Annette Bening) have a shipboard romance, though each is engaged to another, then plan to meet three months later to get married, until a tragic accident jeopardizes their future. Director Glenn Gordon Caron's sumptuous, postcard-pretty melodrama is sweetly old-fashioned in its execution, though it ultimately disappoints in the superficial development of the characters. Romantic complications and an instance of rough language. A-II (PG-13)

Love Always (1997) While mulling a marriage proposal, a young woman (Marisa Ryan) hitchhikes across the country and meets a number of oddballs along the way before returning to answer her suitor. Despite its earnest tone, director Jude Pauline Eberhard's quirky road movie does little more than sketch in the characters in a narrative too episodic to be very involving. Bedroom scene with brief nudity, intermittent rough language, and occasional profanity. A-III (R)

Love and Anarchy (1974) Seriocomic Italian story of an anarchist (Giancarlo Giannini) who decides to avenge a friend murdered by Fascists by journeying to Rome to assassinate Mussolini, staying with a prostitute (Mariangela Melato) whose life has been ruined by Blackshirts. Directed by Lina Wertmuller, the movie's vulgar humor clashes uneasily with the serious tragedy being played out. Some ribald bordello scenes are certainly not glamorized and anything but attractive. A-IV (R)

Love and Death (1975) Ambitious and delightful spoof of Russian literature with Woody Allen turning his wit on the most turgid aspects of Dostoevski and Tolstoy, mocking both the characters and the heavy philosophy. It's a rather rarefied comedy trying perhaps a little too hard to be naughty and nice, funny and ferocious. Given the context and some knowledge of the subject of the satire, it should not offend mature viewers. A-III (PG)

Love and Death on Long Island (1998) Wryly observed tale of a fusty English author (John Hurt) whose crazy crush on a young movie star (Jason Priestly) prompts him to visit America and change his old-fashioned ways while trying to ingratiate himself with the gullible actor. Director Richard Kwietniowski depicts an aging recluse awakening to the contemporary outside world in poignant terms that are gently humorous. A live-in relationship, veiled homosexual reference, minimal profanity, and an instance of rough language. A-III (PG-13)

Love and Human Remains (1995) Bleak portrait of promiscuous single adults, both gay and straight, who listlessly engage in loveless couplings, unaware that a serial killer of young women is in their midst. Canadian director Denys Arcand's empty look at dissolute young adults fails to redeem itself with a tacked-on veneer of caring camaraderie in the final minutes. Brief but recurring violence including a suicide, numerous sexual encounters with nudity, recreational drug use, and much rough language. O (R)

Love and Marriage (1966): Italian movie presents

a quartet of stories making fun of marital fidelity. O (br)

Love and Money (1982) Silver magnate (Klaus Kinski) hires a troubleshooter (Ray Sharkey) to persuade a Latin-American dictator (Armand Assante) to give back his mines. Scripted by Sharkey and directed by James Toback, it's a dreadful little movie with the depth of a television pilot. Prolonged and extravagant sex scenes. O (R)

Love and Pain and the Whole Damn Thing (1973) Aging, ailing, inhibited English spinster (Maggie Smith) meets an inarticulate young American (Timothy Bottoms) on a bus tour of Spain, and the summer friendship turns into a love affair. Director Alan J. Pakula succeeds with poignant comic sequences as the unlikely pair get to know each other, but the romantic ending turns the movie into routine soap-opera. A-III (R/PG)

Love at First Bite (1979) Dracula (George Hamilton) comes to New York and falls in love with a glamorous model (Susan St. James) in this uneven, essentially one-joke comedy directed by Stan Dragoti. Several graphic lovemaking scenes, and blacks are made the butt of some jokes. O (PG)

Love at Large (1990) Entertaining romantic spoof of 1940s private-eye movies tracks the exploits of a rumpled gumshoe (Tom Berenger) who's supposed to be following the sinister boyfriend of a mysterious femme fatale (Anne Archer) but mistakenly trails the wrong man (Ted Levine). Writer-director Alan Rudolph has a ball with these offbeat characters whose love lives are a mess of contradictions and lost causes. Much sexual innuendo, a subplot about bigamy, and comic-book violence. A-III (R)

Love at the Top (1975) Frothy, stylish French comedy that bounces from slapstick to vitriolic satire in telling the story of a young man (Jean-Louis Trintignant) climbing the ladder of success by exploiting a long line of women. Director Michel Deville has his tongue firmly in cheek, but some viewers may find the darkness of the comedy too bleak, the general amorality of the characters offensive, and the casual nudity too pervasive. A-IV (R)

Love Bug, The (1969) Disney comedy about a sentient Volkswagon named Herbie who adopts a has-been, egotistic racing driver (Dean Jones) and drives him to victory and the altar (with Michele Lee). Mildly diverting fantasy from director Robert Stevenson, but it's mostly for the kids. A-I (G)

Love Child (1982) Amy Madigan makes an impressive screen debut as Terry Jean Moore, a troubled, unloved teenager who undergoes a remarkable transformation by learning to love. Thrown into prison, she becomes pregnant by a prison guard (Beau Bridges) and fights for her right to keep her baby. The film is worth seeing for Miss Madigan's performance. Director Larry Peerce's fact-based somewhat sentimental drama has a relatively graphic scene involving sex and nudity. A-IV (R)

Love Crazy (1941) Wacky romantic comedy in which a silly misunderstanding leads wife Myrna Loy into a divorce suit, which husband William Powell stalls by feigning insanity, then has to escape from an asylum to save his spouse from a would-be suitor (Jack Carson). Director Jack Conway has problems meshing the frantic proceedings with the droll, sophisticated style of the two leads, but Powell manages to be funny even when acting cuckoo or masquerading as his own sister. Zany treatment of domestic relations. A-II (br)

Love Crimes (1992) Sleazy would-be thriller has a Georgia prosecutor (Sean Young) using herself as bait to nail a man (Patrick Bergin) posing as a famous photographer who attacks women after getting them to pose nude. With blank performances and an undeveloped plot, director Lizzie Borden presents nothing more than a pointless, dehumanizing peep-show. Much nudity, violence against women, and recurring rough language. O (R)

Love Doctors, The (1971) These doctors run a friendly neighborhood sex-laboratory, where they conduct clinical sex experiments involving various combinations of men, women, and machines. Thoroughly cheap and offensive. O (X/R appeal)

Love Field (1992) A well-intentioned but interfering white woman (Michelle Pfeiffer) en-route to JFK's funeral in 1963 ends up protecting a black man (Dennis Haysbert) and his little girl (Stephanie McFadden) from federal authorities after she mistakenly reports him as a kidnapper. Director Jonathan Kaplan injects this interracial road movie with drama and humor, then damages its credibility by unnecessarily developing an unconvincing romantic angle. An ambiguous sexual situation and brief violence. A-III (PG-13)

Love Finds Andy Hardy (1938) Winding up with two dates (Ann Rutherford and Lana Turner) for the high-school Christmas ball, Andy (Mickey Rooney) is saved from disaster by a new girl in town (Judy Garland). One of the better efforts in the Hardy series, director George B. Seitz's family comedy gets help from songs by Garland, especially her Clark Gable ballad. A-I (br)

Love God?, The (1969) Leaden comedy in which the editor (Don Knotts) of a bankrupt bird-watching magazine becomes a sex symbol when tricked into selling his fourth-class mailing permit to a publisher of pornography. Director Nat Hiken makes up in tastelessness what the satire lacks in wit, making obscenity legislation, civil liberties, and public morality all seem as silly as the movie itself. A-III (M/PG-13)

Love Has Many Faces (1965) Tawdry sudser about the unhappy life of a rich heiress (Lana Turner) married to a womanizer (Cliff Robertson) and pursued by a gigolo (Hugh O'Brian). Directed by Alexander Singer, the thin plot is mired in the empty-headed antics of middle-aged socialites and greedy beach-boys in the glitzy Acapulco resort setting. Sexual situations, implied affairs, and sexual innuendo. A-III (br)

Love in Our Time (1969) Pseudo-documentary purports to explore contemporary sexual mores in Britain by examining the cases of eight volunteer couples. Director Elkan Allen employs graphic re-enactments of marital problems which focus on cruel and unusual sex acts. O (X)

Love in the Afternoon (1957) Overlong, undernourished romantic bauble follows the improbable escapades of a 19-year-old Parisian music student (Audrey Hepburn) in winning the affections of a rich American roué (Gary Cooper). Director Billy Wilder gets an appealing performance from Hepburn as the "susceptible" young thing, but Cooper never seems comfortable as the aging womanizer, and the only thing sophisticated about this story of illicit trysts is the decor of the Ritz Hotel suite in which they take place. Comic treatment of sexual relationships. A-III (br)

Love Is a Funny Thing (1970) French romance about a film composer (Jean-Paul Belmondo) and a film actress (Annie Giradot) who meet on a Hollywood set and initiate a casual affair. The actress admits the situation to her husband in Paris, not knowing that for the composer it's all a game, and she is being taken for a ride. Directed by Claude Lelouch, there's some funny spoofing of Hollywood, but the story moves too slowly in parts and the characterizations too facile to be either effective or affecting. A-III (PG)

Love Is a Many-Splendored Thing (1955) Slickly superficial tearjerker set in 1949 Hong Kong, where a Eurasian doctor (Jennifer Jones) with a Chinese passport has an affair with a married American reporter (William Holden) until he's killed covering the outbreak of the Korean War. Directed by Henry King, the soggy multicultural proceedings are given a glossy treatment which skirts the surface of the moral and racial issues involved. Sexual situations and a benign view of adultery. A-III (br)

love jones (1997) Slow-moving story of a young African-American couple (Nia Long and Lorenz Tate) who have sex on their first date, then go through several break-ups before realizing it's love, not lust, they feel for each other. Writer-director Theodore Witcher explores the emotional immaturity of two young people, but their self-absorbed lives are of only minimal interest, and the outcome is predictable. Restrained sexual encounters with fleeting nudity, recurring rough language, and an instance of profanity. A-III (R)

Love Laughs at Andy Hardy (1946) Army vet Andy (Mickey Rooney) goes to college on the GI Bill, but is crushed when his heart-throb (Bonita Granville) marries another man. Director Willis Goldbeck evokes few smiles in overseeing the demise of a series that outlasted its popularity. Mild romantic complications. A-I (br)

Love Letter, The (1999) Lightweight tale set in a New England village where romantic complications ensue among the residents (including Kate Capshaw, Tom Selleck, Tom Everett Scott, and Ellen DeGeneres) when several of them believe they are the intended recipient of an anonymous love letter. Directed by Peter Ho-Sun Chan, the comedy's charms are minor and its resolution weakly dramatized. An off-screen affair, references to a same-sex relationship, fleeting nudity, and a few instances of rough language. A-IV (PG-13)

Love Letters (1945) Contrived romance of a soldier (Joseph Cotten) and the girl (Jennifer Jones) he has wooed through letters written for his buddy during the war. Directed by William Dieterle, the muddled plot revolves around his comrade's murder and the girl's loss of memory. Phony sentimentality. A-II (br)

Love Letters (1984) Jamie Lee Curtis plays a disc jockey who becomes involved in an obsessive affair with a married man. She is inspired to risk all for love, it seems, by the discovery of some old letters that indicate that her dead mother also had a great love in her life. Contrived, sentimental film directed by Amy Jones has extensive nudity and graphic sexuality. O (R)

Love Machine, The (1971) Screen version of Jacqueline Susann's raunchy novel about high-powered sex and corporate intrigue is just as raunchy with John Phillip Law as the ruthless young executive, Robert Ryan as his corporate head, David Hemmings as his swishy confidant, and Dyan Cannon as only one of the innumerable mistresses who help him earn his mechanical nickname. Directed by Jack Haley Jr., it is laughably stupid and banal, qualities that only partially relieve the boredom. O (R)

Love Me Tender (1956) Muddled tale of a Confederate trooper (Richard Egan) arriving home after the Civil War to find his girlfriend (Debra Paget) married to his youngest brother (Elvis Presley) which leads to misunderstandings, then bloodshed. Directed by Robert D. Webb, the melodrama grows increasingly contrived as federal agents vie with ex-Rebs to find a stolen Union payroll, while Presley sings a few tunes before turning into a jealous husband. Stylized violence and sexual situations. A-III (br)

Love Nest (1951) Slight domestic comedy about an Army veteran (William Lundigan) whose wife (June Haver) has bought a run-down apartment house with all kinds of problems, including a tenant who's an aging Lothario (Frank Fay). Directed by Joseph M. Newman, the situation meanders fitfully and to little comic effect, with Marilyn Monroe and Jack Paar wasted in bit parts. Romantic complications. A-II (br)

Love Object, The (1971) Graphic demonstration of what a pretty but basically untalented young woman must do in order to get her start in the New York Theater. The producers have recruited Kim Pope, a pretty but basically untalented young woman who seems to know what she must do in order to get into movies. O (R)

Love on the Dole (1941) Dated social melodrama set in a 1930 English mill-town, where a working-class family struggles to make ends meet until the daughter (Deborah Kerr) marries a wealthy bookie

(Frank Cellier) after her young man (Clifford Evans) loses his job, postpones their wedding, then is killed trying to stop his fellow workers from rioting. Directed by John Baxter, the story of a family trying to survive the deepening Depression is brought to life by a good cast and some credible situations involving issues of social justice and human dignity. Brief violence, a teenage pregnancy, and a loveless marriage. A-II (br)

Love on the Run (1979) Francois Truffaut's fifth film about Antoine (Jean-Pierre Leaud), now feckless and boring at age 33, in the midst of an affair and about to get a divorce from his wife (Claude Jade). Shallow and vapid exercise in middle-aged melodrama, whose point seems to be the inevitability of divorce. A-III (nr)

Love Potion #9 (1992) Comic complications result when two scientists (Tate Donovan and Sandra Bullock) use themselves as guinea pigs in testing a magic love-potion obtained from a Gypsy (Anne Bancroft). Writer-producer-director Dale Launer's romantic fantasy begins agreeably enough but rather quickly flattens out into a banal, contrived comedy. Frequent sexual innuendo with implied affairs. A-III (PG-13)

Love Serenade (1997) Offbeat comedy set in a backwater Australian town, where two man-starved sisters (Miranda Otto and Rebecca Frith) compete for the love of the new guy in town (George Shevtsov), a silky-sounding deejay who warns them he's an incorrigible Lothario, but learns too late how seriously they take a love affair. Writer-director Shirley Barrett stuffs her quirky tale with eccentric characters who have a certain amount of deadpan charm, but the melodramatic climax will leave viewers scratching their heads. Fleeting violence, restrained sex scenes with brief nudity, and a morally ambiguous conclusion. A-IV (R)

Love Songs (1986) French drama about a woman (Catherine Deneuve) who balances the responsibilities of motherhood with her biological needs by sexually exploiting a younger man (Chris Lambert), whom she coldly leaves when she decides to go back to her husband. Directed by Elie Chouraqui, the movie treats infidelity not as a moral issue but rather as a device to explore some muddled ideas about the nature of the family bond from a feminist perspective. Justifies casual sex. O (nr)

Love Story (1970) Supersuds screen version of Erich Segal's romantic melodrama about a rich youth (Ryan O'Neal) and rough-talking baker's daughter (Ali MacGraw) whose Harvard-Radcliffe courtship and marriage survive their social and cultural differences until her early death from some sort of dread ailment. Director Arthur Hiller manipulates viewer emotions skillfully and shamelessly in a sentimental, old-fashioned tear-jerker, updated with some rude language. A-III (GP)

Love! Valour! Compassion! (1997) Eight gay men, two of whom (Jason Alexander and John Glover) are HIV positive, gather at a lakeside country home for summer holiday weekends as sexual relationships among them develop or deteriorate by summer's end. Director Joe Mantello depicts the lifestyles of active homosexuals with a sentimentality bordering on the soggy, especially when AIDS strikes the group. Scenes of homosexual activity, intermittent frontal nudity, some profanity, and recurring rough language. O (R)

Love Walked In (1998) Muddled crime story in which a failed lounge-singer (Denis Leary) plans to blackmail a wealthy married man (Terence Stamp) by getting his adored wife (Aitana Sanchez Gijon) to seduce him, but is unprepared for the dire consequences this has on his own marriage. Director Juan J. Campanella superficially explores several crises of conscience in a downbeat narrative hampered by an intrusive subplot parallelling these crises with those of imaginary pulp-fiction characters. A sexual encounter with nudity, brief violence, and frequent rough language. A-III (R)

Love Without Pity (1991) Living off his drug-dealing teenage brother (Jean Marie Rolin), a shiftless Parisian (Hippolyte Giradot) listlessly pursues an affair with a brainy interpreter (Mireille Perrier). French writer-director Eric Rochant sympathetically portrays the smugly self-absorbed brothers without offering any hope for their improvement in this dark and sullen study of alienated youth who are society's parasites. Subtitles. Casual depiction of drug use, drug dealing and petty thievery, implied sexual encounters, and occasional rough language. O (R)

Loved One, The (1965) Disjointed satire on life and death in America as a penniless Brit (Robert Morse) arrives in Los Angeles, where an uncle (John Gielgud) working in the movie industry promptly commits suicide, leaving the nephew to arrange his burial in a glitzy cemetary run by a phony minister (Jonathan Winters). Directed by Tony Richardson from Evelyn Waugh's novel, the bizarre narrative is a jumble of cynical situations, including the nephew's romance with a lady embalmer (Anjanette Comer) who's sweet on her repulsive boss (Rod Steiger), but the proceedings are tiresomely overdone, sometimes gross, and not very amusing. Sexual situations and innuendoes. A-IV (br)

Lovely Way to Die, A (1968) B-grade thriller concerning an ex-cop (Kirk Douglas) hired by a district attorney (Eli Wallach) as a bodyguard for a New York socialite (Sylvia Koscina) accused of murdering her husband. Directed by David Lowell Rich, the proceedings are crudely violent and sexually suggestive. O (br)

Lover, The (1992) Empty, soft-core tale of the steamy affair between a bored 15-year-old schoolgirl (Jane March) and an idle rich Chinese (Tony Leung) in 1920s French Indochina. Derived from Marguerite Duras's novel and directed by Jean-Jacques Annaud, the result is little more than a lethargic exercise in voyeurism. Numerous explicit sexual couplings, occasional drug abuse, fleeting violence, and some racial slurs. O (R)

Lover Come Back (1961) Tiresome romantic comedy directed by Delbert Mann in which a Madison Avenue executive (Doris Day) is romanced by an unscrupulous rival (Rock Hudson) masquerading as the shy inventor of a new product which she desperately wants as an advertising account. Crass romantic complications and unfunny sexist humor. A-III (br)

Loverboy (1989) Tasteless comedy about a dopey college student (Patrick Dempsey) who earns his fall tuition by parlaying his summer pizza-delivery route into a sex-for-hire service to unhappy Hollywood wives (Barbara Carrera, Kirstie Alley, and Carrie Fisher). Directed by Joan Micklin Silver, the movie never seems to question the morality of its promiscuous proceedings. O (PG-13)

Lovers (1992) Fact-based melodrama set in mid-1950s Spain, where a manipulative landlady (Victoria Abril) seduces her young border (Jorge Sanz), gradually convincing him to rob his innocent fiancé (Maribel Verdu) of her life savings and her life. Director Vincente Aranda's depiction of desperate lust taken to murderous extremes plays up the erotic sex scenes, virtually ignoring the tragic human consequences of sexual obsession. Subtitles. Some graphic sex scenes with nudity and brief violence. O (nr)

Lovers and Other Strangers (1970) Seriocomic view of love and marriage told through a series of vignettes of the unhappy experiences of those taking part in the wedding of a young couple (Michael Brandon and Bonnie Bedelia). Directed by Cy Howard, the bittersweet currents that underlie the slick, surface witticisms seem to suggest that even as characters deny their love for one another, they share something deeper than a sexual attraction. A-IV (R/GP)

Loves and Times of Scaramouche, The (1976) Moronic Italian slapstick comedy directed by Enzo Castellari with Michael Sarrazin in the title role as a farcical rogue whose sexual exploits, primarily with Ursula Andress, are embroiled in the intrigues of Napoleon's court. Exploitative nudity. O (PG)

Loves of a Blonde (1966) Czechoslovakian movie about the lesson in life that a shy young girl learns from her first disillusioning experience with romance. Director Milos Forman's otherwise sensitive treatment indulges in an unnecessarily graphic seduction sequence. O (br)

Loves of Carmen, The (1948) Pedestrian version of the story made famous by Bizet's opera is set in 19th-century Seville, where a garrison corporal (Glenn Ford) falls for the title Gypsy beauty (Rita Hayworth), then kills his colonel (Arnold Moss) in a duel, and deserts to become a bandit leader after killing the Gypsy's husband (Victor Jory), with a double tragedy for the finale. Directed by Charles Vidor, the heavy melodramatics of the plot are unrelieved by the picture's colorful settings, and the love story is woodenly unconvincing. Stylized violence and tragic romantic complications. A-II (br)

Loves of Isadora, The (1969) Spectacular and poignant dramatization of the life of Isadora Duncan, one of modern dance's daring pioneers and free spirits. Director Karel Reisz focuses on the colorful (and ultimately tragic) career of the artist, with special emphasis on her vigorous and unorthodox romantic life. Vanessa Redgrave carries the title role, and her dancing is surprisingly graceful and appealing. Some sexually frank dialogue and suggestive visuals. A-III (PG)

Lovesick (1983) Dudley Moore plays a married psychiatrist on Manhattan's Upper East Side who falls in love with a patient (Elizabeth McGovern), which isn't a problem because his wife is having an affair with a deranged painter. Predictable and unfunny romantic comedy directed by Marshall Brickman takes a benign view of adultery. A-III (PG)

Lovin' Molly (1974) Adaptation of the Larry McMurtry Western novel in which the earth-mother of the title (Blythe Danner), who lives and loves with the same abandon, gives her favors freely to two men (Anthony Perkins and Beau Bridges) before and after her marriage to a third. Director Sidney Lumet focuses most on her two lovers, thus leaving a good deal of Molly's motivation obscure, at best. Some nudity and much earthy language. A-IV (R)

Loving (1970) Flawed but interesting study of a commercial illustrator (George Segal), who fancies the ladies and himself, as an artist condemned to drawing trucks and who finally goes overboard when, during the course of a party, he is monitored on closed circuit television making love to a neighbor's wife. Directed by Irvin Kershner, the movie succeeds best in placing its aimless hero in the context of affluent, materialistic suburbia. Needlessly extended sex scene. O (R)

Loving Couples (1980) Director Jack Smight's comedy about mate swapping, featuring James Coburn, Shirley MacLaine, Susan Sarandon, and Stephen Collins, is only intermittently funny. Though it is innocuous for the most part, its implication that such behavior can have a therapeutic effect on a marriage is objectionable. O (PG)

Loving You (1957) Glossy musical in which a savvy press-agent (Lizabeth Scott) gets her ex-husband (Wendell Corey) to hire a country boy (Elvis Presley) for his band, then uses her publicity skills to build the lad into a popular rock-singer whose appeal to teenage girls makes him the center of a national controversy. Directed by Hal Kanter, the hokey plot focuses on the agent's manipulation of both the troubled singer and her ex-husband with shallow results, though enough songs to satisfy Presley fans. Sexual situations and romantic complications. A-III (br)

Low Life, The (1996) Wryly comic story of a frustrated would-be writer (Rory Cochrane) struggling with bizarre temp jobs, a desperately friendly roommate (Sean Astin), and a oddball girlfriend (Kyra Sedgwick). Directed by George Hickenlooper, the inconclusive narrative vaguely focuses on five floundering twenty-somethings hard-pressed to convert their college diplomas into successful careers. An implied sexual encounter, an instance of recreational drug use, and some profanity and rough language. A-III (R)

Loyola, the Soldier Saint (1952) Spanish production dramatizing the life of the founder of the Jesuits, it follows Ignatius (Rafael Duran) from his youth in the Spanish court and brave deeds as a soldier through his religious conversion, studies for the priesthood, and establishment of the Society of Jesus. Directed by Jose Diaz Morales, the English adaptation features a narration by Jesuit Father Alfred J. Barrett of Fordham University, who bridges the scenario's episodic development, and, while the result is not great screen drama, it holds interest as a simple testimony to the faith of an earlier generation of Catholics. Dubbed. A-I (br)

Lt. Robin Crusoe, U.S.N. (1966) Dick Van Dyke stars as a navy pilot marooned on a Pacific Island in this mindless Disney comedy directed by Byron Paul without the slightest subtlety of any sort. A-I (br)

Lucas (1986) Bright 14-year-old boy nearly kills himself trying to impress his best and only friend, a 16-year-old girl who is attracted instead to one of the school's football stars. This teen drama offers thoughtful and sensitive characterizations and insightful depiction of high-school socializing. Its gentle tone is slightly jarred by some foul language and locker-room hi-jinks. A-II (PG-13)

Lucia (1974) Unusual Cuban movie with three different stories told from the perspective of three different women in three entirely distinct styles are united by the theme of Cuban revolutions in 1895 against the colonial Spanish rulers, in 1933 against the dictator Machado, and finally the Castro revolution in the 1960s. Director Humberto Solas demonstrates not only technical virtuosity, but his real accomplishment is in the vigor with which he expresses the humanity of his characters. Some shocking brutalities and some confusing historical material. A-IV (nr)

Luck of Ginger Coffey, The (1964) Splendid adaptation of Brian Moore's novel set in Montreal, where an irresponsible dreamer (Robert Shaw) goes on a spree after being fired from his newspaper job, gets arrested, and, facing the laughter in court the next morning, begins to realize how he has failed his wife (Mary Ure). Director Irvin Kershner succeeds in a probing character study of human weaknesses that is presented with feeling but without pity. Domestic strife and some coarse earthiness. A-III (br)

Luck of the Irish, The (1948) When an Irish-American reporter (Tyrone Power) happens to help a leprechaun (Cecil Kellaway) recover a pot of gold, the friendly old fellow reciprocates by turning up in New York to save his benefactor from working for an unsavory publisher (Lee J. Cobb) and to help him wed a proper colleen (Anne Baxter). Henry Koster directs the sentimental blarney with a leaden hand and little imagination, though Kellaway gives an endearingly droll performance as one of the wee people. It's a long sit for children and a matter of taste for others. A-I (br)

Luckiest Man in the World, The (1989) When a wealthy man (Philip Bosco) who has spent his life in quest of power and selfish pleasures is jolted into realizing the harm he has caused family, friends, mistress, business partner, and employees, his attempt to make amends are left to being determined off-camera by his lifelong victims. Playwright Frank D. Gilroy concocts a somewhat pedestrian look at one nasty man's search for redemption. Rough language laced with sexual vulgarities. A-III (nr)

Lucky Lady (1976) Failed crime-melodrama spoof in which smalltime 1920s bootleggers (Gene Hackman, Burt Reynolds, and Liza Minelli), at war with rival mobsters and the US Coast Guard, find time to engage in some kinky sex. Director Stanley Donen seems to have choreographed all the action to a musical whose songs have been edited out. Much sexual innuendo and frequent profanity. O (PG)

Lucky Losers (1950) Mediocre slapstick comedy directed by William Beaudine in which the Bowery Boys (Leo Gorcey, Huntz Hall, and company) help a TV reporter (Gabriel Dell) get the goods on a gambler (Lyle Talbot) who bumped off the stockbroker who had given them jobs. Comic violence and mild sexual innuendo. A-II (br)

Lucky Luciano (1974) Francesco Rosi's dramatization of the most wily of America's wily Mafiosi never manages to bring the facts of Luciano's life into focus, especially with Gian Maria Volonte's detached performance in the title role. The result is a disjointed and confusing portrait of a complex figure, ineffective as a movie entertainment and as history. Stylized violence and profanity. A-III (R)

Lucky Me (1954) Pleasant formula musical in which a superstitious singer (Doris Day) with a stranded revue-troupe (Phil Silvers, Nancy Walker, and Eddie Foy, Jr.) gets lucky when a big-time songwriter (Robert Cummings) falls for her, but misunderstandings get in the way, until, many complications later, they all head for Broadway. Directed by Jack Donohue, the likeable cast works hard in trying to put over a thinly contrived story and give some fresh appeal to lackluster musical numbers. Romantic complications. A-I (br)

Lucky Stiff, The (1949) Far-fetched murder mystery in which a nightclub singer (Dorothy Lamour) is convicted of murder, then is secretly vindicated by a lawyer (Brian Donlevy) who gets the authorities to falsely announce her execution so he can use the now-freed singer as a "ghost" to trap the real killer. Produced by Jack Benny and directed by Lewis R. Foster, the whimsical tone of the labored proceedings falls disappointingly flat, with a good cast done in by the story's heavy-handed treatment. Stylized violence and sexual innuendo. A-II (br)

Lucy Gallant (1955) Sober sudser directed by Robert Parrish in which a woman (Jane Wyman), stranded in a Texas oil boom-town, devotes her energies to building a local fashion-center rather than accept the romantic interest of the area's leading oil tycoon (Charlton Heston), until the final reel. Thin romance keyed to the attraction of opposites. A-I (br)

Ludwig (1973) Director Luchino Visconti presents the story of the mad German ruler (Helmut Berger) of the 19th-century Austrian Reich as a companion piece to his depiction of the madness of the Third Reich in **The Damned**. Severed from any political or social purpose, the work is a pointless exercise in pictorial opulence and rococo style, with questionable implications that latent homosexuality was the reason for Ludwig's problems. A-IV (R/PG)

Lullaby of Broadway (1951) Formula musical in which the daughter of a once-famous singer (Gladys George) almost throws away the chance of becoming the star of a Broadway musical after learning her mom has hit the skids. Directed by David Butler, the hackneyed story line sets up some vintage 1930s songs, but the production numbers are surprisingly flat. Romantic complications. A-II (br)

Lulu Belle (1948) Lackluster tale directed by Leslie Fenton in which a conniving 1890s singer (Dorothy Lamour) romances a series of men (notably George Montgomery, Albert Dekker, and Otto Kruger) as steppingstones to Broadway stardom until she and her current lover are shot. Implied sexual affairs. A-III (br)

Lulu the Tool (1975) Italian dramatization of a political theme illustrating the dehumanization of a worker (Gian Maria Volonte) being driven mad by his assembly-line job. Director Elio Petri's movie is a cry of moral outrage, a reminder that people are more than machines. There is strong material in its depiction of economic injustice, particularly brutish living conditions, with some vulgar language and a pathetic seduction scene some may find offensive. A-IV (nr)

Lumière (1976) Subtle French exploration of the varieties of femininity as mirrored by four actresses (Jeanne Moreau, Lucia Bose, Francine Rachette, and Caroline Cartier) who share their insecurities about men, career, and family. Written and directed by Jeanne Moreau, the psycho-social portrait exudes a cool detachment concerning adult themes of love, seduction, suicide, and ambition. A-III (R)

Luna (1979) Italian director Bernardo Bertolucci treats the subject of incest in the story of a recently widowed opera star (Jill Clayburgh) who drags her 15-year-old son (Matthew Barry) off on an Italian tour. A sullen, self-indulgent movie, it is an unmitigated disaster for all involved. Some violence and graphic sexual scenes. O (R)

Lupo! (1971) Israeli comedy revolving around an honest, earthy man who acts from the heart without attention to protocol or official regulations, thereby embarrassing his daughter and friends. It is a refreshingly entertaining, low-key comedy with quiet humor and some charm. A-II (G)

Lust for a Vampire (1971) Teacher Ralph Bates eyes comely student Yutte Stensgaard at a finishing school for young ladies, but she has only fangs for him. This film is at best a teasing corruption of the vampire genre, introducing some graphic situations of casual nudity and a touch of lesbianism. O (R)

Lust for Gold (1949) Tough-minded Western about Arizona's Lost Dutchman Mine, whose location was known only to the hard-bitten prospector (Glenn Ford) who had killed its owners, then taken up with a married woman (Ida Lupino) who wanted it all for herself, with grizzly results. Directed by S. Sylvan Simon, the unsavory story of the mine's past is framed by a modern murder mystery in which a distant relative (William Prince) of the Dutchman arrives to search for the lost mine in an area where other treasure hunters have recently been killed. Theme of greed employing stylized violence and sexual innuendo. A-III (br)

Lust for Life (1956) Kirk Douglas gives an intense performance as Dutch artist Vincent Van Gogh (1853-90) struggling in poverty to learn his craft and perfect his art, then suffering through a mental breakdown to achieve his best works, with his genius unrecognized until after his death. Directed by Vincente Minnelli from Norman Corwin's adaptation of the Irving Stone novel, the result does well in re-creating the artist's times as well as his artistic influences (notably Gaughin, in Anthony Quinn's Oscar-winning performance), but has a more difficult time trying to get inside the artist's mind and creative vision. Stylized violence and sexual innuendo. A-II (br)

Lust in the Dust (1985) Director Paul Bartel's attempt at a satirical Western is relentlessly tasteless and unfunny. Among other things, its crude humor is directed at women and religious groups. O (R)

Luv (1968) Uneven, occasionally tasteless screen version of Murray Schisgal's Broadway comedy about the marital mix-ups of a New York couple (Peter Falk and Elaine May) and a talkative loser (Jack Lemmon). Director Clive Donner tries everything from burlesque to satire, but is unable to elicit much more than stock reactions from its stock situations about love and marriage. A-IV (br)

Luxury Liner (1948) Dated musical melodrama directed by Richard Whorf with a boatload of romantics singing at the drop of a hat while the captain (George Brent) has his hands full handling a manipulative daughter (Jane Powell) who wants him to marry a lovely passenger (Frances Gifford). Innocent romantic misunderstandings. A-I (br)

Lydia (1941) An aging Boston spinster (Merle Oberon), who has devoted her life to a school for the blind, recalls her past during a reunion with four former beaus, one of whom (Joseph Cotten) still loves her, while the falseness of another (Alan Marshal) becomes clear. Directed by Julien Duvivier and based on his 1937 movie, **Un Carnet du Bal**, the romantic melodrama has some good moments but not enough to justify this elaborate, overlong production. A-II (br)

M. Butterfly (1993) A French diplomat (Jeremy Irons) in 1964 China is drawn into a secretive affair with a Chinese opera singer, unaware his lover is actually a male (John Lone) spying for the Chinese government, which results in the Frenchman's conviction for espionage in Paris years later. Neither Irons nor Lone is able to make his character believable in director David Cronenberg's fact-based movie, which fails to make the situation credible and leaves many questions unanswered. An extramarital affair with a few discreet bedroom scenes, brief nudity, a suicide, and an instance of rough language. A-III (R)

M*A*S*H (1970) Antiwar comedy about a Mobile Army Surgical Hospital during the Korean War, where a trio of skilled battle surgeons (Donald Sutherland, Elliott Gould, and Tom Skerritt) maintain their sanity by engaging in crazy hijinks outside the operating room. Robert Altman directs Ring Lardner, Jr.'s, episodic screenplay with an uneven mixture of comic styles, leaning heavily on irreverence and ridicule of authority figures. Good cast also includes Robert Duvall as a pious hypocrite and Sally Kellerman as the head nurse. Gory operating room sequences and sexually oriented humor. A-IV (PG)

Ma and Pa Kettle (1949) The first of nine comedies featuring the hillbilly couple from **The Egg and I**, this one has phlegmatic Pa (Percy Kilbride) win a luxury house in a tobacco slogan contest, but, when he's accused of plagiarism, it's up to pragmatic Ma (Marjorie Main) to keep them from being evicted. Director Charles Lamont has a field day with the house's futuristic gadgets and furnishings, but the best humor comes from the droll handling of the slapstick material by the two veteran character actors. Broad, old-fashioned family fare. A-I (br)

Ma Saison Préférée (1996) French character study of a lonely, hostile doctor (Daniel Auteuil) trying to reconnect emotionally with his estranged married sister (Catherine Deneuve) after their acid-tongued mother's failing health requires them to decide how to care for her. Director Andre Techine explores in exquisite detail the painful, ever-shifting love-hate relationships between parents, children, and siblings, holding out hope but no easy answers to matters of universal concern. Subtitles. Fleeting bedroom scenes, brief nudity, and occasional rough language. A-III (nr)

Mac (1993) Like his Italian-immigrant father before him, a master carpenter (John Turturro) demands perfection in his craft and from his younger carpenter brothers (Michael Badalucco and Carl Capotorto), alienating them by assuming the role of benevolent dictator within the family as well as in the family homebuilding business. As also directed by Turturro, the sometimes shrill movie salutes a sadly vanishing era when a man was respected more for the quality of his work than the size of his paycheck. Minor violence and sexual innuendo, brief nudity, and frequent rough language. A-II (R)

Macao (1952) Contrived crime melodrama set in the Portuguese colony on China's coast, where an American expatriate (Robert Mitchum) gets involved with a singer (Jane Russell) whose hardened boss (Brad Dexter) mistakes him for a detective (William Bendix) after him for a stateside crime. Directed by Josef von Sternberg, the thin plot offers little beyond an exotic setting, plenty of sinister atmosphere, and amoral characters. Stylized violence, menace, and sexual innuendo. A-III (br)

MacArthur (1977) Gregory Peck plays the title role in this sprawling screen biography of WW II hero General Douglas MacArthur, giving equal time to both sides of his public image as ruthless egotist and noble patriot but without providing any key to the real man. Capable if unspectacular dramatization directed by Joseph Sargent, it's basically a one-man show with the lesser roles devoid of substance. Restrained wartime violence. A-II (PG)

MacArthur's Children (1985) The changes in the life of a Japanese fishing village under the American occupation are seen through the wondering eyes of a fifth-grader (Takaya Yamauchi), whose teacher (Masako Natsume) is a war widow lusted after by her brother-in-law. Though the narrative is episodic and melodramatic, director Masahiro Shinoda excels at showing the human impact of Japan's military defeat and occupation as the villagers strive to retain their traditional values while accommodating those imported from America, including democracy, coeducation, swing music, and, especially, baseball. Subtitles. Implied rape, several discreet sexual references, and a few adolescent vulgarities. A-III (PG)

MacDonald of the Canadian Mounties (see: **Pony Soldier**)

MacKenna's Gold (1969) Gregory Peck stars as a former prospector, now marshal, forced by outlaw Omar Sharif to lead his gang to a hidden Valley of Gold sacred to the Indians but which Peck insists doesn't exist. Interminable complications set in as gold fever corrupts all in a story of cruelty, betrayal, and vengeance. J. Lee Thompson directs an episodic work whose theme of universal greed is morally unappealing and dramatically boring. Frequent violence and brief nudity. O (M)

Macaroni (1985) Breezy Italian comedy in which an uptight American (Jack Lemmon) on a business trip to Naples is confronted by the brother (Marcello Mastroianni) of a woman with whom the American had had a wartime romance, and, in the process of fulfilling the forgotten woman's expectations, the two men become friends. Under Ettore Scola's deft direction, the cheerful proceedings result in a charming little slice of Neapolitan life. Mildly profane language. A-III (PG)

Macbeth (1972) One of Shakespeare's most violent dramas has been visualized on the screen in an extremely realistic manner, turning the tragedy's verbal imagery of evil acts and brutal deeds into a real-life horror show that is neither convincing as human experience nor dramatically necessary. Yet director Roman Polanski's version of the play does have its virtues in being faithful to the text, in creating the primitive time period in Welsh and Northumberland locations, and in a very capable supporting cast for the unfortunately miscast leads (Jon Finch in the title role and Francesca Annis as Lady Macbeth). A mixed-bag with some graphic violence and brief nudity. A-IV (R)

Machine Gun McCain (1970) Paroled convict John Cassavetes pulls off a one-man heist of a Las Vegas gambling casino and is subsequently tracked down by the Syndicate, who disapprove of such private initiatives. Mediocre Italian production directed by Giuliano Montaldo with cast mostly from Italian B-grade movies. Some violence and ethnic stereotyping. A-III (PG)

Macho Callahan (1970) After a gutsy escape from a grisly Confederate prison, outlaw David Janssen kills the husband of Jean Seberg, who puts up a reward and then hunts him down herself. She finds him irresistible, but their relationship is finally terminated when his past and the bounty hunters catch up with him. Bernard L. Kowalski misdirects a twisted exercise in brutality and violent sex. O (R)

Mack, The (1973) Black exploitation movie about an ex-con (Max Julien) who claws his way to the top in the mink-coat, customized-limo world of a big-time ghetto pimp in Detroit. Directed by Michael Campus, the shoddy production views prostitution as an economic necessity. Excessive violence and sexual references. O (R)

Mack the Knife (1989) Cheesy, tedious adaptation of *The Threepenny Opera*, the 1929 Brecht-Weill musical about the downfall of MacHeath (Raul Julia), a despicable womanizer and criminal in London's underworld of beggars, whores, murderers, and thieves at the time of Queen Victoria's coronation. Writer-director Menahem Golan misses the point of the original's social commentary by stuffing this forgettable film with unimaginative musical numbers, a gray-on-gray color scheme, and overacting. Some sexual innuendo, crude language, and violence. A-III (PG-13)

Mackintosh & T.J. (1976) Returning to the screen after an absence of more than 20 years, Roy Rogers is back in the saddle as a washed-up rodeo cowboy of stern moral principles who befriends a young boy (Clay O'Brien in a good performance). Amiable, old-fashioned Western entertainment directed by Marvin J. Chomsky, it has an absurd sub-plot involving a sex maniac, but nothing that would be too strong for most teenagers. A-II (PG)

Mackintosh Man, The (1973) Paul Newman stars in a suspense thriller about a plan to capture a master spy who is a British politician. Though directed by John Huston and filmed on quite enchanting Irish and Maltese locations, it is no more than routine spy fare until the climax, which emphasizes the indistinguishable morality of spies, whatever their allegiance. A-III (PG)

Macon County Line (1974) Cluttered suspense thriller about brothers (Alan and Jesse Vint) driving through the South during the 1950s with a hitchhiker (Cheryl Waters) who find themselves wrongly accused of murdering the wife of a county deputy (Max Baer) and flee for their lives from his bloody rampage. Director Richard Compton supplies the gritty effects, but writer-producer Baer is responsible for the bizarre twist-ending to this tangled tale, supposedly based on a true incident. Excessive violence and exploitative nudity. O (R)

Macunaima (1972) Brazilian satire about a modern Don Quixote who rambles through a series of often-contradictory adventures which take him from primitive jungle to industrialized metropolis and back again. Told in crude but colorful folkloric style, with a melange of symbolic characters and unrelated episodes, the point of it all seems to be that poor nations destroy themselves in their quest for commercial growth. Written and directed by Joaquim Pedro de Andrade, the movie might be likened to the theater of the absurd, but some casual nudity and lewd sight gags prove more offensive than humorous. O (nr)

Mad About Music (1938) Sweetly sappy, gently funny story of a 14-year-old (Deanna Durbin) whose movie-star mom (Gail Patrick) keeps hidden from the press in a Swiss school until the lonely girl inveigles a proper Englishman (Herbert Marshall) into pretending to be her father, with happy results. Director Norman Taurog centers the sentiment on the girl's unhappiness at the boarding school, but Deanna's winsome singing and cheerful innocence, especially her penchant for spinning tall tales with crossed fingers, carry the picture. Entertaining nonsense with plenty of heart and not a few smiles. A-I (br)

Mad Adventures of "Rabbi" Jacob, The (1974) Madcap is the word for this zany French production which begins on New York's Lower East Side, from which Rabbi Jacob departs for Paris to attend the bar mitzvah of a favored nephew. What happens after that is a delightful, non-stop romp with Louis de Funes as an idiotic anti-Semite whose prejudices lead him into, among other things, a bubble-gum vat and a rabbinical disguise. Under the deceptively casual direction of Gerard Oury, bigotry is thoroughly ridiculed with very controlled and funny slapstick humor. The result is a comedy that the whole family can enjoy. A-I (G)

Mad City (1997) Dreary drama in which a fired museum guard (John Travolta) impulsively takes his boss and visiting children hostage, then unwittingly allows an ambitious TV reporter (Dustin Hoffman) to manipulate the situation to advance his flagging career. Director Costa-Gavras offers nothing new or insightful in this drawn-out tale showing the media's role in shaping breaking news. Brief violence, occasional profanity, and an instance of rough language. A-III (PG-13)

Mad Dog (1976) Writer-director Philippe Mora's ragged account of the career of a 19th-century Australian outlaw (Dennis Hopper) squanders a good recreation of the era because of its incoherent narrative, undue attention to the effects of violence, and some brief nudity. O (R)

Mad Dog and Glory (1993) After a nasty loanshark (Bill Murray) sends a beautiful debtor (Uma Thurman) to spend a week with the timid cop (Robert De Niro) who saved his life, the sleazy shyster is enraged because the cop falls in love with her. Director John McNaughton employs a slickly sick sense of humor in a mean-spirited comedy replete with casual violence and women who are willingly victimized. Some brutal violence, a demeaning and sexist depiction of women, an extended sexual encounter, and much rough language. O (R)

Mad Dog Time (1996) Lumbering black comedy in which three rival gangsters (Jeff Goldblum, Gabriel Byrne, and Kyle MacLachlan) shoot it out in trying to take over the mob after their boss (Richard Dreyfuss) is released from a sanitarium. Writer-director Larry Bishop relies on sleek visuals to mask the failings of the dull narrative and the dreary macho posturings of stereotyped characters. Jokey treatment of numerous cold-blooded murders, implied sexual encounters, some profanity, and much rough language. O (R)

Mad Dogs and Englishmen (1971) Performance documentary of 1970 American tour by Joe Cocker's musical group. Director Pierre Adidge also spends some time documenting the communal lifestyle of Cocker's troupe as a warmly sympathetic, but doubtless for many, shockingly irresponsible experiment in human relations. Rather graphic description of a sexual encounter by a groupie, and some flashes of nudity, as well as the musicians' nonconformist lifestyle, require an adult perspective. A-III (nr)

Mad Love (1935) Uneven horror movie in which a brilliant surgeon (Peter Lorre) replaces the smashed hands of a famous pianist (Colin Clive) by grafting on those of a killer (Edward Brophy), with murderous results. Though there are some memorable moments in director Karl Freund's version of the oft-told tale of hands that have "a life of their own," the focus here is on the bald-headed, pop-eyed surgeon's obsession with the pianist's wife (Frances Drake), whose rejection drives him bonkers and leaves viewers unmoved by his downfall. Menacing situations and sexual innuendo. A-III (br)

Mad Love (1995) Sappy teen road-movie in which a high-school senior (Chris O'Donnell) becomes infatuated with a suicidal student (Drew Barrymore), breaks her out of a psychiatric hospital, and heads for Mexico in a stolen car, before realizing she does in fact require professional care. Director Antonia Bird's manipulative cautionary tale romanticizes the lovers' odyssey and glosses over the consequences of their actions in superficial attempts at poignancy. Fleeting love scenes, some menace, brief violence, and an instance of rough language. A-IV (PG-13)

Mad Magician, The (1954) After being thwarted in his attempt to become a stage magician, an inventor of magic tricks (Vincent Price) goes berserk, kills his employer and a rival magician, then impersonates them until a policeman (Patrick O'Neal) gets wise. Directed by John Brahm, the weak thriller has some grisly moments, especially with a crematorium trick, but the gimmicky plot holds little interest. Stylized violence and romantic complications. A-II (br)

Mad Max (1980) Australian action melodrama set in the near future when the world has lurched a little further towards chaos, and nomadic motorcyclists and a brutal police force fight it out on desert roads. Mel Gibson stars as the decent cop who tries to fight within the system, until his wife and daughter are brutally killed and he goes on a bloody rampage. Director George Miller stages the action sequences quite impressively, but characterizations count for nothing and the poor dubbing of American voices is distracting. Excessively graphic violence. O (R)

Mad Max Beyond Thunderdome (1985) Solitary, two-fisted roamer of the post-Armageddon Australian Outback, Mad Max (Mel Gibson) chances upon a backward settlement, where he is forced to fight in its arena (the Thunderdome), goes on to becomes a hero figure for a tribe of lost children, and then has a final showdown with the settlers, involving the usual collection of bizarre vehicles. With the backgrounds showing the appalling consequence of nuclear holocaust, there is more than a touch of solemnity to the proceedings. Directed by George Miller and George Ogilvie, it's all rather violent, but not excessively so, and action fans will find it fairly intelligent entertainment. A-III (PG-13)

Mad Miss Manton, The (1938) Minor screwball comedy in which a rebellious socialite (Barbara Stanwyck) pursues a murderer despite interference from an amorous newspaper editor (Henry Fonda) and an irascible police detective (Sam Levene). Directed by Leigh Jason, the mystery plot takes a backseat to the opposites-attract romance, and the comic turns of a talented cast, including Hattie McDaniel and Grady Sutton. Comic menace and mild romantic situations. A-I (br)

Mad Monster Party? (1967) Animated horror spoof with Dr. Frankenstein (voice of Boris Karloff) hosting a gathering of movie monsters in order to name his successor. Produced by Arthur Rankin, Jr., and directed by Jules Bass, the result is more silly than scary. Mild menace and stylized violence. A-II (br)

Mad Room, The (1969) After having killed their parents, two children committed to a home for the mentally insane are released as teenagers (Barbara

Sammeth and Michael Burns) in the custody of their older sister who lives with her disagreeable, unsuspecting employer. The outcome of this psychological thriller is predictably dire, but writer-director Bernard Girard's disappointing adaptation of a real chiller, **Ladies in Retirement**, is clumsy and only infrequently establishes the required mood of suspense. Restrained violence. A-III (M)

Mad Wednesday (see: **The Sin of Harold Diddlebock**)

Madame Bovary (1991) Faithful adaptation of Gustave Flaubert's 1856 novel about a restless Frenchwoman (Isabelle Huppert) who, bored in her marriage to a doltish physician (Jean-Francois Balmer), precipitates her own downfall by adulterous infatuations and compulsive expenditures. As adapted and directed by Claude Chabrol, the melodramatic story offers a visually engaging but emotionally distant picture of a relentlessly self-absorbed woman. Subtitles. Restrained treatment of extramarital affairs and a suicide. A-III (PG-13)

Madame Butterfly (1996) International co-production of Puccini's tragic opera set in turn-of-the-century Nagasaki, where a callow American naval officer (Richard Troxell) marries, then abandons, his 15-year-old Japanese bride (Ying Huang), only to return to claim their little son for his new American wife to raise. Director Frederic Mitterrand opens up the stage-bound opera format by using outdoor location shooting in a visually lovely film which should be music to opera lovers' ears. Subtitles. Marital desertion and a culturally condoned suicide. A-III (nr)

Madame Rosa (1978) Memorable performance by Simone Signoret as an aging former prostitute and survivor of Auschwitz who makes a living of sorts by running a foster home for the children of prostitutes in her sixth-floor walkup in a rundown Parisian neighborhood. As her health deteriorates, she develops a relationship of need with a 14-year-old Algerian boy (Samy Ben Youb). French production directed by Moshe Mizrahi, its Arab-Jewish jokes quickly wear thin, and its evocation of the horror of Auschwitz and persecution is far too superficial. Mature theme and atmosphere. A-III (PG)

Madame Sousatzka (1988) Madame Sousatzka (Shirley MacLaine) is an eccentric musical *artiste* who achieves her greatest glory as a teacher, not performer. Past middle age, she focuses on her talented piano students, in this case a virtuoso 15-year-old Indian boy (Navin Chowdhry). MacLaine is terrific in this rich character role warmly directed by John Schlesinger. Off-camera adulterous affair and some rough language. A-III (PG-13)

Madame X (1966) Hokey tearjerker in which a shop-girl (Lana Turner) marries a wealthy lawyer (John Forsythe) whose mother (Constance Bennett) blackmails her into leaving husband and baby son, then many bad years later she winds up on trial for killing a sleazy con-man (Burgess Meredith), with her defense lawyer (Keir Dullea) turning out to be her son who grew up believing his mother dead. Directed by David Lowell Rich, the glossy production only emphasizes the lack of genuine emotion in this artificial romantic clunker. Sexual situations and alcoholic excess. A-III (br)

Maddalena (1971) Italian soap opera about a passionate woman (Lisa Gastoni) and her destructive love for a priest (Eric Woofe) contents itself with wallowing in extensive nudity, pulp psychology, and phony pathos. Talented Polish director Jerry Kawalerowicz has turned a potentially interesting theme into a boring feature that has little to offer but sensationalism. O (R)

Made for Each Other (1939) Classy sudser in which a young lawyer (James Stewart) and his bride (Carole Lombard) move in with his meddlesome mother (Lucile Watson) as he struggles to get ahead in a fusty law firm (headed by Charles Coburn), but his career hopes turn sour, then his baby son falls deathly ill. Directed by John Cromwell, the sentimental plot is shamelessly contrived, but an agreeable cast helps put over the story's winning mix of humor and pathos, until the last reel's race against time as an airplane tries to get through a snowstorm with serum to save the baby's life. Domestic tensions over financial worries and a life-threatening situation. A-II (br)

Made for Each Other (1971) Italian boy and Jewish girl find each other at a group-therapy session and shout and fight their way across the city into matrimony. The film's few virtues and many faults are all attributable to Renee Taylor and Joseph Bologna, who both wrote and star in what one may assume is something of a real-life experience. As directed by Robert B. Bean, the movie's contrast of ethnic value systems and traditions provides some humor but cloaks its lack of depth in some puerile sentimentality. A-III (PG)

Made in America (1993) Clunky romantic comedy in which a resourceful African-American teen (Nia Long) discovers that her sperm-donor father is a white used-car salesman (Ted Danson), a revelation that infuriates her mother (Whoopi Goldberg), until she discovers that he's not as obnoxious as he appears. Director Richard Benjamin's one-joke premise is stretched to the limit in a predictable, formula sitcom built around lamely contrived relationships. Some sexual innuendo, fleeting nudity, and a few racial stereotypes. A-III (PG-13)

Made in Heaven (1987) Failed romantic fantasy about a youth (Timothy Hutton) who dies and goes to heaven, falls in love with an unborn soul (Kelly McGillis), and then pursues her when she is sent to earth. Director Alan Rudolph's fantasy lacks imagination, and the romance lacks any appeal or interest. Some restrained love scenes and rough language. A-III (PG)

Made in Italy (1967) Series of semi-documentary vignettes of Italian life, exploring such topics as work, women, customs, the family, politics, and religion. The episodes, which feature some leading Italian and

French performers, are directed by Nanni Loy with humor, affection, and pathos. Standout is Anna Magnani as a mother determined to get her family across an auto-jammed highway, a triumph both hilarious and moving. Older adolescents might enjoy this beautifully photographed, very human work. A-III (br)

Madeleine (1949) In 1857 Glasgow, a young woman (Ann Todd) from a respectable family is put on trial, charged with poisoning a handsome but poor French clerk (Ivan Desny) to whom she had secretly been engaged. Director David Lean's disappointing dramatization of a classic murder trial, whose outcome turns on the Scottish verdict of "not proven," spends a great deal of time setting up the ambiguities of the case but leaves viewers frustrated with the flatly inconclusive ending. Unsavory romantic liaison and a sexual situation. A-III (br)

Madeline (1998) Sweet-natured tale from the children's books by Ludwig Bemelman in which the adventurous title orphan (Hatty Jones), who lives in a 1956 Parisian boarding school run by a devoted nun (Frances McDormand), sets out to save the school from being closed, only to find herself kidnapped by circus performers. Directed by Daisy von Scherler Mayer, the story and characters are warmly engaging, and some will be charmed by its nostalgic picture of obedient schoolchildren in a simpler era. Mild menace. A-I (PG)

Madhouse (1974) Undistinguished horror melodrama, but some fun because its story line is about a faded horror-movie star (Vincent Price) whose attempts to get a leading part in a new TV horror series are thwarted by a fellow actor (Peter Cushing), who starts killing off Price's friends and leaving evidence implicating Price as the murderer. Directed by Jim Clark, the plot is a jumble, not helped much by the inclusion of a number of clips from old horror movies, but there are enough grisly murders for the horror trade. A-III (PG)

Madhouse (1990) Humorless comedy in which houseguests from Hell (actually New Jersey) descend upon a Los Angeles couple (John Larroquette and Kirstie Alley) who have just settled into their first real home. Writer-director Tom Ropelewski leaves no crass stone unturned as the houseguests systematically turn their hosts into raving maniacs. Some suggestive sexual situations, vulgar jokes, and cat abuse. A-III (PG-13)

Madigan (1968) Fast-moving crime thriller featuring Richard Widmark and Harry Guardino as New York City detectives who spend a couple of frenzied days trying to redeem themselves by recapturing the psychotic killer they let escape. Vividly directed by Donald Siegel, the focus is on the details of routine police work rather than on resolving its numerous plot complications and moral ambiguities. Some tough violence. A-III (br)

Madigan's Millions (1969) Botched comedy with Dustin Hoffman playing a bumbling US treasury agent sent to locate a million dollars smuggled into Italy by deported gangster Cesar Romero. Ineptly directed by Stanley Preger, the silly plot has a few amusing moments, but the rest is woefully unfunny. A-II (G)

Madness of King George, The (1994) Farce mixes with historical drama in this period piece set in 1788 England, where the manic behavior of George III (Nigel Hawthorne) enables his pompous son (Rupert Everett) to be named regent, while the queen (Helen Mirren) fumes, and a strong-willed doctor (Ian Holm) uses intimidation and restraints to curb the king's outbursts so he may be restored to the throne. Hawthorne's vigorous performance as the erratic king gradually reveals his touchingly frail humanity in director Nicholas Hytner's sprightly re-creation of royal plotting and court intrigues. Some crude sexual innuendo and intermittent toilet humor. A-III (PG-13)

Mado (1978) Long, rambling tale of a pure-of-heart prostitute (Ottavia Piccolo) whose devotion to her working-class friends and lack of greed are a constant reproach to her most enamored patron, a wealthy businessman (Michel Piccoli). The inconsequential French comedy directed by Claude Sautet gets muddled in corrupt business deals, but has the good sense to drop them for a country outing, a driving rainstorm, and huge quantities of mud in some dim metaphorical resolution. Sexual situations and some gratuitous nudity. O (nr)

Madonna: Truth or Dare (1991) Self-serving documentary-style footage of the rock star's 1990 Blond Ambition concert tour, focusing mostly on her outrageous backstage pronouncements and manipulative encounters with family and tour members. As directed by Alek Keshishian, the result is a boring, self-obsessed descent into vulgar exhibitionism that, far from a honest revelation of the pop icon, is just one more calculating pose. Incessantly crude sexual innuendo with some homosexual references, brief nudity, and much rough language. O (R)

Madron (1971) Low-budget Western about an Indian fighter (Richard Boone) who rescues a nun (Leslie Caron) left for dead by Apaches after a stagecoach attack. Together they wend their way through the desert, fighting off Indians and outlaws, until eventually Sister lets her long hair down and seems to anticipate a love scene that never fully materializes. As directed by Jerry Hopper, the principals play their sharply contrasting roles with an undeserved verve, and the ultimate discretions of the silly script render the movie an innocuous exercise. Some violence and tasteless treatment of religious elements. A-III (GP)

Madwoman of Chaillot, The (1969) Katharine Hepburn, Richard Chamberlain, and Danny Kaye play slightly daft Parisian idealists who rally the poor and simple of the city to foil an insane plot to destroy Paris for the sake of oil deposits beneath its streets. Director Bryan Forbes has made a beautiful-looking but sluggish screen version of the delightful Jean Giradoux play in which the mad are really sane and the supposed sane are quite mad. Disappointing but has plenty of good moments. A-III (G)

Mafia (1969) Italian crime melodrama with Lee J. Cobb as the head of the local syndicate controlling a Sicilian town, where an uncooperative businessman is murdered and the husband of Claudia Cardinale disappears. The efforts of the local police to solve the crimes are thwarted in an involved plot sluggishly directed by Damiano Damiani. Violence. A-III (M)

Mafia! (1998) Comic misfire parodies numerous gangster movies, particularly **The Godfather**, in chronicling how the younger son (Jay Mohr) of a klutzy Sicilian mobster (Lloyd Bridges) eventually takes his father's place as underworld boss. Director Jim Abrahams delivers many goofy sight gags, but the humor often falls flat by becoming too literal in its depiction of the formula plot. Comic treatment of violence, some sexual innuendo, crude toilet humor, ethnic stereotyping, and an instance of rough language. A-III (PG-13)

Magic (1978) Anthony Hopkins stars in this dull and brutal melodrama about an unbalanced ventriloquist who tends to get into arguments with his dummy. Burgess Meredith plays his manager who inadvertently sets off a series of tragic events for all concerned, including Ann-Margaret as an unhappily married woman. Director Richard Attenborough falls far short of the modest goal of making an entertaining thriller. Violence, a bedroom sequence, and a sympathetic attitude towards adultery. O (R)

Magic Christian, The (1969) Screen version of Terry Southern's novel about a wealthy tycoon (Peter Sellers) who sets out to prove that money means everything and everyone has his price. Directed by Joseph McGrath, this spoof of all things establishment has some humorous situations, but the satirical intent of the movie is largely unrealized. Some purple patches of homosexual innuendo, nudity, and off-color language. O (PG)

Magic Flute, The (1975) Director Ingmar Bergman presents this opera by Wolfgang Amadeus Mozart as an actual performance on a cramped 18th-century stage, boldly taking viewers into a world of illusion, stagecraft, and mystery. Originally produced for Swedish television, its stress on the theatricality of Mozart's fairytale operatics is to the advantage of a pretty silly libretto. Bergman's austere yet ingratiating visual style suitably complements Mozart's beautifully intricate music. It is a classic that might serve as a good introduction to opera for young people, though parents should be aware that it contains some sexual allusions and a brief close-up of an erotic drawing. A-III (G)

Magic Garden of Stanley Sweetheart, The (1970) Exploitative melodrama about a college student (Don Johnson) who gradually retreats from reality as he becomes dependent upon sex and drugs. Director Leonard Horn stages an interminable series of explicit sexual encounters and pot parties without providing the least insight into the youth's problems or reasons for his downward climb into sexual aberrations and drugged lethargy. O (R)

Magic in the Water (1995) Muddled adventure-fantasy in which a divorced dad (Mark Harmon) takes his two youngsters on a backwoods vacation, where they encounter a lake monster trying to warn humans about toxic wastes poisoning the water. Director Rick Stevenson finds some genuine warmth in the family relationships and a bit of humor from quirky rural characters, but there is more confusion than magic in a jumbled plot involving Native American myths and a monster who snacks on Oreo cookies. Scenes of menace to children, mystifying rituals, and a few vulgar expressions. A-II (PG)

Magic of Lassie, The (1978) The celebrated collie returns to foil the bad guy (Parnell Roberts) in his attempt to steal James Stewart's ranch. Good production of a standard plot and solid supporting cast includes Mickey Rooney and Alice Faye. Though director Don Chaffey elevates Lassie's human qualities to new heights of absurdity, younger viewers will take much delight in the adventures of this canine movie legend. A-I (G)

Magic of the Kite, The (1971) Children's adventure movie, with beautiful location photography in France and China, follows the odyssey of a young lad and his little sister in search of the owner of a magic kite. The imaginative French production (dubbed in English) features flying bedsteads, a colorful Chinese magician, and two charming youngsters, presented with enough flair and fantasy to captivate the small fry. A-I (G)

Magic Sword, The (1962) Halting medieval fantasy in which the foster son (Gary Lockwood) of a good witch (Estelle Winwood) sets off to rescue a princess (Anne Helm) from being fed to a two-headed dragon by a villainous wizard (Basil Rathbone). Unimaginatively directed by Bert I. Gordon, the threadbare story features some lackluster special effects but not much else of interest. Stylized violence and assorted villainy. A-II (br)

Magic Town (1947) Uneven fable in which a maverick pollster (James Stewart) secretly sets up shop in a small town that's a microcosm of national opinion, but when the local paper's editor (Jane Wyman) exposes his polling activities, the citizens become self-conscious, and the town goes from boom to bust. Director William A. Wellman does well with the small-town setting and characters but overdoes the pollster's sense of guilt at deceiving the town, and his subsequent attempts to make things right become maudlin and unconvincing. Human foibles and deceit. A-II (br)

Magician of Lublin (1979) Failed screen version of the Issac Bashevis Singer novel about an irreligious, woman-chasing, Jewish magician (Alan Arkin) in turn-of-the-century Poland who convinces a Warsaw theater manager (Lou Jacobi) that he can fly, but then squanders the money he receives on a countess (Louise Fletcher). Director Menachem Golan's crude and plodding effort misses the religious theme of the original, and Arkin is badly miscast as the magnetic, erotic, and ultimately spiritually tormented hero. Some extravagant nudity and graphic sexuality. O (R)

Magnetic Monster, The (1953) Effective little chiller in which government scientists (Richard Carlson and King Donovan) track down a radioactive element, discover its growing magnetic power and size, then seek to destroy it with a powerful electric generator deep in a Nova Scotia mine shaft. Directed by Curt Siodmak, the hokey premise works up considerable suspense in the desperate race to stop the deadly element's growth, with the special effects in the concluding sequence especially gripping. Stylized violence and fantasy menace. A-I (br)

Magnificent Ambersons, The (1942) Sturdy saga of American life circa 1900 from the Booth Tarkington novel about the arrogant son (Tim Holt) of a wealthy Midwestern family who keeps his widowed mother (Delores Costello) from marrying a rising auto-maker (Joseph Cotton), then gets his comeuppance by failing to adapt to changing circumstances. Director Orson Welles succeeds in a vivid period re-creation with convincing performances from a strong cast, though flawed by the narrative's uneven pace resulting from a studio re-edit of Welles's original version. Serious treatment of a selfish individual's foolish pride and its tragic consequences. A-II (br)

Magnificent Obsession (1935) Sentimental melodrama from the Lloyd C. Douglas novel in which a rich ne'er-do-well (Robert Taylor) indirectly causes a car accident blinding a woman (Irene Dunne), whom he comes to love so deeply that he spends six years to become a surgeon and restore her sight. Directed by John M. Stahl, the story portrays the man's transformation as motivated by the Gospel message to help others, though the contrived proceedings are more about romantic gestures than religious idealism. Romantic complications. A-II (br)

Magnificent Obsession (1954) Sappy remake of the 1935 tearjerker in which a playboy (Rock Hudson) devotes himself to helping others after causing an accident blinding the woman he loves (Jane Wyman). Director Douglas Sirk emphasizes the artificial sentimentality of the sudsy script, though the cast tries gamely not to notice. High-minded romance but flatly unconvincing. A-II (br)

Magnificent Seven Ride!, The (1972) After his wife is kidnapped, raped, and murdered, Lee Van Cleef sets out to find those responsible, and, when the trail leads to a large and vicious band of renegades, he gathers his old comrades, the Magnificent Seven, five of whom are in prison. Director George McCowan's sequel is a standard Western, though the climactic showdown, as might be expected, is violent in the extreme. A-III (PG)

Magnum Force (1973) Clint Eastwood returns as San Francisco detective "Dirty Harry" Callahan, this time taking on a group of renegade rookie cops who are systematically murdering the city's mobsters. Harry stops them by taking the law into his own hands, though viewers may have difficulty distinguishing between his brand of fascism and theirs. Ted Post directs an irresponsible movie celebrating the vigilante spirit. Graphic violence and incidental sexual references. O (R)

Magus, The (1968) British teacher (Michael Caine), escaping the marriage plans of his mistress (Anna Karina), comes to a Greek island, where he happens upon a practitioner of the occult (Anthony Quinn). As the young teacher becomes sexually involved with one of the magician's followers (Candice Bergen), the movie shifts from reality to self-indulgent fantasy. Director Guy Green's screen version of the John Fowles novel is not only pretentious but hopelessly muddled and ultimately senseless. Explicit sex and nudity. O (PG)

Mahanagar (see: **The Big City**)

Mahler (1976) British production about the Austrian composer constructed out of a series of recollections triggered in Mahler's mind by his triumphant return to Vienna just before his death in 1911. Attempting to show the source of the composer's creative inspiration, director Ken Russell succeeds in linking a personality to a body of music, though there is an excess of Jewish stereotyping and references to the proto-Nazi tendencies of the period. A-IV (PG)

Mahogany (1975) Talented Diana Ross is wasted in a story about a black woman's rise from sales clerk in Chicago to famous model and fashion designer in Rome, where she becomes disillusioned and returns to Chicago and the arms of her rejected lover (Billy Dee Williams). Directed by Berry Gordy, this Cinderella variation starts well enough but soon becomes mired in soap opera histrionics and sexual stereotyping. A-III (PG)

Maid of Salem (1937) Puritan melodrama set in 1692 Massachusetts, where a rebel from Virginia (Fred MacMurray) is hiding from pursuers, then falls in love with a local woman (Claudette Colbert) whom he helps escape being hanged as a witch. Director Frank Lloyd provides a credible picture of colonial life but does a better job evoking the hysteria of the period's witchcraft trials than the growing romance between the principals. Stylized violence and menacing situations. A-II (br)

Maid to Order (1987) Spoiled Beverly Hills heiress (Ally Sheedy) learns a lesson in humility and caring when forced to work as a maid for a zany, garish couple (Dick Shawn and Valerie Perrine). Director Amy Jones sets the appropriate tone of fantasy for this romantic fable which has a brief moment of comic nudity and some rough language. A-II (PG)

Maid's Night Out (1938) Inane romantic comedy about a rich man's son (Allan Lane) wooing a rich woman's daughter (Joan Fontaine), both under the impression the other works for a living. Directed by Ben Holmes, the situation is too contrived to be amusing, but some laughs are supplied by Billy Gilbert as a fishmonger and Cecil Kellaway as a butler who knows better than his betters. Dated nostalgia of unlikely appeal to youngsters. A-I (br)

Maiden for a Prince, A (1967) Based on a historical incident, this bawdy Italian comedy in which the virility of a prince is put to an absurd test by his prospective in-laws satirizes Renaissance manners and morals. Some viewers may not find the subject particularly amusing or appropriate screen entertainment. A-IV (br)

Maids, The (1975) Screen version of the Jean Genet play about two maids (Glenda Jackson and Susannah York) who, whenever their mistress (Vivian Merchant) is absent, act out their hatred of her in little dramas of revolt which always climax in her murder. The last time they go into their act, one of them really dies, or so it seems. Directed by Christopher Miles, three talented actresses are wasted in a hopeless effort to find some meaning in a boring, repetitive drama that takes perverse pleasure in sadomasochistic cruelties. A-IV (PG)

Maidstone (1971) Novelist Norman Mailer made this movie by having a group of actors and non-actors improvise dialogue and action around a story of a movie director (Mailer) who decides to run for president. The result, unfortunately, is a tedious, self-conscious vanity production in which nothing much happens, unless one considers Rip Torn's violent onscreen fight with Mailer notable. Some graphic nudity and rough language. O (nr)

Mail Order Bride (1964) Uneven Western in which a retired lawman (Buddy Ebsen) tries to get a dead friend's wild son (Keir Dullea) to settle down by importing a needy widow (Lois Nettleton) and her young boy from Kansas City, but it will take more than marriage to make a man out of the callow lad. Writer-director Burt Kennedy sets up an intriguing situation with strong characters but then goes sentimental until the baldly contrived ending. Some stylized violence and numerous sexual situations and references. A-III (br)

Main Chance (1966) British crime story in which a gambler outwits a group of international jewel smugglers and makes off with a fortune in diamonds. Director John Knight proves there is no honor among thieves rather smartly but tends to glamorize the amorality of the card-sharp hero. A-III (br)

Main Event, The (1979) Barbra Streisand, a high-pressure perfume executive, finds that her accountant has absconded with her funds, leaving her but a single asset — the contract of a reluctant prizefighter, Ryan O'Neal. Attempting to recoup her losses, she forces him into the ring, and their antagonism soon transmutes itself into true love. Erratic and not very funny comedy directed by Howard Zieff. Several sexually suggestive scenes. A-III (PG)

Maitresse (1976) French movie about a love affair between a country lout (Gerard Depardieu) and a city girl (Bulle Ogier), who works very hard at her chosen profession in which, clothed all in leather, she whips wealthy masochistic clients and provides whatever they request in brisk, businesslike fashion. Director Barbet Schroeder records these sessions with plodding, uncritical fidelity, showing far less interest in developing any credibility to the love affair. Tedious, ill-conceived movie with baldly explicit scenes of sadomasochism. O (R)

Major and the Minor, The (1942) Wacky comedy in which a woman (Ginger Rogers), lacking enough money for a full-fare train ticket, gets the children's rate by pretending to be an 11-year-old, then has to continue the disguise when she's befriended on the journey by an Army officer (Ray Milland) from a boys military academy, with increasingly giddy but mostly good-natured results. Director Billy Wilder sustains the humor of the absurd premise until the sentimental ending, abetted by a capable cast gamely going through the antic proceedings. Comic misunderstandings and romantic complications. A-II (br)

Major Barbara (1941) Good-natured British satire about the title Salvation Army officer (Wendy Hiller) whose cheerful dedication wins many converts, including a hardened Limehouse tough (Robert Newton), but moral scruples lead her to resign when the Army accepts a large donation from her munitions millionaire father (Robert Morley), who then invites her fiancé (Rex Harrison) to be his successor. Directed by Gabriel Pascal from Bernard Shaw's adaptation of his own play, the stagy proceedings are paced by some droll action scenes and wickedly witty exchanges between the enlightened armaments manufacturer, his idealistic daughter, and her philosophic fiancé. Several scenes of violence directed against women and cynical comments about marriage and religion. A-III (br)

Major Dundee (1965) Muddled Western in which a glory-seeking cavalry officer (Charlton Heston) takes a command of misfits and Confederate prisoners-of-war on a raid across the Mexican border to destroy a band of rampaging Apaches who have taken refuge there. Directed by Sam Peckinpah, the Civil War setting makes for all kinds of complications and unconvincing characterizations, though the action scenes are well-done, if implausible. Frontier violence. A-II (br)

Major League (1989) Lighthearted comedy about misfit Cleveland Indian baseball players, who rally for one last hurrah when they learn the team's new owner (Margaret Whitton) is trying to engineer a losing season in order to move the franchise to Miami. Although strapped with a feel-good plot as old as the hills, writer-director David Ward keeps his action fun and funny with a topnotch cast of losers (Tom Berenger, Charlie Sheen, Corbin Bernsen, Wesley Snipes, and James Gammon). Much locker-room language and implied sexual trysts. A-III (R)

Major League II (1994) By-the-numbers sequel

in which a fictional baseball team returns for a new season saddled with assorted ego problems, leaving it up to the now image-conscious pitcher (Charlie Sheen) and catcher-turned-coach (Tom Berenger) to get them back in focus as long-shot contenders for the World Series. With the script's one-dimensional characters and predictable plotting, director David S. Ward turns in a lifeless sports comedy that vainly strains for contrived laughs. Occasional profanity and ball-field scuffles. A-II (PG)

Major League: Back to the Minors (1998) Forgettable baseball comedy in which novice manager Scott Bakula turns a motley crew of eccentric minor-leaguers into a winning team that goes on to challenge a major-league team. Writer-director John Warren's characters are a mostly genial bunch, but a buffoonish rival manager and the predictable course of events make the movie strike out. Fleeting violence, brief sexual innuendo, occasional profanity, and an instance of rough language. A-III (PG-13)

Major Payne (1995) Tiresome one-joke comedy directed by Nick Castle in which a prematurely retired but combat-obsessed Marine officer (Dayan Wayans) terrifies a motley band of junior ROTC cadets until they win the trophy as the best unit in Virginia. An adult's rough treatment of youngsters, dangerous horseplay, vulgar humor, and coarse language. A-III (PG-13)

Make a Face (1971) Independent production about the lonely existence of a young woman (Karen Sperling, who also produced and directed) near the border of schizophrenia, increasingly losing hold on what is real and what is fantasy. The more deeply troubled she becomes, the more fragmented the movie, and the more erratic and inexplicable are the events. An intriguing concept, it flounders in self-absorbed sexual fantasies and the limitations of low-budget filmmaking. A-IV (nr)

Making It (1971) Kristoffer Tabori plays a high-school Lothario whose aim is to make love with every female around. His irresponsible view of life is made all the worse by the movie's portrayal of adults and life in general as thoroughly rotten, apparently justifying the contempt expressed by the boy's sexual vengeance. Director John Erman plays up the exploitative possibilities of the story at the expense of any moral relevance. Though there is nudity and coarseness, what offends most is the lack of any moral values. O (R)

Making Love (1982) Predictable, uninspired triangle story about a husband (Michael Ontkean) who leaves his wife (Kate Jackson) for another man (Harry Hamlin). Under Arthur Hiller's flat direction, the romantic melodrama manages to work up no emotional power whatsoever, partly because homosexuality (a term that is never used, and the word "gay" appears only once) is presented as nothing more than an acceptable variation of normal sexuality. This attempt to forestall moral implications and human consequences is as obviously fabricated as the rest of the movie. O (R)

Making Mr. Right (1987) Young professional woman (Ann Magnuson) giving up on romance finds true love in the arms of the lifelike android (John Malkovich) she has been hired to program with the required social graces. Director Susan Seidelman's social satire explores sexual issues from a women's viewpoint but lacks a balanced approach to the relative importance of sex and love in a lasting relationship. Some crude language and sexual innuendo. A-III (PG-13)

Making the Grade (1984) Wretched little movie about an obnoxious rich kid who hires a tough city kid to go to prep school for him. Directed by Dorian Walker, it is crude, tasteless, and sexually exploitative. O (R)

Malaya (1949) WW II story begins promisingly, as Spencer Tracy and James Stewart concoct a plan to smuggle rubber out of Japanese-occupied Malaya, then turns into a stale tale of wartime adventure. Director Richard Thorpe wastes a good cast, including Sydney Greenstreet, Valentina Cortese, and Gilbert Roland, in patriotic derring-do that rings hollow today. Stylized violence. A-II (br)

Malcolm (1986) A clever and affable story about a misunderstood young man (Colin Friels) who puts his mechanical abilities to work by teaming up with a pair of small-time felons. An Australian production directed by Nadia Tass and David Parker, it is an entertaining social comedy. Some harsh language and sexual references. A-III (PG-13)

Malcolm X (1972) Documentary based on Malcolm X's autobiography offers some selections from the black liberation leader's book (sensitively read by James Earl Jones) played against stock footage intended to sketch in Malcolm's early years. Its main substance, however, comes from newsreel interviews made after he had become a major public-figure. Produced by Marvin Worth and Arnold Perl, the film suffers from the paucity of visual materials documenting Malcolm's life, but at least the interviews let Malcolm speak for himself, and viewers who wish to know more can read his extraordinary autobiography. A-II (PG)

Malcolm X (1992) Uneven, overlong screen biography of the African-American (1925-65) who rose from a sordid background to become the chief spokesman for the separatist Nation of Islam but, after breaking with its leaders and starting his own movement, was cruelly assassinated. Though director Spike Lee indulgently romanticizes Malcolm's criminal record and rise to national prominence, Denzel Washington's riveting performance in the title role captures the mature Malcolm's charismatic personality, intellectual depth, and oratorical skill in attacking racism in American society. Occasional stylized violence and substance abuse, some sexual references, and minimal rough language. A-III (PG-13)

Male of the Century (1976) French production directed by Claude Berri in which he also stars as the jealous husband whose wife (Juliet Berto) is taken hostage in a bank holdup. The movie flounders between comic vulgarity and soap opera histrionics before a final lunge into a moralistic conclusion about learning to live with our human imperfections. Failure in Gaelic wit and taste in dealing with sexual matters. A-III (nr)

Malice (1993) Convoluted plot involves campus murders and a college dean (Bill Pullman) whose wife (Nicole Kidman) leaves him after a botched hysterectomy, performed by his arrogant doctor-friend (Alex Baldwin). Director Harold Becker mixes unrelated murders with an implausible medical plot, but assembles enough slippery plot twists to fashion an adult escapist thriller of passing interest. Brief violence, a few bedroom scenes with shadowed nudity, and intermittent rough language. A-III (R)

Mallrats (1995) Sophomoric sleaze about two college-age retards (Jeremy London and Jason Lee) running amok in a suburban mall after being rejected by their girlfriends (Claire Forlani and Shannen Doherty). Writer-director Kevin Smith plumbs the gutter for laughs but finds only mindless tedium. Sexual situations, nudity, drug abuse, toilet humor, and constant gross language. O (R)

Maltese Bippy (1969) Feeble horror-comedy in which Dan Rowan and Dick Martin are victims of a conspiracy to steal a priceless gem hidden somewhere in their decaying Victorian mansion near a cemetery with walking corpses. Director Norman Panama seldom achieves anything more than an isolated funny line or sight gag. Mild sexual innuendo. A-II (G)

Maltese Falcon, The (1941) Dashiell Hammett's private detective Sam Spade (Humphrey Bogart) gets involved with a crafty trio of crooks (Mary Astor, Sidney Greenstreet, and Peter Lorre), each trying to out-swindle the other in quest of the priceless statue of the title, but all the hardboiled gumshoe wants is to nab the one who murdered his partner (Jerome Cowan). Writer-director John Huston's classy crime melodrama has taut pacing, snappy dialogue, wry characterizations, and an unsentimental payoff. Though there's some menace and violence, it's mainly a mind-over-muscle caper. A-II (br)

Mama, There's a Man in Your Bed (1990) Wildly romantic French comic-fantasy about the head executive of a yogurt company who falls helplessly in love with the black woman who cleans his firm's offices at night after she reveals the plot that almost causes its financial ruin. Written and directed by Coline Serreau, the comedy has some delicious moments of devious corporate back-stabbing, but the romance is so outrageously unlikely that one can't take it seriously. Subtitles. Though there are several discreet bedroom scenes and brief partial nudity, the movie's moral is clearly that people are more important than material riches. A-IV (nr)

Mambo Kings, The (1992) A failed romance haunts two Cuban brothers (Armand Assante and Antonio Banderas) who arrive in New York in 1952 with dreams of becoming the leading mambo band. Directed by Arne Glimcher, the period movie exudes a Latin beat in capturing the emotional conflicts of the close but radically different siblings. Momentary violence, brief bedroom shots with flashes of nudity, and an instance of rough language. A-III (R)

Mame (1974) Lucille Ball gives a game but disappointing performance as the flamboyant Auntie Mame in director Gene Saks's overblown screen version of the Broadway musical hit. Though the fun of the original is still there, it is obscured by an overly lavish and slow-paced production that robs the material of any spontaneity. Mediocre entertainment at best. A-II (PG)

Man, The (1972) Intelligent adaptation of mushy Irving Wallace novel scores as a melodrama about a black man thrust into the White House by a freak accident. The story concerns no real political issues, but it is absorbing to watch the character of the new president (James Earl Jones in a fine performance) develop from figurehead to forceful chief executive. Rod Serling gets credit for wresting a credible screenplay from the Wallace original, and Joseph Sargent directs with a sure sense of popular entertainment. A-II (G)

Man, a Woman and a Bank, A (1979) Routine bank-heist movie about an engineer (Donald Sutherland) and an old friend (Paul Mazursky) who join forces to rig the workings of the bank's computer and the photographer (Brooke Adams in a bright performance) who is on to them. Directed by Noel Black, the predictable plot moves at a sluggish pace with little to recommend it, save some picturesque views of Vancouver and Macao. Acceptance of casual sex and frequent rough language. A-III (PG)

Man About Town (1939) Flat romantic comedy in which a Broadway producer (Jack Benny) brings his latest musical revue to London, then tries to impress the show's star (Dorothy Lamour) by spending a weekend with the aristocratic wife (Binnie Barnes) of a jealous husband (Edward Arnold). Directed by Mark Sandrich, the comic misunderstandings are tiresomely contrived and ill-suited for Benny's brand of humor, though the musical numbers provide some welcome diversion. Muted sexual innuendo. A-II (br)

Man Afraid (1957) When a minister (George Nader) kills a burglar in self-defense, he and his family are threatened by the dead man's unhinged father (Eduard Franz). Director Harry Keller's interesting but overly contrived melodrama underplays the clergyman's troubled conscience over the slaying while focusing on his vulnerability in increasingly harrowing circumstances. Heavy sledding for youngsters. A-I (br)

Man Alone, A (1955) Routine Western in which a wanted man (Ray Milland) is hidden by the daughter (Mary Murphy) of the local sheriff (Ward Bond) until he proves he's innocent of crimes committed by the town banker (Raymond Burr). Also directed by R. Milland, the familiar story is agreeable enough, but some of the action is less than credible, and the sullen hero's bravado wears thin. Frontier violence and sexual innuendo. A-II (br)

Man and a Woman, A (1967) The soap-opera sudsiness of this tender, optimistic love story about a widowed auto test-driver (Jean-Louis Trintignant) and a widowed script-girl (Anouk Aimee) is enhanced by the lush cinematic style of director Claude Lelouch and a haunting musical background. In a graphic sexual encounter, virtue triumphs in effect, but rather slowly for the sensibilities of some viewers of this dubbed French romance. A-III (br)

Man and a Woman: 20 Years Later, A (1986) Director Claude Lelouch's sequel has none of the charm and appeal of the original. Instead, he has made a glossy-looking movie about filmmaking that has its clever moments but lacks any humanity in its characters. Permissive attitude toward sexual affairs. A-III (PG)

Man and Boy (1972) Western about a black ex-cavalry man (Bill Cosby) who struggles to maintain his homestead in spite of racial tensions after the Civil War. Most of the picture, however, deals with the odyssey of father and young son trying to recover a stolen horse. Directed by E.W. Swackhamer, the racial dimension is handled quite well, and the story has a certain gritty honesty, but the plot has some gaping holes and foggy motivations, especially in a climactic shootout. Some salty dialogue may be inappropriate for preteens. A-II (G)

Man and His Mate (see: **One Million B.C.**)

Man Behind the Gun, The (1952) Muddled tale directed by Felix Feist is set a few years before the Civil War when an undercover Army officer (Randolph Scott) is sent to California to smash a ring of pro-slavery secessionists using the dusty village of Los Angeles as their base. Assorted stylized violence and some sexual situations. A-III (br)

Man Betrayed, A (1941) Uneven melodrama in which a hick lawyer (John Wayne) comes to the big city to investigate the death of a friend, then falls for the daughter (Frances Dee) of the town's corrupt boss (Edward Ellis), who's protecting the murderer (Harold Huber). Directed by John H. Auer, the characters are colorful, but the disjointed plot goes in circles until the lawyer cleans up the town in a ridiculous whirlwind finish. Stylized violence. A-I (br)

Man Bites Dog (1993) Failed black comedy supposedly about media's complicity in society's rising tide of violence follows the daily rounds of a moronic serial killer as recorded by a documentary film crew, who gradually begin helping him commit crimes. Directed by Remy Belvaux, the French-language Belgian production is a slapdash low-budget affair with a lot of brutal mayhem, but little sense or purpose beyond affording novice movie-makers a chance to indulge themselves in a simpleminded, inept exercise trivializing a serious subject. Repellent graphic violence, including a rape, incessant criminal rationalizations too stupid to be amusing, and occasional rough language. O (NC-17)

Man Called Adam, A (1966) Muddled, melodramatic story with Sammy Davis, Jr., as a jazz musician struggling against his own personal problems and society's racial prejudice. Unfortunately, the movie is not helped by director Leo Penn's heavy-handed treatment of its mature themes. Some sexual innuendo. A-III (br)

Man Called Dagger, A (1967) Low-budget spy story about an agent (Jan Murray) who thwarts a scheme by neo-Nazis to conquer the world. Ineptly directed by Richard Rush, it is excessively violent and sexually suggestive. O (br)

Man Called Flintstone, The (1966) Big-screen version of the Hanna-Barbera television cartoon series about the Flintstone family, in which Fred's resemblance to a secret agent results in his being sent to Paris on a spy mission. Harmless slapstick fun, though some adults may find it a bore. A-I (br)

Man Called Horse, A (1970) Richard Harris plays a wealthy Englishman who is captured by Sioux Indians, and, after undergoing a painful and humiliating captivity, wins the respect of his captors and is ultimately accepted as a member of the tribe. Director Elliot Silverstein succeeds to a large extent in attempting to portray Native Americans as something more than Hollywood stereotypes. In doing this, however, the dramatization includes some nudity and a number of scenes of torture, scalping, and painful rites of initiation. A-IV (PG)

Man Called Peter, A (1955) Fact-based dramatization of the life of Peter Marshall (Richard Todd), a Scotsman who became an American minister, rose to the pulpit of a venerable church in the nation's capital, and served as chaplain in the US Senate until his death in 1949. Director Henry Koster follows the clergyman's career in uplifting fashion, grounded in the romantic appeal of his joyful marriage to a loving wife (Jean Peters). Inspirational picture of a Christian pastor. A-I (br)

Man Called Sledge, A (1971) Routine caper-movie with James Garner playing the title character, a hard-bitten, semi-respectable outlaw who'd rather rob than kill, but who has been forced for economic reasons to do both. With sidekick Dennis Weaver, Garner and his gang set out to pull off a fantastic gold heist. As directed by Vic Morrow, however, the story heavily accents the violence, including a brutal rape, which occurs in a desecrated church. O (R)

Man Could Get Killed, A (1966) James Garner plays an innocent American banker who gets embroiled in one mysterious situation after another in this caper spoof featuring Melina Mercouri in an international smuggling ring. There is nothing new here, but what gives the comedy some class is the stylish tongue-in-cheek direction under Ronald Neame and Cliff Owen. Some comic violence. A-II (br)

Man for All Seasons, A (1966) Engrossing drama of the last seven years in the life of Thomas More, Henry VIII's chancellor, who met a martyr's death rather than compromise his conscience during a period of religious turmoil. Robert Bolt's script is masterfully directed by Fred Zinnemann, with a standout performance by Paul Scofield in the title role, among other notable performances from a uniformly fine cast. The historical dramatization achieves an authentic human dimension that makes its 16th-century events more accessible and its issues more universal. Profoundly entertaining, but heavy-going for children. A-I (G)

Man Friday (1976) Defoe's story about two men's survival on a desert island is turned into a moralistic attack on the evils of civilization, as Crusoe (Peter O'Toole) attempts to infect the noble savage Friday (Richard Roundtree) with such ignoble concepts as master and servant, personal property, competition, greed, and sexual guilt. Despite some occasional humor, director Jack Gold cannot sustain credibility in the movie's sophomoric central thesis, let alone its bloody conclusion, which turns the 19th-century adventure classic on its head. A-III (PG)

Man from Colorado, The (1948) After the Civil War, an unstable Union colonel (Glenn Ford) goes completely bonkers as a federal judge who rules the Colorado Territory at the end of a rope, until his best friend (William Holden) turns against him. Directed by Henry Levin, the plot centers on a mining war and the rivalry of the two men over a lady (Ellen Drew), but Ford's portrayal of a psychopath is the movie's chief interest. Much stylized violence. A-II (br)

Man from God's Country (1958) Routine Western directed by Paul Landres in which a former lawman (George Montgomery) tangles with a gang terrorizing local ranchers to keep them from selling land to the railroad. Stylized violence. A-I (br)

Man from Laramie, The (1955) Uneven Western opens with a stranger (James Stewart) arriving in a prairie town on the trail of his brother's killer whom, after repeated run-ins with a local rancher (Donald Crisp), his loco son (Alex Nicol), and devious foreman (Arthur Kennedy), he finally finds selling repeating rifles to Apaches. Directed by Anthony Mann, the plot is familiar, but the action scenes are done with style and conviction, helping sustain interest until the predictable outcome. Stylized violence, some quite nasty, and mild romantic complications. A-II (br)

Man from O.R.G.Y., The (1970) Robert Walker Jr., super-sleuth from the Organization for the Rational Guidance of Youth (ORGY), must uncover three lost ladies of easy virtue whose branded behinds prove them beneficiaries of their deceased madam's will. Directed by James Hill, the movie veers into a series of vicious murders and inane burlesque skits relying heavily on nudity and racial slurs. O (R)

Man from Planet X, The (1951) Minor sci-fi tale in which a humanlike creature from an unknown planet lands on a Scottish island, then is turned against humans by a malevolent scientist (William Schallert). Despite the production's pulp story and low budget, director Edgar G. Ulmer manages to evoke a sense of mystery and foreboding in a thin plot holding little suspense. A-I (br)

Man from Snowy River, The (1983) Australian Western about a young man (Tom Burlinson) who tames a herd of wild horses and wins the love of a spirited young woman (Sigrid Thornton). Kirk Douglas is on hand in a dual role playing twin brothers. The scenery is impressive and so are the horses, but director George Miller fares less well with the humans in this moderately entertaining, but far from inspired movie. Some restrained violence. A-II (PG)

Man from the Alamo, The (1953) Sent from the besieged Alamo to warn of advancing Mexican forces, a Texas rancher (Glenn Ford) finds his own family slaughtered and himself arrested as a cowardly deserter, but escapes to stop gringo renegades (led by Victor Jory) raiding the area disguised as Mexicans. Directed by Budd Boetticher, the contrived plot is largely unconvincing, but what makes it worth watching is Ford's compelling performance as the taciturn, misunderstood man of action. Stylized violence. A-I (br)

Man Hunt (1941) Dandy adaptation of Geoffrey Householder's cat-and-mouse suspense story, "Rogue Male," pits an English sportsman (Walter Pidgeon) against a fanatical Nazi (George Sanders) as a "stalking hunt" of Hitler turns into the real thing. Director Fritz Lang packs a lot of anti-Nazi fervor in a fast-paced narrative featuring Joan Bennett as a cockney waif, John Carradine as a relentless villain, and Roddy McDowall as a brave little cabin-boy. Much menace and stylized violence. A-II (br)

Man in the Attic (1953) Jack the Ripper (Jack Palance) once again terrorizes London's Whitechapel district in this bargain-basement variation on the scenario of **The Lodger,** lethargically directed by Hugo Fregonese. Heavy-handed menace and sexual references. A-III (br)

Man in the Glass Booth, The (1975) Screen version of Robert Shaw's play about a Jewish survivor of the Nazi death camps who becomes a wealthy New York businessman, until arrested and put on trial in Israel as a Nazi war-criminal. Edward Anhalt's script shifts the emphasis from the question of the man's true identity to his motivation in testifying about the irrational prejudice that caused the Holocaust. Though director Arthur Hiller fails to integrate all of the themes, including that of a Christ figure, and Maximilian Shell's performance in the title role is uneven, the movie's effort to evoke a more human response to the enormity of the Nazi crimes is of more than passing merit. Mature themes would be accessible to most older teenagers. A-III (PG)

Man in the Gray Flannel Suit, The (1956) Earnest melodrama based on Sloan Wilson's novel in which a novice broadcasting executive (Gregory Peck), torn between the needs of family and job, faces a crisis with his wife (Jennifer Jones) when he learns he fathered a child in a brief wartime affair. Directed by Nunnally Johnson, the plot is as obvious as the situations are contrived, but fine performances from Fredric March as the unhappy boss and Lee J. Cobb as a kindly judge help keep the picture of interest. Though the story and treatment are dated, the conflict between material success and personal integrity remains valid. A-II (br)

Man in the Iron Mask, The (1998) Lavishly mounted adaptation of Alexandre Dumas's 1850 novel in which the imprisoned twin brother of King Louis XIV (Leonardo DiCaprio in a dual role) is rescued by the three aging Musketeers (Jeremy Irons, John Malkovich, and Gerard Depardieu), while the fourth (Gabriel Byrne) opposes their plan to secretly replace the evil monarch with his identical twin. Director Randall Wallace's historical drama has rousing scenes of derring-do, but is burdened by the king's one-dimensional character and the story's sentimentality. Occasional violence including a suicide and brief rear nudity, as well as sexual situations and references. A-III (PG-13)

Man in the Moon, The (1991) The close relationship between adolescent sisters (Reese Witherspoon and Emily Warfield) in 1950s rural Louisiana comes unglued when both fall in love with the 17-year-old boy (Jason London) who moves in next door. With an assist from Sam Waterston and Tess Harper as the girls' finely drawn parents, director Robert Mulligan captures the period and region in exquisite detail but is especially successful in the warm portrayal of a family coping with heartache and forgiveness. An implied sexual encounter, flash of nudity, and brief violence. A-III (PG-13)

Man in the Saddle (1951) Routine Western in which a small rancher (Randolph Scott) refuses to knuckle under to the strong-arm tactics of a would-be cattle baron (Alexander Knox). Directed by Andre de Toth, the range war is muddled by a romantic triangle though the dour proceedings are enlivened by some robust action scenes, and the outdoor locations are worth a look. Stylized violence. A-II (br)

Man in the Shadow (1957) Dark modern-day tale of a small-town Texas sheriff (Jeff Chandler) who tangles with the area's most powerful resident (Orson Welles) after trailing a murderer to his heavily guarded ranch. Director Jack Arnold turns in a tough-minded picture of a man whose wealth has set him above the law, exploiting his workers and pushing locals around with impunity, until an honest lawman risks his life to see justice done. Some nasty violence and strong menace. A-III (br)

Man in the White Suit, The (1951) When an idealistic scientist (Alec Guinness) invents a fabric which is unsoilable as well as indestructible, the development promises to be a boon for the consumer but threatens to put the entire textile industry out of business. British director Alexander Mackendrick puts a wry spin on the comic complications resulting from the premise as high-minded inventor tries to fend off machinations by management and the antagonism of workers, but adding a memorably wacky note to the mock seriousness of the proceedings are the periodic gurgling sounds of the machine producing the miracle fabric. A-I (br)

Man in the Wilderness (1971) Richard Harris plays a frontiersman abandoned in hostile Indian country by a trapping expedition after being mauled by a bear. Recovering, he treks through the wilds seeking revenge on the expedition's leader (John Huston). Richard C. Sarafian's direction becomes tiresome in cutting back and forth between tracker, Indians, and struggling expedition, and the final confrontation is jarringly anti-climactic. The movie's rewards are in its photography of the great, rugged wilderness conveying nature's power and dignity, as well as several sights along the way, notably the trailside birth of an Indian baby, that have their own stunning, eerie beauty. Considerable violence. A-III (GP)

Man in Uniform, A (1994) When a troubled bank clerk (Tom McCamus) who aspires to be an actor gets his first big break playing the part of a tough cop in a TV crime series, he goes too far in trying to identify with the role by roaming the city streets in his prop uniform but with a real revolver, which leads unsurprisingly to dire results. Canadian writer-director David Wellington aims at the gritty reality behind the glossy screen image of urban violence, but doesn't get too far with the predictable developments and pedestrian treatment of this story of an unhinged actor. Some graphic violence, a flash of nudity, and sporadic rough language. A-III (nr)

Man Inside, The (1990) Crusading journalist (Jurgen Prochnow) infiltrates Germany's leading newspaper to expose its reprehensible practices and its link to a high government official. The interesting, fact-based story is rendered in curiously flat fashion by director Bobby Roth, due chiefly to Prochnow's bloodless performance and stiff, methodical pacing. Some violence and an unmarried live-in relationship. A-III (PG)

Man Is Not a Bird (1974) Excellent Yugoslavian drama about a middle-aged engineer whose work takes him to a small town for a couple of weeks, where he passes the evenings in a brief affair that ends badly. Director Dusan Makavejev creates a picture of people mesmerized by the daily routine of their lives from which they escape only through momentary diversions. Though produced in a socialist country, its mood of quiet desperation could be mirrored in any industrialized country of the world. A-III (nr)

Man Made Monster (1941) Weak thriller directed by George Waggner in which a mad scientist (Lionel Atwill) subjects a patient (Lon Chaney, Jr.) to increasing amounts of electricity, until he literally glows with so much voltage anyone he touches is electrocuted. Stylized violence, threatening situations, and some scary visuals. A-II (br)

Man of a Thousand Faces (1957) Screen biography of silent-movie actor Lon Chaney (James Cagney) from childhood with loving deaf-mute parents and early success in vaudeville, through a troubled marriage to a singer (Dorothy Malone) who leaves him and their young son, to his remarriage (Jane Greer) and Hollywood stardom in a series of eccentric roles. Directed by Joseph Pevney, the scenario is riddled with show-biz cliches, but Cagney and a fine supporting cast (though Robert Evans as Irving Thalberg is a hoot) give some human dimension to the domestic woes and career ambitions of those involved. Mature themes and treatment. A-III (br)

Man of Aran (1934) Jutting from the sea off the western coast of Ireland rise the sheer cliffs of the Aran Islands, whose inhabitants over the centuries have eked out their livelihood fishing and growing potatoes on barren rock heaped with seaweed. Documentary filmmaker Robert Flaherty depicts the life of the islanders as a daily struggle against an incredibly hostile environment, reinforcing the theme with some re-creations of an earlier era and awesome photography of fishermen risking their lives in puny boats awash in violent seas. A-I (br)

Man of Conquest (1939) Halting biography of Texas hero Sam Houston (Richard Dix) who abandons Tennessee politics after his wife (Joan Fontaine) divorces him, then tries to save the Cherokee Nation from exile before moving to Texas, where he leads the new Republic's forces to victory over Santa Anna's Mexican regulars in the 1836 battle of San Jacinto. Directed by George Nicholls, Jr., the figure of Andrew Jackson (Edward Ellis) dominates this populist history, which is long on patriotic dialogue but short on action scenes, Battlefield violence and romantic complications. A-II (br)

Man of Iron (1982) Polish production directed by Andrzej Wajda presents a powerful account of the confrontation between Solidarity labor union and Poland's Communist regime at the Gdansk shipyards which ended in Solidarity's victory in August 1980. Though the mix of real characters and documentary footage with a fictional story-line isn't as smooth as it might be, the result is a dramatic and courageous movie in its own right, one that will have a continuing significance for those concerned about human rights. A-II (PG)

Man of La Mancha (1972) Disappointing screen version of the Dale Wasserman musical about Cervantes transforming his Inquisition cell into the world of Don Quixote preserves enough of the music and lyrics to please most admirers of the original, but just barely. Peter O'Toole in the title role and Sophia Loren as Aldonza/Dulcinea are miscast. Even worse, director Arthur Hiller's tight, literal camera and endless pans work against the romantic poetry of the story, and, by dwelling on its adventure aspects, misses the work's emphasis on the power of ideals and the artistic spirit. Mature themes. A-III (PG)

Man of No Importance, A (1994) Seriocomic tale set in 1960s Dublin, where a bus conductor (Albert Finney) endeavors to stage Oscar Wilde's **Salome** in the parish hall, until gossip of the play's immorality and the unwed pregnancy of the lead (Tara Fitzgerald) dash his hopes and force him to face up to his latent homosexuality. Director Suri Krishnamma's character study of an obsessive bachelor in his fifties starts in whimsical fashion, then grows increasingly dark in heavy-handed attempts to convey the lonely passion of a sexually inexperienced individual driven by yearnings for another man. Sympathetic treatment of homosexual inclinations, a brutal beating, and a brief but intense heterosexual bedroom scene. A-IV (R)

Man of the House (1995) Dreary family sitcom in which a bratty 11-year-old (Jonathan Taylor Thomas) tries to break up the romance between his divorced mom (Farah Fawcett) and the witless fellow (Chevy Chase) who moves in for a premarital tryout. Director James Orr raises few smiles with the inane antics of a nerdy father-son club and a klutzy gangster trio, and the rest is tedium devoted to the unamusing domestic arrangements of the principals. Live-in relationship, some sexual innuendo, comic violence, and occasional coarse language. A-III (PG)

Man on a Swing (1974) The brutal murder of a young girl has the police baffled until a clairvoyant comes forward with some information about the crime that could only be known to the murderer. Good performances by Cliff Robertson as the dogged police chief and Joel Grey as the wildly erratic clairvoyant, but director Frank Perry's drama is full of holes, false clues, and an abrupt ending that will satisfy only those interested in parapsychology and the fact that it is difficult to distinguish genuine mediums from fakers. A-III (PG)

Man on the Eiffel Tower, The (1948) Murky crime-thriller from Georges Simenon's story of a deranged killer (Franchot Tone) trying to throw Paris police inspector Maigret (Charles Laughton) off his trail by implicating a nearly blind vagrant (Burgess Meredith). Also directed by Meredith, the quirky plot gains interest from the Paris locales and eccentric characterizations. Stylized violence and threatening situations. A-II (br)

Man on the Roof (1977) Deceptively simple, straightforward crime thriller about the murder of a police inspector and the subsequent siege of the heavily armed killer who takes to a rooftop and cuts down the policemen attempting his capture. Swedish production directed by Bo Widerberg, its attention to detail and urban environment give the sometimes melodramatic events an emotional impact that places it in a class far above the conventional thriller. Its dramatic credibility is helped also by the performances of a superior cast headed by Carl-Gustaf Lindstedt. Some scenes of graphic violence. A-III (R)

Man They Could Not Hang, The (1939) Plodding, low-budget horror movie directed by Nick Grinde about a mad doctor (Boris Karloff) who's executed for murder, then brought back to life by his own resuscitation device to take revenge on those who sent him to the gallows. Ghoulish concept and treatment. A-III (br)

Man Trouble (1992) Dreadfully dumb comedy about a con-man (Jack Nicholson) who sells an attack dog to a frightened female (Ellen Barkin), then falls in love with her. Director Bob Rafelson has a half-dozen story threads unraveling in this embarrassingly barren comedy of errors. Brief violence and an implied extramarital affair. A-III (PG-13)

Man Who Came Back, The (see: **Swamp Water**)

Man Who Came to Dinner, The (1941) Screen version of the Broadway comedy by George S. Kaufman and Moss Hart in which an acerbic network radio personality (Monty Woolley), forced by a broken hip to spend Christmas with a small-town Ohio family, contrives to keep his secretary (Bette Davis) from getting married, while withering all around him with his insufferable sarcasm. Director William Keighley's stagy production gets sure-fire laughs from the fish-out-of-water situation, witty dialogue, and zany characters (Jimmy Durnate, Reginald Gardiner, and Ann Sheridan), though some viewers may tire of Woolley's irascible egomania and the dated topical humor. Mild sexual innuendo. A-II (br)

Man Who Could Cheat Death, The (1959) Hokey British horror movie directed by Terence Fisher in which a 104-year-old doctor (Anton Diffring) keeps himself young by killing a woman victim every 10 years to obtain a gland needed to retard the aging process. Stylized violence, menacing situations, and romantic complications. A-III (br)

Man Who Could Work Miracles, The (1936) Intriguing fantasy from the H.G. Wells story in which an ordinary British clerk (Roland Young) suddenly finds he has the power to do whatever he wishes, tries to use his gift to better the world, then almost destroys it by turning his power to selfish ends. Directed by Lothar Mendes, the story has its context as a test of human responsibility by the gods, but the British production is content to play around with simple yet effective camera tricks that seem to turn the ordinary into the miraculous. Minor stylized violence. A-II (br)

Man Who Fell to Earth, The (1976) Arty science-fiction movie about a visitor from outer space (David Bowie) who has left his own drought-stricken planet in an effort to save his dying wife and child, but how is never quite clear. Director Nicholas Roeg, a former cameraman, prefers flashy visual effects rather than less picturesque exposition that would better advance the story line and develop characterization. Several scenes of nudity in a sexual context. O (R)

Man Who Knew Too Little, The (1997) Silly spoof set in London in which a dense Bill Murray is mistaken for a hit-man, then along the way nearly blows up various government heads at a gala state dinner. As directed by Jon Amiel, the comedy's screwball shenanigans are stretched pretty thin, but Murray's character retains sympathy as a blissfully unaware dunderhead. Brief slapstick violence, fleeting sexual innuendo, and an instance of profanity. A-III (PG)

Man Who Knew Too Much, The (1934) Compact British thriller in which a vacationing couple (Leslie Banks and Edna Best) learn of a plot to assassinate a foreign dignitary in London, but when their little girl is kidnapped to keep them from going to the police, they set out on their own to find her and stop the assassination. Directed by Alfred Hitchcock, the tension mounts as the trail leads from a dentist's office to a mission in the slums and on to the Albert Hall for a showdown with the gang's sinister leader (Peter Lorre), but the suspense is nicely paced with wry humor, and the incongruous acts of ordinary people in desperate circumstances. Stylized violence and menacing situations. A-II (br)

Man Who Knew Too Much, The (1956) Alfred Hitchcock's laborious remake of his classy 1934 thriller updates the story to French Morocco, where the son of a vacationing American couple (James Stewart and Doris Day) is kidnapped to keep them quiet about a political assassination in London. The bloated story-line dulls the suspense and plays havoc with the pacing, including the pivotal Albert Hall sequence keyed to the orchestra's cymbals, though the sinister chapel run by the conspirators and a comic-relief scene in a taxidermist shop are pure Hitchcock. Stylized violence and assorted dangers. A-I (br)

Man Who Had Power Over Women, The (1970) Rod Taylor stars as the London-based manager of a bratty rock star, but he has grown sick of his lucrative job and a marriage that has soured. When he becomes romantically involved with the wife (Carol White) of his best friend, a happy ending is hard to contrive. As directed by John Kish, the well-acted, potentially interesting melodrama concentrates on the slick and flashy rather than facing up to the moral questions, including abortion, that it raises. A-III (R)

Man Who Haunted Himself, The (1971) Stuffy British executive Roger Moore has no difficulty getting back into the swing of things following a nasty auto accident, but he does develop a problem in trying to cope with a look-alike double who is out to smash Moore's career and marriage. Moore is quite good as the confused businessman, but director Basil Dearden's psychological drama lacks tautness and relies upon too many plot contrivances. Adult situations. A-III (PG)

Man Who Loved Cat Dancing, The (1973) Sarah Miles, running away from her husband in the Old West, is picked up by Burt Reynolds's outlaw band. After being humiliated, menaced, brutalized, and finally raped, she at last finds true love and the strength to kill her husband. Directed by Richard C. Sarafian, the movie never gets below the surface of its inept plot, so burdened is it with complications often bordering on the ridiculous. Long, drawn-out scenes of sexual menace and the implication that rape has served to "liberate" this woman from her sexual fears constitute a male fantasy that should be put to rest. O (PG)

Man Who Loved Women, The (1977) Trivial French production about a man (Charles Denner) whose single passion is his pursuit of women is little more than a loosely tied collection of bland vignettes, which are seldom amusing and never moving. Directed by Francois Truffaut, it is a weak and shallow effort, especially because the activity of its title character is given no moral context whatsoever. Some gratuitous nudity. O (nr)

Man Who Loved Women, The (1983) Burt Reynolds plays a famous sculptor whose insatiable pursuit of women is eventually and quite literally the death of him. The story is told in flashbacks by his psychiatrist (Julie Andrews), incessantly droning on with some of the most banal insights ever set to film. Directed by Blake Edwards, the limp comedy is a poor remake of the 1977 French movie. Some extremely crude sexual sequences. O (R)

Man Who Shot Liberty Valance, The (1962) Provocative Western in which a lawyer (James Stewart) from the East becomes the territory's leading politician after confronting a notorious badman (Lee Marvin), though the legend of the shootout omits the role of a local cowboy (John Wayne). Director John Ford shows the power of myth in shaping the past's meaning as the narrative recounts how the frontier's law of the gun gave way to more civilized notions of justice. Stylized violence, some of it quite brutal. A-II (br)

Man Who Skied Down Everest, The (1976) In 1970, Japanese skier Yuichiro Miura set out from Katmandu, Nepal, for Mt. Everest, where his objective was not to make an ascent to the peak, but to reach a ledge 400 yards short of the crest from which he would ski down to the valley that lay more than a mile below. What happened during this dangerous undertaking may be seen in a splendid Academy Award-winning documentary with a narration adapted from Miura's diary, giving Western viewers some insights into this feat as a quest in achieving harmony with nature. An exciting adventure documentary, filled with dazzling scenic beauty, it is absorbing fare for the entire family, including those unconcerned with the paradoxes of Eastern and Western philosophy. A-I (G)

Man Who Wasn't There, The (1983) Gimmicky 3-D movie about a liquid that makes the drinker (Steve Guttenberg) invisible, free to explore a women's locker room, among other things, while eluding various American and foreign agents. Amateurishly directed by Bruce Malmuth, the movie has little plot, humor, or excitement. In 3-D, a bad movie simply gains another dimension of awfulness. Exploitative nudity. O (R)

Man Who Would Be King, The (1975) Sean Connery and Michael Caine star as highly imperfect heroes in an adaptation of Rudyard Kipling's story about two 19th-century British soldiers who pursue their dangerous dream of founding a kingdom of their own in the remote mountains of northern India. Director John Huston has fashioned a vigorous saga of romantic adventure tinged with realism and some fine acting, including that of Christopher Plummer as Kipling, who, one suspects, would have thoroughly enjoyed the movie version. Some hard-edged violence and sexual references. A-III (PG)

Man with a Plan (1996) Gently satirical pseudo-documentary follows Fred Tuttle, an arthritic and broke 73-year-old Vermont dairy-farmer, as he doggedly pursues a grassroots campaign to win a lucrative seat in Congress. Writer-director John O'Brien makes an entertaining contrast between the entrenched political organization of the smooth incumbent and the refreshing honesty of a crusty senior simply out to find a job. Minimal profanity. A-II (nr)

Man with Connections, The (1970) French anti-war comedy about an enterprising draftee (Guy Bedos) who wins the respect of his military superiors by claiming to be a personal friend of Brigitte Bardot, but even this fails to save him from being sent to the front, where he serves more time in the stockade than in defending French imperialism. Director Claude Berri's lightly humorous, occasionally caustic and witty, account is too loosely plotted and nostalgically self-indulgent to be completely satisfying. A-III (R)

Man with One Red Shoe, The (1985) An innocent bystander (Tom Hanks), mistaken for an enemy agent by the CIA, goes through his daily routine blissfully unaware that he is in mortal danger from various and sundry agents who are following his every move. Directed by Stan Dragoti, this comedy is an innocuous remake of the stylish French farce, **The Tall Blond Man with One Black Shoe**. Comic violence and a bit of sexual innuendo. A-II (PG)

Man with the Glass Eye, The (1972) Confused mystery-yarn about a rash of murders decimating a gang of weird characters who use a vaudeville troupe as a cover for their dealings in white slavery and heroin smuggling. Badly dubbed German import directed by Alfred Vohrer relies on grotesque characterizations in a story punctuated by sex and gore. A-III (PG)

Man with the Golden Arm, The (1955) Dreary screen version of Nelson Algren's novel about a drug addict (Frank Sinatra) whom a friend (Kim Novak) helps to kick the habit by going cold turkey. Producer-director Otto Preminger fails to make either the milieu or the characters credible. Sordid atmosphere and situations. A-III (br)

Man with the Golden Gun, The (1974) Rather tired spy-adventure with James Bond (Roger Moore) as the target for a million-dollar assassin (Christopher Lee) who uses golden bullets. Director Guy Hamilton offers the standard Bond mayhem, including a spectacular auto stunt, but the once brittle and bright double-entendres are now merely tasteless and smutty remarks. Maud Adams and Britt Ekland are the decoratively exploited females. A-III (PG)

Man with the X-Ray Eyes, The (see: **X: The Man with X-Ray Eyes**)

Man with Two Brains, The (1983) Brilliant brain-surgeon (Steve Martin) is married to a woman (Kathleen Turner) who has a beautiful body but loathes him, while the woman who loves him is a body-less brain being kept alive by a mad scientist (David Warner). Guess what happens? Director Carl Reiner has a lot of good fun with such things as Warner's Frankenstein-style layout in a sleek condominium and a very tough Austrian test for drunk drivers, but the silliness does pall after a while. Some rather explicit sexual by-play and nudity. O (R)

Man without a Body, The (1957) Horror clunker in which a rich financier (George Coulouris) dying of a brain tumor steals the head of 16th-century seer Nostradamus (Michael Golden), intending it to replace his own once its dead tissue has been regenerated. Directed by W. Lee Wilder and Charles Saunders, the British production is an inept mix of story elements ranging from the ridiculous to the gross. Ghoulish premise, stylized violence, and sexual innuendo. A-III (br)

Man without a Face, The (1993) A fatherless 12-year-old (Nick Stahl), ignored by his self-centered mother (Margaret Whitton) and harassed by an older half-sister (Fay Masterson), persuades a disfigured recluse (Mel Gibson) to tutor him so he can go to a boarding school, leading to ugly rumors in their coastal Maine community. Also directed by Gibson, the relationship which transforms the lonely child and outcast adult is convincingly rendered in earnestly sentimental terms without substantially detracting from the uplifting narrative. Fleeting bedroom scene, some homosexual innuendo, minor violence, and an instance of rough language. A-III (PG-13)

Man without a Star (1955) Uneven Western adventure in which a top cowboy (Kirk Douglas) on a big spread run by a woman (Jeanne Crain) throws in with some small ranchers to even the odds against them. Directed by King Vidor, the predictable proceedings huff and puff but add up to little. Much stylized violence and some sexual implications. A-III (br)

Man Without a World, The (1992) Using the conventions of the silent-movie era, the work re-creates a nostalgic melodrama of Jewish life in an East European *shtetl* (village), where a simple love story is hopelessly complicated by the arrival of a Gypsy troupe, the exorcism of a wandering spirit from a mad girl, religious and political rivalries, murder, and flight to the big city. Written, produced, and directed by Eleanor Antin, this is a labor of love that pays tribute to the craft of the silent cinema while creating an imaginative memorial for a richly human world snuffed out in the Nazi death camps. Some stylized violence including murder and the brutal rape of a young girl, several seduction scenes, and a few flashes of nudity. A-III (nr)

Man, Woman and Child (1983) Sappy screen version of a soppy novel by Erich Segal about a perfect American couple (Martin Sheen and Blythe Danner) and their two perfect children, all living in perfect bliss until Sheen finds out he is the father of a son conceived during a weak moment while in France a decade earlier. The waif is brought to California, where he turns out to be perfectly irresistible and all ends predictably. Director Dick Richards's slick and manipulative melodrama leaves a soapy aftertaste. Glossy depiction of the affair (in flashbacks). A-III (PG)

Man's Best Friend (1993) Repugnant horror-fantasy written and directed by John Lafia unleashes a genetically engineered guard dog whose killer instincts threaten to disembowel a lightheaded TV reporter (Ally Sheedy), her cloddish live-in boyfriend (Fredric Lehne), a mad vivisectionist (Lance Henriksen), and numerous other victims. Mindless graphic violence, an extended bedroom scene, some coarse language, and occasional profanity. O (R)

Man's Favorite Sport (1964) Failed madcap comedy in which a sporting store's angling expert (Rock Hudson) has to overcome the fact that he has never done any real fishing when forced to compete in a fishing tournament by a press agent (Paula Prentiss) who causes misunderstandings with his fiancé (Charlene Holt). Directed by Howard Hawks, the would-be fisherman has more trouble fending off women than in catching fish, but these generally mirthless complications depend on occasional slapstick routines to supply some smiles. Sexual situations and innuendo. A-III (br)

Manchurian Candidate, The (1962) Fine political spine-tingler with Laurence Harvey playing a Korean War POW transformed by Red Chinese hypnosis into a deadly instrument of assassination before his return to the US during a presidential campaign. By the time an ex-POW buddy (Frank Sinatra in a solid performance) figures out the reason for his strange behavior toward wife and family, a major manhunt and race with time are on. Director John Frankenheimer has fashioned a superior suspense movie with a growing intensity that adults and older teenagers may appreciate. A-III (PG-13)

Mandabi (1970) From Senegal comes a small gem of a tale about a money order (which is what the title means) for a small amount of money sent from France by a hardworking young man to his uncle in Dakar, whose attempts to cash it become an odyssey through the senseless byways of modern bureaucracy. Even when it despairs, the film is balanced by humor and belief in the eventual triumph of human righteousness. Very convincing performances by a non-professional cast in a very professionally made movie directed by Ousmane Sembene. A-II (nr)

Mandela (1997) Engrossing picture of the life of Nelson Mandela from his youth in the Xhosa tribal lands of the Transkei and rise in the leadership of the African National Congress, whose fight against apartheid led to 27 years in prison, the Nobel Peace Prize, and 1994 election as South Africa's first black president. Co-directed by South African filmmakers Jo Menell and Angus Gibson, the documentary interweaves interviews of Mandela, his political colleagues, and several family members with historical footage and contemporary scenes recalling the struggles of a painful past while stressing the need for national reconciliation in a post-apartheid society. Newsreel scenes of violence and the injustices of apartheid. A-II (nr)

Mandingo (1975) Old South plantation-owner (James Mason) runs a "breeding farm" for black slaves, a business allowing his son (Perry King) to take his choice of black women when not off setting up fighting matches for his full-blooded Mandingo slave (Ken Norton), whom his wife (Susan George) takes to sleeping with out of pique at her husband's infidelity. Directed by Richard Fleischer, it's sordid melodramatic trash, forgettable save for its cynical box-office manipulation of racial tensions in sexual contexts. Violence, sadism, nudity, and graphic sex. O (R)

Mangler, The (1995) After an industrial laundry's humongous fold-and-press machine begins ensnaring employees, a cop (Ted Levine) discovers that its miserly owner (Robert Englund) has been hiding a long history of unexplained accidents and becomes convinced the machine must be exorcised or more young females will die. Director Tobe Hooper's inept horror show lurches from one gruesome death to the next, its slack story line just a backdrop for dumb mumbo-jumbo about virgin blood and demonic possession. Excessive gore and violence, some sexual innuendo, and recurring rough language and profanities. O (R)

Manhandled (1949) Twisty crime-thriller about a psychiatrist's secretary (Dorothy Lamour) who gets mixed up with a shady private eye (Dan Duryea), then finds herself framed on a murder rap. Directed by Lewis R. Foster, the plot is no great shakes, but the likeable cast helps sustain interest along the way. Some stylized violence, including a nasty murder by auto. A-III (br)

Manhattan (1979) Successful TV comedy-writer (Woody Allen), whose wife (Meryl Streep) has left him for another woman, is having an affair with a 17-year-old high-school girl (Mariel Hemingway) but then gets involved with the lover (Diane Keaton) of his best friend (Michael Murphy). Greatly aided by romantic black-and-white photography and a lush Gershwin score, director Allen has made a small-but-clever bittersweet comedy about sexual relationships, often amusing, but just as often flat. Though the movie's moral vision puts a premium on being faithful and really caring about people, it seems largely to excuse the sexual weaknesses of its characters. A-IV (R)

Manhattan Melodrama (1934) Boyhood buddies from the slums remain best friends even after one becomes a gangster (Clark Gable) and the other a district attorney (William Powell) who marries his erring pal's girl (Myrna Loy) and later puts him on trial for murder. Directed by W.S. Van Dyke II, the colorful story and breezy performances overcome the many plot contrivances and hokey ending. Stylized violence and sympathetic treatment of a criminal. A-III (br)

Manhattan Murder Mystery (1993) Breezy comic-mystery concerns a husband (Woody Allen) who becomes increasingly nervous when his wife (Diane Keaton) decides their next-door neighbor (Jerry Adler) murdered his wife, and sets out to prove it with the help of their flirtatious, newly divorced buddy (Alan Alda), whom the husband has been trying to distract with a colleague (Anjelica Huston), who prefers the husband. Director Allen amusingly combines a rectangular relationship movie with a rather flimsy mystery, but the result is a good-natured look at the fluctuating fortunes of love and life in the Big Apple. Fleeting violence, a few sexual references, and occasional profanity. A-III (PG)

Manhattan Project, The (1986) Over-long melodrama, loosely based on fact, about a teenager (Christopher Collet) who builds an atomic bomb at home to protest the construction of a nuclear plant near his home. A physicist from the lab (John Lithgow) tries to save the boy — and the New York area — from potential disaster. Failed social commentary, token teen romance, and a single harsh expletive. A-II (PG-13)

Manhunter (1986) The twist in this crime thriller is in following an FBI agent (William Peterson) who uses both imagination and intuition to reconstruct the mind of a serial killer in order to track him down. Director Michael Mann emphasizes the psychological elements of detection rather than resorting to the more conventional means of guns and brawn. Glimpses of grisly photos of murder victims, a bedroom scene, and some foul language. A-III (R)

Manila Calling (1942) WW II morale-booster about the exploits of a group of American and Filipino guerrillas (notably Lloyd Nolan and James Gleason) fighting on after the fall of the Philippines. Directed by Herbert I. Leeds, the hokey action centers on capturing a Japanese mountain base and rescuing some American civilians (notably Carole Landis), then holding out long enough to repair the base's radio transmitter to rally resistance to the invaders. Wartime violence and mild sexual innuendo. A-II (br)

Manitou, The (1978) A 500-year-old Indian medicine-man comes back to life and wreaks all sorts of havoc in this inept and ludicrous horror movie starring Tony Curtis and Susan Strasberg. Director William Girdler's otherwise innocuous effort contains violence and nudity. O (PG)

Mannequin (1987) A stock-boy (Andrew McCarthy) has his life changed when the mannequin he created comes to life (Kim Cattrall) and falls in love with him, while helping to foil a villainous attempt to buy out the store for which he works. Michael Gottlieb directs a romantic fantasy in which Miss Cattrall, an older woman, seduces the younger, seemingly innocent youth. Characterizations stressing the physical aspects of the relationship, sexual references, crude jokes, and poorly executed slapstick comedy. A-III (PG)

Mannequin Two: On the Move (1991) A pretty maiden (Kristy Swanson) wakes up from a thousand-year spell to the adoring gaze of a department-store employee (William Ragsdale) who must rescue her from being restored to her mannequin status and whisked off to a faraway kingdom. Director Stewart Raffill's silly slapstick fantasy is a fairly innocuous sequel but decidedly moronic in content and treatment. Mild sexual innuendo and brief, cartoon-like violence. A-II (PG)

Manny & Lo (1996) An orphaned, pregnant 16-year-old (Aleksa Palladino) and her 11-year-old sister (Scarlett Johansson) run off together from their separate foster-homes and kidnap a baby-store clerk (Mary Kay Place) in hopes she will know how to deliver the infant in their hideout. Writer-director Lisa Krueger finds the humanity, humor, and poignancy in all three's predicaments, but fails to fully flesh-out her characters in the inconclusive narrative. Sexual innuendo, petty thievery, occasional profanity, and recurring rough language. A-III (R)

Manon of the Spring (1987) The conclusion of a two-part adaptation of Marcel Pagnol's novel about French country-life in the early decades of the century details the revenge of a young woman (Emmanuelle Beart) on the farmer who ruined her family and on the community who let him get away with it, as told in the first part, **Jean de Florette**. Directed by Claude Berri, the story of long-overdue retribution builds to a powerful conclusion in which wrongs are righted and justice finally served. Subtitles. Mature treatment and brief nudity. A-III (PG)

Manpower (1941) Slick melodrama in which a bar-hostess (Marlene Dietrich) marries a man (Edward G. Robinson) she doesn't love, then yearns for her husband's buddy (George Raft) who wants nothing to do with her. Director Raoul Walsh convincingly visualizes the dangerous world of men who risk their lives working on high-voltage power-lines, but the story of a woman coming between two pals is too contrived to earn any sympathy. Romantic complications and menacing situations. A-II (br)

Manson (1973) Filmmaker Laurence Merrick's exploitative documentary supposedly examining the social ills behind the crimes committed by the hippie clan led by Charles Manson exposes little more than the director's own cynicism and the morbidity of its intended audience. Relentlessly foul language with occasional matching visuals only further emphasizes this work's moral vacuum. O (R)

Manufacturing Consent: Noam Chomsky and the Media (1993) Dense 167-minute documentary on the life, times, and political commitment of linguistics scholar Chomsky who, since voicing opposition to the Vietnam War in 1969, has written much and spoken often against American foreign policy, transnational economic elite, and abuses of power around the world. Canadian filmmakers Mark Achbar and Peter Wintonick concentrate on Chomsky's analysis of the media as ideological agents of "thought control in a democratic society," with a case study comparing the US press coverage of genocide in Cambodia with that of East Timor. Raises provocative questions about contemporary justice issues. A-II (nr)

Many Rivers to Cross (1955) Western misfire with a Kentucky frontiersman (Robert Taylor) running from the Shawnees and a marriage-minded backwoods maiden (Eleanor Parker). Director Roy Rowland's mangled romantic comedy is a howler that makes everybody look like ancestors of the comic-strip Yokum clan. Stylized violence and sexual references. A-III (br)

Map of the Human Heart (1993) Clash-of-culture melodrama spanning several decades and continents involving an Eskimo (Jackson Scott Lee), a Canadian who is half-Indian (Anne Parillaud), and a WW II pilot (Patrick Bergin) who comes between them. Directed by Vincent Ward, the international production makes good use of stark Arctic settings, the wartime era, and well-observed racial themes, but bogs down in story coincidences and unconvincing romances. Some subtitles. A sexual encounter with fleeting nudity, wartime violence, and minimal rough language. A-III (R)

Mara Maru (1952) Slack adventure features a salvage operator (Errol Flynn), a greedy crook (Raymond Burr), several murders, and a sunken treasure in Manila Bay. Directed by Gordon Douglas, the murky intrigue goes around in circles until ending in the tunnels beneath an old church. Stylized violence. A-II (br)

Mara of the Wilderness (1966) Tall yarn set in northern Alaska, where an orphaned child is raised by wolves, until as a 19-year-old woman (Linda Saunders) she is saved from an evil trapper (Theo Marcuse) by a park ranger (Adam West). Director Frank McDonald's low-budget production hardly does justice either to the world of nature or that of humans. Stylized violence. A-I (br)

Marathon Man (1976) Dustin Hoffman stars as an introspective student who finds himself involved with a terrifying fugitive Nazi (Laurence Olivier). Director John Schlesinger has made a shrewd, hollow, and profoundly anti-human thriller, heavy on violence, and exploiting the tragedy of the Holocaust. O (R)

Marauders, The (1955) Bottom-drawer Western about an Arizona squatter (Jeff Richards) facing a motley gang of paid guns led by a psychopath (Dan Duryea). Directed by Gerald Mayer, the feeble plot is as meaningless as the acting is ludicrous, with a silly ending to boot. Stylized violence and brutality. A-III (br)

March of the Wooden Soldiers (1934) Classic screen version of the Victor Herbert operetta, "Babes in Toyland," features Laurel and Hardy as toyshop workers who rescue the winsome Bo-Peep (Charlotte Henry) from the evil Barnaby (Henry Brandon) and save Toyland from invading Bogeymen. Produced by Hal Roach and directed by Gus Meins and Charles Rogers, the antic silliness of the bumbling duo adds to the fun of a musical fantasy whose nursery rhyme characters, sentimental songs, and fanciful story-line will entertain the youngsters while charming their elders. Delightful family fare. A-I (br)

March or Die (1977) Dick Richards directs a muddled action-adventure epic starring Gene Hackman as a cynical major in the French Foreign Legion who, following action in WW I, is given the task of protecting an archaeological expedition in the Sahara led by Max Von Sydow. Among a cast including Catherine Deneuve, only Terence Hill manages to come out of this cliche-ridden melodrama with any amount of luster. Violence and brutal view of life. A-III (PG)

Marching Along (see: **Stars and Stripes Forever**)

Marco (1974) Disappointing musical treatment of the Marco Polo success story has a number of amusing moments, supplied principally by the uncontrollable mugging of Zero Mostel as the naughty-but-nice Kubla Khan, and Cie Cie Win as his nice-but-naughty warrior-daughter. As the intrepid Marco, Desi Arnaz, Jr.'s, role demands little acting but lots of cheery grinning. Directed by Seymour Robbie, the funny bits and pieces cannot overcome the dull stretches in a drawn-out, generally slack production. Some risqué by-play and mild double-entendres. A-II (G)

Marco the Magnificent (1966) Disappointing adventure movie based on the adventures of Marco Polo (Horst Buchholz) in carrying a message from the pope to Kubla Khan in China. Directed by Denys de La Patellière and Noel Howard, the plodding and episodic script is of less interest than the spectacle and beautiful photography. Some violence. A-II (br)

Margaret's Museum (1997) Offbeat tale set in a 1940s mining town in Nova Scotia, where a feisty young bride (Helena Bonham Carter), whose father had died in the mines, reacts strongly when her new husband (Clive Russell) and younger brother (Craig Olejnik) become miners as well. Director Mort Ransen captures a community's financial dependence on a single industry and the human consequence of this for one family, but the climax is not for the squeamish. Brief nudity, sexual innuendo, recurring profanity, and some rough language. A-III (R)

Margie (1946) Nostalgic comedy set in 1928 with a title 16-year-old (Jeanne Crain) who envies her popular classmate (Barbara Lawrence), disdains the gawky student (Alan Young) who likes her, and develops a crush on the new French teacher (Glenn Langan), though her greatest problem is the elastic band on her bloomers tends to break at critical moments, such as the prom. Directed by Henry King, the saccharine plot mixes humor with sentiment that's firmly anchored by the girl's no-nonsense grandmother (Ester Dale), but what's most enjoyable are the period settings and songs. A-I (br)

Margo (1971) Israeli production about a stodgy university professor (Oded Teomi) who is brought out of his shell by a country girl (Levanna Finkelstein) giving him the maternal care, zest for life, and simple pleasures that his swinging, pseudo-sophisticated wife cannot. Lacking wit and originality, director Menahem Golan's effort simply romanticizes adultery and divorce in sun-drenched Jerusalem, with little rhyme and no reason. O (R)

Maria's Lovers (1985) WW II veteran (John Savage) returns from a prisoner-of-war camp to marry his childhood sweetheart (Nastassia Kinski), but when he can't consummate the marriage, she is courted by a host of suitors. In a ponderous slow-moving melodrama, director Andrei Konchalovsky generates far less emotion than needed to keep it from being a bore. Some too-graphic bedroom sequences. O (R)

Marie (1985) Following the true story of Marie Ragghianti, a divorced mother of three children and the first woman to head the Tennessee Board of Pardons and Paroles, the movie details her courage in refusing to cooperate in the graft and corruption of the governor who appointed her to office. Directed by Roger Donaldson, this inspiring film portrait owes much to a superb performance by Sissy Spacek in the title role. Several scenes of violence. A-II (PG-13)

Marie Antoinette (1938) Historical extravaganza follows the tribulations of the Austrian princess (Norma Shearer) in the court of Louis XV (John Barrymore), married to his dull-witted son (Robert Morley), their eventual succession to the throne, and execution in the French Revolution. Director W.S. Van Dyke II alternates scenes of elaborate spectacle with sympathetic vignettes of the queen, her well-meaning but ineffectual husband Louis XVI, and the queen's lifelong admirer (Tyrone Power), with the treacherous Duke of Orleans (Joseph Schildkraut) hastening their downfall. Long and stodgy, but occasionally moving Hollywood rewrite of history, with plenty of court intrigues and revolutionary violence. A-II (br)

Marie Galante (1934) Murky tale of intrigue as an American undercover agent (Spencer Tracy) gets help from a marooned Frenchwoman (Ketti Gallian) in searching for a saboteur (Sig Rumann), who plans to blow up the US fleet as it passes through the Panama Canal. Directed by Henry King, the muddled plot and seedy tropical characters never jell into a credible espionage thriller, though the fine cast, including singer Helen Morgan, holds interest along the way. Stylized violence, menacing situations, sexual innuendo, and comic racial stereotyping. A-III (br)

Marines Have Landed, The (see: **The Leathernecks Have Landed**)

Marines, Let's Go (1961) Sputtering Korean War tale of Marines (crafty Tom Tryon, sensitive David Hedison, and tough Tom Reese) getting in and out of scrapes while on leave in Japan, before returning to combat heroics against the Chinese Red Army. Directed by Raoul Walsh, the predictable proceedings and formula characters were stale then and are even more tiresome today. Wartime violence, service brawls, excessive drinking, and crass sexual situations. A-III (br)

Marjoe (1972) Documentary look behind the gaudy facade of the evangelical "business" in the Southwest, focusing on the spotted career of itinerant preacher Marjoe Gortner, a young man who began big-time tent-preaching at the age of four and who now, in his mid-twenties, wants to cash in his ministry and expose himself and his fellow evangelist-hustlers. When filmmakers Howard Smith and Sarah Kernochan get away from Marjoe's somewhat suspect self-confessions, they find a chilling system of religious exploitation based on a fundamentalist fear of God, and viewers will have to decide for themselves how unbiased is their portrayal of the dark underside of that old time religion. A-III (PG)

Mark of the Devil (1972) Wretched little horror movie about a 16th-century witch hunter (Herbert Lom) and his young assistant (Udo Kier) who go from town to town searching out evidence of witchcraft. Director Michael Armstrong spends a good deal of time in the torture chamber demonstrating the uses of such instruments as tongue extractors, thumb screws, racks, and spiked chairs, torturing not only a host of hapless actors but also the audience. Extreme violence, a few rapes and some nudity. O (R)

Mark of the Gorilla (1950) Formula adventure directed by William Berke in which Jungle Jim (Johnny Weissmuller) tangles with a gang who don gorilla suits to frighten off visitors while searching for gold buried by Nazis in an African game preserve. Stylized violence. A-I (br)

Mark of the Vampire (1935) Things are not all they seem in this creaky horror variation about a Prague police inspector (Lionel Atwill) and a professor of the occult (Lionel Barrymore) investigating reports that vampires (notably Bela Lugosi and Carol Borland) have taken up residence in a secluded castle. Director Tod Browning has a field day in building a properly scary mood out of the rural mid-European setting in which the story's tense situations occur, but the movie's twist ending may not please all horror fans. Much stylized menace. A-II (br)

Mark of Zorro, The (1940) Dashing tale of Old California in which a well-bred *caballero* (Tyrone Power) turns bandit in order to free Los Angeles from its greedy governor (J. Edward Bromberg) and his ruthless commander (Basil Rathbone). Directed by Rouben Mamoullian, the period action piece is strikingly photographed, with Power easy to take as the Spanish Robin Hood masquerading as a foppish dandy. Some stylized violence and mild romance. A-II (nr)

Marked for Death (1990) Trite action-flick has a burned-out DEA agent (Steven Seagal) retiring to Chicago, where his pal (Keith David) enlists him as a vigilante to blow away a gang of Jamaican drug dealers. Director Dwight H. Little's strictly formula film lacks imagination and credible acting, with little attention to all but sleaze and butchered bodies. Constant violence, intermittent rough language, and recurring nudity. O (R)

Marked Woman (1937) Dated but sturdy crime melodrama in which a nightclub hostess (Bette Davis) blames her criminal boss (Eduardo Ciannelli) for the death of her younger sister (Jane Bryan) and gets her roommates to join in helping the DA (Humphrey Bogart) convict him. Director Lloyd Bacon's formula proceedings retain their edge today principally due the movie's strong portrayal of women's solidarity in the face of male oppression. Stylized violence, menace, and veiled sexual inferences. A-II (br)

Marlene (1984) Unconventional documentary on the life and career of screen star Marlene Dietrich (1902-92) uses the usual movie excerpts and newsreel footage, but spends much time listening to director Maximilian Schell's futile tape-recorded efforts at interviewing the retired actress and his failure to persuade her to appear on camera. With Dietrich dismissing most of his questions as "rubbish," Schell winds up making a documentary in which he co-stars as the frustrated director struggling to win the confidence of a feisty 84-year-old, who stubbornly refuses to participate in the project on any but her own terms. Some subtitles. Mature themes. A-III (nr)

Marlowe (1969) James Garner stars as Raymond Chandler's hardboiled detective Philip Marlowe in a complicated plot involving blackmail and ice-pick murders. Garner's Marlowe relies on whimsy but lacks the essential inner toughness of this school of private eye. Director Paul Bogart and cast (including William Daniels and Jackie Coogan) try hard but can't quite bring the movie off as a cohesive whole. Sensationalistic treatment with nudity in story's conclusion. O (PG)

Marnie (1964) Flawed but masterfully eccentric thriller stars Tippi Hedren as a compulsive thief caught in the act by wise and worldly journalist Sean Connery. Instead of turning her in, he marries the disturbed girl and tries to discover the reasons for her irrational behavior. Director Alfred Hitchcock explores the theme of the redeeming power of love with some compassion, but the treatment is adult. A-III (PG)

Maroc 7 (1967) Agent Gene Barry tracks international jewel thief Cyd Charisse to Morocco, where she plans her next robbery in director Gerry O'Hara's dull and implausible crime story. Excessive sexual innuendo and some violence. O (br)

Marooned (1969) Space mission goes awry when

three astronauts (Gene Hackman, Richard Crenna, and James Franciscus) get stranded on a space station, and ground control (headed by Gregory Peck) tries to get a rescue rocket ready in time to save them. Under the direction of John Sturges, what could have been a gripping adventure yarn bogs down in some fine space and electronic effects that detract interest from the human dimension of the plot, and the moral questions raised by it, such as risking the rescue mission in an unproven craft. A-II (PG)

Marquise of O..., The (1976) French adaptation of the 19th-century novel by Heinrich von Kleist in which a woman (Edith Clever) is rescued from enemy soldiers by a seemingly virtuous count, who takes advantage of her sedated sleep as he guards her through the night. Director Erich Rohmer has fun with the conventions of the time, but does not betray Kleist's characters and their concerns. A-II (PG)

Marriage Came Tumbling Down, The (1968) The focus of this slight but beautifully tender little French movie is Michel Simon's performance as an aging, earthy, yet wise and loving grandfather who helps save his philandering grandson's marriage. Unfortunately, director Jacques Poitrenaud fails to give much substance to the young couple's roles, so that their final reconciliation has small significance. However, the lovely countryside of Provence, and Simon's sensitive and profoundly human characterization makes it well worth viewing. A-II (G)

Marriage-Go-Round, The (1961) Unamusing heavy-handed sex-farce directed by Walter Lang in which an anthropology professor (James Mason) is tempted by the proposal of a nubile Swedish visitor (Julie Newmar) to father her child, with predictable complications when his college-dean wife (Susan Hayward) tumbles to what's going on. Leaden treatment of sexual situations. A-III (br)

Marriage Italian Style (1965) Dark comedy about an amoral man (Marcello Mastroianni) tricked into marrying the woman (Sophia Loren) with whom he has lived for 20 years. Directed by Vittorio de Sica, the movie sparkles with biting satire and sophisticated humor about the battle of the sexes. Subtitles. Centers on sexual innuendo. A-IV (br)

Marriage of a Young Stockbroker, The (1971) Failed satire about a neophyte broker (Richard Benjamin) who is a failure in his attempts to control his compulsive voyeurism, which cause endless professional and marital problems, until his realization at movie's end that he need not be ruled by society's conventions. For all of its humorous digs at social conformity, director Lawrence Turman fails to elicit any sympathy for his alienated young man, whose real problem is a complacent smugness that makes him and the movie a bore. Its treatment of women is consistently demeaning; for example, the sordid scene with a nymphomaniac should have been played for compassion instead of snickers. O (PG)

Marriage of Maria Braun, The (1979) German melodrama about a woman (Hanna Schygulla) whose husband returns from a Russian POW camp after WW II to discover she is having an affair with an American soldier, kills him, and goes to prison. Vowing to have a fortune waiting when he gets out, she rises to be top executive at a textile firm through an affair with its owner. Directed by Rainer Werner Fassbinder, this hard-edged portrait of pragmatic amorality seems to be saying that postwar Germany, like Maria, lost its soul in the struggle for material prosperity. Some rough language and brief nudity. A-IV (R)

Marriage on the Rocks (1965) Clunky romantic comedy in which an over-busy advertising executive (Frank Sinatra) takes his long-suffering wife (Deborah Kerr) on a second honeymoon in Mexico, then a bizarre series of mistakes end in their divorce and her remarriage to his woolly business partner (Dean Martin) before they get back together. Directed by Jack Donohue, the contrived proceedings are sluggishly dragged out, and, despite the talented cast, little of it is amusing. Light treatment of marriage and sexual innuendo. A-III (br)

Married Couple, A (1970) Canadian documentary about the marital games that go on within a troubled Toronto household in which husband and wife act out their inner frustrations and conflicts for the benefit of a movie crew. Directed by Allan King, the film might serve a psychologist or marriage counselor as a point of departure for discussion purposes, but in itself it lacks the coherence to justify the extremities of emotion, rough language, and nudity it displays. A-IV (nr)

Married to It (1993) After a PTA meeting, three vastly dissimilar married couples (Beau Bridges, and Stockard Channing; Mary Stuart Masterson and Robert Sean Leonard; Cybill Shepherd and Ron Silver) instantly bond as close friends and see each other through their marital crises. Director Arthur Hiller's well-intentioned but unconvincing comic-drama affirms commitment in marriage even as it battles lame dialogue and contrived situations. Discreet bedroom scene and frequent rough language. A-III (R)

Married to the Mob (1988) Director Jonathan Demme's antic comedy focuses on a Long Island mob-widow (Michelle Pfeiffer) who tries to start a clean new life with her son on New York's Lower East Side in spite of a lusty mob boss (Dean Stockwell), his jealous wife (Mercedes Ruehl), and a nerdy FBI undercover agent (Matthew Modine). Fine performances make Demme's oddball characters and offbeat subject shine. Some graphic rub-outs handled with a humorous touch, much profanity, and brief nudity within an implied illicit dalliance. A-III (R)

Marry Me, Marry Me (1969) French production about an amiable but aimless young man (Claude Berri) who is so uncertain about marrying his already pregnant sweetheart (Elizabeth Wiener) that he has a quick affair before going through with the ceremony. A fatuous epilogue suggests the hero's fears of marriage to have been unjustified. Also directed by Berri, the story is as aimless as its self-absorbed central character, but in the background are some interesting aspects of Jewish life, especially the wedding feast and a certain sense of sadness at the erosion of Jewish traditions in the affluent, socially permissive present. A-III (PG)

Marrying Kind, The (1952) Engaging melodrama in which a blue-collar couple (Judy Holliday and Aldo Ray) recount the ups and downs of seven years of marriage to a divorce-court judge whose questions force them to rethink their relationship. Director George Cukor gets convincing performances from the principals as seen in flashbacks of a happy marriage buffeted by the tragedy of their son's accidental death. Serious treatment of marital discord. A-II (br)

Marrying Man, The (1991) A playboy (Alec Baldwin) falls for a cabaret singer (Kim Basinger), and despite their differences marries her time and time again. Best moments are attributable to Neil Simon's witty script in this otherwise brisk but fluffy farce directed by Jerry Rees. Acceptance of premarital sex and chauvinist references, some comic violence, and occasional rough language. A-III (R)

Mars Attacks! (1996) Goofy but violent sci-fi picture in which flying saucers full of murderous Martians attack the world and manage to exterminate most US government officials (including president and first lady Jack Nicholson and Glenn Close) before a novel solution saves Earth. Director Tim Burton stretches his affinity for the weird and the whimsical into an ultimately boring shoot-'em-up elaborately spoofing 1950s B-movies. Frequent stylized violence, brief sexual innuendo, and an instance of profanity. A-III (PG-13)

Marshmallow Moon (see: **Aaron Slick from Punkin Crick**)

Martha & Ethel (1995) Warmhearted documentary on two nannies now in their 90s, one a German-born nurse with a strict Catholic upbringing who raised producer-director Jyll Johnstone and her four siblings stressing conformity and discipline, the other a tolerant, affectionate black woman who lovingly looked after co-producer Barbara Ettinger and her five siblings for their divorced mother. The highly personal recollections of each nanny, their grown charges, and now-aged parents provide insights about child rearing, which also reflect how much the American family has changed since mid-century. Discussion of parental abandonment may upset young children. A-II (G)

Marty (1955) Low-key tale of a 34-year-old butcher (Ernest Borgnine) who falls for a shy science teacher (Betsy Blair) despite the disapproval of his mother (Esther Minciotti) and his Bronx buddies. Written by Paddy Chayevsky and directed by Delbert Mann, the story of two lonely people who've come to think of themselves as losers only to discover they're not is told with sincerity and warmth, gaining much credibility from the realistic treatment of its urban ethnic setting. Excellent fare for teens. A-II (br)

Martyr, The (1976) Israeli-German screen biography of a Polish physician and educator, Dr. Janusz Korczak, who in 1942 accompanied a group of wartime orphans to the Warsaw Ghetto and then to the extermination camp of Treblinka, where they all perished together. Directed by Alexander Ford, it is a rather plodding and unimaginative dramatization, but the concluding scene of the children with Dr. Korczak (Leo Genn in a very credible performance) at their head, marching with dignity to the train that will take them to Treblinka, is heartrending and unforgettable. A-II (nr)

Martyrs of Love (1969) Czechoslovakian movie offering three surrealistic episodes on the theme of frustrated desire focusing on the monotonous life of a junior clerk, the aristocratic dreams of a servant girl, and a lonely man's need to feel part of a family. Directed by Jan Nemec, its seriocomic mixture of reality and fantasy is very effective, but many will find its absurd logic and bizarre scenes pointless, if not unsettling. A-III (nr)

Marvin's Room (1996) Poignant drama in which a middle-aged woman (Diane Keaton), after devoting 20 years to caring for her invalid father (Hume Cronyn) and childlike aunt (Gwen Verdon), turns to her estranged sister (Meryl Streep) and volatile nephew (Leonardo DiCaprio) for help when she needs a lifesaving bone-marrow operation. Director Jerry Zaks's testy tale of reluctant reconciliation is beautifully acted, shows delightful spurts of wacky humor, and emerges as a moving portrait of a family's enduring bonds of love. Domestic arguments with instances of rough language and profanity. A-II (PG-13)

Mary, Mary (1963) Failed adaptation of Jean Kerr's stage comedy about a book publisher (Barry Nelson) whose lawyer (Hiram Sherman) insists he meet with his ex-wife (Debbie Reynolds) to go over some tax matters, which become complicated by the arrival of the publisher's fiancé (Diane McBain) and an amorous veteran movie-star (Michael Rennie). Director Mervyn LeRoy does little with the static screen proceedings, allowing the play's comic banter to turn into leaden exchanges that throttle the possibility of finding any charm in this sentimental tale of a divorced couple's reunion. Comic treatment of marriage and a few cuss words. A-II (br)

Mary of Scotland (1936) Literate adaptation of Maxwell Anderson's play recounting the political intrigues against Scotland's Catholic Queen Mary Stuart (Katharine Hepburn), driving her protector Bothwell (Fredric March) into exile, and Mary to the execution block under England's Queen Elizabeth (Florence Eldridge). Director John Ford puts a fine cast through their dramatic set-pieces, with occasional flourishes of pageantry to supply the historical atmosphere. Stylized violence and complicated motivations make it unlikely fare for young children. A-I (br)

Mary Poppins (1964) Walt Disney's musical adaptation of P.L. Travers's children's classic about the primly perfect nanny of the title (Julie Andrews), who uses her magical powers and common sense to straighten out the disorderly children and preoccupied parents of a London household at the turn of the century. Director Robert Stevenson fancifully integrates songs, dance numbers, animated characters, and marvelous special effects into the live-action story, which features a bright performance by Dick Van Dyke as a Cockney worker who also does a comic turn as a bank president. Entertaining family fantasy. A-I (G)

Mary, Queen of Scots (1971) Historical drama details the downfall of the Scottish queen (Vanessa Redgrave) in a 16th-century power struggle with Elizabeth of England (Glenda Jackson). Charles Jarrott directs the fascinating story of two strong women, both utterly egotistical but otherwise completely opposite personalities, slugging it out dramatically and politically in a contest of wits and wills. Besides a slice of history, the movie's value is to afford two accomplished actresses the opportunity to play against each another. A-II (PG-13)

Mary Reilly (1996) Dour tale in which the timorous victim of an abused childhood (Julia Roberts) finds safety working as a chambermaid for kindly Dr. Jekyll (John Malkovich in the dual role), until his murderous associate Mr. Hyde turns up, provoking in her both dread and an unwanted physical attraction. Directed by Stephen Frears, this version of the Stevenson classic presents a drawn-out and relentlessly gloomy picture of the duality of good and evil and Victorian sexual repression. Some gruesome violence and recurring sexual innuendo. A-III (R)

Mary Shelley's Frankenstein (1994) Opulent version of the horror classic in which the obsessed Dr. Frankenstein (Kenneth Branagh) lives to regret his reanimation experiment when the hideous but intelligent creature (Robert De Niro) sadly but savagely wreaks revenge on his creator — with some surprising, if gruesome, departures from the original. Also directed by Branagh, the suspenseful treatment alternates the horrific with the doctor's impassioned love for his beautiful adopted sister (Helena Bonham-Carter), thereby adding a human dimension to the old science-tampering-with-nature story, a cautionary fable of continuing relevance in an age of genetic engineering. Some intense and gory violence as well as brief shadowy nudity. A-IV (R)

Masala (1993) Failed surrealist drama about an alienated Indian youth (Srinivas Krishna) who was raised in Canada, but feels an outsider both in the New World and among the Hindu community of Toronto. Also produced, written, and directed by Krishna, the result is multicultural confusion that does best with the comic incongruities of immigrant life but lacks narrative coherence and dramatic substance. An explicit bedroom scene, numerous sexual references, some irreligious remarks, and sporadic rough language. O (nr)

Mask (1985) Sentimental, slow-moving story of a youth with a deformed face who makes a happy life for himself with the help of an understanding mother (Cher). Director Peter Bogdanovich offers a relatively benign view of the lifesty1e of a motorcycle gang, involving drug abuse and sexual promiscuity. A-IV (PG-13)

Mask, The (1961) Slack horror tale in which a psychiatrist (Paul Stevens) is driven to murder after putting on an ancient Aztec mask sent to him by a suicidal patient. Directed by Julian Roffman, the Canadian production has a couple of murders and several nightmare sequences, but the pedestrian plot and wooden acting don't help matters. Hokey violence and murky menace. A-II (br)

Mask, The (1994) Cartoonish fantasy in which a nerdy guy (Jim Carrey) dons a mask whose magical powers turn him into a green-faced, crime-fighting superhero out to rescue a sultry torch-singer (Cameron Diaz) from a gang of bankrobberbers. Director Charles Russell's wacky special-effects comedy generally hits its broad marks thanks to Carrey's zany impersonations, lightning-speed sight gags, and overall madcap nuttiness. Much cartoon-style violence and minimal gutter language. A-III (PG-13)

Mask of Fu Manchu, The (1932) Creaky atmospheric thriller from Sax Rohmer's potboiler about a British agent (Lewis Stone) trying to stop criminal mastermind Fu Manchu (Boris Karloff) and his fiendish daughter (Myrna Loy) from using the sword and death mask of Genghis Khan to start an Asian war. Directed by Charles Brabin, the diabolical cunning of the Oriental principals is so outlandish that it provides more chuckles than chills. Stylized violence, romantic complications, and the pulp fantasy of a "yellow peril." A-III (br)

Mask of Zorro, The (1998) Spirited swashbuckler set in old California in which an aging Zorro (Anthony Hopkins) trains his fiery replacement (Antonio Banderas) to defeat the tyrant who 20 years earlier stole Zorro's infant daughter, now a dazzling beauty (Catherine Zeta Jones) in love with the new masked avenger. Director Martin Campbell combines old-fashioned derring-do with a game cast in a zesty adventure pitting dauntless heroes against daunting villains. Much stylized violence, mild sexual innuendo, and fleeting rear nudity. A-II (PG-13)

Masquerade (1965) Twisty thriller in which an American (Cliff Robertson) hired by a British agent (Jack Hawkins) to guard a young Arab prince hiding in Spain finds he's on his own when the boy is kidnapped, and his rescue attempts are stymied by rival secret agents. Directed by Basil Dearden, the premise here is that no one can be trusted, something the American learns the hard way, while viewers enjoy the picturesque settings and colorful characters. Some stylized violence and much menace. A-II (br)

Masquerade (1988) Thriller using the old romantic plot about a naive, young heiress (Meg Tilly) set upon by gold-diggers has all sorts of plot twists and characters who are not what they seem. A handsome rogue (Rob Lowe) becomes the love of the heiress's life amidst a lovely beach setting in the Hamptons, an eerie score by John Barry, and Bob Swaim's fine direction. Unfortunately marred by a few scenes of graphic violence and several explicit sexual encounters. O (R)

Mass Appeal (1984) Screen version of Bill C. Davis's stage comedy about the pastor (Jack Lemmon) of an affluent suburban parish who is assigned to take an outspoken young seminary student (Zeljko Ivanek) under his wing. Davis's play is really about two characters much alike in everything but age who have suffered through unhappy childhoods and never established a good relationship with their families. For them the priesthood is a refuge from the harsh complexities of life. Since the inaccuracies about the Catholic Church (and there are many) are innocuous, this is for adults and adolescents. A-II (PG)

Massacre in Rome (1973) On March 23, 1944, Italian partisans attacked a column of SS police troops marching through the center of Rome and killed 33 of them. Within 24 hours, 335 Italians were dead, executed in reprisal on the direct orders of Hitler. Director George Pan Cosmatos effectively sets up this specific moment in history and the motivations of the various characters involved, capably performed by a strong cast including Richard Burton, Marcello Mastrioanni, and Leo McKern. The provocative recreation, based on the book by Robert Katz, avoids the easy oversimplifications of most such movies to pose troubling issues of moral responsibility for wartime atrocities that deserve thoughtful consideration by its audience. A-III (PG)

Massacre River (1949) Western time-waster directed by John Rawlins is set on an Army post, where a young officer (Guy Madison) falls for a woman (Carole Matthews) who runs a saloon, flees a murder charge, and is pursued by his onetime best friend (Rory Calhoun). Frontier violence and romantic complications. A-II (br)

Master Gunfighter, The (1975) American gunslinger and samurai-sword fighter (Tom Laughlin) marries into an aristocratic Spanish family in old California, but has to fight their son (Ron O'Neal) when he takes to stealing gold and killing Indians in order to pay the Yankee taxes on the family hacienda. Directed by Frank Laughlin, the result is a tedious, pretentious, badly acted but lushly produced Western, whose theme of anti-violence is conveyed mostly through violence. A-III (PG)

Master Minds (1949) Formula slapstick comedy directed by Jean Yarbrough in which Leo Gorcey and the other Bowery Boys use Sach (Huntz Hall) as a carnival fortuneteller, until he's kidnapped by a mad doctor (Alan Napier) who wants to switch Sach's brain with that of a monster (Glenn Strange). Hokey menace. A-I (br)

Master of Ballantrae, The (1953) Sprawling historical adventure from Robert Louis Stevenson's tale of a Scottish noble (Errol Flynn) who in 1745 joins the cause of Bonnie Prince Charlie, until the English victory at Culloden forces him into exile and piracy before returning a wealthy man to claim his title from his younger brother (Anthony Steel). Directed by William Keighley, the story is full of colorful characters, especially Roger Livesey's wry Irish rebel, and there are some vigorous action sequences, but the movie never rises beyond the level of costume melodrama. Period violence. A-I (br)

Master of the World (1961) Jules Verne fantasy set in 1868, when a US federal agent (Charles Bronson) and several companions are taken captive aboard a heavily armed flying-ship built entirely of paper whose inventor (Vincent Price) is set on forcing nations to disarm or perish. Directed by William Witney, the flying machine is as ingenious a contraption as Captain Nemo's submarine, and the journey is almost as interesting with the agent's efforts to foil the inventor's destructive course. Menacing situations. A-I (br)

Master Race, The (1944) WW II melodrama focuses on the search for a Nazi fanatic (George Coulouris) hiding among the civilians in a Belgian town liberated by the Americans. Director Herbert J. Biberman's low-budget production reflects the fear that Germany's defeat might not end a future Nazi threat. Some stylized violence and menace. A-II (br)

Mastermind (1970) Comedy misfire filmed in Japan with Zero Mostel as a Kyoto police inspector investigating a series of murders involving an android doll (Felix Silla), Nazi war criminals, Israeli agents, an American spy (Bradford Dillman), and a nightclub owner (Keiko Kishi). Directed by Alex March, the disjointed proceedings make little sense, the comedy is flat, and the inspector's recurring daydream of being a samurai super-warrior is tiresome. Stylized violence and sexual innuendo. A-II (G)

Masterminds (1997) Dopey thriller in which a team of armed, high-tech thugs (led by Patrick Stewart) take over a posh children's academy aiming to make a fortune in ransom money but are continually thwarted by a teen hacker (Vincent Kartheiser) hidden in their midst. Directed by Roger Christian, the poorly plotted story features much gunfire and explosions that unrealistically hurt no one as the teen turns into a thoroughly unbelievable superhero. Much stylized violence, an instance of video piracy, and several uses of profanity. A-III (PG-13)

Masters of Menace (1990) Loutish comedy about a spacey biker (David Rasche) and his moronic motorcycle gang trashing the landscape as they flee a court order and overzealous cops. Director Daniel Raskov's sophomoric exercise in crudity can't be taken seriously by adults but may be by some adolescents. A-III (PG-13)

Masters of the Universe (1987) Live-action sci-fi fantasy based on the Mattel toys and TV cartoon series about the ongoing conflict between heroic warrior He-Man (Dolph Lundgren) and power-crazed Skeletor (Frank Langella). Gary Goddard directs using ample comic-book stylized violence in this purely escapist zap-fest that might adversely affect the very young. A-II (PG)

Masterson of Kansas (1954) Dodge City sheriff Bat Masterson (George Montgomery) averts an Indian uprising by saving an innocent man from the gallows. Director William Castle goes through the motions with a transparent plot pitting a few lawmen against scheming, gun-happy cattlemen. Stylized violence. A-I (br)

Matador (1988) Director Pedro Almodovar's slick, seriocomic look at two kinky individuals — a high-class lawyer (Assumpta Serna) and a retired matador (Nacho Martinez) — whose respected positions in Madrid society cloak their search for a deadly sexual high. Despite serious-minded philosophical and political asides on the connections between sex and death, the film includes explicit, often violent sexual encounters, much nudity, and profanity. Subtitles. O (nr)

Match Factory Girl, The (1992) Ignored and exploited at home and dehumanized by her assembly-line job, a love-starved young woman (Kati Outinen) exacts merciless revenge after she spends the night with a man (Vesa Vierikko) who then cruelly rejects her. Finnish writer-director Aki Kaurismaki pointedly evokes the misery of a loveless existence in a dark drama with bleakly comic undertones. Subtitles. An implied sexual encounter and several poisonings. A-III (nr)

Matchless (1968) Steely-eyed Patrick O'Neal is an espionage agent of passing skill in this intermittently comic spy melodrama with an invisible man gimmick. He gets by with a little help from secret agent Ira Furstenburg and the stupidity of heavies Donald Pleasence and Henry Silva. Italian production directed by Alberto Lattuada has some violence, but its suggestive costuming and situations are excessive. O (br)

Matchmaker, The (1958) Romantic comedy from Thornton Wilder's play about an 1884 New York matrimonial agent (Shirley Booth) who snares a Yonkers merchant (Paul Ford) after his prospective bride (Shirley MacLaine) is swept off her feet by the merchant's head-clerk (Anthony Perkins). Directed by Joseph Anthony, the stagy proceedings have the characters speak directly to the audience on occasion, but the performances are winning, and the period humor is sweetly good-natured. Romantic complications. A-I (br)

Matchmaker, The (1997) Weak romantic-comedy set in Ireland, where a US senator's aide (Janeane Garofalo) researching the politician's Irish roots finds herself beset by a professional matchmaker (Milo O'Shea) hoping to interest her in a local bartender (David O' Hara). Directed by Mark Joffe, the flimsy story is overly contrived, but the authentic Irish settings and crafty characters provide some entertaining compensations. Implied premarital encounter, fleeting violence, and recurring profanity and rough language. A-III (R)

Matewan (1987) Arriving in the coal-fields of West Virginia after WW I, a union organizer (Chris Cooper) tries to help the miners win a bitter, bloody strike. Written and directed by John Sayles, the fact-based movie is admirable in its idealistic picture of the workers' solidarity in standing together against the company's reliance upon force. Some graphic violence and a verbal account of a sexual assault. A-III (PG-13)

Matilda (1978) Elliott Gould plays a seedy promoter who discovers a down-at-the-heels kangaroo act, and with the help of sportswriter Robert Mitchum steers the beast to a bout with the heavyweight champion of the world. Director Daniel Mann's mirthless, blindingly dumb comedy is an embarrassment to sit through. The realistic violence of the final boxing match is not the sort of thing most parents would want their younger children exposed to. A-II (PG)

Matilda (1996) Dark children's fantasy from the Roald Dahl story in which a book-loving six-year-old (Mara Wilson) develops magical powers to cope with neglectful, self-centered parents (Danny DeVito and Rhea Perlman) and a vicious school principal, encouraged along the way by a shy but caring teacher (Embeth Davidtz). Directed by DeVito, the picture busily mixes some mean-spirited humor with a gentle affirmation of the joys of reading. Frequent scenes of children in physical danger and a few crude expressions. A-II (PG)

Matinee (1993) Nostalgic period-comedy set in Key West during the Cuban missile crisis, as a horror movie director (John Goodman) tries out his gimmick-laden monster movies on an audience of kids already jumpy about a possible nuclear attack on the area. Joe Dante directs a flighty and fitfully funny look back at the era of radiation-mutation movies and backyard fallout shelters. Brief menace to children and comic treatment of monster movie violence. A-II (PG)

Matinee Idol, The (1928) Breezy silent comedy in which a Broadway revue's black-face star (Johnny Walker) finds a rural tent-show's Civil War melodrama so hilariously awful, he adds it to his revue without realizing how much the audience's laughter will pain the unsophisticated troupe, especially its appealing star (Bessie Love). Directed by Frank Capra, the picture's good-natured humor and unpretentious settings can't quite overcome the contrived situation or lessen the humiliation of the rustic players. Romantic complications and comic roughhousing. A-II (br)

Mating of Millie, The (1948) Sappy romantic comedy in which a single woman (Evelyn Keyes) seeking a husband in order to adopt an orphan, falls for a bachelor (Glenn Ford) who insists he's not the marrying kind. Directed by Henry Levin, the coy romance and its predictable outcome is as dated as its disapproving attitude toward single parents. A-II (br)

Matrix, The (1999) Virtually incoherent sci-fi tale in which a tiny band of cyber-rebels (led by Keanu Reeves and Laurence Fishburne) do battle with virtually indestructible humanoid killers set on destroying every last vestige of humanity in the twenty-second century. As directed by the Wachowski brothers, the action movie's violence is glorified, glamorized, and made to look exciting with eye-popping special effects. Excessive violence and profanity. O (R)

Mattei Affair, The (1973) Enrico Mattei, head of the state's oil cartel, was perhaps the most powerful man in Italy when he died under mysterious circumstances in a plane crash in 1962. In following his career and in examining the contradictory evidence about the crash, this Italian dramatization is as dynamic as Mattei himself, played by Gian Maria Volonte with the complete assurance of the self-confident man who relishes competition. Implicit throughout director Francesco Rosi's fast-moving, impressionistic re-creation are questions about the wider issues of social justice that are seldom raised in the ruthless battle to control the world's oil resources. Some scenes of stylized violence. A-III (R)

Matter of Days, A (1969) French student-activist studying in Prague, believing the Czech liberalization to be tainted with bourgeois materialism, returns to Paris during the May 1968 student riots. Though the Soviet invasion a few months after the completion of the movie proved her political views wrongheaded, the drama is of some interest for its picture of 1960s youth with their easy comradeship, their insatiable quest for new values, and their inevitable sexual candor. A-IV (R)

Matter of Innocence, A (1967) Failed British adaptation of a Noel Coward story about a young girl (Hayley Mills) being raised by her reprobate uncle (Trevor Howard). Guy Green's heavy-handed direction makes even more offensive scenes of her learning about sex, alcohol, and larceny. O (br)

Matter of Time, A (1976) Well-intentioned but hopelessly sentimental and disjointed treatment of the Cinderella theme defeats the best efforts of Liza Minnelli, Ingrid Bergman, and Charles Boyer. Directed by Vincente Minnelli, the inept Italian production has some occasional rough language and a comically meant attempted-rape scene. A-III (PG)

Maurie (1973) Fact-based dramatization of Cincinnati Royals basketball player Jack Twyman (Bo Svenson), who devoted himself to caring for teammate Maurice Stokes (Bernie Casey) after a 1957 head injury during a game resulted in total paralysis. The result is a saga of determination, love, and endless hours of pain from expensive treatments which gradually brought back his powers of speech and partial control of body movement. Though director Daniel Mann's movie is slow, it is never tedious in recounting, without sentimentality but plenty of honest emotion, the story of teammates who summoned the inner strength necessary to surmount a time of deep crisis. A-I (G)

Maverick (1994) Spirited Western in which a high-stakes, winner-takes-all card game onboard a paddlewheeler attracts a gun-toting gambler (Mel Gibson), the light-fingered lady (Jodie Foster) who has lifted his wallet, and a veteran lawman (James Garner) hired to keep the assorted disreputable players from cheating their way to claiming the half-million-dollar pot. Richard Donner directs an appealing cast of doublecrossing critters in a featherweight but crowd-pleasing, near-spoof of Western conventions, in which substance is gleefully tossed aside in favor of style and escapist fun. Some stylized violence, a brief, discreet bedroom scene, and a few coarse expressions. A-III (PG)

Max Dugan Returns (1983) A long-absent father (Jason Robards) turns up at the home of his daughter (Marsha Mason), an impoverished widow with a teenage son (Matthew Broderick). He has only six months to live, is remorseful, and also has more than a half-million in cold cash of dubious origin neatly packed in one of his suitcases. Bland, contrived comedy written by Neil Simon and directed by Herbert Ross, it is mildly amusing thanks to the skill and personality of its performers. Some mild verbal vulgarities and a fuzzy moral stance towards stealing, but it's basically innocuous. A-II (PG)

Max Havelaar (1979) Dutch adventure-drama about a brave and exuberantly idealistic government official (Peter Faber) in mid-19th century Java who almost single-handedly takes on the entrenched exploiters of the native population, until the authorities finally send him back to Holland. Director Fons Rademakers has succeeded admirably in his re-creation of a bygone and little-known era, with Faber giving a vital, wholly convincing performance as the anti-colonial hero. Engrossing and largely entertaining, but with several instances of brutal violence. A-III (R)

Maxie (1985) A young couple (Glenn Close and Mandy Patinkin) rent a house that had once belonged to a promising Hollywood starlet named Maxie (Close in dual role). Seeing her second chance at stardom, Maxie's spirit inhabits the wife's body with comic results. Directed by Paul Aaron, the movie almost succeeds in reviving the madcap verve of the 1930s screwball comedies. Several restrained bedroom scenes. A-III (PG)

Maximum Overdrive (1986) Writer-director Stephen King's malevolent allegory about strange disturbances which turn every machine and truck in a small town into a murderous entity is preoccupied with the demonic. Virtually nonstop images of death and destruction, gore, violence, and profanity. O (R)

Maximum Risk (1996) Brutal action-movie in which a French sharpshooter (Jean-Claude Van Damme) pursues the killers of his American-raised identical-twin brother who had been involved with Russian gangsters and corrupt FBI agents. Directed by Ringo Lam, the numbskull plot is barely held together by recurring scenes of mindless mayhem in explosive car crashes, ear-splitting shootouts, and bone-crunching confrontations. Much murderous violence, brief sex encounter, fleeting nudity, and occasional rough language. O (R)

May Fools (1990) While the turmoil of the May 1968 students' strike in Paris spreads, greedy relatives gather in the picturesque French countryside when the family matriarch dies, and her distraught son (Michel Piccoli) fears they will insist on selling his lifelong home as part of the estate. Not one of director Louis Malle's most insightful works, the film nonetheless is evocative of the gentler, bygone lifestyle of the rural bourgeoisie, and intermittently droll as the family members feverishly pursue the dead woman's belongings. Several explicit sexual references, including a lesbian relationship, and partial female nudity. A-IV (R)

Maya (1966) American boy (Jay North) discovers mystery in India when he visits his big-game hunter father (Clint Walker). John Berry directs the action adventure in a simple, fast-moving manner that emphasizes the sights and sounds of a fabled land. For the younger members of the family. A-I (br)

Maybe ... Maybe Not (1996) Vacuous sex-farce in which an unfaithful clod (Til Schweiger) moves in with a wistful homosexual (Joachim Krol) while his pregnant girlfriend fumes. Writer-director Sonke Wortmann's German production plays the gender confusions and sexual mixups for laughs at the expense of both straights and gays, but there is nothing funny about its amoral treatment of promiscuity. Subtitles. Explicit sexual references, restrained sex scenes, and rough language. O (R)

Mayerling (1968) Mushy, overlong, lavishly costumed tearjerker starring Catherine Deneuve and Omar Sharif in the story of the tragic royal romance between Austrian Crown Prince Rudolph and his young mistress, which ends in double suicide in the royal lodge at Mayerling in 1889. British production directed by Terence Young has all the trappings of a good soap-opera version of the life and leisure of the ruling class, but comes up boring and emotionally empty. A-III (PG/PG-13)

Maze, The (1953) Dim horror story directed by William Cameron Menzies is set in a gloomy Scottish castle, whose new baronet (Richard Carlson) is distraught after learning the terrible secret of an amphibious monster kept hidden by his family for 200 years. Menacing atmosphere builds to hokey climax. A-II (br)

McCabe and Mrs. Miller (1971) Warren Beatty and Julie Christie star in a Western examining the reality of American frontier life in a story about a petty gambler who opens a brothel in a boom-town, and it becomes so successful that Eastern business interests decide to take it over. Director Robert Altman's effort has many interesting segments but fails to come together as a cohesive whole. Rough language and some graphic nudity in brothel scenes. O (R)

McConnell Story, The (1955) Thin tribute to a WW II Army Air Force navigator (Alan Ladd) who trains after the war to be a jet-fighter pilot, becomes an ace in the Korean War, then takes a job as a military test-pilot, with tragic results. Directed by Gordon Douglas, the patriotic proceedings also take note of how the pilot's supportive wife (June Allyson) stands by him during various crises and long absences. Wartime violence. A-I (br)

McCullochs, The (1975) Strong, self-made trucking magnate (Forrest Tucker) has built a successful career but at the expense of not spending enough time with his growing children and their problems. Produced, written, and directed by Max Baer, this sentimental chronicle of family life in the early 1950s offers no new insights into its characters or their times. Some macho brawling and boozing. A-III (PG)

McHale's Navy (1964) Popular TV comedy-series (1962-66) comes to the big screen with a story in which the conniving Commander McHale (Ernest Brognine) of the PT-73, while stationed on a South Seas island, leads his wacky crew in a scheme to win a horserace by generating a smoke-screen to hide the track. Directed by Edward J. Montagne, it's a simple mix of bungling characters awash in slapstick situations and resulting confusions. For the undemanding. A-I (br)

McHale's Navy (1997) Inept sequel to the 1950s TV comedy-series features Tom Arnold as a retired naval officer whose expertise in covert operations helps destroy the Caribbean base of an ex-Soviet terrorist (Tim Curry). Directed by Bryan Spicer, Arnold's charmless character is unamusing, the dumb antics of his klutzy crew are tiresome, and the mirthless plot is scuttled by heavy-duty menace and special-effects mayhem. Considerable stylized violence and some crude sexual innuendo. A-III (PG)

McHale's Navy Joins the Air Force (1965) Dippy sequel directed by Edward J. Montagne in which PT-73's Ensign Parker (Tim Conway) masquerades as an Air Force pilot, then becomes a national hero when he spots the hidden Japanese fleet. Broad comedy with silly characters and slapstick situations. A-I (br)

McKenzie Break, The (1970) Absorbing though familiar WW II story manages to avoid most of the cliches inherent in prison-camp pictures. Centered around two strong personalities (Brian Keith, a hardboiled career officer sent to quell a riotous prison-camp for Nazi officers, and Helmut Griem, an indomitable German officer fomenting trouble to cover-up escape attempts), director Lamont Johnson's movie is nicely paced, with strong performances, a credible script, and an attempt at characterization uncommon in this type of story. Tight, coherent, and thoroughly intelligent contest of wills. Some violence. A-III (GP)

McLintock! (1963) Western comedy about a cantankerous cattle-baron (John Wayne) who spends his time battling with his estranged wife (Maureen O'Hara), uppity homesteaders, unhappy Indians, and a college-educated daughter (Stefanie Powers) who's courted by an earnest cowhand (Patrick Wayne) and a clumsy oaf (Jerry Van Dyke). Directed by Andrew V. McLaglen, the result is a colorful collection of hard-hitting brawls and verbal squabbles, with an ending modeled on Shakespeare's "The Taming of the Shrew." Comic violence and marital strife. A-I (br)

McMasters, The (1970) After the Civil War, black Union soldier Brock Peters returns to his former, aging employer Burl Ives, who makes him co-owner of his ranch, an act of friendship which incites the bigotry of the neighboring ranchers led by ex-Confederate officer Jack Palance. To further complicate matters, the local downtrodden Indians help out with the ranch chores and give Peters a squaw (Nancy Kwan). The inevitable showdown is long and violent. A conventional Western ably directed by Alf Kjellin, what makes it noteworthy is its attempt to deal with a theme of interracial justice. A-III (PG)

McQ (1974) John Wayne stars as a Seattle policeman so determined to nail a notorious drug-dealer that he turns in his badge and initiates justice on his own terms. Director John Sturges offers the usual brand of Wayne frontier justice updated to an urban setting. Violence and some sexual references. A-III (PG)

Me (1970) Quiet, unpretentious French drama about a 10-year-old boy (Michel Terrazon), an unwanted child shuttled from foster home to foster home, never fully trusted, loved, or understood. By movie's end, though he has been returned to the institution, he has at last experienced affection and friendship from an aged grandmother who has taken the time to break through his defensive shell. Maurice Pialat's direction is restrained and unsentimental, while gently probing beneath the surface of events with a rare understanding of childhood and human nature in general. In distancing his subject matter he has re-created an all-too-real world of loneliness and hope, for the tender chords he strikes are at the heart of the human condition. A-II (nr)

Me and the Mob (1994) Amateurish comedy in which an inept New York writer (James Lorinz) goes to work for his mobster uncle (Tony Darrow) in order to write a crime expose, but proves just as hapless at crime as at writing, and is soon risking his neck by wearing a wire to betray his partners in crime. Producer-director Frank Rainone's ham-handed effort quickly falls flat as the script is confined to lame Mafia stereotypes of wise-guys spouting endless macho gutter-talk. An extended sex scene, intermittent violence intended for comic effect, and continuous rough language. O (R)

Me, Natalie (1969) Patty Duke plays an unhappy but spunky teenage "ugly duckling" struggling to fend for herself in New York's Greenwich Village. Directed by Fred Coe, the movie either overstrains for laughs or settles for the cliches of sentimental melodrama, such as her affair with a married architect (James Farentino). Some entertaining moments but few serious insights. A-III (PG)

Mean Frank, Crazy Tony (1977) Mediocre Italian production about a deported American gang-lord (Lee Van Cleef) who teams up with a bumbling, would-be gangster (Tony Lo Bianco) to knock over a really nasty mobster. Though director Michele Lupo treats the story in tongue-in-cheek fashion, there is still a great deal of graphic violence. O (R)

Mean Season, The (1985) A psychotic killer (Richard Jordan) stalks Miami and chats occasionally with the reporter (Kurt Russell) covering his crimes. A melodrama directed by Philip Borsos with ciphers for characters, it is of no more consequence than a ride on a roller coaster. Some bloody violence, premarital sex, and brief nudity. A-III (R)

Mean Streets (1973) Robert De Niro and Harvey Keitel star in director Martin Scorsese's drama about small-time crime in New York's Little Italy. The drama has moments of power and effectiveness, mostly in its depiction of an authentic ethnic neighborhood, but it too often degenerates into a kind of bizarre freak show. Some intense violence, nudity, and rough language. A-IV (R)

Meanest Man in the World, The (1943) In this creaky adaptation of a play by George M. Cohan, radio-comedian Jack Benny plays an unsuccessful lawyer besieged by clients after a newspaper story reporting that he took candy from a child. Director Sidney Lanfield's low-budget comedy yields few laughs, despite a hard-working cast including Eddie Anderson as Benny's servant and Priscilla Lane as the romantic interest, with results only of interest to Benny fans and social historians. Mild romantic complications. A-II (br)

Meatballs (1979) Bill Murray cavorts as the director of a haplessly ill-organized summer camp. Canadian production ineptly directed by Ivan Reitman contains some relatively mild off-color jokes and sex-oriented pranks. A-III (PG)

Mechanic, The (1972) Twisted, ironic, somewhat depressing chiller about a cynical, cold-blooded Mafia hit-man (Charles Bronson) who takes on an apprentice (Jan-Michael Vincent). Betrayal is in the wind, however, but from what direction isn't clear until the twist ending. Director Michael Winner has turned out a slick, suspenseful, and not very pleasant crime movie. Several grisly murders. A-III (PG)

Medea (1971) Italian dramatization of the Medea myth, going beyond the confines of Euripides' tragedy by sketching in some of the background of a violent time and place. The focus, however, is on the title character, and as performed by Maria Callas, the evil of this witch-goddess figure becomes increasingly palpable. Though some may fault the film for its departures from the classic tradition, few will deny the power of director Pier Paolo Pasolini's visualization of the ancient Greek world. A-III (nr)

Medicine Ball Caravan (1971) Documentary directed by Francois Reichenbach recording the travels of a musical troupe (B.B. King, Alice Cooper, Delaney and Bonnie, etc.) across the US during the summer of 1970, promoting peace, love, and music. Judging from the evidence on the screen, one would conclude that all counte-rculturists know how to do is freak out, hassle with the fuzz, and swim naked. Most of this is merely irritating, but viewers should know that Warner Brothers paid for both the tour and the movie, which features many of their slower-selling recording artists, another example of the movie medium's potential as an instrument of commercial exploitation. A-IV (R)

Medicine Man (1992) Belabored drama has Sean Connery as an eccentric medical researcher in the endangered Brazilian rainforest, forced to enlist the help of an unwelcome assistant (Lorraine Bracco) sent from the States to check up on him. Lush cinematography and Connery's considerable screen presence do not compensate for a tedious script and Bracco's dreadfully shrill performance. Some tribal nudity, very brief violence, and an instance of rough language. A-II (PG-13)

Mediterraneo (1992) Stranded on a remote Greek island during WW II, eight Italian soldiers lay down their arms and embrace the peaceful life of the villagers. Director Gabriele Salvatores's charmingly simplistic and bittersweet comedy positions war as a man-made folly in light of our shared humanity. Some sexual innuendo with implied encounters, occasional nudity, and minimal rough language. A-III (nr)

Medium Cool (1969) Television-news cameraman (Robert Forster) has no interest in the effect of the stories he covers until he falls in love with a young widow (Verna Bloom), whom he helps search for her runaway son in the midst of the violence and confusion of police-yippie confrontations during the 1968 Chicago Democratic Convention. Director Haskell Wexler's powerful movie intertwines staged drama and documentary footage in a convincing, seamless style that gives point to the work's probing into the ethics of news coverage. It is unfortunate that a bedroom romp with total nudity mars a significant attempt to question the role the media play in the violence of today's society. O (X/R)

Medusa Touch, The (1978) Richard Burton plays a man who can destroy others just by willing their death, a telekinetic power that psychiatrist Lee Remick discovers to her horror. Though the plot device is extremely implausible, director Jack Gold makes the most of it in turning out a well-acted, superior thriller. Some rather frightening violence and occasional anti-God rantings. A-III (PG)

Meet Boston Blackie (1941) First in a mystery series based on a character created by Jack Boyle, with Chester Morris as the reformed thief of the title who breaks up a spy ring headed by the Mechanical Man (Michael Hand) in a seaside amusement park. Directed by Robert Florey, the formula plot is paced by Blackie's playful banter with Inspector Farady (Richard Lane) who wants to arrest him for a jewelry heist, some comic relief from Blackie's dim pal, Runt (Charles Wagenheim), and a bit of romance (Rochelle Hudson). Stylized violence and menacing situations. A-I (br)

Meet Joe Black (1998) Dull romantic fantasy in which Death takes human form (Brad Pitt) and delays claiming a media magnate (Anthony Hopkins) in order to experience life on earth, including falling in love with the alarmed millionaire's vulnerable daughter (Claire Forlani). Suggested by the 1920s play "Death Takes a Holiday," and directed by Martin Brest, the soggy proceedings limp along for three interminable hours, offering only opulent visuals to distract from the shallow characterizations. Fleetingly intense violence, a discreet sexual encounter, occasional profanity, and an instance of rough language. A-III (PG-13)

Meet John Doe (1941) An unassuming hobo (Gary Cooper) is hired to embody the average American, but when he discovers that his media-created popularity is being used to further the ambitions of a homegrown Fascist politician (Edward Arnold), he decides to commit suicide. Director Frank Capra plumbs the darker side of the American character in an interesting but ultimately heavy-handed story about the dangers of media manipulation. A-II (br)

Meet Me at the Fair (1952) Middling musical romance directed by Douglas Sirk is set in 1904, when the head (Dan Dailey) of a patent-medicine show comes to the aid of a woman (Diana Lynn) determined to save an orphanage from being closed by the corrupt politician (Hugh O'Brian) to whom she's engaged. Wholesome fare with a saccharine flavor. A-I (br)

Meet Me in St. Louis (1944) Nostalgic musical placed in St. Louis on the eve of the 1903 World's Fair celebrates the old-fashioned virtues of close-knit family life, as domestic complications beset parents (Leon Ames and Mary Astor), grandpa (Henry Davenport), teenage daughter (Judy Garland), and the boy next door (Tom Drake). Director Vincente Minnelli lightens the sentiment with good-natured humor, Judy's numbers include "The Trolley Song" and "Have Yourself a Merry Little Christmas," and tiny Margaret O'Brien steals the show with her Halloween pranks. Appealing family fare. A-I (nr)

Meet the Applegates (1991) Giant bugs disguised as typical Americans (Ed Begley Jr. and Stockard Channing) plot the meltdown of an Ohio nuclear-plant to protest the destruction of the Brazilian rainforest that is their home. Directed by Michael Lehmann, the initially amusing satire soon nosedives into ugly stereotypes and unamusing tastelessness. Rape scene, several extramarital encounters, recreational drug use, cartoon violence, constant off-color references, and intermittent rough language. O (R)

Meet the Deedles (1998) Sophomoric comedy in which dopey twin brothers (Paul Walker and Steve Van Wormer) save Yellowstone National Park from being undermined by prairie-dog tunnels. Directed by Steve Boyum, the vacuous enterprise offers a disjointed series of skits alternating between dumb-and-dumber routines, toilet gags, and life-threatening stunts. Mindless comic violence, sexual innuendo, crude language, and gross humor. A-III (PG)

Meet Wally Sparks (1997) Dreary comedy in which a trashy TV talk-show host (Rodney Dangerfield) tries to discredit a Southern governor (David Ogden Stiers) whose family-values speeches are hurting his ratings. Director Peter Baldwin's low-budget, poorly edited movie is an appropriately shabby vehicle for Dangerfield's leering one-liners. Much crude sexual humor, brief nudity, some comic violence, and an instance of rough language. A-III (R)

Meeting Venus (1991) An international production of Wagner's "Tannhauser" in the Paris Opera House presents its little-known Hungarian conductor (Niels Arestrup) with a slew of petty problems, not the least of which is an unexpected love affair with a volatile diva (Glenn Close). Hungarian director Istvan Szabo offers scattered but shallow charms in a movie intended as a metaphor for the problems facing European unification. An adulterous affair, assorted references to sexual promiscuity, and a brief shot of drug abuse. A-III (PG-13)

Meetings with Remarkable Men (1979) Surface treatment of the formative years of Russian mystic G.I. Gurdjieff, who before WW I discovered, hidden deep in the Asian hinterlands, an ancient monastic order in whose keeping were the secrets of the universe and the meaning of life. Directed by Peter Brooks, the natural spectacle of the rugged mountainous landscape of Afghanistan is more remarkable than any of the movie's portentous encounters or pretentious dialogue. A-III (G)

Megaforce (1982) Tongue-in-cheek adventure about an elite force put together by the nations of the free world to combat oppression. Directed by Hal Needham, it has a solid plot and there is a certain charm in its lack of pretension. Barry Bostwick carries off the hero's role with panache and just a touch of self-mockery, while Henry Silva, less burdened than he usually is as the heavy, gets a chance to lighten things up as a not-too-bad villain. Despite much cannon and rocket fire, there's not a drop of blood spilled or even an elbow dislocated during all the spectacular derring-do. Several mild double-entendres. A-II (PG)

Mel Brooks' History of the World, Part 1 (1981) Taking a buffoonish tour through history from the Missing Link to the French Revolution is this episodic series of sketches that offer a few scattered laughs but are otherwise mired in unremitting vulgarity and witless low humor. Director Mel Brooks has nothing on his mind but garnering laughs at any cost, but meaning no harm is not the same as doing no harm, as in a musical sequence about the persecution of Jews at the hands of the Spanish Inquisition and a sketch with Brooks as a waiter at the Last Supper. Slapstick violence, sexual situations, bathroom humor, and coarse language. O (R)

Melo (1988) Dated French period-piece about a tragic love affair in which the wife (Sabine Azema) of a mediocre pianist (Pierre Arditi) falls in love with a concert violinist who is her husband's best friend (Andre Dussollier). Based on Henry Bernstein's 1929 play, director Alain Resnais's movie emphasizes its stage origins by stylized acting and theatrical effects that some may find needlessly affected and historically remote. Mature subject and treatment. A-III (nr)

Melody (1971) Unpretentious little movie about two London schoolboys (Mark Lester and Jack Wild) whose friendship is threatened when one of them develops a crush on 11-year-old Melody (Tracy Hyde). Puppy-love leads to the announcement of their plans to marry, confounding parents, and ending in a free-for-all at school between students and teachers. Sensitively directed by Waris Hussein, the engaging story of fantasy and romance presents a child's view of the adult world with much humor and gentle ironies that will appeal as much to parents as to preteens. A-II (G)

Melody Time (1948) Another of Walt Disney's feature-length variety shows with songs, stories, and musical interludes presented in cel animation, live-action photography, and sometimes a mixture of both. The music segments vary from the lively to the lyric, with visuals to match, but more memorable are the stories of itinerant planter Johnny Appleseed, exuberant young tugboat Little Toot, and, best of all, the tall-tales of Western folk hero Pecos Bill as earnestly told by singing cowboy Roy Rogers. An enjoyable family diversion. A-I (br)

Melvin and Howard (1980) A supreme American loser and a supreme American winner forge a bond based upon mutual respect in this touching comedy about a gas-station attendant (Paul LeMat) who discovers he is among the heirs of eccentric millionaire Howard Hughes (Jason Robards). Director Jonathan Demme's movie makes viewers feel a little better about this crazy, mixedup, but unique and quite wonderful country of ours. Some incidental nudity and some profanity. A-III (PG)

Member of the Wedding, The (1952) Stagy yet evocative portrait of adolescent turmoil from Carson McCuller's story about a lonely 12-year-old (Julie Harris) whose only friends are her widowed father's housekeeper (Ethel Waters) and an eight-year-old boy from next door (Brandon de Wilde). Director Fred Zinnemann succeeds well with the trio's kitchen dialogues, but the larger picture of the girl's uneasy relations with father, relatives, and peers, as well as her coming-of-age experiences in the finale, are less than convincing. Intense yet insightful picture of teenage anxieties. A-II (br)

Memoirs of a River (1992) Fact-based drama of a simple Jewish logger (Sandor Gaspar) and other innocents, both Christians and Jews, who face torture and death during an outburst of anti-Semitic violence in the Austro-Hungarian Empire of 1882. Written and directed by Judit Elek, the Hungarian production gets off to a slow, somewhat confusing, start in establishing the historical circumstances, then becomes a riveting account of the terror unleashed by the spread of a rumor about a Jewish ritual murder of a Christian child. Much tension and some grizzly scenes of torture and brutalization. A-III (nr)

Memoirs of an Invisible Man (1992) Strained comedy about a West Coast businessman (Chevy Chase) accidentally made invisible who, with his girlfriend (Daryl Hannah) in tow, is on the run from a power-crazed government agent (Sam Neill). The funny moments tend to vanish quickly in director John Carpenter's awkward romantic comedy. Restrained bedroom scene, occasional sexual innuendo, stylized comic violence, and an instance of rough language. A-III (PG-13)

Memories of Me (1988) Cardiac surgeon (Billy Crystal), felled by his own heart attack, decides to head West and make peace with his dad (Alan King), a lifelong movie extra and embarrassment. It takes the surgeon's girlfriend (JoBeth Williams) and another critical illness to bring them to play the roles of father and son for the first time in their lives. Uninspired direction by Henry Winkler and a too-facile ending do not detract from the entertaining performances and touching concept. Rough language, sexual references, and a brief premarital sex scene. A-III (PG-13)

Memories of Underdevelopment (1973) Cuban production directed by Tomas Gutierrez Alea about the day-to-day recollections of an upper-middle-class Cuban (Sergio Corrieri) who refused to join his family's flight from Castro by emigrating to Miami, but who also refuses to take part in a revolution that is distasteful to him personally and intellectually. Seen through the eyes of this alienated outsider are the changes taking place under the Marxist regime, but the movie's relaxed, sometimes comic, presentation of revolutionary deficiencies helps give its picture of present Cuban life a sense of credibility instead of propaganda. A-III (nr)

Memory of Justice, The (1976) Documentary on the Nuremberg Trials of Nazi war criminals and whether they established a legal precedent for judging the wartime conduct of all nations. After an extensive examination of the Nuremberg process for trying crimes against humanity, producer-director Marcel Ophuls goes on to ask some uncomfortable questions about offenses committed by the Allies during the WW II and the Occupation, the conduct of the French military during the Algerian War, and Americans during the Vietnam War. Ophuls brings patient intelligence and concern for human dignity to a four-and-a-half-hour demonstration of the difficulty in but the necessity of establishing accountable standards of international conduct. Unflinching look at death camp atrocities and an unnecessary use of nudity. A-IV (PG)

Memphis Belle (1990) Fact-based WW II drama about a B-17 bomber and its 10-man crew embarking on their final and most dangerous mission over Nazi Germany. Director Michael Caton-Jones turns in an unabashedly old-fashioned aerial war-movie that, while offering nothing fresh or original, does convey the extreme pressures and fears faced by young soldiers. Wartime violence, mild sexual innuendo, and minimal rough language. A-II (PG-13)

Men (1986) Another round in the battle of the sexes is provided in this German production about a woman who, tired of her successful businessman-husband, has an affair with a nonconformist musician. The husband moves in with his wife's lover and slowly transforms him into a hardworking ad agency executive, thereby saving his marriage. Director Doris Dorria's comedy of manners and morals concentrates more on the male camaraderie of the odd-couple relationship than on the wife's infidelity. Mild sexual innuendo. A-III (nr)

Men, The (1950) Brooding in a Veteran Administration Hospital, a bitter WW II paraplegic (Marlon Brando) resists all attempts at rehabilitation for civilian life until a dedicated doctor (Everrett Sloane) and his loving fiancé (Teresa Wright) make him face the future. Directed in semi-documentary style by Fred Zinnemann, the story amply demonstrates the psychological dimensions of devastating injuries, but it is Brando's powerful, convincing performance that makes the movie a vivid experience. A-II (br)

Men at Work (1990) Feeble action-comedy about two garbage men (Emilio Estevez and Charlie Sheen) who get stuck with the corpse of a corrupt politician while trying to find his murderer, a sleazy toxic-waste kingpin (John Getz). Also written and directed by Estevez, the result is a sophomoric vanity production, relying on antiestablishment posturing rather than any substantive social perspective in its condescending depiction of blue-collar workers, minorities, police officers, and fears of pollution. Cartoon violence, occasional profanity, bathroom humor, and vulgar situations. A-III (PG-13)

Men Don't Leave (1990) Realistic, unsentimental portrait of a family in crisis after the sudden death of her husband leaves the mother (Jessica Lange) and her two young sons to cope with the shock, grief, and change of lifestyle that result. Director Paul Brickman shows the difficulty of their struggle to survive as a family in a financially strapped environment, a situation made believably poignant by a fine cast. Though the sexual involvement of the 17-year-old son is inappropriate for younger adolescents, parents may wish to share this otherwise relevant film with their older offspring. Some sexual situations and rough language. A-III (PG-13)

Men in Black (1997) Zany sci-fi comedy in which a brassy New York City cop (Will Smith) is recruited by a taciturn government agent (Tommy Lee Jones) who monitors extraterrestrial activity in the city to prevent a ferocious alien in human disguise form destroying planet Earth. Direction by Barry Sonnenfeld and apt pairing of Smith and Jones mixes understated hip-humor with witty creature puppetry and amusing special effects. Some cartoon-like comic violence and a few instances of profanity. A-III (PG-13)

Men in War (1957) Separated from their overrun battalion in 1950 Korea, a lieutenant (Robert Ryan) heads his mauled platoon back toward the US lines, picking up a shell-shocked colonel (Robert Keith) and his driver (Aldo Ray) on the way, but their path is blocked by an enemy entrenchment. Directed by Anthony Mann, the small-scale situation promises a character study of individuals under growing stress but disappointingly little emerges beyond the usual stereotypes. Some nasty wartime violence. A-II (br)

Men in White (1934) Dated medical melodrama from the Sidney Kingsley play about a dedicated intern (Clark Gable) whose plans for further studies are complicated by a rich socialite (Myrna Loy) and a lonely nurse (Elizabeth Allan). Directed by Richard Boleslawski, its idealized treatment of dedicated doctors is cloying, despite a tragic romantic subplot. Veiled reference to abortion. A-III (br)

Men of Respect (1991) When a Bronx Mafia don (Rod Steiger) is murdered by his own lieutenant (John Turturro), a torrent of mob reprisals engulfs the killer and his manipulative wife (Katherine Borowitz). Director William Reilly's updated version of "MacBeth" scores on acting and intrigue, but its chosen form of lurid melodrama yields little moral insight. Some grisly violence, intermittent rough language, and momentary nudity. A-IV (R)

Men of the Fighting Lady (1954) US aircraft carrier's doctor (Walter Pidgeon) recounts the brave acts of its fighter pilots (Van Johnson, Frank Lovejoy, Keenan Wynn, etc.) during the Korean War. Directed by Andrew Marton, the routine All-American script is helped by filming aboard an actual carrier and much use of official combat footage. Wartime violence. A-I (br)

Men with Guns (1998) Powerful drama of a troubled Latin-American country, where an idealistic physician (Federico Luppi) sets out to visit the novice doctors he had trained to care for the rural poor, but he despairs after finding they have been killed or driven off by soldiers or guerrillas, though his selfless example comes to inspire others. Writer-director John Sayles explores the spiritual strengths and human weaknesses of people struggling to survive the calamities of civil war. Subtitles. Brief violence and occasional rough language. A-III (R)

Menace II Society (1993) Ultra-violent drama set in Watts unreels the fate of an African-American youth (Tyrin Turner) who learns the drug trade early on, graduates to murder, but is almost saved by a good woman (Jada Pinkett) before becoming just another statistic of revenge-motivated, drive-by shootings. In allowing the fatalistic youth to rationalize his murderous behavior, directors Allen and Albert Hughes leave the impression that society, not the individual, must take full blame for spiraling crime in the inner city. A nihilistic view of life, excessively graphic bloodshed, a brief bedroom scene, many degrading sexist references, and incessant rough language. O (R)

Ménage (1986) French import about a couple who have their marriage turned inside out when a homosexual friend falls for the husband (Michel Blanc), who will do anything for his wife (Miou-Miou) who, it turns out, is infatuated with the friend (Gerard Depardieu). Director Bertrand Blier's gentle bedroom farce turns nasty as it depicts the treachery, deceit, and brutality inevitable in the situation. Nudity, explicit sex, and rough language. O (nr)

Mephisto (1982) Hungarian-German production directed by Istvan Szabo is an extremely interesting film about the temptation of power. A provincial German actor (Klaus Maria Brandauer) whose forte, ironically enough, is playing the great tempter Mephisto, allows himself to be taken under the wing of a prominent member of the rising Nazi party, and, when they come to power, becomes director of the Berlin National Theatre. The film lacks dramatic force, but it is nonetheless fascinating, especially Brandauer's brilliant performance as the goodhearted but feckless hero. Some rather graphic nudity. A-IV (R)

Mephisto Waltz, The (1971) Mediocre horror movie in which a dying master-pianist (Curt Jurgens) befriends a young journalist (Alan Alda) in whose body he intends to continue his existence as a follower of Satan. Once this is established, the suspense is over, and the rest is a tiresome exercise in hokey witchcraft rituals. Director Paul Wendkos works hard to create the reality of his occult world, but what was needed was a little subtlety and imaginative suggestion. Some violence. A-III (R)

Mercenary, The (1970) Loosely plotted Italian spoof of spaghetti Westerns revolving around the waxing and waning fortunes of a taco-brained Mexican revolutionary (Tony Musante) and a stoic soldier-for-hire (Franco Nero), who is pitted against the sinister arch-villain of the piece (Jack Palance). Musante garners most of the laughs as the grinning fool of a would-be general leading an equally inept, rag-tag band of peasants. Directed by Sergio Corbucci, the frequently hilarious goings-on should not be taken too seriously, especially all the shooting and bright-red paint splattering everyone. Brief nudity. A-III (GP)

Merchant of Four Seasons, The (1973) German drama about a misfit who after many failures in life becomes as a fruit peddler, but his family's malice and his wife's infidelity destroy his last spark of independence. Director Rainer Werner Fassbinder offers a depressing but valid picture of the dehumanizing effects of modern society's materialistic values upon the human spirit. Subtitles. Graphic sexual encounter. A-IV (nr)

Mercury Rising (1998) Lackluster thriller in which a renegade FBI agent (Bruce Willis) goes on the run with a nine-year-old autistic boy (Miko Hughes) who's been targeted for death after inadvertently breaking into a top-secret government computer-file. Director Harold Becker's glossy action story is elaborately but unconvincingly plotted, resulting in a routine, formula chase-film. Recurring violence, intermittent profanity, and some rough language. A-III (R)

Mercy (1996) Dark drama of a wealthy, self-obsessed lawyer (John Rubenstein) forced to own up to his grievous failings after his 11-year-old daughter (Rhea Silver-Smith) is kidnapped by a vengeful teenaged girl (Amber Kain) whom he had rejected after a casual sexual encounter. Writer-director Richard Shepard's unpleasant but revealing character study probes the arrogance of a selfish man and the damage his actions inflict on all around him. Brief violence, sexual references, and much rough language, as well as profanity. A-III (R)

Mermaids (1990) An adolescent girl (Winona Ryder), troubled by her attraction to a 26-year-old man (Michael Schoeffling), is even more embarrassed by her flamboyant single mom (Cher), who has taken up with the local shoe-store owner (Bob Hoskins). The baldly contrived story-line in director Richard Benjamin's limp comedy trivializes a young girl's religious leanings while managing to make her promiscuous mom seem hip. Acceptance of promiscuous and premarital sexual relationships. O (PG-13)

Merrill's Marauders (1963) Fact-based WW II saga of a US force of infantry volunteers fighting behind Japanese lines in Burma under Gen. Frank Merrill (Jeff Chandler), who agonizes over the need to push his men to their limits. Directed by Samuel Fuller, the narrative alternates well-staged battle scenes with the deteriorating condition of the unit as it dwindles from 3,000 to 100 able-bodied soldiers. Strong wartime violence. A-I (br)

Merry Christmas, Mr. Lawrence (1983) David Bowie and Tom Conti star in an English-Japanese production about the clash of cultures in a Japanese camp for British prisoners during WW II. At war's end, with the Japanese prisoners of the British, there is an indication that perhaps humanity can bridge such cultural chasms. The subject is almost a movie cliche and others have done it much better. Directed by Nagisa Oshima, the movie features much hard-edged samurai-code violence and an ambivalent attitude toward homosexuality. A-IV (R)

Merry Go Round (1976) Starring Senta Berger and Helmut Berger, this is an inane, tedious, badly dubbed remake of the turn-of-the-century Schnitzler play about a series of sexual relationships coming full circle. O (R)

Merry War, A (1998) Uneven British satire adapted from George Orwell's 1936 novel *Keep the Aspidistra Flying* in which a bright young man (Richard E. Grant) quits his job in a London ad agency to earn his living as a poet, but winds up a pauper until sorting out his priorities when his sweetheart (Helena Bonham Carter) becomes pregnant. Directed by Robert Bierman, the young man's obstinate idealism makes him an increasingly unlikable character, though the whimsical situations arising from this are quite amusing and lead to an ironical but heartwarming ending. Sexual situations including an unwed pregnancy, a comic scene of inebriation, and an instance of profanity. A-III (nr)

Merry Wives of Windsor, The (1966) Undistinguished British production of Otto Nocolai's opera based on Shakespeare's comedy about the buffoonish Falstaff (American bass Norman Foster) who is made sport of by two mischievous wives. Directed by George Tressler, it might be of interest to students of music but not drama. A-II (br)

Message, The (see: **Mohammad, Messenger of God**)

Message from Space (1978) Mediocre Japanese production offering a pint-sized variation on the **Star Wars** theme, with some plucky youngsters teaming up with an old-timer (Vic Morrow) to save the universe from intergalactic villains. Other familiar elements include a captive princess dressed in white, a cute little robot, two hotshot pilots, and some bargain-basement mysticism. Directed by Kinji Fukasaku, the special effects are satisfactory, though the story line is cluttered and the comic relief not very amusing. A-II (PG)

Message in a Bottle (1999) Gauzy romance in which a widowed boat-builder (Kevin Costner) from North Carolina's Outer Banks is torn between stubbornly clinging to the memory of his adored wife or taking a chance on love again with a Chicago single mom (Robin Wright Penn). As directed by Luis Mandoki, the saccharine-drenched narrative crawls along despite pretty visuals, appealing performances, and uplifting themes about loss, hope, and renewal. A discreet bedroom scene, fleeting violence, and occasional profanity. A-III (PG-13)

Meteor (1979) Sean Connery and Natalie Wood star as scientists attempting to deflect a huge meteor heading for the earth and whose impact might bring on another Ice Age, among other calamities. Though laden with disaster-movie cliches, director Ronald Neame makes the premise into surprisingly good entertainment, thanks to a good cast and several plot twists more sophisticated than is usual for this kind of movie. Some profanity. A-III (PG)

Meteor Man, The (1993) Comic-book adventures of a mild inner-city schoolteacher (Peter Townsend) who, after being hit by a meteor, finds he has superhuman powers which he uses to help his neighbors clear the 'hood of hoodlums and drug traffickers. Also written and directed by Townsend, the superhero fantasy is played for good-natured laughs, with a solid supporting cast (including Bill Cosby, James Earl Jones, Robert Guillaume, and Marla Gibbs) and plenty of rap music. Fantasy violence in a realistic context of street crime. A-II (PG)

Metro (1997) Tedious action-thriller in which a foul-mouthed San Francisco cop (Eddie Murphy) tracks down a foul-mouthed psychotic killer (Michael Wincott), then tracks him down again after he escapes jail. Directed by Thomas Carter, the formula plot puts its one-dimensional characters through overly contrived situations of intense menace and bloody mayhem. Excessive violence, a flash of nudity, and recurring rough language. O (R)

Metroland (1999) A hedonistic bachelor (Lee Ross) returns to London in the late 1970s determined to get his now-married best friend (Christopher Bale) to leave his wife (Emily Watson) and resume their swinging lifestyle, going as far as bringing in a seductress, and making repeated passes at the man's wife. Though belabored in exposition, director Philip Saville's character-driven drama explores commitment, friendship, manipulation, and envy with a few insights along the way. Several sexual encounters with nudity, brief recreational drug abuse, fleeting violence, occasional profanity, and intermittent rough language. A-IV (nr)

Metropolis (1926) Silent classic of a future society ruled by an aristocracy living in luxury above ground while the workers suffer miserably underground, comforted only by the religious faith of a young woman (Brigitte Helm), in whose likeness a sinister scientist (Rudolf Klein-Rogge) fashions a robot inciting the workers to rebel, but all ends in reconciliation. Directed by Fritz Lang, the story's melodramatic turns and woolly finale may be dated, but not its vivid pictorial sense, grandly expressionistic décor, and theme of social justice. Bleak picture of exploited workers, stylized violence, and some sexual innuendo. A-II (br)

Metropolitan (1990) An outsider (Edward Clements) who claims to detest social snobbism is admitted to the nightly Manhattan soirees of seven wealthy youngsters and soon finds his life revolving around them. Whit Stillman's directorial debut is marked by a lighthearted comedy of manners, which is well-acted and enlivened by witty dialogue, but leaves many unanswered questions about the privileged characters' pointless partying and aimless lifestyles. References to promiscuous relationships. A-III (PG-13)

Mexican Spitfire (1939) Dated slapstick farce directed by Leslie Goodwins in which a Mexican singer (Lupe Velez) marries an American lawyer (Donald Woods), whose uncle (Leon Errol) tries to help out the young couple by impersonating an English lord, with predictable comic chaos. Romantic complications and ethnic stereotyping. A-II (br)

Mexican Spitfire Out West (1940) Routine series-comedy directed by Leslie Goodwins in which a domestic spat brings Carmelita (Lupe Velez) to Reno, where her uncle Max (Leon Errol) tries to get her back to her husband (Donald Woods) by masquerading as an English lord. Comic marital mix-ups. A-II (br)

Miami Blues (1990) Colorful black-comedy tracks the battle of wills between a seedy homicide detective (Fred Ward) and a psychopathic ex-San Quentin inmate (Alec Baldwin) who cross paths in Miami. Director George Armitage makes the most of these losers on the fringe of a cotton-candy world, and his actors, especially Jennifer Jason Leigh as the part-time prostitute with a yen for marriage, is bright and often surprising. Some grisly violence, several highly suggestive sexual encounters with some nudity, and occasional rough language. A-IV (R)

Miami Rhapsody (1995) Frivolous bedroom farce in which a struggling but ambitious writer (Sarah Jessica Parker) accepts a marriage proposal, then gets cold feet upon learning her parents (Mia Farrow and Paul Mazursky) and siblings (Kevin Pollak and Carla Gugino) are all involved in extramarital affairs. Writer-director David Frankel copies Woody Allen's ethnic humor and wry dialogue in a mildly amusing tale of betrayals, reconciliations, and belated recognition of the virtues of fidelity. Live-in relationships, numerous sexual references, and an instance of rough language. A-III (PG-13)

Miami Story, The (1954) Standard crime-tale of reformed hood (Barry Sullivan) aiding citizen's committee to smash a syndicate boss (Luther Adler). Directed by Fred F. Sears, it features the usual stylized violence. A-II (br)

Michael (1996) Fantasy misfire in which a slovenly angel (John Travolta) encourages romance between two lonely reporters (William Hurt and Andie MacDowell) who are collaborating on a splashy tabloid story about him. Directed by Nora Ephron, the ill-conceived tale is a charmless, supposedly comic concoction of one-dimensional characters who are romantically inspired by a smug celestial character more fallen than angelic. Implied sex, comically intended violence, and a mild profanity. A-III (PG)

Michael and Helga (1969) Soporific German sex-education movie uses impersonal diagrams and silly dramatizations to treat too many complicated biological, psychological, and social aspects of its subject, so that it tends to confuse more than enlighten viewers. Much too diffuse for parents to use in acquainting their offspring about the facts of life. A-IV (R)

Michael Collins (1996) Sweeping, emotionally engrossing account of the man (Liam Neeson) who masterminded the armed Republican struggle to free Ireland from 700 years of British rule, but in signing the treaty creating the Irish Free State split the Republican movement, which resulted in civil war and his own death in 1922. Writer-director Neil Jordan's dramatization rehabilitates Collins's leading role in achieving Irish independence while splendidly re-creating the crowded events and assorted gallery of heroes and villains which make the times fascinating both as history and human drama. Terrorist violence, rough language, and occasional profanity. A-III (R)

Mickey One (1965) Muddy tale of a small-time stand-up comic (Warren Beatty) on the run from some threatening mobsters without ever learning precisely why they are after him. Director Arthur Penn succeeds best with the moody location filming in Chicago, but the volatile theme of alienation dead-ends in a murky, undefined plot. Some stylized violence and much menace. A-III (br)

Micki and Maude (1985) Broadcast journalist (Dudley Moore) marries his pregnant mistress (Any Irving) before divorcing his pregnant wife (Ann Reinking) because he loves them both. Director Blake Edwards comes up with a few funny moments, but the sentimental treatment of the situation make the movie's attempts at farce unsatisfactory, if not dishonest. Sympathetic depiction of adultery. O (PG-13)

Midas Run (1969) British secret-service officer (Fred Astaire) concocts an elaborate scheme to hijack a large gold shipment he is supposed to be guarding. Jumbled script and plodding direction by Alf Kjellin make the caper tiresome long before the end. Lengthy and over-drawn scene of lovemaking. O (PG)

Middle Age Crazy (1980) Successful contractor (Bruce Dern) with a gorgeous wife (Ann-Margret), a son who loves and admires him, a beautiful home, and a host of friends, but, in an oft-told story, as he approaches 40, things start to fall apart for him. Directed by John Trent, it has fine performances from its principals, and the familiar situation is treated with an unusual moral sense that makes it well worth seeing. Mature theme with some rough language and harsh satire. A-III (R)

Middle of the World, The (1975) Swiss drama about a bright, married engineer (Phillipe Leotard), chosen by party regulars to run for office, who pursues an indiscrete affair with a young waitress (Olimpia Carlisi) until she rejects his callous use of her. Directed by Alain Tanner, the movie proves a wise, humane parable about a comfortable, materialistic society that has lost its soul and sense of the dignity of the individual. It is somewhat ironic, however, that the narrative, in making a strong statement against the exploitation of women, is itself guilty of using an unnecessary amount of nudity in detailing the adulterous affair. O (nr)

Midnight (1939) Dizzy romantic comedy set in Paris, where a penniless American showgirl (Claudette Colbert) aids a rich aristocrat (John Barrymore) by pretending to be an Hungarian countess, until a cabdriver (Don Ameche) shows up claiming to be the count. Directed by Mitchell Leisen from a script by Billy Wilder and Charles Brackett, the bubbly results are wacky fun, with lightheaded characters, charmingly romantic twists, and good-natured social satire. Romantic complications. A-II (br)

Midnight Clear, A (1992) Highly stylized antiwar movie focuses on the insane outburst of violence engulfing a reconnaissance squad (including Ethan Hawke, Ayre Gross, and Gary Sinise) in the Ardennes Forest in December 1944, when an equally small unit of German soldiers tries to arrange a surrender. Adapted from William Wharton's novel by director Keith Gordon, the action is more symbolic than credible, though admirable in using an isolated snowbound setting to suggest a surreal situation transcending all wars. Graphic wartime violence, a highly romanticized sexual encounter, and minimal rough language. A-III (R)

Midnight Cowboy (1969) A Texas bumpkin (Jon Voight) comes to New York City expecting to make his fortune as stud to what he believes are its endless supply of lonely women. In trying to cope with reality of urban life, he relies on his friendship with another loser, a small-time con-artist (Dustin Hoffman) crippled physically and emotionally with a hopeless dream of escaping to the sun. Director John Schlesinger treats with compassion this odyssey of two alienated outcasts blindly groping for some redemptive human fellowship in a society that values sex and money more than human beings. Some may find its realistic depiction of a sordid environment, with a graphic sexual encounter and a brutal outburst of violence, quite reprehensible. Others will find merit in its attempt to recognize the resilience of the human spirit and the dignity of the individual. Challenging fare, not for the casual viewer. A-IV (X/R)

Midnight Crossing (1988) Trashy adventure-story, ineptly directed by Roger Holzberg, about a man (Daniel Travanti) who returns to retrieve a fortune in stolen money he had helped hide 30 years before on an island off Cuba. The ranks of those who become involved are decimated by greed, lies, attempted murder, and a storm at sea. Some bloody violence, some brief but graphic sexual scenes, with fleeting nudity and incidental profanity. A-III (R)

Midnight Express (1978) Wildly melodramatic movie directed by Alan Parker about the imprisonment of an American youth in a Turkish prison for narcotics smuggling wallows in bloody violence and cruelty, an indulgence hardly justified by its human rights plea. Further marred by sexual references and nudity. O (R)

Midnight in the Garden of Good and Evil (1997) Superficial courtroom drama as told by a reporter (John Cusack) covering the murder trial of a wealthy Savannah antiques dealer (Kevin Spacey), who claims he shot his homosexual boyfriend in self-defense. Director Clint Eastwood does little with the central question of the defendant's guilt or innocence, concentrating instead on numerous eccentric characters who add flavor but no substance to the drawn-out proceedings. Brief violence, much sexual innuendo, some rough language, and recurring profanity. A-III (R)

Midnight Lace (1960) Doris Day screams, cries, whines, and whimpers her way through this suspense thriller as a rich American married to a suave Englishman (Rex Harrison) living happily in London, until a series of threatening telephone calls turns her into a basket case. Directed by David Miller, the slickly done, highly manipulative affair depends largely on one's tolerance for women-in-peril situations. Much menace heightened by a little stylized violence. A-II (br)

Midnight Madness (1980) Rival teams of college students compete in a dead-of-the-night treasure hunt in this slapdash effort at zany comedy written and directed by David Wechter and Michael Nankin. The laughs are few and the goings-on get tiresome. Some mild sexual innuendo in the dialogue. A-II (PG)

Midnight Man, The (1974) Burt Lancaster plays a brutal ex-cop employed as security chief for a Midwestern college campus with a bisexual counselor (Susan Clark), a sex-pot student (Catherine Bache) who gets murdered, and a corrupt sheriff (Harris Yulin). Director Roland Kibbee's confused plot is full of numbing twists and inconsistencies, leaving little justification for its violence and sexual references. O (R)

Midnight Run (1988) An embezzler (Charles Grodin), on the run from mobsters and the law, is nabbed in New York by a bounty-hunter (Robert De Niro) who attempts to escort him back to Los Angeles alive to collect $100,000. With humor and some sentiment, director Martin Brest charts the growing camaraderie between this odd couple as they dodge dangers along the way. Much profanity and some comic-book violence. A-III (R)

Midnight Story, The (1957) Intriguing mystery about the murder of a kindly San Francisco priest who a young cop (Tony Curtis) suspects was committed by a local fisherman (Gilbert Roland), but while searching for proof, he comes to respect him as a good family man, then falls in love with his cousin from Italy (Marisa Pavan). Director Joseph Pevney handles the changing relationship between determined cop and unsuspecting quarry with sympathy, strengthened by the strong family flavor of the Italian-American setting. Themes of trust and betrayal, brief violence, and mild romantic complications. A-II (br)

Midsummer Night's Dream, A (1967) The New York City Ballet in its first feature-length presentation, conceived and choreographed by the company's artistic director, George Balanchine, with Suzanne Farrell as Titania, Edward Villella as Oberon, and Arthur Mitchell as Puck. A treat for those who could not otherwise see this lavish, seldom-performed ballet with the music of Felix Mendelssohn. A-I (br)

Midsummer Night's Sex Comedy, A (1982) Woody Allen directs and stars in a slight little comedy of manners set in a Victorian house in rural New York at the turn of the century. Mia Farrow, Jose Ferrer, and Mary Steenburgen are among the three couples who switch, or consider switching, partners in the course of a summer's day and night. There are few jokes, and just about all of them are about sex. Mature subject matter. A-III (PG)

Midway (1976) Charlton Heston, Henry Fonda, and Glenn Ford head an all-star cast in this occasionally effective re-creation of the most decisive naval battle of WW II. Unfortunately, director Jack Smight is unable to overcome the shallow fictional subplots that supposedly were meant to add human interest but which instead blunt the emotional potential of historical material capable of standing on its own. Wartime violence and some rough language. A-II (PG)

Midwinter's Tale, A (1996) An out-of-work English actor (Michael Maloney) sets out to direct and star in a small-town shoestring production of "Hamlet" to be staged on Christmas Eve in an abandoned church, despite the bickering of an eccentric cast of misfits. Writer-director Kenneth Branagh turns in an unpretentious comic valentine to struggling actors and the-show-must-go-on tradition. Sexual references and some rough language. A-III (R)

Mighty, The (1998) Touching drama in which a gifted, deformed schoolboy (Kieran Culkin) befriends a slow-witted oversized classmate (Elden Henson), and their bonding helps each face daunting personal problems on their horizons. Director Peter Chelsom weaves a tale of psychological and physical impairment into a story of hope that triumphs over loss. Brief violence, some menace, and an instance of profanity. A-II (PG-13)

Mighty Aphrodite (1995) Thin seriocomic tale of an adoptive father (Woody Allen) who learns his son's biological mother (Mira Sorvino) is a hapless prostitute and decides to find an unsuspecting guy to marry her. Writer-director Allen develops little more than a shallow veneer of humor and threadbare dramatic conflict in a slack story of mismatched romances. Fleeting bedroom scenes, numerous sexual references, and recurring rough language. A-III (R)

Mighty Barnum, The (1934) The ups and downs of P.T. Barnum (Wallace Beery) are chronicled in this story of how he came to establish the Greatest Show on Earth with the help of his adroit partner Bailey (Adophe Menjou). Directed by Walter Lang, the action is certainly colorful, though Beery's broad performance makes the showman appear to be more foolish, and certainly more gullible, than any of his patrons. Romantic complications. A-II (br)

Mighty Ducks, The (1992) Loud, obnoxious story of a mean yuppie lawyer (Emilio Estevez) and a bunch of nasty juveniles being transformed by working together to win a peewee hockey championship. Director Stephen Herek's oft-told tale of the character-building potential of team sports offers bogus characters in bogus situations that earn little sympathy or respect before the predictably bogus outcome. Bone-crunching violence of a contact sport, nasty youthful pranks, and coarse language. A-II (PG)

Mighty Joe Young (1949) Sentimental adventure-fantasy in which an enterprising nightclub owner (Robert Armstrong) brings a young woman (Terry Moore) and her pet, the giant gorilla of the title, from Africa to New York, where the oversized beast goes berserk, is ordered destroyed, but escapes in time to save children trapped in a burning orphanage. Directed by Ernest B. Schoedsack, the contrived story-line will appeal to youngsters and others willing to enjoy the sympathetic antics of this mild-mannered descendent of King Kong (as animated here by Willis O'Brien and Ray Harryhausen). Hokey stylized violence. A-I (br)

Mighty Joe Young (1998) In this entertaining remake of the genial 1949 monster fantasy, a giant-sized ape is saved from South African poachers and relocated to a stateside nature preserve by a devoted young benefactor (Charlize Theron), then escapes its confines and becomes a danger to the local populace. Directed by Ron Underwood, the hokey adventure is fairly tame, but the visuals are impressive as the huge animal interacts with puny humans. Brief violence and sporadic mayhem. A-II (PG)

Mighty Morphin Power Rangers: The Movie (1995) Formula TV action fare for underdeveloped minds comes to the big screen as the series's six teenage Rangers blast off to a distant planet to find a new source of power with the aid of a bikini-clad warrior (Gabrielle Fitzpatrick), then return home to use it against a 6,000-year-old demon (Paul Freeman) bent on covering the world in purple ooze. Director Bryan Spicer paces the thin comic-book story of earnest youths vs. wisecracking monster with gobs of martial-arts violence, special-effects destruction, dark humor, New Age mumbo-jumbo, and a few vulgarities. A-II (PG)

Mighty Quinn, The (1989) The murder of a white businessman on an exotic Caribbean island pits an honest chief of police (Denzel Washington) against white and black powerbrokers who would like to pin the murder on a local ne'er-do-well (Robert Townsend). Director Carl Schenkel dilutes the suspense with meandering subplots that enhance the film's local color but do nothing for the crime at hand. Some grisly violence, rough language, and sexual innuendo. A-III (R)

Mikado, The (1967) Gilbert and Sullivan's timeless comic operetta about the son who defies his emperor father and wins his love, Yum-Yum, in a wonderful stage production of Japanese make-believe. Pleasant story, lovely costuming, wit, laughter, and song by the D'Oyly Carte Opera Company adds up to excellent entertainment for everyone. A-I (br)

Mike's Murder (1984) When Debra Winger's boyfriend, Mike (Mark Keyloun), is murdered, she investigates and learns about the drug trade and the seamy side of Los Angeles life. Winger has little to do in a listless melodrama, written and directed by James Bridges, that is as flat as its title. A-III (R)

Mikey and Nicky (1977) Nicky (John Cassavetes) is a bookie who steals some money from his boss and, fearing he is marked for death, contacts the only man he can trust to help him, his boyhood friend Mikey (Peter Falk). Writer-director Elaine May follows their odyssey through the course of one wild evening, but the complications encountered along the way are entirely predictable, buoyed only by the strong performances of the principals. Some violence, rough language, and a frank treatment of sex. A-III (R)

Milagro Beanfield War, The (1988) Honest but flawed attempt to depict the cultural strength of a poor Hispanic community in the Southwest when it bands together against greedy Anglo land developers. Directed by Robert Redford, the feel-good plot is rendered in broad, melodramatic strokes, saving most of its energies for illustrating the foibles of a large cast of colorful characters, among them Chick Vennera, Christopher Walken, Sonia Braga, and John Heard. Some violence, rough language, and muted sexual references. A-III (R)

Mildred Pierce (1945) Misplaced ambition fuels James M. Cain's dark story of a driven woman (Joan Crawford) who shucks a useless husband (Jack Carson) in rising from waitress to head a restaurant chain, then falls for a scoundrel (Zachary Scott) who turns his attentions to her adolescent daughter (Ann Blyth). Directed by Michael Curtiz, it's an acerbic tale of how obsession with material success ultimately destroys its misguided heroine, not the least of whose mistakes is raising her only child to be a spoiled brat. Mature theme and treatment. A-III (br)

Miles from Home (1988) Two brothers (Richard Gere and Kevin Anderson) burn down their Iowa farm rather than turn it over to the bank, but the shock of losing their family's once-proud farmstead leads them to a life of aimlessness, one step ahead of the cops. Gary Sinise directs a heartbreaking story of two young men whose rising reputation as folk heroes doesn't ease their sense of family loss. Adult themes and some rough language. A-III (R)

Milestones (1975) Fictional documentary about what happened to those involved in the protest movements of the 1960s, whose failed efforts at changing the nature of the American politics and society led them inward, banding together in little groups for mutual support and survival. Interweaving the activities of some 50 characters may be confusing for those uninterested in political alienation, but filmmakers Robert Kramer and John Douglas have documented how a lost segment of a generation sees itself that has importance for future historians. Unconventional views, some nudity, and a graphic birth-sequence make this mature fare. A-IV (nr)

Milk and Honey (1989) Leaving her native Jamaica for work as a nanny in Toronto, a poor woman (Josette Simon) and her young son hope for eventual citizenship, but bigotry and immigration red-tape lead them into an underground life of fear and deceit. Canadian directors Rebecca Yates and Glen Salzman deliver a sensitive, carefully etched study of one black woman's determination to make a better life without compromising her dignity or values. Some vulgar sexual innuendoes. A-III (nr)

Milk Money (1994) Truly dumb picture of a seventh grader (Michael Patrick Carter) who brings a prostitute (Melanie Griffith) home hoping that his widowed father (Ed Harris) will marry her. Though aimed at youngsters, director Richard Benjamin's adult fairytale reeks of phony romantic notions about prostitution and is cheapened by recurring scenes of leering adolescents. Discreet bedroom scene, numerous sexual situations and double entendres, minor violence, and intermittent profanity. A-III (PG-13)

Milky Way, The (1969) French production about the pilgrimage of two men to the Spanish shrine of St. James the Apostle along the route known as "the Milky Way." It is an extraordinary journey of faith, ranging not only from place to place, but from century to century, as the pilgrims encounter advocates of past heresies and those who are orthodox believers. Director Luis Bunuel presents a lively mixture of pious Christian traditions and superstitious beliefs through an episodic and absurdly humorous series of adventures that challenge the serious viewer with its ambiguous reflections on the relevance of religion in contemporary life. Subtitles. Sexual situations and anti-clerical jibes. A-IV (PG)

Mill on the Floss, The (1937) Creaky dramatization of the George Eliot novel about a mill owner's daughter (Geraldine Fitzgerald) in 1830s England who, despite the warnings of her brother (James Mason), falls in love with the son (Frank Lawton) of the lawyer who had ruined their father. Director Tim Whelan's lame costume drama is a series of handsome scenes which never jell into a dramatically convincing whole. A-I (br)

Millennium (1989) Inept science-fiction excursion a thousand years into the future, from which time travelers return to the 20th century seeking to retrieve an object left behind on a previous visit. Veteran director Michael Anderson tries to work up some tension in a muddled plot involving a romance between an air-crash investigator (Kris Kristofferson) and a traveler from the 30th century. Some fairly graphic violence and several restrained sex scenes. A-III (PG-13)

Miller's Crossing (1990) Tough Prohibition-era gangster movie about a mob war in which the right-hand man (Gabriel Byrne) of the city's top boss (Albert Finney) goes to work for the opposition after the two have a falling-out over a woman (Marcia Gay Harden). Written, produced, and directed by the brothers Joel and Ethan Coen, the hardboiled story has some interesting twists about personal loyalty and the criminal code, the melodramatic performances and the period setting go well together, and the hard-edged violence is neatly stylized for the most part. Considerable violence and menace, references to illicit sexual relationships, and occasional profanity. A-IV (R)

Millhouse: A White Comedy (1971) Documentary on the life and career of Richard Millhouse Nixon begins with Nixon's 1962 "last" press conference, and then returns to his origins and six political crises (including the famous 1956 "Checkers" speech), his role in the 1964 campaign, and finally his election as president in 1968. Based solely on newsreel footage (and a few out-takes), the satiric intent of director Emile de Antonio's partisan selection of material can only amuse anti-Nixonites, but will not convince his supporters of the shallowness and ineptness that de Antonio finds in the visual record. Lack of explanatory historical background limits its usefulness for young viewers. A-III (G)

Million Dollar Legs (1932) Zany comedy opens in the depressed country of Klopstokia, where an American salesman (Jack Oakie) falls for the daughter (Susan Fleming) of its president (W.C. Fields), then discovers all its citizens are super-athletes and brings a team to Los Angeles to compete in the Olympics. Directed by Edward Cline, the funny business includes some hilarious sight gags, and Fields shines both as a statesman who Indian-wrestles his obstinate cabinet (led by Hugh Herbert) and as an Olympic weightlifter who overcomes the efforts of a siren (Lyda Roberti) hired to demoralize the team. Mild sexual innuendo. A-II (br)

Million Dollar Mermaid (1952) Loosely based on the life of Annette Kellerman, the Australian swimmer (Esther Williams) imported by a carnival showman (Victor Mature) to turn-of-the-century America, where she raises eyebrows in a one-piece bathing suit, becomes the aquatic star of New York's Hippodrome, whose owner (David Brian) wants to marry her, then goes to Hollywood, where she's injured making a silent movie. Director Mervyn LeRoy's episodic success-story moves briskly along, abetted by a charming romantic subplot and several eye-filling water ballets staged by Busby Berkeley. Sentimental but easy-to-take family fare. A-I (br)

Million Dollar Mystery (1987) Fluffy comedy-adventure filled with car chases and demolition features an ensemble cast of new faces on a greedy search for $4 million in hidden payoff money. Director Richard Fleischer makes the most of the stark southwest landscape, shot exquisitely by Jack Cardiff as backdrop for the slapstick antics and dangerous stunts which form the substance of the movie. Some coarse language and sexual sight gags are brief and restrained. A-II (PG)

Millionaire for Christy, A (1951) Dated romantic-comedy in which a lawyer's secretary (Eleanor Parker) is sent to inform a man (Fred MacMurray) he has inherited $2 million, then gets carried away by her desire to marry him first. Directed by George Marshall, the complications caused by the gold-digging secretary are too calculated to be sympathetic, let alone amusing. Devious romantic complications and sexual innuendo. A-III (br)

Millionairess, The (1960) Botched romantic-comedy set in London, where a pampered Italian heiress (Sophia Loren) takes a fancy to an idealistic Hindu doctor (Peter Sellers), but he disdains her money, then rejects her love, until she becomes more spiritual and he becomes more materialistic. Directed by Anthony Asquith from a play by George Bernard Shaw, the result is a heavy-handed vehicle for its Italian star whose seductive appeal gets lost in a witless script and a blizzard of elegant costumes, leaving the burden of the comedy to Sellers whose dialect routines grow tiresome. Sexual situations and innuendo. A-III (br)

Mimic (1997) Creepy horror film in which husband-and-wife scientists (Jeremy Northam and Mira Sorvino) desperately try to eradicate a colony of human-sized killer insects breeding in the subway tunnels of New York City, where homeless people have become their first victims. Director Guillermo Del Toro's monster movie provides periodic jolts through scary special effects, but suspense ultimately gives way to formula storytelling. Recurring fantasy violence with occasional rough language and profanity. A-III (R)

Mind of Mr. Soames, The (1970) Offbeat story about the education of a 30-year-old man (Terence Stamp) who, until a delicate brain operation restores consciousness, has been in a coma since birth. A compassionate physician (Robert Vaughn), realizing the man-child's need for tenderness and the simple pleasures of childhood, opposes the unyielding authoritarian rigors of the neurophysiological hospital staff in whose charge he has been placed. Though raising some provocative questions about the learning process and responsibility, director Alan Cooke's work is too episodic and diffuse to provide many insights in the matter. A-II (PG)

Mini-Skirt Mob, The (1968) Honeymooning couple (Ross Hagen and Sherry Jackson) are terrorized by motorcycle gang in a tawdry action film directed by Maury Dexter. Excessive sadistic violence and sexual innuendo. O (br)

Ministry of Fear (1944) Moody version of Graham Greene's novel about an Englishman (Ray Milland) who stumbles onto a Nazi spy ring during the London Blitz, then finds himself framed for murder and on the run from the police. Directed by Fritz Lang, it's a nightmare situation with an innocent man uncertain of what he's gotten into or whom he can trust. Much menace, some stylized violence, and murky references to a mercy killing. A-III (br)

Minnie and Moskowitz (1972) Improbable romance of a zany parking-lot attendant (Seymour Cassel) and a museum assistant (Gena Rowlands), carried on in shouting matches throughout Los Angeles. Minnie with her history of failed masochistic relationships and Moskowitz with his utter lack of direction are so unsuited for each other that the ending is sheer Hollywood romantic fantasy. Director John Cassavetes in characteristic improvisational style has made a wry, harshly shot, but warmly acted contemporary version of the old saw about the attraction between opposites. Some rough language and sexual references. A-III (PG)

Minute to Pray, a Second to Die, A (1968) Routine Italian Western directed by Franco Giraldi about an outlaw hero (Alex Cord) who, fearing he has epilepsy, tries to go straight. Much standard violence. A-III (br)

Miracle, The (1991) A motherless teenager (Niall Byrne) in Bray, an Irish seaside resort town, finds himself strongly attracted to a visiting US actress (Beverly D'Angelo) old enough to be his mother, despite the vehement objections of his alcoholic father (Donal McCann). Irish-born writer-director Neil Jordan's inconclusive melodrama toys with incest and is overwhelmed by its drawn-out predictability, though the setting and some nice performances provide marginal interest. Brief sexual encounter, occasional rough language, and minor violence. A-III (R)

Miracle in Milan (1951) Marvelous Italian fable about an unspoiled youth (Francesco Golisano)who leaves the orphanage in which he was raised and, on the outskirts of post-WW II Milan, chances upon an encampment of homeless people, whose impoverished lives are transformed by his simple, unassuming joy of life. Directed by Vittorio de Sica, the movie looks beyond the miserable conditions of poverty to see the humanity of the poor, pokes satire at the rich, and ends in the happy fantasy of a fairytale. Subtitles. A-II (nr)

Miracle in the Rain (1954) Unabashedly sentimental tale of a WW II romance between a shy Manhattan secretary (Jane Wyman) and a genial, upbeat soldier (Van Johnson), whose death in combat leaves her devastated until seeing him in a vision on the steps of St. Patrick's Cathedral. Directed by Rudolph Maté from a story by Ben Hecht, the whirlwind romance is charmingly acted, then turns into a manipulative tearjerker with a spiritually uplifting ending satisfying romantics, though others may find it emotionally empty. Romantic complications and assorted domestic problems. A-II (br)

Miracle Mile (1989) Writer-director Steve DeJarnatt's woefully ill-conceived story about a promising romance between two strangers (Anthony Edwards and Mare Winningham) loses its quirky appeal when it diverts from giddy romance to far-fetched doomsday thriller played out on the mean streets of Los Angeles. Much gratuitous, grisly violence exploiting the horror of a pending nuclear disaster, and profanity laced with sexual vulgarities. O (R)

Miracle of Fatima (see: **The Miracle of Our Lady of Fatima**)

Miracle of Marcelino, The (1955) A foundling left at a Franciscan monastery in 19th-century Spain is spoiled by the attention of all the monks who raise him until, as a mischievous five-year-old (Pablito Calvo), the lad's disobedience leads to a miraculous encounter with the crucified Christ. Directed by Ladislao Vajda, the Spanish production's story of childhood innocence and the power of faith is told simply but with sincerity and good humor. Dubbed in English, the movie's miracle may tax the credibility of some, but all can enjoy its picture of a child in unusual circumstances. A-I (nr)

Miracle of Morgan's Creek, The (1944) Wacky WW II comedy in which a small-town girl (Betty

Hutton) sneaks out of the house to go to a dance for servicemen, gets drunk, and wakes up with vague memories of having gotten married, then discovers she's pregnant. Writer-director Preston Sturges plays the situation for all it's worth and then some, especially in the reactions of her irate father (William Demarest) and the local lad (Eddie Bracken) who loves her, though parents are unlikely to be amused. Comic treatment of unwed pregnancy and a truckload of sexual innuendo. A-III (br)

Miracle of Our Lady of Fatima, The (1952) When a young girl reports seeing a vision of the Blessed Mother in 1917 Portugal, she is harassed, then arrested by atheistic government officials, but nothing can stop the crowds of faithful from coming to the site in expectation of a miracle. Directed by John Brahm, the religious story is treated with reverence, yet is dramatically interesting with such characters as the good-hearted thief (Gilbert Roland) who helps her. Inspirational fare. A-I (br)

Miracle of Saint Therese (1959) Engrossing French production dramatizing the life of the saint known as the Little Flower, who entered the Carmelite cloister at Lisieux at the age of 14, died of tuberculosis in 1897 at age 24, and was canonized in 1925. Director Andre Haguet makes a serious, largely successful attempt to picture the saint's life within her religious community and the meaning of her "little way" to spiritual perfection, with a winning performance by France Descaut in the title role, and fine use of the visuals to convey the period and the interior life of a young woman who became a saint. Dubbed. A-I (br)

Miracle of the Bells, The (1948) Sticky cardboard tale of a parish priest (Frank Sinatra) presiding over the burial of a former movie star in a played-out mining town, where a media-hyped "miracle" rejuvenates the community. Director Irving Pichel stumbles through the contrived story until an unconvincing ending few will find inspirational. Good intentions but bogus results. A-I (br)

Miracle of the White Stallions (1963) Disney drama about the WW II attempt to smuggle the Spanish Riding School's prize Lipizzan stallions out of Vienna before the city is occupied by the Russians. Directed by Arthur Hiller, the precision-riding sequences show the great training of these famed horses, though their evacuation by military trucks is delayed somewhat by a bloodless battle sequence at the Czech border. Worthwhile family fare. A-I (br)

Miracle on 34th Street (1947) Familiar seasonal favorite follows a department-store Santa (Edmund Gwenn) as he strives to convince a lonely little girl (Natalie Wood) that he's the genuine article, despite the objections of her rigidly pragmatic mother (Maureen O'Hara) and a court trial that hinges on the US Post Office. Director George Seaton's amusing romantic fantasy has its sentimental moments while spreading a reasonable amount of holiday cheer, largely due Gwenn's charming performance as Kris Kringle. Problems of single parenthood. A-II (br)

Miracle on 34th Street (1994) Sweetly updated remake of the 1947 holiday classic about the department-store Santa (Richard Attenborough) who believes he is actually Santa Claus and ends up in court defending his claim, in the process winning over the cynical mom (Elizabeth Perkins) who hired him and her dubious five-year-old (Mara Wilson). Director Les Mayfield's gently values-centered but sluggishly paced family movie stresses faith in things unseen, hope for the future, and a generous loving spirit that underlies the true meaning of Christmas. A-I (PG)

Miracle Woman, The (1931) Dated drama in which an embittered minister's daughter (Barbara Stanwyck) falls in with a cynical grifter (Sam Hardy) who turns her into a big-time evangelist, until she's reformed by the love of a blind composer (David Manners). Directed by Frank R. Capra, the expose of a fake faith-healer is softened by the sentimental romance, but the two strands never quite jell, despite fine performances and a number of memorable scenes, especially the roaring finale as fire consumes a packed tabernacle. Exploiting people's religious faith, sexual situations, and romantic complications. A-III (br)

Mirage (1965) Gregory Peck plays an amnesia victim who is being stalked by a killer, Diane Baker is a woman out of his past, Walter Matthau is a private detective, and, shrouded in the background, is a world peace organization. Directed by Edward Dmytryk, the ingredients of this suspense-filled puzzle may be familiar, but their solution is intriguing and nicely integrated in the New York setting. A-II (br)

Mirror Crack'd, The (1980) Agatha Christie mystery with Miss Marple (Angela Landsbury) solving a murder committed while an American movie company is on location in England. Despite a valiant cast (Tony Curtis, Rock Hudson, Kim Novak, and Elizabeth Taylor), director Guy Hamilton fails to supply any pace, style, or suspense to the proceedings. Some mild profanity and stylized violence. A-II (PG)

Mirror Has Two Faces, The (1996) Drawn-out romantic comedy in which a frumpy college professor (Barbra Streisand) accepts the platonic marriage proposal of a handsome math teacher (Jeff Bridges), then sets about trying to seduce her husband. Also directed by Streisand, the glossy proceedings are mildly amusing but highly predictable in what some may see as essentially a vanity production. Sexual innuendo and a few instances of profanity as well as rough language. A-III (PG-13)

Mirrors (1977) Failed horror tale directed by Noel Black in which a woman (Kitty Winn), while vacationing in New Orleans, comes to fear she is the target of an occult group, then seeks help from a doctor (Peter Donat) who appears to believe her incredible story. Psychological fears and supernatural menace. A-III (PG)

Misadventures of Mr. Wilt, The (1990) Black comedy about a Walter Mitty-like college professor (Griff

Rhys Jones) caught in a bizarre set of circumstances involving his missing wife (Alison Steadman) and a dimwitted police inspector (Mel Smith) who's convinced that the prof has murdered her. Directed by Michael Tuchner, the British farce is intermittently amusing and has some wit, though much depends on one's tolerance for rude humor, saucy situations, and outrageous misunderstandings, caused mostly by an inflatable woman-sized doll of the sex-shop variety. Some rough language and sexual references not all adults will find suitable as a means of ridicule. A-IV (nr)

Mischief (1985) The class nerd (Doug McKeon) and a cool newcomer (Chris Nash) team up to pursue girls in a small-town high school in 1950s Ohio. Directed by Mel Damski, it's a sloppily executed affair in which all adults are depicted as semi-morons, and its idea of humor is obscene language and boys peering up girl's dresses. Excessively graphic bedroom scene. O (R)

Misery (1990) Injured in a car crash, a romance novelist (James Caan) is rescued by his Number One fan (Kathy Bates) who keeps him in her remote farmhouse and becomes his deadly tormentor. Stephen King's horror story becomes a tautly edited, gripping psychological thriller in the hands of director Rob Reiner, who coaxes topnotch performances from the chilling Bates, the terrorized Caan, and a crafty sheriff (Richard Farnsworth). Climactic graphic violence and minimal rough language. A-III (R)

Misfits, The (1961) After getting a Reno divorce, a free but lonely woman (Marilyn Monroe) takes up with a cowboy (Clark Gable) and other inveterate loners (Eli Wallach, Montgomery Clift, and Thelma Ritter), then is appalled by a roundup of wild horses. Written by Arthur Miller and directed by John Huston, the theme seems to have something to do with the fear of being trapped in romantic relationships, though the treatment is obscure, if not muddled. Some sexual inferences. A-III (br)

Mishima: A Life in Four Chapters (1985) Writer-director Paul Schrader attempts to do justice to the complex and flamboyant Japanese writer Yukio Mishima, who committed suicide by military ritual in 1970. The result is flat and listless, an illustrated slide lecture that doesn't come close to capturing the enigmatic Mishima. Brief nudity and violence. A-III (R)

Miss Firecracker (1989) Lifetime outcast (Holly Hunter), living in the shadow of her beautiful older cousin (Mary Steenburgen), tries to win her town's annual Fourth of July beauty pageant. Adapted by Beth Henley from her play and directed by Thomas Schlamme, the result reveals an eye and ear for life lived off the beaten track in the Deep South, and its characters never lack dignity, no matter how wacky or how unrealistic their hopes and dreams. Some sexual innuendo and minimal fisticuffs. A-III (PG)

Miss Grant Takes Richmond (1949) Dippy comedy in which a gambler (William Holden) hires a secretarial-school novice (Lucille Ball) as part of a cover operation, then is undone by her zeal to make good. Directed by Lloyd Bacon, the funny business with Ball's dumb but honest secretary is ably abetted by a solid supporting cast, but the contrived situation becomes tiresome. Comic treatment of illegal activities. A-II (br)

Miss Mary (1986) British governess (Julie Christie) recalls the years she spent in Buenos Aires caring for the children of a wealthy family. The real interest of this Argentinean production, directed by Maria Luisa Bemberg, is its depiction of the politically confused and socially demoralized climate prior to the Peron dictatorship. Mature themes including several sexual encounters. A-III (R)

Missile to the Moon (1959) Low-budget sci-fi clunker from director Richard Cunha about scientists taking two escaped convicts on a space-shot to the moon, where they discover a dying city of women in an underground cave. Unconvincing menace and sexual innuendo. A-II (br)

Missing (1982) Director Costa-Gavras in his first American movie presents a taut and powerful drama based upon an actual event, that of an American father's search for his son, a 31-year-old writer living with his wife in a Latin-American country, who has disappeared in the midst of the brutal repression following a right-wing coup. Jack Lemmon and Sissy Spacek are outstanding as the concerned father and his daughter-in-law, with John Shea giving capable support as the missing man. Significant and absorbing work on a topical and important theme of human rights. General atmosphere of menace, a depiction of the aftermath of bloodshed, and occasional profanity. A-II (PG)

Missing in Action (1984) Chuck Norris stars in a hokey, derivative movie directed by Joseph Vito about a commando operation mounted to rescue Americans still held prisoner in Vietnam. Gene Hackman did it better in **Uncommon Valor**. Graphic wartime violence, rough language, and Asian stereotyping. A-III (R)

Missing in Action 2: The Beginning (1985) In a sequel with even more violence than its violent predecessor, this time around the blank-faced hero (Chuck Norris) is a prisoner-of-war in Vietnam a few years prior to the original. Directed by Lance Hool, this run-of-the-mill war movie overdoses on graphic depictions of brutality and sadism. O (R)

Missing Women (1951) Crime programmer directed by Philip Ford in which a woman victim (Penny Edwards) of car robbers talks her way into the gang, then busts it. Stylized violence and life-threatening situations. A-II (br)

Mission, The (1986) In the 1750s, the large and prosperous Jesuit Indian missions of South America were divided between Spain and Portugal. In retelling these events, Robert Bolt's screenplay focuses not on the religious but on the sociopolitical dimension of the colonial era and its injustices. The epic production is visually splendid, but Roland Joffe's direction is erratic and bogs down in contrasting a non-violent priest (Jermey Irons) and one (Robert De Niro) who leads the Indians against a colonial army. Although flawed, the work recalls a past that provides a context for current Latin-American struggles. Violence and ethnographic nudity. A-III (PG)

Mission: Impossible (1996) Framed as a traitor, a top US spy (Tom Cruise) must evade capture by the CIA, identify the real culprit, and prevent a list of American spies from falling into enemy hands. Based on the vintage TV series, director Brian De Palma's sleek action-thriller has an impossibly complicated plot, but its exciting action scenes, special effects, and swift pacing make it high-style escapist entertainment. Some stylized violence and occasional profanity. A-III (PG-13)

Missionary, The (1982) Writer-producer Michael Palin (of the Monty Python troupe) also stars as the Rev. Charles Fortescue, a missionary sent to the slums of London by his bishop (Denholm Elliot) to open up a home for fallen women, and with Lady Ames (Maggie Smith) as his patron, he has great success. Unfortunately, there is a rather snide quality to the comedy's religious and social criticism, and there is one incredibly crude exchange between Mr. Fortescue and a tough prostitute. Some obscene language. O (R)

Mississippi (1935) Affable period melodrama with comedy supplied by W.C. Fields as a showboat captain and some Rodgers-and-Hart songs crooned by pistol-packing Bing Crosby, who plays the Singing Killer. Director Edward Sutherland succeeds far better with Fields's comedy routines than Crosby's romantic problems with two sisters (Joan Bennett and Gail Patrick). Some comic violence. A-II (br)

Mississippi Burning (1988) Fictionalized version of the 1964 murder of three young civil-rights activists in Mississippi focuses on the conflict between two FBI agents (Gene Hackman and Willem Dafoe) over how to handle the investigation. Director Alan Parker powerfully re-creates the brutal racist climate of the times, but the questionable vigilante tactics used to crack the case may confuse those unfamiliar with the real events. Unrelenting atmosphere of violence and racist rhetoric, together with much profanity. A-IV (R)

Mississippi Gambler (1953) Stale tale of a poor but honest Southerner (Tyrone Power) who, with the financial backing of a frontier adventurer (John McIntire), makes his fortune as a riverboat gambler and wins the heart of a New Orleans belle (Piper Laurie). Directed by Rudolph Maté, the colorful atmosphere of the pre-Civil War setting proves of more interest than does the lackluster scenario. An assortment of dishonest characters, romantic entanglements, and a duel of "honor." A-III (br)

Mississippi Masala (1992) Upbeat interracial love story involving a young woman (Sarita Choudhury) with family roots in India and an enterprising African-American (Denzel Washington) whose romance is opposed by the families and friends of both. Only a sluggish pace detracts from director Mira Nair's warmhearted exploration of racial taboos and family values. Very brief bedroom scene with a flash of nudity, momentary violence, and minimal rough language. A-III (R)

Mississippi Mermaid (1970) Disappointing French melodrama about the mail-order bride (Catherine Deneuve) of a rich planter in the tropics (Jean-Paul Belmondo) who proves to be an imposter when she cleans out his bank account and disappears — but not for very long. A minor effort from director Francois Truffaut, it pays tribute to the old Hollywood action-adventures, while at the same time satirizing them with an incredibly absurd plot made worse by being badly dubbed into English. For Truffaut fans only. Brief nudity. A-III (GP)

Missouri Breaks, The (1976) Jack Nicholson heads a band of rustlers, and Marlon Brando is the ruthless killer hired to hunt them down. Director Arthur Penn's failed Western is full of loose ends and fey dialogue, an embarrassing muddlement that lumbers to a brutal conclusion for want of anything better to do. Excessive violence. O (PG)

Mister Buddwing (1966) Forgettable melodrama about an amnesia victim (James Garner) whose career ambitions and marital woes are shown in flashbacks and dreams as his memory returns. Directed by Delbert Mann, the story is needlessly confusing in the use of three actresses in the role of his wife, and the result doesn't add up to much. Mature sexual themes including abortion. A-III (br)

Mister Johnson (1991) In 1923 British West Africa, a native clerk (Maynard Eziashi) who fancies himself a true English gentleman, wrecks his cherished relationship with his British boss (Pierce Brosnan) by his carefree thieving ways. Bruce Beresford directs a charmingly realized period-piece full of wry observation of British colonialism, but the effect is marred by some cardboard characters and ponderous pacing. Minimal stylized violence and some racial epithets. A-II (PG-13)

Mister Roberts (1955) The conflicts between the bored crew and mean-spirited captain (James Cagney) of a cargo ship in the South Pacific during the waning months of WW II are tempered by the executive officer of the title (Henry Fonda), who jeopardizes his long-sought transfer to combat duty in order to get the crew a long-overdue shore leave. Directed by John Ford and Mervyn LeRoy, the result largely overcomes its stage origins, thanks to vigorous staging of the shipboard antics, as well as memorable lead performances abetted by William Powell as the ship's sage doctor and Jack Lemmon as its callow laundry-and-morale officer. Broad sexual innuendo. A-III (br)

Mister V (see: **Pimpernel Smith**)

Mistress (1992) Flat satire of the movie business centers around the compromises made by a failed producer-director team (Martin Landau and Robert Wuhl) when three backers (Robert De Niro, Danny Aiello, and Eli Wallach) of their proposed movie insist their girlfriends be given starring roles. Director Barry Primus's sluggish mix of comedy and drama is damaged by stale characterizations and lead actor Wuhl's dull performance. Much sexual innuendo and some rough language. A-III (R)

Misty (1961) Nicely told tale of children (David Ladd and Pam Smith) who devote themselves to training a wild pony captured on Chincoteague, an island off the coast of Virginia. Produced by Robert B. Radnitz and directed by James B. Clark, the youngsters are appealing, the history of the island's wild horses is interesting, and the result is superior family entertainment. A-I (br)

Misunderstood (1984) Gene Hackman plays a widower who is slow to come to terms with his loss and make a new life for himself and his two young sons (Henry Thomas and Huckleberry Fox). Director Jerry Schatzberg's picture is pleasant enough, with competent acting and exotic settings (Tunisia), but there are no dramatic sparks to speak of until a contrived tearjerker of an ending. Some vulgar language. A-II (PG)

Mitchell (1975) Los Angeles police detective (Joe Don Baker) pursues two suave lawyers (Martin Balsam and John Saxon) mixed up in the heroin trade by using unorthodox methods that look suspiciously like police brutality. Directed by Andrew V. McLaglen, it's a fairly silly, slapped-together affair whose thin plot is nothing more than an excuse to string together a series of routine chases. Most, but not all, of the rough stuff is kept off-camera, substituting instead some sexual exploitation scenes. O (R)

Mixed Company (1974) Joseph Bologna and Barbara Harris star in a sentimental comedy-drama about a couple who decide to augment their family, which already includes three children, with three more, each from a different race. Melville Shavelson directs a good-natured movie that carefully avoids any realistic situations of racial tension. Mildly entertaining, sometimes funny and touching, it seems like something made for television except for its strong language. A-III (PG)

Mixed Nuts (1994) Threadbare comedy takes place on Christmas Eve at a phone-in suicide prevention center, where a trio of eccentrics (Steve Martin, Rita Wilson, and Madeline Kahn) take lots of kooky calls while being visited by a stream of oddballs (including Juliette Lewis, Anthony LaPaglia, and Liev Schreiber) seeking holiday cheer. Writer-director Nora Ephron's contrived attempt at screwball comedy frequently looks like amateur night, due to a leaden script which wastes the comic talents of all involved. Accidental violence played for laughs, intermittent sexual innuendo, and a fleeting glimpse of nudity. A-III (PG-13)

M'Liss (1936) Sentimental Western tale from the Bret Harte story in which the spunky girl of the title (Anne Shirley) is saved from the orphanage after the death of her alcoholic widowed father (Guy Kibbee) by the support of his saloon friends and her schoolteacher (John Beal), whose concern for her turns to love. Directed by George Nicholls, Jr., the colorful characters and the 1880s setting help compensate for a wispy story of a frontier community taking care of its own. A-I (br)

Mo' Better Blues (1990) Self-absorbed jazz trumpeter (Denzel Washington) remains loyal to his inept manager (Spike Lee) while studiously avoiding commitment to either of his impatient lovers (Joie Lee and Cynda Williams), until his manager's gambling ways change all of their lives. Lee also produced, wrote, and directed this tale of interwoven relationships, which features Washington's finely shaded performance as a character who gradually comes to terms with his egotism. Much casual use of rough language, fairly explicit treatment of sexual relationships, and a graphic scene of gut-wrenching violence. A-IV (R)

Mo' Money (1992) A con-artist (Damon Wayans) disappoints his younger brother (Marlon Wayans) by taking a straight job at a credit-card company to impress a girl (Stacey Dash), then gets involved in a big-time scam ripping off the firm. Director Peter Macdonald's sluggish and predictable comedy pulverizes the work ethic while it exalts stealing as the only cool way to beat the system. Grand theft glamorized, some exploitative violence, sexist attitudes with implied encounters, recurring rough language, and racial stereotyping. O (R)

Mob, The (1951) Standard crime thriller in which a tough cop (Broderick Crawford) goes undercover as a longshoreman in order to get the goods on a waterfront mob (Ernest Borgnine, Neville Brand, and others). Directed by Robert Parrish, there's some fanciful action along the way, with colorful characters (notably, Richard Kiley) but few surprises. Menace and stylized violence. A-II (br)

Mobsters (1991) Glossy Prohibition-era gangster movie follows the bloody rise to power of young thugs Lucky Luciano, Meyer Lansky, Bugsy Siegel, and Frank Costello (Christian Slater, Patrick Dempsey, Richard Grieco, and Costas Mandylor) by murdering the two reigning dons (Anthony Quinn and Michael Gambon). Director Michael Karbelnikoff glamorizes the killers all through this humdrum rehash of far better gangster movies of yesteryear. Excessive violence, uncritical portrayal of murderers, much rough language, a restrained bedroom scene, and occasional nudity. O (R)

Moby Dick (1930) Early talkie loosely drawn from the Melville novel has Captain Ahab (John Barrymore) lose leg and fiancé (Joan Bennett), then dedicate himself to killing the white whale responsible for his misfortunes, after which he returns to find his love has not forgotten him. Directed by Lloyd Bacon, the romantic subplot detracts from the epic sea yarn of man vs. blind beast, though what survives of Melville is credibly visualized, with enough raw energy and rugged action to make it memorable. Stylized violence, the dangers of life at sea, and romantic complications. A-II (br)

Moby Dick (1956) Uneven adaptation of the Herman Melville classic follows the vengeful course of Captain Ahab (miscast Gregory Peck) in quest of the great white whale. Co-scripted by Ray Bradbury and director John Huston, it captures well the details of 19th-century whaling life, but the voyage of the Pequod at the center of the story is curiously slack and largely uninvolving. Stylized violence. A-I (br)

Moby Dick (1998) Faithful adaptation of Herman Melville's epic novel about the hunt for the great white whale of the title follows the doomed voyage of a 19th-century Nantucket whaler under Captain Ahab (Patrick Stewart), whose quest for personal revenge against the dumb sea beast results in disaster. Directed by Franc Roddam, the British-Australian TV co-production succeeds best as a sea spectacle with convincing action sequences, but the drama is less effective because of erratic characterizations and heavily accented dialogue. Scenes depicting the bloody business of whaling and the brutish character of some employed in it. A-II (PG)

Mod Squad, The (1999) Inept crime picture based on a 30-year-old TV series about three young criminals (Claire Danes, Omar Epps, and Giovanni Ribisi) given a second chance to work undercover for the police, then find themselves battling corrupt cops linked to a drug gang. Directed by Scott Silver, the plot is as stale as the picture's premise, but making matters even worse are surly cardboard characters in formula proceedings that prove dramatically inane and emotionally inert. Hokey violence, sexual situations, recurring rough language, and occasional profanity. A-III (R)

Model Shop, The (1969) French romantic drama about a brief encounter between an alienated Los Angeles dropout (Gary Lockwood) and an attractive model (Anouk Aimee) who takes him to bed, tells him her life story, and he gives her money for her fare back to France. Though beautifully produced and mildly appealing, the movie lacks the charm and novelty of director Jacques Demy's earlier works and their unabashed romantic exuberance. A-III (PG)

Modern Problems (1981) Chevy Chase plays an air-traffic controller possessed of extrasensory powers, which are put to no good use in a dreary, slipshod comedy that intersperses long, boring stretches with only a few patches of fitful humor. Directed and co-written by Ken Shapiro, it has some vulgarity and incidental sexual by-play. A-III (PG)

Modern Romance (1981) Obsessive and insecure film editor (Albert Brooks) has an on-again, off-again relationship with his girlfriend (Kathryn Harrold), but he can't break this recurring cycle of misery. Also written and directed by Brooks, it is a sometimes very funny movie, but suffers from a lack of structure and too much Brooks. Still, two hilarious sequences in the cutting-room might make some viewers willing to forgive the movie's frequent slow stretches. Some brief semi-nudity, occasional rough language, and a muddled view of sexual morality. A-III (R)

Modern Times (1936) Charlie Chaplin's insightful fable of man versus machine centers in the artificiality of industrialized society and the anxieties caused by the Depression, as Charlie dances his way through the hazards of an assembly-line job. A model of silent comedic technique and refined slapstick humor, the movie marks the last appearance of the Little Tramp character, as Charlie takes his final walk down the long empty road, this time in the company of Paulette Goddard, who adds an element of freshness to the plot's old-fashioned romance. A-I (G)

Moderns, The (1988) Set in Paris in 1926, this romantic drama follows the travails of some American expatriates, chief among them a struggling painter (Keith Carradine), his estranged wife (Linda Fiorentino), her nouveau-riche companion (John Lone), and a frustrated society columnist (Wallace Shawn). Director Alan Rudolph re-creates a wonderful sense of the period and the artistic millieu that flourished then. Some nudity, brief violence, and implications of sexual hedonism. A-III (nr)

Modesty Blaise (1966) Monica Vitti, Terence Stamp, and Dirk Bogarde in a plot about a shipment of diamonds that is merely an excuse for a series of impossible adventures and characters that parody the cliches of popular culture. The opulent sets, costumes, and gadgets are stylishly photographed, and the dialogue and situations are outrageously exaggerated. Director Joseph Losey obviously enjoyed spoofing areas of the dark world that he has treated seriously so often before. A-III (br)

Mogambo (1953) Lightweight romantic adventure in which a veteran African hunter (Clark Gable) takes a client on a safari in the jungles of Kenya, then falls for his wife (Grace Kelly) until a stranded American entertainer (Ava Gardner) brings him to his senses. Director John Ford finds more romance in the exotic African settings than in the unconvincing Gable-Kelly relationship, though the humorous treatment keeps it from cloying. Romantic triangle and sexual innuendo. A-III (br)

Mohammad, Messenger of God (1977) Dramatic re-creation of the years from 610 A.D., when Mohammad was driven from Mecca for claiming to have received a new religion from the Angel Gabriel, to 630, when the victory of Islam was assured. The best feature of this religious epic directed by Moustapha Akkad is its sincerity in recounting the birth of Islam and some of the essential tenets of the Moslem religion. An international cast includes Anthony Quinn, Irene Papas, and Michael Ansara. Some scenes of restrained violence. A-II (PG)

Mohawk (1956) Colonial adventure set in the Mohawk Valley, where a frontier artist (Scott Brady) falls for the daughter (Rita Gam) of an Iroquois chief

(Ted de Corsia), while a crazed settler (John Hoyt) tries to stir an Indian war. Directed by Kurt Neumann, the story is more interested in the painter's romantic inclinations than the growing tension between settlers and Indians, with many of the action scenes using footage from 1939's Drums Along the Mohawk. Frontier violence and romantic complications. A-II (br)

Mole People, The (1956) Adventure clunker introduced by USC English prof Frank C. Baxter tells of archaeologists (John Agar and Hugh Beaumont) who discover an ancient Sumerian ruin on an Asian mountaintop, then are taken captive by its builders' descendents who had been driven by earthquakes to live in an underground city. Directed by Virgil Vogel, the ludicrous proceedings include some unconvincing menace from the burrowing creatures of the title, who have been enslaved by the Sumerians. Menacing situations. A-I (br)

Moll Flanders (1996) Uplifting costume drama based on the heroine (Robin Wright) of Daniel DeFoe's 1722 novel who triumphs over illegitimacy, poverty, prostitution, and the loss of her husband and baby in her struggle to carve a place for herself in a scornful, class-conscious world. Writer-director Pen Densham embroiders the original story with additional melodramatics, but never loses sight of the characters' humanity as they choose love and hope over despair. Fleeting bedroom scenes with nudity, brief violence, and minimal profanity. A-III (PG-13)

Molly (1950) When Molly Goldberg (Gertrude Berg) plays matchmaker, it threatens a business deal made by her husband Jake (Philip Loeb). Walter Hart directs the TV cast of "The Goldbergs," which began as a daytime radio-serial about the domestic ups-and-downs of a loving Jewish family in the Bronx. Though its production values are rudimentary, its picture of family life still has charm. A-I (br)

Molly Maguires, The (1970) Fact-based, hard-hitting drama set in the Pennsylvania coal-mining fields during the 1880s, when the mine owners hire an undercover agent (Richard Harris) to ferret out the leaders (Sean Connery and Anthony Zerbe) of a secret band of miners known as the Molly Maguires, who resort to terrorist tactics to force better pay and working conditions. Director Martin Ritt has made a thoughtful movie about the futility of using violence to redress injustices. More menace than bloodshed. A-II (PG)

Mom and Dad Save the World (1992) Silly sci-fi comedy about a far-distant planet's dictator (Jon Lovitz) who magnetically draws a suburban California couple (Teri Garr and Jeffrey Jones) to his kingdom, planning to force the wife to marry him. A witless script and Greg Beeman's heavy-handed direction produce a contrived, artificial spoof that quickly fizzles. A few off-color references. A-II (PG)

Moment by Moment (1978) Middle-aged Beverly Hills housewife (Lily Tomlin) succumbs to the charms of a young drifter (John Travolta). Devoid of dramatic action, save for scenes of lovemaking punctuated by little spats of no consequence, writer-director Jane Wagner's movie has hardly a glimmer of wit, intelligence, or credibility. Graphic and glossy depiction of adultery. O (R)

Mommie Dearest (1981) Faye Dunaway plays Joan Crawford in this unpleasant screen version of the harsh biography written by her adopted daughter, Christina. Director Frank Perry alternates heavy doses of sensation and sentimentality without really getting at anything that might make its subject credible. Only occasionally does the episodic and overlong movie rise above the level of verge-of-hysteria soap opera. Some brief but graphic violence, rough language, and vulgarity. A-III (PG)

Mon Homme (1997) Strained comical account of a happy streetwalker (Anouk Grinberg) who falls for a vagrant (Gerard Lanvin) and makes him her pimp, unaware he's cheating on her with a manicurist (Valeria Bruni Tedeschi) he is greedily pushing into prostitution. Writer-director Bertrand Blier's sexist comedy views women as mindless playthings willing to be debased and abused in their desperation to hold onto a man. Subtitles. Benign view of promiscuity, several sexual encounters tinged with violence, full nudity, some rough language, and an instance of profanity. O (nr)

Mona Lisa (1986) Love-starved small-time tough (Bob Hoskins in a memorable performance) falls in love with the prostitute (Cathy Tyson) he chauffeurs around town, only to be victimized by his own blind trust and devotion. This British production's depiction of underworld violence, deception, and betrayal leads nowhere. Brutal violence, brief nudity, and some profanity. O (R)

Money from Home (1953) Witless comedy directed by George Marshall in which a crooning sharpster (Dean Martin) tries to square a gambling debt by fixing a horserace through the substitution of his dimwitted cousin (Jerry Lewis) for the English jockey (Richard Haydn) imported to ride the favorite in a grueling steeplechase. Bungling underworld types and comic treatment of inebriation. A-I (br)

Money Jungle, The (1968) Routine detective melodrama about a private eye (John Ericson) who is hired to solve the mysterious murders of four geologists working aboard an off-shore oil rig. Intriguing but predictable plot competently directed by Francis D. Lyon. Violence. A-III (br)

Money Madness (1948) Lame crime-tale directed by Peter Stewart in which a waitress (Frances Rafferty) marries a pleasant-seeming stranger, who turns out to be a trigger-happy bankrobberber (Hugh Beaumont), with predictable results. Stylized violence and much menace. A-II (br)

Money Man (1993) Documentary follows self-proclaimed artist J.S.G. Boggs as he painstakingly creates counterfeit currency, which he then tries to get people to accept at face value, not as legal tender, but as a works of art. Writer-director Philip Haas looks at this dubious art form mainly through the perspective of Boggs, striking more of a whimsical note than a balanced look at whether he is in fact an artist or a con-artist. Some morally ambiguous situations. A-III (nr)

Money, Money, Money (1973) Amusing but overlong French comedy about a ragtag band of con-artists, petty thieves, bankrobberbers, and other paunchy, middle-aged underworld types (among them, Lino Ventura, Jacques Brel, and Charles Denner) adapt to changing times by turning to kidnapping political figures and extorting high ransoms from embarrassed governments. Directed by Claude Lelouch, the source of the comedy is how the inept misfits complement each other's foolishness and become so rich and successful that they themselves are kidnapped. The Gallic humor, including a Tahitian vacation among semi-clad native beauties, may escape some viewers. A-III (PG)

Money Pit, The (1986) A young engaged couple (Tom Hanks and Shelley Long) buy a mansion and suffer humorous consequences when trying to fix it up. The strained comedy resorts to heavy doses of slapstick, and the deteriorating condition of the house comes to mirror their increasingly exasperated relationship. Some sexually suggestive scenes are handled within the context of their successful efforts to build trust and strengthen commitment. A-II (PG)

Money Talks (1972) Using the same formula as his popular "Candid Camera" TV show, director Allen Funt presents a series of trite sketches and allegedly spontaneous routines designed to show how ordinary people react to situations involving money. Among the offerings, one can watch men pluck, with varying degrees of hesitancy, a dollar bill taped to the backside of a sweet young thing, or listen to Funt interview his pretty three-year-old daughter, who openly exhibits a preference for being rich. At least she's candid about it. A-II (PG)

Money Talks (1997) Mirthlessly violent comedy in which a street hustler (Chris Tucker) and a TV reporter (Charlie Sheen) are chased by the police while a gang of French diamond smugglers shoots up Los Angeles. Directed by Brett Ratner, the contrived proceedings creep along with lame but loud comedy routines and even louder gunfire, demolition-derby car chases, and assorted pyrotechnics. Excessive violence, sexual innuendo, and rough language. O (R)

Money Train (1995) Jokey buddy movie in which the lifelong friendship of two New York City transit cops is complicated by their competing for the same woman (Jennifer Lopez), then is further tested when one (Woody Harrelson) decides to pay off his gambling debts by hijacking a subway car loaded with cash, while the other (Wesley Snipes) tries to keep his partner from being caught. Director Joseph Ruben presents a violent, morally bankrupt action movie in which thieves take on the stature of heroes worthy of admiration. Uncritical depiction of crime, considerable graphic violence, a bedroom scene, and constant rough language. O (R)

Money, Women and Guns (1958) Routine Western directed by Richard H. Bartlett in which a detective (Jock Mahoney) is hired to locate the heirs of a bushwhacked miner, then determine if one of them is the murderer. Frontier violence. A-I (br)

Mongolian Tale, A (1997) Wistful story of the Mongolian Steppes, where a caring old woman raises an unrelated boy and girl, but their plan to marry ends when the boy is sent to school in the city, then the two meet a dozen years later and reflect on the unexpected paths their lives took. Chinese director Xie Fei's poetic tale of love and loss is simple, yet moving in its lyrical exploration of universal themes. Subtitles. Mild sexual innuendo, brief violence, and minimal rough language. A-II (nr)

Monitors, The (1969) Failed satire about a police force of the future which relies on thought control to bring peace and order in a society beset by violence, brutality, and rapaciousness. Directed by Jack Shea, a talented cast headed by Guy Stockwell, Susan Oliver, and Keenan Wynn try desperately but fail to find anything humorous in a plot both tedious and inane. A-III (M)

Monkey Business (1931) The four Marx Brothers (Groucho, Chico, Harpo, and Zeppo) cause all manner of havoc as stowaways aboard an ocean-liner and even more among some gangsters ashore. Directed by Norman Z. McLeod, the manic absurdity of the wacky sight gags and verbal mayhem keep the nonsensical situation from growing tiresome. Slapstick comedy and zany dialogue, including absurd double entendres. A-I (br)

Monkey Business (1952) Halting comedy about an absentminded chemist (Cary Grant) working on a youth-producing drug in a research lab, where a chimpanzee concocts an effective youth formula of his own which is unwittingly tested out on the chemist and his wife (Ginger Rogers). Director Howard Hawks has a top comedy cast, but the silly reversions to childhood are too thin to generate enough laughs to be very memorable. Suspicions of infidelity and other sexual innuendo. A-III (br)

Monkey Hustle, The (1977) Black exploitation comedy about some supposedly loveable con-artists who rally an inner-city neighborhood threatened by highway construction. Director Arthur Marks gets some good acting (Yaphet Kotto, Rosalind Cash, Kirk Calloway, and Randy Brooks) but not much else. Some rough language and a frank treatment of sexual matters. A-III (PG)

Monkey Shines: An Experiment in Fear (1988) Director George Romero's attempt to upgrade his exploitation image flops with this tasteless effort that sees a lab-tortured monkey turn killer after being trained to serve the needs of a paraplegic (Jason Beghe). Graphic injection scenes, grisly murders and mayhem, much menace, and an explicit kinky-sex scene. O (R)

Monkey Trouble (1994) When a lonely little girl (Thora Birch) finds a runaway monkey, she hides it from her parents (Mimi Rogers and Christopher McDonald), unaware that it has been trained to be a pickpocket and in housebreaking by an organ-grinding Gypsy (Harvey Keitel) hot on its trail. Franco Amurri directs a sweet, lively family comedy in which a youngster develops a sense of responsibility in caring for her hidden charge and reforming its behavior. Some bathroom humor and mild menace. A-II (PG)

Monkeys Go Home (1967) Disney comedy in which ex-GI Dean Jones inherits an olive farm in France, retrains four Space Program astro-chimps to help out when a shortage of local olive-pickers develops, and outwits a conniving real-estate man with the aid of a refreshing lass (Yvette Mimieux) and the village priest (Maurice Chevalier). Andrew V. McLaglen directs a slapdash plot with monkey-shines galore that will appeal more to youngsters than their parents. A-I (br)

Monolith Monsters, The (1957) Mild sci-fi thriller set in the Southwest, where local folks (notably Lola Albright, Grant Williams, and Les Tremayne) confront a meteorite's trail of fist-sized black rocks which turn people to stone and grow to the size of skyscrapers when touched by water — and rain is in the forecast. Directed by John Sherwood, the initial situation is intriguing, then is stretched out in pedestrian fashion until the pace picks up again in a salty ending. Menacing situations. A-I (br)

Monsieur Hire (1990) Intriguing psychological puzzler about a pathetic loner (Michel Blanc) who spends his nights spying on a young woman (Sandrine Bonnaire) in an apartment across the way, but when he meets and falls in love with her, the results are tragic. Directed by Patrice Leconte, the French production subtly unfolds a strange, obsessive love story that starts with a murder investigation and ends plumbing the depths of a desperate soul. Subtitles. Mature themes in a highly charged erotic atmosphere. A-III (PG-13)

Monsieur Verdoux (1947) Written, produced, and directed by Charles Chaplin, the fact-based black comedy stars Chaplin in the title role as a French Bluebeard who marries wealthy women, then murders them for their money. Though his first serious role disappointed audiences of its day, Chaplin as a performer was never better in the subtlety of gesture and expression. There is much sharp wit in the script along with some great slapstick, notably from Martha Raye who proves impervious to all murderous stratagems. Its criticism of society's hypocrisy, however, is often strained and its attempts to punctuate serious themes with humor is uneven. A-III (nr)

Monsieur Vincent (1947) Lucid, moving account of St. Vincent de Paul's work among the poor and the oppressed in 17th-century France, from his first labors in a plague-ravaged village and his appeals to the conscience of the aristocracy, to the founding of an order devoted to charitable works and his death in 1660. Director Maurice Cloche portrays the poverty of the times and the cruelty of the regime in starkly convincing fashion, providing a solid historical framework within which Pierre Fresnay's performance in the title role shines with a warm compassion and spiritual intensity which most viewers will find irresistibly compelling. Subtitles. High on the list of great religious movies. A-I (br)

Monsignor (1982) Christopher Reeve plays an American priest with a graduate degree in finance who rises in the church hierarchy when he gets the Vatican involved with the Mafia, but who pauses on the ladder of success to have an affair with a Carmelite postulant (Genevieve Bujold). Directed by Frank Perry, its melodramatic account of an ambitious cleric is so simplemindedly wrongheaded that it would be howlingly funny if it were not so grossly insulting to clergymen and institutional religion. Some gratuitous nudity. O (R)

Monster, The (1996) Screwball Italian comedy of mistaken identity in which a petty crook (Roberto Benigni) becomes a suspect in the hunt for a crazed sex-,murderer, then is set up by a beautiful woman (Nicoletta Braschi) who is actually an undercover cop. Director Benigni keeps up a fitfully funny pace, mixing raciness with sheer silliness as the hapless dope manages to avoid entrapment by the overeager police and a pompous psychologist (Michel Blanc). Subtitles. Vulgar sexual innuendo, minimal rough language, and an instance of profanity. A-III (nr)

Monster in a Box (1992) Monologuist Spalding Gray relates how writer's block chained him to a monster — the huge, autobiographical manuscript which he toted around for years before completing. As directed by Nick Broomfield, writer Gray's darkly funny one-man show generally overcomes the limitations of its form to engage audiences with lively storytelling and sharp observations. Mild sexual innuendo and references to his mother's suicide. A-II (PG-13)

Monster Meets the Gorilla, The (see: **The Boys from Brooklyn**)

Monster of Piedras Blancas, The (1958) Lethargic low-budget thriller directed by Irvin Berwick in which panicky villagers fear being devoured by a prehistoric amphibious reptile living in a cave beneath a lighthouse. Menacing situations and a few scary visuals. A-II (br)

Monster on the Campus (1958) Low-budget thriller in which a college biology teacher (Arthur Franz) turns into a rampaging prehistoric ape-man after scratching his hand on an ancient species of fish. Though the action is efficiently directed by Jack Arnold, the story's premise of evolution in reverse proves an overly pedestrian device for setting up the professor's murderous forays. Stylized violence with some intense menace. A-III (br)

Monster Squad, The (1987) Preteens foil Count Dracula's attempt to destroy an amulet bearing positive energy in this visually stunning mock-horror flick from writer-director Fred Dekker. Lots of fun and frolic but explosively realistic demise of the monsters may chill the very young. A-II (PG-13)

Monster That Challenged the World, The (1957) The title threat is a brood of gigantic killer crustaceans unleashed by an earthquake near a nuclear research center at California's Salton Sea. Trying to destroy these caterpillar-like monsters before they spread across the globe is an earnest naval officer (Tim Holt) whose attempts fail to work up much interest in a feeble effort directed by Arnold Laven. Scary situations with a few mild frights. A-I (br)

Monster Walks, The (1932) Creaky antique thriller directed by Frank Strayer in which a doctor (Rex Lease) tries to save his fiancé (Vera Reynolds) from being murdered while staying in a spooky house inhabited by her paralytic uncle (Sheldon Lewis), a surly handyman (Mischa Auer), a frightened chauffeur (Willie Best), and a howling ape locked in the basement. Feeble menace, some off-screen violence, and black stereotyping. A-II (br)

Monster Zero (1970) Routine Japanese science-fiction fantasy in which the title monster, Ghidrah, teamed with Godzilla and Rodan, attempt to conquer Earth for their masters on Planet X, while Nick Adams leads a force of astronauts out to stop them. Directed by Inoshiro Honda, the movie's special effects will hold the attention of young viewers while grown-ups will chuckle at the anthropomorphic monsters. A-I (G)

Montana (1950) Routine Western directed by Ray Enright brings an Australian sheepherder (Errol Flynn) to 1879 Montana, where the range is ruled by big cattle-ranchers, one of whom happens to be a woman (Alexis Smith) whose loyalties become hopelessly muddled when the ranchers declare all-out war on the sheepherders. Stylized violence and romantic complications. A-I (br)

Montana Belle (1952) Western outlaw Belle Starr (Jane Russell) is wooed by several members of the Dalton Gang (Scott Brady and Forrest Tucker), but she opts to marry a professional gambler (George Brent), then has to join her old pals in a bank robbery to save her beau's life. Directed by Allan Dwan, the script's focus on the contrived romantic angle proves tiresome, with little relief provided by occasional gunplay and Russell's singing. Stylized violence and sexual situations. A-III (br)

Montana Territory (1952) Routine Western directed by Ray Nazarro in which a band of gold robbers in 1863 Montana are headed by a corrupt sheriff (Preston Foster) who uses an upright youth (Lon McCallister) to fend off local vigilantes. Frontier violence. A-I (br)

Monte Walsh (1970) Once the Wild West was tamed, cowboys like Monte Walsh (Lee Marvin) found it hard to adapt to the demands of society. Jeanne Moreau and Jack Palance join Marvin in strong performances in a seriocomic study of ordinary cowpokes put out of work by a changing cattle industry that director William Fraker makes interesting despite a weak and aimless script with a hopelessly melodramatic climax. Some Hollywood heroics featuring fist fights and gun play. A-III (PG)

Monterey Pop (1969) Eye-staggering, ear-popping souvenir of the June 1967 Monterey music festival briefly captures the spirit of an age and a generation. The performers include The Mamas and the Papas, Jefferson Airplane, The Who, Janis Joplin, Jimi Hendrix, and Ravi Shankar, who closes the concert with his extraordinary sitar playing. Some sexually suggestive lyrics and gestures. A-III (nr)

Month by the Lake, A (1995) Slight but charming romance from a story by H.E. Bates focuses on the shifting, often comical, relationship between two middle-aged Britons (Vanessa Redgrave and Edward Fox) at an Italian resort on Lake Como in May 1937. Director John Irvin tries to turn what is little more than an anecdote about a self-sufficient spinster and a dim, self-important businessman into something more substantial by its evocation of a world whose innocence was lost in WW II. Brief scene of an attempted rape. A-III (PG)

Monty Python and the Holy Grail (1975) Departing from their BBC television format of unconnected skits, the Python comedy troupe zero in on the single subject of King Arthur and his dimwitted knights of the roundabout table. Directed by the Python's Terry Gilliam and Terry Jones, the episodic narrative strings together a series of gags, most of which are allowed to cross the threshold of boredom and then repeated to test one's patience further. Their brand of irreverent humor is an acquired taste, appealing to those who can find amusement in the concept of a feisty knight whose extremities are being lopped off one by one, gamely urging a superior but reluctant opponent to fight on. Comic violence and sexual references. A-III (PG)

Monty Python's Life of Brian (see: **Life of Brian**)

Monty Python's The Meaning of Life (1983) The Python troupe (John Cleese, Terry Gilliam, Eric Idle, Michael Palin, and Terry Jones, who also directed) breaks new ground, not in terms of satire, but of grossness for its own sake. There are indeed some very funny moments, but much of it is vile bile, the product of bright, well-bred but naughty boys who bear a lot of minor grudges, but lack the satiric ability to do a proper job on their targets. Graphic nudity and an attack on formal religion. O (R)

Moon Is Blue, The (1953) Lame sex-farce in which a young woman (Maggie McNamara) spends an evening in the apartment of an architect (William Holden), with constant interruptions from a lecherous neighbor (David Niven) and his aggrieved daughter (Dawn Addams). Directed by Otto Preminger, the stagy situation relies on the woman's frank references to sex being taken as an indication of promiscuity, which leads to a series of stupid rather than amusing developments, ending unconvincingly in traditional romance. Sexual situations and references. A-III (br)

Moon over Miami (1941) Romantic-comedy fluff directed by Walter Lang in which two sisters (Betty Grable and Carole Landis) and their aunt (Charlotte Greenwood) pool a meager inheritance to stay in a rich resort in hopes of nabbing wealthy husbands (Don Ameche and Robert Cummings). Mercenary attitudes, romantic complications, and sexual innuendo. A-III (br)

Moon Over Parador (1988) American actor in a Caribbean country (Richard Dreyfuss), strong-armed by the local chief of police (Raul Julia) into impersonating its newly deceased dictator, soon grows to love the power trip and the dead leader's mistress (Sonia Braga). Writer-director Paul Mazursky never quite decides whether he's making a slapstick comedy about the vicissitudes of the acting profession or a satire about Latin-American politics with unfocused and unfunny results. Lusty, clothed bedroom scene and other sexual innuendo played for laughs. A-III (PG-13)

Moon Zero Two (1969) British science-fiction yarn in which a woman (Catherine von Schell) enlists the aid of a space pilot (James Olson) to find her brother, who is missing from his mining claim on the moon. Directed by Roy Ward Baker, the plot is that of a conventional claim-jumping Western with good special effects and little violence. A-II (G)

Moonlight and Valentino (1995) Feminist drama in which a grieving widow (Elizabeth Perkins) gradually puts her life back together with the help of her best friend (Whoopi Goldberg), her college-age sister (Gwyneth Paltrow), and her mellowing ex-stepmother (Kathleen Turner). Directed by David Anspaugh, the situation is deeply emotional, but the story is contrived and the treatment is cerebral, with results that are more sentimental than convincing. Adult themes, including sexual situations, occasional profanity, and rough language. A-III (R)

Moonraker (1979) British agent James Bond (Roger Moore) teams up with a CIA operative (Lois Chiles) to save the world from a deadly shower launched from outer space by a madman (Michael Lonsdale). Director Lewis Gilbert offers the usual Bond fare with the usual mix of stylized sex and violence. A-III (PG)

Moonshine War, The (1970) Internal-revenue agent Patrick McGoohan and a murderous gang led by Richard Widmark go after poor country moonshiner Alan Alda, who has inherited 150 barrels of perfect "white lightning" from his dear departed dad. Director Richard Quine conveys a sense of Depression-era nostalgia, but heavy-handedly injects farcical sex-vignettes and a slapstick parody of mass killing to conclude a pointless plot. A- III (PG)

Moonstruck (1987) Charming romantic comedy set in an Italian-American neighborhood in Brooklyn, where a widow (Cher) accepts the proposal of a fastidious bachelor (Danny Aiello) but falls in love with his darkly emotional younger brother (Nicolas Cage). Director Norman Jewison concentrates more on the comedy of character than on incident, and the result is pleasantly amusing, emotionally operatic, and humanly uplifting. Several restrained scenes implying sex, but the movie's moral perspective is implicit throughout. A-III (PG)

Moonwalk One (1973) Documentary recording man's first visit to the moon on Apollo II in 1969 is first-rate in explaining the technology of space flight, as well as imparting some of the wonderment and sense of history involved in this accomplishment. NASA-produced film, directed by Theo Kamecke, is a fine tribute to a scientific achievement that is truly awesome. A-I (G)

More American Graffiti (1979) Auto racing, Vietnam combat, peace demonstrations, and Flower Children constitute the four facets of the sequel whose characters are now a few years older, have gone their separate ways, but have still kept in touch. The acting (Bo Hopkins, Ron Howard, Candy Clark, and Paul Le Mat) is quite good, but director B.W.L. Norton's effort seems simply to trade on late-1960s nostalgia without any of the wit and feeling of the original. Some rough language, the use of drugs, and the shallow treatment of serious issues, such as the Vietnam conflict. A-III (PG)

More Dead Than Alive (1969) Standard Western about a notorious gunfighter (Clint Walker) who gives up his trade by becoming a sharpshooter in a travelling sideshow (run by Vincent Price) but is gunned down by the son of one of his former victims. Directed by Robert Sparr, the melodrama's anti-violence message is unconvincing, especially in view of its excessively gory visual effects. A-III (PG)

More Than a Miracle (1967) Uneven Italian-French romance set in the 17th century, in which a Spanish prince (Omar Sharif) marries a Cinderella (Sophia Loren), with witches and saints helping matters along. The episodic story-line with none-too-noble nobles and the all-too-common commoners, the bawdy earthiness of a few incidents, and director Francesco Rosi's association of witchcraft with religion makes it all pretty hard to swallow. A-III (br)

More the Merrier, The (1943) Zestful WW II comedy set in overcrowded Washington, D.C., where a patriotic government worker (Jean Arthur) takes in an elderly male boarder (Charles Coburn) who turns matchmaker by subletting his half of the apartment to an eligible bachelor (Joel McCrea) bound for overseas duty. Director George Stevens makes the contrived situation sparkle with sight gags and witty dialogue, but the gay wartime romance sours in a last-minute quickie marriage which the bride is assured can be easily annulled. Romantic complications with a questionable resolution. A-III (br)

Morgan! (1966) Young London nonconformist (David Warner), likeable but hard to understand, tries to win back his estranged wife (Vanessa Redgrave) but increasingly gets lost in his own fantasies, shown by scenes from old movies and camera effects. Director Karel Reisz has achieved a strange mixture of comedy and social comment, effectively brought off by the fine performances of the principals. A-III (br)

Morgan the Pirate (1961) Muscle-bound Steve Reeves plays the English buccaneer preying on sevteenth-century Spanish galleons in a badly dubbed Italian production directed energetically but aimlessly by Andre de Toth. The stylized violent action takes a back seat to sexual situations and innuendo. A-III (br)

Morgan Stewart's Coming Home (1987) Jon Cryer is the wise son and Lynn Redgrave is the overly sophisticated, domineering mother and political power-broker who make a loving compromise when the family is duped by the father's unscrupulous campaign manager in pseudonymous director Alan Smithee's comedy of manners and teen coming-of-age story. Two shower-room sight gags and some concluding rough language are brief and restrained comic asides in this movie which shows that patience and understanding help rebuild family ties. A-II (PG-13)

Morire Gratis (1969) Italian production about a sculptor (Franco Angeli) driving a load of narcotics from Rome to Paris and the woman he picks up along the way (Karen Blanguernon). Director Sandro Franchina prepares for the journey's inevitable tragic ending with a number of scenes of violence encountered along the way. Though it raises moral questions, it lacks depth and its perspective tends to be pessimistic. A-IV (nr)

Morituri (1965) Murky WW II espionage thriller about an unwilling German pacifist (Marlon Brando) forced by a British agent (Trevor Howard) to undertake the disablement of a Nazi freighter (captained by Yul Brynner) on the high seas. Director Bernhard Wicki gets plenty of tension aboard ship but never seems quite certain whether he's making an action picture or some kind of allegorical statement on war. Stylized violence, drug use, and sexual situations. A-III (br)

Morning After, The (1986) A fading actress (Jane Fonda), prone to one-night stands and alcoholic blackouts, wakes up one morning in bed with a dead man. Director Sidney Lumet's thriller solves the murder mystery, but it's a rather empty exercise in style without substance. Implied sex and some rough language. A-III (R)

Morning Glory (1933) Dated melodrama from Zoe Akins's play about a would-be actress from Vermont (Katharine Hepburn) whose wildly romantic dreams of Broadway stardom turn off a cynical producer (Adolphe Menjou) but win the heart of a rising playwright (Douglas Fairbanks, Jr.) and the chance to make good. Directed by Lowell Sherman, the backstage story may interest drama buffs, but others will have to settle for Hepburn's Oscar-winning performance as the vulnerable, idealistic young woman. Romantic complications, including an off-screen sexual liaison. A-III (br)

Mortal Kombat (1995) Martial-arts fantasy based on a video game in which the mythic god of thunder (Christopher Lambert) enlists three mortals in the fight to save Earth from monstrous creatures conjured up by a diabolical sorcerer (Cary-Hiroyuki Tagawa). Directed by Paul Anderson, the adolescent good-vs.-evil yarn blends elaborately staged fights with eye-popping special effects for visually exciting though generally mindless escapist fare. Much highly stylized violence. A-III (PG-13)

Mortal Kombat Annihilation (1997) Bone-crunching sequel in which four muscle-bound humans engage in continual battles with evil, shape-shifting warlords intent on demolishing planet Earth. Directed by John R. Leonetti, might makes right is the wrongheaded message of this martial-arts extravaganza of deadly combat pitting father against son, mother against daughter, and brother against brother. Much nasty fantasy-violence and a theme of killing family members. O (PG-13)

Mortal Storm, The (1940) Effective melodrama showing how Hitler's coming to power in 1933 Germany destroys the family of a Jewish university professor (Frank Morgan) who winds up in a concentration camp while his daughter (Margaret Sullavan) gets help from an anti-Nazi student (James Stewart) in trying to cross the border to safety in Austria. Directed by Frank Borzage, the sentimental story-line tugs at the heart over the family's tribulations while evoking scorn for those (like Robert Young) who join the Party, then grow troubled by its excesses. Stylized violence and racist oppression. A-II (br)

Mortal Thoughts (1991) Two best friends (Demi Moore and Glenne Headly) come under close scrutiny by a police detective (Harvey Keitel) when they try to cover up the accidental killing of one's husband (Bruce Willis). Fine acting generally compensates for director Alan Rudolph's unduly drawn-out suspense movie of female friendship and betrayal. Some gory violence, abuse of women, and much rough language. A-III (R)

Moscow on the Hudson (1984) Robin Williams stars as a jazz-playing Russian musician who falls in love with a department-store sales-clerk and finds a safe haven and the American Dream in New York City. Somewhat funny and vulnerable performance by Williams fails to save director Paul Mazursky's comic study of defection and exile in a movie that resorts to some nude bedroom scenes to heat up the action. O (R)

Moses (1976) Theatrical version of a European television mini-series on the Book of Exodus has serious shortcomings in its level of acting, especially Burt Lancaster's soporific performance as Moses, as well as in the script's plodding rationalizations of the appearance of the divine in human events. Directed by Gianfranco De Bosio, the dramatization is unconvincing, its secular interpretation of the Bible story lacks depth, and its spectacle is low-budget and unimaginative. Some brief but graphic violence. A-III (PG)

Mosquito Coast, The (1986) Dissatisfied with the

ills of modern civilization, an American intellectual (Harrison Ford) takes his family to a tropical wilderness but finds that life in this new Eden is no better than that which he fled. Adapted from Paul Theroux's novel and directed by Peter Weir, the movie's rather cynical outlook makes it less entertaining than thought-provoking fare. Mature themes. A-III (PG)

Mosquito Squadron (1970) WW II adventure with David McCallum leading a squadron of RAF fighter-bombers across the channel to destroy the Nazi center developing a super V-2 rocket and save one bomb to open up the POW-packed chateau next door. Director Boris Sagal handles the heroics as melodramatically as possible so that even the model planes used in re-creating the air battles seem to be overacting. A-I (G)

Most Beautiful Age, The (1970) Low-keyed Czechoslovakian drama about the generation gap in various levels of society set in a sculpture studio, where the interplay between students, teachers, models, and visitors occasion humorous, ironic, and even tragic observations on the human condition. Director Jaroslav Papousek has an eye for detail that lends substance and depth to the film and makes it a rewarding entertainment. Mature themes. A-III (nr)

Most Dangerous Game, The (1932) Creaky but still effective thriller in which a big-game hunter (Joel McCrea) and a wispy socialite (Fay Wray) are shipwrecked on an uncharted island, then find themselves the prey of a mad Russian count (Leslie Banks) who hunts humans instead of animals. Directed by Ernest B. Schoedsack and Irving Pichel, the acting is melodramatic but in keeping with the eerie situation and its steadily mounting menace until the final chase's gripping climax. Threatening situations with some stylized violence and mild sexual undertones. A-II (br)

Most Wanted (1997) Murky thriller in which a fugitive Marine sergeant (Keenen Ivory Wayans) is framed by a power-mad general (Jon Voight) for the murder of the president's wife. Director David Glenn Hogan's convoluted conspiracy plot becomes increasingly far-fetched as the narrative strains to showcase constant action-scenes. Intermittent violence, fleeting nudity, occasional profanity, and some rough language. A-III (R)

Motel Hell (1980) Totally unappetizing horror movie with Rory Calhoun as a motel keeper whose sideline is selling smoked meat made out of humans whose vocal cords have been cut while being fattened before butchering. The grisly horror story is made all the more repugnant because director Kevin Connor apparently thinks it's a comedy. Excessively graphic violence and some nudity. O (R)

Mother (see: **The Toy Grabbers**)

Mother (1996) Thin comedy about a twice-divorced man (Albert Brooks) who decides his problems with women stem from his strained relationship with his mother (Debbie Reynolds) and so moves back home with mom in hopes of resolving their differences. Also written and directed by Brooks, the situation has some funny moments, and Reynolds gives an endearing performance, but much of the humor is obvious and the sentimental ending too contrived to be satisfying. Family tensions, benign view of extramarital sex, and occasional profanity. A-III (PG-13)

Mother and the Whore, The (1974) Provocative French drama about the self-deceptions of a pseudo-intellectual (Jean-Pierre Leaud) who, though kept by an older woman (Bernadette Lafont), gets involved with a young nurse (Francoise Lebrun) bent on marriage. The ambivalent, shifting relationships between the three are seen as basically dishonest, showing especially the man as a perpetual adolescent torn between the two aspects of the title. Director Jean Eustache has chosen a documentary approach to his material, filming in the less fashionable bistros and tenements frequented by his characters, using rough street language and explicit depiction of sexual relationships, challenging viewers about the contradictions of modern lifestyles. A-IV (nr)

Mother Carey's Children (1938) Slight turn-of-the-century sudser directed by Rowland V. Lee centers on a poor small-town widow (Fay Bainter) and her innocent brood (notably Anne Shirley and Ruby Keeler) as they try to save their rented home from a hardhearted buyer (Margaret Hamilton). The period characters have charm, though largely smothered in plot contrivances and idealistic hokum. A-I (br)

Mother, Jugs & Speed (1976) Bill Cosby, Raquel Welch, and Harvey Keitel respectively play the title characters in a failed comedy about a private ambulance-service on the verge of bankruptcy and locked in a frantic rivalry with a competing service. Director Peter Yates stages some spectacular scenes of violent action, but none of it comes off as particularly amusing. Crude, tasteless, and vulgar, especially in its sexual references. O (PG)

Mother Night (1996) Unconvincingly complicated tale from Kurt Vonnegut's novel about an American spy (Nick Nolte) in Nazi Germany, who after the war is regarded as a traitor because the government refuses to acknowledge his secret role. Directed by Keith Gordon, the heavy-handed result depicts events in Nazi Germany with little moral perspective and even less psychological credibility, leaving questions of individual responsibility and collective guilt underdeveloped and without much dramatic impact. Complex themes and some bedroom scenes with nudity. A-III (R)

Mother Teresa (1986) Feature documentary by Ann and Jeanette Petrie on the life and work of a Catholic nun in India, whose tireless efforts for the poorest of the poor earned her the Nobel Peace Prize and recognition as a media star and secular saint. Inspirational portrait of a contemporary woman. A-I (nr)

Mother Wore Tights (1947) Nostalgic story of a husband-and-wife vaudeville team who decide mom (Betty Grable) stay at home to raise their two young daughters while dad (Dan Dailey) continues his song-

and-dance act on the road, thereby causing predictable complications. Directed by Walter Lang, the vignettes of family life in the early part of the century are charmingly presented and nicely paced by a series of easy-to-take musical numbers. A-I (br)

Mother's Boys (1994) Having abandoned her husband (Peter Gallagher) and three young sons several years earlier, a disturbed woman (Jamie Lee Curtis) abruptly returns, obsessed with reclaiming her role as wife and mother despite her husband's plans to remarry. Yves Simoneau directs a routine thriller whose sinister atmosphere lingers listlessly right up to an unconvincing, melodramatic finish. Some sexual innuendo, fleeting nudity, brief violence, and several instances of rough language. A-III (R)

Mother's Day (1980) Bloody shocker about a demented mother and her two cretinous sons who wreak all sorts of horrors on three young women. Poorly written and amateurishly directed by Charles Kaufman, it features excessively graphic violence and some nudity. O (PG)

Mothra (1962) Dubbed Japanese monster-movie directed by Inoshiro Hondo, in which a pair of tiny princesses are taken from their island home to Tokyo which is nearly leveled by a giant caterpillar in rescuing them, before turning into a butterfly to carry them home. Much destruction of miniature models. A-I (br)

Moulin Rouge (1952) Shallow dramatization of the driven, unhappy life of French artist Henri Toulouse-Lautrec (Jose Ferrer) from his early sketches of Paris night-life in 1890 to his growing fame by the time of his death in 1900. Despite the heavy-handed focus on the artist's stunted legs as the cause of his compulsive drinking and complicated relations with women (guttersnipe Colette Marchand and model Suzanne Flon), the picture has interest in director John Huston's vibrant depiction of a changing cultural epoch bursting with talent, energy, and commercialism. Sexual situations. A-III (br)

Mountain, The (1956) Unconvincing melodrama in which a retired mountain-climber (Spencer Tracy) helps his greedy younger brother (Robert Wagner) reach a wrecked airliner in the Alps but refuses to help him rob the dead and, instead, rescues the plane's sole survivor (Anna Kashfi). Directed by Edward Dmytryk, the mountain-climbing sequences are nerve-wracking, but the relationship between the simple, decent older man and his nasty, spoiled sibling makes no sense and undermines the story's dramatic credibility. Menacing situations and confusing motivations. A-I (br)

Mountain Family Robinson (1979) After building a cabin on a mining claim in the Colorado Rockies, the family is informed that unless they mine their claim, they will lose their home. Though director John Cotter's simplistic plotting and saccharine characters are overly familiar, its vistas of nature and abundance of wildlife will satisfy young viewers. A-I (G)

Mountain Men, The (1980) Charlton Heston plays a trapper who has outlived his era with the decline of the fur trade and arrival of wagon trains of settlers in the Old West. Richard Lang's leaden direction of a cliched script centering on a Blackfoot warrior's attempt to revenge himself on the trapper for taking his squaw flounders in graphic violence, an extended rape scene, and foul-mouthed profanity. O (R)

Mountain Road, The (1960) James Stewart plays a demolitions expert who tries to block a Japanese offensive in 1944 China by blowing up a refugee-clogged road. Directed by Daniel Mann, the story is earnest and well-crafted but rather pointless. Stylized violence. A-II (br)

Mountains of the Moon (1990) Epic docudrama recounts the 19th-century expeditions to discover the source of the Nile made by British explorers Richard Burton (Patrick Bergin) and John Hanning Speke (Iain Glen). Director Bob Rafelson's period piece ably reflects the obsession of the explorers and the beauty as well as savagery of the African wilderness. Its masterful mix of entertainment, education, and biography may be accessible for older adolescents, though integrated in the context are intense scenes of violence, some nudity, and an implication of homosexuality. A-III (R)

Mourning Becomes Electra (1947) Failed screen version of Eugene O'Neill's play updating Sophocles's tragic story from ancient Greece to post-Civil War New England, where a Yankee general (Raymond Massey) is killed by his unfaithful wife (Katina Paxinou), with their offspring (Rosalind Russell and Michael Redgrave) plotting a revenge that ends in the family's destruction. Adapted by director Dudley Nichols, the dour result is an overlong, static dialogue piece which defies all efforts of its talented cast to bring to life. Stylized violence, including murders and suicides, and off-screen infidelity. A-II (br)

Mouse, The (1997) Fact-based but flat-footed account of how prizefighter Bruce "The Mouse" Strauss (John Savage) made a career of losing boxing matches across the country, until a computer linking the state boxing commissions put him out of business and saved his marriage. Writer-director Dan Adams tries to turn the gritty world of the fight game into a sentimental comedy about loveable eccentrics, but the brutal beatings suffered by the punch-drunk boxer get in the way of any amusement. Considerable pugilistic violence, sexual situations, coarse expressions, and a few instances of rough language. A-III (nr)

Mouse and His Child, A (1978) Animated feature about the adventures of a mechanical mouse and his son in the forbidding world outside of their toy store, where their friends help them defeat their chief persecutor, a rat (voiced by Peter Ustinov), and gain self-winding status. Directed by Fred Wolf, the movie has its bright and clever moments, but is too often serious, if not downright somber, with many of the jokes and references not at all relevant for youngsters and too juvenile for adults. A-I (G)

Mouse Hunt ((1997) Madcap comedy in which two impoverished brothers (Nathan Lane and Lee Evans) inherit a historic mansion, then plan to auction it off for millions if they can just rid it of an elusive mouse that is bringing the house down around their heads. Directed in episodic fashion by Gore Verbinski, the result offers some zany, occasionally over-the-top comic mayhem as the resourceful rodent foils the humans' every trap. Much slapstick violence, mild toilet humor, and fleeting sexual innuendo. A-II (PG)

Mouse That Roared, The (1959) Wry British comedy about the tiny, bankrupt duchy of Grand Fenwick, whose prime minister (Peter Sellers) convinces the grand duchess (also Sellers) to declare war on the US, then surrender and accept post-war aid. Director Jack Arnold keeps the comic premise bubbling along as Fenwick's general (Sellers again), unaware of the plan, invades New York, and captures a scientist's new secret weapon. The political satire is less amusing today, but Sellers's triple performance and the clever sight gags are as funny as ever. A-I (br)

Mouth to Mouth (1997) Spanish sex-farce in which an aspiring actor (Javier Bardem), while waiting for his big break in an upcoming American movie, takes a temporary job in a phone sex-shop, which ultimately involves him in a murder plot. Directed by Manuel Gomez Pereira, the overly contrived result works best in its satiric jabs at the actor's selfish agent and the arrogant movie producers, but is less successful in poking fun at the sordid business of selling sex fantasies over the telephone. Subtitles. Sexual humor, including several jokey sexual encounters, a flash of a homosexual video, and some rough language. A-IV (R)

Move (1970) Dimwitted comedy about a professional dog-walker and occasional porno pulp-writer (Elliott Gould), in the midst of moving wife (Paula Prentiss), St. Bernard, and their belongings to another apartment, dashes headlong from one unfunny non-crisis to another, including a casual dalliance with a model (Genevieve Waite). Directed by Stuart Rosenberg, the vulgar level of humor reaches rock bottom with a shot of Gould urinating in the kitchen sink to spite the landlord. Sexual references and nudity. O (R)

Move Over, Darling (1963) Lackluster romantic comedy in which a woman (Doris Day) marooned on a desert island for five years returns to find she has been declared legally dead, and her husband (James Garner) has just wed a new wife (Polly Bergen). Directed by Michael Gordon, this pale remake of **My Favorite Wife** bogs down in unamusing confrontations between characters who lack the zestful sophisticated wit that gave the original its appeal. Much sexual innuendo. A-III (br)

Movers and Shakers (1985) A limp satire on Hollywood movie-making, written and produced by actor Charles Grodin (who also stars) and directed by William Asher. Some mild vulgarities and some tasteless humor. A-II (PG-13)

Movie Movie (1978) Producer-director Stanley Donen has contributed a comic valentine to 1930s Hollywood movies by re-creating a modern version of the era's double features, pairing a black-and-white boxing melodrama and a musical in color, using virtually the same cast for both (George C. Scott, Trish Van Devere, Eli Wallach, Art Carney, and others). The gentle parody captures well the innocent fantasies of a less sophisticated age, not to make fun of past movie conventions but to enjoy them in a more knowing way. Some ring violence and a sensuous nightclub dance. A-II (PG)

Moving Violations (1985) The feeble premise for director Neal Israel's failed comedy is the gathering together of some diverse types who must attend driving school to get back their licenses. Heavy emphasis on sexually oriented humor. O (PG-13)

Mr. & Mrs. Bridge (1990) Fascinating portrait of a WW II-era, upper-crust Kansas City family, dominated by a rigidly narrow-minded father (Paul Newman), whose submissive wife (Joanne Woodward) is at a loss to draw emotional warmth from her husband or three grown children. Director James Ivory's film is a minor masterpiece of superb characterizations and extraordinary performances, accentuated by fine dialogue and rich imagery. Instances of promiscuity and fleeting shot of female nude photos. A-III (PG-13)

Mr. Arkadin (1955) Slapdash thriller in which a mystery man of enormous wealth (Orson Welles) hires a shady American (Robert Arden) to investigate his obscure origins, but as soon as his old associates are located, they turn up dead. Also written and directed by Welles, the low-budget production is seeped in a cryptic atmosphere which makes the individual sequences interesting, but the pieces don't add up to much in the weak finale. Stylized violence, sinister menace, and sexual innuendo. A-III (br)

Mr. Baseball (1992) When a fading major-league player (Tom Selleck) is traded to a Japanese team, his flippant attitudes antagonize his new club's team-spirited manager (Ken Takakura) and the player's fiery girlfriend (Aya Takanashi). Fred Schepisi directs a comedy of clashing cultures that drops the ball with its superficially developed one-joke premise. Some subtitles. Benign attitude toward premarital sex, a few off-color references. and some male rear nudity. A-III (PG-13)

Mr. Billion (1976) Poor Italian mechanic (Terence Hill) inherits the controlling interest in a vast American corporation, provided he can reach San Francisco by a certain day. Villainous Jackie Gleason hires Valerine Perrine to impede him, but, predictably enough, she switches sides. Pleasant and diverting, if more than slightly sappy, comedy directed by Jonathan Kaplan. Some limited violence. A-II (PG)

Mr. Blandings Builds His Dream House (1948) Wry view of postwar middle-class yearnings as seen in the rising discontent of a $15,000-a-year Madison Avenue executive (Cary Grant) and his wife (Myrna Loy) at life with two daughters in a cramped four-room city apartment and their escalating woes after they decide to move to a country house in Connecticut. Director H.C. Potter's droll satire of a first-time property owner's bewildered encounters with real-estate agents, architects, and contractors has plenty of funny business, compounded by the know-it-all comments of the family's lawyer and bachelor friend (Melvyn Douglas). Domestic squabbles and misunderstandings. A-II (br)

Mr. Deeds Goes to Town (1936) When a small-town writer of greeting-card verses (Gary Cooper) inherits a fortune, he moves to New York City, where he is made into a front-page laughing-stock by a two-timing reporter (Jean Arthur) and his plans to help the poor embroil him in a sanity hearing. Director Frank Capra deftly juggles romance and humor in this entertaining Depression-era tale of an ordinary American whose homespun virtues triumph over big-city cynicism and greed. A-II (nr)

Mr. Destiny (1990) Anemic fantasy about an average Joe (Jim Belushi) whose life is magically reinvented by a bartender (Michael Caine), so that suddenly he finds himself wealthy, married to the prom queen, and, as the despised president of a business, longing for his old life. Sluggishly directed by James Orr, the flat comedy is harmless but insipid entertainment without wit, grace, or mirth. Minor stylized violence, mild sexual innuendo, and a few vulgar expressions. A-II (PG-13)

Mr. Hobbs Takes a Vacation (1962) Uneven comedy in which a St. Louis banker (James Stewart) makes the best of things when his wife (Maureen O'Hara) insists on using a friend's West Coast beach-house for a holiday with their two children and two grown daughters with their spouses and offspring. Directed by Henry Koster, the comic complications range from the saccharine (Fabian romances their 14-year-old daughter) to the heartwarming (a father-son sailboat misadventure), with some daffy interludes along the way (notably birdwatcher John McGiver and wife Marie Wilson). A-I (br)

Mr. Holland's Opus (1996) Satisfying drama in which an aspiring composer reluctantly takes a job as a high-school music-teacher (Richard Dreyfuss) in order to support a wife and deaf son and spends his life inspiring generations of adolescents with his dedication and love of music. Helped by Dreyfuss's fine performance, director Stephen Herek's sentimental tale of a good man stresses old-fashioned virtues, as well as the importance of good teachers and of the arts in developing young minds. Mild sexual innuendo and fleeting profanity. A-II (PG)

Mr. Imperium (1951) Dated musical fluff about a brief romance in 1930s Italy between a vacationing Ruritanian prince (Ezio Pinza) and an American showgirl (Lana Turner), who becomes a top Hollywood star after WW II, while he's a king-in-exile pondering abdication to co-star in her next movie. Directed by Don Hartman, the weak story and cardboard characters hold little interest, despite some pleasantly forgettable songs. Romantic complications. A-II (br)

Mr. Jones (1993) Downbeat drama in which a manic-depressive (Richard Gere) resists taking medication or opening up to a psychiatrist (Lena Olin) who unprofessionally allows herself to fall in love with him. Gere's nuanced performance elicits much sympathy for those afflicted with mental illness, but the point of director Mike Figgis's uneven movie is unclear and further muddled by the glossy romance between doctor and patient. Fleeting violence, a suicide, sexual innuendo, and frequent rough language. A-III (R)

Mr. Klein (1977) French drama about a dealer in art objects (Alain Delon) who buys family heirlooms from Jews needing cash to escape the Nazi terror, but then he himself is mistaken for a Jew and handed over to the Germans, as were 13,000 others on what is known as Black Thursday, July 16, 1942. Directed with great sensitivity by Joseph Losey, it is exceptional in viewing the Holocaust as a universal experience, as meaningful to gentiles as to Jews. The nature of the theme, and some incidental nudity, make this a film for serious viewers. A-III (PG)

Mr. Love (1986) In this quirky British romance, a timid gardener (Barry Jackson) who is caught in an unhappy 28-year marriage decides he must find love at least once before he dies. Director Roy Battersby's gentle satire implies that the self-indulgence of one's passions justifies infidelity. Romanticization of immoral behavior. O (PG-13)

Mr. Magoo (1997) Feeble live-action comedy in which the near-sighted Magoo (Leslie Nielsen) is pursued by thieves and federal agents after unknowingly walking off with a priceless stolen ruby. Directed by Stanley Tong from a story based on the popular cartoon character, the thin premise occasions few amusing sight gags while floundering in a dull series of slapstick kick-boxing confrontations. Mild sexual innuendo and frequent comic violence. A-II (PG)

Mr. Majestyk (1974) Charles Bronson stars as an embattled ex-convict determined to protect his farm from the inroads of mob-instigated labor problems. Director Richard Fleischer helps divert attention from an overly familiar story by making the most of the scenic Colorado hills and desert locations. Some violence and strong language. A-III (PG)

Mr. Mom (1983) When a father of three (Michael Keaton) loses his job, he takes over the household chores while his wife (Teri Garr) goes back to work. In handling the comic complications of the role-reversal plot, director Stan Dragoti is helped greatly by the likeable leads, who manage to turn saccharine-coated problems into genial comedy. Toys with but firmly rejects several plot-lines leading toward infidelity. A-II (PG)

Mr. Moto Takes a Chance (1938) Lively adventure in the jungles of French Indochina, where the title's Japanese detective (Peter Lorre) poses as an archeologist, then as an ancient guru while searching for an arsenal of weapons to be used in a native uprising. Directed by Norman Foster, the far-fetched and often tongue-in-cheek proceedings end in a pitched battle involving an aviatrix (Rochelle Hudson) working for British intelligence, an American newsreel crew (Robert Kent and Chick Chandler), the region's pompous prince (J. Edward Bromberg), and the surly rebel leader (George Regas). Stylized violence. A-I (br)

Mr. Moto Takes a Vacation (1939) The eighth and final episode in the mystery series with John P. Marquand's Japanese detective (Peter Lorre), who this time is guarding the crown worn by the Queen of Sheba while it's on exhibition in a San Francisco museum. Directed by Norman Foster, the case pits Moto against an international thief who's also a master of disguise, with suspects including curator Lionel Atwill, philanthropist Joseph Schildkraut, and clumsy Englishman John Davidson. Off-screen murder and mild menace. A-I (br)

Mr. Moto's Gamble (1937) While teaching a police crime-class, the genial Japanese detective (Peter Lorre) helps a homicide detective (Harold Huber) solve the murder of a prizefighter whose death in the ring caused heavy losses for a gambling syndicate. Directed by James Tinling, the gritty setting offers plenty of menace and a multitude of suspects, with comic relief supplied by an ex-boxer (Maxie Rosenbloom) and Charlie Chan's son (Keye Luke). Some tense violence, including gory boxing scenes. A-II (br)

Mr. Moto's Last Warning (1939) This time Moto (Peter Lorre) uses a double to thwart some ruthless saboteurs (Ricardo Cortez, George Sanders, and John Carradine) whose target is the Suez Canal. Directed by Norman Foster, the film has some neat plot-twists with double agents and cover identities, plenty of action, and the usual comic relief (Robert Coote). Stylized violence. A-I (br)

Mr. Music (1950) Lackluster musical comedy directed by Richard Haydn concerns a lazy veteran songwriter (Bing Crosby) whose producer (Charles Coburn) hires a no-nonsense college grad (Nancy Olson) to oversee his work schedule, the result of which is a hit musical and a May-December romance. Silly romantic complications. A-II (br)

Mr. Nice Guy (1998) Overdone martial-arts extravaganza in which an Australian TV chef from Hong Kong (Jackie Chan) finds himself pursued by a drug lord (Richard Norton), then decides to fight back and single-handedly demolishes his entire gang. Directed by Samo Hung, the plot serves up one breathless chase after another through Melbourne's streets, buildings, and surrounding environs, but with nothing else going on, the fast-paced action is too contrived to be anything more than tiresome. Much stylized violence, menace, sexual innuendo, and coarse language. A-III (PG-13)

Mr. North (1988) Smarty-pants Yale grad (Anthony Edwards) raises havoc among the wealthy citizens of 1926 Newport, R.I., because of his peculiar talent for giving electric shocks. Based on Thornton Wilder's last novel, the breezy, technically uneven movie is directed by Danny Huston, son of the late director John Huston, who is credited as producer. Lively character performances but some vulgar references. A-II (PG)

Mr. Peabody and the Mermaid (1948) Uneven comic fantasy in which a very proper 50-year-old Bostonian (William Powell) confides to a psychiatrist how he came to be enchanted by an attractively mute mermaid (Ann Blyth) while vacationing in the Caribbean with his wife (Irene Hervey). Directed by Irving Pichel, the saucy situation has its moments, but nothing untoward happens in what is treated as an absurd but harmless midlife hallucination. Mild romantic yearnings. A-II (br)

Mr. Quilp (1975) Uninspired British musical version of Charles Dickens's *The Old Curiosity Shop*, about the villainous usurer Quilp (Anthony Newley), the put-upon Little Nell, and her improvident grandfather (David Warner). Directed by Michael Tuchner, it is a colorless, undistinguished effort which substitutes sweetness and light for Dicken's gritty melodrama. It may divert the very young but won't satisfy their older siblings and parents. A-I (G)

Mr. Ricco (1975) Routine police thriller about a San Francisco lawyer (Dean Martin) who gets his client off a murder rap but comes to regret it when he winds up in the middle between the authorities and a black-activist cell. Directed by Paul Bogart, the movie has some suspense, occasionally clever dialogue, and a good supporting cast, but there's nothing here that hasn't been seen before. A-III (PG)

Mr. Sardonicus (1961) Penny-dreadful directed by William Castle is set in 19th-century Europe, where a cruel count (Guy Rolfe), his twisted face hidden behind a mask, contrives with the help of a henchman (Oscar Homolka) to force a British doctor (Ronald Lewis) into curing for his deformity. Sinister situations with some brutality and a grave-robbing sequence. A-II (br)

Mr. Saturday Night (1992) Bittersweet comedy traces the career of a caustic stand-up comedian (Billy Crystal) whose insatiable need for center stage hurts his neglected family and brother-manager (David Paymer). Also produced and directed by Crystal, despite many good comic moments, it proves a long haul with a nasty central character who stubbornly resists insights until the overly sentimental ending. Some rough language, minor violence, and numerous off-color jokes. A-III (R)

Mr. Smith Goes to Washington (1939) Classic piece of Americana, in which an idealistic junior senator (James Stewart) stages a one-man filibuster to stop the corrupt machinations of his political mentor (Claude Rains). Director Frank Capra's paean to American democracy has a solid plot, fine acting from a memorable cast, including Jean Arthur and

Thomas Mitchell, as well as a lot of heartfelt patriotic sentiment that few will find dated. A-II (br)

Mr. Wonderful (1993) Flat romantic tale of a cash-strapped blue-collar worker (Matt Dillon) seeking to set up his ex-wife (Annabella Sciorra) with eligible men in hopes of ending his alimony payments, though they secretly still care for each other. Director Anthony Minghella's contrived movie limps along to its forgone conclusion while relying on lame stereotypes of its Italian-Catholic characters. Implied sexual encounters, a violent workplace accident, and occasional rough language. A-III PG-13

Mr. Wong, Detective (1938) The first in a short-lived, low-budget series featuring Boris Karloff as James Lee Wong, a Chinese-American detective in San Francisco, who here helps a police inspector (Grant Withers) solve several murders committed by shattering glass bulbs containing poisonous gas as police sirens wail in the background. Directed by William Nigh, the intriguing mystery plot was used again in the 1948 Charlie Chan entry **Docks of New Orleans**. Mild menace. A-I (br)

Mr. Wrong (1996) Uneven comedy in which a career woman (Ellen DeGeneres) is swept into an affair by a handsome, wealthy stranger (Bill Pullman) only to discover he's a nutcase obsessed with marrying her, despite all efforts to get rid of him - and his jealous ex-girlfriend (Joan Cusack). Directed by Nick Castle, the contrived narrative serves primarily as a vehicle for Ms. DeGeneres's low-key comic talents. Brief slapstick violence, sexual innuendo, and crude references. A-III (PG-13)

Mrs. Brown (1997) Fact-based historical drama explores the close personal relationship that developed between the reclusive widowed Queen Victoria (Judi Dench) and her gruff groomsman (Billy Connolly) who bullied her out of years of mourning at Scotland's Balmoral Castle and back to her royal duties in London at a time when the monarchy was falling into public disfavor. Director John Madden's detailed period-piece is an absorbing character study of an imperious monarch's emotional fragility and the ambiguous motivations of her loyal servant. Fleeting male nudity and brief violence. A-III (PG)

Mrs. Brown, You've Got a Lovely Daughter (1968) Delightful British comedy in which some working-class youths turn to performing professionally to support a racing greyhound named Mrs. Brown, whose puppy gets lost during an unfortunate expedition to London. The plot, however, is only a nonsensical peg on which to hang a number of pleasant songs by the teenage pop-singing group Herman's Hermits, who here display some irresistible high spirits plus an off-beat decency and good sense. A-I (br)

Mrs. Dalloway (1998) Engaging adaptation of the Virginia Woolf novel about the middle-aged title character (Vanessa Redgrave) preparing for a dinner party in 1923 London while thinking about her youth (Natascha McElhone) and how she rejected an enthusiastic suitor (Alan Cox) to marry a man more socially acceptable. Directed by Marleen Gorris, the elegant British production moves flawlessly from the present to Mrs. Dalloway's recollections of the past, using two different sets of characters to make it work, though some may find the insular world inhabited by the characters too claustrophobic for comfort. Wartime violence, a suicide, sexual innuendo, and brief nudity. A-III (PG-13)

Mrs. Doubtfire (1993) Limited by court order to seeing his three children only once a week, a resourceful father (Robin Williams) disguises himself as a matronly British housekeeper, gets hired by his estranged wife (Sally Field), then tries to dissuade her from romance with a wealthy former beau (Pierce Brosnan). Directed by Chris Columbus, the sweet but one-joke comedy is carried by Williams, who manages to make the zany situation both hilarious and heartfelt. Frequent though mild sexual innuendo. A-II (PG-13)

Mrs. Parker and the Vicious Circle (1994) Dark depiction of the life of writer Dorothy Parker (Jennifer Jason Leigh), focusing on her close relationship with humorist Robert Benchley (Campbell Scott) and other members of the famed Algonquin Hotel Round Table luncheons in the 1920s and '30s, which helped sustain her emotionally through failed marriages and a doomed affair with playwright Charles MacArthur (Matthew Broderick). Director Alan Rudolph's joyless dramatization captures some of the acerbic wit of the Round Table's celebrities, but is unrelievedly grim in its portrait of a talented woman turned bitter by years of professional insecurity and self-loathing. A few brief bedroom scenes with nudity, frequent alcohol abuse, a suicide attempt, and occasional rough language. A-III (R)

Mrs. Pollifax: Spy (1971) Rosalind Russell plays a woman free of family commitments who satisfies a lifelong ambition to become a spy by joining the CIA and winding up imprisoned with accomplice Darren McGavin on an Albanian mountaintop, from which she must effect a daring escape. Director Leslie Martinson's adventure spoof is laced with warm humor and clever situations and features a winsome performance by its star in her last screen appearance. A-II (G)

Mrs. Soffel (1985) Turn-of-the-century story of a woman (Diane Keaton), married to a prison warden (Edward Herrmann), who falls in love with a condemned convict (Mel Gibson) and helps him escape. Director Gillian Armstrong's powerful, well-acted movie balances sympathy for its doomed principals with a clear-eyed depiction of the devastation caused by the wife's betrayal of her family and herself. Adultery, though clearly depicted as wrong, is a major plot element. A-IV (PG-13)

Mrs. Winterbourne (1996) After surviving a train wreck, an unwed pregnant teenager (Ricki Lake) is mistakenly thought to be the widowed daughter-in-law of a wealthy matron (Shirley MacLaine), whose son (Brendan Fraser) promptly falls in love with his bogus sister-in-law. Director Richard Benjamin's sappy mistaken-identity tale fills this contrived Cinderella story with cardboard characters and cheap sentiments. A live-in relationship, fleeting violence, recurring profanity, and minimal rough language. A-III (PG-13)

Much Ado About Nothing (1993) While a pair of tart-tongued sparring partners (Kenneth Branagh and Emma Thompson) are tricked into confessing mutual love, the wedding of two other lovebirds (Robert Sean Leonard and Kate Beckinsale) seems doomed when the maiden is falsely accused of foul betrayal. Director Branagh's screen adaptation of Shakespeare's lusty comedy is a fresh and playful romp over the rocky road to love, enhanced by period Italian countryside settings and a breathless pace culminating in a heady tribute to chastity and marital vows. Brief group nudity and a fleeting bedroom scene. A-III (PG-13)

Mulan (1998) Boisterous animated tale set in ancient China, where a rebellious daughter (voice of Ming-Na Wen) disguises herself as a man to fight invading Huns in place of her sickly father. Directors Barry Cook and Tony Bancroft meld sumptuous visuals with contrived humor (from Eddie Murphy as a sassy dragon) in a musical tale of female empowerment in which romance plays second fiddle to issues of self-identity, honor, and patriotism. A-I (G)

Mulholland Falls (1996) Investigating the bizarre murder of a call-girl (Jennifer Connelly) with whom he had once had a brief affair, a 1950s Los Angeles detective (Nick Nolte) runs up against a covert government conspiracy to conceal the facts in the case. Director Lee Tamahori's stylish melodrama is rich in period atmosphere but the weak plot is derivative of 1974's **Chinatown** without the benefit of its intelligent screenplay. Recurring brutal violence, several bedroom scenes with nudity, frequent profanity, and minimal rough language. A-IV (R)

Multiplicity (1996) Sex-themed comic fantasy in which a too-busy family man (Michael Keaton) is secretly cloned three times, giving him more time at home and on the job, but creating romantic complications with his flirtatious wife (Andie MacDowell). Keaton skillfully individualizes the four identical-looking characters, but director Harold Ramis's mildly amusing comedy is limited by the script's single-joke premise. Heavy sexual innuendo, several crude references, and minimal profanity. A-III (PG-13)

Mummy, The (1932) Eerie fantasy classic in which the 3,700-year-old mummy of an Egyptian high-priest (Boris Karloff) comes to life in a London museum, then tries to make off with a Englishwoman (Zita Johann) resembling the princess he had once loved. Imaginatively directed by Karl Freund, the creepy premise proves effective even though only Karloff's piercing eyes are seen through the mummy's burial wrappings, with a lengthy flashback to the thwarted love story in ancient Karnak supplying the mummy's motivation for his desperate activities in the present. Stylized violence, menace, and romantic complications. A-II (br)

Mummy, The (1959) Slack British remake of the 1932 original about the vengeance taken by a 4,000-year-old mummy (Christopher Lee) on the archeologists (notably Peter Cushing) who violated the tomb of which it was the guardian. Directed by Terence Fisher, the narrative plods along with little action or tension until the mummy shows up in 1898 England. Some stylized violence and menace. A-II (br)

Mummy, The (1999) Spirited horror adventure set in 1920s Egypt, where a treasure-hunting Yank (Brendan Fraser) and an archaeological librarian (Rachel Weisz) inadvertently revive a 3,000 year-old mummy (Arnold Vosloo) whose evil powers of destruction seemingly know no bounds. Writer-director Stephen Sommers stuffs the lavishly shot action movie with spooky special effects and a comical tone that generally adds up to rousing, old-fashioned entertainment. Recurring stylized violence and fleeting partial nudity. A-III (PG-13)

Mummy's Boys (1936) Formula comedy directed by Fred Guiol in which a pair of ditch-diggers (Bert Wheeler and Robert Woolsey) are hired to excavate an Egyptian pharaoh's tomb in order to put back a treasure whose curse is killing off the archaeologists who took it. Comic menace and period racial stereotyping. A-I (br)

Mummy's Curse, The (1944) Formula horror sequel directed by Leslie Goodwins has a pair of Egyptian priests (John Coe and Martin Kosleck) searching the Louisiana bayous for the ancient mummy (Lon Chaney) and his beloved princess (Virginia Christine), leaving a number of Cajun victims in their wake. Fantasy violence and menace. A-II (br)

Mummy's Ghost, The (1944) Weak horror sequel directed by Reginald LeBorg in which the mummy Kharis (Lon Channey, Jr.) returns with a new priest-guardian (John Carradine) to retrieve Princess Ananka's mummy from a Massachusetts museum, but they find her reincarnation (Ramsay Ames) instead. Hokey chills and menace. A-II (br)

Mummy's Hand, The (1940) Horror sequel to The Mummy has a penniless American archaeologist (Dick Foran) and his breezy pal (Wallace Ford) talk a magician (Cecil Kellaway) into financing a search for the lost tomb of an Egyptian princess, but uncover instead the living mummy, Kharis (Tom Tyler), who has been guarding the princess for 3,000 years. Directed by Christy Cabanne, the eerie proceedings are paced with some cheerful comedy and the unpretentious results prove quite entertaining. Stylized violence, threatening situations, and some scary visuals. A-II (br)

Mummy's Shroud, The (1967) Plodding horror movie directed by John Gilling follows the fate of a 1920 British expedition after it returns to Cairo with the remains of a pharaoh's son. Intermittent hokey menace with the usual stylized violence. A-II (br)

Mummy's Tomb, The (1942) Formula horror sequel directed by Harold Young in which an Egyptian priest (Turhan Bey) accompanies the mummy Kharis (Lon Chaney, Jr.) to Massachusetts, where they seek revenge on the defilers (Dick Foran and Wallace Ford) of the princess's tomb. Stylized violence and some gruesome visuals. A-II (br)

Mumsy, Nanny, Sonny and Girly (1970) The odd quartet of the title live in an out-of-the-way Victorian mansion, to which they lure unsuspecting strangers to play "games" with them, which end in their being murdered in one ghoulish way or another. British horror movie directed by Freddie Francis, it lacks any story development or suspense, fails to elicit sympathy for its loony protagonists, and falls flat as comedy, though the dialogue is frequently unintentionally amusing. Violence. A-III (R)

Munster Go Home (1966) Big-screen version of a popular TV horror/comedy series in which the Munster family inherit a English manor but have to eject the gang of counterfeiters occupying it. Earl Bellamy directs the TV cast (Fred Gwynne, Yvonne De Carlo, Al Lewis) with less attention to the plot than the gags. Mildly entertaining but mostly for the show's fans. A-I (br)

Muppet Christmas Carol, The (1992) In this sprightly version of Charles Dickens's A Christmas Carol, Muppets Kermit, Miss Piggy, the Great Gonzo, Rizzo the Rat, and Fozzie Bear have incidental roles as Michael Caine portrays skinflint Ebenezer Scrooge, who is visited by the spirits of Christmas Past, Present, and Future so he can learn the true spirit of Christmas. Director Brian Henson retells the holiday classic with delightful musical numbers, though with less frenzied fun than the usual Muppet outings. A-I (G)

Muppet Movie, The (1979) After a chance encounter with Hollywood talent scout Dom DeLuise, Kermit the Frog abandons his soggy swamp for a movie career, taking the entire Muppet crew on a heartwarming cross-country jaunt, but it is Miss Piggy who saves the day by getting Kermit his Hollywood audition. In their first appearance on the big screen, Jim Henson's Muppet characters seem right at home, and director James Frawley's location filming gives them the world as a stage. Charming and delightful entertainment for all. A-I (G)

Muppets Take Manhattan, The (1984) Kermit and Miss Piggy emulate Mickey Rooney and Judy Garland in this spoof of old-time Hollywood musicals. Under Frank Oz's direction, the third screen outing of Jim Henson's Muppets offers some highly entertaining musical numbers, much witty comedy, and a lot of fun. Highly recommended for family viewing. A-I (G)

Muppet Treasure Island (1996) Daffy mix of people and puppets cavort on sand and sea as a plucky lad (Kevin Bishop) outsmarts a treasure-hungry pirate (Tim Curry) with a little help from dauntless Kermit and starry-eyed Miss Piggy. Director Brian Henson's musical take on the Robert Louis Stevenson adventure classic is goofily entertaining in sporadic, tongue-in-cheek spurts. A-I (G)

Murder (1930) Creaky but interesting mystery in which a single juror (Herbert Marshall) refuses to join the others in convicting a young actress (Norah Baring) on trial for murder, then tries to prove her innocence by reenacting the crime. Directed by Alfred Hitchcock, the mystery involves a number of colorful suspects among a seedy theatrical troupe, but the events leading up to the homicide are often murky and the solution is not completely satisfying. Sexual situations and innuendo. A-III (br)

Murder Ahoy (1964) Agatha Christie's sleuthing Miss Marple (Margaret Rutherford) finds the solution to a murder committed ashore by going on board a naval training ship, where her snooping unsettles crew and captain (Lionel Jeffries). Directed by George Pollock, the mystery formula has been diluted with too much feeble comedy, and even Rutherford seems bored by the lackluster proceedings. Minimal stylized violence. A-I (br)

Murder at 1600 (1997) Murky thriller in which a police detective (Wesley Snipes) and a Secret Service agent (Diane Lane) put their lives and careers at risk while trying to expose the cover-up of a young woman's murder in the White House. Directed by Dwight Little, it takes some elaborate plotting to set up the sinister situation, but then the story gives way to increasingly formula action and unconvincing suspense. Shadowy bedroom scene with fleeting nudity, intermittent violence, occasional profanity, and some rough language. A-III (R)

Murder at the Gallop (1963) When a wealthy old man dies, Miss Marple (Margaret Rutherford) suspects murder, and her investigation of the beneficiaries leads to a reclusive relative (Flora Robson) and some members of the local horse-set, notably its blustering, autocratic leader (Robert Morley). Directed by George Pollock from an Agatha Christie mystery, the horse-club setting furnishes a number of sinister characters, as well as some deliciously amusing horseplay between the rubbery-faced Rutherford and the grimacing Morley before the killer is finally exposed. Enjoyable mystery fare with some menacing moments. A-I (br)

Murder by Contract (1958) Hard-bitten underworld thriller tracks the rise of a cold-blooded syndicate killer (Vince Edwards), then bogs down in an extended account of how things go wrong when he is sent to Los Angeles to silence a closely guarded government witness (Caprice Toriel). Director Irving Lerner's brisk, chilling start slowly congeals into a conventional crime melodrama that ultimately turns on a sentimental flaw in the hit-man's psyche. Sordid criminal atmosphere and stylized violence. A-III (br)

Murder by Death (1976) Eccentric criminologist (Truman Capote) invites five master detectives and assistants (including David Niven, Maggie Smith, Eileen Brennan, and James Coco) to his sinister mansion, intending to confound them with a crime they cannot solve. Neil Simon's script owes much to Agatha Christie's Ten Little Indians, but its attempt to spoof whodunit movies is badly wide of the mark. Director Robert Moore fails to find much humor in the flimsy plot, multiple inconsistencies, and flat dialogue. Even the broad performances of a capable cast don't help matters much (Alec Guinness is wasted in a butler part). Adult and frequently vulgar humor. A-III (PG)

Murder by Decree (1979) Sherlock Holmes meets Jack the Ripper in this handsome, expensively mounted period-piece in which Holmes (Christopher Plummer) and Dr. Watson (James Mason) trace a series of murders to a high personage in Queen Victoria's England. Directed by Bob Clark, a preposterous and incredibly untidy plot is overcome by the fine acting of the principals supported by such nonpareils as John Gielgud and Anthony Quayle. Harmless but somewhat violent and gory entertainment not meant for younger viewers. A- III (PG)

Murder by Television (1935) Creaky murder mystery directed by Clifford Sanforth starts with the death of an inventor while testing a revolutionary television transmitter, then bogs down in tiresome red herrings and gassy police interrogations of the suspects, among whom is Bela Lugosi in a dual role. Dull period piece with some racial stereotyping. A-II (nr)

Murder, He Says (1945) Eccentric comedy in which an opinion pollster (Fred MacMurray) is forcefully detained by a murderous family of hayseeds headed by a wacky inventor (Porter Hall) and his bullwhip-wielding wife (Marjorie Main) as they search for a fortune hidden in a backwoods house. Though the plot is as nonsensical as the silly rhyme holding the secret to the treasure, director George Marshall has a lot of fun with the zany characters and screwball situations. Comic violence and mild romance. A-II (br)

Murder in the First (1995) Gritty, loosely fact-based prison-courtroom drama set in 1941, in which a novice lawyer (Christian Slater) defends his timid Alcatraz client (Kevin Bacon), who is accused of murdering a fellow convict, by arguing that years of inhumane solitary confinement and brutal beatings by the associate warden (Gary Oldman) transformed his previously nonviolent client into a murderer. Director Marc Rocco's powerful tale of institutional abuse of power is strengthened by superior performances, although its high moral tone regarding prisoner's human rights comes across somewhat heavy-handededly. Several scenes of vicious beatings with shadowy nudity and a gory stabbing, a fleeting suggestion of masturbation, an attempted sexual encounter, and recurring rough language. A-III (R)

Murder, Inc. (1960) Fact-based drama of the crime syndicate's top hit-man (Peter Falk) in the 1930s who was himself murdered in the 1940s after making a deal with the New York DA (Henry Morgan) to testify against Brooklyn mob-boss Lepke (David J. Stewart). Directed by Burt Balaban and Stuart Rosenberg, the gangster era is depicted convincingly enough, though the narrative is handicapped by focusing on two peripheral characters (Stuart Whitman and May Britt) who fail to generate much human interest. Restrained depiction of vicious murders and underworld brutality. A-III (br)

Murder Is My Beat (1955) Hokey crime story directed by Edgar G. Ulmer in which a police detective (Paul Langton) goes off with a convicted killer (Barbara Payton) in order to prove her innocence by finding the real murderer. Stylized violence and sexual situations. A-III (br)

Murder Most Foul (1964) Agatha Christie's Miss Marple (Margaret Rutherford) causes a hung jury in a murder trial and then tracks the real killer to a theatrical troupe headed by a ham actor (Ron Moody). Directed by George Pollack, there are the usual assortment of suspects and red herrings, but the stage setting is rather fun and gives Rutherford the opportunity to recite "The Shooting of Dan McGrew." Enjoyable mystery fare and the violence is minimal. A-I (br)

Murder, My Sweet (1944) Raymond Chandler's hardboiled detective, Philip Marlowe (Dick Powell), sets out to find a missing person, but the trail leads to a widening mystery involving a stolen jade necklace, a blackmail ring, and assorted mayhem. Directed by Edward Dmytryk, the crime story offers a lot of gritty atmosphere, tough characters (Claire Trevor, Mike Mazurki and Otto Kruger), imaginative plot twists, and snappy period dialogue. Justice prevails over all the stylized violence. A-II (br)

Murder on a Bridle Path (1936) Pedestrian murder-mystery with schoolteacher Hildegarde Withers (Helen Broderick in the role created by Edna May Oliver) helping New York City homicide inspector Oscar Piper (James Gleason) catch the killer of a socialite horseback-riding in Central Park. Directed by Edward Killy and William Hamilton, the plot and characters earn little interest, the red herrings are artificial, and the solution proves disappointing, despite some sinister thrills in the climax. Some stylized violence and racial stereotyping. A-I (br)

Murder on a Honeymoon (1935) Once again, prim schoolteacher Hildegarde Withers (Edna May Oliver) and NYPD inspector Oscar Piper (James Gleason) join forces in solving the case of a stolen corpse on Catalina Island. Directed by Lloyd Corrigan, the gangland murder mystery is secondary to the comical bickering between sleuths, with the amateur always one step ahead of the professional. Some stylized violence, considerable menace, and comic racial stereotyping. A-II (br)

Murder on Approval (1956) Mediocre crime story directed by Bernard Knowles in which an American private detective (Tom Conway) goes to London to investigate a swindle involving a rare Barbados postage stamp. Stylized violence and sexual innuendo. A-II (br)

Murder on the Blackboard (1934) Mystery series with sardonic schoolmarm Hildegarde Withers (Edna May Oliver) teaming with NYPD inspector Oscar Piper (James Gleason), this time on the case of a murdered music teacher (Barbara Fritchie). Director George Archainbaud turns the school into an ominous setting whose suspects include fellow teachers Bruce Cabot and Gertrude Michael, principal Tully Marshall, and janitor Fredrik Vogeding, but the fun comes from the banter between the amateur sleuth and the hardboiled cop. Mystery menace and sexual innuendo. A-II (br)

Murder on the Orient Express (1974) Stylish screen version of the Agatha Christie mystery with Belgian detective Hercule Poirot (Albert Finney) solving the murder of a man (Richard Widmark) whom everyone on the train apparently had good reason to kill. Set in the 1930s, director Sidney Lumet emphasizes the elegance of the period, has an enthusiastic all-star cast (Ingrid Bergman, Wendy Hiller, Vanessa Redgrave, Lauen Bacall, John Gielgud, et al.) and is faithful to the original's wit and verve. Exceptionally well-done escapist entertainment for those who enjoy murder mysteries, but the murder here is rather brutal and definitely not for preteens. A-II (PG)

Murder Over New York (1940) Formula mystery in which Charlie Chan (Sidney Toler) teams with a New York cop (Donald MacBride) in solving the murder of a British secret agent (Frederick Worlock). Directed by Harry Lachman, the film's suspects include the dead man's friend (Ricardo Cortez), his butler (Leyland Hodgson), a British official (Melville Cooper), and an American financier (Kane Richmond), with comic relief from Chan's Number Two Son (Sen Yung). Stylized violence and mild ethnic stereotyping. A-II (br)

Murder She Said (1962) Dandy Agatha Christie mystery in which amateur detective Miss Marple (Margaret Rutherford) sees a murder committed on a passing train, but the police aren't interested, and so she investigates on her own by taking a job as maid on the estate where she figures the body was ditched. Directed by George Pollock, the suspects in the puzzling case include the estate's irascible owner (James Robertson Justice), his bickering relatives, and a visiting doctor (Arthur Kennedy), with the resourceful Marple getting out of some dangerous scrapes before trapping the killer. Menacing situations mixed with humor. A-I (br)

Murderer's Row (1966) Dean Martin as Matt Helm, the poor man's James Bond, who specializes less in espionage than in booze and broads. Its plot about a kidnapped scientist is meant to be a spoof of spy-spoof movies but offers little more than a leer-filled bag of crude sexual innuendo and puerile naughtiness, with Martin's lumbering characterization providing a paltry few unintentional guffaws. O (br)

Murders in the Rue Morgue (1932) Creaky horror tale set in 19th-century Paris, where a medical student (Leon Ames) saves his girlfriend from a mad scientist (Bela Lugosi) who's seeking a bride for his giant ape. Directed by Robert Florey, this version of the Edgar Allan Poe story involves some crackpot notions of evolution, but the narrative builds considerable tension from its eerie atmosphere and stark expressionistic visuals. Some nasty violence, menacing situations, and sexual innuendo. A-III (br)

Murders in the Rue Morgue (1971) Poor adaptation of the Poe story, with a wooden performance by Jason Robards matched by those of Christine Kaufmann and Herbert Lom. Director Gordon Hessler provides little tension in what was intended as a horror story, though he keeps the makeup artists and special-effects department busy with a plethora of acid murders, decapitations, and dream sequences. A-III (PG)

Muriel's Wedding (1995) Obsessed with fantasies of her wedding day, a young woman (Toni Collette), lacking self-esteem, excitedly rushes into an arranged marriage, abandoning her wheelchair-bound roommate (Rachel Griffiths) in the process, only to come to her senses after a family tragedy. Despite the infectiously buoyant tone of the proceedings, Australian writer-director P.J. Hogan's giddy comedy-drama never digs deeply into the title character's development as a person until the undeserved feel-good ending. Discreet bedroom scenes, fleeting nudity, and a few instances of rough language. A-III (R)

Murmur of the Heart (1971) French drama about the sexual maturing of a precocious adolescent in an upper middle-class family, whose comfortable materialism is more offensive than the youth's sexual initiation in a brothel or the salvation-through-incest resolution of the story. Directed by Louis Malle, the movie has some light humor and fine performances but depicts the sexual and social antics of the disinterested father (Daniel Gelin), the disorganized mother (Lea Massari), and their three parasitic sons as both healthy and amusing. Amoral treatment of sexual promiscuity and a bogus sense of social values. O (nr)

Murph the Surf (see: **Live a Little, Steal a Lot**)

Murphy's Law (1986) A ruthless felon (Carrie Snodgrass), determined to even the score with the men who sent her to prison, goes on a killing spree for which she frames a cop (Charles Bronson). J. Lee Thompson's direction succeeds only in exploiting vulgarity and violence for simplistic shock value. Profanity and nudity further mar the Bronson vehicle. O (R)

Murphy's Romance (1986) It isn't until movie's end that Sally Field, in the role of a divorcée, and James Garner, as a widower twice her age, realize that all their previous bickering means that they're in love, long after all but middle-aged romantics will have lost interest. Intruding into director Martin Ritt's mostly genial fantasy romance is some rough language and an inconsistent view of sexual morality. A-III (PG-13)

Murphy's War (1971) Offbeat drama about merchant seaman Peter O'Toole, sole survivor of a German submarine attack off South America near the end of WW II, who is picked up by barge owner Philippe Noiret and patched up by Quaker missionary Sian Phillips. O'Toole seeks to sink the U-boat by bombs from an ancient airplane, ramming it with the old barge, and is still at it when the war ends. Director Peter Yates fails to make his implausible revenge tale exciting, let alone interesting. Some intense scenes of wartime violence. A-III (GP)

Muscle Beach Party (1964) Sun-baked youth comedy in which an Italian contessa (Luciana Paluzzi) goes after a muscle-bound he-man (Rock Stevens aka Peter Lupus), then falls for a surfer (Frankie Avalon) who ultimately turns back to his girlfriend (Annette Funicello). Directed by William Asher, the banal proceedings terminate in a massive brawl halted sternly by Peter Lorre in his last screen appearance. Slapstick violence and sexual innuendo. A-II (br)

Music Box (1989) Prominent Chicago attorney (Jessica Lange) successfully defends her father (Armin Mueller-Stahl) against accusations of WW II crimes committed in his native Hungary, but then a startling cycle of events suggests that he may, in fact, be guilty. Instead of exploring the daughter's dilemma whether to believe his denials or turn him in, director Costa-Gavras spends most of the movie on tedious, surprisingly suspenseless courtroom proceedings that do, however, raise some justice issues worth pondering. Rough language and explicit courtroom testimony about a gang rape and other wartime atrocities. A-III (PG-13)

Music in Manhattan (1944) Formula romantic comedy directed by John H. Auer in which a Broadway singer (Anne Shirley), mistakenly identified as the wife of a war hero, tries to straighten matters out by marrying him so she can get an annulment in this reworking of the 1937 **Shall We Dance**. Comic treatment of marriage. A-II (br)

Music in the Air (1934) Weak musical directed by Joe May offers unmemorable songs by Oscar Hammerstein II and Jerome Kern in a story set in Bavaria, where Munich's top singer (Gloria Swanson) and her temperamental male lead (John Boles) mount an operetta with the unlikely help of Alpine rustics (Douglass Montgomery and June Lang). Romantic situations and misunderstandings. A-II (br)

Music Lovers, The (1971) British production about the tormented life of 19th-century Russian composer Peter Ilyich Tchaikovsky (Richard Chamberlain) places too much stress on trying to link his music to his sexual disorientation and unconsummated marriage to a woman (Glenda Jackson), who, in a grisly set of sequences, goes quite mad. Directed by Ken Russell with characteristic visual extravagance and narrative weaknesses, the movie's Freudian approach is questionable, but its interplay with realism and surrealism, objectivity and subjectivity, succeeds to a surprising degree. Mature themes and some nudity. A-IV (R)

Music Man, The (1962) Rousing screen version of Meredith Willson's Broadway musical about Professor Harold Hill (Robert Preston), a smooth-talking con-man who tries to swindle an Iowa community by spinning dreams of a school marching-band, but love pushes larceny out of his heart when he falls for the town librarian (Shirley Jones). Directed by Morton Da Costa, the show revolves around the irrepressibly energetic Preston, supported by a strong cast (Pert Kelton, Paul Ford, and little Ronny Howard), nostalgic bits of 1912 Iowa corn, and Willson's lovely yet lively song-and-dance numbers, including the show-stopping "76 Trombones." Fine family fare, though a bit long for small attention spans. A-I (G)

Music of Chance, The (1993) Seedy gambler James Spader and ex-firefighter Mandy Patinkin lose all in a high-stakes card game to eccentric millionaires Charles Durning and Joel Grey, then set to working off their debt by building a massive stone wall on the winners' secluded estate under the watchful eyes of smilingly sinister groundskeeper M. Emmet Walsh. Directed by Philip Haas, the psychological tale of cunning characters trying to outfox each other is interesting to watch but leads nowhere, and in the end seems pointless. An implied sexual encounter, several off-screen beatings, and intermittent rough language. A-III (R)

Music Teacher, The (1989) Turn-of-the-century story about an opera star (Jose Van Dam) who retires at the peak of his career to become the singing teacher of two unlikely young students (Anne Roussel and Philippe Volter). Belgian director Gerard Corbiau fashions the movie around opera singer Van Dam, and the result will entrance opera buffs with its wall-to-wall music but may distance others with its passionless, ambiguous character study. Implied sexual encounter. A-III (PG)

Mustang Country (1976) Joel McCrea plays an aging cowboy who is joined by a little Indian boy (Demetri Mina) in attempting to capture a wild horse while eluding a three-toed grizzly, the villain of the piece because he kills more than he eats. Directed by John Champion, the result is a predictable wildlife adventure movie for family viewers, but one that youngsters will especially enjoy. A-I (G)

Mutations, The (1974) Disagreeable British horror movie about a mad doctor (Donald Pleasence) whose attempt to create a new form of life that is both plant and animal requires experimental candidates that a sadistic freak-show owner (Tom Baker) helpfully supplies. Humorlessly directed by Jack Cardiff, the movie's collection of human mutants varies from the merely gruesome to the baldly disgusting, with a layer of coy nudity to add the final insult. O (R)

Mute Witness (1995) Overwrought thriller about a mute special-effects technician (Marina Sudina) with an American production filming in a dilapidated Moscow studio, where late one night she stumbles on the making of a snuff film, then flees being killed by a Russian porno ring. Writer-director Anthony Waller's manipulative exercise in terror places its voiceless heroine in precarious situations marked more by violent special effects than credible suspense. Flashes of graphic violence and brief nudity, much menace, and occasional rough language. A-IV (R)

Mutiny on the Bounty (1935) Classic sea-adventure aboard the H.M.S. Bounty on a voyage to Tahiti in 1787 under cruel Captain Bligh (Charles Laughton), whose savage mistreatment of the crew finally drives chief officer Fletcher Christian (Clark Gable) to take command of the ship. Director Frank Lloyd gives a rousing account of life at sea under the strict discipline and harsh conditions of the era, but does even better with the human drama propelling this fact-based yarn of duty, comradeship, and divided loyalties in the face of injustice. Stylized violence and a romantic situations. A-II (br)

Mutiny on the Bounty (1962) The remake is a much more handsome production than the original but, despite Trevor Howard's steely performance as the notorious Captain Bligh, Marlon Brando sinks the enterprise by turning Fletcher Christian into an effete snob rather than a leader of men. Director Lewis Milestone turns an exciting story of conflict between duty and humanity into a good-looking but leaden exercise. Sexual innuendo and stylized violence. A-II (br)

My American Cousin (1986) A Canadian pre-adolescent (Margaret Langrick) is lifted out of the boring doldrums of 1950s Vancouver when her teenaged American cousin (John Wildman) visits her staid and conventional family. Writer-director Sandy Wilson scores with a light and tender reminiscence of puppy love and awakening excitement with the world outside the home. Although there are some scenes of passionate cuddling, it is an essentially innocent treatment of youthful affection. A-II (PG)

My Best Friend Is a Vampire (1988) Humorless comedy in which a nerdish but likeable teenager (Robert Sean Leonard) is seduced and bitten by a new neighbor who turns out to be a vampire. Much offensive sexist humor, some profanity, and disconcerting visuals of the newly vampired teen biting necks and guzzling blood. O (PG)

My Best Friend's Wedding (1997) Dismayed that her longtime pal and former lover (Dermot Mulroney) is about to marry someone (Cameron Diaz) he just met, a restaurant critic (Julia Roberts) decides she wants him back and connives to stop the wedding. Director P. J. Hogan's muddled romantic triangle offers little more than a gooey confection of bogus emotions on beautiful faces. Some sexual references and a risqué sight gag, a crude expression, and an instance of rough language. A-III (PG-13)

My Blood Runs Cold (1965) Pedestrian melodrama about a wealthy 21-year-old (Joey Heatherton), who a mysterious stranger (Troy Donahue) convinces is the reincarnation of her great-grandmother and he's her long-lost lover, until their romance is chilled by news of an escaped homicidal maniac. Directed by William Conrad, the hokey proceedings hold little suspense and less interest. More menace than violence and romantic situations. A-II (br)

My Bloody Valentine (1981) Low-budget Canadian exploitation movie about a demented coal-miner who stalks his attractive young victims with a pick-ax on Valentine's Day. Directed by George Mihalka, the absurd plot offers only violence and vast amounts of flowing blood. O (R)

My Blue Heaven (1990) Big-city mob informant (Steve Martin), relocated to the suburbs by the Witness Protection Program, masterminds a romance between an FBI agent (Rick Moranis) and an assistant district attorney (Joan Cusack), while they have their hands full trying to reform the happy-go-lucky hoodlum. Director Herbert Ross turns in a minor-league comedy notable chiefly for Martin's riotous performance as the tough New Yorker bored to death by laid-back Californians. Cartoon-style shoot-outs, comic treatment of theft and bigamy, and an instance of rough language. A-II (PG-13)

My Bodyguard (1980) Young transfer-student (Chris Makepeace), bullied by a neighborhood gang of toughs, hires a hulking, brooding classmate (Adam Baldwin) to act as his bodyguard. Some effective moments, but it takes some uncertain turns before reaching a violent and far-fetched conclusion. Some sexual references, and its simplistic solving of a problem by resorting to violence makes it dubious fare for young viewers. A-III (PG)

My Boyfriend's Back (1993) Witless comedy about a love-struck teen (Andrew Lowery) who comes back from the dead as a reluctant flesh-eating zombie so he can go to the prom with the girl (Traci Lind) he died saving during a botched convenience store hold-up. Director Bob Balaban maintains a sophomoric level of horror-comedy that might amuse 10-year-olds, were it not for the adult level of the double entendres. Comic depiction of violence and much sexual innuendo. A-III (PG-13)

My Brilliant Career (1980) Bright Australian dramatization of a autobiographical novel about a young farm girl (Judy Davis in a dazzling performance) raised in poverty but determined to make a life of her own as a writer at the turn of the century. Gillian Armstrong directs a work that besides being very funny, very human, very touching and always entertaining, is a tribute to the human spirit and the artistic imagination. Exhilarating family fare. A-I (G)

My Cousin Rachel (1952) Intriguing psychological puzzler from the Daphne du Maurier story about a young Englishman (Richard Burton) who falls in love with an appealing but enigmatic woman (Olivia de Havilland), then comes to fear she is trying to kill him. Director Henry Koster evokes a suitably eerie atmosphere from the Victorian setting on the rugged Cornish coast, but the ambiguous treatment of the title character becomes tiresome, then concludes disappointingly with many loose ends. Romantic complications and unanswered questions. A-II (br)

My Cousin Vinny (1992) Tough-talking comedy has New York college students Ralph Macchio and Mitchell Whitfield improbably charged with murder in the deep South, then defended by rookie Brooklyn lawyer Joe Pesci, with a little help from girlfriend Marisa Tomei. Relying on blue-collar and Southern stereotypes, director Jonathan Lynn fashions a fitfully funny, fish-out-of-water courtroom comedy. Much rough language, a few double entendres, and an implied premarital relationship. A-III (R)

My Darling Clementine (1946) Poetic Western follows Wyatt Earp (Henry Fonda) after he becomes sheriff of Tombstone in 1882, befriends Doc Holliday (Victor Mature), and takes on the Clanton gang (led by Walter Brennan) at the OK Corral. Director John Ford builds an evocative picture of a pioneer community and the people who helped build it, largely through a series of vignettes beautifully photographed by Joseph MacDonald. Stylized violence and romantic complications. A-II (br)

My Dear Secretary (1948) Dim romantic comedy written and directed by Charles Martin in which a philandering author (Kirk Douglas) marries his high-minded secretary (Laraine Day), who proceeds to give him a few lessons in the art of writing as well as the value of fidelity. Sexual situations and innuendo. A-III (br)

My Demon Lover (1987) Scott Valentine plays a youth under a curse that makes him turn into a beast whenever he thinks about sex. A noble act frees him into the arms of true love, but director Charles Loventhal exploits sexual situations and bedroom scenes for one-joke humor about demonic violence. O (PG-13)

My Fair Lady (1964) Screen version of the Lerner and Loewe musical based on George Bernard Shaw's play "Pygmalion," in which an egotistical professor (Rex Harrison) makes a bet that he can transform the Cockney speech and manners of a London flower girl (Audrey Hepburn) well enough for her to pass for a lady at the upcoming Royal Ball. Predictably, it is not always the professor who gives the lessons. George Cukor's nimble direction, Cecil Beaton's stunning sets and costumes, the charming performances, and the wonderful music add up to splendid family entertainment. A-I (G)

My Family — Mi Familia (1995) Mexican-American family saga set in Los Angeles from the 1920s to the 1980s follows the parents and their six children (including Jimmy Smits, Edward James Olmos, and Esai Morales) as they endure separations, tragic deaths, and brushes with the law, leaving one son embittered while others find solace in their religious faith. Director Gregory Nava's ambitious, sprawling movie leans towards melodramatic treatment but still emerges as a vibrant account of a Latino family pursuing the American dream. Some violence, fleeting bedroom scenes, brief nudity, and recurring rough language. A-III (R)

My Father, My Master (1977) Somber Italian production about a Sardinian youth, an illiterate shepherd, until military service opens his eyes to a wider world, studies for a high-school diploma, and eventually obtains a degree in linguistics. Directed by Paolo and Vittorio Taviani, the emphasis is on the simple but backward life of rustic peasants, where the family patriarch has total authority. The cruel beatings that the lad endured as a child and the dark and violent passions that permeate the culture in which he grew up make it a film for none but mature viewers. A-IV (nr)

My Father the Hero (1994) A divorced dad (Gerard Depardieu), vacationing in the Bahamas with his 14-year-old daughter (Katherine Heigl), plays along with her attempt to make a 17-year-old (Dalton James) jealous by pretending to be her lover. Though the characters are essentially sweet-natured, director Steve Miner's wrongheaded comedy is unamusingly premised on creating sympathy for a father who abdicates his responsibility to provide moral guidance for his confused young daughter. Sympathetic depiction of deceit, sexual innuendo, and fleeting rear nudity. A-III (PG)

My Father's Glory (1991) At the turn of the century, a young lad from Marseilles (Julien Ciamaca) spends an idyllic summer with his family in rustic Provence learning about nature's wonders from a local boy (Joris Molinas) and about life from his schoolteacher father (Philippe Caubere). Directed by Yves Robert and based on the reminiscences of French author Marcel Pagnol, the result is a lyrical, conflict-free tribute to family life in a simpler, bygone era (companion to **My Mother's Castle**). Subtitles. Brief shot of nude boys. A-I (G)

My Favorite Blonde (1942) Very funny WW II spy caper in which a British agent (Madeleine Carroll) uses a vaudevillian (Bob Hope) with a penguin act to elude Nazi pursuers (led by George Zucco) while crossing the country with secret orders for a US bomber group bound for Britain. Directed by Sidney Lanfield, Hope keeps the laughs coming as the cowardly hero who blunders his way out of various Nazi traps, though he's less successful in keeping Percy the Penguin from stealing his scenes. Comic thrills and menacing situations. A-I (br)

My Favorite Brunette (1947) Bob Hope is in top comic form as a baby photographer mistaken for a private eye by a desperate woman (Dorothy Lamour) on the run from crooks (Charles Dingle, Peter Lorre, Jack La Rue, and Lon Chaney, Jr.) after her uncle's uranium mine. Director Elliott Nugent paces the comedy with suitable menace and suspense, amusing cameos (Bing Crosby and Alan Ladd), and some very funny routines. Stylized violence and romantic situations. A-II (br)

My Favorite Martian (1999) Dopey comedy based on the 1960s sitcom in which a TV newsman (Jeff Daniels) tries to help an alien (Christopher Lloyd) return to Mars before the government can snatch and study him. Director Donald Petrie overuses special effects throughout the frantic proceedings, which make the movie wacky but never witty. Some slapstick violence, fleeting rear nudity, occasional sexual innuendo, toilet humor, and a few instances of profanity. A-III (PG)

My Favorite Season (see: **Ma Saison Préférée**)

My Favorite Spy (1951) Middling comedy in which a stand-up comic (Bob Hope), sent to Morocco to impersonate a lookalike spy, out-bluffs the villains to get the goods and the real spy's girl (Hedy Lamarr). Directed by Norman Z. McLeod, the vehicle is not one of Hope's best, but there are enough laughs to pass the time until the madcap chase wind-up. Some stylized violence and double entendres. A-II (br)

My Favorite Year (1982) Peter O'Toole plays a fading movie star who agrees to appear on a show in the early days of television comedy, and a young gag-writer (Mark Linn-Baker) is assigned to keep the drunken, womanizing actor in line. Director Richard Benjamin's comedy is bright and entertaining as long as talented, charming O'Toole is on screen, but when he's off, the picture quietly dies. Because the humor revolves around the hero's pursuit of women and the bottle, as well as some rather vulgar gags, it is not for younger viewers. A-III (PG)

My Fellow Americans (1996) While attempting to uncover the facts behind a burgeoning political scandal, two bickering former presidents (Jack Lemmon and James Garner) find themselves pursued by government hit-men. Director Peter Segal's inane escapist comedy is surprisingly dark and vulgar in spots, but some may enjoy the two veteran actors one-upping each other throughout the preposterous narrative. Some violence and profanity, fleeting bedroom scenes, frequent sexual innuendo, and an instance of rough language. A-III (PG-13)

My Friend Flicka (1943) After a horse rancher (Preston Foster) gives his young son (Roddy McDowall) a wild colt to care for as his own, the untamed horse causes much grief to both, until ultimately responding to the boy's steadfast love and devotion. Directed by Harold Schuster, there's nothing fancy about this heartwarming family story of a youngster's growth in responsibility, but most viewers will find the boy's adventures with his colt in the scenic wilds of the ranch reason enough to watch. Fine family fare but especially appealing for children. A-I (br)

My Friend Irma (1949) Halting comedy from the title radio-series about dumb-blonde Irma (Marie Wilson), whose dead-beat boyfriend (John Lund) tries to turn orange juice salesmen (Dean Martin and Jerry Lewis) into nightclub entertainers, while Irma's roommate (Diana Lynn) hopes to marry her new boss (Don Defore). Directed by George Marshall, Irma's dim antics get lost in an overly busy plot whose frantic mix-ups are only intermittently amusing. Comic conniving and romantic complications. A-II (br)

My Friend Irma Goes West (1950) Dean Martin and Jerry Lewis pep up a tired plot taking them, the daffy blonde of the title (Marie Wilson), her chiseling boyfriend (John Lund), and her long-suffering roommate (Diana Lynn) from New York to Hollywood via Las Vegas. Director Hal Walker does little to maintain flagging interest in the meager, predictable proceedings. Some leering sexual innuendo and sexist references. A-III (br)

My Friends (1976) Italian comedy concerning the juvenile pranks of four middle-aged practical jokers for whom nothing is sacred except their own bond of camaraderie. Their idea of a good time, for example, is to go to the railroad station and slap the faces of people looking out the windows of departing trains. Directed by Mario Monicello, the movie's attitude towards people in general, and women in particular, is downright nasty, with nudity and vulgar language compounding the tastelessness. O (PG)

My Gal Sal (1942) Colorful biography of songwriter Paul Dresser (Victor Mature), who leaves home in Indiana to join a patent-medicine show, then goes to New York in the Gay Nineties to write some hit numbers for the Broadway singer of the title (Rita Hayworth), with whom he has a rocky romance. Directed by Irving Cummings from Theodore Dreiser's book about his older brother, the result is a nostalgic excursion into an earlier, less sophisticated era of show business, whose sentimental ballads are still sung today. Romantic complications. A-II (br)

My Geisha (1962) Practical joke turns sour when a Hollywood director (Yves Montand) films Puccini's opera "Madame Butterfly" in Japan, unaware that the geisha he has chosen for the title role is actually his movie-star wife (Shirley MacLaine) and the only reason his studio producer (Edward G. Robinson) is backing the project. Director Jack Cardiff starts with a lightweight comic premise that becomes mere silliness by taking MacLaine's masquerade seriously, though the picturesque Japanese locales and culture offer some compensations. Marital differences and occasional sexual innuendo. A-II (br)

My Giant (1998) Sweet-natured but cloying comedy in which a failed talent-agent (Billy Crystal) thinks he has found his ticket to the big time when he discovers a nearly eight-foot-tall Romanian (Gheorghe Muresan) and lures the gentle giant to America by promising to reunite him with a childhood sweetheart. Directed by Michael Lehmann, the comic proceedings suffer from excessive sentimentality, especially when the manipulative agent suddenly puts his client's needs first. Fleeting violence and occasional profanity. A-II (PG)

My Girl (1991) Heartwarming drama in which an imaginative 11-year-old (Anna Chlumsky), whose widowed father (Dan Aykroyd) operates a funeral parlor out of their home, confronts some of her worst fears when her dad's attention is drawn to the new cosmetologist (Jamie Lee Curtis) and she loses her best friend (Macaulay Culkin). Director Howard Zieff handles childhood traumas with humor and sensitivity in an evocative story of memorable characters and life-affirming relationships. Brief but disturbing sequence of a juvenile's death, discreet scene about menstruation, and a drug reference. A-II (PG)

My Girl 2 (1994) Visiting Los Angeles to find out more about her late mother, a 13-year-old (Anna Chlumsky) is befriended by a teenage boy (Austin O'Brien) who helps the girl hunt down clues to her mom's mysterious past. Director Howard Zieff's sentimental sequel features two appealing youngsters in a slight story-line whose affirmation of family values includes some adult situations. A live-in relationship. A-III (PG)

My Left Foot (1989) Powerful dramatization of the life of Irish writer-artist Christy Brown (1932-81), born with cerebral palsy to a large, impoverished Catholic family, shows his triumph over physical disabilities as the creative intelligence bottled up inside his young, twisted body finds expression, thanks in large part to his mother's love and encouragement. Jim Sheridan's sensitive, unsentimental direction and brilliant acting by Hugh O'Conor and Daniel Day-Lewis as the young and the adult Christy provide a testament to the power of the spirit over adversity and a tribute to a mother's unquestioning belief in her child. Some violence, rough language, and sexual innuendo. A-III (R)

My Life (1993) High-powered but terminally ill business executive (Michael Keaton) experiences emotional and spiritual healing during the process of making an autobiographical video for his pregnant wife (Nicole Kidman) to show their unborn son in later years. Writer-director Bruce Joel Rubin shows the personal growth of a man who has repressed his feelings until coming to terms with his impending death in a drama that resists tugging on the tear-ducts until the closing scenes. Family confrontations and an instance of rough language. A-II (PG-13)

My Life as a Dog (1988) When his mother becomes seriously ill, a fatherless 12-year-old (Anton Glanzelius) finds himself packed off to spend the summer with his uncle in the country, where he comes to feel at home amidst the colorful characters living and working nearby. Swedish director Lasse Hallstrom delivers a lovely, spirited, and hopeful movie about how people survive life's tragedies and loneliness. Subtitles. Fleeting shot of a nude model and several scenes depicting children's curiosity about sex. A-III (nr)

My Love Has Been Burning (1979) Elegant Japanese production about a pioneer for women's rights in the 1890s. Kinuyo Tanaka plays the daughter of a wealthy family, who through bitter personal experience of male domination of society becomes a dedicated feminist who founds a school for the education of women. Directed in 1949 by Kenji Mizoguchi, it is a feminist tract more than a credible drama, but one that has considerable historical interest in terms of the development of women's rights in Japan. A-II (nr)

My Lover, My Son (1970) Failed British melodrama dealing with the sexual attraction a mother (Romy Schneider) develops for her understandably confused adolescent son (Dennis Waterman). Directed by John Newland, whose main object seems to be gaudiness, the screenplay all but drowns its principals in cheap melodramatic thrills, and neither the mother's ultimate comeuppance nor the son's more natural romance with a local girl can save the movie from deserved oblivion. O (R)

My Man Godfrey (1936) Classic screwball comedy in which an empty-headed socialite (Carole Lombard) wins a posh scavenger hunt with the help of a jobless, homeless "forgotten man" (William Powell), who's then hired as butler for her wacky rich family and in the process transforms them and himself. Director Gregory La Cava has a lot of fun with a top cast, but the Depression-era story is treated with social conscience as well as comic wit in its portrayal of a person's worth as more than wealth or position. Some romantic situations. A-I (br)

My Man Godfrey (1957) Updated version of the 1936 comedy now features an illegal Austrian immigrant (David Niven) as the new butler who transforms a wacky household's impetuous daughter (June Allyson), her nasty sister (Marta Hyer), their dotty mom (Jesse Royce Landis), and long-suffering father (Robert Keith). Directed by Henry Koster, the comic proceedings are slickly contrived but lack the heartwarming sentiment of the original Depression-era situations. Sexual innuendo and romantic complications. A-II (br)

My Michael (1976) Screen version of the Amos Oz novel, set in Israel during the 1950s, about a marriage that has withered because it never had a chance to grow. Understanding how the young couple's life together goes on unraveling in estrangement and alienation is possible only if seen as reflecting the embattled Israeli state, not at war, but certainly not at peace, in their own land. While all the dimensions of this ambitious theme are not completely realized, director Don Wolman had made a challenging drama about the special complexities of Israeli life that is worth the attention of serious moviegoers. A-III (nr)

My Mother's Castle (1991) Continuing the story of **My Father's Glory**, a young boy in pre-WW I Marseilles (Julien Ciamaca) has his first case of puppy love, and his schoolteacher father (Philippe Caubere) risks his job by sneaking the family across private property to shorten their miles-long walk to a summer weekend cottage in Provence. French author Marcel Pagnol's joyous childhood memories are beautifully realized under Yves Robert's direction, which casts a kindly eye on its characters' well-observed foibles. Subtitles. Ambivalent discussion of father's atheism. A-II (PG)

My Name Is Joe (1999) Wrenching drama set in a deprived Glascow neighborhood, where a recovering alcoholic (Peter Mullan) and a community health-worker (Louise Goodall) fall in love, but his misguided efforts to help a young couple stay off drugs jeopardize his romance and leads to tragedy. Director Ken Loach captures the desperate humanity of substance abusers trying to go straight, but the narrative is weakened by scattering its focus on too many issues left unresolved. Subtitles. Brief criminal activity and violence including suicide, an implied affair with fleeting nudity, substance abuse, much rough language, and intermittent profanity. A-III (R)

My Name Is Julia Ross (1945) Minor mystery thriller in which a London secretary (Nina Foch) is hired to work in the home of a wealthy woman (Dame May Whitty) and her sinister son (George Macready), then awakens from a drugged sleep to find them holding her prisoner in a seaside mansion in Cornwall. Director Joseph H. Lewis sets up the premise in intriguing fashion, but as the motive for these strange events becomes clear, interest wanes until the hurried, disappointing conclusion. Much menace and threatening situations. A-II (br)

My Name Is Nobody (1974) Henry Fonda and Terence Hill star in a lavish spoof of spaghetti Westerns, produced by Sergio Leone and directed by Tonino Valeria. Fonda is a laconic, aging marshal with the reputation of being the fastest gun in the West. Actually the sly, kinetic Hill is faster, and saves the lawman from any number of mishaps on his last assignment before retirement. Though there are some charming comic bits, the movie's one-joke concept can only be characterized as a good-natured waste of time. A-II (PG)

My Neighbor Totoro (1993) Mildly entertaining animated feature from Japan recounts the adventures of two small girls when their family moves to an old rural house, where they discover, among other things, the fat, furry creature of the title whose magical powers at first frighten, then delight them. Directed by Hayao Miyazaki, the 1988 production does best with its fantasy of spirit creatures, some spooky but most benign, and there are some lovely vistas of nature, especially when Totoro flies them over the countryside, but like the dubbing, the story-line is rather forced and artificial. Some fun for the very young and those young in spirit. A-I (G)

My New Gun (1992) Subservient housewife (Diane Lane) bullied by obnoxious husband (Stephen Collins) into keeping a handgun for protection becomes romantically entangled with a strange neighbor (James LeGros), who steals the weapon to protect his goofy mom (Tess Harper). Writer-director Stacy Cochran's stab at sly, suburban satire is a minor effort showcasing amusingly quirky characters in wry situations. Implied affair, comic violence, and occasional rough language. A-III (nr)

My Night at Maud's (1970) After resolving to marry a religiously devout student (Marie-Christine Barrault) he has never met, a 34-year-old engineer (Jean-Louis Trintignant) happens to meet a sensuous woman (Francoise Fabian) with whom he spends the night in talking about everything, from literature and mathematics to politics and religion. Intriguing French movie directed by Eric Rohmer, the intellectual talkathon focuses on the cerebral quest for life's meaning while indicating the difficulty of people to live up to the practical aspects of idealism and dogma, whether Christian or Marxist. The third in Rohmer's series of Six Moral Tales, it has the ambiguity of real life and is a perfect discussion piece. A-III (GP)

My Old Man's Place (see: **Glory Boy**)

My Outlaw Brother (1951) Routine Western directed by Elliott Nugent is set in Mexico, where a Texas Ranger (Robert Preston) on the trail of a bandit helps a greenhorn from Manhattan (Mickey Rooney) find his older brother (Robert Stack), who happens to be very close to the bandit. Stylized violence and sexual innuendo. A-II (br)

My Own Private Idaho (1991) Perverted tale of two young male prostitutes (River Phoenix and Keanu Reeves) who hustle their way from the Northwest to Italy in a futile search for one's homicidal mom. Writer-director Gus Van Sant's disjointed story is a smug and ugly commentary on friendship and family life. Frequent sordid sexual references and allusions to incest, brief shots of gay and heterosexual encounters with momentary nudity, and much rough language. O (R)

My Side of the Mountain (1969) Toronto youth journeys into the Quebec wilderness to prove that he can take care of himself, adapts quite easily to life in the forest, and is befriended by a migrant folk-singer (Theodore Bikel) who eventually rescues him during a snowstorm. Produced by Robert B. Radnitz and directed by James B. Clarke, its intriguing story has substance instead of cliches, in addition to magnificent photography capturing the beauty of its natural setting. Intelligent family fare whose spirit of adventure and youthful independence can be enjoyed by all. A-I (G)

My Sister Eileen (1942) Amusing period piece from Ruth McKinney's story about a promising writer (Rosalind Russell) and the aspiring actress of the title (Janet Blair) who leave Ohio to seek their fortune in New York City where they rent a $45-a-month basement apartment with a constant stream of eccentric visitors, including an ex-college football star (Wayne Morris), some Brazilian naval cadets, and a smitten magazine editor (Brian Aherne). Directed by Alexander Hall, the whimsical misadventures of two innocents in the big city are still pleasing despite the dated situations. Mild sexual innuendo. A-II (br)

My Sister Eileen (1955) Updated musical version of the 1942 comedy with two sisters from Ohio coming to New York to seek careers as a writer (Betty Garrett) and an actress (Janet Leigh), with wacky results involving their Greenwich Village basement apartment, a contingent of Brazilian naval cadets, a smug magazine editor (Jack Lemmon), and a shy soda jerk (Bob Fosse). Directed by Richard Quine, the updating makes the romantic proceedings considerably less innocent, though the songs and dance numbers add an agreeable dimension to the entertainment. Sexual situations and much innuendo. A-III (br)

My Son Alone (see: **American Empire**)

My Son, the Hero (1963) Dubbed Italian production directed by Ducio Tessari is set in the ancient kingdom of Crete, whose wicked ruler (Pedro Armendariz) is challenged by the righteous Titans. Pale escapist fare. A-I (br)

My Stepmother Is an Alien (1988) Cosmic clinker in which a shapely alien (Kim Basinger) saucers to Earth to find and conquer the scientist (Dan Aykroyd) who is zapping her planet with his zany experiments. Director Richard Benjamin's humorless comedy becomes lurid in depicting her sexual attempts to distract her homeland's tormentor. Explicit seduction scenes, much sexual innuendo, and a child's encouragement of her parent's sexual misconduct. O (PG-13)

My Sweet Charlie (1970) Two fugitives — a frightened pregnant girl thrown out by her family (Patty Duke) and a black lawyer (Al Freeman Jr.) on the run for killing a white man in self defense — find themselves taking refuge in a vacant Southern beach-house. The relationship has nothing to do with sex or sensationalism, but with basic emotions of fear and prejudice that ultimately lead to honesty and recognition of each other as human beings. Director Lamont Johnson avoids melodramatic sentimentality, helped by sharp performances from his two principals and an intelligent script based on David Westheimer's novel. One of those rare made-for-television movies that earned subsequent distribution to movie theaters, it still has something relevant to say about ordinary people as well as social justice. A-II (G)

My Sweet Little Village (1987) Czech director Jiri Menzel creates a gentle fable about fellowship and brotherhood in a tiny worker's commune. Imbedded in the narrative is a sly comment upon socialist ideals and an affirmation of the joys of a simple rural life. A-II (PG)

My Uncle Antoine (1972) Canadian movie centering on a Christmas Eve during the 1940s, when an adolescent gets his first glimpse of adulthood after he and his inebriated uncle lose a corpse they are transporting to the funeral parlor during a snowstorm and arrive home in the early morning to chance upon his aunt's act of infidelity. Directed by Claude Jutra, the film looks with clarity and compassion at the world of a small French-Canadian mining village and its vibrant community of characters seen in a montage of portraiture and vignette. Though rooted in a specific ethnic tradition, its perspective is universal enough to strike chords celebrating our common humanity. A-III (nr)

My Way (1974) Muddled South African melodrama about the highly strained relations within the family of a success-driven building contractor (Joe Stewardson), a former marathon runner who demands success from his three sons, and the predictable conflicts and lapses that result. Directed by Emil Nofal, it is notable only for its complete absence of blacks, even in crowd scenes. Domestic violence. A-III (PG)

Myra Breckinridge (1970) Screen version of Gore Vidal's novel about a sex-change operation turns satire into burlesque, and, in trying to show how society has accepted the false values of Hollywood image-making, makes gross caricatures out of the notable (John Huston and Mae West) and less than notable (Rex Reed). Directed by Michael Sarne, the treatment is thoroughly distasteful and at times repulsive. Sexual innuendo, nudity, vulgar sight gags, and rough language predominate. O (R)

Mysterious Island (1961) Escaping a Confederate prison in an observation balloon, five men (led by Michael Craig and Gary Merrill) wind up on a Pacific island, where they encounter giant-sized animals, a shipwrecked Englishwoman (Joan Greenwood), and her niece, pirates, an erupting volcano, and the helping hand of Captain Nemo (Herbert Lom). Director Cy Enfield's sequel to Jules Verne's *20,000 Leagues under the Sea* is a rousing adventure tale with intriguing plot twists and imaginative special effects by Ray Harryhausen, but the ending flags. Despite the usual stylized violence and menace, the result is exciting family fare with an antiwar message. A-I (br)

Mysterious Island of Captain Nemo, The (1974) The famed Nautilus of Jules Verne has been dry-docked and is being used solely as a kind of plush houseboat by the mysterious Captain Nemo (Omar Sharif), who deters visitors by blasting them from afar with his robot ray-guns. Curiously disjointed European co-production directed by Juan Antonio Bardem and Henri Colpi mixes a thin plot and some lovely scenery with a torrent of mushy dialogue and low-grade acting that results in less than enthralling children's fare. A-I (G)

Mysterious Mr. Moto (1938) John P. Marquand's Japanese detective (Peter Lorre) turns up as a prisoner on Devil's Island, from which he escapes with a British convict (Leon Ames) who takes him to London, where Moto thwarts a gang of assassins. Directed by Norman Foster, the crime plot offers some fun as Moto matches wits with the British police while masquerading as a member of the underworld. Stylized violence. A-I (br)

Mysterious Mr. Wong, The (1935) Low-budget, tongue-in-cheek thriller directed by William Nigh is set in Manhattan's Chinatown, where a newspaper reporter (Wallace Ford) links a series of murders to a master criminal (Bela Lugosi) seeking the twelfth coin of Confucius, which, according to legend, gives its owner the power to rule China. Eerie atmosphere and period stereotypes. A-II (br)

Mystery Broadcast (1943) Unpretentious mystery directed by George Sherman in which the writer (Ruth

Terry) of a radio crime series announces next week's program will name the killer in an unsolved murder case, then gets help from the show's sound-effects director (Mary Treen) and a rival radio detective (Frank Albertson) in accomplishing her purpose. Stylized violence and menacing situations. A-II (br)

Mystery Date (1991) Bloated suspense comedy has a naive young fellow (Ethan Hawke) mistaken for his hotly pursued criminal older brother (Brian McNamara) while trying to impress his perplexed date (Teri Polo). As the number of situations and characters increase, director Jonathan Wacks's muddled movie sinks into oblivion. Recurring nasty menace with some violence and dead bodies. A-III (PG-13)

Mystery of Kaspar Hauser, The (1975) Compelling German drama about the discovery in the town square one morning in 1828 of a teenage boy capable of speaking but a few words, barely able to walk, and apparently without any experience of human society. The mystery of his origins was never solved, but he became an object of curiosity, exhibited in a sideshow, and studied by scientists and philosophers until his equally mysterious murder in 1833. Director Werner Herzog is not interested in rational explanations of these fact-based events but in portraying the injustices committed against a totally innocent outsider by a complacent, self-satisfied society. A-III (nr)

Mystery of Monster Island (1981) English-language version of a multinational production in which a wealthy American (Peter Cushing) buys a volcanic island that a ruthless rival (Terence Stamp) knows is rich in gold deposits, then sends his young nephew to survey it, though most of his time is spent fighting off cannibals, monsters, and marauders. Directed by A. Piquer Simon and based on a Jules Verne story, the fanciful proceedings are rather erratic and make little sense, until a less-than-surprising finale. Stylized violence, fantasy menace, and mild sexual innuendo. A-II (nr)

Mystery of Rampo, The (1995) After the government bans his novel in which a wife kills her husband, an aging Japanese author (Naoto Takenaka) meets a woman (Michiko Hada) who was acquitted of murdering her mate, and this sets him to work on a new story blending the novel's wife with her real counterpart and himself as a dapper detective (Masahiro Motoki). Director Kazuyoshi Okuyama explores the creative process of a writer's imagination, intermingling fantasy with reality and the past with the present in an intriguing work of exquisite visual beauty. Subtitles. Restrained violence, a cross-dresser, and a scene with partial nudity. A-III (R)

Mystery of the Mary Celeste (see: **Phantom Ship**)

Mystery of Thug Island, The (1966) Failed European adventure story ineptly directed by Nino Battiferri, with Guy Madison fighting an outlaw-cult operating under the direction of a pseudo-goddess in India. Stylized violence. A-II (br)

Mystery Train (1989) Writer-director Jim Jarmusch has concocted a trio of lightly comic tales set on the back-streets of Memphis that offhandedly invoke the memory and spirit of Elvis Presley. An offbeat road picture in which locals and foreigners mix in search of themselves and the ghost of Elvis. Some violence, sexual innuendo, and profanity. A-III (R)

Mystic Pizza (1988) Three young Portuguese-American women (Julia Roberts, Annabeth Gish, and Lili Taylor) live in the seaport town of Mystic, Conn., and work in a pizza parlor known for its secret pizza-sauce and warmhearted owner (Conchata Ferrell). Directed by Donald Petrie, the coming-of-age story might work as a TV series minus the focus on the girls' indiscriminate sex lives. Much explicit sex banter and off-camera sex. O (R)

Myth of Fingerprints, The (1997) Prickly family relationships and tenuous romantic involvements are at stake when four adult children (including Noah Wylie and Julianne Moore) return to rural Maine for a tense Thanksgiving weekend with their gentle mother (Blythe Danner) and coldly critical father (Roy Scheider). Writer-director Bart Freundlich's keenly observed character study reflects how young adults continue to be affected by parental figures as they struggle to form lasting love relationships. Discreet sexual encounters, brief recreational drug use, some rough language, and much profanity. A-III (R)

Nada Gang, The (1974) French production about a small motley band of political extremists whose kidnapping of the American ambassador leads authorities to use extreme counter-terrorist tactics, ultimately forcing the band's fanatic leader (Fabrio Testi) to conclude that violence from the left is as self-defeating as from the right. Directed by Claude Chabrol, the individual characterizations of a fine cast overcome stereotyped roles to involve viewers in the movie's obvious anti-terrorist message. Violent action and atmosphere. A-IV (nr)

Nadine (1987) Warmhearted comedy romance about zany, fumbling couple (Kim Basinger and Jeff Bridges) whose marriage is reconciled after dangerously failed attempts to exploit profit from a set of highway plans. Writer-director Robert Benton's Southern gentility shows brightly through Basinger's frothy portrait of a 1950s working-class woman. A-II (PG)

Naked (1993) Seamy picture of a wild-eyed vagrant (David Thewlis) who steals a car in Manchester to drop in on a former girlfriend (Lesley Sharp) in London, where he beds her spaced-out roommate (Katrin Cartlidge), then takes to roaming the streets until beaten up by hoodlums, which brings him back to be patched up by the girlfriend, only to make off with a large sum of money. Writer-director Mike Leigh looks at the dark side of human nature in his portrait of young man gone bad but gives no insight into the cause for his self-destructive behavior or that of the other characters. Graphic sex scenes, stylized violence, and recurring rough language. O (nr)

Naked Alibi (1954) Uneven crime thriller in which a detective (Sterling Hayden) is thrown off the force for hassling a suspected cop-killer (Gene Barry), then goes after him on his own until the suspect's abused girlfriend (Gloria Grahame) tells him where the murder weapon is hidden in a church. Directed by Jerry Hopper, much of the action is cliched and unconvincing, though Grahame's performance as a lost innocent provides some sorely lacking heart. Stylized violence, much menace, and an implied sexual relationship. A-III (br)

Naked Among the Wolves (1967) Tender German movie about a little Jewish boy smuggled by a prisoner into a concentration camp where the child's survival becomes a symbol of the struggle between the inmates and their Nazi guards shortly before the camp's liberation by American troops. Directed by Frank Beyer, the movie has warmth, compassion, and optimism about the survival of the human spirit even in the most inhuman of circumstances. Restrained treatment of Nazi atrocities. A-II (br)

Naked and the Dead, The (1958) Standard WW II tale of US troops battling on a Pacific island under an arrogant commander (Raymond Massey) who sends a quarrelsome aide (Cliff Robertson) on a patrol behind Japanese lines, which succeeds, despite a crazed sergeant (Aldo Ray), in getting information resulting in an American victory. Directed by Raoul Walsh from the Norman Mailer novel, the realistic battlefield scenes feature the usual military stereotypes, except for Ray's round-the-bend non-com who shoots prisoners and takes their gold fillings. Wartime violence, a few racial epithets, and some sexual innuendo. A-II (br)

Naked Ape, The (1973) Failed screen version of the popular anthropology book by Desmond Morris uses live-action segments and cartoon fantasies to illustrate the human evolution from the primate order, with emphasis on pair-mating. Adapted and directed by David Driver, it is a mish-mash of mindless shards seeking desperately to congeal into a whole, though Victoria Principal and Johnny Crawford are attractive as naked apes going bananas over each other. Inept treatment of an inert movie property relies on heavy-handed sexual humor. A-III (PG)

Naked City, The (1948) Crime picture filmed on the streets of New York City follows the painstaking methods of a veteran homicide detective (Barry Fitzgerald) in linking the murder of a model to a gang of jewel thieves. Directed by Jules Dassin, the bustling city landscapes add a human dimension to the drama of a sordid murder investigation with occasional narration by producer Mark Hellinger and a thrilling chase-climax atop the Williamsburg Bridge. Stylized violence. A-II (br)

Naked Dawn, The (1955) Dark Western in which a philosophical Mexican bandit (Arthur Kennedy) enlists the aid of a greedy peasant (Eugene Iglesias) whose wife (Betta St. John) falls for the badman, with disastrous consequences. Directed by Edgar G. Ulmer, the plot takes some quirky turns, but the familiar story and stereotyped characters hold little interest. Stylized violence and sexual situations. A-III (br)

Naked Edge, The (1961) Failed British thriller directed by Michael Anderson in which a wife (Deborah Kerr) suspects her rich husband (Gary Cooper) is guilty of murder, a situation fraught with irrational perils which grow tiresome, then become irritating. Some violence and considerable menace. A-II (br)

Naked Gun: From the Files of Police Squad, The (1988) Silly comedy abounds in this nutty farce about the bumbling attempts of a LA police lieutenant (Leslie Nielsen) to clear the tarnished name of his partner (O.J. Simpson) and save the life of Queen Elizabeth II (Jeannette Charles). Director David Zucker's parody of classic detective yarns is for those who enjoy mindless pratfalls, chases. and other sight gags. Some particularly vulgar bathroom and sexual humor. A-III (PG-13)

Naked Gun 2 1/2: The Smell of Fear, The (1991)

The comic misadventures of a bumbling cop (Leslie Nielsen) continue as he discovers that a business magnate (Robert Goulet) who's subverting the government's energy policy is also stealing his girlfriend (Priscilla Presley). The sight gags are fast and scattershot in director David Zucker's slapstick sequel that is mostly harmless nonsense with only occasional lapses in taste. Intermittent sexual innuendo, mildly vulgar humor, comic violence, and minimal rough language. A-III (PG-13)

Naked Gun 33 1/3: The Final Insult (1994) Despite the misgivings of his bride (Priscilla Presley), a retired cop (Leslie Nielsen) goes undercover, befriending a terrorist (Fred Ward) intent on bombing the Academy Awards ceremony. Director Peter Seagal's unpretentious, cheerfully nutty sequel continues the madcap misadventures of the loony lieutenant with fast-paced pratfalls, merry mix-ups, and silly sight gags that poke fun at famous scenes from other movies. Violence played for laughs, some irreverent humor, and double entendres, as well as several instances of profanity. A-III (PG-13)

Naked Hearts (1970) French production about a group of aimless boys who band together for kicks and occasionally get into trouble, with the focus on one boy more sensitive, yet ultimately as irresponsible, as his companions. French director Edouard Luntz captures a mood of loneliness and frustration, emphasized by harsh black-and-white photography of an alienating industrialized environment with its factory smoke stacks, seedy tenements, and dirty streets. The reality of characters and situations requires a mature perspective. A-III (nr)

Naked in New York (1994) In New York to prepare his first play for an off-Broadway opening, a novice playwright (Eric Stoltz) becomes mired in problems while his photographer girlfriend (Mary-Louise Parker) in New England frets about their cooling relationship. Director Dan Algrant's comic drama of a young couple starting careers while juggling long-distance romance offers occasional moments of low-key humor but doesn't deliver much insight on the situation. A couple of restrained bedroom scenes, brief nudity, and intermittent rough language. A-III (R)

Naked Jungle, The (1954) Turn-of-the-century romantic thriller centers on a sour plantation owner (Charlton Heston) who imports a mail-order bride (Eleanor Parker) to his South American backwater, then faces the fight of his life trying to save his lands from an invasion of soldier ants. Directed by Byron Haskin, the climax pitting Heston against a ferocious army of insects is edge-of-the-seat fare, thanks to George Pal's convincing special effects. Initial romantic complications swept away by the growing menace of a natural disaster. A-II (br)

Naked Lunch (1991) Punk adaptation of William S. Burrough's bizarre 1959 novel about a drug-abusing insect exterminator (Peter Weller) who kills his cheating wife (Judy Davis) and subsequently experiences grotesque hallucinations relating to his sexual identity, writing ambitions, and substance addiction. Writer-director David Cronenberg's unpalatable, surreal procession of depraved humans and hideous monsters attempts sly, counterculture humor, but delivers only pointless and boring excess. Gross sexual imagery, much homosexual innuendo, and drug abuse, extramarital encounters, occasional violence, and some rough language. O (R)

Naked Prey, The (1965) Brutal picture of 19th-century Africa in which natives cruelly massacre a hunting safari, then give its guide (Cornel Wilde) a headstart before sending their best warriors to hunt him down for sport. Also produced and directed by Wilde, the life-and-death action is vigorous, the tactics of surviving in the savage wilderness are inventive, but the result proves little more than an ultimately disappointing exercise in menace. Savage violence and racial stereotyping. A-III (br)

Naked Runner, The (1967) Frank Sinatra plays an American exile and ex-sharpshooter manipulated by British intelligence agents to kill an enemy agent in this suspenseful but wildly improbable yarn taken from the Francis Clifford novel. Director Sidney J. Furie is most concerned with the official ruthlessness that reduces people to instruments of power, and, though the plot may be muddled, it is an interesting premise. Some violence. A-III (br)

Naked Spur, The (1953) Bounty hunter (James Stewart), aided by an old sourdough (Millard Mitchell) and a cashiered Army officer (Ralph Meeker), gets his man (Robert Ryan), but bringing him in for the reward is complicated by the badman's girl (Janet Leigh) and a band of Indians. Director Anthony Mann's tough-minded Western centers on the theme of greed, abetted by an effective performance from Ryan as the smiling outlaw who turns his three captors against each other. Some stylized violence and much menace. A-II (br)

Naked Tango (1991) Baroque potboiler set in 1920s Argentina, where a young bride (Mathilda May) of an old judge (Fernando Rey) assumes a new identity in a bordello, where she becomes obsessed with a tango-mad killer (Vincent D'Onofrio). Writer-director Leonard Schrader crams his lurid melodrama with violent and voyeuristic images and little else of note. Callous exploitation of women, rape scene, recurring nudity, gory violence, and minimal rough language. O (R)

Name of the Rose, The (1986) Darkly envisioned murder-mystery set in a medieval monastery features a Franciscan friar (Sean Connery) who uses logic to uncover the cause of a mysterious death among a Fellini-like assortment of grotesque and repulsive monks, all of whom appear to be either homicidal or homosexual. A freak show is all that emerges from this badly bungled adaptation of Umberto Eco's intriguing novel. Explicit sex scene, violence, and burnings at the stake. O (R)

Namu, the Killer Whale (1966) Simple story of a

fishing village set in an ocean cove, where a visiting naturalist (Robert Lansing) proves to the local fishermen that killer whales are dangerous only if attacked. Directed by Laslo Benedek, it is wholesome children's fare, and parents can enjoy the beautiful ocean setting, if not its pleasant but unremarkable tale. A-I (br)

Nanami (1969) Japanese story about two young people groping toward pure love despite their sordid environment starts well, but their plight and aspirations are soon overpowered by arbitrary and confused melodrama and director Susumu Hani's lack of restraint in several sex scenes. O (nr)

Nanny, The (1965) British thriller with Bette Davis playing the self-effacing nanny of a troubled 10-year-old (William Dix) in a rich household where murderous acts occur and things are not what they seem. Directed by Seth Holt, the plot is too contrived to be entirely satisfying, though the sharpening conflict between the nanny and the youngster more than holds attention. Violence involving children, menacing situations, and a back-street abortion figures in the motivation. A-III (br)

Nanook of the North (1922) Following a year in the life of a nomadic Eskimo family, the documentary begins with Nanook's annual visit to a Hudson Bay trading post, where he barters his furs for supplies, then packs the family back to the tundra to hunt for more, despite the harsh elements and the hardships of the vast icy wastes. Filmmaker Robert Flaherty finds humor as well as drama in the daily rounds of the Arctic family and their many travails, including the threat of starvation when Nanook gets lost in a blizzard. The result is a richly human experience that has more to do with poetry than with journalistic reportage. A-I (br)

Napoleon (1927) Epic silent chronicle of Napoleon Bonaparte (Albert Dieudonne) from his student days at a military academy through his rise as an officer during the Revolution and Reign of Terror, until ending in 1796 when the Directory puts him in command of the army invading Italy. Directed by Abel Gance, the episodic narrative is heavily melodramatic, yet the sheer exuberance of the actors and the monumental staging of the action carry viewers along in richly visual experience made memorable by Gance's innovative use of portable cameras and triple screens. This reconstructed print runs 235 minutes, with music composed by Carmine Coppola. Stylized violence and brief sexual innuendo. A-II (br)

Napoleon (1997) Colorful talking-animal picture of a young puppy (voice of Jamie Croft) in Sydney, Australia, who gets carried away by hot-air balloons into the outback, where he learns the wonders and dangers of the wilderness while making his way home with the help of some friendly animals. Directed by Mario Andreacchio, the puppy's adventures include some scary moments along the way, but his mostly happy encounters with an exotic variety of Australian wildlife will appeal especially to young children and animal lovers. A-I (G)

Napoleon and Samantha (1972) Disney comedy about a young man (Michael Douglas) who gets involved with an orphaned little boy (Johnny Whitaker), his pet lion, and his seven-year-old playmate (Jodie Foster). Among the problems are the burial of the boy's grandfather (Will Geer) and a menacing homicidal maniac. The movie could do without the latter, but Geer's death is handled in a sensitive manner that provides a gentle lesson about the passage from life. Appealing performances from Geer and the children under the competent direction of Bernard McEveety make it an enjoyable family movie. A-I (G)

Narrow Margin, The (1952) Tightly wound thriller takes place aboard a Chicago-to-Los Angeles train carrying a hardboiled cop (Charles McGraw), the reluctant witness (Marie Windsor) he's escorting back to testify against the mob, and some gunmen sent to silence her. Director Richard Fleischer makes the trip a suspenseful one, with plenty of edgy menace, a bit of comic relief, and topped off by an edge-of-the-seat surprise finish. Threatening situations and stylized violence. A-II (br)

Narrow Margin (1990) Two mob hit-men (James B. Sikking and Nigel Bennett) close in on a Deputy DA (Gene Hackman) who is concealing a murder witness (Anne Archer) aboard a Vancouver-bound train. Written, photographed, and directed by Peter Hyams, this remake of a 1952 movie is a sleek, compact thriller that, save for one overly violent shoot-out early on, concentrates on stylish visuals, convincing acting, and razor-sharp editing to tell its suspenseful story. Intermittent menace, some violence, and minimal rough language. A-III (R)

Nashville (1975) Robert Altman's ambitious backstage epic about the careers of the people who make the capital city of country music come alive is a consistently entertaining, at times enlightening, look at an uniquely American phenomenon. Unfortunately, in reaching for something more — an indictment of sorts of contemporary America — Altman lapses into a series of cliches regarding political elections, violence, Vietnam, etc., that are quite unworthy of his film at its best. Fine performances by Ronee Blakley, Henry Gibson, Lily Tomlin, Michael Murphy, and many others in a large and talented cast. Some of the subject matter and its naturalistic treatment make this a movie not for casual viewers. A-IV (R)

Nashville Girl (see: **New Girl in Town**)

Nasty Girl, The (1990) Dark German comedy about a woman (Lena Stolze) who starts out to write a short essay on her Bavarian town during the Nazi era, but, when encountering a collective amnesia on the part of those who lived through the period and denied access to the town records, she becomes obsessed with the need to find the truth. Writer-director Michael Verhoeven uses a variety of comic techniques and dramatic styles in telling his fact-based story which has more to do with modern Germany than with the Third Reich. Subtitles. Mature themes, some racial epithets, and a flash of nudity. A-III (PG-13)

Nasty Habits (1977) Clumsy screen version of **The Abbess of Crewe,** Muriel Spark's satire paralleling the Watergate scandal with wiretapping in a Philadelphia convent. Directed by Michael Lindsay-Hogg, with Glenda Jackson as the autocratic abbess and Sandy Dennis as her kooky aide, the movie's jabs at institutional power vary from slapstick to long, talky sketches and occasional tastelessness. Though the film goes out of its way to insist that this order of nuns is not officially recognized, some may find the treatment of women religious and convent life offensive. A-IV (PG)

National Lampoon's Animal House (1978) After being expelled from college, the members of a rowdy fraternity get revenge on the school's administration and a rival fraternity by disrupting the homecoming parade. Directed by John Landis, the mindless, unfunny exercise in grossness tries to pass itself off as an anti-establishment comedy, despite reserving some of its most tasteless jibes for blacks and women. Exploitative sex and nudity. O (R)

National Lampoon's Christmas Vacation (1989) In the third Griswold family saga, dizzy dad Clark (Chevy Chase) aims to create an old-fashioned Christmas at home despite his clumsy pratfalls and short-fuse patience pushed to the limit by wife (Beverly D'Angelo), kids, in-laws, and assorted relatives. Director Jeremiah S. Chechik keeps the gags moving quickly past the double entendres and gets some laughs from Clark's bumbling attempts to enjoy Christmas. Some rough language laced with vulgarities and sexual innuendoes. A-III (PG-13)

National Lampoon's Class Reunion (1982) The tenth annual reunion of the class of '72 at Lizzie Borden High School is enlivened by a prowling homicidal maniac. Director Michael Miller's comedy is not even mildly funny in its reliance on extremely coarse humor and some nudity. O (R)

National Lampoon's European Vacation (1985) The family that cavorted their way across America on their first film vacation does so again, this time in Europe. Chevy Chase and Beverly D'Angelo repeat their roles as the parents in a movie that is witless, vulgar, unfunny, and in consistently bad taste. Nudity and sexually oriented humor. O (PG-13)

National Lampoon's Loaded Weapon 1 (1993) Freewheeling spoof of recent violent action blockbusters teams a burnt-out cop (Emilio Estevez) with a ready-to-retire partner (Samuel L. Jackson) on a murder-drug conspiracy case of ludicrous proportions. Writer-director Gene Quintano keeps up a stream of sight gags, ditzy dialogue, and star cameos that wryly mock the excesses of macho action movies. Much cartoonish violence, numerous off-color and sexual references, and a flash of nudity. A-III (PG-13)

National Lampoon's Senior Trip (1995) Noxious adolescent offal directed by Kelly Makin in which brain-dead high-school students trash Washington, DC, in a witless display of idiocy purporting to be comedy. There's nothing funny about this snickering depiction of teens engaging in drugs, booze, sex, criminal acts, and assorted rough language. O (R)

National Lampoon's Vacation (1983) Chevy Chase stars in this comic saga of a family's misadventures driving from Chicago to a California amusement park. As in any trip, there are moments of fun and humor and long stretches of dull, tedious travel. Directed by Harold Ramis, there is some tasteless humor involving a corpse, some sexual innuendo. and brief nudity. A-III (R)

National Velvet (1944) Warmly sentimental story of an English country girl (Elizabeth Taylor) who sets her heart on entering her spirited horse, Pie, in the Grand National Steeplechase, England's most challenging race, and with the help of an ex-jockey (Mickey Rooney) and supportive parents (Anne Revere and Donald Crisp), her great expectations are finally realized. Directed by Clarence Brown, it is a fine picture of youthful ambition and determination fostered within a caring, loving home. A family classic with special appeal for youngsters. A-I (br)

Natural, The (1984) Screen version of the Bernard Malamud novel about a phenomenal baseball player (Robert Redford) is as much a fable about the temptations of worldly glory and the flesh as it is a red-blooded sports saga. Directed by Barry Levinson, it has a strong supporting cast (Robert Duvall, Glenn Close, Wilford Brimley) but muddles the story's underlying themes of self-deceit, evil, and mortality. Promiscuity figures in the plot but is treated with restraint. A-II (PG)

Natural Born Killers (1994) Having gleefully shot down scores of victims on a murder spree, a psychotic couple (Woody Harrelson and Juliette Lewis) achieve media celebrity, and their popularity is only enhanced by their capture and subsequent escape during a deadly prison riot broadcast live by a sleazy tabloid journalist (Robert Downey, Jr.) who ultimately joins in the blood-fest. Director Oliver Stone's attempt to satirize the media's pandering to the public's fascination with mass murderers is itself steeped in the same sensationalistic, romanticized portrayal of dehumanizing violence in a movie whose bizarre mixture of cinema styles intensifies the murderous events rather than distances the viewer from them. Unrelenting images of gory violence, flashes of nudity, and much rough language. O (R)

Natural Enemies (1979) Successful magazine editor (Hal Holbrook) decides to shoot his wife (Louise Fletcher) and three teenage children, but his best friend (Jose Ferrer) tries desperately to argue him out of it. Written, produced, and directed by Jeff Kanew, this story of marital breakdown is a cold and superficial exercise. Needlessly explicit brothel scene which includes partial nudity. O (R)

Navajo Joe (1967) Fed by the hatred of their half-breed leader, a gang of outlaws become compulsive Indian-killers until one heroic Indian (Burt Reynolds) outwits and destroys most of them when they try to rob a train. Routine spaghetti Western directed by Sergio Corbucci has an excess of wanton killings, brutality, and sadism. O (br)

Navigator: An Odyssey Across Time, The (1989) New Zealand director Vincent Ward weaves a visually exquisite but muddled tale traveling from the 14th century to modern times and back again. The imaginative but demanding fable concerns a nine-year-old English lad (Hamish McFarlane) whose visions of a church steeple in a strange new world send him on a journey to the 20th century to save his medieval village from the Black Death. The role of faith is obvious and some may see connections with AIDS, but the rest is tenuous. Some intense menace and scenes of death. A-III (PG)

Navy SEALs (1990) US Navy anti-terrorist team (headed by Charlie Sheen and Michael Biehn) is sent into war-torn Beirut to neutralize a cache of stolen American Stinger missiles. Director Lewis Teague delivers a standard action yarn packed with macho stereotypes, daredevil stunts, ferocious explosions, and predictable casualties and triumphs. Much violence and rough language. A-III ((R)

Nazarin (1968) Mexican story set in 1905 when a young priest comes into disfavor with his inflexible religious superiors, the civil authorities, and even the poor among whom he tries to live a life of simplicity, poverty, and charity. Though director Luis Bunuel's work is not very optimistic about the possibility of idealism winning over the world, it's not critical of religion, only pious hypocrisy. Subtitles. Perplexing themes. A-III (br)

Nea (1978) When a rich and nasty 16-year-old girl (Ann Zacharias) writes a successful erotic novel, her lover-editor (Sammy Frey) claims credit, and she exacts a cruel revenge. French director Nelly Kaplan evidently had social satire in mind, but the movie's exploitation of sex is more in evidence than any wit or insight. O (R)

Neanderthal Man, The (1953) Horror clunker directed by E.A. Dupont in which a scientist (Robert Shayne) finds a way to turn pet cats into saber-toothed tigers, then uses the formula to turns himself into a prehistoric man, with predictable results. Stylized violence and hokey menace. A-II (br)

Nebraskan, The (1953) Bare-bones Western about an Army scout (Phil Carey) who helps avert a Sioux uprising by saving the chief's son. Directed by Fred F. Sears, it's forgettable dime-novel stuff with phony action and one-dimensional characters. Frontier violence and Indian stereotypes. A-II (br)

Necessary Roughness (1991) Formula football comedy about a hopeless Texas college team whose coaches (Hector Elizondo and Robert Loggia) recruit a 34-year-old freshman (Scott Bakula) to be their star quarterback. Director Stan Dragoti manages to extract some laughs from an otherwise routinely contrived storyline. Implied sexual affair, some slapstick violence, and minimal rough language. A-III (PG)

Necromancy (1972) Pamela Franklin finds herself the latest candidate to play at witchcraft in a creepy little California village owned and completely dominated by Orson Welles, toy manufacturer and master of the occult. Written, produced, and directed by Bert I. Gordon, it's not very scary but is slightly amusing in its ineptness and desperate attempts at plot twists and shocks. Innocuous save for some brief nudity and a nasty attack by rats. A-III (PG)

Ned Kelly (1970) Uneven but engrossing British production about an Irish outlaw gang led by Kelly, whose exploits in 1870s Australia grew in legend after betrayal by one of their own led to their capture and execution by the Crown. Mick Jagger in the tile role gives a successful portrayal as the embittered, hardened man-child outlaw. Tony Richardson's bold and sweeping direction, the beautifully muted color photography, and the bittersweet ballads about the now-folk hero sung by Waylon Jennings (and composed by Shel Silverstein) are more than enough to recommend it. Some fairly graphic violence. A-III (PG)

Needful Things (1993) Disguised as a sympathetic antiques shopowner, the devil (Max von Sydow) goes about slyly manipulating the good people of a New England town to go on an ugly killing spree, until the sheriff (Ed Harris) calls them to their senses and the devil smugly goes on his merry way. Fraser C. Heston directs this adaptation of a Stephen King novel, a boring and mean-spirited horror-comedy whose glib message is that evil will always triumph in the end. Recurring nasty violence, mindless mayhem, and frequent rough language. O (R)

Negotiator, The (1998) Convoluted thriller in which a Chicago police negotiator (Samuel L. Jackson), accused of stealing department pension funds, tries to clear himself by taking hostage the detective (J.T. Walsh) heading the investigation, then persuades a negotiator (Kevin Spacey) from outside the precinct to help him prove his innocence. Directed by F. Gary Gray, the overly contrived proceedings are filled with hokey action, vague motivations, and stereotyped characters who lose interest long before the formula ending. Considerable violence with some gore, life-threatening situations, recurring rough language, and occasional profanity. A-IV (R)

Neighbors (1981) Director John G. Avildsen's screen version of Thomas Berger's black comedy about a staid suburbanite (John Belushi) who is driven crazy by a looney neighbor (Dan Aykroyd) is a muddled, dismal failure devoid of both laughs and insight. Senseless scene of seduction, much sexual innuendo, and unusually crude language. O (R)

Neil Simon's The Odd Couple II (1998) Genial comedy sequel in which fastidious Felix (Jack Lemmon) and cantankerous Oscar (Walter Matthau) are reunited after 30 years when they acrimoniously travel together to a family wedding, but keep getting arrested along the way. Directed by Howard Deutsch from Neil Simon's screenplay, the veteran actors' practiced ease at delivering zesty one-liners is the main attraction. Mild sexual innuendo, occasional profanity, and a few instances of rough language. A-III (PG-13)

Nell (1994) A woman (Jodie Foster) living completely on her own in a remote wilderness area of North Carolina, and speaking what seems only gibberish, is terrified when discovered by a caring physician (Liam Neeson) who, with the help of a research-minded psychologist (Natasha Richardson), tries to communicate with her and prepare her for the likelihood of court-ordered institutionalization. Directed by Michael Apted, the beautifully photographed, sensitively acted, story deals with the simple wisdom of innocence, though sluggish pacing and logical inconsistencies diminish the narrative's fable-like qualities. Shadowy skinny-dipping, a flash of nudity, brief sexual references, minimal profanity, and an instance of rough language. A-III (PG-13)

Nelly & Monsieur Arnaud (1996) A shy Parisienne (Emanuelle Beart) is torn between committing to an overeager editor (Jean-Hugues Anglade) she is dating or acknowledging her growing feelings for her boss, an adoring author (Michel Serrault) 40 years her senior. Director Claude Sautet's melancholy romantic triangle delicately explores the emotional landscape of fragile relationships among young, middle-aged, and elderly characters. Subtitles. An implied sexual affair. A-III (nr)

Nelson Affair, The (1973) Boudoir history of Admiral Lord Nelson's (Peter Finch) scandalous behavior with his beloved and presumably bewitching mistress Lady Emma Hamilton (Glenda Jackson in an eccentric performance). Scripted by Terence Rattigan and directed by James Cellan Jones, it is a literate, if somewhat bland, treatment of the stormy love affair. A-III (PG)

Nelson Touch, The (see: **Corvette K-225**)

Neptune Factor, The (1973) Ben Gazzara heads the rescue submarine racing to recover the men trapped in an undersea research lab by a volcanic eruption in the North Atlantic. Canadian production directed by Daniel Petrie, the routine underwater adventure relies heavily on the special sub's scientific gadgetry and the exotic deep-sea creatures which will engage the interest of younger viewers, but adults may prefer staying on dry land. A-I (G)

Nest of Vipers (1979) Italian production about a callow piano student (Christian Borromeo) who has an affair with the mother (Senta Berger) of a fellow student and then abandons her for a beautiful young heiress (Ornella Muti). Director Tonino Cervi's story of jealousy and revenge is mired in graphically depicting the affairs as well as others including incest, lesbianism, and homosexuality. O (R)

Net, The (1995) On the run from a hired killer (Jeremy Northam), a computer expert (Sandra Bullock) has to fend for herself in keeping criminals from getting a computer disc crucial to the security systems of the entire federal government. Director Irwin Winkler's sleek techno-thriller combines standard chase fare with the woman-in-peril formula for a mildly suspenseful, but unexceptional, melodrama. Brief spurts of violence, an implied sexual encounter, and an instance of rough language. A-III (PG-13)

Network (1976) When a TV anchorman (Peter Finch) has a breakdown and rants and raves on camera, his ratings soar, and an ambitious network executive (Faye Dunaway) centers a new program concept around him over the protests of a more humane executive (William Holden). Written by Paddy Chayefsky and directed by Sidney Lumet, the heavy-handed satire on the evils of television and its effects on the public misses as often as is on target. Needless subplot involves an adulterous affair with an explicit scene of lovemaking. O (R)

Nevada Smith (1966) Well-made Western about a youth (Steve McQueen) who, after his mother and father are tortured to death by three outlaws looking for gold, tracks them down, killing them one by one. Directed by Henry Hathaway, the revenge story is told in very violent fashion and there are some sexual references. A-III (br)

Nevadan, The (1950) Cat-and-mouse Western in which an escaped gold-robber (Forrest Tucker) gets some help from a mysterious stranger (Randolph Scott) in recovering his stolen loot, despite a gang of hijackers (led by cracked George Macready). Director Gordon Douglas gets the tale of delayed justice off to an intriguing start, then bogs down in some muted romance (Dorothy Malone) before the rousing finish in an abandoned gold mine. Stylized violence. A-I (br)

Never a Dull Moment (1950) After marrying a rodeo cowboy (Fred MacMurray), a New York songwriter (Irene Dunne) tries to adjust to life on a small western ranch with the widower's two young daughters, boisterous local ranchers, and an ornery neighbor (William Demarest) who controls the water rights. Director George Marshall's cheerful but entirely artificial comedy has some good moments, but not enough to justify the title. Domestic misunderstandings. A-II (br)

Never a Dull Moment (1968) Well-paced gangster spoof in which a TV actor (Dick Van Dyke) is mistaken for a killer by a colorful mob of would-be art thieves (led by Edward G. Robinson), then plays along by resorting to tough-guy mannerisms while looking for a chance to escape. Directed by Jerry Paris, the Disney production is a likeable bit of light entertainment that will go down as easily with parents as with their children. Comic menace. A-I (G)

Never Been Kissed (1999) Drippy romantic comedy in which a 25-year old rookie reporter (Drew Barrymore) goes undercover as a high-school senior to write about teen life and ends up reliving her adolescent insecurities before winning the heart of her English teacher (Michael Vartan). Barrymore's clunky performance further sinks director Raja Gosnell's contrived coming-of-age tale. Implied affairs, sex references, a sex-education scene involving condoms, and occasional profanity. A-III (PG-13)

Never Cry Wolf (1983) Government naturalist (Charles Martin Smith), sent to the Canadian Arctic to determine if wolves are responsible for decimating the once-abundant caribou herds, learns instead a lesson in survival and self-knowledge. Director Carrol Ballard's fact-based Disney drama allows the viewer to feel the wonder and excitement of the wilderness with insightful humor and stunning visuals. Some scenes of Smith eating mice and going naked in barren Arctic landsacpe. A-II (PG)

Never Give an Inch (see: **Sometimes a Great Notion**)

Never Let Me Go (1953) Fanciful Cold War clunker in which an American reporter (Clark Gable) is expelled from the USSR but returns to smuggle his Russian ballerina/bride (Gene Tierney) to freedom in a sailboat piloted by a British seaman (Bernard Miles). Director Delmer Daves takes a pedestrian look at Soviet intransigence in a dated romantic adventure of possible interest to social historians. Ideological stereotypes and dangerous doings. A-I (br)

Never Say Die (1939) Frenetic comedy set in a Swiss spa, where an American millionaire (Bob Hope), mistakenly told he has only 30 days to live, jilts a gun-toting socialite (Gale Sondergaard) to wed an oil-man's daughter (Martha Raye) who's unhappily betrothed to a penniless count (Alan Mowbray), intending to leave her a wealthy widow able to marry the man she loves — a Texas bus driver (Andy Devine). Directed by Elliott Nugent and co-authored by Preston Sturges, its good cast provides occasional splashes of humor, but the wacky characters and zany situations grow increasingly tiresome. Romantic complications galore and some sexual innuendo. A-III (br)

Never Say Goodbye (1956) Soapy romance about a doctor (Rock Hudson) with the American occupation forces in postwar Vienna who marries an Austrian pianist (Cornell Borchers), but when she disappears in the Soviet zone, he returns to the US with their two-year-old daughter, until years later his wife suddenly turns up. Director Jerry Hopper's remake of **This Love of Ours** offers some glossy Viennese locales but is even more sentimental and contrived than the original. A-I (br)

Never Say Never Again (1983) Aging agent 007 (Sean Connery), shunted aside by a new chief, is called back to retrieve two nuclear warheads stolen by a charming and sinister villain (Klaus Maria Brandauer). Director Irvin Kershner's version of the Bond mystique goes overboard in treating violence as spectacle and promiscuity as hyperactive heroism. O (PG)

Never So Few (1959) Hokey, overlong WW II tale in which an American officer (Frank Sinatra) makes questionable command decisions while leading a guerrilla unit in Japanese-held Burma, then is court-martialed for killing a maverick Chinese warlord. Directed by John Sturges, the ponderous narrative glamorizes the self-righteous officer's exploits in the field and on leave in Calcutta wooing an undercover agent (Gina Lollobrigida) before the movie's simplistic resolution. Wartime violence, sexual situations, and muddled treatment of moral issues. A-III (br)

Never Steal Anything Small (1959) Musical comedy misfire about a petty New York hood (James Cagney) who takes over a longshoresman's local, then hijacks a shipment of Swiss watches to finance his election as union head. Director Charles Lederer can't quite make Cagney's cynical character likeable, especially his underhanded attempts to woo a sweet innocent (Shirley Jones) by breaking up her marriage. Romantic complications and comic treatment of union corruption. A-III (br)

Never Talk to Strangers (1995) Failed thriller about a criminal psychologist (Rebecca De Mornay) assigned to assess the sanity of an accused serial killer (Harry Dean Stanton) while spending her nights with a new heartthrob (Antonio Banderas) whom she comes to suspect is trying to kill her. Director Peter Hall plods through a kinky but predictable plot whose twist ending will surprise few viewers. Some gory violence, graphic sex scenes, and occasional profanity and rough language. O (R)

Never to Love (see: 1940's **A Bill of Divorcement**)

Never Too Late (1965) Uneven adaptation of the Broadway comedy about a couple who late in life have another child and the complications this causes in their lives. Under Bud Yorkin's direction, Paul Ford is practically the whole show as he tries in his hard-hearted but soft-headed way to cope with the situation. A-III (br)

Never Wave at a WAC (1952) Lame comedy in which a daffy socialite (Rosalind Russell) joins the Women's Army Corps to get on the staff of her officer-boyfriend in Paris, but can't make it through basic training because of interference from her still-caring ex-husband (Paul Douglas). Directed by Norman Z. McLeod, the comedy is almost as flat as the romance, though trainee Marie Wilson adds a certain zest, and some may find it of interest as a vintage recruiting poster for "girls" seeking a military career. Battling ex-spouses and sexual innuendo. A-III (br)

NeverEnding Story, The (1984) While hiding out from class bullies, a schoolboy reads a storybook that propels him into its fantasy world where his imagination runs wild and his courage is tested. German director Wolfgang Peterson delivers a work filled with murky metaphysical references, vividly grotesque creatures, and a concluding literary-inspired act of retribution that adults may appreciate more than younger viewers, although there is more than enough fairytale ambiance to hold their interest. A-I (PG)

NeverEnding Story II: The Next Chapter, The (1991) A young boy (Jonathan Brandis) enters a fairytale storybook to help the characters save their planet from an evil sorceress (Clarissa Burt). Though director George Miller's fantasy-adventure sequel is visually captivating, its bland story line holds little interest for adults and its monsters might scare preschoolers. Some menacing characters and fantasy violence. A-I (PG)

New Adventures of Pippi Longstocking, The (1988) Cheesy, cloying English-language adaptation of the Astrid Lindgren children's books sees high-spirited Pippi (Tami Erin) housed briefly in an orphanage after being washed overboard from her father's (John Schuck) ship. Peppy music, bad acting, and unimaginative direction by Ken Annakin. A-I (G)

New Centurions, The (1972) Screen version of Joseph Wambaugh's novel about a veteran police sergeant (George C. Scott) who schools a rookie cop (Stacy Keach) in handling Los Angeles street crime. Director Richard Fleischer's diffuse and episodic melodrama reduces characters and social issues to simple good-guy, bad-guy dramatics. Some bleary-eyed nightclub philosophizing comparing the collapse of law and order in Rome to present society (presumably symbolized by a topless dancer in the background) is the key to the movie's easy sympathies for the police taking the law into their own hands. Violent action and atmosphere. A-IV (R)

New Girl in Town (1977) Sympathetic account of the rise of a young woman (Monica Gayle) to stardom in the world of country-western music. Under the direction of Gus Trikonis, however, the heroine spends a great deal of time taking off her clothes on camera, making doubtful the movie's sincerity of purpose. O (R)

New Jack City (1991) Ruthless -leader (Wesley Snipes) muscles in on Harlem's drug traffic, while two honest cops (Ice T and Judd Nelson) fight the system to bring him to justice. Director and co-star Mario Van Peebles makes an anti-drug statement by exploiting the seamiest aspects of drug addiction in the ghetto. Excessive violence, sexual exploitation, some nudity, and incessant rough language. O (R)

New Kind of Love, A (1963) Slickly artificial romantic comedy from writer-director Melville Shavelson brings a lovelorn fashion designer (Joanne Woodward) together with a womanizing newsman (Paul Newman) in Paris, where she gets his interest by pretending to be a prostitute, among other lame contrivances. Game cast in a phony plot whose comic sexual innuendoes and situations are largely unamusing and, at times, tasteless. A-III (br)

New Land, The (1973) Sequel to **The Emigrants** continues its story of a Swedish family (Max von Sydow and Liv Ullmann) after they and a small band of farmers arrive in the Minnesota wilderness of the 1850s and set to work establishing homesteads, cultivating the land, raising their families, and acclimatizing themselves to life in the New Land. Superbly directed by Jan Troell, the historical re-creation is an extraordinary achievement in conveying a sense of the pioneer spirit out of which our nation grew. A-II (PG)

New Leaf, A (1971) A slick, money-grubbing cad (Walter Matthau) courts and marries a wealthy spinster (Elaine May) whose passion is botany. She comes to love him dearly, but undeservedly, as he tries various schemes to kill her, until an increasing glimmer of affection rises in his own heart. Witty and fast-paced comedy, also written and directed by May, is frequently hilarious and often biting in its moral satire. A-III (G)

New Life, A (1988) Workaholic Wall Street broker (Alan Alda) and wife (Ann-Margret) split up after 26 years of marriage and nervously enter into the singles' scene and commitment to difficult new relationships. Writer-director Alda takes full advantage of the seriocomic elements found in the somewhat predictable plot that benefits from fine acting and characterizations. Some rough language and discreet nudity in several sexual situations. A-III (PG-13)

New Moon (1940) One of the sillier Nelson Eddy-Jeanette MacDonald costume musicals is set during the French Revolution, when a nobleman-turned-pirate (Eddy) captures a ship bearing an aristocrat's daughter (MacDonald) who spurns his love until marooned on an uninhabited island. Directed by Robert Z. Leonard, the turns of plot are outlandish, but the romance is sappily endearing, backed by Sigmund Romberg-Oscar Hammerstein songs including "Stout-Hearted Men" and "Lover, Come Back to Me." Some romantic mush with unlikely appeal for youngsters. A-I (br)

New York, New York (1977) Nostalgic musical romance about a 1940s showbiz couple (Liza Minnelli and Robert De Niro) who seek stardom and pay the price in an adulterous affair, drugs, and alcohol abuse before achieving success. Directed by Martin Scorsese, the big-budget musical is technically impressive but dramatically off-key in its depiction of the trials and tribulations of marriage. A-III (PG)

New York Stories (1989) Inspired trilogy of dramatic vignettes filmed in and about New York City offers director Martin Scorsese's sobering look at the end of a May-December love affair; director Francis Coppola's whimsical tale about a 12-year-old girl living in a ritzy hotel; and the show's highlight, director Woody Allen's hilarious piece in which a nagging Jewish mom gets the best of her neurotic adult son. Some sexual banter and suggestions of illicit liaisons. A-III (PG)

Newman's Law (1974) George Peppard plays an incorruptible Los Angeles cop who, on the verge of arresting a drug ring, is framed on a drug charge, causing him to go off on his own to clear his record and knock off the villains to boot. Directed by Richard Heffron, the routine crime plot moves swiftly to its predictable bloody climax whose justification — taking the law into one's own hands — would be troubling if it were not here so unbelievable. Some violence and rough language. A-III (PG)

Newsfront (1979) Australian production about the

lives and careers of a veteran newsreel cameraman (Bill Hunter) and his assistant (Chris Haywood) from 1948 to 1956, when the nightly television news made the weekly newsreel redundant. Writer-director Philip Noyce pays more attention to the craft of the newsreel and its content during the era of its glory than to the private lives of its characters, who receive rather soap-opera treatment in marital problems and love affairs. Interesting re-creation but shallow human dimension. A-III (PG)

Newsies (1992) Run-of-the-mill musical about New York City newsboys (including Christian Bale and David Moscow) going on strike in 1899 to protest higher newspaper prices decreed by publisher Joseph Pulitzer (Robert Duvall). Though it offers some skillful choreography and a sprightly musical score, director Kenny Ortega develops little dramatic interest in the characters or their predicaments. Brief violence. A-II (PG)

Newton Boys, The (1998) Fact-based story of four fun-loving brothers (Matthew McConaughey, Ethan Hawke, Vincent D'Onofrio, and Skeet Ulrich) who quit their hardscrabble Texas farm in 1919 to make a living robbing banks, until they get greedy and pull a $3 million mail train robbery in 1924 Chicago. Directed by Richard Linklater, the result has interest in its credible re-creation of the period but fails to earn any sympathy, let alone admiration, for the boys and their criminal exploits that the movie tries so hard to arouse. Some gory violence, sexual innuendo, comic treatment of crime, and occasional profanity. A-III (PG-13)

Next Man, The (1976) Spoiled rich girl (Cornelia Sharpe) works as an assassin for a terrorist group, seducing and liquidating her victims in exotic corners of the world, but meets her match in a visionary Arab diplomat (Sean Connery). Director Richard C. Sarafian's mediocre, high gloss thriller offers little besides mindless violence, some gratuitous nudity, and a brutal ending. O (R)

Next Karate Kid, The (1994) By teaching her mental as well as physical discipline, a wise karate master (Pat Morita) helps to channel the anger of a recently orphaned high-school girl (Hilary Swank) who is being harassed by school bullies. Director Christopher Cain downplays martial-arts bouts in favor of stressing the young woman's learning to cope with adversity in a values-centered, if fanciful, youth film. Brief violence. A-II (PG)

Next of Kin (1989) Savvy Chicago cop (Patrick Swayze) is torn between the law and his family's backwoods code of justice when his older brother (Liam Neeson) comes to town to avenge the murder of their younger brother (Bill Paxton) by the mob. Director John Irvin attempts to contrast the feuding ethics of hillbilly and mobster clans, but the movie's numerous plot gaps, ethnic caricatures, and deterioration into vigilantism weaken the effort. Much profanity and some scenes of grisly violence. O (R)

Next Stop, Greenwich Village (1976) Jewish youth (Lenny Baker) leaves his blue-collar Brooklyn neighborhood in 1953 to seek fame as an actor in Greenwich Village. His growth both on the stage and as a person is chronicled by director Paul Mazursky in a series of incidents that are often quite amusing and sometimes extremely touching. Though soft and sentimental in its portrayal of the young man and overly nostalgic about the era, the movie is positive in its assertions of values and sense of ethnic roots. One notable exception is its acceptance of abortion. A-IV (R)

Next Stop, Wonderland (1998) Off-beat comedy about romance in the 1990s follows a bright Boston nurse (Hope Davis) seeking a serious relationship via a personal-ad column and a serious-minded plumber (Alan Gelfant) studying to become a marine biologist, whose paths frequently cross until accidentally meeting as kindred spirits just before movie's end. Directed by Brad Anderson, the parallel development of the two stories overplays the nurse's wry interviews with the sorry collection of men answering her ad while underplaying the plumber's problems with a loan shark, but the result pokes fun at current sexual mores and plunks for a more old-fashioned notion of romance. Ambiguous view of unmarried sexual relationships, much rough language, and occasional profanity. A-IV (R)

Next Summer (1986) In a story about three generations and how each defines the nature of loving relationships, this French production features an impressive cast, including Claudia Cardinale, Jean-Louis Trintignant, Philippe Noiret, and Fanny Ardant. Directed with charm and humor by Nadine Trintignant, each member of this family saga is shown grappling with the many facets of love, sex, and marriage from the perspective of strengthening or weakening family ties. Adult theme. A-III (nr)

Next Time We Love (1936) Episodic tearjerker in which a struggling young couple grow apart when wife (Margaret Sullavan) finds success on Broadway, and husband (James Stewart) makes good as a foreign correspondent, while their best friend (Ray Milland) waits in the wings burning a torch for the wife. Director Edward H. Griffith relies upon a talented cast to sustain a highly artifical plot that's resolved by terminal illness. Contrived marital woes and misunderstandings. A-II (br)

Next Voice You Hear, The (1950) The lives of an average American worker (James Whitmore), his pregnant wife (Nancy Davis), and their young son are transformed when they hear God speaking to the world on the radio. Directed by William Wellman, the intriguing and well-intentioned concept falls flat because of the banality of the radio message directing people to perform "miracles" of "peace and loving kindness" and the clumsy day-by-day portrayal of how the father gradually changes over the course of a week. It's not silly, but it's not very credible. A-I (nr)

Niagara Niagara (1998) Tortured tale of runaway

teen-lovers (Robin Tunney and Henry Thomas) turns into tragedy when the girl runs out of her Tourette's Syndrome medication and substitutes liquor and pills in a vain attempt to take the edge off her wild outbursts. Directed by Bob Gosse, the formula road movie evokes some sympathy for the afflicted teen in what is otherwise a tired story of outcasts on the run. Brief sexual encounters, much substance abuse, frequent profanity, and continuous rough language. A-IV (R)

Nice Girl Like Me, A (1969) Boring British melodrama about an unwed mother (Barbara Ferris) who conceives one child in Paris, another in Venice, and acquires a third infant when it is dumped in her arms by a desperate Italian mother. Directed by Desmond Davis, there is a lot of lush photography of European cities and pastoral landscapes, but the story lacks any social or moral perspective that might have given it some significance. A-III (PG)

Nicholas and Alexandra (1971) British epic offers the spectacle of glittering palaces, splendid pageantry, and larger-than-life characters in ornate costumes but misses the historical context making understandable why this couple were the last of the Romanovs to rule Russia. Directed by Franklin J. Schaffner, the focus is on the domestic lives of the tsar (Michael Jayston) and tsarina (Janet Suzman), with occasional fragmentary scenes indicating the revolutionary events that were to sweep away the entire epoch. Grand-scale romance set against a turbulent but fuzzy background, with only Rasputin's rampant sexuality to give children pause, though all will wince at his brutal murder. A-II (PG)

Nicholas Nickleby (1947) Memorable adaptation of the Charles Dickens novel in which a young man (Derek Bond) in 1830 England saves a youth (Aubrey Woods) from a brutal boys school while struggling to protect his mother and sister from his miserly, conniving uncle (Cedric Hardwicke). Director Alberto Cavalcanti embroiders the desperate proceedings with zestful visuals of the period setting and its quirky assortment of characters. Some frightening ordeals for young viewers. A-I (br)

Nick and Jane (1997) Lame romantic comedy in which a New York businesswoman (Dana Wheeler-Nicholson) tries to make her womanizing boyfriend (John Dossett) jealous by paying a sensitive cabbie (James McCaffrey) to masquerade as her lover, with unsurprising results. Writer-director Richard Mauro strings out a weak plot with a collection of odd-ball characters, such as the cabbie's rapper roommate (Gedde Watanabe) and transvestite neighbor (Clinton Leupp), but the result is an urban fantasy that delivers a few giggles but lacks any romantic charm. Sexual situations, gay stereotypes, and occasional rough language. A-IV (R)

Nick of Time (1995) Nasty little thriller about the desperate plight of a mild accountant (Johnny Depp) whose six-year-old daughter will be killed unless he assassinates California's governor (Marsha Mason) in the next 90 minutes. Directed by John Badham, the suspense wears thin as the harebrained proceedings are dragged out until the time limit expires in bloody mayhem intended as a feel-good ending. Some hard-edged violence, much menace, and intermittent rough language. A-III (R)

Nickel Ride, The (1975) Aging, small-time operator (Jason Miller) gets into a tight spot trying to put together a deal for the crime syndicate and tries to avoid his inevitable fate. Though the narrative is somewhat muddled, director Richard Mulligan's treatment of the central issue of the man's survival is taut and powerfully done, with nicely nuanced characterizations and atmosphere of menace. Element of human compassion elevates it above standard crime movie. A-III (PG)

Nickelodeon (1977) Mildly humorous slapstick drama about the pioneer days of silent films stars Ryan O'Neal as young lawyer turned writer-director and Burt Reynolds as his star. Director Peter Bogdanovich's story has some amusing moments but is rather thin in dramatic developments, leaving the main focus on movie memorabilia. A-II (PG)

Night and the City (1992) A second-rate lawyer (Robert De Niro) invites disaster by borrowing money from the jealous husband (Cliff Gorman) of his girlfriend (Jessica Lange) to put on a boxing tournament in a venue controlled by a crooked promoter (Alan King). Writer-director Irwin Winkler's profane, edgy movie captures the hustling spirit of New York City lowlifes while leaving their intersecting relationships too vague to be dramatically satisfying. An adulterous relationship, brief violence, some sexual innuendo, and much rough language, including racial slurs. A-III (R)

Night at the Bijou, A (see: **The Three Stooges Follies**)

Night at the Roxbury, A (1998) Witless comedy about two nerdy brothers (Will Ferrell and Chris Kattan) who haunt local nightclubs, until they stumble onto romance and success in spite of themselves. Directed by John Fortenberry, the brainless proceedings feature gratingly irksome characters whose dumb antics are thuddingly dull. Implied affairs, a discreet sexual encounter, crude expressions, and a few instances of profanity. A-III (PG-13)

Night Caller (1975) Unsavory French production about a police inspector (Jean-Paul Belmondo) whose methods in trying to catch some bankrobbers and a deranged serial murderer are both brutal and lack any sense of legal niceties. Director Henri Verneuil's disjointed crime thriller lacks any elements of tension or suspense. Violence, rough language, and elements of sexual perversion. O (R)

Night Crossing (1982) Disney fact-based drama about two families (John Hurt, Jane Alexander, Beau Bridges, and Glynnis O'Connor) who make their way to freedom from East Germany by way of a hot-air balloon. While there are some moments of suspense and entertainment, director Delbert Mann doesn't deal adequately with the foreign setting, culture, and people. Nevertheless, it provides the family audience with a harrowing reminder of the price of freedom. A-I (PG)

Night Digger, The (1971) British psychological thriller about an aging spinster (Patricia Neal), long dominated by a tyrannical adoptive mother, who falls in love with a psychotic killer twenty years her junior (Nicholas Clay). Good acting gives credibility to a rather preposterous situation, allowing director Alistair Reid the intriguing opportunity to probe into the darker corners of the human mind and soul. The result is a mixed bag, caught somewhere between a taut chiller and a human interest story. Some flashbacks indicating the killer's twisted sexuality and several grisly murders with oppressive sexual overtones. A-IV (R)

Night Eyes (1990) Security guard (Andrew Stevens) falls for the rich divorcée (Tanya Roberts) he's guarding and winds being made the patsy in a murder case. Ineptly directed by Jag Mundrha, the story is made out of cardboard with characters to match. Graphic sex scenes with some nudity, occasional violence, and rough language. O (R)

Night Falls on Manhattan (1997) Brooding drama in which an idealistic District Attorney (Andy Garcia) learns that falsified evidence resulted in his winning a conviction against a murderous drug dealer, and that his beloved father (Ian Holm) may have been one of the dirty cops involved. Writer-director Sidney Lumet probes the moral complexities of a flawed justice system and conflicting loyalties in an uneven but thoughtful tale of innocence corrupted. Brief violence, implied pre-marital affair, recurring profanity, and much rough language. A-III (R)

Night Flier, The (see: **Stephen King's The Night Flier**)

Night Flight from Moscow (1973) Convoluted espionage story about a glowering Russian spy (Yul Brynner) who defects to the West and the CIA official (Henry Fonda) whose task is to determine whether the defector is an honest turncoat or a double agent. French production directed by Henri Verneuil has interesting details about counter-intelligence methods, but the slow pace of the international yarn makes it a yawner. Some violence. A-III (PG)

Night Full of Rain, A (1978) The unhappy marriage of a rich American (Candice Bergen) and an Italian Communist journalist (Giancarlo Giannini) forms the basis for director Lina Wertmuller's story of their violent meeting and courtship told in flashbacks. Some nudity, sexual byplay, and crudities. O (R)

Night Game (1989) Tedious serial-killer thriller unfolds in a colorful Gulf Coast setting with a burned-out cop (Roy Scheider), his ill-suited fiancee (Karen Young), and an implausible scenario about a maniac who kills young blonds whenever the Houston Astros's star pitcher wins a game. Director Peter Masterson strikes out on this one. Some profanity, menace, and grisly shots of mutilated corpses. A-III (R)

Night Games (1980) Ludicrous and inept melodrama about a wife (Cindy Pickett), traumatized by a girlhood assault, who is cured of her frigidity by having sex with a stranger dressed in feathers. Listlessly directed by Roger Vadim, the acting is embarrassingly bad. Nudity and graphic sexuality abound. O (R)

Night Has a Thousand Eyes (1948) Unusual mystery from Cornell Woolrich's story about a man (Edward G. Robinson) whose unwanted gift of seeing into the future proves a curse, until he puts it to use trying to save an heiress (Gail Russell) from being murdered. Director John Farrow works up some eerie atmosphere for a plot mixing the paranormal into a murder mystery with quite diverting results. Stylized violence and theme of clairvoyance. A-II (br)

Night Has Eyes, The (1942) Romantic British chiller in which schoolteachers (Joyce Howard and Tucker McGuire) trace a missing friend to the Yorkshire moors, where they stumble upon a spooky mansion inhabited by a strange composer (James Mason) and two servants (Wilfrid Lawson and Mary Clare). Written and directed by Leslie Arliss, the plot's suspense doesn't measure up to the eerie atmosphere of the fog-shrouded setting and Mason's wild-eyed portrayal of a shattered veteran of the Spanish Civil War. Menacing situations. A-II (br)

Night in Casablanca, A (1946) Tame Marx Brothers comedy has Groucho managing the hotel where Sig Ruman and other fugitive Nazis have stashed stolen loot, but, when they try to escape with it, Chico and Harpo ground their plane. Directed by Archie L. Mayo, the script is awfully thin and the old zany flair of the Brothers's antics is barely visible. Comic violence and mild sexual innuendo. A-II (br)

Night in Heaven, A (1983) Married schoolteacher (Lesley Ann Warren) has an affair with a student (Christopher Atkins) who works as a male exotic dancer. Directed by John Avildsen, the crude effort emphasizes nudity and graphic sex while disparaging marital fidelity. O (R)

Night Moves (1975) Gene Hackman plays a Los Angeles private eye who traces a 16-year-old runaway to Florida living with her stepfather and his mistress who are both involved in a smuggling operation. Director Arthur Penn's muddled, badly acted detective melodrama features some brutal murders and resorts to sexual exploitation, especially of the girl, to keep things moving. O (R)

Night Must Fall (1937) Chilling suspense picture from the Emlyn Williams play in which a drifter (Robert Montgomery) charms a wealthy old lady (May Whitty) into giving him a job, until her secretary (Rosalind Russell) comes to suspect he is the one being sought by the police for a series of murders in the area. Directed by Richard Thorpe, the suspense mounts quite effectively in a taut story made convincing by Montgomery's compelling performance as a psycopathic killer. More menace than violence A-II (br)

Night of Bloody Horror (1970) Gross horror movie about a mother who mummifies dead members of the family and her manic-depressive son suspected of three sensational murders. Producer-director Joy N. Houck, Jr., while suggesting these may have been cases of accidental fratricide and paternal suicide, concentrates on explicit lovemaking, ax-wielding, and quarts of bloodletting. O (nr)

Night of Counting the Years, The (1975) Unusual Egyptian production about a poor village whose livelihood depends upon periodically selling archaeological treasures they have discovered in an unlooted royal tomb ingeniously hidden in the rocky heights above the Valley of the Kings on the Upper Nile. Writer-director Shadi Abdelsalam links the grandeur and beauty of the age of the pharaohs with the stark poverty of their black-robed descendents in a brilliantly photographed drama filled with many poetic and lyric passages evoking a sense of mystery appropriate to the land of the Sphinx. A-II (nr)

Night of Dark Shadows (1971) Spooky doings in a sequel to **House of Dark Shadows** center around Quentin (David Selby), the last of the Collins heirs, who returns to the family mansion with his bride (Kate Jackson) and falls victim to reincarnations of his ancestors. Producer-director Dan Curtis dredges up a bushel of scary chestnuts for those who enjoy such things. Minimal gore but some sexual allusions suggest an adult perspective. A-III (GP)

Night of the Big Heat (see: **Island of the Burning Damned**)

Night of the Blood Monster (1972) British cut-rate costume melodrama with Christopher Lee as a lecherous witch hunter under James II. Lee gets his just desserts when William of Orange invades and wins the throne. Directed by Jess Franco, this is a talkie with a lot of posturing and little action. The sex and violence are mostly implied by using victims of rape and torture as background decoration. A-III (PG)

Night of the Comet (1984) Two teenage California Valley girls (Catherine Mary Stewart and Kelli Maroney) survive the passing of a comet which has reduced nearly everyone else to red dust. There are some bright moments in this tongue-in-cheek disaster thriller from director Thom Eberhardt, but silly zombie attacks and a benign view of one of the girls' promiscuity mars the movie's value as simple diversion. O (PG-13)

Night of the Executioners (see: **The Cop**)

Night of the Following Day, The (1969) Failed crime melodrama in which four Americans (Marlon Brando, Richard Boone, Jess Hahn, and Rita Moreno) concoct a scheme to kidnap a wealthy youth (Pamela Franklin) on her arrival in France. Directed by Hubert Cornfield, the plot is implausible, and the characterizations are wildly unconvincing. Some violence, sex, and graphic drug use. A-III (R)

Night of the Generals, The (1967) A detective story without much mystery, but unusual because the suspects are WW II German Army generals (Donald Pleasence, Charles Gray, and Peter O'Toole). Detective Omar Shariff plods along after his man with amiable determination, but director Anatole Litvak's straightforward narrative does not arouse much interest. Some brutal violence. A-III (br)

Night of the Grizzly, The (1966) Unpretentious Western directed by Joseph Pevney about a ranch family (Clint Walker and MartaToren) who are trying to raise livestock on a range at the foot of the Rockies, but their ranch draws an enormous grizzly bear who eludes every effort to trap him. Wholesome outdoor adventure fare for the family. A-I (br)

Night of the Hunter, The (1955) Powerful chiller from David Grubb's novel in which a beserk backwoods preacher (Robert Mitchum) learns of money stolen by a dying convict, marries his widow (Shelley Winters) to find it, then pursues her two frightened youngsters until they find sanctuary with a frail but resourceful matron (Lillian Gish). The only movie directed by actor Charles Laughton, the dark tale of suspense builds a truly frightening picture of a homicidal fanatic whose righteous facade is finally shattered by the innocence of children and the common sense of a determined woman. Much menace, some stylized violence, and muted sexual references. A-III (nr)

Night of the Juggler (1980) Psychotic (Cliff Gorman) kidnaps the teenage daughter of an ex-policeman (James Brolin), and the desperate father tracks down the killer himself, a chase that takes him into a very rough and sordid part of town. Director Robert Butler's moderately exciting thriller is marred by graphic violence, rough language, and gratuitous nudity. O (R)

Night of the Lepus (1972) Zoologists Stuart Whitman and Janet Leigh, experimenting with hormones to reduce the rabbit population, accidentally produce a whole Arizona desert full of rabid cottontails as big as cattle, who terrorize the countryside. Directed by William F. Claxton, the monster bunnies loom large on miniature sets, but not large enough to hide the inanities of the script. Still, this hare-raising tale delivers more chuckles than chills. A-II (PG)

Night of the Living Dead, The (1968) Low-budget horror movie whose plot centers on a group of strangers barricaded in a farmhouse while radiation-animated corpses who feed off the living try to storm in for their prey. Directed by George Romero, the unpolished look of the production (grainy black-and-white photography and use of local Pittsburgh residents) has a makeshift quality helping to sustain the dimension of nightmarish unreality. Every once in a while, there is some unconscious humor, which nicely relieves the tension and helped earn its cult reputation. Several fleeting but graphic scenes of ghouls gnawing on various parts of the anatomy. A-III (nr)

Night of the Living Dead (1990) Color remake of the 1969 low-budget cult classic about flesh-eating zombies converging on a rural farmhouse with six frantic adults and one injured child trapped inside. Director Tom Savini's rehash of George Romero's original stomach-wrencher is superior only in its production values, but its nihilistic conclusion is much nastier. Grisly violence, momentary rear nudity, and minimal rough language. O (R)

Night of the Shooting Stars, The (1983) In the chaotic final days of WW II, some Italian peasants flee their villages and hide out in the woods, trying to avoid both retreating German soldiers and vengeful Fascists. Directed and written by Paolo and Vittorio Taviani, the narrative is seen through the perspective of a six-year-old girl who, years later, relates her impressions of war's absurdities to her young son. Visually stunning, often lyric, essay on hope and human resilience. Brief, but intense violence. A-II (R)

Night of the Witches (1970) Failed horror movie about a venal preacher, a naive young man, and a cult of astrologers who kill people with bad horoscopes. Keith Erik Burt directs a tiresome exercise, relying solely upon sexual innuendo for energy. O (PG)

Night on Earth (1992) Amusing look at five distinctly different cab rides occuring on the same night in Los Angeles, New York, Paris, Rome, and Helsinki. With delightful performances from Gena Rowlands, Winona Ryder, and Armin Mueller-Stahl, these wry anecdotes by writer-producer-director Jim Jarmusch playfully capture the universal nature of people despite differing cultures. Some subtitles. Numerous sexual references and recurring rough language. A-III (R)

Night Passage (1957) Accordion-playing troubleshooter (James Stewart), hired to protect a railroad payroll from Colorado train-robbers, comes up against his outlaw younger brother (Audie Murphy). Director James Neilsen's predictable Western works up some interest in the moral struggle between good and bad siblings and its effect on an impressionable youth (Brandon de Wilde). Some menace and stylized violence. A-I (br)

Night Patrol (1985) Stupid hijinks in the police department are the sole feature of this vulgar, sexually exploitative clone of **Police Academy**. O (R)

Night People (1954) Tense Cold War drama set in Berlin, where a US officer (Gregory Peck) must consider swapping two East German refugees for the GI son of an Ohio businessman (Broderick Crawford) being held by the Russians. Written, produced, and directed by Nunnally Johnson, there is plenty of international intrigue, and Peck's performance is impeccable, but the situation is convoluted and the treatment less than involving. Some stylized violence and sexual innuendo. A-II (br)

Night Porter, The (1974) Dirk Bogarde plays the porter in a Viennese hotel who resumes the sadomasochistic relationship he began years before with a woman inmate (Charlotte Rampling) of a concentration camp where he was a Nazi officer. Director Liliana Cavani claustrophobically dissects the terror and thrill of a renewed and sick lust that both know will ultimately destroy them. Though done with some artistic integrity, this exercise in abnormal psychology lacks dramatic coherence or human insight. Several explicit scenes of a sexual nature involving nudity and sadistic brutality. O (R)

Night Shift (1982) Night crew at the New York City morgue (Henry Winkler and Michael Keaton) turn the place into a call-girl service. The situation allows for little but smirks, and the few laughs are sight gags mainly about life in the big city. Under Ron Howard's heavy-handed direction, Winkler is overshadowed by Keaton's fine performance as a frenetic zany. Romanticizes prostitution and some brief nudity. O (R)

Night Song (1947) Romantic tearjerker in which a San Francisco heiress (Merle Oberon) falls in love with an embittered blind pianist (Dana Andrews), wins his confidence by pretending to be blind herself, then persuades him to submit a concerto in a competition she creates so he can use the prize money for an operation to restore his sight. Directed by John Cromwell, the contrived proceedings are helped along by the pianist's breezy pal (Hoagy Carmichael) and the woman's sensible aunt (Ethel Barrymore), until the tears finally end. Unlikely fare for any but confirmed romantics. A-I (br)

Night Stalker, The (1987) Demented crime melodrama about an alcoholic vice-squad detective (Charles Napier) on the trail of a psychopathic serial killer of hookers. Director Max Kleven's tired plot features an excess of bloody violence, nude corpses, and profanity. O (R)

Night the Lights Went Out in Georgia, The (1981) Dennis Quaid and Kristy McNichol play a brother and sister who dream of being big-time country-western singers in Nashville but face the predictable problems of earning a living in a small Georgia town. Director Ron Maxwell's attempt to cash in on the hit song of the title is mediocre at best. A-III (PG)

Night the World Exploded, The (1957) Pulp doomsday tale about a scientist (William Leslie) and his assistant (Kathryn Grant) seeking the cause of increasing underground pressures which threaten to blow up the world. Directed by Fred F. Sears, the plot is hilariously hokey and the acting wooden, but it may please viewers looking for a simpleminded exercise in the absurd. A-I (br)

Night They Raided Minsky's, The (1968) Because this film celebrates the crude lustiness that characterized burlesque in the 1920s, some may find it an honest relief from the present era's over-glamorization of sex. As directed by William Friedkin, the movie's standout performance is by Norman Wisdom as a sad little comic, with Bert Lahr's last movie appearance adding some pathos and nostalgia to the proceedings. Unfortunately, however, the long-awaited "accident" that led to the first striptease gets most of the emphasis. O (PG)

Night to Remember, A (1958) Vivid British dramatization of the tragic end to the 1912 maiden voyage of the *Titanic*, the so-called unsinkable luxury liner after it hit an iceberg in the North Atlantic and went down with some 1,400 victims, leaving only 705 survivors. Directed by Roy Ward Baker from Eric Ambler's adaptation of Walter Lord's book, the story of the voyage is told through numerous vignettes of the passengers, both famous and ordinary, with one of the ship's officers (Kenneth More) providing some narrative continuity, especially during the scenes of panic, confusion, and resignation aboard the sinking vessel, whose end moves viewers with its sense of human loss. Menacing situations mixed with uplifting ones. A-I (br)

Night Train to Munich (1940) Classy British espionage caper in which a Czech inventor and his daughter (Margaret Lockwood) are snatched from England by a nasty Nazi agent (Paul von Henreid), then rescued from a heavily guarded German train by a daredevil British operative (Rex Harrison). Director Carol Reed paces the cat-and-mouse thriller with some twisty plot turns, comic byplay (notably Basil Radford and Naunton Wayne as woolly English travelers), and suspenseful action, including a shootout atop the Swiss Alps. Stylized violence and mild romance. A-II (br)

Night Visitor, The (1971) A double murder disrupts a quiet Scandinavian countryside, and the man under suspicion (Per Oscarsson) tells the police inspector (Trevor Howard) that the murders could only have been done by his brother-in-law (Max von Sydow) who resides in an escape-proof cell in an insane asylum. Directed by Laslo Benedek, this modern Gothic tale uses von Sydow's gymnastic skills and menacing presence to achieve a near-perfect combination of thriller and mystery. Some violence. A-III (PG)

Night Watch (1973) Disappointing British murder melodrama revolves around whether Elizabeth Taylor is actually mad, or only pretends to be, in order to avenge herself on husband Lawrence Harvey for plotting to get her enormous wealth by doing away with her and marrying Billie Whitelaw. Under Brian Hutton's uncertain direction, Taylor's performance is a monotonous mixture of screechy emotional outbursts and frumphish attempts at feline sensuality, even as the muddled plot lurches towards its throat-slitting climax. A-III (PG)

Night We Never Met, The (1993) Time-sharing a Manhattan apartment with two men she has never met, a married woman (Annabella Sciorra) decides to have an affair with one of them (Matthew Broderick) but accidentally sleeps with the wrong guy (Kevin Anderson). Writer-director Warren Leight's dreary mistaken-identity comedy takes a contrived situation and beats it to death with charmless characters and numbingly dumb dialogue. Benign treatment of casual sex, brief nudity, heavy drinking, and some rough language. O (R)

Night Zoo (1988) French-Canadian crime movie about an ex-con (Gilles Maheu) trying to stay alive in Montreal's sleazy underworld while being pursued by two drug-dealing cops he has doublecrossed. Written and directed by Jean-Claude Lauzon, its hard-edged depiction of criminal excesses is softened somewhat by a subplot involving a growing reconciliation between the ex-con and his father (Roger Le Bel in a fine performance). Excessively violent treatment, several explicit sex scenes, and rough language. O (nr)

Nightbreed (1990) A young man (Craig Sheffer) and his girlfirend (Anne Bobby) race to save a legendary city of dead souls from invading human nut-cases, including a psycho psychoanalyst (David Cronenberg), a Fascist cop (Charles Haid), and a spineless priest (Malcolm Smith). Writer-director Clive Barker's muddled horror movie features a haphazard collection of gruesome freaks, nightmare imagery, and makeup wizardry. Excessive images of grisly human slaughter, some profanity, and nudity. O (R)

Nightcomers, The (1972) Based on the Victorian characters in Henry James's supernatural story, "The Turn of the Screw," the movie ends where the original began and imagines the dark events transpiring between the groundskeeper (Marlon Brando) and his mistress (Stephanie Beacham) that leave two very troubled children for the new governess who arrives at the beginning of the James story. Director Michael Winner dramatizes literally the perverse tendencies and violent events (bizarre sadomasochistic games) which only lurked beneath the surface of the original James story. Climactic gore, nudity in a sexual context, and a theme of evil in innocence. O (R)

Nightfall (1956) Tough crime thriller of an innocent man (Aldo Ray) pursued by a cop (James Gregory) who wants him for murder and a bankrobber (Brian Keith) who wants the loot he's lost. Director Jacques Tourneur makes it all the more intriguing by doling out the story with flashbacks as needed, and the cast makes it seem convincing enough. Stylized violence. A-II (br)

Nighthawks (1981) Intense thriller with Sylvester Stallone playing a New York City policeman assigned to an anti-terrorist unit whose mettle is tested by a clever and utterly ruthless German terrorist (Rutger Hauer). Director Bruce Malmuth fails to invest any human dimension in all the violence and counter-violence that transpires, using the situation merely as the basis for exciting melodrama. Brutal violence and rough language. A-III (R)

Nightjohn (1996) A young girl slave (Allison Jones) on a cotton plantation in the 1830s faces the wrath of her cruel master (Beau Bridges) after secretly being taught to read by the title character (Carl Lumbly), who's determined to bring the power of literacy to his oppressed people. Directed by Charles Burnett, the television production gets strong performances from a largely African-American cast in a drama portraying the painful injustices of slavery and one man's attempt to transcend its inhumanity. Some intense scenes of physical and spiritual violence. A-II (PG-13)

Nightmare (1956) Gripping thriller set in New Orleans, where a jazz-band clarinetist (Kevin McCarthy) awakens from a nightmare convinced he's killed a man, then gets his cop brother-in-law (Edward G. Robinson) to investigate, and the trail leads to a hypnotist. Director Maxwell Shane's remake of **Fear in the Night** is generally better acted and certainly better crafted than the first time around, with more memorable results. Stylized violence, threatening situations, and sexual innuendo. A-III (br)

Nightmare Before Christmas, The (1993) Minor fantasy of the macabre, with puppet animation telling the tale of Halloweentown's skeleton king replacing the kidnapped Santa Claus to spread Christmas fear with scary toys, until stopped by a missile, then returning home to free Santa in time to make his accustomed rounds. Producer Tim Burton's story centers in the dark world of hobgoblins and monsters suddenly intruding on the bright expectations of St. Nick's annual visit, but the narrative proves tiresome in padding out the thin concept, despite all its stylish puppetry and ghoulish humor. Considerable menace and threatening atmosphere. A-II (PG)

Nightmare Castle (1966) Dubbed Italian horror movie directed by Allen Grunewald in which a mad doctor (Paul Miller) experimenting on rejuvenation by blood transfusions kills his unfaithful wife (Barbara Steele), then tries to put her sister (Steele again) in an insane asylum, until undone by ghosts and an honorable physician (Lawrence Clift). Some gory visuals, menacing atmosphere, and sexual innuendo. A-III (br)

Nightmare in Wax (1969) Old-fashioned horror movie about a psychotic wax-museum curator (Cameron Mitchell) who seeks vengeance on some old associates for having humiliated and disfigured him. Director Bud Townsend bridges the gaps in the story line with a little morbid humor, some mild horror, and playful settings. A-II (M)

Nightmare on Elm Street, A (1984) Freddie, a long-dead child murderer, haunts the dreams of some high-school students, who also die from them. Directed by Wes Craven, the horror movie relies on graphic gore, sexual references, and images of uncaring parents for the purpose of eliciting shock and irreverent humor. O (R)

Nightmare On Elm Street, Part 2: Freddy's Revenge, A (1985) Foiled in the original, the slashing monster returns in this sequel, directed by Jack Sholder, to again take possession of a teenager so that he can do some further cutting-up. More blood and gore mixed with sexual titillation aimed at teenagers. O (R)

Nightmare on Elm Street 3: Dream Warriors, A (1987) A group of youngsters are terrorized in their dreams by a restless, evil phantom who returns to avenge his fiery death at the hands of their parents. Director Chuck Russell's worn-out plot relies on gory special effects and sadistic violence, with no other purpose but to shock. O (R)

Nightmare on Elm Street 4: The Dream Master, A (1988) Another inept sequel about a child murderer (Robert Englund) who takes revenge for his death by invading the dreams of his teenage victims. Directed by Renny Harlin, the plot is an unhealthy brew of gruesome, gory visuals with some nudity and rough language. O (R)

Nightmare on Elm Street 5: The Dream Child, A (1989) Freddy Krueger (Robert Englund) is back, stalking teenage Alice (Lisa Wilcox) through the dreams of her unborn, illegitimate child. Directed by Stephen Hopkins, there are gruesome flashbacks recalling Freddy's conception and birth as the son of a nun raped by psychos in an insane asylum, as well as Freddy's usual sadistic teen-stalking. O (R)

Nights of Cabiria (1957) Bittersweet drama in which a Roman streetwalker (Giulietta Masina), longing for marriage and respectability, overcomes her despair at being victimized by a man (Francois Perier) she trusted would wed her and resumes her search for happiness. Director Federico Fellini's compassionate theme of an individual's lonely quest for a place in the world concludes with hope and a sense of spiritual transcendence, largely due Masina's compelling performance as the streetwise yet innocent waif who accepts life with all its good and evil. Subtitles. Mature themes. A-III (br)

Nightwatch (1998) Edgy thriller in which a law student (Ewan McGregor) working nights as a morgue attendant finds he's been framed for the murder of several prostitutes when an investigating detective (Nick Nolte) uncovers evidence tying him to the crimes. Director Ole Bornedal sustains the picture's ominous atmosphere and sense of dread, until an implausible ending ruins its credibility. Some violence and rough language, sexual situations, brief corpse nudity, and occasional profanity. A-III (R)

Nightwing (1979) An Indian deputy sheriff (Nick Mancuso), the deputy's girlfriend (Kathryn Harrold), and an obsessed scientist (David Warner) team up to track down and destroy a colony of ravenous, plague-bearing vampire bats. Director Arthur Hiller's modest thriller relies on an interesting mix of Indian mysticism and scientific facts, but the action leads only to an anticlimax. Rather graphic violence and the use of drugs for religious purposes. A-III (PG)

Nijinsky (1980) Biographical dramatization about legendary ballet dancer Vaslav Nijinsky (George de la Pena) and impresario Sergei Diaghilev (Alan Bates) places less emphasis upon ballet itself than upon their master-protégé relationship and its homosexual dimension. Director Herbert Ross presents an elegant re-creation of pre-WW I Europe, and the acting is of high order, but some may find the pace of the drama far too languid, and others will be uncomfortable with the frank, if non-explicit, manner in which the homosexual relationship is depicted. Graphic but brief scene of heterosexual lovemaking. A-IV (R)

Nina Takes a Lover (1995) Shallow, fragmentary tale of a neglected wife (Laura San Giocomo) who has an affair with a Welsh photographer (Paul Rhys), but it turns out that infidelity is not her game. Writer-director Alan Jacobs plays out the situation in tedious fashion, then tries to make it seem meaningful by a radical twist in the story line, which only acerbates the inadequacies of the exercise. Sexual situations, a restrained sex scene, a flash of nudity, a couple of profanities, and some rough language. A-IV (R)

9 1/2 Weeks (1986) Director Adrian Lyne delivers a passionless expression of erotic fantasy in his sexually explicit depiction of a sadomasochistic love affair between an art gallery manager (Kim Basinger) and a financier (Mickey Rourke). Nudity and simulated sexual activity. O (R)

Nine Lives of Fritz the Cat, The (1974) Based on R. Crumb's comic-strip adventures of a funky feline whose primitive vulgarity and social irreverence some found refreshing, this inept animated version by Robert Taylor throws together a batch of disjointed and unimaginative episodes in a manner too literal and witless to be taken as satire. Its excesses of racial animosity and sexual exploitation go beyond questions of taste and tend to be socially destructive rather than purgative. O (R)

Nine Months (1995) When his pregnant girlfriend (Julianne Moore) leaves him because of his ambivalence about parenthood, a self-centered child psychologist (Hugh Grant) sets out to convince her that he wants both marriage and a family. Writer-director Chris Columbus's contrived situation comedy delivers spotty laughs on its way to a feel-good ending of marital commitment. Several restrained bedroom scenes, frequent sexual innuendo, minor slapstick violence, and occasional profanity and rough language. A-III (PG-13)

9.30.55 (see: **24 Hours of the Rebel**)

9 to 5 (1980) Dolly Parton, Jane Fonda, and Lily Tomlin play a trio of harrassed and exploited secretaries who rise up in revolt against an autocratic boss (Dabney Coleman). Director Colin Higgins's promising satire becomes sheer silliness, and then begins to drag fearfully. Some rough language, a scene of pot-smoking, and sexually oriented dream sequence in which the theme of male dominance is inverted. A-III (PG)

1918 (1985) Mortality presses in upon ordinary happiness in a small Texas town as WW I is coming to an end in Europe and a killer flu epidemic rages at home. Written by Horton Foote and directed by Ken Harrison, it is an excellent movie that catches in wonderfully evocative fashion the terror and beauty of daily life. Though the setting is a vanished era, it nonetheless gives some rich insights into one's own life. There is nothing in it harmful to youngsters, but only children of a certain level of maturity will be able to appreciate it. A-I (nr)

1984 (1984) Uninspired screen version of George Orwell's foreboding vision of a totalitarian state crushing the individual rights of its hapless citizens loses here both the original's passionate idealism and sense of immediacy. Director Michael Radford's drily somber work lacks the sense of human nobility that is the story's thematic core, but it does offer a nuanced performance by Richard Burton as a Big Brother surrogate and John Hurt as the rewriter of history. Some violence and brief nudity. A-III (R)

1941 (1979) Japanese submarine sighted off the coast of southern California in the early days of WW II starts a panic with rumors of an invasion. Director Steven Spielberg wastes the comic talents of Dan Aykroyd and John Belushi in a vulgar, tedious, supremely unfunny comedy. Sexual connotations abound and there is some slapstick nudity. O (PG)

1900 (1977) Sprawling, disjointed narrative spanning 70 years of Italian history seen through the eyes of two men born in 1901, one an aristocrat (Robert De Niro), the other a Marxist (Gerard Depardieu). Director Bernardo Bertolucci's view of history lacks dramatic force and the human frame of reference is chiefly sex and politics. Extravangant depiction of violence and exploitation of nudity. O (R)

1969 (1988) This sentimental reflection on the pivotal year of the Vietnam War era follows two small-town 19-year-olds (Kiefer Sutherland and Robert Downey, Jr.) who as college students struggle to balance their fears about the draft with their desire to enjoy their last summer of teenage freedom. Writer-director Ernest Thompson's contrived memory play fails to flesh out his one-dimensional characters or inject the story with anything more than superfical period-hype. Locker-room language, full frontal nudity in a brief, non-sexual way, and some drug abuse. A-III (R)

90 Days (1986) A young Canadian has three months in which to decide if he will marry the Korean woman he has sent for via a mail-order service. Director Giles Walker's small Canadian comedy explores the pitfalls of the male ego with charm and subtlety while showing that happiness and commitment can develope without premarital sex. A few harsh expletives and running gag about artificial insemination. A-III (nr)

99 and 44/100% Dead (1974) Silly, badly done gang-war movie starring Chuck Conners, Richard Harris, Edmond O'Brien, and Bradford Dillman as various mobster types. Directed by John Frankenheimer, the movie fails to be either a serious crime melodrama or a comic-strip crime spoof, and consequently leaves the audience feeling uncomfortable about its realistic scenes of shootouts and sadistic brutality. A-III (PG)

99 Women (1969) Crude European exploitation movie, directed by Jess Franco, centers on the more sordid aspects of life in a women's prison and is merely an excuse to portray nudity and perversion. O (R)

92 in the Shade (1975) Peter Fonda and Warren Oates play fishing-boat owners competing for the tourist trade in the Florida Keys. The only element that works in this failed comedy by writer-director

Thomas McGuane is Fonda's madcap father (William Hickey) and goatish grandfather (Burgess Meredith, who spends most of his time ogling Sylvia Miles). Some exploitative sexual elements. O (R)

Ninth Configuration, The (1980) Stacy Keach plays a government psychologist trying to determine if the inmates of an asylum housed in a Californian Gothic castle are really psychological casualties of the Vietnam War or fakes. Writer-director William Blatty attempts to explore more than the nature of mental illness by introducing such issues as the existence of God, but the drama gets mired down in the more graphic aspects of insanity and unorthodox therapy. Disturbing and provocative movie with suicide as a plot device, some extreme violence, and rough language. A-IV (R)

Nixon (1995) Overlong, meandering view of the tortured, contradictory personality of Richard M. Nixon (Anthony Hopkins), whose checkered political career comes to an end in the disgrace of the Watergate cover-up. Director Oliver Stone's interpretation of Nixon's character is a work of historical fiction, combining facts and conjecture in a narrative which pays homage to **Citizen Kane** by seeking the key to the man in his experiences as a boy. Devious political machinations, sexual references, much profanity, and some rough language. A-III (R)

No Blade of Grass (1970) Ecological disaster destroys all varieties of grasses and drives a London family to flee to a relative's farm in the north. Along the way the father (Nigel Davenport) kills anyone who stands in his way, but when they finally arrive at the farm they are faced with the father's brother waving a machine gun against unwelcome guests. Unsubtle melodrama directed by Cornel Wilde bludgeons viewers with assorted violence, blood, and gore, a motorcycle gang rape, and a very realistic birth sequence. Cruelly cynical conception of the anarchy and inhumanity resulting from the spectre of doomsday. O (R)

No Deposit, No Return (1976) Disney movie with a better-than-average cast (David Niven, Herschel Bernardi, and Darren McGavin) about two kids who stage their own kidnapping in order to join their mother in Hong Kong. Director Norman Tokar's plot is as old as O'Henry's "The Ransom of Red Chief," but that won't bother youngsters. A-I (G)

No Down Payment (1957) Soapy melodrama about young couples in a middle-class Los Angeles suburb, where a wife (Sheree North) tries to straighten out an alcoholic husband (Tony Randall), a grocery-store manager (Pat Hingle) grapples with the suburb's racial restrictions, and an embittered ex-GI (Cameron Mitchell) lashes out at his wife (Joanne Woodward), then assaults his next-door neighbor (Patricia Owens). Director Martin Ritt tries to use the sudsy story of the couples to reflect the materialistic discontents and confusions arising from America's post-war prosperity, but the social message gets lost in the personal melodrama. Stylized violence, including an off-screen rape, sexual innuendo, racial bias, and domestic conflicts. A-II (br)

No Drums, No Bugles (1971) Small, unpretentious Civil War drama about a West Virginia farmer (Martin Sheen) who, rather than take up arms, leaves his wife and child for a solitary three-year self-imposed confinement in the backwoods. The substance of the movie is taken up with his techniques for survival in the forest through the changing seasons, and Sheen makes it an absorbing experience in a *tour de force* performance. Written, produced, and directed by Clyde Ware, it is not a tract against the evils of war but a comment on the sacrifices that must be made by those who place themselves outside the accepted standards of the community. Some motivations are unclear, and an ambiguous ending make it best suited for an adult audience, but it is certainly one that could be appreciated by older teenagers. A-III (G)

No Escape (1994) Convicted of murder and sentenced to life on a remote island inhabited solely by condemned felons, an ex-Marine (Ray Liotta) joins forces with a small colony of peaceable convicts who live in constant danger from a larger band (led by Stuart Wilson) who murder for sport. Director Martin Campbell's macho action flick goes through the motions of pitting reformed cons against evil cons, but its focus is essentially on gory battles-to-the-death in which men are reduced to the level of beasts. Excessive graphic violence, much mindless mayhem, and a few instances of rough language. O (R)

No Highway in the Sky (1951) Fretful American scientist (James Stewart) aboard a British jet-liner warns a jittery movie star (Marlene Dietrich), a sensible stewardess (Glynis Johns), and a stern pilot (Niall MacGinnis) that metal fatigue will soon cause the plane's tail section to disintegrate. Director Henry Koster's plodding treatment of the distressing premise results in a disappointing mix of fitful tensions and sentimental characterizations. Life-threatening situations and mild romantic complications. A-II (br)

No Holds Barred (1989) Strongman Hulk Hogan grunts, winks, and stomps through his role as a TV-superstar wrestler fending off bids from a sleazy rival network. Directed in gratuitous fashion by Thomas J. Wright, the movie's dumb material includes black stereotyping, excessive comic-book violence, some rough language, and vulgar bathroom humor. O (PG-13)

No Man Is an Island (1962) Fact-based WW II story of an American soldier (Jeffrey Hunter) who flees into the jungle when Japanese soldiers occupy Guam, then is kept hidden by friendly islanders, until US forces return three years later. Written and directed by John Monks, Jr., and Richard Goldstone, the action consists largely of the American's narrow escapes from Japanese patrols and the dangerous risks taken by those sheltering him. Wartime violence and menacing situations. A-I (br)

No Man of Her Own (1932) Amusing romantic melodrama in which a crooked New York gambler (Clark Gable) marries a small-town librarian (Carole

Lombard) on the flip of a coin, then becomes intrigued with the notion of going straight. Director Wesley Ruggles keeps the situation light and lively with snappy dialogue, a dandy supporting cast (notably Grant Mitchell, Elizabeth Patterson, and J. Farrell MacDonald), and the sparks generated by the principals. Some sexual innuendo and criminal activity. A-III (br)

No Man of Her Own (1950) Melodramatic tale in which a desperate unwed mother (Barbara Stanwyck) assumes the identity of a wealthy woman killed in a train wreck, then faces exposure unless she pays off her blackmailing ex-boyfriend (Lyle Bettger). Director Mitchell Leisen drags out the contrived suds as the woman's plight deepens, until a sordid murder solves her immediate problems. Moral complications arising from the deception and some nasty menace. A-III (br)

No Mercy (1986) Chicago cop (Richard Gere) avenges the murder of a fellow officer by using a beautiful Cajun (Kim Basinger) as the bait to smoke out and kill a crime boss of the Louisiana bayous. Director Richard Pearce's nasty, brutish thriller with implied sexual and explicit physical violence and excessive profanity. O (R)

No Name on the Bullet (1959) Talkative Western in which a notorious hired gun (Audie Murphy) rides into a small town, then does little but play chess with the local doctor (Charles Drake), while fear about whom he's come to kill takes its toll on the citizenry. Director Jack Arnold has difficulty sustaining suspense in the far-fetched proceedings and their stereotyped characters. Stylized violence and sexual innunedo. A-III (br)

No Sleep Till Dawn (see: **Bombers B-52**)

No Small Affair (1984) When a 16-year-old boy (Jon Cryer) gives a boost to the career of a young singer (Demi Moore), she takes him to bed in gratitude. Director Jerry Schatzberg's limp romantic comedy is filled with unpleasant characters in an uninvolving plot. Endorses sexual promiscuity. O (R)

No Time for Breakfast (1978) French tearjerker about a witty, vivacious woman (Annie Girardot), senior physician at a Paris hospital, an ideal wife and extraordinary mother, who has an affair and develops a cancer, which goes into remission when family ties are restored. Director Jean-Louis Bertucelli coats the fact-based story with melodramatic overtones. Casual acceptance of infidelity and a nude bathtub scene. O (nr)

No Time for Love (1943) Uneven romantic comedy in which a sophisticated New York magazine photographer (Claudette Colbert) gives a tunnel construction-worker (Fred MacMurray) a job after he's fired because of her, then is swept off her feet by his uncomplicated, no-nonsense manly virtues. Directed by Mitchell Leisen, the fish-out-of-water situations have some wit, but the romantic developments seem even more contrived today than they did then. Romantic complications. A-II (br)

No Time for Sergeants (1958) Drafted into the Army, a Southern yokel (Andy Griffith) gets through boot camp only with the desperate assistance of his long-suffering sergeant (Myron McCormick). Director Mervyn LeRoy's one-joke comedy hinges on Griffith's hilarious performance as the well-intentioned rube, which finally wears out its welcome in a tiresome, overlong ending. Wholesome service comedy except for a vulgar latrine routine and minimal fisticuffs. A-I (br)

No Way Out (1950) Earnest social melodrama in which a white extremist (Richard Widmark) determines to incite a race riot by charging a black doctor (Sidney Poitier) killed his brother. Directed by Joseph L. Mankiewicz, the period proceedings seem overly contrived today, though hold interest because of the movie's frank treatment of racial hatred and strong performances from a cast including Stephen McNally as a color-blind physician, Linda Darnell as an unwitting victim of events, and Ossie Davis and Ruby Dee as the embattled doctor's relatives. Social justice theme depicted with stylized violence, much menace ,and repugnant racial epithets. A-III (br)

No Way Out (1975) Predictable Italian crime melodrama about what happens to a decent, hard-working family man (Alain Delon) when he tries to retire from his job as a Mafia hit-man. Director Duccio Tessari's dreary, mediocre movie deals in the standard violence of the genre, though women are treated especially brutally, and there is a gratuitous lesbian scene. O (R)

No Way Out (1987) Three-way power struggle erupts when a high-ranking politico (Gene Hackman) and his chief counsel (Will Patton) try to cover up the accidental death of a party girl (Sean Young) unknowingly shared by the politician's CIA liaison officer (Kevin Costner). Director Roger Donaldson's taut tale of betrayal and the abuse of power is marred by a fairly graphic lovemaking scene. A-III (R)

No Way to Treat a Lady (1968) Rod Steiger plays a madman with a severe mother complex who changes disguises for five compulsive murders, while a likeable police detective (George Segal) tries to outwit him. Director Jack Smight provides an effective mixture of adult comedy, pyschodrama, and an upbeat love story. A-III (br)

Nobody Waved Goodbye (1965) Perceptive Canadian drama about a know-it-all adolescent (Peter Kastner), whose mounting troubles with middle-class parents, teachers, and pregnant girlfriend (Julie Biggs) end with his running away. Directed in semi-documentary fashion by Don Owen, the result has a sense of spontaneity and unpretentious realism that makes it convincing both as drama and as social commentary. Assorted problems of a troubled youth. A-II (br)

Nobody's Fool (1986) Abandoned by her boyfriend when she becomes pregnant, a teenager (Rosanna Arquette) is befriended by a local theater director

(Eric Roberts) who helps her refocus her life after giving up her baby for adoption. Directed by Evelyn Purcell, the movie is more about building one's self-esteem and trust than about sexual relationships. Implied sexual encounter and brief scene of violence. A-II (PG-13)

Nobody's Fool (1994) Quirky story set in wintry upstate New York, where an incorrigible aging loser (Paul Newman) looks after his ailing former grammar-school teacher (Jessica Tandy) while starting to build a long-overdue relationship with his estranged son and grandson, though romantically pursued by the neglected wife (Melanie Griffith) of his construction-company boss (Bruce Willis). Writer-director Robert Benton juggles nearly a dozen small-town relationships with realism and humor in a movie small in scope but large in heart as it explores friendship, hope, and the ever-present possibility of personal growth. Some partial nudity, sexual references, and minimal rough language. A-III (R)

Nocturne (1946) Sluggish crime thriller directed by Edwin L. Marin in which a police detective (George Raft) sets out to prove that the suicide of a womanizing songwriter was really a case of murder, but the convoluted plot with its multitude of suspects (led by Lynn Bari and Joseph Pevney) becomes dull mystery fare. Stylized violence, occasional menace, and implied romantic liaisons. A-II (br)

Noises Off (1992) On the opening night of a Broadway comedy, its panicked director (Michael Caine) recalls the chaotic road-show rehearsals, while the backstage infighting of the cast (Carol Burnett, John Ritter, Christopher Reeve, and Denholm Elliott) noisily spills onstage. Peter Bogdanovich directs an overwrought, British-inspired sex farce of split-second timing whose frantic pranks and pratfalls entertain for a while, then are repeated to death. Some sexual innuendo, double entendres, and an instance of rough language. A-III (PG-13)

Nomads (1986) A French anthropologist (Pierce Brosnan) is tormented by punkrocker demons who invade his Los Angeles home. After the evil spirits are transferred at his death to his doctor (Lesley-Anne Down), the malevolent punkrockers scare her out of California. Profanity, brief nudity, and scenes of violence. O (R)

None But the Brave (1965) Frank Sinatra directs as well as stars in this anti-war movie set in WW II on an out-of-the-way Pacific island, where the crew of a downed American plane is pitted against a small Japanese outpost. The story's message of brotherhood is clearly stated but a bit too violently. A-II (nr)

None But the Lonely Heart (1944) Darkly muddled story of a British drifter (Cary Grant), who returns to his home in the London slums to look after his dying mother (Ethyl Barrymore), but can't resist the easy money offered by a local mobster (George Coulouris). Written and directed by Clifford Odets, not even the square-jawed Grant can make the shallow lead sympathetic, though Barrymore copped an Oscar for her shining performance as his long-suffering yet ever hopeful mom. Brief stylized violence. A-II (br)

Noose Hangs High, The (1948) Routine comedy caper with Bud Abbott and Lou Costello on the run from a murderous bookie (Joseph Calleia) after losing the money he gave them to pay off a mysterious bettor (Leon Errol). Director Charles Barton keeps the weak proceedings afloat with Errol's dippy antics and the boy's reprise of some old patter routines. Comic menace. A-I (br)

Norma Rae (1979) Inspiring drama with Sally Field in the title role as an Alabama textile worker recruited by a tenacious labor organizer (Ron Liebman) to help rally her exploited coworkers into forming a union in the face of tough tactics by an unenlightened management. Director Martin Ritt's dramatic expose of injustices in the workplace gives viewers some characters and a cause to cheer about. Absorbing, thoughtful entertainment, but there are some frank references to sexual misconduct. A-III (PG)

Norman ... Is That You? (1976) Failed situation comedy about a father (Redd Foxx) who discovers that his son is a homosexual. Though the visual elements are restrained, director George Schlatter's movie stereotypes blacks, women, and homosexuals, conveys a smug contempt for parental authority and affection and exploits a serious theme in a witless manner. O (PG)

Norseman, The (1978) Viking chieftain (Lee Majors) leads his men to the shores of the New World to rescue his father (Mel Ferrer) held prisoner by the Indians. Director Charles B. Pierce's low-budget, low-IQ saga presents Indians as the treacherous, bloodthirsty stereotypes that one would have thought had passed from the screen forever. Generous amount of violence and bloodshed. A-III (PG)

North (1994) Flawed comic fantasy in which a neglected 11-year-old (Elijah Wood) wins the legal right to choose new parents, then travels the globe to audition prospective couples, only to discover there's no place like home. Though there are several whimsical moments, and Wood is splendid in the role, director Rob Reiner's fitful narrative is marked by lame humor and resorts to a dumb murder conspiracy against the boy to set up the hackneyed ending. Intermittent menace to a child. A-II (PG)

North Avenue Irregulars, The (1979) Standard Disney comedy about a minister (Edward Herrmann) who takes over a failing parish in a small town and, along with other revitalizing measures, mobilizes a predictablly zany collection of church women to put some illegal gamblers out of business. Director Bruce Bilson concludes the action with a car-crunching slapstick chase. Fair family fun, but less-than-appealing view of women. A-I (G)

North by Northwest (1959) Stylish tongue-in-cheek thriller in which a suave advertising executive (Cary Grant), mistaken for a spy by foreign agents (James Mason and Martin Landau), and suspected of murder by the police, is chased from the United Nations to Mount Rushmore, with some time out along the way for romance with a double agent (Eva Marie Saint). Though the plot is only an excuse for some dandy suspense sequences (most memorable, the deadly crop-dusting plane in the middle of nowhere), director Alfred Hitchcock is at his most playful in manipulating the innocent hero and the viewer through an intricate maze of menace. Stylized violence and discreet sexual references. A-III (br)

North Country (1972) Ron Hayes is a bush pilot who delivers mail-and-supplies to those rugged individualists who have chosen to live off the land in the lonely, lovely wilds of Alaska. Functioning as a filmmaker in his spare time, Hayes conceived and photographed this documentary view of the modern pioneer on America's last frontier. Its blending of scenery, rare wildlife, and the people who live in the land of the Eskimo make an outdoor adventure that is unusually satsifying family fare. A-I (G)

North Dallas Forty (1979) Nick Nolte and Mac Davis star as professional football players who love the game but not what commercialism has done to it. Nolte is excellent, and director Ted Kotcheff's expose of the hypocrisy and violence of professional sports has some very effective moments, especially the effects of drug abuse, but its focus becomes obscured in promiscuous sex and the athletes' propensity for pranks. Some nudity and much rough language. O (R)

North to Alaska (1960) Robust adventure story set in 1900 Nome, where a trio of gold prospectors (John Wayne, Stewart Granger, and Fabian) make a big strike, then have to defend it against a slick claim-jumper (Ernie Kovacs), while dealing with a Frenchwoman (Capucine) who only has marriage on her mind. Director Henry Hathaway alternates the full-blooded action sequences with on-going romantic misunderstandings between the principals. Stylized violence and sexual innuendo. A-III (br)

North West Mounted Police (1940) Colorful though far-fetched adventure in Canada's Northwest Territories, where a Mountie (Robert Preston) teams with a Texas Ranger (Gary Cooper) to stop the 1885 Rail Rebellion of the mixed-blooded Metis and the Cree Indians. Producer-director Cecil B. DeMille's tribute to the thin line of the early RCMP gets lost in bogus subplots, thick accents, and silly personal romances. Stylized violence and romantic complications. A-II (br)

Northwest Frontier (see: **Flame Over India**)

Northwest Passage (1940) Colorful, large-scale adaptation of Kenneth Roberts's novel about a rugged company of colonial backwoodsmen led by Captain Robert Rogers (Spencer Tracy) deep into hostile country to destroy an enemy stronghold during the French and Indian War. Directed by King Vidor, the narrative's violent frontier action is well-paced with humor and pathos, mainly involving two novice Rangers (Walter Brennan and Robert Young), but in celebrating the brave exploits of a tiny band of colonial patriots against a wilderness foe, the movie is woefully dated in its depiction of Indians as brutal savages. Though there is much good in this historical adventure, its violence and ethnic stereotypes make it questionable fare for young children. A-I (nr)

Northwest Rangers (1942) Routine Yukon adventure directed by Joseph Newman follows boyhood chums growing up on opposite sides of the law, the one (William Lundigan) becoming a Canadian Mountie, and the other (James Craig) a professional gambler — both, of course, in love with the same woman (Patricia Dane). Stylized violence and mild romantic complications. A-I (br)

Northwest Stampede (1948) Modest outdoor adventure directed by Albert S. Rogell is set in the Canadian Rockies, where a lady ranch-foreman (Joan Leslie) competes against her new boss (James Craig) in the Calgary Stampede's six-day rodeo in an attempt to keep him from selling the ranch and its herd of horses. A-I (br)

Norwood (1970) Corny but entertaining Glen Campbell vehicle following his misadventures after military service as he innocently transports some stolen cars to New York, has a one-night stand with a pretty hippie in Greenwich Village, meets Kim Darby on a bus and brings her back to his Southern home along with a midget and a performing rooster. Campbell's fans will enjoy the romp, though some may be put off by the salty dialogue and tasteless but brief situations. A-III (G)

Nosferatu (1922) Silent horror classic loosely based on Bram Stoker's novel *Dracula* centers on the vampire count (Max Schreck) who leaves his sinister castle in the Carpathian mountains to sail on a doomed ship bringing him to 1838 Bremen, where his dark deeds are undone by a brave young woman and the first light of dawn. Directed by F.W. Murnau, the German production is most notable for its eerie portrayal of the vampire in images, which seem to personify evil and dread in a movie even more remarkable for having been filmed mostly on location rather than in the controlled confines of a studio. Stylized violence and menace. A-II (br)

Nosferatu the Vampyre (1979) Slow but stylish German version of the vampire legend, patterned on F.W. Murnau's 1922 classic film, relies upon mood and atmosphere to create an eerie sense of evil and terror rather than resorting to the cheap tricks and shock effects. Under Werner Herzog's direction, Klaus Kinski is suitably malevolent in the title role, with Isabelle Adjani and Bruno Ganz offering fine support. English-language version. The overt sexual references and nightmarish quality of the visuals make it unsuitable for youngsters. A-III (PG)

Nostradamus (1994) Historical mismash about the 16th-century French physician-seer (Tcheky Karyo) who is tutored in the occult arts by a secret practitioner (F. Murray Abraham), then is saved from the Inquisition by the Queen of France (Amanda Plummer), and goes on to compile a series of murky prophecies which continue to confound unwary readers. Directed by Roger Christian, the unfocused narrative goes from one incident to another without defining character or historical context, and the result is sheer confusion. Period violence, sexual situations,, and anticlerical views. A-IV (R)

Not as a Stranger (1955) Fitful melodrama about a blonde nurse with a terrible Swedish accent (Olivia de Havilland) who marries an impoverished medical student (Robert Mitchum), pays his way through school, and, when he begins practice as a rural doctor, helps him face his arrogance, fallibility, and attraction to another woman (Gloria Grahame). Producer-director Stanley Kramer does best with the travails of medical school, but matters get soapier after the doctor hangs up his shingle. Mature themes. A-III (br)

Not in This Town (1997) Stirring fact-based drama in which an ordinary housewife (Kathy Baker), shaken by acts of violence against Jews and other minorities in 1993 Billings, Mont., stirs her community into taking action to stop such crimes of hate. Directed by Donald Wrye, the television movie presents an absorbing account of how one woman's efforts gained support from those of many faiths in uniting the town against racists and hatemongers, with successful results that leave viewers a little more thoughtful about the nature of hate crimes and how to stop them. Some racist violence and rhetoric. A-II (PG-13)

Not on Your Life (1966) Spanish-made black comedy about a good-natured Madrid undertaker (Nino Manfredi) who is persuaded to take the vacant post of state executioner. Directed by Luis Berlanga, the mostly genial movie satirizes government bureaucracy, human foibles, and, quite grimly, capital punishment. A-III (br)

Not Without My Daughter (1990) An American wife (Sally Field) attempts to escape fanatically fundamentalist Iran with her little girl (Sheila Rosenthal) after her husband, an Iranian-born doctor (Alfred Molina), tricks her into a one-way trip to the virulently anti-American country. As directed by Brian Gilbert, the main character's compelling, fact-based story is a real eye-opener, with a bravura performance by Miss Field, but marred by the cartoonish depiction of most of the Iranians in the film. Scenes of domestic violence. A-II (PG-13)

Nothing But a Man (1965) Black railroad worker (Ivan Dixon) tires of life on the rails and settles down in a southern town, where he and his wife (Abbey Lincoln) are confronted by a hostile community that deprives him of one job after another. Directed by Michael Roemer and Robert Young, the movie is episodic and anything but slick, yet it has the ring of documentary reality, as well as a story of human dignity that has universal implications. Some intense violence and a few profanities. A-III (br)

Nothing But the Truth (1941) Routine comedy in which a dim Florida stockbrocker (Bob Hope) bets to tell only the truth for the next 24 hours, wagering the charity money entrusted to him by the featherbrained daughter (Paulette Goddard) of his nasty boss (Edward Arnold). Directed by Elliott Nugent, the comic premise gets sidetracked in mildly amusing subplots, while Hope's desperate antics to avoid being caught in a lie raise some giggles but no real laughs. Comic deceptions and mild sexual innuendo. A-II (br)

Nothing But Trouble (1991) A decrepit, demented judge (Dan Aykroyd) and his police-chief grandson (John Candy) detain a guileless couple (Chevy Chase and Demi Moore) speeding through their zany little burg. Aykroyd's script and direction is heavy-handed and muddled, resulting in an uneven mishmash of mindless comic mayhem. Slapstick violence, brief sexual innuendo, and minimal rough language. A-II (PG-13)

Nothing by Chance (1975) A group of pilots try to recapture the pre-war barnstorming days in which biplanes toured rural America giving farmers and townspeople the opportunity of experiencing the pleasures of open-cockpit flight. Though it has some picturesque aerial photography, William Barnett's documentary will disappoint nostalgia and aviation buffs because of its concentration on the touring pilots and a pretentious narration written by Richard Bach. A-I (G)

Nothing in Common (1986) A wonderfully witty and wise portrait of a young ad-agency superstar (Tom Hanks) who must settle accounts with his divorcing parents (Jackie Gleason and Eva Marie Saint) before it's too late. Director Garry Marshall's seriocomic movie features warm and insightful performances by the three principals as they try to reconcile their differences. Some profanity and sexual scenes. A-III (PG)

Nothing Personal (1980) Romantic screwball comedy about a militant college professor (Donald Sutherland) who goes to Washington to battle a giant corporation bent on the slaughter of baby seals. The insincere social commentary is overpowered by a seduction scene in which Suzanne Sommers as the helpful lawyer futher obscures Sutherland's motives. A-III (PG)

Nothing Personal (1997) Strong but dramatically muddled story in which a daylight bombing of a pub by the IRA leads to a night of reprisals by a Protestant paramilitary group in 1975 Belfast, with the narrative focusing on a Protestant gunman (James Frain), his crazed, trigger-happy subordinate (Ian Hart), and a hapless Catholic (John Lynch) they chance upon. Directed by Thaddeus O'Sullivan from Daniel Momin's script, the drama has too many coincidences to be entirely satisfying, but its moral outrage at the men of violence, Catholic as well as Protestant, is entirely clear. Much graphic violence, a dour sex scene, occasional profanity, and much rough language. A-IV (nr)

Nothing Sacred (1937) Classic screwball comedy in which a New York reporter (Fredric March) convinces his editor (Walter Connelly) to bring a dying Vermont woman (Carole Lombard) to town as a circulation stunt, but, after she captures the city's heart, learns he's been hoaxed by a perfectly healthy specimen. Directed by William A. Wellman from a script by Ben Hecht, the wacky characters and their outrageous deceptions are highly amusing in a story satirizing the shabby tricks of tabloid journalism. Much duplicity with occasional comic violence and sexual innuendo. A-II (br)

Nothing to Lose (1997) Coarse comedy in which a bumbling carjacker (Martin Lawrence) helps a despondent ad executive (Tim Robbins) rob his boss of a fortune, then the ad-man has second thoughts, and insists they try to return the money before its absence is discovered. Writer-director Steve Oedekerk's manipulative buddy plot goes for cheap laughs while implying circumstances may justify grand theft. Ambivalent attitude toward crime, comic treatment of violence, a fleeting sexual encounter, and constant rough language. A-IV (R)

Notorious (1946) Classy suspense tale in which a US agent (Cary Grant) wins over the troubled daughter (Ingrid Bergman) of a Nazi war criminal, then persuades her to wed a Nazi big-wig (Claude Rains) hiding in Rio de Janeiro in order to find out what he and his pals are plotting. Directed by Alfred Hitchcock from a script by Ben Hecht, the tension mounts as Bergman discovers a cache of uranium in the wine cellar, then tries to escape being killed, but the plot's romantic angle is chilled by Grant putting Bergman's life at risk to get the goods on Rains. Menacing situations and romantic complications. A-II (br)

Notorious Gentleman (1945) Satiric British tale of a 1930s upper-class idler (Rex Harrison) who leads a self-indulgent life sponging off others, until the irony of a hero's death in WW II. Directed by Sidney Gilliat, Harrison's witty but unlikeable opportunist reflects the turmoil of British life between the wars. Amoral attitudes and anti-social behavior. A-III (br)

Notorious Landlady, The (1962) Dark comedy about a newcomer (Jack Lemmon) to the American Embassy in London who rents an apartment from a mystery woman (Kim Novak) suspected of having murdered her husband. Director Richard Quine gets some good sight gags out of an anemic story-line which picks up energy only towards the end, when the diplomat risks his career trying to clear the landlady's name. Occasional stylized violence and romantic situations. A-III (br)

Notorious Lone Wolf, The (1946) Routine mystery directed by D. Ross Lederman, in which the title private detective (Gerald Mohr) returns from soldiering in WW II, then is suspected of stealing a priceless sapphire from an Eastern potentate (John Abbott), to whom he returns it after finding the crooks responsible. Menacing situations and sexual innuendo. A-II (br)

Notting Hill (1999) Gauzy romantic comedy in which a Hollywood movie star (Julia Roberts) and a timid London bookseller (Hugh Grant) fall in love, but he is too intimidated by her fame to pursue the relationship. As directed by Roger Michell, the contrived crowd-pleaser is long on stunning smiles and sugary sentiment but short on realistic romance. An off-screen sexual encounter, sexual references, occasional profanity, and minimal rough language. A-III (PG-13)

Now and Then (1995) Four friends from childhood (Rita Wilson, Demi Moore, Rosie O'Donnell, and Melanie Griffith) recall how they helped each other face personal problems when they were 12 in 1970 suburbia. Director Lesli Linka Glatter casts a rosy glow over reminiscences of being on the cusp of adolescence, but with scant story and little character development, the result is a sweet but shallow salute to supportive female friendships. Fleeting nudity and some sexual references. A-III (PG-13)

Now, Voyager (1942) Classy tearjerker follows a repressed Bostonian spinster (Bette Davis) from a sanatorium, where she gains some self-confidence, to an ocean cruise, where she falls for an unhappily married man (Paul Henreid), but sublimates her love for him by giving a home to his love-starved preteen daughter. Directed by Irving Rapper, Davis's transformation from milksop to socialite is winning, Gladys Cooper makes a fine ogre as her domineering mother, and Henreid's routine in lighting two cigarettes is classic Hollywood smaltz. The doomed love affair is handled most discreetly. A-II (br)

Now You See Him, Now You Don't (1972) Although apple-cheeked college boy Kurt Russell doesn't know how he invented a chemical that makes people invisible, he does realize it will come in handy against gangster Cesar Romero. Robert Butler directed the carefully homogenized Disney production which, although morally unimpeachable, nonetheless continues the Disney tradition of setting ususally inane comedies in a safe, largely white, middle-class context whose values, if they exist at all, are purely material, bereft of any spiritual or even social dimension. A-I (G)

Nowhere to Run (1993) Formula movie about an escaped con (Jean-Claude Van Damme) coming to the aid of a widow (Rosanna Arquette) with small children who is being forced to sell her land to a murderously corrupt real-estate developer (Joss Ackland). Director Robert Harmon's attempts to turn action-movie star Van Damme into a brooding romantic hero fall flat in this routine tale of cardboard good guys and bad guys. Intermittent violence, fleeting bedroom scene, brief nudity, and minimal rough language. A-III (R)

Nude Bomb, The (see: **The Return of Maxwell Smart**)

Nueba Yol (1996) Seriocomic tale of a determined optimist (Luisito Marti) from Santo Domingo seeking his fortune in New York City, where, despite formidable obstacles, he finds work and even makes wedding plans before becoming a victim of urban violence, though his dream of a better life lingers on. Written and directed by Angel Muniz, the Dominican production playfully contrasts an alien's image of the US with the actual reality, but its major merit is Marti's ingratiating performance as a wry but compassionate pilgrim in a foreign land. Mostly subtitles. Ambiguous treatment of illegal immigrants, stylized violence involving drug traffickers, and a few instances of rough language. A-III (nr)

Number One (1969) Charlton Heston plays an aging, once-great quarterback who, after some humilitating failures on the field, is emotionally torn over retiring. His inability to communicate with his career-oriented wife (Jessica Walter) leads to a one-night stand with a more-than-cooperative lady sports-enthusiast. Director Tom Gries does as well as he can with a story that offers not enough football for the fans and not enough human interest for non-fans. A-III (PG)

Number Seventeen (1932) Quirky British thriller opens with a hapless drifter (comic actor Leon M. Lion) breaking into an empty house, where he stumbles upon a corpse, then tries to hide when a gang of jewel thieves arrive, but ultimately winds up on a runaway train hurtling toward the channel ferry for a smash finale. Directed by Alfred Hitchcock, the situation offers plenty of opportunity for shadowy menace and macabre humor, but the action never developes into a satisfying plot. Much tension and some violence, including a train wreck. A-II (br)

Nun, The (1971) French dramatization of Diderot's 18th-century novel about a young girl (Anna Karina), forced by her mother into the convent, who in desperation escapes with a discontented priest ,and ultimately destroys herself. Although the narrative's exaggerations and stereotyped characters and situations may annoy or disturb some, director Jacques Rivette's main theme is the arbitrary exercise of power, which in the historical context of this period is not without interest. Mature themes. A-IV (PG)

Nun at the Crossroads (1970) When a Belgian nun (Rosanna Schiaffino) becomes pregnant after being raped during a 1960s uprising in the Congo, her stern superiors in Brussels prefer that she leave the convent, and so she brings up the child alone while engaging in missionary work as a laywoman. Italian-Spanish co-production directed by Julio Buchs with a heavy hand and little help from a generally unconvincing cast. Superficial melodrama. A-III (PG)

Nun's Story, The (1959) Sent by her religious community to be a nurse in the Belgian Congo, a young nun (Audrey Hepburn) resists her feelings of love for the doctor (Peter Finch) with whom she works, returns to Belgium, and, after struggling with the routine of convent life, leaves for the world beyond the wall. Sensitively directed by Fred Zinnemann, the fact-based story focuses on the interior conflict between the nun's idealism and her growing sense of her own needs as an individual. Convincing portrayal of religious life as a vocation requiring more than good intentions. A-II (nr)

Nuns on the Run (1990) Lightweight British comedy about two genially daft gangsters (Eric Idle and Robbie Coltrane) who masquerade as Catholic sisters while using a convent as a hide-out from the police and two rival gangs. Written and directed by Jonathan Lynn, the ridiculous situation of men in religious drag offers much irreverent though good-natured humor that may rub some the wrong way, while providing others with some healthy laughter about Catholic life and foibles. A-IV (PG-13)

Nunzio (1978) Often moving story of a retarded young man (David Proval) whose loving mother (Morgana King) indulges his fantasies of being Superman, while his tough truckdriver brother (James Andronica) tries to protect him from abuse in their ethnic Brooklyn neighborhood. Director Paul Williams's concentrates on character and setting, gradually building through incident and dialogue a convincing picture of the love that binds a family together. Unfortunately, a needlessly graphic rape scene, omitted from the original release, has been inserted subsequently. O (PG/R)

Nutcracker, The (see **George Balanchine's The Nutcracker**)

Nutcracker Prince, The (1990) Animated fantasy about a young girl helping a lad who was transformed into a nutcracker toy-soldier to break the spell he's under and vanquish the wicked Mouseking. Uninspired animation from director Paul Schibli's Lacewood Productions neither enhances Tchaikovsky's famous ballet score nor brings to life Hoffman's classic story, but children may be amused by the fairytale. Minor menace and an evil-looking Mouseking. A-I (G)

Nutcracker, The Motion Picture (1986) Tchaikovsky's fairytale ballet, a perennial Christmas favorite, has been given a darker interpretation as representing a young girl's sensual daydreams that are part of the fears and doubts of coming of age. Performed by the Pacific Northwest Ballet, the movie version's psychological implications will elude younger members of the family. A-II (PG/G appeal)

Nuts (1987) Barbra Streisand stars as a high-priced prostitute charged with manslaughter but whose competency to stand trial is at issue. Director Martin Ritt's highly contrived courtroom drama spends more time trying to manipulate the emotions of viewers than it does in trying to probe the issues facing women in a male-dominated society. Much sexually explicit language and references. A-IV (R)

Nutty Professor, The (1963) Halting comedy in which a klutzy chemistry teacher (Jerry Lewis) tries to impress an attractive coed (Stella Stevens) by concocting a potion transforming him into a hip campus-idol. Also directed by Lewis, the humor in the Jekyll-Hyde premise is mostly of the manic variety prized by Lewis fans, though others may be considerably less amused by the slapstick proceedings and sentimental silliness. Romantic complications. A-I (br)

Nutty Professor, The (1996) Thin Jekyll-and-Hyde comedy in which an obese university professor (Eddie Murphy) swallows an experimental weight-reduction formula turning him into a manic, skinny Romeo intent on romancing his alter-ego's girlfriend (Jada Pinkett). Director Tom Shadyac's lame remake of the 1963 Jerry Lewis comedy features Murphy in seven roles, the humor of which is lost in tasteless body-function jokes and unremarkable special effects. Frequent sexual references, fleeting violence, some racial ephitets, and much crude toilet humor. A-III (PG-13)

O

O. Henry's Full House (1952) Uneven dramatizations of five O. Henry short stories, each with its own director, cast, and introduction by author John Steinbeck, and all with characteristic twist-endings. What works best is Charles Laughton's performance as the vagrant in "The Cop and the Anthem" (director Henry Koster), and Fred Allen and Oscar Levant as the hapless kidnappers of a rural Alabama youth in "The Ransom of Red Chief" (director Howard Hawks). The others feature cop Dale Robertson and killer Richard Widmark in "The Clarion Call" (director Henry Hathaway); Anne Baxter as a critically ill woman in "The Last Leaf" (director Jean Negulesco); Jeanne Crain and Farley Granger as the loving couple in "The Gift of the Magi" (director Henry King). Some stylized violence. A-II (br)

O Lucky Man! (1973) British surreal allegory about a young innocent (Malcolm McDowell), whose attempts to succeed in a world he can't understand result in an absurd series of misadventures involving Ralph Richardson, Rachel Roberts, Arthur Lowe, and Mona Washbourne. The targets of director Lindsay Anderson's satiric jabs include corrupt officials, military xenophobia, medical experimentation, sex clubs, and a host of other aspects of irrational social activity. Some will find its narrative disjointed and senseless, while others will welcome its pro-human, pro-individual stance. It is quite discreet in handling sex and violence, using such scenes only to make a point. A-IV (R)

O.S.S. (1946) Flat, unconvincing WW II espionage tale directed by Irving Pichel follows the daring deeds and mortal dangers of a team of US agents (notably Alan Ladd and Geraldine Fitzgerald) gathering intelligence and sabotaging German installations in occupied France. Patriotic bravado midst wartime violence and menace of unlikely interest to children. A-I (br)

Object of Beauty, The (1991) The relationship of a high-living American couple (John Malkovich and Andie MacDowell), stranded in their London hotel suite without funds, is tested when their only hope for conversion to quick cash — a Henry Moore sculpture — is stolen by the maid (Rudi Davies). Writer-director Michael Lindsay-Hogg dishes out a mildly entertaining send-up of the materialistic yuppie mentality, but it's so vaguely focused that the performers appear to waft through their roles without conviction. Acceptance of extramarital relations and insurance fraud, a flash of nudity, and minimal rough language. A-III (R)

Object of My Affection, The (1998) Failed romantic comedy in which a pregnant social-worker (Jennifer Aniston) falls in love with a homosexual teacher (Paul Rudd) who only wants to be her friend, with unhappy results. Directed by Nicholas Hytner from Wendy Wasserstein's script, the movie places its charmless characters in a repetitive series of unconvincing situations which never get beyond moral muddlement. Benign attitude toward sex outside of marriage, numerous sexual situations, rough language, and profanity. O (R)

Objective, Burma! (1945) After parachuting into Burma to blow up a Japanese radar station, a US Army captain (Errol Flynn) is left with 36 men and a war correspondent (Henry Hull) to fight their way back through the jungle until rescued by invading Allied forces. Directed by Raoul Walsh, the melodrama holds up better than many other WW II morale-boosters, because it downplays the phony heroics to emphasize the human cost of the mission. Wartime violence and racial stereotyping. A-II (br)

Oblomov (1981) Russian dramatization of Ivan Goncharov's 19th-century novel about an absentee landlord who has made sloth his life's work. Oleg Tabakov is excellent in the title as the lazy hero, whose pampered upbringing leaves him ill-prepared for even the moderate rigors of adulthood as a member of a privileged class. Director Nikita Mikhalkov puts too much effort into atmospheric effects and not enough into moving the overlong story forward. Still, the marvelous re-creation of late 19th-century Russian life is engrossing and worth seeing. A-II (nr)

Oblong Box, The (1969) Weak British horror movie loosely based on an Edgar Allen Poe story in which a man (Alastair Williamson), horribly disfigured by an African spell, is kept locked up by his brother (Vincent Price), but when he breaks out, terrible things happen in the neighborhood. Directed by Gordon Hessler, the hazy narrative relies solely on visuals of blood and gore for effect, with little attempt at building suspense. A-III (M)

Obsession (1976) On a business trip to Italy, widower Cliff Robertson falls in love with Genevieve Bujold because she resembles his wife, who, along with their daughter, had been killed in a kidnapping 15 years before. This sets up a plot reminiscent of Hitchcock's **Vertigo**, but director Brian De Palma attempts to pump romance into Robertson's Italian affair and an absurd conclusion make the result a disappointing miscalculation. Some violence and a muted incest theme. A-III (PG)

Obsession (see: **The Hidden Room**)

Ocean's Eleven (1960) Slack crime caper in which a group of WW II paratroop veterans (Frank Sinatra, Dean Martin, Sammy Davis, Jr., Peter Lawford, Richard Conte, et al.) join in simultaneously robbing five Las Vegas casinos, then lose the loot in a ghoulish twist ending. Producer-director Lewis Milestone drags out the proceedings with less than witty dialogue by the principals and misuse of cameos (notably George Raft, Red Skelton, and Angie Dickinson). Rationalization of robbery. A-III (br)

October Sky (1999) Uplifting tale set in 1957 rural West Virginia, where a miner's son (Jake Gyllenhaal) defies his father's (Chris Cooper) insistence he come work in the mines and instead enlists three schoolmates to help build a functioning rocket in hopes of winning a college scholarship. Director Joe Johnston's atmospheric, fact-based drama captures the impoverished community, familial conflicts, and the dogged ambition of youngsters to persevere and better themselves with higher education. A mining tragedy, fleeting parental abuse, and a few muttered profanities. A-II (PG)

Octopussy (1983) Super-agent James Bond (Roger Moore) is once again on the trail of an international conspiracy, this time involving an East German circus, a maverick Soviet general, an Asian dealer in counterfeit gems, and an Oriental ring of women. Like previous Bond outings, the plot is less important than director John Glen's tongue-in-cheek treatment of the unflappable, fantasy hero surrounded by curvaceous women, cartoon violence, mechanical gimmickry, and exotic locales. The venerable formula succeeds only intermittently, partly because of heavy-handed double entendres and sexual encounters. A-III (PG)

Odd Couple, The (1968) Two men separated from their wives and sharing an apartment discover what incompatibility is all about. One is obsessively neat (Jack Lemmon), and the other is a compulsive slob (Walter Matthau). The story is a nice twist on the adjustments people have to make in life as well as marriage, and both principals take good advantage of the comic potential of teaming a disparate pair. Director Gene Sacs relies on Neil Simon's adaptation of his own stage play and the result is often hilarious comedy. Some sexual references. A-III (G)

Odd Man Out (1947) After being shot and left behind in the bungled robbery of a Belfast firm, a mortally wounded IRA leader (James Mason) spends the night seeking shelter from a variety of people until finally cornered by the Ulster police. Directed by Carol Reed, the movie features a strong cast, many from the Abbey Theatre, in a challenging story that is less about the dying fugitive than about the few who try to help him, the many who don't want to get involved, and the several who only want to use him for their own ends. Stylized violence, including a murder and a suicide. A-III (br)

Ode to Billy Joe (1976) Based on a popular Bobbie Gentry song about two Mississippi Delta teenagers (Robby Benson and Glynnis O'Connor) whose brief romance, in the long-ago summer of 1953, ends in tragedy when the boy throws himself off the Tallahatchie Bridge. Not even the considerable charm of the acting nor the beauty of the Delta setting can help director Max Baer overcome the thin, contrived plot and insufferably cute dialogue. A-III (R/PG)

Odessa File, The (1974) Screen version of the Frederick Forsyth thriller about a German journalist (Jon Voight) who seeks to track down a Nazi war criminal (Maximilian Schell) and comes into conflict with the dreaded Odessa, a secret Nazi organization bent on regaining power. Too heavy and slow-moving to be a really effective melodrama, director Ronald Neame has made a run-of-the-mill entertainment with serious overtones. Some violence. A-III (PG)

Odyssey, The (1997) Homer's saga of ancient Greece follows the misadventures of King Odysseus (Armand Assante) on his long voyage home to Ithaca after the Trojan War, arriving just in time to save his faithful wife, Penelope (Greta Sacchi), from a dangerous pack of greedy suitors. Directed by Andrei Konchalovsky, the 165-minute TV production retells the classic story with gusto, and, though the acting doesn't measure up to the imaginative use of special effects in creating the tale's mythic monsters and sea disasters, the result is a grand adventure-fantasy parents might enjoy sharing with their older teenagers, despite some graphic violence and strong sexual innuendo. A-III (PG-13)

Oedipus, the King (1968) Static British version of the Greek tragedy by Sophocles features Christopher Plummer and Lilli Palmer under the direction of Philip Saville. A-II (G)

Of Human Bondage (1934) Tragic romance from W. Somerset Maugham's novel about a wealthy English medical student (Leslie Howard) whose infatuation for a devious waitress (Bette Davis) ruins his life. Directed by John Cromwell, the story creaks, but the performances are still compelling, especially Davis's heartless heartbreaker. Sexual situations and innuendo. A-III (br)

Of Human Hearts (1938) Creaky sentimental melodrama in which a son (James Stewart) leaves his backwoods Ohio home and preacher father (Walter Huston) to study medicine, then becomes a surgeon in the Union Army, where an encounter with President Lincoln (John Carradine) makes him realize he's neglected his aged mother (Beulah Bondi). Director Clarence Brown does better re-creating frontier life than he does with the story of the callow son's belated appreciation of his parents. Interesting Americana but stale melodramatics. A-I (br)

Of Mice and Men (1992) Flat version of the John Steinbeck novel in which a Depression-era migrant (Gary Sinise) looks after a simpleminded, trouble-prone buddy (John Malkovich) until the poor soul accidentally kills someone. Also directed by Sinise, the story is still powerful in its depiction of those on the margins of society struggling to survive hard times, but the result here is somewhat stagy and lacking in emotional impact. Some brutal violence, including murder in the plot resolution, and occasional coarse language. A-III (PG-13)

Off Beat (1986) Judge Reinhold plays a loser who impersonates a New York police officer, foils a bank robbery, and falls in love with a female cop (Meg Tilly) while rehearsing for a police dance-benefit. A weak romantic comedy with a narrow range of emotions and an improbable story line. Brief nudity and some harsh language. A-III (PG)

Off Limits (1953) Tricked into joining the Army, a prizefight manager (Bob Hope) is assigned to the military police, then ordered to make a boxer out of a lightweight recruit (Mickey Rooney) whose aunt (Marilyn Maxwell) disapproves. Directed by George Marshall, the two veteran comics wring few laughs out of a tired service-comedy whose outlandish situations were thin even then. Comic violence and mild romantic complications. A-I (br)

Off Limits (1988) A salt 'n' pepper military-police team (William Dafoe and Gregory Hines) in 1968 Saigon stumble into a series of sadomasochistic murders of prostitutes and are stymied at every turn by cover-up attempts when their prime suspects prove to be high-ranking Army officers. Directed by Christopher Crowe, the movie fails to take its cliched storyline beyond the chase to explore its larger implications within the Vietnam War. Many scenes of extreme violence, wall-to-wall profanity, some nudity, and several suggestive scenes with prostitutes. O (R)

Offence, The (1973) Veteran London police detective (Sean Connery), in interrogating a man picked up for the rape-murder of a number of schoolgirls, pummels the taunting suspect to death, and his world crumbles. Director Sidney Lumet compassionately explores the man's psychological and spiritual disintegration through flashbacks and flash-forwards, actual events, and fragmentary memories of the detective's past experiences. Casual moviegoers may find it a difficult, distasteful experience, but it has value as a picture of the results of constant exposure to violence and sordid criminality that are a part of law enforcement. Challenging but thoughtful mature fare. A-III (R)

Office Space (1999) Sly comedy in which three downtrodden office buddies conspire to rip off their soulless corporation, then relent, just as another disgruntled employee feels driven to desperate measures. While somewhat predictable, writer-director Mike Judge comically captures the atmosphere of numbing corporate environments where disposable workers are at the mercy of bureaucratic policies and power-mad superiors. Fleeting nudity, brief sexual references, gangsta rap lyrics with recurring rough language and racial slurs, and a few instances of profanity. A-III (R)

Officer and a Gentleman, An (1982) Bitter loner (Richard Gere) enters officer-candidate school with the dream of becoming a Navy pilot, but he and a buddy (David Keith) are given a hard time by a tough drill sergeant (Louis Gossett Jr.) and further complicate their lives by getting involved with two local women (Debra Winger and Lisa Blount). Though a suicide puts a pall over the proceedings, director Taylor Hackford's romance is old-fashioned enough to contrive a happy ending, but not enough to avoid steamy sex scenes and rough language. O (R)

Official Story, The (1985) An upper-class Argentine wife (Norma Aleandro), whose wealthy husband is a friend of the powerful, begins to suspect that her adopted daughter might be the child of a mother victimized by the rightwing government's reign of terror five years before. The Argentinian production, directed and co-scripted by Luis Puenzo, is a extraordinary work that subordinates politics to human characterizations of anguish and nobility. Some brief violence and rough language. A-II (nr)

Oh Dad, Poor Dad, Mama's Hung You in the Closet and I'm Feeling So Sad (1966) Failed screen version of Arthur Kopit's play about an overpowering mother (Rosalind Russell) and her inhibited son (Robert Morse). Richard Quine's direction of the black comedy tends to be more offensive than funny, and some of the tasteless treatment plays with the prurient. O (br)

Oh, God! (1977) California supermarket-manager (John Denver) becomes a middle-class Moses when chosen by God (George Burns) to tell the world that he is alive and well. As might be expected, no one believes him and complications arise. The gentle comedy, written and directed by Carl Reiner, has its heart in the right place and provides some effective moments, Burns and Denver both being very appealing performers. Reiner's idea of a nonsectarian God who denies original sin, pronounces morality to be entirely subjective, and says that Jesus is his son only in the sense that God is the father of all presents a special problem for parents of young viewers who might not understand the fantasy nature of the comedy. Moreover, while sparing other religious groups, the movie makes a Billy Graham-style evangelist into a gross caricature. A-III (PG)

Oh, God! Book II (1980) George Burns returns as the Almighty, his comic timing as quasi-omnipotent as ever. This time he teams up with an 11-year-old schoolgirl, whom he persuades to launch an ad campaign promoting him. Directed by Gilbert Cates, it is entertaining, if only mildly funny fare. Though there is less of the secular humanism that marred the original, the concept of Burns as God together with a bit of mild vulgarity may not suit all tastes. A-II (PG)

Oh, God! You Devil (1984) George Burns is back as the Divinity with an infinite number of one-liners. This time he gets to double as the devil and play poker for an errant soul. Director Paul Bogart fashions a comedy that is only mildly amusing and what humor there is comes from Burns. A few sexual references in the dialogue, but otherwise innocuous. A-II (PG)

Oh, Heavenly Dog (1980) A murdered detective (Chevy Chase) is reincarnated as a lovable mutt (Benji) whose mission is to solve the crime. Jane Seymour provides some romantic interest. Director Joe Camp's canine movie is sometimes amusing, but slow-paced, overly cute, and, in general, pretty tepid stuff. Some double entendres and a significant amount of profane language. A-III (PG)

Oh! Susanna (1951) Mediocre Western directed by Joseph Kane is set in the Black Hills during the 1875 gold strike on Indian land, which a US cavalry officer (Rod Cameron) tries to protect from an eager horde of whites, while his glory-seeking superior (Forrest Tucker) prepares to lead his command into battle against the Sioux. Frontier violence and anti-Indian attitudes. A-II (br)

Oh! What a Lovely War (1969) British musical version of WW I covers events from Sarajevo to America's entrance in the conflict as told in a series of sketches conveying the mood, motives, and attitudes of the British government, military, clergy, common soldier, and the folks at home. Directed by Richard Attenborough, with a large and talented British cast, the ambitious but largely successful work intermixes song and comedy with the ugly reality of the battlefield. Its anti-war perspective emphasizes the futility and waste of a war in which a generation of young men sacrificed their lives. A-II (G)

Oklahoma! (1955) Director Fred Zinnemann's stunning, delightful, yet surprisingly serious adaptation of the classic Rodgers and Hammerstein musical is set in the relatively innocent days when Oklahoma was getting ready to join the Union and everything was up-to-date in Kansas City. Shirley Jones is absolutely winsome as the fresh-as-milk farm girl, Gordon MacRae almost outsmarts himself as her cowpoke-beau, and Rod Steiger is downright malevolent as would-be suitor Jud Fry. The plot is corny as all get-out, the music and dance numbers charming and memorable, but the melodrama tends to be a tad too heavy. A-II (br)

Oklahoma Crude (1973) Turn-of-the-century man-hating oil prospector (Faye Dunaway) reluctantly accepts help from her ne'er-do-well father (John Mills) and a drifter (George C. Scott) in order to keep the big oil-combine's enforcer (Jack Palance) from jumping her claim. Her wildcat well, naturally, comes up a gusher, as does her emotional turnabout toward reformed daddy and newfound friend. Directed by Stanley Kramer, there's plenty of old-fashioned action and melodrama here, making fairly solid entertainment for adults who don't mind some Oklahoma crude violence and language. A-III (PG)

Oklahoma Kid, The (1939) Enjoyable Western in which the cheerful outlaw of the title (James Cagney) tracks down the villain (Humphrey Bogart) who incited a Tulsa mob to lynch his law-abiding father (Hugh Sothern), then marries his dead brother's sweetheart (Rosemary Lane). Directed by Lloyd Bacon, the story is strictly routine, but Cagney makes it fun with his tongue-in-cheek performance as a tough hombre who croons a Spanish lullaby to quiet a baby, hides under a mannequin's hoop-skirt, and holds a barroom at bay while singing "I Don't Want to Play in Your Yard." Frontier violence and romantic complications. A-II (br)

Oklahoman, The (1957) Unpretentious Western about a widowed doctor (Joel McCrea) who settles in the Oklahoma Territory of 1870, hires an Indian girl (Gloria Talbott) to care for his young daughter despite malicious gossip, then helps protect the girl's father (Michael Pate) from a local gang who've discovered oil on the Indian's land. Directed by Francis D. Lyon, the honest doctor proves a straight-shooter, not only in besting the villains, but also in romancing a widowed rancher (Barbara Hale). Frontier violence. A-I (br)

Old Acquaintance (1943) Soapy melodrama from John Van Druten's play about a serious-minded writer (Bette Davis) and her lifelong friend (Miriam Hopkins), an empty-headed novelist whose husband (John Loder) leaves her, then becomes a bone of contention between the two women. Directed by Vincent Sherman, the episodic story stretches from the Jazz Age to WW II, but the hackneyed situations are of less interest than the scene-stealing between two strong actresses. Romantic complications involving divorce and a sexual situation. A-III (br)

Old Boyfriends (1979) Recently divorced woman in her 30s (Talia Shire) tries to make sense out of her life by hitting the road in her Firebird and looking up old boyfriends (Richard Jordan and John Belushi). A third, she discovers, has died in Vietnam, and she quickly transfers her affections to his mentally disturbed younger brother (Keith Carradine). Directed by Joan Tewkesbury, the dreary story suffers from the same malaise that afflicts the heroine. Some rough language and adult situations. A-III (R)

Old Curiosity Shop, The (see: **Mr. Quilp**)

Old Dark House, The (1932) Creaky chills from J.B. Priestley's novel set on a stormy night in Wales, where five travelers (notably Raymond Massey, Melvyn Douglas, and Charles Laughton) seek shelter in a crumbling, candlelit manor whose strange owners (Ernest Thesiger and Eva Moore) and deaf-mute butler (Boris Karloff) guard a dark family secret. Director James Whale lightens the ominous atmosphere with a romantic subplot (Douglas and Lillian Bond), but the real fun lies in the scary setting with its eerie shadows, macabre characters, and fears of what's hidden in the dark. Playful exercise in menace with some stylized violence and sexual situations. A-III (br)

Old Dark House, The (1963) Inept mix of comedy and mystery set in a dilapidated manor on the English moors, where an American visitor (Tom Poston) finds its eccentric occupants (Robert Morley, Joyce Grenfell, Mervyn Johns, John Bull, and others) being murdered one by one. Directed by William Castle, this comic version of the J.B. Priestley novel is full of silly perils and wacky characters, but the results are more tiresome than amusing. Stylized violence, comic menace, and romantic complications. A-II (br)

Old Dracula (1976) Director Clive Donner's spoof of the classic horror tale portrays women as sex objects and becomes little more than a sex farce using brief nudity and crude sight gags for humor. Unfortunately, the presence of David Niven in the cast may arouse unwarranted expectations that the movie offers more than cheap thrills. O (PG)

Old-Fashioned Way, The (1934) Nostalgic comedy in which the Great McGonigle (W.C. Fields) takes his debt-ridden theatrical troupe to a small town, inveigles a would-be singer (Jan Duggan) to finance their performance of "The Drunkard," then skips town, leaving his daughter (Judith Allen) behind to wed a suitable suitor. Directed by William Beaudine, the comic proceedings make good use of the 1890s setting, with Fields leading the laughter as the waspish impresario who adroitly cons sheriffs, loathes children (Baby leRoy), and stops the show with his incredible juggling act. Comic insults. A-II (br)

Old Gringo (1989) Lumpy adaptation of the Carlos Fuentes novel about three very different rebels — a repressed American schoolteacher (Jane Fonda), noted American writer Ambrose Bierce (Gregory Peck), and a general in Pancho Villa's army (Jimmy Smits) — whose path cross in 1913 during the Mexican Revolution. Directed by Luis Puenzo, the movie sacrifices substance for style, and the intriguing protagonists can't make up for its confusing depiction of the era. Lengthy, grisly battle scene, point-blank murders, and discreetly filmed sexual encounters with fleeting nudity. A-III (R)

Old Gun, The (1976) French WW II drama about a doctor (Philippe Noiret) who sends his wife and child to the countryside far from the fighting, but on a visit finds that they have been killed in a massacre by a Nazi unit that becomes the target for his revenge. Director Robert Enrico's use of flashbacks recalling details of the doctor's marriage may be sentimental, but they are effective in conveying the outrage that motivates his vengeance. Strong images of wartime violence. A-III (R)

Old Man and the Sea, The (1958) Lyric version of Ernest Hemingway's story of an aged Cuban fisherman (Spencer Tracy) who's gone three months without catching a fish, then lands a giant marlin after an exhausting two-day battle, only to lose it to swarms of hungry sharks. Director John Sturges's handsome, if studio-bound, picture on the theme of man vs. the elements features a compelling performance from Tracy, though the cultural context is weak, and the fisherman's interior reflections tend to platitudes. The ferocious shark sequences may frighten youngsters, but the portrayal of the old man's grace in coping with adversity is for all. A-I (br)

Old Yeller (1958) Dorothy McGuire, Fess Parker, and Chuck Connors star in this Disney movie about a lovable mongrel that proves a loyal, selfless companion for the youngsters of a frontier Texas family. Directed by Robert Stevenson, the nostalgic fun is mixed with some poignant moments that may be tough going for young children. A-I (G)

Oliver! (1968) Rousing British musical drawn from Charles Dickens's **Oliver Twist**, but bearing little resemblance to the original in adapter Lionel Bart's borrowing only the chief characters and turning them loose in what amounts to a colorful, swirling-stomping-singing Cockney street-show. As Fagin, rubber-faced Ron Moody carries most of the burden, with Mark Lester perfectly winning as Oliver, Jack Wild stealing scene after scene (along with handy wallets), and Harry Secombe as a bumbling Mr. Bumble. Under Carol Reed's direction, it all adds up to delightful fare for the entire family. A-I (G)

Oliver & Company (1988) Colorful, toe-tapping animated musical frolic updates Charles Dickens's **Oliver Twist** to New York City where an orphaned kitten named Oliver (voice of Joey Lawrence) gets caught up in the shenanigans of a human con-artist (voice of Dom DeLuise) and his rowdy band of rogue dogs who steal for him, including the terrier Dodger (voice of Billy Joel). Directed by George Scribner, it's a children's movie that parents can enjoy, with just the right balance between pathos, action, comedy, and music. Some menace from animated Dobermans and peril on an elevated subway track. A-I (G)

Oliver Twist (1933) Uneven version of Charles Dickens's novel about the young title orphan (Dickie Moore) who flees a county workhouse for London, where the Artful Dodger (Sonny Ray) brings him to Fagin (Irving Pichel) to learn the "game" of picking pockets before his true origins are revealed. Directed by William J. Cowen, the streamlined narrative works well enough, though the characterizations are superficial at best. Stylized violence and menacing situations. A-II (br)

Oliver's Story (1979) Listless romantic melodrama, a sequel to **Love Story**, takes up the life of widowed Oliver Barrett (Ryan O'Neal), whose father-in-law (Edward Binns) urges to start anew, which he does by having an affair with a rich WASP (Candice Bergen). Director John Korty has difficulty fleshing out the characterizations of the two principals in their ambiguous affair which ultimately becomes tiresome. A-III (PG)

Olivier Olivier (1993) Discovered on the streets of Paris six years after having disappeared in the French countryside, a 15-year-old boy (Gregoire Colin) is returned to this jubilant mother (Brigitte Rouan), though his older sister (Marina Golovine) sullenly suspects that the youth is not her brother. Writer-director Agnieszka Holland fashions an eerie tale of complex familial relationships that range from unhealthy emotions to unconditional love as the family members struggle to sustain one another. Subtitles. Mature themes, including child molestation and possible incest, several sexual encounters, brief nudity, fleeting violence, and minimal rough language. A-IV (R)

Omar Khayyam (1957) Persia's 11th-century poet-astronomer (Cornel Wilde) helps the son (John Derek) of the shah (Raymond Massey) defeat a secret cult of assassins led by a power-mad court official (Michael Rennie). Director William Dieterle's lackluster costume picture suffers from a predictable plot and unconvincing action. Stylized violence and period sexism. A-I (br)

Omega Man, The (1971) Post-nuclear holocaust

movie about the apparently last healthy man on earth (Charlton Heston) wandering around downtown Los Angeles by day, and by night trying to fend off bands of radiation-diseased ghouls. Directed by Boris Sagal, the situation becomes little more than a shallow, garden-variety romantic melodrama, with the hero teaming up with some refugee kids hanging out in the hills, and the only untainted woman around (Rosalind Cash) with whom he has some coyly ludicrous love scenes. A-III (PG)

Omegans, The (1967) Dreary clunker set in the jungles of Malaya, where a painter (Lucien Pan) takes revenge on his wife (Ingrid Pitt) and guide (Keith Larson) after learning they plan to kill him. Producer-director W. Lee Wilder goes nowhere with a dull plot featuring a jungle waterfall emitting deadly omega rays. Stylized violence and implied adultery. A-III (br)

Omen, The (1976) The American ambassador to Great Britain (Gregory Peck) finds himself the foster-father of the anti-Christ in director Richard Donner's slick, expensively mounted, but essentially trashy, horror show. Though it refers to Scripture and religious beliefs, its only interest in religion is in terms of its exploitation potential. Some intense violence. O (R)

Omen II (see: **Damien—Omen II**)

On a Clear Day You Can See Forever (1970) Screen version of a Lerner-Lane musical about a Brooklyn coed (Barbra Streisand) who is cursed with ESP and memories of a past incarnation as a 19th-century coquette, with whom her psychiatrist-teacher (Yves Montand) falls in love. Under Vincent Minnelli's direction, Streisand shines, but the rest is glossy romantic fluff. Brief seduction scene. A-II (G)

On Any Sunday (1971) Written, produced, directed, and narrated by Bruce Brown, this enthralling documentary on motorcycle racing may popularize this endurance sport in the same way that Brown's **The Endless Summer** glorified surfing. Filmed in five countries, the emphasis is on the action and the racers, including top professionals Mert Lawwill and Malcom Smith, as well as actor Steve McQueen. A-I (G)

On Borrowed Time (1939) Intriguing fantasy in which a feisty grandpa (Lionel Barrymore) tricks Death, known here as Mr. Brink (Cedric Hardwicks), into an apple tree, which holds him fast while the old man tries to keep his little orphaned grandson (Bobs Watson) from falling into the clutches of a dreaded spinster-aunt (Eily Malyon). Director Harold S. Bucquet gets prime performances from the two leads, and though the treatment is as dated as the period, the story's redemptive themes are as refreshing as ever. A-II (br)

On Dangerous Ground (1951) In helping a rural sheriff catch a schoolgirl's murderer, a tough, troubled city detective (Robert Ryan) recognizes his own rage in that of the dead child's father (Ward Bond), then feels affinity with the loneliness of the culprit's blind sister (Ida Lupino). Director Nicholas Ray's ambitious attempt to portray the moral regeneration of a hardened cop is weakened by the artificial melodramatics of a contrived, unconvincing plot. Some stylized violence and unsavory criminal atmosphere. A-II (br)

On Deadly Ground (1994) Realizing his ruthless oil industrialist boss (Michael Caine) is knowingly contaminating the Alaskan wilderness and risking many lives in the process, an explosives expert (Steven Seagal) decides to blow up the central pumping-station, with the help of an Inuit woman (Joan Chen) bent on avenging her father's murder. Also directed by Seagal, he self-servingly presents his violent character as an indestructible hero, but the absurd script is unbelievable, its attempts at Native American mysticism shallow, and its passionate environmental closing speech preceded by countless scenes of glossy mayhem and murder. Numerous scenes of brutal violence and gory deaths, some nudity, and much rough language. O (R)

On Golden Pond (1981) Warm movie about the bickering relationship of an aging couple (Katherine Hepburn and Henry Fonda) at the lakeside vacation-home where they have spent their summers for four decades. Visiting is their divorced, middle-aged only child (Jane Fonda), forever at odds with her cantankerous father. Directed by Mark Rydell, the sentimental story revolves around Henry Fonda, who gives a fine performance (his last), despite the shallow, caricature-like nature of the role. Too much of the humor leans upon the device of putting vulgarities in the mouth of either the old man or a 13-year-old boy visitor. A-III (PG)

On Her Majesty's Secret Service (1969) This caper takes James Bond (George Lazenby) to the Swiss Alps, where he uncovers an insidious plan to threaten the world with genetic extinction. Director Peter Hunt makes a conscious effort to outdo its predecessors in scope, excitement, and visual effects, but only succeeds in presenting more of the same formula of fantasy sex and violence. A-III (PG)

On Moonlight Bay (1951) Pleasant nostalgia from Booth Tarkington's **Penrod** stories about a 1917 Indiana family whose bemused parents (Leon Ames and Rosemary DeCamp) try to keep up with their mischievous grade-school son and his big sister (Doris Day), who's in love with the college boy (Gordon MacRae) across the street. Director Roy Del Ruth relaxes with the mundane distractions of small-town life, the sweet innocence of period songs, and the uncertain course of young love. Undemanding family fare. A-I (br)

On the Avenue (1937) Musical fluff about a socialite (Madeleine Carroll) falling in love with a Broadway musical star (Dick Powell), despite his lead in a new show which pokes fun at her stuffy family. Directed by Roy Del Ruth, the on-again, off-again romance meanders amiably through an uneven collection of Irving Berlin songs, with Alice Faye and the Ritz Brothers notable in supporting roles. Romantic complications. A-II (br)

On the Beach (1959) Sturdy doomsday scenario in which the human race faces annihilation as radioactive fallout from nuclear explosions sweeps around the world, finally reaching Australia after an American submarine commander (Gregory Peck) reports finding no signs of life anywhere else. Directed by Stanley Kramer from Nevil Shute's novel, the tale relies chiefly on how various characters (notably Fred Astaire, Ava Gardner, and Anthony Perkins) face their impending doom, though the treatment rarely probes beyond the melodramatic. Sobering look at the human consequences of nuclear disaster, with situations involving radiation sickness, death, and instances of suicide. A-III (br)

On the Edge (1986) Bruce Dern plays a long-distance runner, who 20 years after being unjustly denied a chance at Olympic competition, determines to prove his talent and integrity in the toughest race of his career. Filmed on location in the beautiful Mill Valley region of northern California, the movie is an impressionistic, somewhat rambling essay on the male-jock mentality. Some partial nudity and brief profanity. A-II (PG-13)

On the Nickel (1980) Ralph Waite stars in this story (which he also wrote and directed) of the Los Angeles Skid Row, known as "The Nickel," a place where society's dropouts drown their despair in alcohol. While an admirable attempt to define the helplessness of these unfortunates, the movie is far too long, the action quite repetitive, and the use of comic relief is unfortunate. Depiction of sordid environment is not too strong for older teenagers. A-III (R)

On the Right Track (1981) A small boy (Gary Coleman), who lives in a locker at Chicago's Union Station, makes a living as a shoeshine boy with a psychic ability to pick winning horses. Directed by Lee Phillips, the cluttered plot of this thin comedy throws the whole burden upon the young actor, and some may find his charm not enough to sustain it. Adult romantic complications are inappropriate in a movie aimed at children. A-III (PG)

On the Town (1949) Bright and breezy musical about three sailors (Gene Kelly, Frank Sinatra, and Jules Munshin) who find romance (Vera-Ellen, Betty Garnett, and Ann Miller, respectively) on a 24-hour shore-leave in New York City. Imaginatively directed by Kelly and Stanley Donen, the story line is sweetly lightheaded, yet sturdy enough to hold together daffy comedy routines, agreeable songs, energetic dance numbers, and colorful NYC locations. Romantic situations. A-II (br)

On the Waterfront (1954) Classic labor film about a punched-out boxer (Marlon Brando) who, despite the machinations of his shifty brother (Rod Steiger) and with some encouragement from the woman (Eva Marie Saint) he loves as well as a waterfront priest (Karl Malden), decides to stand up to the criminal boss (Lee J. Cobb) of a corrupt union of dock-workers. Budd Schulberg's fact-based script is directed by Elia Kazan with stand-out performances and a gritty realism grounded in a working-class milieu, abetted by Leonard Bernstein's rousing score and Boris Kauffman's atmospheric photography. Much menace and some violence. A-II (nr)

On the Yard (1979) Screen version of Malcolm Brady's prison novel centers on a wheeler-dealer (Thomas Waites) who rules over the other inmates, until a determined rival inmate (John Heard) brings about his downfall. Subplots involve a prisoner desperate for parole (Mike Kellin) and the obsession of another (Joe Grifasi) to escape in a balloon he is secretly building. Raphael D. Silver's direction is too uncertain and his characterizations too sketchy to achieve anything more than a realistic depiction of the violent world of prison. A-III (R)

On Valentine's Day (1986) After shocking a small Southern town with their elopement, a young couple find reconciliation with their parents and friends. Horton Foote's contemplative little movie covers wide-ranging emotional ground in its exploration of small-town intimacies and the erosion of traditions through careful characterizations of one family. The semi-autobiographical narrative is propelled, albeit slowly, by a spirit of unbridled loyalty and devotion tinged with a sense of loss for pre-WW I ways of life. A brief but brutal suicide scene. A-II (PG)

Once Around (1990) Love-struck, middle-aged salesman (Richard Dreyfuss) takes a young bride (Holly Hunter), whose parents (Danny Aiello and Gena Rowlands) and sister (Laura San Giacomo) can't stomach his overbearing ways. Despite a positive message, the touching moments in director Lasse Hallstrom's family drama are diluted by heavy-handed characterizations, sappy dialogue, and drawn-out situations. Acceptance of premarital sex, vulgar jokes, and casual rough language. A-III (R)

Once a Thief (1965) Listless crime story of an ex-crook (Alain Delon) who has married (Ann-Margret) and settled down, but is hounded by the police (Van Heflin) and a gangster brother (Jack Palance) needing his help for a big-time robbery. Director Ralph Nelson gets good performances and uses the San Francisco settings well, but the loosely plotted proceedings are entirely predictable. Stylized violence and drug usage. A-III (br)

Once Before I Die (1966) John Derek and Ursula Andress spend much of their time together in this attempt at a WW II thriller, making love just out of range of the camera and the advancing Japanese tanks and artillery. Derek gets killed, but Andress carries on, ultimately giving significance to the coy title by taking a young soldier into her arms one fateful night. Overblown and undernourished. O (br)

Once Bitten (1985) A vampire (ineptly played by Lauren Hutton) must find a teenage virgin male in order to preserve her youth. He in turn must lose his virginity to escape the curse of the undead. Lots of tasteless humor and mindless sexual innuendo. O (PG-13)

Once in Paris (1978) Frank D. Gilroy wrote, produced, and directed this romance about the relationship between a screenwriter (Wayne Rodgers), an heiress (Gayle Hunnicut), and a chauffeur (Jack Lenoir). Filmed in Paris, the lame and languid story condones infidelity and adultery. O (R/PG appeal)

Once Is Not Enough (see: **Jacqueline Susann's Once Is Not Enough**)

Once More My Darling (1949) Lumpy screwball comedy about a movie actor (Robert Montgomery) aiding the military to nab an international jewel thief by pretending to woo the man's 19-year-old Hollywood girlfriend (Ann Blyth). Also directed by Montgomery, the humor depends largely upon one's empathy for Blyth in the role of a kooky romantic innocent. Mild sexual innuendo. A-II (br)

Once Upon a Crime (1992) Limp comedy revolves around five innocent Americans (John Candy, James Belushi, Cybill Shepherd, Sean Young, and Richard Lewis) suspected of murdering a wealthy dowager in Monte Carlo. Eugene Levy's directorial debut is a forgettable, failed farce, filled with overly broad acting and predictable situations. Some comic violence and brief sexual innuendo. A-II (PG)

Once Upon a Forest (1993) Animated tale in which three animal youngsters — a hedgehog, a mole, and a wood-mouse — face various dangers in obtaining herbs from a distant meadow needed to cure their sick badger friend. Director Charles Grosvenor turns in a blandly sweet Hanna-Barbera production that ambles along rather listlessly, save for one highly engaging musical number, "He's Gone — He's Back." Best for the very young. A-I (G)

Once Upon a Honeymoon (1942) Halting romantic comedy in which a US radio correspondent (Cary Grant) in 1938 Vienna tries to convince a one-time American burlesque performer (Ginger Rogers) to leave her titled Austrian husband (Walter Slezak) because he's a Nazi agent, then the two fall in love as they flee Hitler's conquest of Europe. Director Leo McCarey mixes a lighthearted comic treatment of the slickly romantic plot with wartime newsreel footage and waxy Nazi villains, but the result is embarrassingly shallow and pretentious. Wartime violence, some sexual innuendo, and light treatment of marriage. A-III (br)

Once Upon a Horse ... (1958) Feeble Western comedy in which would-be badmen (TV comics Dick Martin and Dan Rowan) rustle a herd of cattle, then try to sell them back to their owner (Martha Hyer), but the price of beef is so low nobody wants them, and the sheriff (Leif Erickson) won't let the boys leave town without them. Written, produced, and directed by Hal Kanter, the laughs are meager in this slapdash grab-bag of slapstick gags, tired spoofs, and witless shenanigans, including a painful dentist routine. Comic violence and romantic situations. A-II (br)

Once Upon a Time in America (1984) Italian director Sergio Leone has attempted to make an American urban-crime epic, but his melodramatic tale of Jewish gangsters (Robert De Niro and James Woods) is dull and lifeless in spanning 30 years in the lives of characters impossible to be concerned about, not only because their actions are so brutal, but also because their motivations never rise above the most elemental. Excessive violence and a crude and brutalizing depiction of sex. O (R)

Once Upon a Time in the West (1969) Any movie with such a plainly mythic title can't be all bad, and this one really isn't bad at all. Epic, stately spaghetti Western directed by Sergio Leone, its wispy plot concerns hired killer Henry Fonda's pursuit of outlaw Charles Bronson and widow Claudia Cardinale's land, but it contains a whole encyclopedia of Western cliches and stereotypes that are irresistible for Western buffs. Others may enjoy it as a knowing spoof but one that is overlong and featuring some rather intense violence. A-III (PG)

Once Upon a Time ... When We Were Colored (1996) Growing up in rural Mississippi after WW II, a black youth is nourished by the love and support of an extended family, and, despite all the injustices of a segregated society, never loses pride in his race or hope in the American dream of equality. Director Tim Reid gets fine performances from a seasoned cast (headed by Al Freeman, Jr.) in depicting a closely knit black community taking care of its own in the face of social exclusion and economic exploitation just before the struggle for civil rights becomes a national issue in the 1960s. Racial tensions, some stylized violence, and sexual references including a childbirth scene. A-II (PG)

Once Were Warriors (1995) Harrowing tale of abuse within a Maori family living in urban New Zealand, where a hard-drinking husband (Temuera Morrison) habitually brutalizes his long-suffering wife (Rena Owen) until one of their troubled children (Mamaengaroa Kerr-Bell) meets with tragedy, awakening the wife to challenge her spouse, while finding spiritual solace in her Maori roots and help from her long-estranged relations. Director Lee Tamahori's horrific portrayal of domestic abuse clearly condemns the cycle of physical and psychological violence that destroys family life. Vicious spousal beatings and barroom brawls, restrained treatment of a rape, an off-screen suicide, fleeting nudity, and continuous rough language. A-IV (R)

Once You Kiss a Stranger (1969) Failed thriller about a psychopathic young woman (Carol Lynley) who murders one golf-pro in order to blackmail a competing pro (Paul Burke) into murdering her psychiatrist. Mindless script ineptly directed by Robert Sparr. A-III (M)

One and Only, The (1978) Henry Winkler plays a boorish college dropout in the 1950s who goes to New York to become a Broadway star, but, to avoid starvation, he becomes a wrestler and wins fame and fortune in the ring. Director Carl Reiner tries very hard for the proper blend of humor and nostalgia, but his egotistical hero lacks the essential charm the role intended. The lightweight comedy has a heavy load of crude sexual and scatological references. A-III (PG)

One and Only Genuine Original Family Band, The (1968) Uneven Disney musical about a family (grampa Walter Brennan, Janet Blair, Buddy Ebsen, and eight kids) who emigrate from Nebraska to the Dakota territory just in time to get embroiled in partisan politics over Dakota's proposed statehood and the presidential race between Grover Cleveland and Benjamin Harrison. Behind its over-cute tendencies and over-sentimental songs by the Sherman brothers, the movie has some infectious high spirits, but director Michael O'Herlihy might have done a better job mining the genuine lode of Americana to be found in the book by Laura Van Nuys. A-I (G)

One Body Too Many (1944) Creaky comic thriller directed by Frank McDonald centers on a meek insurance-salesman (Jack Haley) spending the night in a spooky mansion with the relatives and servants (Bela Lugosi as the sinister butler) of its late owner, whose strange will has driven one of them to murder. Ominous atmosphere with few scares and even fewer laughs. A-II (br)

One Brief Summer (1972) Talky British soap opera about a middle-aged financier (Clifford Evans) who carries on a torrid romance with a 17-year-old girl (Felicity Gibson) vacationing on his estate. Director John Mackenzie photographs the boring affair in musty blue hues and glazes the superficial characterizations with bits of gratuitous nudity and kinky eroticism. O (R)

One Crazy Summer (1986) Absurdist comedy replete with tiresome bathroom humor, some profane gestures, and vulgar sight gags has a group of high-school grads saving the ancestral home of a streetwise girl (Demi Moore) from a ruthless developer and his son. Taking place on Nantucket Island, the movie is essentially pulp entertainment, vapid enough to cause goof-ball behavior in the young and immature. A-III (PG)

One Day in the Life of Ivan Denisovich (1971) British screen version of Russian novelist Alexander Solzhenitsyn's account, based on his own experience, of what daily life meant to a prisoner of a forced-labor camp in the Soviet penal system. Directed by Casper Wrede, Tom Courtney excels in the title role, conveying the feeling of a prisoner trying to survive each day by keeping alive the hope of freedom. A powerful indictment of Soviet oppression, it is filled with gloomy images of human suffering and hardship, but it also details the little victories which lessened the pain of injustice. A-II (G)

One Desire (1955) Sudsy period romance directed by Jerry Hopper is chiefly of interest for Anne Baxter's strong performance as a reformed woman with a shady past in the post-bellum South, where her love for a former gambler (Rock Hudson) is spurned by his ambition to wed a banker's daughter (Julia Adams). Romantic hokum. A-II (br)

One Foot in Heaven (1941) Heartwarming tale of a Methodist minister (Fredric March) and his devoted, self-sacrificing wife (Martha Scott) from their first parsonage in 1904 Iowa, through a military chaplaincy in WW I, to serving a divisive congregation in 1920s Denver. Directed by Irving Rapper with Dr. Norman Vincent Peale as technical advisor, the picture succeeds in blending the spiritual with the temporal in good-humored fashion, including the minister's unexpected reaction to seeing his first movie, a silent Western with William S. Hart. A-I (br)

One False Move (1992) After murdering six people in LA, two icy-veined killers (Billy Bob Thornton and Michael Beach) follow a girlfriend accomplice (Cynda Williams) to her Arkansas hometown, whose action-starved sheriff (Bill Paxton) awaits their arrival with mixed emotions. Carl Franklin directs a realistically violent drama that raises some serious questions about contemporary race-relations and the spread of crime to rural areas. Intermittent graphic violence, occasional drug abuse, and some rough language. A-IV (R)

One Fine Day (1996) Frantic romantic comedy in which two overworked single parents (Michelle Pfeiffer and George Clooney) meet one morning and decide to alternate babysitting shifts in order to finish crucial job assignments due that day. Director Michael Hoffman relies on star power to carry an otherwise predictable story, whose chief merit is showing children as the real victims of economically stressed one-parent families. Sexual references and minimal profanity. A-III (PG)

One Flew Over the Cuckoo's Nest (1975) Screen version of the Ken Keasy novel about an abortive rebellion in a mental institution led by a drifter (Jack Nicholson) feigning mental illness to avoid being sent to a prison farm. Director Milos Forman's smooth, low-keyed movie about life in an asylum is filled with colorful, often amusing incidents and characterizations, but the central confrontation between the sane drifter and the repressed and repressing nurse (Louise Fletcher) is too contrived to evoke a strong emotional response. Some violence, very rough dialogue, and an incident presenting loveless sexual intercourse as therapeutic. A-IV (R)

One from the Heart (1982) Teri Garr and Frederic Forrest fall out of love and back into it in this lavishly produced musical that seems more interested in its technical effects than in its story of a young couple's relationship. Directed by Francis Ford Coppola, the result is artificial and tedious. Some partial nudity, sexual by-play, and profanity. A-III (R)

One Good Cop (1991) When a widowed New York City narcotics detective (Anthony LaPaglia) meets a violent death, his partner (Michael Keaton) boldly steals a cache of drug money so he can afford to adopt his dead pal's three little girls. Writer-director Heywood Gould's intense action drama savagely juxtaposes wrenching scenes of tenderness with horrific violence, wrapping up the story with a morally questionable fantasy ending. Considerable violence with recurring rough language and drug abuse. A-IV (R)

100 Men and a Girl (1937) Charming Depression-era musical in which an enthusiastic youngster (Deanna Durbin) persuades her jobless trombonist father (Adolphe Menjou) to form an orchestra of unemployed musicians, then sets about securing the backing of a radio sponsor (Eugene Pallette) and a famous conductor (Leopold Stokowski). Directed by Henry Koster, the sentimental story about the innocence of youth goes down easily, with plenty of humor and good music, as well as a measure of hope in hard times. A-I (br)

101 Dalmatians (1961) Puppy parents Pongo and Perdita (voices of Rod Taylor and Cate Bauer) rush to rescue their offspring from the evil Cruella DeVil (voice of Betty Lou Gerson), who has stolen 99 puppies to make a polka-dot fur coat. Walt Disney's animated canine-caper, with art direction and production design by Ken Anderson, maintains its appeal as heartwarming family entertainment. A-I (G)

101 Dalmatians (1996) Charming live-action remake of the 1961 Disney cartoon in which English pets and barnyard animals unite to rescue a litter of precious puppies from being turned into a polka-dotted fur coat for wicked fashion-plate Cruella DeVil (Glenn Close). Directed by Stephen Herek, the endearing family story proceeds at a bracing pace, with an amusingly over-the-top caricature by Close, fairytale-like visuals, and a sprinkling of slapstick confrontations. A-I (G)

100 Rifles (1969) Arizona deputy (Jim Brown) tracks a bankrobber (Burt Reynolds) into Mexico, where ultimately he takes a leading part in an uprising by the Yaqui Indians against the central government. Director Tom Gries pulls out all the stops in orchestrating the horse opera's violence, ranging from fistfights to total massacre. Overemphasis on brutal action wastes potential of plot and characters. O (PG)

187 (1997) What begins as a fairly convincing picture of a dedicated high-school science teacher (Samuel L. Jackson) confronting dangerously disruptive students and uncaring school administrators turns into a crudely melodramatic thriller when the harassed teacher goes haywire and begins killing his tormentors. Directed by Kevin Reynolds, the story of a good man being pushed too far loses credibility as well as sympathy when the script pushes the violence too far after he becomes a mad avenger. Intense violence, menacing situations, a flash of nudity, much rough language, and occasional profanity. A-IV (R)

One Is a Lonely Number (1972) Intelligent soap opera about a housewife (Trish Van Devere), devastated by a bitter divorce from a philandering husband, who gets some inspiration and hope from a kindly old grocer (Melvyn Douglas). Director Mel Stuart's treatment vacillates between being simplistic and tough, harsh and sentimental, but there are some worthwhile insights along with all the superficialities. A-IV (PG)

One in a Million (1936) In her movie debut, Sonja Henie stars as a Swiss skater whose Winter Olympics gold medal is jeopardized by charges of her having skated professionally for an American promoter (Adolph Menjou), but a love-smitten newsman (Don Ameche) clears her name and makes her fortune. Director Sidney Lanfield surrounds the Danish star with a seasoned cast and some comic relief from the Ritz Brothers among others, but the lackluster plot has aged rather badly. Wholesome period entertainment. A-I (br)

One Little Indian (1973) Above-average Disney adventure set in the Old West about a US Calvary corporal (James Gardner) on the run from an unjust court martial, a white boy being raised by the Indians, and a pretty widow lady (Vera Miles) who helps both of them. Directed by Bernard McEveety, what makes the movie of more than average interest is that the corporal's predicament is for disobeying orders by defending Indian women and children during a no-prisoner raid. What makes it fun is that his escape across the desert is by camel, a temperamental beast responsible for much of the film's comedy. A-I (G)

One Magic Christmas (1985) Failed Disney movie directed by Philip Borsos lets materialistic values predominate in a story starring Mary Steenburgen and Gary Basaraba supposedly learning about "the true spirit" of Christmas. A-II (G)

One Million B.C. (1940) An anthropologist (Conrad Nagel) uses prehistoric cave-drawings to tell the story of a petulant hunter (Victor Mature) expelled from the Rock People, then given refuge by a woman (Carole Landis) of the more advanced Shell People, with their eventual union joining the two groups. Directed by Hal Roach and Hal Roach, Jr., the acting is as primitive as the situations pitting humans against lizards posing as dinosaurs, but the corny results are still watchable and not a little interesting. Stylized violence and veiled sexual innuendo. A-I (br)

$1,000,000 Duck (1971) Disney situation comedy about a Peking duck who lays golden eggs, but when its owners (Sandy Duncan and Dean Jones) try to turn them into cash, they get in trouble with the Treasury Department. Director Vincent McEveety offers standard animal antics and climactic chase sequence that will divert, if not delight preteens. A-I (G)

One Million Years B.C. (1966) Prehistoric tale in which an outcast (John Richardson) from the Rock People is rescued by a woman (Raquel Welsh) of the Shell People, then after much grunting and bouts with dinosaurs and other posturing, the two clans are united by an earthquake. Directed by Don Chaffey, the narrative draws heavily from 1940's **One Million B.C.**, but the result is visually much more polished, especially in the special effects provided by Ray Harryhausen. Stylized violence and scanty costumes. A-II (br)

One Minute to Zero (1952) An Army colonel (Robert Mitchum) wins the heart of a UN relief worker (Ann Blyth) during the US retreat in the early months of the Korean War. Directed by Tay Garnett, the patriotic but plodding tale includes some implausible derring-do and the colonel's firing on Korean refugees being used as a shield by infiltrating enemy troops. Wartime violence. A-I (br)

One More Saturday Night (1986) Director Dennis Klein overcomes a weak script and subject matter to provide an affectionate glance at the adaptability and resourcefulness of less-than-articulate teenagers (and some adults) who struggle during a typical weekend date-night in contemporary suburbia. Some rough language and a brief instance of nudity in a sexual context are offset by honest and objective performances. A-III (R)

One More Time (1970) In a sequel to **Salt and Pepper**, comedy duo Peter Lawford and Sammy Davis, Jr., chase about the English countryside in a contrived and irrelevant diamond-smuggling plot that is terribly forced and unfunny. Directed by Jerry Lewis, the timing of all the gags is off, the plot predictable, and the dialogue stupid. Some sexual innuendo. A-III (PG)

One More Train to Rob (1971) Slack Western with George Peppard as ex-con returned to take revenge on his partner (John Vernon), who doublecrossed him by not only taking the gold but also his girlfriend (Diana Muldaur). Director Andrew V. McLaglen offers more cliches than action, but its bawdy language and violent situations are not for youngsters. A-III (GP)

One Night at Dinner (1971) Italian production about a dramatist (Jean-Louis Trintignant) who decides to base his next play on the personal affairs of his seductive wife (Florinda Bolkan), his friend (Tony Musante) who is pursuing her, and the bisexual stage star (Lino Capolicchio) on whose affections they both trade. Directed by Giuseppe Patroni Griffi, the movie tries to justify infidelity and promiscuity but offers only teasing eroticism. O (R)

One Night Stand (1997) While on a business trip, a husband (Wesley Snipes) spends the night with a married woman (Nastassja Kinski), but their chance liaison has unexpected consequences when the two married couples are brought together by a mutual friend (Robert Downey, Jr.) dying of AIDS. Directed by Mike Figgis, the movie starts with pretensions of being a sensitive, serious drama, but ends up as a tacky tale of listless mate-swapping. Some graphic sexual encounters with nudity, a casual attitude towards adultery, much rough language, and an instance of profanity. O (R)

One of Our Aircraft Is Missing (1942) Hit during a raid on Nazi Germany, a British bomber crew (Godfrey Tearle, Eric Portman, Bernard Miles, and others) bail out over Holland and are helped by Dutch patriots (including Peter Ustinov as a local priest) to reach the coast and embark for England. Directed by Michael Powell and Emeric Pressberger, the airmen's predicament behind enemy lines is tense but lightened by occasional humor, some of it directed at British conceits. Wartime violence. A-I (br)

One of Our Dinosaurs Is Missing (1975) Walt Disney romp set in London during the 1920s with a gang of nannies, headed by Helen Hayes, and a clutch of Oriental villains, led by Peter Ustinov, vying with each to recover a secret Chinese formula hidden in a dinosaur skeleton. Directed by Robert Stevenson, the slapstick affair will appeal to the very young, but the Oriental stereotypes may not amuse adults. A-I (G)

One of Our Spies Is Missing (1966) Slack spy-caper directed by E. Darrell Hallenbeck follows the TV formula of "The Man from U.N.C.L.E." series as super-agents Robert Vaughn and David McCallum try to save an aged British politician (Maurice Evans) from a rejuvenation scheme. The usual stylized violence. A-II (br)

One on One (1977) Robby Benson stars as a hotshot basketball player recruited by a college coach who tries to make him give up his scholarship when he doesn't measure up to expectations. Directed by Lamont Johnson, the cluttered story-line makes only a token gesture towards exposing the corruption of college sports. Glossy, sympathetic depiction of a casual sexual relationship. O (PG)

One Potato, Two Potato (1964) Sincere melodrama about the problems faced by a shy divorcée (Barbara Barrie) after she marries a black coworker (Bernie Hamilton). Director Larry Peerce's low-budget movie is flawed dramatically but raises some important questions about the problems facing an interracial couple. A-II (br)

One Spy Too Many (1966) Secret gas is stolen from an Army testing unit and agents Solo (Robert Vaughn) and Kuryakin (David McCallum) set off in pursuit of the thief (Rip Torn). Directed by Joseph Sargent, the third movie derived from the TV series "The Man from U.N.C.L.E." is one too many. Stylized violence. A-II (br)

One Step to Hell (1968) South African potboiler directed by Sandy Howard about the exploits of a lone police officer (Ty Hardin) as he tramps through the bush after a gang of killers. Considerable stylized violence, some of it quite nasty, and sexual situations. A-III (br)

One Third of a Nation (1939) Dated but still interesting social drama set in the slums of New York, where the young brother (Sidney Lumet) of a millinery worker (Sylvia Sidney) is crippled by a fire in a tenement whose young millionaire-owner (Lief Erikson) is so appalled by the tragedy, he determines to replace his slum properties with modern housing. Directed by Dudley Murphy, the movie's idealistic message isn't helped by the awkwardly contrived story, though the actors give some flavor to stereotyped roles, and there are some strong expressionistic scenes, especially the boy's conversations with the hated tenement house. Stylized violence, muted sexual innuendo, and romantic complications. A-II (br)

1000 Convicts and a Woman (1971) When the trusty warden's lusty daughter (Alexandra Hay) comes home from school on holiday, all manner of havoc breaks loose on dad's normally quiet prison farm. The exploitation movie's ridiculous ineptness fails to mitigate the unsubtle titillation. O (R)

One Touch of Venus (1948) Pedestrian romantic fantasy in which a statue of Venus comes to life (Ava Gardner) when kissed by a department-store clerk (Robert Walker), whose attempts to escape her romantic powers engender love between fellow clerks (Dick Haymes and Olga San Juan) and the store's owner (Tom Conway) and his secretary (Eve Arden). Directed by William A. Seiter, the silly premise is helped by some comic dialogue and occasional Kurt Weill songs, but the result is decidedly earthbound. Sexual situations amidst all the romantic complications. A-III (br)

One Tough Cop (1998) Lackluster melodrama in which an New York City cop (Stephen Baldwin) tries to do his job while saddled with an alcoholic partner (Chris Penn) and under pressure to help nail his lifelong best friend, a known Mafioso. Director Bruno Barreto lionizes the conflicted cop as a victim of callous police bureaucracy in an otherwise routine police procedural. Some violence, implied affairs, occasional profanity, and much rough language. A-III (R)

One Trick Pony (1980) Singer-composer Paul Simon stars as a band leader whose marriage is on the rocks and whose group is breaking up. An ambitious movie, directed by Robert M. Young and written by Simon, it is very knowing about the tensions in the popular-music industry between those who run the business and those who provide the talent, but less sure about the personal problems of those involved. Several sexually explicit scenes, nudity, and gross language. O (R)

One True Thing (1998) Contemporary family drama in which a grown daughter (Renee Zellweger) reluctantly puts her writing career on hold when summoned home by her father (William Hurt) to care for her cancer-stricken mother (Meryl Streep) and, in the process, acquires a deeper understanding of her parents and of herself. Directed by Carl Franklin, the movie is rooted in the traditional values of home and family relationships, though the story unfolds under the cloud of an investigation into the mother's death from an overdose of medication. A tragic death, some sexual references, several scenes of inebriation, and occasional use of rough language and profanity. A-III (R)

One, Two, Three (1961) Madcap Cold War farce set in divided Berlin, where a Coca Cola executive (James Cagney) tries to negotiate a franchise deal with the Russians, then finds his career on the line when his boss's 17-year-old daughter (Pamela Tiffin) turns up married to a Communist East Berliner (Horst Buchholz). Director Billy Wilder has intermittent fun with East-West rivalries and Prussian manners, but the picture really centers in Cagney's energetic, wise-cracking performance as the quick-thinking, fast-talking pragmatist who's equal to any occasion. Much bawdy humor and sexist attitudes on both sides of the Iron Curtain. A-III (br)

One Woman or Two (1987) Ex-model (Sigourney Weaver) impersonates a patroness of the sciences (Dr. Ruth Westheimer) to escape a pesky ex-lover. Gerard Depardieu and Michael Aumont are the duped scientists who discover the remains of a two-million-year-old woman as well as the deception. The conclusion of director Daniel Vigne's dizzy romantic comedy has brief nudity in a sexual context. A-III (PG-13)

Onion Field, The (1979) Two petty criminals (James Woods and Franklyn Seales) kidnap two policemen, brutally murdering one of them (Ted Danson), and the consequences nearly destroy the surviving officer (John Savage) in this somber, slow-moving, but gripping movie version of Joseph Wambaugh's novel. Director Harold Becker conveys the grim reality of police work and the varied, intensely human character of those involved on both sides of the law. Violence, rough language, and frank depiction of the seamy details of criminal life. A-IV (R)

Only Angels Have Wings (1939) A stranded American entertainer (Jean Arthur) gets stuck on the leader (Cary Grant) of a bunch of daring aviators trying to win a government contract flying the mail over a dangerous South American route. Director Howard Hawks's classic picture of men whose bond of camaraderie transcends the dangers of their profession is conveyed by a fine cast including Noah Berry Jr. and Allyn Joselyn as devil-may-care pilots, Thomas Mitchell as the flier with failing eyesight, and Richard Barthlemess as a disgraced pilot trying to prove himself. A-II (br)

Only Game in Town, The (1970) Two lonely people in Las Vegas, a mixed-up compulsive gambler (Warren Beatty) and a hefty chorus girl (Elizabeth Taylor), meet by chance, take up residence together, and ultimately fall in love. Though overlong and lacking comic flair, director George Stevens's movie offers some interesting delineations of character and excursions into motive and meaning, but never with any real depth or emotion. A-III (PG)

Only the Lonely (1991) A 38-year-old Chicago cop (John Candy) vacillates in his struggle to free himself from the manipulative domination of his mother (Maureen O'Hara) as he seeks a last chance at love with a shy mortuary cosmetician (Ally Sheedy). Writer-director Chris Columbus scores with a topnotch cast in a warmhearted story that casts a wry eye on Irish-Catholic mores. Implied premarital sexual encounter, minimal slapstick violence, flash of nudity, a few ethnic slurs, and an instance of rough language. A-III (PG-13)

Only Two Can Play (1962) Uneven satire set in Wales, where a married librarian (Peter Sellers) seeks a promotion by wooing the wife (Mai Zetterling) of the library board's chairman, then rejects the position before it costs him his marriage. Directed by Sidney Gilliat from the Kingsley Amis novel, the story pokes fun at the idle rich, bureaucrats, and other mediocrities, especially the non-hero, who's willing to commit adultery to get ahead, but can't because of comic circumstances that eventually cause him to reconsider. Sexual situations and innuendo. A-III (br)

Only When I Larf (1968) Three con-artists (Richard Attenborough, David Hemmings, and Alexandra Stewart) pull some neat capers on a variety of victims, ranging from gullible New York stock-speculators to army officers from an emerging African nation. For the most part Basil Deardon directs the international swindles with a light, witty touch, but in following the novel by Len Deighton, there are some slow moments with a love triangle and assorted jabs at contemporary social values. A-III (G)

Only When I Laugh (1981) Marsha Mason plays a successful actress who is a reformed alcoholic whom circumstances conspire to push to the brink once more. Contributing to her problems are her daughter (Kristy McNichol), a homosexual actor (James Coco), and a rich man's wife (Joan Hackett) who is pathologically afraid of growing old. Written by Neil Simon and directed by Glenn Jordan, it's a moderately entertaining blend of laughs and seriousness. Aside from some occasional foul language, the contrived plot is innocuous. A-II (R)

Only You (1994) Contrived romantic comedy in which a Pittsburgh bride-to-be (Marisa Tomei) impulsively takes off for Italy in determined pursuit of a stranger whom she believes is destined to marry her, but, along the way, she meets a love-struck shoe salesman (Robert Downey, Jr.) who insists he's the man for her. Director Norman Jewison's frothy confection is shot though with fairy dust of appeal to diehard romantics but which others may dismiss as sheer sentimentality in an implausible love story. Mild sexual innuendo. A-II (PG)

Open City (1945) Composite picture of the resistance movement in German-occupied Rome, focusing on an underground leader (Marcello Pagliero) hidden by a widow (Anna Magnani) until he's betrayed to the Gestapo, then tortured and executed along with a partisan priest (Aldo Fabrizi). Director Roberto Rossellini began filming while German troops were still in the city, and the result has a documentary quality giving a sense of immediacy to the period portrayal of events by a cast whose naturalistic acting captures the fervor and determination of diverse social types united in their opposition to Fascism. Subtitles. Wartime violence and some intense torture scenes. A-III (br)

Open Doors (1991) Ignoring public outcry and pressures from the Fascist regime in 1937 Italy, a judge (Gian Maria Volonte) refuses to mete out the death penalty to a fired civil servant (Ennio Fantastichini) convicted of murdering his wife, ex-boss, and his replacement. Director Gianni Amelio evokes strong performances from the leads, but the snail-like pace of the film and its exploration of capital punishment is generally unsatisfying. Subtitles. Restrained depiction of a triple murder and adulterous references. A-III (nr)

Open Season (1974) Grisly plot about three war buddies (Peter Fonda, John Phillip Law, and Richard Lynch) who, on their annual people-hunting trip, kidnap a couple (Albert Mendoza and Cornelia Sharp) for a week of rape and mayhem before the father (William Holden) of a previous victim puts a revengeful stop to it. Directed by Peter Collinson, the exercise in sadism has nothing to redeem it. O (R)

Open Your Eyes (1999) Confusing Spanish thriller in which a young man (Eduardo Noriega), facially disfigured in a car crash that apparently kills his jealous lover, finds himself in a psychiatric prison accused of murder and uncertain of what is real or imagined. Director Alejandro Amenabar's futuristic fantasy becomes increasingly dense as virtual reality and cryogenics are used to explain the man's mental deterioration. Subtitles. Some violence, a few sexual encounters with nudity, and recurring rough language. A-IV (R)

Opening Night (1978) Director John Cassavetes explores the terrors of aging in the story of a popular stage-actress facing her first role as an older woman, and the prospect of a future limited to character parts. Gena Rowlands's performance as a woman on the edge is universal in capturing the dread and fear of a person making the passage to a new stage in life. An exceptional supporting cast (Joan Blondell, Paul Stewart, and Ben Gazarra) is pushed to the limits of their craft. Mature themes. A-III (nr)

Operation Condor (1997) Comedy-action tale of a secret agent (Jackie Chan) who is assisted by three bickering women in searching for Nazi gold buried in the Sahara as various villains track the quartet's every move. Also directed by Chan, the dubbed 1991 production uses the nonsensical plot as a vehicle for tongue-in-cheek displays of bold stunts and martial-arts feats. Much comic-book violence, sexual references, and brief nudity. A-III (PG-13)

Operation Crossbow (1965) Colorful adventure story about an Allied espionage mission to destroy German long-range missiles in the final days of WW II. Directed by Michael Anderson, there's plenty of tension and interesting characterizations from an international cast headed by George Peppard, Tom Courtney, Sophia Loren, and Lilli Palmer. Wartime violence. A-I (br)

Operation Dumbo Drop (1995) Two cantankerous Green Berets (Danny Glover and Ray Liotta) in war-torn 1968 Vietnam are assigned to transport an orphaned boy and his ornery elephant across hundreds of miles of Viet Cong-infiltrated territory to raise morale in a village outpost. Director Simon

Wincer's fact-based story strains the limited comic elements of moving the big beast while also stressing multiracial harmony in earnest, heavy-handed terms. Some restrained military shootouts, a brief sexual reference, and instances of scatological humor. A-II (PG)

Operation Kid Brother (1967) Inept spy spoof about an international scheme to hypnotize the world's great powers into surrendering most of their gold reserves to a gang of crooks. Neil Connery, Sean's younger brother, apparently was never told that he was acting in a take-off, and hence he doesn't. A-II (br)

Operation Leontine (1973) In this zany French spoof of the crime genre, Francoise Rosay plays a feared former gang-leader who emerges from retirement for one last caper and outwits and outguns all her gangster opponents. Directed by Michel Audiard, the stylish, well-acted movie adds up to little more than a collection of sight gags (some quite hilarious) and adult fantasies revolving around rival gangs doublecrossing one another. A-III (M)

Operation Pacific (1951) Thin WW II melodrama directed by George Waggner in which a submarine captain (John Wayne) battles the Japanese Imperial Fleet while trying to win back the wife (Patricia Neal) who divorced him just before the war. Wartime violence, shore leave shenanigans, and romantic interludes. A-II (br)

Operation Petticoat (1959) Belabored WW II comedy aboard a patched-up submarine whose captain (Cary Grant) depends upon a cunning officer (Tony Curtis) to find the parts to keep it running, despite the complications caused after evacuating five Army nurses from a Japanese-threatened island. Directed by Blake Edwards, the best jokes come from the frantic efforts to keep the broken-down sub operational, with the usual sexist jokes occasioned by the nurses in close quarters with the crew. Much sexual innuendo. A-III (br)

Operation S.N.A.F.U. (1974) Failed WW II comedy about some unwilling Allied soldiers (Jason Robards, Martin Landau, and Peter Falk) sent into German-held Sicily to destroy artillery positions impeding a sea-borne invasion. Filmed in Italy and Yugoslavia, director Nanni Loy's slapstick treatment of a cornball plot is rarely amusing. Some rough language and raunchy humor. A-III (nr)

Operation Thunderbolt (1978) Director Menahem Golan's dramatization of the heroic rescue by Israeli commandos of the Jewish hostages at Entebbe Airport perhaps errs on the side of being too scrupulous in avoiding the sensational. Thus there is considerable plodding and skimping on characterization, but the subject itself has enough excitement and heroism to make it an entertaining and quite moving viewing experience. A-II (PG)

Ophélia (1974) Modern version of "Hamlet" attempts to make the audience question its initial sympathy for the title character (Andre Jocelyn) and prepare it for an ending which Shakespeare never envisioned. Director Claude Chabrol turns the original into a study of destructive obsessions involving such themes as family tensions, middle-class materialism, the sense of the irreparable, and emotional ambivalence. While not entirely successful, the adaptation has brilliance and imagination. A-II (nr)

Opium War, The (1978) Chinese production about the early 19th-century imperial commissioner sent from Peking to put a stop to the opium trade at the port of Canton but who instead sets off a war between China and Great Britain. Director Chen Chun-li's highly romanticized and stylized dramatization gives only sketchy details of the conflict but is worth seeing for its spectacle and sheer novelty, if nothing else. A-II (nr)

Opportunity Knocks (1990) Humorless rags-to-riches comedy about a Chicago con-artist (Dana Carvey) who falls for the daughter (Julia Campbell) of his rich victim (Robert Loggia). Uninspired direction by Donald Petrie and a hackneyed script do little for TV comic Carvey's first starring vehicle on the big screen. Some comic-book violence and bathroom humor. A-II (PG-13)

Opposite of Sex, The (1998) Seriocomic tale concerning the unstable sexual relationships of a pregnant 16-year-old (Christina Ricci), her homosexual half-brother (Martin Donovan), his bisexual lover (Ivan Sergei), and a family friend (Lisa Kudrow), some of whom begin to reflect on the need for a relationship to be based on something more fulfilling than sexual gratification. Writer-director Don Roos tries to make the lumpy proceedings seem amusingly madcap rather than contrived, but the effort gets lost in convoluted subplots and a superficial ending. Stylized violence, comic treatment of sexual situations, a troubled childbirth scene, some rough language, and occasional profanity. A-IV (R)

Optimists, The (1973) Aged ex-vaudevillian (Peter Sellers), reduced to entertaining on the London streets with his scruffy little trained dog Bella, gradually develops a cherished friendship with two young slum children (played delightfully by Donna Mullande and John Chaffey). The British production, warmly directed by Anthony Simmons, has much to say about the world of children and the importance of the magical and the incongruous in their world. Meaningful family entertainment. A-I (PG)

Orca (1977) Shark-hunter Richard Harris decides to go after bigger game and, in attempting to catch a male killer-whale, kills its mate, a pregnant female, thus incurring the wrath of the male. Charlotte Rampling is on hand as a whale specialist who seems to have a soft spot in her heart for big brutes of all sorts. Director Michael Anderson's seafaring adventure has some scenic beauty, but its story is mediocre entertainment at best. Some rather graphic violence. A-III (PG)

Orchestra Rehearsal (1979) Italian production about an orchestra whose members are constantly being distracted by one another and the inane questions of a television crew. A union dispute leads to violence and ultimately chaos. Director Federico Fellini's failed fable about the tension between authority and the individual becomes a disjointed series of gags and jabs at music, nationality, television, art, sports, sex, and other perennial favorites. Minor work from a great director. A-III (R)

Orchestra Wives (1942) Lightheaded romantic melodrama from the big-band era revolves around a small-town girl (Ann Rutherford) who marries a trumpet player (George Montgomery), tries to adjust to life on the road with the bored, catty wives of other band members, then calls it quits after being led to believe her mate is having an affair with the band's lead singer (Lynn Bari). Director Archie Mayo tries to cover the weak story-line by concentrating on the flip lifestyle of the musicians, but the movie's chief asset is the smooth sound of Glenn Miller's band performing vintage hits from the era. Domestic tensions and references to marital infidelity. A-III (br)

Ordet (1954) Challenging Danish production about different kinds of faith and various sorts of miracles, one of which restores a dead woman to life. Directed by Carl Dreyer, the austere narrative centers on a farming family troubled by the madness of a son (Preben Lerdorff Rye) who believes he is Jesus Christ until, regaining his balance, his faith in God achieves the miracle which brings the story to a positive though less-than-convincing conclusion some may find disappointingly ambiguous. Mature themes. A-III (br)

Ordinary People (1980) Donald Sutherland and Mary Tyler Moore give fine performances as confused and troubled parents trying to cope with the psychological aftershocks that result when the older of two sons dies in a boating accident, and the surviving son (Timothy Hutton) attempts suicide. Directed by Robert Redford, the movie hints that the characters' complacent and wholly materialistic environment may have contributed to the family's instability, but these aspects remain underdeveloped. The problems are very real, but the movie is strangely cool and distanced from them. Due to the heaviness of the theme and some instances of rough language, it is for mature viewers. A-III (R)

Oregon Passage (1957) Hokey Western directed by Paul Landres is set in an 1871 outpost, where a cavalry officer (John Ericson) rescues a missionary-educated Indian maid (Lola Albright) taken captive by a band of hostiles, then has to save the fort not only from Indian attacks but the blunders of a new commanding officer. Stylized violence, some quite nasty, and mild romance. A-II (br)

Orfeu Negro (see: **Black Orpheus**)

Organization, The (1971) Sidney Poitier in a third outing as Lt. Virgil Tibbs of the 1967 movie, **In the Heat of the Night**, finds himself involved in a situation where the police are using extra-legal methods to apprehend a gang trafficking in heroin. Directed by Don Medford, the thriller concentrates on chase scenes without any attempt at characterization or addressing the moral and legal issues inherent in the plot. Physical and psychological violence. A-III (R/PG-13)

Organizer, The (1964) Prime Italian import about underpaid factory workers in turn-of-the-century Turin, as they try to form a union with the help of a teacher-turned-labor organizer (Marcello Mastroianni). Directed by Mario Monicelli, the production is steeped in a sense of social justice, clearly showing management's exploitation of the workers and the blighted lives of their impoverished families. Subtitles. Earthy treatment and vulgar language. A-III (br)

Orgazmo (1998) Inept one-joke sex farce about a clean-cut Mormon youth (Trey Parker) who becomes a porno-movie star, then rebels against his sleazy producer (Michael Dean Jacobs). Also written and directed by Parker, the low-budget proceedings are as excruciatingly witless as the raunchy humor is appallingly unfunny. Simulated sex acts, explicit sexual dialogue, occasional nudity, stylized violence, religious gibes, recurring rough language, and some profanity. O (NC-17)

Original Gangstas (1996) Five middle-aged former gang-members (including Fred Williamson, Jim Brown, and Pam Grier) reunite as vigilantes to mow down a murderous gang of vicious thugs terrorizing their old neighborhood. Director Larry Cohen exploits violence by depicting it as an exciting means of wielding power and commanding respect. Much revenge-themed mayhem, fleeting nudity, brief sexual innuendo, and constant rough language. O (R)

Orlando (1993) British adaptation of Virginia Woolf's feminist fantasy about the curious experiences of an Elizabethan noble (Tilda Swinton) who lives for 400 years, the first 200 as a man and the next 200 as a woman. Adapted and directed by Sally Potter, the result is always pretty to look at but not particularly amusing or enlightening, as the centuries roll by slowly with few insights on the unequal social conditions that till recently had been women's traditional lot. Momentary frontal nudity and a few circumspect scenes of lovemaking. A-III (PG-13)

Orpheus (1949) Startlingly designed, exquisitely photographed version of the classic myth about the relationship between love and death visualized with haunting beauty in this French movie directed by artist and poet Jean Cocteau. A-II (br)

Oscar (1991) The efforts of a Prohibition-era gangster (Sylvester Stallone) to turn over a new leaf are continuously complicated by skeptical cops, greedy bankers, his larcenous accountant (Vincent Spano), and his scheming daughter (Marisa Tomei). Director John Landis's attempt at farce is only modestly entertaining with generally unfunny performances and methodical pacing. Very mild sexual innuendo. A-II (PG)

Oscar, The (1966) One-dimensional story of the efforts of a psychopath (Stephen Boyd) to achieve

Hollywood stardom has all the empty glitter of Tinsel Town, but director Russell Rouse goes to excess in sexual suggestiveness. O (br)

Oscar and Lucinda (1997) Quirky story set in Victorian-era Australia, where an English preacher (Ralph Fiennes) and an idealistic heiress (Cate Blanchett) are drawn to each other by their scandal-causing love of gambling. Director Gillian Armstrong's lushly photographed period piece over-emphasizes the characters' comical eccentricities before abruptly switching to bizarre melodramatics. Brief but intense violence including suicide and a sexual encounter. A-III (R)

Osterman Weekend, The (1983) Screen version of Robert Ludlum's espionage thriller about a television talk-show host (Rutger Hauer) who is used by a CIA agent (John Hurt) in a ruse to discredit the head of intelligence (Burt Lancaster). Directed by Sam Peckinpah, the convoluted plot serves up a thoroughly distasteful stew of gratuitous violence and sex, with not a trace of human feeling. O (R)

Otello (1986) Franco Zeffirelli's lavish production of the Verdi opera, with Placido Domingo in the title role, emphasizes the visuals at the expense of the rather depressing libretto, based on Shakespeare's play about jealousy leading to murder and suicide. A-II (PG)

Othello (1966) British adaptation of Shakespeare's play, with Laurence Olivier as the epileptic general whose jealousy and passion destroy him, abetted by Frank Finlay as Iago and Maggie Smith as Desdemona. Directed by Stuart Burge, it is a photographed performance in which simple stage backgrounds, stage movements, and camera close-ups focus all attention on the lead actor and Shakespeare's language. A-II (br)

Othello (1995) Compact version of William Shakespeare's tragedy set in a Venetian fortress on Cyprus where, in 1570, the villainous Iago (Kenneth Branagh) plots the downfall of its commander, Othello (Laurence Fishburne), by causing him to doubt the fidelity of his innocent bride, Desdemona (Irene Jacob). Adapter-director Oliver Parker places Iago at center stage in smirking asides to the audience as his devious scheme builds suspicion and jealousy into bloody havoc. Stylized violence, sexual encounters, and a flash of nudity. A-III (R)

Other, The (1972) Sleepy Connecticut farm in the summer of 1935 is the setting for a tale of horror and suspense involving the possession of an innocent child by the evil spirit of his dead twin. Director Robert Mulligan gets the proper atmosphere, but the story, based on the Thomas Tryon novel, gets so convoluted in the deaths of family members that it becomes a bit unbelievable and more than a touch too gruesome. A-III (PG)

Other People's Money (1991) Disappointing comedy stars Danny DeVito as a Wall Street corporate raider in love with the lawyer (Penelope Ann Miller) representing the New England company he is trying to wrest from its benevolent chief-exec (Gregory Peck). Director Norman Jewison blunts the potential for rich social commentary by stressing the unconvincing romance. Some crude sexual references and minimal rough language. A-III (R)

Other Side of Midnight, The (1977) Screen version of Sidney Sheldon novel about a poor French girl (Marie-France Pisier), jilted and left pregnant by a romantic American WW II pilot (John Beck), who becomes the mistress of a Greek tycoon (Raf Vallone) and seeks revenge on the faithless American. Directed Charles Jarrott's vulgar, trashy melodrama features a great deal of nudity and explicit sex. O (R)

Other Side of the Mountain, The (1975) Good telling of fact-based story about young skier Jill Kinmont (Marilyn Hassett) who, completely paralyzed from the chest down after a 1956 fall in pre-Olympic competition, overcame her handicap to make a new life for herself as a grade-school teacher. Director Larry Peerce at times veers into sentimentality, but for the most refrains from tampering with the emotional power inherent in the story of an individual's achievement over cruel odds. Very appealing young cast also includes Belinda J. Montgomery and Beau Bridges. A-II (PG)

Other Side of the Mountain, Part II, The (1978) Sequel to the movie about paralyzed skier Jill Kinmont (Marilyn Hassett) takes up the events leading to her marriage to John Boothe (Timothy Bottoms). Though lacking the drama of the original, director Larry Peerce's movie is consistently entertaining and, at times, quite moving, chiefly because of Hassett's superb performance. Brief sequence involving premarital sex. A-III (PG)

Other Sister, The (1999) Sentimental romance follows the struggles of two mentally challenged young adults (Juliette Lewis and Giovanni Ribisi) to live productive, independent lives despite the woman's overprotective mother (Diane Keaton), who opposes their marriage plans. While director Garry Marshall poignantly conveys the difficulties of mainstreaming, the often awkward humor in the story makes the movie seem more manipulative than intended. A discreetly suggested premarital affair, an implied lesbian relationship, and brief alcohol abuse. A-III (PG-13)

Other Voices (1970) Documentary by David Sawyer and Robert Elfstrom details the confrontational "verbal shock" therapy used on mentally ill patients at the Delaware Valley Mental Foundation. Suicide prevention is a primary objective of the treatment, but the movie's realistic observation of the private lives of these patients offers the lay audience little insight into the complexity of the social and moral problems of mental-health care. A-IV (nr)

Otley (1969) Sardonic British satire about a drifter (Tom Courtenay) who muddles his way into the middle of an espionage caper, winds up being pursued by two rival spy-organizations, and falls for a temptress with ambiguous allegiances (Romy

Schneider). Directed by Brian Clement, the story gets lost in its own intrigues, but Courtenay holds it together with a likeable comic performance and some sharp comments on the times and people's lack of integrity. A-III (PG)

Our Betters (1933) Dated high-society fluff from Somerset Maugham's play about an American hardware heiress (Constance Bennett) who marries an English lord (Alan Mowbray), then discovers he's squandered her money on another woman and turns to a wealthy American businessman (Minor Watson) until he catches her with a gigolo (Gilbert Roland). Directed by George Cukor, the picture's satire of British manners and morals was considered naughty in its day but is now little more than cold mutton, though there are some droll subsidiary characters, notably an aging American duchess (Violet Kemble-Cooper). Sexual situations and innuendo. A-III (br)

Our Hearts Were Growing Up (1946) Thin sequel to **Our Hearts Were Young and Gay**, with brash Cornelia (Gail Russell) and dizzy Emily (Diana Lynn) leaving their prim women's college to join their boyfriends at the Princeton-Harvard football game, where they get mixed up with bemused bootleggers (Brian Donlevy and William Demarest). Directed by William D. Russell, the pair's misadventures in the Jazz Age offer some period fun but are otherwise only mildly amusing. A-I (br)

Our Hearts Were Young and Gay (1944) Slight but engaging comedy from Cornelia Otis Skinner's tale of the misadventures she (Gail Russell) and college chum Emily Kimbrough (Diana Lynn) encounter on a trip to Europe in the 1920s, the highlight of which is being locked overnight in Notre Dame's belltower. Directed by Lewis Allen, the predicaments of the young ladies are delightfully innocent in keeping with period proprieties, with a capable supporting cast (notably Charles Ruggles and Dorothy Gish as Skinner's parents) adding to the fun. The silliness of the situations will amuse youngsters while their elders are more likely to be charmed by the period characters. A-I (br)

Our Latin Thing (1972) Latino-music documentary filmed in and around New York City's Cheetah nightery, the Leon Gast production fills the screen with people enjoying the vibrant sounds of Johnny Pacheco, Willie Colon, El Conde, and many other performers (there are no subtitles for the Spanish lyrics). Though partly a plug for the record company issuing works by these performing artists, it stands on its own as a lively, appealing musical celebration of life. A-II (nr)

Our Little Girl (1935) Low-budget Shirley Temple vehicle directed by John Robertson has the charming moppet run away from her troubled home, thereby saving her miserable parents (Rosemary Ames and Joel McCrea) from a divorce neither really wants. Heavy-handed domestic strife. A-II (PG)

Our Man Flint (1966) Spy spoof with James Coburn as an agent with an eye more for the ladies than the job in hand has been directed by Daniel Mann with a heavy emphasis on sexually suggestive situations and references. O (br)

Our Miss Brooks (1956) Flat adaptation of the popular radio comedy-series about the title's high-school English teacher (Eve Arden) and her hopes of wedding the school's handsome but unromantic biology instructor (Robert Rockwell). Director Al Lewis gets few laughs from a disjointed script that largely wastes Arden's comic talents, though tyrannical principal Gale Gordon and dizzy student Richard Crenna provide some amusing diversions. Romantic situations and mild sexual innuendo. A-II (br)

Our Mother's House (1967) Disturbing British movie about seven children who, to avoid being sent to an orphanage, bury their deceased mother secretly and hold séances in which they continue to invoke her advice. When their long-absent father (Dirk Bogarde) turns up and announces he is going to sell "our mother's house," the children deal forcefully with the situation. Director Jack Clayton effectively tells a rather chilling parable of the influence, for good or evil, exercised on children by their elders. A-III (br)

Our Relations (1936) Stan Laurel and Oliver Hardy find their troubles doubled when their long-lost twin brothers, Alf and Bert, turn up as sailors fleeing an irascible shipmate (James Finlayson) and an irate captain (Sidney Toler) after a pearl ring in their keeping. Director Harry Lachman has some droll fun crisscrossing the two sets of twins as each gets blamed for what the other has done until a hilarious climax involving concrete boots. A-I (br)

Our Time (1974) Set unconvincingly in 1955, this film coyly depicts the frantic sexual experimentation of two WASP schoolgirls (Pamela Sue Martin and Betsy Slade), which for one leads to abortion and death. Directed by Peter Hyams, the tearjerker's contrast between the good girl who pays with her life for making a mistake and the more calculating, unscathed friend conveys a sour, halfhearted lesson in life. A-IV (PG)

Our Town (1940) Fine adaptation of Thornton Wilder's play about two families in a small New Hampshire town circa WW I, centering on the romance between the daughter (Martha Scott) of one family and the son (William Holden) of the other. Directed by Sam Wood, the result is prime Americana, with the narrator (Frank Craven) pointing out the virtues of the community and the values of its individual members. The whole family can enjoy this look back at a simpler age and more wholesome way of life. A-I (br)

Our Very Own (1950) Soggy melodrama directed by David Miller in which a high-school senior (Ann Blyth) suddenly learns she's an adopted child, has a hard time adjusting to the revelation, seeks out her biological mother (Ann Dvorak), then embraces the parents who raised her (Jane Wyatt and Donald Cook). Superficial treatment of illegitimacy. A-II (br)

Our Winning Season (1978) High-school senior

(Scott Jacoby) trains earnestly to win the mile run in the season's finale, but in the interim the movie marks time with a string of less-than-compelling vignettes of school life. Director Joe Rubin's only attempt at deeper significance involves an affair between the hero's best friend and his sister before the friend goes off to die in Vietnam. Banal in every department. A-III (PG)

Out Cold (1989) Offbeat black comedy about two California butchers (John Lithgow and Bruce McGill) whose longtime business partnership ends abruptly when one is frozen to death in a meat locker by his wife (Teri Garr), who also bumps off the nitwit gumshoe (Randy Quaid) she has hired to track her philandering husband. Director Malcom Mowbray understates just about everything in this humorless effort, except his cliched characters. Casual treatment of adultery, some flashes of nudity, and profanity. A-III (R)

Out for Justice (1991) Enraged at the murder of his partner by a bully (William Forsythe) from their childhood, a Brooklyn cop (Steven Seagal) sets out to kill the killer before the police or the Mafia can get to him. Director John Flynn's gritty urban story of vigilante vengeance wallows in excessive violence, sexual exploitation of women, incessant rough language, recreational drug use, and brief nudity. O (R)

Out of Africa (1985) Slow-moving narrative and beautiful photography characterize this dramatization of storyteller Isek Dinesen's (Meryl Streep) years as a plantation owner in East Africa and her love affair with a hunter (Robert Redford). Produced and directed by Sydney Pollack, the movie celebrates the mystique of Africa rather than the muddled romance of its two main characters. Romanticized treatment of adultery. A-IV (PG)

Out of Bounds (1986) An Iowa farm-boy (Anthony Michael Hall) is hunted by drug peddlers, police, and corrupt narks when he picks up the wrong bag upon arriving in Los Angeles to visit his brother. Derivative script and melodramatic treatment. Profanity and needlessly extended violence and bloodshed. O (R)

Out of It (1969) Story of a shy adolescent (Barry Gordon) who is inept in dealing with girls has some funny and perceptive moments but not enough substance for a feature-length movie. Director Paul Williams makes things worse by pretentious and obtrusive camera techniques. A-III (PG)

Out of Sight (1966) Spies vie with rock-music group in director Lennie Weinrib's innocuous entry for the youth market. A-II (br)

Out of Sight (1998) Giddy crime-caper from Elmore Leonard's novel about a federal marshal (Jennifer Lopez) torn between romancing or arresting a charming con-man (George Clooney) who is about to pull off a diamond heist with traitorous partners. Steven Soderbergh's stylish direction of the result doesn't compensate for the highly contrived plot and shallow characterizations. Some nasty violence, jokey treatment of criminal activity, an implied sexual encounter, occasional profanity, and much rough language. A-IV (R)

Out of the Past (1947) Stylishly dark crime-thriller in which a private eye (Robert Mitchum) is hired to find the doublecrossing girlfriend (Jane Greer) of a big-time gambler (Kirk Douglas), but falls in love with her instead — until she double-crosses him on a murder rap. Director Jacques Tourneur keeps viewers off balance with a twisty plot that begins in a small town, where the detective is hiding out until this sordid past catches up with him, and he's forced to protect himself from his former associates. Stylized violence and romantic complications. A-II (br)

Out-of-Towners, The (1970) Midwestern couple (Jack Lemmon and Sandy Dennis) on a business trip to New York City try to cope with a hilarious series of mishaps, including a garbage strike, a snafu with hotel reservations, a rainy night in Central Park, a mugging to go with it, the siege of the Cuban UN embassy, and a stolen-car chase. Arthur Hiller's spirited direction of Neil Simon's script provides lots of fun at the expense of big-city life for family viewers. A-I (G)

Out-of-Towners, The (1999) Sluggish comedy updates Neil Simon's 1970 screenplay in which a middle-aged Ohio couple (Steve Martin and Goldie Hawn) go to New York City for a job interview and are immediately mugged, leaving them penniless, homeless, and increasingly desperate to survive the city's nighttime perils. Director Sam Weisman has a game cast, including transvestite hotel manager John Cleese, but the script proves only fitfully funny, lacking a consistently madcap quality. Sexual references and situations. A-III (PG-13)

Out on a Limb (1992) Action-comedy clunker in which a hapless yuppie (Matthew Broderick) finds himself up to his neck in murderous mayhem while visiting his kid sister (Courtney Peldon) in a remote logging town. Director Francis Verber's numbingly sophomoric plot strings together an odd assortment of klutzy characters, silly shootouts, and crashing cars. Much mindless slapstick violence. A-III (PG)

Out to Sea (1997) Thin formula comedy in which two cranky elders, an inveterate schemer (Walter Matthau) and his long-suffering honest pal (Jack Lemmon), find unexpected romance while working as dancing partners aboard a cruise-liner. Amiably directed by Martha Coolidge, it's good-natured vehicle for a veteran comedy team backed by a supporting cast of other veterans (notably Gloria DeHaven, Elaine Stritch, and Donald O'Connor), who add to the fun of this light-hearted, light-weight sentimental comedy. Sexual situations and innuendoes as well as coarse language. A-III (PG-13)

Out West with the Hardys (1938) Judge Hardy (Lewis Stone) takes wife (Fay Holden), daughter Marian (Cecilia Parker), and son Andy (Mickey Rooney) on an excursion in a typical episode of the Hardy family series directed by George B. Seitz. A-I (br)

Outback (1971) On his way from a backcountry one-room schoolhouse to Sydney for the Christmas holidays, a naive young teacher (Gary Bond) falls in with a depraved and besotted one-time doctor (Donald Pleasance) who insists on showing him some of the perverse ways he passes his time, the highlight of which is a drunken kangaroo-hunt slaughtering the defenseless animals for amusement. Directed by Ted Kotcheff, this is a disturbing picture of life in Australia's outback which, unfortunately, provides little positive insight to justify its tasteless language and brutal visuals. A-IV (R)

Outbreak (1995) As a deadly, highly contagious African virus tears through a California town, a team of government virologists (Dustin Hoffman, Renee Russo, Cuba Gooding, Jr., and Kevin Spacey) race against time to produce an antidote before their military superiors (Donald Sutherland and Morgan Freeman) solve the containment problem by vaporizing the entire town. Despite some irrational behavior by several characters, director Wolfgang Petersen's action-packed medical thriller builds considerable suspense as the ominously realistic scenario unfolds. Some military violence, shots of diseased victims, and intermittent rough language. A-III (R)

Outfit, The (1974) Two born losers, an ex-con (Robert Duvall) and an ex-torpedo (Joe Don Baker), team up to take over the gang (headed by Robert Ryan), methodically mowing their way up the mob ranks and robbing syndicate operations for ready cash. An action-packed, B-grade, old-time gangster movie with plenty of violence, but under John Flynn's direction there is such a dreamlike 1950s nostalgia coating the entire proceedings, that none of it can be taken seriously. A-III (PG)

Outland (1981) It's high noon on a moon of Jupiter, with Sean Connery playing a beleaguered federal marshal involved in an old-fashioned Western shootout with a team of killers sent to stop his investigation of Peter Boyle's deadly mining operation. Written and directed by Peter Hyams, the sci-fi movie lacks energy and imagination but does have a sympathetic depiction of the friendship that grows between the marshal and space-doctor Frances Sternhagen. Moderately entertaining but has scenes of intense violence. A-III (R)

Outlaw, The (1950) Flat-footed Western in which Billy the Kid (miscast Jack Beutel) gets some help from Doc Holliday (Walter Huston) and a sullen half-breed beauty (Jane Russell) in eluding the implacable lawman Pat Garrett (Thomas Mitchell). Producer-director Howard Hughes paces the slack action with some hard-breathing romance, which seems today seems more ridiculous than sexy, though was controversial when the film was first released in 1943, then withdrawn and re-edited for the 1950 version. Frontier violence and sexual situations. A-III (br)

Outlaw Blues (1977) Peter Fonda and Susan Saint James star in a comic chase-adventure about a singer-songwriter on the run after being framed for a crime. Directed by Richard T. Heffron, it is an amiable and fairly entertaining movie, but the romantic relationship between the principals is rich in sexual innuendo. A-III (PG)

Outlaw Josey Wales, The (1976) At the outbreak of the Civil War, Northern guerrillas slay the wife and young son of a Missouri farmer (Clint Eastwood, who also directs), leaving him for dead. He settles the score by wreaking havoc as a Confederate guerrilla who befriends a strange assortment of colorful characters along the way. Graphic scene of attempted rape and lack of any moral perspective to balance the unremitting slaughter. O (PG)

Outpost in Morocco (1949) Wooden desert-adventure with a French Foreign Legion captain (George Raft) romancing the daughter (Marie Windsor) of a sheik (Eduard Franz) who is preparing to massacre the local French garrison. Directed by Robert Florey, the location photography makes use of Legion facilities and units, though little else is notable about the movie, save a scene with French officer Akim Tamiroff praying for a miracle. Stylized violence and implied sexual liaisons. A-III (br)

Outrage, The (1964) Embarrassingly bad Western in which a cynical drifter (Edward G. Robinson) listens to various versions of events given in the trial of a Mexican bandit (miscast Paul Newman) for the hold-up of a Southern rancher (Laurence Harvey) and the rape of his wife (Claire Bloom). Director Martin Ritt's wrong-headed attempt to Westernize "Rashomon," the powerful Japanese story about subjective perceptions of reality, fails on its own dramatic terms, as well as lacking the depth and cultural relevance of the original. Mature theme and treatment. A-III (br)

Outrageous! (1977) Canadian production about a young mental patient (Hollis McLaren) who escapes and takes refuge with a homosexual hairdresser (Craig Russell) who helps her to cope with the demons of her schizophrenia, and she, in turn, encourages him to embark upon a new career as a satiric female impersonator. Director Richard Benner's movie is alive with humor, vitality, and warmth, thanks to some witty dialogue and two superb performances by the principals. Frank, thoroughly objective presentation of the homosexual subculture. A-IV (R)

Outrageous Fortune (1987) Arthur Hiller directs Bette Midler and Shelley Long as aspiring actresses who single-mindedly seek revenge when they learn that they have been betrayed by the same man with whom each is having an affair. Negative stereotyping of women, a casual attitude toward sex, and rough language leave no room for genuine comedy. O (R)

Outriders, The (1950) After escaping from a Union prison-camp, three Confederate soldiers (Joel McCrea, Barry Sullivan, and James Whitmore) are dragooned into leading a wagon train bearing Yankee gold into a Rebel ambush. Directed by Roy Rowland, the routine Western action is less interesting than the interplay between the characters and their dubious loyalties. Stylized violence. A-II (br)

Outside Chance of Maximilian Glick, The (1989) When his family in a rural Canadian town of the 1960s squashes his friendship with a Catholic girl (Fairuza Balk) who is his partner in a piano competition, a 12-year-old Jewish youth (Noam Zylberman) is troubled by the hypocrisy and prejudice that he discovers within the local Jewish and Christian communities. Directed by Allen Goldstein, the slickly produced story too easily resolves the issue of ingrained religious prejudice, though it does not sugarcoat the Jewish point of view and clearly evokes the confusion faced by children too young to understand or accept the concept of prejudice. Fine for interfaith parent-child audiences. A-I (G)

Outside Man, The (1973) Jean-Louis Trintignant plays a hired killer brought to Los Angeles to knock off a mob biggie, but then finds himself being hunted by an equally faceless killer. Ann-Margret is cast as a friend-of-a-friend who gets dragged into the confusion by her pretty heels, and Roy Scheider plays the sadistic silent type on Trintignant's tail. Director Jacques Deray's intriguing melodrama of a stranger in a strange land is packed with sly comic touches and has restrained, but continuous, tension and violence. A-III (PG)

Outsider, The (1980) Thriller about an Irish-American youth (Craig Wasson) who leaves his affluent Detroit family to fight in Belfast with the provisional IRA. Blinded by the love of an Irish girl (Patricia Quinn), he is unaware that he is being used as a pawn in their dangerous game. Director Tony Luraschi gets excellent performances from a fine Irish and English cast. The movie shows the grimy details of life in war-torn Belfast and is a thoughtful commentary on the victimized people of Ulster and the injustices on both sides. A-III (R)

Outsiders, The (1983) Screen version of S.E. Hinton's novel about three youths (Matt Dillon, C. Thomas Howell, and Ralph Macchio) growing up in Tulsa, Okla., during the 1960s. Director Francis Coppola's fragile mood-piece can't quite connect the youth's violent ways with their discussions of **Gone with the Wind** and Robert Frost's poetry. The violence in a fight between rival gangs is very pronounced. A-III (PG)

Outward Bound (1930) Creaky version of the Sutton Vane play set aboard a fog-shrouded oceanliner carrying only seven passengers (notably Leslie Howard, Montagu Love, Alison Skipworth, and young lovers Helen Chandler and Douglas Fairbanks, Jr.), all of whom finally grasp that they are dead and bound for the hereafter, where they face an examination. Director Robert Milton's stagy handling of the portentous premise benefits from some good performances, but the allegory is thin and often treacly. Sympathetic treatment of unwed lovers and their suicide. A-III (br)

Over-Exposed (1956) Weak programmer directed by Lewis Seiler follows an ambitious young photographer (Cleo Moore) who wants to get to the top fast by turning to blackmail but is saved from ruin by her reporter-boyfriend (Richard Crenna). Some stylized violence. A-II (br)

Over the Brooklyn Bridge (1984) Brooklyn luncheonette owner (Elliott Gould) yearns to open a restaurant in Manhattan, but his rich uncle won't come across with the financing unless he gives up his WASP girlfriend (Margaux Hemingway) and marries a nice Jewish girl (Carol Kane). Director Menahem Golan's failed ethnic comedy-drama is embarrassingly bad on all counts. Much sexually oriented humor and some rough language. A-III (R)

Over the Top (1987) A truck driver (Sylvester Stallone) tries to win back the son he abandoned by showing off his physical prowess. Limp, unconvincing drama directed by Menahem Golan says little about the nature of father-son relationships and opts instead for the goofy contortions of an arm-wrestling championship. Some mildly vulgar language and momentary violence are evident. A-II (PG)

Overboard (1987) When a rich lady (Goldie Hawn) suffers amnesia, a rough carpenter (Kurt Russell) claims her as his wife and the mother of his four unruly children. Directed by Garry Marshall, the tasteless sex-farce relies on the suggestiveness of a situation that makes light of adultery and uses vulgar language and references. O (PG)

Overcoat, The (1965) Fine adaptation of the Gogol short story of a poor clerk (Roland Bykov) in desperate need of a new coat to get through the Russian winter. Director Aleksei Batalov's 1959 production runs its inevitably tragic course with genuine pathos, some gentle humor, and much satire poked at office bureaucracy. A-II (br)

Overlanders, The (1946) Fearing a Japanese invasion of northern Australia in 1943, a small band of riders (headed by Chips Rafferty) herd 1,000 head of cattle 1,500 miles to Queensland. Writer-director Harry Watt's fact-based story convincingly details the physical and spiritual courage needed to overcome the dangers of the drive across desert wasteland and mountainous terrain. Epic cattle drive with an Aussie accent. A-I (br)

Overseas (1991) The lives of three French sisters (Nicole Garcia, Marianne Basler, and Brigitte Rouan) are individually portrayed as each copes with domestic crises in the midst of the 1950s Algerian War. Also directed by Rouan, the lyrical tri-part story builds interest as the war takes its sobering toll on the stalwart sisters and their loved ones. Subtitles. Momentary violence and fleeting nudity. A-III (nr)

Owl and the Pussycat, The (1970) Barbra Streisand plays a would-be model working as a part-time hooker, and George Segal is a would-be writer working in a bookstore who, when both are kicked out of their apartments, find themselves the oddest of bedfellows. Director Herbert Ross undercuts the situation's potential for lighthearted comedy by giving it an overly realistic treatment, emphasizing its acceptance of casual sex. O (R/PG)

Ox, The (1992) Fact-based Swedish period-piece begins in 1868, when a young man (Stellan Skarsgard) is sentenced to life imprisonment for slaughtering his employer's ox to feed his starving family, but the village vicar (Max Von Sydow) perseveres in a years-long effort to get him released and restored to his tormented wife (Ewa Froling). Director Sven Nykvist's drama of justice and compassion captures the diverse humanity of its characters with spare dialogue, expert acting, and achingly beautiful images. Subtitles. Minor violence and an implied sexual encounter. A-III (nr)

Oxford Blues (1984) Director Robert Boris badly bungles this remake of **A Yank at Oxford** (1938) by making its hero (Rob Lowe) such a dislikable heel that most American viewers probably will cheer for the British when he takes on the upper-class establishment. Favorable attitude toward sexual promiscuity. O (PG-13)

PCU (1994) Witless, brain-dead comedy about a politically correct university whose shrewish president (Jessica Walter) overlooks protesting radical groups while seeking to expel a party-minded pack of students (led by Jeremy Piven) plotting her downfall. Instead of topical satire, director Hart Bochner has little to offer but a feeble collection of sophomoric students and their lame shenanigans. Fleeting violence, some sexual references, brief recreational drug use, and an instance of rough language. A-III (PG-13)

PT 109 (1963) Drawn-out account of future President John F. Kennedy (Cliff Robertson) as a torpedo-boat skipper in the South Pacific, where he saves his marooned crew after their ship is rammed by a Japanese destroyer. Director Leslie H. Martinson turns the wartime action into standard all-American heroics whose chief interest is Robertson's likeable performance in the impossible role of a flawless character. Wartime violence. A-I (br)

Pacific Heights (1990) After moving into their newly purchased Victorian home, a young couple (Melanie Griffith and Matthew Modine) rent its studio to a devious sociopath (Michael Keaton) who twists the law in hopes of wresting the house's ownership from them. Director John Schlesinger's psychological thriller is full of dark doings and murky motivation, but only the good performances lift it beyond run-of-the-mill fare. Some violence, acceptance of premarital sex, brief nudity, and occasional rough language. A-III (R)

Pacific Liner (1939) Static melodrama directed by Lew Landers about an outbreak of cholera among the crew of a 1932 American ocean-liner, which the ship's doctor (Chester Morris) tries to keep from spreading to the passengers, while the engineer (Victor McLaglen) pushes a diminishing number of coal-stokers to keep the engines turning to reach port. Stylized violence, menacing situations, and sexual innuendo. A-II (br)

Pacific Vibrations (1971) Producer-director John Severson's documentary presents a colorful and musically pulsating portrait of the West Coast surfer. His treatment, however, tries a bit too hard to de-emphasize the joyousness of this obviously fun sport and tries to elevate it into something of sociological significance and ecological importance in the battle to save the California coastline. Some discussion of hedonistic lifestyles. A-II (G)

Pack Up Your Troubles (1932) Stan Laurel and Oliver Hardy are up to their usual tricks as WW I doughboys whose blunders at the front capture a German position, then return home to help a dead buddy's little girl find her grandparents. Directed by George Marshall and Raymond McCarey, the disjointed plot isn't much but serves up enough funny business for the boys to keep viewers laughing at their muddled antics. Slapstick violence and domestic complications. A-II (br)

Package, The (1989) In an otherwise middling espionage thriller, Gene Hackman gives a sterling performance as an Army sergeant whose search for an escaped prisoner uncovers an international military conspiracy. Director Andrew Davis fails to evoke much suspense in proceedings which ultimately target a world leader for assassination, but gets a truly sinister performance from Tommy Lee Jones as Hackman's principal adversary. Some intense violence and profanity. A-III (R)

Pad and How to Use It, The (1966) Weak sex-comedy adapted from a Peter Shaffer play about an inept young man (Brian Bedford) and his pursuit of a swinger (Julie Sommars). Directed by Brian G. Hutton, it makes extensive use of sexual innuendo. A-III (br)

Paddy (1970) Irish production about a supposedly likeable but totally irresponsible Dublin lad (Des Cave) who alternately services a middle-aged widow (Judy Cornwell), indulges in occasional orgies, and fathers a child with a girlfriend (Dearbhla Molloy), whom he abandons. Directed by Daniel Haller, the episodic movie wanders about aimlessly, uncertain of its theme, statement, or sympathies in telling the story of an immature teenager. O (PG)

Pagemaster, The (1994) Bland, mostly animated tale starts with a fearful boy (Macaulay Culkin) wandering into a library, where the librarian (Christopher Lloyd) magically turns into a wizard, providing the young worrywart with experiences of adventure, horror and fantasy which leave him a braver lad for having faced up to his fears. Director Maurice Hunt animated effort is a tame affair which preaches the value of reading without offering young viewers much in the way of wonder or imagination. A-I (G)

Pain in the A—, A (1975) French farce in which a professional assassin (Lino Ventura) checks into a hotel to carry out a job, but the bungling attempts at suicide by the man in the next room (Jacques Brel) distract him with a series of frenetic mishaps. Director Edouard Molinaro keeps things moving at a good pace, with some fine comic moments, until the one-joke situation finally wears thin. Subtitles. Brief but graphic violence and a comically intended nude scene. A-III (PG)

Paint Your Wagon (1969) Screen adaptation of the Lerner and Loewe musical about two mining partners (Lee Marvin and Clint Eastwood) who "marry" the discarded second wife (Jean Seberg) of a pioneer Mormon, though monogamy triumphs in the end. Director Josh Logan's lavish production has plenty of lush scenery and swirling action to go with the lively songs and dances, but it's all pretty earthbound entertainment. Some frontier humor and ambiance are not for all tastes. A-III (M)

Painted Hills, The (1951) Western adventure starring Lassie as the canine pal of a prospector (Paul Kelly) who strikes gold, then is murdered by his partner (Bruce Cowling), though the courageous collie prevents him from getting away with the crime. Directed by Harold F. Kress, the simple story of a dog's devotion to her master has plenty of country charm to balance the threatening situations facing a young boy (Gary Gray) who happens to discover the murder. A-I (br)

Painters Painting (1973) Documentary on the postwar rise and influence of New York as a center of the art world, it consists mainly of interviews with many of those who contributed to this development, from de Kooning to Warhol, as well as some prominent art dealers and collectors. Produced and directed by Emile De Antonio, it is a valuable resource for the history of contemporary American art. A-I (nr)

Painting the Clouds with Sunshine (1951) Lackluster musical directed by David Butler in which a trio of women singers (Virginia Mayo, Lucille Norman, and Virginia Gibson) seeking husbands in Las Vegas find themselves pursued by a singer (Dennis Morgan), a rich hoofer (Gene Nelson), and the hoofer's prim cousin (Tom Conway). Romantic complications. A-II (br)

Pajama Game, The (1957) Successful adaptation of the Broadway musical about pajama-factory workers ready to strike over a pay raise until their union representative (Doris Day) falls for the factory's new manager (John Raitt). Directed by George Abbott and Stanley Donen, the intrusion of romance into a labor-management dispute has interest, but what works best are the Richard Adler-Jerry Ross songs, including "7-1/2 Cents," "Hernando's Hideaway," "Hey There," "Once-a-Year Day," and Carol Haney's specialty number, "Steam Heat." Sexual situations and innuendo. A-III (br)

Pajama Party (1964) Lame **Beach Party** fare directed by Don Weis gets nowhere with a nonsensical plot involving an extraterrestrial infiltrator (Tommy Kirk) preparing the way for a Martian invasion, a crook (Jesse White) whose Indian guide (Buster Keaton) tries to rob a wealthy widow (Elsa Lanchester), a biker gang (led by Harvey Lembeck), and aging teenagers (Annette Funicello and Jody McCrea). Slapstick violence and heavy sexual innuendo. A-III (br)

Palaces of a Queen (1967) Documentary tour of Buckingham Palace, St. James Palace, Windsor Castle, Kensington Palace, and the Palace of Holyroodhouse in Edinburgh, showing the art treasures, architecture, and furnishings of a royal way of life long past. Directed by Michael Ingrams and narrated by Sir Michael Redgrave, it is an agreeable way to renew a sense of history, though most youngsters will find it a long sit. A-I (br)

Pale Flower (1974) This 1964 Japanese-gangster melodrama tells the story of a hit-man (Ryo Ikebe) who gets out of prison, meets a beautiful but compulsive gambler, pulls another job, and returns to jail. Director Masahiro Shinoda builds up the alienated ambiance of the Tokyo criminal underworld into an exotic but convincing picture of crime familiar the world over. A-III (nr)

Pale Rider (1985) Clint Eastwood plays a mysterious stranger who helps a group of embattled miners in their struggle with a brutal magnate determined to take over their claims. In all essentials a remake of **Shane** updated by resort to a little sex and a lot more violence. O (R)

Paleface, The (1948) Wild West comedy in which a tenderfoot with a mail-order degree in dentistry (Bob Hope) is tricked into marrying Calamity Jane (Jane Russell), who uses his dental practice as a cover while searching for a gang supplying guns to the Indians. Directed by Norman Z. McLeod, the comic action is fueled by zany sight gags and zippy one-liners, with Hope in top form as the cowardly hero, and there's even an amusing, Oscar-winning song, "Buttons and Bows." Stylized violence and sexual innuendo. A-II (br)

Pallbearer, The (1996) Comic misfire about a well-meaning wimp (David Schwimmer) who's persuaded to eulogize a high-school classmate he doesn't even remember, then is seduced by the deceased's grief-stricken mother (Barbara Hershey), though he's only interested in wooing a former classmate (Gwyneth Paltrow). Directed by Matt Reeves, the script gives trite treatment to the personal crossroads faced by the title character and his twenty-something pals. Fleeting bedroom scenes, recurring profanity, and an instance of rough language. A-III (PG-13)

Palm Beach Story, The (1942) Daffy romantic comedy in which a wife (Claudette Colbert) tries to help her penniless inventor-husband (Joel McCrea) by leaving him for a millionaire (Rudy Vallee) who has a marriage-minded sister (Mary Astor), but the husband's only concern is getting his wife back. Written and directed by Preston Sturges, the comic premise sets up a wacky variety of witty confusions and funny incidental characters, but the empty-headed, conniving wife adds a sour note to the otherwise entirely frivolous proceedings. Comic treatment of marriage. A-III (br)

Palm Springs Weekend (1963) Dated romantic comedy set in the title desert resort, where Easter-vacationing college students (Troy Donahue, Jerry Van Dyke, Connie Stevens, and others) team up with a movie stuntman (Ty Hardin), a troubled playboy (Robert Conrad), and the local police-chief's daughter (Stefanie Powers). Directed by Norman Taurog, the formula plot has no surprises, though some of the frothy mating games go seriously sour. Stylized violence with a youth gang and sexual situations. A-III (br)

Palmetto (1998) Absurd thriller in which an embittered ex-con (Woody Harrelson) is ensnared by a seductive woman (Elisabeth Shue) in an elaborate kidnapping scheme that leaves him framed for murder. Directed by Volker Schlondorff, the glaring lapses in logic reduce this film noir to mere pulp. Some violence, discreet sexual encounters, much rough language, and occasional profanity. A-III (R)

Palomino, The (1950) Simple story of a cattleman's son (Jerome Courtland) who helps save a Chicano horse-ranch by finding its prize palomino and the thieves who stole it. Directed by Ray Novarro, the thin plot and perfunctory acting won't keep youngsters from enjoying the antics of a palomino colt and the majesty of its sire. A-I (br)

Palooka (1934) Wacky comedy in which the dim farm-boy of the title (Stuart Erwin) knocks out the middleweight boxing champ (William Cagney), then falls for a gold digger (Lupe Velez) and ignores the advice of his manager (Jimmy Durante) and his mother (Marjorie Rambeau) about a rematch with the ex-champ. Directed by Ben Stoloff, the humor revolves around the naive rustic whose invincible innocence stymies all the sharpsters trying to exploit him. Stylized ring violence, heavy drinking, and sexual innuendo. A-III (br)

Palookaville (1996) Low-key comedy about three jobless Jersey City losers who halfheartedly plan robberies to pay the bills but bungle their every attempt. Director Alan Taylor maintains a consistently wry tone as the basic humanity of its would-be felons keeps the trio reluctantly on the straight and narrow. Fleeting sexual innuendo, brief nudity, and recurring rough language with profanity. A-III (R)

Pancho Villa (1973) Telly Savalas plays the Mexican revolutionary as a blithering idiot who forces his advocates to watch home movies of his exploits when he is not abusing women or cynically executing opponents. Director Gene Martin occasionally interrupts the juvenile horseplay to stage some tiresome shootouts and a head-on train collision. There's more entertainment in Villa's encyclopedia entry. A-III (PG)

Pandora and the Flying Dutchman (1952) Dark romantic fantasy set in a 1930s Spanish port where an American beauty (Ava Gardner) spurns several lovers (notably Nigel Patrick and Mario Cabre) to sail off with a mysterious sea-captain (James Mason). Writer-director Albert Lewin delivers a visually pretty but mawkishly pretentious melodrama based on the legend of a Dutch captain doomed to wander the seas in a ghost ship until he finds a woman willing to die for him. Sexual situations and stylized violence, including a gory bullfight. A-III (br)

Panic in Needle Park, The (1971) Grim and harshly realistic love story about a wasted junkie (Al Pacino) struggling to survive in New York City's underworld of drugs, and his doomed romance with the girl (Kitty Winn) he introduces to hard drugs and who then turns tricks to feed their habit. Directed by Jerry Schatzberg, the drama convincingly shows the horrors of drug addiction and its toll on human potential. Much brutality and foul language, with graphic depiction of heroin injections and occasional nudity. A-III (R/PG)

Panic in the Streets (1950) Gripping thriller about a medical officer (Richard Widmark) in New Orleans to track down carriers of a deadly plague before it blossoms into a runaway epidemic, but he needs police help when the trail leads to some murderous street criminals (Jack Palance and Zero Mostel). Director Elia Kazan combines fine performances, striking location photography, and a credible story to heighten the tension over the city's plight until an edge-of-the-seat chase through waterfront locales nabs the carriers. Stylized violence, menacing situations, and marital discord. A-III (br)

Panther (1995) Sketchy dramatization recounts the rise of the Black Panther movement in 1967 Oakland as seen through the eyes of a fictional recruit (Kadeem Hardison) who becomes a confidant of Panther leader Huey Newton (Marcus Chong), then a double agent for both police and Panthers, until the FBI destabilizes the movement by flooding the ghetto with cheap drugs. Scripted by Melvin Van Peebles and directed by his son, Mario, the result simplifies both the era's politics and the movement's ideology by spending most of its time depicting the racist brutality of the police and the Panther's turn to arms in self-defense. Graphic depictions of bloody confrontations between white policemen and African Americans, drug trafficking, and recurring rough language. A-IV (R)

Papa's Delicate Condition (1963) Nostalgic melodrama about a turn-of-the-century Texas family whose railroad executive father (Jackie Gleason) does strange things, such as buying a circus, when he overimbibes — the condition of the title. Directed by George Marshall, the potential charm of the family story is often stifled by scenes overindulging the star for whom this served as a vehicle. Comic intemperance. A-I (br)

Paper, The (1994) City-news editor (Michael Keaton) of a New York tabloid battles the managing editor (Glenn Close) over the front-page coverage of a racially charged murder while struggling with the wishes of his very pregnant, neglected wife (Marisa Tomei) to take a less demanding job offered by an arrogant competitor (Spalding Gray). Director Ron Howard's ensemble comedy-drama conveys the frantic pressures of one fractious day in a big-city newsroom, but its stressed-out characters are too sketchily drawn to involve viewers in their assorted personal crises. Brief violence, some adulterous innuendo, and frequent rough language. A-III (R)

Paper Chase, The (1973) First-year Harvard law student Hart (Timothy Bottoms) quickly finds himself torn between the cool, cruel competitive life of the intellect, personified in distinguished law contracts professor Kingsfield (John Houseman, who steals the show), and the warm, sensuous, spontaneous life of the body, personified in Kingsfield's daughter (Lindsay Wagner). Director James Bridges conveys well the pressures of campus life, especially in Hart's study-group with students whose varied personalities and weaknesses represent a cross-section of humanity. Mature treatment, although accessible for older teenagers. A-III (PG)

Paper Lion (1968) Alan Alda stars as journalist George Plimpton investigating the world of professional football by actually playing quarterback for the Detroit Lions. Directed by Alex March, it's a fairly interesting football movie for those who don't normally follow the sport. A-I (G)

Paper Mask (1992) Murky psychological drama has an ambitious hospital orderly (Paul McGann) successfully assuming the identity of a deceased doctor until his nurse-girlfriend (Amanda Donohue) learns the truth and must decide what to do. British producer-director Christopher Morahan's initially interesting tale of deadly deception steadily falters until its flimsy conclusion. Brief bedroom shots with nudity and minimal violence. A-III (R)

Paper Moon (1973) Entertaining period comedy in which a bumbling con-man (Ryan O'Neal) finds himself saddled with a nine-year-old girl (Tatum O'Neal) who proves to be more adept at his profession than he is. Directed by Peter Bogdanovich, there is occasional rough language and adult references. A-III (PG)

Paper Tiger (1976) David Niven plays a mild-mannered schoolteacher tutoring the young son of a Japanese official (Toshiro Mifune) when terrorists strike and kidnap both of them. Although the film is sentimental and poorly directed by Ken Annakin, it conveys effectively the influence upon a youngster of an imaginative adult who proves hero is when put to the test. The movie's realistic treatment of terrorist violence may adversely affect its intended preteen audience. A-II (PG)

Paper Wedding, The (1991) An unplanned romance develops when a Canadian immigration official suspects that a Montreal schoolteacher (Genevieve Bujold) has married a swarthy dishwasher (Manuel Aranguiz) in order to save him from political persecution back in Chile. Director Michel Brault's unpretentious movie is a slight but rather sweet love story that gradually brings out the best in its varied characters. Subtitles. An extramarital affair and flash of nudity. A-III (nr)

Paperback Romance (1997) Charmless story set in Australia, where a writer of erotic romances (Gia Carides) tries to disguise a physical disability while pursuing an engaged jeweler (Anthony LaPaglia), whose shady dealings lead the police to investigate her. Writer-director Ben Lewin's clumsy romantic comedy relies heavily on pratfalls in a poorly contrived narrative filled with unconvincing, one-dimensional characters. Fleeting bedroom scenes with nudity and a cavalier treatment of grand theft. A-III (R)

Paperhouse (1989) Troubled by her mother's minimal attention and her father's lengthy absences, an 11-year-old (Charlotte Burke) is consumed with her drawings of an odd, isolated house inhabited by a crippled boy (Elliott Spiers), which are translated into frightening dreams when she comes down with a fever. British director Bernard Rose imbues his haunting psychological drama with riveting, surreal visuals, some unanswered questions, and a far-fetched ending. Intense climatic violence, ongoing menace, and some rough language. A-III (PG-13)

Papillon (1973) Steve McQueen and Dustin Hoffman star in this generally entertaining drama of one man's daring attempts to escape from Devil's Island, an inhumane penal system designed to break both body and spirit. Director Franklin Schaffner neatly balances adventure and spectacle with a vivid depiction of the horrors of prison life. Viewers may not appreciate some of the brutality and references to masturbation and homosexuality, yet such scenes are necessary to the factual description of the convict's world and are in no way sensationalized. A-III (PG)

Parade (1974) French comedian Jacques Tati serves up some of his classic pantomime routines, including a one-man tennis match, as part of a one-ring circus featuring everything from horseback riders to magic acts and a comic chorus of acrobats. Also written and directed by Tati, the uneven result is more a comic variety show than traditional circus entertainment, but what makes it special is the bemusing byplay backstage and in the audience, especially among the children in attendance. Though there are a few words in French and some in English, the show depends entirely on the visuals. Genial family fun. A-I (nr)

Parades (1972) Muddled film-within-a-film story follows the making of a documentary about a pacifist soldier's suicide, which triggers a riot and the massacre of protesting students outside a military stockade. Though well-intentioned, director Robert J. Siegel's dramatization is artificial and unconvincing, while the issues it raises are treated inadequately. Some sadistic violence and coarse language. A-III (R)

Paradine Case, The (1948) Courtroom misfire from director Alfred Hitchcock in which an English barrister (Gregory Peck) becomes so enthralled with a client (Valli) charged with poisoning her wealthy husband that he tries to prove the man's valet (Louis Jourdan) was the murderer. The pedestrian proceedings are centered in the lawyer's infatuation and the hurt this causes his wife (Ann Todd), but the result is oddly unemotional and, despite an excellent cast, largely uninteresting. Sexual references. A-II (br)

Paradise (1982) Two teenagers (Phoebe Cates and Willie Aames) survive an attack on their caravan and find bliss in various lushly appointed oases in director Stuart Gillard's shoddy, trashy little movie that attempts to do the **Blue Lagoon** number with camels. Exploitative nudity and graphic sex. O (R)

Paradise (1991) Touching story of a young boy (Elijah Wood) who comes to live with an emotionally estranged couple (Melanie Griffith and Don Johnson) mired in individual grief over the loss of their toddler son. Writer-director Mary Agnes

Donoghue's well-acted picture interweaves several stories about relationships for an evocative look at childhood fears and adult pain. Fleeting shot of a sexual encounter, glimpse of nudity, and several sexual references. A-III (PG-13)

Paradise Alley (1978) Sylvester Stallone (who also wrote and directed), stars as one of three tough brothers from the New York slums trying for big money in the wrestling ring in the 1940s. Rivalry between brothers and the machinations of a petty gangster (Kevin Conway) complicate matters. Though the movie has a few good moments, it never rises above the level of pulp melodrama and sometimes sinks to that of a cartoon. The violence of the wrestling sequences make this mature viewing fare. A-III (PG)

Paradise, Hawaiian Style (1966) Innocuous Elvis Presley vehicle directed by Michael Moore in another Hawaiian musical romance. A-I (br)

Paradise Lost: The Child Murders at Robin Hood Hills (1996) Unsettling documentary chronicles the 1994 Arkansas murder trials of three teenage boys accused of killing three eight-year-old boys as part of a satanic ritual. Producer-directors Joe Berlinger and Bruce Sinofsky's record of the trials includes the raw emotions of the accused and the victims' families in a provocative account raising questions about the evidence and the verdicts. Shots of nude corpses, graphic descriptions of mutilation, and sexual references. A-III (nr)

Paradise Road (1997) A group of European women (led by Glenn Close and Pauline Collins) form a vocal orchestra to keep up their spirits while struggling to survive the deprivations and brutalities of a Japanese prison camp in the Dutch East Indies during WW II. Writer-director Bruce Beresford's fact-based dramatization of the women's ordeal succeeds in showing the bleak conditions of camp life, but even the main characters are treated as little more than stereotypes, and the triumph of the vocal orchestra seems hollow in comparison to the women's tragic circumstances. Numerous scenes of brutality, sexual references, and flashes of nudity. A-III (R)

Parallax View, The (1974) Gripping thriller about an unorthodox reporter (Warren Beatty) whose investigation of a senator's assassination leads him to suspect that the murder was the work of a nationwide conspiracy. Though it's bit too contrived, director Alan Pakula keeps the action tense and taut until the sudden, smashing climax. The result is a first-rate suspense chiller that makes clever use of a number of political conspiracy theories without pretending to be a serious statement on the subject. Some violence and rough language. A-III (R)

Parasite (1982) Robert Glaudini plays a scientist with nothing better to do than developing creatures that fasten onto people, propagate, and burst out at odd moments through various sections of their victim's anatomy. Directed by Charles Band, it is a loathsome exercise in nausea. Excessively graphic sex and violence. O (R)

Paratrooper (1953) Routine war story with an angry young Yank (Alan Ladd) joining an elite British airborne unit in 1940 and his difficulties with the outfit, until proving his leadership on the battlefield. Director Terence Young is helped by a fine stiff-upper-lip cast (Leo Genn, Harry Andrews, and Stanley Baker) but is hampered by the script's focus on the American's struggle with his personal problems. Wartime violence. A-I (br)

Pardon Mon Affaire (1977) French sex farce about a middle-aged man (Jean Rochefort) who is encouraged by his friends to seduce a beautiful model (Anny Duperey), and his infidelity leads to a comic expose in full view of television-news cameras. Director Yves Robert has a difficult time striking the proper balance between the comic and the serious in a story devoted to an adulterous situation. O (PG)

Pardon My Past (1945) Returning GI (Fred MacMurray) gets into heaps of trouble when mistaken for a dissolute lookalike playboy with an estranged wife and a large debt owed an impatient bookie. Directed by Leslie Fenton, the mistaken-identity plot generates some weak smiles with occasional heart-tugs from a romantic subplot involving Marguerite Chapman. Romantic complications. A-II (br)

Parent Trap, The (1961) Identical twins (Hayley Mills), raised separately by parents (Maureen O'Hara and Brian Keith) who split up shortly after their birth, learn of the other's existence at summer camp, and concoct an elaborate scheme to get Mom and Dad back together again. Typical sentimental Walt Disney family comedy, with parents having the IQ of domestic pets and no match for precocious youngsters. Still, it's genial and mostly heartwarming, with good acting thrown in for good measure. A-I (br)

Parent Trap, The (1998) Slow-paced but often charming re-make of the 1961 tale of 11-year-old identical twin sisters (Lindsay Lohan as both) whose parents had divorced when they were infants, one going to England with the mother (Natasha Richardson), while the other remained in California with the father (Dennis Quaid), until the sisters finally meet in summer camp, then switch places on their return home and set to work reuniting their parents. Directed by Nancy Myers, the sentimental premise yields a number of heartwarming moments, and the mischievous antics of the twins provides some comic relief, but the feel-good results are superficial at best. Some unamusing pranks and a scene of amateur ear-piercing. A-II (PG)

Parenthood (1989) Disappointing comedy-drama about four generations of one troubled American family, centering on a 35-year-old (Steve Martin) and his father (Jason Robards). Director Ron Howard catalogs some very real problems faced by modern single- and two-parent households, but, much like sitcoms, the vignettes have no depth or follow-through. Much sexual innuendo, vulgar language, and some female stereotyping. A-III (PG-13)

Parents (1989) Corny satire of 1950s suburbia

employs a grisly theme of cannibalism as practiced by a supposedly perfect mom (Mary Beth Hurt) and dad (Randy Quaid), whose morose son (Bryan Madorsky) turns out to be the only sane one in the family. Director Bob Balaban carefully creates a sense of menace in picture postcard 1950s America, but destroys it all with an unpalatably bloody ending. Much climactic gore and stomach-turning implications of suburban cannibalism. O (R)

Paris After Dark (1943) Hokey WW II morale-booster directed by Leonide Moguy about a French doctor (George Sanders) who works for the Resistance, his anti-Nazi nurse (Brenda Marshall), and her husband (Philip Dorn), who returns from a German prison camp a broken man but winds up a Free French hero. Stylized violence, including a Nazi massacre of hostages and the grisly murder of an informer. A-II (br)

Paris Blues (1961) Expatriate jazz musicians Paul Newman and Sidney Poitier pair up with tourists Joanne Woodward and Diahann Carroll, sharing the sights of Paris and their beds. Director Martin Ritt's bittersweet romance has a fine jazz score but bogs down in self-conscious soul-searching about love, musical genius, and race relations. Implied sexual relationships. A-III (br)

Paris Holiday (1958) Leaden comedy about an American comedian (Bob Hope) whose life is threatened when he goes to France to buy a hot script. Directed by Gerd Oswald, the international cast (Fernandel, Anita Ekberg, and Marta Hyer) never jells in a slapdash narrative whose highlight is Hope's stay in a mental clinic. Occasional slapstick violence and double entendres. A-I (br)

Paris, Texas (1984) Father and son are reunited, and then son and mother are reunited, as dad rides off into the sunset. Directed by Wim Wenders, it is a pretentious and boring effort with a hero (Harry Dean Stanton) who at first won't talk and then won't stop talking. Some rough language. A-II (R)

Paris Vu Par ... (see: **Six in Paris**)

Paris — When It Sizzles (1964) Failed romantic comedy set in Paris, where an American screenwriter (William Holden) and a typist (Audrey Hepburn) work out a script by imagining themselves as characters in a crime thriller, which inevitably turns into a love story. Directed by Richard Quine, the contrived situations are more heavy-handed than lighthearted, and the hammy results have little wit and less charm. Sexual innuendo. A-III (br)

Park Avenue Logger (1937) Adventure programmer directed by David Howard in which a millionaire's son (George O'Brien) becomes a logger in his father's Oregon lumber mill to learn the business, then saves it from some corrupt employees (notably Ward Bond). Stylized violence. A-I (br)

Parrish (1961) Dreary potboiler in which a young man (Troy Donahue) goes to work for the Connecticut tobacco grower (Karl Malden) whom his mother (Claudette Colbert) has married, then quits his unscrupulous stepfather to work for his less wealthy but more honorable rival (Dean Jagger). Directed by Delmer Daves, the soapy proceedings are awash in inept plotting, overripe acting, and unconvincing situations, especially the young man's romantic appeal to a variety of local women. Sexual situations and innuendo. A-III (br)

Part 2, Sounder (1976) Tepid sequel continuing the story of a black family of sharecroppers in the rural Louisiana of the 1930s focuses on how the father (Harold Sylvester) rallies his neighbors to build a new school that will keep the teacher (Annazette Chase) from leaving for a better job in the North. Produced, as was the original, by Robert B. Radnitz and directed by William A. Graham, the plot is disappointingly predictable, but some fine acting, the beauty of the setting, and its earnest sense of humanity make it above-average family entertainment. A-I (G)

Part 2, Walking Tall (1975) Sequel, far more restrained and low key than its violent predecessor, picks up the story of Sheriff Buford Pusser as he searches for the criminals who killed his wife, but, by sequel's end, the man responsible is still at liberty. Capably directed by Earl Bellamy, Svenson's characterization of the fighting sheriff is much more credible than the melodramatic script. A-III (PG)

Partner (1974) Heavy-handed Italian production about a schizophrenic drama teacher (Pierre Clementi) whose other personality is that of a violent revolutionary. Directed by Bernardo Bertolucci in the heat of the political upheavals of 1968, the drama tries to relate art to politics, making an unconvincing statement about revolution as a creative act. Suicide figures into the abstract plot-line. A-III (nr)

Parson and the Outlaw, The (1957) After hanging up his guns for good, Billy the Kid (Anthony Dexter) comes out shooting when his preacher friend (Buddy Rogers) is ruthlessly gunned down. Directed by Oliver Drake, it's a clunker despite the hardworking cast (including Sonny Tufts, Bob Steele and Marie Windsor). Stylized violence overcomes pacifist premise. A-II (br)

Partners (1982) Ryan O'Neal and John Hurt star as detectives, one of them homosexual, who are assigned to pose as a homosexual couple in order to investigate a murder in a stupid comedy directed by James Burrows. O'Neal and Hurt struggle admirably with an underdeveloped script that turns homosexual and heterosexual characters alike into insulting stereotypes. Exploitative nudity. O (R)

Party, The (1968) Well-meaning, disaster-prone actor from India (Peter Sellers), instead of receiving a pink slip for his unwitting sabotage on a remake of **Gunga Din**, gets an invitation to the producer's home for a pretentious Hollywood party that he turns into total chaos. Director Blake Edwards borrows liberally from the situations and sight gags of silent slapstick, but in the thin, one-joke context of a hopeless bungler, the hilarity soon gives way to tedious repetitiousness, especially in a prolonged and tasteless bathroom sequence. A-III (br)

Party Girl (1958) Mediocre crime film set in Prohibition-era Chicago, where a mobster's mouthpiece (Robert Taylor) turns on his boss (Lee J. Cobb) in order to save his showgirl-lover (Cyd Charisse). Director Nicholas Ray finds few fresh angles in a hackneyed story of shifting loyalties. Nasty stylized violence and sexual innuendo. A-III (br)

Party Girl (1995) Marginally amusing tale in which an empty-headed 23-year-old New Yorker (Parker Posey) turns from the funky nightlife scene toward maturity when her scathingly critical godmother (Sasha von Scherler) hires her as a library clerk. Director Daisy von Scherler Mayer wryly de-glamorizes the dissolute world of after-hours partying while her bubble-headed heroine undergoes a positive transformation. Flippant treatment of substance abuse and petty thievery, an implied sexual encounter, brief nudity, and much rough language. A-IV (R)

Pascali's Island (1988) Adaptation of Barry Unsworth's novel set on an Aegean island in 1908, where a Turkish spy (Ben Kingsley) comes under the spell of a fast-talking but secretive British archaeologist (Charles Dance). Director James Dearden slowly unfolds his plot of a man who has dealt so long in deceit that he ultimately cannot trust those who would save his life. Fleeting nudity and a bloody climax. A-III (PG-13)

Passage, The (1979) WW II story about a fiendish Nazi (Malcolm McDowell) who pursues an escaping scientist (James Mason) and his family across the Pyrenees, where they get help from a stalwart Basque guide (Anthony Quinn). Mediocre British production directed by J. Lee Thompson, it is filled to excess with sadistic violence and brutality. O (R)

Passage to India, A (1984) Screen version of the E.M. Forster classic about the inability of two diverse cultures to have any but perilous contact in the British-ruled India of the 1920s as seen in a story centering around a question of rape. Though painstakingly crafted by director David Lean and superbly acted by an outstanding cast (Judy Davis, Victor Banerjee, Dame Peggy Ashcroft, James Fox, and Alec Guinness), the movie fails to dramatize convincingly the mysticism at the heart of its theme. Flawed but culturally rich entertainment. A-II (PG)

Passage West (1951) Tedious tale in which escaped convicts from a Utah prison hijack a wagon-train of Christian homesteaders bound for California, but by trail's end the pioneer preacher (Dennis O'Keefe) has transformed the convict's leader (John Payne). Writer-director Lewis R. Foster stages a potentially interesting situation in unconvincing fashion with a gold-strike ending that's pure hokum. Stylized violence and minor romantic complications. A-II (br)

Passed Away (1992) Ensemble comedy concerns the reunion of a bickering Irish-American family (Pamela Reed, Bob Hoskins, William Petersen, and Frances McDormand) upon the sudden death of their father (Jack Warden). Writer-director Charlie Peters turns in a fitfully funny movie whose one-dimensional characters are entirely predictable. Frequent sexual innuendo and an instance of rough language. A-III (PG-13)

Passenger, The (1970) Polish production about two women who meet by accident on an ocean liner, triggering memories of their days in a concentration camp together: one a Nazi officer, the other a prisoner. Both stories are related subjectively in flashback, and their differing perspectives become both fascinating and disturbing. Although director Andrej Munk died before the movie's completion, what he did accomplish are brilliant fragments in a compelling exploration of human motivation and justification. A-III (nr)

Passenger, The (1975) Empty Italian drama in which a TV journalist (Jack Nicholson), exasperated by an assignment in North Africa and acting on impulse, switches passport photos with a European who dies of a heart attack and finds that he has assumed the identity of an international gunrunner. Director Michelangelo Antonioni has made a visually stunning work, yet its plot contrivances are more irritating than mysterious, and its delving into the interior of its characters is without interest. A-III (PG)

Passenger 57 (1992) Standard action yarn pits a ruthless British terrorist (Bruce Payne) against an airline security expert (Wesley Snipes) onboard a hijacked L-1011 as the lives of 200 passengers hang in the balance. Director Kevin Hooks delivers a fast-moving, somewhat muddled plot in which violence is an inevitable but not unduly glamorized ingredient. Much menace with frequent violence and some rough language. A-III (R)

Passion (1954) When the Mexican authorities refuse to arrest the gang who murdered his family in Old California, a 19th-century ranchero (Cornel Wilde) sets out on his own to bring them to justice, with a little help from the sister (Yvonne De Carlo) of his dead bride. Directed by Allan Dwan, the formula plot and stereotyped characters are enlivened by some good action sequences and the colorful Hispanic settings. Stylized violence and a common-law marriage. A-II (br)

Passion Fish (1992) A former TV soap-opera star (Mary McDonnell), embittered by an accident that left her a paraplegic, is cared for by a no-nonsense nurse (Alfre Woodard) who is secretly battling her own demons. Writer-director John Sayles's intimate portrait of the anguished, interior struggles of two women is unsentimental and affecting when not bogged down by its sleepy pace. An implied sexual encounter and intermittent rough language. A-III (R)

Passion of Anna, The (1970) Swedish production about a human cipher (Max von Sydow), living hermit-like on a small island, who becomes friendly with a cynical architect (Erland Josephson), his wife (Bibi Andersson), and their close friend Anna (Liv Ullmann). Eventually he and Anna share their loneliness, then part even more hopeless than when they first met. Director Ingmar Bergman's bleak vision of people unable to find salvation from existential despair questions the meaning of life. A suicide and brief shots of mutilated animals combined with the moral ambiguity of the brief affair make this adult fare. A-III (R)

Passion of Joan of Arc, The (1928) Silent screen masterpiece portraying the heresy trial, confession, recantation, and execution of the Maid of Orleans (Maria Falconetti) in a performance of such emotional power that it still stands as the most convincing portrayal of spirituality on celluloid. Directed by Carl Dreyer, the work is essentially the interior epic of a soul, consisting largely of close-ups of Joan's face and those of her interrogators accomplished in a fashion which is never static, as the camera explores the inner struggle between human frailties and spiritual strength. Some duplicitous churchmen, medicinal bloodletting, and a restrained torture scene. A-II (br)

Passover Plot, The (1977) Dramatization of a book by biblical archaeologist Hugh J. Schonfield presents Jesus as a good and pious man who believed himself to be the Messiah, but his plan to fake his death by Roman crucifixion failed, leaving his disciples to invent the story of his resurrection. Directed by Michael Campos, the movie is deeply flawed in narrative construction, acting, and production values, but many Christians will find its muddled attempt to demythologize the Gospels repugnant. O (PG)

Passport to Pimlico (1949) Upon learning that a medieval document found in a WW II bomb-crater makes London's Pimlico district a part of Burgundy, the residents (led by Stanley Holloway, Margaret Rutherford, and Hermione Baddeley) promptly form their own government, declare an end to post-war rationing, and enter into negotiations with the British Foreign Office. Scripted by T.E.B. Clarke and directed by Henry Cornelius, the scenario takes matters to hilarious extremes, as Whitehall diplomacy is outwitted by the spunky tactics of beleaguered Pimlico in a delightful comedy of ordinary folk showing up the weaknesses of officialdom. A-I (br)

Pastime (1991) Old-fashioned sports story set in the mid-1950s, when an over-the-hill minor-league baseball pitcher (William Russ) befriends an insecure black rookie (Glenn Plummer) ignored by his teammates. Directed by Robin B. Armstrong, the heartwarming if simplistic story of black and white heroes and villains is soft on dramatic tension but strong on sentiment and values. Brief fisticuffs and a veiled sexual reference. A-I (PG)

Pat and Mike (1952) Offbeat romantic comedy teams veteran sports-promoter Mike (Spencer Tracy) with top amateur-athlete Pat (Katharine Hepburn), who's aces in any competition except when her beau (William Ching) is watching. Directed by George Cukor, it's Hepburn's picture, with Tracy cheering her on as she goes through her winning paces, including a scene in which Pat saves Mike from two thugs. Feminist twist on the battle of the sexes. A-II (br)

Pat Garrett and Billy the Kid (1973) The story of Garrett (James Coburn), in the hire of ruthless cattlemen, tracking down his old saddle-mate Billy (Kris Kristofferson) is intended to show the slow passing of the Western frontier in the 1880s. The end result is a ponderous and depressing study of men whose time has passed. It's a familiar theme for director Sam Peckinpah who, once again, cannot resist graphic depictions of blood-spattered killings and various characters' rough use of women. O (R)

Patch Adams (1998) Fact-based comedy-drama about an idealistic medical student (Robin Williams) whose belief in the healing power of humor leads him to risk dismissal from medical school by opening a nontraditional clinic. Director Tom Shadyac's unsubtle treatment of the unabashedly sentimental story is held together mainly by Williams's ingratiating performance and his character's appealing concept of holistic medicine. An off-screen violent tragedy, fleeting nudity, and a few coarse words, as well as double entendres. A-III (PG-13)

Patch of Blue, A (1965) A blind girl (Elizabeth Hartman), living in a dismal tenement, falls in love with the gentle black neighbor (Sidney Poitier) who befriends her, despite the shrill opposition of her mother (Shelley Winters). Director Guy Green takes an honest look at racial relations, avoids most of the obvious cliches, and scores some points for human values. Mature theme. A-III (br)

Paternity (1981) Callous egomaniac (Burt Reynolds) decides he wants a son and interviews prospective surrogate mothers. Beverly D'Angelo, a musician working as a waitress, gets the job and foolishly falls in love with the boor. Directed by David Steinberg, the ill-conceived romantic plot results in a slack and listless comedy of sexual politics with a false female stereotype and some rough language. A-III (PG)

Pathfinder, The (1952) James Fenimore Cooper's title character (George Montgomery) offers to guide a French force in the American wilderness of 1754 in order to betray them to the English. Director Sidney Solkow's low-budget effort turns the frontier into the usual stereotyped entertainment, however with notably unconvincing action scenes. Stylized violence. A-I (br)

Paths of Glory (1957) The terrible slaughter of WW I is re-created in this fact-based story of a French colonel (Kirk Douglas) who tries to save his men from being court-martialed for cowardice in a failed attack that should never have been ordered. Director Stanley Kubrick's anti-war classic contrasts the horrors of trench warfare at the front with the indifference and incompetence of the generals (Adolphe Menjou and George Macready) safely quartered in the rear. Graphic battlefield violence and a harrowing execution by firing squad. A-II (nr)

Patrick (1979) Tacky little thriller from Australia about a young man (Robert Thompson) who, while being kept alive on a support system, develops a "seventh sense" that enables him to perform all sorts of disgusting stunts when he becomes attached to a pretty nurse (Susan Penhaligon). Directed by Richard Franklin, it is a painful experience in every respect, with violence and a graphic depiction of some alleged medical techniques. A-III (PG)

Patriot Games (1992) Suspenseful thriller from Tom Clancy's novel about an ex-CIA agent (Harrison Ford) who returns to the fold to protect his wife and child (Anne Archer and Thora Birch) from a revenge-crazed IRA terrorist (Sean Bean). Director Phillip Noyce rivets attention on the family's vulnerability but doesn't shield viewers from brutal terrorist executions and violent shootouts. Much violence, a brief bedroom scene, and minimal rough language. A-IV (R)

Patsy, The (1964) After a famous comedian dies in an accident, his staff (John Carradine, Peter Lorre, Everett Sloane, Keenan Wynn, and Ina Balin) decide to turn a hotel bellboy (Jerry Lewis) into his successor. Also written and directed by Lewis, the slack plot and klutzy slapstick action can only appeal to fans of the star's goonish brand of comedy. Mild slapstick violence. A-I (br)

Patterns (1956) Thoughtful drama in which a callous corporation head (Everett Sloane) tries to force an aging executive (Ed Begley) to retire by bringing in a younger man (Van Heflin), but the newcomer has his own ideas about what's best for the company. Adapted by Rod Serling from his teleplay and directed by Fielder Cook, the result is a credible picture of conflict in the executive suite as corporate greed and bottom-line policies are challenged by a more human style of business management. Unlikely fare for children. A-I (br)

Patterns of Power (see: **Patterns**)

Patti Rocks (1988) Boring, pretentious, and ultimately repellent movie in which a married clod (Chris Mulkey) cajoles a friend (John Jenkins) into joining him in trying to persuade his pregnant, out-of-town girlfriend to have an abortion. Director David Burton Morris takes an interminable car-ride with two foul-mouthed sexists that finally ends with a romp in the girlfriend's bed. Unremittingly rough language and simulated sex. O (R)

Patton (1970) George C. Scott's complex portrayal of WW II general George S. Patton conveys a paradoxical, multifaceted character whose love of the fray and intense will to win was grounded in a deep-seated hatred of war itself. Director Franklin Schaffner's powerful dramatization is neither a glorification of war nor an anti-war tract but pays homage to a career officer who, unfortunately, could only achieve his destiny in wartime. Violence and profanity within a realistic context. A-II (PG)

Patty Hearst (1988) The 1974 kidnapping of heiress Patty Hearst (Natasha Richardson) from her Berkeley campus apartment by the Symbionese Liberation Army is told from her point of view in an intense docudrama directed by Paul Schrader. Richardson's mesmerizing performance conveys the brutality and brainwashing Hearst had to endure. Much conscienceless violence, a continuing sense of menace, and wall-to-wall profanity. A-IV (R)

Paul and Michelle (1974) Noxious sequel to **Friends** returns to the perils of Paul (Sean Bury) who finds Michelle (Anicee Alvina) living with their young daughter and an understanding American (Keir Dullea). They fly off to Paris to resume their lives in a morass of sickly sweet dialogue, carefully photographed nudity, Michelle's abortion of the American's baby, Paul's fat allowance being cut off by Daddy, and they separate yet again. Directed by Lewis Gilbert, it is sheer exploitation without pretense of moral perspective. O (R)

Paula (1952) Soggy tearjerker in which the barren wife (Loretta Young) of a college professor (Kent Smith) accidentally runs down a young orphan (Thomas Rettig) leaving him unable to speak, but, with the help of her doctor (Alexander Knox), she adopts the mute boy and teaches him to speak again. Directed by Rudolph Maté, the melodramatic contrivances keep getting in the way of Young's showy display of surface emotion. Delicate treatment of infertility and a youth's protracted trauma. A-II (br)

Paulie (1998) Frail comedy follows the mischievous misadventures of a wisecracking parrot (voice of Jay Mohr) who crisscrosses the country in search of the little girl who first owned him. Director John Roberts surrounds the talkative bird with goodhearted people (including Gena Rowlands and Tony Shalhoub) and one cardboard villain (Bruce Davison) in a sweet, colorful story of modest appeal. A rude expression and a muttered instance of profanity. A-II (PG)

Pauline at the Beach (1983) French comedy about six oddly assorted lovers and would-be lovers who pursue and flee one another at a seaside resort in Brittany in late summer, while talking endlessly about the nature of love. As with director Eric Rohmer's better movies, it is never dull, never less than diverting, but is satisfied with clever surfaces rather than underlying meaning. Extremely mature subject matter. A-IV (R)

Pawnbroker, The (1966) Holocaust survivor (Rod Steiger) runs a pawnshop in Harlem, where his past experiences of oppression are intermingled with the present realities facing the oppressed inhabitants of a black ghetto. Directed by Sidney Lumet, the movie proves a powerful, effective parable on human solidarity and the painful consequences of injustice. Mature theme and treatment. A-III (br)

Pawnee (1957) Western tale of a white youth who's raised as the son of a Pawnee chief (George Montgomery), then has an identity crisis when a wagon train of settlers is attacked by some of his fellow braves. Directed by George Waggner, the situation of a man caught between two worlds offers interesting possibilities, but the personal conflict is secondary to the plot's superficial action. Frontier violence. A-I (br)

Payback (1999) Violent action movie in which a thief (Mel Gibson), cheated of his share of a heist and left for dead, survives to return for the money, murdering one and all who get in the way of his revenge mission. Director Brian Hegeland depicts sadistic violence in a jokey fashion that suggests the killer is a super-cool hero for ending up with the booty, a blonde, and a batch of bodies underfoot. Numerous brutal beatings and killings, sadomasochistic sexual situations, drug abuse, intermittent profanity, and much rough language. O (R)

Payday (1973) Gritty study of second-rate country-western singer (Rip Torn) a whose career has peaked without his even knowing it, and whose life is about to go right over the edge in a series of one-night stands, cheap motel rooms, good bourbon, popped uppers and downers, and a ragged assortment of groupies and hangers-on. Director Daryl Duke's picture of the tormented, self-destructive anti-hero on a lonesome road with nothing at the end has the tragic sense of reality. Some rough language and brief nudity. A-IV (R)

Payment in Blood (1969) Dreary Italian Western set right after the Civil War, when disbanded military freebooters (led by Guy Madison) terrorized the Southwest. Director E.G. Rowland's badly staged violence and even worse acting is a tiresome bore. A-III (R)

Peace Killers, The (1971) Brutal motorcycle gang makes war on a commune of peaceful pot-smokers when one of the gang's women trades in her backseat on a cycle for a snug little sleeping bag at the commune. Directed by Douglas Schwartz, the resulting reprisals would make grown men blanch at scenes of utter brutality, torture, gang rape, and general mayhem. O (R)

Peacemaker, The (1997) Frantic thriller teams an aggressive military-intelligence agent (George Clooney) with a nuclear physicist (Nicole Kidman) in tracking stolen nukes across continents, until they come face-to-face with a madman intent on setting off a doomsday bomb in midtown Manhattan. Director Mimi Leder packs the rushed narrative with car chases and shoot-'em-ups, resulting in an emotionally sterile story of bogus thrills. Frequent violence, intermittent rough language, and a few instances of profanity. A-III (R)

Peach Thief (1969) Disappointing Bulgarian import tells a WW I story about a frustrated young wife (Nevena Kokanova) who has a foredoomed affair with a Serbian prisoner-of-war (Rade Markovich). The meager and predictable story lacks individuality and human resonance. A-III (nr)

Pearl of Death, The (1944) Updated version of Conan Doyle's **The Six Napoleons**, with Sherlock Holmes (Basil Rathbone) and Dr. Watson (Nigel Bruce) out to retrieve the fabled Borgia Pearl from a master criminal (Miles Mander) and devious accomplice (Evelyn Ankers). Directed by Roy William Neill, the mystery has some dandy twists, not least a monstrous killer (Rondo Hatton) who breaks the backs of his victims' as well as their china bric-a-brac. Fairly intense for young children. A-I (br)

Pearl of the South Pacific (1955) Turgid tale directed by Allan Dwan follows a greedy trio (Virginia Mayo, Dennis Morgan, and David Farrar) to a remote island in search of black pearls, but the natives kill one of them and convert the other two to their happy way of life. Stylized violence, romantic complications, and idealized island paradise. A-II (br)

Pebble and the Penguin, The (1995) Amiable animated tale in which a stuttering, love-struck penguin (voice of Martin Short) seeks, with the grudging aid of a resourceful pal (voice of James Belushi), to return to his true love (voice of Annie Golden) after being tossed into the churning sea by a romantic rival (voice of Tim Curry). The Don Bluth production is a peppy, colorful treat for preschoolers, though adults may not be as engaged by the thin story and routine music numbers by Barry Manilow. A-I (G)

Peck's Bad Boy (1934) Sentimental tale directed by Edward F. Cline in which a "regular" young lad (Jackie Cooper) runs away from home after his nasty aunt (Dorothy Peterson) comes for an extended visit, and her mean son reveals the boy was adopted as a baby by his beloved widower dad (Thomas Meighan). Dated treatment but still of interest for young viewers. A-I (br)

Pecker (1998) Generally sweet-natured satire about a Baltimore amateur photographer (Edward Furlong) whose sudden discovery by the New York art world brings intrusive, unwanted limelight to his working-class family and girlfriend (Christina Ricci), and prompts him to turn his back on fame and fortune. Writer-director John Waters's skimpy tale tosses innocent characters into raunchy settings with carefree abandon calculated to amuse more than offend, but the comic returns are slight. A discreet sexual encounter, striptease scene with fleeting nudity, indulgent treatment of shoplifting, comically intended use of a religious statue, occasional rough language, and minimal profanity. A-IV (R)

Pedestrian, The (1974) Demanding German drama about an aging industrialist (Gustav Rudolf Sellner) who is tortured by guilt and the fear that his secret crime as a Nazi officer responsible for an atrocity is about to be made public because of the digging and sifting into the incident by a German news-magazine. Director Maximilian Schell questions what might be called a moral statute of limitations in his complex probing of personal and collective guilt. Strong subject not for casual moviegoers. A-III (PG)

Pee Wee's Big Adventure (1985) Comic personality Pee Wee Herman's search for his stolen bike takes him on a madcap chase from the Alamo in Texas to Hollywood. Directed by Tim Burton, the humor is puerile with occasional slapstick violence. A-II (PG)

Peggy Sue Got Married (1986) A middle-aged mom (Kathleen Turner), about to be divorced from her unfaithful husband (Nicolas Cage), relives her past when she faints at a class reunion and discovers that the person she was, and has become, are one and the same. Director Francis Ford Coppola carefully controls the sentimental romanticism inherent in this story showing the continuum of values through the course of an individual's life. Brief scene of lovemaking and some coarse language. A-II (PG-13)

Pelican Brief, The (1993) With her life in grave danger after figuring out who was behind the assassination of two Supreme Court justices, a New Orleans law student (Julia Roberts) turns to a investigative reporter (Denzel Washington) to get her incriminating brief in print. Abetted by exceptional performances from a fine supporting cast, director Alan J. Pakula's spiky thriller maintains suspense despite a convoluted plot. Some restrained violence and an instance of rough language. A-III (PG-13)

Pelle the Conqueror (1988) Unsentimental Danish production follows a turn-of-the-century elderly widower (Max von Sydow) and his young son (Pelle Hvenegaard) from their arrival on Danish shores in search of a better life to their many hardships as stable-hands on a farm. Directed by Bille August, this is long and grim, but imbued with a strong feel for the landscape and low level of humanity on the farm, as well as the life-sustaining love of a father for his young son. Subtitles. Brief, graphic images implying the results of incest, infanticide, castration, some violence, and vulgar language. A-III (nr)

Pendulum (1969) George Peppard, Jean Seberg, and Richard Kiley star in a fast-paced crime thriller about a dedicated cop (Peppard) who, within the space of a few weeks, finds himself on both sides of the issues surrounding civil rights of accused criminals. With strong performances and fine location photography of the nation's capital, director George Schaefer's work poses some tough questions about law enforcement and the justice system, providing enough material for viewers to draw their own conclusions. A-II (M)

Penguin Pool Murder, The (1932) The first in a comic mystery-series teaming schoolmarm Hildegarde Withers (Edna May Oliver) with New York City police inspector Oscar Piper (James Gleason) in solving the murder of a stockbroker found floating in the municipal aquarium's penguin tank. Directed by George Archainbaud, the case has some interesting suspects (Mae Clark, Robert Armstrong, and Donald Cook) but the fun comes from the comic banter between the sharp teacher and tough cop, who decide to wed in an ending forgotten in subsequent sequels. Stylized violence and implied love triangle. A-II (br)

Penitentiary (1980) A young black (Leon Issac Kennedy), wrongly convicted and set to prison, takes up boxing and battles his way to vindication. The mediocre melodrama, written and directed by Jamaa Fanaka, provides an excessively graphic depiction of the corruption, brutality, and homosexuality pervading prison life. O (R)

Penitentiary II (1982) Young convict (Leon Isaac Kennedy) gains freedom and respectability by his boxing skills. Director Jamaa Fanaka's sequel, however, falls far short of the barely competent standards of the original. Repulsive, brutal mess with excessive violence. O (R)

Penitentiary III (1987) A boxer (Leon Isaac Kennedy) fights his way out of a prison dominated by a wealthy degenerate inmate (Tony Geary), but can't overcome the nightmarish plot absurdities and writer-director Jamaa Fanaka's near farcical excesses of violence and brutality. O (R)

Penn & Teller Get Killed (1989) Pointless black comedy enmeshes the comic magicians Penn and Teller in a web of self-inspired practical jokes that become more and more macabre, until they backfire and snuff them out. Directed by Arthur Penn, the schoolboy gags involve lots of fake blood and grisly pranks. Cavalier attitude toward death and suicide, much profanity, and some sexual innuendo. A-III (R)

Penn of Pennsylvania (see: **Courageous Mr. Penn**)

Pennies from Heaven (1981) Comedian Steve Martin plays a straight role in this almost unqualified disaster. As an unsuccessful peddler of sheet music in the Depression era, Martin is beastly to women and takes refuge from harsh reality by imagining lavish Busby Berkley-style production numbers. Neither director Herbert Ross nor writer Dennis Potter seem to have any idea how to adapt the story and concept for a feature movie. Besides the amorality of the hero, the plot contains scenes dealing with prostitution and abortion. A-III (R)

Penny Serenade (1941) Sentimental tale of a childless couple (Irene Dunne and Cary Grant) who adopt a baby girl, love her as their own, then are devastated by her sudden death six years later, leaving them tortured by grief and on the verge of divorce. Director George Stevens keeps the tragic story of adoptive parents from turning into a tearjerker by making their romance brightly believable and well-paced with gentle humor, genuine emotions, and some honest tears, all of which is put across by a fine cast. Domestic tensions. A-II (br)

Penthouse, The (1967) Failed adaptation of a play by C. Scott Forbes in which two psychopaths keep a man (Terence Morgan) and his mistress (Suzy Kendall) prisoner in their penthouse apartment, the woman in the bedroom and the man tied to a chair. Director Peter Collinson's attempt to make a statement about hypocrisy and disillusionment fails because of its contrived and melodramatic treatment and becomes little more than a tiresome exercise in sadism. O (br)

People Against O'Hara, The (1951) Aging lawyer who's a recovering alcoholic (Spencer Tracy) agrees to defend a neighborhood youth (James Arness) accused of murder, but when the trial goes badly, he puts his career on the line by bribing a witness. Director John Sturges's slack courtroom drama is less interesting than Tracy's arresting portrayal of a faltering veteran doing his best for a client he knows is innocent. Legal complications involving a lawyer's unethical conduct. A-II (br)

People Next Door, The (1970) J.P. Miller's adaptation of his award-winning television play about a middle-class teenager (Deborah Winters) who grooves with the boys and trips on LSD to escape the reality of her hypocritical parents (Eli Wallach and Julie Harris). Drearily moralizing, one-dimensional melodrama contrasts parents who drink and hide their sexual indiscretions with youngsters who smoke dope and flaunt theirs. Director David Greene's treatment fosters false stereotypes, uses unnecessary nudity, and fails to deal adequately with the serious problem of drug abuse in suburbia. O (R)

People of the Wind (1976) British documentary follows the annual trek of a nomadic tribe in southern Iran, which each spring must bring their sheep and cattle from winter quarters to fresh grazing-lands on a journey through perilous mountain terrain. Directed by Anthony Howarth, it is the record of a fiercely independent people who accept such dangers as the price of remaining free from the influences of the outside world. A-I (nr)

People That Time Forgot, The (1977) Rescue attempt on a prehistoric island brings viewers back to the same ice-bound fastness teeming with prehistoric monsters and cavemen depicted in **The Land That Time Forgot**. Directed by Kevin Connor, the British production is lackluster, with tepid acting from Patrick Wayne and Doug McClure, but its silly special effects may amuse youngsters. A-II (PG)

People Under the Stairs, The (1991) Revolting horror comedy in which a ghetto kid (Brandon Adams) gets trapped in a creaky mansion populated by a cannibalistic couple (Everett McGill and Wendy Robie), their abused daughter (A.J. Langer), and a cellar full of rampaging ghouls. Writer-director Wes Craven wallows in gore and sick humor about child abuse in a drawn-out, badly acted terror-tale. Excessive violence, some racial slurs, sexual references, and occasional rough language. O (R)

People vs. Larry Flynt, The (1996) Romanticized account of the rise of self-described pornographer Larry Flint (Woody Harrelson) from strip-club owner to multimillionaire smut-publisher, whose lawyer (Edward Norton) wins a Supreme Court decision upholding the media's prerogative to ridicule public figures as a constitutional right of free speech. Director Milos Forman turns Flynt into a poster boy for the First Amendment while depicting all those opposed to flesh-peddling as narrow-minded prudes. Sexual encounters and references, recurring nudity, substance abuse, brief violence, much rough language, and occasional profanity. O (R)

Pepe (1960) Tedious sentimental hokum starring Mexican comic Cantinflas as the hick groom of a stud stallion bought by a has-been Hollywood director (Dan Dailey) who restarts his career when Pepe comes up with a fresh new star (Shirley Jones) and enough money to produce a movie after spending a night gambling in Las Vegas. Directed by George Sidney, the leaden script is cluttered with several dozen Hollywood-star cameos, mediocre songs, and uninspired dance numbers, but most disappointing is Cantinflas, whose role as a rustic simpleton draws few smiles. A-I (br)

Pepi, Luci, Bom (1992) Vicious black comedy centers on the gleefully sadomasochistic activities of three women (Carmen Maura, Eva Siva, and Olvido Gara). Written and directed by Pedro Almodovar, this 1980 Spanish production celebrates the abuse of women and treats rape as a joke. Subtitles. Scenes of rape and other violence, sexual encounters with nudity, recreational drug use, and occasional rough language. O (nr)

Peppermint Soda (1979) French production about two sisters in 1963, one of whom is 15 and trying to cope with love, politics, and anti-Semitism, while her 13-year-old sister wants to follow her example but is not quite ready. Directed by Diane Kurys, the beautifully made movie is about people in the midst of life, but many viewers may find the pace too leisurely for enjoyment. A-III (nr)

Perceval (1978) Stylized French production based on the medieval romance about the knight (Fabrice Luchini) who joins King Arthur's court, fails to claim the Holy Grail when he has the chance, and is punished for his ignorance. Directed by Erich Rohmer, the visuals beautifully evoke the world of the Middle Ages and its code of chivalry, as well as the conflict in Christendom between the spiritual and temporal. A-II (nr)

Percy (1971) Witless British sex farce about a young man (Hywel Bennett) with a genital transplant that fascinates both the medical world and several young ladies who discover his new acquisition. Directed by Ralph Thomas, its snickering tone is even more offensive than such scenes as a nurse doing a striptease to test his convalescence. O (R)

Perez Family, The (1995) A Cuban refugee (Alfred Molina) in the 1980 Mariel boatlift to Miami seeks to rejoin the wife (Anjelica Huston) and daughter (Trini Alvarado) he's not seen in 20 years, but instead is processed through immigration as the husband of a part-time prostitute (Marisa Tomei) intent on creating a bogus family in order to stay in the States. Director Mira Nair plays the initial confusions mainly for laughs, then bogs down in soggy contrivances as romance blossoms between the two refugees, as well as between Molina's wife and a Miami policeman (Chazz Palminteri). Sexual situations, flashes of nudity, crude gestures, and occasional rough language. A-IV (R)

Perfect (1985) Rolling Stone reporter (John Travolta) becomes involved with an aerobics instructor (Jamie Lee Curtis) while researching a story on health clubs. Director Jim Bridges's muddled and pretentious movie offers a favorable view of promiscuity and includes a thoroughly distasteful sequence with a male stripper. O (R)

Perfect Candidate, A (1996) Behind-the-scenes account of the 1994 Virginia senatorial campaign between Republican challenger Oliver North, the former Marine officer best known for his part in the Iran-Contra scandal, and incumbent Democratic Sen. Charles Robb. Produced and directed by R.J. Cutler and David Van Taylor, the documentary has no narration, and viewers are on their own in forming judgments about the candidates, their political views, and campaign strategies, which turn the race into a classic of negative campaigning. Mean-spirited character assassination and a few instances of rough language. A-II (nr)

Perfect Couple, A (1979) Middle-aged, browbeaten son of a wealthy, conservative Greek family (Paul Dooley) uses a computer-dating service, which matches him with an aspiring rock-singer (Marta Heflin). They surmount all difficulties, proving that director Robert Altman has a heart, and the title is not ironically meant. The film does have some cheerful moments, and the acting is quite good, but the whole thing is so inconsequential that it often seems in danger of evaporating. A-III (PG)

Perfect Friday (1970) British caper-movie tries to liven up the muddled plot revolving around bank-teller Stanley Baker's clever bank robbery with an incoherently staccato narrative, false plot twists, and shots of accomplice Ursula Andress undressed. Director Peter Hall's sense of timing and humor is as badly off the mark as the movie's sense of moral perspective. O (R)

Perfect Furlough, The (1958) Predictable farce directed by Blake Edwards in which a conniving Army corporal (Tony Curtis) wins a vacation in Paris with a movie star (Linda Cristal), then tries to outwit the military psychologist (Janet Leigh) assigned to keep him out of trouble. Much sexual innuendo. A-III (br)

Perfect Murder, A (1998) Glossy thriller in which a heartless husband (Michael Douglas) plots to have his rich trophy-wife (Gwyneth Paltrow) killed by her ex-con lover (Viggo Mortensen), but all goes murderously awry. Directed by Andrew Davis, this remake of Hitchcock's 1954 **Dial M for Murder** retains the twisty plot, but by adding adultery and more violence to the mix, the result is dramatically unconvincing. Fleeting sexual encounter, brief but intense violence, and some rough language, as well as profanity. A-III (R)

Perfect Specimen, The (1937) Predictable romantic comedy directed by Michael Curtiz in which a rich young man (Errol Flynn) is shielded from the world by his stern grandmother (May Robson), until he runs off with a free-spirited young woman (Joan Blondell) and proves he's perfectly capable of managing on his own. Romantic complications. A-I (br)

Perfect Weapon, The (1991) Seeking the gangland slayer (James Hong) of his mentor (Mako), a kenpo karate expert (Jeff Speakman) is tricked into thinking the killer's arch-rival is the guilty party. Director Mark DiSalle's standard action-yarn is a yawn that could pass for an episode of a TV private-eye series, simply stretched out to accommodate more karate bouts. Intermittent martial-arts violence and an isolated instance of rough language and drug use. A-III (R)

Perfect World, A (1993) Hard-edged adult thriller about an escaped convict (Kevin Costner) taking a seven-year-old hostage (T.J. Lowther) on a blood-splattered ride as he tries to elude the pursuit of a veteran Texas Ranger (Clint Eastwood) and a young criminologist (Laura Dern). Also directed by Eastwood, the story's tension revolves around the menacing situations in which the young boy is placed as he witnesses deadly violence and then participates in it. Intense menace to a child, graphic violence, sexual references, and coarse language. A-III (R/PG-13 on appeal)

Perfectly Normal (1991) A young loner (Michael Riley) jettisons his plans to build a house when a flamboyant stranger (Robbie Coltrane) persuades him to spend his inheritance on a restaurant, where the two would sing Italian operas to the clientele. Director Yves Simoneau's offbeat, fitfully funny comedy endearingly portrays eccentric characters who happily change each other for the better. Restrained love scene with brief nudity and some rough language. A-III (R)

Performance (1970) A hood (James Fox) on the run from the mob takes refuge with a temporarily retired pop-singer (Mick Jagger) awaiting the return of his inspiration in the company of several fans (Anita Pallenberg and Michele Breton). Bizarre British drama directed by Don Cammell and Nicholas Roeg is a pseudo-sophisticate's vision of evil, with the kind of slick gimmickry that promises revelations but never rises above its shallow fascination with the perversities it supposedly explores. It's a morass of unrelieved violence, drug use, sex, and grotesque immoralities. O (R)

Perils of Gwendoline, The (1985) Coy, flyblown adventure movie, by French director Just Jaeckin, about a trio of explorers in a land ruled by warrior women. Obviously meant to be satirical and sexy, it's merely distasteful and boring. O (R)

Perils of Pauline, The (1947) Musical comedy about silent-screen heroine Pearl White (Betty Hutton), who leaves a New York sweat-shop to join a theatrical troupe and winds up in Hollywood as the queen of cliff-hanging serials, but they lose popularity after WW I and she ends a heroic cripple. Directed by George Marshall, the result is colorful escapist entertainment, though its depiction of the era is largely hokum, and her unrequited love for a self-centered actor (John Lund) may be too gooey for some tastes. A-I (br)

Perils of P.K., The (1986) Amateurish, low-budget sex-farce centering around a neurotic middle-aged woman recounting her sexual daydreams and memories to a psychiatrist. Vulgar sight gags and crude gestures, foul language, and off-color sexual jokes. O (R)

Permanent Record (1988) The repercussions of a popular high-school senior's suicide are followed as the boy's friends attempt to deal with their grief, rage, guilt, and bewilderment over his senseless death. Director Marisa Silver sensitively explores the emotional turmoil experienced by adolescents in facing such a tragedy, though the movie is weakened by a pat resolution. Unsettling theme, incidental drug and alcohol abuse, and some profanity. A-III (PG-13)

Persecution and Assassination of Jean-Paul Marat As Performed by the Inmates of the Asylum of Charenton under the Direction of the Marquis De Sade, The (1967) The play by Peter Weiss examines the conflict between the political autocracy of the French revolutionary Marat and the social anarchy of De Sade. Peter Brooks directs the Royal Shakespeare Company in a screen version that is not so much a record of its staging and performances as it is a surprisingly good movie that never quite overcomes the weaknesses of its material. Complex, sometimes shocking, the drama's criticism of social, political, and religious conventions will agitate some, but give others a number of insights into the conflict between freedom and authority. A-IV (br)

Persona (1967) Swedish drama about an actress (Liv Ullmann) who suddenly cannot speak, fails to respond to psychiatric treatment, and is sent to a seaside villa for a rest in the care of a talkative, sympathetic nurse (Bibi Andersson). There the two women seem to change roles, and their personal identities become strangely intermingled. Directed by Ingmar Bergman, it is intensely personal, largely obscure, and not a little disturbing. A-IV (br)

Personal Best (1982) Two female track-stars (Mariel Hemingway and Patrice Donnelly) carry on a homosexual affair in a dull, unbelievably crude, and relentlessly simpleminded movie written and directed by Robert Towne. Excessive nudity. O (R)

Personal Journey with Martin Scorsese through American Movies, A (1994) After recalling the Hollywood movies that most impressed him as a youth, director Scorsese focuses on the Westerns, gangster films, and musicals as the American contribution to world cinema, then turns in the second part to the great directors of the silent era, concluding with a program devoted to Hollywood rebels from D.W. Griffith to Billy Wilder. Produced by Florence Dauman for the British Film Institute, the three-volume documentary runs 3 hours, 46 minutes, offering a choice collection of film excerpts to illustrate Scorsese's idiosyncratic selection of Hollywood's most important movies, from the early silents to the 1960s, intermixing venerable screen-classics with trashy B-movies, whose influence on the director helps explain the uneven quality of his own body of work. Stylized violence, sexual innuendo, and instances of rough language and profanity. A-III (nr)

Personal Services (1987) Wry British sex-farce about a waitress (Julie Walters) who turns to running a brothel catering to the whims of the upper class. Despite some barbs at the hypocrisy of the toffs, director Terry Jones insists on romanticizing an immoral profession. Kinky sex, arrogant bawdiness, and nudity are used as sources of humor. O (R)

Persuasion (1995) Artful adaptation of Jane Austen's 1818 novel about an upper-class Englishwoman (Amanda Root) who secretly regrets having rejected an impoverished seaman (Ciaran Hinds) years earlier, just as he is too proud to admit his feelings for her now that he is prosperous and ready to settle down. Director Roger Michell captures the look of the era and its rigid class-distinctions, while delicately exploring the repressed yearnings of the would-be lovers. Romantic complications and a few accident-related injuries. A-II (PG)

Pest, The (1997) Annoying comedy in which a hyperactive Hispanic crook (John Leguizamo) is hunted by a lunatic German (Jeffrey Jones) who mounts human heads of assorted nationalities in his trophy room. Directed by Paul Miller as a one-man show for Leguizamo's frantic antics, its witless stereotyping has something to offend everyone. Comic violence, scatological humor, ethnic stereotyping, fleeting nudity, and occasional profanity. A-III (PG-13)

Pet Sematary (1989) Failed horror movie about a Maine family living near a dangerous highway and two cemeteries — one for family pets and the other for those who want their loved ones to return from the dead. Adapted by Stephen King from his bestseller and directed by Mary Lambert, the movie is peppered with loose ends and gratuitous climactic gore. While relevant questions about the finality of death are raised by the family's six-year-old (Blaze Berdahl), her toddler brother's afterlife transformation into a gruesome slasher is depicted in horrific, graphic detail. O (R)

Pet Sematary Two (1992) Buried on supposedly cursed ground by teenaged buddies (Edward Furlong and Jason McGuire), a vicious stepfather (Clancy Brown) and a dog return as fiendish zombies on a murderous rampage. Mary Lambert directs a drawn-out and consistently predictable horror sequel with a death-affirming theme. Numerous grisly killings, brief nudity, and some rough language. O (R)

Pete Kelly's Blues (1955) Prohibition-era crime drama in which a Kansas City jazz trumpeter (Jack Webb) tangles with a local mobster (Edmond O'Brien) who's abusing the singer (Peggy Lee) he's made his mistress. Also directed by Webb, the movie has interest in its depiction of the period jazz scene, but the story's melodramatics are flat and unconvincing. Some hard-edged brutality and gritty underworld setting. A-III (br)

Pete 'n' Tillie (1972) Awkward and at times grating seriocomedy in which Pete (Walter Matthau) meets Tillie (Carol Burnett) in sunny California, bed down, get married, raise a son, only to lose him to leukemia, separate, and finally re-unite. Director Martin Ritt proceeds with a wildly inappropriate mixture of sardonic humor, slapstick, stark tragedy, heavy melodrama, and cheap soap operatics. Lapses in taste include an excessive amount of profanity and a shrill bit of blasphemy. A-IV (PG)

Pete Seeger ... A Song and a Stone (1972) Documentary on one of the bedrock figures of American folk-song shows him in performance and conversation about his music and its relation to such issues as ecology. The stone in the title represents the only weapon Seeger has ever carried, a little one he keeps in his banjo, symbolic of breaking Establishment windows. Seeger's songs and his little stone are at the core of this engaging and rewarding work directed by Robert Elfstrom. A-II (nr)

Pete's Dragon (1977) Pete, a young orphan (Sean Marshall), and Elliot, an amiable dragon, are befriended by a lighthouse-keeper's daughter (Helen Reddy) in a small Maine fishing village at the turn of the century. Disney musical fantasy, directed by Don Chaffey, combines live-action with animation. The dragon's ability to become invisible is the chief source of humor in a slow-moving picture that also features Mickey Rooney, Red Buttons, and Shelley Winters. A-I (G)

Peter Ibbetson (1935) Strange romantic fantasy of separated childhood sweethearts whose chance meeting years later results in the title character (Gary Cooper) being wrongly sentenced to life imprisonment for killing her husband (John Halliday), though Peter and his beloved Mimsy (Ann Harding) are thereafter united in their dreams and eventually in death. Directed by Henry Hathaway from George du Maurier's novel, the stilted 19th-century proceedings are elegantly photographed, but the spiritual bond linking the couple's dreams depends entirely on the viewer's willingness to suspend disbelief. Romantic complications. A-II (br)

Peter Pan (1953) Walt Disney's animated feature is a delightful adaptation of Sir James M. Barrie's 1904 play about an impish 12-year-old boy (voice of Bobby Driscoll) who refuses to grow up. Directed by Hamilton Luske, Clyde Geronimi, and Wildred Jackson, it offers dreamy fantasy panoramas of London and Never Never Land, along with the antics of feisty pixie Tinker Bell and mostly unmemorable songs. Some dated sexist (jealous women) and racial (Native Americans) stereotypes are used in wrong-headed attempts at humor. A-I (G)

Peter Rabbit and Tales of Beatrix Potter (1971) British ballet production conjures up Beatrix Potter's delicate animal fables, and through Frederick Ashton's choreography enables them to dance and pantomime their way into the hearts of story lovers. Director Reginald Mills frees the work from the stage by photographing it in a picturesque English countryside and patterns the costumes on the soft, cuddly textures and pale pastels of the famous Potter sketches. A beautiful way to introduce youngsters to the world of Peter Rabbit and the art of the ballet. A-I (G)

Peter's Friends (1992) British seriocomedy about six university classmates (Kenneth Branagh, Emma Thompson, Stephen Fry, Alphponsia Emmanuel, Hugh Laurie, and Imelda Staunton) who, a decade after graduation, reunite at an English manor for a New Year's weekend of carefree catching-up and unexpected soul-searching. Producer-director Branagh's derivative situation is sporadically entertaining as it charts the shifting personal relationships of friends who are each facing turning points in their lives. Fleeting bedroom shot, flash of rear nudity, and frequent rough language. A-III (R)

Petty Girl, The (1950) Musical comedy clunker directed by Henry Levin in which a would-be serious artist (Robert Cummings) pursues a strait-laced college instructor (Joan Caulfield) who eventually rebels against her moralistic colleagues, then convinces him to embark on a successful career painting images of scantily clad women. Heavy sexual innuendo. A-III (br)

Petulia (1968) An affair between a discontented wife (Julie Christie) and a divorced doctor (George C. Scott) is ended when her husband (Richard Chamberlain) finds out and brutally beats her. In picturing a sick society, director Richard Lester follows the story's alienated characters as they check in and out of a San Francisco hospital, where it is easier to mend broken bodies than damaged lives. The humor is dark, but the effect is stunning. A-III (R)

Peyton Place (1957) Trashy soap opera from the Grace Metalious novel about the bedroom affairs of a hypocritical small town in Maine, until culminating in the trial of a young woman (Hope Lange) for murdering her stepfather (Arthur Kennedy). Director Mark Robson dresses up the one-note scenario in a glossy production that makes it seem all the more tawdry. Muted treatment of a variety of sexual wrongdoing, stylized violence, and a veiled reference to abortion. A-III (br)

Phantasm (1979) Dreadfully amateurish attempt to cross comedy with horror in a story about two brothers in a graveyard battle with brown-robed dwarfs and a fiendish undertaker on the lookout for bodies, dead or alive. Directed by Don Coscarelli, the movie employs excessive violence, gore, and nudity. O (R)

Phantasm II (1988) Two teenagers (James Le Gros and Paula Irvine) and a middle-aged cohort (Reggie Bannister) track and attempt to kill a ghoulish mortician (Angus Scrimm) who can't get his fill of corpses. Director Don Coscarelli's sequel has no redeeming qualities. Excessive blood and gore, some profanity, and a kinky sex scene. O (R)

Phantom, The (1996) The comic-book jungle hero of the title (Billy Zane) is a mysterious masked figure who sets out to prevent an evil millionaire (Treat Williams) from securing three magical skulls which have the power to rule the world. Directed by Simon Wincer, the fantasy adventure is set in the 1930s and features a colorful collection of dashing heroes, mustachioed villains, and desperate damsels in distress. Some stylized violence and frequent menace. A-II (PG)

Phantom Creeps, The (1939) Feature version of a 13-episode serial directed by Ford Beebe and Saul A. Goodkind in which a mad scientist (Bela Lugosi) plans to use the power derived from a meteorite fragment to rule the world, but a gang of foreign spies gets in the way before an American government agent (Robert Kent) puts an end to the silly proceedings. Fantasy violence and menace. A-II (br)

Phantom Lady (1944) Intriguing crime thriller in which an engineer (Alan Curtis) is convicted of murdering his wife until cleared by his faithful secretary (Ella Raines), who finally locates a missing witness, thereby flushing the real killer (Franchot Tone). Director Robert Siodmak ratchets the suspense as the secretary comes to rely for help on a man who viewers already know is the unbalanced killer. More menace than violence. A-II (br)

Phantom of Liberty, The (1974) French production freely shifts through a series of loosely connected vignettes beginning as a costume drama set in Toledo during the Napoleanic era, returning to contemporary scenes of political, social, and religious satire. Directed by Luis Bunuel, the narrative's general complexity, as well as its anti-clerical references, casual nudity, and mature sexual motifs, make this surrealistic work not for all audiences. A-IV (R)

Phantom of Terror, The (see: **The Bird with the Crystal Plumage**)

Phantom of the Opera, The (1925) Silent horror classic in which a mad composer with a hideously deformed face (Lon Chaney) lives in the vast cellars beneath the Paris Opera House, where he helps a young singer (Mary Philbin) become a star, then abducts her because she loves another (Norman Kerry). Director Rupert Julian wraps the Opera House in a sinister atmosphere of shadowy visuals, secret passages, and subterranean chambers, but the real fright doesn't come until late in the proceedings, when the grotesque visage behind the Phantom's mask is finally unveiled. Stylized violence, much menace, and muted sexual innuendo. A-II (br)

Phantom of the Opera, The (1943) His face disfigured by acid, an embittered musician (Claude Rains) hides behind a mask in the cavernous rooms beneath the Paris Opera, from which he terrorizes the company into making his protégé (Susanna Foster) a star despite her love for a weak tenor (Nelson Eddy). Director Arthur Lubin's lush period costumer lavishes more attention on stilted opera scenes than the sinister activities of the menacing phantom. Some stylized violence and moody atmosphere but few scares. A-II (br)

Phantom of the Opera, The (1962) Disappointing British version of the horror story about an embittered masked composer (Herbert Lom) living in the subterranean cellars of a London opera house, where he helps a young singer (Heather Sears) succeed, but she spurns his love for that of another (Edward De Souza). Directed by Terence Fisher, the elaborate opera-house settings furnish some eerie moments, but the attempt to make the Phantom a more sympathetic character than previously turns a sinister tale into a relatively bland one. Stylized violence and romantic complications. A-I (br)

Phantom of the Paradise (1974) Loosely based on **The Phantom of the Opera**, the updated version is about an aspiring rock composer (William Finley) whose face is mutilated by a recording press, and his rock cantata on the Faust legend is stolen by a ruthless music producer (Paul Williams) who wants it for the opening of his new house, the Paradise. The composer seeks revenge by terrorizing those working in the Paradise in an effort to have his one love (Jessica Harper) sing his cantata. Director Brian De Palma uses the almost surrealistic plot to concoct a unique combination of horror and comedy, avoiding excess while making some incisive comments about the state of modern music. A-III (PG)

Phantom of the Rue Morgue (1954) Tame version of the Edgar Allan Poe story about a series of murders in 19th-century Paris, leading the police (Claude Dauphin) to a zoology professor (Karl Malden) and a trained ape. Director Roy Del Ruth gets only mild menace out of the creaky situation and the performances are uniformly wooden. Some stylized violence and tense moments. A-II (br)

Phantom Planet, The (1961) Sci-fi clunker directed by William Marshall in which a spaceship is forced to land on an asteroid, where its captain (Dean Fredericks) soon shrinks to the same minute size as its wee human-shaped inhabitants, then helps them fight an alien monster before being rescued by a search party. Unconvincing menace. A-I (br)

Phantom Ship (1935) Creaky British melodrama based on the 1872 mystery of the US brig Mary Celeste, discovered derelict on the high seas with no clues as to what had happened to its crew. In speculating on what might have occurred, writer-director Denison Clift imagines the doomed ship sailed by a mutinous crew (notably one-armed Bela Lugosi), though the movie's sinister atmosphere and heavy-handed portents of disaster have little to do with the ultimate outcome involving a revengeful lunatic. Stylized violence and contrived menace. A-II (br)

Phantom Tollbooth (1970) When a tollbooth appears in his bedroom, a rather listless youngster (Butch Patrick) escapes through it into a world of fantasy, where he meets an assortment of allegorical figures and learns the value of using time well and making the most of his schooling. Director Chuck Jones's feature-length cartoon makes playful, intelligent use of visual metaphors and clever word-turns that may motivate some youngsters' interest in reading and writing. A-I (G)

Phantoms (1998) Dreary horror movie pitting a shape-shifting monster against a small-town sheriff (Ben Affleck), two sisters (Rose McGowan and Joanna Going), and an eccentric professor (Peter O'Toole) who holds the key to destroying the deadly menace. Director Joe Chappelle uses familiar cliches to advance the narrative, but neglects to build the suspense necessary to make the fright formula work. Recurring fantasy violence, some profanity, and occasional rough language. A-III (R)

Phar Lap (1984) Rousing, wholesome entertainment from Australia about a famous Depression-era racehorse who meets a tragic end. Though not especially dramatic, director Simon Wincer's work with Tom Burlinson, Martin Vaughan, and Ron Liebman is nonetheless interesting family entertainment. A-I (PG)

Phase IV (1974) Sci-fi tale of the world being taken over by ants acting out of mass instinct. The photographic techniques somehow make the ants and their colony a much more believable world than that of the cast of human characters (Nigel Davenport, Michael Murphy, and Lynne Frederick). Although artist-director Saul Bass's ending is a little muddled, getting there is half the fun. A-II (PG)

Phat Beach (1996) Puerile comedy in which a smooth-talking Romeo (Brian Hooks) persuades his overweight buddy (Jermaine Hopkins) to head for a week-long beach party with bikini-clad bimbos. Director Doug Ellin's lame jiggle-show is little more than a mindless male fantasy about women as anonymous playthings. Sexist humor, crude sexual references, nudity, a brief sexual encounter, fleeting drug use, some profanity, and much rough language. O (R)

Phedre (1973) Marie Bell, the legendary actress of the Comedie Francaise, plays the tragic queen in Racine's 17th-century version of the Greek myth of Theseus, the prince torn between two loves. Director Pierre Jourdan has tried to do more than record a stage performance, yet the play is necessarily artificial and stage-bound. Though the English subtitles give only a suggestion of Racine's complicated romantic verse, the work is of interest to students of French culture and drama. A-II (PG)

Phenix City Story, The (1955) Fact-based dramatization of how an Alabama town long ruled by a gambling syndicate gets national attention when its boss (Edward Andres) orders the murder of a local reform candidate (John McIntire), and the victim's son (Richard Kiley) seeks the intervention of the state militia. Directed by Phil Karlson, the movie opens with a real reporter interviewing Phenix City residents, then switches to a semi-documentary style that is fairly realistic, despite some melodramatic flourishes. Stylized violence, some of it quite nasty, and sexual innuendo. A-III (br)

Phenomenon (1996) Sentimental tale about a small-town mechanic (John Travolta) whose simple life and love for a wary single mom (Kyra Sedgwick) are suddenly turned upside down when he becomes an overnight genius with telekinetic powers. Director Jon Turteltaub keeps the focus steadily on the human element and positive emotions in this charmingly bittersweet though somewhat schmaltzy movie. Mild sexual innuendo, fleeting nudity, and occasional profanity. A-III (PG)

Phffft! (1954) Leaden romantic comedy about a couple (Judy Holliday and Jack Lemmon) who get divorced for no good reason, then can't adjust to the complications of single life, and decide to get back together. Director Mark Robson gets no laughs from his heavy-handed treatment of the mating game, which here has little to do with love, much less fidelity. Recurring sexual references. A-III (br)

Philadelphia (1993) After abruptly being fired for incompetence, a homosexual lawyer (Tom Hanks) dying of AIDS hires an attorney (Denzel Washington) to sue his former boss (Jason Robards) for discrimination. Directed by Jonathan Demme, the emotionally manipulative script and Hanks's restrained, powerful performance reduce complex social issues to the personal level of one victim's humanity and search for justice. Sympathetic depiction of gay relationships, fleeting nudity, and a few sexist and sexual slurs. A-IV (PG-13)

Philadelphia Experiment, The (1984) Routine time-travel adventure with Michael Paré and Bobby Di Cicco playing WW II sailors projected into the present. Directed by Stewart Raffill, the result is innocuous and moderately entertaining. A-II (PG)

Phone Call from a Stranger (1952) Thin tale in which a survivor (Gary Merrill) of a airplane crash visits the families of three passengers (actress Shelley Winters, salesman Keenan Wynn, and alcoholic doctor Michael Rennie) he had met on the flight but who did not survive it. Directed by Jean Negulesco, the only thing the stories have in common is the caller, and the only one that stands on its own is that featuring Bette Davis as Wynn's quadriplegic wife. Sexual innuendo and implied infidelity. A-III (br)

Phynx, The (1970) Intended as a satire of both foreign intrigue movies and popular music, director Lee H. Katzin's story about a group of rock musicians who are sent to Albania to rescue some American show people is merely dull and boring, save for the brief appearances of some famous performers of the past (Ruby Keeler, Dorothy Lamour, Busby Berkely, Leo Gorcey, Huntz Hall, and many others). Some slapstick violence and sexual references. A-III (PG)

Physical Evidence (1989) A hard-living, veteran detective (Burt Reynolds), accused of murdering a crook known to have had many enemies, is represented by a yuppie public defender (Theresa Russell) who's stymied in her efforts to clear her client. Director Michael Crichton fails to rev up his derivative scenario with thrills or star chemistry. Some profanity and bloody violence. A-III (R)

Piaf — The Early Years (1982) Disappointing dramatization of French singer Edith Piaf's life from her birth in 1915, through her formative years in the seedy underworld of criminals and prostitutes who helped her eke out a living as a street singer, until her success as a top Paris entertainer in the 1930s. Director Guy Casaril has trouble maintaining interest in the muddled continuity of the narrative, but Brigitte Ariel in the title role is moderately successful in overcoming this handicap. Rather romantic treatment of Piaf's affairs of the heart. A-III (PG)

Piano, The (1993) A Scottish mute woman (Holly Hunter) with a nine-year-old child (Anna Paquin) arrives in 19th-century New Zealand bush-country for an arranged marriage, but, after her new husband (Sam Neill) sells her beloved piano, she and its new owner (Harvey Keitel) fall in love. Writer-director Jane Campion's striking film explores the intensity of sexual desire and love without placing it in a moral context. Brief bedroom scene with full nudity, fleeting violence, and an instance of rough language. A-IV (R)

Pickpocket (1969) Alienated youth turns to petty crime as a kind of lark, but, not very good at it, he is caught and sent to prison, where he is visited by a young woman who cares for him and will be waiting when he is released. French production directed by Robert Bresson in 1956, the work has nothing to do with crime thrillers but is an austere look at a lost soul and his possible chance of redemption. Challenging but worthwhile fare for reflective viewers. A-II (nr)

Pickup Artist, The (1987) Unintelligent late-teen romance about an aggressive womanizer (Robert Downey) and promiscuous museum guide (Molly Ringwald) who take a tumble in the front seat, solve father Dennis Hopper's gambling debt to tough Harvey Keitel, and find true love without much happiness or a solution to their bad habits. Director James Toback indulges in TV superficiality and tired stereotyping in this lazy tale which endorses gambling and recreational sex. A-III (PG-13)

Pickup on 101 (1972) College coed (Lesley Warren) heading toward a New Mexico commune and a rock guitarist (Martin Sheen) on his way to Los Angeles are brought together on the road by a an old hobo (Jack Albertson), whose redemptive quality brings the young couple to transcend their own selfishness and learn that love means more than sex. Director John Florea has a script loaded with simplistic and pietistic preachments, but at least it tries for something a bit more substantial than the usual sentimental romance. A-III (PG)

Pickup on South Street (1953) Run-of-the-mill crime caper turns into a counterespionage case when a New York pickpocket (Richard Widmark) filches a wallet containing government secrets on microfilm, then finds himself caught in the middle between a Communist spy ring (led by Richard Kiley) and a squad of G-men. Writer-director Samuel Fuller loads the far-fetched plot with violence, especially directed at women (Jean Peters and Thelma Ritter), with a hokey ending lauding the nasty crook as a hero after he nails the Communists. Hard-edged violence and sexual situations. A-III (br)

Picnic at Hanging Rock (1979) On a sunny St. Valentine's Day in 1900, a group of Australian schoolgirls go off on a picnic to a strange and foreboding place called Hanging Rock, where three of the girls and one teacher disappear without a trace. Director Peter Weir's fact-based, never-solved mystery creates an eerie, otherworldly atmosphere as the girls explore the ledges and recesses of the ancient rock formation. The somberness of the theme and an emphasis on suppressed sexuality make it mature fare. A-III (PG)

Picture Bride (1995) Fact-based story of Japanese laborers on a 1918 Hawaiian sugarcane plantation, where a homesick teenager (Youki Kudoh) arrives as a mail-order bride but refuses to let her much-older husband (Akira Takayama) touch her, until loneliness and tragedy bring the couple together. Writer-director Kayo Hatta delicately unfolds a lyrical story about a past generation of Japanese who endured culture shock, harsh living conditions, and meager wages to begin families in an alien land. Partially subtitled. Several restrained bedroom scenes. A-III (PG-13)

Picture Mommy Dead (1966) Suspense melodrama about a young heiress (Susan Gordon) who returns to the house where her mother had burned to death many years before, and, in the company of her father and stepmother (Don Ameche and Martha Hyer), strange things begin happening to her. Director Bert I. Gordon tries to do something with all the frights and hallucinations contained in the script, but the result borders on the absurd. Stylized violence. A-III (br)

Picture Perfect (1997) Sour romantic comedy about a conniving woman (Jennifer Aniston) who concocts a fantasy fiancé in order to win a job promotion and the man of her dreams (Kevin Bacon), then realizes she loves another (Jay Mohr) and tries to undo the harm caused by her deception. Directed by Glenn Gordon Caron, the proceedings are clumsily contrived from start to finish, with plot complications that are too obvious to be amusing, and an empty-headed heroine who invites little sympathy. Tawdry sexual situations, jokes about serious sexual matters, and occasional profanity. A-IV (PG-13)

Piece of Pleasure, A (1976) French drama about a "liberated" husband (Paul Gegauff, who also wrote the script) who pushes his less-educated wife (Danielle Gegauff) into a chaos of sexual experimentation with predictably tragic results. That people are capable of destroying themselves by their own self-deceptions may sound like a fairly banal theme, but director Claude Chabrol presents it as a harrowing truth, with a level of human involvement, yet distancing itself from their excesses. A-IV (R)

Piece of the Action, A (1977) Two smooth con-men (Bill Cosby and Sidney Poitier) are blackmailed by a retired police detective (James Earl Jones) into working for a youth center devoted to educating ghetto youngsters and getting them jobs. Directed by Poitier, the comedy-melodrama quickly exhausts the situation and is only mildly entertaining. Strong language and a muddled sense of morality (the two criminals show no signs of remorse, and Poitier lives in unwedded bliss). A-III (PG)

Pieces of Dreams (1970) A troubled, lonely pastor (Robert Forster), out of touch with his people and bored with the routine chores of parish life, leaves the priesthood and marries a divorced social-worker (Lauren Hutton). Director Daniel Haller fails to get inside the personal world of his characters and their spiritual conflicts, leaving one with the impression that the priest's ultimate decision was motivated by little more than a tumble in the hay. A-IV (PG)

Pied Piper, The (1972) British production filmed in Germany by French director Jacques Demy results in a confused retelling of the medieval tale about the piper (folksinger Donovan), who comes to save the hamlet of Hamelin from the Black Plague by leading a parade of rodents down to the river to drown but, unpaid, returns to spirit the town's children away to a happier clime. It mixes childlike fantasy with such a cluttered picture of the people and artifacts of medieval life that its simple story-line is often difficult to follow. A-II (G)

Pierrot le Fou (1969) Unconventional French melodrama about a man and a woman (Jean-Paul Belmondo and Anna Karina) whose relationship is based upon misunderstandings and boredom. Director Jean-Luc Godard's highly subjective, stream-of-consciousness lacks narrative coherence, yet conveys the need people have for ideals in a world of absurdity. A-IV (nr)

Pigeons (1971) Trite and silly story about aimless urban youth, here a yuppie New York cab driver (Jordan Christopher) who falls for a cute neighbor (Jill O'Hara), but their romance withers on a trip to the suburbs to meet his neurotic folks. Directed by John Dexter, the story is overly familiar and the treatment overly cute. Some relatively innocuous nudity. A-III (R)

Pigskin Parade (1936) Dated fun in a musical comedy about a losing Texas college coach (Jack Haley) whose wife (Patsy Kelly) finds him a farmer (Stuart Erwin) who can toss a football a country mile just in time for the big game with Yale. Directed by David Butler, the zany proceedings over turning the reluctant farmer into a college boy are intermittently amusing, with occasional songs by Judy Garland and the Yacht Club Boys. A-I (br)

Pillars of the Sky (1956) Wooden Western set in 1868 Oregon, where a veteran sergeant (Jeff Chandler) and a missionary (Ward Bond) try to avert the massacre of a cavalry troop ordered to open a road through Indian territory protected from whites by treaty. Director George Marshall does little more than a routine job with a frontier conflict, whose chief interest comes from the fact that the Indians are peaceful Christian converts turned into hostiles by the violation of their treaty rights. Stylized violence and complications arising from a wife's suspected infidelity. A-II (br)

Pillow Book, The (1997) Bizarre tale in which a Japanese woman (Vivian Wu), obsessed with painting calligraphy on her lovers' nude bodies, who exacts revenge on a scornful publisher (Yoshi Oida) by enticing his bisexual lover (Ewan McGregor) into a relationship that culminates in suicide and murder. Writer-director Peter Greenaway's sensual imagery becomes boringly repetitive as the narrative becomes increasingly grotesque and visually graphic. Subtitles. Some gory violence, a variety of sexual encounters, and much frontal nudity. O (nr)

Pillow Talk (1959) Slick but sappy romantic comedy in which an interior decorator (Doris Day) berates an amorous songwriter (Rock Hudson) for hogging their shared telephone party-line, but his days as a bachelor are doomed after he foolishly trifles with her affections. Directed by Michael Gordon, the contrived situation is decked out in plush settings with comic support by Tony Randall and Thelma Ritter, but the weak results don't justify the effort. Comic treatment of sexual situations. A-III (br)

Pilot #5 (1943) Dated WW II flag-waver about an American pilot (Franchot Tone) setting off against a Japanese aircraft carrier in the unit's last plane, while his comrades (Gene Kelly, Van Johnson, etc.) recall in flashback his pre-war troubles with a local political boss. Director George Sidney's woodenly patriotic melodrama is of only limited historical interest. Wartime violence. A-I (br)

Pimpernel Smith (1941) The Scarlet Pimpernel rides again, this time in the spring of 1939, as a British archeologist (Leslie Howard) helps anti-Nazis escape Germany, despite the fiendish efforts of a Gestapo chief (Francis L. Sullivan). Also directed by Howard, the cat-and-mouse thrills still hold up, as does much of the low-key humor, though some patriotic rhetoric dates it as a period piece. A-I (br)

Pin (1991) A disturbed young man (David Hewlett), who believes a ventriloquist's dummy to be real, goes over the edge when the boyfriend (John Ferguson) of his sister (Cyndy Preston) suggests he be committed. Director Sandor Stern's drawn-out thriller is a low-budget, predictable affair of little tension or distinction. Brief violence, references to promiscuity and abortion, and momentary nudity. A-III (nr)

Ping Pong (1987) Young Chinese law-clerk (Lucy Sheen) rediscovers her cultural roots and inadvertently reunites a fragmented family while executing the will of a wealthy Chinese businessman. British import from director Po Chih Leong deals affectionately with the social and cultural pressures that alienate westernized foreign nationals and erode their family ties. Charming but slow-moving portrait. A-I (nr)

Pink Cadillac (1989) A bail bondsman's skip-tracer (Clint Eastwood) falls for his prey, a dizzy bail jumper and devoted mom (Bernadette Peters) wrongfully arrested for hiding her husband's counterfeit cash. On the run from the law and her husband's white-supremacist gang of ex-cons, the duo manage to put a little life into a suspenseless scenario sluggishly directed by Buddy Van Horn. Much comic-book violence, some rough language, and a brief sexual encounter. A-III (PG-13)

Pink Floyd (1974) The musical group of the title in a sophisticated, heavily electronic rock concert that their fans will appreciate, though others may be put off by the intensity of sound and artiness of image (most of it was filmed in an amphitheater amid the ruins of Pompeii). Directed by Alan Parker, it features Bob Geldof, Christine Hargreaves, James Laurenson, Eleanor David, and Bob Hoskins. A-II (G)

Pink Jungle, The (1968) Amusing comedy-adventure with a twist ending in which a photographer (James Garner) and pretty model (Eva Renzi) helicopter into a Latin-American jungle for a lipstick ad layout, are mistaken for spies, and get involved with a flamboyant wheeler-dealer (George Kennedy) searching for a lost diamond mine. Directed by Delbert Mann, it's generally fast-paced and funny, if a trifle condescending toward that nameless Latin government, and Kennedy nearly steals the show. A-II (br)

Pink Panther, The (1964) Farcical comedy introducing the accident-prone French policeman Inspector Clouseau (Peter Sellers), in Switzerland on the trail of a suspected English jewel thief (David Niven) after the fabled gem of the title. Directed by Blake Edwards, the comic caper complications are broad and zesty, ranging from unsubtle sight gags and silly puns to bedroom hanky-panky, with the clumsy antics of the dim Clouseau amusing enough to sustain six sequels. Slapstick violence, sexual situations, and double entendres. A-III (br)

Pink Panther Strikes Again, The (1977) Peter Sellers returns as Inspector Clouseau, but the one-joke nature of his success through bungling has worn rather thin, especially the running gag of karate assaults by his Oriental servant. The plot revolves around the machinations of Clouseau's former superior (Herbert Lom) who, driven mad by the constant incompetence of his underling, has gotten control of a doomsday machine. Director Blake Edwards achieves some good comic bits but mainly relies on slapstick violence and sexually derived humor. A-III (PG)

Pink Telephone, The (1977) French production about an American conglomerate (run by Michel Lonsdale) which tries to induce an aging French factory-owner (Pierre Mondy) to sell out by setting him up with a call girl (Mireille Darc), with whom he falls in love. Director Edouard Molinaro and writer Francis Verber resist a pat sentimental and moralistic ending and concentrate on illustrating the lack of values operating in an amoral environment. Well-acted and directed, the movie's adult theme contains brief nudity and rough language. A-IV (R)

Pinocchio (1940) Walt Disney's animated classic about a wooden-headed puppet (voice of Dick Jones) who wants to be a real boy but keeps getting into trouble by listening to foxy Honest John (voice of Walter Catlett) instead of appointed conscience Jiminy Cricket (voice of Cliff Edwards). The fantasy quality of the story is made all the more delightful by superb animation and such lovely songs as "When You Wish Upon a Star," though small fry may get some frights on Pleasure Island and in the sea depths with Monstro the Whale. One of Disney's grandest contributions to family entertainment. A-I (G)

Pinup Girl (1944) Inane wartime morale-booster directed by Bruce Humberstone involves a dizzy small-town secretary (Betty Grable) who thinks it's her patriotic duty to romance men in uniform, until she gets serious about a Guadacanal naval hero (John Harvey) who thinks she's a Broadway musical star. Silly romantic complications. A-II (br)

Pipe Dreams (1976) Going to Alaska in an attempt to win back her estranged husband, a woman (Gladys Knight) gets involved in breaking up a teenage prostitution ring. The failed romantic melodrama is poorly directed and carelessly edited by Stephen Verona. Some violence, rough language, and a scene of an attempted abortion. A-III (PG)

Pippi Longstocking (1997) In this animated adventure, the spunky nine-year-old girl of the title (voice of Melissa Altro) awaits her father's return from being lost at sea while engaging in amusing encounters with neighboring children, an interfering busybody, and a pair of bumbling burglars. Directed by Clive Smith, the production has colorful but unexceptional cartooning, though Pippi's carefree hijinks should delight young viewers and lead some to the books recounting other of her adventures. A-I(G)

Pirate, The (1948) Stylish musical romance set in the 18th century on a Caribbean island, where a traveling performer (Gene Kelly) woos a well-bred señorita (Judy Garland) by pretending to be the dashing pirate she secretly admires. Directed by Vincente Minnelli, the stage-bound story is an uneasy mix of comedy and sentimentality, though the sets, costumes, and choreography are lovely to look at, and the Cole Porter songs easy to take, especially the "Be a Clown" finale. Romantic situations. A-II (br)

Pirate Movie, The (1982) Incompetent movie musical revolves around contemporary characters (Kristy McNichol and Christopher Atkins) who find themselves in the world of Gilbert and Sullivan's "The Pirates of Penzance." Filmed in Australia by director Ken Annakin, the movie desperately tries to evoke laughter at any cost, relying mainly on pratfalls, vulgar language, and crude double-entendres, but nothing can save it from its own ineptitudes. A-III (PG)

Pirates (1986) Director Roman Polanski's obsessively detailed and ornamental portrait of the era when galleons feared ships flying the Jolly Roger features

Walter Matthau as an irascible pirate captain determined to possess a solid gold throne. Unfortunately, the overblown action epic leaves little room to develop a somewhat whimsical plot. Vulgarity, brutality and disproportionate amounts of realistically staged sea battles. A-III (PG)

Pirates of Blood River, The (1961) Pulp British adventure yarn about a 17th-century Huguenot colony being invaded by pirates (led by Christopher Lee) searching for treasure. Directed by John Gilling, the hokey proceedings make as little sense as the bad acting. Stylized violence. A-II (br)

Pirates of Penzance, The (1983) Screen adaptation of a New York stage version of the Gilbert and Sullivan operetta has a fine cast headed by George Rose, whose rendition of "A Modern Major General" is easily the best moment, Linda Ronstadt as Mabel, and Kevin Kline as the Pirate King. Directed by Wilford Leach, it is good family entertainment, though some may find it much too stage-bound. A-I (G)

Pirates of Tripoli, The (1955) Lackluster romantic adventure in which an Arabian princess (Patricia Medina) is put back on her throne by a pirate captain (Paul Henreid). Directed without conviction by Felix Feist, it's escapist entertainment for the undemanding. Swashbuckling violence and romantic complications. A-II (br)

Pirosmani (1978) Russian import about an obscure Georgian painter whose work has grown in stature since his death in 1919. Director Georgy Shengelaya employs beautifully stark images to show how the artist's imagination was rooted in his rural environment and time period, one that is rather exotic because so unfamiliar. His kind of folk art appealed to the common people because of its traditional ethnic and religious themes and symbolism. A-II (nr)

Pittsburgh (1942) Sprawling melodrama in which coal miners (John Wayne and Randolph Scott) become partners in a small company that grows into a coal and steel empire, then drift apart over a woman (Marlene Dietrich) and differing ambitions, until WW II reunites them in running a war plant. Directed by Lewis Seiler, the improbable plot transforms working stiffs into business leaders undone by Wayne's greed but brought together again in a patriotic finale joining capital and labor in the war effort. Stylized violence and romantic complications. A-II (br)

Pixote (1982) Harrowing and poignant Brazilian drama about a gang of nomad boys in Rio and the terrible things they do to survive. Directed by Hector Babenco, this powerful movie is definitely not for the faint of heart or weak of stomach because it involves sordid violence and graphic sexuality. A-IV (nr)

Pizza Triangle, The (1970) Stylish Italian satire about a tragic love affair involving a Marxist bricklayer (Marcello Mastroianni) who leaves his wife for a cemetery flower-peddler (Monica Vitti) and then becomes insanely jealous when she in turn falls in love with a pizza cook (Giancarlo Giannini). Director Ettore Scola is not interested in his hackneyed romantic plot except as a device supporting a pastiche of comic styles and sensibilities poking fun at movie cliches and stereotypes, as well as Italian life and institutions. Some rough language. A-III (R)

Place Called Glory, A (1966) Undistinguished Western directed by Ralph Gideon with Lex Barker as a gunfighter who joins a pal in cleaning out a town full of bad men. Stylized violence. A-II (br)

Place for Lovers, A (1969) Lovely American (Faye Dunaway) initiates an affair with a romantic Italian (Marcello Mastroianni) who learns only after falling hopelessly in love that she is doomed by a fatal disease. Directed by Vittorio De Sica, the melodrama's amoral approach to love and life is handled in a heavy, pretentious manner. A-III (R)

Places in the Heart (1984) Sally Fields plays a young widow struggling to keep her family together and her integrity intact after her husband's death in rural Texas during the Depression. Under Robert Benton's direction, Field's performance winningly conveys a character of strong faith and good will in the face of adversity. A-II (PG)

Place in the World, A (1994) Slow-paced drama set in rural Argentina, where a 12-year-old boy (Gaston Batyi) tries to understand the complex relationship between a visiting Spanish geologist (Jose Sacristan) and his idealistic parents (Federico Luppi and Cecilia Roth) who run a farming cooperative with an activist nun (Leonor Benedetto). Believable characterizations and well-realized themes of personal and social commitment shine through producer-director Adolfo Aristarain's dialogue-clogged work. Subtitles. Misguided act of violence, a scene of drunkenness, and an instance of rough language. A-III (nr)

Plague of the Zombies, The (1966) Routine British horror movie directed by John Gilling about a man (Andre Morell) who can turn people into the walking dead. Restrained gore. A-II (br)

Plainsman, The (1936) Wild and woolly Western adventure yarn in which Wild Bill Hickok (Gary Cooper) teams up with Calamity Jane (Jean Arthur) and Buffalo Bill Cody (James Ellison) to stop a traitor (Charles Bickford) from selling repeating rifles to the Indians. A rousing and often agreeable entertainment directed by Cecil B. DeMille, the result has plenty of outdoor action but little sense of Western history. Woefully stereotyped Indians and stylized violence. A-I (br)

Plainsman, The (1966) Director David Lowell Rich's undistinguished remake of the 1936 original features Don Murray as Hickok, Abby Dalton as Calamity Jane, and not much more. For patient youngsters and undemanding adults. A-I (br)

Plainsman and the Lady (1946) Standard Western directed by Joe Kane in which a veteran frontiersman (William Elliott) and his sidekick (Andy Clyde) help the Pony Express get started, then win the gratitude of its founder's daughter (Vera Ralston) by stopping an underhanded rival (Joseph Schildkraut) from putting it out of business. Frontier violence and an unfaithful wife. A-II (br)

Plan 9 from Outer Space (1956) Totally inept sci-fi clunker directed by Edward D. Wood, Jr., in which cut-rate aliens spend several nights resurrecting corpses while a hooded figure (Bela Lugosi) watches, then the aliens depart in tin saucers to end the dreary proceedings. A few ludicrous, no-frills frights. A-II (br)

Planes, Trains and Automobiles (1987) Steve Martin plays a hapless traveler trying to get from New York to Chicago in time to have Thanksgiving with his family but, among other disasters and discomforts, planes are grounded, trains break down, and automobiles catch fire. Adding to the disagreeable experiences of the journey is fellow traveler John Candy in director John Hughes's comedy which, though uneven, does have its truly hilarious moments. Some very rough language and sexual references. A-III (R)

Planet of the Apes (1968) Charlton Heston plays the leader of a space expedition who lands his craft on an unnamed planet in the constellation of Orion, where he discovers a civilization of apes trying to domesticate a species of human beings. Director Franklin J. Schaffner's entertaining screen version of Pierre Boulle's novel is an allegorical warning to a destruction-prone world. Some violence and mature themes. A-III (G)

Plastic Dome of Norma Jean, The (1974) The media's inevitable victimization of the personalities that they create is the theme of this story about a young woman (Sharon Henesy) whose gift of clairvoyance is used to popularize an exceptionally undistinguished rock group. The script and direction by Juleen Compton prove simply inadequate to the ambitions of what proves to be a terribly flawed movie. Mature themes. A-III (nr)

Plato's Run (1997) Formula action-melodrama set in southern Florida, where a former CIA agent (Gary Busey) is hired to get some escaped prisoners out of Cuba, then has to rescue his teen daughter from the clutches of a ruthless crime boss (Roy Scheider), with unconvincing results. Writer-director James Becket offers no fresh angles on a drearily predictable plot marked by hammy acting. Assorted violence, menacing situations, sexual innuendo, and occasional rough language. A-III (R)

Platoon (1986) The Vietnam War as experienced by a raw recruit (Charlie Sheen) is evoked with relentless realism in scenes of battle and brutality in writer-director Oliver Stone's haunting reminiscence of its horrors and inhumanity. Its excessive violence, unrelenting profanity, and graphic depiction of representative atrocities are stomach-churning, but serve as a corrective to Rambo-style romanticizations of the war. A-IV (R)

Play Dirty (1969) British WW II story about a motley collection of criminals sent behind German lines in North Africa under the command of an inexperienced but decent officer (Michael Caine). Andre de Toth's direction emphasizes the ugly realities of survival in the desert, but its anti-war message suffers from overkill and borders on a cynical destruction of all values. Strong graphic violence. A-III (PG)

Play It Again, Sam (1972) Woody Allen plays a balding, bespectacled loser who grooves on Humphrey Bogart movies (and even conjures Bogey up for on-the-spot advice in touchy situations). When his beautiful, brainy wife (Susan Anspach) walks out on him, his best friends (Diane Keaton and Tony Roberts) devote themselves to setting up blind dates (Jennifer Salt, Viva, and Joy Bang). A very funny comedy directed by Herbert Ross, it's not a family film, but one most older teens and adults will thoroughly enjoy for some witty insights into the mating game. A-III (PG)

Play It As It Lays (1972) Failed exploration of contemporary womanhood and decadent movie industry folk based on the Joan Didion novel. Tuesday Weld is the unsuccessful actress, neglected wife, and mother on a Hollywood odyssey into self-realization. Director Frank Perry envisions life as a crap-game, but doesn't see beyond the superficial characters whose confusion he portrays. A suicide and marital problems are central to the plot. A-IV (R)

Play Misty for Me (1971) Slick disk-jockey (Clint Eastwood) has a near-tragic romantic involvement with one of his fans, a severely disturbed woman (Jessica Walter) who is given to very dangerous fits of jealousy. Also directed by Eastwood, his performance is less wooden than usual though still lethargic, and it is up to Walter to supply the spark, here of manic menace. Gripping but flawed psychodrama lacks any sense of the moral implications of the situation. Violence and gore with brief nudity. A-IV (R)

Player's Club, The (1998) Cheap exploitation piece about a single mother (LisaRaye) working her way through college as a nude dancer in the sleazy bar of the title. Written and directed by rap-singer Ice Cube, the bogus story is little more than a transparent pretext for exhibiting nude dancers, a variety of sexual encounters, and acts of violence in and around the club. Numerous sex scenes, nudity, violence including a rape, frequent rough language, and occasional profanity. O (R)

Playboys, The (1992) An Irish village in the 1950s is beset by scandal when a middle-aged constable (Albert Finney) and a traveling theatrical troupe's leading man (Aidan Quinn) compete for the affections of a fiercely independent unwed mother (Robin Wright). Director Gillies MacKinnon's romantic triangle is sensitively played out without glossing over the moral considerations of the woman's predicament. A few discreet sexual encounters, a suicide, and brief fisticuffs. A-III (PG-13)

Player, The (1992) Incisive satire of the Hollywood moviemaking scene revolves around a studio executive (Tim Robbins) whose murder of an insulting screenwriter (Vincent D'Onofrio) concerns him less than the continual power plays inherent in his job. Director Robert Altman deftly skewers Hollywood's shallowness with sharply observed characterizations brimming with cynical wisdom. Momentary violence, a discreet encounter, flashes of nudity, and some rough language. A-III (R)

Players (1979) Ali MacGraw plays the contented, middle-aged mistress of magnate Maximilian Schell, but she falls in love with young tennis-hustler Dean-Paul Martin and has to choose between security and romance. Directed by Anthony Harvey, the turgid melodrama deals in simplistic love-hate characterizations consistent with its muddled conclusion. Condones an illicit sexual relationship. O (PG)

Playing by Heart (1999) Talky romantic drama follows the troubled relationships of five separate couples until they all come together at a marriage-renewal ceremony, by which time each couple has begun to resolve their difficulties. Some of their problems turn out to be more interesting than writer-director Willard Carroll's contrivances to reveal surprise connections among the characters. Implied affairs and discreet sexual situations, brief alcohol abuse, occasional profanity, and intermittent rough language. A-III (R)

Playing for Keeps (1986) A teenager elicits the help of friends to convert a dilapidated hotel his mom has inherited, foiling attempts by unscrupulous real-estate agents to convert the site into a secret toxic-waste dump. Predictable and simplistic in plot, the movie highlights matter-of-fact acceptance and depictions of casual sex-relations between the kids. O (PG-13)

Playing God (1997) Dreary melodrama in which a drug-addicted ex-doctor (David Duchovny) comes under the sway of a psychotic mobster (Timothy Hutton), then tries to double-cross him, with bloody results. Drably mounted and lifelessly acted, director Any Wilson's gore-soaked proceedings offer nothing beyond numbing murders and assorted mayhem. Excessive violence, substance abuse, constant rough language, and some profanity. O (R)

Playtime (1973) Monsieur Hulot (Jacques Tati) wanders through various vignettes with characteristic absentmindedness, totally unsurprised by any absurdity that crosses his path. The 1967 French comedy is a loose collection of anecdotes about the depersonalized steel-and-glass environments comprising the urban landscape, a Parisian maze which writer-producer-director Tati treats with the humor of the urban commonplace. A-I (nr)

Plaza Suite (1971) Walter Matthau plays the central character in each of three segments about successive occupants of the same suite in New York's famed Plaza Hotel. Directed by Arthur Hiller, derived from the Broadway play by Neil Simon, the lame comedy matches Matthau's penchant for mugging with Simon's middlebrow humor resulting in only a passing diversion. Mature themes. A-III (PG)

Pleasantville (1998) Empty-headed comic fantasy in which two contemporary teens (Tobey Maguire and Reese Witherspoon) are zapped into a 1958 black-and-white family sitcom, where their freewheeling attitudes start changing everything in previously perfect Pleasantville. Writer-director Gary Ross sets up some amusing if obvious culture clashes, but his depiction of the repressed '50s vs. the supposedly enlightened '90s is jarringly simplistic and heavy-handed. Implied infidelity, masturbation and teen sex, fleeting violence, occasional profanity, and an instance of rough language. A-IV (PG-13)

Please Don't Eat the Daisies (1960) Overwrought screen version of Jean Kerr's amusingly anecdotal book of family life as wife (Doris Day) of New York drama-critic Walter (David Niven). Director Walter Lang gets few smiles from the frenetic goings-on in a household of busy parents, rambunctious boys, longsuffering maid (Patsy Kelly), and neurotic dog during the transition from cramped city apartment to affluent suburban home. Domestic misunderstandings and mild sexual innuendo. A-II (br)

Pleasure of His Company, The (1961) Romantic comedy fluff from the play by Cornelia Otis Skinner and Samuel Taylor in which an aging playboy (Fred Astaire) unexpectedly shows up for the wedding of his daughter (Debbie Reynolds) and cheerfully tries to charm his ex-wife (Lilli Palmer), while scorning her new husband (Gary Merrill). Directed by George Seaton, the static situation is helped by lively performances and lush San Francisco backgrounds, but they're not enough to sustain the flashes of wit along the way to the picture's pat conclusion. Comic treatment of marriage. A-II (br)

Plenty (1985) Impressionistic chronicle of the growing disillusionment and mental instability of an English woman (Meryl Streep), a heroine of the French Resistance, over the course of the two decades following WW II. Directed by Fred Schepisi, the sole bright spot in this cold, tedious, unfocused, and intellectually muddled movie is John Gielgud's performance as a befuddled but honorable diplomat. Some fairly graphic bedroom scenes. A-IV (R)

Plot Against Harry, The (1990) Originally filmed in 1969, the whimsical tale tells of a small-time Jewish numbers-racketeer (Martin Priest) who loses his Bronx turf after a nine-month stint in prison. Director Michael Roemer's slice of Jewish Americana and New York mob-life uses black-and-white photography to capture the environment as well as the humorous situation of a has-been whose family tries to steer him straight. Minimal rough language and some casual involvement with prostitutes. A-III (nr)

Plunderers, The (1948) Routine Western directed by Joseph Kane in which an undercover Army officer (Rod Cameron) falls for a classy saloon-singer (Ilona Massey) after joining the gang of a soft-hearted outlaw (Forrest Tucker), but before he can arrange their capture a Sioux uprising intervenes. Frontier violence and a sham marriage. A-II (br)

Plunderers of Painted Flats (1959) Formula Western directed by Albert C. Gannaway in which a retired gunslinger (Edmund Lowe) sides with sod-busters (led by Skip Homeier) against a vicious landbaron (George Macready) and his hired gunman (John Carroll), with three mail-order brides (Corinne Calvet, Bea Benadaret, and Madge Kennedy) caught in the middle. Some nasty frontier violence and sexual innuendo. A-III (br)

Plymouth Adventure (1952) Hokey history of the Pilgrims' voyage to the New World aboard the *Mayflower*, whose hard-drinking, double-dealing captain (Spencer Tracy) pursues the wife (Gene Tierney) of the colony's leader (Leo Genn), then blames himself for her suicide. Director Clarence Brown's talky script, sporadic action, and melodramatic treatment add up to disappointing results. Stylized violence, including an off-screen suicide. A-II (br)

Pocahontas (1995) Visually lovely animation romanticizes the historical story of Native-American princess Pocohantas (voice of Irene Bedard) and English captain John Smith (voice of Mel Gibson) whose life she saved in 1607 Jamestown, as conflicts between Indians and settlers threaten to boil over. While not Disney's finest achievement, directors Mike Gabriel and Eric Goldberg's exceptional imagery and simple narrative stress respecting nature and appreciating how different cultures can learn from each other and live in harmony. A-I (G)

Pocket Money (1972) Slight but often amusing contemporary Western in which a down-on-his-luck cattleman (Paul Newman) is hired by a shady operator (Strother Martin) to buy rodeo bulls in Mexico, enlists the help of an old friend (Lee Marvin) to bring them back, but encounters some double-dealing along the way. Directed by Stuart Rosenberg, the meandering buddy movie has some fine rodeo action and occasional adult humor. A-III (PG)

Pocketful of Miracles, A (1961) Colorful Damon Runyon story about how a band of Manhattan hoods and grifters (headed by Glenn Ford) turn poor old Apple Annie (Bette Davis) into a socialite so her daughter can marry into a wealthy family. Director Frank Capra's last movie is an embarrassingly sentimental remake of his 1933 **Lady for a Day** and, despite the fine cast, seems little but silly. An elaborate deception and mild sexual innuendo. A-II (nr)

Poetic Justice (1993) A beautician (Janet Jackson) mourning her murdered boyfriend cautiously allows herself to open up to a South Central LA postal-worker (Tupac Shakur) while they are on a trip to Oakland with a shrilly argumentative couple (Regina King and Joe Torry) — until more deadly violence nearly deep-sixes the new couple's budding romance. Writer-director John Singleton focuses on the relationships of four foul-mouthed and often boring characters, but the ultimate message is that love is possible and worthwhile, even in the most menacing environments. Some nasty violence, a discreet sexual encounter, coarse sexual references, and constant rough language. A-IV (R)

Point Blank (1967) Doublecrossed in a robbery by a friend who takes not only the loot and his wife but also leaves him for dead, tough guy Lee Marvin comes back to uncover an underworld connection, which he destroys man by man until all responsible are dead. Director John Boorman's brutally violent and illogical crime thriller is handled with a technical virtuosity that is sometimes effective but frequently pretentious and overblown in its graphic depiction of violence. O (br)

Point Break (1991) Ultra-violent action thriller in which a rookie FBI agent (Keanu Reeves) befriends a surfer-guru (Patrick Swayze) suspected of masterminding a string of California bank robberies. Director Kathryn Bigelow's splashy surfing footage and razzle-dazzle camerawork don't erase the plot inconsistencies, hackneyed romantic subplot, or uncritical portrayal of extremely macho behavior. Excessive violence and rough language, implied promiscuity, suicide, and brief nudity. O (R)

Point of No Return (1993) A convicted killer (Bridget Fonda), turned into a skilled assassin by a government agent (Gabriel Byrne) for a covert organization, takes on a high-risk mission hoping if she succeeds to be allowed to retire and wed her lover (Dermot Mulroney), who knows nothing of her past. Director John Badham shortchanges the supposed reformation of the central character for a steady stream of graphic violence. Excessive violence, brief bedroom shots, fleeting nudity, and much rough language. O (R)

Point of Terror (1971) Pop singer (Peter Carpenter) plays up to the lusting wife of the crippled owner of a record company, but, when she refuses to marry him after he kills her spouse, he switches his affections to her comely daughter, who has reaped the lioness's share of Daddy's inheritance. The sordid melodrama depends totally upon crude sensationalism for cheap thrills. O (R)

Poison Ivy (1992) Sleazy melodrama about a conniving high-school girl (Drew Barrymore) who moves into her friend's (Sara Gilbert) home, where she seduces the girl's father (Tom Skerritt), murders her mother (Cheryl Ladd), and drives her distraught friend into a killing rage. Director Katt Shea's death-embracing movie is darkly atmospheric but comes up short on intelligence and moral perspective. Several adulterous encounters with brief nudity, occasional violence, alcohol abuse, and some rough language. O (R)

Police Academy (1984) Reluctant police recruit (Stephen Guttenberg) finds that law enforcement can be fun in this dismal, failed comedy directed by Hugh Wilson. It relies heavily on sexually oriented humor, some nudity, and rough language to convey its crude message of social irresponsibility. O (R)

Police Academy 2: Their First Assignment (1985) Sequel directed by Jerry Paris is somewhat less vulgar than the original but vulgar enough, as well as altogether lackluster and unfunny. Sexually oriented humor. A-III (PG-13)

Police Academy 3: Back in Training (1986) Police recruits try to save the prestige of the training academy's aging director in a tasteless movie, whose failed humor is derived chiefly through sadistic violence, lewd jokes, and slapstick stunts. O (PG)

Police Academy 4: Citizens on Patrol (1987) Limp plot and lame script with unfunny Keystone Cop slapstick antics by Steve Guttenberg, Bobcat Goldwait, and company is featured in this edition, which deals with the academy's post-graduate project involving a citizens' action-group. Tame in language and sexual references, director Jim Drake's movie emphasizes aerial and ballooning chase sequences. Mild-mannered but sophomoric entertainment. A-III (PG)

Police Academy 5: Assignment Miami Beach (1988) The Police Academy graduates return to honor soon-to-be-retired Commandant Lassard (George Gaynes) as Policeman of the Decade at a police-chief's convention in Miami Beach. Directed by Alan Myerson, the boys and girls in blue frolic on the beach and, among other things, foil a kidnapping plot. Dumb but innocuous fun, though some brief sexist visuals. A-II (PG)

Policy Academy 6: City Under Siege (1989) The crackpot cop-squad is back, this time to rid the city of an insidious gang of thieves. Though the gals and guys in blue have more dignity this time around, director Peter Bonerz's tired sequel provides more than enough time to snooze and schmooze. Minimal vulgar references and some comic-book violence. A-II (PG)

Police Call 9000 (see: **Detroit 9000**)

Police Connection, The (see: **Badge 373**)

Policeman, The (1972) Israeli import features Shay K. Ophir as a Jaffa policeman, whose 20-year career is distinguished only by its lack of arrests. Learning that Ophir is about to be fired, some crooks stage a heist to save his job. Director Ephraim Kishon uses a number of sweet, light, and warm moments to celebrate human solidarity. A-II (nr)

Policewoman (1974) Sondra Currie and her squad of distaff detectives turn the underworld upside down by outdoing their brothers in blue. Director Lee Frost's mindless female crime-topper movie offers a variety of wild fights, hints of sadism, endless car chases, undeleted expletives, and a sprinkling of coy nudity. O (R)

Polish Wedding (1998) Muddled tale of a Polish-American family headed by a baker (Gabriel Byrne) who works nights, his wife (Lena Olin) who's having an affair with a businessman, their unwed pregnant daughter (Claire Danes), her cop-lover (Adam Trese), and assorted other family members. Writer-director Theresa Connelly's thin script focuses on the wife's preoccupation with love, sex, and motherhood as mirrored in the experiences of her daughter, with the rest of the clan serving mainly as comic relief, and the ribald treatment of sexual scenes laboriously overdone. Numerous sexual situations, ethnic stereotyping, some profanity, and occasional rough language. A-IV (PG-13)

Pollyanna (1960) Heartwarming Disney dramatization of the Eleanor Porter children's classic about a turn-of-the-century orphan (Hayley Mills) who comes to live with her stern New England aunt (Jane Wyman), then proceeds to brighten the lives of all in the vicinity with her sunny disposition and penchant for looking on the bright side. Director David Swift has the benefit of Mills's sweet performance with a contrasting cast of grumps (notably Wyman, Adolphe Menjou, and Karl Malden), though youngsters may find the proceedings overlong and their elders put off by the sugarcoated treatment. A-I (G)

Poltergeist (1982) Suburban couple (Jobeth Williams and Craig T. Nelson) find their cozy existence disturbed when their five-year-old daughter gets trapped in the television screen, and a parapsychologist (Beatrice Straight) is called in to retrieve her. Along the way to the burial grounds, producer Steven Spielberg and director Tobe Hooper treat viewers to some special-effects violence and gore, teenage sexuality, and a benign look at Mom and Dad smoking marijuana at bedtime. O (R/PG appeal)

Poltergeist II: The Other Side (1986) Angry spirits led by a demonic minister (Julian Beck) return to torment and terrorize the Freeling family just when they thought it was safe to leave grandma's house. The family has become more cynical, and the effects less frightening but more disgusting, in this sequel. The Vomit Creature sequence may be too gruesome for the very young in an otherwise mild-mannered Gothic tale. A-II (PG-13)

Poltergeist III (1988) Impossibly silly sequel sees little Carol Anne (Heather O'Rourke) spending some time in a Chicago high-rise with her mother's sister (Nancy Allen), her new husband (Tom Skerritt), and his teenage daughter (Lara Flynn Boyle). The potential of their glass-and-mirrored high-tech environs are utilized by the ghouls who continue to hound the little girl in a far-fetched and gruesome movie directed by Gary Sherman. Much grisly violence and frightening special effects that are specially aimed at destroying a youngster and some teenagers. O (PG-13)

Polyester (1981) Saga relating the sorrows of Francine Fishpaw, an overweight suburban matron (played by female impersonator Divine) and the man (Tab Hunter) who seems to be the answer to her dreams. Baltimore writer-director John Waters often shows real satirical flair, but he too often tries to get laughs by appealing to the sadistic streak in an audience. Romantic homosexual aspect figures in the plot. O (R)

Ponette (1997) French production in which a four-year-old French girl (Victoire Thivisol) whose mother has been killed in a car crash is confused by adult attempts to comfort her with platitudes about heaven, because she adamantly expects her mother will return to her. Writer-director Jacques Doillon convincingly captures a toddler's innocent perspective, but the picture's preoccupation with the tearful child's abject misery becomes tiresome. Subtitles. Conflicting ideas about God and the afterlife. A-II (nr)

Pony Express (1953) Standard Western heroics with Buffalo Bill Cody (Charlton Heston) and Wild Bill Hickok (Forrest Tucker) fighting off badmen and Indians to open the route for riders carrying the mail from Missouri to California. Directed by Jerry Hopper, the action features some fanciful derring-do, but the ladies (Rhonda Fleming and Jan Sterling) are purely decorative, and expect no surprises along the way. Frontier violence and mild romantic complications. A-II (br)

Pony Soldier (1952) Fair Western set in Canada's Northwest Territories, where in 1876 a Mountie constable (Tyrone Power) and his reluctant half-breed guide (Thomas Gomez) rescue some white captives from a band of Cree renegades (led by Cameron Mitchell). Director Joseph M. Newman delivers a credible story of how the Mountie on his own in a vast wilderness relies on reason rather than force in persuading the Crees to keep the peace. Frontier violence. A-I (br)

Poor Cow (1968) British story of life in London's slums, where an impoverished, too-young mother (Carol White) drifts into degrading situations, even posing for lecherous amateur photographers, while her husband (John Bindon) and lover (Terence Stamp) are in prison. Directed by Kenneth Loach, the stuff of social protest is certainly here, but artistic discipline is lacking in such matters as a gory scene of childbirth and several erotic sequences whose point is less dramatic than exploitative. O (br)

Poor Little Rich Girl (1936) Dated but enduring Shirley Temple vehicle in which she pretends to be an orphan, gets taken in by a song-and-dance vaudeville team (Jack Haley and Alice Faye), then charms a crusty soap-manufacturer (Claude Gillingwater) into sponsoring their radio show. Directed by Irving Cummings, little Shirley troupes through the formula sentiment in winning fashion, though the bald plot-contrivances may hinder the enjoyment of some viewers. A-I (G)

Popcorn (1969) Loud, cluttered documentary with pop-music groups, such as the Vanilla Fudge, the Rolling Stones, the Bee Gees, and a host of others, performing amid psychedelic lights and wildly fast editing. Some extremely fleeting nudity and a suggestive performance involving Jimi Hendrix make it inappropriate for youngsters. A-III (G)

Popcorn (1991) Film students (Tom Villard and Jill Schoelen) and their teacher (Tony Roberts) stage an all-night horror film-fest, which is punctuated by as much mayhem and murder off-screen as on. Director Mark Herrier's attempt to create a campy spoof mostly bombs out with a convoluted plot, corny dialogue, and choppy editing — which just may make it a cult favorite on video. Some violence and minimal rough language. A-III (R)

Pope Joan (1972) Legendary tale of a ninth-century woman (Liv Ullmann) who disguised herself as a man and worked her way up to the papacy. Directed by Michael Anderson, the British production is both a dramatic clunker and an historical yawner which fails to convey any sense of the life and experience of Christianity in the early Middle Ages. Graphic rape scene and the suggestion of lesbianism in the convent. A-IV (PG)

Pope Must Die, The (1991) Flaccid British farce in which a bumbling country priest (Robbie Coltrane) is mistakenly named pope, only to discover an unholy alliance of cardinals and crooks as well as a pre-seminary girlfriend (Beverly D'Angelo), who announces he has a rock-musician son. Director Peter Richardson's witless spoof of Vatican officialdom is a one-joke affair that grows tiresome with silly sight gags, one-liners, and incongruities so outrageous that they cannot be taken seriously, yet done in such bad taste as to offend many. Some rough language, comic violence, and sexual references with a flash of nudity. A-IV (R)

Pope of Greenwich Village, The (1984) Two amateur hustlers (Mickey Rourke and Eric Roberts) run afoul of both the mob and corrupt police. Though it lacks dramatic power, director Stuart Rosenberg's movie presents a sensitive study of a streetwise collection of characters made interesting because of good acting and perceptive script. Some scenes of restrained sex and violence. A-III (R)

Popeye (1980) Disappointing attempt to bring Popeye and the Thimble Theater gang to the screen is clever and sometimes mildly amusing, but never very funny. Robin Williams works valiantly as the hero, but neither director Robert Altman nor writer Jules Feiffer have given him much to do. The songs and dances are leaden and witless. Some slightly naughty visuals and expletives dragged in for no good purpose. A-II (PG)

Popi (1969) Puerto Rican widower (Alan Arkin), struggling to give his sons something of a decent life amidst the slums of New York City, finds that he can't make it even with his three jobs as handyman, busboy, and hospital orderly. Director Arthur Hiller skirts sentimental melodrama and Arkin's comic lightness keeps viewers engaged in a potentially tragic story, the point of which is that there are no fantasy solutions to the hard realities of poverty. Some brutal aspects of slum life. A-II (G)

Pork Chop Hill (1959) Fine Korean War picture in which an Army lieutenant (Gregory Peck) follows orders to retake an overrun position, but loses most of his company in the process, then is ordered to hold the hill with his handful of survivors against a Chinese counterattack. Directed by Lewis Milestone, the combat scenes are grimly realistic and convincingly acted, but the battle takes on added meaning by being shown as having no military value except as a bargaining chip in the final phase of the 1953 cease-fire negotiations. Wartime violence. A-I (br)

Porky's (1982) Sex-obsessed adolescents cavort at a Florida high school during the Eisenhower era.

Director Bob Clark's extended dirty joke is made even more offensive by some ill-advised stabs at seriousness. Witlessly vulgar movie with much nudity, graphic sexuality, and an almost non-stop flow of verbal obscenities. O (R)

Porky's II: The Next Day (1983) Sequel dishes up more of the same elaborate but boring hijinks of sex-crazed Florida high-school boys, most of whom look old enough to play their teachers. Directed again by Bob Clark, it differs from the original only in having an even more muddled and disjointed story-line. Excessive nudity and scabrous dialogue. O (R)

Porky's Revenge (1985) The old gang at Angel Beach High who now look old enough, if not bright enough, to be out of graduate school, are at it again. This effort directed by James Komack, like the previous ones, is beneath contempt. Exploitative nudity and tedious, mindless vulgarity. O (R)

Portnoy's Complaint (1972) Sneering, caustic, and self-defeating adaptation of the Philip Roth novel about the sexual fetishes and fixations of a Jewish youth (Richard Benjamin). Produced and directed by Ernest Lehman, its social satire is an extraordinarily repulsive mix of vulgar sight gags, crude bathroom humor, sexual escapades, and profanity that add up to a demeaning stereotyped portrait of Jewish family life. O (R)

Portrait of a Lady, The (1996) Brooding version of the Henry James novel in which a young but spirited American (Nicole Kidman) in 1872 England inherits a fortune, and, forsaking suitors, she sets off on a journey of self-discovery until manipulated into marrying the malevolent brother (John Malkovich) of an opportunistic friend (Barbara Hershey). Director Jane Campion provides a credible re-creation of the Victorian world as the uneasy setting for James's tortured melodrama of an American innocent made wiser by her ordeals among corrupt sophisticates. Domestic violence, suggestions of incest, a flash of nudity, and multiple romantic complications. A-III (PG-13)

Portrait of the Artist As a Young Man, A (1979) Screen version of James Joyce's autobiographical novel about his aesthetic and philosophical development during his school and university years before departing for Paris. Director Joseph Strick's uninspired, talky drama has a number of good performances, the most memorable of which is John Gielgud as the Jesuit retreat-master delivering the famous sermon on hell. The tension between religious faith and literary aspirations is at the heart of the adaptation and is treated in serious and mature fashion. A-IV (nr)

Poseidon Adventure, The (1972) Massive tidal wave overturns ocean-liner, leaving just enough survivors to exemplify every stereotype and cliche expected by disaster-movie fans. Gene Hackman plays a liberal minister leading his instant flock of Hollywood stars to the deepest part of the overturned hull, where there is an air pocket and chance of escape. Ronald Neame directs the mushy but occasionally gripping tale for viewers seeking escapist fare. Stylized violence, a few sexual references, and some profanity. A-III (PG)

Posse (1975) Kirk Douglas plays a politically ambitious US marshal in late 19th-century Texas who battles outlaws by means of his own well-trained, fanatically loyal posse, but runs into trouble when he brings in a popular train-robber (Bruce Dern). Also directed by Douglas, the simplistic morality tale is heavy-handed in its use of violence and offensive in a needless bit of sexual exploitation. O (PG)

Posse (1993) Returning from fighting in the Spanish-American War in 1898 Cuba, a small band of African-American soldiers (headed by Mario Van Peebles) and a white comrade (Stephen Baldwin) head West to settle a score with the sheriff (Richard Jordan) who murdered their leader's peace-loving father. Also directed by Van Peebles, the movie certainly doesn't skimp on shootouts and portrays vigilante justice uncritically, but it also reminds viewers of the not-insignificant presence of African-American settlers in the development of the West and of the particular hardships they encountered. Much stylized violence, a bedroom scene, brief nudity, and some rough language. A-IV (R)

Posse from Hell (1961) Cliched Western directed by Herbert Coleman follows a small posse of misfits led by a bitter deputy (Audie Murphy) as they hunt down four killers who escaped from prison, held up a bank, and fled with a woman hostage (Zohra Lampert). Frontier violence and veiled references to rape. A-II (br)

Possessed (1947) Murky melodrama in which a troubled woman (Joan Crawford) is rejected by her lover (Van Heflin), then marries a wealthy widower (Raymond Massey) in hopes of winning him back, only to go bonkers when he turns to another. Directed by Curtis Bernhardt, the convoluted story is told in flashbacks as the woman is treated by a psychiatrist, but the main interest is Crawford's vintage performance in a split-personality role. Heavy-handed treatment of an emotionally unstable person, romantic complications, and some stylized violence. A-II (br)

Possession of Joel Delaney, The (1972) Strained horror movie with some pretensions to social commentary tells the story of an affluent New York divorcée (Shirley MacLaine) and her brother (Michael Hordern), seemingly possessed by the malevolent soul of a dead Puerto Rican youth who had brutally murdered several women. The social dimension shows the cultural gulf between the Park Avenue rich and those living in Spanish Harlem. Director Waris Hussein resorts to shock tactics, considerably lessening the intensity of his film's serious subject matter by punctuating action with beheaded nude bodies and a climax that is as berserk as poor Joel. A-IV (R)

Postcards from the Edge (1990) Dramatic comedy about a young actress (Meryl Streep) forced to confront longstanding conflicts with her hard-drinking movie-star mom (Shirley MacLaine), in whose care she is released following drug rehabilitation. Written by actress Carrie Fisher and directed by Mike Nichols, the stylishly mounted look at mother-daughter relationships features splendid performances by the two leads representing the old and the new Hollywood. Comic treatment of drug and alcohol abuse, intermittent rough language, and several references to promiscuous relationships. A-III (R)

Postman, The (see: **Il Postino**)

Postman, The (1997) Set in a lawless post-apocalyptic society, where isolated towns are at the mercy of a murderous army of thieves (led by Will Patton), a wandering loner (Kevin Costner) assumes the uniform and role of a dead US postman, which has the unexpected effect of motivating the people to resist their oppressors and fight to restore democracy. Also directed by Costner, the movie's narrative is far-fetched but emotionally involving, appealing to sentimental notions of patriotism while overly idealizing the title character. Recurring violence, a sexual encounter with nudity, fleeting substance abuse, some profanity, and an instance of rough language. A-III (R)

Postman Always Rings Twice, The (1946) Gritty crime tale from James M. Cain's novel in which a tough drifter (John Garfield) takes a job in a roadside diner, falls for the unhappy wife (Lana Turner) of its good-natured owner (Cecil Kellaway), whom they determine to murder, then face the law and retribution. Directed by Tay Garnett, the sexual attraction motivating the horrendous crime is effectively depicted without any explicit visuals, but the murder's aftermath grows increasingly contrived and emotionally hollow. Stylized violence, including cold-blooded murder, an adulterous relationship, and much sexual innuendo. A-III (br)

Postman Always Rings Twice, The (1981) Failed adaptation of James M. Cain's bleak, Depression-era tale of passion and retribution, as an adulterous couple (Jessica Lange and Jack Nicholson) conspire to kill the woman's husband. Directed by Bob Rafelson, the slow-moving, uninvolving picture devotes most of its energy to conveying the sadomasochistic relationship between the two principals, neither of whom give very convincing performances. Excessively graphic display of sex. O (R)

Pot o' Gold (1941) Sentimental tale in which a bankrupt music-store owner (James Stewart) is taken in by some unemployed musicians (led by Horace Heidt), then manages to get them on a radio show sponsored by his mean but very rich uncle (Charles Winninger). Director George Marshall gives pedestrian treatment to the artificial plot and its formula characters with results that are even less convincing than Stewart's singing and harmonica playing. A-I (br)

Pound (1970) Absurdist social satire in which the actors assume the roles of dogs waiting in the city pound to be destroyed. These sad, lonely, unfulfilled social outcasts are potential elements for a meaningful exploration of one or another aspect of the human condition. Unfortunately, director Robert Downey's improvisational approach lacks any insight, and the content consists of little else but gross crudities played simply for irreverent and tasteless humor in a style that is more asinine than canine. O (X)

Powder (1995) Thin tale of an orphaned, albino teenager (Sean Patrick Flanery) whose supernormal powers make him a bizarre misfit in the normal world, though they inspire respectful awe in an educator (Mary Steenburgen), a science teacher (Jeff Goldblum), and the local sheriff (Lance Henriksen). Writer-director Victor Salva works hard at visualizing a character with powers beyond human ken but never develops the situation far beyond people's fear of what they don't understand. Some violent special effects, menacing situations, a flash of bare buttocks, and occasional profanity. A-III (PG-13)

Power (1986) Richard Gere stars as a public-relations expert and power broker in this glamorized depiction of the media process which creates and manipulates the image of politicians. The drama asserts that television is the major influence in molding public opinion. The narrative is spotted with a profanity unnecessary for characterization. O (R)

Power, The (1967) As his colleagues die mysteriously, scientist George Hamilton has to discover which of those involved in his pain-resistance experiment is a super-intelligent being. The thriller has an interesting premise, but suspense drains off through credibility gaps in the plot and Byron Haskin's slack direction. Benign attitude toward premarital sex. A-III (br)

Power of One, The (1992) Touching drama about a white orphan's experiences growing up English in South Africa at the time the German-speaking Afrikaners were gaining enough political power to make apartheid the law of the land in 1948. Under John G. Avildsen's less-than-subtle direction, the action scenes of boxing bouts and racial bloodshed threaten to overshadow the inspirational story of the young boy developing courage and a keen sense of social justice. Frequent bloody violence and racial slurs. A-II (PG-13)

Powwow Highway (1989) A philosophical conflict emerges on a journey from Montana to New Mexico between two Native Americans, one of whom (A. Martinez) dismisses Cheyenne tradition and culture as irrelevant in pulling the tribe up from Third World poverty, while the other (Gary Farmer) cherishes Cheyenne legends and longs to become a spiritual warrior. Though director Jonathan Wacks injects little suspense into his low-key road picture, it highlights the personal and political struggles being waged within the Native American community to regain and sustain their fast-disappearing culture. Some profanity, violence, and a flash of nudity. A-III (R)

Practical Magic (1998) Fantasy, horror, and sappy

romance collide when sister-witches (Sandra Bullock and Nicole Kidman) kill one's abusive boyfriend in self-defense, who then returns from the dead to bedevil their lives. Director Griffin Dunne's jumbled proceedings make no narrative sense, tossing together contrived comedy, pretty faces, and picturesque settings with less-than-magical results. Some brief violence, an implied affair, substance abuse, crude expressions, and minimal profanity. A-III (PG-13)

Practice Makes Perfect (1980) Jean Rochefort plays a famous pianist, a conceited self-centered woman-chaser, who gets a mild comeuppance when he tries to abandon his second wife (Nicole Garcia) and their three children by running off with the granddaughter (Catherine Le Prince) of an old flame (Danielle Darrieux). French sex-farce directed by Philippe de Broca, it's all very light, very sentimental, and passably droll for adults who enjoy such fare. A-III (nr)

Prancer (1989) Sweet-natured Christmas story about a spirited eight-year-old farm girl (Rebecca Harrell) who cares for an injured reindeer, believing it is one of Santa's team. While this "E.T." clone may have its fill of cranky adults and earnest moments, John Hancock's direction has a feel for rural community life that will please older viewers, while younger ones will love the reindeer and the praise lavished on the spunky heroine for revitalizing the town's Christmas spirit. A-I (G)

Prayer for the Dying, A (1987) A political assassin (Mickey Rourke) seeks redemption while fleeing killers from the IRA to which he belonged, a mobster (Alan Bates) who wants his services, and the police. A priest (Bob Hoskins) helps and comforts him in director Mike Hodges's heavy-handed drama saved by Rourke's skintight portrayal. Some violence and profanity cut with black humor. A-III (R)

Preacher's Wife, The (1996) Charming remake of the 1948 fantasy **The Bishop's Wife**, in which an angel (Denzel Washington) is sent to help the discouraged Baptist minister (Courtney B. Vance) of a struggling inner-city church and his neglected wife (Whitney Houston) rediscover romance in their marriage. Director Penny Marshall's slow-paced, sentimental story about the values of faith and hope is enlivened by an engaging cast and vibrant gospel songs. Romantic complications. A-II (PG)

Predator (1987) Elite commando rescue-team, on a mission into the Latin-American tropics, becomes the prey of a superhuman predator, who fights it out to the death with Arnold Sshwarzenegger. Director John McTiernan builds suspense in his nightmarish depiction of the hunt, but the landscape is strewn with skinned, bloodied victims. Profuse profanity and gruesome stylized violence. A-III (R)

Predator 2 (1990) Sci-fi horror tale set in 1997 Los Angeles, where a hotheaded cop (Danny Glover) ignores the hands-off orders of a top federal-agent (Gary Busey) and vows to personally exterminate the powerful alien-killer (Kevin Peter Hall) who has slaughtered his colleagues. In spite of clever lighting and special effects, director Stephen Hopkins cuts straight to the jugular with no pretense at character build-up in a grisly blood-fest devoid of human dimension. Excessive, graphic violence, full frontal nudity, and continuous rough language. O (R).

Prefontaine (1997) Fact-based story of distance runner Steve Prefontaine (Jared Leto), who set track records at the University of Oregon, competed unsuccessfully in the 1972 Munich Olympics, then became an activist for the rights of amateur athletes until his death in a 1975 auto accident. Directed by Steve James, the dramatization of the athlete's obsession to become a track star gains credibility from the use of newsreel footage and re-creations, but the story is thin on the human dimension of the characters and offers little for those uninterested in athletic competitions. Some stylized violence and a few instances of rough language and profanity. A-II (PG-13)

Prehistoric Women (1967) Clunky adventure fantasy follows a British hunter (Michael Latimer) into a time warp, where he is taken prisoner by a Stone Age clan of women whose totem is a white rhinoceros. British writer-director Michael Carreras turns the pulp situation primarily into a showcase for an assortment of scantily clad starlets (led by Martine Beswick and Edina Ronay). Stylized violence and much sexual innuendo. A-III (br)

Prelude to a Kiss (1992) When they kiss at her wedding, a bride (Meg Ryan) and an elderly stranger (Sydney Walker) magically switch personalities, leaving the groom (Alec Baldwin) to figure out how to get the woman he loves out of the old man's body. Director Norman Rene's featherweight fantasy barely sustains a contrived romantic comedy about the transcending power of love. An implied premarital relationship. A-III (PG-13)

Premonition, The (1976) Unconvincing thriller concerns a parapsychologist's attempt to find a missing child through the foster mother's psychic contact with the child's dead mother. Though it has some eerie moments and suggests some gory horrors, one doesn't have to be clairvoyant to perceive how badly director Robert Allen Schnitzer has missed the mark. A-III (PG)

President's Analyst, The (1968) James Coburn plays shrink to the commander-in-chief, who develops a case of the jitters when the revelations that relieve the president's tensions also happen to be state secrets. But he also discovers that he is being pursued by agents and double-agents who alternately want him to keep the lid on or blow it off. Director Theodore J. Flicker's comedy has some adult humor. A-III (br)

President's Lady, The (1953) Tangled historical romance in which rising Tennessee politician Andrew Jackson (Charlton Heston) weds a divorced woman (Susan Hayward) before learning the divorce had not been finalized, then re-weds her when it is, and goes on to be elected president despite being branded an adulterer by his political opponents. Directed by Henry Levin from the Irving Stone novel, the slick Hollywood production turns history into bad melodrama and the actors into cardboard characters. Frontier violence and romanticized marital mix-ups. A-III (br)

Presidio, The (1988) An army officer (Sean Connery) based at the Presidio and a San Francisco police inspector (Mark Harmon) who once served under him jointly investigate a murder on the base, but their past conflicts and the cop's brewing relationship with the officer's sexy daughter (Meg Ryan) complicate matters. Director-cinematographer Peter Hyams handles the car pile-ups better than he does the actors and their relationships. Several intense chase sequences culminating in brutal death and destruction, much profanity, and a fairly explicit sexual encounter. O (R)

Presumed Innocent (1990) A prosecuting attorney (Harrison Ford) becomes the prime suspect in his own investigation of a sensational murder case in which the victim (Greta Scacchi) was a colleague as well as his ex-lover. Director Alan J. Pakula's darkly absorbing courtroom drama weaves an intricate plot around adultery and criminal complicity, while presenting a disturbing picture of the manipulation of the criminal justice system by those who administer it. Ambiguous treatment of the justice theme, some scenes of an adulterous relationship, and occasional rough language. A-IV (R)

Pretty Baby (1978) The story of a 12-year-old girl (Brooke Shields), born and raised in a house of prostitution, who eventually marries historical figure E.J. Bellocq (Keith Carridine), a photographer who first came to photograph her mother (Susan Sarandon). Director Louis Malle's listless, dubiously nostalgic tour of a bordello relies on extravagant nudity and the flagrant exploitation of a 12-year-old girl. O (R)

Pretty Boy Floyd (1960) Clunky low-budget gangster picture directed by Herbert J. Leder follows the Prohibition-era rise and fall of the title New York criminal (John Ericson). Much stylized violence, some of it quite nasty. A-III (br)

Pretty in Pink (1986) Self-sufficient, self-assured teenager (Molly Ringwald) goes to the junior prom alone when let down by the boy who was to take her. Director John Hughes provides a positive portrayal of a teenager who maintains a wholesome sense of her own identity despite the peer pressures and scorn of some of her classmates. Sexual innuendo and harsh language. A-III (PG-13)

Pretty Maids All in a Row (1971) Failed sex farce stars Rock Hudson as a high-school guidance counselor who cures the coeds' hang-ups by couch therapy, and solves sophomore John David Carson's perpetual erection by introducing him to teacher-sexpot Angie Dickinson. As some of the pretty coeds wind up as corpses, super-sleuth Telly Savalas questions the student counselor's methods. Directed by Roger Vadim, there is little comedy or mystery in a work whose sole purpose seems to be to exploit sex. O (R)

Pretty Poison (1968) Psychological terror movie about a mad youth running murderously amok is only routine, but director Noel Black has gotten subtle and chilling characterizations from Anthony Perkins as a crazed killer and Tuesday Weld as the perverse teenage nymph who inspires him. A-III (R)

Pretty Woman (1990) Entertaining romantic confection about a smarmy corporate raider (Richard Gere) and a feisty street-walker (Julia Roberts) who fall in love against their better judgment and are transformed into good, wholesome people. The contemporary fairytale, a meld of Pygmalion and Cinderella, shines due to its likeable characterizations and sentimental touches injected by director Garry Marshall. Strictly adult comedy fare with a romanticized view of prostitution, several suggestive sexual encounters, and some rough language laced with sexual innuendo. A-III (R)

Prettykill (1987) When the life of a New York call-girl (Season Hubley) is threatened by the schizophrenic Southern charmer (Suzanne Snyder) she has taken under her wing, she seeks help from her long-time boyfriend, a police detective (David Birney). Director George Kaczender's failed thriller plays more like a distorted caricature of a romance. Unwholesome mix of sex and violence, with some nudity. O (R)

Price Above Rubies, A (1998) Uneven tale in which the wife (Renee Zellweger) of a Torah scholar becomes discontented with her life in a Hasidic community in Brooklyn, then is seduced by her brother-in-law and his offer of a job in his Manhattan jewelry store, where she embarks upon a new life. Writer-director Boaz Yakin treats the woman's conflicts with Orthodox Jewish traditions seriously, but the story of her painful path to liberation is overly contrived and often taxes credibility. Explicit sexual situations, fleeting nudity, and instances of profanity and rough language. A-IV (R) — (Miramax, rental)

Price of Fear, The (1956) Twisty crime tale about a canine-racetrack owner (Lex Barker) on the run from racketeers, while falling for a woman (Merle Oberon) who has set him up to take the blame for her hit-and-run accident. Director Abner Biberman wrings easy menace from contrived situations, but the characters are flat and motivations unconvincing. Stylized violence and romantic complications. A-II (br)

Prick Up Your Ears (1987) Harshly realistic depiction of the doomed love affair between British playwright Joe Orton (Gary Oldman) and collaborator Kenneth Halliwell (Alfred Molina). Uncompromising direction by Stephen Frears dwells too vividly on the details of sordid homosexual encounters and a concluding bloody murder and suicide scene. Vanessa Redgrave co-stars in the British production, which has brief male nudity and vulgar language. O (R)

Pride of St. Louis, The (1952) The life and times

of baseball pitcher Jerome "Dizzy" Dean (Dan Dailey), whose Arkansas twang and garbled syntax make him a beloved sports-announcer after his glory years on the mound for the Cardinals during the 1930s. Directed by Harmon Jones, Daily gives a likeable performance as the clowning ballplayer, whose biggest fan is his wife (Joanne Dru), while the pitching career of his brother "Daffy" (Richard Crenna) becomes one of his major concerns. A-I (br)

Pride of the Bowery (1941) Routine East Side Kids comedy in which Danny (Bobby Jordan) gets the gang to join the Civilian Conservation Corps to make $22 a month, while they help Muggs (Leo Gorcey) train for a boxing match. Directed by Joseph H. Lewis, the thin plot has Muggs blamed for another's theft, the boxing scenes are ridiculous, but the footage filmed at a CCC camp has historical interest. Loud and brassy slapstick. A-I (br)

Pride of the Marines (1945) Fact-based story of Marine Al Schmid (John Garfield), whose injuries in the battle for Guadalcanal result in blindness, which he fears will make him a burden to the hometown girl (Eleanor Parker) waiting to marry him, but she knows better. Directed by Delmer Daves, the situation develops along the lines of a conventional tearjerker, but the personable cast helps make the uncertainties of the characters humanly compelling. Wartime violence and its anguishing consequences A-II (br)

Pride of the Yankees, The (1942) Fine drama of New York Yankee first baseman Lou Gehrig (Gary Cooper), who never missed a game in 14 years of outstanding play until forced to retire in 1939 by an incurable disease, which has since borne his name. Directed by Sam Wood, the result has interest beyond the story of a baseball hero, because it captures the universal qualities of character and spirit underlying the career of a man who gave his unfailing best for team, fans, and family. Memorable movie even for those who don't like baseball. A-I (br)

Priest (1995) Flawed British drama probes the conflict between religious ideals and human frailties in a story set in a working-class Catholic parish, where a young curate tries to live a life of celibacy, yet initiates several homosexual encounters, partly out of torment at his helplessness in stopping a case of incest revealed in confession. Director Antonia Bird provides a credible picture of a lonely priest in a busy parish, though its emphasis on his struggles with his own sexuality strangely lacks any notion of sin, and the ambiguous ending in an emotionally powerful scene of reconciliation leaves matters unresolved. Serious treatment of a very troubling subject, depictions of homosexual acts, and occasional crude language. A-IV (R)

Priest and the Girl, The (1973) The story told by this 1966 Brazilian drama is of a young priest, overwhelmed by the poverty and injustice of the backward community to which he has been sent, blindly runs away in the company of a sensual young girl who looks to him for protection from her brutal guardian. Director Joaquim Pedro de Andrade's slow-moving study of spiritual aridity is less concerned with his two central characters than in the barren lives of the people who inhabit a desolate part of the world. A-III (nr)

Priest's Wife, The (1971) Careless Italian romp stars Sophia Loren as a suicidal pop-singer and Marcello Matroianni as the priest who becomes the object of her attentions. What begins as a rather lighthearted spoof of the issue of priestly celibacy ends up as a humorless and bitter indictment of Church law. While the viewer is mercifully spared the visual aspects of the pair's sexual relationship, director Dino Risi's irreverent and occasionally tasteless humor is more an insult to one's intelligence than to one's religious convictions. A-IV (PG)

Primal Fear (1996) Clunky thriller from William Diehl's novel in which a hotshot Chicago lawyer (Richard Gere) defends a youth (Edward Norton) charged with killing a Catholic prelate who had sexually abused him, but the trial's result is a cynical mockery of justice. Directed by Gregory Hoblit, the manipulative proceedings posture a great deal about truth and justice, but the result is only an empty exercise in cheap thrills. Graphic scenes of sex and of violence, as well as a cynical exploitation of a religious figure. O (R)

Primary Colors (1998) Political satire involving a charismatic southern governor (John Travolta), whose campaign for his party's presidential nomination is threatened by allegations of extramarital affairs. Directed by Mike Nichols from Elaine May's script, the candidate's character is given superficial treatment, though some keen observations are made along the way on the political process and ethical compromises. Fleeting violence including a suicide, various implied affairs, recurring profanity, and much rough language. A-III (R)

Prime Cut (1972) Tough slice-of-crime melodrama about a hired killer (Lee Marvin) sent to extol tribute from a doublecrossing Kansas City gangster (Gene Hackman) who sells beef and women. As directed by Michael Ritchie, the fast-paced action becomes a senseless nightmare of white slavery, drugs, and meatpacking treated with blood, gore, nudity, and foul language. O (R)

Prime of Miss Jean Brodie, The (1969) Poignant screen version of Muriel Spark's novel about a bright, demanding teacher (Maggie Smith) who doesn't fit the mold of a conservative girls' academy in 1930s Edinburgh, where she teaches her devoted, unquestioning "gurrls," until one of them (Pamela Franklin) betrays her confidence by posing in the nude for the art teacher. Director Ronald Neame handles the moral ambiguities of the situation with great sensitivity, leaving viewers to consider an inspiring teacher's powerful influence on the young, for both good and bad. A-III (PG)

Primrose Path (1940) Erratic sudser in which a

genial go-getter (Joel McCrea) weds a young woman (Ginger Rogers), then stalks off after learning her father (Miles Mander) is an alcoholic and her mother (Marjorie Rambeau) lives off other men. Directed by Gregory LaCava, the contrived plot starts with some sunny humor, then turns increasingly maudlin until an unearned happy ending. Veiled treatment of prostitution and sexual innuendo. A-III (br)

Prince and the Pauper, The (1937) Durable version of the Mark Twain classic in which an English prince (Bobby Mauch) switches places with a lookalike urchin (Billy Mauch) for a lark that could prove fatal unless a would-be usurper (Claude Rains) is undone by a mettlesome commoner (Errol Flynn). Director William Keighley's melodramatic style only slows the pace of the boys' misadventures after swapping the dangers of the Tudor court for the squalor of the London slums and vice versa. For all the aristocratic villainy and stylized violence, the period adventure is grand fun for family viewers. A-I (br)

Prince and the Showgirl, The (1957) Fluffy romantic comedy from Terence Rattigan's play about the urbane regent (Laurence Olivier) of a Balkan kingdom who arrives in London for the 1911 coronation of George V and falls for a dizzy American chorus-girl (Marilyn Monroe). Also directed by Olivier, the contrast between the cynical prince and the not-so-innocent starlet is obvious but fun, with some witty jabs at stuffy English characters (notably Richard Wattis) and daffy asides by the Balkan Queen Mother (Sybil Thorndike who steals every scene she's in). Sexual situations and innuendo. A-III (br)

Prince of Darkness (1987) Failed horror movie in which a priest (Donald Pleasence) discovers a secret vault in a Los Angeles church containing a cosmic force that if let loose will become the Son of Darkness. Directed self-indulgently by John Carpenter, the boring and pretentious movie talks itself to death but sprinkles in enough blood-and-gore scenes and vomiting zombies to bludgeon moral sensibilities. O (R)

Prince of Foxes (1949) Tale of intrigue and adventure in 1500 Italy, where an ambitious courtier (Tyrone Power) tries to save the lands of an aged noble (Felix Aylmer) and his lady (Wanda Hendrix) from conquest by the notorious Cesare Borgia (Orson Welles). Director Henry King's elegant costume melodrama has some interesting twists as well as spectacular location photography of fortified castles and other period settings. Stylized violence, duplicity, and romantic complications. A-II (br)

Prince of the City (1981) Treat Williams plays a New York City detective who, tormented by guilt, comes forward to cooperate with federal authorities investigating police corruption. Director Sidney Lumet succeeds in portraying the human complexity in this flawed but gripping drama that has some of the inexorable force of Greek tragedy. Williams is particularly fine among a strong cast giving many excellent performances. Though the violence is extremely restrained, a somber and difficult theme with much rough language. A-III (R)

Prince of Egypt, The (1998) The biblical story of Moses (voice of Val Kilmer) is retold in a beautifully crafted animated feature that focuses on the oppression of the Israelites in Egypt and God's selection of Moses to lead them to the Promised Land, though younger children may find it an overwhelming experience with some harrowing scenes. Directed by Brenda Chapman, Steve Hickner and Simon Wells, the result is an impressive animated spectacle re-creating its biblical-era story in compelling fashion, marred only by the artificiality of Stephen Schwartz's songs. Some emotionally intense scenes. A-II (PG)

Prince of Tides, The (1991) Hoping to help his suicidal sister, an estranged husband (Nick Nolte) relates their troubled family history to her psychiatrist (Barbra Streisand), and the two become romantically involved, profoundly affecting each other and both of their families. Also produced and directed by Streisand, the emotionally complex drama muddies the question of infidelity, but is rich in themes of interpersonal communication and familial forgiveness. Momentary but violent rape scene, discreet bedroom scenes, adulterous and homosexual references, and some rough language. A-IV (R)

Prince Who Was a Thief, The (1951) Arabian Nights baloney about a prince (Tony Curtis) who was stolen as a baby and raised by a thief (Everett Sloane), but then discovers his true identity because of a pretty pickpocket (Piper Laurie), and fights to take his rightful place on the throne. Directed by Rudolph Maté from a story by Theodore Dreiser, the action varies from the silly to the ludicrous, with performances to match, though the ridiculous proceedings may be enjoyed by those seeking escapist fun. Some sexual innuendo. A-II (br)

Princes in Exile (1991) A 17-year-old boy (Zachary Ansley) finds romance and a new attitude at a summer camp for youngsters struggling with cancer. Humor and hope come shining through this moving film from Canadian director Giles Walker, who keeps excess sentimentality at bay with honest performances from its young cast. Disturbing subject matter which may be frightening to small children and mild sexual references. A-II (PG)

Princess, The (see: **A Time in the Sun**)

Princess and the Goblin, The (1994) Animated version of George MacDonald's 1872 fairytale in which a sheltered young princess (voice of Sally Ann Marsh) and a plucky boy (voice of Peter Murray) upset the plans of evil underground goblins to conquer the unsuspecting people of the kingdom. Director Jozsef Gemes's Welsh-Hungarian production features two youngsters learning to overcome their fears as they face the grotesque creatures, but otherwise has little charm, catchy music, or humor to hold audience interest. A-I (G)

Princess and the Pirate, The (1944) Madcap comedy in which a ham actor (Bob Hope) helps a runaway princess (Virginia Mayo) escape capture by a notorious pirate known as the Hook (Victor McLaglen), then both wind up in a pirate haven whose governor (Walter Slezak) takes them prisoner, only to be later recaptured by the Hook. Director David Butler keeps the slapstick proceedings merrily afloat with Hope's comic blunderings, zany asides, and hilarious impersonation of the Hook, though Walter Brennan as a toothless tattooer almost steals the picture. Stylized violence and sexual innuendo. A-II (br)

Princess Bride, The (1987) Affectionate, lighthearted parody of medieval romance, as a young beauty (Robin Wright) is saved from a forced marriage to a nasty prince (Chris Sarandon) by a farm boy-turned-pirate (Cary Elwes). Directed by Rob Reiner from William Goldman's script, the comic proceedings are marked with verbal wit and some silly turns by Mandy Patinkin, Wallace Shawn, and Billy Crystal. Some comic-book violence. A-II (PG)

Princess Caraboo (1994) Delightful fact-based tale set in early 19th-century England, where an exotically dressed young woman (Phoebe Cates) speaking no English is found on the wayside and is embraced by the upper classes, who believe she is a shipwrecked Javanese princess, until a love-truck reporter (Stephen Rea) uncovers her true background. Director Michael Austin turns in a deft comedy that skewers the pretension of the British upper-crust and features masterful comic performances by John Lithgow and Kevin Kline in smaller roles. Mild sexual innuendo. A-II (PG)

Princess Comes Across, The (1936) Fitful comedy combining murder and romance aboard an ocean-liner, whose passengers include a girl from Brooklyn (Carole Lombard) trying to get to Hollywood by masquerading as a princess from Sweden, a band leader (Fred MacMurray) aware of the ruse but sweet on its perpetrator, top detectives from around the world, and an escaped killer. Director William K. Howard can't quite make it all work, but Lombard has a lot of fun spoofing Garbo, and Alison Skipworth shines as her brassy lady-in-waiting. Mild romance and some menace. A-I (br)

Princess Yang Kwei Fei (1972) One of the most beautiful color movies ever made, this 1955 Japanese production retells a Chinese legend about a graceful princess who dies for her emperor and whose love lives on after death. Directed by Kenji Mizoguchi, the narrative is slow and measured, but the interest lies less in its traditional story than in the beauty and grace of its presentation, done with an artistry that is genuine and universal. A-II (nr)

Principal, The (1987) Rowdy, inept teacher (James Belushi) becomes a dedicated administrator who takes it upon himself to tame the drug-dealing felons who rule an inner-city high school. Director Christopher Cain milks an improbable plot for violence and brutality, failing to provide a balanced forum for the real and pressing issues of crime in the schools. O (R)

Prison Guard (1973) Surrealistic Czech drama about institutional dehumanization tells the story of a young prison guard in the 1920s, whose experiences teach him that brutality is the best way to deal with prisoners. Having previously taken out his frustrations on his dog, the guard turns to beating the inmates when one of them runs off with his wife. Director Ivan Renc's characters are strange and disturbing inhabitants of a bleak terrain that corresponds to the barrenness of their lives. A-III (nr)

Prisoner of Second Avenue, The (1975) Uneven screen version of Neil Simon's Broadway comedy about a middle-aged New Yorker (Jack Lemmon) who loses his job, gets mugged while his apartment is robbed, and endures all sorts of other urban traumas with the help of his sensible, down-to-earth wife (Anne Bancroft). Direector Melvin Frank pumps up all the life possible in a script hinged on situations that are not very amusing and wisecracks that are only occasionally witty. Intermittent profanity. A-III (PG)

Prisoner of Shark Island, The (1936) Sentenced to life imprisonment for setting the broken leg of Lincoln's assassin, Dr. Samuel Mudd (Warner Baxter) is sent to an island fortress off the Florida coast, where he earns a pardon after risking his life to save others during a yellow-fever epidemic. Director John Ford's fact-based story of a doctor who became an innocent victim of his times achieves considerable impact from its credible evocation of the period and its human context. Miscarriage of justice and brutal mistreatment. A-I (br)

Prisoner of the Mountains (1997) Two Russian soldiers (Oleg Menshikov and Sergei Bodrov, Jr.) held hostage by Chechan villagers, come to know one another and their Muslim captors as their fate hangs in the balance. Directed by Sergei Bodrov from a Tolstoy short story, the quietly powerful tale of shared humanity and the insanity of war is starkly beautiful as well as emotionally engrossing. Subtitles. Brief violence and nudity as well as occasional rough language. A-III (R)

Prisoner of Zenda, The (1937) Grand romantic adventure from the Anthony Hope novel of a mythical central European kingdom, where a vacationing Englishman (Ronald Colman) saves the throne of his distant royal cousin (also Colman) who's been kidnapped by a villainous stepbrother (Raymond Massey) and his chief henchman (Douglas Fairbanks, Jr.). Directed by John Cromwell, the late 19th-century setting nicely suits the tale of loyalty and honor amid court intrigues, desperate forays, and the bittersweet romance of commoner and princess (Madeleine Carroll). Some stylized violence and romantic complications. A-I (br)

Prisoner of Zenda, The (1952) Color remake of the 1937 version has Stewart Granger in the dual role as the Englishman who saves a lookalike European crown-prince from a ruthless usurper (James Mason), then loses his heart to the king's intended bride

(Deborah Kerr). Director Richard Thorpe's turn-of-the-century costume romance has plenty of regal spectacle, though the bittersweet love story is somewhat stilted, and Mason nearly steals the show as the nasty plotter whose downfall in the big action-finish is entirely satisfying. Some stylized violence and romantic complications. A-I (br)

Prisoner of Zenda (1979) Peter Sellers plays the dual role of the foppish King Rudolph of Ruritania and the stout-hearted Englishman who takes his place to foil a plot against the throne. Under Richard Quine's direction, the action and pageantry in gorgeous settings are treated realistically rather than as fantasy, so that the result falls between two stools, being neither funny, nor romantic enough. A-II (PG)

Prisoners of the Sun (1991) International political considerations after WW II impede the efforts of a tenacious lawyer (Bryan Brown) to bring to trial the Japanese officers responsible for the torture and execution of more than 300 Australian prisoners-of-war. Directed by Stephen Wallace, the earnest, fact-based drama suffers from lugubrious pacing and uninvolving characters but poses some intriguing moral questions about justice. Some wartime violence and an instance of rough language. A-II (R)

Private Benjamin (1980) When her husband dies on their wedding night, the distraught bride (Goldie Hawn) joins the New Army as an impossibly inept recruit, whom boot camp changes into a person able to look after herself, until she meets a rich, handsome French doctor. Some good laughs from old military jokes updated to the coed Army, with Eileen Brennan especially funny as a wacky martinet. Sexual morality is ridiculed in a number of scenes, and there is brief nudity and some rough language. O (R)

Private Buckaroo (1942) Patriotic musical follows Harry James and his orchestra after they're drafted into the Army, go through basic training, and perform in camp shows, until embarking overseas. Directed by Edward F. Cline, the proceedings are thin on comedy (Shemp Howard trying to keep girlfriend Mary Wickes from Joe E. Lewis) but worth seeing for vintage performances by James, the Andrews Sisters, singer Dick Foran, and comic turns by Donald O'Connor and Peggy Ryan. A-I (br)

Private Eyes (1981) Anemic little slapstick comedy stars Tim Conway and Don Knotts as a Sherlock Holmes-Dr. Watson duo solving a murder in a spooky old house. Director Lang Elliot serves up all the predictable comic cliches of the genre, but none of them are very funny. Several mild vulgarisms. A-II (PG)

Private Function, A (1985) With rationing in effect at the end of WW II, an English couple (Michael Palin and Maggie Smith) steal the pig that local dignitaries are secretly fattening up for a banquet celebrating Princess Elizabeth's wedding. The English comedy, directed by Malcolm Mowbray, is slow-moving and leans heavily on vulgar humor some may find offensive. Restrained bedroom scene. A-III (R)

Private Hell 36 (1954) Familiar but well-done crime tale of two cops, who get help from a club singer (Ida Lupino) in locating a bundle of stolen cash, then keep some of it for themselves, until one (Howard Duff) has a crisis of conscience, but the other (Steve Cochran) doesn't. Directed by Don Siegel, the story of good cops tempted by easy money is handled realistically and gains interest from sympathetic performances. Stylized violence and romantic complications. A-II (br)

Private Lessons (1981) Housekeeper Sylvia Kristel gives the master's teenage son a hands-on course in sex. Directed by Alan Myerson, it's a failed little exploitation comedy with nudity and graphic sex. O (R)

Private Life of Sherlock Holmes, The (1970) Plodding spy melodrama without much mystery to it takes some extreme liberties with the Conan Doyle character by making the Victorian detective not only a cocaine addict, but sexually ambiguous as well. Directed with a heavy hand by Billy Wilder, the lightweight case involves Holmes (Robert Stephens) and Dr. Watson (Colin Blakely) in the search for the missing husband of a mysterious woman (Genevieve Page), with some assistance from Holmes's brother, Mycroft (Christopher Lee). Lacking lightness and imagination, it will irritate Holmes's fans and disappoint others. Some sexual innuendo. A-III (GP/PG-13)

Private Navy of Sgt. O'Farrell, The (1968) Unfunny WW II comedy set on a Pacific island, where O'Farrell (Bob Hope) tries to raise moral on an Army-Navy base by importing some nurses, who turn out to be all male, except for Phyllis Diller. Director Frank Tashlin can't get much out of the situation except to parody some other films. A-II (G)

Private Parts (1973) Creepy, campy, sex-and-horror movie about a teenage girl who becomes a more or less willing victim to an assortment of sinister types inhabiting a creaky flea-bag hotel managed by her crazed aunt. Directed by Paul Bartel, nudity and cheap thrills abound. O (R)

Private Parts (1997) Vulgar comic treatment of the career and personal life of trash-talk radio host Howard Stern (playing himself). Directed by Betty Thomas, the self-serving vehicle promotes Stern as a fearless iconoclast on the air but a faithful family man at home. Fleeting violence, benign view of recreational drug use, many crude sexual references, frequent nudity, and much rough language. O (R)

Private School (1983) Self-described comedy is no more than a B-grade sexploitation movie, from the vulgar lyrics of the opening song to the closing scene where the graduating class simultaneously indulges in an obscene gesture to their headmistress. Directed by Noel Black, it consists of an unremitting stream of sexual scenes, jokes, and dialogue. O (R)

Privates on Parade (1984) Uneven British satire about a motley collection of misfit soldiers who, under the flamboyant leadership of a homosexual director (Dennis Quilty), put on a variety show for troops fighting Communist guerrillas in 1948 Malaya and, thanks to invincible stupidity of their unit commander (John Cleese), become directly involved in the conflict. Director Michael Blakemore scores enough satiric hits to overcome its excess of double entendres, a bit of blasphemy, a brief bedroom scene involving nudity, and its abundance of homosexual references. A-III (R)

Privilege (1967) Uneven British cautionary tale about the use of the mass media to manipulate and control public opinion, as seen in the case if a pop-singing star (Paul Jones). Directed by Peter Watkins, there is more flash than substance, so that its unfocused indignation blunts its criticism and ultimately leaves viewers without a constructive point of view. A-IV (br)

Prize of Gold, A (1955) Muddled crime caper set in post-war Berlin, where an American Army Air Force sergeant (Richard Widmark) falls for a German woman (Mai Zetterling) caring for a group of orphans, then determines to hijack a shipment of stolen Nazi gold to finance their relocation in Brazil. Directed by Mark Robson, the hokey plot tries to gain sympathy for the soldier because of his unselfish motivation for the crime, but it's not very convincing. Some nasty violence and sexual innuendo. A-III (br)

Prizzi's Honor (1985) Middle-aged man (Jack Nicholson) falls in love with a beautiful and mysterious woman (Kathleen Turner) and she with him. It turns out they are both in the same line of work, but since that happens to be killing people, it makes for complications once they're married. Though this very black comedy is directed with great skill and flair by John Huston, its level of violence is extremely mature fare and not suited to everybody's taste. A-IV (R)

Problem Child (1990) Dumb one-joke comedy in which a would-be dad (John Ritter) and his social-climbing wife (Amy Yasbeck) adopt a sweet-looking seven-year-old (Michael Oliver), unaware that he is the bane of the nuns at the orphanage and that his pen-pal is an escaped killer. Directed by Dennis Dugan, the comic fantasy rarely rises above the level of nasty, often vulgar, pranks and overblown characterizations, except for the performances by Ritter and the youngster. Stylized violence intended for comic effect, crude expressions, and bathroom humor. A-II (PG)

Problem Child 2 (1991) After moving to a new town, bratty Junior (Michael Oliver) runs into an even brattier girl (Ivyann Schwan) as he tries to prevent his divorced dad (John Ritter) from having any dates. Director Brian Levant's sequel is mired in shrill toilet-humor and dangerously unfunny pranks. Brief adolescent sexual innuendo, much coarse humor, and mindless comic-book violence. A-III (PG-13)

Prodigal, The (1955) Inept biblical drama directed by Richard Thorpe in which the prodigal son (Edmund Purdom) of a prosperous Hebrew family squanders his inheritance in Damascus pursing the high priestess (Lana Turner) of a pagan god, with predictable results. Unconvincing violence and sexual situations. A-III (br)

Prodigal, The (1983) Produced by the Rev. Billy Graham's organization, the movie is a modern retelling of the parable about the repentance of a man who squandered his inheritance, but, despite some fine acting and good intentions, it doesn't quite come together as persuasive drama. Its shortcomings, however, do not keep it from being inspirational family entertainment. A-II (PG)

Producers, The (1967) Farce about an accountant (Gene Wilder) who gets involved with would-be producer (Zero Mostel) of a buoyant musical based on the life of Hitler. Some of the laughs are a little sick around the edges, but those who don't mind bawdy and blatant satire should survive the experience. Director Mel Brooks gets a brilliant comic performance from Mostel, well supported by Wilder. Matter of comic taste. O (br)

Professional, The (1994) Graphically violent tale in which a hit-man (Jean Reno) rescues a 12-year-old girl (Natalie Portman) whose drug-dealing family has been slaughtered by a corrupt DEA official (Gary Oldman) and agrees to teach her how to kill people for a living. Writer-director Luc Besson assaults the eyes with frequent gory shootouts while pretentiously trying to make a moral hero out of a killer who murders for profit. Excessive grisly violence, brief drug abuse, and much rough language. O (R)

Professional Sweetheart (1933) Flimsy show-biz comedy in which a national radio-singer (Ginger Rogers) marries a rustic fan from Kentucky (Norman Foster) to be rid of the morality clause in her contract, but the chump believes she's on the level and takes her to his home in the hills to reform her. Directed by William A. Seiter, the frothy period proceedings have gone quite flat, though there's some goofy fun along the way with the singer's press agent (Frank McHugh) and rival sponsors (Gregory Ratoff and Edgar Kennedy). Sexual situations and innuendo, with a "comic" scene of the groom knocking out his hysterical bride. A-III (br)

Professionals, The (1966) Four soldiers of fortune (Lee Marvin, Burt Lancaster, Woody Strode, and Robert Ryan) are hired to rescue a woman (Claudia Cardinale) being held for ransom by a Mexican bandit (Jack Palance). What raises this above the level of the average action-adventure movie is the stylish manner and steady pace of director Richard Brooks's homage to the specials skills of a group. Some brutal violence, coarse language, and several sensuous scenes. A-III (br)

Professor Beware (1938) Uneven comedy in which an Egyptologist (Harold Lloyd) escapes misunderstandings with a movie starlet (Phyllis Welch) and the police by riding the rails from Los Angeles to New York, where he intends joining an expedition to the Pyramids in search of a lost tablet. Directed by

Elliott Nugent, the plot is woefully thin but picks up along the way as Lloyd is befriended by con-men Raymond Walburn and Lionel Stander. Dated amusement of interest mainly for Lloyd fans and students of slapstick comedy. A-I (br)

Program, The (1993) Predictable tale of a college football coach (James Caan) and his team of troublesome players, including an alcoholic quarterback (Craig Sheffer), a steroid-taking defensive tackle (Andrew Bryniarski), and a freshman tailback (Omar Epps). Directed by David S. Ward, the story portrays the multiple ills of collegiate sports while focusing its sympathies on those involved in breaking the rules. Bone-crunching violence on the field, an attempted rape, substance abuse, and occasional rough language. A-III (R)

Project X (1968) Futuristic, science-fiction reconstruction of the 22nd century, in which the quality of life has drastically changed, but the ideological tensions between East and West have persisted. In the end, it turns out that the movie's pretensions and sometimes effective special effects are used for nothing more than a routine secret-agent melodrama that might as well have taken place in the present. A-II (br)

Project X (1987) Unpleasant military monkey business is challenged by altruistic recruit with a social conscience (Matthew Broderick) in this story about lovable chimps used for flight-simulation testing. His attempt to help them escape nearly causes a nuclear disaster. Director Jonathan Kaplan's lightweight tale of youthful idealism vs. duty is shareable family entertainment, though there is a touch of rough language. A-II (PG)

Projectionist, The (1971) Chuck McCann runs the projector in a New York movie theater and is given to lapsing into movie-based fantasies in which he becomes Capt. Flash, has conversations with Bogart, feasts in Babylon, shoots down Ming's spaceship, and cavorts with King Kong. Directed by Harry Hurwitz, its collection of movie nostalgia is somewhat self-indulgent but should delight the buffs and has enough off-beat comedy for the uninitiated to enjoy. Some brief sexual fantasies. A-III (GP)

Prologue (1970) Stilted, uneven, and technically inferior study of war dissenters during the riots at the Chicago Democratic Convention in 1968. Directed from a Canadian perspective by Robin Spry, the black-and-white semi-documentary pretentiously contrasts the brutality of the police with gentle lovemakers in a commune. Gratuitous nudity. O (nr)

Prom Night (1980) Mad killer seeks revenge by stalking high-school students on the night of the big dance and slashing their throats whenever they stray from the dance floor. Directed by Paul Lynch, the horror story is more dumb than nasty, but some of its grisly scenes are excessively graphic. O (R)

Promise, The (1979) Silly tearjerker about a woman (Kathleen Quinlan), disfigured in an auto accident, who is separated from her lover (Stephen Collins) when his wealthy mother (Beatrice Straight) offers to pay for expensive plastic surgery, provided she never see her son again. Directed by Gilbert Cates, the sentimental, overwrought melodrama has a permissive attitude about premarital sex. A-III (PG)

Promise at Dawn (1970) French adaptation of novelist Romain Gary's memoir of his boyhood days and aspirations living with his loving mother (Melina Mercouri) in the Leningrad of the 1920s. Directed by Jules Dassin, these poignant recollections become a buoyantly human portrait, rich in the cultural humor and solid values that stoke the human spirit's inexhaustible striving for identity and achievement. A scene dealing with the young man's sexual awakening and his mother's response require a mature perspective. A-III (GP)

Promise Her Anything (1966) Mediocre romantic comedy about a recent widow (Leslie Caron), on the lookout for a new father for her young son, settles first on her boss (Robert Cummings), but then finds true love with a low-budget moviemaker (Warren Beatty). Director Arthur Hiller's predictable story offers little new in an old scenario. A-III (br)

Promised Lands (1974) Directed by Susan Sontag, this documentary about Israel at the time of the October War proves a poetic and moving meditation on the tragedy of a nation's struggle for existence in a land claimed by others. From its opening shots of the diverse cultural traditions that co-exist in Israel to its concluding episode of a soldier being treated for battle trauma, the film's images connect again and again with the precise detail or telling scene to express the bewildering complexity of the problems facing this beleaguered state. A-II (nr)

Promises in the Dark (1979) Counterpointing the decline of a 17-year-old terminal-cancer patient (Kathleen Beller) with her doctor's (Marsha Mason) renewed interest in romance after the experience of bitter divorce, producer-director Jerome Hellman offers us a sentimental melodrama that contains scattered bits of insight. The movie does not go too deeply into the complex moral problems it raises, notably the cutting off of life-sustaining systems when life ceases to be viable. A-IV (PG)

Proof (1992) Absorbing psychological drama about a blind, emotionally fragile photographer (Hugo Weaving), his new friend (Russell Crowe) who describes the content of his photos, and a jealous housekeeper (Genevieve Picot) who is determined to wreck their friendship. Writer-director Jocelyn Moorhouse builds an eerily suspenseful story out of the strange dynamics motivating this odd triangle of troubled adults learning to relate to one another. Fleeting sexual encounter, flash of nudity, and minimal rough language. A-III (R)

Prophecy (1979) When a health-department doctor (Robert Foxworth) takes his pregnant wife (Talia Shire) on an assignment checking the environmental effects of a paper mill in the Maine woods, they become the target of an exceptionally ill-tempered mutant. Everything about director John Frankenheimer's ecological shocker is so ludicrous and inept that it overwhelms the ecological message it's supposedly plugging. Some intense violence. A-III (PG)

Prophecy, The (1995) Clumsy horror fantasy in which a Los Angeles cop (Elias Koteas) gets caught in the conflict between a good angel (Eric Stoltz) and an evil one (Christopher Walken) over a lost soul hiding within a young girl who's taken refuge in a Native-American village. Writer-director Gregory Widen establishes a pseudo-religious veneer to the ominous proceedings, which never make much sense beyond some elementary frights and bits of gore. Fairly graphic violence, muddled religious references, and occasional rough language. A-IV (R)

Proposition, The (1998) Melodramatic clunker set in 1935 Boston, where a wealthy Catholic couple hire a young man (Neil Patrick Harris) to impregnate the wife (Madeleine Stowe) because the husband (William Hurt) is sterile, with the wildly disastrous results including a parish priest (Kenneth Branagh) who becomes romantically involved with the wife as well. Directed by Lesli Linka Glatter, the talented cast is left hopelessly adrift in a badly scripted tearjerker that never achieves a shred of credibility. Superficial treatment of moral issues, discreet sexual encounters, and an off-screen murder. A-IV (R)

Protector, The (1985) Two New York policemen (Jackie Chan and Danny Aiello) wreak havoc in Hong Kong, where they have gone to break up a drug ring in a mindlessly violent movie written and directed by James Glickenhaus. Besides the violence there is some exploitative nudity. O (R)

Protocol (1984) Dizzy cocktail waitress (Goldie Hawn) becomes a national heroine when she thwarts the assassination of a visiting Arab leader, which gives some nasty State Department types the idea of using her as a diplomatic pawn. Directed by Herbert Ross, it's a routine comedy vehicle for its star, who would be better if the role was just a bit less lovable and cute. Sexually oriented humor, including depicting Arabs throughout as over-sexed buffoons. A-II (PG)

Proud Rebel, The (1958) Coming to the Midwest in search of a doctor able to cure his mute son (David Ladd), an ex-Confederate officer (Alan Ladd) gets caught in a land war between a mean sheep farmer (Dean Jagger) and a spinster farmer (Olivia de Havilland). Directed by Michael Curtiz, the post-Civil War conflict between the adults is heavy-going at times, but the boy and his smart sheep dog will appeal to the youngsters. Some stylized violence, with several scenes quite harrowing for children. A-I (br)

Providence (1977) Uneven British drama about a 78-year-old novelist (John Gielgud) trying to come up with a story interweaving fantasies about his son (Dirk Bogarde), his son's wife (Ellen Burstyn), her friend (David Warner), and his son's imaginary mistress (Elaine Stritch). Director Alain Resnais fails to create any consistent emotional mood for scriptwriter David Mercer's indulgent jumping back and forth in time and space to indicate a failing imagination. Gielgud's character is not only foul-mouthed and lecherous, but is excessively graphic in his complaints about failing bodily functions set against unpleasant shots of his autopsy. O (R)

Prudence and the Pill (1968) Brittle British comedy with Deborah Kerr and David Niven dealing with the advent and repercussions of the contraceptive pill in a manner that overlooks the basic issues of premarital sex, adultery, and divorce. When two households take to underhanded pill-swapping for various reasons, the final result is two marriages, two divorces, and remarriages and babies under every cabbage leaf. In spite of few smiles, director Fielder Cook gets them by ignoring the emotional upheaval that such finagling would produce. O (R)

Psychic Killer (1976) Lightweight horror movie about a man (Jim Hutton) who projects mental powers to avenge his unjust incarceration in a mental institution. Director Raymond Danton uses parapsychology to explain the plot's series of gruesome murders, but nothing can justify their bloody detail, the nudity, or the movie's resolution in vigilante justice. O (PG)

Psycho (1960) Classic thriller from the Robert Bloch story in which a private detective (Martin Balsam) tracks a missing person (Janet Leigh) to a lonely, back-roads motel, whose affable but high-strung manager (Anthony Perkins) seems strangely preoccupied with the demands of his invalid mother in the eerie Victorian house atop a nearby hill. Director Alfred Hitchcock starts the proceedings with an impulsive theft, then smoothly switching gears, turns the ordinary into a scary, sinister nightmare with a compulsive murderer on the loose at the motel. Strong adult fare with much suspense, brief but shocking violence, most notably in the motel shower scene, and some sexual references. A-III (br)

Psycho (1998) Faithful re-make of the 1960 black-and-white Hitchcock thriller in which a doomed young woman (Anne Heche) vanishes from the Bates Motel, drawing suspicion on its secretive owner (Vince Vaughn). Director Gus Van Sant adds color and a new cast, retaining the sleek storytelling and slow build-up of suspense much as in the original shocker. Some violence with gore, implied masturbation, a premarital affair, and brief nudity. A-III (R)

Psycho II (1983) Norman Bates (Anthony Perkins) is declared sane and comes home after more than 20 years in a mental institution. This time poor Norman is the victim of a mother and daughter (Vera Miles and Meg Tilly) who are determined to push him over the edge again so that he has to be recommitted. Director Richard Franklin diminishes tensions by the broad in-joke quality of the whole enterprise, but the conclusion is explicitly graphic in its bloody violence. O (R)

Psycho III (1986) Tony Perkins directs and stars in this intense, brutally sardonic drama in which Norman Bates once again goes over the edge, providing the audience with a parade of gruesomely victimized women in various states of undress. Excessive mix of sex and violence. O (R)

Psychopath, The (1966) Mild British mystery thriller directed by Freddie Francis in which the investigation of four murders leads a London police inspection (Patrick Wymark) to the strange house of widow (Margaret Johnston) confined to a wheelchair. Stylized violence. A-II (br)

Psych-Out (1968) Cliched story of hippie life in San Francisco's Haight-Ashbury district, with Susan Strasberg as a deaf teenage runaway and Dean Stockwell as a freaked-out guru. Director Richard Rush tries to balance his picture of the dropout lifestyle, but conventional society is shown as responsible for such alienation. Confused treatment of violence, sex, and drugs. A-III (br)

Psychout for Murder (1971) Rossano Brazzi plays the head of a wealthy but depraved Italian family and has a luscious offspring (Adrienne La Russa) whose heart, deep down inside, only belongs to Daddy. Directed by Edward Ross, its sordid story of revenge and incest has no redeeming elements. O (R)

Public Enemy (1931) Classic gangster melodrama about a young hoodlum (James Cagney) during Prohibition who rises up the gang ladder until a mob war shows that he "ain't so tough." Directed by William A. Wellman, Cagney gives his definitive performance as the cocky tough in an era of lawlessness spawned by the demand for illegal booze. Stylized violence and implied promiscuous relationships. A-III (br)

Public Eye (1972) Witty British production about an insecure newlywed (Michael Jayston) who hires a private eye (Topol) to tail his capricious wife (Mia Farrow). Detective and wife flirt innocently after they discover a bond of attraction in their mutually unorthodox personalities. Director Carol Reed proves his adeptness at handling romantic comedy as he blends the sprightly performances of the three stars with a sumptuous tour of London. A-II (G)

Public Eye, The (1992) A lonely freelance tabloid photographer (Joe Pesci) in 1942 New York City tries to help a glamorous nightclub owner (Barbara Hershey) from a mob takeover, then stumbles on a syndicate plot to control wartime gas rationing. Writer-director Howard Franklin weaves together a gangster story and an intriguing character study in a downbeat picture with more gritty style than substance. Some stylized violence, several grisly corpse shots, discreet sexual innuendo, and minimal rough language. A-III (R)

Puerto Rican Mambo, The (1992) Incisive humor highlights the monologues and skits of stand-up comedian Luis Caballero, who bemoans what he perceives to be the lowly status of Puerto Ricans in this country. Produced and directed by co-star Ben Model, the increasingly amusing look at common ethnic stereotypes channels Caballero's frustrations into wry, insightful commentary. Mild sexual references and minimal rough language. A-II (nr)

Pufnstuf (1970) Director Hollingsworth Morse's merry romp of song, dance, and adventure features young Jack Wild as a human visitor to the magical land of Living Island, home of a dotty assortment of colorful stuffed animals overseen by their gentle dragon of a mayor, the Hon. H.R. Pufnstuf. Kids will enjoy the antics, although the flute-napping Witchiepoo (Billie Hayes) makes up in decibels what she lacks in scariness. Grown-ups might enjoy it too, especially those who like the idea of an absent-minded owl who sounds like Ed Wynn, a blind bat-messenger who keeps banging into walls, and a cheerful lion who does a pretty good turn at W.C. Fields. A-I (G)

Pulp (1972) Michael Caine plays a hack author hired to ghost-write the memoirs of aging gangster-movie actor Mickey Rooney, but soon discovers himself in the middle of a murder caper not unlike the plots of any number of his own cheap novels. Though occasionally very funny, director Michael Hodges cannot sustain his spoof on old Hollywood crime movies as a coherent whole. Some mature references. A-III (PG)

Pulp Fiction (1994) Ultra-violent tale of vicious killers and assorted lowlifes (notably John Travolta, Samuel L. Jackson, Bruce Willis, Uma Thurman, Tim Roth, and Amanda Plummer) whose paths murderously intersect during a 24-hour period in Los Angeles. Writer-director Quentin Tarantino finds much slick, cynical humor and a twisted code of honor among characters for whom life is cheap and crime is a profitable lark. Much gory violence and positive depictions of drug use, a homosexual rape, fleeting nudity, many racial slurs, and much rough language. O (R)

Pump Up the Volume (1990) Painfully shy teenager (Christian Slater) secretly develops a hip alter-ego as Hard Harry during his nightly broadcasts on a pirate radio-band, and the show's influence on his impressionable peers turns the entire community on its ear. Written and directed by Allan Moyle, the plot touches on teenage problems of loneliness, emerging sexuality, alienation, and suicide, though its insensitivity in treatment of these important issues is likely to prove more of a barrier for some than a bridge to meaningful insights. Positive depiction of radio piracy, simulated masturbation, frequent rough language, and a flash of nudity. A-IV (R)

Pumping Iron (1977) Unassuming documentary about the world of bodybuilders, singling out for major consideration Austrian-born Arnold Schwarzenegger, six-time winner of the "Mr. Olympia" title. Directed by George Butler and Robert Fiore, the film has some human touches that are entertaining and sometimes moving, but its adulation of Schwarzenegger's limited view of life and his blunt advocacy of hedonism makes this questionable material for younger viewers. A-III (PG)

Pumping Iron II: The Women (1985) Mostly boring documentary by George Butler and Charles Gaines (who also made the original) about women bodybuilders participating in Las Vegas competition. Snide approach to its subject leaves a bad taste. Some brief partial nudity and a general air of vulgarity. A-III (nr)

Punchline (1988) A frustrated New Jersey housewife (Sally Field) and a manic medical student (Tom Hanks) aspire to become stand-up comics in a seedy Manhattan comedy club. Writer-director David Seltzer fails to bring the two into focus as unlikely friends, though each creates a quirky but interesting characterization. Much profanity, sexually explicit humor and vulgarities, including a male comic dressed as a nun. A-IV (R)

Punishment Park (1971) Social drama imagines a kangaroo court of conservative Americans conducting the trials of an assortment of conscientious objectors, hippies, and peaceniks in a tent on the edge of the Mojave Desert, whose heat is part of the terrors awaiting those sentenced for punishment. Directed by Peter Watkins, the nearsighted political tract about repression and dissent is steeped in brutality and foul language, which antagonize rather than inspire, provoke disdain rather than assent. A-IV (R)

Puppet Masters, The (1994) Government agents Donald Sutherland and Eric Thal turn to scientists Julie Warner and Will Patton in a race against time to rescue the good citizens of Iowa, who are rapidly being turned into automatons by aliens bent on enslaving the world. Stuart Orme's by-the-numbers direction of the Robert A. Heinlein story results in an unremarkable blend of science fiction and horror reminiscent of such movies as **Alien** and **Invasion of the Body Snatchers** but lacking their elements of suspense. Intermittent violence, brief rear nudity, and an instance of rough language. A-III (R)

Puppet on a Chain (1972) British adaptation of the Alistair MacLean novel about Interpol agents (Sven-Bertil Taube and Barabara Parkins) assigned to uncover the Amsterdam drug connection. Directed by Geoffrey Reeve, the movie's high point is a speedboat chase through the canals of Amsterdam, but the rest of it goes from run-of-the-mill to dull. Some sadistic violence is not redeemed by its sophomoric preaching on the fate of a teenage drug addict who figures in the plot. A-III (PG)

Pure Country (1992) Flat story of a disillusioned country singer (George Strait) who falls in love with a rancher (Isabel Glasser) while on the lam from a possessive manager (Lesley Ann Warren) and her bookings of huge, impersonal concerts. Corny dialogue and Christopher Cain's consistently drab direction reduce this vehicle for country star Strait to little more than trite schmaltz backed by a fine soundtrack. Minor sexual innuendo, an instance of drunkenness, and brief fisticuffs. A-II (PG)

Pure Formality, A (1995) Found dazed and running from a nearby murder site, a novelist (Gerard Depardieu) is closely questioned in a crumbling police station by a sly inspector (Roman Polanski) who, over the course of a storm-tossed, candlelit night, gets the author to reveal shameful secrets. Finely acted and mystery-drenched, director Giuseppe Tornatore's intriguing, surreal drama is left open to interpretation as it explores the subtle nature of memory in submerging the recollection of past failures. Subtitles. Some violence and fleeting nudity. A-III (PG-13)

Pure Luck (1991) Amiable but lame comedy teaming a detective (Danny Glover) with an accident-prone accountant (Martin Short) who careen across Mexico in search of a missing amnesiac (Sheila Kelley). The many mishaps and pratfalls eventually wear thin in director Nadia Tass's faint-hearted attempt at slapstick. Minor violence, minimal profanity, and a discreet sexual allusion. A-II (PG)

Purlie Victorious (see: **Gone Are the Days**)

Purple Hearts (1984) Mediocre Vietnam War soap opera about the efforts of a Navy doctor (Ken Wahl) and nurse (Cheryl Ladd) to resolve all the obstacles that stand in the way of the inevitable clinch. Directed by Sidney J. Furie, the movie's sentiments are about as genuine as the contrived and improbable dialogue that passes here for the utterances of brave men under fire. Premarital sex figures in the theme, and there is one restrained bedroom scene, in addition to some very rough language. A-III (R)

Purple Noon (1960) Stylish French thriller set in Italy, where a manipulative American (Alain Delon), hired to get an industrialist's playboy son back to the States, kills him instead, then assumes his identity and plots to win over the dead man's girlfriend (Marie Laforet) as well. Directed by Rene Clement from Patricia Highsmith's novel, the sleek suspense drama relies greatly on Delon's sinister charm to carry the fairly simple narrative to its ironic conclusion. Subtitles. Brief violence and some sexual innuendo. A-III (PG-13)

Purple Rain (1984) Rock star Prince's film debut features graphic sex, nudity, and an outrageous treatment of women that goes beyond anything demanded by plot considerations. O (R)

Purple Rose of Cairo, The (1985) Woody Allen comedy about a Depression-era housewife (Mia Farrow), married to an insensitive brute (Danny Aiello), whose only solace is going to the movies. One day, while watching a romance, its handsome young hero (Jeff Daniels) steps out of the screen into the audience and tells her that he loves her. There are some good moments and some laughs, but the comedy is not especially inspired and its rather grim, realistic mood suggests pretensions to seriousness that the movie is incapable of supporting. A-II (PG)

Pursuit of D.B. Cooper, The (1981) Slapdash chase-comedy, inspired by a successful 1971 airplane hijacking and robbery, is such mediocre fare that even as capable an actor as Robert Duvall looks bad in his role of determined insurance investigator. Treat Williams fares even worse as the happy-go-lucky criminal who is less than endearing. Though director Roger Spottiswoode's movie plays on a cartoon level, its benign attitude toward crime and an amorous sequence are adult material. A-III (PG)

Pursuit of Happiness (1971) Failed melodrama about a campus dropout (Michael Sarrazin), who turns his back on both his WASP background and synthetic college radicals, winds up in jail, and in the end decides to escape to Canada with his girlfriend (Barbara Hershey). Directed by Robert Mulligan, the manipulative plot loads the deck against society, making it to blame for the problems of its misguided, misunderstood young man. There are some real issues here, but they are treated only superficially. Several silly nude scenes. A-IV (GP)

Pursuit of the Graf Spee (1957) Earnest, overlong dramatization of the 1939 battle between three British cruisers and the German pocket-battleship of the title, which seeks repairs in the neutral port of Montevideo, hoping to depart before the British Atlantic fleet can get there. Written, produced, and directed by Michael Powell and Emeric Pressburger, events are viewed mainly through British eyes (John Gregson, Anthony Quayle, Bernard Lee, Ian Hunter, et al.), with occasional scenes portraying the German captain (Peter Finch) as a gallant foe, but the result is a disappointing collection of action cliches dressed up with patriotic asides by cardboard characters. Brief wartime violence submerged in period dialogue, of little interest for children. A-I (br)

Pushing Hands (1995) Gentle clash-of-cultures comedy in which a retired martial-arts master (Sihung Lung) leaves Beijing for New York to live with his son (Bo Z. Wang) and American daughter-in-law (Deb Snyder), but feeling he's in the way, moves to Chinatown, where a new job and a possible romance restores his sense of self. Writer-director Ang Lee's well-observed tale of strained family relationships and the challenges of aging in a youth-oriented society consistently uses wryly understated humor to reveal the humanity of the characters. Partially subtitled. Minor violence and an instance of profanity. A-II (nr)

Pushing Tin (1999) Quirky comedy in which the intense professional rivalry between two air-traffic controllers (John Cusack and Billy Bob Thornton) spills over into their personal lives to threaten their respective marriages (to Cate Blanchett and Angelina Jolie). Briskly directed by Mike Newell, the characters' finely tuned performances poke fun at the macho world of controllers, whose split-second decisions mean life or death in the skies. Brief violence, theme of infidelity, fleeting nudity, and some profanity and rough language. A-III (R)

Puss in Boots (1988) Lackluster live-action musical version of the children's story about an ingenious cat (Christopher Walken) who gets his penniless young master (Jason Connery) engaged to the king's daughter (Carmela Marner), then installs them in a castle after disposing of its owner, a ferocious ogre. Directed by Eugene Marner, the result is a charmless misfire. A-I (G)

Pussycat, Pussycat, I Love You (1970) Utterly dismissable sex-farce about a writer (Ian McShane) who cheats on his wife (Anne Calder-Marshall) and her retaliation in kind. Written and directed by Rod Amateau, it is a totally inept production devoid of any but sophomoric humor. The theme involves adultery, with some nudity, and tasteless sight gags. O (PG)

Putney Swope (1969) Uneven satire in which blacks take over a Madison Avenue advertising agency and, despite their ban on alcohol, cigarette, and war-toy advertising, their basic philosophy is as money-oriented as their white predecessors. Director Robert Downey's off-beat, irreverent humor uses a machine-gun barrage of complex irony and slapstick imagery, only some of which hit their intended targets. Very casual approach to sex, some scenes of extensive nudity, and rough language. O (R)

Puttin' on the Ritz (1930) Creaky musical in which a song plugger (Harry Richman) rises to Broadway stardom as a singer, opens his own nightclub, then goes blind from bad booze, while his neglected wife (Joan Bennett) becomes the toast of Broadway. Directed by Edward H. Sloman, the inane story emphasizes high society's hedonism and disdain for Prohibition, though its period production-numbers of Irving Berlin songs are its main interest today. Sexual situations and heavy drinking. A-III (br)

Puzzle of a Downfall Child (1970) Tired melodrama starring Faye Dunaway in the story of a fashion model's rise to the top, where she leads a life of illusion and delusion. The tale has been told too many times and in too many better versions than this particularly hollow attempt by director Jerry Schatzberg. Some nudity and sexual references. A-III (R)

Pygmalion (1938) Droll screen version of Bernard Shaw's play in which a testy professor of phonetics (Leslie Howard) bets a colleague (Scott Sunderland) he can teach a London flower-peddler (Wendy Hiller) to speak proper English, but in the process transforms her into a proper lady who proves to have a mind of her own. Co-directed by Anthony Asquith and Leslie Howard, the battle between bullying teacher and struggling student has plenty of witty dialogue and even wittier visuals, with the comic proceedings put over by a fine cast, including Wilfrid Lawson as a victim of "middle-class morality." Romantic complications and occasional coarse language. A-II (br)

Pygmy Island (1950) Formula adventure directed by William Berke pits Jungle Jim (Johnny Weissmuller) and the US Army against a foreign agent (Steve Geray) whose men are raiding pygmy territory in quest of a plant whose tactile strength makes it of military importance. Stylized violence. A-I (br)

Pyromaniac's Love Story, A (1995) Romantic-comedy clunker in which two guys (William Baldwin and John Leguizamo) claim credit for torching a bakery in order to impress their girlfriends (Erika Eleniak and Sadie Frost), while the long-married bakery owners (Joan Plowright and Armin Mueller-Stahl) also separately claim to have set the blaze. Director Joshua Brand's charmless movie flames out with a leaden script, dopey characterizations, and transparently phony whimsy. Flippant treatment of arson. A-III (PG)

Pyx, The (1973) Montreal hooker (Karen Black) falls to her death from a high rise, clutching a pyx (a container holding communion wafers) and wearing an inverted cross around her neck. Investigating her death, a detective (Christopher Plummer) uncovers a strange underworld where drugs, prostitution, and religious perversion go hand in hand. Directed by Harvey Hart, the occult mystery's treatment of the diabolic makes a fairly intriguing horror fantasy, though its inversion of religious symbols is disturbing and at times repulsive. A-IV R

Q (1982) Failed horror movie about the feeding habits of a giant predatory bird, once an Aztec God, but now reduced to living in a cramped nest in the peak of the Chrysler Building and grabbing a bite wherever she can. David Carradine, Candy Clark, and Michael Moriarty are featured in this lackluster, ludicrous chiller produced and directed by Larry Cohen. Some disgusting violence, brief nudity, and much foul language. O (R)

Q & A (1990) Blatantly racist New York cop (Nick Nolte) murders a Hispanic hood and gets a reputable district attorney (Patrick O'Neal) to push for an open-and-shut case of justifiable homicide. Writer-director Sidney Lumet tautly follows the investigation of the case by an idealistic assistant DA (Timothy Hutton), who uncovers a chain of sleazy witnesses and high-level judicial corruption. Intense profanity, including racial and ethnic slurs, and vulgar sexual references, much grisly violence, and graphic scenes involving sexual come-ons. A-IV (R)

Q Planes (see: **Clouds over Europe**)

Quackser Fortune Has a Cousin in the Bronx (1970) He also has an unusual profession collecting horse manure in the Dublin streets for sale to gardening ladies, an offbeat girlfriend (Margot Kidder), and all of the bluff humor, warmth, rascality, and pathos too often assigned to movie Irishmen. Fortunately, Quackser (so dubbed because of the duck sounds he made as a wee babe) is played by Gene Wilder, and without him, director Waris Hussein's movie would be just another charming but slight slice of Irish life. Some fairly graphic love scenes make it adult fare. A-III (R/PG)

Quadrophenia (1979) British musical (whose title comes from The Who album that serves as the score) re-creates in gritty, vital fashion the world of the Mods and the Rockers, rival youth-gangs of the 1960s who affected different versions of rebellion against the values of their working-class parents. Director Frank Roddam fails to offer any perspective on the characters and environment he has so skillfully evoked. and the movie ends in an anarchistic, morally ambiguous scene. Graphic depiction of drug abuse and sexual promiscuity. as well as rough language. A-IV (R)

Quantez (1957) Pedestrian Western in which fleeing bankrobbers shelter in a deserted border town, then have a falling-out, which leaves the survivors (Fred MacMurray, John Gavin, and Dorothy Malone) to face attacking Apaches on their own. Director Harry Keller goes nowhere with the contrived plot and cardboard characters, though Charles Barton has some choice scenes as an itinerant peddler. Stylized violence and sexual innuendo. A-II (br)

Quarrel, The (1992) Two old friends from eastern Europe, a Yiddish writer (R.H. Thomson) and a Hasidic rabbi (Saul Rubinek), meet by chance in 1948 Montreal and resume their pre-war disputations about God, Jewish identity, and the mystery of evil as personified by the Nazis. Directed by Eli Cohen, the outdoor setting on Montreal's Mount Royal gives some visual relief to the deftly performed series of verbal exchanges ranging from the intensely cerebral to the deeply emotional, as the rabbi tries to persuade the writer to return to his orthodox religious roots. Some complicated but universal questions of faith and a discreetly handled sexual reference. A-II (nr)

Quatermass and the Pit (see: **Five Million Years to Earth**)

Queen Bee (1955) Outlandish melodrama stars Joan Crawford as a wealthy, domineering businesswoman who makes life miserable for her alcoholic husband (Barry Sullivan), ex-lover (John Ireland), and assorted friends and relations. Writer-director Ranald MacDougall's venomous portrait of a snarling, matronly egoist is ridiculously contrived and as unconvincing as the story's trite moral. Stylized violence, including suicide, and intermittent sexual references. A-III (br)

Queen Margot (1994) Densely crowded historical drama from the Alexandre Dumas novel begins in 1572 Paris, where the Protestant Henry of Navarre (Daniel Auteuil) weds the Catholic king's sister, Margot (Isabelle Adjani), but the king's mother, the devious Catherine of Medici (Virna Lisi), uses the occasion to unleash the St. Bartholomew's Day massacre of Protestants, from which Margot saves her wounded lover (Vincent Perez) who survives to help rally the Protestant forces. Directed by Patrice Chereau, the lavish production re-creates this turbulent period of religious wars on a grand scale with much blood-splattered spectacle, but the complexities of the era's political intrigues overwhelm Dumas's romantic tale of doomed lovers. Subtitles. Much graphic violence, several extended sexual encounters, and flashes of nudity. A-IV (R)

Queen of Blood (1966) Routine horror movie written and directed by Curtis Harrington features a futuristic gimmick and stars Basil Rathbone and John Saxon. A-I (br)

Queen of Hearts (1989) British love story and sweeping family saga about an Italian couple (Anita Zagaria and Joseph Long) who run off to London to marry, raise a family, and flourish as owners of a café, until their past comes back to haunt them. Told through the eyes of their endearing youngest son (Ian Hawkes), the movie is a warm comedy-drama filled with many surprises. Director Jon Amiel nicely connects old and young, past and present, and shows the power of the family bond to transcend sorrow. Minimal violence, some menace, and sexual innuendo. A-III (PG)

Queen of Outer Space (1958) Low-budget sci-fi clunker directed by Edward Bernds, with US astronauts (led by Eric Fleming) arriving on Venus in 1985 to find the planet ruled by women, among whom are man-loving rebels (led by Zsa Zsa Gabor) who free the spacemen and overthrow their male-hating queen (Laurie Mitchell). Dated sexist twaddle. A-III (br)

Queens Logic (1991) Longtime friends in a New York City neighborhood reexamine their relationships when one couple (Joe Mantegna and Linda Fiorentino) separate, and the wedding of another couple (Chloe Webb and Ken Olin) is jeopardized. Steve Rash's direction of this ensemble cast produces a few good characterizations, though it is hampered by its talky, drawn-out predictability. A live-in relationship, some rough language, and a shadowy flash of nudity. A-III (R)

Quentin Durward (1955) Indifferent adaptation of Sir Walter Scott's novel about an adventurous Scot (Robert Taylor) righting wrongs in the French court of Louis XI (Robert Morley). Directed by Richard Thorpe, the costumed derring-do only occasionally comes to life, though there's plenty of 15th-century pageantry to watch. Stylized violence. A-II (br)

Quest, The (1996) While a skilled street-fighter (Jean-Claude Van Damme) competes in a martial-arts championship in 1928 Tibet, his suave con-artist manager (Roger Moore) plots to steal the first-prize — a solid-gold dragon. Also directed by Van Damme, the result is little more than a series of bone-crunching bouts surrounded by a flimsy plot with one-dimensional characters. Recurring martial-arts violence and an instance of profanity. A-III (PG-13)

Quest for Camelot (1998) Animated fantasy in which a young girl grows up to help a blind youth save King Arthur (voice of Pierce Brosnan) from a false knight (voice of Gary Oldman) with evil powers. Directed by Frederick Du Chan, the movie features numerous violent encounters on a perilous journey to Camelot, which is no longer the feudal Christian city of legend but is portrayed instead as a stronghold of democracy on the outskirts of Stonehenge. Heavy fantasy violence and much menace. A-II (G)

Quest for Fire (1982) Ludicrously serious prehistoric adventure tale about three warriors (Everett McGill, Ron Perlman, and Nameer Eli-Kadi) whose search for fire when that of their clan has been extinguished by a marauding band of Neanderthals leads to a humanizing encounter with a more culturally advanced girl (Rae Dawn Chong), who helps them learn to laugh and even fall in love. Directed by Jean-Jacques Annaud who co-scripted with Gerard Brach, its attempts at authenticity are made even more ludicrous by brutal sex-scenes, violent combat, and other assorted caveman antics. O (R)

Quick and the Dead, The (1995) Revenge-themed Western in which a female gunslinger (Sharon Stone) arrives in town to compete in a quick-draw, shoot-to-the-death contest, intent on gunning down the sadistic town tyrant (Gene Hackman) who had her lawman father lynched years earlier. Director Sam Raimi's flashy but cynically ludicrous shoot-'em-up amounts to nothing more than redundant stagings of stylized shootouts that greatly glamorize guns and killing. Justification of murderous revenge, numerous deadly gunfights, some sexual innuendo, and fleeting partial nudity. O (R)

Quick, Before It Melts (1964) Witless comedy directed by Delbert Mann in which a magazine reporter (Robert Morse) and photographer (George Maharis) doing a story on US operations in Antarctica inveigle the commander into allowing a planeful of women to tour the ice-bound base. Comic violence and heavy-handed sexual situations. A-III (br)

Quick Change (1990) Disguised as a clown, Bill Murray and accomplices Geena Davis and Randy Quaid pull off an ingenious million-dollar bank robbery in the Big Apple, only to find that their complicated caper was a breeze compared to getting to the airport. Co-directed by Murray and Howard Franklin, the result is a sporadically funny attempt at screwball comedy, with the madness of New York City serving as a backdrop for understated performances by Murray and Davis, abetted by Quaid's slapstick goofiness. Some rough language, references to an unmarried sexual relationship, and crime treated as a lark. A-III (R)

Quick Gun, The (1964) A reformed gunslinger (Audie Murphy) is treated as an outcast in his hometown until he saves it from a band of desperados (led by Ted de Corsia). Director Sidney Salkow's slack Western has no particular merit or interest. Stylized violence. A-II (br)

Quicksand (1950) Small but effective thriller in which a cocky garage-mechanic (Mickey Rooney) dumps a nice girl (Barbara Bates) for a sharp cookie with a shady past (Jeanne Cagney), then hits the skids after she gets him to rob a penny-arcade owner (Peter Lorre). Directed by Irving Pichel, Rooney holds attention as the two-bit tough guy who gets deeper and deeper in trouble until an unexpected conclusion. Stylized violence, sexual innuendo, and an escalating series of crimes. A-III (br)

Quicksilver (1986) Ill-conceived youth movie in which a young stockbroker (Kevin Bacon) has a run of bad luck, quits the market to become a bicycle courier, and saves his new working-class friends from dope pushers, loan sharks, and dead-end jobs. Directed by Tom Donnelly, it is a phony picture of a teenage hero demonstrating that immaturity and juvenile behavior can lead to success. A-III (PG)

Quiet Cool (1986) When a gang of dope addicts brutally murder a peaceful family, they themselves are hunted down and killed in an extraordinarily violent and sadistic manner. The crude and bloody story encourages vigilantism. O (R)

Quiet Days in Clichy (1970) Screen version of a Henry Miller novel about the dehumanized sexual adventures of two writers down and out in Paris. The result is human debasement, made all the worse by an irrelevant scatological music-lyric soundtrack supplied by Country Joe McDonald. O (nr)

Quiet Earth, The (1986) New Zealand scientist (Bruno Lawrence) awakes one morning to discover that he is the last man alive after a US celestial experiment goes haywire. Director Geoff Murphy's quaint science-fiction mystery has some suspense and a warning against tampering with the laws of nature. Several scenes with nudity. A-III (nr)

Quiet Gun, The (1957) Sluggish Western directed by William F. Claxton in which a sheriff (Forrest Tucker) arrests the men who lynched a rancher, then goes after the nasty cowboy (Lee Van Cleef) who instigated the lynching in order to get the rancher's land. Frontier violence and implied adultery. A-III (br)

Quiet Man, The (1952) When a retired Irish-American boxer (John Wayne) buys a plot of Irish land and courts a lovely colleen (Maureen O'Hara) to go with it, his stubborn bride insists he collect her dowry from her mean-spirited brother (Victor McLaglen). Director John Ford's grand celebration of all-too-familiar Irish stereotypes, ranging from a fondness for spirits to the love of a good fight, is delivered with much broad humor, but the movie's universal appeal lies in the robust romance at the heart of the good-natured, old-fashioned story. Comic violence. A-II (br)

Quiet Place in the Country, A (1970) When a troubled abstract-expressionist artist (Franco Nero) is placed in an institution (a nice quiet place in the country) by his mistress (Vanessa Redgrave), his madness crystallizes into an object of tediousness rather than of possible interest. Director Elio Petri chooses to use tricky nude-shots and violent erotic dreams to hold attention, but the movie crumbles as it goes all out for slick sensationalism. O (R)

Quiet Room, The (1997) Australian drama in which a seven-year-old girl (Chloe Ferguson) stops speaking as a response to her battling parents' imminent separation. Writer-director Rolf de Heer has the child voice her thoughts to the audience, offering insights into the fear, anger, and stress felt by a youngster when divorce looms, although the uncompromising nature of the film is not for those seeking buoyant entertainment. Serious treatment of marital discord and an instance of profanity. A-II (PG)

Quigley Down Under (1990) An American cowboy (Tom Selleck), hired as a sharpshooter in the 1860s Australian outback, turns against his villainous boss (Alan Rickman) in defense of the native aborigines and a slightly mad young woman (Laura San Giacomo). Director Simon Wincer gives a fresh spin to the traditional Western and backs it with interesting plot developments, credible performances, and breathtaking Australian locales. Intermittent violent shootouts, occasional menace, and shots with tribal nudity. A-II (PG-13)

Quiller Memorandum, The (1967) Resurgence of Nazism in post-war Germany is the background for this spy story with George Segal, Max von Sydow, Senta Berger, and Alec Guinness in a cameo. Director Michael Anderson gets some suspenseful moments in a convoluted thriller that is spun out beyond its limits. A-III (br)

Quintet (1979) Director Robert Altman's failed futuristic fable about six citizens of an ice-bound, dying world engaged in a lethal cat-and-mouse game of survival that gives the movie its title. Paul Newman, Bibi Andersson, Fernando Rey, and Vittorio Gassman head the fur-swathed cast of an ambitious but hapless attempt to philosophize about the meaning of life. Graphic depiction of brutal killings. O (R)

Quiz Show (1994) Fact-based retelling of the late 195s television scandal in which quiz contestants are fed answers beforehand, until a disgruntled loser (John Turturro) spills the beans to a Congressional investigator (Rob Morrow) about the show's corrupt producer (David Paymer) and a much-admired winner (Ralph Fiennes), who reluctantly confess to betraying the public trust, while the network and sponsor escape official blame. Producer-director Robert Redford dramatically captures the contrasting personalities involved and the manner in which basic ethical considerations got shoved aside in favor of personal and corporate greed. Questions of moral integrity and minimal rough language. A-II (PG-13)

Quo Vadis (1951) After a Roman general (Robert Taylor) falls in love with a Christian maid (Deborah Kerr), the situation is complicated by the loony emperor deciding to burn Rome and blame the Christians. In director Mervyn LeRoy's version of the Henryk Sienkiewicz novel, the epic production overpowers the pallid love story, and is less interested in the conflict between Christianity and paganism than that between the mad Nero (Peter Ustinov) and his rationalist advisor (Leo Genn). A mixed bag of religious fervor and pagan frolics, there's a lengthy suicide scene, some sexual innuendo, and stylized violence. A-I (br)

R.P.M. (1970) When Gary Lockwood and fellow foul-mouthed students take over the campus-administration building, college president Anthony Quinn (hopelessly miscast) gets them to stop the agitation, but a million-dollar computer has been damaged, and the police intervene with brutal force. Erich Segal's script is a mishmash of easy problems and stereotyped solutions, ploddingly directed by Stanley Kramer. Unconvincing melodrama about student unrest, with much violence and sexual situations. A-IV (R)

Ra Expeditions, The (1972) Documentary record of anthropologist Thor Heyerdahl's voyage from Africa to the Americas in a papyrus-reed boat called the Ra, the name of an Egyptian god. Using a reed craft of early Mediterranean design, Heyerdahl set out to demonstrate that such a ship could stand the long voyage between hemispheres, and does on a second try. Produced and directed by Lennart Ehrenberg, the documentary enables a vicarious sharing of adventure on high seas. A-I (G)

Rabbit, Run (1971) Failed screen version of John Updike's dark and brooding novel probing the shadowed corners of the mind of an irresponsible young man (James Caan) who persists in chasing illusions and women with equal fervor, resulting in a ruined marriage and shattered dreams. Director Jack Smight dissipates the novel's passionate intensity by concentrating on the surface level of the action. Graphic sexual depictions. O (R)

Rabbit Test (1978) Failed sex-farce about the world's first pregnant man is comedienne Joan Rivers's debut as a director. Posing a feminist satire, the effort lacks the wit and satiric nuance that might have saved it from being ploddingly tasteless and offensive. Unfunny jokes about religious beliefs are scattered throughout this indelicate comedy. O (PG)

Rabid (1977) Canadian production about a young woman (porno star Marilyn Chambers) who undergoes plastic surgery, only to find herself turned into a vampire who soon has a good portion of the population of Montreal going green in the face, frothing at the mouth, and biting one another. Directed by David Cronenberg, it's a nauseating, gory piece of trash. O (R)

Race for Your Life, Charlie Brown (1977) Feature cartoon based on the Charles M. Schulz comic strip which tells of the adventures and perils that the Peanuts characters encounter while spending the summer at a wilderness camp out West. Though little of the subtlety of Schulz at his best is represented, the movie will entertain younger children. A-I (G)

Race Street (1948) Routine crime-story directed by Edwin L. Marin in which a San Francisco gambler (George Raft), about to retire and wed (Marilyn Maxwell), gets some unwanted help from a friendly cop (William Bendix) when a protection racket (headed by Frank Faylen) moves in and kills his best friend (Henry Morgan). Underworld violence and treachery. A-II (br)

Race with the Devil (1975) Businessmen (Warren Oates and Peter Fonda) on a vacation trip with their wives inadvertently come upon some Satanists at their rituals and then are pursued across Texas by the vengeful cultists. Directed by Jack Starrett, the silly horror movie has a bad script, a few scares, and some bloodshed. A-III (PG)

Rachel and the Stranger (1948) A widower (William Holden), raising a son on the Kentucky frontier, marries a bonds-woman (Loretta Young), but only appreciates her when his best friend (Robert Mitchum) tries to win her affections. Directed by Norman Foster, the odd triangle leads Young to reject both men as wanting a servant rather than a wife, but a Shawnee attack resolves the dilemma. Quasi-feminist theme with conventional romantic ending. A-II (br)

Rachel, Rachel (1968) Joanne Woodward plays a painfully lonely, somewhat repressed schoolteacher in a small Midwestern town, where she fears becoming a dowdy spinster. When an old school-chum (James Olson) visits, she falls hopelessly in love and has a brief, intense affair that ends harshly and with bitterness. Director Paul Newman receives excellent performances from a fine cast in a story that is touchingly poignant and deeply human. Mature theme. A-III (R)

Racing with the Moon (1984) Likable teenager (Sean Penn), finishing high school during WW II, falls for a winsome California beauty (Elizabeth McGovern), and both try to get money for a friend's abortion. Nostalgic romance from director Richard Benjamin captures the atmosphere and the mood of the period, but concentrates too heavily on the sexual nature of youthful relationships. Some nudity and a benign view of premarital sex. O (R/PG appeal)

Rack, The (1956) Back from a North Korean prisoner-of-war camp, an Army officer (Paul Newman) refuses to defend himself when put on trial for collaborating with the enemy, despite the anguish of his career-officer father (Walter Pidgeon) and the endeavors of a discerning military lawyer (Edmond O'Brien). Adapted from Rod Serling's TV drama and directed by Arnold Laven, the treatment is slick and melodramatic, save for Newman's powerful performance as the tormented, withdrawn soldier. Demanding fare for children. A-I (br)

Racket, The (1951) Tired crime-melodrama in which an honest cop (Robert Mitchum) and a cynical racketeer (Robert Ryan) try to knock each other off, despite having been boyhood friends and sharing a common enemy in the syndicate now running the town. Directed by John Cromwell, the proceedings are earnest but predictable with an unsurprising pat ending. Some nasty violence. A-II (br)

Rad (1986) Talia Shire stars in her own production of a story about a teenage bike-enthusiast who overcomes an unscrupulous businessman's plot to keep him from winning a national championship race. Directed by Hal Needham, it is a pretentious and simplistic tale, and its execution is graceless and unrewarding. Several obscene gestures by Ray Walston in a cameo role and some rough language by a little girl seem quite unnecessary. A-II (PG)

Radio Days (1987) Writer-director Woody Allen celebrates the positive impact of radio on the lives of a New York family in the story of two women (Dianne Wiest and Mia Farrow) seeking romance via different paths. This nostalgic look at the 1940s indicates that the values of that era have been lost, and even the fond memories are fading. A-II (PG)

Radio Flyer (1992) Sensitive but jumbled drama about two kid brothers (Elijah Wood and Joseph Mazello) who build a wagon that can fly so the younger boy can escape their brutally abusive, alcoholic stepfather (Adam Baldwin). Director Richard Donner mixes a serious story about child abuse with elements of magical fantasy that don't successfully mesh. Continual menace to children and momentary graphic violence. A-II (PG-13)

Radio City Revels (1938) Thin comedy directed by Ben Stoloff in which a songwriter from the hills of Arkansas (Bob Burns) comes to the big city in hopes of finding success, but instead is taken in by a second-rate composer (Jack Oakie) who copies the songs the yokel sings in his sleep and sells them under his own name. A-I (br)

Radioactive Dreams (1986) Two youths leave their bomb shelters after 15 years to explore the post-nuclear world outside. Passing through a desolate and bleak landscape, they encounter a vile assortment of mutants and perverted road-life. Many visual effects are used by director Albert Pyun simply to frame violence, brutality, nudity, and profanity. O (R)

Radioland Murders (1994) Opening night in 1939 Chicago for a new radio-network proves wildly eventful when the head writer (Brian Benben) frantically struggles to keep the on-microphone actors supplied with dialogue, while trying to reconcile with his estranged wife (Mary Stuart Masterson) and elude police after him for a series of murders that begin in the station after it signs on the air. Director Mel Smith's chaotic comedy is a case of overkill with a script too stuffed with incident and an immense cast that is largely wasted in scrambled comic misfires. Several murders played for laughs, some sexual innuendo, and a flash of partial nudity. A-III (PG)

Rafferty and the Gold Dust Twins (1975) Bumbling Los Angeles driving-test examiner (Alan Arkin) is kidnapped by roving hippies (Sally Kellerman and Mackenzie Phillips) and forced at gunpoint to drive them to New Orleans. Directed by Dick Richards, everything about this predictable heart-tug road movie is bogus, including the realistic language and frequently sordid situations. O (R)

Raffles (1930) Ronald Colman turns on the charm as the gentleman thief who steals a valuable necklace to help a needy pal, then has to outwit Scotland Yard's bulldog sleuth (David Torrence). Directed by Harry D'Arrast and George Fitzmaurice, the picture of an honorable crook is dated and its treatment creaky, but still fun for all that. A-II (br)

Raffles (1940) Playful gentleman thief (David Niven) steals a jeweled necklace from under the nose of a Scotland Yard inspector (Dudley Digges) and the chase is on. Directed by Sam Wood, Niven's bright performance as the light-fingered Raffles sparkles in its stuffy British society setting, but the period plot fairly creaks and the action is disappointingly slack. Justice prevails implicitly. A-II (br)

Raga (1971) American documentary provides a historical introduction to the musical heritage of India and Ravi Shankar's part in introducing it to Western audiences. Produced and directed by Howard Worth, the account is filled with insights about the individual and the cultural diffusion engendered by modern world communications. A-I (nr)

Rage (1966) Muddled melodrama set in a remote area of Mexico, where an alcoholic doctor (Glenn Ford) is bitten by a dog with rabies, then delivers a poor woman's baby, before racing the clock to get the serum needed to save his life. Directed by Gilberto Gazcon, the dubbed Mexican production is hardly credible, especially with Stella Stevens's role as the doctor's would-be girlfriend. Much menace, a complicated childbirth, and some sexual innuendo. A-III (br)

Rage (1972) After camping out with his boy one night, an Arizona sheep-farmer (George C. Scott) wakes to the horror of finding his son and flock dying in convulsions. When he finally learns that a secret military test of nerve gas is responsible, he goes berserk and sets out to destroy those he considers responsible. The story of a decent man crushed by a technocracy unconcerned with the individual is told by Scott in his debut as a director in purely melodramatic terms with two-dimensional figures and plot contrivances. Yet it is close enough to reality to trouble any viewer's complacency, though its violent conclusion undercuts the meaning of what precedes these scenes of destruction. A-III (PG)

Rage: Carrie 2, The (1999) Nasty horror film in which callous high-schoolers taunt an emotionally fragile classmate (Emily Bergl) who eventually turns her telekinetic powers on them with murderous ferocity. Director Katt Shea's sequel exploits teen angst, peer pressure, and sexist attitudes to deliver a bloodbath of cheap thrills. Gory multiple killings, a sexual encounter, much implied promiscuity, brief nudity, some rough language, and a few instances of profanity. O (R)

Rage at Dawn (1955) Slack Western directed by Tim Whelan has an undercover lawman (Randolph Scott) join an outlaw band of brothers (led by Forrest Tucker) in order to get the goods on corrupt officials in 1866 Indiana. Stylized violence, including a lynching. A-I (br)

Rage in Harlem, A (1991) Toting a trunkful of stolen gold, a scheming sexpot (Robin Givens) hooks up with a gullible chump (Forest Whitaker) but is tracked down by her furious ex-lover and partner in crime (Badja Djola). Bill Duke directs an overproduced potboiler awash in brutal characterizations and sleazy situations. Excessive, gory violence, some promiscuity, nudity, and much rough language. O (R)

Rage in Heaven (1941) Labored adaptation of the James Hilton novel in which a cracked millionaire (Robert Montgomery) kills himself so that it appears he has been murdered by a friend (George Sanders) who he suspects is in love with his wife (Ingrid Bergman). Directed by W.S. Van Dyke II, the fine cast seems hopelessly adrift in this static, unconvincing melodrama. Unsettling atmosphere and a suicide. A-II (br)

Rage of Paris, The (1938) Flimsy romantic comedy directed by Henry Koster in which a Frenchwoman (Danielle Darrieux) stranded in New York agrees to trick a millionaire (Louis Hayward) into marriage, then falls for his even wealthier friend (Douglas Fairbanks, Jr.). Romantic situations and some sexual innuendo. A-III (br)

Raggedy Ann and Andy (1977) Feature-length musical cartoon inspired by the long-time childhood favorites is, unfortunately, distinguished more by the technical excellence of Richard Williams's animation than by any real creative verve or even sense of imagination. The songs are mostly forgettable and there is no story line of any significance to keep children's attention. A-I (G)

Raggedy Man (1981) A young divorcée (Sissy Spacek) in a small Texas town during the Second World War has a brief romance with a sailor passing through (Eric Roberts) and fends off the unwelcome attentions of two local louts who threaten her and her two boys. Director Jack Fisk fails badly in the attempt to mix childlike whimsy, light romance, and Gothic terror. Some violence and premarital sex are central to the plot. A-III (PG)

Raging Bull (1980) Hard-edged, uncompromising portrait of former middleweight boxing champ, Jake La Motta (Robert De Niro in an outstanding performance) and his agonizing relationship with his second wife (Cathy Moriarity) and his brother (Joe Pesci). Director Martin Scorsese's stark black-and-white treatment conveys La Motta's often grim, violently hostile personality, which, the film suggests, was born of sexual problems. Brutal fight scenes, a graphic bedroom sequence, and rough language. A-III (R)

Raging Tide, The (1951) Uneven crime melodrama in which a San Francisco hood (Richard Conte) escapes a pursuing police detective (Stephen McNally) by hiding out on a fishing trawler whose captain (Charles Bickford) treats him like a son. Directed by George Sherman, the situation is redemptive, but the characters remain largely undeveloped, and the plotting overly contrived. Stylized violence and romantic complications. A-II (br)

Ragman's Daughter, The (1974) British bittersweet romance between a young tough who steals out of need and his hopelessly middle-class girl friend who does it for kicks. Scripted by Alan Sillitoe and directed by Harold Becker, the predictable plot lacks energy and drive as well as credibility. A-III (nr)

Ragtime (1981) Loose, sporadically effective adaptation of the E.L. Doctorow patchwork novel about some representative Americans at the turn of the century. Notable among them are James Cagney as the police commissioner of New York City, and a black piano-player (Harold E. Rollins, Jr.) who turns into a revolutionary combating social injustice. Directed by Milos Forman, it succeeds as a lavish historical recreation but gets low grades in the matter of credible characterization. An excessively extended sequence involving partial nudity and some rough language. A-IV (PG)

Raid, The (1954) Fact-based Civil War account of how the Vermont border-town of St. Albans was sacked in 1864 by Confederate soldiers, who mounted the attack from Canada after escaping from Union prison camps. Directed by Hugo Fregonese, the story centers on the Reb officer (Van Heflin) who spends some days reconnoitering the town disguised as a Canadian, then leads the raid despite having been befriended by many of the townspeople. Wartime violence and the conflict between military duty and human compassion. A-I (br)

Raid on Rommel (1971) WW II adventure gasps along with Richard Burton's commandos as they fight Rommel's Afrika Korps across the Sahara and through Tobruk to an awaiting rescue unit, leaving a path of mayhem and devastation in their wake. Directed by Henry Hathaway, the action sequences are made up of stock footage and darkened sequences lifted from the 1966 **Tobruk**. Ludicrous desert-action histrionics. A-III (PG)

Raiders, The (1963) Muddled Western directed by Herschel Daugherty in which Wild Bill Hickok (Robert Culp) and Buffalo Bill Cody (James McMullan) try to help desperate Texas ranchers (led by Brian Keith) avoid bloodshed on a cattle drive through hostile country to the railhead in Abilene, Kansas. Frontier violence and justice questions. A-II (br)

Raiders of the Lost Ark (1981) Tongue-in-cheek action melodrama about Indiana Jones, an archeologist-adventurer (Harrison Ford), and his feisty girlfriend (Karen Allen), who save the biblical Ark of the Covenant for the good old USA despite the worst efforts of a clutch of Nazi villains. Director Steven Spielberg's attempt to recapture the excitement of the old movie serials becomes tiresome and repetitious in its reliance upon constant action. Intense violence, gruesome special effects, and a questionable use of something as sacred as the Ark as a source of destructive power. A-III (PG)

Railroad Man, The (1965) Series of misfortunes

plague a working-class family in Italy after WW II. The sincerity of the characterizations more than outweigh the contrivances of the plot. Pietro Germi both directs and stars as the head of the family, but it is a child actor (Eduardo Nevola) who will steal the affection of even the most cynical viewer. A-II (br)

Rails into Laramie (1954) Standard Western in which an Army troubleshooter (John Payne) is sent to clean up the corruption that has halted the building of the transcontinental railroad in 1869 Wyoming. Directed by Jesse Hibbs, the story pits noble troubleshooter against devious troublemaker (Dan Duryea) who eludes justice until tried by the first all-woman jury in US history. Stylized violence and romantic complications. A-II (br)

Railway Children, The (1971) Three children (Jenny Agutter, Sally Thomsett, and Gary Warren) and their mother (Dinah Sheridan) are forced to move from their comfy Victorian mansion to an austere cottage in the country along the railway tracks, while they wait expectantly for their daddy to be cleared of false charges. Directed by Lionel Jeffries, the entire production is colored with an instinctive, childlike innocence and loyalty, providing viewers of all ages with a warming and reassuring conviction that even in the most adverse times hope and love can, indeed must, exist. A-I (G)

Rain (1932) Stilted but still powerful version of Somerset Maugham's South Seas story of Sadie Thompson (Joan Crawford), a hard-as-nails prostitute waiting out a monsoon on Pago Pago, where she attracts both a US Marine (William Gargan) and a missionary (Walter Huston) whose efforts to reform her lead to his own terrible downfall. Director Lewis Milestone generates the story's sexual tension through suggestion rather than overt action, with the confrontations between Crawford and Huston deeply charged with emotion. Sexual situations and references as well as an off-screen suicide. A-III (br)

Rain for a Dusty Summer (1972) Humberto Almazan, a popular Mexican actor who retired from the screen at the age of 35 to become a missionary priest, returns to portray Father Miguel Pro, a Mexican priest whose ministry during a time of religious oppression in the 1920s made him a folk hero and, ultimately, a martyr. Unfortunately, Arthur Lubin's heavy-handed direction of an oversimplified, melodramatic script makes the religious theme appear absurd and prevents a talented cast (including Ernest Borgnine as the dictator) from developing any but superficial characterizations, especially with the flat, expressionless dubbing of the mostly Spanish-speaking cast. Restrained violence. A-II (GP)

Rain Man (1988) A shady Los Angeles car-dealer (Tom Cruise) loses the family inheritance to an older brother (Dustin Hoffman) who suffers from irreversible autistic savant syndrome and has been institutionalized most of his life. On a cross-country auto journey, the younger brother drops his plans for a custody battle when he learns to love his brother despite his disability. Under Barry Levinson's direction, the brothers' intense and sometimes comical interaction during the life-affirming journey is wonderful, but the rest of the movie is less satisfying and detracts from the character study. Much profanity, a few intense but brief emotionally unhinged outbursts by the autistic protagonist, and a fleeting off-camera sex scene. A-III (R)

Rain or Shine (1930) Sentimental comedy in which the young owner (Louise Fazenda) of a failing circus depends upon a savvy manager (Joe Cook) to keep it running — even putting on a show almost by himself when the performers strike over unpaid salaries. Director Frank R. Capra builds the movie around the multi-talented Cook, who flawlessly performs a variety of circus acts while proving equally adept in nonsensical dialogues with comic Tom Howard and pantomimes with clown Dave Chasen. Some crude humor and a bit of sexual innuendo. A-II (br)

Rain People, The (1969) Shirley Knight plays a pregnant woman fleeing husband and home to come to terms with her womanhood and incomplete sense of fulfillment. Written and directed by Francis Ford Coppola, the movie's theme of flight from responsibility is treated with poetic intensity and subtle nuance. Some violence and sexual references. A-III (PG)

Rain Without Thunder (1993) Dreary talking-heads feature offers a series of repetitious interviews about the case of a woman (Ali Thomas) convicted of fetal murder in the year 2042 after a Constitutional amendment has made abortion illegal. Instead of a movie, writer-director Gary Bennett has made a cheap propaganda piece substituting cardboard figures for human beings and straw arguments for conflicting moral principles. Unfairly caricatures the moral issue of abortion. O (PG-13)

Rainbow, The (1989) British adaptation of the 1915 D.H. Lawrence novel about the sexual and political awakening of an adolescent girl (Sammi Davis) occasioned by her maverick swimming instructor (Amanda Donohoe). Despite writer-director Ken Russell's uncharacteristically restrained treatment of the material, there are several needlessly explicit depictions of heterosexual and lesbian encounters. O (R)

Rainbow Brite and the Star Stealer (1985) In her film debut, Rainbow Brite, the creation of toy manufacturers, must save the universe from destruction. Not strong on imagination or substance, but lots of color and action designed to sell dolls to the toddler crowd. A- I (G)

Raining Stones (1994) Gritty British social drama about an unemployed Catholic (Bruce Jones) who's determined to buy his daughter a First Communion dress but, unable to find enough odd jobs to pay for it, borrows the money from a loan shark who terrorizes his family when he can't repay it. Director Ken Loach explores working-class life in semi-documentary fashion, finding universal appeal in the story of a good but muddled family-man whose struggles to find work are often humorous, though they have serious consequences reflecting social-justice issues. Passing sexual references, occasional profanity, and assorted rough language. A-III (nr)

Rainmaker, The (see: **John Grisham's The Rainmaker**)

Rains Came, The (1939) Soggy romantic melodrama set in a remote Indian principality, where some Western visitors endure monsoon, earthquake, and cholera, resulting in the moral transformation of a dissolute painter (George Brent) helped by the love of a missionary's daughter (Brenda Joyce) and of a cynical socialite (Mryna Loy) inspired by a noble Indian physician (Tyrone Power). Director Clarence Brown uses the exotic setting to make the stock characters almost as interesting as the spectacular catastrophes they face, though the script's dated colonial attitudes may put some viewers' teeth on edge. Romantic situations and ethnic stereotyping. A-II (br)

Rains of Ranchipur, The (1955) Romantic clunker set in modern India, where the rich American wife (Lana Turner) of an English lord (Michael Rennie) wins the love of an idealistic Hindu doctor (Richard Burton), until an earthquake makes her realize she can't compete with his dedication to helping those in need. Directed by Jean Negulesco, this updated version of **The Rains Came** flounders in pedestrian action, unconvincing characters, and shallow emotions, with even the scenes of devastation wrought by earthquake and flood rousing little interest. Natural disasters and romantic complications. A-II (br)

Raintree County (1957) Epic misfire about a Hoosier youth (Montgomery Clift), his hometown sweetheart (Eva Maria Saint), and the troubled Southern belle (Elizabeth Taylor) he marries on the eve of the Civil War. Directed by Edward Dmytryk, the tragic romance unfolds in a muddled, overlong narrative, which, despite lyric interludes and interesting period detail, flounders in its focus on the unbalanced wife's lethal obsessions with race. Wartime violence and suicide in the plot resolution. A-II (br)

Raise the Red Lantern (1992) Exquisitely mounted period-piece about a young Chinese bride (Gong Li) who competes daily with her husband's three other wives to win his favor and establish preeminence in the household. Director Zhang Yimou's tragic story of women reduced to treachery to maintain self-esteem is depicted in the context of a closed, tyrannical society. Subtitles. Much sexual innuendo and malicious intrigue. A-III (PG)

Raise the Titanic! (1980) Failed action melodrama with Jason Robards and Richard Jordan in a story about attempts by American and Russian soldiers of fortune to recover rare minerals from the sunken luxury-liner. Director Jerry Jameson's lackluster underwater adventure is unbelievably lethargic and muddleheaded. A-II (PG)

Raisin in the Sun, A (1961) Fine screen version of the Lorraine Hansberry play about a young black man in a Chicago slum (Sidney Poitier) whose ambitions to get ahead in the world come into conflict with the values of his mother (Claudia McNeil in a remarkable performance). What keeps this story about the evils of racial segregation from being dated is that director Daniel Petrie and a very capable cast have focused their energies on depicting human aspirations common to all and transcending limits of plot and period. A-II (br)

Raising Arizona (1987) Nicolas Cage and Holly Hunter play a simpleminded childless couple who kidnap one of a set of quintuplets to raise as their own in this madcap comedy from the Coen brothers, Joel and Ethan. Stridently effective parody of socially conscious drama has some vulgar and brutal moments played with deadpan intensity by Cage and a host of crude and profane heavies, perfectly restrained at the borderline of good taste. A-III (PG-13)

Raising Cain (1992) An unfaithful wife (Lolita Davidovich) suspects her eccentric husband (John Lithgow) when neighborhood women and their toddlers, including her own, begin disappearing. Writer-director Brian de Palma parodies his own and other horror movies in a clunky mix of comedy and terror that never meshes individual scenes into a cohesive whole. Intermittent violence, a discreet sexual encounter, and occasional rough language. A-III (R)

Rake's Progress, The (see **Notorious Gentleman**)

Rambling Rose (1991) A kindly Southern family (headed by Robert Duvall and Diane Ladd) in 1935 takes in an abused 19-year-old (Laura Dern) whose promiscuous habits cause continual problems in the community. Directed by Martha Coolidge, the story begins playfully, but sensitive performances and the lead character's eventual maturity make this an uncommon and wistful movie. Discreet scene of foreplay by teenagers, numerous references to promiscuity, and a flash of nudity. A-IV (R)

Rambo (see: **First Blood**)

Rambo: First Blood Part II (1985) Rambo (Sylvester Stallone) is released from prison to undertake a secret mission to free Americans still being held in Vietnam and, after much slaughter, does so only to face the traitor who wanted the mission to fail. Playing shamelessly upon the fears and hopes of the relatives of MIA's, this comic-strip movie features excessive violence. O (R)

Rambo III (1988) One-man wrecking crew John Rambo (Sylvester Stallone) returns to the battlefield, this time in Afghanistan, to save his mentor, Col. Trautman (Richard Crenna), from certain death at the hands of his Soviet captors. Directed by Peter MacDonald, the movie's plot is as simplistic as its politics, and Stallone's performance is notable only for some self-mocking humor. Excessive violence and rough language. O (R)

Rampage (1992) When a particularly perverse serial-murderer (Alex McArthur) pleads insanity at his California trial, the young prosecutor (Michael Biehn) argues that society will only be safe from this mad killer if he is given the death penalty. Writer-director William Friedkin's courtroom drama centers on the slow, tortuous processes of the law rather than the gruesome details of the sadistic crimes, though it becomes increasingly clear that the movie is weighted on the side of capital punishment. Restrained depiction of grisly killings, the desecration of a church, and the bizarre ravings of a sick mind. A-III (R)

Rampage at Apache Wells (1966) Hokey German-produced Western from a Karl May story about the heroics of veteran frontiersman Old Surehand (Stewart Granger) in saving a wagon train from attack by Indians stirred up by an evil oil-baron. Harald Philipp directs the melodramatics with a heavy hand, and the ludicrous results are not helped by inept dubbing. Stylized violence and silly frontier stereotypes. A-II (br)

Ramparts of Clay (1971) French director Jean-Louis Bertucelli uses scenes of everyday life in a small Tunisian village at the edge of the Sahara to tell the story of a young woman (Leila Schenna) who can no longer accept the old patterns in which she has been raised. This is a beautiful work showing the dignity of a simple way of life, while conscious of the irreversible forces that will transform it. A-II (GP)

Ramrod (1947) Routine Western directed by Andre de Toth in which a manipulative woman rancher (Veronica Lake) goads a larger rancher (Preston Foster) into a range war, costing the lives of a top hand (Don DeFore), the local sheriff (Donald Crisp), and others before her honest foreman (Joel McCrea) stops it, then quits her for another (Arleen Whelan). Some nasty violence and romantic complications. A-II (br)

Ran (1985) Samurai version of Shakespeare's "King Lear" by director Akira Kurosawa is, unfortunately, little more than an opulently staged historical pageant, lacking pathos and tragic force. Many battle scenes, but the violence is stylized. A-II (R)

Rancho Deluxe (1975) Jeff Bridges and Sam Waterson star as footloose and free-spirited modern rustlers finally apprehended by a bumbling Slim Pickens. Director Frank Perry's unfunny comedy is further undone by nudity and graphic sexuality. O (R)

Random Harvest (1942) Romantic melodrama in which a shell-shocked English officer (Ronald Colman) escapes an asylum at the end of WW I, marries a loving music-hall singer (Greer Garson), then forgets his new life when a head injury restores his pre-war memory, and he returns to run the family business, until his wife sees his picture in a newspaper. Directed by Mervyn LeRoy from James Hilton's novel, the contrived proceedings are kept from becoming too maudlin by a compelling cast and interesting period-settings, but the sentimental results seem largely bogus today. Romantic complications. A-II (br)

Ransom (1956) Talky, flat-footed suspensor in which a wealthy executive (Glenn Ford) and his hysterical wife (Donna Reed) agonize about the morality, as well as practicality, of paying kidnappers to return his young son. Director Alex Segal's serious but simple-minded picture suggests that there would be no kidnappings if no one paid ransom, but the concept is lost in the melodramatics of the harrowing situation. Much soul-searching and emotional duress. A-II (br)

Ransom (1996) Fearing his kidnapped son will be killed anyway, an enraged father (Mel Gibson) spurns the FBI's advice to pay the ransom money and offers it instead to anyone who can identify the abductors (led by Gary Sinise) as he races against time to locate the boy. Director Ron Howard's taut action thriller twists and turns suspensefully, although its point-blank violence is disturbingly realistic. Several gory killings, deadly menace to a child, frequent profanity, and much rough language. A-IV (R)

Rapa Nui (1994) Overblown melodrama set on Easter Island shortly before its first contact with Europeans follows two brawny natives (Jason Scott Lee and Esai Morales) as they compete in brutal physical ordeals to become leader of the island's clans and win the hand of the beautiful woman (Sandrine Holt) they both love. Directed by Kevin Reynolds, the story plays on the level of trite romance with uninvolving, undeveloped characters, the result being a visually striking but otherwise barren fiction. Some gruesome violence, much ethnographic nudity, and a premarital sexual relationship. A-III (R)

Rape of Love (1979) Difficult French drama about an attractive, self-possessed, and quite intelligent young nurse (Nathalie Nell) who is abducted by four men and brutally raped. Directed by Yannick Bellon, it is a serious attempt to deal with a detestable crime of violence and its consequences, not only for the victim, her fiancé, family, and friends, but also for the rapists and society as a whole. Despite its good intentions, however, the rape scene is unnecessarily graphic and extended. O (nr)

Rapid Fire (1992) Having witnessed a mob murder, a college student (Brandon Lee) is betrayed in the federal witness protection program and reluctantly relies on two Chicago cops (Powers Boothe and Kate Hodge) and his own martial-arts skills to stay alive. Dwight H. Little directs a graphic action yarn that does a slick job of exploiting murderous violence as exciting entertainment. Excessive violence, a brief sexual encounter, occasional nudity, and much rough language. O (R)

Rappin' (1985) A young ex-convict adept at rapping (the street art of fast-talking) comes to the aid of the urban poor victimized by nasty landlords and the like. The actors, under Joel Silberg's direction, are personable, but the flimsy story is nothing but a frame for a skill that's not likely to enthrall most viewers. A-II (PG)

Rapture, The (1991) Wooden tale of a depressed woman (Mimi Rogers) who tires of trying to fill the emptiness of her life with meaningless sexual encounters, joins a pseudo-Christian cult, and becomes a deranged religious fanatic. Writer-director Michael Tolkin's blankly superficial treatment of the subject results in an unpalatable brew of sex, religious rhetoric, and irrational psychology. Excessively graphic depictions of sexual encounters, eccentric interpretations of biblical texts, and occasional rough language. O (R)

Rare Breed, The (1966) Languid Western in which an English widow (Maureen O'Hara) and her grown daughter (Juliet Mills) arrive in 1884 Texas to deliver a prize Hereford bull purchased for a Scottish rancher (Brian Keith), but he's interested only in the widow, and it's up to a veteran cowpuncher (James Stewart) to prove the bull's value in improving the longhorn breed of cattle. Directed by Andrew V. McLaglen, the narrative relies mainly on the comic potential of upper-class ladies coping with the rugged ways of the range, enlivened by occasional fistfights, shootouts, and a stampede. Frontier violence and mild romance. A-I (br)

Rascal (1969) A boy (Bill Mumy), a dog, and a mischievous raccoon spend a summer together in Small Town, USA, in the innocent days just before WW I. Director Norman Tokar keeps the action lively (especially that of Rascal, the raccoon) and the sentiment wholesome in this Disney production celebrating the virtues of rural America. A-I (G)

Rashomon (1951) Medieval Japanese story in which a bandit (Toshiro Mifune) is charged with murdering a samurai and raping his wife, but the three (the samurai speaks through a medium) give contradictory accounts, to which is added a yet different version of events as witnessed by a woodcutter (Takashi Shimura). Director Akira Kurosawa makes brilliant use of the actors and the sunlit forest setting in flashbacks restaging the four versions of the crime, but the result is less about the relativity of truth than about the human capacity for evil and deceit, a theme which ends on a hopeful note as the woodcutter rescues an abandoned baby. Subtitles. Stylized violence and sexual situations. A-III (br)

Raspad (1992) Harrowing political drama, set during and just after the Soviet nuclear-reactor explosion at Chernobyl in April 1986, follows a skeptical reporter (Sergei Shakurov) around as the official government continues to deny the enormity of the disaster. Director Mikhail Belikov compellingly converts a tragic incident in history into deeply-felt personal statement resonating with moral outrage. Subtitles. Somber theme and flashes of nudity. A-II (nr)

Rasputin (1966) Failed British dramatization of a sinister monk (Christopher Lee) in the Czar's court before the Russian Revolution. Directed by Don Sharp, the evil actions depicted are excessive in their visual detail. O (br)

Rat's Tale, A (1998) Disappointing family fantasy in which a pair of enterprising rats save their community from a new rodent poison by finding an antidote in the flowers of a long-lost magical garden hidden in the subterranean rock beneath Manhattan. Directed by Michael F. Huse, the German production mixes live-action American actors and settings with beautifully crafted German marionettes and studio backgrounds, but the thin story of talking animals and magical powers is too belabored to hold much interest or charm. A-I (G)

Ratboy (1986) A boy whose facial deformity makes him look like a rodent becomes exploited for monetary gain. Directed by actress Sandra Locke (who also plays a leading role as one of those taking advantage of the boy), this version of the beauty-and-the beast fable lacks any convincing insight and relies upon conventional plot devices, including negative stereotyping of black Los Angelinos and people in the entertainment business. Liberal sprinklings of profanity. A-III (PG-13)

Raven, The (1935) Grisly horror movie in which a surgeon (Bela Lugosi) goes batty after being rejected by a woman (Irene Ware) whose life he saved, then seeks his revenge with the help of an escaped killer (Boris Karloff), who needs the doctor to repair his disfigured face. Directed by Louis Friedlander (aka Lew Landers), the contrived proceedings grow ridiculously overwrought as the sadistic surgeon imprisons the woman and her loved ones in a torture chamber inspired by Edgar Allan Poe stories. Stylized violence, menacing situations, and some gruesome visuals. A-III (br)

Raven, The (1963) Edgar Allan Poe's poem is turned into a comic fantasy involving a serious conjuror (Vincent Price) and an inept colleague (Peter Lorre) who combine their magical powers in a duel to the death against a power-mad wizard (Boris Karloff). Directed by Roger Corman, the thin story offers some off-beat humor, mainly from Lorre's manic son (Jack Nichoson), but things turn lively once the duel of magic gets underway. Supernatural hokum. A-I (br)

Ravenous (1999) Grisly thriller set in the 1847 Sierra Nevadas, where a tiny group of soldiers (including Guy Pearce and Jeffrey Jones) are set upon by a cunning stranger (Robert Carlyle) claiming to have fled a cannibalistic killer in the area, but it is he who has devoured numerous pioneers and now turns on the unwary soldiers. Director Antonia Bird's repulsive tale is made all the more stomach-churning by its graphic visuals, giddy music, and jokey tone completely at odds with the continual slaughters. Excessive violence and gore, desecration of corpses, fleeting nudity, and occasional profanity. O (R)

Raw Deal (1986) Fueled by pride and a promise, a small-town sheriff (Arnold Schwarzenegger) massacres an entire crime syndicate in a bloody shootout providing a primitive brand of justice on the behalf of the slain son of his former FBI buddy (Darren McGavin). The excessive violence isn't justified by plot or characterization. O (R)

Raw Edge (1956) Muddled Western set in 1842 Oregon, where a cowboy (Rory Calhoun) takes on the cattle baron (Herbert Rudley) who murdered his brother, then saves the villain's wife (Yvonne De

Carlo) when she's threatened by a lustful gunman (Neville Brand) during an Indian uprising. Directed by John Sherwood, the dire proceedings are often desperate but mostly senseless. Nasty violence including a lynching and attempted sexual assaults. A-III (br)

Raw Wind in Eden (1958) Hokey romantic adventure in which an American playgirl (Esther Williams) crash-lands on an isolated Mediterranean island inhabited by a mysterious American (Jeff Chandler) who wants to be alone. Directed by Richard Wilson, the bogus situation goes nowhere until a climactic shootout resolves matters predictably. Romantic complications and sexual innuendo. A-III (br)

Rawhide (1938) Low-budget Western in which NY Yankee Lou Gehrig quits baseball to join his sister (Evalyn Knapp) in buying a ranch, but once there, he runs into a protection racket which he busts with the help of a singing cowboy-lawyer (Smith Ballew), then returns to the peace and quiet of the Yankee ball park. Directed by Ray Taylor, there's some two-fisted action, but Gehrig's genial tenderfoot is the whole show and worth seeing. A-I (br)

Rawhide (1951) Suspenseful Western set in an Arizona stagecoach relay-station, where the attendant (Tyrone Power), a mother (Susan Hayward), and her toddler are held prisoner by escaped convicts (led by Hugh Marlowe) waiting to rob a gold shipment on an incoming stage. Director Henry Hathaway establishes the station's isolation and the helplessness of the captives, then tightens the tension as the two try to escape in time to warn the stage. Frontier violence and mounting menace. A-II (br)

Rawhide Years, The (1956) Middling Western in which a riverboat gambler (Tony Curtis) is framed for murder, then tracks down those responsible (Peter Van Eyck and William Demarest), with a little help from a down-on-his-luck gunman (Arthur Kennedy). Director Rudolph Maté tries to make Curtis credible as an action hero but succeeds better with the colorful Western backgrounds and hard-bitten frontier types who made it dangerous. Stylized violence and romantic complications. A-II (br)

Razor in the Flesh (1974) Brazilian drama about a prostitute tormented by her pimp, who in turn is taunted by a homosexual, until the roles are reversed and attacker becomes victim, and the story becomes a parable about the interchangeable roles of oppressor and oppressed. Directed by Braz Chediak, the movie is about characters living at the last extremities of humanity, vividly reacting with the desperation of those who can only hurt others and themselves, because they have nothing left to hope for. As a reminder of our common human fragility, it cuts to the bone. A-IV (nr)

Razor's Edge, The (1946) Glossy adaptation of W. Somerset Maugham's story of an American (Tyrone Power) who returns from WW I convinced there is more to life than attaining wealth, quits his society friends for Paris to rethink his goals, then winds up in India seeking spiritual wisdom. Directed by Edmund Goulding, the man's growing idealism leads him to give up the love of a socialite (Gene Tierney) and devote himself instead to helping a deeply troubled woman (Anne Baxter), but the result of all this selflessness adds up to little more than a slickly contrived tearjerker. Romantic complications and vague spiritual yearnings. A-II (br)

Razor's Edge, The (1984) The path to salvation is hard in this ill-conceived and shallow remake of the 1946 version of the W. Somerset Maugham novel. Bill Murray plays a WW I veteran who travels in Europe to find the meaning of life and some measure of inner peace. Under the direction of John Byrum, Murray has difficulty displaying the emotion and sensitivity required by the role. Empty parable with some harsh language. A-III (PG-13)

Re-Animator (1985) In this abysmal effort, a zealous young scientist (Jeffrey Combs) develops a serum to raise the dead. Directed by Stuart Gordon, it's an abundantly gory affair made all the more revolting by its attempts at grisly humor. O (R rating surrendered by distributor and no longer applies)

Reaching for the Moon (1931) Slack Depression-era comedy about a financial tycoon (Douglas Fairbanks) who pursues a flighty socialite (Bebe Daniels) on an England-bound liner, then learns she's engaged and he's been wiped out on Wall Street. Directed by Edmund Goulding, Fairbanks flounders in a flat role that invites little sympathy and offers few opportunities for his athletic talents, except some silly pranks after drinking an especially potent cocktail. Sexual situations and innuendoes. A-III (br)

Ready to Wear (1994) In this overlong, overripe jape at the phony pretensions of the fashion industry, the apparent murder of the head (Jean-Pierre Cassel) of Paris's biggest fashion show is mourned by his mistress (Anouk Aimee), applauded by his estranged wife (Sophia Loren), and shrugged off by the chief suspect (Marcello Mastroianni), while the show goes on its silly, inconsequential way. Robert Altman directs an empty film about a hollow profession, squandering an embarrassingly large cast in a slapdash series of unconnected shaggy-dog stories about characters with whom one wouldn't want to spend five minutes, let alone over two hours. Extended scenes with full nudity, much sexual promiscuity, some rough language, and occasional profanity. O (R)

Real Blonde, The (1998) Scattershot romantic comedy about a fashion makeup artist (Catherine Keener) and her live-in love, a struggling actor (Matthew Modine), whose relationship is tested by new romantic interests. Writer-director Tom DiCillo is better at mocking the superficial worlds of fashion and entertainment than in developing interesting central characters. Sexual situations with occasional nudity, frequent rough language, and intermittent profanity. A-IV (R)

Real Genius (1985) When a college science-whiz (Val Kilmer) and his fellow students discover they have been tricked by their professor (William Atherton) into helping create a laser weapon for the military establishment, they revolt and destroy their work. Director Martha Coolidge is unable to get any laughs from this failed satire on higher education. Some vulgar language and sexual promiscuity A-III (PG)

Real Glory, The (1939) Training Filipino recruits to defend their land against invading Moros, a handful of American soldiers (notably Gary Cooper, David Niven, and Broderick Crawford) help their "little brothers" learn to fight a fanatic enemy while also having to contend with a cholera outbreak. Director Henry Hathaway builds plenty of tension in the plight of the remote island outpost and stages some classy battle scenes, but the patriotic melodrama seems dated hokum today, not least because of its patronizing attitude toward the Philippine people. Stylized violence, some of it rather grisly. A-I (br)

Real Life (1979) Episodic comedy, written and directed by comedian Albert Brooks, in which he plays the role of a moviemaker who wants to capture on film the life of a real American family, a Phoenix veterinarian (Charles Grodin), his wife (Francis Lee McCain), and their two children. While frequently hilarious, with a touch of black humor, many of the jokes are adult in nature, but probably not too strong for older teenagers. A-III (PG)

Real McCoy, The (1993) When her little boy is kidnapped by criminals who need her expertise, a paroled bankrobber (Kim Basinger) is forced to attempt one more treacherous bank job, with the help of her inept assistant (Val Kilmer). Russell Mulcahy directs a dull and plodding comedy of no originality and completely lacking romantic sparks between the couple. Intermittent violence, an uncritical attitude toward ill-gotten gain, and an instance of rough language. A-III (PG-13)

Reality Bites (1994) While searching for a job, a novice filmmaker (Winona Ryder) becomes romantically involved with an ambitious TV-programmer (Ben Stiller), much to the disgust of her lethargic musician-friend (Ethan Hawke) who can't express his own romantic feelings for her. Also directed by Stiller, the movie takes a mildly comic look at the twenty-something generation caught between trying to juggle confusing adult relationships and starting careers in an economy with few opportunities. Implied premarital affairs. A-III (PG-13)

Reap the Wild Wind (1942) In this 19th-century adventure yarn, a sea captain (John Wayne) and a maritime lawyer (Ray Milland) fall for the same damsel (Paulette Goddard) while fighting a pirate wrecker-salvager (Raymond Massey) operating off the Florida Keys. Director Cecil B. DeMille depicts the era of sailing ships in colorful fashion with some rousing action sequences, including Wayne's battle with a giant squid, but the narrative frequently bogs down in fitful romance and soggy soul-searching. Some menace and stylized violence. A-I (br)

Rear Window (1954) Stylish thriller in which a Manhattan photographer (James Stewart), immobilized by a broken leg, idly passes the time watching his neighbors across the way until witnessing a murder, then uses his girlfriend (Grace Kelly) to catch the killer (Raymond Burr). Director Alfred Hitchcock gradually notches the level of suspense to fever pitch in the conclusion. Much menace and a stylized act of violence. A-II (br)

Rebecca (1940) Daphne du Maurier's classic tale of mystery and romance tells of the remarriage of a wealthy British widower (Laurence Olivier) whose young bride (Joan Fontaine) is intimidated by the great estate of Manderley and its disapproving housekeeper (Judith Anderson) until she discovers the truth about the death of her husband's former wife. Alfred Hitchcock's first movie to be directed in the US is slow and deliberate in turning Manderley into a sinister setting whose empty halls reverberate with the echoes of her brooding husband's deceased wife. Though more romantic than mysterious, it's effectiveness as an eerie exercise in suspense might rattle the very young. A-II (br)

Rebecca of Sunnybrook Farm (1938) Pedestrian Shirley Temple vehicle gives her the role of a "self-reliant" motherless child whose country aunt (Helen Westley) won't hear of her becoming a radio star, until talent wins out. Directed by Allan Dwan, the predictable plot complications keep getting in the way of mild romance (Randolph Scott and Gloria Stuart), pale comedy (Slim Summerville, Jack Haley, and William Demarest), and Shirley's singing and hoofing with Bill Robinson. Dated but innocent fun. A-I (G)

Rebel with a Cause (see **The Loneliness of the Long Distance Runner**)

Rebel Without a Cause (1955) Unconvincing tale of teenage angst portrays troubled Los Angeles youths (James Dean, Natalie Wood, and Sal Mineo), whose alienation from affluent parents propels them into dangerous scrapes that eventually end in tragedy. Directed by Nicholas Ray, the picture's intended theme is more substantial than its clumsy execution and self-serving picture of adults as hypocritical and uncaring. Stylized violence. A-II (br)

Rebellion in Patagonia (1977) When armed violence broke out in 1921 between the landowners and striking workers of Patagonia, Argentina's southernmost state, the government intervened by sending in troops to help the landowners crush the workers. Large-scale Argentinean re-creation directed by Hector Olivera has much colorful action with hard-riding gaucho bands pitted against columns of soldiers in vintage autos. There are, however, some strong scenes of violence illustrating the inequities of power and class. A-III (nr)

Reckless (1984) Pretentious, slow-moving account of star-crossed teenaged lovers (Aidan Quinn and Daryl Hannah) in a grimy, impoverished steel town treads numbingly familiar ground. Director James

Foley has found no way to recharge the old formula, nor has writer Chris Columbus discovered anything of significance. Aimed at a teenage audience, it has an abundance of nudity and graphic sex. O (R)

Reckoning, The (1970) Nicol Williamson gives a brilliant performance as a London businessman who drinks too much, drives too fast, uses and abuses women, ruins business rivals, and even commits murder to avenge his father's death back in the Liverpool slum where he grew up. It is a portrait of a ruthless, amoral fellow, and yet director Jack Gold's fast-moving action melodrama takes a reckoning, not only of him, but of a society that rewards his brand of cut-throat tactics in life as well as the business world. A disturbing movie not intended as escapist fare. A-IV (R)

Red (1994) Elusive but compelling tale in which a Swiss fashion-model (Irene Jacob) with an ebbing long-distance romance strikes up a friendship with a retired judge (Jean-Louis Trintignant) whose life had been blighted as a young man when the woman he loved chose another, precisely the situation confronting a novice jurist (Jean-Pierre Lorit) who happens to be the model's neighbor, though the two don't meet until later drawn together by an act of fate. Preceded by **Blue** and **White**, the concluding portion of director Krzysztof Kieslowski's **Three Colors** trilogy involves the viewer in the intertwining lives of three lonely individuals as it probes the connections between people and their place within a rational but uncertain universe. Subtitles. Mature themes with a fleeting but intense bedroom scene. A-III (R)

Red and the White, The (1969) Hungarian dramatization about the confused struggles between Communists and anti-Communists that broke out in eastern Europe after the Russian Revolution. Director Miklos Jancso's picture of a violent era, when a man's shirt was worth more than his life, is set against the bleak but hauntingly beautiful Volga countryside. A-III (nr)

Red Badge of Courage, The (1951) Powerful though uneven dramatization of Stephen Crane's novel about an Ohio youth (Audie Murphy) coming of age in combat during the Civil War. Brutally truncated by the studio before its release, what remains of director John Huston's effort is a strong, naturalistic re-creation of the period's bloody warfare of attrition and the human cost for those who fought it. The battlefield violence is strong fare for youngsters. A-I (br)

Red Ball Express (1952) Standard WW II story of an Army unit of misfits (led by Jeff Chandler) formed after Normandy to move supplies to the front lines in truck convoys that often have to fight their way through bypassed enemy pockets. Directed by Budd Boetticher, the action is energetic and purposeful, though the characters (including Alex Nicol, Hugh O'Brien, and Sidney Poiter) are the usual cross-section of comic, sentimental, and heroic types. Wartime violence. A-I (br)

Red Beard (1969) Japanese character study of a 19th-century doctor (Toshiro Mifune) who must be incredibly tough and unbending in running a clinic for the poor, and yet be tender and loving in his ministry to those who need his care. Director Akira Kurosawa's movie conveys the complexities of compassion in the person of this hardheaded, single-minded doctor made credible by Mifune's great performance. Realist depictions of the period's crude operating facilities. A-III (nr)

Red Beret, The (see: **Paratrooper**)

Red Blood of Courage (1935) Adventure programmer directed by Jack English in which an undercover Canadian Mountie (Kermit Maynard) saves a woman (Ann Sheridan) being held hostage by a gang after her uncle's oil-rich land. Stylized violence. A-I (br)

Red Corner (1997) Framed after a one-night stand for rape and murder, an American lawyer (Richard Gere) in China must rely on a government-appointed defense attorney (Bai Ling) to save him from imminent execution, but uncovering the facts puts her own life in jeopardy. Director Jon Avnet's dense political thriller hinges on a barely credible plot twist, but manages to maintain suspenseful momentum up to a mushy conclusion. Some gory violence, a fleeting sexual encounter, and brief nudity. A-III (R)

Red Dawn (1984) Director John Milius presents a preposterous and heavy-handed war movie with the premise that the United States has been invaded by Russian and Cuban troops. A group of teenage Rambos (led by Patrick Swayze and C. Thomas Howell) take up guerrilla warfare to preserve the integrity of America. Because of its violence and its glorification of the macho rather than patriotism, it is not for immature viewers. A-III (PG-13)

Red Desert, The (1965) Vague Italian mood-piece about a troubled woman (Monica Vitti) living in the industrial city of Ravenna who struggles to find human warmth and hope in a seemingly alienated world. Directed by Michelangelo Antonioni, the unconventional narrative is more concerned with interior feelings than the exposition of events, and many may find its images of disorientation irritatingly abstract and meaningless. Subtitles. Needlessly detailed treatment of sexual matters. A-IV (br)

Red Dragon, The (1945) Routine Charlie Chan mystery directed by Phil Rosen with the Chinese-American detective (Sidney Toler) in Mexico City helping a local cop (Fortunio Bonanova) solve a series of murders involving atomic secrets and the rare Chinese ink of the title. Comic racial stereotypes with Chan's Number Three son (Benson Fong) and chauffeur (Willie Best). A-I (br)

Red Dragon: The Pursuit of Hannibal Lecter (see: **Manhunter**)

Red Heat (1988) Buddy-cop action thriller pairing a tight-lipped Soviet cop (Arnold Schwarzenegger) with a loud-mouthed Chicago cop (Jim Belushi) in a manhunt for a Soviet drug smuggler (Ed O'Ross) on the streets of Chicago. Directed by Walter Hill, the movie's international dimension adds nothing to the tired, overly familiar formula plot. Excessive violence and foul language. O (R)

Red, Hot and Blue (1949) Tiresome, silly musical directed by John Farrow features Betty Hutton belting out some Frank Loesser tunes ("Where Are You Now That I Need You") as a would-be showgirl from Ohio, whose dizzy schemes for publicity get her kidnapped by New York gangsters, then rescued by boyfriend Victor Mature, a struggling Broadway director. Mild showbiz romance with some comic violence. A-II (br)

Red House, The (1947) Tangled psychological thriller about a crippled farmer (Edward G. Robinson) trying to save his adopted daughter (Allene Roberts) from discovering the terrible truth about her parent's death which lies hidden deep in a nearby woods. Writer-director Delmer Daves creates a suitably eerie atmosphere for a plot that never quite delivers the intended impact. Some stylized violence and romantic complications present and past. A-II (br)

Red Line 7000 (1965) Episodic story of racing-car drivers (James Caan, John Robert Crawford, and James Ward) and the women in their lives (Marianna Hill, Gail Hire, and Laura Devon respectively). Director Howard Hawks fails to get much emotion out of cardboard characters, whose romantic involvements are of less interest than the newsreel footage of auto races such as the Daytona 500, which furnish the movie's only real excitement. Racing accidents and sexual situations. A-III (br)

Red Mantle, The (see: **Hagbard and Signe**)

Red Pony, The (1949) Uneven adaptation of John Steinbeck's story about a young boy (Peter Miles) growing up on a California ranch, where he wrongly blames the death of a beloved colt on the hired hand (Robert Mitchum) until reconciled to its loss by the promise of another. Director Lewis Milestone does better with the troubled family relationships (aloof mom Myrna Loy, browbeaten dad Shepperd Strudwick, and overbearing grandpa Louis Calhern) than the youngster's world and the ranch hand's surrogate role in it. Some harrowing moments, including the boy's hand-to-hand battle with a buzzard. A-I (br)

Red Psalm (1973) Hungarian import uses a 19th-century peasant revolt as a socialist hymn celebrating the collective power of the people in their continuing struggle against oppression. Director Miklos Jancso's lyric flow of images is choreographed to a symphony of folk song, and the movie's poetic strength is rooted in its agrarian setting and Eastern European folk traditions. Some may be offended by the work's appropriation of religious symbolism in a revolutionary context. A-IV (nr)

Red River (1948) Western classic in which a hard-bitten Texas rancher (John Wayne) stakes his future on getting his herd to Abilene, but on the way he pushes his riders so hard they turn against him in a revolt led by his foster son (Montgomery Clift). Director Howard Hawks raises the story of a rugged cattle-drive to epic proportion with sweeping action scenes, colorful characters, numerous mishaps along the trail, and, at its center, the conflict between the rancher and the grown man he's raised from a boy. Harsh period violence and a sexual situation. A-III (br)

Red Rock West (1994) Mistaken for a hired killer, an honest drifter (Nicolas Cage) gets caught between a husband (J.T. Walsh) and wife (Lara Flynn Boyle), each plotting to murder the other, but things get really complicated when the actual hit-man (Dennis Hopper) shows up. John Dahl directs an atmospheric and quirky suspense thriller whose plot coincidences are totally unconvincing but add some wry humor. Brief violence, fleeting bedroom scene, and much rough language. A-III (R)

Red Scorpion (1989) Violence-saturated action adventure set in an obscure African country, where a deadly Soviet super-agent (Dolph Ludgren) is saved from death by kindly bushmen and is transformed into a good guy who sees firsthand how his fellow Russians are cruelly decimating the native rebels. Director Joseph Zito fills his desert landscape with long, tedious chase and battle sequences, grisly violence, gruesome torture scenes, and much profanity. O (R)

Red Shoes, The (1948) Life imitates art in the romantic tragedy of a dedicated ballerina (Moira Shearer) in a company whose manipulative impresario (Anton Walbrook) forces her to choose between her love for a talented composer (Marius Goring) and her dedication to dancing. Written, produced, and directed by Michael Powell and Emeric Pressburger, the convincing portrayal of the ballet world, on-stage and off, proves of more interest than the star-crossed romance and its relation to the title ballet which is the movie's thematic center. Suicide in the plot resolution. A-III (br)

Red Sky at Morning (1971) Mindless WW II coming-of-age story set in New Mexico, where a callow youth (Richard Thomas) lusts after a plump schoolmate (Catherine Burns) while his boozy mother (Claire Bloom) needs help fending off amorous "uncles." Directed by James Goldstone, the plot's serious level is hindered by the melodramatic treatment, with moral insights getting lost in the shuffle. A-III (PG)

Red Sonja (1985) Plodding, lackluster sword-and-sorcery movie directed by Richard Fleischer and starring muscleman Arnold Schwarzenegger, who helps out a woman warrior intent on vengeance. The only bright spots are bits of unintentional humor. Some violence. A-III (PG-13)

Red Sun (1972) The gimmick for this bloody European Western teams a hard-bitten cowboy (Charles Bronson) with an inscrutable samurai warrior (Toshiro Mifune) in order to track down an outlaw (Alain Delon) who doublecrossed the cowboy and dishonored the samurai. Along for the ride is a superfluous prostitute (Ursula Andress). Granted the fantasy plot, director Terence Young treats the derring-do with too little whimsical flair and too much prosaic gore. A-III (GP)

Red Sun Rising (1993) Sluggish martial-arts picture directed by Francis Megahy follows a Japanese cop (Don Wilson) who tracks a gangster (Soon-Teck Oh) to Los Angeles, then teams with a woman cop (Terry Farrell) and his former teacher (Mako) to stop the villain from selling military weapons to rival street-gangs. Stylized violence, ninja psychic powers, sexual situations, and occasional rough language and profanity. A-III (R)

Red Sundown (1956) Formula Western directed by Jack Arnold in which a reformed badman (Rory Calhoun) helps the local sheriff (Dean Jagger) reform a lawless town. Stylized violence and menacing situations. A-II (br)

Red Tent, The (1971) Ambitious Italian-Russian re-creation of the crash of an Italian dirigible over the North Pole in the spring of 1928. Under the command of General Umberto Nobile (Peter Finch), the crew pitches a red tent hoping to be spotted by rescuers, while three of their members go in search of help. Directed by Mikhail K. Kalatozov, the classic adventure of man vs. nature aspires to epic height but blunders with a frame device of Nobile's tortured memories and feelings of failure. Grueling picture of struggle for survival that has one of the leading characters (Sean Connery) committing suicide. A-III (G)

Red Violin, The (1999) Sumptuous drama spans more than 300 years, as an exquisitely handmade violin passes from its grief-stricken maker in 1681 Italy, to a child prodigy in Vienna a century later, a passionate virtuoso in late 1800s England, a disgraced music teacher during Mao's Cultural Revolution, and on to an eventful auction in contemporary Montreal. Enhanced by the movie's haunting music track, director Francois Girard orchestrates the numerous stories with dramatic flair and fine visual details, although the pace is halting. Some subtitles. Instances of theft, a fleeting sexual encounter, brief nudity, momentary opium use, and a few instances of profanity. A-III (nr)

Red, White and Blue (1971) Taking as its pretext the 1971 Report of the Commission on Obscenity and Pornography, the exploitation documentary even gives the president's commissioners a minute or two of interview time before getting to explicit illustrations of the report's subject. O (X)

Redhead and the Cowboy, The (1950) Far-fetched Western adventure directed by Leslie Fenton follows a Confederate courier (Rhonda Fleming) making her way through Union territory with the help of a genial cowpoke (Glenn Ford) and a Yankee undercover agent (Exdmond O'Brien) until she reaches the hide-out of a rebel guerrilla leader (Alan Reed). Stylized violence and romantic complications. A-II (br)

Redhead from Wyoming, The (1952) Stale Western directed by Lee Sholem in which a sheriff (Alex Nicol) teams with the title casino-owner (Maureen O'Hara) to stop an ambitious crook (William Bishop) from starting a range war. Frontier violence and romantic complications. A-II (br)

Reds (1981) Epic-scale re-creation of the turbulent life and times of radical American journalist John Reed (Warren Beatty), best known for his sympathetic coverage of the 1917 Russian Revolution. Also written and directed by Beatty, the production intelligently balances the sheer spectacle of events with Reed's involvement in them and his personal relations with others, especially his wife (Diane Keaton). Benign view of adultery and revolutionary politics. A-III (R/PG appeal)

Reed: Insurgent Mexico (1974) John Reed, the American newspaper correspondent who gained fame through his reports on the Russian Revolution, had previously covered Mexico in the revolutionary chaos of 1913-1914. Reconstructing this period is a Mexican movie following Reed's sojourn with various rebel units, his struggle to maintain his objectivity about events in the face of his inclinations to side with the oppressed, and his symbolic act of solidarity with the revolution that ends the movie. The result has the feeling of an historical document as well as a convincing character study of an idealist. A-II (nr)

Reefer Madness (1936) Reissue of a movie antique about the evils of marijuana has appeal today apparently because it is so easy to laugh at, but also perhaps because it all seems so familiar. It underscores the point, however, that preachy exaggeration is the worst kind of propaganda. A-III (PG)

Ref, The (1994) Escaping from the cops on Christmas Eve, a jewel thief (Denis Leary) takes a battling married couple (Judy Davis and Kevin Spacey) hostage in their home, pretending to be their marriage counselor when relatives arrive for dinner. Ted Demme's comedy of barbs is at times wickedly funny, but its one-joke premise gradually runs out of steam before the fuzzy ending. Fleeting violence, a dysfunctional family, some sexual innuendo, and much rough language. A-III (R)

Reflection of Fear, A (1973) Failed Gothic horror-movie about a disturbed young woman (Sandra Locke) who lives with her mother (Mary Ure) in a sinister mansion, where a series of gruesome murders take place when her estranged father (Robert Shaw) pays a call. Directed by William Fraker, it has a good cast, moody atmosphere, but muddled script, with a ludicrous conclusion. Heavy-handed sexual implications. A-III (PG)

Reflections in a Golden Eye (1967) Screen version of the Carson McCullers's novel about the twisted relationships and abnormal inclinations of a homosexual Army officer (Marlon Brando). Directed by John Huston, the movie's treatment of its various characters communicates little insight or compassion. Exploitative nudity. O (br)

Regarding Henry (1991) Inspirational drama about a high-rolling Manhattan attorney (Harison Ford) who loses nearly all his memory and motor functions after a brain injury, and must reacquaint himself with his very neglected wife and 11-year-old daughter (Annette Bening and Mikki Allen). The positive message in director Mike Nichols well-acted drama is undercut by the snail-like pace of its leaden, overly manipulative script. A brief scene of violence, some adulterous references, and an instance of rough language. A-III (PG-13)

Regeneration (1998) Absorbing WW I story of a psychologist (Jonathan Pryce) in a British psychiatric hospital who in 1917 is assigned to rid poet Siegfried Sassoon (James Wilby) of his anti-war views and return him to combat duty. Directed by Gillies Mackinnon, the movie centers in therapy sessions and casual conversations between the two about the lunacy of war and its cost to the human spirit, but these dialogue scenes are paced and given deeper meaning by flashbacks to the horrors of the battlefield, their traumatic effect on other patients, and the treatment they receive to mend their broken psyches. Graphic battlefield scenes, disturbed psychiatric patients, sexual situations, brief nudity, and a profane expletive. A-III (R)

Reg'lar Fellers (1941) Weak formula comedy directed by Arthur Dreifuss and based on Gene Byrnes's comic strip about a bunch of small-town kids (Carl "Alfalfa" Switzer, Billy Lee, and others) who busy themselves on makeshift inventions, which come in handy when they try to save a mean old lady (Sarah Padden) from big-city swindlers. Dated amusement. A-I (br)

Reincarnate, The (1971) Creepy 8,000-year-old man (Jack Creley) convinces a reluctant young sculptor (Jay Reynolds) to give up his body when he explains that a mind transplant involves the deflowering of a young virgin. Wooden acting and leaden script detailing the intricacies and advantages of reincarnation result in occult balderdash, seasoned with some coy titillation. A-III (R/GP appeal)

Reincarnation of Peter Pound, The (1975) Young man (Michael Sarrazin) dreams of his own murder in a previous life and falls in love with the woman (Jennifer O'Neill) who was his daughter in that life. Director J. Lee Thompson's muddled story has frequent nudity and graphic sex scenes. O (R)

Reivers, The (1969) Screen version of William Faulkner's last novel about a 12-year-old boy (Mitch Vogel) from a small Southern town in 1905 who is introduced to some of the realities of the adult world when taken on a trip to Memphis by a devil-may-care cousin (Steve McQueen). Director Mark Rydell has created a rich bit of Americana that owes as much to Mark Twain as to Faulkner, but its story of growth towards manhood may be perplexing for youngsters, especially a lengthy brothel sequence. A-III (M)

Relentless (1948) Routine Western in which a horse-breeder (Robert Young) leaves a prize colt in the care of an itinerant peddler (Marguerite Chapman) while eluding a posse as he tries to track down the claim-jumper (Barton MacLane) who framed him for a triple murder. Director George Sherman paces the action with some cute antics from the colt and low-key romance between the preoccupied wanted man and the patient woman who helps him. Frontier violence. A-I (br)

Relentless (1989) Los Angeles serial-killer (Judd Nelson) goes on the rampage, slaughtering victims who share his name, while a mismatched detective duo (Leo Rossi and Robert Loggia) bicker their way to a far-fetched capture, though not before viewers witness the psycho's sadism up-close. Director William Lustig has too many plot-lines to deal with and ends up exploiting the violence and the killer's abusive upbringing. Much grisly sadistic violence and profanity. O (R)

Relic, The (1997) Gruesome horror flick in which a genetically altered creature goes on a murderous rampage at a gala museum-party, while a homicide detective (Tom Sizemore) and a biologist (Penelope Ann Miller) at the gathering work to kill it before they all die. After much murky plotting, director Peter Hyams's dark monster-movie delivers a final half-hour of suspenseful jolts. Graphic fantasy violence with shots of severed heads, some rough language, and intermittent profanity. A-III (R)

Reluctant Astronaut, The (1967) Halting comedy directed by Edward J. Montagne features Don Knotts as a janitor in a space training-center, where he briefly overcomes his fear of heights to take a solo flight in a space capsule whose automated control system is not quite foolproof. Silly misunderstandings and deceptions. A-I (br)

Remains of the Day, The (1993) Having utterly sacrificed his personal life in the service of an English lord (James Fox) who ended up as a disgraced Nazi sympathizer, an aging English butler (Anthony Hopkins) journeys to the west of England in 1958, hoping to rehire and possibly risk romance with the spirited housekeeper (Emma Thompson) whose love he dutifully spurned decades earlier. James Ivory meticulously directs a splendid portrait of personal tragedy as a selfless man sadly comes to realize that in his unquestioned devotion to his master, he has missed out on the all the best things in life. A few emotional confrontations. A-II (PG)

Remarkable Andrew, The (1942) Patriotic whimsy with the ghost of Andrew Jackson (Brian Donlevy) coming to the aid of his namesake (William Holden), an honest bookkeeper accused of embezzlement by corrupt officials (Porter Hall, et al.) after he finds a discrepancy in the city accounts. Director Stuart Heisler treats the thin proceedings in lighthearted fashion, but the fantasy elements can't overcome the predictable civics lesson at its core. A-I (br)

Remarkable Mr. Kipps, The (1941) When a lowly drapper's apprentice (Michael Redgrave) in Edwardian England inherits a fortune, his childhood sweetheart (Phyllis Calvert) saves him from being turned into a snob by a socialite (Diana Wynyard).

Director Carol Reed scores with this leisurely paced, finely detailed version of H.G. Wells's gentle comedy of manners about a easy-going commoner's sudden rise in society. A bit of a stretch for youngsters. A-I (br)

Remember My Name (1979) Woman (Geraldine Chaplin), sent to prison for trying to kill her husband's mistress, returns to harass her now ex-husband (Anthony Perkins) and his new wife (Berry Berenson), at first from a distance, but then moves in for closer encounters of various kinds. The melodrama is rather flat and listless, further dragged down by mannered performances and the uninspired direction of Alan Rudolph. Rough language and adult situations. A-III (R)

Remember the Night (1940) Wryly sentimental romance has a New York prosecutor (Fred MacMurray) spend the Christmas recess by taking an accused jewelry-store shoplifter (Barbara Stanwyck) to his mother's home in Indiana, where they fall in love, then return to face the music in court. Director Mitchell Leisen keeps the romance bright and amusing, yet gives it substance with a warm depiction of the Hoosier homestead (Beulah Bondi, Elizabeth Patterson, and Sterling Holloway) and its homespun values. Innocent romantic situations and legal complications. A-II (br)

Reminiscences of a Journey to Lithuania (1974) Independent filmmaker Jonas Mekas's record of a visit to the land of his birth is as informal as a family album and as filled with warmth and affection. Mekas serves as an always enthusiastic guide to this celebration of his past through the present, and his unpretentious pleasure at showing his family bonds will most likely stimulate remembrances of one's own immigrant roots. A-I (nr)

Remo Williams: The Adventure Begins (1985) A New York policeman (Fred Ward) who was apparently slain in an encounter with muggers has actually been given a new identity as a member of a secret organization dedicated to seeing that justice is done despite a defective legal system. Though amoral in concept, director Guy Hamilton's movie is so divorced from reality that it is for the most part inoffensive. Aside from a brutal opening scene, the violence is muted. A-III (PG-13)

Renaissance Man (1994) Appealing comedy-drama in which a jobless adman (Danny DeVito), hired by the Army to teach basic English skills to semiliterate recruits, succeeds in getting them to read Shakespeare, despite interference from their skeptical drill-sergeant (Gregory Hines). Director Penny Marshall maintains a consistent level of genuine humor throughout a script peppered with self-help themes sandwiched between the laughs. An instance of rough language. A-II (PG-13)

Renaldo & Clara (1978) Singer Bob Dylan makes his debut as a movie director by taking footage from one of his concert tours and interspersing it with some absurd and awkward episodes acted out in improvisational style by himself, his wife, and friends (Sam Shepard, Ronee Blakley, Joni Mitchell, Arlo Guthrie, and Joan Baez). The result is a tedious, dismal exercise in self-indulgence. Although there is some rough language, like much of the other dialogue, it is almost unintelligible. A-III (R)

Rendezvous in Paris (1996) Three droll anecdotes of the mating game involve a law student (Clara Bellar) and her unfaithful boyfriend; a woman (Aurore Rauscher) who insists on meeting a suitor in out-of-the-way parks; and a painter (Michael Kraft) infatuated with a woman (Benedicte Loyen) he follows into a museum. Writer-director Eric Rohmer playfully spins each tale around the fragile, uncertain relationships between intelligent people with more on their minds than sex. Subtitles. Mature themes. A-III (nr)

Renegades (1946) Routine Western directed by George Sherman follows the travails of an outlaw's honest son (Larry Parks) and the woman (Evelyn Keyes) who sticks up for him. Stylized violence. A-II (br)

Renegades (1989) An undercover cop (Kiefer Sutherland) and a Native American (Lou Diamond Phillips) uneasily join forces to nab some murderous jewel thieves. The two leads are appealing, and the stunts are hair-raising, but the story line is implausible, and director Jack Sholder does little with a promising Indian subplot. Some profanity, several cold-blooded murders, and intense comic book chases. A-III (R)

Renfrew on the Great White Trail (1933) Routine adventure directed by Al Herman in which the singing Canadian Mountie of the title (James Newill) investigates several murders committed at a trading post, then gets his man after a harrowing dog-sled chase. Stylized violence. A-I (br)

Rent-a-Cop (1988) Sleazy crime picture in which a Chicago ex-cop (Burt Reynolds) joins forces with a reformed prostitute (Liza Minnelli) to nab a mad-dog killer (James Remar) working for a drug lord (John Stanton). Directed by Jerry London, the formula plot is awash in repulsive characters with sour results. Gory violence, sexual situations, profanity, and rough language. O (R)

Replacement Killers, The (1998) Bullet-riddled action movie in which a hit-man (Chow Yun-Fat) finds himself targeted for death after refusing an assignment, then unwittingly ensnares a shady lady (Mira Sorvino) in his desperate attempts at flight. Directed by Antoine Fuqua, the mindless story merely shuffles its flat, unsympathetic characters from one bloody shootout to the next with boring predictability. Excessive violence, some rough language, and a few instances of profanity. O (R)

Replay (1978) When a young woman (Marie-Jose Nat) loses her memory in an auto crash, her loving husband (Victor Lanoux) seems overly solicitous in his efforts to help her regain her past. Director Michel Drach's psychological melodrama provides little more than some modest diversion, adult in theme, with infidelity figuring as a minor element in the plot. A-III (nr)

Repo Man (1984) Absurdist mix of social satire and sci-fi thrills is tied to the story of an aimless youth (Emilio Estevez) learning the tricks of the auto-repossession trade from a hardened pro (Harry Dean Stanton), but their quirky misadventures end in wild pursuit of a stolen car with radioactive aliens in the trunk. Writer-director Alex Cox lumbers along erratically with a scenario aiming pot-shots at mindless consumerism and urban subcultures but without substantial results. Gritty violence, sexual situations, and rough language. A-III (R)

Report from China (1971) Japanese documentary filmed in 1966-67 during the flux of the Cultural Revolution shows the total faith of the Chinese leadership in the efficacy of ideology to solve their many economic and social ills as well as their willingness to sacrifice everything for the future. A-I (nr)

Report on the Party and the Guests, A (1968) A friendly outing in the woods is disrupted when some menacing strangers escort the group of picnickers to a lakeside party, where they are commanded to enjoy themselves. When one escapes the party, his friends join in the deadly pursuit. Czechoslovakian director Jan Nemec's parable on freedom and force has a threatening atmosphere of restraint and absurdity that makes for some very unsettling viewing, which is the reason it was originally banned by Communist officials. A-III (br)

Report to the Commissioner (1975) Violent urban drama about a young detective (Michael Moriarity) and his baptism of fire as a member of a New York City undercover narcotics-squad. Directed by Milton Katselas, the movie is partially successful in conveying its complex vision of a claustrophobic urban hell. Sordid backgrounds and incidents. A-III (PG)

Reprisal! (1956) Buying a small ranch in an area where killing Indians is considered sport, a half-Indian cowboy (Guy Madison) has to choose sides. Directed by George Sherman, the action plot is nothing out of the ordinary, but its pro-Indian slant is emotionally engaging, though not fully realized. Stylized violence. A-II (br)

Reptile, The (1966) Minor British horror movie directed by John Gilling unfolds 19th-century tale of an Englishwoman (Jacqueline Pearce) who returns from travels in Borneo cursed with the power of periodically turning into a deadly human cobra. Stylized violence and mild hokey effects. A-II (br)

Reptilicus (1962) Formula monster movie directed by Sidney Pink in which a giant prehistoric reptile is regenerated by Danish scientists, then escapes to run amok in Copenhagen. Hokey animated monster and special-effects destruction. A-I (br)

Requiem for a Heavyweight (1962) Gritty drama in which a social worker (Julie Harris) tries to help a punched-out prizefighter (Anthony Quinn) find a new line of work, until stymied by his manager (Jackie Gleason) who plans to square his debts by turning the boxer into a clownish wrestler. Directed by Ralph Nelson from Rod Serling's TV script, the result is an emotionally strong picture of a broken-down boxer trying to retain some human dignity after 17 years in the ring. Brutal boxing scenes and corrupt aspects of the fight game. A-II (br)

Requiem for a Secret Agent (1965) Dubbed Italian clunker directed by Sergio Sollimo in which a US spy agency hires a freelance agent (Stewart Granger) to nail an ex-Nazi (Peter Van Eyck) operating in Tangiers. Stylized violence and an implied sexual encounter. A-III (br)

Requiem for Dominic (1991) A Romanian expatriate (Felix Mitterer) returns to his homeland during the December 1989 Revolution to help a wounded friend (August Schmolozer) but discovers the man is dying in police custody after being falsely accused as a terrorist. Using actual footage from the Revolution, director Robert Dornhelm's disjointed dramatization personalizes Romania's political oppression through the fact-based story of a committed Christian who shows remarkable compassion on his deathbed. Subtitles. Graphic views of massacred and naked corpses. A-III (R)

Rescue, The (1988) Implausible fantasy about five youngsters whose larkish, bloodless rescue of their Navy fathers from a North Korean prison camp might have been pulled off by the Hardy Boys, but not by these ragtag Navy brats. Director Ferdinand Fairfax jumps from one far-fetched turn to another, with little sense of menace or suspense until the improbable climax. Some rough language and comic-book violence. A-II (PG)

Rescuers, The (1977) Disney animated feature in which two tiny members of the International Rescue Aid Society of mice are dispatched to save an orphan girl from the clutches of wicked Madame Medusa, ensconced in her lair on a Mississippi sternwheeler beached in the dark Louisiana swamps. Director Wolfgang Reitherman paces the action rather smartly, though some scenes may be a bit scary for the very young. All others, however, will find it entertaining enough, helped along by an imaginative assortment of human and animal characters as well as several pleasant songs. A-I (G)

Rescuers Down Under, The (1990) Animated tale of a little Australian boy and a beautiful eagle who must be saved from the snares of an evil poacher by Bernard and Miss Bianca, two top mouse-agents. Directors Hendel Butoy and Mike Gabriel have created a delightful family fantasy, a captivating eyeful that never flags and is filled with good humor and innocent charm. Several moments of danger and menace. A-I (G).

Rescuers: Stories of Courage — Two Women (1997) Fact-based dramatization about two Catholic women who risk their lives to save Jews during World War II, one of whom is a Polish governess (Elizabeth

Perkins) who protects her late employer's only child from Nazi roundups, then raises him as a Jew, the other a Frenchwoman (Sela Ward) who hides a Jewish family in the attic of her home until the liberation. Directed by Peter Bogdanovich, the Showtime cable movie convincingly re-creates the terrors of the era in which these desperate activities took place, poignantly evoking the human drama in each story with fine performances from the two leads. Heart-wrenching depiction of the plight of Holocaust victims, considerable menace, and an instance of rough language. A-II (PG-13)

Reservoir Dogs (1992) Inept low-budget movie about bungling gangsters (Harvey Keitel among them) featuring incessant rough language and gory brutalities that are pretentiously meant to be outrageous but only dull the sensibilities of unfortunate viewers of the aptly titled woofer written and directed by Quentin Tarantino. O (R)

Restless Natives (1986) Lighthearted comedy features exquisite scenic backgrounds of the Scottish highlands in an implausible story about two youths (Joe Mullaney and Vincent Friell) who devise an outlandish scam to extort money from tourists in the hope of gaining financial security before they hit the ripe old age of 20. Their only potential problem is a vacationing CIA agent (Ned Beatty). Director Michael Hoffman concentrates on the relationship between the two friends rather than the flimsy plot and its twist ending. A-II (PG)

Restless Years, The (1958) Inane teenage sudser directed by Helmut Kautner centers on a withdrawn adolescent (Sandra Dee) whose overly protective mother (Teresa Wright) tries to shield her from making the same mistake she had made at her age, while a new classmate (John Saxon) befriends the girl and defies a bunch of small-town hypocrites. Muted sexual innuendoes and references to illegitimacy. A-II (br)

Restoration (1995) Elaborate but uneven costume drama in which a frivolous physician (Robert Downey Jr.) in the 17th-century court of King Charles II (Sam Neill) reluctantly finds his humanity by treating London's poor after being tossed out of court on a royal whim. Director Michael Hoffman switches gears rather awkwardly in going from bedroom farce to a more substantial drama of personal transformation. Fleeting bedroom scenes with nudity and frequent references to sexual court intrigues. A-III (R)

Resurrection (1980) Engrossing but flawed drama about a woman (Ellen Burstyn) who discovers that she has the power to heal people after barely surviving a tragic accident in which she loses her husband. The screenplay by Lewis John Carlino sets up a fascinating situation, but neither Carlino nor director Daniel Petrie is able to work it out in satisfactory fashion. The spiritual side of faith-healing is dealt with in very unimaginative fashion showing the afterlife, for example, as being, quite literally, the light at the end of the tunnel. Theme and language require a mature perspective. A-III (PG)

Return from Witch Mountain (1978) The further adventures of the two castaway space children from **Escape to Witch Mountain**, with Tony falling into the villainous hands of Christopher Lee and Bette Davis who are intent on using the boy's powers for personal gain. Tia, with the aid of the lovable kind of street gang that exists nowhere outside of Disney films, rescues him in the nick of time. The sequel, directed by John Hough, is a movie that younger children will enjoy. A-I (G)

Return of a Man Called Horse, The (1976) Sequel finds bored English nobleman (Richard Harris) back in South Dakota when his adopted Indian tribe needs a leader. After another gruesome purification ceremony consisting of mind-altering drugs and of having bones inserted into his chest, he leads his tribe to victory over their enemies. Director Irvin Kershner delivers a serious film, entertaining and beautifully photographed, but its emphasis on violence makes this decidedly mature fare. A-III (PG)

Return of Count Yorga, The (1971) Though this time the gentlemanly ghoul (Robert Quarry) falls in love (his one weakness), most of his time is spent preying upon a neighboring orphanage. The sequel is properly amusing and frightening, with director Bob Kelljan sprinkling the proceedings with enough blood, however, to warrant caution for young or squeamish viewers. A-II (GP)

Return of Dracula, The (1958) Offbeat horror tale in which the legendary vampire (Francis Lederer) flees pursuers in post-World War II eastern Europe by emigrating to California, where he's taken in by the unsuspecting relatives of the man he killed for his identity papers. Directed by Paul Landres, the hokey proceedings generate little suspense though the genial small-town setting provides some eerie moments, and Lederer's modern-day Dracula exudes sinister intensity. Stylized violence and menacing situations. A-II (br)

Return of Frank James, The (1940) Dandy sequel to **Jesse James**, largely with the same cast and settings, follows Frank as he sets out to avenge his brother's death by killing the cowardly Ford brothers (John Carradine and Charles Tannen), then gets sidetracked by a Denver reporter (Gene Tierney) from whom he learns his black farmhand (Robert Whitman) is to be hanged as his accomplice unless he returns. Director Fitz Lang gets a fine performance from Fonda as the reformed outlaw who wrestles with his conscience over revenging a past wrong or saving an innocent life, then puts his life at risk in the taut trial sequence in the dramatic finale. Brief stylized violence, some muddled motives, and several period racial expressions. A-II (br)

Return of Jack Slade, The (1955) Uneven Western directed by Harold Schuster in which the title outlaw's son (John Ericson) tries to atone for his father's crimes by joining the notorious Hole in the

Wall gang in 1886 Wyoming, then luring them into an ambush set up by Pinkerton agents. Stylized violence and sexual innuendo. A-II (br)

Return of Jafar, The (1994) Peppy animated sequel to **Aladdin** in which the evil wizard of the title (voice of Jonathan Freeman) escapes from the magic lamp and attempts to seize power by forcing reformed parrot Iago (voice of Gilbert Gottfried) to betray Aladdin (voice of Scott Weinger) and the princess (voice of Linda Larkin). Directed by Tad Stones, Toby Shelton, and Alan Zaslove, the result lacks the original's superior animation and the inspired humor of Robin Williams, but delivers zippy pacing to the story's misadventures along with some mildly enjoyable musical numbers. A-I (G)

Return of Martin Guerre, The (1983) Engrossing, fact-based French production about a 16th-century peasant who abandons his wife and disappears from his native village to reappear some eight years later, much improved in every way, and accepted by his wife and most of the villagers. A few years later, a squabble over property provokes the accusation that he's an imposter, and a trial with tragic results ensues. Written by Jean-Claude Carriere and directed by Daniel Vigne, the movie is partly a mystery, but most of all a love story that most adults will find intriguing entertainment. Brief nudity and sexual references. A-III (nr)

Return of Maxwell Smart, The (1980) TV's secret agent Maxwell Smart (Don Adams) is assigned to thwart a villain (Vittorio Gassman) who has developed a bomb capable of destroying all the clothing in the world. Director Clive Donner's woefully inept and dull comedy relies on sexual innuendo. A-III (PG)

Return of Mr. Moto, The (1965) Muddled mystery in which the Japanese detective (miscast Henry Silva) helps Scotland Yard unmask an international conspiracy to control Mideast oil production. Directed by Ernest Morris, the low-budget picture goes nowhere with its dull formula plot and lackluster cast. Stylized violence and sexual innuendo. A-II (br)

Return of Sabata (1972) Frank Kramer (alias Gianfranco Parolini) directs this third installment in the spaghetti Western series spoofing spaghetti Westerns. This time the sooty-suited hero with the twitching nostrils (Lee Van Cleef) matches wits and weapons with the Irish boss of a cardboard Texas town whose citizens are being taxed to the tune of a million dollars. Sabata comes to the rescue and sneers at the audience as he rides away from his bordello beauty and a cast full of sloppily dubbed characters. A-III (PG)

Return of Swamp Thing, The (1989) Forgettable sequel in which the crime-busting human plant (Dick Durock), a former scientist who keeps the bayou safe for kids and damsels in distress, falls for the stepdaughter (Heather Locklear) of a gene-tampering scientist (Louis Jourdan). Directed by Jim Wynorski, the cheesy sets and sleepwalking actors negate the good stuff, which includes clever makeup and the heroic antics of the asparagus stalk with a heart of gold. Some sexual innuendo, rough language, and much comic-book violence. A-III (PG-13)

Return of the Badmen (1948) Pioneering Oklahoma settler (Randolph Scott) takes on the worst of the Old West's outlaws, the nastiest of whom is the Sundance Kid (Robert Ryan). There's some comic relief (Gabby Hayes), and the hero gets the girl (Jacqueline White) in the last reel, but otherwise director Ray Enright's shoot-'em-up is strictly routine action fare. Frontier violence. A-I (br)

Return of the Fly (1959) Thin sequel in which the son (Brett Halsey) of the Montreal scientist whose molecular structure got mixed with that of a housefly continues his father's experiments, with similar botched results, until his uncle (Vincent Price) intervenes. Directed by Edward L. Bernds, the hokey plot and mediocre special effects hold little interest. Some stylized violence and occasional menace. A-II (br)

Return of the Gunfighter (1966) Retired gunslinger (Robert Taylor) sets out to find the murderers of a Mexican couple who were his friends, taking along their daughter (Ana Martin) to identify them, as well as a wounded cowboy (Chad Everett) he meets along the way. Director James Neilson's formula Western has some good action sequences, a respect for the Mexican settlers of the Southwest, and a strong performance from Taylor. Frontier violence. A-I (br)

Return of the Jedi (1983) In the third installment of the Star Wars trilogy, Luke Skywalker (Mark Hamill) has a revealing confrontation with Darth Vader, Princess Leia (Carrie Fisher) and Han Solo (Harrison Ford) finally get somewhere with their romance, Billy Dee Williams saves the day with his air support, and R2D2 and C3PO steal some major scenes. Directed by Richard Marquand, it's fun for action fans, but the violence and tension from some of the nasty characters (Jabba the Hutt is not only scary, but disgusting) may be too intense for the younger crowd. A-II (PG)

Return of the Living Dead (1985) Written and directed by Dan O'Bannon, this is yet another tedious variation on the horror movie theme of the dead coming to life and devouring the living. Nudity, violence, and bloody gore. O (R)

Return of the Musketeers, The (1989) Flabby seriocomic sequel directed by Richard Lester picks up the story 20 years later, with D'Artagnan (Michael York) and his aging comrades (Oliver Reed, Frank Finlay, and Richard Chamberlain) trying to stop Cromwell's execution of Charles II, thwart the court intrigues of Cardinal Mazarin (Philippe Noiret), and escape the vengeance of Lady de Winter's daughter (Kim Cattral). Aimless mix of mock heroism and cardboard villainy with stylized violence, sexual situations, and religious hypocrites. A-III (PG)

Return of the Pink Panther, The (1975) The Pink Panther, the sacred jewel of the Middle East kingdom of Lugash, has been stolen again, and only Inspector Clouseau (Peter Sellers) can get retrieve it. Directed by Blake Edwards, the comedy is relatively innocent, and, thanks to Sellers, has more then a few funny moments. Some slapstick violence. A-II (G)

Return of the Secaucus Seven, The (1980) Nothing much happens except a weekend of talking during a reunion of seven friends who, as college students on a 1960s protest march, once spent a night together in jail in Secaucus, N.J. Written and directed by John Sayles on a shoestring budget, the movie won't satisfy everyone, but the dialogue is bright, and some of the insights are clever. The frankness of the language, especially about sex, would rule out younger viewers. A-III (R)

Return of the Seven (1966) Director Burt Kennedy's shallow, violent sequel to John Sturges's 1960 **The Magnificent Seven**, lacks original's flair and high-powered sense of adventure. Yul Brynner, Robert Fuller ,and Jordan Christopher are three of the deadly septet, leading a small parade back to a little Mexican town, where one of their companions is being held prisoner. A-III (br)

Return of the Soldier, The (1985) Wealthy middle-aged man (Alan Bates) returns from WW I with a case of selective amnesia. Forgotten are the years with his spoiled, ill-tempered wife (Julie Christie); remembered instead is his first love, a working-class woman (Glenda Jackson) now grown quite dowdy and, like himself, married. Well-acted English production directed by Alan Bridges from the Rebecca West novel, but the period piece is very slight and its neat resolution is unsatisfying. A-II (nr)

Return of the Streetfighter, The (1975) Japanese karate action-film, the villain being the American heading the Mafia branch in the Far East. Minimal production values and excessive violence. O (R)

Return of the Tall Blond Man with the One Black Shoe, The (1976) French production in which Pierre Richard again stars as the concert violinist mistaken for a super-spy and unaware that he is the object of assassination attempts. This time the action takes place in Rio de Janiero, with the lovely Mireille Darc on hand as decoration, but director Yves Robert's comic touch is not nearly as deft as it was in the original. Restrained violence. A-III (nr)

Return of the Vampire, The (1943) Minor horror tale about a vampire (Bela Lugosi) who was buried with a spike through his heart in 1918 London, then is unearthed by a bomb in the 1941 Blitz and seeks revenge on the daughter (Nina Foch) of the doctor who did him in. Directed by Lew Landers, there are a few eerie scenes in an otherwise pedestrian story with a muddled subplot about a wolf-man under the vampire's spell, and weak comic relief from the bemused Scotland Yard chief (Miles Mander). Stylized violence and hokey menace. A-II (br)

Return to Macon County (1975) Two young men (Nick Nolte and Don Johnson) bound for California in a souped-up car pick up a chunky girl who constantly smiles when she is not pointing a large pistol at people and sometimes even when she is. Director Richard Compton's thin, aimless youth movie dips into sexual exploitation for want of anything better to do. O (PG)

Return to Paradise (1998) Flawed tale of an American (Joaquin Phoenix) facing execution in Malaysia on a drug conviction, unless his lawyer (Anne Heche) can convince his buddies (Vince Vaughn and David Conrad) to return and serve three years in prison for their part in buying the drugs. Director Joseph Ruben allows a premise meant to explore difficult moral choices to gradually descend into overwrought melodrama. Brief violence and recreational drug abuse, an implied affair, recurring profanity, and much rough language. A-III (R)

Return to Snowy River (1988) Enterprising horse rancher (Tom Burlinson) in 19th-century Australia must overcome an aristocratic blackguard (Nicholas Eadie) to wed the daughter (Sigrid Thornton) of an American settler (Brian Dennehy). Director Geoff Burrowes's sequel to **The Man from Snowy River** is filled with picturesque scenery and spirited horses, but the human narrative is thin and the action sluggish. Stylized violence, including some fierce hand-to-hand combat, and romantic situations. A-II (PG)

Return to Oz (1985) Grim, joyless sequel to the grand Judy Garland original that attempts to make up for its lack of warmth and imagination by substituting an abundance of special effects. The scariness of some of the latter are inappropriate for pre-teenagers. A-II (PG)

Return to Peyton Place (1961) Imitation sudser with a lifeless script ineptly directed by Jose Ferrer has the illegitimate daughter (Carol Lynley) of an adulteress (Eleanor Parker) write a bestselling novel about the peccadilloes of the folks in her home town. Sexual references. A-III (br)

Return to the Blue Lagoon (1991) Insipid fantasy in which once again a boy and girl (Brian Krause and Milla Jovovich) come of age while stranded on an uninhabited South Pacific island. Producer-director William A. Graham handles the adolescents' emerging sexuality with a self-performed wedding ceremony and a lamely predictable story line that languidly repeats the 1980 original. Brief scenes of violence and a few shots of partial nudity. A-III (PG-13)

Reuben, Reuben (1983) Alcoholic, womanizing Scottish poet (Tom Conti) sponges his way through the New England campus circuit in director Robert Ellis Miller's uneven social satire which details the slow disintegration of a creative soul. The script is very literate and Conti's performance is exquisite, but his several sexual conquests compound the movie's already muddled moral perspective. A-III (R)

Revenge (1990) Intriguing but ultimately muddled tale of a newly retired Navy pilot (Kevin Costner) who is implausibly lured into an affair with the wife (Madeleine Stowe) of his best friend, a ruthless Mexican powerbroker (Anthony Quinn). Directed by Tony Scott, the exotic Mexican locale takes precedence over character development in this story of male friendship, betrayal, and retribution. Some brutally graphic violence, several scenes involving adultery, a rape, and incidental rough language. A-III (R)

Revenge of the Creature (1955) Thin sequel to **The Creature from the Black Lagoon** has the captured Gill Man taken from the Amazon to a Florida theme park, where he's angered by a scientist (John Agar), then breaks loose, terrifies crowds of visitors, and escapes with a park official (Lori Nelson). Directed by Jack Arnold, the hokey proceedings finally work up some mild tension as the prehistoric creature is hunted down, but without evoking the sympathy generated by the original. A-I (br)

Revenge of the Nerds (1984) Misfit college freshmen (Robert Carradine and Anthony Edwards) form a fraternity to protect themselves and fight the persecution of college jocks. The underdog heroes' attitude toward women is as reprehensible as that of their tormentors. Director Jeff Kanew's farce is full of vulgarities, much nudity, and the romantic treatment of what is in effect rape. O (R)

Revenge of the Nerds II: Nerds in Paradise (1987) Director Joe Roth's silly sequel has the goofy Tri Lambdas seeking to retrieve their integrity at a fraternity conference in Fort Lauderdale. Though its theme is not to judge others on surface values, it reinforces false stereotypes of women, bad habits, and vulgarity via peek-a-boo nudity, slapstick humor, and crude sight gags. A-III (PG-13)

Revenge of the Ninja (1983) Japanese warrior (Sho Kosugi) comes to the United States, where he makes short order of an illegal drug operation and battles old enemies. Directed by Sam Firstenberg, the action is mostly of the martia- arts variety, but a number of weapons are used in achieving an extremely bloody victory. Excessive violence and gore. O (R)

Revenge of the Pink Panther (1978) Peter Sellers romps again as the bumbling Inspector Clouseau who gains glory, inadvertently as usual, by breaking up an international drug ring headed by Robert Webber, thanks to some timely help from Webber's mistress, Dyan Cannon. Directed by Blake Edwards, the plot is cluttered and noticeably less scintillating than its predecessors. Some sexual innuendo. A-III (PG)

Revengers, The (1972) William Holden stars as a rancher who, after his family is slaughtered by renegade Indians, dedicates his life to avenging them, and, with the help of a second-string wild bunch (including Ernest Borgnine and Woody Strode), he kills just about everyone who crosses his path until gentled by an Irish spinster (Susan Hayward). Directed by Daniel Mann, this violent and bloody Western has a totally unmotivated ending. A-III (PG)

Reversal of Fortune (1990) Fact-based re-creation of the successful appeal by a Harvard law professor (Ron Silver) of the conviction of Claus von Bulow (Jeremy Irons) for the attempted murder of his socialite wife (Glenn Close). Director Barbet Schroeder's wickedly witty film offers several possible scenarios for the victim's two comas and details how the case was won legally, without resolving the question of von Bulow's innocence. Adulterous relationships and occasional rough language. A-III (R)

Revolution (1986) Director Hugh Hudson's epic treatment of the American Revolution is grand spectacle but lacks a credible human dimension. What it offers, instead, are underdeveloped characters (notably Al Pacino in the central role) and episodic plot contrivances. Violent battle scenes. A-II (PG)

Revolutionary, The (1970) College student (Jon Voight) moves from a radical student movement, to a socialist worker's organization, to a short-lived stint in the army, and, finally, to an anarchists' bomb plot. The result is less the story of a young man's political radicalization than it is the meanderings of a social misfit. Paul Williams's low-keyed direction tends to level rather than highlight plot development and leaves too many significant questions unanswered. A-III (GP)

Reward, The (1965) On the arid, sun-drenched plains of Mexico, a small band of bounty hunters are destroyed by their greed and moral decay. Director Serge Bourguignon's story of death in the desert makes its point about life by turning the desperate journey of the last survivor (Max Von Sydow) to reach a lake into the quest for a moral oasis. A-II (br)

Rhapsody in August (1991) Three generations of a Japanese family in Nagasaki react quite differently to a surprise visit by an US relative (Richard Gere) who has come to remember the family patriarch, who was killed in the American bombing of the city 45 years earlier. Writer-director Akira Kurosawa presents a poignant look at the futility of war through the eyes of the elderly who remember, the middle-aged who prefer to forget, and children who are curious about their past. Subtitles. References to the horror of mass death and destruction caused by the A-bomb. A-II (PG)

Rhapsody in Blue (1945) Long but mostly engaging tribute to composer George Gershwin (1898-1937), from his early success with Broadway show tunes to his more serious works, including the title concert piece, with Robert Alda playing the composer as a driven musical genius whose ambition leaves no room for love (Joan Leslie and Alexis Smith). Directed by Irving Rapper, the Hollywood version of Gershwin's life is well-crafted melodrama, and the plentiful musical portions are first-rate. Romantic complications. A-II (br)

Rhinestone (1984) Embarrassingly bad romantic match-up in which Dolly Parton tries to make a country-western singer out of tough New York cabby Sylvester Stallone. Director Bob Clark's unfunny musical comedy exploits Parton's physical attributes and musical abilities but merely makes Stallone look silly. Vulgar dialogue and benign view of casual sex. A-III (PG)

Rhubarb (1951) Lightweight comedy in which the

scrappy cat of the title inherits a millionaire's estate, including a major-league baseball club, with the will's acerbic executor (Ray Milland) fending off nasty interlopers as the team heads for the pennant, and his fiancé (Jan Sterling) develops an allergy to cats. Director Arthur Lubin turns the daffy premise into a slowmoving vehicle for mostly minor amusements. Some mean-spirited skullduggery. A-II (br)

Rhyme & Reason (1997) Documentary celebrating almost 20 years of rap music and the hip-hop subculture as commented on by some 70 performers from Ice-T to Dr. Dre and the late Tupac Shakur. Directed by Peter Spirer, the result is basically self-promotional, providing an uncritical view of rap as a form of social protest using verbal violence and sexually explicit lyrics to express the oppression of ghetto life, an explanation which will not satisfy those who reject rap as socially irresponsible. Recurring violent rhetoric and sexual expletives. A-IV (R)

Rhythm on the River (1940) Tuneful nostalgia from director Victor Schertzinger in the slight tale of an established songwriter (Basil Rathbone) who buys his compositions from unknowns, two of whom (Bing Crosby and Mary Martin) fall for each other while trying to establish independent songwriting careers. Creaky but cheery musical with a quite charming romance. A-I (br)

Rich and Famous (1981) Screen version of the John Van Druten play about two very different women (Candice Bergen and Jacqueline Bisset), both writers, who preserve a friendship for more than two decades, despite the strains caused by emulation and jealousy. Directed by George Cukor, the glossy soap-opera pays more attention to its glamorous locations than to the human dimension of its story. The sole redeeming feature is good acting by the principals. General air of vapid amorality and two graphic sexual sequences. O (R)

Rich and Strange (1932) Whimsical tale in which a London couple use an inheritance to take a cruise to the Far East, where the wife (Joan Barry) is charmed by a genial plantation-owner (Percy Marmont), while the husband (Henry Kendall) is fleeced by a phony princess (Betty Amman), then they get shipwrecked on the return voyage and arrive home with a new appreciation of ordinary life. Director Alfred Hitchcock treats the proceedings with tongue firmly in cheek, adding a few bizarre touches and some grisly humor along the way, with still-enjoyable results. Stylized violence, implied infidelity, and some rude language. A-III (br)

Rich in Love (1993) A Southern teenager (Kathryn Erbe) puzzles over life and love after her mother (Jill Clayburgh) deserts her father (Albert Finney) without explanation, and her pregnant sister (Suzy Amis) moves back home, unsure whether she wants to stay married to her new husband (Kyle MacLachlan). Director Bruce Beresford unveils richly textured characters caught between the pain of change and the mundane joys of family living. Implied extra-marital relationships. A-III (PG-13)

Rich Kids (1979) Uneven melodrama about the effect of divorce on two adolescents (Trini Alvarado and Jeremy Levy), whose wealthy and adulterous parents (John Lithgow and Kathryn Walker) seem unconcerned about their offspring. The two teenagers spend a weekend together in an exotically appointed bachelor apartment. The situation leads to an angry, recriminatory adult confrontation, involving spouses current and former, lovers, friends, and one or two relatively innocent bystanders Directed by Robert Young, the movie raises, but doesn't probe too deeply into, questions of parental responsibility, and glosses over the sexual implications of the young people's weekend together. A-III (PG)

Rich Man's Wife, The (1996) Preposterous thriller in which an unfaithful wife (Halle Berry) fears being implicated in the murder of her philandering husband (Christopher McDonald) by a homicidal maniac (Peter Greene) who wants a share of the widow's inheritance. Writer-director Amy Holden Jones drags out a tawdry tale of the devious deeds of unsympathetic characters in a clumsy, slow-moving plot taxing credibility and viewers' patience. Some strong scenes of violence, threatening situations, marital infidelity, and occasional rough language. A-III (R)

Richard (1972) Political spoof with little satirical bite blending newsreel footage with staged segments in order to trace Richard Nixon's journey from whipping cookie-batter of an evening in Whittier, Calif., to fireside reminiscences at the White House. Directed by Lorees Yerby and Harry Hurwitz, the resulting lampoon, more than anything else, provides proof that this is a free country. A-III (PG)

Richard Pryor Live on Sunset Strip (1982) Standup comic performance, with the usual obscenities and scatological references, though Pryor is in a mellower, more humane mood than in his previous performance movie. Under Joe Layton's direction, Pryor's humor and his perception of human nature are usually on target and often extremely funny, but his sexually oriented jokes and vulgar language may offend those unfamiliar with his style. A-IV (R)

Richard III (1995) Wildly imaginative updating of Shakespeare's play to 1930s Britain, where civil war brings a new monarch to the throne coveted by his duplicitous brother, the Duke of Glouster (Ian McKellan), who sets out to gain it through murder. Directed by Richard Loncraine, the result places Shakespeare's Elizabethan language and medieval subject in a 20th-century context of Fascist movements and absolute dictatorships that give fresh significance to the play's portrait of an autocratic villain. Stylized violence and sexual references. A-III (R)

Richest Girl in the World, The (1934) Eccentric romantic comedy in which an heiress (Miriam Hopkins) changes places with her private secretary (Fay Wray) in order to test the real intentions of a would-be suitor (Joel McCrea). Director William A. Seiter keeps the implausible situations light and mostly fun, with a fine cast making all the duplicity seem almost credible. Sexual situations. A-III (br)

Richie Rich (1994) Uninspired comedy about a lonely but plucky 12-year-old (Macaulay Culkin) who conspires to outwit a nasty businessman (John Larroquette) out to steal his inheritance when the boy's parents (Edward Herrmann and Christine Ebersole) are presumed dead after their private jet blows up. Director Donald Petrie's formula comedy has few surprises and only minor amusements for easily satisfied viewers. Some mock comic violence, occasional double entendres, and a crude expression. A-II (PG)

Ricochet (1991) Hard-edged revenge drama pits a hero cop-turned-prosecutor (Denzel Washington) against an escaped psychopath (John Lithgow) who frames him for murder and involvement in kiddie porn. Solid action-scenes and chilling performances are outweighed by director Russell Mulcahy's emphasis on killings and sexual violence. Excessive violence, the repeated use of a graphic rape scene, and much rough language. O (R)

Riddle of the Sands, The (1984) British melodrama about two chaps from Oxford who accidentally uncover German preparations for an invasion of England in 1901. Michael York and Simon MacCorkindale are fine as the stuffy pair who prove their mettle once the going gets tough, but they can't save a languid movie that lacks even a good villain. Director Tony Maylam succeeds best with the period atmosphere, but its intrigue and derring-do are only mildly diverting. A-II (PG)

Ride a Crooked Trail (1958) Routine Western directed by Jesse Hibbs in which an outlaw (Audie Murphy) turns honest after a small-town judge (Walter Matthau) mistakes him for a famed lawman and appoints him marshal, whereupon he tracks down a bankrobber (Henry Silva) and weds a former accomplice (Gia Scala). Stylized violence and sexual innuendo. A-II (br)

Ride a Wild Pony (1976) Colorful Disney adventure, set in the Australian outback before WW I, in which a poor lad attempts to recover his pony after it has come into the possession of a spoiled cripple, the little daughter of the town's wealthiest family. It is up to the horse, in the satisfying conclusion, to decide for one child or the other. Better than average children's movie, directed by Don Chaffey with some good touches of reality and a solid theme of human selflessness. A-I (G)

Ride Beyond Vengeance (1966) After a long absence, a buffalo hunter (Chuck Connors) returns home with a sizable sum of money, and then revenges on the three who steal it from him. Directed by Bernard McEveety, it is a tough, almost cynical story of human greed and brutality. Much violence. A-III (br)

Ride Clear of Diablo (1954) Standard Western directed by Jesse Hibbs with a straight-shooting cowboy (Audie Murphy) trailing the rustlers who murdered his father and brother, but, along the way, he becomes a sheriff's deputy and arrests the area's worst badman (Dan Duryea), whom he wrongly accuses of the crime. Stylized violence and muddled seriocomic plot. A-II (br)

Ride Lonesome (1959) Strong Western in which a bounty hunter (Randolph Scott) tracks down a killer (James Best), then uses him as bait to bring his outlaw brother (Lee Van Cleef) to justice for a grisly crime committed years before. Director Budd Boetticher notches the suspense by having the bounty hunter joined on the trail by an abandoned wife (Karen Steele) and a couple of cowboys (Pernell Roberts and James Coburn) with their own designs on the killer. Stylized violence and considerable menace. A-I (br)

Ride the High Country (1962) Hired by a bank to escort a gold shipment from a mining camp in the Sierra Mountains, a retired lawman (Joel McCrea) takes along an old friend (Randolph Scott) who has his own plans for the ore. Director Sam Peckinpah's off-beat Western mixes in a farmer's daughter (Mariette Hartley), a novice gunfighter (Ronald Starr), and a brawling brood of brothers, but the focus is on the two veteran cowboys and their differing notions of duty and honor. Some stylized violence, sexual references, and ribald humor. A-III (br)

Ride the Pink Horse (1947) Atmospheric crime story set in a New Mexico town during a fiesta, when a war profiteer (Fred Clark) doublecrosses and almost kills a cynical Army vet (Robert Montgomery) who's saved by a Indian girl (Wanda Hendrix), a Mexican merry-go-round operator (Thomas Gomez), and a wry FBI agent (Art Smith). Also directed by Montgomery, the plot is full of holes, but the colorful characters make the situation of more than usual interest. Stylized violence. A-II (br)

Ride the Wild Surf (1964) Innocuous tale of college-age beach buddies (Fabian, Tab Hunter, and Peter Brown) finding high waves and low-voltage romance (Shelley Fabares, Barbara Hunt, and Barbara Eden, respectively) on a New Year's vacation in Hawaii. Directed by Don Taylor, the picturesque locales and surfboard action make up for the generally inept dramatic proceedings. Innocent but shallow escapist fare that children are likely to find simply tedious. A-I (br)

Ride to Hangman's Tree, The (1967) Formula Western directed by Alan Rafkin in which a robber (James Farentino) of Wells Fargo gold shipments is forced to split the loot with an ex-partner (Jack Lord), though the result is far less interesting than **Black Bart**, the 1948 movie upon which it is based. Stylized violence and some heavy sexual innuendo. A-III (br)

Ride, Vaquero (1953) A Mexican bandit leader (Anthony Quinn) grows testy when his lifelong friend and top-gun (Robert Taylor) sides with a Texas rancher (Howard Keel) and his wife (Ava Gardner) against his former comrades. Director John Farrow's quirky little melodrama has its interesting moments, among them the local priest (Kurt Kasznar) taking a hand in the action, and Taylor's stinging rejection of Gardner's advances. Stylized violence and romantic complications. A-II (br)

Rider on the Rain (1970) Intriguing French mystery thriller about a newlywed (Marlene Jobert) who kills her attacker and then is afraid to tell husband, friends, or the police. After she has disposed of the body, a stranger (Charles Bronson) begins to badger her about it, and a neatly matched duel of wits ensues. Director Rene Clement has hit the mark with this suspenseful melodrama, with plenty of moody atmosphere and engaging characterizations. The tribulations of the heroine are not for the youngsters. A-III (GP)

Riders of the Northwest Mounted (1943) Low-budget adventure picture follows a Canadian Mountie (Russell Hayden) on the trail of a gang of fur robbers. Directed by William Berke, the formula story has some picturesque scenery, the singing of Bob Wills and his Texas Playboys, and comic relief by Dub Taylor. Stylized violence. A-I (br)

Ridicule (1996) Lush costume drama set at the court of Versailles in 1783 as an altruistic country engineer (Charles Berling) discovers he must first bed the king's cunning mistress (Fanny Ardent) and develop the art of witty sarcasm before he can win the king's ear. Directed by Patrice Leconte, the satirical period-piece focuses on the rampant decadence and superficiality of court life that culminated a few years later in the French Revolution. Subtitles. Brief violence including a suicide, fleeting bedroom scenes, and gratuitous frontal male nudity. A-IV (R)

Riding High (1950) Happy-go-lucky racehorse owner (Bing Crosby) stakes his future on a horse he's raised from a colt, and, with the help of its trainer (Clarence Muse) and a rooster mascot, he wins the big race and the daughter (Colleen Gray) of an ulcer-ridden tycoon (Charles Bickford). Despite period updating and some songs, director Frank Capra's remake of his 1934 **Broadway Bill** over-sentimentalizes the slim plot, though a talented veteran cast (Oliver Hardy, Margaret Hamilton, James Gleason, Raymond Walburn, William Demarest, Gene Lockhart, and Douglass Dumbrille) provides some amusement. Romantic complications leading to divorce. A-III (br)

Riding Shotgun (1954) Western misfire directed by Andre de Toth in which a town suspects a stagecoach guard (Randolph Scott) is in cahoots with a notorious outlaw gang, but he escapes being lynched in time to save them from the outlaws. Stylized violence. A-I (br)

Riff-Raff (1993) Gritty look at what Britain's double-digit unemployment statistics mean in the life of one out-of work laborer (Robert Carlyle) who takes a low-paying job on a nonunion construction project, becomes a squatter in a vacant apartment complex, and falls for an untalented, unrealistic would-be singer (Emer McCourt). Using a largely nonprofessional cast whose accents require subtitles, director Ken Loach gets a good measure of blue-collar reality in a variation on the old story of greedy employers, exploited workers, and the struggle for economic justice. Its treatment of justice themes includes a devastating accident, a premarital relationship, drug use, crude humor, and much rough language. A-III (R)

Right On! (1971) Documentary of performances by a talented but angry rock group, The Original Last Poets (Gylan Kain, David Nelson, and Felipe Luciano), whose songs echo the pain and frustration of ghetto life and insist on racial pride as the means for redeeming the future. By filming the group in New York slums framed by the Manhattan skyline, director Herbert Danska finds the visual equivalent to their music. Some violent and vulgar lyrics, but motivated by a sense of hope rather than hopelessness. A-IV (nr)

Right Stuff, The (1983) Screen version of Tom Wolfe's book about the original seven astronauts is an extraordinary tribute to the pioneers of the US space program, notably Chuck Yeager (Sam Shepard), Alan Shepard (Scott Glenn), and John Glenn (Ed Harris). Director Philip Kaufman captures the gallant endeavor in a style that's at once respectful yet exuberant, lavishly entertaining, and very inspiring. Unfortunately, a scene involving masturbation, intended as a bit of comic relief during a sequence of laboratory tests, is mature fare. A-III (R/PG appeal)

Rikky and Pete (1988) Australian road picture pairing a brother-sister team (Stephen Kearney and Nina Landis) who leave their wealthy family in Melbourne to start a new life in a mining town in the Australian outback. Director Nadia Tass gets some offhand humor in scenes featuring Pete's Rube Goldberg inventions, but the focus is on Rikky, who is the stronger of the two and protective of her spacey brother. Brief nudity and much rough language. A-III (R)

Rikyu (1991) A 16th-century Japanese warlord (Tsutomu Yamazaki) and his tea master (Rentaro Mikuni) perfect the art of the tea ceremony while clashing over the warlord's burgeoning political ambitions. Exquisite delicacy and simplicity mark director Hiroshi Teshigahara's homage to Japanese culture, with powerful performances from the two opposed characters. Subtitles. Suicide within a cultural perspective. A-II (nr)

Ring, The (1952) Small but effective picture of a Mexican-American youth (Lalo Rios) who sets out to help his family by becoming a prizefighter, but, despite the efforts of a veteran trainer (Gerald Mohr), he gets beaten to a pulp and quits the ring to look elsewhere for success. Directed by Kurt Neumann, the movie presents a positive view of Latinos while showing the seamy side of the fight game. Violent boxing scenes. A-II (br)

Ring of Bright Water (1969) London clerk (Bill Travers) leaves his computerized job to move to a small cottage in the Scottish highlands with an otter. Unpretentious British story directed by Jack Couffer proves intelligent, entertaining family fare. A-I (G)

Ring of Fire (1961) Combination crime-and-disaster thriller starts with a police officer (David Janssen) being taken hostage by marauding teenagers (Frank Gorshin and Joyce Taylor), who are captured in the Oregon wilderness where one of their cigarettes causes a forest fire which threatens to engulf a nearby town. Writer-director Andrew L. Stone's busy scenario shifts abruptly from the nasty teen menaces to the low-budget conflagration, ending with Janssen at the throttle of a trainload of panicked townspeople in the fiery climax. Much menace, some stylized violence, and occasional sexual innuendo. A-III (br)

Ringmaster (1998) Tawdry tale of two sets of dim characters who bring their tangled sexual problems to the TV talk-show hosted by master of insincerities Jerry Springer, with the results predictably featuring scenes of sex and violence on and off the show. Directed by Neil Abramson, this low-budget promo for the TV talk-show is a tedious exercise in sexual exploitation and human manipulation. Numerous sexual encounters, some nudity, physical and verbal violence, much rough language. and occasional profanity. O (R)

Rings Around the World (1966) Compilation movie showing famous circus acts from various countries produced and directed by Gilbert Cates and narrated by Don Ameche. A-I (br)

Rio Bravo (1959) Long-winded but pungent Western in which a seasoned sheriff (John Wayne) tries to keep a killer (Claude Aikens) from being busted out of jail by his brother's army of gunslingers, with only a drunken deputy (Dean Martin), an elderly cripple (Walter Brennan), a callow cowboy (Ricky Nelson), and a saloon hostess (Angie Dickinson) to back him up. Director Howard Hawks savors the desperate situation and its collection of oddball characters as the tension builds to the long-delayed slam-bang conclusion. Assorted stylized violence and sexual innuendo. A-III (br)

Rio Conchos (1964) Ponderous Western in which an Army officer (Stuart Whitman) heads into Mexico with a black sergeant (Jim Brown), a hardened Apache killer (Richard Boone), and a convicted murderer (Tony Franciosa) seeking to recover 2,000 stolen repeating rifles before they wind up in the hands of Apache hostiles. Directed by Gordon Douglas, there's plenty of rugged action, but it's all as wildly improbable as the plans of the mad Confederate colonel (Edmond O'Brien) who stole the rifles to arm the Apaches for an invasion of 1867 Texas. Nasty frontier violence, brutality, and sexual situations. A-III (br)

Rio Grande (1950) Veteran cavalry officer (John Wayne) commanding a frontier outpost has his hands full when his estranged wife (Maureen O'Hara) arrives with their West Point son (Claude Jarman, Jr.), but the untested youth proves his mettle on a raid across the Mexican border to rescue children captured by the Apaches. Director John Ford plays the commander's domestic problems for laughs, but turns grimly serious in the climactic border raid. Stylized violence. A-I (br)

Rio Lobo (1970) Stylish Western with John Wayne as a Civil War veteran pursuing two traitors for hijacking an army payroll, and not perturbed in the least by a small army of hired gunslingers, nor a final thunderous shootout with an entire town taking part. Under Howard Hawks's deft direction, there is plenty of rough horseplay and tongue-in-cheek references to Wayne's overweight condition and old age in general. Violence, both physical and psychological, and some adult sexual references. A-III (G)

Riot (1968) Set within the grime and frustration of prison life is a realistic drama in which an inmate (James Brown), unwittingly caught up in fast-moving events, assumes leadership of a full-scale revolt by the entire prison. Director Buzz Kulik's movie is by no means casual entertainment, but it is very knowing about prison life and injustices. Several violent, bloody sequences bolster the dramatic action, and the dialogue is a bit rough. A-IV (R/GP)

Riot in Juvenile Prison (1959) Tough juvenile delinquent Scott Marlowe is no match for crusading penal reformer Jerome Thor in director Edward L. Cahn's dreary low-budget clunker. Stylized violence and sexual innuendo. A-III (br)

Ripper, The (1997) Flatfooted melodrama in which a Scotland Yard inspector (Patrick Bergin) romances a poor working-girl (Gabrielle Anwar), then uses her as bait to nab a serial killer of prostitutes in the East End slums of 1888 London. Directed by Janet Myers, the TV movie is a tired variation on the familiar story of Jack the Ripper, who is here identified as a member of the royal family, but the unimaginative plot gets lost in detailing the Victorian snobbery which keeps the inspector from solving the lurid case. Some brief graphic violence and occasional profanity. A-III (R)

Rise and Fall of Legs Diamond, The (1960) Formula gangster movie directed by Budd Boetticher follows the ruthless methods by which its title character (Ray Danton) comes to rule the mobs of Prohibition-era New York, then is cut down by a syndicate organizing crime on a national basis in the 1930s. Stylized violence, some of it quite nasty, and sexual situations. A-III (br)

Rise of Catherine the Great, The (see: **Catherine the Great**)

Rise of Louis XIV, The (1970) French historical dramatization meticulously traces the gradual assumption of power by the Sun King, from the time he assumed the crown to his undercutting the nobility by enticing them to spend their lives in the frivolous splendors of the court at Versailles. Directed by Roberto Rossellini, the re-creation of the period is beautifully exquisite and painstakingly detailed, but those uninterested in history may find the pace interminably slow. A-I (G)

Rising Sun (1993) Investigating a sex murder in a Japanese-owned building, two Los Angeles police detectives (Sean Connery and Wesley Snipes) run up against a complex cover-up involving a politically sensitive sale of an American company to Japanese businessmen who must avoid scandal at all costs. Director Philip Kaufman's coldly stylish and wholly cynical thriller from Michael Crichton's novel exploits sexual violence against women in a story presenting a disturbing view of Japanese commerce on our shores. Repeated replay of a taped graphic sex killing, some nasty violence, recurring nudity, and much rough language. O (R)

Risky Business (1983) Enterprising young prostitute (Rebecca De Mornay) persuades a high-school senior (Tom Cruise), while his affluent parents are away on vacation, to turn his plush Chicago home into a bordello for his classmates. Written and directed by Paul Brickman, it is much slicker than similar exploitation movies aimed at teenagers, but it is appallingly crass in its celebration of promiscuity. Nudity and graphic sexuality as well as a benign view of deceit, manipulation, and sexual indulgence. O (R)

Rita, Sue and Bob Too (1987) British sex-farce posing as ribald social-satire about two lower-class teenagers sexually exploited by a married man who in turn ruin his already failing marriage and then exploit him. Director Alan Clarke displays a callous hand in his graphic depiction of sex with minors, including nudity and profanity. O (R)

Ritz, The (1976) Screen version of a mediocre Broadway comedy about an Italian-American businessman from Cleveland (Jack Weston) hiding out from a murderous brother-in-law (Jerry Stiller) in a homosexual bathhouse, where he is pursued by an off-key Puerto Rican singer (Rita Moreno) who thinks he is a Hollywood producer. Directed by Richard Lester, it's an ugly, disagreeable attempt at farce. Ethnic stereotyping and some foul language O (R)

Rivals (1972) Clunker about an Oedipal 10-year-old brat (Scott Jacoby) who is so fatally jealous of his widowed mother (Joan Hackett) and her childish second husband (Robert Klein) that he makes a humiliating mess of trying to have sex with his dumb but nubile babysitter. Director Krishna Shah is hopelessly adrift in dealing with the esoteric lifestyles of Americans with too much money. Repugnant trash. O (R)

River, The (1984) Ernest but dull effort to dramatize the plight of the American farmer tells the story of a farm family (Mel Gibson and Sissy Spacek) who must battle nature, bill collectors, and public indifference in their struggle to hold on to their land and livelihood. The characters simply do not come alive in an unfocused script directed by Mark Rydell. Some violent encounters and a restrained bedroom scene. A-II (PG-13)

River Lady (1948) Muddled romantic adventure directed by George Sherman in which the owner (Yvonne De Carlo) of a gambling riverboat uses a slick agent (Dan Duryea) to create a logging syndicate until stopped by her former logger beau (Rod Cameron) who forms a combine of independent loggers. Stylized violence and romantic complications. A-II (br)

River Niger, The (1976) Powerful drama about a black American's struggle to forge his own identity out of a tragic history of blacks as the eternally displaced persons of our nation. Though director Krishna Shah fails to overcome the stage origins of the work, this does lessen the value of its hopeful message about the choices facing our society, its moving portrait of closely knit family life, and the strong performances of James Earl Jones, Cicely Tyson, and Glynn Turman. Mature themes. A-III R)

River of No Return (1954) Slack Western in which a backcountry farmer (Robert Mitchum) saves his son (Tommy Rettig) and a saloon singer (Marilyn Monroe) from rampaging Indians by rafting downstream to safety in a town where he confronts the crooked gambler (Rory Calhoun) who had run out on them. Directed by Otto Preminger, the rugged raft scenes work up considerable tension, but the rest of the picture is a letdown over the contrived relationships of cardboard characters. Frontier violence, romantic complications, and sexual innuendo. A-III (br)

River Runs Through It, A (1992) Meditative reflections on the experiences of a youth (Craig Sheffer) growing up in rural Montana in the first part of the century, chiefly comprising his relationship with his rebellious younger brother (Brad Pitt), minister father (Tom Skerritt), and the great outdoors. Directed by Robert Redford, the tone of the episodic narrative is earnest, the pace leisurely, and the result largely dependent upon how one relates to the poetry of nature. Some scenes of inebriation and discreet sexual references, several shots of rear nudity, teens in a life-threatening situation, and occasional profanity. A-III (PG)

River Wild, The (1994) Taut outdoors thriller in which a former river-guide (Meryl Streep) on a whitewater rafting vacation with her non-athletic husband (David Strathairn) and young son (Joseph Mazzello) is forced to take two fugitives (Kevin Bacon and John C. Riley) down a deadly stretch of river, knowing the two will kill her and her family even if they survive the trip down the rapids. Director Curtis Hanson underplays the characterizations but maintains edgy suspense as the woman becomes increasingly resourceful in her efforts to save her loved ones. Frequent menace and brief shots of brutal violence. A-III (PG-13)

River's Edge (1987) The callous sex-killing of a young high-school girl is viewed by her apathetic peers as an occasion for protective support of her psychopathic boyfriend, who becomes the equally innocent victim of an adult psychotic (Dennis Hopper). Director Tim Hunter's picture of several troubled youths downplays emotional and spiritual issues in favor of surface sensationalism, including permissive teen sex, nudity, and profanity. O (R)

Riverrun (1970) When a seagoing father (John McLiam) visits the sheep farm where his daughter (Louise Ober) and her young man (Mark Jenkins) live, he is at first amused by their attempt to get back to nature and escape the dehumanization of city life, but when he learns that she is pregnant and not formally married, he is determined to take her away. Written and directed by John Korty, the contrivances of romantic melodrama are evident, but the generational theme of value systems is handled sensitively and treated with honesty. A-III (R)

Road House (1948) Bleak sudser about a singer (Ida Lupino) who comes between best friends when her boss, the roadhouse owner (Richard Widmark), pursues her, while she prefers the arms of his manager (Cornel Wilde). Directed by Jean Negulesco, the contrived story is less interesting than the flawed characters, one of whom is driven bonkers by the unbalanced triangle. Stylized violence, some intense menace, and sexual innuendo. A-III (br)

Road House (1989) College-educated bouncer (Patrick Swayze) cleans up a nasty nightclub in Missouri, only to incur the wrath of the town's sleazy kingpin (Ben Gazzara). In director Rowdy Herrington's modern-day Western, women are the resident playthings, and men the resident idiots. Interminable fisticuffs, graphic sexual encounters, nudity, and endorsement of vigilantism. O (R)

Road Movie (1974) Wildly exaggerated melodrama about two truck-drivers (Robert Drivas and Barry Bostwick) whose friendship is shattered when they pick up a fuel-stop prostitute (Regina Baff) in a story that ends with the destruction of the truck and the death of one of them. Directed by Joseph Strick, whatever intentions the movie had as social commentary on the dangers of the road is undone by the movie's meanness of characters and their rough language. A-III (nr)

Road Show (1941) Comic misfire directed by Hal Roach in which an eccentric millionaire (John Hubbard) escapes a mental asylum with the help of an inmate (Adolphe Menjou), then is hidden by the softhearted owner (Carole Landis) of a failing carnival, with predictable results. Romantic complications, slapstick violence, and a comic black stereotype (Willie Best). A-II (br)

Road to Bali (1953) Fitful comedy in which a hapless pair of entertainers (Bing Crosby and Bob Hope) try diving for sunken treasure in the South Seas, then vie for the affections of an island princess (Dorothy Lamour) while saving her from court intrigues, cannibals, and an erupting volcano. Directed by Hal Walker, the sixth **Road** picture sputters along on a haphazard mix of silly situations, daffy one-liners, and cameos by Jane Russell, Humphrey Bogart, and Martin and Lewis. Menacing situations and mild sexual innuendo. A-II (br)

Road to Denver, The (1955) Routine Western directed by Joe Kane in which a Texas cowboy (John Payne) becomes a partner in a Colorado stage-line, then is confronted by his trigger-happy younger brother (Skip Homeier) who's working for the competition (Lee J. Cobb). Stylized violence and romantic complications. A-II (br)

Road to Glory, The (1936) Creaky WW I tale about a battle-fatigued French captain (Warner Baxter) who leads his company, among whom is his aged father (Lionel Barrymore), in a 1916 offensive which costs him his eyesight, then learns his Red Cross girlfriend (June Lang) loves a lieutenant (Fredric March), and returns to the front, where his father guides him on a suicide mission. Director Howard Hawks struggles with the credibility of the plot's contrived melodramatics but excels in vivid scenes of trench warfare and the gallows humor of combat soldiers. Battlefield violence and muted sexual innuendo. A-II (br)

Road to Hong Kong, The (1962) In the seventh and final **Road** picture, Bing Crosby and Bob Hope play con-artists kidnapped in the Orient by an agent (Joan Collins) of a would-be world dictator (Robert Morley), and they wind up on a one-way rocket-trip to the moon. Directed by Norman Panama, the low-budget British production doesn't give the veteran duo much to work with, though occasionally the old boys put some new life in the stale proceedings. Stylized violence and a few mild double-entendres. A-I (br)

Road to Morocco (1942) Wacky comic romp in which castaways Bing Crosby and Bob Hope land in a desert kingdom, vie to wed its princess (Dorothy Lamour), and wind up captives of a rebel Arab chieftain (Anthony Quinn). Directed by David Butler, the third **Road** comedy continues the pair's genial buffoonery as small-time hustlers trying to woo Lamour amidst throwaway gags, one-liners, talking camels, and occasional songs. Some mild sexual innuendo. A-II (br)

Road to Rio (1947) After accidentally torching a carnival, a hapless pair of musicians (Bing Crosby and Bob Hope) stow away on a Brazilian-bound ocean-liner, where they befriend an heiress (Dorothy Lamour) hypnotized by her wicked aunt (Gale Sondergaard). Directed by Norman Z. McLeod, the fifth **Road** comedy continues the series' tradition of zany plots strewn with wisecracks, sight gags, and musical interludes, this time including the Andrews Sisters and the three manic Wiere Brothers. Silly but fun. A-I (br)

Road to Salina (1971) Dreadfully pretentious European production set in the middle of a baked salt-flat, where Lana Turner runs a gas-station/cafe and mistakes Robert Walker for her runaway son. Her daughter (Mimsy Farmer) goes along with the situation by engaging in a sexual relationship that had originally sent the son packing. Directed by Georges Lautner, the muddled incest theme is conveyed with many arty scenes of graphic lovemaking. O (R)

Road to Singapore (1940) Romantic comedy about

a scandal-ridden playboy (Bing Crosby) who hides out with a dim but trusted chum (Bob Hope) in a Far Eastern backwater, where both fall for a local maid (Dorothy Lamour). Directed by Victor Schertzinger, the thin plot wasn't very funny, but the Crosby-Hope by-play sparked enough laughs to engender their own series in the **Road** comedies that followed. Some sexual innuendo. A-II (br)

Road to Utopia (1945) Bing Crosby and Bob Hope con their way to the Alaskan gold fields, where they foil crooks (Douglass Dumbrille and Jack La Rue) trying to steal a rich mine from its rightful owner (Dorothy Lamour). Directed by Hal Walker, the boys are in fine form masquerading as a pair of wanted killers, with Robert Benchley's addled commentary adding to the zany proceedings. Some sexual innuendo. A-II (br)

Road to Wellville, The (1994) Unappetizing satire about the bizarre digestive and sexual practices at a loosely fact-based turn-of-the-century Battle Creek health-spa run by corn-flakes inventor Dr. Kellogg (Anthony Hopkins) centers on the antics of a confused married couple (Matthew Broderick and Bridget Fonda), a would-be cereal tycoon (John Cusack), and the fanatical doctor's lunatic son (Dana Carvey). Director Alan Parker's failed comedy plumbs the depths of repellent scatological humor as cardboard characters drone on endlessly about their private bodily functions. Recurring nudity, an adulterous situation, continuous toilet humor, an accidental electrocution, and an instance of rough language. A-III (R)

Road to Zanzibar (1941) Zany fun with a pair of con-men (Bing Crosby and Bob Hope) whose witless schemes leave them stranded in Africa, until they join a jungle safari with two Brooklyn entertainers (Dorothy Lamour and Una Merkel) in quest of a rich hunter. Directed by Victor Schertzinger, the second **Road** picture relies on the boys' shenanigans to carry the weak plot, and they do so in amusing fashion. Some sexual innuendo. A-II (br)

Road Warrior, The (1982) Set in a post-nuclear wasteland, this Australian action thriller pits a surviving outpost of civilization clustered around a still-functioning oil refinery against the barbarian horde who need gasoline for their motley assortment of vehicles. Max (Mel Gibson), a wandering loner, is chosen to deliver the gas through hostile lines. Except for director George Miller's stylish use of the setting, there is little in this blood-and-gore epic to occupy the mind. Excessive violence. O (R)

Roadhouse Murder, The (1932) Sappy melodrama directed by J. Walter Ruben in which a cub reporter (Eric Linden) stumbles on a double murder, plants evidence of his own guilt so he can write front-page stories about being hunted by the police, then is captured, tried, and convicted after the real murderer (Bruce Cabot) steals the evidence that would clear him. Stylized violence and romantic complications. A-II (br)

Roadie (1980) Failed spoof of rock-music's subculture follows the misadventures of a country bumpkin (rock singer Meatloaf) who is convinced by a wacky groupie to become a "roadie," or general roustabout and handyman, for a traveling rock-group. Director Alan Rudolph offers few good sight gags and plenty of bad ones, with lots of ear-numbing music. Some jokes about sex and drugs. A-III (PG)

Roadside Prophets (1992) Shapeless road movie follows a loner (John Doe) as he motorcycles through the Nevada desert meeting assorted oddballs and outcasts along the way, including a would-be friend (Adam Horovitz) who stubbornly trails him. Writer-director Abbe Wool needles the establishment with minimal wit and drab counterculture twaddle. Implied sexual encounter, fleeting violence, nudity, occasional substance abuse, and recurring rough language. A-III (R)

Rob Roy (1995) Romantic tale of the struggle for justice waged by the title's 18th-century Scottish highlander (Liam Neeson) who becomes a fugitive after the money loaned to him by a venal nobleman (John Hurt) is stolen by a ruthless thief (Tim Roth) who also violated Rob's wife (Jessica Lange). Although overlong and ponderously directed by Michael Caton-Jones, the result succeeds better as the personal story of a loving couple than as a sweeping historical epic. Some sexual innuendo and intermittent violence, including a restrained rape scene and an off-screen suicide. A-III (R)

Robbery (1967) Fact-based British thriller about the hijacking of the Royal Mail train with three millions pounds in cash and the escape of the robbery's mastermind (Stanley Baker) from the police dragnet. Director Peter Yates builds a lot of excitement and suspense, with a refreshingly minimum amount of violence. A-II (br)

Robe, The (1953) Reverent but plodding Gospel-era story from the Lloyd C. Douglas novel about a Roman tribune (Richard Burton) whose gambling wins Christ's robe at the Crucifixion, then fears the robe's power to bewitch him, until later becoming a Christian martyr in Rome. Directed by Henry Koster, the fictional tale is sincere but dramatically less than convincing in story line and performances ranging from wooden to scenery-chewing, with the resulting inspiration more in the eye of the beholder than on the screen. Stylized violence and veiled sexual references. A-I (br)

Robert A. Heinlein's The Puppet Masters (see: **Puppet Masters, The**)

Robert et Robert (1980) Slight French comedy about two hapless and, apparently, hopeless bachelors (Jacques Villeret and Charles Denner) who meet while enlisting aid from a computerized matrimonial service and find themselves banding together against a hostile world. Directed by Claude Lelouch, the two principals are forced to fall back upon their quirks of character to keep the humor going. Mature theme and treatment. A-III (nr)

Robin and Marian (1976) Disappointing British addition to the Robin Hood legend set some 20 years after his youthful adventures in Sherwood Forest. Robin (Sean Connery) and his now-melancholy men rescue Maid Marian (Audrey Hepburn) from a convent and the clutches of the dastardly Sheriff of Nottingham (Robert Shaw). Under Richard Lester's direction the performances are very good, but the mood of the piece is confused, halfway between genuine romance and clumsy demythologizing. Some violence, crude humor, and a sympathetically viewed suicide. A-III (PG)

Robin and the Seven Hoods (1964) Uneven gangster spoof set in 1928 Chicago, where the top mob (headed by Peter Falk) tries to crush a smaller gang (led by Frank Sinatra) which gains public sympathy by donating its loot to charitable organizations. Directed by Gordon Douglas, the silly Robin Hood gimmick adds little to the sprawling comedy's hit-or-miss humor from a cast including Dean Martin, Sammy Davis, Jr., Edward G. Robinson, Bing Crosby, and Barbara Rush. Comic violence and underworld activities. A-II (br)

Robin Hood (1973) Disney feature cartoon offers a humorous version of the exploits of the English folk-hero who robbed from the undeserving rich to give to the exploited poor. The cast consists of crisply drawn animals, who lend themselves to such characterizations as Robin being a crafty fox and King John as an anemic lion. Older viewers will appreciate the classic Disney-style animation under the direction of Wolfgang Reitherman, while younger viewers enjoy the comic derring-do. A-I (G)

Robin Hood: Men in Tights (1993) Mel Brooks's wacky send-up of the Sherwood Forest legend has the band of singing, prancing Merry Men attempting to rescue the captured Robin Hood (Cary Elwes), while Maid Marian (Amy Yasbeck) reluctantly agrees to marry the dastardly Sheriff of Rottingham (Roger Rees) to save him. As co-written, produced, and directed by Brooks, the goofy spoof has moments of refreshing lunacy, as well as his trademark brand of tasteless jokes that make this a hit-and-miss affair. Much comic violence and some crude humor. A-III (PG-13)

Robin Hood: Prince of Thieves (1991) Returning from the Crusades, Robin Hood (Kevin Costner) and his Moorish protector (Morgan Freeman) join the outlaws of Sherwood Forest in defiance of the cunning Sheriff of Nottingham (Alan Rickman) and his plans to marry Maid Marian (Mary Elizabeth Mastrantonio). Director Kevin Reynolds gives a frenzied, fresh spin to the oft-told tale, which, despite many scattered flaws, boasts glorious cinematography and production design in addition to fine performances, especially Rickman's campy villain. Some gory violence and mild sexual innuendo. A-II (PG-13)

Robin Hood of El Dorado, The (1936) Creaky Hollywood saga of California's legendary 19th-century Hispanic outlaw, Joaquin Murrieta (Warner Baxter), who becomes a bandit after gringo goldminers kill his wife and drunken Americanos lynch his brother. Director William Wellman romanticizes the bandits and their exploits in a plot muddled by unresolved notions of justice and revenge that ultimately have tragic consequences. Considerable stylized violence and menace in treating the theme of an oppressed minority. A-III (br)

Robinson Crusoe and the Tiger (1972) Amateurish Spanish version of the Daniel Defoe classic tale of shipwreck and survival, with Crusoe played by Hugo Stiglitz who double-takes his way through various episodes of being chased by everything from sharks and panthers to bats and tigers. Directed by Rene Cardona Jr., its stagy camerawork and droning narration may put the small fry to sleep. A-I (G)

Robinson Crusoe on Mars (1964) Engaging sci-fi variation on the Defoe story with an astronaut (Paul Mantee) marooned on Mars with only a monkey as company, then rescuing a human-like slave (Vic Lundin) from an alien spaceship. Directed by Byron Haskin, the story is told in imaginative fashion holding interest to the end which is a new beginning. A-I (br)

Robinson Crusoeland (see: **Utopia**)

RoboCop (1987) Futuristic urban crime-drama about a good Detroit cop (Peter Weller) shot up by hoods and recycled into a robotized part-man, part-machine programmed to rid the streets of crime. Dutch director Paul Verhoeven doesn't spare any blood and gore in his relentlessly graphic depiction of violent law enforcement tactics used against equally violent criminals. Conveys a dangerous ends-justifies-the-means brand of justice. O (R)

RoboCop 2 (1990) About to be relegated to the junk heap, RoboCop (Peter Weller) struggles to maintain his identity while searching for Detroit's drug lord (Tom Noonan), whose demonic mind is being used by an evil corporation to create a far worse enemy: RoboCop 2. Directed by Irvin Kershner, the story is overwhelmed by an endless avalanche of explosive special effects and machine gun mayhem, with the particularly objectionable use of a preteen portrayed as a hardened criminal. Excessive violence, intense menace, and rough language. O (R)

RoboCop 3 (1993) Slack but violent sequel in which the part-human cop (Robert John Burke) joins Detroit's citizen rebels who have gone underground to fight the systematic destruction of their homes by the powerful development corporation that runs the beleaguered city. Directed by Fred Dekker, the long, unrelieved formula tale offers little more than wall-to-wall bullets and bloodshed. Much mindless mayhem and gratuitous violence. O (PG-13)

Rock, The (1996) Violent action thriller involves the down-to-the wire efforts of a FBI chemicals expert (Nicolas Cage) and a former Alcatraz prisoner (Sean Connery) to defeat a disgruntled military hero (Ed Harris) from detonating poison-gas rockets aimed at vaporizing San Francisco. Director Michael Bay's slickly manipulative macho-fantasy exaggerates murderous mayhem in a drawn-out exercise glorifying violence as he-man heroics. Excessive violence, brief bedroom scene, and constant rough language. O (R)

Rock Island Trail (1950) Uneven Western directed by Joseph Kane in which an Illinois railroad owner (Forrest Tucker) bridges the Mississippi, then pushes his line across Iowa, despite acts of sabotage caused by a riverboat company owner (Bruce Cabot). Frontier violence. A-I (br)

Rock-a-Bye Baby (1958) Weak Jerry Lewis vehicle directed by Frank Tashlin has the befuddled comic playing nursemaid to the infant triplets of a former girlfriend (Marilyn Maxwell), now a voluptuous Hollywood star trying to keep her marriage and motherhood hidden from the public. Occasional fun for those willing to overlook all the sappy contrivances. A-I (br)

Rock-a-Doodle (1992) In a story combining animation with live action, a runaway rooster (voice of Glen Campbell) finds fame as an Elvis impersonator but doesn't forget his barnyard pals when they need him. Director Don Bluth turns out a busy musical fairytale that holds some fun for the kiddies while being tolerable for adults. A-I (G)

Rock 'n' Roll High School Forever (1991) Doltish teen comedy written and directed by Deborah Brock pits student-vulgarian Corey Feldman against school-disciplinarian Mary Woronos in a battle marked by gross physical hijinks, tasteless sexual situations, and crude language. A-III (PG-13)

Rocket Gilbraltar (1988) Limply sentimental story of a family gathering to celebrate the 77th birthday of the clan's patriarch (Burt Lancaster), whose grown children are self-absorbed yuppies with mid-career problems, but whose young grandchildren (notably Macaulay Culkin) heed his wish for burial at sea in a Viking's funeral. Director Daniel Petrie's romanticized version of life and death in a wealthy American suburb looks good, but is empty of substance, both cerebral and emotional. Soggy human values, maudlin treatment of death, and a benign view of promiscuity. A-III (PG)

Rocket Man, The (1954) Low-budget fantasy about an orphan (George Winslow) whose magic rocket-gun saves the town orphanage from a crooked politician. Directed by Oscar Rudolph, the juvenile story offers little except veterans Spring Byington and Charles Coburn as small-town types. A-I (br)

Rocketeer, The (1991) Dumb story set in 1938 Los Angeles, where a gangster (Paul Sorvino) and a movie-star-turned-Nazi (Timothy Dalton) conspire to recover a stolen rocket-powered backpack from a daredevil pilot (Bill Campbell) by kidnapping his girlfriend (Jennifer Connelly). Director Joe Johnston's lively but cornball adventure features amusing special effects, which help offset the hero's colorless personality. Sporadic comic-book violence. A-II (PG)

RocketMan (1997) Dull comedy in which an annoyingly infantile computer nerd (Harland Williams) saves the day while aboard a space mission to Mars that goes awry. Directed by Stuart Gillard, the charmless proceedings are reduced to a series of clumsy pratfalls and rude body-function humor. Mild menace and toilet humor. A-II (PG)

Rocking Horse Winner, The (1950) Unsettling British adaptation of D.H. Lawrence's story about a young boy (John Howard Davies) trying to help his spendthrift mother (Valerie Hobson) by getting winning tips on horse races from frenzied rides on his rocking horse. Writer-director Anthony Pelissier handles the boy's attempt to shoulder responsibility for his careless mother's financial needs, but his strange system for picking winners turns the ending into uneasy fantasy. Parental neglect and its tragic result. A-II (br)

Rocky (1976) Underdog Philadelphia club-fighter Rocky Balboa (Sylvester Stallone) has a shot at the heavyweight championship with the help of a tough, old trainer (Burgess Meredith). Director John Avildsen concentrates on the gritty, back-street quality of life in the old neighborhood and the relationship that grows between Rocky and the introverted sister (Talia Shire) of his best friend (Burt Young). The bloody brutality of the prizefight game is abundantly evident. A-III (PG)

Rocky II (1979) Writer-director Sylvester Stallone stars as the prizefighter unable to settle down with a new wife (Talia Shire), house, and baby. Low on cash and brains, he accepts a rematch with Apollo Creed (Carl Weathers), the undefeated champ whom he almost beat in the first film. Though the sequel is formula entertainment with its theme of the victorious underdog, the movie clearly celebrates the violence of the ring, assigning value as much to the brutal sport as to its likeable hero's will and determination. A-III (PG)

Rocky III (1982) Apollo Creed (Carl Weathers) trains his former opponent (Sylvester Stallone) so that he can hold on to his title against a snarling and vicious challenger (Mr. T.). Also written and directed by Stallone, it may not be a knockout but it is good, solid entertainment. The carnage in the ring, though of briefer duration than previously, is still very intense. A-III (PG)

Rocky IV (1985) Sylvester Stallone gets back in the ring for the fight of his life against a Russian Olympic boxing machine (Dolph Lundgren). Stallone directs himself fighting to avenge the death of Apollo Creed (Carl Weathers) while regaining American honor. The sensitive may find the fight scenes too brutal. A-III (PG)

Rocky V (1990) When brain damage forces Rocky (Sylvester Stallone) to retire from the ring, he tries a new career as a manager, but in the process neglects his wife (Talia Shire) and son (Sage Stallone), until a startling blow from his protégé (Tommy Morrison) brings him to his senses. As scripted by Stallone and directed by John Avildsen, there's still energy and brutality left in the sequel formula, which this round concentrates on preserving family values despite the loss of material goods. Graphic boxing violence. A-III (PG-13)

Rocky Horror Picture Show, The (1975) An engaged couple (Susan Sarandon and Barry Bostwick), stranded on a back-road late at night, wander into an eerie mansion, where they join in the kinky games of a Transylvanian transvestite (Tim Curry) and his weird band of followers. Directed by Tim Sharman, this clumsy adaptation of a campy British musical spoofs old horror movies while trashing traditional values in a tiresome display of bad taste and moral vacuity. Excessive emphasis on sexual license and some scenes of violence. O (R)

Rocky Mountain (1950) Once again, Errol Flynn dies with his boots on, this time when Shoshone Indians massacre his column of Confederate cavalry (including Guinn Williams and Slim Pickens) in California to stir up trouble just before the end of the Civil War. Under William Keighley's lackluster direction, the grimly stirring finale can't save the talky, slow-paced narrative preceding it. Stylized violence and an unconvincing tribute to a lost cause. A-I (br)

Rodan (1957) Dubbed Japanese monster movie with Inoshiro Honda directing ugly-looking mega-creatures stirred from prehistoric slumber by H-bomb tests and decked out in rubber suits, the most threatening of which are the two pterodactyls of the title whose flapping wings cause typhoon-force winds. Formula menace and stylized violence, mostly in the destruction of scale-model miniatures. A-II (br)

Roger & Me (1989) Arresting documentary on the economically depressed city of Flint, Mich., once the prosperous bastion of good old-fashioned capitalism, and now a town with 30,000 unemployed autoworkers due to General Motors's plant closings. Written, produced, and directed by Michael Moore, a Flint native, the work's subjective treatment contains much irony and black humor as it documents the city's decline and pitiful attempts to rejuvenate itself while trying to bring GM chairman Roger Smith face-to-face with the results of these layoffs. Some profanity laced with vulgar ethnic and sexist references and the gratuitous inclusion of a rabbit's slaughter and skinning. A-III (R)

Roger Corman's Frankenstein Unbound (1990) Campy sci-fi horror yarn in which a scientist from the future (John Hurt) zooms back to the 19th century for a perilous confrontation with Dr. Frankenstein (Raul Julia) and his gabby monster (Nick Brimble). Director Roger Corman jumbles genres, using gore for comic effect, in this silly but eye-catching update of the monster myth. Stylized grisly violence and a casual attitude toward promiscuity. A-III (R)

Rogue Cop (1955) Hardboiled story of a veteran police-detective (Robert Taylor) who's on the mob's payroll until they kill his younger cop-brother and he pays them back in kind. Directed by Roy Rowland, the result is an overly familiar crime-does-not-pay story with few interesting details and no surprises. Nasty stylized violence and some sexual innuendo. A-III (br)

Roller Boogie (1980) Spoiled little rich girl (Linda Blair) flees parents and promising career as flutist for the joys of the roller-skating rink. Director Mark L. Lester forgets the plot to focus on scenes of nubile youngsters in scanty costumes skating and dancing to disco rhythms. The boring exercise in coed velocity has little to offer its intended teenage audience. A-III (PG)

Rollerball (1975) The title refers to a brutal game invented by the rulers of a future society in order to keep their subjects docile by watching the violence of others. When one of the star players (James Caan) begins attracting his own followers, he is ordered to retire, but instead leads a revolt. Directed by Norman Jewison, the movie has little to offer except the lavish violence of the game and then of the revolt, thereby exploiting what supposedly it intended to condemn. O (R)

Rollercoaster (1977) Slack thriller about an extortionist (Timothy Bottoms) who plants bombs on rollercoasters and the safety inspector (George Segal) who chases him across the country. Directed by James Goldstone, the movie's sole aim is visceral excitement unhindered by any larger concerns, including the risk entailed by putting such an idea into the public consciousness. Graphically depicted rollercoaster crash. A-III (PG)

Rolling Thunder (1977) When a returned Vietnam prisoner-of-war (William Devane) finds that his wife and son have been murdered during a robbery, he sets out to exact a bloody vengeance. Written by Paul Schrader and directed by John Flynn, the movie's mayhem and slaughter exploits the serious issue of the problems of returned prisoners-of-war. Its reverence for guns approaches fetishism. O (R)

Rollover (1981) Slick romantic melodrama about a bank-president's widow (Jane Fonda) who uncovers fraud in the international monetary system after Arab financiers decide not to redeposit (rollover) their huge sums in her bank, and her boyfriend (Kris Kristofferson) tries to save the day. Directed by Alan J. Pakula, the plot is so contrived that the proceedings are hard to take. Several restrained sex scenes and some rough language. A-III (R)

Roma, Citta Aperta (see: **Open City**)

Roman Holiday (1953) Charming romantic comedy in which a young princess (Audrey Hepburn) on an official visit to Rome slips away from her stuffy entourage to see the sights in the company of two American reporters (Gregory Peck and Eddie Albert), one of whom inevitably falls for her. Directed by William Wyler, the plot begins as lighthearted fluff, proceeds with warm camaraderie along the avenues and byways of the Eternal City, then turns serious as romance blossoms until the bittersweet ending. Romantic situations. A-II (nr)

Roman Scandals (1933) After a vivid dream about being a slave in ancient Rome plotting against a corrupt emperor (Edward Arnold), a jobless menial (Eddie Cantor) awakens to save his small town from a corrupt mayor. Directed by Frank Tuttle, the musical comedy has some good gags and funny routines featuring racing chariots, laughing gas, and poisoned food, but several outlandish production numbers featuring slave girls fall flat. Sexual innuendo and a period black-face routine. A-III (br)

Roman Spring of Mrs. Stone, The (1961) When her rich husband dies, an aging Broadway actress (Vivien Leigh) retires to Rome, meets the wrong people (notably Lotte Lenya), and takes an Italian gigolo (miscast Warren Beatty) as her lover until he turns to a younger woman (Jill St. John). Directed by Jose Quintero from the Tennessee Williams novel, the shallow proceedings are beautifully photographed, but the characters and situations are largely unconvincing, despite Leigh's poignant performance in the title role. Sexual situations. A-III (br)

Romance of a Horsethief (1971) Folk-tale set in a Polish village near the German border in 1904, where most of the peasants subsist by selling stolen horses to the Imperial German Cavalry. When the local Cossack commander (Yul Brynner) requisitions all horses and conscripts the young men for the Czar's war against Japan, some of the villagers (Eli Wallach, David Opatoshu, and Lainie Kazan) turn the tables on the Russian officer. Director Abraham Polonsky tells the tale in lively farcical fashion, but some indulgent nudity and rough verbal exchanges between wily Wallach and his mistress Kazan spoil what should have a lighthearted adventure. O (GP)

Romancing the Stone (1984) Sedate novelist (Kathleen Turner) finds herself plunged into wild adventure when she goes to Colombia to ransom her kidnapped sister, but a handsome American adventurer (Michael Douglas) turns up to save her at fairly regular intervals. Directed by Robert Zemeckis, the exotic romance strives hard for, but never achieves, a tongue-in-cheek style to take the realistic edge off the action and allow for laughs. Some graphic violence, rough language, and partial nudity in a bedroom scene. A-III (PG)

Romantic Comedy (1983) Mediocre screen version of Bernard Slade's play about a successful Broadway playwriting team (Dudley Moore and Mary Steenburgen), whose professionalism takes a decade or so to ripen into romance. As directed by Arthur Hiller, the movie is not very romantic or comic, but the charm of the principals makes it a shade less unbearable. Though adultery figures in the plot, it is not condoned, and the whole enterprise is rather innocuous. A-II (PG)

Romantic Englishwoman, The (1975) Starts out in a Central European spa and quickly goes from Baden-Baden to worse in a continental triangle involving Michael Caine, Helmut Berger, and Glenda Jackson. Very British production directed by Joseph Losey attempts to be civilized and very arch, but aside from an occasional joke that comes off, it is a pretentious nothing. Sexual situations and some nudity. O (R)

Rome Adventure (1962) Romantic clunker about a young American (Suzanne Pleshette) in Rome to see the sights while looking for a job, then finds true love with an art student (Troy Donahue), until his former flame (Angie Dickinson) turns up to reclaim him. Writer-director Delmer Daves pours on the treacle shamelessly, but the only romance going on here is the camera's love affair with the beautiful Italian landscapes and grand cultural monuments. Romantic complications and sexual innuendo. A-III (br)

Romeo and Juliet (see: **William Shakespeare's Romeo and Juliet**)

Romeo and Juliet (1968) Director Franco Zeffirelli's somewhat free interpretation of Shakespeare's tragedy of young love offers much energetic action in a stylish production with teenaged Olivia Hussey and Leonard Whiting in the title roles. Brief nude scene. A-IV (G/PG)

Romeo Is Bleeding (1994) Crooked New York cop (Gary Oldman), doubling as a mob informer-hit-man for big bucks, gets in way over his head when he falls for a sexually voracious murderess (Lena Olin) he's been ordered to kill. Director Peter Medak sensationalizes a host of vicious characters in a garish, blood-drenched potboiler about soulless killers-for-hire. Much grisly violence, seamy sexual encounters, recurring nudity, and constant rough language. O (R)

Romero (1989) Powerful dramatization of the last three years in the life of Archbishop Oscar Romero of San Salvador, whose condemnation of human-rights abuses led to his assassination in 1980. Director John Duigan gets a brilliant performance from Raul Julia, who invests the title role with an intense spiritual dimension that makes credible Romero's courage in condemning the immorality of a ruthless regime. Its graphic scenes of violence are not for the immature, though most adolescents will understand the justice issues involved. A-II (PG-13)

Romper Stomper (1993) Sour Australian production follows a group of skinheads who spout white-supremacist slogans while brutalizing Asians and others in and around Melbourne. Writer-director Geoffrey Wright's dreary story of society's rejects and dropouts turning into Neo-Nazi thugs leads nowhere and proves as aimless as the mayhem and destruction it spends all its energy depicting. Excessive violence, explicit sex-scenes, racist rhetoric, and occasional rough language. O (NC-17/R)

Romy and Michele's High School Reunion (1997) Thin comedy about two blonde airheads returning for their tenth class-reunion and trying to prove they are as bright as everyone else. Directed by David Mirkin, the feather-brained situation is tiresomely padded out with sophomoric jokes and unamusing sexual references. Some restrained sex scenes, crude discussions of sexual subjects, and frequent rough language with a blatant instance of profanity. O (R)

Ronja, Robbersdaughter (1986) Swedish import directed by Tage Danielsson features two children reacting to the selfish insensitivity of their feuding families in a medieval forest setting. Exemplary for its insight and understanding about the feelings of children in relation to parental weaknesses, the movie has two brief scenes of nudity, treated innocently and humorously, in an otherwise delightfully entertaining feature for children. A-I (nr)

Ronin (1998) Well-crafted action thriller in which a band of professional gunmen (including Robert De Niro, Jean Reno, and Stellan Skarsgard) are hired to hijack a metal case, but the plan goes awry when one of them escapes with it and leads them on a chase across France. Veteran director John Frankehimer turns in a taut, fast-paced crime caper filled with shootouts, car chases, murky international intrigue, and picturesque French locales, all of which will be enjoyed by fans of old-fashioned action movies. Much stylized violence, some rough language, and occasional profanity. A-III (R)

Rooftops (1989) Fantasy about New York City street-kids who use a form of martial arts called combat dancing to defend their turf from crack dealers. Included are a thwarted love affair between a white boy and a Hispanic girl (Jason Gedrick and Troy Beyer), some comic relief by a graffiti artist (Alexis Cruz), and dastardly deeds by a crack dealer (Eddie Velez). Despite its anti-drug message and some energized music and dance, veteran director Robert Wise's urban fairytale is no **West Side Story**. Much profanity, some intense violence, and a fleeting, graphic sexual encounter. A-III (R)

Rookie, The (1990) Determined to avenge the murder of his partner, a grizzled detective (Clint Eastwood) is hell-bent on nailing the auto thieves responsible (Raul Julia and Sonia Braga) with or without the help of the new rookie (Charlie Sheen) assigned to him. Also directed by Eastwood, the inane action movie lacks imagination or interest while portraying cops as deliberate killers. Intermittent violence condoning vigilante justice, a sordid sex-encounter, and much rough language. O (R)

Rookie of the Year (1993) Lightweight but mostly enjoyable comedy, with a 12-year-old youth (Thomas Ian Nicholas) becoming the star pitcher for the Chicago Cubs after his broken arm heals in a fashion enabling him to throw 103-mph fastballs. Director Daniel Stern pins most of the laughs on the incongruity of a youngster competing successfully with big leaguers, though adults may find the predictable results of this boyhood fantasy rather mechanical little-league entertainment. Mild sexual innuendo involving adults. A-II (PG)

Room Service (1938) The Marx Brothers romp in a frenetic Broadway comedy set in a hotel, where a penniless producer (Groucho) tries to land a financial backer for his new play while fending off an exasperated manager (Donald MacBride) out to evict him and his entire company from their unpaid rooms. Director William A. Seiter parlays the situation into farcical fun with the madcap antics of Chico and Harpo abetted by Lucille Ball, Frank Albertson, Philip Loeb, and Ann Miller. Slapstick rowdiness not for all tastes. A-I (br)

Room with a View (1986) Radiant romance set in Edwardian England depicts a love triangle resolved when the petulant heroine (Helena Bonham-Carter) chooses the good commoner over the wealthy toff. James Ivory directs from an adaptation of the E.M. Forester story of manners and self-determination. Scene of male nudity is a satiric comment on post-Victorian prudishness. A-III (nr)

Roommates (1971) Greenwich Village roommates (Dan Mason and Harvey Marks), with girlfriends who come and go, seemingly available to either, spend a good deal of their time on the street, much of it waiting to cross at intersections. Written and directed by Jack Baran, the material is so thin, so shallow, so uninspired and banal, that perhaps its deepest insight is realizing how long it takes a New York traffic light to change. Casual sex scenes. A-IV (R)

Roommates, The (1973) Five permissive college girls vacationing at a California resort become romantically involved with various available males (ranging from a timid teenager to an implacable ex-husband), seemingly undeterred by the news of a perverted killer on the loose. Written and directed by Arthur Marks, the relationships are mere contrivances pandering to prurient taste. O (R)

Roommates (1995) Sweetly sentimental tale in which an elderly Polish-American baker (Peter Falk) raises his six-year-old orphaned grandson, shares a room with the grown man (D.B. Sweeney) as he completes his medical studies, then at age 100 moves in with him, his social-worker wife (Julianne Moore), and two small children. Though occasionally contrived, director Peter Yates presents a credible picture of a feisty, yet very loving, 30-year relationship, despite the difficulty of both men to express their emotions. An implied premarital affair and a few profanities. A-III (PG)

Rooster Cogburn (1975) Two Hollywood institutions, John Wayne and Katharine Hepburn, spoof one another's on-screen, off-screen images in a Western set against some beautifully photographed Oregon locales. Directed by Stuart Millar, it's a self-indulgent exercise, but, for all that, many will still find its stars most engaging performers, though youngsters likely will find it pretty tame fare. A-II (PG)

Rope (1948) Psychotic college students (Farley Granger and John Dall) murder a classmate, place his body in a chest, then hold a party for friends, including an astute professor (James Stewart). Filming the action in a single take without cuts except to change film rolls, director Alfred Hitchcock's failed experiment results in a stagy, unconvincing drama loosely based on the Leopold-Loeb case. Grisly subject and treatment may be inappropriate for younger adolescents. A-II (br)

Rope of Sand (1949) Tangled tale of an American adventurer (Burt Lancaster) stumbling upon a cache of gems in a South African diamond-concession whose crafty manager (Claude Rains) and brutal security chief (Paul Henreid) try to force him to reveal their hiding place. Director William Dieterle lards the desperate proceedings with seedy characters, murky atmosphere, and improbable romance (Corinne Calvet). Stylized violence, including some nasty brutality, a revenge subplot, and sexual situations. A-III (br)

Rosalie Goes Shopping (1990) The loving Bavarian wife (Marianne Saegebrecht) of an Arkansas crop-duster (Brad Davis) is a compulsive shopper who sinks deeper and deeper into debt, despite her talent for forgery and credit juggling. Director Percy Adlon's whimsical comedy about American consumerism uses its likeable heroine to poke fun at materialism as the way to economic disaster. A suggestive sexual situation and a theme satirizing the joys of greed and petty theft. A-III (PG)

Rosary Murders, The (1987) Resourceful priest (Donald Sutherland) tries to stop the mysterious serial-killer of priests and nuns in his Detroit parish, while wrestling with his conscience about revealing the clues obtained in the psychopath's confession. Eerie crime melodrama from director Fred Walton illustrates the rigors and dedication of the religious life, but has several chilling murder scenes — one involving the nude body of a novice — and brief profanity. A-III (R)

Rose, The (1979) Glossy romantic tragedy about a flamboyant, whiskey-swilling rock star of the late 1960s (Bette Midler), someone much like Janis Joplin. When she finds a man she really loves (Frederic Forrest), the blow of losing him shatters whatever stability she has left. Fine performance by Midler and the capable direction of Mark Rydell convey with some force how too much success can alienate one from all those values that give significance to life. Sympathetic depiction of illicit sexual relationships, drug and alcohol indulgence, and some very rough language. A-IV (R)

Rose of Washington Square (1939) In a romantic melodrama loosely paralleling events in singer Fanny Brice's life, a promising vocalist (Alice Faye) marries a suave crook (Tyrone Power), becomes a Broadway star thanks to a former partner (Al Jolson), then sticks by her weak-willed husband when he's sent to prison. Directed by Gregory Ratoff, the Prohibition-era sudser is saved by Faye's cheerful singing, Jolson's enthusiastic performance, and Power's handsome insincerity. Romantic complications. A-II (br)

Rose Tattoo, The (1955) Overwrought Tennessee Williams's drama set in a Southern port town, where an emotive Sicilian widow (Anna Magnani) learns of her late husband's infidelity, takes up with a thick-headed but goodhearted truck driver (Burt Lancaster), and lets her teen daughter (Marisa Pavan) marry a sailor. Directed by Daniel Mann, the adaptation is stagy and overacted, but the relationships are validly drawn with some spicy ethnic flavoring. Mature themes. A-III (br)

Rosebud (1975) Failed, boring thriller about Middle East terrorists holding five teenage girls captive aboard the title pleasure-yacht until rescued by CIA and Israeli agents (Peter O'Toole and Cliff Gorman). Directed by Otto Preminger, the movie is a plodding succession of sequences in which each minor bit of action is talked to death in frequently redundant dialogue. Some violence, sexual innuendo, and murky politics. A-III (PG)

Roseland (1977) Three nostalgic stories set in the venerable Manhattan ballroom telling of a widow (Teresa Wright) whose dancing partner (Lou Jacobi) helps her forget her dead husband; a charming gigolo (Christopher Walken) who appeals to a dancing instructor (Helen Gallagher) and a recent divorcée (Geraldine Chaplin); and an elderly German woman (Lilia Skala) who dreams of winning a dance contest despite the shortcomings of her partner (David Thomas). Directed by James Ivory, the romantic movie provides a lightly diverting, affectionate look at human foibles. A-II (PG)

Rosemary's Baby (1968) Modern-day horror story about a young husband (John Cassavetes) who turns his wife (Mia Farrow), body and soul, over to the next-door neighbors, a coven of witches (led by Ruth Gordon and Sidney Blackmer) so she can become the mother of Satan incarnate. Directed by Roman Polanski, the production values are topnotch and performances completely chilling, but the movie's inverted Christian elements denigrate religious beliefs. Brief nudity. O (R)

Rosie (1967) Wealthy widow (Rosalind Russell) alarms her heirs with her spending sprees, and, to protect their inheritance, they have her committed to a high-security rest-home from which she is rescued by the loyal family lawyer (Brian Aherne). Directed by David Lowell Rich, the material may be predictable, but the two veteran leads make it work. Some mature treatment. A-III (br)

Rosewood (1997) Fact-based drama about a thriving black town burned to the ground in 1923 Florida after a mob of neighboring whites react murderously to a white woman's lie about being beaten by a black man. Director John Singleton unfortunately weakens his dramatization of a tragic episode in American race-relations by relying on melodramatic action and shallow characterizations, including a reluctant white sympathizer (Jon Voight) and two blacks (Ving Rhames and Don Cheadle) reduced to cartoon superheroes. Much racial violence, a few discreet sex scenes, and many racial epithets. A-III (R)

Rough Cut (1980) Fluffy, implausible romantic comedy about a Scotland Yard inspector (David Niven) who blackmails a high-society kleptomaniac (Lesley-Anne Down) to set up her jewel-thief lover (Burt Reynolds) so he can be arrested. Directed by Donald Siegal, the film's pervasive amorality and sexual references make it adult fare. A-III (PG)

Rough Night in Jericho (1967) Stale Western in which a retired marshal (John McIntire) and his ex-deputy (George Peppard) help a stage-line owner (Jean Simmons) battle the callous boss (Dean Martin) of a lawless town. Directed by Arnold Laven, the cliched plot is paced by a rough assortment of shootings, beatings, and a lynching, but none of it is very convincing, especially Martin's swaggering villain. Gory violence, sexual situations, and alcohol abuse. A-III (br)

Round Midnight (1986) Musical tribute to the expatriate black-American jazz musicians who went to Paris to perform in the late 1950s. Director Bertrand Tavernier centers the story on the friendship between a tenor saxophonist (Dexter Gordon) and a young Frenchman (Francois Cluzet), deriving much charm and appeal by interweaving original jazz performances with allusions to the art, craft, and personalities of the period's jazz scene. Some harsh language. A-II (R)

Round-Up, The (1969) Hungarian production dramatizing the aftermath of the failed 1848 Revolution against the Austro-Hungarian empire and the ruthless repression of all who took part in it. Director Miklos Jancso's haunting black-and-white images of the prisoners' isolation and the pressures to betray others provide a strong experience of political oppression and conflicting national ambitions. Subtitles. Some physical, but mostly psychological, violence and brief nudity. A-IV (nr)

Rounders (1998) Flawed drama in which a card-shark becomes a law student (Matt Damon), then is lured back into illegal gambling when the life of his ex-con pal (Edward Norton) is threatened by huge poker debts. Despite Damon's taut performance, director John Dahl deals a losing hand with an unconvincing narrative drawn out to a weak conclusion. Fleeting violence, some sexual references, brief nudity, drug abuse, much rough language, and recurring profanity. A-IV (R)

Rounders, The (1965) Contemporary Western comedy in which two veteran cowpokes (Glenn Ford and Henry Fonda) spend the winter rounding-up strays for a miserly rancher (Chill Wills), then come to town with an unrideable roan horse with which they aim to make a fortune in the annual rodeo. Writer-director Burt Kennedy does best with the leisurely portrait of amiable yet diehard cowboys, but the flimsy story-line veers from the sentimental to the bogus, as in their encounter with a pair of would-be showgirls. Comic sexual situations. A-III (br)

Roustabout (1964) Minor star vehicle with Elvis Presley as a cynical, out-of-work singer hired by the owner (Barbara Stanwyck) of a struggling carnival, but he causes trouble when he falls for the daughter (Joan Freeman) of the outfit's mean manager (Leif Ericson). Directed by John Rich, the carnival background holds some interest, but the formula plot and the surly singer's redemption are strictly routine. A couple of fistfights and sexual innuendo. A-II (PG)

Roxanne (1987) Written and performed by Steve Martin, this contemporary version of Cyrano de Bergerac is an unfunny combination of slapstick, physical comedy, and perfunctory sexual tease. Director Fred Schepisi offers only a vanity production for a remarkably untalented Daryl Hannah, whose portrayal of young womanhood is caught between 1960s mindless love-child and a seductive Botticelli Venus. Slapstick violence, dumb jokes, and casual acceptance of premarital sex defeat any sense of romantic idealism. A-III (PG)

Royal African Rifles, The (1953) When a shipment of machine guns is stolen en route to British forces in East Africa at the start of World War I, the naval officer (Louis Hayward) from whom they were taken treks off into the jungle to get them before the Germans do. Directed by Lesley Selander, it's a minor adventure yarn with more talk than action, though an African corporal (Roy Glenn) proves the most interesting character. A-I (br)

Royal Flash (1975) Disappointing tongue-in-cheek adventure in which the English hero (Malcolm McDowell) incurs the wrath of Otto von Bismarck (Oliver Reed) and gets involved in the 19th-century maneuvering to unite the German states under the Prussian king. Directed by Richard Lester, the action drags and the humor is forced rather than inventive. Romantic situations and restrained violence. A-III (PG)

Royal Hunt of the Sun (1969) Disappointing screen version of Peter Shaffer's play about the clash of cultures when 16th-century Spanish adventurers under Pizarro (Robert Shaw) invaded the empire of the Incas ruled by Atahuallpa (Christopher Plummer). Directed by Irving Lerner, the narrative is little more than a series of encounters between the two principals who give highly mannered stage performances. A-III (G)

Royal Wedding (1951) Genial musical in which a brother-sister song-and-dance duo (Fred Astaire and Jane Powell) take their show to London on the eve of Queen Elizabeth II's wedding, then get caught up in the spirit of the occasion and find mates of their own in a dancer (Sarah Churchill) and an aristocrat (Peter Lawford). Directed by Stanley Donen, the lightweight plot is helped by some pleasant songs and agreeable dance numbers, but what's most memorable is the eye-popping sequence in which Astaire dances on the walls and ceiling of his hotel room. Romantic complications. A-II (br)

Ruby (1977) Murdered gangster comes back to haunt his killers, all of whom work at a Florida drive-in owned by the dead man's mistress (Piper Laurie). Directed by Curtis Harrington, the absurd and slipshod horror movie tries to shock with excessively violent and crude visual effects. O (R)

Ruby (1992) Fictional account of what Dallas nightclub owner Jack Ruby (Danny Aiello) knew of a conspiracy between the CIA and organized crime to assassinate President Kennedy. Director John MacKenzie re-creates the era well enough, but the script is of the wild-eyed variety. Stylized violence, sexual situations, drug-dealing, and rough language. A-III (R)

Ruby Gentry (1952) Hokey potboiler set in tidewater North Carolina, where a swamp girl (Jennifer Jones) is dumped by her ambitious boyriend (Charlton Heston), then marries the town's richest citizen (Karl Malden), whose death gives her the wealth to ruin her snooty detractors and try to win back the now-married boyfriend, with tragic results. Directed by King Vidor, the story of a woman wronged by social prejudices and her self-destructive revenge is highly contrived and mired in tawdry romantic complications. Stylized violence and sexual situations. A-III (br)

Ruby in Paradise (1993) Leaving the confines of rural Tennessee, a reflective young woman (Ashley Judd) becomes a store clerk in a Florida resort-town, where she struggles to maintain her independence despite the unwanted attentions of the store-owner's playboy son (Bentley Mitchum) and being romanced by a gentle nurseryman (Todd Field). Writer-director Victor Nunez' modest drama gradually explores the inner life of a solemn young woman, unsure she can survive on her own but unwilling to trust a knight in shining armor to take care of her. A few discreet bedroom scenes, brief shots of topless dancers, and a shoplifting incident. A-III (R)

Rudy (1993) Earnestly portrayed true story of Daniel Ruettiger (Sean Astin), a youth so determined to play football for Notre Dame in the '70s he overcame his slight physical stature, mediocre athletic ability, poor grades, and lack of emotional or financial support from his family to gain admission to the university and wear the uniform of the Fighting Irish. David Anspaugh's narrowly focused direction results in an inspirational but overly sentimental story in which one can admire the young man's bulldog tenacity, yet find the movie rather humorless. Numerous football field skirmishes. A-II (PG)

Rudyard Kipling's The Jungle Book (1994) Fanciful tale set in 19th-century India, where a young man (Jason Scott Lee), raised by animals when lost in the jungle as a child, falls in love with the engaged daughter (Lena Headey) of a British colonel (Sam Neill), then must rescue them from the villainy of her cunning fiancé (Cary Elwes), who's after a fabulous treasure buried in the jungle. Director Stephen Sommers fashions a fast-paced, nature-loving adventure from Kipling's short stories, despite some obvious overacting and stereotypical characters. Several intense scenes of danger involving wild animals and gunfire. A-II (PG)

Rudyard Kipling's The Second Jungle Book: Mowgli and Baloo (1997) The live-action adventures of Mowgli (Jamie Williams), Kipling's wild boy of 1890s India, involve an American (Bill Campbell) who wants to bring him back as a P.T. Barnum circus attraction, his evil uncle (Gulshan Grover) who wants to kill him, a dotty old solider (Roddy McDowall), and a variety of jungle animals, some friendly, some murderous, and others given to monkeyshines. Directed by Duncan McLachlan, the jungle action-fantasy does well with the wonders of nature, but the plot meanders fitfully along until the boy's harrowing escapes in a lost city for the story's big but bumpy finish. Many scenes of menace, some quite frightening, and occasional slapstick violence. A-II (PG)

Ruggles of Red Gap (1935) Droll tale of a British butler (Charles Laughton) transplanted to the Wild West after an American cattle-baron (Charlie Ruggles) wins his services in a poker game with an English lord (Roland Young). Director Leo McCarey pokes fun at the social pretensions of the newly rich cattleman's wife (Mary Boland), while centering the comedy on Laughton's gradual transformation from straitlaced servant to red-blooded frontier patriot. The comic situation and performances hold up better than the sentimental theme. A-I (br)

Rugrats Movie, The (1998) Animated tale based on the children's TV series in which five frisky toddlers get lost in a scary forest while trying to return the crybaby infant brother of one of them to the baby hospital. Directors Norton Virgien and Igor Kovalyov have the tykes survive assorted dangers and misadventures as they discover the meaning of friendship and helping the helpless. A-I (G)

Rulers of the Sea (1939) Dated but watchable story of how a sea captain (Douglas Fairbanks, Jr.) and a machinist (Will Fyffe) join forces in making the first steamship crossing of the Atlantic in 1838. Director Frank Lloyd shows how the hazards and uncertainties of voyages under sail caused merchants to back the development of a steam-driven vessel, though the characters involved in its achievement are sentimentalized in standard Hollywood fashion. A-I (br)

Ruling Class, The (1972) Screen version of Peter Barnes's play satirizing the British upper classes in a story about the demented Earl of Gurney (Peter O'Toole in a madcap virtuoso performance) who, once he is cured of believing he is God, assumes the identity of Jack the Ripper. Directed by Peter Medak, the loony black comedy even has some hilarious song and dance numbers, but the nonsense goes on much too long and becomes repetitive. Some may take the casebook condition of claiming to be the deity as irreverent, but religion is not at all under attack here. A-IV (PG)

Rumble Fish (1983) Failed screen version of a C.E. Hinton novel, with Matt Dillon giving an overwrought Brando imitation as a teenager trying to live up to the bad reputation of his brother (Mickey Rourke) and drunken father (Dennis Hopper). Director Francis Ford Coppola's confusing portrait of a youth struggling to regain self-esteem is marred by gang-war violence, some nudity, and brief but graphic sex. O (R)

Rumble in the Bronx (1996) Inane action flick

about a Chinese martial-arts expert (Jackie Chan) who runs into a dangerous biker gang while visiting New York, and ends up persuading them to help him foil a big diamond robbery. Directed by Stanley Tong, the lame script is an uneasy blend of Chan's slapstick-brand of martial arts with more realistic bone-crunching confrontations. Recurring violence, fleeting nudity, and several instances of rough language. A-III (R)

Run (1991) A resourceful law student (Patrick Dempsey) flees for his life, pursued by the mob and corrupt cops, after being innocently involved in the death of the son of a gang leader (Ken Pogue). Director Geoff Burrowes delivers a fast track of action and suspense abetted by Dempsey's winning performance and the movie's gallows humor. Considerable violence in a realistic, non-gratuitous context, and minimal rough language. A-IV (R)

Run After Me — Until I Catch You (1979) Soggy French farce about the owner of a canine beauty-parlor (Annie Girardot) and her romance with a tax collector (Jean-Pierre Marielle). Director Robert Pouret makes a feeble attempt to show that middle-aged people can be as romantic, foolish, and funny as any other age group. Adult situations. A-III (PG)

Run Before the Wind (1972) New York art director (Jean Yves) races a sailboat from San Francisco to Tokyo in a semi-documentary that captures the breathtaking ocean vistas and challenging duties of the 6,000-mile contest. Written, produced, and directed by Brud Talbot, the movie becomes exploitation fare by punctuating the voyage with a series of sexually graphic daydreams. O (R)

Run for Cover (1955) Disappointing Western in which an ex-con (James Cagney) becomes the sheriff of a small town, earns the love of a good woman (Viveca Lindfors), then is betrayed by the crippled youth (John Derek) he's dedicated himself to helping. Directed by Nicholas Ray, the contrived action and thin characterizations give little conviction to the scenario's theme of misplaced loyalties and corrupted innocence. Frontier violence with murky themes. A-III (br)

Run for the Sun (1956) Exotic chase-thriller about an author-adventurer (Richard Widmark) and a journalist (Jane Greer) whose plane crashes in a Mexican jungle, where they are rescued by fugitive Nazis (Trevor Howard and Peter Van Eyck) from whom they try to escape. Director Roy Boulting spends too much time setting up the premise, but once the couple flee into the jungle, the proceedings become quite harrowing. Stylized violence and much tension. A-II (br)

Run of the Arrow (1957) After the Civil War, an unreconstructed rebel (Rod Steiger) moves West, joins a Sioux tribe (whose chief is Charles Bronson), and tries to avert a war with Army troops (led by Ralph Meeker). Written, produced, and directed by Samuel Fuller, the ambitious scenario is largely unrealized on the screen, partly because of its disjointed treatment of themes including regional rivalries, Native American tribalism, and the foibles of ordinary people. Much stylized violence, some of it quite bloody. A-II (br)

Run of the Country, The (1995) Dark coming-of-age story in which an 18-year-old Irish lad (Matt Keeslar) quarrels with his policeman father (Albert Finney), moves in with a rural roughneck (Anthony Brophy), and gets a girl (Victoria Smurfit) pregnant, before finally taking some tentative steps towards maturity. Directed by Peter Yates, the adolescent's eccentric misadventures mix comedy with tragedy, but the depiction of growing up on the border with the North is too fragmented to add up to a convincing whole. Some violence, strong sexual situations, brief nudity, occasional profanity, and rough language. A-IV (R)

Run the Wild River (1971) Shooting the rapids in huge, rubber pontoons is a rugged way to find adventure, the challenge here taking the form of a river in southern Mexico that had never been run before. The thrills are real enough, with boats bouncing off rocks and swirling in the foaming waters, but too much footage is devoted to travelogue excursions into the surrounding countryside to pad out a documentary short into a full-length feature. A-I (nr)

Run Wild, Run Free (1969) British story in which a mute country-child (Mark Lester) is befriended by a retired Army officer (John Mills), who teaches him to train a falcon and tame a wild colt, with predictable but quite satisfying results. Directed by Richard C. Sarafian, the story has appeal for adults as well as children both for its human qualities and the delights of nature. A-I (G)

Runaround, The (1946) Hired to find a millionaire's eloping daughter, a private detective (Rod Cameron) has his hands full trying to bring the protesting woman (Ella Raines) back home while eluding his former boss (Broderick Crawford), who wants the reward for himself. Directed by Charles Lamont, the cross-country romance is secondary to the comic flimflam between the rival detectives, with a trick ending appropriate to the title. Stylized violence and mild romance. A-II (br)

Runaway (1984) Silly science-fiction vehicle for Tom Selleck, who plays a futuristic cop on the runaway squad, a branch of the police force assigned to corralling robots that have run amok. Directed by Michael Crichton, its unintentionally funny high-tech mayhem provides passable entertainment for action fans. Some violence and brief nudity. A-III (PG-13)

Runaway Train (1985) Alaskan train, whose steely-black locomotive is hurtling out of control, carries two escaped convicts (Jon Voight and Eric Roberts) along with a napping railroad-worker (Rebecca DeMornay). Directed by Andrei Konchalovsky and based on a screenplay by Akira Kurosawa, something has been lost in the translation. Senseless plot, excessive violence, and coarse language. O (R)

Runner Stumbles, The (1979) Fact-based story of a gifted but morose pastor (Dick Van Dyke) of a small-town parish in the 1920s, who is accused of murdering a young nun (Kathleen Quinlan) to whom he had shown special attention. Director Stanley Kramer delicately tries to avoid the sensational, but its superficial treatment of the Catholic context, sketchy characterizations, and a bizarre climax add up to a disappointing muddle. Because it deals with the emotional involvement of a priest and nun under extremely melodramatic circumstances, it is mature viewing fare that some may find distasteful. A-IV (PG)

Running (1979) Aging marathon-runner (Michael Douglas), who has a reputation for choking up in the clutch both in running and in life, resolves to vindicate himself and win back his estranged wife (Susan Anspach) by making it to the Olympics. Directed by Steven Hillard Stern, the grimly determined athlete featured in the foreground proves less compelling than the pageantry of Montreal's Olympics in the background. Some foul language. A-III (PG)

Running Man, The (1963) Halting suspense story in which an English pilot (Laurence Harvey) fakes his death, then rejoins his wife (Lee Remick) in Spain after she collects the insurance money, but they fear arrest when the insurance agent (Alan Bates) who investigated the claim turns up. Director Carol Reed makes good use of colorful Spanish locations to pace a cat-and-mouse tale that never measures up to its potential. Menacing situations and an implied sexual encounter. A-III (br)

Running on Empty (1988) After injuring a janitor in college bombing as a protest against the Vietnam War, a couple (Judd Hirsch and Christine Lahti) have been on the run from the FBI for 15 years, but problems arise when their 17-year-old son (River Phoenix) wants to go to college and lead a normal life under his own identity. Director Sidney Lumet presents a universal family crisis within the context of an unusual family whose children have been forced to carry the burden of their parents' crime of conscience. Rough language and an implied teenage sexual liaison. A-III (R)

Running Scared (1986) Director Peter Hyams's rough-edged action comedy about veteran Chicago undercover cops (Billy Crystal and Gregory Hines) making their last drug-bust before early retirement to the good life in Key West is waylaid by violence, harsh language, brief nudity, and ethnic stereotyping. O (R)

Rush (1991) Two romantically involved cops in a narcotics unit (Jennifer Jason Leigh and Jason Patric) use drugs to protect their cover as junkies, then struggle with addiction and their superiors' illegal demands to frame a suspect (Gregg Allman). Novice director Lili Fini Zanuck presents a gritty, harrowing look at the drug netherworld and the moral ambiguities of the war against drugs. Graphic shots of drug abuse, occasional violence including a suicide, brief bedroom scenes with a flash of nudity, and frequent rough language. A-IV (R)

Rush Hour (1998) Mindless action tale of a cocky Los Angeles police detective (Chris Tucker) forced to team with a Chinese cop (Jackie Chan) when the Chinese Consul's young daughter is kidnapped by Asia's top crime-lord. Director Brett Ratner depicts the deadly menace and brutal violence as exciting and the kind of jokey fun that has no consequences. Recurring violence, nasty menace to a child, a few racial slurs, and intermittent profanity. O (PG-13)

Rushmore (1998) Offbeat comedy about a hyperactive 15-year-old (Jason Schwartzman) whose crush on a widowed schoolteacher (Olivia Williams) leads him to extremes in trying to stop his closest friend, a married millionaire (Bill Murray), from romancing her. Directed by Wes Anderson, the bittersweet tale of teenage angst is helped by performances which aptly blend humor with pathos as the youth learns about rejection and forgiveness. Brief violence, an implied affair, a few crass sexual references, and a flash of nude pin-ups, a scene of underage drinking, occasional rough language, and minimal profanity. A-III (R)

Russia House, The (1990) A Russian woman (Michelle Pfeiffer) sends a politically sensitive manuscript written by her former lover (Klaus Maria Brandauer) to a British publisher (Sean Connery) who falls for her while checking out the document's authenticity for Allied intelligence agencies. Director Fred Schepisi's version of the John le Carre novel lacks a sense of urgency and the romance is flat, leaving only Connery's performance and scenic Russian locations to hold interest. Mild sexual innuendo and occasional rough language. A-III (R)

Russian Adventure (1966) Picturesque Russian travelogue showing scenes of cities and countryside, the Bolshoi Ballet and the Moscow State Circus, but anyone hoping to learn more about what life in the Soviet Union is like will be disappointed. A-I (br)

Russian Roulette (1975) Mediocre Canadian melodrama about the attempted assassination of a Soviet leader visiting Vancouver in which a Mountie (George Segal) becomes the unwitting tool of both Russian and Canadian counter-intelligence. Directed by Lou Lombardo, the plot is too convoluted for its own good, but it's diverting, especially the lovely location photography. Some violence. A-III (PG)

Russians Are Coming, the Russians Are Coming, The (1966) Inspired farce built around the accidental grounding of a Russian submarine off the coast of Cape Cod. Producer-director Norman Jewison ably handles a fine cast including Alan Arkin, Carl Reiner, Eva Marie Saint, Jonathan Winters, and Paul Ford. The movie's satire can be appreciated at several levels and will be enjoyed by the whole family. A-I (br)

Rustler's Rhapsody (1985) Spoof of the singing cowboy movies, written and directed by Hugh Wilson and starring Tom Berenger, starts out promisingly enough, but soon goes flat. A-II (PG)

Ruthless (1948) Trite account of how an impoverished youth (Zachary Scott) rises to great wealth by exploiting friends (Louis Hayward and Diana Lynn) and crushing business rivals (notably Sidney Greenstreet). Directed by Edgar G. Ulmer, the story of a man who loses his soul in material pursuits has an obvious moral, but it's too contrived to be convincing. A career built on betrayal and deceit, including marital infidelity. A-III (br)

Ruthless People (1986) Corrupt garment-industry magnate (Danny DeVito) is delighted when his wife (Bette Midler) is kidnapped by a couple (Helen Slater and Judge Reinhold) he has wronged, but the three become friends and hatch a scheme to ruin the magnate. The hostility and profanity in this movie directed by Jim Abrahams, David Zucker, and Jerry Zucker is excessive, and the use of nudity in a sight gag in a movie produced by the Disney subsidiary Touchstone virtually defiles the memory of the man whose name is synonymous with family entertainment. O (R)

Ryan's Daughter (1970) Rural Irish schoolteacher Robert Mitchum marries simmering Sarah Miles, who later develops a mad passion for British officer Christopher Jones in a huge, sweeping drama set along the ruggedly beautiful coast of Dingle during the explosive time of the 1916 Easter Rebellion. Written by Robert Bolt and directed by David Lean, the story of political upheaval and lustful passions has village pastor Trevor Howard as a figure of reconciliation. The result proves a rather confused moral drama on a theme of adultery. Stylized violence and brief nudity. A-III (PG/R)

Ryder P.I. (1986) Inept, humorless parody of a TV detective-show starring Bob Nelson relies on silliness and gross humor for a few laughs. Sexually derived vulgarities pervade the sophomoric narrative. A-III (PG-13)

S

S.O.B. (1981) Hollywood producer (Richard Mulligan) attempts to transform his multi-million dollar flop into a box-office winner by persuading its star, who's also his wife (Julie Andrews), to forsake her wholesome screen image and bare her breasts on camera. Directed by Blake Edwards, the satiric comedy has some very funny moments, but they do not soften the movie's basically cynical outlook and amoral perspective which exploits its audience in the same way as the moviemakers it criticizes. Some sequences involving nudity. O (R)

S*P*Y*S (1974) Failed comedy with Elliott Gould and Donald Sutherland as inept CIA agents who, after fouling up a defection by murdering two Russian agents, are on the run as marked men sought by both sides. Blankly directed by Irvin Kershner, the comedy is low, witless, and frequently tasteless. A-III (PG)

SSSSSSSS (1973) Unpretentious thriller about a rather nice but quite mad zoologist (Strother Martin) who is working on a serum to transform people into snakes because reptiles, being cold-blooded, will not be affected when pollution shrouds earth from the sun. Director Bernard Kowalski capitalizes on Martin's fondly dotty performance rather than his experiments with deadly cobras. Viewers with a phobia for snakes should be warned away, but the less squeamish will find it an engaging, at times witty, entertainment. A-III (PG)

Sabata (1970) Sharp-eyed marksman (Lee Van Cleef) wipes out a couple of hundred baddies in record time in this tongue-in-cheek Italian Western directed by Frank Kramer. Superficially little above the cartoon level of derring-do, what makes it fun is the skill with which its stunts are conceived and executed and the wry wit with which it regards its own shaggy story. Stylized violence. A-III (GP)

Saboteur (1942) Accused of sabotage, a war plant-worker (Robert Cummings) flees the police to hunt down the real culprit (Norman Lloyd). and, with the help of a spunky blonde (Priscilla Lane), traps him atop the Statue of Liberty. Director Alfred Hitchcock's uneven thriller delivers the usual goosebumps as the cross-country chase leads to a homegrown nest of spies (led by Otto Kruger), though the proceedings are slowed by much wartime flag-waving. More menace than violence. A-II (br)

Saboteur, Code Name Morituri, The (see: **Morituri**)

Sabre and the Arrow, The (see: **Last of the Comanches**)

Sabrina (1995) Gauzy romantic fantasy in which a workaholic billionaire (Harrison Ford) falls in love with his chauffeur's daughter (Julia Ormond) while trying to distract her from an infatuation with his engaged brother (Greg Kinnear). Director Sydney Pollack's long but lush re-make of the 1954 Audrey Hepburn version is featherweight fluff laboriously plumped up with contrived romantic emotions. Fleeting violence and very mild sexual references. A-II (PG)

Sacco & Vanzetti (1971) European co-production about two Italian immigrants, cobbler Sacco (Riccardo Cucciolla) and fishmonger Vanzetti (Gian Maria Volonte), who were convicted of murder and, despite protests that this was a miscarriage of justice, executed in 1927 by the State of Massachusetts. Director Giuliano Montaldo centers not on the question of their guilt but on the judicial process in a trial tainted by prejudice and perjury because of the pair's anarchist views. The mostly courtroom dramatization is uneven, but much of it works extremely well. Accessible for most older teenagers. A-III (GP)

Sacrifice, The (1986) Swedish production in which a group of adults and one child pass through a night of confusion and fear, including portents of a nuclear-devastated landscape. Director Andrei Tarkovsky's murky religious allegory about an aging writer's bargaining with God to save others relies upon long silences, ritualized dialogue, and beautiful but static photography. Subtitles. A very personal film about love and compassion, its effect is strangely cold and distant. A-III (PG)

Saddle the Wind (1958) Gassy psychological Western in which a reformed gunfighter (Robert Taylor) is forced into a final showdown with his wild kid-brother (John Cassavetes). Directed by Robert Parrish, the sibling rivalry adds little to an otherwise standard plot that is scant on outdoor action. Stylized violence. A-II (br)

Saddles and Sagebrush (1943) Grade-B Western with Russell Hayden as a straight-shooter who sides with homesteaders against a cattle baron's hired guns. Director William Berke paces the formula action plot with the singing of Bob Wills and Dub Taylor's comic relief. Stylized violence. A-I (br)

Safari (1956) Pale adventure in which a big-game hunter (Victor Mature) guides a nasty British aristocrat (Roland Culver) and his shapely American fiancé (Janet Leigh) into the Kenyan bush to bag a lion, then are beset by Mau Mau terrorists. Directed by Terence Young, the story tries to mesh hunting scenes and campfire romance with colonial politics and period atrocities, with unconvincing results. Stylized violence and romantic complications. A-II (br)

Safe (1995) Convinced she's being harmed by chemicals in the air, a physically and emotionally frail California housewife (Julianne Moore) leaves her baffled husband (Xander Berkeley) for treatment at a New Age complex in the desert, where she seeks to renew her sense of self. Writer-director Todd Haynes's spare and snail-paced tale is largely uninvolving, since the key character remains a blank, though the narrative raises concerns about environmentally caused illness. Discreet marital encounter and minimal rough language. A-III (R)

Safe Passage (1994) A middle-aged woman (Susan Sarandon) is joined by her estranged husband (Sam Shepard) and six grown sons when a seventh son, a Marine in the Mideast, is reported missing after a terrorist bombing and, while awaiting further news, vent long-standing familial frustrations. Although director Robert Allan Ackerman's earnest kitchen-sink drama deals with numerous prickly personal problems and family relationships, its doggedly glum tone and lethargic pacing blunt its examination of the enduring strength of family ties. Several sexual references, brief recreational drug use, occasional profanity, and minimal rough language. A-III (PG-13)

Safe Place, A (1971) Tuesday Weld plays a New Yorker who spends most of her time in and around Central Park, remembering her past and fantasizing about the present, though no reason is ever indicated why this young woman is so tied to her childhood. Written and directed by Henry Jaglom, the movie has no substance beyond its self-conscious attempt to reflect the way a disoriented mind copes with the passage of time. A-III (GP)

Saga of Death Valley (1940) Years after his father's murder, a cowboy (Roy Rogers) avenges his death and finds his long-lost kid brother in a low-budget but effective Western directed by Joseph Kane. Unpretentious action fare with frontier violence. A-I (br)

Saga of Hemp Brown, The (1958) Sluggish Western directed by Richard Carlson in which an Army officer (Rory Calhoun) is court-martialed for losing the post payroll to outlaws, then gets some help from a showgirl (Beverly Garland) in tracking down the man (John Larch) who stole it. Frontier violence. A-I (br)

Sahara (1943) Sturdy WW II melodrama follows an American tank-commander (Humphrey Bogart) as he picks up an international cast of survivors (Rex Ingram, J. Carrol Naish, Kurt Kreuger, etc.) to make a stand at a waterhole in the desert war against Rommel. Directed by Zoltan Korda, the action is as uncomplicated as the tone is patriotic, with good ensemble acting and a big finish. Wartime violence. A-I (br)

Sail a Crooked Ship (1962) Witless comedy directed by Irving Brecher in which a bankrobber (Ernie Kovacs) and accomplices (Frank Gorshin and Carolyn Jones) try to make a getaway in a broken-down cargo ship, shanghaiing those aboard (Robert Wagner, Delores Hart, and Frankie Avalon) in the process. Comic crime-caper with considerable sexual innuendo. A-III (br)

Sailor Beware (1951) Feeble Dean Martin-Jerry Lewis comedy in which the boys join the Navy, train in San Diego, and ship out on a submarine to Honolulu, where Lewis wins a bet by kissing Corinne Calvet. Director Hal Walker's remake of **The Fleet's In** (1942) is mainly flat and mostly unamusing, with Lewis especially grating in exaggerated routines only fans may find funny. Mild sexual innuendo. A-I (br)

Sailor of the King (1953) Escaping from captivity on a German raider when it anchors at a remote island for repairs, a Canadian sharpshooter (Jeffrey Hunter) wins the Victoria Cross by pinning down its crew with rifle fire until the British Navy arrives. C.S. Forester's intriguing story of naval action and personal courage in WW II suffers from Roy Boulting's pedestrian direction and a romantic subplot involving the lad's parents (Wendy Hiller and Michael Rennie). Wartime violence and discreet treatment of a premarital relationship. A-II (br)

Sailor Who Fell from Grace with the Sea, The (1976) Failed adaptation of Yukio Mishima's novel in which a sailor (Kris Kristofferson) decides to give up the sea and marry a wealthy widow (Sarah Miles), but a gang of schoolboys take drastic action to prevent him from betraying his manly career. Writer-director Lewis John Carlino has turned this into a glossy, sentimental love story ruined by a bunch of rotten kids. Ludicrous, excessive sex scenes. O (R)

Saint, The (1997) The updated title character of the Leslie Charteris mysteries of the 1930s is a sly thief (Val Kilmer) who assumes numerous identities in trying to save one of his intended victims (Elizabeth Shue) from a power-mad Russian seeking her revolutionary energy-formula. Directed by Philip Noyce, the action story is slickly produced and provides undemanding escapist entertainment, although the one-dimensional characters are less than engaging. Some stylized violence, implied affairs, and an instance of profanity. A-III (PG-13)

Saint in London, The (1939) Enjoyable series entry with Simon Templar (George Sanders) returning to London to help the British secret service nab an espionage ring before it escapes with a fortune in the new currency of a foreign government. Directed by John Paddy Carstairs and filmed in England, the twisty plot is played more for humor than suspense, and the mix of British and American character actors proves surprisingly congenial. Stylized violence. A-I (br)

Saint in New York, The (1938) Breezy crime caper with Leslie Charteris's crime-fighting Englishman, Simon Templar (Louis Heyward), summoned to Manhattan to stop a crime wave, which he briskly does by nabbing Mr. Big with the help of a mystery woman (Kay Sutton). Directed by Ben Holmes, the first in the series has some dapper humor, a lot of narrow escapes, several killings, and a little romance. Stylized underworld violence, with vigilante overtones. A-II (br)

Saint in Palm Springs, The (1941) Weak series entry directed by Jack Hively in which the reformed gentleman crook of the title (George Sanders) gets help from a former pickpocket (Paul Guilfoyle) in protecting the owner (Wendy Barrie) of three extremely rare postage-stamps from a ruthless gang of thieves. Stylized violence. A-I (br)

Saint Jack (1979) Screen version of the Paul Theroux novel about an expatriate American (Ben Gazzara) who makes his way with flare and humor as a procurer in modern-day Singapore but balks at blackmailing a visiting US senator. Director Peter Bogdanovich's rather thin and slow-paced melodrama shows far too benign an attitude toward the hero's character and profession, and it also has one quite suggestive sequence. O (R)

Saint Joan (1957) Screen version of George Bernard Shaw's play about the French heroine (Jean Seberg) whose voices led her to take up arms for her king against the English, who put her to death as a heretic. Adapted by Graham Greene and directed by Otto Preminger, the result is flat and static, but Shaw's jabs at authority, secular and religious, emerge often enough to make it interesting. A-II (br)

Saint Meets the Tiger, The (1943) Weak series entry set in England, where debonair crime-fighter Simon Templar (miscast Hugh Sinclair) tangles with a gang of gold smugglers operating in Cornwall. Directed by Paul Stein, the British cast give game performances in hackneyed roles, with the thin script providing little challenge either for them or the audience. Stylized violence. A-I (br)

Saint of Fort Washington, The (1993) Impoverished Vietnam vet (Danny Glover) and the fragile, schizophrenic youth (Matt Dillon) he has befriended plan to rent a small apartment by washing car windshields until victimized by a vicious thug (Ving Rhames) who preys on New York City's homeless. Director Tim Hunter's realistic portrait of homeless men trying to reestablish themselves is heartbreaking, but the characters are simplistically portrayed as angels or devils. Brief violence and some rough language. A-II (R)

Saint Strikes Back, The (1939) Routine crime caper directed by John Farrow with the sardonic crime-buster (George Sanders) in San Francisco tangling with a safecracker (Barry Fitzgerald), a criminologist (Jerome Cowen) and others while helping a desperate women (Wendy Barrie) clear her late father's name. The usual stylized violence and romantic posturing. A-II (br)

Saint Takes Over, The (1940) Twisty crime-series mystery directed by Jack Hively in which the title crime-fighter (George Sanders) sets out to prove a police pal (Jonathan Hale) was framed on a bribery rap by a gang of racetrack fixers, but matters get complicated when the gang begins to be murdered one by one. Stylized violence and romantic situations. A-II (br)

Saint's Double Trouble, The (1940) Cheery but convoluted crime caper directed by Jack Hively, with George Sanders in the dual role of crime-buster Simon Templar and a lookalike Philadelphia crime boss whose confederate (Bela Lugosi) has hidden stolen gems in the wrappings of an Egyptian mummy. The stylized violence includes a couple of murders and some menacing moments. A-I (br)

Saint's Vacation, The (1941) Change of pace for the mystery series in a story directed by Leslie Fenton, with Hugh Sinclair playing the role as a very English Simon Templar on holiday in France, where he comes into possession of a box whose secret is sought by a cunning spy (Cecil Parker) as well as the head of British intelligence (Felix Aylmer). The usual stylized violence. A-I (br)

Salaam Bombay! (1988) After coming to Bombay to earn the 500 rupees needed by his mother to pay a debt, a 10-year-old country lad struggles to keep from being swallowed up in the sordid slums of an overcrowded city. Directed with warm humanity and some humor by Mira Nair, her work manages to avoid both sentimentality and cynicism in relating a sympathetic tale of hope amidst squalor and injustice. Though the subtitled movie affirms the human dignity of India's poor and homeless, there are several restrained scenes in a brothel, a few drug transactions, and some violence, including a knifing. A-II (nr)

Salesman (1969) Documentary showing the day-to-day life of four door-to-door Bible salesmen who work the Boston area and then start a campaign in Florida. It is not about the commercialization of religion or the tricks of the trade, though viewers will see a little bit of both. It is essentially about the effect of this trade upon these individuals and their relations with others. Directed by Albert and David Maysles, it is a rare picture of people seen through the perspective of their line of work. A-II (G)

Sallah (1965) Israeli comedy about a Jewish immigrant from the Orient (Haym Topol) who outsmarts the bureaucratic system in its attempts to integrate him and his large family into their new community. Writer-director Ephraim Kishon has created a highly amusing satire that succeeds best with its outrageous sight gags and Topol's larger-than-life performance in the title role as the wily alien. Subtitles. A-II (nr)

Sally and Saint Anne (1952) Sentimental hokum about an Irish-American family whose bedridden grandfather (Edmund Gwenn) finally bests their greedy landlord (John McIntire), with some help from his granddaughter (Ann Blyth) and her saintly patron. Directed by Rudolph Maté, the halting story and stereotyped characters add up to bogus proceedings made even worse by attempting to add an inspirational note to the failed enterprise. Hokey romantic complications. A-I (br)

Salo (1977) Italian sex-fantasy directed by Pier Paolo Pasolini set in the Fascist state during the final days of WW II, when four officials decide to finish their lives by perversely victimizing a group of boys and girls rounded up by their thuggish guards. O (nr)

Salome (1953) Fanciful biblical charade in which the title character (Rita Hayworth) dances for Herod (Charles Laughton), who rewards her mother, Herodias (Judith Anderson), with the head of John the Baptist (Alan Badel), after which Salome walks off with her centurion lover (Stewart Granger) to follow the Nazarene. Directed by William Dieterle, the contrived proceedings are colorful but have little to do with the Gospel account, and Hayworth's performance is lovely to look at but is unconvincing as a dramatic character. Stylized violence, sexual situations, and lusty innuendo. A-III (br)

Salome, Where She Danced (1945) Ludicrous romantic adventure in which an Austrian dancer (Yvonne De Carlo) caught spying on the Prussians escapes to 1868 San Francisco with the help of a US newsman (Rod Cameron), then complicates her chance for stardom by falling for a Western outlaw (David Bruce). Directed by Charles Lamont, the absurd proceedings are played straight, which makes them unintentionally comic, but no less dim. Stylized violence and dance sequences more silly than provocative. A-III (br)

Salome's Last Dance (1988) In yet another of his flamboyant films about eccentric artists, writer-director Ken Russell zeroes in on Oscar Wilde (Nicholas Grace), who watches as his friends (Imogene Millais-Scott, Stratford Johns, and Glenda Jackson) stage a performance of his banned play "Salome." Wall-to-wall nudity, rough language of a sexual nature, and much implied and some exhibited sexual activity. O (R)

Salsa (1988) Latino-dance movie about a young Puerto Rican-American (Robby Rosa) who dreams of winning a local salsa contest in East Los Angeles, but is distracted by the social blossoming of his teenage sister (Magali Alvarado) and by his new partner (Miranda Garrison). Director Boaz Davidson's minimal plot and weak acting are overshadowed by dazzling salsa numbers choreographed by Kenny Ortega. Some sexually suggestive dancing inappropriate for children or younger adolescents. A-II (PG)

Salt and Pepper (1968) Witless British espionage spoof about night-club owners (Sammy Davis Jr. and Peter Lawford) who get mixed up in a plot against the government. Directed by Richard Donner, the mostly unfunny proceedings depend largely on sexually oriented dialogue and situations. O (G)

Salut Cousin! (1997) The seriocomic adventures of an Algerian youth (Gad Elmaleh) on a trip to Paris revolve around his sometimes bizarre experiences with his aspiring rap-singer cousin (Mess Hattou), an encounter with skinheads, visits with Algerian expatriates, and his unexpected romance with a black woman (Magaly Berdy). Directed by Merzak Allouache, the movie looks at Paris through Algerian eyes showing the cultural conflicts between the innocent visitor and his urbanized cousin, while also reflecting the abhorrence of Algeria's Islamic terrorists. Subtitles. A sexual situation, brief nudity, rough language and a profanity. A-III (nr)

Salut L'Artiste (1976) Charming French trifle directed by Yves Robert about a second-rate actor (Marcello Mastroianni), who thinks his Italian accent robs him of good roles, and his mistress (Francoise Fabian), who knows his frailties only too well. Incidental nudity. A-IV (nr)

Salvador (1987) Out-of-work photojournalist (James Woods) takes his buddy (James Belushi) on a trek to Latin America for fun and games, but finds instead the harsh realities of civil war and militarism's reckless disregard for the value of human life. Profuse profanity and extensive depiction of war atrocities make director Oliver Stone's political essay palatable only for the thick-skinned and tough-minded. A-IV (R)

Salzburg Connection, The (1972) Fitful screen version of a Helen MacInnes novel of international intrigue, as various agents (Barry Newman, Karen Jensen, and Klaus-Maria Brandauer) vie to find a chest containing the names of WW II Nazi collaborators hidden on the bottom of a sinister Alpine lake. Directed by Lee Katzin, aside from some sparkling but occasionally violent action sequences, the escapist adventure has little but the beautiful setting of Salzburg and the surrounding Austrian Alps to recommend it. A-III (PG)

Sam Whiskey (1969) Angie Dickinson tries to protect the family name by seducing Burt Reynolds into retrieving some gold bars stolen by her dead husband and returning them to the US Mint before the theft is discovered. Directed by Arnold Laven, the movie's sense of morality displays the same lightheadedness as that of the heroine. Some nudity. O (PG)

Sam's Son (1985) Hollywood producer returns to his hometown for a premiere and recalls his loving father, who always had faith in him. Writer-director Michael Landon's first feature is very sentimental, unabashedly uplifting entertainment and succeeds in large part because of some good acting. A-II (PG)

Sambizanga (1973) Effective Angolan-made drama about the colonial injustices that led to their struggle for independence from Portuguese rule, as seen in the story of a wife's search for her husband, taken by the police in a dawn raid on their village. Directed by Sarah Maldoror, it is a sophisticated study of simple people, oppressed but beginning to learn the possibility of alternatives. The enemy is presented as colonialism and not race (whites are among the revolutionaries and blacks among the police). A-II (nr)

Same Time, Next Year (1978) Screen version of Bernard Slade's slick comedy of extramarital bliss, in which an accountant from New Jersey (Alan Alda) meets a demure housewife (Ellen Burstyn) at a California seaside resort in 1951, and they begin an affair that continues for the next 26 years, limited to a single weekend each year. Directed by Robert Mulligan, there is a moderate amount of cleverness and amusing lines, but, though the fantasy-level of the proceedings makes somewhat less offensive the condoning of this particular brand of adultery, there remains something intrinsically offensive about the premise of the movie. O (PG)

Samson and Delilah (1949) Flatfooted biblical epic from producer-director Cecil B. DeMille lumbers along, with Victor Mature rarely credible as the Israelite hero, Hedy Lamarr less than subtle as the pagan seductress, and a labored spectacle hardly worth the effort. Stylized violence and sexual innuendo. A-II (br)

San Antone (1953) Meandering Western in which a Texas rancher (Rod Cameron) takes a herd of cattle into Mexico to ransom some ex-Rebs being held by a guerrilla leader (Rodolfo Acosta) fighting Maximillian because one of them is the coward (Forrest Tucker) who killed his father at the end of the Civil War. Directed by Joseph Kane, the colorful proceedings also include a spiteful Texas belle (Arleen Whelan) who tries to break up the rancher's romance with the rebel's sister (Katy Jurado). Stylized violence, romantic complications, and ethnic bigots. A-II (br)

San Antonio (1945) Routine Western in which a Texas cowboy (Errol Flynn) falls for a saloon singer (Alexis Smith), then gets the goods on the crooked saloon-owner (Victor Francen) and a corrupt land agent (Paul Kelly). Directed by David Butler, the formula plot is helped by a well-mounted production and a picturesque nighttime shootout in the Alamo for the climax. Frontier violence and mild sexual innuendo. A-II (br)

San Francisco (1936) Robust romantic melodrama set on the eve of 'Frisco's 1906 earthquake, as Barbary Coast saloon-owner Clark Gable vies with Nob Hill swell Jack Holt for the affections of opera singer Jeanette MacDonald, with local priest Spencer Tracy trying to safeguard her best interests. Director W.S. Van Dyke II's colorful period piece has a grand cast in a formula plot whose romantic complications are resolved and ennobled by the quake's destructive magnitude in a finale that still ranks among the most memorable of screen disasters. Not especially suited for children, though enduring, old-fashioned entertainment for the rest of the family. A-I (br)

San Quentin (1946) Predictable crime story directed by Gordon M. Douglas has an ex-con (Lawrence Tierney) jeopardizing his parole in order to save a prison-reform program by tracking down an escaped con (Barton MacLane) who used it to make his getaway. Criminal menace and stylized violence. A-II (br)

Sand Pebbles, The (1966) Steve McQueen stars as a hard-bitten member of the crew of an American gunboat assigned to Chinese waters in 1926 to protect US commercial interests by its presence during a time of social and political unrest. Director Robert Wise manages to sustain interest and suspense almost to the end of this convoluted epic, which is mostly a serious, sometimes grim study of the causes and effects of intervention by one country in the affairs of another. Some rather intense violence. A-III (M)

Sandakan 8 (1977) Japanese movie about a feminist (Komaki Kurihara) researching the life of an old woman (Kinuyo Tanaka) who as a girl had been sold into prostitution at the beginning of the century. Director Kei Kumai has made a work of some cultural and historical value, gets superb performances but his feminist message is rather preachy and somewhat sentimental. Mature themes. A-III (R)

Sandlot, The (1993) An adult recalls how baseball influenced his life in the summer of 1962, when, as a newcomer in town, the 11-year-old boy (Tom Guiry) makes friends with a scruffy gang of youngsters who introduce him to the national pastime's craft and lore by playing their hearts out every day on a sandlot behind whose left-field fence lurks a fearsome canine. Director David Mickey Evans's strained portrayal of the events of that summer rarely measures up to the narrator's supposed fond memories of them, and its packaging of sentimentalized nostalgia is too superficial to provide any genuine insights into preteen friendships, fears, anxieties, and sexual awakenings. Some fantasy menace, occasional coarse language, and a few mild sexual references. A-II (PG)

Sands of Iwo Jima (1949) John Wayne gives a standout performance as a tough Marine sergeant leading his men (Forrest Tucker, John Agar, and Richard Jaeckel, among them) against the Japanese in one of the bloodiest campaigns in the Pacific. Director Allan Dwan's movie of men in battle is a fairly realistic portrayal of island warfare and the not-so-easy courage of those who fought it. A-II (br)

Sands of the Kalahari (1966) British melodrama about the struggle for survival of the six survivors of a plane crash in the African desert, among them the usual assortment of good (Harry Andrews) and bad (Nigel Davenport), hard (Stanley Baker) and soft (Theodore Bikel) stereotypes. Directed by Cy Enfield, the lone woman passenger (Susannah York) is almost raped, and the proceedings are grim, thirsty going. A-III (br)

Sangaree (1953) Wooden costume-romance directed by Edward Ludwig is set at the end of the Revolutionary War, when the dying owner of a rich Georgia plantation places it in the charge of a bond-servant's son (Fernando Lamas), who keeps it going despite plague, pirates, local schemers, and the scorn of the late owner's haughty, aristocratic daughter (Arlene Dahl). Occasional violence and sexual situations. A-III (br)

Santa Claus Conquers the Martians (1964) Silly twaddle directed by Nicholas Webster has jolly old Santa (John Call) and two earthling tots being whisked to Mars in order to bring Christmas cheer to sober-sided Martian youngsters. Low-budget clunker awash in humbug sentimentality. A-I (br)

Santa Claus: The Movie (1985) The story of Santa Claus (David Huddleston) gets off to a good start but slows down to a crawl when a subplot about a disillusioned elf (Dudley Moore) and a wicked 20th-century toy maker (John Lithgow) is introduced. The beautiful cinematography of the North Pole and Santa's workshop is wasted on an ultimately silly and forgettable story. A-II (PG)

Santa Clause, The (1994) Magically transformed into Santa Claus when he dons a Santa costume, a divorced dad (Tim Allen) takes a sleigh ride to the North Pole and back with his awed young son (Eric Lloyd), whose boisterous account of the experience moves his mom and step-dad (Wendy Crewson and Judge Reinhold) to seek to protect the child from a man they suspect has gone bonkers. Director John Pasquin's cutesy comic-fantasy is blandly amusing without reaching any discernible level of wit or adding anything new to the enduring Santa Claus legend. A vituperative relationship between divorced parents and occasional toilet humor. A-II (PG)

Santa Fe (1951) After the Civil War, four brothers from Virginia head West, where the eldest (Randolph Scott) takes a job with the Santa Fe Railroad, while the others join an outlaw band whose chief target is their brother's employer. Directed by Irving Pichel, the railroad setting adds some interest to a routine plot of brothers on opposite sides of the law. Frontier violence. A-I (br)

Santa Fe Passage (1955) Tangled Western in which an Indian-hating trail guide (John Payne) leads a wagon trainload of rifles through hostile Kiowa country, but along the way falls for the fiancé (Faith Domergue) of his boss (Rod Cameron) until learning her mother was a Kiowa. Directed by William Witney, the formula story has several big action-scenes, a bit of comic relief (Slim Pickens), a longwinded romance, and plenty of rugged Utah landscapes. Frontier violence and an anti-prejudice theme. A-I (br)

Santa Fe Satan (see: **Catch My Soul**)

Santa Fe Trail (1940) West Point graduate Jeb Stuart (Errol Flynn) goes after abolitionist firebrand John Brown (Raymond Massey) while vying with a former classmate, George Armstrong Custer (Ronald Reagan), for the affections of the same woman (Olivia de Havilland). Director Michael Curtiz is hampered by a weak script, though some of the action scenes still hold interest. Stylized violence. A-I (br)

Sapphire (1959) Engrossing British murder-mystery with an unflappable Scotland Yard inspector (Nigel Patrick) on the trail of the murderer of a mulatto music-student (Yvonne Mitchell) who made many enemies when she began passing for white. Director Basil Dearden follows the case suspect by suspect, but the real quest is uncovering British class divisions and racial barriers. Implied sexual liaisons and bigoted racial attitudes. A-III (br)

Saraband (1948) Historical dramatization of the 17th-century love affair between a dashing Swedish mercenary (Stewart Granger) and the unhappy princess of Hanover (Joan Greenwood), whose philandering husband (Peter Bull) has her lover killed and his wife imprisoned before moving to England in 1694 to be crowned King George I. Directed by Basil Dearden, the lavish period re-creation is lovely to look at, but the characters are mostly cardboard and the romantic tragedy is lost in a confusing tangle of devious court intrigues. Stylized violence and sexual situations. A-III (br)

Saraband for Dead Lovers (see: **Saraband**)

Saracen Blade, The (1954) Dull, predictable tale of a medieval Italian serf (Ricardo Montalban) who rises to knighthood, then seeks to avenge his father's murder by an evil noble (Michael Ansara). Director William Castle alternates low-budget battles with lackluster derring-do and soapy romance. Stylized violence and sexual innuendo. A-III (br)

Sarafina! (1992) Inspired by the arrest of a teacher (Whoopi Goldberg) for encouraging black pride among her students, a teenage girl (Leleti Khumalo) confronts the oppression of South Africa's racist policies in beleaguered Soweto Township in 1986. Directed by Darrell James Roodt, this vibrant musical makes a strongly human as well as political statement about racial injustice, though the abrupt cuts from brutal military killings to the schoolchildren's joyous musical numbers are distractingly ineffective. Frequent violence, including beatings, shootings and torture of youngsters, and a murderous act of retaliation by adolescents. A-III (PG-13)

Saratoga (1937) Romantic comedy in which the granddaughter (Jean Harlow) of a horse-breeder (Lionel Barrymore) falls for a racetrack bookie (Clark Gable) who's trying to take her Wall Street fiancé (Walter Pidgeon) to the cleaners, until the big race clarifies matters in the final reel. Directed by Jack Conway, the breezy plot is cheerfully unconvincing, sustained mainly by a good cast in colorful roles, especially Gable's big-hearted lug with his habitual line, "I love ya," though Harlow's pretending to smoke a cigar brings the biggest laugh. Romantic complications. A-I (br)

Saskatchewan (1954) A Royal Canadian Mountie (Alan Ladd) disobeys orders as the only way to keep the Cree nation from joining the Sioux after the Custer massacre. Director Raoul Walsh wastes the interesting period story and its colorful Canadian locales in a formula romance between the Mountie and a woman (Shelley Winters) he rescues along the way. Frontier violence and wooden romance. A-II (br)

Sasquatch (1978) Pseudo-documentary about a motley expedition's venture into the wilds of British Columbia in search of the legendary ape-like creature called Sasquatch by the Indians. The acting is atrocious and the general tone is one of tedium, which some stock footage of wildlife and scenic views does little to alleviate. A-I (G)

Sasuke Against the Wind (1973) Japanese samurai movie about warring feudal clans whose loyalties shift back and forth, while ninja (samurai spies) sow dissension and mistrust among their enemies. Director Masahiro Shinoda portrays the ninja as figures of moral ambiguity, men in any period of history using violence and corruption for "higher" ends. The visually beautiful black-and-white action film has some strong violence serving to open up the question of moral values in a violent world. A-III (nr)

Satan Bug, The (1965) Weak espionage thriller about US security agents (George Maharis and Dana Andrews) tracking down a deadly virus stolen from a government chemical-warfare lab by a mad fanatic (Richard Basehart). Director John Sturges plods through the dim doomsday plot with little conviction and even less suspense. Stylized violence and intermittent menace. A-II (br)

Satan Met a Lady (1936) Wild and woolly version of Dashiell Hammett's *The Maltese Falcon* changes hardboiled private eye Sam Spade into wise-cracking, money-hungry Ted Shane (Warren William), snookered by a doublecrossing blonde (Bette Davis) into joining the search for the fabled eighth-century, jewel-laden Horn of Roland. Director William Dieterle plays the story for screwball comedy with many good moments, from its cast of eccentric crooks (notably Alison Skipworth and Arthur Treacher) as well as Shane's wacky secretary (Marie Wilson), but the result never quite jells into a consistent whole. Some stylized violence and sexual innuendo. A-II (br)

Satan's Sadists (1971) Clean-cut ex-marine (Gary Kent) battles in his own merciless manner a gang of motorcycle maniacs (led by Russ Tamblyn) in order to save a mindless coed (Jackie Taylor). Directed by Al Adamson, the crude proceedings are excessively violent. O (R)

Satisfaction (1988) Lightweight teen-saga starring TV actress Justine Bateman as the leader of a high-school rock band made up of four girls and one boy — all misfits until they play a summer gig at a yuppie beach-resort. Director Joan Freeman updates a tired subject with some good music but unappealing characters. Implied sex scene, drug abuse by a principal character, and much profanity. A-III (PG-13)

Saturday Morning (1971) Dated documentary recording a group-encounter session, with 20 southern California teenagers talking, at times quite crudely, among themselves about parents, sex, and love. Directed by Kent Mackenzie, what emerges from their statements is general confusion and uncertainty about their identity and social roles. Perhaps useful for group-discussion purposes but without some mature guide, it can only further confuse young viewers. A-III (R/GP appeal)

Saturday Night at the Baths (1975) Low-budget movie about the initiation into homosexuality of a young pianist hired to play at a mecca for homosexuals in New York City. The quality of its inspiration and characterization is more sad than gay. O (R)

Saturday Night Fever (1978) Brooklyn youth (John Travolta) works hard six days a week and escapes into the magic time of Saturday night at the local discotheque, where he is the king of the dance floor and girls are readily available. The movie's dramatic tension comes from the youth's gradually becoming aware of the emptiness of his life. Directed by John Badham, this vivid portrayal of blue-collar youth at play is filled with coarse language and sexual references, but it comes to grips with some fundamental and extremely painful moral and social problems. A-IV (R/PG)

Saturn 3 (1980) Mediocre British science-fiction movie with Kirk Douglas and Farrah Fawcett living in tranquility aboard a deep-space station, until psychotic Harvey Keitel drops in with a robot named Hector who kills people that disagree with him. Directed by Stanley Donen, this has a very violent finale and some nudity in a sexual context. O (R)

Savage! (1973) American mercenary (James Iglehardt) brings along his carnival gir friends when he joins rebels in their struggle to overthrow sadistic military leaders in an obscure jungle country. Director Cirio H. Santiago exploits the women for casual sex and steers hundreds of puppet soldiers into bloody massacres. Terrible rubbish. O (R)

Savage, The (1952) Involving Western in which an orphaned white youth (Charlton Heston) is raised as the son of a Sioux chief, then faces divided loyalties when the US orders the tribe onto a reservation. Directed by George Marshall, the clash-of-cultures theme is too patly resolved, but the Indian lore and South Dakota locales are interesting enough. Some stylized violence. A-I (br)

Savage Guns, The (1961) Clunky Western directed by Michael Carreras follows a worn-out veteran gunfighter (Richard Basehart) who comes to Mexico hoping to hang up his guns for good, but instead finds himself in the middle of a land war. Lots of stylized killings and assorted mayhem before the good guys win. A-II (br)

Savage Is Loose, The (1974) Soggy melodrama about a shipwrecked family stranded on a remote island, where their young son grows to adolescence, and his sexual longings lead him to taunt his father (George C. Scott) to mortal combat, with winner-take-all, meaning Mom (Trish Van Devere). Also produced and directed by Scott, the plodding narrative is dramatically unconvincing, while its treatment of incest is exploitative and the story's resolution morally unsupportable. The movie could be severely disturbing to youngsters, particularly those wrestling with their own growing awareness of sexuality. O (R)

Savage Island (1985) Director Edward Muller's story of women behind bars in the tropics is filled with violence and graphic sex. O (R)

Savage Messiah (1972) Uneven British screen biography of Henri Gaudier-Brzeska (Scott Anthony), a young French painter who came to London in 1910, began his career in a great burst of energy, and died at the age of 23 in the trenches of WW I. Director Ken Russell makes convincing the young artist's brother-sister relationship with an older woman (Dorothy Tutin) who inspires his love and artistic endeavors. In placing the figure in his times, however, Russell strays over the edge of taste in some scenes at the decadent Vortex Club and in depicting at great length the crass vulgarity of a naked society-girl. O (R)

Savage Nights (1994) Aware he has AIDS, a bisexual Parisian (Cyril Collard) deliberately initiates volatile, life-threatening affairs with a tough punk (Carlos Lopez) and a teenage girl (Romane Bohringer) whose possessive love edges her towards madness. Also written and directed by Collard, the corrosive drama gives sympathetic treatment to characters who are obsessed with their own sexual gratification, regardless of the consequences for others. Subtitles. Some brutal violence, including scenes of self-mutilation and sadism, numerous sexual encounters, and brief nudity. O (nr)

Savage Wild, The (1970) George Eastman wrote, produced, directed, and stars in a documentary providing a remarkably vivid portrait of the lives and habits of three Alaskan wolves which he caught as cubs and photographed over a period of two years before releasing them in the wilds. Young audiences will relate to the director's daughter who shares in the raising of the cubs, though they may be slightly alarmed at seeing the grown wolves hunting down and devouring a caribou. A-I (G)

Savage Wilderness (see: **The Last Frontier**)

Savages (1972) Failed fable in which a primitive tribe is civilized in one day by the decaying remains of a higher culture, and then that night falls back into barbarism. Director James Ivory tries an allegorical form and satiric style clearly foreign to his previous compassionate intercultural studies, and the result is a hodgepodge of individual scenes that fail to mesh into a consistent whole. Some bizarre sexual scenes. O (nr)

Save the Children (1973) Documentary directed by Stan Lathan records the vibrant performances at the 1972 PUSH (People United to Save Humanity) Expo's celebration of the black musical heritage, from basic gospel through classic rhythm-and-blues to the soul sound and polished nightclub swinging. The final segment is in Rev. Jesse Jackson's church, where he preaches the message of saving children and all sorts of other people in a way that has a compelling effect upon the congregation and, deservedly, the viewer. A-I (G)

Save the Tiger (1973) Harried West Coast clothing executive (Jack Lemmon) goes through a personal and business crisis over a 36-hour period and discovers that there is nothing left to believe in. Directed by John G. Avildsen, the movie is not without interest or rewards, and it is especially good at conveying a sense of the American Everyman caught in the pressure-cooker of gritty, everyday life. The problem is that the character has no other values than his material affluence, and his fear of losing it evokes only pity rather than sympathy. A-III (R)

Saving Private Ryan (1998) Riveting war drama set during and immediately after D-Day 1944, when seven soldiers, led by their captain (Tom Hanks), are ordered to go behind German enemy lines to rescue a GI (Matt Damon) whose three brothers had been killed in action the previous week. Director Steven Spielberg brilliantly re-creates the horror and chaos of warfare, never losing sight of the soldiers' humanity, savagery, and patriotism, even as they question the justification of their mission. Graphic battlefield violence with gore, some profanity, and recurring rough language. A-III (R)

Say Amen, Somebody (1982) Feature documentary shows how African-American gospel music grew from the churches of the 1940s to the concert halls and hit records of today. Director George T. Nierenberg focuses on Thomas A. Dorsey, a blues composer who became the father of gospel in Chicago, and Willie Mae Ford Smith, one of the era's leading singers, with plenty of examples to demonstrate gospel's universal appeal. A-I (G)

Say Anything (1989) Charming teen love-story between a misfit jock (John Cusack) and a beautiful brain (Ione Skye) that also addresses problematic issues of open communication, honesty, and trust between a parent and child. Written and directed by Cameron Crowe, the film portrays teens sensitively, with minimal profanity, some solid relationships, and no blaring filler music. Though the girl ultimately has sex (off-screen) with her boyfriend, she discusses the pressures to do so with her father (John Mahoney), who does not condone the situation. A-III (PG-13)

Say Hello to Yesterday (1971) Through the course of a single sunny day, a British suburban matron (Jean Simmons) is encountered, pursued, and seduced by an obnoxious, devil-may-care youth (Leonard Whiting). Directed by Alvin Rakoff, the unwholesome story of a brief encounter offers implausible characters in a shallow plot about a superficial relationship whose inevitable denouement is a slightly ludicrous bedroom scene. O (PG)

Say One for Me (1959) Artificial melodrama about a parish priest (Bing Crosby) in an off-Broadway church who sings a little and reforms a few show-people (Robert Wagner, Debbie Reynolds, and Ray Walston). Directed by Frank Tashlin, the proceedings are contrived, and the sentiment is somewhat hollow. A-II (br)

Sayonara (1957) Well-intentioned but heavy-handed adaptation of the James Mitchener novel, in which a US Air Force major (Marlon Brando) stationed in Japan bucks the military's non-fraternization policy to woo a popular entertainer (Miko Taka). Directed by Joshua Logan, the cultural tour is lovely, but the East-meets-West romance is forced, and a tragic subplot with an enlisted man (Red Buttons) and his Japanese bride (Miyoshi Umeki) is unconvincing. Veiled sexual inferences and an off-screen double suicide. A-II (br)

Scalawag (1973) Middling pirate adventure based loosely on Robert Louis Stevenson stars peg-legged Kirk Douglas (who also directs) as he sails along the California coast robbing gold-laden merchantmen, as well as hobbling upon the hardscrabble coastal area where Mark Lester and his pretty sister are trying to maintain a faltering homestead. There's old-fashioned romance, doublecrosses, and a climactic fight deep inside a cave holding a fortune in gold doubloons. What's not old-fashioned is a clumsy rape attempt played for laughs. A-II (G)

Scalpel (1978) Plastic surgeon remakes the face of a beaten-up go-go dancer to resemble that of his runaway daughter in order to cash in on a five-million dollar will left in his daughter's name. Directed by John Grissmer, the movie indulges in some gore, has a casual attitude toward the value of human life, and uses nudity and titillating references to incest. O (PG)

Scalphunters, The (1968) Frontier trapper (Burt Lancaster) sets out to retrieve his winter haul of furs stolen by Indians, who in return have left him with a runaway slave (Ossie Davis), a situation further complicated when white scalp-hunters take the furs from the Indians. Directed by Sidney Pollack, the Western narrative is well-researched and scores some telling points on racial prejudice ,but the result chiefly demonstrates what a fine actor Davis can be. Some violence. A-II (nr)

Scandal (1989) Based on the notorious 1963 Profumo affair that toppled the Macmillan government, this British production sketches in the story of teenage sexual playmate, Christine Keeler (Joanne Whalley-Kilmer), and her platonic mentor, society osteopath Stephen Ward (John Hurt). Directed by Michael Caton-Jones, the movie has not a single character to stir human empathy, nor does it provide any insight into its sordid proceedings. Much nudity, sexual promiscuity, drug abuse, and violence. O (R)

Scandal at Scourie (1953) Norman Corwin's story about a childless Protestant couple (Greer Garson and Walter Pidgeon) in a small Ontario town who adopt a French-Canadian orphan (Donna Corcoran) promising to continue her Catholic upbringing, but this becomes a political as well as religious issue dividing the mostly Protestant community. Jean Negulesco directs the sentimental yet sturdy turn-of-the-century story with warm intelligence and a strong sense of family values, abetted by Garson's winning performance, but it all turns to mush in a disappointingly soggy ending. Religious misunderstandings and intimations of illegitimacy. A-II (br)

Scandalous (1984) Television journalist (Robert Hays), working on an expose of an uncle-niece team of con-artists (John Gielgud and Pamela Stephenson), suddenly finds himself accused of murdering his unloving but rich spouse. Director Rob Cohen's mishmash of a plot becomes a wasted effort for all concerned. Some adult humor. A-III (PG)

Scandalous John (1971) Irascible, unpredictable old man (Brian Keith), dreaming of the old days when he and the West were young and exciting, begins imagining himself a Western Don Quixote, and the man (Alfonso Arua) hired to care for him becomes his jovial Sancho Panza as the two do battle against some land developers. Keith faultlessly treads the narrow line between comic madness and pathos in a thoroughly delightful Disney production directed by Robert Butler. A-I (G)

Scanners (1981) Repellent Canadian horror movie about the super-intelligent people of the title, whose highly developed brains can cause such things as heads to explode when they put their minds to it. Directed by David Cronenberg, the flimsy plot about tracking down some deviant scanners is only an excuse for gory special effects of explicit violence. O (R)

Scarecrow (1973) Uneven buddy movie about two drifters (Gene Hackman and Al Pacino) who meet on a Western road, throw in together, and decide to go back East to open a car-wash. What follows is an odyssey of hitchhiking and hopping freights from one tank-town to another, and some of their encounters with American low-lifes are quite gross. Directed by Jerry Schatzberg, the two principals give solid performances of the mismatched characters, but the movie is more discouraging than illuminating in its portrayal of the male bond. Tawdry details abound, and among the sordid incidents are a brutal rape attempt, a savage prison beating, and a brief but graphic encounter with a prostitute. O (R)

Scarecrow in a Garden of Cucumbers (1972) Amateurish musical-comedy spoof about a star-struck Kansan (female impersonator Holly Woodlawn) who encounters the expected variety of vulgar New York City types in quest of Broadway fame. Film-school graduate Robert J. Kaplan gets a failing grade for his purported direction. A-III (nr)

Scared Stiff (1953) Uneven comedy in which a nightclub singer (Dean Martin) and his busboy pal (Jerry Lewis) flee from a killer by hiding out on a cruise ship, where they get involved with a woman (Lizabeth Scott) who has inherited a spooky castle on an island off the Cuban coast. Directed by George Marshall, this pale remake of Bob Hope's **The Ghost Breakers** has some diverting moments but none of the eerie suspense of the original. A-I (br)

Scared to Death (1947) Anemic low-budget thriller directed by Christy Cabanne in which a green mask plays a part in the death of the estranged wife (Molly Lamont) of a sinister doctor (George Zucco) in a former mental asylum whose visitors include a mysterious magician (Bela Lugosi) and a comic-relief private-eye (Nat Pengleton). Hokey tension with few, if any, scary moments. A-II (br)

Scarface (1983) Repellent remake of Howard Hawk's 1932 gangster classic is set in present-day Miami, where a Cuban immigrant and hardened criminal (Al Pacino) make it in no time from the bottom rung to the top in the drug rackets. Director Brian De Palma's ugly, turgid, foul-mouthed, and violent movie owes little to the original and is classic only in the sense of its crude self-indulgence. Perversely excessive violence. O (X/R appeal)

Scarlet Angel (1952) Formula melodrama in which a New Orleans saloon hostess (Yvonne De Carlo) promises a dying woman to take her baby to the woman's wealthy San Francisco in-laws, then assumes the dead woman's identity until blackmailers threaten to reveal her past. Directed by Sidney Salkow, the post-Civil War setting adds a bit of color to a predictable plot, with romantic interest provided by a Yankee sea-captain (Rock Hudson). Stylized violence, veiled sexual innuendo, and a series of deceptions. A-III (br)

Scarlet Blade, The (see **The Crimson Blade**)

Scarlet Claw, The (1944) Eerie mystery with Sherlock Holmes (Basil Rathbone) and Dr. Watson (Nigel Bruce) in a remote, fog-shrouded French-Canadian village on the trail of a revenge killer whose victims are found with their throats ripped out by a garden claw. Directed by Roy William Neill, this one has plenty of suspense abetted by an unsettling atmosphere and a fine cast of suspects (including Gerald Hamer, Paul Cavanagh, and Arthur Hohl. Verbal description of grisly murders and much menace. A-II (br)

Scarlet Letter, The (1934) Uneven dramatization of Nathaniel Hawthorne's tale of Puritan Massachusetts, where the mother (Colleen Moore) of an illegitimate child refuses to reveal her lover is the local minister (Hardie Albright), then matters are further complicated by the secret return of her supposed dead husband (Henry B. Walthall). Directed by Robert G. Vignola, the 17th-century morality tale is given earnest treatment, though the attempt to lighten matters with comic relief from two bumpkins (Allan Hale and William W. Kent) only gets in the way. Themes of infidelity, hypocrisy, guilt, and revenge. A-II (br)

Scarlet Letter, The (1995) Badly flawed adaptation of the Nathaniel Hawthorne classic set in 1666 Puritan Massachusetts, where an unfaithful wife (Demi Moore) is held up to public scorn while pregnant with an illegitimate child sired by a local minister (Gary Oldman), whom she refuses to name. Director Roland Joffe fills the screen with bogus emotion, undercutting the novel's observations by adding ludicrous characters and an absurdly happy ending. Some gory violence, a shadowy sexual encounter, and intermittent fleeting nudity. A-III (R)

Scarlet Street (1945) Gritty crime tale in which a middle-aged, unhappily married cashier (Edward G. Robinson) is fleeced by a pretty young hustler (Joan Bennett), whom he kills in a rage after learning the truth, then lets her cocky boyfriend (Dan Duryea) take the rap, with an epilogue showing the ruined cashier being driven bonkers by remorse. Directed by Fritz Lang, the story has some neat plot twists involving the cashier's artistic ability and a wife who's a widow, but the focus is on the cruelty of the grifters and the gullibility of their victim, with results that are heavily melodramatic. Stylized violence, sexual situations, and criminal duplicity. A-III (br)

Scars of Dracula (1971) Nearby villagers are unable to help three young people trapped in the castle lair of Dracula (Christopher Lee), but two of them survive after a bolt of lightening finally destroys the monster. British production directed by Roy Ward Baker is one of the less interesting of the Dracula movies. Though less frightening than tedious, its visualization of bloodlust makes it inappropriate for youngsters. A-III (R)

Scavenger Hunt (1980) Uninvolving plot about a rich eccentric (Vincent Price) whose will decrees that his fortune go to the heir that scores the most points in a scavenger hunt. Robert Morley, as his lawyer, manages to give the only dignified performance in this excruciatingly silly movie directed by Michael Schultz. A-II (PG)

Scavengers, The (1970) Demented, racist captain (Jonathan Bliss) spurs his mangy band of Confederates on to rape and murder as they commandeer a Civil War-torn Kentucky town to capture a Union gold shipment. Director R.L. Frost treats the gross killings and sexual abuse with repulsive intensity. O (R)

Scenes from a Mall (1991) The 16th wedding anniversary of a wealthy couple (Bette Midler and Woody Allen) is marked by guiltily shared secrets, recriminations, and eventual insight about their honest feelings toward each other. Produced and directed by Paul Mazursky, it's a realistic story of limited wry humor that would work better as a radio play since the visual medium is wasted here. Adulterous references and minimal rough language. A-III (R)

Scenes from a Marriage (1974) Episodic Swedish drama about a middle-aged couple (Liv Ullmann and Erland Josephson) who after ten years of a seemingly ideal marriage, get divorced when the husband falls in love with a younger woman. Seven years later, though married to different partners, they drift into an affair with each other, relatively happy in their newfound discovery of themselves. Written, produced, and directed by Ingmar Bergman, the movie uses exterior moments in the couple's relationship to tellingly reveal the interior pain and loneliness that constitute the motivation for their actions. Some may object to its depiction of the intimate details of married life, but, for many, it will hit the mark for honesty and truth in showing the frail attempts by which one individual reaches out to another. A-IV (PG)

Scenes from the Class Struggle in Beverly Hills (1989) Shamelessly acid satire and sex farce focusing on a weekend with a recently widowed ex-sitcom star (Jacqueline Bisset), her family, neighbors, and servants, all of whom are bored and sexually frustrated. Sex partners are swapped and bartered; clothes, sets, and music are deliberately lush, and peccadilloes are decadently warped. Though Paul Bartel's direction is sharp, and the production and acting credits are top-notch, the explicit sexual focus and raw language will offend many. Nudity and lewd behavior. O (R)

Scent of a Woman, The (1976) Director Dino Risi's tedious, sentimental, and often distasteful account of a blinded Italian army-officer (Vittorio Gassman) who journeys from Turin to Naples to carry out a suicide pact with a fellow officer but is redeemed by the love of a young woman. Excessive nudity and graphic sex. O (R)

Scent of a Woman (1992) A high-school student (Chris O'Donnell), needing to earn some extra money, accompanies a blind, retired military officer (Al Pacino) for Thanksgiving weekend in New York City, where the despairing ex-soldier intends to live it up before killing himself. Bo Goldman's literate script and an exceptionally nuanced performance from Pacino allow producer-director Martin Brest to orchestrate an ultimately satisfying drama of human failings transformed by renewed hope. An implied sexual encounter, momentary violence, several coarse sexual references, and recurring rough language. A-III (R)

Scent of Green Papaya, The (1994) Languid, delicately told tale of a 10-year-old Vietnamese girl servant (Lu Man San) in a 1951 Saigon household and her transfer 10 years later to a home whose master (Vuong Hoa Hoi) decides to marry her (Tran Nu Yen-Khe). Writer-director Tran Anh Hung's Vietnamese production narrowly focuses on the gentle girl's serenity and delight in her daily life without directly alluding to the country's troubled political climate. Subtitles. Some sexual innuendo. A-III (nr)

Schlindler's List (1993) Sobering account of an opportunistic German businessman (Liam Neeson) who comes to occupied Poland to make his fortune by exploiting Jewish capital and labor but, after witnessing the increasing barbarism of Nazi racial policies and the sadistic perversions of the local concentration-camp commandant (Ralph Fiennes), he risks his life by using his talents for manipulation to save the Jews in his employ. Director Steven Spielberg painstakingly re-stages the appalling history of the Holocaust on an epic scale that gives horrifying dimension to one man's attempt to save a few innocent lives, but the narrative provides little insight in the German's moral transformation or the individual lives of his slave laborers. Realistically graphic treatment of an infamous historical period and its crimes against humanity, a few discreet sexual scenes, and occasional rough language. A-III (R)

School Daze (1988) Fraternity hijinks and political conflicts divide students during homecoming weekend at fictional, all-black Mission College. Writer-producer-director Spike Lee's musical comedy features rousing dance numbers, lackluster music, and politicized lyrics highlighting differences between blacks on their own turf but unlikely to appeal to a wide audience. Explicit sex scenes and much street language. O (R)

School Ties (1992) A 1950s working-class high-school senior (Brendan Fraser) gets a football scholarship to an posh prep-school, where he finds friendship and acceptance — until a jealous teammate (Matt Damon) reveals the newcomer is Jewish. Director Robert Mandel orchestrates a fine ensemble movie that dramatically explores the harmful effects of anti-Semitism. Minor fisticuffs, a few sexual references, and brief rear nudity. A-II (PG-13)

Scorchy (1976) Narcotics agent Connie Stevens is ever eager to give her all in the fight against crime. Much sex, much mayhem, no intelligence. O (R)

Scorpio (1973) Good espionage thriller about a CIA agent (Burt Lancaster) who senses his number is up and tries to disappear with his wife and the money he has made selling classified information. Director Michael Winner fills in the plot, which has enough twists to satisfy spy buffs, with plenty of solid action and fast-paced excitement. The amoral world of espionage stories is very evident here, and the cynicism of its characters is not for anyone who might take them seriously. A-III (PG)

Scott Joplin (1977) Screen biography of the gifted black ragtime composer (Billy Dee Williams) does not gloss over the less entertaining aspects of his career and grim death. Thanks to some good performances, the colorful backgrounds of the era, and, above all, Joplin's music, it is an enjoyable and at times affecting movie in spite of the self-conscious direction of Jeremy Paul Kagan. A-II (PG)

Scott of the Antarctic (1948) Stiff-upper-lip tribute to the British expedition under Captain Robert Falcon Scott (John Mills) which sets out in 1911 to be the first to reach the South Pole, though Norwegian explorer Roald Amundsen eventually beats them to it. Directed by Charles Frend, the British production painstakingly re-creates the hardships and dangers of trekking through the frozen terrain and the courage needed to endure them, though the proceedings are laboriously slow-going, and the expedition's fate may distress some young viewers. A-I (br)

Scout, The (1994) Down-on-his-luck baseball scout (Albert Brooks) in the hinterlands of Mexico discovers a phenomenal switch-hitting pitcher (Brendan Fraser) who, after being signed by the New York Yankees, is diagnosed by a psychiatrist (Dianne Wiest) as repressing terrible memories of childhood abuse and is badly in need of therapy. Director Michael Ritchie begins with a lightweight but good-natured comic premise, then turns darkly serious by focusing on the player's emotional instability and its potential consequences until copping-out in a slick feel-good finale. Some heavy menace, a few sexual references, and some profanity. A-III (PG-13)

Scratch Harry (1969) Although its plot had some potential for making valid comments on marriage and social values, it loses dramatic perspective on its amoral characters with the introduction of an extended lesbian sequence, a completely gratuitous lovemaking episode, and sporadic nudity. O (R)

Scream (1996) Trashy horror flick in which a pair of crazed teenage killers set off a bloodbath among local high-school students which grows to engulf their small town in terror and death. Director Wes Craven's tale of bloodlust taken to gruesome extremes is thoroughly repugnant. Excessive violence, fleeting bedroom scene, recurring profanity, and much rough language. O (R)

Scream 2 (1997) Formula slice-and-dice sequel with a college co-ed (Neve Campbell) threatened by a masked killer slashing people to death, much as in the original. Directed by Wes Craven, the only thing going on in the movie besides the bloodshed is endless speculation over the killer's identity. Excessive violence, sexual references, recurring rough language, and occasional profanity. O (R)

Scream and Scream Again (1970) British horror movie in which Vincent Price plays a mad doctor assembling living organs to create a master race. Director Gordon Hessler's thriller leaves little to the imagination by dwelling at length on violence, blood, and gore. O (PG)

Scream, Blacula, Scream (1973) Sequel in which Blacula (William Marshall) rises from the dust to put the bite on the brothers and sisters of Los Angeles, but he winds up on the wrong end of a voodoo pin-sticking spree when he tangles with sexy Pam Grier. Director Bob Kelljan's campy B-grade horror movie has fanged ghouls coming out of the woodwork at the eerie mansion where much of the action, including a gory climax, takes place. A-III (PG)

Scream in the Dark, A (1943) Slack comic mystery directed by George Sherman in which a novice private-eye (Robert Lowery) and his dim partner (Edward Brophy) take on a divorce case which comes to involve four corpses, one of them headless, and a killer who uses an umbrella with a spring blade in its tip. Stylized violence, light treatment of marriage, and sexual innuendo. A-III (br)

Scream of Terror, The (see: **Point of Terror**)

Screamers (1996) Grim sci-fi thriller set on a war-ravaged planet, where the remaining survivors (Peter Weller, Jennifer Rubin, and others) struggle to stay alive while suspecting one of them is actually a robot programmed to kill human beings. Director Christian Duguay's atmospheric visuals compensate for a sluggish pace and minimal suspense until the final minutes. Stylized violence with intermittent profanity and rough language. A-III (R)

Screwballs (1983) Mindless, unfunny comedy about five high-school students and their pursuit of the one unattainable girl at their school. Director Rafal Zielinski's focus is totally on sex with excessive reliance upon nudity as a source of humor. O (R)

Scrooge (1935) Truncated but effective version of Dickens's *A Christmas Carol*, with impressive performances from Seymour Hicks in the title role and Donald Calthrop as Bob Cratchit, though the only ghost to be seen is the robust figure of Christmas Present (Oscar Asche). Director Henry Edwards delivers an atmospheric picture of 1840s London emphasizing the oppressive gulf between rich and poor bridged by Dickens's fable of helping others. A-I (br)

Scrooge (for 1951 version, see: **A Christmas Carol**)

Scrooge (1970) British musical version of Dickens's *A Christmas Carol* concentrates on poor old misanthropic Scrooge (Albert Finney), a thoroughly craven humbug whose disagreeableness is never believable and hence all the more fun to watch. Directed by Ronald Neame, it is a light, intelligent, and very amusing effort which wisely concentrates on the plot, using song and dance sparingly but well. The acting by the ghosts (Alec Guinness, Edith Evans, and Kenneth More) is especially imaginative, and the mood of the film is closely tied to Ronald Searle's delightful caricatures appearing with the credits. It's a movie for those who still have enough of the child within them to be able to relax and enjoy an old-fashioned bit of make-believe. A-I (G)

Scrooged (1988) The youngest, nastiest network president in the history of television (Bill Murray) is forced to live through his own "Christmas Carol" until redeemed in the end from his crass materialistic view of programming and life in general. Director Richard Donner satirizes the TV-ratings game and other mindless yuppie aspirations with savvy technical effects, a large cast of notable comic performers, and lots of one-liners. The satiric humor, however, is laced with vulgarities and sexual innuendo, as well as locker-room language and brief nudity. A-IV (PG-13)

Scuba (1973) Documentary follows six young diving enthusiasts in the Caribbean as they search the ocean floor for buried treasure, feed fish, and visit the decaying hulks of ancient wrecks. Narrated by Lloyd Bridges and directed by Ambrose Gaines, there is some quite engaging underwater photography of sea life that provides an experience of nature's beauty. A-I (G)

Sea Chase, The (1955) Convoluted saga of a German tramp-steamer whose anti-Nazi captain (John Wayne) evades internment at WW II's start by slipping out of an Australian port, then eluding the British Navy until reaching European waters. Director John Farrow turns a compelling sea-adventure into turgid melodrama as the captain warms to the German spy (Lana Turner) aboard ship while harassed by a fanatical Nazi (Lyle Bettger) among his officers. Wartime violence, including the off-screen murder of unarmed seamen and an implied suicide, as well as some tepid romance. A-III (br)

Sea Devils (1937) Dated manly hokum directed by Ben Stoloff in which a Coast Guard officer (Victor McLaglen) tries to keep a womanizing sailor (Preston Foster) from wooing his daughter (Ida Lupino) while pushing a steady seaman (Donald Woods) to marry her, then all three men prove heroes on sea duty, though two die in the process. Much brawling, some life-threatening situations, and romantic complications. A-I (br)

Sea Gull, The (1968) Screen version of Chekhov's play about a *dacha* full of characters (Simone Signoret, Vanessa Redgrave, James Mason, and David Warner) quietly destroying themselves and one another through lovelessness and infatuation for the wrong people. Director Sidney Lumet brings a fresh eye to the play's tensions and impending sense of tragedy, but some will find it rather static and overlong. A-III (G)

Sea Gypsies, The (1978) Handsome widower (Robert Logan), his two young daughters, a woman photographer (Mikki Jamison-Olsen), and a little black stowaway set off on a round-the-world sailing trip, but the boat sinks off the coast of Alaska, and the movie becomes a family-style Robinson Crusoe adventure. Needless to say, everyone cooperates to cope with the forbidding terrain and climate and the incursions of hostile animals. Writer-director Stewart Raffill has made a pleasant and unpretentious entertainment for the whole family. Very young children, however, might be frightened by skillfully done scenes involving unfriendly animals. A-I (G)

Sea Hawk, The (1940) Classic Hollywood swashbuckler about an Elizabethan privateer whose raids on the Spanish Main end when its crew is captured and chained to the oars of an enemy galleon, until their dashing captain (Errol Flynn) leads them to take over the ship and sail to London to warn the Queen (Flora Robson) of the impending attack by the Spanish Armada. Action director Michael Curtiz handles the swordplay and sea battles with gusto, abetted by a colorful host of Warner Bros. character actors (Alan Hale, Donald Crisp, Henry Daniell, Una O'Connor, among others) and a sweeping musical score by Erich Wolfgang Korngold. First-class entertainment for action fans, but its romanticized version of history with anti-Spanish stereotypes and sanitized violence need to be clarified for young viewers. A-I (br)

Sea of Grass, The (1947) Draggy, episodic Western from Conrad Richter's novel about a strong-willed cattle baron (Spencer Tracy) who tries to keep farmers from settling on his range, forces his wife (Katharine Hepburn) to leave when he suspects her of infidelity, then is finally broken when his son (Robert Walker) dies defending his father's honor. Directed by Elia Kazan, the socioeconomic conflict between cattle-ranchers and crop-growers proves more interesting than the personal story of a marriage floundering in misunderstandings and unspoken feelings. Some stylized violence and references to illegitimacy. A-II (br)

Sea of Love (1989) Nasty crime thriller about a hard-drinking, morose New York City cop (Al Pacino) who, while tracking down a serial sex killer through the personal columns, falls madly in love with his principal suspect (Ellen Barkin). As directed by Harold Becker, the cat-and-mouse situation is so convoluted and dragged out that one loses patience long before the killer is unmasked. Excessive violence, the sexual nature of the murders, several graphic sex scenes, and much rough language. O (R)

Sea Pirate, The (1967) Mediocre Italian adventure-movie about the crew of a corsair who turn to piracy when the French take all the booty, one-half of which, according to the unwritten code of the high seas, belongs to the crew. Directed by Roy Rowland, its story of an outlaw hero (Gerald Barray) is leagues away from the Robin Hood legend, but its swashbuckling violence is relatively innocuous. A-II (br)

Sea Wife (1957) Fanciful WW II tale of four survivors of a ship torpedoed in the Pacific, but as the days stretch into weeks without rescue, one of them (Richard Burton) begins falling in love with the only woman survivor (Joan Collins), unaware she is a nun. Directed by Bob McNaught, the British production has a strong subplot pitting a racist (Basil Sydney) against a black survivor (Cy Grant), but the ending is what's most memorable as Burton passes by without recognizing Collins in her religious garb, leading to the closing line: "No one ever looks at the face of a nun." Stylized violence, romantic complications, and racist attitudes. A-II (br)

Sea Wolf, The (1941) Gripping turn-of-the-century yarn from the Jack London story about the despotic captain of a rogue sailing-ship confronted by three reluctant passengers — a shipwrecked journalist (Alexander Knox), a fugitive from justice (Ida Lupino), and a shanghaied sailor (John Garfield). Directed by Michael Curtiz, the brooding tale of desperation centers in the battle of wills between the ruthless captain, who's going blind, and the humane writer, who's outraged at the unjust conditions aboard the brutal vessel, conveyed by a properly rough atmosphere and effective character roles (Gene Lockhart as the ship's drunken doctor and Barry Fitzgerald as a cheerful informer). Harsh stylized violence, including a suicide. A-II (br)

Sea Wolves, The (1981) Fact-based WW II story about some overage, overweight British civilians in India who steal into the neutral harbor of Goa to destroy a German freighter. Director Andrew V. McLaglen focuses not on the gallantry of the amateur commandos but on the derring-do of two intelligence agents (Gregory Peck and Robert Moore) who prepare the way. Preposterous subplot involves a dalliance between Moore and a beautiful German spy (Barbara Kellerman). Some violence, vulgar language, and incidental nudity. A-III (PG)

Sealed Lips (see: **After Tonight**)

Seance on a Wet Afternoon (1964) Intelligent British mystery thriller about a neurotic medium (Kim Stanley), her weak but compassionate husband (Richard Attenborough), and the kidnapping of a small child. Director Bryan Forbes builds a stark, somber atmosphere as riveting as it is disquieting, in a work that has a lot of psychological tension but no cheap thrills. A-II (br)

Search, The (1948) Stationed in post-war Germany, an American solider (Montgomery Clift) tries to find the relatives of a street urchin (Ivan Jandl) he has befriended, while the boy's mother (Jarmila Novotna) desperately searches for her missing child. Director Fred Zinnemann's picture of WW II's displaced persons is entirely credible in its treatment of their problems and genuinely moving in its respect for the human dignity of all involved. A-I (br)

Search for Signs of Intelligent Life in the Universe, The (1991) In the movie version of her one-woman play, Lily Tomlin tartly interprets a dozen characters who have been affected by the woman's movement during the last two decades. Jane Wagner's stage-play looks dated, and John Bailey's artsy direction softens its impact, but Miss Tomlin still delivers a performance with considerable wit and some insight into modern relationships. Several sex, drug, and suicide references. A-III (PG-13)

Search for Solutions, The (1980) Extremely well-done inquiry into the scientific method of problem-solving is designed to stimulate the interest of youngsters. Director Michael Jackson and producer James C. Crimmins lead the viewer through an imaginative and thoughtful odyssey which is part dramatization, part newscast, part interview, and part straight documentary. Very entertaining as well as informative. A-I (G)

Searchers, The (1956) Returning from the Civil War, a seasoned Westerner (John Wayne) stops to visit his brother's family but, after an Indian war-party raids the ranch, kills the family, and abducts his young niece (Natalie Wood), he sets out to rescue her in a quest that spans many years and a variety of frontier experiences that mellow the aging man of action. Classic Western directed by John Ford, its themes of pioneer-versus-Indian and civilization-versus-the freedom of nature are conveyed through the rich and often surprisingly warm interplay of its diverse characters amid the striking landscapes of Monument Valley. Fairly balanced view of Native Americans and some frontier violence. A-II (br)

Searching for Bobby Fischer (1993) Fact-based story of the struggle of a seven-year-old (Max Pomeranc) to become a champion chess-player without becoming as obsessed by winning as are his sportswriter dad (Joe Mantegna) and single-minded tutor (Ben Kingsley). Director Steve Zaillian nicely captures the conflict between well-meaning adults and the sweet-natured child in a dark-hued, sluggishly paced movie that nonetheless has good points to make about respecting the individuality of a child. Adults in heated conflict over a child's development. A-II (PG)

Searching Wind, The (1946) Dated melodrama from the Lillian Hellman play about a romantic triangle involving a decent but weak-kneed US diplomat (Robert Young) in Europe between the world wars, the freedom-loving journalist (Sylvia Sidney) who spurns him as an advocate of compromise with Fascist regimes, and the rich, frivolous socialite (Ann Richards) he comes to regret marrying. Making good use of the period preceding WW II, director William Dieterle gives some needed weight to a talky script whose hindsight-wisdom belabors the obvious. Contrived, artificial romantic complications. A-III (br)

Sebastian (1967) British satire about the re-humanization of a mathematical genius (Dirk Bogarde) who is so obsessed with his government work that he barely notices that all of his assistants are pretty young women, until the prettiest among them (Susannah York) ultimately manages to make him look up from his desk and try a little tenderness. Slightly marred by cliche visits to a discotheque and an LSD-type freak-out, but has some genuinely witty dialogue and Bogarde's topnotch acting. A-III (br)

Second Best (1994) Earnestly told tale of a lonely middle-aged Welsh postmaster (William Hurt) determined to adopt an emotionally scarred 10-year-old (Chris Cleary Miles) who only wants to be reunited with his long-imprisoned father (Keith Allen). Director Chris Menges plumbs the emotional landscape of the would-be father and seething child to unlock the possibilities of trust and gradual love in their relationship, though the movie's funereal pace and depressing content require considerable patience. An off-screen suicide and the child's angry acts of self-mutilation. A-II (PG-13)

Second Chance (1953) Fighting exhibition bouts in South America, a US boxer (Robert Mitchum) helps a gangster's ex-girlfriend (Linda Darnell) escape the twisted killer (Jack Palance) sent to silence her. Directed by Rudolph Maté, it's strictly a formula thriller until the final reel's showdown aboard a mountain cable-car stalled high above the valley below. Stylized violence, menacing situations, and sexual innuendo. A-II (br)

Second Chorus (1940) Labored musical comedy in which ex-collegian trumpet-players (Fred Astaire and Burgess Meredith) vie for a job with Artie Shaw's band while pursuing his secretary (Paulette Goddard) and alienating his potential financial-backer (Charles Butterworth). Directed by H.C. Potter, the contrived proceedings afford occasional merriment and good period music but is otherwise disappointingly lame. A-I (br)

Second Greatest Sex, The (1955) Clunky musical comedy about feuding towns in 1880 Kansas, whose exasperated womenfolk (led by Jeanne Crain) refuse to have anything to do with their men (led by George Nader) until they stop fighting. Directed by George Marshall, the convoluted proceedings and mediocre songs have little appeal and less originality in a theme originating in the ancient Greek tale of Lysistrata. Sexual innuendo. A-III (br)

Second Gun, The (1973) Tedious documentary attempts to prove that Sen. Robert F. Kennedy was assassinated not by Sirhan B. Sirhan, the man convicted of the murder, but by a nearby security guard. Director Gerard Alcan raises some intriguing questions but hardly supplies enough convincing evidence, and his argument requires some maturity to sort things out and place them in proper perspective. A-III (PG)

Second Hand Hearts (1981) Barbara Harris plays a widow with three children, and Robert Blake is a self-described bum who marries her in a drunken stupor but awakes to face up to his responsibilities, and they try to find happiness as a family. The comedy's heart, secondhand or otherwise, is in the right place, but it suffers from an uncertainty of tone under Hal Ashby's direction. Some vulgarities and a homosexual encounter. A-III (PG)

Second Jungle Book: Mowgli and Baloo, The (see: **Rudyard Kipling's The Second Jungle Book: Mowgli and Baloo**)

Second Sight (1989) Dim-bulb comedy about a goofy team of gumshoes (John Larroquette and Stuart

Pankin) tracking down the kidnapped cardinal of Boston with the help of a psychic (Bronson Pinchot) and a feisty nun (Bess Armstrong) who ultimately leaves the convent to tame the duo's male chauvinist (Larroquette). Directed by Joel Zwick, the result is silly and senseless. Some rough language and mild sexual innuendo. A-III (PG)

Second Woman, The (1950) Flat mystery thriller directed by James V. Kern in which an architect (Robert Young) seems to be coming unhinged by a series of misfortunes, until his girlfriend (Betsy Drake) helps him find their cause. Stylized violence and menacing atmosphere. A-II (br)

Seconds (1966) Middle-aged banker (Rock Hudson), fed up with his deadening routine, pays a mysterious organization to provide a new identity, but he finds his new life not what he expected. Directed by John Frankenheimer, it's intriguing mystery with a troubling ending. Sexually exploitative sequence. O (R)

Secret, The (1975) French thriller about a man (Jean-Louis Trintignant) who escapes from a psychiatric ward and is given refuge by a couple (Philippe Noiret and Marlene Jobert) after telling them that he is hiding from government agents ordered to kill him. Directed by Robert Enrico, the suspense and red herrings are handled rather clumsily, but the skillful acting and characterizations keep one's attention to the chilling climax. Some violence and sexual implications. A-III (nr)

Secret Admirer (1985) A girl's anonymous loveletters to a boy who is her best friend keep falling into the wrong hands, including those of their respective parents, making for all sorts of complications in this inept teenage comedy from director David Greenwalt. Benign view of teenage drinking and promiscuity, brief nudity, and some harsh language. O (R)

Secret Agent Fireball (1966) Mediocre Italian spy-melodrama directed by Martin Donan about an American agent (Richard Harrison) assigned to Europe to protect an international scientific project. Stylized violence. A-II (br)

Secret Agent Super Dragon (1966) Routine European-made spy melodrama directed by Calvin J. Padgett about a CIA agent (Ray Danton) who foils the plans of an underground group to control the world through a drug that turns people into human robots. Stylized violence and mild sexual innuendo. A-III (br)

Secret Cave, The (see: **The Black Pearl**)

Secret Ceremony (1968) Morbid, disquieting melodrama about the unhealthy relationship between a middle-aged prostitute (Elizabeth Taylor) and a retarded girl (Mia Farrow), who, though they need help, cannot help each other. Directed by Joseph Losey, its story has a heavy touch of madness, incest, suicide, and sexual shenanigans introduced by Robert Mitchum's uninvited presence. A-IV (R)

Secret Four, The (see: **Kansas City Confidential**)

Secret Friends (1992) Lumbering, stream-of-consciousness fantasies and memories enable a train-bound amnesiac (Alan Bates) to piece together who he is and why he has violent sexual thoughts about his wife (Gina Bellman). Writer-director Dennis Potter's trite conclusions regarding the power of guilt and sexual repression are hardly worth the time spent witnessing Ms. Bellman's hammy acting and one-dimensional characterization. Briefly violent flashbacks, much sexual suggestiveness, and minimal rough language. A-III (nr)

Secret Garden, The (1949) Durable version of the Frances Hodgson Burnett children's classic about an orphaned girl (Margaret O'Brien) given a home in the remote Yorkshire mansion of her sour uncle (Herbert Marshall), then discovers a hidden garden whose secret transforms her 10-year-old cousin (Dean Stockwell) and others. Directed by Fred M. Wilcox, the eerie mansion and past family tragedies are balanced by the girl's spunk and the healing powers of nature. A-I (br)

Secret Garden, The (1993) Winning dramatization of Frances Hodgson Burnett's children's classic about a little Victorian orphan-girl (Kate Maberly) who comes to live in her uncle's remote manor on the English moors, where she uncovers the mystery of a locked garden, transforms her sickly cousin (Heydon Prowse), and wins the friendship of a local country-lad (Andrew Knott). Directed by Agnieszka Holland, the appealing tale of three lonely children discovering the wonder and joy of life in tending a long-neglected garden is vividly told through evocative visuals ranging from the forbidding gloom of the manor to the enchanting beauty of the natural world outside. A rich experience for all members of the family. A-I (G)

Secret Life of an American Wife, The (1968) Failed satire in which a bored suburban housewife (Anne Jackson) tries to convince a movie star (Walter Matthau) that she's a high-priced call-girl. Directed by George Axelrod, the situation is not only unfunny, but its blatant toying with adultery is punctuated by tasteless sight gags and language. O (R)

Secret Life of Walter Mitty, The (1947) Uneven Danny Kaye vehicle from James Thurber's story of a mild-mannered proofreader of pulp magazines whose daydreams of glory turn perilously real when he helps a young woman (Virginia Mayo) save Holland's national treasures from a gang of cutthroats (led by Boris Karloff). Director Norman Z. McLeod turns Thurber's witty whimsy into broad comedy featuring frantic buffoonery, much mugging, and a couple of Kaye's distinctive patter-songs. Some comic violence and menace. A-I (br)

Secret of Magic Island (1964) Real, not cartoon, domestic animals, employed with remarkable skill, are the only performers in this simple fairytale, which will be of special interest to animal lovers and the very young. A-I (br)

Secret of My Success, The (1987) Ambitious college-educated Kansas farm-boy (Michael J. Fox) takes the sexual route to the top of the corporate ladder as a mail-boy impersonating an executive in a madcap comedy about business ethics and the new American dream of instant achievement. Helen Slater is the love interest, and Margaret Whitton plays the amorous woman who gets him to the top. Director Herbert Ross goes the bedroom-humor route dependent upon sexual innuendo, negative stereotypes of women, and acceptance of adultery. O (PG-13)

Secret of NIMH, The (1982) Uneven animated feature about a mother mouse who, anxious to save her family and home from a farmer's plow, seeks help from some rats with human intelligence gained inadvertently when they were subjected to various experiments at the National Institute for Mental Health (NIMH). Though director Don Bluth's graphics have the style and texture of the Walt Disney classics, unfortunately it lacks both a compelling story and a strong central character. It is on balance better than average family entertainment, with some scary moments for the very young. A-I (G)

Secret of Roan Inish, The (1995) Wispy Irish tale in which a young girl (Jeni Courtney), whose baby brother had been carried off to sea from the island of the title, happens to hear the legend of an ancestor who married a Selkie, a creature half-woman, half-seal, and becomes convinced her brother is still alive. Writer-director John Sayles capitalizes on a fine Irish cast, lyric locales, and moody seascapes to create a compelling mythic-fantasy about the bonds of family, the mysteries of nature, and the power of the human imagination. A youngster in perilous circumstances and a wee bit of profanity. A-II (PG)

Secret of Santa Vittoria, The (1969) Anthony Quinn and Anna Magnani star in an adaptation of Robert Crichton's comic novel about an Italian village hiding its prize wine from the Germans during WW II. Directed by Stanley Kramer, it's broad in style, but its characters are warm and the plot is entertaining. A-II (PG)

Secret of the Purple Reef, The (1960) Convoluted action tale directed by William N. Witney is set in the Caribbean, where two brothers (Jeff Richards and Richard Chamberlain) tangle with a shady character (Peter Falk) and his gang while searching the islands for their missing father and his boat. Stylized violence and sexual innuendo. A-II (br)

Secret of the Sword, The (1985) Animated feature starring He-Man, a hero who has progressed from toy to movie star. The plot has to do with He-Man's quest for his long-lost twin sister, She-Ra. Too unsubstantial to sustain a feature-length movie, and the animation is entirely non-distinctive. A-I (G)

Secret Policeman's Other Ball, The (1982) Filmed record of two London revues that the British Monty Python troupe did for Amnesty International. Some of the skits are very funny, but the rock interludes are undistinguished. Only for the most avid Python fans. Some sexually oriented humor and occasional rough language. A-III (R)

Secret Rites (1971) Italian pseudo-documentary collection of what it describes as "weird practices" from around the world. Others would call it a bizarre, vulgar, and sensationalistic peep-show, presented by director Ramiro Arango without pretext of cultural context or sociological significance. O (R)

Secret Service of the Air (1939) Low-budget programmer about a pilot (Ronald Reagan) recruited by the US Secret Service to infiltrate a gang flying aliens across the Mexican border. Directed by Noel Smith, it's standard action fare, chiefly of interest as the first of three 1939 quickies with Reagan as agent Brass Bancroft. Some stylized violence. A-I (br)

Secret War of Harry Frigg, The (1968) Grinning Paul Newman fills the title role in this off-base Army comedy about a private who's only adept at escaping from the base stockade, a skill which gets him promoted to the rank of brigadier general in order to help spring a covey of fellow generals from an Italian POW camp. Directed by Jack Smight, it's an unfunny clunker in which even Newman looks bad. A-II (br)

Secret Ways, The (1961) Standard Cold War fiction directed by Phil Karlson in which an American adventurer (Richard Widmark) endeavors to get an underground patriot (Walter Rilla) and his spirited daughter (Sonja Ziemann) out of communist Hungary. Stylized violence and highly unlikely derring-do. A-II (br)

Secret World, The (1969) Tree-house-centered world of an 11-year-old boy is the secret world of the title, but is not the central interest of this French movie. Instead it is the youth's random consideration of the relationships between his uncle, his mistress, and his wife. Between the uncle's mistress and the youngster grows an ambiguous friendship which turns out to be a modified mother-son relationship, sought by the boy who has lost his real mother in a car accident. A-III (PG)

Secretary, The (1972) Amateurish melodrama about a broker who encourages his wife's affair with his best friend, while he enjoys the charms of his secretary and her pot-smoking friends. Written, produced, and directed by William Diehl Jr., it is blatantly sex-oriented entertainment. O (R)

Secrets (1979) Young couple (Jacqueline Bisset and Robert Powell) revitalize their sagging marriage with an afternoon of therapeutic adultery — she with a Swedish businessman, he with a woman executive. Trivial, low-budget movie directed by Philip Saville insults the intelligence while exploiting nudity and condoning adultery. O (R)

Secrets & Lies (1996) Powerful British drama in which an adopted black woman learns she was the illegitimate daughter of a white woman who at first denies being her mother, then comes to like her as a person, and eventually invites her to a family gathering, where one painful truth leads to a number of others. Director Mike Leigh uses the credibly contrived situation to examine the flawed humanity of each of the characters, as well as their family relationships, social aspirations, and racial attitudes. Sexual situations and references, much domestic tension, and occasional rough language. A-III (R)

Secuestro: The Story of a Kidnapping (1994) Documentary chronicling the three months of financial negotiations by a Columbian father after his 20-year-old daughter was kidnapped and held chained in a suburban bedroom until her ransom was delivered. Director Camila Motta dispassionately presents the drawn-out story of her family's ordeal in a troubled society where kidnapping is so commonplace the police recommend paying only a fraction of the ransom price demanded. Momentary menace and an atmosphere of potential deadly violence. Subtitles. A-II (nr)

Seduction, The (1982) Failed suspense thriller about a mentally disturbed young man (Andrew Stevens) who pursues and terrorizes a beautiful Los Angeles television newswoman (Morgan Fairchild). Directed by David Schmoeller, it's a deadly dull affair that exploits the subject with a great deal of nudity. O (R)

Seduction of Joe Tynan, The (1979) Failed melodrama about the moral disintegration of an ambitious politician (Alan Alda) whose affair with a beautiful civil-rights lawyer (Meryl Streep) almost destroys his marriage and career. Directed by Jerry Schatzberg, the story borders on soap opera despite some good acting. Though the adultery is presented as wrong, it is depicted quite vividly in some bedroom scenes, and there is also vulgar and profane language. A-III (R)

Seduction of Mimi, The (1974) Italian satire about a Sicilian metal-worker (Giancarlo Giannini) who gets fired for voting against the bosses, works hard at a factory in Turin, is promoted back to his hometown, but, in seeking revenge for his wife's unfaithfulness, gets unwanted help from the Mafia and becomes trapped forever serving those he had originally opposed. Written and directed by Lina Wertmuller, the theme of the poor being exploited by the powerful is entirely serious, but the treatment is in hilarious black-comedy style. Some excesses in sexual treatment and language. O (R)

See No Evil (1971) Effective British thriller about a blind woman (Mia Farrow) who awakes to discover that everyone in the household has been slaughtered and panics when she realizes that the killer will return to recover some incriminating evidence. Though director Richard Fleischer doesn't play quite fair in his emotional manipulations, he achieves some high-intensity terror found in the best of Hitchcock. The violence is more implicit than explicit, but its aura of psychological horror is not meant for youngsters to handle. A-III (GP)

See No Evil, Hear No Evil (1989) When a deaf newsstand-proprietor (Gene Wilder) and his blind employee (Richard Pryor) are mistakenly arrested for a murder they've witnessed, they engage in some comic hijinks to prove their innocence and nab the real murderers. Director Arthur Hiller's hilarious buddy-movie manages, despite a flimsy plot and Pryor's excessive profanity, to keep the characters lovable and to score some points about physical disabilities. Slapstick violence, some sexual innuendo, and brief nudity. A-III (R)

See You in the Morning (1989) Heavy-handed story of the remarriage of a woman (Alice Krige) whose husband commits suicide and a man (Jeff Bridges) whose wife divorces him and how they deal with the children, as well as the psychological baggage, from their first marriages. Director Alan J. Pakula tries to get more than a superficial grip on the pain and humor of such blended families, but it's chockfull of precious, pretentious moments that it could well have done without. Adult situations and some rough language. A-III (PG-13)

Seems Like Old Times (1980) Offbeat romance about a liberal lawyer (Goldie Hawn) whose ex-husband (Chevy Chase) seeks her help when he becomes a fugitive mistakenly wanted for bank robbery, even though she is married to a stuffy district attorney (Charles Grodin). Predictable comedy, written by Neil Simon and directed by Jay Sandrich, is a guileless, innocent adult entertainment that succeeds in delivering a large number of laughs. Some bedroom pranks and occasional profanities. A-III (PG)

Seizure (1975) Turgid Canadian chiller about a horror writer-illustrator whose imaginings become real when a group of weekend visitors arrive at his eerie estate and a series of gruesome murders ensue, everything from knifings to head crushings. Directed by Oliver Stone, the ridiculous plot renders the contrived and clumsily handled violence relatively innocuous. A-III (PG)

Selena (1997) Musical biography of vivacious Mexican-American Selena Quintanilla Perez (Jennifer Lopez) who grows up under the guidance of her strict father (Edward James Olmos) to become a leading Tejano singer on the verge of mainstream stardom when she is tragically murdered at age 23. Written and directed by Gregory Nava, the picture of a close and loving Latino family is treated with such heavy-handed earnestness that it ends up being more than a little dull, despite Lopez and Olmos's best efforts. Momentary mild language and brief domestic tension. A-II (PG)

Seminole (1953) Routine Western directed by Budd Boetticher is set in 1835 Florida, where a West Point graduate (Rock Hudson) tries to keep his bellicose commander (Richard Carlson) from inciting the peaceful Indian leader Osceola (Anthony Quinn) to war. Stylized violence and muddled treatment of justice issues. A-II (br)

Seminole Uprising (1955) Inept Western directed by Earl Bellamy follows the far-fetched efforts of an Army officer (George Montgomery) to capture a Seminole chief (John Picard) who has led his warriors from Florida to 1855 Texas. Stylized violence and Indian stereotyping, though a theme of mixed races is treated sympathetically. A-I (br)

Semi-Tough (1977) Burt Reynolds and Kris Kristofferson star in a comedy about pro-football players and their playmates. Directed by Michael Ritchie, it has some genuinely funny moments, but its satiric focus is unclear, often turning nasty, and for humor relying on foul language and nudity. O (R)

Send Me No Flowers (1964) Flimsy romantic comedy sputters along with a hypochondriac (Rock Hudson) mistakenly convinced he has only a few weeks to live and obsessed with finding a second husband for his future widow (Doris Day), who interprets his odd behavior as evidence of an affair. Director Norman Jewison plays the anemic proceedings as broad farce, but the only laughs come from the supporting cast (Tony Randall, Paul Lynde, and Edward Andrews). Silly romantic misunderstandings. A-II (br)

Sender, The (1982) Horror clunker about a troubled amnesiac (Zeliko Ivanel) in the care of a pretty psychiatrist (Kathryn Harrold), given to wearing provocative clothing, who discovers that her patient has the deadly power to transmit his nightmares to other people. Directed by Roger Christian, this incoherent and violent movie contains gore, sexual innuendo, and flirts with blasphemy. O (R)

Sense and Sensibility (1995) Splendid adaptation of Jane Austen's 1795 tale of two devoted but emotionally dissimilar sisters (Emma Thompson and Kate Winslet) who endure unexpected heartbreak only to eventually triumph in securing suitable husbands. Director Ang Lee's spirited period-piece offers frequent subtle humor in its wry observation of the characters and social conventions of the day. Romantic complications. A-II (PG)

Sense of Loss, A (1972) In his disturbing documentary about the violent strife in Northern Ireland, Marcel Ophuls examines the conflict by allowing its inhabitants, from all corners and levels, to speak for themselves. The result is a document that addresses with chilling directness a situation apparently beyond control of political forces and national aims and, indeed, very nearly beyond rational comprehension. A-II (nr)

Senseless (1998) Feeble college comedy about an economics major (Marlon Wayans) whose determination to win a student competition for a plum Wall Street job brings him to rely on the help of an experimental sense-enhancing drug, with tiresomely unamusing results. Directed by Penelope Spheeris, the charmless story-line unfolds in a labored series of sophomoric sight gags and skits, most of them involving low humor and dim-witted characters. Explicit sexual situations, fleeting rear nudity, bathroom humor, and crude language. A-IV (R)

Senso (1970) Set in the 19th century during the time of Garibaldi, this 1954 Italian melodrama relates the story of a passionately indiscreet countess (Alida Valli) and an unscrupulous lieutenant (Farley Granger). Directed by Luchino Visconti, the movie probes the relationship of personal and class attitudes, love, and infidelity, evoking the ambivalence and decadence of a society in transition. A-III (nr)

Sensual Man, The (1977) Giancarlo Giannini is wasted in this muddled movie about the sexual misadventures of the lustful son of a noble Sicilian family. Writer-director Marco Vicario has taken Vitaliano Brancati's acclaimed novel, one of whose themes was the linking of sexual exploitation with the economic and social, and made a fatuous and tedious movie that itself exploits sex. O (R)

Sentinel, The (1977) Young couple (Christina Raines and Chris Sarandon) experiences terror and unnatural phenomena in a New York brownstone. Although director Michael Winner's horror movie purports to depict a struggle between good and evil, it deals in gross violence and nudity. O (R)

Separate Beds (see: **The Wheeler Dealers**)

Separate Peace, A (1972) Faithful screen version of the novel by John Knowles, set in a New England prep school just before WW II, in which a shy and studious student (Parker Stevenson) leaves adolescence forever behind after inadvertently causing the death of his gregarious and athletic roommate (John Heyl). Directed by Larry Peerce, the film captures the spirit of the original in its ambiguous statement about the effect of the past in the formation of the mature adult. A-II (PG)

September Affair (1950) Slick tale of a romantic triangle involving a successful engineer (Joseph Cotton) who leaves his wife (Jessica Tandy) and son for Italy and a mid-life crisis with a pianist (Joan Fontaine) after both are reported dead in a plane crash. Director William Dieterle pulls out all the emotional stops with romantic music and picturesque sites in Rome, Naples, and Florence, but the wistful love story is strictly a formula affair, and its reaffirmation of the bonds of marriage rings hollow. Discreet treatment of an unmarried relationship. A-III (br)

September 30, 1955 (see: **24 Hours of the Rebel**)

Serafino (1970) Earthy Italian comedy about the misadventures, mainly amorous, of a lustful but dense shepherd (Adriano Celentano) who is almost snared by his beautiful cousin (Ottavia Piccolo) but escapes marriage at the cost of his lean inheritance. Director Pietro Germi departs from his usual sophisticated brand of satire for a gritty, sweaty, extremely loud comedy with only modest results. Bawdy humor and coarse language. A-III (GP)

Serail (1976) Stylish French movie about a novelist who buys a chateau because he is intrigued by the odd behavior of its housekeeper (Leslie Caron), its owner (Marie-France Pisier), and its apparent ghost (Bulle Ogier). Written and directed by Eduardo de Gregorio, the mystery deepens until, at last, the mood shifts from suspense to horror. A sequence employs sexually explicit dialogue as unnecessary as it is offensive. O (R)

Serenade (1956) Sappy tearjerker in which a California vineyard worker (Mario Lanza) becomes an opera singer as the protégé of a socialite (Joan Fontaine), then goes into a career tailspin when she loses interest in him, but the love of a good woman (Sarita Montiel) puts him back on top. Directed by Anthony Mann, the hokey script ranges from the silly to the ludicrous, but the real disappointment is Lanza's erratic singing performance. Unlikely children's fare. A-I (br)

Sergeant, The (1968) Outwardly tough but inwardly unstable Army sergeant (Rod Steiger) gets into real trouble when a young recruit (John Phillip Law) challenges his latent-homosexual superior. Director John Flynn helps enhance Steiger's fine performance by carefully creating the bleak post-war Army environment with effective detail. Solid, finely wrought, adult drama. A-III (R)

Sergeant Rutledge (1960) Credible Western in which the black trooper of the title (Woody Strode) faces a court martial charged with murder and rape. Director John Ford tells the story in flashbacks as the court examines the evidence, with Strode coming across as a strong figure of considerable integrity. Stylized violence in well-treated theme of racial prejudice. A-II (br)

Sergeant Ryker (1968) Korean War story of a soldier (Lee Marvin) accused of collaborating with enemy but who insists he was following the orders of an officer now dead. Directed by Buzz Kulik, the courtroom drama raises a number of moral questions about responsibility in wartime. A-II (br)

Sergeant York (1941) In the dark months preceding America's entry into WW II, Gary Cooper had one of his best roles as Alvin C. York, a backwoodsman from the Tennessee hills who wrestled with his religious conviction that killing was immoral to become a battlefield hero in WW I. Director Howard Hawks succeeds best in evoking the honest, homespun virtues of rural America but is less convincing in portraying the moral conflict between pacifism and patriotism. Though its resolution may seem dated today, the issue remains basically unchanged in our nuclear age. Wartime violence. A-I (br)

Serial (1980) Cynical social satire about the effects of experimenting with hedonistic lifestyles and the narcissistic search for cures by a California couple (Martin Mull and Tuesday Weld) and their rebellious teenage daughter (Jennifer McAlister). Directed by Bill Persky, the movie lacks the intelligence and integrity to carry off the satire and settles instead for sexual orgies, nudity, rough language, and easy stereotypes. O (R)

Serial Mom (1994) Absurdist social satire in which a suburban matron (Kathleen Turner) goes around nonchalantly killing people who offend her sense of decorum, then is put on trial, while her adolescents (Ricki Lake and Matthew Lillard) cheerfully capitalize on her media celebrity. Writer-director John Waters skewers current media fascination with mass murderers, but in such exaggerated style that the campy black humor is sometimes overwhelmed by a gross depiction of violence more troubling than funny. Several nasty murders, some brief nudity, occasional sexual innuendo, an obscene phone-call, and recurring rough language. A-IV (R)

Serpent, The (see: **Night Flight from Moscow**)

Serpent and the Rainbow, The (1988) Failed horror movie about an American anthropologist in Haiti (Bill Pullman), whose quest to learn the voodoo secret of turning people into zombies leads to his being buried alive. Director Wes Craven is anything but subtle in his depiction of occult practices and rituals. Excessively gory visuals and graphic bedroom scene. O (R)

Serpent's Egg, The (1978) Director Ingmar Bergman's story of an American Jew (David Carradine), stranded in Berlin in 1923 with the German economy in total collapse and anti-Semitism on the rise, is a dramatic muddlement which seems to be aiming at some sort of political commentary, but failing badly. The somberness of its atmosphere and its vivid depictions of the squalor of the times make it decidedly mature fare. A-IV (R)

Serpico (1973) Screen version of the life and hard times of Frank Serpico (Al Pacino), the New York City patrolman whose disclosure of deep and insidious corruption within the police force went unheard until he told the press, after which a commission was set up to reform the department. Director Sidney Lumet's movie is gritty and uncompromising, convincingly realistic, yet engrossing in its human drama and tension. Its theme of corruption is unpleasantly graphic, and some will find its implications frightening. A-IV (R)

Servant and Mistress (1978) French melodrama about a man (Victor Lanoux) who comes to claim his inheritance when his wealthy uncle dies but finds that the entire estate has been left to the maid (Andrea Ferreol). Seeking revenge, she gives him the option of leaving without a penny or staying on as her servant. Director Bruno Gantillon's well-acted but tedious parable on the misuse of power in human relations is seriously offensive in several scenes of sexuality. O (nr)

Set It Off (1996) Trashy crime story in which four downtrodden black women (Jada Pinkett, Queen Latifah, Vivica A. Fox, and Kimberly Elise) turn to robbing Los Angeles banks, partly out of anger at an oppressive society, but mostly to get enough money to start new lives. Though director F. Gary Gray strives to justify the gang's crimes by depicting the injustices that drive them to armed robbery, the result is another glamorized version of violence in the 'hood. Extreme violence, a lesbian relationship, brief nudity, and much rough language. O (R)

Set-Up, The (1949) Classic picture of the fight game in which an aging boxer (Robert Ryan) refuses to take a dive in a bout his manager has agreed to fix and suffers the consequences when he scores a KO. Directed by Robert Wise, the brutality inside the ring is reflected in the bloodlust of the spectators and the hard cases who make their living off prizefights. Ryan brings an inner sense of dignity to the role, as does Audrey Totter as his caring wife. The violence is brutal but meaningful. A-III (br)

Seven (1995) Gruesome thriller about a veteran homicide-detective (Morgan Freeman) and his cocky new partner (Brad Pitt) on the trail of a serial killer, each of whose tortured victims represents one of the seven deadly sins. David Fincher directs a pointless exercise in shock value as increasingly horrific murders come full circle to ensnare the detectives as well as the killer. Muddled theme of religious fanaticism, intermittent violence, graphic shots of mutilated corpses with full nudity, base sexual references, and much rough language. O (R)

Seven Alone (1975) Disappointing re-creation of a historical incident that took place in 1843, when seven children, led by their 14-year-old brother (Stewart Peterson), traveled a good portion of the Oregon Trail on their own after losing their parents. Earl Bellamy's uncertain direction lacks the feel of pioneer realities and stereotypes the Indians. Let the children watch if there is nothing else to see, but don't expect a great deal. A-I (G)

Seven Angry Men (1955) Historical dramatization about anti-slavery crusader John Brown (Raymond Massey) starts in 1856 Kansas, where he fights for its entry into the Union as a free state, then goes to 1859 Virginia, where he seizes the military arsenal at Harper's Ferry and is sentenced to hang for treason. Director Charles Marquis Warren portrays Brown as a man compelled by what he believes to be his divine mission to free the slaves, though his cruel use of violence appalls some of his supporters and causes dissension among his six sons (notably Jeffrey Hunter). Unlikely fare for children. A-I (br)

Seven Beauties (1976) Italian tragicomedy about a petty crook (Giancarlo Giannini) in 1930s Naples, who bungles a murder, gets drafted in WW II, deserts while being shipped to the Russian front, is interned in a concentration camp, but survives, having learned nothing. Director Lina Wertmuller's vision, though dark and stormy, is also permeated with a love for the beauty and richness of life. Some grisly violence and an earthy treatment of sex. A-IV (R)

Seven Brides for Seven Brothers (1954) Western musical about Oregon pioneers who, when their brother (Howard Keel) brings home a bride (Jane Powell), go out and kidnap some local belles. Directed by Stanley Donen, the zest of the music, dancing, and story carry the movie in highly enjoyable fashion. A-II (br)

Seven Cities of Gold (1955) Plodding melodrama about Spanish conquistadors hunting for Indian gold with the good Padre Junipero Serra (Michael Rennie) trying to avert bloodshed. Directed by Robert D. Webb, it's a well-intentioned but shallow historical adventure. A-I (br)

Seven Days in May (1964) When a top American general (Burt Lancaster) plots to take over the government to stop the president (Fredric March) from signing a disarmament agreement with the Russians, a loyal Army colonel (Kirk Douglas) tries to avert the coup. Director John Frankenheimer's suspense thriller is thoroughly involving, credibly done, and provides some food for thought. Much tension and some menace. A-II (br)

Seven Days Leave (1942) Witless comedy directed by Tim Whelan with some music (Ginny Sims, Les Brown's orchestra, and others) and a meandering plot about a soldier (Victor Mature) who learns he will inherit a fortune if he marries a Civil War general's descendant (Lucille Ball) before the week is up. Romantic complications and some sexist humor. A-I (br)

Seven Days to Noon (1950) Excellent British thriller about a deranged scientist (Barry Jones) who threatens to destroy London with an atomic bomb unless the world disarms. Directed by Roy and John Boulting, the plot is neatly worked out, the acting is first rate, and the suspense has real point. A-II (br)

711 Ocean Drive (1950) Uneven crime story in which a smart telephone-linesman (Edmond O'Brien) finds easy money modernizing a wire service for California bookies, but, after he's on easy street running the operation, a national syndicate moves in, and he tries to get out with a big score. Director Joseph M. Newman's pedestrian script derives interest from a credible cast and good location photography, especially a climactic chase atop and inside Boulder Dam. Criminal atmosphere and stylized violence. A-II (br)

Seven Faces of Dr. Lao (1964) Diverting entertainment focusing on a traveling circus owned by the mysterious Dr. Lao (Tony Randall, who also plays seven other roles) whose performances work strange effects on his audience in a town of the Old West. Director George Pal's fantasy has imaginative special effects, and its story should intrigue youngsters and amuse adults. A-I (br)

Seven Golden Men (1969) Routine Italian heist movie about the intricate maneuvers used to get into a bank vault, steal the loot, and then lose it in a series of doublecrosses. Director Marco Vacario's crime movie is not a spoof, though it does have some humor, and some personable crooks (Philippe Leroy, Gastone Moschin, Jose Suarez, and Rossana Podesta). A-II (G)

Seven Keys to Baldpate (1947) Tongue-in-cheek thriller in which a genial author (Philip Terry) sets out to write a mystery story in a country inn that's been closed for the winter, but arrives to find it occupied by an odd assortment of characters (Eduardo Ciannelli, Margaret Lindsay, Arthur Shields, and others) engaged in sinister activities. Directed by Lew Landers from George M. Cohan's adaptation of an Earl Derr Biggers story, the mysterious goings-on are creaky and the treatment is melodramatic, but the premise is still amusing and the contrivances mostly fun. A-I (br)

Seven Little Foys, The (1955) Bob Hope plays Eddie Foy, popular turn-of-the-century vaudeville star, who, after the death of his forbearing wife (Milly Vitale), creates a stage act featuring his seven young children. Director Melville Shavelson does well with the show-biz setting, including a zesty turn by James Cagney as George M. Cohan, but Foy as an absentee father remains largely unsympathetic, until the end when he takes the kids on the road to keep the family together. A-II (br)

Seven Miles from Alcatraz (1942) Dated thriller in which convicts (James Craig and Frank Jenks) escape the island prison during a wartime blackout, cross San Francisco Bay, and reach a lighthouse being used by a Nazi spy-ring to relay military secrets to a nearby submarine. Directed by Edward Dmytryk, the low-budget adventure is contrived to the patriotic theme that even crooks have a part to play in the fight against Hitler. More menace than violence. A-II (br)

Seven Minutes, The (1971) Numbingly sensationalistic rendering of Irving Wallace's novel about a California pornography trial has all the depth of a Hollywood press release and all the titillation of an arcade peep-show. Director Russ Meyer's characters are uniformly stereotypes, the relevant issues are hopelessly obscured, and there is some explicit sexual action. O (R/PG)

Seven Percent Solution, The (1976) Sigmund Freud (Nichol Williamson) meets Sherlock Holmes (Alan Arkin) in a stylish and mostly entertaining mystery directed by Herbert Ross. An incidental brothel scene and some frightening images that occur while Holmes is suffering from narcotic withdrawal symptoms are not for youngsters. A-III (PG)

Seven Samurai (1954) Medieval Japanese adventure-saga in which a veteran samurai (Takashi Shimura) agrees to protect a small farming village from a band of bandits, then selects five other samurai and a determined peasant youth (Toshiro Mifune) to join him in fortifying the village and training its inhabitants to defend it against the much larger bandit force. Directed by Akira Kurosawa, the result is partly a character study of idealistic samurai, partly a lyric tribute to the enduring virtues of farm life, but mostly a well-plotted, fast-paced action epic based on the element of surprise, individual heroism, and the unified spirit of a group fighting for its very survival. Subtitles. Stylized battlefield violence, much menace, and several sexual situations. A-III (br)

Seven Seas to Calais (1962) Plodding swashbuckler with privateer Francis Drake (Rod Taylor) plundering the Spanish Main, being knighted for it by Queen Elizabeth (Irene Worth), then going on to defeat the Spanish Armada. Director Rudolph Maté trudges through tired historical cliches with no particular sense of adventure and disappointing action scenes. Stylized violence and devious period politics. A-I (br)

Seven Sinners (1940) Marlene Dietrich stars as a cabaret singer in a seedy South Seas port, where her charms provoke a battle royal between a dangerous gangster (Oscar Homolka) and a US naval officer (John Wayne). Action director Tay Garnett expends a lot of energy staging massive brawls, but there's plenty of comic relief (Billy Gilbert, Mischa Auer, and Broderick Crawford), as well as Dietrich's alluring yet sympathetic performance. Much stylized violence and muted sexual innuendo. A-III (br)

Seven-Ups, The (1974) Action-packed but hackneyed story of a special police-unit, headed by Roy Scheider, that gets in the middle of an elaborate gangland war. Directed by Phil D'Antoni, New York City is well-used as the battleground where cop and criminal shoot it out, and where it is hard to tell the hunter from the hunted. Elaborate and intense car chases and an assortment of other special-effects violence. A-III (PG)

Seven Waves Away (see: **Abandon Ship!**)

Seven Ways from Sundown (1960) Routine Western in which a novice Texas Ranger (Audie Murphy) teams with a seasoned veteran (John McIntire) to track down a feared gunman (Barry Sullivan), then comes to like the captured desperado despite his resolve to bring him to justice. Directed by Harry Keller, the formula proceedings are enlivened by the shifting relationship between the young lawman and the wily outlaw. Frontier violence and convoluted relationships. A-II (br)

7 Women (1966) Uneven melodrama set in 1935 China, where a rural Christian mission compound staffed by women (headed by Margaret Leighton) is captured by a barbarous Mongolian war lord (Mike Mazurki) who takes a fancy to its tough American doctor (Anne Bancroft), with the other women's fate hanging on how she handles the situation. Director John Ford's last picture focuses on the shifting relationships between the women as danger heightens, but fails, except for Bancroft, to make anything more of the characters than stereotypes, with disappointingly predictable results. Stylized violence, sexual situations, and a murder-suicide in the plot resolution. A-III (br)

Seven Years in Tibet (1997) Flawed, fact-based dramatization about the transformation of an arrogant Nazi mountain-climber (Brad Pitt) who in 1942 escapes a British internment camp in the Himalayas and walks 1,500 miles to the holy city of Lhasa, Tibet, where he befriends, then tutors, the teenage Dalai Lama (Jamyang Wangchuk) and, in the process, becomes spiritually centered himself. Directed by Jean-Jacques Annaud, the scenic vistas are visually stunning, but the lead character's inner regeneration is dramatically unconvincing. Brief battlefield violence and a gory mountaineering accident. A-II (PG-13)

1776 (1972) Entertaining screen version of the popular Broadway musical by Sherman Edwards and Peter Stone about the travails of the Continental Congress in forging the Declaration of Independence utilizes most of the original cast, from William Daniels's John

Adams to Howard Da Silva's Benjamin Franklin. Director Peter Hunt, who also directed the stage musical, relies on the original staging rather than trying for any big-screen effects, and it works well in mixing some light, diverting entertainment with some serious asides, such as slavery and marital loneliness. A-II (G)

7th Cavalry (1956) Strictly formula Western directed by Joseph H. Lewis in which a cavalry officer (Randolph Scott) returns from leave to learn of his troop's massacre at the Little Big Horn, then, to prove he's not a coward, volunteers to bring back the bodies of Custer and his officers. Frontier violence. A-I (br)

Seventh Chamber of Edith Stein, The (1996) Dense but compelling dramatization of the complex life of the title German philosopher (Maia Morgenstern), who was born a Jew in 1891, baptized a Catholic in 1922, gained fame as teacher, writer, and lecturer until being barred from academic life by the Nazis in 1933, then entered the Carmelite Order, and devoted herself to writing on spiritual subjects until her arrest as a Jew and death in Auschwitz in 1942. Directed by Marta Meszaros and filmed in Hungary, the French-language production portrays Nazi anti-Semitism as the historical reality underlying the interior drama of Stein's spiritual struggle to integrate her Jewish heritage and Catholic faith with her philosophical training and mystical calling in a life leading beyond a martyr's death to beatification in 1987. Subtitles. Period violence and some intense scenes of personal anguish. A-II (nr)

Seventh Continent, The (1968) Czech-Yugoslav children's fantasy about a magical island which becomes the refuge for all the youngsters of the world who are ignored and forgotten by their busy parents, leaving the adult world behind in squabbles about how their children can be gotten back. Directed by Dustan Vukotic, it has a number of highly imaginative scenes and good special effects but tends to dwell too long on the tiresome adults. A-I (br)

Seventh Seal (1956) Intense medieval morality tale about a disillusioned knight (Max Von Sydow) returning from the Crusades to a plague-ravaged land, where he forestalls Death (Bengt Ekerot) by wagering his life on a game of chess, during the course of which he saves a traveling player named Joseph (Nils Poppe), his wife Mary (Bibi Andersson), and their infant son. Swedish director Ingmar Bergman convincingly re-creates the religious context of the Middle Ages, but the knight's quest to find meaning in a world of physical suffering and spiritual emptiness has less to do with religious faith than with the contemporary search for the life's meaning in our own age of doubt and uncertainty. Subtitles. Recurring images of death, some stylized violence, and instances of religious fanaticism. A-III (br)

Seventh Sign, The (1988) Although the Apocalypse appears to be near at hand, a pregnant woman (Demi Moore) finds she has the power to stop it. Director Carl Schultz's convoluted thriller makes glossy, ultimately exploitative use of the New Testament's Book of Revelation. Several scenes of intense violence involving the woman and some brief nudity. O (R)

Seventh Victim, The (1943) Murky thriller in which a young woman (Kim Hunter) arrives in New York City to find her missing sister, then learns she's become involved with a cult of devil worshippers who have condemned her to death as a traitor. Produced by Val Lewton and directed by Mark Robson, the story establishes an unsettling atmosphere, but the sinister implications of the plot are too nebulous to make much of an impact. Minimal stylized violence, much suspense, and a suicide in the plot's resolution. A-III (br)

7th Voyage of Sinbad, The (1958) Exciting Arabian Nights adventure with Sinbad (Kerwin Matthews) battling a one-eyed Cyclops, a two-headed Roc, a ferocious dragon, and a sword-wielding skeleton in order to rescue a princess (Kathryn Grant) from a wicked magician (Torin Thatcher). Director Nathan Juran teams with special-effects artist Ray Harryhausen to create a satisfying action fantasy that will enthrall youngsters without boring their parents. Some scary scenes with menace and stylized violence. A-I (G)

Severed Head, A (1971) Failed British adaptation of the Iris Murdoch novel purports to be a sophisticated comedy of manners about the savagely civilized exercise of mixing and matching mates (among them, Lee Remick, Richard Attenborough, Claire Bloom, and Clive Revill). Among all the soap-opera forsaking of partners, director Dick Clement forsakes taste with some unnecessarily bare anatomy. A-IV (R)

Sex Crimes (1993) Writer-director M.L. Behrman's inept thriller has zero production values in a disjointed story about a hokey TV-reporter (Margot Hope) on the trail of perverted serial killers (Jack Klarr and Dave Schiesser). Graphic sex and violence with sporadic rough language. O (nr)

Sex Drugs Rock & Roll (1991) Overlong but occasionally incisive one-man show, with Eric Bogosian acting out ten characters caught up in their separate mini-dramas. As written by Bogosian and directed by John McNaughton, this filmed stage-play is well-acted by Bogosian, but his insights into his smug, braggardly characters soon repeat themselves. Positive drug references within a satirical framework, allusions to promiscuity, and frequent rough language. A-III (R)

sex, lies, and videotape (1989) In this quirky contemporary morality tale, the relationships between an unhappy wife (Andie MacDowell), her philandering husband (Peter Gallagher), and her spiteful sister (Laura San Giacomo), who is having an affair with the husband, are thrown up for grabs by the arrival of a visitor (James Spader) who is obsessed with videotaping women talking about their sexual experiences. Written and directed by Steven Soderbergh, the result is more or less morally satisfying, as self-deceptions are unmasked and more positive relationships are initiated. Mature themes with some graphic sexual language and several suggestive scenes. A-IV (R)

Sextette (1979) Mae West plays a glamorous movie star whose wedding night with husband number six is interrupted by former husbands and the need to rescue a summit conference near shambles. Director Ken Hughes's farce is insufferably boring and, as might be expected, overflowing with an abundance of double entendres. A-III (PG)

Sgt. Bilko (1996) The money-making schemes of an Army supply-sergeant (Steve Martin) and his loyal underlings are jeopardized when a major (Phil Hartman) with a grudge against the sergeant turns up on base to expose Bilko's scams — and steal his fiancé. With only a wafer-thin narrative, director Jonathan Lynn relies heavily on Martin to carry off this genial but unremarkable movie adaptation of the 1950s TV sitcom. Comic depiction of gambling and minimal rude expressions. A-II (PG)

Sgt. Pepper's Lonely Hearts Club Band (1978) Peter Frampton and the Bee Gees attempt to turn the Beatles's famous music album into a movie in which they play small-town musicians temporarily corrupted by becoming Los Angeles rock stars. When they learn that baddies have despoiled their hometown, they return to right all wrongs. Director Michael Schultz gets more the feel of an animated cartoon than a live-action, and George Burns does some narration since the movie has no dialogue. Some suggestive gestures and lyrics as well as pot smoking and the use of cocaine. A-III (PG)

Shadow, The (1994) Empty adaptation of the pulp-novel radio series in which a 1930s playboy and secret crime-fighter (Alec Baldwin) joins forces with his mind-reading girlfriend (Penelope Ann Miller) to prevent a power-mad villain (John Lone) from detonating a catastrophic bomb in Manhattan. Director Russell Mulcahy's plodding adventure fantasy is awash in glamorous art-deco décor, but its throwaway plot fails to come to grips with the title character's dual nature. Some stylized but nasty violence and fleeting sexual innuendo. A-III (PG-13)

Shadow Conspiracy (1997) Slick thriller in which a top presidential aide (Charlie Sheen) becomes the target of an assassin while working with the White House chief of staff (Donald Sutherland) to find the high-level officials plotting to topple the government. Directed by George P. Cosmatos, the chase scenes are skillfully executed, but the story's muddled plot becomes increasingly less than credible. Numerous stylized murders, occasional profanity, and intermittent rough language. A-III (R)

Shadow of a Doubt (1943) Young girl (Teresa Wright) begins to suspect that her favorite uncle (Joseph Cotton) is wanted for a series of murders. Director Alfred Hitchcock unfolds his usual dark doings in the commonplace setting of small-town America's solid citizenry with uncommonly suspenseful results. A classic psychological thriller rich in visual understatement rather than shocking graphics. A-II (br)

Shadow of the Hawk, The (1976) Terribly amateurish movie about an Indian medicine man (Chief Dan George) who wants his grandson (Jan-Michael Vincent), an IBM executive, to take over his practice and ward off the evil that threatens the tribe. Canadian production directed by George McCowan, the story is awfully far-fetched and not particularly scary. A-II (PG)

Shadow of the Thin Man (1941) Intriguing mystery sequel in which retired San Francisco sleuth Nick Charles (William Powell) helps a homicide detective (Sam Levene) solve several murders tied to a gambling syndicate, while wife Nora (Myrna Loy) befriends one of the suspects (Barry Nelson) and his girlfriend (Donna Reed). Directed by Major W.S. Van Dyke II, the plot employs numerous criminal types, including Stella Adler as a gold-digger, but matters are lightened by some witty domestic scenes with three-year-old Nicky, Jr. Stylized violence and menacing situations. A-II (br)

Shadow of the Wolf (1993) When an Eskimo hunter (Lou Diamond Phillips) kills a drunken white trader in the Far North of 1935, he and his wife (Jennifer Tilly) flee their village to live in the vast Arctic wilderness on their own, but they cannot escape the curse of his shaman father (Toshiro Mifune) and the inexorable pursuit of white justice. In this beautifully photographed Canadian production based on the novel by Yves Theriault and directed by Jacques Dorfmann, the story of the individual hunter's struggle with the elements gets lost in the larger story of a native people's eroding culture, but dwarfing all is the awesome splendor of this isolated, inhospitable, frozen world. Some stylized violence, including savage native customs, several sexual situations with fleeting nudity, and a few instances of profanity. A-III (PG-13)

Shadow Strikes, The (1937) Creaky mystery directed by Lynn Shores and based on the Street and Smith pulp-magazine hero, Lamont Cranston, who secretly fights crime in the guise of the mysterious Shadow. Here Cranston (Rod La Rocque) impersonates a big-time lawyer to get the goods on a blackmailer (Cy Kendall), while also solving a murder along the way with some comic-relief help from his bumbling English butler (Norman Ainsley). Menacing situations. A-I (br)

Shadowlands (1993) Fact-based story of Anglican writer and Oxford don C.S. Lewis (Anthony Hopkins), whose closely guarded scholarly seclusion is unsettled late in life by one of his readers, a divorced American writer (Debra Winger) who stirs the lifelong bachelor to discover the friendship of a woman, then the emotional fulfillment of marriage, and finally the pain of loss when she dies of cancer. Director Richard Attenborough's 1950s period piece explores the gradual transformation of a man who has devoted his life to intellectual pursuits, until his heart is touched by a woman whose death plunges him in dark despair that challenges the consolation of his Christian faith. The tragic ending to this romantic story raises questions of life's true meaning. A-II (PG)

Shadows (1960) Low-budget picture of two black musicians (Ben Carruthers and Hugh Hurd) whose light-skinned sister (Lelia Goldoni) comes for a visit after graduating from college, then is seduced by a white writer (Anthony Ray) who scrams after learning her race. Directed by John Cassavetes, the Manhattan settings and cultural mix provide a realistic backdrop for situations improvised with some credibility by a talented cast, though the characters' problems are left unresolved. Some nasty violence, sexual situations, and crude language. A-III (br)

Shadows and Fog (1992) Drafted by vigilantes hunting a strangler in a 1920s European town, a timid clerk (Woody Allen) wanders the nighttime streets afraid of his own shadow until befriending a jilted circus performer (Mia Farrow) whose spunk inspires him. Using atmospheric black-and-white photography reminiscent of German silent movies, writer-director Allen creates a spooky story of chance meetings that hits as often as it misses with its forays into wry humor and philosophical musings. Some stylized violence and sexual innuendo. A-III (PG-13)

Shadows Over Chinatown (1946) Formula mystery with Charlie Chan (Sidney Toler) getting help from the San Francisco Missing Persons Bureau in nabbing a gang murdering people for their insurance. Directed by Terry Morse, a mysterious pickpocket (Jack Norton) adds some interest to the proceedings, with the usual comic relief from Chan's chauffeur (Mantan Moreland) and Number Two Son (Victor Sen Young, aka Yung). Menacing situations. A-I (br)

Shadrach (1998) Depression-era tale of an impoverished rural Virginia family (headed by Harvey Keitel and Andie MacDowell) that takes in a 99-year-old former slave (John Franklin Sawyer), who wants to be buried on the grounds of their ancestors' plantation where he grew up. Based on a William Styron short story and seen through the eyes of a 10-year-old boy, director Susanna Styron's slowly paced movie is a poignant portrait of hardscrabble folk reaching out to help a stranger die with dignity. Some alcohol abuse, fleeting sexual innuendo, juvenile skinny-dipping, and constant profanity. A-III (PG-13)

Shaft (1971) Director Gordon Parks adroitly uses New York City as the backdrop for what is really only a routine, if fast-paced and savvy, detective story involving a private eye (Richard Roundtree) and the police department in a power struggle between a black mobster (Moses Gunn) and the Mafia to control the drug, prostitution, and numbers racket in Harlem. Some sharp and vicious violence, brief nudity, and realistic street language. A-III (R)

Shaft in Africa (1973) John Shaft (Richard Roundtree) is taken out of Harlem by an African diplomat who requires his services to break up a contemporary slave-ring being run by a depraved Arab (Frank Finlay). Directed by John Guillermin, the plot is merely a pretext for indulging in graphic violence, explicit nudity, and extremely crude dialogue. O (R)

Shaft's Big Score (1972) When a big-time Harlem numbers operator dies, there is a scramble by black and white mobsters to take over the racket. Director Gordon Parks has turned his sequel into black exploitation, once again using Richard Roundtree as his hip private-detective, but this time smothering him in both easy (and often nude) women and gimmicky situations. Abundance of explicit violence and nudity. O (R)

Shag: The Movie (1989) Nostalgic, feel-good story, set in 1963, tracks the last weekend fling of four recent high-school grads (Page Hannah, Bridget Fonda, Annabeth Gish, and Phoebe Cates) at Myrtle Beach, S.C., where boys, the annual Sun Fun Festival, and a shag dance-contest are attractions. When one loses her virginity and breaks her engagement, the stage is set for an agonizing moral dilemma, despite the cartoon plot. Director Zelda Barron respects her young subjects, who giggle a lot about sex but have mostly harmless things on their minds. Some locker-room language laced with mild sexual vulgarities. A-III (PG)

Shaggy D.A., The (1977) Disney sequel has the now grownup hero (Dean Jones) a crusading district attorney candidate running against a crooked incumbent (Keenan Wynn) and severely inconvenienced by his sudden transformations. Directed by Robert Stevenson, the humor is very broad and the slapstick heavy-handed, even by Disney standards. All but very young children will likely be bored much of the time. A-I (G)

Shaggy Dog, The (1959) Disney comedy directed by Charles Barton in which a magic ring causes a teenager (Tommy Kirk) to be transformed into a big, bushy dog every now and then. The comic premise will appeal to youngsters, if not their parents. A-I (br)

Shake Hands with the Devil (1959) In the 1920s, an American student (Don Murray) in Ireland gets drawn into the struggle against British rule by a tough rebel leader (James Cagney). Director Michael Anderson is less interested in the issues of the conflict than in the human casualties caused by a spiraling cycle of violence. Some stylized violence and considerable tension. A-II (br)

Shakedown (1988) Another buddy crime-buster movie in which a flaky legal-aid attorney (Peter Weller) and a vigilante plainclothes detective (Sam Elliot) attempt to snare some crooked New York City cops who live high on the hog by stealing from drug dealers. With little chemistry between the leads, director James Glickenhaus relies on intense chase scenes and graphic violence. Gritty scenes within a posh drug-club and a grim 42nd Street sex parlor featuring frontal nudity and much street language. O (R)

Shakes the Clown (1992) A womanizing alcoholic

clown (Bobcat Goldthwait) is framed for the drug-related murder of his boss (Paul Dooley) by a rival clown (Tom Kenny). Also written and directed by Goldthwait, the poorly made black comedy wallows in the spiritual emptiness of the characters and is unredeemed by a phony righteous ending. Sporadic nasty violence, incessant rough language, numerous sexual references, and recreational drug use. O (R)

Shakespeare in Love (1998) Spirited farce in which young Will Shakespeare (Joseph Fiennes) has problems writing "Romeo and Juliet" until he falls for a passionate beauty (Gwyneth Paltrow) who is engaged to a callous nobleman (Colin Firth) but disguises herself as a boy to play the role of Romeo. Director John Madden's rousing play-within-a-film is a zesty concoction of mistaken identities, outsized egos, and doomed romance served up with contemporary humor. Brief comic violence, sexual encounters with nudity, and occasional double entendres. A-III (R)

Shakespeare Wallah (1966) Director James Ivory's gentle study of the old and the new in modern India centers around an itinerant group of Shakespearean actors who find it difficult to bridge the gap between the old Anglo-Indian past and the changing values of the new India. One of the highlights is its ironic contrast between the romantic notions of a young English actress (Felicity Kendal) and the materialism of an Indian movie star to whom she is attracted. Utterly disarming picture of a culture in transition, though with some mature situations. A-III (br)

Shakiest Gun in the West, The (1968) Western comedy in which Don Knotts stars as a dentist who bungles his way to becoming a hero. Directed by Alan Rafkin, it's a pint-sized version of Bob Hope's **Paleface**, but not nearly as amusing. A-I (br)

Shalako (1968) Unconvincing Western about an aristocratic hunting expedition caught poaching on Apache land and rescued by a wily Indian-fighter (Sean Connery). Director Edward Dmytryk handles the episodic action quite clumsily and the contrived love interest is ridiculous. Stylized violence. A-III (PG)

Shall We Dance (1937) Thin musical comedy in which a ballet dancer (Fred Astaire) and a musical-revue star (Ginger Rogers) team for a Broadway show, then get married in name only to avoid a scandal, but true love predictably wins out in the end. Directed by Mark Sandrich, the fluffy story creaks with contrived comic complications and show business eccentrics, but the song-and-dance numbers provide some first-rate entertainment. A-I (br)

Shall We Dance? (1997) Charming Japanese film in which a restless married businessman (Koji Yakusho) secretly takes ballroom-dancing lessons because he's attracted to one of the instructors (Tamiyo Kusakari), but instead of having an affair, he benefits from the supportive friendships that develop among the students and teachers. Writer-director Masayuki Suo deftly uses the social nature of ballroom dancing to explore with gentle humor the contradictions of a culture which frowns upon emotional displays by males. Subtitles. Some sexual references. A-II (PG)

Shallow Grave (1995) Macabre thriller in which three young professionals (Kerry Fox, Christopher Eccleston, and Ewan McGregor) sharing a flat in Edinburgh take in a roommate who soon overdoses, leaving a suitcase full of cash which the three decide to keep after disposing of the body, but their sudden wealth has deadly consequences. Director Danny Boyle alternates unsettling humor with menacing visuals as the tension mounts between the bright, self-absorbed trio, whose greed drives them to ghoulish deeds in guarding the money from the dead man's colleagues and eventually each other. Some graphic violence, images suggesting dismemberment, much menace, fleeting nudity, and occasional rough language. A-IV (R)

Shame (1969) Bleak Swedish drama about a couple (Liv Ullmann and Max Von Sydow) who escape a civil war by living on an island, where they torment one another until the war drives them to a lifeboat drifting to sea. Director Ingmar Bergman's theme is the responsibility, personal and societal, for the kind of self-destruction imaged by civil war. Subtitles. Very intense, introspective picture, but powerfully told and worth seeing despite some scenes of violence. A-III (R)

Shame (1988) Woman barrister skilled in the martial arts (Deborra-Lee Furness) motorcycles into a rural Australian town whose men-folk think nothing of molesting and raping women as a group sport. Director Steve Jodrell's heroine uses the time-honored methods of macho screen-stars to right these wrongs. Rough language with sexual connotations, a continuing sense of menace. and an intense grisly climax. A-III (R)

Shameless Old Lady, The (1966) Gently satiric French story of an old lady (Sylvie), widowed in her seventies, who is clear-sighted enough not to let her offspring take charge of her affairs, but uses her small estate to enjoy the final months of her life. Directed by Rene Allio, it is an objective yet tender look at old age and the passive role assigned to it by social convention. A-II (br)

Shampoo (1975) Warren Beatty stars as a Beverly Hills hairdresser who becomes involved with his clients, especially Julie Christie, Goldie Hawn, and Lee Grant. Directed by Hal Ashby, it is mindless fare as much devoid of humor as of humanity. Verbal obscenities and graphic depiction of sexual misbehavior. O (R)

Shamus (1973) Tough private eye from Brooklyn (Burt Reynolds) gets embroiled in a nasty little adventure involving diamond-heisting, gunrunning, and doublecrossing doublecrossers. Directed by Buzz Kulik, the shallow plot's fast-paced action is done with some genial humor, which helps diffuse numerous savage beatings and several restrained sex-scenes. A-III (PG)

Shane (1953) Classic Western about a former gunfighter (Alan Ladd) who is befriended by a farm family (Van Heflin, Jean Arthur, and young Brandon De Wilde), then saves them from being run off their land by a rancher's hired gun (Jack Palance). Directed by George Stevens, it's an epic tale of the conflict over land-rights pitting the cattlemen's six-shooters against the homesteaders' moral fortitude and family roots. Stylized frontier violence. A-II (br)

Shanghai Chest, The (1948) Formula Charlie Chan mystery directed by William Beaudine pits the Chinese-American detective (Roland Winters) against a murderer in an insurance scam, with the usual comic relief supplied by Chan's chauffeur (Mantan Moreland) and Number Two son (Victor Sen Yung). Mild racial stereotyping. A-I (br)

Shanghai Killers, The (1973) Routine martial-arts programmer from Hong Kong in which the warrior swords go snicker-snack, and the studio crew throw rubber hands and arms and buckets of blood around with wild abandon, all in service of the usual senseless violence. O (R)

Shanghai Surprise (1986) Sean Penn and Madonna give woefully inadequate performances in a supposedly romantic adventure set in 1930s China involving a search for a lost shipment of opium intended for wounded soldiers in a mission hospital. Brutal violence, sex scenes, and profanity. A-III (PG-13)

Shanghai Triad (1995) Gangster tale set in 1930s China chronicles the power struggle between a Chinese crime boss, his trusted assistant, and the beautiful mistress (Gong Li) they share, as seen through the naive eyes of her 14-year-old servant-boy. Director Zhang Yimou captures the emptiness of ill-gotten material wealth in a powerful story of evil characters, their betrayals, and reprisals. Subtitles. Some stylized violence, sexual innuendo, and rough language. A-III (R)

Shanks (1974) Odd but inept chiller starring French mime Marcel Marceau in the dual role of an ancient scientist and his deaf-mute assistant in a story-within-a-story involving an electronic device which can restore the dead to life. Directed by William Castle, the disjointed segments of the generally aimless and confused plot are introduced by title cards which don't help a bit. Some gruesome and violent visuals. A-III (PG)

Sharks' Treasure (1975) Not-very-exciting movie about diving for sunken treasure and a boat hijacking by murderous escaped convicts. Directed by Cornel Wilde (who also stars), it's routine adventure fare, save for a homosexual reference in the plot. A-III (PG)

Sharky's Machine (1981) Burt Reynolds (who also directed) plays a tough and aggressive Atlanta detective demoted for over-zealousness to the vice squad, where he cracks down on prostitutes and drug-dealers. Though the crime movie has some good moments (such as burly policeman Bernie Casey being a Zen devotee) and is consistently entertaining until its lackluster conclusion, the action includes a harrowing and far-fetched torture scene, some other graphic violence, and very crude language. A-III (R)

Shattered (1991) Convoluted thriller in which a wealthy land-developer (Tom Berenger), suffering from amnesia after a near-fatal car crash, enlists a cagey gumshoe (Bob Hoskins) to determine if his adulterous wife (Greta Scacchi) set up the accident. Writer-director Wolfgang Petersen spins an intricate tale of treachery and deceit greatly abetted by Hoskins's colorful characterization. Brief but recurring adulterous shots with nudity, momentary violence, and some rough language. A-III (R)

Shattered Image (1998) Violently surreal tale in which a wealthy bride (Anne Parillaud) on her honeymoon can't decide whether her husband (William Baldwin) is plotting to kill her, or whether she's actually a professional hit-woman and he's her next target. Though director Raul Ruiz wraps the dreamlike proceedings in an atmosphere of sinister mystery, the result is simply a tawdry potboiler littered with lurid scenes of real or imagined murders. Recurring violence, sexual encounters with nudity, and some rough language. O (nr)

Shawshank Redemption, The (1994) Gritty prison drama begins in 1946, when a quiet banker (Tim Robbins) is wrongly convicted of murder, then spends the next two decades inside a brutal and corruptly run penitentiary, where he has positive effects on the hapless inmates, especially another lifer (Morgan Freeman), before his unexpected departure. Director Frank Darabont does not spare viewers the dehumanizing ugliness of life behind bars in a story notable for its portrayal of a man who inspired hope in others while coping with the injustice done to him. Some graphic prison violence and suicides, crude sexual innuendo, brief nudity, and much rough language. A-IV (R)

She (1965) Slim escapist entertainment from H. Rider Haggard's novel of adventurers (Peter Cushing, Christopher Lee, and John Richardson) exploring the African desert in search of a hidden city, a lost civilization, and an eternal female (Ursula Andress). Director Robert Day adds nothing new to the old story of derring-do in quest of the fantastic. Stylized violence and romantic situations. A-II (br)

She-Creature, The (1956) Feeble thriller directed by Edward L. Cahn in which a financier (Tom Conway) becomes partners with a strange mesmerist (Chester Morris) whose hypnotized assistant (Marla English) recalls various reincarnations until turning into a prehistoric sea monster. Stylized violence and menacing situations. A-II (br)

She-Devil (1989) Plodding comic fantasy about the revenge of a wife (Roseanne Barr) on her philandering husband (Ed Begley Jr.) and his rich mistress (Meryl Streep). Produced and directed by Susan Seidelman, the comic premise is handled so methodically that it quickly loses interest, except for Streep's broadly funny performance as an empty-headed, outrageously pretentious, author of romance novels. Some profanity and several sex-scenes intended as satire. A-III (PG-13)

She Wore a Yellow Ribbon (1949) Superior Western about a frontier outpost, where a veteran cavalry officer (John Wayne) averts an Indian war on the eve of his mandatory retirement. Director John Ford's tribute to the horse soldiers who pacified the Western wilderness makes glorious use of Monument Valley in framing the action and warmly depicts the details of garrison life. Frontier violence. A-I (br)

She's All That (1999) Predictable teen romance in which a handsome senior (Freddie Prinze, Jr.), after being dumped by his glamorous girlfriend (Jodi Lyn O'Keefe), bets he can transform the class loner (Rachael Leigh Cook) into a popular beauty by prom night. Director Robert Iscove's derivative comedy is all too familiar, and the self-absorbed adolescents prove uninteresting. An implied affair, some sexual references, brief alcohol abuse, and a few instances of profanity and of rough language. A-III (PG-13)

She's Gotta Have It (1986) A seriocomic movie about a strong-willed, independent black woman (Tracy Camila Johns) who confounds three egocentric males. Director Spike Lee brings imagination and vitality to this low budget, black-and-white feature that offers some interesting characterizations with an accomplished all-black cast. Explicitly depicted sexual encounters, nudity, and one scene of sexual brutality. O (R)

She's Having a Baby (1988) Writer-producer-director John Hughes's coming-of-age comedy about a young man (Kevin Bacon) who must learn to face the responsibilities of married life before he and his wife (Elizabeth McGovern) have a baby. Fantasy sequences comically reflect Jake's inner turmoil, but the technique is overused to the detriment of the narrative. Sexual situations within marriage, fleeting nudity, and some profanity. A-III (PG-13)

She's Out of Control (1989) Mindless, one-joke film about an overly protective single father (Tony Danza) who lies and spies on his 15-year-old daughter (Ami Dolenz) when she begins dating. Directed by Stan Dragoti, there are no subtleties in this picture of a distrustful parent-child relationship. Some sexually vulgar innuendoes. A-III (PG)

She's So Lovely (1997) Gritty, unappealing story of a woman (Robin Wright Penn) who's torn between her first husband (Sean Penn), who's just been released from a 10-year stay in a psychiatric asylum, and her present husband (John Travolta), who has provided a good home for her and their three children. Directed by Nick Cassavetes from a script by his late father, John Cassavetes, the arbitrary love story involves three unlikable people in sordid situations that evoke little sympathy, though there are occasional flashes of wit and originality sprinkled throughout. Some violence including an off-screen rape, sexual references, occasional profanity, and much rough language. A-IV (R)

She's the One (1996) Talky domestic comedy in which two Irish-Catholic brothers face marital break-ups when the younger, fiercely competitive brother (Mike McGlone) begins cheating on his wife with the former fiancé of his newly married brother (Ed Burns). Also written and directed by Burns, the lightweight story explores issues of commitment vs. selfishness with airy charm, but scant substance. Theme of infidelity, numerous sexual references, and frequent rough language, as well as profanity. A-III (R)

She's Working Her Way Through College (1952) Lackluster musical about a dancer (Virginia Mayo) who quits burlesque to go to college, then faces expulsion over her past, until a downtrodden professor (Ronald Reagan) rallies the students in her support. Directed by Bruce Humberstone, the predictable proceedings include a hypocritical college trustee (Roland Winters), the former beau (Don DeFore) of the prof's wife (Phyllis Thaxter), and a musical football-star (Gene Nelson), though the highlight is Reagan's game but inept performance in a comic drunk scene. Sexual situations and marital misunderstandings. A-III (br)

Sheba Baby (1975) Avenging black woman (Pam Grier) annihilates an army of hoods of various hues. Directed by William Girdler, it is a tasteless fantasy of sex and violence, though handled with some restraint. A-III (PG)

Sheena (1984) Comic-book jungle drama about a female Tarzan named Sheena (Tanya Roberts) who runs through Africa scantily clad in animal skins, pursued by a romantic TV-reporter (Ted Wass). Directed by John Guillermin, it is so bad that it provokes laughter in all the wrong places. Extensive nudity. O (PG)

Sheepman, The (1958) Genial Western comedy in which an ornery cowboy (Glenn Ford) establishes a sheep ranch in the middle of cattle country, then unmasks the region's biggest rancher (Leslie Nielsen) as a crook, thereby winning over the local cattlemen and the man's fiancé (Shirley MacLaine). Director George Marshall paces the good-natured narrative with Ford's quirky characterization as an experienced gunman who would rather talk things out than engage in a shootout. A-I (br)

Shelia Levine Is Dead and Living in New York (1975) Failed screen version of Gail Parent's acerbically witty novel about a small-town girl (Jeannie Berlin) who escapes to New York in search of meaning and marriage, finds a doctor (Roy Scheider), and convinces him that country virtues are better than urban sophistication. Not only are the principals miscast, but director Sidney Furie is out of his element in working with a script that has the deadly mediocre level of TV situation-comedy. A-III (PG)

Sheltering Sky, The (1990) Visiting North Africa in the late 1940s, a troubled married couple (Debra Winger and John Malkovich) and their traveling companion (Campbell Scott) take a trip into the Sahara, where they encounter typhoid fever, infidelity, and madness. Director Bernardo Bertolucci's bleak journey into the void is a roadmap to despair given some poignancy by the beautifully photographed desert environment that devours the characters in this intense and harrowing film. A number of graphic adulterous liaisons with brief shots of full nudity. O (R)

Shenandoah (1965) Civil War story of a Virginia family patriarch (James Stewart) whose opposition to slavery keeps him out of the war until one of his sons is captured, and he fights his way through Union lines trying to find him. Director Andrew McLaglen does best with the action scenes showing the futile havoc of war but is less effective in portraying its consequences on the family and its members. Wartime violence. A-I (br)

Shepherd of the Hills (1941) Creaky rural saga set in the Ozarks, where revenue agents pursue moonshiners while a mysterious stranger (Harry Carey) wins over the suspicious mountain folk, except for a troubled young woodsman (John Wayne) who vows to kill him despite the protests of the girl (Betty Field) who loves the boy. Director Henry Hathaway establishes the isolated backwoods setting convincingly, but the melodramatic story of tangled family relationships does not date well, and the result is chiefly of interest for its good cast. Stylized violence and domestic strife. A-II (br)

Sheriff of Fractured Jaw, The (1959) Leaden Western spoof directed by Raoul Walsh delivers a mirthless misfire, with Kenneth Moore as an English gunsalesman pressed into service to protect a frontier town from warring ranchers (Bruce Cabot and William Campbell), with only Jayne Mansfield and a motley band of Indians for support. Stylized violence and mild sexual innuendo. A-II (br)

Sherlock Holmes and the Secret Code (see: **Dressed to Kill**)

Sherlock Holmes and the Secret Weapon (1942) Dated mystery directed by Roy William Neill in which Holmes (Basil Rathbone) takes a hand in WW II by smuggling a bombsight inventor (William Post, Jr.) out of Switzerland, only to lose him in England to kidnappers led by Professor Moriarty (Lionel Atwill). Stylized violence, including a scene of torture. A-II (br)

Sherlock Holmes and the Spider Woman (see: **The Spider Woman**)

Sherlock Holmes and the Voice of Terror (1942) Called in by British intelligence to silence short-wave broadcasts of Nazi sabotage, Holmes (Basil Rathbone) and Watson (Nigel Bruce) succeed with some help from the London underworld and a patriotic widow (Evelyn Ankers). Directed by John Rawlins, it's an interesting period-piece, with colorful atmosphere and a good supporting cast (Thomas Gomez, Reginald Denny, and Henry Daniell). Wartime menace. A-II (br)

Sherlock Holmes Faces Death (1943) Intriguing entry in the updated Conan Doyle detective series, with Holmes (Basil Rathbone) and Watson (Nigel Bruce) after a killer (Arthur Margetson) in a creaky English manor being used by convalescent Allied officers. With a script based on **The Musgrave Ritual**, director Roy William Neill works up a lot of sinister atmosphere in the story of murdered brothers and a chess riddle involving a secret family-inheritance. Menacing situations. A-I (br)

Sherlock Holmes in Washington (1943) Fair WW II mystery in which Holmes (Basil Rathbone) and Watson (Nigel Bruce) search the US capital for a missing British secret document which must be found before it falls into the hands of a Nazi spy-ring (led by George Zucco). Directed by Roy William Neill, the plot involves the use of microfilm and a book of matches, with Watson providing the usual comic relief amidst the patriotic fervor of the period. A-I (br)

Shiloh (1997) After lying to his stern but loving father (Michael Moriarty) in order to save an abused puppy from its cruel master (Scott Wilson), an 11-year-old lad (Blake Heron) learns the painful consequences of dishonesty. Writer-director Dale Rosenbloom uses the appealing bond of boy and dog to probe the father-son relationship in a meaningful way, but the narrative is too slow-paced and repetitive to be entirely successful as drama. Strong threat of animal abuse and domestic tensions. A-II (PG)

Shinbone Alley (1971) Disappointing cartoon version of the Broadway musical based on Don Marquis's classic "archy and mehitabel" about the cockroach chronicler of the irrepressible alley-cat whose spirit has transmigrated from Cleopatra. Directed by John D. Wilson, with the central characters voiced by Eddie Bracken and Carol Channing, the result simply lacks the elemental zest and witty irony of the Marquis original. A-I (G)

Shine (1996) Remarkable fact-based story of an Australian musical prodigy who suffers a mental collapse as a youth (Noah Taylor) because of his iron-willed father (Armin Mueller-Stahl), then resumes a brilliant career as classical pianist in middle age after he (Geoffrey Rush) weds an understanding woman (Lynn Redgrave). Director Scott Hicks gives a universal dimension to this story of the damage done by a father's possessive, destructive love being undone by a woman's patient, redemptive love. Domestic violence, a fleeting bedroom scene and brief nudity. A-III (PG-13)

Shining, The (1980) Disappointing screen version of the Stephen King novel is a haunted house movie on a grand scale, with Jack Nicholson as a writer who takes the job of winter caretaker of a hotel resort in the Colorado Rockies, accompanied by wife (Shelley Duvall) and young son (Danny Lloyd). Tormented and manipulated by the evil lurking in the massive hotel (the scene of a brutal axe-murder), he is taken to the brink of madness and tries to kill his family. Director Stanley Kubrick's ponderous horror movie is predictable and slow-paced in building to its violent climax. Graphic violence, a needlessly extended erotic sequence, and some rough language. O (R)

Shining Through (1992) Blandly romantic WW II espionage tale follows an OSS Colonel (Michael Douglas) into Nazi Germany to rescue his spy-girlfriend (Melanie Griffith) who's trying to get crucial war plans from a high-ranking German officer (Liam Neeson). Though the actors try their best, they cannot overcome the plot implausibilities underlying writer-director David Seltzer's slack wartime love story. Brief violence and fleeting bedroom scene. A-III (R)

Ship of Fools (1965) Abby Mann's flawed yet powerful adaptation of Katherine Anne Porter's allegorical novel centers on the foibles and self-delusions of some two-dozen passengers (including Vivien Leigh, Oskar Werner, Simone Signoret, Jose Ferrer, and Lee Marvin) on a German liner sailing from Mexico to its home port in 1933, the year Hitler came to power. Though producer-director Stanley Kramer is not always successful in giving dramatic credibility to the truncated stories of the numerous characters, he does manage to convey the inability of most to comprehend the Nazi menace, as well as to suggest through the narrator (Michael Dunn) that viewers may discover something of themselves in this portrayal of human frailty. Some anti-Semitic references and sexual situations. A-III (br)

Ship of Lost Men, The (1929) Silent German melodrama aboard a creaky old windjammer bound for Brazil with contraband cargo and a cruel captain (Fritz Kortner) whose mistreated crew mutiny, then turn against an unwilling American passenger and a downed woman-pilot (Marlene Dietrich) he rescued from the sea. Written and directed by Maurice Tourneur, the murky story shows the self-destructive nature of violence with appropriate visual force, mixing realistic shots of the sailing ship with darkly menacing interiors and occasionally surrealistic images. Periodic violence, threatening situations, and sexual innuendo. A-III (br)

Shipwrecked (1991) Young Norwegian lad (Stian Smestad) goes to sea as a cabin-boy, but his ship is shanghaied by pirates, then wrecked by a tropical storm, and the boy is washed overboard to wind up on a deserted island, where he finds the pirates' treasure and frees his shipmates from their fearsome captor (Gabriel Byrne). Directed by Nils Gaup, the 19th-century adventure of a youth coping in a man's world has the excitement of an ocean voyage under full sail and the inventiveness of a 14-year-old Robinson Crusoe, but the personal level tends to get lost in the narrative's constant action. Much menace and some frightening moments for young children. A-I (PG)

Shirley Valentine (1989) In a British comedy of some wit and intelligence, a 42-year-old Liverpool housewife (Pauline Collins) leaves hubby and grown children for a two-week holiday in Greece, where she meets a clay-footed womanizer (Tom Conti) but rediscovers on her own a long-submerged zest for life. Adapted from his own stage-play by Willy Russell and directed a bit too literally by Lewis Gilbert, the adult comedy about a spunky middle-aged woman has a lot of heart and a memorable title performance. Some mature themes, fleeting nudity, and comic use of a sexual expletive. A-III (R)

Shoah (1985) Death-camp survivors, former Nazi officials and Poles living in the vicinity of the extermination sites, are interviewed by producer-director Claude Lanzmann in this French documentary on the Holocaust. Although it does not show any photographs of Hitler's mass murder of European Jewry, the survivors' oral history of events is powerful and often shocking, all the more so because it personalizes the horror of the camps. Subtitled and more than nine hours in length, the work is a valuable educational resource on the Holocaust. A-II (nr)

Shock to the System, A (1990) Mild-mannered Manhattan ad executive (Michael Caine) finds that he can easily murder his demanding wife (Swoosie Kurtz) and yuppie colleague (Peter Riegert), among others who stand in his way. With flat direction by Jan Egleson, the movie balances uncomfortably between a satiric black comedy and a serial-murder drama, providing a view of moral corruption that would be utterly distasteful if not for Caine's fine performance. Condones murder as an acceptable means to an end, a jokey on-screen suicide, some rough language, and sexual innuendoes. O (R)

Shock Troops (1968) French-Italian production about a group of French resistance fighters in WW II who raid a German prison to rescue 12 men sentenced to death but find that they have saved one man too many (Michel Piccoli) and suspect he may be a spy. Directed by Costa-Gavras, the story is much like other movies about the French Resistance, though its action scenes are almost documentary-like in effect. Wartime violence and brutality. A-III (R)

Shocker (1989) When a TV repairman (Mitch Pileggi) is electrocuted for murdering entire families, he is sucked into the TV airwaves, from which he returns to slash more families until freeze-framed by a telepathic college-football hero (Peter Berg). Writer-director Wes Craven mixes black humor and simpleminded satire with much profanity and grisly mass murders. O (R)

Shocking Miss Pilgrim, The (1947) Mild musical comedy set in 1874, when Boston's first woman typist (Betty Grable) has a hard time keeping her job with a sexist boss (Dick Haynes), who ultimately proposes marriage. Writer-director George Seaton tries to have some fun playing both sides of the street, but neither feminists nor chauvinists are likely to be amused, though some may enjoy the Gershwin music. Bland romantic complications and dated treatment of gender roles. A-I (br)

Shoes of the Fisherman, The (1968) Uneven screen version of the Morris L. West novel about a Russian bishop (Anthony Quinn) who becomes pope and decides that the Vatican's wealth be given to the world's poor. Directed by Michael Anderson, the point of the story gets lost in a series of murky subplots involving international intrigue. The religious pageantry is eye-catching but conveyed largely on a superficial level. A-I (br)

Shogun Assassin (1980) Samurai swordsman wields his blade tirelessly in dispatching legions of assassins in this campy Americanized version of a Japanese martial-arts movie directed by Kenji Jisumi. Narrated by a child, the action is a visual ballet of incessant violence and bloodshed. O (R)

Shoot (1976) Painfully well-intentioned diatribe directed by Harvey Hart against the cult of guns has a preposterous story of two groups of hunters who, because of an accidental shooting death, begin an armed war against each other. Much violence. A-III (R)

Shoot the Moon (1982) Successful Hollywood writer (Albert Finney) walks out on his wife (Diane Keaton) and four young daughters in director Alan Parker's account of sometimes savage martial strife. Though there are some effective touches, the movie withholds so much vital information about the principals that it becomes irritating and pretentious. Some intense violence and very rough language. A-III (R)

Shoot to Kill (1988) Taut, at times harrowing, thriller about a street-smart FBI agent (Sidney Poitier) and a woods-wise guide (Tom Berenger) who learn to trust each other in the course of tracking down a psychotic killer. Director Roger Spottiswoode handles the action scenes effectively, but the relationship between the two principals is too contrived to be entirely convincing. Some brief but intense violence and considerable menace. A-III (R)

Shooting Party, The (1985) In the fall of 1913, some aristocrats gather at the estate of a nobleman (James Mason) to do a bit of shooting and carry on some romantic intrigues on the eve of the war that would end their world forever. Alan Bridges directs a thoughtful and entertaining film, if a bit slow-moving and predictable at times. Superbly acted but contains a rather explicit bedroom scene. A-IV (nr)

Shootist, The (1976) Uneven Western directed by Don Siegel in which a legendary gunfighter (John Wayne), told by a doctor (James Stewart) that he is dying of cancer, engages in a final shoot-out. The movie's glossing-over of the hero's various moral failings makes it mature fare. A-III (PG)

Shootout (1971) Familiar revenge plot about a stoic ex-con (Gregory Peck) on his way to settle accounts with a doublecrossing partner starts going astray when he is detained by a dependent widow (Pat Quinn) and a homeless waif (Dawn Lyn) who may be his daughter by a prostitute. Director Henry Hathaway leaves family audiences far behind with some sadistic violence, including a gang rape in a brothel and coarse language out of the mouth of a nine-year-old. Grim stuff. O (GP)

Shoot-Out at Medicine Bend (1957) Routine Western directed by Richard L. Bare in which an ex-Army officer (Randolph Scott) masquerades as a Quaker in order to get the goods on a man (James Craig) selling defective guns to settlers beset by Indian raids. Frontier violence. A-I (br)

Shop Around the Corner, The (1940) Delightful romantic comedy set in a Budapest department store, where two clerks (James Stewart and Margaret Sullavan) nurture a mutual dislike of the other while each exchanges love letters with a lonely heart's pen-pal until ultimately discovering they have been corresponding with each other. Director Ernst Lubitsch treats the workaday friction between the clerks with some wry humor while building sympathy for both, then brings them together in an emotionally satisfying conclusion that has charmed viewers ever since. Romantic complications. A-II (br)

Shop on Main Street, The (1966) Czechoslovakian tragicomedy of life under a puppet Nazi regime sensitively details the unusual friendship that develops between a simple man (Josef Kroner) and an elderly Jewish widow (Ida Kaminska) over whose button shop he has been appointed "Aryan Controller." Director Jan Kadar draws the situation with a loving sense of human character that helps underscore the movie's condemnation of moral passivity in the face of inhumanity. Subtitles. A-III (br)

Short Circuit (1986) Number Five is a lovable robot who acquires human attributes after being struck by lightning and befriended by Ally Sheedy, an ill-tempered snack-wagon operator. Steve Guttenberg plays Number Five's inventor in this routine romance from director John Badham. Some suggestive comments and mild profanity are lost in the context of chase scenes. A-I (PG)

Short Circuit 2 (1988) Robot Number Five returns as Johnny Five to help a friend (Fisher Stevens) launch a toy-robot company, but gets caught up in all sorts of mayhem, including a jewel heist. Directed by Kenneth Johnson, the loveable erector-set steals the show, but some harrowing attacks on the robot may upset very young children. Rough language. A-II (PG)

Short Cuts (1993) Long, sprawling narrative intertwines the troubled lives and eccentric experiences of nine families numbering 21 major characters (among them, Andie MacDowell, Bruce Davison, Jack Lemmon, Matthew Modine, Anne Archer, Tim Robbins, and Lily Tomlin) over the course of several days in a Los Angeles suburb. Loosely based on short stories by Raymond Carver and directed by Robert Altman, the result is a messy collage of egocentric lives, arbitrarily thrown together through overlapping story lines, whose flawed characters and dysfunctional behavior turn into a dreary sideshow of human frailties. Extramarital affairs, explicit discussions of sex, nudity, violence, substance abuse, and rough language. O (R)

Short Eyes (1977) Screen version of Miguel Pinero's play about prison life tells the story of a man (Bruce Davison), accused of molesting a little girl, who is thrust into a volatile environment where the other prisoners subject him to systematic and brutal harassment as someone who is lower than them. Directed by Robert M. Young, the movie's strength is in the almost overpowering realism of its mood and setting and the compelling personalities of its characters. Although the rough language, the violence and the threatening atmosphere are thoroughly justified in content, the movie is not for everyone. A-IV (R)

Short Time (1990) Mildly amusing comedy about a Seattle police officer who, after being mistakenly told he has only a few weeks to live, sets out to be killed in the line of duty so his ex-wife can collect his insurance and send his son to Harvard. Directed by Gregg Champion, the one-joke comedy is an uneasy melange of slapstick humor, melodramatic sentimentality, and action stunts, but its chief asset is Dabney Coleman, who knows how to wring a good laugh from slim material. Mature theme, some hard-edged violence, a bedroom scene, and needless profanity. A-III (PG-13)

Shot in the Dark, A (1964) French police inspector Clouseau (Peter Sellers) drives his superior (Herbert Lom) 'round the bend during a murder case involving a pretty maid (Elke Sommer) whom his bungling, accident-prone subordinate keeps trying to prove is innocent. Director Blake Edwards has fun with a farcical plot and characters to match, but its parade of sight gags (including a nudist colony) is overlong and mostly self-indulgent. Slapstick violence and much sexual innuendo. A-III (br)

Shout, The (1979) Intriguing psychological thriller about a mysterious stranger (Alan Bates) who threatens the husband (John Hurt) of a woman (Susannah York) he wants to take; the stranger has the lethal power of a shout capable of killing everything within hearing distance, a mystical technique learned during a long stay among Australian aborigines. British production directed by Jerzy Skolimowski, it is beautifully photographed and performed, but it cannot sustain its fragile premise. Mature treatment. A-III (R)

Shout (1991) Lame 1950s youth drama set in a delinquent boys' home, where a rebellious teen (James Walters) defies the man in charge (Richard Jordan), pursues his daughter (Heather Graham), and conspires with a music teacher (John Travolta) to form a forbidden rock 'n' roll band. Director Jeffrey Hornaday milks familiar anti-authority and coming-of-age themes for a plastic story lacking dramatic or even musical energy. A brief bedroom scene with adolescents and momentary violence. A-III (PG-13)

Shout at the Devil (1976) Comedy about a boozy buccaneer (Lee Marvin) in WW I southeast Africa who cons upright Briton (Roger Moore) into a little elephant-tusk poaching on German territory suddenly turns nasty when Moore's wife is brutalized and his infant daughter burned to death by German forces. Directed by Michael Klinger, the movie has a blood-and-gore conclusion. A-III (PG)

Show Boat (1936) Fine version of the Jerome Kern-Oscar Hammerstein musical about the daughter (Irene Dunne) of a Mississippi riverboat captain (Charles Winninger) and her stormy marriage to an inveterate gambler (Allan Jones), which is counterpointed by a tragic subplot involving a mulatto singer (Helen Morgan). Director James Whale gets some real feeling out of the sentimental melodrama with a talented cast and a convincing turn-of-the-century setting that helps make the nostalgic musical as much a part of Americana as Paul Robeson's deckhand singing "Old Man River." Period depiction of race relations and domestic difficulties. A-II (nr)

Show Boat (1951) Glossy remake of the Kern-Hammerstein musical from Edna Ferber's novel about a turn-of-the-century Mississippi riverboat troupe whose ingenue (Kathryn Grayson) weds a dashing, unreliable gambler (Howard Keel), with their troubled marriage finding counterpoint in the tragic victimization of the troupe's mulatto star (Ava Gardner). Director George Sidney's rousing period entertainment has lovely songs, zestful dance numbers, and comic relief from riverboat captain Joe E. Brown, but short-changes the romance and soft-pedals the era's racial bigotry. Romantic complications and justice issues. A-II (br)

Show of Force, A (1990) Plodding political thriller centers on a San Juan television reporter (Amy Irving) who puts her life in danger tracking evidence of apparent collusion between US and Puerto Rican officials in the deaths of two men at a communications facility. Brazilian director Bruno Barreto depicts the controversial 1978 slayings as being staged by a repressive government in an effort to discredit the local independence movement, but its murky, disjointed treatment strains credibility, despite good performances by Andy Garcia as the prosecutor and Lou Diamond Phillips as a double agent. Several strong scenes of graphic violence, much menace and minimal rough language. A-III (R)

Showdown (1973) Saddle-worn tale of two boyhood chums whose trails diverge, but intertwine years later when one of them, an outlaw on the run (Dean Martin) seeks refuge from a one-time girlfriend (Susan Clark), now the wife of the other, an upright sheriff (Rock Hudson). George Seaton directs the B-grade Western with deadly earnestness, relieved only by some foggy flashbacks of the pair's boyhood escapades and a few good action scenes. A-II (PG)

Showdown, The (1950) Revenge Western in which an ex-lawman (William Elliott) seeks his brother's murderer among the cowpunchers (Harry Morgan, Peter Graves, and others) working for a Texas rancher (Walter Brennan) and a saloon owner (Marie Windsor). Directed by Dorrell and Stuart McGowan, the hard-bitten proceedings center on the hero's determination to avenge his brother's death until the last reel softens his resolve. Frontier violence, theme of personal retribution, and some sexual innuendo. A-III (br)

Showdown at Abilene (1956) Convoluted Western in which Abilene's sheriff (Jock Mahoney) returns from the Civil War guilt-ridden and unable to fire a gun, then finds his girl (Martha Hyer) about to marry a friend (Lyle Bettger) who's become a cattle baron driving local farmers off their land. Directed by Charles Haas, the situation's potential is wasted in muddy motivations as the plot grows increasingly contrived. Stylized violence and some nasty brutality. A-III (br)

Showdown at Boot Hill (1958) Routine Western directed by Gene Fowler, Jr., in which a bounty hunter (Charles Bronson) kills his quarry in self-defense, then has to face the dead man's friends in a frontier town with no one willing to take his side except a lonely waitress who wants to reform him. Several shootouts and an attempt at vigilante justice. A-II (br)

Showgirls (1995) Relentlessly sleazy potboiler about a hardened Vegas stripper (Elizabeth Berkley) who graduates to performing in a casino's topless show, then steals the star spot by incapacitating its lead dancer. Director Paul Verhoeven's sexist depiction of women is a mindless exercise in sneering, leering voyeurism. A brutal gang rape, simulated sex acts, much exploitative nudity, drug abuse, and rough language. O (NC-17/R)

Shriek in the Night, A (1933) Creaky murder mystery directed by Albert Ray in which rival newspaper reporters (Ginger Rogers and Lyle Talbot) covering a murder case finally join forces when one of them (Rogers) is targeted by the mad killer. Stylized violence, menace, and sexual situations. A-III (br)

Shrike, The (1955) Twisted psychological drama in which a successful stage director (Jose Ferrer) goes into a professional tailspin after marrying a would-be actress (June Allyson), leaves her for another women (Joy Page), then tries to commit suicide, and winds up in a mental ward. Also directed by Ferrer, the situation tentatively suggests that the man is the victim of a manipulative wife, then reverses course in assessing blame and potential cure. Discreet treatment of domestic problems and troubled individuals. A-II (br)

Shut My Big Mouth (1942) Wacky Western directed by Charles Barton features comedian Joe E. Lewis as a meek horticulturist mistakenly made sheriff of a town beset by outlaws (Victor Jory, Forrest Tucker, and Lloyd Bridges) whom he befuddles by, among other things, dressing as a woman and making allies of a local Indian tribe. Slapstick violence, comic menace, and mild sexual innuendo. A-II (br)

Shuttered Room, The (1967) British suspense thriller directed by David Greene about a couple (Carol Lynley and Gig Young) who journey to a New England island to take possession of the house where the wife grew up, but find themselves harassed by the islanders and warned of a dire evil in the house. Excessive violence, a near-rape, and scenes with semi-nudity. O (br)

Shy People (1988) Brash New York writer (Jill Clayburgh) and nymphet daughter (Martha Plimpton) come upon some sinister goings-on in a Louisiana bayou while visiting a distant relative (Barbara Hershey) and her four wild sons. Director Andrei Konchalovsky fills the hothouse drama with American stereotypes. Some intense violence, drug abuse, an explicit striptease sequence, and teen sexual promiscuity. O (R)

Sibling Rivalry (1990) When a frustrated housewife's (Kirstie Alley) one instance of infidelity kills the guy (Sam Elliott), she makes a hapless salesman (Bill Pullman) think he's responsible, and together they concoct a suicide scene which leads to further complications. Director Carl Reiner's minor screwball comedy wedges a tasteless scene among several madcap moments animated by the leads' flair for physical comedy. Comic treatment of extramarital sex and minimal profanity. A-III (PG-13)

Sicilian, The (1987) Failed screen version of the Mario Puzo novel focuses on Salvatore Giuliano (Christopher Lambert), a historical figure whose rebellion against Sicily's Mafia, landowners, and churchmen ended in 1950 with his murder. Directed by Michael Cimino, the movie is muddled and disjointed, with a narrative that is often ludicrous and lacking in a sense of the area's culture and history. Graphic violence, brief nudity, and some rough language. A-IV (R)

Sicilian Clan, The (1970) Epic French heist tale is a duel of wits and guts between white-maned crime patriarch (Jean Gabin) and ambitious Paris hood (Alain Delon) over an impossibly complicated plane hijack of a fortune in jewels, with frustrated but persistent police inspector (Lino Ventura) keeping one step behind all the way. Directed by Henri Verneuil, the briskly paced story of honor among thieves has a number of superior action-sequences, from an ingenious jail escape at the start to a grandly anticlimactic shootout. A-III (GP)

Sid and Nancy (1987) All the sordid details of physical and spiritual disintegration are celebrated in this harsh and excessively explicit portrait of the sadistic, self-destructive lives of British punk-rock music-star Sid Vicious and his American girlfriend, Nancy. Without care for the reasons behind Sid's tragic self-destruction, the film is masochistically exploitative. O (R)

Siddhartha (1973) Screen version of Hermann Hesse's novel about a Brahmin's son, Siddhartha (Shashi Kapoor), who rebels at his father's asceticism, rejects the message of various holy-men, is disappointed with the pleasures of sex and the rewards of business, but finally discovers enlightenment in nature and the unity of life. Written, produced, and directed by Conrad Rooks, the movie attempts to create a mystic experience, rendering the abstract and sometimes ponderous philosophizing of the text into the sheer beauty of poetic imagery, ably supplied by Sven Nykvist's camera. Some will find it an uplifting experience, while others will see only an album of pretty pictures. Restrained but erotic sex scene. A-III (R)

Sidecar Racers (1975) Young American (Ben Murphy), at loose ends in Australia, becomes involved in the hazardous sport of sidecar motorcycle-racing. Directed by Earl Bellamy, it's an innocuous, mildly diverting action movie, but some romantic complications are not for the youngsters. A-III (PG)

Sidekicks (1993) Corny tale of asthmatic teen student of karate (Jonathan Brandis) who daydreams of rescuing damsels in distress alongside karate hero Chuck Norris (playing himself), then finds himself partnered with his idol at a competition. Director Aaron Norris depicts his brother Chuck as an awesome good guy in this dull and predictable vanity production that caters to teen macho fantasies. Stylized martial-arts violence and periodic menace. A-III (PG)

Sidewalk Stories (1989) The story of a homeless New York City street artist (Charles Lane) and the two-year-old waif (Nicole Alysia) he shelters is told in a virtually silent, black-and-white movie that depends upon the eloquent body-language of the actors and an energetic musical score by Marc Marder. Lane also wrote, produced, and directed this Chaplinesque tale of two black outcasts which presents a poignant if sentimentalized view of the plight of the homeless. Brief frontal nudity in an erotic dream-sequence and some comic-book violence. A-III (R)

Sidewalks of London (1938) Bittersweet tale in which a London street performer (Charles Laughton) keeps a waif (Vivien Leigh) out of trouble by teaching her his trade, then she becomes a music-hall star with the help of an admirer (Rex Harrison) and, years later, tries to repay her old teacher when she discovers he's fallen on hard times. Directed by Tim Whelan, the sentimental story is secondary to the bright performances of Laughton and Leigh. Veiled sexual innuendo. A-II (br)

Sidewinder 1 (1977) Mediocre motorcycle-racing movie directed by Earl Bellamy in which engineer Alex Cord develops a new cycle and goes into partnership with driver Michael Parks to refine it. An extramarital relationship makes it adult fare. A-III (PG)

Siege, The (1998) Shrill action movie in which an FBI agent (Denzel Washington) and a slippery CIA operative (Annette Bening) join forces to locate Brooklyn-based Arab terrorists responsible for a series of deadly bombings that have left New York City under marital law enforced by a fanatical general (Bruce Willis). Director Edward Zwick's densely plotted thriller raises provocative questions about democracy and racism, which prove more interesting than the explosive story at hand. Some intense violence and mayhem, brief sexual innuendo, and intermittent rough language. A-III (R)

Siege of the Saxons (1963) When King Arthur (Mark Dignam) is slain by a Cornish usurper (Ronald Howard) in league with Saxony, his daughter (Janette Scott) is rescued by a forest outlaw (Ronald Lewis), proclaimed Camelot's queen by Merlin (John Laurie), and routs England's foes. Director Nathan Juran's cut-rate British production muddles through the outlandish proceedings with the help of action scenes lifted straight out of **The Black Knight** (1954). Clunky Arthurian tale with stylized violence. A-I (br)

Sierra (1950) Tangled Western in which a man (Dean Jagger) wrongly accused of murder escapes into the mountains with his son (Audie Murphy), where they complicate their lives by rescuing a woman lawyer (Wanda Hendrix) lost in the wilds. Directed by Alfred E. Green, the unconvincing story meanders along listlessly, though the tedium is relieved occasionally by songs from Burl Ives. Frontier violence. A-I (br)

Sierra Baron (1958) Disappointing Western set in California after its 1848 acquisition by the US enables a crooked American (Steve Brodie) to sell land belonging to a Mexican don (Rick Jason) who holds out with the help of a Texas gunslinger (Brian Keith), until his Spanish title is recognized by the new government. Directed by James B. Clark, the formula proceedings rarely measure up to the subject's rich potential. Frontier violence. A-I (br)

Sierra Stranger (1957) Formula Western about a cowboy (Howard Duff) who rides into the middle of a dispute over a mining claim and winds up on the wrong side. Directed by Lee Sholem, the plot is tired and the action tiresome. Stylized violence and mild romance. A-II (br)

Sign of the Cross, The (1932) After Nero (Charles Laughton) condemns the Christians for his burning of Rome in 64 A.D., the city's prefect (Fredric March) promptly falls in love with one (Elissa Landi), but when his efforts to save her are blocked by jealous empress Poppaea (Claudette Colbert), the tribune joins his beloved for a martyr's death in the arena. Producer-director Cecil B. DeMille lavishes more creative imagination on scenes of Roman debauchery and brutality than on the inspirational story of early Christian martyrs, though the result is impressive as historical spectacle, especially the arena sequences. The 1944 reissue opens with a prologue in liberated Rome as WW II military chaplains set the scene. Much period violence, menace, and sexual innuendo. A-III (br)

Sign of the Pagan (1954) Talky historical melodrama in which Attila the Hun (Jack Palance) leads the barbarians in a march on Rome, but turns away after a meeting with Pope Leo I (Maroni Olsen), then tangles with a Roman legion (led by Jeff Chandler), and is killed by a Christian captive. Directed by Douglas Sirk, this Hollywood version of history oversimplifies the triumph of Christian idealism over barbarian superstitions and wastes time on a romantic subplot involving Chandler's centurion with a Byzantine princess. Stylized violence and romantic complications. A-II (br)

Signs of Life (1989) Sketchy drama about the impending closure of a venerable New England family's boat-building business and the effects on its elderly owner (Arthur Kennedy), assorted employees, and hangers-on. Directed by John David Coles, its inconsequential narrative hints at the occult, includes a botched suicide, a near-drowning, and a pointless robbery. Some rough language and a brief sexual encounter. A-III (PG-13)

Silence of the Lambs, The (1991) An FBI trainee (Jodie Foster) seeks the identity of a psychotic serial-killer (Ted Levine) from a brilliantly manipulative psychiatrist (Anthony Hopkins), himself an imprisoned multiple-murderer. Jonathan Demme directs a riveting thriller eliciting superb performances from Foster and Hopkins while attempting a straightforward treatment of repugnant subject-matter by focusing on the novice agent's dedication to her assignment. Some intense violence and graphic shots of mutilated bodies, a flash of nudity, and occasional rough language. A-IV (R)

Silence of the North (1981) Fact-based Canadian story of a spunky 1920s farm woman (Ellen Burstyn) who, after her husband (Tom Skerritt) perishes trapping in the Northwest Territories, moves to Calgary to raise her three children during the Depression. Director Allan Winton King succeeds in showing the fearsome beauty of Canada's northern wilderness, but the human drama of pioneer folk is smothered in low-key, dull performances. The deadly menace of a hostile environment and a few instances of profanity. A-II (PG)

Silencers, The (1966) Shabby imitation spy-spoof of James Bond spy-adventure movies, with Dean Martin playing Matt Helm, freelance super-spy who spends much of his time cracking heads and getting his own bent occasionally. When not thus engaged, he chases an assortment of comely female spies around the set. The comic level is uniformly low and so is the moral tone of the action. O (br)

Silent Death (see: **Voodoo Island**)

Silent Fall (1994) Psychological thriller in which a troubled child-psychiatrist (Richard Dreyfuss) attempts to learn the identity of a murderer from an autistic nine-year-old boy (Ben Faulkner) who was the sole eyewitness to the stabbing deaths of his parents and is now being cared for by his distraught 18-year-old sister (Liv Tyler). Director Bruce Beresford's poorly developed whodunit suffers from its halting pace until it slams into a lurid, overwrought solution, which is in turn capped off by a pat and patently unconvincing finale. A gory murder site, references to incest and adultery, and some rough language. A-III (R)

Silent Movie (1976) Writer-director Mel Brooks stars as a washed-up director who gets the head of his studio (Sid Caesar) to let him make a silent comedy provided he can get Hollywood's biggest stars to participate. The result is sometimes funny, sometimes not, but it is harmless fun and less vulgar than other Brooks's comedies. Adult humor. A-III (PG)

Silent Night, Deadly Night (1984) Maniac dressed in a Santa Claus costume uses an axe to kill people. Dreadfully produced exploitative horror suggests that director Charles Sellier, Jr., should think about another line of work. Excessive gory violence. O (R)

Silent Night, Evil Night (see: **Black Christmas**)

Silent Partner, The (1979) Dull bank-teller (Elliott Gould) keeps out a large cache of money for himself during a bank holdup, but the robber (Christopher Plummer) is a cunning sadist who doesn't like being made a fool of. What follows includes a brutal murder and a savage beating. Directed by Daryl Duke, the film is cleverly done and well-acted, but the cheap, corrosive cynicism that permeates it, together with the sex and violence inserted to jolt the audience, is seriously offensive. O (R)

Silent Rage (1982) Small-town sheriff (martial-arts whiz Chuck Norris) confronts a seemingly indestructible superman fashioned by an irresponsible scientist. Directed by Michael Miller, it is an utterly inconsequential effort of deadening predictability. Considerable violence, though stylized, and some fleeting nudity. A-III (R)

Silent Running (1972) Above-average tale of ecological disaster in the not-too-distant future, where the commander (Bruce Dern) of a space-ark refuses the order to destroy its precious cargo of plant life that can no longer grow on earth. Directed by Douglas Trumbull, the sci-fi effects are good, and the story's theme of humanity's relationship to the environment is thoughtful. Unfortunately, the weak storyline ends in the confusion of madness and restrained mayhem. A-II (GP/G)

Silent Stranger, The (see: **Step Down to Terror**)

Silk Stockings (1957) Belabored musical updating the 1939 romantic comedy, **Ninotchka**, has a Soviet commissar (Cyd Charisse) arriving in Paris to replace three faltering comrades (Peter Lorre, Jules Munshin, and Sam Wanamaker), then falling for a capitalist movie-producer (Fred Astaire.). Despite spirited Cole Porter songs, director Rouben Mamoulien fails to convey any romantic sparks between the Astaire-Charisse duo, and the flashy production numbers fail to pep up the lethargic proceedings. Sexual innuendo. A-III (br)

Silken Skin (see: **The Soft Skin**)

Silkwood (1983) Fact-based story of Karen Silkwood (Meryl Streep), a worker in a plutonium processing factory who died in a 1974 auto accident, on her way to tell a reporter what she knew about unsafe conditions in the plant. The movie does not confront the question of whether this was indeed an accident or a murder committed to prevent her evidence from being revealed. Instead, director Mike Nichols has invested a great deal of labor and care in depicting something of Silkwood's independent lifestyle on the job and in relations to her roommate (Cher) and boyfriend (Kurt Russell). The result is a nicely crafted disappointment. A-III (R)

Silver Bears (1978) Michael Caine stars in this leaden-paced, largely unfunny comedy of international intrigue involving a hoax about a silver mine. Directed by Ivan Passer, it affects a sympathetic attitude towards adultery. O (PG)

Silver Bullet (1985) A small town is terrorized by a maniacal killer, coincidentally enough, only when the moon is full. When most of the members of a posse formed to track down the killer are annihilated, it is left to a 12-year-old handicapped boy to convince the town that the killer is a werewolf. Based on a Stephen King novella, director Daniel Attias takes liberties with Hollywood werewolf conventions that may offend hard-core Lon Chaney fans. Graphic violence with gory murder sequences, as well as some vulgar language. O (R)

Silver Chalice, The (1954) Biblical clunker from Thomas B. Costain's novel in which an artist (Paul Newman) from Corinth comes to Rome to consult Peter the Apostle (Lorne Greene) about the chalice he's making to hold the cup Christ used at the Last Supper, but a fanatic revolutionary (Joseph Wiseman) and a mad magician (Jack Palance) are intent on its destruction. Directed by Victor Saville, the pot boils over as the callow artist is torn between a pious Christian (Pier Angeli) and an impious hussy (Virginia Mayo), while trying to claim his stolen inheritance and protect the chalice from being stolen. Violence, intrigue, and romantic complications. A-II (br)

Silver Lode (1954) Bogus marshal (Dan Duryea) turns the title town against its leading citizen (John Payne) in a dreary Western directed by Allan Dwan, who compounds the artificiality of the revenge plot with lots of unconvincing action. Stylized violence and intermittent menace. A-II (br)

Silver Streak (1976) Gene Wilder and Jill Clayburgh battle a ruthless gang of killers aboard a transcontinental train, aided by Richard Pryor, whose comic talents give the movie a much-needed lift when he appears halfway through. Directed by Arthur Hiller, it is moderately entertaining but has some unnecessary profanity and a rather crude love scene. A-III (PG)

Silverado (1985) Big, gaudy Western, as artificial as its title, in which four strangers meet on the road to Silverado and unite to fight evil and injustice. One problem, among the many that afflict the movie, is that director Lawrence Kasdan fails to make the bad guys seem very formidable competition. Nor can one find much to cheer about in the four lackluster heroes weighed down by a convoluted and contrived story-line and a tone that wavers between spoof and dead seriousness. Some moderate violence. A-II (PG-13)

Simon (1980) Anemic satire about a mischievous group of scientists (headed by Austin Pendleton) who brainwash an eccentric philosophy teacher (Alan Arkin) into believing he is from outer space. Written and directed by Marshall Brickman, the acting is good, but the laughs are few and far between. Some sexual innuendo and a feeble thrust at organized religion. A-III (PG)

Simon Birch (1998) Old-fashioned tale of friendship between two 12-year-old boys in 1964 Smalltown, USA, one (Joseph Mazzello) seeking the identity of his father, while the other (Ian Michael Smith), afflicted with dwarfism, is convinced God has put him on earth to do something heroic. Suggested by John Irving's 1989 novel *A Prayer for Owen Meany*, writer-director Mark Steven Johnson's well-meaning attempt to explore faith through the eyes of a doomed child has tender moments, but its uplifting message is delivered with a heavy hand. Scene of extreme menace to children, sexual references, a few rude expressions, and minimal profanity. A-II (PG)

Simon of the Desert (1969) Surrealistic Mexican fantasy about a hermit (Claudio Brook) who, like his fifth-century namesake Simeon Stylites, exiles himself to the top of a pillar in the wilderness living in prayer, doing penance, and working miracles, but constantly at war with himself, his followers, and the devil (Silvia Pinal). Director Luis Bunuel's satiric foray into the sacred and the profane deals in paradox and the contradictions inherent in human nature. His ironic wit and uncomfortable insights will be appreciated most by those willing to reconcile the movie's ambiguities with their own beliefs. A-IV (nr)

Simon the Swiss (1971) French crime thriller about a petty crook (Jean-Louis Trintignant) who thinks he's pulled off the perfect crime when he kidnaps a bank clerk's small child and gets the bank to pay a fortune in ransom. Director Claude Lelouch's plot has all kinds of intricate turns and twists and the likable hero is anything but a Robin Hood. Intelligent entertainment with much psychological tension and some physical violence. A-III (G)

Simple Men (1992) Disjointed story of an unsuccessful criminal (Robert Burke) and his college-student younger brother (William Sage) who are given a place to stay by a Long Island inn-keeper (Karen Sillas) while searching for their outlaw father. Written and directed by Hal Hartley, the situation provides a stage for eccentric characters with throwaway dialogue that is by turns comical and mock-philosophic, suggesting insights which never materialize. Some stylized violence, sexual references, and occasional rough language. A-III (R)

Simple Plan, A (1998) Menacing drama in which two brothers (Bill Paxton and Billy Bob Thornton) and a buddy (Brent Briscoe) stumble upon a snow-covered plane wreck with a cache of four-million dollars and decide to keep it, then grow suspicious of one another as they try to hide their guilty secret from the police. Director Sam Raimi's cautionary tale turns into an edgy thriller as ordinary Joes become increasingly corrupted by the desire for immense wealth. Intermittent violence, fleeting nudity, some profanity, and recurring rough language. A-III (R)

Simple Story, A (1980) Moody French portrait of a divorced woman (Romy Schneider) in middle-aged crisis and agonizing over whether to have an abortion or raise her child. Directed by Claude Sautet, the movie avoids sentimental melodramatics in favor of thoughtful, sensitive probing of life's moral priorities. A-III (nr)

Simple Twist of Fate, A (1994) Poignant updating of George Eliot's 1861 novel *Silas Marner*, in which a miserly divorced carpenter (Steve Martin) is transformed into a loving foster-father after adopting an abandoned baby, only to face losing her at age 11 when her wealthy biological father (Gabriel Byrne) sues to regain custody of the child. Also written by Martin and directed by Gillies MacKinnon, the handsomely shot drama presents well-developed characters who gradually come to terms with past mistakes in an uplifting story of love and acceptance. Negative depiction of drug abuse, mild sexual references, and an instance of profanity. A-II (PG-13)

Simple Wish, A (1997) Weak comic fantasy in which an inept male fairy-godmother (Martin Short) has trouble granting the wish of a little girl (Mara Wilson) that her dad (Robert Pastorelli) win the lead in a Broadway musical. Directed by Michael Ritchie, the innocuous fun comes from the amusing special effects rather than the frantic antics of Short's klutzy character. Mild menace and a few crude words. A-II (PG)

Simply Irresistible (1999) Leaden romantic fantasy in which a small-time New York restaurant owner (Sarah Michelle Gellar) and a swank department-store executive (Sean Patrick Flanery) are brought together by a magical force endowing her with extraordinary culinary skills that literally sweep him off his feet. Directed by Mark Tarlov, the unimaginative premise fails to spark any magic in the appeal of the two leads and the resulting romantic complications are too labored to be much more than occasionally amusing. Sexual innuendo, crude language, and some profanity. A-III (PG-13)

Sin of Adam and Eve, The (1973) Writer-producer-director Michael Zachary's literal visualization of Genesis uses an off-screen narrator to add some sensual embellishments to the Biblical text, while on-screen bare, healthy primates George Rivers and Candy Wilson explore an Eden which seems to have been culled from the Burpee Seed Catalogue. O (R)

Sin of Harold Diddlebock, The (1947) Interesting comedy opens with footage from **The Freshman** (1925) showing how college go-getter Harold Lloyd's football prowess wins him a job as an accountant at an ad agency, but, still at the same job 20 years later, Harold finds himself fired, takes his first drink, wins a fortune gambling, and buys a circus, none of which he can remember when he awakens a day later, though the aftermath turns him back into a go-getter. Writer-director Preston Sturges comes up with an intriguing story-line and lots of visual funny business for Lloyd who is equally good in exchanges of droll dialogue, but the comedy is poorly paced and the result is disappointingly uneven. Some menacing moments and comic inebriation. A-II (br)

Sin Takes a Holiday (1930) Stiff romantic comedy in which a New York divorce lawyer (Kenneth MacKenna) avoids being forced into marriage by wedding his secretary (Constance Bennett) in name only, then sending her to travel in Europe, where a friendly bachelor (Basil Rathbone) turns her into the toast of French society, with predictable results. Directed by Paul L. Stein, the dated proceedings are flatly contrived and too obvious to be amusing. Implied adultery and shallow treatment of love and marriage. A-III (br)

Sinbad and the Eye of the Tiger (1977) Slow-paced bit of leaden whimsy follows a voyage of Sinbad (Patrick Wayne) to the polar regions to free a prince from a witch's spell. The acting is undistinguished, Sam Wanamaker's direction is haphazard, and only a few special effects merit anything more than passing interest. A-II (G)

Since You Went Away (1944) When her husband is called up in WW II, a woman (Claudette Colbert) makes ends meet by taking in a boarder (Monty Woolley), is cheered by occasional visits from a family friend (Joseph Cotten), and finally becomes a shipyard welder, while her 17-year-old daughter (Jennifer Jones) gets engaged to a soldier, and a younger daughter (Shirley Temple) tends a victory garden. Directed by John Cromwell, the patriotic tribute to the home-front is done in epic fashion, though the sentimentalized situations and idealized characters may seem rather hollow today. A-I (br)

Sinful Davey (1969) Tongue-in-cheek adventure movie about an 18th-century Scottish laddie (John Hurt) who deserts the English army and embarks upon a career as a highwayman. Director John Huston relies upon an abundance of misadventures, escapes, and turnabouts in a stylish action-story done in fun. Some explicit romantic interludes. A-III (PG)

Sing (1989) Poorly focused, reality-based fantasy about Brooklyn's annual high-school performance competitions uses a cliched story of romance between a good girl (Jessica Steen) and a petty hood (Peter Dobson) who is turned around by a tough-minded new teacher (Lorraine Bracco). Director Richard Baskin depends on music-video flourishes to divert attention from his derivative scenario, but gets help from a cast of energized teens, a subplot about community pride, and an anti-drug message. Some rough language and sexually suggestive dancing. A-III (PG-13)

Singapore (1947) Soggy melodrama directed by John Brahm follows the return of an American smuggler (Fred MacMurray) to the title colonial outpost after WW II to recover a hidden cache of pearls, but the quest is complicated by a shrewd British policeman (Richard Haydn), a greedy crook (Thomas Gomez), and the American's love for a woman (Ava Gardner) he thought killed in an air raid but who survived, afflicted with amnesia and married to another. Some stylized violence and hokey romantic complications on the rocky road to divorce. A-III (br)

Singin' in the Rain (1951) Engaging musical spoof of early Hollywood, as a silent-movie star (Gene Kelly) makes the transition into talking pictures with some help from a loyal pal (Donald O'Connor) and a talented young singer (Debbie Reynolds) who dubs the voice of the star's shrill leading-lady (Jean Hagen). Directed by Kelly and Stanley Donen, the period nostalgia is served up as lighthearted fun, with the Kelly-Reynolds romance sweetly in the background, while the plot rolls along with fine songs, zestful comedy routines and lovely production numbers, from O'Connor's solo "Make 'Em Laugh" to Kelly's memorable title number. Minor sexual innuendo. A-II (br)

Singing Nun, The (1966) Hollywood's tribute to the joyful spirit of a young Dominican nun is colorful, sentimental, and lively, though Henry Koster's glossy direction is out of tune with the reality of a basically interior story about the difficulty of secular fame for a member of a religious community. Greer Garson as the mother superior turns in a well-balanced performance, while Debbie Reynolds sings prettily, and Agnes Moorehead provides comic relief. There is some pleasant amusement, a little uplift, and the music of "Soeur Sourire" is well worth hearing. A-I (br)

Single White Female (1992) After tossing out her unfaithful fiancé (Steven Weber), a young Manhattanite (Bridget Fonda) takes in a shy roommate (Jennifer Jason Leigh) who quickly turns out to be a cunning murderess. Producer-director Barbet Schroeder's tired slasher movie turns a plausible concept into a mindless exercise in sensational violence. Excessive violence, brief sexual encounters, some nudity, and occasional rough language. O (R)

Singles (1992) Romantic comedy centers on several romances among the twenty-something tenants (including Bridget Fonda, Scott Campbell, Kyra Sedgwick, and Matt Dillon) of a small and homey Seattle apartment building. Writer-director Cameron Crowe takes a genial but superficial look at the emotional rollercoaster of the dating wars with sympathetic, marriage-minded characters. Restrained scene of a sexual encounter, a benign attitude toward premarital affairs, and an instance of rough language. A-III (PG-13)

Sink the Bismarck! (1960) Stirring dramatization of the 1941 British naval victory over the title German battleship after it slips into the North Atlantic, easily defeats the first British warships encountered, then becomes a sitting duck when its rudder is disabled by a carrier plane's torpedo. Directed by Lewis Gilbert, the sea action is inter-cut with the personal drama involving the Admiralty's director of operations (Kenneth More), his assistant (Dana Wynter), the officers of the ships following his orders, and the Nazi admiral (Karel Stepanek) commanding the Bismarck. Wartime violence. A-I (br)

Sinners' Holiday (see: **Christmas Eve**)

Sins of Rachel Cade, The (1961) Sudsy melodrama in which an American nurse (Angie Dickinson) takes charge of a Protestant mission in the Belgian Congo in 1939, wins over the natives and the local Belgian administrator (Peter Finch), but falls in love with a wounded WW II pilot (Roger Moore), who leaves her pregnant. Director Gordan Douglas plods through the narrative with little concern for either the African setting or the title character's moral struggles, which are depicted as little more than hypocrisy. Muddled theme of an unwed pregnancy and religious, as well as African, stereotypes. A-III (br)

Sirens (1994) Coyly pretentious Australian tale of a clergyman (Hugh Grant) and his prim wife (Tara Fitzgerald), who loses some of her sexual inhibitions when they spend a few days with an artist (Sam Neill) and his entourage of models. Writer-director John Duigan's listless, highly romanticized proceedings center on models cavorting in various stages of undress, while the wife gradually awakens to lust in what ultimately proves only a glossy exercise in voyeurism. Sexual promiscuity and much nudity. O (R)

Sirocco (1951) Murky tale of a cynical American gunrunner (Humphrey Bogart) supplying arms to Syrian rebels in 1925 Damascus, where he uses the girlfriend (Marta Toren) of a French intelligence-officer (Lee J. Cobb) to avoid arrest, then tries to save the officer from capture by the rebels. Directed by Curtis Bernhardt, the meandering plot is thick with ominous intrigues, but the unsavory characters fail to gain interest, let alone sympathy. Stylized violence, menacing situations, and sexual innuendo. A-III (br)

Sister Act (1992) Having witnessed a mob rubout, a Reno lounge-singer (Whoopi Goldberg) hides out in a cloistered San Francisco convent disguised as a nun and horrifies Mother Superior (Maggie Smith) by turning their choir into a local sensation and getting the nuns involved in their neighborhood. Director Emile Ardolino parlays Goldberg's sassiness into a lively comedy that treats nuns both as comic figures and spirited, caring individuals with a positive lifestyle. References to an extramarital affair and brief comic violence. A-III (PG)

Sister Act 2: Back in the Habit (1993) Fair comedy sequel in which the Las Vegas singer (Whoopi Goldberg) is back in a nun's habit, hoping to save a Catholic high school from closing by transforming a bunch of unruly students into a vibrant choir in time to win the all-state competition. Though lacking the novel premise of the original and off-kilter in its goofy depiction of several priests, director Bill Duke's moderately amusing comedy stresses positive values for youngsters. Mild sexual innuendo, comic treatment of religious characters, and an instance of profanity. A-II (PG)

Sister Kenny (1946) Stodgy fact-based dramatization about the title Australian nurse (Rosalind Russell) who discovers an effective method for treating polio victims on the eve of WW I, but the country's medical organizations refuse to adopt it until she is invited to the United States and proves its worth during WW II. Directed by Dudley Nichols, the production is first-rate, but the script suffers from too much windy sincerity and not enough effective dramatization of character and situation. A-I (br)

Sisters (1973) Failed horror thriller about a Staten Island reporter (Jennifer Salt) who happens to observe a bloody murder in a neighboring apartment house occupied by a schizophrenic Siamese twin (Margot Kidder) and her mad doctor-husband (Bill Finley). Assisting her investigation is a bumbling, comic-relief detective (Charles Durning). Directed by Brian De Palma, the movie's mixture of mindless comedy and visceral gore presumes an audience willing to participate in such voyeuristic displays of violence. O (R)

Sitting Bull (1954) Failed Western tale of a cavalry officer (Dale Robertson) whose friendship with the Sioux chief (J. Carrol Naish) leads to a court martial after Custer's Last Stand. Directed by Sidney Salkow, the mawkish story mauls American history and frontier stereotypes to no discernable advantage. Frontier violence. A-I (br)

Sitting Ducks (1980) Two bumbling con-men (Michael Emil and Zach Norman) steal some mob gambling receipts and flee to Miami with two women who have been hired to bump them off. Amateurish sex-farce directed by Henry Jaglom gets off to a good start but becomes progressively less amusing as it wears on. Demeaning treatment of sex and some rough language. O (R)

Sitting Pretty (1948) Period comedy in which busy suburban parents (Robert Young and Maureen O'Hara) engage the services of a live-in babysitter (Clifton Webb), a self-proclaimed genius who proves more than capable of handling not only the children, but any crisis along the way. Directed by Walter Lang, the whole show is Webb's imperious performance as the unflappable Mr. Belvedere, who is more than superior to any situation, including nosy neighbors. Some muted sexual inferences. A-II (br)

Situation Hopeless — But Not Serious (1965) Failed black comedy of two downed American fliers (Robert Redford and Michael Connors) taken prisoner in 1944 by a lonely German clerk (Alec Guinness) and held captive in his cellar until six years after WW II's end. Director Gottfried Reinhardt concentrates on the ludicrous humor of the situation rather than the characters and their relationships, with little to show for it except adding to the Guinness gallery of odd characterizations. Uneasy humor in a desperate situation. A-II (br)

Six Bridges to Cross (1955) Crime picture of the uneasy friendship that develops between a dedicated Boston cop (George Nader) and a shrewd but engaging juvenile delinquent (Tony Curtis), whose crimes escalate into a 1950s multi-million dollar heist. Directed by Joseph Pevney, the torturous relationship between law-enforcer and law-breaker plays out unconvincingly, though the Boston locations and gritty criminal action add a realistic veneer to the proceedings. Stylized violence and ambiguous treatment of a criminal. A-III (br)

Six Days, Seven Nights (1998) Mildly comic adventure in which a tropical-island pilot (Harrison Ford) and his high-strung passenger (Anne Heche) crash-land on an abandoned isle, where they must fend off pirates from the sea and their unwanted mutual attraction. Director Ivan Reitman's tired formula is made palatable by the airy banter between appealing performers in an otherwise predictable popcorn movie. Brief violence, some sexual innuendo, recurring profanity, and an instance of rough language. A-III (PG-13)

Six Degrees of Separation (1993) New York art-dealer (Donald Sutherland) and wife (Stockard Channing) recount to their amused upper-crust friends how a troubled homosexual youth (Will Smith), by pretending to be Sidney Poitier's son, insinuated himself into their lives hoping to become part of their privileged world. Based on John Guare's play and directed by Fred Schepisi, the deftly acted movie uncomfortably mixes scathing satire about patronizing rich folk with the murky plight of a lost, delusional young man. Fleeting homosexual encounter with a flash of frontal nudity, brief violence including suicide, and occasional rough language. A-III (R)

Six in Paris (1969) Light, colorful, and entertaining compilation of short vignettes by six French directors (Jean-Luc Godard, Jean-Daniel Pollet, Jean Rouch, Jean Douchet, Claude Chabrol, and Eric Rohmer). Despite the assortment of stories and styles, they cohere nicely and leave viewers with a memorable experience of several interesting Parisian characters. Mature themes and treatment. A-III (nr)

Six O'Clock News (1997) Impelled by TV's nightly news-reports of random violence from crime and natural disasters, documentary filmmaker Ross McElwee began visiting victims of the violence to record what had happened and how they were coping with the aftermath. The result is a series of human-interest stories strung together in the form of a video diary, with McElwee's wry comments and philosophical musings on human mortality but without achieving its stated aim of trying to make some sense of life's painful, inexplicable tragedies. News footage of crime scenes and disaster areas, as well as discussions of violent events. A-II (nr)

Six Pack (1982) Kenny Rodgers plays a fading racecar driver who becomes the surrogate father of six needy orphans. Pretty soon he's back on top with the kids as his pit crew, and he even decides to marry Erin Gray, whom he favors with his presence every few months. Directed by Daniel Petrie, it's sheer, contrived mediocrity from start to finish. Foul language out of the mouths of babes and a benign attitude toward casual sex. A-III (PG)

Six-Pack Annie (1975) Young girl (Lindsay Bloom) becomes a prostitute in order to save her aunt's restaurant from foreclosure. Directed by Graydon F. David, the tedious, flat movie is as consistently vulgar as it is unfunny. O (R)

633 Squadron (1964) Routine WW II story directed by Walter Grauman has an American (Cliff

Robertson) heading a squadron of British bombers on a raid to destroy a mountain-sheltered German war factory in Norway. Stylized violence and hokey heroics. A-II (br)

Six Ways to Sunday (1999) Unfunny crime comedy follows the rise of a violent mama's boy (Norman Reedus) within a mob of Jewish gangsters as he deals with his sexual inadequacies, a smother-mother (Deborah Harry), and a talent for killing friends and foes alike. Writer-director Adam Bernstein substitutes a lamely jokey tone for any insights into the disturbed individual at the story's center. Numerous gory killings, a suicide, implied incest, sexual situations with nudity, intermittent profanity, and constant rough language. O (R)

Six Weeks (1982) Congressional candidate (Dudley Moore) befriends a youngster dying of leukemia (Katherine Healy), who persuades her wealthy mother (Mary Tyler Moore) to back his campaign, but when she succumbs to his charm, he reciprocates and his marriage is in jeopardy. Director Tony Bill's romance is outrageously sentimental, totally detached from both political and human realities, and cloyingly smug in its hedonistic values. A-III (PG)

Sixteen Candles (1984) A girl (Molly Ringwald) is devastated when her family, in the throes of preparing for her older sister's marriage, forgets about her 16th birthday. Were that not enough, she is pursued by a skinny freshman (Anthony Michael Hall) while longing for a handsome, unattainable senior (Michael Schoeffling). Director John Hughes's old-fashioned comedy about the anguish of adolescence is updated, alas, by a dose of foul language, pervasive vulgarity, some shower-room nudity, and a benign view of casual sex. Some other not-so-bright spots include nasty stereotyping of Orientals and Italians and some National Lampoon-style laughs at the expense of a girl in a body brace. O (PG)

Sixth Man, The (1997) Lame comic fantasy in which a college-basketball star (Kadeem Hardison) dies in mid-season, but his spirit returns to help his brother (Marlon Wayans) lead their underrated team to the championship. Directed by Randall Miller, the cliched sports-story offers no surprises, and the one-joke premise of a ghostly sixth player seen only by his brother delivers few giggles before growing tiresome. Player's death during a game, strong sexual innuendo, and coarse language. A-III (PG-13)

Skateboard (1978) Down-on-his-luck agent (Allen Garfield) extricates himself from the clutches of a loan shark by becoming a skateboard entrepreneur. Directed by George Gage, it is a very bad little movie hastily and cheaply slapped together to cash in on a fad; it is also offensive in its benign attitude towards teenage promiscuity and drinking. O (PG)

Skatetown, U.S.A. (1979) Ho-hum homage to the fad of disco roller-skating pits nice young man against tough dude in competing for the big skating-crown. Written, produced, and directed by William Levey, the undernourished story-line constantly halts for unfunny comic sketches (Ruth Buzzey and Flip Wilson), undistinguished songs, and skating numbers. Frequently sleazy mood and abundance of marijuana consumption in the background, and sometimes the foreground, make it highly dubious fare for any but mature viewers. A-III (PG)

Skezag (1971) Well-intended but amateurish documentary about drug abuse goes on endlessly with New York addicts using street language describing the scene. In the last sequence, however, filmmakers Joel Freedman and Phil Messina revisit an addict who is now a walking dead man, hollow of soul and poisoned of body, conveying most effectively what had been missing so incessantly in the preceding footage. Those last few minutes say more than anyone needs to know about the white powder that destroys so many young Americans. A-IV (nr)

Ski Bum, The (1970) Failed screen version of a Romain Gary novel about a young drifter (Zalman King) hanging around a Colorado winter resort who becomes embroiled in a crooked business scheme, is roundly doublecrossed, and left emotionally shattered by the experience. Directed by Bruce Clark, the plot is episodic and underdeveloped, the characters are superficial, and their motivations often enigmatic. A confused morality underpins the story. O (R)

Ski Fever (1969) Ski instructor (Martin Milner) at an Austrian ski lodge finds his contract requires him to socialize with the guests, and, by the time of the movie's romantic fade-out, he has teamed up with one of them (Claudia Martin). Directed by Curt Siodmak, it's an inept story built around some footage of the Austrian Giant Slalom, but not even ski enthusiasts will find it worth seeing. A-III (M)

Ski Party (1965) Formula **Beach Party** fare set in a ski resort, where two dim college youths (Frankie Avalon and Dwayne Hickman) hope to learn how to get dates by masquerading as British co-eds. Directed by Alan Rafkin, the unamusingly contrived proceedings are best forgotten. Some menacing situations and sexual innuendo. A-II (br)

Ski Patrol (1990) The schemes of a sleazy land-developer (Martin Mull) to take over a trendy ski resort run owned by a popular old-timer (Ray Walston) are thwarted by its dauntless young staff of ski patrollers, whose talents also include dancing, singing, and partying. Director Richard Correll combines his paint-by-numbers cast with dumb, vulgar hijinks to concoct a basically innocuous sophomoric comedy highlighted by snazzy ski-togs and funky daredevil skiing. Minor sexual innuendoes, bathroom humor, and incidental rough language. A-II (PG)

Skidoo (1969) Retired thug (Jackie Gleason) is ordered by his old boss (Groucho Marx) to rub out a loquacious friend (Mickey Rooney) safely ensconced in prison. Directed by Otto Preminger, it is a mixture of inert comedy and ponderous satire, done in consistently bad taste, with some lecherous dialogue and sexual shenanigans. O (M)

Skin Deep (1989) Menopausal male saga about a famous writer (John Ritter) suffering simultaneously from alcoholism, writer's block, and an obsession to bed every nubile female who crosses his path. Written and directed by Blake Edwards, the movie lacks any moral insight in following the Lothario from one pointless liaison to another, while romanticizing his lust for sex and alcohol. Some nudity and much profanity. O (R)

Skin Game, The (1932) Dated melodrama from John Galsworthy's play about the bitter antagonism between a family of English aristocrats and their new neighbor, a wealthy businessman (Edmund Gwenn) buying up the surrounding countryside to turn into an industrial park. Directed by Alfred Hitchcock, the conflict is dramatically static and largely uninteresting, except for some sharp montages depicting the era's social changes and a romantic subplot involving class divisions. Suicide in plot resolution. A-III (br)

Skin Game (1971) In the pre-Civil War border states, a cunning con-artist (James Garner) makes the rounds selling his slave (Lou Gossett) and then waiting with the cash for him to escape and proceed to the next con, until another crook (Susan Clark) adds a new dimension of confusion. Director Paul Bogart blends large doses of improbability with pinches of reality to keep the interracial swindle skimming along its superficial surface, only touching on the serious for comic effect. A-III (GP)

Skull, The (1965) Weak British horror story about a student of the occult (Peter Cushing) who becomes obsessed by the evil powers of the Marquis de Sade's skull. Directed by Freddie Francis, the trappings of black magic and witchcraft are as hokey as the action is clunky. Stylized violence and creaky menace. A-II (br)

Skullduggery (1970) Witless, at times tasteless, comedy about an anthropologist (Susan Clark) whose New Guinea expedition is led by their guide (Burt Reynolds) into uncharted territory, where they discover a species of apes that manifest distinctly human qualities. Directed by Gordon Douglas, the question of whether the creatures are indeed human is kicked around in aimless fashion, matched by banal dialogue and half-dimensional characterizations. Reference to bestiality. A-III (PG)

Sky Bandits (1986) A British production set in WW I France tells the comic adventures of two bankrobbers (Scotty McGinnis and Jeff Osterhage), who join the army to avoid prison and blunder their way through the war in a series of stolen airplanes. Directed by Zoran Perisic, the charm of this elegantly photographed movie derives from high-spirited performances and fanciful sets, props, and special effects. A post-bedroom scene and some very stylized wartime violence. A-II (PG)

Sky Dragon, The (1949) Formula mystery directed by Lesley Selander in which Honolulu detective Charlie Chan (Roland Winters) gets some help from his Number One Son (Keye Luke) in solving the case of a money shipment stolen from an airliner while its passengers and crew were knocked out by drugged coffee. Notable only as the last in the Monogram Chan series. Stylized violence. A-I (br)

Sky Riders (1976) Routine melodrama about the rescue of a family kidnapped by terrorists through the intervention of some daring hang-gliding enthusiasts is distinguished only by some spectacular aerial photography. Directed by Douglas Hickox, the movie's violent elements include the terrorists' threatening of a small child. A-III (PG)

Sky's the Limit, The (1943) Lightweight musical romance in which a WW II ace with the Flying Tigers (Fred Astaire) spends a 10-day leave back in the States pretending to be a civilian while trying to romance a magazine photographer (Joan Leslie), who's only interested in getting a war assignment overseas. Directed by Edward H. Griffith, there are several pleasant song-and-dance numbers, but Leslie is no Rogers, and Astaire can't carry the weak story by himself, despite some help from Robert Benchley. A-I (br)

Skyjacked (1972) Effective thriller about an American airliner hijacked to Russia. Captain Charlton Heston keeps his planeload of problem characters under control on a flight chockfull of dangerous situations, ending in a shootout at Moscow airport. John Guillermin directs with emphasis upon suspense rather than trying to develop characterization or the numerous subplots. Unpretentious escapist entertainment. A-II (PG)

Slams, The (1973) Super-bad, super-cool Jim Brown is in the penitentiary but has stashed away $1.5 million in Mafia drug-money for his planned breakout to escape to the Caribbean with girlfriend Judy Pace. Directed by Jonathan Kaplan, the brutal and sadistic action is as relentless and explicit as the prison language, which consists largely of racial, sexual, and just plain mean insults. O (R)

Slap, The (1976) Lightweight comedy drama, a sort of updated **Father of the Bride**, in which such talented actors as Lino Ventura, Annie Giradot, and Isabelle Adjani struggle gallantly with an aimless script more suited to American television than a French feature. Sexual innuendo. A-III (PG)

Slap Shot (1977) Paul Newman stars as an aging player-coach who rejuvenates an inept bush-league hockey team by introducing the wonders of dirty playing to his charges. Directed by George Roy Hill. the playing is but one of the dirty elements in a crude, foul-mouthed comedy. Some nudity. O (R)

Slappy and the Stinkers (1998) Feeble family-comedy about five seven-year-olds known at school as the Stinkers, who sneak Slappy the sea-lion out of an aquarium, but before they can free it into the ocean, Slappy is stolen by a villain who intends selling it to a Bulgarian circus. Directed by Barnet Kellman, the result is a mirthless slapstick comedy of "cute" kids outsmarting dopey adults, but the property damage and bodily harm caused by the Stinkers's antics is rarely amusing and anything but cute. Slapstick violence, bathroom humor, and crude language. A-II (PG)

Slaughter (1972) Black exploitation story of an ex-Green Beret (Jim Brown) who pummels his way into an international conspiracy and becomes the unwilling employee of the US government. Directed by Jack Starrett, the production values are minimal, with the emphasis on the hero's biceps and his winning ways with knuckles and bullets. Excessively graphic violence and sex. O (R)

Slaughter of the Innocents (1993) Exploitative thriller in which an FBI agent (Scott Glenn) gets some help from his grade-school son in tracking down a serial killer in the badlands of Utah. Writer-director James Glickenhaus concocts synthetic thrills from the demented acts of pseudo-religious cultists and a white supremacist, but the super-cop's encouragement of his computer whiz-kid's precocious interest in crime is as appalling as it is unconvincing. Some grisly graphics, children in peril, and occasional profanity and rough language. O (R)

Slaughter on Tenth Avenue (1957) Earnest crime-buster drama in which the murder of a New York longshoreman (Mickey Shaughnessy) causes a dedicated lawyer (Richard Egan) to risk life and career in linking the crime to a mobster (Walter Matthau) controlling a corrupt waterfront union. Directed by Arnold Laven, the predictable story-line is helped along by interesting character bits (Jan Sterling, Sam Levene, Charles McGraw, and Dan Duryea) and realistic dock scenes with longshoremen and union goons. Stylized violence and menacing atmosphere. A-II (br)

Slaughter's Big Rip-Off (1973) Big, bad Jim Brown mows his way through the Los Angeles branch of the syndicate (headed by Ed McMahon) and plows through a number of willing female sex-objects. Directed by Gordon Douglas, rip-off is the operative word in this cheap sex-and-violence exploitation job. O (R)

Slaughterhouse Five (1972) Uneven screen version of Kurt Vonnegut, Jr.'s, time-tripping novel about the progress of a soldier (Michael Sacks) from POW chaplain's assistant, to witness at the 1945 firebombing of Dresden, to post-war participant in the American Way of Life, and, at last, the captive of a Hollywood starlet (Valerie Perrine), the girl of his erotic dreams. Directed by George Roy Hill, the wildly seriocomic satire on American manners and mores is mostly on target and the acting is first-rate, though its hero's helplessness in dropping in and out of time tends to be confusing and, at times, incoherent. Marred by unnecessary nudity. A-IV (R)

Slaughterhouse Rock (1988) Even some funny moments can't save this teen horror-movie set on Alcatraz Island, which a local student (Nicholas Celozzi) and friends visit one night to confront the source of his bad dreams — the marauding ghost of a cannibal who once inhabited the island. Directed by Dimitri Logothetis, it's an amateurish production with a nonsensical plot. Much gore and violence, several nude scenes, an attempted rape, and some profanity. O (R)

Slave Girls (see: **Prehistoric Women**)

Slave of Love, A (1978) Movie company in the Crimea grinds out melodramatic romances, seemingly oblivious to the Bolshevik revolution sweeping across 1917 Russia. In the end, the company's empty-headed but beautiful star (Elena Solovei) joins her cameraman in smuggling out film of czarist atrocities in the area. Gorgeously photographed and engagingly acted, director Nikita Mikhalkov's nostalgic tribute to the silent movies and their age of innocence is an enjoyable experience in spite of perfunctory Soviet propaganda. A-III (nr)

Slaves (1969) Inept melodrama about a hardworking slave (Ossie Davis) unjustly sold to a bad master (Stephen Boyd) whose mistreatment drives him to foment a slave uprising. Director Herbert Biberman depends largely upon dialogue rather than visuals to convey the historical reality of the terrible injustices of slavery. It is an important subject and it is unfortunate that it has been done poorly. Several scenes with nudity. A-III (R)

Slaves of New York (1989) Director James Ivory's unsuccessful satire of the contemporary downtown Manhattan art scene works overtime to reproduce its chaotic glitz, but fails to provide more than superficial commentary on the hedonistic, narcissistic denizens of this throwaway subculture. Satiric glamorization of sexual promiscuity and drug abuse, brief nudity, and some profanity. O (R)

Slayground (1984) The getaway car in a robbery crashes into a limousine, killing the young daughter of a millionaire, who retaliates by hiring a professional hit-man to track down the gang's leader (Peter Coyote), a sensitive fellow already badly upset by the tragic turn of events. British production directed by Terry Bedford is a run-of-the-mill chase movie with some pretentious literary overtones. Stylized violence. A-III (R)

Sleep My Love (1948) Formula thriller in which a New Yorker (Don Ameche) plans to marry his mistress (Hazel Brooks) after killing his wealthy wife (Claudette Colbert) by staging a fatal "accident," but the scheme begins unraveling when a Boston visitor (Robert Cummings) sticks his nose in. Directed by Douglas Sirk, the predictable plot belabors the obvious as the capable cast go through the motions portraying stereotyped characters. Stylized violence and menacing situations. A-II (br)

Sleep with Me (1994) An impulsive one-night stand between a new bride (Meg Tilly) and the best friend (Craig Sheffer) of her husband (Eric Stoltz) deals a possibly fatal blow to their marriage, as the three continually air their pent-up feelings at a series of social gatherings. Written as six vignettes by separate authors, and sluggishly directed by Rory Kelly, the cynical thirty-something comedy assumes a hip and knowing air about sex, drugs, and relationships, but fails to address the problems that are shown to be created by casual sex. Positive depiction of drug and alcohol abuse, brief bedroom scenes with nudity, crude sexual references, and constant rough language. O (R)

Sleeper (1973) Typically wacky Woody Allen spoof on contemporary society's pop foibles in a plot casting Woody as a chap who goes into the hospital for routine surgery and wakes up 200 years from now in a world gone mad, with people dependent upon electronic gadgets (most of which don't work). Without an identity, he becomes tapped to lead a revolution and soon finds that his new friends are often more dangerous than his intended enemies. The humor is rapid-fire, mainly of the one-liner and sight-gag variety, and his satirical targets include just about every institution or group on the scene. A-III (PG)

Sleepers (1996) Overblown drama of four inner-city boys who grow up to take revenge on the sadistic guards (led by Kevin Bacon) who abused them in reform school, with two of the four getting away with murder on the perjured testimony of their parish priest (Robert De Niro). Writer-director Barry Levinson's manipulative crime picture romanticizes the bond of friendship between Catholic youths from a working-class neighborhood, then depicts their brutalizing imprisonment in disturbingly realistic detail, with the payoff years later in a dramatically unconvincing murder trial which nonetheless raises morally ambiguous justice issues. Harrowing scenes of teen inmates subjected to sadistic violence and sexual abuse, cold-blooded murders, vigilante justice, and habitual rough language. A-IV (R)

Sleeping Beauty (1959) Animated children's tale in which a bad fairy casts a spell on the Princess Aurora (voice of Mary Costa) causing eternal sleep until her true love, Prince Philip (voice of Bill Shirley), gets some help from a trio of good fairies in overcoming a ferocious dragon and awakening the princess. Directed by Clyde Geronomi with music from the Tchaikovsky ballet, this classic story of love conquering evil remains Walt Disney's last great achievement of storytelling in fully detailed animation. Fine family entertainment. A-I (G)

Sleeping City, The (1950) Standard crime melodrama set in New York City's Bellevue Hospital, where a detective (Richard Conte) assumes the identity of an interne in order to solve some murders linked to the peddling of drugs among the hospital staff. Directed by George Sherman, the story gets some realistic dramatic tension from being filmed in and around the large metropolitan hospital, but the plot bogs down in the cop's romance with a nurse (Coleen Gray), conventional police work, and criminal stereotypes. Stylized violence, romantic complications, and drug dealing. A-II (br)

Sleeping Tiger, The (1954) Turgid melodrama in which a London psychiatrist (Alexander Knox) attempts to treat a young thug (Dirk Bogarde) by taking him into his home, but the cunning, resentful youth proceeds to seduce his benefactor's troubled American wife (Alexis Smith), among other nasty deeds. Directed by Victor Hanbury (aka Joseph Losey), the unconvincing proceedings are unredeemed by a tragic ending. Much menace and sexual situations. A-III (br)

Sleeping with the Enemy (1991) When a psychotically jealous husband (Patrick Bergin) discovers his abused wife (Julia Roberts) has faked her own death to escape him, he tracks her down and finds her in the arms of her new love (Kevin Anderson). Director Joe Ruben's sleek thriller efficiently creates suspense by making full use of Robert's beautifully played vulnerability, but falters with a needless cliche at the end. Some violence, restrained marital encounter, and minimal rough language. A-III (R)

Sleepless in Seattle (1993) After hearing a Seattle widower (Tom Hanks and his boy [Ross Malinger]) on a syndicated radio talk-show on Christmas Eve, a young reporter (Meg Ryan) feels irresistibly drawn to the man, even though she is engaged and lives in Baltimore. Director Nora Ephron turns in a highly appealing, if unabashedly romantic, love story about singles and families, liberally sprinkled with comic moments. Some mild sexual references and a live-in relationship. A-III (PG)

Sleepwalkers (see: **Stephen King's Sleepwalkers**)

Slender Thread, The (1966) A telephone is the only means by which a psychology student (Sidney Poitier) can hope to save a woman (Anne Bancroft) who has taken an overdose of barbiturates. Director Sydney Pollack's story has an overabundance of contrivances, but the acting of the principals makes it all seem urgent and worth the emotional involvement. A-II (br)

Sleuth (1972) Stylish screen version of Anthony Shaffer's play about an urbane detective-story writer (Laurence Olivier) who invites his wife's lover (Michael Caine) to his mansion, and the two engage in a game of wits which becomes progressively more deadly. Directed by Joseph Mankiewicz, the intricately plotted thriller is carried off by the tautly balanced performances of the two principals, but attentive viewers will see through the mystery early on. Some sharp tension and suspense make it mature fare. A-III (PG)

Sliding Doors (1998) Halting romantic fantasy set in London develops two scenarios showing alternate versions of what might happen in the life of a woman (Gwyneth Paltrow in a dual role) if she boards a departing subway train, or misses it and has to take the next one. Writer-director Peter Howitt sets up a playfully imaginative premise that becomes increasingly predictable as the one prospers after getting rid of a parasitic lover, while the other doesn't. Sexual situations, including a live-in relationship and a bedroom scene, some crude language, and occasional profanity. A-III (PG-13)

Slightly Honorable (1940) Screwball caper in which a hotshot lawyer (Pat O'Brien), aided by a dim assistant (Broderick Crawford), tries to solve a murder case in which he and a crooked politician (Edward Arnold) are prime suspects. Directed by Tay Garnett, the action is treated with comic gusto, especially the lawyer's problems with an under-aged female (Ruth Terry), but the mystery gets lost in red herrings and an unsatisfying twist ending. Stylized violence and much sexual innuendo. A-III (br)

Slim (1937) After a veteran lineman (Pat O'Brien) befriends an inexperienced novice (Henry Fonda) working on high-voltage wiring jobs, a woman (Margaret Lindsay) comes between the two pals, who are a team on and off construction sites. Director Ray Enright convincingly pictures the dangers of a lineman's job and the camaraderie among those who do it for a living, but the story dates badly with its view of a man's world in which women are only a distraction. Occasional stylized violence, menace, and romantic yearning. A-I (br)

Slim Carter (1957) Sentimental tale directed by Richard H. Bartlett in which a Hollywood publicist (Julie Adams) helps create the Western cowboy-star of the title (Jock Mahoney), but it takes a precocious orphan (Tim Hovey) to bring them together. Some stylized violence. A-I (br)

Sling Blade (1996) Challenging picture of a mentally retarded man (Billy Bob Thornton) after his release from the asylum to which he had been committed as a boy for murdering his mother and her lover. Upon his return to his Southern hometown, he's befriended by a boy (Lucas Black) and his widowed mom (Natalie Canerday), until her abusive boyfriend (Dwight Yoakam) threatens them all. Also written and directed by Thornton, the portrayal of the retarded man earns sympathy through its gentle, sometimes humorous, depiction of his simple, common-sense approach to difficulties, though its dark ending is appropriately disturbing. Some chilling off-screen violence, alcohol abuse, and occasional rough language. A-III (R)

Slingshot, The (1994) Showing the resilience of youth is this Swedish tale of a 10-year-old boy growing up in 1920s Stockholm, where he suffers the scorn of classmates and teachers because of his Jewish mother and socialist father, tries to earn money to buy a bike by selling slingshots fashioned out of condoms, and winds up in reform school for something he didn't do, yet survives it all without his spirit being crushed. Director Ake Sandgren evokes the period tensions of the adult world as seen through the innocent, wondering eyes of a boy too young to comprehend them, but precocious and enterprising enough to get into troubles beyond his age. Subtitles. Religious prejudice, stylized violence, sexual references, comic treatment of condoms, and occasional profanity. A-IV (R)

Slipper and the Rose, The (1976) Richard Chamberlain and Gemma Craven star in a pleasant and very entertaining British version of the Cinderella story, as directed by Bryan Forbes. A-I (G)

Slither (1973) Offbeat comedy adventure about a dense ex-con (James Caan) and his equally bumbling partner (Peter Boyle) who wend their way across rural California in search of a hidden stash of embezzled cash. Directed by Howard Zieff, there's plenty of fun along the way as the inept pair try to figure out the secret of the loot's location, but the chuckles trail off badly with a twist ending. Some rough language. A-III (PG)

Sliver (1993) Boring potboiler about a book editor (Sharon Stone) moving into a death-plagued Manhattan high-rise, where, after becoming sexually involved with the owner (William Baldwin), she learns he is secretly videotaping the private activities of all his tenants and may have murdered some of them. Under Phillip Noyce's lifeless direction, the story lacks suspense, focusing instead on the sexual proclivities of fuzzy, shallow characters of interest only to voyeurs. Several graphic sex scenes, recurring nudity, many sexist references, some violence, and intermittent rough language. O (R)

Slow Dancing in the Big City (1978) Tough, streetwise columnist for a New York newspaper (Paul Sorvino) falls in love with a beautiful Canadian dancer (Anne Ditchburn) who is making her debut at Lincoln Center but is afraid it might be her finale. Thanks to an appealing performance by Sorvino, the movie has a few good moments, but, as directed by John G. Avildsen, its blatant sentimentality, its contrived plot, and its shallow characterizations prevent it from being anything more than mediocre entertainment. A-II (PG)

Slugger's Wife, The (1985) Failed Neil Simon comedy about a baseball star (Michael O'Keefe) married to a rock singer (Rebecca DeMornay). Some sexually oriented scenes and a rather benign view of premarital sex. A-III (PG-13)

Slums of Beverly Hills (1998) Lethargic coming-of-age tale set in 1976, when a 15-year-old girl (Natasha Lyonne) learns about life from her hard-up divorced dad (Alan Arkin) and about sex from her mixed-up older cousin (Marisa Tomei) as well as the neighborhood pot-dealer (Kevin Corrigan). Written and directed by Tamara Jenkins, what might have been a slight but whimsical series of anecdotes is pumped up into a glossy picture about charmless characters and their unamusing antics. An exploitative sex-scene involving a vibrator, sexual references, some nudity, drug usage, rough language, and profanity. O (R)

Small Change (1976) Episodic French seriocomedy about the natural innocence of childhood that protects youngsters from being overwhelmed by the harsher realities of life. Director Francois Truffaut offers older viewers a chance to rediscover their own childhood as well as being more sympathetic to the needs of youngsters who depend upon them. Excellent movie for parents to share with their youngsters. A-II (PG)

Small Circle of Friends, A (1980) Radcliffe coed (Karen Allen) becomes the mistress of two Harvard students (Brad Davis and Jameson Parker) during the late 1960s campus anti-war activities. Director Rob Cohen's trio appear less committed to the protest movement than to indulging their selfish egos. Benign view of illicit sex and some graphic visuals of sexual activity. O (R)

Small Faces (1996) Living in a working-class ghetto in 1968 Glasgow, three adolescent brothers find themselves increasingly in danger from a local gang after its hot-tempered leader is accidentally injured by the youngest brother. Director Gillies MacKinnon shifts unexpectedly from a droll coming-of-age tale into a darker examination of a brutalizing social environment and the violence it breeds. Some violence, mild sexual innuendo, brief nudity, and occasional use of profanity and rough language. A-III (R)

Small Soldiers (1998) Mean-spirited fantasy mixes live action and animation in a story of toy soldiers coming to life bent on destroying rival peaceful toys, but in the process the aggressors also target two families housing the enemy toys. Appallingly, the humans become just as violent as the computer-generated toys in director Joe Dante's cynical parody of macho heroics. Recurring fantasy mayhem and brief drug references. A-IV (PG-13)

Small Town Girl (1953) Thin musical romance in which the wholesome daughter (Jane Powell) of a suburban magistrate (Robert Keith) transforms a rich city wastrel (Farley Granger), whom her father sentenced to a month in jail for speeding through town, thus saving him from a mercenary New York musical star (Ann Miller). Directed by Leslie Kardos, the artificial proceedings are entirely forgettable both dramatically and musically. Innocuous time-waster. A-I (br)

Small Town in Texas, A (1976) Young convict (Timothy Bottoms) gets out of prison and returns home to find himself harassed by the corrupt sheriff who framed him. Director Jack Starrett's mindlessly violent chase movie is of no interest. O (R)

Smallest Show on Earth, The (1957) Engaging British comedy in which a young couple (Bill Travers and Virginia McKenna) inherit a decrepit movie theater known to locals as "the fleapit," then join longtime employees (Margaret Rutherford, Peter Sellers, and Miles Mander) in trying to put it back on its feet. Director Basil Dearden smooths over the contrived plot with some very funny character bits, a nostalgia for old movies, and the quirky ways of the exhibition business. Mild sexual references. A-II (br)

Smart Woman (1948) Soapy romance directed by Edward A. Blatt in which a special prosecutor (Brian Aherne) out to nail a ring of corrupt officials falls for the criminal attorney (Constance Bennett), who's defending them to keep a blackmailer (Barry Sullivan) from revealing her past. Stylized violence and romantic complications. A-III (br)

Smartest Girl in Town (1936) Minor romantic comedy directed by Joseph Santley in which a model (Ann Sothern), intent on snaring a rich suitor, spurns the attentions of a millionaire (Gene Raymond) she mistakes for an inept male model. Good supporting cast (Helen Broderick and Eric Blore) abet the romantic mix-ups. A-II (br)

Smash-Up: The Story of a Woman (1947) Sudsy, dated tale of a nightclub singer (Susan Hayward) whose songwriter husband (Lee Bowman) becomes a big radio-star while she declines into alcoholism during his long absences and fears of losing him to his glamorous production assistant (Marsha Hunt). Director Stuart Heisler focuses on the woman's insecurities as wife and mother in a plush home with too many servants to feel needed, a plight inviting little sympathy, despite Hayward's emotionally wringing performance. Marital problems and a child in a life-threatening situation. A-II (br)

Smashing the Money Ring (1939) Standard B-budget programmer in which secret service operative Brass Bancroft (Ronald Reagan) masquerades as a convict in order to get the goods on a counterfeiting gang using the prison print-shop. Directed by Terry Morse, the thin-bare plot paces the forgettable action with occasional comic relief from Eddie Foy, Jr., as a gabby federal agent. Stylized violence. A-II (br)

Smashing Time (1968) English musical satire on London's Mod Scene which draws two country girls (Rita Tushingham and Lynn Redgrave) who become overnight successes, but disillusioned with fame, return home. Directed by Desmond Davis, the movie is an uncomfortable mixture of realism and stylization, superficial plot, and slapstick treatment. A-III (br)

Smic Smac Smoc (1972) French romantic comedy about three Marseilles dock-workers (Charles Gerard, Jean Collomb, and Amidou), one of whom decides to marry the baker's maid (Catherine Allegret), and the other two host a wacky wedding-day celebration that lands all the revelers in the clink. Unpretentious little movie with plenty of charm and smiles, directed by Claude Lelouch with a few of his friends, including composer Francis Lai as a blind accordionist playing lush themes from earlier Lelouch movies. Some earthy dialogue. A-III (GP)

Smile (1975) Facile car-salesman (Bruce Dern) is a judge in the American Miss beauty contest, who, by its end, begins to realize that his philosophy of life has been as empty as that of the contest. Director Michael Ritchie's satire affects a snickering, superior attitude towards the people it pictures as crass and ludicrous, and itself becomes nothing more than a peep show, lacking in a sense of humanity which might have redeemed its dabbling in voyeurism. Sexual situations. O (PG)

Smile Like Yours, A (1997) Bogus romantic comedy about a childless couple (Greg Kinnear and Lauren Holly) whose visits to a fertility clinic prove unsuccessful, and their marriage begins to unravel as misunderstandings escalate into tearful separation, then predictable reconciliation. Directed by Keith

Samples, the sentimental proceedings alternate crocodile tears with uneasy leers, none of which proves particularly amusing as the formula plot grows increasingly tiresome. A bedroom scene, sexual situations, comic treatment of fertility problems, and an instance of rough language. A-IV (R)

Smile Orange (1976) Comedy directed by Trevor Rhone set in Jamaica about a black waiter and his encounters with American tourists results in some satiric but good-natured thrusts at human nature whether black, white, or brown. Its paper-thin story, however, grows increasingly silly, and some exploitative nudity could easily have been done without. O (PG)

Smilin' Through (1941) Glossy Victorian sudser in which an Englishman (Brian Aherne) devotes himself to raising an orphaned niece (Jeanette MacDonald), then is embittered when she falls for the son (Gene Raymond) of the man who had killed the Englishman's bride on their wedding day. Directed by Frank Borzage, the fanciful romantic melodrama counterpoints the young people's courtship with the uncle's tragic love, all sweetly embellished by MacDonald's rendering of period ballads. Heavy sledding for youngsters. A-I (br)

Smilla's Sense of Snow (1997) Convinced the death of a little Inuit boy in her Copenhagen apartment building was murder, a reclusive mathematician (Julia Ormand) is aided by a mysterious neighbor (Gabriel Byrne) in uncovering a fantastic conspiracy going back three decades that puts their lives in danger. Director Bille August creates a remarkable tale, whose visuals are filled with mystery and echoes of a native culture being exploited for reasons involving a jarring plunge into the realms of melodramatic science fiction. Brief sexual innuendo, some violence, and intermittent rough language. A-III (R)

Smith (1969) Contemporary Western about a cattle rancher (Glenn Ford) who champions an Indian accused of murder. Unusually good Disney effort dealing with racial intolerance and the need for people of different cultures to get along together, though director Michael O'Herlihy's sentimental lack of realism mars the central trial sequences. Good family setting with warmly likable characters. A-I (G)

Smoke (1995) Quirky tale in which a Brooklyn cigar-store owner (Harvey Keitel) helps an old flame (Stockard Channing) and a grieving widower (William Hurt) who, in turn, befriends a troubled adolescent (Harold Perrineau). Director Wayne Wang allows this offbeat relationship story to ebb and flow, but, in spite of frequent gutter-language, its humanistic values are never far from the surface. Momentary violence, some sexual references, ambiguous treatment of a theft, and recurring rough language. A-III (R)

Smoke Signal (1955) Routine Western directed by Jerry Hopper is set in 1868, when a renegade Army officer (Dana Andrews) helps a small cavalry-outpost escape Ute attackers by getting the post's survivors, including a widow (Piper Laurie), to a boat and heading down the Grand Canyon's rapids-filled Colorado River. Frontier violence. A-I (br)

Smoke Signals (1998) Engaging story about a pair of 22-year-old Native-American men (Adam Beach and Evan Adams) making the journey from the reservation to Phoenix, where one is to pick up his estranged father's ashes from a caring native woman (Irene Bedard), who explains why the guilt-ridden father left his tribe. Director Chris Eyre explores Indian culture with sly wit and a keen eye for pain and anger, tempered by healing forgiveness. Fleeting violence and an instance of profanity. A-II (PG-13)

Smokey and the Bandit (1977) Burt Reynolds, Sally Fields, and Jackie Gleason star in this chase comedy about a daredevil trucker pursued by a state trooper. Director Hal Needham's action comedy has little humor and lots of elaborate but boring car crashes. Some rough language, many vulgarities, and suggestion of premarital sex. A-III (PG)

Smokey and the Bandit II (1980) Burt Reynolds, Sally Field, and Jackie Gleason do it again in a sequel which, like the original, is essentially a live-action version of a Road Runner cartoon. Directed by Hal Needham, this time the plot involves trucking a pregnant elephant over several state lines, with the usual car chases and crashes, an abundance of crude sexual references, and vulgar language. A-III (PG)

Smokey and the Bandit, Part 3 (1983) Burt Reynolds makes but the briefest of appearances in this sequel about a trucker (Jerry Reed) racing the clock to transport a plastic replica of a shark on time,in spite of being pursued by a loudmouthed sheriff (Jackie Gleason). Director Dick Lowry's chase farce hits new lows in moral as well as entertainment terms. Demeaning sexual humor and foul language. O (PG)

Smoky (1966) Fess Parker stars in a nicely done family-type Western based on the Will James novel about a rancher and an outlaw mustang stallion. Directed by George Sherman, it affords plenty of outdoor action for all. A-I (br)

Smooth Talk (1986) Written and directed by Joyce Chopra, it is the story of a maturing teenage girl (Laura Dern) who places herse1f in a dangerous situation when a soft-spoken stranger (Treat Williams) talks her into accepting him as her first lover. The movie seems to accept this as a reasonable introduction to womanhood. O (PG-13)

Smugglers' Cove (1948) Formula slapstick comedy directed by William Beaudine in which the Bowery Boys (led by Leo Gorcey) smash a gang (led by Martin Kosleck) using a manor on the Long Island seacoast to smuggle aliens into the country. Comic violence. A-I (br)

Snake Eyes (1998) Glossy thriller in which the lifelong friendship of a corrupt cop (Nicolas Cage) and a Navy officer (Gary Sinese) is tested while investigating the assassination of the secretary of defense at a championship prizefight. Director Brian de Palma's implausible conspiracy plot is more slippery than suspenseful as it twists its way to a conclusion involving the hardly credible redemption of a key character. Intermittent violence, some sexual innuendo, minimal rough language, and frequent profanity. A-III (R)

Snake Pit, The (1948) Earnest story of a woman (Olivia de Havilland) who suffers a nervous breakdown, but slowly recovers during the course of treatment she receives from a dedicated psychiatrist (Leo Genn) in an overcrowded state mental institution. Directed by Anatole Litvak, the movie's sympathetic treatment of a mental case broke new ground in its day but seems dated now. Stylized depiction of various psychotic conditions and the use of shock treatment. A-II (br)

Snapper, The (1993) Upset Irish parents (Colm Meaney and Ruth McCabe) stand by their pregnant 20-year-old daughter (Tina Kellegher) when she refuses to name the father, whom gossipy neighbors suspect is a middle-aged married man (Pat Laffan). Director Stephen Frears's failed comedy presents a boisterous family coping to maintain dignity under fire, but while the parents are sympathetic, their immature daughter is not, and her predicament tends to be trivialized. Brief bedroom scenes, minor violence, frequent rough language, and much heavy drinking. A-III (R)

Sneakers (1992) Duped into giving top-secret computer information to the mob, an eccentric team of security experts (including Robert Redford, Sidney Poitier, and Dan Aykroyd) risk their lives in attempting to retrieve it for the government. Director Phil Alden Robinson's high-tech comic-flavored caper frequently bogs down in glaring script implausibilities. Light-hearted attitude toward computer crime, brief violence, a sexual reference, and minimal rough language. A-III (PG-13)

Sniper (1993) Lethargic action thriller teams a Marine sniper (Tom Berenger) with a novice intelligence agent (Billy Zane) in sloughing through the Panamanian jungle on a covert mission to assassinate a rebel leader. Director Luis Llosa fails to build much interest in the personal antagonism between the two assassins, focusing instead on the deadly fantasy of Americans licensed to kill on behalf of some shady US government officials. Sanctions assassins as heroes, some graphic violence, and occasional rough language. O (R)

Sniper's Ridge (1961) Limp Korean War picture directed by John Bushelman in which a frontline US Army unit (Jack Ging, Stanley Clements, John Goddard, and others) is at war with itself more than the enemy on the eve of the armistice ending the fighting. Wartime violence. A-II (br)

Snoopy, Come Home (1972) Disappointing animated feature from the Peanuts gang of Charles M. Schulz uses a lot of aimless skits to pad out a saccharine story of Snoopy's visit to his original owner, a little girl who lies ailing in the hospital. Directed by Bill Melendez, the result lacks author Schulz's characteristic humor and intelligence in dealing with the little joys and anxieties of childhood. A-I (G)

Snow Job (1972) Failed caper movie involves ex-ski champion Jean-Claude Killy in the robbery of a posh ski-resort high in the Italian Alps, from which he skies down the impossible slope of an adjacent glacier in a heart-thumping display of skiing skills and thrills, some of which are pretty terrifying. Aside from that, director George Englund can't do much with a silly plot, shallow characterizations, and the star's impressive lack of acting talent. A-III (G)

Snow White and the Seven Dwarfs (1937) Walt Disney's first feature-length fairytale remains an amazingly fresh and inventive landmark in the history of movie animation. Sequences such as Snow White's flight from the terrifying queen, the antics of the dwarfs, and the forest animals racing to the rescue through a frightening storm retain their original vitality and impact. Disney's combination of sentiment, laughter, and excitement makes the movie an especially satisfying entertainment for every age. A-I (G)

Snow White and the Three Stooges (1961) Silly slapstick fairytale directed by Walter Lang in which the aging Stooges (Moe Howard, Larry Fine, and Joe de Rita) save both Snow White (Carol Heiss) and Prince Charming (Edson Stroll) from the evil queen (Patricia Medina). Mild fantasy menace. A-I (br)

Snowball Express (1972) Big-city accountant (Dean Jones) leaves his boring job to run a tumbledown Colorado ski-resort hotel inherited from a distant relative, and his enthusiasm is enjoyably infectious as he wins out over avalanches, bank foreclosures, burst water pipes, and other impossible odds. Above-average Disney comedy directed by Norman Tokar has some very funny moments, a fine supporting cast, and a story that should hold the interest of the entire family. A-I (G)

Snows of Kilimanjaro, The (1952) Slack dramatization of Ernest Hemingway's story in which a famed author (Gregory Peck) recalls the women in his life (Susan Hayward, Ava Gardner, and Hildegard Neff) as he lies wounded on an African safari. Director Henry King does better with the flashbacks to colorful French and Spanish locales between the wars than with the thin characters and their unconvincing romances. Romantic complications including marital infidelity. A-III (br)

So Big (1953) Edna Ferber's period family-saga about an independent woman (Jane Wyman), who, after the death of her husband (Sterling Hayden), builds a successful truck-farming business near Chicago, then tries to save her architect son (Steve Forrest) from getting involved with the wrong society set. Directed by Robert Wise, Wyman's performance is good enough to almost make this manipulative melodrama worth watching. Preteens will find the later portions heavy-going. A-I (br)

So Evil My Love (1948) Dark tale of crime and deceit set in Victorian London, where a missionary's widow (Ann Todd) is wooed by a suave, cynical criminal (Ray Milland) wanting her to purloin some incriminating letters from a wealthy friend (Geraldine Fitzgerald) in a blackmail scheme ending in murder. Directed by Lewis Allen, the villain's duplicity is so overdrawn it taxes credibility while lessening sympathy for the starry-eyed widow and her final revenge. Stylized murders, moody menace, and romantic complications. A-II (br)

So Fine (1981) Meek college-professor (Ryan O'Neal) comes out of his shell to save his father's garment business by accidentally inventing jeans with transparent seats, but gets into trouble through a reluctant affair with a gangster's wife (Mariangela Melato). Written and directed by Andrew Bergman, the vulgar and mostly unfunny comedy tries to get laughs from overt sexuality and obscene language. O (R)

So I Married an Axe Murderer (1993) Sophomoric comedy in which a young man (Mike Myers) suspects his bride (Nancy Travis) is a notorious murderess who has axed her last three husbands to death. Director Thomas Schlamme lets a slightly amusing situation lurch out of control as it careens towards a contrived and hammy climax. Some comic violence, a live-in relationship, momentary rear nudity, and an instance of rough language. A-III (PG-13)

So Proudly We Hail (1943) Maudlin morale booster about Army nurses (Claudette Colbert, Paulette Goddard, Veronica Lake, and others) caring for the wounded during the battle of Bataan, then the siege of Corregidor, all the while fearing capture by the Japanese. Directed by Mark Sandrich, the emphasis is on the heroism of the Americans and their Filipino allies against the overwhelming forces of an inhuman enemy, relieved only by some battlefield romances (George Reeves and Sonny Tufts). Wartime violence and patriotic rhetoric. A-II (br)

So This Is Paris (1955) Pedestrian musical about three sailors (Tony Curtis, Gene Nelson, and Paul Gilbert) on shore leave in Paris, where they try to raise money for some orphaned children in the care of an American singer (Gloria De Haven). Directed by Richard Quine, the thin story-ine is paced by some indifferent songs and mediocre dance numbers, but there is surprisingly little charm to the characters, and the humor is largely unamusing. Wartime violence and sexual innuendo. A-III (br)

Soapdish (1991) The interlocking personal lives of a soap-opera cast and crew (Sally Field, Kevin Kline, Whoppi Goldberg, Elisabeth Shue, and Robert Downey, Jr.) get progressively crazier than their daily TV melodrama. Some good satirical lines and a sharp ensemble cast make director Michael Hoffman's fitfully funny spoof more zany than racy. Frequent bawdy innuendo and minimal rough language. A-III (PG-13)

Socrates (1971) Italian director Roberto Rossellini re-creates the life of the Greek philosopher, drawing heavily on the works of Plato and other traditional sources for script and setting. In the title role, Jean Sylvere is quite acceptable, and the drama of his trial and subsequent death becomes increasingly involving and poignant. However, so much philosophy reduced to English subtitles for 120 minutes becomes essentially a rapid-reading exercise. A-I (nr)

Sofie (1993) Slow but graceful story of a close-knit Jewish family in late 19th-century Copenhagen, where their only daughter (Karen-Lise Mynster) falls in love with a gentile artist (Jesper Christensen), but dutifully marries a dull, seemingly prosperous Jewish merchant (Torben Zeller) to please her parents (Erland Josephson and Ghita Norby) and preserve the family's Jewish heritage. Director Liv Ullmann unfolds an episodic tale of family life, treating each character with equal compassion, while focusing on the daughter's struggle to find happiness within the confines of her parents' world. Subtitles. Some sexual innuendo and a traumatic scene with nudity. A-III (nr)

Soft Skin, The (1965) Quiet yet absorbing story examining the relationship of a middle-aged publisher (Jean Desailly) to his wife and to a lovely airline stewardess. In this mature and sensitive work, director Francois Truffaut takes a rather commonplace situation and gives it a moral weight that becomes extremely involving. Subtitles. Theme of marital infidelity. A-III (br)

Sol Madrid (1968) Routine crime melodrama directed by Brian G. Hutton in which an undercover agent (David McCallum) is sent to Mexico to break up a narcotics ring which he does by using a gangster's girlfriend as bait. Some fairly heavy violence. A-III (br)

Solarbabies (1986) Sci-fi escapist fantasy about a group of rebellious adolescents who escape from a state-run orphanage of the distant future and he1p save their planet from destruction. Silly plot, but imaginative special effects from director Alan Johnson who doesn't help matters by trying to enliven the action with stylized violence. A-II (PG-13)

Soldier (1998) Failed sci-fi fantasy set on a planetary garbage-dump, where a veteran soldier (Kurt Russell) is nursed back to health by a lost colony of space pioneers, whom he then saves from annihilation by a battalion of genetically engineered soldiers. Directed by Paul Anderson, the thin plot is so predictable, and the characters take themselves so seriously that the unimaginative futuristic story of a hardened solider rediscovering his human qualities seems even more ridiculous than it is. Much special-effects violence, including some gore, and instances of rough language and profanity. A-III (R)

Soldier Blue (1970) Based on the notorious 1864 Sand Creek Massacre of some 500 Cheyenne braves, women, and children by the US Cavalry, the account begins with a tedious romance between a soldier (Peter Strauss) and a former Indian captive (Candice Bergen), who, when she learns of the impending attack on the Indian village, tries to prevent the slaughter. Director Ralph Nelson's well-intentioned attempt to confront a military atrocity becomes itself a brutalizing experience by wallowing in graphic depictions of bloodshed and rape. Excessive, stomach-wrenching violence. O (R)

Soldier in Skirts (see: **Triple Echo**)

Soldier of Fortune (1955) Far-fetched adventure directed by Edward Dmytryk in which a major Hong Kong smuggler (Clark Gable) defies a local police-official (Michael Rennie) in order to help an American (Susan Hayward), with whom he is smitten, get her missing husband (Gene Barry) out of Red China. Stylized violence and romantic complications peppered with anti-Communist rhetoric. A-III (br)

Soldier of Orange (1979) Dutch production about a wealthy, aristocratic young student (Rutger Hauer in a superb performance) who is caught up in the catastrophe of the Nazi invasion and becomes a hero of the Resistance. Directed by Paul Verhoeven, it is at its best as an old-fashioned war movie fortified with a credibility and heightened emotions that are above the usual. Too often, however, it indulges in showy stunts that have a jarring effect, and its depiction of sexuality is excessively graphic. O (R)

Soldiers Three (1951) Pale imitation-Kipling tale of British privates (Stewart Granger, Robert Newton, and Cyril Cusak) in imperial India, where their sophomoric antics help put down a rebellion to the satisfaction of their regimental commander (Walter Pidgeon). Director Tay Garnett's treatment of all these mock-heroics flounders erratically, and the trio's supposed camaraderie is painfully artificial and belabored. Stylized violence. A-II (br)

Soldier's Daughter Never Cries, A (1998) Fact-based drama about the troubled family of a 1960s American author (Kris Kristofferson), who after years of living in Paris, returns to the States, where his 15-year-old daughter (Leelee Sobieski) seeks to be popular with boys by promiscuous behavior. Director James Ivory sensitively explores the effects of culture shock on a close-knit family, but the father's glib sexual permissiveness toward his teenage daughter is the picture's most troubling aspect. Tolerant view of premarital sex, fleeting violence, occasional profanity, and intermittent rough language. A-IV (R)

Soldier's Story, A (1984) When a black sergeant (Adolph Caesar) is murdered at an Army camp in 1944, the investigating officer (Howard Rollins, Jr.,) discovers that the victim was a ruthless tyrant who had been well-hated by his men. Director Norman Jewison's fine production looks at racial prejudice from a number of perspectives with unusually effective results. Some violence and rough language. A-II (PG)

Soleil-O (1973) Young accountant from a former French-African colony (Robert Linesol) arrives in Paris looking for work, but finds instead racism, ranging from the subtle to the blatant, becomes increasingly bewildered, and finally ends on the brink of violent despair. Mauritanian production written and directed by Mel Hondo, its use of ironic humor and lively music keeps the plight of the black emigrant-worker from becoming totally depressing. A-III (nr)

Solid Gold Cadillac, The (1956) Delightful comedy about a small shareholder (Judy Holliday) in a large corporation who ejects its corrupt board of directors through the proxies of other small shareholders and the savvy of an honest business executive (Paul Douglas). Directed by Richard Quine, Holliday's eccentric brand of comedy is perfectly suited to this populist tale of ordinary people triumphing over corporate sharks. Mild romantic complications. A-II (br)

Solo (1996) Secretly developed by the US military, a warrior android (Mario Van Peebles) goes AWOL in a Central American jungle to aid peasants fighting off murderous guerrillas while dodging a team of military exterminators. Director Norberto Barba's male-power fantasy is little more than a vanity vehicle for the muscular Van Peebles. Intermittent violence, fleeting nudity, and occasional profanity. A-III (PG-13)

Solomon and Sheba (1959) Thin gruel derived from the biblical story of Israel's wise king (Yul Brynner) seduced by a pagan queen (Gina Lollabrigida), while his elder brother (George Sanders) plots to seize the throne. Director King Vidor's last movie proves a disappointing spectacle with a soapy plot, wooden acting, and only a few large-scale action sequences, notably the blinding of Egyptian forces by the burnished shields of the Israelites and a ludicrous pagan orgy. Stylized violence and sexual situations. A-III (br)

Some Call It Loving (1973) Pretentious hothouse fantasy about a musician (Zalman King) who buys a Sleeping Beauty from a sideshow, wakes the sleeper (Tisa Farrow), and has her join him and his strange companions (Carol White and Veroncia Anderson) in perverse games. Directed by James B. Harris, it's a glossy exercise in voyeurism, and its leering attitude toward women and sex is degrading. O (R)

Some Came Running (1958) Overblown melodrama from James Jones's novel about an ex-GI novelist with writer's block (Frank Sinatra) returning to his Indiana hometown, where he embarrasses his successful brother (Arthur Kennedy) by taking up with a gambler (Dean Martin) and a prostitute (Shirley MacLaine), then falls for an upright English teacher (Marta Hyer). Directed by Vincente Minnelli, Sinatra tries to gain sympathy in the role of a surly but misunderstood hero, though the proceedings are too contrived to sustain interest. Stylized violence, alcoholic excess, and sexual situations. A-III (br)

Some Girls Do (1971) Bulldog Drummond (Richard Johnson) returns as an anemic James Bond imitation with a gaggle of gorgeous girls on a secret island-hideout from which the baddies plan to rule the world with a super-destructive weapon. Lackluster British movie directed by Ralph Thomas goes one step further in reducing women to objects by making them mechanical dummies activated by a convenient off/on switch behind the ear. A-III (G)

Some Kind of a Nut (1969) When a bank-teller (Dick Van Dyke) grows a beard, his boss takes it as a sign of nonconformity and orders him to shave it off. As fellow employees and associates choose sides in the course of the dispute, the hero rediscovers the sterling qualities of his about-to-be ex-wife (Angie Dickinson). Director Garson Kanin fails in his attempt at a whimsical examination of a man's search for integrity and individuality. A-III (PG)

Some Kind of Hero (1982) Returned Vietnam prisoner-of-war (Richard Pryor) finds himself neck-deep in trouble when a high-priced prostitute (Margot Kidder) falls in love with him, and he gets involved with organized crime. Ill-assorted mix of comedy and melodrama, which director Michael Pressman is unable to organize into any semblance of unity. Some graphic sex, cheap thrills, and low humor. O (R)

Some Kind of Wonderful (1987) A confused teenager (Eric Stoltz) struggles against authority figures and shallow advice from parents and schoolmates in overcoming his insecurities while asserting his nonconformist aspirations. Director John Hughes's adolescent soap-opera passively accepts teen sex as a natural outcome of rapid physical and underdeveloped emotional maturity, as well as subtly undermining trust in the values of the adult world. A-III (PG-13)

Some Mother's Son (1996) Fact-based story spans 1979-81 in troubled Northern Ireland, where a mother (Helen Mirren) opposed to violence is befriended by a fervent IRA supporter (Fionnula Flanagan) after both their imprisoned sons (Aidan Gillen and David O'Hara) join in a hunger strike to the death to protest inhumane conditions in their Ulster prison. Director Terry George stresses the human anguish resulting from the continuing struggle between IRA gunmen prepared to die for their cause and a brutal government bureaucracy determined to crush the republican spirit. Some violence, intermittent profanity, and rough language. A-III (R)

Some of My Best Friends Are ... (1971) Mervyn Nelson's documentary on the patrons of a gay bar borders on exploitation of its subject through demeaning cliche and stereotype that contribute nothing of understanding nor insight into homosexuality and how it affects these men's lives. O (R)

Somebody Killed Her Husband (1978) Innocuous bit of fluff in which a bumbling but charming clerk (Jeff Bridges) in Macy's toy department falls in love with a beautiful customer (Farrah Fawcett), who soon becomes a widow when somebody kills her husband. Directed by Lamont Johnson, it's a fairly entertaining mystery-comedy except for its benign view of adultery. A-III (PG)

Someone Behind the Door (1971) Plodding murder-melodrama about a neurologist (Anthony Perkins) who plans to kill his wife's lover by using an escaped lunatic (Charles Bronson), but the plan goes badly awry. Directed by Nicolas Gessner, the dull and static movie contains a rape scene that is ludicrous despite its ferocity. A-III (GP)

Someone Else's America (1996) Bittersweet story of a kindhearted Spanish immigrant (Tom Conti) who shares his cramped Brooklyn digs with an illegal Yugoslav alien (Miki Manojlovic), whose relations begin showing up on their doorstep without green cards. Director Goran Paskaljevic tenderly depicts a multi-ethnic neighborhood whose inhabitants generously help each other cope and care for their families. Brief violence, occasional rough language, and minimal profanity. A-III (R)

Someone to Watch Over Me (1987) Failed romantic-thriller in which a police detective (Tom Berenger) falls in love with the rich socialite (Mimi Rogers) he is supposed to be protecting from a killer, conveniently forgetting that he is already married to a good woman (Lorraine Bracco). Director Ridley Scott's muddled tearjerker is equally slack as a suspense thriller. Excessive violence, lush treatment of adultery, and much rough language. O (R)

Something Big (1971) Failed Western spoof about an outlaw (Dean Martin) who abducts the wife (Honor Blackman) of a US Cavalry officer (Brian Keith) in order to trade her for a Gattling gun so he can mow down an army of Mexican bandits and take their hoard of stolen treasure. Directed by Andrew V. McLaglen, the comedy consists of overacting and double entendre, and the action is of the tired fantasy variety. A-III (GP)

Something for Everyone (1970) Bleak comedy about an aspiring footman (Michael York), in the employ of an enchanting countess (Angela Lansbury), who decides that the swiftest path to noble rank is through the bedroom, with a few slayings along the way. Directed by Harold Prince, there are a few pleasant moments in this adult fairytale, but not nearly enough for most tastes. Stylized sex and violence. A-IV (R)

Something Short of Paradise (1979) On-again, off-again comedy romance between the manager of a New York art-cinema (David Steinberg) and a journalist (Susan Sarandon) develops rather slowly, hampered by a needlessly complex flashback structure. As directed by David Helpern, the result is only moderately entertaining. The nature of the relationship between the two lovers makes it adult fare. A-III (PG)

Something to Sing About (1937) Silly but unpretentious romantic comedy in which a bandleader (James Cagney) returns from his honeymoon to discover he's an overnight Hollywood sensation with a movie contract that forces him to pretend he's not married. Directed by Victor Schertzinger, the Cagney vehicle is entirely predictable but provides a lot of light, fluffy fun, especially the period music. A-I (br)

Something to Talk About (1995) After discovering her husband (Dennis Quaid) has been unfaithful, a Southern wife and mother (Julia Roberts) re-evaluates her life and family relationships, a painful process which leads her own mother (Gena Rowlands) to finally confront her tyrannical husband (Robert Duvall) about his own philandering. Director Lasse Hallstrom elicits strong performances in an ensemble work written by Callie Khouri whose sassy, comedic script makes well-considered points about marital communication, the value of family, and eventual forgiveness. Confrontations about infidelity, fleeting violence, and intermittent profanity, as well as rough language. A-III (R)

Something Wicked This Way Comes (1983) Disney adaptation of the Ray Bradbury story about a strange traveling-carnival that disrupts life in a small Illinois town sometime in the 1920s. The evil carnival-master (Jonathan Pryce) fulfills people's desires, but in a way that costs them dearly. When two adventurous boys (Vidal Peterson and Shawn Carson) tumble to the carnival master's secret, they become the special object of his malevolence. Jack Clayton directs all this with just the right blend of tension and human warmth, but some of the special effects are definitely not for younger viewers. A-II (PG)

Something Wild (1986) Eccentric young woman (Melanie Griffith) seduces a corruptible yuppie (Jeff Daniels) into a kinky romance based on mutual deception, but, when her husband (Ray Liotta) gets out of prison, the affair becomes deadly. Although indicating the moral bankruptcy of the central characters, director Jonathan Demme's emphasis on the sexual nature of their relationship results in just another male sex-fantasy. Nudity in a sexual context, brutal violence, and profanity. O (R)

Sometimes a Great Notion (1971) Muddled screen-version of the Ken Kesey novel about a family of independent Oregon loggers whose reliance on rugged individualism makes them defy a strike action called by their fellow loggers, and this has dire, far-reaching consequences. Directed by Paul Newman, who also stars as the family's leader, the story's action is effectively presented, notably the difficulty and dangers of logging, and is extremely well-acted. However, the movie's sympathies about its larger theme of individualism versus society and changing conditions are ambiguous, if not confused, especially in its final, vulgar gesture of defiance. Heavy-going even for adults. A-IV (GP)

Somewhere in the Night (1946) Twisty mystery in which a WW II vet suffering from amnesia (John Hodiak) gets some help from a nightclub singer (Nancy Guild), her boss (Richard Conte), and a friendly cop (Lloyd Nolan), while searching for his true identity. Directed by Joseph L. Mankiewicz, the plot grows increasingly contrived in linking the vet to a four-year-old murder, missing Nazi , and various thugs, before he learns who he really is. Stylized violence and romantic complications. A-II (br)

Somewhere in Time (1980) Young playwright (Christopher Reeve) wills himself back several generations into the past to meet the famous actress (Jane Seymour) with whose portrait he has fallen in love. Directed by Jeannot Szwarc, the sentimental romance and its lovely images (filmed on Mackinac Island) are for incurable romantics only. A-II (PG)

Sommersby (1993) An abusive husband (Richard Gere) is so changed for the better after years in a Civil War POW camp that his wife (Jodie Foster) is sure he is an imposter, but plays along until their happiness is shattered when he is tried for murder. Director Jon Amiel's mystery-laden period-romance is an engrossing tale of a man's struggle for personal integrity and the positive effects that has on all around him. Mature themes with brief violence and very discreet marital encounters. A-III (PG-13)

Son-in-Law (1993) Airhead comedy in which a coed (Carla Gugino) brings a freaky college chum (Pauly Shore) home for the Thanksgiving weekend to her straitlaced farm family, with the two pretending to be engaged to save her from accepting the marriage proposal of a longtime boyfriend. Director Steve Rash fails to sustain the one-joke premise of Shore as a fish out of water in heartland America, with the humor wholly dependent on anti-authoritarian, often vulgar, stabs at humor. Mild sexual innuendo, fleeting nudity, momentary violence, and many crude remarks. A-III (PG-13)

Son of Ali Baba (1952) Muddled, often silly Arabian Nights adventure directed by Kurt Neumann in which the fun-loving title character (Tony Curtis) gets serious enough to save a beautiful princess (Piper Laurie) and his father's fortune from Baghdad's wicked caliph (Victor Jory) and even nastier son (Hugh O'Brian). Tiresome bosh with the usual stylized violence and mild sexual innuendo. A-II (br)

Son of Blob (1972) Once again the creeping crimson mass has fun overrunning Small Town USA, sparing no one in its path, until a fearless couple (Robert Walker, Jr., and Gwynne Gilford) remember the chilling device used by Steve McQueen to stop the blob in the original. Directed by Larry Hagman, the object this time is to glean smiles instead of screams from undemanding viewers, who are helped by delightful cameos from the likes of Godfrey Cambridge and Shelley Berman. Fantasy violence. A-II (GP)

Son of Dracula (1943) Creeky horror tale in which the Hungarian Count Alucard (Lon Chaney, Jr.), a backward relative of Dracula, comes to the United States with plans to take over an isolated southern mansion by marrying its owner (Louise Allbritton), but she turns out to have some plans of her own. Directed by Robert Siodmak, the overwrought proceedings feature a sappy leading man (Robert Paige), some eerie special effects, and the usual vampire lore. Stylized violence and menacing situations. A-II (br)

Son of Flubber (1963) Silly Disney sequel directed by Robert Stevenson continues the experiments of the wacky inventor (Fred MacMurray) from **The Absent Minded Professor**, the havoc this time caused by trying to control the weather and, along the way, win a football game. Slapdash comic situations result in few laughs, even for the undemanding. A-I (br)

Son of Frankenstein (1939) Stylish horror movie in which the baron's son (Basil Rathbone) sets out to vindicate his late father's name by repairing the defective brain of the monster (Boris Karloff), but before he can do so, his father's crazed old helper (Bela Lugosi) orders the creature to kill unfriendly villagers. Directed by Rowland V. Lee, the sinister proceedings are helped by eerie expressionistic sets and memorable characterizations, especially Lugosi's broken-necked schemer, Karloff's troubled monster, and Lionel Atwill's police inspector with a mechanical right-arm. More menace than violence, with a child's life at stake in the suspenseful conclusion. A-II (br)

Son of Fury (1942) Moody 18th-century adventure tale of an English orphan (Roddy McDowall) raised as a servant by his villainous uncle (George Sanders), but when grown (Tyrone Power) runs away to the South Seas, falls in love with a native woman (Gene Tierney), harvests a fortune in pearls, and returns to claim his rightful inheritance. Director John Cromwell delivers a well-crafted period-piece with a great supporting cast (Elsa Lanchester, John Carradine, and Dudley Digges), but the wronged hero's brooding over past injustices grows tiresome. Stylized violence and romantic complications. A-II (br)

Son of Godzilla (1969) Dubbed Japanese production directed by Jun Fukuda has the old monster come to the rescue of a baby Godzilla attacked by gigantic insects on a radioactive Pacific island. Inane plot and cheesy special-effects violence. A-II (br)

Son of Kong, The (1933) Satisfying sequel starts with King Kong's discoverer (Robert Armstrong) escaping New York lawsuits to return to Skull Island, where the giant ape's young son helps him find a lost treasure, then saves his life when the island is convulsed by an earthquake and sinks into the sea. Director Ernest B. Schoedsack's adventure-fantasy features exotic settings and colorful characters, including a spunky orphaned singer (Helen Mack), but the action is thin and largely tongue-in-cheek, including animator Willis O'Brien's goodhearted monster. Mild suspense and restrained violence. A-I (br)

Son of Lassie (1945) The title's Laddie tracks his Yorkshire owner (Peter Lawford) to a RAF airbase, is snuck aboard a reconnaissance flight which is shot down over German-occupied Norway, and, after they get separated, the faithful collie overcomes all obstacles to rejoin his master. Directed by S. Sylvan Simon, Laddie's incredible adventures among the Nazis must have seemed silly even to WW II audiences, though the picture's main appeal is seeing a handsome, well-trained dog go through his paces. Wartime heroics. A-I (br)

Son of Monte Cristo, The (1940) Routine costume-adventure directed by Rowland V. Lee with the title character (Louis Hayward) stopping off in an 1865 Balkan duchy to help a band of patriots restore their rightful ruler (Joan Bennett) by overthrowing a nasty usurper (George Sanders). Swashbuckling action and mild romance. A-I (br)

Son of Paleface (1952) Searching out West for his father's hidden treasure, a Harvard man (Bob Hope) gets mixed up with a lady outlaw (Jane Russell) and a government agent (Roy Rogers). Directed by Frank Tashlin, the **Paleface** sequel has its comic moments, but doesn't measure up to the original. Some stylized violence and mild sexual innuendo. A-II (br)

Son of the Pink Panther (1993) Unaware he is the illegitimate son of the late, great Inspector Clouseau, a bumbling gendarme (Roberto Benigni) assigned to aid the police chief (Herbert Lom) recover a kidnapped princess (Debrah Farentino) only further complicates the case with his accident-prone shenanigans. Director Blake Edwards poorly utilizes the comic talents of Benigni by recycling pranks and pratfalls from seven previous Panther outings while neglecting to develop a believable or interesting plot. Occasional sexual innuendo and some nasty violence played for laughs. A-III (PG)

Son of the Shark (1995) Abused by an alcoholic father, two preteen runaways (Ludovic Vandendaele and Erick Da Silva) vent their rage by embarking on nightly campaigns of theft and vandalism, then escape from foster homes and more punitive environments, each time returning to wreak further havoc on their coastal community. French writer-director Agnes Merlet paints a bleak though poignant portrait of unloved, violence-prone siblings whom society has tried but failed to help. Subtitles. Constant juvenile menace and crime, fleeting nudity, occasional crude remarks, and some rough language. A-III (nr)

Sonatine (1998) Violent Japanese tale of an aging, world-weary gangster (Takeshi Kitano), whose boss sends him to settle a mob turf-war in a distant locale, where he comes to realize he has been betrayed and turns to taking revenge on his former colleagues. Also written and directed by Kitano, the story centers on a series of bloody killings, which are given a disturbingly comic edge until the proceedings culminate in a nihilistic bloodbath and suicide. Subtitles. Much gory violence, sexual situations with fleeting nudity, and frequent rough language. O (R)

Song of Bernadette, The (1943) Durable adaptation of the Franz Werfel novel about Bernadette Soubirous (Jennifer Jones), the French schoolgirl who in 1858 saw apparitions of the Virgin Mary at a grotto near Lourdes, but news of this is initially discredited by her stern pastor (Charles Bickford), the town prosecutor (Vincent Price), and an envious teacher (Gladys Cooper). Directed by Henry King, the story of a young girl's faith withstanding the disbelief of her elders is made dramatically convincing by a fine cast, evocative photography, and largely unsentimental treatment. A-I (br)

Song of Norway (1970) Huge, panoramic biographical portrait of composer Edvard Grieg (Toralv

Maurstad), filmed in the natural splendor of his beautiful Norway. Part of the saga involves the two women in his life: the heiress who rejects his love and then tries to buy him back (Christina Schollin), and the patient admirer and singer of his works whom he eventually marries (Florence Henderson). Written and directed by Andrew Stone, the result is a stunning musical postcard, but its personal drama does not measure up to its magnificent location photography. Still, it offers more than enough wholesome entertainment to satisfy most family viewers. A-I (G)

Song of Scheherazade (1947) Hokey but colorful story of Russian naval cadet Rimsky-Korsakov (Jean-Pierre Aumont), who falls for an exotic dancing-girl (Yvonne De Carlo) while on shore leave in 1865 Turkey, and, despite the admonitions of his strict commander (Brian Donlevy), goes off to become a great composer. Director Walter Reisch's musical spectacle has some visual interest, but the characters are never more than wooden and the fanciful plot is sluggishly contrived. A-I (br)

Song of the Islands (1942) Breezy romantic comedy set in Hawaii, where the visiting son (Victor Mature) of a Chicago millionaire (George Barbier) falls in love with the daughter (Betty Grable) of an Irish-American beachcomber (Thomas Mitchell), but their romance is cut short by the wrath of their respective fathers. Director Walter Lang paces the proceedings with some agreeable songs, Hawaiian dance numbers, and comic relief from Jack Oakie, Hilo Hattie, and Billy Gilbert. Romantic complications. A-II (br)

Song of the Open Road (1944) Routine programmer notable for Jane Powell's screen debut as a 14-year-old singing star who runs away from her Hollywood studio to join a group of teenagers doing their bit for the war effort by harvesting farm produce . Directed by S. Sylvan Simon, the pedestrian plot ends rather listlessly in the orange groves of Pamona, Calif., but it marks the beginning of the genial young singer's acting career. A-I (br)

Song of the South (1946) James Baskett gives a winning performance as Uncle Remus, the wise old storyteller who helps a youngster (Bobby Driscoll) understand the ways of the world through folktales about Brer Rabbit and his friends. The Disney version of Joel Chandler Harris's tales from the mythic Old South is a warm and zestful mixture of animation and live action that most parents will enjoy as much as the youngsters. A-I (G)

Song to Remember, A (1944) Slick Hollywood biography of composer Frederick Chopin (1810-49), who escapes Czarist oppression in Warsaw to find fame and love in Paris with writer George Sand (Merle Oberon), until his death on a concert tour raising money for Polish independence. Directed by Charles Walters, the result focuses on Chopin's nationalism as nurtured by his music teacher (Paul Muni) with little attention to his struggles and achievements as an artist. Discreet depiction of an unmarried relationship. A-II (br)

Song without End (1960) Elegant but overblown biography of Hungarian composer Franz Liszt (1811-86) centers on his unhappy affairs with a French countess (Genevieve Page), then a Russian princess (Capucine), ultimately ending in retirement to a monastery. Directed by Charles Vidor and completed by George Cukor, the result never gets beneath the surface of the characters or the glossy veneer of the Romantic Age, though the music is splendid, and Dirk Bogarde's portrayal of Liszt offers an unusual mix of the pious and the profane. Discreet treatment of sexual relationships. A-II (br)

Sons of Katie Elder, The (1965) John Wayne stars as the eldest of four brothers (Dean Martin, Earl Holliman, and Michael Anderson, Jr.) who reunite at the funeral of their mother, then set out to get the land-grabber (James Gregory) who killed their father and stole the family ranch. Directed by Henry Hathaway, the story is overly familiar as well as overlong, but Wayne is in top form as the mythic Western hero who prevails against injustice. Some fairly intense stylized violence. A-I (br)

Sophie's Choice (1982) Plodding screen version of William Styron's novel about a Polish survivor of Auschwitz (Meryl Streep) who in 1947 has found refuge in a garish pink boarding-house in Brooklyn with her lover (Kevin Kline), an American Jew of mercurial temperament. A young, inexperienced Southern writer (Peter MacNichol) gets caught up in their lives, their lies, and their secrets (including one that gives the story its title). Director Alan J.Pakula gets good performances and tries to keep the sluggish narrative moving, but in the end it seems hardly worth the effort. Suicide figures in the plot and there is some brief nudity and rough language. A-III (R)

Sorcerer (1977) Four down-and-outers (Roy Scheider, Bruno Cremer, Francisco Rabal, and Amidou) in a South American backwater seize the chance to drive trucks loaded with dynamite over some 200 miles of jungle road in order to put out a burning oil well. Director William Friedkin sketches in the background of each of the four, unlike the original 1953 French movie **The Wages of Fear** upon which it is based, but in doing so diffuses the impact of the dangerous truck ride. Occasional violence and a scene showing the victims of the oil well explosion. A-III (PG)

Sorcerers, The (1967) Hokey British horror movie directed by Michael Reeves has an old man (Boris Karloff) invent a machine enabling him and his aged wife (Catherine Lacey) to control the mind and actions of a young man (Ian Ogilvy), then becomes horrified by the wife's commanding the youth to kill. Stylized violence and sexual innuendo. A-III (br)

Sorrento Beach (see: **Hotel Sorrento**)

Sorrow and the Pity, The (1972) Classic documentary directed by Marcel Ophuls examines France during the German Occupation and replaces the legend of popular resistance with the fact of complicity by large sections of society. Focusing on the town of

Clermont-Ferrand, Ophuls uses it as a measure of the nation's collaboration with the Nazis. The object is not to judge the inhabitants of the village, but to show how easy it is for people in crisis to accept tyranny and yet believe that they are free. A-II (PG)

Sorry, Wrong Number (1948) Uneven thriller from Lucille Fletcher's taut, half-hour radio play about a wealthy, bedridden neurotic (Barbara Stanwyck) who accidentally learns her husband (Burt Lancaster) has hired someone to kill her in the next few hours. Directed by Anatole Litvak, the adaptation spends more time on flashbacks providing the motivation for the crime than on the suspenseful situation of the helpless woman whose life hangs on a telephone line. Much tension and vicious criminals. A-II (br)

Soul Food (1997) Spirited ensemble-drama follows the near-rupture of the ties that bind three married sisters (Vanessa L. Williams, Vivica Fox, and Nia Long) in an extended African-American family after their peacekeeping matriarch goes into a diabetic coma. Writer-director George Tillman, Jr.'s, comedic drama is contrived and sentimental, but ends up as a testament to the loving relationships that families are all about. Fleeting violence, brief bedroom scenes, occasional profanity, and recurring rough language. A-III (R)

Soul Man (1986) Youth from a wealthy family finds a way to pay for his Harvard Law School education by means of a minority-student scholarship when he takes pills that blacken the color of his skin. This disappointing youth-oriented comedy fails to deliver any insightful social satire save some foul one-liners. Instead, it affirms the materialistic aspirations of young people, faces issues of racial prejudice only , and is accepting of promiscuous sex and false social values. O (PG-13)

Soul of Nigger Charley, The (1973) Lame sequel to **The Legend of Nigger Charley** finds the two ex-slaves (Fred Williamson and D'Urville Martin) up against some Confederate aristocrats who are trying to re-create the Old South in Mexico. Director Larry Spangler places the emphasis squarely on the action sequences with lots of special-effects bullet impacts. A-III (R)

Soul Soldier (1972) Low-budget story of the mostly-black 10th Cavalry of Fort Davis, Texas, and their heroism against the Indians on the Western frontier concentrates on foolishness at the fort rather than fortitude in the field. Directed by John Cardos, the shoddy production wastes a capable cast (Rafer Johnson, Lincoln Kilpatrick, Janee Michelle, Cesar Romero, and Robert Dix) in sexual hijinks and violent heroics. O (R/GP)

Soul to Soul (1971) In celebration of its 14th year as an independent African nation, Ghana sponsored a music festival featuring a number of America's top black rock, jazz, and blues performers, including Wilson Pickett, Ike and Tina Turner, Roberta Flack, Santana, and many others. Denis Sanders's fine documentary follows the performers to Ghana, conveys some of their reflections on their participation, but mostly encapsulates the festival in a joyous musical entertainment that is universal in its appeal. A-I (G)

Souls at Sea (1937) Unusual yarn about an 1842 Yankee seaman (Gary Cooper) working secretly with the British to smash the African slave-trade, but complications arise when he is unjustly put on trial for cowardice during a sea disaster. Directed by Henry Hathaway, the movie establishes the seaman's motivation with some strong opening scenes of the brutal conditions aboard an American slave-ship, then shifts into a conventional melodrama focusing on the seaman's romance with the sister (Frances Dee) of a British traitor (Henry Wilcoxon) and his loyalty to an erring shipmate (George Raft). Some fairly intense stylized violence. A-II (br)

Sound and the Fury, The (1959) Disappointing adaptation of the William Faulkner novel about an adopted son (Yul Brynner) trying to repair the fallen fortunes of a once-proud Mississippi family while raising the illegitimate daughter (Joanne Woodward) one of them (Margaret Leighton) left behind. Directed by Martin Ritt, the choppy narrative centers on the adolescent girl's troubled path to maturity, but the proceedings are often murky and burdened with ill-defined characters and portentous dialogue. Sexual situations and implied promiscuous relationships. A-III (br)

Sound of Music, The (1965) Particularly fine screen version of the Rodgers and Hammerstein musical about the formative years of the Trapp Family Singers in Austria between the two world wars. Its interesting story, solid cast (headed by Julie Andrews and Christopher Plummer), lovely music and intelligent lyrics, colorful scenery, and pleasant fantasy will entertain the mind and enliven the spirit. Directed by Robert Wise, the movie has held up over the years as thoroughly refreshing family entertainment. A-I (G)

Sounder (1972) Appealing story of a black family of Louisiana sharecroppers struggling to survive against natural and human odds during the early days of the Depression. When the father (Paul Winfield) is jailed for stealing food, his wife (Cicely Tyson) and three children (Kevin Hooks is the eldest) are left to crop the sugar cane on their own. The boy's subsequent odyssey to find the labor camp where his father is being held provides additional drama. Produced by Robert B. Radnitz and directed by Martin Ritt, it captures the humanity of the characters and a fine, distanced sense of its sleepy Southern locale. The movie earns a deep emotional response from its audience because its story and characters are believable. Not only a valid examination of the black experience in America, it is also a fine family experience. A-I (G)

Sounder, Part II (see: **Part II, Sounder**)

Soup for One (1982) Nice young man (Saul Rubinek) wanders through New York's frenetic singles scene in search of the ideal wife in this sometimes bright, but more often erratic and awkward, romantic comedy written and directed by Jonathan Kaufer. Some of the jokes are more mean-spirited than genuinely satiric, and its rather heavy dependence on nudity for comic relief makes this unsuitable entertainment. O (R)

Soupçon (1980) Celebrating their 25th wedding anniversary, a couple (Jean Carmet and Marie Dubois) declare to their surprised family that they are separating. Both discover in the end that growing old together is perhaps better than chasing illusions of freedom. French production directed by Jean Charles Tacchella is a Gallic bit of whimsy with some nicely turned characterizations and a frank treatment of sex. A-III (nr)

South Central (1992) While in prison for killing a drug dealer, a member (Glenn Plummer) of a powerful black gang is reformed by a fellow inmate (Carl Lumbly) and emerges to save his young son from being turned into a criminal by the gang's leader (Byron Keith Minns). In depicting the rise of a vicious street gang in a Los Angeles ghetto, writer-director Steve Anderson is a lot more convincing than in showing the moral transformation of a bitter man into a caring father. Much graphic violence, some sexual situations and references, drug abuse, and rough language. A-IV (R)

South Pacific (1958) Clunky screen version of the hit Rodgers and Hammerstein musical from James A. Mitchener's tales of a 1943 Navy base, where a nurse (Mitzi Gaynor) falls for a French planter (Rossano Brazzi), and a Marine lieutenant (John Kerr) yearns for a Polynesian maid (France Nuyen). Directed by Joshua Logan, the leads fail to score either with the songs or the dramatic action, and the use of color filters to set the mood for key scenes only emphasizes the movie's artificiality. Sexual situations and innuendo. A-III (br)

South Sea Sinner (1950) Halting melodrama directed by Bruce Humberstone in which a sick sailor (Macdonald Carey) is hospitalized on a Pacific island, where a crooked cafe-owner (Luther Adler) identifies him as a man wanted for aiding the Japanese during the war, but a goodhearted singer (Shelley Winters) helps prove his innocence. Sexual situations and innuendo. A-III (br)

Southern Comfort (1981) Louisiana National Guardsmen become lost in the bayous and run afoul of vengeful Cajuns, in this grim, somber, altogether pretentious melodrama directed by Walter Hill. Aside from some spectacular cinematography by Andrew Laszlo, it has little to recommend it, though Powers Boothe makes an effective screen debut as one of the hapless guardsmen. Violence and rough language. A-III (R)

Southern Star, The (1969) Fortune-hunter George Segal and girlfriend Ursula Andress trek across Africa's jungles in pursuit of a diamond thief, but are themselves pursued by a crook who wants both the prize diamond and the girl. Directed by Sidney Hayers, there's lots of cliched action done in tongue-in-cheek fashion, including Orson Welles as an effeminate outlaw, but there is no reason for its excessively graphic violence. O (PG)

Southern Yankee, A (1948) Mild Civil War comedy with Red Skelton as a bungling St. Louis hotel porter who accidentally captures a Confederate spy, then is sent back South in his place carrying bogus Union plans. Director Edward Sedgwick centers the visual humor on Skelton's goofy clowning as the timid hero, abetted by suitable villains (Brian Donlevy and John Ireland) and a minor love-interest (Arlene Dahl). Comic menace and a stylized battle scene. A-I (br)

Southerner, The (1945) A year in the life of a Texas sharecropper (Zachary Scott) who works hard to support his wife (Betty Field), two children, and grandmother (Beulah Bondi), until his first harvest is wiped out by a flashflood, and he considers quitting the land to become a factory worker. Directed by Jean Renoir, the location photography gives a semi-documentary flavor to this portrait of simple, homespun characters whose sense of independence and self-reliance sustain them through the hardships and insecurities of farm life. A-I (br)

Soylent Green (1973) Charlton Heston plays a New York City cop in the year 2022, when lack of food forces people to subsist on a mysterious substance called Soylent Green, the secret of which Heston discovers after the voluntary death of his assistant (Edward G. Robinson). For all its posturing about ecological and moral disaster, it's no more than a routine detective movie with a slick and shallow futuristic setting. A-III (PG)

Space Jam (1996) Madcap mix of live action and animation, as basketball star Michael Jordan joins Bugs Bunny, Tweety Bird, and the rest of the Looney Tune gang in a basketball match against animated aliens bent on winning the right to relocate the Looney Tuners back to their planet forever. As directed by Joe Pytka, the human and cartoon elements blend well together for a lighthearted, wacky tale of hoop-dreams come true. Some comic violence. A-II (PG)

Spaceballs (1987) Space-fantasy parody from writer-director Mel Brooks is a takeoff of **Star Wars**, with Rick Moranis and John Candy supplying most of the character spoofs. Brooks plays a dual role in a technically polished, but rather self-indulgent, farce offering an assortment of movie-industry jokes, mild slapstick, sexual innuendo, ethnic stereotypes, and vulgar language. A-III (PG)

Spacecamp (1986) Kate Capshaw portrays an astronaut who takes a team of teenagers through training exercises at the National Aeronautics and Space Administration's facility of the same name in Huntsville, Ala. The youngsters are put to the test of courage and determination when they are accidentally launched in a space shuttle by an affectionate robot. Director Harry Winer offers a somewhat inspiring and informative promo for the space program that youngsters will find engaging. A-I (PG)

Spaced Invaders (1990) Mildly diverting children's comedy about five bumbling, diminutive Martians who mistakenly invade Earth on Halloween, but have trouble convincing people that they're really aliens and not trick-or-treating youngsters. Director Patrick Read Johnson's one-joke movie has so-so special effects and some broad humor, notably from Royal Dano as an old codger who saves the day. Some scenes of menace that may frighten the very young. A-II (PG)

Spacehunter: Adventures in the Forbidden Zone (1983) Failed sci-fi fantasy about three 21st-century damsels in distress who are rescued from a perverted mutant by the driver of a futuristic junk-mobile (Peter Strauss). Directed by Lamont Johnson, this 3-D adventure is only for those who are amused by stupidity and mediocrity. Mild violence. A-II (PG)

Spanish Cape Mystery, The (1935) Routine murder mystery directed by Lewis D. Collins in which detective Ellery Queen (Donald Cook) falls for a pert young lady (Helen Twelvetrees) while figuring out who has been killing off her relatives during a family gathering at her rich father's seaside estate. Mild menace and off-screen mayhem. A-I (br)

Spanish Gardener, The (1956) Affecting tale of a young lad (Jon Whiteley) whose cold, unhappy father (Michael Hordern) is the British consul in a Spanish coastal town, where his gardener (Dirk Bogarde) befriends the affection-starved youngster. Directed by Philip Leacock from the A.J. Cronin novel, the picture of a child's rejection of his father for treating his friend unjustly is quietly drawn and quite touching in its resolution. Domestic tensions. A-I (br)

Spanish Main, The (1945) Energetic swashbuckler in which a dashing Dutch pirate (Paul Henreid) wins the love of a haughty aristocrat (Maureen O'Hara) who's betrothed to the pirate's archenemy, the villainous viceroy of Cartegena (Walter Slezak). Directed by Frank Borzage, there's plenty of romance, double-dealing intrigue, and colorful action with battling galleons, crossed swords, and a dangerous lady pirate (Binnie Barnes). Stylized violence and mild sexual innuendo. A-II (br)

Spanish Prisoner, The (1998) An invention worth a vast fortune sets in deadly motion an industrial espionage tale in which the inventor (Campbell Scott) is caught between his suspicious boss (Ben Gazzara) and a mysterious acquaintance (Steve Martin), whose helpful advice may get the inventor framed for murder. Writer-director David Mamet unfolds a devilishly serpentine plot too far-fetched to be credible but thoroughly engrossing for its unexpected surprises. Brief violence and fleeting sexual innuendo. A-III (PG)

Sparkle (1976) Absurdly melodramatic story of a Harlem girl (Irene Cara) who gains success as a singer. In spite of Cara's strong performance, Sam O'Steen's direction cannot make credible the anticlimactic crime elements grafted onto the plot. Restrained depiction of drugs and sex. A-III (PG)

Sparkler (1999) Offbeat comedy in which an unlikely friendship develops between a sweet-natured housewife (Park Overall) fleeing her faithless husband of 15 years and three young men hoping to win their way out of debt in Vegas. Director Darren Stein finds the heart in the main characters despite the tawdry surroundings of sleaze bars and their lowlife inhabitants. A fairly graphic sexual encounter, brief violence, nudity, and sexual references, as well as recurring rough language and profanity. A-IV (nr)

Spartacus (1960) While two corrupt politicians (Laurence Olivier and Charles Laughton) vie for power in Rome, the enslaved title gladiator (Kirk Douglas) escapes his owner (Peter Ustinov) to lead a great slave-revolt that shakes the ancient world. Directed by Stanley Kubrick from Howard Fast's novel, the result is an epic spectacle that re-creates the first century B.C. with flair and vigor, though the personal drama seldom measures up to the historical significance of the period's events. Vivid gladiatorial combat, battlefield violence, and veiled sexual innuendo. A-III (PG-13)

Spawn (1997) Clunky live-action cartoon in which the Devil's emissary (John Leguizamo) orders the head (Martin Sheen) of a covert government agency to murder his top agent (Michael Jai White), who then is given superhuman powers to lead the forces of evil, but instead joins the forces of good (led by Nicol Williamson). Directed by Mark Dippe from a comic book by Todd McFarlane, it's a flimsy fantasy at best, serving mainly as a vehicle for grandstanding special effects that are big but emotionally sterile, the result being a tiresome exercise in unimaginative mythmaking. Considerable special-effects violence, menacing situations, and some devilish vulgarity. A-III (PG-13)

Spawn of the North (1938) Rugged sea-adventure set in 1890s Alaska, where a fisherman (Henry Fonda) and his best friend (George Raft) both fall for the same woman (Dorothy Lamour), then find themselves on opposite sides in a fishing war with a crafty Russian poacher (Akim Tamiroff). Director Henry Hathaway excels in picturing the workaday world of the fishermen, but the melodramatic plot is far less convincing, despite well-staged sea battles against the poachers, and a good cast including John Barrymore as a newspaperman. Some hard-edged violence and romantic complications. A-III (br)

Speaking Parts (1990) Chilling, obtuse story of four people (Michael McManus, Arsinee Khanjian, Gabrielle Rose, and David Hemblen) who use video to connect with themselves and others. Canadian writer-director Atom Egoyan depicts a world of passive voyeurs so lulled by the use of video technology that their lives are emotional vacuums. Some profanity, much sexual innuendo, and a graphic masturbation scene. O (nr)

Special Day, A (1977) The day of the title is that of Hitler's state visit to Rome, which is used as the background and counterpoint to an encounter between a downtrodden wife (Sophia Loren) and a harassed homosexual (Marcello Mastroiani), who has been fired from the government radio station and faces even graver measures. Directed by Ettore Scola, the movie focuses not on the moral aspect of the wife's being unfaithful to her brutal husband, but upon the human anguish of the two principals. A-IV (nr)

Special Delivery (1976) Failed comedy melodrama about a bankrobber (Bo Svenson) and a kooky young woman (Cybill Shepherd) teaming up to recover some loot stashed in a mail box. Directed by Paul Wendkos, it is a jumble of many styles and plots, none of them very good. Some sexual innuendo. A-III (PG)

Special Investigator (1936) Crime programmer directed by Louis King in which a Chicago mouthpiece (Richard Dix) goes to a Nevada mining town as an undercover FBI agent in order to get the goods on the gangster (J. Carrol Naish) who killed his brother, but matters get complicated when he falls for the criminal's sister (Margaret Callahan). Stylized violence. A-I (br)

Special Section (1975) Story of injustices rendered by a special court instituted by France's Vichy government to satisfy the demands of their Nazi conquerors. Directed by Costa-Gavras, the movie is loosely episodic and lacking in characterization but excels in its re-creation of the period. As a result one can learn a little bit of history and be fairly entertained but moved hardly at all. A-II (PG)

Specialist, The (1975) Overwrought soap opera about rival lawyers (Adam West and John Anderson) in a small town who get involved in a case of entrapment and blackmail. Directed by Hikmet Avedis, it has a great deal of nudity, probably meant to take one's mind off a talky, determinedly simpleminded script. O (R)

Specialist, The (1994) A former CIA explosives expert (Sylvester Stallone), hiding from a murderous colleague (James Woods), is lured into the open by an icy seductress (Sharon Stone), who persuades him to murder a trio who slaughtered her parents years earlier. Every character is despicable in director Luis Llosa's atrociously acted, totally trashy, soft-core revenge melodrama, in which brutal violence is seen as the immediate solution to any conflict. Excessive violence, positive depiction of revenge murders, extended sex-scene, nudity, and much rough language. O (R)

Species (1995) Sexually violent potboiler blends horror and science fiction as a government team (led by Ben Kingsley) is sent into Los Angeles to exterminate a murderous half-human, half-alien predator (Natasha Henstridge) who is fully bent on reproducing her deadly kind. Director Roger Donaldson's sleazy chase-thriller relies on special effects for shock value, but nothing can save the one-dimensional characters and nonsensical narrative from terminal boredom. Excessive violence, graphic sexual encounters, much nudity, and intermittent rough language. O (R)

Species II (1998) Pedestrian but gory sci-fi sequel in which an astronaut (Justin Lazard) returns from Mars unaware he is carrying an alien creature in his body, which soon takes control, compulsively mating with women who die after bearing alien offspring, until the monster is tracked down by a team of alien-slayers (Michael Madsen and Marg Helgenberger). Directed by Peter Medak, the boring, unimaginative story is as senseless as its one-dimensional characters, though the bloody visuals of the monster skewering people with its tentacles are particularly noxious in the mating scenes. Graphic images combining sex and violence, some nudity, rough language, and profanity. O (R)

Spectre of Edgar Allan Poe, The (1974) Inept low-budget horror movie about E.A. Poe (Robert Walker, Jr.) who delivers his deranged true-love Lenore (Mary Grover) into the hands of the mad Dr. Grimaldi (Cesar Romero), whose asylum is an authentically creepy Southern mansion. Written and directed by Mohy Quandour, the silly script is treated so seriously that it becomes unintentionally quite funny. A-II (PG)

Speechless (1994) Frothy romantic comedy about two political speechwriters (Michael Keaton and Geena Davis) on opposing senatorial campaigns and their attempts to outsmart each other on the job while secretly romancing each other after hours. Directed by Ron Underwood, the sympathetic characters, snappy dialogue, and sprightly comic timing carry this strictly featherweight effort. Restrained bedroom scene and an instance of rough language. A-III (PG-13)

Speed (1994) Determined to save a busload of terrified passengers, a Los Angeles SWAT team cop (Keanu Reeves) leaps onboard a city bus that has been rigged by a psychotic explosives-expert (Dennis Hopper) to blow up if it goes less than 50 mph. Despite the ludicrous escapist plot that ultimately goes over the top in turns of impossible heroics, director Jan De Bont's nonstop action-movie concentrates more on the steel-willed cop's efforts to prevent mass murder than on the mayhem committed by the crazed maniac. Intermittent violence, intense explosions, and frequent rough language. A-III (R)

Speed 2: Cruise Control (1997) On a Caribbean cruise, an LA cop (Jason Patric) gets sidetracked from proposing to his girlfriend (Sandra Bullock) when a passenger (Willem Dafoe), who happens to be a psychotic computer-whiz, programs the ship to collide with an oil-tanker. Director Jan De Bont's hectic action sequel focuses on constant shipboard perils and giant special-effects, but fails to work up much empathy for its colorless characters. Intermittent violence and an implied affair. A-III (PG-13)

Speedway (1968) Routine Elvis Presley musical in which he plays a stockcar racer involved with leading lady Nancy Sinatra and the Internal Revenue Service. Director Norman Taurog keeps the action adventure moving at a pedestrian pace. A-II (G)

Spellbound (1945) Stylish psychological thriller about a psychiatrist (Ingrid Bergman) who falls for an amnesiac (Gregory Peck) accused of murder, but whom she's sure can be cleared once she's helped him recover his memory. Director Alfred Hitchcock uses some of Salvador Dali's surrealistic imagery to indicate Bergman's probes of Peck's subconscious, but the tightly wound plot takes much too long in its unraveling. A few chills and much unsettling tension. A-II (br)

Spencer's Mountain (1963) Thin family-saga from Earl Hamner, Jr.'s, novel about a salt-of-the-earth father (Henry Fonda) who works in the local quarry to provide for his large brood but has to sacrifice the house he's promised his wife (Maureen O'Hara) in order to send their eldest (James MacArthur) to college. Directed by Delmer Daves, the movie's chief asset is the rugged Wyoming locales, but the stereotyped family is as bogus as their script-full of problems. Some sexual situations and innuendo. A-III (br)

Spetters (1981) Dutch import about three young men with little else on their minds except motorcycle racing, sex, and idolizing race-champ Rutger Hauer. Directed by Paul Verhoeven, the movie reflects the confused values of a segment of contemporary youth but adds nothing of significance to the subject. Some graphic nudity and sexually explicit scenes. O (R)

Sphere (1998) Sci-fi thriller in which scientists (including Dustin Hoffman, Sharon Stone, and Samuel L. Jackson) grapple with what may be a malevolent, extraterrestrial life-force just outside the deep-sea station in which they are trapped. Directed by Barry Levinson, the intriguing start gives way to murky developments which undercut the suspense and lead the scientists to end their predicament in disappointing fashion. Some stylized violence and intermittent profanity. A-III (PG-13)

Sphinx, The (1981) Beautiful Egyptologist (Lesley-Anne Down) with pluck and luck, eludes hordes of Levantine villains and discovers a cache of ancient treasures stolen by grave-robbers. The thoroughly muddled thriller, based on a novel by Robin Cook and directed by Franklin J. Schaffner, is so badly done that it will have viewers giggling halfway through and hooting in derision by the end. Some unnecessary violence. A-III (PG)

Spice World (1998) In this feature-length music video, the Spice Girls (Emma Bunton, Geri Halliwell, Melanie Brown, Melanie Chisholm, and Victoria Adams) sing a few songs while being chased around London by the media and mobs of their fans. Director Bob Spiers tries to make the action seem lively and spontaneous, interjecting some flashbacks of the Girls's origins and a couple of surreal dreams, but the witless results are clumsily contrived and the self-promotion of the singing group is too obvious to hold interest for any but their fans. Sexual innuendo, a childbirth scene, and some rude remarks. A-III (PG)

Spices (1989) Indian production set in colonial times tells the story of a feisty married woman (Smita Patil) who refuses to submit to the sexual demands of a visiting tax-collector (Naseeruddin Shah) but is pressured by male and female villagers to do so lest the whole village be punished. Directed by Ketan Mehta, this small, technically flawed movie is notable not only for exploring the subservient role of Indian women during this period, but also the very essence of oppression, and the potential price of bucking the status quo. Some rough language, sexual innuendo, and comic-book violence. A-III (nr)

Spider, The (see: **Earth vs. the Spider**)

Spider Woman, The (1944) Intriguing entry in the updated detective series has Sherlock Holmes (Basil Rathbone) fake his own death, then join Dr. Watson (Nigel Bruce) in tracking down the mastermind (Gale Sondergard) behind an insurance scheme using a spider whose venom is so painful it drives its victims to suicide. Directed by Roy William Neill, the plot is a bit creaky, but Sondergard's zesty, resourceful criminal is the best villain of the series. A-I (br)

Spider's Stratagem, The (1973) Intriguing Italian mystery about a man (Giulio Brogi) returning to the town where 30 years earlier his father had been murdered by local Fascists and learns more than he wants to know about those responsible. Directed by Bernardo Bertolucci, the well-crafted movie is a satisfying mystery story, yet there is substance in its treatment of corruption in the Mussolini era. Mature theme. A-III (nr)

Spies Like Us (1985) Chevy Chase and Dan Aykroyd sink to the lowest common denominator in a vain attempt to get laughs in this mindless and meandering comedy about two incompetent federal agents who are chosen to be decoys in an international spy-ring. Much coarse language and sexual innuendo with brief nudity in a sexual context. O (PG)

Spike of Bensonhurst (1988) A young boxer (Sasha Mitchell) gets into trouble with low-level mob antics in the Italian neighborhood of Bensonhurst, Brooklyn. Director Paul Morrissey's attempt at broad satire fails on all counts save a comic turn by Ernest Borgnine as a mob boss. Ethnic stereotypes, profanity, irresponsible treatment of sex, pregnancy, and drug abuse. O (R)

Spikes Gang, The (1974) Formula Western about a bankrobber (Lee Marvin) who initiates a trio of wide-eyed youngsters (Gary Grimes, Ron Howard, and Charlie Martin Smith) into a life of crime and then betrays them. Directed by Richard Fleischer, the B-grade screenplay offers the usual violence and a distasteful scene involving religious articles. A-IV (PG)

Spinout (1966) Innocuous Elvis Presley vehicle directed by Norman Taurog in which the singer escapes the clutches of three women who want to marry him. Preteens may find it boring but not Presley fans. A-I (br)

Spiral Road, The (1962) Plodding saga from Jan de Hertog's novel of the 1930s Dutch East Indies colonial medical-service in which an ambitious novice doctor (Rock Hudson) treks through the bush with a famous leprosy specialist (Burl Ives), marries his

Dutch sweetheart (Gena Rowlands), and almost loses his sanity combating a jungle witch-doctor. Directed by Robert Mulligan, the story of how a doctor regains his faith in God and humanity gets lost in a banal script and lots of bad acting. Jungle menace, off-screen infidelity, and a drunken party. A-II (br)

Spiral Staircase, The (1946) Moody suspense thriller set in 1906 New England, as a serial killer stalks the mute servant (Dorothy McGuire) of a bedridden old lady (Ethel Barrymore) who shares an eerie country house with her son (Gordon Oliver), stepson (George Brent), a cook (Elsa Lanchester), and a caretaker (Rhys Williams). Directed by Robert Siodmak, the sinister proceedings take place during a long, stormy night, as fear gradually mounts into terror after the mad stalker finally emerges from the shadows. Stylized violence and frightening situations. A-II (br)

Spirit of St. Louis, The (1957) Meticulous but lengthy re-creation follows the thoughts and reflections of Charles Lindbergh (James Stewart) while making aviation history in 1927 as the pilot of the first nonstop flight from New York to Paris. Directed by Billy Wilder, Stewart manages to hold viewer interest on the solo flight across the Atlantic, partly because of the journey's dangers en route, but mostly because of the character's courage and determination in accomplishing this feat of early aviation. Some threatening situations. A-I (br)

Spirit of the Beehive, The (1976) Spanish movie set in 1940 deals with two children growing up in the aftermath of the Civil War. Directed by Victor Erice, it is one of those rare films that captures something of the secret world of childhood, with its strange notions and innocent rituals, yet also mirrors the adult world and its way of dealing with terrible realities. A-II (nr)

Spirits of the Dead (1969) Trilogy of short stories by Edgar Allen Poe as told by three European directors. Roger Vadim's medieval tale of a decadent heiress (Jane Fonda) who kills her cousin (Peter Fonda) is dull, but Louis Malle's story of a corrupt man (Alain Delon) pursued by his righteous double overdoses on nudity and sadistic violence. In a class by itself is Federico Fellini's **Toby Dammit**, about an alcoholic English actor (Terrence Stamp) who comes to Rome to star in a Western. It's a small gem, capturing the grotesquely surrealistic, grim, and ironic humor of Poe's "Never Bet the Devil Your Head." O (R)

Spiritualist, The (1948) Eerie mystery in which a phony psychic (Turhan Bey) convinces a rich widow (Lynn Bari) to commune with her late husband (Donald Curtis), but the scam takes a deadly twist threatening not only the psychic and the widow, but her worried fiancé (Richard Carlson) and younger sister (Cathy O'Donnell) as well. Directed by Bernard Vorhaus, the contrived plot works up some sinister situations and spooky effects which might frighten young children, but offer their elders a moderately diverting tale with a few chills along the way. A-I (br)

Spite Marriage (1929) Buster Keaton, the great stoic-master of silent comedy, plays an actor married out of spite by a jilted actress (Dorothy Sebastian) whose affection he finally wins after overcoming all manner of surrealistic complications. Directed by Edward Sedgwick, Keaton makes the best out of a heavy-handed plot, but his comic efforts seem forced and lack the easy air of spontaneity that marked his best work. A-I (br)

Spitfire (1934) Curious yet appealing backwoods melodrama about a free-spirited mountain lass (Katharine Hepburn) who's romanced by a married engineer (Robert Young) constructing a nearby dam, while his wiser colleague (Ralph Bellamy) respects her natural virtues and protects her when she is denounced as a witch by superstitious locals. Directed by John Cromwell, the rustic story of a simple woman and her faith in the healing powers of prayer is treated with sincerity, though some may find Hepburn's spunky yet fey performance a distraction. Romantic complications. A-II (br)

Spitfire (1942) British homage to R.J. Mitchell (Leslie Howard), the designer of the title WW II fighter plane which the RAF used to win the Battle of Britain in the air war against the German Luftwaffe. Also produced and directed by Howard, the biographical story is told by Mitchell's test pilot (David Niven) with a patriotic fervor that makes the idealized characters of less interest today than the historical period in which they served. Dated inspirational portrait and wartime violence. A-I (br)

Spitfire Grill, The (1996) Engrossing picture of a troubled young woman (Alison Elliott) coming to a small town in Maine for a fresh start in life which seems possible after she's befriended by a couple of local women (Ellen Burstyn and Marcia Gay Harden) but her growing sense of belonging ends in a tragedy which sobers the community and helps transform it. Written and directed by Lee David Zlotoff, the emotionally involving story is told with realism, the characters are warmly human, and, despite some melodramatic turns, the result is heartfelt drama with a genuinely uplifting conclusion. Some menace, a tragic death, and a reference to the sexual abuse of a minor resulting in murder. A-II (PG-13)

Splash (1984) Mediocre Disney romantic comedy about a mermaid (Daryl Hannah) who falls in love with a human (Tom Hanks). Directed by Ron Howard, the Disney production is modestly successful as escapist entertainment, with slapstick chase-scenes and klutzy over-acting. Brief nudity and sexual references. A-III (PG)

Split, The (1968) Inept crime movie directed by Gordon Fleming about a gang's robbery of a box-office during a big sporting-event. Gratuitous brutality and graphic sexual treatment. O (R)

Split Image (1982) Bright young man (Michael O'Keefe) falls in love with a young girl (Karen Allen) and is entrapped by a religious cult (headed by Peter Fonda), but his desperate parents hire a seedy deprogrammer (James Woods) to win him back. Director Ted Kotcheff's flashy, melodramatic, and highly superficial treatment of a serious social problem may serve some adolescents as a cautionary tale. Some rough language. A-II (R)

Split Second (1992) Violent thriller concerns the efforts of an obsessed cop (Rutger Hauer), his murdered partner's widow (Kim Cattrall), and his new partner (Neil Duncan) to kill an inhuman marauding beast that is clawing out the hearts of its victims. A formula macho-action film drenched in buckets of blood amounts to grisly garbage from director Tony Maylan. Excessive violence, brief nudity, many crass sexual references, and much rough language. O (R)

Splitface (see: 1945's **Dick Tracy**)

Spoilers, The (1942) Robust adventure directed by Ray Enright is set in Alaska, where partners (John Wayne and Harry Carey) try to save their gold mine from a slick schemer (Randolph Scott) and a crooked judge (Samuel S. Hinds), with a casino owner (Marlene Dietrich) and one of her dealers (Richard Barthlemess) eventually taking a hand. Stylized shootouts, barroom brawls, and romantic complications. A-II (br)

Spoilers, The (1955) Lackluster remake directed by Jesse Hibbs, with 1899 Alaska gold-mine owner Jeff Chandler fighting crafty claim-jumper Rory Calhoon, while getting help along the way from partner John McIntire and jealous saloon-owner Anne Baxter. Stylized violence, including an extended barroom brawl, and mild sexual innuendo. A-II (br)

Spook Busters (1946) Formula slapstick comedy with the Bowery Boys (Leo Gorcey, Huntz Hall, Bobby Jordan, etc.) working as insect exterminators in a magician's old mansion, where they get spooked by trick doors and secret passages until trapped in the cellar laboratory of a mad brain-surgeon (Douglass Dumbrille). Directed by William Beaudine, the silly proceedings offer some tame action-comedy. A-I (br)

Spook Who Sat by the Door, The (1973) Black exploitation movie about a token, black CIA agent (Lawrence Cook) who returns to his Chicago home, where he raises and trains a street army intended first to turn the ghetto into a riot zone, and then to take over the city, the state, the nation, the world! Directed by Ivan Dixon, it starts as wry comedy but turns vicious halfway through when it begins taking its message of violent revolution seriously. Dreary abundance of racial cliches and stereotypes. A-III (PG)

Spooks Run Wild (1941) Slapstick comedy with the East Side Kids (notably Leo Gorcey, Bobby Jordan, and Huntz Hall) in a summer camp for the underprivileged, from which they sneak off for town one night and chance upon a decrepit mansion occupied by a sinister magician (Bela Lugosi), whom they fear is the vampire killer stalking the area. Directed by Phil Rosen, the scary setting and menacing situations in the dark old house are played strictly for laughs, though the killer's capture has some harrowing moments. A-I (br)

Sporting Club, The (1971) Failed version of Thomas McGuane's novel about an exclusive club of Detroit's wealthiest citizens and their alienated offspring and servants who try to wreck it. Directed by Larry Peerce, the movie lacks the wit, imagination, and sensitivity needed to suggest, rather than simply depict, the terrible heritage of sex and violence it supposedly is condemning. O (R)

Spot (see: **Dogpound Shuffle**)

Spring Fever (1983) Undernourished story of a Florida tennis tournament for teenage girls stars Susan Anton and Jessica Walters as tennis mothers, with Carling Bassett as the daughter struggling to be a champ. Innocuous little movie directed by Joseph L. Scanlan, a love affair figures in the plot. A-III (PG)

Springfield Rifle (1952) Sluggish Civil War tale directed by Andre de Toth, with a Union officer (Gary Cooper) working undercover to expose a ring of traitors (led by Paul Kelly) supplying the Confederate Army with stolen Yankee horses. Murky plot with stylized violence. A-I (br)

Springtime in the Rockies (1942) Standard musical comedy directed by Irving Cummings has a Broadway singer (John Payne) pursue his once co-star and fiancé (Betty Grable) to a Canadian resort, where she is performing with a former partner (Cesar Romero). The romantic complications of the thin plot are outpaced by the droll antics of the supporting cast (Edward Everett Horton, Carmen Miranda, and Charlotte Greenwood). A-I (br)

Sprung (1997) Mindless low-budget sex comedy about an African-American couple (Tisha Campbell and Rusty Cundieff) who move in together, then break up because of nasty friends (Paula Jai Parker and Joe Torry), but ultimately get back together. Also directed by Cundieff, there is nothing original or amusing here, and, though there's occasional talk of love, the action is focused mostly on sex. Exploitative sex scenes, explicit sexual references, rough language, and profanity. O (R)

Spy Hard (1996) Flat comedy in which a bumbling Secret Service agent (Leslie Nielsen) teams with a younger, more agile agent (Nicollette Sheridan) to rescue hostages held by a power-mad general (Andy Griffith). Directed by Rick Friedberg, the flimsy plot strings together fitfully funny skits and sight gags spoofing mostly other action movies. Much cartoon-like violence, implied affairs, double entendres, and fleeting nudity. A-III (PG-13)

Spy in Your Eye (1966) Routine Italian spy caper directed by Vittorio Sala, whose chief gimmick is a mini-camera placed by enemy agents in the glass eye of an American colonel (Dana Andrews) by which they monitor what the Americans are up to. Mild violence and derring-do. A-II (br)

Spy Who Came in from the Cold, The (1966) Sobering screen version of the John Le Carre novel about a shabby British spy (Richard Burton) whose cynicism grows as his assignment in Berlin becomes a maze of betrayals and counter-betrayals. Director Martin Ritt's spy movie is not an escapist adventure, but one that demonstrates the loss of humanity on the part of those who treat people only as means of achieving their ends. A-III (br)

Spy Who Loved Me, The (1977) Roger Moore and Barbara Bach stars as James Bond and a beautiful Russian spy who find themselves united against the usual all-powerful villain bent upon a free enterprise conquest of the world and who employs a steel-toothed henchman named Jaws (Richard Kiel). Styled sex and violence. A-III (PG)

Spy with a Cold Nose, The (1967) Minor British spy spoof about the bumbling antics of some secret agents (Laurence Harvey and Lionel Jeffries). Directed by Daniel Petrie, the humor is mild and the plot slight. A-III (br)

Spy with My Face, The (1966) Formula spy caper out of "The Man from U.N.C.L.E." TV series sees its top agent, Napoleon Solo (Robert Vaughn), kidnapped and replaced by a perfect double in a plot to steal the plans for a new super-weapon. Directed by John Newland, the cliched plot is as tiresome as Solo's swaggering womanizing. Stylized violence and snickering sexual innuendo. A-III (br)

Spysmasher Returns (1942) Choppy feature edited from a serial based on the title comic-book character of an American (Kane Richmond) who returns from fighting Nazis in occupied France to take on a Nazi spy-ring in the States, getting help along the way from his identical twin brother. Directed by William Witney, Spysmasher's fantasy heroics are about as convincing as his caped uniform and aviator goggles. Stylized violence and hokey menace. A-I (br)

Square Dance (1987) Young girl with religious convictions (Winona Ryder) forsakes the custody of her cranky grandpa to live with her tragically flawed mother (Jane Alexander). She overcomes disillusionment with the adult world while expressing the inner strength and grace that propel her with loving enthusiasm toward womanhood. Sexual references and some rough dialogue do not dim the luster of director Dan Petrie's joyous affirmation of the beauty and wisdom of youthful innocence. A-II (PG-13)

Square Jungle, The (1955) Lumpy story of a 'Frisco grocery clerk (Tony Curtis) who decides to become a boxer, learns the ropes from a savvy trainer (Ernest Borgnine), and wins the middleweight title, then goes to pieces when he almost kills an opponent in the ring. Directed by Jerry Hopper, the story starts well, then becomes predictable as it builds to a sentimental ending, helped by Joe Louis, no less. Pugilistic violence and a drunken binge. A-II (br)

Squeeze (1997) Gritty tale of three ghetto youths (Tyrone Burton, Eddie Cutanda, and Phuong Duong) who court danger by stealing from a drug-dealer, then are torn between joining a rival drug gang or trying to go straight under the guidance of a caring youth worker. Writer-director Robert Patton-Spruill uses the sole perspective of the three teen dropouts to offer an overly sympathetic portrait of kids at risk in a violent but not particularly insightful story. Intermittent violence, crude sexual remarks, drug abuse, and continuous rough language. A-III (R)

Squeeze, The (1987) Struggling set-designer and compulsive gambler (Michael Keaton) teams up with a process server (Rae Dawn Chong) to confound and foil a scam defrauding the New York lottery with a magnetic box he finds and then loses to corporate thugs. Mild-mannered comedy directed by Roger Young has little else save Keaton's charm, which lessens the casual acceptance of his dangerously amoral behavior. Comic seduction scene and some violence are adult fare. A-III (PG-13)

Squeeze Play (1981) Rival community softball teams, with husbands on one side and wives on the other, battle for the playoffs. Amateurish movie directed by Samuel Weil, it contains graphic sex, nudity, and unrelieved profanity. O (R)

Squirm (1976) Low-budget horror movie directed by Jeff Lieberman about an invasion of killer worms that almost wipes out a small Southern town. Disgusting scenes of violence. O (R)

St. Benny the Dip (1951) Feeble fable in which a trio of grifters (Dick Haynes, Lionel Stander, and Roland Young) escape the police by posing as clergymen, then are transformed when they reopen a Skid Row mission. Director Edgar G. Ulmer muddles through a cliched inspirational plot whose humdrum proceedings waste a cast including Nina Foch as the romantic interest and Freddie Bartholomew as a hopelessly dim cleric. Criminal misdeeds and romantic situations. A-II (br)

St. Elmo's Fire (1985) Seven friends cope with the world after graduating from Georgetown University. Director Joel Schumacher's cast of characters consists almost entirely of shallow, boring, self-absorbed individuals, and their mostly favorable view of sexual promiscuity is in keeping with the amoral atmosphere that pervades the movie. O (R)

St. Ives (1976) Formula detective mystery directed by J. Lee Thompson with Charles Bronson as a retired journalist who becomes a go-between in a scheme to recover some stolen papers has too many gaping holes in the plot for even this kind of light entertainment. Some incidental sex and violence. A-III (PG)

St. Louis Blues (1958) Biography of composer W.C. Handy (1873-1958) revolves around the estrangement between the young Handy (Nat King Cole) and his minister father (Juano Hernandez) over the son's writing blues music rather than sacred music, though he finds encouragement from his aunt (Pearl Bailey), girlfriend (Ruby Dee), and a rising singer (Eartha Kitt). Director Allen Reisner plods through the melodramatic script with little attention to the period or its bigotry, though the music and its performers are what really matter here. Despite domestic tensions, the sympathetic portrayal of a black artist's struggle for recognition is worthwhile fare. A-I (br)

St. Louis Kid, The (1934) Breezy action melodrama features a truck driver (James Cagney) who has to clear himself of a murder charge during a dairy farmer's strike. Directed by Ray Enright, Cagney is in top form as the cocky, wisecracking charmer who wins the girl (Patricia Ellis), outwits the goons, and saves his fists by using his head to knock out opponents. Stylized violence. A-II (br)

St. Valentine's Day Massacre, The (1967) Bloody re-creation of one of the more lurid episodes in American gangland history, when Chicago's Al Capone (Jason Robards) wiped out some of his competitors. Directed by Roger Corman, the acting is overdone, but, then, so too is the violence. A-III (br)

Stage Door (1937) Seriocomic classic set in a Broadway boarding house for aspiring actresses (Ginger Rogers, Gail Patrick, Eve Arden, Lucille Ball, et al.) who keep up their spirits with zany hijinks while waiting for a successful part. Director Gregory La Cava smartly paces heartbreak with comedy, while skewering a predatory producer (Adolphe Menjou) along the way, yet ends paying tribute to the theatrical art as a stage novice (Katharine Hepburn) becomes a star in a performance inspired by a dead actress (Andrea Leeds). Romantic situations and off-screen suicide. A-II (br)

Stage Door Canteen (1943) Patriotic WW II souvenir with a multitude of show-business personalities serving meals and entertaining troops on leave in New York City. Directed by Frank Borzage, a lame romance between a soldier and a canteen hostess keeps getting in the way of the bands, singers, walk-ons, and star-turns, notably by Edgar Bergen, Ray Bolger, and Gypsy Rose Lee in a mock striptease. Some sexual situations and innuendo. A-III (br)

Stage Fright (1950) Stodgy thriller in which a London drama student (Jane Wyman) helps a friend (Richard Todd) accused of murder escape the police, then tries to trap the music star (Marlene Dietrich) he says did it but, instead, falls for the confused detective (Michael Wilding) working on the case. Directed by Alfred Hitchcock, the muddled plot works up little tension and less romance, though some whimsical characters (Alastair Sim, Sibyl Thorndike, and Kay Walsh) and Dietrich's grandstanding provide a bit of fun along the way. More menace than violence and some sexual innuendo. A-II (br)

Stage to Thunder Rock (1964) Contrived Western directed by William F. Claxton interweaves the story of a struggling pioneer family (Lon Chaney, Jr., Anne Seymour, and Marilyn Maxwell) with that of a veteran sheriff (Barry Sullivan) forced to arrest the outlaw son of the man who raised him (Keenan Wynn). Stylized violence and muted references to prostitution. A-II (br)

Stagecoach (1939) In this Western classic, a cowboy (John Wayne) wanted by the law on trumped-up charges joins an odd assortment of passengers (Claire Trevor, Thomas Mitchell, Donald Meek, John Carradine, and others) on the stage to Lordsburg in the midst of an Apache uprising. Directed by John Ford, the characters are a microcosm of frontier types, each of whom has a different reason for the journey, whose dangers are played out against the majestic vistas of Monument Valley, with a brilliantly staged Indian attack and a final showdown on the streets of Lordsburg bringing the story to a rousing finish. Stylized violence. A-II (br)

Stagecoach (1966) Poor remake of the Western classic about an oddly assorted group (Alex Cord, Bing Crosby, Van Heflin, Slim Pickens) crowded in a stagecoach under Indian attack. Directed by Gordon Douglas, there are some good action-scenes to enliven the ride, but the characterizations are embarrassingly bad. A-II (br)

Stagecoach to Fury (1956) Routine Western directed by William Claxton in which Mexican bandits hold a stagecoach guard (Forrest Tucker) and some passengers (notably Mari Blanchard and Wallace Ford) hostage while waiting to rob a incoming gold shipment, with unsurprising results. Stylized violence and sexual innuendo. A-II (br)

Staircase (1969) The terrible loneliness of two homosexuals (Richard Burton and Rex Harrison) is the subject of Charles Dyer's adaptation of his own play, told basically in a series of bickering arguments about their fears, vanity, and lack of future. Directed by Stanley Donen, the earnest examination of each man's desperate dependence upon the other fails as entertainment and falls short as a truly insightful human document, partly because two expert actors are more intent on portraying homosexuals than creating two believable human beings. A-IV (R)

Stakeout (1987) Voyeurism turns into romance when a cop on surveillance (Richard Dreyfuss) falls for the target of his perusal, a escaped con's girl (Madeline Stowe). Director John Badham offers little mystery and in-depth characterization in this mundane depiction of a simple love affair. Some violence, a sex scene, and brief nudity. A-III (R)

Stalag 17 (1953) Seriocomic WW II tale of a German POW camp holding some 600 captured US airmen, among whom is a cynical opportunist (William Holden), whose profitable bartering with the guards causes his comrades to suspect that he's the informer who's been betraying their escape plans to the Nazi commandant (Otto Preminger). Director Billy Wilder turns the bleak prisoner-of-war situation into a zesty black comedy, mixing slapstick hijinks with tense drama as the prisoners puzzle over the mysterious identity of the informer in their midst. Stylized violence and some sexual innuendo. A-II (br)

Stalingrad (1995) The crushing Soviet defeat of Hitler's overextended Wehrmacht is depicted through the horrific experiences of a seasoned infantry platoon under a green lieutenant (Thomas Kretschmann) on the outskirts of Stalingrad from September 1942 until the exhausted survivors surrender in January

1943. Directed by Joseph Vilsmaier, the German production vividly re-creates the terrible carnage of war as seen by frontline troops but, despite its epic scale, rarely rises above other similar portrayals of war's inhumanity. Subtitles. Gory battlefield violence, the execution of civilians, and an implied rape. A-III (nr)

Stalking Moon, The (1968) Above-average Western in which an Apache (Nathaniel Narcisco), feared for his cruelty, follows the trail of those who have taken his young son and leaves his own path of dead settlers, while a former Army scout (Gregory Peck), who has the boy, waits on his ranch for the inevitable arrival of his menacing pursuer. Directed by Richard Mulligan, the Western has some physical violence, but its cat-and-mouse story is plotted almost totally for its suspense potential, which it achieves with some intelligence. A-I (G)

Stampede (1949) Old-fashioned Western directed by Lesley Selander pits homesteaders (notably Gale Storm) against a big rancher (Rod Cameron), as the local sheriff (Johnny Mack Brown) tries to keep a crooked land-agent from breaking the peace. Stylized violence. A-I (br)

Stand and Deliver (1988) Quietly affecting movie about an extraordinary real-life math teacher (Edward James Olmos) in an East Los Angeles high school who transforms a rowdy class of Hispanics into calculus whiz-kids. When test administrators question his students' high grades, the teacher fights back with charges of discrimination. Inspiring story, fine acting by the leads, and deft direction by Ramon Menendez. Some profanity in a realistic context. A-II (PG)

Stand at Apache River, The (1953) Sluggish Western directed by Lee Sholem pits a sheriff (Stephen McNally), his wounded prisoner (Russell Johnson), an Army colonel (Hugh Marlowe), a bride-to-be (Julie Adams), and several other frontier-types against a hostile Apache band (led by Edgar Barrier). Frontier violence and muddled justice issues. A-I (br)

Stand By Me (1986) The power of this drama lies in the simple, profound truths four boys learn about themselves while on a journey through the backwoods of their rural hometown in the late 1950s. Director Rob Reiner's preteen coming-of-age picture carefully avoids excess while focusing upon simple tests of patience, courage, caring, and the joys of male camaraderie. Some harsh language, uncharacteristic of the times, and brief violence, but it is an experience some parents might wish to share with their youngsters. A-III (R)

Stand-In (1937) Dated comedy in which a Wall Street banker (Leslie Howard) tries to save a movie studio from bankruptcy with the help of a cheerful stand-in (Joan Blondell) and a veteran director (Humphrey Bogart). Director Tay Garnett's playful spoof of the Hollywood studio system still has amusing moments, but what remains impressive is Howard's deliciously wry performance as the staid financier who learns that people are more important than making money. Little to interest youngsters, but fun for veteran movie-goers. A-I (br)

Stand Up and Be Counted (1972) Journalist Jacqueline Bisset is assigned to cover the Women's Liberation Movement in her home town and finds plenty of fodder within her own family. Idiotic comedy directed by Jackie Cooper not only belittles women in its contrived episodes involving shrill maidens and audacious matrons, but also insults the viewer's intelligence by its parade of unsavory situations and its very explicit sexual banter. O (PG)

Stand Up and Cheer (1934) Musical comedy about the Depression blues starts with the president adding a Secretary of Amusement (Warner Baxter) to his Cabinet in order to regenerate the nation's morale. Directed by Hamilton MacFadden, the curious concept sputters along on the enthusiastic energy of various vaudeville acts, but the showstopper is little Shirley Temple's big finale with James Dunn in the production number, "Baby, Take a Bow." Dated fun, but Stepin Fetchit's comic turn as a servile black is a period-movie convention embarrassing today. A-I (PG)

Stanley (1972) The title critter is a very agile rattlesnake used by a very disturbed Seminole Indian (Chris Robinson) to dispose of a lot of people who annoy him. Produced and directed by William Grefe, the script tosses serpents and victims together guilelessly to evoke clumsy guffaws more than sincere shudders. Some sexual insinuations and vulgar language. A-III (PG)

Stanley & Iris (1990) When an illiterate factory-worker (Robert De Niro) asks a friendly co-worker (Jane Fonda) to teach him to read, they fall in love, find fulfillment, and go on presumably to live happily ever after. Despite credible performances rooted in a working-class environment, director Martin Ritt's socially conscious melodrama goes about achieving its intention to be uplifting in too obvious fashion to be satisfying. Brief but meaningful treatment of a teen pregnancy and a few instances of profanity. A-II (PG-13)

Stanley and Livingstone (1939) Fine dramatization of the 1871-72 trek into British East Africa made by New York reporter Henry M. Stanley (Spencer Tracy) to find missing missionary-explorer Livingstone (Cedric Hardwicke), then faces disbelief upon his return. Directed by Henry King, there's plenty of action from the opening in 1870 Wyoming, through the African safari sequences, to the London meeting of the Royal Geographic Society, but the drama centers in first-rate performances of the title characters. Stylized violence, including scenes depicting the injustice of the slave trade. A-I (br)

Star, The (1952) After three years without a job, a former movie-star (Bette Davis) gets a chance at a supporting role, but her ego gets in the way. Directed by Stuart Heisler, Davis runs the gamut of emotions, lacerating her agent (Warner Anderson), charming a veteran producer (Minor Watson), smothering her child (Natalie Wood), and scorning the man (Sterling Hayden) who loves her, but the melodramatic results are hardly worth the effort. Romantic complications, sexual innuendo, and delusional behavior. A-III (br)

Star! (1968) Lovely, lively musical based on the life of British stage star Gertrude Lawrence, who is portrayed as a very nice, very talented, very ambitious, and very tough lady. Making the role her own is Julie Andrews, whose bright characterization and fine singing are front and center in director Robert Wise's polished re-creation of British life from WW I through WW II, giving the proceedings a historical perspective both interesting and illuminating. Romantic complications. A-II (G)

Star Chamber, The (1983) When a judge (Michael Douglas), disillusioned by the legal technicalities that force him to free defendants he considers guilty, joins a secret group who execute those who have escaped the penalty of the law, he finally comes to realize they are no better than criminals. Director Peter Hyams's plodding, contrived, and muddled story at least raises some questions about crime, law, and vigilante justice. Some brutal violence and much profanity. A-III (R)

Star Dust (1940) Pleasantly amusing Hollywood fluff involving a movie talent-scout (Robert Young) who signs up two young hopefuls (Linda Darnell and John Payne), then has to trick the studio into giving them contracts. Directed by Walter Lang, the title aptly describes this movie-fan fantasy, but the story's seriocomic treatment has enough heart to sustain interest in the outcome. A-I (br)

Star 80 (1983) Fact-based story of Dorothy Stratten, Playboy playmate and budding movie star (Mariel Hemingway), who was murdered by her husband (Eric Roberts). Though director Bob Fosse is rather superficial in the characterizations and lets the playboy philosophy get off much too easily, the movie is grimly moral in its implications about the consequences of promiscuity. The nature of its theme and frequent nudity, though never in a genuinely erotic context, make it very mature fare. A-IV (R)

Star in the Dust (1956) Muddled Western directed by Charles Haas in which a sheriff (John Agar) prepares to hang a hired gunman (Richard Boone), though he has to fight off the cattlemen (led by Leif Erickson) who paid him, as well as a lynching party of farmers whose sons he killed. Stylized violence and sexual innuendo. A-II (br)

Star Is Born, A (1976) Third version of the durable classic about the incompatibility between career and marriage proves little more than a starring vehicle for Barbra Streisand as a rock music superstar going to the top of the charts as the career of her husband (Kris Kristofferson) is sinking into oblivion. Director Frank Pierson develops little depth to their relationship, and the romantic interludes are silly (though they do provide some relief from the din of the Muzak rock score). Coarse language and vulgar characters. A-III (R)

Star Kid (1998) Thin adventure fantasy in which a 12-year-old boy (Joseph Mazzello) climbs inside the shell of an alien android and uses its superhuman strength to take revenge on a school bully, then is confronted by a ferocious spider-like invader from outer space. Written and directed by Manny Coto, the movie's premise of controlling a powerful robot may appeal to young boys, though most others will find the formula plot as tiresome as the derivative special effects. Fantasy violence, menacing situations, bathroom humor, and few coarse words. A-II (PG)

Star Maker, The (1996) Promising fame and fortune, a phony talent-scout (Sergio Castellitto) cons naive Sicilians in 1953 to pay him for bogus screentests, but his past catches up with him just as he begins to fall in love with a vulnerable, star-struck teenager (Tiziana Lodato). Despite the movie's contrived sense of whimsy, director Giuseppe Tornatore spins a dark story of a cad whose belated conversion to unselfish love may or may not strike a redemptive note with viewers. Subtitles. A few fairly explicit sexual encounters, brief full female nudity, and occasional rough language. A-IV (R)

Star of Midnight (1935) Convoluted murder mystery in which a debonair lawyer (William Powell) on the trail of a missing woman finds a corpse instead, then discovers the killer while trying to dodge an insistent girlfriend (Ginger Rogers). Directed by Stephen Roberts, the dim plot has less interest than the colorful characters and their flow of wisecracks. Stylized violence and romantic complications. A-II (br)

Star Spangled Girl (1971) Mediocre adaptation of Neil Simon's Broadway comedy about the ideological clash between a little gal from Way Down South (Sandy Duncan) and a pair of radical Los Angeles underground newspapermen (Todd Susman and Tony Roberts). Directed by Jerry Paris, the only bright thing about the so-so comic romance is Duncan's cute performance. A-II (G)

Star Spangled Rhythm (1942) Chaotic WW II frolic revolves around a sailor (Eddie Bracken) bringing his buddies to a Hollywood studio, which his father (Victor Moore) pretends to run with the help of a telephone operator (Betty Hutton) sweet on his son. Filmed on the Paramount lot by director George Marshall, the picture ends with Bing Crosby, Bob Hope, Dorothy Lamour, Veronica Lake, Alan Ladd, and many of the studio's other players putting on a show for the fleet. Dated wartime entertainment laden with double entendres. A-III (br)

Star Trek: The Motion Picture (1980) The familiar faces of TV's Starship Enterprise crew are back with William Shatner, now an admiral, and Leonard Nimoy as Spock, to do battle with an ominous alien adversary. Directed by Robert Wise, the heart of the movie is its spectacular special effects with the characters in a supporting role. Trekkies, nevertheless, will find it nostalgic entertainment, but youngsters may find it a long sit. A-I (G)

Star Trek II: The Wrath of Khan (1982) Capt. Kirk (William Shatner), promoted to a desk job, makes it back to the helm of the Enterprise in time to confront a flamboyant villain (Ricardo Montalban). Director Nicholas Meyer's sequel attempts to be droll and lively but is only slightly more entertaining than its dull and ponderous predecessor. Torture sequence involving the insertion of parasites into the ears of victims is rather strong, but the action is otherwise innocuous. A-II (PG)

Star Trek III: The Search for Spock (1984) Considerably better than its two predecessors, the sequel involves the efforts of Admiral James Kirk (William Shatner) and his crew to return to the planet Genesis, resting place of Capt. Spock (Leonard Nimoy), who gave his life to save the Enterprise in the last outing, on the chance that he might somehow be restored to life. Some heavy-breathing Klingon pirates (led by Christopher Lloyd) try to prevent this, but all obstacles are surmounted for the grand climax on Vulcan (presided over by Judith Anderson). Harve Bennett's intelligent script and Nimoy's capable direction prove that it is possible to be both entertaining and civilized. A-II (PG)

Star Trek IV: The Voyage Home (1986) Admiral Kirk (William Shatner) and the Enterprise crew travel back to 1986 San Francisco to retrieve two humpbacked whales that may be the key to saving Earth from alien destruction. Director Leonard Nimoy makes an entertaining mix out of sci-fi fantasy, ecological advocacy, and satiric jabs at contemporary pop culture. Documentary footage of whales being slaughtered and a few coarse words bring home some of the realities of environmental waste. A-II (PG)

Star Trek V: The Final Frontier (1989) Messianic Vulcan (Laurence Luckinbill) hog-ties the Enterprise's crew and other interplanetary hams, setting a course through the Great Barrier for a meeting with God. Directed by William Shatner, the narrative is suspenseless and overwrought with senseless Klingon attacks. Best scenes feature comedic banter between crew members. Minimal rough language, silly comic-book violence. A-II (PG)

Star Trek VI: The Undiscovered Country (1991) A peace conference between the Federation and the treacherous Klingons is threatened when Captain Kirk and Dr. McCoy (William Shatner and DeForest Kelley) are framed for the assassination of the Klingon negotiator (David Warner), leaving Spock (Leonard Nimoy) to ferret out the traitor in their midst. Superior production values and a peppy pace make director Nicholas Meyer's sci-fi adventure genial entertainment in spite of its aging characters and familiar situations. Some laser shootouts and explosions. A-II (PG)

Star Trek: First Contact (1996) Headed by its bold captain (Patrick Stewart), the 24th-century Starship Enterprise battles an onboard invasion by killer aliens while racing back to the year 2063, where a crisis on planet Earth could terminate humankind. Director Jonathan Frakes weaves together two separate stories for a sci-fi tale of old-fashioned adventure jazzed up with futuristic visuals. Some stylized violence and fleeting sexual innuendo. A-II (PG-13)

Star Trek Generations (1994) Sequel joins Starship Enterprise captains from different centuries (William Shatner and Patrick Stewart) in trying to stop a villainous alien (Malcolm McDowell) whose tampering with an energy field would result in millions of deaths. Director David Carson's ambitious sci-fi saga is heavy on the kind of action, plotting, special effects, and technobabble that "Trekkies" relish, but other moviegoers may find less than stellar entertainment. Stylized space battles, some fistfights, and a crude expression. A-II (PG)

Star Trek: Insurrection (1998) Lively addition to the series, in which Captain Picard (Patrick Stewart) and the Enterprise crew defy their superiors in order to save an endangered race on a distant planet whose atmosphere provides eternal youth to its inhabitants. Director Jonathan Frakes maintains a brisk pace, alternating sci-fi action with humor and romantic subplots for a modestly entertaining tale of courage tested and true. Intermittent fantasy violence, romantic complications, and a few coarse words. A-II (PG)

Star Wars (1977) Set in a galaxy other than our own, a desperate struggle takes place between evil usurpers of empire and a dedicated band of rebels (Carrie Fisher, Mark Hamill, Harrison Ford, and Alec Guinness). Written and directed by George Lucas, the outcome never is in doubt, because the movie's conventions are as old-fashioned as its story of good triumphing over evil. The special effects are stunning, the characters imaginative, and the narrative intriguing. Much stylized violence. A-II (PG)

Star Wars: Episode I The Phantom Menace (1999) Prequel to the **Star Wars** trilogy, in which two Jedi knights (Liam Neeson and Ewan McGregor) out to save the planet Naboo from Federation invaders enlist the help of a young boy (Jake Lloyd) who will eventually become the evil Darth Vader. By emphasizing fantastical creatures and myriad special effects, writer-director George Lucas loses the movie's human dimension, achieving only visual spectacle. Sci-fi sword-fights and battle sequences. A-II (PG)

Stars and Bars (1988) Dismal comic misfire tracking the misfortunes of an Englishman (Daniel Day-Lewis) in Georgia trying to make a deal with the loony owner (Harry Dean-Stanton) of a lost Renoir painting. Directed by Pat O'Connor, the senseless proceedings are wildly unamusing, and the star's antics in the buff are simply an embarrassment. Slapstick violence, crude sexual situations, extended nudity, and occasional rough language. O (R)

Stars and Stripes Forever (1952) Episodic story of John Philip Sousa (Clifton Webb) from his years conducting the US Marine Corps band to his success as a music composer whose rousing marches make the Sousa Band an international favorite. Directed by Henry Koster, the late 19th-century era is as interesting as the characters, with Webb's stiff yet likeable performance ably abetted by Ruth Hussey as his bemused wife, but it's Sousa's irresistibly upbeat music which paces the action and makes the result grandly entertaining. A-I (br)

Starchaser (1985) Young Orin uses a magic sword to free his people from enslavement by a wicked despot. This animated 3-D movie is passable entertainment for juveniles except for an abundance of cartoon violence. A-II (PG)

Stardust (1975) Sequel to **That'll Be the Day**, a British movie about a would-be rock star (David Essex), has him forming a Beatles-like group and becoming as superstar. Directed by Michael Apted, the result has a slickness and pace that are engaging, though it is a bit heavy in showing the corrupt consequences brought about by sudden fame and fortune. A-III (R)

Stardust Memories (1980) Dry autobiographical parody from director Woody Allen focuses upon a writer-director (Allen) suffering from middle-class, middle-aged neuroses that come with success. The true confession-style work is only fitfully funny, and its serious flights of fantasy stop far short of anything with depth. Satirical treatment of promiscuous relationships and frequent profanity. A-III (PG)

Stargate (1994) Woodenly acted sci-fi tale in which an Egyptologist (James Spader) accompanies a military reconnaissance team (led by Kurt Russell) to another planet, where they discover an enslaved civilization whose evil ruler (Jaye Davidson) is prepared to destroy the visitors and explode their mother planet. Director Roland Emmerich relies on lavish production design and exceptional special effects to maintain interest in a derivative story that depends on tired movie cliches to advance its jumbled narrative. Some physical brutality, stylized shootouts, fleeting sexual innuendo, and an instance of profanity. A-III (PG-13)

Starman (1984) Alien from another planet (Jeff Bridges) takes on the human form of the much-mourned husband of a young widow (Karen Allen). Director John Carpenter does fairly well in creating the mood of a sci-fi fantasy, though he resorts to such scenes as the ever-popular car chase for excitement. Some violence and a restrained bedroom scene. A-II (PG)

Stars Fell on Henrietta, The (1995) After persuading an impoverished 1935 farm family (headed by Aidan Quinn and Frances Farmer) that oil lies beneath their shriveled crops in the Texas dust-bowl, a failed wildcatter (Robert Duvall) robs a wealthy oilman (Brian Dennehy) to take a chance on striking a gusher before the bank repossesses the farm. Director James Keach's atmospheric character study holds modest charms as Depression-era adversity tests the humanity of the story's hardscrabble characters. Ambiguous treatment of theft and brief violence. A-III (PG)

Starship Invasions (1978) Inept, ludicrous, boring Canadian movie directed by Ed Hunt about good and bad flying saucers locked in a battle upon which the fate of Earth depends. Violence and tasteless depiction of experiments on human beings. A-III (PG)

Starship Troopers (1997) Mindless sci-fi fantasy about teenage recruits (notably Casper Van Dien and Denise Richards) fighting to save Earth and their militaristic society from an invasion of giant bugs. Directed by Paul Verhoevan, the sophomoric story of teen romance and military bloodlust is a tiresome special-effects bore. Excessive violence, a sexual encounter, nudity, coarse language, and a sexual expletive. O (R)

Starstruck (1983) Australian musical comedy about the staging of a New Year's Eve show by a young woman (Jo Kennedy) and her cousin (Ross O'Donovan) to raise money to save the family's pub. Directed by Gillian Armstrong, it is good light entertainment, but, unfortunately, because of its benign view of casual sex and brief nudity, it cannot be recommended for youngsters. A-III (PG)

Start the Revolution Without Me (1970) Fumbled period comedy about two sets of twins (Gene Wilder and Donald Sutherland), one pair aristocratic and the other of peasant stock, who get switched at birth and, years later, get mixed up again during the French Revolution, when those raised as noble twins become confused with the cowardly peasant twins, who are unwilling members of the revolting mob led by Jack McGowran. Though the situation is promising, Bud Yorkin's direction is remarkably dull, with heavy slapstick routines, inane dialogue, and poorly staged attempt at spoofing the old swashbuckler movies. A-III (PG)

Starting Over (1979) Divorced man (Burt Reynolds) finds himself drawn to a nice, sensible, but rightly wary schoolteacher (Jill Clayburgh). The problem is that he is still strongly attached to his former wife (Candice Bergen), who now shows up wanting to give it another try. Directed by Alan J. Pakula, the movie is often very funny, largely due to Reynolds's engaging performance, but it grows repetitive, and its humor doesn't blend easily with its more serious concerns. Occasional foul language and some sexual references. A-III (R)

State Fair (1945) Agreeable musical about a farm family's visit to the Iowa State Fair, where dad Charles Winninger expects his entry to win the hog competition, mom Fay Bainter hopes her fortified mincemeat will get a blue ribbon, son Dick Haymes falls for married singer Vivian Blaine, and daughter Jeanne Crain finds romance with newspaper reporter Dana Andrews. Directed by Walter Lang, the fairground proceedings are good-natured, the cast has considerable charm, and the songs by Rodgers and Hammerstein add some zest to the fun and poignancy to the romance. A-I (br)

State Fair (1962) Flat version of the Rodgers and Hammerstein musical about a Texas family's annual fair visit, where dad (Tom Ewell) enters his prize hog, mom (Alice Faye) competes with her brandied mincemeat, son (Pat Boone) vies for a showgirl (Ann-Margaret), and daughter (Pamela Tiffin) interests a flip TV-reporter (Bobby Darin). Directed by Jose Ferrer, the folksy sentiment is largely cornpone, the romance is artificial, and even the songs seem out of place. Youthful romantic complications. A-II (br)

State of Grace (1990) An undercover cop (Sean Penn) is torn between betrayal and duty when assigned to infiltrate a murderous gang headed by two brothers with whom he had grown up and whose sister (Robin Wright) now falls in love with him. Director Phil Joanou focuses on brutality and casual slaughter without regard for plot or characterization in a synthetic, unconvincing crime melodrama. Excessive violence and rough language, positive treatment of macho, anti-feminist attitudes, and brief nudity. O (R)

State of Siege (1973) Fact-based political drama about an American official (Yves Montand) who in 1970 was kidnapped, accused of being a police specialist in torture, and murdered by Uruguayan terrorists. Directed by Costa-Gavras, the movie accepts revolutionary change as necessary but demonstrates the futility of political terrorism, both by those who have power and those who want it. Excessively graphic scene of torture. A-IV (nr)

State of the Union (1948) Campaigning for the Republican presidential nomination, a self-made millionaire (Spencer Tracy) fights for his political principles with his estranged wife (Katherine Hepburn), his campaign advisor (Van Johnson,) and his chief backer (Angela Landsbury). Directed by Frank Capra, the political and domestic battlefields are rendered with wit, intelligence, and plenty of good humor. A-II (br)

State Penitentiary (1950) Director Lew Landers's low-budget quickie features Warner Baxter as a wronged convict who escapes from prison to prove his innocence. Stylized violence and a muddled plot about justice. A-II (br)

Station, The (1992) Sluggish Italian drama about a night in a lonely train station, where the timid stationmaster (Sergio Rubini) is called on to protect a beautiful young woman (Margherita Buy) from the increasingly violent attempts of her furious fiancé (Ennio Fantastichini) to drag her home. Also directed by Rubini, the narrative alternates long static stretches with sudden horror while gradually revealing the engaged couple's essentially gentle natures. Subtitles. Intermittent violence and some rough language. A-III (nr)

Station West (1948) Offbeat Western tale in which an undercover military agent (Dick Powell), on the trail of a gold-robber who murdered two soldiers, nails the culprit by getting a job with a shady outfit run by a woman (Jane Greer). Directed by Sidney Lanfield, the killer's identity isn't too difficult to figure out, but the situation and tough-guy dialogue hold interest along the way. Stylized violence. A-I (br)

Statue, The (1971) Drearily unfunny one-line joke about the relative size of male organs, belonging in this case to a Nobel Prize-winner (David Niven) and the man who modeled for the lower portion of a large nude statue of the prize-winner. British production directed by Rod Amateau is an exercise in high-density witlessness. O (R)

Stavisky (1975) French production set in the Depression of the 1930s presents an emotionally engaging character study of the era's best-known swindler, Serge Alexandre Stavisky (Jean-Paul Belmondo), whose destruction mirrors the collapse of capitalism and the rise of Fascism. Directed by Alain Resnais, the powerful visuals and flawless narrative flow make it rewarding viewing, whatever the value of its historical insights about a past world. Mature themes. A-III (PG)

Stay As You Are (1980) A married man in his 50s (Marcello Mastroianni) falls in love with a teenage girl (Natassia Kinski), who he discovers may be his own daughter. Directed by Alberto Lattuada, the story goes nowhere and evaporates into a series of arty sequences that seem to come from a fashion magazine. Exploitation of the incest theme and extravagant nudity. O (nr)

Stay Away, Joe (1968) Poor Elvis Presley vehicle in which he plays a contemporary Indian who rides a lot of bucking broncos, chases a lot of pretty girls, and sings a lot of songs. He also gets in a number of fights trying to get a good deal from the government for his southwestern Indian tribe. Directed by Peter Tewksbury, besides the miscasting of Burgess Meredith, Joan Blondell, and Katy Jurado, the Indian stereotypes are ludicrous. A-III (PG)

Stay Hungry (1976) Muddled story in which Jeff Bridges plays a youth hired by some crooks to dicker the owners of a Southern health spa out of their property but instead befriends its muscleman (Arnold Schwarzenegger) and his ex-girl friend (Sally Field). Directed by Bob Rafelson, the murky plot resorts to an unhealthy mix of sex and violence. O (R)

Stay Tuned (1992) Silly satire about a Seattle couple (John Ritter and Pam Dawber) who must survive 24 hours in the netherworld, where the devil (Jeffrey Jones) projects them into the deadly programs offered on "Hellvision." Peter Hyams's anything-goes direction ends up going haywire, as the visual gags flag and the nonsensical plot lurches out of control. Some mindless comic violence and occasional nasty menace. A-III (PG)

Staying Alive (1983) The disco king of **Saturday Night Fever** (John Travolta) goes from chorus boy to star with the help of the two women in his life (Cynthia Rhodes and Finola Hughes). Director Sylvester Stallone's sequel is a loud, vulgar bit of mediocre entertainment, not at all moving and with no semblance of the bothersome demands of reality. Benign attitude toward casual sex. A-III (PG)

Staying Together (1989) Three young men (Tim Quill, Dermot Mulroney, and Sean Astin) must decide their future when their father suddenly closes the family restaurant and retires. Directed by Lee

Grant, the badly scripted family saga focuses on the brothers' senseless sexual conquests rather than the implications of the family crisis. Several sexually suggestive encounters including nudity and some profanity. O (R)

Steagle, The (1971) Uneven comic fantasy set during the 1962 Cuban missile crisis, when a professor (Richard Benjamin) throws caution to the winds by flying off to Chicago for a tryst with his former girlfriend's daughter, on to a Las Vegas romp with a couple of frisky stewardesses and a minister, and then to Hollywood for a climactic movie shootout. Written and directed by Paul Sylbert, the movie lacks consistency in its attempts at comedy and satire, too often settling for much that is crudely vulgar and sexually exploitative. Some religious implications that are tasteless if not offensive. O (R)

Steal Big, Steal Little (1995) Comic misfire about identical twin-brothers (both played by Andy Garcia) pitted against each other when their adoptive mother leaves a vast Santa Barbara, Calif., estate to one son, prompting the other to desperate measures to wrest it from him. Director Andrew Davis relies on contrived whimsy and weak romantic complications in an overlong story that eventually affirms family loyalty and marital fidelity. Minor violence, references to adultery, and a few profanities. A-III (PG-13)

Stealing Beauty (1996) Staying in a Tuscan villa with the friends of her late mother, a 19-year-old American (Liv Tyler) becomes the subject of intense interest when it becomes common knowledge she is quietly seeking a partner with whom to lose her virginity. Director Bernardo Bertolucci lavishes endless attention upon the physical beauty of the teenager and the lush landscape in a frivolous but essentially empty coming-of-age movie. Several sexual encounters, some full nudity, casual drug use, and intermittent profanity and rough language. A-IV (R)

Stealing Home (1988) Flashbacks detail the lifelong infatuation of a washed-up baseball player (Mark Harmon) with an older family friend (Jodie Foster) whose suicide brings him home to bury her ashes and ultimately put the pieces of his life back together. Writer-directors Steve Kampmann and Will Aldis fail to develop the girl's character beyond that of an unattainable fantasy-figure in a soapy melodrama. Brief nudity and several scenes of sexual promiscuity, one including a minor and an adult. A-III (PG-13)

Steel (1997) The comic-book exploits of an ex-Army officer (basketball star Shaquille O'Neal) who clads himself in an armored suit to battle criminals using powerful electronic weapons. Directed by Kenneth Johnson, the superhero proceedings are as ridiculously overdone as the destructive violence, though the action is paced with some good-natured humor. Much fantasy violence and coarse language. A-III (PG-13)

Steel Helmet, The (1951) Hard-bitten Korean War tale in which a veteran sergeant (Gene Evans) helps a green lieutenant (Steve Brodie) set up an observation post in a Buddhist temple, then leads its defense when the enemy attacks in force. Writer-director Samuel Fuller hinges the formula military proceedings on the tough-minded noncom who proves no less vulnerable to the emotional stress of battle than the others. Wartime violence, including the shooting of a captured soldier. A-II (br)

Steel Lady, The (1953) Stranded while looking for oil in the Sahara Desert, four adventurers (Rod Cameron, John Dehner, Tab Hunter, and Anthony Caruso) come upon an abandoned German tank with a fortune in jewels stolen from an Arab tribe that wants them back. Directed by E.A. Dupont, the low-budget production is a routine exercise in stereotyped characters and contrived situations. Some menace and stylized violence. A-I (br)

Steel Magnolias (1989) Some sassy Southern belles (Dolly Parton, Shirley MacLaine, Olympia Dukakis, and Daryl Hannah) share the joys and sorrows of a friend (Sally Field) and her headstrong, diabetic daughter (Julia Roberts) in comic and supportive banter at the beauty shop and during key events involving marriage, birth, and death. Adapted by Robert Harling from his play and directed by Herb Ross, the movie is a rollicking tearjerker with polished performances and a refreshing focus on women-friends who are more seasoned than sexy. Some sexual innuendo. A-III (PG)

Steel Town (1952) In order to learn the business, a steel magnate's nephew (John Lund) gets a job in a steel mill, falls for the girlfriend (Ann Sheridan) of a co-worker (Howard Duff), then becomes a hero by saving her father's life in a mill accident. Directed by George Sherman, the romantic plot is predictable, but the mill setting and blue-collar characters add interest. Dangerous situations and romantic complications. A-II (br)

Steele Justice (1987) Troubled and vengeful Vietnam veteran (Martin Kove) blasts away a good portion of the Vietnamese underworld dealing in drugs and extortion. Director Robert Boris's tabloid depiction of ruthless crime offers little except equally bloody retribution. Lame acting and dialogue coupled with excessive violence and ethnic stereotyping add up to exploitation. O (R)

Steelyard Blues (1973) Donald Sutherland, Jane Fonda, and Peter Boyle romp aimlessly in a lightweight, adolescent fantasy about three losers who dream of flying away in a reconditioned WW II bomber to find a land without jails. Directed by Alan Myerson, there are some occasional laughs to be had among the elaborate gags and frantic comedy conveying sociopolitical banalities about being free in today's restrictive society. Worth seeing for some momentary diversion, but not worth a moment's thought. A-III (PG)

Stella (1990) Third remake of Olive Higgins Prouty's teary novel about the self-sacrifices of an unwed mother (Bette Midler) for her daughter (Trini Alvarado). Though Midler is both touching and raucous in the title role, and the period is updated to the present, director John Erman's melodrama is saddled with one-dimensional characters, some far-fetched bits of business, and a weepy fairytale ending. Its portrayal of strong, selfless parenting and a teen's refusal to be coerced into a sexual relationship are positive images for older adolescents. Some rough language, sexual vulgarities, and brief violence. A-III (PG-13)

Stella Dallas (1937) Sentimental tale of a small-town wife (Barbara Stanwyck) whose husband (John Boles) gets a good job in New York while she stays behind raising their daughter (Anne Shirley), until she realizes the youngster will have a better life with her father and his new wife. Director King Vidor's classic tearjerker about a mother's love and self-sacrifice has a well-plotted script, neatly defined class distinctions, and a standout performance by Stanwyck. Some domestic strife. A-II (br)

Step Down to Terror (1958) Failed thriller about a psychopathic murderer (Charles Drake) returning to his small hometown, where his sister-in-law (Colleen Miller) comes to suspect he is the man sought by a detective (Rod Taylor). Director Harry Keller's pale reworking of Hitchcock's **Shadow of a Doubt** is flat and unconvincing. Hokey menace. A-II (br)

Step Lively (1944) Genial musical version of **Room Service**, the madcap comedy about a small-town playwright (Frank Sinatra) showing up in New York, where his penniless producer (George Murphy) and the play's cast have been living on credit in a hotel whose manager (Walter Slezak) demands immediate payment. Director Tim Whelan keeps the wacky proceedings good-natured, though the pace is slowed considerably by production numbers with bland songs from Sammy Cahn and Jule Styne. Some mild romance. A-II (br)

Stepfather, The (1987) Chilling portrait of a psychopath (Terry O'Quinn) who slaughters his family, changes his identity, and remarries, only to be inspired once again to kill. Director Joseph Rubin's suspense thriller touches upon the precarious nature of modern relationships and mutual trust but gets carried away with brutality, bloody murder, and some brief nudity. O (R)

Stepfather II (1989) Cut-rate horror sequel directed by Jeff Burr follows the further exploits of a family serial-killer (Terry O'Quinn) who escapes from an asylum, then poses as a suburban psychologist while wooing a divorcée (Meg Foster) and slaughtering those who get in his way. Much graphic mayhem, a simulated sex scene, and some rough language. O (R)

Stepfather III (1992) Dreary formula sequel directed by Guy Magar with the deranged family killer (Robert Wrightman) running murderously amok in suburbia while married to one divorcée (Priscilla Barnes) and courting another (Season Hubley). Much graphic violence, some sex scenes, and occasional rough language. O (R)

Stepford Wives, The (1975) Katherine Ross stars in this failed thriller about suburban wives behaving like docile, mindless windup dolls. Directed by Bryan Forbes, the harder it tries to be frightening and sinister, the more laughable it becomes. Adult hokum because of language and some visuals. A-III (PG)

Stephen King's Graveyard Shift (1990) A drifter (David Andrews) joins an overnight crew hired to clean out a rat-infested factory basement that is also home to a huge bat-like monster that devours trespassers. Director Ralph S. Singleton's inane horror film is more repelling than frightening, virtually abandoning story line and characterization in favor of blood, guts, and rodents. Excessive gore and violence with intermittent rough language. O (R)

Stephen King's Sleepwalkers (1992) Lurid horror movie about an incestuous mother (Alice Krige) and son (Brian Krause) who are shape-shifting ghouls intent on sucking the life out of a virginal high-school girl (Madchen Amick). Director Mick Garris exploits sexual violence and extracts needless gore from a gruesome and perverse script. Incestuous bedroom scene, excessive violence, and some rough language. O (R)

Stephen King's The Night Flier (1998) Tedious horror story about a cynical reporter (Miguel Ferrar) hot on the trail of a vampire killer who lands his plane on lonely, backcountry airstrips, then drains the blood from his victims. Directed by Mark Pavia, the concept of the supernatural marauder is too thin to be sustained in this overlong feature which ends in an overdone blood bath. Excessive violence, menacing situations, occasional profanity, and rough language. O (R)

Stephen King's Thinner (1996) Steadily losing weight because of a Gypsy's curse, a frantic lawyer (Robert John Burke) takes increasingly desperate measures to get the curse lifted. Directed by Tom Holland, the thin premise soon turns into a formula revenge-themed horror story with nasty Gypsy stereotypes. Some gory violence, brief sexual innuendo, fleeting nudity, occasional profanity, and recurring rough language. A-III (R)

Stepmom (1998) Pointed drama in which a devoted but seriously ill mother (Susan Sarandon) must learn to accept her ex-husband's glamorous young fiancé (Julia Roberts), whose parenting skills are less than the mother wants for her two impressionable youngsters. Directed by Chris Columbus, the heartfelt tale is anchored by Sarandon's searing performance as it explores the painful aftermath of divorce for children and adults alike. A live-in relationship, sexual references, and an instance of rough language. A-III (PG-13)

Stepmother, The (1972) Pretentious story about the tenuous friendships and nebulous liaisons which cause much unhappiness for a devout, temperamental architect (Alejando Rey) and all those around him. Written, produced, and directed by Hikmet L. Avedis, the movie indulges in the stale techniques of hazy flashbacks and freeze-frames while attempting to keep viewers awake by tossing in some perfunctory nudity and a few murders. O (R)

Steppenwolf (1974) Max von Sydow stars as Herman Hesse's alienated outsider whose life illustrates industrial society's need to reconcile the spiritual and physical through people's re-establishing contact between the body and the soul. Writer-director Fred Haines fails to establish the character as anything more than a poor social misfit in what proves to be little more than a pictorialization of Hesse's text. Questionable sexual sequence. A-IV (R)

Stepping Out (1991) A past-her-prime tap-dance teacher (Liza Minnelli) gamely tries to prepare eight fumbling adult students for their professional debut while evaluating a longtime love affair in light of her unexpected pregnancy. Producer-director Lewis Gilbert infuses a very human drama with many charming comic moments for a warmhearted look at distinctly different individuals affecting each other for the better. A live-in relationship and momentary violence. A-III (PG)

Sterile Cuckoo, The (1969) Off-beat look at college romance in which a coed (Liza Minelli) comes out of her alienated shell to pursue a naive freshman (Wendell Burton) and involves him in obligations and responsibilities beyond his ability or desire to assume. Director Alan J. Pakula has made a little film with small pretensions about young people's growth to self-awareness and responsible relationships. Some restrained sexual scenes. A-IV (R)

Stevie (1981) British screen biography of English poet Stevie Smith (Glenda Jackson), the tough but sensitive spinster who lived just about all of her life in the same row-house in a London suburb with her loving maiden-aunt (Mona Washbourne). Based on Hugh Whitemore's play and directed by Robert Enders, the movie's warmly sympathetic portrayal of these two women is unusually intelligent and articulate. It also proves to be highly entertaining fare, thanks largely to their memorable, very human performances. A-II (PG)

Stewardesses, The (1970) Stilted staging, slushy sound, and indolent editing ground this plot-less 3-D picture of a flock of mini-dressed airline hostesses who indulge in sexual adventures between flights. Excessive nudity. O (X/R)

Stick (1985) Burt Reynolds, playing an ex-convict, runs into some nasty people in Miami, makes mincemeat of them, and lives happily ever after. Director Reynolds's screen version of the Elmore Leonard novel turns the gritty original into a glossy and cartoonish star-vehicle. Excessively graphic violence and amoral tone mark this vanity production. O (R)

Sticky Fingers (1988) Lightweight comedy about two erstwhile musicians (Helen Slater and Melanie Mayron) sharing both a New York flat and a lot of trouble after spending money left in their keeping by a friend who turns out to be involved in drugs. Directed by Catlin Adams, the bickering, bubble-headed roommates grow increasingly tiresome, and their predicament isn't worth the bother. Some crude language and sexual references, as well as a benign attitude toward drugs. A-III (PG-13)

Stiletto (1969) Cynical, fast-paced crime melodrama about a playboy (Alex Cord) who is called upon to repay a mobster for saving his life and finds himself hopelessly involved in the mob's criminal activities. Directed by Bernard Kowalski, the movie's overriding theme of brute force against force presents a pessimistic, unnerving view of life. Merciless violence and some nudity. O (R)

Still Crazy (1999) Uneven British spoof in which former band members of Strange Fruit, a rock group that broke up in the 1970s, try to overcome old antagonisms for a comeback concert tour in the 1990s. Directed by Brian Gibson, the proceedings focus on the fictitious band's behind-the-scenes activities and the flawed characters of its members (Stephen Rea, Billy Connolly, Timothy Spall, and Bill Nighy) but the treatment is more sentimental than satirical, and the uneven results are only mildly amusing. Sexual situations and references, a flash of nudity, drug and alcohol abuse, recurring rough language, and occasional profanity. A-IV (R)

Still of the Night (1982) New York psychiatrist (Roy Scheider) is irresistibly drawn to a mysterious woman (Meryl Streep) who may have murdered one of his patients and may make him her next victim. Director Robert Benton's attempt at Hitchcock-style suspense has no sense of emotion or reality and none of Hitchcock's stylish virtues. Murky plot and stylized violence are not for the youngsters. A-II (PG)

Sting, The (1973) Robert Redford and Paul Newman team up as two Chicago con-men who concoct an elaborate scheme involving a phony betting-parlor to get revenge on New York gangster Robert Shaw while turning a handsome profit. Director George Roy Hill's action comedy is solid entertainment, though some might find it more than a little contrived. The Depression-era setting includes a house of prostitution. A-III (PG)

Sting II, The (1983) Dreadfully inept sequel written by David S. Ward and directed by Jeremy Paul Kagan has Jackie Gleason and Mac Davis essay the roles originated by Newman and Redford. A movie to be avoided at all cost. Some sexually oriented humor. A-III (PG)

Stingray (1978) Two callow youths buy a car, unaware that it contains a large quantity of heroin and money, and are pursued by a murderous trio, led by a woman disguised as a nun. Richard Taylor directs the movie-long car chase interspersed with brawls and brutal killings of various sorts. Violence and low moral tone. O (PG)

Stir Crazy (1980) Failed comedy about two losers from New York (Gene Wilder and Richard Pryor) who find themselves doing time in a southwestern prison after being framed on a bankrobbery charge. Bruce Jay Friedman's script directed by Sidney Poitier relies on vulgar jokes and crude sight gags that quickly wear thin. Lewd scene in a go-go bar and frequent profanity. O (R)

Stolen Children (see: **Il Ladro di Bambini**)

Stolen Kisses (1969) French director Francois Truffaut carries on the story of young Antoine Doinel (Jean-Pierre Leaud) from **The Four Hundred Blows** (1959), who here takes faltering steps towards maturity in a series of jobs, gets involved with an older woman (Delphine Seyrig), but finally squares himself with his girlfriend. His haphazard misadventures are told in a relaxed episodic manner, and Truffaut ends with the implication that Antoine has finally grown up. Some sexual situations and brief nudity. A-IV (R)

Stolen Life, A (1946) Slick sudser in which a goodhearted woman (Bette Davis) falls for a lighthousekeeper (Glenn Ford), but he instead marries her nasty identical twin who soon dies in a boating accident, which leads the woman to foolishly assume her sister's identity, though she's too honest to carry it off. Directed by Curtis Bernhardt, the hokey plot becomes increasingly implausible, though Davis's zesty performance in the dual role of good and evil twins is worth seeing. Romantic complications. A-II (br)

Stone Boy, The (1984) Thoughtful study of a rural family-tragedy as bereaved parents (Robert Duvall and Glenn Close) try to come to terms with the death of their teenage son, accidentally shot by his younger brother (Jason Preston). The father's decision to let the boy work out his trauma on his own is a bit hard to take, but otherwise, director Chris Cain's fine, quiet movie is well worth seeing. Some relatively mild profanity used by the boy's grandfather in an attempt to jar his grandson out of his sense of isolation. A-II (PG)

Stone Cold (1991) The FBI persuades a suspended Alabama cop (Brian Bosworth) to infiltrate a deadly motorcycle gang whose leader (Lance Henriksen) has been orchestrating religious and political murders throughout Mississippi. Director Craig R. Baxley's macho bloodbath is couched in the tough, sexist credo of the outlaw bikers who wallow in promiscuity, endless explosions, and multiple murders. Excessive violence and rough language, women degraded as sex objects, and occasional nudity. O (R)

Stone Killer, The (1973) Sprawling crime epic about a tough cop (Charles Bronson) on the trail of a Sicilian mobster (Martin Balsam) who plans to use some Vietnam vets to assassinate the non-Sicilian gang that took over the New York underworld. Directed by Michael Winner, the film's core theme is the nearly interchangeable identities of police and criminal as they act out their respective vicious roles within a society pictured on the verge of collapse. Heavy violence. A-IV (R)

Stooge, The (1953) Lackluster tale of a singer (Dean Martin) who hits the big time in 1930 vaudeville after hiring a comic foil (Jerry Lewis) for his act, then falls on his face when he decides to go it alone, despite the warnings of his wife (Polly Bergen) and agent (Eddie Mayehoff). Directed by Norman Taurog, the plot is painfully predictable, and Lewis's comic antics tend to get mired in saccharine sentimentality. A scene of inebriation. A-I (br)

Stoolie, The (1974) Seedy, smalltime hustler (nightclub comic Jackie Mason) is a police informer who takes the funds intended to set up a crook and flees to Miami, where he finds true love (Marcia Jean Kurtz) just as the cops catch up with him. Directed by John Avildsen, the old-fashioned melodrama is long on romance and short on logic and credibility, but does have good characterizations and gritty, realistic locales. A-III (PG)

Stop! Or My Mom Will Shoot (1992) Witless comedy has a meddling mom (Estelle Getty) endlessly fussing over her police-sergeant son (Sylvester Stallone) and his neglected girlfriend (JoBeth Williams) while becoming his unwanted partner in a homicide investigation. Genial performances can't rescue director Roger Spottiswoode's one-joke sitcom from its flaccid predictability. Occasional violence and mild profanity. A-II (PG-13)

Stop the World — I Want to Get Off (1966) British musical about an average man (Tony Tanner) who marries his employer's daughter, has a couple of kids and a few affairs, winds up with a title and the realization that he has never loved anyone but himself. Director Philip Saville photographs the stage production rather than turning it into a movie. A-III (br)

Stork Club, The (1945) Frivolous musical comedy in which a hatcheck girl (Betty Hutton) saves an elderly millionaire (Barry Fitzgerald) from drowning, then he rewards her anonymously with expensive gifts, which cause misunderstandings when her Marine boyfriend (Don DeFore) returns from the Pacific. Directed by Hal Walker, Fitzgerald and lawyer Robert Benchley have a lot of fun with a thin premise that only makes Hutton and company look uncomfortably slow-witted. Romantic complications. A-II (br)

Storm in a Teacup (1937) When an old woman (Sara Allgood) in a Scottish town refuses to buy a license for her pet dog, the mayor (Cecil Parker) orders it impounded, then faces a national crusade to save the dog instigated by an English reporter (Rex Harrison) who, in the process, wins the heart of the mayor's daughter (Vivien Leigh). Directed by Victor Saville and Ian Dalrymple, the droll British comedy has plenty of fun with the situation as well as class differences, political ambitions, and English-Scottish tensions, but some of the dialogue is a bit thick for American ears. Incidental comic treatment of marital infidelity. A-II (br)

Stormy Monday (1988) Intriguing thriller set in Newcastle, England, tracks the shady tactics used by a crooked American entrepreneur (Tommy Lee Jones) to control the city's waterfront nightclub district. His principal stumbling blocks include a hardboiled jazz-club owner (Sting), a reformed party-girl (Melanie

Griffith), and her young Irish boyfriend (Sean Bean). Written, directed, and scored by Mike Figgis, the fine acting, gorgeous cinematography, and incredible jazz-blues score make this a haunting film. Some brief scenes of violence and a few scenes with fleeting nudity. A-III (R)

Stormy Weather (1943) All-black musical centers on a dancer (Bill Robinson) as he recalls 25 years in show business, starting with his entertaining fellow soldiers in WW I, and ending with his performing for WW II troops and reunion with the love of his life (Lena Horne). Director Andrew Stone's loosely constructed, disappointedly thin narrative serves mainly to provide the backdrop for a lively revue of performances by the considerable black talent of the day, including Fats Waller, Cab Calloway, the Nicholas Brothers, and Katherine Dunham's dance troupe. This record of the period's segregated artists is offset by its use of black stereotypes. A-II (nr)

Story of a Love Affair (1975) Italian melodrama about a woman (Lucia Bose) who joins her former lover in causing the death of her jealous industrialist husband with tragic consequences. Made in 1950 by director Michelangelo Antonnioni, the chief interest in the work is its focus on the social disparity between the luxury-loving wife and her jobless husband making the conclusion inevitable. A-III (nr)

Story of a Teenager, The (1975) A high-school football-star tries to make a home for his kid brother, but their alcoholic father tragically interferes. The film is well-intended as a look at the pressures of adolescence, but its script is simply too melodramatic and its treatment woefully inadequate to the task. Some intense violence. A-III (PG)

Story of a Woman (1970) Romantic tripe about a Swedish pianist studying in Rome (Bibi Andersson) who has an affair, but when she discovers her lover (James Farentino) is already married, returns to Stockholm, and marries an American (Robert Stack). Years later back in Rome, she must choose between her husband and child and her passion for her former lover. Directed by Leonardo Bercovici, this dull, boring effort has an excessively graphic bedroom scene. O (R)

Story of Adele H., The (1976) French romance of a 19th-century woman (Isabelle Adjani), the daughter of Victor Hugo, who exhausted her health in pursuing a worthless cad around the world, was brought back to France and lived under constant care for another 40 years, keeping a journal devoted to her obsessive passion. Director Francois Truffaut's adaptation of the journal is done with a fine blend of detachment, compassion, and respect for a woman who wasted her life in one sense and yet, in another, through the journal, turned it into a creative act. A-III (PG)

Story of Boys and Girls, The (1991) At a sumptuous feast in 1936 Italy celebrating the engagement of a young couple (Lucrezia Lante Della Rovere and Davide Bechini) from different social classes, the intrigues and secret frustrations of the two families surface. By giving equal weight to more than 30 characters, writer-director Pupi Avati turns the sprawling narrative into an unfocused collection of slice-of-life vignettes. Subtitles. Numerous sexual references. A-III (nr)

Story of Christiane F. (1982) German drama about a 13-year-old girl (Natja Brunkhorst) who drifts into drug addiction because of the squalid environment in which she lives. Director Ulrich Edel's coldly clinical yet lurid account of the hell of drug abuse lacks a moral perspective adequate to the horrific events it matter-of-factly chronicles. Innumerable scenes of needles being thrust into arms and its depiction of sexual activity make this extremely mature fare. A-IV (nr)

Story of Gilbert and Sullivan, The (1953) British dramatization begins in 1875, with composer Arthur Sullivan (Maurice Evans) teaming with librettist William Gilbert (Robert Morley) to write comic operas for producer Rubert D'Oyly Carte (Peter Finch), but their happy collaboration ends some 15 years later over Sullivan's yearning to write more serious music. Directed by Sidney Gilliat, the Victorian settings are quite charming and the characters are certainly interesting, but what's most appealing are the many excerpts of their works as performed by the D'Oyly Carte Company (notably Martyn Green). A-I (br)

Story of Qiu Ju, The (1993) A pregnant peasant-wife (Gong Li) adamantly seeks justice at increasingly distant and higher levels of Red Chinese bureaucracy when her village chief (Lei Lao Sheng) remains unrepentant after having angrily kicked her husband (Lui Peiqi) in the groin. Building tragic irony with exquisite simplicity, director Zhang Yimou captures the humanity and uncompromising spirit of a powerless woman pursuing justice despite the lethargy of officialdom and the scorn of her village. An instance of rough language. A-II (nr)

Story of Sin (1976) Walerian Borowczyk's screen version of Stefan Zeromski's novel about a hopeless love affair beautifully evokes its turn-of-the-century era but wallows in passionate despair and focuses on the erotic elements of the story. O (R)

Story of Vernon and Irene Castle, The (1939) Nostalgic musical biography of a vaudevillian (Fred Astaire) and his bride (Ginger Rogers), who in 1911 team as ballroom dancers and become international favorites before Vernon's tragic death as an aviator in WW I. Director H.C. Potter's warm portrait of a loving couple is paced by elegant dance numbers, period songs, and occasional comic relief (Edna May Oliver, Walter Brennan, and Lew Fields). Old-fashioned family fare. A-I (br)

Story of Women (1988) Grim French production about a poor, uneducated, but coldly ambitious woman (Isabelle Huppert) who is executed for performing abortions during the German occupation of WW II. Director Claude Chabrol uses the wartime setting to distance the subject from the controversy of today, treating the narrative in a somber, unemotional fashion that forces the viewer to confront the moral and social dimensions of abortion without the comfort of any easy answers. Subtitles. Challenging, at times unsettling, fare that requires discernment. A-IV (nr)

Story on Page One, The (1959) Trite courtroom drama of a lawyer (Tony Franciosa) defending a woman (Rita Hayworth) accused of plotting with her lover (Gig Young) to kill her husband. Written and directed by Clifford Odets, it's the old story of an abused wife seeking a sympathetic shoulder, but the trial scenes are flat and unconvincing, especially the defense lawyer's swaggering examination of the lover's manipulative mother (Mildred Dinnock). Tawdry situations. A-III (br)

Storyville (1992) A third-generation New Orleans politician (James Spader) running for Congress is unwittingly drawn into a murder investigation, while his uncle (Jason Robards) discourages him from prying further into a lingering family scandal about parish mineral-rights that ended in his father's suicide. Director Mark Frost's potboiler is fairly engrossing melodrama, though it is awash in Southern and political stereotypes. Some violence, an adulterous encounter, occasional nudity, and intermittent rough language. A-III (R)

Stowaway (1936) After her missionary parents die in war-torn China, a little girl (Shirley Temple) makes her way to Shanghai, winds up by accident on a US-bound ocean-liner, and helps a rich idler (Robert Young) and an earnest maiden (Alice Faye) find true love after they wed to adopt the child who otherwise will be deported. Directed by William A. Seiter, the hokey vehicle relies entirely on the child-star's appeal as a spunky orphan who is fluent in Chinese, sings like a seasoned professional, and knows more proverbs than Charlie Chan. Convoluted romantic complications. A-II (G)

Straight Talk (1992) Reluctantly posing as a professional psychotherapist, a big-hearted Southerner (Dolly Parton) becomes Chicago's leading radio talk-show personality, unaware that her reporter boyfriend (James Woods) is writing an expose about her. Directed by Barnet Kellman, the character's wholesome, down-home philosophy is smothered in a vanity production featuring a music track composed and sung by its star. Implied sexual relationships. A-III (PG)

Straight Time (1978) Dustin Hoffman plays an ex-con who, when pressured by a cynical parole-officer (Emmet Walsh), gives up on going straight and re-enters the criminal underworld. Directed by Ulu Grosbard, there is not enough in the script to involve the viewer with the characters, and while the fine acting and austere texture of the movie earn respect, one cannot really care about what happens to anybody in the story. The violence and rough language are part of the context, but the gratuitous nudity is not. O (R)

Straight to Hell (1987) Madcap spoof of a spaghetti Western, this farcical celebrity showcase from director Alex Cox mixes madness and mayhem with touches of sexual seduction and teasing to evoke a sense of the Theater of the Absurd. Cameo cast including Joe Strummer, Elvis Costello, and Courtney Love are all bandits trying to survive in a zany town. Some violence and sexual sight gags are not for youngsters. A-III (R)

Strait-Jacket (1964) Cheap horror show in which an axe-murderer (Joan Crawford) is released after 20 years in an asylum to live with her daughter (Diane Baker), but soon after she arrives, there are some more axe-victims. Written by Robert Bloch and directed by William Castle, the result is highly manipulative in creating an eerie atmosphere and sense of dread that is undercut by a contrived, unsatisfying resolution. Much menace and some special-effects violence. A-III (br)

Strange Adventure, A (1956) Formula crime caper directed by William Witney in which a teen hot-rodder (Ben Cooper) is tricked by a bad woman (Marla English) into driving the getaway car for a pair of gun-happy robbers, then captures them with the help of a good woman (Joan Evans). Some nasty violence, much menace, and recurring sexual innuendo. A-III (br)

Strange Affair, The (1968) Failed British crime melodrama about corruption in the London police department in connection with a pornography ring. Directed by David Greene, the slow and contrived plot makes sensationalistic use of violence and nudity. O (R)

Strange Affair of Uncle Harry, The (1945) Creaky melodrama about a man (George Sanders) who lives with his two sisters, but when one of them (Geraldine Fitzgerald) breaks up his engagement to a coworker (Ella Raines), he decides to poison her. Directed by Robert Siodmak, the slow-paced story generates little interest until the tale's twist ending. Threatening situations and mild sexual innuendo. A-II (br)

Strange Bedfellows (1964) Thin but frantic romantic comedy in which a London-based oil executive (Rock Hudson) reconciles with his flighty estranged wife (Gina Lollobrigida) in order to get a promotion in his staid company, then she insists on playing Lady Godiva in a left-wing protest at the American Embassy. Directed by Melvin Frank, the sour comedy falls flat on all counts except for the scenes with Terry-Thomas as an undertaker. Sexual situations and innuendo. A-III (br)

Strange Behavior (1981) Offbeat horror movie about the revenge of a mad scientist, set in the kind of small Midwestern town inextricably bound up with this genre. What makes it unusual is that the town was re-created rather well in New Zealand by director Michael Laughlin, who got a few American actors (Michael Murphy and Louise Fletcher) to journey there. Unfortunately, the story piles on the gruesome details of violent deaths to a needlessly excessive degree. O (R)

Strange Brew (1983) The comic duo of Doug and

Bob McKenzie (Dave Thomas and Rick Moranis, who also directed) lampoon Canada mercilessly as a land of rubes and rustics in an intentionally incoherent plot about a brewery run by arch-villain Max von Sydow, with Paul Dooley as his cowardly lackey. Chiefly serving as a vehicle for the McKenzie pair of spaced-out zanies, whose substance addiction happens to be beer, the comedy is a random collection of stale sight gags and boisterous stupidities that grow increasingly tiresome. Course language and a visual sexual reference. A-III (PG)

Strange Days (1995) Dreary thriller set in violence-racked Los Angeles on the eve of the year 2000, when a sleazy hawker (Ralph Fiennes) of illegal virtual-reality software finds himself and his ex-girlfriend (Juliette Lewis) stalked by a psychotic serial-killer. Directed by Kathryn Bigelow, the senseless plot relies on shock effects for interest rather than characters with some dimension of humanity, or a story with some semblance of credibility. Repellant violence, simulated sex acts, nudity, racial epithets, profanity, and rough language. O (R)

Strange Deception (see: **The Accused**)

Strange Invaders (1983) Some less-than-cuddly E.T.'s descend upon Centreville, Ill., one night in the 1950s, and stay on in human form for a quarter of a century wearing the same-style clothes as when they first arrived, something quickly noted by a professor (Pal LeMat) who arrives there looking for his missing wife. The silly plot is somewhat engaging, but director Michael Laughlin's handling of it is plodding and uninspired. Some messy special-effects when the aliens strip off their human exteriors to reveal their true life-forms. A-II (PG)

Strange Lady in Town (1955) Western misfire in which a red-haired lady doctor (Greer Garson) arrives in 1880 Sante Fe, is befriended by the tomboy daughter (Lois Smith) of the town's resident doctor (Dana Andrews) whom she alienates by treating his patients, then is ostracized because of her Army-renegade brother (Cameron Mitchell). Directed by Mervyn LeRoy, the plot complications keep getting in the way of a budding romance between the rival doctors, though the tiresome results still have interest because of the story's feminist angle. Stylized violence and romantic complications. A-II (br)

Strange Love of Martha Ivers, The (1946) Darkly contrived tale in which a troubled heiress (Barbara Stanwyck) and her weakling husband (Kirk Douglas) fear a childhood friend (Van Heflin) who disappeared on the night the woman murdered her wealthy aunt (Judith Anderson), then suddenly turns up in town with a girlfriend (Lizabeth Scott). Though the story is full of cheese, director Lewis Milestone maintains interest in the characters, especially Stanwyck's twisted, tortured lady of the title, and Heflin's tough, breezy gambler who knows all the angles. Stylized violence, including a double suicide, and abundant romantic complications. A-III (br)

Strange Shadows in an Empty Room (1977) Director Martin Herbert's frantic exercise in mindless violence about a detective trying to find the murderer of his sister. The Italian production was filmed in Montreal with second-string American leads, and there is not another nice thing to say about it. Nudity, brutality and sheer nastiness. O (R)

Strange Triangle (1946) Contrived story of murder told in flashback by a bank examiner (Preston Foster) who fell for an attractive nuisance (Signe Hasso) with larceny in her heart and a bank director (John Shepperd) under her thumb. Directed by Ray McCarey, the results are hardly worth the effort. Off-screen shooting and mild romantic situations. A-II (br)

Strange Vengeance of Rosalie, The (1972) Botched contemporary horror story about a traveling salesman (Ken Howard) who is tricked by a young girl (Bonnie Bedelia) into visiting her dead grandfather's hovel in a deserted Western wasteland and then breaks his leg to keep him there. Director Jack Starrett dissipates the terror of the situation with a subplot about a menacing motorcycle hood (Anthony Zerbe) who harasses the girl both for her grandfather's hidden gold and her body. A-III (R/PG)

Strange Woman, The (1946) Muddled melodrama begins in 1824 Maine, where a poor but ambitious woman (Hedy Lamarr) marries a rich but elderly merchant (Gene Lockhart), tries to entice his son (Louis Hayward) to kill him, then marries an enterprising logger (George Sanders) who soon gets wise. Directed by Edgar G. Ulmer, the period picture of a woman driven by contradictory impulses is rarely anything more than tedious. Romantic complications. A-II (br)

Strangeland (see: **Dee Snider's Strangeland**)

Stranger, The (1946) Atmospheric thriller set in a small Connecticut town, where a government agent (Edward G. Robinson) tries to persuade the bride (Loretta Young) of a prep-school teacher (Orson Welles) that her husband is an escaped Nazi war-criminal. Also directed by Welles, the sunny small-town setting heightens the cat-and-mouse tension of the ensuing manhunt, which concludes in the clock-works high aloft a church steeple. Some menace and stylized violence. A-II (br)

Stranger, The (1968) Italian-French adaptation of the Albert Camus novel about the senseless murder of an Arab tough by a Frenchman (Marcello Mastroianni) and his subsequent trial and conviction for the crime. Directed by Luchino Visconti, it is a painstaking and often beautiful translation of the Nobel Prize Winner's object lesson in existential absurdity. A-IV (br)

Stranger Among Us, A (1992) Investigating the murder of a diamond-cutter in New York City's Hasidic community, a cynical detective (Melanie Griffith) is drawn to the sect's spirituality — and its leading Hasidic scholar (Eric Thal). Director Sidney Lumet enriches a standard murder mystery-romance with a sensitive and uplifting look at a little-known religious group. Brief scenes of violence and mild sexual references. A-II (PG-13)

Stranger and the Gunfighter, The (1976) Italian production directed by Anthony Dawson about a gunslinger (Lee Van Cleef) and a kung-fu master (Lo Lieh) who team up to find a lost fortune, clues to which are tattooed on four former mistresses of the deceased owner. Intended as a comic mixture of sex and violence, the result is offensive. O (PG)

Stranger in My Arms, A (1959) Turgid sudser directed by Helmut Kautner in which a Korean War pilot (Jeff Chandler) visits the wealthy family of a fallen comrade, learns why he was suicidal after meeting the dead man's manipulative mother (Mary Astor), then falls in love with his sweetly naive widow (June Allyson). Wartime violence, including an off-screen suicide, and romantic complications. A-II (br)

Stranger in the House (see: **Black Christmas**)

Stranger in Town, A (1967) Sadistic Italian Western directed by Vance Lewis in which a stranger in Mexico (Tony Anthony) makes a deal with a bandit gang to help steal a shipment of gold, but when they take it all, he follows and picks them off one by one, until he has all the loot. Cynical treatment employs brutal, sadistic violence. O (R)

Stranger Is Watching, A (1982) Rapist-murderer (Rip Torn) kidnaps a young girl (Shawn Von Schreiber) and a television newswoman (Kate Mulgrew) and holds them prisoner beneath New York's Grand Central Station. Director Sean Cunningham's dull, plodding thriller is derived from a novel by Mary Higgins Clark. Because of violence, rough language, and the sordid nature of the story, it is not for young viewers. A-III (R)

Stranger on the Third Floor (1940) Stylish low-budget thriller in which a reporter (John McGuire) testifies against a man (Elisha Cook, Jr.) in a murder trial, then discovers that a sinister drifter (Peter Lorre) is really the killer, but finding him puts his fiancé (Margaret Tallichet) in jeopardy. Director Boris Ingster relies on dark, moody visuals to create an eerie atmosphere, with Lorre especially effective as the deranged, misunderstood menace. Threatening situations. A-II (br)

Stranger Returns, The (1968) Standard Italian Western directed by Vance Lewis in which a lone stranger (Tony Anthony) sees bandits rob a stagecoach and kill all its passengers, then follows them, and exterminates the lot. Much cruelty and violence. A-III (R)

Stranger Wore a Gun, The (1953) Muddled Western directed by Andre de Toth has an ex-Confederate spy (Randolph Scott) join, then smash, a gang of Arizona stagecoach-robbers (led by George Macready) after engineering a deadly shootout with a rival gang (led by Alfonso Bedoya). Stylized violence. A-I (br)

Stranger's Return, The (1933) Dated rural melodrama in which a woman (Miriam Hopkins) deserted by her husband returns to the family farm, convinces her 85-year-old grandfather (Lionel Barrymore) she has farming in her blood, though she antagonizes her other relatives, and is pursued by a married neighbor (Franchot Tone). Directed by King Vidor, the rustic setting is a lot more interesting than the slow-paced plot and the interplay between stock characters. Romantic complications. A-II (br)

Strangers in Good Company (1991) On a day's outing in the Quebec countryside, a group of elderly women find themselves stranded when their bus breaks down, and they have to spend the night in an abandoned farmhouse. By placing non-actors in this bare-bones situation, Canadian director Cynthia Scott comes up with a convincing portrait of seven old women — among them, a nun, a lesbian, and a Mohawk Indian matriarch — who pass the time while waiting to be rescued by exchanging reminiscences of their past lives and sharing common concerns about their present circumstances. Simple yet compelling evocation of the mixed blessings of old age, though young children may find some of it confusing. A-II (PG)

Strangers on a Train (1951) Uneasy thriller about the aftermath of a chance conversation between a tennis player (Farley Granger) and a rich psychopath (Robert Walker), who proposes that each kill the person the other wishes were dead. Despite the script's ragged plotting, director Alfred Hitchcock makes the concept of "crossover" murders chillingly plausible, fueled by Walker's edgy performance, Farley's inept innocence, and a frightening finale in an amusement park. Faithless wife, stylized violence, and mounting menace. A-III (br)

Strapless (1990) Fortyish American doctor (Blair Brown), living in England and supporting her fun-loving younger sister, lets down her emotional barriers and marries a mysterious stranger, who then disappears. Writer-director David Hare has concocted a moodily intriguing film whose gentle pace allows the viewer to take an intimate look at a repressed woman's midlife crisis and how it affects those whom she loves. Several instances of rough language, momentary flashes of nudity, and a glimpse of a casual sexual encounter. A-III (R)

Stratton Story, The (1949) Fact-based dramatization of baseball's Monty Stratton (James Stewart), a Texas farm-youth who becomes a star pitcher for the Chicago White Sox until losing a leg in a hunting accident, then tries for a comeback pitching with an artificial leg. Directed by Sam Wood, Stewart gives a fine performance on and off the field, with solid assists from wife June Allyson, mother Agnes Moorehead, and pitching scout Frank Morgan. Convincing depiction of a successful athlete overcoming the despair of a devastating disability. A-I (br)

Straw Dogs (1971) Introverted American mathematician (Dustin Hoffman) takes his sabbatical in the small English village where his wife (Susan George) grew up, and in her boredom, she begins to flirt with her former admirers, leading ultimately to a brutalizing double rape. The movie ends in a bloodbath precipitated by the husband's refusal to let a mob invade his home to lynch an injured man who has taken refuge there. Director Sam Peckinpah benefits from some uncommonly good acting, but the characters are contrived stereotypes who would be more at home in a Western movie than the English countryside. As with the rape scene, the attack on the house is particularly brutal and vicious, wallowing in an excess of violence that the plot supposedly condemns. O (R)

Strawberry and Chocolate (1995) Sluggish comedy-drama set in Cuba, where a homosexual artist (Jorge Perugorria) befriends a straight-laced student (Vladimir Cruz) unaware the youth is being pressured to report him as a likely political subversive. Directed by Tomas Gutierrez Alea and Juan Carlos Tabio, the Cuban production overcomes dramatic weaknesses and drab visuals in portraying the contradictions of institutionalized homophobia. Subtitles. Fleeting nudity in a heterosexual bedroom scene and in beefcake photos, arguments about homosexuality, and occasional rough language. A-IV (R)

Strawberry Roan, The (1948) When a rancher's son (Dick Jones) is injured by a wild stallion, the foreman (Gene Autry) is ordered to destroy the horse, but, instead, secretly tames it for the boy to ride, certain this will effect his recovery. Directed by John English, the sentimental story benefits from the colorful Arizona scenery and exciting sequences featuring Autry's horse, Champion, in the roan's role. Still pleases youngsters and horse-lovers. A-I (br)

Strawberry Statement, The (1970) Phony screen version of James Kunen's novel purports to be about the radicalizing of a college student (Bruce Davison) who, drawn into participating in a campus sit-in by a pretty revolutionary (Kim Darby), winds up being gassed and bludgeoned when the police and national guard brutalize the protestors. Stuart Hagmann's gimmicky direction calls more attention to itself than to the social and political issues which the movie supposedly is addressing. Further clouding matters is the movie's emphasis on sex and the heavy-handed stylized violence of the riot sequence. O (R)

Streamers (1983) Screen version of David Rabe's play about barracks tension exploding into violence during the early days of the Vietnam War creates sympathy for its characters (Matthew Modine, Michael Wright, and Mitchell Lichtenstein), though the presentation itself remains too stage-bound. Directed by Robert Altman, the essential problem with the movie, as with the play, is the attempt to load melodrama with heavy philosophical significance. Admirable intentions but disappointing results. Some violence and rough language. A-III (R)

Street Fighter (1994) Tedious comic-book adventure in which a beefy colonel (Jean-Claude Van Damme) leads an international expeditionary force against the southeast Asian stronghold of a military megalomaniac (Raul Julia). Inspired by a video game, writer-director Steven E. de Souza has come up with a laborious assortment of make-believe violence that is as pointless and uninvolving as the stick characters perpetrating it. Mindless, though bloodless, violence and occasional coarse language. A-III (PG-13)

Street Fighter, The (1975) Japanese martial-arts movie revolving around a missing oil-heiress and a repulsive thug (Sonny Chiba) who undertakes her rescue. Superior special effects but excessively violent. O (X/R)

Street People (1976) Aimless, shamelessly derivative gangster movie directed by Maurizio Lucidi in which Roger Moore and Stacy Keach take on a cast of dubbed-in Italian heavies. Some nudity, but most offensive is its mindless brutality. O (R)

Street Scene (1931) Dated but still interesting social drama in which residents of a Manhattan tenement seeking relief from a heat wave sit on the front stoop exchanging gossip and banter, then in the quiet of the next morning one of the tenants (David Landau) shoots his wife and a married bill-collector he suspects is her lover, with tragic consequences for their unmarried daughter (Sylvia Sidney). Directed by King Vidor from Elmer Rice's Pulitzer Prize-winning play, the result mixes static dialogue scenes with eloquent visuals of an ethnically mixed neighborhood and the Depression-era problems of its inhabitants. Stylized violence and sexual innuendo. A-III (br)

Street Smart (1987) Magazine reporter (Christopher Reeve) writes a fictitious account of a pimp's daily activities, passes it off as fact, and becomes embroiled in a dilemma when his article is subpoenaed as evidence in the murder trial of a real pimp (Morgan Freeman). Director Jerry Schatzberg's few insights on the subject are lost in a plot featuring mindless revenge, instances of brutality, acceptance of fornication, brief nudity, and rough language. O (R)

Street with No Name, The (1948) In a story described as "from the files of the FBI," a G-man (Mark Stevens) goes undercover to worm his way into a gang run by a murderous psychopath (Richard Widmark), who tries to kill him after learning his real identity from a corrupt police official. Director William Keighley's semi-documentary approach uses some actual FBI facilities and personnel, but this doesn't add any greater credibility to the formula crime story or the actors' melodramatics. Stylized violence and threatening situations. A-II (br)

Streetcar Named Desire, A (1951) Screen version of Tennessee Williams's play about the tensions that develop when an emotionally unstable widow (Vivien Leigh) arrives in New Orleans and moves in with her younger sister (Kim Hunter), whose coarse husband (Marlon Brando) resents his sister-in-law's aristocratic pretentious, learns of her shady past, and destroys her chance to marry his friend (Karl Malden). Director Elia Kazan probes the loneliness as well as the volatile passions that nearly consume the drama's all-too-human characters. Mature themes with much sexual innuendo. A-III (PG)

Streets of Fire (1984) Listless, boring rock 'n' roll

story about a brooding outsider of a hero (Michael Paré) who rescues a rock star (Diane Lane) from a gang of bikers with the help of a straight-shooting female sidekick (Amy Madigan). Written and directed by Walter Hill, it turns out to be another tedious, stylized celebration of the macho mystique. Violence and a homosexual dance-sequence. A-III (R/PG)

Streets of Gold (1986) A Jewish émigré (Klaus Maria Brandauer) from the Soviet Union, where he had once been an Olympic contender, gets some measure of satisfaction from teaching two Brooklyn street-kids the art of boxing so they can compete with a visiting Soviet boxing team. In a well-intentioned but predictable plot following the underdog formula, the movie weakly affirms believing in oneself and one's talents. Profanity and violence in and out of the ring by the principals provide no positive role models for youngsters. A-III (R)

Streets of Laredo (1949) Standard Western directed by Leslie Fenton features a friendly trio of bandits, two of whom (William Holden and William Bendix) escape a posse by joining the Texas Rangers, then find they like the work until ordered to arrest their former partner (Macdonald Carey), now a famous outlaw. Frontier violence and romantic complications. A-II (br)

Streetwalkin' (1985) A prostitute tries to escape from her pimp in this sordid little movie exploiting sex and violence while having pretensions as social commentary. O (R)

Strictly Ballroom (1993) Old-fashioned success story of an Australian youth (Paul Mercurio), with his own ideas about dance-steps, teaming with an ugly-duckling novice (Tara Morice) to compete for the championship in a traditional ballroom-dancing contest. Directed by Baz Luhrmann, the outcome of all this is as obvious as the eventual romance between the two principals is inevitable, but the movie's pleasure comes along the way in watching the energy and determination of the young dancers and their innocence in confronting unsympathetic parents and manipulative contest organizers. Mild sexual references, domestic difficulties, and several instances of profanity. A-II (PG)

Strictly Business (1991) Predictable romantic comedy about young African-Americans in which a mailroom clerk (Tommy Davidson) helps an executive (Joseph C. Phillips) win over the clerk's gorgeous friend (Halle Berry) in exchange for a spot in the management-training program. Only the lively music in director Kevin Hooks's uninspired movie relieves the flatness of the uniformly one-dimensional characters. A few discreet bedroom scenes, occasional sexual references, racial slurs, and momentary violence. A-III (PG-13)

Strike It Rich (1990) British adaptation of the Graham Greene novella, **Loser Takes All**, this fairytale bonbon charts the romantic ups and downs of a divorced London accountant (Robert Lindsay) and a demure younger woman (Molly Ringwald) he meets on a bus. Writer-director James Scott nicely re-creates the look of a 1950s comedy of manners as the couple marry in Monte Carlo, while he tries to parlay a "perfect system" at the roulette table into millions. Slight but refreshingly refined exploration of values and the role of chance in romance. Minimal sexual innuendo. A-II (PG)

Strike Me Pink (1936) Weak comedy about an amusement park's meek manager (Eddie Cantor) and his problems fending off a gangster (Brian Donlevy) and his crooked slot-machines. Directed by Norman Taurog, Cantor's goofy routines fail to score any big laughs in this lackluster vehicle. Some stylized violence and romantic complications. A-II (br)

Strike Up the Band (1940) Bouncy teen musical in which a high-school band-leader (Mickey Rooney), set on winning a network-radio competition of new bands, gets the gang (including Judy Garland) to put on a show raising the fare to New York to perform for contest judge Paul Whiteman. Director Busby Berkeley paces the story's youthful enthusiasm and high hopes with refreshing musical numbers and an idealized view of small-town life and values. Pleasant fun from an optimistic past. A-I (br)

Striking Distance (1993) Former homicide detective (Bruce Willis), demoted to the Pittsburgh police river-patrol alongside a duplicitous female partner (Sarah Jessica Parker), continues to pursue the serial killer he believes murdered his father (John Mahoney), much to the chagrin of his uncle (Dennis Farina), the homicide chief. Director Rowdy Herrington steadily builds suspense in this whodunit, then throws in every cliche in the book in an overwrought climax of absurdly melodramatic proportions. Recurring violence, a fleeting bedroom scene, and much rough language. A-III (R)

Stripes (1981) After bungling their way though basic military-training, Bill Murray and his troop of losers create havoc in Czechoslovakia. Director Ivan Reitman's mediocre hit-or-miss comedy has only scattered laughs and an occasional serious bit at odds with the rest. Extravagant use of nudity, sexual promiscuity, and rough language. O (R)

Stripper (1986) Pseudo-documentary on a striptease competition is an exploitation movie about women who are paid to display their bodies to voyeurs. O (R)

Striptease (1996) Lame sex-comedy about the infatuation of a brainless, oversexed congressman (Burt Reynolds) with a dancer (Demi Moore) in a sleazy strip-joint. Directed by Andrew Bergman, the listless jumble of one-note characters and situations is wedged in between numerous striptease routines. Women depicted as sex objects, frequent nudity, off-screen murders, substance abuse, profanity, and rough language. O (R)

Striptease Lady (see: **Lady of Burlesque**)

Stroker Ace (1983) Race-car driver (Burt Reynolds) wants to break his contract representing a fried-chicken franchiser (Ned Beatty) and to seduce a principled young woman (Loni Anderson). Director Hal Needham's action comedy has plenty of racing sequences, including several crashes, and humor with a minimum of subtlety. Occasional strong language and one relatively mild bedroom scene, but, all in all, it's fairly good escapist entertainment for mature viewers. A-III (PG)

Strong Man, The (1926) Classic silent comedy with vacant-faced Harry Langdon as a Belgian veteran in America searching for the woman who had been his WW I pen-pal. Directed by Frank Capra, Langdon's childish innocent survives much comic adversity until he reaches a town run by bootleggers, brings down the house as the stand-in for a vaudeville strongman-act, and achieves his romantic quest, thereby proving love is blind. Slapstick violence, criminal menace, and mild sexual innuendo. A-II (br)

Strongest Man in the World, The (1974) Two college students (Kurt Russell and Joe Flynn) accidentally concoct a formula that gives people unlimited strength. Plodding, poorly scripted Disney comedy directed by Vincent McEveety. A-I (G)

Stroszek (1977) Slight German tale of three Berliners (a street musician, a hapless prostitute, and their landlord) who go off to join the landlord's son in Wisconsin, but their hope in the American dream proves to be an empty one. Writer-director Werner Herzog seems to just let things happen, and the result is often little more than a home movie with artistic pretensions. Mature themes. A-III (nr)

Stuart Saves His Family (1995) Mild-mannered comedy in which the struggling host (Al Franken) of a self-help talk show is continually faced with crisis situations involving his own highly dysfunctional family of alcoholics, depressives, and overeaters. Directed by Harold Ramis and based on Franken's "Saturday Night Live" TV character, the movie gently mocks New Age psychobabble, and ends up being sweetly touching as various family members come to grips with their addictions. Mild sexual innuendo, fleeting violence, substance abuse, occasional profanity, and an instance of rough language. A-III (PG-13)

Stuck on You (1984) A palimony suit serves as the peg on which to hang a series of vulgar, unfunny skits in this low-budget comedy directed by Michael Herz and Samuel Weil. Much nudity. O (R)

Stud, The (1979) Directed by Quentin Masters and written by Jackie Collins, this embarrassingly sordid British production stars Joan Collins in a story detailing the rise and fall of a working-class youth (Oliver Tobias), whose only salable asset is his body. O (R)

Study in Scarlet, A (1933) Sherlock Holmes (Reginald Owen) and Dr. Watson (Warburton Gamble) solve a series of murders involving a fortune in gems stolen from China. Directed by Edwin L. Marin, Owen makes a worthy Holmes, and, though the mystery isn't Conan Doyle, it's intriguing enough to hold interest. Creaky stylized violence and Oriental stereotypes. A-II (br)

Stunt Man, The (1980) Fugitive from the police (Steve Railsback) is hidden by a manic movie-director (Peter O'Toole) on condition that he do some dangerous stunts, but he makes a mistake by falling for its star (Barbara Hershey). Directed by Richard Rush, the movie-within-a-movie plot starts well, but soon becomes repetitious and drags considerably thereafter. Graphic depiction of sex with extensive nudity. O (R)

Stupids, The (1996) Lame-brained comedy in which a moronic family of four (headed by Tom Arnold) inadvertently foils a plot to sell illegal arms but remains none the wiser. Directed by John Landis, the movie has some amusing visuals, but the thin, slapstick story is simply dumb without being especially funny. Comic violence. A-II (PG)

Subject Was Roses, The (1968) Fine drama about a Bronx Irish family's domestic crisis succeeds far beyond the limitations of its basically one-set story. Starring Patricia Neal and Jack Albertson as the parents, and Martin Sheen as their serviceman son, the movie probes the love and hate that alternately bind the three together and tear them apart. Adapted from Frank Gilroy's Broadway drama, the movie contains intimate touches of family life, its joys and its frustrations, and is masterful in its revelation of human nature, jealousy, and love. Mature themes. A-III (G)

Submarine Command (1951) After WW II, a career officer (William Holden), troubled by feelings of guilt over his commander's death, buries himself in a Navy desk-job and shamefully neglects his wife (Nancy Olson), until given a chance to prove his courage as a sub commander in the Korean War. Directed by John Farrow, the on-shore melodramatics of the moody officer grow increasingly tiresome, though the underwater action sequences still have interest. Wartime violence and domestic tensions. A-II (br)

Submarine X-1 (1968) British WW II story directed by William Graham about the training of submarines crews for an experimental mini-sub under a harsh and disliked commander (James Caan). The underwater sequences with the miniature submarines will be enjoyed by youngsters, and the only violence is the sinking of a German battleship. A-I (G)

Substance of Fire, The (1996) Brooding drama about an aging Jewish publisher (Ron Rifkin) whose concentration on Holocaust-themed books is bankrupting his company despite practical advice from his three concerned children (Tony Goldwyn, Sarah Jessica Parker, and Timothy Hutton). Director Daniel Sullivan explores themes of guilt, independence, and failed familial relationships in a sluggish, talky film that fails to transcend its stage-play roots. Some sexual innuendo, intermittent rough language, and minimal profanity. A-III (R)

Substitute, The (1996) Formula action-thriller in which a between-jobs military mercenary (Tom Berenger) tames an unruly Florida high-school class, then breaks up a gang of drug smugglers using the school as their base of operations. Directed by Robert Mandel, the cliched characters go through the motions required by a tired scenario of vigilante justice. Excessive violence and menace, a scene with nude dancers, and considerable rough language. O (R)

Suburban Commando (1991) Mindless sci-fi fantasy has an intergalactic warrior (Hulk Hogan) crash-landing on Earth, where a downtrodden architect (Christopher Lloyd) helps him right wrongs and outsmart a pair of pursuing interplanetary bounty-hunters. Burt Kennedy directs a silly movie pitting a superhero against klutzy villains in a slapstick comedy of no distinction. Much comic violence. A-II (PG)

Such a Gorgeous Kid Like Me (1973) Lighthearted French farce about a sociologist (Claude Brasseur) whose research brings him to do a prison interview with a beautiful but amoral murderess (Bernadette Lafont). Enamored, he eventually proves her innocence, but she in turn frames him for her latest murder and becomes a media celebrity. Directed by Francois Truffaut, the comedy bubbles brightly, the plot's twists and turns are delightful, and, best of all, it has a feeling for humanity that cloaks even the worst of its characters with an elemental dignity. Some strong language and sexual escapades. A-III (R)

Such Good Friends (1971) Director Otto Preminger has transformed Lois Gould's sly, satirical novel about the seamy underside of New York's cocktail party set into a souped-up sexual soap-opera. The movie is a series of melodramatic tableaux that become progressively cheaper in their depiction of the harsh discoveries a youngish wife (Dyan Cannon) makes about her dying husband (Lawrence Luckinbill) and her own series of sexual adventures, past and present. O (R)

Sucker, The (1966) Funny French comedy directed by Gerard Oury in which a smuggler (Louis de Funes) hires a sucker (Bourvil) to drive him from Naples to Bourdeaux, but when the booby learns that the car is loaded with drugs, gold, and jewels, he outsmarts the crooks. Some sexual innuendo. A-III (br)

Sudan (1945) Lame adventure fantasy directed by John Rawlins, with Maria Montez as a young queen in ancient Egypt who's sold into slavery by an evil usurper (George Zucco), then rescued by itinerant thieves (Jon Hall and Andy Devine) with the help of a rebel leader (Turhan Bey). Stylized violence, including a torture scene, and mild romance. A-II (br)

Sudden Death (1985) Female **Death Wish** variant in which a young woman (Denise Coward) buys a gun after being raped and goes hunting without a license. The woefully inept movie dangerously attempts to find an audience by suggesting vigilantism, yet its central interest is an exploitation of sex and violence. O (R)

Sudden Death (1995) Formula thriller pitting a fire inspector (Jean-Claude Van Damme) against a corrupt government-agent (Powers Boothe) who will blow up a crowded sports arena unless he gets a $1.7 billion payoff. Directed by Peter Hyams, the narrative generates little suspense as people are killed with dreary regularity until the predictably heroic conclusion. Excessive violence and brutality, fleeting nudity, and recurring rough language. O (R)

Sudden Fear (1952) Slickly contrived thriller in which a wealthy playwright (Joan Crawford) weds a struggling actor (Jack Palance), then discovers he has a girlfriend (Gloria Grahame), and they plan to murder her. Directed by David Miller, the slow-starting narrative quickens the pace after the menaced writer devises her own counter-plot with growing suspense as matters spin out of control in the tense climax. Menacing situations and implied marital infidelity. A-II (br)

Sudden Impact (1983) Dirty Harry (Clint Eastwood who also directs) is back, this time in picturesque Santa Cruz to halt a series of gruesome shootings that prove to be the work of a gang-rape victim (Sondra Locke) exacting vengeance upon those who brutalized her. With the two having so much in common, the outcome is entirely predictable. Excessive violence and the espousal of an end-justifies-the-means outlook. O (R)

Sudden Terror (1971) Above-average British thriller about a youngster (Mark Lester) living on a Mediterranean island who happens to see a policeman shoot the visiting president of an African nation. Afraid of going to the police and unable to convince his grandfather (Lionel Jeffries) that he is telling the truth, the boy is left to the mercy of the murderer in a violent chase crisscrossing the island. Director John Hough offers a mixture of suspense and sly British humor, with a decided Hitchcock flair. Series of violent murders and grisly auto smash-ups. A-III (GP)

Sudden Wealth of the Poor People of Kombach, The (1974) Fact-based German dramatization set in the early 19th century, when a group of simple peasants rob a tax-collector but are quickly apprehended, since they are the only ones buying goods in an area where everyone else is starving. Director Volker Schlondorff's excellent visual re-creation foreshadows the violent struggles for social justice that break out in Europe a few decades later. A-III (nr)

Suddenly (1954) Modest thriller in which a small band of assassins (led by Frank Sinatra) take captive a family (including Nancy Gates and James Gleason) whose house is on the route to be taken by the US president. Director Lewis Allen builds the tension in realistic detail, especially the gunmen's threatening treatment of the family and the suspicions of the local lawman (Sterling Hayden). Much menace and some stylized violence. A-II (br)

Suddenly, Last Summer (1959) Uneven adaptation of Tennessee Williams's play in which an aging Southern heiress (Katharine Hepburn) tries to induce a neurosurgeon (Montgomery Clift) to perform a lobotomy on a niece (Elizabeth Taylor) traumatized by the bizarre death of the aunt's son. Directed by Joseph L. Mankiewicz, the cast is hard-put sustaining interest in the slowly unfolding tale of a mother's unnatural love for her son and a young woman's hysterical repression of witnessing death and degradation in 1937 Spain. Veiled references to homosexuality, cannibalism, and loss of virginity, as well as restrained depictions of a mental asylum. A-IV (br)

Sued for Libel (1939) Formula murder-mystery directed by Leslie Goodwins concerns the producer (Kent Taylor) of a radio news-show and a newspaper reporter (Linda Hayes) who join forces to find a killer. Dated but colorful period background, with some silly magic tricks and occasional menace. A-I (br)

Suez (1938) Stodgy biographical melodrama based on the life of Ferdinand de Lesseps (Tyrone Power), the French builder of the Suez Canal. Directed by Allan Dwan, the result has little to do with history, but the Hollywood version is certainly colorful and heroic, developing two platonic romances (aristocratic Loretta Young and plebeian Annabella) while waffling the international issues delaying the canal's completion. A-II (br)

Sugar Hill (1974) Ludicrous horror film about a black woman (Marki Bey) who uses voodoo to summon a horde of moss-covered, chrome-eyed zombies to hack to pieces the murderers of her husband. The hacking is bloody enough to be sure, but Paul Maslansky's direction, not to mention the dialogue, the makeup, and the acting, is so inept that the entire effort comes off as something of a caricature. A-III (PG)

Sugar Hill (1994) Wanting to begin an honest life down South with his love (Theresa Randle), a Harlem drug-dealer (Wesley Snipes) vacillates while he and his volatile brother-partner (Michael Wright) get trapped in a deadly drug turf-war with tragic consequences for his family. Underlying director Leon Ichaso's often violent melodrama is a powerful anti-drugs-and-guns message, which comes through in the movie's anguished portrait of families destroyed by the scourge of crime and addiction. Intermittent intense violence, some harrowing scenes of drug use, and much rough language. A-IV (R)

Sugarland Express, The (1974) Young wife (Goldie Hawn) breaks her small-time criminal hubby (William Atherton) out of a Texas jail, helps him steal a state-trooper's car and, with its cop (Michael Saks) as hostage, the unlikely trio pick up a mass following of local lawmen. With the news media reporting the caravan's every turn, public sentiment builds up enough to make the edgy wife-husband team into the stuff of legend, inevitably ending in tragedy. Director Steven Spielberg's fact-based story has the feel of real people with very real needs and flaws, achieved by unusually fine performances from the principals. Much tension and some heavy violence. A-III (PG)

Suicide Club, The (1988) A bored, depressed Long Island heiress (Mariel Hemingway) becomes involved with some equally bored overage yuppies whose costume parties end with terminal card-games, the winner of which must guzzle a fatal dose of sherry. Directed by James Bruce, the story drowns in a sea of angst, artsy cinematography, somber music, and meaningless dialogue. Acceptance of suicide and implications of incest. A-III (R)

Suicide Squadron (see: **Dangerous Moonlight**)

Sullivan's Travels (1942) Wacky comedy about a lightweight Hollywood director (Joel McCrea) who wants to make a serious movie on the struggles of poor people, sets out to research the subject dressed in rags, and winds up on a chain-gang, where he learns the universal value of laughter. While satirically whaling the tar out of Hollywood and its pretensions, writer-director Preston Sturges uses the comic misadventures of the director's sojourn into the real world to demonstrate the refreshing attributes of a good laugh. Some menace and minor romantic complications. A-II (br)

Sullivans, The (1944) Enlisting in the Navy the day after Pearl Harbor, five brothers insist on being assigned to the same ship and die together when it's torpedoed off Guadalcanal in 1942. Director Lloyd Bacon's fact-based dramatization centers on the youth's close-knit, working-class family in Waterloo, Ia., and their loyalty to each other and to country. Simply told with considerable emotional impact, despite wartime flag-waving. A-I (br)

Summer and Smoke (1961) Leaden version of the Tennessee Williams play set in 1916 Mississippi, where a minister's daughter (Geraldine Page) pines for a rakish medical-student (Laurence Harvey) who reforms, then breaks her heart by proposing to another. Directed by Peter Glenville, the glossy production undercuts the story of a lonely woman's romantic yearnings by concentrating on the student's flashy escapades and subsequent reformation, with unconvincingly melodramatic results. Sexual situations and innuendo. A-III (br)

Summer House, The (1993) The wedding preparations of a listless young Englishwoman (Lena Headey) engaged to a pompous cad (David Threlfall) take unexpected turns when a flamboyant friend (Jeanne Moreau) of the bride's mother (Julie Walters) arrives from Egypt and connives to prevent the couple's marriage. Director Waris Hussein's strained comedy revolves around casual adultery and alcohol abuse as means of solving life's problems. Glamorization of promiscuity and drunkenness. O (nr)

Summer Lovers (1982) Given an Aegean holiday as a graduation present, a callow youth (Peter Gallagher) takes his girlfriend (Daryl Hannah) to a picturesque Greek island, where a French archaeologist (Valerie Quennessen) teaches them that threesomes have more fun than couples. Achieving the emotional level of a tourism poster, writer-director Randall Kleiser's movie is an experience in boredom of appeal only to desperate voyeurs. Excessive nudity. O (R)

Summer Of '42 (1971) Sticky little romantic melodrama about three foul-mouthed teens who come of age during the first summer of WW II in a lush Cape Cod setting. Of the three, the focus is on the quiet-but-deep dreamer (Gary Grimes) and his interest in the fetching form of the grief-stricken war-widow (Jennifer O'Neill) who invites him to share her bed. Director Robert Mulligan tries to balance all the nostalgia with a little honesty in depicting the limbo of loneliness and longing between adolescence and manhood but stumbles at the end. Mature theme. A-IV (R/PG)

Summer of '64 (see: **The Girls on the Beach**)

Summer Paradise (1978) Swedish movie about four generations of a family who gather to spend the summer in a comfortable old house in beautiful natural surroundings becomes an intricate study of their relationships, lives, careers, and values. Director Gunnel Lindblom uses her family setting to offer a sharp, passionate but non-doctrinaire critique of modern society, not least of its targets being abortion, mercy killing, and the pill. Unnecessary use of nudity in a manner quite incidental to the movie's themes and development. A-IV (nr)

Summer Place, A (1959) Soap operatics run amok in this tale paralleling the woes of teenage lovers (Sandra Dee and Troy Donahue) with those of their divorced parents (Dorothy McGuire and Richard Egan). Adapted from Sloan Wilson's romantic potboiler by writer-director Delmer Daves, the result is glossy trash relieved only by the natural beauty of the Maine-island setting of the title. Sexual situations and a shallow view of love and marriage. A-III (br)

Summer Rental (1985) Innocuous little comedy, directed by Carl Reiner, about a family's Florida vacation simply doesn't have enough humorous material to be worth the effort. Some fairly vulgar sequences say little about family ties or vacationing. A-II (PG)

Summer School (1987) A gym teacher (Mark Harmon) becomes a reluctant remedial-English instructor whose non-conformist tactics finally produce positive results with a group of impudent teenagers forced to spend their summer in school. The deals which are struck between teacher and student in writer-director Carl Reiner's light comedy address social and sexual issues requiring a mature perspective. A-III (PG-13)

Summer Stock (1950) Pleasant musical comedy in which a farm girl (Judy Garland) reluctantly lets a theatrical troupe (headed by Gene Kelly) use her barn to put on a musical revue, then winds up the show's star. Directed by Charles Walters, there's not much plot, but it's got plenty of music, notably Garland singing "Get Happy" and Kelly building a tap-dance around a squeaky floorboard and some newspaper pages, paced with intermittent comedy from the likes of Eddie Bracken, Phil Silvers, and Marjorie Main. Enjoyable family fare. A-I (br)

Summer Wishes, Winter Dreams (1973) Character study of a woman (Joanne Woodward) whose mother's death initiates a midlife crisis which, despite her understanding husband (Martin Balsam), nearly sweeps her away. Woodward's moving performance reveals the private agony of a lonely, desperate woman who has allowed life to slip past her because of her refusal to deal with its realities but who tries to struggle for a new understanding of self and a renewed need for others. Gilbert Cates's sensitive direction shows an understanding for the subtleties of intimate relationships, their pain, and love. A-III (PG)

Summerdog (1977) Mild little comedy about a family who fall in love with a dog that attaches itself to them on their summer vacation. The problem, happily overcome of course, is how to bring him home when their landlord does not allow pets. There is some lovely photography, but it is a movie for younger and less demanding viewers. A-I (G)

Summertime (1955) Katharine Hepburn plays a spinster on a vacation in Venice who becomes enchanted with a handsome Italian (Rosanno Brazzi), but, when she learns he is married, cuts her vacation short and returns home, a sadder but wiser person. British production directed by David Lean is a classic romantic melodrama, faultlessly told with charming, bittersweet humor and the eye-filling, Renaissance splendor of the city of canals. A-III (br)

Summertime Killer (1973) Formula revenge tale about a young man (Christopher Mitchum) who kidnaps the daughter (Olivia Hussey) of a member of the gang that killed his father and then falls in love with her while being trailed to Lisbon by a crooked cop (Karl Malden). Director Antonio Isasi makes the most of motorcycle chases in the picturesque Portuguese countryside but has much less success with tracking a largely incoherent plot. Amoral characters and situations. A-III (PG)

Summertree (1971) Hollow melodrama about a talented guitarist (Michael Douglas) who, drafted before he can enroll in music school, disillusioned by the woman he loves (Brenda Vaccaro), and prevented by his parents (Jack Warden and Barbara Bel Geddes) from escaping to Canada, becomes another victim of the Vietnam era. Directed by Anthony Newley, the characters and their experiences don't add up, and its unearned sentimentality trivializes a serious subject. Especially soft-headed is a nude love-scene with ludicrous super-impositions of luxuriant vegetation. A-III (PG)

Sun Also Rises, The (1957) Uneven adaptation of the Ernest Hemingway novel about alienated American expatriates in 1922 Paris, where an impotent war-veteran (Tyrone Power) encounters his former love (Ava Gardner), then go off to Spain with her fiancé (Errol Flynn) and his friends (Eddie Albert and Mel Ferrar) to see the running of the bulls. Directed by Henry King, the location photography is an eyeful, but the plodding narrative provides little insight into troubled characters who overindulge variously in drink, cryptic banter, brave gestures, and self-pity. Stylized violence and implied sexual relationships. A-III (br)

Sun Comes Up, The (1949) Sentimental story in which a widowed concert-singer (Jeanette MacDonald) mourns the death of her young son by brooding alone in a backwoods cabin, where her boy's dog, Lassie, attracts an orphaned lad (Claude Jarman, Jr.) greatly in need of a mother's love. Directed by Richard Thorpe from a story by Marjorie Kinnan Rawling, Lassie is as appealing as ever, but what steals the show is the country setting and the wry humor of its homespun characters. Good family fare. A-I (br)

Sun Never Sets, The (1939) Dated Hollywood salute to the British Empire in the story of brothers (Basil Rathbone and Douglas Fairbanks, Jr.) working for the colonial service in an African outpost, where they uncover a plot by a mad scientist (Lionel Atwill) to foment a world war. Director Rowland V. Lee's moldy melodrama offers stiff-upper-lip characters in a feeble plot of flag-waving contrivances. Stylized violence and colonial attitudes. A-II (br)

Sun Valley Serenade (1941) Uneven musical in which a music arranger (John Payne) sponsors a war refugee and winds up being responsible for a grown Norwegian imp (Sonja Henie) who complicates his love life (Lynn Bari) by tagging along when his band is hired by the Idaho mountain resort of the title. Directed by H. Bruce Humberstone, the soggily contrived romance and thin comic-relief (Milton Berle and Joan Davis) are less memorable than the vintage music of Glenn Miller's band ("In the Mood" and "Chattanooga Choo-Choo"), tap-dancing by the Nicholas Brothers, and Henie's ice-skating routines. Silly romantic complications. A-II (br)

Sunburn (1979) Insurance investigator (Charles Grodin) hires a model (Farrah Fawcett) to act as his wife while in Acapulco on a murder-suicide case with a $5 million pay-out. Joined by a retired sleuth (Art Carney), the trio pull off the solution with lots of assistance from scenery, costumes, and sneaky tactics. Directed by Richard C. Sarafian, it's simple escapist fare with well-intentioned bunglers bringing more cunning crooks to justice. A-II (PG)

Sunchaser (1996) Pretentious clunker in which a smug Los Angeles physician (Woody Harrelson) is forced at gunpoint to drive a dying 16-year-old killer (Jon Seda) to Arizona in quest of a cure by a Navaho medicine-man, and, by journey's end, the doctor is himself transformed. Director Michael Cimino's unconvincing attempt to concoct a mythic story of spiritual regeneration out of dreary stereotypes and trite New Age platitudes is annoying in its shallow depiction of characters, motivations, and the social realities of different cultures. Much menace, some brutal violence, and incessant rough language. A-IV (R)

Sunday (1997) Downbeat drama in which an emotionally unstable actress (Lisa Harrow) mistakes a homeless man (David Suchet) for a movie director, takes him home and into her bed, staunchly refusing to accept the truth about his identity as they pass the remainder of the day together. Director Jonathan Nossiter probes the loneliness of two unemployed mid-lifers at a crossroads, but after establishing their genuine desperation the narrative essentially goes nowhere. A bedroom scene, intermittent full frontal nudity, some profanity, and much rough language. A-IV (nr)

Sunday, Bloody Sunday (1971) British stiff-upper-lip triangle between a successful middle-aged physician (Peter Finch), an attractive divorcée (Glenda Jackson), and a young, pleasant, but uncommitted art-designer (Murray Head) whose companionship and affections the two older people knowingly, if regretfully, share. Directed by John Schlesinger, the locale is contemporary London, peopled by middle-class ciphers who live in a world bereft of hope and spiritual freedom. Sensitive, nuanced portrayal of tortured relationships but morally ambiguous in its conclusion. Details of the homosexual relationship are restrained but central to the plot. A-IV (R)

Sunday in the Country (1976) Dull, predictable Canadian movie about a seemingly mild-mannered farmer (Ernest Borgnine) who takes the law into his own hands in brutal fashion. O (R)

Sunday in the Country, A (1985) Warm, insightful French production about a Sunday in the spring of 1912, when an aged artist (Louis Ducreux) in his country home near Paris is visited by his dull son, even duller wife, and their three lively children, then are joined by the painter's unmarried daughter (Sabine Azema), who is the old man's delight. Though nothing out of the ordinary occurs, director Bertrand Tavernier's marvelously discerning study of family relationships probes the bafflements and complexities of human love and ambition. Subtitles. Various levels of enjoyment for all ages. A-I (G)

Sunday Lovers (1981) Failed omnibus movie about the amorous adventures of four middle-aged men in four different countries presented in separate episodes directed by Bryan Forbes, Edouard Molinaro, Dino Risi, and Gene Wilder. The segments range from mediocre to dismal, with Wilder's being the worst. Prolonged nude love-scene. O (R)

Sunday's Children (1994) Beneath a family's seemingly idyllic summer vacation in the Swedish countryside of the 1920s are simmering tensions, especially between an eight-year-old boy (Henrik Linnros) and the volatile minister-father (Thommy Berggren) he both idolizes and fears. Scripted by Ingmar Bergman and directed by his son, Daniel, the autobiographical drama exquisitely captures the fine details of daily life in a bygone era while providing insights about the lifelong effects a parent's behavior can have on his offspring. Subtitles. Familial tensions, some violence, including a suicide, brief nudity, and occasional profanity. A-III (nr)

Sundown (1941) Flag-waving colonial adventure in which the commander (Bruce Cabot) of a British outpost in Kenya's interior gets help from an American hunter (Harry Carey) and an Arab trader's daughter (Gene Tierney) in stopping a Nazi plot to arm a native uprising. Director Henry Hathaway convey the tensions of a remote frontier-post more credibly than the bogus heroism displayed in the big action finish. Stylized violence and African stereotypes. A-II (br)

Sundowners, The (1950) Routine Western directed by George Templeton in which a Texas rancher (Robert Sterling) fights off rustlers with the help of a laughing outlaw (Robert Preston) who proves a bad influence on the rancher's kid-brother (John Barrymore, Jr.). Frontier violence, including several nasty murders. A-II (br)

Sundowners, The (1960) Excellent story about the joys and hardships of an itinerant Australian sheepherder (Robert Mitchum) whose passion for the unencumbered life is in direct conflict with the yearnings of his wife (Deborah Kerr) to settle down. Directed by Fred Zinnemann, the movie's characters and its locale are finely evoked in a story that is part outdoors adventure and part domestic-drama. A-II (br)

Sunflower (1970) Italian tearjerker about a newly married couple (Sophia Loren and Marcello Mastroianni) whose life is disrupted when he is sent to the Russian front during WW II. When he does not return, she journeys to Russia, and finds him married and with a child. Eventually following her back to Milan, he learns she is now in love with someone else. Directed by Vittorio De Sica, the movie is not essentially concerned with such matters as marital commitment and fidelity, and younger adolescents are likely to misunderstand the moral ambiguities of the story's human complications. A-III (G)

Sunnyside (1979) A tough street-fighter (Joey Travolta) wants to stop gang warfare and start a new life. Haphazardly directed by Timothy Galfas, the movie brutalizes viewers with incessant violence. O (R)

Sunny Side Up (1929) Creaky musical romance in which a Long Island swell (Charles Farrell), charmed by a jobless Manhattan lass (Janet Gaynor) at a Fourth of July block party, invites her and her friends back home with him, but she leaves in a huff after being insulted by his posh set, making it all the more difficult for him to win her back. Directed by David Butler, the slow-paced romance is less interesting than its sharply comic contrast between the working poor and the idle rich on the eve of the Depression, though this early talkie didn't help the careers of its two silent-film stars, who prove game non-singers at best. Sexual situations and references. A-III (br)

Sunrise at Campobello (1960) Engaging historical dramatization begins with Franklin Delano Roosevelt (Ralph Bellamy) being struck down by polio in 1921, his unsuccessful struggle to regain the use of his legs, and his decision to return to active politics by nominating Alfred E. Smith at the 1924 Democratic Convention. Scripted by producer Dore Schary from his own play and directed by Vincent J. Donehue, in the film politics take second place to the resilient character of the crippled Roosevelt and the variety of support he receives from the family's inner circle of wife Eleanor (Greer Garson), Franklin's mother (Ann Shoemaker), and political adviser Louis Howe (Hume Cronyn). Fine portrait of a family coping with illness and party politics. A-II (br)

Sunset (1988) Witless, period buddy movie set in 1929 Hollywood, where the unlikely sleuthing team of cowboy-movie star Tom Mix (Bruce Willis) and marshal Wyatt Earp (James Garner) uncover a bundle of dirty linen in the movie capital. In this bomb directed by Blake Edwards, colorful characters meander through a vapid, humorless plot. Several scenes of violence, some profanity, brief nudity, and implied kinky-sex in a brothel. A-III (R)

Sunset Park (1996) A novice high-school basketball coach (Rhea Perlman) struggles to gain respect from her losing inner-city team of hostile players and in the process pushes them to be the best they can be on and off the court. Director Steve Gomer's familiarly uplifting tale of athletic teamwork transforming troubled youth is offset by the coach lying to a judge in court to give a player an alibi. Recurring profanity and crude expressions, minimal rough language, some sexual innuendo, and fleeting violence. A-IV (R)

Sunshine Boys, The (1975) Good screen version of the Neil Simon comedy about an old vaudeville team (George Burns and Walter Matthau), long separated, who are brought together, despite their antagonism, for one last performance. Director Herbert Ross gets an excellent performance from Burns, and though Matthau overacts, there are enough laughs to provide an evening's entertainment. Some rough language. A-III (PG)

Super, The (1991) Shrill comedy concerns a convicted slum-landlord (Joe Pesci) forced to live in the same rat-infested building with his own tenants. Director Rod Daniel ruins an amusing concept with clanky, heavy-handed humor and trite stick figures throughout. Much rough language and some base sexual references. A-III (R)

Super Cops, The (1974) Fact-based story about two New York City detectives, nicknamed Batman (Ron Liebman) and Robin (David Selby), whose turf is a Brooklyn ghetto and its liver-colored tenements, gaudy pimp-dope dealer hangouts, and crime-ridden streets. As directed by Gordon Parks, there is an undeniable vigor in this fast-paced movie and great appeal in its two central figures and solid supporting cast. However, it goes to excess in its graphic violence, coarse street humor, and relentlessly foul language. O (R/PG)

Super Mario Bros. (1993) Frenetic fantasy adventure with two Brooklyn plumbers (Bob Hoskins and John Leguizamo) falling into another dimension, where they rescue a princess (Samantha Mathis) from an evil lizard-king (Dennis Hopper) descended from dinosaurs who plan to conquer Earth. Attempting to capitalize on a popular video-game, Rocky Morton and Annabel Jankel direct a dopey live-action plot of mirthless mayhem and chase sequences whose jazzy special effects only momentarily lift the level of interest. Some menace and comic violence. A-II (PG)

Super Sleuth (1937) Breezy comedy with a wacky movie-detective (Jack Oakie) out to nab a real-life killer (Eduardo Ciannelli), despite interference from an LA cop (Edgar Kennedy) and the studio's savvy publicist (Ann Sothern). Directed by Ben Stoloff, the actors have a lot of fun with a plot that is less a mystery than a Hollywood spoof. Stylized violence and comic menace. A-I (br)

Super Stooges Versus the Wonder Women (1974) Inept Italian adventure fantasy about a band of Amazons who meet their match in a trio of super heroes. Director Al Bradley's low-grade sword-and-sandals action offers inane buffoonery, poorly staged battles, and minor skirmishes, both military and romantic. A-III (PG)

Superargo and the Faceless Giants (1971) Mad doctor (Guy Madison) turns abducted athletes into bankrobbing robots until foiled by Superargo (Ken Wood), retired wrestler and masked mystic, indomitable in crimson bulletproof costume, together with ray-gun and super-car. Directed by Paul Maxwell, it's a throwback to the simple spills and thrills of the old Saturday matinee serials but lacks their corny charm. A-I (G)

Superbeast (1972) Shoestring Philippine horror movie about ape-like mutants resulting from the botched attempts of a mad doctor (Craig Littler) in reconditioning hardened criminals on his jungle river island outside Manila. Director George Schenck botches a plot derived from any number of older, better movies, with his only innovation being the use of some stock medical footage of a cadaver's dissection. A-III (R)

Supercop (1996) Bone-crunching pulp adventure follows a Hong Kong policeman (Jackie Chan) teamed with a mainland Chinese policewoman (Michelle Khan) as they go undercover to nab a top drug-lord (Ken Tsang). Directed by Stanley Tong, the dubbed production revels in the comic-book exploits of its genial, self-deprecating hero in an action fantasy keyed to martial-arts stunt work and special-effects destruction, including a wild chase finale. Tongue-in-cheek fantasy violence. A-III (R)

Superdad (1974) West Coast teenagers have their summer beach-party fun interrupted by a dumb but well-meaning father (Bob Crane) who opposes his daughter's (Kathleen Cody) involvement with a directionless youth (Kurt Russell). Though intended as the usual lightweight Disney family fare, director Vincent McEveety's picture of family life and values is a tasteless mixture of middle-class affluence, alienation, and artificiality. A-II (G)

Superfly (1972) Black exploitation movie about a tough, cool drug-dealer (Ron O'Neal) who is planning one last deal so he can make a killing and get out, but the police (all white) and a New York City commissioner want in. Directed by Gordon Parks, Jr., the super antics of affluent criminals glamorize these fantasy characters as viable, attractive figures to be admired. Excessive violence and sex. O (R)

Superfly T.N.T. (1973) Middling sequel takes the ex-drug dealer (Ron O'Neal, who also directed) from Harlem to Rome, where he pitches in with his special brand of hustling know-how in order to help an emerging West African nation. The role has taken on some fairly human characteristics, but, unfortunately, the change gets lost in the context of a static story offering little but glamorous location photography and mildly violent action. A-III (R)

Supergirl (1984) Superman's cousin (Helen Slater) does battle with a wicked witch, the fate of mankind depending upon the outcome. Faye Dunaway and Brenda Vaccaro are among the nasties in a wooden film directed by Jeannot Szwarc. Restrained attempted-rape scene and some profanity. A-II (PG)

Superman (1978) The Man of Steel (Christopher Reeve) is brought to Earth from the dying planet Krypton, nurtured by the kindhearted Kents, and becomes a reporter in Metropolis, where he meets Lois Lane (Margot Kidder). As Superman, he encounters evil in the person of master criminal Lex Luthor (Gene Hackman) and his cronies (Ned Beatty and Valerie Perrine). Fun-filled comic-book fantasy adventure directed by Richard Donner has some pyrotechnics that may be too intense for the very young. A-II (PG)

Superman II (1981) Exciting, romantic, and often very funny sequel has three nasty villains from Krypton show up to wreak havoc just as Superman (Christopher Reeve) gives up his powers in order to make love to an ordinary mortal (Margot Kidder). Directed by Richard Lester, the special effects, especially the climatic battle between superhero and super-villains above the streets of New York, are very effective. Unfortunately, some of the violence is rather intense and the sympathetic portrayal of premarital sex between the principals makes it inappropriate for youngsters. A-III (PG)

Superman III (1983) Weak sequel which fails to mesh two plots, the first involving the return of Superman (Christopher Reeve) to Smallville for his high-school reunion, and the second concerning a ruthless tycoon (Robert Vaughn) disrupting the world economy with the aid of an incompetent dishwasher-turned-computer-wizard (Richard Pryor). Directed by Richard Lester, it's a muddled, unfocused effort that keeps promising to develop into something entertaining but never quite does. Realistic fight sequence and Superman's bad conduct while under the baleful influence of Kryptonite rule out younger viewers. A-II (PG)

Superman IV: The Quest for Peace (1987) The Man of Steel (Christopher Reeve) battles his evil clone created by Lex Luthor (Gene Hackman) in this even-tempered sequel which features an appearance by Mariel Hemingway as a romantic rival to Lois Lane (Margot Kidder). Director Sidney J. Furie stages a violent conflict which may be too intense for the very young. A-II (PG)

Supernatural (1933) Creaky chiller in which a fake spiritualist (Alan Dinehart) sets out to con an heiress (Carole Lombard), then learns too late she is possessed by the spirit of an executed murderess (Vivienne Osborne). Directed by Victor Halperin, the contrived proceedings are matched by melodramatic performances, though there are some eerie moments along the way. Stylized violence, much menace, and sexual situations. A-III (br)

Superstar: The Life and Times of Andy Warhol (1991) Impressionistic biography of the late pop artist follows his controversial course through the art wars of the 1960s and 1970s to his enjoyment of being recognized in the 1980s as a star personality in his own right. Written, produced, and directed by Chuck Workman, the documentary uses contrasting views of Warhol's family, friends, and associates to further Warhol's reputation as an enigma in the midst of the confusions and contradictions of contemporary American culture. Some references to the promiscuous lifestyles of the period and several flashes of frontal nudity. A-III (nr)

Support Your Local Gunfighter (1971) James Garner plays an ingenuous con-man who tricks a small town divided by rival mine-operators into believing that an innocuous rummy (Jack Elam) is a dangerous gunslinger. Under Burt Kennedy's direction, the amiable Western comedy meanders its way through predictable but amusing plot twists and cliches before reaching its long-overdue happy ending. A-II (G)

Support Your Local Sheriff (1969) Gentle Western spoof set in a lawless boom-town whose leading citizens hire a quiet drifter (James Garner) to be sheriff, and he proceeds to tame the town through a series of clever and non-lethal maneuvers. Garner is past master at this kind of genial characterization, and his performance combines neatly with Burt Kennedy's deft, off-beat direction to make a very solid comedy. Joan Hackett supplies the daffy romantic interest and Walter Brennan, Jack Elam, and Bruce Dern are excellent in support. A-I (G)

Suppose They Gave a War and Nobody Came? (1970) Witless, unfunny slapstick comedy about a skirmish that develops between US military units and the paramilitary units of a town near an Army base somewhere in the Southwest. Viewers should receive Purple Hearts, and director Hy Averback should be court-martialed. Most of the senseless violence is between machines with nary a drop of spilt blood. A-III (PG)

Sure Thing, The (1985) Two college freshmen (John Cusack and Daphne Zuniga) share a ride to California. He's got a date with a "sure thing" and she's going to join her fiancé. What results is mildly amusing. Director Rob Reiner's movie is about romance instead of sex, a refreshing concept for a teenage movie, yet it accepts promiscuity as a way of life for most young people. A comically intended scene involving a sex act occurring in the background further lessens its suitability for youngsters. A-III (PG-13)

Surrender (1987) Old-fashioned romantic comedy updated for the sexually explicit 1980s, with the story of a writer (Michael Caine) who believes all women to be greedy until he finds one (Sally Field) who does not seem interested in whether he has any money. Written and directed by Jerry Belson, it has some sharp satire on contemporary materialism and a few good sight gags, but its matter-of-fact acceptance of extramarital relationships is objectionable. O (PG)

Survive (1976) Poorly made, badly dubbed Mexican movie about a plane crash in the Andes whose survivors are forced to eat the flesh of those who were killed in order to survive until rescued. As directed by Rene Cardona, Jr., the moral issues involved in the situation are beyond the range of this cheap exploitation effort. A-III (R)

Surviving Picasso (1996) Well-crafted dramatization of the personal life of aging artist Pablo Picasso (Anthony Hopkins) as recalled by ex-mistress Francoise Gilot (Natascha McElhone) who became his companion in 1943, bore two of his children, and endured his erratic behavior until leaving him 10 years later over his affair with another woman. Directed by James Ivory, the movie is worth seeing for its evocative visualization of the artist's times and associates, though the story of a failed relationship lacks emotional substance, and the character of Picasso never adds up to more than that of a gifted egoist. Restrained portrayal of love affairs, sexual references, and brief frontal nudity. A-III (R)

Survivors, The (1983) When a young executive (Robin Williams) and the manager of a gas station (Walter Matthau) thwart the holdup of a diner by a robber (Jerry Reed), they spend the rest of the movie trying to survive the crook's relentless pursuit. Director Michael Ritchie's social satire attempts a bit too much, especially in terms of a sagging American economy, but it is nonetheless an often hilarious, consistently entertaining movie. Some adult humor. A-III (R)

Susan Slept Here (1954) Tasteless romantic comedy in which a 17-year-old juvenile delinquent (Debbie Reynolds) spends an unchaperoned Christmas with a cynical screenwriter (Dick Powell) doing research on a story of troubled youth, then complicates his life by falling in love with him. Director Frank Tashlin drags out the contrived situation with over-cute, largely unfunny stabs at humor, including the writer's Oscar (voice of Ken Carpenter) serving as narrator. Much sexual innuendo. A-III (br)

Susannah of the Mounties (1939) Western vehicle for Shirley Temple as an 1880s orphan rescued from a massacred wagon-train by a Royal Canadian Mountie (Randolph Scott) during a time of Blackfoot Indian raids on the Canadian Pacific Railroad. Directed by William A. Seiter, the highlight comes with little Shirley rescuing Scott from being burned at the stake when she points out the traitorous Indian (Victor Jory) behind all the troubles. Frontier violence with phony but well-intended Indian stereotypes. A-I (PG)

Suspect, The (1944) Chilling suspense tale set in 1902 London, where a middle-aged husband (Charles Laughton) stages a fatal "accident" for his shrewish wife (Rosalind Ivan) in order to wed another woman (Ella Raines), then has to kill a blackmailer (Henry Daniell) to keep him from going to the Scotland Yard detective (Stanley C. Ridges) investigating the case. Director Robert Siodmak uses shadowy gas-lit interiors to reflect the inner turmoil of an ordinary man who turns to murder, then is undone by its consequences. Off-screen murders, marital discord, and an abusive alcoholic. A-II (br)

Suspect (1987) Good suspense story of murder and corruption in the nation's capital stars Cher as a public defender who proves her indigent client innocent, with some assistance from a juror (Dennis Quaid) who has a romantic interest in her. Directed by Peter Yates, the center of the movie is the character played extremely well by Cher, who conveys the strength, intelligence, dedication, and appeal of the role. Some graphic violence and a lot of moody tension and menace. A-III (R)

Suspicion (1941) Suspense tale in which a shy Englishwoman (Joan Fontaine) is swept off her feet by a dashing charmer (Cary Grant) then, learning after their marriage of his large debts, comes to fear that he is planning to murder her for the insurance. Director Alfred Hitchcock starts with a sunny love story that grows increasingly sinister as the wife's suspicions deepen until the letdown of a slapdash ending. Mounting tension and menace. A-II (br)

Swamp Thing (1982) Lightweight monster movie in which a botanist on a secret government project is accidentally turned into a superhuman vegetable (Dick Durock), then grows fond of a government agent (Adrienne Barbeau) who keeps getting in his way while battling gunmen sent by a crazed scientist (Louis Jourdan) to find his research records. Writer-director Wes Craven has some fun with the green crime-busting monster but wastes too much time on clumsily staged rough stuff and the tongue-in-cheek villain. Stylized violence, sexual innuendo, and coarse language. A-III (PG)

Swamp Water (1941) Backwoods tale of a Georgia youth (Dana Andrews) who discovers an escaped killer (Walter Brennan) hiding in the Okefenokee Swamp but agrees to be his silent partner in trapping animals and selling their pelts, then falls for the fugitive's daughter (Anne Baxter) and sets out to prove her father was wrongly convicted by finding the real killer. Directed by Jean Renoir, the slow-paced story has interest in its depiction of the genial country setting and its folksy rural characters, though the dramatic action finally heats up as the facts about the past miscarriage of justice come to light and lead to a showdown between the guilty and the innocent in the treacherous backwaters of the great swamp. Stylized violence and romantic complications. A-II (br)

Swan Princess, The (1994) Animated children's tale of a beautiful princess (voice of Michele Nicastro) changed into a swan by an evil sorcerer (voice of Jack Palance), while a valiant prince (voice of Howard McGillin) attempts to find her and break the spell. Directed by Richard Rich, the lovely graphics are animated in the style of Disney's **Beauty and the Beast**, with the heavily romantic story paced by some lighthearted humor supplied by a frog-puffin-turtle trio assisting in the rescue of the bewitched princess. A-I (G)

Swan Princess: Escape from Castle Mountain, The (1997) Animated sequel to the 1994 original continues the story of the fairytale prince and princess (voices of Douglas Sills and Michelle Nicastro) who here are threatened by a villainous wizard after a magic ball containing evil powers which is hidden in their castle. Directed by Richard Rich, there is nothing very imaginative about the story, the cartooning, or the songs, though its fantasy elements will keep young children entertained. A-I (G)

Swappers, The (1970) Pseudo-documentary about affluent middle-class marrieds in Britain who trade mates in sexual games supposedly to heal marital problems or at least provide a thrilling diversion from them. Patent sex exploitation. O (R)

Swarm, The (1978) Air Force General Richard Widmark and scientist Michael Caine try to stop the progress of billions of perturbed killer bees and save the lives of the usual collection of aged and aging actors who assemble for such disaster movies. Since Widmark and Caine spend most of the movie trying to out-shout each other, the bees, not surprisingly, almost prevail. Director Irwin Allen's effort would be silly if it were not so inane. A-II (PG)

Swashbuckler (1976) Witless pirate movie directed by James Goldstone that, in a mistaken attempt to combine tongue-in-cheek action with straight melodrama, is so achingly bad that a competent cast (Robert Shaw, James Earl Jones, Peter Boyle) can do nothing to make it bearable. Some brief nudity. A-III (PG)

Swedish Fly Girls (see: **Christa**)

Sweepings (1933) After the 1871 Chicago Fire, a merchant (Lionel Barrymore) spends his life building a great department store in the Loop, then is sorely disappointed when his spoiled children (William Gargan, Gloria Stuart, George Meeker, and Eric Linden) show no interest in taking over the family enterprise. Directed by John Cromwell, the episodic family saga contrasts the hard-working father with his profligate offspring as well as his own shabby treatment of the loyal assistant (Gregory Ratoff) who helped make the store a success. Stylized violence, drunken excesses, and sexual situations. A-III (br)

Sweet Charity (1969) Overblown screen version of Broadway musical about a dance-hall hostess (Shirley MacLaine) who gets the romantic runaround from a series of guys who try to break her heart of gold. But her spirit is buoyant and there is true love around the corner (John McMartin). Directed by Bob Fosse, it tries so hard it gets tiresome. A-II (G)

Sweet Dreams (1985) Moving and entertaining biography of country-western singer Patsy Cline (Jessica Lange), whose career was cut short in a 1963 plane crash. Director Karel Reisz concentrates on characterization rather than showbiz glitter, and there is some fine acting, but the movie's episodic structure undercuts its dramatic impact. Some vulgar language and vividly displayed passion, loving as well as violent, mark the relationship between the heroine and her husband. A-III (PG-13)

Sweet Hearts Dance (1988) Fairly innocuous slice of romantic Americana set in small-town Vermont tracks the temporary midlife breakdown of a 15-year marriage (Don Johnson and Susan Sarandon) and the efforts of their kids and friends to get them back together. Nice performances, but director Robert Greenwald provides a stronger portrait of male bonding than marriage. Locker-room language, implied infidelity as well as premarital sex, and brief flashes of nudity. A-III (R)

Sweet Hereafter, The (1997) When a rural Canadian town is devastated by a tragic school-bus accident, a big-city lawyer (Ian Holm) arrives to represent those whose children were killed or injured, but his pursuit of the facts in the case comes to divide the community, until the testimony of a teen (Sarah Polly) injured in the accident destroys the basis of the lawyer's suit. Writer-director Atom Egoyan parallels the lawyer's own sense of loss over his drug-addicted daughter with the bereavement of the town's residents and their tangled relationships with their children and each other, as the community struggles to bring closure to their grief. Stylized violence, sexual situations, brief nudity, and occasional rough language. A-III (R)

Sweet Jesus, Preacher Man (1973) Low-budget black exploitation movie about a criminal (Roger E. Mosley) who poses as the new pastor of a small congregation (after incinerating the real clergyman) in order to double-cross a white racketeer. Director Henning Schellerup has a flair for confusing characters and situations in dimly lit scenes. Excessive violence, some explicit sex, and rough language. O (R)

Sweet Liberty (1986) The lighthearted vehicle written and directed by Alan Alda is a disappointingly shallow view of the sexual and professional frustrations of an amiable historian (Alda) whose book is being made into a movie. The comic touches don't override the movie's celebration of permissive casual sex with several partners as an acceptable route to mutual trust and devotion. O (PG)

Sweet Light in a Dark Room (1966) Czechoslovakian drama set in Nazi-occupied Prague, where a student makes an attempt to help a Jewish girl hide from the deportations. Director Jiri Weiss maintains a grim wartime atmosphere, and his two young principals (Dana Smutna and Ivan Mistrik) are credible in a life-and-death situation. A-II (br)

Sweet Lorraine (1987) Young woman (Trini Alvarado) rediscovers family ties and a sense of belonging while working for her grandmother (Maureen Stapleton) during a summer at a resort hotel. Director Steve Gomer mixes nostalgia with delicate romance in a family story marred only by some harsh language in a kitchen scene. A-II (PG-13)

Sweet Nothing (1996) Grim chronicle of the descent of a Wall Street office-worker (Michael Imperioli) into a desperate crack addict and dealer who loses his wife (Mira Sorvino), children, and nearly his life to his addiction. Directed by Gary Winick, the fact-based drama contrasts the addict's rationalization of his drug habit with the reality of its self-destructive effects. Brief violence, fleeting porn-video footage, frequent drug abuse, and much rough language. A-III (R)

Sweet November (1968) Sappy romance about a woman (Sandy Dennis) who is in the habit of changing male roommates each month, and November happens to be Anthony Newley's turn. The reason for living life in joyous monthly installments is because the woman is dying of the standard Hollywood non-disfiguring but incurable disease. Directed by Robert Ellis Miller, there is some gentle humor at work in the script, but the basic theme of the movie is unacceptable, even though given mild treatment. O (br)

Sweet Revenge (1977) Stockard Channing plays a tough teenage car-thief and Sam Waterson is the good-natured lawyer who constantly comes to her rescue only to be rewarded with contempt for his efforts. Director Jerry Schatzberg attempts to carry off a kind of conversion of his heroine at the end of this run-of-the-mill comedy melodrama, but its morality (she sets fire to a valuable car bought with stolen money) is highly ambiguous. A-III (PG)

Sweet Ride, The (1968) Trashy tangled tale having to do with the wasted lives and energies of a pack of Malibu beach-bums (such as Tony Franciosa and Michael Sarrazin) and their assorted girlfriends (most notably, Jacqueline Bisset). Directed by Harvey Hart, its sexual misadventures are not redeemed by one character's sudden moral awakening. O (R)

Sweetie (1990) Surreal, off-kilter Australian drama about two bizarre sisters — one thin, sour, and inhibited (Karen Colston), the other schizophrenic, plump, and insatiable for food, sex, and attention (Genevieve Lemon). Directed by Jane Campion, it's an uncomfortable, unconventional study of adult female-sibling rivalry and the long-standing ties that bind and choke off all that is good and healthy in a family. Scenes of graphic sexuality and psychological breakdown may be disturbing to some, yet the work's unusual artistic and family vision warrants serious attention. Nudity and rough language. A-IV (R)

Swept Away (by an Unusual Destiny in the Blue

Sea of August (1975) Italian satire about a spoiled rich woman (Mariangela Melato) marooned on a deserted island with proletarian brute (Giancarlo Giannini). Directed by Lina Wertmuller, the battle of the sexes between classes gets swept away in some extensive depictions of lovemaking. O (R)

Swept from the Sea (1998) Engrossing drama from Joseph Conrad's story in which a Ukrainian immigrant (Vincent Perez) bound for America in the 1890s is shipwrecked on the rugged English coast of Cornwall, where he courts a lonely servant girl (Rachel Weisz), and they wed to live in blissful isolation from their hostile neighbors, until tragedy strikes. Directed by Beeban Kidron, the British production succeeds as a lyric love-story of two strangers clinging to each other in an alien land, told with feeling for its characters and lushly photographed landscapes, with enough period detail to satisfy even those who ordinarily disdain movie romantics. Some stylized violence, a restrained sexual encounter, an illegitimate birth, and occasional profanity. A-III (PG-13)

Swimmer, The (1968) Adaptation of the John Cheever story about a middle-aged suburbanite (Burt Lancaster) who swims home through the pools of his affluent neighbors, a journey recalling his wasted life. Directed by Frank Perry, the swim is a long one, and the recollections, especially of past affairs, lead to only a banal conclusion. A-III (PG)

Swimming to Cambodia (1987) Moderately interesting monologue written and delivered by actor Spalding Gray, who sits at a desk talking about his personal reflections on life and his profession, mostly centered on what he experienced in Thailand during the filming of **The Killing Fields** (1984). Director Jonathan Demme makes a straightforward record of Gray's stage performance, punctuated by fades, a few film-clips, and a modest variety of camera positions. Some graphic descriptions of Khmer Rouge atrocities in Cambodia, a few sexual references including a brief account of prostitution in Bangkok, and some rough language. A-III (nr)

Swimming with Sharks (1995) Dark comedy about the Hollywood food-chain, as a nasty studio executive (Kevin Spacey) is taken hostage and brutalized by his crazed assistant (Frank Whaley) who's driven to murder when his writer-girlfriend (Michelle Forbes) shows up. Writer-director George Huang uses flashbacks to show the assistant's gradual demoralization by his manic boss, but goes overboard in depicting the man's revenge and ironic aftermath. Some vicious violence, sexual situations, and rough language, as well as profanity. A-IV (R)

Swindle, The (see **Il Bidone**)

Swindle, The (1998) Lightweight Gallic Suspense story of two con-artists at a Swiss resort to fleece a dentist's convention, but when the younger one (Isabelle Huppert) latches onto a gold courier, her cautious partner (Michel Serrault) plays along on a scam that leads to a Caribbean resort and a gang of deadly professionals. Writer-director Claude Chabrol's twisty plot puts his petty thieves out of their league and in fear of their lives in a scam of big-time operators, though the larger question is whether the two are trying to con one another. Subtitles. Stylized violence, criminal activities, and occasional rough language. A-III (nr)

Swing High, Swing Low (1937) Uneven romantic melodrama in which a fun-loving trumpet player (Fred MacMurray) weds a wise-cracking singer (Carole Lombard) while both are stranded in Panama City, then gets a gig in New York, becomes a big hit, and forgets his wife until he hits the skids. Director Mitchell Leisen can't save the sentimental story from turning into a tearjerker, despite high-spirited characters and some very funny situations. Romantic complications. A-II (br)

Swing Kids (1993) The friendship of two music-loving adolescents (Robert Sean Leonard and Christian Bale) in 1939 Hamburg is savagely torn apart when they reluctantly join the Hitler Youth, and one buys into the racist Nazi philosophy. Despite its good intentions, director Thomas Carter's manipulative drama is a thoroughly artificial-looking Hollywood version of anti-Semitism in pre-war Germany. Some stylized violence, racial and ethnic slurs, and an instance of rough language. A-II (PG-13)

Swing Shift (1984) Young housewife (Goldie Hawn) takes a job in an aircraft factory after her husband (Ed Harris) enlists in the Navy at the start of WW II. Making friends with an independent young woman (Christine Lahti), she eventually falls into an affair with a personable young man exempt from service (Kurt Russell). Directed by Jonathan Demme, the flawed but superbly acted and often quite moving movie recaptures the hopes and fears, the aspirations and idealism, of a now-vanished era. Though sympathetic in its depiction of adulterous conduct, it clearly shows that adultery is harmful. Occasional rough language. A-III (PG)

Swing Time (1936) Down-on-his-luck hoofer (Fred Astaire) rides the rails to New York City, teams with a comely dance instructor (Ginger Rogers), and they score as the town's top dancing duo in such numbers as "Waltz in Swing Time" and Astaire's solo showstopper, "Bojangles of Harlem." Director George Stevens keeps the pair's romantic misunderstandings light and lively, gets strong comic relief from Victor Moore and Helen Broderick, and effortlessly stages such songs as "A Fine Romance" and "The Way You Look Tonight." Elegant entertainment for all but the very young. A-I (br)

Swinger, The (1966) Good girl (Ann-Margaret) poses as a bad girl in order to sell some of her stories to a sex magazine. Directed by George Sidney, it is a silly exercise in titillation. O (br)

Swingers (1996) Lame look at the egocentric lives of several young men (Jon Favreau, Vince Vaughn, and Ron Livingston) whose search for work in Hollywood seems limited to party-going and bar-hopping looking for showbiz contacts and available women. Director Doug Liman tries to give a comic tone to the aimless proceedings, but the material is too thin to be amusing, and the characters are too wrapped up in themselves to be interesting. Sexual situations, heavy drinking, and much rough language with some profanity. A-III (R)

Swiss Family Robinson (1960) Good Disney version of the classic adventure about a shipwrecked family (headed by John Mills and Dorothy McGuire) living in a tree-house on a deserted island learning to survive offers an engrossing picture of family devotion and solidarity. Nicely directed by Ken Annakin, much of the fun for children will come from the delightful and inventive conveniences the family builds and their relationships with the island's wildlife including an elephant, turtle, and ostrich. A-I (G)

Swiss Miss (1938) As American boobs selling mousetraps in Switzerland, Stan Laurel and Oliver Hardy provoke some smiles in a bland story about the misunderstandings between a Viennese composer (Walter Woolf King) and his leading singer (Della Lind). Directed by John G. Blystone, the comedy involves Stan and Ollie with an irascible cook, a faithful St. Bernard, a bubbly pipe-organ, and a perplexed gorilla on an Alpine footbridge. A-I (br)

Switch (1991) Murdered by a trio of his enraged ex-lovers, an incorrigible male chauvinist (Perry King) is returned to earth as a female (Ellen Barkin) to mend his ways, or it's hell for him. Writer-director Blake Edwards's one-joke comedy does not sustain the humor beyond obvious, vulgar situations and its contrived, last-minute pro-life message is thoroughly unconvincing. Blatant sexist attitudes, barroom brawls played for laughs, recurring rough language, frequent sexual innuendo, some recreational substance abuse, and brief nudity. O (R)

Switchback (1997) Grim thriller in which a relentless FBI agent (Dennis Quaid) tracks a cunning serial-killer (Danny Glover) who has kidnapped the agent's child while on a cross-country killing spree. Glover's chilling portrayal of an unpredictable psychopath helps compensate for the far-fetched plotting in writer-director Jeb Stuart's somewhat gory tale. Intermittent violence, nude pin-up photos, and occasional profanity. A-III (R)

Switching Channels (1988) Failed adaptation of **The Front Page**, updated to a 1980s TV newsroom, tracks the love-hate relationship between a star newswoman (Kathleen Turner) and her ex-husband boss (Burt Reynolds), with a foppish lover (Christopher Reeve) in the wings. Weak chemistry between lead actors and clumsy direction by Ted Kotcheff. Some rough language. A-II (PG)

Swoon (1992) Bizarre, arty dramatization of the 1924 Leopold-and-Loeb murder case stars Craig Chester and Daniel Schlachet as college students convicted of the thrill-killing of a young Chicago boy. Looking like an extended music video, writer-director Tom Kalin's low-budget movie is more concerned with playing up the homophobic and anti-Semitic prejudices of the 1920s than in offering a balanced or insightful examination of the crime and its consequences. A few discreet homosexual bedroom shots, two off-camera murders, and minimal rough language. A-III (nr)

Sword in the Desert (1949) Small but effective melodrama in which a US sea-captain (Dana Andrews) smuggles a group of refugees into 1947 Palestine, then gets caught up in the Jewish underground's struggle against the British forces controlling the country. Directed by George Sherman, the picture contrasts the idealism of the underground fighters (Jeff Chandler, Stephen McNally, Marta Toren, and Liam Redmond) with the captain's initial cynicism, which by story's end has been transformed in the good will of Christmas Eve on the road to Bethlehem. Stylized violence. A-II (br)

Sword in the Stone, The (1963) Disney cartoon version of the Arthurian legend of a young squire who, with the help of a wizard, becomes the king of England by pulling a sword from a boulder. Directed by Wolfgang Reitherman and featuring the voices of Sebastian Cabot, Karl Swenson, and Rickie Sorenson, the movie is pleasant viewing for children but offers little for older members of the family. A-I (br)

Sylvester (1985) The story of a girl and her horse. Good acting by Melissa Gilbert and Richard Farnsworth as a gruff but lovable trainer, but little else to recommend this cliched tale directed by Tim Hunter. Vulgar language, a graphic near-rape, and implied premarital sex propel the narrative out of its romantic framework. A-III (PG)

Symphony for a Massacre (1965) Low-budget but well-executed French crime story of five thieves trying to figure out which among them is responsible for stealing their loot. Director Jacques Deray works out the seriocomic plot neatly with fine performances from Michel Auclair, Claude Dauphin, and Charles Vanel. Subtitles. Stylized violence and sexual situations. A-III (br)

Synanon (1965) Edmond O'Brien, Chuck Connors, Eartha Kitt, and Richard Conte star in a movie about the work of Synanon House, a haven for the cure of drug addiction near Santa Monica, Calif. Directed by Richard Quine, the movie's problem lies in exploiting too many side stories to the detriment of making understandable the problems with which it deals. A-III (br)

T

T-Men (1947) Gritty tale of Treasury Department agents (Dennis O'Keefe and Alfred Ryder) infiltrating a Los Angeles counterfeiting ring by masquerading as gangsters from Detroit. Directed by Anthony Mann, the story is narrated in semi-documentary style as the undercover agents try to get the goods on hardened criminals (notably Charles McGraw, who kills informer Wallace Ford in a steam bath), with tension mounting from moody visuals and credible plot twists. Stylized violence in realistic underworld situations not for young children. A-I (br)

THX 1138 (1971) In a futuristic underground world, a minor technician named THX 1138 (Robert Duvall) rebels against its sterile, dehumanizing conditions and tries to escape through a maze of electronic devices and guard robots to the unknown outside world. Director George Lucas creates a terrifying technological future out of the materials of today, but it is difficult to empathize with the story's dehumanized characters who have been stripped of all sensitivity and emotion. Though the movie is visually extraordinary and its story has substance, a rather explicit love scene and an extended sequence with a nude dancer limit its audience. A-IV (GP)

TNT Jackson (1975) Standard black exploitation movie directed by Cirio Santiago, with Jeanne Bell as a martial-arts addict. Excessive violence and nudity. O (R)

T.R. Baskin (1971) Bright, ambitious woman from a small Ohio town (Candice Bergen) has a hard time adjusting to life in Chicago, especially creepy blind-dates and swinging-singles places. Among the men who disappoint her is a children's book editor (James Caan). By movie's end the audience will have lost interest in all the contrived nonsense that director Herbert Ross puts his confused heroine through. A-III (GP)

Table for Five (1983) Failed tearjerker in which a divorced husband (Jon Voight) takes his three children on a Mediterranean cruise, during which his ex-wife (Millie Perkins) dies in an accident, and the children's stepfather (Richard Crenna) starts showing up at ports of call demanding custody of the still-unknowing children. Directed by David Seltzer, the sentimental hokum seems interminable. Shipboard romance with a lovely Frenchwoman (Marie-Christine Barrault) is adult fare. A-III (R)

Tail Spin (1939) Routine aviation picture about women pilots competing in the Cleveland Air Show's Powder Puff Race, among whom are a socialite (Constance Bennett) and a waitress (Alice Faye) vying for the same man (Kane Richmond). Directed by Roy Del Ruth, there's some comic relief (Joan Davis) but a lot of bad melodrama, including a crash (Edward Norris) and the suicide of the dead pilot's wife (Nancy Kelly). Romantic triangle and muddled treatment of suicide. A-III (br)

Taipan (1986) Rambling epic soap-opera leaves out the history, drama, and details of the economic exploitation of China during the 1840s, when British traders dominated the opium and tea trades, centering instead on the sexual exploitation of bare-breasted Chinese women. Based on James Clavell's bestseller about a Scotsman (Bryan Brown) who loses, then regains, control of a lucrative Hong Kong trading post, the photography of actual Chinese locales is picturesque, but Daryl Duke's direction is ponderous. Much nudity, sexual activity, and brutality. O (R)

Take, The (1974) Billie Dee Williams stars as a cop who's tough on the mob, but takes money from them on the side in a muddled detective thriller which tries to create a complex environment, where cops and crooks are interchangeable, and money makes the world go 'round. Unfortunately, director Robert Hartford-Davis never bothers to explain the two sides of Williams's character or what the action is really all about, especially why the mob is attacking Paloma, N.M. A-III (PG)

Take a Girl Like You (1970) British production about an innocent young teacher (Hayley Mills) being pursued by her landlord (John Bird) and fellow teacher (Oliver Reed), both nasty, rather than romantic, types. Directed by Jonathan Miller, the heavy-handed melodrama deals in the corrupting influence of swingers and their world of casual sex. O (R)

Take a Hard Ride (1975) Routine Western about a wrangler (Jim Brown), entrusted by his dying boss (Dana Andrews) to bring his widow the money from the sale of a herd, who forms an uncertain alliance with a devil-may-care gambler (Fred Williamson) as various villains pop out of the sagebrush on the way home. Directed by Anthony Dawson, it's bland and harmless, save for a lot of unimaginative chases and gunfights. A-II (PG)

Take a Letter, Darling (1942) Stylish romantic comedy in which a no-nonsense career woman (Rosalind Russell) hires a starving artist (Fred MacMurray) as a male secretary, but their strictly business relationship takes a romantic turn with some amusing help from her woolly business partner (Robert Benchley) and a tobacco millionaire (Macdonald Carey). Director Mitchell Leisen finds heart as well as smiles in the shifting relationship while having some fun along the way with period conventions, gender roles, and the advertising game. Romantic complications. A-II (br)

Take Down (1979) Small-town teacher (Edward Herrmann) becomes the reluctant coach of the high school's game-but-inept wrestling team and has to motivate the one youngster (Lorenzo Lamas) who could boost it to the championship. Though the plot is entirely predictable, director Keith Merrill gives it some heart, and his handling of the young cast makes it fun. Wholesome teen entertainment. A-II (PG)

Take Her, She's Mine (1963) Failed comedy about the silly troubles an inept dad (James Stewart) gets into while trying to protect his college daughter (Sandra Dee) from amorous lads here and in France. Directed by Henry Koster, the generation-gap proceedings are dully contrived and tiresomely executed, with Stewart particularly ill-used as the lame-brained parent whose blundering antics arouse few smiles and less sympathy. Comic violence and tasteless sexual innuendo. A-III (br)

Take It All (1966) French-Canadian production directed by Claude Jutra about an immoral young man's sexual experiences is offensive in its suggestive treatment in spite of its superficial condemnation of the hero. O (br)

Take Me Out to the Ball Game (1949) Genial musical comedy about a turn-of-the-century baseball club whose new owner is a woman (Esther Williams), despite which the team heads for the World Series, until its star shortstop (Gene Kelly) gets sidetracked by a crafty gambler (Edward Arnold). Director Busby Berkeley combines the colorful period setting with some zestful song-and-dance numbers in dressing up a romantic plot pairing Kelly with Williams, and infielder Frank Sinatra with assertive showgirl Betty Garrett. Smoothly contrived, easy-to-take family fare. A-I (br)

Take One False Step (1949) Minor chase-thriller with a New York educator (William Powell) on the run from LA policemen (James Gleason and Sheldon Leonard) certain he's the mystery man in the case of a missing blonde (Shelley Winters). Directed by Chester Erskine, the flabby plot is helped by some bemused humor and interesting turns, including the educator being bitten by a dog he fears has rabies. Some stylized violence and sexual innuendo. A-II (br)

Take the High Ground (1953) Korean War vet (Richard Widmark) proves tough drill-sergeant pushing draftees through 16 grueling weeks of basic training at Fort Bliss, Tx. Director Richard Brooks covers the routine chores of boot camp in pedestrian fashion as the sour sergeant mellows, thanks to a good buddy (Karl Malden) and a girlfriend (Elaine Stewart). Manly posturing and romantic complications. A-II (br)

Take the Money and Run (1969) Woody Allen stars as the world's least-dangerous criminal, botching bank jobs and terrorizing no one but himself. Also directed by Allen, it's an entertaining romp through many fields and styles of humor, one-line witticisms, subtle jokes, and sight gags galore. Some sexual references and a few profanities. A-III (PG)

Taking Care of Business (1990) Tame comedy about an escaped con (James Belushi) who blithely assumes the identity of a stuffy corporate executive (Charles Grodin) after finding his appointment book, credit cards, and keys to an ocean-side mansion. Under Arthur Hiller's direction, the two leads work hard at creating characters likeable enough to overcome the predictable mistaken-identity plot. A brief sexual encounter, a flash of nudity, some slapstick violence, and minimal rough language. A-III (R)

Taking of Pelham One Two Three, The (1974) New York City transit policeman (Walter Matthau) has to outwit a heavily armed band of desperate men (led by Robert Shaw) who have seized control of a subway train and are holding its passengers hostage for ransom. Director Joseph Sergent's rattling-good action movie keeps the mood claustrophobic, the suspense tightly wound, and paced with just the right amount of comic relief. The cast is topnotch, all of whom hit the mark as New York types. The only distraction is its relentlessly crude language which, unlike the subway, never stops. A-III (R)

Taking Off (1971) Uneven satire on the generation gap in suburbia follows the frantic search of parents (Buck Henry and Lynn Carlin) for their teenaged daughter, who they think has run away when, in fact, she has only gone to the big city for a rock-music audition. Directed by Milos Forman, the parents come off worse than the kids, partly because they're older and should know better. It is mostly a series of outrageous burlesques, some riotously funny, others merely outrageous or excessive, such as a strip-poker scene and one with youngsters singing an Elizabethan-style ballad with obscene lyrics. A-IV (R)

Talent for the Game (1991) Well-worn baseball story of a big-league scout (Edward James Olmos) discovering a natural fastball pitcher in the Idaho hinterlands, then fighting to save the untried novice's career when he's put on the mound as a publicity stunt. Directed by Robert M. Young, the story's theme contrasts those who love the sport with the new breed who regard baseball as just another business. Mild treatment of a romantic affair and minimal coarse language. A-III (PG)

Tales from the Crypt (1972) Touring a subterranean burial ground, five sightseers find themselves locked in with the crypt-keeper (Sir Ralph Richardson), who reveals to them the horrible fate that awaits each. Solid British horror movie has a good cast (Peter Cushing, Ian Hendry, Patrick Magee, Nigel Patrick, and Joan Collins) and five fairly intriguing tales which Freddie Francis directs with some verve, a lot of polish, and even restraint in the visuals. A-III (PG)

Tales from the Crypt, Part II (see: **The Vault of Horror**)

Tales from the Crypt Presents Bordello of Blood (1996) Schlocky horror flick in which a cynical private eye (Dennis Miller) stumbles on a funeral home that by night is a brothel whose prostitutes are actually vampires. Producer-director Gilbert Adler's never-ending parade of silicon sirens, crass humor, and bloodied body parts belongs in the video trashbin. Countless gory killings, much nudity, some profanity, and frequent rough language. O (R)

Tales from the Crypt Presents Demon Knight (1995) Trashy horror flick in which a satanic creature (Billy Zane) leads assorted goo-drenched demons on a night-long murderous assault upon the inhabitants of a boarding house, in which a newcomer (William Sadler) guards a sacred relic to keep it from falling into demonic hands which would bring humanity's destruction. Mindless mayhem rules the night in this poorly crafted splatter-movie whose dumb dialogue and phony spiritual mumbo-jumbo are patently pathetic. Intermittent nudity, a bedroom scene, much carnage, and recurring rough language. O (R)

Tales from the Darkside: The Movie (1990) Clunky horror movie in which a boy delays being served up as dinner by diverting the murderous cook (Deborah Harry) with hackneyed stories of death and doom meted out by an avenging mummy, a diabolical black cat, and a lonely monster. Director John Harrison's classy production values and camerawork serve only to dress up an abundance of gory dismemberments and eviscerations. Excessive violence, a sexually promiscuous scene, and some rough language. O (R)

Tales from the Hood (1995) When a trio of inner-city youths go to a funeral home to buy a cache of drugs found by a mortician (Clarence Williams III), he regales them with supernatural tales of vengeance on racist cops, a white-supremacist politician, an African-American guilty of domestic abuse, and a ghetto drug-dealer. Director Rusty Cundieff's feeble exercise in horror spends more time evoking outrage at injustices visited on African-Americans by whites as well as blacks than in trying to create an atmosphere of terror and dread. Excessive violence, occasional profanity, and intermittent rough language. O (R)

Tales of Terror (1962) Uneven trilogy of Edgar Allan Poe stories presents "Morella," in which a dying woman (Maggie Pierce) discovers her dead mother (Lenona Gage) still lives; "The Black Cat," in which a drunken husband (Peter Lorre) walls up his wife (Joyce Jameson) and her lover (Vincent Price); and "The Facts in the Case of M. Valdemer," about a hypnotist (Basil Rathbone) keeping a dying man's brain alive after death. Directed by Roger Corman, the best of the trio is "The Black Cat," though each has the eerie mood of Poe's dark fantasies. Frightening scenes. A-II (br)

Tales That Witness Madness (1973) Failed British terror movie with Donald Pleasance as a psychiatrist explaining four case histories (involving Kim Novak, Peter McEnery, Suzy Kendall, Georgia Brown, and Joan Collins) which in the end boil down to a padded cell for the good doctor. Directed by Freddie Francis, neither the frights nor the occasional nudity are worthy of comment or the viewer's time. A-III (R)

Talk of the Town, The (1942) Egalitarian romantic comedy in which a schoolteacher (Jean Arthur) rents her house to a stuffy legal scholar (Ronald Colman) who discovers a suspected arsonist (Cary Grant) hiding in the attic, then decides to help the fugitive prove his innocence in court. Directed by George Stevens, the comedy has some delicious madcap moments as the teacher finds herself emotionally caught between the two men, but the picture's patriotic themes for WW II audiences have worn less well. Stylized violence and romantic complications. A-II (br)

Talk Radio (1988) Fictional story of a radio talk-show host (Eric Bogosian) who makes his living verbally abusing the lonely, livid, or just plain loony souls who call in nightly to bait him. Directed by Oliver Stone, it is an intense indictment of the irresponsible individuals who often host this type of shock radio and raises questions about providing a forum for off-the-wall listeners. The language of the radio host is explicitly vulgar, involving sexual, racial, and ethnic slurs, and is laced with much profanity. There's also a brief but extremely graphic murder scene. A-IV (R)

Tall Blond Man with One Black Shoe, The (1973) Entertaining French farce about a violinist (Pierre Richard) who becomes the pawn in a struggle between two counterespionage factions for no other reason than that he absentmindedly happens to be wearing an unmatched pair of shoes. Richard's droll performance as a man oblivious to all the assassination attempts surrounding his daily routine is neatly abetted by the comic efforts of Bernard Blier, Jean Rochefort, and Mireille Darc. Director Yves Robert turns in an amusing, at time hilarious, comedy of errors carried off in high style. Some sexual innuendoes. A-III (PG)

Tall Guy, The (1990) Just when a hapless American actor (Jeff Goldblum) becomes the hit of the London stage in a tasteless musical, his budding romance with a starchy English nurse (Emma Thompson) hits the rocks. Director Mel Smith's comedy is an uneven mix of satire and sex farce, sprinkled with amusing moments, thanks in large part to Goldblum's bumbling but sympathetic performance. Comical treatment of promiscuity, occasional brief nudity, and minimal rough language. A-III (R)

Tall Man Riding (1955) Routine Western directed by Lesley Selander in which a cowboy (Randolph Scott) returns to square accounts with a rancher who had wronged him, then steps in to save him and his daughter (Dorothy Malone) from a vicious gang of landgrabbers. Stylized violence and sexual innuendo. A-II (br)

Tall Men, The (1955) Overblown Western in which an ex-Reb (Clark Gable) and his nasty brother (Cameron Mitchell) join a rancher (Robert Ryan) on a cattle drive from Texas to Montana during which they battle blizzards, Sioux attacks, and misunderstandings over a woman (Jane Russell) rescued along the way. Directed by Raoul Walsh, the formula story bogs down in cliched action and stereotyped characters, with unsurprising results. Frontier violence and sexual situations. A-III (br)

Tall Story (1960) Romantic fluff from the Howard Lindsay-Russel Crouse play in which a serious-minded college-basketball star (Anthony Perkins) proves no match for a conniving, marriage-minded co-ed (Jane Fonda). Produced and directed by Joshua

Logan, the thin proceedings generate few laughs in poking fun at college athletics, hypocritical academics, and students' raging hormones. Sexual situations and innuendo. A-III (br)

Tall Stranger, The (1957) Murky Western directed by Thomas Carr, in which a Union officer (Joel McCrea) returning home after the Civil War is saved from a bushwhacker (Michael Ansara) by a wagon-train of settlers, whom he in turn saves from being massacred in a war between a Colorado cattle-baron and a ruthless band of rustlers. Shootouts, fistfights, a woman fighting off an attacker, and an endangered child. A-II (br)

Tall T, The (1957) Credible Western in which a cowboy (Randolph Scott) foils the plans of ruthless stagecoach bandits (Richard Boone, Henry Silva, and Skip Homeier) to ransom a mine-owner's daughter (Maureen O'Sullivan). Director Budd Boetticher establishes the murderous nature of the bandits early on, then builds the tension while waiting for the ransom, until the cowboy takes on the trio in the final shootout. Stylized violence and menace. A-II (br)

Tall Tale: The Unbelievable Adventures of Pecos Bill (1995) Largely unimaginative fantasy-adventure set the West of 1905, where a 12-year-old boy (Nick Stahl) conjures up a trio of legendary folk-heroes (Patrick Swayze, Oliver Platt, and Roger Aaron Brown) to save the family farm from villainous land-grabbers. Director Jeremiah Chechik's scenic yarn features trite preachments about family values, although the narrative often resorts to brawn and bullets to solve problems. Frequent stylized violence and fleeting sexual innuendo. A-II (PG)

Tall Target, The (1951) Engrossing thriller set in 1861 aboard a Washington-bound train, as New York City detective John Kennedy (Dick Powell) tries to thwart an assassination plot to kill president-elect Lincoln. Director Anthony Mann keeps the suspense tight and the period details add interest, but the ending is a bit of a letdown. Stylized violence. A-I (br)

Tall Women, The (1967) Spanish Western directed by Sidney Pink about a wagon train of women facing hostile Indians on the wild frontier has excessive violence and sexual innuendo. O (br)

Tam Lin (1971) Domineering, aging millionaire (Ava Gardner), living on a sinister Scottish estate with a coven of coed decadents, keeps her current paramour (Ian McShane) in line by showing him a few grisly snapshots of what happened to past lovers whose attentions wandered. Hothouse melodrama is best summed up as a soggy misfire by novice director Roddy McDowall. A-III (GP)

Tamarind Seed, The (1974) Russian spy (Omar Sharif) falls in love with a secretary in the British Foreign Office (Julie Andrews), and their romance becomes hopelessly entangled in international intrigue. Directed by Blake Edwards, its fine cast and gorgeous location photography are wasted by a script that misses both as love story and as spy thriller. A-III (PG)

Taming of the Shrew, The (1967) Sparkling but noisy adaptation of the Shakespeare play, with bravura performances by Elizabeth Taylor as the comely shrew and Richard Burton as the rowdy tamer. Director Franco Zeffirelli's inventive staging preserves the flavor of the original but never seems firmly in control of the action or the actors. Mature treatment. A-III (br)

Tammy and the Bachelor (1957) Sappy romantic comedy in which the innocent teenager of the title (Debbie Reynolds), raised by her grandfather (Walter Brennan) in a bayou backwater, knocks the socks off the scion (Leslie Nielsen) of a once-wealthy family. Directed by Joseph Pevney, the silly situation and insufferable homespun wisdom of the heroine were stale then and haven't gotten any fresher since. Sugary confection not for all tastes. A-I (br)

Tammy and the Doctor (1963) The third outing of the homespun lass from the Mississippi bayous sees Tammy (Sandra Dee) as a nurse's aide spreading her country wisdom among the staff (Peter Fonda, Macdonald Carey, and Margaret Lindsay) and patients (Beulah Bondi and Reginald Owen) of a Los Angeles hospital. Directed by Harry Keller, the hokey script offers bland situations and plenty of bogus sentimentality, though youngsters may be amused by the silly goings-on. A-I (br)

Tammy Tell Me True (1961) This time around Tammy (Sandra Dee) hikes across the swamp to enroll in a nearby college, where she helps a rich old lady (Beulah Bondi), saves the marriage of a dean (Virginia Grey), and snags a bemused professor (John Gavin). Director Harry Keller's sugary concoction of contrived situations mistakes the virtue of simplicity for the bane of banality. Bland family fare. A-I (br)

Tampico (1944) Minor WW II espionage thriller in which the captain (Edward G. Robinson) of an oil-tanker marries a survivor (Lynn Bari) of a torpedoed ship, then suspects she's a Nazi agent. Directed by Lothar Mendes, there's little action, and the identity of the traitor is wildly implausible. Wartime violence. A-II (br)

Tampopo (1987) Wry Japanese satire in which a young widow's unsuccessful noodle business is transformed by a burly truck-driver is laced with comic asides relating food to passion, commerce, and art. Director Juzo Itami's droll, earthy farce has several sexually suggestive scenes, one with partial nudity, which mars the basically innocent appeal of the story. A-III (nr)

Tanganyika (1954) Far-fetched adventure directed by Andre de Toth is set in 1903 British East Africa, where an American timber-contractor (Van Heflin) goes after an escaped killer (Jeff Morrow) who's behind a native revolt, but the manhunt is slowed in rescuing a wounded traveler (Howard Duff) and the survivors of a massacre (Ruth Roman and two children). Stylized violence. A-I (br)

Tango & Cash (1989) Ultra-violent super-cop saga

featuring an unlikely pair of Los Angeles detectives (Sylvester Stallone and Kurt Russell) who dislike each other's style but wind up working together to nail the criminal mastermind (Jack Palance) behind their being framed for murder. Directed by Andrei Konchalovsky, the result is a sophomoric exercise in rock 'em-sock 'em macho violence and bloodletting. Excessive violence, insulting sexual references, rough language. O (R)

Tango Bar (1989) Beautifully filmed and choreographed anthology of tango dancing set in Argentina and framed by the personal and political musings of a fictional trio of cabaret performers (Raul Julia, Ruben Juarez, and Valeria Lynch). Keeping the love triangle and repressive politics in the background, Puerto Rican director Marcos Zurinaga concentrates on the trio's songs and monologues about the history and evolution of the tango, as well as staging some breathtaking tango numbers plus clips of tango dancing from Hollywood and foreign movies. Subtitles. Implied sexual relationships. A-III (nr)

Tank (1984) Career Army sergeant uses a Sherman tank to rescue his unjustly arrested son from a vicious southern sheriff (G.D. Spradlin) and then heads for the state line, stirring the sympathy of the nation. Audience reaction to director Marvin Chomsky's movie is likely to be much less spectacular, because after the breakout, the story becomes increasingly silly and unentertaining. Some violence and rough language. A-III (PG)

Tank Force (1958) WW II clunker directed by Terence Young is set in the Libyan Desert, where some captured Australian soldiers (notably Victor Mature, Leo Genn, and Anthony Newley) make their escape, then are recaptured by pro-German Arab nomads, only to escape again. The wartime violence makes it unlikely children's fare. A-I (br)

Tap (1989) An entertaining look at the redemption of a talented tap-dancer (Gregory Hines) who took a wrong turn and must choose between a potentially low-paying, rewarding career as a dancer and a lucrative life of crime. Writer-director Nick Castle creates a respectful tribute to this American art-form and is especially mindful of tap's black roots. A lusty kissing scene, brief heavily shadowed nudity within a fleeting sexual encounter, and some locker-room language. A-III (PG-13)

Taps (1981) High-minded teenage cadets take control of a military boarding-school when they learn the authorities are going to close it. George C. Scott does his usual fine job as the officer who inspires the boys to make their stand, and Timothy Hutton is good as the insurgent leader. Directed by Harold Becker, the rather implausible youth-in-revolt drama fails to make its story of courage and leadership very credible. Some violence and coarse language. A-II (PG)

Tarantula (1955) Effective monster fantasy in which a scientist (Leo G. Carroll) experimenting on a growth nutrient becomes grotesquely disfigured, then dies, while a spider injected with the nutrient escapes into the Arizona desert, grows bigger than a house, and heads for town, until stopped by the local doctor (John Agar) and some jet-fighters. Director Jack Arnold gets plenty of menace from the low-budget production, though the scientific experiments at the beginning are more frightening than the rampages of the special-effects monster. Stylized violence and menacing situations. A-I (br)

Target (1985) A middle-aged father (Gene Hackman) gains the admiration of his son (Matt Dillon) when his wife (Gayle Hunnicutt) is kidnapped on a European trip, and dull old Dad, who has a secret CIA past, becomes transformed into a super-agent as the two attempt to find Mom. Directed by Arthur Penn, but so preposterous that it skirts parody in spots, it is, nonetheless, entertaining fantasy fare, especially for fathers weary of feeling like Rodney Dangerfield. A bit of rough language and some violence. A-II (R)

Target Unknown (1951) Standard WW II tale of a 1944 B-26 bomber crew (led by Mark Stevens), whose German captors (led by Robert Douglas) use devious means to learn of an upcoming raid. Directed by George Sherman, the cat-and-mouse game between German interrogators and US airmen holds interest, until the Americans escape in a melodramatic attempt to use the French underground to contact their airbase and stop the raid. Wartime violence. A-I (br)

Target Zero (1955) Contrived Korean War story in which a US infantry patrol (led by Richard Conte) comes across a nurse (Peggy Castle) as well as a British tank while fighting their way back through enemy lines. Director Harmon Jones plods through an unconvincing plot whose wartime heroics aren't helped much by pretentious dialogue and an improbable romance. Battlefield violence. A-I (br)

Targets (1968) Modest crime thriller concerning a psychopathic killer (Tim O'Kelly), on the loose with an arsenal of weapons, and a retired movie actor (Boris Karloff), who confront each other in a drive-in movie theater. Written and directed by Peter Bogdanovich, the contrast between the horror of reality and that of fantasy don't quite come off, partly because Karloff in his few scenes steals the film. Some stylized violence but no insights. A-III (R/PG)

Tartu (see: **The Adventures of Tartu**)

Tarzan (1999) Ferocious animated tale about an orphaned human baby raised by a jungle gorilla (voice of Glenn Close) who as an adult (voice of Tony Goldywn) encounters his first humans, including a duplicitous hunter (voice of Brian Blessed) intent on capturing his beloved ape family, and spunky Jane (voice of Minnie Driver), who tempts Tarzan to return to civilization. Based on Edgar Rice Burrough's characters dating back to 1912, the animation by directors Kevin Lima and Chris Buck is accomplished, and the characters appealing, but several fast-paced action scenes of predatory violence are too intense for younger children. Intensely menacing hunting scenes. A-II (G)

Tarzan and His Mate (1934) Dandy sequel to 1932's **Tarzan, the Ape Man** concerns the return of the safari guide (Neil Hamilton) to the African escarpment hoping to bring Jane (Maureen O'Sullivan) back to civilization, though his partner (Paul Kavanagh) wants only the ivory in the elephant's graveyard and shoots Tarzan (Johnny Weissmuller) to get it. Directed by Cedric Gibbons, the jungle adventure features battles with fierce native tribes, animals ranging from friendly to murderous, and the contentment of the loving couple in their primitive paradise. Stylized violence, incidental nudity, sexual innuendo, and African stereotyping. A-III (br)

Tarzan and the Amazons (1945) Thin jungle adventure directed by Kurt Neumann in which Boy (Johnny Sheffield) guides an archaeologist (Henry Stephenson) to a lost city of women warriors, whose priestess (Maria Ouspenskaya) spares their lives, then greedy expedition members (Barton MacLane and J.M. Kerrigan) loot the city, until Tarzan (Johnny Weissmuller) comes to the rescue. Stylized violence. A-I (br)

Tarzan and the Great River (1967) Tarzan (Mike Henry) journeys to the upper reaches of the Amazon to put a halt to some occult goings-on by a tribe of headhunting terrorists. Directed by Robert Day, it's an exciting enough adventure, if all-too-familiar for older members of the family. A-I (G)

Tarzan and the Green Goddess (1938) Slapdash feature version of a serial directed by Edward Kull with Tarzan (Herman Brix, aka Bruce Bennett) in the jungles of Guatemala trying to recover a sacred Mayan idol in which is hidden the formula for a super-explosive. Hokey stylized violence. A-I (br)

Tarzan and the Huntress (1947) Formula jungle adventure directed by Kurt Neumann in which Tarzan (Johnny Weissmuller) saves Jane (Brenda Joyce) and Boy (Johnny Sheffield) from the murderous guide (Barton MacLane) of a zoological expedition that has far exceeded its agreed quota of animal specimens. Stylized violence and mild sexual innuendo. A-II (br)

Tarzan and the Jungle Boy (1968) Newspaperwoman comes looking for a youngster lost years before in the jungle and runs into a slew of obstacles, including some unfriendly natives (led by Rafter Johnson). Tarzan (Mike Henry) flexes his muscles and puts everything right in director Robert Day's routine adventure. A-I (G)

Tarzan and the Leopard Woman (1946) Formula jungle adventure directed by Kurt Neumann in which Tarzan (Johnny Weissmuller), Jane (Brenda Joyce) and Boy (Johnny Sheffield) are taken captive by a murderous leopard-cult led by a woman (Acquanetta) fighting colonial rule, with Cheetah coming to the rescue for a Samson-like finale. Stylized violence and threatening situations. A-II (br)

Tarzan and the Lost City (1998) Lackluster tale teams the Ape Man (Casper Van Dien) with his fiancé (Jane March) as they help a jungle tribe prevent a band of mercenaries from plundering their sacred treasures. Directed by Carl Schenkel, the tame, humorless movie has little sense of adventure but plenty of beefcake shots of the title actor. Sporadic stylized violence. A-II (PG)

Tarzan and the Lost Safari (1957) Standard jungle adventure directed by Bruce Humberstone has Tarzan (Gordon Scott) save the five occupants of a downed airplane from being turned over to a hostile tribe by a greedy hunter (Robert Beatty). Stylized violence. A-I (br)

Tarzan and the Mermaids (1948) Exotic adventure directed by Robert Florey in which Johnny Weissmuller makes his 12th and final appearance as Tarzan, this time rescuing a woman (Linda Christian) from the high priest (George Zucco) of a bogus god worshiped by her island people, until the Ape Man reveals their "god" is only a greedy mortal after their pearls. Stylized violence. A-I (br)

Tarzan and the She-Devil (1953) Formula jungle adventure directed by Kurt Neumann with Tarzan (Lex Barker) saving Jane (Joyce MacKenzie) and a herd of elephants from nasty ivory poachers (Raymond Burr, Tom Conway, and Monique Van Vooren). Stylized violence. A-I (br)

Tarzan and the Slave Girl (1950) Hokey jungle adventure directed by Lee Sholem in which Tarzan (Lex Barker) tracks some kidnapped women to a hidden city, where he frees the captives while saving Jane (Vanessa Brown) and a jungle nurse (Denise Darcel) from being entombed alive, then helps a doctor (Arthur Shields) cure the city of a deadly disease. Stylized violence and brutality. A-II (br)

Tarzan and the Trappers (1958) Pulp adventure directed by Charles Haas and Sandy Howard in which Tarzan (Gordon Scott) captures a poacher, then thwarts a greedy group of treasure hunters seeking a lost city. Comic-book heroics with hokey violence. A-I (br)

Tarzan and the Valley of Gold (1966) Standard jungle adventure directed by Robert Day with Tarzan (Mike Henry) getting involved with some spies. A-I (br)

Tarzan Escapes (1936) Familiar African adventure in which Jane (Maureen O'Sullivan) is visited by London cousins, who want her to return with them just long enough to collect her inheritance, but their guide (John Buckler) is more interested in capturing Tarzan and selling him as a sideshow attraction. Directed by Richard Thorpe, a number of previous encounters with animals and native tribes are reused here with the new story-line woven around them with agreeable results. Stylized violence. A-I (br)

Tarzan Finds a Son! (1939) Enjoyable adventure in which Tarzan (Johnny Weissmuller) and Jane (Maureen O'Sullivan) rescue a baby boy from a crashed airplane, then five years later have to save him (Johnnie Sheffield) from greedy relatives (Ian Hunter and Frieda Inescort) after his inheritance. Director Richard Thorpe paces the sunny scenes of happy jungle life with the harsh realities of the wild and the deceit of civilized outsiders. Stylized violence and menacing situations. A-I (br)

Tarzan Goes to India (1962) Formula adventure featuring picturesque Indian locales, where Tarzan (Jock Mahoney) befriends an orphaned boy, then uses the lad's elephant to lead a herd of rogue elephants through a mountain pass, before they are drowned by the opening of a new dam. Directed by John Guillermin, the pedestrian plot has scant interest save for the scenery and the thundering herd of elephants. Some stylized violence. A-I (br)

Tarzan the Ape Man (1959) Director Joseph M. Newman's flat remake of the 1932 original features a lethargic performance by Dennis Miller in the title role and an anemic portrayal of Jane by Johanna Barnes. Stale wildlife adventure. A-I (br)

Tarzan, the Ape Man (1981) Embarrassingly inept version of the jungle hero's adventures, with Miles O'Keeffe in the title role, Bo Derek in various stages of undress, and the ape in the cast the only character to emerge with any dignity from a debacle directed by John Derek. O (R)

Tarzan the Fearless (1933) Feature version of a serial directed by Robert F. Hill in which a woman (Jacqueline Wells) on a safari to find her missing father is saved from Arab slavers by Tarzan (Buster Crabbe), who then rescues her father from a vengeful priest (Mischa Auer) guarding the statue of an Egyptian god whose fingers are embedded with priceless emeralds. Stylized violence and sexual innuendo. A-II (br)

Tarzan the Magnificent (1960) Standard action adventure directed by Robert Day in which Tarzan (Gordon Scott) captures a killer (Jock Mahoney) in the jungles of Kenya, and, despite ambushes by his murderous father (John Carradine) and three brothers, takes him and some stranded travelers (notably Lionel Jeffries, Betta St. John, and Alexandra Stewart) to the nearest police post. Stylized violence, some of it quite nasty. A-II (br)

Tarzan Triumphs (1943) WW II adventure in which Tarzan (Johnny Weissmuller) and Boy (Johnny Sheffield) help a woman (Frances Gifford) free her jungle village from Nazi paratroopers after oil and jewels. Directed by William Thiele, Tarzan kills a number of paratroopers without resorting to firearms, though Boy shoots one with a pistol, and Cheetah uses a machine gun to get another. Stylized violence, including Nazi brutality. A-I (br)

Tarzan's Deadly Silence (1970) The Ape Man (Ron Ely), despite being temporarily deafened by an explosion, saves a native tribe from the exploitation of a megalomaniac trying to set up a jungle empire. Directed by Robert L. Friend, it's the usual wilderness adventure, though fans may be disappointed that there is no Jane and no blood-curdling jungle call. Directed by Robert L. Friend. A-I (G)

Tarzan's Desert Mystery (1943) Routine adventure in which Tarzan (Johnny Weissmuller) and Boy (Johnny Sheffield) save a woman magician (Nancy Kelly) from Nazi agents (Otto Kruger and Joe Sawyer), avert a war between desert tribes, and fight off a giant spider, while gathering medicinal plants requested by Jane, now an Army nurse. Directed by William Thiele, the contrived proceedings plod along rather aimlessly until the predictable ending. A-I (br)

Tarzan's Fight for Life (1958) Formula jungle adventure directed by Bruce Humberstone with Tarzan (Gordon Scott) helping a dedicated white doctor save his bush hospital from a tribal witch doctor (James Edwards) and a renegade band of warriors (led by Woody Strode). Stylized violence. A-I (br)

Tarzan's Greatest Adventure (1959) Routine action adventure filmed in Africa with an articulate Tarzan (Gordon Scott) tracking a band of killers (Anthony Quayle, Niall MacGinnis, and Sean Connery) on their way to a hidden diamond mine. Directed by John Guillermin, the proceedings are rather sluggish, until the action heats up in a fairly nasty showdown. Stylized violence and psychopathic criminals. A-II (br)

Tarzan's Hidden Jungle (1955) Standard adventure directed by Harold Schuster with Tarzan (Gordon Scott) saving a UN doctor (Peter Van Eyck) and his nurse (Vera Miles) from an unfriendly tribe (headed by Rex Ingram) stirred up by murderous poachers (led by Jack Elam). Stylized violence and mild sexual innuendo. A-II (br)

Tarzan's Jungle Rebellion (1970) Archaeologist (Sam Jaffe) searching for a lost civilization, a native looking for a sacred statue to establish his rule over the jungle, and a group simply after gold come up against the lord of the jungle (Ron Ely). Director William Whitney follows the formula without much conviction. A-I (G)

Tarzan's Magic Fountain (1949) Fanciful jungle adventure directed by Lee Sholem in which Tarzan (Lex Barker) tries to keep greedy outsiders (Albert Dekker and Charles Drake) from finding a hidden mountain city, whose waters restore youth and heal the sick, though Jane (Brenda Joyce) complicates matters by trying to guide an aviatrix (Evelyn Ankers) and her husband (Alan Napier) there. Stylized violence. A-I (br)

Tarzan's New York Adventure (1942) Enterprising series entry with Tarzan (Johnny Weissmuller), Jane (Maureen O'Sullivan), and Chita off to New York to find Boy (Johnny Sheffield) after he's abducted from the escarpment to perform in a circus. Directed by Richard Thorpe, Tarzan takes civilization in stride as he climbs down a skyscraper's exterior, dives off the Brooklyn Bridge, and leads a troop of circus elephants to the rescue. Menacing situations. A-I (br)

Tarzan's Peril (1951) Routine jungle adventure in which Tarzan (Lex Barker) rescues an African queen (Dorothy Dandridge) and her people from a warring tribe, then hunts down the villain (George Macready) who sold them rifles and has taken Jane (Virginia Huston) hostage. Directed by Byron Haskin, the movie drags between action sequences, though

Barker's Tarzan is a rather personable fellow. Stylized violence. A-I (br)

Tarzan's Revenge (1938) Routine jungle adventure with Tarzan (Glenn Morris) rescuing a woman (Eleanor Holm) on safari with her parents (George Barbier and Hedda Hopper) from an Arab prince (C. Henry Gordon) who has paid the safari guide (Joe Sawyer) to kidnap her. Directed by D. Ross Lederman, the situations are more humorous than dangerous, though there's a tense battle on a rope bridge across a chasm, and by movie's end Tarzan has found a mate. Some stylized violence. A-I (br)

Tarzan's Savage Fury (1952) Formula jungle adventure directed by Cyril Endfield in which Jane (Dorothy Hart) persuades Tarzan (Lex Barker) to guide a thief (Patric Knowles) posing as his cousin, Lord Greystoke, across the desert to the land of a fierce tribe rich in diamonds. Stylized violence. A-I (br)

Tarzan's Secret Treasure (1941) Routine jungle adventure directed by Richard Thorpe in which Tarzan (Johnny Weissmuller) has to save Jane (Maureen O'Sullivan) and Boy (Johnny Sheffield) after they're kidnapped by a ruthless gold hunter (Tom Conway), then captured by a savage tribe. Stylized violence. A-I (br)

Tarzan's Three Challenges (1963) Exotic adventure with Tarzan (Jock Mahoney), leaving Africa for Thailand, where he saves the young boy chosen by Buddhist monks to be the country's spiritual leader from being killed by the king's wicked brother (Woody Strode). Directed by Robert Day, the Thai locales are a welcome change to the usual jungle setting, though the action remains much the same. Stylized violence. A-I (br)

Task Force (1949) On the eve of his retirement, an admiral (Gary Cooper) recalls his part in the struggle after WW I to prove to the Navy the importance of aircraft carriers, his marriage to a fellow pilot's widow (Jane Wyatt), and his role in the battles of Midway and Okinawa. Written and directed by Delmer Daves, the personal story is most interesting in the early years of carrier development, then gets lost in the WW II battle-scenes. Wartime violence and patriotic sloganeering. A-I (br)

Taste the Black Earth (1971) Polish dramatization of the 1920 uprising against the Germans occupying the coal-mining region of Silesia is shown through the eyes of a young lad who refuses to let his six older brothers go to battle without him. Written and directed by Kazimierz Kutz, the movie is less a historical narrative than a patriotic ballad told with great feeling, much visual poetry, and emphasis on the absurdities of civilians pitted against soldiers. A-II (nr)

Taste the Blood of Dracula (1970) Disappointing British horror movie wastes its first half on a ridiculous club dabbling in sex and Satanism, while the remainder is routine-to-inferior vampire lore in which Dracula (Christopher Lee) has only one big scene. Directed by Peter Sasdy, it offers only some slack suspense and almost no psychological terror. A-III (PG)

Tatie Danielle (1991) Wickedly dark comedy about a sly 82-year-old widow (Tsilla Chelton) who moves in with her nephew's family and proceeds to make their lives miserable while appearing to be frail and helpless. French production directed by Etienne Chatiliez deftly blends wit and satire while questioning preconceptions about the elderly and skewering adults who patronize them. Subtitles. Occasional sexual innuendo, brief bedroom shot of a married couple, and a few vulgar expressions. A-III (PG-13)

Tattered Dress, The (1957) Melodramatic clunker directed by Jack Arnold, in which a top New York lawyer (Jeff Chandler) is charged by a vengeful Nevada cop (Jack Carson) with bribing a juror (Gail Russell) in a local murder case, with the outcome reuniting lawyer and estranged wife (Jeanne Crain). Some stylized violence and heavy sexual innuendo. A-III (br)

Tattoo (1981) Bruce Dern plays a man obsessed with the mystique of tattooing who kidnaps model Maud Adams and proceeds to decorate her body with the fervor of a graffiti artist embroidering his own subway car, until the contrived plot suddenly turns perverted hero into expert lover. Directed by Bob Brooks, the dreary, pretentious story lacks any credible sense of logic. Some nudity and graphic sexuality. O (R)

Tattooed Swordswoman, The (1974) Japanese *Yakuza* (gangster) movie about an imprisoned woman's dream, which after her release comes back to haunt her. Director Teyuo Ishii's effort has more of interest than the usual spectacular swordplay, because it vividly incorporates elements of supernatural horror within its traditional revenge plot. A-III (nr)

Taxi Blues (1991) Set in present-day Moscow, an embittered cabdriver (Pyotr Zaichenko) reluctantly befriends a self-destructive Jewish saxophone player (Pyotr Mamonov) whose alcoholism causes continual crises. Writer-director Pavel Longuine's character study of two vastly divergent personalities touches on class conflicts, alienation, and anti-Semitism in Russia's troubled society with compassion, rude humor, and unaccustomed frankness. Subtitles. Brief scene of fairly graphic sexual relations, partial nudity, minimal violence, and vulgar expressions. A-IV (nr)

Taxi Driver (1976) Disturbing portrait of a troubled New York cabby (Robert De Niro), apparently traumatized by service in Vietnam, lost in his macho fantasies and infatuated with a political worker (Cybill Shepherd), whose rejection triggers his suppressed rage into an orgy of killings. Director Martin Scorsese's excursion into urban alienation and irrational violence lacks a distancing objectivity, and its attempts to shock are excessively graphic in scenes of bloodshed. O (R)

Taxing Woman, A (1988) A woman tax-collector (Nobuko Miyamoto) faces her biggest case in trying to crack the sleazy operation of an adult-hotel scion (Tsutomu Yamazaki), which leads to various comical interactions. Director Juzo Itami delivers a sometimes amusing, but overlong, satire on tax evasion, which in Japan apparently is fast becoming a national pastime. Subtitles. Several graphic sexual encounters with nudity, a brief sequence involving the physical battering of a woman, and some rough language. O (nr)

Taxing Woman's Return, A (1989) Sequel picks up the career of the feisty Japanese tax-inspector (Nobuko Miyamoto) as she investigates a bogus fundamentalist religious sect headed by a charismatic influence-peddler (Rentaro Mikuni). Written and directed by Juzo Itami, the sharp satire of Japanese tax-crimes shows the conflicting roles of women in modern Japan and underscores how exploitative bogus "religions" can be. Some rough language, grisly violence, and adultery. A-IV (nr)

Taza, Son of Cochise (1954) Formula Western directed by Douglas Sirk has the title character (Rock Hudson) struggling to fulfill the peace treaty signed by his dead Apache father (uncredited Jeff Chandler), while his younger brother (Bart Roberts) conspires to join a warring band of Apaches led by Geronimo. Frontier violence and Indian stereotypes. A-I (br)

Tea and Sympathy (1956) Dated coming-of-age melodrama in which an effeminate college freshman (John Kerr) suffers all kinds of humiliations from manly fellow students, until his house-master's wife (Deborah Kerr) decides to act as a surrogate love-partner. Directed by Vincente Minnelli from Robert Anderson's adaptation of his own play, the stagy proceedings are overlong and dramatically unconvincing. Sexual situations. A-III (br)

Tea for Two (1950) Slack, unimaginative backstage musical loosely based on "No, No, Nanette" and directed by David Butler is set in the 1920s, with a frantic producer (Billy De Wolfe) after a socialite (Doris Day) to back his new show, of which she becomes the star singing duets with its songwriter (Gordon MacRae). Mild sexual innuendo. A-II (br)

Tea with Mussolini (1999) Warmly nostalgic tale in which some matronly English art-lovers (notably Maggie Smith, Joan Plowright, and Judi Dench) residing in 1930s Florence come to care for an abandoned boy, who returns as a teenager to help when they are interned as enemy aliens during World War II. Directed by Franco Zeffirelli, the semi-autobiographical picture shows how the Italian youth comes to appreciate English culture, but what succeeds best is its gently humorous depiction of the women's eccentric circle, which includes two brassy Americans (Cher and Lily Tomlin) and how they manage to survive the tragic circumstances of wartime Italy. Some threatening situations, sexual references, and a few instances of coarse language. A-II (PG)

Teachers (1984) Nick Nolte stars as a harassed but effective and idealistic teacher in a zoo-like high school. Directed by Arthur Hiller, the crude, disjointed effort seems just another teenage exploitation movie. Rough language, nudity, and a sympathetic view of abortion. O (R)

Tear in the Ocean, A (1973) The remnant of the Nazi onslaught of a peaceful Hassidic community in Poland joins the local resistance-group operating from the country estate of an idealistic nobleman (Armand Abplanalp), but the ultimate result is tragedy, as the Poles themselves turn on their Jewish allies during the count's absence. Written, produced, and directed by Henri Glaeser, the complex movie views the Holocaust from a variety of perspectives, challenging viewers with its questions rather than comforting them with facile answers. A-II (nr)

Ted & Venus (1991) Sour comedy about a would-be poet (Bud Cort) whose obsessive pursuit of a wary social-worker (Kim Adams) ends in death when his infatuation proves unstoppable. Fledgling director Cort stars in a pathetic vehicle whose sick humor seems pointless except to put casual sex in an appealing light. Positive portrayal of promiscuity with some gratuitous nudity, violence, and rough language. O (R)

Teen Witch (1989) Sappy little story about a teen (Robyn Lively) who learns that she is a witch, uses her magic powers to become the most popular girl in school, but discovers that what she really wants is to be liked for herself. Directed by Dorian Walker, there is nothing magical about the inane plot or its trite treatment. A sexually suggestive scene and a number of sexual references. A-III (PG-13)

Teen Wolf (1985) High-school lad (Michael J. Fox) becomes a big man on campus and a basketball star when he discovers that he is a werewolf in this moderately funny teenage comedy. Directed by Rod Daniel, the movie is marred by jokes about alcohol and drugs, as well as some vulgarity and sexually oriented humor. A-III (PG)

Teen Wolf Too (1987) Mild sequel in which the younger cousin (Jason Bateman) of the high-school student in the original **Teen Wolf** goes to college and becomes a boxing champ when he discovers his cousin's condition runs in the family. Directed by Christopher Leitch, it is more tiresome than silly, except for the violence of its boxing scenes and a benign attitude towards casual sex. A-III (PG)

Teenage Caveman (1958) Low-budget adventure directed by Roger Corman in which the title Neanderthal character (Robert Vaughn) rebels against the law of his clan and ventures into the land beyond the river, with a sci-fi ending. Stylized violence and menacing situations. A-II (br)

Teenage Frankenstein (see: **I Was a Teenage Frankenstein**)

Teenage Mother (1973) Sleazy movie about the social and sexual rivalries of a class of inane high-school students and how they are corrupted by a health instructor. Directed by Jerry Gross, the movie's scenes of rape and seduction are restrained but not

some documentary footage showing the ghastly details of a forceps delivery of a baby. O (GP)

Teenage Mutant Ninja Turtles (1990) Live-action feature movie debut of the half-human, half-turtle cartoon heroes who do battle with a rogue Japanese ninja society to win back their kidnapped rat-mentor, Splinter. Though music video-maker Steve Barron's direction is amateurish, Jim Henson's turtle costumes expand the frolicking foursome to entertaining life-sized creatures. Much comic-book violence involving bashing and smashing human and turtle bodies and some mild rough language. A-II (PG)

Teenage Mutant Ninja Turtles II: The Secret of the Ooze (1991) This time rat-mentor Splinter and the feisty foursome are out to recapture the last vial of a dangerously toxic ooze from the clutches of the evil Shredder (Francois Chau) and his ninja thugs. Director Michael Pressman uses nonstop kung-fu battles to disguise the amateur-hour plot, and Jim Henson's workshop furnishes two new monsters to keep the eyes entertained up to a point. Considerable slapstick martial-arts violence. A-II (PG)

Teenage Mutant Ninja Turtles III (1993) Lifeless sequel has the four teen-turtles hurtled back in time to feudal Japan to rescue a friend (Paige Turco) and save a war-torn village. Writer-director Stuart Gillard relies on the turtle's established popularity instead of developing something more than a sophomoric story without liveliness, wit, or whimsy. Some ethnic stereotyping and several cartoon-like fight scenes. A-II (PG)

Telefon (1977) Russian agent (Charles Bronson) is sent to the US to eliminate a fanatical maverick comrade (Donald Pleasence) who is bent upon activating a long-discarded sabotage scheme. Mediocre thriller made more bearable by a lavish production, Don Siegel's smooth direction, and Lee Remick's personable performance as an American double-agent. Some graphic violence. A-III (PG)

Tell Me a Riddle (1980) Melvyn Douglas and Lila Kedrova play an elderly Jewish immigrant couple, at odds for decades, who are reconciled while visiting their granddaughter (Brooke Adams). Although the fine acting is at times quite moving, Lee Grant's direction of a script awkwardly updating the 1961 story by Tillie Olsen is often clumsy. Somber theme and an implied acceptance of abortion. A-III (PG)

Tell Me That You Love Me, Junie Moon (1970) Screen version of Marjorie Kellogg's novel about a disfigured woman (Liza Minnelli), an epileptic (Ken Howard), and a paralyzed homosexual (Robert Moore), who band together to live on their own. Director Otto Preminger's treatment dredges up a dozen sicknesses and perversions with consistent shallowness and lack of understanding, winding up with a limp moral of love conquers all. A-IV (R/GP)

Tell Them Willie Boy Is Here (1969) Reservation Indian (Robert Blake) at the turn of the century is caught between tribal tradition and the white man's law when he kills the father of his sweetheart (Katharine Ross). The clash of two cultures, the injustice of the dominant one, and the human fallibility on both sides are themes left largely unexplored in director Abraham Polonsky's drama, which spends more time on the abrasive relationship between the fair-minded sheriff (Robert Redford) and the frustrated reservation doctor (Susan Clark). The result is no more than an average Western chase-movie with an unhappy ending. A-III (PG)

Temp, The (1993) All-too-obvious thriller concerns a devious secretarial fill-in (Lara Flynn Boyle) whose ambitions to advance her cookie-company boss (Timothy Hutton) and then herself include killing her way to the top. Director Tom Holland lets Hutton stumble around while the murderous leading-lady and co-star Faye Dunaway chew the scenery in this unappetizing, cookie-cutter formula entertainment. Some stylized violence, sexual innuendo, and rough language. A-III (R)

Tempest (1982) Famous architect (John Cassevetes), beset with faddish mid-life crisis, flees wife (Gena Rowlands) and job to an idyllic Greek isle with his daughter (Molly Ringwald) and mistress (Susan Sarandon). Director Paul Mazursky's updating of Shakespeare's autumnal comedy is sometimes charming, certainly never dull, but fails to overcome the handicap of its boorish, unappealing hero. Some frank references to sexual matters, including adultery, and rough language. A-III (PG)

Temptation (1946) Sluggish melodrama about an unfaithful wife (Merle Oberon) whose lover (Charles Korvin) persuades her to poison her rich husband (George Brent), but she has a change of heart and poisons the lover instead. Directed by Irving Pichel, the dour story gains some interest from its setting in 1900 Egypt, where archeologist Brent is excavating a pharaoh's tomb, but it's not enough to save the picture. Stylized violence, menace, and implied sexual relationships. A-III (br)

Tempter, The (1978) Italian version of **The Exorcist**, whose theme of demonic possession is crudely handled by director Alberto de Martino with improbable appearances by Mel Ferrer and Arthur Kennedy, nauseating special effects, and heavy doses of brutal violence and dumb sex. O (R)

Temptress Moon (1997) Opulent melodrama set in 1920s Shanghai, where a thieving gigolo (Leslie Cheung) returns to the decaying estate of his childhood and becomes romantically involved with his opium-addicted cousin (Gong Li), despite the protestations of her love-struck servant (Kevin Lin). While director Chen Kaige's dreamy tale of deceit and intrigue is lovely to look at, its narrative is confusing and emotionally chilly. Subtitles. Fleeting violence, restrained bedroom scenes, drug abuse, and an instance of rough language. A-III (R)

10 (1979) Successful middle-aged composer (Dudley Moore) abandons his mature lover (Julie Andrews) to pursue a young beauty (Bo Derek), even though she happens to be on her honeymoon. Directed by Blake Edwards, the sometimes funny comedy tries to have it both ways by indulging the same male sex-fantasies that supposedly it is satirizing. Frequent nudity, shaky morality, and rough language. O (R)

10 Things I Hate About You (1999) Crude high-school comedy in which a surly senior (Heath Ledger) is paid to take out a hostile student (Julia Stiles) so that her younger sister (Larisa Oleynik) will then be allowed to date as well. As lamely directed by Gil Junger, adults are hapless or horrible, and adolescents have only one thing on their minds. Brief violence, some crass sexual references, and some underage drinking. A-III (PG-13)

Ten Commandments, The (1956) Less an inspirational story based on biblical sources than a dramatic vehicle with a sense of history, director Cecil B. DeMille's epic production offers some spectacular re-creations, excellent technical effects, and good acting from a fine cast, including Charlton Heston as Moses, Yul Brynner, Anne Baxter, Edward G. Robinson, and many other stars of the era. A-I (G)

Ten Days' Wonder (1972) Complex French suspenseful drama based on an Ellery Queen mystery about a man (Anthony Perkins) who suspects that he has committed murder during a recent mental blackout. Director Claude Chabrol is less interested in the fairly simple mystery than in exploring the relationship between the strange characters (including Orson Welles and Marlene Jobert) living on the man's country estate, the decadent atmosphere that pervades his household, and the sense of impending disaster that mounts throughout the film (and it is a shocker). Mature theme. A-III (R/PG)

Ten from Your Show of Shows (1973) Top comedy in some choice cuts from the classic Sid Caesar television show of the early 1950s, when Sid, Imogene Coca, Carl Reiner, and Howie Morris had as much fun doing their wacky bits as viewers have ever since. For those looking for lots of laughs dished up with a heaping spoonful of plain old nostalgia, this is unsurpassed entertainment. A-I (G)

Ten Little Indians (1966) Director George Pollack's routine remake of the classic Agatha Christie movie mystery **And Then There Were None** (1945) has a good cast (Hugh O'Brian, Wilfrid Hyde-White, Stanley Holloway, Leo Genn, and Dennis Price) and a still-intriguing plot. Stylized violence. A-III (br)

Ten Little Indians (1975) Stylish version of the Agatha Christie mystery in which ten strangers (including Oliver Reed, Stephane Audran, Elke Sommer, and Richard Attenborough) confess to past crimes before falling victim to swift punishment. Director Peter Collinson moves the action from a remote island to a Byzantine hotel in the middle of a desert and introduces a variant ending written by Dudley Nichols. Restrained violence. A-II (PG)

Ten Little Niggers (see: **And Then There Were None**)

10 Rillington Place (1971) Superior fact-based drama about a 1952 British murderer of six women (Richard Attenborough in a brilliant performance as a quite ordinary person about whom something is not quite right) who was apprehended only after the husband (John Hurt) of one of the victims had been hanged for his wife's murder. Directed by Richard Fleischer, the emphasis is on the death of an innocent man and the nonentity who was capable of such brutal crimes. In the end it leaves viewers pondering the human inadequacies of the judicial system. A-III (GP)

Ten Tall Men (1951) Burt Lancaster leads a motley group of French Foreign Legionnaires against the Riffs before they can unite to attack an undermanned garrison town. Directed by Willis Goldbeck, the only thing tall here is the tale, which shifts back and forth between straight adventure and spoof. Stylized violence and sexual innuendo. A-III (br)

10:30 P.M. Summer (1966) Director Jules Dassin's depiction of the complete alienation of an individual (Melina Mercouri) presents a degrading view of life, with some grossly indecent visuals. O (br)

10 to Midnight (1983) Retrograde thriller about a police sergeant (Charles Bronson) who, discharged for falsifying evidence against the man terrorizing his daughter (Lisa Eilbacher), sets out on his own to stop the handsome psycho (Andrew Stevens) who kills his victims while in the nude. Directed by J. Lee Thompson, the movie's treatment of violence, nudity, and graphic sex is thoroughly objectionable. O (R)

Ten Wanted Men (1955) Western potboiler in which a prosperous Arizona rancher (Randolph Scott) tries to avoid bloodshed when confronted by a rival rancher (Richard Boone) and his gang of hired gunslingers, but in the end has to rely on his six-shooter and some dynamite. Directed by Bruce Humberstone, the final shootouts are even less credible than the rest of the contrived proceedings. Nasty stylized violence, including cold-blooded murders, and some heavy-handed sexual innuendo. A-III (br)

Tenant, The (1976) Mediocre French thriller in which a meek clerk (Roman Polanski, who also directed) rents a room in a rather sinister Paris apartment house, learns that the former occupant threw herself out of the window, and, with increasing paranoia, comes to believe his own life is in danger. Some chilling and effective moments lead only to a disappointing anti-climax. Its theme of madness, depicted with some slashing knives and bouncing heads, are adult fare. A-III (R)

Tenchu! (1972) During the civil wars of the 186O's, assassin bands of samurai roamed Japan eliminating political opponents and their followers. This film by Hideo Gosha traces the exploits of one such group and the trouble its leader (Tatsuya Nikadai) has in manipulating his most devoted cutthroat (Shintaro Katsu). The result is a lush production that is little more than a routine exercise in the futility of violence. A-III (nr)

Tender Comrade (1943) Dated WW II sudser

about four war-plant workers (Ginger Rogers, Ruth Hussey, Kim Hunter, and Patricia Collinge) who share expenses in renting a house while their men are in service. Director Edward Dmytryk's attempt to dramatize the home-front centers on Rogers and her thoughts of soldier-hubby Robert Ryan, but the result is clogged with patriotic rhetoric that rings hollow to post-war ears. Chiefly of interest for its idealized version of the domestic problems of the period. A-II (br)

Tender Mercies (1983) Down-on-his-luck country-western singer (Robert Duvall), whose drinking broke up his first marriage, meets and weds a young widow (Tess Harper) who runs a ramshackle motel with her young son (Allan Hubbard). Director Bruce Beresford gets feeling performances from his cast, most especially Duvall in one of his best roles, and treats in a refreshingly uncynical, matter-of-fact manner the widow's strong religious convictions and her quiet pride when she sees her son and husband baptized. A rare movie, tough and gentle, inspiring and immensely entertaining, but the serious nature of the story is more appropriate for adults and older adolescents. A-II (PG)

Tender Moment, The (1971) Failed French romantic melodrama about a teenager (Renaud Verley) and an older woman (Nathalie Delon) who fall in love, have an affair, and separate when the man with whom the woman had been living returns. Director Michel Boisrond's story is not one of lost innocence (the boy has been sleeping with a housemaid, even "lending" her to classmates), and his older paramour is presented as something of a nymphomaniac, so that the result celebrates nothing but the sexual imperative. O (GP)

Tender Trap, The (1955) Soppy romantic comedy about a New York theatrical agent (Frank Sinatra) who enjoys being a bachelor playing the field, until he falls for a singer (Debbie Reynolds) who won't settle for anything but marriage. Director Charles Walters tries to keep it bright and breezy, but what works best is the bittersweet romance between one of the agent's girlfriends (Celeste Holm) and a married pal (David Wayne). The playboy philosophy flunks out. A-III (br)

Tender Warrior, The (1972) Filmed in Georgia, this portrait of a modern Huck Finn provides fine matinee fare for the small fry. The boy (Charles Lee) keeps tabs on all the wild animals of his domain, who respond when he calls them by name. Directed by Stewart Raffill, the photography beautifully captures the swamplands teeming with wildlife as background for this simple story. A-I (G)

Tennessee's Partner (1955) Formula Western directed by Allan Dwan uneasily links a cowpoke (Ronald Reagan), a gambler (John Payne), and the proprietor of a fancy house (Rhonda Fleming) in a dusty gold-mining town. Stylized violence, romantic complications, and sexual innuendo. A-III (br)

Tension (1949) Clumsy crime thriller directed by John Berry in which a meek pharmacist (Richard Basehart) plots to kill the lover of his two-timing wife (Audrey Totter), then is accused of the murder when someone else beats him to it. Sexual situations and considerable menace. A-III (br)

Tension at Table Rock (1956) Forgettable Western about a good badman (Richard Egan) who helps a gun-shy sheriff (Cameron Mitchell) clean up a crooked town. Directed by Charles Marquis Warren, the cliched plot is not worth the effort the actors put into it. Stylized violence. A-II (br)

Tentacles (1977) Poor Italian imitation of the marine-menace formula substitutes a giant octopus for rogue shark. John Huston, Shelley Winters, and Henry Fonda are out-acted by several killer whales in a story that is more tedious than threatening. Director Oliver Hellman's special effects are unconvincing, except for the grisly visuals of a bloody victim. Some needless profanity. A-III (PG)

Teorema (1969) Paradoxical Italian drama about the isolated world of a comfortable middle-class family which is transformed by sexual intimacy with a mysterious visitor (Terence Stamp). Director Pier Paolo Pasolini's theme is the corruption of material values, but he approaches it in such coldly intellectual style that one is uninvolved in the events. Though the use of sex is symbolic and not graphically depicted, some viewers will reject its appropriateness as a plot premise. A-IV (nr)

Tequila Sunrise (1988) Slickly produced detective yarn about a Los Angeles cop (Kurt Russell) who uses a restaurant owner (Michelle Pfeiffer) as a pawn to trap an old friend (Mel Gibson) who's attempting to quit the drug-smuggling racket and his notorious Latin-American dealer (Raul Julia). Writer-director Robert Towne entangles his attractive cast in a confusing plot that reaches incoherence by the time of the movie's improbable ending. Some rough language, a discreetly filmed sex-scene, and an intense climax. A-III (R)

Teresa the Thief (1979) Italian drama about a woman's tragic life (Monica Vitti) after being abandoned to the streets by an abusive father at age 11, made pregnant by a man who marries her just to escape military service, and finally left to a life of prisons and mental institutions. Director Carlo Di Palma only partially achieves the intended blend of pathos and comedy, and the movie's graphic, slice-of-life naturalism is mature fare. A-III (nr)

Term of Trial (1963) Middle-aged schoolmaster (Laurence Olivier), happily married (to Simone Signoret), finds himself pursued by a schoolgirl (Sarah Miles) who works out a nasty trap for him, oblivious to its tragic consequences. Solid adult drama directed by Peter Glenville, with fine performances from all three principals. A-III (br)

Terminal Man, The (1974) George Segal plays a scientist given to violent seizures, who has his brain hooked to a computer to control them, but short-circuits turn him into a menace for what appears to be most of southern California. Director Mike Hodges's version of Michael Crichton's novel takes a ridiculous concept to extremes. Much hokey violence. A-III (PG)

Terminal Velocity (1994) Routine action movie in which a skydiving instructor (Charlie Sheen) gets entangled with a beautiful, manipulative former KGB agent (Nastassja Kinski) in Arizona tracking a shipment of gold bullion, while Russian criminals pursue her with lethal intent. Director Deran Sarafian's empty escapist fare features a nonsensical narrative embroidered with a gimmicky series of death-defying skydiving rescues. Intermittent nasty violence and an instance of rough language. A-III (PG-13)

Terminator, The (1984) Violent sci-fi movie in which a killing machine in the shape of a man (Arnold Schwarzenegger) comes back from the future to assassinate a young waitress destined otherwise to bear a son who will lead the humans to victory over android rule of a post-nuclear world. James Cameron directs the action in taut, suspenseful fashion, but its violence is overdone, and a bedroom scene goes much further than necessary. O (R)

Terminator 2: Judgment Day (1991) With the fate of the planet depending on the survival of a plucky lad (Edward Furlong), his ferociously strong mother (Linda Hamilton) escapes a psycho ward to protect him, while two rival cyborg-terminators (Arnold Schwarzenegger and Robert Patrick) arrive from the future to tip the scales. Producer-director James Cameron's flashy sequel to his 1984 sci-fi fantasy has some stunning special effects, but the threadbare story-line merely showcases overblown scenes of callous butchery. Excessive violence and some rough language. O (R)

Terms of Endearment (1983) Uneven comedy about a mother-daughter relationship, that of a wealthy, imperious Houston widow (Shirley MacLaine) and her only child (Debra Winger), who marries a man her mother detests. The mother herself becomes involved with the wrong sort of man, in the person of a lecherous, dissipated former astronaut (Jack Nicholson), a confrontation of opposites that is sometimes very funny. Though consistently amusing, there is something uncomfortable about the way in which director James L. Brooks invites laughter at his characters for three-quarters of the way, and then demands empathy for them in the tearjerker conclusion. Some fairly graphic references to sexual activity and a benign attitude toward sex outside of marriage. A-III (PG)

Terror, The (1963) Thin chiller directed by Roger Corman mixes a lot of moody photography with a halting narrative about a French officer (Jack Nicholson) separated from his unit during the Napoleonic Wars, who is lured into a spooky castle on the Baltic Sea by the apparently dead wife of its resident count (Boris Karloff). Supernatural hokum. A-II (br)

Terror by Night (1946) Intriguing mystery aboard an express train to Scotland, with Sherlock Holmes (Basil Rathbone) and Dr. Watson (Nigel Bruce) solving a locked-compartment murder and the theft of a precious jewel, the Star of Rhodesia. Directed by Roy William O'Neill, the combination of mild humor, elementary deductions, eccentric red-herrings, and modest thrills make it one of the better examples of this 1942-46 series. Some menace and stylized violence. A-I (br)

Terror from the Year 5000 (1958) Sci-fi dud directed by Robert J. Gurney, Jr., in which a scientific experiment succeeds in breaking the time barrier by bringing back a deformed mutant (Salome Jens) from the radioactive world of Earth 3,000 years in the future. Stylized violence and some sexual innuendo. A-II (br)

Terror House (see: **The Night Has Eyes**)

Terror in the Aisles (1984) Director Andrew J. Kuehn's haphazard compilation of excerpts from horror movies concentrates on the period from **Psycho** (1960) to **Halloween** (1980), but the result is little more than a frivolous jumble of fright scenes joined by writer Margery Doppelt's inane commentary. Gory violence, sexual situations, fleeting nudity, and occasional rough language. A-IV (R)

Terror in the Wax Museum (1973) Dotty John Carradine's wax dummies appear to come to life and re-enact their grisly crimes in turn-of-the-century London. Director Georg Fenady's plot is as creaky as the museum's backstairs, and the suspense is as phony as the dummies, but for undemanding horror fans it provides some lightweight diversion. A-II (PG)

Terror of Mechagodzilla (1975) Muddled Japanese monster movie directed by Inoshiro Honda with a revengeful scientist aiding aliens in their plan to conquer Earth through his control of the sea-monster Titanosaurus and a mechanical Godzilla, until the real Godzilla gums up the works. Dubbed American version. Stylized violence and a human turned into a troubled cyborg. A-II (nr)

Terror on a Train (1953) Canadian demolitions expert (Glenn Ford) works through the night trying to find and defuse a bomb on a British munitions train, while the police evacuate the area and seek the saboteur. Director Ted Tetzlaff's tight little exercise in suspense is balanced by the stiff-upper-lip demeanor of British officials and civilians. Much tension. A-I (br)

Terrorists, The (1975) A group of political terrorists seize a British ambassador in Scandinavia and demand the release of their comrades from a British prison, something which the country's head of security (Sean Connery) sets out to thwart. Directed by Caspar Wrede, the suspense and excitement are well-maintained, though in a chilly, abstract manner, that makes the ironic ending arbitrary and disappointing. Some violence and much threatened violence. A-III (PG)

Terry Whitmore, for Example (1969) Vietnam deserter Whitmore, a 21-year-old black Marine corporal from Memphis who was wounded and awarded the Bronze Star, explains his reasons for deserting the Corps in an oral-history documentary filmed in Sweden by Bill Brodie. Viewers will have to determine how typical were his experiences and motivation, but his account does not seem to have any political axe to grind. Explicit description of a sexual encounter. A-IV (nr)

Tess (1980) British screen version of the Thomas Hardy novel about the young Wessex woman (Nastassia Kinski) whose life is irrevocably changed when her father discovers that the family are the impoverished descendants of a noble line. Directed by Roman Polanski, it is an always beautiful, at times powerful, drama whose somber theme of a woman doomed by class and circumstance is not for younger viewers. A-II (R)

Tess of the Storm Country (1960) Artificial melodrama clumsily unfolds as a Scottish lass (Diane Baker) moves to an American farm, sides with those protesting a local chemical plant, then falls for an upright Mennonite neighbor. Director Paul Guilfoyle squanders the beautiful rural setting in stilted scenes with cardboard characters of little emotional interest. Superficial depiction of a religious sect and discreet treatment of an unwed pregnancy. A-II (br)

Test of Love, A (1985) A courageous teacher (Angela Punch McGregor) takes an institution to court to effect the release of a bright child suffering from cerebral palsy who has been diagnosed as severely retarded. Fine Australian production directed by Gil Brealey offers solid entertainment and is immensely inspiring. A-II (PG)

Testament (1983) A family in a small American community attempts to cope with the aftermath of a nuclear war in this grim but extraordinary movie about a mother (Jane Alexander) who tries to make life go on for her three children after her husband (William Devane) perishes in the nuclear strike. The warmth and compassion she embodies vivifies and makes moving a story that otherwise might be unbearable. Director Lynne Littman spares the audience most of the more horrific results of nuclear disaster, but what it shows and what it implies are unsettling enough. The subject matter and a restrained bedroom scene are more suited for adults and older adolescents. A-II (PG)

Tex (1982) Good Disney version of S.E. Hinton's story about two teenage brothers, one earnest and responsible (Jim Metzler), one amiable but somewhat feckless (Matt Dillon), who attempt to cope with life while living by themselves on a rundown ranch outside Tulsa. Though director Tim Hunter's plot is overloaded with incident and occasionally veers into extravagant melodrama, its virtues outweigh its flaws, making it entertaining and sometimes moving. Restrained scene of teenage sexual discovery and some jocular references to sex and drugs. A-II (PG)

Texas (1941) Dandy Western about a genial pair of ex-Rebs (William Holden and Glenn Ford) who wind up on opposite sides in a war between ranchers and rustlers, as well as rivals courting the same gal (Claire Trevor). Director George Marshall turns the formula plot into robust entertainment with plenty of frontier action, paced by zesty humor, intriguing plot twists, and off-beat characters (local booster George Bancroft and laconic dentist Edgar Buchanan). Vigorous stylized violence and underhanded dealings. A-II (br)

Texas Across the River (1966) Spanish nobleman (Alain Delon) has trouble adjusting to the ways of the Old West, especially those of an outlandish cowboy (Dean Martin) and his peculiar Indian companion (Joey Bishop). Director Michael Gordon makes no pretense of a plot but strings together a series of humorous mishaps spoofing Western conventions. Threadbare but mostly innocuous comedy. A-I (br)

Texas Carnival (1951) Flat romantic comedy about a small-time carnival concessionaire (Red Skelton) being mistaken for an oil millionaire (Keenan Wynn), with predictable results. Directed by Charles Walters, the comic possibilities of the situation wear out quickly, and, except for some tacked-on musical numbers, the rest of the cast (Esther Williams, Ann Miller, and Howard Keel) have little to do. Mild romantic complications. A-II (br)

Texas Chainsaw Massacre, The (1974) Fiendish butcher out in the Texas bush country carves up four or five (it is difficult to determine the sum from the scattered parts) outdoors adventurers and then goes on a wild rampage of slaughter with chainsaw and other instruments of destruction, including a meat hook. Directed by Tobe Hooper, what is more dehumanizing than all the violence is that the treatment seems to regard it as amusing. O (R)

Texas Chainsaw Massacre, Part II, The (1986) Grotesque parody of the blood-and-gore genre of horror films features a leather-faced maniac twitching riotously in the air each time he approaches a new victim with his chainsaw. Making it even worse is director Tobe Hooper's vain attempt to distance the viewer from the movie's sadistic action through misconceived comic exaggeration. Gory violence, often in a sexual context. O (R)

Texas Chainsaw Massacre: The Next Generation (1997) Repulsive horror yarn in which a sadistic quartet of rural psychopaths (led by Matthew McConaughey) torture and murder teens on prom night with only one survivor (Renee Zellweger). Writer-director Kim Henkel's sick sequel to its 1974 and '86 predecessors borders on the depraved with its continual display of jokey graphic mayhem. Excessive violence, a flash of nudity, much profanity, and recurring rough language. O (R)

Texas Lady (1955) Thin Western directed by Tim Whelan is set in an 1885 Texas town whose newspaper's new owner (Claudette Colbert) gets into serious trouble with the nasty cattle-baron (Ray Collins) who owns everything in the vicinity, then gets some help from a Mississippi riverboat gambler (Barry Sullivan). Frontier violence. A-I (br)

Texas Rangers, The (1951) Low-budget oater directed by Phil Karlson with George Montgomery and Noah Berry, Jr., tricking an unlikely collection of legendary badmen — Sam Bass, John Wesley Hardin, Butch Cassidy, the Sundance Kid, and many others — into robbing a gold train with the Rangers waiting in ambush. Hokey plot with formula frontier action. A-I (br)

Texas Terror (1935) Formula Western directed by R.N. Bradbury features John Wayne as a former lawman who helps a murdered rancher's daughter (Lucille Brown) fend off rustlers, while his Indian friends aid in capturing her dad's killer. Frontier violence. A-I (br)

Texasville (1990) When the former high-school sweetheart (Cybill Shepherd) of a nearly broke Texas oilman (Jeff Bridges) arrives back in town, she flirts with her old beau but is more successful in winning over the man's unhappy wife (Annie Potts) and unruly children. Director Peter Bogdanovich's sequel to **The Last Picture Show** is less a touching reunion story than a lame putdown of family life and values wrapped up in a rambling soap opera with little structure, less wit, and no dramatic tension. O (R)

Texican, The (1966) Plodding formula Western in which an outlaw (Audie Murphy) leaves his Mexican refuge to avenge his brother's murder by the vicious boss (Broderick Crawford) of a corrupt border town. Directed by Lesley Selander and filmed in Spain, the dubbed dialogue is as clunky as the phony action. Stylized violence. A-II (br)

Thank God, It's Friday (1978) Youth exploitation movie about the problems that develop one Friday night at a disco, set against a blaring background of frenetic music. Directed by Robert Klane, it juggles a dozen or so stereotyped characters, and, though the pace is lively, the comedy is tiresome and repetitious. Some failed jokes about sex and drugs. A-III (PG)

Thank You All Very Much (1969) British melodrama in which a young woman (Sandy Dennis) living alone in London becomes pregnant as the result of her first and only sexual experience, decides against abortion, and becomes an unwed mother. Director Waris Hussein does well in depicting the life of Londoners and is sensitive to the young woman's situation, but the treatment is superficial and makes no attempt to understand the woman and her future. A-III (PG)

Thank You and Goodnight! (1992) Fact-based account of a young woman (Jan Oxenberg) coming to terms with the terminal illness of her grandmother (Mae Joffe) who looks back on her life as family and friends comfort her. Writer-producer-star-director Oxenberg uses actual family members and precariously balances a humorously philosophical attitude toward life and death with emotionally honest scenes of pain and loss. A skeptical attitude toward the afterlife. A-II (nr)

Thank You, Jeeves (1936) Diverting fun with P.G. Wodehouse's sterling butler, Jeeves (Arthur Treacher), who here saves his asinine employer (David Niven) from a gang of spies. Directed by Arthur Greville Collins, the comedy is light and breezy escapist fare. Mild comic violence. A-I (br)

Thank You, Mr. Moto (1937) Intriguing entry in the mystery series, with Japanese detective Moto (Peter Lorre) in China to search for an ancient scroll showing the burial site of Genghis Khan and his treasures. Director Norman Foster uses the Oriental setting to provide a sinister atmosphere for a plot involving an American tourist (Jayne Regan), a White Russian count (Sig Ruman), the mother (Pauline Frederick) of a Chinese prince (Philip Ahn), and a ruthless gang leader (Sidney Blackmer). More menace than violence. A-I (br)

That Championship Season (1982) Jason Miller directs his own adaptation of his prize-winning play about four middle-aged men (Bruce Dern, Paul Sorvino, Stacy Keach, and Martin Sheen) who gather with their former coach (Robert Mitchum) to celebrate the 24th anniversary of winning the state high-school basketball championship. As the evening of drinking wears on, the guilty secrets of each come out, but before they do, most viewers will have lost interest. Some strong language. A-III (R)

That Cold Day in the Park (1969) Failed psychological melodrama in which a lonely spinster (Sandy Dennis) invites a drifter (Michael Burns) in out of the rain for a hot meal and goes to bizarre lengths trying to get him into bed. Director Robert Altman juxtaposes two unbelievable characters in a series of impossibly phony situations that lead to no insights about social alienation but only to morbid, sexually explicit sensationalism. O (R)

That Darn Cat (1966) Disney live-action adventure comedy in which Hayley Mills gets FBI agent Dean Jones to follow the trail of a mischievous cat who is the only clue to the whereabouts of a kidnapped bank-teller. Robert Stevenson directs the antics, but it is the cat who steals the show. Amusing for youngsters and not too hard on parents either. A-I (G)

That Darn Cat (1997) Convinced her cat has found a clue to the whereabouts of a kidnapping victim, an alienated teen (Christina Ricci) enlists the help of a hapless FBI agent (Doug E. Doug) in solving the crime by following the frisky feline around town. Director Bob Spiers's shoddy remake of the 1965 comedy overdoes the resulting mayhem and chaos in a mistaken attempt at humor. Frequent slapstick violence. A-II (PG)

That Hamilton Woman (1941) Fact-based historical romance recounts the ill-fated extramarital affair between Lady Hamilton (Vivian Leigh), the low-born wife of the British ambassador to Naples (Alan Mowbray), and Lord Nelson (Laurence Olivier), the admiral who crushed Napoleon's fleet at Trafalgar. While director Alexander Korda treats the characters sympathetically, their romance is placed within the context of the times, which hopelessly doomed their affair to unhappiness. Wartime violence and discreet treatment of marital infidelity. A-II (br)

That Kind of Woman (1959) Contrived sudser begins in June 1944 aboard a Miami-to-New York train, where a small-town Army private (Tab Hunter) falls for the glamorous mistress (Sophia Loren) of a rich war-contractor (George Sanders), then spends his leave trying to convince her to marry him. Director Sidney Lumet gets an appealing performance from Loren, as well as from Barbara Nichols and Jack Warden in a parallel subplot, but Hunter fails to make the grade, and the situation never fulfills its promise. Probes the relationship between love and sex. A-III (br)

That Lady in Ermine (1948) Failed romantic comedy in which a tiny 1861 principality is occupied by Hungarian hussars, whose dour colonel (Douglas Fairbanks, Jr.) mellows after falling for its ruling countess (Betty Grable), while her husband (Cesar Romero) flits around disguised as a Gypsy. Directed by Ernst Lubitsch (who died during its production), the situation yields little comedy and even less whimsy, especially some heavy-handed musical fantasy sequences involving the countess' ancestors. Sexual situations and innuendo. A-III (br)

That Man Bolt (1973) Fred Williamson stars as the super-smooth courier of valuables for well-heeled international clients, but this trip he's doublecrossed by his employers, and he works out a nifty cross of his own. Directed by Henry Levin, it has plenty of action, often quite violent, but relieved by whimsical staging, and there's some sexual innuendo. A-III (R)

That Man from Rio (1964) French production with Jean-Paul Belmondo and Francois Dorleac in an hilarious spoof of stereotype characters and stock situations that typify mystery-adventure movies. Directed by Philippe de Broca with real Gallic flair, the comedy is first-class entertainment. A-II (br)

That Night (1993) Coming-of-age melodrama seen from the perspective of a starry-eyed 10-year old (Eliza Dushku), who idolizes her 17-year-old neighbor (Juliette Lewis) and tries to reunite her with her boyfriend (C. Thomas Howell) after the teen is quietly shipped off to a Catholic home for unwed mothers in the early '60s. Writer-director Craig Bolotin tries to present a sympathetic portrait of teen passion colliding with painful realities, but his formulaic treatment of cardboard characters is heavy-handed and muddled by the child's simplistic point of view towards the lovers. A premarital relationship, many sexual references, fleeting violence, and an instance of profanity. A-III (PG-13)

That Night in Rio (1941) Glossy musical comedy set in Rio de Janeiro, where an American nightclub entertainer (Don Ameche) gets in trouble with his girlfriend (Carmen Miranda) when he's hired to impersonate a count (also Ameche), whom he resembles so closely even the countess (Alice Faye) can't tell them apart. Directed by Irving Cummings, the comedy of mistaken identities wears increasingly thin, though the cast is generally entertaining, and the Brazilian novelty numbers are diverting. Sexual situations and innuendo. A-III (br)

That Obscure Object of Desire (1977) Disappointing French production in which a wealthy middle-aged Parisian (Fernando Rey) falls hopelessly in love with a young Spanish woman (alternately played by Carole Bouquet and Angela Molina) who leads him a merry chase. Director Luis Bunuel's surrealistic treatment of the romantic situation makes shallow attempts at social commentary. Excessive use of nudity. O (R)

That Old Feeling (1997) Reunited at their daughter's wedding, a bitterly divorced couple (Bette Midler and Dennis Farina) in stable second marriages impulsively surrender to passion, then spend the next two days trying to evade facing their horrified spouses and shocked daughter as they ponder what to do next. Director Carl Reiner lampoons matrimony in a farcical story tailor-made for Midler's brassy acting style. Comic treatment of adultery and instances of profanity and rough language. A-IV (PG-13)

That Thing You Do! (1996) Warmhearted comedy in which four clean-cut teens from Erie, Pa., form a rock'n'roll band in 1964, then briefly rocket towards the top of the pop charts under the savvy guidance of their record-label manager (Tom Hanks). Also written and directed by Hanks, the thin story brims with youthful exuberance in a vivid picture of a more innocent era. A few rude expressions. A-II (PG)

That Touch of Mink (1962) Flat romantic comedy in which a nice young woman (Doris Day) succumbs to the charms of a wealthy philanderer (Cary Grant), then backs off until he's willing to marry her. Directed by Delbert Mann, the glossy proceedings are slickly contrived, relatively witless, and, despite the tacked-on ending, lack any deeper sense of romance than sex and dollar signs. Sexual situations and innuendo. A-III (br)

That Uncertain Feeling (1941) Droll comedy in which a dull insurance executive (Melvyn Douglas) agrees to give his dippy wife (Merle Oberon) a divorce after she gets involved with an eccentric pianist (Burgess Meredith), then proceeds to win her back on his own terms. Producer-director Ernst Lubitsch has some witty fun with the idle rich who can afford to turn minor problems into major ones, but Meredith steals the show as a wacky egoist. Comic treatment of marriage and sexual innuendo. A-III (br)

That Was Then, This Is Now (1985) From the work of novelist S.E. Hinton, the bard of misunderstood youth, comes a story of two boys (Craig Sheffer and Emilio Estevez) who hang out together wondering about the meaning of it all, until one falls in love and gets a job, while the other wallows yet deeper in self-pity. Directed by Christopher Cain, the movie is so dull and pretentious that it is painful to watch. Benign view of premarital sex. O (R)

That'll Be the Day (1975) British drama, based loosely on the formation of the Beatles rock group, tells the story of an young man (David Essex) who is helped to find some direction in his life by a casual friend (Ringo Starr, in a non-musical role). Director Claude Whatham's movie is raw, often ragged, but full of feeling and compassion, and it will interest both rock fans and those who like unvarnished pictures of unwashed types. A-III (PG)

That's Dancing! (1985) A film compilation of great moments in dancing from the film musicals of the 1930s to the recent past. Produced by Jack Haley, Jr., the movie is very entertaining, but real fans will note some significant omissions and yearn for more extended selections. A-I (G)

That's Entertainment! (1974) Singing, dancing historical survey of the best of the MGM musicals charms the eye and ear with romantic fantasy. Written, produced, and directed by Jack Haley, Jr., the selection of excerpts from these musicals demonstrates effortlessly why their appeal endures from generation to generation. A-I (G)

That's Entertainment, Part 2 (1976) Fred Astaire and Gene Kelly (who also directs) serve as hosts for this anthology from Hollywood's musical past, though there are brief glimpses of such comedians as the Marx Brothers, Jimmy Durante, Laurel and Hardy, and Abbott and Costello, as well as a sequence devoted to the films of Spencer Tracy and Katherine Hepburn. Highly enjoyable, but not up to the original's consistent quality. A-I (G)

That's Entertainment! III (1994) Yet more excerpts from MGM musicals, this time featuring the studio's gallery of stars in offbeat and unusual production numbers, as well as some musical routines that landed on the cutting-room floor. Producer-directors Bud Friedgen and Michael J. Sheridan's compilation of less-familiar footage from the golden age of Hollywood musicals is lively and engaging family fare with special appeal for nostalgic adults. A-I (G)

That's Life (1986) Fumbling, self-centered husband (Jack Lemmon), preoccupied with thoughts of old age and death, is insensitive to the needs of his wife (Julie Andrews) as she awaits the results of a cancer test. Director Blake Edwards uses sexual encounters as a source of comic relief in an exploration of family ties that has few genuine moments. His infidelity is treated as a symptom of an inner insecurity left unresolved and overshadowed by the image of a strong woman and mother who absorbs all family ills. Brief nudity. A-III (PG-13)

That's My Boy (1951) Lame comedy in which a dim father (Eddie Mayehoff) who was a college-football hero wants his hypochondriac son (Jerry Lewis) to do the same and gets the team's star (Dean Martin) to show him how, but they have a falling out over a co-ed (Marion Marshall). Directed by Hal Walker, the proceedings are more sentimental than comic, though Lewis's antics raise an occasional giggle. Scenes of inebriation. A-II (br)

That's Right — You're Wrong (1939) Dated musical comedy in which band leader Kay Kyser comes to Hollywood to make a movie, but when the studio producer (Adolphe Menjou) can't come up with a suitable script, he and the gang return to their radio show. A-I (br)

Theatre of Blood (1973) Gruesome British chiller has its genuinely amusing moments, as a B-grade Shakespearean actor (Vincent Price) takes his revenge on the stuffy circle of London critics who thwarted his career. Each execution is conducted through a re-enactment of the murder scene from one of the Bard's tragedies in which the critic had lambasted Price's performance. Director Douglas Hickox stages the action with a distinct flair, and the cast of British character actors is marvelous. The gore becomes a bit tacky at times, but horror fans will find it has a touch of class. A-III (R)

Their Secret Affair (see: **Top Secret Affair**)

Thelma & Louise (1991) Two girlfriends from Arkansas (Susan Sarandon and Geena Davis), intent on a carefree getaway weekend in a '66 Thunderbird, find themselves dodging police all the way to Arizona after one murders an attempted rapist. Director Ridley Scott's flashy road movie makes the two women highly appealing but glamorizes their willing, sometimes gleefully made, choices to break the law and escape the consequences. Rationalization of murder and suicide, casual marital infidelity, brief but graphic attempted-rape scene, and intermittent rough language. O (R)

Thelma Jordan (see: **The Files on Thelma Jordan**)

Thelonious Monk: Straight, No Chaser (1989) Straight-forward documentary on the eccentric black jazz-pianist and composer gives plenty of screen time to his music but not enough to his biography. Director Charlotte Zwerin incorporates much black-and-white footage of Monk shot by cinematographer Christian Blackwood during a 1967-68 world tour, which will delight jazz buffs but will not enlighten those who want to know more about the musician whose reputation has continued to grow since his death in 1982. Some profanity and sexual innuendo. A-III (PG-13)

Them! (1954) Durable science-fiction thriller, with steady through incredulous lawmen (James Whitmore and James Arness) helping a scientist (Edmond Gwenn) track the spread of deadly giant ants from New Mexico to the storm drains under Los Angeles. Director Gordon Douglas plays on period fears of organic mutations stemming from radiation released in A-bomb tests, and the results are suitably tense, even though the movie's 12-foot ants are more threatening off-screen than on. Some stylized violence and considerable suspense. A-I (br)

Theodora Goes Wild (1936) Wacky romantic comedy in which a young woman (Irene Dunne) shocks her prim Connecticut hometown by revealing she's the author of a risqué bestseller, then goes after the married heel (Melvyn Douglas) who wooed her only to return to his wealthy wife. Director Richard

Boleslawski makes an easy target of small-town hypocrisy and gets some funny results from the slapstick situations of a plot whose theme of self-liberation from social convention proves more sentimental than subversive. Shallow treatment of marriage. A-III (br)

Theory of Flight, The (1998) Seriocomic misfire in which a feisty, terminally ill paraplegic (Helena Bonham Carter) is so determined to experience sexual intimacy before death that her daily caretaker (Kenneth Branagh) sets out to rob a bank to pay for the services of a dashing gigolo. While striving to emphasize the characters' humanity, director Paul Greengrass fails to mesh comedy with tragedy as the situation becomes increasingly bizarre and contrived. Discreet bedroom scenes, several sexual references, fleeting background shots of Internet pornography, and much rough language. A-IV (R)

There Was a Crooked Man (1970) Offbeat Western about a reform-minded warden (Henry Fonda) who rises to the moral challenge of a convict renegade (Kirk Douglas) to practice what he preaches about rehabilitation and trust. The twist ending has to do with a race to the death for a secret pile of Spanish gold. Directed by Joseph L. Mankiewicz, it's corny but effective, if occasionally violent and tasteless, as the two leads ham up a storm. A-III (R)

There's a Girl in My Soup (1970) Disappointing screen version of the popular London play about a sex-obsessed TV gourmet (Peter Sellers) whose free-wheeling amorous affairs grind to a halt when he tries to introduce an uninhibited hippie (Goldie Hawn) into his more sumptuous world. Director Roy Boulting's far-fetched, frequently tasteless humor, coupled with the compromising situations of a belabored script, thwart the comic talents of Sellers and Hawn. O (R)

There's Always Tomorrow (1956) Soapy tale of a mid-life crisis, as a good family man (Fred MacMurray) feels neglected by wife (Joan Bennett) and offspring, then turns to a former employee (Barbara Stanwyck) who is now a successful fashion-designer. Directed by Douglas Sirk, the sentimental proceedings gain some interest from sincere performances by a good cast, but the predictable outcome is never in doubt. Considerations of infidelity. A-II (br)

There's No Business Like Show Business (1954) Overblown musical spanning the life of a vaudevillian couple (Ethel Merman and Dan Dailey) from 1919 to WW II, during which their three offspring become, variously, a musical star (Mitzi Gaynor), a talented hoofer (Donald O'Connor) on the skids because of a woman (Marilyn Monroe), and a smiling, singing priest (Johnnie Ray). Directed by Walter Lang, the episodic family saga consists of little more than show-biz stereotypes linking a medley of Irving Berlin songs and big production numbers which are the movie's primary purpose. Some sexual innuendo and romantic complications. A-III (br)

There's Something About Mary (1998) Crude screwball comedy in which an ordinary guy (Ben Stiller), a sneaky private eye (Matt Dillon), and assorted misfits all compete for the affections of an incredibly naive but attractive young surgeon (Cameron Diaz). Directed by Peter and Bobby Farrelly, the picture's sense of humor runs the gamut from outrageous dopey to offensively vulgar, but the goofy story's basically sentimental center prevents it from becoming thoroughly repulsive. Some comic violence, gross sexual innuendo, fleeting nudity, intermittent profanity, and much rough language. A-IV (R)

Thérèse (1986) French dramatization of the life of St. Thérèse de Lisieux from age 15, when she joined a cloistered convent of Carmelite nuns, to her death there nine years later of tuberculosis. Director Alain Cavalier's impressionistic account of the young woman (luminously played by Catherine Mouchet) who found personal joy, spiritual liberation, and the sanctity of selfless simplicity within the restrictive traditions of an austere religious community will challenge contemporary viewers and confound some. The young may find its picture of 19th-century religious life more confusing than inspiring. A-III (nr)

Thermidor (1971) Italian documentary about 19th-century European nationalism and the competition for empire that resulted in the bloodbath of the First World War. Director Tinto Brass relies heavily on the narration to make all the wars and internal strife understandable, but it's a complex period, and casual viewers may find it a struggle. History teachers, however, might make good use of its dramatic visuals. A-II (nr)

These Three (1936) Pooling their meager resources after college, two friends (Miriam Hopkins and Merle Oberon) open a school in a small town but face ruin because of lies about their relations with the local doctor (Joel McCrea) spread by a malicious student (Bonita Granville). Adapted from Lillian Hellman's play and directed by William Wyler, the result offers an absorbing tale of people's willingness to believe the worst about others. Menacing situations. A-II (br)

They All Laughed (1981) Screwball comedy is aggressively unfunny as it follows the antics of four private detectives, some beautiful women, and other odd assortments of New Yorkers (among whom are Audrey Hepburn, Ben Gazzara, John Ritter, and Dorothy Stratten). Written and directed Peter Bogdanovich, the plot is thin to the point of transparency. Illicit sexual relationships. A-III (PG)

They Call Her One Eye (1974) Scandinavian exploitation import about a woman (Christina Lindberg) forced into prostitution who finally takes a sadistic revenge on the vice ring who enslaved her as a prostitute. Absurd sex and violence. O (R)

They Call Me Mister Tibbs! (1970) Routine sequel to **In the Heat of the Night** finds its homicide specialist (Sidney Poitier) slithering through slimy red-herrings to fish out the strangler of an overworked call-girl. The bright spots in the plodding crime melodrama are with his wife (Barbara McNair), though he finds the growing pains of his son almost as troublesome as the murder case. Director Gordon Douglas provides plenty of slam-bang action, including the movie's opening sequence depicting a sadistic sex-slaughter and clinical police-work in more graphic terms than a lay audience might wish. A-IV (GP/R)

They Call Me Trinity (1971) Italian Western spoof stars the grinning Terence Hill as the grimiest, laziest, fastest outlaw gun on the frontier, who is drawn into a conflict involving evil rancher Farley Granger and some pacifist Mormon farmers. He and his brother (Bud Spencer), posing as a lawman, radicalize the farmers and teach them a primitive form of martial arts in time for the climactic showdown. Directed by E.B. Clucher, the shooting and mayhem are comically genial rather than the usual cynical violence of the genre. A-III (G)

They Came from Beyond Space (1967) British sci-fi clunker in which meteorites carrying invisible life-forms land in Cornwall and inhabit the bodies of those who come to investigate, except for a scientist (Robert Hutton) who's protected by a silver plate in his head. Directed by Freddie Francis, the slack proceedings eventually lead to the Master of the Moon (Michael Gough) in a suitably silly ending. Hokey violence. A-I (br)

They Came from Within (1976) Canadian science-fiction movie about parasites that take over the inhabitants of an apartment building. Directed by David Cronenberg, the amateurish effort is disgusting in its exploitation of gory violence, sex, and nudity. O (R)

They Came to Cordura (1959) During the US Army pursuit of Pancho Villa's raiders into 1916 Mexico, a brooding major (Gary Cooper) returns to HQ with five Medal of Honor candidates (Van Heflin, Tab Hunter, Richard Cote, Michael Callan, and Dick York), as well as an American resident (Rita Hayworth) charged with aiding the enemy, but their journey is filled with disasters from without and within their ranks. Director Robert Rossen probes the nature of courage and the limits of endurance in this gritty but uneven tale that gradually brings out the worst in all the characters until the unconvincing finish. Some stylized violence, much menace, and occasional sexual innuendo and situations. A-III (br)

They Came to Rob Las Vegas (1969) Elke Sommer joins Gary Lockwood in pulling off a spectacular plan to hijack an armored car carrying the mob's casino loot as it speeds across the Nevada desert. European co-production directed by Antonio Isasi has an imaginative heist plot that only works sporadically because unsavory subplots with sex and violence keep getting in the way. A-III (R)

They Died with Their Boots On (1941) Sprawling spectacle follows the career of George Armstrong Custer (Errol Flynn) from West Point to the battlefields of the Civil War, marriage to a financier's daughter (Olivia de Havilland) and into legend fighting the Indians of the western plains. Director Raoul Walsh holds the episodic picture together with an ingratiating performance by Flynn and picturesque action sequences, notably at the Little Big Horn. Though this version of the Custer myth makes grand entertainment, it should not be mistaken for history. A-I (br)

They Don't Wear Black Tie (1983) Fine Brazilian movie about how a wildcat strike disrupts the domestic life of a working-class family in Sao Paulo. Directed by Leon Hirszman, the essential drama is played out on the family level, leading to a tragic clash between the father, who supports the strike, and his son, who believes people should go their own way. Not a very entertaining movie, but one that provides some insights into the human reality behind the headlines of Latin-American strife. Some nudity and rough language. A-IV (nr)

They Flew Alone (see **Wings and the Woman**)

They Got Me Covered (1943) Fired for incompetence, a dim-witted reporter (Bob Hope) stumbles upon a Nazi spy-ring in Washington, DC, then gets help from a lovely colleague (Dorothy Lamour) in his bumbling efforts to nab the ringleaders (Otto Preminger and Eduardo Ciannelli). Director David Butler keys the comedy to Hope's brand of buffoonery, but the wartime plot is dated by heavy-handed patriotic asides. Comic menace and mild sexual innuendo. A-II (br)

They Live (1988) An alien race disguised as yuppies lull Americans into submission through subliminal media advertising. Director John Carpenter's biting satire of the fundamentalist right is a bust due to bad casting (wrestler Roddy Piper stars) and a poor script. Mindless violence, much profanity. O (R)

They Live by Night (1949) After the seasoned criminals (Howard da Silva and Jay C. Flippen) with whom he's escaped prison are killed, an inexperienced young man (Farley Granger) and the girl (Cathy O'Donnell) he married on the spur of the moment try to escape a police dragnet. Director Nicholas Ray's portrait of a youth caught in the quagmire of crime is realistic enough, but the formula plot never strays far from its predictable course. Stylized violence and criminal acts. A-III (br)

They Made Me a Criminal (1939) Dated melodrama in which a boxing champ (John Garfield), framed for the murder of a reporter, hides out on an Arizona date-farm set up to rehabilitate wayward youths (the Dead End Kids), until a hard-bitten New York cop (Claude Rains) spots his photograph. Directed by Busby Berkeley, it's an old story of a heel turned into a hero by the love of a good woman (Gloria Dickson) and the expectations of others, but it's done well and still effective. Stylized violence and mild romance. A-II (br)

They Met in Bombay (1941) Brisk romantic comedy in which rival jewel-thieves (Clark Gable and Rosalind Russell) join forces to flee Bombay police by stowing aboard a tramp steamer (captained by Peter Lorre) which docks in Hong Kong just as Japanese forces close in. Director Clarence Brown's lighthearted crime caper turns serious when Gable, masquerading as a British officer, is ordered to head a relief column evacuating foreign nationals from the mainland. Grand larceny redeemed by wartime heroics and mild romance. A-II (br)

They Might Be Giants (1971) George C. Scott plays a demented New York judge who believes himself to be Sherlock Holmes, and Joanne Woodward is a psychiatrist named Watson enlisted to bring him back to his senses. Between the promising opening scenes and the closing shot in front of a Central Park underpass, where the principals bravely face the dread Dr. Moriarity, director Anthony Harvey has supplied too many slack spots and unconnected parts to justify the question of whether the judge or society are the more insane. A-III (G)

They Only Kill Their Masters (1972) James Garner gives a wry performance as a small-time peace officer who's dumb like a fox, involved in a nasty murder case that unpeels some of the respectable veneer on his little coastal town. Displaced divorcée Katharine Ross finds a place not only in bachelor Gardner's bed but on his list of murder suspects as well. Director James Goldstone can't decide whether to play it straight or go for laughs and winds up doing neither well. A-III (PG)

They Passed This Way (see: **Four Faces West**)

They Rode West (1954) Routine Western about an Army doctor (Robert Francis) who averts an Indian uprising by treating the sick members of the tribe despite the orders of a superior (Phil Carey). Directed by Phil Karlson, it's well-intentioned but unconvincing, especially in its portrayal of Indian life and lore. Stylized violence. A-I (br)

They Shall Have Music (1939) Sentimental melodrama features violinist Jascha Heifetz coming to the rescue of a bankrupt music-school for the children of New York's slums. Directed by Archie Mayo, there's plenty of classical music and a game cast (Joel McCrea, Andrea Leeds, and Walter Brennan), but the manipulative script keeps tripping over its own bathos. High-minded but artificial inspirational fare. A-I (br)

They Shoot Horses, Don't They? (1969) Marathon dances were a popular form of distraction from the desperate times of the Depression, the period recreated by director Sydney Pollack's picture of exhausted contestants (Jane Fonda, Michael Sarrazin, Red Buttons, and Susannah York) trying to stay on their feet under the cruel urging of the master of ceremonies to win the $1,500 pot at the end of the musical rainbow. Sometimes depressing and not at all pleasant, the result captures the grimy texture of an agonized era. A-III (PG)

They Were Expendable (1945) Arriving in the Philippines just before Pearl Harbor, a squadron of PT boats (led by Robert Montgomery and John Wayne) manages, despite heavy losses, to sink two Japanese cruisers and evacuate senior officers from Corregidor before meeting its end. In this grim but idealistic and involving portrait of men in war, director John Ford, Captain USNR, pays tribute to those whose sacrifice against overwhelming forces gained time for the US to prepare a counter-offensive in the Pacific. Wartime violence. A-I (br)

They Won't Believe Me (1947) Convoluted melodrama in which a philandering husband (Robert Young) stands trial for murdering his wealthy wife (Rita Johnson), though he maintains he only hid her already dead body because his girlfriend (Susan Hayward) had just been identified as his wife after dying in a fiery auto accident. Director Irving Pichel gets a convincing performance from Young as a coldly calculating cad, but the contrived proceedings don't make much sense, even after the twist ending. Offscreen violence and marital infidelity. A-III (br)

Thief (1981) After a long prison term, a skilled safecracker (James Caan) wants to pull a couple of big jobs and retire on the proceeds, but, when he deals with a mob leader (Robert Prosky), he discovers too late that there is no way out of mob connections. Written and directed by Michael Mann, the emotional depth in Caan's characterization places it far above the usual standard of crime movie, though the story may be too grim for some tastes. A lot of tension, some violence, and rough language. A-III (R)

Thief, The (1998) Bittersweet drama set in 1952 Stalinist Russia, where a vulnerable war widow (Ekaterina Rednikova) and her six-year-old son (Misha Philipchuk) become involved with a con-man (Vladimir Mashkov) who passes them off as his family to win the trust of unsuspecting victims. Writer-director Pavel Chukhrai's skillfully told tale unfolds from the perspective of the child whose adoration of the father figure ultimately turns violent when mother and son feel betrayed. Subtitles. Brief instances of violence, discreet sexual encounters, brief full nudity, and minimal rough language. A-III (R)

Thief and the Cobbler, The (see: **Arabian Knight**)

Thief of Bagdad, The (1940) Grand adventure fantasy about an Arabian prince (John Justin) who, helped by a little thief (Sabu) and a gigantic genie (Rex Ingram), overcomes a series of obstacles conjured up by a wicked magician (Conrad Veidt) in order to wed the beautiful princess (June Duprez). Produced by Alexander Korda with fanciful Middle Eastern set designs by his brother Vincent, the result is filled with magic spells, wonderful transformations, and such marvels as a winged horse and flying carpet. Delightful family fun. A-I (br)

Thief of Baghdad (1961) Plodding variation on the Arabian Nights story about a goodhearted vagabond (Steve Reeves) who overcomes a host of obstacles to find the blue rose that will free the sultan's daughter (Georgia Moll) from an evil spell. Director Arthur Lubin plays much of this for laughs, and the result is only sporadically entertaining. Italian production dubbed in English. Stylized violence. A-I (br)

Thief of Damascus (1952) Inept adventure clunker directed by Will Jason is set in ancient Persia, where the sultan's throne is saved by a turncoat general (Paul Henried) in league with cut-rate versions of Sinbad (Lon Chaney, Jr.), Aladdin, Ali Baba, and Scheherezade. Witless script with a motley variety of stylized violence and sexual innuendo. A-III (br)

Thief of Hearts (1984) Slick, chrome-plated little melodrama about a burglar (Steven Bauer) who falls in love with a woman (Barbara Williams) whose intimate diaries were part of the loot he took from her house. Some serious possibilities of the story lose out to a blaring, obtrusive score and director Douglas Day Stewart's fondness for nudity and graphic sex. O (R)

Thief of Paris, The (1967) Fair French satire in which its 19th-century antihero (Jean-Paul Belmondo) recalls the motives and circumstances that caused his career as a thief. Directed by Louis Malle, the movie's slow pace is offset by some intelligent criticism of middle-class hypocrisy and some appropriate period costuming and sets. A-III (br)

Thief Who Came to Dinner, The (1973) Pretentious heist movie about a computer engineer (Ryan O'Neal) who starts a new career robbing the safes of Houston's finest families and leaving behind a chessman as his trademark. On his trail is a dogged insurance investigator (Warren Oates) who knows but can't prove it. Listlessly directed by Bud Yorkin, the movie never catches fire and begins to irritate with its repetitious comments about society's hypocrisy. A-III (PG)

Thieves (see: **Les Voleurs**)

Thieves (1977) Often affecting and funny story of an upwardly mobile Manhattan couple (Charles Grodin and Marlo Thomas) whose impending divorce gets sidetracked by the heroine's wild-eyed cabby father (Irwin Corey) and other assorted characters, including the police. Directed by John Berry, the comedy is saved from being too-cute and self-conscious by some exceptionally good acting. Infidelity and abortion figure in the plot (though not favorably), and there is frequent use of blasphemous expletives. A-III (PG)

Thieves Like Us (1974) Set in the deep South of the 1930s, the story concerns a trio of escaped convicts (Keith Carradine, Bert Remsen, and John Schuck) who take to smalltime bank-robbing. Director Robert Altman's back-roads ballad with conventional bloody ending is long on sleepy Southern atmosphere and earthy humor, but short on engaging characterizations (save Shelley Duvall's tender-waif performance) and narrative. A-III (R)

Thin Blue Line, The (1988) The 1976 murder of a Dallas policeman is the basis for this compelling documentary which uses some dramatized footage to reexamine the crime and explore the fine line between guilt and innocence. Director Errol Morris provides a chilling look at the man unjustly convicted of the murder, the man who fingered him, and the legal eagles responsible for a muddled conviction. Some rough language and repeated murder dramatizations. A-III (nr)

Thin Ice (1937) Alpine-resort star ice-skater (Sonja Henie) falls in love with a prince (Tyrone Power) masquerading as a reporter. Directed by Sidney Lanfield, the romantic comedy's thin plot does not deter from the charming performances of the two principals, the beauty of the skating, and comic relief by Joan Davis, Raymond Walburn, Arthur Treacher, Alan Hale, and Sig Ruman. Innocent romantic misunderstandings. A-I (br)

Thin Line Between Love & Hate, A (1996) Failed comedy thriller in which a conceited Lothario (Martin Lawrence) cheats on one woman too many (Lynn Whitfield), then finds she's out to murder him and his current flame (Regina King). Also directed by Lawrence, the lame fatal-attraction plot fizzles while Lawrence carries on with crude, misogynistic tirades that are not in the least amusing. Blatant sexist humor, a bedroom encounter with nudity, some violence, and constant rough language. O (R)

Thin Man, The (1934) Classic murder mystery from the Dashiell Hammett story of private detective Nick Charles (William Powell) announcing his retirement after marrying rich socialite Nora (Myrna Loy), then getting involved in trying to help a young woman (Maureen O'Sullivan) find her missing father, the eccentric inventor of the title (Edward Ellis). Director W.S. Van Dyke II paces the suspenseful plot with numerous suspicious characters, witty dialogue, and affectionate kidding between happily married Nick and Nora. Menacing atmosphere, some stylized violence, hardboiled types, and heavy drinking. A-II (br)

Thin Man Goes Home, The (1944) Genial mystery sequel in which private eye Nick Charles (William Powell) takes wife Nora (Myrna Loy) for a visit with his small-town parents (Harry Davenport and Lucile Watson), then gives the town's police chief (Donald MacBride) a hand in solving the murder of a local painter in a case involving wartime espionage. Directed by Richard Thorpe, the mystery takes a back seat to the varied reactions of the townsfolk to Nick's return, with a running gag about his switch from hard liquor to apple cider. Stylized violence and references to an illegitimate birth. A-II (br)

Thin Red Line, The (1998) Eloquent meditation on the insanity of warfare takes place as WW II American soldiers (notably Sean Penn, Ben Chaplin, Nick Nolte, and Jim Caviezel) battle the Japanese forces entrenched on Guadalcanal while reflecting on what brought each to this once-peaceful tropical paradise. Based on the James Jones novel, director Terrence Malick's lengthy philosophical drama views war as a desecration to all living things be they human, animal, or vegetable. Graphic battlefield violence, fleeting nudity, and recurring rough language and profanity. A-III (R)

Thing, The (1951) Arctic expedition (led by Kenneth Tobey) digs a flying saucer out of the ice, but its thawed occupant turns out to be an alien monster (James Arness) that feeds on human blood. Nicely crafted sci-fi thriller produced by Howard Hawks and directed by Christian Nyby, the conflict is not only with the monster from outer space but between the soldiers and the scientists in the frozen outpost. Growing sense of menace and suspense builds to a violent climax and final warning to "watch the skies." A-II (br)

Thing, The (1982) Director John Carpenter's brutal, simpleminded remake of the classic 1951 horror movie in which a research group in Antarctica struggles with a protean monster from outer space features Kurt Russell, A. Wilford Brimley, Richard Dysart, and Richard Masur. Excessive violence and appalling lack of respect for mangled human remains. O (R)

Thing That Couldn't Die, The (1958) Horror cheapie directed by William Cowan concerns what happens after a chest buried by Sir Francis Drake in 1579 is dug up on a California ranch and found to contain the still-living head of a warlock (Robin Hughes) whose evil eyes give him power over onlookers. Stylized violence and supernatural hokum. A-II (br)

Thing with Two Heads, The (1972) Racial bigot (Ray Milland) awakens to find his pale head attached to the hulking black frame of a condemned convict (Rosie Grier) who, buying time to prove his innocence, has volunteered his body for the dying Milland. Director Lee Frost forsakes all hope of evoking horror and simply joins the cast in having some dumb fun. A-II (PG)

Things Are Tough All Over (1982) Inept comedy with Cheech Marin and Thomas Chong driving a money-laden car from Chicago to Las Vegas for two rich Arabs, whose roles they also take. Directed by Tom Avildsen, it has the usual problem of beating jokes into the ground, but happily, the emphasis on narcotics has been dropped this time, though there is still the customary foul language, coarse humor, and a brief bit of nudity. O (R)

Things Change (1988) When a Chicago shoeshine man (Don Ameche) agrees to take the murder rap for a lookalike mob boss, his bungling mob babysitter (Joe Mantegna) takes him on a fantasy weekend to Lake Tahoe. Directed by David Mamet, this fictional slice of mob life entertains adults without relying on sex, violence, or special effects. Fine acting, spare dialogue, an improbable pair of buddies, and an ironic look at honor among thieves. Some rough language and brief violence. A-III (PG)

Things of Life (1970) Slow-moving French portrait of a middle-aged engineer (Michel Piccoli) torn between conflicting feelings toward his estranged wife, his mistress, and his own shaky dreams. Director Claude Sautet juggles together a convoluted tangle of flashes forward and backward, but the slickly confected pastry reveals a definite soap-opera base. A-III (GP)

Things to Do in Denver When You're Dead (1995) Violent tale in which an ex-con (Andy Garcia) tries to save his buddies after a botched job puts them on the hit-list of a vengeful mobster (Christopher Walken). Director Gary Fleder's crime thriller gives heroic treatment to the ex-con as a decent, selfless pal, despite his decision to murder an innocent relative of the mobster. Recurring graphic violence, fleeting bedroom scenes, and constant rough language. O (R)

Think Dirty (1978) Bumbling, good-natured, happily married adman (Marty Feldman) is ordered to launch a lewd ad-campaign selling porridge. Feldman, directing his own screenplay, is more interested in laughs than in sexual titillation, but the humor is often heavy-handed, and there is some nudity thrown in for bad measure. O (R)

Think Fast, Mr. Moto (1937) In the first of eight mysteries with Peter Lorre playing the Japanese detective created by John P. Marquand, a murder in San Francisco leads Moto to Shanghai, where he smashes a smuggling ring (led by Sig Ruman). Director Norman Foster paces the action with some comedy and mild romance, but lifting it out of the ordinary is Lorre's performance as the wry, wily sleuth. A-I (br)

Thinner (see: **Stephen King's Thinner**)

Third Animation Celebration, The (1991) Ninety-five minutes of recent animated shorts from the US and eight other countries, using techniques from traditional line-drawings to clay animation and computer graphics. Producer Terry Thoren's selection stresses offbeat humor, clever satire, and fast-moving visuals for an entertaining overview of what's happening in animation around the world. Minor cartoon violence and close-ups of an anatomically accurate male figure. A-II (nr)

Third Man, The (1949) Classic mystery thriller about an American writer of pulp Westerns (Joseph Cotton) searching the British sector of post-war Vienna for clues in the death of his old school chum, Harry Lime (Orson Welles). Directed by Carol Reed from a script by Graham Greene, the engrossing result offers a fascinating study in contrasts between the unscrupulous Lime and his naive friend, skillfully abetted by a superior supporting cast (Alida Valli, Trevor Howard, Bernard Lee, and Wilford Hyde-White), Robert Krasker's moody photography and the distinctive zither music of Anton Karas. A-II (br)

Third Secret, The (1964) Plodding British murder mystery directed by Charles Crichton has a London-based US TV-reporter (miscast Stephen Boyd) seeking to find a psychiatrist's killer while befriending the dead man's young daughter (Pamela Franklin). Much pretentious psychological musings, stylized violence, and sexual innuendo. A-III (br)

13 Ghosts (1960) Silly horror movie about the frights and scares encountered by a meek paleontologist (Charles Herbert), his wife (Rosemary DeCamp), and two offspring when they inherit a haunted house with a spooky housekeeper (Margaret Hamilton) and a hidden treasure. Director William Castle provides an eerie soundtrack, but neither the superimposed spooks nor the threadbare plot are likely to frighten anyone. Some occult trappings and supernatural menaces. A-I (br)

13 Rue Madeleine (1946) Taut WW II story starts in a US espionage school, with a tough veteran (James Cagney) training a new group of agents (including Annabella, Richard Conte,and Frank Latimore), one of whom proves to be a Nazi spy who jeopardizes an important mission. Director Henry Hathaway treats the material in sober, semi-documentary fashion, though Cagney's exploits to protect his agents in France tax credibility. Wartime violence and moral question of suicide by captured agents. A-III (br)

13 West Street (1962) Nasty little thriller in which a rocket engineer (Alan Ladd), after recovering from a senselessly brutal beating by five teens, gives up on the LA police detective (Rod Steiger) investigating the case and goes after the delinquents himself. Directed by Philip Leacock, the story of a citizen determined to take the law into his own hands gets increasingly muddled until its contrived ending. Much menace and some stylized violence. A-II (br)

Thirteen Women (1932) Half-baked hokum about a half-caste Oriental (Myrna Loy) bent on murdering the dozen members (notably Irene Dunne) of a school sorority from which she had been excluded years before. Directed by George Archainbaud, the revenge plot mixes in elements of the occult and hypnotism along with the racially motivated murders, but what makes the melodrama even more ludicrous is the bad acting from a good cast. Stylized violence and Asian stereotyping. A-III (br)

Thirteenth Floor, The (1999) Densely plotted sci-fi thriller involving a murder in parallel worlds, including 1937-era Los Angeles and the present, with characters (Armin Mueller-Stahl, Craig Bierko, and Vincent D'Onofrio) slipping between dimensions as they search for one true reality. Director Josef Resnak's convoluted tale plays intriguing mind games until the weakly constructed climax goes over the top, then imposes a pat conclusion. Sporadic nasty violence, some sexual innuendo, intermittent rough language, and a few instances of profanity. A-III (R)

30-Foot Bride of Candy Rock, The (1959) Woefully inept comedy about a garbage man (Lou Costello) whose girlfriend (Dorothy Provine) suddenly grows giant-sized, panicking town and Pentagon. Director Sidney Miller's loud, unfunny script and cheezy effects make Costello's last movie a sorry exercise. Minimal entertainment. A-I (br)

Thirty Seconds over Tokyo (1944) WW II morale booster depicting the 1942 raid on Tokyo by an Army squadron of B-25 bombers led by Lt. Col. James H. Doolittle (Spencer Tracy) which was launched from an aircraft carrier with only enough fuel to land in China. Directed by Mervyn LeRoy, the movie centers on the pilot's training, the brief low-level raid itself, and the difficulties facing survivors in occupied China, with human interest focused on one of the pilots (Van Johnson) and his pregnant wife (Phyllis Thaxter). Wartime violence, anti-Japanese rhetoric, and some sexual innuendo. A-II (br)

39 Steps, The (1935) Classic spy thriller about an innocent but resourceful Canadian (Robert Donat) pursued across Scotland by the police and a sinister gang of foreign agents, while handcuffed for a time to a woman (Madeleine Carroll) who believes him to be a murderer. Director Alfred Hitchcock has a lot of fun concocting surprising visual twists to the fast-paced suspense story, relieved by occasional comic turns of plot and a charming romance that begins in mutual antagonism. Some stylized violence, much menace, and mild romantic references. A-II (br)

Thirty-Nine Steps, The (1980) Lackluster British version of John Buchan's classic espionage yarn, made famous by the Hitchcock movie, about the pursuit both by police and nasty spies of an innocent man (Robert Powell) who has seemingly stumbled onto the plans to start WW I. Directed by Don Sharp, the 1914 setting is fine, the acting is excellent, but the brisk action is by now routine. Stylized violence. A-II (PG)

36 Fillette (1989) Sullen 14-year-old (Delphine Zentout) on summer holiday with her family plays cat-and-mouse sexual games with a much older man and finally loses her virginity to a peer. French director Catherine Breillat's irresponsible portrait of teenage angst features a depressing protagonist, her explicit sexual encounters with a middle-aged Lothario, and sexually vulgar language. Much nudity. O (nr)

36 Hours (1965) Neat suspense thriller about a fantastic plot by German intelligence to get information about the Allied invasion. Directed by George Seaton with Rod Taylor, Eva Marie Saint, and James Garner, the gimmicks are entertaining, and most viewers will excuse its melodramatic conclusion. A-II (br)

This Beast Must Die (see: **This Man Must Die**)

This Boy's Life (1993) Powerful coming-of-age drama set in the 1950s Pacific Northwest, where a young teen (Leonardo DiCaprio) faces daily jeopardy after his mother (Ellen Barkin) marries an emotionally abusive mechanic (Robert De Niro) who rules his backwater roost with an iron fist. Adapted from Tobias Wolff's memoirs and directed by Michael Caton-Jones, the searing performances and an undercurrent of sardonic wit convey both the boy's traumatic adolescence and his determination to survive the stepfather's monstrous mistreatment. Some scenes of intense physical and verbal abuse, a brief bedroom scene, and frequent rough language. A-III (R)

This Gun for Hire (1942) Interesting Americanized version of Graham Greene's novel about a professional hit-man (Alan Ladd) whose search for a double-crosser (Laird Cregar) leads to a wartime traitor. Directed by Frank Tuttle, the dark doings are brightened by a good woman (Veronica Lake) who shows some kindness to the hard-bitten gunman. Stylized violence. A-II (br)

This Happy Feeling (1958) Thin romantic comedy in which an aging actor (Curt Jurgens) gets a new lease on life from a bright young woman (Debbie Reynolds) who finds him more attractive than a neighbor (John Saxon) her own age. Writer-director Blake Edwards gets few laughs from a situation which proves more silly than charming. Sexual situations and innuendo. A-III (br)

This Is Elvis (1981) Complete but somewhat superficial look at superstar Elvis Presley using a documentary format with candid shots, home footage, scenes from television appearances, and dramatic action, all pointing to the image of a man being devoured by his fans. Best are the 38 Presley songs presented. Some sexual innuendo make the movie less suitable for youngsters. A-III (PG)

This Is My Father (1999) Melancholy romance set in 1939 rural Ireland, where a vivacious 17-year-old (Moya Farrelly) and a dirt-poor farmer (Aidan Quinn) fall in love and must face the wrath of her wealthy alcoholic mother, disapproving priests, and scornful villagers, driving the couple to desperate action. Writer-director Paul Quinn's muted tale explores loneliness and despair against the backdrop of class and religious strictures of the era. Fleeting violence, a discreet sexual encounter, and occasional profanity and rough language. A-III (R)

This Is My Life (1992) Two young daughters (Samantha Mathis and Gaby Hoffmann) become resentful when the growing success of their single mom (Julie Kavner) as a stand-up comedienne starts taking her away from home. Director and co-writer Nora Ephron's lighthearted, mildly insightful treatment of a working mother's frustrations and those of her daughters masks a drama common to many single-parent families. Brief bedroom scene with a parent's casual acceptance of her adolescent son's sexual activity and several sexual references. A-III (PG-13)

This Is Spinal Tap (1984) Mock documentary on the last, inglorious American tour of an aging English heavy-metal group whose fame is long gone makes the grade as a subtle, sometimes very funny, satire both on rock groups and on the documentaries made about them. The four principals (Rob Reiner as the director and Michael McKean, Christopher Guest, and Harry Shearer as the not over-bright leaders of the group) also collaborated on the script. Reiner tripled as director. There is a great deal of crude language and many sexual references in the dialogue and lyrics, but these are essential to the satirical nature of the movie. A-II (R)

This Is the Army (1943) Patriotic musical using Irving Berlin's songs from his WW I Army show as recycled for a WW II edition. Director Michael Curtiz blends fact and fancy by restaging the 1917 original with a cast headed by George Murphy, and then films the new version with the 1943 Army cast headed by Ronald Reagan as Murphy's son. Standout is Berlin singing one of his own numbers, but the flag-waving rhetoric keeps getting in the way of the music and comedy. A-I (br)

This Island Earth (1958) Fanciful sci-fi thriller with US scientists (Faith Domergue and Rex Reason) being shanghaied to a distant galaxy by a kindly alien (Jeff Morrow) whose planet desperately needs new energy-sources to shield it from the ceaseless bombardments of an enemy planet. Directed by Joseph Newman, the story begins with a mysterious secret project, then carries the action to a war-scarred, dying planet imaginatively suggested by modest but well-done special effects. More menace and suspense than violence. A-I (br)

This Land Is Mine (1943) Patriotic tale of a town in Nazi-occupied Europe, where an introverted schoolteacher (Charles Laughton) refuses to collaborate with the Fascist authorities (headed by Walter Slezak) after learning his mother (Una O'Connor) informed on the partisan brother (Kent Smith) of the woman (Maureen O'Hara) he loves. Directed by Jean Renoir, the movie's anti-Nazi aims are accomplished not through the melodramatics of the contrived plot, but through the earnest acting of a good cast. Stylized violence. A-II (br)

This Love of Ours (1945) Soggy tearjerker in which a French doctor (Charles Korvin), convinced his wife (Merle Oberon) is having an affair, takes their three-year-old daughter to America, then 10 years later meets her again by chance and learns how terribly wrong he had been. Directed by William Dieterle, the contrived plot unfolds in flashbacks, which fail to distract from the shallowness of the hokey proceedings. Marital misunderstandings and an attempted suicide. A-II (br)

This Man Must Die (1970) Superior French suspenseful drama follows a father (Michel Duchaussoy) in tracking down the hit-and-run driver (Jean Yanne) who killed his son, but he finds that retribution is not so simple. Director Claude Chabrol convincingly portrays the father's cold determination in seeking revenge but is more interested in the wider circle of guilt that this incurs. Some sexual situations. A-III (GP)

This Property Is Condemned (1966) Trashy soap opera about a young woman (Natalie Wood) in a small Southern railroad-town during the Depression who falls in love with the man (Robert Redford) sent by the railroad company to fire most of its workers. Directed by Sydney Pollack, the movie is excessively suggestive in its treatment of sexual situations. O (br)

This Savage Land (1968) Pioneer Ohio widower (Barry Sullivan) brings his family to settle in Kansas after the Civil War, but they are harassed by Southern vigilantes in Vincent McEveety's rather pedestrian Western. Stylized violence. A-II (br)

This Special Friendship (1967) French story of a homosexual attraction between two boys in a strict Catholic boarding-school in the 1920s ends in tragedy. Directed by Jean Delannoy in sensitive and thoughtful fashion, it leaves the viewer to judge the nature of the relationship and the way in which the school authorities dealt with it. Mature fare. A-III (br)

This Time I'll Make You Rich (1975) Totally undistinguished formula kung-fu action adventure produced in Hong Kong by Joseph E. Levine. Restrained violence. A-III (PG)

This Woman Is Dangerous (1952) Soapy crime tale in which a hot-headed gangster (David Brian) gets jealous when his fancy moll (Joan Crawford) goes to a distant clinic for an operation to save her eyesight, then learns the surgeon (Dennis Morgan) has fallen in love with her. Directed by Felix Feist, the contrived plot and formula characters develop in predictable fashion, except for a bizarre scene in which a hospital operating-room is turned into a shooting gallery. Some nasty violence, including several cold-blooded murders, and romantic complications. A-III (br)

Thomas Crown Affair, The (1968) Steve McQueen plays a wealthy, clever Bostonian who gets away with two perfect bank robberies before meeting his match in insurance investigator Faye Dunaway, and two engage in a totally amoral game of cat and mouse that ends in a love match, with the law left holding the bag. In director Norman Jewison's smoothly calculated, slickly executed work, it seems that crime pays quite well. O (R)

Thomasine and Bushrod (1974) Vonetta McGee and Max Julien play a black Bonnie and Clyde duo fighting racial oppression and injustice in the West of 1911. Though it has all the now-standard cliches of period cars, a redneck sheriff (George Murdock), bank robberies, news accounts, and a bloody finale, director Gordon Parks, Jr., fails to make the characters credible or the situations plausible. A-III (PG)

Thoroughly Modern Millie (1967) In a musical spoof of the Roaring Twenties, Julie Andrews and Mary Tyler Moore seek careers and romance in New York City with the help of handsome John Gavin and debonair James Fox. Director George Roy Hill's irreverent lark gets some good support from Bea Lillie and Carol Channing, some songs that characterize the period, and a fast-moving script that has something for everybody. A-I (G)

Those Calloways (1965) Predictable Disney movie in which a backwoods family (Brian Keith, Vera Miles, Brandon De Wilde) tries to keep hunters from shooting the Canadian geese that migrate through their area. Directed by Norman Tokar, the outdoors sequences are fine, especially those of the wild geese. A-I (br)

Those Daring Young Men in Their Jaunty Jalopies (1969) The Monte Carlo Rally in the early part of the century served as an endurance test for cars, and in many respects this movie about the rally proves to be much the same kind of test for viewers. Director Ken Annakin has a large cast of comedians (best are Peter Cook and Dudley Moore), but the tired formula-racing action is unfunny, though it does some tasteless off-color jokes. Vintage car-fanciers might enjoy it. A-II (G)

Those Endearing Young Charms (1945) WW II romance in which a sensible New York shop-girl (Laraine Day) falls for a cynical bomber pilot (Robert Young) out for a good time before returning overseas, then gets serious just before his leave is up. Directed by Lewis Allen, the contrived situation has some human interest, though the pilot is an unlikable heel whose last-minute transformation is unearned. Romantic complications. A-II (br)

Those Fantastic Flying Fools (1967) Phineas T. Barnum (Burl Ives), straight from bankruptcy in the US, arrives in Victorian England ready to construct the first rocket-ship to the moon. Director Don Sharp can't do much with a script riddled with cliches, but the obvious and predictable slapstick difficulties of building the rocket may prove diverting fun for the very young. A-I (br)

Those Lips, Those Eyes (1980) Sentimental look at summer theater in a 1951 Cleveland suburb, where a college student (Thomas Hulce) takes a job as a prop man and gets so carried away with show business and one of the dancers (Glynnis O'Conner) that he wants to go to New York, much to the anguish of his father (Jerry Stiller). Directed by Michael Pressman, the nostalgia is unfortunately marred by some explicit nudity in a bedroom scene, compounded by the movie's rather benign attitude toward casual sex. O (R)

Those Magnificent Men in Their Flying Machines (1965) Early vintage aircraft are the real stars and source of fun in this colorful comedy spectacular about a 1910 air race from England to France. Good musical score, tongue-in-cheek script, and international cast including Alberto Sordi, Gert Frobe, Jean-Pierre Cassell, Terry-Thomas, and Red Skelton, are some of the reasons for the success of this entertainment package from director Ken Annakin. A-I (G)

Thousand Acres, A (1997) Earnest but slow-moving sudser in which two sisters (Jessica Lange and Michelle Pfeiffer) battle their nasty, aged father (Jason Robards) and younger sister (Jennifer Jason Leigh) over the ownership of a rich Iowa farm. Directed by Jocelyn Moorhouse, the overly contrived story of a family in conflict fails to generate much sympathy from its dour collection of dark family secrets and insufferable male stereotypes. Recollections of child sexual abuse, adulterous relationships, a flash of nudity, and a few instances of rough language and profanity. A-III (R)

Thousand Clowns, A (1966) Screen version of Herb Gardner's Broadway comedy about a cheerful eccentric (Jason Robards) who has withdrawn from society to live as he pleases, until a social worker (Barbara Harris) perks his romantic interest and he must decide how to adjust to the demands of responsibility. Producer-director Fred Coe retains the good-natured wit and feeling for people in its humorous digs at social conformity, though the closer it strives for contemporary relevance, the more it loses its shield of fantasy and romantic innocence. Mature treatment. A-III (br)

1,000 Plane Raid, The (1969) Routine WW II picture directed by Boris Sagal in which a US bomber pilot (Christopher George) proposes a massive joint American-British air strike, then is ordered to lead such a raid against a heavily fortified German submarine factory. Stylized violence and sexual situations. A-III (G)

Three (1969) Three young people (Robie Porter, Sam Waterston, Charlotte Rampling) spend a summer touring Europe and come to know one another and themselves better. There's not much plot or action, but there's plenty of gorgeous scenery and some shallow characterizations intended to show the subtle development of human relationships and self-awareness. A-III (PG)

Three Amigos (1986) Steve Martin stars in and produces, but doesn't dominate, this pictorially grand but sometimes brutal Western parody about three silent-screen actors playing silly *caballeros* in a Mexican village that mistakes them for hired gunmen. Chevy Chase and Martin Short supply the slapstick and wit for director John Landis, whose interest seems rooted in the physical comedy and dangerous stunts. Stylized violence and some rough language. A-II (PG)

Three Brothers (1982) French-Italian drama in which three brothers, whose lives have taken divergent paths, return to their native village in southern Italy when their mother dies. Director Francesco Rosi's warmly human study of family bonds has fine acting, especially Charles Vanel's awesome presence as their peasant father, and many touching moments, mostly in flashbacks. Despite its many virtues, the story fails to come together as a whole, and the result is a disappointment. A-II (PG)

Three Caballeros, The (1945) Walt Disney's colorful celebration of our neighbors to the South follows Donald Duck's tuneful trip to Latin America. Among the animated characters that he meets are Jose Carioca and Panchito, who teach him about their customs and culture. Informative as well as good fun. A-I (G)

Three Came Home (1950) Interned by the Japanese after the fall of Borneo, an American writer (Claudette Colbert) looks after her young son (Mark Kuening) while enduring the deprivations and humiliations of a prison camp, until reunited with her husband (Patric Knowles) at war's end. Director Jean Negulesco suggests more than he shows of the hardships shared by the women prisoners, whose fear of their captors is epitomized in the misunderstandings between the level-headed heroine and the camp's commander (Sessue Hayakawa). Much tension and some stylized violence. A-II (br)

Three Came to Kill (1960) Low-budget crime tale directed by Edward L. Cahn, in which two professional killers (Cameron Mitchell and Steve Brodie) and the man (Jan Arvan) who hired them hold a family prisoner, while using their home adjacent to the Los Angeles airport in an attempt to blow up an airliner carrying a Middle Eastern leader. The scenes of stylized violence and menace are balanced by the efforts of dedicated law officers and the bravery of the family's father (John Lupton). A-I (br)

Three Cases of Murder (1954) Dull trilogy of murder stories opens with Roderick Wilkinson's fantasy about an art museum, where people live inside the paintings (director Wendy Toye); an inane Brett Halliday mystery about the murder of a woman who comes between two lifelong chums (director David Eady); and concludes with W. Somerset Maugham's tale of a British foreign secretary tormented by dreams of killing a political rival (director George More O'Ferrall). Only this last effort shows any imagination in plot construction or character development as the conflict builds between domineering government official (Orson Welles) and sneering opponent (Alan Badel). Some deadly menace and minimal stylized violence. A-II (br)

Three Coins in the Fountain (1954) Sentimental tale of three American women sharing an apartment in Rome, where, after making a wish for romance at the Trevi Fountain, one (Maggie McNamara) snares an Italian prince (Louis Jourdan), another (Jean Peters) reforms a handsome hustler (Rossano Brazzi), while the third (Dorothy McGuire) mellows her testy boss. Directed by Jean Negulesco, the soppy proceedings benefit greatly from some well-paced humor, a heart-throbbing theme song, and truly magnificent location photography. Romantic complications. A-II (br)

Three Comrades (1938) Sentimental adaptation of the Erich Maria Remarque novel in which a trio of German front-line veterans (Robert Taylor, Robert Young, and Franchot Tone), struggle to make a living after WW I, take a fragile young woman (Margaret Sullavan) under their wing, then learn she is dying of tuberculosis. While director Frank Borzage concentrates on the veterans' camaraderie and tender friendship with the woman, viewers today are likely to be more interested in the movie's depiction of post-war Germany's poverty and despair as the breeding ground of Fascism. Stylized violence, including a suicide. A-III (br)

Three Days of the Condor (1975) CIA agent (Robert Redford), on the run from assassins who may be fellow agents, happens on a woman (Faye Dunaway) who lends him at first reluctant, then enthusiastic, assistance. Directed by Sydney Pollack, it's a slickly done but shallow movie whose heroics are implausible, and whose idealism is more than a little inconsistent. Some violence, occasional rough language and a love affair between the two principals. A-III (R)

Three Faces of Eve, The (1957) Sober fact-based dramatization, introduced by journalist Alistair

Cooke, portrays the struggle within a prim Georgia housewife (Joanne Woodward) as she tries, with the help of a psychiatrist (Lee J. Cobb), to resolve the conflict between her multiple personalities. Written, produced, and directed by Nunnally Johnson, the case study of a psychiatric condition achieves a credible human dimension, thanks primarily to Woodward's touching *tour-de-force* performance. Psychological abnormalities and domestic upheavals. A-III (br)

Three Faces West (1940) Dated but interesting melodrama in which a refugee Austrian physician (Charles Coburn) and his daughter (Sigrid Gurie) settle in a Midwest farming community beset by dust storms, then join a local farm-leader (John Wayne) in persuading their neighbors to migrate to new lands in Oregon. Directed by Bernard Vorhaus, the movie portrays refugees as an asset for the nation, with Coburn's warm performance as the caring doctor putting the point over convincingly. A-I (br)

Three for the Road (1987) Director B.W.L. Norton's teen comedy-romance disguised as rebellious-youth road-movie features Charlie Sheen as an aspiring politician who delivers a senator's troubled daughter (Kerri Green) to a prison-like school. Falling in love, he helps her to escape into the custody of her estranged mom (Sally Kellerman), whose change of heart resolves the movie's conflict between duty and conscience. Some rough language and mildly permissive attitude toward teen romance. A-II (PG)

Three Fugitives (1989) Writer-director Francis Veber's English-language version of his 1986 French movie about a novice robber (Martin Short) who takes a hostage (Nick Nolte) in a bank heist, and then the pair of misfits spend the rest of the film trying to extricate themselves from each other and the cops. Also on the lam is the robber's tiny, troubled daughter (Sarah Rowland Doroff) who adds implausible, sentimentalized heart to this nutty slapstick comedy. Much rough language and intense comic book violence. A-III (PG-13)

Three Godfathers (1948) After robbing a bank, an outlaw trio (John Wayne, Pedro Armendariz, and Harry Carey, Jr.) pause to help a dying woman (Mildred Natwick) deliver her infant son on Christmas Eve, then take the babe with them as they are pursued across a desert wasteland. Dedicated by director John Ford to Western actor Harry Carey, Sr., the story may be unabashedly sentimental and the action romanticized, but its lyrical images and religious resonances celebrate the myth of the Old West and its rugged heroes with good hearts. Off-screen suicide of one of the principals. A-II (br)

Three Guys Named Mike (1951) Dated romantic comedy directed by Charles Walters, in which airline stewardess Jane Wyman is pursued by pilot Howard Keel, advertising-man Barry Sullivan, and science-professor Van Johnson, while she mulls which of the title trio to marry. Of interest mainly as a sociological artifact. A-II (br)

Three Hours to Kill (1954) Static Western directed by Alfred Werker, in which a man (Dana Andrews) escapes being lynched for a murder he didn't commit, then returns years later to clear his name by finding the real killer. Stylized violence and romantic complications. A-II (br)

300 Spartans, The (1962) Pedestrian account of Persia's invasion of Greece in 480 B.C. focuses on the confrontation between the mighty forces of King Xerxes (David Farrar) and a small band of Spartans (led by Richard Egan) guarding the pass at Thermopylae, just before the decisive defeat of the Persian fleet by the Athenians (led by Ralph Richardson). Rudolph Maté directs a lifeless script full of cardboard characters and high-school rhetoric about the virtues of democracy and the need for unity, though interest picks up once the battle at the pass is joined with convincing action scenes. Battlefield violence. A-I (br)

Three in the Attic (1969) Grade-B youth sex fantasy in which a three-timing college student (Christopher Jones) is abducted by the wronged trio (Yvette Mimieux, Judy Page, and Maggie Thrett) and punished with having to indulge them incessantly in the sorority-house attic. Producer-director Richard Wilson rings the changes on a thoroughly tasteless situation. O (R)

Three in the Cellar (see: **Up in the Cellar**)

Three into Two Won't Go (1969) British drama about a couple (Rod Steiger and Claire Bloom) whose marriage is in serious trouble because of the husband's habit of picking up women on his business trips. Directed by Peter Hall, the movie's dramatic potential in probing the problems of married life is, unfortunately, undermined by focus on the prurient antics of the husband's latest misadventure (Judy Geeson). O (R)

Three Little Girls in Blue (1946) Formula musical directed by Bruce Humberstone in which three farm-girl sisters (June Haver, Vivian Blaine, and Vera-Ellen) aim to find rich husbands in 1902 Atlantic City, with predictable results. Romantic complications. A-I (br)

Three Lives (1971) Author Kate Millet's documentary consists of interviews with three women, who, in a series of separate monologues, express the message of women's liberation and, among other things, the male influences in their lives. Its plain and simple technique adds rather than detracts from credibility of the three, who seem to epitomize the personal commitment that women's lib requires of those who espouse it. Some strong language. A-III (nr)

Three Lives and Only One Death (1996) Surrealist tale of a man (Marcello Mastroianni) who leads four lives, as a travelling salesman, a professor, a butler, and a dying businessman whose wandering mind suggests the link between the four personalities. Chilean director Raul Ruiz's elegant French production recounts stories about each man in turn, involving them in absurd events with characters to match, though there is no logical connection between them other than as imaginative variations on the human possibilities of a fictional character. Subtitles. Sexual situations and innuendo. A-III (nr)

Three Men and a Baby (1987) The carefree life of three bachelors (Tom Selleck, Steve Guttenberg, and Ted Danson) changes when they become responsible for an infant girl fathered by one of them. Director Leonard Nimoy gets a few genuine laughs out of the situation, but the entertainment level is pretty flat. Benign view of casual sex. A-III (PG)

Three Men and a Cradle (1986) French comedy in which three single, macho males confront their shallow emptiness when an unexpected visitor, a baby, changes their lifestyle and elicits feelings of tenderness and devotion. Writer-director Coline Serreau's film is uplifting, even inspirational, for male audiences in its demonstration that tenderness is an important aspect of manliness. A-II (PG-13)

Three Men and a Little Lady (1990) Three bachelors (Tom Selleck, Ted Danson, and Steve Guttenberg) take drastic action when Sylvia (Nancy Travis) announces she and little Mary (Robin Weisman) will no longer be living with them, as she is marrying and returning to England. Director Emile Ardolino's sprightly sequel tries hard to be a screwball comedy with an old-fashioned romance thrown in, but the likeable performers never quite capture the fun of the baby situation in the original. Very mild sexual innuendo. A-II (PG)

Three Musketeers, The (1935) Serviceable version of Alexandre Dumas's adventure saga, in which provincial youth D'Artagnan (Walter Abel) joins Parisian musketeers Athos (Paul Lukas), Porthos (Maroni Olson), and Aramis (Onslow Stevens) in saving the French throne from the intrigues of Cardinal Richelieu (Nigel de Brulier) and his agents (Ian Keith and Margot Grahame). Directed by Rowland V. Lee, the plot is streamlined to its essential conflict of fidelity vs. treachery, with some fanciful swordplay, chaste romance (Heather Angel), and a game performance by the miscast Abel. Stylized violence and romantic folly. A-II (br)

Three Musketeers, The (1939) The Dumas adventure classic survives surprising well in this musical comedy version starring Don Ameche as D'Artagnan, with the Ritz Brothers clowning around as the counterfeit trio of the title. Director Allan Dwan mixes the action and romance with agreeable songs and daffy comic relief. Stylized violence and court intrigues. A-II (br)

Three Musketeers, The (1948) Stylish but uneven adaptation of the Dumas classic, with a frenetic D'Artagnan (Gene Kelly), a tormented Athos (Van Heflin), an oily Richelieu (Vincent Price), and a steamy Milady (Lana Turner). Director George Sidney stages the swashbuckling derring-do with showy flair, but the story of saving the French throne tends to drag in comparison. Considerable stylized violence and sexual innuendo. A-III (br)

Three Musketeers, The (1974) Satiric British version of the Dumas classic zestfully follows the shambling trail of the raw and foolish D'Artagnan (Michael York) in his quest to become one of the Musketeers (Oliver Reed, Richard Chamberlain, and Frank Finlay). Directed by Richard Lester, it is an energetic swashbuckler in the grand style, offering an entertaining mix of romantic adventure and slapstick comedy, even if the frenetic humor sometimes wears a bit thin. Some restrained sexual innuendo. A-II (PG)

Three Musketeers, The (1993) Trashy comic-book adaptation of the Alexandre Dumas tale of a country lad (Chris O'Donnell) joining a rollicking trio of musketeers (Kiefer Sutherland, Charlie Sheen, and Oliver Pratt) to save the throne of France from the wicked Cardinal Richelieu (Tim Curry). Director Stephen Herek's heavy-handed attempts to portray lighthearted heroes trouncing atrocious comic villains turn a durable adventure classic into campy, often mean-spirited comedy. Much stylized violence, sexual references, and jokey treatment of religion. A-III (PG)

3 Ninjas (1992) Thoroughly contrived comedy follows the three young sons of a neglectful FBI dad (Alan McRae) as they outsmart an arms-dealer (Rand Kingsley), thanks to martial-arts training by their grandpa (Victor Wong). Directed by Jon Turtletaub, the manipulative formula movie tries to make the youngsters' brutalizing of adults seem hysterically funny, despite inept plot and poor acting. Frequent comic violence and some toilet humor. A-III (PG)

3 Ninjas: High Noon at Mega Mountain (1998) Boring sequel in which four youngsters use their martial-arts skills and computer savvy to outwit a band of terrorists (led by Loni Anderson) holding them and many others hostage in a theme park. Director Sean McNamara showcases constant physical aggression in this predictable and juvenile macho fantasy. Much slapstick violence. A-III (PG)

3 Ninjas Kick Back (1994) Uninspired sequel in which the three ninja-loving youngsters (Max Elliott Slade, Sean Fox, and Evan Bonifant) land in Japan to rescue their grandfather (Victor Wong) from an evil rival bent on stealing the old man's ceremonial dagger. Director Charles T. Kanganis adds a perky girl-ninja to the formula but limits the entertainment to unconvincing bouts between the four children and dozens of adult opponents, with always predictable results. Martial-arts violence and some menace. A-II (PG)

Three of Hearts (1993) A bizarre triangle develops when a male escort (William Baldwin) falls for a bisexual teacher (Sherilyn Fenn) he has been hired to romance and dump, in hopes she will then return to the lesbian nurse (Kelly Lynch) she left behind. Director Yurek Bogayevicz's uneven movie stresses the humanity, not the sexuality, of its characters, especially the gigolo who gradually gains self-respect and rejects his sleazy lifestyle. An uncritical treatment of homosexuality, brief bedroom scenes, fleeting nudity, minor violence, and recurring rough language. A-IV (R)

Three on a Couch (1966) Jerry Lewis directs himself in the story of an inventive fellow using his wits and several disguises (including that of a female) in order to win the heart of his psychiatrist fiancé (Janet Leigh), who keeps postponing the wedding date because she claims her patients need her more. Typical Lewis vehicle though with more than usual sexual innuendo. A-III (br)

Three on a Match (1932) Period melodrama in which a bored wife (Anne Dvorak) abandons her rich husband (Warren William) for a flashy gambler who loses all her money, then holds her young son for ransom, until the desperate woman pays with her life to save the child. Directed by Mervyn LeRoy, some contrast is provided by the woman's childhood chums, a showgirl (Joan Blondell) and a secretary (Bette Davis), but most notable is its use of newsreels and newspapers to root the story in the social context of the Prohibition and Depression eras. Stylized violence, marital infidelity, and implied drug addiction. A-III (br)

3 Ring Circus (1954) Two Army buddies get menial jobs in a circus, and, after much blundering, one (Dean Martin) becomes the manager and the other (Jerry Lewis) its top clown. Directed by Joseph Pevney, the colorful circus acts and a good supporting cast (Joanne Dru, Zsa Zsa Gabor, Wallace Ford, and Elsa Lanchester) help make up for Dean's singing and Lewis's mugging. Small children may enjoy it. A-I (br)

Three Seasons (1999) Lyrical drama loosely weaves together four stories set in present-day Vietnam, where impoverished natives struggle to survive and make emotional connections, and an ex-Marine (Harvey Kietel) returns to find his Amerasian daughter. Exquisite cinematography enhances writer-director Tony Bui's humanist tale of courage and kindness overcoming a hardscrabble existence. Subtitles. Some sexual innuendo. A-II (PG-13)

Three Sisters, The (1969) Russian adaptation of the Chekhov play about a 19th-century family whose financial reverses keep them in a remote garrison town, each of them overwhelmed by the sense of frustrated desires and the ultimate hopelessness of their fate. Writer-director Sergei Samsonov is faithful to the original by centering the movie on characterization and mood rather than on dramatic plot. A-II (nr)

Three Smart Girls (1936) In her screen debut, Deanna Durbin plays the youngest of three sisters (Barbara Read and Nan Gray are the others) who hope to reunite their divorced parents by saving their father (Charles Winniger) from marrying a gold-digger (Binnie Barnes). Director Henry Koster's sentimental comedy relies on the old wheeze of mistaken identities (Ray Milland and Mischa Auer), the mischievous conniving of the teen sisters, and young Durbin's singing talents. Wholesome but dated entertainment. A-I (br)

Three Stooges Follies, The (1974) Entertaining collection of WW II-vintage movie short-subjects, headlining the Stooges's Neanderthal variety of slapstick humor, an acquired taste perhaps best left uncultivated. On the other hand, this package of instant nostalgia includes a Buster Keaton short, a wartime serial with Batman and Robin fighting a Japanese spy-ring, and a rousing finale with Kate Smith singing a flag-waving medley of patriotic songs. All in glorious black-and-white. A-I (G)

Three Stooges Go Around the World in a Daze, The (1963) Mediocre slapstick comedy directed by Norman Maurer, in which Phileas Fogg III (Jay Sheffield) sets out from London to circle the globe in 80 days without spending a farthing, but he needs help from his Stooge servants (Moe Howard, Larry Fine, and Joe De Rita) to foil attempts to disrupt the journey. Comic violence. A-I (br)

Three Stooges in Orbit, The (1962) Halting slapstick comedy directed by Edward Bernds in which the Stooges (Moe Howard, Larry Fine, and Joe De Rita) try to help the inventor (Emil Sitka) of a flying submarine by tangling with Martians sent to steal the contraption. Slapstick violence. A-I (br)

Three Stooges Meet Hercules (1962) Slack slapstick comedy directed by Edward Bernds follows the time-traveling Stooges (Moe Howard, Larry Fine, and Joe De Rita) to ancient Greece, where they irritate Hercules by helping Ulysses, save Rhodes from a two-headed Cyclops,, work as galley slaves, then flee for their lives in a chariot chase, before returning home to Ithaca, N.Y. Comic violence. A-I (br)

Three Stripes in the Sun (1955) Gentle clash-of-cultures tale concerns a sergeant (Aldo Ray) stationed in 1949 Osaka, where he overcomes his hostility to the Japanese in helping the Sisters of Charity rebuild an orphanage, then falls in love with a helpful interpreter (Mitsuko Tamura). Written and directed by Richard Murphy, the fact-based story has its sentimental moments but is mostly clear-eyed in its account of interracial misunderstandings and healings. Youngsters may need some help with the cultural barriers separating the two principals. A-I (br)

3:10 to Yuma (1957) Intelligent, well-crafted Western in which a small Arizona rancher (Van Heflin) in need of ready cash takes the job of delivering a captured badman (Glenn Ford) to the federal marshal on the next train, but, as they await its arrival, the outlaw's band of a ruthless gunmen show up to free him. Director Delmer Daves concentrates on the shifting relationship between the decent family man and his cynical prisoner in a psychological war of wit and nerve, until the suspenseful situation erupts in the final showdown. Stylized violence, much menace, and an implied sexual encounter. A-II (br)

Three the Hard Way (1974) Black exploitation movie about three superheroes (Jim Brown, Fred Williamson, and Jim Kelly) who join in tracking down a villain plotting to put a serum in America's drinking water that will kill only blacks. Ineptly directed by Gordon Parks Jr., the movie's plot premise borders on the socially irresponsible. Some brutal as well as sadistic violence. O (R)

Three Tough Guys (1974) Hard-hitting priest (Lino Ventura) and a down-at-the-heels detective (Isaac Hayes) join forces in solving a bank robbery that has cost the one a parishioner and the other his job. The plot's trail of corpses is fairly routine, but one can enjoy the fine performances of the two principals. Italian production directed by Duccio Tessari makes intelligent use of Chicago's architecture and lakefront, often making the background more interesting to watch than any of the fantasy violence that clutters the view. A-III (PG)

Three Violent People (1956) Returning home after the Civil War, a Texas rancher (Charlton Heston) marries a lady with a shady past (Anne Baxter), fends off land-grabbing carpetbaggers (Bruce Bennett and Forrest Tucker), and feuds with his resentful, one-armed brother (Tom Tryon). Director Rudolph Mate's formula Western limps fitfully along with predictable plot complications, cliched action, and stereotyped characters. Stylized violence, domestic strife, and muted sexual allusions. A-II (br)

Three Warriors (1977) Native-American (Lois Red Elk) returns to the reservation with her young son, who learns about his people's customs and heritage from his grandfather, assisted by a lame horse and a good-natured forest ranger (Randy Quaid) who's chasing rustlers. In the context of credible acting, the beautiful cinematography of Bruce Surtees and the sensitive direction of Keith Merrill, it is a good family movie that parents can enjoy as much as their children. A-I (G)

Three Wishes (1995) Fable-like drama about a young boy (Joseph Mazzello) in 1955 suburbia, who hopes his widowed mom (Mary Elizabeth Mastrantonio) will marry the kind-hearted drifter (Patrick Swayze) who has come into their lives as the result of an accident. Director Martha Coolidge spins a charming, well-observed story of decent people coping with life's problems, but the story is weakened by a subplot in which a sickly younger brother comes to believe he has magical powers. Fleeting nudity and a crude expression. A-II (PG)

3 Women (1977) Director Robert Altman explores the friendship between two single women (Shelley Duvall and Sissy Spacek), unskilled workers in a geriatric facility, and an unhappily married artist (Janice Rule) whose work on a grotesque mural keeps her on the periphery until the movie's bleak, simplistic resolution, which brings the three together in a strong, sexless relationship. Though thoughtful in its character study of the women, promiscuity figures in the plot, and the camera's obsession with the exaggerated sexual characteristics of the mural's semi-human figures make it questionable fare. A-IV (PG)

Three Worlds of Gulliver, The (1960) Slack adaptation of Swift's novel about Dr. Lemuel Gulliver (Kerwin Matthews) who leaves 18th-century England for adventures among the small folk of Lilliput and the giants of Brobdingnag. Co-written and directed by Jack Sher, the scenario varies from the sluggish to the slapdash, the acting is largely charmless, and Ray Harryhausen's special effects are bargain-basement affairs. Disappointing fantasy except for the very young. A-I (br)

Threesome (1994) Accidentally assigned to share college-dorm quarters with a leering stud (Stephen Baldwin) and a latent homosexual (Josh Charles), a promiscuous young woman (Lara Flynn Boyle) seduces both, then the trio together explore the limits of lust. Writer-director Andrew Fleming's boring, inept exercise in soft-core male fantasies reduces its vacuous characters to mindless sex-objects. Trivialization of sexuality, simulated sex, considerable nudity, and much rough language. O (R)

Threshold (1983) Canadian drama about an American heart specialist (Donald Sutherland) and an eccentric but brilliant research biologist (Jeff Goldblum) who join forces to develop an artificial heart. Director Richard Pearce successfully avoids all the melodramatic cliches inherent in the situation and the result is a good, if not especially inspired, movie. A-II (PG)

Through the Olive Trees (1995) While making a movie in a remote mountainous area of Iran, the director casts two young locals as a married couple, unaware that the man is actually the girl's rejected suitor, which causes problems as the would-be groom attempts to woo the impassive adolescent between takes. In this Iranian production, writer-director Abbas Kiarostami delivers a small gem of human comedy, disarmingly unpretentious in interweaving the tedious process of filmmaking with the droll situation of an earnest young suitor steadfastly ignoring the continuous indifference of his prospective bride until a romantic, if inconclusive, ending. Subtitles. Humorous romantic complications. A-II (G)

Throw Momma from the Train (1987) After seeing Hitchcock's **Strangers on a Train**, a dim-witted student sets out to kill the hated ex-wife of his adult-education writing-instructor (Billy Crystal), mistakenly expecting his domineering mother to be killed by the teacher in return. Also directed by DeVito, the broad performance of Anne Ramsey as the mother is so outrageous that it cannot be taken seriously, but the rest of the humor pales in comparison. Black comedy treatment of a murder plot and a casual attitude toward sex. A-III (PG-13)

Thumb Tripping (1972) Two idealistic college students (Meg Foster and Michael Burns) waste their summer (and the viewer's time) hitchhiking East from Big Sur and meet bigots, thugs, and perverts along the way. Directed by Quentin Martin, the treatment of the episodes is explicit in both visuals and language, but far more offensive is the movie's smug attitude toward its finally disillusioned youngsters. O (R)

Thunder Across the Pacific (see: **The Wild Blue Yonder**)

Thunder Alley (1967) Suspended race-car driver (Fabian) takes a job as stunt driver while trying to prove his innocence. Directed by Richard Rush, the routine action film is marred by scenes of casual sex. O (br)

Thunder and Lightning (1977) Mediocre chase thriller in which a hippie moonshiner and his girl (David Caradine and Kate Jackson) race across the Florida Everglades with tough Northeastern bootleggers in hot pursuit. Daring stunts, failed humor, and lame dialogue dominate in a movie directed by Corey Allen. Gratuitous use of slapstick violence and nudity. O (PG)

Thunder in the Sun (1959) Mediocre Western follows a wagon train of French Basques heading for California with a precious cargo of grapevines, beset by the hazards of the trail in crossing a desert without water, a prairie fire, an Indian attack, and a hard-drinking guide (Jeff Chandler) who takes a fancy to the wife (Susan Hayward) of the group's leader (Jacques Bergerac). Though bringing a bit of ethnic color to the frontier setting, writer-director Russell Rouse focuses mostly on the wife's determined rejection of the guide's unwanted advances until being widowed by the script. Frontier violence and romantic complications. A-II (br)

Thunder of Drums, A (1961) Wooden Western about a frontier outpost under the command of a veteran officer (Richard Boone) whose feuding subordinates (George Hamilton and Richard Chamberlain) are of little help in defending the Montana Territory against Indian raids. Director Joseph M. Newman fails to work up much interest in any of the characters and even less in the badly staged climactic battle. Some hard-edged violence, Indian stereotyping, and a romantic triangle. A-III (br)

Thunder on the Hill (1951) Stilted murder mystery set in an English convent hospital, where a convicted murderess (Ann Blyth) and her police guards are marooned by a flood, while one of the nuns (Claudette Colbert) tries to prove the prisoner's innocence. Director Douglas Sirk fails to work up much suspense despite the plot's many contrivances and uses the convent setting for little more than pious atmosphere and nun stereotypes (Gladys Cooper and Connie Gilchrist). Implied marital infidelity and brief menace. A-II (br)

Thunder Over the Plains (1953) Standard Randolph Scott vehicle directed by Andre de Toth is set in post-bellum Texas, where a loyal Union officer (Scott) overcomes a callow fellow officer (Lex Barker) to save a rebel leader (Charles McGraw) from hanging for a murder committed by a greedy carpetbagger. Stylized violence and a scene of unwanted romantic advances. A-I (br)

Thunderbirds Are Go (1967) British space fantasy uses animated puppets to tell the story of the Thunderbirds International Rescue unit, who are on the job when sabotage wrecks a flight to Mars. Lots of action and noise as well as imaginative puppetwork and special effects. Should engage the seven to 13 crowd, and parents won't get too bored in the process. A-I (br)

Thunderbolt and Lightfoot (1974) Clint Eastwood and Jeff Bridges play a pair of bungling bankrobbers teamed up with former gang-members George Kennedy and Geoffrey Lewis. The character study of good and bad criminals is couched in amoral terms, with viewers expected to sympathize with the first two. Instead of settling for a solid, albeit fantasy-prone, action adventure, director Michael Cimino goes for cheap thrills with needless nudity and profanity, bringing it to a close with some downright ugly, savage deaths. O (R)

Thunderheart (1992) Murder investigation on a South Dakota reservation in the late 1970s forces a yuppie FBI agent (Val Kilmer) to confront his Native-American heritage when he is presented with conflicting evidence by his superior (Sam Shepherd) and a tribal police-officer (Graham Greene). Director Michael Apted's intriguing look at Native-American spirituality, reservation living conditions, and governmental indifference gets trapped inside a stagnant mystery thriller. Recurring rough language, a few grisly shots of dead bodies, and several shootouts. A-III (R)

Thunder in the City (1937) On a vacation in London, a high-powered American advertising executive (Edward G. Robinson) uses his promotional talents to help a hard-up distant relative sell shares in a questionable mining company. British director Marion Gering pokes some gentle fun at the outspoken US go-getter as well as his stuffy English peers (including Ralph Richardson and Nigel Bruce), but the satiric effect has faded with the years. Tough sledding for small fry. A-I (br)

Thunder in the East (1953) Stilted political melodrama pits an American gunrunner (Alan Ladd) against the pacifist leader (Charles Boyer) of a small state in northern India who refuses to use force to stop an uprising after the 1947 British withdrawal. Director Charles Vidor gets a credible performance from Boyer but wastes a good cast (notably a blind Deborah Kerr as the love interest) in an empty exercise undermining the concept of non-violence. Stylized violence and much menace. A-II (br)

Thursday's Child (1943) Thoughtful British melodrama about a 12-year-old girl (Sally Ann Howes) who becomes a child movie-star and how this affects her family and her own plans for the future. Writer-director Rodney Ackland de-glamorizes the movie business effectively, gets solid performances from a good cast (including Wilfrid Lawson, Stewart Granger, and Felix Aylmer), and ends on a positive, though realistic, note. Romantic situations. A-II (br)

Tick ... Tick ... Tick ... (1970) Using their newly acquired voting privileges, the blacks of a small Southern county elect one of their own (Jim Brown) as sheriff, and, after some stereotyped black and white hostilities, a crisis unites both races behind their sheriff, and the ending indicates a rosy future of racial harmony. Shallow treatment by director Ralph Nelson of a serious subject. A-III (G)

Ticket to Heaven (1981) Well-made Canadian movie about the efforts to rescue a young man (Nick Mancuso) who left his Toronto home and turned up in San Francisco, gaunt-cheeked and hollow-eyed, selling flowers on a street corner as a member of a religious cult. Directed by Ralph L. Thomas, the dramatization has unusual credibility and will be of special interest to teenagers and concerned parents. A-II (PG)

Ticket to Tomahawk (1950) Uneven Western comedy in which a traveling salesman (Dan Dailey) and a sheriff's granddaughter (Anne Baxter) help establish a railroad line in 1876 Colorado, despite rampaging Arapaho braves and a gunslinger (Rory Calhoun) working for a stagecoach competitor. Director Richard Sales makes the most of the colorful characters and picturesque Rocky Mountain locales, but the thin plot meanders fitfully along until its predictable ending. Frontier violence and mild romance. A-I (br)

Tickle Me (1965) Thin star-vehicle, with Elvis Presley as an out-of-work singing cowboy who gets a job at a women's health-ranch, falls for a staff member (Jocelyn Lane), and helps her search for the fortune left by her grandfather. Directed by Norman Taurog, Elvis charms the ladies with some crooning, brawling, and rodeo riding, but the real fun is saved for the mildly spooky finale in a ghost town. Sexual innuendo. A-II (br)

Tidal Wave (1975) Clumsy Americanized version of a Japanese disaster movie directed by Shiro Mariano is not only episodic and lacking any sense of pace, but it is badly dubbed and cluttered with unconvincing inserts of Lorne Greene as a UN delegate. Though one gets bored of the same old shot of lava flowing into the sea, several scenes are too graphic for very young viewers. A-III (PG)

Tie Me Up! Tie Me Down! (1990) Released mental patient (Antonio Banderas) binds and gags an actress (Victoria Abril), holding her prisoner in her apartment until she falls in love with him. Writer-director Pedro Almodovar's Spanish production tries to parlay a sick male sexual fantasy into a kinky sex-comedy, but there is nothing amusing in seeing a woman's brutal victimization. Perverse theme and extended depictions of sex acts. O (NC-17)

Tie That Binds, The (1995) Trashy thriller in which crazed fugitives from the police (Keith Carradine and Daryl Hannah) attempt to recover their six-year-old daughter by killing the couple (Vincent Spano and Moira Kelly) planning to adopt her. Director Wesley Strick turns in a trite, formula tale of one-note characters in a plot thick with grotesque tortures and murders. Recurring gory violence and brutal beatings, intense menace to a child, and several instances of rough language. O (R)

Tiger Makes Out, The (1967) Postman Eli Wallach decides one day to revolt against bureaucratic routine, kidnaps suburban housewife Anne Jackson, and she undertakes to educate her captor. Directed by Arthur Hiller, the subsequent action tends to be overdone, but what is enjoyable are the excellent performances of the two principals. A-III (br)

Tiger Shark (1932) When one of his crew is killed by sharks, a San Diego fishing captain (Edward G. Robinson) looks after the dead man's troubled daughter (Zita Johann), who eventually agrees to marry him out of gratitude, then falls for his closest friend (Richard Arlen), but a shark resolves the situation. Directed by Howard Hawks, the fishing sequences and the ever-present sharks establish a realistic context for Robinson's compelling performance as the gruff, good-hearted Portuguese fisherman, but the triangle plot is heavily melodramatic and its outcome predictable. Fierce shark attacks and romantic complications. A-II (br)

Tight Spot (1955) Potential government witness (Ginger Rogers) against a crime boss (Lorne Greene) holes up in a New York hotel room while the federal prosecutor (Edward G. Robinson) tries to persuade her to testify, and a swarm of policemen (led by Brian Keith) try to keep her from being killed by the mob. Director Phil Karlson's classy crime melodrama paces the suspense with some nifty curves and a sassy performance by Rogers as a one-time shady lady with a chance to be a gangbuster. Stylized violence and mild sexual innuendo. A-II (br)

Tightrope (1984) Clint Eastwood plays a New Orleans police detective searching for a sadistic killer whose aberrant sexual proclivities he fears he might share. Written and directed by Richard Tuggle, the movie embodies an interesting theme, but the execution of it falls short, even though Eastwood's performance is one of his best. The sex and violence loom much too large. O (R)

Tiko and the Shark (1966) Harmless, sometimes charming, story of the romance between a Polynesian boy and girl, the lad's friendship with a shark, and their role in the activities of an island fishing village. Directed by Falco Quilici, the movie's simple story and gorgeous photography should appeal to youngsters. A-I (br)

'Til There Was You (1997) Drawn-out romantic comedy which tracks the failed romances of a ghostwriter (Jeanne Tripplehorn) and an architect (Dylan McDermott) who almost meet each other countless times before finally connecting at movie's end. Directed by Scott Winnant, the romantic comedy is clumsily contrived to keep the would-be sweethearts apart yet in close proximity for years on end. Premarital affairs, some crude expressions, and an instance of rough language. A-III (PG-13)

Till Marriage Do Us Part (1979) Italian sex comedy directed by Luigi Comencini deals with the many tribulations endured by a noble Sicilian lady (Laura Antonelli), who discovers on her wedding night that her husband is, in fact, her brother. Excessive nudity and graphic sexuality. O (R)

Till the End of Time (1946) Sudsy tearjerker about returning WW II vets centers on an ex-Marine (Guy

Madison) and a troubled war widow (Dorothy Malone) who tries to help him adjust to civilian life. Director Edward Dmytryk delivers a soppy melodrama that winds up in a patriotic barroom brawl between some vets and group of hometown bigots. Dated period romance. A-II (br)

Timberjack (1955) Routine adventure directed by Joe Kane in which a Montana lumber company is being driven into bankruptcy by a ruthless rival (Brian Keith), until the owner's son (Sterling Hayden) arrives to stop the villain, with some help from the local saloon-owner (Vera Ralston) and her tipsy father (Adolphe Menjou). Much stylized violence. A-I (br)

Time After Time (1979) H.G. Wells (Malcolm McDowell) uses a time machine to pursue Jack the Ripper (David Warner) to modern-day San Francisco, where the author and a liberated woman executive (Mary Steenburgen) get involved in a duel of wits with the mad killer. Director Nicholas Meyer's romantic thriller is moderately entertaining, especially the satiric asides about modern technology, but it has some rather violent touches involving the Ripper's crimes, some profanity, and implied premarital sex. A-III (PG)

Time Bandits (1981) Witty British comedy about a gang of greedy but good-hearted dwarfs who steal a map of creation from the Supreme Being (Ralph Richardson) and use it to bring an adventurous lad into a variety of historical epochs, meeting Napoleon (Ian Holm), Greek warrior Agamemnon (Sean Connery), and Robin Hood (John Cleese). Directed by Terry Gilliam, it is sometimes amusing and always intelligent, but its appeal for youngsters is spoiled by typical Monty Python vulgarities and black humor, some of it violent. A-III (PG)

Time Bomb (see **Terror on a Train**)

Time for Burning, A (1967) Extraordinary documentary of what happened when a pastor tried to get his all-white congregation to meet with nearby blacks. Produced by the Lutheran Film Associates and directed by William Jersey, it is a moving document of troubled times and the need for human understanding. A-I (br)

Time for Killing, A (see: **The Long Ride Home**)

Time in the Sun, A (1969) Sensitive Swedish drama about a young journalist (Lars Passgard) who pursues and wins the woman (Grynet Molvig) of his dreams, despite the fact that she is fatally afflicted with Hodgkin's disease. Director Ake Falck invests a good deal of human warmth in an unusual story of married life, human suffering, and the healing power of love. Restrained lovemaking scene. A-III (R)

Time Lost and Time Remembered (1966) Unhappily married woman (Sarah Miles) returns to her home town in the west of Ireland to find the boy she loved now engaged to another. Director Desmond Davis evokes beautifully the Irish atmosphere and locale, but the story is somewhat sentimentalized. Mature themes. A-III (br)

Time Machine, The (1960) Imaginative adaptation of H.G. Wells's fanciful tale of an English inventor (Rod Taylor) who travels from 1900 into the distant future, where he tries to rally an oppressed people against their loathsome overlords, the radiation-damaged Morlocks. Directed by George Pal, the special effects may not be very elaborate, but they're effective enough to convey the fantastic nature of the sci-fi scenario and its underlying anti-war theme. Some stylized violence. A-II (br)

Time of Destiny, A (1988) Old-fashioned romantic melodrama set during WW II in San Diego and Italy traces the catastrophic effects on the family of a wealthy Basque-American rancher when he interferes in the elopement of his favorite daughter (Melissa Leo) with a young penniless soldier (Timothy Hutton). The filmmakers, Gregory Nava and Anna Thomas (**El Norte**), handle the themes of young love, revenge, and Old World values with operatic relish. A few scenes of intense violence and some profanity. A-III (PG-13)

Time of Roses (1970) Tangled tale from Finland about a supposedly perfect society in 2012 whose government manipulates the news, unaware of a plot to expose its deceptive methods through a television documentary about a woman who died in 1976. Directed by Rista Jarva, the movie's intriguing and challenging themes are treated with a cerebral aloofness that leaves the viewer uninvolved and unmoved. A-III (nr)

Time of the Gypsies (1990) Yugoslavian import tells of a Gypsy adolescent (Davor Dujmovic) who is lured to his destruction after poverty and his sister's illness force the boy to seek help from the richest, most corrupt Gypsy in town. Relying on a largely non-professional cast, director Emir Kusturica provides some insight into Gypsy myth, morality, and family life. Subtitles. Some violence, sexually suggestive scenes with nudity, and the rape of a minor. A-III (R)

Time of Their Lives, The (1946) Killed mistakenly as traitors in the Revolutionary War, two ghosts (Lou Costello and Marjorie Reynolds) cause comic havoc for the residents (Bud Abbott, Binnie Barnes, and Gale Sondergaard) of a country estate, until proof of their loyalty is found. Directed by Charles Barton, this classy Abbott and Costello effort replaces the usual string of gags with a real story that has plenty of charm and engaging humor with simple yet amusing special effects. The spirits and their predicament, as well as a spooky séance scene, may scare very young children. A-II (br)

Time of Your Life, The (1948) Static version of William Saroyan's play set in a San Francisco bar whose easy-going owner (William Bendix) enjoys his eccentric clientele, including a philosophical lounger (James Cagney), his dim go-fer (Wayne Morris), a lonely woman (Jeanne Cagney), a dancer (Paul Draper), and a woolly teller-of-tall-tales (James Barton). Under H.C. Potter's direction, the scenes sputter unevenly without ever jelling into a whole, though Saroyan's exotic characters certainly hold attention. A scene of stylized violence and some sexual inferences. A-II (br)

Time to Kill, A (1996) A novice Southern white lawyer (Matthew McConaughey) and an enterprising law student (Sandra Bullock) collaborate to defend an African-American father (Samuel L. Jackson) who has killed the two thugs who raped and nearly murdered his 10-year-old daughter. Adapted from John Grisham's bestseller, director Joel Schumacher's solid but slick courtroom melodrama provides engrossing entertainment while oversimplifying race relations and the revenge-based murders. Ambiguous treatment of justice issues, disturbing violence including an off-screen rape, and crude language with racial epithets. A-IV (R)

Time to Love and a Time to Die, A (1958) Flat romance from Erich Maria Remarque's novel, in which a German soldier (miscast John Gavin) on leave from the Russian front in the spring of 1944, finds his city in ruins, searches for his missing parents, witnesses Nazi oppression, and marries one of its victims (Lilo Pulver), before returning to the front. Director Douglas Sirk's picture of the moral dilemma facing decent Germans under an evil regime gets lost in unconvincing drama, though the result has some interest as social history. Wartime violence and Nazi excesses. A-II (br)

Time to Remember, A (1988) A young boy (Ruben Gomez) regains his voice when he has a vision of the Madonna during Christmas Midnight Mass. Directed by Tom Travers, the well-intended but inept and saccharine melodrama offers some wholesome, if shallow, entertainment for undemanding viewers. A-I (G)

Time to Sing, A (1968) Country-music comedy about a farm boy (Hank Williams, Jr.) who becomes a singing star despite many obstacles in a cliched, sentimental, but tuneful picture directed by Arthur Dreifuss. For those who enjoy the country-music sound. A-I (br)

Time without Pity (1956) Heavy British thriller in which a recovering alcoholic (Michael Redgrave) arrives in London the day before his son (Alex McCowen) is to be executed for murder, then races the clock seeking new evidence for a stay of execution. Directed by Joseph Losey from the Emlyn Williams play against capital punishment, the intriguing premise bogs down in frantic interrogations, overwrought encounters, and ominous visuals, but the game cast manages to hold interest until the desperate conclusion. Stylized violence, implied sexual affairs, and justice questions. A-III (br)

Timecop (1994) Ultra-violent action movie set in the year 2004, when a widowed cop (Jean-Claude Van Damme) time-travels back to the 1990s to prevent a murderous politician (Ron Silver) from manipulating the future while also saving his own wife (Mia Sara) from being murdered. Director Peter Hyams goes through the motions in a tired, boring story overstuffed with earsplitting martial-arts battles, constant deadly shootouts, and jazzy special effects amounting only to a stream of mindless mayhem. Excessive violence, some nudity, and frequent rough language. O (R)

Timerider (1983) Motorcycle racer (Fred Ward) finds himself whisked back in time to the late 19th century, where he gets mixed up with some lowlifes of various sorts. Directed by William Dear, it is a simple-minded attempt to combine science fiction and the Western with little result. Considerable, though restrained, sex and violence. A-III (PG)

Tin Cup (1996) An underachieving golf pro (Kevin Costner) enters the US Open in order to win the love of a psychologist (Renee Russo) who is the girlfriend of his longtime golf rival (Don Johnson). Director Ron Shelton's low-key romantic comedy offers a genial cast of characters in a drawn-out story which fails to generate sufficient romantic or comedic momentum. A discreet sexual encounter, fleeting nudity, and frequent rough language, as well as profanity. A-III (R)

Tin Drum, The (1980) German adaptation of Gunter Grass's satiric novel about a boy (David Bennent) who, in protest against the absurd world of adults, decides to stop growing on his third birthday and shows his anguish at events by beating on a tin drum. Directed by Volker Schlondorff, the work is a serious attempt to show the moral and political corruption of the 1930s that led to Germany's defeat in the cataclysm of WW II. Though it has moments of brilliance, it founders on trying to accommodate its vivid, often gross, slice-of-life realism to some abrupt and arbitrary excursions into absurdity. Crudely graphic treatment of sex, especially in scenes with the 13-year-old Bennent. O (R)

Tin Men (1987) Danny DeVito and Richard Dreyfuss are 1960s aluminum-siding salesman obsessed with getting even with each other over a car accident. Barbara Hershey plays DeVito's estranged wife, who becomes fair game for vindictive seduction by Dreyfuss in director Barry Levinson's wry and ribald comedy whose main sources of humor, unfortunately, are adultery and profanity. O (R)

Tin Pan Alley (1940) Standard musical in which struggling song publishers (John Payne and Jack Oakie) in 1915 New York get singing sisters (Alice Faye and Betty Grable) to plug their songs, but Grable soon leaves to become a star, and Faye follows after the overly ambitious Payne breaks her heart, then all four are reunited as the boys go off to fight in WW I. Directed by Walter Lang, the soggy romance is bolstered by the colorful period backgrounds, enjoyable songs, and a running gag with Oakie struggling to find words for a tune which finally becomes "K-K-K-Katy." Romantic complications. A-II (br)

Tin Star, The (1957) Solid Western in which a veteran bounty-hunter (Henry Fonda) helps a young sheriff (Anthony Perkins) capture a pair of outlaws and stop a lynching. The laconic hero and his grudging protégé are fully developed as likeable individuals in an involving, well-paced, and low-keyed story, scripted by Dudley Nichols and directed by Anthony Mann, of frontier justice. Some stylized violence. A-I (br)

Tingler, The (1959) Creaky horror hokum from producer-director William Castle, with Vincent Price as a doctor who discovers that fear triggers a physical substance in the body powerful enough to fracture the spine unless neutralized by screaming. Ridiculous concept in a dull plot with some tongue-in-cheek menace and a few cut-rate frights. A-II (br)

Tip-Off, The (1931) Breezy adventure directed by Albert Rogell, in which a radio repairman (Eddie Quillan) falls for a gangster's unhappy girlfriend (Joan Peers), then steals her away from the mob with the help of a middleweight boxer (Robert Armstrong) and his sassy fiancé (Ginger Rogers). Stylized violence and some heavy sexual innuendo. A-III (br)

Titanic (1953) Uneven dramatization of the 1912 sinking of the "unsinkable" title ocean-liner bogs down in the shipboard strife between a rich dandy (Clifton Webb) and his estranged wife (Barbara Stanwyck), though it achieves tragic proportions after the ship's hull is ripped open by an iceberg. Director Jean Negulesco spends most of the movie developing characters, who only become compelling in their varied reactions to the ship's disaster and lack of lifeboats for all the passengers. Marital discord and life-threatening situations. A-II (br)

Titanic (1996) The epic 1912 disaster which took over 1,500 lives in the sinking of the title luxury-liner is recounted mainly in the story of a torrid shipboard romance between two first-class passengers (Catherine Zeta Jones and Peter Gallagher) and the wooing of a Danish immigrant (Marilu Henner) by a young thief (Mike Doyle) in the steerage section. Directed by Robert Lieberman, the 165-minute TV-production largely wastes the human drama inherent in the historic tragedy by focusing on banal fictional characters provided by an inept script, though the re-creation of the majestic vessel and the terrible fate of so many of its passengers is still awesome. Fearsome body count, much menace, and some sexual encounters. A-III (PG-13)

Titanic (1997) Lavish re-creation of the 1912 sea disaster begins with an exploration of the sunken luxury-liner today, then follows its fateful voyage keyed to the improbable shipboard romance between a first-class passenger (Kate Winslet) and one in steerage (Leonardo DiCaprio), until an iceberg sends the ship and over 1,500 people to the bottom. Writer-producer James Cameron reduces the human dimension of the tragedy to a paltry soap opera about two love-struck youths, though the special effects re-creating the human drama aboard the sinking vessel are truly spectacular. Agonizing death scenes on a massive scale, sexual situations, brief nudity, and sporadic rough language and profanity. A-III (PG-13)

Titans (see: **My Son, the Hero**)

Titicut Follies (1967) Emotionally wrenching documentary looks unblinkingly and without commentary at the appalling conditions of life for inmates at Massachusetts's Bridgewater State Hospital for the Criminally Insane. Produced, directed, and edited by Frederick Wiseman, its impressionistic picture of this state institution ranges from a musical entertainment put on by staff and inmates, to scenes from the ward for the profoundly disturbed where inmates are housed without clothing, as well as a staff meeting with an inmate who claims to have been wrongly committed. Though some adults may find certain scenes quite distressing, it is important that the public be aware of such conditions and, indeed, an afterward states that Bridgewater has since changed. Scenes of brutalizing conditions, some frontal male nudity, and occasional rough language. A-IV (nr)

To Be Free (1973) Psychiatrist tries hypnotism as short-cut therapy for a sexually confused young woman, with obviously dire consequences for them both. Director Ned Bosnick's banal plot is treated with gimmicky camera techniques and a soft-core approach to sexual anomalies. O (R)

To Be or Not To Be (1942) Classic WW II comedy about a Polish actor (Jack Benny) whose impersonation of a murdered Nazi spy hoodwinks Warsaw's bumbling Gestapo chief (Sig Ruman) and saves his wife (Carole Lombard), his theater company, and the Polish underground. Director Ernst Lubitsch, a master of sophisticated comedy, finds much humor and some wit in what is essentially a darkly menacing wartime subject, and Benny, teamed with Lombard, was never better or funnier. Restrained violence and a sexual innuendo or two. A-II (br)

To Be or Not to Be (1983) Director Mel Brooks fails in his attempt to remake the 1942 Ernst Lubitsch black comedy about a Warsaw drama troupe who outwit the Nazis and save the Polish underground, with himself and Anne Bancroft in the roles created by Jack Benny and Carole Lombard. Unfortunately, Brooks has neither the sophisticated wit of Lubitsch nor Benny's subtlety and sense of timing. Instead his humor runs from crude slapstick to bad taste, trivializing the Nazis, and there is nothing intrinsically amusing about the Gestapo, however klutzy, however roly-poly. A-II (PG)

To Catch a Thief (1955) Fluffy romantic thriller set on the French Riviera, where a string of jewel robberies have the local *gendarmes* chasing a one-time cat burglar (Cary Grant), who uses an heiress (Grace Kelly) to catch the real crook. Alfred Hitchcock directs the chic proceedings with his usual flair for the eccentric and off-beat, but there's more romance than suspense. Some stylized violence and veiled sexual references. A-II (br)

To Commit a Murder (1969) French spy thriller in which an agent (Louis Jourdan) either has to prevent a noted scientist from defecting to Red China or kill him and his accomplice (Edmond O'Brien). Directed by Edouard Molinaro, the formula plot is neatly packaged and moderately entertaining. Some violence. A-III (PG)

To Die For (1995) Black comedy in which an ambitious small-town TV weather forecaster (Nicole Kidman) begins filming a documentary about three teenagers, then persuades them to murder her husband in order to make the film sensational enough to attract TV and movie sales. Director Gus Van Sant's biting satire lampoons the pursuit of fame and the media's avid coverage of killers while tending to trivialize a murderous act of vengeance that climaxes the story. Ambiguous treatment of revenge murder, brief violence, a few bedroom encounters, and intermittent rough language. A-IV (R)

To Die in Madrid (1966) Excellent French documentary by Niclole Stephane and Frederic Rossif describes the bitter struggle that was the Spanish Civil War. Fine editing and a poetic commentary by Madeleine Chapsal help re-create the anguished emotions of 1936-39 and derive some significance from the tragic war. A-II (br)

To Die of Love (1972) Fact-based French drama about a teacher (Annie Girardot) who falls in love with a 17-year-old student (Bruno Pradal) and wants to marry him, but, harassed by officials, she commits suicide. Directed by Andre Cayatte, the movie is more concerned with the impersonal bureaucratic system responsible for the tragedy than it is with the two main characters. Those viewing it as nothing more than a love story will find it romanticizing a relationship that the movie does not even try to make dramatically credible. A-IV (GP)

To Each His Own (1946) Slick tearjerker about a WW I unwed mother (Olivia de Havilland) who gives up her baby boy, then watches from afar as he grows into manhood (John Lund) until they meet by chance during WW II. Directed by Mitchell Leisen, the flashback form of the narrative is mightily contrived and emotionally manipulative, but de Havilland makes the mother's heartache seem real enough. A-II (br)

To Find a Man (1972) Self-centered Catholic girl (Pamela Martin) finds herself pregnant and returns home for the Christmas holidays to find an abortionist with some help from the boy next door (Darren O'Connor). The trouble with director Buzz Kulik's mediocre effort is its shallow treatment of adolescent values and acceptance of abortion as natural in a society where everything, including morality, is disposable. O (R/GP)

To Gillian on Her 37th Birthday (1996) Soapy tale of a widower (Peter Gallagher) who can't get over the death of his wife (Michelle Pfeiffer) until he comes to realize his obsession with keeping her memory alive is harming his relationship with his teenage daughter (Claire Danes). Scripted by David E. Kelley and directed by Michael Pressman, the hokey proceedings are too thin to sustain emotional credibility in the characters and their problems, especially the husband's soppy conversations with his late wife's apparition. Morbid obsession, sexual innuendo, a teen's excessive drinking, and some rough language. A-III (PG-13)

To Have and Have Not (1944) Lively adventure from Ernest Hemingway's novel set in the Caribbean, where the American captain (Humphrey Bogart) of a charter fishing-boat throws in with the Free French resistance after being pushed around by Vichy agents in 1940 Martinique, while managing to find romance along the way with a slim adventuress (Lauren Bacall). Directed by Howard Hawks from a script by Jules Furthman and William Faulkner, the melodramatic action is secondary to the romantic subplot and interesting cast of stereotypes, notably Walter Brennan's drink-addled seaman and his recurring question: "Was you ever bit by a dead bee?" Stylized violence and sexual innuendo. A-II (br)

To Hell and Back (1955) Audie Murphy plays himself in the Hollywood version of how he came to be the most decorated US soldier in WW II. Directed by Jesse Hibbs, Murphy seems less self-conscious on the battlefield than off in portraying himself as a soft-spoken, patriotic Texas boy who enlists at 16, then proceeds to win medals fighting through North Africa, Sicily, Italy, and France. Wartime violence and heroics, as well as several muted sexual references. A-II (br)

To Kill a Mockingbird (1962) When a Southern lawyer (Gregory Peck) undertakes the defense of a black man (Brock Peters) accused of rape, he has to help his young children cope with the town's racial hostilities and their own fears of a retarded neighbor (Robert Duvall). In this fine adaptation of the Harper Lee novel, director Robert Mulligan evokes a nostalgic picture of small-town life as seen mostly through the eyes of a youngster whose father is a reassuring figure of integrity in the confusing world of adults. Excellent for discussions of racial prejudice. A-II (nr)

To Kill a Priest (1989) Uneven fictionalized drama based on actual events in 1984 Poland, when Father Jerzy Popieluszko, a popular pro-Solidarity activist (Christopher Lambert), was murdered by state security police on the orders of a captain (Ed Harris) obsessed by his conviction that the priest is a dangerous subversive. Filmed in France in the English language by Polish director Agnieszka Holland, the movie contrasts the spiritual power and national appeal of the priest with the wavering Marxist dedication of the psychologically troubled officer. The work succeeds best in its depiction of the historical context — an armed government at war with its own people and their faith. Some hard-edged violence, a bedroom scene, and several instances of rough language. A-III (R)

To Live (1994) A Chinese couple (Ge You and Gong Li) struggle to raise two children while coping with tumultuous personal and political upheavals during the civil war of the 1940s through three decades of poverty under the repressive reign of Chairman Mao and the excesses of the Cultural Revolution. Director Zhang Yimou's rich tapestry of bittersweet family life affords heartfelt insights into the universal will to live and to nurture one's family. Subtitles. Some gory corpses and a young woman's death in childbirth. A-II (nr)

To Live and Die in L.A. (1985) Director William Friedkin attempts to make a southern California version of the **French Connection** in this story of two Treasury agents (William Petersen and John Pankow) pursuing a vicious counterfeiter (Willem Dafoe). The result, however, has no more depth than an extended music video. Brutal and so amoral that it's hard to tell the good guys from the bad. O (R)

To Sir with Love (1967) Warm British melodrama about an American (Sidney Poitier) who takes a teaching job in London, where he tries to turn teenage students from a Cockney slum into ladies and gentlemen. Though the story offers some pat solutions for real problems and the student transformations seem over-swift, director James Clavell gets winning performances from Poitier and his fine supporting cast to show aspects of life, love, and adolescence that American audiences will find familiar, despite the accent. A-II (br)

To Sleep with Anger (1990) Tensions within a black middle-class family escalate when a boyhood pal from the deep South (Danny Glover) shows up on the Los Angeles doorstep of the family patriarch (Paul Butler) and slyly insinuates himself into the family circle. Glover's multi-layered performance and a fine ensemble cast help director Charles Burnett meld comedy and drama into a cohesive whole contrasting the servile ways of the rural South with modern urban life. Mild violence and a few vulgarities. A-II (PG)

To Trap a Spy (1966) Movie version of the TV spy series, "The Man from U.N.C.L.E.," features Robert Vaughn going through his paces as a super-agent with little help from the sets, the gimmicks, or director Don Medford. Violence and sexual innuendo. A-III (br)

To Wong Foo, Thanks for Everything! Julie Newmar (1995) Weak but warmhearted comedy in which three drag-queens (Wesley Snipes, Patrick Swayze, John Leguizamo) driving to Hollywood have motor trouble in rural Nebraska, where they make friends with the startled townspeople by helping several resolve personal problems. Director Beeban Kidron elicits some chuckles from the fish-out-of-water antics of the goofy trio, but the situations are highly contrived and continually predictable. Breezy depiction of cross-dressing, mild sexual references, and minor violence. A-III (PG-13)

Tobor the Great (1954) Hokey sci-fi tale directed by Lee Sholem in which a scientist (Taylor Holmes) invents the title robot, which has extrasensory perception enabling it to pilot the first space rocket, then he and his 11-year-old grandson (Billy Chapin) are abducted by Red agents (led by Steven Geray) until the trusty Tabor comes to their rescue. A-I (br)

Tobruk (1967) WW II story about a British commando column (Rock Hudson, George Peppard, Nigel Green) disguised as a German convoy bringing Allied prisoners through the desert into the German base of Tobruk to destroy its oil stockpiles. Directed by Arthur Hiller, the straightforward action narrative alludes to the absurdity of war and has an interesting sub-plot dealing with anti-Semitism. It brings a measure of intelligence to the usual mindless war formula. Stylized violence. A-II (br)

Toby Tyler, Or Ten Weeks with a Circus (1960) Sturdy little Disney production about the turn-of-the-century adventures of an orphan (Kevin Corcoran) when he runs away from aunt and uncle to join a traveling one-ring circus. The earnest little fellow makes a lot of friends, the most notable being a mischievous monkey. Pleasant, uncomplicated story, directed by Charles Barton, though its main appeal is to youngsters. A-I (br)

Today We Kill ... Tomorrow We Die! (1971) Poor Italian Western about a rancher (Montgomery Ford) who recruits four gunslingers to wipe out the gang responsible for the rape-murder of his wife. Director Tonino Cervi's production values are laughable, but the violence is not. A-III (GP)

Todd Killings, The (1971) Lurid fact-based melodrama about a perverse killer (Robert F. Lyons) who sexually assaulted and mutilated a number of teenage girls in Tucson, Ariz. Directed by Barry Shear, the movie dwells on the sensational aspects of the case and as a result is quite sordid in its details. O (R)

Together (1971) Pseudo-documentary promotes a summertime romp at the estate of a self-proclaimed pioneer in sexual guidance. Filmmakers Roger Murphy and Sean C. Cunningham encounter uninhibited and unclad couples who explicate and demonstrate their host's theories of tactile therapy. O (R)

Together Brothers (1974) Good action movie, filmed in steamy Galveston, Tex., with a cast largely of unknowns, it involves a black street-gang tracking down the killer of a cop who treated them fairly. Director William A. Graham gets some extraordinarily sensitive character portrayals and conveys a feel for the ramshackle black ghettos of Galveston. Though there is a minimum of street language, the sudden, concluding violence is adult fare. A-III (PG)

Tokoloshe (1971) Uneven South African production about a winsome Bantu youngster (Saul Pelle) who escapes the curse of the evil spirit of the title through his mother's intervention and reaches safety in Johannesburg. Directed by Peter Prowse, the sequences in the city unfortunately lack the narrative interest and sense of conviction found in the earlier portions of the movie. A-I (G)

Tokyo Joe (1949) Returning to Japan, where he had built a business before the war, a former Army officer (Humphrey Bogart) is blackmailed into helping a gang of war criminals in order to save his ex-wife (Florence Marley) and child. Directed by Stuart

Heisler, the convoluted proceedings unfold awkwardly and never quite jell into a satisfying whole. Stylized violence and heavy romantic complications. A-III (br)

Tokyo Story (1972) Elderly couple on their first visit to the Tokyo homes of their children meet only disguised rejection except, ironically, for the kindness of their dead son's wife. When the mother dies shortly upon returning to their country village, it is only the widowed daughter-in-law who shows any real feeling of loss. Director Yasujiro Ozu's eloquent treatment of old age makes it a uniquely moving hymn to life. A-I (nr)

Tom and Huck (1995) Sluggish tale of Tom Sawyer (Jonathan Taylor Thomas) and Huckleberry Finn (Brad Renfro) out to rescue the town drunk from being wrongly hanged for murder while preventing the killer from absconding with stolen gold. Directed by Peter Hewitt, the weak script results in a colorless narrative with no surprises and little adventure. Some violence, frequent menace, and a profanity. A-II (PG)

Tom and Jerry — The Movie (1993) When their home is demolished, the mischievous cartoon cat-and-mouse duo must take to the mean streets, where they rescue a poor little rich girl from the clutches of a greedy aunt who's after her trust fund. Producer-director Phil Roman's adventuresome animated tale of the scrappy twosome will hold the small fry, while some of the six musical numbers sprinkled throughout this amiable cartoon may entertain grown-ups as well. A-I (G)

Tom & Viv (1994) Literate portrait of the turbulent marriage of American-born, British-based poet T.S. Eliot (Willem Dafoe) to first wife Vivien Haigh-Wood (Miranda Richardson) from 1914 through Viv's growing mood swings which in 1936 cause Tom to have her committed to an institution, where she remained until her death in 1947. Brian Gilbert directs this adaptation of Michael Hasting's controversial play portraying Vivien as a true collaborator on Eliot's poetry, as well as a tragic victim of his social ambitions and inability to discuss intimate personal problems, notably her hormonal imbalance. Harrowing depiction of a troubled marital relationship and some sexual innuendo. A-III (PG-13)

Tom Brown's School Days (1940) Sturdy version of the Thomas Hughes novel about the troubles of a new boy (Jimmy Lydon) in 19th-century England's Rugby, where he's tormented by the house bully (Billy Halop), then ostracized mistakenly as a tattletale by classmates, but makes it through thanks to the school's reformist headmaster (Cedric Hardwicke). Director Robert Stevenson provides a robust period picture of life in a boys' boarding school and the struggle to end the tyranny of the older students. A-I (br)

Tom, Dick and Harry (1941) Daffy comedy in which a telephone operator (Ginger Rogers) has strange dreams about her persistent suitors — a rich socialite (Alan Marshal), a car salesman (George Murphy), and a genial dreamer (Burgess Meredith) — with her choice coming as no surprise. Director Garson Kanin has a lot of fun with the attitudes of the time, especially in the wacky dream sequences, but the love story's sentimentality wears less well. Romantic complications. A-II (br)

Tom Horn (1980) Frontier hero at the end of his career (Steve McQueen) is hired by a group of ranchers to stop some rustlers, a job he performs with such murderous zeal that they decide to get rid of him by framing him for murder. Though director William Wiard fails to provide much dramatic steam, McQueen's solid performance raises the material a notch above the standard Western. Some graphic violence. A-III (R)

Tom Jones (1963) Zestful adaptation of Henry Fielding's classic novel about the misadventures, largely amorous, of a young man (Albert Finney) among the high- and low-born of 18th-century England. Director Tony Richardson treats the melodramatic proceedings with a droll combination of mock heroics, antic slapstick, bawdy asides, and much social satire. Though the humor is often coarse, and the bloodlust of a deer hunt is brutally graphic, it succeeds largely as a period comedy of manners and morals. A-IV (br)

Tom Sawyer (1973) Reader's Digest musical adaptation of the Mark Twain classic, with Johnny Whitaker as Tom, Jeff East as Huck, Jodie Foster as Becky, and Celeste Holm as Aunt Polly. Directed by Don Taylor, the movie is a quite diverting, though undistinguished bit, of nostalgia that, if it misses the wit and cultural perceptions of the original, succeeds nonetheless in being continually engaging. Young viewers will be delighted. A-I (G)

Tom Thumb (1958) Amiable retelling of the Brothers Grimm fairytale about a woodsman and his wife (Bernard Miles and Jessie Matthews) whose thumb-sized son (Russ Tamblyn) thwarts the scheme of a comic pair of villains (Terry-Thomas and Peter Sellers) to rob the village treasury. Director George Pal mixes a variety of animation and special effects with occasional lyrics sung by Peggy Lee to fashion a pleasant fantasy that will amuse children and pacify parents, though of less appeal for more demanding viewers. A-I (br)

Tomahawk (1951) Routine Western directed by George Sherman is set in 1866 Wyoming, where frontiersman Jim Bridger (Van Heflin) saves an enterprising entertainer (Yvonne de Carlo), as well as an Army garrison (under Preston Foster) from Sioux warriors stirred up by a cowardly soldier (Alex Nicol). Frontier violence. A-I (br)

Tomahawk and the Cross, The (see: **Pillars of the Sky**)

Tomb of Ligeia, The (1965) Moody chills from the Edgar Allan Poe story in which a morose widower (Vincent Price) in Victorian England leaves off mourning his late wife (Elizabeth Shepherd) to wed a bright young lady (also Shepherd) who soon fears the first wife's unearthly presence in the form of a black cat. Directed by Roger Corman, the eerie tale of hypnotism and the undead doesn't quite hold together, but the nighttime antics in the widower's creepy old abbey certainly hold attention. Supernatural menace. A-II (br)

Tomboy (1940) Minor rural romance directed by Robert McGowan in which a brassy Chicago girl (Marcia Mae Jones) is enrolled in a country school, where she takes up the cause of a farm-boy classmate (Jackie Moran) who's overworked by his mean-spirited uncle. A-I (br)

Tombstone (1993) Bloody retelling of the legendary events of 1879 in an Arizona town, where a gang of murderous outlaws (led by Michael Biehn and Powers Boothe) come up against the new sheriff Wyatt Earp (Kurt Russell), his brothers (Sam Elliott, Bill Paxton), and Doc Holliday (Val Kilmer) who have decided to wipe them out. George P. Cosmatos directs a glossy dud filled with shootouts between wooden characters mouthing cliches while attired in high-fashion Western duds. Excessive violence including numerous grisly murders, acceptance of cold-blooded murder, recurring substance abuse, and an instance of rough language. O (R)

Tommy (1975) British adaptation of Peter Townshend's rock opera about a pinball wizard (Roger Daltrey) who becomes a religious guru and ends as a rejected mystic calling out for a new consciousness. Though the performances of Eric Clapton, Elton John, and Tina Turner are excellent, director Ken Russell's treatment is ludicrously out of control, obscuring the sense of the opera by an undue emphasis on visual pyrotechnics that is not dramatic but destructive. Satiric jabs at religion are excessive if taken literally. A-IV (PG)

Tommy Boy (1995) Derivative comedy in which a porky, likable dimwit (Chris Farley) battles the machinations of his late dad's scheming bride (Bo Derek) while trying to save the family business from a hostile takeover, getting grudging help from a clever employee (David Spade). Director Peter Segal's innocuous buddy movie offers only a few funny moments sandwiched between endless fat jokes. Some slapstick violence, minor sexual innuendo, a few crude remarks, and minimal profanity. A-III (PG)

Tomorrow (1972) Winter watchman (Robert Duvall) for a backwoods Mississippi sawmill gives shelter to a pregnant woman (Olga Bellin) abandoned by her husband. As the winter passes, he falls in love with her, but she dies shortly after her child is born. Adapted from a William Faulkner story by Horton Foote and directed by Joseph Anthony, the material is sparse, even tedious, but the characters — the taciturn man of the land and the worn-out woman — convey a genuine sense of the American rural ethic. A-II (PG)

Tomorrow Never Dies (1997) The 18th James Bond movie finds super-agent 007 (Pierce Brosnan) out to prevent a maniacal missile-bearing media magnate (Jonathan Pryce) from instigating a war between England and China in order to boost ratings for his new global news network. Directed by Roger Spottiswoode, the explosive action is virtually non-stop, bypassing Bond's supposed suave sophistication in favor of numbingly mindless mayhem. Excessive violence, sexual innuendo, and fleeting profanity. O (PG-13)

Tonight and Every Night (1945) Wartime morale booster pays tribute to the brave cast and stagehands of a London music hall who put on five performances a day throughout the Blitz, even living in the theater during the worst of the bombing, though the revue's American star (Rita Hayworth) finds time for romance with an RAF pilot (Lee Bowman). Directed by Victor Saville, the musical numbers are bright but unmemorable, and the cardboard romance becomes tiresome long before the bittersweet patriotic ending. Sexual situations and innuendo. A-III (br)

Tonka the Comanche (1958) Director Lewis R. Foster's mildly entertaining Disney movie is set in the Old West, where a young Indian (Sal Mineo) captures a wild stallion, loses him, and then gets him back again. A-I (br)

Tony Rome (1967) Frank Sinatra stars as a Miami private eye who displays a nice sense of values and humor as his work takes him deeper and deeper into the corrupt layers of the resort town. Directed by Gordon Douglas, its sporadic gunplay and fistfights are standard, but some of the subject matter is sordid, and some of the language is rough. A-III (br)

Too Beautiful for You (1990) Wealthy Frenchman (Gerard Depardieu) shocks his beautiful wife (Carole Bouquet) and their friends by falling madly in love with a plain, plump woman (Josiane Balasko). Director Bertrand Blier twists the cliches of marital infidelity and French film convention with this serio-comic farce that mixes fantasy with reality, and raises, but does not answer, philosophical questions about love, infidelity, and the nature of sexual attraction. Subtitles. Some sexually explicit dialogue. A-IV (R)

Too Late Blues (1962) Ambitious jazz bandleader (Bobby Darrin) falls for a novice singer (Stella Stevens), goes haywire when they break up, and leaves the band cold to go it alone, though his envious agent (Everett Chambers) sets him up for a fall. Directed by John Cassavetes, the camaraderie between the musicians and their circle makes a convincing background for a story which has many fine scenes but never quite jells as a dramatic whole. Some stylized violence, notably a drunken brawl, and sexual situations. A-III (br)

Too Late the Hero (1970) Routine WW II movie set on a small Pacific island, where an Allied patrol (notably Cliff Robertson and Michael Caine) makes its way through the jungle to blow up a Japanese radio transmitter, then returns back to base. Director Robert Aldrich offers the usual amount of bloody violence in glossy color, but all except hardened action buffs will find it disappointing. Some hard-edged wartime violence. A-III (GP)

Too Many Girls (1940) Sappy Rodgers and Hart

musical in which collegiate football stars (Richard Carlson, Eddie Bracken, Hal LeRoy, and Desi Arnaz), hired as bodyguards for a millionaire's daughter (Lucille Ball) attending Pottawatomie College in New Mexico, transform the small school into a football powerhouse. Director George Abbott stages the sophomoric proceedings in stilted fashion, pausing occasionally for forgettable songs (Frances Langford) and dance numbers (Ann Miller) whose energy seems misplaced. Considerable emphasis on double entendres. A-III (br)

Too Much Sun (1991) The fortune left in an old man's will galvanizes various money-grabbers, including the man's gay son (Eric Idle), his lesbian daughter (Andrea Martin), and his unscrupulous parish priest (Jim Haynie). Director Robert Downey's sex farce mocks gays and religious in a lame attempt at outrageous humor that never gets beyond tasteless twaddle. Promiscuous encounters, heavy homosexual innuendo, and much rough language. O (R)

Too Much Too Soon (1958) In this account of the troubled life of Diana Barrymore (Dorothy Malone), she leaves her domineering mother, writer Michael Strange (Neva Patterson), for an acting career in Hollywood but fails badly, then sees her father, John Barrymore (Errol Flynn), die of alcoholism, and becomes one herself. Directed by Art Napoleon, the glossy proceedings have little depth and are mostly unconvincing, except for Flynn's compelling performance as a gifted actor who's lost his bearings. Violence, sexual situations, and alcoholic excess. A-III (br)

Too Outrageous (1987) Low-budget Canadian production about a homosexual (Craig Russell) whose career as a female impersonator leads to a chance at television stardom if he will change his act, but he prefers to remain the way he is. Written and directed by Dick Benner, the movie condones, but does not glamorize, homosexual relationships. O (R)

Tootsie (1982) Very funny movie about an unemployed actor (Dustin Hoffman) who dresses up as a woman to get a part in a TV soap-opera, but his success in the role complicates matters when he falls in love with the show's beautiful co-star (Jessica Lange). Director Sydney Pollack's romantic comedy makes some witty points about being a woman in a man's world. Adult sexual humor. A-III (PG)

Top Dog (1995) Dumb action-comedy in which a San Diego cop (Chuck Norris) investigating a bloodthirsty band of neo-Nazi terrorists is assigned a shaggy canine partner who sniffs out clues about the imminent bombing of a gathering of religious leaders. Director Aaron Norris does little but inter-cut cutesy, unrelated doggy tricks with standard martial-arts violence and gunfights, but this feeble attempt at humor does not make the results any less violent. Intermittent violence and an instance of profanity. A-III (PG-13)

Top Gun (1986) The bravado of a Navy hot-shot jet pilot (Tom Cruise) wins the grudging admiration of his comrades, the affection of his female flight-instructor (Kelly McGillis), and audience commendation for his patriotic hip-shooting heroism. Director Tony Scott's high-flying celebration of peacetime military training is mostly a hollow exercise in macho derring-do. Fairly restrained bedroom scene, brief nudity, and incidental profanity. A-III (PG)

Top Hat (1935) Stylish musical romance between a hoofer (Fred Astaire) and a socialite (Ginger Rogers) starts with comic misunderstandings in London, then go on to ever more zany encounters in Venice. Director Mark Sandrich keeps the lightweight proceedings on the boil, with only the dance routines and Irving Berlin songs providing any substance. Sexual innuendo and frivolous treatment of marriage. A-III (br)

Top of the Heap (1972) Black policeman in Washington, DC, (Christopher St. John, who also wrote, produced, and directed) works with racist, bribe-taking fellow officers, and off the job his wife browbeats him, his daughter experiments with sex and drugs, and even his boozy mistress mocks him with abandon. He proves as nasty as anyone else in a movie that goes out of its way to alienate viewers with needless, salacious nudity and an endless barrage of gutter epithets. O (R)

Top o' the Morning (1949) Thin slice of stereotyped Irish whimsy, as a Manhattan insurance investigator (Bing Crosby) comes to Cork to recover the stolen Blarney Stone, then falls for the daughter (Ann Blyth) of a cranky village policeman (Barry Fitzgerald) whose dim assistant (Hume Cronyn) keeps gumming up the works. Directed by David Miller, the lighthearted proceedings are darkened by the strange prophecies of a local wise woman (Eileen Crowe) and a heavy-handed conclusion involving murder, though there are enough Irish songs to keep a viewer's eyes shining. A-I (br)

Top Secret (1984) Creators of **Airplane** (Jim Abrahams, David Zucker, and Jerry Zucker) have set out to parody movies of international intrigue. But this time they haven't gotten it right, and most of the jokes misfire. Some sexually oriented humor. A-III (PG)

Top Secret Affair (1957) Glossy romantic comedy in which a magazine publisher (Susan Hayward) sets out to trash the reputation of an Army general (Kirk Douglas) to keep him from getting a diplomatic post, then falls in love with him. Directed by H.C. Potter, the on-again, off-again romance becomes increasingly tiresome, though Hayward's bright performance almost makes it work. Sexual situations. A-III (br)

Topaz (1969) Alfred Hitchcock's adaptation of the pulpy Leon Uris novel about high-powered espionage and counter-spying in a variety of exotic locales. The dialogue is mostly banal and the action largely unconvincing, but there are occasional glimmers of the Hitchcock touch in subtle plot twists here and blind alleys there. Diverting if ultimately disappointing. Some physical and psychological violence and a lot of confusing intrigue. A-III (PG)

Topaze (1933) Droll comedy from Marcel Pagnol's

play in which a poor but honest Paris schoolteacher (John Barrymore) becomes a wealthy man after turning the tables on the baron (Reginald Mason) who duped him into promoting a shoddy product. Directed by Harry d'Abbadie d'Arrast, the story's humor stems from Barrymore's tongue-in-cheek portrayal of the meek academic who learns to enjoy the rewards of dishonesty. An unfaithful husband and sexual innuendo. A-III (br)

Topkapi (1964) Entertaining adaptation of Eric Ambler's comic thriller in which a bungling two-bit con-man (Peter Ustinov) becomes part of a fantastic plot to steal a priceless jeweled dagger from the Istanbul Museum. Directed with gusto by Jules Dassin, the suspenseful caper is pulled off in sparkling style by a cast including Melina Mercouri, Maximillian Schell, and Robert Morley, but they are all upstaged by a little bird. Some stylized violence and mild sexual innuendo. A-III (br)

Topo Gigio (1966) Delightful little movie about a small talking mouse who outwits a wicked magician to save his friends. Young children will love it, and the puppet characterization is droll enough to please their parents. A-I (br)

Topper Returns (1941) Zany sequel with Topper (Roland Young) reluctantly aiding a ghost (Joan Blondell) solve her own murder in the spooky mansion of her to girlfriend (Carole Landis), whose ailing father (H.B. Warner) is in the care of a sinister doctor (George Zucco). Director Roy Del Ruth mixes perilous situations involving a cloaked mystery figure, sliding panels, and hidden passages with the wacky goings-on of a very funny cast (Billie Burke, Eddie Rochester, Patsy Kelly, Donald McBride, and Dennis O'Keefe). Comic menace. A-II (br)

Tora! Tora! Tora! (1970) Huge, sprawling, and occasionally unfocused wartime epic based on the events leading up to the surprise Japanese attack on Pearl Harbor. Director Richard Fleischer alternates American and Japanese points of view as the one side goes about its daily routines, unsuspecting of the deadly assault that the other side is preparing. The Japanese segments are the more interesting in showing less-known aspects of a strategy that some realized would start an unwinnable war. A-I (G)

Torch Song (1953) Slick romantic melodrama in which a tough-as-nails musical star (Joan Crawford) comes to realize that she's only human when she falls for a blind pianist (Michael Wilding) unintimidated by her success or tantrums. Directed by Charles Walters, the vehicle provides a chance for Crawford to strut in the musical routines (including a blackface number) while showing off her emotional range in the character's change of heart. For incurable romantics. A-II (br)

Torch Song Trilogy (1988) Screen version of Harvey Fierstein's play about a homosexual (Fierstein) who works as a female impersonator in a drag revue and his unfulfilling love life and ongoing mother-son conflicts. Directed by Paul Bogart, the movie compassionately and often raucously shows the common threads that connect heterosexual and homosexual family relationships, courtship, and love, but its validation of homosexuality and depiction of promiscuity in the 1970s is disturbing, especially in light of the AIDS epidemic. A few fleeting scenes of male kissing and discreet touching, a scene of a brutal beating, much rough language with homosexual innuendoes, and a few bawdy musical drag numbers. O (R)

Torchlight (1985) The destruction of a successful businessman and loving husband (Steve Railsback) by cocaine is a serious and important theme, but director Tom Wright's treatment is so uninspired and at times ludicrous that the movie fails even as a cautionary tale. Explicit depiction of drug taking. A-III (R)

Torn Apart (1990) Trite romance about an Israeli youth (Adrian Pasdar) and a Palestinian girl (Cecilia Peck) who defy the wishes of their families, only to be sacrificed to the political conflict that engulfs them. Director Jack Fisher fails to develop the characters as individuals, and the narrative never gets beyond a superficial examination of Mid-East tensions and the human realities behind them. Intermittent scenes of bloodshed and violence, and a restrained scene of sexual passion. A-III (R)

Torn Curtain (1966) Slack Alfred Hitchcock suspense thriller about an American physicist (Paul Newman) who pretends to defect to East Germany in order to get some secret information. The predictable plot is further marred by a detailed treatment of a realistically brutal killing. O (br)

Torpedo Alley (1953) Routine service drama from director Lew Landers in which a guilt-ridden WW II Navy pilot (Mark Stevens) flops in civilian life, then tries to pull himself together by re-enlisting in the Navy, and graduates from submarine school in time to become a hero in the Korean War. Wartime violence. A-I (br)

Torpedo Run (1958) Turgid war movie directed by Joseph Pevney, with Glenn Ford as a troubled submarine skipper chasing a Japanese aircraft carrier across the Pacific, intent on sinking it to avenge the deaths of his wife and daughter. Standard wartime heroics and underwater dangers. A-I (br)

Torrent (1926) Creaky silent melodrama from the Blasco Ibanez novel about star-crossed lovers in Spain as a wealthy mama's boy (Ricardo Cortez) comes to regret breaking his vows of love to a poor country girl (Greta Garbo) after she goes to Paris and becomes a famous opera star. Directed by Monta Bell, the picture's highlight is a torrential flood, but it's not enough to save this soggy tale of unrequited love between a weak hero and a strong heroine. Romantic complications. A-II (br)

Torrents of Spring (1990) Visually lovely, emotionally bland version of Ivan Turgenev's novel about a 19th-century Russian nobleman (Timothy Hutton) traveling in Germany who becomes engaged to a sweet Italian immigrant (Valeria Golino), but then falls passionately in love with the wanton wife (Nastassja Kinski) of an old school chum. Director Jerzy Skolimowski fails to clearly delineate the time and place of this oddly cast, multi-national movie whose one-dimensional characters undercut its cautionary tale of misdirected love. Lengthy, clothed sexual liaison. A-III (nr)

Torrid Zone (1940) Tough-guy romantic comedy set in Latin America, where the cynical manager (Pat O'Brien) of a banana export-company uses a stranded nightclub entertainer (Ann Sheridan) to keep his top troubleshooter (James Cagney) from taking a job in Chicago. Directed by William Keighley, the shifting Cagney-Sheridan romance takes a backseat to the movie's he-man heroics and adolescent pranks that seem less amusing today than then. Stylized violence, ethnic stereotypes, and sexual innuendo. A-III (br)

Torture Dungeon (1970) Bungled medieval tale about a duke's problems in ensuring an heir for his kingdom, preoccupied as he is in dispatching his peers of both sexes by prolonged torture or sudden death. Played apparently for laughs, the movie is far from funny in its own preoccupation with nudity and acts of swift, bloody violence. O (R)

Torture Garden (1967) Five visitors to a carnival fright-show run by Dr. Diablo (Burgess Meredith) are given warning visions of the inner evil within each. Written by Robert Bloch and directed by Freddie Francis, the omnibus is more hokey than scary, though the episode about a collector (Jack Palance) of Edgar Allen Poe memorabilia has at least a suitably sinister atmosphere. Fanciful but unconvincing scenes of violence. A-II (br)

Total Recall (1990) Ultra-violent sci-fi thriller about a man (Arnold Schwarzenegger) who has to travel to Mars to discover why his wife (Sharon Stone), as well as total strangers, are trying to kill him. Director Paul Verhoeven's intricate plot exposes an ugly futuristic society where human life warrants no respect, women are manipulative sexual playthings, and the only solution to injustice is massive bloodshed. Excessive violence, sexual exploitation, including nudity, and rough language. O (R)

Toto le Heros (1992) Believing he was switched in the hospital nursery with a neighborhood boy who then led a privileged life, an embittered old man (Michel Bouquet) recalls his lifelong envy and fantasies about killing the man who "stole" his life. Using flashbacks and fantasies, Belgian writer-director Jaco Van Dormael imaginatively captures an entire life-span, from a child's innocence to a crusty old codger who finally learns to accept the mixed blessings of the life he has led. Subtitles. An implied affair, brief violence, and momentary nudity. A-III (PG-13)

Touch (1997) Botched satire from Elmore Leonard's novel about a Catholic stigmatic (Skeet Ulrich) whose healing powers attract the attention of a one-time bogus faith-healer (Christopher Walken), but his plans to exploit those powers for profit go awry when the miracle worker falls in love with the con-man's confederate (Bridget Fonda). Scripted and directed by Paul Schrader, the heavy-handed narrative drifts along, aimlessly following the eccentric types who make up the tiresome plot, but even worse is the movie's negative attitude to institutional religion. Jaundiced views of religion, sexual situations, rear nudity, coarse language, and occasional profanity. O (R)

Touch, The (1971) Failed English-language production written and directed by Ingmar Bergman, the story is of a love triangle involving a busy, sensitive husband (Max von Sydow), his uncertain wife (Bibi Andersson), and her importunate, apparently unbalanced, and unfeeling lover (Elliott Gould). Though it has flashes of Bergman's mastery in handling themes of alienation and searching, Gould is a classic case of miscasting, and his performance makes the whole affair seem no more than campy soap opera. Ambiguous attitude towards adultery. A-IV (R)

Touch and Go (1975) French WW II comedy about a French deserter (Michel Picoli), an inept British officer (Michael York), and the wife of the Swiss consul (Marlene Jobart) who find themselves fleeing for their lives from Nazis who are certain they are spies. Director Philippe de Broca's comedy is full of sight gags, absurd situations, and broad humor that not everyone appreciates. His insistence upon the wartime vulnerability of his characters, however, makes the laughter at their ridiculous adventures somewhat uneasy. A-III (nr)

Touch and Go (1987) Improbable romance of a star pro-hockey player (Michael Keaton) and a down-and-out Hispanic single parent (Maria Conchita Alonzo) who meet when the hockey star drags her son, who helped mug him, home. Simplistic, forced characterizations with no understanding of parenthood, some foul language, and a semi-nude bedroom scene type this as adult fare. A-III (R)

Touch of Class, A (1973) London-based American executive (George Segal) and a British career woman (Glenda Jackson) meet, a love affair ensues, and then the man's vacationing wife, kids, and in-laws return unexpectedly, bringing all the inevitable and predictable complications that follow. Director Melvin Frank's central problem is that his stars don't seem very comfortable as a romantic couple, a feeling many will share about a comedy whose theme is adultery. Frank tries to keep it light and witty, but, after a tasteless bedroom scene, the froth goes flat, and only a stale aftertaste remains. Some scatological epithets. A-III (PG)

Touch of Evil (1958) Stylish crime thriller about a Mexican policeman (Charlton Heston) whose American bride (Janet Leigh) becomes a foil in the criminal machinations of a top border-town cop (Orson Welles). Also directed by Welles, the dark, moody narrative has plenty of menace and occasional nasty violence, but succeeds best as a character study of a warped crime-buster who metes out justice by placing himself above the law. A-III (PG-13)

Touched by Love (1980) Fact-based story about a young nurse (Deborah Raffin) who takes it upon herself to bring a teenage victim of cerebral palsy (Diane Lane) out of her deep depression, partly through an extraordinary exchange of letters with Elvis Presley. Directed by Gus Trikonis, the acting is very credible, and the story is told with just the right balance of emotion and sentimentality. Rare, immensely enjoyable family movie. A-I (PG)

Tough (1974) Preteen (Dion Gosset) has problems with his parents, teachers, and, finally, the police. Nothing unusual about this picture of the generation gap, except that the family are middle-class blacks living in the suburbs and suffering the same problems as many of their white neighbors. Written, produced, and directed by Horace Jackson, regrettably the characterizations and plot situations are too thinly drawn for either credibility or insight, and the principals rarely rise above stereotypes. A-I (G)

Tough Enough (1983) Violent clunker in which a would-be country-western singer (Dennis Quaid) seeks publicity by entering a series of brutal boxing matches put on by a crafty promoter (Warren Oates). Nothing much happens in the way of characterization or plot, as director Richard Fleischer puts all the emphasis on the fights themselves, depicting the brutal encounters in loving detail. Considerable violence. A-III (R)

Tough Guys (1986) Silly and somewhat crude comedy exploiting the seasoned acting talents of Burt Lancaster and Kirk Douglas, who star as thieves released after 30 years in prison into a society neglectful and uncaring about its senior citizens. Bemused by the disordered world that confronts them, the proud old-timers decide to pull off one more caper just to show that they can. Unseemly sexual encounter and much harsh language. A-III (PG)

Toughest Man in Arizona (1952) Western potboiler directed by R.G. Springsteen in which the singing marshal (Vaughn Monroe) of 1881 Tombstone rescues a woman (Joan Leslie) from Apache raiders, then goes after an outlaw (Victor Jory) in league with her telegrapher husband (Harry Morgan). Stylized violence and sexual innuendo. A-II (br)

Tous les Matins du Monde (1992) An aged royal-court musician (Gerard Depardieu) in 17th-century France ruefully recalls his fiery relationship as a cocky young student (Guillaume Depardieu) with his purist teacher (Jean-Pierre Marielle), who shunned him when he discovered the young man's affair with his daughter (Anne Brochet). In a movie of painstaking pace, sublime baroque soundtrack, and graceful performances of restrained passion, director Alain Corneau contrasts the approaches of two musicians to their art — the master who saw music as a source of spiritual consolation and the youth as a means to achieve worldly ambitions. Subtitles. A sexual encounter with brief nudity and a suicide. A-III (nr)

Tout Va Bien (1973) Muddled French story of a factory strike, with a great deal of ideological debate from all sides. Director Jean-Luc Godard's return to the narrative form and the use of actors (Jane Fonda and Yves Montand) have little appeal except for those interested in political cinema. A-III (nr)

Tower of London (1939) Static dramatization drawn from English history follows the course of murder and intrigue leading to the usurpation of the throne by the villainous Richard III (Basil Rathbone) and his defeat by Henry Tudor (Ralph Forbes) in 1483. Director Rowland V. Lee's leaden treatment adds little interest, except for the diabolical relish with which the royal executioner (Boris Karloff) carries out Richard's dirty work, such as drowning the Duke of Clarence (Vincent Price) in a wine vat. Stylized violence, including a torture sequence. A-II (br)

Towering Inferno (1974) A 135-story office and residential tower goes up in smoke, trapping hundreds of Hollywood extras and a score of past and present stars. Director John Gillermin's disaster movie is weak in plot and characterization, but stunningly realistic in its special effects of death and destruction. A-III (PG)

Town Called Hell, A (1971) Mexico in 1895 is the setting for a series of slaughters between revolutionary guerrillas (led by Robert Shaw) and government soldiers (led by Telly Savalas), who torture and execute various peasants and prisoners. Directed by Robert Parrish, the movie is unrelenting in its emphasis on violence and senseless punishment. O (R)

Town Tamer (1965) Formula Western directed by Lesley Selander has an aging lawman (Dana Andrews) working on his own to clean up a corrupt town run by a gambler (Bruce Cabot) aided by a crooked judge (Pat O'Brien) and an ambivalent marshal (Lyle Bettger). Matters worsen when the townspeople (led by Lon Chaney and Richard Arlen) turn to vigilante justice. Stylized violence, including an abused wife. A-II (br)

Town That Dreaded Sundown, The (1977) Tedious, solemn, and embarrassingly inept fact-based movie, featuring Ben Johnson and Andrew Prine, about the summer-long rampage of a homicidal maniac in 1940s Texarkana, Ark. Directed by Charles B. Pierce, the movie's depiction of brutal atrocities is all the more disagreeable when the ending states that the killer was never apprehended. O (R)

Toy, The (1979) French comedy about the spoiled 10-year-old son of a tyrannical tycoon (Michel Bouquet) who, told he can have any toy he wants in a store owned by his father, points to a hapless writer in his father's employ. The writer (Pierre Richard) goes along with the joke, develops a warm relationship with the boy, and helps bring about the father's comeuppance. Mild, innocuous entertainment. A-II (PG)

Toy, The (1982) Dreary adaptation of a mediocre French comedy about a poor journalist (Richard Pryor) so desperate for money that he lets a ruthless tycoon (Jackie Gleason) hire him to be the playmate of his spoiled, affection-starved son. The talents of everyone in the movie are wasted in an embarrassingly failed comedy. Directed by Richard Donner. Some comically intended scenes with sexual implications. A-III (PG)

Toy Grabbers, The (1971) Toy company head (Julie Newmar) wants the services of a talented toy-maker (Wally Cox) and entrusts the task to her imbecilic son (Victor Buono) who uses a string of seductive beauties to secure a contract. From there, writer-producer-director Don Joslyn veers into black comedy, adding crude touches that do little to compensate for all the nudity employed in this odious ode to motherhood. O (R/GP/R)

Toy Soldiers (1991) Led by a Colombian drug-czar's son (Andrew Divoff), a dozen heavily armed terrorists take over an elite boys' prep school in New England, where the most troublesome student (Sean Astin) covertly organizes a high-risk counterattack. Director Daniel Petrie, Jr.'s fast-moving formula action-movie features a thoroughly likable young cast, plus a good performance from Louis Gossett, Jr., but all it adds up to is empty escapist fare. Some gratuitous violence, a flash of nudity, fleeting sexual references, and intermittent rough language. A-III (R)

Toy Story (1995) Toys come to life when humans aren't looking in this animated fantasy about the rivalry between a cowboy doll (voiced by Tom Hanks) and a flashy plastic spaceman (voiced by Tim Allen), whose subsequent misadventures teach them a lesson in friendship. Director John Lasseter makes good use of computer animation in a slim but imaginative tale featuring the frantic antics of mischievous playthings, though little ones may be frightened by some scenes of a nasty child who enjoys destroying toys. A-I (G)

Toy Tiger (1956) Artificial comedy directed by Jerry Hopper in which a disgruntled commercial artist (Jeff Chandler) is inveigled into pretending to be the explorer-father of a wan boarding-school lad (Tim Hovey) whose widowed mom (Laraine Day) is too busy to visit him. Weak remake of **Mad About Music** (1938) but with none of its charm. A-I (br)

Toys (1992) The suspicions of a gentle brother (Robin Williams) and sister (Joan Cusack) are aroused when their career-officer uncle (Michael Gambon) inherits their father's toy factory, bringing in his militaristic son (LL Cool J) to begin secretly creating miniature deadly weapons disguised as toys. Director Barry Levinson's madly uneven movie practically cancels itself out by starting with dreamlike visual delights and ending in a morass of mirthless mayhem. Much menace, an off-screen sexual encounter, and some suggestive remarks. A-III (PG-13)

Toys Are Not for Children (1972) Marcia Forbes sleepwalks through her starring role as a young woman afflicted with an Electra complex, obsessively searching for dear old daddy. Though not quite soft-core pornography, there are enough visuals and coarse language to offend everyone. O (R)

Traces of Red (1992) Womanizing Palm Beach police detective (James Belushi), investigating a series of lurid sex killings, himself becomes a prime suspect, as do in turn his wealthy lover (Lorraine Bracco), his cop partner (Tony Goldwyn), and his politically ambitious brother (William Russ). Director Andy Wolk turns in a sleazy potboiler weighted down by obvious plot contrivances and Ms. Bracco's stilted acting. Acceptance of sexual promiscuity, including several depictions of sex encounters, brief nudity, some violence, and frequent rough language. O (R)

Track 29 (1988) An affluent North Carolina housewife (Therese Russell) spends her days drinking and hallucinating about the son (Gary Oldman) she as a teen had given up for adoption, while her physician husband (Christopher Lloyd) dallies with his nurse (Sandra Bernhard) and dabbles with his computer-operated toy-train set. British director Nicolas Roeg concocts an alien view of America in a surreal black comedy that makes little distinction between fantasy and reality. Much vulgar language, explicit sexual encounters of a kinky and incestuous nature, some nudity, and a gory fantasy climax. O (R)

Trackdown (1976) Vicious vigilante potboiler in which a Montana rancher (Robert Mitchum) comes to Los Angeles to wreak havoc among the scum who have brutalized his young runaway sister (Karen Lamm). Directed by Richard T. Heffron, the brutalization is dwelt upon with sickening detail that would be intolerable even in a movie dealing seriously with the social problems that this one cynically exploits. Excessive violence, sexual perversion, nudity, and some racist attitudes. O (R)

Tracks (1979) Jumpy Army sergeant (Dennis Hopper), escorting home the body of a Vietnam comrade, finds himself drawn to a college girl (Taryn Power), but his problems seem to stem more from an unrequited love for mama than the horrors of Vietnam. Directed by Henry Jaglom, the soppy, self-indulgent movie is less ambiguous than it is pointless. Excessive nudity. O (R)

Trader Horn (1973) Inept romantic adventure directed by Reza Badiyi is set in WW I Africa, where a veteran hunter (Rod Taylor) dodges British and German forces while guiding a Frenchman (Jean Sorel) to a lost platinum mine and falling in love with the man's wife (Anne Heywood) along the way. Romantic situations, stylized violence, and menace from stock jungle-footage. A-III (PG)

Trading Places (1983) Caustic streetwise con-man (Eddie Murphy) switches roles with a wealthy snob in a brokerage firm (Dan Aykroyd) in a less-than-noble experiment concocted by the two billionaire brothers who own the firm. The elaborate game of greed provides some insight into aspects of prejudice, but director John Landis relies too often on nudity, vulgarity, and profanity as sources of humor. O (R)

Traffic (1972) Fine French comedy from director Jacques Tati, who returns in his comic character of Monsieur Hulot in a story following the series of mishaps that occur as he shepherds a station-wagon camper from Paris to Amsterdam for an automobile show. There is no need for dialogue (grunts and groans suffice) because the situations are as universal as the visual gags that develop from them. The comedy is relaxed, refreshing, and even the habitually grouchy will get a few belly-laughs. A-I (G)

Tragedy of a Ridiculous Man (1982) Italian drama about a wealthy factory-owner (Ugo Tognazzi) whose son is kidnapped by political terrorists. Directed by Bernardo Bertolucci, the movie's modest premise provided a chance to come to grips with the realities of contemporary terrorism, but instead it tries to make obscurity and ambiguity do duty for profundity. One is never quite sure what's going on, and neither is Bertolucci. Some wholly gratuitous nudity. O (PG)

Trail of the Pink Panther (1982) Collection of outtakes and reprises of earlier movies in the series stitched together with some flat and uninspired new material using the gimmick of a TV reporter trying to find out what Inspector Clouseau was really like. It's a poor excuse for a movie, though if writer-director Blake Edwards only intended to show how much the late Peter Sellers is missed, he's succeeded admirably. Brief nudity and some sexually oriented humor. A-III (PG)

Train, The (1965) Resistance leader (Burt Lancaster) tries to stop a Nazi colonel (Paul Scofield) from taking a train loaded with French art treasures into Germany during the last days of the Occupation. Directed by John Frankenheimer, the overlong story has some exciting action with spectacular train wrecks and a monumental scheme of deception, yet never probes whether works of art are worth more than human lives. Much tension and stylized violence. A-I (br)

Train Robbers, The (1973) Good Western about a poor widow (Ann-Margret) who gets a tough hombre (John Wayne) and a couple of his pals (Ben Johnson and Rod Taylor) to go to Mexico to retrieve a fortune in stolen gold and bring it back past hordes of outlaws. Along the way there's plenty of entertaining action, slowed only by a few too many reflections on the old days. Director Burt Kennedy's witty dialogue and light touch keep this melodramatic tale moving at a fast and breezy clip. A-II (PG)

Trainspotting (1996) Episodic excursion into the aimless world of drug addicts, alcoholics, and misfits in Scotland, as recounted by one of them (Ewan McGregor), who lapses in and out of his heroin habit until stealing a satchel of money from his buddies, supposedly to start a life of middle-class respectability. Directed by Danny Boyle, the British production presents a glib account of the blighted lives of alienated youths whose repugnant activities are played alternately for shock value or comic effect, neither of which touches the painful reality of this self-destructive subculture. Graphic depictions of drug highs and lows, explicit sex scenes, some intense violence, and constant rough language. O (R)

Traitor's Gate (1966) Uneven British thriller directed by Freddie Francis about an attempt to steal the crown jewels from the Tower of London has a complicated plot with some violence and a restrained striptease scene. A-II (br)

Traitors, The (1974) Argentinean drama paralleling the corruption of a Peronist union leader who sells out the workers with the growth of a revolutionary group determined to destroy him and the ruling class he has come to represent. The fictional story easily encompasses the realities the country's social, economic, and political history, and viewers may find it a helpful introduction to the complexities of Latin-American political developments. A-III (nr)

Tramplers, The (1966) Leaden-paced Italian Western ineptly directed by Albert Band about a family feud which ultimately drives the father (Joseph Cotten) insane. Stylized violence. A-II (br)

Transylvania 6-5000 (1985) Two bumbling reporters (Jeff Go1dblum and Ed Begley, Jr.) for a tabloid magazine get hot on the trail of the Frankenstein monster and some of his friends. Director Rudy DeLuca works hard, but there are few laughs, even for viewers in a very silly mood. Some mild sexually oriented jokes. A-II (PG)

Trap, The (1947) Anemic Charlie Chan mystery directed by Howard Bretherton brings the Chinese-American detective (Sidney Toler) to a boardinghouse in Malibu Beach, where a troupe of showgirls are being stalked by a murderer. Comic racial stereotyping of Chan's chauffeur (Mantan Moreland) and Number Two son (Victor Sen Yung). A-I (br)

Trapeze (1956) Lackluster romantic triangle develops in a French circus when a veteran aerialist (Burt Lancaster) and his apprentice (Tony Curtis) break in a wily novice (Gina Lollobrigida) who vies for stardom by playing one against the other. Director Carol Reed captures the color of the circus setting while stressing the dangers of a high-wire act but gets little amorous tension from this unconvincing trio. Romantic complications grow to murderous proportions. A-III (br)

Trapped in Paradise (1994) Knuckleheaded comedy in which three bank-robbing brothers (Nicolas Cage, Jon Lovitz, and Dana Carvey) can't seem to escape the kindness of strangers in the small town they've just robbed until they become so guilt-ridden they return their booty. Writer-director George Gallo stitches together a series of lame skits, a contrived romance, and a frantically slapstick climax that add up to minimal entertainment. Brief, comically treated violence with intermittent profanities and crude expressions. A-III (PG-13)

Trash (1970) Apt title for director Andy Warhol's listless story of a heroin addict (Joe Dallesandro) whose habit has rendered him listless and impotent, while his transvestite lover (Holly Woodlawn) has a passion for scrounging in garbage heaps. Total nudity, graphic drug use, and gutter language. O (nr)

Traveling Executioner, The (1970) Clunker about

an itinerant with an electric chair (Stacy Keach) who makes the rounds of Southern prisons in the 1920s until a beautiful murderess (Mariana Hill) seduces him into helping her escape, the plan misfires, and he winds up being strapped into his device. Directed by Jack Smight, the unfunny black comedy suffers from Keach's grotesque performance and an excess of sexual scenes and references. O (R)

Traveller (1997) The title refers to an American clan of Gypsies originally from the British Isles who take in the son (Mark Wahlberg) of a former traveler, but his mentor (Bill Paxton) in learning the trade of conning people falls for a single mom (Julianna Margulies), then joins a sharp outsider (James Gammon) in a big-money scam that puts all their lives at risk. Directed by Jack Green, the narrative develops slowly while building sympathy for its characters, then erupts with hard-edged violence in a less-than-satisfying ending. Graphic violence, sexual situations, Gypsy stereotyping, and occasional rough language. A-IV (R)

Travels with My Aunt (1972) Primly proper British accountant (Alec McCowen) is suddenly whisked off to Paris by his wildly eccentric aunt (Maggie Smith) and finds himself an accessory in drug smuggling and other illegal activities that he comes to find exhilarating. Smith is badly miscast, and director George Cukor is given to mounting grandiose but leaden set pieces that turn Graham Greene's light comedy into a heavy fantasy that will strike some as vulgar farce. A-IV (PG)

Treason (see: **Guilty of Treason**)

Treasure Island (1934) The classic Hollywood version of the Robert Louis Stevenson adventure saga, with Wallace Berry outstanding as Long John Silver and Jackie Cooper as the stout-hearted Jim Hawkins. Directed by Victor Fleming, it is still enjoyable family fare, though youngsters may be disappointed by its black-and-white photography. A-I (br)

Treasure Island (1950) The Disney version of the Stevenson adventure classic stars Robert Newton as a scenery-chewing Long John Silver, with little Bobby Driscoll as a suitably serious Jim Hawkins. Directed by Byron Haskin, the action gets fairly intense at times, but the kids will love it. A-I (G)

Treasure Island (1972) Disappointing British screen version of the R.L. Stevenson classic, with Orson Welles garbling the role of Long John Silver. Director John Hough takes a rather uninspired literal approach to the high adventure of the novel, the characters are but cardboard caricatures, and the cast simply read their lines against the pretty Spanish coast. Nonetheless, the little ones will still enjoy this classic tale of buried treasure. A-I (G)

Treasure of Lost Canyon, The (1952) Uneven family adventure from Robert Louis Stevenson's yarn about an orphan (Tommy Ivo), his adopted parents (William Powell and Rosemary DeCamp), a crooked lawyer, and a Spanish treasure chest. Director Ted Tetzlaff gets disappointing results from all this, though Powell's performance adds considerable humor and the mystery of the youth's origins offer some compensations. Best for preschoolers. A-I (br)

Treasure of Matecumbe (1976) Routine Walt Disney adventure about two boys (Johnny Doran and Billy Attmore) and some buried treasure in the exotic Florida Keys. Directed by Vincent McEveety, the search goes on a bit too long, but younger viewers should enjoy the locale and the Huck Finn hijinks. A-I (G)

Treasure of Pancho Villa, The (1955) Plodding adventure in 1915 Mexico, where an American gunman (Rory Calhoun) teams with a revolutionary (Gilbert Roland) to hijack a government gold train, then trek into the mountains to deliver the loot to Villa, while fighting off pursuing soldiers. Directed by George Sherman, the plot complications include a greedy traitor (Joseph Calleia) and a patriotic American schoolteacher (Shelley Winters), though the outcome is hardly worth the effort. Considerable stylized violence. A-II (br)

Treasure of San Gennaro, The (1968) Italian heist-spoof in which two American gangsters (Harry Guardino and Senta Berger) come to Naples to rob its cathedral of a fortune in jewels and enlist the help of a goodhearted, somewhat dim, local crook (Nino Manfredi). During the course of the thoroughly wacky, bungled theft, director Dino Risi builds a consistently amusing, often hilarious, satiric comedy on Neapolitan manners and mores. A-II (br)

Treasure of the Four Crowns, The (1983) Dreadful Spanish-made 3-D movie about a Mission Impossible attempt, led by Tony Anthony, to recover some crowns having mystical powers from the hands of the villainous head of a cult. Directed by Fernando Baldi with the emphasis upon things whizzing out at the viewer and murkily photographed, it achieves intense boredom and eyestrain. Some violence. A-II (PG)

Treasure of the Sierra Madre, The (1948) A trio of down-on-their-luck Americans in Mexico (Humphrey Bogart, Walter Huston, and Tim Holt) pool their stakes to prospect for gold in the mountainous backcountry, stumble upon a rich vein of ore, and then face dissension over dividing their sudden wealth and getting it past a local band of murderous cutthroats. Director John Huston's suspenseful adventure tale features standout performances by his father, Walter, as a happy-go-lucky veteran prospector and Bogart as a penny-ante drifter driven over the edge by greed. Some intense menace. A-II (br)

Tree Grows in Brooklyn, A (1945) Solid adaptation of Betty Smith's novel about a young girl (Peggy Ann Garner) growing up in a working-class Brooklyn neighborhood around 1900. Under Elia Kazan's sensitive direction, the movie chronicles her troubled family's hand-to-mouth existence, with father (James Dunn) mostly unemployed, often-inebriated mother (Dorothy McGuire) holding the household together, and the kids experiencing the various pains and joys of being young during hard times. Warmly evocative picture of family life, though a bit heavy for youngsters. A-II (br)

Tree of Liberty (see: **The Howards of Virginia**)

Tree of Wooden Clogs, The (1979) Quiet, richly textured Italian drama about the lives of four peasant families who work as tenant farmers on a Lombardy estate at the end of the last century. Beginning with the fall harvest and ending with the spring planting, the movie depicts the everyday life of rural people who endure with human dignity in spite of the oppressive system which exploits their labor. Written, photographed and directed by Ermanno Olmi, this is a loving portrait of ordinary life in an age of social injustice. Some tense scenes. A-II (nr)

Tremors (1990) When some huge, reptilian underground monsters suddenly begin gobbling up the locals in and around a desolate Nevada desert town, two losers (Kevin Bacon and Fred Ward) helm a monster-bashing survival team. Director Ron Underwood splatters a lot of comic-book gore in this send-up of 1950s sci-fi flicks, which might have been innocuous fun if it hadn't also been strewn with so much locker-room language. A-III (PG-13)

Trenchcoat (1983) Poor Disney comedy about a would-be mystery-story writer (Margot Kidder) who runs into all sorts of nasty people during a vacation on Malta. The script is matched in ineptness only by the direction of Michael Tuchner, which underscores everything that would have been better passed over as quickly as possible. Some moderate violence and a few mild vulgarities. A-II (PG)

Trespass (1992) Senseless thriller about two white firemen (Bill Paxton and William Sadler) searching for stolen loot in a long-abandoned factory, where they are trapped after being discovered witnessing a brutal slaying by a gang of black drug-dealers (headed by Ice-T). Directed by Walter Hill, the situation grows increasingly preposterous as the graphic violence escalates until it exhausts itself in a cheap, throwaway ending. Excessive violence and incessant rough language. O (R)

Trial, The (1963) Nightmarish tale of anxiety and alienation from the Franz Kafka novel in which Joseph K. (Anthony Perkins), a junior office-manager in a nameless European city, is arrested for an unspecified crime, but can learn nothing about the case from his lawyer (Orson Welles) or court officials before facing his executioners in an apocalyptic ending. Also written and directed by Welles, the surreal proceedings are filled with dark images and labyrinthine visuals of a hapless individual caught in an impersonal, bureaucratic legal system, though much of this vivid excursion into the absurd remains troublingly obscure. Some stylized violence, menacing situations, sexual innuendo, and an instance of profanity. A-III (br)

Trial, The (1993) Slack British adaptation of the Franz Kafka novel about Josef K. (Kyle MacLachlan), a bank official in Prague making various futile attempts to defend himself from charges of a crime that is never specified. Director David Jones can't blend the surreal aspects of the labyrinthine narrative with the sparkling setting of turn-of-the-century Prague, though some of the minor roles are effective, especially Anthony Hopkins as the austere prison chaplain and Jason Robards as an aged, roguish lawyer. Some fairly restrained sex scenes. A-III (nr)

Trial and Error (1997) Feeble courtroom comedy in which an actor (Michael Richards) tries to help a drunken lawyer (Jeff Daniels) by taking his place in a trial which drags witlessly on, until the actor falls for the prosecutor (Jessica Steen) and the lawyer beds a dreamy waitress (Charlize Theron). Director Jonathan Lynn treats the lightweight material in laborious, heavy-handed fashion, though the chief drawbacks are the charmless principals, who prove as bogus as the trial and as shallow as the plot. Sexual situations and occasional profanity. A-III (PG-13)

Trial by Jury (1994) Derivative melodrama in which a mobster (Armand Assante) on trial for murder has a corrupt ex-cop (William Hurt) intimidate a juror (Joanne Whalley-Kilmer) by threatening the life of her child unless she votes to acquit him. As directed by Heywood Gould, the narrative steadily disintegrates into a cliche-ridden gangster movie as the frightened woman cooperates, then resorts to murder in order to guarantee her family's continued safety. Intermittent violence, some sexual innuendo, and occasional rough language. A-III (R)

Trial of Billy Jack, The (1974) Using the same mixture of violence and simple-minded idealism that marked the original **Billy Jack**, co-writer/director/star Tom Laughlin's sequel offers as an alternative to contemporary injustices only a shallow romanticism that has little relevance to the real world. A-IV (PG)

Trial of Joan of Arc, The (1965) Based on the actual trial transcript, the courtroom conflict between the Maid of Orleans and her judges is presented objectively with impersonal camerawork that builds in stark intensity to the catharsis of the inevitable burning at the stake. Director Robert Bresson's 1962 French production succeeds in making an overly familiar story freshly interesting, partly through the use of non-professional actors who give the impression of actually undergoing the trial process and not just playing at it. Subtitles. Heavy-going for children. A-I (br)

Trial of the Catonsville Nine, The (1972) Screen version of Rev. Daniel Berrigan's play about the 1968 trial of nine Vietnam War protestors who readily admitted burning draft records in Catonsville, Md., using the trial as a forum to argue against the war's morality. Handsomely photographed by Haskell Wexler, the movie employs the same cast and director (Gordon Davidson) as the stage version. Producer Gregory Peck deserves credit for preserving on film this particular aspect of the peace movement. A-II (PG)

Trial without Jury (1950) Feeble mystery directed by Philip Ford in which a playwright (Robert

Rockwell) tries to solve the murder of his Los Angeles producer by staging a play based on the killing in hopes this will unnerve the culprit enough to make a slip. Stylized violence and sexual innuendo. A-II (br)

Tribute (1980) Screen version of the Bernard Slade play about a lecherous, incorrigibly non-serious, but lovable press agent (Jack Lemmon) who, knowing he has but a short time to live, tries to make peace with his priggish son (Robby Benson) and remarried ex-wife (Lee Remick). Directed by Bob Clark, it is civilized entertainment, but not nearly as moving or funny as it was meant to be. Brief nudity and some rough language. A-III (PG)

Tribute to a Bad Man (1956) Dark, brooding Western about a pioneer rancher (James Cagney) who rules the range with an iron hand until his hard heart is softened by an Eastern tenderfoot (Don Dubbins) and a strong, loving woman (Irene Pappas). Directed by Robert Wise, the flawed plot is of less interest than the character study of a man who comes to realize that people mean more than possessions. Stylized violence and implied live-in relationship. A-II (br)

Trick Baby (1972) Gritty street movie about two Philadelphia con-artists, one of whom is black (Mel Stewart), while the other (Kiel Martin) insists he was born black and only looks white. Together they are truly democratic in hustling everyone, regardless of race. Director Larry Yust makes an entertaining game of watching them keep one step ahead of the cops and the avenging mob, though its genial air of amorality, some nudity, and rough language limit its audience considerably. A-IV (R)

Trigger Effect, The (1996) Grim tale of an increasingly desperate husband (Kyle MacLachlan), wife (Elisabeth Shue), baby, and family friend (Dermot Mulroney) who, fearing for their safety during a prolonged, widespread power failure and subsequent looting, take to the road, where they encounter more danger. Writer-director David Koepp's thriller is an atmospheric but overly murky story of ordinary people driven to lawlessness by their fears. Some violence, mild sexual innuendo, recurring rough language, and a few instances of profanity. A-III (R)

Trigger Happy (see: **Mad Dog Time**)

Trilogy (1969) Theatrical adaptation of three television plays, written by Truman Capote and directed by Frank Perry, consists of "Miriam," about a retired nurse (Mildred Natwick); "Among the Paths to Eden," about an aging spinster (Maureen Stapleton); and "A Christmas Memory," about the elderly relative (Geraldine Page) of an orphaned boy (narrated by Capote). Creatively made and beautifully acted, the work reaffirms the delight to be found in ordinary lives and people when they are observed by a humane sensibility. Some intense scenes. A-II (G)

Trinity Is Still My Name (1972) Terence Hill repeats his role as the vagabond outlaw Trinity, as does Bud Spencer as his ornery, hulking brother. Director E.B. Clucher plays everything for laughs, and the hijinks are refreshingly in good humor. The fun is constant, no one gets killed, and there's not even a shot fired. A few risqué lines will zoom right over the heads of youngsters. A-II (G)

Trip, The (1967) Director Roger Corman's movie about the psychedelic experiences of LSD presents a one-sided, excitement-laden view of the drug's effects. The result serves not to enlighten, but to expose impressionable viewers to the temptation of dangerous experimentation. Exploitative use of sexual imagery. O (br)

Trip to Bountiful, The (1986) Geraldine Page gives a memorable performance as a feisty old woman who can't stand living with her daughter-in-law and, when her son refuses to take her, sets off by herself to see her hometown of Bountiful, Tex. On this journey to a place that is now a ghost town, the viewer comes to respect the indomitable spirit of a strong personality who refuses to give up in spite of waning physical strength. John Masterson directs Horton Foote's story with dignity and compassion, though some of the old woman's difficulties might be upsetting to the very young. A-II (PG)

Trippin'(1999) Crude high-school comedy about an aimless, daydreaming senior (Deon Richmond), who pretends to be college-bound to impress a serious classmate (Maia Campbell) and ends up following her lead. Director David Raynr allows the lad's puerile fantasies to perpetuate negative racial stereotypes only to be clumsily overcome in the narrative with preachy warnings about staying in school. Fleeting comic violence, sexual situations with brief nudity, repeated racial slurs, much rough language, and an instance of profanity. A-IV (R)

Triple Cross (1967) Lengthy, fact-based WW II espionage movie is a vehicle for Christopher Plummer as Eddie Chapman, a safecracker and opportunist who worked both sides of the Channel as double agent for Germany and England. Director Terence Young's complicated plot tries too hard for effects that seem more often cynical than ironic. Restrained bedroom scenes. A-III (br)

Triple Echo (1973) Fetid British drama about a woman (Glenda Jackson) whose husband is in a WW II POW camp and an Army deserter (Brian Deacon), whom she dresses up as a woman and passes off as her sister, until a lecherous army sergeant (Oliver Reed) discovers the deception. Director Michael Apted's talented cast tries so hard to make this credible, but can't overcome an overwhelming sense of disbelief. It all seems a rather pointless exercise in the byways of sexual ambivalence and self-identity. O (R)

Tristana (1970) Spanish production about an innocent young woman (Catherine Deneuve) who, after being seduced by her guardian (Fernando Rey), runs away with a painter, only to return to torment her former guardian in his old age. Surrealist director Luis Bunuel is in top form in this story of an ironic reversal of roles that rests on such themes as middle-class materialism, anti-clericalism, human deformity, and the dead hand of convention. Bunuel is a moralist rather than a realist, and his sense of evil and dark humor are not for casual viewers. A-III (GP)

Triumph of Hercules, The (1964) Dubbed Italian production directed by Alberto De Martino has the muscle-bound hero (Dan Vadis) save the kingdom of Mycenae from a witch's son and her magic men of gold. Pulp time-waster with comic-book violence. A-III (br)

Triumph of Sherlock Holmes, The (1935) Creaky but watchable adaptation of Conan Doyle's **The Valley of Fear**, with the retired Baker Street detective (Arthur Wontner) joining Dr. Watson (Ian Fleming) to solve a murder case involving a secret society of Pennsylvania coal-miners and the nefarious Professor Moriarty (Lyn Harding). Directed by Leslie S. Hiscott, the British production is comfortably stodgy except for the overblown melodramatics in flashbacks to US-labor troubles. Stylized violence and menacing situations. A-II (br)

Triumph of the Spirit (1989) Grim, unrelenting Holocaust drama, set almost entirely within the Auschwitz death camp where it was filmed, re-creates the fact-based story of a Greek Jew and champion boxer, Salamo Arouch (Willem Dafoe), whose survival hinged on his ability to win some 200 fights held to entertain the SS guards. Realistically directed by Robert M. Young, the fine cast includes Wendy Gazelle as Salamo's girlfriend and Edward James Olmos as a Gypsy inmate. Some particularly grisly concentration camp scenes of torture, murder, and degradation. A-III (R)

Trog (1970) Low-budget British monster movie in which the head of a research laboratory (Joan Crawford) subdues, studies, and educates a rather ludicrous ape-man that is eventually killed by the local townspeople because of fear and superstition. Director Freddie Francis treats the story as a serious, if heavy-handed, plea for human understanding, but the result is only slow and melodramatic entertainment. A-II (GP)

Trojan Eddie (1997) Downbeat Irish tale of an ex-con (Stephen Rea) whose brutal boss (Richard Harris) suspects he has helped his employer's conniving bride run off with a younger man and a fortune in wedding gifts. Directed by Gillies Mackinnon, the story's characters are a murky mix of ne'er-do-wells slyly seeking to make money by any means or resigned to dashed dreams. Some violence, brief nudity, intermittent profanity, and much rough language. A-III (nr)

Trojan Women, The (1971) Directed by Michael Cacoyannis, this adaptation of Euripides' tragedy about the shattering effect of war on society is faithful to the original and frequently flamboyant. In spite of the stately acting of Katharine Hepburn as Hecuba the Trojan queen, and Irene Papas as Helen, the cause of the war, the result is of more interest to the student of ancient Greek drama than the casual moviegoer. A-III (GP)

Troma's War (1988) Sleazy exploitation movie about the perils facing a band of ditzy tourists when their plane crash lands on a Caribbean island infested with terrorists out to overthrow the United States. Directed by Michael Herz and Samuel Weil, this truly awful parody of the **Airport** genre profanes everything from motherhood to religion and AIDS. Wall-to-wall oozing gore and slice 'n' dice violence, as well as sexual and bathroom vulgarities. O (R)

Tron (1982) Disney high-tech sci-fi adventure in which three heroes (Jeff Bridges, Cindy Morgan, and Bruce Boxleitner), on the trail of a greedy villain (David Warner), get caught in the workings of a computerized video game. Fortunately, director Steven Lisberger has treated the material with a certain amount of humor, but how much you enjoy it depends upon your enthusiasm for the special effects, which are the movie's reason for being. Some violence, and also the clear implication that the heroine has gone to bed with both of her heroic companions. A-III (PG)

Troop Beverly Hills (1989) Faced with a pending divorce and an empty life of shopping and party-going, a Beverly Hills matron (Shelly Long) decides to dedicate her time to her daughter's floundering Wilderness Girls troop. This lightweight satire of materialism works mainly because of Long's spunky performance and Jeff Kanew's spirited direction. Fleeting rough language and minimal sexual innuendo. A-II (PG)

Trooper Hook (1957) Uneven but interesting Western in which a seasoned sergeant (Joel McCrea) is detailed to escort an Apache captive (Barbara Stanwyck) and her son fathered by the chief back to the husband (John Dehner) who thought her dead. Director Charles Marquis Warren handles the period's racial bigotry with some sensitivity, but the sluggish action is not very convincing. Frontier violence and sexual innuendo. A-II (br)

Tropic of Cancer (1970) Screen version of Henry Miller's long-banned autobiographical novel about an impoverished expatriate writer (Rip Torn) and his chiefly sexual exploits in the Paris of the early 1930s. Directed by Joseph Strick, the movie's most serious failure is not its shallow characterization of the writer, nor its crude images and cruder language, but its overall disregard of women as no more than sex objects. O (X)

Trouble Along the Way (1953) Overly sentimental tale in which a down-on-his-luck coach (John Wayne) is hired by the aging rector (Charles Coburn) of a small Catholic college to field a winning football team, or else the financially troubled school will be closed. Directed by Michael Curtiz, the plot is darkened by the coach's problems convincing a juvenile caseworker (Donna Reed) to leave his 11-year-old daughter in his custody rather than that of his ex-wife (Marie Windsor), though the treatment is paced by humorous Catholic stereotypes. Strife between ex-spouses and questionable collegiate sports practices. A-II (br)

Trouble in Mind (1986) Unlikable crime melodrama directed by Alan Rudolph about a cynical ex-cop (Kris Kristofferson) who tries to help a young punk in trouble (Keith Carradine) but gets romantically involved with two women (Genevieve Bujold and Lori Singer). Excessive violence and sex scenes. O (R)

Trouble Makers (1948) Routine Bowery Boys caper in which Slip (Leo Gorcey) and Sach (Huntz Hall) help a rookie cop (Gabriel Dell) nab a killer and his gang (including Lionel Stander). Some slapstick violence. A-I (br)

Trouble Man (1972) Slick black action-movie about a super-tough, super-cool dude (Robert Hooks) who is being used by one black gambling-ring to wipe out another, but when he catches on they all go down in a series of shootouts. Directed by Ivan Dixon, its violent action and constant rough language, despite coy restraint in several sex scenes, is for undemanding but hardy adults. A-III (R)

Trouble with Angels, The (1966) Episodic screen version of Jane Trahey's comic recollections of life in a Catholic girl's boarding-school revolves around the finely balanced battle of wit and will between the girls and the nuns. Rosalind Russell is in top form as the mother superior who squelches the adolescent mischief concocted by Hayley Mills and June Harding. Save for a few mawkish scenes, director Ida Lupino has made the sentimental comedy seem amusingly fresh and enjoyable. A-I (PG)

Trouble with Girls, The (1969) The Chautauqua show, a bit of Americana that was part carnival, part educational forum, serves as a the background for an Elvis Presley movie set in the 1920s. Peter Tewksbury has not helped matters much by directing the picture as if it were all high camp, and the plot bogs down in some heavy dramatics about a local murder, but, on the whole, it's a relaxed venture into nostalgia. A-III (G)

Troublesome Creek: A Midwestern (1997) Uplifting documentary chronicles how a long-married Iowa farm couple decide, with the help of their six grown children, to auction off their livestock, machinery, and household possessions to pay off their bank debt without losing their land, which one son will farm to continue a century-old family tradition. Filmmakers Jeanne Jordan and Steven Ascher sensitively profile Jordan's fine, upstanding parents and supportive siblings in an emotionally resonant story typifying the gradual demise of farming as a viable way of life in America. Adult financial entanglements. A-II (nr)

Truck Turner (1974) Los Angeles tracker of bail-jumpers (Isaac Hayes) is kept busy looking for pimps, prostitutes, dope dealers, and other low types while trying to keep his feisty girlfriend (Annazette Chase) out of prison. Director Jonathan Kaplan's work is so relentlessly awful, in terms of both quality and its view of humanity, that its excessive violence is almost beside the point. O (R)

Truce, The (1998) Sobering fact-based drama follows the grueling journey of Holocaust survivor Primo Levi (John Turturro) from Auschwitz in early 1945 over nine arduous months through war-ravaged Eastern Europe, before he reaches his home in Italy. Based on Levi's 1962 memoir and directed by Francesco Rosi, the movie conveys his painful transition from being treated like a beast of burden to feeling human once more, but the characters' deadened emotions make the slowly paced movie less than involving. Brief violence, discreet sexual situations, and occasional rough language. A-III (R)

True Believer (1989) Formerly idealistic lawyer (James Woods), who now makes easy money defending drug-dealers, takes the case of a young Korean (Yuji Okumoto) unjustly incarcerated for a Chinatown murder, thereby restoring the lawyer's waning self-respect and integrity. An intriguing premise, a flamboyant performance by Woods, and classy direction by Joseph Ruben often make this courtroom thriller quite diverting. Some grisly violence, intense menace, and rough language. A-III (R)

True Colors (1991) Ambition threatens the friendship of two law students (John Cusack and James Spader) when one steals the other's girlfriend (Imogen Stubbs) to further his political ambitions by working for her father (Richard Widmark), a powerful senator. Director Herbert Ross gets some sharp performances in an engrossing, if over-baked, tale of greed, betrayal, and revenge. Restrained premarital encounters, intermittent rough language, and minimal violence. A-III (R)

True Confession (1937) Dark comedy in which the highly imaginative wife (Carole Lombard) of a struggling lawyer (Fred MacMurray) is charged with a murder she didn't commit, but lets her husband plead she acted in self-defense to save her honor. Directed by Wesley Ruggles, the murder case is fairly heavy-handed, especially John Barrymore's role as a cynical onlooker, but Lombard's bright performance as the wife with her tongue in her cheek is undercut by MacMurray's dour portrayal of the husband. Uneasy comic predicaments. A-II (br)

True Confessions (1981) Uneven screen version of John Gregory Dunne's novel about troubled brothers in late 1940s Los Angeles, the one (Robert De Niro) being a monsignor adept at political infighting, and the other (Robert Duvall) a tough police sergeant intent on solving the murder of a prostitute. Director Ulu Grosbard uses the crime as the core of this interesting but only moderately effective melodrama intertwining religion, politics, and crime. Because of its relentless concentration upon the seamy side of things (brothels, morgues, and a pornographic film), some adults may find it unsuitable entertainment. A-IV (R)

True Crime (1999) Tautly paced drama in which a disgraced, womanizing reporter (Clint Eastwood), newly assigned to cover the execution of a black man (Isaiah Washington) at midnight, races against time to turn up evidence to support his belief in the man's innocence. As produced and directed by Eastwood, the character studies of both men prove absorbing, but the climax is flawed by trite plot contrivances. Brief violence, sympathetic treatment of adultery, much rough language, and recurring profanity. A-IV (R)

True Grit (1969) Rousing Western adventure based on the Charles Portis novel about a justice-minded little gal with true grit (Kim Darby) who tracks down her father's killer with the aid of a gruff overweight US marshal (John Wayne) and an over-eager Texas Ranger (Glenn Campbell). Directed with gusto by Henry Hathaway, their adventures and scrapes with death are furious and action-packed, though leavened nicely with human touches and good humor. Because of some stylized violence, young children may need the support of older members of the family. A-I (G)

True Identity (1991) A young black actor (Lenny Henry) disguises himself as a white man to keep from being killed after accidentally learning the secret identity of a mob kingpin (Frank Langella). Director Charles Lane gets some mileage out of this mildly diverting combination of gangland spoof and racial farce, but it's more a showcase for Henry, with its one-joke premise stretched to the breaking point. Comic violence, implied promiscuity, and intermittent rough language. A-III (R)

True Lies (1994) Overblown action fantasy in which a US super-spy (Arnold Schwarzenegger) finds his tranquil domestic life suddenly shattered when his wife (Jamie Lee Curtis), then daughter (Eliza Dusku), are taken hostage by a gang of fanatical terrorists armed with nuclear weapons. Director James Cameron throttles the picture's mix of comedy and suspense by overplaying every scene to the point of tedium, including all the special-effects violence and unsavory sexual situations. Excessive violence, snickering treatment of sex, and occasional rough language. O (R)

True Love (1989) Low-budget independent comedy charting the rocky road to marital bliss taken by a young, Italian-American Bronx couple (Annabella Sciorra and Ron Eldard), whose well-meaning family and friends, as well as their own naivety, play havoc with their upcoming nuptials. Directed by Nancy Savoca, the result is true-to-life, consistently fresh, and lightly satirical without being judgmental. Much profanity laced with sexual vulgarities and implied premarital sex. A-III (R)

True Romance (1993) Brutally violent tale of a call-girl bride (Patricia Arquette) and her reckless groom (Christian Slater) on the run from police and gangsters while trying to peddle a suitcase full of cocaine stolen from the woman's murdered pimp. Director Tony Scott fills the screen with recurring scenes of graphic gore and mayhem in a story conveying the abhorrent message that murder is "cool" and crime pays handsomely. Excessive violence, a bedroom scene with nudity, recreational drug use, many racial slurs, and constant rough language. O (R)

True Stories (1986) Director David Byrne presents a sociological vision of arcane Americana in this whimsical movie about the style, spirit, and substance of small-town life in the Southwest. With Byrne himself serving as a somewhat sardonic on-screen commentator, the movie offers a series of documentary vignettes of more or less ordinary town activities. Driven by an eclectic musical score, the result is a wholesome and innocent post-modern version of "Our Town." A-II (PG)

Truly, Madly, Deeply (1991) An Englishwoman (Juliet Stevenson) is emotionally paralyzed long after the sudden death of her lover (Alan Rickman), until his ghost materializes, thereby enabling her to end their relationship and open herself to new possibilities. Anthony Minghella wrote and directed this gentle, rather mawkish romance, enlivened by its eccentric humor and sensitive performances. Discreet treatment of sexual relationships. A-III (PG)

Truman (1995) Based on David McCullough's Pulitzer Prize-winning biography, this 135-minute television dramatization treats the life and times of Harry S Truman in episodic fashion as he makes his way from Independence, Mo., to the White House, and back. Directed by Frank Pierson, the re-creation of far-ranging events is held together by Gary Sinise's likeable performance in portraying Truman as a man with no high opinion of his own abilities, yet striving mightily to measure up to the responsibilities of the land's highest office. Wartime violence, racial bigotry, and occasional profanity. A-II (PG)

Truman Show, The (1998) Beguiling fantasy in which a 30-year-old man (Jim Carrey) eventually discovers his life from day one has been secretly televised 24 hours a day, and all the people in his tranquil island community, such as his parents and wife, are paid actors. Director Peter Weir's bracing tale is emotionally involving while only scratching the surface of its moral themes concerning blatant media intrusion and control. Mature theme, marital discord, and a few instances of profanity. A-III (PG)

Trust (1991) Mean-spirited attempt at black comedy in which a pregnant teenager considering abortion (Adrienne Shelly) brings home a volatile stranger (Martin Donovan), but her mother (Merritt Nelson) and sister (Edie Falco) react with extreme treachery. Writer-director Hal Hartley presents a vicious vision of middle-class family life with no insights but plenty of nasty role models. Casual attitude toward abortion, poisonous parental figures, minor violence, and intermittent rough language. O (R)

Truth about Cats & Dogs, The (1996) Insecure about her looks, a radio talk-show host (Janeane Garofalo) persuades her gorgeous girlfriend (Uma Thurman) to impersonate her when an admiring radio fan (Ben Chaplin) asks her out. Director Michael Lehmann's contrived, mistaken-identity comedy essentially stresses the value of friendship, love, and inner beauty, although it is marred by a gratuitous phone-sex scene. Implied masturbation, some sexual innuendo, occasional profanity, and an instance of rough language. A-IV (PG-13)

Truth about Spring, The (1965) Despite different social backgrounds, an adolescent tomboy (Haley Mills) and a young Harvard graduate (James MacArthur) find romance while searching the Caribbean for sunken pirate treasure. Directed by Richard Thorpe, the comedy adventure is set aboard a sailing ship whose captain (John Mills) and rascally crew (Lionel Jeffries, Harry Andres, and Niall MacGinnis) abet the growing friendship between the charming young couple. Gentle, old-fashioned entertainment. A-I (br)

Trygon Factor, The (1968) Muddled British mystery directed by Cyril Frankel in which a Scotland Yard inspector (Stewart Granger) traces a series of unsolved robberies to a bogus order of nuns. Violence. A-III (br)

Tsar to Lenin (1971) Documentary on the Russian Revolution presents rare footage of the royal family, the Bolshevik leaders, the complicated events of the February and October revolutions, and the subsequent terrors of the Civil War. Valuable as this footage is, the movie is relatively unsophisticated in the use it makes of it. A-I (nr)

Tucker: The Man and His Dream (1988) Dramatized portrait of the maverick (Jeff Bridges) whose innovative automobile designs challenged the lackluster product of Detroit's car industry after WW II. Director Francis Coppola has a hard time blending the documentary and dramatic aspects of his scenario, and ends up portraying his subject in mostly one-dimensional terms, with moral issues (good guys vs. bad guys) treated in similar black-and-white fashion as well. Mild rough language. A-II (PG)

Tuff Turf (1985) WASP golden-boy finds himself at inner-city high school and makes things even tougher for himself by going after the girlfriend of a gang leader. Mindless youth exploitation movie directed by Fritz Kiersch with a blaring musical score and some scenes of despicable violence. O (R)

Tulsa (1949) During the 1920s, a cattleman's daughter (Susan Hayward) gambles on a wildcat oil well, strikes it rich, then almost loses all before being saved by conservation-minded friends (Robert Preston and Pedro Armendariz). Directed by Stuart Heisler, the romance is more in the building of an oil empire than in the heroine's life, but the real conflict is between oil derricks and grazing cattle. Some fisticuffs and an oil field burning out of control. A-I (br)

Tumbleweed (1953) Standard Western directed by Nathan Juran in which a cowboy (Audie Murphy), mistakenly blamed for the Indian massacre of a wagon train, escapes a posse while trying to get proof of his innocence, which is finally established by the strange horse of the title. Frontier violence. A-I (br)

Tune, The (1992) Fanciful animated story in which a struggling songwriter on his way to the office to meet a deadline gets sidetracked in a surreal world of wacky characters, who give him the inspiration for a hit tune. Director Bill Plympton's slyly witty tale boasts a distinctive visual style and 10 whimsical songs, but its helter-skelter procession of events seems padded to accommodate a feature-length running time. Some cartoon violence. A-II (nr)

Tune in Tomorrow ... (1990) Comedy set in the 1950s about a flamboyant writer of radio soap-operas (Peter Falk) who manipulates a romance between a novice news-writer (Keanu Reeves) and his 35-year-old aunt by marriage (Barbara Hershey) as grist for his sudsy scripts. Director Jon Amiel orchestrates an offbeat but overproduced comic fantasy that is enlivened by Falk and Hershey's feisty performances, great period costumes, and vibrant New Orleans setting. Some make-believe violence, mild sexual innuendo, and minimal rough language. A-III (PG-13)

Tunnelvision (1976) Sick satire about television programming of the future features Howard Hesseman, Betty Thomas, Chevy Chase, and Larraine Newman. Directed by Neal Israel and Brad Swirnoff, it offers a series of degrading, detestable, and altogether unfunny vignettes. O (R)

Turbo: A Power Rangers Movie (1997) Inane action fantasy from the children's TV series has the teen rangers trying to stop a power-mad Valkyrie (Hilary Shepard Turner) and a volcano monster from wreaking havoc on the entire universe. As clumsily directed by David Winning and Shuki Levy, the lame result is a choppy mix of formula mythic-characters, derivative situations, and extended martial-arts battles. Special-effects violence and stylized mayhem. A-II (PG)

Turbulence (1997) Formula thriller in which a terrified flight attendant (Lauren Holly) locks herself in a jumbo jet's cockpit hoping to land the storm-tossed aircraft after a crazed serial killer (Ray Liotta) shoots the pilots. Director Robert Butler's frantic melodrama eventually becomes unintentionally funny with its overwrought damsel-in-distress cliches. Intermittent violence, recurring rough language, and occasional profanity. A-III (R)

Turk 182 (1985) In rescuing a little girl from a burning building , an off-duty New York fireman (Robert Urich) is badly injured. When he's refused compensation, his young brother (Timothy Hutton) embarks on a campaign for justice by embarrassing the mayor with graffiti signed "Turk 182," his injured brother's nickname and badge number. A crude, noisy movie directed by Bob Clark with pretensions to folk-epic grandeur. Sexual promiscuity. O (PG-13)

Turner & Hooch (1989) Diverting man-and-beast comedy about a small-town cop (Tom Hanks) who takes in the nasty, drooling watchdog of a murder victim (John McIntire), becomes fond of the overgrown pet, and the mismatched duo end up solving the murder. Scenes pairing the ugly dog with handsome Hanks are amusing, and the pooch enables the cop to fall in love with the local veterinarian (Mare Winningham). Director Roger Spottiswoode manages to make the lightweight tale entertaining and somewhat affecting. Brief but intense violence, an implied sexual encounter, and minimal locker-room language. A-III (PG)

Turning Point, The (1952) Above-average crime melodrama follows a tough-minded journalist (William Holden) who can't resist helping an idealistic special prosecutor (Edmond O'Brien) break a crime-syndicate boss (Ed Begley). Director William Dieterle's shady underworld characters make credible foes for the lawmen, with taut action scenes, especially a hitman (Neville Brand) seeking his target in a crowded prizefight arena. Stylized violence. A-II (br)

Turning Point, The (1977) Shirley MacLaine and Anne Bancroft star as one-time rival ballerinas who renew their feud when MacLaine's daughter (Leslie Browne) joins Bancroft's troupe. Directed by Herbert Ross, the old-fashioned sentimental melodrama is set against the glamorous world of ballet, with plenty of grand dance sequences. Brief nudity and a benign attitude toward illicit sex. A-III (PG)

Turtle Diary (1986) Adaptation of playwright Harold Pinter's story of an author (Glenda Jackson) and a bookseller (Ben Kingsley) who are brought together by their mutual aspiration to free three sea turtles from the London aquarium. Director John Irvin's delicate, contemplative narrative is a testament to gentle souls who set simple goals and celebrate small, private victories. Brief but intense scene of violence. A-II (PG)

Twelfth Night (1996) Screen version of Shakespeare's comedy of mistaken identities in which a shipwrecked woman (Imogen Stubbs) disguises herself as a man in a foreign country whose ruler (Toby Stephens) and the countess (Helena Bonham Carter) he hopes to wed are both taken in by her male impersonation, which becomes complicated by her falling in love with the ruler, while the countess falls in love with her. Adapted and directed by Trevor Nunn, the droll fantasy of mixed-up lovers is highly amusing, often charming, and paced by a madcap subplot, but the real enjoyment is in watching a talented cast having fun with nonsensical roles. Mild sexual innuendo. A-II (PG)

12 Angry Men (1957) When a jury begin its deliberations on the guilt or innocence of a youth accused of murdering his father, one man (Henry Fonda) insists they re-examine the evidence before rendering their verdict. Directed by Sidney Lumet, the result is an absorbing character study of the jurors (a brilliant ensemble of character actors, including E.G. Marshall, Lee J. Cobb, Jack Klugman, Martin Balsam, and Jack Warden), the preconceptions they bring to the case, and the human dynamics of the jury system. Some intense moments. A-I (br)

Twelve Chairs, The (1970) Uneven comedy set in the Soviet Union of 1927, when a deposed nobleman (Ron Moody) learns that the family jewels were hidden in a confiscated dining-room chair, but his search is complicated by a suave con-artist (Frank Langella) and a greedy priest (Dom DeLuise). Written and directed by Mel Brooks, the comedy depends upon old-fashioned mugging and slapstick spiked with some modern cynicism, but by the end the farce turns to bathos and disappointment. A-III (GP/G appeal)

Twelve Chairs, The (1973) Soviet cinema is not known for its levity or wit, and yet both are in evidence in this large-scale extravaganza in the picaresque adventures of a grasping ex-aristocrat (A. Gomiashvili) and a conniving proletarian (S. Filippov) who are forced to work together in searching for a fortune hidden in a chair seized during the Revolution. Directed by Leonid Gaidai, it is a good-humored and often hilarious picture of the flaws and strengths that made up life in the Soviet Union of the 1920s, and the ending has considerably more bite than the boisterous 1970 Mel Brooks version. A-II (nr)

12 Monkeys (1995) Convoluted sci-fi tale set in 2035, when the few survivors of a 1997 killer virus seek to learn the cause of the epidemic by sending an expendable criminal (Bruce Willis) back in time to 1996, where a psychiatrist (Madeleine Stowe) helps in tracking the mysterious gang of the title (led by Brad Pitt). Directed by Terry Gilliam, the elaborate narrative gets lost in quirky byways and nasty turns which only obscure what is essentially the story of a youth witnessing his own death as a time-traveler. Some nasty violence, sexual situations, and rough language. A-IV (R)

Twelve O'Clock High (1949) Tense WW II story of a US B-17 bomber group based in England whose commander (Gary Merrill) is relieved for fretting over casualty rates, but the straight-laced officer (Gregory Peck) who succeeds him eventually cracks under the emotional strain of ordering men to risk their lives flying hazardous daylight missions. Director Henry King's character study of men in war has a strong supporting cast (notably Dean Jagger, Millard Mitchell, and Hugh Marlowe), a thoughtful script, and stunning wartime footage of air combat. Much psychological tension. A-I (br)

20 Dates (1999) Documentary-like chronicle in which a two-person camera crew follow filmmaker Myles Berkowitz (playing himself) around on 20 dates as he searches for, and surprisingly finds, Ms. Right. The contrived results are occasionally amusing despite Berkowitz's whiny personality and the shameless hidden-camera tactics he sometimes employs. An implied sexual encounter, some crass sexual references, much rough language, and an instance of profanity. A-III (R)

25th Hour, The (1967) Well-intentioned European co-production showing how senseless coincidences and petty officials separate a Romanian peasant (Anthony Quinn) from his wife (Virna Lisi) during WW II. Their ultimate reunion as a beaten family of displaced persons demonstrates the devastating effects of war on the innocent. Director Henri Verneuil has a worthy theme, but the plot contrivances are thin and the production is flat and plodding. A-II (br)

24 Hours of the Rebel (1977) Mediocre story about the effect the news of actor James Dean's death has upon a group of college students in a small Arkansas town who seem to find movies more real than their own lives. Written and directed by James Bridges, the movie fails to build much sympathy for its two principal characters (Richard Thomas and Deborah Benson) or explain why they are drawn so compulsively to Dean's screen persona. Several scenes of youthful sexual explorations and vulgar language. A-III (PG)

20 Million Miles to Earth (1957) Weak sci-fi effort from director Nathan Juran in which a specimen of life brought from Venus by US astronauts escapes when their spaceship crashes, then grows to monstrous size (thanks to Ray Harryhausen's animated models) and runs amok in Rome until cornered in the Coliseum. Some special-effects violence and menacing situations. A-I (br)

29th Street (1991) The fractious relationship between a shiftless but uncommonly lucky young man (Anthony LaPaglia) and his debt-ridden father (Danny Aiello) reaches crisis level when the son becomes a six-million-dollar lottery finalist. Writer-director George Gallo turns in a shrill comedy that affirms family ties with stereotypical characters and sledgehammer humor. Benign depiction of car insurance fraud and much rough language. A-III (R)

Twenty-One (1991) Trashy comedy in which a smugly promiscuous 21-year-old swinger (Patsy Kensit) recounts her meaningless sexual adventures in London before heading to New York for more of the same. Co-writer-director Don Boyd presents only crass, self-involved characters in a tasteless and repelling movie not worthy of 21 seconds' viewing. Positive attitude toward promiscuity, several bedroom scenes with brief nudity, shots of drug mainlining, and much rough language. O (R)

20,000 Leagues Under the Sea (1954) Marvelous Disney version of the classic Jules Verne sea yarn about a marauding red-eyed monster sinking 19th-century ships some of whose survivors (Kirk Douglas, Paul Lukas, and Peter Lorre) are taken aboard the submarine Nautilus by the embittered Captain Nemo (James Mason), who wants to rule the seas. Directed by Richard Fleischer, the story is great fun for all ages and the special effects are really special. A-I (G)

Twice in a Lifetime (1985) This is a big, glossy valentine to adultery, in which a 50-year old steelworker (Gene Hackman) falls in love with a barmaid (Ann-Margret) and leaves his wife (Ellen Burstyn) and children. Directed by Bud Yorkin, the movie lacks authentic characters and motivation, relying instead upon a dense sentimental smokescreen in its attempts to justify the husband's wholly selfish actions. O (R)

Twice-Told Tales (1963) Vincent Price stars in Nathaniel Hawthorne stories of love beyond the grave ("Dr. Heidigger's Experiment"), a father's obsessive protectiveness ("Rappaccini's Daughter"), and a Puritan family curse ("The House of the Seven Gables"). Directed by Sidney Salkow, the adaptations are largely flat and unimaginative, though the last evokes something of the eerie atmosphere intended by Hawthorne. Stylized violence and romantic complications. A-II (br)

Twice Upon a Yesterday (1999) Breezy romantic fable in which the clock is magically turned back so that a cheating boyfriend (Douglas Henshall) can have a second chance with his girlfriend (Lena Headey), only to discover that she too had begun a clandestine affair. Director Maria Ripoll's bittersweet tale follows four characters who learn that love can't flourish in an atmosphere of betrayal and deceit. Brief sexual encounter, a live-in relationship, intermittent rough language, and a few instances of profanity. A-III (R)

Twilight (1998) Flawed suspense story in which a retired private eye (Paul Newman) becomes involved with the wife (Susan Sarandon) of his terminally ill friend (Gene Hackman) while trying to figure out their part in the long-unsolved murder of her first husband. Director Robert Benton's twisty mystery is ably abetted by a veteran cast (including James Garner) whose skillful performances distract from a major plot contrivance. Intermittent violence, implied sexual encounters, brief nudity, some rough language, and recurring profanity. A-III (R)

Twilight for the Gods (1958) Halting South Sea adventure from Ernest K. Gann's story of assorted troubles aboard a leaky two-masted sailing ship, whose hapless captain (Rock Hudson) dallies with a mysterious passenger (Cyd Charisse), while the fretful crew (Arthur Kennedy, Wallace Ford, and Charles McGraw) ponder mutiny. Director Joseph Pevney tries to build some suspense as the dangers of the voyage mount, but the soggy romance and contrived plot sink the effort. Some menace and sexual situations. A-III (br)

Twilight of the Golds (1997) Earnest drama about a Jewish family whose grown son (Brendan Fraser) is gay and whose married daughter (Jennifer Beals) ponders abortion after learning that her fetus carries a gene supposedly linked to homosexuality. Director Ross Marks insightfully explores fractured relationships as family members confront homophobic attitudes, struggle to accept or forgive one another, and embrace unconditional love. Serious treatment of an abortion decision, brief male kissing, occasional profanity, and an instance of rough language. A-III (PG-13)

Twilight People (1972) The title refers to the gruesome results of a mad doctor (Charles Macaulay) in trying to create a new breed of humans, but his experiments have yielded only a bat man, a panther woman, a wolf girl, and assorted other odd hybrids. Low-budget Philippine production directed by Eddie Romero, the childish story goes from the utterly unbelievable to the ludicrous, but its violent conclusion is not for the youngsters. A-III (PG)

Twilight Time (1983) Shapeless, sentimental Yugoslavian production directed by Goran Paskaljevic centers on an old man (Karl Malden) returning from America to spend his remaining years in his mountain village, where he winds up caring for two young grandchildren with the help of a friendly schoolteacher (Jodi Thelen). Dubbed in English. The slow-paced narrative offers few insights into another culture. A-II (PG)

Twilight Zone — The Movie (1983) Anthology movie, inspired by the popular 1960s television series, is made up of five separate episodes by four different directors, and only the one about an airline passenger (John Lithgow) who spots and odd-looking creature sitting on the wing, rises above mediocrity. Some frightening effects here, and in three of the other four segments, make it inappropriate fare for younger viewers. A-II (PG)

Twilight's Last Gleaming (1977) Burt Lancaster plays a cashiered Air Force general who seizes control of a nuclear missile-launching site in an attempt to alter government policies. director Robert Aldrich, not known for his subtlety, has made an extremely clumsy, if well-intentioned movie, whose ham-handed approach to a complex moral issue, as well as its extreme, if sporadic, violence and rough language make it questionable fare at best. O (R)

Twin Peaks: Fire Walk with Me (1992) The characters from the "Twin Peaks" TV series appear in a big-screen clunker about events leading up to the murder of promiscuous, drug-addicted teenager Laura Palmer (Sheryl Lee). Director David Lynch's sleazy, self-indulgent horror show goes nowhere slowly, spending an endless 134 minutes revealing nothing of interest beyond Ms. Lee's inability to act. Numerous perverse sexual situations, some of them violent, several bloody murders, frequent drug and alcohol abuse, recurring nudity, and rough language. O (R)

Twinkle, Twinkle, Killer Kane (see: **The Ninth Configuration**)

Twins (1988) Often hilarious tale of twin brothers separated at birth but reunited 35 years later, after the big guy (Arnold Schwarzenegger) has been raised to be sound of mind and body on a South Pacific island, while the little guy (Danny DeVito) grew up in an orphanage where he began his sleazy life of petty crime and womanizing. Though sluggishly directed by Ivan Reitman, the two actors manage to carry this tale of mismatched twins who learn to love and trust each other so that, in the end, goodness, family, and marriage triumph over greed, gluttony, and sexual promiscuity. Some violent cartoon fisticuffs and graphic rub-outs mostly played for laughs, as well as some locker-room language and promiscuous behavior. A-III (PG)

Twins of Evil (1972) British horror movie about a 17th-century witch-hunter (Peter Cushing) whose voluptuous twin nieces catch the eye of a depraved devil-worshipper (Damien Thomas), and soon one of them is drawn into his evil sphere, but Cushing is unable to tell which is the witch. Directed by John Hough, it's an exercise in pumped-up suspense with more than usual reliance on graphic gore, nudity, and a spot of kinky eroticism. O (R)

Twist Around the Clock (1961) Formula musical directed by Oscar Rudolph in which a music agent (John Cronin) attends a country dance, discovers the Twist, and promotes it into a national dance craze, with the aid of Clay Cole's band, the Marcels, Chubby Checker, Dion, and Vicki Spencer. Romantic complications. A-II (br)

Twist of Fate (1954) Tawdry melodrama directed by David Miller is set on the French Riviera, where a former US entertainer (Ginger Rogers) falls for a French artist (Jacques Bergerac) whom her obsessive British lover (Stanley Baker) mistakes for a third-rate thief (Herbert Lom), with dire consequences. Stylized violence, contrived menace, and the sudsy heroine's implied affair with a married man. A-III (br)

Twist of Sand, A (1968) Returning to the African coast where years before he had sunk a Nazi sub and massacred its crew, a British sea captain (Richard Johnson) and his partners (Jeremy Kemp and Honor Blackman) retrieve a fortune in diamonds, but one of them wants it all. Directed by Don Chaffey, the crime caper has plenty of atmosphere but suffers from a hokey plot and an overly contrived ending. Much menace and some nasty violence. A-II (br)

Twist and Shout (1986) Danish import about two teenagers experiencing the pains of growing up in the 1960s without any parental guidance to help them cope with their adolescent sexual desires and the tragic consequences that result. Nudity, sexual encounters, and graphic depiction of abortion. O (R)

Twisted Nerve (1969) British psychological thriller about an unstable young man (Hywel Bennett) who gradually loses control of his faculties and becomes a homicidal maniac. Directed by Roy Boulting, the plot tries to integrate the effects of heredity and environment upon the youth, but the sexual nature of the problems touched upon in the course of the movie make it adult fare. A-III (PG)

Twisted Obsession (1990) American screenwriter (Jeff Goldblum) living in Paris is lured into a web of deceit and infidelity by the teenage sister (Liza Walker) of the director (Dexter Fletcher) with whom he is working. Filmed in dark, murky fashion by director Fernando Trueba, the minimal plot serves little purpose but to exploit the innocent appeal of a young actress depicted as an experienced sexual manipulator. Exploitative use of nudity, some restrained scenes of sexual activity, and occasional rough language. O (R)

Twister (1996) As a series of killer tornadoes bears down on their puny van, meteorologists Helen Hunt and Bill Paxton forget their marital woes in hopes of making a scientific breakthrough — and escaping with their lives. Director Jan De Bont's jolting special-effects thriller hits a brick wall each time the danger subsides and the script's one-dimensional characters return to the fore. Much meteorological mayhem and recurring casual profanity. A-III (PG-13)

Two Bits (1995) Spiritually uplifting Depression-era story about a 12-year-old boy (Jerry Barone) trying to earn a quarter to go to the movies, though worried his aging Italian grandfather (Al Pacino) may die that very day. Director James Foley sensitively captures the period's economic hardships and generous gestures of the neighbors, as well as the child's love for his widowed mom (Mary Elizabeth Mastrantonio) and grandpa. Mild sexual innuendo and a neighborhood suicide. A-II (PG-13)

2 Days in the Valley (1996) Slickly cynical tale of a brutal slaying by two hit-men (Danny Aiello and James Spader) who proceed to involve a number of others (including Teri Hatcher, Glenne Headly, Eric Stoltz, and Paul Mazursky) in the crime's bloody aftermath. Writer-director John Herzfeld's contrived, pulpy story is an unpalatable concoction of sadistic violence and sick humor. Much gory violence, sex encounter with nudity, occasional profanity, and much rough language. O (R)

Two English Girls (1972) Director Francois Truffaut has made the perfect companion movie for his previous **Jules and Jim**. The situation this time is neatly reversed, with the man (Jean-Pierre Leaud) in love with two sisters and unable to make a commitment to either. Some viewers will find the situation completely amoral, and often ridiculously romantic. But as a picture of life at the turn of the century, with its very formal etiquette, suppressed emotions, and artificial manners, it couldn't be better. A-IV (nr)

Two Flags West (1950) Rambling tale of captured Confederate troopers (led by Joseph Cotten) released from a Union prison in 1864 to fight Indians in New Mexico, then are driven to the point of desertion by their Reb-hating commander (Jeff Chandler). Directed by Robert Wise, the script is cluttered with undeveloped plot turns and stereotyped characters, but the rugged location photography is excellent, and the action scenes are well-staged, especially the climactic attack on Fort Thorn. Frontier violence. A-I (br)

Two for the Road (1967) Producer-director Stanley Donen's saga about a modern marriage on wheels that skids dangerously but doesn't quite crack up, teams Audrey Hepburn and Albert Finney as the troubled couple. By following the pair on their various jaunts through Europe, Donen provides both a fluid vehicle for narrative development, as well as strikingly scenic backgrounds. A-III (br)

Two for the Seesaw (1962) Glum drama from William Gibson's play about a morose lawyer (Robert Mitchum) who leaves Nebraska for a fresh start in New York after separating from his wife, falls for a wacky dance-teacher (Shirley MacLaine) from the Bronx, then broods over whether to marry her. Director Robert Wise treats the lawyer's mid-life crisis with undeserved sympathy, dampened further by his unlikely romance with the free-spirited dancer, and a sentimental ending that leaves viewers flat. Troubled personal relationships. A-III (br)

Two Gentlemen Sharing (1969) Failed British drama about a white Londoner (Robin Phillips) and an upwardly mobile black from the West Indies (Hal Frederick) who share a London mews apartment, have their separate problems, and end with one discovering his homosexuality and the other returning to Jamaica. Director Ted Kotcheff's treatment lacks any subtlety, especially in several lovemaking scenes. A-III (R)

Two Girls and a Guy (1998) Shrill exploitation clunker in which three emotionally distraught people exhaust themselves shouting foul-mouthed recriminations at each other, before two wind up having sex, while the third muses on the possibilities of a threesome. Writer-director James Toback has come up with a shoddy piece of merchandise whose idea of dramatic conflict is verbal assault and sexual promiscuity without any insight into the characters or what they have gone through. Exploitative sexual themes and situations, constant rough language, and occasional profanity. O (R/NC-17)

200 Cigarettes (1999) Strained comedy set in Greenwich Village on New Year's Eve 1981, as a dozen young adults and two teenage girls desperately try to sexually connect with members of the opposite sex. Writer-director Risa Bramon Garcia's narcissistic characters and the threadbare story-line translate into a tiresomely drawn-out take on the battle of the sexes. Benign view of promiscuity and substance abuse, recurring profanity, and constant rough language. O (R)

200 Motels (1971) Written, produced, and directed by Frank Zappa, the title refers to the bleak digs occupied by touring groups such as Zappa's The Mothers of Invention during the course of an average year. It features, however, rough language and a smutty lyric, explained with glee by a pair of semi-nude groupies, as well as a raunchy cartoon sequence depicting the sleazy side of life. O (R)

Two Jakes, The (1990) Sequel to **Chinatown** (1974) has its Los Angeles private eye (Jack Nicholson) haunted by painful memories of a previous case while trying to uncover the real reasons why his client (Harvey Keitel) killed the man having an affair with his wife (Meg Tilly). Also directed by Nicholson, the well-crafted performances and lushly atmospheric setting gets bogged down from the start with too many characters and an overly intricate plot. Sporadic violence, restrained sexual depictions, and occasional rough language. A-III (R)

Two If by Sea (1996) A dull-witted thief (Denis Leary) with a stolen Matisse hides out with his girlfriend (Sandra Bullock) for a weekend in a unoccupied seaside mansion, where they pretend to know the absent owner to a suspicious neighbor who has something to hide himself. Bill Bennett directs a vacuous comedy of all-too convenient coincidences in which gutter language is a poor substitute for wit. A lame rejection of a life of crime, implied affair, and much rough language and profanity. A-III (R)

Two-Lane Blacktop (1971) Introspective young man (folk-rock singer James Taylor) who lives on the road in his 1955 Chevy coupe races the owner of a Pontiac GTO (Warren Oastes) in a back-roads tour across America. Director Monte Hillman's low-key approach does not romanticize his drifters of the road but along the way shows some of the reasons why they have opted out of the mainstream. Some realistic street language, A-III (R)

Two Men and a Girl (see: 1947's **Honeymoon**)

Two Men of Karamoja (1974) Documentary account of seven months of conflict and change in Uganda's Kidepo Valley National Park, as the British chief warden prepares to turn the preserve over to a native warden. Directed by Natalie and Eugene Jones, the movie examines not only the park's wildlife problems but its native population, whose tribal structures are changing with the times. Much of this ethnographic material is best suited for adults and older adolescents. A-III (R/PG appeal)

Two Minute Warning (1976) Gathered in the Los Angeles Coliseum are an assortment of disaster veterans (Charlton Heston, John Cassavetes, Martin Balsam, and David Jansen) and 100,000 extras; when a sniper is spotted, the police move in, and the arena is turned into a Roman forum of bloodshed and graphic violence. Directed by Larry Peerce the mindless fantasy plays on fears and anxieties of random senseless violence in extreme fashion. O (R)

Two Moon Junction (1988) Slick soap opera about a rich Southern belle (Sherilyn Fenn) set upon marrying a rich young yuppie (Martin Hewitt), but not before being lustfully distracted by a carnal worker (Richard Tyson). Although artfully photographed, with gorgeous plantation settings and a solid supporting cast (Louise Fletcher, Burl Ives, and Kristy McNichol), writer-director Zalman King comes up with nothing more than glorified soft porn. A sequence of extreme violence, several scenes with frontal nudity, explicit sexual encounters, and much locker-room language. O (R)

Two Much (1996) Failed comedy in which a con-artist (Antonio Banderas) becomes engaged to a wealthy divorcée (Melanie Griffith), then woos her brainy sister (Daryl Hannah) by pretending to be his own brother. Directed by Fernando Trueba, the lame proceedings are listlessly contrived, leadenly performed, and rely more on sexual innuendo than comic wit. Sexual situations and references with occasional coarse language. A-III (PG-13)

Two Mules for Sister Sara (1970) Prostitute masquerading as a nun (Shirley MacLaine) in order to help Mexican rebels is joined by cowboy loner (Clint Eastwood) in undertaking the capture of a French garrison, and they fall in love. Directed by Don Siegel, there are some good action sequences, but the comic irreverences (a supposed nun smoking, drinking, and cursing like a trooper), like the movie, are not to be taken seriously. A-III (PG)

Two of a Kind (1983) John Travolta and Olivia Newton-John have the misfortune to star in a dreadful movie about God's sending a quartet of angels to earth to try and reform two nasty people. Written and directed by John Herzfield, it is for the most part innocuous, except for some profanity. A-III (PG)

Two of Us, The (1968) Excellent French story of a little Jewish boy (Alain Cohen) who is hidden from the Nazis on a remote farm in occupied France by an elderly anti-Semite (Michael Simon). Directed by Claude Berri, the movie is a very touching, gentle sort of comedy, told simply through an accumulation of incidents rather than a tightly knit plot. Everyone can identify with and enjoy the warm, human relationship between the old man and the young lad. A-I (br)

Two or Three Things I Know About Her (1970) Director Jean-Luc Godard's paean to Paris (the "her" in the title) follows the fragmentary story of a part-time prostitute (Marina Vlady), but Raoul Coutar's camera is focused on the ever-changing face of a modern city. Though the movie is heavily laced with philosophical asides and interruptions, it is often amusing, at times illuminating, and always stunningly beautiful in its picture of a great city. A-III (nr)

Two People (1973) Trivial romantic claptrap about a Vietnam deserter (Peter Fonda) and a jaded divorcée (Lindsay Wagner) who meet in Marrakech, talk their way to Casablanca, make love in Paris, and finally fly to New York, where he is going to turn himself in. Directed by Robert Wise, the budding romance is totally unmotivated, and certainly made no more credible by a ridiculously over-extended, semi-nude love scene. A-IV (R)

Two Rode Together (1961) On a mission to rescue women and children taken captive by Comanches, an idealistic cavalry officer (Richard Widmark) bickers along the way with a frontier marshal (James Stewart) who's only interested in the reward offered by the captives' families. Director John Ford uses the conflict between these familiar Western character types to take a darker, less poetic view of the tragic confrontation between the forces of civilization and the waning powers of a less developed native culture. Some stylized violence. A-II (br)

2001: A Space Odyssey (1968) Director Stanley Kubrick's epic work, co-written with Arthur C. Clarke, is both science fiction and metaphysical poetry, using an unconventional mixture of visuals and music to bridge humanity's reconstructed past, identifiable present, and projected future, all tied together by the recurring image of a monolith as symbol of a superhuman existence. The central narrative follows the struggle of two astronauts (Keir Dullea and Gary Lockwood) to wrest control of their spacecraft from HAL, a talking computer (voice of Douglas Rain), on a half-billion-mile trip to Jupiter and the unknown. For young people and imaginative adults, but too long, deep, and intense for children. A-II (G)

2010 (1985) Sequel to **2001: A Space Odyssey**, in which Roy Scheider leads a joint American-Soviet probe of Jupiter to discover the fate of the spacecraft sent there in the original. Writer-director Peter Hyams overwhelms the story with spectacular special effects, but young people especially should find it an engaging voyage into space. A-I (PG)

2000 Years Later (1969) Weak satire in which an ancient Roman (John Abbott), sent by the god Mercury, fails to warn society of the consequences of its moral corruption. Bert Tenser's low-budget, amateurish production, lacking any moral focus of its own, merely exaggerates and exploits the more obviously decadent elements of the day. O (R)

Two Years Before the Mast (1946) Stodgy dramatization of the account written in 1840 by Richard Henry Dana (Brian Donlevy) describing the brutal conditions and unjust treatment he witnessed as a seaman aboard a US merchant ship, whose crew is finally driven to mutiny against their cruel captain (Howard da Silva). Though saddled with a script focusing on the travails of the ship-owner's shanghaied son (Alan Ladd), director John Farrow manages to convey the harsh realities of a sailor's life in the age of sail. Restrained depictions of brutality in a human-rights context. A-I (br)

Twonky, The (1953) Comic sci-fi misfire written and directed by Arch Oboler, in which a college professor (Han Conried) finds his new TV-set is actually a robotic machine from the future which proceeds to take charge of his life, until the professor rebels. Slapstick violence and sexual innuendo. A-II (br)

Tycoon (1947) Long but intriguing drama in which an American engineer (John Wayne) is hired by a South American aristocrat (Cedric Hardwicke) to build a railroad tunnel through a mountain, then makes an enemy of his powerful employer by wooing his daughter (Laraine Day). Director Richard Wallace alternates the hard, dangerous work of construction with the cultural differences dividing engineer and employer, not least of which are differing notion of romance and marriage. Some stylized violence and romantic complications. A-II (br)

U

UHF (1989) Pop culture satirist "Weird Al" Yankovic stars as a loser with a vivid imagination who takes over as manager of a family-owned TV station and concocts offbeat shows to save it from bankruptcy. Director Jay Levey's slim story-line relies on silly slapstick parodies, though a tasteless animal-kingdom show may encourage kids to mishandle pets. Minimal rough language, vulgar antics, and non-menacing cartoon violence played for laughs. A-II (PG-13)

U.S. Marshals (1998) Pale spin-off from the 1993 thriller **The Fugitive**, with its iron-willed lawman (Tommy Lee Jones) doggedly pursuing a escaped murder suspect (Wesley Snipes) who is out to find whoever framed him. Directed by Stuart Baird, the action is nonstop, but the thin characterizations and hokey plot are unmemorable. Gory violence, occasional profanity, and an instance of rough language. A-III (PG-13)

U-Turn (1997) Gore-soaked tale of a grungy gambler (Sean Penn) whose car breaks down in an Arizona desert town, whose vicious residents variously beat, rob, and lure him into committing murder. Directed by Oliver Stone, the repugnant result wallows in gleeful killings, sordid lust, and murderous greed. Excessive violence, numerous explicit sexual encounters with nudity, continuous profanity, and constant rough language. O (R)

U2: Rattle and Hum (1988) A feature-length concert documentary on U2, the popular Irish rock-band with a conscience. Directed in uninspired fashion by fan Phil Joanou, it's a montage of U2's record-breaking 1987 American performances, backstage rap, and rehearsal, much of which is shot in grainy black and white. Fans will love this, but it won't enlighten those unfamiliar with U2's political concerns. Mild rough language. A-II (PG-13)

Ugly, The (1998) Repulsive slasher movie in which an incarcerated serial killer (Paolo Rotondo) describes his abused childhood to a naive psychiatrist (Rebecca Hobbs), then gleefully recounts numerous killing sprees, which are depicted in gory flashbacks. Writer-director Scott Reynolds offers a bogus character study which serves only as a vehicle for scenes of sadism and bloodshed. Excessive violence, sexual situations, and intermittent rough language. O (nr/R)

Ugly American, The (1963) Muddled Cold War tale set in a Southeast Asian country, where the new US Ambassador (Marlon Brando) learns the hard way that nationalism is not the same as communism. Produced and directed by George Englund, the Asian locales are authentic, but the plot is more political lecture than human drama, and Brando is disappointing as the know-it-all American humbled by events. Stylized violence and political posturing. A-I (br)

Ugly Dachshund, The (1966) Disney comedy about a Great Dane puppy who gets mixed in with a litter of dachshunds but wins a place with the family of Dean Jones and Suzanne Pleshette. Directed by Norman Tokar, it is for dog lovers and small children. A-I (br)

Ugly Ones, The (1968) Sordid Italian-Spanish Western directed by Eugenio Martin about a bounty hunter (Richard Wyler) on the trail of a depraved Mexican bandit (Tomas Milian). It revels in protracted scenes of violence and brutality. O (R)

Ulee's Gold (1997) Finely detailed character study of an aging Florida beekeeper (Peter Fonda) turns into a suspenseful melodrama when he takes on a pair of murderous thugs who threaten to harm his daughter-in-law (Christine Dunford) and two young granddaughters. Writer-director Victor Nunez has created a small picture of ordinary people and everyday life which, though flawed by some gritty melodramatics, has real human substance centered principally in Fonda's performance as a man whose simple, down-home virtues are tested by irrational forces from the world outside. Some scenes of violence and harrowing menace, drug abuse, and occasional profanity. A-III (R)

Ulysses (1967) Director Joseph Strick's adaptation of the James Joyce classic makes a static movie, but it may be of interest to those who have studied the Irish author's work. Those unfamiliar with the novel are likely not only to find the movie incomprehensible but its verbal treatment of sexual and religious matters to be offensive. A-IV (br)

Ulysses' Gaze (1997) The search for some missing reels of film shot in the Balkans before WW I leads a Greek-American filmmaker (Harvey Keitel) to film archives in Greece and Albania, then on to those in Bucharest, Belgrade, and finally war-torn Sarajevo on an epic journey that becomes a personal quest for his lost roots. Directed by Theo Angelopoulos, the 1995 Greek-French-Italian co-production presents a fascinating cultural panorama of the Balkans, emphasizing its recent history of Soviet domination ending in national conflicts, but the searcher's personal drama is told in a murky mix of present realities, uncertain memories of the past, and surreal flights of fancy that never jell into a coherent character. Wartime violence, sexual situations, and brief male nudity. A-III (nr)

Ulzana's Raid (1972) Tracking a band of raiding Apaches are a hardened scout (Burt Lancaster), his Indian sidekick (Jorge Luke), and a greenhorn officer fresh out of West Point (Bruce Davison), unsure of himself and his religious inhibitions about the brutal methods used to hunt and destroy the Indians. On the action level, director Robert Aldrich's Western works fairly well, but it raises moral questions of justice and retribution that require more than well-staged fight scenes and good location photography. The violent visuals of frontier savagery borders on the exploitative. A-IV (R)

Umbrellas of Cherbourg, The (1965) Everybody sings instead of talks in this romantic French musical about a brief, ecstatic love affair, and the mature reflections of the lovers when they meet years later. With music by Michel Legrand and lyrics by director Jacques Demy, the bittersweet story of heedless youth and the pragmatic demands of maturity are lovely but fragile and not to everyone's taste. Subtitles. Mature theme. A-III (br)

Un Air de Famille (1998) A French family's birthday gathering becomes the occasion for less merriment than searing emotional confrontations among the six adults which force each of them to see themselves anew for better or worse. As directed by Cedric Klapisch, the slow pacing and claustrophobic cafe setting eventually give way to insightful character studies laced with dry wit and an emphasis on each person's humanity. Subtitles. A few sexual references and some rough language. A-III (nr)

Un Couer en Hiver (1993) French character study of a man (Daniel Auteuil) who perversely steals the affections of a concert violinist (Emmanuelle Beart) with whom his business partner (Andre Dussollier) is in love, then coldly rejects her because he is unable to love anyone, including himself. Director Claude Sautet's strange portrait of an individual untouched by passion is all the more chilling set in the soulful world of music and the emotional lives of musicians, but the result of all this is itself empty of feeling. Subtitles. Discreet treatment of sexual relationships and passing reference to a mercy killing. A-III (nr)

Unbearable Lightness of Being, The (1988) Adapted from a novel about a womanizing brain surgeon (Daniel Day-Lewis) and his relationship with two women in particular — an artistic free spirit (Lena Olin) and his wife (Juliette Binoche) — before, during, and after the Russian invasion of Czechoslovakia in 1968. Directed by Philip Kaufman, it is a moving evocation of the period and its effect on the protagonists. The movie's remarkable performances, however, are marred by numerous scenes of graphic nudity and explicit sex. O (R)

Unbelievable Truth, The (1990) A rebellious daughter (Adrienne Shelly) is attracted to an ex-con (Robert Burke) who works in her father's garage and is rumored to be a mass murderer. Writer-director Hal Hartley delivers a clumsy, drawn-out tale peopled with minimally interesting characters, save for the laconic ex-con who turns out to have more integrity than the respectable citizens around him. Some rough language and references to teen sex. A-III (R)

Uncle, The (1966) Warm British movie about the groping, confused efforts of a seven-year-old lad to cope with the mysteries of birth, death, and growing up over the course of a summer. Directed by Desmond Davis, the movie is unusual in its realistic depiction of a wholesome childhood set within the context of happy family life. Though about the world of a child, young children may find some of its aspects perplexing. A-II (br)

Uncle Buck (1989) Limited laughs in a situation comedy involving a cloddish bachelor looking after his brother's three children for a couple of days. Directed by John Hughes, it is little more than a vehicle for John Candy's comic talents as a screen buffoon with a heart of gold. Some sexual situations, double entendres, and vulgar language. A-III (PG)

Uncle Harry (see: **The Strange Affair of Uncle Harry**)

Uncle Joe Shannon (1979) Burt Young stars in his own screenplay about a trumpet player who hits the skids after the tragic death of his wife and young son but regains his self-esteem and starts on the road back when he becomes the unofficial guardian of a young boy. Directed by Joseph C. Hanwright, the result is mawkish melodrama chock-full of embarrassingly bad moments. A-II (PG)

Uncle Tom's Cabin (1977) Sincere but woefully inept retelling of the famous Harriet Beecher Stowe classic, unfortunately contains some crass exploitation scenes. Though the main part of the movie was apparently made abroad, the American distributors seem to have clumsily inserted scenes of sex and brutality utterly at variance with the rest of the narrative. O (R)

Uncle Vanya (1972) Brooding Soviet version of Anton Chekhov's play takes place in the claustrophobic rooms of a dilapidated manor, where Vanya (Innokenty Smoktunovsky), the estate's caretaker, despairs at his wasted life, and the local doctor (Sergei Bondarchuk) is the only character who sees the absurd social injustices of his time. Writer-director Andrei Mikhalkov-Konchalovsky evokes the impoverished spirit of pre-Revolutionary Russia by alternating scenes of one-tone sepia with those of muted color, and the result will affect all who care about the depths of human feelings. A-II (nr)

Uncommon Valor (1983) Wealthy Texas oil man (Robert Stack), whose son is a Vietnam War MIA, hires a Marine colonel (Gene Hackman) to rescue him and his comrades, among them the colonel's own son. Though it has a fairly literate script by Joe Gayton, director Ted Kotcheff does not do much to lift it above the level of routine action adventure. Violence and the heroic depiction of a native drug-dealer who gives his all for the American cause. A-III (R)

Unconquered (1947) Cliched colonial adventure follows a Virginian militia captain (Gary Cooper) through the wilderness as he tries to keep a treacherous white trader (Howard da Silva) from uniting the Indian nations to drive the English out of the Ohio territory. Producer-director Cecil B. DeMille burdens the frontier conflict with a contrived love interest as the two men vie for a bond servant (Paulette Goddard), whom the captain rescues from a sinister Seneca hostile (Boris Karloff) in a supremely silly scene involving a compass. Frontier violence, romantic complications, and Indian stereotypes. A-II (br)

Undead, The (1957) Low-budget hokum directed by Roger Corman in which a psychic researcher leads a woman under hypnosis to relive her previous life as an accused witch in medieval France, then somehow joins her there, with disastrous results. Stylized violence, sexual innuendo, and tongue-in-cheek treatment of witchcraft and reincarnation. A-III (br)

Undefeated, The (1969) Post-Civil War story in which a group of Confederate families (led by Rock Hudson) heading for asylum in Mexico under Emperor Maximillian join forces with a former Union officer (John Wayne) bringing a herd of horses south of the border as they fight off Mexican bandits and get embroiled in the Mexican Civil War. Directed by Andrew V. McLaglen, it's an unpretentious, old-fashioned cowboy movie that can be enjoyed by any who like Western action and adventure. A-I (G)

Under Fire (1983) American photojournalist (Nick Nolte) covering the Sandinista revolution in Nicaragua loses his sense of detachment at seeing the brutality of the Somoza regime and agrees to fake a story suggested by his lover and fellow journalist (Joanna Cassidy). Directed by Ron Shelton and Clayton Frohman, the powerful and extremely entertaining film conveys the feel of guerrilla warfare, especially in an urban environment, with uncanny force. Violence and rough language. A-III (R)

Under Milk Wood (1973) British dramatization of the Dylan Thomas poem-play, with Richard Burton and Ryan Davies as the two narrators who pass through the little Welsh seacoast town of Llareggub and share the lives of its inhabitants with the viewer much as did the Stage Manager in **Our Town**. Directed by Andrew Sinclair, its great compression of incidents involving some 60 actors in a fast-paced, impressionistic scenario does not lend itself to casual viewing. Several scenes of unabashed sensuality and earthiness. A-IV (R/PG)

Under Siege (1992) Two traitors (Tommy Lee Jones and Gary Busey) hijack the USS Missouri, planning to sell its nuclear arsenal to the highest bidder, unaware that the ship's cook (Steven Seagal) is an ex-Navy SEAL bent on outsmarting them. While director Andrew Davis's action yarn is fairly engrossing, it is fueled by graphic violence treated as heroic and exciting. Excessive violence, a flash of nudity, and occasional rough language. O (R)

Under Siege 2: Dark Territory (1995) Violent action sequel in which the former Navy SEAL of the original (Steven Seagal) takes on a whole trainload of murderous terrorists (led by Eric Bogosian and Everett McGill) who plan to obliterate Washington, DC, with an armed satellite for a billion-dollar payoff from a foreign country. Director Geoff Murphy orchestrates the mindless stream of murder and mayhem surrounding the invincible Seagal, who barely musses his hair while surviving dozens of deadly encounters. Excessive violence, brief sexual innuendo, and constant rough language. O (R)

Under Suspicion (1992) A private eye (Liam Neeson), suspected of murdering both his wife (Maggie O'Neill) and a client, develops an affair with another suspect — the client's mistress (Laura San Giacomo). Writer-director Simon Moore's amoral but engrossing thriller is done in by its cynical treatment of lurid situations. Adulterous and homosexual encounters with recurring nudity, some violence, and minimal rough language. O (R)

Under the Cherry Moon (1986) Rock star Prince and his comic sidekick Jerome Benton try to resurrect the age of Valentino's sensual mystique in this shimmering black-and-white male fantasy about black American gigolos trying to strike it rich in the beautiful resort city of Nice, France. The movie's preoccupation with sex distorts the meaning of a loving relationship. A-III (PG-13)

Under the Domin Tree (1996) Israeli dramatization set in a 1953 boarding school for teenagers orphaned in the Holocaust focuses on the stories of a few who make some strides coping with a painful past, adjusting to the present, and learning to face the future with hope symbolized by the title's sturdy little tree. Directed by Eli Cohen from Gila Almagor's autobiographical book, the series of small personal dramas is treated in such halting fashion that they fail to jell in a convincing whole. Subtitles. The problems of troubled adolescents. A-II (nr)

Under the Rainbow (1981) Legendary off-screen drunken carousing by the diminutive actors playing Munchkins in **The Wizard of Oz** (1938) becomes the central premise of a dim comedy burdened by slapstick subplots and a predictable romance between a Secret Service agent (Chevy Chase) and a movie studio assistant (Carrie Fisher). Director Steve Rash lavishes his energies on re-creating the Depression era, but the movie's many sight gags fall embarrassingly flat. Coarse language, double entendres, and bawdy situations, as well as tasteless stereotyping of little people. A-III (PG)

Under the Volcano (1984) Screen version of the Malcolm Lowry novel about an alcoholic English diplomat serving in Mexico (Albert Finney) is an impressive work but fails to convey the inner drama that gave such tragic force to the original, despite Finney's powerful performance. Nevertheless, director John Huston's effort is well worth seeing, though its adult treatment includes a vicious, sordid scene in a brothel. A-III (R)

Under the Yum Yum Tree (1963) Dreary sex farce in which a college couple (Dean Jones and Carol Lynley) share an apartment in a celibate trial marriage beset by the leering interference of their lecherous landlord (Jack Lemmon). Directed by David Swift, the stale one-joke comedy becomes tedious long before the predictable ending. Lame comic treatment of sexual situations and endless innuendo. A-IV (br)

Under Two Flags (1936) Escapist adventure with the French Foreign Legion as a suave English enlistee (Ronald Colman) attracts the interest of a visiting Englishwoman (Rosalind Russell), the love of an Arab cafe singer (Claudette Colbert), and the enmity of his commanding officer (Victor McLaglen). Directed by Frank Lloyd from the Ouida novel, the romantic angle is somewhat silly fun, and there are some good action sequences, including the climactic desert battle between Arab horsemen and outnumbered legionnaires. Stylized violence and romantic complications. A-II (br)

Undercover Blues (1993) While vacationing in New Orleans, husband-and-wife espionage agents (Kathleen Turner and Dennis Quaid) reluctantly agree to a dangerous, top-secret assignment, taking along their baby girl as they dodge curious cops, a persistent mugger (Stanley Tucci), and assorted armed goons. Director Herbert Ross imitates the breezy style of the **Thin Man** movies, but his formula comedy is overwhelmed by klutzy, cardboard characters and a wrongheaded assumption that bullets and babies make for a laugh-fest. Intermittent violence played for laughs and an instance of rough language. A-III (PG-13)

Undercovers Hero (1975) Peter Sellers plays six roles, ranging from a British intelligence agent to Adolf Hitler, in a sex farce about how WW II was really won in a Paris bordello run by Lila Kedrova. Directed by Roy Boulting, the thoroughly inane script works on the same low level of wit as the pun of the title. O (R)

Underground (1970) B-grade WW II movie about the abduction of a Nazi general by the French underground (led by Robert Goulet). Little attempt is made to advance sympathy for either side in a weak story with confusing flashbacks, lackluster action photography, and elements of sex and torture. A-III (PG)

Underground (1976) Documentary about what happened to some of those who were radicalized by the failure of the protest movements of the 1960s. Directed by Emile de Antonio, Mary Lampson, and Haskell Wexler, the film consists essentially of a group interview with five surviving members of the Weather Underground, who went into hiding after the explosion of their New York bomb factory in 1970. A tragic part of American history. A-III (nr)

Underneath, The (1995) Intriguing but uneven remake of the 1949 crime thriller **Criss Cross**, in which a two-bit gambler (Peter Gallagher) tries to win back his ex-wife (Alison Elliott) from her shady new lover (William Fichtner) by concocting an armored-car heist, which backfires on the participants in unexpected ways. Director Steven Soderbergh goes for psychological depth over lurid melodrama, but this is undermined by confusing flashbacks and flash-forwards that disrupt the narrative flow. Some violence, brief shadowy bedroom scene, fleeting nudity, and occasional rough language. A-III (R)

Underwater (1955) Feeble Caribbean adventure directed by John Sturges finds treasure hunters (Gilbert Roland, Richard Egan, and Jane Russell) vying with larcenous locals in trying to salvage the gold aboard a sunken 17th-century Spanish galleon. Stylized violence and romantic situations. A-III (br)

Underwater City, The (1962) Pseudo-scientific hokum about an experimental base built on the bottom of the ocean by a would-be space engineer (William Lundigan). Director Frank MacDonald's corny scenario and cheesy model work are a boring waste of time. Mild menace and stylized violence. A-I (br)

Underworld (1997) Dark but dizzy crime clunker about an ex-con (Denis Leary) spending Father's Day mowing down those responsible for shooting his mob-boss father, while taking a former pal (Joe Mantegna) along for the ride to determine if he was in on the hit. Directed by Roger Christian, the phony characters and gory revenge killings add up to little more than another empty exercise in mindless mayhem. Graphic violence, flashes of nudity, sexual situations, and recurring rough language. O (R)

Underworld, U.S.A. (1961) Brutal crime melodrama in which an ex-convict (Cliff Robertson) joins a syndicate run by the men who murdered his father in order to take revenge on them. Directed by Samuel Fuller, the plot is hokey, but the criminal environment is realistic, and the action tough-minded. Much stylized violence and menace. A-III (br)

Une Femme Douce (1971) French drama about a woman (Dominique Sanda) who commits suicide and her husband (Guy Frangin) who tries to find out why. Director Robert Bresson's investigation is really into the emptiness of middle-class lives in which material objects consume people's entire interest to the detriment of interpersonal relationships. Sparse and demanding, it is a very interior film whose text is the ambiguous surface of reality. A-III (nr)

Unearthly, The (1957) Weak horror hokum directed by Brooke L. Peters concerns a mad doctor (John Carradine) whose experiments to achieve eternal youth leave a number of dead, deformed, and comatose patients. Some scary visuals, hokey menace, and brief violence. A-II (br)

Unfaithfully Yours (1948) Black comedy in which a symphony-orchestra conductor (Rex Harrison) suspects his wife (Linda Darnell) is unfaithful and imagines three scenarios in which he takes his revenge. Writer-director Preston Sturges fills the dark proceedings with some hilarious moments, but the conductor's fumbling attempts at murder are not among them. Fantasy violence. A-II (br)

Unfaithfully Yours (1984) Symphony conductor (Dudley Moore) wrongly suspects his wife (Natassja Kinski) of being unfaithful and fantasizes revenge while on the podium. Director Howard Zieff's expensively mounted comedy is not anywhere near as funny as the 1948 Preston Sturges original. Though otherwise innocuous, it is marred by an ill-conceived shower scene and excessive bedroom sequence. O (PG)

Unfinished Business (1941) Halting romantic comedy in which a would-be singer (Irene Dunne) from a small Ohio town comes to New York, has her heart broken by a rich bounder (Preston Foster), then marries his alcoholic kid brother (Robert Montgomery) for a lark, but both fall in love, though it takes him a while to grasp the implications. Directed by Gregory LaCava, the sputtering plot is kept afloat by the antics of a talented supporting cast (Ester Dale, Eugene Palette, Walter Catlett, and others) until the sentimental ending. Comic treatment of marriage leads to a more serious view of the matter. A-II (br)

Unfinished Dance, The (1947) A young girl (Margaret O'Brien) maliciously causes an accident ending the career of a ballerina (Cyd Charisse), but the child's remorse helps rectify the damage done. Directed by Henry Koster, the sugary story has little to offer but its ballet setting and dance numbers. A-I (br)

Unforgettable (1996) Overwrought thriller in which a medical examiner (Ray Liotta) tries to track down his wife's real killer by injecting himself with her spinal fluid in hopes of discovering her final memory of the attack. Director John Dahl captures the edgy desperation of the doctor's ghoulish quest, but the far-fetched narrative disintegrates in complicated revelations of adultery, police, and multiple murders. Grisly violent flashbacks, morgue-slab nudity, and frequent rough language. A-III (R)

Unforgiven, The (1960) Muddled Western saga of a pioneer Texas family (widow Lillian Gish and sons Burt Lancaster and Audie Murphy) deserted by their neighbors when their grown daughter (Audrey Hepburn) is accused of being an orphaned Kiowa Indian raised from infancy as one of their own. Directed by John Huston, the theme of frontier racial hostility develops slowly, then grows increasingly ponderous until swept away in the fiery climax of the family's desperate stand against a band of Kiowa attackers. Uneven treatment of a serious theme and stylized violence. A-II (nr)

Unforgiven (1992) A reformed gunfighter (Clint Eastwood) and his former partner (Morgan Freeman) join a novice bounty-hunter (Jaimz Woolvett) to hunt down two cowboys wanted for cutting up a prostitute, but find a despotic sheriff (Gene Hackman) squarely in their way. Also produced and directed by Eastwood, the richly textured movie demythologizes the Western hero while portraying the main character's moral downfall as tragic. Intermittent violence motivated by revenge and vigilante justice, fleeting bedroom shots, an uncritical acceptance of prostitution, and occasional rough language. A-IV (R)

Unguarded Moment, The (1956) Contrived thriller about a police detective (George Nader) trying to protect a high-school teacher (Esther Williams) from a mixed-up student (John Saxon) and his dotty dad (Edward Andrews). Directed by Harry Keller, the school setting is as bogus as the teacher's attempts to help a dangerous student who needs professional care. Stylized violence and sexual innuendo. A-II (br)

Unholy Rollers, The (1972) The rise of a young roller-skater (Claudia Jennings) into the big-time roller derby involves women slugging it out like animals in one small-town rink after another, shown with an excess of breast-bashing, groin-stomping visuals. Directed by Vernon Zimmerman, the movie's off-camera commentary is provided by a pair of ringside announcers using tongue-in-cheek burlesque humor. O (R)

Unhook the Stars (1996) A lonely widow (Gena Rowlands) discovers a new perspective on life by taking in a shy six-year-old while his troubled, brassy mother (Marisa Tomei) works a split shift. Nick Cassavetes directs a gentle, sentimental tale of intergenerational friendship, family reconciliation, and hard-won self-reliance. Much rough language and occasional profanity. A-III (R)

Unidentified Flying Objects (1956) Earnest but dull account of the first reports of flying saucers in 1947 and the inconclusive results of military investigations of subsequent UFO sightings. Directed by Winston Jones, the re-created interviews and brief film footage of supposed UFOs tax one's credulity, though may be of interest to social historians. A-I (br)

Unidentified Flying Oddball (1979) Good Disney comedy about an American space scientist (Dennis Dugan) and his look-alike robot, who land in King Arthur's Court and save the monarch (Kenneth More) from being overthrown by Merlin (Ron Moody) and Sir Mordred (Jim Dale). Russ Mayberry directs the proceedings with proper charm and ingenuous good humor, leaving family audiences happier for the viewing. A-I (G)

Uninhibited, The (1968) Mediocre Spanish drama about a group of dropouts from life trying to rekindle some sense of direction and responsibility. Directed by Juan Antonio Bardem, the movie's theme has merit, but its amoral setting and treatment may offend some adult viewers. A-IV (br)

Uninvited, The (1944) A writer (Ray Milland) and his sister (Ruth Hussey) move into a house apparently haunted by the troubled spirit of the mother of a young woman (Gail Russell) who once lived there. Director Lewis Allen's intriguing ghost story revolves around solving the mystery of the mother's death in a movie buttressed by the whimsical attitude of the skeptical writer and a number of spooky effects. Some mild scares and restless spirits. A-II (br)

Union Station (1950) Effective crime thriller in which an alert citizen (Nancy Olsen) tips a railroad detective (William Holden) to what turns out to be the kidnapping of a millionaire's blind daughter (Allene Roberts), with the crowded train station serving as the ransom point. Director Rudolph Maté keeps the tension high as the search for the desperate kidnapper (Lyle Bettger) widens through the city until the final showdown in the station's labyrinthine tunnels. Stylized violence and much menace. A-II (br)

Universal Soldier (1992) Two soldiers (Jean-

Claude Van Damme and Dolph Lundgren), who killed each other in Vietnam but were secretly regenerated by the government for use as mindless killing machines, turn on one another with brute force. Director Roland Emmerich makes a repulsive movie out of constant images of degradation, death, and phony heroics. Excessive violence, some nudity, and much rough language. O (R)

Unknown, The (1927) Sinister silent movie set in Spain, where a performer faking armlessness (Lon Chaney) in a gypsy circus has his arms amputated, hoping to wed a woman (Joan Crawford) who can't stand being pawed by men, then goes berserk when she decides to marry the troupe's strong-man (Norman Kerry). Directed by Tod Browning, the plot's bizarre twists don't stand up as well today as does Chaney's performance in using his feet to accomplish what hands normally do, whether throwing knives, playing a guitar, or simply twiddling his big toes. Violent situations and considerable menace. A-III (br)

Unlawful Entry (1992) Violent thriller centers on a psychotic cop (Ray Liotta) whose obsession with a married woman (Madeleine Stowe) leads him to frame her husband (Kurt Russell) for a drug felony. Jonathan Kaplan directs a transparent plot geared to set up a bloodthirsty ending that justifies murder. Several sexual encounters with nudity, recurring violence, and much rough language. O (R)

Unman, Wittering and Zigo (1971) Group of British schoolboys murder their teacher and threaten to do likewise to his replacement (David Hemmings) unless he goes along with their plans. Hemmings doesn't believe them at first, and by the time he does, no one else will. This juxtaposition of innocence and corruption is powerful material, but director John Mackenzie loses control of it early on in the film, making several scenes involving sex ludicrous and dramatically implausible. A-III (GP)

Unmarried Woman, An (1978) Jill Clayburgh stars as a reasonably happy wife who is forced to begin a new life when her husband (Michael Murphy) deserts her and their teenage daughter for a younger woman. Though it supposedly is about the trauma and suffering of a woman struggling to forge a new identity, writer-director Paul Mazursky's work is a bit too slick and sentimental to be very moving or very convincing. Extremely well-acted and relatively sincere effort contains some rough language, nudity, and one needlessly graphic lovemaking scene. O (R)

Unsinkable Molly Brown, The (1964) Ponderous screen version of Meredith Willson's stage musical about a Colorado backwoods tomboy (Debbie Reynolds) who, after a stint singing in a frontier bar, marries a rich miner (Harve Presnell), but is snubbed by Denver society until she's accepted by European nobility and survives the Titanic. Director Charles Walters tries to keep the narrative bright and lighthearted, but Molly's elitist hankerings never square with her free-spirited, egalitarian manner, a central flaw compounded by lackluster songs and flatfooted production numbers. Some romantic complications, sexual innuendo, and occasional crude language. A-II (br)

Unstrung Heroes (1995) Bittersweet comedy about a 12-year-old who moves in with his very eccentric uncles during the terminal illness of his adored mom (Andie MacDowell) cared for at home by his emotionally stressed dad (John Turturro). Directed by Diane Keaton, the sensitive performances and distinctive characters keep the mother's loss from becoming maudlin as the child learns from his uncles the importance of family and his Jewish faith in coping with life and death. The death of a parent and occasional cursing. A-II (PG)

Unsuspected, The (1947) Convoluted mystery in which the suave host (Claude Rains) of a radio crime-show is puzzled by his secretary's murder, then is visited by a man (Michael North) claiming to be the husband of his dead ward (Joan Caulfield), who soon turns up very much alive. Directed by Michael Curtiz, the murky proceedings don't add up to much until the murderer's scheme is finally revealed, but it's not enough to save the picture. Stylized violence, menace, and domestic tensions. A-II (br)

Untamed (1955) Convoluted romance directed by Henry King is set in 19th-century South Africa, where an Irish immigrant (Susan Hayward) gets involved with a Boer leader (Tyrone Power) despite Zulu attacks and English animosity. Stylized violence and sexual situations. A-III (br)

Untamed Frontier (1952) Western clunker directed by Hugo Fregonese involves a Texas cattleman's dissolute son (Scott Brady), the waitress (Shelley Winters) he marries to keep from testifying against him in a murder trial, and his tough, upright cousin (Joseph Cotten) who feels sorry for her. Frontier violence and muted sexual innuendo. A-II (br)

Untamed Heart (1993) Bogus sentiments litter this unlikely tale of romance between a Minneapolis waitress (Marisa Tomei) and a taciturn loner (Christian Slater) who grew up in an orphanage with a serious heart-condition. Producer-director Tony Bill gets likeable performances from Tomei and Rosie Perez as her co-worker, but the main event with Slater is hopelessly contrived and maudlin to boot. Some sexual situations and references, an attempted rape, and occasional rough language. A-III (PG-13)

Until September (1984) Young American in Paris (Karen Allen) becomes involved with a suave Frenchman quite capable of juggling a wife, two children, and a mistress, but she wants to play for keeps. Director Richard Marquand's limp and uninventive romance falls back upon abundant nudity in a vain attempt to sustain interest. Benign view of adultery. O (R)

Until the End of the World (1991) Vaguely futuristic road movie in which a thrill-seeking woman (Solveig Dommartin) joins a wanted man (William Hurt) on a mysterious mission around the world, one step ahead of her ex-boyfriend (Sam Neill) and assorted bounty hunters. German director Wim Wenders gets the strange, overly long narrative off to a good start, but the incidents along the way fail to sustain emotional involvement or intellectual interest. Momentary violence, brief bedroom shots with fleeting nudity, and minimal rough language. A-III (R)

Untouchables, The (1987) Brian De Palma, not known for directorial subtleties, provides an almost camp parody of the TV original, as federal agent Eliot Ness (Kevin Costner), portrayed as an inept family man, gets the goods on infamous Chicago gang boss Al Capone (Robert De Niro). The violence is dreamlike and distanced in a highly stylized crime-stopper movie which has some harsh language and brutal intensity. A-III (R)

Unzipped (1995) Documentary portrait of New York fashion designer Isaac Mizrahi as he muses on his career and the fashions of past and present while working on a new line of clothes to be presented in his fall 1994 collection. Though director Douglas Keeve's leisurely, behind-the-scenes look at the fashion business is helped considerably by Mizrahi's self-deprecating sense of humor, the result is little more than an insider's view of the self-absorbed world of high fashion. Occasional sexual references and some rough language. A-III (R)

Up Close & Personal (1996) Romantic fluff about a novice TV-journalist (Michelle Pfeiffer) and a veteran correspondent (Robert Redford) who becomes a bullying mentor, then marries her as his career spirals downward, while she is groomed for a network-anchor spot. Directed by Jon Avnet, the romance is credibly developed within the tension-filled world of live news, resulting in a bittersweet, sentimental crowd-pleaser. Several restrained bedroom scenes, brief violence, and minimal rough language. A-III (PG-13)

Up Front (1951) WW II comedy brings cartoonist Bill Mauldin's GI characters to the screen, with grouch Willie (Tom Ewall) in Naples to get dim Joe (David Wayne), his wounded buddy, out of the hospital and back to their frontline unit, despite Italian bootleggers, black marketers, and a corps of military police. Directed by Alexander Hall, the weak storyline is strong enough to serve Mauldin's humorous view of the combat soldier's disdain for Army bureaucracy and those serving behind the lines. Wartime violence and confusion. A-I (br)

Up in Arms (1944) WW II musical features draftee Danny Kaye with pals Dana Andrews, Dinah Shore, and Constance Dowling aboard a troop ship bound for the Pacific, where he becomes an improbable hero. Directed by Elliott Nugent, Kaye's patter songs in his screen debut were then a welcome novelty, but the movie's disjointed narrative and heavy-handed slapstick have not worn well. Romantic complications and brief comic violence. A-II (br)

Up in Smoke (1978) Utterly mindless comedy about two California pot-heads (counterculture figures Cheech Marin and Tommy Chong), who travel to Tijuana in search of some marijuana and subsequent pursuit by a bumbling narcotics cop (Stacey Keach). Director Lou Adler's jokes, when not witless cliches about the pleasures of the drug culture, depend heavily on the titillating and the scatological. O (R)

Up in the Cellar (1970) Deprived of a college scholarship by a discerning computer, a youth (Wes Stern) seeks revenge on the college's pompous president (Larry Hagman) by seducing his wife, daughter, and black mistress/secretary. Though a number of director Ted Flicker's well-deserved jabs sting the college administration scene, the light touch never gets funny enough, and the moral tone never gets high enough to save this slipshod attempt at adult entertainment. O (R)

Up Periscope (1959) Routine WW II derring-do directed by Gordon Douglas, in which a troubled submarine captain (Edmond O'Brien) ferries a Navy frogman (James Garner) to a South Pacific island, where he sneaks ashore to make photographic copies of a Japanese code-book. Wartime violence and romantic complications. A-I (br)

Up the Academy (1980) Tedious, sophomoric romp set in a military academy ruled by a sadistic headmaster (Ron Leibman, who wisely had his name taken off the credits). Though director Robert Downey's visuals are restrained, the movie makes excessive use of sexual innuendo, rough language, and all-around vulgarity. O (R)

Up the Creek (1984) Four college losers (Tim Matheson, Jennifer Runyon, Stephen Furst, and Dan Monahan) battle military cadets and intense preppies to win a raft race in another exercise in brain-dead humor. Directed by Robert Butler, the movie contains abundant nudity and crude sexual humor. O (R)

Up the Down Staircase (1967) Screen version of Bel Kaufman's novel about a dedicated young teacher (Sandy Dennis) overwhelmed by school regulations, supply shortages, overcrowding, disciplinary problems, and some misguided colleagues, but who manages to do some real teaching in spite of it all. Director Robert Mulligan's realistic drama about the problems of a big-city high school is helped by some humor and a fine supporting cast. A-II (br)

Up the Junction (1968) Peter Collinson directs the British story of a rich woman (Suzy Kendall) seeking to find some sense of purpose in the slums of Battersea. It will impress some viewers as an honest essay in social realism, while striking others as patronizing and banal. Casual moviegoers may find its coarse and vulgar language offensive. A-IV (br)

Up the MacGregors (1967) Forgettable Italian-Spanish Western directed by Dario Sabatello is routine Saturday matinee fare. Mild violence. A-II (br)

Up the Sandbox (1972) Seriocomic story of a somewhat mad Manhattan housewife (Barbra Streisand) who finds herself experiencing an acute identity crisis and creates a soaring fantasy life that enables her to escape a myriad of troubles and even transcend them. Directed by Irvin Kershner, the housewife's struggle for liberation is what makes the film, despite its cinematic flaws in some of the flights of fantasy (including an abortion clinic), engagingly healthy and at times quite wise. A-IV (R)

Up Tight (1968) Updated version of **The Informer** (1936) replaces the IRA with a black-revolutionary group, one of whom is wanted for murder and is betrayed for the reward by a former member of the group (Julian Mayfield). Directed by Jules Dassin, the movie has raw power and plenty of tension but oversimplifies the issues facing black Americans after Martin Luther King, Jr.'s, assassination. Mature themes. A-III (PG)

Upstairs and Downstairs (1961) Uneven British comedy about the problems of a young couple (Michael Craig and Anne Haywood) in hiring reliable domestic help. Directed by Ralph Thomas, the highlights include an alcoholic maid (Joan Hickson), a retired couple who rob the bank next door, and a nubile Swedish *au pair* girl (Mylene Demongeot). Much sexual innuendo. A-III (br)

Uptown Saturday Night (1974) Sidney Poitier and Bill Cosby play a couple of would-be sharpies who get caught in the middle of a Harlem gang war when they try to enlist the services of gangster Harry Belafonte to get back the money stolen from them. Also directed by Poitier, it's a pleasantly entertaining, good-natured comedy with some good acting. A-III (PG)

Uranus (1991) An innocent barkeep (Gerard Depardieu) is implicated when two compassionate Frenchmen (Philippe Noiret and Jean-Pierre Marielle) hide a Nazi collaborator (Gerard Desarthe) immediately after WW II. Writer-dirctor Claude Berri uncovers many sides of the human condition in this tragicomedy, which has Depardieu's over-the-top performance as its centerpiece. Subtitles. Brief violence, discreet references to sexual liaisons, and occasional rough language. A-III (nr)

Urban Cowboy (1980) John Travolta plays a rural Texan who comes to the big city of Houston to find work and becomes romantically involved with Debra Winger in a honky-tonk saloon whose feature attraction is a mechanical bronco. Directed by James Bridges, it's a boring, embarrassingly adolescent movie celebrating the masculine virtues of hard drinking, fighting, and wenching. O (PG)

Urban Legend (1998) Gory horror tale in which a college coed (Alicia Witt) realizes she and her friends are in imminent danger from a serial killer stalking the campus and executing students by duplicating grisly folkloric legends. Director Jamie Blanks surrenders an offbeat premise and initial suspense to a barrage of over-the-top grotesque slaughters by the end. Excessive violence, fleeting sexual encounter, crude innuendo, some profanity, and intermittent rough language. O (R)

Used Cars (1980) Nasty supposed comedy about rival car-dealers with Kurt Russell, Jack Warden, Deborah Harmon, and Andrew Duncan. Directed by Robert Zemeckis, there is nothing funny about the totally amoral and tasteless story which also employs nudity and rough language. O (R)

Used People (1992) After secretly admiring her for the past 23 years, an impassioned Italian widower (Marcello Mastroianni) pursues an emotionally repressed, newly bereaved Jewish widow (Shirley MacLaine) in 1969 Queens, encouraging her in the process to embrace life and reconcile with her divorced daughters (Kathy Bates and Marcia Gay Harden). Director Beeban Kidron's genial ethnic comedy features an appealing cast in a heartwarming story, but the script works overtime extracting comedy from dysfunctional family relationships. Brief bedroom scene and an instance of rough language. A-III (R)

Usual Suspects, The (1995) Gritty crime tale told in flashback to a hard-nosed cop (Chazz Palminteri) by the surviving member (Kevin Spacey) of a motley band of thieves (including Gabriel Byrne and Stephen Baldwin) who pull off a heist with far-reaching consequences. Director Bryan Singer builds a moody story of shifting identities and diabolical deceit from a bewildering plot and taut ensemble performances. Recurring stylized violence and much rough language. A-III (R)

Utamaro and His Five Women (1972) Encapsulating the vision of an 18th-century Japanese artist, known especially for his prints of beautiful women, director Kenji Mizoguchi's movie succeeds admirably is showing an artist's view of his world. It is a paean to a vital classicism, both in subject and technique, idealizing a society in which people worked and lived in a harmony unknown in modern times. A-III (nr)

Utopia (1950) The final entry for the comedy team of Stan Laurel and Oliver Hardy unhappily is this muddled French-Italian comedy in which the boys inherit a South Seas island which is overrun by adventurers after uranium is discovered. Directed by Leo Joannon, the script is as haphazard as the production, though the aging comics manage to wring some smiles from the unpromising material. Stylized violence and sexual innuendo. A-II (br)

Utz (1993) An American art dealer (Peter Riegert) arrives in Prague to purchase a priceless collection of Meissen porcelain and in the process learns about the late owner's (Armin Mueller-Stahl) unconventional life and strange relationship with his devoted housekeeper (Brenda Fricker). Dutch director George Sluizer fashions a multi-layered but emotionally alienating story of obsessive and eccentric characters. Subtitles. Some sexual innuendo and a distant shot of nudity. A-III (nr)

V.I.P.s, The (1963) Minor-league **Grand Hotel** set in a London airport, where anxious characters fretfully waiting for a flight delayed by fog conditions. As the fog deepens, the plot diddles with the tax problems of movie mogul Orson Welles, the merger being fought by tractor manufacturer Rod Taylor and devoted secretary Maggie Smith, the flat bank-book of duchess Margaret Rutherford ,and the discomforts of pampered wife Liz Taylor at leaving tycoon-husband Richard Burton for continental hustler Louis Jourdan. Director Anthony Asquith's glossy treatment of this soap-opera stew turns it into grade-A trash, of interest mainly to students of bad taste. A-III (br)

V.I. Warshawski (1991) Hard-boiled Chicago private eye (Kathleen Turner in the title role) gets stuck with a scrappy 13-year-old (Angela Goethals) when her father is killed and the girl becomes the next murder target. Turner's tough, sassy, and supremely confident performance is at the center of director Jeff Kanew's standard suspense movie that keeps the action going full tilt, even when the plot becomes opaque. Mostly stylized violence, recurring sexual references, and intermittent rough language. A-III (R)

Vagabond (1986) French director Agnes Varda offers a somber, flawed observation of spiritual and moral decay as a young female drifter's last days are recounted by the people she's met on the road to self-effacement. As a vision of alienated youth, the movie depicts casual sex as symptomatic of spiritual disintegration with much more emotional ground to be explored. Simple yet profound, although a potentially confusing work. A-III (nr)

Vagabond King, The (1956) Lackluster adaptation of the Rudolph Friml operetta in which rebel poet Francois Villon (Italian tenor Oreste) wins the love of a noblewoman (Kathryn Grayson) by rousing the people of Paris to save Louis XI (Walter Hampden) from the invading forces of Burgundy. Directed by Michael Curtiz, the pedestrian proceedings are interrupted occasionally by songs and a few dance numbers, but the result is largely unmemorable. Stylized violence. A-I (br)

Valachi Papers, The (1972) Charles Bronson plays the role of Joe Valachi, the late Mafia informer whose revelations formed the book by Peter Maas upon which the movie is based. Director Terence Young has passed up the opportunity to provide a rare glimpse inside the workings of organized crime in order to produce one more straight action movie, filled with brutality and sudden violence. Several scenes of gangland inhumanity require a strong stomach. A-IV (R/PG)

Valdez Is Coming (1971) Tedious Western in which a Mexican-American deputy (Burt Lancaster) tries to collect some money for an Indian widow from those who had mistakenly shot her husband and then goes after the rancher responsible. Directed by Edwin Sherin, the heavy-handed plot development contains much violence and smatterings of sex and near-nudity. A-III (GP)

Valentino (1977) British director Ken Russell's screen biography of Rudolph Valentino (Rudolf Nureyev) is a boring, overdone piece of pretentious trash having only the remotest connection with the famous movie star's life. Nudity and graphic sexuality. O (R)

Valentino Returns (1989) Lackluster 1950s coming-of-age drama about the frustrations of a young adult male (Barry Tubb) searching for sex on a typical Saturday night in his pink Cadillac. First-time director Peter Hoffman's effort fizzles into small-town vignettes that lack punch. Some rough language laced with sexual vulgarities, implied promiscuity, and some nudity. A-III (R)

Valerie and Her Week of Wonders (1974) Czechoslovakian fantasy in which a 13-year-old girl's daydreaming transforms her ordinary world into one filled with strange adventures, bizarre characters, and the first vague stirrings of sexual awareness. Directed by Jaromil Jires, the setting is a picturesque village at the turn of the century, affording lush imagery, striking compositions, colorful costuming, and ornamental detail that lend themselves easily to a surrealistic picture of a young adolescent's imagination. Literal-minded viewers may be confused by the movie's lack of narrative guideposts, but the juxtaposition of religious and Freudian symbolism invites deeper psychological probing by those so inclined. A-IV (nr)

Valley Girl (1983) San Fernando Valley girl (Deborah Foreman) throws over her handsome but dumb Valley boyfriend in favor of a punk rocker from Hollywood (Nicolas Cage), much to the consternation of her friends. Directed by Martha Coolige, this Romeo and Juliet variation makes some gestures in the direction of satire, but essentially is another teen exploitation movie, with graphic nudity and rough language. O (R)

Valley of Gwangi, The (1969) A group of riders from a Wild West show (headed by James Franciscus) go in search of a major attraction in a hidden Mexican valle,y where prehistoric monsters survive protected from the outside world by a band of mysterious gypsies. Directed by James O'Connolly, the far-fetched adventure depends mostly on Ray Harryhausen's special effects and one's own imagination. A-I (G)

Valley of Mystery (1967) Airliner crash-lands in South American jungle among whose perils are a tribe of headhunters, but the pilot (Richard Egan) manages to keep the survivors alive until rescued by helicopters. Director Josef Leytes turns a routine adventure story into a slack melodrama of little interest. Stylized violence. A-II (br)

Valley of the Dolls (1967) Trashy melodrama based on a trashy novel about decadence in the world of show business and the deleterious effects of gulping pep and sleeping pills. Directed by Mark Robson, the insight is nil, most of the acting is embarrassingly bad, and it elicits only pained disbelief at its amateurishness and a few laughs where none was intended. O (br)

Valley of the Dragons (1961) Minor sci-fi adventure from the Jules Verne story "Career of the Comet" is set in 1881, when a Frenchman (Cesare Danova) and an Irishman (Sean McClory) are swept up by a comet which, on a previous pass of Earth some 100,000 years before, had picked up examples of prehistoric life. Director Edward Bernds lends little credibility to the proceedings, but Verne's audacious premise is sufficiently diverting for those who don't mind bargain-basement cavemen and dinosaurs. Stylized violence and mild thrills. A-I (br)

Valley of the Kings (1954) American archeologist (Robert Taylor) helps an Englishwoman (Eleanor Parker) search for evidence proving the biblical account of Joseph's sojourn in the land of the pharaohs. Director Robert Pirosh muddies matters with murderous conniving by greedy traffickers in antiquities, but the result is worth seeing for its grand vistas of famous sites in ancient Egypt. Some menace and stylized violence. A-II (br)

Valley of the Sun (1941) Odd-ball Western in which an Army scout (James Craig) averts an Apache uprising by exposing a corrupt Indian agent (Dean Jagger) while wooing the sidewinder's girlfriend (Lucille Ball). Director George Marshall mixes in a lot of rough humor with the low-budget action and flavorsome romancing. Some positive Indian stereotyping and a bit of stylized violence. A-I (br)

Valmont (1989) Visually lush but emotionally empty adaptation of the 18th-century novel *Les Liaisons Dangereuses*, the story centers on the sexual intrigues among a circle of French aristocrats, notably the title character (Colin Firth) and his one-time paramour (Annette Bening). Though director Milos Forman tries to humanize these upper-class libertines, he seems more interested in re-creating the rich opulence and frivolous style of a world that disappeared with the French Revolution. Restrained treatment of immoral relationships. A-III (R)

Vampire Bat, The (1933) Creaky horror story of a German village fearing a vampire is in its midst, as a mad doctor (Lionel Atwill) leaves victims drained of blood needed for his experiments. Director Frank Strayer does better with the spooky atmosphere than the sinister proceedings in a weak script notable only for a cast including Melvyn Douglas, Fay Wray, and Dwight Frye. Stylized violence and menacing situations. A-II (br)

Vampire Circus (1972) British horror movie in which a traveling troupe of Gypsy vampires (Adrienne Corri and Anthony Corlan) visit a Serbian village to revive a dead count who had been killed there 15 years before. Director Robert Young tries to make up for the script's lack of wit and suspense with a fair sprinkling of incidental sex, but with little success. A-III (R/PG)

Vampire in Brooklyn (1995) Unamusing horror parody in which a wary New York City cop (Angela Bassett) is romantically pursued by a suave vampire (Eddie Murphy) intent on getting her to willingly join the undead. Director Wes Craven's flat mix of horror, comedy, and grisly special effects is about as comatose as its title character before sunset. Some gory violence played for laughs, scene of a mock preacher convincing his flock evil is good, and much rough language. A-IV (R)

Vampire's Kiss (1989) After picking up a vampire (Jennifer Beals) in a singles' bar, a New York yuppie (Nicolas Cage) turns into a blood-sucking vampire by night and a manic monster terrorizing his young secretary (Maria Conchita Alonso) by day. Directed by Robert Bierman, the misogynist movie depicts men as sorry victims of women who exist only to lure men to self-destruction. Much profanity and promiscuity, laced with flashes of nudity, and bloody sexual encounters. O (R)

Vampires (see: **John Carpenter's Vampires**)

Van, The (1977) Gawky youth (Stuart Getz) becomes a Don Juan when he buys a van in this shoddy low-budget sex-exploitation movie directed by Sam Grossman. O (R)

Van, The (1997) To support their families, two unemployed Dublin pals (Colm Meaney and Donal O'Kelly) partner in selling fish and chips out of a truck, but the demands of running a business bring their lifelong friendship to the breaking point. Director Stephen Frears finds much good-natured humor in the men's disorganized venture — and the strength of their wives to remain emotionally supportive of their well-meaning but hapless husbands. Fleeting nudity, momentary violence, some profanity, and frequent rough language. A-III (R)

Van Gogh (1992) Laborious depiction of the final days of the suicidal artist (Jacques Dutronc) living in the suburbs of 1890s Paris, where he distracts himself with an alleged affair with the daughter (Alexandra London) of his benefactor (Gerard Sety). Maurice Pialat's tedious direction and Dutronc's stony performance only reveal surface details of the artist's mundane existence without adequately conveying his mental state or the scores of paintings he feverishly finished in his final days. Implied affairs and some nudity. Subtitles. A-III (R)

Vanishing, The (1991) Three years after the disappearance of his wife (Johanna Ter Steege), the husband (Gene Bervoets) is contacted by the abductor (Bernard-Pierre Donnadieu) and eventually learns her fate — as well as meets his own. Directed by George Sluizer, the Dutch-French production is an unsettling and far-fetched psychological study in which the good guy is no match for the seemingly normal sociopath he's pitted against. Subtitles. Much menace and occasional restrained violence. A-III (R)

Vanishing, The (1993) Flat Hollywood remake by Dutch director George Sluizer of his own eerie 1991 foreign thriller pitting a methodic maniac (Jeff Bridges) against a young man (Kiefer Sutherland) obsessed with finding his long-missing girlfriend (Sandra Bullock), even if it means losing his new love (Nancy Travis) or his own life. In bowing to alleged American preferences for action over emotional complexity, Sluizer strips the narrative of the suspense and mounting sense of dread that made the original so memorable. Brief but intense climatic violence, a live-in relationship, and minimal rough language. A-III (R)

Vanishing Point (1971) Speed demon (Barry Newman) attempts to outrun the police of four states aided by a blind disc-jockey (Cleavon Little) who monitors police frequencies. Directed by Richard C. Sarafian, the plot is aimless, marked by a number of hair-raising near-crackups and some gratuitous nudity. O (GP/R)

Vanishing Westerner, The (1950) Formula Western directed by Philip Ford in which a pair of lawmen (Monte Hale and Paul Hurst) pose as wanted killers to get the goods on a slick gang of murderous robbers. Frontier violence. A-I (br)

Vanishing Wilderness (1974) Slow-moving, incoherent parade of unrelated wildlife scenes, directed by Arthur Dubs and Heinz Seilmann, with an obnoxiously cute narration by Rex Allen. It ranks low on the scale of well-made nature documentaries. A-I (G)

Vanquished, The (1953) Post-bellum clunker directed by Edward Ludwig has an ex-Confederate officer (John Payne) return to his Union-occupied hometown to get enough evidence to convict its corrupt administrator (Lyle Bettger) but winds up, instead, on the run from a trumped-up murder charge. Stylized violence, romantic situations, and reconstruction woes. A-II (br)

Vanya on 42nd Street (1994) Playwright David Mamet's stripped-down version of "Uncle Vanya," Anton Chekhov's 1899 play about the troubled relations within a Russian family living on a poor country estate, is performed under Andre Gregory's direction in a rehearsal held in a once-grand, now-dilapidated Broadway theatre. Giving a contemporary edge to the work's themes of regret and hope, director Louis Malle shifts between the real world and the theatrical, showing the company off-stage as well as on, thereby capturing the transformation of the actors into the play's characters, notably Wallace Shawn's embittered Vanya, Larry Pine's idealistic doctor, and Brooke Smith as Vanya's yearning niece. Domestic tensions and romantic complications. A-II (PG)

Variety Girl (1947) Thin tale saluting the philanthropic work of the movie industry's Variety Clubs as a couple of would-be starlets (singer Mary Hatcher and comic Olga San Juan) seek a career at Paramount Pictures. Directed by George Marshall, the result is of interest chiefly for cameos by the studio's roster of stars (Bing Crosby, Bob Hope, Gary Cooper, Barbara Stanwyck, and many more), as well as directors Cecil B. DeMille and Marshall. A-I (br)

Variety Lights (1950) Delightful Italian comedy about a traveling theatrical troupe whose frustrated star (Peppino De Flippo) drops his fiancé (Giulietta Masina) when a novice actress (Carla Del Poggio) joins the troupe. Directed by Federico Fellini and Alberto Lattuada, the world of small-time show people is filled with infectious good humor, much whimsy, and some pathos. Subtitles. Romantic complications. A-III (br)

Varsity Blues (1999) Hokey formula tale in which a high-school football team (led by James Van Der Beek) gets rid of its mean, dishonest coach at halftime in the championship game. Directed by Brian Robbins, the bogus proceedings are devoted largely to the teens' activities off the field, especially their drunken escapades and quest for sex. Sexual situations, nudity, alcohol abuse, intermittent rough language, and occasional profanity. O (R)

Vault of Horror, The (1973) Unimaginative British horror movie offers five tales, interwoven with vampires, voodoo, murder, and torture, with a cast including Daniel Massey, Terry-Thomas, Glynis Johns, and Curt Jurgens. Directed by Roy Ward Baker, there is too much emphasis on mutilation and blood for younger viewers, and not enough psychological terror to chill the hearts and imaginations of horror devotees. A-III (R/PG)

Vegas Vacation (1997) Witless comedy with Chevy Chase and Beverly D'Angelo as the parents of two teenagers on the loose in a Las Vegas gambling resort. Directed by Stephen Kessler, the family's misadventures are mostly dull, entirely predictable, and woefully unamusing. Comic sexual innuendo, the allure of gambling, and mild profanity. A-III (PG)

Veils of Bagdad, The (1953) Tired Arabian Nights tale directed by George Sherman, in which a seeming carefree adventurer (Victor Mature) in 1560 Baghdad woos a married woman (Virginia Field) as well as a dancing girl (Mari Blanchard) in order to learn what they know about a plot against the Ottoman emperor, Suleiman. Period violence including a torture sequence, romantic complications, and sexual innuendo. A-III (br)

Velvet Goldmine (1998) Nihilistic tale boringly details the rise and demise of two decadent rockers (Jonathan Rhys Meyers and Ewan McGregor) who become lovers during the London-New York glitter-rock scene of the early 1970s. Writer-director Todd Haynes's empty tale of excess and self-indulgence goes nowhere in between numerous raw musical performances. Glamorization of bisexual lifestyles, full frontal nudity, sexual situations, substance abuse, occasional profanity, and recurring rough language. O (R)

Velvet Touch, The (1948) Psychological drama in

which a Broadway actress (Rosalind Russell) kills her manipulative producer (Leon Ames), then matches wits with the policeman (Sydney Greenstreet) investigating the murder. Director John Gage does well with a fine cast and dandy backstage settings, but stumbles in dragging out a less-than-perfect crime story. An act of deadly violence, much tension, and some romantic complications. A-II (br)

Velvet Vampire, The (1971) Low-budget horror about newlyweds (Michael Blodgett and Sherry Miles) who come for a weekend in a desert hotel whose hostess (Celeste Yarnall) is desperate for new blood. Director Stephanie Rothman requires hardly a stitch of clothing for the atrocious acting of all participants in this silly exercise. O (R)

Vengeance of Fu Manchu, The (1967) Master criminal Fu Manchu (Christopher Lee) sets out to murder all the world's chiefs of police and, through plastic surgery, replace them with his own men but is foiled by Scotland Yard's Nayland Smith (Douglas Wilmer). Directed by Jeremy Summers, the British production's weak story makes middling adventure entertainment. Stylized violence. A-II (br)

Vengeance of She, The (1968) Weak British adventure fantasy based on characters created by H. Rider Haggard in which an occult power compels a young woman (Olinka Berova) to journey to a hidden city in North Africa to become the lost queen of its ruler (John Richardson). Directed by Cliff Owen, the action is pedestrian, and the plot mistakes silliness for imagination. Mild violence. A-II (G)

Vengeance Valley (1951) Below-par Western in which a ranch foreman (Burt Lancaster) protects his shiftless half-brother (Robert Walker) until the nasty lad's treachery leads to a final showdown between them. Directed by Richard Thorpe, the drearily detailed plot of mistaken loyalties is relieved only by occasional scenes of cowboy life on the open range. Stylized violence and an unwed-mother subplot. A-II (br)

Venice-Venice (1992) Frail, talky story in which a self-consumed director (Henry Jaglom), promoting his movie at the Venice Film Festival, becomes involved with an adoring Parisian journalist (Nelly Allard) who follows him home to Venice, Calif., to pursue their relationship. Also written and directed by Jaglom, the thin plot is given some interest by inter-cutting remarks from a variety of women who feel betrayed by Hollywood movies that led them to believe life would be filled with glamour and perfect romance. Benign attitude towards unmarried intimacy and some rough language. A-III (R)

Venom (1982) Deadly snake cavorts about a household taken over by ruthless international terrorists in this mediocre and far-fetched melodrama directed by Piers Haggard. A fine cast, including Klaus Kinski, Nicol Williamson, Oliver Reed, Sarah Miles, and Sterling Hayden, is wasted in a mindless effort that features violence and some restrained sexual activity. A-III (R)

Verdict, The (1982) When a drunken wreck of a lawyer (Paul Newman) presses a medical malpractice suit against a Boston Catholic hospital represented by a powerful attorney (James Mason), he overcomes his personal problems by relying upon his heart instead of his mind during the extended court battle. Though director Sidney Lumet's script has a faulty perspective on Church procedures, Newman's performance outweighs such defects. The sexual aspects of the story are done with the greatest restraint, but it does contain some foul language from one of its characters. A-II (R)

Verites et Mensonges (see: **F for Fake**)

Veronico Cruz (1990) This Argentinean film tracks the life of a shepherd boy (Gonzalo Morales) whose isolation in a remote region is lifted by a new schoolteacher (Juan Jose Camero) who ultimately brings the boy to the city to search for his political-dissident father. Director and co-writer Miguel Pereira captures well the indigenous population, the stark landscape, and the encroachment of the outside world, including political turmoil from revolving military dictatorships and the Falklands War. English subtitles. Incidental rough language, and some brief but intense political interrogations. A-II (nr)

Veronique (1976) Warm, sensitive French movie follows a perceptive 13-year-old girl's not-especially-eventful summer. Director Claudine Ghuilmain fulfills her modest aims in showing the youngster's experiences and some misunderstandings in what is little more than a string of vignettes best appreciated by adult viewers. A-III (nr)

Vertigo (1958) Fine suspense thriller from Alfred Hitchcock in the tale of a retired detective (James Stewart) called back for a private investigation of a seemingly shady lady (Kim Novak). Naturally they fall in love and land in high danger. Jimmy gulps and stammers a lot, Kim just smolders, and Hitch masterfully pulls the strings. A-II (PG)

Very Bad Things (1998) Sick black comedy in which five buddies accidentally kill a prostitute during a bachelor party, then turn murderously on each other and innocent bystanders to keep from being discovered. Writer-director Peter Berg's smirky attempts at graveyard humor miss the mark as the movie steadily descends into an orgy of grisly killings. Recurring gory violence, a sexual encounter, prolonged nudity, recreational drug use, as well as constant profanity and rough language. O (R)

Very Brady Sequel, A (1996) The lives of the every-bouncy Brady Bunch are turned upside down when mom (Shelley Long) and dad (Gray Cole) welcome into their home a devious con-man (Tim Matheson) claiming to be her presumed-dead first husband. Director Arlene Sanford makes feeble, goofy fun of the sprightly, stuck-in-the-'70s family, who remain blissfully unaware they are in the nastier '90s. Numerous double entendres, fleeting comic violence, and an instance of profanity. A-III (PG-13)

Very Curious Girl, A (1970) French social satire

about the revenge a young gypsy (Bernadette Lafont) takes on the people of a small village who have exploited her and her mother. Director Claude Makovski has elicited strong and convincing performances from a cast mainly of villagers and peasants in creating a strange atmosphere of a primitive morality based on ignorance, simplicity, and superstition. A-IV (R)

Very Happy Alexander (1969) Elegant French comedy about middle-aged rebellion, in which a browbeaten husband (Philippe Noiret) scandalizes his neighbors by leading a life of lazy indolence after the death of his finger-snapping wife. He finds a soulmate in a shiftless woman (Marlene Jobert), but when she snaps her fingers, he leaves her at the altar. Directed by Yves Robert, it is essentially a bucolic poem in which Noiret's warm, human performance makes convincing the urge to return to the unregimented life of Eden. A-II (nr)

Very Natural Thing, A (1974) Young man leaves the monastic life, becomes a high-school teacher, and takes a male lover whose promiscuity eventually results in a breakup. Director Chistopher Larkin's movie is a sincere and obviously deeply felt effort to present the moral dilemmas of a homosexual relationship, but it is painfully naive about film technique and embarrassingly romantic about its theme. Several nude scenes of male grapplings. O (R)

Vibes (1988) Three spirited performers can't save this muddled mess about two psychics (Cyndi Lauper and Jeff Goldblum lured to Ecuador by a seedy adventurer (Peter Falk) hoping to psyche out hidden Incan treasure. Director Ken Kwapis misuses many comic lines as well as his talented cast. Some sexual innuendo and minimal rough language. A-III (PG)

Vice Squad (1982) Prostitute (Season Hubley) is saved from the clutches of a brutal pimp (Wings Hauser) by a stalwart policeman (Gary Hanson) in a loathsome, unremittingly brutal, and squalid movie directed by Gary A. Sherman. O (R)

Victor/Victoria (1982) Unemployed singer (Julie Andrews) dresses up as a man in order to get a job as a female impersonator and soon is the toast of 1934 Paris. Helping her along the way is an aging homosexual (Robert Preston), and complicating her life is a Chicago nightclub owner (James Garner). Directed by Blake Edwards, the humor is fitful, more slapstick than witty, and the situation stretches itself thin long before movie's end. Benign attitude toward homosexuality, though given the farcical context, unlikely to blur the moral outlook of adults. A-IV (PG)

Victors, The (1963) Uneven series of vignettes about an American infantry squad (George Peppard, George Hamilton, Vince Edwards, and others) led by a tough but decent sergeant (Eli Wallach) from 1942 London to 1946 Berlin, focusing on some bittersweet romantic encounters (Jeanne Moreau, Melina Mercouri, Romy Schneider, Elke Sommer, and Senta Berger) along the way. Written, produced, and directed by Carl Foreman, the picture's anti-war theme dispenses with battlefield heroics, showing instead a deserter's execution, black soldiers attacked by white racists, surrendering Germans killed by a French unit, and civilian victims of the conflict. Wartime violence and sexual situations. A-III (br)

Victory (1981) WW II story about a soccer game staged for propaganda purposes between a crack German team and a ragtag group of Allied prisoners of war (Michael Caine, Sylvester Stallone, and legendary Brazilian soccer star Pele, among others), who use the match to effect an escape from the packed Paris stadium where they are playing. Effectively directed by John Huston, the result is a sports movie with some taut wartime suspense. Solid entertainment for the whole family. A-I (PG)

Videodrome (1983) Seedy operator of a sleazy television station (James Woods) gets hooked on the unrelenting sadomasochism of a program called Videodrome, which is actually a sinister plot against humanity carried out by some villains steeped, like the movie itself, in ill-digested media theories of Marshall McLuhan. Written and directed by David Cronenberg, there are some hints of satire, but no hint of intelligence or perspective, and its imagination is as dull as it is perverse. Sadomasochistic sex and exceedingly gory violence. O (R)

Vietnam, Texas (1990) Trashy drama about a Catholic priest (Robert Ginty) who battles a gang of Vietnamese refugees in Houston to find the daughter he fathered as a soldier during the Vietnam War. Also directed by Ginty, the inept result is an unsatisfying mixture of ambiguous idealism and lethal mayhem. Hard-edged violence, references to prostitution, and occasional rough language. A-III (R)

View to a Kill, A (1985) In another 007 adventure for the perpetually adolescent, James Bond (Roger Moore) is pitted against a rather pallid villain (Christopher Walken) who wants to remove all competition for his new computer chip by inducing an earthquake that will obliterate Silicon Valley. Director John Glen's pulp action-adventure fantasy has excessive violence and a benign view of promiscuity. O (PG)

Vigilante (1983) Brutal variation on the theme of the good guys getting fed up and taking the law into their own hands features Robert Forster joining forces with some vigilantes after his family is attacked by degenerate punks. Directed by William Lustig, the proceedings are cynically exploitative and incredibly violent. O (R)

Vikings, The (1958) Energetic re-creation of the Norse sea raids on England during the Dark Ages pits a Viking leader (Ernest Borgnine) and his son (Kirk Douglas) against an English princess (Janet Leigh) and the escaped slave who becomes her champion (Tony Curtis). Directed by Richard Fleischer, the story is romanticized hokum, but the action is full-blooded and the performances colorful. Much stylized bloodshed and carnage, as well as some sexual references. A-III (br)

Villa Rides (1968) Buzz Kulik directs a dismissible,

violent Western, starring Yul Brynner as the menacing Mexican revolutionary and Robert Mitchum as a tough American gunrunner. Kulik ignores the historical complexity of the period and emphasizes its violence, with men being lined up and slaughtered, *ad nauseam*. O (R)

Village of Dreams (1998) Lyric Japanese movie about eight-year-old identical-twin brothers whose family in 1948 moves to a rural village, where, treated as outsiders, the lonely boys spend their free time exploring the surrounding countryside, whose wonders spark their imagination and drawing abilities, eventually leading both to successful careers as artists. Director Yoichi Higashi has created a compelling, impressionistic picture of childhood, beautifully photographed with often poetic, sometimes surreal, imagery as the brothers engage in pranks, enjoy fishing and skinny dipping, experience the cruelty of other children, and have brief encounters with the spirits of nature and Japanese mythology. Subtitles. Sexual references and occasional nudity. A-III (nr)

Village of the Damned (1960) Eerie chiller from John Wyndham's novel *The Midwich Cuckoos* centers in a rural English town, where a strange brood of children are born with extraterrestrial powers that threaten their parents (notably George Sanders and Barbara Shelley) and the world. Director Wolf Rilla builds the suspense to considerable lengths without recourse to special effects — except the alien light in the children's eyes. Menacing atmosphere and some stylized violence. A-II (br)

Village of the Damned (1995) Trashy remake of a British chiller updates the setting to a rural American village, where nine children born with alien powers conspire to take over the world, despite the efforts of a doctor (Christopher Reeve), a scientist (Kirstie Alley), and other distraught adults. Director John Carpenter fails to build any narrative interest in the situation or characters, relying instead on periodic outbursts of violence and special effects. Some menace and intermittent violence, including several suicides, and a difficult childbirth scene. A-III (R)

Village of the Giants (1965) Sophomoric sci-fi clunker about some beach party-goers (Beau Bridges, Trisha Sterling, et al.) who take over a town after growing to giant-size, thanks to a juvenile scientist (Ronny Howard). Director Bert I. Gordon's inane story and bargain-basement special effects are embarrassingly bad. Sexual innuendo. A-III (br)

Villain (1971) Nasty excursion into the lower depths of the British underworld, in which a smalltime homosexual hood (Richard Burton) carves up a stool pigeon, blackmails a lusty member of Parliament, and bungles a payroll heist, while on his case is a rumpled Scotland Yard detective (Nigel Davenport) who exacts his just desserts, but just barely. Directed by Michael Tuchner, the acting is very good, the action and plot only routine, but the overall tint of moral decay and degradation is suffocating. O (R)

Villain, The (1979) Kirk Douglas, Ann-Margret, and Arnold Schwarzenegger toil through director Hal Needham's spoof of Western outlaws and other heavies to no avail. One is left with the impression of watching a live-action version of a Road Runner cartoon for no apparent reason. Vulgar language and suggestive gowns. A-III (PG)

Vincent & Theo (1990) Emotionally charged biography chronicles the troubled lives and early deaths of frustrated artist Vincent Van Gogh (Tim Roth) and Theo (Paul Rhys), his singularly devoted younger brother who supported him to the end. Director Robert Altman's handsomely mounted film uses a bright palette of sumptuous colors as a backdrop for the dark side of the brothers' symbiotic relationship, portrayed with convincing intensity by Roth and Rhys. Restrained treatment of promiscuous relationships, occasional studio scenes with nude models, some violence, and the artist's suicide. A-III (PG-13)

Vincent, François, Paul and the Others (1976) Disappointing French import deals with the crisis of middle age in a series of loosely strung-together sketches exhibiting little but the Gallic charm of such performers as Yves Montand, Michel Piccoli, Serge Reggiani, and Stephane Audran. Directed by Claude Sautet, it is not much of a movie but, for those interested, the performances are worth observing. A-III (nr)

Violent Four, The (1968) Italian crime melodrama about a gang of ruthless bankrobbers (led by Gian, Maria Volonte, and Tomas Milian) who are so successful that the police call in troops to hunt them down. Directed by Carlo Lizzani, the clumsy and overlong narrative uses a forced semi-documentary style and suffers from tired images out of American gangster movies. Much violence. A-III (M)

Violent Men, The (1955) Muddled, unconvincing Western directed by Rudolph Maté pits law-abiding small rancher (Glenn Ford) against unscrupulous cattle baron (Edward G. Robinson), whose faithless wife (Barbara Stanwyck) is in cahoots with crippled hubby's snarling hired gun (Brian Keith). Pacifism loses out to the usual stylized violence. A-II (br)

Violets Are Blue (1986) Kevin Kline plays the big fish in a small pond who slips in and out of an extramarital relationship with his former sweetheart (Sissy Spacek), who has returned home on vacation after being away for 13 years. Infidelity is treated as an egocentricity, not a moral breakdown. The script tends also to celebrate characters without conscience, as its anti-hero gets his old flame out of his system without any consequences. Director Jack Fisk's movie romanticizes adultery. O (PG-13)

Violette (1978) Fact-based French dramatization of a 1933 case, in which a 14-year-old girl (Isabelle Hupert) decided that she would be happier as an orphan and poisoned her parents, but her mother (Stephane Audran) survived to become her most vehement accuser. Whatever political, social, or artistic implications this somber event may have remain obscure, because director Claude Chabrol centers on the depiction of the heroine's promiscuity as the motivation for her callous crime. A-IV (R)

Virgin and the Gypsy, The (1970) British adaptation of the D.H. Lawrence story about two sisters who return from a French finishing-school to their father's country rectory, where one is content to settle down, and the other (Joanna Shimkus) falls in love with a Gypsy (Franco Nero). Directed by Christopher Miles, the re-creation of the 1925 English countryside is lovely to look at, though the dated romantic story doesn't quite fare as well. Brief nudity and a resolution some may mistake as an endorsement of promiscuity. A-IV (R)

Virgin Queen, The (1955) Bette Davis returns to the regal role she played so memorably in **The Private Lives of Elizabeth and Essex** (1939), her problems this time involving the dour Sir Walter Raleigh (Richard Todd) rather than the buoyant Essex (Errol Flynn). Unfortunately, Henry Koster's heavy-handed direction of a slack script has little interest except for the dramatic antics of the veteran actress. A-I (br)

Virgin Soldiers (1970) Group of bumbling, ill-suited young British draftees (Hywel Bennett, Nigel Davenport, and Jack Sheperd) in a 1951 Malayan transit camp are initiated into the arts of love and war. Directed by John Dexter, the central failure of the movie is its inability to decide whether or not to take itself seriously, and the result is a curiously flat, not very amusing, string of incidents. Some violence, bloodshed, a sequence with a Singapore prostitute, and two sexual encounters. A-III (R)

Virility (1976) One more satire on Sicilian honor, this one about a father's frantic efforts to prove to the rumor mongers that his son is not a homosexual. There is nothing light or subtle about Paola Cavara's direction of the film's offensive material. O (R)

Virtuosity (1995) An ex-cop (Denzel Washington) and a criminal psychologist (Kelly Lynch) attempt to track down and terminate the computer model of a serial killer (Russell Crowe) which has sprung from virtual reality into murderous real life in 1999 Los Angeles. Director Brett Leonard's glossy action movie delivers some startling computerized special effects, but pumps up the bizarre narrative with wall-to-wall violence and nearly nonstop mindless mayhem. Excessive violence, brief sexual innuendo, deadly menace to a child, and recurring profanity and rough language. O (R)

Virus (1999) Murky monster movie in which the crew (led by Jamie Lee Curtis, William Baldwin, and Donald Sutherland) of a sinking tugboat seek refuge onboard a mysteriously empty Soviet vessel, only to discover murderous alien life-forms onboard that interpret human life as a virus to be destroyed. Director John Bruno allows by-the-book shootouts between humans and robot-like creatures to grow tiresome in an often ludicrous special-effects thriller. Some gory sci-fi violence, occasional profanity, and intermittent rough language. A-III (R)

Viscount, The (1967) Failed European spy movie directed by Maurice Cloche features excessive brutality and sexual suggestiveness. O (br)

Vision Quest (1985) A gung-ho high-school wrestler (Matthew Modine) is distracted from his goal of a state championship and a scholarship by a sultry young woman (Linda Fiorentino). What happens is, like its young hero, a bore in a movie directed by Harold Becker with a blaring soundtrack and rough language typical of such youth films. Though there is no nudity, characters talk about sex and its desirability constantly, presenting a benign view of fornication. O (R)

Visions of Eight (1973) Eight directors (Arthur Penn, Kon Ichikawa, Milos Forman, Claude Lelouch, John Schlesinger, Mai Zetterling, Michael Pfleghar, and Juri Ozerov) offer eight different views of the 1972 Munich Olympics. Despite the inevitable unevenness, it is a rewarding experience affording viewer's a different, more personal perspective of a familiar sports competition. A-I (G)

Visions of Light: The Art of Cinematography (1993) Illuminating documentary about the art and the craft of the cinematographer as practiced by its masters since the turn of the century. using interviews with leading cinematographers of today as well as excerpts from some 125 movies, directors Arnold Glassman, Todd McCarthy, and Stuart Samuels illustrate how creative camerawork is not dependent upon the medium's technological changes. Fleeting nude shot and a brutal boxing match. A-II (nr)

Visit to a Chief's Son (1974) American anthropologist (Richard Mulligan) brings his teenage son (Philip Hodgdon) to Kenya on a trip studying and photographing the Masai tribes, and their lives become enmeshed in those of the people they have come to visit. Directed by Lamont Johnson, this cross-cultural tale of how a father and his son achieve a healthy relationship in the picturesque African veldt is a good family experience, though some parents may not appreciate a brief skinny-dip in the wilds. A-II (G)

Visiting Hours (1982) Minimal Canadian effort at a horror movie with Lee Grant playing a woman terrorized by beefy maniac Michael Ironside. Directed by Jean Claude Lord, the stupid plot is frequently revolting and has not a single redeeming quality. O (R)

Visitors, The (1971) Two recent parolees from prison for rape and murder committed in Vietnam visit a third vet who testified against them at their trial, now living on a farm with his common-law wife, and after interminable tension, the final, inevitable scenes of rape and violence occur. Directed by Elia Kazan, the story's pessimism is as deep and dark as its moral perspective is shallow and glossy. O (R)

Visitors, The (1996) Fanciful Gallic farce in which a brave knight (Jean Reno) and his cloddish squire (Christian Clavier) are magically transported from the 12th century to contemporary France, where they cope with culture shock, meet some of their descendents, and contrive to return to their own time. Directed by Jean-Marie Poire, the comedy is largely slapstick, mixed with mistaken identities and misunderstandings, though the absurd proceedings prompt some thoughtful reflections on past and present. Subtitles. Slapstick violence, sexual references, vulgarities, and minimal rough language. A-III (R)

Vital Signs (1990) Sudsy melodrama about five medical students (most notably, Adrian Pasdar and Jack Gwaltney) trying to make the grade as doctors while dealing with their personal problems, chiefly those of the heart. Directed by Marisa Silver, the movie fails to generate anything but surface interest in its youthful characters, and the daily round of critical cases in a teaching hospital will be of interest only to inveterate fans of medical programs. Several sexual encounters, one of which is depicted graphically enough in the shadows of a medical supply room. A-III (R)

Viva Italia (1978) Bland anthology film featuring several stories done by directors Mario Monicelli, Dino Risi, and Ettore Scola, with such stars as Vittorio Gassman, Alberto Sordi, and Ugo Tognazzi. Most of the incidents are comic, ranging from moderately amusing to boring and tasteless, with the serious vignettes faring not much better. Coarse language and humor. A-III (R)

Viva Knievel (1977) Flamboyant motorcycle stuntman Evel Knievel gets the chance to play himself in a rather innocent and sentimental little melodrama which presents its folk hero as instrumental in reuniting a father and his young son as well as thwarting a gang of narcotics smugglers. Directed by Gordon Douglas, it is for the young and very undemanding. A-II (PG)

Viva la Muerte (1973) Written and directed by avant-garde playwright Fernando Arrabal, this is an impassioned, surrealistic expression of growing up during the Spanish Civil War. The movie's central experience (which is autobiographical) concerns a youngster's growing realization that his mother has betrayed his father into the hands of the local Fascists. Some viewers will be repelled by its emotional ferocity and pervasive imagery of seduction, mutilation, degradation, and sexual fantasies. O (nr)

Viva Las Vegas (1964) Breezy Elvis Presley vehicle in which he plays a race-car driver who falls for a Las Vegas resort employee (Ann-Margret) while trying to line up a car for the big race. Directed by George Sidney, the romantic story-line is less interesting than the colorful Nevada scenery. Sexual innuendo. A-III (br)

Viva Maria! (1965) Erratic French farce in which an Irish anarchist (Brigitte Bardot) escapes police in 1907 Central America by teaming with a touring performer (Jeanne Moreau) in a strip-tease act billed as the Two Marias, which masks their leadership of a revolution against an oppressive regime. Director Louis Malle's big-budget comic fiasco belabors the obvious as the sleight, whimsical plot flounders in overdone slapstick, clumsy satire, and bad taste. Dubbed. Comic violence, sexual situations, and much innuendo. A-IV (br)

Viva Max (1969) Peter Ustinov plays a bumbling Mexican general who recaptures the Alamo with a hundred equally bumbling soldiers, while Jonathan Winters as a National Guard general mainly battles the witless script. Director Jerry Paris simply misses the mark in trying to expand a single gag into a feature comedy. A-I (G)

Vivacious Lady (1938) Slight romantic comedy about a college prof (James Stewart) who can't bring himself to tell his stuffy father (Charles Coburn) that he's gotten married to a showgirl (Ginger Rogers). Directed by George Stevens, the plot complications stemming from this flimsy premise tax credibility, but are often amusing and occasionally hilarious. Some comic brawling and inebriation as a source of humor. A-II (br)

Vladimir and Rosa (1971) Low budget, politically committed French film dealing with the 1969 Chicago Conspiracy Trial as part of the process in changing the capitalistic system. Director Jean-Luc Godard's work possesses a coherence of style and content (and even some humor) but, as political propaganda, it is preaching only to the already converted. A-IV (nr)

Vogues of 1938 (1937) Creaky but colorful melodrama in which a New York fashion designer (Warner Baxter) gives a modeling job to the ex-fiancé (Joan Bennett) of a wealthy cad (Alan Mowbray), who seeks revenge by bankrolling a rival designer (Misha Auer). Directed by Irving Cummings, the halting proceedings include a tepid romance between the model and her married boss, as well as period fashion shows, several musical numbers, and a keepsake thimble bringing good luck. Romantic situations, sexual innuendo, and light treatment of marriage. A-III (br)

Voice in the Mirror (1958) Predictable story in which an alcoholic (Richard Egan), supported by wife (Julie London) and cranky doctor (Walter Matthau), finds the strength to face his addiction by turning to God, admitting his weakness and helping others (notably Arthur O'Connell). Directed by Harry Keller, the theme is effectively presented, though the narrative tends to repeat the obvious, and the characters are little more than stereotypes. Cautionary tale of some merit for older adolescents. A-II (br)

Voices (1979) Young singer (Michael Ontkean) and a deaf girl (Amy Irving) who wants to be a dancer fall in love, but the story is slight and the dialogue often ludicrous. A subplot involving the hero's raucous all-male family is so awkwardly handled by director Robert Markowitz that it is at best a distraction. Ambiguous view of premarital sex and a suggestive dance sequence. A-III (PG)

Voices of Sarafina (1989) Documentary focusing on the rehearsal, performance and backstage action surrounding the hit Broadway musical "Sarafina!," in which the troupe of black teenagers from South Africa discuss and enact their struggles growing up under the repression of apartheid. Directed by Nigel Noble, it's an eloquent introduction to the role played by South African youngsters in the struggle for black liberation. Some violently staged numbers may be too intense for young children. A-II (nr)

Volcano (1977) Director Donald Brittain's documentary reconstructs the life of Malcom Lowry, author of *Under the Volcano*, who died from an overdose of sleeping pills in 1957, relying upon interviews with family, friends, and associates and by visiting places where he had lived in England, the United States, Mexico, and Canada. The short passages read by Richard Burton from his novel are too few for one to gain any sense of the work's literary merit, but anyone interested in literature or in people will find it a fascinating experience of life on the edge. A-II (nr)

Volcano (1997) Formula disaster movie, with Tommy Lee Jones as head of the Los Angeles emergency office desperately trying to mobilize the city to stem the flow of lava which threatens to engulf it. Directed by Mick Jackson, the lame story focuses on trying to save people, while the special-effects department concocts scenes of fiery destruction which will surely frighten the young and impressionable. Scenes depicting massive destruction of property with mostly off-screen loss of life and occasional profanity. A-III (PG-13)

Volere Volare (1993) Silly Italian sex farce about a bashful cartoon sound-technician (Maurizio Nichetti) whose dates with a mysterious woman of the night (Angela Finocchiaro) are complicated by the fact that he is gradually turning into a cartoon character himself. Written and directed by Nichette and Guido Manuli, the irreverent mix of slapstick live action and zany animation eventually substitutes raciness for originality. Subtitles. Much sexual innuendo and fleeting nudity. A-III (R)

Volunteers (1985) Supposedly madcap adventures of Peace Corps volunteers (John Candy and Tom Hanks) in the jungles of Thailand range from dull to vapid in a mindless comedy directed by Nicholas Meyer. Some nudity and vulgarity are the sole, albeit offensive, punctuations in a simplistic story about evading a gambling debt. O (R)

Von Richthofen and Brown (1971) Anti-war extravaganza makes camera fodder out of the air aces of WW I (John Phillip Law and Don Stroud are the opposing aviators of the title). Though director Roger Corman's movie has stilted dialogue and wooden acting, it is saved by the excellence of its biplane footage. The planes dominate the screen, making an interesting contrast to more familiar scenes of modern warfare's carefully programmed annihilation of distant, dehumanized enemies. A-II (GP/PG-13)

Von Ryan's Express (1965) Fast-paced WW II action thriller focuses on some prisoners-of-war (with Frank Sinatra as their leader) who escape by train through the Italian Alps into Switzerland. Directed by Mark Robson, the movie has a fine international supporting cast and moments of high excitement, though some scenes are played too heavily for laughs and patriotism. A-I (br)

Voodoo Island (1957) Slack thriller directed by Reginald LeBorg, in which a TV debunker of paranormal phenomena (Boris Karloff) investigates reports of people mysteriously disappearing on a Pacific island and finds the place contains huge carnivorous plants and a sinister native tribe. Unconvincing scares. A-I (br)

Voodoo Woman (1957) Horror hokum directed by Edward L. Cahn, in which a mad doctor (Tom Conway) living with a jungle tribe combines science with voodoo to turn a murderous gold digger (Marla English) into a deadly monster, despite the best efforts of her intrepid guide (Mike "Touch" Connors). Hokey violence and hoodoo voodoo. A-II (br)

Voyage of Silence (1968) Impressive French drama about the victimization of illegal Portuguese workers who slip across the border seeking work in France. Directed by Christian de Chalogne, it shows the aloofness of society and its institutions in the face of suffering and exploitation. An important work on social justice. A-II (br)

Voyage of the Damned (1977) Fact-based story about a German ship carrying some 900 Jewish refugees on the eve of WW II who were denied entry by Cuba and the United States. Director Stuart Rosenberg has turned the tragedy into sluggish melodrama with a disjointed script and an all-star cast (including Faye Dunaway, Oskar Werner, and Max Von Sydow). Frank treatment of a couple's marital problems. A-III (PG)

Voyage to Grand Tartarie (1978) Failed French satire in which a young man (Jean-Luc Bideau), whose wife is the victim of a random killing, drops everything and embarks on a wild, eccentric journey through France beset with all sorts of social, political, spiritual, and physical ills. Director Jean-Charles Tacchella's effort lacks both humor and perception, as well as making excessive use of nudity. O (nr)

Voyage to the Bottom of the Sea (1961) Uneven thriller in which the commander (Walter Pidgeon) of the Navy's first atomic-powered submarine is beset by sabotage, mutiny, and hostile subs while trying to launch a nuclear missile to destroy a freak radiation belt before it turns Earth into a cinder. Producer-director Irwin Allen wastes little time on the credibility of the situation, focusing instead on the melodramatic action and race against time to save the planet. Undemanding escapist fare. A-I (br)

Voyeur (1991) Bizarre Dutch melodrama involves a 31-year-old recluse (Alex van Warmerdam), his overprotective mother, frustrated father (Olga Zuiderhoek and Henri Garcin), and a nude dancer (Annet Malherbe) who seduces both men. There's little point to the sick behavior of the wildly dysfunctional family in writer-director-star van Warmerdam's self-indulgent and perverse black comedy. Subtitles. Frequent adulterous and promiscuous situations with nudity and some violence. O (nr)

Vukovar (1996) When her Serbian groom is drafted, a pregnant Croat bride is forced to fend for herself after her parents are killed in the escalating Bosnian war that turns lifelong friends into deadly foes. Shot entirely in the war-torn city of the title, director Boro Draskovic's Yugoslav production is a documentary-like drama putting a human face on the conflict's innocent victims caught up in the irrational violence of ethnic hatreds. Subtitles. Much wartime violence including brutal rapes, a restrained bedroom scene, and brief frontal nudity. A-III (nr)

Vulture, The (1967) Canadian horror clunker written and directed by Lawrence Huntington is set in Cornwall, England, where a scientist (Robert Hatton) battles a mad doctor (Akim Tamiroff) who through "nuclear transmutation" has been changing himself into a half-man, half-bird to carry out a 200-year-old family curse. Weak menace and references to witchcraft. A-I (br)

W (1974) Ridiculous B-grade suspense thriller in which Twiggy plods through her role as the nervous heroine being terrorized by her mad ex-husband (Dirk Benedict) who has escaped from prison after his conviction for her murder. Directed by Richard Quine, the senseless plot is only an excuse for putting a vulnerable young woman at the mercy of a maniacal sadist. Some feeble psychological and physical violence. A-III (PG)

W.C. Fields and Me (1976) Directed by Arthur Hiller, this story of the romance between the Hollywood comedian (Rod Steiger) and Carlotta Monti (Valerie Perrine) distorts the people and events of an era shamelessly and has a tone of leering vulgarity that destroys any pretense of serious intent. O (PG)

WUSA (1970) Confused political melodrama about the right-wing owner (Pat Hingle) of a New Orleans radio station, its liberal disc jockey (Paul Newman), his waitress girlfriend (Joanne Woodward), and a manic social-worker (Tony Perkins). Director Stuart Rosenberg toys with ill-formed notions of political polarization and reduces them to cliches in a nearly incoherent plot. A-III (PG)

W.W. and the Dixie Dancekings (1975) Burt Reynolds plays a professional con-man who takes in hand a hapless group of country musicians. Director John G. Avildsen's comedy is often hilarious and is marked by fine acting. One scene at a drive-in is adult fare. A-III (PG)

Wabash Avenue (1950) Thin but lavish musical recreating 1890s Chicago, where a down-on-his-luck promoter (Victor Mature) plans to take over a plush Loop barroom from a former partner (Phil Harris) by wooing its star singing-attraction (Betty Grable). Directed by Henry Koster, the proceedings center in the mean-spirited rivalry between the two men for both saloon and singer, but the comic treatment is largely unamusing, leaving the entertainment to the vintage songs and colorful production numbers. Barroom brawls, scenes of inebriation, and heavy sexual innuendo. A-III (br)

Wackiest Ship in the Army, The (1960) Comic drama in which a Navy lieutenant (Jack Lemmon) takes a broken-down sailing ship with an inexperienced crew on a 1943 mission to the South Pacific, where they land an Australian observer (Chips Rafferty) on a Japanese-held island just before the Battle of the Bismarck Sea. Director Richard Murphy plays the action for laughs, most of which are good-natured except for some unfunny scenes of hand-to-hand combat. Wartime violence. A-I (br)

Wacky World of Mother Goose (1968) Animated fantasy in which Mother Goose (voice of Margaret Rutherford) leaves all her nursery-rhyme characters to visit her sister on the moon, then has to return to rescue them from imprisonment by a wicked count. Very young children may enjoy all the movie's repetitions, but parents will find it rather dull and unimaginative. A-I (br)

Waco (1966) Routine Western directed by R.G. Springsteen, in which a gunslinger (Howard Keel) is reformed by his former girlfriend (Jane Russell) and her minister husband (Wendell Corey). Stylized violence. A-II (br)

Wag the Dog (1997) Political satire in which a savvy spin-doctor (Robert De Niro) and an egotistical Hollywood producer (Dustin Hoffman) combine forces to distract attention from a presidential sex scandal by creating the appearance of a breaking war for the president to bring to a victorious end. Despite the far-fetched plot premise, director Barry Levinson keenly skewers electoral politics, Hollywood, and the voracious media, with Hoffman's producer the standout performance. Sexual references, an off-screen homicide, recurring rough language, and occasional profanity. A-III (R)

Wages of Fear, The (1953) Stranded in Central America, four down-on-their-luck Europeans (Yves Montand, Charles Vanel, Folco Lulli, and Peter Van Eyck) jump at the money offered to drive two truckloads of volatile nitroglycerine over primitive roads crossing mountains and jungle to blow out a fire raging in an American-owned oilfield. French director Henri-Georges Clouzot's classic thriller builds the suspense as the dangers of the fearsome journey take their toll on the desperate drivers. Subtitles. Extreme menace, brief stylized violence, and sordid situations of life among the impoverished. A-III (br)

Wagon Master (1950) Lyric Western about a Mormon wagon train whose leader (Ward Bond) hires a pair of genial cowboys (Ben Johnson and Harry Carey, Jr.) to guide them to Utah, encountering along the way a broken-down patent-medicine show (Alan Mowbray and Joanne Dru), a band of Navajo Indians, and some vicious killers on the run from a posse. Director John Ford's poetic homage to the pioneer spirit is imbued with the natural grandeur of the terrain, as well as an appreciation of the faith needed to journey into the wilderness, and the courage required to withstand the perils of the trail. Frontier violence. A-I (br)

Wagons East! (1994) Failed comedy in which homesick pioneers (notably Richard Lewis, Ellen Greene, and John C. McGinley) hire a drunken wagon-master (John Candy) to lead them back East to the comforts of civilization. Saddled with a one-joke script, director Peter Markle extracts few zesty zingers from a series of tiresome, tasteless one-liners. Brief comic violence, frequent sexual innuendo, toilet humor, crude female and gay stereotypes, and a few instances of profanity. A-III (PG-13)

Wagons West (1952) Routine oater directed by Ford Beebe with a veteran wagon-master (Rod Cameron) shepherding a train of pilgrims from Missouri to

California while romancing one of the company (Peggy Castle) and stopping a gang selling rifles to Cheyenne renegades. Stylized violence. A-I (br)

Wait Until Dark (1967) Taut thriller from Frederick Knott's play about a recently blinded housewife (Audrey Hepburn) alone in her apartment when it's invaded by crazed thugs (Alan Arkin, Richard Crenna, and Jack Weston) in search of a doll containing a cache of heroin. Directed by Terence Young, the harrowing plight of the sightless woman is depicted so convincingly that it turns a contrived situation into a gripping melodrama of suspense. Not for the nervous or the younger members of the family. A-II (br)

Waiting for Caroline (1969) Canadian version of the old story about the girl (Alexandra Stewart) who can't make up her mind which of her two lovers to marry and in the end gets neither. Writer-director Ron Kelly is more interested in social comment than making the characters interesting, let alone credible. Some nudity. O (nr)

Waiting for Guffman (1997) Minor comedy set in a fictional Missouri city, where a temperamental director (Christopher Guest) attempts to stage what he hopes will be a Broadway-bound musical, despite the dubious talents of his amateur cast (including Catherine O'Hara, Parker Posey, and Eugene Levy). Also directed by Guest, the movie is done in documentary style, using the conventions of filming a story within a story to bring out the subtle humor of ordinary folk getting caught up in aggrandizing their 15 minutes of fame. Some crude sexual references and a few instances of rough language. A-III (R)

Waiting for the Light (1990) A single mother of two (Teri Garr) struggles to make a go of an old diner, until an apparition staged by her eccentric aunt (Shirley MacLaine) is mistaken for a miracle and draws crowds to the sight. Lackadaisical direction by Christopher Monger results in a sluggish, too-pat comedy enlivened by MacLaine's zesty performance but lacking the wry satire the story calls for. Minor violence and some vulgar expressions. A-II (PG)

Waiting to Exhale (1995) Glossy romantic saga of African-American women friends (Whitney Houston, Angela Bassett, Loretta Devine, and Lela Rochon) and their love affairs during the course of a turbulent year of change for each of them. Director Forest Whitaker's sassy but emotionally manipulative adaptation of the Terry McMillan novel pays tribute to supportive female friendships but presents their affairs as the means to find Mr. Right. Several bedroom scenes, minor substance abuse, and recurring rough language. A-IV (R)

Wake Island (1942) Above-average WW II picture of the small Marine garrison on a tiny Pacific island overwhelmed at war's start by a Japanese naval taskforce. Directed by John Farrow, the script downplays the heroics of the doomed outpost's seasoned commander (Brian Donlevy) and under-strength force comprising the usual cross-section of American types, including a civilian contractor (William Bendix) who joins in the desperate proceedings. Wartime violence and Japanese stereotypes. A-I (br)

Wake Me When It's Over (1960) Thin service comedy about a US air base on a tiny island in the Pacific after WW II whose manic commander (Ernie Kovacs) puts a private (Dick Shawn) in charge of constructing a luxury hotel out of discarded military materials. Directed by Mervyn LeRoy, the dim proceedings are meant to be wacky but are too dragged out to be anything but tiresome. Mild sexual innuendo. A-II (br)

Wake of the Red Witch (1948) Convoluted South Seas adventure, in which a 19th-century skipper (John Wayne) scuttles a boatload of gold bullion belonging to a shipping magnate (Luther Adler) who had robbed him of his love (Gail Russell) and a fortune in pearls. Directed by Edward Ludwig, the action scenes are vigorous, with colorful characters and exotic locales, but the fitful plot keeps getting in the way of the escapist fun. Stylized violence and romantic complications. A-II (br)

Wake Up and Live (1937) Dated but still enjoyable comedy directed by Sidney Lanfield, in which a radio commentator (Walter Winchell) vies with a band leader (Ben Bernie) over a mystery singer (Jack Haley) whose voice has gone on the air while practicing with a singing star (Alice Faye) who's trying to cure his fear of microphones. Romantic complications. A-I (br)

Waking Ned Devine (1998) Wry Irish comedy in which the residents of a tiny village conspire to divide a seven-million-pound lotto by passing off one of their own as the winner after the actual ticket-owner died from the shock. Writer-director Kirk Jones plays up the slyness of the villagers in amusing, understated fashion without losing sight of their humanity and sense of community. Mild alcohol abuse, fleeting rear nudity, and minor profanity. A-III (PG)

Walk, Don't Run (1966) Cary Grant is the main attraction in this genial situation comedy about a rooming shortage during the Tokyo Olympics, where he serves as matchmaker for room-mates Samantha Eggar and Jim Hutton. Director Charles Walters brings off the sight gags and zany dialogue in relaxed style. A-III (br)

Walk in the Clouds, A (1995) Stylish but highly contrived romance set at the end of WW II, when a married vet (Keanu Reeves) undertakes to help an unwed pregnant woman (Aitana Sanchez-Gijon) face the wrath of her Mexican-American father (Giancarlo Giannini) by pretending to be her husband. Lyrically directed by Alfonso Arau, their subsequent romance unfolds on the wealthy vineyard estate of the woman's loving family, but the plot contrivances detract from the story's celebration of traditional values and feel-good ending. Plot hinged on deceit, some violent wartime flashbacks, and several sexual situations. A-III (PG-13)

Walk in the Shadow (1966) Good British movie of rights in conflict when a father's religious beliefs cause him to refuse a blood transfusion for his daughter, and her death results in his being put on trial. Director Basil Dearden builds the situation with precision and fairness to all concerned, until, after the verdict, it reveals its own point of view. A-II (br)

Walk in the Spring Rain, A (1970) Happily married professor (Fritz Weaver) takes a sabbatical to write a book in the Great Smoky Mountains, where his wife (Ingrid Bergman) finds herself falling in love with the kind, earthy handyman (Anthony Quinn). Directed by Guy Green, it's a slow-moving, old-fashioned sentimental melodrama that romantics will love and others dismiss as a tearjerker. A-III (PG)

Walk in the Sun, A (1945) WW II classic follows an American infantry platoon as it lands in 1943 Salerno, Italy, then moves from the beach in carrying out its orders to take a farmhouse six miles inland. Director Lewis Milestone's strong but poignant depiction of men in war is put over by fine performances from an ensemble cast headed by Dana Andrews, Richard Conte, John Ireland, and Lloyd Bridges, and backed by brutally realistic combat scenes whose sense of human loss is punctuated by the soldiers' ironic refrain, "Nobody dies." Wartime violence. A-I (br)

Walk on the Moon, A (1999) Sensitive drama explores the effects of adultery on a Jewish family in 1969, when the husband (Liev Schrieber) discovers his wife (Diane Lane) is having an affair while spending the summer in the Catskills with her two children and mother-in-law. Director Tony Goldwyn presents credible characters forced to re-evaluate marital commitment vs. personal fulfillment in a turbulent era of changing values. Theme of infidelity, fleeting violence, brief nudity, recreational drug use, some rough language, and a few instances of profanity. A-III (R)

Walk Proud (1979) Sensitive but inarticulate Chicano youth (Robby Benson), trapped in a morass of machismo and gang warfare in Los Angeles, tries to go straight when he falls in love with a dentist's daughter. Under Robert Collins's direction, Benson is just not credible as a Chicano, and he and his gang are a singularly elderly collection of teenagers. Some violence. A-III (PG)

Walk the Proud Land (1956) Thoughtful Western about Indian agent John Clum (Audie Murphy), who orders the military off the San Carlos reservation, then trains a force of Apache police to keep the peace and eventually uses them to capture the elusive Geronimo (Jay Silverheels) and his band of raiders. Directed by Jesse Hibbs, the fact-based story presents a sympathetic account of the Apache nation's plight in 1880s Arizona, with Murphy especially good as a devout Christian determined to end the unjust treatment of an oppressed people. Frontier violence. A-I (br)

Walk with Love and Death, A (1969) Failed medieval romance about two young lovers (Anjelica Huston and Assaf Dayan) caught in the midst of a peasant's war and doomed to death either by knight's sword or serf's cudgel. Directed by John Huston, the dark atmosphere of feudalism is convincing but little else is, especially the acting of its two young principals. Mature theme and treatment. A-III (PG)

Walkabout (1971) Australian story of a lovely teenager (Jenny Agutter) and her six-year-old brother (Lucien John) who, stranded deep in the wilderness after their father commits suicide, are rescued by a young aborigine (David Gumpilil) who leads them to eventual safety. Nicolas Roeg does better with his stunning location photography than he does with his heavy-handed direction of a movie that practically shouts out its theme of noble savagery. Extended nude swimming scene and the aborigine's suicide are questionable elements. A-IV (R/GP appeal)

Walker (1987) Mangled story of William Walker, the American adventurer who overthrew the Nicaraguan government in 1855 and set up his own corrupt regime until deposed two years later. The potential drama of these historical events is ignored by director Alex Cox, who treats the events instead in an exaggerated style closer to slapstick than satire or surrealism. Muddled treatment of a past episode of contemporary political significance, much graphic violence, and some sexual references. A-IV (R)

Walking and Talking (1996) Two lifelong women friends are nearly split asunder when one (Anne Heche) announces she's engaged, and the other (Catherine Keener), feeling left out, pursues a weird video-store clerk (Kevin Corrigan). Writer-director Nicole Holofcener looks indulgently on the romantic insecurities of the twenty-something crowd while affirming essential bonds of love as well as friendship. Implied affairs, occasional profanity, and some rough language. A-III (R)

Walking Dead, The (1995) When their unit is cut to pieces on a mission to rescue POWs in 1972 Vietnam, four African-American Marines (Joe Morton, Eddie Griffin, Allen Payne, and Vonte Sweet) confront themselves as well as the enemy in their struggle to survive. Written and directed by Preston A. Whitmore II, the movie uses the havoc of a failed military operation to present flashbacks showing what motivated each to enlist, but the result is too superficial to succeed, either on the action level or as personal drama, let alone social commentary. Graphic violence on the battlefield and in civilian flashbacks, a sexual situation, drug abuse, occasional profanity, and extremely rough language. O (R)

Walking Hills, The (1949) Contemporary Western in which an odd assortment of characters (headed by Randolph Scott, Edgar Buchanan, John Ireland, Arthur Kennedy, and Ella Raines) join in searching for a fortune in gold carried by a wagon train lost crossing Death Valley in 1852. Director John Sturges's melodramatic but intriguing tale is fueled by greed, personal rivalries, and guilty pasts, with plenty of moody atmosphere from endlessly shifting desert dunes and lonesome ballads performed by Josh

White. Some moral muddlement and stylized violence. A-II (br)

Walking Stick, The (1970) Young girl crippled with polio (Samantha Eggar) is courted and won by a persistent young artist (David Hemmings) who is obviously not as sincere in his affections as he appears. Director Eric Till proceeds with such a heavy hand that any subtleties are lost in a welter of dramatic close-ups and romantic bursts of color photography. A-III (PG)

Walking Tall (1973) Fact-based story of Tennessee sheriff Buford Pusser (Joe Don Baker), who walks tall and clubs freely in his campaign to close down rural vice in the county where he lives, as well as root out the accommodating political corruption that allows the vice to flourish. Nice objectives, but the means used to achieve them in director Phil Karlson's dramatization are ignoble, ugly, and downright vicious. Super-violent rendering of a noxious vigilante message. O (R)

Walking Tall, Part II (see: **Part II, Walking Tall**)

Walkover (1969) Polish drama directed by Jerzy Skolimowski carries on the story of **Identification Marks: None**, whose young hero is now making a meager living as a boxer unable to get a factory job. Scheduled to fight a tough ring-opponent, he flees town, but returns to face the challenge, and presumably the challenge of life in a socialist state. Its theme of alienation and its episodic presentation serve to disorient the viewer, but the work leads to a positive conclusion of self-awareness. A-II (nr)

Wall in Jerusalem, A (1972) Excellent documentary account of the birth of the state of Israel in 1948, and its struggle for survival ever since, limits itself chiefly to political history, detailing various major events and the leaders who participated in them. Director Frederic Rossif's compilation of archival footage makes a fascinating visual chronicle, and Richard Burton's narration lets the images communicate the emotion while it understates the facts. A-I (nr)

Wall Street (1987) An earnest young stockbroker (Charlie Sheen) wants to make an honest million, but a financial wheeler-dealer (Michael Douglas) teaches him that there are easier ways to make money than working for it. Directed by Oliver Stone, the cautionary tale does a creditable job in showing how part of the financial community has made greed a way of life, but is somewhat unconvincing in its dramatization of the corruption of an innocent and his ultimate redemption. Several scenes depicting sexual activity and some very rough language. A-IV (R)

Wanda (1971) Low-budget but impressive portrait of a woman, a nobody wandering through life conditioned to being badly used by others, who meets an insecure petty thief (Michael Higgins), and the two go off together, leaving viewers hoping this relationship will turn out better than her other experiences. Directed by and starring Barbara Loden, the movie succeeds in making an unvarnished plea for understanding the needs of isolated, impoverished human beings. A-III (GP)

Wanda Nevada (1979) Laid-back gambler (Peter Fonda, who also directs) wins an orphan (Brooke Shields) in a poker game and then goes hunting for gold with her in the Grand Canyon. Indian ghosts and a couple of flesh-and-blood villains complicate matters, but not enough to make things interesting. Some violence and the unresolved nature of the relationship between the two principals make this aimless movie adult fare. A-III (PG)

Wanderer, The (1969) French screen version of the Alain-Fournier novel about the romantic illusions of youth melting into the realities and responsibilities of adulthood in a story focusing on the one boy in the class who never quite matures and ultimately brings tragedy to those he loves most. Director Jean-Gabriel Albicocco has beautifully filmed the simple, turn-of-the-century narrative, conveying well the adult narrator's glow of nostalgia for those youthful years. Subtitles. A-II (G)

Wanderers, The (1979) Screen version of the novel by Richard Price about a group of Italian teenagers growing up in the Bronx in 1963 has a lot of vitality and some good acting (Ken Wahl, John Friedrich, Karen Allen). Philip Kaufman's direction, however, is too pretentious to stir any real emotional response in a movie that lacks a significant context. Violence, sexual references, and foul language. O (R)

Wannsee Conference, The (1987) German dramatization of the meeting held on January 20, 1942, at which the final decision was made by the Nazi leadership to exterminate all European Jews. Directed by Heinz Schirk, it is an historical document filled with anti-Semitic statements, but the brutish manner of the participants shows them clearly as racists. Mature theme and treatment. A-III (nr)

Wanted Dead or Alive (1987) Bounty hunter (Rutger Hauer) tracks down a ruthless international terrorist (Gene Simmons), but is then set up as bait, loses his best friend, and his lover, which impels him to inflict a terrible vengeance on those responsible. Its rough language, bloodshed, and brutality are not redeemed by director Gary Sherman's eye-for-an-eye brand of justice. O (R)

War, The (1994) Affecting anti-war parable set in 1970 rural Mississippi, where a guilt-ridden Vietnam vet (Kevin Costner) encourages his young son and daughter (Elijah Wood and Lexi Randall) to befriend, rather than fight, neighborhood bullies bent on taking over their prized tree house. Director Jon Avnet connects the children's increasingly physical skirmishes with the wartime experiences of the emotionally scarred father. Handsomely shot and delicately acted, the movie suffers from the script's stridently preachy tone as the two children learn valuable life lessons from caring parents. Flashbacks of battlefield violence, escalating juvenile violence and menace, as well as minimal profanity. A-II (PG-13)

War and Peace (1956) Episodic Hollywood version of Leo Tolstoy's epic novel centers on Russian aristocrats (Mel Ferrer, Audrey Hepburn, and Henry Fonda) caught up in the Napoleonic Wars. Directed by King Vidor, the US-Italian co-production muddles through the human dimension of events, but excels in its reenactment of military movements and historic battles, especially Napoleon's retreat from Moscow through the devastation of a Russian winter. Stylized violence and muted romance. A-I (br)

War and Peace (1968) Massive Russian version of the Tolstoy novel, originally released in three parts, evokes both the feeling of an era (1805 Russia threatened by Napoleon's march east) and Tolstoy's vision of individuals and destiny. Directed by and starring Sergei Bondarchuk as the contemplative Pierre, the movie in its sweep and detail provides an absorbing visual rendition of a great classic. A-I (GP)

War Arrow (1953) Standard Western fare, with a cavalry officer (Jeff Chandler) training a band of Seminole Indians to fight Kiowa hostiles in Texas, despite interference from his Indian-hating superior (John McIntire). Director George Sherman does better with the action scenes, including an all-out attack on the fort, than with a romantic subplot involving the hero with an apparent widow (Maureen O'Hara) and an Indian maid (Suzan Ball). A-I (br)

War at Home, The (1996) Sluggish story of a traumatized Vietnam vet (Emilio Estevez) returning to 1972 Texas as a psychological time-bomb, increasingly consumed by inner rage though his parents (Kathy Bates and Martin Sheen) expect him to get on with life and stop thinking about those he unwillingly killed. Also directed by Estevez, the talky drama illustrates that war can destroy many more lives than those taken on the battlefield. Scenes of wartime violence and frequent profanity and rough language. A-III (R)

War Between Men and Women, The (1972) Caustic cartoonist with failing eyesight (Jack Lemmon) hates women, children, and dogs, and naturally succumbs to the charms of a divorcée (Barbara Harris) who has three children and a terrier. Losing his sight completely, he is overtaken by a bout of self-pity that cuts him off from wife and children. Written and directed by Melville Shavelson, it tries to wring humor and pathos out of a human tragedy by using casual profanity, misanthropic wit, and finally cloying sentimentality. A-III (PG)

War Between the Planets (1971) Italian sci-fi programmer about the choleric commander (Jack Stuart) of a space expedition whose mission is to destroy a gaseous asteroid that is causing tidal waves and other catastrophic destruction on Earth. Director Anthony Dawson tries to compensate for his undernourished script by using low-budget special effects, but they don't hide the fact that this is a colossal clunker. A-I (G)

War Devils, The (1973) Routine Italian action movie with Guy Madison leading a squadron of US paratroopers behind German lines in Tunisia, but he turns the mission into a personal battle between himself and the German commander (Van Tenney). Director Bert Albertini serves up WW II according to the war-is-fun formula with a lot of special-effects flourishes. A-III (PG)

War Game, The (1967) British docudrama about the effects of nuclear warfare on a civilian population features nonprofessionals in realistically simulated scenes. Produced, written, and directed by Peter Watkins, the movie gets considerable shock value from its hypothetical events, but in making the unthinkable appear possible, it raises important questions of public concern. A-III (br)

War Games (see: **Suppose They Gave a War and Nobody Came?**)

War-Gods of the Deep (1965) Convoluted adventure fantasy set on the English seacoast in the early 1900s, when the search for a missing woman (Susan Hart) leads a scientist (Tab Hunter) to discover an ancient undersea city inhabited by gill-people and ruled by a smuggler (Vincent Price) who hasn't aged a day since his arrival in 1803. Directed by Jacques Tourneur from a poem by Edgar Allan Poe, the mystery of the city and its strange inhabitants is overshadowed by a nearby underwater volcano which is about to explode. Stylized violence and menace. A-II (br)

War Hunt (1962) Posted to a frontline infantry unit in 1953 Korea, a green recruit (Robert Redford) comes to fear for the safety of an orphaned Korean boy looked after by a combat-crazed veteran (John Saxon) who slips behind enemy lines on nightly killing sprees. Director Denis Sanders probes the psychological damage of war in this chilling portrait of a psychotic soldier whose dangerously bizarre behavior is considered commendable rather than abnormal by his superiors. Combat violence and perilous situations. A-II (br)

The War Lover (1962) Uneven version of the John Hersey novel set in 1943 England, where a daredevil American B-24 bomber pilot (Steve McQueen) grows increasingly psychopathic, while his conscientious co-pilot (Robert Wagner) finds comfort in an affair with an Englishwoman (Shirley Anne Field). Director Philip Leacock does better with the dangers of daylight bombing raids than with the story of the conflict between a social misfit who enjoys employing his destructive talents in the military and a subordinate who has a normal fear of dying. Wartime violence and discreet depiction of an affair. A-III (br)

War of the Buttons (1994) Remake of the 1962 French movie is set in Ireland, where the boys of a one village (led by Gregg Fitzgerald) battle those of a neighboring village (led by John Coffey), with each side trying to outdo the other in youthful bravado, including cutting the buttons off captives' clothing and once fighting in the buff. Directed by John Roberts and filmed entirely in West Cork, the picture captures the innocent seriousness of the rival bands, but the treatment falters in a mix of whimsy, social consciousness, and youthful self-importance. Stylized violence, flashes of rear nudity, and some coarse language. A-III (PG)

War of the Colossal Beast (1958) Director Bert I. Gordon's clunky sequel to his 1957 sci-fi monster entry **The Amazing Colossal Man**, has the presumed dead 60-foot radiation victim turn up in Mexico, then brought back to Los Angeles for treatment, but instead he goes berserk, until tangling with high-voltage power lines. Stylized violence and life-menacing situations. A-II (br)

War of the Gargantuas (1970) Below-average Japanese monster movie about a scientist (Russ Tamblyn) whose experiments on a baby ape go awry, and it and a companion grow large enough to crush the city of Tokyo. Director Inoshiro Honda relies on nature and the special-effects crew to resolve the difficulty, while leaving a few cardboard buildings standing for a sequel. A-I (G)

War of the Planets (1965) Dubbed Italian sci-fi adventure directed by Anthony Dawson offers a muddled, lackluster story, in which a space station captain (Tony Russell) saves Earth, along with his girlfriend (Lisa Gastoni), from a mass of extraterrestrial green vapor seeking to inhabit human bodies. Silly special-effects violence. A-II (br)

War of the Roses, The (1989) Black comedy on the battle of the sexes has a divorce lawyer (Danny DeVito) telling the story of a couple (Michael Douglas and Kathleen Turner) who go from happy penury to wealthy discontent, and then divorce proceedings that turn into a horror show as they fight over house and possessions. As director, DeVito does a good job satirizing the anger and greed of divorce settlements, but has little sensitivity to the problems underlying the break-up. Nasty cartoon-like marital violence, brief but explicit sexual encounters, and some rough language. A-IV (R)

War of the Wildcats (1943) Boisterous Western romance directed by Albert S. Rogell is set in 1900 Oklahoma, where an enterprising cowboy (John Wayne) goes into the oil business in order to compete with a local tycoon (Albert Dekker) for the affections of an ambitious woman author (Martha Scott). Stylized violence and romantic complications. A-II (br)

War of the Worlds, The (1953) First-rate version of H.G. Wells's sci-fi classic about Martians invading Earth with deadly heat-rays, from whose destructive path through California flee nuclear physicist Gene Barry and companion Ann Robinson, until the aliens meet with the unexpected. Produced by George Pal and directed by Byron Haskin, the apocalyptic tale is tautly told with often frightening effect, thanks to its superior model work and astonishing special effects. Some religious dimension, much menace, and stylized violence. A-I (G)

War Paint (1953) Trekking through the desert with a peace treaty promised to an Indian chief, a cavalry officer (Robert Stack) copes with all manner of problems as his small column of troopers is decimated from without and within. Directed by Lesley Selander, the deadly journey is outlandishly contrived, though it gains some interest by being filmed appropriately in Death Valley. Stylized violence, including the attempted rape of a captured Indian woman. A-III (br)

War Room, The (1993) Human-interest documentary centers on the political strategies used by George Stephanopoulos and James Carville during the 1992 presidential campaign to get Bill Clinton elected. In low-key but entertaining fashion, directors D.A. Pennebaker and Chris Hegedus capture the very different styles of the two men in deflecting issues of the candidate's personal character to concentrate on a weak national economy as the reason to vote for change. Discreet sexual references and an off-screen instance of rough language. A-II (PG)

War Wagon, The (1967) Familiar Western story about a super-tough hombre (John Wayne) just out of jail and bent on robbing a gold shipment belonging to the villain (Bruce Cabot) who framed him and now has hired a gunman (Kirk Douglas) to kill him. Director Burt Kennedy mixes some comedy into the rough, he-man action, but the result is nothing out of the ordinary. Stylized violence. A-II (br)

Warehouse (1974) Strange Japanese story of a blind sculptor who kidnaps a beautiful model and imprisons her in his hidden studio, where she becomes as obsessed as he with tactile sensations, leading to tragedy for both. As an allegory on the consequences of enslavement to the senses, director Yasuzo Masumura's treatment will please neither hedonist nor puritan, but its technical virtuosity in creating the intensely physical world of a mad artist does have some interest. A-IV (nr)

WarGames (1983) Good teen suspense thriller about a high-school computer-wiz (Matthew Broderick) who breaks into a government nuclear-strategy computer and starts playing a war game whose logical conclusion is nuclear Armageddon. Directed by John Badham, the story loses much of its momentum when the program's designer (John Wood) is tracked down and points out the just desserts of human folly just before the slack conclusion. A few vulgar expletives. A-II (PG)

Warlock (1959) Muddled Western in which the title town hires a pair of gunmen (Henry Fonda and Anthony Quinn) to enforce the law, then a former outlaw (Richard Widmark) takes the vacant job of sheriff, and comes up against both the hired guns and his old gang. Director Edward Dmytryk's variation on law-and-order themes is tangled with complications that add nothing to the basic plot of justice prevailing at the end of a six-shooter. Stylized shootouts and some romantic complications. A-II (br)

Warlock (1991) A time traveler (Richard E. Grant) from the 17th century enlists the aid of a spunky California girl (Lori Singer) to defeat a male witch (Julian Sands) on the verge of destroying humanity.

Strong performances and a steady build-up of suspense bolster producer-director Steve Miner's preposterous tale of black magic mumbo-jumbo. Some stylized violence and minimal rough language. A-III (R)

Warlords of Atlantis (1978) Innocuous British adventure with two young scientists (Doug McClure and Peter Gilmore) who find themselves in the power of the rulers of an undersea kingdom, where they encounter a beautiful and apparently ageless princess (Cyd Charisse). Directed by Kevin Connor, there's plenty of paper-maché monsters, wooden dialogue, and leaden comic relief. A-II (PG)

Warm December, A (1973) Black doctor (Sidney Poitier) is racing motorcycles on a vacation in England when he runs across the gorgeous niece of an African ambassador (Ester Anderson), falls in love, but then learns she is dying of sickle-cell anemia. Also directed by Poitier, the romantic melodrama is laid on with a sledgehammer to the tune of **Love Story**, and its entertainment appeal is limited to devotees of the TV soaps. A-III (PG)

Warning Shot (1966) Story begins interestingly as a social drama about a policeman (David Janssen) who kills a highly regarded public figure. From there the movie turns into a routine detective thriller directed by Buzz Kulik with little suspense but more than a little violence. A-II (br)

Warning Sign (1985) An accident in a genetic engineering lab where biological-warfare experiments are being carried on causes those inside to be transformed into crazed zombies, save for a lone security guard (Kathleen Quinlan). Written and directed by Hal Barwood, it is a run-of-the-mill exercise in gory violence. O (R)

Warpath (1951) Civil War veteran (Edmond O'Brien) enlists in the Seventh Cavalry to track down his girlfriend's killers (Forrest Tucker and Dean Jagger), becomes a heroic Indian-fighter, and warns Custer that the Sioux are massing for an attack, before riding off with his new love (Polly Bergen). Director Byron Haskin's routine Western has an earnest cast and some mildly interesting plot twists. Frontier violence and Indian stereotypes. A-I (br)

Warrior Empress, The (1960) Dubbed Italian clunker directed by Pietro Francisci is set in ancient Greece, where a rebel (Kerwin Matthews) fights an unjust king while wooing his poetic niece, Sappho (Tina Louise). Stylized violence, sexual innuendo, and bevies of scantily clad maidens. A-III (br)

Warriors, The (1955) While leading the English forces defending Aquitaine during the 100 Years Wars, Edward Prince of Wales (Errol Flynn) takes time out to rescue a lady (Joanne Dru) abducted by a French nobleman (Peter Finch). Directed by Henry Levin, the colorful British production has a good cast and well-mounted action sequences, though it takes itself more seriously than the story warrants. Much derring-do and stylized battle scenes. A-I (br)

Warriors, The (1979) Screen version of Sol Yurick's novel about a youth gang trying to make their way back to their own neighborhood through a New York City in which every hand is turned against them. Directed by Walter Hill, the gang's sordid adventures are of even less interest than its one-dimensional characters and their stilted dialogue. Constant violence and glorification of vicious behavior. O (R)

Warriors of Virtue (1997) Martial-arts fantasy in which an American teenager (Mario Yedidia) finds himself transported to a mythical kingdom of warring kung-fu masters, as a villainous warlord (Angus Macfadyen) tries to conquer a peaceable land led by the wise Master Chung (Chao-Li Chi). Directed by Ronny Yu, the good master's words of wisdom get lost in the fury of the fantasy action, but the formula story doesn't measure up to the imaginative sets and costuming in a production filmed mainly in China's Beijing Film Studios. Some stylized violence, much menace, and a vulgar expression. A-II (PG)

Wash, The (1988) Poignant chronicle of the end of a long-term Japanese-American marriage in which the wife (Nobu McCarthy) is quietly determined to forge a new, happy life for herself after years of being ignored and belittled by her husband (Mako). Director Michael Toshiyuki Uno does a wonderfully restrained job of exploring the fears that plague the couple and their grown children in coming to terms with the marriage's dissolution. Incidental rough language, a fairly explicit sexual encounter within marriage, and implications of cohabitation outside marriage. A-III (nr)

Washington Square (1997) Sobering dramatization of Henry James's tale in which a plain young heiress (Jennifer Jason Leigh) is eager to marry an attentive suitor (Ben Chaplin), even though her brutally honest father (Albert Finney) denounces him as a gold-digger and vows to disinherit her. Director Agnieszka Holland stresses the woman's hard-won sense of self-esteem despite male rejection, but the solemn pace and a clumsy attempt to make her aunt (Vanessa Redgrave) a comic figure diminish the story's emotional impact. A theme of false love, as well as a brief scene of gore. A-II (PG)

Washington Story (1952) Assigned to do a hatchet job on novice congressman Van Johnson, journalist Patricia Neal has a change of heart when he stands up for the national interest. Written and directed by Robert Pirosh, it's less a drama than a patriotic civics lesson, chiefly of interest for its picture of the relatively unsophisticated trappings of yesteryear's federal government. A-I (br)

Wasp Woman, The (1960) Flimsy horror quickie directed by Roger Corman has an aging cosmetics queen (Susan Cabot) seek youthful transformation from wasp enzymes processed by a quack doctor (Michael Mark), with predictable results. Mild stylized violence and silly wasp-woman mask. A-II (br)

Watched! (1974) Interesting independent production about a drug-case prosecutor (Stacy Keach) who is set up by his own agents after he begins to have second thoughts about the legality of their surveillance methods. Written and directed by John Parsons, the movie suggests that bugging has become a way of life in America, with some well-executed scenes of extra-legal surveillance techniques. A-III (R)

Watcher in the Woods, The (1980) Mediocre Disney suspense thriller in which an American teenager (Lynn-Holly Johnson) staying in a gloomy English country house tries to solve the mystery of what happened to the teenage girl who disappeared from the house 30 years before. Directed by John Hough, the script and its mystery are rather banal, but the movie does have its frightening moments. Though too scary for preteens, its primary appeal is to younger teenagers. A-II (PG)

Water (1986) This adult comedy is funnier on paper, as Michael Caine stars as the frustrated governor of an underdeveloped island nation in the Caribbean. Prosperity and independence are achieved only after diuretic mineral water and oil are discovered at a defunct US drilling rig. Ethnic jokes, TV sitcom-style humor, and sexual innuendo predominate as **Water** oozes rather than bubbles. A-III (PG-13)

Waterboy, The (1998) Slack sports comedy in which a dim-witted water-boy (Adam Sandler) for a Southern college's losing football team becomes their star player despite the fierce objections of his wild-eyed Cajun mama (Kathy Bates). As directed by Frank Coraci, Sandler's sweetly stupid character is just one of many Southern stereotypes in a halting comedy where brute strength is valued above all. Bruising athletic competitions, brief alcohol abuse and sexual innuendo, fleeting nudity, crude expressions, and an instance of rough language. A-III (PG-13)

Waterdance, The (1992) Insightful drama of a newly wheelchair-bound writer (Eric Stoltz) in a multiracial rehabilitation center, where he must deal with two battling patients (Wesley Snipes and William Forsythe) and a decision regarding his married girlfriend (Helen Hunt). Co-directed by Neal Jimenez and Michael Steinberg and based on Jimenez's experiences, the movie is an emotionally honest and exceptionally well-acted look at four distinct personalities, each at a turning point in their lives. Some discreet bedroom encounters, brief nudity, and occasional rough language. A-III (R)

Waterhole No. 3 (1967) When the fastest con-artist in the West (James Coburn) lifts a thief's wallet containing a map to a cache of stolen gold, he lights out for the loot with the robber in pursuit and the Army pursuing him. Directed by William Graham, the tone of the movie is coarse, bawdy, and frequently just plain crude. O (br)

Waterland (1992) A middle-aged history teacher (Jeremy Irons) recounts to his class his own troubled adolescent history, and the resulting guilt that weighs so heavily on his rocky marriage to a woman (Sinead Cusack) who is suffering a nervous breakdown. Stephen Gyllenhaal directs a rambling, unwieldy story of dark sexual secrets, madness, and murder whose tragic elements are dissipated by the jarring flashbacks. Much discussion of sexual matters, a discreet sexual encounter, and some nudity. A-III (R)

Waterloo (1971) Stately, grandiose set piece re-creates Napoleon's return from exile on Elba to his final defeat at Waterloo. Director Sergei Bondarchuk reduces the two principal opponents, Napoleon (Rod Steiger) and Wellington (Christopher Plummer), to little more than historical caricatures speaking the famous epigrams attributed to them. Yet the movie comes alive in the broad, colorful sweep of action sequences showing an epic moment in European history. A-II (G)

Waterloo Bridge (1940) Soapy romantic tragedy of WW I, as a Scottish captain (Robert Taylor) and a London ballet student (Vivien Leigh) fall in love, but before they can wed he's sent to the front, then reported dead, and she turns to prostitution, until he turns up at war's end, and her shame drives her to suicide. Directed by Mervyn LeRoy from Robert E. Sherwood's play, the contrived proceedings haven't worn well, though the moody photography and a strong supporting cast (notably Lucile Watson and Virginia Field) at least make it watchable. Romantic complications, veiled treatment of prostitution, and suicide in the plot resolution. A-III (br)

Watermelon Man (1970) When a mindlessly bigoted white (Godfrey Cambridge) one night turns black, he undergoes the indignities and injustices of white America. Unfortunately, in dealing with all-too-familiar racial stereotypes (sexual, musical, commercial), director Melvin Van Peebles's satire is crude, embarrassing, and at times consciously offensive. Though terribly uneven, it at least attempts to deal with the festering ulcer of everyday racial prejudice. A-IV (R)

Watership Down (1978) British animated adaptation of Richard Adams's popular novel about a band of brave rabbits making a dangerous journey in search of a new home has been done with taste and intelligence under Martin Rosen's direction. Some of the voices belong to John Hurt, Ralph Richardson, Denholm Elliot, and Harry Andrews, with Zero Mostel providing comic relief as a zany German seagull. Some scenes may be too intense for younger children. A-II (PG)

Waterworld (1995) In a waterlogged future where scattered bands of people subsist on man-made atolls, a mutant fish-man (Kevin Costner) reluctantly gives refuge aboard his uniquely rigged sailboat to a woman (Jeanne Tripplehorn) and a child with a mysterious tattoo sought by a murderous pirate gang (under Dennis Hopper) because it supposedly shows the location of a hidden patch of dry land. Aside from a visually bleak vision of humans struggling for survival in an aquatic world, director Kevin Reynolds's shallow action picture offers little more than formula chase fare with a decided mean streak and badly underwritten characters. Recurring violence, partial nudity, sexual innuendo, profanity, and an instance of rough language. A-IV (PG-13)

Wattstax (1973) Exciting documentary directed by Mel Stuart with rock, jazz, and general all-around soul performers (Issac Hayes, The Staple Singers, Bar-Kays), centering around the black experience and, in particular, the Los Angeles community of Watts. Giving it continuity is a funny but sad and, at times, raunchy commentary by Richard Pryor. A-III (R)

Way Ahead, The (1944) WW II saga of British draftees (Stanley Holloway, James Donald, John Laurie, and many others) grousing their way through boot camp while being gradually transformed under the guidance of a dedicated officer (David Niven) into a crack infantry unit sent to fight in North Africa. Directed by Carol Reed, the movie's patriotic intentions wear well, principally because its group portrait is grounded in convincing individual details, though the heroics in the concluding battle sequence seem today surprisingly hollow. Wartime violence. A-II (br)

Way Out West (1937) Entrusted with delivering the deed for a gold mine to a poor orphan, Stan Laurel and Oliver Hardy trace her to a frontier town, where they run afoul an outrageously crooked innkeeper (James Finlayson). Directed by James Horne, the situation sets up some prime comedy routines as well as a couple of country tunes and a dance number by the boys that's truly elegant. Genial fun for all. A-I (br)

Way, Way Out! (1966) Jerry Lewis movie about a trip to the moon is preoccupied with sex in its dialogue, costuming, and situations. O (br)

Way We Live Now, The (1970) Advertising agency director (Nicholas Pryor), separated from his wife, has long conversations with himself and imaginary famous visitors, but his time is mostly given to stalking and bedding women. Written, produced, directed, and photographed by Barry Brown, the incessant talk is pretentious, and the long string of sexual adventures tedious and exploitative. O (R)

Way We Were, The (1973) Robert Redford and Barbra Streisand as ill-matched lovers in a seriocomic story sweeping from Ivy League idylls in the late 1930s into WW II and on to Hollywood in the postwar era of blacklisting. There is just too much material here for anyone to put into a coherent shape, and director Sydney Pollack succumbs to the temptation of trivializing the period and their events in favor of the sheer glamour of it all. It's slick and shallow, but romantics may find it diverting. A-III (PG)

Way West, The (1967) Fairly good pioneer Western with Kirk Douglas as a harried wagon-master trying to get a wagon train of Western settlers through the mountains and past Indian perils. Director Andrew V. McLaglen gets rugged acting support from Richard Widmark and Robert Mitchum, with Lola Albright on hand for the boys to fight over. A-III (br)

Wayne's World (1992) Dopey comedy about two bumblers (Mike Myers and Dana Carvey) whose cable-access talk show is threatened by a smarmy producer (Rob Lowe). Director Penelope Spheeris stretches what was originally a "Saturday Night Live" TV skit into 95 mindless minutes of numbing nonsense. Sexist attitudes, implied premarital encounter, some sexual innuendo, and toilet humor. A-III (PG-13)

Wayne's World 2 (1993) Inane comedy sequel in which overgrown adolescents Wayne and Garth (Mike Myers and Dana Carvey) juggle trouble with girlfriends (Tia Carrere and Kim Basinger) while throwing a Woodstock-like rock concert without performers or ticket sales. Director Stephen Surjik simply cranks up the sophomoric humor, adding spoofs of other movies to liven up the lads' lame repertoire of airhead asides. Frequent sexual innuendo, recurring rear nudity, minor violence, and occasional profanity. A-III (PG-13)

We All Loved Each Other So Much (1977) Warm and moving Italian comedy about three men (Vittorio Gassman, Nino Manfredi, and Stefano Satta Flores) who love the same woman (Stefania Sandrelli) at one time or another, with varying degrees of intensity, over the course of three decades. Directed by Ettore Scola, it is a rare, wise, and entertaining movie on the theme of love and friendship. A-II (PG)

We Dive at Dawn (1943) Taut WW II picture in which a British submarine tracks a German battleship into the enemy waters of the Baltic, then runs out of fuel after torpedoing it. Director Anthony Asquith turns the action story into a character study of men in war, focusing on the sub's capable captain (John Mills) and two seamen (Eric Portman and Niall MacGinnis) with very different marital problems. Wartime violence and domestic misunderstandings. A-II (br)

We Live Again (1934) Hollywood version of Leo Tolstoy's novel *Resurrection*, about a Russian prince (Fredric March) who learns years later that he has ruined the life of a peasant girl (Anna Sten) on his aunt's estates by leaving her pregnant, then tries to atone by joining her when she is sent to Siberia for a crime of which she is innocent. Director Rouben Mamoulian evokes both the beauty of the Russian spirit and the injustices of the czarist regime, but the characters and their emotions are melodramatically thin. Muddled treatment of an idealistic theme. A-II (br)

We Will All Meet in Paradise (1978) Thin French comedy about the life and times of four overaged, overindulged, middle-class Dead End Kids (Jean Rochfort, Claude Brasseur, Guy Bedos, and Victor Lanoux) as they go through a round of sophomoric escapades. Directed by Yves Robert, the result is a tepid comedy of manners whose sole merit is the considerable charm of the performers. Adultery figures in the plot. A-III (PG)

We're Back! A Dinosaur's Story (1993) Magically transported to present-day New York City, four friendly dinos are saved by a gruff street-urchin and a lonely little girl when an evil circus-master changes them into snarling monsters. Steven Spielberg's animated production of Hudson Talbott's children's story sacrifices much of its charm and character appeal for an overabundance of busy and noisy misadventures that may delight children a lot more than their elders. A-I (G)

We're No Angels (1955) Minor comedy in which bumbling convicts (Humphrey Bogart, Peter Ustinov, and Aldo Ray) delay their escape from Devil's Island to save a kindly but inefficient French shopkeeper and his wife (Leo G. Carroll and Joan Bennett) from the machinations of a crafty relative (Basil Rathbone). Director Michael Curtiz gets some laughs from the unlikely antics of the good-hearted cons, but the plot's intended whimsy falls flat. Devious deeds aplenty. A-II (br)

We're No Angels (1989) Heavy-handed comic misadventure in which two escaped convicts (Robert De Niro and Sean Penn) hide out in a monastery pretending to be priests while they figure out a way to cross the border into Canada. David Mamet's script has plenty of comic possibilities in contrasting the spiritual impoverishment of the two earthbound clods with the faith and innocence of the unworldly community of monks, but director Neil Jordan plays the piece so broadly that the result may appear to some as an irreverent farce, questionable in taste and treatment of religion. Some sexual references, several scenes of hard-edged violence, and a bemused, agnostic attitude toward religion. A-IV (PG-13)

We're Rich Again (1934) Wacky Depression comedy in which a stock-market casualty (Grant Mitchell) hopes to recoup his fortune after his daughter (Joan Marsh) marries a millionaire (Reginald Denny), but when her dizzy country-cousin (Marian Nixon) arrives for the wedding, chaos follows. Directed by William A. Seiter, the zany proceedings feature running gags with a polo-playing grandmother (Edna May Oliver) and a frustrated process-server (Edgar Kennedy), but the thin plot belabors the obvious. Light treatment of marriage and sexual innuendo. A-III (br)

Weapons of the Spirit (1989) Pierre Sauvage is a Jew who survived the Holocaust only because he happened to be born in 1944 in Le Chambon-sur-Lignon, a French town which provided safe harbor for some 5,000 Jews during WW II. Returning to this largely Protestant community to make a documentary about those remaining strong-minded Christian farmers, educators, and clergy who risked their lives as an act of faith against Nazi racism, Sauvage examines how and why they managed to get away with their massive unorganized opposition when other French resistance fighters faced reprisals. The result is a moving tribute to human solidarity and a reminder of the power of Christian teachings. A-II (nr)

Web, The (1947) Tricky crime story in which a brassy lawyer (Edmund O'Brien) is hired to protect a threatened industrialist (Vincent Price), then shoots an armed intruder in what a veteran cop (William Bendix) suspects is a case of murder linked to a million-dollar swindle. Directed by Michael Gordon, the plot takes some devious turns as the lawyer tries to clear himself of the murder rap with the help of the industrialist's secretary (Ella Raines). Stylized violence and callous deceptions. A-II (br)

Wedding, A (1978) Some 20 major characters, and perhaps twice as many minor ones, assemble for a satiric assault on the extravagance of a wedding in a family recently risen to affluence. With no central plot worth mentioning, director Robert Altman lets the action go in every direction at once, much of it revolving around the many skeletons in the family closet. The actors (among them Lillian Gish, John Cromwell, Vittorio Gassman, Dina Merrill, Howard Duff, Carol Burnett, and Paul Dooley) are better than the material in this extremely uneven effort that is further marred by sexual goings-on and gratuitous nudity. O (R)

Wedding Banquet (1993) A gay couple in New York decides to help a Chinese friend (May Chin) get a green card by having one of them (Winston Chao) marry her in name only, but wind up living together when the groom's elderly parents (Sihung Lung and Ah-Leh Gua) arrive from Taiwan for a prolonged stay with the newlyweds. Director Ang Lee stresses the human side of the comic complications in a bittersweet comedy of manners. A sympathetic portrayal of a gay live-in relationship, fleeting nudity, and occasional rough language. A-IV (R)

Wedding Bell Blues (1997) Weakly contrived tale of three single women (Illeana Douglas, Paulina Porizkova, and Julie Warner) who impulsively decide to find husbands overnight in Las Vegas, then file for divorce the next day just so they can say they were married before age 30. Director Dana Lustig tries to make the instant romances seem comically poignant in what gradually ends up a mushy tale that affirms female friendship and marital commitment. Off-screen marital encounters, sexual references which include an abortion, and occasional profanity. A-IV (R)

Wedding Gift, The (1994) Maudlin British drama about a woman (Julie Walters) whose crippling disease completely baffles doctors as it progressively worsens, until she finds her devoted husband (Jim Broadbent) a suitable replacement (Sian Thomas), then dies an apparent suicide. Directed by Richard Loncraine, the fact-based BBC production centers in the pathos of the wife's weakening condition and her determination, abetted by husband, to keep up flagging spirits by making jokes about it, then cops out in the end by sentimentalizing her terminal act of matchmaking. Ambiguity of the wife's death, a flash of nudity, and occasional profanity. A-III (PG-13)

Wedding in Blood (1974) Disappointing French crime story about a couple (Stephane Audran and Michel Piccoli) who, drawn together by an almost incendiary passion, conspire to murder their spouses. Instead of trying to create a truly chilling horror movie out of this story of forbidden desire and desperate murder, director Claude Chabrol uses it to express his moralistic views on the middle class and their loss of values. A-III (PG)

Wedding in White (1973) Hard-edged but compassionate Canadian drama set in a small town during WW II tells the story of a father (Donald Pleasence) who, learning his teenage daughter (Carol Kane) is pregnant after an assault by a drunken soldier, persuades his best friend (Leo Phillips), a bachelor in his mid-fifties, to marry the girl, thereby saving the family reputation. Director William Fruet uses the situation to focus on the limited horizons and narrow attitudes of small-town life, which proves just as much a closed society as the nearby prisoner-of-war camp where the father works. A-IV (R)

Wedding Night (1970) Irish movie about a young Catholic woman (Tessa Wyatt) whose fears of sex and pregnancy make her unable to consummate her marriage. Directed by Piers Haggard, the story is told in strong and pointed discussions of the contraceptive pill, morality, the medical profession, and an uncomprehending husband. Thoughtful drama about a deeply emotional subject, but it offers no positive solutions. A-IV (PG)

Wedding Party, The (1969) Unsure about marrying his fiancé (Jill Clayburgh), a prospective bridegroom (Charles Pfluger) tries a variety of ruses to call off the wedding. Directed by Cynthia Munroe, Brian De Palma, and Wilford Leach, the low-budget black-and-white production tries all kinds of camera tricks, but can't save its hodge-podge of comedy, satire, and fantasy. A-III (nr)

Wedding Singer, The (1998) Sappy romantic comedy set in the suburbs of 1985 New York, where a jilted fiancé (Adam Sandler) falls for a sweet waitress (Drew Barrymore), then discovers she is about to marry a crass playboy. Directed by Frank Coraci, the contrived comedy pokes heavy-handed fun at 1980s fads and fashions, but the bland proceedings remain largely lifeless. Implied affairs, fleeting violence, occasional profanity, and an instance of rough language. A-III (PG-13)

Wednesday's Child (1972) British dramatization of the gradual psychic destruction of a young woman (Sandy Ratcliff) by her repressive working-class parents and by the behaviorist theories practiced on her in a government-run mental hospital. Written by David Mercer and directed by Kenneth Loach, the result is a plea for respect for the individuality of the person that is a powerfully moving, incontrovertible statement. A-III (nr)

Wee Willie Winkie (1937) Unlikely but likeable Shirley Temple vehicle from a Rudyard Kipling story in which she stars as the American granddaughter of the crusty British commander (C. Aubrey Smith) in northern India, where she has a glorious time playing a soldier of the queen under the tutelage of a seasoned sergeant (Victor McLaglen), then stops a border uprising by befriending the local rebel chief (Cesar Romero). Director John Ford gets some lively humor from the ranks of the military post, together with a few good battle scenes, but does best with Shirley parading around in her kilted uniform and the by-play with the burly McLaglen. Colonial rhetoric doesn't impede the sentimental fun. A-I (PG)

Week-End with Father (1951) Sentimental family comedy in which a widower (Van Heflin) with two young girls courts a widow (Patricia Neal) with two young boys, but their spoiled offspring do their best to break them up, then have a change of heart, and conspire to bring them back together. Directed by Douglas Sirk, the formula proceedings are mired in contrived misunderstandings and slapstick situations, mostly in a summer-camp setting which is as bogus as the story. Synthetic fare. A-I (br)

Weekend (1968) Apocalyptic French vision of modern civilization's self-destruction is constructed out of a disjointed narrative of motorized mayhem, dehumanized people, and mindless revolution. Directed by Jean-Luc Godard, the movie's attempts to shock and its static militant speeches become simplistic attacks on traditional morality and existing social values. O (nr)

Weekend at Bernie's (1989) Silly, one-joke farce about two witless, low-level executives (Andrew McCarthy and Jonathan Silverman) who hide the fact that their boss (Terry Kiser) has been murdered so they can take advantage of his weekend beach-house invitation. Director Ted Kotcheff knocks the conscienceless, self-absorbed hedonists who don't notice that their host is dead, but the main focus is on how easy it is to lie to get whatever you want in the way of materialistic ambitions. Alcohol and drug abuse, sexual innuendoes, and implied necrophilia. O (PG-13)

Weekend at Bernie's II (1993) Moronic sequel set in the Caribbean, where two junior executives (Andrew McCarthy and Jonathan Silverman) pass off the corpse of their boss (Terry Kiser) as alive so they can get the funds he embezzled to clear their reputations. Writer-director Robert Klane's witless comedy resorts to a voodoo subplot in which the corpse becomes a dancing zombie, but nothing can save a script that was already dead on arrival. Disrespectful treatment of a dead person, some mild sexual innuendo, and tasteless gallows humor. A-III (PG)

Weekend at Dunkirk (1966) French sergeant (Jean-Paul Belmondo), among the mass of troops trapped by the Germans in the Dunkirk pocket in June 1940, has to decide whether to try to escape with the British, desert and return home, or stay and be captured. Directed by Henri Verneuil, the beaches of Dunkirk were a bitter French defeat, and this movie is a grim picture of war without any of the usual movie heroics. A-III (br)

Weekend in Havana (1941) Lightweight musical comedy in which a steamship official (John Payne) escorts a disgruntled passenger (Alice Faye) on a free trip to Cuba, where she's romanced by a con-man (Cesar Romero) whose girlfriend (Carmen Miranda) raises a storm before all ends happily. Directed by Walter Lang, the fluffy tale of a shop-girl's dream vacation has some amusing moments, but not enough to make it memorable entertainment. Romantic complications. A-II (br)

Weekend Murders (1972) Routine Italian mystery movie in which the relatives (among them, Anna Moffo) of a deceased British earl gather at his plush estate to learn of their legacies, fall prey to grisly pranks, sexual dalliances, and ultimately five murders. The real villain of the piece is director Michele Lupo, who indulges in acute camera angles, and wears out his zoom lens in a supreme display of technique over talent. A-III (R)

Weekend Pass (1984) Four sailors just out of boot camp hit Los Angeles on a weekend pass in this mediocre effort. Writer-director Lawrence Bassoff has put a variety of Los Angeles backgrounds to good use, but his script is thoroughly pedestrian. Although veering toward romantic wholesomeness, some graphic, utterly gratuitous nudity in an early cabaret sequence is highly offensive. O (R)

Weird Science (1985) Two high-school nerds conjure up their idea of the perfect woman (Kelly LeBrock) on a computer and have all their dreams of popularity and wild adventure fulfilled. Essentially a one-joke affair, written with an excess of rough language, and directed with too many sexual inferences by John Hughes, it's a vulgar, mediocre effort which does a hard sell of promiscuity to teenagers. O (PG-13)

Welcome Home (1989) Shot down over Cambodia in 1970, an Air Force flyer (Kris Kristofferson) is officially declared dead, but 17 years later, when illness separates him from his new Cambodian family, he returns to the States to renew ties with the American family he left behind. As directed by Franklin J. Schaffner, this weepy melodrama fails to shed light on the very real problems facing Vietnam veterans and their kin. Some profanity and an adulterous sexual encounter. A-III (R)

Welcome Home Roxy Carmichael (1990) A small town anticipates the return of their one Hollywood celebrity, but none more eagerly than her former beau (Jeff Daniels), now a family man, and an alienated 15-year-old (Winona Ryder) who suspects Roxy may secretly be her mom. Director Jim Abrahams takes a basically frivolous story, and, helped by Ryder's fine performance, develops it with charm, warmth, and a small dose of insight about human relationships. References to a premarital relationship, minimal vulgar expressions, and a flash of nudity. A-II (PG-13)

Welcome Home, Soldier Boys (1972) Four Vietnam vets (Joe Don Baker, Alan Vint, Paul Koslo, and Elliott Street) pull into the sleepy hamlet of Hope, N.M., gang-rape a girl, kill everyone in town, and then burn it to the ground. Directed by Richard Compton, the gruesome and ultimately cynical movie contributes nothing to understanding the problems of Vietnam veterans. O (R)

Welcome to L.A. (1977) Listless and pretentious account of the amorous adventures of a young songwriter (Keith Carradine) whose charm is such that women jostle and trample one another in a mad rush to enjoy his favor. Writer-director Alan Rudolph's unsurprising message is that sex without love is unrewarding, and that Los Angeles has some sort of monopoly on self-deception. Gratuitous nudity. O (R)

Welcome to Sarajevo (1997) Fact-based story of a world-weary British TV journalist (Stephen Dillane) who grimly reports on civilian massacres in war-torn 1992 Sarajevo, then attempts to smuggle a 10-year-old girl back with him when he returns to London. By focusing on the touching story of one child's fate, director Michael Winterbottom's semi-documentary hits home emotionally in decrying the insanity of genocide. Some violence, numerous gory corpses, fleeting nudity, and occasional rough language. A-III (R)

Welcome to the Club (1971) Generally witless comedy about a naive Quaker morale officer (Brian Foley) who attempts to integrate a postwar Hiroshima officer's club, and comes off more as a fool than as a nice guy going through some sobering disillusionment. Directed by William Shenson, the result is rather depressing, and, whatever its good intentions in trying to satirize both the military and bigotry, it contains considerable offensiveness, notably foul language. O (R)

Welcome to the Dollhouse (1996) Painfully funny story of a geeky 11-year-old suburban girl (Heather Matarazzo) and her efforts to become popular, which are continually undermined by her mom, siblings, and taunting classmates. Writer-director Todd Solondz insightfully and unsentimentally captures the seventh grader's nightmare existence, which just a little kindness from those around could dramatically change for the better. Fleeting violence, some sexual references, and recurring rough language. A-III (R)

Wells Fargo (1937) Interesting saga of the title overland express as portrayed in the exploits of its field agent (Joel McCrea), who forges the line from New York to St. Louis in the 1840s, establishes an office in 1850 San Francisco, then constructs a series of relay stations from Missouri to California on the eve of the Civil War. Directed by Frank Lloyd, the story is paced by frontier action and colorful pioneer lore, but the agent's marriage to a Southern belle (Frances Dee) adds some dark melodramatics that cloud the last portion of the picture. Stylized violence and domestic strife. A-I (br)

Went the Day Well? (1942) Small but intriguing British picture of what might happen if German paratroopers dressed as British soldiers took control of a rural English village to prepare the way for an invasion. Directed by Alberto Cavalcanti from a Graham Greene story, the story focuses on how the villagers come to suspect the deception and begin to fight back while trying to alert the Home Guard. Wartime violence involving civilians. A-II (br)

Werewolf, The (1956) Pedestrian monster fantasy directed by Fred F. Sears has a poor fellow (Steven

Ritch) roaming the US countryside after being turned into a wolf-man by a botched radiation experiment. Stylized violence and unconvincing chills. A-II (br)

Werewolf of London (1935) Creaky but still effective monster tale in which a botanist (Henry Hull) is bitten by a werewolf while searching for a rare flower in Tibet, then returns to London with the plant, only to learn too late its bloom is an antidote to becoming a wolf-man. Directed by Stuart Walker, the twisty plot has the Tibetan werewolf (Warner Oland) turn up as a respected professor who steals the blooms for himself, leaving London to be terrorized by the botanist-wolf-man during the four nights of the full moon. Stylized fantasy violence and menace. A-II (br)

Wes Craven's New Nightmare (1994) In the sevebth of the **Nightmare on Elm Street** horror series, an actress (Heather Langenkamp) and her little boy (Miko Hughes) begin having violent nightmares, which trigger the return of maniac Freddy Krueger (Robert Englund) who makes repeated attempts at killing them. Writer-director Wes Craven unreels a trite series of mother-and-child-in-peril situations in a suspenseless sequel featuring smug cameo appearances by the director and his studio boss. Some horror-fantasy violence, frequent menace to a child, and a few instances of rough language. A-III (R)

West Point Story, The (1950) Strained musical romance in which a down-on-his-luck Broadway director (James Cagney) is required to live as a cadet while staging the military academy's annual revue (headed by Gordon MacRae), with some help from his devoted assistant (Virginia Mayo) and a friendly movie star (Doris Day). Directed by Roy Del Ruth, the dim plot's contrived romances are strictly formula fare, with only the academy setting and Cagney's energetic song-and-dance numbers to hold interest. Comic violence, romantic complications, and much duplicity. A-II (br)

West Side Story (1961) Rousing Broadway musical, with choreography by Jerome Robbins and music by Leonard Bernstein, is a contemporary, inner-city adaptation of the classic Romeo and Juliet theme, with Richard Beymer and Natalie Wood playing the star-crossed lovers set apart ethnically and by their opposing street-gang backgrounds. Directed by Robert Wise, the picture captures the grit of life in the city's lower depths, with glimmers of hope and elements of tragedy in a delicate balance, carried along by song and the dance numbers that pulsate with energy and verve. Some of the social issues, relationships, and street language, however, require a mature perspective. A-III (br)

Westbound (1959) Standard Western about a Union officer (Randolph Scott) put in charge of a stagecoach line carrying California gold past Confederate sympathizers (led by Andrew Duggan). Directed by Budd Boetticher, it offers the usual brand of heroics and villainy but little else. Stylized violence. A-I (br)

Western Union (1941) A reformed outlaw (Randolph Scott) and a rich tenderfoot (Robert Young) help a Western Union engineer (Dean Jagger) fight off Indians and Confederate raiders (headed by Barton MacLane) while stringing the last link in the telegraph line connecting the east and west coasts in 1861. The heroic theme is directed by Fritz Lang, with plenty of Western action and colorful characters galore, including Slim Summerville's comically fearful cook. Frontier violence and Indian stereotypes. A-I (br)

Westerner, The (1940) Cowboy Gary Cooper sides with the sod-busters against the cattlemen led by Roy Bean (Walter Brennan), the hanging judge of Vinegaroon, Tex. Directed by William Wellman, the situation is familiar but flavorsome and wryly fashioned, particularly Brennan's performance as the ornery judge whose ideal is the English singer, Lily Langtry. Periodic stylized violence. A-I (br)

Westward the Women (1951) Distaff Western chronicles the adventures of 140 women (Denise Darcel, Marilyn Erskine, Hope Emerson, et. al.) recruited in Chicago as prospective brides for California settlers, making their way cross-country in a wagon train led by a tough but increasingly bemused wagon-master (Robert Taylor). Directed by William A. Wellman, there are plenty of dangers and some losses along the trail, but the trek's sentimental ending is never in doubt. Stylized frontier violence and mild sexual references. A-II (br)

Westworld (1973) James Brolin and Richard Benjamin vacation in a futuristic resort where, during the fun and games, a Western gunslinger robot (Yul Brynner) malfunctions, turns on the vacationers, and starts to stalk them. Unfortunately, after about ten minutes, writer-director Michael Crichton has explored all the subtleties of the one-idea situation. Some ludicrous nonsense about "willing" female robots. A-III (PG)

Wetherby (1985) Vanessa Redgrave plays a schoolteacher in a small town who becomes the indirect victim of an act of violence that seems to be wholly unprovoked. But was it? This superbly acted but somewhat thin and contrived murder mystery, written and directed by playwright David Hare, explores the question of suicide in a careful, literate, and sometimes compelling fashion. Good entertainment for mature viewers, although there is some violence and a few fairly restrained bedroom scenes. A-III (R)

Whales of August, The (1987) Two aged sisters (Bette Davis and Lillian Gish), sharing a cottage on an island off the coast of Maine, rely upon each other, since one is blind but wealthy, and the other is poor but kind. Director Lindsay Anderson's picture of old age and sibling rivalries is finely told through mood and characterization, and though sentimental, it is full of heart and small truths. Some incidental profanity. A-II (PG)

What? (1973) Innocent young woman (Sydne Rome) wanders into the house of an eccentric millionaire (Hugh Griffith) and is assaulted by various perverted characters, stripped of her identity as well as her clothes, and spends the rest of the movie in various stages of undress. Director Roman Polanski apparently intended this bizarre Alice in Wonderland story to be amusing, but its gross sexual activity and extensive nudity, as well as some violently scabrous language, make it anything but. O (X/R)

What a Way to Go! (1964) Deadly one-joke comedy told in flashbacks, as psychiatrist Bob Cummings listens to widow Shirley MacLaine explain how the untimely demise of husbands Dick Van Dyke, Paul Newman, Robert Mitchum, and Gene Kelly left her enormously wealthy, but all she wants is penniless janitor Dean Martin. Directed by J. Lee Thompson, the lumbering production glitters with period costuming and décor, but the witless plot and humor are painfully heavy-handed. Much sexual innuendo. A-III (br)

What About Bob? (1991) Multi-phobic kook (Bill Murray) drives his shrink (Richard Dreyfuss) bonkers by tagging along on the doctor's family vacation at a New Hampshire lake. Frank Oz's relaxed direction picks up speed halfway through, providing ample lightweight laughs in predictable predicaments. Some mildly vulgar expressions and cartoonish violence. A-II (PG)

What Am I Bid? (1967) The son of a country-music star decides to forgo cattle auctioneering and launch his own singing career is the thin story line used to showcase some old and new talent in the world of country and western music. Written and directed by Gene Nash, it's pleasant if unimaginative entertainment. A-I (br)

What Became of Jack and Jill? (1972) Paul Nicholas and Vanessa Howard are the title characters who gruesomely plot the death of Jack's 78-year-old grandmother (Mona Washbourne) so they can enjoy London with the old lady's money. The moral of this rather improbable, mediocre little horror is offset by director Bill Blain's sleazy resort to a lot of ogling, pawing, and some attic sex. O (GP)

What Did You Do in the War, Daddy? (1966) The combination of bosomy Italian girls and a local wine festival sidetrack a platoon of invading GIs (Dick Shawn, Carroll O'Connor, James Coburn, Cameron Mitchell, and Aldo Ray) who are supposed to be out after Nazi troops. Directed by Blake Edwards, vulgarity and dumb sight gags are the order of the day in a movie presumably showing that war isn't hellish at all but just a lot of off-color fun. O (br)

What Do You Say to a Naked Lady? (1970) Allen Funt employs the familiar hidden camera techniques of the TV show, except that here he focuses on nudity as a supposed source of humor. Unfortunately, the use of unsuspecting victims confronted with completely naked men and women walking out of office elevators or flagging down taxis shows no more maturity or insight than the silly pranks on the TV show. O (X/R)

What Dreams May Come (1998) Gooey afterlife fantasy in which a doctor (Robin Williams) killed in a car crash is reunited with his deceased children in the hereafter, then chooses to seek out his artist wife (Annabella Sciorra) in hell following her suicide. While director Vincent Ward's painterly visuals are exquisite, the incoherent treatment of afterlife reunions renders the movie largely unappealing. A suicide, theme of reincarnation, and minimal profanity and rough language. A-III (PG-13)

What Happened Was ... (1994) Unsettling two-person drama about a middle-aged paralegal (Tom Noonan) and a thirtyish secretary (Karen Sillas) in the same firm whose awkward first date begins with dinner in her Manhattan studio and ends up revealing both as very troubled adults, quite unlike the workaday personalities they project. Also written and directed by Noonan, the dramatic situation is intriguing as a reflection of the loneliness of urban life and the individual's need to have some sense of belonging. Concerns regarding emotional intimacy, some sex and drug references, and occasional rough language. A-III (R)

What Lola Wants (see: **Damn Yankees**)

What Price Glory (1952) Stagy remake of the 1926 original, with Captain James Cagney and Sergeant Dan Dailey as brawling Marines in WW I France, where they battle over a barmaid (Corinne Calvet) before going back into the line. Director John Ford lets the romance slide in favor of manly horseplay and military heroics, with disappointing results. Wartime violence and romantic tomfoolery. A-II (br)

What Price Hollywood? (1932) Alcoholic movie director (Lowell Sherman) turns a waitress into a top star (Constance Bennett) who marries a handsome stuffed shirt (Neil Hamilton), with predictable results. Director George Cukor's dated period piece plays the Hollywood scene first for laughs, then tragedy, with a good supporting cast including Gregory Ratoff, Eddie Anderson, and Louise Beavers. Mild black stereotyping, romantic complications, and a suicide. A-III (br)

What's Eating Gilbert Grape (1993) A compassionate stranger (Juliette Lewis) helps a frustrated young man (Johnny Depp) deal with the burden of heading a dysfunctional household consisting of his mom (Darlene Cates), who's a 500-pound recluse, and his mentally disabled younger brother (Leonardo DiCaprio), who is often a danger to himself. Though the narrative sometimes ambles and rambles, director Lasse Hallstrom's offbeat, often downbeat, drama features finely honed performances and a poignant script that never insults the emotional, mental, or physical frailties of its characters. An implied affair and brief violence. A-III (PG-13)

What's Good for the Goose (1970) Failed British movie in which a glum bank manager (Norman Wisdom) is introduced to the psychedelic world of free love, loud music, and general aimlessness by an uninhibited hitchhiker (Sally Geeson) who is always ready to disrobe and jump into bed. Directed by Menahem Golan, the movie's attempt to pass this off as social comment fails to overcome the exploitative elements that predominate. O (R)

What's Love Got to Do with It (1993) Musical biography of rock singer Tina Turner (played by Angela Bassett) focusing on her rise to fame and troubled marriage to abusive husband Ike (Laurence Fishburne), until she left him and established a solo career. Director Brian Gibson serves up a spirited but ultimately superficial look at the entertainer, offsetting the ugly hysterics of a violent relationship with glossy musical set-pieces. A discreet bedroom scene, some intense domestic violence, occasional recreational drug use, and recurring rough language. A-III (R)

What's New Pussycat? (1965) Wacky plot about a demented psychiatrist (Peter Sellers) whose efforts to sort out his hectic life bring him into contact with an inordinate number of loony types (Peter O'Toole, Paula Prentiss, Capuchine, Woody Allen, and Ursula Andress) running free and easy, in and around Paris. Directed by Clive Donner, the laughs in this attempt at screwball comedy are only intermittent, and their taste level is abysmally low. O (br)

What's So Bad About Feeling Good (1968) Colorful tropical bird infects the rude, scowling citizens of New York City with a mysterious happiness virus, and within hours everyone is smiling and polite to one another, including George Peppard and Mary Tyler Moore playing reformed hippies. But when New Yorkers also quit gambling, smoking, and drinking, the government develops an antidote to protect their tax revenues. Produced and directed by George Seaton, it's an amusing little satire on urban life that some may find infectious. Romantic complications. A-III (br)

What's the Matter with Helen? (1971) Two mothers (Debbie Reynolds and Shelley Winters) with a troubled past start a dance school for children in 1930s Hollywood, until poor Shelley goes bonkers and puts her entire rabbit warren to the knife. Director Curtis Harrington has a lot of fun with the gaudy period settings and fashions, but mixes in a bit too much blood and gore for younger viewers, but they wouldn't appreciate Reynolds's tap dances and tangos anyway. A-III (GP)

What's Up, Doc? (1972) Funny, stylish, and entertaining comedy loosely strings two plots together, one involving a group of four identical valises, the other following a kooky student (Barbra Streisand) in her zany pursuit of an absentminded college professor (Ryan O'Neal) who has come to San Francisco with his persistent fiancé (Madeline Kahn) to receive a research grant. Produced and directed by Peter Bogdanovich, this throwback to the Hollywood screwball comedies of the 1930s is great fun for family audiences. A-I (G)

What's Up Tiger Lily? (1966) Woody Allen's reediting and dubbing of a Japanese spy movie is at times amusing, often self-conscious, but mostly tiresome. Some smutty dialogue and visuals. O (br)

Whatever (1998) Downbeat coming-of-age story of two high-school seniors (Liza Weil and Chad Morgan) from dysfunctional families who sneak out to drug parties and try casual sex, but end up going in very different directions. Writer-director Susan Skoog captures the adolescent angst of rudderless girls lacking parental guidance, but the unsentimental narrative is flawed by one girl's sudden transformation. Brief violence, teen promiscuity, much substance abuse, frequent rough language, fleeting nudity, and occasional profanity. A-IV (R)

Whatever Happened to Aunt Alice? (1969) Suspense thriller with Geraldine Page as a widow, left without any observable means of income, who combines murder and gardening as profitable pastimes in bilking a series of housekeepers out of their life savings. Routine chiller directed by Lee H. Katzin. A-II (PG)

Whatever Happened to Baby Jane? (1962) Overdone chiller in which a child movie star is now a dotty middle-aged woman (Bette Davis) living in a crumbling Hollywood mansion with her hated sister (Joan Crawford) who was a popular movie actress, until an accident left her an invalid dependent upon her sibling whom she comes to fear intends to kill her. Directed by Robert Aldrich, the slow-paced proceedings focus on the conflict between the sisters, with Davis snarling out of control as Crawford calculates her options, though the situation grows tiresome long before the twist ending. Stylized violence, some of it quite nasty, and intense sibling rivalries. A-III (br)

Wheel of Fortune (see: **A Man Betrayed**)

Wheeler Dealers, The (1963) Romantic comedy about a cunning Texas high-roller (James Garner) who falls for a Wall Street broker (Lee Remick), then is indicted for helping her sell stock in a product that went out with high-button shoes. Director Arthur Hiller's comic treatment of stock-market hijinks is no longer as wacky as it once seemed, though the characters still please. Romantic situations. A-II (br)

When a Man Loves a Woman (1994) After an airline pilot (Andy Garcia) discovers that his wife (Meg Ryan) has become a secret alcoholic, they get professional help, but each must learn to change destructive behavior patterns in order to save their marriage and nurture their two small daughters. Despite its sometimes soggy treatment, director Luis Mandoki's inspirational drama is credible in its depiction of the tragic consequences of alcoholism on a family and its wrenching struggle for recovery. Scenes of drunkenness with fleeting nudity and minor violence as well as intermittent rough language. A-III (R)

When a Stranger Calls (1979) Homicidal maniac (Tony Beckley) stalks a babysitter (Carol Kane) in this plodding, mediocre thriller directed by Fred Walton. Some intense violence and the impending threat of violence are adult fare. A-III (R)

When Dinosaurs Ruled the Earth (1971) British

production directed by Val Guest is a few cuts above the average prehistoric monster movie which, aside from some Hollywood bikinis on the cave-women, has some authentic-looking overgrown reptiles, birds, and dinosaurs. It's an enjoyable movie for the youngsters, not too scary, and colorful enough to hold short attention spans. A-I (G)

When Eight Bells Toll (1971) British adaptation of an Alistair MacLean novel about a Bond-type government agent (Anthony Hopkins) and his gentle partner (Corin Redgrave), who are dispatched to the Western Highland lochs to find out what lies behind the disappearance of several gold-carrying ships. Directed by Etienne Perier, the plot employs masterful twists and cross currents, but though handled with restraint, it is adult fare both in story and treatment. A-III (GP)

When Father Was Away on Business (1985) Yugoslavian production set in the time of Tito's break with the Soviet Union has a plot following a philandering husband who is denounced by his mistress as a political deviant and ends up in a labor camp. This warm human comedy by director Emir Kusturica ends in the resolution of personal problems and political differences during a madcap wedding feast of family forgiveness. Some coarse language and partial nudity are treated with restraint. A-III (R)

When Harry Met Sally ... (1989) Story of the unlikely ways people connect with suitable marriage partners focuses on the comic and touching travails of one couple (Billy Crystal and Meg Ryan) over a dozen years as they wander in and out of each other's lives. Director Rob Reiner's comedy about love, commitment, sex, and friendship inter-cuts distracting testimonials from elderly couples about how they met. Though there is much graphic talk about sex and love in Yuppieland, and an indiscreet spoof of female orgasm, the movie demonstrates that true love and commitment are still here to stay. Implied sexual promiscuity. A-IV (R)

When Night Is Falling (1995) A solemn young woman (Pascale Bussieres) on the verge of marriage to a Protestant theology professor (Henry Czerny) chooses instead to join a traveling circus to be with her lesbian lover (Rachel Crawford). Writer-director Patricia Rozema's romanticized lesbian love story heavy-handedly presents the young teacher's crisis in faith, marriage, and career as no match for the exotic creature who awakens latent homosexual desires. Positive portrayal of homosexuality, extended sex scenes with nudity, and occasional rough language. O (nr)

When Strangers Marry (1944) Twisty crime tale in which a bride (Kim Hunter) gets some help from a former beau (Robert Mitchum) when she comes to suspect her secretive husband (Dean Jagger) is a murderer. Directed by William Castle, the plot is overly contrived, but the characters invite sympathy and most viewers will be unsurprised by the trick ending. Menacing situations and romantic complications. A-II (br)

When the Cat's Away (1997) Seriocomic tale of a lonely Parisian (Garance Clavel) who gets lots of help searching for her lost cat, particularly from older women, but others prove more interested in romance than locating the missing feline, until the picture's sweetly hopeful ending. Writer-director Cedric Klapisch's wistful story of a single woman whose search for a pet turns into a quest for the right man to share her life is treated earnestly, yet with humor, in an odd series of unsuitable encounters before a real prospect finally turns up. Subtitles. Several restrained sex scenes, sexual references, coarse expressions, and occasional rough language. A-III (R)

When the Daltons Rode (1940) Forced off their land by a crooked developer (George Bancroft), the Dalton brothers (Broderick Crawford, Brian Donlevy, and Stewart Irwin) become feared outlaws, though a steadfast friend (Randolph Scott) tries to clear their name. Directed by George Marshall, the old story is played for all its worth until the final demise of the Dalton Gang in a Kansas City shootout. Stylized violence. A-II (br)

When the Legends Die (1972) Above average Western in which a sharp rodeo-hustler (Richard Widmark) takes in an 18-year-old Ute Indian (Frederic Forrest) and teaches him the tricks of the trade, but the youth does not see the value in taking money from suckers and returns to the reservation, sadder but wiser. Produced and directed by Stuart Millar, the fine character study of the two principals is chiefly what is of interest here, and not its commonplace message. Implied sexual affair. A-III (PG)

When the West Was Young (1933) Western movie from a Zane Gray story about a bushwhacked surveyor (Randolph Scott) who helps a horse rancher (J. Farrell McDonald) and his ward (Sally Blaine) fight off an outlaw gang. Director Henry Hathaway embellishes the simple action tale with colorful details and an appealing romantic subplot. Frontier violence. A-I (br)

When the Whales Came (1989) Some 70 years after an 1844 legend about a curse befalling England's Scilly Isles for slaughtering a pack of beached whales, a deaf hermit (Paul Scofield) manages to successfully warn neighboring islanders to lay off some newly beached whales. In a tedious adaptation of Michael Morpurgo's children's book, director Clive Rees lets a lovely story with the gentle hermit, two island children, and an ecological theme get bogged down in boring extraneous action and predictable period caricatures. Occasional menace involving parental abuse and minimal rough language. A-II (PG)

Where There's Life (1947) Minor screwball comedy in which a New York radio announcer (Bob Hope) learns he's next in line to the throne of a tiny European country after a royal emissary (Signe Hasso) arrives to protect him from a band of rebels (headed by George Zucco) sent to kill him. Directed by Sidney Lanfield, Hope is in good form as the frantic announcer whose pursuers include his hapless fiancé

(Vera Marshe) and her irascible policeman brother (William Bendix). Comic menace and mild sexual innuendo. A-II (br)

When Time Ran Out (1980) Paul Newman, Jacqueline Bisset, Burgess Meredith, Ernest Borgnine, and other unfortunates are trapped on a Pacific island when the local volcano lets go. Directed by James Goldstone, the disaster epic is so dreadful that it could have put an end to the disaster epic once and for all. A-II (PG)

When Trumpets Fade (1998) WW II tale of an embittered private (Ron Eldard) who becomes a hero in spite of himself when his infantry unit is mauled by the German Wehrmacht during the 1944-45 Battle of the Hurtgen Forest along the Belgian-German border. Directed by John Irvin, the television production re-creates the inhuman carnage of the battlefield with special-effects realism, but its anti-war story never gets beyond the usual movie stereotypes of men in war, especially the heroic anti-hero at its center. Gory battlefield violence, coarse humor, numerous sexual expletives, and occasional profanity. A-III (R)

When Worlds Collide (1951) With Earth doomed to destruction by an onrushing star, scientists build a rocket ship to serve as a new Noah's ark, hoping to continue the human race on a new planet. Director Rudolph Mate's doomsday scenario is about as convincing as the wooden romance between Barbara Rush and Richard Derr, though the special effects by producer George Pal help build some interest in the desperate situation. Apocalyptic fantasy which may trouble young children. A-II (br)

When You Comin' Back, Red Ryder? (1979) A half-crazed Vietnam vet (Marjoe Gortner) and his hippie girlfriend (Candy Clark) terrorize and humiliate five people (notably Lee Grant and Pat Hingle) in a roadside diner in a desolate region of New Mexico. Though there are some credible performances in this adaptation of Mark Medoff's play directed by Milton Katselas, its psychological as well as physical violence and frequent sexual crudities destroy whatever social comment may have been intended. O (R)

Where Angels Fear to Tread (1992) Satiric comedy filters through tragedy in E.M. Forster's turn-of-the-century story of a wealthy English widow (Helen Mirren) who impulsively marries a penniless young Italian (Giovanni Guidelli) against the wishes of her in-laws. As directed by Charles Sturridge, the cultural clash between fiery Italian and straight-laced Britons affords several well-observed character studies. Brief violence. A-II (PG)

Where Angels Go ... Trouble Follows! (1968) Weak sequel to **The Trouble with Angels** in which a liberal young nun (Stella Stevens) tries to update the convent boarding-school under a traditionalist Mother Superior (Rosalind Russell) by leading a busload of nuns and students to a peace rally. Directed by James Neilson, the old pros in the cast (Binnie Barnes, Mary Wickes, Van Johnson, Robert Taylor, and others) overcome the painfully contrived story and turn it into light, unsophisticated entertainment. A-I (G)

Where Danger Lives (1950) Dark, muddled tale of a doctor (Robert Mitchum) on the run from the police with the wife (Faith Domergue) of the man (Claude Rains) he believes he killed. Directed by John Farrow, the tension is artificial in a situation that has little interest. Stylized violence and romantic complications. A-II (br)

Where Does It Hurt? (1972) Failed comedy about a slick California hospital whose administrator (Peter Sellers) divides his time between fleecing unwitting patients and molesting the pretty females on the staff. Directed by Rod Amateau, the result is not only unfunny, but unrelentingly tasteless and offensive. O (R)

Where Eagles Dare (1969) A spy-counter-spy melodrama set in the Bavarian Alps during WW II pits Richard Burton, Clint Eastwood, and Mary Ure against what must be half the German army ensconced in a castle literally inaccessible except by cable car. Brian Hutton directs the Alistair MacLean script which consists of an interminable, totally implausible series of killings, escapes, and pyrotechnic displays. A-III (PG)

Where It's At (1969) Las Vegas casino owner (David Janssen) teaches his disinterested son (Robert Drivas) the tricks of exploiting the tourist trade, but the lad beats his father at his own game, gains control of the casino, and then hands it back, realizing it is his father's whole life but will never be his. Director Garson Kanin tries to gloss over a most implausible script by resorting to some sexual diversions. O (R)

Where Love Has Gone (1964) Trashy sudser from Harold Robbins's novel about an artist (Susan Hayward) who divorces her war-hero husband (Michael Connors) after he's driven to drink by her domineering mom (Bette Davis), then takes a series of lovers, until their 15-year-old daughter (Joey Heatherton) murders one of them. Directed by Edward Dmytryk, the soapy proceedings are dressed up in a glossy production whose shallow characters waste the talents of the cast. Stylized violence including a suicide and much sexual innuendo. A-III (br)

Where the Boys Are '84 (1984) Four women college students (Lisa Hartman, Lorna Luft, Wendy Schaal, and Lynn-Holly Johnson) go to Fort Lauderdale for the spring break and carry on like amateur hookers, but viewers are supposed to believe its very wholesome and therapeutic. Director Hy Averback's updating of a silly 1960 movie contains nudity, sexually oriented humor ,and an appalling moral outlook. O (R)

Where the Buffalo Roam (1980) Bill Murray portrays famed underground journalist Hunter S. Thompson, who seems to have derived much of his inspiration from drugs and alcohol. Director Art Linson tries to blend serious social concern with outrageous comedy but is only intermittently successful. Rough language and use of drugs. A-III (PG)

Where the Heart Is (1990) Pointless, humorless farce about a wealthy demolitions expert (Dabney Coleman) who attempts to teach his three grown but spoiled offspring a lesson in self-sufficiency by leaving them stranded in an abandoned Brooklyn tenement. Director John Boorman shows little sensitivity to family responsibilities and is offensively crass in dealing with minority issues and the reality of homelessness. Some nudity in the context of artwork, rough language, and sexual innuendoes. A-III (R)

Where the Lilies Bloom (1974) Four sturdy Appalachian children keep the death of their widowed father a secret so the state won't take them away to an orphan's home and provide for themselves out of the profits of "wildcrafting" (collecting and preparing certain herbs and wild flowers prized for their medicinal qualities). The Robert B. Radnitz production directed by William A. Graham tells its story of youngsters learning to care for themselves in the adult world with warm humor and genuine sensitivity for the conditions of life for the rural poor. A rare and satisfying entertainment for the entire family. A-I (G)

Where the Sidewalk Ends (1950) Quirky crime story of a hardened cop (Dana Andrews) who accidentally kills a suspect, then falls for the dead man's girlfriend (Gene Tierney) while trying to pin the murder on a slippery mobster (Gary Merrill). Director Otto Preminger diverts attention from the improbable plot twists by focusing on the gritty atmosphere and matching characterizations. Stylized violence and troubled relationships. A-II (br)

Where Were You When the Lights Went Out? (1968) Typical Doris Day vehicle revolving around a woman's honor seemingly compromised but untarnished in the final reel. The only novelty here is that the story is placed in the context of the 1965 power failure that darkened New York City, and director Hy Averback does get some good comic bits from Robert Morse and Terry-Thomas, who are caught up in the contrived circumstances of the plot during the Great Blackout. A-III (PG)

Where's Charley? (1952) Cheerful musical adaptation of "Charley's Aunt," the creaky stage farce about an Oxford undergraduate (Ray Bolger) who is forced by circumstances to impersonate his friend's dotty old aunt from Brazil ("where the nuts come from"). Directed by David Butler and filmed in Britain, the action is rather stilted, but the songs by Frank Loesser and George Abbott range from good to delightful, notably "Once in Love with Amy," with Bolger's song-and-dance numbers providing the movie's highlights. Romantic complications. A-I (br)

Where's Jack? (1969) British adventure story set in 18th-century London about a locksmith's apprentice (Tommy Steele) turned thief and highwayman by necessity and a popular hero by virtue of his incredible escapes from prison. Director James Clavell carefully ensures that the cruelty and violence of the period do not overpower the human values of loyalty and comradeship that are at its heart. A-II (G)

Where's Poppa? (1970) New York lawyer (George Segal) tries to cope with his senile mother (Ruth Gordon) by hiring a nurse (Trish Van Devere) to care for her. Directed by Carl Reiner, the situation becomes a black-humored nightmare, with gags involving rape, muggings, nursing homes, and other human ills, going beyond the line of tastelessness. O (R)

Which Way Is Up? (1977) A poor fruit-picker (Richard Pryor) suddenly finds himself the chosen tool of the powerful and in a position to be rewarded amply for his subservience. Directed by Michael Schultz and adapted from Lina Wertmuller's **The Seduction of Mimi**, the serious nature of the comedy is fatally undercut by Pryor's too-broad performance. Excessive reliance on foul language and sex to get laughs. O (R)

Which Way to the Front? (1970) Jerry Lewis directs as well as stars as a man who, when rejected by the army in WW II, forms his own little fighting force composed of similar rejects, defeats the Axis in Europe, and proceeds to win the war in the Pacific. Some isolated skits are funny, but on the whole, the poor timing and dull material make the comic fantasy seem interminable. Fantasy violence. A-II (G)

Whiffs (1975) Elliott Gould plays a medically discharged Army private whose use as a chemical warfare guinea pig has, among other ill effects, left him impotent. Gould gets his revenge, and cures his malady, by using stolen Army gas to disable an entire town and clean out its banks. Director Ted Post does nothing to redeem a singularly unfunny and tasteless screenplay, many of whose failed jokes have to do with the hero's sexual incapacity. O (PG)

While You Were Sleeping (1995) Endearing screwball comedy in which the family of a comatose yuppie (Peter Gallagher) mistakenly believes he's engaged to a Chicago El token attendant (Sandra Bullock), who's actually attracted to the man's gentle brother (Bill Pullman), though neither will admit they're falling in love. Director Jon Turteltaub strengthens a predictable love story by fleshing it out with appealing characterizations of the brothers' big-hearted Catholic family and their wise Jewish neighbor (Jack Warden). Mild sexual innuendo and minimal profanity. A-III (PG)

Whisperers, The (1967) Dame Edith Evans gives a brilliant performance as an impoverished old woman, beset by loneliness and physical infirmity, victimized and abandoned by an unfeeling husband and son, and finding her only comfort in the world of her imagination. Directed by Bryan Forbes, it is a compassionate examination of the struggles of old age and achieved without false sentimentality. A-II (br)

Whispering Smith (1948) Off-beat Western in which a soft-spoken railroad troubleshooter (Alan Ladd) has to go after his best friend (Robert Preston) when he teams up with a crook (Donald Crisp). Directed by Leslie Fenton, the railroad setting has some interest as does the soured friendship, though the story's treatment is fairly routine. Frontier violence. A-I (br)

Whispers in the Dark (1992) Lurid, violent melodrama has a psychiatrist (Annabella Sciorra) seeking help from her mentor (Alan Alda) after one of her patients (Deborah Unger) is murdered and her lover (Jamey Sheridan) and another patient (John Leguizamo) become prime suspects. Writer-director Christopher Crowe exploits sexual violence against women in a manipulative, tawdry potboiler. Recurring violence and nudity, graphic photos of tortured women, sexually explicit dialogue and situations, and much rough language. O (R)

Whistle Blower, The (1987) Veteran spy Michael Caine finds a way to avenge the death of his son, a British intelligence agent, without jeopardizing his position in the international club of spy organizations. British director Simon Langton's murder mystery has a plot device concerning infidelity and a far more subtle, pulpy, and pernicious political bite, which may confuse youngsters and certainly annoy sophisticated adults. A-III (PG)

Whistle Stop (1946) Unrewarding tale of a woman (Ava Gardner) who revisits the hick town in which she grew up, then finds herself caught between the surly loafer (George Raft) she was once sweet on and a smooth-but-hardened club owner (Tom Conway). Director Leonide Moguy focuses on the feuding males and their criminal pursuits, including attempted robbery and murder, leaving scant time for the story's romantic intentions. Stylized violence and sordid atmosphere. A-III (br)

Whistling in the Dark (1941) Dated but still amusing comedy in which a mild-mannered radio actor (Red Skelton) plays the role of a brilliant detective so well, he's kidnapped by the leader (Conrad Veidt) of a bogus cult who wants him to devise a foolproof way to murder a wealthy cult member. Directed by Sylvan Simon, the silly radio-era proceedings provide a solid comedy vehicle for the bumbling, good-natured antics of Skelton in his first starring role. Mild comic menace. A-I (br)

White (1994) Left penniless and homeless when divorced by his beautiful French bride (Julie Delpy) on the grounds of impotence, a Polish hairdresser (Zbigniew Zamachowski) amasses a fortune in Warsaw in hopes of luring her there for a devious reconciliation. Directed by Krzysztof Kieslowski, the murky and underdeveloped characterizations result in an ambiguous black comedy in which love is subjugated to power, greed, and sexual prowess. Subtitles. Some violence, a few bedroom scenes, and instances of rough language. A-III (R)

White Balloon, The (1996) A seven-year-old girl living in Teheran goes to buy a plump goldfish for the Islamic New Year's celebration, but loses the money down a street-side grate and enlists the aid of harried passersby to retrieve it before nightfall. Producer-director Jafar Panahi's Iranian production tells its simple tale in real time from the youngster's perspective, with much of its appeal coming from the varied reactions of those called upon to help the child. Subtitles. Distraught youngster. A-II (nr)

White Buffalo, The (1977) Ponderous Western in which nightmares of a charging white buffalo bring Wild Bill Hickok (Charles Bronson) to the Black Hills in 1874, where, after a respite with an old friend (Kim Novak) and shootouts with old enemies, he teams with Sioux chief Crazy Horse (Will Sampson) in quest of a four-legged Moby Dick. Directed by J. Lee Thompson, the characters brood a good deal between vigorous spurts of action, with picturesque Dakota locales helping distract attention from the pretentious dialogue and phony-looking beast. Stylized violence, a sexual encounter, course expressions, and several profanities. A-III (PG)

White Christmas (1954) Cheerful but synthetic musical comedy about two WW II veterans (Bing Crosby and Danny Kaye) who use their popularity as entertainers to make a success out of the winter resort opened by their wartime commander (Dean Jagger). Directed by Michael Curtiz, the post-war feel-good plot is less memorable than Kaye's clowning and Crosby's crooning of the title song among other Irving Berlin numbers originally written for the earlier, better **Holiday Inn** (1942) pairing Crosby with Fred Astaire. While not a classic, it offers some good family entertainment. A-I (br)

White Cliffs of Dover, The (1943) Dated patriotic sudser about an American tourist (Irene Dunne) whose whirlwind marriage to an English aristocrat (Alan Marshal) ends with his death in WW I, but their child (Roddy McDowell) inherits the title and grows to become a military casualty (Peter Lawford) in WW II. Directed by Clarence Brown, it's an earnest, well-crafted sermon on Anglo-American relations, with too little humor and too much bathos to be convincing. Of some interest as a period piece. A-II (br)

White Comanche (1968) Dubbed European production directed by Gilbert Lee Kay has William Shatner playing twin brothers born of a captive white woman and a Comanche brave — one raised by whites, the other by Indians — until they meet on opposite sides in a range war that the local sheriff (Joseph Cotten) has been unable to stop. Hokey plot and treatment paced with assorted stylized violence, including an off-screen rape. A-III (br)

White Dawn, The (1974) Challenging fact-based story of three whalers (Warren Oates, Tomothy Bottoms, and Lou Gossett) marooned in the 1890s on Baffin Island, 700 miles below the North Pole, are taken in by local Eskimos, but their initial warm relationship degenerates into mistrust and finally vengeance as the two alien cultures threaten each other. Directed by Philip Kaufman, the corrupting influence of civilization on the savage innocence of the natives is depicted in realistic, often grisly, detail, and

Eskimo sexual customs are treated without sensation or exploitation. A-III (R/PG)

White Fang (1991) While hunting for gold with an older prospector (Klaus Maria Brandauer) on the Alaskan frontier in 1898, a youth (Ethan Hawke) befriends a snarling, attack-trained wolf-dog that helps them fend off marauders. Director Randal Kleiser's version of the Jack London novel combines authentic Alaskan settings, untamed wildlife, and a mildly suspenseful adventure to make diverting family fare for all but young children. Much simulated violence to animals and menace to humans. A-II (PG)

White Fang 2: Myth of the White Wolf (1994) Accompanied by his wolf-dog, a young gold-miner (Scott Bairstow) in 1906 Alaska sets out to find food for a starving Native American tribe, falls in love with their princess (Charmaine Craig), and uncovers a dastardly plot against them. Director Ken Olin's scenic but uninspired sequel to Jack London's tale of a lad and his canine in the wilderness is a standard outdoors adventure with scenery-chewing stick villains and pat solutions involving aboriginal mysticism. Some stylized violence. A-II (PG)

White Hunter, Black Heart (1990) Egotistical director (Clint Eastwood) persuades a writer friend (Jeff Fahey) to collaborate on making a movie in Africa, but once there the director's obsession with killing a bull elephant puts the entire project in jeopardy. Eastwood also produced and directed this blandly uninvolving adaptation of a novel about director John Huston's experiences while filming **The African Queen**, but the result is best enjoyed for its on-location cinematography. Minimal violence and vulgar expressions. A-II (PG)

White Lightning (1973) Routine country melodrama in which hard-driving Arkansas moonshiner (Burt Reynolds) is paroled from prison in order to get the goods on a county sheriff (Ned Beatty) who is not only taking graft but also murdered Reynolds's kid brother. Crisply directed by Joseph Sargent, the fragmented story of rough backwoods codes and justice is of less interest than the high-powered car chases that keep the dust swirling on those backcountry roads. Some romantic escapades. A-III (PG)

White Line Fever (1975) Young trucker Jan-Michael Vincent fights corruption in director Jonathan Kaplan's passably entertaining, though needlessly violent, action movie. Benign attitude toward vigilantism. A-III (PG)

White Man's Burden (1995) Race-reversal story in which an unjustly fired white man (John Travolta) rashly kidnaps his company's African-American owner (Harry Belafonte), unsure what to do next, as each begins to gradually open up to the other's different perceptions of life. Writer-director Desmond Nakano flips racial stereotypes in a heavy-handed yet thought-provoking narrative that has occasional insights on the irrationality of prejudice. Brief violence and much rough language. A-III (R)

White Men Can't Jump (1992) While trying to hold onto his hot-tempered girlfriend (Rosie Perez) and elude loan sharks, a white basketball player and small-time con-artist (Woody Harrelson) meets his match in a black street-hustler (Wesley Snipes) who joins in on his scams. Writer-director Ron Shelton drops the ball early on in this shrill comedy of pointlessly tiresome macho posturing. Continual rough language, brief bedroom shots, much gambling, and some nasty menace. A-III (R)

White Mischief (1988) Fact-based story of the debauched lifestyles of wealthy British colonists living near Nairobi, Kenya, in 1940-41, and the doomed adulterous affair between a rogue earl (Charles Dance) and the beautiful young wife (Greta Scacchi) of an aged landowner (Joss Ackland). Director Michael Radford depicts an exotic, decadent society whose people exhibit few morals, little political or social conscience, and no remorse. Treatment includes graphic sexual scenes, much explicit sexual language, and some intense violence. O (R)

White Nights (1985) Excellent dance sequences highlight this contrived story of a dissident American tap-dancer (Gregory Hines) and a Russian ballet star (Mikhail Baryshnikov) who join forces in escaping from the Soviet Union. Director Taylor Hackford gets little suspense from a muddled plot clogged with political posturing, but Twyla Tharp's choreography generates some cultural excitement for those interested. Some romantic complications and coarse language. A-II (PG-13)

White Palace (1990) A 27-year-old yuppie (James Spader) is embarrassed by his affair with a common and much older waitress (Susan Sarandon) who insists on brutal honesty in their relationship. Luis Mandoki directs a moderately interesting story of a couple who find sex before love and then struggle to overcome age and class differences in hopes of surviving as a couple. Emphasis on an unmarried sexual relationship, some partial nudity, and minimal rough language. A-IV (R)

White Sands (1992) Investigating a man's mysterious death by assuming his identity, a persistent New Mexico cop (Willem Dafoe) finds himself up against a slippery arms-dealer (Mickey Rourke), a seductive heiress (Mary Elizabeth Mastrantonio), and a quicksilver FBI agent (Samuel L. Jackson). Roger Donaldson directs a well-acted thriller marred by a dense, confusing story-line. Recurring violence, a sexually suggestive scene with momentary nudity, and frequent rough language. A-III (R)

White Sister (1973) Uneven Italian melodrama about the Mother Superior (Sophia Loren) of a hospital in northern Italy whose confrontations with one of the male staff (Adriano Celentano), a lusty malingerer and a communist to boot, leads inevitably to a rather idealized romance, very platonic, but serious enough to make both parties come to mature decisions about their lives. Director Alberto Lattuada plays it broadly, offering some pithy comic moments in the best tradition of Italian social comedy, but not enough to overcome the story's underlying sentimentality. A-III (R)

White Squall (1996) Fact-based account of a 1961 voyage in which the skipper (Jeff Bridges) of a floating prep school takes a dozen adolescent lads on an around-the-world cruise, until a freak storm drowns some of the students and crew, leading to a maritime inquiry into the skipper's culpability. Director Ridley Scott's sluggish character study finally gives way to harrowing scenes of the storm's violence, its tragic results, and the sober reflections of the survivors. Some sexual innuendo and crude references, fleeting violence, and intermittent profanity. A-III (PG-13)

White Squaw, The (1956) Low-budget Western directed by Ray Nazarro in which a mixed-blood Sioux woman (May Wynn) gets some help from a cowboy (David Brian) in trying to stop an Indian-hating rancher from driving her people off their lands on a Wyoming reservation. Stylized violence, including an attempted sexual assault. A-II (br)

White Tower, The (1950) While vacationing in Switzerland, an American (Glenn Ford) joins a party of climbers (Alida Valli, Claude Rains, Oscar Homolka, and Lloyd Bridges) trying to scale an unconquered peak. Directed by Ted Tetzlaff, the Alpine grandeur of the location climbing sequences far surpass the pretentious studio-bound character study of who will make it to the top. Much danger and some stylized violence. A-I (br)

White Zombie, The (1932) Dated but still eerie tale of the living dead set in Haiti, where a dissolute plantation owner (Robert Frazer) pays a voodoo master (Bela Lugosi) to turn a beautiful visitor (Madge Bellamy) into a zombie, and all seems lost, until the power of love proves stronger than that of evil. Director Victor Halperin's nightmarish fantasy succeeds as an atmospheric chiller, despite the melodramatic treatment and technical limitation of early sound movies. Scary visuals, sexual situations, and supernatural hooey. A-III (br)

Who Done It? (1942) Comic murder mystery with Bud Abbott and Lou Costello as soda jerks who turn detectives when the head of a radio network is murdered, and, despite a series of blunders, they capture the killer atop a New York skyscraper. Directed by Erle C. Kenton, the boys are in good form, and the frantic chases are helped by a good cast (including secretary Mary Wickes and cops William Gargan and William Bendix). Slapstick violence. A-I (br)

Who Framed Roger Rabbit (1988) Down-and-out 1940s Hollywood gumshoe (Bob Hoskins) attempts to clear the name of murder suspect Roger Rabbit, a cartoon stunt-clown. Director Robert Zemeckis and animator Richard Williams achieve a seamless interaction of animated and human characters in this touching, hilarious movie. Some scary threats of violence and humorous sexual references. A-II (PG)

Who Is Harry Kellerman and Why Is He Saying Those Terrible Things About Me? (1971) Wealthy composer-singer of pop hits (Dustin Hoffman) is a 40-year-old schizophrenic whose life is being pulled apart by personal and business problems, and to top it all off, some guy named Harry Kellerman is calling all of his girlfriends and saying "terrible things" about him. Directed by Ulu Grosbard, the confused psychodrama is too introverted, too slick, and too specialized to appeal to a wide audience. Adult themes, brief nudity, and some rough language. A-III (R)

Who Is Killing the Great Chefs of Europe? (1978) Screen version of the novel by Nan and Ivan Lyons about an epicurean publisher (Robert Morley) of a gourmet magazine, from whose list of the world's best chefs are being murdered one by one in the manner of the preparation of their specialty. Ted Kotcheff's heavy-handed direction doesn't help a talented cast including Jacqueline Bisset, Jean-Pierre Cassel, Philippe Noiret, Jean Rochefort, and George Segal. Some violent visuals and much tasteless humor. A-III (PG)

Who Killed Doc Robbin? (1948) Dated family fare from producer Hal Roach and director Bernard Carr features a gang of kids (including Larry Olsen, Eilene Janssen, and Gerald Perreau) trying to find the missing part to an atomic energy machine in a spooky mansion with hidden passages and a hokey gorilla. Comic black stereotyping. A-I (br)

Who Killed Mary What's'ername? (1971) No one really much cares, except a rich, diabetic, former boxing-champ (Red Buttons) who sets out to track down the killer of a Greenwich Village hooker. Director Ernie Pintoff doesn't seem able to cope with the twisted plots and tangled lines of this rather sordid mystery story. A-III (GP)

Who Says I Can't Ride a Rainbow? (1971) Fact-based story of Barney Morovitz (Jack Klugman), founder of PONY foundation, a homemade zoo in a rundown section of New York's Greenwich Village, who has to frantically relocate his enterprise after Big Business encroaches upon his cherished patch of ground. Directed by Edward Mann, besides the sincere acting of all involved, its chief merit is that it cares about youngsters, especially kids of different races who grow up together on the cold concrete streets of a big city. A-I (G)

Who Shot Patakango? (1990) Bouncy, nostalgia-drenched look at life in a Brooklyn vocational high school in 1957 borrows freely from **West Side Story**, with a working-class youth falling for an affluent suburban girl while trying to prevent an outside gang from inciting violence at his interracial school. Filmmakers Robert and Halle Brooks convey the vitality and innocence of the era, but their treatment of student life is sophomoric and sugar-coated. Some petty thievery played for laughs, sporadic minor violence, and a sexually ambiguous scene. A-III (nr)

Who Slew Auntie Roo? (1972) The best aspect of this garden-variety horror movie is its integration of the familiar Hansel and Gretel story with the on-screen tale, set in the turn-of-the-century English countryside, in which orphaned Mark Lester and Chloe Franks have been taken in by Shelley Winters, who in Lester's eyes is trying to fatten them up. Though Ralph Richardson and Lionel Jeffries steal some colorful moments in bit parts, under Curtis Harrington's direction most of the picture is drab and slow-moving. Some scenes may be too intense for younger viewers. A-II (GP)

Who'll Stop the Rain? (1978) Hard-edged screen version of a Robert Stone novel about a Vietnam war correspondent (Michael Moriarty) who sends his wife (Tuesday Weld) two kilos of heroin, but things go awry, and the wife, assisted by an old Marine buddy (Nick Nolte), are off on an existential odyssey, trailed by ugly thugs and corrupt policemen. Director Karel Reisz explores an America as full of dope, death, and depravity as the Vietnam which had generated the illicit cargo. Adult themes, drug use, and strong language. A-III (R)

Who's Afraid of Virginia Woolf? (1966) Director Mike Nichols's adaptation of the Edward Albee play amounts to a high-then-low-level encounter-group session involving two college faculty couples who thrash out their bitterness and frustrations during a semi-drunken evening. The main event features Richard Burton and Elizabeth Taylor, who are old veterans of marital bouts, while George Segal and Sandy Dennis are rank amateurs, and as the tension mounts and they begin going for each other's throats (verbally), the air turns rather blue. The very nature of the movie, with its rough language and unsavory slice of married life and human relationships, needs an adult's perception for full comprehension and understanding. It is definitely not an entertainment for the casual viewer. A-IV (br)

Who's Been Sleeping in My Bed? (1963) Vapid sexist comedy directed by Daniel Mann in which a soap-opera star (Dean Martin) is pursued by the wives (Elizabeth Fraser and Jill St. John) of his poker pals (Martin Balsam and Louis Nye), while his fiancé (Elizabeth Montgomery) engages in desperate tactics to get him to marry her. Inane sexual situations and innuendo. A-III (br)

Who's Harry Crumb? (1989) Dim-witted detective (John Candy) is enabled by good intentions and dumb luck to find a kidnapped heiress. Candy is dandy, but director Paul Flaherty has a field day with his larkish depiction of adultery. Sexually suggestive encounters and some rough language laced with sexual vulgarities. O (PG-13)

Who's Minding the Mint? (1967) Labored comedy about a needy US Mint employee (Jim Hutton), whose scheme to print money after hours relies on one too many hare-brained confederates (Jamie Farr). Directed by Howard Morris, the cast of thieves (Walter Brennan, Dorothy Provine, Milton Berle, Jack Gilford, Joey Bishop, Bob Denver, and Victor Buono) is better than the material. Comic treatment of crime. A-II (br)

Who's Minding the Store? (1963) Jerry Lewis comedy in which he makes a shambles of an entire department store, while in the process boosting sales and winning the girl (Jill St. John). Directed by Frank Tashlin, it's the usual slapstick affair with a good supporting cast (Agnes Moorehead, John McGiver, and Ray Walston) and plenty of sight gags, including an exploding golf machine. Strictly for Lewis fans. A-I (br)

Who's That Girl (1987) Dull and lifeless vanity production showcasing music idol Madonna as an ex-con trying to vindicate herself while ruining the marriage plans of her escort (Griffin Dunne). Director James Foley is unable to tone down the hard edge of the essentially irresponsible role model his star awkwardly creates in this failed action comedy of interest only to diehard fans. A-III (PG)

Who's That Knocking at My Door? (1969) Potentially interesting but unrealized attempt to show an Italian American youth's re-examination of his emotionally religious upbringing in relation to his sexual hang-ups. Director Martin Scorsese handles the subject with little depth or conviction and goes to extremes with a lengthy erotic montage. O (R)

Who's the Man? (1993) Bumbling Harlem barbers (comics Doctre Dre and Ed Lover) become rookie cops, then set out to solve the murder of their ex-boss (Jim Moody), whose barbershop is firebombed when he refuses to sell to a ruthless developer. Director Ted Demme overloads a goofy, hip-hop comedy by abruptly changing gears, tossing in the social concerns of the inner city without giving them the serious treatment they deserve. Occasional violence, some ethnic stereotyping, a few crude sexual references, and minimal rough language. A-III (R)

Whole Town's Talking, The (1935) Lively crime tale in which a timid accountant looks so much like a notorious gangster (Edward G. Robinson in a dual role) the police give him an ID pass, which the criminal forces him to share, until the worm turns to free a feisty co-worker (Jean Arthur) taken hostage by the gangster. Directed by John Ford, the humorously contrived plot mixes the comic menace with occasional edgy violence, but the main attraction is Robinson's dual performance as tough guy and milksop, often in the same frame. Stylized violence, threatening situations, and mild sexual innuendo. A-II (br)

Whole Truth, The (1992) Boring, longwinded, and utterly predictable account of two singles (Dyan Kane and Dan Cohen) who get together, break up, and then reunite. Also written and co-directed by Cohen, the shallow vanity production lacks romantic credibility and comic sensibility. Superficial treatment of a serious subject and occasional profanity. A-III (nr)

Whole Wide World, The (1996) Fact-based story of a 1930s Texas schoolteacher (Renee Zellweger) whose aspirations to be a writer lead her to seek out a reclusive local author of pulp fantasy tales (Vincent D'Onofrio), and their mutual interests grow into an ill-fated romance due to the man's dependence on his mother. Director Dan Ireland evokes the period well and gets strong performances from the leads, but the picture fails to distinguish between creative genius and dysfunctional personality, leaving viewers unmoved by what is intended as a poignant conclusion. Off-screen suicide, unsettling romantic complications, and occasional profanity. A-III (PG)

Wholly Moses (1980) Boring Biblical comedy in which the brother-in-law of Moses (Dudley Moore) believes he is the one entrusted with a mission from God. Directed by Gary Weis, its attempts at humor can best be described as tiresome, mirthless, and witless. Occasional vulgar jokes and some incidental irreverence. A-III (PG)

Whoopee! (1930) Primitive color version of the Ziegfeld stage musical, with Eddie Cantor as a nervous wreck vacationing on a lazy Western dude ranch until finding himself pursued by a posse, while helping the rancher's daughter reach her outcast boyfriend on an Indian reservation. Directed by Thornton Freeland, the hokey plot provides the comic context for Cantor's goofy clowning and corny one-liners, abetted by Gus Kahn's songs (notably "Making Whoopee") and Busby Berkeley's splashy production numbers. Some sexual innuendo and period comedy conventions that give offense today, including Native-American stereotypes and a black-face routine. A-III (br)

Whore (1991) A prostitute (Theresa Russell) provides those interested with a detailed account of the tricks of the trade and its degradations. Directed by Ken Russell, the low-budget production is tedious and unenlightening. Excessively graphic in its descriptions and simulations of sex acts, as well as occasional violence and profanity. O (NC-17)

Whose Life Is It, Anyway? (1981) Brilliant, witty sculptor (Richard Dreyfuss), paralyzed from an auto accident and dependent upon a dialysis machine and constant medication, retains a lawyer to force the hospital to release him, an action that will result in his speedy death. Directed by John Badham, the movie pits the patient's reasons for being allowed to die against his doctor's (John Cassavetes) determination to keep him alive at all costs. The treatment of the theme, as well as a nude sequence, make this questionable adult fare. A-IV (R)

Why? (1972) Italian morality tale about a family vacation that turns into a nightmare when the father (Alberto Sordi) is arrested for an unspecified crime, shunted from prison to prison, until finally accused of murdering a man he's never even heard of. By the time the mistake is cleared up and he is released, he is a broken man. Director Nanni Loy allows nothing to be overstated, but omits none of the harrowing details that indict a society that permits such bureaucratic indifference and brutal prison conditions to exist. A-III (PG)

Why Anna? (see: **Diary of a Schizophrenic Girl**)

Why Do Fools Fall in Love (1998) Musical melodrama misfires in the story of a rock'n'roll singer (Larenz Tate) who dies of a drug overdose in 1985, leaving three wives (Vivica A. Fox, Halle Berry, and Lela Rochon) to fight over a fortune in unpaid royalties. Directed by Gregory Nava, the result succeeds better in its re-creation of rock'n'roll's beginnings in the mid-1950s than in the flashbacks portraying the bickering widows' very different recollections of the same man who never becomes more than a cipher for viewers. Intense physical and psychological violence, explicit sexual situations, recurring rough language, and some profanity. A-IV (R)

Why Does Herr H. Run Amok? (1978) Tedious German melodrama about a hard-working, inoffensive husband who suddenly goes over the edge and murders his wife and children and some other people unfortunate enough to be within reach at the moment. Director Rainer Werner Fassbinder does not answer the question his title poses but simply records the events that end in such violent tragedy. A-III (nr)

Why Not! (1979) Thin French comedy directed by Coline Serreau deals with the lives and domestic habits of a cozy trio (Sami Frey, Mario Gonzales, and Christine Murillo) whose sleeping arrangements are quite complicated. Though the focus is not exclusively on sex, and there is an occasional droll sequence, its use of nudity and benign attitude towards moral anarchy are offensive. O (nr)

Why Would I Lie? (1980) Social worker (Treat Williams), who's also a compulsive liar, adopts a young boy (Gabriel Swann) and then tries to reunite him with his ex-con mother (Lisa Eichhorn). Directed by Larry Peerce, the pointless plot contains vulgarity, profanity, and a warm endorsement of promiscuity. O (PG)

Wichita (1955) Credible law-and-order Western directed by Jacques Tourneur portrays Wyatt Earp (Joel McCrea) as a mild-mannered frontiersman whose prowess with a gun leads him to reluctantly accept the job of keeping the peace in a booming cattle town. Anti-violence theme with considerable stylized violence. A-I (br)

Wicked Dreams of Paula Schultz, The (1968) Low burlesque about an East German woman decathlon champ (Elke Sommer) who tries to defect to the West rather than be sent to work in a tractor factory. Directed by George Marshall, the feeble attempts at humor resort to some very crudely contrived calendar-art shots and sequences, a lesbian joke, and other misguided attempts at humor. O (br)

Wicked Lady, The (1983) Thoroughly inept remake of a 1945 British Restoration-era movie about a bored English noblewoman (Faye Dunaway) who turns to highway robbery for diversion. Under Michael Winner's aimless direction, not only does Dunaway give a poor performance, but also cast adrift are Alan Bates, John Gielgud, Denholm Elliott, and Prunella Scales. Abundant nudity and crass vulgarity. O (R)

Wicked Stepmother (1989) Clunky horror spoof in which a modern-day witch (Bette Davis) and her equally diabolical confederate (Barbara Carraras) steal people's money after reducing them to the size of six-inch dolls, until stymied by a dedicated policeman (Tom Bosley). With Davis having only a few scenes, writer-director Larry Cohen tries to pad out the time with a jokey script and ludicrous acting. Some sexual references and occasional profanity. A-III (PG-13)

Wicked, Wicked (1973) Clumsy thriller about the hunt for a psycho (Randolph Roberts) who murders blondes checking into an old seaside resort whose new singer (Tiffany Bolling) sports a blonde wig. Written, produced, and directed by Richard L. Bare, the movie uses an ineffective split-screen process. Restrained sex and violence. A-III (PG)

Wicker Man, The (1980) British melodrama in which a police sergeant (Edward Woodward) is called to a small island off the west coast of Scotland to investigate the disappearance of a child whom, he finds, has been made a human sacrifice in a pagan rite. Directed by Robin Hardy, the movie shows signs of intelligence and sophistication, but its tragic ending is unprepared for by what has gone before. Excessive nudity. O (R)

Wide Awake (1998) Disarming tale of a nine-year-old Catholic schoolboy (Joseph Cross) whose depression over the death of his grandpa (Robert Loggia) leads him to search for signs that God and heaven really exist. Writer-director M. Night Shyamalan deftly captures the child's sincerity and suggests the caring presence of God in the boy's daily life as he comes to terms with his loss. Vivid depiction of juvenile grief and a few crude words. A-II (PG)

Wide Sargasso Sea (1993) Passions cool between a proper 1840s English gentleman (Nathaniel Parker) and his sensuous Jamaican bride (Karina Lombard) when he suspects she is using voodoo to bewitch him. Director John Duigan's turgid romance rarely ventures beyond the couple's melodramatic bedroom hysterics which end unhappily. Some simulated sex and frequent nudity. O (NC-17)

Widow Couderc, The (1974) Complex French melodrama set in the 1930s in which a killer (Alain Delon) hides out working on the farm of a widow (Simone Signoret), but life is so peaceful there that he begins thinking of it as home, until someone in the small, inbred rural community calls the attention of the police to the outsider. Director Pierre Granier-Deferre's picture of country life contrasts human frailty with the beauty of the natural order, lust with love, and death with life in a way which may discomfort some but evoke a sympathetic response in others. A-IV (nr)

Widows' Peak (1994) Whimsical period piece set in a 1926 Irish village, where scandal erupts when the arrival of a glamorous young widow (Natasha Richardson) upsets the delicate balance between an eccentric spinster (Mia Farrow) and the village's gossipy widows (led by Joan Plowright). Director John Irvin pours on the blarney in a fairly entertaining concoction that blends the hint of a murder mystery into a deftly acted comedy of manners. Some mild sexual references. A-II (PG)

Wifemistress (1979) Italian sex comedy in which a rich merchant (Marcello Mastroianni), implicated in a crime and forced into hiding in a building across the street from his home, observes the erotic as well as humanitarian activities of his formerly repressed wife (Laura Antonelli), who thinks he is dead. Directed by Marco Vicario, it is little more than a tepid and uninspired period comedy whose simplistic anti-religious views and frequent nudity are offensive. O (R)

Wilby Conspiracy, The (1975) Sidney Poitier and Michael Caine star in a political-chase melodrama set against the background of apartheid South Africa, but Nicol Williamson steals the show as a coolie fanatic policeman. Director Ralph Nelson's movie is taut and well-acted, but it is marred by some unnecessary sexual hijinks and a violent conclusion that sets up a moral problem beyond its depth. O (PG)

Wild America (1997) Unaware their 12-year-old brother (Jonathan Taylor Thomas) has hidden himself in their station wagon, two Arkansas teens (Devon Sawa and Scott Bairstow) set out to cross the country filming wildlife footage of endangered predators as they go in hope of both adventure and fame as documentary filmmakers. Directed by William Dear, the fact-based tale of these high-spirited lads has several scary moments in the bush, but otherwise their tame adventures are less effectively staged. Scenes with menacing animals, mild sexual innuendo, and a profanity. A-II (PG)

Wild and the Innocent, The (1959) Uneven Western in which a young trapper (Audie Murphy) picks up a runaway girl (Sandra Dee) on the trail to Casper, Wy., to sell his pelts, but there he falls for a fancy lady (Joanne Dru) whom he tries to reform, then has to rescue the runaway from the town's corrupt sheriff (Gilbert Roland). Directed by Jack Sher, the innocence of the two country bumpkins in the big, bad city is depicted with some sympathetic amusement, though the plotting is contrived and the ending heavy-handed. Stylized violence and veiled sexual innuendo. A-II (br)

Wild Angels, The (1966) Motorcycle gang movie with Peter Fonda and directed by Roger Corma is excessively violent, and its theme of social protest is bogus. O (br)

Wild at Heart (1990) Madly in love, a reckless couple (Nicolas Cage and Laura Dern) tear across the Deep South on the run from the law and killers hired by the girl's obsessive mother (Diane Ladd). Writer-director David Lynch captures the lovers' sensual passion, but the movie's sluggish pace is accentuated by a tiresome parade of psychotic characters, revolting images, and violent episodes that turn an upbeat ending into self-indulgent sham. Excessive violence, graphic sexual content, and much rough language. O (R)

Wild Bill (1995) Leaden Western depicting some of the shootouts which made Wild Bill Hickok (Jeff

Bridges) a feared gunfighter until confronted in 1876 by an inept youth (David Arquette) determined to avenge his mother's mistreatment by Wild Bill. Writer-director Walter Hill whizzes through Hickok's early exploits, then bogs down in a prolonged series of bizarre events, including opium dreams, hired assassins, and sex on a barroom table, before he is finally gunned down in Deadwood Gulch. Much stylized violence, a constrained sex scene, sexual innuendo, and coarse language. A-IV (R)

Wild Blue Yonder, The (1951) Routine WW II story directed by Allan Dwan centers on the camaraderie among the first group of pilots (Wendell Corey, Forrest Tucker, Phil Harris, and others) assigned in 1943 to fly the new B-29 bomber against Japanese targets in the Pacific. Wartime violence. A-I (br)

Wild Bunch, The (1969) William Holden and Ernest Borgnine star in director Sam Peckinpah's violent and unglamorized account of the end of an outlaw band who had outlived the frontier era. Though its intentions are to show the ugly reality underlying the Western movie myth, the general viewer is apt to find the work's brutality and several sexual scenes quite excessive. A-IV (R)

Wild Child, The (1970) Exceptional French dramatization about a young boy who was found in 1798 living as an animal in a forest and the doctor who, rather than place in an asylum, took him into his own home for more intense care. Director Francois Truffaut (who also plays the doctor) creates an austerity of image, settings, and music (Vivaldi) to mirror the child's alienation and gradual response to the doctor's openness. Most of all, the moving drama is an affirmation of the tireless efforts of educators to overcome environmental handicaps and an act of faith that humanity will survive in spite of itself. A-II (PG)

Wild Country, The (1971) Pittsburgh family (Steve Forrest, Vera Miles, Ron Howard, and Clint Howard) arrives in the Wyoming territory of the 1880s full of hope and fervor of the early settlers, but their farm is below expectations, their water supply jeopardized by cattlemen, and a devastating cyclone nearly destroys their homestead. Above-average Disney production directed by Robert Totten provides a wholesome, quality adventure story for solid family entertainment. A-I (G)

Wild Duck, The (1977) Pallid German adaptation of the Ibsen classic. Director Hans W. Geissendorfer unwisely opens up the play to the extent of showing Hedvig's cherished wild duck, but has made a much more critical mistake in casting a fat and clownish actor (Peter Kern) as the feckless but attractive Hjalmar. A-II (nr)

Wild Geese, The (1978) Richard Burton, assisted by Roger Moore, Richard Harris, and Hardy Kruger, lead a mercenary army to Africa to rescue a democratic African leader (Winston Ntshona). Although director Andrew V. McLaglen has a talented cast, a literate script, and some well-photographed action sequences, the complexity of its racial and political context are beyond the movie's capability to treat responsibly. The graphic nature of its brutal violence and accompanying rough language are excessive. O (R)

Wild Heart, The (1950) Dark tale of romance in 1897 Shropshire, where a wild country girl (Jennifer Jones) marries the local minister (Cyril Cusack), then is seduced by a devil-may-care squire (David Farrar), but ultimately returns contritely to her husband for a tragic ending. Directed by Michael Powell and Emeric Pressberger, the story's strange nature-girl is more than coy, but less than convincing, in her muddled ways, though the rustic setting of the Welsh-English border country is suitably moody, and its local folkways hold interest. Sexual situations. A-III (br)

Wild Hearts Can't Be Broken (1991) During the Great Depression, a blind 15-year-old orphan (Gabrielle Anwar) convinces a crusty stunt-show owner (Cliff Robertson) that she can ride a speeding stallion and leap into a pool of water as their new horse-diver — from 40 feet above Atlantic City's famed Steel Pier. Director Steve Miner's spunky heroine overcomes various obstacles and a harrowing tragedy in an inspiring, fact-based movie that shimmers in sun-drenched cinematography. Fine family fare. A-I (G)

Wild Heritage (1958) Mild frontier tale of two pioneer families headed by widows (Maureen O'Sullivan and Jeanette Nolan) who settle in a Western valley where they share a small herd of cattle, learn to fight rustlers, and are befriended by a helpful lawyer (Will Rogers, Jr.). Directed by Charles Haas, the uneven narrative centers on fatherless teenagers having to shoulder adult responsibilities, in particular, learning to handle a gun for an inevitable shootout with a pair of local badmen. Stylized violence. A-I (br)

Wild in the Country (1961) Soapy melodrama in which a troubled country youth (Elvis Presley) courts a nice girl (Millie Perkins) while pursued by a single mom (Tuesday Weld), then falls in love with an older woman (Hope Lange) who encourages him to become a writer. Directed by Philip Dunne from a script by Clifford Odets, the story is little more than glossy trash, though the cast is better than the roles, and the sentimental ending is classic hokum. Stylized violence, including a suicide attempt, romantic complications, and sexual innuendo. A-III (br)

Wild in the Sky (1972) Brandon de Wilde and two fellow draft-dodgers escape jail by commandeering a SAC bomber captained by Robert Lansing and try to make it to Cuba, as General Keenan Wynn back at SAC headquarters issues insane orders to stop them. Directed by William T. Naud, this low-budget flying Ship of Fools tries to work both the hijack and anti-war angles but is consistent only in its cheap vulgarities and exploitation of serious themes. O (GP)

Wild in the Streets (1968) Young pop-singer (Chris Jones) mobilizes America's youth, gets elected president, and puts everyone over 30 into concentration camps. Director Barry Shear tries to satirize the youth culture of the 1960s while exploiting it as well, but it is the kind of free-from-responsibility fantasy that is not good for adolescents. A-III (R/GP)

Wild Is the Wind (1957) Tangled romantic melodrama in which a prosperous Nevada sheep-rancher (Anthony Quinn) marries his dead wife's sister (Anna Magnani), but she rebels at his expectations of her being like her sister rather than being herself and turns for affection to the rancher's adopted son (Tony Franciosa). Directed by George Cukor, there are some high-powered naturalistic performances, but the contrived proceedings lessen their emotional impact and the story's credibility. Sexual situations and an extended sequence of a lamb's birth. A-III (br)

Wild Life, The (1984) Dreary sequel to **Fast Times At Ridgemont High** shows what happens to Eric Stoltz after he graduates and moves into a swinging-singles apartment complex. Directed by Art Linson, the proceedings feature the same sort of benignly viewed sexual amorality which permeated the first movie. Nudity and rough language. O (R)

Wild North, The (1952) Rugged outdoor adventure in Canada's frozen backcountry, where a Mountie (Wendell Corey) gets his man — a French-Canadian hunter (Stewart Granger) accused of murder — then needs his help to survive a series of disasters on the trail back. Directed by Andrew Marton, the plot is more than a little contrived, but the vigorous action is in keeping with the remote setting and the shifting relationship between captor and captive has a satisfying human dimension. Much menace and some brutal violence, notably an attack by starving wolves. A-II (br)

Wild One, The (1953) Motorcycle gang (headed by Marlon Brando) stops off in a small California town, and, after being joined by a rival gang (led by Lee Marvin), the bikers go on a rampage trashing the town and terrorizing its inhabitants. Directed by Laslo Benedek, the work has dated badly in subject and style, especially the romantic subplot with Mary Murphy, but there is still some edge in its early look at the violence in American counter-cultures. Much menace and stylized violence, including vigilante action. A-III (br)

Wild Orchid (1990) Boring voyeuristic exercise in titillation over the sexual awakening of an innocent young woman (Carre Otis) by a sleazy international operator (Mickey Rourke). Director Zalman King's hothouse fantasy about unappealing characters offers unrelieved tedium except for travelogue views of Rio de Janeiro and its environs. Several simulated sex acts. O (R)

Wild Orchid 2: Two Shades of Blue (1992) Dreary sex drama about a teenager (Nina Siemaszko) lured into very lucrative prostitution after the death of her addict father (Tom Skeritt). Writer-director Zalman King can't imbue this soft-core peep show with any redeeming qualities. Prostitution glamorized, much nudity, brief violence, drug abuse, and some rough language. O (R)

Wild Pack, The (1972) Produced, directed, and written by Hall Bartlett from a novel by Jorge Amado, the movie follows the fates of a gang of homeless children in Bahia, Brazil, as they struggle to survive on the fringes and in the slums of an indifferent South American society. It unfortunately clutters its statement of revolutionary protest with a romantic subplot and a graphic rape sequence. O (nr)

Wild Party, The (1975) Part musical, part study of late 1920s Hollywood decadence, and part compassionate character study of a silent-film comedian (James Coco) ruined by the coming of sound pictures. Directed by James Ivory, these diverse elements fail to fuse, and the result is an aimless, repetitious, and more than a little distasteful melodrama. Excessive sexual display. O (R)

Wild Racers, The (1968) American race-car driver (Fabian) gets a shot at the Grand Prix circuit and leaves behind a trail of a compliant women. Director Dan Haller intercuts stock racing-footage with numerous suggestive situations in the story of a man who values machines more than human beings. O (br)

Wild Reeds (1995) Coming-of-age tale set in 1962 rural France at the end of the Algerian war, when two boys and a girl confront issues of sex, class, and politics after a French-Algerian youth is placed in their high-school senior class. Andre Techine directs a slow yet sensitive story of youths facing adult realities during a turbulent period in French politics and society. Subtitles. Restrained portrayal of sexual encounters, brief nudity, sexual references, and an instance of rough language. A-III (nr)

Wild River (1960) Uneven 1930s story about an official (Montgomery Clift) from the Tennessee Valley Authority who tries to get an old woman (Jo Van Fleet) to leave her island home before it's flooded by a new dam, but falls for the woman's granddaughter (Lee Remick) in the process. Director Elia Kazan evokes the hard times of the Depression era and racial inequalities in the rural South, but the contrived love story only weakens the movie's theme of individual rights in conflict with the common good. Some stylized violence and an implied sexual relationship. A-III (br)

Wild Rovers (1971) William Holden and Ryan O'Neal are quite effective in this flawed but engagingly bittersweet study of ordinary cowpokes who dream of owning a little ranchero down in Mexico, rob a Montana bank, and head toward the distant border. Written and directed by Blake Edwards, the characterizations are its strong point, the plot rather shaky and slow-moving, and the resolution is a downer. Some brutal violence and a gratuitous bordello scene. A-III (GP)

Wild Season (1968) Belgian movie about the life of North Sea fishermen centers around a young boy who tries to prove to his father that he can be just as good a man as was the son lost at sea. Directed by Emil Nofal, the natural elements surpass the labored efforts of the actors, but younger audiences will enjoy the outdoor adventure aspects of the story without much concern about character motivations. A-I (nr)

Wild Seed, The (1965) A drifter (Michael Parks) reluctantly helps a young runaway (Celia Kaye) cross the country to find her father, but she gives up the search when they decide to get married. Directed by Brian Hutton, the contrived situation of the journey yields little interior growth in the two young people and the conclusion is not promising. Mature theme. A-III (br)

Wild Strawberries (1958) During the day on which he is to be awarded an honorary degree from a nearby university, a 78-year-old retired scholar (Victor Sjostrom in a masterful performance) is visited with dreams and reveries about his past life, especially his failures and disappointments in personal relationships. Swedish director Ingmar Bergman brilliantly develops the man's interior journey from pangs of regret and anxiety to a refreshing sense of peace and reconciliation summed up in blissful images of his happy youth. One of the great films about aging that touches universal chords in all viewers. English subtitles. A-III (br)

Wild Thing (1987) Orphaned child (Rob Knepper) grows up essentially on his own in the bowels of a deserted inner-city hovel and one day avenges his parents' death at the hands of ruthless drug-dealers while saving a young social worker (Kathleen Quinlan). Director Mac Reid uses the thematic razor's edge of revenge to mutilate scriptwriter John Sayles's childlike fable. Restrained violence and a scene of implied sex lessen the urban Tarzan yarn's suitability for youngsters. A-III (PG-13)

Wild Things (1998) Trashy potboiler in which a police detective (Kevin Bacon) investigates the rape accusations of two high-school seniors (Denise Richards and Neve Campbell) against their guidance counselor (Matt Dillon), then suspects all three are in cahoots to split the civil-suit settlement once the counselor is exonerated. Director John McNaughton's steamy soap opera twists into ludicrous triple crosses before smugly rewarding the most vile of the conspirators. Sporadic violence, various sexual encounters, full nudity, substance abuse, recurring profanity, and much rough language. O (R)

Wild Westerners, The (1962) Low-budget oater directed by Oscar Rudolph is set in 1864 Montana, where a US marshal (James Philbrook) is tricked into marrying a stranded showgirl (Nancy Kovack), then falls in love with her while rounding up a gang of gold thieves. Frontier violence and romantic complications. A-I (br)

Wildcats (1986) Goldie Hawn stars in this failed comedy about a woman coach of an inner-city high-school football team. Excessive amounts of streetwise profanity, brief nudity, and a scene involving simulated fornication make this vanity production by director Michael Ritchie off-limits for its intended youthful audience. O (R)

Wilder Napalm (1993) Seriocomic misfire about the showdown between two brothers, both born with telekinetic powers to make objects burst into flame, when the older (Arliss Howard) tries to keep the younger (Dennis Quaid) from exploiting this power to gain fame, fortune, and his brother's free-spirited wife (Debra Winger). Directed by Glenn Gordon Caron, the movie generates little interest as the conflict between the brothers over whether their unique power is a gift or a curse is slowly dragged out until the climactic fiery confrontation, with only occasional comic diversions to pass the time. Some special-effects violence, sexual situations, and coarse language. A-III (PG-13)

Wilderness Family, Part 2, The (see: **The Further Adventures of the Wilderness Family**)

Wilderness Journey (1972) In the far north, a 12-year-old Eskimo lad (Tony Tucker Williams) embarks on a courageous canoe journey to find his father (Richard Stitt), a hunting-party guide whose assistance is needed back home. The boy's adventure is made suspenseful and engrossing by Chuck D. Keen's superlative photography of the region and its wildlife and by the reverent narration explaining the tradition of the boy's ancestors. Directed by Ford Beebe, whose career in films dates back to 1914, the movie is splendid family entertainment. A-I (G)

Will Penny (1967) Fine Western about an illiterate, aging, but still capable cowhand (Charlton Heston) who, after the fall roundup, is sent to tend the cattle wintering in the hills, where he gives shelter to a lost pioneer woman (Joan Hackett) and her son until the spring thaw. Director Tom Gries has achieved a realistic portrait of a cowboy whose code of morality reflects the rigors of frontier life, the shortage of marriageable women, and the rudimentary nature of early Western justice. Some sadistic violence. A-III (br)

Will the Real Norman Mailer Please Stand Up? (1970) Low-budget documentary gives a rather interesting and fairly objective account of the life and times of popular author Norman Mailer, centering on his views and activities related to the anti-Vietnam movement. Unfortunately, the result provides little more than a superficial understanding of this enigmatic public figure, and the rather amateurish production further detracts from its value. A-III (nr)

Willard (1971) Horror fantasy about a psychotic young man (Bruce Davidson) who, after the death of his mother (Elsa Lanchester), trains an army of rats to exact revenge for the injustices heaped upon him and his family by a businessman (Ernest Borgnine), but alas, he trains the little beasties all too well. Tighter editing and pacing might have given director Daniel Mann a first-class horror movie, but, as it is, animal trainer Moe Di Sesso runs away with the prize for his direction of the rats. A-II (GP)

William Shakespeare's A Midsummer Night's Dream (1999) Fanciful adaptation of the Bard's comedy is updated to 1900 Tuscany in a magical forest where the fairy Puck (Stanley Tucci) causes all manner of romantic mix-ups overnight, casting spells on mismatched young lovers (including Christian Bale and Calista Flockhart), an aspiring actor (Kevin Kline), and the fairy queen (Michelle Pfeiffer). Some cast members excel while others do not in articulating Shakespearean dialogue in writer-director Michael Hoffman's whimsical adaptation whose luminous visuals look sprinkled with fairy dust. Romantic complications and fleeting nudity. A-III (PG-13)

William Shakespeare's Romeo and Juliet (1996) Ambitious adaptation of the classic tale of star-crossed lovers (Leonardo Di Caprio and Claire Danes) remains literally faithful to the original while updating the story to a contemporary US urban setting. Director Baz Luhrmann's flawed but never dull adaptation is visually operatic, highly stylized — and jarringly wedded to Shakespeare's Elizabethan language. Several violent deaths and romanticized suicides. A-III (PG-13)

Willie and Joe Back at the Front (see: **Back at the Front**)

Willie & Phil (1980) Writer-director Paul Mazursky's tale of a three-sided friendship begins with the 1970 meeting of Willie (Michael Ontkean) and Phil (Ray Sharkey) as they come out of a screening of Truffaut's triangle movie **Jules and Jim**, the inspiration for Mazursky's work. The trio is completed a few days later when they meet free-spirited Jeannette (Margot Kidder), and the movie follows their shifting relationships over the entire decade of the 1970s. Mazursky has created three charming characters and places their quest for meaning and fulfillment within the context of the ethnic, moral, and religious traditions each represents. However, the nature and treatment of the theme makes this strictly mature viewing. A-III (R)

Willie Dynamite (1974) Big city's most successful pimp (Roscoe Orman) vies with a reformed-hooker-turned-social-worker (Diana Sands) over the girls he tries to keep on the street, while she tries to get them off. Directed by Gilbert Moses, it is a lifeless, aimless, and meaningless attempt to blend outright black exploitation material with a sober examination of the psychology of the pimp and his women. The result is largely a waste of time. O (R)

Willow (1988) Fantasy adventure in which the tiny hero of the title (Warwick Davis) attempts at all odds to protect the baby girl prophesized to bring the downfall of the wicked sorceress (Jean Marsh) who rules the land. Directed by Ron Howard from a story by George Lucas, the tale is jam-packed with strangely shaped and oddly sized characters, forbidding medieval sets, and a complex plot. Breathtaking chases, dramatic sword-fights, and fearsome creatures may rattle the small fry. A-II (PG)

Willy Wonka and the Chocolate Factory (1971) Screen version of Roald Dahl's children's story about a candy manufacturer (Gene Wilder) who conducts an electrifying tour of his factory for the five lucky children who learn that greed and selfishness can be their own reward. Even the punishments, occasionally a bit gruesome for younger children, are in good fun. Director Mel Stuart manages to avoid the cloying sentimentality of similar children's movies, though it's never quite as magical as one would have hoped. A-I (G)

Wilson (1944) Historical dramatization follows the career of Woodrow E. Wilson (Alexander Knox) from New Jersey college president to US president during WW I and his tragic final years rallying support for the League of Nations. Directed by Henry King, the picture succeeds best as an elaborate, convincingly detailed re-creation of the period, but, with political events taking precedence over the human drama, the result is rather lifeless despite a fine cast including Charles Coburn, Cedric Hardwicke, Geraldine Fitzgerald, and Thomas Mitchell. A-I (br)

Winchester '73 (1950) After his prize rifle is stolen, a determined cowboy (James Stewart) sets out to find it and the man (Stephen McNally) who took it. Director Anthony Mann's meandering but energetic Western follows the trail through chance encounters with homesteaders, Indians, and outlaws before the final showdown reveals the personal nature of the cowboy's persistent quest. Stylized violence. A-II (br)

Wind (1992) After losing the America's Cup to Australia, a young sailboat skipper (Matthew Modine) teams with his ex-fiancé (Jennifer Grey) and her boyfriend (Stellan Skarsgard) to build a new boat for the rematch Down Under. Carroll Ballard directs a splendidly photographed but otherwise ordinary root-for-the-underdog picture that works best in the racing sequences. Implied premarital affairs. A-III (PG-13)

Wind and the Lion, The (1975) Writer-director John Milius takes some liberties with the 1904 incident in which Teddy Roosevelt (Brian Keith) thundered against a Moroccan brigand (Sean Connery) for kidnapping an American citizen (Candice Bergen). The historical facts are more interesting than this artificial romance/bogus adventure movie that glamorizes weapons and their use. Violence. A-III (PG)

Wind from the East (1972) French director Jean-Luc Godard's first directly political work, this 1969 effort fails both as a movie and as Maoist propaganda. Basically a film of ideas, its dialectical progress fitfully winds down to a final call for total revolution, but it is unlikely to persuade viewers to accept its convictions. A-IV (nr)

Wind in the Willows, The (1997) Charming live-action tale set in an English meadow, where timid Mole (Steve Coogan), kindly Rat (Eric Idle), and bold Badger (Nicol Williamson) must save reckless Toad (Terry Jones) from losing his country estate to evil Weasels. Also written and directed by Jones, this adaptation of Kenneth Grahame's 1908 children's classic is enhanced by an endearing cast, sprightly songs, lovely visuals, and a delightful sense of whimsy, which despite moments of menace translates into appealing family entertainment. A-I (PG)

Window, The (1949) Gritty thriller in which a young lad (Bobby Driscoll) witnesses a murder, but his parents (Arthur Kennedy and Barbara Hale) refuse to believe their highly imaginative son, until the murderer (Paul Stewart) corners him in an abandoned building. Director Ted Tetzlaff's minor suspense classic about the boy who cried wolf once too often gains considerable credibility from its working-class setting and creditable characters. Mounting tension and life-threatening situations. A-I (br)

Window to Paris (1995) Chaotic Russian fantasy in which the residents of a St. Petersburg apartment building discover a magical window through which they step daily into Paris, amassing consumer goods to take home, though a music teacher (Sergei Dontsov) dallies with an eccentric Parisian (Agnes Soral), and his young students refuse to return to their dreary city. Director Yuri Mamin carries the whimsical elements of the time-space warp to belabored extremes in a clash-of-cultures comedy haphazardly combining romance and political satire. Subtitles. Fleeting full nudity, occasional drunkenness, minor violence, and a few instances of rough language. A-III (PG-13)

Windows (1980) Failed thriller about a psychotic, homicidal lesbian (Elizabeth Ashley) who cherishes an unholy and, at times, quite noisy passion for a mousy friend (Talia Shire). Director Gordon Willis leaves his actresses to their own devices in the heavy-breathing and crying department while he devotes his energies to getting some exquisite views of the Manhattan skyline and landmarks. A brutal scene involving sexual assault is needlessly graphic. O (R)

Winds of the Wasteland (1936) Low-budget Western directed by Mack V. Wright tells of former Pony Express riders (John Wayne and Lane Chandler) who turn a ghost town into a growing community by bringing in a telegraph line and winning the area's mail contract from a dishonest competitor (Douglas Cosgrave) in an exciting stagecoach race. Frontier violence. A-I (br)

Windwalker (1981) A dying Cheyenne patriarch (Trevor Howard) yearns to see once again the son who was kidnapped by hostile Crows when he was an infant. Aside from the miscasting of Howard, director Keith Merrill has created an extremely authentic picture of Indian life told in an unusually absorbing story. Because of the violence and conflict essential to the plot, it is not suited to very young children, but for older ones, the dignity with which it portrays Indians and their culture recommends it highly. A-II (PG)

Windy City (1984) Written and directed by Armyan Bernstein, this story of young men growing up on the north side of Chicago with their dreams unrealized has some good acting (John Shea, Kate Capshaw, Josh Mostel, and Jim Borrelli) but can't overcome the handicaps of banal dialogue and sketchy characterizations. Considerable violence and gore. A-III (R)

Wing and a Prayer (1944) Dated WW II morale booster directed by Henry Hathaway pays tribute to the officers (Charles Bickford and Don Ameche) and pilots (Dana Andrews, William Eythe, Henry Morgan, and others) of an aircraft carrier during the Battle of Midway. Wartime violence and patriotic heroics. A-II (br)

Wing Commander (1999) Uninvolving space adventure set 600 years in the future, as a handful of interplanetary pilots (including Freddie Prinze, Jr., and Saffron Burrows) attempt to short circuit an invasion of Earth by a malevolent alien species. Director Chris Roberts adapts his line of Wing Commander computer games to the big screen with routine special effects, standard spaceship shootouts, and corny dialogue that add up to a sci-fi cipher. Frequent stylized fantasy violence, an implied sexual encounter, and a few crude references. A-III (PG-13)

Wings (1927) Silent-screen epic about two young men (Buddy Rogers and Richard Allen), in love with the same girl (Jobyna Ralston), who wind up in the same flying squadron during WW I, where their rivalry turns to friendship, until one of them is accidentally killed by the other. Clara Bow is the girl-next-door who follows Rogers to France as a nurse. Directed by William Wellman, it's a classic adventure film with a refreshing sense of innocence unembarrassed by any doubts about the justice of the actions of the principals. Stylized violence and romantic complications. A-II (br)

Wings and the Woman (1941) British wartime morale-booster about 1930s record-setting aviatrix Amy Johnson (Anna Neagle) and her aviator husband Jim Mollison (Robert Newton). Produced and directed by Herbert Wilcox, the fact-based story treats the dangers facing the era's pilots in proper stiff-upper-lip fashion, ending in a patriotic flourish lauding the role of women in the war effort. A-II (br)

Wings of Desire (1988) Art-house film follows the lonely work of two angels (Bruno Ganz and Otto Sander) who wander about and above Berlin listening to the joys and travails of people in libraries, a circus, and even on an American movie-set (starring Peter Falk as himself). One angel chooses to shed his wings for the chance of expressing human emotions and love for a woman. German director Wim Wenders is by turns ponderous, playful, reflective, and philosophic. Subtitles. Some sexually suggestive material, fleeting nudity, and some profanity. A-IV (PG-13)

Wings of Eagles, The (1957) Uneven but colorful bio of Frank "Spig" Wead (John Wayne), a pioneering naval aviator in the 1920s who became a writer after a spine injury in the 1930s. Director John Ford's sentimental tribute to the Navy has plenty of romanticized action and broad humor, with a solid cast including Maureen O'Hara as Wead's wife, Dan Dailey as his orderly, and Ward Bond as a Ford-like movie director. Much drinking and brawling, as well as some domestic strife. A-I (br)

Wings of the Dove, The (1997) Lovely rendering of Henry James's 1902 novel in which a young Englishwoman (Helena Bonham Carter) urges her impoverished lover (Linus Roache) to court the dying American heiress (Alison Elliott) they have befriended in hopes she will leave him her fortune. Under Iain Softley's astute direction, the myriad ways of the human heart delicately unfold in this fine character study. A few sexual encounters and brief nudity. A-III (R)

Wings of the Hawk (1953) Routine adventure in 1911 Mexico, where an American mining engineer (Van Heflin) tries to protect his gold strike by siding with the rebels against corrupt government forces (led by George Dolenz). Directed by Budd Boetticher, the story bogs down in the bickering among the rebels until they unite in the final showdown with the local military. Stylized violence. A-II (br)

Winner, The (1997) Uninvolving crime tale of a naive do-gooder (Vincent D'Onofrio) on a weekly winning streak in Las Vegas and how a manipulative lounge singer (Rebecca DeMornay), his estranged brother (Michael Madsen), and other lowlifes attempt to separate him from his winnings. Director Alex Cox trots out a half-dozen quirky, one-dimensional characters in a failed attempt to mix film *noir* with hip comedy. Some murderous violence, a fleeting sexual encounter, and frequent profanity, as well as rough language. A-III (R)

Winners, The (see: **My Way**)

Winning (1969) Paul Newman is ruggedly impressive as a race-car driver whose obsession with the track leads his neglected wife (Joanne Woodward) to dally with his chief competitor (Robert Wagner). Directed by James Goldstone, the movie is as slick and quick as the race cars that provide its action thrills, and its message boils down to the fact that sometimes winning is really losing. A-III (PG)

Winning Team, The (1952) Dramatized story of baseball pitcher Grover Cleveland Alexander (Ronald Reagan), a Nebraska farmer whose major-league career begins in 1911, then collapses in 1925 due to medical problems complicated by drinking binges, until given the chance to help the St. Louis Cardinals win the 1926 World Series. Directed by Lewis Seiler, the story holds interest, though the human drama is surprisingly flat, despite the emotional support given Alexander by his wife (Doris Day) and loyal friend, Cardinal player-manager Rogers Hornsby (Frank Lovejoy). A-I (br)

Winning Way, The (see: **The All-American**)

Winslow Boy, The (1999) Eloquent adaptation of Terence Rattigan's stage play in which a father (Nigel Hawthorne) in 1910 London believes the naval academy has wrongly expelled his 14-year-old son for stealing a five-shilling postal order, and at great cost, especially to his daughter (Rebecca Pidgeon), he engages a prominent lawyer (Jeremy Northam) to prove the lad's innocence. Writer-director David Mamet unfolds the story through elegant dialogue and a marvelous cast of characters, honing and sharpening, but not changing, Rattigan's period piece about British justice upholding the rights of a citizen against the power of the state. Heavy sledding for preschoolers. A-I (G)

Winter Guest, The (1997) Talky drama set on a bitterly cold day in a Scottish seaside town explores relationships between an elderly mother (Phyllida Law) and her widowed daughter (Emma Thompson), a pair of amorous teenagers, a couple of funeral-loving spinsters, and two boys playing hooky. Writer-director Alan Rickman's moody set-piece deals with themes of grief, friendship, and coming-of-age in lyrical but lethargic fashion. Sexual references and situations, brief nudity, frequent profanity, and much rough language. A-III (R)

Winter Kills (1979) Failed screen version of Richard Condon's novel about the brother (Jeff Bridges) of an assassinated US president who, years later, discovers that the actual assassin was not the man accused but another who was the agent of a vast and intricate conspiracy. Nothing makes much sense in this ill-conceived and badly executed melodrama, directed by William Richert, which exploits memories of a tragic moment in American history. Some scenes of graphic sex. O (R)

Winter People (1989) Melodramatic tale of love and revenge unfolds in the snowy hills of North Carolina during the Depression, when an honorable city man (Kurt Russell) tries to protect an unfortunate country woman (Kelly McGillis) from the wild mountain man who fathered her illegitimate child. Directed by Ted Kotcheff, its family feud subplot, while key to the suspense, is poorly realized, and its lush rural landscapes are wasted in an implausible period plot. Some rough language, a grisly bear hunt, and several scenes of sadistic violence. A-III (PG-13)

Winter Soldier (1972) During the winter of 1971, 200 men calling themselves Vietnam Veterans Against the War, sat before members of the press in Detroit and ruefully related their military experiences. The Pentagon refuted none of their testimony, which found its way into the Congressional Record. Eighteen anonymous friends of the veterans preserved the recollections of some of these men in a documentary which eminently deserves to be seen as part of the record of a very troubled time in the history of our nation. A-III (nr)

Winter Wind (1970) Hungarian director Miklos Jancso relates an incident about a Croatian anarchist in the 1930s who is considered a hero by his followers, but only after they have destroyed him. The film is not for casual viewers but those interested in foreign films or European politics will find it worth seeing. A-III (nr)

Winterset (1936) Depression-era drama from Maxwell Anderson's play in which a young drifter (Burgess Meredith) finds the gangster (Eduardo Ciannelli) who years before had committed the crime for which the youth's anarchist father (John Carradine) was executed. Directed by Alfred Santell, the theatrical style of the adaptation fairly creaks, but the justice theme and characterizations of good people in hard times still hold interest. Some stylized violence. A-II (br)

Wired (1989) Muddled movie about the self-destruction of media personality John Belushi (Michael Chiklis) who died of a drug overdose in 1982. Director Larry Peerce fails to mesh diverse and contradictory elements of a narrative told largely in flashbacks, but the movie's anti-drug stance is clearly unambiguous. Graphic depictions of substance abuse and much foul language. A-III (R)

Wisdom (1986) Ridiculous teenage Bonnie-and-Clyde team (Emilio Estevez and Demi Moore) show their defiance of adult authority and social injustice by destroying mortgage records. The vanity production, written and directed by Estevez, centers on an unhealthy preoccupation with guns and violence, along with profanity and casual sex. O (R)

Wise Blood (1980) Screen version of Flannery O'Connor's novel about a God-haunted young man (Brad Dourif) who on his way to Taulkinham, Tenn., to preach a new religion, meets such bizarre characters as a failed preacher pretending he is blind (Harry Dean Stanton), his mildly depraved daughter (Amy Wright), and a jovial evangelist (Ned Beatty). Director John Huston has made a powerful and provocative movie whose spiritual implications are as compelling as its artistic excellence. The incidental violence and moral complexity are more appropriate for adult viewers. A-III (PG)

Wise Guys (1986) Brian De Palma's brash and audacious parody of the gangster film relies too heavily upon profanity and violence as source of humor. Although Danny De Vito and Joe Piscopo create frantically likable but bungling small-time hoods, their stereotyped characterizations, along with others in the film, are likely to give offense to some Italian and Jewish viewers. O (R)

Wish You Were Here (1987) British director David Leland's sensitive, bittersweet evocation of a youngster's coming of age in a 1950s English coastal town focuses upon her sexual initiation, disappointments with her father, and encounters with the male-dominated working-class society of the period. The sexually explicit but emotionally accurate portrait of a young woman's discovery of self-worth and meaning deals responsibly with the issue of abortion, though takes a benign attitude toward birth control. Brief nudity and some vulgar language. A-III (R)

Wishing Machine, The (1970) Czechoslovakian children's story about two boys whose visit to an industrial fair leads them to imagine they can make a trip to the moon. Written and directed by Josef Pinkava, the movie (dubbed into English) has imaginative visuals and a pleasant story that small children will enjoy because it is, from beginning to end, entirely made for them. A-I (G)

Wishmaster (1997) Monster movie in which a powerful evil spirit can conquer the world if, after taking human form (Andrew Divoff), it's able to persuade a vulnerable young woman (Tammy Lauren) to make three wishes. Director Robert Kurtzman uses some imaginative visuals and special effects to enliven an otherwise routine horror film. Much fantasy violence, some of it gory, recurring rough language, and a few instances of profanity. A-III (R)

Witchboard (1987) The bloody consequences of fooling around with a Quija board are demonstrated in this horror tale of a young woman (Tawny Kitaen) whose jousts with an evil spirit manage to get her former boyfriend killed and her current lover nearly dismembered. Writer-director Kevin Tenney's story of the supernatural presents all its gory excesses and vulgarities in broad daylight. O (R)

Witches, The (1990) Uneven adaptation of Roald Dahl's contemporary fairytale in which a grandmother (Mai Zetterling) helps her nine-year-old grandson (Jasen Fisher) thwart the plans of the Grand High Witch (Anjelica Huston) to turn all of Britain's children into mice. Produced by Jim Henson and directed by Nicolas Roeg, the fantasy starts well and has some cute mice puppetry, but bogs down in the frenetic flamboyance of a witches' convention in a posh British spa. Some intense menace, several discreet sexual references, and an instance of profanity. A-II (PG)

Witches of Eastwick, The (1987) Jack Nicholson plays a devil summoned via the wishful thinking of three lonely, frustrated women (Cher, Susan Sarandon, and Michelle Pfeiffer) who allow themselves to be seduced and impregnated while living a life of reckless abandon at the demon's mansion. In director George Miller's version of John Updike's sardonic, allegorical novel about the battle of the sexes, the action is entirely on the sexual level, obscuring other dimensions of its theme while trying to find humor in vulgar excesses, promiscuous behavior, and sexually derived profanity. O (R)

Witches' Brew (1980) Jokey horror story about a college psychology professor (Richard Benjamin) who laughs at his wife (Teri Garr) for dabbling in witchcraft, then is terrified when a dying witch (Lana Turner) tries to switch places with her. Directed by Richard Shorr and Herbert L. Strock, the comic menace is too fitful to be funny and too contrived to be frightening. Eerie witchcraft rituals, a hokey supernatural monster, and sexual situations. A-III (PG)

Witchmaker, The (1971) Psychology professor (Alvy Moore) stupidly leads his students into the Louisiana swamplands to investigate a series of occult-oriented murders, where they succumb to spells cast by a maniacal fiend (John Lodge) who drains his victims' blood for use in satanic orgies. Written, produced and directed by William O. Brown, the feeble horror concoction keeps the camera at a distance from the mayhem. A-III (M/R)

With a Song in My Heart (1952) Glossy screen biography of singer Jane Froman (Susan Hayward) and her successful struggle to make a comeback after being crippled in a plane crash during WW II. Despite director Walter Lang's sudsy treatment of marital woes (hubby David Wayne supplanted by true love Rory Calhoun) and extensive hospital stays (made bearable by wisecracking nurse Thelma Ritter), the movie's main appeal is its large offering of period songs with Froman's voice on the soundtrack. Marital misunderstandings and divorce. A-III (br)

With Honors (1994) When a self-involved Harvard senior (Brendan Fraser) accidentally loses a crucial term-paper, he gets it back from a cantankerous homeless man (Joe Pesci) by providing him with a place to sleep during the frigid winter nights, out of which develops an unlikely bond between privileged student and witty indigent. Director Alek Keshishian's poignant story unreels in earnest if methodical fashion as the student and his three roommates admirably — and predictably— come to care for the unfortunate stranger, who in turn has some wisdom to share from the school of hard knocks. Fleeting bedroom scene, occasional sexual references, and a few instances of profanity. A-III (PG-13)

With Six You Get Egg Roll (1968) Doris Day plays a widow in coveralls with three sons, and Brian Keith is a widower with one daughter who try to keep their courtship a secret from the children, and then get them to all act in harmony as part of the new family. Director Howard Morris is not only stuck with a contrived and saccharine situation, with four over-cute children, but the movie gags on attempts at slapstick humor. The result is the kind of entertainment film that gives family pictures a bad name. A-II (G)

Withnail and I (1987) British drama about two struggling young actors (Richard E. Grant and Paul McGann) who, at the end of the 1960s hippie era, spend a weekend on the country estate of the wealthy uncle of one of them. Their friendship dissolves in remorseful recognition of the hurt they cause their host (Richard Griffiths) by preying upon his homosexual tendencies. Director Bruce Robinson's movie is spotted with harsh language and some drug and sexual references, but manages to convey a kind of elegiac farewell to the excesses of the times. A-III (R)

Without a Clue (1988) This bit of British comic fluff reverses the roles of Sherlock Holmes and Dr. Watson by having Watson (Ben Kingsley) be secretly the super-sleuth who writes stories about the fictional Holmes. To cover his tracks, Watson hires a third-rate actor (Michael Caine) to impersonate Holmes, but the actor's ineptitude and liberties with wine, women, and song drive Watson to distraction. As directed by Thom Eberhardt, their comic relationship wears thin, but there are some hilarious moments. Fleeting violence with humorous undertones and mild sexual innuendo. A-II (PG)

Without a Trace (1983) Fact-based story of a six-year-old boy who is kidnapped on the way to school in New York City, and his mother (Kate Nelligan) who convinces a police detective (Judd Hirsch) to stay on the case even when it looks as if there is no hope. Thanks largely to the performances of Hirsh and Nelligan, there are some good moments, but for the rest, director Stanley Jaffe's effort remains a flat and uninspired story, sorely lacking any real dramatic development, and with a ludicrous sentimental ending. Some strong language. A-II (PG)

Without Apparent Motive (1972) Tough, ruthless detective (Jean-Louis Trintignant) must flush out a madman who has been going about the picturesque city of Nice popping off one victim after another with his sniper's rifle. Nearly every encounter in director Philippe Labro's movie has sex simmering just below the surface, and, as the story builds towards climax and resolution, twisted sexual relations not surprisingly provide all the keys. A-III (PG)

Without Limits (1998) Uneven dramatization based on the life of track star Steve Prefontaine (Billy Crudup) and his University of Oregon coach, Bill Bowerman (Donald Sutherland), as the young athlete breaks records in collegiate meets, but breaks his heart losing in the 1972 Munich Olympics, then, after refocusing his efforts to compete in the 1976 Olympics, dies in a tragic auto accident. Directed by Richard Towne, the story of a talented athlete who insisted on winning his way will interest sports fans, but the human character portrayed on the screen is a quirky, self-centered rebel with a cause few non-fans are likely to find appealing. Explicit sexual situations, brief rear nudity. rough language, and profanity. A-III (PG-13)

Without Reservations (1946) Slight but amusing romantic comedy in which a novelist (Claudette Colbert) meets a Marine pilot (John Wayne) on a cross-country train journey, decides he'd be perfect as the hero in the movie version of her bestseller, but hides her identity because he hated the book. Director Mervyn LeRoy gets the story off to a bright start, but has trouble sustaining the contrived plot to its predictable conclusion, though the travelers' silly misadventures provide laughs along the way, and there are some droll jabs directed at Hollywood. Romantic situations. A-II (br)

Without You I'm Nothing (1990) Loosely structured version of Sandra Bernhard's one-woman show allows the comedienne to badmouth current pop idols, the political scene, commercial products, and anything resembling conventional behavior. Directed by John Boskovich, the result is emotionally uninvolving, with drawn-out musical numbers and sketches whose barbed humor and cold delivery accomplish little more than alienating the audience. Scenes of sexual exploitation with nudity, much rough language, and a positive portrayal of drug use. O (R)

Witness (1985) Tough Philadelphia police detective (Harrison Ford) hides out among the Amish to protect his life and that of a young boy who witnessed a murder committed by a corrupt fellow detective. He and the boy's widowed mother (Kelly McGillis) are drawn to each other despite their different worlds.

Director Peter Weir gets excellent performances in a good romantic melodrama that also offers some relatively thoughtful reflections on violence and non-violence. Some graphic violence and brief nudity are handled as restrained, but essential, plot devices. A-IV (R)

Witness for the Prosecution (1957) Twisty Agatha Christie courtroom puzzler in which British barrister Charles Laughton defends accused lady-killer Tyrone Power in a murder trial complicated by mysterious title character Marlene Dietrich and a double surprise ending. Director Billy Wilder plays the case's red herrings for all they're worth, helped by solid comic relief from the on-going feud between ailing lawyer Laughton and dictatorial nurse Elsa Lanchester. Implications of marital infidelity and stylized violence. A-II (br)

Wives and Lovers (1963) Flat satire of marital woes caused by the sudden success of a struggling writer (Van Johnson) whose wife (Janet Leigh) has a fling with an actor (Jeremy Slate) when she suspects her husband of having an affair with his agent (Martha Hyer). Director John Rich wrings little humor out of a contrived situation that grows tiresome as the bogus misunderstandings escalate until the counterfeit sentimental ending. Sexual situations. A-III (br)

Wiz, The (1978) Diana Ross stars as Dorothy, the girl who flies over the rainbow in a black musical version of **The Wizard of Oz**. Chasing Toto into a snowstorm in Harlem, she winds up on the yellow-brick road with the Scarecrow (Michael Jackson), the Tinman (Nipsey Russell), and the Cowardly Lion (Ted Ross) on their way to meet the Wiz (Richard Pryor). Directed by Sidney Lumet, it has lavishly staged musical numbers, opulent costumes, and colorful settings, but is overlong, and its humor seems addressed more to adults and teenagers than younger viewers. A-II (G)

Wizard, The (1989) Small-fry version of **Rain Man** tracks the exploits of a 13-year-old (Fred Savage) who kidnaps his emotionally disturbed nine-year-old brother (Luke Edwards) from an institution to enter him in a video-game championship for a crass feel-good ending. Directed by Todd Holland, the sentimental, far-fetched plot plugs everything from Nintendo games to the Universal City Studios tour. Some rough language and an unfortunate gag about child molestation. A-II (PG)

Wizard of Loneliness, The (1988) Bitter, precocious 12-year-old (Lukas Haas), forced to live with his grandparents in Vermont after his mother's death while his father's off fighting WW II, finally overcomes his resentment and accepts the unconditional love offered by an uncritical grandfather (John Randolph), gently seductive aunt (Lea Thompson), and tiny cousin (Jeremiah Warner). Director Jenny Bowen gets some fine acting in a richly detailed family drama based on a semi-autobiographical novel by John Nichols. Much rough language from the youthful protagonist, a clothed but intense sexual encounter, an assault on a child, and a graphic murder scene. A-III (PG-13)

Wizard of Oz, The (1939) Dorothy rides her tornado to the magic land over the rainbow in director Victor Fleming's classic that skyrocketed Judy Garland's career and has given generations of families prime entertainment again and again. The 50th-anniversary edition has 17 minutes of material not included in the original release. A-I (G)

Wizard of Speed and Time, The (1990) A special-effects artist (Mike Jittlov) tries to crack the big time in Hollywood only to come up against some sleazy TV producers who take advantage of him. Also written and directed by Jittlov, this amateurish bit of self-promotion is badly written and acted, though youngsters may enjoy the zany special effects. Some sexual innuendo. A-II (PG)

Wizards (1977) Animated feature starts with a thermonuclear destruction of human life on earth, then jumps to the far-distant future, in which mutants inhabit radioactive lands, and elves and fairies live in the uncontaminated area where are born twin wizards who battle for the future of the planet. It is animator Ralph Bakshi's most polished effort with bold, imaginative graphics and effective integration of live action footage. A number of violent visuals. A-III (PG)

Wolf (1994) Bitten by a dying wolf he's accidentally run over, a Manhattan book editor (Jack Nicholson) fears he is turning into a fanged beast capable of attacking his estranged wife (Kate Nelligan), traitorous colleague (James Spader), or new love interest (Michelle Pfeiffer). Director Mike Nichols's elegant take on a classic monster-myth may not scare anyone but will engross viewers in Nicholson's performance as the anguished wolf-man trying to cling to his diminishing humanity. Brief but intense violence, implied affairs, and intermittent rough language. A-III (R)

Wolf Call (1939) Low-budget adventure directed by George Waggner in which a playboy (John Carroll) is sent by his father to look over an Alaskan radium mine, routs the crooks running the place, hires a backwoods chemist to refine the ore at low cost, and stays on to sing duets with a local Indian maid (Movita). Mild menace. A-I (br)

Wolf Man, The (1941) Creaky screen-monster classic in which the son (Lon Chaney, Jr.) of an English lord (Claude Rains) is bitten by a werewolf (Bela Lugosi), but only realizes his fate when transformed into a human beast at the next full moon. Director George Waggner excels in creating a fearful atmosphere out of nighttime shadows and misty moors, with Chaney winning sympathy as the man who loathes what he becomes, and the venerable Maria Ouspenskaya adding some dignity to the proceedings as the wise Gypsy matriarch who tries to help the tormented victim. Menacing situation and stylized violence. A-II (br)

Wolfen (1981) Murky thriller in which a hardboiled,

nearly burnt-out detective (Albert Finney) investigating three brutal murders links them to some menacing wolf-like creatures seen roaming the streets of New York. Directed by Michael Wadleigh with some spectacular camera effects, the story suggests that these preternatural creatures are punishment for the sins of a rapacious society, but its sense of moral indignation doesn't justify the violence and graphic depiction of blood and gore. A-III (R)

Woman at Her Window, A (1978) Slack French 1930s political drama in which an Austrian woman (Romy Schneider) tries to help a Communist fugitive (Victor Lanoux) escape the secret police in Athens by involving her husband (Umberto Orsini) and a wealthy friend (Philippe Noiret). Director Pierre Granier-Deferre's narrative is needlessly complex and muddled, though it has compelling acting and some philosophical depth. Several scenes of police brutality. A-III (nr)

Woman Destroyed, A (see: **Smash-Up: The Story of a Woman**)

Woman in Green, The (1945) Convoluted mystery with Sherlock Holmes (Basil Rathbone) and Dr. Watson (Nigel Bruce) on the trail of the trail of the nefarious master criminal, Professor Moriarty (Henry Daniell), who this time heads a blackmail scheme employing hypnosis and murder. Under Roy William O'Neill's direction, Holmes faces death by auto fumes, an assassin's bullet, and a walk off a ledge high above the street before the case is closed. Some fairly effective menace and minimal stylized violence. A-I (br)

Woman in Hiding (1949) Minor thriller in which a wealthy bride (Ida Lupino) flees her murderous husband (Stephen McNally), then seeks help from a friendly war vet (Howard Duff) and her husband's ex-flame (Peggy Dow). Directed by Michael Gordon, the cat-and-mouse game is too contrived to build much suspense, though there are some good bits, notably a raucous hotel convention. Stylized violence and menace. A-II (br)

Woman in Red, The (1984) Gene Wilder directs and also stars as a philandering advertising manager who pursues a beautiful model (Kelly Le Brock) while keeping his wife (Judith Ivy) in the dark. It is an ill-conceived and clumsily executed attempt to recast a French farce about adultery (**Pardon Mon Affaire**) in an American mold. Nudity and a benign attitude toward illicit sex. O (PG-13)

Woman Next Door, The (1981) Weak French romantic melodrama about a happily married couple who move next door to another happily married couple, but, as it happens, the wife who has just moved in (Fanny Ardant) and the husband next door (Gerald Depardieu) had had a stormy love affair seven years before, and soon the two are off and running again. Director Francois Truffaut handles this material with his usual adroitness, but to little purpose in a story that proves banal and unmoving, with some questionable amorous sequences. A-IV (R)

Woman Obsessed (1959) Turgid sudser from the Canadian northwest, where a farmer's widow (Susan Hayward) marries her brawny, inarticulate hired man (Stephen Boyd) but comes to regret it. Directed by Henry Hathaway, the picturesque locales of the setting are a lot easier to watch than the cliched story of a woman's soured romance. Domestic misunderstandings and natural catastrophes. A-II (br)

Woman of Dolwyn (see: **The Last Days of Dolwyn**)

Woman of Straw (1964) Intriguing British mystery in which the cunning nephew (Sean Connery) of an aged, irascible millionaire (Ralph Richardson) convinces a beguiling nurse (Gina Lollobrigida) to marry the old man in order to get a share of his wealth. Director Basil Dearden sets up the mercenary situation convincingly, then bogs down in some improbable plot twists for a disappointing ending, though Richardson's roguish performance is worth catching. Some grisly situations, amoral characters, and sexual innuendo. A-III (br)

Woman of the Ganges (1974) French writer Marguerite Duras's story of a man at a resort during its winter off-season where he meets, or perhaps imagines that he meets, the woman of the title whom he had loved in India long ago. Also directed by Duras, the highly verbal movie takes place not on the screen, but in the mind of the beholder willing to plumb its blend of time, memory, and illusion. A-III (nr)

Woman Times Seven (1967) Italian potpourri of comedy, farce, and pathos is directed by Vittorio De Sica, with Shirley MacLaine as the heroine of each episode. It is needlessly marred by one tasteless and provocative sequence. O (br)

Woman Under the Influence, A (1974) The woman of the title (Gena Rowlands) is a mother of three small children in the middle of a nervous breakdown, while her husband (Peter Falk), a rough, callous, but loving man, is totally unable to cope with the situation. Directed by John Cassavetes in his characteristic improvisational style, the result is full of the small realities and individual details that make up ordinary human experience, but it is short on the sort of heightened drama one expects from a conventional movie narrative. A-III (R)

Woman's Decision, A (1977) Sensitive, extremely well-acted Polish triangle story whose heroine (Maya Komorowska) is married to a wonderful husband (Piotr Franczewski), has an affectionate son and a modern apartment in Warsaw, but finds herself wanting to give it all up for the company of a footloose man (Marek Piwowski). Directed by Krzystof Zanussi, it is a perceptive study of the interior struggle each of the characters undergoes during the course of the narrative. A-III (nr)

Woman's Secret, A (1949) Transparent sudser in which a radio singer (Gloria Graham) is shot, and her dour manager (Maureen O'Hara) is arrested for the deed, while their mutual friend, a debonair songwriter (Melvyn Douglas), seeks the truth, along with a cop (Jay C. Flippen) whose wife (Mary Philips) knows a romantic triangle when she sees one. Despite the capable cast, director Nicholas Ray makes matters seem even duller than they actually are in numerous flashbacks slowly explaining the obvious. Brief violence and romantic complications. A-II (br)

Woman's Tale, A (1992) Somber drama about an elderly, cancer-ridden woman (Sheila Florance) who, with her devoted young nurse (Gosia Dobrowolska) at her side, grittily determines to extract all the enjoyment she can from her final days. Though director Paul Cox elicits moving performances from both women, the life-affirming theme is delivered with belabored heavy-handedness. Uncritical attitude toward the nurse's extramarital affair and brief nudity. A-III (PG-13)

Woman's Vengeance, A (1947) When a rich Englishwoman is poisoned, her unfaithful husband (Charles Boyer) is convicted and sentenced to death, though a physician (Cedric Hardwicke) suspects the wife's best friend (Jessica Tandy) is guilty. Directed by Zoltan Korda, the murky plot gains interest from solid performances by the cast and moody period photography. Romantic complications. A-II (br)

Women, The (1939) Lavish screen version of Clare Boothe's satiric play in which a New York socialite (Norma Shearer), whose husband has fallen for a calculating gold-digger (Joan Crawford), goes to Reno for a divorce, then returns home to pick up the pieces. Directed by George Cukor, the all-female cast (Rosalind Russell, Paulette Goddard, Mary Boland, and many others) provides a comic compendium of feminine stereotypes and caustic comments on the battle of the sexes, much of which is unflattering to women, but it is the unseen males who get the worst of it. Comic treatment of sex and marriage. A-III (br)

Women (1978) Sensitive Hungarian character study of an unlikely and slowly developing friendship between the wife of a successful engineer (Marina Vlady) and a factory worker (Lili Monori) whose husband is an alcoholic. The melodramatic plot and its soap-opera problems simply provide the background against which director Marta Meszaros explores the human needs that draw these two women together despite their differences in character, education, and social position. Mature themes. A-III (nr)

Women in Love (1970) British adaptation of the D.H. Lawrence novel about the gradual involvement of two couples, one (Alan Bates and Glenda Jackson) having a rather healthy though incomplete relationship, while the other (Oliver Reed and Jennie Linden) tragically ends in suicide. Directed by Ken Russell, the acting is first-rate, the photography almost too beautiful, and the treatment of the convoluted relationships remains on the superficial level of the physical. Lengthy naked wrestling match between the men is more symbolic than erotic. O (R)

Women in Revolt (1972) Three women from different social levels (female impersonators Candy Darling, Holly Woodlawn, and Jackie Curtis) get caught up in the Women's Liberation Movement. Typical of the poor film quality and sexual explicitness of Andy Warhol's efforts in the past, it makes men, women, and sex look ridiculous, ugly, and perverted. O (nr)

Women on the Verge of a Nervous Breakdown (1988) After an actress (Carmen Maura) is deserted by her live-in lover (Fernando Guillen), she attempts to face down the coward before he leaves town with another woman. Written and directed by Pedro Almodovar, this Spanish farce explores without exploitation the comic vicissitudes of male-female relationships. Subtitles. Some rough language and a benign attitude toward sex and pregnancy outside of marriage. A-IV (R)

Women's Prison (1955) Tawdry programmer directed by Lewis Seiler in which the warden (Ida Lupino) of the women's division in a prison also housing male inmates is a sadist who is finally put in a straightjacket by the prison doctor (Howard Duff) after her brutality causes a riot. Much stylized violence and sexual innuendo. A-III (br)

Won Ton Ton, the Dog Who Saved Hollywood (1976) Director Michael Winner's wretchedly thrown-together slapstick comedy about a wonder dog of the old silent-movie era is made all the more tasteless by seeing performers one once admired in a series of painfully inane cameos. It is definitely not for young viewers. O (PG)

Wonder Man (1945) Sappy Danny Kaye vehicle in which he doubles as a murdered nightclub comic whose spirit inhabits the body of his scholarly twin brother, thereby confounding police, gangsters, and the brothers' girlfriends (Virginia Mayo and Vera-Ellen). Directed by Bruce Humberstone, there are a couple of good song-and-dance numbers and some funny routines, but the phantom-brother gimmick wears thin. Minimal stylized violence. A-II (br)

Wonderful Country, The (1959) Convoluted Western directed by Robert Parrish centers on an American (Robert Mitchum) who's made a career as a gunslinger in 1880s Mexico, but the love of a good woman (Julie London) and the assassination of his boss (Pedro Armendariz) lead him back to the States to join the Texas Rangers. Stylized violence and sexual references. A-III (br)

Wonderful Crook, The (1977) Off-beat French comedy about a good-natured, but inept, young man (Gerald Depardieu) who, in order to pay the employees' wages of his family's furniture business, undertakes a series of holdups and falls in love with one of his victims (Marlene Jobert). Neither his wife (Dominique Labourier) nor his employees suspect his double life, until the police arrive to arrest him. Directed by Claude Goretta, the movie details in a warmly humorous manner the complications that can arise from a simplistic notion of "doing good." Brief nudity and vulgar language. A-III (nr)

Wonderful, Horrible Life of Leni Riefenstahl, The (1993) Absorbing account of how German movie director Riefenstahl came to make **The Triumph of the Will** (1934), the powerful Nazi propaganda film which made her unemployable after WW II, though she never joined the Nazi Party, nor was ever accused of being anti-Semitic. Written and directed by Ray Mueller, the subtitled German production also interviews the 90-year-old Riefenstahl about her subsequent career as a photographer, yet keeps returning to the question of how an artist, no matter how disinterested in politics, could have been so blind to the evils of a repressive regime. The subject of a moviemaker's social responsibility has importance for more than film students. A-II (nr)

Wonderful World of the Brothers Grimm, The (1962) Lavish but plodding Cinerama production interweaving the story of the 19th-century German brothers (Laurence Harvey and Karl Boehm) with dramatizations of three of the many folk tales they popularized despite personal adversities. Co-directed by George Pal and Henry Levin, the Rhineland locales and period settings are better realized than either the biographical material or the special effects used in the fairytales. Intermittently diverting for youngsters, though a long sit for their elders. A-I (G)

Wonders of Aladdin, The (1961) Embarrassingly inept comic adventure, with Donald O'Connor as an over-aged Aladdin, and Vittorio de Sica as a cut-rate genie, all mixed up in the old story of a magic lamp. Directed by Mario Bava and Henry Levin, this dubbed Italian misfire suffers from an impoverished script and threadbare fantasy effects. Much sexual innuendo and comic violence, including a sadistic torture scene. A-III (br)

Woo (1998) Dopey comedy crudely chronicles a madcap blind date between a cautious law student (Tommy Davidson) and an impetuous beauty (Jada Pinkett Smith) who attracts trouble wherever they go. Director Daisy Von Scherler Mayer's lame battle-of-the-sexes comedy is a tiresome collection of witless pranks and dumb jokes. Brief violence, much sexist humor, racial slurs, sexual innuendo, fleeting nudity, occasional profanity, and frequent rough language. A-IV (R)

Wooden Man's Bride, The (1995) In 1920s China, a woman (Wang Lan) whose groom is accidentally killed on their wedding day is forced by her mother-in-law (Wang Yumei) to live as a married woman with a wooden statue of her dead spouse, until the kindly servant (Chang Shih) she comes to love resorts to desperate means to free her. Director Huang Jianxin's visually haunting melodrama explores a harsh feudal society in which the honor-bound but inwardly seething characters eventually rebel against the old lady in order to marry. Subtitles. Some gory violence, fleeting nudity, and an instance of rough language. A-III (nr)

Wooden Soldiers (see: **March of the Wooden Soldiers**)

Woodstock (1970) Documentary about the landmark musical event that brought together a half-million young people to hear a parade of such talented performers as Richie Havens, Joan Baez, Country Joe and the Fish, The Who, Sha-na-na, Arlo Guthrie, Crosby Stills and Nash, Joe Cocker, and so on. Directed by Michael Wadleigh, it is dazzling in image and sound, but as a record of this particular music festival, it concentrates on the positive themes of love and peace, giving scant attention to the drugs and commercialism that for many marred the event. Brief nudity, and some rough language and lyrics. A-IV (R)

Work Is a Four Letter Word (1968) British comedy about a man (David Warner) who grows mushrooms that have a narcotic effect. Directed by Peter Hall, its premise is better than the results. A-III (br)

Working Girl (1988) A 30-year-old secretary (Melanie Griffith) with the training and dreams to make it big as a Wall Street stockbroker is held back by sexist male bosses and a treacherous female boss (Sigourney Weaver), but when she transforms herself into a polished professional, her appealing vulnerability attracts the right boss (Philip Bosco) and suitor (Harrison Ford). Directed by Mike Nichols, the upbeat story balances its women-in-the-workplace concerns with a delightful Cinderella story that will entertain and enlighten even diehard anti-feminists. Much rough language laced with sexual innuendo and some frontal nudity within brief graphic sexual situations. A-IV (R)

World According to Garp, The (1982) Uneven screen version of John Irving's novel about a fragile writer (Robin Williams) overwhelmed by catastrophes, bizarre events, and his indomitable mother (Glenn Close). Under George Roy Hill's direction, Williams by going all out to turn the character into a lovable schnook makes his problems seem even crueler and more arbitrary than they might have been. Some nudity and graphic sexual references. A-III (R)

World Apart, A (1988) Fact-based drama set in 1963 South Africa concerns an anti-apartheid white journalist (Barbara Hershey) and her inability to give her three young daughters the same love and devotion she channels into the political arena. British director Chris Menges skirts over the political and social issues to focus on the mother-daughter conflict. Some emotional and physical political violence, an off-camera suicide attempt, and the suffering caused one of the daughters because of her parents' political activities. A-II (PG)

World in His Arms, The (1952) Romantic adventure with a Yankee sea captain (Gregory Peck) who's grown so rich poaching seals in Russian-owned Alaska that he decides to buy it from the czar, but along the way falls for a Russian countess (Ann Blyth), battles a Portuguese freebooter (Anthony Quinn), and is captured by a Russian gunboat. Director Raoul Walsh submerges the 19th-century romance in high-seas derring-do and imperial despotism, with the action sputtering to a bogus ending. Stylized violence and romantic complications. A-I (br)

World of Buckminster Fuller, The (1974) Educational documentary directed by Robert Snyder provides a coherent outline of Fuller's basic concepts, as well as a personal portrait of a humanist who put his scientific knowledge to the task of considering the present under the aspects of the future, rather than from the conventional wisdom of the past. A-I (nr)

World of Hans Christian Andersen, The (1971) Feature-length cartoon about the childhood of young Hans and where he got some of the ideas for his highly imaginative fairytales. The animation is colorful and creative, though stylistically comparable to Saturday morning TV shows. It provides a wonderful world of fantasy to absorb the small fry at a matinee. A-I (G)

World of Henry Orient, The (1964) Peter Sellers stars in a wacky comedy about a fair-to-middling concert pianist whose pursuit of extracurricular love (Paula Prentiss) is foiled by the unwitting but persistent efforts of two teenage girls, who just may be his only fans in all the world. Directed by George Roy Hill, the acting is very good, the comedy nicely paced, and the romantic element only in the background. A-II (br)

World of Susie Wong, The (1961) Exotic but unappetizing tale of the rough life and times of a Hong Kong lady of the night, toned down from Paul Osborn's play in the Hollywood version starring Nancy Kwan as Susie and William Holden as her American love-interest. Directed by Richard Quine, its plush production of a sentimental romance may have some interest for hardy adults, but not for youngsters or those with reservations about a drama which unfolds, for the most part, in a seamy brothel. O (br)

World Without End (1956) Fanciful sci-fi adventure as the first manned space-flight speeds out of control through time, returning to Earth in the year 2508 A.D. to find the survivors of a nuclear holocaust living underground, while human mutants rule the planet's radioactive surface. Writer-director Edward Bernds focuses on the efforts of the spaceship's crew (notably Hugh Marlowe and Rod Taylor) to get the survivors to quit their unhealthy subterranean city and retake the now radiation-free surface from the mutants. Fantasy violence. A-I (br)

World Without Sun (1964) Documentary made by oceanaut Jacques-Yves Cousteau details the human conquest of underwater space. It is an opportunity to see and experience an incredibly beautiful part of creation, till now hidden from human eyes. A-I (br)

World's Greatest Athlete, The (1973) Frustrated coach (John Amos) vacationing in Africa discovers a Tarzan-like jungle youth (Jan-Michael Vincent) and brings him to his sunny California campus, where he starts making a shambles of the record books. It is the Disney studio's special-effects men who save the day for sports, as well as for parents, who with their children will have to take the yawns along with the laughs in this matinee special directed by Robert Scheerer. A-I (G)

World's Greatest Lover, The (1977) Failed comedy written and directed by Gene Wilder, who also stars as a hapless oaf who goes to Hollywood in the 1920s hoping to win a studio-sponsored world's greatest lover contest. The direction is inept, the writing shows no vestige of wit or originality, and Wilder's performance is loud, vulgar, and supremely unfunny. Boring, but its low level of humor is not for young viewers. A-III (PG)

Worth Winning (1989) Adolescent male fantasy about a shallow Philadelphia TV-weatherman (Mark Harmon) who bets a friend (Mark Blum) that he can propose marriage to three women (chosen by the friend) in three months and be accepted by each. The heel gets his comeuppance, but director Will Mackenzie treats him more sympathetically than the three female guinea-pigs (Maria Holvoe, Madeleine Stowe, and Lesley Ann Warren) in a sexist exercise demeaning to women. Sexual promiscuity including adultery and some profanity laced with sexual vulgarities. O (PG-13)

Woyzeck (1979) Stark German adaptation of Georg Buchner's 19th-century play about a much-abused soldier (Klaus Kinski) in a small garrison town who goes mad and brutally murders the woman (Eva Mattes) he has been too poor to marry. Directed by Werner Herzog, the story of a man's alienation and descent into irrationality is powerfully acted, and its dark mood unrelieved. A-III (nr)

Wraith, The (1986) A brutally murdered teenager (Charlie Sheen) returns as an avenging angel to race to their deaths the depraved auto gang that has killed him. A deadly supernatural demolition derby filmed on the picturesque highways of Arizona sells violence, vengeance, and a few sexual inferences with foul language to a youth market already overburdened with negative role models. A-III (PG-13)

Wrath of God, The (1972) Hard-drinking, gun-toting renegade priest (Robert Mitchum) joins forces with two other fugitive misfits to erase a fanatical madman-rancher in Central America during the revolutionary 1920s. Directed by Ralph Nelson, the result is downright painful in some sections, embarrassing and simply ludicrous in others. Some heavy violence. A-IV (PG)

Wreck of the Mary Deare, The (1959) What starts as a dandy mystery goes sour after a salvager (Charlton Heston) boards a floundering, storm-tossed freighter and discovers it abandoned by all but the captain (Gary Cooper), who insists he is still in command of the vessel. From there on, matters pale considerably as director Michael Anderson plods through the captain's trial by a maritime court, with entirely predictable results. Some stylized violence. A-I (br)

Wrecking Crew, The (1968) The only funny aspect of this limp spy-spoof is watching Dean Martin lumber through it as super-agent Matt Helm entrusted to guard a gold shipment from Denmark to London, giving rise to jokes about Danish pastries (one of whom is Elke Sommer). Directed by Phil Karlson, the level of crude sexual humor is beneath adolescent interest. O (PG)

Wrestling Ernest Hemingway (1993) Slow-moving, sentimental portrait of the unlikely friendship that develops between two lonely old men — a foul-mouthed, lecherous former sea captain (Richard Harris) and an introverted retired barber from Cuba (Robert Duvall). Directed by Randa Haines, it's an actor's feast, with Harris chewing up whatever scenery he can find, while Duvall concentrates on being slow and deliberate in everything, including his Hispanic accent, though Sandra Bullock's performance as a friendly waitress is brightly refreshing. Some lengthy discussions of love and sex, flashes of rear nudity, and occasional rough language. A-III (PG-13)

Written on the Wind (1956) Soapy sudser about the troubled life and death of a weak-willed Texas oil tycoon (Robert Stack), the strong wife (Lauren Bacall) who tries to reform him, and his best friend (Rock Hudson) who secretly loves her while disdaining the love offered him by the oil man's dissolute sister (Dorothy Malone). Director Douglas Sirk's trashy exercise in sentimental melodrama is slickly contrived and mindlessly boring. Much alcohol abuse, some stylized violence, and veiled sexual references. A-II (br)

Wrong Box, The (1966) British black comedy revolves around the bumbling attempts of someone to kill off members of a family in order to obtain a large inheritance. Directed by Bryan Forbes, the script is not very sharp, but the acting of John Mills, Ralph Richardson, Michael Caine, and Peter Sellers is first-rate. The most hilarious performance, a classic of its kind, belongs to Wilfred Lawson as the old family retainer. A-II (br)

Wrong Guys, The (1988) Often entertaining story about a wilderness reunion of a pack of onetime Cub Scouts who are threatened by their old neighborhood bullies and an escaped con who wields a mighty range of weaponry. Director Danny Bilson is aided by a cast of young, stand-up comics (Louie Anderson, Richard Lewis, Richard Belzer, Franklyn Ajay, and Tim Thomerson) who have their own particular comic shticks. Mild profanity. A-II (PG)

Wrong Is Right (1982) Failed black comedy in which Sean Connery plays a television news commentator who finds himself in the middle of a struggle between an American president (George Grizzard), his political rival (Leslie Nielsen), Arab terrorists, and assorted villains to gain possession of two suitcases containing nuclear bombs. Writer-director Richard Brooks tries to satirize amorality in high places, but the humor is flat and the story terribly jumbled. Graphic violence. A-III (R)

Wrong Move, The (1978) Tedious, empty German drama in which a moody would-be writer (Rudiger Vogler), who doesn't like people and has no interest in politics, takes a rambling journey through West Germany. Written by Peter Hanke and directed by Wim Wenders, the random incidents and various characters met along the way occasion little interest for the young man and less for the viewer. Mature themes. A-III (nr)

Wrongfully Accused (1998) Uneven comedy in which a gullible violinist (Leslie Nielsen) becomes a fugitive from justice while hunting down the terrorists who got him framed for murder. Writer-director Pat Proft uses Nielsen's deadpan delivery to spoof up **The Fugitive** and other movies with goofy sight gags, comical props, and silly situations that are fitfully funny. Slapstick violence, sexual situations, and minimal profanity. A-III (PG-13)

Wuthering Heights (1939) Classic romantic melodrama from the Emily Brontë novel about the doomed love between Cathy (Merle Oberon), a Yorkshire doctor's daughter, and Heathcliff (Laurence Olivier), the downtrodden orphan who grows up with her, then runs away to make his fortune, only to return to find Cathy wed to another (David Niven) and his riches meaningless without her. Directed by William Wyler, the well-crafted melodrama succeeds in evoking the fierce passion of Heathcliff's tormented yearnings for his lost love, which allow him no peace until their spirits are united after death. Physical and mental cruelties, romantic obsessions, and a spite marriage. A-III (br)

Wuthering Heights (1970) Good British version of the Emily Brontë romantic classic of tragic love on the moors stars Anna Calder-Marshall as Cathy and Timothy Dalton as Heathcliff. Director Robert Fuest has made a conscious effort to enable young viewers to identify with the doomed pair, but in doing so, he has softened the rough edges of the characters and the malevolent nature of their relationship. Good cast and fine creation of mood and period. A-II (G)

Wyatt Earp (1994) Violent, over-long, revenge-themed Western in which reluctant lawmen Wyatt Earp (Kevin Costner) and two of his brothers (Linden Ashby and Michael Madsen) dole out six-shooter justice in lawless towns of the Old West, until, joined by buddy Doc Holliday (Dennis Quaid), they track down and willfully execute the Clanton-McLaury gang who dared defy them. Though visually impressive, director Lawrence Kasdan's shallow treatment of the characters centers in the depiction of Earp as a remorseless cold-blooded figure who is ultimately elevated to heroically triumphant stature. Much gory violence, justification of murders, discreet bedroom scene, fleeting nude photo, and an instance of rough language. O (PG-13)

Wyoming (1947) Routine Western directed by Joe Kane in which a pioneer ranching family (William Elliott and Vera Ralston) build a large spread after the Civil War, then get involved in a range war when homesteaders start moving into the area. Frontier violence. A-I (br)

Wyoming Kid, The (see: **Cheyenne**)

Wyoming Mail (1950) Routine Western directed by Reginald LeBorg in which an undercover government agent (Stephen McNally) passes himself off as an escaped convict in order to join a gang of mail train-robbers (notably Ed Begley, Howard da Silva,

James Arness, and Richard Jaeckel), then bring them to justice. Stylized violence. A-I (br)

Wyoming Renegades (1955) Murky tale of an ex-outlaw (Phil Carey) who tries to go straight but has to shoot it out with Butch Cassidy's Wild Bunch before his reformation is accepted by his neighbors. Directed by Fred F. Sears, it's a tired exercise in overly familiar territory. Stylized violence. A-I (br)

X-15 (1961) Routine service melodrama directed by Richard D. Donner in which an Air Force pilot (Charles Bronson) breaks a speed record, then joins the program testing the experimental craft of the title which is being developed for manned space-flights. Tense moments for test pilots and their families. A-I (br)

X Files, The (1998) Meandering story based on the title TV-series in which two stubborn FBI agents (Gillian Anderson and David Duchovny) stumble upon a global conspiracy involving frozen aliens, a mutating virus, and the possible colonization of Earth by extraterrestrials. Directed by Rob Bowman, the result is little more than a two-hour series episode with the usual murky visuals of menacing aliens amidst elaborate theories of government and corporate conspiracies which are never resolved. Brief violence, menacing situations, occasional profanity, and an instance of rough language. A-III (PG-13)

X — The Man with X-Ray Eyes (1963) Failed sci-fi chiller directed by Roger Corman in which a doctor (Ray Milland) develops a drug enabling the human eye to see through physical objects, but his obsession to perfect the drug leads to murder, flight, and into hiding as a carnival mind-reader, then a faith healer, until the police chase him into a Christian revival tent for a gruesome "moral" ending. Stylized violence, menacing situations, and occasional sexual innuendo. A-II (br)

X the Unknown (1956) British sci-fi thriller pits a nuclear scientist (Dean Jagger) against a mysterious radioactive ooze which threatens a Scottish community after bursting from beneath the earth's crust in search of more radiation. Directed by Leslie Norman, the suspense mounts as the unseen deadly force takes its toll of victims, then deflates in a pat conclusion with disappointing visuals of the slimy blob. More menace than violence. A-I (br)

X, Y & Zee (1972) Shrill British sex melodrama involving a self-destructive, affluent, childless couple (Elizabeth Taylor and Michael Caine) and an attractive widow (Susannah York) with whom the husband falls in love and the wife tries to seduce in order to thwart the interest of her errant spouse. Directed by Brian G. Hutton, the perverse triangle is a vulgar, one-dimensional affair with brief nudity and considerable abusive language. O (R/PG)

Xala (1975) Black African satire, filmed in Senegal, about a prosperous businessman who takes a third wife but, unable to consummate the marriage, is convinced someone has cursed him with a spell of impotence and spends all his money seeking the help of witch doctors. Director Ousmane Sembene's metaphor of impotence is vividly applied to the neo-colonialist values of the African middle class which is the movie's main target. A-III (nr)

Xanadu (1980) Olivia Newton-John sings her way through her role as a materialized Greek muse who inspires a middle-aged musician (Gene Kelly) and a young artist (Michael Beck) to become partners in a nightclub. Directed by Robert Greenwald, the movie offers little but special effects, optical devices, and a few vulgar dance numbers in what is essentially an illustrated sound-track album. A-II (PG)

Xiu Xiu: The Sent-Down Girl (1999) In the waning days of China's Cultural Revolution, a young girl (Lu Lu) sent by the government to learn horse-herding techniques on the remote western plains alongside a stoic herder (Lopsang) eventually allows local officials to use her sexually in hopes of getting permission to return home. Director Joan Chen's bleakly poetic melodrama captures the desperate loss of innocence and ensuing tragedy as symbolic of so many lives disrupted or destroyed in that era. Subtitles. Brief violence including suicidal behavior, some sexual encounters with nudity, and an instance of rough language. A-IV (R

Yaaba (1989) Two youngsters befriend an old woman who lives as an outcast on the outskirts of their tiny village in the African country of Burkina Faso. Director Idrissa Ouedraogo's beautifully photographed movie shows the virtues, as well as the foibles, of the villagers in warmly human terms evoking a certain sense of kinship on the part of interested viewers, though those looking for casual entertainment are likely to be disappointed. English subtitles. Some youngsters may be confused or perplexed by aspects of this very different culture. A-II (nr)

Yakuza, The (1975) Robert Mitchum plays an American back in Japan, where he had served in the Occupation, to help get back a friend's kidnapped daughter (Keiko Kishi) by having a top gangster (Ken Takadura) repay the favor he owes the American. Though Mitchum is able to rise above the inane story with some dignity, director Sydney Pollack's Japanese gangster movie (which is what the title means) proves silly as well as repugnant in its exotic brutality and simple-minded concept of manhood. A-III (R)

Yank in the R.A.F., A (1941) Stale WW II tale of a hotshot American pilot (Tyrone Power) enlisting in the Royal Air Force only because a former girlfriend (Betty Grable) has taken a job in London, but he loses her to his squadron leader (John Sutton) until proving his heroism in the skies over Dunkirk. Directed by Henry King, what has dated badly is the romantic appeal of Power's character as a supposedly charming heel, but the wartime setting provides some agreeable humor, and the scenes re-creating the desperate evacuation of Dunkirk are first-rate. Wartime violence and romantic complications. A-I (br)

Yankee Buccaneer (1952) Historical hokum directed by Frederick de Cordova revolves around the captain (Jeff Chandler) of a US Navy vessel ordered to masquerade as a pirate ship in order to locate a fleet of buccaneers plundering the Caribbean, with further complications stemming from his ornery second officer (Scott Brady), a Portuguese countess (Suzan Ball), and the area's Spanish governor (Howard da Silva). Stylized violence. A-I (br)

Yankee Doodle Dandy (1942) Born on the Fourth of July, George M. Cohan melded patriotism with Irish charm in his rise from song-and-dance vaudevillian to leading Broadway songwriter and producer in a career celebrated by this nostalgic, flag-waving musical starring James Cagney as the feisty entertainer. Directed by Michael Curtiz, it features a grand collection of Cohan's best-remembered songs, as well as Cagney at the top of his form, singing and dancing his way to an Academy Award for the year's best performance. Fine family fare. A-I (br)

Yankee Pasha (1954) Anemic romantic adventure directed by Joseph Pevney in which a sharpshooting American frontiersman (Jeff Chandler) pursues the kidnappers of his girlfriend (Rhonda Fleming) to Morocco, then rescues her from a dastardly Barbary pirate (Bart Roberts). Stylized violence and romantic complications. A-II (br)

Yanks (1979) Overlong but beautifully photographed re-creation of a worn and ravaged England during WW II offers the thin story of two English women (Vanessa Redgrave and Lisa Eichhorn) and two American soldiers (William Devane and Richard Gere) told in terms of parallel romances. Directed by John Schlesinger, the story suffers from a slow-moving pace and lack of focus, which leaves it without much dramatic force. Adultery figures in the plot, with some profane language and some bedroom scenes. A-III (R)

Year My Voice Broke, The (1988) Coming-of-age drama set in Australia in 1962 tells of a 15-year-old's (Noah Taylor) infatuation with his 16-year-old childhood friend (Loene Carmen), who has set her eyes on a wilder lad (Ben Mendelsohn) for her first sexual involvement, forcing the younger boy to stand by and watch her ruin her life. Writer-director John Duigan's sensitive, non-exploitative handling of puberty results in a touching portrayal of boy-girl friendship and first love. Some rough language and the implications of sex and pregnancy outside marriage. A-III (PG-13)

Year of Living Dangerously, The (1983) Murky story set in 1965 Indonesia, where a newly arrived Australian correspondent (Mel Gibson) comes to depend upon an Asian news-photographer (Linda Hunt in a male role) for information about an impending revolution, but along the way the Aussie's attention is distracted by a torrid love affair with a British intelligence agent (Sigourney Weaver). Director Peter Weir re-creates the place and chaotic period very effectively, but characterizations are sketchy, and the action lacks coherence. Though the film has compassion for the poor and oppressed, the sexual relationship makes it mature fare. A-III (PG)

Year of the Comet (1992) Contrived chase story of a mismatched couple (Penelope Ann Miller and Tim Daly) on the run from assorted villains (led by Louis Jourdan) while trying to deliver a priceless bottle of Napoleonic wine to an auction. Producer-director Peter Yates's sprightly and visually delightful caper is all but ruined by its self-consciously precious tone. Occasional stylized violence and discreet sexual innuendo with a flash of nudity. A-III (PG-13)

Year of the Dragon (1985) A police captain and Vietnam veteran (Mickey Rourke) wages war against a dapper but ruthlessly deadly Chinatown gang-lord (John Lone). Directed by Michael Cimino, and written by Oliver Stone, the film is muddled almost to the point of incoherence by extreme amounts of profanity and violence, while being pointedly racist and sexist. O (R)

Year of the Gun (1991) Standard political thriller set in 1978 terrorist-ravaged Rome, where a naive American reporter (Andrew McCarthy) becomes involved with an Italian divorcée (Valeria Golino), a university professor (John Pankow), and an aggressive photojournalist (Sharon Stone) who is convinced the reporter is her ticket inside the Red Brigades terrorist organization. Routine performances dilute director John Frankenheimer's shadowy story of personal ambition and surprise betrayals, interestingly set against the political backdrop of President Aldo Moro's kidnapping and murder. A few bedroom scenes with nudity, sporadic brutal violence, and some rough language. A-III (R)

Year of the Quiet Sun, A (1985) An American soldier (Scott Wilson) and a Polish widow (Maja Komorowska) fall in love, despite their lack of a common language in Russian-occupied Poland in the grim days following WW II. Under the masterful direction of Krzysztof Zanussi, the Polish production probes into the tragic complications arising from a relationship foundering over cultural differences. Sensitive treatment of serious matters. A-II (PG)

Year of the Woman (1973) Pretentious documentary on the politicization of women's rights adds, unfortunately, little enlightenment about the subject. It suffers not only from missed opportunities to demonstrate systematic injustice, but from the misuse of interviews with articulate individuals, edited mainly to serve the needs of filmmaker Sandra Hochman. A-IV (nr)

Yearling, The (1946) A young boy's attachment to an orphaned fawn relieves the loneliness of life in the Florida wilderness but brings grief as the deer grows to threaten the family's crops in this classic version of the Marjorie Kinnon Rawlings story. With credible performances by Gregory Peck and Jane Wyman as the parents, and Claude Jarman, Jr., as the youth, director Clarence Brown has fashioned a genuine portrait of rural American life, as well as a sincere celebration of family values. A-I (G)

Years of Lightning, Day of Drums (1966) Celebratory documentary about the promise of President Kennedy's years in office as seen from the perspective of his tragic assassination and burial. It recalls vividly the feeling of personal loss experienced by people around the world during that terrible November in 1963. A-I (br)

Yellow Cab Man, The (1950) Comedy of errors about an accident-prone inventor (Red Skelton) whose secret formula for unbreakable glass makes him the target of a crooked lawyer (Edward Arnold) and a bogus psychologist (Walter Slezak), until his girlfriend (Gloria de Haven) and a veteran cab-driver (James Gleason) come to the rescue. Under Jack Donohue's direction, Skelton mugs his way through the comic complications, including dream sequences using photographer Weegee's distorted urban images, and a big-chase finish that turns a home furnishings exhibition into a shambles. Some comic violence and psychological duress. A-I (br)

Yellow Rolls-Royce, The (1965) Slickly elegant romantic melodrama in which the automobile of the title passes from an English aristocrat (Rex Harrison) in Ascot to an American gangster (George C. Scott) in Florence and a Scandanavian heiress (Ingrid Bergman) in Yugoslavia. Directed by Anthony Asquith, the film's love interests are Jeanne Moreau, Shirley MacLaine, and Omar Sharif, respectively, but only the third tale has any weight, and that scarcely memorable. Sexual situations and some stylized violence. A-IV (br)

Yellow Submarine (1968) Wonderful animated feature for young and old, with music from the Beatles's Sergeant Pepper album, follows the adventures of John, George, Paul, and Ringo to the never-never-world of Pepperland, where they find that the Blue Meanies are overrunning its lovely terrain. Director George Dunning's animation is a wonder, the music a delight, and, of course, Sgt. Pepper and his Lonelyhearts Club Marching Band get their peaceful land back at the end, and those Blue Meanies are not all that mean. A-I (G)

Yellow Tomahawk, The (1954) Cliched Western directed by Lesley Selander is set in Wyoming, where a former Army scout (Rory Calhoun) tries to save a cavalry outpost from Cheyenne warriors seeking revenge on its commander (Warner Anderson) for his part in the Sand Creek Massacre. Frontier violence and some unsavory characters. A-II (br)

Yellowbeard (1983) Several of the Monty Python troupe join forces with Cheech and Chong, Susannah York, James Mason, Peter Boyle, Madeline Kahn, and the late Marty Feldman in this leaden, stultifyingly unfunny pirate spoof directed by Mel Damski..Brief nudity and an abundance of coarse jokes. A-III (PG)

Yellowstone Kelly (1959) Clumsy Western directed by Gordon Douglas places the title Montana trapper (Clint Walker) and his helper (Edd Byrnes) in the middle of a tribal dispute between the Sioux over a captured Arapaho woman, while an inexperienced Army major prepares to drive the Sioux back to the Dakotas. Frontier violence and romantic complications. A-I (br)

Yentl (1983) Barbra Streisand musical in which she stars in the title role as an intelligent Jewish woman living in Eastern Europe at the turn of the century who dresses as a man in order to study in a *yeshiva* (male religious school), and finds herself attracted to a student (Mandy Patinkin) already engaged to be married. When the engagement is called off, Yentl is persuaded to become the bridegroom instead, but all is resolved when she leaves the handsome student and his beloved by emigrating to America and less-restrictive educational prerequisites. Streisand, who also produced, directed, and co-authored the script, is on center stage for almost the entire length of the movie, a bit much for all but her most avid fans. Yentl's mock marriage to another woman makes the movie inappropriate for young viewers. A-III (PG)

Yes, Giorgio (1982) Operatic tenor Luciano Pavarotti makes his film debut as a great opera star who, despite his wife in Italy, has a love affair with a beautiful American doctor (Kathryn Harrold) during a tour of the US. Pavarotti's singing would be enough to recommend it, except that director Franklin J. Schaffner's supremely silly movie takes a benign attitude toward the adulterous affair, which is not just incidental, but the main focus of the plot throughout. O (PG)

Yesterday's Enemy (1959) While sloughing through the Burmese jungle in 1942, a squad of British soldiers (led by Stanley Baker) execute some villagers to get information about the Japanese invaders, then ironically face the same treatment when captured by the Japanese. Directed by Val Guest, the tough-minded WW II drama effectively raises moral questions of military expediency and basic human rights. Much tension amid wartime violence. A-III (br)

Yo Yo (1967) French comedy about a millionaire's son (Pierre Etaix) who, after his father is ruined in the Depression, becomes a renowned clown, makes a fortune in the novelty business, but ultimately rejects the grand, yet lonely, style of life in which he had been raised. Also directed by Etaix, the episodic tale is told mainly through sight gags and visual humor that bears comparison with the antics of Keaton, Chaplin, and Lloyd. A-II (br)

Yog — Monster from Space (1971) Japanese monster moviemaker Ishiro Honda has picked the farthest recesses of his brain to create an elephantine octopus with a mitre-shaped head. The sight of this super-squid might thrill moppets, but older kids may yawn and yearn for more imaginative stuff, and they are right. A-I (G)

Yolanda and the Thief (1945) Odd musical romance set in a mythical South American country, where an 18-year-old convent-raised heiress (Lucille Bremer) is duped by an American con-man (Fred Astaire) posing as her guardian angel, until his conscience gets in the way. Directed by Vicente Minnelli, the story's silly premise never gets off the ground, though the songs and dance numbers are fanciful enough, and there's a bit of fantasy involving a real angel (Leon Ames). Romantic complications. A-II (br)

You Are What You Eat (1968) Pseudo-documentary about the youth counter-culture of the 1960s presents a montage of disjointed scenes of the so-called love generation engaged in various sexual activities, pot smoking, rock-song gatherings, and street happenings, sprinkled with scenes of the cult heroes of the period. Directed by Barry Feinstein, it tries to be outrageous, but is mostly tasteless and vulgar. Some exploitative nudity. O (br)

You Belong to My Heart (see: **Mr. Imperium**)

You Came Along (1945) Three combat pilots (Robert Cummings, Don DeFore, and Charles Drake) clown their way across the country on a WW II bond-drive in a romantic comedy which turns serious when one of them (Cummings) determines to marry their tour guide (Lizabeth Scott) despite his terminal medical condition. Directed by John Farrow, there's plenty of fun along the way, but what period audiences saw as an uplifting ending seems maudlin and heavy-handed today. A-I (br)

You Can't Beat Love (1937) Dated situation comedy about a wealthy playboy (Preston Foster) who runs for mayor on a bet, then falls for his opponent's daughter (Joan Fontaine). Directed by Christy Cabanne, the comedy gets heavy-handed on the issue of municipal corruption, but Paul Hurst scores as a tough union-leader aiming to become chief of police. A-I (br)

You Can't Cheat an Honest Man (1939) Uneven comedy about a hard-up circus owner (W.C. Fields) whose constant flimflams keep him in trouble with the law, until his daughter (Constance Moore) decides to marry a man wealthy enough to pay his debts. Directed by George Marshall, the comic proceedings include ventriloquist Edgar Bergen and his wooden pal, Charlie McCarthy, but the funniest scenes belong to Fields, whose imaginative antics turn the circus into a fun house and transform a high-society party into a chaotic shambles at picture's end. Slapstick humor and comic invective. A-I (br)

You Can't Run Away from It (1956) Dim musical version of **It Happened One Night**, with exasperated reporter Jack Lemmon helping spoiled heiress June Allyson elude domineering father Charles Bickford. Producer-director Dick Powell's mirthless remake of a classic romantic comedy has all the appeal of a flat tire. Sexual situations and innuendo. A-III (br)

You Can't Sleep Here (see: **I Was a Male War Bride**)

You Can't Take It with You (1938) Solid adaptation of the George Kaufman-Moss Hart screwball comedy about an impoverished family of eccentrics whose daughter (Jean Arthur) falls for a rich man's son (James Stewart). Directed by Frank Capra, the zany guests of the wacky household come and go, as the family's head (Lionel Barrymore) tries to convince the rich man (Edward Arnold) that happiness has nothing to do with money. That sentiment may seem less convincing today than in the Depression, but the cheerfully uninhibited antics of this house of sage fools are still very funny indeed. A-I (br)

You Can't Steal Love (see: **Live a Little, Steal a Lot**)

You Can't Win 'Em All (1970) Tony Curtis and Charles Bronson cavort through post-WW I Turkey as a pair of roguish mercenaries, periodically betraying each other for the least whiff of beauty or booty. Director Peter Collison's tired, formula adventure features Turkey's matinee idol, Fikret Hakan, but the real star of this turkey is a beautiful old steam-engine, lovingly photographed against a picturesque Turkish locations. A-II (PG)

You Gotta Stay Happy (1948) Slack romantic comedy in which a mixed-up heiress (Joan Fontaine) runs out on her wedding night and falls for a diffident pilot (James Stewart), who lets her come along on a cross-country air-cargo flight, with predictable results. Directed by H.C. Potter, the off-beat proceedings have some amusing moments, but much of the humor is forced, and the romance lacks the intended charm. Sexual situations and innuendo. A-III (br)

You Light Up My Life (1977) Young singer-composer (Didi Conn) breaks away from the smothering influence of her comedian father and comes to New York, determined to rely on no one but herself. Director Joseph Brooks neatly packaged bit of nothing fails to hold its thin story line together, despite Conn's good performance. An incident of premarital sex is presented as a moral lapse which the heroine immediately regrets. A-II (PG)

You Never Can Tell (1951) Daffy off-beat comedy in which a dog, poisoned after inheriting a fortune, is sent back from "beastatory" in human form as a private investigator (Dick Powell) to find his poisoner (Charles Drake). Director Lou Breslow treats the fantasy premise in leaden fashion, though this doesn't impede the dizzy humor with the private eye's penchant for snacking on dog biscuits while his fellow "manimal" (Joyce Holden), a former horse, out-races automobiles on occasion. Those in the mood for silliness will not be disappointed. A-I (br)

You Only Live Twice (1967) Sean Connery in his fifth appearance as James Bond goes through the motions of tracking down some mission space-capsules amidst oriental intrigue in Japan, and finally bests his arch-foe Blofeld (Donald Pleasence). The Agent 007 formula of impersonal sex and violence has worn thin, with the result that director Lewis Gilbert's Bond movie is just another mediocre spy thriller. A-III (GP)

You Only Love Once (1969) Unpretentious French romance depicting the loving relationship of a couple (Karen Blanguernon and Frederic de Pasquale) from first fancy to marriage, parenthood, estrangement, and reconciliation. Directed by Dirk Sanders, it is a gay, moody, colorful expression of the simple things in real life, often having the effect of a lilting visual ballet, and is well-worth seeing for its vision of the constancy of love. A-II (G)

You So Crazy (1994) Martin Lawrence demonstrates his limited talents as a stand-up comic in a series of rambling, very raunchy monologues devoted almost exclusively to sex in an unamusing, unenlightening, and unimaginative performance recorded by director Thomas Schlamme. Trivialization of sexuality, explicit language, and unrelenting use of sexual expletives. O (NC-17)

You Talkin' to Me? (1987) By dyeing his hair blonde, struggling New York actor (Jim Youngs) meets tanned California girl (Faith Ford), whose Disney-like daddy (James Noble) casts him as the evangelical host of a family TV-show. Director Charles Winkler uncovers some further inbred elements of the Hollywood scene but doesn't explore them. Racial violence and some profanity. A-III (R)

You'll Find Out (1940) Creaky vehicle for radio personality Kay Kyser, who takes his orchestra, including comic Ish Kabibble and vocalist Ginny Simms, to a debutante's isolated mansion, where they spend a stormy night amidst sinister goings-on with ominous visitors (Boris Karloff, Peter Lorre, and Bela Lugosi). Director David Butler's spooky comedy mixes silly period humor with tepid menace and hokey suspense. Unmemorable save for the period music. A-I (br)

You'll Like My Mother (1972) When her husband is killed in Vietnam, the pregnant widow (Patty Duke) visits her mother-in-law but is met with unaccountable hostility, is troubled by a menacing man lurking in the shadows, and gradually realizes she is being kept a prisoner in the creaky old mansion. Directed by Lamont Johnson, the twisting plot of this tight little mystery thriller offers a goodly number of chills and shocks. A-III (PG)

You're a Big Boy Now (1967) Wacky comedy about young man (Peter Kaster) who, in trying to make the transition from adolescence to independence from overbearing father (Rip Torn) and clinging mother (Geraldine Page), gets his own apartment and becomes infatuated with an actress (Elizabeth Hartman). Directed by Francis Ford Coppola, its exaggerated comic style does not always succeed, especially with some of the erotic elements. A-IV (br)

You're Lying (1973) Powerful Swedish semi-documentary indictment of the inadequacies and outright injustices existing in a penal system that prides itself on being the best in the world. Directed by Vilgot Sjoman, it demonstrates the contradictions between official policy and the actual practice of using prisons to effect social rehabilitation, as well as society's indifference to how its prisons actually operate. Excessively explicit treatment of sexual matters. O (nr)

You're My Everything (1949) Boston socialite (Anne Baxter) and vaudeville song-and-dance man (Dan Dailey) marry, make it big in early movies, then argue about whether to let their daughter (Shari Robinson) become a Shirley Temple-like child star. Director Walter Lang gets some brisk fun with old Hollywood nostalgia, but the characters are superficial, and the domestic situations syrupy. Few bright spots for youngsters. A-I (br)

You're Never Too Young (1955) Silly comedy in which Jerry Lewis escapes a murderer by getting on a train dressed in an 11-year-old's sailor suit with a ticket bought by a teacher (Dean Martin) returning to his post in a girl's academy. In a tiresome remake of **The Major and the Minor**, director Norman Taurog drags out the mirthless proceedings in slack fashion, save for Lewis's frenetic mugging. Mild romantic complications and sexual innuendo. A-II (br)

You're Only Young Once (1938) Judge Hardy (Lewis Stone) and family vacation at the seashore, with romantic complications furnished by son Andy (Mickey Rooney) and daughter Marian (Cecilia Parker). Director George B. Seitz's pleasant but lightweight entry in the Hardy series is notable chiefly for its period picture of fun at a family resort. A-I (br)

You're Telling Me! (1934) W.C. Fields comedy in which he plays a hard-drinking small-town inventor whose bad luck is changed by a chance encounter with a foreign princess (Adrienne Ames). Directed by Erle C. Kenton, the plot's not much, but Fields makes what's there hilarious, especially a classic comic routine on the golf links. Intemperance and malicious gossip as sources of humor. A-II (br)

You've Got Mail (1998) Breezy romantic comedy in which two rival Manhattan booksellers (Tom Hanks and Meg Ryan) trade barbs, unaware they are falling in love with each other through anonymous e-mail messages. Director Nora Ephron turns in a romantic trifle made enjoyable by the winning chemistry between its appealing stars. Implied affairs and an instance of profanity. A-III (PG)

You've Got to Walk It Like You Talk It or You'll Lose That Beat (1971) Director Peter Locke's low-budget story of a confused young man in search of himself (Zalman King) is a witless attempt to satirize the Establishment, but all that emerges is a stupefying amount of visual and verbal crudity. O (nr)

Young Americans (1967) Semi-documentary on a national tour of teenage singers presenting a program of show tunes, spirituals, folk songs, and traditional melodies. Written and directed by Alex Grasshoff, the material is blended into a pleasant story of the personal interaction between the talented young musicians and the reaction of audiences to the troupe's humor and enthusiasm. A-I (br)

Young and Innocent (1937) British mystery in which a jobless writer (Derrick de Marney) is arrested for the murder of a screen actress, then escapes to prove his innocence with the help of the local constable's daughter (Nova Pilbeam). Directed by Alfred Hitchcock, the couple's flight from the police is paced with grit and humor, eventually culminating in the capture of the killer, who's playing the drums in a hotel dance band and whose blinking eyes give him away to the audience before the pursuers get wise. Stylized violence and menacing situations. A-II (br)

Young Animals, The (1968) Crudely contrived story of Mexican-American teenagers trying to win acceptance and equal rights in a California small-town high school. Exploitative treatment of violence and teenage sexual relations. O (PG)

Young at Heart (1955) Slick sudser in which the daughter (Doris Day) of a music teacher (Robert Keith) calls off her wedding to a promising composer (Gig Young) because she thinks her sister (Elizabeth Fraser) is in love with the guy, then marries an embittered musician (Frank Sinatra) who proves to be suicidal. Directed by Gordon Douglas, this musical version of Fannie Hurst's **Four Daughters** has some good songs, including the title number, but lays on the sentiment with a trowel, and only Sinatra fans will appreciate the saccharine ending. Romantic complications and a suicide attempt. A-II (br)

Young Billy Young (1969) Standard Western about the new marshal (Robert Mitchum) of a lawless town, who takes the job in order to avenge the killing of his son, while befriending a wild youth (Robert Walker) who reminds him of his dead boy. Directed by Burt Kennedy, the story is entirely predictable, and the relationship between the older man and the youth is never explored with any depth. Some rather bloody shoot-outs. A-II (G)

Young Cassidy (1965) Somewhat fictionalized biography of young Sean O'Casey (Rod Taylor) explores the background of poverty, ignorance, injustice, and rebellion in Ireland that was to shape the playwright's dramatic vision. Directed by Jack Cardiff and John Ford, the British production is rich in period detail and attains some human dimension but is rather romanticized in its picture of Irish life. Some stylized violence and sexual references. A-III (br)

Young Couple, A (1971) Familiar French tale of a young couple (Anna Gael and Alain Libolt) who marry, enjoy a rich party-going life, but separate when the self-centered wife and the husband cannot reconcile their different visions of life. Directed by Rene Gainville, it is a well-made but somewhat fleeting portrait of early married life and the consequences of infidelity. A-III (nr)

Young Dillinger (1965) Clunky crime melodrama in which Dillinger (Nick Adams) is caught after robbing a safe with the help of his girlfriend (Mary Ann Mobley), then escapes custody to form his own gang, and is hunted down by the FBI. Directed by Terry O. Moore, the Depression-era action is woefully unconvincing, and the crime-does-not-pay ending is a bad joke. Nasty violence and common-law marriage. A-III (br)

Young Doctors in Love (1982) Stupid spoof of doctor movies and soap operas intermixes sketches and sight gags with a narrative line about the adventures of first-year interns. Directed by Gary Marshall, this has a few good laughs along the way, but excessive vulgarity sours the humor. Some nudity. O (R)

Young Einstein (1989) Wacky Australian comedy links the physicist who gave us the theory of relativity to the origins of rock'n'roll music. Writer, director, editor, co-producer, and star Yahoo Serious pratfalls his way through an eccentric interpretation of Einstein's youth, taking Monty Python-esque liberties, and introducing a comedy persona rivaling that of Pee-Wee Herman. Shower scene with rear male nudity and minimal sexual innuendo. A-II (PG)

Young Frankenstein (1974) Director Mel Brooks's spoof of the venerable horror classic stars Gene Wilder as an American doctor who inherits the family's Transylvanian estate, with Peter Boyle as the monster whose prodigious sexual appetite provides the one-liner for the movie. Bright spots are Marty Feldman, whose pop-eyes are upstaged by his shifting hump, and Cloris Leachman as the housekeeper whose name causes horses to whinny. Though generally amusing, with some clever bits, and occasionally hilarious moments, it features much vulgarity, verbal and otherwise. A-IV (PG)

Young Girls of Rochefort, The (1967) French musical romance in which false values are nicely ribbed, star-crossed lovers are united, and everyday dreams come true when a fair comes to town, and two local girls (Catherine Deneuve and Francoise Dorleac) join in the fun. Directed by Jacques Demy, the production has some simple charm, but suffers from a static setting, lack of continuity, and a surfeit of nonprofessional singing. A-II (br)

Young Guns, The (1956) Formula Western set in 1897 Wyoming, where the son (Russ Tamblyn) of an executed outlaw tires of being treated as an outcast and joins a wild bunch of young toughs, then has to decide whether to be their leader or go straight as urged by an outlaw's daughter (Gloria Talbott). Directed by Albert Band, there are no surprises here, except for a pretentious foreword equating the story's young gunmen with the juvenile delinquents of its own day. Stylized violence, some of it quite nasty. A-III (br)

Young Guns (1988) The young Billy the Kid (Emilio Estevez) teams up with a group known as the Regulators to avenge the murder of his mentor, a good-guy cattle rancher (Terence Stamp). Director Christopher Cain depicts Billy and his buddies (Kiefer Sutherland, Charlie Sheen, Lou Diamond Phillips) cavorting like Robin Hood's merry band as they destroy a corrupt rancher and his murderous gang. Some intense violence and bloodshed, much profanity, a sequence glorifying drug use, and implications of sexual impropriety. A-III (R)

Young Guns II (1990) Claiming to be Billy the Kid, a grizzled old cowboy (Emilio Estevez) recounts in flashback what really happened after his one-time friend, Pat Garrett (William Petersen), put on a sheriff's badge and set out to kill the Kid and his gang. Director Geoff Murphy's spirited sequel has some good performances and eye-catching scenery, but tends to idealize the outlaws as hip and funny true-blue buddies — especially troubling as they introduce a young teen to their lusty, lawless way of life. Some gory violence, implied sexual liaisons, several shots of rear nudity, and occasional profanity. A-III (PG-13)

Young Lions, The (1958) Flawed adaptation of Irwin Shaw's novel about three soldiers in WW II France — a brash Broadway entertainer afraid he's a coward (Dean Martin), an American Jew plagued by home-grown anti-Semites (Montgomery Clift), and a German officer disillusioned by Nazi inhumanity (Marlon Brando). Director Edward Dmytryk plods through a fitfully interesting but overlong script, whose good intentions are largely undone by Martin's inept performance and Clift's limp portrayal of victim-turned-hero, though Brando commands attention as an ambiguous idealist. Wartime violence and sexual situations. A-III (br)

Young Man with a Horn (1950) Uneven melodrama of a poor but musically gifted youth (Kirk Douglas) who is taught to play the trumpet by a jazz master (Juan Hernandez), achieves success with a popular dance band, then falls for a rich, neurotic woman (Lauren Bacall) who takes the joy out of his life and music, leaving him a self-destructive has-been, except to his friends (Hoagy Carmichael and Doris Day). Directed by Michael Curtiz, the episodic story is musically effective with Harry James dubbing the horn work, but the characters' personal lives are thinly written and dramatically unconvincing. Some stylized violence and emotional outbursts. A-II (br)

Young Mr. Lincoln (1939) Henry Fonda gives a warm, ingratiating performance as the young country lawyer whose self-deprecating wit and common-sense intelligence are put to the test in defending an innocent youth charged with murder. Director John Ford is at his best in this leisurely slice of Americana that gains stature in credibly foreshadowing the home-spun virtues which would soon propel young Abe into Illinois politics and the White House. Durable family fare that is as meaningful as it is entertaining. A-I (br)

Young People (1940) Tired Shirley Temple vehicle in which the moppet actress plays an orphan whose vaudevillian foster-parents (Jack Oakie and Charlotte Greenwood) retire to an unfriendly town. Despite some lively song-and-dance numbers, director Allan Dwan fails to find any fresh angles on the formula plot and stereotyped characters. Best for the young and undemanding. A-I (G)

Young Philadelphians, The (1959) Slick melodrama in which a poor law-student (Paul Newman) loses a rich girlfriend (Barbara Rush), then becomes a high-priced lawyer by cultivating the wife (Alexis Smith) of a partner (Otto Kruger) in a leading law firm, acquiring the account of a wealthy dowager (Billie Burke), and winning acquittal for a buddy (Robert Vaughn) in a murder trial. Directed by Vincent Sherman, the soapy story mixes the greed and sexual intrigues of the mainline set with the struggles of a young man to reach the top on his own terms. Sexual situations. A-III (br)

Young Poisoner's Handbook, The (1996) Uneven black comedy in which a chemistry-obsessed London teen (Hugh O'Conor) spends eight years in a mental asylum after poisoning his stepmother (Ruth Sheen), then is released only to resume experimenting with lethal poisons on unsuspecting co-workers. Directed by Benjamin Ross, the fact-based events are viewed mostly from the poisoner's warped perspective, resulting in some mean-spirited humor about the tragic loss of innocent lives caused by a lunatic would-be scientist. Stylized death scenes and some rough language. A-III (nr)

Young Rebel (1967) European co-production directed by Vincent Sherman in which the young Cervantes (Horst Buchholz) serves as secretary to the cardinal (Louis Jourdan) negotiating a truce with a Turkish emissary (Jose Ferrer), then becomes a hero in the Battle of Lepanto, but is later captured and held prisoner in Algiers until ransomed. The disjointed English-language version has much action but little insight into the character of the man who wrote *Don Quixote*. Period violence and sexual innuendo. A-II (PG)

Young Runaways, The (1968) Contrived story of three teenagers who flee abusive home situations and find their fate on their own even worse. Director Arthur Dreifuss treats a significant social subject in a superficial manner, leaving viewers with no clear insight into the reasons or solutions of the problem. Mature themes. A-III (R)

Young Sherlock Holmes (1985) A series of fatal accidents in Victorian London baffle the police, but not a student named Sherlock Holmes (Nicolas Rowe) and his school chum John Watson (Alan Cox). Directed by Barry Levinson, Chris Columbus's script gives a convincing account of Holmes's early schooldays that is entirely in keeping with the character of the master sleuth found in the pages of Arthur Conan Doyle's classic stories. The special effects are spectacular, but never gory or overdone, though some nightmare sequences may frighten young children. A-II (PG-13)

Young Tom Edison (1940) Hollywood version of the inventor's youth in a small Midwestern town features Mickey Rooney, whose curiosity about how and why things work constantly get him in trouble, until his ingenuity saves his mother's life and stops a train wreck. Directed by Norman Taurog, the script is emotionally manipulative but goes down easily enough, thanks to a good cast and credible period production. While inspirational fare for youngsters, some of their elders may find the sentimental exercise rather cloying. A-I (br)

Young Winston (1972) British dramatization of Churchill's memoir *My Early Life* retells uncritically his own version of his formative years from war correspondent in the Boer War to Parliament, with Simon Ward in the title role. Directed by Richard Attenborough, it excels as a panorama of life in the Empire before WW I, through a succession of tableaux of balls and battles, of parliamentary debates and family discourses. Although not a perfect film, it is a film of idealism and very enjoyable on a number of levels. A-II (PG)

Youngblood (1978) Black youth (Bryan O'Dell) joins a street gang for self-protection, and, when the gang takes on the local drug organization, he finds himself on a collision course with his older brother. It is an excessively violent movie whose morality is as muddled as its story line. O (R)

Youngblood (1986) Rob Lowe stars as the young and talented amateur hockey player who must come to terms with the violence of his sport and his determination to be a winner. When turning the other cheek doesn't work, he learns how to be tough, but still proves he can outclass the brutes. Nevertheless, he can't resist a final display of macho combat to satisfy his critics. Brutality, an explicit nude sex-scene, and ambivalent values ruin a simple tale about sports ethics for youngsters. O (R)

Younger Brothers, The (1949) Routine Western in which paroled outlaw Cole Younger (Wayne Morris) and his three brothers try to go straight, despite an old friend (Janis Page) who wants them to join her gang and an ex-lawman (Fred Clark) who wants them dead. Director Edwin L. Marin's weak shoot-'em-up is filled with cliches, though the double-take bank robbery in the finale is one for the books. Stylized gunplay and fisticuffs. A-II (br)

Younger Generation, The (1929) Sentimental tale from Fannie Hurst's novel about a Jewish family (headed by Jean Hersholt) moving from Manhattan's Lower East Side into a plush Fifth Avenue apartment after their son (Ricardo Cortez) becomes a wealthy antique dealer, but they move out again when he proves ashamed of them and his ethnic identity. Directed by Frank R. Capra, it's essentially a silent movie with a few dialogue sequences, but the result is eloquent enough in universalizing the pain of immigrant parents over offspring who reject their family heritage. Domestic strife. A-II (br)

Your Friends & Neighbors (1998) Sordid series of sketches involving six dim individuals whose unsatisfying sexual relationships have become the source of frustration, anger, and resentment. Writer-director Neil LaBute puts his cast of self-centered characters through the torments of sexual disappointments and misalliances, but the result becomes tediously monotonous and lacks any moral perspective. Numerous sexually explicit situations and dialogue, recurring rough language, and occasional profanity. O (R)

Your Three Minutes Are Up (1973) Unemployed swinger (Ron Liebman) initiates his younger, hardworking buddy (Beau Bridges) into a series of con-games that at first seem easy and fun, but they threaten the young man's approaching marriage (to Janet Margolin), and in the end events take an ugly turn. Director Douglas Schwartz introduces some heavy-handed and explicit sex scenes, which only compound the problem of its murky underlying morality. O (R)

Your Turn, My Turn (1979) Unpleasant French comedy romance stars Marlene Jobert as the mother of an eight-year-old boy who meets Philip Leotard, the father of a nine-year-old girl, and though encumbered by their perceptive children, they begin an adulterous affair. Directed by Francoise Leterrier, the movie's Gallic view of life is not especially amusing despite its frothy treatment. Benign attitude towards adultery. O (nr)

Yours, Mine and Ours (1968) Fact-based story of a Navy widower (Henry Fonda) and a Navy widow (Lucille Ball) who fall in love, get married, and merge their 18 children into one big, happy family. Director Melville Shavelson's comedy has predictable but genuinely funny complications, such as an interrupted honeymoon, identity crises, bathroom lineups, troop-movement planning, and economy-sizing. Underneath all the broad humor is a gently moving story that manages to keep in touch with human reality. Truly a family picture. A-I (br)

Yukon Flight (1939) Adventure programmer directed by Ralph Staub in which singing Sgt. Renfrew (James Newill) of the Royal Mounted Police teams with a airplane pilot (Warren Hull) to stop a crooked air-cargo service which is cheating gold-miners of the true value of their ore shipments. Stylized violence. A-I (br)

Z (1969) When a leftist minister (Yves Montand) in the Greek government is assassinated, the investigating magistrate (Jean-Louis Trintignant) tries to untangle the shadowy affair in order to find those responsible. The French dramatization directed by Costa-Gavras is a taut political thriller that goes beyond Greek politics and party labels because it is interested in justice and critical of any system of government that justifies criminal acts and violence in attaining its objectives. A-II (PG)

Z.P.G. (see: **Zero Population Growth**)

Zabriskie Point (1970) Taking its title from a promontory that overlooks Death Valley, director Michelangelo Antonioni's first movie about America is critical of its ill-treatment of youth and its self-cannibalism through violence and material excess, topped off in an explosive finale. Yet, because the message is expressed largely via cliches, all that it underscores is that perhaps middle-aged filmmakers should avoid making youth-oriented movies about other cultures. Some excessive sexual scenes. O (R)

Zachariah (1971) Director George Englund updates the Western with rock music, hippie garb, the search for identity, and a plea for peace, all laced together with self-parody and an incurable romanticism. The two heroes (Don Johnson and John Rubenstein) show the audience that peace, love, and friendship are possible in a world of violence, hate, and mistrust. Hokey as it sounds, the movie works if given a chance, and its overriding values and goals cannot be dismissed too lightly. Stylized violence, sexual innuendo, drug references, and coarse language. A-III (PG)

Zandy's Bride (1974) Gene Hackman plays a rough-and-tough Western rancher circa 1870 who is finally mellowed by Liv Ullmann, his mail-order bride from Minnesota. Though the narrative is disappointingly little more than a disorganized series of scenes between two extreme character types, director Jan Troell re-creates the frontier era with authority, gets excellent performances from his principals, and conveys some insights into human relations. Adult material, including a rape. A-III (PG)

Zarak (1957) Plodding potboiler directed by Terence Young pits a 19th-century British officer (Michael Wilding) against the noble Afghan rebel of the title (Victor Mature) who, among his other problems, has wed a sultry dancer (Anita Ekberg) from his late father's harem. Assorted stylized violence and sexual situations. A-III (br)

Zardoz (1974) British science-fiction fantasy set in 2293, when technology has given the power of eternal life to a single enclave of humans whose paradise is penetrated and ultimately destroyed by a barbarian (Sean Connery) from the outlands. Director John Boorman's vision of the shapelessness of things to come needs a road map simply to follow the plot and sort out its intended parables. Some violence, confused religious references, and brief nudity. A-III (R)

Zatoichi Meets Yojimbo (1972) Japanese movie hero Zatoichi (Shintaro Katsu) is a blind masseur whose skill with a stick sword makes him invulnerable to the gangs of cut-throats and samurai bands which inhabit the medieval milieu of his films. Director Kihachi Okamoto pits Zatoichi against Toshiro Mifune's classical characterization of the samurai professional turned free agent in an action fantasy about a violent world where death is only as real as the special-effects man can make it. A-III (nr)

Zatoichi: The Blind Swordsman (see: **Zatoichi's Conspiracy**)

Zatoichi's Conspiracy (1974) Director Kimiyoshi Yasuda is back with another adventure of Zatoichi (Shintaro Katsu), the blind, flabby masseur whose exploits with a cane-sword make him the terror of criminals and equal to a samurai squad. Zatoichi is visiting his hometown just as it is taken over by a vicious crook in league with the corrupt bailiff of the district. There is the final showdown in a crescendo of special effects. A-III (PG)

Zebra in the Kitchen (1965) A lot of silliness occurs when a town is overrun by wild animals freed from the local zoo by a young lad (Jay North) opposed to caging animals. But no harm is done, thanks to the zoo's dedicated director (Martin Milner) and head keeper (Andy Devine). Director Ivan Tors mixes in some mild-mannered slapstick along with the message of treating animals humanely, but its contrived cuteness is not for all tastes. A-I (G)

Zebrahead (1992) Violence flares when a white senior (Michael Rapaport) in a predominantly black Detroit high school engages in an interracial romance with the cousin (N'Bushe Wright) of his best friend (DeShonn Castle). Writer-director Anthony Drazan's sobering look at teenage and adult racial prejudice dramatizes in a low-keyed manner the tragic effects of senseless casual violence. Implied sexual encounters, brief violence, a few crude sexual references, and occasional rough language. A-III (R)

Zelig (1983) Director Woody Allen spoofs the American obsession with celebrity in this comedy about an obscure clerk (also Allen) in the 1920s who wants so desperately to fit in that he develops a malady transforming him physically and mentally into a person quite like whomever he happens to be with. A mildly amusing comedy in which the camerawork of Gordon Willis weaves the Zelig saga into actual historical footage, making for some good sight gags. A-II (PG)

Zelly and Me (1988) Sensitive movie set in 1950s Virginia tells the story of a wealthy, orphaned 11-year-old (Alexandra Johnes) who is emotionally abused by her grandmother (Glynis Johns) and loved unconditionally by her governess (Isabella Rossellini). Writer-director Tina Rathborne explores the gentle child's heartbreaking attempts to cope with her grandmother's volatile and irrational demands. Some intense scenes of emotional abuse and humiliation may be disturbing to very young children. A-II (PG)

Zentropa (1992) Absorbing story of a naive American (Jean-Marc Barr) working in postwar Germany who becomes ensnared between an alluring seductress (Barbara Sukowa) and a manipulative colonel (Eddie Constantine) with the American Occupation. Impressive technique and style surpass the substance of Danish director Lars Von Trier's surreal tale of multiple deceptions. Some subtitles. A discreet sexual encounter, brief violence ,and an instance of rough language. A-III (nr)

Zeppelin (1971) While the Kaiser's dirigibles bomb London from heights out of range of early WW I biplanes, British intelligence decides to slip a spy into the Zeppelin works, where he learns of a secret mission to destroy British morale decisively. Director Etienne Perier's old-fashioned tale of wartime adventure features a good cast (Michael York, Marius Goring, Elke Sommer, and Alexandra Stewart) and action laced with humor, suspense, and some quite good special-effects work. Wartime violence. A-I (G)

Zero Effect (1998) Offbeat tale of a reclusive private eye (Bill Pullman) who falls for a suspect (Kim Dickens) in a blackmailing case, then fears she is in danger from his ruthless client (Ryan O'Neal). Writer-director Jake Kasdan gets so bogged down in detailing the eccentricities of his quirky characters that the resolution of the case becomes almost incidental. An implied sexual encounter, intermittent profanity, and recurring rough language. A-III (R)

Zero Population Growth (1972) In some brave new world of the future, joy has gone out of life because childbirth has been made punishable by death, though Oliver Reed and Geraldine Chaplin risk all to procreate. Directed by Michael Campus, the movie pretends to be an indictment of 20th-century decadence, but is simply a rather plodding exercise whose outcome is ridiculously anticlimactic. Adult theme. A-III (PG)

Zeus and Roxanne (1997) A dog and a dolphin form an unlikely friendship while the dog's widowed owner (Steve Guttenberg) and a single mom (Kathleen Quinlan) who happens to be a scientist studying the dolphin are nudged towards love and marriage by their enterprising children. Director George Miller accentuates the postcard-pretty Caribbean setting, but the romance is highly contrived, and the cuteness of the animals relentlessly stressed. Brief intense menace. A-II (PG)

Zig Zag (1970) George Kennedy plays a man dying of a brain tumor who sets himself up to be convicted of an unsolved crime and arranges through a lawyer (Eli Wallach) that his wife (Anne Jackson) receive the reward offered by the insurance company. Directed by Richard Colla, the story's plot complications become a jumble of events, and the incredibly contrived ending makes it not worth the effort. A-II (GP)

Zig Zag (1976) Catherine Deneuve and Bernadette Lafont play slightly talented showgirls eager to get ahead, in an erratic French movie directed by Laszlo Szabo, which attempts to tell a tragicomic story against the background of a seedy entertainment world. Graphic sexual depiction. O (R)

Zita (1968) Evocative but flawed French movie of a young girl (Joanna Shimkus) trying to accept the trauma of her beloved aunt's impending death. Though beautifully directed by Robert Enrico, the story is susceptible to the interpretation that maturity is achieved through casual sex. O (M)

Zombies of Mora Tau (1957) Dull horror tale directed by Edward Cahn in which a woman (Allison Hayes) on a salvaging expedition after a sunken fortune in diamonds becomes one of the walking dead who guard the treasure. Supernatural hooey with no surprises and few frights. A-III (br)

Zombies on Broadway (1945) Low-budget comic thriller directed by Gordon Douglas has a pair of dippy press agents (Wally Brown and Alan Carney) scouring a remote Caribbean island for a zombie demanded by a nightclub owner (Sheldon Leonard), then find themselves the guests of a mad scientist (Bela Lugosi) who's an expert on the walking dead. Comic menace with a few scary moments. A-II (br)

Zorba the Greek (1965) Anthony Quinn embodies the zestful, warmly human title-character who helps his withdrawn English employer (Alan Bates) learn to enjoy life in spite of its imperfections, including sad encounters along the way with a lonely widow (Irene Papas) and an elderly courtesan (Lila Kedrova). Directed by Michael Cacoyannis, the realistic depiction of harsh living conditions on the island of Crete is transformed by the movie's joyful affirmation of life. Some brutish coarseness and sexual references. A-IV (br)

Zorro, The Gay Blade (1981) George Hamilton plays the son of Zorro, the legendary righter of wrongs and champion of oppressed peasants in Old California, with a twin brother (Hamilton again) who is a foppish homosexual. Directed by Peter Medak, the one-joke comedy has a lackluster plot, slow pacing, and the smiles are few and far between. Occasional mild vulgarity, and the homosexual aspect is amiably farcical. A-II (PG)

Zulu (1964) Vivid re-creation of the 1879 battle at Rorke's Drift in Africa's Natal, where a small British outpost (led by Stanley Baker and Michael Caine) is beset by some 4,000 Zulus in desperate hand-to-hand combat on the day after other Zulu warriors have massacred an entire British field force of 1,200 soldiers. Directed by Cy Endfield, the military action is well-staged and played with conviction by a strong British cast and numerous Zulus, though the stirring results are marred by some early scenes disparaging a Christian missionary (Jack Hawkins) and his daughter (Ulla Jacobsson). Intense battlefield violence and brief ethnographic nudity. A-III (br)

A Choice Collection of Family Movies

Not all movies listed below will suit all tastes but there is enough variety to leave no one unsatisfied. Please use the capsule review to help in selecting appropriate fare for your family.

ADVENTURE

Adventures of Marco Polo, The (1938)
Adventures of the Wilderness Family, The (1975)
Adventures of Tom Sawyer, The (1938)
Antarctica (1984)
Arabian Adventure (1979)
Around the World in 80 Days (1956)
Boy Ten Feet Tall, A (1965)
Captains Courageous (1937)
Elephant Boy (1937)
Flight of the Doves (1971)
Heidi (1937)
Hero's Island (1962)
His Majesty O'Keefe (1954)
Huckleberry Finn (1939)
Kidnapped (1960)
King Solomon's Mines (1950)
Little Lord Fauntleroy (1936)
Lost Horizon (1937)
Maya (1966)
Mutiny on the Bounty (1935)
Mysterious Island (1961)
Prince and the Pauper, The (1937)
Prisoner of Zenda, The (1937)
Scott of the Antarctic (1948)
Sea Gypsies, The (1978)
Shipwrecked (1991)
Swiss Family Robinson (1960)
Tarzan's New York Adventure (1942) - series
Treasure Island (1934)
Treasure of Lost Canyon, The (1952)
Wilderness Journey (1972)

ANIMALS

Adventures of Milo and Otis, The (1989)
Air Bud (1997)
Bear, The (1989)
Benji (1974)
Biscuit Eater, The (1940)
Black Beauty (1971)
Black Stallion, The (1979)
Born Free (1966)
Brighty of the Grand Canyon (1967)
Brother of the Wind (1975)
Christian the Lion (1977)
Clarence the Cross-eyed Lion (1965)
Digby, the Biggest Dog in the World (1974)
Dog of Flanders, A (1959)
Elephant Called Slowly, An (1971)
Flipper (1963)
Free Willy (1993)
Gentle Giant (1967)
George! (1973)
Homeward Bound: The Incredible Journey (1993)
The Incredible Journey (1963)
It's Showtime (1976)
Kelly and Me (1957)
Lad: A Dog (1962)
Lassie Come Home (1943)
My Friend Flicka (1943)
Namu, The Killer Whale (1966)
National Velvet (1944)
Phar Lap (1984)
Ring of Bright Water (1969)
Tender Warrior, The (1972)

ANIMATION

Adventures of Mark Twain, The (1986)
Aladdin (1992)
Alice in Wonderland (1951)
All Dogs Go to Heaven (1989)
American Tail, An (1986)
Anastasia (1997)
Babar: The Movie (1989)
Bambi (1942)
Boy Named Charlie Brown, A (1969) - series
Bug's Life, A (1998)
Care Bears Adventure in Wonderland (1987)
Charlotte's Web (1973)
Cinderella (1949)
Dumbo (1941)
Fantasia (1940)
Ferngully ... The Last Rainforest (1992)
Gulliver's Travels (1939)
Gulliver's Travels Beyond the Moon (1966)
Gumby (1996)
Hercules (1997)
Hunchback of Notre Dame, The (1996)
Jungle Book, The (1967)
Land Before Time, The (1988)
Last Unicorn, The (1982)
Lion King, The (1994)
Little Nemo: Adventures in Slumberland (1992)
Madeline (1998)
Mulan (1998)
My Neighbor Totoro (1993)
101 Dalmatians (1961)
Peter Pan (1953)
Phantom Tollbooth, The (1970)

Pinocchio (1940)
Pippi Longstocking (1997)
Pocahontas (1995)
Prince of Egypt, The (1998)
Rugrats Movie, The (1998)
Secret of NIMH, The (1982)
Sleeping Beauty (1959)
Snow White and the Seven Dwarfs (1937)
Swan Princess, The (1994)
Toy Story (1995)
World of Hans Christian Anderson, The (1971)
Yellow Submarine (1968)

FANTASY

Alias Nick Beal (1949)
Babe (1995)
Barney's Great Adventure: The Movie (1998)
Blue Bird, The (1940)
Captain Nemo and the Underwater City (1970)
Christmas Carol, A (1951)
Connecticut Yankee in King Arthur's Court, A (1949)
Dark Crystal, The (1983)
Daydreamer, The (1966)
E.T. The Extra-Terrestrial (1982)
Fantastic Voyage (1966)
Glass Slipper, The (1955)
Golden Voyage of Sinbad, The (1974)
Hans Christian Andersen (1952)
Heaven Can Wait (1943)
Here Comes Mr. Jordan (1941)
Horn Blows at Midnight, The (1945)
It's a Wonderful Life (1946)
Jack the Giant Killer (1961)
Journey to the Center of the Earth (1959)
Labyrinth (1986)
Luck of the Irish, The (1948)
March of the Wooden Soldiers (1934)
Mary Poppins (1964)
Master of the World (1961)
Miracle in Milan (1951)
Muppet Movie, The (1979) - series
NeverEnding Story, The (1984)
On Borrowed Time (1939)
Peter Rabbit and Tales of Beatrix Potter (1971)
Pufnstuf (1970)
Seven Faces of Dr. Lao (1964)
7th Voyage of Sinbad, The (1958)
Thief of Bagdad, The (1940)
Tom Thumb (1958)
20,000 Leagues Under the Sea (1954)
Voyage to the Bottom of the Sea (1961)
War of the Worlds, The (1953)
Willy Wonka and the Chocolate Factory (1971)
Wind in the Willows, The (1997)
Wizard of Oz, The (1939)
You Never Can Tell (1951)

DARK FANTASIES

Cat People (1942)
Dead of Night (1945)
Devil and Daniel Webster, The (1941)
Dr. Jekyll and Mr. Hyde (1941)
Fly, The (1958)
Haunting, The (1963)
House of Wax (1953)
Invisible Man, The (1933)
Island of Lost Souls (1932)
Uninvited, The (1944)

MONSTERS

Beast of Hollow Mountain, The (1956)
Bride of Frankenstein (1935)
Creature From the Black Lagoon, The (1954)
Dracula (1931)
Frankenstein (1931)
Godzilla, King of the Monsters (1956)
Gorgo (1961)
It Came from Beneath the Sea (1955)
Jurassic Park (1983)
King Kong (1933)
Mighty Joe Young (1949)
Mummy, The (1932)
Son of Kong, The (1933)
Tarantula (1955)
Werewolf of London (1935)
Wolf Man, The (1941)

SCIENCE FICTION

Blob, The (1958)
Close Encounters of the Third Kind (1977)
Day of the Triffids, The (1963)
Day the Earth Stood Still, The (1951)
Destination Moon (1950)
Dr. Who and the Daleks (1966)
Fahrenheit 451 (1966)
First Men in the Moon (1964)
Flight of the Navigator (1986)
Forbidden Planet (1956)
Incredible Shrinking Man, The (1957)
Invaders from Mars (1953)
Invasion of the Body Snatchers (1956)
It Came from Outer Space (1953)
Kronos (1957)
Last Starfighter, The (1984)
Robinson Crusoe on Mars (1964)
Star Trek: The Motion Picture (1980)
Star Wars (1977)
Them! (1954)
Thing, The (1951)
This Island Earth (1958)
Time Machine, The (1960)
2001: A Space Odyssey (1968)
Village of the Damned (1960)
World Without End (1956)
X the Unknown (1956)

MUSICALS

Anchors Aweigh (1945)
Annie (1982)
Annie Get Your Gun (1950)

Band Wagon, The (1953)
Carousel (1956)
Damsel in Distress, A (1937)
Fiddler on the Roof (1971)
Finian's Rainbow (1968)
Harvey Girls, The (1946)
Hello Dolly! (1969)
In the Good Old Summertime (1949)
King and I, The (1956)
Knickerbocker Holiday (1944)
Meet Me in St. Louis (1944)
Music Man, The (1962)
My Fair Lady (1964)
Oh! What a Lovely War (1969)
Oklahoma! (1955)
Oliver! (1968)
On the Town (1949)
Royal Wedding (1951)
Scrooge (1970)
Seven Brides for Seven Brothers (1954)
1776 (1972)
Show Boat (1936)
Singin' in the Rain (1951)
Sound of Music, The (1965)
State Fair (1945)
Take Me Out to the Ball Game (1949)
That's Entertainment (1974)
Where's Charley? (1952)
Wiz, The (1978)

COMEDY

Abbott and Costello in Hollywood (1945) - series
Addams Family, The (1991)
Andy Hardy Gets Spring Fever (1939) - series
Arsenic and Old Lace (1944)
Bedtime for Bonzo (1951)
Blondie (1938) - series
Bringing Up Baby (1938)
Brother Orchid (1940)
Cat Ballou (1965)
Cheaper by the Dozen (1950)
Christmas Story, A (1983)
Court Jester, The (1955)
Dude Goes West, The (1948)
Egg and I, The (1947)
Farmer's Daughter, The (1947)
Father of the Bride (1950)
Ferris Bueller's Day Off (1986)
George of the Jungle (1997)
Ghost Breakers, The (1940)
Gone Are the Days (1963)
Great Man Votes, The (1939)
Great McGinty, The (1940)
Happiest Days of Your Life, The (1950)
Help! (1965)
Holiday (1938)
Home Alone (1990)
International House (1933)
It Happened One Night (1934)
Lavender Hill Mob, The (1951)
Major and the Minor, The (1942)
Man in the White Suit, The (1951)
Margie (1946)
Midnight (1939)
Million Dollar Legs (1932)
Mouse That Roared, The (1959)
Murder, He Says (1945)
My Man Godfrey (1936)
My Sister Eileen (1942)
Nothing Sacred (1937)
Our Hearts Were Young and Gay (1944)
Paleface, The (1948)
Princess and the Pirate, The (1944)
Road to Singapore (1940) - series
Ruggles of Red Gap (1935)
Russians Are Coming, The Russians Are Coming, The (1966)
Solid Gold Cadillac, The (1956)
Sullivan's Travels (1942)
Three Smart Girls (1936)
Trouble with Angels, The (1966)
Way Out West (1937)
Whistling in the Dark (1941)
Yours, Mine, and Ours (1968)

DRAMA

All Mine to Give (1957)
And Now Miguel (1966)
Anne of Green Gables (1934)
Avalon (1990)
Billy Budd (1962)
Birdman of Alcatraz (1962)
Boy of Two Worlds (1970)
Boys Town (1938)
Breaking Away (1979)
Browning Version, The (1951)
By the Light of the Silvery Moon (1953)
Casablanca (1942)
Citizen Kane (1941)
Conrack (1974)
Crossfire (1947)
80 Steps to Jonah (1969)
84 Charing Cross Road (1987)
Gateway (1938)
Goodbye, Mr. Chips (1939)
Great Santini, The (1980)
Happy Years, The (1950)
Holiday Affair (1949)
How Green Was My Valley (1941)
I Remember Mama (1948)
Inn of the Sixth Happiness (1958)
Karate Kid, The (1984)
Little Princess, The (1939)
Little Women (1933)
Miracle on 34th Street (1947)
Mr. Mom (1983)
Night to Remember, A (1958)
Old Man and the Sea, The (1958)
100 Men and a Girl (1937)
Our Town (1940)

Quiet Man, The (1952)
Red Pony, The (1949)
San Francisco (1936)
Secret Garden, The (1949)
Seven Angry Men (1955)
Sounder (1972)
Spitfire Grill, The (1996)
Stand and Deliver (1988)
Tom Brown's School Days (1940)
Treasure of the Sierra Madre, The (1948)
Tree Grows in Brooklyn, A (1945)
Two Years Before the Mast (1946)
Where the Lilies Bloom (1974)
Yearling, The (1946)

MYSTERY

Adventures of Sherlock Holmes, The (1939) - series
And Then There Were None (1945)
Boston Blackie and the Law (1946) - series
Charlie Chan at the Opera (1936) - series
Detective, The (1954)
Dinner at the Ritz (1937)
Ex-Mrs. Bradford, The (1936)
Falcon in Danger, The (1943) - series
Gambit (1966)
Maltese Falcon, The (1941)
Mr. Moto Takes a Chance (1938) - series
Murder Ahoy (1964) - series
My Name Is Julia Ross (1945)
Saint in New York, The (1938)
Seven Keys to Baldpate (1947)
Thin Man, The (1934) - series
Wreck of the Mary Deare, The (1959)
Young Sherlock Holmes, The (1985)

THRILLERS

Birds, The (1963)
D.O.A. (1950)
Detective Story (1951)
Flame Over India (1959)
High Wind in Jamaica (1965)
Lady Vanishes, The (1938)
Most Dangerous Game, The (1932)
Naked Jungle, The (1954)
Narrow Margin (1952)
Phantom of the Opera, The (1943)
Rear Window (1954)
Shadow of a Doubt (1943)
Spiral Staircase, The (1946)
Tall Target, The (1951)
Third Man, The (1949)
39 Steps, The (1935)
Union Station (1950)
Window, The (1949)

SPORTS

Bang the Drum Slowly (1973)
Chariots of Fire (1981)
Fear Strikes Out (1957)
Field of Dreams (1989)
Harlem Globetrotters, The (1951)
Hoosiers (1987)
It Happens Every Spring (1949)
Jackie Robinson Story, The (1950)
Joe Louis Story, The (1953)
Knute Rockne, All American (1940)
League of Their Own, A (1992)
Natural, The (1984)
Paper Lion (1968)
Pastime (1991)
Pride of the Yankees, The (1942)
Rhubarb (1951)
Stratton Story, The (1949)

WESTERNS

Apache (1954)
Arizona (1940)
Big Trail, The (1930)
Broken Arrow (1950)
Cheyenne Autumn (1964)
Cimarron (1960)
Cowboy (1958)
Deerslayer, The (1957)
Fighting Kentuckian, The (1949)
Fort Apache (1948)
High Noon (1952)
Hondo (1953)
Jeremiah Johnson (1972)
Jesse James (1939)
McLintock! (1963)
My Darling Clementine (1946)
North West Mounted Police (1940)
Pony Soldier (1952)
Rio Grande (1950)
Searchers, The (1956)
Shane (1953)
She Wore a Yellow Ribbon (1949)
Stagecoach (1939)
They Died with Their Boots On (1941)
3:10 to Yuma (1957)
True Grit (1969)
Wagon Master (1950)
Will Penny (1968)

WAR

All Quiet on the Western Front (1930)
Battleground (1949)
Bell for Adano, A (1945)
Bridge on the River Kwai, The (1957)
Bridges at Toko-Ri, The (1954)
Caine Mutiny, The (1954)
Captive Heart, The (1946)
Cruel Sea, The (1953)
The Dam Busters (1954)
Dawn Patrol, The (1930)
Desert Fox, The (1951)
Destination Tokyo (1943)
Enemy Below, The (1957)
5 Fingers (1952)
Go for Broke! (1951)

Great Escape, The (1963)
Guadalcanal Diary (1943)
Hell in the Pacific (1968)
Home of the Brave (1949)
Longest Day, The (1962)
Men in War (1957)
Merrill's Marauders (1963)
Objective, Burma! (1945)
Paths of Glory (1957)
Patton (1970)
Pork Chop Hill (1959)
Pride of the Marines (1945)
Sergeant York (1941)
So Proudly We Hail (1943)
Sullivans, The (1944)
Task Force (1949)
They Were Expendable (1945)
Thirty Seconds over Tokyo (1944)
Three Came Home (1950)
Twelve O'Clock High (1949)

PERIOD HEROICS

Adventures of Robin Hood, The (1938)
African Queen, The (1951)
Beau Geste (1939)
Ben-Hur (1959)
Black Rose, The (1950)
Black Shield of Falworth, The (1954)
Captain Blood (1935)
Captain Horatio Hornblower (1951)
Crimson Pirate, The (1952)
Damn the Defiant! (1962)
Drums (1938)
Flame and the Arrow, The (1950)
Four Feathers, The (1939)
Gone With the Wind (1939)
Gunga Din (1939)
Horse Soldiers, The (1959)
Hunchback of Notre Dame, The (1939)
Ivanhoe (1952)
Lives of a Bengal Lancer (1935)
Lost Patrol, The (1934)
Mark of Zorro, The (1940)
Master of Ballantrae, The (1953)
Sea Hawk, The (1940)
Three Musketeers, The (1935)

BIOGRAPHY

Adventures of Mark Twain, The (1944)
Anastasia (1956)
Cromwell (1970)
Daniel Boone (1936)
Diary of Anne Frank, The (1959)
Edison, the Man (1940)
First Texan, The (1956)
Gandhi (1982)
Give 'em Hell, Harry (1976)
Houdini (1953)
Joe Hill (1971)
Lawrence of Arabia (1963)
Life of Emile Zola, The (1937)
Nicholas and Alexandra (1971)
Prisoner of Shark Island, The (1936)
Young Mr. Lincoln (1939)
Young Tom Edison (1940)

RELIGIOUS

And There Came a Man (1968)
Bernadette (1987)
Bible, The (1966)
Brother Sun, Sister Moon (1973)
Entertaining Angels: The Dorothy Day Story (1996)
Flowers of St. Francis, The (1950)
Francis of Assisi (1961)
Gospel According to St. Matthew, The (1966)
Gospel Road (1973)
Greatest Story Ever Told, The (1965)
Green Pastures, The (1936)
Joan of Arc (1948)
Loyola, the Soldier Saint (1952)
Man for All Seasons, A (1966)
Miracle of Our Lady of Fatima, The (1952)
Miracle of Saint Therese (1959)
Monsieur Vincent (1947)
Robe, The (1953)
Romero (1989)
Saint Joan (1957)
Seventh Chamber of Edith Stein, The (1996)
Song of Bernadette, The (1943)
Ten Commandments, The (1956)
Trial of Joan of Arc, The (1965)

STORIES OF FAITH

Angel in My Pocket (1968)
Assisi Underground, The (1984)
Bells of St. Mary's, The (1945)
Chosen, The (1982)
Count Three and Pray (1955)
Cross and the Switchblade, The (1970)
Deep Six, The (1958)
Demetrius and the Gladiators (1954)
Devil at 4 O'Clock, The (1961)
Fighting Father Dunne (1948)
Fighting 69th, The (1940)
Friendly Persuasion (1956)
Fugitive, The (1947)
Garden of Allah, The (1936)
Going My Way (1945)
Guilty of Treason (1950)
Hand in Hand (1960)
Heaven Knows, Mr. Allison (1957)
I Confess (1953)
Joni (1982)
Keys of the Kingdom, The (1944)
Left Hand of God, The (1955)
Lilies of the Field (1963)
Man Called Peter, A (1955)
Miracle in the Rain (1954)
Miracle of Marcelino, The (1955)
Miracle of the Bells, The (1948)

Nun's Story, The (1959)
One Foot in Heaven (1941)
Quo Vadis (1951)
Rain for a Dusty Summer (1972)
Sally and Saint Anne (1952)
Scandal at Scourie (1953)
Sea Wife (1957)
Singing Nun, The (1966)
Trouble Along the Way (1953)
Two of Us, The (1968)
Walk in the Shadow (1966)

MORAL ISSUES

Abandon Ship! (1957)
Ace in the Hole (1951)
Bad Day at Black Rock (1955)
Ballad of Gregorio Cortez, The (1983)
Boat Is Full, The (1981)
Boomerang (1947)
Call Northside 777 (1948)
China Syndrome, The (1979)
Cry, the Beloved Country (1952)
Count Five and Die (1958)
Days of Wine and Roses (1962)
Driving Miss Daisy (1989)
Fail Safe (1964)
Fury (1936)
Gentlemen's Agreement (1947)
Ghosts of Mississippi (1996)
Grapes of Wrath, The (1940)
Intruder in the Dust (1949)
Kundun (1997)
Long Walk Home, The (1990)
Missing (1982)
On the Waterfront (1954)
Raisin in the Sun, A (1961)
Seven Days in May (1964)
Seven Days to Noon (1950)
Snake Pit, The (1948)
Soldier's Story, A (1984)
Testament (1983)
To Kill a Mockingbird (1962)
Trial of the Catonsville Nine, The (1972)
Z (1969)

HISTORICAL

Agony and the Ecstasy, The (1965)
Alexander the Great (1956)
Amadeus (1984)
Barbarian and the Geisha, The (1958)
Buccaneer, The (1938)
Charge of the Light Brigade, The (1936)
Clive of India (1935)
Crusades, The (1935)
Cry Freedom (1987)
Emigrants, The (1972)
55 Days at Peking (1963)
Helen of Troy (1955)
Henry VIII and His Six Wives (1974)
Howards of Virginia, The (1940)
Lady Godiva (1955)
Marie Antoinette (1938)
Molly Maguires, The (1970)
New Land, The (1973)
Suez (1938)
Waterloo (1971)
Wilson (1944)
Young Winston (1972)

LITERATURE

As You Like It (1936)
Barabbas (1962)
Bostonians, The (1984)
Call of the Wild, The (1935)
Cyrano de Bergerac (1950)
Daisy Miller (1974)
David Copperfield (1935)
Dead, The (1987)
Devil's Disciple, The (1959)
Doctor Zhivago (1965)
Doll's House, A (1973)
Emma (1996)
Ethan Frome (1993)
Europeans, The (1979)
Far from the Madding Crowd (1967)
Glass Menagerie, The (1950)
The Hairy Ape (1944)
Hamlet (1969)
Heart Is a Lonely Hunter, The (1968)
Heiress, The (1949)
Henry V (1945)
House of the Seven Gables, The (1940)
Islands in the Stream (1977)
Jane Eyre (1944)
King Lear (1971)
Les Miserables (1936)
Lord Jim (1965)
Magnificent Ambersons, The (1942)
Nicholas Nickleby (1947)
O. Henry's Full House (1952)
One Day in the Life of Ivan Denisovich (1971)
Othello (1966)
Overcoat, The (1965)
Passage to India, A (1984)
Pygmalion (1938)
Sense and Sensibility (1995)
Tess (1980)
Twelfth Night (1996)
Uncle Vanya (1972)
War and Peace (1956)
Washington Square (1997)
Wuthering Heights (1939)

DOCUMENTARIES

NATURE

African Elephant, The (1971)
American Wilderness (1973)
Animals Are Beautiful People (1975)
Blue Water, White Death (1971)
Cougar Country (1972)
Cry of the Wild (1974)
Glacier Fox, The (1979)
High, Wild and Free (1968)
Leopard Son, The (1996)
North Country (1972)
Savage Wild, The (1970)
Scuba (1973)
World Without Sun (1964)

CULTURE AND THE ARTS

Arthur Rubenstein — Love of Life (1975)
Children of Theatre Street, The (1978)
Chronicle of Anna Magdelena Bach, The (1969)
Clowns, The (1971)
Don Quixote (1973)
Evening with the Royal Ballet, An (1965)
First Position (1973)
Homage to Chagall: The Colours of Love (1977)
I Am a Dancer (1973)
La Boheme (1965)
Midsummer Night's Dream, A (1967)
Nutcracker, the Motion Picture (1986)
Raga (1971)
Visions of Light: The Art of Cinematography (1993)
Voices of Sarafina! (1989)

PEOPLE

Anne Frank Remembered (1996)
Ben-Gurion Remembers (1973)
Cousin Bobby (1992)
Film Portrait (1974)
Finest Hours, The (1964)
Holy Outlaw, The (1971)
I.F. Stone's Weekly (1973)
Listen Up: The Lives of Quincy Jones (1990)
Malcolm X (1972)
Mother Teresa (1986)
Reminiscences of a Journey to Lithuania (1974)
Salesman (1969)
World of Buckminster Fuller, The (1974)
Years of Lightning, Day of Drums (1966)

EVENTS & ISSUES

American Dream (1992)
Brief History of Time, A (1992)
Dear America: Letters Home from Vietnam (1988)
Famine Within, The (1992)
Fire on the Mountain (1996)
Four Days in November (1964)
4 Little Girls (1997)
Freedom on My Mind (1994)
Gizmo (1980)
Guns of August, The (1965)
Harlan County, U.S.A. (1977)
Hoop Dreams (1994)
In the Land of the Deaf (1994)
In the Year of the Pig (1969)
Incident at Oglala (1992)
Kon Tiki (1951)
Manufacturing Consent: Noam Chomsky and the Media (1993)
People of the Wind (1976)
Ra Expeditions, The (1972)
Search for Solutions (1980)
Sense of Loss, A (1972)
Shoah (1985)
Sorrow and the Pity, The (1972)
Time for Burning, A (1967)
To Die in Madrid (1966)
Tsar to Lenin (1971)
Wall in Jerusalem, A (1972)
Weapons of the Spirit (1989)

POP MUSIC PERFORMANCES

Concert for Bangladesh (1972)
Don't Look Back (1967)
Elvis: That's the Way It Is (1970)
Johnny Cash: The Man, His World, His Music (1970)
Keep on Rockin' (1974)
Let It Be (1970)
Let the Good Times Roll (1973)
Our Latin Thing (1972)
Pink Floyd (1974)
Save the Children (1973)
Soul to Soul (1971)
Young Americans (1967)

SPORTS & RECREATION

Black Rodeo (1972)
Endless Summer, The (1966)
Goal! (1967)
Visions of Eight (1973)